Archaic Societies

Archaic Societies

Diversity and Complexity across the Midcontinent

edited by

Thomas E. Emerson, Dale L. McElrath, and Andrew C. Fortier

State University of New York Press
Albany, New York

Published by
State University of New York Press, Albany

Printed in the United States of America

For information, contact State University of New York Press, Albany, NY
www.sunypress.edu

Production by Eileen Meehan
Marketing by Anne M. Valentine

Library of Congress Cataloging-in-Publication Data

Archaic societies : diversity and complexity across the midcontinent / edited by Thomas E. Emerson, Dale L. McElrath, and Andrew C. Fortier.
p. cm.
Includes bibliographical references and index.
ISBN 978-1-4384-2701-0 (hardcover : alk. paper) 1. Paleo-Indians--North America. 2. Hunting and gathering societies--North America. 3. Archaeology--North America. I. Emerson, Thomas E., 1945- II. McElrath, Dale L., 1949- III. Fortier, Andrew C., 1947-
E77.9.A7 2009
970.01--dc22

2008047545

10 9 8 7 6 5 4 3 2 1

Table of Contents

Part 5. The Great Lakes

Part 6. Concluding Comments

Figures

Tables

Preface

The 2004 Urbana Archaic Working Conference

Archaic societies have come into much sharper focus over the last several decades, due in no small part to the efforts of researchers associated with cultural resource management investigations. The broad evolutionary and environmental sequences available from the rockshelter work of the mid-twentieth century have been fleshed out and refined by data gathered from significant excavations at open-air villages, campsites and cemeteries. One result of this effort has been to demonstrate that there are serious problems with the cultural framework in many areas, even in fairly recent sequences such as the American Bottom chronology established only twenty years ago. In particular, the unsystematic application of an ecological and evolutionary framework envisioning a regionally identifiable group with steadily growing population sizes, gradual improvements in technological proficiency and increasingly complex levels of social interaction leading to later agricultural economies has come in question in American Bottom research. Instead, we see wholesale population replacements, shifting cultural alliances, periods of depopulation, and shifting levels of social complexity throughout the archaeological record of the American Bottom, including the Archaic period. A review of papers at several recent Midwestern conferences suggests that regional scholars are developing new regional chronologies, as well as revaluating existing subsistence and social models of Archaic lifeways. The Archaic Working Conference that was held in Urbana in December, 2004 sought to foster a greater level of interaction and understanding among regional scholars.

The conference format was similar to several that have been hosted by the organizers and other regional scholars in the past (e.g., Late Woodland—Emerson, McElrath and Fortier; Early Woodland—Farnsworth and Emerson; French Colonial—Walthall and Emerson; Mississippian—Emerson and Lewis, and several others). Each of these conferences involved a select group of scholars delivering papers on their area of regional expertise, and each conference resulted in one or more published volumes. Combined with the paper presentations and discussion was the opportunity to examine large artifact assemblages made available by participating regional specialists. This informal small meeting format provides a favorable environment for the free exchange of ideas and examination of relevant diagnostic material, a situation that can no longer be achieved, even at regional conferences.

We asked participants to come with a prepared manuscript. It has been our experience that presentations and discussion are far more productive if presenters have written drafts at the time of the conference, although presentation time (approximately 30 minutes) may only allow a summary to be delivered; extemporaneous talks from outlines, although stimulating, do not provide the level of detail that is necessary for a productive conference.

We viewed this conference as an opportunity to capture the disparate "gray literature" on Archaic materials. Much of this information is known only to a few researchers or has been published in reports that are poorly circulated. Presenters are limited only by the requirement that it is necessary to present the baseline information on the cultural chronology, artifact assemblages and lifestyles of the Archaic societies in their region; beyond the mandate of a solid grounding in material culture and context, their theoretical bend, be it selectionist, processualist, post-processualist, or historical processualist was up to them—it was an opportunity to move beyond the "rocks" and "environment" explanations of Archaic societies. In anticipation that we all faced similar definitional and interpretational conundrums in the Midcontinental Archaic, we provided a series of topics that had proven to be of concern to regional archaeologists. We believed that a coordinated discussion of these issues might provide new insights into this, the longest, recognized period of human history in the Eastern Woodlands.

One of the concerns of all conference organizers is bringing together a diverse yet representational body of regional researchers. We have found in past instance that a working group of about twenty to thirty is large enough to provide a broad spectrum of theoretical and evidential perspectives. Larger groups of individuals become unwieldy and there is a loss of intimacy and informality. We took our usual approach to organizing such a working conference by selecting a key set of individuals who had regional expertise and a demonstrated record of publication. We asked them to serve as coordinators for a specific region or topic. In this capacity we suggested that they identify and contact colleagues that they felt could contribute to their effort. In some cases they invited these individuals to participate as co-authors but that was a decision we left up to the coordinators.

With these considerations in mind, we assembled a group of individuals who had demonstrated a commanding research interest in Archaic studies for their respective regions or states; or, who were currently working with large Archaic data sets from specific sites or localities, or specific topics. The volume and participants might be thought of as "Illinois centric" because of our heavy reliance on data from our own state. We unashamedly point to the importance of the major rivers that both define and traverse this state, along with the level of research activities and funding that have been invested in the Illinois River Valley, American Bottom, and Southern Illinois, along with the number of published site reports and availability of synthesized data. In fact, we suggest that Illinois can be seen as the birthplace of the modern Archaic site report with the publication of Howard Winter's Riverton Culture in 1968. Illinois also came to the forefront of Archaic research with the systematic radiocarbon dating studies of Modoc in the 1950s, and the ground-breaking efforts at the stratified open air site at Koster in the 1970s. With these efforts in mind, we eagerly accepted the offer by Ahler and Koldehoff (this volume) to summarize the results of a return to Modoc in the 1980s, and a re-examination of the Koster work by Wiant and his co-authors (this volume). Before leaving Illinois we would call attention to the effort by Nolan and Fishel to deal with the Archaic of western Illinois. There are no comparable regional studies that we are aware of that approach the level of detail accomplished by these researchers in examining over 3500 Archaic sites to establish a fine-grained, temporally sensitive distribution as study of Archaic phases, complexes, horizons and point types. It has provided information at the regional level that is the "horizontal" equivalent of the best examples of "vertical" analyses of deeply stratified sites anywhere in North America.

In choosing individuals from adjoining states we were fortunate enough to entice individuals who were in a position to deal with datasets at a comprehensive state level (i.e., Wisconsin, Michigan, Ohio, Kentucky) or appropriate sub-state regional level (i.e., eastern Iowa, southern and eastern Missouri). We were unable to find equivalent researchers who were willing to deal comprehensively with either Missouri or Indiana; but we were fortunate in attracting researchers who were currently involved in major site locality projects for both southern Indiana (Stafford and Cantin, this volume), and the Ozark region of Missouri (Ray et al., this volume).

We also thought it appropriate to bracket the major Midwestern study area with overviews that served to provide a Midcontinental backdrop perspective on our understanding of Archaic period research. In this effort we were successful in enlisting the aid of researchers in the southeast (Kidder and Sassaman, this volume) and our colleagues from Canada (Ellis et al., this volume). Their contributions are effective in highlighting the level and scope of interaction and possible boundary maintenance by populations during the Archaic period.

Also valuable in placing the midcontinental Archaic in context are the insightful overviews provided on fauna (Styles and McMillan, this volume), flora (Simon, this volume), mortuary patterns (Milner et al. this volume), and theory (Emerson and McElrath, this volume). These reviews help put the individual regional and site contributions in a broad context.

We envisioned several broad themes that we asked all authors to discuss in their papers. These included a) the appropriateness of the correlation in your region between archaic cultural change and climatic/environmental change, b) the validity of existing Archaic taxonomies in your region (e.g., is there really a Middle Archaic), c) the actual (rather than extrapolated) archaeological evidence for an Archaic sequence in your region, and d) the soundness of the standard hunting and gathering, seasonal-round models when compared to the actual archaeological record in your region (or do such models actually prejudice our interpretations of the data).

Presenters were encouraged to utilize regional survey and excavation material to touch on some of the following issues:

- What constitutes the earliest recognizable Early Archaic manifestation in your area, and how is it technologically distinct from the late Paleoindian occupation?
- Do you recognize formally defined Early Archaic phases or view these manifestations (Theban, Kirk, Bifurcate etc.) more generally as traditions or horizons?
- What marks the Early-Middle Archaic transition? Are there regionally specific radiocarbon dates and archaeological data that support this transition?
- Do you view the Hypsithermal as a relevant backdrop for explaining the Early/Middle Archaic transition? Do you have regional data that allows a fine-grained reconstruction of the effects of this climatic episode on native vegetation, animal life and human society in your area?
- Do you recognize a Middle and Late Archaic break? When did this occur and what are the criteria used for recognizing this break? Also, what are the social and technological diagnostics that signal this switch.
- What constitutes sedentism, and when does it occur in your area? Was sedentism an ongoing trend or does it vary from locality to locality or even fluctuate within your locality? Do you equate this with the postulated switch from foraging to collecting?
- Do you equate specific diagnostic projectile points with identifiable groups, thereby recognizing regional boundaries between "societies" in the Middle or Late Archaic?
- Do you have representative dated assemblages/contexts for cultural events within your study region or must you extrapolate from other regions?
- Do you believe that the lack of specific diagnostic projectile point types that may be recognized in neighboring areas, but not your own, is based on real divisions or is related to differences in nomenclature?
- Are there diagnostics other than projectile points (scrapers, drills, bifaces, groundstone implements) that are temporally sensitive in your area?
- Are there recognizably distinct, temporally sensitive methods of biface manufacture in your area?
- Is the appearance of Early Woodland in your area simply the addition of ceramics to a Late Archaic material

assemblage, or does it represent actual population as well as technological replacement?

- We have recently seen the appearance of spectacular Archaic complexity in the Southeast and the Lower Mississippi River valley. Is the Archaic of the Western Great Lakes more complex than we have previously admitted?
- Think about the social, religious and political ramifications of your data. What are the implications of the formalized Archaic mortuary complexes, especially those that are associated with the Late Archaic societies?

With these suggestions in mind three-dozen researchers and a number of guests gathered at the University of Illinois on December 2, 2004 for an intense two-day session in which nineteen oral presentations were given. The conference concluded with an afternoon workshop session in which hundreds of artifacts from various Archaic contexts were displayed and discussed. Saturated, and in some cases inundated, with this deluge of new information authors were sent off with the admonition to revisit their preliminary draft presentations and to consider and, as appropriate, incorporate the new ideas, new data, and divergent theories into a final draft manuscript by early summer 2005. The majority of contributors were able to meet this deadline some, however, were as much as a year late. Fortunately this did not interfere with the editorial and production aspects of the volume and while we waited we were able to edit the chapters in hand. Consequently, over the last two years, with the dedicated work of the editors, copy editor, graphic designer, production manager, and authors this massive, nearly 900-page volume, has moved towards final completion. We thank everyone involved in this process but we are especially grateful to Dr. Gary Dunham, Director of SUNY Press, for making this great effort finally come to fruition.

Thomas E. Emerson, Dale L. McElrath, Andrew C. Fortier

Organized by the Illinois Transportation Archaeological Research Program (ITARP), University of Illinois at Urbana-Champaign.

Acknowledgments

To host a conference of this magnitude and complexity and to turn that effort into a published volume is an immense undertaking that can only be accomplished with the support, cooperation, and enthusiasm of many parties, in this case, the conference participants and contributors, the staffs of the Illinois Transportation Archaeological Research Program (ITARP), the Levis Faculty Center at the University of Illinois at Urbana–Champaign (UIUC), the Illinois Department of Transportation (IDOT) Cultural Resources Section, and the State University of New York (SUNY) Press. The assembly, formatting, and production of a 23-chapter volume, an impressive final compendium covering more than 8,000 years of prehistory, is not an easy undertaking. Fortunately, in this project, the task was seamlessly executed by Michael Lewis, ITARP Production Manager, and copyeditor and indexing assistant Linda Forman. We, the organizers and editors, owe much to those many people who contributed to make this effort a success, and we thank them all. We also would also like to acknowledge the financial and logistical support of the UIUC and ITARP that made this project possible.

2004 Archaic Conference Participants, Urbana, Illinois: *Bottom to Top, L to R:* Andrew C. Fortier, Dale L. McElrath, Rochelle Lurie, Bonnie W. Styles, Thomas E. Emerson, John A. Walthall, Mary L. Simon, Jane E. Buikstra, Larry Conrad, R. Bruce McMillan, Jack H. Ray, Matthew P. Purtill, Richard L. Fishel, Kenneth E. Sassaman, George R. Milner, Tristram R. Kidder, Richard W. Jefferies, William A. Lovis, Joe B. Thompson, David J. Nolan, Scott J. Demel, Douglas Kullen, David W. Benn, Thomas C. Pleger, C. Russell Stafford, Neal H. Lopinot, Mark Cantin, Christopher Ellis, Kenneth B. Farnsworth, James B. Stoltman, Brad Koldehoff, Brian M. Butler, Michael D. Wiant

Part 1

An Archaic Overview

1

An Introduction to the Archaic Societies of the Midcontinent

Dale L. McElrath, Andrew C. Fortier, and Thomas E. Emerson

Archaic Themes

In our position as editors, we sometimes felt, as the various authors submitted their chapters, that we were privileged recipients of pieces of an intricate mail-order puzzle. From this vantage point, we were able to see commonalities that would have been far less obvious to the volume's individual contributors. Although the individual authors are of differing opinions and scholarly persuasions concerning major factual and many theoretical issues confronting Archaic studies, they are surprisingly evenhanded in presenting and summarizing the available regional data. Most have gone to extraordinary efforts to integrate gray literature and unpublished site reports and to use available site records to develop a comprehensive, if not always temporally representative, framework. In this introduction, we examine some of the issues that dominate the discussions and explore both the truisms and conundrums that have fettered attempts to reconstruct Archaic lifestyles. We have developed opinions that are sometimes at odds with those of our colleagues. We are especially concerned in this chapter with identifying positions that may have questionable foundations—positions that obscure rather than elucidate patterns that are essential for reconstructing the history of Archaic societies.

Ideally, our call for contributions to this conference and volume would have resulted in regionally balanced summaries of Archaic-period developments based on the natural physiographic regions within which related groups might have been expected to develop. Such an approach would have enabled construction of an overarching chronological framework for relating Archaic social and technological developments, as has been attempted, for example, for the Woodland and Mississippian periods (e.g., Emerson and Lewis 1991; Emerson et al. 2000; Farnsworth and Emerson 1986). The nature of the available archaeological data and the configuration of researchers' study areas, however, are somewhat at odds with this aim. Although the arbitrary political boundaries of midwestern states were of no relevance for the coming and going of Archaic peoples, they are of paramount relevance for shaping the research scope of institutionally affiliated archaeologists. The quantity and quality of Archaic research, therefore, for multiple historical reasons, have varied considerably from state to state.

As we assembled these many contributions on the Archaic period in the Midcontinent, it became clear to us that three themes dominate, either implicitly or explicitly, all of the chapters and that they are fundamental to interpreting or, we should perhaps say, reinterpreting Archaic societies. First and foremost among these issues is the establishment of basic relative and absolute chronologies; the second is the essential question of the meaning of material culture, often summarized as the "points equal people" debate; and the third is the relationship of culture, climate, and landscape. These are hardly new issues and we are not the first to discuss them, but we highlight them here because of their central importance for Archaic research, interpretation, and theorizing. In the following sections of this introduction, we explore in some detail the implications of these issues for interpreting the past.

Dating the Archaic

There can be no doubt that the development of radiocarbon dating has revolutionized, and continues to revolutionize, understanding of the archaeological record, no more so than in the case of the Archaic. The picture changed dramatically from the late 1940s, when the Archaic was formally recognized and thought to comprise a few thousand years of prehistory, to the late 1950s, when its antiquity was appreciated for the first time. The large number of radiocarbon dates (exceeding 1,000) gathered in this volume testifies to the value placed on this tool by researchers. However, given the extensive time span and expansive area of Archaic manifestations, even this number must be viewed as inadequate to properly document the sequence of cultural developments and events that unfolded. Also, researchers are realizing that radiocarbon dating has limitations that prevent achieving the tight chronological controls that are necessary to answer many of the questions they pose.

Although advances in radiocarbon dating have overcome initial concerns with, for example, dating bone and shell or C_4 plants such as corn, the process is still plagued by contamination of samples, issues of context, and variation between labs and, surprisingly, in results between specific techniques (i.e., conventional vs. AMS dating; see Fortier et al. 2006). In addition, variations in atmospheric carbon have generated problems that were not apparent at first glance. So, archaeologists not only are faced with issues of sampling and instrument limitations in the accuracy of sample measurement but also with the fact that samples of substantially differing ages can each have multiple "intercepts." Whereas archaeologists once operated under the (mistaken) assumption that dates could be reliably compared with one another within the latitude offered by statistically measurable confidence limits, they must now contend with the reality that dates can be easily "flipped" depending on which intercepts one "accepts." The dilemma has been compounded by the most recent version of a standard calibration scheme used by researchers in the Midwest (CALIB 5.0). While this version is, no doubt, more realistic and accurate in its results than previous versions, the system generates differing probabilities for assigning a date to specific time frames, thereby precluding convenient presentation in text form and complicating any attempt to summarize information from multiple dates. These difficulties explain the reluctance of contributors to this volume to adopt CALIB 5.0, even though they were offered the opportunity to do so prior to final submission of their chapters. The calibration dilemma has caused some (e.g., Ahler and Koldehoff, this volume; Ray et al., this volume) to prefer the original uncalibrated dates as simpler and offering greater clarity (with relative accuracy), at the expense of obfuscating precision.

Whatever the shortcomings of the radiocarbon dating method, it is clear that this method still provides the main vehicle for establishing and comparing the timing of cultural developments between and within regions. It is also clear that researchers are only beginning to determine the ages of the various Archaic manifestations that typify the Midcontinent. Using the American Bottom in the Mississippi River valley of western Illinois as a test case, we note that, while the 9,000-year-long Archaic period is estimated to represent approximately 75 percent of the post-Paleoindian archaeological record, less than 20 percent of the radiocarbon date assays are for this time span. While other regions and states may present more balanced results, the number of authors in this volume who indicate that their regions of study lack basic chronological frameworks suggests that the American Bottom region is, in fact, at least marginally ahead of the curve in terms of Archaic radiometric documentation.

We suspect that, in large part, this is due to the scholarly focus on later time periods and ceramic-producing groups. In this case, the cultural-evolutionary paradigm acts as a two-edged sword; not only are the later time periods viewed as the pinnacle of cultural development and complexity but the earlier periods are also conceived of as simpler, more uniform, and therefore easier to characterize. Because the Archaic period is viewed monolithically, that is, in terms of "homogeneous long-term trends," more attention has been given to dating later periods, characterized in terms of cultural dynamics or emergences and collapses. As long as this perspective prevails, there is little incentive to create detailed histories of Archaic people. Because of this, researchers find it acceptable to extrapolate dates and interpretations from neighboring, or even distant, regions to "fill in" local sequences of cultural expressions; given such practices, one should not be surprised to find broad homogeneity characterizing interpretations of the archaeological record of the Archaic period.

To some degree, such generalizations result from the paucity of Archaic archaeological manifestations. The factors of time and preservation have taken their toll on Archaic remains. Archaic sites often yield substantially fewer features containing diagnostics and datable charcoal than do their later counterparts. This accounts for the large number of Archaic dates that have been generated for features (e.g., Lovis, this volume) and stratigraphic levels (e.g., Ahler and Koldehoff, this volume) without associated diagnostic material. Much of the Archaic chronology is built on the radiocarbon dating of geomorphological rather than cultural units, with all of the uncertainties such contexts engender. This testifies to the need to excavate larger samples from Archaic-period sites to generate sufficient cultural material for dating. In our experience, only one out of 10 or 20 (or in some cases one out of 100 or 200) pit features at open-air Archaic sites yields diagnostics. Furthermore, Archaic pits are usually shallow, small processing features that seldom served as trash repositories, and they contain little charcoal. Given these factors, then, greater effort must be made to collect datable material from the few features that are capable of providing reliable and contextually secure diagnostic material.

Regardless of the reason, there can be little doubt that many Archaic-period material expressions remain poorly dated at the regional level. Examples in Illinois that come to mind involve well-recognized point traditions or horizons (e.g., Kirk, Table Rock, Hardin Barbed, Smith Basal Notched, Fox Valley Barbed, and Merkle side-barbed, among others), for which there are no known dates from single-component sites or stratigraphic levels in which these point types dominate. If culture-historical reconstructions and histories rest on constructing chronologies, establishing spatially delineated social boundaries, and, most importantly, identifying regional population stability and movements, then the vagaries of the dating methods employed thus far have left considerable latitude for interpretation of the archaeological record.

Dividing the Archaic

When it became available in the early 1950s, the radiocarbon dating method provided a major boost to understanding Archaic culture history. It confirmed archaeologists' suspicions that aceramic sites represented groups that existed prior to the ceramic-using Woodland lifestyle. More importantly, no longer were interregional comparisons completely dependent on the vagaries of trait distribution analysis to establish cultural associations and contemporaneity. For the first time, small sites with modest assemblages could be reasonably dated. This resulted in a major reappraisal of the age of and variability present among Archaic cultures. Although Ritchie proposed a comprehensive division of the Archaic period, it was Fowler (1959a, 1959b) who struggled with subdividing materials spanning the entire Archaic period from a single site (Modoc Rock Shelter). In the end, he did so arbitrarily by dividing a 6,000-year period of occupation (i.e., 8000–2000 B.C. uncalibrated) into three subperiods of equal 2,000-year units. This division suited his research focus since he was primarily interested in identifying subsistence trends through time (on the basis of artifacts and faunal and floral data) for the various periods of rockshelter use. Although Fowler (1959a, 1959b) created his divisions arbitrarily for intrasite comparative purposes, his ability to recognize substantive differences between them led him to propose three periods of Archaic use of the Modoc site area: (1) a period of initial occupation, (2) a period of localization, and (3) a period of specialization. Once he had identified these subdivisions, he sought to refine the dating involved, incorporating available Archaic dates from throughout the Midwest. He suggested that the initial occupation dated prior to 8000 B.C. and that the period of specialization began about 3500 B.C.

Because he published extensive comparisons between Modoc and sites in eastern Missouri (Graham Cave and Logan), southern Illinois (Faulkner and Ferry), and Kentucky (Green River sites), these divisions represented, for the Midwest at least, the beginnings of the Early, Middle, and Late tripartite division of the Archaic (even though Fowler did not use these designations). Researchers have struggled ever since with the chronological boundaries assigned to these divisions and the associated lifestyles. For example, Cook (1976), using the established date of 3500 B.C. for the beginning of the Late Archaic in the lower Illinois River valley, defined and characterized two sequential phases, Helton and Titterington, at the famous Koster site. However, presumably because major differences were observed between these two phases in subsistence and settlement patterning, later researchers used the end of the Helton phase to denote the conclusion of the Middle Archaic and the beginning of the Titterington phase (ca. 2500 B.C.) to signal the beginning of the Late Archaic. The problem researchers encounter outside the valley in using this criterion is that the Titterington phase has a very limited distribution in Illinois (many argue that it represents an intrusion from the west; e.g., see McElrath et al. ch. 11, this volume), and they have struggled to find equivalent-age materials. The issue is further complicated by the appearance of the Matanzas point (the hallmark of the Helton phase) much later in Indiana and its use there well into the Late Archaic period (Stafford and Cantin, this volume).

Subsequent Archaic studies in Illinois provided further impetus to the concept that the Early, Middle, and Late subdivisions represented logical divisions of directional trends, especially after Brown and Vierra (1983) published their Middle Archaic model (themes that Brown [1985, 1986] further explored and that we discuss below). This provided the basis for a seemingly perfect marriage of data and theory by taking the Koster site stratigraphic data and wedding it to a hypothesized switch from residential mobility to logistical mobility. This built on Binford's (1980) influential article on the relationship between resource distribution and hunter-gatherer settlement patterning. An indication of the impact of Brown and Vierra's and Binford's articles on midcontinental Archaic research is that they are both cited by many of the contributors to this volume.

Brown used the schema suggested by Binford of a continuum of hunter-gatherer subsistence-settlement strategies that related consumers to available resources, and he transmogrified this concept into a cultural-evolutionary model. Thus, whereas Fowler (1959a, 1959b) had assumed, at least for purposes of discussion, that the environment between 8000 and 2000 B.C. was essentially stable, Brown (1985; Brown and Vierra 1983), using more recent data developed at Koster (e.g., Butzer 1977, 1978; Hajic 1981) and elsewhere in the Midwest (King 1981), attempted to relate the archaeological record in the lower Illinois Valley to rather dramatic changes in riverine geomorphology combined with vegetational changes purportedly associated with the Hypsithermal climatic episode. In the resultant reconstruction, populations were both forced off the upland prairie regions by deteriorating climatic conditions associated with a drying episode and attracted to enhanced aquatic resources in the floodplain associated with the development of meandering river channels. This "push-pull" reorientation of populations has assumed the dominant role in explaining population distribution in the Midwest, just as the switch from residential mobility to logistical mobility (à la Binford) has become a dominant explanation for significant changes in the archaeological record throughout the Midcontinent (although the timing of this event is viewed as regionally variable).

One might expect that the broad perspective gained by incorporating data at the midcontinental level in this volume would provide a comprehensive regional basis on which to divide the Archaic into consistent, comparable, yet regionally sensitive diachronic units. In our judgment this is not feasible at this juncture because every region has a historically rooted rationale for its own temporal divisions, and, at least in some cases, rationality has less to do with it than does the force of tradition. It seems reasonable to divide such a lengthy period (which is now seen as extending for at least eight millennia) into manageable subdivisions, and virtually all contributors to this volume make use of a tripartite schema of some sort. This triple division has become the de facto temporal framework and will no doubt continue to be, despite its problems, for the foreseeable future.

It seems reasonable, therefore, to retain the tripartite system as an arbitrary division of the Archaic for purposes of identifying the time frame with which one is dealing; but, at the same time, it seems unwise to link temporal boundaries to perceived technological "progress," adaptational "advances," or changing climatic episodes for the simple reason that, to the extent that any of these factors influenced human actions, they were, by definition, regionally experienced and highly variable. Virtually all of the technological innovations that have been enlisted to define the Archaic either by inclusion or exclusion (e.g., the inception of the bow and arrow, agriculture, pottery, sedentism, political complexity, mound building, etc.) have proven to be, if not outright inapplicable, at least equivocal. It is no longer feasible to view the Archaic at any supraregional level as exhibiting broad trends that can be used to characterize temporal subdivisions representing isomorphic units, even if one allows for the time-transgressive expression of effects associated with south-to-north vegetational shifts resulting from glacial retreats, and west-to-east changes triggered by an advancing prairie. Indeed, the Archaic seems to have been far more complex than either its name or the previous attempts at overviews have intimated.

Projectile Point Style, Form, and Function

Archaic-period research begs the question, how do scholars establish local or regional sequences and determine historic trajectories for Archaic-period societies? The answer is, of course, that they use "diagnostics" (usually projectile point types) from surface sites to establish the relative intensity of local and regional occupations and the settlement systems employed; the presumed dates of the various diagnostics are usually assigned in the Midwest on the basis of relative dates and radiocarbon determinations generated from other areas, particularly the Midsouth and Southeast. This dependence on surface diagnostics raises a host of inevitable and very thorny issues concerning the nature and reliability of projectile point typologies and the validity of types as chronological markers. In fact, the "hafted biface," as researchers now prefer to call the projectile point, has been viewed with mixed feelings and today has a problematic place in archaeological research.

The use of projectile point types by midwestern cultural resource management (CRM) archaeologists has persisted because types have proven valuable for recognizing chronological and cultural units and because they facilitate communication among researchers. The idea of types may also prove useful in new analytical approaches involving the concepts of communities of practice and the *châine opératoire*. While we do not wish to relive or, worse, rekindle the typology debates of the mid-twentieth century, we briefly explore the historical development of the point-type debate and new perspectives that may serve to resolve some of the more contentious issues that were once considered irresolvable.

One philosophical aspect of the typology issue that was hotly debated in the 1950s concerned the nature of types. Some theoreticians argued that types existed in the real world and simply awaited discovery (Spaulding 1953), whereas others argued that they were arbitrarily imposed (Rouse 1960). Perhaps because a new generation of scientists has turned its attention to phenomena, such as certain life-forms and subatomic particles, that defy conventional classification, increasingly, researchers in many fields have accepted that all categories are humanly constructed and, therefore, by definition, are arbitrarily imposed on the unsuspecting "real" world (Tschauner 1994). If one accepts this premise, then the only measure of the validity of a defined type or classification system is how useful the categories prove for advancing understanding of the subject matter. It also means that the essentialism that purportedly undercuts the usefulness of artifact types (Lyman et al. 1997) is of equal concern for all organizing schema used by archaeologists (be they artifact types, political types, settlement types, subsistence types, ethnic types, or selectionist traits).

Whereas previous conceptualizations of artifact typologies analogized them as "mental templates" representing ideals that were shared by social groups and that producers strove to replicate, practice theory recognizes that they are the products of communities of practice, that is, interacting individuals who are involved in their production. Although the two concepts appear superficially similar, the latter is more flexible and less abstract because it explicitly acknowledges the method (human agency) by which the knowledge of tool production was transmitted between generations. In terms of our discussion, it recognizes that a teacher-student (i.e., master-novitiate) relationship provided the context for training successive generations of flintknappers in the "correct" way to perform a task (in this case, producing hafted bifaces). Correct performance involved not only the basic mechanical aspects and the chaîne opératoire of tool production but also the religious and symbolic implications that imbued the process with meaning. Many idiosyncratic elements of point production were also transmitted, involving the appropriate blade shape, stem treatment, hafting method, refurbishing sequence, and so on. Obviously, the subject of training was not limited to the production of hafted bifaces but, rather, included a multifaceted catechism of lithic tool manufacture; raw material acquisition; weapon production; techniques of tracking, trapping, killing, and processing game; and the general wisdom and special lore necessary for defending and supplying the individual, family, or corporate group with food.

Much attention has been focused on how hafted bifaces inform archaeologists about activities undertaken (i.e., function) or group interaction (form or style). The neutral term *hafted biface* became popular after Stanley Ahler convincingly argued, on the basis of his examination of a sample of 114 projectile points from a single level (Stratum 2) at Rodgers shelter in Missouri, that the belief that points served as tips for projectiles is not always consistent with evidence from use-wear analysis. He further addressed the issue of whether the morphological variability in the Rodgers assemblage was due to "mental templates" derived from ethnic preferences or, as he surmised, from functional distinctions. Ahler (1970:118–121) arrived at a series of conclusions that have typically been characterized as supporting functional categories as opposed to "formal" or cultural categories, although Ahler himself was more cautious in describing his results. Among other things, he discovered functional categories that crosscut some formal categories and formal categories that fulfilled more than one function, suggesting they contained more than one tool "type." Ahler was also able to replicate many of the wear patterns evident in the sample assemblage and provide insight into some of the activities undertaken by the tool users. Among other things, he suggested that heavy serration was correlated with sawing or slicing and that, by contrast, beveling was not related to function (i.e., tool use) but, rather, was the result of resharpening. Eastern Woodland specialists have largely accepted these conclusions, while often ignoring other of Ahler's insights, for example, that "gross morphological" formal categories were better supported by factor analysis than the refined formal categories based on "objective" criteria (Ahler 1970:119).

Weapon Systems

Ahler may have been one of the first of the New Archaeologists to address point typology and function, but he and contemporary lithic researchers were not the first to confront the problem of discerning the uses of stone projectile points; nor are today's researchers the first to struggle over the form versus function dilemma. The great artist and anthropologist William Henry Holmes, who documented many of the lithic quarry sites and flintknapping techniques used in North America, observed in a symposium on "Arrows and Arrow-Makers" that "it is not possible, in all cases to distinguish points made for the arrow from those made and employed for projectiles thrown by the hand, or throwing stick, or from those intended to be hafted and used as knives, daggers, drills, and the like. It is not unlikely that many points were alternately used for a number of purposes as necessity demanded" (1891:49). In the same symposium, Thomas Wilson, another important student of the stone projectile point, reinforced this observation with his own. "The arrow-heads, spear-heads, and knives of the prehistoric races have such likeness of form, style, and size that a line of division between the three is practically impossible" (Wilson 1891:58). The problem was expressed even earlier by Haldeman in a consideration of "unsymmetric arrow-heads." He observed that, "while irregularities would interfere with the function of arrows, all these objects are not to be regarded as arrow-heads, some of the larger kinds being for spears, while others are probably borers, ... scrapers ... and knives" (Haldeman 1879:292).

The fundamental question concerning the weapon system represented by projectile points from archaeological contexts persisted into the twentieth century, when systematic excavations began to yield stratigraphic results that could be used to separate and relatively date artifact assemblages. Turn-of the-century attempts to solve the problem, as they are today, were based on observations made on ethnographic and archaeological collections and on experimentation and replication. Willoughby (1902) scoured the literature and museum collections to identify prehistoric knives that were still hafted onto handles. He discovered several from California, Colorado, Oregon, and Ohio as well as examples from dry caves in northern Mexico (state of Coahuila). He noted that the stone blades were "of the common typical forms (leaf-shaped, triangular, stemmed and notched) usually found in a collection of chipped implements" (Willoughby 1902:3). He further observed that the blades were affixed to wooden handles sometimes using only gum, sometimes only cords (either plant cordage or animal sinew), and sometimes both. He concluded by enumerating the various uses that researchers today ascribe to projectile points and observed that "the greater number of the implements of the common types, of lengths varying from about two inches to seven inches, were probably used as knife blades" (Willoughby 1902:6). Despite these early observations, which continued to be upheld by the recovery of additional specimens from dry cave sites in the Southwest (e.g., Guernsey and Kidder 1921), archaeologists to this day hold out hope that the geometry of the hafting element will eventually be proven to vary according to the specific weapon system in use. To further pour cold water on this idea, we offer the example of late prehistoric arrowpoints (e.g., Justice 1987), which display all of the hafting-element shapes that are present among earlier hafted bifaces, with the possible exception of fluting.

Aside from the function of projectile points, early researchers speculated on the rationale for such attributes as beveling, serration, and barbs. By the late nineteenth century, the process of stone tool production had been demystified through direct observation of tool production by native flintknappers (Redding 1879; Wilson 1899) and by some researchers' mastery of stone tool production techniques (e.g., Cushing 1895). Researchers began to examine the individual elements of stone tools, in particular, hafted bifaces, to debate the functional merit of individual characteristics. For example, Haldeman (1879) suggested that barbs, especially the single barbs associated with "unsymmetric points" might be related to fish gigging. Fox addressed the issue of serration, noting that, although characteristic of tools from North America, Europe, and Japan, its widespread occurrence was probably not the result of diffusion or migration, and he observed that

> the mode of working flint and other materials which flake off with conchoidal fracture, by taking off flakes and leaving facets from the edge alternately on opposite sides, naturally produces a more or less serrated edge, in consequence of the projection of the edges between the facets. A perfectly serrated edge, therefore, appears to me to be a refinement of workmanship produced by deepening the facets, which might or might not have been produced independently in different countries. [1875:319]

Similar arguments were presented for the "spiraling" or beveling that was noted on points. Beveling was popularly thought to impart a spinning or "rifling" motion to the dart or arrow in flight (Fairbank 1864; Hough 1891; Wilson 1899). This notion was disputed by accomplished practitioners to the degree that, by the mid-twentieth century, reference to "rotary points" brought derision from one flintknapper: "The fable that beveled points were made in that manner to spin an arrow in flight is in the same category as that fable about the Mound Builders tempered copper, and the one about chipping arrow heads from red-hot flint with an icicle. Let us forget them or leave them to the writers of filler pieces for the Sunday Supplement" (Smith 1953:270). The assertion that beveling imparts important flight characteristics, however, continues to be asserted by some researchers today (i.e., O'Brien and Wood 1998:96).

Like modern researchers, these early pioneers were also fascinated by the relationship between the spear-thrower and the bow and arrow. Otis Mason (1885) published a study of North American spear-throwers in the collections of the National Museum, and in 1891, Zelia Nuttall published her influential study of the atlatl, based on an analysis of Mexican codices. Interest increased considerably when several ethnographic spear-throwers, collected along the western coast of North America during the Vancouver expedition in the late eighteenth century (1790–1795), came to light when the expedition collection was donated to the British Museum almost a hundred years later (Read 1892). The discovery of ethnographic specimens was followed quickly by reports of archaeological specimens from Colorado (Mason 1893) and Florida (Cushing 1897). Like their modern counterparts (e.g., Vanderhook 1998), early researchers also experimented with the efficiency and accuracy of the atlatl weapon system.

These discoveries spurred debates over the antiquity and possible multiple inventions of the bow and arrow, which was clearly the weapon of choice in subarctic and temperate North America at the time of European expansion. Sporadic discoveries of archaeological atlatls were made throughout the early twentieth century, leaving little doubt as to the ubiquity (cf. Kellar 1955) and, to some extent, the antiquity of the spear-thrower. By 1940, when Fenenga and Wheat (1940:222) reported on one specimen recovered from the Baylor Rock Shelter in Texas, they were able to list multiple southwestern examples, from Arizona, Oklahoma, New Mexico, Mexico (Chihuahua), and Texas. Once the spear-thrower was shown to have been widespread and important in North America, the discussion eventually shifted to practical considerations involving the identification of archaeological correlates of this weapon system, since few regions outside the Southwest enjoyed favorable preservation conditions.

Fenenga (1953) was the first to formally employ weight to distinguish between atlatl and arrow points. In fact, size had already been recognized as a potential criterion for sorting atlatl points from arrowheads, and archaeologists had been informally using it for years to classify specimens. Baker and Kidder (1937) dated the transition from spear-thrower to bow and arrow in the Southwest to Basket Maker II times and noted the absence, in general, of arrow-sized points from "respectably ancient deposits." This prompted a response from Browne (1938, 1940), an avid archer and hunter, concerning the optimal size of arrow points. Browne had experimented extensively with stone points and had concluded that there was considerable overlap between atlatl and arrow points, in terms of both overall size and haft-element size. He used stone points exceeding 5 cm in length, including archaeological specimens from the Signal Butte I, Sheep Mountain, and Pictograph Cave sites, and was able to shoot arrows tipped with these points to distances of 175–200 yds (Browne 1938). He lamented that he was not able to test a Folsom point from the Lindenmeier site, suggesting that, "if ever there was a point that was made for efficient bow and arrow shooting, it is the Folsom point" (Browne 1938:359).

Elements of this long debate have been resolved to some degree in recent times; Thomas (1978) did what researchers had done almost a century earlier and examined museum specimens in an attempt to distinguish spear from arrow points. He developed a statistical method of separating them that proved accurate 86 percent of the time. His method was based on his examination of over 100 archaeological hafted arrowheads but only 10 dart points attached to foreshafts. Shott (1997) extended the hafted-dart sample size to 39 by visiting several more North American museums. On the basis of his larger dart population, he was able to demonstrate that simply measuring shoulder width was as effective as the more complex statistical methods employed by Thomas (1978) to distinguish between arrow and dart points. Researchers quickly realized, however, that, while shoulder width might be a reasonably accurate guide for distinguishing between isolated dart and arrow points from surface survey, it would not serve to resolve the issue of the antiquity of the bow and arrow if both systems operated contemporaneously (Corliss 1980; Shott 1997).

In addition to the stone tips of darts, researchers have also attempted to identify "adjuncts" to the spear-thrower that might be considered *cartes de visites* in the absence of preserved specimens of the spear-thrower itself. Occasionally, bone spurs have been recovered that are interpreted as the hooks that were attached to the distal end of the throwing stick and that served as the point of contact with the base of the dart shaft during launch (Goslin 1944). While bone is only slightly more likely to be preserved than wood, the recovery of such hooks in linear association with ground bannerstones and stone points in Late Archaic burials in the Midsouth (Webb 1946; Webb and Haag 1939) led most researchers to conclude that the exotically shaped bannerstones served as spear-thrower weights. Atlatl weights of copper, galena, and stone were soon identified in archaeological context (sometimes associated with burials) throughout North America (e.g., Butler and Osborne 1959; Neuman 1967). Other archaeological atlatl adjuncts that were recognized included shell or stone "spurs" from California (Riddell and McGeein 1969) and U-shaped shell "fingerhooks" from northern Mexico (Ekholm 1962). In the Eastern Woodlands, the bannerstone (e.g., Winters 1961) and, eventually, the "boatstone" and "birdstone" of the Northeast (Griffin 1967) became synonymous with the atlatl. The earliest occurrence of the bannerstone (i.e., Middle Archaic) was thought by some (e.g., Griffin 1967, 1968) to date the invention of the spear-thrower.

These circumstantial associations seemed to generate confidence among Eastern Woodlands scholars that the artifacts involved were functional parts of an atlatl weapon assembly. However attempts to prove the functional advantage of attaching a weight to a spear-thrower were considerably less supportive; for example, Hill (1948) suggested only "some" improvement using a weight with lightweight darts; Peets (1960) was unable to demonstrate any advantage; Mau (1963) suggested improved distance throws; Howard (1974) suggested no improvement; Palter (1976) suggested diminished throwing capacity; and Raymond (1986) suggested no improvement in distance but potentially improved accuracy. Although the jury is still out on the subject, the one thing that is beyond doubt is that weights are not necessary for competent and reliable use of the spear-thrower as a hunting and warring device. Notably, none of the ethnohistoric or ethnographic atlatl examples on record involved use of a weight (Palter 1976); however, small "fetish" stones (often turquoise or hematite) and related symbolically charged paraphernalia (usually animal teeth) were sometimes attached near the proximal end presumably to confer a spiritual, if not a functional, advantage to the operator (Palter 1976). In any event, the presence or absence of atlatl weights, if, indeed, the artifacts so identified operated as such, cannot be argued as proof of the antiquity of this weapon.

The past couple of decades have seen a renewed emphasis on the study of projectile technology on a worldwide basis (e.g., contributors to Knecht 1997), one aspect of which has been an attempt to identify archaeological correlates of specific weapon systems. Christenson (1986) has provided a comprehensive review of attempts at relating hafted-biface attributes to appropriate weapon systems, noting that several ethnographic, archaeological, and experimental studies support a relationship between stem width and haft diameter that may have implications for distinguishing different weapon systems. In an impressive, commanding grasp of both the physical principles governing projectile flight and the knowledge gained through experimentation with artifacts, he assessed how information about projectile accuracy, killing power, range, and durability can be used to functionally decode archaeological hafted bifaces. He used a surface-collected sample from the Sangamon Valley of Illinois to explore these issues and examined technological developments in the context of a generalized temporal framework. Although Christenson found that hafted bifaces dating to certain periods seem to conform to predicted trends, he encountered problems in recognizing long-term technological trends; in particular, the larger hafted bifaces associated with the Early and Middle Woodland periods counter an expected trend of decreasing point size through time. We would add to this the observation that, in the American Bottom, the average sizes of points from dated context are erratic through time, sometimes oscillating wildly, as exemplified by the hypertrophic Titterington points and the diminutive Riverton point types, the latter only a few hundred years later than the former (contra Shott 1996; cf. McElrath et al. ch. 11, this volume).

We have embarked on this history of the study of Archaic weapon technology and the functional and typological aspects of hafted bifaces to highlight several issues that we consider to be of paramount importance, especially in a volume dedicated to Archaic societies. First, after almost a century and a half of directed research by some of the best minds, past and present, in the discipline, the categorization of hafted bifaces either by form or by function remains problematic. Disciplinary consensus has emerged on occasion. For instance, archaeologists seem to have concluded that projectile points are better viewed as hafted bifaces, because they were often used as knives (e.g., Ahler 1970; Finkelstein 1937; Haldeman 1879; Holmes 1891; Nance 1971; Odell 1994; Willoughby 1902; Wilson 1899). Points of consensus, however, are few.

Archaeologists are unable to convincingly distinguish between the tips of arrows and the tips of atlatl darts or to determine whether the bow and arrow or the spear-thrower is a technologically or functionally superior weapon system, whether groups used multiple weapon systems contemporaneously, or whether hafted-biface morphological form was generated by ethnic practices or simple functionality or both. Inability to answer these simple real-world questions has a dramatic impact on interpretations of the past.

Take, for example, the inability to identify the morphological characteristics of arrow versus dart points. This precludes archaeologists from determining the individual histories of these two weapon systems in the New World. It leads to a lack of consensus on such topics as the date of the introduction of the bow and arrow in North American prehistory. If, for example, one were to poll current views on when the bow and arrow was introduced or reinvented in North America, one would find the following opinions: Paleoindian (Amick 1994; Patterson 1994), Early Archaic (Byers 1959; Shott 1997), Late Archaic (Bradbury 1997; Nassaney and Pyle 1999), Middle Woodland (Justice 1987), and Late Woodland (Hall 1977, 1980; McElrath et al. 2000). The best that can be said from written historic accounts is that both systems existed at contact in the Western Hemisphere. An equally diverse set of archaeologists could be called on to dispute related topics, such as whether there were single versus multiple inventions of the bow and arrow or whether it was technologically superior to the spear-thrower.

It would appear that well over a century of functional analysis has resolved little about the relationship between stone points and their counterpart weapon systems. In reviewing the current literature, we note that researchers are of two opinions. The optimistic scenario is perhaps best expressed by Christenson, who passionately argues that the pursuit of several lines of research "will ultimately lead to the development of numerous general and specific models of projectile design" (1986:123–124). In seeming contradiction, Shott concludes that, "leaving aside other possible uses of chipped-stone bifaces, we cannot with certainty classify archaeological unknowns as dart or arrow points, and we will never attain such an impossible goal" (1997:99). Although these views may seem an unusual segue into the next topic, which concerns the use of hafted bifaces as spatially and temporally sensitive group-identity markers, we argue that it is the reconciliation of these two seemingly contradictory statements that will provide the foundation for building a more productive and realistic understanding of the place of Archaic people and the social role of technology, in the history of the Eastern Woodlands.

We begin by pointing out that we have presented the two quotes in the previous paragraph out of context. Christenson is referring to interpreting a sequence of points from a specific region (the Sangamon River valley of Illinois), whereas Shott is referring to the overlap in archaeological hafted dart and arrow point metrics that reduces to 85 percent the reliability that unhafted projectile points can be correctly assigned to either class, thereby leaving considerable room for doubt about the assignment of any given specimen. This is relevant because researchers interested in identifying early (indeed, the earliest) use of the bow and arrow will find this objective difficult to achieve if the bow and arrow was used in tandem with the atlatl system. Still, one can view this state of affairs from the perspective of the glass half full rather than half empty. After all, Shott points out, regarding the 85 percent level of accuracy, "Considering the problematics of archaeological inference, this is not a bad average." It goes to the core, however, of what questions archaeology and archaeologists may be capable of addressing.

Of course, a large part of the uncertainty in hafted-biface studies comes from applying modern engineering concepts of specialization and optimal efficiency to prehistoric systems of technology that were, in fact, extremely flexible and technologically forgiving, especially when used in combination with a variety of hunting techniques (e.g., communal drives, netting, and perhaps even poisoning). The minimal requirement of a stone point hafted on a shaft is that it allow the shaft to be propelled a "reasonable" distance, with sufficient force, accuracy, and penetrating power to kill or cripple the target, whether a person or an animal. Despite impressions to the contrary presented by modern researchers, this minimum requirement is met by a wide array of shapes and sizes of "points" (witness the multitude of shapes and sizes of stone, bone, wood, teeth, antler, and other materials that bedeck the business end of historic arrow and spear shafts). The "significant" engineering parameters of projectile points may, in fact, be limited to broad principles; for example, beyond a certain threshold, a point may simply be too large or heavy to be propelled by a bow. Clearly almost no point is too small to be placed on the piercing end of an atlatl or spear shaft. This suggests that studies based on the principle of functional optimization may, again, be misdirected when applied to ancient tradition-bound technologies.

Are Points People?

Moving beyond the concept of functional optimization, we consider the demonstrable relevance of projectile point types as group-identity markers and their importance in documenting group interaction across space and through time. The early pioneers involved in relating projectile points with their counterpart weapon systems were also concerned about classifying projectile points into logical categories. To some extent, this was no doubt a reflection of the museum mentality that favors classification as an organizational device, but it is also clear that early researchers entertained the idea that similarities in form indicated historical and social relationships. For example, Fox (1875) argued that stone point styles from sites in Patagonia were more similar to North American forms than Old World types, suggesting historical relationships within the New World. The issue of classificatory types was such a common concern in the nineteenth century that

Wilson complained about the complexity of the classification systems that had been employed by his contemporaries, suggesting that they were "too complex, the divisions have been too close, and the distinctions not sufficiently broad to be popular. A classification of infinitesimal divisions, with slight differences, difficult to distinguish and still more difficult to remember, will never be satisfactory or acceptable" (1891:58). He went on to propose a simplified system that included three shape categories: leaf shaped, triangular, and stemmed, with each shape type including up to three subclasses. He further identified a "peculiar" category made up of beveled, serrated, and bifurcated specimens and examples with "extremely long barbs usually squared at the ends." Obviously, "lumpers" and "splitters" have a long tradition in archaeological studies.

We credit a fellow American Bottom researcher, Robert McCormick Adams, with popularizing the term *diagnostic* to refer to point types that were spatially or temporally restrictive or both. He noted that "several valuable classifications of flint points have been formulated but few of these have attempted to distinguish between those points having diagnostic value, and the numerous forms which are found rather indiscriminately over a large series of cultures and which may or may not have value as cultural determinants" (Adams 1940:72). Adams may have been the first to explicitly lay out criteria to be considered in developing point types. He suggested that a classification system might "include a description of form, technique of chipping, type of chipping scars, and the nature of flint or chert used in its manufacture" (Adams 1940:72). The examples he chose as diagnostic for the Eastern Woodlands were all Woodland or late prehistoric forms; no Archaic examples were considered illustrative. This highlights a problem that persists today, that is, that many Archaic projectile point types cannot confidently be associated with other "cultural traits" that could be used to establish their diagnostic value. So, many Archaic point "types" were created simply on the basis of morphological similarity rather than on cultural and chronological contextual associations. Is it a surprise, then, that many of these types are suspect as valid cultural indicators or even as morphological units?

By the 1930s, researchers were beginning to promote "taxonomic systems" of classes and types of projectile points (e.g., Finkelstein 1937). As with other artifact categories, many researchers believed that projectile point types existed and awaited discovery (Smith 1954). By the 1960s, the analytical power of computers was seen as the key to sorting out the myriad of metric and nonmetric data necessary to scientifically describe and objectively categorize stone tools (Krieger 1964; Weyer 1964), an unfortunate trend that continues to this day. The classification of projectile point types very quickly became caught up in the debate over artifact types, in general (see Lyman et al. 1997). An even more unfortunate fate was in store for types when they were equated with "norms" (Binford 1965) and were swept up in the normative-substantivist debates (cf. Lyman and O'Brien 2004). Ironically, although Binford equated "type" with "norm" and treated both as four-letter words not to be used in social discourse, it was the New Archaeologists who undeniably incorporated norms into their methodological approach to model building (cf. Lyman and O'Brien 2004).

One outcome of the processualist approach to artifact analysis was the famous "style or form versus function" or "tale of two caves" debates between Binford and Bordes (Bordes 1972) in the 1970s; in the Old World, the argument centered on the implications of variability among Mousterian lithic assemblages, but in North America it signaled the start of a major reassessment of how archaeology should be conducted. The scholarly free-for-all that resulted directly and indirectly affected midcontinental Archaic studies, partly because Binford learned (and taught) much of his archaeology in the Midwest but also because the debate thrust hunter-gatherers into the limelight. The North American Archaic became the darling of the Americanist New Archaeologists. Efforts to persuade archaeologists that the miscreant type concept was so heavily laden with flaws that it could not be usefully applied largely succeeded. This only served to drive the use of types underground; while researchers in the Midwest openly talked about and used types for purposes of communication, in published reports they tried to objectify their analyses by using arbitrary biface categories (e.g., Class Ia, Ib, II, etc.). This attempt at sidestepping the issue actually made it worse for those attempting to compare reported assemblages, because of the confusing overabundance of artificially labeled categories to be considered. Meanwhile, CRM archaeology was steadily amassing evidence that supported the affiliation of specific point types with specific regions, periods, and even societies. The premature announcement of the death of point types was eerily similar to the conclusion reached by engineering studies that bumblebees, by virtue of their poor body weight-to-wing ratio, were not actually capable of flight. During the 1970s and 1980s, the chronological and cultural validity of projectile point types was being demonstrated as was the value of culture history (e.g., Bareis and Porter 1984).

We might point out that recognizing "communities of practice" as the underlying rationale for the existence of types should clarify one aspect of the archaeological record, but it will do so at the expense of the traditional functionalist approaches cited above. At issue is the central role accorded to the master-novice relationship and the impact this relationship has on shaping material culture. This holds major significance for the debate concerning the antiquity of the bow and arrow. Typically, in ethnographic hunting and gathering societies, the teacher charged with the training of a student in the necessary lore of hunting will gift the student with a "toy" set of weapons (or perhaps several sets throughout his childhood and early adolescence) to allow him to develop the complex motor skills required to skillfully operate weapons as an adult. Archaeologically, this would be reflected in "undersized" stone tools, appropriate to the size of the person being trained. In the case of spears or darts, the small hafted bifaces would easily fall into the size range of arrowpoints. Most midwestern archaeologists have encountered diminutive examples of all of the commonly recognized Archaic forms and have privately speculated that they served as teaching toys. Such points would only account for a small number of the points used by the average hunter throughout his lifetime, but this scenario certainly highlights the concerns that some researchers have expressed (Corliss 1980; Shott 1997) concerning the reliability of distinguishing between arrow and dart points.

As proof of the validity of types, we offer the success that has been achieved in the recognition of contextually and chronologically based projectile point types or styles. In fact, time and the accumulation of data tend to favor resolution of issues surrounding the viability of point types. Few archaeologists now dispute the priority of fluted points in the Eastern Woodlands sequence and North America, in general. The 14 point types Scully (1951) identified for the central Mississippi Valley are still recognized as valid today, even if researchers have modified their associations on the basis of new information; for example, several types originally identified as Late Archaic or Early Woodland are now recognized as indisputably Early Archaic (i.e., Hardin Barbed, St. Charles, Graham Cave Notched). Points that had been assigned to a broad Late Archaic–Early Woodland time span have recently proven to be restricted, on the basis of good contextual data, to one or the other period, at least in some regions (e.g., Emerson and Fortier 1986). Other examples abound. Dalton points were once chronologically grouped with side-notched varieties because of their co-occurrence in mixed deposits in cave and rockshelter sites, but their unique occurrence on open-air sites in the Southeast led to their recognition as an earlier horizon marker (Goodyear 1982). Kramer points, which were thought to bridge the Terminal Archaic–Early Woodland transition, are now definitively associated exclusively with Early Woodland times (in fact, with one specific Early Woodland culture—Marion), at least in the Midwest. The straight- and expanding-stemmed, barbed varieties (e.g., Dyroff, Springly, Mo-Pac) that were thought to persist from Archaic times into the Early Woodland in Illinois (Linder 1974) are now recognized as restricted to the terminal Late Archaic (McElrath et al. 1984). Contracting-stemmed points have been historically difficult to employ as cultural identifiers because they seem to reappear often in the archaeological record, having been found in the Eastern Woodlands and on the Plains in contexts dating from about 6000 B.C. to A.D. 500. In specific localities, however, they seem to be restricted in their affiliation to narrow periods or specific cultural associations. For example, in the American Bottom Archaic sequence, they are largely restricted to a single Late Archaic phase (i.e., Mule Road). They reappear in Early Woodland contexts, in which they are associated with Black Sand and Florence-phase sites, but not with Marion-phase sites (Emerson and Fortier 1986; Farnsworth 1986), and they are common in Middle Woodland contexts but may be more temporally and regionally sensitive than previously thought (Fortier 2001).

Archaeologists are also beginning to recognize significant boundaries in the distribution of particular point types; for example, the classic Dalton variety is arguably restricted to the central Mississippi Valley (Koldehoff and Walthall, this volume). We are even beginning to recognize contemporary (ethnic?) boundaries or interface zones between point types, as in the case of the McLean point type of the Falling Springs phase of the American Bottom and the side-notched Hemphill and Godar types in the central Illinois Valley (McElrath et al. ch. 11, this volume; Nolan and Fishel, this volume). Stafford and Cantin (this volume) suggest a possible boundary between the Brewerton Eared variety of the Ohio River valley and the Matanzas types of the southern Indiana hill country.

This is not to imply that the pursuit of types has not been without missteps, setbacks, or failures, many of which have involved grouping points by a single apparent morphological trait, usually centering on the haft element. The failure to conduct careful typological examinations and to rely on secure collections from chronologically and contextually secure deposits has led to much confusion. For example, in the Midwest, the common assumption that side-notched points can be reliably assigned to the Middle Archaic period (O'Brien and Warren 1983) has largely been disproved (Nolan and Fishel, this volume). Contracting-stemmed points are a perennial focus of examination in the effort to develop explicit criteria to formularize a method of objectively sorting surface-collected materials into various named Archaic and Woodland types. Such studies seldom yield publishable results; as is the case for side notching, the tendency is to resort to a functional explanation for the contracting base shape (Boszhardt 2002; Musil 1988).

It is important to recognize that projectile point types do not form a classification scheme that can be invalidated or undermined because a given point type proves not to be a useful indicator of age or cultural affiliation. We recognize that each type must stand on its own and that some are more useful and restrictive, either temporally or spatially, than others are. Also, we reject any attempt to mathematically define or recognize point types on the basis of a uniform set of criteria. A single trait, such as a distinctive haft element (e.g., Turkey-tail), shoulder element (e.g., Table Rock), blade shape (e.g., Wadlow), barb shape (e.g., Calf Creek), or unusual composite shape (e.g., Fox River Valley), may be sufficient to define a category; more often, multiple factors, such as frequency of heat treatment, method of resharpening, degree and placement of grinding, and material preference play significant roles in contributing to the recognition of distinct types. Again, the criteria for accepting a type (or variety) as useful rests solely on the degree to which the point can be reliably associated with a group or time period on the basis of excavated, contextually secure materials.

The suggestion that projectile point types are subjective is absolutely correct; all attempts at lithic categorization are subjective. Researchers have recently recognized that debitage types are not easily replicated or necessarily logically bounded

(Shott 1994). Degree of thermal alteration of chert has always been difficult to define, and even assignment of chert to bedrock formations is not without difficulty (McElrath and Emerson 2000). Still, experienced regional practitioners who are accustomed to identifying the projectile point types that occur in their region will achieve and share a consistency rate of identification that matches the success rate that lithic use-wear analysts have demonstrated with blind testing (Odell and Odell-Vereecken 1980).

Whatever misgivings researchers may have had in the past concerning the concept of projectile point types, it is clear that the universality and heuristic value of types as cultural markers outweighs the shortcomings accruing to small pointed stones with few distinguishing comparative traits. Many contributors to this volume have endorsed hafted bifaces as ethnic or cultural markers to varying degrees (e.g., McElrath et al.; Ray et al.; Stafford and Cantin; Nolan and Fishel; cf. Ahler and Koldehoff; Butler; Purtill; and Wiant et al.). In fact, the projectile point has assumed a preeminent role in assigning time and cultural affiliation, to judge by the contributions. For example, in their summary of western Illinois Archaic prehistory, Nolan and Fishel (this volume) list 62 radiocarbon dates from 29 sites, but the database they draw from of sites with chronological parameters exceeds 4,000 locations (Dave Nolan, pers. comm. 2005), indicating that over 99 percent of the sites are given a temporal assignment on the basis of diagnostic projectile point type present.

Most researchers now recognize the falsity of the form-versus-function dichotomy that developed during the twentieth century and accept the two aspects as complementary sides of the same "biface" (Christenson 1986; Odell 1994, 1996; Shott 1997). The cultural-evolutionary paradigm that artificially postulates a trend of continually increasing efficiency precludes the independent study of point styles and forms since those who endorse that paradigm seek answers that are, to a large extent, predetermined by the model. We see the projectile point form as a very forgiving, functionally diverse, and variable tool that was documented in the ethnohistoric record as having served, at a minimum, as a piercing weapon for hunting and war, as a butchering and cutting tool, and as a scraping implement. Functionalist studies that impose modern standards of tool specificity onto the past establish false parameters by which to measure tool selection. Point shape was more likely dictated by hafting needs and cultural preferences than by standards of physics and functionality. We further argue that only by adopting a theoretical stance that allows for the stereoscopic perspective necessary to integrate form and function will archaeologists contribute to a meaningful, three-dimensional reconstruction of the history of Archaic societies. The basic documentation of the growth, spread, and interaction of Archaic social groups in a culture-historical framework (homology) is the fundamental and necessary precondition for any contextually meaningful discussion of the role of environment and technology (analogy) among the apparently diverse trajectories undertaken by those societies.

The incomplete and sometimes contradictory nature of the evidence surrounding formal stone tool uses and associated weapon systems precludes data-based conclusions that lead to a grand narrative theme. The narrative themes that have been employed in the literature were in place prior to the collection of the data that are marshaled to dispute the issues. So, for example, the argument that the bow and arrow system is technologically superior to and, therefore, replaced the atlatl and dart as a preferred weapon system exists in the absence of conclusive data from the prehistoric record; instead, the evidence cited in support of the argument is selected on the basis of its conformity to the paradigm. We believe that most researchers quickly overlook this in the heat of debate. Even more problematic are the subtle, unexpressed biases inherent in the Western outlook. In particular, we argue that the concepts or, more accurately, the assumptions of the inevitability of technological progress and innovation and the accepted importance of "newer, better" devices are so ingrained in the Western world view that they have become the accepted scientific explanation for whatever archaeological phenomenon is thought to require illumination.

Earth, Wind, Fire, and Water and the Archaic Landscape

The study of climate change and culture-climate relationships has been an integral part of Holocene research for at least a century and was especially emphasized in the New Archaeology. Climates change because of natural forcing mechanisms such as variations in solar output, increases in carbon dioxide and methane gases, volcanic aerosols, and rapid deglaciation, which creates changes in oceanic water temperatures (Webb et al. 2004). The relationship between climate change and fluvial response is unpredictable and variable (Knox 1985; Van Nest 1997). Understanding the episodic nature of rainfall, erosion, and flooding, especially in regard to human habitation in river valleys, is, however, an important aspect of Archaic research as is documenting the relationship between landscape evolution and climatic change at the local level during the Holocene. In fact, large-magnitude flooding in river valleys likely had more direct impact on landscape modification and human environments than broader regional changes in climate (e.g., Kidder 2006; Kidder and Sassaman, this volume).

Biotic communities, which form the sources for human subsistence, are directly shaped by the inherent characteristics of prevailing air masses, wind patterns, and resulting weather conditions. Evidence of regional climate change based on reconstructions of vegetation patterns comes largely from pollen cores (King 1981; Webb et al. 2004; Wright 1968). In the Midcontinent, the advance and contraction of the Prairie Peninsula has been a major area of research (Transeau 1935). Early characterizations of this movement (King 1981; Wright 1968) were based primarily on pollen sequences derived from the northern periphery of the prairie. However, recent research has broadened perspectives through additional sequences from virtually all of the states bordering the Prairie Peninsula (cf. Styles and McMillan, this volume). The scenario recorded by pollen has been corroborated by additional data sets, including macrofossil remains (Baker et al. 1992), and by stable isotope analysis of speleothem calcite from cave sites (Denniston et al. 1999; Dorale et al. 1992). Faunal (Styles and McMillan, this volume) and floral (Simon, this volume) data from cultural contexts have also provided information on species availability useful for local environmental reconstruction. The emerging picture of Holocene climate change in the Midwest is assuming a much sharper focus, and we refer the reader to the excellent summary of this data by Styles and McMillan (this volume).

Despite the considerable strides being made, local environmental conditions usually still must be extrapolated from regional data. For example, the Illinois River valley, which has generated climate and culture-change models, has not been sampled by pollen cores (Van Nest 1997). As a result, there is little direct evidence for vegetation or climate change in this area during the Archaic. Botanical evidence from the Koster site is derived from carbonized wood fragments, and it is through these remains that researchers have argued for minimal direct climatic effect on floral communities in this locality during the Hypsithermal. The general absence of pollen data in the southern portion of the Midwest is striking, leading researchers to rely more heavily on faunal remains to reconstruct ancient environments for specific locales (Klippel 1971; McMillan and Klippel 1981; Styles and McMillan, this volume). Lower Illinois River valley geomorphologists have also often utilized landscape deposition and alluviation rates to model landform changes and, by extension, changes in vegetation and climate (Hajic 1990). The data from which researchers reconstruct climate and vegetation during the Holocene are, at best, indicators of broad regional patterns. Debates continue about the specific effects of climate change on vegetation in many localities because of the uneven nature of the data. Geomorphic data are usually modeled on such an expansive scale that they are of limited use in understanding and interpreting local conditions that would have had significant impacts on human populations. It is apparent that when this very incomplete environmental record is considered in conjunction with the very limited archaeological evidence, researchers need to proceed with some caution when proposing human-climate relationships in the Midwest.

Rather than attempt a comprehensive review of the posited climatic shifts that potentially impacted midcontinental Archaic populations, we highlight several aspects of the climate-landscape connection that not only may have affected the life histories of prehistoric native groups but also may have altered or structured the appearance of the archaeological record. There has been a trend in recent years, largely in response to the perceived trend toward environmental determinism, to discount the environment as a relevant factor influencing the historical trajectories of human groups. While it is true that some researchers have accorded the environment unwarranted preeminence and treated it as a prime mover in shaping human behavior, there is little doubt it is a relevant factor in human decision making.

A distinction must be drawn, however, between long-term meteorological shifts that operated over millennia (e.g., the Hypsithermal) versus short-term calamitous events (flooding, volcanoes, earthquakes, mudslides, natural dam breaches, tsunamis, regional droughts, etc.). For the most part, longer-term climatic shifts had little perceptible year-to-year impact on the lifestyles of groups who occupied and exploited the environmental niches that were gradually impacted. Life-threatening catastrophic events involving days, months, several years, or decades, however, would have focused the attention of indigenous populations in ways that were direct and immediate, perhaps instilling patterns in the corporate memory that lasted for generations. It is important to note that both of these categories of events affected the ultimate disposition of the archaeological record, but only the latter impacted the real-life histories of native groups at the individual or transgenerational level.

Researchers also need to be cognizant that in many cases human practices in conjunction with specific environmental settings become key factors in long-term landscape modification. Perhaps the most profound impact on the landscape initiated by nonindustrial human practice is through the use of fire. The maintenance of prairie-forest ecotonal zones through the use of fire has been proposed in the past (Abrams 1992; Grimm 1984; Guyette and Cutter 1991; Nelson et al. 2004; Sauer 1950; Van Nest 1997). Palynologists generally view the effect of fire on the landscape as the result of natural causes; from their standpoint, fire was not utilized by Native Americans until after they became slash-and-burn corn agriculturalists (McAndrews 1988). However, the ethnographic record in North America indicates that the use of fire was not restricted to agriculturalists (Barrett and Arno 1982; Sauer 1950; Van Nest 1997:352; Wright 1973), and recent research has largely tipped the scale in favor of human burning practices having characterized the earliest periods of occupation in the Midcontinent (Styles and McMillan, this volume).

There is little doubt that the Hypsithermal episode initiated a drying effect resulting in the expansion of the Prairie Peninsula; at the same time, however, the drying impact favored xeric forest expansion at the expense of mesic forested areas and would have made midwestern woodlands even more susceptible to impact by anthropogenic burning. The prevailing westerly winds and the general lack of relief over much of the Midwest ensured the rapid spread of fires from west to east. Not only did human intervention hasten prairie expansion but it also prolonged the episode of expansion and slowed what would have been the natural reversal of this process when a wetter climatic regime returned. More important, however, was the net effect on resources of economic value to human groups. As Styles and McMillan (this volume) point out, the expansion of the Prairie Peninsula opened up and expanded the woodland-prairie interface, making it a more suitable habitat for animals (rabbit, squirrel, deer, turkey, etc.) that were of interest to humans. So, not only were the quantity and variety of floodplain resources improved as a result of climatic change associated with the Hypsithermal, but upland resources surrounding the advancing prairie also were enriched. We believe that the growth and economic enhancement of a large area of the prairie-woodland ecotone during mid-Holocene times have been ignored by those suggesting a net deterioration of the resources of the greater Prairie Peninsula. While some areas would, no doubt, have become economically less productive (e.g., tallgrass prairie), other areas would have been substantially enhanced. Importantly, this would have unfolded at such a "glacial" pace that it would not have been perceptible to indigenous populations (Simon, this volume); it would have had little impact on the real-life histories of individual native groups.

Nevertheless, such a time-transgressive phenomenon would have contributed to the ultimate shape of the archaeological record. For example, if Early Archaic groups regularly hunted animals that preferred the open savannas associated with timber-grass ecotones, their collective multigenerational campsites and hunting losses would have accumulated in the archaeological record in such a way as to mimic the movement of the forest edge as it retreated (e.g., Conrad 1981). Moreover, the advance and retreat of the prairie edge would have triggered several landscape-altering events that would, in turn, have reconfigured the archaeological record. The episodic erosion and infilling of stream valleys routinely erases or buries traces of human occupation, and to the extent that such phenomena are temporally restricted at the regional level, the net effect is to erase evidence of specific periods of occupation or specialized components of settlement systems. Geomorphologists in Iowa (Bettis and Hajic 1995) have demonstrated the role that geomorphic and soil processes have played in the Midwest to disguise the nature of the archaeological record.

Archaeologists are just beginning to appreciate the importance of water-level history on the modern disposition of the Archaic portion of the archaeological record. Griffin (1967), in his classic summary of Eastern Woodlands prehistory, recognized that many coastal Middle Archaic sites are now underwater. Kidder and Sassaman (this volume) indicate that mid-Holocene rising sea levels drowned many coastal Early Archaic sites and occluded the entire chapter on subsistence and settlement for this period along the coast. The drowning of Archaic sites is not limited to the seacoast. If anything, because of their association with glacial events, the interior Great Lakes have experienced significant and complex water-level histories. Lovis (this volume) paints a vivid picture of alternating higher and lower lake levels for the Michigan-Huron and Superior basins (by comparison with today). Such reconstructions are complicated by the distinctive histories of each lake basin, one often experiencing high water levels at the same time that the other underwent low-water episodes. Lovis notes that at the inception of the Early Archaic, the Michigan-Huron basin was at its lowest and that all of the initial Early Archaic settlements that were within several miles of the coast are now submerged. This picture is further complicated by water levels that were, at times, higher than those prevailing today, resulting in "coastal" sites occurring at locations deep in the interior of Michigan, not to mention that the alternately submerged and exposed sites have undergone complex geomorphic histories often resulting in burial by deposition of sediments.

In addition to the drowning of many Early Archaic sites, the fluvial activities associated with river valleys have buried many sites from later periods beneath often-thick layers of sediment. Kidder and Sassaman cite the example of the Nolan site, a Middle Archaic mound complex on the modern floodplain of the Mississippi River that is buried by up to 5 m of alluvium. The only Early and Middle Archaic open-air sites in the American Bottom floodplain that have been investigated were buried by a meter or more of alluvium. In the lower Illinois River valley, Archaic deposits at the Koster site exceed 10 m in depth, and remains of all three subperiods have been buried by a combination of alluvial and colluvial processes (Brown and Vierra 1983). More recently, archaeologists have come to appreciate that many sites in upland settings may have been buried by a combination of wind-borne loess and other soil processes (Abbott 1987; Benn and Thompson, this volume; Bettis and Hajic 1995; Van Nest 1997), and Lurie et al. (this volume) identify a series of factors that have caused the burial of sites in the glaciated topography typifying northeastern Illinois.

It is important to distinguish between those gradual, time-transgressive climatic events that may have resulted in a gradual shift in the location of settlements through time (rising or falling sea levels) or the location where hunting activities took place (expanding prairie-woodland ecotones) from events with a certain urgency, like the unexpected onset of a period of catastrophic floods, that would have immediately affected the locations of villages and fishing stations, if not associated lifestyles. Even the latter events may not have affected the overall lifestyle of native groups unless the resources they depended on were seriously degraded by such catastrophes. An example of the latter involves the episode of increased flooding and overall cooling of the temperatures in eastern North America at the end of the Archaic (see Kidder 2006; Kidder and Sassaman, this volume). The degree to which such events disrupted established social networks and the extent to which they can, in turn, be deciphered from the existing archaeological record vary considerably; but the occurrence of such history-altering episodes cannot be ignored by cultural evolutionists who seek to explain every perceived social development as a step toward social integration and complexity. It is important to disentangle the *historical trajectories* of specific native groups from the background of *reconfigured archaeological records* that are the inevitable result of landscape evolution. This is the peculiar task of the archaeologist, who, by undertaking it, will shed light on issues of concern to social scientists, such as anthropology, economics, social interaction, technology, and the growth of complex societies.

Concluding Remarks

In this chapter, we have discussed three domains of Archaic research—chronology and taxonomy; projectile technology, function, and style; and climate and landscapes—and the many-layered issues embedded in their interpretation. These topics, in various forms and guises, have dictated the course of Archaic research for generations. The impressive growth of Archaic databases resulting from CRM research has only served to highlight the commanding role that these themes play in attempts to understand the nature of early indigenous societies in North America. The contributors to this volume, each to a differing degree, have been forced to confront these themes in the course of their research. Climate change, landscape evolution, and their subsistence implications, for instance, have been central to much Archaic research. For topical specialists, changes in climate form the organizational frame (Styles and McMillan), or at least the backdrop, for population studies (Milner et al.) or establishing the context of diet choices (Simon). For those examining culture change, as interpreted from deep stratigraphic sequences (Ahler and Koldehoff; Ray et al.; Stafford and Cantin; Wiant et al.), reconstructing environmental conditions is key to understanding not only the geomorphological determinants of site contexts but also the habitats encountered by the human occupants of sites and those occupants' lifeways. For those attempting regional summaries, the environment is of concern for understanding broad-scale populations movements, local and regional adaptations, and habitat preferences of successive populations.

Problems associated with dating artifacts, recognizing contemporary assemblages, and taxonomic organization of material remains have proven more difficult to resolve than one might have imagined, despite the advent of radiocarbon dating. In addition to the limitations of ^{14}C dating (which were magnified with the advent of calibration programs), the problems inherent in determining secure archaeological context and meaningful associations (especially in deep sites such as Modoc [Ahler and Koldehoff, this volume] and Koster [Wiant et al., this volume]) still plague archaeologists. These concerns are increased when one considers that most artifacts are dated only by association. Because of these constraints, archaeologists have made only erratic progress in transforming diagnostic artifact markers into reliable regional chronologies. These problems are exacerbated by the sad state of artifact typologies, especially hafted-biface categories—which are all too often indiscriminately correlated, dated, identified, and modified to the extent that they become unusable for defining cultural and chronological contexts. The use of artifact typologies to identify technological or cultural traditions is further hampered by researchers' inability to understand the relationship of points and people. As we discussed above at length, archaeology as a discipline has yet to come to terms with issues as seemingly straightforward as hafted-biface function, chronological associations, styles, delivery systems, and so forth. The lack of detailed chronologies and cultural associations is most critically felt by researchers reconstructing social landscape use on the basis of distribution patterns of surface-collected diagnostics (e.g., Nolan and Fishel, this volume).

All of the above factors and more play into the essential taxonomic divisions of the Archaic period promoted by various archaeologists. These divisions, in turn, recursively dominate the interpretation of what the Archaic "means." It has become increasingly popular to use perceived climatic and landscape changes to demark changes in Archaic cultures. Whether they are intended to or not, these climatic shifts all too often become the primary variables in creating cultural (i.e., material and subsistence) change. In a broad sense, such scenarios provide a reassuring picture of cultural adaptations marching through time in lockstep with climatic shifts. Yet, as is apparent from the evidence we have presented above (as well as from the chapters in this volume by Kidder and Sassaman; Lovis; and Styles and McMillan), while there have been significant, indeed, almost catastrophic landscape changes in some regions, many landscapes remained almost unchanged in terms of their habitability through the Archaic. There is no doubt that environmental conditions do create boundary conditions for human subsistence and habitation, but we contend, and many of the authors in this volume illustrate, these parameters are extremely broad and more often serve as enabling rather than delimiting factors.

The specialists invited to participate in this volume have had to cope with and, to some extent, overcome the problems just enumerated to impart as complete a picture as possible of Archaic developments in their specific regions or topics of interest. Despite the often-unstated misgivings researchers may have about their respective data sets, it seems midwestern archaeologists are collectively on the threshold of a breakthrough in the construction of a new baseline for Archaic research. We believe that the careful reader will discern in the following chapters a somewhat inchoate framework of the early history of native social developments and interaction in the Midcontinent. We also believe that this beginning will serve to encourage future researchers to break out of the neo-evolutionary straightjacket within which Archaic studies have all too often been confined.

References Cited

Abbott, Larry R.
1987 *Archaeological Investigations at the Kewanee Site (11-HY-126), Henry County, Illinois.* Research Reports 27. Resource Investigation Program, Department of Anthropology, University of Illinois, Urbana.

Abrams, Marc D.
1992 Fire and Development of Oak Forest. *Bioscience* 42:346–353.

Adams, Robert McCormick
1940 Diagnostic Flint Points. *American Antiquity* 6:72–75.

Ahler, Stanley A.
1970 *Projectile Point Form and Function at Rodgers Shelter, Missouri.* Research Series 8. Missouri Archaeological Society Columbia.

Amick, Daniel S.
1994 Technological Organization and the Structure of Inference in Lithic Analysis: An Examination of Folsom Hunting Behavior in the American Southwest. In *The Organization of North American Chipped Stone Tool Technologies*, edited by Philip J. Carr, pp. 9–34. Archaeological Series 7. International Monographs in Prehistory, Ann Arbor, Michigan.

Baker, Richard G., Louis J. Maher, Craig A. Chumbley, and Kent L. Van Zant
1992 Patterns of Holocene Environmental Change in Midwestern United States. *Quaternary Research* 37:379–389.

Baker, W. E., and A. V. Kidder
1937 A Spear Thrower from Oklahoma. *American Antiquity* 3:51–52.

Bareis, Charles J., and James W. Porter (editors)
1984 *American Bottom Archaeology: A Summary of the FAI-270 Project Contribution to the Culture History of the Mississippi River Valley.* University of Illinois Press, Urbana.

Barrett, Stephen W., and Stephen F. Arno
1982 Indian Fires as an Ecological Influence in the Northern Rockies. *Journal of Forestry* 80:647–651.

Bettis, E. Arthur, III, and Edwin Hajic
1995 *Landscape Development and the Location of Evidence of Archaic Cultures in the Upper Midwest.* Special Paper 297. Geological Society of America, Boulder, Colorado.

Binford, Lewis R.
1965 Archaeological Systematics and the Study of Culture Process. *American Antiquity* 31:203–210.
1980 Willow Smoke and Dogs' Tails: Hunter-Gatherer Settlement Systems and Archaeological Site Formation. *American Antiquity* 45:4–20.

Bordes, François
1972 *A Tale of Two Caves.* Harper and Row, New York.

Boszhardt, Robert F.
2002 Contracting Stemmed: What's the Point? *Midcontinental Journal of Archaeology* 27:35–67.

Bradbury, Andrew P.
1997 The Bow and Arrow in the Eastern Woodlands: Evidence for an Archaic Origin. *North American Archaeologist* 18:207–233.

Brown, James A.
1985 Long-Term Trends to Sedentism and the Emergence of Complexity in the American Midwest. In *Prehistoric Hunter-Gatherers: The Emergence of Cultural Complexity*, edited by T. Douglas Price and James A. Brown, pp. 201–231. Academic Press, New York.
1986 Food for Thought: Where Has Subsistence Analysis Gotten Us? In *Foraging, Collecting, and Harvesting: Archaic Period Subsistence and Settlement in the Eastern Woodlands*, edited by Sarah W. Neusius, pp. 315–327. Occasional Papers 6. Center for Archaeological Investigations, Southern Illinois University, Carbondale.

Brown, James A., and Robert K. Vierra
1983 What Happened in the Middle Archaic? Introduction to an Ecological Approach to Koster Site Archaeology. In *Archaic Hunters and Gatherers in the American Midwest*, edited by James L. Phillips and James A. Brown, pp. 165–196. Academic Press, New York.

Browne, Jim
1938 Antiquity of the Bow. *American Antiquity* 3:358–359.
1940 Projectile Points. *American Antiquity* 5:209–213.

Butler, B. Robert, and Douglas Osborne
1959 Archaeological Evidence for the Use of Atlatl Weights in the Northwest. *American Antiquity* 25:215–224.

Butzer, Karl W.
1977 *Geomorphology of the Lower Illinois Valley as a Spatial-Temporal Context for the Koster Archaic Site.* Reports of Investigations 34. Illinois State Museum, Springfield.
1978 Changing Holocene Environments at the Koster Site: A Geo-Archaeological Perspective. *American Antiquity* 43:408–413.

Byers, Douglas S.
1959 The Eastern Archaic: Some Problems and Hypotheses. *American Antiquity* 24:233–256.

Christenson, Andrew L.
1986 Projectile Point Size and Projectile Aerodynamics: An Exploratory Study. *Plains Anthropologist* 31:109–128.

Conrad, Lawrence A.
1981 *An Introduction to the Archaeology of West Central Illinois: A Preliminary Archaeological Survey of the Canton to Quincy Corridor for the Proposed FAP 407 Highway Project.* Reports of Investigations 2. Archaeological Research Laboratory, Western Illinois University, Macomb.

Cook, Thomas Genn
1976 *Koster: An Artifact Analysis of Two Archaic Phases in West-central Illinois.* Prehistoric Records 1, Koster Research Reports 3. Northwestern Archaeological Project, Evanston, Illinois.

Corliss, David W.
1980 Arrowpoint or Dart Point: An Uninteresting Answer to a Tiresome Question. *American Antiquity* 45:351–352.

Cushing, Frank Hamilton
1895 The Arrow. *American Anthropologist* 8:307–349.
1897 Exploration of Ancient Key-Dweller Remains on the Gulf Coast of Florida. *Proceedings of the American Philosophical Society* 35:329–432.

Denniston, Rhawn F., Luis A. Gonzalez, Holmes A. Semken Jr., Yemane Asmerom, Richard G. Baker, Heather Recelli-Snyder, Mark K. Reagan, and E. Arthur Bettis III
1999 Integrating Stalagmite, Vertebrate, and Pollen Sequences to Investigate Holocene Vegetation and Climate Change in the Southern Midwestern United States. *Quaternary Research* 52:381–387.

Dorale, Jeffrey A., Luis A. Gonzalez, Mark K. Reagan, David A. Pickett, Michael T. Murrell, and Richard G. Baker
1992 A High-Resolution Record of Holocene Climate Change in Speleothem Calcite from Cold Water Cave, Northeast Iowa. *Science* 259:1626–1630.

Ekholm, Gordon F.
1962 U-Shaped "Ornaments" Identified as Finger-Loops from Atlatls. *American Antiquity* 28:181–185.

Emerson, Thomas E., and Andrew C. Fortier
1986 Early Woodland Cultural Variation, Subsistence, and Settlement in the American Bottom. In *Early Woodland Archeology*, edited by Kenneth B. Farnsworth and Thomas E. Emerson, pp. 475–522. Kampsville Seminars in Archeology 2. Center for American Archeology, Kampsville, Illinois.

Emerson, Thomas E., and R. Barry Lewis (editors)
1991 *Cahokia and the Hinterlands: Middle Mississippian Cultures of the Midwest*. University of Illinois Press, Urbana.

Emerson, Thomas E., Dale L. McElrath, and Andrew C. Fortier (editors)
2000 *Late Woodland Societies: Tradition and Transformation across the Midcontinent*. University of Nebraska Press, Lincoln.

Fairbank, Frederick Royston
1864 Some Flint Arrow-Heads from Canada. *Journal of the Anthropological Society of London* 2:lxiv–lxv.

Farnsworth, Kenneth B.
1986 Black Sand Culture Origin and Distribution. In *Early Woodland Archeology*, edited by Kenneth B. Farnsworth and Thomas E. Emerson. Kampsville Seminars in Archeology 2. Center for American Archeology, Kampsville, Illinois.

Farnsworth, Kenneth B. and Thomas E. Emerson (editors)
1986 *Early Woodland Archeology*. Kampsville Seminars in Archeology 2. Center for American Archeology, Kampsville, Illinois.

Fenenga, Franklin
1953 The Weights of Chipped Stone Points: A Clue to Their Functions. *Southwestern Journal of Anthropology* 9:309–323.

Fenenga, Franklin, and Joe Ben Wheat
1940 An Atlatl from the Baylor Rock Shelter, Culbertson County, Texas. *American Antiquity* 3:221–223.

Finkelstein, J. Joe
1937 A Suggested Projectile Point Classification. *American Antiquity* 2:197–203.

Fortier, Andrew C.
2001 A Tradition of Discontinuity: American Bottom Early and Middle Woodland Culture History Reexamined. In *The Archaeology of Traditions: Agency and History Before and After Columbus*, edited by Timothy R. Pauketat, pp. 174–194. University Press of Florida, Gainesville.

Fortier, Andrew C., Thomas E. Emerson, and Dale L. McElrath
2006 Calibrating and Reassessing American Bottom Culture History. *Southeastern Archaeology*, in press.

Fowler, Melvin L.
1959a *Summary Report of Modoc Rock Shelter 1952, 1953, 1955, 1956*. Reports of Investigations 8. Illinois State Museum, Springfield.
1959b Modoc Rock Shelter: An Early Archaic Site in Southern Illinois. *American Antiquity* 24:257–270.

Fox, A. Lane
1875 On a Series of About Two Hundred Flint and Chert Arrowheads, Flakes, Thumbflints, and Borers, from the Rio Negro, Patagonia; with Some Remarks on the Stability of Form Observable in Stone Implements. *The Journal of the Anthropological Institute of Great Britain and Ireland* 4:311–323.

Goodyear, Albert C.
1982 The Chronological Position of the Dalton Horizon in the Southeastern United States. *American Antiquity* 47:382–395.

Goslin, Robert
1944 A Bone Atlatl Hook from Ohio. *American Antiquity* 10:204–205.

Griffin, James B.
1967 Eastern North American Archaeology: A Summary. *Science* 156:175–191.
1968 Observations on Illinois Prehistory in the Late Pleistocene and Early Recent Times. In *The Quaternary of Illinois: A Symposium in Observance of the Centennial of the University of Illinois*, edited by Robert E. Bergstrom, pp. 123–137. Special Publication 14. University of Illinois College of Agriculture, Urbana.

Grimm, Eric C.
1984 Fire and Other Factors Controlling the Big Woods Vegetation of Minnesota in the Mid-Nineteenth Century. *Ecological Monographs* 54:381–311.

Guernsey, Samuel James, and Alfred Vincent Kidder
1921 *Basketmaker Caves of Northeastern Arizona*. Papers of the Peabody Museum of American Archaeology and Ethnology 8(1). Harvard University, Cambridge, Massachusetts.

Guyette, Richard P., and Bruce E. Cutter
1991 Tree-Ring Analysis of Fire History of a Post Oak Savanna in the Missouri Ozarks. *Natural Areas Journal* 11:93–99.

Hajic, Edwin
1981 Geology and Paleopedology of the Koster Archeological Site, Greene County, Illinois. Master's thesis, Department of Geology, University of Illinois.
1990 *Koster Site Archeology I: Stratigraphy and Landscape Evolution*. Research Series 8. Center for American Archeology, Kampsville, Illinois.

Haldeman, S. S.
1879 On Unsymmetric Arrow-Heads and Allied Forms. *The American Naturalist* 13:292–294.

Hall, Robert L.
1977 An Anthropocentric Perspective for Eastern United States Prehistory. *American Antiquity* 42:499–518.

1980 An Interpretation of the Two-Climax Model of Illinois Prehistory. In *Early Native Americans*, edited by David Browman, pp. 401–462. Mouton, The Hague.

Hill, Malcom W.
1948 The Atlatl or Throwing Stick: A Recent Study of Atlatls in Use with Darts of Varying Sizes. *Tennessee Archaeologist* 4:37–44.

Holmes, W. H.
1891 Manufacture of Stone Arrow-Points. In *Arrows and Arrow-Makers*, by Otis T. Mason, W. H. Holmes, Thomas Wilson, Walter Hough, Weston Flint, W. J. Hoffman, and John G. Bourke. *American Anthropologist* 4:49–58.
1919 *Handbook of Aboriginal American Antiquities: Part I, Introductory, the Lithic Industries*. Bulletin 60. Bureau of American Ethnology, Smithsonian Institution, Washington, D.C.

Hough, Walter
1891 Arrow Feathering and Pointing. In *Arrows and Arrow-Makers*, by Otis T. Mason, W. H. Holmes, Thomas Wilson, Walter Hough, Weston Flint, W. J. Hoffman, and John G. Bourke. *American Anthropologist* 4:60–63.

Howard, Calvin D.
1974 The Atlatl: Function and Performance. *American Antiquity* 39:102–104.

Justice, Noel D.
1987 *Stone Age Spear and Arrow Points of the Midcontinental and Eastern United States*. Indiana University Press, Bloomington.

Kellar, James H.
1955 *The Atlatl in North America*. Prehistory Research Series 3(3). Indiana Historical Society, Indianapolis.

Kidder, Tristram R.
2006 Climate Change and the Archaic to Woodland Transition (3000–2500 cal B.P.) in the Mississippi River Basin. *American Antiquity* 71:195–231.

King, James E.
1981 Late Quaternary Vegetational History of Illinois. *Ecological Monographs* 51:43–62.

Klippel, Walter E.
1971 Prehistory and Environmental Change along the Southern Border of the Prairie Peninsula during the Archaic Period. Ph.D. dissertation, Department of Anthropology, University of Missouri.

Knecht, Heidi (editor)
1997 *Projectile Technology*. Plenum Press, New York.

Knox, James C.
1985 Responses of Floods to Holocene Climatic Change in the Upper Mississippi Valley. *Quaternary Research* 23:287–300.

Krieger, Alex D.
1964 New World Lithic Typology Project: Part II. *American Antiquity* 29:489–493.

Linder, Jean
1974 The Jean Rita Site: An Early Woodland Occupation in Monroe County, Illinois. *The Wisconsin Archeologist* 55:99–162.

Lyman, R. Lee, and Michael J. O'Brien
2004 A History of Normative Theory in Americanist Archaeology. *Journal of Archaeological Method and Theory* 11:369–396.

Lyman, R. Lee, Michael J. O'Brien, and Robert Dunnell
1997 *The Rise and Fall of Culture History*. Plenum Press, New York.

Mason, Otis T.
1885 Throwing-Sticks in the National Museum. *Report of the United States National Museum for 1884*, pt. 2, pp. 279–289. Government Printing Office, Washington, D.C.
1893 Throwing Sticks. *Science* 22:152–153.

Mason, Otis T., W. H. Holmes, Thomas Wilson, Walter Hough, Weston Flint, W. J. Hoffman, and John G. Bourke
1891 Arrows and Arrow-Makers. *American Anthropologist* 4:45–74.

Mau, Clayton
1963 Experiments with the Spear Thrower. *New York State Archaeological Association Bulletin* 29:1–13.

McAndrews, J. H.
1988 Human Disturbance of North American Forest and Grasslands: The Fossil Pollen Record. In *Vegetation History*, edited by Brian Huntley and Thompson Webb III, pp. 673–697. Kluwer Academic Publishers, Dordrecht, the Netherlands.

McElrath, Dale L., and Thomas E. Emerson
2000 Toward an "Intrinsic Characteristics" Approach to Chert Raw Material Classification: An American Bottom Example. *Midcontinental Journal of Archaeology* 25:215–244.

McElrath, Dale L., Thomas E. Emerson, and Andrew C. Fortier
2000 Social Evolution or Social Response? A Fresh Look at the "Good Grey Cultures" after Four Decades of Research in the Midwest. In *Late Woodland Societies: Tradition and Transformation across the Midcontinent*, edited by Thomas E. Emerson, Dale L. McElrath, and Andrew C. Fortier, pp. 3–36. University of Nebraska Press, Lincoln.

McElrath, Dale L., Thomas E. Emerson, Andrew C. Fortier, and James L. Phillips
1984 Late Archaic Period. In *American Bottom Archaeology: A Summary of the FAI-270 Project Contributions to the Culture History of the Mississippi River Valley*, edited by Charles J. Bareis and James W. Porter, pp. 34–58. University of Illinois, Urbana.

McMillan, Bruce R., and Walter E. Klippel
1981 Post-Glacial Environmental Change and Hunting-Gathering Societies of the Southern Prairie Peninsula. *Journal of Archaeological Science* 8:215–245.

Musil, Robert R.
1988 Functional Efficiency and Technological Change: A Hafting Tradition Model for Prehistoric North America. In *Early Human Occupation in Far Western North America: The Clovis-Archaic Interface*, edited by Judith A. Willig, C. Melvin Aikens, and John L. Fagan, pp. 373–387. Anthropological Papers 21. Nevada State Museum, Carson City.

Nance, J. D.
1971 Functional Interpretation from Microscopic Analysis. *American Antiquity* 36:361–366.

Nassaney, Michael S., and Kendra Pyle
1999 The Adoption of the Bow and Arrow in Eastern North America: A View from Central Arkansas. *American Antiquity* 64:243–263.

Nelson, David, Feng Sheng Hu, and Eric C. Grimm
2004 Dynamics of Middle-Holocene Climate, Vegetation, and Fire on the Northern Prairie Peninsula. *AMQUA 2004: American Quaternary Association Program and Abstracts of the 18th Biennial Meeting*. University of Kansas, Lawrence.
Neuman, Robert
1967 Atlatl Weights from Certain Sites on the Northern and Central Great Plains. *American Antiquity* 32:36–53.
Nuttall, Zelia
1891 The Atlatl or Spear-Thrower of the Ancient Mexicans. *Archaeological and Ethnological Papers of the Peabody Museum* 1(3):173–197. Harvard University, Cambridge, Massachusetts.
O'Brien, Michael J., and Robert E. Warren
1983 An Archaic Projectile Point Sequence from the Southern Prairie Peninsula: The Pigeon Roost Site. In *Archaic Hunters and Gatherers in the American Midwest*, edited by James L. Phillips and James A. Brown, pp. 71–98. Academic Press, New York.
O'Brien, Michael J., and W. Raymond Wood
1998 *The Prehistory of Missouri*. University of Missouri Press, Columbia.
Odell, George H.
1994 Prehistoric Hafting and Mobility in the North American Midcontinent: Examples from Illinois. *Journal of Anthropological Archaeology* 13:51–73.
1996 *Stone Tools and Mobility in the Illinois Valley: From Hunter-Gatherer Camps to Agricultural Villages*. Archaeological Series 10. International Monographs in Prehistory, Ann Arbor, Michigan.
Odell, George H., and Frieda Odell-Vereecken
1980 Verifying the Reliability of Lithic Use-Wear Assessments by "Blind Tests": The Low-Power Approach. *Journal of Field Archaeology* 7:87–120.
Palter, John L.
1976 A New Approach to the Significance of the "Weighted" Spear Thrower. *American Antiquity* 41:500–510.
Patterson, Leland W.
1994 Identification of Unifacial Arrow Points. *Journal of the Houston Archaeological Society* 108:19–24.
Peets, Orville H.
1960 Experiments in the Use of Atlatl Weights. *American Antiquity* 26:108–110.
Raymond, Anan
1986 Experiments in the Function and Performance of the Weighted Atlatl. *World Anthropology* 18:153–177.
Read, Charles H.
1892 An Account of a Collection of Ethnographical Specimens Formed during Vancouver's Voyage in the Pacific Ocean, 1790–1895. *The Journal of the Anthropological Institute of Great Britain and Ireland* 21:99–105.
Redding, B. B.
1879 How Our Ancestors in the Stone Age Made Their Implements. *The American Naturalist* 13:667–674.
Riddell, Francis A., and Donald F. McGeein
1969 Atlatl Spurs from California. *American Antiquity* 34:474–478.
Rouse, Irving
1960 The Classification of Artifacts in Archaeology. *American Antiquity* 25:313–323.
Sauer, Carl O.
1950 Grassland Climax, Fire and Man. *Journal of Range Management* 3:16–21.
Scully, Edward G.
1951 Some Central Mississippi Valley Projectile Point Types. Unpublished manuscript, Museum of Anthropology, University of Michigan, Ann Arbor.
Shott, Michael J.
1994 Size and Form in the Analysis of Flake Debris: Review and Recent Approaches. *Journal of Archaeological Method and Theory* 1:69–110.
1996 Innovation in Prehistory: A Case Study from the American Bottom. In *Stone Tools: Theoretical Insights into Human Prehistory*, edited by George H. Odell, pp. 279–309. Plenum Press, New York.
1997 Stones and Shafts Redux: The Metric Discrimination of Chipped-Stone Dart and Arrow Points. *American Antiquity* 62:86–101.
Smith, Arthur George
1953 Beveled or "Rotary" Points. *American Antiquity* 18:269–270.
Smith, Marian W.
1954 Attributes and the Discovery of Projectile Point Types: With Data from the Columbia-Fraser Region. *American Antiquity* 20:15–26.
Spaulding, Albert C.
1953 Statistical Techniques for the Discovery of Artifact Types. *American Antiquity* 18:305–313.
Thomas, David Hurst
1978 Arrowheads and Atlatl Darts: How the Stone Got the Shaft. *American Antiquity* 43:461–472.
Transeau, Edgar N.
1935 The Prairie Peninsula. *Ecology* 16:426–437.
Tschauner, Hartmut
1994 Archaeological Systematics and Cultural Evolution: Retrieving the Honour of Culture History. *Man* 29:77–93.
Van Nest, Julieanne
1997 Late Quaternary Geology, Archeology and Vegetation in West-Central Illinois: A Study of Geoarcheology. Ph.D. dissertation, Department of Geology, University of Iowa.
Vanderhook, Richard
1998 The Atlatl and Dart. Master's thesis, Department of Anthropology, University of Illinois.
Webb, Thompson, III, Bryan Shuman, and John W. Williams
2004 Climatically Forced Vegetation Dynamics in Eastern North America during the Late Quaternary Period. In *The Quaternary Period in the United States*, edited by A. R. Gillespie, S. C. Porter, and B. F. Atwater, pp. 459–478. Elsevier, Amsterdam.
Webb, William
1946 Indian Knoll. *Reports in Anthropology and Archaeology* 4(3, pt. 1):111–365. Department of Anthropology and Archaeology, University of Kentucky, Lexington.
Webb, William S., and William G. Haag
1939 The Chiggersville Shell Heap in Ohio County. *Reports in Anthropology and Archaeology*4:1–62. Department of Anthropology and Archaeology, University of Kentucky, Lexington.

1940 Cypress Creek Villages, Sites 11 and 12, McLean County, Kentucky. *Reports in Anthropology and Archaeology* 4:63–110. University of Kentucky, Department of Anthropology and Archaeology, Lexington.

Weyer, Edward M.

1964 New World Lithic Typology Project: Part I. *American Antiquity* 29:487–489.

Willoughby, Charles C.

1902 Prehistoric Hafted Flint Knives. *The American Naturalist* 36:1–6.

Wilson, Thomas

1891 Form of Ancient Arrow-Heads. In *Arrows and Arrow-Makers*, by Otis T. Mason, W. H. Holmes, Thomas Wilson, Walter Hough, Weston Flint, W. J. Hoffman, and John G. Bourke. *American Anthropologist* 4:58–60.

1899 Arrowpoints, Spearheads, and Knives of Prehistoric Times. In *Annual Report of the Smithsonian Institution for 1897*, pp. 811–988. Smithsonian Institution, Washington, D.C.

Winters, Howard D.

1961 The Archaic Period. In *Illinois Archaeology*, pp. 9–16. Bulletin 1. Illinois Archaeological Survey, Urbana.

Wright, Henry E., Jr.

1968 History of the Prairie Peninsula. In *The Quaternary of Illinois: A Symposium in Observance of the Centennial of the University of Illinois*, edited by Robert E. Bergstrom, pp. 129–134. Special Publication 14. University of Illinois College of Agriculture, Urbana.

1973 *Patterns of Indian Burning in California: Ecology and Ethnohistory*. Ballena Press, Ramona, California.

2

The Eastern Woodlands Archaic and the Tyranny of Theory

Thomas E. Emerson and Dale L. McElrath

The Archaic of ... the Great Lakes area represents a rather monotonous cultural pattern through time. Current data do not permit close-knit arguments as to culture change and specific activities dictated by local environmental circumstances or cultural predilections. While, obviously, it would be nice to establish some empathetic relationship with actual people involved in the Archaic, this is impossible, because dead men tell no tales. What we are left with is an essentially boring situation in which, as far as I can tell, only those devoted to the investigation of minutiae could be interested.

—Olaf Prufer

This is an exciting time to be studying Archaic societies in eastern North America. A wealth of new data provides evidence that this was a time of unprecedented social, political, economic, and technological variability.

—Tristram R. Kidder and Kenneth E. Sassaman

Theories, and those who craft them, prosper best with ambiguous and limited data sets.

—Thomas E. Emerson

Introduction

The first of these three epigraphs concerning Archaic studies embodies a common perspective in the North American Midcontinent. Indeed, archaeologists, as well as the public, in general, have seldom shown the passion for the lengthy Archaic period that they demonstrate for either the Paleoindian period or the later ceramic-bearing periods. To paraphrase the cliché about the Late Woodland period, one might characterize the Archaic period as incorporating the "other good gray cultures" of the Eastern Woodlands. This disinterest seems counterintuitive since the Archaic period has yielded prolific assemblages, spectacular artifacts, and, as any knowledgeable collector can attest, the most commonly recovered artifacts on the landscape. The third epigraph focuses on one of the major problems facing Archaic-period studies—the domination of theorizing and the paucity of data.

Is it the ubiquity of Archaic material remains that contributes to the period's neglect, or is a more fundamental scholarly bias at play? To be sure, both archaeologists and the public often succumb to the hyperbole that can be attached to artifacts, styles, and sites touted as the "earliest," "largest," "most complex," "most sophisticated," and so on, superlatives that are seldom applied to Archaic sites or artifacts. In fact, Prufer suggests that, "if the human element involved in the study of real, live people is removed, the material remains of such 'Archaic-style' folk as the Australian aborigines or the Bushmen of the Kalahari Desert would be just as uninteresting as the study of the Archaic of northeastern Ohio" (2001:195). Indeed, we believe that it is this conception of the Archaic peoples of the Eastern Woodlands as the social equivalents of modern hunter-gatherers that has contributed to declining interest in the Archaic period in the Midcontinent. If so, this is, indeed, ironic because it was scholars' confidence that North American Archaic societies constituted a laboratory for hunter-gatherer studies that put those societies in the spotlight several decades ago.

From the earliest times in North American archaeology, interest focused on large sites with obvious or elaborately constructed earthworks or mound centers and spectacular artifacts. In areas where these archaeological sites had not been destroyed by urban, industrial, or agricultural development, they were investigated during the Depression-era Works Progress Administration (WPA) program. In the Midsouth, WPA excavations explored spectacular Archaic sites such as the Green River shell middens (e.g., Webb 1946; see also Jefferies, this volume; Milner et al., this volume). During the 1970s and 1980s, when the foundation was laid for the long-term public financial support of what had been largely "salvage" archaeology up to that time, a fundamental shift occurred in archaeologists' understanding of what constituted "significant" information from prehistoric sites. The emphasis placed on the study of hunter-gatherers and their settlement patterns correlated with a new cultural resource management (CRM) appreciation of the small site as an essential element of the archaeological record. In the name of cultural ecology and processualism, New Archaeologists scoured the landscape for the spoor of hunter-gatherers no less diligently than the latter had searched for evidence of game movement, good locations for plant gathering, or productive fishing stations. The New Archaeologists were armed with more advanced weapons than their WPA predecessors, among which were an absolute dating method, a soil flotation technique, and a mandate to scientifically sample the landscape. Carbon dating could relate sites of similar age across the landscape, flotation could provide evidence for reconstructing the relative importance of plant and animal foods in the diet, and the sampled landscape could reveal whole settlement patterns and systems—or so researchers thought.

Like most scholarly movements (not to be confused with fads), the processualism of the 1970s and 1980s has been followed by a counterreformation, and archaeological interest has shifted away from the sterile scientism that typified some processualist thought. Contributors to this volume span the spectrum of archaeological theory, some eschewing processualism while others continue to embrace it. However, we suggest the Archaic record, as currently known, is largely resistant to many processualist modes of analysis. All too often Archaic societies have been abandoned to the neo-evolutionists, who have adopted them as the necessary basic building blocks in ancient North Americans' advance to social complexity. Thus, to rephrase the situation and to address Prufer's concerns, we believe that, after cultural ecologists breathed life into the Archaic, it was left conceptually adrift until it was embraced by neo-evolutionists and transmogrified into a taxon to do the heavy lifting for the complex societies that necessarily followed. In this overview, we endeavor to historicize the Archaic so that it can fulfill the panegyric offered by Kidder and Sassaman and assume its rightful place in the history of midcontinental North America's native peoples.

Perhaps because of the breadth and depth of Archaic occupation in the Midcontinent, the presentation of data has often been implicitly centered on a neo-evolutionary model of cultural change that has served to frame the research and shape the results. The outcome of our research in Illinois has caused us to question the validity of this model as well as others for later periods, and our colleagues' presentations in this volume have reinforced our suspicions about the tyrannical nature of the neo-evolutionary paradigm. Because models have been so inextricably woven into discussions of the Archaic, we think it useful to untangle and examine their individual threads prior to suggesting what the data gathered thus far might indicate about the early history of native groups in the midcontinental United States.

Defining the Archaic

Since its formal conception and introduction by William Ritchie (1932a, 1932b, 1936, 1944:235–309) in the 1930s, the *Archaic pattern* has presented a persistent and apparently irresolvable conundrum to North America's Eastern Woodland archaeologists. Early reactions reveal a less than enthusiastic reception to the concept by key figures in regional archaeology, such as William S. Webb (Webb and Haag 1939, 1940), William Haag (1942:214), James Griffin (1946:42), William Sears (1948), and Richard MacNeish (1948:243). However, histories of early archaeological practice (Byers 1959b; Stoltman 1992) illustrate that, by the late 1940s and early 1950s, the identification of "Archaic" components had become widespread in the professional literature. It was clear that the utility of the term in giving conceptual form and structure to prepottery or nonpottery assemblages overcame any perceived typological and taxonomic weaknesses.

Why is it that the Woodland and Mississippian patterns (Deuel 1935; McKern 1939) quickly established themselves as bulwarks of Eastern Woodland taxonomy while the intrinsic validity of the Archaic pattern continues to be debated nearly three-quarters of a century after its introduction? The answer to that question may lie in its retention of those inherent weaknesses that were apparent to early critics. The failure to address those flaws still haunts current archaeological conceptions of the Archaic. With this in mind, it is useful to revisit the original definitions and usage of the Archaic pattern and the contemporaneous critiques of early commentators.

In defining an Archaic pattern, William Ritchie codified and expanded on what earlier excavators had already begun to recognize in the field—that assemblages of stone and bone tools were being recovered that were apparently preceramic. Such preceramic assemblages were tentatively assigned to a period preceding the newly recognized Woodland pattern. Without the advantage of radiocarbon dating or sealed stratigraphic sequences, early twentieth-century investigators could do little more than guess at the real age of such materials. What these early assemblages seemed to share, however, was a *lack* of ceramics and an *absence* of agricultural products (Ritchie 1932a). Such assemblages were, therefore, defined as "Archaic" more by default than by design. Increasingly, as archaeologists excavated and analyzed preceramic assemblages, they concluded that the remains represented traces of semisedentary peoples who lived by hunting, fishing, gathering, and collecting (e.g., Webb and DeJarnette 1942). By the time Sears negatively commented on the validity of the Archaic pattern, he was able to summarize it in terms that generally still characterize it today—"a complex which is non-ceramic, non-horticultural, old, and has a hunter-fisher-collector culture pattern" (1948:123).

Of the early criticisms expressed by opponents of the Archaic pattern, some have stood the test of time, while others have faded with additional research. For example, Griffin (1946:42–43) declined to use the term *Archaic* because he believed the Lamoka type assemblages represented a culture that was insufficiently primitive and too late chronologically to be "archaic." It seems evident from his discussion that he equated the term *archaic* with the pre-Neolithic period of Eurasia. Perhaps this is why he ultimately subsumed the known Archaic components into his Paleoindian cultures (Griffin 1946:42–43, Figure 3). Sears (1948:123) objected on the same grounds to the use of *Archaic* for cultures that he saw as too recent to deserve that appellation (assumed to be about A.D. 500 at the time he wrote). Obviously, in some sense these writers conceptualized "archaic" very much in the term's dictionary definition as "out of use, obsolete, having characteristics of an earlier more primitive time." The advent of radiocarbon dating eliminated the chronological objection and revealed the long span of preceramic occupation of the eastern United States.

More telling has been the objection that the Archaic pattern was defined in the negative, that is, by the absence of certain cultural traits (e.g., Sears 1948:123–124). At a practical level, these negative traits could be so broadly applied as to be meaningless for recognizing true Archaic assemblages. Scholars were cognizant that functional variation among sites could account for the absence of traits such as pottery or evidence of horticulture. They raised the concern that the remains of, for example, non-ceramic-using or highly mobile groups might be miscategorized as Archaic when they actually were associated with one of the later cultural patterns. Sears (1948:123–124) further stressed that, in the Midwest Taxonomic System classification, except for the presence of pottery, the Archaic and Woodland patterns were indistinguishable, suggesting the Archaic classification had questionable utility and, in fact, might be deceptive. The problem of classification was exacerbated by the tendency of researchers in the West and Southeast to appropriate the Archaic terminology and apply it to inappropriate assemblages (Byers 1959b:231–232). Running through these early discussions was an undertone questioning the actual taxonomic status of the Archaic—was it a time framework, a technological or evolutionary stage, or something altogether different? By 1955, research on Archaic-pattern assemblages seemed to be in such a state of confusion that there was an attempt to bring order to the issue by holding the first Archaic Conference in conjunction with the Society for American Archaeology (SAA) meeting in Bloomington, Indiana. From this conference emerged the initial attempt at a synthesis of the Archaic of North America (Baerreis 1959; Byers 1959a, 1959b; Fowler 1959; Kelley 1959; Meighan 1959).

For midcontinental archaeologists, one of the most important outcomes of the 1955 conference was the publication of Melvin Fowler's (1959) Modoc Rock Shelter sequence and his initial discussion of the Archaic stage in this region. Expanding on Willey and Phillips's (1955:740–747) technological definition, Fowler (1959:257) conceived of an Archaic "stage" that involved progressive technological development, adaptation to and utilization of local fauna and flora, subsistence practices based on collecting, and a community patterning best described as "Restricted Wandering" or even "Central-Based Wandering" settlement. The Modoc excavations also added an important dimension of great time depth to the regional Archaic stage through the demonstrable presence of deeply stratified deposits and very early radiocarbon dates. Modoc Rock Shelter appeared to support many of the early assumptions about Archaic lifestyles and continues, in many respects for some scholars, to represent the quintessential definition of the Archaic in the Midcontinent (e.g., Ahler and Koldehoff, this volume).

In the last half-century, the Archaic has become a well-worn and integral part of the Eastern Woodlands cultural chronology—although many of the criticisms of early detractors remain unresolved. Some of the early questions have become even more pertinent now that archaeologists recognize that horticulture and ceramics occurred within some Archaic cultures and that some societies were socially and politically complex and perhaps even sedentary. While the cultural and economic criteria for defining Archaic societies have become less clear, the parameter of time has been clarified and the long span validated by the multiple absolute dating technologies that are now widely available.

James Stoltman (e.g., 1978, 1992) has evaluated the continuing ambiguity of the Archaic concept as a taxonomic unit in his review of Eastern Woodland Archaic archaeological literature. His discussion underscores the generally casual attitude of midcontinental archaeologists toward taxonomic issues. He notes that, while the majority of practitioners appear to conceive of the Archaic as a fixed *period* of time, following James Griffin's (1952, 1967) early presentation of the concept, in reality its specific chronological boundaries shift from geographical region to region (e.g., see the various chapters in this volume). Given that shifting chronological boundaries are incompatible with the taxonomic definition of a period, Stoltman concludes that, despite what many researchers say, "*in practice*, the Archaic concept functions as a stage, not a period" (1992:109). Adding to the taxonomic uncertainty, in the late 1960s Gordon Willey (1966:247ff.) introduced the concept of a geographically circumscribed Eastern Woodlands Archaic *tradition* with implied historical and cultural group continuity. In contradistinction to Willey's tradition, it is not uncommon in the Eastern Woodlands to find references to a widespread Archaic *horizon*, both within and across regions. In this volume, all of these terms (*period, stage, tradition*, and *horizon*) appear in discussions of the regional Archaic cultures in the Midcontinent.

Whatever shape the concept of the Archaic assumes, whether a specific chronological period, a technological or social stage of development, a subsistence economy, or a long-term cultural-historical pattern of evolutionary development, archaeologists must be able to define its unique characteristics if it is to be a useful tool for understanding the past, a point Sears made (1948) nearly 60 years ago. It is this ability to define "difference" that was originally called into question by Sears and that still resonates today—perhaps even more strongly than it did in the early twentieth century.

In his assessment of the Archaic tradition as a meaningful formal taxon in the Eastern Woodlands, Stoltman (1992:111–114) characterizes its distinctive properties as consisting of the appearance of stemmed and notched spear points, generalized hunting and gathering subsistence practices, and the lack of ceramic containers. He contends that Archaic-tradition stone technology is recognizably distinct from that of Paleoindian times and that a distinctive shift took place in subsistence practices from the early big-game hunters to the later generalized Archaic foragers. While recognizing the presence of horticulture in Late Archaic times, he accepts Willey and Phillips's (1958:108) argument that plant cultivation only became a critical factor in the cultural-neo-evolutionary sequence when populations became dependent on its produce.

This effectively removes horticulture (or the lack thereof) as a defining Archaic criterion. The absence of pottery, which was a crucial variable in the original definition, seems to have become less important with the documented occurrence of stone vessels and early-fiber tempered wares in Late Archaic societies. Such a shift seems to us to seriously impinge on the utility of a definition that depended on the Archaic being "prepottery."

Stoltman concludes by offering a new conception of the Archaic that he believes represents a general consensus of current archaeological practitioners. He defines the Eastern Woodland Archaic as including those "cultures with Foraging or Cultivating ecosystem types (see Stoltman and Baerreis 1983) whose technological inventories are characterized by the presence of post-Paleoindian projectile point styles and the absence of true Woodland pottery" (Stoltman 1992:114). Little remains of Ritchie's *Archaic pattern* in this modern retelling.

We contend that, even 70-plus years after the *Archaic pattern* first emerged as a formal taxon in Eastern Woodlands prehistory, its definition continues to elude researchers. In fact, one could easily say that, in terms of definitional clarity, the Archaic has regressed rather than progressed. In the 1930s, archaeologists "knew" that Archaic societies did not make pottery, did not practice horticulture, and were hunting and gathering folk and that they preceded the Woodland pattern and were of some antiquity. Intervening years of research have demonstrated that, in contradistinction to earlier beliefs, the transition between big-game-hunting and Archaic foraging lifestyles is less clear than once thought. Some "archaic" groups did make and use pottery, did practice horticulture, and were likely socially and politically complex, even to the extent of engaging in monumental construction. Only the relative age of Archaic societies has been preserved intact (although greatly modified in absolute time and span).

One implicit conceptualization that has been transmitted through time virtually unaffected by the vagaries of research and theorizing is that the Archaic pattern is a reflection of a primitive stage in a cultural-neo-evolutionary sequence. As noted above, the common meaning of the *archaic* label itself was inherent in the archaeological definition—to be archaic was to be technologically and socially primitive. In fact, some of the objections to the term by Griffin and Sears related to the fact that the then-representative assemblages (e.g., Late Archaic Lamoka) were not "archaic" or "primitive" enough to fit into their evolutionary schema. More than anything else, the Archaic concept reflects the persistence of a neo-evolutionary stage framework that underlies and is tightly interwoven with much of eastern North American archaeology. This genre of thinking typically correlates attributes such as progressive technological improvements and subsistence efficiency with increasing social, economic, and political complexity, beginning with the earliest and simplest big-game hunters and ending with the late prehistoric chiefdoms or, in some scenarios, historic-period native confederacies (Muller 1997). Despite the profession's long inability to satisfactorily "define" the Archaic, it persists as a taxon because it fills a necessary developmental niche in the neo-evolutionary perspective of North American native societies. One might conclude that the Archaic theme is sustained more by theory than by data—a perspective that is supported by many of the chapters in this volume, which repeatedly demonstrate just how sparse the factual base is for many current theoretical constructions.

Archaic Theory and Truisms

To state, as we have above, that the Archaic taxon is definitionally ambiguous is not to say that no conceptual consensus exists among researchers as to what is appropriately "archaic." We believe that many points of consensus, so-called Archaic truisms, may be of doubtful validity or, at the very least, should be seriously questioned rather than simply accepted. The challenge to Archaic-period researchers is to recognize and confront unproven assumptions. Most archaeologists would probably not characterize Archaic-period research as being dominated by theoreticians. It is more likely to be thought of as the exclusive realm of paleoecologists, geomorphologists, archaeozoologists, archaeobotanists, lithic specialists, and their like. It is usually associated with "real science" and seen as a fieldwork endeavor enmeshed in site-formation processes and geomorphological deep trenches with complex stratigraphies interpreted against a backdrop of geoarchaeological and paleoclimatological issues.

Yet we contend that Archaic-period research involves some of the most theory-dependent archaeology being practiced in North America. The reasons seem clear to us. Because of preservation difficulties, sheer age, and the often-limited material signature of the small societies involved, Archaic assemblages tend to be restricted in diversity and are often contextually ambiguous. Theories, and those who craft them, prosper best with ambiguous and limited data sets. Large data sets from many sites with good cultural and chronological context limit the creative abilities and flexibility of theorists. The relative scarcity of data-rich assemblages makes the Archaic period a prime location for theoretical endeavors. Nowhere is this better or more completely expressed than in such issues as sedentism, mobility, cultural evolution, technological progressivism, adaptationism, environmental determinism, and the like. Not only are Archaic studies dominated by theory but that theory is also restricted almost entirely to a single paradigm—adaptation (i.e., Emerson and McElrath 2001).

Modern archaeological field investigations seem overburdened with theoretical baggage and often collect relatively few substantive data. We propose that some of the blame for this must rest squarely on the predominance in such research of behaviorist assumptions combined with an overriding neo-evolutionary paradigm. A behaviorist approach diminishes the importance of variation, categorizing it as idiosyncratic, and assumes that virtually any "sample" is representative of the behavior of the studied group as a whole. These typically inadequate samples can only confirm what is already known—they are seldom of sufficient vigor to actually challenge models. Such approaches are an unfortunate legacy of the New Archaeology, in which methodology took precedence over data. When this research approach is incorporated into a neo-evolutionary paradigm with its adaptationist assumptions about the relationship among key cultural variables, it is difficult for the research results to ever be at variance with the model. Such research agendas are more about filling in the details than about challenging the paradigm.

Theorizing the Archaic

From its earliest conception, the Archaic pattern was believed to represent the material vestiges of societies with hunter-gatherer lifestyles. Such people were presumed to have lived in small groups and have possessed a technologically unpretentious material culture. For archaeologists, the question was one of recognizing such prehistoric communities from the nominal material deposits. Beardsley et al. (1956) first systematically explored the connection between social, political, and economic variables and what they called "community mobility and patterning" in a seminal theoretical initiative sponsored by the SAA. Defining a "community" essentially as a group of people representing an "economically self-sufficient corporate unit" that is "politically independent and self-conscious," Beardsley and his colleagues (1956:133) were convinced that community mobility should be differentially reflected in archaeological residues. They believed a comprehensive examination of these residues would reveal the distinctive *community pattern* of a society and provide insights into its (to them) clearly interrelated economic, sociopolitical, and religious features. A series of these community patterns was identified that reflected, in a stage-like progression, an increase in economic, social, and political complexity.

On the bottom rung of the community-pattern stages envisioned by the SAA symposium participants (Beardsley et al. 1956) were Free Wandering folk hypothesized to have followed a lifestyle linked to the hunting of large mammals and foraging for locally abundant resources. Earlier Paleoindian societies were thought to have been Free Wandering. Lifestyles in the newly recognized Archaic pattern were generally thought to resemble a pattern either of Restricted Wandering or Central-Based Wandering. Archaeologists postulated that with the advent of the Restricted Wandering pattern, groups settled into distinct and perhaps defended territories. They might have followed a seasonal round or a less regimented schedule depending on the distribution and form of the exploited resources. This adaptation was usually attributed to later Paleoindian and the earliest Archaic groups. In the subsequent stage of Central-Based Wandering, people began to spend at least part of the year at a central settlement to which they may or may not have annually returned. The realization of such a pattern required storable wild foods, a locally abundant food source such as fish, and incipient agriculture. The succeeding Semi-Permanent Sedentary community pattern, in which participants lived in a sedentary village that moved in its entirety every several years, represented the advent of fully agricultural economies (although with some exceptions; see below).

For the first several decades after their conception, Archaic-pattern societies were primarily recognized as being *nonceramic* and *nonagricultural*; however, these societies were not necessarily characterized as being either socially or technologically simple. Beardsley et al. (1956) recognized such groups as the Australian Aborigines, the Kalahari Bushmen, the subarctic Athabascans, and the Shoshone as examples of Restricted Wanderers. Other groups such as the northern and central California natives, the Interior Salish, and many Siberian maritime groups were categorized as Central-Based Wanderers. Importantly, the researchers further acknowledged (Beardsley et al. 1956:150–151) that some hunter-gatherer societies with access to a rich and steady resource base (such as the classic exceptions to nearly every rule, the Northwest Coast societies) might have possessed a Semi-Permanent Sedentary community pattern. From their published discussions, it is apparent that Beardsley and his colleagues recognized that hunter-gatherer societies possessed diverse subsistence economies, participated in a wide range of social and political systems, and practiced diverse forms of community mobility.

Modern Hunter and Gatherer Analogs and Simple Societies

Initially, researchers did not envision hunter and gatherer societies as especially simple and certainly not as a one-dimensional social type. Yet by the 1970s, such economies had become pigeonholed, at least in the archaeological literature, as those of small, egalitarian, highly mobile groups living in marginal environments. So one might with some justification ask, what changed? What happened to that earlier rich, multilayered view such that it was replaced by what many think of today as stereotypic hunters and gatherers—those small bands of highly mobile folks idealized in the Bushman societies of Africa? Within a decade of the early attempts to correlate archaeological residues and hunter-gatherers, the character of such research was transformed by a burst of anthropological interest in modern hunting and gathering groups. The benchmark publication relating to this transformation was Lee and DeVore's *Man the Hunter* (1968). Peter Rowley-Conwy (2001) suggests that *Man the Hunter*, in combination with the conceptualization of "the original affluent society" in *Stone Age Economics* (Sahlins 1972), revolutionized the way anthropology, and ultimately archaeology, thought about hunters and gatherers. These works tapped into dominant social themes of the 1960s, including the multifaceted environmental movement that accentuated humans living at one with nature and the ever-continuing Romantic theme of the "noble savage." These influential works and the many similar studies that followed served to create a public image of hunters and gatherers as living a generally peaceful and tranquil existence, in relative ease and plenty, in tune with their environment. They also presented such hunters and gatherers as timeless, living virtually fossilized lifestyles from time immemorial, perpetually uninfluenced by surrounding complex societies.

What emerged from Lee and DeVore's research agenda (1968b:11–12, cited in Rowley-Conwy 2001:39–40) was a powerful image of small, highly mobile groups characterized as possessing an egalitarian social system and minimal personal property, living in bands that sporadically aggregated and between which individuals might move at will, and lacking territorial rights or claims, food-storage capabilities, and an attachment to any particular landscape. Lee and DeVore's work generated a revival in hunter and gatherer studies in anthropology as well as in ecology and human biology. The initial reaction was a flourishing research agenda that focused passionately on environmentally and ecologically related variables. Given the new field studies, it seemed self-evident that hunting and gathering societies were tightly integrated with their host environments and were best studied in that context. This new focus effectively disenfranchised the vast majority of historic hunting and gathering societies in the world and focused attention on very specialized adaptations to marginal environments as representing *all* such societies. This tendency to accept a particularly narrow spectrum of hunting and gathering practices as representative of the whole was widely adopted in archaeological studies and was unquestionably the predominant view until very recently.

Binford's New Archaeology paradigm, his concentration on the principal role of the environment in influencing human actions, and his fieldwork with Arctic Eskimos typified these trends. An effective expression of this perspective emerged in 1980 in his "Willow Smoke and Dogs' Tails" article—a work that continues to provide an important model for archaeological studies of hunters and gatherers. On the face of it, Binford's premise was straightforward—different patterns of human mobility were linked to different patterns of resource distribution and utilization, and these could be recognized in the material patterning in the archaeological record. Groups he labeled "foragers" moved their residences to the location of the resources. They made daily foraging trips from their mobile residential bases to obtain needed food resources. Populations who possessed a stable residential base and made long-range logistical trips to collect and process resources for transport back to the settlement he referred to as "collectors." They traditionally practiced food storage. Although he stressed that these dichotomized types simply represent two extremes of a virtually continuous array of mobility variations, they are most often employed by analysts as oppositions.

For Binford, hunting and gathering is all about high mobility, environmental constraints, and differential resource distribution. In his memorable "Garden of Eden" quote, Binford (1980:19) contends that human societies do not remain in a fixed location unless *compelled to do so by extraneous forces*—such as differential resource distribution or increasing population density. From this perspective, the world of hunters and gatherers is a world in constant movement. Yet Binford's own data suggest the universality of his assumption is questionable.

In a less often cited section of "Willow Smoke and Dogs' Tails," Binford elaborates on his environment–resource distribution–mobility correlation by looking at the big picture. He presents data that suggest his Garden of Eden "rejection" scenario may be somewhat overstated. His examination of a north-to-south transect of hunting and gathering societies in the Northern Hemisphere of the New World strongly reinforces his point that tropical-forest peoples are among the most resource deprived, resulting in small populations and high group mobility. What his data also coincidentally show is that more than three-quarters of historically documented hunting and gathering groups in temperate zones lived in fixed settlements for some part of the year. His analysis makes it apparent that in areas that are *not* characterized by highly differentiated resource distributions, populations are inclined to be less mobile. In cases in which rich, dependable resources such as large volumes of nuts or fish are available or where food storage is possible, long-term residential villages are possible and are perhaps even the dominant form of settlement. As Binford (1980:17) himself notes, any factor that restricts residential mobility (e.g., hostile neighbors or the attraction of stable resources) will produce a responsive increase in logistically organized production, that is, residential stability or sedentism. Binford stresses the mobility side of this equation, namely, that people must be forced to be less mobile. We suggest that an equally valid view is that people must be forced to be mobile and that Binford's assumption of universal mobility and his rejection of the Garden of Eden premise might not fully apply to the temperate zones of North America that midcontinental archaeologists study.

The seven plus decades since the recognition of preceramic archaic hunting, gathering, and collecting economies in the North American archaeological record have seen a tremendous expansion in understanding of the basic subsistence economy that was the primary lifestyle for most of human prehistory. As is the case in most instances of expanding research frontiers, much of the recent work has raised questions about earlier assumptions. However, in some cases, ongoing work has verified earlier suppositions. For example, the famous "Kalahari" debates in the 1980s justifiably questioned the validity of Lee and DeVore's model of timeless hunters and gatherers (e.g., Barnard 2004). From that revisionist debate came a more balanced picture of modern hunter and gatherer groups as marginalized societies existing in a complex web of interactions based on dominance by and resistance to surrounding agriculturalists and state-level societies. With the decline of the universalist vision of hunters and gatherers as economically simple, socially and politically egalitarian peoples, archaeologists were encouraged to refocus on issues of complexity and diversity that had been acknowledged decades earlier (i.e., Beardsley et al. 1956).

Adaptationism and Cultural Evolution

The interpretative assumptions in cultural neo-evolutionary and adaptationist theories that are associated with modern hunter-gatherer analogs promote a belief in a directional, progressive, and irreversible movement from simple to complex societies. In fact, as Rowley-Conwy quips, such perspectives presume that "there was a time *before* complexity emerged: a time, therefore, of *universal simplicity*" (2001:44, emphasis added). Several maxims can generally be correlated with what one might call the "original simplicity" model. These include (1) a view that there is a universal directional neo-evolutionary trend from simple to complex, (2) that the transition between social states of organization occurs gradually, (3) that the path to complexity is irreversible, and (4) that these trends are (often) linked within a framework that sees society as a "system" in stasis that can only be affected by an external force, typically, environmental change. Such maxims should not be accepted at face value.

The presumption of potential hunter-gatherer complexity has yet to make significant inroads in neo-evolutionary thinking. Of course, that evolutionary change is progressive, directed toward greater complexity, and irreversible is, on the face of it, refutable. In fact, the acceptance of such preconceptions would likely be denied by most of the scholars who implicitly incorporate them into their archaeological reconstructions and analyses. Yet it remains a dominant theorem in hunter-gatherer archaeological studies (e.g., see the lower Illinois River valley studies cited below; see other commentary by Ames 1991; Emerson and McElrath 2001; Pluciennik 2001; Rowley-Conwy 2001; Trigger 1989; Willey and Sabloff 1973, 1980). This is unfortunate, for, as Ames points out, these notions are detrimental to understanding the past because they "obscure the very dynamic of culture change that archaeologists seek to understand" (1991:109).

Also pervasive in hunter and gatherer research is an approach that weaves human society into the ecology of the past and investigates it as simply one more species in the biota on the landscape. In its most recent incarnation, such a view can be linked to White's (1959) conflation of culture with environmental adaptation. This attitude was influential in the New Archaeology, which identified environmental factors as the prime movers in human culture change. The traditional characterization of environmental change as inherently gradual promotes a view of cultural change as equally gradual, as people react to the incremental shifts in environmental stimuli.

The adaptationist paradigm is becoming increasingly questionable given the mounting evidence from field archaeology for the discontinuous nature of past patterns of sedentism and mobility, the clear demonstration of early complexity sometimes followed by episodes of simpler lifestyles, the lack of convincing verification for the synchronization of cultural and environmental change, the perceived importance of human culture as a variable in understanding even Archaic societies, and the new focus on studying the historical trajectories of these societies and, to some extent, eschewing the broad behavioral and universal explanations so important to the adaptationist approach. It is time for archaeologists to return to the actual material remains of Archaic societies and to make the practices reflected in those remains the focus of study. This will be a difficult task for an area of study in which theory has taken pride of place for so long that archaeological evidence has become almost secondary. It is critical that Archaic research shift from creating elegant models based on ecological and economic principles, modern hunter and gatherer studies, and neo-evolutionary agendas to a detailed study of the actual remains of early North American hunter-gather societies. Perhaps they have something to say.

Settlement and Mobility

Many of the suppositions concerning Archaic societies, especially regarding social organization and subsistence, spring directly from conceptualizations of mobility and settlement. The implicit correlations between mobility, sedentism, complexity, and progressive evolutionary change are so interwoven and all pervasive as to be all but impossible to disentangle in adaptationist theory. The typical characterizations of Archaic settlement patterns are replete with inherent assumptions of high residential mobility. The validity of these characterizations depends greatly on how one defines a sedentary or mobile way of life (Emerson 1999:189–191).

Archaic studies are not alone in suffering from a lack of precision regarding the definition of residence and mobility, and these concepts are subjects of ongoing debate in the literature (e.g., Ames 1991; Bocek 1991; Eder 1984; Gregg 1988; Kelly 1995; Rafferty 1985). Beardsley and his colleagues (1956) provided one of the earliest categorizations of settlement permanence by creating a model of group mobility that ran the gamut from sedentary to nomadic (with various degrees of each) lifeways. These broadly defined stages of community patterning, however, were hard to identify in the archaeological record. When the distinction between residential and logistical mobility was recognized (e.g., Binford 1980; Hitchcock 1982), it enabled archaeologists to correlate the material remains at sites with facets of human mobility. This critical differentiation involves identifying the movement of a group's residential base from an individual's or a task group's movements to and from the primary settlement. Binford describes this lifestyle continuum as ranging from residentially mobile groups of foragers to those living in fairly stable settlements of collectors.

Such conceptual differentiation contributes to Eder's (1984:838) penetrating observation that *sedentism* should be thought of as a threshold property of social groups, while *mobility* is best seen as a continuous variable that is an attribute of individuals. Such a distinction is crucial for comprehending modern observations that show sedentism and mobility do not covary (cf. Eder 1984; Kelly 1995). For example, one conceivably might have populations in which individual mobility actually increases at the same time residential mobility decreases. With the uncoupling of mobility and sedentism, it becomes possible to recognize the appearance of sedentism and, coincidentally, to independently observe variations in the frequency and constitution of mobility patterns (Eder 1984:848).

A fairly common definition of sedentism focuses on the idea of year-round occupation of a site (e.g., Eder 1984; Kelly 1995; Rafferty 1985; Rice 1975). A review of the literature makes it clear that most archaeologists simply sidestep the definitional issue by continuing to use *sedentism* in a relative sense as measuring one group's residential mobility against another's. It is the kind of considerations noted above that causes some scholars to categorize sedentism as a threshold event rather than as a gradualist continuum. Viewed as a threshold, sedentism takes on a very different meaning than it does when thought of as a continuum; for example, this perspective makes it impossible for a people to be "semisedentary." Part of the dispute is definitional. For Rafferty (1985), anything less than year-round use of a site by a social group is, by definition, nonsedentary. Brown and Vierra (1983:168) adhere to a similar definition. In this approach, sedentism is an absolute property of social groups rather than a continuous variable, as is individual mobility (i.e., Eder 1984:845). This type of rigid either-or approach is not of much utility in understanding the development or implications of sedentism in Archaic lifeways, or, in fact, in any society.

A simple "time of occupation" criterion does not adequately define the complex trajectory of changes inherent in sedentism, and those changes are what archaeologists seek to explain. The significant aspects of sedentism are the important economic, social, and political alterations it engenders within a previously residentially mobile society. Consequently, a less didactic but much more satisfying answer to the threshold question is one that highlights the dramatic social and political changes that accompany the long-term coresidence of numerous families. All too often, research on the viability of long-term residence focuses on the capacity of environmental resources to support sedentary populations. While, clearly, a minimum resource base is required for sedentism to be viable, a more serious impediment lies in the inability of band-level social and political mechanisms to provide ways that ensure the successful long-term interaction and stability of a sedentary group.

The consequences of adopting a sedentary way of life can be varied. Keeley (1988, in Kelly 1995:58) observes that multifamily populations living in stable residences for at least five months a year have an increased population density, depend more on stored food, and have greater wealth distinctions than more mobile populations. If these observations are valid, they mean that individuals who continue to coreside in a village that moves as a unit from place to place throughout the year develop the social and political characteristics of "sedentism." Other potential side effects of a sedentary lifestyle include increasing fecundity and shifting patterns of male and female interaction and offspring enculturation (i.e., Kelly 1995:58–59). Sedentism may even generate conceptualizations of the landscape that are different from those of mobile hunters and gatherers (Meillassoux 1973). Sedentary populations, even when absent from their place of residence, show a cultural attachment to it and treat the land differently than those who simply pass through it (Kelly 1995:45).

A review of current thinking on sedentism shows that the concept, as defined in its most rigid form, is difficult to implement in an archaeological study. It is misguided to focus on the spatial and chronological parameters of sedentism when one is actually interested in its social and political ramifications. Keeley's (1988) study indicates that human social groups experience the social, political, and economic effects of aggregation after a minimal period of five months. Thus, social groups who aggregate for at least half of each year on a consistent basis or who coreside in sufficiently large population clusters (*regardless of their degree of residential mobility*) will feel the political and social effects of sedentism. To identify such a pattern archaeologically is possible.

An Adaptationist Case Study—The Lower Illinois River Valley Model Examined

The lower Illinois River valley articles of Brown and Vierra (1983; Brown 1985, 1986) epitomize the "adaptationist" research trend in Archaic-period hunter and gatherer studies (Emerson and McElrath 2001). This approach remains central in many midcontinental studies of Archaic-period topics. Such models interpret the Archaic as a period of ahistorical, unbounded human societies that, as a result of economic rationalism and increasingly functionally efficient environmental adaptations, move through a framework of progressive, gradualistic evolutionary changes toward greater sedentism and increased complexity (Emerson and McElrath 2001:202–204). As is typical in the adaptationist school of culture change, humans play the role of "reactors" rather than actors.

Binford's forager-collector template has seen wide service as an explanatory device in Archaic studies in North America. While there is no evidence that Binford viewed his mobility model as in any way evolutionary, others clearly have. In the forefront of those who have are Brown and Vierra (1983), who weave together a blend of adaptationist factors to create a functionally satisfying explanation of shifting Archaic settlement patterns in the Illinois River valley. Brown and Vierra (1983:168–169) observe that, as settlement forms move from a highly mobile to a sedentary pattern, food acquisition logically depends less on residential mobility and increasingly on logistical mobility. Since they *know* earlier groups were more mobile than later groups, that is, that there was a trend toward sedentism, and since they assume population stability through time, their interpretations add a diachronic flavor to Binford's typology, producing a unidirectional neo-evolutionary shift from residential to logistical mobility. The product of these assumptions is a picture of an apparently inevitable and irreversible multithousand-year progression from mobile to sedentary lifeways in the lower Illinois Valley.

In an elaboration on the rise of sedentism in the lower Illinois River valley, Brown (1985) reconfirms his commitment to the premise that adaptationist factors are the key to understanding the rise of sedentism and complexity. In creating his model of the emergence of sedentism, Brown (1986) follows Binford in assuming that human societies must be forced out of a pattern of high residential mobility (their *natural* state) toward a more residentially stable pattern (their *unnatural* state). In these discussions, he acknowledges that in situ populations, following a risk-management strategy (another rationalist economic strategy) and reacting to external variations in environment and population density, might have a role in the development of sedentism and complexity.

The lower Illinois River valley model includes a perception of innate human aggressiveness (Byers 2004:163–167). Brown (1986) assumes that humans are forced into a restricted territorial mode by the pressure of increasing populations and their inability to peacefully interact. He contends that a capacity for nonviolent intersociety interaction developed only at the end of the Middle Archaic and was marked by the appearance and circulation of exotica (minerals, cherts, worked chert and bone, etc.). As Byers (2004:164–167), however, points out, Walthall and Koldehoff (1998) have demonstrated that Dalton people were circulating hypertrophic Sloan points, very probably to facilitate intergroup reciprocity, by cal 9000 B.C. Furthermore, the recent recovery of hypertrophic Paleoindian blades suggests such mechanisms may have been in place by the time the first immigrants entered the New World (Gramley 1993). Consequently, mechanisms of intergroup interaction and peaceful reciprocity can be presumed to have existed long before Middle Archaic times, and their lack cannot be used to explain the inability of peoples to peacefully interact or to demonstrate the "forced" nature of sedentism.

Paradoxically, the lower Illinois Valley model also envisions a world in which populations, while reacting to locally manifest environmental factors, were almost mythically stable during the course of many-millennia-long evolutionary processes. This concept of culture change stands in stark contradiction to the other classic adaptationist concept of small, highly mobile bands of hunters and gatherers who eschewed territories. One would expect such groups to have roamed widely across the Midcontinent, or at least to have frequently crossed the upland divides between river valleys and have moved freely up and down those valleys. How does a model that incorporates high rates of residential mobility articulate with the New Archaeology's assumptions of in situ evolution of stable populations over the long durée? We suspect that they are essentially incompatible. In fact, the evidence presented in this volume suggests the Archaic was a period typified by population movements, some possibly over great distances; by the abandonment of some environmental zones, perhaps some regions; by pioneering movements of populations into newly emerging landscapes; and probably by the first clashes of divergent cultures. The adaptationist image of stable Archaic populations who passively accepted technological and stylistic innovations does not fit well with the emerging picture provided by archaeology (see also Milner 2004).

When cultural change in adaptationist models does not respond in the proper manner to environmental change, this can lead to interpretive convolutions. The lower Illinois River valley model hypothesizes that the enrichment of the available floodplain resources during the Hypsithermal pulled local populations from the uplands to the floodplains, thus evoking a major shift in both resource utilization and settlement patterns (e.g., Brown 1985, 1986; Brown and Vierra 1983). Yet, as even the model's proponents note, the shift of local societies from residential mobility to residential stability, that is, to a situation in which they employed a logistical resource-collection strategy to take full advantage of the plentiful clustered resources, took millennia to come into its own (Brown 1985:220–221). In other words, in one of the prime examples of adaptationist modeling, neither human society nor environmental causation appears to be functioning properly. As Byers observes, the archaeological record has failed to produce what the theoretical approach predicted: "the rapid working out of the adaptive process to its optimal conclusion, this being fully domesticated subsistence integrated with fully tethered settlement, that is, sedentary farming regimes" (2004:161). The failure of the lower Illinois River valley people to fall into line with the model is explained away as the result of hunter-gatherer conservatism (Brown 1986:317–318). Employing risk-management and gaming strategies, these Archaic people determined it to be to their advantage to remain mobile until local population pressure began to make productive resource patches scarce. At that point, they picked a patch and reluctantly settled down, often only to later drop their sedentary mode and resume a pattern of residential mobility. The consequence of this pattern was a long, drawn-out trend toward sedentism (see Byers 2004:163). Between-group accommodation and negotiation are envisioned as impossible because Middle Archaic peoples are said to have lacked "tokens of intergroup exchange" (Brown 1985:223), a view that Byers (2004:165–166) demonstrated is untenable.

Byers (2004:166–167) further argues that the lower Illinois River valley model of long-term shifting from sedentism to mobility and back again seems unlikely. While some groups, after settling in on a resource patch, may have "remobilized," it is unlikely that all would have. This means that selected groups would rather quickly have become entrenched in prime locations on the floodplain, thereby eliminating the viable options for other undecided residentially mobile groups. This process would rapidly have excluded those still-mobile groups from the area. Consequently, while the establishment of territorial groups might have taken generations, it would hardly have taken millennia, making the explanation for the lag of social response to environmental change improbable.

Moving Hunter-Gatherers Toward Complexity

The last two decades have reawakened archaeologists to the broader multiplicity of social, political, and economic variables contained within the hunting and gathering spectrum. This increasing comprehension has expanded to form an entirely new direction of research conducted under the rubric of hunter-gatherer complexity (e.g., Price and Brown 1985). Archaeologists now know that hunter-gatherer societies can be extremely complex, may be hierarchically structured, and can inhabit settlements for long periods of time, engage in monumental constructions, organize significant efforts in the "production and management" of wild food sources and incipient domestication, and maintain large population clusters. This change has not only altered the picture of prehistoric hunting and gathering populations but it has also required an entirely new theoretical base to pursue their investigation. This new theorizing, most clearly articulated in historical processualism, places its emphasis on comprehending the historical trajectories of groups and on envisioning peoples as actors rather than reactors. It privileges the material record over idealist neo-evolutionary trends, accumulating large and rich data sets, and understanding power, gender relations, resistance, and accommodation (Sassaman 2001, 2005).

Nowhere have the remains of Archaic-pattern people been so "vocal" on the subject of complexity as on the south Atlantic coast and in the lower Mississippi River valley, with the discovery of Middle Archaic monumental mound constructions (Gibson and Carr 2004; Kidder and Sassaman, this volume; Russo 1994, 1996; Saunders et al. 1994; Saunders et al. 1997). Given the recognition that these mounds provide precedence for the previously anomalous Late Archaic Poverty Point complex (e.g., Gibson 1996, 2000), it is difficult to ignore a several-millennia-long tradition of Archaic mound building in the southeastern United States (Anderson 2004; Kidder and Sassaman, this volume). Not only did these societies "mound" dirt and shell in a systematic manner but there is also good reason to suspect that some Louisiana sites, such as Watson Brake, Caney, Frenchman's Bend, and Insley, represent planned complexes expressing "proportional and geometric" spatial regularities; this activity suggests relatively complex associated political and social organization (Sassaman and Heckenberger 2004:220–231). Contemporaneous ring shell mounds on the Atlantic coast, while not usually constructed in complex groupings, also suggest hierarchical social and political structure (Russo 2004).

Despite its now more than decade-old revelation, the evidence that Archaic people were "mound builders" seems to have had little impact on the conventional wisdom of traditional archaeology—early New World inhabitants continue to be perceived as essentially "simple folk." This is due in part to an inherent archaeological conservatism that categorizes incompatible data as "idiosyncratic exceptions to the rule" and ignores them or explains them away and to a not unhealthy skepticism that delays acceptance of new data and ideas until they are "proven." Initially, there was a reasonable hesitation on the part of many to accept the purposeful construction of mounds as dating to Middle Archaic times. The careful work of researchers such as Saunders et al. (1997), Russo (1994), and many others has now demonstrated beyond a doubt that the identification of some mounds as Archaic constructions is correct. No one can doubt that these early societies built mounds, so the issue for current skeptics becomes one of doubting the social or political significance of the monumental construction process. The debate over the material and behavioral correlates of political, social, and economic complexity far exceeds the space available to reprise it here (see discussions of various aspects of the debate in Anderson 2004; Crothers 2004; Milner 2004; Milner and Jefferies 1998; Sassaman and Heckenberger 2004; Saunders 2004). However, the systematic construction of monumental forms does require "formal" conceptions of planning and organization and perceptions of time and space that would seem at a premium among the ephemeral band-level societies that some scholars envision as populating the Middle Archaic period. Can it be possible that the Archaic peoples of the New World failed to understand and conform to the neo-evolutionary sociopolitical models that are so frequently applied to them? (Anderson 2004).

The movement of human societies into the New World, whether Clovis bands, coastal maritime hunters and fishers, or unknown pre-Clovis groups, occurred very late in terms of human history. Those initial pioneers carried with them long-standing social, political, and economic traditions. How well these cultural practices survived the lengthy movement by generations across and down the hemisphere is unknowable. But the first immigrants came from Eurasian backgrounds with well-established patterns of human social and economic interactions probably couched in terms of exchange and ritual. So why should archaeologists not expect to find evidence of Paleoindian ritual objects that were created specifically to facilitate intersocietal exchange, interaction, and marriage and to soothe intergroup tensions and hostilities? The first concrete evidence of such social signifiers in North America might be hypertrophic Clovis points such as the Rutz point or the magnificent points recovered from the East Wenatchee cache in Washington (Gramly 1993). It may not be simple coincidence that the hypertrophic point phenomenon is recognized by Walthall and Koldehoff (1998) in their slightly later Dalton-era "Cult of the Long Blade" and again by Brookes (1997) in his Middle Archaic "Benton" analogy.

Oversized stone blades appear in the archaeological records dating throughout Paleoindian and Archaic times, sometimes associated with items such as bone pins, bannerstones, beads, and other unusual items or materials. Most archaeologists think such items were involved in practices that facilitated social, economic, and political relationships between spatially disparate groups. Essentially they are interpreted as having served to make possible those large population agglomerations so necessary to keep these scattered societies viable, that is, simply to maintain a breeding population. How far are such large social, presumably non-kin gatherings from what social typologies hold to be loosely bound tribal clusterings? So even in a neo-evolutionary paradigm, one must accept the presence of social and perhaps even political complexity as a necessary aspect of very early population continuity.

The evidence for monumental constructions, large permanent-appearing settlements, and exploitation patterns suggesting a rich resource base is becoming increasingly common in Archaic contexts in the Eastern Woodlands (e.g., see Gibson and Carr 2004 and various chapters in this volume). However, only in the last few years have researchers begun to seriously question the generally pervasive conventional models of regional unilinear culture history, perhaps expressed most elegantly by Bruce Smith in his 1986 summary of Eastern Woodlands prehistory. The emergence of apparent "complexity" in the Archaic period, of course, raises serious concerns about the entire reconstruction of Eastern Woodlands social and political history. It also calls into question the comfortable correlations that the discipline has long promoted between such variables as hunting and gathering and mobile lifestyles, agriculture and complexity, monumental constructions and political control, and so forth. Archaeologists such as David Anderson (e.g., 2002, 2004) and Kenneth Sassaman (e.g., 2001, 2005; Sassaman and Heckenberger 2004) have recently questioned Archaic-period political and social reconstructions and found them wanting. They contend that it is not unreasonable to envision at least a moderate level of sociopolitical organization in parts of the region by the Middle Archaic period.

Why not Early or Middle Archaic political and social complexity that in neo-evolutionary terms is usually described as tribal?[1] What factors trigger tribal patterns of organization? Traditional explanations of tribal origins are generally tied to environmental causal factors such as resource shortages resulting from either uncertainty of access or general scarcity. In this sense, tribal alliances are thought of as "risk-minimization strategies" to circumvent scarcities (e.g., Braun and Plog 1982). As Anderson (2002:248) notes, most explanations rely on increased population pressure on resources or environmental stress as causing unreliability in resource availability and therefore view "complexity" as inevitable when that threshold point is reached. Traditionally, such a threshold is not conceived of as having come into existence until the Woodland period in the Eastern Woodlands (Bender 1985; Braun and Plog 1982).

Such tribalization models stress, to some degree, outmoded concepts of hunter-gatherer behavior patterned after modern marginalized groups such as the Kung Bushman (as discussed earlier). By implication, early human societies are seen as *naturally* existing in small band-level groups that essentially had to be forced into associating within larger macroband or tribal groups. However, other factors than food shortages can promote population clustering and increased levels of political organization, for example, intergroup violence (Anderson 2002:248; Milner 2004). Not only does such violence promote population clustering but it also encourages the creation of ethnic identities (e.g., Anderson 2002; Emerson 1999; Emerson and McElrath 2001; Sassaman 2001) that are supportive in the context of intergroup conflict as well as individual group survival. One would also assume that larger groups facilitate access to reproductive partners, economic success, and personal safety and longevity. In preindustrial societies, population size, to a large extent, equals power—the relative size of one's group directly empowers its members. Therefore, where resources allowed (we would argue in much of the temperate zone), there was arguably momentum to gather group members into sizable clusters of population—large enough to support loosely organized tribal forms.

As new archaeologically focused studies have demonstrated (e.g., the papers in Parkinson 2002a), tribal patterns of organization have much to offer social groups in terms of adaptive postures. Tribal forms are extremely fluid and flexible in regard to population size; political, social, and economic levels of integration; spatial bounding; mobility; and longevity (Anderson 2002, 2004; Fowles 2002; Parkinson 2002b). This plasticity is what makes them of prime value to their members as well as rather nebulous to scholars who seek to study them. It is reasonable to assume that tribal patterns of organization have an extremely long history in human societies, in the New World perhaps coming in as part and parcel of the original inhabitants' social and political repertoire.

Summary

Archaic studies suffer as much from the paucity of appropriate theorizing as from a paucity of large, contextually sound data sets. The dominance of the adaptationist paradigm has structured (and continues to structure) virtually all Archaic research. Through the decades, this has led considerable numbers of researchers into interpretive dead ends and has discouraged studies of Archaic social and political development. When joined with the precepts of the New Archaeology, for example, interpretations acknowledging even the potential of population movements fell into theoretical disfavor. Instead, archaeologists postulated a prehistoric landscape in which populations apparently were established in perpetuity. These populations were conceived of as evolving in situ, and there was little acknowledgment that population exchange, movement, interaction, or depopulation could play any role in altering the stability of local societies. Meaningful culture modification within this stultified social landscape could only be initiated by environmental change. This fit well within a perspective that saw technological change as an adaptationist mechanism geared to increasingly efficient human exploitation of the environment (à la White 1959).

This model of environmentally driven change also fit well with a tendency to conceive of "culture" as a monolithic, ahistorical analytical unit (Marcus and Fischer 1986). Such a perspective obscures individuals, factions, and communities from consideration, and, consequently, social interaction (except in the almost extraneous sense of exchange, etc.) cannot be considered a force of change. It eliminates the possibility of modeling social agency even of collectivities. This view of cultural unity, especially when coupled to perceptions of band-level hunter-gathering societies, did not encourage models of social or political diversity in Archaic societies. Only recently have archaeologists considered the possibility that more complex political forms such as tribes may have been present in the Archaic period (e.g., Anderson 2002).

Perhaps more than for any other cultural context, researchers have had to struggle with the dilemma of the relationship of Archaic material culture to social formations. To some extent, this is due to the limited artifact inventories of such groups—how does one link a cluster of points to ethnicity, political communities, or family groups? Do the stylistically similar stone tools recovered from Archaic sites represent the distinctive signatures of related social groups? Or are these simply functionally specific tools that owe their similar morphological form to the similar tasks being performed? And how much variety is there in Archaic tool assemblages? Did projectile points and large knife styles come and go like the length of women's skirts in the modern fashion world? Did a woman in Archaic society have a choice of formal knives and points to perform her daily tasks? Some stratified sites seem to suggest the contemporaneous use of multiple biface styles that had chronologically different use spans. But in open-air sites, where the probability of multiple occupations and component mixing is statistically much lower than in rockshelters (Walthall 1998), it seems that the old equation "points equal people" often holds true (e.g., Ray et al., this volume). We also note that Archaic caches recovered in the Midcontinent tend to be mostly limited to a single point style. How archaeologists determine contemporaneity of point styles is critical in determining how they interpret the past.

Archaeologists have begun to recognize the dangers of using modern and ethnohistoric hunter-gatherer data as direct analogs to model Archaic lifestyles. Significant disadvantages include the lifestyle modifications of such groups that resulted from their marginal positions vis-à-vis environmental resources and their political and social relations with complex societies. The emphasis by modern hunter-gatherer subsistence and settlement research in marginal environments has encouraged the development of a series of theoretical positions heavily influenced by the boundary conditions encountered. Such research has tended to incorporate assumptions of economic rationality, optimal foraging, technological progress and efficiency, functionalism, and behavioralism. When such models have been applied to the study of Archaic subsistence practices, they have carried the same theoretical assumptions with them. It is not clear that these are applicable to ancient prehistoric hunter-gatherers. Added to these concerns is the inappropriate application of subsistence and social models derived from such marginalized groups to the prehistoric inhabitants of temperate zones. The environmental richness of the temperate woodlands of the Midcontinent of North America minimized the necessity of significant seasonal movements to exploit widely spaced resource patches (Binford [1980] notwithstanding).

The conceptual issues in Archaic-period research outlined above suggest the wide range of challenges currently facing scholars of the period. It is perhaps fortunate that many of these challenges simply require all of us to be more intellectually open. One crucial change involves a basic adjustment of perspective: we need to be willing to accept and explore models of political and social complexity outside of the neo-evolutionary paradigm. We cannot simply accept the Archaic template of small bands of seasonally mobile hunters and gatherers as a given. This requires us, when interpreting our data, to decouple the traditional linkage of the environment, subsistence economy, and sociopolitical organization and to consider the impact of such factors as ethnicity, tribalism, incipient complexity, multiple populations, migrations, and historical process. An essential part of this consideration is the large-scale recovery and identification of the all-important material correlates of such factors that allow us to define them in an archaeological context.

Endnote

1. We do not participate here in the seemingly endless anthropological debates decrying the evils of social typologies. We see no reason not to use such long-standing terms as *bands*, *tribes*, or *chiefdoms* to communicate approximate levels of social organization. It seems to us the outcry against such terms is appropriate when they become explanations but is overdrawn when the terms are used as general descriptors.

References Cited

Ames, Kenneth M.
1991 Sedentism: A Temporal Shift or a Transitional Change in Hunter-Gatherer Mobility Patterns? In *Between Bands and States*, edited by Susan A. Gregg, pp. 108–134. Occasional Papers 9. Center for Archaeological Investigations, Southern Illinois University, Carbondale.

Anderson, David G.
2002 The Evolution of Tribal Social Organization in the Southeast. In *The Archaeology of Tribal Societies*, edited by William A. Parkinson, pp. 246–277. Archaeological Series 15. International Monographs in Prehistory, Ann Arbor, Michigan.
2004 Archaic Mounds and the Archaeology of Southeastern Tribal Societies. In *Signs of Power: The Rise of Complexity in the Southeast*, edited by Jon L. Gibson and Philip J. Carr, pp. 270–299. University of Alabama Press, Tuscaloosa.

Baerreis, David A.
1959 The Archaic as Seen from the Ozark Region. *American Antiquity* 24:270–275.

Barnard, Alan
2004 Hunter-Gatherers in History, Archeology, and Anthropology: Introductory Essay. In *Hunter-Gatherers in History, Archeology, and Anthropology*, edited by Alan Barnard, pp. 1–13. Berg, Oxford.

Beardsley, R. K., Preston Holder, A. D. Kreiger, B. J. Meggars, and John Rinaldo
1956 *Functional and Evolutionary Implications of Community Patterning.* Memoir 11. Society for American Archaeology, Salt Lake City, Utah.

Bender, Barbara
1985 Emergent Tribal Formation in the American Midcontinent. *American Antiquity* 50:52–62.

Binford, Lewis R.
1980 Willow Smoke and Dogs' Tails: Hunter-Gatherer Settlement Systems and Archaeological Site Formation. *American Antiquity* 45:4–20.

Bocek, Barbara
1991 Prehistoric Settlement Pattern and Social Organization on the San Francisco Peninsula, California. In *Between Bands and States*, edited by Susan A. Gregg, pp. 58–86. Occasional Papers 9. Center for Archaeological Investigations, Southern Illinois University, Carbondale.

Braun, David P., and Stephen Plog
1982 Evolution of "Tribal" Social Networks: Theory and Prehistoric North American Evidence. *American Antiquity* 47:504–526.

Brookes, Samuel O.
1997 Aspects of the Middle Archaic: The Atassa. In *Results of Recent Archaeological Investigations in the Greater Mid-South: Proceedings of the 17th Annual Mid-South Archaeological Conference, Memphis, Tennessee, June 29–30, 1996*, edited by Charles H. McNutt. Occasional Paper 18. Anthropological Research Center, University of Memphis, Memphis, Tennessee.

Brown, James A.
1985 Long-Term Trends to Sedentism and the Emergence of Complexity in the American Midwest. In *Prehistoric Hunter-Gatherers: The Emergence of Cultural Complexity*, edited by T. Douglas Price and James A. Brown, pp. 201–231. Academic Press, New York.
1986 Food for Thought: Where Has Subsistence Analysis Gotten Us? In *Foraging, Collecting, and Harvesting: Archaic Period Subsistence and Settlement in the Eastern Woodlands*, edited by Sarah W. Neusius, pp. 315–327. Occasional Papers 6. Center for Archaeological Investigations, Southern Illinois University, Carbondale.

Brown, James A., and Robert K. Vierra
1983 What Happened in the Middle Archaic? Introduction to an Ecological Approach to Koster Site Archaeology. In *Archaic Hunters and Gatherers in the American Midwest*, edited by James L. Phillips and James A. Brown, pp. 165–196. Academic Press, New York.

Byers, A. Martin
2004 *The Ohio Hopewell Episode: Paradigm Lost and Paradigm Gained.* University of Akron Press, Akron, Ohio.

Byers, Douglas S.
1959a An Introduction to Five Papers on the Archaic Stage. *American Antiquity* 24:229–232.

1959b The Eastern Archaic: Some Problems and Hypotheses. *American Antiquity* 24:233–256.

Crothers, George M.
2004 The Green River in Comparison to the Lower Mississippi Valley during the Archaic: To Build Mounds or Not to Build Mounds. In *Signs of Power: The Rise to Complexity in the Southeast*, edited by Jon L. Gibson and Philip J. Carr, pp. 86–96. University of Alabama Press, Tuscaloosa.

Deuel, Thorne
1935 Basic Cultures of the Mississippi Valley. *American Anthropologist* 37:429–445.

Eder, James F.
1984 The Impact of Subsistence Change on Mobility and Settlement Pattern in a Tropical Forest Foraging Economy: Some Implications for Archeology. *American Anthropologist* 86:837–853.

Emerson, Thomas E.
1999 The Keeshin Farm Site and the Rock River Langford Tradition. In *The Keeshin Farm Site and the Rock River Langford Tradition in Northern Illinois*, pp. 187–205. Transportation Archaeological Research Reports 7. Illinois Transportation Archaeological Research Program, University of Illinois at Urbana–Champaign.

Emerson, Thomas E., and Dale L. McElrath
2001 Interpreting Discontinuity and Historical Process in Midcontinental Late Archaic and Early Woodland Societies. In *The Archaeology of Tradition: Agency and History Before and After Columbus*, edited by Timothy R. Pauketat, pp. 195–217. University Press of Florida, Gainesville.

Fowler, Melvin L.
1959 *Summary Report of Modoc Rock Shelter: 1952, 1953, 1955, 1956*. Reports of Investigations 8. Illinois State Museum, Springfield.

Fowles, Severin M.
2002 From Social Type to Social Process: Placing "Tribe" in a Historical Framework. In *The Archaeology of Tribal Societies*, edited by William A. Parkinson, pp. 13–33. International Monographs in Prehistory, Ann Arbor, Michigan.

Gibson, Jon L.
1996 Poverty Point and Greater Southeastern Prehistory: The Culture That Did Not Fit. In *Archaeology of the Mid-Holocene Southeast*, edited by Kenneth E. Sassaman and David G. Anderson. University Press of Florida, Gainesville.
2000 *The Ancient Mounds of Poverty Point: Place of Rings*. University Press of Florida, Gainesvlle.

Gibson, Jon L., and Philip J. Carr (editors)
2004 *Signs of Power: The Rise of Complexity in the Southeast*. University of Alabama Press, Tuscaloosa.

Gramly, Richard Michael
1993 *The Richey Clovis Cache: Earliest Americans on the Columbia River*. Persimmon Press, Buffalo, New York.

Gregg, Susan A. (editor)
1988 *Foragers and Farmers: Population Interaction and Agricultural Expansion in Northern Europe*. University of Chicago Press, Chicago.

Griffin, James B.
1946 Cultural Change and Continuity in Eastern United States Archaeology. In *Man in Northeastern North America*, edited by Frederick Johnson, pp. 37–95. Papers of the Robert S. Peabody Foundation for Archaeology 3. Andover, Massachusetts.
1952 Culture Periods in Eastern United States Archaeology. In *Archaeology of Eastern United States*, edited by James B. Griffin, pp. 352–364. University of Chicago Press, Chicago.
1967 Eastern North American Archaeology: A Summary. *Science* 156:175–191.

Haag, William G.
1942 Early Horizons in the Southeast. *American Antiquity* 7:207–222.

Hitchcock, Robert K.
1982 Patterns of Sedentism among the Basarwa of Eastern Botswana. In *Politics and History in Band Society*, edited by Eleanor Leacock and Richard Lee, pp. 223–267. Cambridge University Press, Cambridge, England.

Keeley, Lawrence H.
1988 Hunter-Gatherer Economic Complexity and "Population Pressure": A Cross-Cultural Analysis. *Journal of Anthropological Archaeology* 7:373–411.

Kelley, J. Charles
1959 The Desert Cultures and the Balcones Phase: Archaic Manifestations in the Southwest and Texas. *American Antiquity* 24:276–288.

Kelly, Robert L.
1995 *The Foraging Spectrum: Diversity in Hunter-Gatherer Lifeways*. Smithsonian Institution Press, Washington, D.C.

Lee, Richard B., and Irven DeVore (editors)
1968 *Man the Hunter*. Aldine, Chicago.

MacNeish, Richard S.
1948 The Pre-Pottery Faulkner Site of Southern Illinois. *American Antiquity* 13:232–243.

Marcus, George E., and Michael M. J. Fischer
1986 *Anthropology as Cultural Critique: An Experimental Moment in the Human Sciences*. University of Chicago Press, Chicago.

McKern, William C.
1939 The Midwest Taxonomic Method as an Aid to Archaeological Culture Study. *American Antiquity* 4:301–313.

Meighan, Clement W.
1959 Californian Cultures and the Concept of an Archaic Stage. *American Antiquity* 24:289–305.

Meillassoux, Claude
1973 On the Mode of Production of the Hunting Band. In *French Perspectives in African Studies*, edited by Pierre Alexandre, pp. 187–203. Oxford University Press, Oxford.

Milner, George R.
2004 Old Mounds, Ancient Hunter-Gatherers, and Modern Archaeologists. In *Signs of Power: The Rise of Complexity in the Southeast*, edited by Jon L. Gibson and Philip J. Carr, pp. 300–315. University of Alabama Press, Tuscaloosa.

Milner, George R., and Richard W. Jefferies
1998 The Read Archaic Shell Midden in Kentucky. *Southeastern Archaeology* 17:117–132.

Muller, Jon
1997 *Mississippian Political Economy*. Plenum Publishing, New York.

Parkinson, William A.

2002a (editor) *The Archaeology of Tribal Societies.* Archaeological Series 15. International Monographs in Prehistory, Ann Arbor, Michigan.

2002b Introduction: Archaeology and Tribal Societies. In *The Archaeology of Tribal Societies*, edited by William A. Parkinson, pp. 1–12. Archaeological Series 15. International Monographs in Prehistory, Ann Arbor, Michigan.

Pluciennik, Mark

2001 Archaeology, Anthropology, and Subsistence. *Journal of the Royal Anthropological Institute* (n.s.) 7:741–758.

Price, T. Douglas, and James A. Brown (editors)

1985 *Prehistoric Hunter-Gatherers: The Emergence of Cultural Complexity.* Academic Press, New York.

Prufer, Olaf H.

2001 The Archaic of Northeastern Ohio. In *Archaic Transitions in Ohio and Kentucky Prehistory*, edited by Olaf H. Prufer, Sara E. Pedde, and Richard S. Meindl, pp. 183–209. Kent State University Press, Kent, Ohio.

Rafferty, James E.

1985 The Archaeological Record of Sedentariness: Recognition, Development, and Implications. In *Advances in Archaeological Method and Theory*, vol. 8, edited by Michael Schiffer, pp. 113–156. Academic Press, New York.

Rice, Glen

1975 A Systematic Explanation in a Change in Mogollon Settlement Patterns. Ph.D. dissertation, Department of Anthropology, University of Washington, Seattle.

Ritchie, William A.

1932a The Algonkin Sequence in New York. *American Anthropologist* 34:406–414.

1932b The Lamoka Lake Site: The Type Station of the Archaic Algonkin Period in New York. *Researches and Transactions of the New York State Archaeological Association* 7:79–134. Rochester.

1936 New Evidence Relating to the Archaic Occupation of New York. *Researches and Transactions of the New York State Archaeological Association* 8:1–23. Rochester.

1944 *The Pre-Iroquoian Occupations of New York State.* Rochester Museum of Arts and Sciences, Rochester, New York.

Rowley-Conwy, Peter

2001 Time, Change and the Archaeology of Hunter-Gatherers: How Original Is the "Original Affluent Society." In *Hunter-Gatherers: An Interdisciplinary Perspective*, edited by Catherine Panter-Brick, Robert H. Layton, and Peter Rowley-Conwy, pp. 39–72. Cambridge University Press, Cambridge, England.

Russo, Michael

1994 A Brief Introduction to the Study of Archaic Mounds in the Southeast. *Southeastern Archaeology* 13:89–93.

1996 Southeastern Preceramic Archaic Ceremonial Mounds. In *Archaeology of the Mid-Holocene Southeast*, edited by Kenneth E. Sassaman and David G. Anderson, pp. 177–199. University Press of Florida, Gainesville.

2004 Measuring Shell Rings for Social Inequality. In *Signs of Power: The Rise of Cultural Complexity in the Southeast*, edited by Jon L. Gibson and Philip J. Carr, pp. 26–70. University of Alabama Press, Tuscaloosa.

Sahlins, Marshall A.

1972 *Stone Age Economics.* Aldine, Chicago.

Sassaman, Kenneth E.

2001 Hunter-Gatherers and Traditions of Resistance. In *The Archaeology of Traditions: Agency and History Before and After Columbus* edited by Timothy R. Pauketat, pp. 218–236. University Press of Florida, Gainesville.

2005 Poverty Point as Structure, Event, Process. *Journal of Archaeological Method and Theory* 12:335–364.

Sassaman, Kenneth E., and Michael J. Heckenberger

2004 Crossing the Symbolic Rubicon in the Southeast. In *Signs of Power: The Rise of Complexity in the Southeast*, edited by Jon L. Gibson and Philip J. Carr, pp. 214–233. University of Alabama Press, Tuscaloosa.

Saunders, Joe

2004 Are We Fixing the Same Mistake Again? In *Signs of Power: The Rise of Complexity in the Southeast*, edited by Jon L. Gibson and Philip J. Carr, pp. 146–161. University of Alabama Press, Tuscaloosa.

Saunders, Joe, Rolfe D. Mandel, Roger T. Saucier, E. Thurman Allen, C. T. Hallmark, Jay K. Johnson, Edwin H. Jackson, Charles M. Allen, Gary L. Stringer, Douglas S. Frink, James K. Feathers, Stephen Williams, Kristen J. Gremillion, Malcolm F. Vidrine, and Roca B. Jones

1997 A Mound Complex in Louisiana at 5400–5000 Years Before the Present. *Science* 277:1796–1799.

Saunders, Joe, Allen Thurman, and Roger T. Saucier

1994 Four Archaic? Mound Complexes in Northeast Louisiana. *Southeastern Archaeology* 13:134–153.

Sears, William H.

1948 What Is the Archaic? *American Antiquity* 14:122–124.

Smith, Bruce D.

1986 The Archaeology of the Southeastern United States: From Dalton to de Soto, 10,500–500 B.P. In *Advances in World Archaeology*, vol. 5, edited by Fred Wendorf and Angela E. Close, pp. 1–92. Academic Press, New York.

Stoltman, James B.

1978 Temporal Models in Prehistory: An Example from Eastern North America. *Current Anthropology* 19:703–746.

1992 The Concept of Archaic in Eastern North America Prehistory. *Revista de Arqueología Americana* 5:101–118.

Stoltman, James B., and David A. Baerreis

1983 The Evolution of Human Ecosystems in the Eastern United States. In *Late-Quaternary Environments of the United States: 2. The Holocene*, edited by H. E. Wright Jr., pp. 252–268. University of Minnesota Press, Minneapolis.

Trigger, Bruce G.

1989 *A History of Archaeological Thought.* Cambridge University Press, Cambridge, England.

Walthall, John A.

1998 Rockshelters and Hunter-Gatherer Adaptations to the Pleistocene/Holocene Transition. *American Antiquity* 63:223–238.

Walthall, John A., and Brad Koldehoff

1998 Hunter-Gatherer Interaction and Alliance Formation: Dalton and the Cult of the Long Blade. *Plains Anthropologist* 43:257–273.

Webb, William

1946 Indian Knoll, Site Oh2, Ohio County, Kentucky. *Reports in Anthropology and Archaeology* 4(3):115–365. Department of Anthropology and Archaeology, University of Kentucky, Lexington.

Webb, William S., and David L. DeJarnette

1942 *An Archaeological Survey of Pickwick Basin in the Adjacent Portions of the States of Alabama, Mississippi and Tennessee.* Bulletin 129. Bureau of American Ethnology, Washington, D.C.

Webb, William S. and William G. Haag

1939 The Chiggerville Site, Site 1, Ohio County, Kentucky. *Reports in Anthropology and Archaeology* 4(1):1–62. Department of Anthropology and Archaeology, University of Kentucky, Lexington.

1940 Cypress Creek Villages, Sites 11 and 12, McLean County, Kentucky. *Reports in Anthropology and Archaeology* 4(2):67–110. Department of Anthropology and Archaeology, University of Kentucky, Lexington.

White, Leslie A.

1959 *The Evolution of Culture.* McGraw-Hill, New York.

Willey, Gordon R.

1966 *An Introduction to American Archaeology: 1. North and Middle America.* Prentice-Hall, Englewood Cliffs, New Jersey.

Willey, Gordon R., and Philip Phillips

1955 Method and Theory in American Archeology II: Historical Developmental Interpretation. *American Anthropologist* 57:723–819.

1958 *Method and Theory in American Archaeology.* University of Chicago Press, Chicago.

Willey, Gordon R., and Jeremy A. Sabloff

1973 *A History of American Archaeology.* W. H. Freeman, San Francisco.

1980 *A History of American Archaeology.* 2nd ed. W. H. Freeman, San Francisco.

3

Archaic Faunal Exploitation in the Prairie Peninsula and Surrounding Regions of the Midcontinent

Bonnie W. Styles and R. Bruce McMillan

Introduction

In this chapter, we contrast Archaic-period faunal exploitation strategies in different ecological settings across the Prairie Peninsula and into the deciduous forests to the east. To facilitate this discussion, we have defined a series of biogeographic regions that include the tallgrass prairie of the Prairie-Plains border; the open forests, savannas, and prairie patches of the Ozark Highland; the riverine environments of the great river valleys—the Mississippi and Illinois rivers; the prairies and groves of the Grand Prairie of Illinois; the eastern deciduous forests of Indiana, Ohio, and Michigan; and the northern pine-hardwood forests and littoral environments of the western Great Lakes (e.g., Bailey et al. 1994; Kuchler 1975). Critical for understanding faunal exploitation in this region is the time-transgressive development of the Prairie Peninsula, including the mid-Holocene expansion of the prairie, the opening of the forest, and the development of productive aquatic ecosystems in some major river valleys.

Landscapes varied dramatically across geographic space and through time, affecting the availability of animal resources. North-to-south variation ranged from the northern mixed conifer-hardwood forests of southern Ontario to the cypress swamps of southern Illinois, the prairies of western Iowa, and the eastern deciduous forest in Indiana and Ohio. The diverse area considered here crosscuts numerous physiographic divisions and provinces: the Central Lowlands (the Wisconsin Driftless Area, Till Plains, Dissected Till Plains, and Eastern and Western Lake sections), and the Interior Highlands (Ozark Highland) (Fenneman 1946). These landforms contributed to differences within and between the major ecological regions. Faunal availability varied across these diverse regions (e.g., Semken 1983; Shelford 1963).

We quantitatively examined faunal data for 48 Archaic components from 19 archaeological sites with satisfactory faunal preservation (Figure 3.1). For this study, we used pre-

Figure 3.1. Study area and Archaic sites used in the quantitative analyses of faunal exploitation.

settlement vegetation as a baseline from which to assess how the vegetation may have differed from region to region. Our assessments of environmental change for the early and middle Holocene are also informed by recent studies of fossil pollen and charcoal from lakes and fens in the Midwest.

Throughout this chapter, all dates are given in calibrated years before present (cal yr B.P.). Radiocarbon (^{14}C) ages are converted to calibrated ages utilizing IntCal04 (Reimer et al. 2004), available at http://www.calib.org. Table 3.1 presents the calibrated ages for ^{14}C dates at 100-year intervals. For the purposes of this discussion, we divide the Holocene epoch into the early Holocene (12,500–8900 cal yr B.P.), the middle Holocene (8900–5700 cal yr B.P.), and the late Holocene (post-5700 cal yr B.P.).

Holocene Evolution of Midwestern Biomes

Climate and a Changing Biota

Post-Pleistocene environmental changes contributed to variation in the resources available to Archaic hunters and foragers. Issues related to ecosystem evolution identified as important for understanding human use of fauna are the development of grassland and forest habitats, the stabilization of river systems, and changes in Great Lakes water levels. Rapid warming at the

Table 3.1. Chart for Converting Radiocarbon Dates in Radiocarbon Years B.P. (^{14}C Yr B.P.) to Calendar Years B.P. (Cal Yr B.P.).

^{14}C Yr B.P.	Cal Yr B.P.	^{14}C Yr B.P.	Cal Yr B.P.	^{14}C Yr B.P.	Cal Yr B.P.
100	109	4000	4479	7900	8693
200	177	4100	4608	8000	8881
300	389	4200	4738	8100	9022
400	480	4300	4856	8200	9162
500	526	4400	4960	8300	9335
600	605	4500	5167	8400	9448
700	666	4600	5320	8500	9509
800	712	4700	5391	8600	9545
900	827	4800	5512	8700	9633
1000	927	4900	5627	8800	9822
1100	1005	5000	5723	8900	10,034
1200	1123	5100	5810	9000	10,200
1300	1245	5200	5951	9100	10,242
1400	1309	5300	6083	9200	10,347
1500	1379	5400	6235	9300	10,512
1600	1471	5500	6297	9400	10,631
1700	1603	5600	6364	9500	10,752
1800	1736	5700	6477	9600	10,926
1900	1849	5800	6605	9700	11,163
2000	1949	5900	6715	9800	11,221
2100	2072	6000	6839	9900	11,279
2200	2238	6100	6968	10,000	11,468
2300	2335	6200	7086	10,100	11,711
2400	2419	6300	7220	10,200	11,908
2500	2582	6400	7336	10,300	12,083
2600	2744	6500	7425	10,400	12,276
2700	2797	6600	7493	10,500	12,518
2800	2903	6700	7574	10,600	12,688
2900	3035	6800	7640	10,700	12,780
3000	3201	6900	7723	10,800	12,831
3100	3334	7000	7843	10,900	12,870
3200	3418	7100	7940	11,000	12,919
3300	3523	7200	8001	11,100	13,010
3400	3651	7300	8105	11,200	13,110
3500	3771	7400	8250	11,300	13,188
3600	3906	7500	8343	11,400	13,262
3700	4037	7600	8400	11,500	13,339
3800	4187	7700	8482	–	–
3900	4344	7800	8578	–	–

Note: Conversions made using IntCal04 (Reimer et al. 2004).

end of the Pleistocene contributed to establishment of biotic communities that differed with the geographic expression of each region. Vegetation changed in structure and composition as dictated by climate and local edaphic features and by the differential response of individual taxa to climate change (Webb et al. 2004:472). The position and seasonal variation in air masses played a major role in the distribution of vegetation (e.g., Bryson 1966). The interplay between the Arctic, Pacific, and Gulf air masses as well as the circulation of ocean currents affected temperature, precipitation, and vegetation.

Shifts in the ranges of certain vertebrate species or increases in the abundance of specific taxa have been used to interpret changing landscape conditions. Climatically induced expansion of the prairie during the early Holocene pushed the prairie-forest ecotone eastward and opened and changed the composition of the mesic deciduous forests. The early Holocene deciduous forest was ultimately transformed into a more xeric and open oak-hickory association interspersed with prairie outliers and smaller patches that covered the interfluves and south-facing slopes.

With the opening of the arboreal vegetation, anthropogenic fire undoubtedly became a significant factor in maintaining, if not expanding, the parklandlike environment within forested areas, eliminating woody undergrowth and replacing the understory with grasses and forbs. Fire-scar studies in the Ozarks demonstrate that frequent fires maintained this vegetational regime. The biota was transformed by climate during the early to mid-Holocene but was maintained and further changed through human agency for the next several millennia (Cutter and Guyette 1994; Guyette and Cutter 1991). How far back in time the landscape was truly transformed by human intervention is still speculative, but charcoal-influx studies of wetland basins with stratigraphic records spanning the Holocene suggest that the human burning of midwestern landscapes may be as ancient as the period of major prairie expansion itself (Nelson 2005:53–54; Nelson et al. 2004:54).

From eastern Kansas to central Illinois expansion of the prairie from west to east was time transgressive. When patches of upland prairie first became established is still a question, but this probably occurred by the end of the Younger Dryas (10,650 cal yr B.P.), if not earlier. On the basis of his work along the South Fork of the Big Nemaha River in southeastern Nebraska, Baker (2000) presents evidence that prairie was well established on the thinly timbered uplands by 9800 cal yr B.P. By 9500 cal yr B.P. the full-blown development of the prairie was well underway as upland forests disappeared and riparian trees became sparse. During this time, alluvial fans began to aggrade rapidly in the valleys (Baker et al. 2000). This period of maximum aridity lasted for about three millennia. After ca. 6500 cal yr B.P., droughts apparently became more intermittent, aggradation of fans slowed, and riparian forests returned to the valleys (Baker et al. 2000).

South of the Missouri River along the western margins of the Ozark Highland in southwest Missouri, the collective appearance of grassland animals (bison, pronghorn, jack rabbit, plains pocket mouse, and prairie chicken) in the deposits of Rodgers Shelter by 9500 cal yr. B.P. argues for a change from a more mesic forested environment to a drier landscape wherein uplands and valley interfluves supported prairie (McMillan 1976:229; McMillan and Klippel 1981:230). After their initial appearance, prairie taxa increased so that by 9000 cal yr B.P. the greatest numbers of prairie taxa were present. This faunal evidence suggests that maximal expansion of prairie into the western Ozarks occurred during the two millennia after 9000 cal yr B.P. (McMillan and Klippel 1981). This interpretation is supported by subsequent faunal studies from Ozark sites (Purdue 1982; Purdue and Styles 1987; Wolverton 2002, 2005) and by analysis of temporal clinal variation in small mammals—eastern cottontail (*Sylvilagus floridanus*), gray squirrel (*Sciurus carolinensis*), and fox squirrel (*Sciurus niger*) (Purdue 1980). More recently, Denniston and colleagues (Denniston et al. 2000; Denniston et al. 1999) have reported the results of carbon isotopic research on speleothems from caves in the Ozark Highland, a record they then compared with pollen records from Cupola Pond (Smith 1984) and Oldfield Swamp (King and Allen 1977) and with the vertebrate biostratigraphic sequences at Rodgers Shelter and Modoc Rock Shelter. The speleothem data, which provide an independent proxy for vegetation, support the interpretation of steppelike conditions in the Ozark Highland between approximately 9000 and 1500 cal yr B.P. (Denniston et al. 1999:381).

Holocene pollen records from artesian spring deposits in western Missouri are discontinuous and incomplete (King 1982, 1988), even though some of the same springs yielded pollen records that aided in constructing vegetation models for the late Wisconsin (King 1973). Pollen and plant macrofossils from organic-rich alluvial sediments from along the lower Sac River in southwest Missouri provide some tentative results for comparison with the Rodgers Shelter faunal data (Baker et al. 2005). These data suggest that by 9000 cal yr B.P., percentages of nonarboreal pollen (NAP) were high and were increasing and that percentages of oak (*Quercus*) and maple (*Acer*) pollen were relatively low. Big bluestem (*Andropogon gerardii*) and Indian grass (*Sorghastrum nutans*) macrofossils were present (Baker et al. 2005:35–36). After 7300 cal yr B.P., Baker et al. (2005:34) suggest, there was a return to a higher percentage of deciduous trees, with more diversity in the riparian forest and recolonizaton of the more mesic habitats along valleys by sugar maple (*Acer saccharum*) and American elm (*Ulmus americana*). Macrofossils from prairie plants were still abundant, indicating that the uplands were a mosaic of forest and prairie. Historical records indicate that the presettlement vegetation of the uplands was primarily prairie and oak savannah, while the steeper valley slopes and floodplains were dominated by dense deciduous forest (Jacobson and Primm 1997:12). Although tree cover probably thinned and receded down ravines and valley slopes during the mid-Holocene, faunal evidence suggests that throughout this period arboreal vegetation continued to cover the valley floors.

On the northern border of the Prairie Peninsula in Minnesota, the late Wisconsin spruce forest was replaced with an elm-dominated mesic assemblage (Webb et al. 1983:161). This transition began around 11,400 cal yr B.P. and lasted until ca. 9000 cal yr B.P. This mesic vegetation assemblage indicates that the northern Midwest was slightly cooler and more moist than during later parts of the Holocene. Prairie advanced eastward following the early Holocene mesic phase and was fully developed in Minnesota by 9000 cal yr B.P., then retreated ca. 4500 cal yr B.P. with the onset of a cooler, wetter climate that favored arboreal vegetation (McAndrews 1966:67; Webb et al. 1983:162). Once prairie was established, fire became an important factor in maintaining the mosaic of prairie and forest along the prairie-forest ecotone (Grimm 1984).

Pollen, plant macrofossils, and carbon isotopic ($\delta^{13}C$) values for alluvial organic matter in samples collected along Roberts Creek in northeast Iowa, when compared with carbon isotopic values in speleothem calcite from Coldwater Cave 60 km northwest of Roberts Creek, provide a multiproxy record of Holocene environments that suggests a steep climatic gradient across Iowa. Prairie did not reach this area in northeastern Iowa until sometime between 6300 and 6000 cal yr B.P. (Baker et al. 1996; Baker et al. 1998; Chumbley et al. 1990; Dorale et al. 1992). A similar record obtained from Mud Creek indicates that deciduous forest was extant in east-central Iowa at 6300 cal yr B.P. (Baker et al. 1990). These records indicate that prairie existed for much of the next three millennia, until ca. 3500 cal yr B.P., when oak savanna returned. Baker et al. (1992:387) suggest that fires may have played an important role in maintaining savanna-like vegetation following the amelioration of climate after the peak dry conditions of the mid-Holocene.

In southern Wisconsin, Baker et al. (1992:386) suggest, a xeric oak (*Quercus*) forest replaced mesic deciduous forest by 6300 cal yr B.P. Grimm et al. (2001:339–340) propose that prairie began replacing the elm-oak forest slightly earlier, sometime between 6800 and 6300 cal yr B.P. Grimm and Jacobson (2004:392–393) stress that mesic forest prevailed in the driftless region of southeastern Minnesota and northeastern Iowa during the driest part of the prairie period in central Minnesota. They cite the stable-isotope data from cave speleothems and plant fossil data to support a model that fixes the position of the prairie-forest border along a sharp gradient between southeastern Minnesota and northeastern Iowa between 8000 and 6000 cal yr B.P. After 6000 cal yr B.P., the prairie expanded eastward, forested areas opened, and more xeric trees (oaks) replaced mesic-adapted vegetation. A mosaic of prairie, savanna, and open forest was created across this region, dictated in part by areas of relief and firebreaks.

Recent research has helped clarify the timing of the development and expansion of prairie into the glacially modified landscapes of Illinois. Since the 1960s, most researchers have followed the model proposed by H. E. Wright Jr. (1968), which posited gradual warming and desiccation beginning on the western edge of the tallgrass prairies in South Dakota and gradually spreading east, reaching its maximum extent between 9000 and 4500 cal yr B.P. During the late Holocene, cooler climate gradually returned to the Midwest, reversing the expansion of the Prairie Peninsula. King (1980, 1981), in his interpretation of stratigraphic pollen sequences from Volo and Chatsworth bogs in northeast and east-central Illinois, supported Wright's model and suggested that prairie vegetation was established in Illinois between ca. 9500 and 8700 cal yr B.P. Wright's general model for the Prairie Peninsula and King's work in northern and east-central Illinois established a paradigm for the vegetational history of the Prairie Peninsula in Illinois. Webb et al. (1983) refined this model on the basis of data from 49 pollen-bearing sites from throughout the northern Prairie Peninsula. They constructed isofrequency contours for prairie-forb pollen at millennial intervals between 11,200 and 6800 cal yr B.P. and suggested that the 20 percent isopoll for prairie-forb pollen intersected northeastern Illinois ca. 8800 cal yr B.P. They observe, however, that prairie-forb pollen decreased at Chatsworth Bog between 8800 and 7800 cal yr B.P., indicating a shift back to greater percentages of arboreal components. Prairie forbs did not increase in abundance until 6800–3200 cal yr B.P., a period when prairie forbs were actually decreasing further west (Webb et al. 1983:147).

Baker and his colleagues at the University of Iowa continued to refine this model, questioning whether or not prairie expansion in eastern Iowa, Illinois, and southern Wisconsin was as early and as extensive as some previous authors had claimed (Baker et al. 1992:380). Examining data from fossil-pollen sites along the axis of the Prairie Peninsula, they note the virtual absence in sites in Ohio and Indiana of "such prairie-indicator taxa as *Ambrosia* (ragweed), *Artemisia* (wormwood), Chenopodiineae (goosefoot family and related taxa), Poaceae (grass family), and Asteraceae (sunflower family)" (Baker et al. 1992:380). They observe that Chatsworth Bog exhibits relatively insignificant increases in these prairie elements. Baker et al. (1992) conclude that the climatic signal recorded for Roberts Creek (eastern Iowa) indicates that prairie supplanted mesic deciduous forest in eastern Iowa and northern Illinois only after 6300 cal yr B.P. and that in southern Wisconsin (Devil's Lake and Lima Bog) a xeric oak (*Quercus*) forest replaced mesic deciduous forest after that same time. Grimm et al. (2001:339) subsequently placed the expansion of prairie in eastern Iowa, southern Wisconsin, and Illinois between 6800 and 6300 cal yr B.P., where it replaced forest dominated by elm (*Ulmus*) and oak (*Quercus*).

Recent work is beginning to establish a more precise timing for the development of prairie in Illinois. Paleoecological research at Nelson Lake in Kane County and Chatsworth Bog in Livingston County in the heart of the Grand Prairie suggests that a period of drought occurred ca. 9000 cal yr B.P., when C_4 grasses began replacing the elm-dominated arboreal vegetation. The records at both Nelson Lake and Chatsworth

Bog show increases of NAP from ca. 5 percent at 11,500 cal yr B.P. to ca. 35 percent by 9000 cal yr B.P., suggesting that prairie was expanding as the climate became progressively drier (Nelson 2005; Nelson et al. 2004; Nelson et al. 2006). This initial prairie pulse lasted about 1,500 years. After ca. 7700 cal yr B.P. at Chatsworth Bog and ca. 7300 cal yr B.P. at Nelson Lake, trees again increased, including fire-sensitive taxa such as *Ulmus* (Nelson et al. 2006:2533). During the driest phase of the mid-Holocene (after ca. 6200 cal yr B.P.) NAP increased to ca. 50 percent and C_4 plants were abundant, marking the full development of prairie in Illinois (Nelson et al. 2006:2533). Grimm and Jacobson (2004:392–393) conclude that the prairie initially expanded about 9000 cal yr B.P., then retreated, and then expanded again in northern Illinois, with prairie reaching its maximum extent between 6800 and 3200 cal yr B.P. This "maximum prairie period" was then followed by a period of more moderate climate with increased precipitation. Significantly, once prairie was established in Illinois, this grassland biome persisted with the aid of fire into the Historic period.

Transeau's map of the Prairie Peninsula shows that prairie historically extended east into northwestern Indiana, especially between the Kankakee and Wabash River drainages, with outliers as far east as west-central Ohio and southern Michigan (Transeau 1935:Figure 1). But, overall, the geographic region encompassed by Indiana, Ohio, and southern Michigan was covered by deciduous forests, grading into mixed deciduous-conifer forests to the north. These forests were dynamic throughout the Holocene, with mesic and xeric arboreal species responding individualistically to climatic shifts in temperature or moisture. Kapp (1999:53) has presented a model of changing vegetation for southern Michigan and northern Indiana that is based on the work by Williams (1974) at Pretty Lake in northern Indiana. His summary identifies an early Holocene mesic forest established between 10,700 and 9500 cal yr B.P. that was supplanted by oak savanna and prairie after a period of warming and drying that culminated between 9500 and 8100 cal yr B.P. After 8100 cal yr B.P., the mesic forest returned, following a regime of greater effective moisture, as recorded by increases in beech (*Fagus*) pollen in cores from Pretty Lake (Williams 1974) and Clear Lake (Bailey 1972). This increase marked the beginning of a warm, moist period that was dated ca. 6800–5200 cal yr B.P. After 5200 cal yr B.P., the climate shifted back to a drier regime and reached maximum warmth and dryness. During this interval, prairie expanded and the oak-hickory forest opened (Kapp 1999:53). Kapp (1999:53) identified two prairie phases, with a mesic arboreal phase sandwiched between them. The latter "prairie phase," with scattered stands of open oak-hickory forest and C_4 plants, was the period of peak dryness. This bimodal pattern was first seen in Illinois (Nelson et al. 2004). Given the more refined AMS dating for the Illinois sites, the dates given by Kapp (1999:53) for the initial prairie phase (as well as the dates for the onset of the succeeding mesic-forest phase) seem too early. We would expect the timing of these vegetation changes to be more in concert with those in Illinois. However, some transgressive time lapse would be anticipated further east. Redating the cores from Pretty Lake and Clear Lake would help clarify this issue.

The Holocene pollen record for Ohio is somewhat sketchy, but that from the East Twin Lake site in eastern Ohio (Shane 1989) indicates that the early Holocene deciduous forest was dominated by oak, followed by an interval in the mid-Holocene when beech (*Fagus*) became far more common. Following this mesic interval, climate became warmer and drier after 5000 cal yr B.P. Prairie outliers probably became established in western Ohio at this time. This drier climatic regime would have favored opening of the forest, which was no doubt aided by fire.

River Systems and the Great Lakes

River systems changed dramatically during the Holocene (e.g., Hajic 1990; Knox 1985, 1993), and these changes were not synchronous or unidirectional in their effects on aquatic resources (e.g., Styles 1995, in press). At the end of the Pleistocene, impounded meltwater at the margins of the Laurentide ice sheet overtopped or burst through moraines, causing enormous river floods (Montgomery and Wohl 2004:225). Catastrophic meltwater megafloods flowed down the Mississippi River until 12,900 cal yr B.P., when meltwater, bolstered by a release of water from proglacial Lake Agassiz, was redirected eastward through the now-exposed Hudson and St. Lawrence rivers (Clark et al. 2001:283; Montgomery and Wohl 2004:225–226). This influx of cold water into the Atlantic Ocean forced the abrupt climatic cooling associated with the Younger Dryas between 12,900 and 11,400 cal yr B.P. (Clark et al. 2001:283). Redirection of meltwater through different drainage systems occurred both before and after this time (Clark et al. 2001:284). As meltwater floods subsided and sea levels rose in the Holocene, many streams aggraded.

During the Holocene, climate changes continued to affect levels of discharge and sediment transport and deposition (Montgomery and Wohl 2004:226). For example, the Mississippi and the Illinois rivers ultimately evolved from braided, glacial-outwash streams to meandering streams with flood-basin and oxbow lakes, a change that occurred earlier in the Mississippi River valley (Hajic 1990, 1991). These productive, shallow lakes developed in the Illinois and Mississippi floodplains during the mid-Holocene and provided optimal habitat for spawning fish (Hill 1975; Styles 1986). Annual floods restocked the lakes (e.g., Styles 1981). There is evidence for periodic, Holocene megafloods in the Mississippi River basin (e.g., Brown et al. 1999; Knox 1985, 1993). Geologists are refining the timing of major, possibly episodic Holocene flood events, which are ultimately related to changes in continental precipitation (Brown et al. 1999). For example, Knox (1985) has documented periods of large

Mississippi River floods between 6800–5700 cal yr B.P. and 3500–2000 cal yr B.P. that resulted in channel migration and removal of floodplain alluvium. The impacts of these floods on floodplain habitats, settlement practices, and subsistence strategies are subjects for further research. On the western edge of the study area along the southern border of the Prairie Peninsula and in the central Ozark Highland, fluvial evolution took a different course. Changes in mid-Holocene aridity reduced water flow in small streams in these areas, leading to degradation of habitat for some aquatic species (e.g., Klippel et al. 1982; Warren 1995, 1996).

The configuration, connectivity, and water levels in the Great Lakes changed dramatically as post-Pleistocene deglaciation progressed (Larson and Schaetz 2001). Differential isostatic deformation of the lake basins, catastrophic overflows from proglacial Lake Agassiz, drainage of the lakes variously through northern and southern outlets, channel downcutting, and Holocene climate changes all affected lake levels and areas (e.g., Larsen 1999:28–30; Larson and Schaetz 2001). Water levels rose and fell dramatically in the Great Lakes during the Holocene. Larsen (1999:27–29) provides the following summary of Holocene changes in the Great Lakes: In the early Holocene around 11,300 cal yr B.P., the Lake Superior basin was still covered with glacial ice. Separate lakes occupied deep basins of Lakes Huron and Michigan, and water levels in the Lake Michigan, Huron, Erie, and Ontario basins were lower than their modern levels (Chippewa and Stanley low levels). Lake levels rose, and Michigan and Huron became connected around 9000 cal yr B.P. (pre-Nipissing transgression), but lake levels were still lower than modern ones. Studies of terraces indicate that lake levels were high at 5100 cal yr B.P. (Nipissing I), 4500 cal yr B.P. (Nipissing II), and 3400 cal yr B.P. (Algoma). Lake levels in the Michigan, Huron, and Superior basins were higher than today during these intervals; lake levels in the Erie and Ontario basins were also high, but were still lower than modern levels. Periods of low water, although with higher levels than recorded for the modern lakes, and shorter-term fluctuations in lake levels also occurred. Around 2,000 years ago, Lake Superior was separated from Michigan and Huron. Climate change was probably the primary cause of lake-level fluctuations during the Nipissing and Algoma stages and over the last 2,000 years (Larsen 1999:29). Lake levels in the Holocene varied by as much as 24 to 30 m, which affected plant and animal communities and the rivers that flowed into the lakes (Kapp 1999:41; Lovis 1986; Robertson 1987; Robertson et al. 1999:97).

Faunal Records from Archaic Sites

We have organized our discussions of faunal data under six biogeographic regions (Table 3.2) where Holocene ecosystem evolution has differed because of climate variation, physiography, and edaphic factors as well as time transgression in climate-induced change across the Midcontinent. These issues affect resource patterning and availability on both a local and regional scale.

As a prelude to our quantitative analyses, we present a general discussion of what is known about faunal exploitation and subsistence for each of the geographic regions. Multiple sites with Archaic components containing faunal remains are mentioned in the text, but only 19 sites yielded samples large enough for comparative analyses. The dearth of faunal data for Archaic sites can be attributed to poor preservation in many depositional situations or, in some instances, to early excavations in which recovery techniques and identification of remains failed to meet modern standards. Furthermore, our intent was not to provide a compendium of all Archaic sites that have produced faunal remains. Instead, we discuss sites that aid in clarifying the regional pattern for faunal exploitation, and from those we have selected 19 sites for quantitative analysis. The 48 Archaic components analyzed herein clearly demonstrate different trajectories of regional faunal exploitation that are closely linked to differences in resource availability through time and space across the midwestern landscape.

Western Prairie Peninsula

The western Prairie Peninsula, as defined here, includes the western portions of Minnesota, Iowa, and Missouri, essentially the western portions of the Prairie Peninsula shown on Transeau's (1935) map. Two sites just west of these state boundaries have been included because they contained faunal records useful for comparison with sites further east. These are the Logan Creek site (Sheehan 1998; Widga 2003), in eastern Nebraska just west of the Missouri River, and the Coffey site (Schmits 1978, 1980), situated on the east bank of the Big Blue River in northeastern Kansas. Both sites are located in the tallgrass prairie (e.g., Bailey et al. 1994).

Several Archaic sites in western Iowa have produced faunal assemblages dominated by bison. These are sites that occur along the Little Sioux River in northeastern Iowa and along Pony Creek in the southwestern part of the state. Additional sites that are related to this complex occur in western Minnesota, along the St. Croix River on the Minnesota-Wisconsin line, and in eastern North Dakota just west of the Minnesota state line. Kay (1998:176) has termed this series of sites the "Logan Creek complex," after the Logan Creek site, while others simply refer to it as "Prairie Archaic" (e.g., Tatum 1980:159). Sites included here are Cherokee Sewer, Simonsen, Ocheyedan, Hill, and Lungren in Iowa (Anderson et al. 1980:262); Itasca (Shay 1971) and Granite Falls (Kuehn 2000) in Minnesota; Rustad (Michlovic and Running 2005) and Smilden-Rostberg (Larson and Penny 1991) in North Dakota; and, potentially, Interstate Park (Palmer 1954; Pond 1937) and Nye (Eddy and Jenks 1935) in Wisconsin. Recent research on the Interstate Park collection and records has suggested, however, that the

Table 3.2. Archaic Sites with Faunal Records Analyzed for this Study.

Region	Site	Location, Presettlement Vegetation	Cal Yr B.P.	Period Context ^{14}C Yr B.P. (Component)	References
Western Border Prairie Peninsula	Cherokee Sewer	Iowa, tallgrass prairie	9400	late Early Archaic Horizon III 8400 B.P. (EA2)	Pyle 1980; Semken 1974; Whittaker 1998
	Cherokee Sewer		8300–8000	middle Middle Archaic Horizon II 7450–7200 B.P. (MA2a)	
	Cherokee Sewer		7200	middle Middle Archaic Horizon I 6350 B.P. (MA2b)	
	Logan Creek	Nebraska, tallgrass prairie	7900	middle Middle Archaic Zone D 7070 B.P. (MA2a)	Widga 2003
	Logan Creek		7800	middle Middle Archaic Zone C 7020 B.P. (MA2b)	
	Logan Creek		7200	middle Middle Archaic Zone B 6340 B.P. (MA2c)	
	Logan Creek		6800	late Middle Archaic Zone A 6020 B.P. (MA3)	
	Coffey	northeastern Kansas; Big Blue River; tallgrass prairie	6100	late Middle Archaic Horizon III-8 5270 B.P. (MA3a)	Schmits 1978
	Coffey		5900	late Middle Archaic Horizon III-7 5175 B.P. (MA3b)	
	Coffey		5900	late Middle Archaic Horizon III-5 5163 B.P. (MA3c)	
Ozark Highland	Rodgers Shelter	west-central Missouri, Pomme de Terre River; southern edge of Prairie Peninsula; prairie parkland	12,500–10,800	early Early Archaic, Dalton Shelter levels 21–24 Main Excavation levels 36–41 10,500–9500 B.P. (EA1)	Klippel et al. 1982; Parmalee et al. 1976; Purdue 1982
	Rodgers Shelter		9600–9000	late Early Archaic Shelter level 19 Main Excavation levels 19–25 8600–8100 B.P. (EA2)	

Table 3.2. Archaic Sites with Faunal Records Analyzed for this Study, continued.

Region	Site	Location, Presettlement Vegetation	Cal Yr B.P.	Period Context ^{14}C Yr B.P. (Component)	References
Ozark Highland	Rodgers Shelter		7600–6000	late Middle Archaic Shelter level 11 Main Excavation levels 11–14 6700–5200 B.P. (MA3)	
	Rodgers Shelter		3900–2600	Late Archaic Levels 3–4 3600–2500 B.P. (LA)	
	Little Freeman Cave	central Missouri; Big Piney River, northern Ozark Highlands; deciduous forest	9400	late Early Archaic Unit 3, Stratum 4 8400 B.P. (EA2)	Styles and White 1997
	Little Freeman Cave		6600	late Middle Archaic Unit 3, Stratum 3 5800 B.P. (MA3)	
Ozark Highland (Northern Border)	Graham Cave	northern Missouri; Loutre River; dissected hill country; deciduous forest	11,200–10,200	Early Archaic Natural Level 4 Arbitrary Level Zone IV (Level 5B) 9700–9000 B.P. (EA1)	Klippel 1971
	Graham Cave		8700	early Middle Archaic Natural Level 3 Arbitrary Level Zone III (Level 3B) 7900 B.P. (MA1)	
	Graham Cave		8400	late Middle Archaic/Late Archaic Natural Level 2 Arbitrary Level Zone II (Level 2A) 7600–? B.P. (MA–LA)	
Illinois and Mississippi River valleys	Napoleon Hollow	west-central Illinois; Illinois River valley; deciduous forest	7800–7500	middle Middle Archaic Napoleon component 7000–6630 B.P. (MA2)	Styles 1992
	Napoleon Hollow		7000–5700	late Middle Archaic Helton component 6130–5010 B.P. (MA3)	
	Koster		9200–8400	early Middle Archaic Horizons 10B, 10A, 9C/D, 8F, 8E 8200–7600 B.P. (MA1)	
	Koster		8100–7700	middle Middle Archaic Horizons 8D, 8C, 8B, 8A 7300–6850 B.P. (MA2)	

Table 3.2. Archaic Sites with Faunal Records Analyzed for this Study, continued.

Region	Site	Location, Presettlement Vegetation	Cal Yr B.P.	Period Context ^{14}C Yr B.P. (Component)	References
Illinois and Mississippi River valleys	Koster		6500–5600	late Middle Archaic Horizons 6 lower, 6 main 5700–4900 B.P. (MA3)	
	Modoc Rock Shelter	west-southern Illinois; Mississippi River valley; deciduous forest	9500–9200	Early Archaic Central Shelter Strata 30–31, 28, 23/26, 20/21, 15–19, 14 8500–8200 B.P. (EA2)	Styles and White 1991; Thorson and Styles 1992
	Modoc Rock Shelter		8900–8000	early Middle Archaic Central Shelter Strata 12/13, 11/ 10, 9, 7/8, 6 8000–7200 B.P. (MA1)	
	Modoc Rock Shelter		7600–7100	middle Middle Archaic Central Shelter Strata 5, 4, 3, 2, 1; 6800–6200 B.P. (MA2)	
	Modoc Rock Shelter		6400–6000	late Middle Archaic Central Shelter Strata A, A2 5600–5200 B.P. (MA3)	
	Modoc Rock Shelter		5400–4900	early Late Archaic Central Shelter Strata B, 9E, 8 E/C 4700–4300 B.P. (LA1)	
Grand Prairie Illinois	Pabst	central Illinois; tallgrass prairie		Late Archaic (LA)	Lewis 1979
Eastern Deciduous Forest	Riverton	eastern Illinois; Wabash River valley; deciduous forest		Late Archaic (LA)	Parmalee 1969:139–144; Winters 1969
	Swan Island	eastern Illinois; Wabash River valley; deciduous forest		Late Archaic (LA)	Parmalee 1969:139–144; Winters 1969
	Robeson Hills	eastern Illinois; Wabash River valley; deciduous forest		Late Archaic (LA)	Parmalee 1969:139–144; Winters 1969
	Black Earth		6200	late Middle Archaic Area A, 3C 5400 B.P. (MA3b)	
	Black Earth		5800	late Middle Archaic Area A, 3B 5120 B.P. (MA3c)	
	Black Earth		5600	late Middle Archaic Area A, 3A 4860 B.P. (MA3d)	

Table 3.2. Archaic Sites with Faunal Records Analyzed for this Study, continued.

Region	Site	Location, Presettlement Vegetation	Cal Yr B.P.	Period Context ^{14}C Yr B.P. (Component)	References
Eastern Deciduous Forest	Bluegrass	southwestern Indiana upland; upper reaches of a tributary to the Ohio River	6100–5700	late Middle Archaic 5300–5000 B.P. (MA3)	Stafford et al. 2000
	Railway Museum	western Kentucky; Ohio River valley; deciduous forest		Late Archaic (LA)	Yerkes and Machuga 1994:194–229
	Raddatz Rockshelter	southern Wisconsin; deciduous forest		Early Archaic Level 12 (EA)	Cleland 1966:98–108; Parmalee 1959:83–90; Wittry 1959a:33–69
	Raddatz Rockshelter		5950	Middle Archaic Levels 5–11 5200 B.P. (MA)	Boszhardt 1977
	Raddatz Rockshelter			Late Archaic Levels 3–4 (LA)	
	Durst Rockshelter	southern Wisconsin; deciduous forest		Middle Archaic Zone VI (MA)	Parmalee 1960:11–17; Wittry 1959b:137–267
	Durst Rockshelter			Late Archaic Zone V (LA)	
Great Lakes	Weber I	northern Michigan; Saginaw Valley; deciduous forest	7100–5300	late Middle Archaic Zone II 6200–4600 B.P. (MA3)	Monaghan et al. 1986; Smith 1989; Smith and Egan 1990
	Weber I		3200	late Late Archaic Zone I 3000–2900 B.P. (LA2)	

remains at this locality represent a natural death assemblage (Hawley et al. 2007), and Hill has informed us that Nye may represent multiple localities within the St. Croix River valley. All of these archaeological sites date between 9500 and 7000 cal yr B.P., except for the two later components at Logan Creek, which date to 6850 and 6000 cal yr B.P., respectively. Summary statements for this complex of Early to Middle Archaic sites have been published by Caldwell and Henning (1978:12–122), Anderson and Semken (1980), Kay (1998:174–177), and Frison (2001:144–145).

Collectively, these sites range from kill sites to processing camps and seasonal habitations, but all seem to have been occupied by hunter-forager bands that shared a common tradition. Although bison hunting seemed to have been a focus, some sites show a broader range of fauna, indicating that, at least seasonally, other animals provided important supplements to the diet. Since many of these sites are bison kill sites or meat processing camps, one would not expect to find much diversity in the fauna. In camps that spanned multiple seasons, such as has been suggested for the Itasca site in north-central Minnesota (Shay 1971:64–65), faunal diversity is greater. According to Shay (1971:64–65), the Itasca site occupation includes a fall bison kill and processing camp but also a spring camp focused on fishing. Widga (2006:58), who recently examined the fauna from the Itasca site, interprets the bison kill as representing more than a single event on the basis of additional ^{14}C dates on purified collagen from bison bone. He also argues that the fish and aquatic turtle remains represent natural accumulations that are unrelated to the archaeological assemblage. Widga based his argument on a lack of burning and modification of fish and turtle bones. However, we offer a word of caution in that bones in food refuse are often unburned or lack modification.

The Itasca site was historically situated in jack-pine barrens with larger openings supporting bluestem prairie. Forty kilometers to the west was the border with the continuous tallgrass prairie. The site report did not present faunal tallies separately by component, so only a gross assessment is possible. Even so, the composition of the Middle Archaic fauna at this site appears to reflect its setting along a shallow bay of Lake Itasca. Remains from fish, including walleye, northern pike, suckers, bass, other sunfish, and minnows dominate the assemblage. They contribute 62 percent of the vertebrate number of identified specimens (NISP) (Shay 1971), but a question has now been raised as to whether these remains represent cultural or natural accumulation. Bison remains far outnumber other mammalian taxa, and recent dates (7970–7790 cal yr B.P. and 8519–8179 cal yr B.P.) suggest more than one death event (Widga 2006:58). Proximal prairie patches may have been larger, and the prairie border may have been closer to the site during the middle Holocene (McAndrews 1966).

Plains archaeologists have characterized these groups as broad-spectrum hunter-gatherers (Caldwell and Henning 1978; Mayer-Oakes 1959; Wedel 1961, 1986) and specialized bison hunters (Reeves 1973) and, more recently, have recognized the use of a mix of strategies (Frison 1991; Sheehan 1998). Nevertheless, the availability of bison as a high-quality, high-quantity subsistence item provides a nice contrast to adaptations by Archaic foragers farther east. We selected two sites from this region—Cherokee Sewer and Logan Creek—for our analysis and for comparison with other sites across the Midwest.

The Cherokee Sewer site lies in the tallgrass prairie along the western border of the Prairie Peninsula in northwestern Iowa. It is situated along the Little Sioux River, but evidence for exploitation of aquatic resources is limited to a few scraps of fish bone. Bison dominate the Early and Middle Archaic components at this site. Other prairie taxa include prairie vole, plains pocket gopher, and ground squirrel, but bison contributed by far the most bones and, by inference, the most meat. Both components are interpreted as winter processing sites for bison killed in close proximity (Tatum and Shutler 1980:251), and, thus, they provide only a partial view of Early and Middle Archaic subsistence strategies in the region.

The Logan Creek site is located along the western border of the Prairie Peninsula in tallgrass prairie in eastern Nebraska. We compare the site's middle Holocene assemblages to Middle Archaic patterns in this chapter on the basis of the age of the site, but they are considered Early Archaic by Plains anthropologists. The faunal remains are primarily associated with short-term bison processing camps. However, the component dated to 7800 cal yr B.P. is slightly more diverse and may represent a longer stay at a processing site (Widga 2003:161). The fauna is dominated by bison and includes numerous other prairie species, including pronghorn, bison, plains pocket gopher, ground squirrel, blacktail prairie dog, jack rabbit, and badger.

In addition to the Prairie Archaic sites described above, we also selected a site from northeastern Kansas that had good faunal preservation. The Coffey site is located in tallgrass prairie along the western border of the Prairie Peninsula. Bones from bison and fish dominate the late Middle Archaic deposits at Coffey (Schmits 1978). Fish bones are surprisingly abundant at this prairie site. This pattern no doubt reflects its location on the Big Blue River, which was the likely source of the ducks, geese, and softshell turtle, in addition to the fish (including numerous catfish). The Coffey site is a unique site in the tallgrass prairie because of the productivity of the Big Blue River. The Big Blue River is a tributary to the Kansas River, which is also known for rich fish resources. On the basis of a variety of archaeological evidence, the Coffey site is considered a base camp (Schmits 1978:155) and, thus, provides a more complete view of the subsistence system in this region. Not surprising, given its location, the three mid-Holocene components at the Coffey site show high proportions of bone from prairie species, primarily from bison, but also including thirteen-lined ground squirrel and plains pocket gopher. The floodplain near the site is forested today, but this riparian habitat may have been reduced during the mid-Holocene.

Another site complements the pattern of bison procurement at these prairie sites. The Sutter site, dating between 8350 and 8900 cal yr B.P. (Katz 1973:168), was located on a small tributary at some distance from a major stream. The location is about 90 km southeast of the Coffey site and contained two large, stained features strewn with bison bones. The site report presented no quantitative faunal analysis, but the inventory consisted mostly of bison elements and a bone each of rabbit and bird. The site is interpreted as a bison processing camp adjacent to a marshy area where, the site investigator believes, the animals were dispatched (Katz 1971:15–17). We added this site because the early Middle Archaic projectile point styles at Sutter are comparable to points from Rodgers Shelter to the southeast, where a modicum of prairie species representing this period was recovered.

The Stigenwalt site in southeastern Kansas provides a contrast with bison procurement and processing sites of the eastern Plains. This settlement contained an Early to Middle Archaic faunal assemblage that more closely resembled the pattern of broad-spectrum, small-mammal procurement described for the Middle Archaic in the western Ozark Highland (McMillan and Klippel 1981; Parmalee et al. 1976; Purdue 1982). The site is approximately 80 km west of the Kansas-Missouri border in Labette County, located on the Osage Plains (Fenneman 1917; Schoewe 1949:276). A buried stratigraphic unit within a small alluvial/colluvial fan along the valley margin of Big Hill Creek contained this cultural horizon (Mandel 1990; Thies 1990:51–65). Radiocarbon dates (Thies 1990:109) calibrated to 9800–9000 cal yr B.P. and 8400–8250 cal yr B.P. provide ages for the top and base of the stratigraphic unit in two discrete areas of the site, allowing separation of the fauna into late Early Archaic and early Middle Archaic components. Rabbits (*Lepus* and *Syvilagus*) and small rodents constitute the majority of the fauna in both these assemblages (Finnegan and West 1990); however, lagomorphs and rodents, which represent 82 percent of the NISP

of the Archaic components, the overall faunal composition suggests that Early Holocene and mid-Holocene hunters took deer, squirrel, eastern cottontail, other small mammals, and birds (Styles and White 1997). They made little use of fish in these settlements. Changes in species composition and diversity of freshwater mussels for other cave sites in the same region (Miller Cave and Sadies's Cave) suggest that the magnitude of streams was reduced in the mid-Holocene (Warren 1995, 1996). The faunal subsistence base was diverse for these occupations, similar to the case at Rodgers Shelter.

A second cave site, Tick Creek Cave, is located on a small tributary of the Gasconade River just 32 km northeast of Little Freeman Cave. The cave is situated between rolling uplands that historically supported a mosaic of prairie and forest and a more dissected forested hill country bordering the Gasconade River. Excavations carried out by amateurs in the early 1960s (Roberts 1965) unearthed Archaic and Woodland components that contained extensive deposits of faunal subsistence remains. Paul Parmalee (1965) identified 31,590 bones from Tick Creek Cave, of which deer accounted for more than 75 percent of the mammal bone from all levels. Although the site was excavated in 6-inch levels within 5-foot-square units, the amateurs lacked the experience to sort out postdepositional disturbances, and, thus, mixing was a serious problem. Because of this problem, the site has largely been ignored by most analysts.

Parmalee (1965:4–8) used the simplified breakdown of materials into "Woodland" and "Archaic" categories provided by the excavators to report the fauna. This system for sorting the fauna was patently flawed, and the chronological implications of the fauna, as reported, have very little meaning. Having said this, we still regard Tick Creek Cave as an important site given the sheer volume of faunal remains. McMillan (1963) examined two of the excavation units and plotted the faunal remains by level. Chipped- and ground-stone artifacts from the total excavation were also plotted by level, an exercise that demonstrated that, despite some mixing, there is superposition of cultural materials. Early, Middle, and Late Archaic and Late Woodland materials (as determined by projectile point styles and presence or absence of ceramics) sort out in the appropriate sequence. Given the relative superposition of these components, one can say with some confidence that most of the faunal deposit is representative of the Archaic components, not Woodland, as reported by Parmalee (1965:4–8). In fact, a rich Middle and Late Archaic deposit is represented by extensive remains of white-tailed deer. White-tailed deer remains are so prevalent that this high-rank prey species must have been locally abundant in the extensive edge areas in this region. In addition to deer remains, which made up ca. 78 percent of the fauna, turkey, raccoon, cottontail, and box turtle were also important (McMillan 1963:159–160). As the forested landscape of the interior Ozarks opened during the mid-Holocene, areas of optimal habitat for deer were created, to which Archaic hunters and foragers would have been attracted. Tick Creek Cave, like Graham Cave (Klippel 1971), provides evidence for a coalescence of Middle Archaic hunters and foragers into these resource-rich ecological settings during the mid-Holocene, areas that, because of their relative resource potential, were preferred after 9000 cal yr. B.P. (McMillan and Styles 1979).

At Graham Cave, located near the Loutre River on the northern border of the Ozark Highland in the forested, dissected hill country just south of Missouri's till plain, the pattern is different from that in the more xeric prairie-parkland settings to the southwest. At this site, deer and eastern cottontail increased in abundance and gray squirrel declined in the mid-Holocene (Klippel 1971), a testimony to the opening of the forest. As McMillan and Klippel (1981) and Styles and Klippel (1996) have argued, opening of the forest, perhaps aided by fire, would have improved habitat for open-forest and edge-loving species, such as white-tailed deer. Fish remains are scarce at this cave site, and few prairie elements are present. Plains pocket gopher occurs in the early mid-Holocene and badger (three elements) is reported for one of the early Holocene levels (5A). No western-restricted grassland forms are noted for Graham Cave; however, Wolverton (2002:202) reports a single bison element (a left femur fragment dated to 7850 cal yr B.P.) from nearby Arnold Research Cave. On the basis of data from Rodgers Shelter and Arnold Research Cave, Wolverton (2005:101) argues that foraging efficiency increased from the middle to the late Holocene as hunters in the Ozark Highland relied more heavily on high-rank prey (i.e., deer, which had increased in abundance).

Illinois and Mississippi River Valleys

Excavations at deeply stratified archaeological sites with excellent bone preservation in the lower Illinois and central Mississippi River valleys provide an excellent record of changing patterns of human use of faunal resources throughout the Archaic period. Both valleys are historically characterized by rich aquatic habitats, including large rivers, tributary streams, and flood-basin lakes and sloughs. Flood-basin lakes were naturally restocked with fish during spring floods and were critical to the productivity of these river systems (Styles 1981). The lakes offered excellent fish habitat, and many fish species moved into their shallow waters to spawn in the spring and early summer. The rivers and lakes supported great numbers of freshwater drum, catfish, suckers, walleye, pike, rock bass, black bass, small sunfish, crappies, gizzard shad, bowfin, and gars as well as beaver, muskrat, river otter, and mink. The lakes also sustained large waterfowl populations during their spring and fall migrations along the Mississippi Flyway. In addition to the waterfowl, herons and other wading birds, grebes, rails, and American coot would have been available in aquatic habitats as well as turtles and freshwater mussels. Terrestrial environments in the floodplains and adjacent uplands were also rich in animal resources (Styles 1981). Nineteenth-century terrestrial environments included a variety of animals of potential economic importance, such as white-tailed deer, raccoon, turkey, prairie chicken, and passenger pigeon. This landscape also sustained a wide range of medium and small-bodied animals such as opossum, wolves, coyote, gray fox, bobcat, striped skunk, woodchuck, tree squirrels, ground squirrels, eastern cottontail, numerous small rodents, and box turtles. Large mammals that are less often recorded in historical accounts and archaeological sites, such as elk, or wapiti (*Cervus elaphus*), and black bear (*Ursus americanus*), may not have been abundant in prehistory, and small herds of bison (*Bison bison*), although present in the early and middle Holocene in Illinois (McMillan 2006) probably did not expand significantly until the late prehistoric period (e.g., Griffin and Wray 1945; Purdue and Styles 1986, 1987). Even then, herds were much smaller than those to the west of the Mississippi River.

As noted above, several studies have demonstrated climatic, geomorphic, and vegetation change during the mid-Holocene (e.g., Grimm and Jacobson 2004; Hajic 1990; King 1981; King and Allen 1977; Styles 1985). During this dry period, tallgrass prairie expanded in Illinois, creating a mosaic of grasslands and deciduous forest, and the forest became more open. Prairie reached maximal extent between 6800 and 3200 cal yr B.P. (Grimm and Jacobson 2004:392–393). The aquatic environments of the Illinois and Mississippi River valleys, like the terrestrial environments, changed through time as the rivers evolved from braided to meandering streams (Hajic 1990, 1991). All of these changes had impacts on human subsistence, settlement, and mobility strategies (Brown 1985; Brown and Vierra 1983; Styles et al. 1983).

The Koster and Napoleon Hollow sites in the lower Illinois River valley and Modoc Rock Shelter, located at the base of the bluffs in the Mississippi River valley in southern Illinois, occurred in deciduous forest settings surrounded by upland and floodplain prairies. During the middle Holocene, forests became more open and prairies expanded. Quantitative analyses of faunal remains from these sites document environmental and subsistence changes during the Archaic period. Deer dominates the middle Holocene deposits at the Napoleon Hollow site (Styles 1992), which is similar to the pattern for the Koster site. Also similar to the Koster pattern, fish increased dramatically in the middle Holocene levels. Mid-Holocene deposits at Napoleon Hollow did not include any prairie taxa. Deer and squirrel abound in the early Holocene deposits at the Koster site (Neusius 1982). Deer increased dramatically in the early middle Holocene levels—again linked to the opening of the forest. A dramatic increase in fish occurred in the late middle Holocene deposits dating to around 6,500 cal yr B.P. Increases in quiet-water mussels and fish and in dabbling ducks have been linked by Styles (1986) and Hill (1975) to the emergence of shallow backwater lakes in the floodplain. Prairie elements are rare at Koster, limited to single elements from badger and plains pocket gopher in early Holocene and a few prairie chicken bones in middle Holocene contexts.

The early Holocene deposits at Modoc Rock Shelter are similar to those at Graham Cave and Rodgers Shelter in the high representation of small mammals. Tree squirrels are especially abundant and have been linked to the closed, mesic forests of the early Holocene (e.g., Styles et al. 1983; Styles and Klippel 1996). Representation of squirrel declines and deer increases in the mid-Holocene levels—testimony to the opening of the forest. As was argued for Graham Cave, we suspect that human use of fire contributed to the opening of the forest and actually improved habitat for deer. Fish are relatively abundant in the early middle Holocene levels. Appearance of quiet-water fish suggests that shallow backwater lakes were emerging by about 8900 cal yr B.P. (Styles and White 1991). No western-restricted grassland forms are noted, but prairie species (badger, spotted skunk, and plains pocket gopher) occur in middle Holocene deposits. Representation of prairie fauna increases in late mid-Holocene and persists in the late Holocene deposits. Maintenance of prairie habitat in the more mesic late Holocene was probably due in part to anthropogenic fires.

Overall, human reliance on freshwater mussels increased at about 8300 cal yr B.P. in the lower Illinois River valley in association with stabilization of river systems—a prerequisite for the bottom stability required for the establishment of productive mussel beds, with a subsequent shift at around 6500 cal yr B.P. to more quiet-water species correlated with the emergence of shallow flood-basin lakes (Hajic 1981; Styles 1986). As the lakes matured, reliance on fish increased, and use of mussels declined. A similar pattern of initial reliance on mussels and gastropods during the middle Holocene, followed by decreased importance in later time periods, has also been documented in the Mississippi River valley and across the Midsouth (e.g., Styles and Klippel 1996).

Human reliance on fish increased through time (Styles 1994, 1995, 2000:90). In the lower Illinois River valley, an increase in the importance of fish, particularly quiet-water species, occurred by 6500 cal yr B.P. and has been linked to the development of shallow flood-basin lakes (Hill 1975; Styles 1986), which were both naturally restocked during annual floods and easy to harvest as their depth decreased in summer and fall (Styles 1981, 1986). A similar increase in utilization of quiet-water species such as bowfin occurred earlier (around 8900 cal yr B.P.) along the central Mississippi River (Ahler and Styles 1998), again, at the same time for which independent geomorphic data indicate the development of meandering river systems and associated flood-basin lakes (Hajic 1991). Numerous fish species are represented in Archaic settlements, and small individuals predominate in these sites and throughout the prehistoric record in the Illinois and Mississippi River valleys, suggesting that nonselective procurement technologies, such as nets, traps, or poisoning, were used (e.g., Styles 1986:147; Styles et al. 1983:288). Species composition and body-size distribution suggest that these technologies were already present in the Early Archaic (Styles et al. 1983:288).

Archaic hunters made greater use of white-tailed deer during the middle Holocene. In the lower Illinois River valley, for example, reliance on white-tailed deer increased in the Middle Archaic (e.g., Neusius 1982) and then showed a general decline (Styles 1994, 2000:90). In the central Mississippi River valley the proportional use of deer initially increased at the Early to Middle Archaic transition around 8900 cal yr B.P. (Styles 2000:90). Increased use of deer in base-camp occupations at Koster and Modoc Rock Shelter has been linked to opening of the forest and incorporation of logistic mobility to exploit deer (Neusius 1982; Styles et al. 1983).

The relative abundance of squirrel (Sciuridae) bones is greatest in Early Archaic components in both valleys and then declines in later Archaic-period contexts (Styles 1995). McMillan and Klippel (1981) and Styles and Klippel (1996) have attributed the abundance of squirrels, particularly gray squirrels (*Sciurus carolinensis*), in early Holocene components to the closed and more mesic nature of early Holocene forests in the Prairie Peninsula. The use of a broader variety of mammals, including those that would not be considered high-ranking prey, could reflect the lower faunal productivity of early Holocene environments.

Use of waterfowl and other birds associated with aquatic habitats generally increased through time in the lower Illinois River valley. An increase in dabbling ducks, similar to the increases noted above for quiet-water mussels and fish, in late Middle Archaic contexts at the Koster site has been linked to development of shallow backwater lakes (Hill 1975). Proportional representation of waterbirds in the central Mississippi River valley is generally higher than for the lower Illinois River valley and does not show a clear temporal trend.

In the lower Illinois River valley, a general temporal decline is apparent in the abundance of bones from birds associated with terrestrial habitats (e.g., turkey, prairie chicken, and passerine birds). In the central Mississippi River valley, the pattern is bimodal. The relative abundance of turkey bones, similar to that for most terrestrial resources, shows a general decline through time. Contrary to the predictions of some economic models, turkey never comprises more than a minor portion of vertebrate assemblages in either river valley. Prairie chicken remains are recovered in relatively low numbers in middle Holocene and later sites. Passenger pigeon bones occur in numerous prehistoric sites but are not abundant (e.g., Parmalee 1958:173). Passerine birds are not abundant in Archaic contexts in the lower Illinois or central Mississippi River valley.

Most of the variation in the Illinois and Mississippi River valleys is caused by changes in the relative proportions of squirrels, deer, and fish (Styles 1995, in press). Several studies in the western United States have successfully demonstrated that body size serves as a good proxy for prey rank (Bayham 1979, 1982; Broughton 1994) and suggest that relative abundances of large- and small-bodied prey in archaeological assemblages can be used to measure "selective efficiency" (Broughton 1994:503). These techniques based on body size are useful for assessing changes in mammal exploitation in the Illinois and Mississippi River valleys but are hampered by the great productivity of fish in such environments. Fish, although individually small, can be harvested in large numbers and emerge as a first-line resource in most models, including those based on optimal foraging theory.

Optimal models of diet predict that a decrease in resource abundance will be accompanied by an increase in search time and a resultant increase in diet breadth. An increase in resource abundance will be accompanied by a decrease in diet breadth (i.e., greater selectivity) (Bettinger 1987:133). Most researchers recognize that individual decision making at the point of encounter (Bettinger 1987:133), the division of labor (Jochim 1988), and choice guided by nonsubsistence motives played roles in faunal exploitation and that all strategies accommodated use of second-line and lower-ranked prey.

Following Broughton (1994:506), Styles (1995, in press) developed several indexes to examine the contributions of taxa with different body sizes, in this case, squirrels, deer, and fish in the Illinois and Mississippi River valleys. The Squirrel Index [squirrel NISP / (squirrel + deer NISP) X 100] provides an example of the contribution of low-ranking squirrels as compared with that of high-ranking white-tailed deer. There is a clear decrease in the representation of squirrel at the early to middle Holocene transition as compared with deer, which, according to many, would reflect an increase in foraging efficiency. The Deer Index [deer NISP / (deer + squirrel NISP) X 100] shows the increase in deer relative to squirrel in the middle Holocene and its dominance over squirrel throughout later prehistory. As argued throughout this chapter, squirrel may have been more abundant and deer may have been less abundant in the mesic, closed forests of the early Holocene than in the more open mid-Holocene forests in many areas of the Prairie Peninsula and the eastern deciduous forest. Assessments of selective efficiency must consider the effects of changes in resource abundance. In this case, the mid-Holocene increase in selective efficiency, as manifested by greater reliance on white-tailed deer, was facilitated by environmental change as well as by the likely incorporation of logistic mobility to hunt deer.

The Fish Index [fish NISP / (fish NISP + deer NISP) X 100] (Styles 1995, in press) shows that the proportion of fish relative to deer was greater in the Mississippi River valley than in the lower Illinois River valley, especially in the early Holocene, possibly because of the earlier emergence of productive flood-basin lakes in the Mississippi Valley. Fish and deer were both abundant, and their relative proportions converged in the late middle Holocene in both valleys. Fish generally increased in abundance relative to deer in the late Holocene in both valleys. As noted before, we do not think that this change reflects technological change.

A comparison of faunal assemblages from sites in the Illinois and Mississippi River valleys based on a detrended correspondence analysis shows clear similarity between sites of similar time periods in the two regions (Styles 2000:90, in press). The Archaic site components cluster by time, indicating strong patterning in the faunal data. The two Early Archaic components share a high representation of other terrestrial mammals, specifically, squirrels. The Middle and Late Archaic components cluster primarily on the basis of the high representation of deer. The correspondence analysis highlights the differences in faunal exploitation through time. There is good correspondence between the major shifts in faunal exploitation and recorded shifts in botanical exploitation (e.g., Asch and Asch 1985; Johannessen 1984, 1993; Styles 1994). The Early Archaic sites are characterized by the utilization of a diverse mix of nuts. The Middle and Late Archaic sites show a dominance of hickory nuts.

Early Holocene inhabitants of the lower Illinois and central Mississippi River valleys exploited a diverse assortment of animals, especially white-tailed deer and squirrels. The transformation of the patterning of the biota of the mid-Holocene landscape provided new opportunities for hunters and gatherers in the Mississippi and Illinois River valleys. The formation of flood-basin lakes and a patchy prairie-forest mosaic provided optimal environments for fish and white-tailed deer, and mid-Holocene populations made greater use of these resources, indicating greater selective efficiency and possible changes in mobility strategies to capitalize on these productive resources. The timing and nature of the effects of environmental changes varied slightly from region to region as did the timing of changes in human subsistence practices and settlement strategies (Styles 1995, in press). In this case, the similarities between the two large river valleys are remarkable.

Grand Prairie of Illinois

The Grand Prairie, an extensive area of tallgrass prairie, historically covered the flat till plains that characterize much of the central Illinois landscape. Gallery forests occurred along larger tributaries and on moraines. During the more mesic early Holocene, elm and oak forests were more broadly distributed than suggested for the middle or late Holocene. Distributions of Early Archaic sites suggest that small stream valleys that historically supported prairie were likely forested (e.g., Klippel and Maddox 1977). Sediment did not accumulate rapidly in these upland settings, and, consequently, they were not conducive to the preservation of bone. Although prairie developed in northern Illinois as early as 8000 cal yr B.P., it subsequently retreated, and then expanded again around 7000 cal yr B.P. Prairie reached maximal extent between 6800 and 3200 cal yr B.P. (Grimm and Jacobson 2004:392).

The Pabst site provides a lone record for Archaic faunal exploitation in the Grand Prairie of central Illinois. The site is located along the North Fork of the Salt River, which was forested historically. The fauna from the Late Archaic component at this site suggests that the stream valley was likely forested at the time of occupation, although prairie would have been well established by this time. Bones from deer and other terrestrial mammals dominate the late Holocene assemblage at the Pabst site. The diverse assemblage of mammals includes tree squirrel, eastern cottontail, canids, raccoon, ground squirrels, and plains pocket gopher, and remains from aquatic turtles are relatively abundant (Lewis 1979). Fish are sparsely represented at this site, which Lewis (1979) interpreted as a base camp occupation. Prairie chicken and at least five prairie mammals (elk, badger, ground squirrel, plains pocket gopher, and prairie vole) are represented. The prairie mammals constitute only 3.7 percent of the mammal NISP. A single bison bone was recovered in alluvial sediments immediately overlying the Late Archaic occupation (Lewis 1979:180). Although the Late Archaic inhabitants of this site made some use of prairie animals, they primarily subsisted on white-tailed deer and other denizens of the forest and forest edge. Persistence of prairie and prairie animals in the more mesic late Holocene was likely aided by aboriginal burning.

Eastern Deciduous Forest

Historically, deciduous forest dominated the landscapes to the east, south, and north of the Prairie Peninsula. Prairie outliers were present, however, as far east as west-central Ohio and southern Michigan (Transeau 1935). The forests in this area generally evolved from the more closed mesic forests of the early Holocene to more open woodlands in the middle Holocene. In many respects, terrestrial forest resources would have been similar to those noted for the Illinois and Mississippi River valleys. However, access to prairie resources would have been more limited, and aquatic resources were not as plentiful as in the flood-basin lakes of the Illinois and Mississippi River valleys.

Hunters living in the midwestern deciduous forests to the east, south, and north of the Prairie Peninsula benefited from the opening of the forest in the middle and late Holocene. Late Archaic (ca. 3800–3200 cal yr. B.P.) inhabitants of the Riverton, Swan Island, and Robeson Hills sites along the Wabash River in eastern Illinois lived in a mosaic of deciduous forest and prairie. These Late Archaic sites contain diverse faunal assemblages (Parmalee 1969). White-tailed deer, medium mammals, and box turtles abound. Deer is particularly abundant at the Riverton and Robeson Hills sites, which are interpreted as a base camp and a winter settlement, respectively (Winters 1969). Fish are most abundant at the Swan Island site, which is interpreted as a "transient" spring camp or fall camp or both (Winters 1969), but fish are not particularly abundant at any of these sites, even though they are all located near the Wabash River. They do, however, contain unusually large numbers of freshwater mussels. Excavations at the Robeson Hills site, for example, yielded about 19,000 mussels (Parmalee 1969:143), constituting 97 percent of the total faunal NISP. Elk bones were recovered from all three sites. Prairie taxa included plains pocket gopher at Swan Island and prairie chicken at all three sites. The inhabitants of these sites took deer, medium mammals, box turtles, birds associated with terrestrial habitats, and some fish, and they collected numerous freshwater mussels (Parmalee 1969). The presence of shell middens at the Riverton and Robeson Hills sites has led some authors to group these sites with the Shell Mound Archaic of the Green and Tennessee rivers (Claassen 1996).

The Late Archaic (6400–5600 cal yr B.P.) inhabitants of the Black Earth site in the Saline drainage of southern Illinois just north of the Shawnee Hills, focused their hunting pursuits on white-tailed deer, with collection of aquatic turtles constituting a distant second activity, as indicated by numbers of identified specimens (Breitburg 1982). Deer were probably abundant in the forested environment, which was likely kept open by fire. Aquatic turtles may have been locally abundant in the shallow lake located near the site. Fish remains are rare. A few elements from prairie chicken and plains pocket gopher are the only prairie taxa recovered.

Deer and box turtle dominate the middle Holocene (late Middle Archaic, 6100–5700 cal yr B.P.) fauna from the Bluegrass site, located in the forested uplands of a small tributary to the Ohio River in southwestern Indiana. Remains from aquatic turtle are rare, and no prairie taxa were identified. Stafford et al. (2000) attribute the feasibility of establishing a base camp at this upland locale to the opening of the forest, which increased availability of deer. They further note that the base camp was established in the absence of abundant aquatic resources.

At the Railway Museum site (Anslinger et al. 1994), situated along the Falls of the Ohio River near Louisville, Kentucky, a Late Archaic base camp was established with a faunal subsistence base high in deer, box turtles, and fish (Yerkes and Machuga 1994). No prairie taxa were noted. The representation of fish is much greater than noted for Bluegrass, which is not surprising given the great productivity of this stretch of the Ohio River.

Three sites in Ohio (Purtill, this volume) further illustrate the importance of deer to Late Archaic populations in the eastern deciduous forest. At the Bullskin Creek site, located in southwestern Ohio, deer constitutes about 93 percent of the vertebrate fauna (Purtill, this volume; Slawson 1977). The identified fauna also includes beaver and a few remains of raccoon, opossum, gray fox, eastern cottontail, chipmunk, and gray squirrel. Turtle remains are not common and only include a few elements from softshell and box turtle. Fish remains are rare, and freshwater drum is the only identified fish species. Deer constitutes about 44 percent of the vertebrate assemblage at the Scioto County Home site in southeastern Ohio (Bowen 1987), but Purtill (this volume) suggests that deer abundance is underestimated because many of the bones were classified only as unidentified mammal. The occupants of the site also procured raccoon, squirrel, woodchuck, and other small and medium-sized mammals but in relatively low numbers. Fish and turtles (both box turtles and aquatic turtles) contribute about 13 percent and 9 percent, respectively, of the vertebrate fauna. Fish include freshwater drum, catfish, redhorse sucker, gar, pike, and largemouth bass. The bird assemblage includes a few remains of wild turkey, but most of the bird bones were not identified. Deer contributes 64 percent of the bones at Krill Cave, located in the Allegheny Plateau region of northeastern Ohio (Prufer et al. 1989; Purtill, this volume). The Late Archaic inhabitants of this site also procured raccoon, beaver, woodchuck, bobcat, and other small and medium-sized mammals. In addition, a few remains from dabbling ducks, turkey, passenger pigeon, and hawk are reported. Turtle remains are not common, but both box and painted turtle are present. Fish remains are rare; only freshwater drum was identified.

The Raddatz and Durst rockshelters are in dissected-upland forest settings proximal to prairie patches in southern Wisconsin. Deer dominates in the Early, Middle, and Late Archaic deposits at Raddatz (Cleland 1966). The Early Archaic component is more diverse than the later components, with a greater representation of gray squirrels, perhaps suggesting that the forest was more closed in the early Holocene. It is tempting to argue that the increased focus on deer at the Middle and Late Archaic camps reflects the opening of the forest. The appearance of a few elk elements in the Middle and Late Archaic deposits may also reflect opening of the forest. Faunal composition in the Middle and Late Archaic components at Durst Rockshelter is virtually identical to that at Raddatz in terms of the dominance of deer (Parmalee 1959, 1960). On the basis of his reanalysis of faunal remains from Raddatz Rockshelter, Cleland (1966) proposed that Early Archaic hunters had a focal economy based primarily on white-tailed deer. Data from other rockshelters in this same region suggest that during the Late Archaic period there was a seasonal emphasis on white-tailed-deer hunting (Emerson 1979:285–290; Theler 1987:35–36), leading Theler (2000) and Theler and Boszhardt (2003:212) to caution that short-term encampments (probably fall and winter) at sites such as Raddatz Rockshelter only provide a partial glimpse of the subsistence system. Emerson (2003) has argued, however, on the basis of his analysis of white-tailed-deer mortality profiles and season-of-death information from Raddatz and Durst rockshelters, that Middle and Late Archaic hunters were procuring deer opportunistically year-round. In view of the habitat preferences of animals represented at Raddatz Rockshelter, Cleland (1966) suggested that conditions were cooler and moister in the Early Archaic (early Holocene) and warmer and drier in the Middle Archaic (middle Holocene). Pollen data for Devil's Lake and Lima Bog provide independent evidence that a xeric oak forest replaced mesic deciduous forest in the middle Holocene (Baker et al. 1992:386).

Great Lakes

In many respects, prehistoric faunal availability in the inland areas of the lower Great Lakes region was similar to that noted for the remainder of the interior midwestern United States. Deciduous trees dominated the mixed forests in this area, and white-tailed deer was an important game animal. Prairie openings in the Great Lakes region were smaller than in the Prairie Peninsula. Prairie taxa, such as prairie chicken and bison, were not present, but elk, a denizen of open marshy areas, is commonly reported from archaeological contexts, and may have been relatively abundant. Bison were present on the western fringe of the Great Lakes region and were exploited by the Middle Archaic inhabitants of the Itasca site in north-central Minnesota (Shay 1971). However, as noted above, this site lies within 40 km of the tallgrass-prairie border today, and this border may have been closer to the site area during the middle Holocene. The forested areas of the upper Great Lakes region, including Lake Superior and the northern parts of Lakes Huron and Michigan, include more boreal elements. As one moves north, mixed confer and deciduous forests transition into a conifer-dominated forest (Cleland 1982:765). In the mixed conifer-deciduous forests, white-tailed deer and elk were present but probably not as abundant as in the deciduous-dominated forests. The conifer-dominated forests supported moose and caribou (Cleland 1982:765). Turkey probably occurred in the same habitats as white-tailed deer. Passenger pigeons once nested in the northern part of the Upper Peninsula of Michigan and were also abundant during the spring and fall migrations (Cleland 1966:169).

Fish resources in inland streams in the lower Great Lakes area were similar to, but possibly not as easy to exploit as, those in the large flood-basin lakes of the Illinois and Mississippi River valleys. Freshwater mussels were also considerably less abundant than noted for midwestern streams. However, the Great Lakes themselves offered a unique suite of resources. The lakes are not as productive of fish per unit area as the Illinois and Mississippi rivers and, because of their great size and depth, would have been more difficult to exploit with aboriginal technologies (Cleland 1982:765; Rostlund 1952:65). There were, however, optimal times for harvesting fish. Many lake fish species congregate in shallow waters, and many ascend streams during spring spawning, which would have made them easier to catch during certain seasons (Cleland 1982:766). According to Cleland (1982:766), economically important spring-spawning fish included lake sturgeon (*Acipenser fulvescens*), white sucker (*Catostomus commersoni*), northern redhorse (*Moxostoma macrolepidotum*), channel catfish (*Ictalurus punctatus*), black bullhead (*Ameiurus melas*), brown bullhead (*A. nebulosus*), yellow perch (*Perca flavescens*), walleye (*Sander vitreus),* northern pike (*Esox lucius*), and several species of bass. Many of these species ascend streams to spawn. Important fall-spawning species included lake trout (*Salvelinus namaycush*), lake whitefish (*Coregonus clupeaformis)*, lake herring (*C. artedi*), other varieties of shallow- and deep-water ciscoes, and round whitefish (*Prosopium cylindraceum*). These species congregate in deep waters offshore to spawn. They would have been difficult to procure without the aid of gill nets, which are not documented until later in prehistory (Cleland 1982; Smith 2004). In the game-impoverished upper Great Lakes region, fish would have been an important resource, especially during spring and fall spawning (Cleland 1982:768), and given Archaic-period technology, procurement of spring-spawning fish is more likely.

The importance of geographic variation in resource availability and temporal changes in climate in the mixed deciduous and coniferous forests of the upper Great Lakes has long been recognized (Cleland 1966). Cleland (1966:50) and others have argued that during the Early Archaic period, the spruce, fir, and pine forests of the upper Great Lakes area would have supported moose (*Alces alces*) and woodland caribou (*Rangifer tarandus*).

The nature and timing of Holocene environmental changes in the upper Great Lakes region has been refined since Cleland's (1966) landmark study, but the basic storyline remains the same. During the early Holocene, around 11,500 cal yr B.P., pine forests with some hardwoods covered much of Michigan, and spruce parkland may have been present in the Upper Peninsula (Shott 1999:72). Pine forests with some hardwood trees dominated until about 9500 cal yr B.P. (Kapp 1999:53). Early Holocene (11,500–8900 cal yr B.P.) faunal remains from the Deadman Slough site in northwestern Wisconsin primarily included bones from indeterminate large mammals, but bones from turtles, white-tailed deer, black bear, porcupine, birds, and fish were also present (Kuehn 1998:466). The early Holocene occupants of the Sucices site in the same region (Kuehn 1998) procured turtle and white-tailed deer as well as beaver and fish, the last taxon represented by a single bone. The occupants of both of these sites appear to have had a generalized foraging strategy that incorporated forest and a few freshwater resources (Kuehn 1998).

From approximately 9500 to 8100 cal yr B.P. (or perhaps a little later), the climate became warmer and drier, and oak savanna and prairie developed in southern Michigan and northern Indiana (Kapp 1999:53). By the end of the Early Archaic period (around 8900 cal yr B.P.), hardwood-dominated forests became established across lower Michigan, and terrestrial fauna would have been more similar to that present under modern conditions (Shott 1999:72). Lake levels for Lakes Michigan, Huron, and Erie dropped dramatically in the Early Archaic to 40 to 100 m below current levels, streams entrenched, and fish resources in the lakes and streams draining into the lakes may have been less abundant than today (Shott 1999:72–73).

Lovis (1999) and others have argued that understanding lake stages is critical for interpreting settlement distribution and the development of aquatic resources in the Great Lakes region. He argues that by the middle Holocene, the Great Lakes "were beginning to assume fully their modern shapes and drainages" and that during the mid-Holocene, climate was warmer than present (Lovis 1999:83). Throughout parts of the mid-Holocene, conditions were generally warm and moist (Kapp 1999:53). By 7800 cal yr B.P., or perhaps as early as 8900 cal yr B.P., mixed deciduous forest had become established in the southern Lower Peninsula of Michigan, and more settlements were present in the area (Lovis 1999:86). Water levels in the Great Lakes were high during the middle Holocene but lower than today (Robertson et al. 1999:96). Lovis (1999:85) suggests that productive wetland habitats were developing in the Saginaw basin during the Middle Archaic. No deeply stratified sites with adequate faunal preservation have been reported for this region that would allow tracking of long-term changes in use of fauna from a single locality, but Middle Archaic (7100–5300 cal yr B.P.) and Late Archaic (3200–3000 cal yr B.P.) occupations are present at the Weber I site, located along the Cass River in the Saginaw Valley (Lovis 1999). At the time of occupation, a mixed deciduous forest, including oak, black walnut, butternut, hazelnut, and hickory, was present (Smith and Egan 1990). Prior to the middle to late Holocene transition, the climate became warmer and dryer and open oak forest was established (Kapp 1999:53). Both occupations at Weber I are interpreted as summer–fall residential base camps (Lovis 1999). Deer dominates the fauna for both occupations (Smith 1989; Smith and Egan 1990). Elk and fish are present in both components but are more abundant in the Late Archaic (Smith and Egan 1990). The increase in elk may reflect the opening of the forest, and the increase in fish may reflect higher lake stages in the Late Archaic than in the Middle Archaic. Lovis (1999) and Robertson et al. (1999) note that the Great Lakes were lower in the Middle Archaic than in the Late Archaic, and, thus, sites such as Weber I would have been further inland in Middle than in Late Archaic times.

Resource use has been studied at a series of other sites in the region. For example, Beverley Smith identified remains from white-tailed deer, raccoon, beaver, muskrat, ruffed grouse (*Bonasa umbellus*), black duck (*Anas rubripes*), and fish in the Middle Archaic Bear Creek site in the same county as Weber I and suggested that the site represented a spring logistic camp (Lovis 1999:91). Middle Archaic and Late Archaic settlement systems included residential base camps and logistic camps for the exploitation of both upland and lowland resources (Lovis 1999:94).

Water levels in the Great Lakes fluctuated on both a long-term and short-term basis during the Late Archaic between 5700 and 2600 cal yr B.P. (Larsen 1999; Robertson et al. 1999:95–97). By 5400 cal yr B.P., lake levels (Nipissing I, or Nipissing maximum) were much higher than today, as indicated by archaeological data (Robertson et al. 1999:96). Water levels fell below maximum, but they rose again around 4900 cal yr B.P. (Nipissing II, or Nipissing transgression). Water levels were also high from 4500 to 3200 cal yr B.P. (Algoma stage) but were lower than noted for the Nipissing stage. Waters levels in the Huron-Michigan lake basin dropped below historical mean levels by 3200 cal yr B.P., the post-Algoma low (Robertson et al. 1999:96). These changes in lake levels had dramatic effects on the availability of land for settlement, aquatic resource productivity, and the visibility of the archaeological record. Human populations dealt with risk and uncertainty by developing flexible settlement and subsistence strategies and incorporating a diverse set of resources (Lovis 1986; Robertson et al. 1999:95). Cleland (1966, 1976) used the term *diffuse* to describe Middle and Late Archaic subsistence patterns in the upper Great Lakes.

Taggart (1967), Keene (1981), Lovis (1986), Robertson (1987), and Egan (1993) all postulate a seasonally mobile settlement system that could accommodate desirable (but perhaps unpredictably available) fish and other wetland and aquatic resources as well as white-tailed deer and a wide range of smaller animals. Keene's (1981:195) linear programming models of Late Archaic subsistence in the Saginaw Valley are regulated by limiting elements (specifically, requirements for hides, calcium, and ascorbic acid) and predict focal exploitation of spawning fish in the spring and deer hunting in the fall, with more "diffuse and variable" procurement during the remainder of the year. At some Late Archaic camps in the Saginaw basin, such as the Feeheley (Cleland 1966:112; Keene 1981; Taggart 1967) and Hart sites (Cleland 1966:113; Keene 1981), fish dominate the faunal assemblages, suggesting a warm-season (spring and/or summer) occupation, while at others, such as the Schmidt site, more species are represented and bones from deer and waterfowl dominate, suggesting a fall occupation (Cleland 1966:116). At the Weber I site, both deer and fish were exploited from the same residential base (Smith and Egan 1990), suggesting considerable variability in the subsistence-settlement system. At the Screaming Loon site in the northern part of the Lower Peninsula of Michigan, Terrance Martin identified remains from indeterminate medium to large mammal, common loon (*Gavia immer*), catfish, bass (*Micropterus* sp.), whitefish or cisco (*Coregonus* sp.), northern pike or pickerel (*Esox* sp.), and bowfin (*Amia calva*) in a series of deposits interpreted as repeated warm-season occupations (Lovis 1990:247).

In southern Ontario, bones from sturgeon, trout, pike, bass, walleye, sucker, catfish, and freshwater drum dominate in the early levels at two Late Archaic sites along Lake Huron (Rocky Ridge and Knechtel I) (Ellis et al. 1990:111). Deer bone increased in the upper levels at these sites, and this increase has been attributed to local environmental change as lake levels dropped. At the Crawford Knoll site, located in the Lake St. Clair Delta, between Lake Huron and Lake Erie in southern Ontario, deer abounds, along with muskrat, turtle, and fish, especially bowfin and freshwater drum (Ellis et al. 1990:112). All of these lakeshore sites are interpreted as spring through fall occupations. Fall and winter camps would have been located in interior environments and presumably would have focused on procurement of deer. Given the locations of Terminal Archaic mortuary sites, settlements may also have been established along rivers to harvest spring-spawning sucker and walleye (Ellis et al. 1990:114). The Late Archaic occupation at the McIntyre site in southeastern Ontario, located on the north shore of Rice Lake, primarily yielded remains from small bullhead, bass, freshwater drum, and sucker, along with white-tailed deer, dog, beaver, muskrat, and bear (Ellis et al. 1990:120; Naylor and Savage 1984:118; Waselkov 1984:152). The site is considered a locus of repeated spring and summer occupations on the basis of the macrofaunal remains (Naylor and Savage 1984:133) and of fall occupations on the basis of analyses of annuli on fish scales recovered through flotation (Waselkov 1984:157). Waselkov (1984:141) suggests that the small size of the fish may indicate procurement with nets, possibly used in combination with a weir.

Fishing technology changed through time in the Great Lakes region, but the degree of change within the Archaic period is debatable. Cleland (1982:768) has argued that by the Late Archaic period in the upper Great Lakes (around 5700 cal yr B.P.), fish were procured through spearing, angling, and use of weirs (documented in Ontario) by societies that primarily relied on hunting. Late Archaic sites attributed to the Old Copper culture have yielded fishhooks, gorges, spears, gaffs, and numerous fish bones (Cleland 1982:768). For the northern Great Lakes, Cleland (1982:773) conservatively has suggested that spearing and angling were used during the Late Archaic. However, he (Cleland 1982:769) notes evidence for earlier use of nets in the Lake Erie and Ontario basins and to the east along the Atlantic Coast. As noted above, recovery of small fish in Late Archaic camps at the McIntyre site in southern Ontario (Waselkov 1984) may indicate early use of netting technology in this area. Net sinkers have been recovered from even earlier contexts, including Middle Archaic components of the Harry's Farm site in New Jersey (Kraft 1986:58). Thousands of net sinkers preserved in the Late Archaic component from the Lamoka Lake site in north-central New York suggest that net fishing was in use in the lower Great Lakes by at least this time (Cleland 1982:769). In addition to net sinkers, Late Archaic sites in New York have yielded bone and copper fishhooks, fish spears, harpoons, and gorges. On the basis of the recovery of perishables (cordage and other preserved fibers), net sinkers, and fish remains, Petersen et al. (1984:199–200) argue that nets were used to exploit fish in eastern North America by at least the beginning of the Early Archaic period. Although weirs were likely used to harvest fish in the Michigan area, especially lake fish when they ascended streams in the spring to spawn, none have been documented in this area. However, to the north and east, evidence is mounting for Late Archaic or even earlier use of weirs (e.g., Petersen et al. 1994).

Geographic Variation and Temporal Changes

To further examine geographic variation and temporal changes in midwestern faunal exploitation, we selected 48 components from 19 sites with adequate faunal preservation for quantitative comparisons. In the following analyses, site components are identified as Early Archaic, Middle Archaic, and Late Archaic on the basis of cultural assignments by regional archaeologists. These broad divisions are grossly subdivided into early Early Archaic (EA1; ca. 12,500–9600 cal yr B.P.), late Early Archaic (EA2; ca. 9600–9000 cal yr B.P.), early Middle Archaic (MA1; ca. 9000–8300 cal yr B.P.), middle Middle Archaic (MA2, ca. 8300–7000 cal yr B.P.), late Middle Archaic (MA3; ca. 7000–5400 cal yr B.P.), early Late Archaic (LA1; ca. 5400–4000 cal yr B.P.), and late Late Archaic (LA2, ca. 4000–2600 cal yr B.P.) based on the ages of the components in our sample. This practice allows us to compare sites of similar age across the transect. If a component spanned a considerable period of time, we assigned it to the subdivision with the most overlap.

We divided the fauna into 12 categories on the basis of habitat and economic criteria: fish, aquatic turtles, terrestrial turtles, birds associated with aquatic habitats, other birds, small mammals (smaller than squirrel), tree squirrel (fox, gray, and red squirrel), rabbit (eastern cottontail, swamp rabbit, and jack rabbit), other medium mammals (ground squirrels to smaller than deer), deer, bison, and other ungulates (elk and pronghorn). Quantitative summaries of fauna are based on NISP. Given that the goal of this analysis is to examine broad differences and changes in the proportional representation of taxa, the use of NISP is appropriate (Grayson 1984:63–67). Analyses are based on the proportion of vertebrate NISP for each faunal category (Table 3.3). Following the methods devised by Styles (1995, in press), we calculated special indexes on the basis of comparative relationships of the NISP for bison, deer, rabbit, squirrel, and fish. The indexes for deer, squirrel, and fish are the same as those developed by Styles (1995, in press) for the lower Illinois and Mississippi River valleys and discussed above. We used the same approach to develop the Bison Index [bison NISP/(bison + deer NISP) x 100] and the Rabbit Index [rabbit NISP/(rabbit + deer NISP) x 100]. The Bison Index allows us to examine the relative importance of this large prairie mammal on the western edge of our study area. The Rabbit Index simultaneously allows us to examine the contribution of a small-bodied mammal that, unlike squirrel, indicates exploitation of more open habitat. Only the Bison Index is appropriate for the Cherokee Sewer and Logan Creek sites because deer is so rare at these bison processing camps that plots of other categories of fauna against deer NISP are meaningless.

Early Holocene Faunal Exploitation (12,500–8900 cal yr B.P.)

Two sites in our sample yielded faunal remains from earliest Holocene contexts—Rodgers Shelter (EA1) and Graham Cave (EA1), both in the Ozark Highland but in very different environmental settings. Deer, rabbit, and other small mammals dominate in the earliest levels at Rodgers Shelter, which are associated with Dalton cultural material

Table 3.3. Proportion of Vertebrate NISP for Each Faunal Category for Site Components Used in the Quantitative Analyses.

Site	Component	Fish	Aquatic Turtle	Terrestrial Turtle	Aquatic Bird	Terrestrial Bird	Small Mammal	Tree Squirrel	Rabbit	Medium Mammal	Deer	Bison	Other Ungulate
Western Border of the Prairie Peninsula													
Cherokee Sewer	EA2	.5	.0	.0	.0	.0	2.0	.0	.0	.0	.5	97.0	.0
Cherokee Sewer	MA2a	.5	.0	.0	.0	.0	5.9	.5	.5	.0	.0	92.8	.0
Cherokee Sewer	MA2b	.0	.0	.0	.0	.0	5.7	.0	.0	12.4	.0	81.4	.5
Logan Creek	MA2a	.0	.4	.0	.4	.0	3.1	.0	.0	1.2	1.5	93.5	.0
Logan Creek	MA2b	.9	.4	.0	.0	.9	18.7	.0	.4	4.9	3.1	60.0	10.7
Logan Creek	MA2c	.2	.0	.0	.0	.1	2.9	.0	.0	1.8	.8	93.9	.3
Logan Creek	MA3	.0	.0	.0	.0	.0	1.6	.0	.8	.0	1.2	96.5	.0
Coffey	MA3a	30.4	1.5	16.9	21.9	15.4	.4	.4	2.7	2.7	3.1	4.6	.0
Coffey	MA3b	26.0	.0	5.8	1.3	.0	.7	.2	.0	.7	1.2	64.3	.0
Coffey	MA3c	41.1	1.3	2.2	14.4	12.5	.6	.0	3	.6	3.1	23.8	.0
Ozark Highland													
Rodgers Shelter	EA1	.4	.0	2.4	4.0	2.8	20.0	12.0	20.4	9.2	28.4	.0	.4
Rodgers Shelter	EA2	2.7	.0	4.1	.2	2.9	17.3	19.5	36.0	7.6	8.5	1.0	.1
Rodgers Shelter	MA1	6.9	.6	5.5	.2	2.7	23.3	15.5	35.7	3.0	6.3	.2	.1
Rodgers Shelter	MA2	2.2	1.8	7.6	.1	2.6	7.2	11.0	38.5	7.2	21.8	.0	.0
Rodgers Shelter	MA3	2.3	1.0	13.4	.1	2.1	12.4	8.9	37.4	6.8	15.5	.0	.1
Little Freeman	EA2	1.7	.0	.0	16.8	14.7	23.3	6.9	15.4	11.3	9.6	.3	.0
Little Freeman	MA3	2.1	1.3	.9	9.9	14.5	20.5	14.6	13.7	4.9	17.6	.0	.0
Northern Border Ozark Highland													
Graham Cave	EA1	.0	.7	.4	.0	4.8	.4	38.1	2.2	18.1	35.3	.0	.0
Graham Cave	MA1	.0	.5	1.6	.2	7.9	.8	17.7	4.0	19.0	48.1	.0	.3
Graham Cave	MA-LA	.2	1.7	5.2	.2	6.0	.6	12.9	7.0	14.5	51.8	.0	.0
Lower Illinois River Valley													
Napoleon Hollow	MA2	8.1	1.6	1.6	.0	1.6	1.2	1.2	1.2	4.9	78.5	.0	.0
Napoleon Hollow	MA3	41.6	7.5	1.1	.9	.7	.4	1.8	1.6	15.0	29.4	.0	.0
Koster	EA2	5.2	1.2	2.0	1.5	3.8	.6	43.8	2.3	7.5	32.2	.0	.0
Koster	MA1	13.2	2.5	5.5	2.6	2.1	2.2	6.0	1.8	1.7	53.4	.0	.0
Koster	MA2	8.9	4.1	9.0	.6	.8	.3	.9	1.4	5.4	68.7	.0	.0
Koster	MA3	39.0	2.9	.8	6.3	2.2	.2	.4	1.4	6.4	4.5	.0	.0
Central Mississippi River Valley													
Modoc	EA2	18.1	2.5	2.9	10.9	11.1	9.5	15.4	6.6	13.1	10.0	.0	0
Modoc	MA1	36.8	3.2	1.8	9.2	7.0	2.8	6.6	3.1	6.3	23.1	.0	.0
Modoc	MA2	31.0	3.7	2.5	7.3	3.8	3.0	5.0	5.1	7.8	30.9	.0	.0
Modoc	MA3	18.4	7.0	5.1	13.1	2.1	4.9	2.5	4.2	7.0	35.8	.0	.0
Modoc	LA1	23.7	7.5	7.5	18.5	2.8	2.3	1.0	3.1	6.7	27.0	.0	.0

Table 3.3. Proportion of Vertebrate NISP for Each Faunal Category for Site Components Used in the Quantitative Analyses, continued.

Site	Component	Fish	Aquatic Turtle	Terrestrial Turtle	Aquatic Bird	Terrestrial Bird	Small Mammal	Tree Squirrel	Rabbit	Medium Mammal	Deer	Bison	Other Ungulate
Grand Prairie of Illinois													
Pabst	LA	1.9	10.9	4.8	1.0	1.1	24.4	2.3	3.0	7.3	43.3	.1	.1
Eastern Deciduous Forest													
Riverton	LA	8.4	4.4	10.3	.2	4.3	.2	5.0	.4	15.3	49.2	.0	2.2
Swan Island	LA	20.8	8.6	9.4	1.8	4.2	1.9	7.6	2.6	10.1	32.9	.0	.3
Robeson Hills	LA	5.3	4.2	2.9	2.2	5.9	.0	1.9	1.4	7.0	69.2	.0	.2
Black Earth	MA3a	2.5	12.3	1.3	4.0	2.1	.1	1.3	.2	2.3	73.9	.0	.0
Black Earth	MA3b	2.4	10.9	2.3	2.6	2.2	.1	.5	.3	2.8	75.8	.0	.0
Black Earth	MA3c	2.2	11.9	1.0	3.1	1.5	.2	.8	.6	3.3	75.5	.0	.0
Black Earth	MA3d	4.4	8.5	1.7	2.4	2.0	.1	.7	.5	2.4	77.2	.0	.0
Bluegrass	MA3	.9	1.9	38.3	.0	.6	.6	9.1	1.4	14.2	33.0	.0	.0
Railway Museum	LA	31.2	2.8	22.1	.7	1.1	5.4	1.4	.2	4.6	30.3	.0	.1
Raddatz	EA	.0	5.0	.0	1.3	21.3	3.8	7.5	1.3	2.5	57.5	.0	.0
Raddatz	MA	.0	1.1	.3	.1	3.2	1.7	.6	.3	3.2	89.0	.0	.6
Raddatz	LA	.0	1.2	.3	.2	2.3	.3	.2	.0	2.3	92.9	.0	.3
Durst	MA	.0	3.1	.2	.0	.7	.7	.0	.0	4.0	90.2	.0	1.1
Durst	LA	.0	1.9	.8	.0	1.0	.0	.2	.2	2.3	93.2	.0	.4
Great Lakes													
Weber I	MA3	1.5	1.1	.0	.4	.0	.0	.0	.0	.7	91.5	.0	4.8
Weber I	LA2	12.2	.9	.0	.0	.0	.0	.0	.0	.9	52.3	.0	33.6

Note: NISP = number of identified specimens.

(Figure 3.2; Table 3.2). Deer is more abundant in the Dalton levels than noted for later occupations, perhaps a result of the more mesic conditions of the early Holocene. The early Holocene forests of the western Ozark Highland were more open than mesic deciduous forests to the east, thus, providing better deer habitat during the earliest part of the Holocene. This situation was short lived, however, for after 10,000 cal yr B.P., more xeric conditions prevailed and the region was invaded by C_4 plants from the west. At Graham Cave to the east, squirrel remains are more numerous than deer remains, a pattern that is then reversed for later occupations (Table 3.2). In this area, the early Holocene forest was denser, as well, but in this case was perhaps too closed to offer optimal habitat for deer, which thrive in open forest.

Six sites in our sample yielded faunal remains associated with the latter part of the early Holocene. Some differences in faunal exploitation are attributable to differences in resource availability across the Midwest. Bison dominates the Cherokee Sewer site assemblage, while deer dominates the assemblage at Raddatz Rock Shelter. If we exclude the bison processing camp at Cherokee Sewer and the possible fall–winter camps at Raddatz, the other early Holocene components show diverse assemblages—many with relatively high frequencies of small mammals such as rabbits or tree squirrels (Figure 3.3). Deer was important, but not as important as it became in the mid-Holocene, when deer populations are inferred to have expanded. On the western edge of the Prairie Peninsula, the decline in deer and increase in rabbits at Rodgers Shelter suggest that warming and drying was already underway. Presence of bison and other prairie taxa lends support to the evidence for warming and drying in this area. The abundance of squirrels, particularly gray squirrels, at sites to the east of Rodgers Shelter suggests that forests there were still somewhat closed.

We examined variation in the body size of prey species across the study area using the Bison, Deer, Rabbit, Squirrel, and Fish indexes (Figures 3.4–3.8). Only a single deer bone was recovered in Early Archaic levels at Cherokee Sewer, so we only plotted the Bison Index for this site. These analyses support the patterns observed in the proportional data. Bison, the largest prey species in our sample, is only present in our westernmost sites and is only important at Cherokee Sewer (Figure 3.4). Deer, the second largest common prey species in the study area, is most abundant at Raddatz Rock Shelter (Figure 3.5). The dominance of deer at this site may reflect a variety of factors, including bias toward recovery of large mammal bones during excavation and a more specialized settlement function (perhaps a fall or winter camp). Rabbits, small mammals associated with more open habitats, are most abundant at sites along the western edge of the Ozark Highland (Figure 3.6), where the environment was already opening but conditions were not optimal for deer. Rabbits are only moderately represented at Modoc Rock Shelter and show even lower numbers in the Illinois and Mississippi River

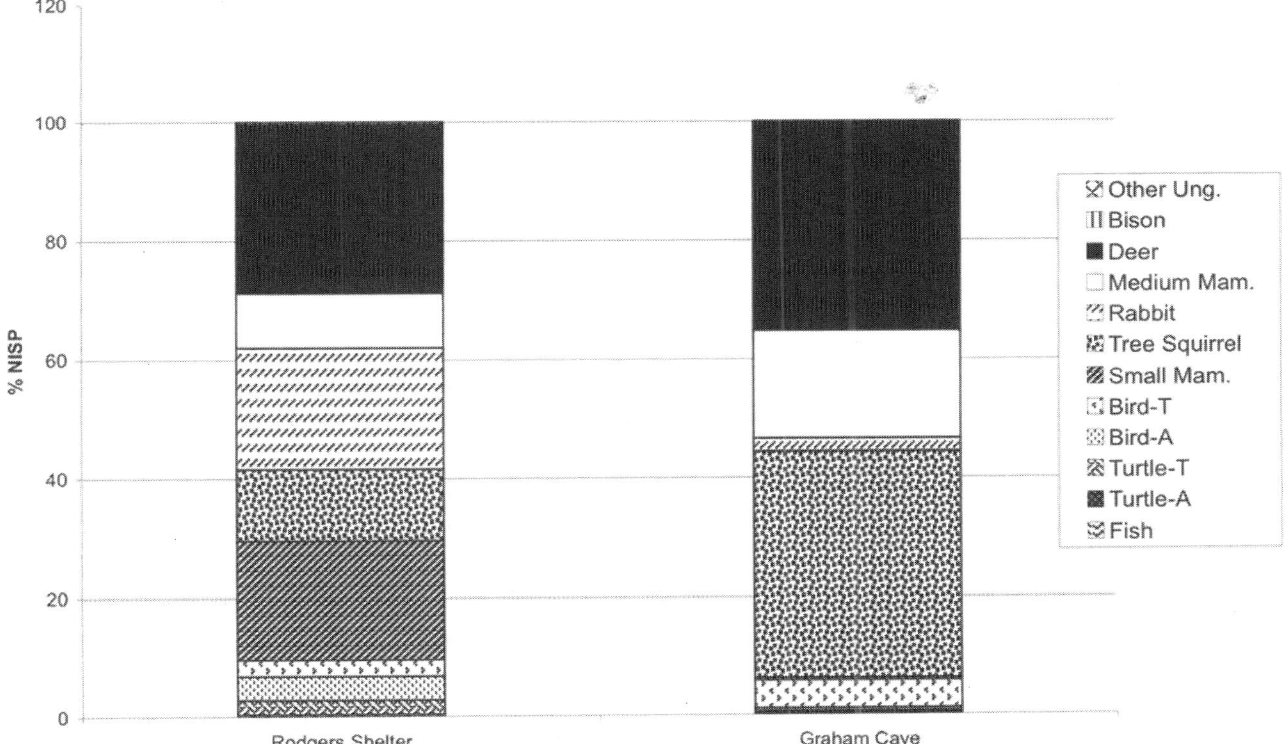

Figure 3.2. Proportion of vertebrate NISP (number of identified specimens) in each faunal category for early early Holocene site components.

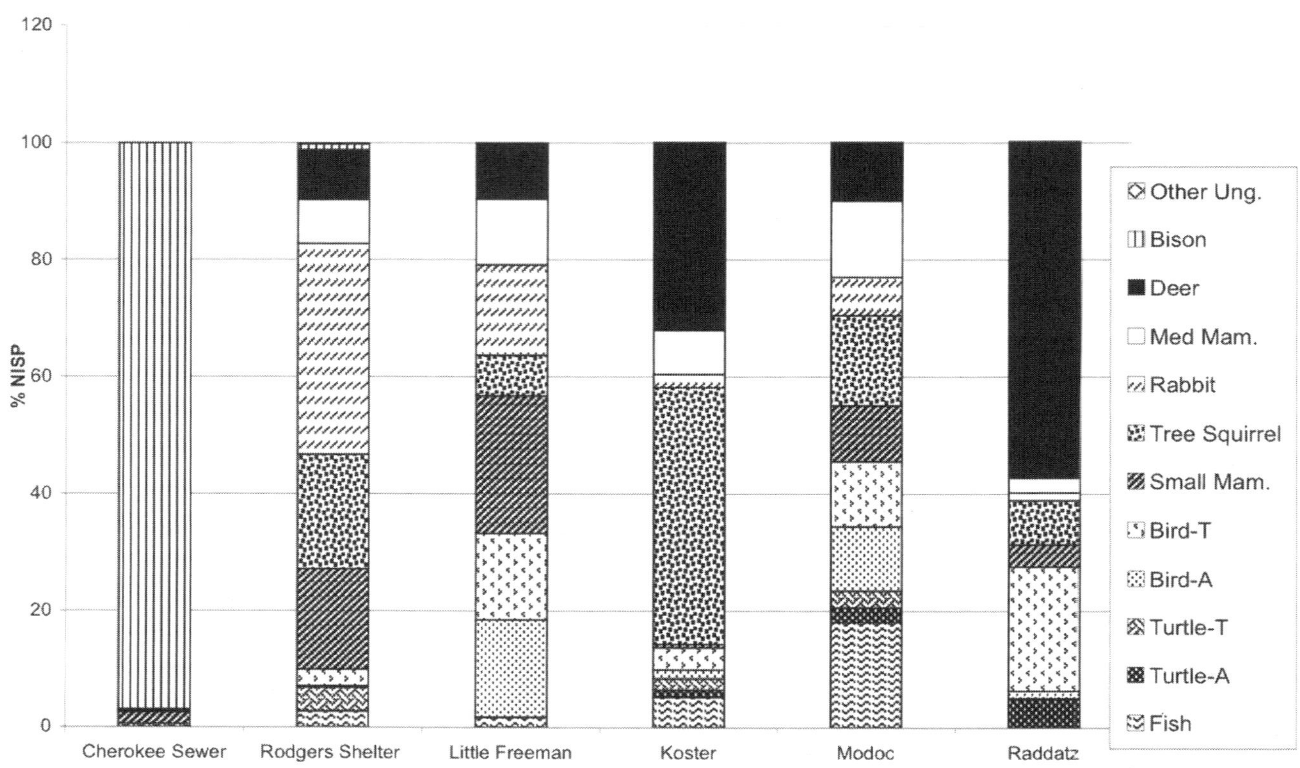

Figure 3.3. Proportion of vertebrate NISP (number of identified specimens) in each faunal category for late early Holocene site components.

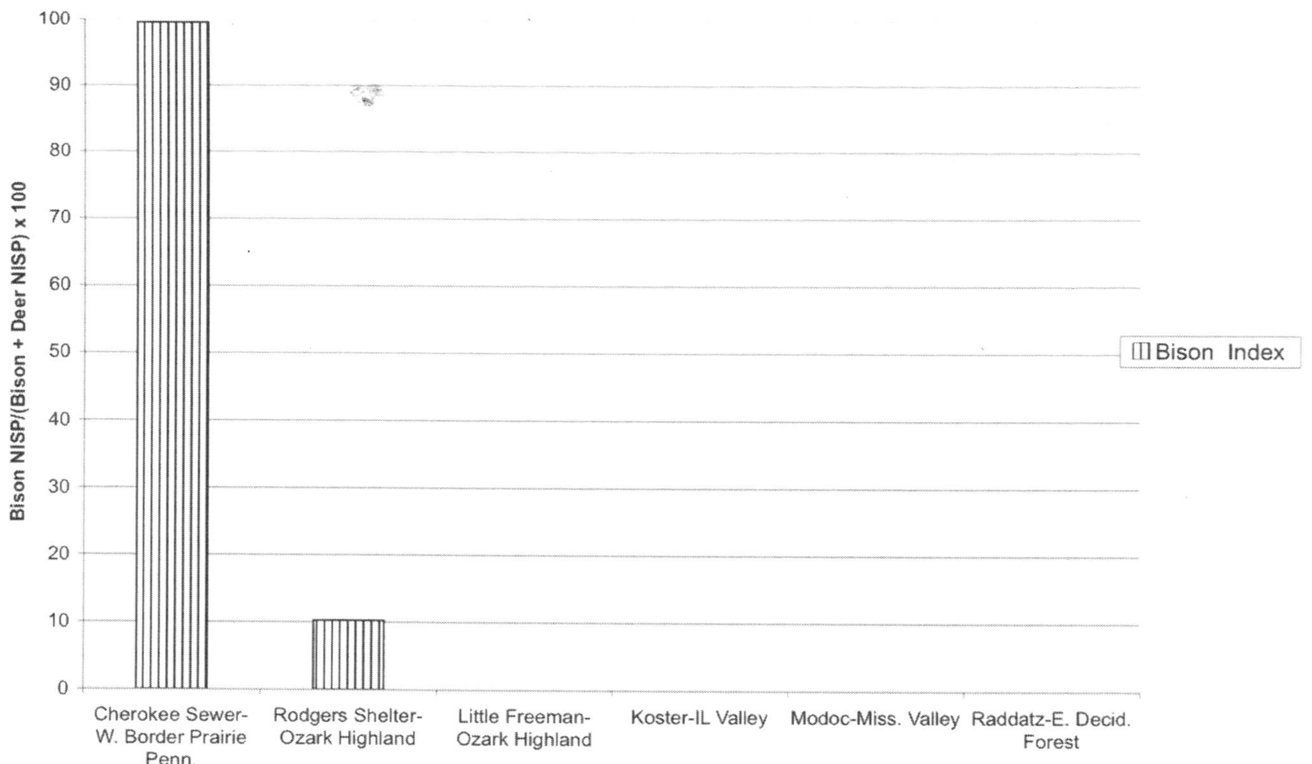

Figure 3.4. Bison index [bison NISP / (bison + deer NISP) x 100] for late early Holocene site components.

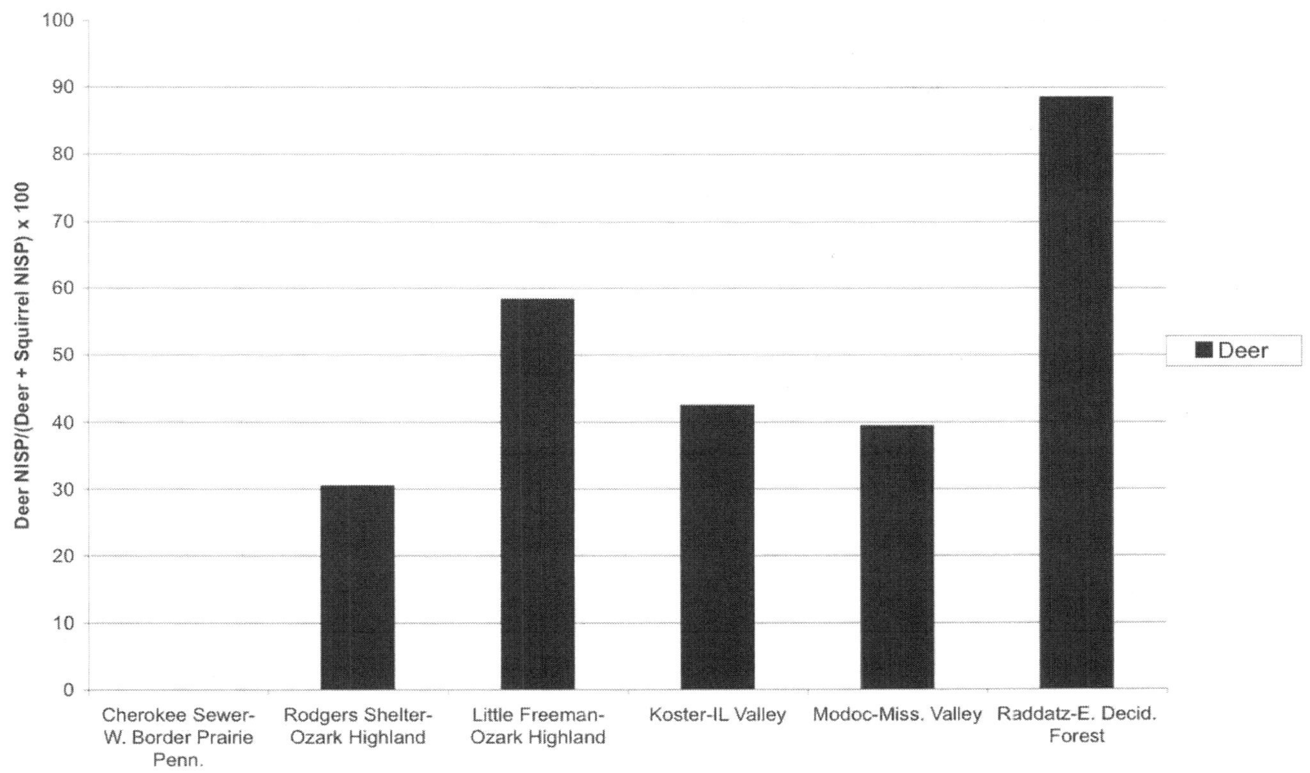

Figure 3.5. Deer index [deer NISP / (deer + squirrel NISP) x 100] for late early Holocene site components.

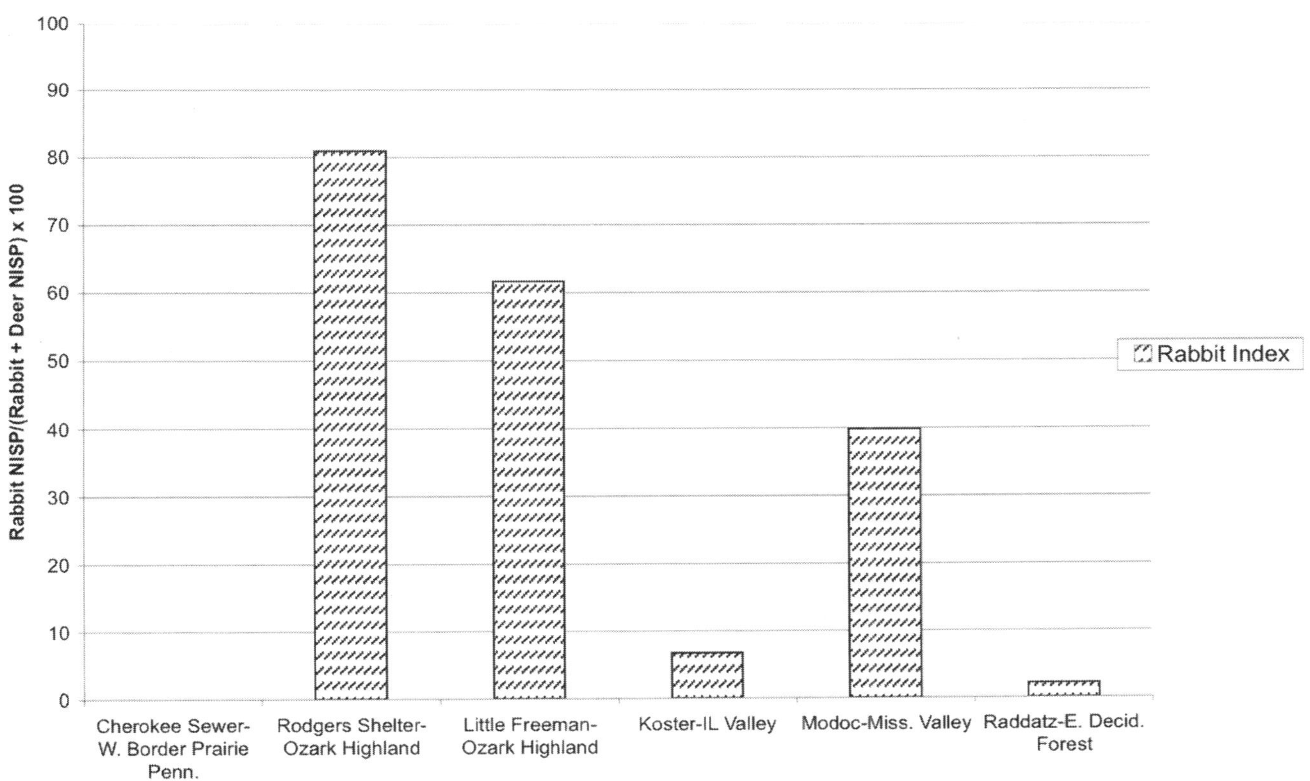

Figure 3.6. Rabbit index [rabbit NISP / (rabbit + deer NISP) x 100] for late early Holocene site components.

valleys and along the northern edge of the Prairie Peninsula, where forests remained closed. Squirrels, denizens of closed forests, are relatively abundant except at Raddatz Rock Shelter (Figure 3.7). We would expect more squirrel remains; as noted above, small mammals may be underestimated at this site because of recovery techniques. Fish are not dominant at any of the sites but are most abundant at Modoc Rock Shelter in the central Mississippi River valley (Figure 3.8).

Middle Holocene Faunal Exploitation (8900–5700 cal yr B.P.)

We divided the middle Holocene into three time slices to tease out time-transgressive effects of mid-Holocene warming and drying. Four sites have faunal-bearing components dated to the early part of the middle Holocene (Figure 3.9). At Rodgers Shelter in the western Ozark Highland, rabbits continue to dominate assemblages and deer shows an even lower representation than in components dating to the latter part of the early Holocene, showing the continuing effects of warming and drying in this setting. The presence of remains from bison, pronghorn, plains pocket mouse, and jack rabbit provide additional support for this interpretation. At Graham Cave, Koster, and Modoc Rock Shelter, deer is more abundant and squirrel is less abundant than in the late early Holocene levels, suggesting that the forest had opened in the northern Ozark Highland, lower Illinois River valley, and Mississippi River valley. Koster and, especially, Modoc Rock Shelter also show increases in the representation of fish. As noted above, the earlier emphasis on fish at Modoc Rock Shelter when compared with Koster has been linked to the earlier development of productive flood-basin lakes in the Mississippi River valley (Styles 2006).

Six site components are dated to the middle segment of the middle Holocene (Figure 3.10). The three middle middle Holocene components at the Logan Creek site were treated as a single sample for these analyses. Bison dominates in the bison processing camps at the Cherokee Sewer and Logan Creek sites on the western edge of our study area. Exploitation of a diverse assortment of small mammals, especially rabbits, continued at Rodgers Shelter. At the Koster site in the lower Illinois River valley, deer increased in abundance over the early part of the middle Holocene and dominates the assemblage. Mussels constitute a greater proportion of the total NISP than in assemblages of other time periods at Koster, and species are associated with a flowing-water habitat. These data suggest that stream systems had stabilized sufficiently for the development of productive mussel beds (Styles 1986). The dominance of deer, and the overall faunal composition at the Napoleon Hollow site, also in the lower Illinois River valley, is very similar to that recorded for Koster. The inhabitants of Modoc Rock Shelter also procured more deer than their early mid-Holocene predecessors did, but subsistence was more

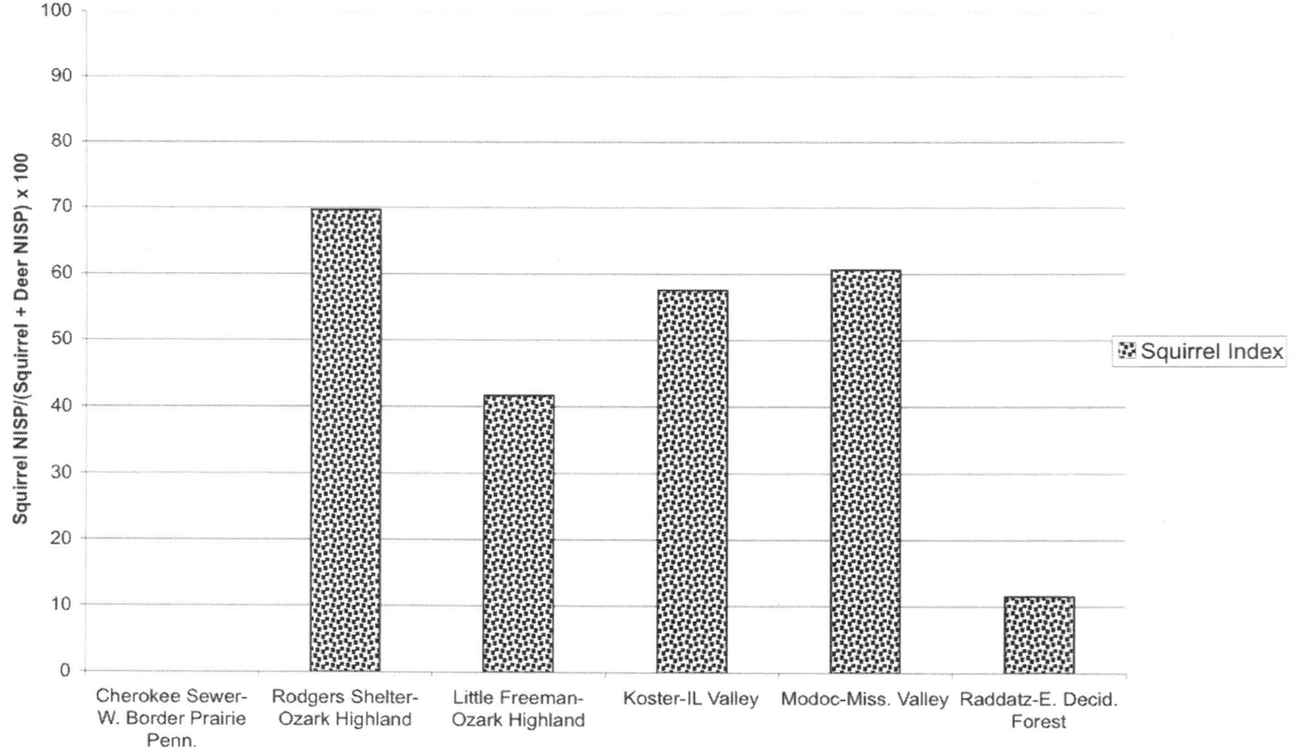

Figure 3.7. Squirrel index [squirrel NISP / (squirrel + deer NISP) x 100] for late early Holocene site components.

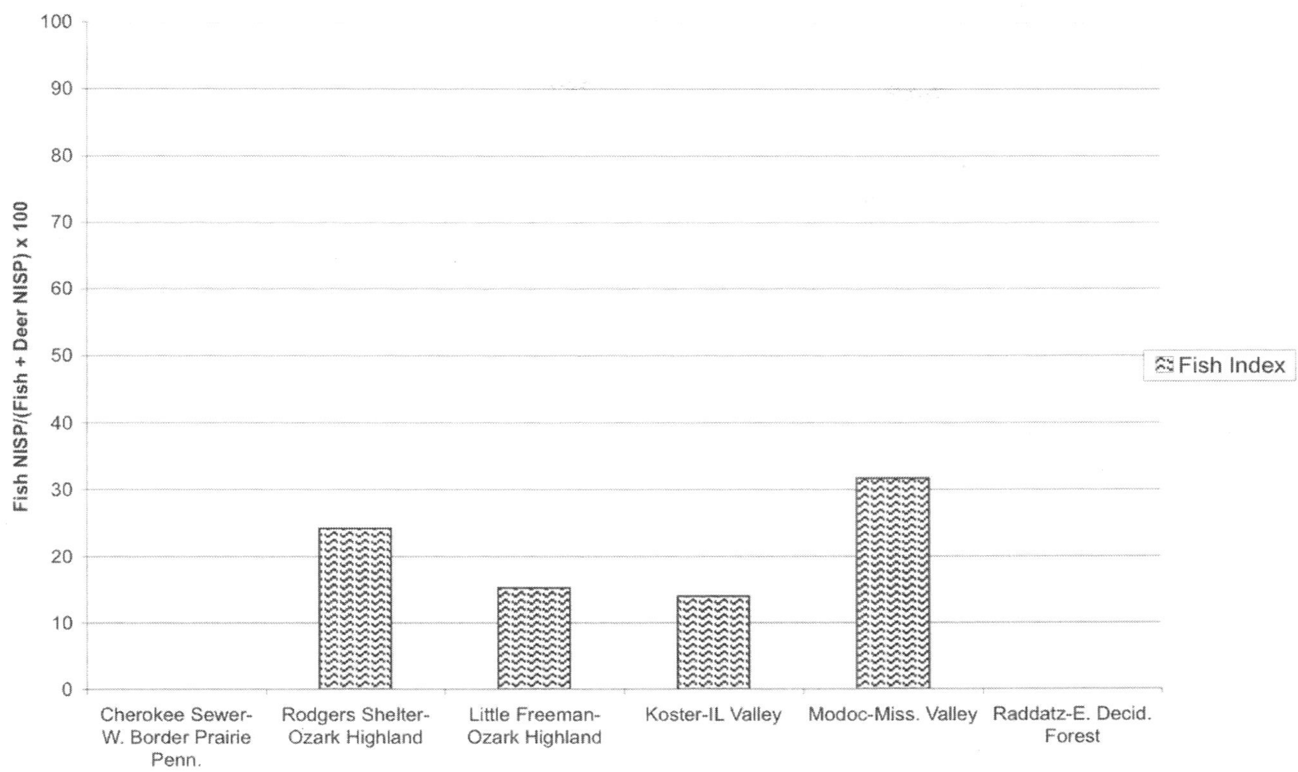

Figure 3.8. Fish index [fish NISP / (fish + deer NISP) x 100] for late early Holocene site components.

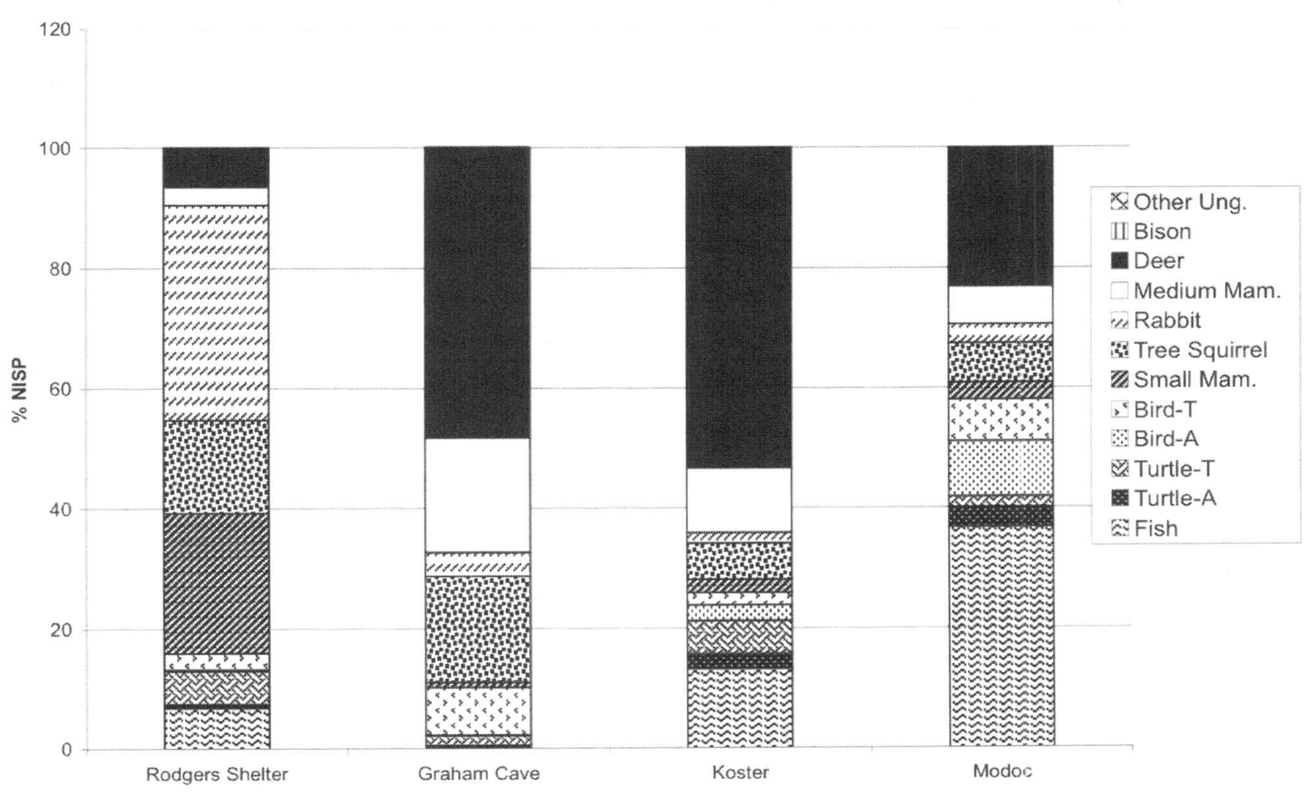

Figure 3.9. Proportion of vertebrate NISP (number of identified specimens) in each faunal category for early middle Holocene site components.

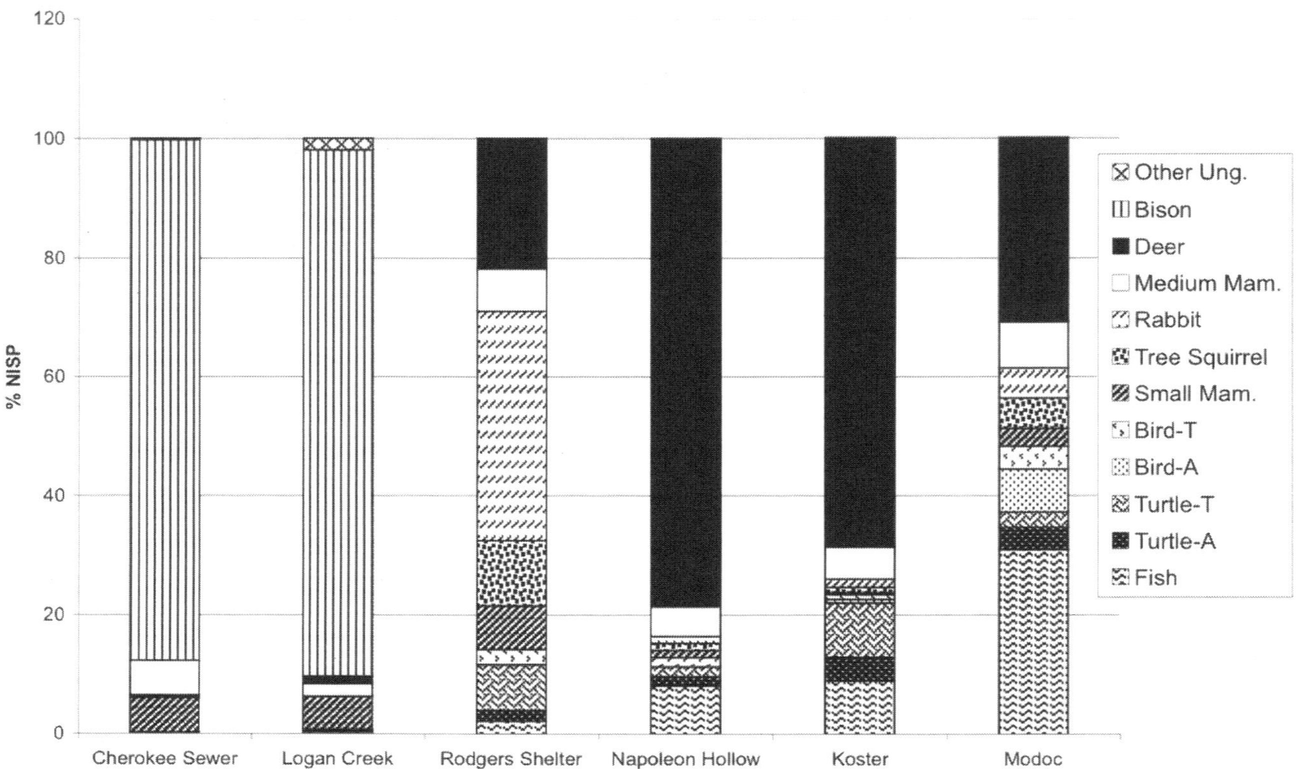

Figure 3.10. Proportion of vertebrate NISP (number of identified specimens) in each faunal category for middle middle Holocene site components.

diverse and included more fishing than in the lower Illinois River valley—again because of the earlier development of the flood-basin lakes in the Mississippi Valley.

Data are more extensive for the latter part of the middle Holocene, and ample evidence exists for regional differences in subsistence pursuits across the Midwest (Figure 3.11). The multiple late middle Holocene components at the Coffey and Black Earth sites were grouped for each site for these analyses. Not surprisingly, bison dominates in the bison processing camp at the Logan Creek site on the western edge of our study area. Bison remains are also abundant at the Coffey site, but remains of locally procured fish are also common at this base camp located adjacent to the Big Blue River. Rodgers Shelter and Little Freeman Cave in the Ozark Highland continue to show diverse assemblages with many small and medium-size mammals. The presence of pronghorn at Rodgers Shelter, a bison bone at Little Freeman Cave, and remains from other prairie taxa at both sites indicates that prairie and savanna-like conditions prevailed. In these more xeric western areas, use of deer was relatively low, but other sites in our study area demonstrate relatively great use of white-tailed deer. Deer is abundant at the Bluegrass site in the forested uplands of southwestern Indiana, but here box turtles contribute more bones than do deer. In many sites in the eastern deciduous forest, such as Black Earth in southern Illinois, Raddatz and Durst in southern Wisconsin, and Weber I in eastern Michigan, deer dominates the assemblages and would have been abundant in the open forest. In the major river valleys and eastern deciduous forest, base and residential camps show high use of deer in the late Middle Archaic.

Fish are abundant in areas with productive aquatic habitats—that is, in the Mississippi and Illinois River valleys. In areas with less productive aquatic habitats, fish are not abundant and dominance by deer is greater. The large sample of components for the late Middle Archaic clearly shows geographic variation in fish use. The relative abundance of fish remains in the late Middle Archaic appears to vary with the productivity of nearby aquatic environments and within the constraints of aboriginal technology. There is no evidence for gill nets, a technology that later led to the development of the inland Great Lakes fishery (e.g., Cleland 1982; Smith 2004). The proportion of fish in late middle Holocene sites of the Illinois River valley is higher than elsewhere, and the presence of quiet-water species in these assemblages suggests that flood-basin lakes had developed in this area by this time. As noted above, increased use of fish occurred earlier in the Mississippi Valley than in the lower Illinois River valley and may relate to an earlier emergence of productive shallow flood-basin lakes in the Mississippi River valley (Styles in press). Increased use of fish in the mid-Holocene reflects increasing productivity with floodplain evolution and also resource intensification by groups living in more sedentary base-camp settlements. Use of small-bodied fish is not seen as a decrease in foraging efficiency because fish can be harvested in great

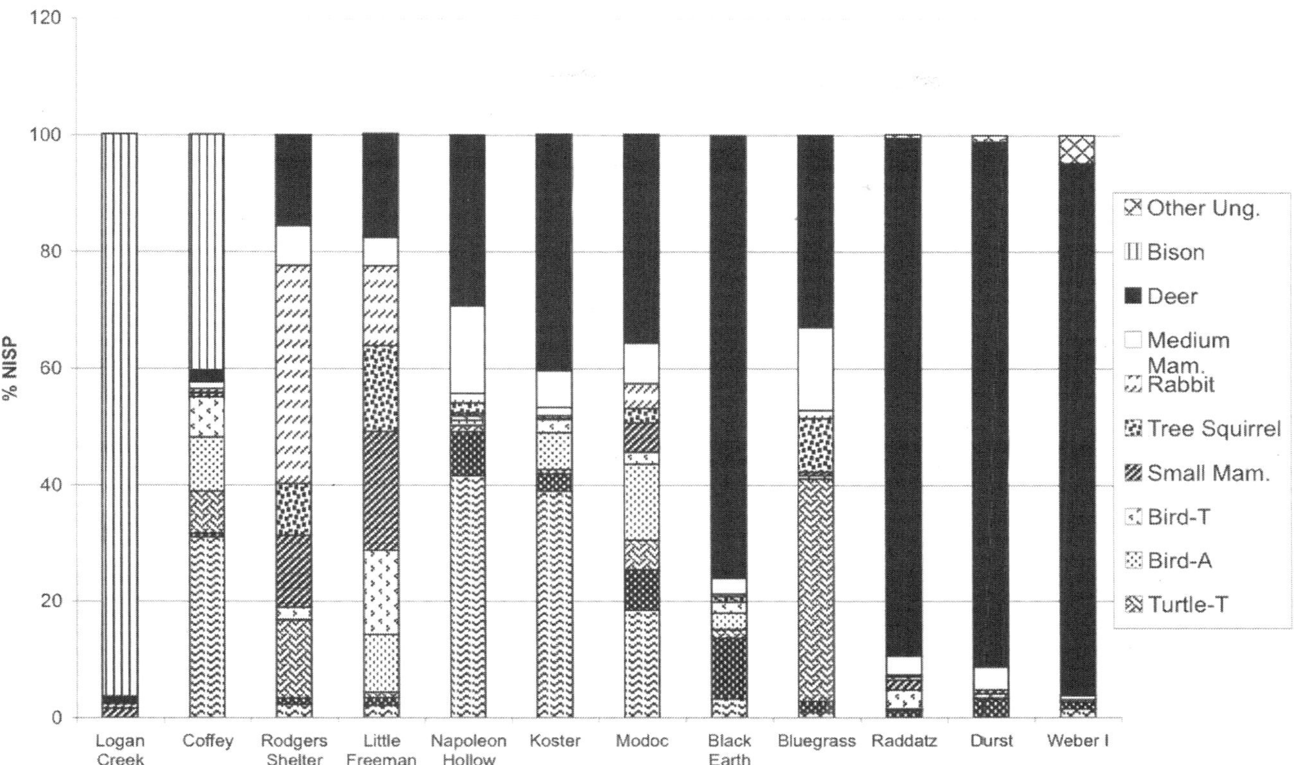

Figure 3.11. Proportion of vertebrate NISP (number of identified specimens) in each faunal category for late middle Holocene site components.

numbers. Use of aquatic resources was much greater in these large river systems with productive flood-basin lakes, but it was not a requirement for the establishment of base camps. Mid-Holocene base-camp occupations were supported by a wide range of subsistence strategies, including bison hunting and fishing in the west, procurement of a diverse mix of small mammals in the Ozark Highland, deer hunting and fishing in the big valleys, and deer hunting across much of the eastern deciduous forest.

Calculation of the faunal indexes supports the interpretations based on the proportional data. Only three deer bones were recovered at the Logan Creek site, so we only calculated the Bison Index for this site. As noted above, these indexes were developed for midwestern sites in the Prairie Peninsula and the eastern deciduous forest and are not effective for our westernmost sites.

The Bison Index (Figure 3.12) demonstrates the importance of bison on the western edge of the study area and the importance of deer across the Prairie Peninsula and into the eastern deciduous forest. The Deer Index (Figure 3.13) highlights the importance of deer across the transect. However, the Coffey site yielded only 25 deer bones and two bones from tree squirrel, so the importance of deer is exaggerated for this site. At many of the base-camp settlements, exploitation of deer was likely facilitated by logistic mobility. The Deer Index and the Squirrel Index show the continued exploitation of squirrel in the Ozark Highland sites of Rodgers Shelter and Little Freeman Cave. The Squirrel and Rabbit indexes (Figures 3.14 and 3.15) show that these small mammals are abundant in late middle Holocene deposits only at Rodgers Shelter and Little Freeman Cave, where foragers continued to subsist on a diverse assortment of mammals. The Fish Index (Figure 3.16) shows that fish continued to be important in the Mississippi River valley and had become much more important in the lower Illinois River valley where flood-basin lakes made fishing more lucrative. The Coffey site shows an intensive use of fish, which would have been locally abundant in the Big Blue River. As noted above, this site occurs in a unique location where a resource-rich stream crosscuts prairie habitat.

Late Holocene Faunal Exploitation (post-5700 cal yr B.P.)

Late Archaic components from the sites in our sample postdate mid-Holocene warming and drying and reveal a continued pattern of regional variation in subsistence pursuits (Figure 3.17). Subsistence pursuits in the early Late Archaic component at Modoc Rock Shelter were similar to those in the late Middle Archaic period. Fish, deer, and birds associated with aquatic habitats were all important. At the Pabst site in the Grand Prairie, deer and small mammals predominated, and few aquatic resources were used. Vertebrate faunal composition is similar overall at the Riverton, Swan Island, and Robeson

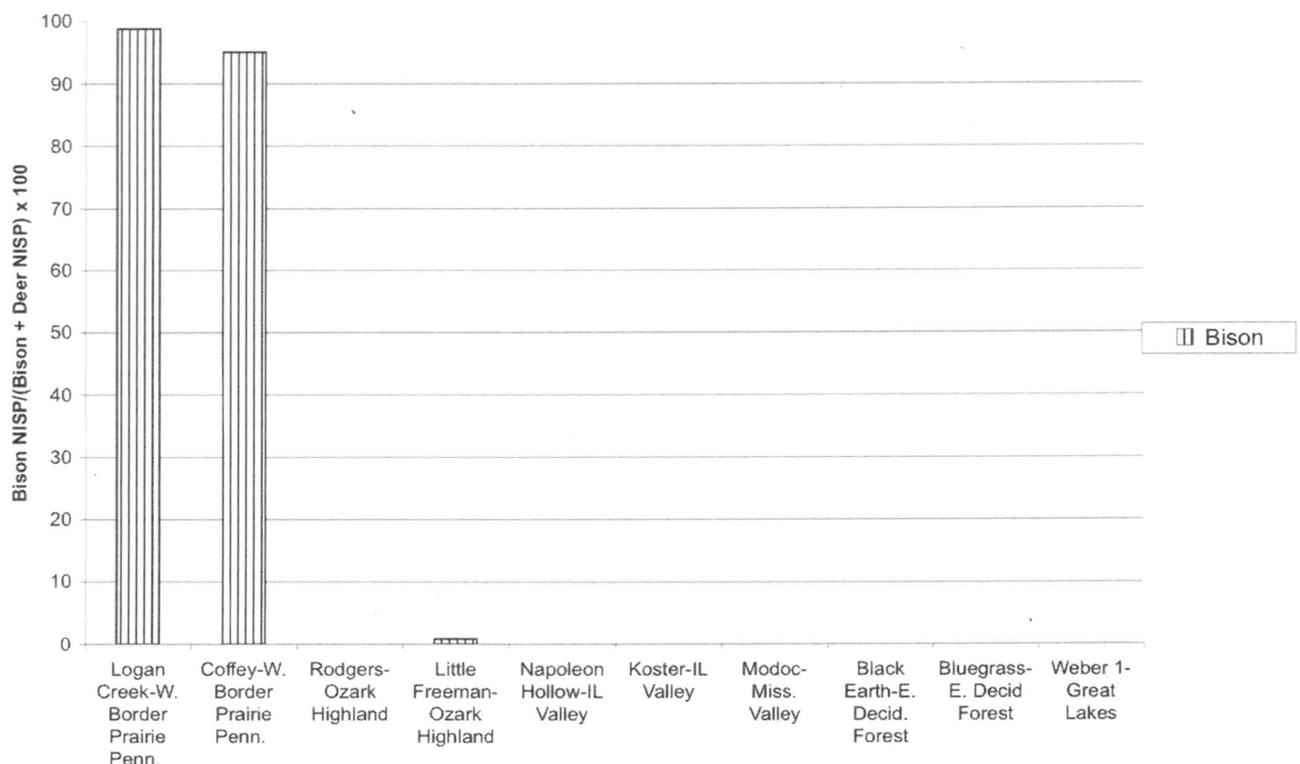

Figure 3.12. Bison index [bison NISP / (bison + deer NISP) x 100] for late middle Holocene site components.

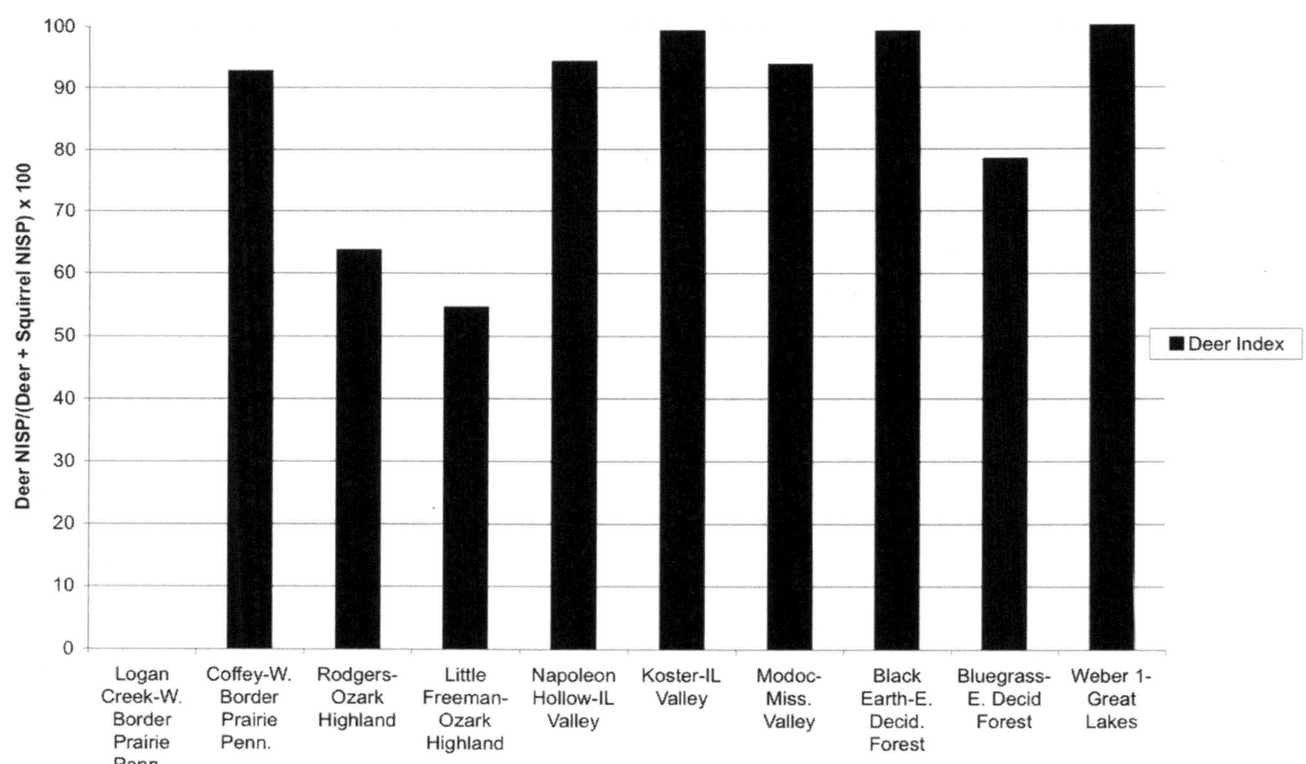

Figure 3.13. Deer index [deer NISP / (deer + squirrel NISP) x 100] for late middle Holocene site components.

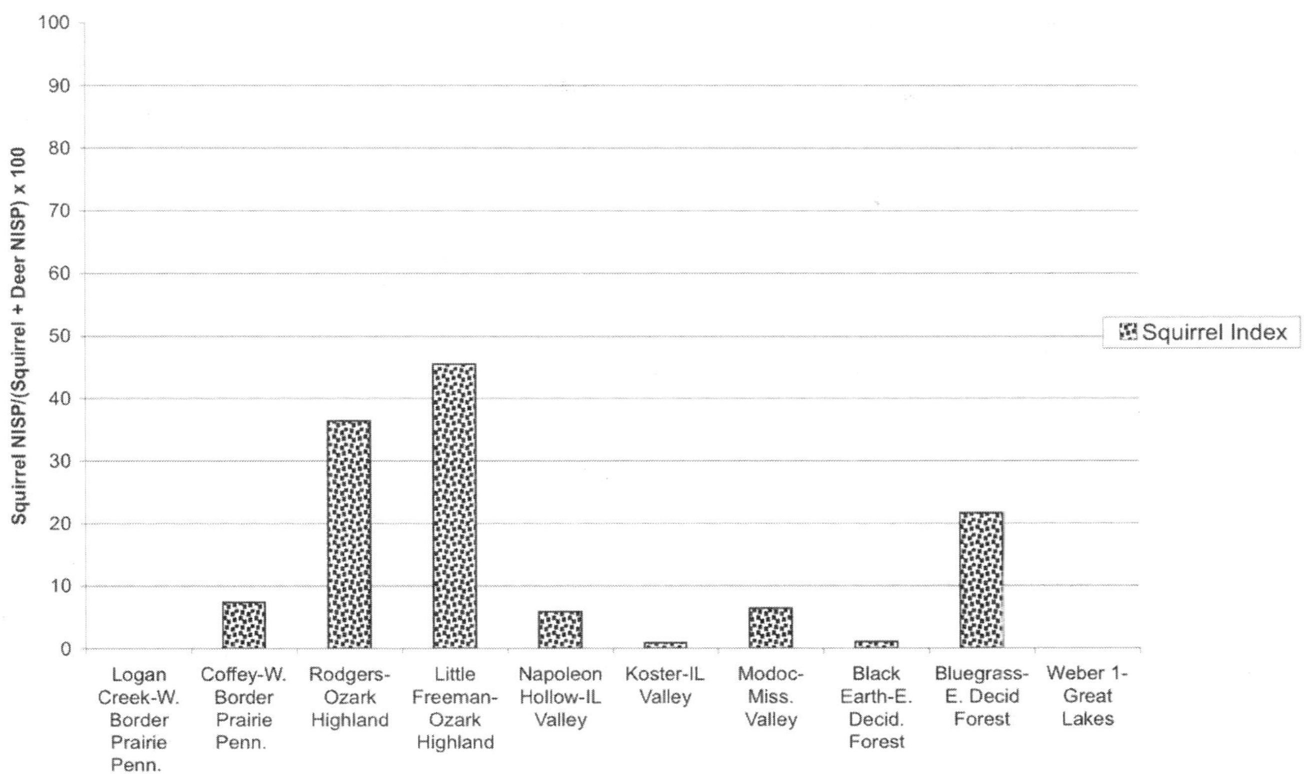

Figure 3.14. Squirrel index [squirrel NISP / (squirrel + deer NISP) x 100] for late middle Holocene site components.

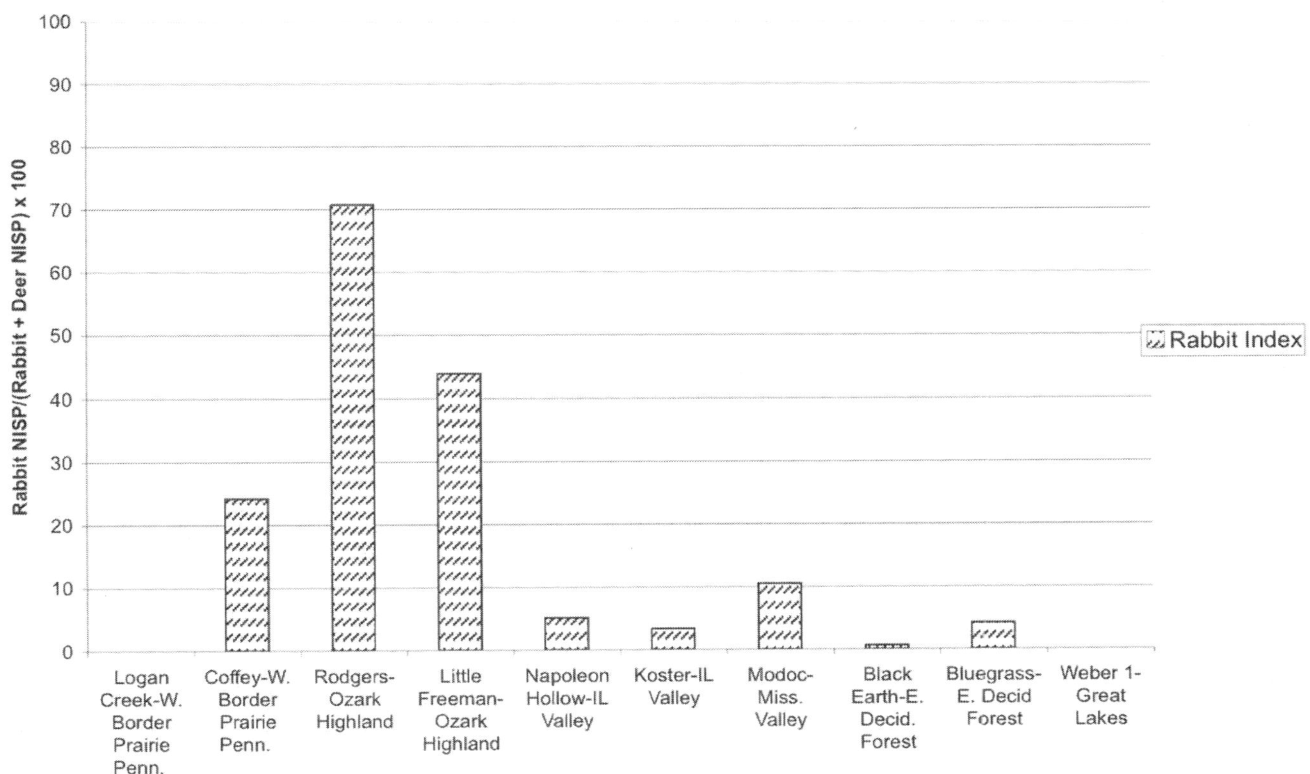

Figure 3.15. Rabbit index [rabbit NISP / (rabbit + deer NISP) x 100] for late middle Holocene site components.

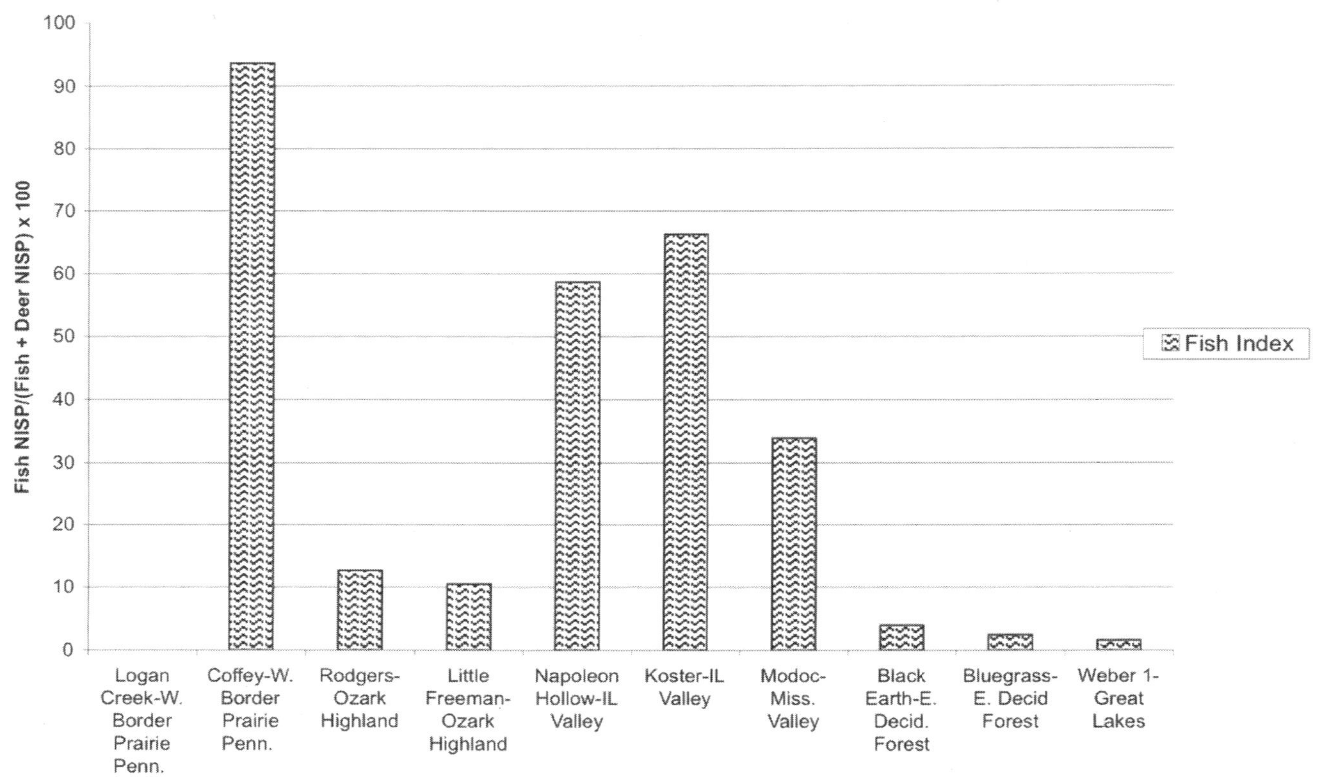

Figure 3.16. Fish index [fish NISP/(fish + deer NISP) x 100] for late-middle Holocene site components.

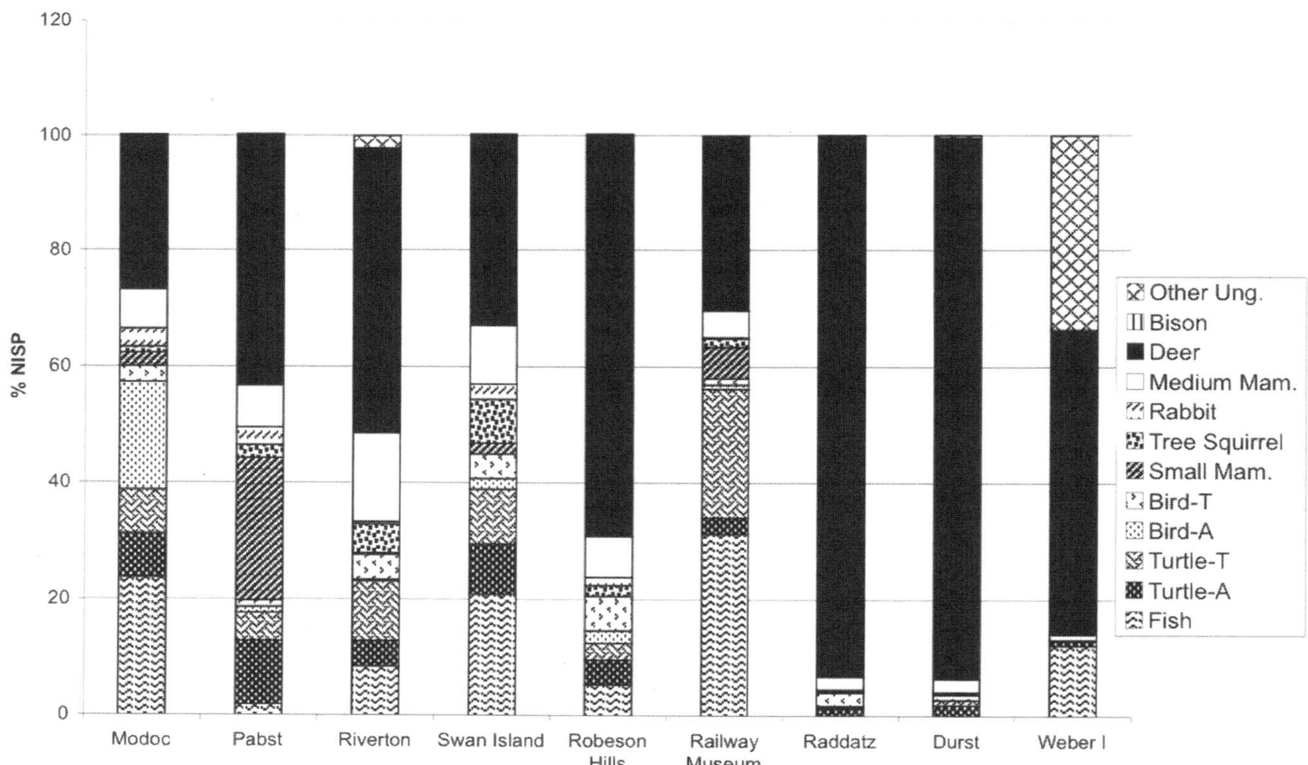

Figure 3.17. Proportion of vertebrate NISP (number of identified specimens) in each faunal category for early late Holocene site components.

Hills sites in the Wabash River valley of Illinois but shows some variation, which has been related to differences in settlement function and seasonality of occupation (Parmalee 1969; Winters 1969). Robeson Hills, possibly a winter settlement, shows the highest proportion of deer. Swan Island, considered a transient spring or fall occupation, or both, shows the highest proportion of fish. Faunal composition at the Riverton site, interpreted as a base camp, is intermediate between the two other sites. Fish remains are not abundant at any of these "Riverton culture" sites. However, freshwater mussels, recovered from shell middens, are particularly abundant at these sites (Parmalee 1969). Riverton and Swan Island show relatively high proportions of box turtles, a pattern shared with the Railway Museum site, situated along the Falls of the Ohio in Kentucky. However, Railway Museum shows even more box turtles and a greater number of fish than the "Riverton culture" sites. Deer dominates in the Late Archaic deposits at Raddatz and Durst rockshelters in southern Wisconsin. However, the function of the occupations at these shelters is poorly understood and may only represent a portion of the broader subsistence round. The Late Archaic component at the Weber I site in the Saginaw Valley of eastern Michigan shows more fish and elk than the mid-Holocene component, perhaps reflecting improvements in aquatic resource productivity with rising lake levels and an opening of the forest in this area.

Spatial and Temporal Patterning

To summarize and evaluate the data, we employed a detrended correspondence analysis (DCA), an ordination technique based on reciprocal averaging. The cases are the Archaic site components, and the variables are the proportions of fauna in our faunal categories. The fauna that appear together in a DCA graph are similar in their proportional representation in the site components. The site components that appear close together in a DCA graph are similar in faunal composition. The first graph (Figure 3.18) shows how the faunal categories group for the first two axes on the basis of the sites in our sample. The first axis separates bison and deer. The second axis primarily separates aquatic taxa (fish, birds associated with aquatic habitats, and aquatic turtles) from terrestrial taxa. The other-ungulate category includes elk and pronghorn, which are insignificant in most of the sites.

The second graph (Figure 3.19) shows how the sites cluster on the basis of the faunal categories. The early Holocene site components (represented as triangles) cluster somewhat by time and fauna—Rodgers Shelter, Little Freeman Cave, Modoc Rock Shelter, Koster, Graham Cave, and Raddatz show a broadly similar, high representation of rabbits, tree squirrels, and other terrestrial mammals. The early Holocene component at Cherokee Sewer is segregated from the others on the basis of the high occurrence of bison at this bison processing camp.

The middle Holocene components, represented as circles (with the numbers 1, 2, 3 representing progressively older components), cluster geographically, showing regionalization in resource availability and procurement strategies. All of the components at Rodgers Shelter cluster with the early Holocene site components, showing the continued exploitation of small mammals in the western Ozark Highland. The mid-Holocene component at Little Freeman Cave also clusters with its early Holocene component, showing the continued use of small mammals at this Ozark Highland site. The middle Holocene

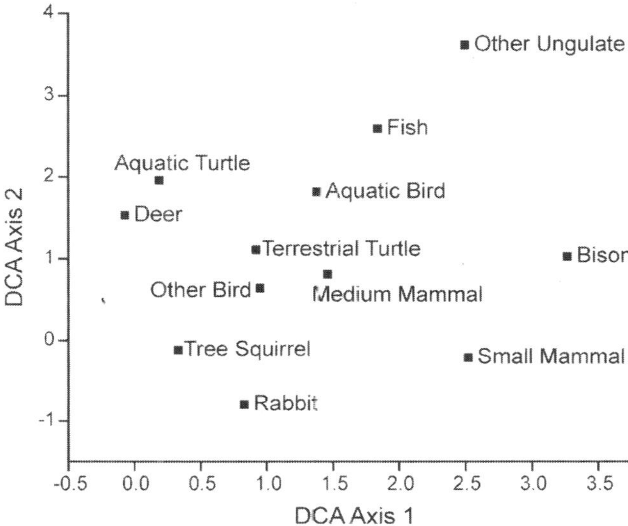

Figure 3.18. Detrended correspondence analysis (DCA) plot of faunal category variables based on patterning in Archaic site components.

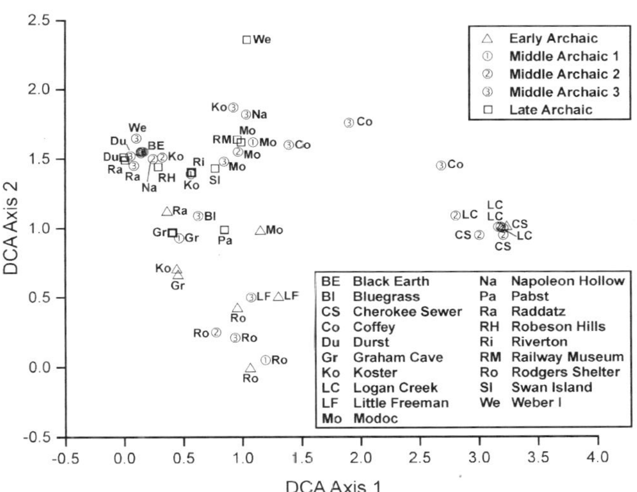

Figure 3.19. Detrended correspondence analysis (DCA) plot of Archaic site components based on patterning in faunal categories. Middle Archaic 1, 2, and 3 represent the early, middle, and late middle Holocene, respectively.

component at Graham Cave is separated from the early Holocene component because of the greater dominance of deer in the middle Holocene component. All of the mid-Holocene components at the Black Earth, Durst, Raddatz, and Weber I sites form a tight cluster, showing the uniform dominance of deer at these sites. The middle Holocene components at Koster and Modoc Rock Shelter and the late mid-Holocene component at Napoleon Hollow cluster—reflecting the high representation of fish in these large river valley sites. The mid-Holocene components at the Coffey site in the tallgrass prairie of northeastern Kansas are intermediate between the large river valley sites and the bison sites, reflecting the more equable representation of fish and bison in these occupations. The mid-Holocene components at Cherokee Sewer and Logan Creek group on the basis of the high representation of bison at these western bison processing camps. The late Holocene, Late Archaic site components (represented by squares) roughly cluster in the upper left-hand quadrant. The differences between these sites primarily reflect variation in the representation of deer, fish, and, in the case of Weber I, elk. They show continued regional differences based on exploitation of locally abundant resources.

Conclusions

The correspondence analysis supports the concept of regional exploitation strategies linked to differences in resource availability across the Prairie Peninsula and into the eastern deciduous forest. These differences in resource availability increased in the mid-Holocene with time-transgressive and differential effects of mid-Holocene warming and drying, the development of aquatic systems, and the evolution of anthropogenic fire in the ecosystem. These landscape changes interplayed with changes in settlement strategies and mobility, leading to regionally different subsistence strategies.

Early Holocene groups in the Midwest primarily subsisted on terrestrial faunal resources, especially white-tailed deer, but also including a diverse assortment of locally available animals, such as gray squirrels, in the dense, mesic forests. Early Archaic groups moved with the seasons, hunting, fishing, and collecting a broad range of resources. The small size of fish recovered at interior sites suggests that nonselective technologies such as netting, trapping, or poisoning were already present, but early Holocene groups for the most part made much less use of aquatic resources than did later groups in the same areas. The presence of white-tailed deer at sites all across the Midwest testifies to the broad distribution and importance of this mammal at many sites. However, along the western border of our study area, bison predominated over deer, and hunters made use of small mammals in addition to deer across much of the Midwest.

Early to mid-Holocene environmental changes exaggerated differences between resource catchments within and outside large river valleys in the midwestern United States and between Great Lakes margins and interior settings. The transformation of the patterning of the biota of the mid-Holocene landscape provided new opportunities for hunters and gatherers across the Midwest, and settlement and subsistence patterns changed in many areas. We see the emergence of greater variability in local subsistence strategies across this broad area. Stabilization of river systems, the formation of flood-basin lakes, and development of a patchy, open forest-prairie mosaic in the Illinois and Mississippi River valleys provided optimal environments for fish and white-tailed deer, and subsistence systems placed more emphasis on these productive resources. Longer-term base-camp occupations were established at the edges of the valleys, often with logistical mobility to exploit other resources.

The timing and nature of the effects of environmental changes varied from region to region as did the timing of changes in human subsistence practices and settlement strategies. Along the western and southern edges of the Prairie Peninsula, forests and prairies became more xeric and stream environments were degraded in the middle Holocene. Middle Holocene peoples in these areas primarily hunted an assortment of small mammals and made less use of deer and little use of aquatic resources. Mid-Holocene climate changes led to the opening of the eastern and northern deciduous forests, which improved habitat for deer across the Midwest and deer and elk to the north. Mid-Holocene populations in prairie-parkland and deciduous forest settings across much of the Midwest made greater use of white-tailed deer and aquatic resources than did early Holocene groups, probably facilitated through incorporation of logistic mobility to procure these productive resources. However, use of aquatic resources was greater in the large river valleys with flood-basin lakes than in other areas of the Midcontinent, even along relatively large rivers. Mid-Holocene stabilization of lake levels and stream systems benefited groups in the Great Lakes area, where a tradition of harvesting spring-spawning lake fish extended back to at least the middle Holocene. A wide variety of subsistence strategies supported seasonally sedentary, base-camp occupations—bison and fish in the tallgrass prairie, small game along the western borders of the Prairie Peninsula, white-tailed deer and fish in the Illinois and Mississippi River valleys, white-tailed deer and other game in the open deciduous forests of the Midcontinent, and spring-spawning lake fish and white-tailed deer in the Great Lakes area. Even with this variability, where sustainable, high-ranked animal resources were available—bison in the prairies, deer in the deciduous forest, and fish in the large river valleys—hunters and foragers tended to focus their economies on these resources, which interplayed with the settlement and mobility strategies of the respective groups.

References Cited

Ahler, Steven R., and Bonnie W. Styles
1998 A Summary of Changes in Archaic Period Subsistence and Site Function at Modoc Rock Shelter. *Illinois Archaeology* 10:110–154.

Anderson, Duane C., and Holmes A. Semken Jr. (editors)
1980 *The Cherokee Excavations: Holocene Ecology and Human Adaptations in Northwestern Iowa*. Academic Press, New York.

Anderson, Duane C., Richard Shutler Jr., and Wayne M. Wendland
1980 The Cherokee Sewer Site and the Cultures of the Atlantic Climatic Episode. In *The Cherokee Excavations: Holocene Ecology and Human Adaptations in Northwestern Iowa*, edited by Duane C. Anderson and Holmes A. Semken Jr., pp. 257–268. Academic Press, New York.

Anslinger, C. Michael, Albert M. Pecora, Charles M. Niquette, and Jonathan P. Kerr
1994 *Salvage Excavations at the Railway Museum Site (15JF630), Jefferson County, Kentucky.* Contract Publication Series 94-15. Cultural Resource Analysts, Hurricane, West Virginia.

Asch, David L., and Nancy B. Asch
1985 Prehistoric Plant Cultivation in West-Central Illinois. In *Prehistoric Food Production in North America*, edited by Richard I. Ford, pp. 149–203. Anthropological Papers 75. Museum of Anthropology, University of Michigan, Ann Arbor.

Bailey, Robert E.
1972 Late- and Postglacial Environmental Changes in Northwestern Indiana. Ph.D. dissertation, Department of Plant Sciences, Indiana University, Bloomington.

Bailey, Robert G., Peter E. Avers, Thomas King, and W. Henry McNab
1994 *Ecoregions and Subregions of the United States* (map). U.S. Department of Agriculture, Forest Service, Washington, D.C.

Baker, Richard G.
2000 Holocene Environments Reconstructed from Plant Macrofossils in Stream Deposits from Southeastern Nebraska, USA. *The Holocene* 10:357–365.

Baker, Richard G., E. Arthur Bettis III, and Patrick Moss
2005 Holocene Pollen and Plant Macrofossils in the Sac River Valley. In *Regional Research and the Archaic Record at the Big Eddy Site (23CE426), Southwest Missouri*, edited by Neal H. Lopinot, Jack H. Ray, and Michael D. Conner, pp. 133–146. Special Publication 4. Center for Archaeological Research, Southwest Missouri State University, Springfield.

Baker, R. G., E. A. Bettis III, D. P. Schwert, D. G. Horton, C. A. Chumbley, L. A. González, and M. K. Reagan
1996 Holocene Paleoenvironments of Northeast Iowa. *Ecological Monographs* 66:203–234.

Baker, Richard G., C. A. Chumbley, P. M. Witinok, and H. K. Kim
1990 Holocene Vegetational Changes in Eastern Iowa. *Journal of the Iowa Academy of Science* 97:167–177.

Baker, Richard G., Glen G. Fredlund, Rolfe D. Mandel, and E. A. Bettis III
2000 Holocene Environments of the Central Great Plains: Multi-Proxy Evidence from Alluvial Sequences, Southeastern Nebraska. *Quaternary International* 67:75–88.

Baker, R. G., L. A. González, M. Raymo, E. A. Bettis III, M. K. Reagan, and J. A. Dorale
1998 Comparison of Multiple Proxy Records of Holocene Environments in the Midwestern United States. *Geology* 26:1131–1134.

Baker, Richard G., Louis J. Maher, Craig A. Chumbley, and Kent L. Van Zant
1992 Patterns of Holocene Environmental Change in the Midwestern United States. *Quaternary Research* 37:379–389.

Bayham, Frank
1979 Factors Influencing the Archaic Pattern of Animal Utilization. *Kiva* 44:219–235.
1982 A Diachronic Analysis of Prehistoric Animal Exploitation at Ventana Cave. Ph.D. dissertation, Department of Anthropology, Arizona State University, Tempe.

Bettinger, Robert L.
1987 Archaeological Approaches to Hunter-Gatherers. *Annual Review of Anthropology* 16:121–142.

Blair, W. F.
1939 Faunal Relationships and Geographic Distribution of Mammals in Oklahoma. *American Midland Naturalist* 22:85–133.

Boszhardt, Robert
1977 Wisconsin Radiocarbon Chronology–1976: A Second Compilation. *The Wisconsin Archeologist* 58:87–143.

Bowen, Jonathan E.
1987 Late Archaic Occupations at the Scioto County Home Site (33SC17). *Ohio Archaeologist* 37(1):15–17.

Breitburg, Emanuel
1982 Analysis of Area A Fauna. In *The Carrier Mills Archaeological Project: Human Adaptation in the Saline Valley, Illinois*, vol. 2, edited by Richard W. Jefferies and Brian M. Butler, pp. 861–957. Research Paper 33. Center for Archaeological Investigations, Southern Illinois University, Carbondale.

Broughton, Jack M.
1994 Late Holocene Resource Intensification in the Sacramento Valley, California: The Vertebrate Evidence. *Journal of Archaeological Science* 21:501–514.

Brown, James A.
1985 Long-term Trends to Sedentism and the Emergence of Complexity in the American Midwest. In *Prehistoric Hunter Gatherers: The Emergence of Cultural Complexity*, edited by T. Douglas Price and James A. Brown, pp. 201–231. Academic Press, New York.

Brown, James A., and Robert K. Vierra
1983 What Happened in the Middle Archaic? Introduction to an Ecological Approach to Koster Site Archaeology. In *Archaic Hunters and Gatherers in the American Midwest*, edited by James L. Phillips and James A. Brown, pp. 165–195. Academic Press, New York.

Brown, Paul, James P. Kennett, and B. Lynn Ingram
1999 Marine Evidence for Episodic Holocene Megafloods in North America and the Northern Gulf of Mexico. *Paleoceanography* 14:498–510.

Bryson, Reid A.
1966 Air Masses, Streamlines, and the Boreal Forest. *Geographical Bulletin* 8:228–269.

Caldwell, Warren, and Dale R. Henning
1978 North American Plains. In *Chronologies in New World Archaeology*, edited by R. E. Taylor and Clement W. Meighan, pp. 113–145. Academic Press, New York.

Chasan, Rebecca
1999 Untitled editorial preface. *Bioscience* 49(1):1.

Chumbley, C. A., R. G. Baker, and E. A. Bettis III
1990 Midwestern Holocene Paleoenvironments Revealed by Floodplain Deposits in Northeastern Iowa. *Science* 249:272–274.

Claassen, Cheryl P.
1996 A Consideration of the Social Organization of the Shell Mound Archaic. In *Archaeology of the Mid-Holocene Southeast*, edited by Kenneth E. Sassaman and David G. Anderson, pp. 235–258. University Press of Florida, Gainesville.

Clark, Peter U., Shawn J. Marshall, Garry K. C. Clarke, Steven W. Hostetler, Joseph M. Licciardi, and James T. Teller
2001 Freshwater Forcing of Abrupt Climate Change during the Last Glaciation. *Science* 293:283–287.

Cleland, Charles E.
1966 *The Prehistoric Animal Ecology and Ethnozoology of the Upper Great Lakes Region*. Anthropological Papers 29. Museum of Anthropology, University of Michigan, Ann Arbor.
1976 The Focal-Diffuse Model: An Evolutionary Perspective on the Prehistoric Cultural Adaptations of the Eastern United. *Midcontinental Journal of Archaeology* 1:59–76.
1982 The Inland Shore Fishery of the Northern Great Lakes: Its Development and Importance in Prehistory. *American Antiquity* 47:761–784.

Cutter, Bruce E., and Richard P. Guyette
1994 Fire Frequency on an Oak-Hickory Ridgetop in the Missouri Ozarks. *The American Midland Naturalist* 132:393–398.

Denniston, Rhawn F., Luis A. González, Yemane Asmerom, Mark K. Reagan, and Heather Recelli-Snyder
2000 Speleothem Carbon Isotopic Records of Holocene Environments in the Ozark Highlands, USA. *Quaternary International* 67:21–27.

Denniston, Rhawn F., Luis A. González, Holmes A. Semken Jr., Yemane Asmerom, Richard G. Baker, Heather Recelli-Snyder, Mark K. Reagan, and E. Arthur Bettis III
1999 Integrating Stalagmite, Vertebrate, and Pollen Sequences to Investigate Holocene Vegetation and Climate Change in the Southern Midwestern United States. *Quaternary Research* 52:381–387.

Dickson, Don R.
1991 *The Albertson Site: A Deeply and Clearly Stratified Ozark Bluff Shelter*. Research Series 41. Arkansas Archeological Survey, Fayetteville.
2003 Albertson Shelter (3BE174) Radiocarbon Dates. *Missouri Archaeological Society Quarterly* 20(1):12–13.

Dorale, Jeffrey A., Luis A. González, Mark K. Reagan, David A. Pickett, Michael T. Murrell, and Richard G. Baker
1992 A High-Resolution Record of Holocene Climate Change in Speleothem Calcite from Cold Water Cave, Northeast Iowa. *Science* 258:1626–1630.

Eddy, Samuel E., and Albert E. Jenks
1935 A Kitchen Midden with Bones of Extinct Animals in the Upper Lakes Area. *Science* 81:535.

Egan, Kathryn C.
1993 Hunter-Gatherer Subsistence Adaptation in the Saginaw Valley, Michigan. Ph.D. dissertation, Department of Anthropology, Michigan Sate University, East Lansing.

Ellis, Chris J., Ian T. Kenyon, and Michael W. Spence
1990 The Archaic. In *The Archaeology of Southern Ontario to A.D. 1650*, edited by Chris J. Ellis and Neal Ferris, pp. 65–124. Occasional Publication 5. London Chapter, Ontario Archaeological Society.

Emerson, Thomas E.
1979 Prehistoric Seasonal Exploitation of White-Tailed Deer in the Driftless Area of Wisconsin: An Example from Brogley Rockshelter (47-GT-156). *The Wisconsin Archeologist* 60:278–292.
2003 Observations on Prehistoric White-Tailed Deer Hunting Practices in Southwestern Wisconsin. *Illinois Archaeology* 15 & 16:12-29.

Fenneman, Nevin M.
1917 Physiographic Subdivision of the United States. *Proceedings of the National Academy of Sciences of the United States of America* 3(1):17–22.
1946 *Physical Divisions of the United States*. U.S. Department of the Interior, Geological Survey, Washington, D.C.

Finnegan, Michael, and Dixie L. West
1990 Faunal Remains from the Stigenwalt Site (Appendix IV). In *The Archeology of the Stigenwalt Site, 14LT351*, by Randall M Thies, pp. 160–184. Contract Archeology Series 7. Kansas State Historical Society, Topeka.

Frison, George C.
1991 *Prehistoric Hunters of the High Plains*. 2nd ed. Academic Press, New York.
2001 Hunting and Gathering Tradition: Northwestern and Central Plains. In *Plains*, edited by Raymond J. DeMallie, pp. 131–145. Handbook of North American Indians vol. 13, pt. 1, W. C. Sturtevant, general editor. Smithsonian Institution, Washington, D.C.

Graham, Mary Ann, and Russell W. Graham
1990 Holocene Records of Martes pennanti and Martes americana in Whiteside County, Northwestern Illinois. *The American Midland Naturalist* 124:81–92.

Grayson, Donald K.
1984 *Quantitative Zooarchaeology: Topics in the Analysis of Archaeological Faunas*. Academic Press, New York.

Griffin, John W., and Donald E. Wray
1945 Bison in Illinois Archaeology. *Transactions of the Illinois State Academy of Science* 38:21–26. Springfield.

Grimm, Eric C.
1984 Fire and Other Factors Controlling the Big Woods Vegetation of Minnesota in the Mid-Nineteenth Century. *Ecological Monographs* 54:291–311.

Grimm, Eric C., and George L. Jacobson Jr.
2004 Late-Quaternary Vegetation History of the Eastern United States. In *The Quaternary Period in the United States,* edited by A. R. Gillespie, S. C. Porter, and B. F. Atwater, pp. 381–402. Elsevier, Amsterdam.
Grimm, Eric C., Socorro Lozano-García, Hermann Behling, and Vera Markgraf
2001 Holocene Vegetation and Climate Variability in the Americas. In *Interhemispheric Climatic Linkages*, edited by Vera Markgraf, pp. 325–370. Academic Press, San Diego, California.
Guyette, Richard P., and Bruce E. Cutter
1991 Tree-Ring Analysis of Fire History of a Post Oak Savanna in the Missouri Ozarks. *Natural Areas Journal* 11:93–99.
Hajic, Edwin R.
1981 *Shallow Subsurface Geology, Geomorphology and Limited Cultural Resource Investigations of the Hartwell Levee and Drainage District, Greene County, Illinois*. Report of Investigation 109. Prepared for the U.S. Army Corps of Engineers, St. Louis. Contract Archeology Program, Center for American Archeology, Kampsville, Illinois.
1990 Late Pleistocene and Holocene Landscape Evolution, Depositional Subsystems, and Stratigraphy in the Lower Illinois River Valley and Adjacent Central Mississippi River Valley. Ph.D. dissertation, Department of Geology, University of Illinois, Urbana-Champaign.
1991 Geomorphology, Stratigraphy, and Landscape Evolution of the Modoc Rock Shelter in the Mississippi Valley. Paper presented at the 56th Annual Meeting of the Society for American Archaeology, New Orleans, Louisiana.
Hawley Marlin F., Matthew G. Hill, and Christopher C. Widga
2007 Recent Research on the Interstate Park Bison Site, Polk County, Northwestern Wisconsin. *Current Research in the Pleistocene* 24.
Hill, Frederick C.
1975 Effects of the Environment on Animal Exploitation by Archaic Inhabitants of the Koster Site, Illinois. Ph.D. dissertation, Department of Biology, University of Louisville, Louisville, Kentucky.
Jacobson, Robert B., and Alexander T. Primm
1997 *Historical Land-Use Changes and Potential Effects on Stream Disturbance in the Ozark Plateaus, Missouri.* Water-Supply Paper 2484. U.S. Geological Survey, Reston, Virginia.
Jochim, Michael A.
1988 Optimal Foraging and the Division of Labor. *American Anthropologist* 90:130–136.
Johannessen, Sissel
1984 Paleoethnobotany. In *American Bottom Archaeology: A Summary of the FAI-270 Project Contribution to the Culture History of the Mississippi River Valley*, edited by Charles J. Bareis and James W. Porter, pp. 197–214. University of Illinois Press, Urbana.
1993 Farmers of the Late Woodland. In *Foraging and Farming in the Eastern Woodlands*, edited by Margaret Scarry, pp. 57–77. University Press of Florida, Gainesville.
Kapp, Ronald O.
1999 Michigan Late Pleistocene, Holocene, and Presettlement Vegetation and Climate. In *Retrieving Michigan's Buried Past: The Archaeology of the Great Lakes State,* edited by John R. Halsey, pp. 31–58. Bulletin 64. Cranbrook Institute of Science, Bloomfield Hills, Michigan.
Katz, Paul R.
1971 Archaeology of the Sutter Site in Northeastern, Kansas. *Plains Anthropologist* 16:1–19.
1973 Radiocarbon Dates from the Sutter Site, Northeastern Kansas. *Plains Anthropologist* 18:167–168.
Kay, Marvin
1998 The Central and Southern Plains Archaic. In *Archaeology on the Great Plains,* edited by W. Raymond Wood, pp. 173–200. University Press of Kansas, Lawrence.
Keene, Arthur S.
1981 *Prehistoric Foraging in a Temperate Forest: A Linear Programming Model.* Academic Press, New York.
King, James E.
1973 Late Pleistocene Palynology and Biogeography of the Western Missouri Ozarks. *Ecological Monographs* 43:539–565.
1980 Post-Pleistocene Vegetational Changes in the Midwestern United States. In *Archaic Prehistory on the Prairie-Plains Border*, edited by Alfred E. Johnson, pp. 3–11. Publications in Anthropology 12. University of Kansas, Lawrence.
1981 Late Quaternary Vegetational History of Illinois. *Ecological Monographs* 51:43–62.
1982 Palynological Investigations at Phillips Spring. In *Holocene Adaptations within the Lower Pomme de Terre River Valley, Missouri*, vol. 3, edited by Marvin Kay, pp. 687–699. Report prepared for the U.S. Army Corps of Engineers, Kansas City District. Illinois State Museum Society, Springfield.
1988 Palynology of Midcontinental Spring Deposits. In *Late Pleistocene and Early Holocene Paleoecology and Archeology of the Eastern Great Lakes Region*, edited by Richard S. Laub, Norton G. Miller, and David W. Steadman, pp. 151–158. Bulletin 33. Buffalo Society of Natural Sciences. Buffalo, New York.
King, James E., and William H. Allen Jr.
1977 A Holocene Vegetation Record from the Mississippi River Valley, Southeastern Missouri. *Quaternary Research* 8:307–323.
Klippel, Walter E.
1971 Prehistory and Environmental Change along the Southern Border of the Prairie Peninsula during the Archaic Period. Ph.D. dissertation, Department of Sociology and Anthropology, University of Missouri, Columbia.
Klippel, Walter E., and James Maddox
1977 The Early Archaic of Willow Branch. *Midcontinental Journal of Archaeology* 2:99–130.
Klippel, Walter E., Gail Celmer, and James R. Purdue
1982 The Holocene Naiad Record at Rodgers Shelter in the Western Ozark Highland of Missouri. In *Holocene Adaptations within the Lower Pomme de Terre River Valley,*

Missouri, edited by Marvin Kay, pp. 155–198. Report prepared for the U.S. Army Corps of Engineers, Kansas City District. Illinois State Museum Society, Springfield.

Knox, James C.

1985 Responses of Floods to Holocene Climatic Change in the Upper Mississippi Valley. *Quaternary Research* 23:287–300.

1993 Large Increases in Flood Magnitude in Response to Modest Changes in Climate. *Nature* 361:430–432.

Kraft, H. C.

1986 *The Lenape: Archaeology, History, and Ethnography*. New Jersey Historical Society, Newark.

Kuchler, A. W.

1975 *Potential Natural Vegetation of the Conterminous United States* (map). 2nd ed. American Geographical Society, New York.

Kuehn, Steven R.

1998 New Evidence for Late Paleoindian-Early Archaic Subsistence Behavior in the Western Great Lakes. *American Antiquity* 63:457–476.

2000 The Granite Falls Site (21YM47), a Prairie Archaic Bison Kill in Southwestern Minnesota. Paper presented at the 2000 Joint Plains Anthropological and Midwest Archaeological Conference, St. Paul, Minnesota.

Larsen, Curtis E.

1999 A Century of Great Lakes Levels Research: Finished or Just Beginning. In *Retrieving Michigan's Buried Past: The Archaeology of the Great Lakes State,* edited by John R. Halsey, pp. 1–30. Bulletin 64. Cranbrook Institute of Science, Bloomfield Hills, Michigan.

Larson, Grahame, and Randall Schaetz

2001 Origin and Evolution of the Great Lakes. *Journal of Great Lakes Research* 21:518–546.

Larson, Thomas K., and D. M. Penny

1991 The Smilden-Rostberg Site: An Early Archaic Component in the Northeastern Plains. Submitted to KBM, Inc. Unpublished report on file, State Historical Society of North Dakota, Bismarck.

Lewis, R. Barry

1979 Hunter-Gatherer Foraging: Some Theoretical Explorations and Archaeological Tests. Ph.D. dissertation, Department of Anthropology, University of Illinois at Urbana-Champaign.

Lovis, William A

1986 Environmental Periodicity, Buffering, and the Archaic Adaptations of the Saginaw Valley of Michigan. In *Foraging, Collecting, and Harvesting: Archaic Period Subsistence in the Eastern Woodlands,* edited by Sarah W. Neusius, pp. 99–116. Occasional Papers 6. Center for Archaeological Investigations, Southern Illinois University, Carbondale.

1990 Screaming Loon: A Post-Nipissing Site on the Devil's Elbow. In *Pilot of the Grand: Papers in Tribute to Richard E. Flanders*, Part I, edited by Terrance J. Martin and Charles E. Cleland, pp. 233–252. *The Michigan Archaeologist* 36(3–4).

1999 The Middle Archaic: Learning to Live in the Woodlands. In *Retrieving Michigan's Buried Past: The Archaeology of the Great Lakes State*, edited by John R. Halsey, pp. 83–94. Bulletin 64. Cranbrook Institute of Science, Bloomfield Hills, Michigan.

Mandel, Rolfe D.

1990 Geomorphology and Stratigraphy of the Stigenwalt Site (Appendix I). In *The Archeology of the Stigenwalt Site, 14LT351*, by Randall M. Thies, pp. 138–148. Contract Archeology Series 7. Kansas State Historical Society, Topeka.

Mayer-Oakes, William J.

1959 Relationship between Plains Early Hunter and Eastern Archaic. *Journal of the Washington Academy of Sciences* 49:146–156.

McAndrews, John H.

1966 Postglacial History of Prairie, Savanna, and Forest in Northwestern Minnesota. *Memoirs of The Torrey Botanical Club* 22(9):1–72.

McMillan, R. Bruce

1963 A Survey and Evaluation of the Archaeology of the Central Gasconade River Valley in Missouri. Master's thesis, Department of Anthropology, University of Missouri, Columbia.

1971 Biophysical Change and Cultural Adaptation at Rodgers Shelter, Missouri. Ph.D. dissertation, Department of Anthropology, University of Colorado at Boulder.

1976 The Dynamics of Cultural and Environmental Change at Rodgers Shelter, Missouri. In *Prehistoric Man and His Environments: A Case Study in the Ozark Highland*, edited by W. Raymond Wood and R. Bruce McMillan, pp. 211–232. Academic Press, New York.

2006 Perspectives on the Biogeography and Archaeology of Bison in Illinois. In *Records of Early Bison in Illinois*, edited by R. Bruce McMillan, pp. 67–147. Scientific Papers 31. Illinois State Museum, Springfield.

McMillan, R. Bruce, and Walter E. Klippel

1981 Post-Glacial Environmental Change and Hunting-Gathering Societies of the Southern Prairie Peninsula. *Journal of Archaeological Science* 8:215–245.

McMillan, R. Bruce, and Bonnie W. Styles

1979 Ecological Approaches to Archaeology in the American Midwest. Paper presented at a Plenary Session on "Ecological Archeology: Techniques Versus Goals," 78th Annual Meeting of the American Anthropological Association, Cincinnati, Ohio.

Medlock, Raymond E.

1978 Ten Mile Rock: Pigs, Peccaries, and People. *The Arkansas Archeologist* 19:1–24.

Michlovic, Michael G., and Garry L. Running IV (editors)

2005 Archaeology and Paleoenvironment at the Rustad Site (32RI775). *Plains Anthropologist* 50 (Memoir 37).

Monaghan, George W., William A. Lovis, and Leslie P. Fay

1986 The Lake Nipissing Transgression in the Saginaw Bay Region, Michigan. *Canadian Journal of Earth Sciences* 23:1851–1854.

Montgomery, David R., and Ellen E. Wohl

2004 Rivers and Riverine Environments. In *The Quaternary of the United States*, edited by A. R. Gillespie, S. C. Porter, and B. F. Atwater, pp. 221–246. Elsevier, Amsterdam.

Naylor, Larry J., and Howard G. Savage
1984 Analysis of the Macro-Faunal Remains from the McIntyre Site, Petersborough County, Ontario. In *The McIntyre Site: Archaeology, Subsistence, and Environment*, edited by Richard B. Johnston, pp. 115–134. Mercury Series Paper 26. Archaeological Survey of Canada, National Museum of Man, Ottawa.

Nelson, David M.
2005 Influence of Aridity and Fire on Holocene Vegetational Patterns in the Tallgrass Prairie Peninsula. Ph.D. dissertation, Department of Plant Biology, University of Illinois at Urbana-Champaign.

Nelson, David M., Feng Sheng Hu, and Eric C. Grimm
2004 Dynamics of Middle-Holocene Climate, Vegetation, and Fire on the Northern Prairie Peninsula. *AMQUA 2004: American Quaternary Association Program and Abstracts of the 18th Biennial Meeting*, pp. 53–55. University of Kansas, Lawrence.

Nelson, David M., Feng Sheng Hu, Eric C. Grimm, B. Brandon Curry, and Jennifer E. Slate
2006 The Influence of Aridity and Fire on Holocene Prairie Communities in the Eastern Prairie Peninsula. *Ecology* 87:2523–2536.

Neusius, Sarah W.
1982 Early-Middle Archaic Subsistence Strategies: Changes in Faunal Exploitation at the Koster Site. Ph.D. dissertation, Department of Anthropology, Northwestern University, Evanston, Illinois.

Palmer, Harris A.
1954 A Review of the Interstate Park, Wisconsin Bison Find. *Proceedings of the Iowa Academy of Science* 61:313–319.

Parmalee, Paul W.
1958 Remains for Rare and Extinct Birds from Illinois Indian Sites. *The Auk* 75:169–176.
1959 Animal Remains from the Raddatz Rockshelter, Sk5, Wisconsin. *The Wisconsin Archeologist* 40:83–90.
1960 Animal Remains from the Durst Rockshelter, Sauk County, Wisconsin. *The Wisconsin Archeologist* 41:11–17.
1965 The Food Economy of Archaic and Woodland Peoples at the Tick Creek Cave Site, Missouri. *The Missouri Archaeologist* 27(1):1–34.
1969 Animal Remains from the Archaic Riverton, Swan Island, and Robeson Hills Sites, Illinois. In *The Riverton Culture*, by Howard D. Winters, pp. 139–144. Monograph 1. Illinois Archaeological Survey, Urbana. Reports of Investigations 13. Illinois State Museum, Springfield.

Parmalee, Paul W., R. Bruce McMillan, and Frances B. King
1976 Changing Subsistence Patterns at Rodgers Shelter. In *Prehistoric Man and His Environments: A Case Study in the Ozark Highland*, edited by W. Raymond Wood and R. Bruce McMillan, pp. 141–162. Academic Press, New York.

Petersen, James B., Nathan D. Hamilton, J. M. Adovasio, and Alan L. McPherron
1984 Netting Technology and the Antiquity of Fish Exploitation in Eastern North America. *Midcontinental Journal of Archaeology* 9:199–225

Petersen, James B., Brian S. Robinson, Daniel F. Belknap, James Stark, and Lawrence K. Kaplan
1994 An Archaic and Woodland Period Fish Weir Complex in Central Maine. *Archaeology of Eastern North America* 22:197–222.

Pond, Alonzo W.
1937 Wisconsin Joins Ranks of Oldest Inhabited Areas in America. *The Wisconsin Archeologist* 17:51–54.

Prufer, Olaf H., Dana A. Long, and Donald Metzger
1989 *Krill Cave: A Stratified Rockshelter in Summit County, Ohio*. Kent State Research Papers in Archaeology 8. Kent State University Press, Kent, Ohio.

Purdue, James R.
1980 Clinal Variation of Some Mammals during the Holocene in Missouri. *Quaternary Research* 13:242–258.
1982 The Environmental Implications of the Fauna Recovered from Rodgers Shelter. In *Holocene Adaptations within the Lower Pomme de Terre River Valley, Missouri*, edited by Marvin Kay, pp. 199–261. Prepared for the U.S. Army Corps of Engineers, Kansas City District. Illinois State Museum Society, Springfield.

Purdue, James R., and Bonnie W. Styles
1986 *Dynamics of Mammalian Distribution in the Holocene of Illinois*. Reports of Investigations 41. Illinois State Museum, Springfield.
1987 Changes in the Mammalian Fauna of Illinois and Missouri during the Late Pleistocene and Holocene. In *Late Quaternary Mammalian Biogeography and Environments of the Great Plains and Prairies*, edited by Russell W. Graham, Holmes A. Semken Jr., and Mary Ann Graham, pp. 144–174. Scientific Papers 22. Illinois State Museum, Springfield.

Pyle, Katherine B.
1980 The Cherokee Sewer Site Large Mammal Fauna. In *The Cherokee Excavations: Holocene Ecology and Human Adaptations in Northwestern Iowa,* edited by Duane C. Anderson and Holmes A. Semken Jr., pp. 171–196. Academic Press, New York.

Reeves, Brian
1973 The Concept of an Altithermal Cultural Hiatus in Northern Plains Prehistory. *American Anthropologist* 75:1221–1253.

Reimer, Paula J. et al. (includes 29 contributors of IntCal Working Group)
2004 IntCal04 Terrestrial Radiocarbon Age Calibration, 0–26 Cal kyr BP. *Radiocarbon* 46:1029–1058.

Risser, Paul G.
1990 Landscape Processes and the Vegetation of the North American Grassland. In *Fire in North American Tallgrass Prairies*, edited by Scott L. Collins and Linda L. Wallace, pp. 133–146. University of Oklahoma Press, Norman.

Roberts, Ralph G.
1965 Tick Creek Cave, an Archaic Site in the Gasconade River Valley of Missouri. *The Missouri Archaeologist* 27(2):1–52.

Robertson, James A.
1987 Inter-Assemblage Variability and Hunter-Gatherer Settlement Systems: A Perspective from the Saginaw Valley of Michigan. Ph.D. dissertation, Department of Anthropology, University of Michigan, Ann Arbor.

Robertson, James A., William A. Lovis, and John R. Halsey
1999 The Late Archaic: Hunter-Gatherers in an Uncertain Environment. In *Retrieving Michigan's Buried Past: The Archaeology of the Great Lakes State*, edited by John R. Halsey, pp. 95–124. Bulletin 64. Cranbrook Institute of Science, Bloomfield Hills, Michigan.
Rostlund, Erhard
1952 *Freshwater Fish and Fishing in Native North America.* University of California Publications in Geography 9. University of California Press, Berkeley.
Schmits, Larry J.
1978 The Coffey Site: Environment and Cultural Adaptation at a Prairie Plains Archaic Site. *Midcontinental Journal of Archaeology* 3:69–185.
1980 Holocene Fluvial History and Depositional Environments at the Coffey Site, Kansas. In *Archaic Prehistory on the Prairie-Plains Border*, edited by Alfred E. Johnson, pp. 79–105. Publications in Anthropology 12. University of Kansas, Lawrence.
Schoewe, Walter H.
1949 The Geography of Kansas. *Transactions of the Kansas Academy of Science* 52(3):261–333.
Semken, Holmes A., Jr.
1974 Microvertebrates from the Cherokee Sewer Site. In *The Cherokee Sewer Site (13CK405): A Preliminary Report of a Stratified Paleo-Indian/Archaic Site in Northwestern Iowa*, pp. 117–129. *Journal of the Iowa Archeological Society* 21.
1983 Holocene Mammalian Biogeography and Climatic Change in the Eastern and Central United States. In *Late-Quaternary Environments of the United States: 2. The Holocene*, edited by H. E. Wright Jr., pp. 182–207. University of Minnesota Press, Minneapolis.
Shane, Linda C. K.
1989 The History of Vegetation, Climate, and Relict Plant Taxa: Palynology of the Gott Fen/Frame Lake Area, Portage Co., Ohio. Final report to the Ohio Department of Natural Resources on 1988 grant. Limnological Research Center, University of Minnesota, Minneapolis. Copy on file North American Pollen Database (NAPD), Illinois State Museum, Springfield.
Shaw, James H., and Tracy S. Carter
1990 Bison Movements in Relation to Fire and Seasonality. *Wildlife Society Bulletin* 18:426–430.
Shay, C. Thomas
1971 *The Itasca Bison Kill Site: An Ecological Analysis.* Minnesota Historical Society, St. Paul.
Sheehan, Michael S.
1998 Early Archaic Diet in the Tallgrass Prairie and Shortgrass Plains: A Comparison. *North American Archaeologist* 19:363–381.
Shelford, Victor E.
1963 *The Ecology of North America.* University of Illinois Press, Urbana.
Shott, Michael J.
1999 The Early Archaic: Life after the Glaciers. In *Retrieving Michigan's Buried Past: The Archaeology of the Great Lakes State*, edited by John R. Halsey, pp. 71–82. Bulletin 64. Cranbrook Institute of Science, Bloomfield Hills, Michigan.
Slawson, Laurie V.
1977 Faunal Analysis: A Study of the Methods and Their Application to the Late Archaic Bullskin Creek Site, 33Ct29, Clement County, Ohio. Master's thesis, Department of Anthropology, University of Cincinnati, Cincinnati, Ohio.
Smith, Beverley A.
1989 Analysis of the Faunal Remains from the Weber I Site. In *Archaeological Investigations at the Weber I (20SA581) and Weber II (20SA582) Sites, Frankenmuth Township, Saginaw County, Michigan*, edited by William Lovis, pp. 143–174. Michigan Cultural Resource Investigations Series 1. Michigan Department of State and Michigan Department of Transportation, Lansing.
2004 The Gill Nets "Native Country." In *An Upper Great Lakes Archaeological Odyssey*, edited by William A. Lovis, pp. 64–84. Wayne State University Press, Detroit.
Smith, Beverley A., and Kathryn C. Egan
1990 Middle and Late Archaic Faunal and Floral Exploitation at the Weber I Site (20Sa581), Michigan. *Ontario Archaeology* 50:39–54.
Smith, Everett N., Jr.
1984 Late-Quaternary Vegetation History at Cupola Pond, Ozark National Scenic Riverways, Southeastern Missouri. Master's thesis. Department of Geology, University of Tennessee, Knoxville.
Stafford, C. Russell, Ronald L. Richards, and C. Michael Anslinger
2000 The Bluegrass Fauna and Changes in Middle Holocene Hunter-Gatherer Foraging in the Southern Midwest. *American Antiquity* 65:317–336.
Styles, Bonnie W.
1981 *Faunal Exploitation and Resource Selection: Early Late Woodland Subsistence in the Lower Illinois Valley.* Scientific Papers 3. Northwestern University Archeological Program, Evanston, Illinois.
1986 Aquatic Exploitation in the Lower Illinois River Valley: The Role of Paleoecological Change. In *Foraging, Collecting, and Harvesting: Archaic Period Subsistence and Settlement in the Eastern Woodlands*, edited by Sarah W. Neusius, pp. 145–174. Occasional Papers 6. Center for Archaeological Investigations, Southern Illinois University, Carbondale.
1992 Archaic Faunal Remains from the Napoleon Hollow Site, Pike County, Illinois. Manuscript on file, Illinois State Museum, Springfield.
1994 The Value of Archaeological Faunal Remains for Paleodietary Reconstruction: A Case Study for the Midwestern United States. In *Paleonutrition: The Diet and Health of Prehistoric Americans*, edited by Kristin D. Sobolik, pp. 34–54. Occasional Papers 22. Center for Archaeological Investigations, Southern Illinois University, Carbondale.
1995 Changing Subsistence Strategies in the Midwestern United States: The View from the Big Valleys. Paper presented at the 60th Annual Meeting of the Society for American Archaeology, Minneapolis, Minnesota.

2000 Late Woodland Faunal Exploitation in the Midwestern United States. In *Late Woodland Societies: Tradition and Transformation across the Midcontinent*, edited by Thomas E. Emerson, Dale L. McElrath, and Andrew C. Fortier, pp. 77–94. University of Nebraska Press, Lincoln.

2006 Northeast Animals. In *Environment, Origins, and Population*, edited by Douglas H. Ubelaker, pp. 412-427. Handbook of North American Indians, vol. 3, W. C. Sturtevant, general editor, Smithsonian Institution, Washington, D.C.

Styles, Bonnie W., Steven R. Ahler, and Melvin L. Fowler

1983 Modoc Rock Shelter Revisited. In *Archaic Hunters and Gatherers in the American Midwest*, edited by James L. Phillips and James A. Brown, pp. 261–297. Academic Press, New York.

Styles, Bonnie W., and Walter E. Klippel

1996 Mid-Holocene Faunal Exploitation in the Southeastern United States. In *Archaeology of the Mid-Holocene Southeast*, edited by Kenneth E. Sassaman and David G. Anderson, pp. 115–133. University Press of Florida, Gainesville.

Styles, Bonnie W., and Karli White

1991 Shifts in Archaic Period Faunal Exploitation in the Mississippi River Valley: Modoc Rock Shelter Revisited. Paper presented at the 56th Annual Meeting of the Society for American Archaeology, New Orleans, Louisiana.

1997 Archaeozoological Assemblage. In *Interdisciplinary Data Recovery at Four Sites in the Ramsey Complex, Fort Leonard Wood, Pulaski County, Missouri*, by Steven R. Ahler, Dawn E. Harn, Margot Neverett, Marjorie B. Schroeder, Bonnie W. Styles, Robert E. Warren, Karli White, James L. Theler, and Robert A. Dunn, pp. 177–205. Technical Report 97-1066-18. Quaternary Studies Program, Illinois State Museum Society, Springfield.

Styles, Thomas R.

1985 *Holocene and Late Pleistocene Geology of the Napoleon Hollow Site in the Lower Illinois River Valley*. Kampsville Archeological Center Research Series 5. Center for American Archeology, Kampsville, Illinois.

Taggart, David W.

1967 Seasonal Patterns in Settlement, Subsistence, and Industries in the Saginaw Late Archaic. *The Michigan Archaeologist* 13:153–170.

Tatum, Lise S.

1980 A Seasonal Subsistence Model for Holocene Bison Hunters on the Eastern Plains of North America. In *The Cherokee Excavations: Holocene Ecology and Human Adaptations in Northwestern Iowa*, edited by Duane C. Anderson and Holmes A. Semken Jr., pp. 149–169. Academic Press, New York.

Tatum, Lise S., and Richard Shutler Jr.

1980 Bone Tool Technology and Subsistence Activity at the Cherokee Sewer Site. In *The Cherokee Excavations: Holocene Ecology and Human Adaptations in Northwestern Iowa*, edited by Duane C. Anderson and Holmes A. Semken Jr., pp. 239–255. Academic Press, New York.

Theler, James L.

1987 *Woodland Tradition Economic Strategies: Animal Resource Utilization in Southwestern Wisconsin and Northeastern Iowa*. Report 17. Office of the State Archaeologist, Unversity of Iowa, Iowa City.

2000 Animal Remains from Native American Archaeological Sites in Western Wisconsin. *Transactions of the Wisconsin Academy of Sciences, Arts and Letters* 88:121–142. Madison.

Theler, James L., and Robert F. Boszhardt

2003 *Twelve Millennia: Archaeology of the Upper Mississippi River Valley*. University of Iowa Press, Iowa City.

Thies, Randall M.

1990 *The Archeology of the Stigenwalt Site, 14LT351*. Contract Archeology Series 7. Kansas State Historical Society, Topeka.

Thorson, Paula J., and Bonnie W. Styles

1992 Analysis of Faunal Remains. In *Late Archaic Components at Modoc Rock Shelter, Randolph County, Illinois*, by Steven R. Ahler, Mary J. Bade, Frances B. King, Bonnie W. Styles, and Paula J. Thorson, pp. 52–80. Reports of Investigations 48. Illinois State Museum, Springfield.

Transeau, Edgar N.

1935 The Prairie Peninsula. *Ecology* 16:423–437.

Warren, Robert E.

1995 *Variation and Change in Freshwater Mussel Faunas from Two Caves in the Northern Ozark Highland, Missouri*. Technical Report 95-954-9. Quaternary Studies Program, Illinois State Museum, Springfield.

1996 *Freshwater Mussels from Little Freeman Cave (23PU65) and Far View Shelter (23PU567), Pulaski County, Missouri*. Technical Report 96-1048-16. Quaternary Studies Program, Illinois State Museum, Springfield.

Waselkov, Gregory A.

1984 Small Faunal Remains from the McIntyre Site. In *The McIntyre Site: Archaeology, Subsistence, and Environment*, edited by Richard B. Johnston, pp. 137–158. Mercury Series Paper 126. Archaeological Survey of Canada, National Museum of Man, Ottawa.

Webb, Thompson, III, Edward J. Cushing, and Herbert E. Wright Jr.

1983 Holocene Changes in the Vegetation of the Midwest. In *Late-Quaternary Environments of the United States: 2. The Holocene*, edited by Herbert E. Wright Jr., pp. 142–165. University of Minnesota Press, Minneapolis.

Webb, Thompson, III, Bryan Shuman, and John W. Williams

2004 Climatically Forced Vegetation Dynamics in Eastern North America during the Late Quaternary Period. In *The Quaternary of the United States*, edited by A. R. Gillespie, S. C. Porter, and B. F. Atwater, pp. 459–478. Elsevier, Amsterdam.

Wedel, Waldo R.

1961 *Prehistoric Man on the Great Plains*. University of Oklahoma Press, Norman.

1986 *Central Plains Prehistory: Holocene Environments and Cultural Change in the Republican River Valley*. University of Nebraska Press, Lincoln.

Widga, Christopher C.

2003 Human Subsistence and Paleoecology in the Middle Holocene Central Great Plains: The Spring Creek (25FT31) and Logan Creek (25BT3) Sites. Master's thesis, Department of Anthropology, University of Kansas, Lawrence.

2006 Bison, Bogs, and Big Bluestem: the Subsistence Ecology of Middle Holocene Hunter-Gatherers in the Eastern Great Plains. Ph.D dissertation, Department of Anthropology, University of Kansas, Lawrence.

Whittaker, William E.

1998 The Cherokee Excavations Revisited: Bison Hunting on the Eastern Plains. *North American Archaeologist* 19:293–316.

Williams, Alice S.

1974 *Late-Glacial–Postglacial Vegetational History of the Pretty Lake Region, Northeastern Indiana: Hydrologic and Biological Studies of Pretty Lake, Indiana.* U.S. Geological Survey Professional Paper 686-B. U. S. Government Printing Office, Washington, D.C.

Winters, Howard D.

1969 *The Riverton Culture: A Second Millennium Occupation in the Central Wabash Valley.* Monograph 1. Illinois Archaeological Survey, Urbana. Reports of Investigations 13. Illinois State Museum, Springfield.

Wittry, Warren L.

1959a The Raddatz Rockshelter, Sk5, Wisconsin. *The Wisconsin Archeologist* 40:33–69.

1959b Archeological Studies of Four Wisconsin Rockshelters. *The Wisconsin Archeologist* 40:137–267.

Wolverton, Steve

2002 Zooarchaeological Evidence of Prairie Taxa in Central Missouri during the Mid-Holocene. *Quaternary Research* 58:200–204.

2005 The Effects of the Hypsithermal on Prehistoric Foraging Efficiency in Missouri. *American Antiquity* 70:91–106.

Wood, W. Raymond, and R. Bruce McMillan (editors)

1976 *Prehistoric Man and His Environments: A Case Study in the Ozark Highland.* Academic Press, New York.

Wright, Herbert E., Jr.

1968 History of the Prairie Peninsula. In *The Quaternary of Illinois: A Symposium in Observance of the Centennial of the University of Illinois*, edited by Robert E. Bergstrom, pp. 78–88. Special Publication 14. University of Illinois College of Agriculture, Urbana.

Yerkes, Richard W., and Pamela T. Machuga

1994 Vertebrate Remains from the Railway Museum Site (15JF630), Jefferson County, Kentucky. In *Salvage Excavations at the Railway Museum Site (15JF630), Jefferson County, Kentucky*, by C. Michael Anslinger, Albert M. Pecora, Charles M. Niquette, and Jonathon P. Kerr, pp. 194–229. Contract Publication Series 94-15. Cultural Resource Analysts, Hurricane, West Virginia.

4

A Regional and Chronological Synthesis of Archaic Period Plant Use in the Midcontinent

Mary L. Simon

By conservative estimate, the Archaic period in the midwestern United States spanned about 7,000 years, or over three times the length of all succeeding prehistoric periods combined. Despite its length, it remains, in many respects and for obvious reasons, poorly known. Mechanical processes, of both human and nonhuman agency, have combined with prehistoric social and demographic factors to minimize its archaeological visibility. This sheer lack of data, particularly of perishable cultural remains, including carbonized plant parts, can be quite discouraging to researchers. Assumptions of cultural homogeneity have further influenced interpretations and have perhaps even engendered disinterest in the seemingly simple societies of the period (see McElrath et al. ch. 1, this volume). However, as the chapters in this volume demonstrate, archaeologists' understanding of this long prehistoric sequence is increasing as is our appreciation of the complexity and variability evinced by Archaic peoples.

Despite the obvious problems, Archaic-period plant studies have benefited both because excavations have provided a greatly expanded database and, equally importantly, because increased analytical rigor has been applied to these data and the results of analyses are increasingly well disseminated. Archaic plant assemblages range in size from only a few virtually unidentifiable fragments of wood or nutshell to fairly substantial and diverse sets that include native domesticates and reflect long-term human occupations. While archaeobotanists tend to focus on the substantial data sets, each new assemblage has the potential to contribute some level of information, particularly when one recognizes that all sites are part of the greater whole that defines the Archaic lifestyle. Recent studies of Archaic-period plant assemblages have focused not only on foodways, which have traditionally been the focus of attention, but also on such diverse topics as paleoecology, landscape management, plant genetics and sytematics, and technologies of use. All these areas of study may come to bear not only on questions relating to subsistence-settlement systems and plant domestication or cultivation issues but also on more abstract, socioeconomic questions about group organization, intergroup contact, and even ritual or belief, the types of issues that are more often addressed with more robust Woodland- and Mississippian-period data sets.

Increased attention to the Archaic period is especially important because, perhaps more so than for any other period of time, understanding of Archaic human-plant relations suffers from biases inherent in all archaeological data recovery. As is well recognized, the archaeobotanical record is the product of both pre- and postdepositional factors. With each filtering activity or process, that record decreases both quantitatively and qualitatively. For the Archaic, biases are well exemplified in the very limited nature of the record as a whole, particularly for earlier millennia. They are also obvious in the persistent dominance throughout the record of dense, readily preserved nutshell. This overriding dominance can (and frequently does) tempt analysts to focus our attention, and our interpretations, almost exclusively on that resource, to the extent that every movement Archaic people made could be attributed to the quest for nut masts. Nuts no doubt played variously important economic roles, but they were not the only plant products available. People living in eastern North America between about 10,000 and 3,000 years ago lived in an incredibly rich environment, with access to a wide variety of plant resources.

The opposite approach to a narrow focus on nut use is to assume that plant use was so inclusive that everything present was being indiscriminately used. While perhaps providing a more realistic picture of the scope of prehistoric plant use, disregarding the archaeobotanical record because of its biases in favor of such an all-inclusive approach is likewise not very informative. Lists of potential or ethnographically documented plant resources in the midwestern United States (e.g., Densmore 1974; Gilmore 1977; King 1984; Scarry 2003; Yanovsky 1936; Yarnell 1964) are excellent resources for those of us studying prehistoric plant use. They also serve to remind us of the limitations of the archaeobotanical record. Nonetheless, however interesting, these lists are inadequate in and of themselves for truly assessing the relationships between people and plants (Ford 1978), which is really at the core of our inquiry.

Some Challenges to Interpreting the Archaic-Period Plant Record

Among the most obvious biases archaeobotanists face is the incomplete nature of the Archaic-period record. We simply do not have much plant-use information from those millennia preceding about 2000 B.C. This is in part a function of factors that we cannot control: differential site preservation and destruction, variability in formation processes, and limited archaeological excavation and flotation sampling are all important limiting variables. Also, at least during the first two-thirds of the Archaic in the Midwest, populations were relatively dispersed and mobile, divided into small groups that left behind only minimal evidence for their presence. While archaeological evidence indicates that, through time, Archaic settlement was characterized by an increasing tendency toward reuse of the same space, this was a long-term and nonsynchronous process. It is entirely probable that any given geographically defined area, even one that became populous later in prehistory, was unoccupied (or only sparsely occupied) for hundreds or perhaps even thousands of years. Consequently, at least some of the so-called gaps in local archaeological sequences probably reflect the actual absence of Archaic occupation. Given the small group size and level of mobility, particularly earlier in the Archaic, there is no reason to expect that every river valley—or any other well-defined geographical area—will harbor long evolutionary Archaic sequences. Our tendency, as archaeologists, has been to try and fill in the gaps by making leaps of inference, but these gaps may, in fact, be meaningful vis-à-vis settlement. Archaic plant-use records reflect changing lifeways, but these lifeways did not necessarily change at the same rate nor were they geographically bounded. The story of Archaic plant use is evolutionary and sequential only on a very grand scale.

While no single site of any time period will provide a complete plant-use record, for mobile Archaic groups, in particular, this incompleteness extends beyond issues of preservation to the fact that individual occupations (sites) represent only one part of a seasonal round. Attempting to model an entire subsistence system on the basis of plant remains recovered from a single site that represents only a "seasonal slice in time" is obviously problematic. Defining all or even most sites that compose a single settlement system may be impossible, but efforts to do so can be productive. A good example is found in the work of Stafford (1991) in the lower Illinois River valley. On the basis of multiple lines of evidence, including the archaeobotanical record, site distribution, and internal site structure, he concluded that Middle Archaic people were logistically, but opportunistically, foraging for nuts into the uplands from base camps located in the floodplain. The opportunistic nature of this system is reflected in the distribution of nut types. Thick-shelled hickory dominates in most cases, but occasionally, as at the Elizabeth site, another nut type, usually black walnut, is exceptionally well represented. In other words, the quest for one kind of resource did not preclude using other resources as available or encountered. Under this scenario, the observable archaeological distribution is not necessarily the result of one group "selecting" black walnut, while others "selected" thick-shelled hickory but, rather, of overall group behavior. This work also suggests that (1) logistical foraging could, indeed, involve a lot of moving about; (2) despite the "pull" of aquatic resources, nut crops were important in Archaic settlement-subsistence strategies; and (3) good nut masts were not entirely predictable, in terms of either location of productive groves or timing of harvest. Unpredictability was ultimately mediated to some extent by human intervention, in particular, landscape clearing to enhance mast production, as proposed by Munson (1986). Nonetheless, it may be that, for the most part, Archaic nut-harvesting strategy involved intentional movement to predictable spaces, rather than opportunistic foraging, at least in many parts of the Midwest.

Another challenge archaeologists face is that the Midwest covers a large geographic area and the Archaic period extended over thousands of years. The period witnessed a general transformation from foraging to collecting to low-level food-production economies (Smith 2001), but changes were not synchronous across the region. Comparisons among and between sites should be approached with the understanding that contemporary sites in different parts of the Midwest need not reflect the same set of behaviors and that even sequential Archaic occupations in the same locale need not be the product of similar activities. Comparisons of archaeobotanical assemblages between and among sites must take into account that sites are located in distinct physical settings, were often occupied for completely different (though usually unknown) purposes, and may have been separated in time by a thousand years or more.

That plant use comprises a complex set of behaviors is, at least on a theoretical basis, well recognized and accepted.

Because assemblages are so limited, it is easy to overlook the potential role that choice or cultural preference had in shaping the observable Archaic archaeobotanical record. Archaic groups had a broad-based subsistence economy, and certainly at times people ate anything they could to avoid starvation, but those times were not necessarily the norm. The Archaic plant record reflects choice or preference and socially defined conventions (e.g., Gremillion and Sobolik 1996) as well as need and availability.

Plants helped shape prehistoric cultures, but prehistoric cultures also shaped plants and plant communities. While acknowledging the presence of rich plant resources, archaeobotanists are gaining better appreciation for the degree to which Archaic people were actually manipulating, whether intentionally or unintentionally, some of the plants that were present in their local environments. People and plants even at this early date did not exist in isolation from one another. This interaction is central to understanding agricultural origins as a coevolutionary process (sensu Rindos 1984). Because the process of domestication can often be recognized in the plant remains themselves, the study of agricultural origins comprises a main focus of Archaic-period research (for recent regional reviews of this topic and for many additional references, see Smith 2001; Smith and Cowan 2003). Plant-use behaviors also have implications for how people distribute themselves on the landscape and, therefore, constitute an integral aspect of settlement-system studies. Furthermore, as is becoming more and more apparent, plant-management activities during Archaic times extended beyond experimentation with weedy annuals to landscape control, including intentional burning, perhaps with the intention of enhancing mast production (Chapman et al. 1982; Delcourt et al. 1998; Munson 1986; Wagner 2003). These behaviors left more-indirect records than that made up of subsistence remains but are equally worthy of study.

Regional midwestern Archaic cultural-historical sequences share several characteristics. Decreased group mobility, increased population density, increased competition for resources, and increased scheduling in resource-procurement practices are particularly relevant to interpretation of plant remains. Although the timing and extent of the transition across the Midwest was variable, traditionally the Archaic period is interpreted as witnessing a shift from residentially mobile foragers to residentially stable, logistically organized collectors. In theory, these two quite distinct settlement strategies should provide distinct archaeobotanical records recognizable on the basis of the nature of the material culture. The reality is quite different. Subsistence-settlement systems can and do vary extensively between the two extremes, and there are many possible permutations. Binford recognizes this, explicitly stating that "we are not talking about two polar types of settlement system ... [but] are discussing a graded series" (1980:12), a fact that archaeologists must keep in mind as we construct our models. The transition to sedentism among groups in the Eastern Woodlands was not consistent across space or through time. Neither are we likely to find close analogues in the ethnographic data.

We also need to carefully define our terms. *Sedentism*, even as used in the above paragraph, is a good example of a word that is fluidly defined along a continuum ranging from year-round occupation of one area by a core group to scheduled seasonal movement by a group through a defined space to designated locales. As discussed by Emerson and McElrath in the second chapter of this volume, sedentism may be better defined as a "condition" necessitating the development of a set of social controls. Archaeologists also must be cautious of automatically "linking" definitions. "Residential foragers" and "logistical collectors" represent two extremes, but the individual components of the two are not mutually exclusive; rather, each word in each term refers to a specific feature of subsistence and settlement strategies. Thus, Stafford defines "logistic foragers" as groups displaying logistically mobile patterns but whose plant-food procurement behaviors also included elements of fortuitous encounter. Likewise, residentially mobile groups may be collectors of well-defined, targeted, and predictable resources. Unlinking terminology provides greater flexibility for describing Archaic economies.

Archaeologists have recognized for some time that the original markers by which we have defined the end of the Archaic, that is, the presence of pottery, settled village life, the use of burial mounds, and the development of agricultural systems, are no longer applicable. In fact, by the beginning of the Woodland period, groups in the Midwest were already growing crops that included true domesticated, or at least "quasi-domesticated," plant species. They are identifiable as such because their seeds display morphological characteristics, particularly increased size and decreased seed-coat thickness, that distinguish them from the seeds produced by their wild progenitors. Most importantly, these characters are genetically controlled. Their presence reflects a long period of human intervention in those plant species' life cycles. Domesticated plants obviously did not suddenly appear at 500 B.C. but, instead, were the result of a long period of manipulation and experimentation, whether intentional or unintentional on the part of human users (for overviews of this process from the perspective of the Eastern Woodlands, see Cowan 1985; Ford 1985; Gremillion 1996; Rindos 1984; Smith 1992a, 1995; Smith and Cowan 2003). Because domestication is a process and not an event, analysts should and do find transitional forms or morphologically mixed populations of some seeds. Identifying these is an important feature of Archaic plant studies.

While domesticated plants are, by definition, cultivated—that is, subject to intentional human manipulation that includes sowing, harvesting, or storing of seed—cultivated plants are not necessarily domesticated. To archaeobotanists, the distinction between domestication and cultivation is common knowledge; to some archaeologists it appears to be less so. Plant cultivation has long been recognized in the archaeobotanical record of the Eastern Woodlands in the presence of plant parts from sites outside a plant's natural range, exceptionally high occurrences of an individual seed type, nonrandom association with remains of domesticated plants, and economic potential or ethnohistorically documented analogues (Asch and Asch 1985a:150–151). Cultivated plants tend to be annual species that can be incorporated into some kind of cropping or gardening system. However, the concept may also extend to woody shrubs (cf. sumac during the late prehistoric in Kentucky; Rossen 1992) and fruit-bearing trees (Munson 1986; cf. hickory masts during the late prehistoric in the American Bottom of Illinois; Rindos and Johannessen 1991).

The Prehistoric Environment in the Midwest

In the absence of human intervention, geographical and climatic factors dictate the distribution and composition of plants and animals in the environment. Resource availability, in turn, provides broad parameters within which people live and which people must either adapt to or surmount. That is, the environment imposes constraints or provides opportunities that people must take into consideration when making lifeway decisions. Natural resource availability is obviously particularly critical for hunter-gatherers, and behavioral models for these groups, particularly those models grounded in foraging theory, rely on accurate reconstructions of resource distribution (e.g., Gremillion 1996; Keene 1981; Neusius 1987; Winterhalder and Goland 1993, 1997; and the many references therein). Forager theory derived from ecological studies of animal foraging behavior posits that people also try to maximize benefits (i.e., food) while minimizing energy output. While archaeologists have pulled back from the environmental determinism of early models, the basic premise that environment is important cannot be disputed. Because of this importance, it is useful to look at both broad vegetative patterns and documented changes therein during the Archaic period.

While major shifts in air circulation patterns that accompanied the final stages of the Wisconsinan glacial retreat produced relatively rapid shifts in vegetation patterns (Jacobson and Grimm 1988), paleoecological studies have demonstrated that, across the Midwest, the transition from postglacial communities to modern plant communities was both temporally and spatially transgressive (Baker et al. 1992; Delcourt and Delcourt 1983, 1987; Webb 1988; Webb and Bartlein 1988; H. E. Wright 1964, 1992). Consequently, while changes across the Midwest were rapid about 10,000 years ago, "modern" deciduous or mixed pine-deciduous forests were developing in the southeastern Midwest by the earliest Holocene, but the same was not true for the northern Midwest until about 5,000 years later. Studies of Archaic lifeways must take into account that the Holocene, if defined as the existence of modern climatic conditions, arrived later with increasing latitude. Early Holocene human adaptation to tundra-boreal forests in southern Michigan was different from contemporaneous adaptations to mixed deciduous forests in Tennessee.

The nature, timing, and, most importantly, the complexity, of shifts in vegetational communities across the Midwest are reviewed in detail by Styles and McMillan (this volume). Of particular interest is their observation that the expansion of the so-called Prairie Peninsula was actually expressed as two "pulses," accompanied by dynamic floral and faunal distributions.

Palynological studies, combined with climate models and principles of plant ecology, provide the basis for generating Holocene paleovegetation maps describing both general plant communities and individual dominant tree taxa in the Midwest through time (Baker et al. 1992; Delcourt and Delcourt 1983, 1987:88–29; Webb 1988). These biome-level plant-community models provide reasonable approximations of general vegetation patterns that are useful for assessing conditions faced by prehistoric groups. However, they are only generalizations depicting large-scale biotic communities moving as units. In reality, community composition and the distributions of individual species therein are quite variable. Borders between communities are fluid and ill defined, and individual species transcend communities, and, if local conditions permit, even persist in refugia long after a "community type" has retreated. Consequently, while analysts may posit modern analogues for prehistoric plant communities, in reality, those communities are unlikely to have been identical in species composition or distribution to modern-day communities (Webb 1988; Webb and Bartlein 1988).

There is little doubt that the environment of the Midwest changed over the course of the Holocene, both in terms of shifts in biotic zones and of changes in landscape physiography, culminating in complex and diverse midwestern ecosystems (see Styles and McMillan, this volume). However, as Dincauze (1996:422) has succinctly noted, general, or biome-level, vegetation models, and, by extension, the interpretations of human adaptation one can draw from them, are elegant in their simplicity because they are based on so few data. Pollen data have provided insights into prehistoric ecology, but they cannot provide all the information needed to develop precise vegetation models, especially on the subregional level. The Archaic midwestern landscape was characterized by a great deal of variability against which to evaluate the Early Archaic plant-use record.

Archaic-Period Plant-Use Records

The Archaic period in the Midwest spanned 7,500 years. To provide necessary structure, in this chapter the Archaic is subdivided into chronologically defined periods using the corrected dates provided by the American Bottom sequence (Fortier et al. 2006). These are the Early Archaic (ca. 8700–6000 B.C.), the Middle Archaic (ca. 6000–4000 B.C.), the Late Archaic (ca. 4000–1400 B.C.), and the terminal Late Archaic (ca. 1400–950 B.C.). Presenting the data in this structured manner is convenient but may obscure the time-transgressive nature of these period designations. For example, one finds cultures described as "Late Archaic" appearing earlier in the southern Midwest than in the north. Radiocarbon dates provided in this chapter are calibrated using the calibration program CALIB rev. 4.3 (Stuiver and Reimer 1993, 2000).

As defined in this chapter, the midwestern United States encompasses midlatitude temperate deciduous forest and grassland biomes bordered on the south and east by the southern pine and eastern mixed mesophytic forests and the Appalachians and Ozarks. The western border corresponds roughly with the short-grass prairie of the Great Plains. The northern border is marked by the presence of the northern hemlock-white pine forests. Sites located in the Tennessee River valley and its tributaries provide some of the oldest open-air botanical assemblages in the Eastern Woodlands and are included in this discussion. Likewise, the Marble Bluff rockshelter in northern Arkansas provides exceptionally early, domesticated forms of native plants. Although these sites are technically outside the Midwest, their botanical assemblages are important because they provide information that has direct bearing on developments in the Midwest.

It would be exceedingly generous to categorize the Archaic-period archaeobotanical database as substantial, but the numbers of reported assemblages are increasing regularly, especially for sites dating after about 1500 B.C. A list of all sites considered in this study and the references consulted are presented in Table 4.1. This list does not constitute an exhaustive inventory of midwestern, Archaic-period plant assemblages. Smaller sites excavated in conjunction with cultural resource management projects (or under other auspices) are no doubt missing. Sites that are included tend to derive from larger or more geographically focused, published studies. In several cases, they are included on the basis of information from secondary contexts, usually regional summary tables. Because of research focus, reports often provide data on specific plant parts, notably annual seeds derived from native crop plants, but sometimes do not include information about other assemblage elements, such as wood. Finally, quantitative comparisons, especially those pertaining to earlier portions of the Archaic, are of questionable value, so the following presentation does not include detailed summary data tables or extensive graphs depicting quantified data.

The Early Archaic Period

While early Holocene, closed-canopy forests developed relatively rapidly across the Midwest, paleoecological records indicate that these communities were not fully modern in composition. Pollen records from across the northern part of the Midwest reflect an early postglacial landscape characterized by a mixed deciduous-boreal forest dominated by spruce, pine, and hemlock as well as deciduous oaks, maples, beeches, and elms (Figure 4.1). Farther south, early Holocene records from sites in northern Ohio reflect the presence of a closed-canopy, oak-dominated forest (Shane et al. 2001), while in eastern Kentucky the Early Archaic Cloudsplitter rockshelter contained both hemlock and spruce, indicative of an early Holocene climate that was both cooler and wetter than today (Jefferies 1990). Similarly, spruce pollen was present with deciduous tree pollen in late Pleistocene spring sites in west-central Missouri (King and Lindsey 1976). Over most of the Midwest, the late Pleistocene and early Holocene marked the beginning of closed-canopy forest development. However, on the basis of palynological and stable carbon isotope data from west-central Missouri, researchers have suggested that this marginal area also witnessed the periodic development of prairie at this early date (Hajic et al. 1998; Webb et al. 1993). This response to episodes of drier conditions is reflected in increases in nonarboreal pollen and in heavy carbon isotope ratios in early Holocene sediments. As Hajic et al. have noted, "Such fluctuations in vegetation should be expected along the

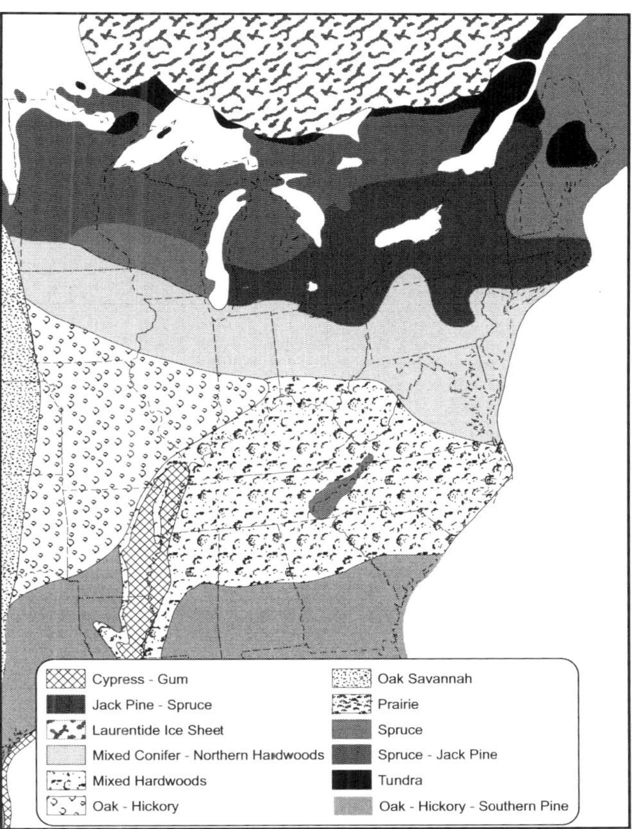

Figure 4.1. Midwest vegetation model at 10,000 B.C. (after Delcourt and Delcourt 1983, 1987).

Table 4.1. Selected Archaic Sites in the Midwest with Plant Remains.

Period	State	Site Name	Reference
Early Archaic	Missouri	Big Eddy	Lopinot 1998
Early Archaic	Missouri	Rodgers Shelter	Parmalee et al. 1976
Early Archaic	Missouri	Fort Leonard Wood rockshelters	Edging n.d.
Early Archaic	Missouri	Pigeon Roost Creek	King 1982
Early Archaic	Illinois	Koster	Asch and Asch 1985a; Asch et al. 1972
Early Archaic	Illinois	Nochta	Parker 1990
Early Archaic	Illinois	Modoc Rock Shelter	Ahler 1984; King 1981a, 1992
Early Archaic	Illinois	Olive Branch	Gramly and Funk 1991
Early Archaic	Indiana	Swan's Landing	E. Smith 1995
Early Archaic	Ohio	Longworth-Gick	Lannie 1979
Early Archaic	Ohio	Deep Shelter	Cowan et al. 1981
Early Archaic	Ohio	Cloudsplitter Rockshelter	Cowan et al. 1981
Early Archaic	Tennessee	Bacon Farm	Chapman 1978; Chapman and Shea 1981
Early Archaic	Tennessee	Rose Island	Chapman 1975; Chapman and Shea 1981
Early Archaic	Tennessee	Icehouse Bottom	Chapman 1973; Chapman and Shea 1981
Early Archaic	Illinois	Hills Branch Rock Shelter	Parker 2000
Middle Archaic	Missouri	Phillips Spring	Kay et al. 1980; King 1980
Middle Archaic	Missouri	Rodgers Shelter	Parmalee et al. 1976
Middle Archaic	Missouri	Fort Leonard Wood rockshelters	Edging n.d.
Middle Archaic	Tennessee	Hayes	Crites 1987
Middle Archaic	Tennessee	Howard	Chapman 1979; Chapman and Shea 1981
Middle Archaic	Tennessee	Bacon Farm	Chapman 1978; Chapman and Shea 1981
Middle Archaic	Tennessee	Rose Island	Chapman 1975; Chapman and Shea 1981
Middle Archaic	Kentucky	Carlston Annis	Crawford 1982; Watson 1985
Middle Archaic	Kentucky	Whalen	Wymer 1987
Middle Archaic	Kentucky	Morrisroe	Wymer 1987
Middle Archaic	Illinois	Fitzgibbons	Hunter 1986
Middle Archaic	Illinois	Little Muddy Rockshelter	Cremin 1992
Middle Archaic	Illinois	Rose Hotel	Parker 1999
Middle Archaic	Illinois	Black Earth	Lopinot 1982, 1984
Middle Archaic	Illinois	Diana	Lopinot 1991
Middle Archaic	Illinois	Strong	Walz 1997
Middle Archaic	Illinois	Cave Creek Rockshelter	Parker 1998b
Middle Archaic	Missouri	Lone Wolf	Hamilton et al. 1986
Middle Archaic	Illinois	Modoc Rock Shelter	Ahler 1984; King 1981a, 1992
Middle Archaic	Illinois	Nochta	Simon 1990
Middle Archaic	Illinois	Ringering	Simon 2000a
Middle Archaic	Illinois	South Roxanna	Parker 1993
Middle Archaic	Illinois	Koster	Asch and Asch 1985a; Asch et al. 1972
Middle Archaic	Illinois	Elledge	Schroeder 1994
Middle Archaic	Illinois	Napoleon Hollow	Asch and Asch 1980
Middle Archaic	Illinois	Elizabeth	Asch and Asch 1988
Middle Archaic	Illinois	Campbell Hollow	Asch and Asch 1985b
Middle Archaic	Illinois	Slim Lake	Schroeder and Asch 1989
Middle Archaic	Illinois	Buckshaw Bridge	Asch and Asch 1987
Middle Archaic	Iowa	Cherokee Sewer	Koeppen and Conrad 1974; Tiffany 1974b
Middle Archaic	Wisconsin	Crow Hollow	Egan-Bruhy 1997
Middle Archaic	Wisconsin	Murphy	Egan 1995
Middle Archaic	Wisconsin	Bobwhite	Finney et al. 1992
Middle Archaic	Michigan	Weber I	Egan 1987; Smith and Egan 1990
Middle Archaic	Michigan	Bear Creek	Lovis and Robertson 1989
Middle Archaic	Wisconsin	Brogley Rock Shelter	Tiffany 1974a
Late Archaic	Missouri	Rodgers Shelter	Parmalee et al. 1976
Late Archaic	Missouri	Boney Spring	Kay 1983
Late Archaic	Missouri	Phillips Spring	Kay et al. 1980; King 1980
Late Archaic	Missouri	Fort Leonard Wood rockshelters	Edging n.d.
Late Archaic	Missouri	Cobb Cave	Benn and Lopinot 1996
Late Archaic	Missouri	Hayden	Wright 1995
Late Archaic	Illinois	American Bottom sites: Monroe County	Go Kart: Johannessen 1984a; Marge: Simon 1996

Table 4.1. Selected Archaic Sites in the Midwest with Plant Remains, continued.

Period	State	Site Name	Reference
Late Archaic	Illinois	American Bottom sites: St. Clair County	McLean: Johannessen 1986; Labras Lake: King 1981b, 1987; Kingfish: Lopinot et al. 1982; Meyer: Parker 1986
Late Archaic	Illinois	Ringering	Simon 2000a
Late Archaic	Iowa	Sand Run West	Lopinot 1987
Late Archaic	Illinois	Cypress Land	Asch and Asch 1986
Late Archaic	Illinois	Brush College	Schroeder 1994
Late Archaic	Illinois	Axedental	Schroeder 1994
Late Archaic	Illinois	Tree Row	Simon 2002
Late Archaic	Illinois	Christianson	Parker 1998a
Late Archaic	Illinois	Crosstown Road	Calentine 2005
Late Archaic	Illinois	Riverton	Yarnell 2004
Late Archaic	Michigan	Schmidt	Egan 1987
Late Archaic	Michigan	Rock Hearth	Parachini 1983
Late Archaic	Michigan	Wymer	Parachini 1983; Robertson et al. 1999
Late Archaic	Ohio	Freeworth	Stothers et al. 2001
Late Archaic	Kentucky	Cloudsplitter Rockshelter	Cowan et al. 1981
Late Archaic	Kentucky	Hedden	Rossen 2000
Late Archaic	Kentucky	Peter Cave	Crawford 1982; Watson 1985
Late Archaic	Kentucky	Bowles	Crawford 1982; Watson 1985
Late Archaic	Kentucky	Haynes	Crothers 1999
Late Archaic	Kentucky	Carlston Annis	Crawford 1982; Watson 1985
Late Archaic	Kentucky	Spadie	Lannie 1979
Late Archaic	Kentucky	Rosenberg	Lannie 1979
Late Archaic	Tennessee	Tellico Reservoir sites	Chapman 1977; Bacon Bend, Iddens, Icehouse Bottom: Chapman 1981; Chapman and Shea 1981
Late Archaic	Tennessee	Normandy Reservoir sites	Banks III, Eoff I: Faulkner et al. 1976; Faulkner and McCollough 1977; Yarnell and Black 1985
Late Archaic	Kentucky	Ward	Bonzani 2001
Late Archaic	Kentucky	Cranks Creek	Bonzani 2004
Late Archaic	Illinois	Koster	Asch and Asch 1985a; Asch et al. 1972
Late Archaic	Kentucky	Highland Creek	cited in Rossen 2000
Late Archaic	Illinois	Napoleon Hollow	Asch and Asch 1980
Late Archaic	Tennessee	Baily	Crites 1988
Late Archaic	Michigan	20By387	Lovis, this volume
Terminal Late Archaic	Illinois	Modoc Rock Shelter	Ahler 1984; King 1981a, 1992
Terminal Late Archaic	Illinois	American Bottom sites: St. Clair County	MoPac: Johannessen 1983; Dyroff: Johannessen 1984b;
Terminal Late Archaic	Illinois	Floyd	Parker 2001
Terminal Late Archaic	Illinois	Ringering	Simon 2000a
Terminal Late Archaic	Illinois	Marge	Simon 1996
Terminal Late Archaic	Illinois	Riverton	Yarnell 2004
Terminal Late Archaic	Michigan	Eidson	Parachini 1983
Terminal Late Archaic	Kentucky	Villier	Lannie 1979
Terminal Late Archaic	Kentucky	Salts Cave	Watson 1985; Yarnell 1969
Terminal Late Archaic	Kentucky	Skidmore	Cowan 1985
Terminal Late Archaic	Kentucky	Cold Oak	Gremillion 1993b, 1998; Ison 1988
Terminal Late Archaic	Kentucky	Hooton Hollow	Crawford 1982; Gremillion 1995
Terminal Late Archaic	Kentucky	Newt Kash	Gremillion 1995, 1997
Terminal Late Archaic	Kentucky	Grayson	Ledbetter and O'Steen 1992
Terminal Late Archaic	Tennessee	Chapman	Crites 1986
Terminal Late Archaic	Tennessee	Hayes	Crites 1988, 1993
Terminal Late Archaic	Tennessee	Aenon Creek	Dixon 1995
Terminal Late Archaic	Tennessee	Higgs	Brewer 1973
Terminal Late Archaic	Illinois	Little Muddy Rockshelter	Cremin 1992
Terminal Late Archaic	Michigan	20By387	Lovis, this volume
Terminal Late Archaic	Michigan	Green Point	H.T. Wright 1964
Terminal Late Archaic	Michigan	Weber I	Egan 1987; Smith and Egan 1990
Terminal Late Archaic	Iowa	Gast Spring	Dunne and Green 1998
Terminal Late Archaic	Missouri	Dirk	Lopinot 2000
Terminal Late Archaic	Minnesota	King Coulee	Perkl 1998

forest-prairie margin in western Missouri" (1998:105). While modern taxa were present at this early date, fully modern distributions were not.

Little substantive information is available for human plant use in the Midwest in this early postglacial landscape. Open-air sites are often ephemeral, either lacking features or with only shallow features characterized by poor plant-part preservation. Sites also may be deeply buried, difficult to access, and lack good contexts from which to collect samples for archaeobotanical analysis. Much of the available information comes from rockshelters. It is tempting to use these assemblages to develop inclusive plant-use models for the Early Archaic. However, these sites typically represent only one small, perhaps specialized, aspect of prehistoric life and so provide limited perspective on Archaic subsistence-settlement strategies. Further, mixing with later Archaic occupations also presents interpretive problems (Walthall 1998). Obviously, we cannot assume that small quantities of plant remains from Early Archaic sites correlate positively with levels of plant use or accurately represent the importance of plant resources.

The distribution of Early Archaic sites considered in this study is presented in Figure 4.2. Included are Dalton occupations that actually predate the Early Archaic as defined above. The Big Eddy site in western Missouri dates to almost 11,000 years ago (Hajic et al. 1998), and the Olive Branch site in southern Illinois is about 1,000 years younger. Both produced small numbers of plant parts. The Olive Branch site had both walnut shell and a wood assemblage that contained oak, maple, elm, and pine. It also yielded a single

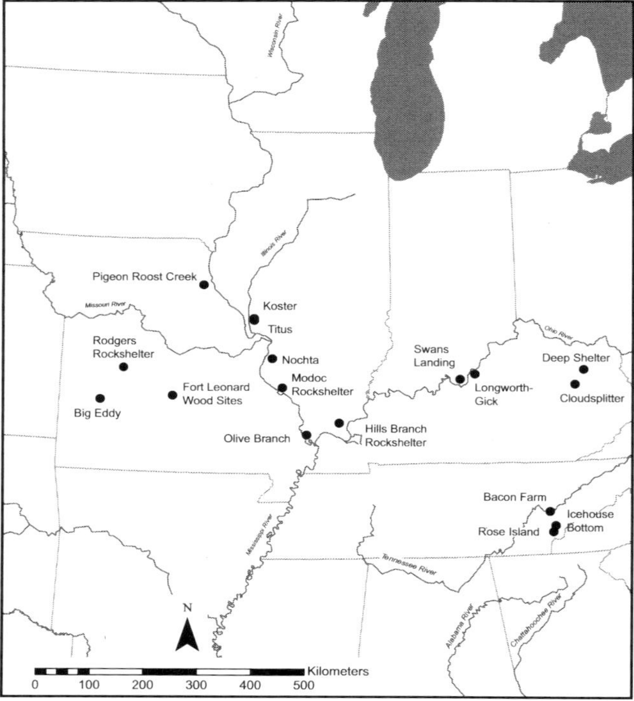

Figure 4.2. Early Archaic sites with analyzed plant remains.

grape seed. The Big Eddy site assemblage also contained grape seed fragments as well as pieces of chenopod testa and one tentatively identified piece of acorn shell. Unidentifiable wood was diffusely distributed among samples. These data are consistent in character with those from the few other Eastern Woodlands Paleoindian data sets reported to date. They provide our oldest evidence to date for subsistence plant use (Lopinot 1998:286).

The Early Archaic record is also limited and includes materials from both open-air and rockshelter occupations. Early Archaic plant assemblages from rockshelters include those from Rodgers in Missouri, Modoc in southwestern Illinois, and Cloudsplitter in eastern Kentucky. Wood samples from the Rodgers shelter recently submitted for AMS determination provided a series of dates that calibrate to around 8500 B.C. (ISGS A-0273, A-0274, A-0311, A-0312, and A-0313). These wood samples were tiny, mostly unidentifiable fragments. The few small pieces that could be identified were from typical deciduous trees: coffee tree or locust and elm.

Early Archaic plant assemblages from open-air sites include those from the poorly understood but well-known Koster site in western Illinois and from a series of sites in the Tennessee River valley (Table 4.1). The latter—Icehouse Bottom, Rose Island, and Bacon Farm—provide some of the earliest substantial plant-use data in the Eastern Woodlands. Other, more recently analyzed assemblages include that from the extensive Nochta site in the American Bottom, from which 39 Early Archaic features were analyzed, and the much smaller assemblages from cave sites at Fort Leonard Wood. Sites containing plant residues are widely distributed across the central and southern parts of the Midwest; however, they are fewer and more ephemeral to the north. While Early Archaic sites are present in the western Lake Erie drainage area (e.g., Stothers et al. 2001), they do not provide macrobotanical assemblages.

Plant-part remains from Early Archaic contexts are small, few, and invariably dominated by wood charcoal and nutshell. The most striking feature of these assemblages is their diversity, especially given the very limited quantities of materials present. Assemblages tend to contain a variety of different wood types, without one or two very strong dominants. Woods vary on a regional basis, and taxa profiles reflect vegetation as modeled by paleoecologists (Delcourt and Delcourt 1983, 1987). In the lower Tennessee River valley, identified wood includes oak, hickory, elm, locust, and some softwood, probably pine. All are typical of the local mixed deciduous and southern pine forests that predominated in the Holocene vegetation in this region. Further north and west, assemblages reflect early Holocene vegetation communities that were, as noted above, slightly different than late Holocene communities. Specifically, hickory wood is less common than it is in later Archaic and all subsequent assemblages, while occasional softwoods attest to remnant northerly taxa. The oldest levels at Koster in western Illinois are dominated by a combination of hardwoods that includes elm, locust, ash, walnut, and oak, but hickory wood is conspicuously absent. Hickory wood is also lacking from the Nochta site Early Archaic assemblage. Plant lists from Rodgers and Modoc include wood charcoal from various deciduous trees, with oak being the most common. Paleoecological studies suggest that, during the Early Archaic, about half of all trees over much of the Midwest were oaks (Delcourt and Delcout 1987:Figure 5.30g, h), while hickory was both less common and more fragmented in distribution than it was in later times (Delcourt and Delcourt 1987:Figure 5.8g, h).

This pattern is repeated in the nutshell record. Thick-shelled hickories are certainly represented in Early Archaic assemblages, but with increasing latitudes, they usually do not dominate to the same extent as in later records. In the southern part of the study area, thick-shelled hickories make up at least 80 percent of the Early Archaic nutshell assemblages from seven of nine sites in the lower Little Tennessee River valley. Further north at Koster, thick-shelled hickory is common, but black walnut, acorn, and pecan attain maximum frequencies relative to hickory late in the Early Archaic sequence. At Modoc, both pecan and black walnut are more abundant than hickory in early levels, while the Early Archaic record at the Longworth-Gick site near the Falls of the Ohio River in Kentucky is dominated by butternut. An exception to this pattern is found at the Nochta site in the American Bottom of Illinois, which contains almost exclusively hickory nutshell, despite the absence of hickory wood.

Like wood, the low counts of hickory shell at early archaeological sites may in part be a function of early Holocene distributions of hickory trees. Following the Delcourts' vegetation models, hickory-tree dissemination across the Midwest lagged somewhat behind that of other deciduous hardwoods, especially oaks, and those hickories that were present were more scattered across the landscape than in later times. Consequently, the patterning in nutshell residues is not a product of random wandering and gathering as encountered but rather could reflect focused collection of resources as dictated by availability. Fewer and widely scattered trees would obviously be less productive than would the more abundant or clustered trees of later times. Under this scenario, Early Archaic groups moved in a scheduled, nonrandom manner across the landscape, exploiting nut trees that were predictable in their habitat preference. Such predictability would be possible because trees are long-lived enough that individual stands would have been known to multiple generations.

Aside from wood and nutshell, the Early Archaic record is quite limited. The only other materials recovered with any regularity, although still quite sporadically, are seeds from fleshy fruits such as sumac, grape, and persimmon. While providing convincing evidence for the presence of these plants in local environments, the counts are so low as to make accidental inclusion a real possibility. Nonetheless, these fruits probably were eaten, and, in the absence of long-term storage, their presence may reflect seasonal use of any given location. Given the limited nature of the record, however, even these very simple observations remain problematical.

Paleoindian and Early Archaic studies are producing increasingly complex, sophisticated models of Early Archaic settlement systems (for reviews, see Anderson et al. 1996 and the chapters in this volume). The Early Archaic, band-macroband settlement model proposed for the greater Southeast posits an Early Archaic system of seasonal shifts between cold-weather, logistically provisioned base camps and warm-weather, short-term residential encampments provisioned through foraging (Anderson 1991, 1996; Anderson and Hanson 1988). Kimball (1996) has likewise suggested that the distribution of Early Archaic sites in the Tellico Reservoir area of Tennessee reflects groups that were logistically mobile at least for a good part of the year. These models have important implications for understanding how Early Archaic people were "mapped onto" regional landscapes. Further, the concepts pertain across the postglacial Eastern Woodlands. The ability to target specific resources implies both that people were familiar with local resource distributions and that resource availability had elements of stability or predictability. Although they lived in a less mature landscape than found further south, Early Archaic groups in the Midwest surely recognized that, even where resources were diffuse, their distribution was governed by habitat preference. People understood the landscape and had set rounds based on this understanding. In fact, familiarity with natural local conditions was prerequisite to their survival. Recent work, including that of Stafford (1994, 2000) in southern Indiana and of University of Illinois researchers at the Nochta site in the American Bottom (Higgins 1990), demonstrates the presence of very extensive, open-air habitation locales, reflecting repeated revisits to a specific area early in the Archaic sequence. Assuming the interpretation is correct, the presence of large storage pits at several Early Archaic sites, including Koster and Cloudsplitter, provides another line of evidence supporting the idea that groups were, in fact, moving across the landscape in a regular, directed manner. These pits characteristically contained abundant burned nutshell fragments that resulted from processing nuts for their edible meats or oils. Although mast production varies on a yearly basis, nut crops would still have been among the most predictable, and storable, resources available to Early Archaic groups.

The Middle Archaic Period

The archaeobotanical record for the Middle Archaic (ca. 6000–4000 B.C.), while not extensive, is stronger than that for the Early Archaic. Traditional Middle Archaic settlement models for the Midwest attribute the increase in archaeological visibility to increasing sedentariness that accompanied mid-Holocene climate change. Climate change promoted both an eastward expansion of prairie and a shift from braided to meandering river regimes in the major river valleys of the central and upper Mississippi River, lower Illinois River, and lower Ohio River regions. The meandering regimes provided conditions suitable for the development of extensive, resource-rich backwater lakes and sloughs in many major floodplains. In Middle Archaic settlement models, these zones are seen as producing abundant, concentrated, predictable resources that were efficient to exploit and, thus, provided the "pull" for populations to move into the bottomlands (cf. Ahler 1993; Brown 1985; Brown and Vierra 1983; Jefferies 1988). At the same time, the mid-Holocene expansion of the resource-poor prairie into formerly forested spaces provided a "push" that directed people toward these same, resource-rich zones.

The presence of large, dense Middle Archaic sites in many major floodplains of the Midwest attests to periodic population aggregations. However, while Middle Holocene changes in resource distribution may have facilitated the process of aggregation or altered its expression those changes did not really cause it. Rather, they presented a new opportunity that people chose to take advantage of.

Middle Archaic archaeobotanical data sets are derived from sites that are spread over a wide geographical area and represent highly variable levels of occupation intensity (Figure 4.3). These include deeply stratified, multicomponent sites such as Koster in the Illinois River valley, extensive, nonstratified floodplain sites like Nochta in the American Bottom, and numerous small camp and rockshelter sites (Table 4.1). Despite their low numbers and their limited macrobotanical assemblages, sites of this period provide the earliest evidence for plant manipulation and even possible cultivation in the Midwest.

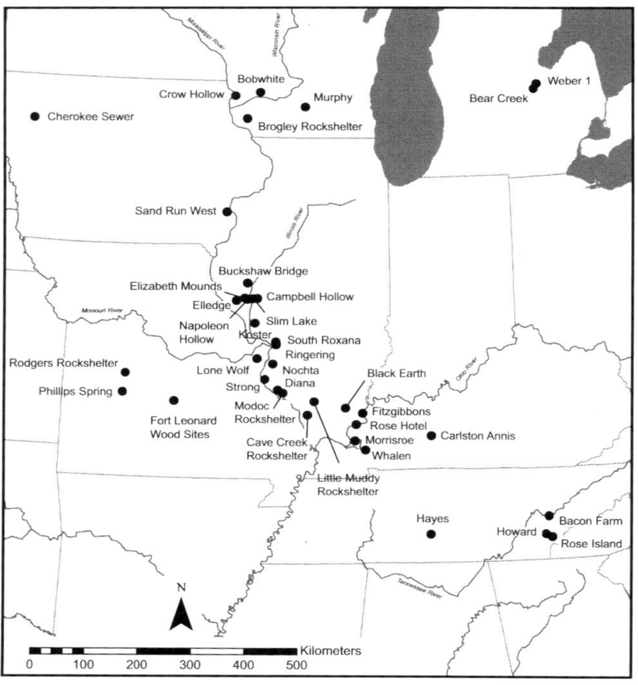

Figure 4.3. Middle Archaic sites with analyzed plant remains.

Not surprisingly, the main plant parts recovered are wood charcoal and nutshell. As was the case for the Early Archaic, Middle Archaic wood-charcoal assemblages are small. They tend to reflect continued exploitation of local forests and to be quite taxonomically diverse. The main change is that hickory-wood charcoal is more common. Although cultural selection cannot be ruled out, assemblages possibly also reflect ongoing changes in resource distribution, as the timing corresponds to the spread of hickory trees, as modeled by Delcourt and Delcourt (1987:Figure 5.8g, h). A similar phenomenon is evident to the south, in the Tennessee River valley. In that locale, the increase in pine reported for Middle Archaic assemblages is coincident with the development of modern oak-hickory-southern pine forests.

Nutshell is the only other plant part that is well preserved in Middle Archaic assemblages. As is true for wood, Middle Archaic nutshell assemblages witness an increase in thick-shelled hickory, again coincident with the range expansion indicated by paleoecological models. Given hickory's abundance in the archaeological record, it is no wonder that optimal foraging theories of the 1980s focused on hickory nuts as a first-line resource; and nuts were undoubtedly important to the diet, even if overrepresented in the record.

Two important caveats must be taken into account in efforts to understand Archaic-period nut use. First, because the shells are so fragile, acorn is undoubtedly underrepresented in the archaeobotanical record. As demonstrated by Lopinot (1984), in terms of actual food value, low counts of acorn shell can translate into relatively large amounts of nutmeat. The same weight of hickory shell represents less nutmeat. Consequently, despite low shell counts and weights in archaeobotanical assemblages, acorns may actually have contributed more to the diet than the low numbers would indicate. Acorn may have been as important as hickory. Lopinot (1984:Tables 6 and 7) illustrates this using data from the lower Tennessee River valley. As he shows, although thick-shelled hickory shell-fragment weights exceed the weights of acorn shell in all cases, actual acorn nutmeats represented are greater for all time periods represented. The six Middle Archaic components he examines have a combined thick-shelled hickory nutmeat estimated weight of 415.1 g; estimated acorn meat weight is 868.2 g. Even if thick-shelled hickory meats remain better represented than acorn, their degree of dominance decreases dramatically. For example, at the Black Earth site, the ratio of thick-shelled hickory to acorn shell is 108.03:1; following conversion, the same ratio for nutmeats is 1.94:1. Similar differences are evident in the Koster and Napoleon Hollow site records (data from Lopinot 1984:Table 43).

Second, as was true for the Early Archaic, many of these individual sites represent not only a slice in archaeological time but also a slice in seasonal time. To truly assess Middle Archaic patterns of plant use, one needs to have all the parts of the seasonal round represented—an objective that is difficult to obtain but is necessary to begin to define subregional use patterns.

Middle Archaic Squashes

The oldest records for plant manipulation in the Midwest are for *Cucurbita pepo*, yellow flowered gourd or, commonly, "squash" (Table 4.2), and date to the Middle Archaic period. Originally, Archaic-period squash was thought to represent a Mesoamerican introduction (Ford 1981; Kay et al. 1980; King 1980), and its presence was attributed to down-the-line trade and intentional propagation of a nonnative species. However, analysts now generally accept that the eastern United States was one of several centers of independent plant domestication and that the early squash in the region represents manipulation of an indigenous species (see Cowan 1997 and Smith et al. 1992 for historical syntheses and arguments relevant to the Midwest).

Recent ecological and genetic studies have both clarified and complicated understanding of the prehistoric origins and use of cucurbits. Protein allozyme analyses indicate that prehistoric squash was most similar to the modern varieties of *Cucurbita pepo* subspecies *ovifera*—either variety *ozarkana* or *texana*, which have modern ranges in riparian habitats of the Ozark Mountains and of central Texas, respectively (Decker 1988; Decker-Walters 1993; Decker-Walters et al. 1993). Given their apparently limited modern distribution, determining the prehistoric range of wild squashes has become an important issue in prehistoric squash studies, as the presence of *Cucurbita pepo* remains from contexts outside the natural range would constitute good evidence for human transport and propagation. The issue remains the subject of some contention (see Asch 1994; Cowan 1997; Cowan and Smith 1993; Smith et al. 1992). Smith et al. argue for the extensive distribution of free-living squashes in prehistoric midwestern river valleys, extending well into Illinois and perhaps even as far to the east as eastern Kentucky (Cowan 1997). More conservatively, Fritz (2000:225) has argued that, while pepo squashes were probably more extensively distributed than indicated in modern floras, extending their range even as far north as the Illinois River valley is problematic (Gail J. Fritz, pers. comm. 2005). However, extensions into the Southeast are supported by recovery of remains in nonarchaeological early Holocene deposits in Florida (Newsom et al. 1993). Asch (1994) suggests that modern plants outside the ranges outlined above, for example, those from the Mississippi River valley in Illinois, are feral escapees. He questions the presence of native squash in Illinois or elsewhere across the central Midwest during the middle Holocene and argues for intentional transport and propagation, true "cultivation," in this locale at this early date.

In any regard, pepo squash clearly was present during the Middle Archaic in the Illinois River valley of western Illinois. The Koster and Napoleon Hollow sites produced rind fragments that have been directly dated to the Middle Archaic and are the oldest securely dated materials reported (Figure 4.3; Table 4.2). Middle Archaic squash has also been identified from the Memorial Park site in Pennsylvania (Hart and Asch Sidell 1997) and the Sharrow site in central Maine (Peterson and Asch Sidell 1996). By most assessments, these locations are so distant from the plant's original range that the fragments must represent transported or even propagated fruits. Additionally, a rind fragment from site 20BY389, in eastern Michigan, has been AMS dated to about 2900 B.C. (date provided by Lovis, this volume). This location is also probably outside the natural range of the plant. While details are still open to debate, the apparent extension of the plant's native range and its consistent recovery from archaeological sites across the Midwest, beginning in the Middle Archaic and extending throughout later prehistory, provide convincing arguments for inferring intentional transport and propagation. Genetic and ecological studies support the contention that these activities focused on a North American native.

The economic function of these early pepo squashes is also the subject of speculation. Early squashes were probably small, thin-shelled fruits (Cowan 1997; Heiser 1985; King 1985) so may have been unsuitable for use as containers or dippers (Cowan 1997). However, because squashes may not have been optimal for these purposes does not preclude such use, especially prior to the widespread adoption of heavy-shelled *Lagenaria* gourds (Heiser 1985) and, ultimately, pottery vessels. The flesh of these early gourds was probably bitter and unpalatable, so the fruits more likely were originally grown for their oily seeds than for the flesh itself (Cowan 1997; King 1985). The recovery of squash seeds from Early Woodland human feces at Salts Cave provides convincing evidence that seeds were, indeed, consumed (Yarnell 1969). Small squashes can successfully serve as fishing net floats (Fritz 1999; Hart et al. 2004), yet another potential economic benefit. Finally, Prentice (1986) has suggested that squashes were shamanistic tools, propagated by specific individuals both to ensure availability and to appropriate the associated power. All of these functions are plausible, and, in fact, David Asch (1994:27) has argued that the first cultivated plants would have been versatile specialty crops, rather than plants grown only for subsistence.

Seeds and Tubers in the Middle Archaic Record

The Middle Archaic record for subsistence plants other than nuts is composed mostly of seeds and underground plant parts. Distribution is spotty and counts are low, but the diversity of plant types represented is quite high. The following is not a comprehensive listing of all non-nutshell subsistence plant parts from Middle Archaic contexts but is an effort to illustrate the variability and consistency of the Middle Archaic record. Unless otherwise noted, references for all sites in this section can be found in Table 4.1.

The numbers and types of carbonized seeds present vary greatly. Among those sites with the highest seed counts and taxonomic diversities are Koster, Napoleon Hollow, and Black Earth; however, even among this group, carbonized seed counts number only into the low hundreds. (The Black Earth site also contained over 8,000 uncarbonized hackberry or sugarberry pits, which Lopinot argues are prehistoric.

Table 4.2. Archaic-Period Squash, Contexts, and Dates.

Period Method	Site	Material	14C Age	Corrected ±	Calibrated Date	Reference
Middle Archaic						
conventional	Koster 1	charcoal in sediment asso. w/27 rind frags	7100	300	5940[a]	Asch and Asch 1985a:Table 6.1
AMS	Anderson	seed	6990	120	5864[a]	Chapman and Watson 1993
conventional	Koster 2	from dispersed charcoal asso. w/rind	7000	80	5858[a]	Asch and Asch 1985a:Table 6.1
AMS	Napoleon Hollow 1	rind	7000	250	5858[a]	Asch and Asch 1985a:Table 6.1
conventional	Koster 3	from dispersed charcoal asso. w/rind	6960	80	5822[a]	Asch and Asch 1985a:Table 6.1
conventional	Koster 4	from dispersed charcoal asso. w/rind	6910	100	5760[a]	Asch and Asch 1985a:Table 6.1
AMS	Koster 5	rind	6860	80	5727	Asch and Asch 1985a:Table 6.1
conventional	Napoleon Hollow 11	from dispersed charcoal asso. w/rind	6730	80	5636	Asch and Asch 1985a:Table 6.1
conventional	Napoleon Hollow 2	from dispersed charcoal asso. w/rind	6630	100	5589[a]	Asch and Asch 1985a:Table 6.1
conventional	Napoleon Hollow 10	rind asso. w/midden charcoal	6030	110	4870	Asch and Asch 1985a:Table 6.1
conventional	Napoleon Hollow 9	from dispersed charcoal asso. w/rind	6080	90	4959	Asch and Asch 1985a:Table 6.1
conventional	Little Freeman Cave	from dispersed charcoal asso. w/rind	5810	130	4690	Edging n.d.
AMS	Carlston Annis	rind	5730	640	4548	Watson 1985
AMS	Sharrow	rind	5694	100	4509[a]	Peterson and Asch Sidell 1996
conventional	Napoleon Hollow 8	from dispersed charcoal asso. w/rind	5670	90	4469	Asch and Asch 1985a:Table 6.1
conventional	Hayes 3	older date from wood associated	5660	190	4473[a]	Crites 1987
AMS	Memorial Park	rind	5404	552	4266[a]	Hart and Asch Sidell 1997
conventional	Little Muddy Rockshelter	from dispersed charcoal asso. w/rind	5480	60	4338	Cremin 1992
conventional	Napoleon Hollow 3	from dispersed charcoal asso. w/rind	5350	70	4182[a]	Asch and Asch 1985a:Table 6.1
AMS	Hayes 1	rind	5340	120	4165[a]	Crites 1987
conventional	Napoleon Hollow 7	from dispersed charcoal asso. w/rind	5280	70	4136	Asch and Asch 1985a:Table 6.1
conventional	Hayes 2	older date from wood associated	5140	185	3962	Crites 1987
conventional	Napoleon Hollow 6	from dispersed charcoal asso. w/rind	5140	40	3962	Asch and Asch 1985a:Table 6.1
AMS	Cloudsplitter 1	rind	5130	60	3960	Cowan 1997
conventional	Modoc	from dispersed charcoal asso. w/blossom scars	4820	130	3640	King 1992
AMS	Cloudsplitter 2	seed	4700	250	3412[a]	Cowan 1997
conventional	Bacon Bend	from dispersed charcoal asso. w/rind	4390	155	2971	Chapman 1981
conventional	Phillips Spring	charcoal asso. w/seeds and rind	4310	70	2906	King 1985
Late Archaic						
AMS	Lagoon	rind	4300	600	2902	Asch and Asch 1985a:Table 6.1
AMS	20BY387	rind			2900[b]	Lovis, this volume
conventional	Phillips Spring	charcoal w/rind	4257	39	2884	Kay et al. 1980
conventional	Phillips Spring	charcoal asso. w/seeds and rind	4240	80	2882	King 1985
conventional	Phillips Spring	charcoal asso. w/seeds and rind	4222	57	2879	King 1985
conventional	Napoleon Hollow 4	from dispersed charcoal asso. w/rind	4060	75	2615[a]	Asch and Asch 1985a:Table 6.1
AMS	Bowles	rind	4060	220	2615[a]	Watson 1985
conventional	Lagoon	from dispersed charcoal asso. w/rind	4030	75	2518	Asch and Asch 1985a:Table 6.1
conventional	Kuhlman	from nutshell asso. w/rind	4010	130	2537[a]	Asch and Asch 1985a:Table 6.1

Table 4.2. Archaic-Period Squash, Contexts, and Dates, continued.

Period Method	Site	Material	14C Age	Corrected ±	Calibrated Date	Reference
Late Archaic (cont.)						
conventional	Lagoon	from dispersed charcoal asso. w/rind	4010	150	2537	Asch and Asch 1985a:Table 6.1
conventional	Phillips Spring	charcoal from pit containing pepo seeds	3995	96	2489	King 1985
conventional	Phillips Spring	charcoal from pit containing pepo seeds	3938	66	2464	King 1985
conventional	Napoleon Hollow 5	from dispersed charcoal asso. w/rind	3920	90	2460	Asch and Asch 1985a:Table 6.1
AMS	Nebo Hill 1	rind	3782	46	2200	Adair 2003
AMS	Nebo Hill 2	rind	3758	46	2169[a]	Adair 2003
conventional	Iddens 1	from dispersed charcoal asso. w/rind	3655	135	1990[a]	Chapman 1981
conventional	Iddens 3	from dispersed charcoal asso. w/rind	3470	75	1761[a]	Chapman 1981
conventional	Peter Cave	charcoal from layer overlying rind frags	3415	105	1714[a]	Watson 1985
conventional	Carlston Annis	from dispersed charcoal asso. w/rind	3330	80	1675	Watson 1985
Terminal Late Archaic						
conventional	Iddens 2	from dispersed charcoal asso. w/rind	3205	145	1478[a]	Chapman 1981
AMS	Cloudsplitter 3	rind	3150	55	1420[a]	Cowan 1997
conventional	Christianson	charcoal from pit at site/ rind	3040	70	1363	on file, ITARP
conventional	Christianson	charcoal from pit at site/ rind	2910	80	1088	on file, ITARP
AMS	Cold Oak	rind	2900	100	1104[a]	Gremillion 1993b
AMS	Memorial Park	rind	2625	45	802	Hart and Asch Sidell 1997
AMS	King Coulee	squash seeds	2530	60	764	Perkl 1998
conventional	Bacon Bend	from dispersed charcoal asso. w/rind	2440	155	458[a]	Chapman 1981
AMS	20BY387	seed			1000[b]	

Note: All dates corrected following Stuiver et al. 1993, 2000.

[a]Denotes multiple calibrated ages obtained, calibrated date presented is midrange of dates at one-sigma level.

[b]Calibrations as presented by Lovis, this volume.

He reports a minimum seed count for other taxa of 292 [Lopinot 1984:325]). Despite the low counts, taxonomic diversities are quite high; at Black Earth, 28 carbonized seed taxa were identified. Smaller assemblages with between six and nine different types of seeds include those from Slim Lake, Diana, Morrisroe, Hayes, and Weber I. As illustrated in Figure 4.3, these eight sites are widely spaced across the Midwest. All are wetland or floodplain oriented and have provided relatively large feature assemblages. The three largest, Koster, Napoleon Hollow, and Black Earth, were probably base camps, and it is logical to assume that long-term habitations and repeatedly occupied locations will have higher counts and diversities of all classes of remains, including seeds. However, site size alone is not an accurate predictor of carbonized seed diversity or quantity. The Nochta site, from which almost 1,000 liters of fill from 63 features were analyzed, yielded only six seed fragments.

Specific identified seed types vary among sites, as dictated by factors that include local environment and human selection. The majority of seeds are derived from fleshy fruits; for example, Yarnell and Black (1985:Table 4) report that this economic class comprises 56 percent of identified seeds from Middle Archaic sites in the greater Southeast, but grasses and annual weeds are also well represented. Many of the identified seeds have ethnohistoric use records (e.g., King 1984; Moerman 1998; Scarry 2003; Yarnell 1964) and presumably functioned in similar ways prehistorically.

Among the most common fleshy-fruit seeds identified in Middle Archaic–period plant-part assemblages are grape, persimmon, sumac, and raspberry or blackberry. Of this group, grape is the only type that can be considered either widespread or abundant. Grape seed records occur from the lower Little Tennessee River valley in the south to the Weber I site in Michigan in the north to Rodgers Shelter in the west. They are especially abundant in the lower Ohio and Tennessee rivers region, where they dominate carbonized seed assemblages from the Morrisroe, Fitzgibbons, and Black Earth sites.

With the exception of a single seed from Napoleon Hollow, Middle Archaic records for persimmon are restricted to latitudes south of the mouth of the Illinois River, coincident with the tree's natural range. It is the second most abundant carbonized seed identified at both Black Earth and Diane and is also reported from Rodgers Shelter to the west. Sumac is reported from several sites in the lower Illinois River valley and from Morrisroe in western Kentucky. Brambles are present at the Weber I site and in lower Little Tennessee River valley sites, but the tiny seeds are infrequent in Middle Archaic components from sites at points in between. One can safely assume that these spotty distributions and low recovery levels underestimate the value of fleshy fruits. At the least, they added variety and flavor to the diet. Recovery is poor in part because, whether fresh or dry, much fruit was probably completely consumed, seeds and all. Even when further processing was involved, as for pemmican or through the addition of fruits to soups or stews, seeds may have been incorporated into the final product and so were, again, ultimately consumed. Finally, many fleshy fruits have uses, especially medicinal, that extend beyond subsistence. This was no doubt recognized and exploited by Archaic period people.

Most of the fleshy-fruit-producing trees, shrubs, and vines are successional species that thrive in clearings, edges, and other disturbed habitats. In view of the increasing sedentism that characterized settlement systems in the Middle Archaic Midwest, some researchers have suggested that the relative abundance of fleshy-fruit seeds in the archaeobotanical record may be a function of anthropogenic disturbance as well as of natural disturbance (Lopinot 1984; Scarry 2003; Wagner 2003). Whether intentionally or unintentionally, repeated revisits to and sustained occupations of a specific place provided conditions that promoted growth of fleshy-fruit-producing plants, which, in turn, would have increased the attractiveness of that place for return visits.

Fragments of underground plant parts—tubers, bulbs, and roots—are almost invariably poorly represented in the archaeobotanical record. Nonetheless, this group of plants was no doubt important. As Scarry (2003:72–73, Table 3.2) has summarized, at least 14 plants native to the southeastern United States produce edible roots and tubers. Several are available year-round, but others are especially valuable because they supply food in the winter and early spring, traditionally lean times of the year. Middle Archaic records provide some evidence for tuber use in the western and northern Midwest. Unidentifiable tuber fragments are present in six samples collected from the Campbell Hollow site in the lower Illinois River valley. Groundnut (*Apios americana*) tuber fragments have been identified in Middle Archaic levels at the Black Earth site in southern Illinois) and from the Lone Wolf site in eastern Missouri. Further north, aquatic tuber fragments are reported from the Bear Creek site assemblage, in the Saginaw Valley of Michigan. At the other geographic extreme, Crites reports one bulb, probably of either wild onion or leek, from a Middle Archaic stratum at the Hayes site in Tennessee, and he notes that a similar item was recovered from the Middle Archaic component at the Ervin site, also in Tennessee (Crites 1987:10).

With increased sedentism comes an increased demand on local environments to supply needed resources. Concurrently, one of the obvious consequences of repeated or sustained occupation is the increased level of disturbance to local "natural" plant communities. As noted above in reference to fleshy fruits, disturbed site margins as well as abandoned site locations provide optimal habitats for early successional plant growth, and, these habitats are quickly colonized by rapidly growing and prolific annuals. Included among these early invasive species in the Eastern Woodlands are goosefoot, erect knotweed, maygrass, little barley, sumpweed, and sunflower, which ultimately constitute the "Eastern Agricultural Complex" of native crop plants. The large settlements of the Middle Archaic and the attendant landscape disturbance provided both the physiographic and the social contexts in which plant manipulation culminating in domestication (i.e., reliance on human intervention for reproduction) could, at least theoretically, have occurred (Smith 1992a).

The processes that ultimately "produced" domesticated plants were neither synchronous nor uniform in scope across the Midwest (Fritz 1990), However, they all involved some kind of interference with a given plant's life cycle. Identifying the first "steps" in this process in the archaeobotanical record is difficult, and, in fact, most early plant manipulation may have been on such a low scale that it falls under the archaeological radar. Middle Archaic assemblages tend to contain more seeds from weedy plants than do Early Archaic sites, but counts are still, for the most part, low. At the very least, these seeds reflect the presence of "weedy" fruiting plants in the areas of human occupation. At most, their presence is the direct result of human processing and consumption activities. The types of weed seeds identified vary among sites, but the most common are chenopod, giant ragweed, amaranth, knotweed, wild bean, and sumpweed. Several of these plants, notably chenopod and amaranth, provide edible greens in addition to seeds, an attribute that no doubt enhanced their desirability and may even have been their initial consumptive focus (Bonzani 2004).

Sumpweed, or marsh elder (*Iva annua*), is the native plant for which the earliest good evidence exists—in the form of seeds that fall outside of the size range for seeds produced by wild plants—for true prehistoric domestication. Although that evidence postdates the Middle Archaic period (Asch and Asch 1978; Smith 1992b), the processes that culminated in domesticated plants must have been in place much earlier. To date, Middle Archaic archaeological records for sumpweed are focused in western and southwestern Illinois. The oldest is from the Koster site in the lower Illinois River valley, dates to about 7,000 years ago, and consists of 23 small seeds derived from wild plants. Small sumpweed seeds are also reported from the Nochta site and Diana site assemblages.

The record for giant ragweed (*Ambrosia trifida*) is strongest in the lower Illinois River valley site assemblages. It is reported from Campbell Hollow, Napoleon Hollow, Koster, Slim Lake, and Buckshaw Bridge. Giant ragweed seeds are also reported from the Diana site. The economic status of this plant remains problematic, although, as outlined below, its abundance and association with recognized cultigens in Late Archaic archaeobotanical assemblages suggest it was among the earliest cultivated plants, at least in some parts of the Midwest. Experimental harvesting efforts reported by Cowan (1985) show that harvest of the seeds is feasible, if not efficient.

Wild bean (*Strophostyles helvola*) is among the most widely distributed seed types in macrobotanical assemblages from Middle Archaic sites. It is reported from Little Tennessee River valley site components and from several sites in southern and into western Illinois. Like giant ragweed, it becomes even more common in Late Archaic–period assemblages, often in association with giant ragweed, chenopodium, and sumpweed.

Carbonized seeds are by no means abundant in Middle Archaic records, especially when compared with later prehistoric counts and ubiquity indexes. Further, data sets are obviously strongest for certain parts of the study area, notably western and southern Illinois and the Little Tennessee River valley. In these areas, the archaeobotanical seed record provides intriguing hints of the time depth and geographic scope of early plant manipulation. Whether the same is true for other parts of the Midwest is simply not yet known.

The Late Archaic Period

The Late Archaic archaeobotanical record is extensive (Figures 4.4 and 4.5) and more complex than are earlier records. Wood and nutshell continue to dominate assemblages, but seeds are increasingly common and provide secure evidence for propagation of selected weedy plant species. Because seed assemblages exhibit such dramatic change throughout the period, the following discussion of this material class is divided into Late Archaic (ca. 4000–1400 B.C.) and terminal Late Archaic (1400–950 B.C.) sections. The wood and nutshell records vary to a lesser extent and with much less subregional complexity so are conflated.

By initial Late Archaic times, or about 5,000 years ago, the vegetation of the Midwest had achieved its pre-European-settlement configuration of oak-hickory and mixed deciduous forests, floodplain marshes or swamps, and open savannah and

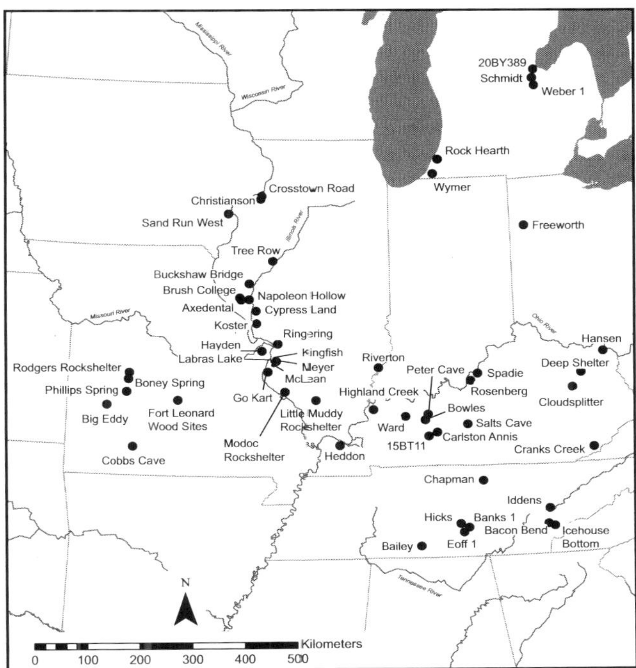

Figure 4.4. Late Archaic sites with analyzed plant remains.

Figure 4.5. Terminal Late Archaic sites with analyzed plant remains.

prairie. Figure 4.6 provides a generalized, and greatly simplified, depiction of this late Holocene vegetation community patterning. Individual plant distributions, of course, fluctuated (and continue to do so), especially along ecotones, but this figure provides a broad contextual model. While causality is not implied, concurrent with the establishment of modern configurations, subregional variability is increasingly evident in both the archaeobotanical record and in other aspects of material culture.

The Late Archaic Wood Record

Wood charcoal is almost always present and is often abundant in Late Archaic archaeobotanical assemblages. Unless otherwise indicated, it is presumed to reflect use of wood as fuel. Given that collection of fuelwood for nonspecific purposes was dictated by economy of effort, a broad congruence between local forest community and archaeobotanical wood charcoal is to be expected (the "firewood indifference hypothesis"; Asch and Asch 1985c:346). This congruence is evident in Archaic-period wood assemblages from across the Midwest on both regional and local scales. In keeping with general Midwest vegetation models, oak and hickory are the most consistently recovered taxa, but quantities and associated wood types vary with location. In the southern Great Lakes area, they are joined by beech and maple, reflecting the local northern forests. Assemblages from sites in the Midsouth add characteristically southern taxa, including dogwood, red bud, and pine. Local-level variability is also evident. For example, in the American Bottom of western Illinois, wood assemblages from Late Archaic sites situated on dry terraces or in the uplands are dominated by oaks and hickories, with fewer counts of secondary taxa, such as walnut and ash. Assemblages from sites situated near lower, wetter parts of the floodplain often contain both a greater variety of wood types and a better representation of moisture-tolerant taxa, such as willow or sycamore, as well as elm, ash, and coffee tree. Forest composition is not, of course, the only environmental or ecological factor affecting wood availability. Species-specific features such as propensity for deadwood "production" or external factors like driftwood availability also come into play. Further, the oak and hickory in assemblages possibly reflect selection for intrinsic properties (specifically, high heat value). However, taken as a whole, the evidence does not point to focused selection of specific wood types; neither is there evidence for large-scale environmental impact that would have affected local supplies and required long-distance collection forays. People may simply have moved on when local wood supplies became depleted—or were perceived to be.

As expected, Late Archaic wood assemblages from many of the most extensively studied sites also tend to have high taxonomic diversities. For example, over 20 different wood types are present in assemblages from Bacon Bend and Iddens on the Little Tennessee River. Assemblages from the large, terminal Late Archaic Prairie Lake–phase (ca. 1500–1000 B.C.) Dyroff and MoPac sites in southwestern Illinois contain 16 and 17 different types of wood, respectively. These assem-

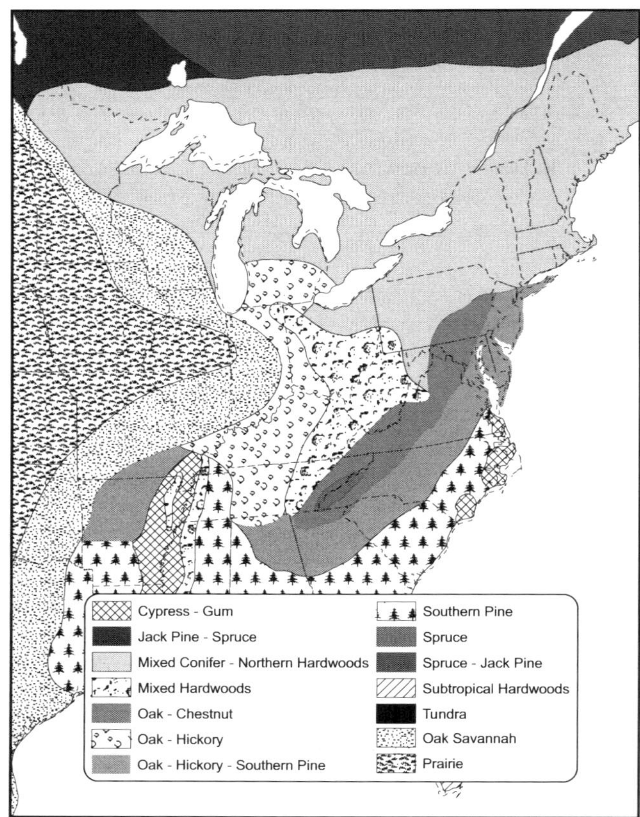

Figure 4.6. Midwest vegetation model at 1000 B.C. (after Delcourt and Delcourt 1983, 1987).

blages provide exceptionally comprehensive records of Late Archaic wood use and reinforce theories of nonselectivity (Johannessen 1984c, 1988).

Because fuel needs vary with different situations, Late Archaic wood records may have more to convey at the individual site or settlement-system level than is encompassed by the firewood-indifference hypothesis. Prehistoric people's fuel requirements and how those needs were met varied not only according to where people were living but also according to the types of activities in which they were engaged and the duration and seasonality of these activities. Because requirements varied, the wood-charcoal assemblages that are the by-products of said activities may also vary. Comparisons of quantitative measurements such as wood densities, feature ubiquity indexes, and taxonomic diversities among "contemporaneous" sites in a given area can potentially contribute to understanding of human impact on local environments, individual site function, and entire settlement systems. These types of studies require quantified and standardized (or standardizable) data.

Late Archaic Nutshell

Nutshell is the most common plant part in most Late Archaic assemblages. Usually, thick-shelled hickory dominates, but black walnut (or black walnut and butternut) or acorn shell fragments sometimes outnumber those of thick-shelled hickory. Hazelnut, pecan, bitternut, and chestnut shells are also represented. As one would expect, large assemblages from large sites usually have higher diversities, and small assemblages from small sites tend to be less diverse. In contrast, absolute quantities, particularly of thick-shelled hickory, may be quite high at small upland sites.

As noted above, acorn was undoubtedly more important in prehistoric economies than is suggested by shell recovery levels alone. Applying Lopinot's (1984) nutshell to nutmeat conversion factors to both data provided by Lopinot and to nutshell weights from an additional 17 Late Archaic sites provides a perhaps more realistic picture of actual nut use (Figure 4.7).

As Figure 4.7 indicates, converted acorn meat weights tend to be higher in the Tennessee River valley area of the Midsouth than they are at other sites across the Midwest. This pattern was originally noted by Lopinot, who interpreted it as reflecting the use of acorns as a "first-line nut resource" (1984:153) in this part of the Midsouth throughout the Archaic period. However, as Figure 4.7 also shows, acorn meat is well represented across the area, especially in terminal Late Archaic assemblages. Not included in this figure are records from the Saginaw Valley in Michigan (Egan 1987:Table 6) and Cold Oak shelter in eastern Kentucky, which further attest to the widespread use of acorn during the Late Archaic period.

Black walnut contributes least to assemblages reported in Figure 4.7. Note, however, that, sites located in the northern part of the study area tend to contain relatively more black-walnut shells than do midlatitude sites. Assemblages from both the Weber I site in the Saginaw Valley and the Rock Hearth site in southwestern Michigan are dominated by black walnut. In addition, Lovis (1986:Table 4-1) lists black walnut or butternut as equaling or exceeding hickory in abundance at

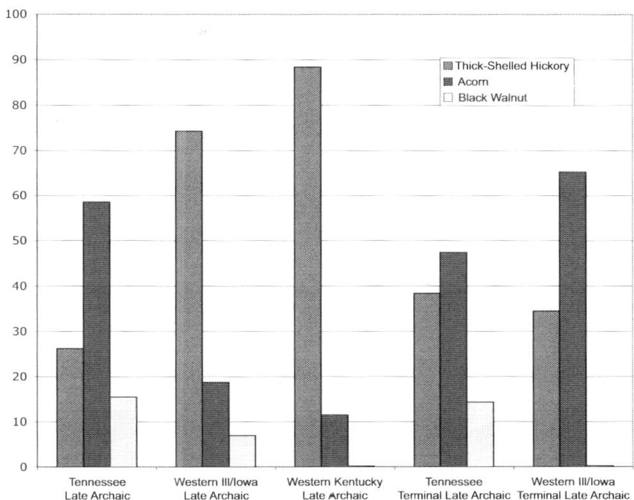

Figure 4.7. Average contributions of nutmeats, estimated on the basis of nutshell weights, to grouped Archaic and terminal Late Archaic assemblages in three parts of the Midwest. (Conversions follow Lopinot 1984:151–153. Nutmeat weight = (x) x (c) x (m), where x = raw shell weight, c = conversion factor, and m = maximum meat:shell ratio; (c) x (m) = 1.32 for thick-shelled hickory, 73.43 for acorn, and .997 for black walnut).

the Schmidt, Feeheley, Kretz, and Hart sites in the Saginaw Valley. Egan (1988:91) interprets this pattern as reflecting opportunistic exploitation of any and all available nut crops in any given year. Availability may also enter in if hickory groves were fewer and more scattered this far north. Given the Michigan pattern, the dominance of thick-shelled hickory in the terminal Late Archaic–Early Woodland occupation at Eidson in southwest Michigan is anomalous. It may reflect seasonal variability in mast production capacities, such that it represents several excellent years of hickory nut production (Parachini 1983) or even increased availability engendered by the more moderate climate of southwestern Michigan.

Not surprisingly, nutshell quantities are also closely tied to occupation intensity and site type. Nutshell diversities for 10 Late Archaic sites in the American Bottom range from only two nut types to seven different types, but three of the four sites with three or fewer shell types are also short-term or specialized encampments. Taken alone, this group would certainly provide a much different picture of Late Archaic nut use than would be obtained by taking into account large sites, such as Go-Kart, which contained seven different nut types. A similar situation is found in the lower Illinois River valley. Upland sites such as Axedental have exceptionally high quantities of thick-shelled hickory, reflecting their function as nut-processing locales. A more complete picture of nut use in this part of Illinois is evident in the recently analyzed assemblage from the Tree Row site, which, despite the abundance of thick-shelled hickory, also produced respectable quantities of black walnut, hazelnut, acorn, and butternut shells.

In light of the variability in the archaeobotanical record, attempts to uniformly characterize nut use across the entire Archaic Midwest are probably not useful. As data accumulate, it is becoming evident that, while Late Archaic groups no doubt were heavy nut users, the nature and extent of this use was not the same in all places. Archaeobotanists working in the lower Illinois River valley have proposed diachronic shifts that involved an increasing focus on thick-shelled hickories through the Middle and into the Late Archaic periods (Asch and Asch 1985b; Stafford 1991). In turn, the terminal Late Archaic witnessed a shift back to increased diversification, structured to meet growing needs of increasingly sedentary groups (Asch and Asch 1986). At the same time, the record from the Saginaw River valley in Michigan is consistently diverse (Egan 1988).

Miscellaneous Plant Parts in the Late Archaic Record

Scarry (2003:Table 3.1) lists 14 plants that produce roots and tubers for which there are ethnohistoric use records from the Eastern Woodlands. Most do not appear in the archaeobotanical record but, by virtue of their presence in indigenous plant communities and their economic potential, are assumed to have been important prehistorically, particularly during the late winter and spring, when resources were scarce. Although still few in number, these plant parts are better represented in Late Archaic assemblages from across the Midwest than in assemblages from earlier times. Hogpeanut tuber fragments are reported from Floyd, Hayden, and ICT in the American Bottom of western Illinois. One unidentifiable terrestrial tuber fragment is reported from Weber I in eastern Michigan. Individual unidentified carbonized bulbs are reported from the Christianson site in far western Illinois and the Riverton site in southeastern Illinois. These few recoveries are quite fortuitous. Tubers and bulbs may have been minimally processed and the plant part consumed in its entirety. Items lost in fires may have quickly ashed or been degraded through mechanical attrition. At the recovery and analytical levels, differences in the nature and scope of archaeological investigations among sites and difficulty in identification may also be factors limiting the record.

Wetland plants are also better represented in later assemblages. Wild rice is not reported from any of the pre–Late Archaic site assemblages listed in Table 4.1, but grains have a sporadic presence in the Late Archaic assemblages. In the western part of this region, they have been reported from the Sand Run site (Figure 4.8 *top*) in the Mississippi River valley and from the Campbell Hollow, Cypress Land, and Napoleon Hollow sites in the lower Illinois River valley. A single feature at the Tree Row site contained over 1,000 grains. Further to the southeast, wild rice has also been reported from the Iddens and Bacon Bend sites, which are in the Tennessee River valley, and from the Carlston Annis site in western Kentucky (Crawford and Smith 2003:Table 6.3). As Crawford and Smith (2003:202) note, ethnohistorically, wild-rice harvesting was usually associated with more northerly groups; however, there is no reason to suppose that the grains were not used across the plant's natural range during prehistoric times.

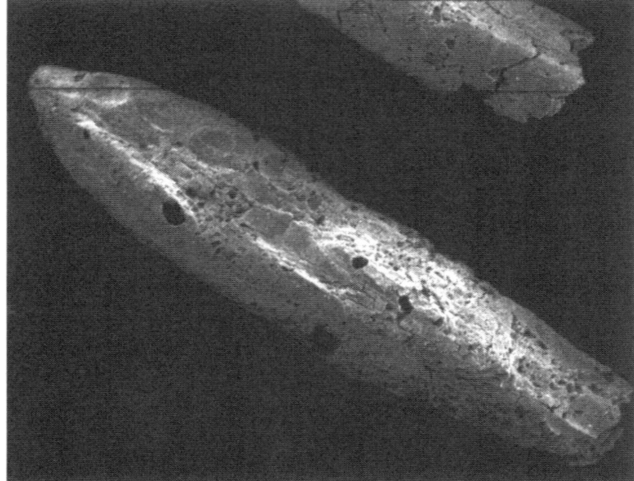

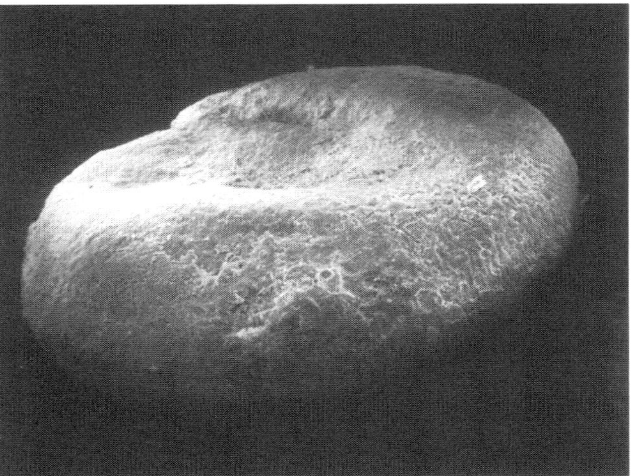

*Figure 4.8. Top: scanning electron micrograph of wild rice (*Zizania aquatica*); bottom: scanning electron micrograph of* Chenopodium berlandieri *showing rounded margin. Both from the Late Archaic–component Sand Run Slough site, eastern Iowa, courtesy of Neal Lopinot, Southwest Missouri State University.*

American lotus seed-coat fragments are quite common, if not abundant, in Late Archaic assemblages from western Illinois. They are reported from the Axendetal, Napoleon Hollow, and Tree Row sites, the last of these producing an exceptionally large collection, with shell pieces identified in 38 percent of the 74 features analyzed. Fragments are also present in assemblages from several sites in the American Bottom area, including Modoc, ICT, Go-Kart, and Floyd. Like acorn shell, which they resemble, lotus seed-coat pieces are usually quite small and fragile so are poorly represented in the large fraction (material that does not pass through a 2-mm-mesh screen) of most flotation samples. As is the case with so many plants, the nutlike seeds are suspected to have been more widely used than is indicated in the archaeobotanical record.

More indirect indicators of wetland resource use include the seeds from wetland sedges and rushes that are found in floodplain site assemblages, including those from Hedden and Bowles in western Kentucky, Iddens in Tennessee, and MoPac, ICT, and Floyd in Illinois. These recoveries may reflect either site location or actual exploitation of the represented plant. In either event, they serve to emphasize the importance of aquatic or semiaquatic resources and wetland locales to Late Archaic groups.

Late Archaic Squash and Gourd

While use of native squashes clearly extended well back into the Archaic period (Table 4.2), by Late Archaic times, manipulation had become even more common, and people in some parts of the Midwest were growing a domesticated form of the plant. Late Archaic pepo squash rind and seeds are well distributed among assemblages from sites across the region, ranging from Phillips Spring in the west to Cloudsplitter in the east, and from the Iddens site in Tennessee to Green Point in Michigan. Most Late Archaic squash remains consist of small, minimally informative rind fragments. However, some pieces exhibit distinct morphological characteristics that are the consequence of human manipulation and that distinguish them from rind fragments produced by wild plants. These characteristics are thickened rinds, warty or lobed rind surfaces, and enlarged seed sizes. Thickened rind has been recognized as a consequence of manipulation for some time. "King's rule," proposed by Frances King in 1985, established a 2-mm baseline thickness for distinguishing domesticated squash from its wild progenitors. Likewise, increased seed size is a well-recognized characteristic of domesticated plants, in general. For squash, Smith (1987) has suggested an 11-mm baseline length as delimiting derivation from domesticated populations. Rind surface characteristics are difficult to determine, especially given the very small size and poor condition of most archaeological fragments. However, warty and lobed forms are not present among wild gourds (Cowan 1997) so, if discernible, may be attributed to human selection.

Cowan (1997) documents these morphological changes in his detailed study of Late Archaic and Early Woodland–period squash remains from the Cumberland Plateau of Kentucky. At Cloudsplitter shelter, thin rind and small seeds are present throughout Late Archaic deposits dating between 4700 and 3000 B.P. (Cowan 1997:69), attesting to the plant's long history of use in this locale. Cowan believes that these earliest Late Archaic squashes were very much like modern wild varieties native to the Ozarks and Texas; that is, they were small, with brittle shells and bitter meat. They were also the objects of cultivation, possibly for their oily seeds, which could have served as a nutritious backup mediating mast-crop failure. Local continuity in manipulation is evident at the Cold Oak shelter. Rind fragments from that site dating to 1040 B.C. (calibrated date from Cowan 1997:Table 4.2) are, on average, greater than 2 mm in thickness and are the only examples I found of Late Archaic materials with a warty surface. Smooth, lobed, and warty forms of squash all appear in assemblages from both Cloudsplitter and Newt Kash that date only a few hundred years later. These Early Woodland domesticated squashes have average rind thicknesses in excess of 2 mm and average seed lengths exceeding the 11-mm baseline (Cowan 1997:Tables 4.3 and 4.4).

If the existence of Archaic gourds in eastern Kentucky is well established, the question of how these materials ended up in upland shelters on the Cumberland Plateau is still unresolved. The uplands of eastern Kentucky are not within the range of modern, wild squashes (Gremillion 1993b), and Smith et al. (1992:Figure 4.7, Table 4.1) report only a single herbarium record for *Cucurbita* sp., from Powell County in eastern Kentucky. The next closest record is far to the west in east-central Illinois. Nonetheless, as suggested by Cowan (1997:69), wild squash may have been part of the prehistoric indigenous flora, in which case in situ domestication is possible. Alternatively, weedy or transitional forms of squash may have been introduced and maintained, whether intentionally or unintentionally, in this area early in prehistory (Gremillion 1993b). The presence of rind fragments from Middle Archaic contexts far to the east, in Pennsylvania, and to the north, in Maine, demonstrates that not only were the fruits subject to human use but they were also subject to human transport at a relatively early date.

Late Archaic squash records are also available from several sites in Missouri. Perhaps the best known is the impressive collection of noncarbonized seed and rind fragments recovered from waterlogged sediments at the Phillips Spring site. King (1985:81) reports that the bulk of these materials were collected from the "squash and gourd zone" dating to about 2884 B.C. (Table 4.2). Included are a series of 65 seeds with a mean length of 10.5 mm and 10 rind fragments that measure between .6 and 1.8 mm in thickness. While they fall just below the established size baselines for domestication, Fritz (1997) believes that these materials might very well have derived from domesticated plants.

Another excellent record is found at the Marble Bluff shelter in Arkansas, where large squash seeds (average length of 11.6 mm) were identified among a cache of crop seeds that includes domesticated forms of other native plants. Seeds in this cache provide radiocarbon dates that indicate deposition about 1,000 years later than the Phillips Spring materials. They make up the oldest securely dated collection yet identified of specimens that consistently exceed the 11-mm baseline length for domesticated plants. As discussed in the following section, like those from Cloudsplitter, the Marble Bluff materials are associated with seeds from other domesticated, or at least quasi-domesticated, Eastern Agricultural crop plants. Unlike Cloudsplitter, however, the Arkansas sites are well within the range of modern (and presumably prehistoric) wild squashes

(Decker 1988; Decker-Walters 1993; Decker-Walters et al. 1993; Smith et al. 1992:Figure 4.7). It is interesting that the oldest records for clearly domesticated fruits are from sites located away from major river valleys, in rugged upland or secondary valley terrain, but it is not surprising that they are from rockshelters that afforded excellent preservation. Perhaps these locales provided the genetic isolation needed to effect permanent change (Gremillion 1993b).

The Late Archaic Seed Record (ca. 4000 to 1400 B.C.)

The increase in both the number and diversity of seeds is no doubt the best-recognized feature of the Late Archaic archaeobotanical record. Factors of redundancy, association, context, and economic potential indicate that many are the product of human use, either of the seeds themselves or of other plant parts, rather than the product of natural seed rain or fruit dispersal. Among the most important are the seeds from weedy annuals, which are rapidly growing, prolific seed producers that thrive in disturbed soil and may provide edible greens as well as seeds. These characteristics would have made them attractive for exploitation, since at least initially, no energy needed to be expended to propagate them, greens could provide early-season resources, and seed harvest provided a supplemental, storable, late-season resource. Their absolute contributions to the total Archaic diet are uncertain, but, as a group, these plants had a long history of use in the Midwest.

Weedy annuals colonized prehistoric sites both through nonhuman mechanisms of seed dispersal and through human dispersal, whether intentional or unintentional. Human dispersal provides a means of effectively extending a plant's range outside its usual habitat. Seeds can be directly introduced to a new area through human collection and transport for consumption (Smith 1992a, 1995) or indirectly introduced through collection of nonseed plant parts, such as greens, for food; through use of other plant parts, such as stems, for technological purposes; or simply fortuitously. Extension beyond the natural range is one mechanism of achieving some measure of genetic isolation, which is a prerequisite for true domestication. As noted above, in some parts of the Midwest, selection processes that could have culminated in the development of domesticated species were already underway by the Middle Archaic (e.g., southwestern Illinois; Lopinot 1991). However, a full 1,500 years separates the earliest Late Archaic records for use of Eastern Agricultural Complex plants and their emergence, as evidenced by morphological change, as quasi domesticates. Further, there is no reason to expect that this process was expressed in the same manner, to the same extent, or at the same time everywhere across the Midwest.

The invasive weedy annuals for which the Archaic-period archaeological records are strongest are the native chenopod (*Chenopodium berlandieri*); sumpweed, or marsh elder (*Iva annua*); maygrass (*Phalaris caroliniana*); and sunflower (*Helianthus annuus*). The other two members of the Eastern Agricultural Complex, erect knotweed (*Polygonum erectum*) and little barley (*Hordeum pusillum*), both of which were ultimately cultivated but not clearly domesticated, are poorly represented. Plants of spatially or temporally limited importance include giant ragweed (*Ambrosia trifida*) and barnyard grass (*Echinochloa muricata*).

Chenopod is by far the most widely distributed of this group. With the exception of central and southern Michigan, chenopod seeds have been identified in Late Archaic samples from across the Midwest. They are especially common in assemblages from sites located along major rivers, notably the Mississippi, Illinois, and Little Tennessee rivers. In addition, chenopods have been identified from sites as far to the west as Big Eddy and Nebo Hill in western Missouri and as far to the south as Iddens and Bacon Bend in Tennessee. Although the seeds are widely distributed, counts tend to be low. Only rarely have more than 100 individual seeds been reported for any one assemblage, and often only a single or a few seeds are represented. For the most part, chenopod seeds from Late Archaic sites exhibit thick, reticulate seed coats and convex margins (although carbonization tends to distort this latter feature) and appear to have been derived from wild plants. However, the Sand Run West site, located along the Mississippi River in eastern Iowa, provided an exceptionally large assemblage that included a few specimens with thinner coats and more rounded margins (Figure 4.8 *bottom*). Lopinot (1987) has suggested that these may derive from incipient domesticated plants, but evaluations are complicated by natural variation in wild seed populations, especially by the presence of so-called red morphs, naturally occurring thin-coated seeds produced in small numbers by wild plants (Asch and Asch 1985a; Smith 1992c). Thin-coated chenopods dating to the Late Archaic–terminal Late Archaic interface, or about 1500 B.C., are also present in the seed assemblage from Cloudsplitter Rockshelter in eastern Kentucky (Gremillion 1994; Smith and Cowan 1987). Testa thickness for a sample of these seeds ranged from 9 to 16 μ, well below the 20-μ maximum for *C. berlandieri* spp. *jonesianum* (Smith and Cowan 1987).

Although distribution is limited, the second most commonly recovered Eastern Agricultural Complex seed is sumpweed. There are no secure records for pre-1500 B.C. sumpweed from Kentucky or Tennessee, although it is a well-recognized component of terminal Late Archaic and Early Woodland assemblages from sites in that region. Moreover, Yarnell and Black (1985:Table 6) do not report it for the Late Archaic in their general synthesis of prehistoric plant foods from the Southeast. In contrast, sumpweed has been reported from over half of all Late Archaic sites located in the Mississippi and Illinois river drainages listed in Table 1.

Through time, archaeological sumpweed achenes from sites across the Midwest display an increase in size that reflects ongoing processes of human manipulation and selection. They ultimately attain sizes that are much larger than those produced by wild plants. Early studies of this archaeological material led to the recognition of a fully domesticated subspecies, *Iva annua* var. *macrocarpa* (Jackson 1960;Yarnell 1972).The earliest evidence of size increase is found in Late Archaic assemblages from sites in the central Mississippi River and Illinois River valley regions. Sumpweed from the Napoleon Hollow, Tree Row, and Axedental sites in the lower Illinois River valley includes examples that are quite large, with average lengths exceeding 4 mm. The Christianson site, farther north along the Mississippi River (Figure 4.4), contained one exceptionally large achene. The estimated original size of 7.2 x 5.45 mm (Parker 1998a) is comparable to sizes from later, terminal Late Archaic and Early Woodland–period populations (Asch and Asch 1978; Yarnell 1978).

However, not all Late Archaic sumpweed collections include large-sized seeds. Specimens from the Sand Run West, Hayden, and McLean sites along the Mississippi River are small, averaging around 3.0 to 3.2 mm in length, well within the range of seeds produced by wild plants. Apparently, along sections of the Illinois and Mississippi River valleys, the process of sumpweed domestication was underway by about 2000 B.C. (Asch and Asch 1985a:159; Parker 1998a). Elsewhere in this same part of the Midwest, use is indicated but genetic response is not. Whether this distribution reflects differential use or response at the local level or simply sampling and recovery biases is not known. While the best data indicate that the genetic change was initiated in the central Mississippi River region of the greater Midwest, there is no recognized hearth of domestication.

Sunflower seeds are more widely distributed than sumpweed. In the southern part of the study area, sunflower is reported from three pre-1500 B.C. components, Iddens in Tennessee and Carlston Annis and Hedden in western Kentucky. Seeds from the latter two sites are reported to be over 5 mm in length (Crawford 1982; Rossen 2000), placing them on the large end of the size range reported for wild plants (Yarnell 1978). A single, large sunflower seed from the Hayes site in central Tennessee has been AMS dated to about 2200 B.C. (Crites 1993) and provides the oldest secure evidence for domestication. As was true for sumpweed in the north, sunflower plants were being manipulated at an early date in the southern Midwest.

Farther north in the Mississippi River valley region, Late Archaic components at the McLean and Sand Run sites contain small sunflower seeds. The Christianson site yielded two seeds, one of which was quite small and one of which was unusually large and whose measurement was corrected to fall within the size range for Early Woodland populations (Parker 1998a). The Titterington component at Napoleon Hollow contained six kernels with an average size that falls in the upper end of the range provided for seeds from wild sunflowers. These latter materials may represent early stages of domestication, but identification as such is not secure (Asch and Asch 1985a:168–169). Assessing prehistoric domestication of sunflower is complicated by the variability in seed size evident among plants or even on one individual plant (Asch and Asch 1985a:164–170; Heiser 1954, 1985). Experimental work has shown that wild plants can produce large achenes, and domesticated plants can produce quite small achenes (Asch and Asch 1985a:Figure 6.5; Heiser 1954:Figure 3; Yarnell 1978:Table 1). Consequently, early stages of domestication are difficult to assess without large collections.

Late Archaic–period maygrass seeds have been reported from only a few sites. The earliest record to date is that from the Bacon Bend site in Tennessee, from which 130 grains were reported. This area is outside (to the east) of the modern natural range of *P. caroliniana*, so these seeds may be the result of intentional or unintentional transport by humans. However, whether the plant was actually being grown in this locale at this early date is not known, as seeds can arrive in a given spot through any number of means. Similarly, one and two grains, respectively, have been reported from the Cranks Creek site in Kentucky and the Go-Kart site in the American Bottom, both of which are also outside the plant's natural range. The former may be contamination from later occupations, while the latter seem more securely provenienced, given the absence of non-Archaic subsurface features. These findings suggest that humans were moving this plant, or at least the seeds of the plant, into new environments at an early date.

The record for giant ragweed is strong in west-central Illinois. In the Illinois River valley region, 38 seeds were recovered from Buckshaw Bridge, and 346, almost all of which were kernels, were identified in the Tree Row site assemblage. Farther south, giant ragweed is present in the McLean and Hayden site assemblages, in the American Bottom region. While no evidence indicates that it was domesticated, recurrences and abundance suggest that by about 1500 B.C., giant ragweed plants were tolerated and perhaps even encouraged by people living in this part of the Midwest (Asch and Asch 1982, 1985a).

The Late Archaic record east of the Tennessee River in Kentucky is different. With the exception of 80 seeds of *C. berlandieri* from the Ward site on the Green River and a single *Chenopodium* sp. specimen from the Cranks Creek site, chenopod, sumpweed, and giant ragweed are absent from sites predating about 1500 B.C. in this area. For sites reported several decades ago, like Spadie and Rosenberger in northern Kentucky (Figure 4.4), this absence may be attributed to the novelty of flotation recovery and analysis of small-scale remains at the time the sites were excavated. Alternatively, as Gremillion has noted (2004:229), neither chenopod nor sumpweed was a common constituent of wild prehistoric plant communities this far east, so their absence could reflect lack of availability. As discussed below, the record from terminal Late Archaic rockshelters in eastern Kentucky indicates that this use pattern changed dramatically over the next several hundred years.

Many early Late Archaic groups across the Midwest included plant cultivation as part of their economic systems. On the basis of Late Archaic data from western Illinois, Nancy and David Asch (1982, 1985a:161), defined a local "Titterington Complex" of cultivated plants comprising chenopod, giant ragweed, and sumpweed as well as sunflower and squash. Elements of this complex, including ragweed, have been recognized in the much earlier, late Middle Archaic (ca. 4000–3700 B.C.; Lopinot 1991:113) assemblage at the Diana site, suggesting its antiquity. This recurrent theme suggests (relatively) continuous occupation and population stability within circumscribed parts of the Midwest. At the same time, this complex appears to be missing from pre-1500 B.C. Late Archaic assemblages from the eastern part of the study area.

The increasing number of weed seeds, and the attention they receive, in the Late Archaic archaeobotanical record can mask the contributions of other plants. Though relative proportions often decline, absolute counts and ubiquity indexes for fleshy-fruit seeds remain at or even above levels in older assemblages. Sumac, grape, and persimmon seeds are especially common. Intentional and unintentional landscape disturbance that was part of changing human settlement systems may have encouraged the growth of pioneering shrubs and trees that provide such edible fleshy fruits. Whether intentionally or not, human behavior increased availability.

The Terminal Late Archaic Seed Record (ca. 1400 to 950 B.C.)

The terminal Late Archaic seed record reflects the presence of low-level food-production economies (Smith 2001) in parts of the Midwest. The record is particularly strong along the eastern and western peripheries, where well-preserved assemblages from rockshelters provide good evidence for morphological change in select seed taxa. In eastern Kentucky, abundant small seeds in the well-preserved assemblages from the Cold Oak, Newt Kash, and Hooton Hollow rockshelters indicate that farming was an integral part of the economy in this region by about 3,000 years ago (Gremillion 1993b, 1994, 1995, 1997, 2004; Smith and Cowan 1987). At Cold Oak, crop seeds, including chenopod, sumpweed, sunflower, and maygrass, constitute about 29 percent of all seeds identified from the terminal Late Archaic component. Both sumpweed and sunflower seeds approach or exceed the size threshold for domesticated plants. Chenopods from Cold Oak include specimens that are thin coated and have truncate margins. Similar thin-coated chenopods have been identified in paleofeces collected from Hooton Hollow and Newt Kash rockshelters (Gremillion 1997); in both cases, they are associated with wild forms. These paleofecal samples also contained ragweed, sunflower, and sumpweed seeds (Gremillion 1997:Table 2). The latter average well over 4 mm in length, placing them within the size range for domesticated specimens. The genetically modified plants that produced these thin-coated chenopod seeds and enlarged sumpweed and sunflower achenes were the consequence of human intervention in the plants' life cycles. Their presence in such large numbers at this early date indicates that the collection, storage, and sowing of seeds from this group of plants were purposeful, ongoing activities in these upland locales. What remains unknown is the.sequence of events that led to their presence. Gremillion (204:229) has suggested that chenopod and sumpweed seeds and their propagation technologies were originally acquired from neighboring groups, since neither plant is native to this upland area.

On the extreme southwestern edge of the study area, the terminal Late Archaic seed assemblage from the Marble Bluff shelter in north Arkansas also contains chenopod, sunflower, and sumpweed. Included are thin-testa chenopod fruits from the domesticated spp. *jonesianum* as well as more typical thick-coated seeds. The size indexes for both the sumpweed and sunflower achenes are exceptionally large, indicating that they, too, are derived from domesticated or quasi-domesticated plants (Fritz 1994). Fritz (1997:45–56) has suggested that the Marble Bluff cache represents seeds that were intentionally selected and stored for future planting. If so, they may be atypically large for this time period but are good indicators of the extent to which changes in seed morphology had occurred by this early date. The Marble Bluff, Hooton Hollow, and Cold Oak collections also contained numerous ragweed seeds associated with these quasi domesticates. These findings greatly extend the geographic range for this complex of Archaic-period cultigens first identified in the late Middle Archaic.

Other records for genetically altered seeds are more diffuse and singular. A single sunflower achene from the Riverton site in Illinois (Figure 4.5) measures 6.8 x 4.3 mm (Yarnell 2004:126), placing it at the lower size limit for domesticated plants. In western Kentucky, chenopod seeds and large sumpweed and sunflower are present in terminal Late Archaic contexts at Salts Cave, although the bulk of this assemblage dates to slightly later in time. Chenopod seeds from the Dirk site in the Missouri bootheel of the central Mississippi River valley are described as having thin testae with rounded to even partially truncated margins, indicative of seeds from genetically altered plants (Lopinot 2000). Finally, the Higgs site in central Tennessee provides domesticated-sized sunflower dating to around 900 B.C. All these reports suggest that terminal Late Archaic plant-management practices were widespread and ongoing across the southern Midwest.

At points north of the Mississippi River and Ohio River confluence, the terminal Late Archaic record for genetically modified crop plants is less extensive, especially for chenopod. This is particularly the case for the terminal Late Archaic Prairie Lake–phase sites in the American Bottom area of Illinois, for which an unusually strong archaeobotanical record is available (Figure 4.5; Table 4.1). While chenopod is among the most commonly identified seed types in these assemblages, morphologically, seeds are much more consistent with those produced by wild plants than with domesticated forms. Except for a single shriveled seed, all the Floyd site specimens exhibit roughened, thick testae and acute margins, as do those from the Ringering site. Relatively large collections from both the ICT and Marge sites are too poorly preserved to definitively characterize, although two "forms," one resembling the wild morph and the other displaying a less reticulated seed coat, may be represented (Lopinot 1983:100–101; Simon 1996).

In view of the record elsewhere in the Midwest and given factors of redundancy, association, and quantity, these seeds may have been intentionally collected from tended or at least tolerated plant stands. Wild stands would have been common in this floodplain area, so, no doubt, cross-pollination with sown stands was ongoing and genetic isolation difficult to achieve. In fact, wild stands were probably also harvested as available, since acquiring food, not developing a domesticated strain, was the intent. Just to the north in the lower Illinois River valley, thin-coated chenopod has not been securely identified from any assemblages predating the Middle Woodland period (Asch and Asch 1985a, 1985c).

Similarly, the few terminal Late Archaic sumpweed achenes from sites in this area are fairly small. The single achene from Dyroff has corrected measurements of 2.8 mm x 2.0 mm (Johannessen 1984b:Table 28). ICT produced numerous achenes (n = 181), ranging in length from 1.5 to 4.5 mm and averaging 2.77 mm (Lopinot 1983:Figure 14). Given the record elsewhere, it is reasonable to assume that these were collected from plants in the initial "stages" of domestication. However, to date, these are the only two terminal Late Archaic sites in the American Bottom with sumpweed, which seems unusual given the relatively large number of analyzed assemblages.

Barnyard grass is common in terminal Late Archaic assemblages from the American Bottom. It is the dominant seed type in the Floyd site assemblage and is present at the Dyroff, MoPac, Ringering, Carr Creek, and Range sites. As Parker has stated, "The abundance and ubiquity of barnyard grass ... is difficult to explain as other then a consequence of deliberate harvest" (2001:123). Like giant ragweed, barnyard grass may have been regularly used at the local level during the Archaic period. During Woodland times, its popularity fell drastically.

Initial evaluation of terminal Late Archaic sites located just to the north along the Mississippi and Illinois rivers indicates that they provide plant-use records that are very similar to those of the Prairie Lake–phase sites. Chenopods from the Gast Spring site in eastern Iowa display rounded margins, characteristic of intermediary or incipient domesticated plants (Dunne and Green 1998). The site also contained little barley, one of very few early records for the plant, and squash as well as barnyard grass. Patterns of plant use in this region mirror other aspects of material culture (Emerson and McElrath 1983; McElrath 1993), retaining a "Midsouth" aspect.

In contrast, the record for terminal Late Archaic seed use, especially for native cultivated plants, is increasingly limited and quite different farther to the north. The Weber I and Eidson sites in Michigan have interesting seed records, but they display very limited evidence that plant cultivation was part of the cultural repertoire. The Weber I site assemblage is unusually large for the time and place and is dominated by seeds from a member of the Brassicaceae (mustard) family. These may well have had economic import, but no evidence suggests that they were part of a garden complex. The few chenopods are of wild form and presumably derive from natural seed rain (Egan 1988). The Eidson site seed assemblage is also large, but Archaic and Woodland components are, for the most part, undifferentiated, so it is of limited value vis-à-vis interpretations of terminal Late Archaic plant use. The most interesting specimen is a single, domesticated-size sunflower seed from good terminal Late Archaic context. This provides the only record for use of cultivated sunflower at this time across the northern half of the Midwest.

Issues and Implications of Archaic Plant Use

The record for Archaic period plant us is obviously incomplete and biased. Nonetheless, within the parameters imposed by pre- and postdepositional factors of use and preservation, archaeobotanists have been able to identify a large number of plant types, all of which (presumably) had some function in the culture and economy of Archaic-period prehistoric peoples. For some areas and some time spans, we have been quite successful in building regional and local "chronologies," or historical sequences of plant use. Compiling detailed inventories of the plant parts present in the archaeobotanical record may not be terribly exciting, but it is a necessary precursor to more involved studies. Publication of detailed analyses of well-provenienced, securely dated assemblages from individual sites or site components is still needed.

Among the best-studied aspects of the Archaic-period record is the development of food-production economies, and of the plants that were important components of those economic systems. By the end of the Middle Archaic, use of three native annuals—chenopod, squash, and sumpweed—extended beyond collection of wild seeds to low-scale interference, whether intentional or inadvertent, with the plants' life cycles. By the end of the terminal Late Archaic, at least two more plants, sunflower and giant ragweed, were added to this complex as was barnyard grass, albeit within a limited area. Concurrently, sumpweed and chenopod plants had undergone genetic alteration, such that seeds from archaeological contexts display morphological features that distinguish them from seeds produced by wild plants. The most readily assessed is the increase in seed size evidenced by sumpweed. Genetically controlled changes in chenopod include a decrease in seed-coat thickness and a "squaring off" or truncation of seed margins. The latter may be attributed to selection for nonshattering habits or synchronous seed germination or both. These characteristics reduce the plant's chances for survival in the wild but enhance the attractiveness of its fruits to humans. Intervention included intentional harvest, storage, and sowing (Smith and Cowan 2003).

Biological, ecological, and cultural factors affect the speed at which changes occur. Hillman and Davies (1999) note that experimental studies suggest that wheat grains may evince morphological changes in response to deliberate planting within a relatively short time period, only 20 to 200 years. A constant level of selective pressure seems unlikely, especially for the Archaic; rather, at least initially, selective pressures were probably more punctuated, with times of focused selection alternating with times when the plants were more or less ignored, or at least infrequently used. Further, over much of the Midwest, constant introgression from wild plants, especially in the case of chenopods, may have precluded establishment of a fully domesticated variety except in a few situations (Gremillion 1993a). Rates of change also vary greatly by species, with some taxa being more malleable than others. Nonetheless, the Hillman and Davies study is important because it shows that, under specific conditions of harvest and storage, genetic change can become established quite rapidly. Theoretically, one should be able to identify "transitional" varieties of ultimately domesticated species in the archaeological record. On a practical level, while manipulation may have a long history, if morphological changes were rapid, intermediaries could be difficult to identify. The idea of rapid change would certainly change expectations of the record (Hastorf 1998).

Further complicating the issue is the lack of continuous local records through which biological changes can be traced. Rather, archaeobotanists piece together sequences on the basis of remains left behind by geographically and temporally disparate groups. Even in areas like the American Bottom of Illinois, from which the sequence is quite strong, there are big gaps in the Archaic-period record. This may reflect the reality of occupation (see above) but is not conducive to identifying processes of domestication.

Many of the most convincing, early records for genetically modified plants come from upland rockshelters or cave sites in the Cumberland Plateau of eastern Kentucky, where large sumpweeds and chenopods appear rather abruptly. This is rugged terrain some distance from broad river valleys characterized by regular fluvial disturbance regimes and colonizing annuals. In light of the floodplain model of plant domestication (Smith 1987, 1992a, 1995), these upland locations provide problematic contexts for domestication processes (Smith and Cowan 2003). Not only are requisite disturbance regimes absent but so, too, are wild progenitors. In fact, modern floral records suggest that *Chenopodium berlandieri* and *Iva annua* are not even native plants in upland eastern Kentucky, where Cloudsplitter, Cold Oak, and Hooton Hollow are located (Gremillion 1993b). Nonetheless, seeds were brought to these shelter sites, presumably for storage (Gremillion 1993b, 1994). The question is, where did they come from?

Gremillion (1993b, 1996, 1998, 2003) has proposed three alternatives: that large seeds were transported to these locations from distant fields of domesticated plants, that they derive from fully domesticated plants transported into the uplands for purposes of propagation, or that they are the progeny of plants that were first introduced to the upland plateau as weedy or transitional forms, not as fully domesticated forms. The last model is especially attractive because it takes into consideration the problems posed by wild plant introgression. The uplands provided a context in which weedy plants could have been propagated in stands that were genetically isolated from wild stands. The area had the added benefit of providing soils that were quite amenable to slash-and-burn agriculture (Ison 1991). Under this scenario, genetic change could have been relatively rapid and well expressed. In fact, upland locations may have been better contexts for final stages of domestication than the alluvial valleys precisely because they provided genetic isolation (Fritz 1990; Gremillion 1993b).

Coevolution provides a conceptual model for how domesticated plants evolved (Rindos 1984). However, as has long been recognized, domestication did not take place in a cultural vacuum. Interest in food production and plant management, culminating in agricultural systems, extends well beyond the Midwest (cf. chapters in Cowan and Watson 1992; Harris and Hillman 1989; Price and Gebauer 1995; as well as the extensive bibliography in Hastorf 1999). For the midwestern United States, early plant manipulation was probably not a response to environmental stress or scarcity (Hayden 1995; B. Smith 1995), even though maximizing efficiency in the event of need is a popular paradigm. At the same time, in some times and places, risk management may have been involved (Gremillion 1993a, 1998, 2004; Keeley 1995), especially during the later stages of the domesticatory process, by which time the potential value of certain plants was well recognized. Socioeconomic competition (Hayden 1995) or the group benefits, whether economic or social, afforded by increased production (Hastorf 1998) could have provided motivation for people to increase crop productive efforts. The desire for individual aggrandizement, to increase individual status, or to provide items for gift exchange (Bender 1978; B. Smith 1995, 2001) may also have motivated people to propagate especially productive subsistence crops or even specialty plants (Asch 1994; Hastorf 1998). The extent to which any of these models applies to the Archaic of the midwestern United States no doubt varies with different situations. In fact, as Watson (1995:22) points out, while human behavior is to some extent predictable, archaeologists are probably remiss in looking for a single covering "law" that explains the transition to agriculture in the Midwest or anywhere else. Different situations demanded different responses. At the same time, the meager archaeobotanical records that are the products of different historical sequences may be quite similar. This is an obvious dilemma, but at least by recognizing it, one can quit looking for single-cause explanations. For the midwestern United States, the Archaic-period plant record has much potential for addressing shifts to a low-level food-production economy in a temperate climate. There is no reason to assume that the sequences in all locales will be identical, and there is still much to be learned about the timing and geographical scale of these developments as well as the environmental and cultural context in which they occurred (Smith and Cowan 2003:106–111).

No single hearth of domestication has been recognized for the midwestern United States (Fritz 1997, 2000; Hastorf 1998; Watson 1985). However, it is not reasonable to assume that domesticated plants arose in every habitable river valley or on every upland plain. The transition to horticultural economies varied greatly both in intensity and in the suites of targeted plants. One must also consider the possibility that cultivated varieties were in some cases introduced and not the products of local development. For example, we have argued that the record for the American Bottom of Illinois was not one of in situ development of a horticultural economy but, rather, one of repeated introductions of both plants and people (Parker and Simon 1994; Simon and Parker 2006). Analysts have to guard against the assumption that the presence of a cultivated plant, even in Archaic-period contexts, is always the result of in situ development (Fortier et al. 2006).

A second aspect of the Archaic plant record that is of particular interest is its ability to contribute to understanding of settlement systems. As the chapters in this volume show, changing patterns of group mobility constitute a major research topic in midwestern archaeology and one in which the quest for food is intimately involved. The relationships between changes in patterns of plant exploitation and spatial tethering are quite complex, particularly if one considers the entire plant record and not just the cultivated plants. It is doubtful that once people actually occupied any part of the Midwest, true "foraging" (if defined as random, exploratory wandering) groups persisted for long. Rather, as McElrath, Fortier, and Emerson argue in chapter 1 of this volume, the Midwest was characterized by population expansion and patterned use of specific microregions. Consequently, the plant record for the Archaic is the result of intentional movements of people on the landscape. For the Southeast, this strategy of "mapping on" to a specific locality may have had very early, Paleoindian-period roots (Anderson 1991, 1996). In the Midwest, the same phenomenon may have occurred once vegetation and climate stabilized to the extent that resources were relatively predictable. The environment of the Midwest changed over the course of the Holocene, both in terms of shifts in biotic zones and changes in landscape physiography, but change was slow. In fact, in terms of individual human generations, changes were probably essentially imperceptible. Consequently, biome-level shifts had little impact on the people occupying different parts of the Midwest during the Archaic, even given that groups moved over extensive territories. No matter how resources were distributed, whether fine or coarse grained, people adjusted their strategies to accommodate availability. They may have moved within a large area, but they were familiar with and understood that area.

Finally, the importance of landscape disturbance must be considered. While it is unreasonable to assume that the prehistoric Eastern Woodlands landscape was completely manufactured (Fritz 2000), people, nevertheless, impacted the places they occupied. Fire, whether intentionally set or not, was a particularly important tool. Fire may have been used for landscape clearance, to drive game, to increase the nut mast, or for yet-undefined purposes during the Archaic period in the Midwest (Styles and McMillan, this volume; Wagner 2003). Tree girdling is another land-clearance and raw-material production technique that has been documented for the late prehistoric Eastern Woodlands (Hammett 2000). Mobile groups moving within a circumscribed territory could easily return to clumps of girdled trees and use the deadwood for numerous tasks, not the least of which was as fuel. However, these important prehistoric behaviors are difficult to identify in the archaeobotanical record, especially for the very distant past.

The manipulation of plants, whether intentionally or unintentionally, has critical consequences for both economic and social systems. At the simplest level, human plant use can be defined as manipulative if it in any way affects a plant's natural cycle. Thus, picking fruit promotes fruit production and clearing ground for a campsite promotes growth of early successional taxa. While Archaic-period plant manipulation may well have originated in these most basic behaviors, it eventually, if inconsistently, expanded beyond them in scope, sophistication, and impact.

The number of analyzed archaeobotanical assemblages from Archaic sites across the Midwest is increasing rapidly. The data they provide are applicable to many areas of study, among which are agricultural origins and the evolution of domesticated plants, settlement systems and increasing sedentism, changes in diet and technology, the development of vegetation models and associated models of resource availability, and assessments of human impact on local landscapes. All of these topics are important, and all have been variously addressed from different perspectives by archaeologists and archaeobotanists working across the Midwest and beyond. While we have perhaps been most successful in outlining a preliminary historical sequence and in identifying important cultivated and ultimately domesticated species, the research potential of archaeobotanical analysis remains enormous.

Acknowledgments

I wish to thank all my colleagues at ITARP for their assistance and advice during the production of this chapter. Dale McElrath, Tom Emerson, and Andy Fortier provided the impetus for its production when they invited me to participate in the Archaic Conference held in Urbana in December 2004. Their support and editorial comments are much appreciated. Mike Farkas and Mike Lewis produced the figures. Mary King and Leighann Calentine helped with data entry and table compilation as well as undertaking the day-to-day management of the ITARP paleoethnobotany lab while I was immersed in the Archaic. Brian Butler and Dick Jefferies provided much needed information about "gray literature" sites in Illinois and Kentucky. Colleagues providing provocative and instructive review include Katie Parker, Gayle Fritz, Neal Lopinot, and Kristin Gremillion. Neal also graciously provided the SEM photographs presented in Figure 4.8. Suggestions and comments from all these individuals have immensely improved readability and content of this chapter. Finally, thanks to Linda Forman for her, as always, excellent technical editing.

References Cited

Adair, Mary
2003 Great Plains Paleoethnobotany. In *People and Plants in Ancient Eastern North America*, edited by Paul E. Minnis, pp. 258–346. Smithsonian Books, Washington, D.C.

Ahler, Steven R.
1984 Archaic Settlement Strategies in the Modoc Locality, Southwest Illinois. Ph.D. dissertation, Department of Anthropology, University of Wisconsin–Milwaukee.
1993 Stratigraphy and Radiocarbon Chronology of Modoc Rock Shelter, Illinois. *American Antiquity* 58:462–489.

Ahler, Steven R., Mary J. Bade, Frances B. King, Bonnie W. Styles, and Paula Thorson
1992 *Late Archaic Components at Modoc Rock Shelter, Randolph County, Illinois*. Reports of Investigations 48. Illinois State Museum, Springfield.

Anderson, David G.
1991 Examining Prehistoric Settlement Distribution in Eastern North America. *Archaeology of Eastern North America* 19:1–22.
1996 Models of Paleoindian and Early Archaic Settlement in the Early Southeast. In *The Paleoindian and Early Archaic Southeast*, edited by David G. Anderson and Kenneth E. Sassaman, pp. 26–57. University of Alabama Press, Tuscaloosa.

Anderson, David G., and Glen T. Hansen
1988 Early Archaic Settlement in the Southeastern United States: A Case Study from the Savannah River Valley. *American Antiquity* 53:262–286.

Anderson, David G., Lisa D. O'Steen, and Kenneth E. Sassaman
1996 Environmental and Chronological Considerations. In *The Paleoindian and Early Archaic Southeast*, edited by David G. Anderson and Kenneth E. Sassaman, pp. 3–15. University of Alabama Press, Tuscaloosa.

Asch, David L.
1994 Aboriginal Specialty Plant Cultivation in Eastern North America: Illinois Prehistory and a Post-Contact Perspective. In *Agricultural Origins and Development in the Midcontinent*, edited by William Green, pp. 25–86. Report 19. Office of the State Archaeologist, University of Iowa, Iowa City.

Asch, David L., and Nancy B. Asch
1982 A Chronology for the Development of Prehistoric Horticulture in Westcentral Illinois. Paper presented at the 47th Annual Meeting of the Society for American Archaeology, Minneapolis, Minnesota.
1985a Prehistoric Plant Cultivation in West Central Illinois. In *Prehistoric Food Production in North America*, edited by Richard I. Ford, pp. 149–203. Anthropological Papers 75. Museum of Anthropology, University of Michigan, Ann Arbor.
1985b Archeobotany of the Campbell Hollow Archaic Occupations. In *The Campbell Hollow Archaic Occupations: A Study of Intrasite Spatial Structure in the Lower Illinois Valley*, edited by C. Russell Stafford, pp. 82–107. Research Series 4. Kampsville Archeological Center, Center for American Archeology, Kampsville, Illinois.
1985c Archeobotany. In *Smiling Dan: Structure and Function at a Middle Woodland Settlement in the Illinois Valley*, edited by Barbara D. Stafford and Mark B. Sant, pp. 327–401. Research Series 2. Kampsville Archeological Center, Center for American Archeology, Kampsville, Illinois.
1987 *Archeobotany of Buckshaw Bridge, an Archaic Site in Brown County, Illinois*. Archeobotanical Laboratory Report 77. Kampsville Archeological Center, Center for American Archeology, Kampsville, Illinois.
1988 Archeobotany of the Sub-Mound 6 Middle Archaic Occupation. In *The Archaic and Woodland Cemeteries at the Elizabeth Site in the Lower Illinois Valley*, edited by Douglas K. Charles, Steven R. Leigh, and Jane E. Buikstra, pp. 296–302. Research Series 7. Kampsville Archeological Center, Center for American Archeology, Kampsville, Illinois.

Asch, Nancy B., and David L. Asch
1978 The Economic Potential of *Iva annua* and Its Prehistoric Importance in the Lower Illinois Valley. In *The Nature and Status of Ethnobotany*, edited by Richard I. Ford, pp. 301–341. Anthropological Papers 67. Museum of Anthropology, University of Michigan, Ann Arbor.
1980 *Archeobotany of Napoleon Hollow, a Multicomponent Site in Pike County, Illinois: Initial Report*. Archeobotanical Laboratory Report 37. Northwestern University Archeological Program, Evanston, Illinois.
1986 Analysis of Plant Remains. In *Cypress Land: A Late Archaic/Early Woodland Site in the Lower Illinois River Floodplain*, edited by Michael D. Conner, pp. 60–72. Technical Reports 2. Kampsville Archeological Center, Center for American Archeology, Kampsville, Illinois.

Asch, Nancy B., Richard I. Ford, and David L. Asch
1972 Paleoethnobotany of the Koster Site: The Archaic Horizons. In *Illinois Valley Archaeological Program Research Papers*, vol. 6, edited by Stuart Struever, pp. 1–34. Reports of Investigations 24. Illinois State Museum, Springfield.

Baker, Richard G., Louis J. Maher, Craig A. Chumbley, and Kent L. Van Zant
1992 Patterns of Holocene Environmental Change in the Midwestern United States. *Quaternary Research* 37:379–389.

Bender, Barbara
1978 Hunter Gatherer to Farmer: A Social Perspective. *World Archaeology* 10:204–222.

Benn, David W., and Neal H. Lopinot
1996 Prehistoric Occupations at Cobb Cave in the Western Ozarks. *The Missouri Archaeologist* 54:53–78.

Binford, Lewis R.
1980 "Willow Smoke and Dogs' Tails": Hunter-Gatherer Settlement Systems and Archaeological Site Formation. *American Antiquity* 45:4–20.

Bonzani, Renee M.
2001 Plant Remains from Test Excavations at the Ward Site. In *Cypress Creek Archaeological Project: Archaic Adaptive Strategies in West Central Kentucky*, edited by Richard W. Jefferies, V. Thompson, and George Milner, pp. 158–174. Report submitted to the National Park Service, U.S. Department of the Interior, Washington D.C. Kentucky Heritage Council, Frankfort.
2004 Botanical Analysis. In *Data Recovery Excavations at the Cranks Creek Site (15Hl58), Harlan County Kentucky*, by Jessica L. Algood, Andrew P. Bradbury, Renee M. Bonzani, Daniel R. Hays, Jonathan P. Kerr, Andrew V. Martin, and Michael D. Richmond. Contract Publication Series 01-118. Cultural Resource Analysts, Lexington, Kentucky.

Brewer, Andrea J.
1973 Analysis of Floral Remains from the Higgs Site (40Lo45). In *Excavation of the Higgs and Doughty Sites I-75 Salvage Archaeology*, edited by M. C. R. McCollough and C. H. Faulkner, pp. 141–144. Miscellaneous Paper 12. Tennessee Archaeological Society, Knoxville.

Brown, James A.
1985 Long-Term Trends to Sedentism and the Emergence of Complexity in the American Midwest. In *Prehistoric Hunter-Gatherers: The Emergence of Cultural Complexity*, edited by T. Douglas Price and James A. Brown, pp. 201–231. Academic Press, New York.

Brown, James A., and Robert K. Vierra
1983 What Happened in the Middle Archaic? In *Archaic Hunters and Gatherers in the American Midwest*, edited by James L. Phillips and James A. Brown, pp. 165–195. Academic Press, New York.

Calentine, Leighann
2005 Plant Remains from the Crosstown Road Site (11Ri693). Report on file, Illinois Transportation Archaeological Research Program, Department of Anthropology, University of Illinois, Champaign.

Chapman, Jefferson
1973 *The Icehouse Bottom Site (40MR23)*. Report of Investigations 13. Department of Anthropology, University of Tennessee, Knoxville.
1975 *The Rose Island Site and the Bifurcate Point Tradition*. Report of Investigations 14. Department of Anthropology, University of Tennessee, Knoxville.
1977 *Archaic Period Research in the Lower Little Tennessee River Valley*. Report of Investigations 18. Department of Anthropology, University of Tennessee, Knoxville.
1978 *The Bacon Farm Site and a Buried Site Reconnaissance*. Report of Investigations 23. Department of Anthropology, University of Tennessee, Knoxville.
1979 *The Howard and Calloway Island Sites*. Report of Investigations 27. Department of Anthropology, University of Tennessee, Knoxville.
1981 *The Bacon Bend and Iddens Sites: The Late Archaic Period in the Lower Little Tennessee River Valley*. Report of Investigations 31. Department of Anthropology, University of Tennessee, Knoxville.

Chapman, Jefferson, Paul A. Delcourt, Patricia A. Cridlebaugh, Andrea B. Shea, and Hazel R. Delcourt
1982 Man-Land Interaction: 10,000 Years of American Indian Impact on Native Ecosystems in the Lower Little Tennessee River Valley, Eastern Tennessee. *Southeastern Archaeology* 1:115–121.

Chapman, Jefferson, and Andrea Brewer Shea
1981 The Archaeobotanical Record: Early Archaic to Contact in the Lower Little Tennessee River Valley. *Tennessee Anthropologist* 6:61–84.

Chapman, Jefferson, and Patty Jo Watson
1993 The Archaic Period and the Flotation Revolution. In *Foraging and Farming in the Eastern Woodlands*, edited by C. Margaret Scarry, pp. 27–38. University Press of Florida, Gainesville.

Cowan, C. Wesley
1985 Understanding the Evolution of Plant Husbandry in Eastern North America: Lessons from Botany, Ethnography, and Archaeology. In *Prehistoric Food Production in Eastern North America*, edited by Richard I. Ford, pp. 205–243. Anthropological Papers 75. Museum of Anthropology, University of Michigan, Ann Arbor.
1997 Evolutionary Changes Associated with the Domestication of *Cucurbita pepo*: Evidence from Eastern Kentucky. In *People, Plants, and Landscapes: Studies in Paleoethnobotany*, edited by Kristen J. Gremillion, pp. 63–85. University of Alabama Press, Tuscaloosa.

Cowan, C. Wesley, H. Edwin Jackson, Katherine Moore, Andrew Nickelhoff, and Tristine L. Smart
1981 The Cloudsplitter Rockshelter, Menifee County Kentucky: A Preliminary Report. *Southeastern Archaeological Conference Bulletin* 24:60–76.

Cowan, C. Wesley, and Bruce D. Smith
1993 New Perspectives on a Wild Gourd in Eastern North America. *Journal of Ethnobiology* 13:17–54.

Cowan, C. Wesley, and Patty Jo Watson (editors)
1992 *The Origins of Agriculture*. Smithsonian Institution Press, Washington, D.C.

Crawford, Gary W.
1982 Late Archaic Plant Remains from West-Central Kentucky: A Summary. *Midcontinental Journal of Archaeology* 7:205–224.

Crawford, Gary W., and David G. Smith
2003 Paleoethnobotany in the Northeast. In *People and Plants in Ancient Eastern North America*, edited by Paul E. Minnis, pp. 172–257. Smithsonian Books, Washington, D.C.

Cremin, William M.
1992 Botanical Analysis. In *The Little Muddy Rock Shelter: A Deeply Stratified Prehistoric Site in the Southern Till Plains of Illinois*, edited by Charles R. Moffat, Brad Koldehoff, William M. Cremin, Terrance J. Martin, Mary Carol Masulis, and Mary R. McCorvie, pp. 375–425. Cultural Resource Management Report 186. American Resources Group, Carbondale, Illinois.

Crites, Gary
1986 Plant Remains. In *The Chapman Site: A Terminal Archaic Settlement in the Middle Cumberland River Drainage of Tennessee*, edited by Charles Bentz, pp. 97–105. Miscellaneous Paper 11. Tennessee Anthropological Association, Knoxville.

1987 Middle and Late Holocene Ethnobotany of the Hayes Site (40ML139): Evidence from Unit 990N918E. *Midcontinental Journal of Archaeology* 12:3–32.

1988 Plant Remains. In *The Baily Site (40GL26): Late Archaic, Middle Woodland, and Historic Settlement and Subsistence in the Lower Elk River Drainage of Tennessee*, edited by Charles Bentz Jr., pp. 279–283. Publications in Archaeology 2. Tennessee Department of Transportation, Environmental Planning Office, Knoxville.

1993 Domesticated Sunflower in Fifth Millennium B.P. Temporal Contexts: New Evidence from Middle Tennessee. *American Antiquity* 58:146–148.

Crothers, George Martin

1999 Prehistoric Hunters and Gatherers, and the Archaic Period Green River Shell Middens of Western Kentucky. Ph.D. dissertation, Department of Anthropology, Washington University, St. Louis, Missouri.

Decker, Deena S.

1988 Origin(s), Evolution, and Systematics of *Cucurbita pepo* (Cucurbitaceae). *Economic Botany* 42:4–15.

Decker-Walters, Deena S.

1993 New Methods for Studying the Origins of New World Domesticates: The Squash Example. In *Foraging and Farming in the Eastern Woodlands*, edited by C. Margaret Scarry, pp. 91–97. University Press of Florida, Gainesville.

Decker-Walters, Deena S., Terrence W. Walters, C. Wesley Cowan, and Bruce D. Smith

1993 Isozymic Characterization of Wild Populations of *Cucurbita pepo*. *Journal of Ethnobiology* 13:55–72.

Delcourt, Paul A., and Hazel R. Delcourt

1983 Late Quaternary Vegetational Dynamics and Community Stability Reconsidered. *Quaternary Research* 19:265–271.

1987 *Long-Term Forest Dynamics of the Temperate Zone: A Case Study of Late Quaternary Forests of Eastern North America*. Springer-Verlag, New York.

Delcourt, Paul A., Hazel R. Delcourt, Cecil R. Ison, William E. Sharp, and Kristen Gremillion

1998 Prehistoric Human Use of Fire, the Eastern Agricultural Complex, and Appalachian Oak-Chestnut Forests: Paleoecology of Cliff Palace Pond, Kentucky. *American Antiquity* 63:263–278.

Densmore, Frances

1974 *How Indians Use Wild Plants for Food, Medicine, and Crafts*. Reprinted, Dover Publications, New York. Originally published 1928 as "Uses of Plants by the Chippewa Indians," Annual Report of the Bureau of American Ethnology 44:273–379, Smithsonian Institution, Washington, D.C.

Dincauze, Dena F.

1996 Modeling Communities and Other Thankless Tasks. In *The Paleoindian and Early Archaic Southeast*, edited by David G. Anderson and Kenneth E. Sassaman, pp. 421–424. University of Alabama Press, Tuscaloosa.

Dixon, Anna R.

1995 Plant Remains. In *The Aenon Creek Site (40Mu493): Late Archaic, Middle Woodland, and Historic Settlement and Subsistence in the Middle Duck River Drainage of Tennessee*, edited by Charles Bentz, pp. 103–115. Publications in Archaeology 1. Tennessee Department of Transportation Environmental Planning Office, Knoxville.

Dunne, Michael T., and William Green

1998 Terminal Archaic and Early Woodland Plant Use at the Gast Spring Site (13LA152), Southeast Iowa. *Midcontinental Journal of Archaeology* 23:45–88.

Edging, Richard

n.d Temporal Variation in Botanical Exploitation Patterns. In The Archaeology of the Northern Ozarks: A Case Study of Marginality, edited by Paul P. Kreisa, Steven R. Ahler, and Richard Edging. Manuscript on file, U.S. Army Construction Engineering Research Laboratory, Champaign, Illinois.

Egan, Kathryn C.

1987 Analysis of the Floral Remains from the Weber I Site (20SA581) Frankenmuth, Michigan. Paper presented at the Midwest Archaeological Conference, Milwaukee, Wisconsin.

1988 Middle and Late Archaic Phytogeography and Floral Exploitation in the Upper Great Lakes. *Midcontinental Journal of Archaeology* 13:81–107.

1995 Appendix IX: Floral Analysis at the River Quarry (47 Da-768) and Murphy/S. Ziegler II (47 Da-739/965) Sites. In *Archaeological Investigations of the Alternate Corridor Alignments for the Proposed Reconstruction of U.S.H. 12 between Middleton and Sauk City, Dane County, Wisconsin*, edited by K. Hamilton, D. Tennessen, S. Slessman, and M. Baumann, pp. 262–287. Research Report in Archaeology 46. Museum Archaeology Program, Wisconsin Historical Society, Madison.

Egan-Bruhy, Kathryn C.

1997 Appendix I: Paleoethnobotanical Analysis: Crow Hollow (47 Cr-598) and Kickapoo Hill (47 Cr-599), Crawford County, Wisconsin. In *Archaeological Investigations at the Bell Center Wetland Mitigation Area, Crawford County, Wisconsin*, edited by S. R. Kuehn, pp. 118–124. Research Report in Archaeology 63. Museum Archaeology Program, Wisconsin Historical Society, Madison.

Emerson, Thomas E., and Dale L. McElrath

1983 A Settlement-Subsistence Model of the Terminal Late Archaic Adaptation in the American Bottom, Illinois. In *Archaic Hunters and Gatherers in the American Midwest*, edited by James L. Phillips and James A. Brown, pp. 219–242. Academic Press, New York.

Faulkner, Charles H., Michael W. Corkran, and Paul W. Parmalee

1976 Report of Floral and Faunal Remains Recovered in 1972 Excavations on the Banks III Site (40CF108). In *Third Report of the Normandy Reservoir Salvage Project*, edited by Major C. R. McCollough and Charles H. Faulkner, pp. 217–238. Report of Investigations 16. Department of Anthropology, University of Tennessee, Knoxville.

Faulkner, Charles H., and Major C. R. McCollough (editors)

1977 *Fourth Report of the Normandy Archaeological Project*. Report of Investigations 19. Department of Anthropology, University of Tennessee, Knoxville.

Finney, Fred A., Scott B. Meyer, and Kathryn E. Parker

1992 *Phase III Archaeological Investigations of a Middle Archaic Raddatz Occupation at the Bobwhite Site (47Ri185), Richland County, Wisconsin*. Research Papers 17(2).

Office of the State Archaeologist, University of Iowa, Iowa City.

Ford, Richard I.

1978 Ethnobotany: Historical Review. In *The Nature and Status of Ethnobotany*, edited by Richard I. Ford, pp. 33–49. Anthropological Papers 67. Museum of Anthropology, University of Michigan, Ann Arbor.

1981 Gardening and Farming before AD 1000: Patterns of Prehistoric Cultivation North of Mexico. *Journal of Ethnobiology* 1:6–27.

1985 The Process of Plant Food Production in Prehistoric North America. In *Prehistoric Food Production in North America*, edited by Richard I. Ford, pp. 1–18. Anthropological Papers 75. Museum of Anthropology, University of Michigan, Ann Arbor.

Fortier, Andrew C., Thomas E. Emerson, and Dale L. McElrath

2006 Calibrating and Reassessing American Bottom Culture History. *Southeastern Archaeology* 25:170-211.

Fritz, Gayle J.

1990 Multiple Pathways to Farming in Precontact Eastern North America. *Journal of World Prehistory* 4:387–435.

1994 In Color and In Time: Prehistoric Ozark Agriculture. In *Agricultural Origins and Development in the Midcontinent*, edited by William Green, pp. 105–126. Report 19. Office of the State Archaeologist, University of Iowa, Iowa City.

1997 A Three Thousand Year Old Cache of Crop Seeds from Marble Bluff, Arkansas. In *People, Plants, and Landscapes: Studies in Paleoethnobotany*, edited by Kristen J. Gremillion, pp. 42–62. University of Alabama Press, Tuscaloosa.

1999 Gender and the Early Cultivation of Gourds in Eastern North America. *American Antiquity* 64:417–430.

2000 Levels of Native Biodiversity in Eastern North America. In *Biodiversity and Native America*, edited by Paul E. Minnis and Wayne J. Elisens, pp. 223–247. University of Oklahoma Press, Norman.

Gilmore, Melvin R.

1977 *Uses of Plants by the Indians of the Missouri River Region*. Reprinted. University of Nebraska Press, Lincoln. Originally published 1919, Annual Report of the Bureau of American Ethnology 33, Smithsonian Institution, Washington, D.C.

Gramly, Michael, and Robert E. Funk

1991 Olive Branch Site: A Large Dalton and Pre-Dalton Encampment at Thebes Gap, Alexander County Illinois. In *The Archaic Period in the Mid-South: Proceedings of the 1989 Mid-South Archaeological Conference*, edited by Charles H. McNutt, pp. 23–34. Archaeological Report 24. Mississippi Department of Archives and History, Jackson.

Gremillion, Kristen J.

1993a Crop and Weed in Prehistoric North America: The *Chenopodium* Example. *American Antiquity* 58:496–509.

1993b Plant Husbandry at the Archaic/Woodland Transition: Evidence from the Cold Oak Shelter, Kentucky. *Midcontinental Journal of Archaeology* 18:161–189.

1994 Evidence of Plant Domestication from Kentucky Caves and Rockshelters. In *Agricultural Origins and Development in the Midcontinent*, edited by William Green, pp. 87–103. Report 19. Office of the State Archaeologist, University of Iowa, Iowa City.

1995 Botanical Contents of Paleofeces from Two Eastern Kentucky Rockshelters. In *Current Archaeological Research in Kentucky*, vol. 3, edited John F. Doershuk, Christopher A. Bergman, and David Pollack, pp. 52–69. Kentucky Heritage Council, Frankfort.

1996 Diffusion and Adoption of Crops in an Evolutionary Perspective. *Journal of Anthropological Archaeology* 15:183–204.

1997 New Perspectives on the Paleoethnobotany of the Newt Kash Shelter. In *People, Plants, and Landscapes: Studies in Paleoethnobotany*, edited by Kristen J. Gremillion, pp. 23–41. University of Alabama Press, Tuscaloosa.

1998 Changing Roles of Wild and Cultivated Plant Resources among Early Farmers of Eastern Kentucky. *Southeastern Archaeology* 17:140–157.

2003 Eastern Woodland Overview. In *People and Plants in Eastern North America*, edited by Paul E. Minnis, pp. 17–49. Smithsonian Books, Washington, D.C.

2004 Seed Processing and the Origins of Food Production in Eastern North America. *American Antiquity* 69:215–233.

Gremillion, Kristen J., and Kristin D. Sobolik

1996 Dietary Variability among Prehistoric Forager-Farmers of Eastern North America. *Current Anthropology* 37:528–539.

Hajic, Edwin R., Rolfe D. Mandel, Jack H. Ray, and Neal H. Lopinot

1998 Geomorphology and Geoarchaeology. In *The 1997 Excavations at the Big Eddy Site (23CE426) in Southwest Missouri*, edited by Jack H. Ray, Neal H. Lopinot, and Michael D. Conner, pp. 74–110. Special Publication. Center for Archaeological Research, Southwest Missouri State University, Springfield.

Hamilton, M. Colleen, Patti Wright, Hanna Stazewski-Kruel, Joseph M. Nixon, and Neal H. Lopinot

1986 *Report of Extensive Archaeological Testing at the Lone Wolf Site, 23SL467, South St. Louis County, Missouri*. Research Report 41. Archaeological Survey, Division of Continuing Education-Extension, University of Missouri, St. Louis.

Hammett, Julia E.

2000 Ethnohistory of Aboriginal Landscapes in the Southeastern United States. In *Biodiversity and Native America*, edited by Paul E. Minnis and Wayne J. Elisens, pp. 248–300. University of Oklahoma Press, Norman.

Harris, David R., and Gordon C. Hillman (editors)

1989 *Foraging and Farming: The Evolution of Plant Exploitation*. Unwin Hyman, London.

Hart, John P., and Nancy Asch Sidell

1997 Additional Evidence for Early Cucurbit Use in the Northern Eastern Woodlands East of the Allegheny Front. *American Antiquity* 62:523–537.

Hart, John P., Robert A. Daniels, and Charles J. Sheviak

2004 Do *Cucurbita pepo* Gourds Float Fishnets? *American Antiquity* 69:141–148.

Hastorf, Christine A.

1998 The Cultural Life of Early Domestic Plant Use. *Antiquity* 72:773–782.

1999 Recent Research in Paleoethnobotany. *Journal of Archaeological Research* 7:55–103.

Hayden, Brian

1995 A New Overview of Domestication. In *Last Hunters First Farmers: New Perspectives on the Transition to Agriculture*, edited by T. Douglas Price and Anne Birgitte Gebauer, pp. 273–346. School of American Research Press, Santa Fe, New Mexico.

Heiser, Charles B., Jr.

1954 Variation and Subspeciation in the Common Sunflower, *Helianthus annuus*. *American Midland Naturalist* 51:287–305.

1985 Some Botanical Considerations of the Early Domesticated Plants North of Mexico. In *Prehistoric Food Production in North America*, edited by Richard I. Ford, pp. 57–72. Anthropological Papers 75. Museum of Anthropology, University of Michigan, Ann Arbor.

Higgins, Michael

1990 *The Nochta Site: The Early, Middle, and Late Archaic Occupations*. American Bottom Archaeology FAI 270 Site Reports 21. University of Illinois Press, Urbana.

Hillman, Gordon C., and M. Stuart Davies

1999 Domestication Rate in Wild Wheats and Barley under Primitive Cultivation: Preliminary Results and Archaeological Implications of Field Measurements of Selection Coefficient. In *Prehistory of Agriculture: New Experimental and Ethnographic Approaches*, edited by Patricia C. Anderson, pp. 70–102. Monograph 40. Institute of Archaeology, University of California, Los Angeles.

Hunter, Andrea

1986 Appendix D. Analysis of Plant Remains. In *Archaeological Excavations at the Fitzgibbons Site, Gallatin County, Illinois*, edited by Cathy A. Robison, pp. 219–234. Research Paper 58. Center for Archaeological Investigations, Southern Illinois University, Carbondale.

Ison, Cecil R.

1988 The Cold Oak Shelter: Providing a Better Understanding of the Terminal Archaic. In *Paleoindian and Archaic Research in Kentucky*, edited by Charles D. Hockensmith, David Pollack, and Thomas N. Sanders, pp. 205–219. Kentucky Heritage Council, Frankfort.

1991 Prehistoric Upland Farming along the Cumberland Plateau. In *Studies in Kentucky Archaeology*, edited by Charles D. Hockensmith, pp. 1–10. Kentucky Heritage Council, Frankfort.

Jackson, R. C.

1960 A Revision of the Genus *Iva* L. *University of Kansas Science Bulletin* 41:793–807.

Jacobson, George L., and Eric C. Grimm

1988 Synchrony of Rapid Change in Late Glacial Vegetation South of the Laurentide Ice Shield. In *Late Pleistocene and Early Holocene Paleoecology and Archeology of the Eastern Great Lakes Region*, edited by R. S. Laub, N. G. Miller, and D. W. Steadman, pp. 31–38. Bulletin 33. Buffalo Society of Natural Sciences, Buffalo, New York.

Jefferies, Richard

1988 Archaic Period Research in Kentucky: Past Accomplishments and Future Directions. In *Paleoindian and Archaic Research in Kentucky*, edited by Charles D. Hockensmith, David Pollack, and Thomas N. Sanders, pp. 85–126. Kentucky Heritage Council, Frankfort.

1990 Archaic Period. In *The Archaeology of Kentucky: Past Accomplishments and Future Directions*, vol. 1, edited by David Pollack, pp. 143–246. State Historic Preservation Comprehensive Plan Report 1. Kentucky Heritage Council, Frankfort.

Johannessen, Sissel

1983 Plant Remains from the Missouri Pacific #2 Site. In *The Missouri Pacific #2 Site (11-S-46)*, edited by Dale L. McElrath and Andrew C. Fortier, pp. 191–207. American Bottom Archaeology FAI-270 Site Reports 3. University of Illinois Press, Urbana.

1984a Plant Remains. In *The Go-Kart North Site*, edited by Andrew C. Fortier, pp. 166–178. American Bottom Archaeology FAI-270 Site Reports 9. University of Illinois Press, Urbana.

1984b Floral Resources and Remains. In *The Dyroff and Levin Sites*, edited by Thomas E. Emerson, pp. 294–307. American Bottom Archaeology FAI-270 Site Reports 9. University of Illinois Press, Urbana.

1984c Paleoethnobotany. In *American Bottom Archaeology: A Summary of the FAI-270 Project Contribution to the Culture History of the Mississippi River Valley*, edited by Charles J. Bareis and James W. Porter, pp. 197–214. University of Illinois Press, Urbana.

1986 Plant Remains. In *The McLean Site (11-S-640)*, edited by Dale L. McElrath, pp. 85–99. American Bottom Archaeology FAI-270 Site Reports 14. University of Illinois Press, Urbana.

1987 Floral Remains. In *The Range Site: Archaic through Late Woodland Occupations*, edited by John E. Kelly, Andrew C. Fortier, Steven J. Ozuk, and Joyce A. Williams, pp. 102–105. American Bottom Archaeology FAI-270 Site Reports 16. University of Illinois Press, Urbana.

1988 Plant Remains and Culture Change: Are Paleoethnobotanical Data Better Than We Think? In *Current Paleoethnobotany*, edited by Christine A. Hastorf and Virginia S. Popper, pp. 145–166. University of Chicago Press, Chicago.

Kay, Marvin

1983 Archaic Period Research in the Ozark Highland. In *Archaic Hunters and Gatherers in the American Midwest*, edited by James L. Phillips and James A. Brown, pp. 41–70. Academic Press, New York.

Kay, Marvin, Frances B. King, and Christine K. Robinson

1980 Cucurbits from Phillips Spring: New Evidence and Interpretation. *American Antiquity* 45:806–822.

Keeley, Lawrence H.

1995 Proto-Agricultural Practices among Hunter-Gatherers: A Cross Cultural Survey. In *Last Hunters First Farmers: New Perspectives on the Prehistoric Transition to Agriculture*, edited by T. Douglas Price and Anne Birgitte Gebauer, pp. 243–272. School of American Research Press, Santa Fe, New Mexico.

Keene, Arthur S.

1981 *Prehistoric Foraging in a Temperate Forest*. Academic Press, New York.

Kimball, Larry R.

1996 Early Archaic Settlement and Technology: Lessons from Tellico. In *The Paleoindian and Early Archaic*

Southeast, edited by David G. Anderson and Kenneth E. Sassaman, pp. 149–186. University of Alabama Press, Tuscaloosa.

King, Frances B.

1980 Plant Remains from Phillips Spring, a Multicomponent Site in the Western Ozark Highland of Missouri. *Plains Anthropologist* 29:217–227.

1981a *Analysis of Plant Remains from the 1980 Excavations at Modoc.* Completion Report to the Department of the Interior, Heritage Conservation and Recreation Service and the Illinois Department of Conservation. Illinois State Museum, Springfield.

1981b Plant Remains from Labras Lake. In *Labras Lake: Investigations into the Prehistoric Occupations of a Mississippi Floodplain Locality in St. Clair County, Illinois*, edited by James L. Phillips and Robert L. Hall, pp. 310–319. Department of Anthropology, University of Illinois at Chicago Circle.

1982 Analysis of Archaeobotanical Remains. In *The Cannon Reservoir Human Ecology Project: An Archaeological Study of Cultural Adaptations in the Southern Prairie Peninsula*, edited by Michael J. O'Brien, Robert E. Warren, and Dennis E. Lewarch, pp. 197–213. Academic Press, New York.

1984 *Plants, People, and Paleoecology.* Scientific Papers 20. Illinois State Museum, Springfield.

1985 Early Cultivated Cucurbits in Eastern North America. In *Prehistoric Food Production in North America*, edited by Richard I. Ford, pp. 73–97. Anthropological Papers 75. Museum of Anthropology, University of Michigan, Ann Arbor.

1987 Bioarchaeology at Labras Lake. In *Prehistoric Life on the Mississippi Floodplain: Stone Tool Use, Settlement Organization, and Subsistence Practices at the Labras Lake Site, Illinois*, edited by Richard W. Yerkes, pp. 95–113. University of Chicago Press, Chicago.

1992 Analysis of Plant Remains. In *Late Archaic Components at Modoc Rock Shelter, Randolph County, Illinois*, edited by Steven R. Ahler, Mary J. Bade, Frances B. King, Bonnie W. Styles, and Paula J. Thorson, pp. 81–92. Reports of Investigations 48. Illinois State Museum, Springfield.

King, James E., and Everett H. Lindsay

1976 Late Quaternary Biotic Records from Spring Deposits in Western Missouri. In *Prehistoric Man and His Environment: A Case Study in the Ozark Highland*, edited W. Raymond Wood and R. Bruce McMillan, pp. 63–78. Academic Press, New York.

Koeppen, Robert C., and Lawrence A. Conrad

1974 An Analysis of Charcoal from the Cherokee Sewer Site. *Journal of the Iowa Archeological Society* 21:145–146.

Lannie, Donna Dean

1979 Ethnobotanical Analysis. In *Excavations at Four Archaic Sites in the Lower Ohio Valley, Jefferson County, Kentucky*, vol. 2, edited by Michael B. Collins, pp. 978–1006. Occasional Papers in Anthropology 1. Department of Anthropology, University of Kentucky, Louisville.

Ledbetter, R. Jerald, and Lisa D. O'Steen

1992 The Grayson Site: Late Archaic and Late Woodland Occupations in the Little Sandy Drainage. In *Current Archaeological Research in Kentucky*, vol. 2, edited by David Pollack and A. Gwynn Henderson, pp. 13–42. Kentucky Heritage Council, Frankfort.

Lopinot, Neal H.

1982 Plant Macroremains and Paleoethnobotanical Implications. In *The Carrier Mills Archaeological Project, Human Adaptation in the Saline Valley, Illinois*, vol. 1, edited by Richard W. Jefferies and Brian M. Butler, pp. 673–860. Research Paper 33. Center for Archaeological Investigations, Southern Illinois University, Carbondale.

1983 Analysis of Flotation Sample Materials from the Late Archaic Horizon. In *The 1982 Excavations at the Cahokia Interpretive Center Tract, St. Clair County, Illinois*, edited by Michael S. Nassaney, Neal H. Lopinot, Brian M. Butler, and Richard W. Jefferies, pp. 77–108. Research Paper 37. Center for Archaeological Investigations, Southern Illinois University, Carbondale.

1984 Archaeobotanical Formation Processes and Late Middle Archaic Human-Plant Interrelationships in the Midcontinental U.S.A. Ph.D. dissertation, Department of Anthropology, Southern Illinois University, Carbondale.

1987 Archaeobotany. In *Archaeology in the Mississippi River Floodplain at Sand Run Slough, Iowa*, by David W. Benn, E. Arthur Bettis III, Arthur Hoppin, Lucretia S. Kelly, Neal H. Lopinot, and David G. Stanley, pp. 203–235. CAR 690. Center for Archaeological Research, Southwest Missouri State University, Springfield.

1991 The Diana Site (11Ri-331), an Archaic and Woodland Settlement in Southwestern Illinois. *Illinois Archaeology* 3:113–202.

1998 Analysis of Flotation Samples. In *The 1997 Excavations at the Big Eddy Site (23CE426) in Southwest Missouri*, edited by Jack H. Ray, Neal H. Lopinot, and Michael D. Conner, pp. 266–287. Special Publication 2. Center for Archaeological Research, Southwest Missouri State University, Springfield.

2000 Late Archaic and Woodland Archaeobotany in Southeast Missouri and Northeast Arkansas: Status, Trends, and Problems. Paper presented at the 57th Southeastern Archaeological Conference, Macon, Georgia.

Lopinot, Neal H., M. Denise Hutto, and David P. Braun

1982 *Archaeological Investigations at the Kingfish Site, St. Clair County, Illinois.* Research Paper 25. Center for Archaeological Investigations, Southern Illinois University, Carbondale.

Lovis, William A.

1986 Environmental Periodicity, Buffering, and Archaic Adaptations of the Saginaw Valley of Michigan. In *Foraging, Collecting, and Harvesting: Archaic Period Subsistence and Settlement in the Eastern Woodlands*, edited by Sarah W. Neusius, pp. 99–116. Occasional Papers 6. Center for Archaeological Investigations, Southern Illinois University, Carbondale.

Lovis, William A., and James A. Robertson

1989 Rethinking the Archaic Chronology of the Saginaw Valley, Michigan. *Midcontinental Journal of Archaeology* 14:226–260.

McElrath, Dale L.

1993 Mule Road: A Newly Defined Late Archaic Phase in the American Bottom. In *Highways to the Past: Essays on Illinois Archaeology in Honor of Charles J. Bareis*, edited by Thomas E. Emerson, Andrew C. Fortier, and Dale L. McElrath, pp. 148–157. *Illinois Archaeology* 5(1–2).

Moerman, Daniel E

1998 *Native American Ethnobotany.* Timber Press, Portland, Oregon.

Munson, Patrick J.

1986 What Happened in the Archaic in the Midwestern United States? *Reviews in Anthropology* 13:276–282.

Neusius, Sarah W. (editor)

1987 *Foraging, Collecting, and Harvesting: Archaic Period Subsistence and Settlement in the Eastern Woodlands.* Occasional Papers 6. Center for Archaeological Investigations, Southern Illinois University, Carbondale.

Newsom, Lee A., S. David Webb, and James S. Dunbar

1993 History and Geographic Distribution of *Cucurbita pepo* Gourds in Florida. *Journal of Ethnobiology* 13:75–97.

Parachini, Kathryn E.

1983 Natural Harvest: Prehistoric Relationships between Man and the Environment in Southwest Michigan. Paper presented at the Midwest Archaeological Conference, Iowa City, Iowa.

Parker, Kathryn E.

1986 Archaeobotany. In *The Meyer Site (11-S-321), a Late Archaic Occupation in the American Bottom,* edited by Andrew C. Fortier, pp. 40–45. FAI 270 Archaeological Mitigation Project Report 72. Department of Anthropology, University of Illinois, Urbana-Champaign.

1990 Early Archaic Archaeobotany. In *The Nochta Site: The Early, Middle, and Late Archaic Occupations,* edited by Michael J. Higgins, pp. 231–236. American Bottom Archaeology FAI 270 Site Reports 21. University of Illinois Press, Urbana.

1993 Plant Remains from Archaeological Testing at the South Roxana Site (11-Ms-66). Report on file, Illinois Transportation Archaeological Research Program, University of Illinois, Champaign.

1998a Macrobotanical Remains from Archaeological Excavations at the Christianson Site (11-Ri-42). Report on file, Illinois Transportation Archaeological Research Program, University of Illinois, Champaign.

1998b Botanical Remains. In *Archaeological Investigations at the Cave Creek Rockshelter (11J-822), Jackson County, Illinois,* by Brian G. DelCastello and Brian M. Butler, pp. 74–76. Technical Report 98-3. Center for Archaeological Investigations, Southern Illinois University, Carbondale.

1999 Prehistoric Botanical Remains. In *Archaeological Investigations at the Rose Hotel (11Hn116), Hardin County, Illinois,* edited by Michael J. Wagner and Brian M. Butler, pp. 395–408. Technical Report 99-3. Center for Archaeological Investigations, Southern Illinois University, Carbondale.

2000 Plant Remains from the Hills Branch Site. In *Archaeological Investigations at Dixon Springs State Park: The Hills Branch Rock Shelter, Pope County, Illinois,* edited by Michael J. Wagner and Brian M. Butler, pp. 145–154. Technical Report 00-2. Center for Archaeological Investigations, Southern Illinois University, Carbondale.

2001 Macrobotanical Remains from Archaeological Excavations at the Floyd Site. In *The Floyd Site: A Terminal Archaic Habitation in the Northern American Bottom,* edited by J. Bryant Evans, pp. 117–126. Transportation Archaeological Research Reports 11. Illinois Transportation Archaeological Research Program, Department of Anthropology, University of Illinois, Urbana-Champaign.

Parker, Kathryn E., and Mary L. Simon

1994 Exploitation and Manipulation: Prehistoric Human-Plant Relationships in the Central Mississippi River Valley. Paper presented at the combined Southeastern Archaeological and Midwest Archaeological Conference, Lexington, Kentucky.

Parmalee, Paul W., R. Bruce McMillan, and Frances B. King

1976 Changing Subsistence Patterns at Rodgers Shelter. In *Prehistoric Man and His Environments: A Case Study in the Ozark Highland,* edited by W. Raymond Wood and R. Bruce McMillan, pp. 141–161. Academic Press, New York.

Perkl, Bradley E.

1998 *Cucurbita pepo* from King Coulee, Southeastern Minnesota. *American Antiquity* 63:279–288.

Petersen, James B., and Nancy Asch Sidell

1996 Mid-Holocene Evidence of *Cucurbita* sp. from Central Maine. *American Antiquity* 61:685–698.

Prentice, Guy

1986 Origins of Plant Domestication in the Eastern United States: Promoting the Individual in Archaeological Theory. *Southeastern Archaeology* 5:103–119.

Price, T. Douglas, and Anne Birgitte Gebauer (editors)

1995 *Last Hunters First Farmers: New Perspectives on the Prehistoric Transition to Agriculture.* School of American Research Press, Santa Fe, New Mexico.

Rindos, David

1984 *The Origins of Agriculture: An Evolutionary Perspective.* Academic Press, New York.

Rindos, David, and Sissel Johannessen

1991 Human-Plant Interaction and Cultural Change in the American Bottom. In *Cahokia and the Hinterlands: Middle Mississippian Cultures of the Midwest,* edited by Thomas E. Emerson and R. Barry Lewis, pp. 35–45. University of Illinois Press, Urbana.

Robertson, James A., William A. Lovis, and John R. Halsey

1999 The Late Archaic: Hunters and Gatherers in an Uncertain Environment. In *Retrieving Michigan's Buried Past: The Archaeology of the Great Lake State,* edited by John R. Halsey, pp. 95–124. Bulletin 64. Cranbrook Institute of Science, Bloomfield Hills, Michigan.

Rossen, Jack

1992 Botanical Remains. In *Fort Ancient Cultural Dynamics in the Middle Ohio Valley,* edited by A. Gwynn Henderson, pp. 189–208. Monographs in World Archaeology 8. Prehistory Press, Madison, Wisconsin.

2000 Archaic Plant Utilization at the Hedden Site, McCracken County, Kentucky. In *Current Archaeological Research in Kentucky,* vol. 6, edited by David Pollack and Kristen J. Gremillion, pp. 1–24. Kentucky Heritage Council, Frankfort.

Scarry, C. Margaret

2003 Patterns of Wild Plant Utilization in the Prehistoric Eastern Woodlands. In *People and Plants in Ancient Eastern North America,* edited by Paul E. Minnis, pp. 50–104. Smithsonian Books, Washington, D.C.

Schroeder, Marjorie B.

1994 Archeobotany. In *Central Illinois Expressway Archeology: Upland Occupations of the Illinois Valley Crossing*, edited by Barbara D. Stafford, pp. 105–120. Technical Report 5. Kampsville Archeological Center, Center for American Archeology, Kampsville, Illinois.

Schroeder, Marjorie B., and David L. Asch

1989 Slim Lake Archeobotany. In *Central Illinois Expressway Archeology: Floodplain Archaic Occupations of the Illinois Valley Crossing*, edited by Barbara D. Stafford, pp. 95–116. Technical Report 4. Kampsville Archeological Center, Center for American Archeology, Kampsville, Illinois.

Shane, Linda C. K., Gordon G. Snyder, and Katherine H. Anderson

2001 Holocene Vegetation and Climate Changes in the Ohio Region. In *Archaic Transitions in Ohio and Kentucky Prehistory*, edited by Olaf H. Prufer, Sara E. Pedde, and Richard S. Meindl, pp. 11–55. Kent State University Press, Kent, Ohio.

Simon, Mary L.

1990 Middle Archaic Archaeobotany. In *The Nochta Site: The Early, Middle, and Late Archaic Occupations*, edited by Michael J. Higgins, pp. 237–260. American Bottom Archaeology FAI 270 Site Reports 21. University of Illinois Press, Urbana.

1996 Late Archaic Plant Remains. In *The Marge Site: Late Archaic and Emergent Mississippian Occupations in the Palmer Creek Locality*, edited by Andrew C. Fortier, pp. 79–94. American Bottom Archaeology FAI-270 Site Reports 27. University of Illinois Press, Urbana.

2000a Plant Remains from the Ringering Site. In *The Ringering Site and the Archaic-Woodland Transition in the American Bottom*, edited by J. Bryant Evans and Madeleine G. Evans, pp. 347–380. Transportation Archaeological Research Reports 8. Illinois Transportation Archaeological Research Program, Department of Anthropology, University of Illinois, Urbana-Champaign.

2000b Regional Variations in Plant Use Strategies in the Midwest during the Late Woodland. In *Late Woodland Societies: Tradition and Transformation across the Midcontinent*, edited by Thomas E. Emerson, Dale L. McElrath, and Andrew C. Fortier, pp. 37–75. University of Nebraska Press, Lincoln.

2002 Plant Remains from the Tree Row Site. Report on file, Illinois Transportation Archaeological Research Program, University of Illinois, Champaign.

Simon Mary L., and Kathryn E. Parker

2006 Prehistoric Plant Use in the American Bottom: New Thoughts and Interpretations. *Southeastern Archaeology* 25:212-257.

Smith, Barbara A., and Kathryn Egan

1990 Middle and Late Archaic Faunal and Floral Exploitation at the Weber I Site (20SA581), Michigan. *Ontario Archaeology* 50:39–54.

Smith, Bruce D.

1987 The Independent Domestication of Indigenous Seed-Bearing Plants in Eastern North America. In *Emergent Horticultural Economies of the Eastern Woodlands*, edited by William F. Keegan, pp. 3–47. Occasional Papers 7. Center for Archaeological Investigations, Southern Illinois University, Carbondale.

1992a The Independent Domestication of Indigenous Seed-Bearing Plants in Eastern North America. In *Rivers of Change: Essays on Early Agriculture in Eastern North America*, edited by Bruce D. Smith, pp. 35–66. Smithsonian Institution Press, Washington, D.C.

1992b The Economic Potential of *Iva annua* in Prehistoric Eastern North America. In *Rivers of Change: Essays on Early Agriculture in Eastern North America*, edited by Bruce D. Smith, pp. 185–200. Smithsonian Institution Press, Washington, D.C.

1992c *Chenopodium berlandieri* ssp. *jonesianum*: Evidence for a Hopewellian Domesticate from Ash Cave, Ohio. In *Rivers of Change: Essays on Early Agriculture in Eastern North America*, edited by Bruce D. Smith, pp. 133–162. Smithsonian Institution Press, Washington, D.C.

1995 Seed Plant Domestication in Eastern North America. In *Last Hunters First Farmers: New Perspectives on the Prehistoric Transition to Agriculture*, edited by T. Douglas Price and Anne Birgitte Gebauer, pp. 193–213. School of American Research Press, Santa Fe, New Mexico.

2001 Low Level Food Production. *Journal of Archaeological Research* 9:1–43.

Smith, Bruce D., and C. Wesley Cowan

1987 Domesticated Chenopodium in Prehistoric Eastern North America: New Accelerator Dates from Eastern Kentucky. *American Antiquity* 52:355–357.

2003 Domesticated Crop Plants and the Evolution of Food Production Economies in Eastern North America. In *People and Plants in Ancient Eastern North America*, edited by Paul E. Minnis, pp. 105–125. Smithsonian Books, Washington, D.C.

Smith, Bruce D., C. Wesley Cowan, and Michael P. Hoffman

1992 Is It an Indigene or a Foreigner? In *Rivers of Change: Essays on Early Agriculture in Eastern North America*, edited by Bruce D. Smith, pp. 67–100. Smithsonian Institution Press, Washington, D.C.

Smith, Edward E., Jr.

1995 The Swan's Landing Site (12Hr304): An Early Archaic (Kirk Horizon) Site in Harrison County, South-Central Indiana. *Midcontinental Journal of Archaeology* 20:192–237.

Stafford, C. Russell

1991 Archaic Period Logistical Foraging Strategies in West-Central Illinois. *Midcontinental Journal of Archaeology* 16:212–246.

1994 Structural Changes in Archaic Landscape Use in the Dissected Uplands of Southwestern Indiana. *American Antiquity* 59:219–237.

2000 The Bluegrass Fauna and Changes in Middle Holocene Hunter-Gatherer Foraging in the Southern Midwest. *American Antiquity* 65:317–336.

Stothers, David M., Timothy J. Abel, and Andrew M. Schneider

2001 Archaic Perspectives in the Western Lake Erie Basin. In *Archaic Transitions in Ohio and Kentucky Prehistory*, edited by Olaf H. Prufer, Sara E. Pedde, and Richard S. Meindl, pp. 290–327. Kent State University Press, Kent, Ohio.

Stuiver, Minze, and Paula J. Reimer
1993 Extended ^{14}C Data Base and Revised CALIB 3.0 ^{14}C Age Calibration Program. *Radiocarbon* 35:215–230.
2000 University of Washington Quaternary Isotope Lab Radiocarbon Calibration Program, Version 4.3. Seattle, Washington.

Tiffany, Joseph A.
1974a An Application of Eigenvector Techniques to the Seed Analysis of the Brogley Rock Shelter (47 GT-156). *The Wisconsin Archeologist* 55:2–42.
1974b Seeds from the Cherokee Sewer Site (13Ck405), Cherokee, Iowa. *Journal of the Iowa Archeological Society* 36:147–154.

Wagner, Gail E.
2003 Eastern Woodlands Anthropogenic Ecology. In *People and Plants in Ancient Eastern North America*, edited by Paul E. Minnis, pp. 126–171. Smithsonian Books, Washington, D.C.

Walthall, John A.
1998 Rockshelters and Hunter-Gatherer Adaptation to the Pleistocene/Holocene Transition. *American Antiquity* 63:223–238.

Walz, Gregory W.
1997 Paleoethnobotanical Analysis. In *Archaeological Investigations for the Relocation of Valmeyer, Monroe County, Illinois, 2: The Strong Site*, edited by Brian Adams, Gregory R. Walz, Paul P. Kreisa, Kevin P. McGowan, Jacqueline M. McDowell, Cynthia L. Balek, and Kristin Hedman, pp. 65–76. Research Report 28. Public Service Archaeology Program, University of Illinois, Urbana-Champaign.

Watson, Patty Jo
1985 The Impact of Early Horticulture in the Upland Drainages of the Midwest and Midsouth. In *Prehistoric Food Production in North America*, edited by Richard I. Ford, pp. 99–147. Anthropological Papers 75. Museum of Anthropology, University of Michigan, Ann Arbor.
1995 Explaining the Transition to Agriculture. In *Last Hunters First Farmers: New Perspectives on the Prehistoric Transition to Agriculture*, edited by T. Douglas Price and Anne Birgitte Gebauer, pp. 21–37. School of American Research Press, Santa Fe, New Mexico.

Webb, Thompson, III
1988 Eastern North America. In *Vegetation History*, edited by B. Huntley and T. Webb III, pp. 385–414. Kluwer Academic, Dordrecht, the Netherlands.

Webb, Thompson, III, and Patrick J. Bartlein
1988 Late Quaternary Climate Change in Eastern North America: The Role of Modeling Experiments and Empirical Studies. In *Late Pleistocene and Early Holocene Paleoecology and Archaeology of the Eastern Great Lakes Region*, edited by R. S. Laub, N. G. Miller, and D. W. Steadman, pp. 31–38. Bulletin 33. Buffalo Society of Natural Sciences, Buffalo, New York.

Webb, Thompson, III, Patrick J. Bartlein, Sandy P. Harrison, and Katharine H. Anderson
1993 Vegetation, Lake Levels, and Climate in Eastern North America for the Past 18,000 Years. In *Global Climates since the Last Glacial Maximum*, edited by H. E. Wright Jr., John E. Kutzbaugh, Thompson Webb III, William F. Ruddiman, F. Alayne Street-Parrot, and Patrick J. Bartlein, pp. 416–467. University of Minnesota Press, Minneapolis.

Winterhalder, Bruce, and Carol Goland
1993 On Population, Foraging Efficiency, and Plant Domestication. *Current Anthropology* 43:710–715.
1997 An Evolutionary Ecology Perspective on Diet Choice, Risk, and Plant Domestication. In *People, Plants, and Landscapes: Studies in Paleoethnobotany*, edited by Kristen J. Gremillion, pp. 123–160. University of Alabama Press, Tuscaloosa.

Wright, Henry T.
1964 A Transitional Archaic Campsite at Green Point (20SA1). *The Michigan Archaeologist* 10:17–22.

Wright, Herbert E.
1964 Aspects of the Early Postglacial Forest Succession in the Great Lakes Region. *Ecology* 45:439–448.
1992 Patterns of Holocene Climatic Change in the Midwestern United States. *Quaternary Research* 38:129–132.

Wright, Patti
1995 Paleoethnobotanical Analysis. In *Data Recovery Investigations at the Hayden Site (23SL36) and the Rabanus Site (23SL859), Chesterfield, St. Louis County, Missouri: New Insights into the Titterington/Sedalia Phase in East-Central Missouri*, edited by Joseph L. Harl, pp. 93–104. Archaeological Services Research Report 182. University of Missouri–St. Louis.

Wymer, Dee Ann
1987 The Paleoethnobotanical Record of the Lower Tennessee-Cumberland Region. *Southeastern Archaeology* 6:124–129.

Yanovsky, Elias
1936 *Food Plants of the North American Indians*. Miscellaneous Publication 237. United States Department of Agriculture, Washington, D.C.

Yarnell, Richard A.
1964 *Aboriginal Relationships between Culture and Plant Life in the Upper Great Lakes Region*. Anthropological Papers 23. Department of Anthropology, University of Michigan, Ann Arbor.
1969 Contents of Human Paleofeces. In *The Prehistory of Salts Cave, Kentucky*, edited by Patty Jo Watson, pp. 41–54. Reports of Investigations 16. Illinois State Museum, Springfield.
1972 *Iva annua* var. *macrocarpa:* Extinct American Cultigen? *American Anthropologist* 74:335–341.
1978 Domestication of Sunflower and Sumpweed in Eastern North America. In *The Nature and Status of Ethnobotany*, edited by Richard I. Ford, pp. 289–299. Anthropological Papers 67. Museum of Anthropology, University of Michigan, Ann Arbor.
2004 Riverton Plant Remains and Terminal Archaic Crops. In *Aboriginal Ritual and Economy in the Eastern Woodlands: Essays in Memory of Howard Dalton Winters*, edited by Anne-Marie Cantwell, Lawrence A. Conrad, and Jonathan E. Reyman, pp. 123–130. Scientific Papers 30. Illinois State Museum, Springfield.

Yarnell, Richard A., and M. Jean Black
1985 Temporal Trends Indicated by a Survey of Archaic and Woodland Plant Food Remains from Southeastern North America. *Southeastern Archaeology* 4:93–106.

5

Archaic Burial Sites in the American Midcontinent

George R. Milner, Jane E. Buikstra, and Michael D. Wiant

Burials—specifically the ways bodies were handled and the objects interred with them—have long been an important part of archaeological definitions of the midcontinental hunter-gatherer societies collectively known as Archaic (Griffin 1952, 1967). Despite such archaeological visibility, it is still difficult to identify systematically variation over time and space in how Archaic people were treated when they died. Most research has focused on single sites rather than entire regions, partly because data are of variable quality and reports of excavations are uneven. Thus, for much of the Midcontinent, little can be said about typical mortuary treatments for different age, sex, and social groups, let alone the range of variation that existed in particular times and places. This situation is unfortunate because the reasons behind such variability were likely related to how people structured their lives.

At this point, it is useful to assess what we think we know, what can be extracted from readily available sources, what cannot be said from a literature survey, and where research should go from here. To do so, we focus on site structure, grave goods, and skeletons, emphasizing geographical patterning in burial practices, the presence (or absence) of formal cemeteries, and the demographic composition of Archaic hunter-gatherer groups.

Published Information

This overview relies mostly on published descriptions of sites, although unpublished material and limited-distribution contract reports are occasionally considered. We focus on Kentucky and Illinois, two states for which abundant information is available, although the geographical coverage extends to other midwestern states and southern Ontario (west of Lake Ontario).

Most contextually documented skeletons were excavated during the first half of the twentieth century. Figure 5.1 shows the distribution of 4,500 skeletons, excluding cremations, according to when they were excavated.[1] These burials represent only a fraction of those that have been found, but they provide a general feel for change over time in the level of archaeological activity. A count by decade, however, does not adequately capture the history of archaeological

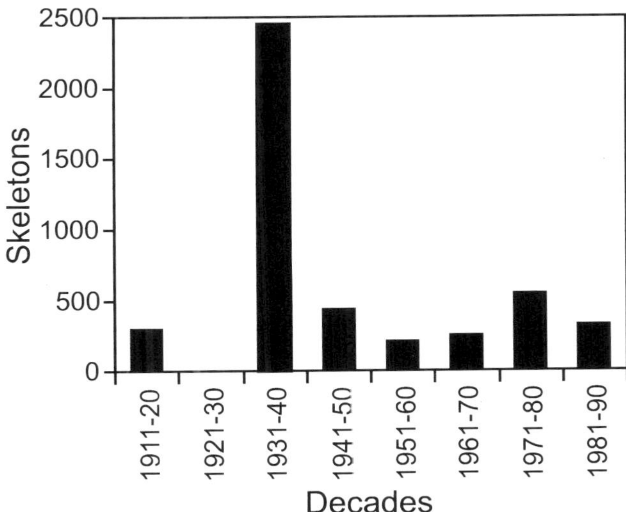

Figure 5.1. Most Archaic skeletons were excavated early in the twentieth century, particularly during the Great Depression.

investigations. Many recent excavations have not yet been reported, so our tally includes few skeletons found during the last decade or so. The most important feature of Figure 5.1 is the disproportionately large number of skeletons from excavations in western Kentucky undertaken during the Great Depression. In fact, well over one-half of the burials in this sample (2,860, or 63.6 percent) were from Kentucky sites excavated between 1937 and 1941. That is why so many years later these particular sites still have much to contribute to current understandings of Archaic peoples.

While published information can be used for broad characterizations of the past, it is seldom suitable for detailed, especially quantitative, comparative studies involving multiple sites. Problems include inadequate chronological controls, inconsistent terms for grave goods and burial positions, uneven reporting of what was found, varied definitions of what items constitute burial goods (as opposed to other inclusions in graves), inaccurate age and sex estimates, and contradictory accounts of the same archaeological contexts.

Difficulties with temporal controls and artifact classifications are common to all areas of archaeology, not just analyses of mortuary remains, and largely result from change over time in research questions, field and analytical methods, and accumulated knowledge about the past. Unfortunately, materials from sites are often described in summary fashion, with disproportionate attention directed toward unusual burials, especially those with aesthetically pleasing artifacts. Thus, determining what belonged to specific individuals is frequently difficult, if not impossible. Even distinguishing intentionally buried artifacts from incidental inclusions in grave fill sometimes verges on the impossible, especially in older reports. The same difficulty exists with projectile points lying next to bones or within thoracic and abdominal cavities. Some of these points may have been embedded in bodies (not all wounds produce detectable bone damage), although determining if that had occurred is difficult to establish from published descriptions. Erroneous assessments of age and sex in the older literature should be of great concern, although this difficulty is not always recognized. Discrepancies in critical information, such as the number of individuals or different burial designations, further complicate the use of previously reported information. Such inconsistencies are inevitable when earlier materials are restudied, although resolving discrepancies is difficult. None of these problems will come as a surprise to researchers who have persevered in the use of published data; in fact, some of them have been identified previously in analyses of Archaic sites (e.g., Winters 1968). So limitations exist on what can be done systematically and rigorously with currently available mortuary data. The only real solution—and it is a feasible but laborious one—is to return to the original field records (notes, maps, and photographs), skeletons, and artifacts when these exist in usable form (e.g., Milner and Jefferies 1998).

Another problem is that many collections have never been fully reported. A related issue is the inadequate dissemination of information about cultural resource management (CRM) projects as well as difficulties in accessing completed project reports. This problem is especially acute when attempts are made to interpret the archaeological record beyond the confines of narrowly defined regions where researchers have had personal involvement.

This situation means that much less can be said from existing materials than one might suppose. Any summary of a large geographical area, such as the Midcontinent, can only include a sample of excavated sites that, in theory, provide valuable perspectives on conditions in the past. Nevertheless, the reports covered here—primarily original site descriptions—are sufficient to highlight strengths and weaknesses in the existing literature. The information presented in this chapter is, within reason, consistently reported in many, but by no means all, publications. That does not mean it is necessarily correct in all respects, although we believe the aggregate picture is a satisfactory basis on which to design future problem-oriented research.

Temporal and Spatial Patterns

Little is known about Early Archaic (ca. 8000–6000 B.C.) burial practices because few skeletons have been found, consistent with a mobile way of life (Walthall 1999). These people presumably buried or otherwise disposed of their dead near typically short-term, ephemeral camps as they moved from one place to another throughout the course of the year. Thus, great accumulations of burials would not be expected—nor have they been found.

A few exceptions, however, can be cited, most notably Horizon 11 at Koster in west-central Illinois. The excavation of deeply buried Horizon 11 yielded skeletons of nine individuals, some showing signs of physical disabilities.[2] Five were flexed adults in pits, some covered with limestone. The rest were infants in shallow, unmarked graves. Nearly all of them were buried near the edge of the midden, the most intensively occupied area. Since both young and old people were present, burial near the camp appears to have been normal for the majority, if not all, of the group members. We hesitate to regard the scattered graves as a formal cemetery because they were not arranged in any obvious pattern, although they were not distributed evenly across the excavated area. This accumulation of bodies is consistent with Horizon 11 being a long-term or frequently occupied base camp, repeatedly visited by people who dug graves as needed, perhaps with some burials put in the vicinity of earlier ones. This site type would become common later during Archaic times at sites such as Koster and Napoleon Hollow that were situated in resource-rich settings (James A. Brown, pers. comm.; Wiant, this volume).

Such sites, perhaps where several bands simultaneously met, were also present elsewhere but were not common. Cremations in small pits at McCullough's Run in southern

Indiana are another example of a group of burials (Cochran 1997). Individuals of all ages had been buried, often more than one individual in a pit, and various artifacts, most notably projectile points, were included with the remains. Red ocher, a common feature of later Archaic burials, was also found. At the Butterfield site, in western Kentucky, many burials were encountered, some of which might be Early Archaic. Nevertheless, most burials, perhaps all of them, probably date to later Archaic components also represented by artifacts in the midden (Jefferies et al. 2005). This ambiguity in dating highlights the need for systematic studies of museum collections to tease apart the temporal associations of graves at sites excavated many years ago.

Much more can be said about mortuary practices from the last half of the Middle Archaic onward because the body of data is incomparably richer (Middle Archaic, ca. 6000–3000 B.C.; Late Archaic, ca. 3000–1000 B.C. or a few centuries later). Mortuary practices appear more varied both spatially and temporally than they were earlier, but such a conclusion is heavily influenced by a far larger sample of graves. More variable burial customs later in Archaic times would be consistent with a greater differentiation in ways of life and the existence of clearly distinguishable regional cultural traditions. Available data, however, are still far from what might be desired because known sites, even including the many poorly described ones, are thinly and unevenly distributed over a long period of time and a broad geographical region. Here we focus on three areas, dictated largely by existing data, that underscore the diversity in Archaic mortuary practices and serve as a first but incomplete approximation of regional patterning. Of course, any such summary, regardless of how the Midcontinent is partitioned, masks considerable variability in mortuary practices that is useful in the reconstruction of life in different times and places.

By the late Middle Archaic, burial practices had changed in many parts of the Midcontinent. Large numbers of skeletons are not uncommon at sites dating from the late fifth to the early first millennium B.C., a strong contrast to earlier sites. These skeletons, regardless of whether they were from formal cemeteries or long-occupied camps, are just one indication of a fundamental shift in hunting-and-gathering ways of life (Brown 1983, 1985; Brown and Vierra 1983; Jefferies 1995; Marquardt and Watson 2005b). For many people, residential mobility had decreased as they increasingly focused on a narrower range of settings with particularly rich mixes of resources, specifically those like shellfish that were not only abundant but also dependable. Yet, despite general trends, neither ways of life nor mortuary customs were uniform across the length and breadth of the Midcontinent.

Lower Ohio River Valley

Among the best-known Archaic sites with burials are the ca. 4500 to 1000 B.C. shell and midden heaps in the lower Ohio River valley, including those along tributaries such as the Green River in western Kentucky. Interest in the people responsible for the Green River sites was initiated by Moore (1916) in the early twentieth century when he dug into several of them, including Indian Knoll. Excavations during the Great Depression, begun in 1934 along the middle Tennessee River, markedly expanded knowledge about Archaic peoples of the Midcontinent (Jefferies, this volume; Milner and Smith 1986; Webb and Haag 1939). William S. Webb, who directed the Kentucky statewide archaeology program, thought the Green River sites in his home state were "complementary to those in Alabama and it is our conviction that in the time sequence they will fit into the Alabama chronology" (Webb 1938). Largely through Webb's influence, the debris heaps of the "riparian culture area of the Green River" were regarded as some of "the most important types of archeological sites in the ethnic areas of Kentucky" (Cotter 1939). Not all of the shell and midden mounds were located along the river, either on its banks or on nearby high ground, although for convenience the sites in the western Kentucky coalfields are referred to here as "Green River sites." They share many characteristics, were mostly excavated as part of New Deal projects, and form a coherent unit, given the geographical scale of this overview. Of 10 sites considered here—Barrett, Butterfield, Carlston Annis, Chiggerville, Indian Knoll, Kirkland, Morris, Parrish Village, Read, and Ward—only one, Butterfield, has a strongly expressed Early Archaic component (Jefferies et al. 2005). The remainder yielded predominately Middle to Late Archaic materials, and most or all of the burials also date to that time.

The Green River skeletons were mostly flexed, typically with legs bent at the hips and knees (Figure 5.2). Of 3,066 individuals described for 10 Green River sites, 76.6 percent were either tightly or loosely flexed (Moore 1916; Rolingson and Schwartz 1966; Webb 1946, 1950a, 1950b, 1951; Webb and Haag 1939, 1940, 1947). Most graves held only a single person, although occasionally more were present. Skeletons were often found in shallow pits, although pit outlines could not always be detected in deposits of shell or organic-rich soil. Pits were easiest to identify when they extended into soil beneath cultural deposits. Nevertheless, excavators noted that some burials were merely placed on the ground or in shallow depressions and then covered by shell and debris-laden soil.

Many skeletons were also disarticulated, and, in some instances, excavators distinguished bones that had been disturbed from those that were intentional reburials resulting from protracted mortuary sequences. Without looking at original field notes, determining what exactly was meant by "disturbed" is often impossible, and some of these remains are perhaps better considered purposefully bundled bones. Nevertheless, the New Deal archaeologists were quite certain that later graves and a habitation-related churning of soil had intruded on earlier but shallowly buried skeletons. At Chiggerville, for example, they noted the "constant digging of the

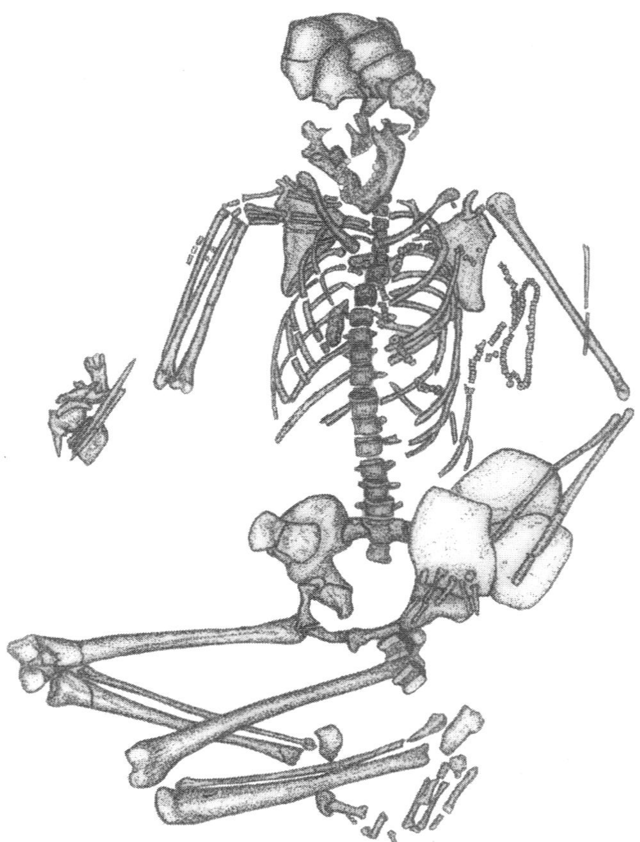

Figure 5.2. Most late Middle to Late Archaic skeletons from the Green River area in Kentucky were partly or fully flexed, much like this individual from the Read shell heap. This individual was buried with an unusually rich array of artifacts, including shell disk beads (left thorax), cut pieces of shell (left hand), atlatl weights (pelvis), and a tool kit (right hand). Drawn from Webb 1950b:Figure 4.A.

aborigines broke many bones and scattered and disturbed many skeletons" (Webb and Haag 1939:12).

Published site plans are often lacking, although comprehensive maps can be compiled from field notes that were generally quite good by the standards of that time. Yet burials clearly were unevenly distributed across at least some of the Green River sites. At Ward, only part of which was excavated, the burials were concentrated in the middle of the midden, rather than on its periphery (Pedde and Prufer 2001; Webb and Haag 1940). At Read, most graves were located on the side of a low shell heap that overlooked the river (Milner and Jefferies 1998). There is a need for further analyses of the vertical and horizontal layout of burials as part of systematic reexaminations of the large Green River collections. At Barrett, for example, a group of ca. 40 burials, many of which were flexed, were buried in one area. It was described as a "very heavy concentration in a very localized area" (Webb and Haag 1947:14, Figure 5C).

Broadly similar burial practices existed beyond the Green River drainage, such as along the lower Ohio River into southern Illinois. Many late Middle to Late Archaic skeletons were found in middens at the Rosenberger and KYANG sites in Kentucky, located in the vicinity of the Falls of the Ohio, as well as at Fitzgibbons in Illinois farther downstream (Bader 1992; Bader and Granger 1989; Conner and Brandon 1986; Granger 1988; Robison 1986; Wolf and Brooks 1979). The Middle to Late Archaic Black Earth site alongside a wetland in the interior of southern Illinois is better known, and here numerous skeletons were found in shallow pits in midden deposits (Jefferies and Lynch 1983; Lynch 1982). Once again, graves usually contained single individuals, although some held more than one. Graves were also scattered across other long-occupied sites in this general area, such as Robeson Hills and Riverton along the lower Wabash River (Winters 1969). They were not restricted to open-air sites as skeletons have been found in habitation deposits at Middle to Late Archaic Modoc Rock Shelter along the Mississippi River, also in Illinois (Anderson 1991; Bade 1992; Fowler 1959).

The southern Illinois sites differ from those in the Green River and the Falls of the Ohio areas in terms of body positioning, specifically flexed versus extended skeletons. At Black Earth, 46 percent of 124 burials were extended (Lynch 1982). Extended skeletons also occurred among the few burials at Robeson Hills in Illinois (Winters 1969). In contrast, only 2.6 percent of the people at the 10 Green River sites were buried that way (Moore 1916; Rolingson and Schwartz 1966; Webb 1946, 1950a, 1950b, 1951; Webb and Haag 1939, 1940, 1947). Likewise, 8.3 percent of 84 burials from Rosenberger with reported body positions were extended, with the rest flexed, and all skeletons at KYANG were flexed, other than those that were disturbed (Bader and Granger 1989; Granger 1988; Wolf and Brooks 1979). Furthermore, one cremation was found among the few burials uncovered at Riverton, a practice that seemingly was more common farther north. Some cremations, however, might have been overlooked in hurried New Deal excavations, which were undertaken in difficult conditions, although it is unlikely many were missed at the Green River sites.

Another difference between the western Kentucky and southern Illinois sites is the number of shell-disk beads, many fashioned from marine shell, at the former as compared with the latter. For unknown reasons, numerous Green River burials had these beads, sometimes long strings of them.

West-Central Illinois and Adjacent Missouri

Prevailing burial patterns were different farther north in western Illinois and adjacent Missouri, where cemeteries separate from habitation sites appear to have been more common. Most of these sites date to Late Archaic times, although some, like Bullseye in west-central Illinois, date to the late Middle Archaic (Buikstra and Charles 1999; Charles 1995; Hassen 1987).

Bullseye is important because its tight cluster of poorly preserved Middle Archaic burials, at least some of which were flexed, represents an early example of a specially designated burial area, in this instance perhaps located near a camp. The richness and diversity of artifacts, most notably atlatl weights, prompted Buikstra and Charles (1999) to suggest that bands congregated there at certain times for various social reasons, including the burial of the dead accompanied by the ostentatious disposal of valued objects.

Other groups of late Middle Archaic burials have been identified in the lower Illinois Valley, as shown by skeletons at Godar, Gibson, Elizabeth, and perhaps Pete Klunk (Mound 14). At Godar, a heavy concentration of artifacts measured ca. 18 m in diameter, within which were burials covered by red ocher and pieces of limestone (Titterington 1950). Bullseye, therefore, is not the only mortuary site associated with large numbers of artifacts. Not all of the Bullseye and Godar artifacts were placed in graves, so whatever took place at those sites extended beyond the mere disposal of bodies. The graves at Gibson, Elizabeth, and Pete Klunk were located on high bluffs above the Illinois River (Albertson and Charles 1988; Buikstra 1981; Charles 1995; Perino 1962, 1968). At Gibson and Pete Klunk, the skeletons were found beneath mounds dating to later periods. Burial features at Elizabeth, located on a bluff-crest knoll, included simple graves as well as a large, shallow basin, within which were dug additional shallow pits for bodies. Earth mixed with fragmentary bones, including burned remains, was located nearby, indicating earlier burials were disturbed when the large basin was dug. People repeatedly returned to this spot for burial purposes, and the character of the cemetery changed over time. Although the field evidence is equivocal, a low pile of earth measuring ca. 8 by 10 m in diameter and .4 m high was possibly added to the knoll while the cemetery was in use. These several sites are significant as they represent early indications of what, by Late Archaic times, had developed into a common pattern in this area: the use of spatially distinct cemeteries, many in prominent locations such as on bluff crests, accompanied by mound building.

During late Middle Archaic times, bodies were also buried in or near camps, as at Napoleon Hollow and Koster (Horizon 6, Helton phase), both in the Illinois Valley (Buikstra 1981). Many of the people buried at Koster were disabled or old. Because they were not interred with everyone else, choices were apparently being made about burial location based on an individual's ability to perform vital community-related tasks. Less effort was spent on people capable of making less of a contribution to group survival.

Burial in a long-occupied place marked by a midden also took place in Late Archaic times at Tree Row (ca. 4400–2300 B.C.), the only such site excavated to date (Hedman and West n.d.; Dale R. McElrath, pers. comm.).[3] Here skeletons were usually flexed, discounting poorly preserved remains where it was not possible to identify body positions. Much like burials in middens elsewhere in the Midcontinent, the Tree Row graves were distributed across the site with little apparent order. Once again, burial apparently took place near camps as deaths occurred, although occasionally people might have been interred near group members whose grave locations were marked or remembered. Tree Row stands out as unusual in the Midcontinent for the lack of items, at least nonperishable artifacts, found with the dead.[4] The reason for the absence of grave offerings is unclear.

Despite the findings at Tree Row, during the Late Archaic period a shift appears to have occurred in burial practices toward mortuary behavior typical of more recent time periods, at least in its spatial dimension. By this time, the separation of burial and habitation areas had become common. Late Archaic cemeteries include Airport, Etley, Hartford Church, Kampsville, Marquette Park, and Pete Klunk (Mound 7) in west-central Illinois and Elm Point, Gronefeld, Hatten, and 23LN11 in northeastern Missouri (Bacon and Miller 1957; Farnsworth 1993; Klepinger and Henning 1976; Perino 1962, 1968; Roper 1978; Titterington 1950). Purposeful mound building took place at some sites, such as seen in a cobble-covered pile ca. 8 m in diameter and .5 m high at Hatten. Here the earliest mortuary events consisted of bone bundles and flexed skeletons placed in shallow depressions dug into a specially prepared floor made by removing a little soil. They were covered by several layers of limestone interspersed with deposits of bones that, for the most part, had been burned.

Mound building with stone and earth also took place at Pete Klunk (Mound 7), where seven crematories along with flexed and bundle burials were excavated (Perino 1962, 1968). Slabs of limestone covered the cremations and most of the other burials. After a period of use, the cemetery was capped by soil and slabs, additional mortuary features, and, finally, still more stones, collectively making a mound ca. 9 m in diameter and 1 m high. Burials, however, were not restricted to the mound.

Limestone slabs over or near skeletons have been found at several other Late Archaic sites: Etley, Hartford Church, Kampsville, and Marquette Park in west-central Illinois and Elm Point, Gronefeld, and 23LN11 in nearby Missouri (Bacon and Miller 1957; Farnsworth 1993; Perino 1962; Titterington 1950). Unfortunately, much less is known about these sites because they were excavated long ago by landowners or amateur archaeologists. Red ocher covered most of the skeletons, so this custom appears to have been more common here than to the south, such as the Green River middens where red ocher was only occasionally found with burials. One of the Illinois sites, Etley, was located on the bluff just south of Godar and consisted of two mounds measuring ca. 15 m by 6 m and .5 m high. Although little is known about the graves, some contained multiple extended interments. Several other sites were also located on high ridgetops, although sites also occurred in floodplain settings. At least some of them were specially designated cemeteries, including the mounds at Etley, hilltop burials at 23LN11, and a ca. 5-m-diameter area at Gronefeld where there were many fine artifacts and poorly preserved bones.

By putting together scattered information, Charles and Buikstra (1983; Charles 1995) have argued that the Late Archaic inhabitants of the main valleys tended to use cemeteries that held many articulated skeletons. They inferred that people in and near resource-rich major valleys used specially designated cemeteries that were physically separated from their camps to mark rights of access to the immediately surrounding areas. Cemeteries farther up smaller streams that feed these rivers, such as Airport, Hatten, and 23LN11, contained more disarticulated skeletons (Bacon and Miller 1957; Klepinger and Henning 1976; Roper 1978). Presumably, some of these remains, perhaps the great majority of them, were carried long distances across a landscape that could not support populations living in quasi-permanent settlements and focusing on concentrated resources. That is, mobile groups carried the remains back to their cemeteries whenever that became possible or at some fixed interval. Periodic interments might be indicated by layers of slabs and skeletal remains, such as at Hatten.

Thus, both near-contemporaneous and temporally distinct mortuary customs were highly variable. Simplifying greatly, Early Archaic people were laid to rest with few objects in graves dug wherever and whenever they were needed. Yet graves still accumulated at repeatedly occupied places, such as Koster Horizon 11. By the late Middle Archaic, people were buried both near camps and some distance away from them in discrete clusters of graves, some of which were in relatively inaccessible but prominent locations such as on bluff tops. Bullseye and Godar—many of the burials at each perhaps date to a relatively narrow period of time marked archaeologically by Godar points—included skeletons and caches of fine artifacts, especially atlatl weights and projectile points. In the Late Archaic, people were often buried with artifacts in discrete cemeteries in the main river valleys and surrounding uplands. Body treatments, however, varied according to differences in ways of life, specifically group mobility. Taking a longer perspective, the elaborate funerary activities in place from late Middle Archaic times onward can be considered precursors of the elaborate mortuary-related ceremonialism that became so well established in western Illinois by the Middle Woodland period ca. 2,000 years ago.

This vignette is not meant to imply unidirectional change in either mortuary practices or ways of life throughout the Archaic into later time horizons.[5] People would have responded to ever-changing natural and social settings, and burial customs, linked to how people structured their lives, changed accordingly. For example, climatic-related transformations in resource distribution and productivity, most obviously the mid-Holocene Climatic Optimum, must have had an effect on humans' interactions with their local surroundings and each other, as they did elsewhere in Illinois (Jefferies 1983). Unfortunately, the current temporal resolution for the lengthy Archaic period is too coarse to determine whether changes over time in mortuary practices and, hence, social systems could be characterized as either gradual or steplike; that is, whether fundamental transformations occurred on time scales of millennia as opposed to a few centuries or even generations. Nor is it possible with the present level of temporal resolution to determine whether changes in burial practices ever alternated between new and old customs.

Elsewhere in the Midcontinent

Various burial practices dominated other parts of the Midcontinent, although information is not nearly as complete for those areas as it is for the lower Ohio Valley, particularly the Green River, and west-central Illinois, principally the central to lower Illinois Valley. Across the upper Midwest, Archaic mortuary sites tended to be small and sparsely distributed, both geographically and temporally (Alex 2000; Arzigian and Stevenson 2003; Ellis et al. 1990; Lovis 1999; Robertson et al. 1999; Stoltman 1997). For example, in a recent comprehensive survey of burial sites in Minnesota, Arzigian and Stevenson (2003) identified only 16 sites that might date to Archaic times, the largest of which yielded just over a dozen burials; most had only one.[6]

Burials from the Early through Late Archaic periods are known from the upper Midwest into Ontario, although later ones are more common, particularly those dating to the Late Archaic, including Old Copper (Alex 2000; Arzigian and Stevenson 2003; Ellis et al. 1990; Ritzenthaler 1946; Ritzenthaler and Wittry 1952; Robertson et al. 1999; Stoltman 1997). The ways the dead were treated varied greatly, as indicated by articulated skeletons, bone bundles, and cremations in graves containing one or more individuals. In southern Ohio, Late Archaic people were buried in camps, including those marked by middens, as well as in spatially distinct burial areas (Bowen 1987; Purtill, this volume). The significance of this variability—that is, whether it reflects temporally or culturally distinct peoples or mortuary programs with separate tracks for different members of these societies—is unknown.

Of special interest are mortuary sites dating to the Late Archaic to Early Woodland transition—those from the end of the second millennium B.C. through much of the subsequent millennium—that are distributed through the upper Midwest into the Northeast (Abel et al. 2001; Alex 2000; Arzigian and Stevenson 2003; Baerreis et al. 1954; Binford 1963a, 1963b; Cunningham 1948; Donaldson and Wortner 1995; Ellis et al. 1990; Faulkner 1960; Green and Schermer 1988; Hruska 1967; Mead and Kingsley 1985; Overstreet 1980; Overstreet et al. 1996; Robertson et al. 1999; Sciulli and Aument 1987; Sciulli and Schuck 2001; Sciulli et al. 1982; Sciulli et al. 1993; Spence 1986; Stevenson et al. 1997; Stothers and Abel 1993). They are commonly referred to as "Red Ocher" or "Glacial Kame," depending on where they are located, whether a site is situated on a glacial knoll, the materials accompanying the burials, and the terms in use when reports were published. A common characteristic is red ocher in graves, although this custom is not restricted to these burials, as ocher also covers skeletons clearly separable temporally, spatially, and culturally. Once again, the ways bodies were handled varied greatly at this time horizon—they included inhumations of intact bodies, bundles of disarticulated bones, and cremations of single or multiple individuals—and often different burial procedures were in contemporaneous use at the same site. Ellis and colleagues (1990) have called attention to the widespread distribution of a few distinctive artifacts, which no doubt obscures variation among these groups; after all, they were scattered across a large area. The same could be said about the use of red ocher, which as indicated previously has a considerable temporal and geographical distribution, although it was certainly used more in some times and places than in others.

Cemeteries and Monuments

One of the most important objectives of Archaic-related mortuary research is the identification of where and when cemeteries first appeared. Here one must be careful not to conflate two separate issues: purposeful burial of the dead and planned cemetery construction.

The former refers to the intentional disposal of a corpse accompanied by activities commemorating the deceased's life, reaffirming social ties and a sense of order among the living, and facilitating the transmission of rights and obligations from one person to another. The last function, in particular, ensures transgenerational continuity in social groups ranging from households to larger descent groups and residential communities. Funerals are typically solemn affairs in which the corpse is handled respectfully according to generally accepted customs, and whatever takes place typically reflects, to a greater or lesser extent, the deceased's place in society. These burial proceedings contrast with a casual or merely expedient disposal of the dead, such as people of low status or nongroup members whose bodies might simply be thrown into a conveniently open pit or on a trash heap.[7]

While corpses can be disposed of in ways that are intentional in the sense described above, they do not necessarily have to be put in formal burial areas—specially designated places for burial where remains are typically arranged according to a set plan. The distinction between simple accumulations of burials in long-occupied places and planned cemeteries is important because ethnographically known sedentary groups commonly used the latter to mark rights of access to essential, spatially fixed resources critical to their survival (Buikstra and Charles 1999; Charles and Buikstra 1983; Goldstein 1976, 1980). But while many such groups used burial grounds for that purpose, not all did so; thus, the absence of a formal cemetery need not mean that a particular group did not exercise rights over key places and restrict access to them. Modern small-scale societies with formal cemeteries typically depend heavily on agriculture, and in the distant past this practice was also probably common among hunter-gatherer-fisher groups that relied on resources with characteristics that mimicked the opportunities and constraints so typical of agriculture. These were plant and animal foods that were spatially fixed and limited in distribution, proved to be highly productive and reliable in most years, required heavy and coordinated investments of labor at certain points in the annual cycle, yielded abundant storable surpluses in average to good years, and provided the means to survive through lean times of the year.

Cemeteries were in place by late Middle Archaic times in west-central Illinois, and were widespread by the Terminal Archaic (Red Ocher and Glacial Kame) across much of the upper Midwest (Alex 2000; Brown 1983; Buikstra and Charles 1999; Charles and Buikstra 1983; Donaldson and Wortner 1995; Green and Schermer 1988; Spence 1986; Stevenson et al. 1997; Stothers and Abel 1993). This development occurred when, generally speaking, people had settled in smaller territories and were using key resources more intensively than their Early and early Middle Archaic predecessors (Brown 1983; Brown and Vierra 1983; Jefferies 1995). It also took place during a period of overall population growth that is archaeologically visible as an increase in sites across much of the Eastern Woodlands beginning about 2000 B.C. (Milner 2004). During these several millennia, considerable regional and temporal variation characterized settlement patterns and site densities as well as the direction, magnitude, and timing of population change. That is, these changes were by no means unidirectional, nor did they occur uniformly across the Midcontinent (e.g., Jefferies 1983). Nonetheless, by the end of the Late Archaic period, ways of life were considerably different from what they were like several thousand or more years earlier.

In commenting on Terminal Archaic burials in southern Ontario, Spence (1986:92) made a useful distinction between cemeteries signifying exclusive access to particular areas and those promoting the integration of "macrobands" to counterbalance fluidity in local group composition. This point highlights an important function of mortuary-related behavior: the transgenerational maintenance and solidification of group identity through shared participation in funerary proceedings, which might stretch out over several years. Promoting group cohesion might even be the principal reason formal burial areas were used in Ontario during the Terminal Archaic, as Spence suggested. More recently, Buikstra and Charles (1999) have argued a similar position for Bullseye, a Helton-phase Middle Archaic site with a rich array of projectile points and atlatl weights. The cemetery, a place for burial as well as ostentatious displays, was likely associated with periodic population aggregations, an important function of which was social transactions solidifying group membership. It would be a mistake, however, to draw too sharp a contrast between community self-identification and resource control that excludes nonmembers because cemeteries could easily serve both functions simultaneously.

For sites with many skeletons, the challenge for archaeologists is to distinguish between accumulations of burials in frequently occupied spots and formal cemeteries (Charles and Buikstra 1983; Ellis et al. 1990; Milner and Jefferies 1998). The latter are of interest because they represent more than the disposal of the dead in a convenient location, typically where people lived. Goldstein (1976, 1980), who looked closely at this issue, emphasizes the dedication of a particular place for burial and cemetery permanence. A detectable internal order to the graves, regardless of the form that it might take (rows or clusters of burials, etc.), is a good indication of a formally recognized and maintained cemetery. It signifies permanence because bodies were brought to a special place and placed in graves arranged according to a fixed plan (minimally, relative to the positions of at least some earlier graves, the positions of which were remembered or marked).

Thus, numerous burials indicate many deaths but not necessarily specially designated cemeteries. This distinction is important because only the latter can be used as an argument that graves collectively represent a territorial marker. The major Green River sites, which often encompassed many graves, serve as an example of confusion over this issue. Claassen (1991, 1992, 1996a, 1996b) has argued that these sites were formal cemeteries marked by the intentional mounding of shell. The traditional view is that these sites were principally settlements occupied repeatedly for many generations. That interpretation is supported by considerable refuse, including stone tools and chipping debris as well as numerous features, particularly caches of artifacts, dog burials, hearths, piles of fire-cracked rock, and pits (Marquardt and Watson 1983, 2005a; Milner and Jefferies 1998; Rolingson and Schwartz 1966; Watson 2005; Webb 1946, 1950a, 1950b, 1951; Webb and Haag 1939, 1940, 1947). In fact, much more debris was encountered in these sites than is apparent from the original excavation reports. For example, animal bones, including pieces cracked into small bits, as if broken for marrow, were rarely collected since they were viewed as inconsequential, although they were certainly present because they were mistakenly packed with human skeletons from the Read shell heap. While the cemetery-as-monument position focuses on shell as a construction material, shell was no doubt usually laid down in lesser amounts than other materials, to judge from the organic-rich soil commonly encountered in excavations (Marquardt and Watson 2004, 2005b; Milner and Jefferies 1998; Webb 1946; Winters 1968). Moreover, the piles were so spread out across such large areas relative to their heights that they would not have been particularly imposing sights from a human's ground-level perspective. They were not the same as the earthen mounds commonly built later in time, many of which were tall relative to their bases and featured steep sides, making them stand out from the surrounding landscape. These intentionally constructed earthen mounds were meant to impress, and they did so by being noticeably human creations, clearly separable from their natural settings. Thus, we concur with Moore, who a century ago had this to say about the most famous Green River site of them all: " 'The Indian Knoll,' it should be remembered, is not, properly speaking, a mound, but a dwelling-site" (1916:464).

Skeletons, artifacts, and field notes (including profiles showing deposits) from one Green River site, Read, have been reexamined (Milner and Jefferies 1998). This work supports the earlier interpretation that the accumulated materials resulted from habitation-related activities. Nothing at all about Read indicates it was a purposefully constructed monument of shell and dirt intended for the burial of the dead or for any other reason. Furthermore, the burials exhibit no discernible order, other than the occasional placement of graves near one another, which could easily represent roughly contemporaneous deaths. So the site does not appear to have consisted of one or more discrete and internally organized cemeteries. That does not mean such cemeteries were entirely absent along the Green River, although a cursory examination of some excavation plan maps supports the original interpretation that these sites, for the most part, contain just the accumulation of burials expected from the long occupation of the debris heaps. However, one site, in particular, might prove to have a demonstrable cemetery. At Barrett, Webb and Haag noted "much burying and reburying in [one] small area;" it was "an unusual feature of shell-midden habitation sites" (1947:14, Figure 5C). It was so unusual it deserved special comment by an archaeological team that had collectively uncovered far more Archaic burials in large excavations than anyone alive today. In short, all Green River sites should be systematically reexamined—everything from skeletons and artifacts to features, their distribution, and site stratigraphy. That would require laborious investigations of paper records, skeletons, and artifacts, not casual perusals of existing reports.

Discrete cemeteries were also not apparent in midden excavations at Black Earth in southern Illinois, Tree Row in west-central Illinois, and Rosenberger in northern Kentucky (Hedman and West n.d.; Jefferies and Lynch 1983; Lynch 1982; Wolf and Brooks 1979). Bodies at these sites, like those in the Green River middens, were carefully placed in purposefully prepared graves. Yet the sheer number and irregular placement of graves, coupled with problems with temporal control, have obscured any clustering that might once have been present. Perhaps a few people were intentionally buried near earlier graves, but no evidence suggests spatially discrete and internally organized burial areas.

Demography

The age and sex of skeletons in excavated samples are critical to an understanding of demographic and social structures, including identifying dependent and fully productive members of societies, as well as the nature of mortuary practices and what they might indicate about the roles of various categories of individuals. Unfortunately, published information on Archaic burials, much of which is several decades old, does not always conform to current standards. To the extent that old assessments of age and sex can be called into question, so, too, can analyses that rely on these data (Rothschild 1979; Winters 1968, 1969). Fortunately, older skeletal collections are beginning to be reexamined, including several from Green River sites (Meindl et al. 2001; Mensforth 1990, 2005; Milner and Jefferies 1998).

Just over 30 years ago, Weiss (1973) noted an overrepresentation of males in his survey of the worldwide osteological literature. Presumably then-current sex-estimation methods contributed to that finding, specifically a fixation on the cranium in preference to the pelvis when assessing sex-related characteristics of adult skeletons.[8] Such bias in sex estimation, while disputed by St. Hoyme and Işcan (1989), has strong implications for analyses based on the older literature. To investigate this issue, we compared information on Archaic skeletons published over the past quarter-century (since 1980) with earlier data. The separation point postdates both Weiss's (1973) observation of a male bias and the initial development of "bioarchaeology" undertaken by a new generation of researchers that laid the groundwork for current studies (Buikstra 1977). In our survey, we see a shift toward more females, hence, a more equal representation of the two sexes, in recent studies when considered in aggregate.[9] Of 876 skeletons enumerated in reports preceding 1980, 56.7 percent were male; in the later reports, 51.7 percent of 646 skeletons were male. Significantly more males than the expected 50 percent were recorded in the early reports, considered collectively ($p < .001$); males were also more common than females in later studies, but the difference in proportions was not statistically significant (one-tailed difference of proportions test, $p > .05$; Blalock 1972:228–230). Furthermore, significantly more males were reported in the earlier studies when the two samples were compared, just as predicted if a shift in sex estimation outcomes accompanied a heavier reliance on the pelvis relative to the cranium (one-tailed difference of proportions test, $p < .05$). Because this shift in the proportions of males is precisely in the right direction—that is, fewer males in later studies—Weiss's (1973) contention that males were erroneously overreported is supported.

This shift in how sex is estimated certainly affects analyses of artifacts associated with men and women. While studies based on old data might correctly identify general trends, any results can be expected to be less clear than if estimates of sex more closely approximated the actual sex of the individuals being examined. Erroneous sex estimates also affect other archaeological interpretations. For example, in part because of the marked disparity in the numbers of adult males and females, Skarland (1939) speculated that female infanticide was practiced at Chiggerville.

Age-at-death distributions and resulting inferences can also be problematic.[10] As is commonly understood, poor preservation can have an effect on the numbers of recognizable skeletons, especially when excavations were conducted hurriedly in often difficult conditions by unskilled laborers, such as during the Great Depression in Kentucky. Fortunately, Depression-era archaeologists had considerable practical experience and tended to notice the effects of differential preservation. For example, a deficit of juveniles at Parrish Village was attributed to poor preservation (Webb 1951). At many sites the small bones of young children, especially infants, were probably commonly missed by excavators, as happened at Modoc Rock Shelter in the 1950s when these bones were often included with nonhuman animal remains (Anderson 1991).

Perceptions about what would be typical of age-at-death distributions in preindustrial populations also affect how skeletal samples are interpreted. With respect to the supposed female infanticide at Chiggerville, Skarland (1939) noted a large number of deaths among "infants" (0–6 years). The proportion of very young people, however, was by no means excessive, and juveniles collectively made up 38.6 percent of the mortality sample. This figure is, in fact, a bit low for a preindustrial society (Howell 1979; Weiss 1973). Presumably young children, especially those who died in the first year, were underrepresented in the excavated sample (to the extent that reported ages reflect actual ages). Here is an instance in which the characteristics of small-scale societies, information widely appreciated by osteologists and archaeologists only after the initial work was done, call into question original conclusions.

Another issue has been debated among osteologists since the 1980s: biases in adult age distributions introduced by standard age-estimation methods (Jackes 2000; Konigsberg and Frankenberg 1994; Milner et al. 2000). In particular, if one assumes that ancient groups should approximate the age-at-death characteristics of historically known populations and widely used demographic models, most paleodemographic studies show too many deaths among young to middle-age adults, with few surviving beyond ca. 50 years. No weight whatsoever should be placed on age-at-death estimates made before the last few decades. But even some more recently analyzed samples do not have nearly enough old adults (ca. 50+ years) if ancient and modern populations share fundamental similarities in mortality experience (Bassett 1982; Klepinger and Henning 1976; Meindl et al. 2001; Mensforth 1990, 2005; Wolf and Brooks 1979). This discrepancy raises the issue of whether paleodemographic estimates in general are essentially correct for ancient small-scale societies, or whether they largely reflect measurement error. We think systematic biases in age estimates are a strong possibility, although others take the opposite view (for discussions of this issue with regard to Archaic populations, see Meindl et al. 2001 and Mensforth 2005).

The considerable social complications posed by high young- to middle-aged adult mortality have escaped the attention of archaeologists, despite Howell's (1982) lucid discussion of such issues in the early 1980s. If mortality in early adulthood was as great as indicated by most paleodemographic studies, including those focusing on midcontinental Archaic groups, then household functions were frequently disrupted by the death of one or both spouses. These individuals had to be replaced quickly, or the risk of death would have increased markedly for survivors, especially young dependents, the infirm, and the elderly (although there would not have been many of the last). Social mechanisms would have been required for the quick replacement of the lost spouse to perform customarily sex-specific tasks essential for family survival.

Although mortality during Archaic times was no doubt high by today's Western standards, we believe what appears to have been excessively high mortality among adults younger than 50 years is in large part a function of the age-estimation methods commonly used. Fortunately, methods are being developed that that can address this issue (Boldsen et al. 2002). They now need to be applied to Archaic skeletal samples, once again necessitating access to invaluable museum collections in order to refine our views of Archaic populations.

Artifacts, Skeletons, and Social Structure

Beyond Single Sites

However important analyses of single sites might be, they provide incomplete pictures of Archaic peoples. For example, to think that closely spaced and temporally overlapping Green River sites were somehow isolated from one another would be a mistake. Considering the mobility of hunter-gatherers, even of people tethered to highly productive places like mussel shoals, any single individual lived at multiple sites during his or her lifetime, being born in one and buried in another. So for purposes such as analyses of burial practices, combining data from several sites might be advisable. This approach will considerably increase sample sizes, an important consideration because many types of artifacts occur infrequently in these sites. But it also comes at a cost—researchers must go back to the original field notes and collections, not rely on more readily accessible published material.

The benefits of examining multiple sites simultaneously are best illustrated by studies in west-central Illinois. A linkage between body treatment and Late Archaic cemetery location has been mentioned above (Charles and Buikstra 1983). Here mortuary practices were likely constrained by the physical environment. People who relied on abundant valley resources could afford to be relatively sedentary, and they buried their dead in nearby cemeteries. Those in the uplands depended on more widely dispersed and less concentrated resources, necessitating more movement, and bodies were consequently skeletonized by the time they were taken to cemeteries for burial, in some instances perhaps on a periodic, prearranged basis. Focusing on single sites can also result in an incomplete picture of the demographic and health-related characteristics of ancient populations. For example, the Middle Archaic Gibson site had an overabundance of adults who died in the third and fourth decades, whereas at Koster just over half of the adults were more than 50 years old. While biased age estimates possibly affected the Gibson mortality distribution, that is not the entire story because the Koster skeletons, examined at roughly the same time as the Gibson skeletons by the same researcher (Buikstra), were decidedly weighted toward the elderly. The Koster people also suffered from debilitating conditions, whereas similarly noticeable ailments were not found at Gibson (Buikstra 1981). So just one of these two sites, analyzed alone, would have produced a skewed picture of Middle Archaic life.

The Koster pattern of personal capability influencing burial location, presumably along with other aspects of the mortuary proceedings, is not an isolated finding. At the late Middle to Late Archaic Read site in Kentucky, the elderly (45+ years) had fewer artifacts than younger adults (15–45 years) (Milner and Jefferies 1998). Similarly, old people at Black Earth possessed a narrower range of artifacts, lacking those classified as "ceremonial" or "ornamental" (Jefferies and Lynch 1983:319). There is, therefore, some reason to believe that impaired abilities resulted in a diminishment of social standing, at least as recognized at death—reflected in expedient burial at Koster, fewer artifacts at Read, and a less diverse array of objects at Black Earth. A similar pattern in which burial treatment was related to physical ability might also have been present at Modoc Rock Shelter during Helton times, as indicated by a small sample of mostly old adults (Anderson 1991).

Significance of Artifacts

Burials, regardless of whether they represented formal cemeteries or accumulations of graves in long-occupied camps, hold considerable potential for providing a better understanding of life in Archaic societies. Future investigations will build on Rothschild's (1979) and Winters's (1968, 1969) work with burial artifacts, but they must also integrate osteological and archaeological data to a greater extent than these pioneering studies. In part that is because age and sex assignments made many decades ago are often likely to be in error.

Concluding that disproportionately large numbers of items mark individuals who enjoyed an unusually high standing in their society is not unreasonable. But what exactly that might imply about the nature of that society is difficult to say. Simplifying greatly, an unequal distribution of items could indicate an egalitarian society in which claims to influential positions were based largely on personal characteristics, such as advanced age or remarkable abilities.[11] Alternatively, one might be tempted to argue that these artifacts signal the presence of a hierarchically organized society based largely on ascribed status in which a few key people enjoyed preferential access to prestige-denoting objects as part of their birthright, such as might be found in chiefdoms.

There are several problems with precipitously concluding that an uneven distribution of ornaments indicates institutionalized social inequality based on principles of descent, especially if observable distinctions among burials are based solely on artifacts. First, high-ranking people in organizationally complex societies, including those commonly called "chiefdoms" and "states," tend to be treated differently from everybody else through a combination of burial goods, body treatment, mortuary facility, and interment (or monument) location (Saxe 1970). The message conveyed is important and intended for a broad audience; as such, it is not subtle, even though not all possible dimensions of variability (artifact, body, grave, or location) may be used to symbolize exalted social positions. Second, little is known about the various meanings that might have been attached to most burial goods, other than some raw materials were more difficult to obtain and certain artifacts more difficult to fashion than others. Third, what variability in the quantity of artifacts associated with single individuals might indicate is unclear. For example, one must demonstrate that burials with many artifacts exceed what can be reasonably expected to occur in the normal course of excavation before attributing great social import to differences in artifact distributions.

We expand on the third point through examining disk beads found with 216 people of all ages from seven Green River sites: Barrett, Carlston Annis, Chiggerville, Indian Knoll, Kirkland, Read, and Ward (Webb 1946, 1950a, 1950b; Webb and Haag 1939, 1940, 1947; Figures 5.3 and 5.4).[12] Disk beads were probably fashioned mostly from marine whelk shells that had passed through numerous hands before reaching Kentucky. They must have been highly valued, if for no other reason than their scarcity. Some relationship probably existed, no matter how indirect and inexact, between the number of beads and an individual's or lineage's social position (a position that was quite likely transitory). That would be consistent with the common use of such ornaments by the members of many different societies in historic times as signs of position and wealth as well as gifts to seal socially and ritually important transactions.

We pooled the Green River data, following the reasoning presented above, and examined all burials for which counts of disk beads are provided in original reports. Most of these people were buried with only a handful of disk beads, but a few had thousands of them. Because of overall sample size, individuals with similar numbers of beads were grouped together by intervals: those with one to five beads, those with six to 10 beads, and so on. All that is intended by Figure 5.4 is a general impression of the data, not great mathematical precision, because the available information displays glaring deficiencies. Most notably, the sample is small and, worse, it is perhaps biased. The very real possibility exists that small numbers of beads, particularly when they occurred singly, were more likely than concentrations of them to have been missed by excavators or simply overlooked when filling out burial forms. Fortunately, difficulties with using published grave lots can be addressed to some extent by going back to original field and inventory records, which remains to be done.

Despite troublesome aspects of these data, the overall distribution—many people with few beads and few people with many of them—approximates a power-law distribution. Power-law distributions characterize diverse physical, biological, and social phenomena in which a few extreme outliers occur relative to the vast majority of cases (for highly readable accounts of this phenomenon accompanied by numerous examples, see Barabási [2002] and Buchanan [2002]; for World Wide Web links, see Albert et al. [1999] and Huberman and Adamic [1999]; for anthropological applications, see Bentley [2003] and Maschner and Bentley [2003]). Some of them, such as the sizes of stream catchments in river drainages, have nothing whatsoever to do with human intentions; others, including the number of links to web pages, result from human

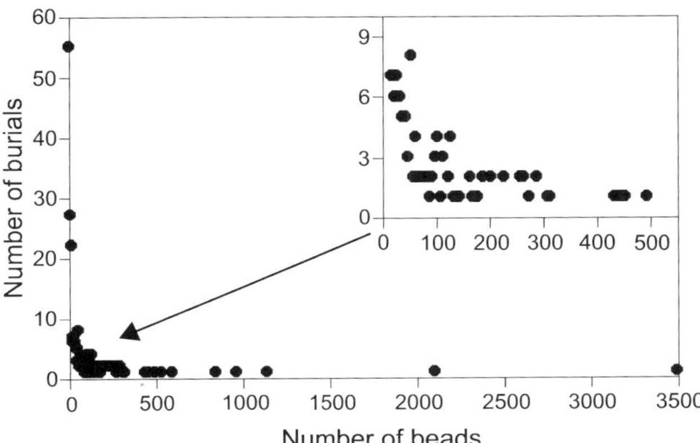

Figure 5.3. The distribution of beads associated with 216 skeletons from late Middle to Late Archaic Green River sites. Inset shows points in the lower left corner of the larger figure.

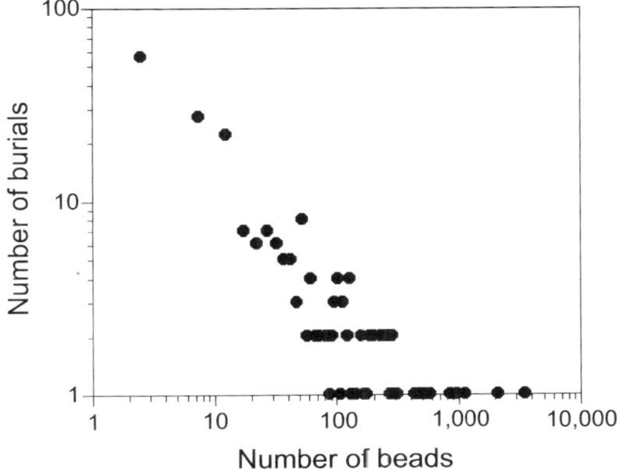

Figure 5.4. The distribution of beads associated with 216 skeletons from late Middle to Late Archaic Green River sites. Axes are plotted using log scales.

actions but cannot be attributed to any organized behavior. The latter example is interesting because, like airline hubs, the network is dominated by a relatively few well-connected nodes with many more links than would occur if the nodes were randomly connected. This organizational feature of complex networks has been shown to occur often in human affairs as well.

Archaeologists must therefore resist the temptation to immediately assign great significance to the discovery of a few individuals with large numbers of artifacts. When samples are sufficiently large, one might expect to find great disparities in the numbers of artifacts—most burials having very few objects while a few have many of them. At least that would be true if the following conditions were met: nonperishable objects were placed with the dead; an adequate sample could be obtained of all group members who died; certain objects denoted positions of prestige, wealth, and influence; reasonably consistent rules were applied for the distribution of these artifacts to people on the basis of their social standing; and the chances of acquiring more objects was positively associated with having some already (i.e., those who were already advantaged tended to do better than their fellows). One might suppose that, during the late Middle to Late Archaic along the Green River, high status was closely linked to the degree to which an individual or descent group managed to forge connections with other people, both members of the local community and outsiders, and thereby accumulate beads. The people with numerous, strong, long-lasting, and frequently reinforced ties to other people were the ones most likely to accumulate the greatest number of marine-shell beads. That would result in a distribution of artifacts more consistent with a network featuring a few key hubs (people) rather than one where each node (person) had an equal chance of connecting with any other one. Considering the inexact relationship expected between social positions and artifact quantities, along with deficiencies in the archaeological information at hand, the existence of any patterning at all in the bead data is nothing short of remarkable.

Thus, it is quite possible the uneven distribution of beads indicates that relatively few people along the Green River were key participants in social networks allowing them to acquire and dispose of valued and rare items. Prized items, most probably used to seal various social transactions, were quite likely passed among separate residential groups by individuals who, through their own abilities and charisma, became major players in social networks. The marine-shell beads, to the extent their uneven distribution reflects differences in interpersonal contacts, did not cross long distances by moving randomly among all members of these societies. Success bred success, and individuals or families that enjoyed the most interconnectedness (imprecisely estimated by the most beads) were the ones with whom new interpersonal connections were preferentially made.

The latter half of the Archaic is known as a time when artifacts, both nonlocal items and stylistically distinctive bone pins, marked the maintenance of ties among neighboring groups, presumably as a safeguard against localized shortfalls in necessary resources (Brown 1985; Jefferies 1996). To judge from the beads, these contacts were for the most part maintained by certain individuals who served as critical nodes in social networks. So it was largely through them that spatially separate groups of people were connected.

The Green River social networks implied by artifact distributions should not be confused with sociopolitical organizations in which a few high-ranking people held positions guaranteed by widely accepted and relatively fixed social institutions that promoted and protected political and economic inequities. As far as the Green River Archaic is concerned, nothing else about the individuals with numerous beads (or other artifacts) makes them stand out from everybody else in terms of body treatment, grave characteristics, and burial location. If they were really separable from other people by virtue of their social rank and political or economic clout, then they also should have been distinguishable from everyone else in terms of other aspects of mortuary behavior. This demonstrates the importance of multiple lines of evidence to make sense of the often ambiguous archaeological record.

By their very nature, some burial offerings, perhaps a minority of them, are informative about the specific nature of interpersonal relations or the roles people (or their families) performed in life. Accurate age and sex estimates, however, are needed before great weight can be placed on statements about the association of certain artifacts with different age and sex groups.

At the recently reanalyzed Read site, for example, atlatls (weights and hooks) from adults for whom sex could be determined were found only with men (Milner and Jefferies 1998). That is not the impression one gets from the earlier literature on the Green River sites, beginning with Webb and Haag (1939). Weights and hooks with women and children were considered puzzling but were perhaps explicable because atlatls, utilitarian items, might have been used in "some form of ceremonial ritual" (Webb 1946:330). Winters, also concerned with this problem, decided that "the roles of females overlapped those of males in some way"—he was unwilling, however, "to evoke a platoon of Amazons, or a succession of Boadiceas defending the Green River mussel beds against the onslaught of intruders" (1968:206–207). If the discrepancy between Read and the original Green River site reports in terms of adults with atlatls is not a result of some peculiarity at Read, it can only result from two problems, both of which are within our ability to resolve through additional studies. First, this difference might be attributable to the use of error-prone sex estimates in older studies. Second, single-site samples such as that from Read might be too small to be representative of broader patterns. These issues can be addressed through the use of better osteological methods and by increasing samples through combining geographically proximate, temporally equivalent, and culturally similar sites.

Intergroup Relations

Artifacts from Archaic burials that generally receive the most attention are those indicative of connections to distant places. Mortuary sites are especially important in studies of exchange systems because much of the exotic material in circulation in the distant past ended up in graves. Broad-based studies of large regions up to and beyond the entire Midwest are needed to identify fully spatial and temporal variability in the distributions of various kinds of artifacts, including nonlocal objects and distinctive artifact forms of both commonly available and exotic materials, as Jefferies (1996) has done for carved bone pins. Here it is sufficient to say that the distributions of two kinds of materials—native copper and marine shell—varied greatly across the Midcontinent during late Middle to Late Archaic times.

Copper was much more common in the upper Midwest than in the lower Ohio Valley, especially during the Late Archaic (including the Terminal Archaic). This distribution, spanning a lengthy period, is largely explicable by proximity to the source since much of the copper presumably originated in upper Michigan (compare Alex 2000; Arzigian and Stevenson 2003; Baerreis et al. 1954; Binford 1963a; Charles et al. 1988; Donaldson and Wortner 1995; Ellis et al. 1990; Faulkner 1960; Green and Schermer 1988; Hruska 1967; Klepinger and Henning 1976; Marquardt and Watson 1983; Moore 1916; Overstreet 1980; Overstreet et al. 1996; Perino 1968; Ritzenthaler 1946; Ritzenthaler and Wittry 1952; Robertson et al. 1999; Robison 1986; Sciulli and Aument 1987; Sciulli and Schuck 2001; Sciulli et al. 1993; Spence 1986; Stevenson et al. 1997; Stoltman 1997; Titterington 1950; Watson 2005; Webb 1946, 1951; Webb and Haag 1947). Here, for once, sampling is not a problem because so many Green River burials have been excavated, and copper so rarely occurs there.

Marine shells—mostly whelk but also marginella and other shells—were another widely distributed and highly valued material found at late Middle to Late Archaic sites, primarily with burials. They were usually fashioned into beads, such as the whelk disk and columella beads in many Green River graves (Marquardt and Watson 2005b; Moore 1916; Watson 2005; Webb 1946, 1950a, 1950b; Webb and Haag 1939, 1940, 1947). In western Kentucky, the disk form was the most common, and the beads were generally regularly shaped, polished, and often occurred in matched sets. Aesthetically speaking, they were every bit as attractive as the numerous beads fashioned in the much later Mississippian chiefdoms, about which so much has been written. Cut sections of shells have also been found, although not as many people were buried with them as with beads. Marine-shell objects, mostly beads and gorgets, from contemporaneous to Terminal Archaic (Red Ocher and Glacial Kame) sites to the north were not nearly as common, although they have been found from the upper Mississippi drainage eastward across the Great Lakes region (Alex 2000; Arzigian and Stevenson 2003; Baerreis et al. 1954; Donaldson and Wortner 1995; Ellis et al. 1990; Green and Schermer 1988; Hruska 1967; Overstreet 1980; Overstreet et al. 1996; Perino 1968; Ritzenthaler and Wittry 1952; Robertson et al. 1999; Sciulli and Schuck 2001; Stevenson et al. 1997; Stothers and Abel 1993). The reason for a markedly uneven regional distribution of marine-shell objects, mostly beads, is not known. Sampling plays a part in it since so many Green River burials have been carefully excavated (New Deal archaeologists were particularly interested in finding and documenting grave goods). It is, however, not the full explanation because enough burials are known elsewhere, such as at Black Earth and Rosenberger, to show that marine-shell objects have not been missed simply because insufficient numbers of graves have been excavated (Driskell 1979; Jefferies and Lynch 1983; Lynch 1982).

Another topic that requires additional attention is the origin and continuity of belief systems indicated by grave goods of presumed ritual significance. Among them are turtle carapace rattles from lower Ohio Valley sites, including Barrett, Carlston Annis, Chiggerville, Indian Knoll, Read, and Ward in Kentucky, and Riverton in Illinois (Moore 1916; Webb 1946, 1950a, 1950b; Webb and Haag 1939, 1940, 1947; Winters 1969). Rattles continued to be used from Archaic times into the historic period, when they were incorporated into various ceremonies, often as part of costumes. Cut upper and lower carnivore jaws similar to those used by Middle Woodland groups indicate that some rituals that were widespread later in time had antecedents in the Archaic period. A few cut carnivore jaws have been discovered at Indian Knoll and the Terminal Archaic Hind site in Ontario, and specially prepared sections of bear crania have been found at the Terminal Archaic Williams site in Ohio and at Hind (Abel et al. 2001; Donaldson and Wortner 1995; Ellis et al. 1990; Sciulli et al. 1982; Stothers and Abel 1993; Webb 1946). While such objects indicate a continuity of beliefs for lengthy periods, their specific meanings and uses no doubt changed over many generations and were not identical in all places.

Conflicts resulting in injury and death also broke out on occasion during the Archaic period (Milner 1999). Stone and antler projectile points deeply embedded in bone were recognized as early as Moore's (1916) excavation at Indian Knoll (Figure 5.5). Most people were presumably killed in conflicts between separate bands rather than in disputes that took place within residential groups. When tensions within a particular group had increased to the point at which disruptive killings took place, the band almost certainly fissioned along kin lines. The bloody conflict likely continued between the newly separated groups, much like those that often took place in near-recent times in small-scale societies. Mutilation of bodies, specifically by scalping and decapitation, is clear evidence of intergroup conflict as opposed to within-group homicide. Fighting among community members was sufficiently disruptive without adding the humiliation and antagonism that followed the desecration of corpses and the flaunting of trophies. Examples of such treatment of bodies have been identified at Ward, Carlston Annis, and Indian Knoll,

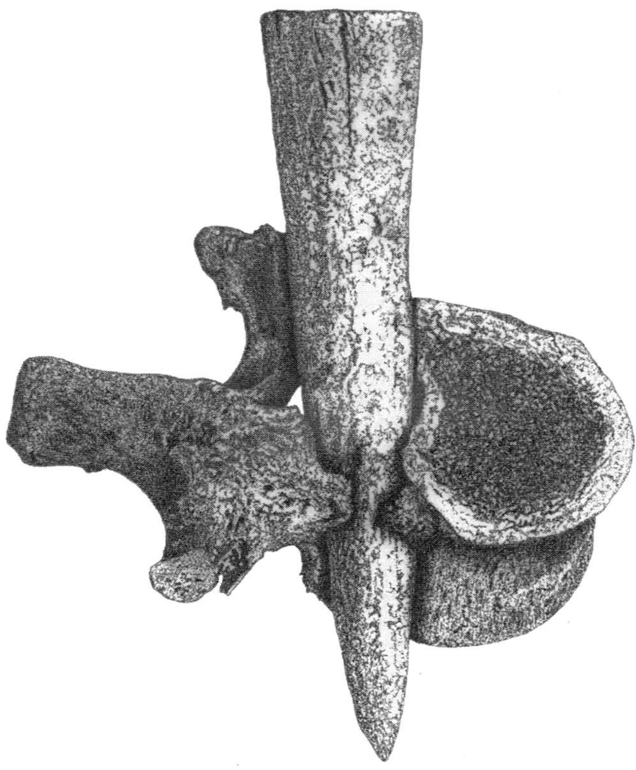

Figure 5.5. An antler point (ca. 10 cm long) was lodged in a lumbar vertebra from C. B. Moore's excavation at Indian Knoll, Kentucky. Drawn from Moore 1916:Figure 20.

and they have also been found in skeletal samples from the large debris heaps along the middle Tennessee River to the south (Mensforth 2001, 2005; Smith 1997).

Conflicts date back at least to the Early Archaic, the oldest period for which skeletons are available for examination. One of the relatively few Kentucky skeletons dating to this period has a projectile point embedded in the vertebral column (DiBlasi 1981). People in the Midcontinent were not the only ones to fight among themselves, as shown by the well-known Kennewick skeleton from the American Northwest (Chatters 2000). Skeletal trauma attributable to warfare has been identified in several late Middle to Late Archaic Green River debris heaps (Mensforth 2001, 2005; Moore 1916; Snow 1948; Watson 2005; Webb 1946, 1950a; Webb and Haag 1940, 1947). An important, unresolved question is whether these individuals were clustered temporally (stratigraphically) or spatially within the Green River middens or were scattered throughout these long-occupied sites. Such information would help determine if attacks punctuated long periods of generally peaceful conditions or if warfare was a feature of much or all of the late Middle and Late Archaic periods.

People in other parts of the Midcontinent were also killed on occasion, particularly during the terminal Late Archaic (Milner 1999). While conflict-related losses of life are known to have been widespread, data are too sparse to say much more than that. Systematic examinations of skeletons will perhaps allow the identification of certain times and places that were more dangerous than others and to relate this variation to differences in natural and social settings.

Individuals showing signs of violent death who were buried in the Green River and Tennessee River debris heaps dominate perceptions about late Middle to Late Archaic conflict. Perhaps conflicts were more likely to break out in these areas than they were elsewhere. At this point, however, the possibility that these river valley sites show the most evidence of conflict simply because they are the ones with disproportionately large numbers of skeletons cannot be excluded.

Estimating the frequency of conflict-related deaths is difficult, beyond noting that counts based on direct skeletal evidence—embedded points and desecrated bodies—surely underestimate warfare casualties. That is because skeletons are frequently incomplete, bones are poorly preserved, and projectile points struck bone in only a minority of cases.[13] Nevertheless, even low frequencies of deaths from intergroup conflicts added just one more element of uncertainty to lives already full of uncertainties. Warfare is likely to have had a broader impact than the immediate loss of life alone. Sudden and unexpected deaths of people who played critical roles in the survival of small groups increased the risk of death for remaining household and community members. Local groups undoubtedly went through periods of growth and decline, despite population size having changed little over the long run across such broadly defined areas as the Midcontinent. Warfare likely played a part in this process, perhaps mostly from mortality crises stemming from the loss of just a few key people, especially if they happened to die at critical points in the annual cycle when their contributions were essential for survival.

Concluding Statements

Given the existing state of knowledge, we advocate three levels of future analysis. All require attention, and work on all three should proceed simultaneously. First, effort should be directed toward single sites, especially more analyses of earlier excavated materials. Second, regional analyses are necessary to identify common features of the cemetery samples and to document variability among them. An argument can be made for combining geographically and temporally proximate collections, such as those from sites along the Green River, for many kinds of analyses. Third, regional patterns should be put into a larger context of occupations across the Midwest and beyond. Whether mortuary customs varied across broad geographical areas, much like the distributions of various contemporaneous point styles, would be important to know. Issues worth examining include precisely how the dead were handled, which likely varied greatly from one place to the next, and how various categories of individuals, those separated by age, sex, and physical ability, were treated. The first topic is likely indicative of largely idiosyncratic historical factors, including which groups had the greatest cultural affinity, regardless of how those close relationships arose. The second one is related to fundamental ways in which societies were organized and people went about making a living.

While there is much that cannot be done with earlier reports, dismissing them is not an option. In fact, the rich information in older reports and collections often goes largely unrecognized, and much of what was once known is simply forgotten in the rush to dig more sites. Findings of earlier surveys and excavations in their entirety, not only the most remarkable discoveries, must be a part of future analyses. We must address a situation not unlike the one 70 years ago when archaeologists were faced with unprecedented amounts of materials from the Great Depression excavations. Their solution, when they availed themselves of it, was the now much-maligned trait list—they had little choice in the matter. Unlike them, we possess the means of organizing and analyzing vast amounts of information. It remains for us to do so in temporally and geographically broad-scale analyses.

The results of our simple bead exercise are encouraging as an example of what can be learned by reexamining old data. The principal conclusion stemming from the bead distribution—that certain people served as critical nodes in networks that encompassed the Green River groups—will come as no surprise to archaeologists dealing with the Archaic period. But demonstrating that was indeed the case is another matter. The most important point is that much more remains to be learned from mortuary-related materials.

Toward this end, we advocate the development of accessible databases based on systematic examinations of old reports and collections, when possible done in tandem. Without making full use of the great efforts of preceding generations of researchers, we will continue to speak from an impoverished knowledge of the past. The databases we advocate must accommodate current research questions while remaining sufficiently open and flexible to allow for those of the future.

Several steps must be taken. First, unambiguous classifications of materials and standardized data-collection methods must be employed for features, artifacts, and skeletons. A model of that approach is the widely used skeletal data collection guidelines developed in the early 1990s (Buikstra and Ubelaker 1994). Second, archaeological reports—including the so-called gray literature, which might just as well be considered unpublished—should be gleaned for the information they contain. Third, collections must be reexamined for critical information that previously was not of interest, was inadequately collected by today's standards, or was not reported in its entirety. Fourth, these data sets should be made available in a publicly accessible format so that all scholars can make use of them. Such tasks are by no means easy, but they are necessary to enable full use of the information that has already been collected and to allow the design of problem-specific projects to address what we do not already know.

In short, old collections contain much new information hidden within them. A case could be made—and in our opinion it would be a strong one indeed—that existing collections are as valuable a resource as much of the material that still remains in the ground. Reanalyses of museum materials that address current research questions and employ up-to-date methods are absolutely essential for interpreting what took place in the distant past. They are necessary to take full advantage of the information on Archaic burials that has been collected and reported with great effort and expense over the past century by numerous archaeologists and osteologists.

Acknowledgments

Published and unpublished sources and field impressions were generously provided by Anne Bader, Donald Cochran, Eve Hargrave, Kris Hedmon, Richard Jefferies, Dale McElrath, and Lori Wright.

Endnotes

1. The burials came from 47 sites. Cremations were not included because estimates of the number of individuals represented are typically not included in original reports.
2. Unpublished information kindly provided by James A. Brown and from notes in the possession of Buikstra and Wiant.
3. All but three of 15 Tree Row radiocarbon estimates postdate 3000 B.C. When these estimates are calibrated, the dates range from 5320 to 2880 B.C. (Dale L. McElrath, pers. comm.).
4. In the absence of associated grave goods, the excavators based cultural affiliation on radiocarbon dates.
5. A similar point has been made for prehistoric hunter-gatherer societies elsewhere in the world (Rowley-Conwy 2001).
6. The 16 Minnesota sites yielded from one to 15 individuals, with a mean of four and a median of one (Arzigian and Stevenson 2003:76).
7. Note that the nature of the deposits where someone was buried does not necessarily indicate anything whatsoever about the intention of the people involved in the funerary proceedings or about the importance of the individual being buried. For example, in the Southwest marked graves that were considered sacred were placed near habitation areas but within trash deposits (Ortiz 1969).
8. All statements about the sex of juveniles in older osteological and archaeological reports can be dismissed without further ado.
9. The older studies included skeletons from Carlston Annis, Chiggerville, Indian Knoll, Morris, Parrish, Read, and Rosenberger in Kentucky; Airport, Modoc Rock Shelter, Pete Klunk, Riverton, and Robeson Hills in Illinois; an unnamed Red Ocher site in Indiana; Riverside in Michigan; Hatten in Missouri; Oconto, Osceola, and Reigh in Wisconsin; and Hind and Milton-Thomazi in Ontario (Faulkner 1960; Katzenberg and Sullivan 1979; Klepinger and Henning 1976; Neumann 1967; Perino 1968; Pfeiffer 1977; Rolingson and Schwartz 1966; Roper 1978; Skarland

1939; Webb 1946, 1950a, 1950b, 1951; Winters 1969; Wolf and Brooks 1979). The post-1980 studies included skeletons from the following sites: Ashworth, Carlston Annis, KYANG, and Read in Kentucky; Black Earth, Bluebell, Elizabeth, Gibson, Koster, Modoc Rock Shelter, and Tree Row in Illinois; Turkey River in Iowa; 20IS46 in Michigan; Boose, Duff, and Kirian-Treglia in Ohio; and Hind, Meredith-Goodall, Sartori, and Schweitzer in Ontario (Anderson 1991; Bade 1992; Bader and Granger 1989; Barondess and Sauer 1985; Buikstra 1981; Charles et al. 1988; DiBlasi 1981; Donaldson and Wortner 1995; Granger 1988; Green and Schermer 1988; Hedman and West n.d.; Lynch 1982; Mensforth 1990; Milner and Jefferies 1998; Sciulli and Aument 1987; Sciulli and Schuck 2001; Sciulli et al. 1993; Varney and Pfeiffer 1995; Wiant and Van Arsdale 2002; Wright 1987).

10. There are additional problems beyond those of immediate interest. For example, at Carlston Annis, altogether too many skeletons are identified as A (Adolescent, 13–17 years) in the burial list, mainly on the basis of field observations (Webb 1950a:275–287). They represent 60 percent of the skeletons from the site, even though this is the age range in which the risk of death is the lowest. Presumably, some confusion arose over what "A" designated, either "Adolescent" or "Adult." That seems to have been the case here because one of the burial photographs clearly shows an adult with fused long-bone epiphyses, although the table lists the skeleton as A (Adolescent). Furthermore, a gross overrepresentation of adolescents was not found in a more recent examination of skeletons from the site (Mensforth 1990).
11. We recognize that in no society are social, political, and economic relationships truly egalitarian. Here the term is applied to societies that lack significant institutionalized inequalities among hierarchically organized groups whose membership is based largely on birthright. That is, a distinction is drawn between societies commonly classified as "bands" and "tribes" versus those labeled "chiefdoms" and "states."
12. Some individuals were omitted because the numbers of beads were not provided in site reports. The bead sample could be increased by examining field notes, as was done for Read, once again underscoring the value of museum materials.
13. On the basis of Indian Wars arrow injuries, the number of casualties under conditions of ideal preservation can be conservatively estimated as triple the number of skeletons with projectile-related bone damage (Milner 2005). While comparable information on spear injuries is unavailable, skeletal evidence for these wounds must likewise underestimate the total number of wounds.

References Cited

Abel, Timothy J., David M. Stothers, and Jason M. Koralewski
2001 The Williams Mortuary Complex: A Transitional Archaic Regional Interaction Center in Northwestern Ohio. In *Archaic Transitions in Ohio and Kentucky Prehistory*, edited by Olaf H. Prufer, Sara E. Pedde, and Richard S. Meindl, pp. 290–327. Kent State University Press, Kent, Ohio.

Albertson, Donald G., and Douglas K. Charles
1988 Archaic Mortuary Component. In *The Archaic and Woodland Cemeteries at the Elizabeth Site in the Lower Illinois Valley*, edited by Douglas K. Charles, Steven R. Leigh, and Jane E. Buikstra, pp. 29–40. Research Series 7. Kampsville Archeological Center, Kampsville, Illinois.

Albert, Réka, Hawoong Jeong, and Albert-László Barabási
1999 Diameter of the World-Wide Web. *Nature* 401:130–131.

Alex, Lynn M.
2000 *Iowa's Archaeological Past*. University of Iowa Press, Iowa City.

Anderson, Eve
1991 New Perspectives on Archaic Mortuary Behavior at Modoc Rockshelter. Paper presented at the 56th Annual Meeting of the Society for American Archaeology, New Orleans, Louisiana.

Arzigian, Constance M., and Katherine P. Stevenson
2003 *Minnesota's Indian Mounds and Burial Sites: A Synthesis of Prehistoric and Early Historic Archaeological Data*. Publication 1. Office of the State Archaeologist, St. Paul, Minnesota.

Bacon, Willard S., and William J. Miller
1957 Notes on the Excavation of a Burial Area in Northeast Missouri. *The Missouri Archaeologist* 19:19–33.

Bade, Mary J.
1992 Human Skeletal Analysis. In *Late Archaic Components at Modoc Rock Shelter, Randolph County, Illinois*, by Steven R. Ahler, Mary J. Bade, Frances B. King, Bonnie W. Styles, and Paula J. Thorson, pp. 130–132. Reports of Investigations 48. Illinois State Museum, Springfield.

Bader, Anne T.
1992 An Analysis of Bone and Antler Tool Use Patterns from the Kentucky Air National Guard Site. Master's thesis, Department of Anthropology, University of Kentucky, Lexington.

Bader, Anne T., and Joseph E. Granger
1989 *Recent Archaeological Investigations on the Kentucky Air National Guard Site (15JF267) Jefferson County, Kentucky*. Granger Consultants, Louisville, Kentucky.

Baerreis, David A., Hiroshi Daifuku, and James E. Lundsted
1954 The Burial Complex of the Reigh Site, Winnebago Cunty, Wisconsin. *The Wisconsin Archeologist* 35:1–35.

Barabási, Albert-László
2002 *Linked: The New Science of Networks*. Perseus, Cambridge, Massachusetts.

Barondess, David A., and Norman J. Sauer
1985 Human Skeletal Remains from 20IS46 a Late Archaic Burial Locale in Eastern Michigan. *The Michigan Archaeologist* 31:82–96.

Bassett, Everett J.
1982 Osteological Analysis of Carrier Mills Burials. In *The Carrier Mills Archaeological Project: Human Adaptation in the Saline Valley, Illinois*, edited by Richard W. Jefferies and Brian M. Butler, pp. 1027–1114. Research Paper 33. Center for Archaeological Investigations, Southern Illinois University, Carbondale.

Bentley, R. Alexander
2003 Scale-Free Network Growth and Social Inequality. In *Complex Systems and Archaeology*, edited by R. Alexander Bentley and Herbert D. G. Maschner, pp. 27–45. University of Utah Press, Salt Lake City.

Binford, Lewis R.
1963a The Hodges Site: A Late Archaic Burial Station. In *Miscellaneous Studies in Typology and Classification*, pp. 124–148. Anthropological Papers 19. Museum of Anthropology, University of Michigan, Ann Arbor.
1963b The Pomranky Site: A Late Archaic Burial Station. In *Miscellaneous Studies in Typology and Classification*, pp. 149–192. Anthropological Papers 19. Museum of Anthropology, University of Michigan, Ann Arbor.

Blalock, Hubert M.
1972 *Social Statistics*. McGraw-Hill, New York.

Boldsen, Jesper L., George R. Milner, Lyle W. Konigsberg, and James W. Wood
2002 Transition Analysis: A New Method for Estimating Age from Skeletons. In *Paleodemography: Age Distributions from Skeletal Samples,* edited by Robert D. Hoppa and James W. Vaupel, pp. 73–106. Cambridge University Press, Cambridge, England.

Bowen, Jonathan E.
1987 Late Archaic Occupations at the Scioto County Home Site (33SC17). *Ohio Archaeologist* 37:15–17.

Brown, James A.
1983 Summary. In *Archaic Hunters and Gatherers in the American Midwest*, edited by James L. Phillips and James A. Brown, pp. 5–10. Academic Press, Orlando, Florida.
1985 Long-Term Trends to Sedentism and the Emergence of Complexity in the American Midwest. In *Prehistoric Hunter-Gatherers: The Emergence of Cultural Complexity*, edited by T. Douglas Price and James A. Brown, pp. 201–231. Academic Press, Orlando, Florida.

Brown, James A., and Robert K. Vierra
1983 What Happened in the Middle Archaic? Introduction to an Ecological Approach to Koster Site Archaeology. In *Archaic Hunters and Gatherers in the American Midwest*, edited by James L. Phillips and James A. Brown, pp. 165–195. Academic Press, New York.

Buchanan, Mark
2002 *Small Worlds and the Groundbreaking Theory of Networks*. W. W. Norton, New York.

Buikstra, Jane E.
1977 Biocultural Dimensions of Archeological Study: A Regional Perspective. In *Biocultural Adaptation in Prehistoric America*, edited by Robert L. Blakely, pp. 67–84. Proceedings of the Southern Anthropological Society 11. University of Georgia Press, Athens.
1981 Mortuary Practices, Palaeodemography and Palaeopathology: A Case Study from the Koster Site (Illinois). In *The Archaeology of Death*, edited by Robert Chapman, Ian Kinnes, and Klavs Randsborg, pp. 123–132. Cambridge University Press, Cambridge, England.

Buikstra, Jane E., and Douglas K. Charles
1999 Centering the Ancestors: Cemeteries, Mounds, and Sacred Landscapes of the Ancient North American Midcontinent. In *Archaeologies of Landscape: Contemporary Perspectives*, edited by Wendy Ashmore and A. Bernard Knapp, pp. 201–228. Blackwell, Malden, Massachusetts.

Buikstra, Jane E., and Douglas H. Ubelaker
1994 *Standards for Data Collection from Human Skeletal Remains*. Research Series 44. Arkansas Archeological Survey, Fayetteville.

Charles, Douglas K.
1995 Diachronic Regional Social Dynamics: Mortuary Sites in the Illinois Valley/American Bottom Region. In *Regional Approaches to Mortuary Analysis*, edited by Lane A. Beck, pp. 77–99. Plenum Press, New York.

Charles, Douglas K., and Jane E. Buikstra
1983 Archaic Mortuary Sites in the Central Mississippi Drainage: Distribution, Structure, and Behavioral Implications. In *Archaic Hunters and Gatherers in the American Midwest*, edited by James L. Phillips and James A. Brown, pp. 117–145. Academic Press, New York.

Charles, Douglas K., Steven R. Leigh, and Donald G. Albertson
1988 Appendix 2: Burial Descriptions. In *The Archaic and Woodland Cemeteries at the Elizabeth Site in the Lower Illinois Valley*, edited by Douglas K. Charles, Steven R. Leigh, and Jane E. Buikstra, pp. 247–274. Research Series 7. Kampsville Archeological Center, Kampsville, Illinois.

Chatters, James C.
2000 The Recovery and First Analysis of an Early Holocene Human Skeleton from Kennewick, Washington. *American Antiquity* 65:291–316.

Claassen, Cheryl P.
1991 Gender, Shellfishing, and the Shell Mound Archaic. In *Engendering Archaeology: Women and Prehistory*, edited by Joan M. Gero and Margaret W. Conkey, pp. 276–300. Blackwell, Oxford, England.
1992 Shell Mounds as Burial Mounds: A Revision of the Shell Mound Archaic. In *Current Archaeological Research in Kentucky*, vol. 2, edited by David Pollack and A. Gwynn Henderson, pp. 1–11. Kentucky Heritage Council, Frankfort.
1996a A Consideration of the Social Organization of the Shell Mound Archaic. In *Archaeology of the Mid-Holocene Southeast*, edited by Kenneth E. Sassaman and David G. Anderson, pp. 235–258. University Press of Florida, Gainesville.
1996b Research Problems with Shells from Green River Shell Matrix Sites. In *Of Caves and Shell Mounds*, edited by Kenneth C. Carstens and Patty Jo Watson, pp. 132–139. University of Alabama Press, Tuscaloosa.

Cochran, Donald R.
1997 *McCullough's Run (12-B-1036): A Prehistoric Cremation Cemetery, Bartholomew County, Indiana*. Archaeological Resources Management Service, Ball State University, Muncie, Indiana.

Conner, Michael D., and Elizabeth Brandon
1986 Analysis of Skeletal Remains. In *Archaeological Excavations at the Fitzgibbons Site, Gallatin County, Illinois*, by Cathy A. Robison, pp. 197–217. Research Paper 53. Center for Archaeological Investigations, Southern Illinois University, Carbondale.

Cotter, John
1939 Letter to Kinkead dated January 2nd. William S. Webb Museum of Anthropology, University of Kentucky, Lexington.

Cunningham, Wilbur M.
1948 *A Study of the Glacial Kame Culture in Michigan, Ohio, and Indiana*. Occasional Contributions 12. Museum of Anthropology, University of Michigan, Ann Arbor.

DiBlasi, Philip J.

1981 A New Assessment of the Archaeological Significance of the Ashworth Site (15BU236). Master's thesis, Interdisciplinary Studies, University of Louisville, Louisville, Kentucky.

Donaldson, William S., and Stanley Wortner

1995 The Hind Site and the Glacial Kame Burial Complex in Ontario. *Ontario Archaeology* 59:5–95.

Driskell, Boyce N.

1979 The Rosenberger Site (15JF18). In *Excavations at Four Archaic Sites in the Lower Ohio Valley Jefferson County, Kentucky*, vol. 2, edited by Michael B. Collins, pp. 697–803. Occasional Papers in Anthropology 1. Department of Anthropology, University of Kentucky, Lexington.

Ellis, Chris J., Ian T. Kenyon, and Michael W. Spence

1990 The Archaic. In *The Archaeology of Southern Ontario to A.D. 1650*, edited by Chris J. Ellis and Neal Ferris, pp. 65–124. Occasional Publications 5. London Chapter, Ontario Archaeological Society.

Farnsworth, Kenneth B.

1993 New Information on 1932 Titterington Salvage Excavations at the Hartford Church Archaic Cemetery. *Illinois Archaeology* 5:141–147.

Faulkner, Charles H.

1960 The Red Ochre Culture: An Early Burial Complex in Northern Indiana. *The Wisconsin Archeologist* 41:35–49.

Fowler, Melvin L.

1959 *Summary Report of Modoc Rock Shelter 1952, 1953, 1955, 1956*. Report of Investigations 8. Illinois State Museum, Springfield.

Goldstein, Lynne G.

1976 Spatial Structure and Social Organization: Regional Manifestations of Mississippian Society. Ph.D. dissertation, Department of Anthropology, Northwestern University, Evanston, Illinois.

1980 *Mississippian Mortuary Practices: A Case Study of Two Cemeteries in the Lower Illinois Valley*. Scientific Papers 4. Northwestern University Archeological Program, Evanston, Illinois.

Granger, Joseph E.

1988 Late/Terminal Archaic Settlement in the Falls of the Ohio River Region of Kentucky: An Examination of Components, Phases, and Clusters. In *Paleoindian and Archaic Research in Kentucky*, edited by Charles D. Hockensmith, David Pollack, and Thomas N. Sanders, pp. 153–203. Kentucky Heritage Council, Frankfort.

Green, William, and Shirley J. Schermer

1988 The Turkey River Mound Group (13CT1). In *Archaeological and Paleoenvironmental Studies in the Turkey River Valley, Northeastern Iowa*, edited by William Green, pp. 131–198. Research Papers 13. Office of the State Archaeologist, University of Iowa, Iowa City.

Griffin, James B.

1952 Culture Periods in Eastern United States Archeology. In *Archeology of Eastern United States*, edited by James B. Griffin, pp. 352–362. University of Chicago Press, Chicago.

1967 Eastern North American Archaeology: A Summary. *Science* 156:175–191.

Hassen, Harold

1987 Preliminary Summary and Interpretations of the 1984 Investigations at the Bullseye Site, 11-Ge-127. In *The Bullseye Site: A Floodplain Archaic Mortuary Site in the Lower Illinois River Valley*, by Harold Hassen and Kenneth B. Farnsworth, pp. 1–12. Reports of Investigations 42. Illinois State Museum, Springfield.

Hedman, Kristin, and Jolee West

n.d. Tree Row Skeletal Remains. Manuscript on file, Illinois Transportation Archaeological Research Program, University of Illinois, Urbana.

Howell, Nancy

1979 *Demography of the Dobe !Kung*. Academic Press, New York.

1982 Village Composition Implied by a Paleodemographic Life Table: The Libben Site. *American Journal of Physical Anthropology* 59:263–269.

Hruska, Robert

1967 The Riverside Site: A Late Archaic Manifestation in Michigan. *The Wisconsin Archeologist* 48:145–260.

Huberman, Bernardo A., and Lada A. Adamic

1999 Growth Dynamics of the World-Wide Web. *Nature* 401:131.

Jackes, Mary

2000 Building the Bases for Paleodemographic Analysis: Adult Age Determination. In *Biological Anthropology of the Human Skeleton*, edited by Shelley R. Saunders and M. Anne Katzenberg, pp. 417–466. Wiley-Liss, New York.

Jefferies, Richard W.

1983 Middle Archaic–Late Archaic Transition in Southern Illinois: An Example from the Carrier Mills Archaeological District. *American Archeology* 3:199–205.

1995 The Status of Archaic Period Research in the Midwestern United States. *Archaeology of Eastern North America* 23:119–144.

1996 Middle Archaic Bone Pins: Evidence of Mid-Holocene Regional-Scale Social Groups in the Southern Midwest. *American Antiquity* 62:464–487.

Jefferies, Richard W., and B. Mark Lynch

1983 Dimensions of Middle Archaic Cultural Adaptation at the Black Earth Site, Saline County, Illinois. In *Archaic Hunters and Gatherers in the American Midwest*, edited by James L. Phillips and James A. Brown, pp. 299–322. Academic Press, New York.

Jefferies, Richard W., Victor D. Thompson, and George R. Milner

2005 Archaic Hunter-Gatherer Landscape Use in West-Central Kentucky. *Journal of Field Archaeology* 30:3–23.

Katzenberg, M. Anne, and Norman C. Sullivan

1979 A Report on the Human Burial from the Milton-Thomazi Site. *Ontario Archaeology* 32:27–34.

Klepinger, Linda, and Dale R. Henning

1976 The Hatten Mound: A Two-Component Burial Site in Northeast Missouri. *The Missouri Archaeologist* 37:92–170.

Konigsberg, Lyle W., and Susan R. Frankenberg

1994 Paleodemography: "Not Quite Dead." *Evolutionary Anthropology* 3:92–105.

Lovis, William A.

1999 The Middle Archaic: Learning to Live in the Woodlands. In *Retrieving Michigan's Buried Past:*

The Archaeology of the Great Lakes State, edited by John R. Halsey, pp. 83–94. Bulletin 64. Cranbrook Institute of Science, Bloomfield Hills, Michigan.

Lynch, B. Mark
1982 Mortuary Behavior in the Carrier Mills Archaeological District. In *The Carrier Mills Archaeological Project: Human Adaptation in the Saline Valley, Illinois*, edited by Richard W. Jefferies and Brian M. Butler, pp. 1115–1231. Research Paper 33. Center for Archaeological Investigations, Southern Illinois University, Carbondale.

Maschner, Herbert D. G., and R. Alexander Bentley
2003 The Power Law of Rank and Household on the North Pacific. In *Complex Systems and Archaeology*, edited by R. Alexander Bentley and Herbert D. G. Maschner, pp. 47–60. University of Utah Press, Salt Lake City.

Marquardt, William H., and Patty Jo Watson
1983 The Shell Mound Archaic of Western Kentucky. In *Archaic Hunters and Gatherers in the American Midwest*, edited by James L. Phillips and James A. Brown, pp. 323–339. Academic Press, New York.

Marquardt, William H., and Patty Jo Watson
2004 The Green River Shell Mound Archaic: Interpretive Trajectories. In *Aboriginal Ritual and Economy in the Eastern Woodlands: Essays in Memory of Howard Dalton Winters*, edited by Anne-Marie Cantwell, Lawrence A. Conrad, and Jonathan E. Reyman, pp. 113-122. Scientific Papers 30. Illinois State Museum, Springfield.

Marquardt, William H., and Patty Jo Watson
2005a SMAP Investigations at the Carlston Annis Site, 15Bt5. In *Archaeology of the Middle Green River Region, Kentucky*, edited by William H. Marquardt and Patty Jo Watson, pp. 87-120. Monograph 5. Institute of Archaeology and Paleoenvironmental Studies, University of Florida, Gainesville.
2005b The Green River Shell Mound Archaic: Conclusions. In *Archaeology of the Middle Green River Region, Kentucky*, edited by William H. Marquardt and Patty Jo Watson, pp. 629-647. Monograph 5. Institute of Archaeology and Paleoenvironmental Studies, University of Florida, Gainesville.

Mead, Barbara, and Robert G. Kingsley
1985 20IS46, a Late Archaic Cemetery in Iosco County, Michigan. *The Michigan Archaeologist* 31:67–81.

Meindl, Richard S., Robert P. Mensforth, and Heather P. York
2001 Mortality, Fertility, and Growth in the Kentucky Late Archaic: The Paleodemography of the Ward Site. In *Archaic Transitions in Ohio and Kentucky Prehistory*, edited by Olaf H. Prufer, Sara E. Pedde, and Richard S. Meindl, pp. 87–109. Kent State University Press, Kent, Ohio.

Mensforth, Robert P.
1990 Paleodemography of the Carlston Annis (Bt-5) Late Archaic Skeletal Population. *American Journal of Physical Anthropology* 82:81–99.
2001 Warfare and Trophy Taking in the Archaic Period. In *Archaic Transitions in Ohio and Kentucky Prehistory*, edited by Olaf H. Prufer, Sara E. Pedde, and Richard S. Meindl, pp. 110–138. Kent State University Press, Kent, Ohio.
2005 Paleodemography of the Skeletal Population from Carlston Annis (15Bt5). In *Archaeology of the Middle Green River Region, Kentucky*, edited by William H. Marquardt and Patty Jo Watson, pp. 453-487. Monograph 5. Institute of Archaeology and Paleoenvironmental Studies, University of Florida, Gainesville.

Milner, George R.
1999 Warfare in Prehistoric and Early Historic Eastern North America. *Journal of Archaeological Research* 7:105–151.
2004 *The Moundbuilders*. Thames and Hudson, London.
2005 Nineteenth Century Arrow Wounds and Perceptions of Prehistoric Warfare. *American Antiquity* 70:144–156.

Milner, George R., and Richard W. Jefferies
1998 The Read Archaic Shell Midden in Kentucky. *Southeastern Archaeology* 17:119–132.

Milner, George R., and Virginia G. Smith
1986 *New Deal Archaeology in Kentucky: Excavations, Collections, and Research.* Occasional Papers in Anthropology 5. Program for Cultural Resource Assessment, University of Kentucky, Lexington.

Milner, George R., James W. Wood, and Jesper L. Boldsen
2000 Paleodemography. In *Biological Anthropology of the Human Skeleton*, edited by Shelley R. Saunders and M. Anne Katzenberg, pp. 467–497. Wiley-Liss, New York.

Moore, Clarence B.
1916 Some Aboriginal Sites on Green River, Kentucky; Certain Aboriginal Sites on Lower Ohio River; Additional Investigation on Mississippi River. *Journal of the Academy of Natural Sciences of Philadelphia* 16:431–511.

Neumann, Holm W.
1967 *The Paleopathology of the Archaic Modoc Rock Shelter Inhabitants.* Reports of Investigations 11. Illinois State Museum, Springfield.

Ortiz, Alfonso
1969 *The Tewa World: Space, Time, Being, and Becoming in a Pueblo Society*. University of Chicago Press, Chicago.

Overstreet, David F.
1980 The Convent Knoll Site (47-WK-327): A Red Ocher Cemetery in Waukesha County, Wisconsin. *The Wisconsin Archeologist* 61:34–90.

Overstreet, David F., Larry Doebert, Gary W. Henschel, Phil Sander, and David Wasion
1996 Two Red Ocher Mortuary Contexts from Southeastern Wisconsin—The Henschel Site (47Sb29), Sheboygan County and the Barnes Creek Site (47Kn41), Kenosha County. *The Wisconsin Archeologist* 77(1–2):36–62.

Pedde, Sara E., and Olaf H. Prufer
2001 The Kentucky Green River Archaic as Seen from the Ward Site. In *Archaic Transitions in Ohio and Kentucky Prehistory*, edited by Olaf H. Prufer, Sara E. Pedde, and Richard S. Meindl, pp. 59–86. Kent State University Press, Kent, Ohio.

Perino, Gregory H.
1962 A Review of Calhoun County, Illinois, Prehistory. *The Wisconsin Archeologist* 43:44–51.

1968 The Pete Klunk Mound Group, Calhoun County, Illinois: The Archaic and Hopewell Occupations. In *Hopewell and Woodland Site Archaeology in Illinois*, pp. 9–128. Bulletin 6. Illinois Archaeological Survey, Urbana.

Pfeiffer, Susan
1977 *The Skeletal Biology of Archaic Populations of the Great Lakes Region*. Mercury Series 64. Archaeological Survey of Canada, National Museum of Man, Ottawa.

Ritzenthaler, Robert
1946 The Osceola Site: An "Old Copper" Site near Potosi, Wisconsin. *The Wisconsin Archeologist* 27:53–70.

Ritzenthaler, Robert E., and Warren L. Wittry
1952 The Oconto Site—An Old Copper Manifestation. *The Wisconsin Archeologist* 33:119–224.

Robertson, James A., William A. Lovis, and John R. Halsey
1999 The Late Archaic: Hunter-Gatherers in an Uncertain Environment. In *Retrieving Michigan's Buried Past: The Archaeology of the Great Lakes State*, edited by John R. Halsey, pp. 95–124. Bulletin 64. Cranbrook Institute of Science, Bloomfield Hills, Michigan.

Robison, Cathy A.
1986 *Archaeological Excavations at the Fitzgibbons Site, Gallatin County, Illinois*. Research Paper 53. Center for Archaeological Investigations, Southern Illinois University, Carbondale.

Rolingson, Martha A., and Douglas W. Schwartz
1966 *Late Paleo-Indian and Early Archaic Manifestations in Western Kentucky*. University of Kentucky Press, Lexington.

Roper, Donna C.
1978 *The Airport Site: A Multicomponent Site in the Sangamon River Drainage*. Papers in Anthropology 4. Illinois State Museum, Springfield.

Rothschild, Nan A.
1979 Mortuary Behavior and Social Organization at Indian Knoll and Dickson Mounds. *American Antiquity* 44:658–675.

Rowley-Conwy, Peter
2001 Time, Change and the Archaeology of Hunter-Gatherers: How Original Is the 'Original Affluent Society'? In *Hunter-Gatherers: An Interdisciplinary Perspective*, edited by Catherine Panter-Brick, Robert H. Layton, and Peter Rowley-Conwy, pp. 39–72. Cambridge University Press, Cambridge, England.

St. Hoyme, Lucile E., and Mehmet Yasar Işçan
1989 Determination of Sex and Race: Accuracy and Assumptions. In *Reconstruction of Life from the Skeletons*, edited by Mehmet Yasar Işçan and Kenneth A. R. Kennedy, pp. 53–93. Alan R. Liss, New York.

Saxe, Arthur A.
1970 Social Dimensions of Mortuary Practices. Ph.D. dissertation, Department of Anthropology, University of Michigan, Ann Arbor.

Sciulli, Paul W., and Bruce W. Aument
1987 Paleodemography of the Duff Site (33LO111), Logan County, Ohio. *Midcontinental Journal of Archaeology* 12:117–144.

Sciulli, Paul W., Bruce W. Aument, and Leonard R. Piotrowski
1982 The Williams (33WO7A) Red Ochre Cemetery: Preliminary Description and Comparative Analysis of Acquired Dental Pathology. *Pennsylvania Archaeologist* 52:17–24.

Sciulli, Paul W., and Ray Schuck
2001 Terminal Late Archaic Mortuary Practices II. The Boose Cemetery. *Pennsylvania Archaeologist* 71:29–42.

Sciulli, Paul W., Ray Schuck, and Myra J. Geisen
1993 Terminal Late Archaic Mortuary Practices at Kirian-Treglia (33AL39). *Pennsylvania Archaeologist* 63:53–63.

Skarland, Ivar
1939 The Skeletal Material. In *The Chiggerville Site: Site 1, Ohio County, Kentucky*, by William S. Webb and William G. Haag, pp. 28–49. Reports in Anthropology 4(1). Department of Anthropology and Archaeology, University of Kentucky, Lexington.

Smith, Maria O.
1997 Osteological Indications of Warfare in the Archaic Period of the Western Tennessee Valley. In *Troubled Times: Violence and Warfare in the Past*, edited by Debra L. Martin and David W. Frayer, pp. 241–265. Gordon and Breach, Amsterdam.

Snow, Charles E.
1948 *Indian Knoll Skeletons of Site Oh 2, Ohio County, Kentucky*. Reports in Anthropology 4(3, pt. 2). Department of Anthropology, University of Kentucky, Lexington.

Spence, Michael W.
1986 Band Structure and Interaction in Early Southern Ontario. *Canadian Journal of Anthropology* 5:83–95.

Stevenson, Katherine P., Robert F. Boszhardt, Charles R. Moffat, Philip H. Salkin, Thomas C. Pleger, James L. Theler, and Constance M. Arzigian
1997 The Woodland Tradition. *The Wisconsin Archeologist* 78:140–201.

Stoltman, James B.
1997 The Archaic Tradition. *The Wisconsin Archeologist* 78:112–139.

Stothers, David M., and Timothy J. Abel
1993 Archaeological Reflections of the Late Archaic and Early Woodland Time Periods in the Western Lake Erie Region. *Archaeology of Eastern North America* 21:25–109.

Titterington, Paul F.
1950 Some Non-Pottery Sites in St. Louis Area. *Illinois State Archaeological Society Journal* 1:19–31.

Varney, Tamara L., and Susan Pfeiffer
1995 The People of the Hind Site. *Ontario Archaeology* 59:96–108.

Walthall, John A.
1999 Mortuary Behavior and Early Holocene Land Use in the North American Midcontinent. *North American Archaeologist* 20:1–30.

Watson, Patty Jo
2005 WPA Excavations in the Middle Green River Area: A Comparative Account. In *Archaeology of the Middle Green River Region, Kentucky*, edited by William H. Marquardt and Patty Jo Watson, pp. 515–628. Monograph 5. Institute of Archaeology and Paleoenvironmental Studies, University of Florida, Gainesville.

Webb, William S.
1938 Letter to Setzler dated August 5th. Webb Papers, Box 4. Library Archives, University of Kentucky, Lexington.

1946 *Indian Knoll: Site Oh 2, Ohio County, Kentucky*. Reports in Anthropology 4(3, pt. 1). Department of Anthropology and Archaeology, University of Kentucky, Lexington.

1950a *The Carlson Annis Mound: Site 5, Butler County, Kentucky*. Reports in Anthropology 7(4). Department of Anthropology, University of Kentucky, Lexington.

1950b *The Read Shell Midden: Site 10, Butler County, Kentucky*. Reports in Anthropology 7(5). Department of Anthropology, University of Kentucky, Lexington.

1951 *The Parrish Village Site: Site 45, Hopkins County, Kentucky*. Reports in Anthropology 7(6). Department of Anthropology, University of Kentucky, Lexington.

Webb, William S., and William G. Haag

1939 *The Chiggerville Site: Site 1, Ohio County, Kentucky*. Reports in Anthropology 4(1). Department of Anthropology and Archaeology, University of Kentucky, Lexington.

1940 *Cypress Creek Villages: Sites 11 and 12, McLean County, Kentucky*. Reports in Anthropology 4(2). Department of Anthropology and Archaeology, University of Kentucky, Lexington.

1947 *Archaic Sites in McLean County, Kentucky*. Reports in Anthropology 7(1). Department of Anthropology, University of Kentucky, Lexington.

Weiss, Kenneth M.

1973 *Demographic Models for Anthropology*. Memoirs 27. Society for American Archaeology, Washington, D.C.

Wiant, Michael D., and Cathy Van Arsdale

2002 Human Remains. In *Bluebell Site (11CT466) Archaeology: The 2001 Excavations*, by William Gordon Howe, Erin Brand, Marjorie B. Schroeder, Bonnie W. Styles, Cathy Van Arsdale, Robert E. Warren, and Michael D. Wiant, pp. 101–104. Technical Report 2002-1467-5. Quaternary Studies Program, Illinois State Museum, Springfield.

Winters, Howard D.

1968 Value Systems and Trade Cycles of the Late Archaic in the Midwest. In *New Perspectives in Archeology*, edited by Sally R. Binford and Lewis R. Binford, pp. 175–221. Aldine, Chicago.

1969 *The Riverton Culture*. Reports of Investigations 13. Illinois State Museum, Springfield.

Wolf, David J., and Robert L. Brooks

1979 The Prehistoric People of the Rosenberger Site. In *Excavations at Four Archaic Sites in the Lower Ohio Valley Jefferson County, Kentucky*, vol. 2, edited by Michael B. Collins, pp. 899–945. Occasional Papers in Anthropology 1. Department of Anthropology, University of Kentucky, Lexington.

Wright, Lori

1987 An Analysis of Early Archaic Skeletal Remains from Horizon 11 at the Koster Site, Illinois. Unpublished manuscript, Center for American Archaeology, Kampsville, Illinois.

6

Dalton and the Early Holocene Midcontinent: Setting the Stage

Brad Koldehoff and John A. Walthall

In eastern North America, the Paleoindian–Archaic transition generally corresponds to the Pleistocene–Holocene interface. During this time, the landforms, drainage systems, and biotic resources of the Midcontinent were reshaped. As the climate warmed and ice sheets melted, late Pleistocene plant and animal communities, which had few modern analogs, were reorganized into the basic biomes of today (Shelford 1963). This reorganization occurred over centuries and moved northward as the ice retreated and weather patterns shifted. Large mammals, like mammoths and mastodons, became extinct in the process. The Mississippi River valley was a conduit for change: initially clogged with sediment discharged by melting glaciers, often in great torrents, it was occupied by a shallow, braided channel, but once the flow of meltwater stopped, the river began to down-cut and meander, creating resource-rich lakes and wetlands. As the meandering river regime migrated up the Mississippi Valley, so did temperate deciduous forest (Delcourt et al. 1999; Graham and Grimm 1990; Grimm and Jacobson 1992; Jacobson et al. 1987; Saucier 1994; see also Styles and McMillan, this volume). With these new, essentially modern habitats came abundant seasonal resources, such as white-tailed deer, wild turkey, fish, waterfowl, and nuts. The utilization of these resources created the core subsistence practices of native populations for millennia, and these practices remained largely unchanged even after the advent of plant cultivation (Simon, this volume; Styles and McMillan, this volume).

We consider the initiation of these subsistence practices, and related land-use patterns and technological developments, as marking the beginning of the Archaic period or tradition.[1] In contrast, in the Paleoindian period or tradition, fluted-point-producing groups encountered now-extinct fauna and lived a more mobile lifestyle, hunting and foraging in a largely vacant and unfamiliar environment. In the central Mississippi Valley (CMV), the new Archaic practices and technologies were geared toward the emerging, seasonal resources of the early Holocene, and they were initiated by Dalton-point-producing groups. However, many researchers classify Dalton not as Early Archaic but as Late Paleoindian, primarily on the basis of point morphology (e.g., Ellis et al. 1998; Goodyear 1999; Morse 1997; Morse and Morse 1996; Morse et al. 1996). Nonetheless, Dalton faunal assemblages, unlike those of Clovis (e.g., Graham and Kay 1988), do not contain extinct mammal remains; instead, Dalton faunal assemblages reflect generalized foraging and hunting practices targeting modern species, such as white-tailed deer (Goodyear 1982, 1999; Styles and McMillan, this volume). Likewise, Dalton tool kits typically contain heavy-duty woodworking tools (chipped-stone adze blades), whereas Clovis (and other fluted-point) tool kits lack such tools. Dalton adzes are significant because they mark the inception of a robust woodworking industry, a key element of subsequent Archaic, Woodland, and Mississippian cultures (Gaertner 1994; Morse and Goodyear 1973; Yerkes and Gaertner 1997). As noted by Morse, adzes were likely used to make "dugout canoes, houses, baskets, wooden bowls, masks, and so forth" (1997:128). This inferred level of cultural elaboration denotes a more settled and localized land-use pattern than that commonly assigned to Paleoindian groups. On the basis of patterns of lithic procurement and inferred patterns of land use and mobility, we have demonstrated that Dalton groups in the CMV were more sedentary and river valley oriented than were Clovis groups

(Koldehoff 2006; Koldehoff and Walthall 2004; Walthall and Koldehoff 1998, 1999).

Therefore, unlike researchers who see continuity between Clovis and Dalton, we see discontinuity, particularly in technology, mobility, and land use. We see Dalton populations in the CMV as founders of a new way of life: Dalton groups were the first to "settle in," to fully occupy and utilize the Holocene landscape and its plant and animal resources, in effect, setting the stage for the entire Archaic period and beyond (Koldehoff and Walthall 2004; Walthall 1998a, 1998b; Walthall and Koldehoff 1998, 1999). Thus, we propose that Caldwell's (1958) notion of "primary forest efficiency" be pushed back to the Early Archaic, which is not a new idea (see Cleland 1966; Fitting 1968). Specifically in the CMV, we think Dalton culture marks the initiation of the Archaic lifestyle. Regional variations and specializations are expected and certainly developed in response to shifts in Holocene environments and to the unfolding of new resource concentrations (e.g., shellfish). However, basic woodland-riverine foraging practices, technologies, and foodways appear to have been established early on in the Holocene by Dalton groups, and these new lifeways differed substantially from those of fluted-point groups.

The conventional starting date for the Holocene is 10,000 RCYBP (see above citations). But, as we discuss later in this chapter, Dalton culture emerged in the CMV and adjacent Ozark Highlands (Figure 6.1) centuries before this date, and its development and expansion appear to have been linked to the northward and westward migration of temperate deciduous forest habitats and resources. Consequently, there may have been a time-transgressive pattern to the spread of Dalton culture, resulting in the development of regionally specific point styles, tool kits, and subsistence practices. While Dalton points may share some morphological and technological attributes with fluted points, Dalton tool kits and land-use patterns in the CMV and Ozarks differ substantially from those of fluted-point groups. These differences are significant and mark the initiation of a new way of life.

In this chapter, we review the arguments for interpreting Dalton culture not as marking the end of the Paleoindian period but as marking the beginning of the Archaic period. In support of this position, we highlight discontinuities in technology, mobility, and land-use patterns between Dalton and fluted-point groups. Focusing more on lifeways than on point morphology, our reconsideration of CMV Dalton is more than an exercise in taxonomy or semantics.

The Dalton Horizon: Continuity or Discontinuity?

Dalton points, regional variants, and related types (Figure 6.2) are hallmarks of the early Holocene Dalton horizon (Goodyear 1982; Tuck 1974). While the exact temporal and cultural

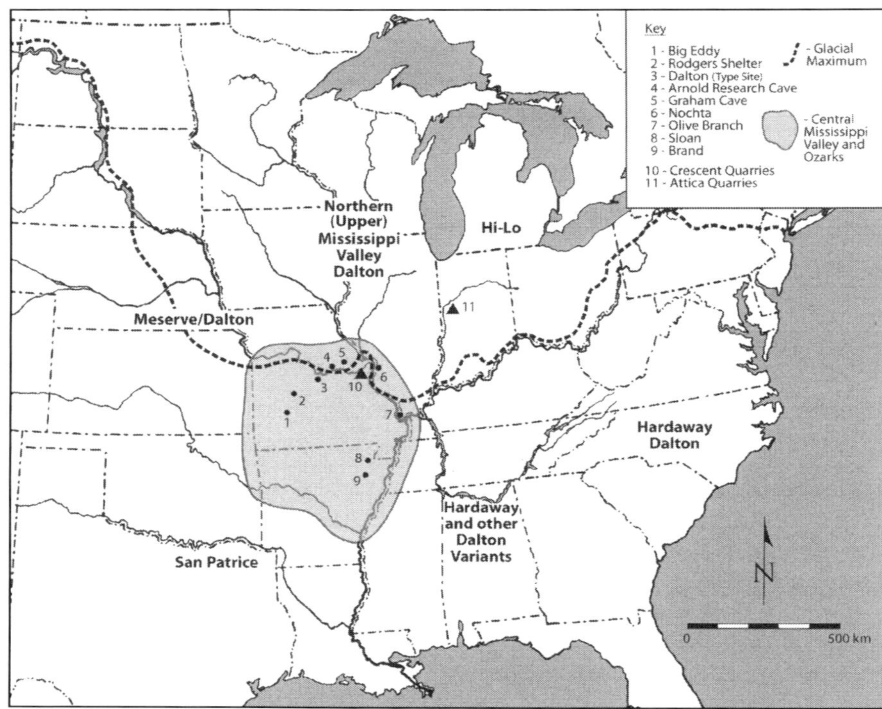

Figure 6.1. Location of the Dalton Heartland, important sites, and related Dalton-horizon complexes.

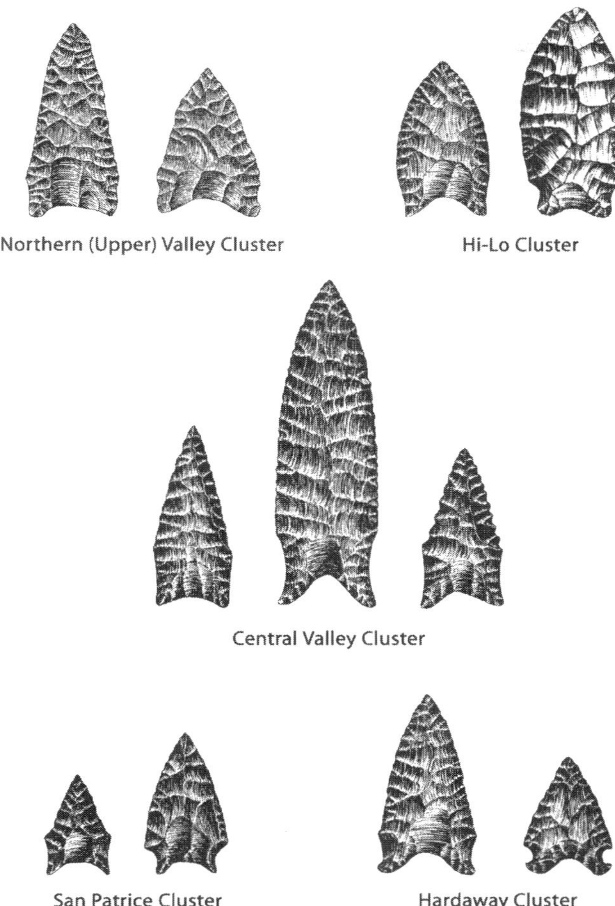

Figure 6.2. Point type clusters of the Dalton horizon.

relationship between these point styles is poorly understood, researchers recognize morphological and technological similarities (Justice 1987; Perino 1985). And while these similarities do not necessarily equal similarities in lifeways, it is significant that these early points and associated tool kits are often the focus of the same debate, that is, whether they are Paleoindian or Early Archaic. For example, the Hi-Lo complex in the Great Lakes is subject to this debate, and Ellis (2004; see also Ellis et al., this volume) presents a cogent argument for interpreting the Hi-Lo complex as a continuation of earlier Paleoindian patterns. Two lines of evidence used by Ellis are particularly convincing and pertinent to our analysis: (1) Hi-Lo lithic procurement duplicated that of earlier fluted-point groups in that it was focused on specific raw materials often procured over considerable distances (200 km), and (2) Hi-Lo tool kits lack heavy-duty woodworking tools, such as adzes and axes, which are commonplace in Archaic assemblages. These two observations indicate an unsettled, highly mobile lifestyle of the kind typically ascribed to Paleoindian groups in the Great Lakes and Northeast. These groups were apparently avid caribou hunters who undertook periodic long-distance settlement relocations and aggregations to intercept migrating caribou herds (Ellis and Deller 1990; Ellis and Lothrop 1989; Jackson and Thacker 1997).[2] Successful hunts likely entailed a communal effort involving several families or related groups, not unlike Plains bison hunts, both recent and ancient (Frison 1991). Fluted-point sites with assemblages dominated by points and tools made from raw materials from distant sources are a strong indicator of such long-distance moves, both on the Plains and in the Great Lakes area (e.g., Amick 1996; Gramly 1984; Hofman 1999; Meltzer 1989; Simons 1997).

Meltzer (1988), partly on the basis of the apparent lack of such sites and lithic-procurement patterns in the Midwest and Southeast, argues for two distinct Paleoindian adaptations in the East: a specialized caribou-hunting pattern for groups operating in northern areas recently deglaciated and dominated by tundra and spruce parkland (particularly the Northeast), and a generalized foraging pattern for groups operating south of this zone, especially in forested regions. The specialized groups, he believes, were derived from the generalized groups, which he also believes were the forebears of the Archaic lifestyle (see also Meltzer and Smith 1986; Smith 1986). While this two-pattern model has gained currency among researchers, Meltzer (1993:304) has recognized that Paleoindian lifeways were more diverse than this. For example, the model is unsupported by midwestern data sets, from Illinois (Koldehoff 1999) to Ohio (Seeman 1994). Although we cannot be certain at this time that fluted-point groups in Illinois were hunting caribou, we are certain that they routinely traveled great distances. For instance, Clovis (or Gainey) groups "retooled" at the Attica quarries along the Wabash Valley in Indiana (Figure 6.1) and traveled across Illinois to the Mississippi Valley, a straight-line distance of more than 300 km (Koldehoff 1999; Koldehoff and Walthall 2004).[3] Caribou hunting in the Midwest may have been part of a multifaceted hunting and gathering lifestyle designed to cope with shifting environmental conditions and subsistence uncertainties during the terminal Pleistocene. High mobility, while characteristic of caribou hunting, was probably a key component of Clovis lifeways, no matter what was being hunted, because mobility was often an effective means of dealing with uncertainty. For example, unfavorable conditions or circumstances could be alleviated by moving to new or better hunting grounds or by visiting neighbors and relatives (see Anderson 1995; Meltzer 2002). And to make such moves, people needed to know where and when herds and friends would be on the landscape, which required mobility and social networks.

The faunal remains from the Kimmswick Clovis-mastodon kill site, south of St. Louis, indicate that an array of both large and small mammals was likely hunted, and while deer remains are represented, caribou remains are not (Graham et al. 1981; Graham and Kay 1988). Their absence may be explained by the site's position in rugged forested terrain along the margin of the Mississippi Valley. Adjacent areas in southern Missouri and southern Illinois are similarly rugged and were largely unglaciated. As proposed by Loebel (2005), Clovis groups may have overwintered in protected, forested areas like these and in the spring moved north to intercept caribou herds heading north to their summer range in what is now Wisconsin. While overwintering in these southern areas, Clovis groups could have encountered caribou, but they likely pursued mastodon, deer, and other forest resources while also retooling with southern cherts (e.g., Cobden/Dongola). Groups farther to the south may have operated within smaller home ranges, similar to Meltzer's original model, but lithic-procurement data from some areas in the Southeast indicate long-distance mobility (see Anderson and Sassaman 1996), reinforcing notions of diversity and flexibility in lifeways as well as the importance of settlement mobility and social networks (Anderson 1995; Meltzer 2002).

The north–south movement of raw materials that is evident in Clovis assemblages from Illinois and Wisconsin can be explained by the seasonal caribou-hunting model (Koldehoff 2006; Koldehoff and Walthall 2004; Loebel 2005). These seasonal movements likely took place within a home range that probably shifted through time. In addition, these movements likely involved annual aggregations, in part for social reasons: small, dispersed populations, like Clovis bands, required periodic gatherings to renew interband contacts and to exchange information and mates. The exchange of fluted points likely occurred at such gatherings, but exchange does not explain tool and debitage assemblages dominated by long-distance raw materials (Meltzer 1989); these assemblages are the result of group movements (Ellis and Lothrop 1989; Tankersley and Isaac 1990). However, unlike the colonization models proposed by Kelly and Todd (1988), Tankersley (1991, 1994), and Anderson (1990, 1996; Anderson and Gillam 2000), these movements appear to have been cyclical within home ranges and tied to key landscape features, such as specific chert sources, overland trails, stream crossings, and well-known landmarks (Koldehoff and Walthall 2004; Loebel 2005). In other words, evidence indicates intimate knowledge of certain resources and landscapes. If Clovis groups were the initial colonizers of the Midcontinent, evidence of their initial settlements and unidirectional movements was overprinted by repeated seasonal cycles of movement and tool transport and discard. Tool assemblages typically represent cumulative or time-averaged measures of mobility patterns (Koldehoff and Walthall 2004; Loebel 2005).

Admittedly, the delineation of lithic-procurement patterns is an imperfect or partial measure of group mobility, but these patterns offer unparalleled insights into the direction, distance, and frequency of movement. Even so, we do not believe that fluted-point groups were "tethered" to specific high-quality lithic sources (Gardner 1974, 1977; Goodyear 1979); rather, they used the best and largest (most predictable) lithic sources available, given their home ranges, mobility patterns, and the character of the "lithic landscape" (see Koldehoff 1999).[4]

The paucity of evidence of similar long-distance movements by CMV Dalton groups indicates little, if any, continuity in patterns of mobility and land use with Clovis groups (Koldehoff and Walthall 2004). The routine use of caves and rockshelters by Dalton populations (and all subsequent groups), in contrast to the near avoidance of such sites by fluted-point groups, indicates differing patterns of land use (Walthall 1998a). The regular use of such natural shelters and local lithic sources indicates a more localized land-use pattern. It also indicates a detailed knowledge of local landscapes, a prerequisite for successful hunting and gathering in patchy, resource-rich woodlands and waterways, a point made by Caldwell (1958) and Fowler (1959a, 1959b) decades ago.

Continuity, however, has been a common interpretive theme. For example, drawing on Gardner's (1974, 1977) influential ideas about continuity, based on his work with the Flint Run complex in Virginia, Meltzer and Smith argue that "in the eastern forests ... there is demonstrable continuity in adaptation from Paleoindian through the Archaic" (1986:5). Focusing on Dalton points and tool kits, Morse, Goodyear, and others argue that Dalton technology was essentially Paleoindian, prompting a Late or Terminal Paleoindian classification (Ellis et al. 1998; Goodyear 1982, 1999; Morse 1997; Morse et al. 1996; Morse and Morse 1983, 1996). Yet Goodyear and Morse recognize that Dalton's environmental context was modern and that, in turn, its subsistence practices were more Archaic than Paleoindian. Goodyear states that "Dalton technology appears to be a somewhat modified Paleoindian toolkit applied to modern or Holocene biota. In this respect, Dalton can be considered the beginning of the early Archaic period in the Southeast" (1999:441). Morse and Morse state that "continuity from the Paleo-Indian period is evident in tool types, whereas affinity with later Archaic expressions is seen in other tools and inferred behaviors" (1983:42). They also state, "There is little doubt that Dalton represents a base out of which the Archaic developed" (Morse and Morse 1983:71).

This mix of traits and interpretations has led some (e.g., MacDonald 1971; McNutt 1996; Stoltman 1978; Tuck 1974) to classify Dalton as transitional. But as Goodyear (1974:102) noted decades ago, this approach does nothing to further understanding of the issue and its implications. In fact, the Dalton question underscores a bigger unresolved question: how should the Archaic be defined (Emerson and McElrath, this volume)? To us, *Archaic* implies more than a temporal or cultural-historical unit; it denotes a lifestyle, one that was focused on exploiting the natural, seasonal bounty of the Holocene woodlands and waterways of eastern North America. This lifestyle revolved around local resources and involved a reliance on wood and woodworking technologies.[5] And, as suggested by Goodyear and the Morses, this lifestyle originated with Dalton culture, probably in the CMV.

Because Dalton sites are particularly abundant in the CMV and the adjacent Ozark Highlands, we consider this area to be the "Dalton Heartland" (Figure 6.1): Dalton populations, with new technologies, such as the adze and the multifunctional Dalton point, may have originated here; if not, they certainly flourished here, leaving behind a rich archaeological record, especially in Ozark rockshelters and on CMV braided-stream terrace remnants. Sites of various sizes and types are particularly common in and along the Mississippi Valley between the Illinois River on the north and the Arkansas River on the south. The largest sites, some of which have produced hundreds of Dalton points and many adzes and other tools, as well as evidence of midden accumulations, roasting pits, and possible houses, appear to be base settlements that may have been occupied year-round and also may have functioned as regional or interregional aggregation sites (Gramly 2002; Higgins 1990; Morse 1975, 1997; Price and Krakker 1975; Redfield and Moselage 1970; Walthall and Koldehoff 1998). Excavations at these and other sites over the past half century have established the age of the Dalton horizon (see below) and have provided insights into land-use patterns and tool kits (e.g., Goodyear 1974, 1982; Kay 1982; Lopinot et al. 1998; Morse 1975, 1997; Price and Krakker 1975; Schiffer 1975; Walthall and Holley 1997). For example, this work has demonstrated that Dalton flake tools and unifaces, while similar to those in Clovis tool kits, were not made from blades struck from formal blade cores, as Clovis examples often were (Morse 1997:136; see also Koldehoff and Walthall 2004).

The careful excavation and analysis of the Sloan site in Arkansas is remarkable not only for providing insights into Dalton tool kits but also for providing insights into Dalton mortuary practices and social networks. The Sloan site is one of the earliest cemeteries in eastern North America (Morse 1997; Walthall 1999), and the extra-large, finely crafted Sloan-style Dalton points found here and elsewhere (Figures 6.3 and 6.4a), often in caches, likely represent items of ritualized exchange that moved through social networks designed to promote and maintain alliances (Walthall and Koldehoff 1998). We believe that the need for such networks arose in the CMV to manage localized subsistence shortfalls and intergroup conflicts stemming from reduced settlement mobility and expanding populations.[6] In most study areas, for example, researchers find five to 10 times more Dalton sites and points than earlier sites and points (e.g., Anderson 1999; Gillam 1996; Koldehoff 2006; Morse 1997; Price and Krakker 1975; Price and Price 1983).

Cemeteries denote a certain level of settlement stability, group identity, and territoriality (Charles and Buikstra 1983; Walthall 1999; see also Milner et al., this volume). Morse (1975, 1997) notes that the CMV during the early Holocene was a "land of opportunity" and that Dalton groups likely occupied base settlements within specific territories. While we do not disagree with this characterization, we do not see Dalton as a Paleoindian climax, as Morse does; rather, we see it as an initial Archaic florescence. Dalton technology, mobility, and land use differed substantially from those of fluted-point groups and, thus, marked the beginning of a new way of life. This new lifestyle, along with the broadening Holocene resource base, particularly in the CMV, provided favorable conditions for population growth and the emergence of social complexity. By 10,000 RCYBP, the CMV was covered by a rich mosaic of lakes, wetlands, and oak-hickory forest (Delcourt et al. 1999; Styles and McMillan, this volume). Immediately to the west, the Ozarks appear to have been especially productive in terms of deer hunting because the area was more open, affording better deer habitat than the mesic, closed-canopy forests east of the Mississippi (Styles and McMillan, this volume). This difference in deer habitat may help to explain the near absence of Dalton-horizon sites along the Wabash and Ohio valleys (Koldehoff 2006; Prufer and Baby 1963; Winters 1967; see also Jefferies, this volume; Stafford and Cantin, this volume). But this area may have been a cultural divide, as well.

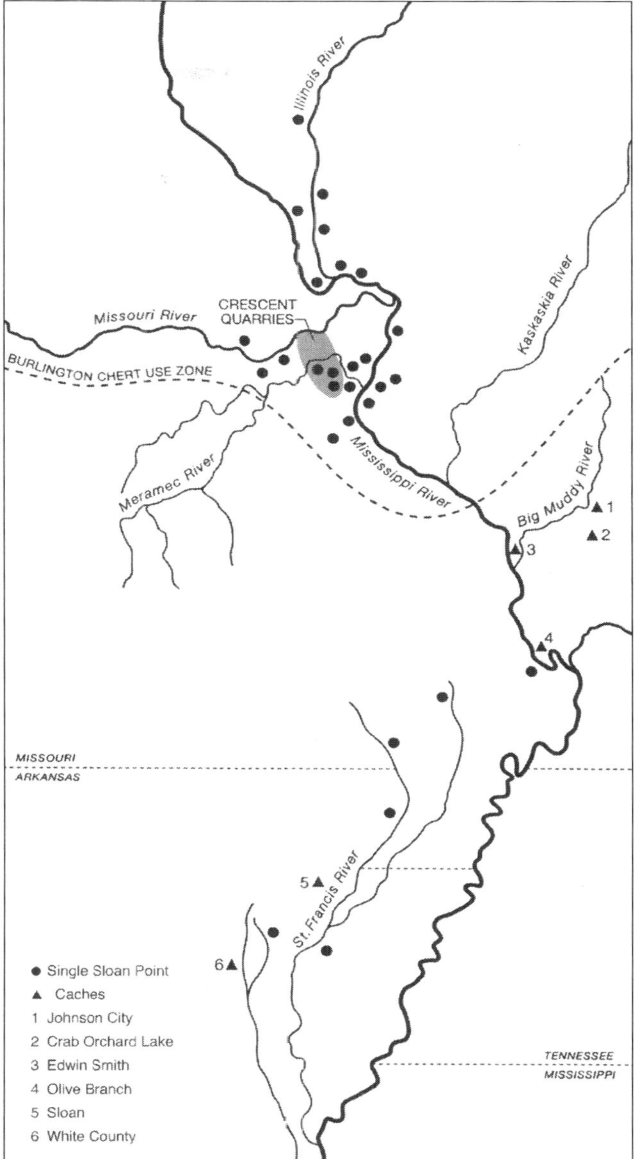

Figure 6.3. Location of the Crescent quarries and Sloan Dalton discoveries in the central Mississippi Valley (after Walthall and Koldehoff 1998:Figure 1).

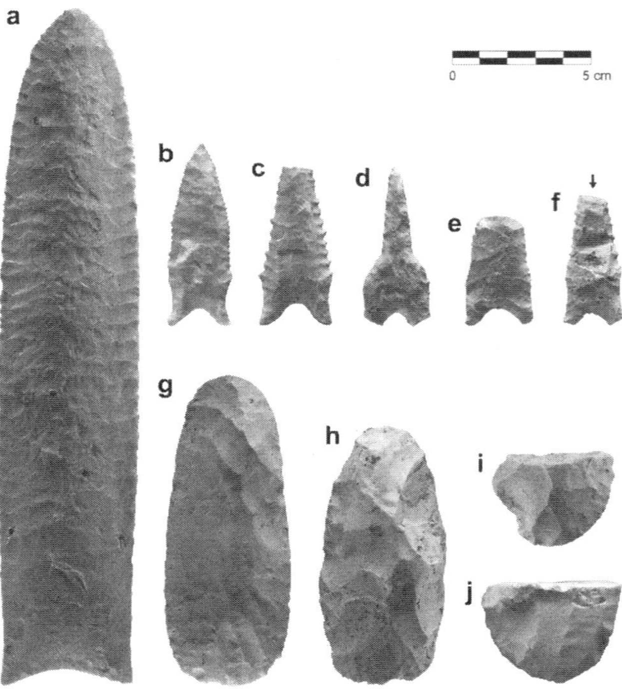

Figure 6.4. Dalton points and adzes from the American Bottom region: a, Sloan Dalton; b, c, points; d, point worked into a drill/awl; e, point worked into an end scraper; f, point with massive distal impact fracture; g, h, adzes; i, adze bit worked into a core; j, adze bit.

The discovery of the Sloan cemetery and the evidence of Dalton exchange are reshaping how researchers view the Early Archaic. Byers (2004:160–167) points out that the evidence of Dalton exchange networks negates prior notions that such networks first appeared in the Middle Archaic, as proposed by Brown (1985; see also Brose 1979). Anderson (2002) and Sassaman (2005) view the Dalton evidence as possible support for the early emergence of tribal formations and assertions of group or individual identity, while Brookes (2004) suggests that Sloan-style Daltons may have been crafted by specialists. Traditional interpretations place developments such as these in the Woodland period, not in the Archaic. These new interpretations are reinforced by discoveries of Middle Archaic mound construction, site planning, and craft production in the lower Mississippi Valley (e.g., Anderson 2002; Brookes 2004; Sassaman 2005).

Few researchers would disagree with the statement that Dalton culture in the Dalton Heartland is one of the better-documented examples of early Holocene human adaptation in eastern North America. The history of Dalton research, however, began neither in the Mississippi Valley nor in the Ozarks but on the Central Plains, at the Meserve site along the Platte River in Nebraska. In 1923 and again in 1931, lanceolate points with concave bases, basal thinning and grinding, and alternately beveled blades (from resharpening) were found in association with the bones of extinct bison (Wormington 1957:113–114). This early discovery has helped perpetuate the idea that Meserve/Dalton points are part of the Paleoindian tradition. Early on, Meserve became an established point type, and similar forms were recognized across the Midwest and Southeast. Chapman (1948), more than a decade later, defined the Dalton type on the basis of specimens collected from eroding sediments exposed in a borrow pit on land owned by Judge Samuel P. Dalton in central Missouri. Shortly thereafter, Dalton (or Meserve) points were excavated from the lower levels of Graham Cave in Missouri (Logan 1952) and Modoc Rock Shelter in Illinois (Fowler 1959a, 1959b), and similar discoveries followed at Arnold Research Cave in Missouri (Shippee 1966), at Stanfield-Worley Bluff Shelter in Alabama (DeJarnette et al. 1962), and at the open-air stratified Hardaway site in North Carolina (Coe 1964). In subsequent decades, similar discoveries were made across the Midwest and the Southeast and continue to be made (see below).

The lanceolate shape of Meserve/Dalton points, not to mention their basal thinning and occasional fluting, is similar to that of Clovis and other fluted-point types. This fact, along with their association, in a few cases, with extinct bison on the Plains, enhances the perception that these points are part of the Paleoindian tradition. Some researchers, in fact, suggest that lanceolate-shaped (unnotched) points are characteristic of the Paleoindian period, with notched points being characteristic of the Archaic (e.g., Ellis et al., this volume). This distinction does not work well in the Ozarks and CMV because lanceolate-shaped Searcy points occur at the end of the Early Archaic sequence, being preceded by numerous notched point types (see Ahler and Koldehoff, this volume; Ray et al., this volume). The routine recovery of Meserve/Dalton points from the lowest level of caves and rockshelters in the Midwest and Southeast, along with rather early but variable radiocarbon dates, confirms an early age for these points. But analysis of the faunal remains from cave and rockshelter deposits indicates a generalized exploitation of a modern environment. The excavations at Rodgers Shelter in Missouri firmly place Dalton in the early Holocene, associated with a generalized foraging lifestyle (Kay 1982; Wood and McMillan 1976). The early radiocarbon dates from the sealed terrace deposits at the shelter were used by Goodyear (1982) to reject later dates from other sites with apparent mixed deposits and to propose a date range of 10,500–9900 RCYBP for the Dalton horizon. Excavations at the Big Eddy site (Lopinot et al. 1998, 2000), an open-air stratified site not far from Rodgers Shelter, produced dates that closely match those from Rodgers Shelter, indicating that "Dalton people occupied the early submember floodplain intermittently over a span of approximately 450 years, from 10,470–10,020 B.P." (Ray 1998:199). In addition, the Dalton occupation is stratified above earlier fluted-point occupations (Clovis/Gainey and Folsom/Sedgewick) and below later Early Archaic occupations.

We accept this date range for the Dalton horizon in the Dalton Heartland, but outside this area similar dates, especially from sealed Dalton deposits, are lacking. For instance, similar dates were obtained from the lowest levels of Dust Cave in Alabama, but the few Dalton points that were recovered were found in association with other early point types, like Quad (Sherwood et al. 2004). The early date range supports the idea that Dalton culture originated in the Ozarks and the adjacent Mississippi Valley. But a time span of 450 years (or longer) seems rather lengthy, which may be explained in part by the limitations of radiocarbon dating, particularly during this time frame, for which there is a radiocarbon plateau (see Fiedel 1999). Because of these early dates and the morphological and technological similarities between Dalton and Clovis (or Gainey) points, the Big Eddy researchers classify the Dalton component, which includes examples of San Patrice points, as Late Paleoindian (Ray et al., this volume; see also Lopinot et al. 1998, 2000). This interpretation is not unlike those of Goodyear and Morse (see above). On the basis of early radiocarbon dates and Bradley's (1997) conclusion that Dalton flaking techniques are similar to those of Clovis, Morse (1997) argues that Dalton technology developed directly from Clovis and that the early part of the Dalton horizon may have overlapped with Folsom on the Plains as well as with a local Folsom expression represented by Sedgewick points. He also suggests that Meserve points were made by groups that hunted bison and occupied a buffer zone between Folsom and Dalton groups (Morse 1997:125).

Wyckoff argues for a possible temporal overlap between Folsom and Dalton in Oklahoma. But he documents strikingly different technological and land-use patterns: Folsom groups primarily occupied the rolling grasslands of western Oklahoma, preferred nonlocal Edwards chert from Texas, rarely recycled points into other tools, did not bevel their points when resharpening, and did not have adzes in their tool kits; by contrast, Dalton groups primarily occupied the Ozark foothills and major stream valleys of eastern Oklahoma, preferred local cherts, routinely recycled points into other tools, beveled their points when resharpening, and had adzes in their tool kits (Wyckoff 1999; Wyckoff and Bartlett 1995). These are the same basic differences that distinguish fluted-point groups and Dalton groups in the CMV, especially in Illinois (Koldehoff and Walthall 2004; Walthall and Koldehoff 1999). In fact, there is a bona fide Folsom presence in central and northern Illinois, an area that has long been part of the Prairie Peninsula, and in this area, Dalton sites are uncommon outside of major steam valleys, particularly east of the Illinois River valley (Conrad 1981; Koldehoff 2006; Munson 1990; Munson and Downs 1968; Nolan 2002; Nolan and Fishel, this volume).

Similar patterns are evident in Kansas, Iowa, and Nebraska, which brings us back to the Meserve site (Hofman 1996; Holven et al. 2005; Morrow and Morrow 1999; Myers and Lambert 1983; see also Benn and Thompson, this volume). Since its discovery, this site and its beveled Dalton-like points have been a source of debate (e.g., Goodyear 1982; Myers and Lambert 1983). In particular, are Meserve points really Dalton points, or are they just resharpened (alternately beveled) Plainview, Allen, or Angostura points? Given the presence of what appear to be CMV Dalton points—and Dalton adzes—in Oklahoma and Iowa (Holven et al. 2005; Wyckoff 1999), we support Myers and Lambert's position that Meserve points are Dalton points and that these points are associated with early Holocene populations that exploited oak-hickory forest habitats as these habitats expanded into the Plains along stream valleys:

> From these fragments of evidence we can hypothesize that peoples with a technology characteristic of the oak-hickory forests were exploiting the westernmost fringes of this habitat. Rather than a primary forest efficiency (Caldwell 1958), they had developed a valley-plains pattern which made use of both the resources of the oak-hickory forests and the large herbivores of the Plains. This valley-plains economic system foreshadowed later Plains Woodland and Plains Village economies in the same sense that primary forest efficiency foreshadowed Woodland and Mississippian patterns in the east. ... People, as we know, adapt to microenvironments. Oak-hickory gallery forests threaded westward across the Plains in the river valleys. So, too, did peoples with Dalton reduction technology exploit the limits of that microenvironment in the Central Plains where they exploited not only the resources of the oak-hickory forest, but also the resources of the Plains which occupied large tracts of land between the forests. [Myers and Lambert 1983:113]

Although Myers and Lambert stipulate that they are not necessarily advocating the movement of people but, rather, a technology, we see both emanating from the Dalton Heartland, advancing westward and northward with the spread of temperate deciduous forest (and its biotic resources) up major stream valleys (see also Johnson 1989). Thus, Meserve points appear to be CMV Dalton points, but more research is needed to better date and define Meserve points and their associated tool kits and land-use patterns. In the upper Mississippi Valley, CMV Dalton points (and adzes) are present but rare, and assemblages are dominated by Dalton points that are shorter, broader, and more triangular in shape. These points are often beveled but not in the same unifacial and alternate pattern that produces the pronounced beveling on CMV Daltons. These points have tentatively been grouped into the Northern (or Upper) Valley cluster (Figure 6.2); Nolan and Fishel (this volume) provide descriptive information. These points resemble some Hi-Lo and Hardaway points, and the best-documented sample is from the Christianson site. Evans and Womac (1998) compare the points from Christianson to Chesrow points, which Ellis (2004) considers to be part of the Hi-Lo complex. Similar points were recovered from the Itasca bison kill site at the headwaters of the Mississippi River in Minnesota (Shay 1971).

Shay points out that bison hunting and deer hunting require different patterns of land use and settlement mobility:

> Seasonally mobile bison herds were most conveniently taken at places where they could be ambushed or driven by groups of hunters. Camps at or near bison kills were most often occupied briefly, which apparently limited the variety of manufacturing and domestic activities carried on. Also, a site convenient for bison hunting may not have been suitable for obtaining other foods. By comparison, the more solitary and restricted habits of deer meant that they could be hunted from site locations chosen primarily for shelter [e.g., rock-shelters] and other reasons. Except for winter yarding, deer are dispersed throughout their habitat. Hunting techniques could include both individual and co-operative efforts. At several sites a variety of plants and animals were exploited in addition to deer. These sites were occupied intermittently throughout the year, permitting a wide range of activities. [Shay 1971:73]

Therefore, like caribou hunting, bison hunting often required long-distance mobility, whereas deer hunting often required considerable short-distance mobility. These two patterns of mobility and land use should be reflected in the lithic raw materials selected for tool production: in general, long-distance mobility provides regular access to nonlocal lithic sources, and short-distance mobility provides regular access to local lithic sources. Accordingly, if two different groups or cultures in the same region practiced similar patterns of land use and mobility, their lithic tool kits should show a similar mix of local and nonlocal raw materials, and if they practiced different patterns, their tool kits should show a different mix of local and nonlocal raw materials.[7]

By examining lithic assemblages from early sites in the CMV (Koldehoff and Walthall 2004), we have shown that Clovis groups routinely procured nonlocal (long-distance) raw materials, while Dalton groups routinely procured local (within 50 km) raw materials (Figure 6.5). As we have just argued, these different patterns represent different lifestyles. The nonlocal materials used by Dalton groups appear to have been procured more by exchange than by seasonal settlement relocations. For example, nonlocal raw materials are typically represented by a few finished Dalton points, rather than entire tool kits. Burlington chert, particularly from the Crescent quarries, was one of the raw materials routinely exchanged by Dalton groups, often in the form of large Sloan-style Dalton points. Morse (1997:14) suggests that the Dalton chert trade was driven as much by sociological needs as by technological needs and that this trade helped to maintain social networks (see also Walthall and Koldehoff 1998).

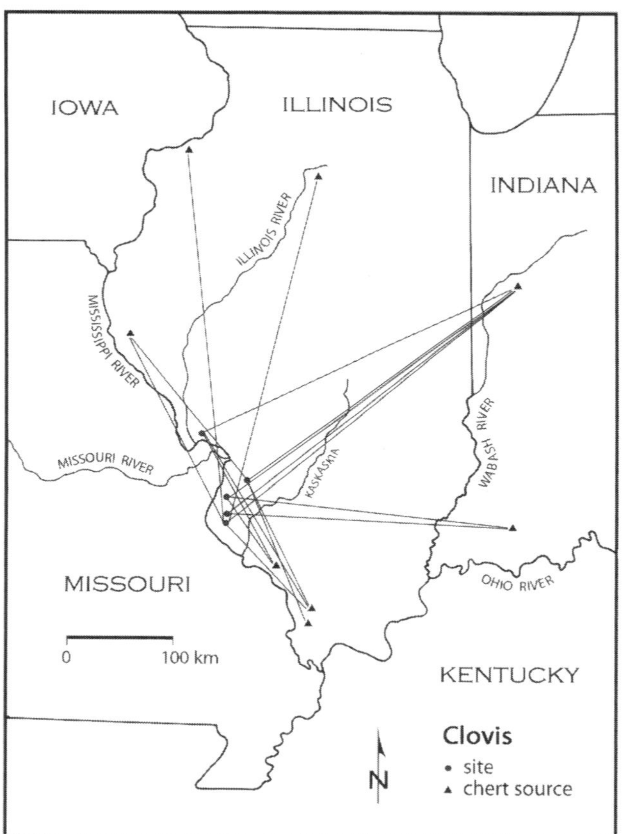

Figure 6.5. Plots of nonlocal (long-distance) raw materials used by Clovis and Dalton groups in the central Mississippi Valley (after Koldehoff and Walthall 2004:Figures 9 and 10).

The local lithic resources used most often by Dalton groups tended to be those with prominent exposures along the margins of the Mississippi Valley (e.g., Mounds/Lafayette, Burlington, and Bailey), which accents the upland-bottomland ecotone focus of Dalton settlement, as noted by Morse (1997:128). These valley-margin chert sources were ideally situated for refurbishing tool kits as groups moved back and forth from the interior uplands to the bottomlands (Koldehoff 2006; Walthall and Koldehoff 1999). Moreover, these chert sources were likely spots for making dugout canoes, given the juxtaposition of ample chert resources, suitable timber (e.g., bald cypress, white oak, and black walnut), and bottomland lakes and streams. The numerous Dalton adzes recovered from the New Valmeyer site complex overlooking the Mississippi Valley lends support to this idea (Koldehoff and Walthall 2004:56–57). Ancient dugout canoes preserved in waterlogged environments across the Midwest and the Southeast, some dating to 7000 RCYBP, "demonstrate an early and well-developed canoe-making tradition that is difficult to distinguish from that of later periods" (Wheeler et al. 2003:546). This tradition, as well as evidence of similarly early and well-developed traditions in woodworking, textiles, and basketry (e.g., Doran 2002; Kuttruff et al. 1998), likely originated with Dalton populations or other early groups in the Southeast, or perhaps with earlier coastal groups (as suggested by McElrath and Emerson, this volume). Dugout canoes represent a considerable investment of time, labor, and material, which denotes a riverine settlement and subsistence focus. In the CMV, dugout canoes were probably an integral part of Dalton life, helping to link communities and provide access to resources. Upland resources and travel along overland trails were also an integral part of Dalton life.

Summary and Conclusions

We have highlighted four differences between Dalton and fluted-point groups that illustrate how Dalton groups in the Dalton Heartland followed a more sedentary and localized lifestyle: (1) Dalton groups regularly used local lithic resources (within 50 km), while fluted-point groups regularly used nonlocal or extraregional resources; (2) Dalton groups routinely occupied rockshelters and caves, while fluted-point groups rarely did; (3) Dalton groups routinely made and used adzes for heavy-duty woodworking, while fluted-point groups rarely did; and (4) Dalton groups routinely beveled their points when resharpening and frequently reworked their points into other tools, while fluted-point groups rarely did. The last distinction reflects differing tool-design strategies shaped by differing hunting practices and mobility patterns: Dalton points were designed to be multifunctional, and their usefulness was extended not only by their repeated resharpening but also by their routine reworking into other tools (e.g., end scrapers and drills/awls; see Figure 6.4); by contrast, fluted points were designed primarily for penetration, for tipping spears. Thus, when resharpened, fluted points were not beveled but were bifacially retipped, and they were rarely reworked into other tools (Ahler and Geib 2000; Ellis 2004; Ellis and Deller 1990; Goodyear 1974; Michie 1973). Thus, Dalton points, like other Early Archaic points, represent flexible, mobile tool kits designed to meet the demands of short-distance mobility patterns.

Hi-Lo points are interesting because they were regularly beveled and reworked into other tools. But if they were used as weapon tips for hunting caribou, as were fluted points, they should not have been treated in this Dalton-like manner. Furthermore, Hi-Lo points are often stemmed or even notched, which Ellis believes to have been a later development, prompting him to interpret Hi-Lo points as a transitional technology between that of fluted points and Early Archaic points (e.g., Kirk Corner Notched):

> Overall, all characteristics of Hi-Lo points, whether it be stemming, notching, thickness, or thicker and more robust ears, can be seen very easily to relate to changes in point use contexts over time. The changes range from a point designed more as a projectile weapon tip in fluted point times, to a point designed to be used for a much broader range of hafted tasks, including continued use as an effective projectile tip. There is no need to invoke a switch to the use of the spear-thrower to explain these changes. [Ellis 2004:75]

His last comment is noteworthy because it refers to the suggestion by some researchers that changes in haft design corresponded to changes in weaponry. For instance, some theorize that fluted points tipped handheld lances and javelins, while Dalton, Hi-Lo, and notched Early Archaic points tipped spears or darts propelled by a spear-thrower. O'Brien and Wood are proponents of this theory and suggest that Dalton beveling was not an edge-maintenance strategy but a design strategy to help in "stabilizing the flight of the dart" (1998:93–96). This idea has no technical merit, having been discounted a century ago (e.g., Fowke 1913; Smith 1953), and it ignores the dynamic nature (or "life cycle") of chipped-stone tools, especially hafted bifaces. The occurrence of similarly massive distal impact fractures on fluted points, Dalton and Hi-Lo points, and notched Early Archaic points (e.g., Figure 6.4f) indicates that a similar delivery system was used: the spear-thrower, which likely arrived in North America with the continent's earliest immigrants (whenever they arrived and wherever they came from). Perishable items, like spear-throwers (made of wood or bone), textiles, and basketry are rare finds, especially in early deposits, which has led some researchers to assume that such technologies developed in later periods, rather than being present early on in the settlement of North America (see Doran 2002).

The bottom line is that the point type clusters that make up the Dalton horizon (Figure 6.2) may, in fact, be related in that they appear to represent a similar transitional technology between that of earlier fluted points and that of later notched points. Even so, this does not mean that they were all part of one uniform adaptation or culture. For example, Hi-Lo groups may have hunted caribou, at least part of the time, and Meserve/Dalton and Upper Valley groups probably hunted bison periodically, while groups in the Dalton Heartland and in the Southeast targeted deer. Therefore, on the basis of technology, mobility, and land use, some groups could be considered Late Paleoindian, for instance, Hi-Lo groups, as argued by Ellis (2004). Groups along the Plains border (Meserve/Dalton) appear to have been hunting bison, but as noted by Myers and Lambert, these valley-plains-oriented groups "foreshadowed later Plains Woodland and Plains Village economies" (1983:113), just as Dalton groups in the CMV foreshadowed later Archaic and Woodland economies. These issues of interpretation beg the question, what is Archaic? Moreover, they underscore the apparent regionalization of early Holocene adaptations. We believe the evidence shows that Dalton groups in the Dalton Heartland represent the very beginning of the Archaic period (or tradition). This interpretation is not unlike those of Morse and Goodyear, but they and others classify Dalton as Late Paleoindian, despite the greater similarities between Dalton technology, mobility, and land use with later Archaic and Woodland patterns than with earlier Clovis (and other fluted-point) patterns.

Whether Dalton technology and lifeways developed directly out of Clovis or intervening groups is hard to determine at this time as is the possible contemporaneity of Dalton with Folsom or Agate Basin. However, the latter is supported to some degree by the early radiocarbon dates for Dalton in the Ozarks. The well-developed stoneworking skills evident in Dalton points suggest a link to Clovis and later Paleoindian groups, but the fine pressure flaking employed by Dalton knappers to finish and resharpen Dalton points is characteristic of Folsom and Agate Basin points rather than Clovis points. Conversely, Dalton culture may have had no direct connection to Clovis or other fluted-point groups; rather, it may have developed from early coastal populations (see McElrath and Emerson, this volume) or perhaps a merging of the two.

A great deal of work remains to be done when it comes to establishing contemporaneity and connectedness of regional manifestations within the Dalton horizon as well as between it and other early cultures and their specific environmental settings. The emerging picture of life in the Dalton Heartland, while still fragmentary, is one of prosperity, population growth, and budding social complexity underwritten by the richness of the expanding resource base of the Midcontinent's early Holocene woodlands and waterways. This picture is substantially more complex than traditional interpretations of the Early Archaic, but it is not unexpected given recent discoveries of Middle Archaic mound construction, site planning, and craft production. Combined, these findings warrant a rethinking of traditional notions of what Archaic is as well as of the pace and uniformity of cultural evolution. No longer can Archaic cultures be viewed as simple hunter-gatherers evolving along a single trajectory, slowly adding new technologies and resources, and gradually becoming more sedentary and more complex.

Acknowledgments

Our interpretations of Dalton culture in the CMV are in large part built on the groundbreaking work of Dan and Phyllis Morse and Al Goodyear. We are indebted to them, particularly for work at the Sloan site and the unique insights it has provided. Our efforts here and elsewhere have benefited from interactions with numerous researchers: Tom Emerson, Dale McElrath, Andy Fortier, Dave Nolan, Tom Loebel, Dan Amick, Jack Ray, Chris Ellis, Steve Ahler, Blaine Ensor, Matt Hill, and Adam Holven. We also acknowledge the late Gregory Perino and the late Howard Winters for their contributions to Archaic research and point typology. The figures were prepared with the expert assistance of Mera Hertel and are used here courtesy of the Illinois Transportation Archaeological Research Program. In Figure 6.2, the majority of the images are taken from Perino (1985), with permission.

Endnotes

1. We use the terms *period* and *tradition* interchangeably here and elsewhere because our primary focus is on lifeways rather than on temporal or taxonomic units. We use the term *horizon* to encompass regional expressions of a similar technology or point type. Specific Dalton phases have been proposed (Gramly 2002; Morse and Morse 1983), but we see no utility in defining phases, given the general lack of fine-grained temporal controls. See Emerson and McElrath (this volume) for an expanded discussion of these terms and their utility.
2. Little hard evidence indicates that Hi-Lo groups hunted caribou, and while Ellis (2004) argues for Hi-Lo being Late Paleoindian rather than Early Archaic, he does not directly argue that Hi-Lo groups were hunting caribou. Moreover, in northern Illinois and southern Wisconsin, Hi-Lo and Upper Valley Dalton points are often made from local rather than long-distance raw materials (Evans and Womac 1998; Tom Loebel, pers. comm. May 4, 2006; Nolan and Fishel, this volume).
3. Some of the fluted points we refer to as "Clovis" may be considered Gainey points by some researchers (see Morrow and Morrow 2002). Other types of fluted points, such as Folsom and Cumberland, are present in the CMV but in much smaller numbers than Clovis.
4. See also Gould and Saggers (1985) for a discussion of the "lithic landscape" concept as well as for a discussion of the possibility that hunter-gatherers procured distant lithic raw materials for reasons unrelated to technology. However, ritual concerns or personal preferences are not likely to have played a major role in Clovis raw material selection.
5. Our definition of the Archaic is not unlike Fowler's (1959a:257).
6. Dalton social networks appear to have been more formal and ritualized than those of fluted-point groups in the CMV (see Walthall and Koldehoff 1998).

7. While we emphasize hunting, and its associated weaponry, as a factor that shaped patterns of land use and lithic procurement, plant foods undoubtedly played a role, one that is often less visible in the archaeological record.

References Cited

Ahler, Stanley A., and Phil R. Geib
2000 Why Flute? Folsom Point Design and Adaptation. *Journal of Archaeological Science* 27:799–820.

Amick, Daniel S.
1996 Regional Patterns of Folsom Mobility and Land Use in the American Southwest. *World Archaeology* 27:411–426.

Anderson, David G.
1990 The Paleoindian Colonization of Eastern North America: A View from the Southeastern United States. In *Early Paleoindian Economies of Eastern North America*, edited by Kenneth B. Tankersley and Barry L. Isaac, pp. 163–216. Research in Economic Anthropology, Supplement 5. JAI Press, Greenwich, Connecticut.
1995 Paleoindian Interaction Networks in the Eastern Woodlands. In *Native American Interactions: Multiscalar Analyses and Interpretations in the Eastern Woodlands*, edited by Michael S. Nassaney and Kenneth E. Sassaman, pp. 3–26. University of Tennessee Press, Knoxville.
1996 Models of Paleoindian and Early Archaic Settlement in the Lower Southeast. In *The Paleoindian and Early Archaic Southeast,* edited by David G. Anderson and Kenneth E. Sassaman, pp. 29–57. University of Alabama Press, Tuscaloosa.
1999 Archaeology in the L'Anguille River Basin, Northeast Arkansas: Large-Scale Survey in the Southeast. In *Arkansas Archaeology: Essays in Honor of Dan and Phyllis Morse*, edited by Robert C. Mainfort Jr. and Marvin D. Jeter, pp. 65–97. University of Arkansas Press, Fayetteville.
2002 The Evolution of Tribal Social Organization in the Southeastern United States. In *The Archaeology of Tribal Societies*, edited by William A. Parkinson, pp. 246–277. Archaeological Series 15. International Monographs in Prehistory, Ann Arbor, Michigan.

Anderson, David G., and J. Christopher Gillam
2000 Paleoindian Colonization of the Americas: Implications from an Examination of Physiography, Demography, and Artifact Distributions. *American Antiquity* 65:43–66.

Anderson, David G., and Kenneth E. Sassaman (editors)
1996 *The Paleoindian and Early Archaic Southeast.* University of Alabama Press, Tuscaloosa.

Bradley, Bruce A.
1997 Sloan Site Biface and Projectile Point Technology. In *Sloan: A Paleoindian Dalton Cemetery in Arkansas*, edited by Dan F. Morse, pp. 53–57. Smithsonian Institution Press, Washington, D.C.

Brookes, Samuel O.
2004 Cultural Complexity in the Middle Archaic of Mississippi. In *Signs of Power: The Rise of Cultural Complexity in the Southeast*, edited by Jon L. Gibson and Philip J. Carr, pp. 98–113. University of Alabama Press, Tuscaloosa.

Brose, David S.
1979 A Speculative Model for the Role of Exchange in the Prehistory of the Eastern Woodlands. In *Hopewellian Archaeology*, edited by David S. Brose and N'omi Greber, pp. 3–8. Kent State University Press, Kent, Ohio.

Brown, James A.
1985 Long-Term Trends to Sedentism and the Emergence of Complexity in the American Midwest. In *Prehistoric Hunter-Gatherers: The Emergence of Cultural Complexity*, edited by T. Douglas Price and James A. Brown, pp. 201–231. Academic Press, New York.

Byers, Martin A.
2004 *The Ohio Hopewell Episode: Paradigm Lost and Paradigm Gained.* University of Akron Press, Akron, Ohio.

Caldwell, Joseph R.
1958 *Trend and Tradition in the Prehistory of the Eastern United States.* Memoir 88. American Anthropological Association, Washington, D.C.

Chapman, Carl H.
1948 A Preliminary Survey of Missouri Archaeology, Part IV: Ancient Cultures and Sequence. *The Missouri Archaeologist* 10(4).

Charles, Douglas K., and Jane E. Buikstra
1983 Archaic Mortuary Sites in the Central Mississippi Drainage: Distribution, Structure, and Behavioral Implications. In *Hunters and Gatherers in the American Midwest*, edited by James L. Phillips and James A. Brown, pp. 117–145. Academic Press, New York.

Cleland, Charles E.
1966 *The Prehistoric Animal Ecology and Ethnozoology of the Great Lakes Region.* Anthropological Papers 29. Museum of Anthropology, University of Michigan, Ann Arbor.

Coe, Joffre L.
1964 *The Formative Cultures of the Carolina Piedmont.* Transactions of the American Philosophical Society 54, pt. 5. Philadelphia.

Conrad, Lawrence A.
1981 *An Introduction to the Archaeology of Upland West Central Illinois: A Preliminary Archaeological Survey of the Canton to Quincy Corridor for the Proposed FAP 407 Highway Project.* Reports of Investigations 2. Archaeological Research Laboratory, Western Illinois University, Macomb.

DeJarnette, David L., E. B. Kurjack, and J. W. Cambron
1962 Stanfield-Worley Bluff Shelter Excavations. *Journal of Alabama Archaeology* 8(1–2).

Delcourt, Paul A., Hazel R. Delcourt, and Roger T. Saucier
1999 Late Quaternary Vegetation Dynamics in the Central Mississippi Valley. In *Arkansas Archaeology: Essays in Honor of Dan and Phyllis Morse*, edited by Robert C. Mainfort Jr. and Marvin D. Jeter, pp. 15–30. University of Arkansas Press, Fayetteville.

Doran, Glen H. (editor)
2002 *Windover: Multidisciplinary Investigations of an Early Archaic Florida Cemetery.* University Press of Florida, Gainesville.

Ellis, Christopher J.
2004 Hi-Lo: An Early Lithic Complex in the Great Lakes Region. In *The Late Palaeo-Indian Great Lakes: Geological and Archaeological Investigations of Late Pleistocene and Early Holocene Environments,* edited by Lawrence J. Jackson and Andrew Hinshelwood, pp. 57–83. Mercury Series Paper 165. Archaeological Survey of Canada, Canadian Museum of Civilization, Gatineau.

Ellis, Christopher J., and D. Brian Deller
1990 Paleo-Indians. In *The Archaeology of Southern Ontario,* edited by Christopher J. Ellis and Neal Ferris, pp. 37–63. Occasional Publication 5. London Chapter, Ontario Archaeological Society.

Ellis, Christopher J., Albert C. Goodyear, Dan F. Morse, and Kenneth B. Tankersley
1998 Archaeology of the Pleistocene–Holocene Transition in Eastern North America. *Quaternary International* 49–50:151–166.

Ellis, Christopher J., and Jonathan C. Lothrop (editors)
1989 *Eastern Paleoindian Lithic Resource Use.* Westview Press, Boulder, Colorado.

Evans, J. Bryant, and Kevin T. Womac
1998 The Christianson Site (11RI42): A Paleoindian Occupation in the Lower Rock River Valley, Illinois. *Illinois Archaeology* 10:331–355.

Fiedel, Stuart J.
1999 Older Than We Thought: Implications of Corrected Radiocarbon Dates for Paleo-Indians. *American Antiquity* 64:95–115.

Fitting, James E.
1968 Environmental Potential and the Postglacial Readaptation in Eastern North America. *American Antiquity* 33:441–445.

Fowke, Gerard
1913 *Prehistoric Objects Classified and Described.* Bulletin 1. Missouri Historical Society, St. Louis.

Fowler, Melvin L.
1959a Modoc Rock Shelter, an Early Archaic Site in Southern Illinois. *American Antiquity* 24:257–275.
1959b *Summary Report of Modoc Rock Shelter, 1952, 1953, 1955, 1956.* Reports of Investigations 8. Illinois State Museum, Springfield.

Frison, George C.
1991 *Prehistoric Hunters of the High Plains.* 2nd ed. Academic Press, New York.

Gaertner, Linda M.
1994 Determining the Function of Dalton Adzes from Northeast Arkansas. *Lithic Technology* 19:97–109.

Gardner, William M.
1974 (editor) *The Flint Run Paleo-Indian Complex: A Preliminary Report 1971–73 Seasons.* Occasional Publication 1. Archeology Laboratory, Department of Anthropology, Catholic University of America, Washington, D.C.
1977 Flint Run Paleoindian Complex and Its Implications for Eastern North American Prehistory. In *Amerinds and Their Paleoenvironments in Eastern North America,* edited by Walter S. Newman and Bert Salwen, pp. 257–263. Annals of the New York Academy of Sciences 288. New York.

Gillam, J. Christopher
1996 A View of Paleoindian Settlement from Crowley's Ridge. *Plains Anthropologist* 1:273–286.

Goodyear, Albert C.
1974 *The Brand Site: A Techno-Functional Study of a Dalton Site in Northeast Arkansas.* Research Series 7. Arkansas Archeological Survey, Fayetteville.
1979 *A Hypothesis for the Use of Cryptocrystalline Raw Materials among Paleo-Indian Groups of North America.* Research Manuscript Series 156. Institute of Archaeology and Anthropology, University of South Carolina, Columbia.
1982 The Chronological Position of the Dalton Horizon in the Southeastern United States. *American Antiquity* 47:383–395.
1999 The Early Holocene Occupation of the Southeastern United States: A Geoarchaeological Summary. In *Ice Age People of North America: Environments, Origins, and Adaptations,* edited by Robert Bonnichsen and Karen L. Turnmire, pp. 432–481. Oregon State University Press, Corvallis.

Gould, Richard A., and Sherry Saggers
1985 Lithic Procurement in Central Australia: A Closer Look at Binford's Idea of Embeddedness in Archaeology. *American Antiquity* 50:117–136.

Graham, Russell W., and Eric C. Grimm
1990 Effects of Global Climate Change on the Patterns of Terrestrial Biological Communities. *Trends in Ecology and Evolution* 5:289–292.

Graham, Russell W., C. Vance Haynes, Donald L. Johnson, and Marvin Kay
1981 Kimmswick: A Clovis-Mastodon Association in Eastern Missouri. *Science* 213:1115–1117.

Graham, Russell W., and Marvin Kay
1988 Taphonomic Comparisons of Cultural and Noncultural Faunal Deposits at the Kimmswick and Barnhart Sites, Jefferson County, Missouri. In *Late Pleistocene and Early Holocene Paleoecology and Archaeology of the Eastern Great Lakes Region,* edited by Richard S. Laub, Norton G. Miller, and David W. Steadman, pp. 227–240. Bulletin 33. Buffalo Society of Natural Sciences, Buffalo, New York.

Gramly, Richard M.
1984 Kill Sites, Killing Grounds and Fluted Points at the Vail Site. *Archaeology of Eastern North American* 12:110–121.
2002 Olive Branch: A Very Early Archaic Site on the Mississippi River. *Amateur Archaeologist* 8(1–2):5–232.

Grimm, Eric C., and George L. Jacobson
1992 Fossil Pollen Evidence from Abrupt Climate Changes during the Past 18,000 Years in Eastern North America. *Climate Dynamics* 6:179–184.

Higgins, Michael J.
1990 *The Nochta Site: The Early, Middle, and Late Archaic Occupations.* American Bottom Archaeology FAI-270 Site Reports 21. University of Illinois Press, Urbana.

Hofman, Jack L.
1996 Early Hunter-Gatherers of the Central Great Plains: Paleoindian and Mesoindian (Archaic) Cultures. In *Archeology and Paleoecology of the Central Great Plains,* edited by Jack L. Hofman, pp. 41–100. Research Series 48. Arkansas Archeological Survey, Fayetteville.

1999 Unbounded Hunters: Folsom Bison Hunting on the Southern Plains circa 10,500 B.P., the Lithic Evidence. In *Le bison: Gibier et moyen de subsistance des hommes du Paléolithique aux Paléoindiens des Grandes Plaines*, edited by Jean-Philip Brugal, Francine David, James G. Enloe, and Jacques Jaubert, pp. 383–415. Actes du Colloque International, Toulouse 1995. Éditions APDCA, Antibes, France.

Holven, Adam C., Erik Otarola-Castillo, and Matthew G. Hill
2005 Dalton in Iowa: The Reece Site. Poster presented at the 51st Annual Midwest Archaeological Conference, Dayton, Ohio.

Jackson, Lawrence J., and Paul T. Thacker (editors)
1997 *Caribou and Reindeer Hunters of the Northern Hemisphere.* Ashgate, Aldershot, England.

Jacobson, George L., Jr., Thompson Webb III, and Eric C. Grimm
1987 Patterns and Rates of Vegetation Change during the Deglaciation of Eastern North America. In *North America and Adjacent Oceans during the Last Deglaciation*, edited by W. F. Ruddiman and H. E. Wright, pp. 277–288. Geological Society of America, Boulder, Colorado.

Johnson, Leroy, Jr.
1989 *Great Plains Interlopers in the Eastern Woodlands during Late Paleoindian Times: The Evidence from Oklahoma, Texas, and Areas Close By.* Office of the State Archaeologist Report 36. Texas Historical Commission, Austin.

Justice, Noel D.
1987 *Stone Age Spear and Arrow Points of the Midcontinental and Eastern United States.* Indiana University Press, Bloomington.

Kay, Marvin
1982 *Holocene Adaptations within the Lower Pomme de Terre River Valley.* Illinois State Museum Society, Springfield.

Kelly, Robert L., and Lawrence C. Todd
1988 Coming into the Country: Early Paleoindian Hunting and Mobility. *American Antiquity* 52:231–244.

Koldehoff, Brad
1999 Attica Chert and Clovis Land Use in Illinois: The Anderson and Perkins Sites. *Illinois Archaeology* 11:1–26.
2006 *Paleoindian and Archaic Settlement and Lithic Procurement in the Illinois Uplands.* Illinois Transportation Archaeological Research Reports 108. Illinois Transportation Archaeological Research Program, University of Illinois, Urbana-Champaign.

Koldehoff, Brad, and John A. Walthall
2004 Settling In: Hunter-Gatherer Mobility during the Pleistocene-Holocene Transition in the Central Mississippi Valley. In *Aboriginal Ritual and Economy in the Eastern Woodlands: Essays in Memory of Howard Dalton Winters*, edited by Anne-Marie Cantwell, Lawrence A. Conrad, and Jonathan E. Reyman, pp. 49–72. Scientific Papers 30. Illinois State Museum, Springfield.

Kuttruff, Jenna T., S. Gail DeHart, and Michael J. O'Brien
1998 7500 Years of Prehistoric Footwear from Arnold Research Cave, Missouri. *Science* 281:72–77.

Loebel, Thomas J.
2005 The Organization of Early Paleoindian Economies in the Western Great Lakes. Ph.D. dissertation, Department of Anthropology, University of Illinois, Chicago.

Logan, Wilfred D.
1952 *Graham Cave: An Archaic Site in Montgomery County, Missouri.* Memoir 2. Missouri Archaeological Society, Columbia.

Lopinot, Neal H., Jack H. Ray, and Michael D. Conner (editors)
1998 *The 1997 Excavations at the Big Eddy Site (23CE426) in Southwestern Missouri.* Special Publication 2. Center for Archaeological Research, Southwestern Missouri State University, Springfield.
2000 *The 1999 Excavations at the Big Eddy Site (23CE426) in Southwestern Missouri.* Special Publication 3. Center for Archaeological Research, Southwestern Missouri State University, Springfield.

MacDonald, George F.
1971 A Review of Research on Paleo-Indian in Eastern North America, 1960–1970. *Arctic Anthropology* 8:32–41.

McNutt, Charles H.
1996 The Central Mississippi Valley: A Summary. In *Prehistory of the Central Mississippi Valley*, edited by Charles H. McNutt, pp. 187–257. University of Alabama Press, Tuscaloosa.

Meltzer, David J.
1988 Late Pleistocene Human Adaptations in Eastern North America. *Journal of World Prehistory* 2:1–52.
1989 Was Stone Exchanged among Eastern North American Paleoindians? In *Eastern Paleoindian Lithic Resource Use*, edited by Christopher J. Ellis and Jonathan C. Lothrop, pp. 11–39. Westview Press, Boulder, Colorado.
1993 Is There a Clovis Adaptation? In *From Kostenki to Clovis: Upper Paleolithic–Paleo-Indian Adaptations*, edited by Olga Soffer and N. D. Praslov, pp. 293–310. Plenum Press, New York.
2002 What Do You Do When No One's Been There Before? Thoughts on the Exploration and Colonization of New Lands. In *The First Americans: The Pleistocene Colonization of the New World*, edited by Nina G. Jablonski, pp. 27–58. Memoir 27. California Academy of Sciences, San Francisco.

Meltzer, David J., and Bruce D. Smith
1986 Paleoindian and Early Archaic Subsistence Strategies in Eastern North America. In *Foraging, Collecting, and Harvesting: Archaic Period Subsistence and Settlement in the Eastern Woodlands*, edited by Sarah W. Neusius, pp. 3–31. Occasional Paper 6. Center for Archaeological Investigations, Southern Illinois University, Carbondale.

Michie, Jim
1973 A Functional Interpretation of the Dalton Projectile Point in South Carolina. *South Carolina Antiquities* 5(2):26–36.

Morrow, Juliet E., and Toby A. Morrow
2002 Exploring the Clovis-Gainey-Folsom Continuum: Technological and Morphological Variation in Midwestern Fluted Points. In *Folsom Technology and Lifeways*, edited by John E. Clark and Michael B. Collins, pp. 141–157. Special Publication 4. Lithic Technology. Department of Anthropology, University of Tulsa, Tulsa, Oklahoma.

Morrow, Toby A., and Juliet E. Morrow
1999 On the Fringe: Folsom Points and Preforms in Iowa. In *Folsom Lithic Technology: Explorations in Structure and Variation*, edited by Daniel S. Amick, pp. 65–81. Archaeological Series 12. International Monographs in Prehistory, Ann Arbor, Michigan.

Morse, Dan F.
1975 Paleo-Indian in the Land of Opportunity: Preliminary Report on the Excavations at the Sloan Site (3GE94). In *The Cache River Archeological Project: An Experiment in Contract Archeology*, assembled by Michael B. Schiffer and John H. House, pp. 135–143. Research Series 8. Arkansas Archeological Survey, Fayetteville
1997 *Sloan: A Paleoindian Dalton Cemetery in Arkansas*. Smithsonian Institution Press, Washington, D.C.

Morse, Dan F., David G. Anderson, and Albert C. Goodyear
1996 The Pleistocene-Holocene Transition in the Eastern United States. In *Humans at the End of the Ice Age: The Archaeology of the Pleistocene-Holocene Transition*, edited by Lawrence G. Straus, Berit V. Eriksen, John M. Erlandson, and David R. Yesner, pp. 319–338. Plenum Press, New York.

Morse, Dan F., and Albert C. Goodyear
1973 The Significance of the Dalton Adz in Northeast Arkansas. *Plains Anthropologist* 19:316–322.

Morse, Dan F., and Phyllis A. Morse
1983 *Archaeology of the Central Mississippi Valley*. Academic Press, New York.
1996 Northeast Arkansas. In *Prehistory of the Central Mississippi Valley*, edited by Charles H. McNutt, pp. 119–135. University of Alabama Press, Tuscaloosa.

Munson, Patrick J.
1990 Folsom Fluted Projectile Points East of the Great Plains and Their Biogeographical Correlates. *North American Archaeologist* 11:255–272.

Munson, Patrick J., and N. L. Downs
1968 A Surface Collection of Plano and Paleo-Indian Projectile Points from Central Illinois. *The Missouri Archaeologist* 30:122–131.

Myers, Thomas P., and Ray Lambert
1983 Meserve Points: Evidence of a Plains-Ward Extension of the Dalton Horizon. *Plains Anthropologist* 28:109–114.

Nolan, David J.
2002 A Distinctive Paleoindian Assemblage from the Central Illinois River Valley. *Illinois Antiquity* 37:3–7.

O'Brien, Michael J., and W. Raymond Wood
1998 *The Prehistory of Missouri*. University of Missouri Press, Columbia.

Perino, Gregory
1985 *Selected Preforms, Points, and Knives of the North American Indians*, vol. 1. Points and Barbs Press, Idabel, Oklahoma.

Price, James E., and James J. Krakker
1975 *Dalton Occupation of the Ozark Border*. Museum Brief 20. Museum of Anthropology, University of Missouri, Columbia.

Price, James E., and Cynthia R. Price
1983 Section 3: Study of Private Artifact Collections. In *Archaeological Investigations in the Ozark National Scenic Riverways, 1981–1982*, by James E. Price, Cynthia R. Price, Roger T. Saucier, and Timothy K. Perttula, pp. 227–293. Project 447. Submitted to the National Park Service, Midwest Archaeological Center, Lincoln, Nebraska. Contract No. CX-6000-1-0054. Center for Archaeological Research, Southwest Missouri State University, Springfield.

Prufer, Olaf H., and Raymond S. Baby
1963 *Palaeo-Indians of Ohio*. Ohio Historical Society, Columbus.

Ray, Jack H.
1998 Cultural Components. In *The 1997 Excavations at the Big Eddy Site (23CE426) in Southwestern Missouri*, edited by Neal H. Lopinot, Jack. H. Ray, and Michael D. Conner, pp. 111–220. Special Publication 2. Center for Archaeological Research, Southwest Missouri State University, Springfield.

Redfield, Alden, and John H. Moselage
1970 The Lace Place, a Dalton Project Site in the Western Lowland in Eastern Arkansas. *The Arkansas Archeologist* 11:21–44.

Sassaman, Kenneth E.
2005 Structure and Practice in the Archaic Southeast. In *North American Archaeology*, edited by Timothy R. Pauketat and Diana DiPaolo Loren, pp. 79–107. Blackwell, Oxford.

Saucier, R. T.
1994 *Geomorphology and Quaternary Geologic History of the Lower Mississippi Valley.* U.S. Army Corps of Engineers, Vicksburg, Mississippi.

Schiffer, Michael B.
1975 Some Further Comments on the Dalton Settlement Pattern Hypothesis. In *The Cache River Archeological Project: An Experiment in Contract Archeology*, assembled by Michael B. Schiffer and John H. House, pp. 103–112. Research Series 8. Arkansas Archeological Survey, Fayetteville.

Seeman, Mark F.
1994 Intercluster Lithic Patterning at Nobles Pond: A Case for "Disembedded" Procurement among Early Paleoindian Societies. *American Antiquity* 59:273–288.

Shay, C. Thomas
1971 *The Itasca Bison Kill Site: An Ecological Analysis.* Minnesota Historical Society, Minneapolis.

Shelford, Victor E.
1963 *The Ecology of North America.* University of Illinois Press, Urbana.

Sherwood, Sarah C., Boyce N. Driskell, Asa R. Randall, and Scott C. Meeks
2004 Chronology and Stratigraphy at Dust Cave, Alabama. *American Antiquity* 69:533–554.

Shippee, J. M.
1966 The Archaeology of Arnold-Research Cave, Callaway County, Missouri. *The Missouri Archaeologist* 28:1–40.

Simons, Donald B.
1997 The Gainey and Butler Sites as Focal Points for Caribou and People. In *Caribou and Reindeer Hunters of the Northern Hemisphere*, edited by Lawrence J. Jackson and Paul T. Thacker, pp. 105–131. Ashgate, Aldershot, England.

Smith, Arthur G.
1953 Beveled or "Rotary" Points. *American Antiquity* 18:269–270.

Smith, Bruce
1986 The Archaeology of the Southeastern United States: From Dalton to de Soto, 10,500–500 B.P. *Advances in World Archaeology* 5:1–92.

Stoltman, James B.
1978 Temporal Models in Prehistory: An Example from Eastern North America. *Current Anthropology* 19:703–746.

Tankersley, Kenneth B.
1991 A Geoarchaeological Investigation of Distribution and Exchange in the Raw Material Economies of Clovis Groups in Eastern North America. In *Raw Material Economies among Prehistoric Hunter-Gatherers*, edited by Anta Montet-White and Steven Holen, pp. 285–304. University of Kansas Press, Lawrence.
1994 Was Clovis a Colonizing Population in Eastern North America? In *The First Discovery of America: Archaeological Evidence of the Early Inhabitants of the Ohio Area*, edited by William S. Dancey, pp. 95–116. Ohio Archaeological Council, Columbus.

Tankersley, Kenneth B., and Barry L. Isaac
1990 *Early Paleoindian Economies of Eastern North America*. Research in Economic Anthropology, Supplement 5. JAI Press, Greenwich, Connecticut.

Tuck, James A.
1974 Early Archaic Horizons in Eastern North America. *Archaeology of Eastern North America* 2:72–80.

Walthall, John A.
1998a Rockshelters and Hunter-Gatherer Adaptation to the Pleistocene/Holocene Transition. *American Antiquity* 63:223–238.
1998b Overwinter Strategy and Early Holocene Hunter-Gatherer Mobility in Temperate Forests. *Midcontinental Journal of Archaeology* 23:1–22.
1999 Mortuary Behavior and Early Holocene Land Use in the North American Midcontinent. *North American Archaeologist* 20:1–30.

Walthall, John A., and George R. Holley
1997 Mobility and Hunter-Gatherer Toolkit Design: Analysis of a Dalton Lithic Cache. *Southeastern Archaeology* 16:152–162.

Walthall, John A., and Brad Koldehoff
1998 Hunter-Gatherer Interaction and Alliance Formation: Dalton and the Cult of the Long Blade. *Plains Anthropologist* 43:257–273.
1999 Across the Divide: Dalton Land Use in the Southern Till Plains. *Illinois Archaeology* 11:27–49.

Wheeler, Ryan J., James J. Miller, Ray M. McGee, Donna Ruhl, Brenda Swann, and Melissa Memory
2003 Archaic Period Canoes from Newnans Lake, Florida. *American Antiquity* 68:533–551.

Winters, Howard D.
1967 *An Archaeological Survey of the Wabash Valley in Illinois.* Reports of Investigation 10. Illinois State Museum, Springfield.

Wood, W. Raymond, and R. Bruce McMillan (editors)
1976 *Prehistoric Man and His Environments: A Case Study in the Ozark Highland.* Academic Press, New York.

Wormington, H. M.
1957 *Ancient Man in North America.* 5th ed. Popular Series 4. Denver Museum of Natural History, Denver, Colorado.

Wyckoff, Don G.
1999 Southern Plains Folsom Lithic Technology: A View from the Edge. In *Folsom Lithic Technology: Explorations in Structure and Variation*, edited by Daniel S. Amick, pp. 39–64. Archaeological Series 12. International Monographs in Prehistory, Ann Arbor, Michigan.

Wyckoff, Don G., and Robert Bartlett
1995 Living on the Edge Late Pleistocene–Early Holocene Cultural Interaction along Southeastern Woodlands–Plains Border. In *Native American Interactions: Multiscalar Analyses and Interpretations in the Eastern Woodlands*, edited by Michael S. Nassaney and Kenneth E. Sassaman, pp. 27–72. University of Tennessee, Knoxville.

Yerkes, Richard W., and Linda M. Gaertner
1997 Microwear Analysis of Dalton Artifacts. In *Sloan: A Paleoindian Dalton Cemetery in Arkansas*, edited by Dan F. Morse, pp. 58–71. Smithsonian Institution Press, Washington, D.C.

Part 2

Stratigraphic Sequences in the Archaic Period

7

Archaic Prehistory of the Western Ozarks of Southwest Missouri

Jack H. Ray, Neal H. Lopinot, and Edwin R. Hajic

Introduction

Until recently, knowledge of Archaic prehistory in southwest Missouri has been based on little systematic and focused geoarchaeological and archaeological surveys and a long history of excavations in sheltered sites, in earthen burial mounds, and in rock cairns, followed by cultural resource management (CRM)–driven mitigation of a handful of open-air sites in both upland and bottomland contexts. In the past, efforts to establish a detailed chronology and understanding of material culture and adaptation have suffered from substantial reliance on sites with mixed deposits, leaving room for generalized discussions of little more than complexes encompassing thousands of years of prehistory and improvised speculation on settlement and subsistence behavior (e.g., the Tick Creek complex [McMillan 1965] and the Rice and James River complexes [C. Chapman 1975]).

One of the major problems in Missouri and in many other states in eastern North America is that relatively few excavated sites have provided sufficient clarity to tease out well-dated Archaic components. At some of the best-known sites in Missouri and elsewhere, various types of projectile points and other residues of past human activities are often found within the same stratigraphic unit or scattered among several units (e.g., at Rodgers Shelter [Kay 1982b; McMillan 1971; Wood and McMillan 1976], Pigeon Roost Creek [O'Brien and Warren 1985], Graham Cave [Klippel 1971; Logan 1952], Modoc Rock Shelter [Ahler 1993; Fowler 1959], Rice Shelter [Bray 1956], Jakie Shelter [Marshall and Chapman 1960], and Standlee Shelter [Bray 1960]). More recent excavations at Albertson Cave (Dickson 1991) and John Paul Cave (Ray 1995, 1997) have supplemented the records resulting from earlier investigations, but these sheltered sites also contain some mixed deposits.

Archaeologists have long been attracted to the caves and rockshelters common in the karstic Ozarks region. This interest continues today in part because of the occasional occurrence of relatively thick stratigraphic records and the sometimes-excellent preservation conditions characterizing such sites. Unfortunately, such sites are behaviorally circumscribed, and the resulting deposits often consist of palimpsests, mixed as the result of intensive use and reuse by humans, rats, mice, and other animals. Although a significant improvement over that presented by C. Chapman (1975), the Archaic projectile point typology and chronology described by O'Brien and Wood (1998:117–149) is still characterized by a good number of errors and much imprecision. Despite their repeated criticisms of interpretations based on the mixed or disturbed Archaic deposits at most sheltered sites, O'Brien and Wood and others continue to rely on those sites in their discussions of the chronology and adaptations of Archaic peoples. In Missouri, these sites include Rodgers Shelter, Graham Cave, Rice Shelter, Standlee Shelter I, and Arnold Research Cave. One should not avoid extant evidence from caves and rockshelters, but those sites having the greatest utility for understanding the past must exhibit relatively unmixed, stratified, single-component, well-dated deposits. In the Midwest and Plains, these characteristics are most likely to occur in alluvial-floodplain, alluvial-fan, and colluvial-slope contexts in which relatively low-energy sedimentation from suspension and sheetflood of largely fine-grain sediment dominates (Hajic 1990; Smith 1983). The Big Eddy site and a few other nearly single-component sites in southwest Missouri offer such contexts. In this chapter, we provide a more precise Archaic projectile point chronology for the western Ozarks and, with that in place, a better basis for understanding human adaptational dynamics in this portion of the Midcontinent.

Physiographic Setting

The western Ozarks of southwest Missouri comprises two physiographic subprovinces (Figure 7.1). Most of this area is occupied by the Springfield Plateau (Bretz 1965; Fenneman 1938). The topography in this subprovince is generally characterized by broad, gently rolling uplands with limited dissection and relatively minor relief. The only exceptions are steep slopes and bluffs along major river valleys. Rock formations are dominated by Mississippian-age cherty limestones in which karst features (e.g., caves, sinkholes, and springs) are well developed. The Springfield Plateau is bordered on the west by the relatively undissected Osage Plains, dominated by prairie plant and animal species. The Eureka Springs Escarpment demarcates the eastern boundary of the Springfield Plateau and the western boundary of the Salem Plateau. Unlike the Springfield Plateau, the topography of the Salem Plateau is quite rugged. It is generally characterized by highly dissected uplands with narrow, winding ridges, steep slopes, and narrow river valleys. Rock formations are dominated by Ordovician-age cherty dolostones, which also contain numerous karst features.

The rock formations in the western Ozarks yield bountiful supplies of lithic resources that were useful to prehistoric peoples. Foremost among these are insoluble siliceous raw materials. Cherts, many of high quality, are especially abundant. Chert is ubiquitous across the landscape, and often three to five different chipped-stone resources occur locally in any given area in southwest Missouri (Ray 2007). In this regard, the western Ozarks contrast significantly with the chert-poor Osage Plains. Other abundant rocks, such as sandstone, siltstone, limestone, dolostone, hematite, and limonite, provided resources for the production of ground-stone equipment and pigments.

The major rivers on the Springfield Plateau have relatively low stream gradients and generally have adopted a meandering pattern. Overbank sheetflood deposits are silt dominated, reflecting the influence of redeposited Late Wisconsin loess derived from erosion of upland surfaces (Johnson et al. 1993). These environmental factors have allowed the development and preservation of extensive late Pleistocene- and Holocene-age low terrace and floodplain sediment assemblages that are 5–7 m or more thick in broad bedrock valleys. The most thoroughly investigated and best-known alluvial stratigraphic unit in southwest Missouri is the Rodgers Shelter Formation, or member (Brakenridge 1981; Hajic et al. 2000; Hajic et al. 1998; Haynes 1976, 1985). Aggradation of alluvial sediments and burial of cultural components in this unit often were

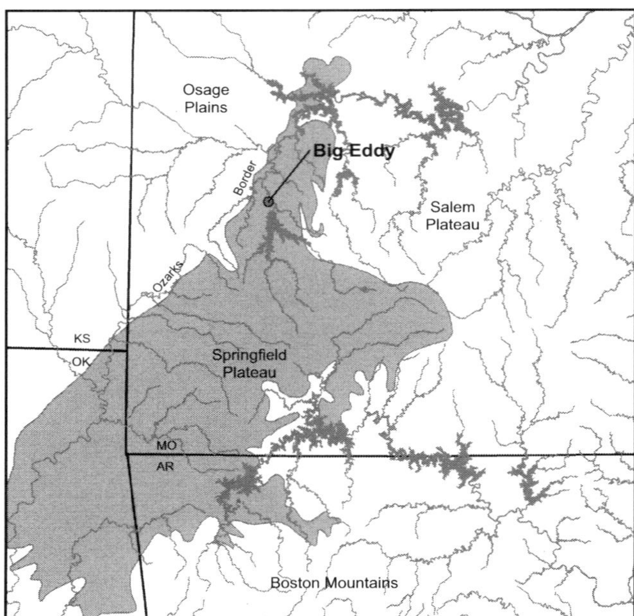

Figure 7.1. Physiographic subprovinces in the western Ozarks.

rapid enough to preserve a natural and cultural stratigraphic record unparalleled in other parts of the Ozarks.

Floodplain formation in bedrock valleys occupied by meandering streams involves both vertical and lateral accretion of overbank deposits (Brakenridge 1984, 1988). As a meander migrates, new sandy point-bar deposits are exposed close to the river, and older, more distal, point-bar deposits are buried by fine, overbank deposits. Through time, as the river migrates, each successive flood deposits a new increment of overbank deposits. Depending on flood magnitudes, existing floodplain and low terrace surfaces also may be draped with overbank sheetflood deposits. The net result of this alluvial sedimentation mode through time is (1) a time-transgressive base to floodplain overbank sequences, with deposits becoming progressively younger in the directions of point-bar growth and meander migration; (2) an isochronous floodplain surface; (3) relatively thick floodplain sheetflood facies; and (4) relatively thin, high floodplain- and terrace-veneer sheetflood facies deposited on higher, older established valley geomorphic surfaces of little or no relief.

At Big Eddy, migration of the Sac River during the late Pleistocene and Holocene resulted in deposition of Rodgers Shelter member alluvium that is divisible into early, middle, and late submembers (Hajic 2005; Hajic et al. 2000; Hajic et al. 1998). Each submember includes a thick floodplain sheetflood facies, and the younger two submembers exhibit a relatively thin floodplain- or terrace-veneer sheetflood facies where they lie atop earlier submembers. Each submember has a moderately expressed soil developed in the top of the submember; thus, two buried soils and paleogeomorphic surfaces are easily recognized in the Rodgers Shelter member at Big Eddy, although at least one additional, subtle buried soil is present in the thick late submember. The early submember was deposited atop a paleo–gravel bar deposit in the central part of the site and dates from about 13,000 to 10,000 RCYBP. It is in this submember that stratified pre-Clovis-age and Paleoindian deposits occur. Shortly after 10,000 RCYBP, as the Sac River migrated westward following a brief hiatus in sedimentation, the middle submember was deposited. The thick floodplain facies of the middle submember (thick middle submember) occurs west of the early submember, whereas a thinner floodplain-veneer facies (thin middle submember) was simultaneously deposited over the early submember. Sedimentation of the middle submember continued until about 4500 RCYBP. Following a hiatus in significant overbank sedimentation that lasted several hundred years, the Sac River migrated farther to the west, and deposits of the late submember began to accumulate. The thick floodplain facies of the late submember (thick late submember) was deposited west of the thick middle submember. A thinner floodplain- and terrace-veneer facies (thin late submember) was deposited atop the thick and thin middle submembers. It is primarily within the thin middle submember and the thick late submember that multiple stratified Early and Late Archaic deposits are represented.

Big Eddy and the One Point–One Culture Concept

The Big Eddy site (23CE426) is located on the west flank of the Ozarks Province in Cedar County, southwest Missouri (Figure 7.2). It is situated along the lower Sac River, a major southern tributary of the Osage River. In comparison with streams draining the southern portion of the Ozarks, the lower Sac River exhibits a low gradient. The broad valley and Holocene history of landscape evolution of a meandering lower Sac River have allowed for the development and preservation of extensive, thick alluvial members dominated by a fine-grain floodplain overbank facies. Although much of this chapter focuses on the Archaic record at the Big Eddy site, the lower Sac River valley hosts a relatively large number of sites with buried Archaic components (Ray and Lopinot 2005a).

The Big Eddy site is best known for its relatively rich and stratified fluted-point and Dalton deposits, but it also provides a relatively complete post-Dalton-San Patrice sequence for at least the Early Archaic and Late Archaic periods. In contrast to other deeply stratified sites in Missouri (e.g., Rodgers Shelter) and elsewhere (e.g., Koster and Modoc Rock Shelter in Illinois), the Big Eddy site is *not* characterized by exceedingly rich Archaic deposits and continuous site use over relatively long spans of time. With the exception of a Dalton-San Patrice and several Late Archaic middens, Big Eddy is, instead, marked primarily by intermittent and spatially scattered site use, often of a relatively specialized and brief character. Bone preservation is very poor and, except for the Late Archaic midden deposits, plant remains are nowhere very abundant.

While Big Eddy lacks the alkaline-charged, artifact-rich deposits characterizing some sites, the intermittent site use, preceded and followed by episodes of sediment accretion, is precisely what makes it such a remarkable resource, particularly with respect to stratigraphic and geochronologic investigations. The integrity and discrete nature of individual artifact-bearing deposits set it apart from many other sites. Pits from one horizon do not intrude into another, and there is limited evidence for significant amounts of natural and cultural syn- and postdepositional disturbances affecting multiple strata. Some postdepositional displacement of artifacts, both vertically and horizontally, surely occurred at Big Eddy, but such natural movements appear to have been negligible overall in comparison with what occurred at most other major sites, especially at cave and rockshelter sites.

The Big Eddy site is quite complex, and a good understanding of that complexity has required substantial geoarchaeological investigation to define, date, and determine the geometry of stratigraphic units, paleogeomorphic surfaces, and depositional environments (Hajic 2005; Hajic et al. 2000; Hajic et al. 1998). The strength of our statements about projectile point chronology and the content of assemblages, for example, is only as good as the strength of our understanding of the contexts from which those artifacts were recovered. In the absence of a competent comprehension of stratigraphy, sedimentology, and history of landscape evolution at Big Eddy, most aspects of the archaeology of this site would be more contentious.

The long-term multidisciplinary research at the Koster site and elsewhere in the lower Illinois River valley, as well as in the American Bottom, provide exceptional model programs for attaining an in-depth understanding of the prehistoric record for a region. To a great extent, we have sought to emulate this model, but in a much smaller way. The growing body of detailed data from the Big Eddy site and the lower Sac River valley is derived from our investigations carried out over a ten-year period. Substantial excavations were undertaken at Big Eddy during 1997, 1999, 2001, 2002, 2005, and 2007. Eleven major block excavations were opened at the site during those six years. The first part of the 1997 field season, the entire 2001 field season, and the first part of the 2002 field season were focused on investigating the Archaic deposits at the site. Five excavation blocks were opened during the 2001 and 2002 field seasons, mostly in an effort to study the Archaic deposits within the middle and late submembers of the Rodgers Shelter member (Figure 7.3). More limited supplemental excavations were undertaken in a sixth block in 2004 to resolve some stratigraphic gaps in our Late Archaic sequence.

The sustained work at Big Eddy facilitated much interaction among researchers in identifying new problems and

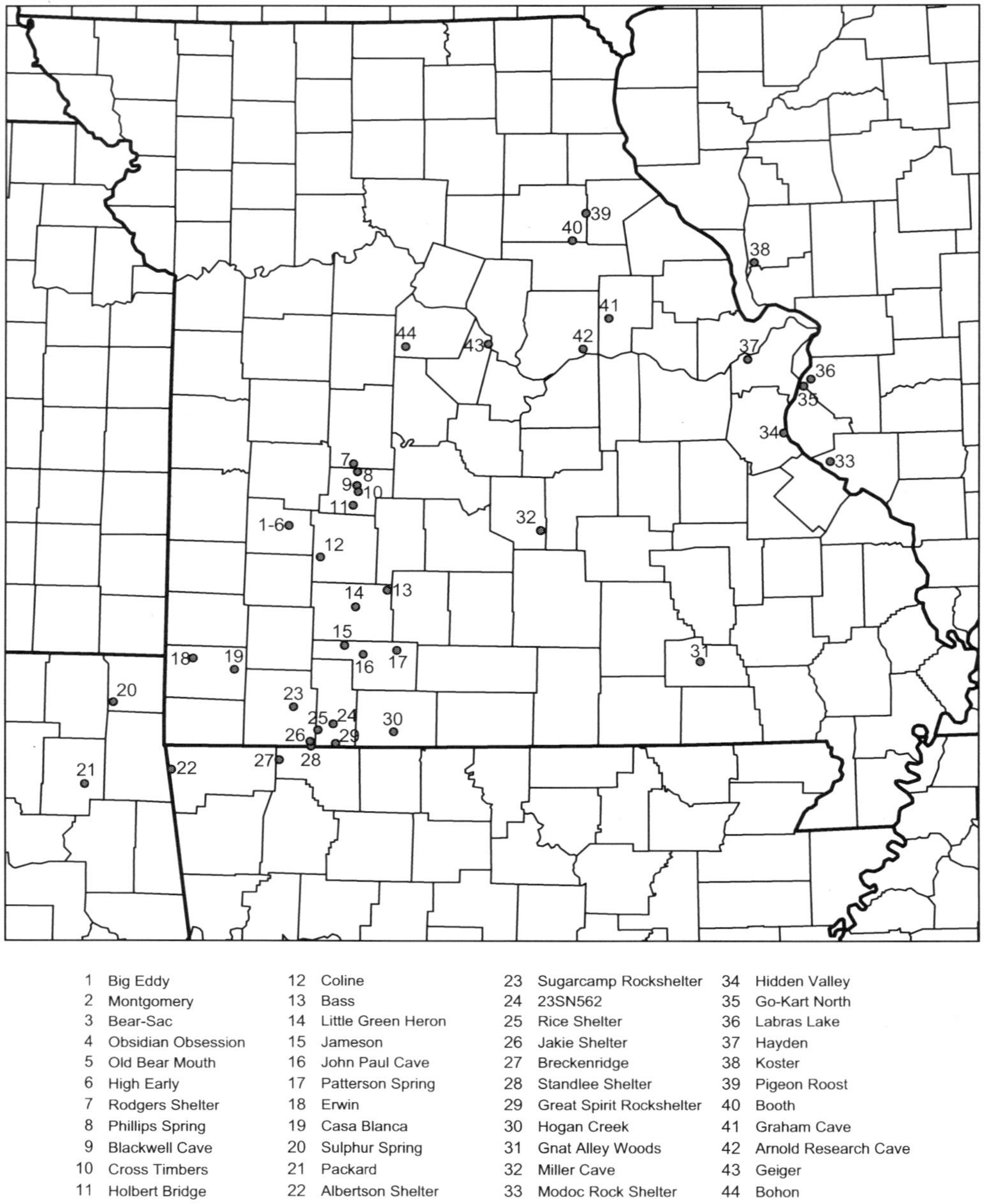

Figure 7.2. Location of Big Eddy and other sites discussed in the text.

questions as well as potential solutions. In comparison with "one-shot" mitigation projects, the multiyear effort at Big Eddy has permitted staged research to address new questions and seek refined or alternative perspectives on older questions. The duration of the Big Eddy project has also permitted a great amount of interaction with local artifact collectors since 1997. During the last ten years, we have examined most of the major private collections pertaining to a 49-km stretch of the lower Sac River, including several containing artifacts from the Big Eddy site (Ray and Lopinot 2005a). Most collectors continue to show us new finds and, if they had not done so systematically before, they have learned to keep detailed locational information, including measurements of the horizontal and vertical locations of in situ diagnostic artifacts eroding from cutbanks.

We do not necessarily ascribe to the concept of "one point–one culture," but the evidence from Big Eddy is indicative of the likelihood that individual styles (or types) of projectile points represent different cultural groups throughout most of Archaic prehistory. At the site level, one could equate a particular Archaic projectile point type to a specific band or other consanguineal or kindred entity (Kinsey 1971). At the regional or pan-regional level, one could view a particular type or, at most, a few similar types

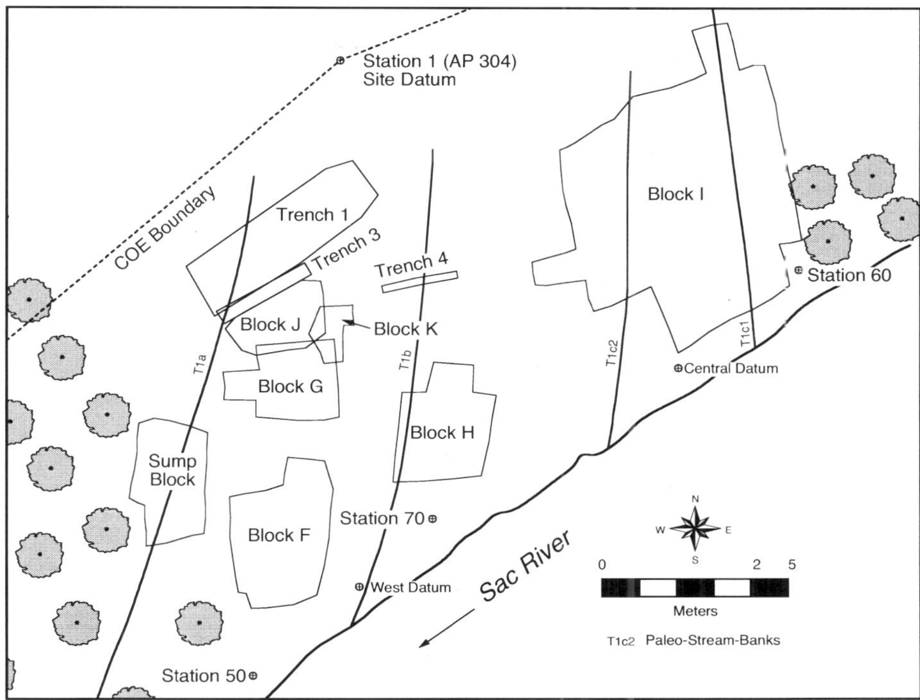

Figure 7.3. Blocks F–K and Trenches 1, 3, and 4 in relation to stream banks T1c, T1b, and T1c1–2 at the Big Eddy site.

as representative of a larger cultural entity, much as Winters (1967, 1969) did with the "Riverton culture" of the Wabash River valley in Illinois and Indiana. In many respects, Big Eddy is similar to the St. Albans site (Broyles 1971) and several sites investigated in the lower Little Tennessee River valley (J. Chapman 1973, 1975, 1977) (also see Stafford and Cantin, this volume). The thick stratigraphic records at these sites demonstrate that component-specific projectile points and assemblage contents are relatively homogeneous. At such sites, projectile points within a single artifact-bearing stratum representing a single component are generally of a single type. In summarizing the importance of sites such as Icehouse Bottom and Rose Island in the Little Tennessee Valley, Chapman remarked:

> Perhaps the most significant aspect of the Icehouse Bottom site for current studies is its stratified artifact assemblage. Although it is apparently passé in the 1970's to be concerned with culture history and assemblages, these are the hard data for model building and processual studies. Too much has been written based on deflated sites and surface manifestations in which there were no controls of the time span represented by the artifacts. It is only with sites such as Icehouse Bottom and Rose Island that diagnostic and less diagnostic artifacts can be placed in perspective. We are still in this "formative" stage of Early and Middle Archaic studies in the eastern United States. [1977:125–126]

In some respects and in many geographic locations, archaeologists remain in this formative stage more than a quarter of a century later.

The Archaic record at Big Eddy is perhaps not as clear in places as one would desire, but it is substantially clearer than at other stratified sites (particularly sheltered sites) investigated in the Missouri Ozarks. Furthermore, the Big Eddy record corroborates the notion of "one point–one culture" to a great extent. The evidence supporting this position is particularly evident within the western part of the site, where the thick late submember hosts relatively well-stratified Late Archaic cultural deposits. Considerable evidence also has been marshaled to reach the same conclusion for the Early Archaic deposits in the thin middle submember. This is particularly true for the Hidden Valley and Graham Cave components but less so for the others, perhaps the result only of small sample size.

Early Archaic

The placement of Dalton in the Late Paleoindian period versus the Early Archaic period is controversial. Technological, settlement, and subsistence evidence can be marshaled to support either argument (see Goodyear 1982; O'Brien and Wood 1998:75–96; Ray and Lopinot 2005c; Sherwood et al. 2004; Walthall and Koldehoff, this volume). Perhaps it is best viewed, following C. Chapman (1975), as intermediate between Paleoindian and Early Archaic. We opt not to address the issue of whether Dalton is a Late Paleoindian or an Early Archaic phenomenon. An extensive discussion of Dalton and San Patrice at Big Eddy is presented in Lopinot et al. (1998:147–211). Here, we begin our discussion of Early Archaic with the post-Dalton record for southwest Missouri. Our original estimate for the end of Dalton site use at Big Eddy was approximately 10,000 RCYBP (Lopinot et al. 1998). On the basis of more radiocarbon ages and the recovery of in situ Dalton and San Patrice artifacts after the 1997 field season, however, we now place the end of Dalton and San Patrice at ca. 9800 RCYBP.

Most of our discussion of Early Archaic manifestations in southwest Missouri is directly related to findings at Big Eddy. The Big Eddy site may not contain the thickest Early Archaic deposits in the Midwest, but it contains a sequence of relatively discrete Early Archaic occupations at different locations (vertically and horizontally) within sediments of early Holocene age. Some occupations lasted longer and produced more artifacts and food remains than others. Habitation surfaces were not stable long enough to produce organic-rich anthrosols, nor were they occupied with enough intensity to produce midden deposits. As a result, individual Early Archaic occupation layers (or components) were not visually discernible in profile. Nevertheless, concentrations of flake debitage and associated preforms, diagnostic artifacts, or cultural features at different levels were sufficient to delineate individual components. These artifact and feature concentrations indicate habitation surfaces that were regularly and rapidly buried by younger increments of overbank sediment. This process resulted in the preservation of single-component deposits largely uncontaminated by artifacts from earlier or later components. Sediments dating to the Early Archaic occur primarily between 160 cm below datum (bd) and 270 cm bd in the central part of the site. Radiocarbon ages obtained from Early Archaic deposits are presented in Table 7.1.

With very few exceptions, only one type of projectile point is associated with each sequential and stratigraphically distinct Early Archaic component. A minimum of eight recognizable Early Archaic components are represented in the stratified deposits at Big Eddy (Ray and Lopinot 2005c). Most of these (Packard, Breckenridge, Graham Cave, Rice Lobed, Hidden Valley, and Searcy) represent indigenous manifestations in the western Ozarks. Two (Scottsbluff and Cache River) represent manifestations that are more common outside the Ozarks, but these manifestiations also occasionally occur in southwest Missouri. The hafted biface forms associated with these components include practically all recognized Early Archaic point types in the western Ozarks except for St. Charles and Hardin, which are rarely found in southwest Missouri. A final type, Jakie, appears to occur in both late Early Archaic and early Middle Archaic temporal contexts, but it is discussed here in the Early Archaic section.

The reader should also note that we have not created a stratigraphic and geochronologic model for the Early Archaic deposits in the central part of the Big Eddy site by simply connecting specimens representing particular point types, regardless of their depths or relative stratigraphic positions. Rather, a holistic model incorporating paleotopographic and paleogeomoprhic surfaces was employed. If one examines only the vertical distribution of various point types, some overlap is evident in their relative depths. For example, a few of the Hidden Valley points were found at the same depths as and deeper than Rice Lobed points. However, The Early Archaic deposits sampled by Block I were not flat; rather, the landscape at the time consisted of an elongated topographic high or alluvial ridge summit trending north–south, with sloping scarps on either side (Figure 7.4). This alluvial ridge was oriented with, and morphologically mimicked in muted form, an underlying paleo-braid bar and topographic high. Taking into account this paleolandscape variability, the distribution of projectile points reflects little if any stratigraphic mixing.

We have divided the Early Archaic period into three subperiods on the basis of stratigraphic data, radiocarbon ages, and the geologic model from Big Eddy, combined with apparent changes in lithic technologies and resource use. These are the early Early Archaic subperiod (ca. 9800–8600 RCYBP), the middle Early Archaic subperiod (ca. 8600–8000 RCYBP), and the late Early Archaic subperiod (ca. 8000–7000 RCYBP). Partly because of the slightly acidic soils and the scant amounts of debris represented for most components at Big Eddy, subsistence and settlement data are quite limited. Thus, any discussion of subsistence must be limited to generalizations derived primarily from sheltered sites with partially mixed strata. In addition, the geoarchaeological model for, and known site occurrences in, the lower Sac River valley indicates that Early Archaic sites are vastly underrepresented in nearly all available survey data for major river valleys. Given these constraints, any discussion of settlement strategies also is limited.

Early Early Archaic (ca. 9800–8600 RCYBP)

Four point types (Packard, Breckenridge, Scottsbluff, and Cache River) and associated lithic assemblages at the Big Eddy site are assigned to the early Early Archaic subperiod. The earliest of these may be partially contemporaneous with or immediate successors of Dalton. Technologically, the Breckenridge type appears to be most closely related to Dalton, as indicated by the presence of beveled blades and random flaking. The Packard, Scottsbluff, and Cache River types differ primarily in the absence of beveled blades and transverse parallel (or collateral) flaking. The manufacturers of all four types selected for Jefferson City chert, the highest-quality local chert resource, and they did not heat treat bifaces.

Table 7.1. Radiocarbon and Calibrated Ages from Archaic Sites in the Western Ozarks.

Site Name	Site Number	Component	Material Dated	Dating Method	Lab Number	RCYBP	Cal B.P. Intercept(s)[1]	Cal B.P. 1 Sigma[1]	Cal B.P. 2 Sigma[1]
Sulphur Spring	34OT100	Afton	antler	AMS	AA-55199	2830 ± 45	2935	2975–2865	3065–2805
Big Eddy	23CE426	Afton	nutshell charcoal	AMS	AA-59419	2890 ± 40	2990	3075–2945	3155–2880
Little Green Heron	23GR535	Kings?	nutshell charcoal	standard	Beta-12658	2940 ± 60	3080	3215–2980	3315–3295, 3275–2905
Little Green Heron	23GR535	Kings?	nutshell charcoal	standard	Beta-11999	2960 ± 60	3135, 3105, 3100	3230–3005	3330–2940
Big Eddy	23CE426	Kings?	wood charcoal	AMS	AA-56587	3060 ± 40	3260	3340–3225	3365–3155
Erwin	23NE212	Kings	charcoal	standard	Beta-69970	3120 ± 60	3355	3385–3260	3460–3200
Big Eddy	23CE426	Kings	wood charcoal	AMS	AA-59420	3160 ± 40	3370	3405–3355	3460–3320
Erwin	23NE212	Kings	charcoal	standard	Beta-69972	3230 ± 60	3455	3485–3375	3585–3345
Big Eddy	23CE426	Kings?	nutshell charcoal	AMS	AA-59425	3335 ± 40	3570	3625–3485	3675–3460
Big Eddy	23CE426	Kings?	charcoal	AMS	AA-59415	3500 ± 55	3815, 3785, 3740	3850–3690	3910–3630
Sugarcamp	23BY629	Williams	nutshell charcoal	standard	Beta-55826	3620 ± 70	3910	4065–4050, 3995–3845	4135–3710
Big Eddy	23CE426	Smith-Etley	nutshell charcoal	AMS	AA-60847	3625 ± 40	3915	3980–3870	4075–4020, 4010–3840
Big Eddy	23CE426	Kings	nutshell charcoal	AMS	AA-59426	3655 ± 35	3970	4065–4040, 4000–3910	4085–3855
Big Eddy	23CE426	Smith-Etley?	wood charcoal	AMS	AA-60624	3765 ± 40	4140	4165–4080	4250–3985
Big Eddy	23CE426	Smith-Etley	wood charcoal	AMS	AA-56588	3835 ± 50	4240	4300–4155	4410–4080
Big Eddy	23CE426	Smith-Etley	charred bark	AMS	AA-59421	3855 ± 40	4255	4360–4195, 4195–4170	4410–4145
Big Eddy	23CE426	Smith-Etley	wood charcoal	AMS	AA-56589	3900 ± 40	4365	4410–4260	4430–4220, 4185–4175
Big Eddy	23CE426	Williams	wood charcoal	AMS	AA-56591	3905 ± 40	4390	4415–4270	4430–4225
Bohon	23CP243	Sedalia	charcoal	standard	unreported	3970 ± 60	4420	4515–4395	4555–4250
Big Eddy	23CE426	Williams	nutshell charcoal	standard	Beta-109009	4020 ± 80	4505, 4475, 4445	4565–4410	4815–4740, 4725–4260
Big Eddy	23CE426	Williams	woodand nutshell	standard	Beta-112984	4040 ± 100	4520	4795–4765, 4630–4410	4835–4240
Big Eddy	23CE426	Smith-Etley	nutshell charcoal	AMS	AA-29018	4125 ± 45	4605	4810–4745, 4715–4545	4830–4515
Big Eddy	23CE426	Smith-Etley	charred bark	AMS	AA-29020	4130 ± 45	4790, 4780, 4720	4815–4745, 4720–4550	4830–4515
Big Eddy	23CE426	Smith-Etley?	wood charcoal	AMS	AA-59422	4180 ± 40	4815, 4740, 4720	4830–4795, 4770–4630	4840–4560
Big Eddy	23CE426	Smith-Etley	wood charcoal	AMS	AA-56590	4410 ± 40	4970	5045–4880	5260–5180, 5065–4860
Big Eddy	23CE426	Smith-Etley?	soil humates	bulk carbon	Tx-9328	4495 ± 55	5265, 5180, 5065	5295–5040	5315–4950, 4920–4890
Kubik	34KA354	Calf Creek	nutshell	AMS	Beta-130710	4600 ± 60	5315	5445–5405, 5325–5290	5465–5220, 5210–5055
Kubik	34KA354	Calf Creek	nutshell	AMS	Beta-142026	5380 ± 30	6190	6255–6240, 6210–6175	6275–6105, 6060–6015
John Paul	23CN758	?	nutshell charcoal	standard	Beta-102270	5790 ± 130	6620	6740–6425	6885–6300
John Paul	23CN758	Jakie/White River	nutshell charcoal	standard	Beta-82219	6000 ± 120	6795	6985–6685	7190–6545
Hogan Creek	23TA601	White River	nutshell charcoal	AMS	AA-29231	6100 ± 50	6960	7010–6885	7165–6790
Hogan Creek	23TA601	White River	nutshell charcoal	AMS	AA-29230	6180 ± 55	7155, 7130, 7025	7185–6985	7245–6905
Hogan Creek	23TA601	White River	nutshell charcoal	AMS	AA-29228	6190 ± 50	7160, 7120, 7065, 7065, 7030	7190–7000	7245–6930

[1] Calendar ages obtained using the CALIB 4.3 version downloaded from http://depts.washington.edu/qil/dloadcalib/

Table 7.1. Radiocarbon and Calibrated Ages from Archaic Sites in the Western Ozarks, continued.

Site Name	Site Number	Component	Material Dated	Dating Method	Lab Number	RCYBP	Cal B.P. Intercept(s)[1]	Cal B.P. 1 Sigma[1]	Cal B.P. 2 Sigma[1]
John Paul	23CN758	Jakie/White River	nutshell charcoal	standard	Beta-102271	6300 ± 180	7245	7420–6985	7565–6740
Great Spirit	23SN866	Hidden Valley?	bone	standard	Beta-70365	7090 ± 90	7935	7970–7810	8045–7700
John Paul	23CN758	Searcy	nutshell charcoal	standard	Beta-102272	7160 ± 180	7960	8165–7795	8350–7655
Big Eddy	23CE426	Hidden Valley	wood charcoal	AMS	AA-56604	7300 ± 50	8125, 8070, 8055	8170–8025	8190–7985
John Paul	23CN758	Searcy	nutshell charcoal	standard	Beta-82220	7540 ± 90	8365	8400–8300, 8275–8270, 8260–8205	8455–8170
Albertson	3BE174	Searcy	wood charcoal?	standard	Beta-127986	7800 ± 80	8580	8635–8450	8955–8935, 8855–8835, 8785–8405
Albertson	3BE174	Rice Lobed	wood charcoal	standard	Beta-127988	8000 ± 90	8985	9015–8660	9110–8595
Casa Blanca	23NE198	Jakie?	wood charcoal	standard	Beta-54304	8140 ± 150	9040	9290–8980, 8805–8805	9480–8605
Big Eddy	23CE426	Rice Lobed	wood charcoal	AMS	AA-29019	8190 ± 60	9115	9265–9030	9385–9369, 9305–9005
Albertson	3BE174	Rice Lobed?	wood charcoal	standard	Beta-127985	8200 ± 100	9135	9300–9015	9455–8985
Big Eddy	23CE426	Graham Cave	nutshell charcoal	AMS	AA-60623	8235 ± 55	9235	9290–9105	9415–9025
Jameson	23CN579	Graham Cave	wood charcoal	AMS	Beta-198069	8320 ± 40	9390, 9360, 9305	9435–9430, 9425–9270	9465–9220
Albertson	3BE174	Rice Lobed?	wood charcoal	standard	Beta-127987	8320 ± 80	9390, 9355, 9305	9455–9245	9505–9065, 9060–9050
Albertson	3BE174	Rice Lobed?	wood charcoal	standard	UGA-3939	8410 ± 245	9460	9560–9080	10,130–9995, 9950–8710
Big Eddy	23CE426	Scottsbluff	wood charcoal	AMS	AA-27479	9525 ± 65	10,735	11,070–10,940, 10,865–10,695	11,135–10,575
Packard	34MY66	Packard	bark charcoal	AMS	AA-3118	9770 ± 80	11,190	11,220–11,155	11,280–11,075, 10,930–10,875
Packard	34MY66	Packard	bark charcoal	AMS	AA-3117	9830 ± 70	11,210	11,245–11,180	11,315–11,155
Packard	34MY66	Packard	bark charcoal	AMS	AA-3116	9880 ± 90	11,230	11,315–11,195	11,565–11,160
Jameson	23CN579	Packard	nutshell charcoal	AMS	Beta-198071	9950 ± 50	11,280	11,530–11,520, 11,340–11,240	11,560–11,215

[1] Calendar ages obtained using the CALIB 4.3 version downloaded from http://depts.washington.edu/qil/dloadcalib/

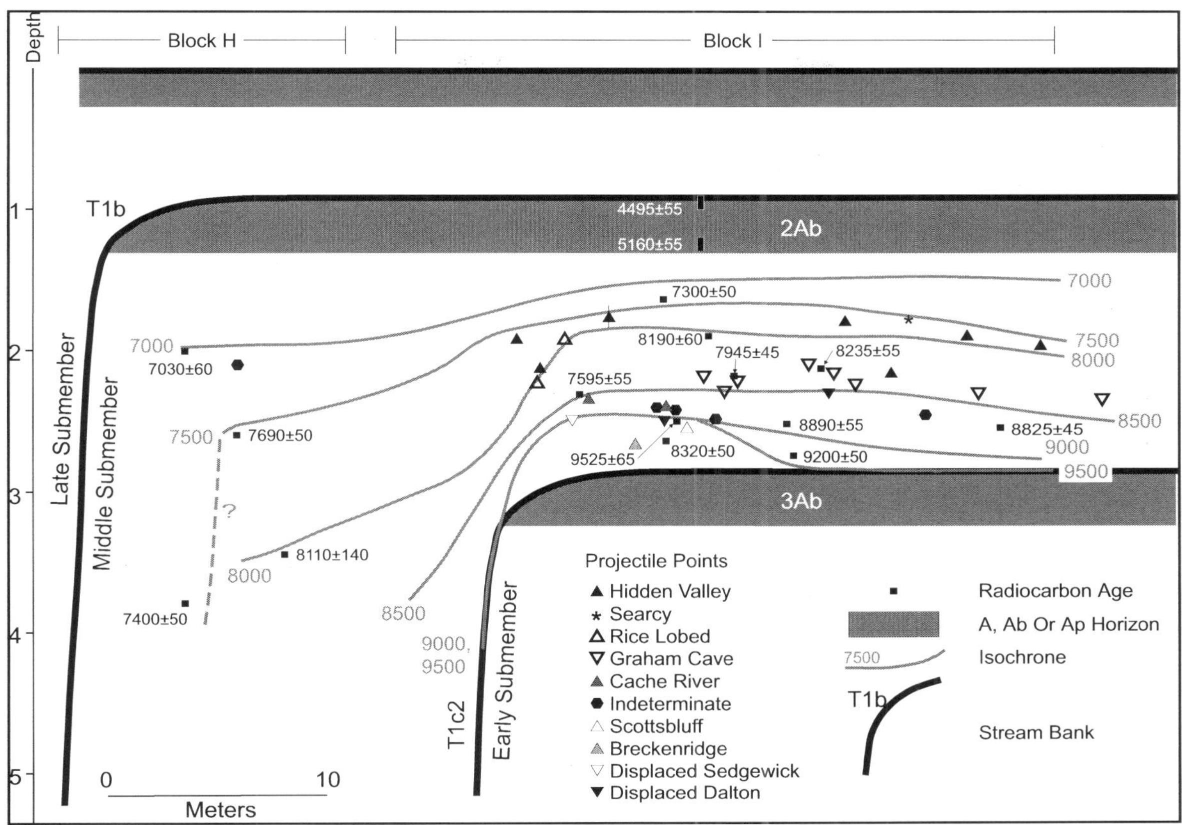

Figure 7.4. Collapsed stratigraphic profile of the middle submember oriented perpendicular to the T1c stream bank and north–south trending alluvial ridge illustrating diagnostic artifacts, radiocarbon ages, and isochrones.

Packard

The Packard point was defined by Wyckoff (1985) as the result of work at the Packard site in northeast Oklahoma. This point type occurs throughout southwest Missouri, but it is not common (Sandstrom and Ray 2004:44). It has a relatively narrow lanceolate shape with the widest portion usually slightly above the midpoint of unresharpened specimens. The stem is ground and contracts slightly toward the base, which may be slightly convex, straight, or slightly concave. These points were not intentionally heat treated. Because they superficially resemble the Agate Basin point type found primarily in the western and central Plains (Frison 1978:31), Packard points are sometimes called "Eastern Agate Basin." Packard points, however, differ from Agate Basin points in that they are thick and have a diamond-shaped cross section (Wyckoff 1985:16). The blade also exhibits transverse parallel flaking that terminates at the midline, often forming a slight medial ridge.

Five Packard points have been found at Big Eddy by private collectors (Figure 7.5). All five were found in disturbed contexts such as cutbank slumpage or nearby gravel deposits. Four are complete but resharpened points that exhibit transverse parallel flaking and thick diamond-shaped cross sections. The recovery of all five Packard points from eroded deposits prior to 1997 and the lack of Packard points from our extensive excavations at the site suggest that the Packard occupation area at the southern end of the Big Eddy site had already eroded into the Sac River prior to our investigations. Therefore, the exact placement of the Packard component in the cultural sequence at Big Eddy is unknown. An approximate stratigraphic location, however, can be extrapolated on

Figure 7.5. Packard points, 23CE426.

the basis of relative and absolute data from two other sites in the southwestern Ozarks.

The age of Packard points has been dated at the deeply stratified Packard site in northeast Oklahoma (Wyckoff 1984, 1985, 1989). Artifacts associated with a Packard complex occurred at a depth of 255 cm to 315 cm below surface and within 3 m horizontally of a hearth (Wyckoff 1984:129–130). Three AMS radiocarbon ages obtained on wood charcoal from the hearth were reported as 9880 ± 90 RCYBP (cal 11,230 B.P.; AA-3116), 9830 ± 70 RCYBP (cal 11,210 B.P.; AA-3117), and 9770 ± 80 RCYBP (cal 11,190 B.P.; AA-3118) (Wyckoff 1989:25). A younger standard radiocarbon age of 9416 ± 193 RCYBP (cal 10,659 B.P.; AA-3119) was believed to be contaminated.

One AMS age recently obtained for the Jameson site (23CN579) on the James River south of Springfield appears to be associated with a Packard point. One Packard point was recovered in situ in a vertical cutbank at a depth of approximately 325 cm below surface. This depth is about 45–75 cm below a Graham Cave component identified in test excavations. A small piece of charred nutshell obtained from sediments just above the Packard point yielded an age of 9950 ± 50 RCYBP (cal 11,280 B.P.; Beta-198071). This AMS age overlaps at two standard deviations with those for two of the three older ages from the Packard site. Relative to the stratigraphic evidence from Big Eddy, an approximate age range of 10,000–9750 RCYBP would place Packard at a depth of about 265–290 cm bd, coeval with the youngest Dalton and San Patrice deposits and the oldest Breckenridge deposits.

Breckenridge

The Breckenridge type (Figure 7.6) appears to be transitional between Dalton points and younger side-notched Early Archaic points (Ray and Lopinot 2005c). The Dalton tradition, which spans the Southeast and Midwest, spawned several distinct varieties. Some of these Dalton varieties include Hardaway, Greenbrier, Colbert, Meserve, and Breckenridge (Bell 1960:50–51; Cambron and Hulse 1975:58; Coe 1964:64; Justice 1987:42–43; Wood 1963:80). Most of these varieties are presumed to be contemporaneous with or slightly later than classic Dalton points, but few from sealed stratigraphic contexts have been adequately dated. The Breckenridge point type was defined by Wood (1963) on the basis of several specimens collected from the lower levels of Breckenridge Shelter in northwest Arkansas. A characteristic attribute of the Breckenridge type is the presence of bevels on the sides of the stem that are oriented in the opposite direction of the bevels on the blade edges (Wood 1963:80).

The Breckenridge component at Big Eddy occurs at approximately 261–268 cm bd in the earliest Early Archaic deposits. It overlies the Dalton and San Patrice horizon and underlies a Scottsbluff component. The component was characterized by a moderate lithic scatter, one knapping debris pile, and a single shallow side-notched projectile point (Figure 7.6a) that resembles the Greenbrier and Breckenridge types. The *Greenbrier* and *Breckenridge* names may designate the same point type (or slight variations thereof), the former on the east and the latter on the west side of the Mississippi River. Accordingly, the term *Breckenridge* is preferred here. Although not pronounced, the characteristic opposing beveling of the blade and stem is evident on the single specimen from the earliest Early Archaic deposits at the Big Eddy site. The broad, shallow side notches, the steeply beveled blade, and the artifact's stratigraphic location only about 5 cm above the top of the Dalton horizon all suggest an affinity with the Dalton tradition.

Figure 7.6. Breckenridge points: a, 23CE426; b, 23LA120; c, 23WB70; d, 23CN57.

The in situ stratigraphic position of the Big Eddy specimen indicates that it may be transitional or intermediate between Dalton and a later Early Archaic point type. An AMS age of 9525 ± 65 RCYBP (cal 10,735 B.P.; AA-27479) was obtained from sediments approximately 15 cm stratigraphically above the Breckenridge point, and an age of 10,185 ± 75 RCYBP (cal 11,920 B.P.; AA-26653) came from sediments approximately 33 cm below the Breckenridge point (Hajic et al. 1998:Table 7.1). These ages suggest an approximate age range of 9800–9700 RCYBP for Breckenridge.

The Breckenridge specimen from Big Eddy may reflect a technological shift from fluted or basally thinned, lanceolate Dalton points to nonfluted and non–basally thinned Early Archaic notched points. The left-beveled blade apparently reflects a shift from resharpening the left side (producing right bevels), which was predominant on Dalton points, to resharpening the right side (producing left bevels), which was predominant during subsequent Early Archaic times. Technological differences, such as a beveled versus a nonbeveled blade and random percussion and pressure flaking versus transverse parallel pressure flaking on the blade, do not suggest an evolutionary relationship between the Breckenridge type and the subsequent Scottsbluff or Cache River types. More likely, the Graham Cave type represents the technological successor to Breckenridge in the Ozarks. It shares attributes such as relative size, thickness, cross-section form, notching, random primary and secondary flaking, and blade resharpening (i.e., beveled and serrated blades). However, current stratigraphic evidence and temporal differences between the Breckenridge and Graham Cave components at Big Eddy do not appear to support a direct Breckenridge-Graham Cave, ancestor-descendant connection.

Scottsbluff

Scottsbluff is a distinctive stemmed point type that is generally found in the Plains area east of the Rocky Mountains, but it also occurs as far east as the Mississippi River valley (Justice 1987:47–48). Scottsbluff points generally exhibit a square stem, although stems may expand slightly and bases may be slightly convex or even slightly concave. Shoulders immediately above the haft usually are slight and never barbed. The blade is never beveled. Perhaps the most characteristic attribute is the transverse parallel pressure flaking that terminates at the midline, producing a biconvex cross section.

In the Plains area, Scottsbluff points are often associated with two point types (Alberta and Eden) that exhibit similar technologies and are included in a Cody complex (Bradley and Frison 1987; Frison 1978; Wormington 1957). Scottsbluff points are occasionally found in the Ozarks, especially along its western border with the Osage Plains (Figure 7.7). At least 12 specimens are documented for Cedar County, and four more are known in nearby counties (Ray and Lopinot 2005a, 2005c). None of the Scottsbluff specimens from southwest Missouri exhibit evidence of intentional heat treatment.

The Scottsbluff component is not well represented at Big Eddy. It occurs at a depth of approximately 251–257 cm bd. It underlies a Cache River component and overlies the Breckenridge component. Two Scottsbluff point fragments have been recovered from Big Eddy (Figure 7.7f, g). One was found out of context (in cutbank slumpage) by a private collector, and the other was found in situ in Block B at a depth of 253 cm bd. Both specimens are broken at the stem-blade juncture. The blades exhibit controlled transverse parallel flaking to the midline and a biconvex cross section. Relatively little debitage and no features were found in association with the Scottsbluff component.

One AMS radiocarbon age was obtained from a wood charcoal fragment found 2 cm above and less than 5 m southwest of the in situ Scottsbluff point. It yielded an age of 9525 ± 65 RCYBP (cal 10,735 B.P.; AA-27479). Radiocarbon ages associated with Cody-complex sites in the Plains are older and younger than the Big Eddy date (Frison 1978:Table 2.2, 1987:105). Superposition of points at Big Eddy indicates Scottsbluff points are younger than Dalton, San Patrice, Packard, and Breckenridge points and that they are older than Cache River and Graham Cave points. We suggest an age range of approximately 9600–9500 RCYBP for Scottsbluff at Big Eddy.

Cache River

The Cache River point type (Figure 7.8) is most common in the Mississippi Alluvial Lowland and adjacent areas of

Figure 7.7. Scottsbluff points: a, d, 23CE519; b, in gravels of the Sac River below 23CE491; c, 23CE444; e, 23CE435; f, g, 23CE426.

Figure 7.8. Cache River points: a, 23WB294; b, c, 23CE426.

northeast Arkansas and southeast Missouri. However, several specimens also have been documented in the western Ozarks (Ray and Lopinot 2005c). Cache River points are typically small and thin dart points compared with other Early Archaic types. They usually are side notched, although some notches may enter the sides at a diagonal angle (Perino 1971:14). The notches are usually small, narrow, and shallow. The stem is squared and short, usually less than 10 mm in length. Blade edges of Cache River points are not beveled. Final flaking across the blade is well executed, and flake scars generally terminate at or near the midline of the point, creating a biconvex cross section.

A Cache River component is represented at approximately 10–18 cm above the Scottsbluff component and directly beneath a substantial Graham Cave component at Big Eddy. At least three Cache River points have been found at Big Eddy. Two were recovered by private collectors out of context, and one was found in situ in Block I. The in situ point was recovered at a depth of 232–236 cm bd. A small, delicate distal fragment with fine, parallel pressure flaking that terminates at the midline appears to represent a fourth Cache River point. It was recovered at a depth of 239 cm bd. Site use was relatively short term and nonintensive, as indicated by the paucity of other recovered lithic artifacts.

Cache River points have not been adequately dated. Nowhere has a radiocarbon age been directly associated with a Cache River component. At Big Eddy, a sample of wood charcoal found at the same depth as and approximately 30 cm north of the in situ Cache River point yielded an aberrant age, apparently associated with a burned root system (Ray and Lopinot 2005c). At present, the age of the Cache River component at Big Eddy can only be interpolated on the basis of radiocarbon ages obtained from the underlying Scottsbluff and overlying Graham Cave components. These dates suggest a range of 9000–8700 RCYBP for Cache River.

Middle Early Archaic (ca. 8600–8000 RCYBP)

Two point types (Graham Cave and Rice Lobed) and associated assemblages at Big Eddy are assigned to the middle Early Archaic subperiod. Manufacturers of both types employed a biface reduction technology similar to Dalton and Breckenridge. They also resharpened the blades of projectile points/knives on alternate sides, producing prominent bevels and did not use heat treatment as an aid to biface reduction. Unlike the makers of early Early Archaic points, they used locally more abundant but poorer-quality Burlington chert.

Graham Cave

Graham Cave points are relatively common in the western Ozarks in comparison with earlier point types. Most investigators in the western Ozarks recognize a technological difference between Graham Cave points associated with the Early Archaic period and smaller side-notched points typical of the Middle Archaic period (C. Chapman 1975; Dickson 2002; O'Brien and Wood 1998:141–144; Ray and Lopinot 2003:9–12; Wyckoff 1984:136). Nevertheless, side-notched points in southwest Missouri often are misidentified. Key differences that distinguish later forms are smaller size, absence of beveling, and the practice of heat treating bifacial preforms (Ray and Lopinot 2003:11–12).

A Graham Cave component is represented at Big Eddy by several in situ diagnostic Graham Cave points (Figure 7.9b–e), multiple lithic features, and light to moderate lithic debris scatters in deposits measuring at least 20 cm in thickness. Most of the Graham Cave points and features were discovered on the level summit of the alluvial ridge, but a few were found at slightly lower elevations on the east side slope (Figure 7.10). Diagnostic artifacts and features delineated upper and lower boundaries of the Graham Cave component at about 210 cm

Figure 7.9. Graham Cave points: a, 23CN57; b–e, 23CE426.

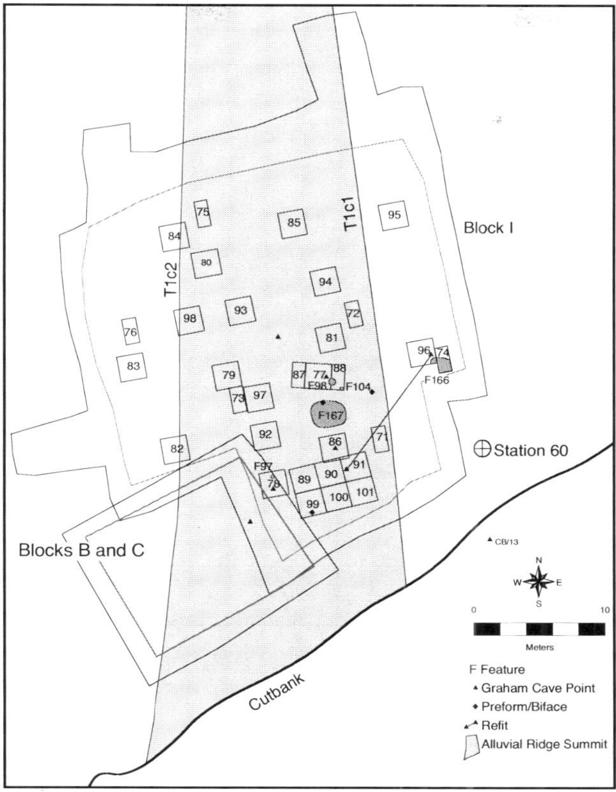

Figure 7.10. Graham Cave component piece plots and features in relation to excavation units and the alluvial ridge summit.

and 230 cm bd, respectively. This 20-cm-thick accumulation of overbank sediments at Big Eddy contained *only* Graham Cave points. On the basis of these findings, the assemblage associated with the Graham Cave points appears to represent a single component. It overlies the Cache River component and underlies a Rice Lobed component.

The Graham Cave component exhibited the highest artifact density of any Early Archaic component at Big Eddy, and Graham Cave is the most common Early Archaic point type recovered from Big Eddy to date (Ray and Lopinot 2005c). Many points exhibit beveled blades (usually left bevels), while some do not. Beveling appears to be directly related to use life and multiple resharpening, or rejuvenation, of dulled blade edges (i.e., pristine or unresharpened specimens are unbeveled, whereas resharpened specimens are beveled). Graham Cave points presumably represent multipurpose tools with variable functions dependent on use life and resharpening. Functional analyses of Graham Cave points from Rodgers Shelter revealed that many were probably used as projectiles (Ahler 1970:105–117), whereas others were used as cutting tools (Kay 1982b:481). At least two unbeveled specimens with distal-end impact fractures from Big Eddy were used as projectile points.

Other chipped-stone tools from the Graham Cave component include large, backed, flake knives, one large, secondary biface with a squared base that appears to be a failed Graham Cave preform, one reworked, broken blade fragment, and four distal and midsection fragments (Ray and Lopinot 2005c). Very little initial reduction debitage (< 2 percent) and no cores are represented in the Graham Cave assemblage. The overwhelming majority of the debitage is composed of biface flakes and flake fragments, indicating that the primary knapping activities involved middle-stage to late-stage biface reduction. Four discrete piles of debitage (knapping features) associated with the Graham Cave component also were composed of middle- and/or late-stage reduction debitage. Most of the chert that was procured and knapped was Burlington. None of the Graham Cave points had been intentionally heat treated. Intentional heat treatment of chert to improve control over flaking, then, was not part of the technology involved in the production of Graham Cave tools at Big Eddy. Nonetheless, three specimens that exhibit evidence of having been thermally altered (two at the distal end only) appear to have been intentionally burned for purposes other than to facilitate tool manufacture.

The recovery of Graham Cave points and other remains vertically throughout the 20-cm increment at Big Eddy suggests that the site was occupied repeatedly. We suspect that the site may have served as a base camp during at least one or more episodes of Graham Cave occupation, but materials other than chipped-stone artifacts do not lend much support to this notion. Non-chipped-stone artifacts were relatively few in number and consisted of one pitted stone, one hammerstone, one faceted and grooved rock, one possible mano, and a few pieces of fire-cracked rock. Ten small calcined bone fragments from an indeterminate medium- to large-size mammal(s) were recovered between 211 cm and 221 cm bd. Finally, the only plant remains recovered by flotation consisted of a single fragment of black walnut shell and small pieces of wood charcoal.

Radiocarbon ages from sheltered sites such as Modoc, Graham Cave, and Rodgers Shelter suggest that Graham Cave points have an age range of a thousand years or more (O'Brien and Wood 1998:142). Open-air sites such as Pigeon Roost Creek and Koster also have produced Graham Cave points. However, other Early Archaic point types with different hafting elements were found in the same horizons as the Graham Cave points at each site (O'Brien and Warren 1985:218–219; Michael Wiant, pers. comm. 2004). Nevertheless, an age of approximately 8500 ± 220 RCYBP (cal 9510 B.P.; TX-3289) was presented for Graham Cave at Pigeon Roost Creek (O'Brien 1985:73; O'Brien and Wood 1998:142), and four radiocarbon ages from Graham Cave–bearing Horizon 11 at Koster form a tight cluster ranging from 8430 ± 90 RCYBP (cal 9475 B.P.; ISGS-230) to 8480 ± 110 RCYBP (cal 9500 B.P.; ISGS-236) (Hajic 1990:Table 2).

Two radiocarbon ages were recently obtained from charred material in alluvial sediments exhibiting a Graham Cave component at the open-air Jameson site (23CN579). A radiocarbon age of 8320 ± 40 RCYBP (cal 9360 B.P.; Beta-198069) was obtained from a fragment of charred acorn meat found less than10 cm above a Graham Cave point and about 11 cm above a Graham Cave preform. A second age obtained from wood charcoal 30 cm below the first radiocarbon sample yielded an apparently aberrant radiocarbon age of 7800 ± 40 RCYBP (cal 8580 B.P.; Beta-198070).

Two AMS radiocarbon ages were obtained for the Graham Cave component at Big Eddy. One wood-charcoal sample (AA-56597) from an apparent natural burn feature yielded an unassociated young age. The other sample, obtained from the single walnut shell fragment, yielded an age of 8230 ± 55 RCYBP (cal 9235 B.P.; AA-60623). This charred nutshell was obtained from a flotation sample collected at 208–219 cm bd in the upper half of the Graham Cave component. On the basis of this radiocarbon age and other stratigraphic data, the lower and upper limits of the Graham Cave component are estimated to be ca. 8600 and 8200 RCYBP.

Rice Lobed

Rice Lobed points are common throughout the Ozarks. They usually exhibit a slightly expanding stem and a slightly concave to straight base (Figure 7.11). The corners of the stem are rounded. When rounded corners occur on specimens with a concave base, the hafted portion of the point exhibits a lobed appearance. Straight-based specimens, however, are not uncommon. The sides of the stem and base are often smoothed by grinding. The point is relatively thick in cross section. Resharpened blade edges are always moderately to steeply beveled and sometimes serrated (Sandstrom and Ray

Figure 7.11. Rice Lobed points: a, 23CE426; b, e, 23CN57; c, 23WB404; d, 23DL187.

2004:56). Bevels often occur on the left side of the blade, but many Rice Lobed points have bevels on the right side. Although resharpened specimens do not possess barbs, pristine or unresharpened specimens may exhibit short barbs (Ahler 1970: Plates 2 and 3; Bray 1956:128; Marshall 1958:107; Sandstrom and Ray 2004:56). Rice Lobed is similar in some respects to certain Early Archaic points in the East, such as Kirk Stemmed (Coe 1964:71) and MacCorkle (Justice 1987:85–86).

The Rice Lobed component at Big Eddy is not as well represented as the underlying Graham Cave component. Nevertheless, nonintensive Rice Lobed occupations appear to have occurred during the deposition of a 20-cm-thick accumulation of overbank sediments between Graham Cave and Hidden Valley occupations. Rice Lobed artifacts occur at approximately 190–210 cm bd on the alluvial ridge summit.

At least two Rice Lobed points have been recovered from Big Eddy. One Rice Lobed point was recovered by a collector from cutbank slumpage during the early 1980s. The other Rice Lobed point was found in stratigraphic context at 188–192 cm bd. This position is just below the base of the Hidden Valley component and about 20 cm above the top of the Graham Cave component. Another projectile point broken at the stem-blade juncture probably represents a third Rice Lobed point. It was found in a trackhoe scrape on the side slope of the alluvial ridge, which is equivalent to a depth of approximately 206 cm bd on the summit of the alluvial ridge. Few other chipped-stone tools and relatively little debitage were recovered from the Rice Lobed component. A low incidence of heat treatment among the debitage and Rice Lobed points from Big Eddy and other sites in the Sac River valley indicates a lack of intentional heat treatment of chipped-stone tools (Ray 2005b).

One AMS radiocarbon age of 8190 ± 60 RCYBP (cal 9115 B.P.; AA-29019) appears to be associated with the Rice Lobed component at Big Eddy. The AMS sample was recovered from a depth of 190–192 cm bd (Ray 1998a:144). Few other sites have yielded reliable dates associated with Rice Lobed points. Perhaps the one with the best dates is Albertson Shelter (Dickson 1991, 2002). Four radiocarbon ages were obtained from Levels 18 and 19: 8320 ± 80 RCYBP (cal 9355 B.P.; Beta-127987), 8410 ± 245 RCYBP (cal 9460 B.P.; UGa-3939), 8200 ± 100 RCYBP (cal 9135 B.P.; Beta-127985), and 8000 ± 90 RCYBP (cal 8985 B.P.; Beta-127988) (Dickson 2003:Table 1). These radiocarbon ages suggest an approximate range of 8400–8000 RCYBP for Rice Lobed. However, one or two of the earliest ages from Albertson Shelter could be associated with a Graham Cave occupation (Dickson 1991:Figure 19k). We suggest an age range of approximately 8200–8000 RCYBP for the Rice Lobed component at Big Eddy.

Late Early Archaic (ca. 8000–7000 RCYBP)

Three point types (Hidden Valley, Searcy, and Jakie) are associated with the late Early Archaic subperiod. They differ from earlier point types in at least three important technological ways. First, they are stemmed rather than corner- or side-notched forms. Two types have contracting stems, and one exhibits an expanding stem. This may reflect a change from hafted points to socketed points (O'Brien and Wood 1998:117). Second, although they are made largely of Burlington chert, unlike earlier forms, many specimens are heat treated. Whether the appearance of thermal pretreatment of stone tools to improve control over flaking, shortly after 8000 RCYBP, was a local innovation or an idea that diffused from a neighboring area is unknown. Third, late Early Archaic forms are bifacially resharpened, rather than resharpened on alternate sides. Bifacial resharpening also reduces the size and prominence of serrations. Bifacial resharpening, however, was not applied to all late Early Archaic point types. It is most common on the Hidden Valley and Jakie types.

Hidden Valley

The Hidden Valley point type generally is conceived of as a relatively large contracting-stemmed point with prominent shoulders and a slightly concave to straight base (C. Chapman 1975:250). The edges of the stem and the base are often, but not always, smoothed by grinding. Resharpened specimens also may exhibit fine serrations and slight bevels on the left side of the blade (Sandstrom and Ray 2004:51). The beveling, however, is never as prominent or as steep as that on other Early Archaic points such as Graham Cave, Rice Lobed, and Searcy. Marshall (1958:112, 171) and C. Chapman (1975:252–253) described a similar point type from southwest Missouri called "Rice Contracting Stemmed." The blades of Rice Contracting Stemmed points differ from Hidden Valley in that they are slightly thicker, shorter, and more narrow and often exhibit prominent alternate bevels. The stems differ in that they frequently are straight and often square stemmed in appearance, whereas the stems of Hidden Valley points are nearly always contracting (Ray and Lopinot 2005c). We believe that Hidden Valley and Rice Contracting Stemmed may have been contemporaneous regional variations on a pan-regional theme for contracting-stemmed to straight-stemmed socketed bifaces. The Ozarks Divide may represent an approximate boundary that separates the Hidden Valley type (north side) from the Rice Contracting Stemmed type (south side).

A well-defined Hidden Valley component at Big Eddy is represented by multiple diagnostic Hidden Valley artifacts (Figure 7.12), multiple lithic features, and at least three well-defined activity areas in deposits measuring about 20 cm in thickness. The Hidden Valley component overlies a Rice Lobed point and is more than 25 cm above the upper limit of the Graham Cave component. The Hidden Valley component also appears to be spatially separate from an apparently contemporaneous Searcy component (Ray and Lopinot 2005c). It is overlain by nearly sterile deposits of Middle Archaic age. On the basis of these stratigraphic distinctions and a lack of mixing with earlier, contemporaneous, and later point types, the assemblage appears to represent a single component.

Figure 7.12. Hidden Valley points, 23CE426.

Diagnostic Hidden Valley artifacts and features were found at variable depths across the level summit and gently sloping sides of the alluvial ridge at Big Eddy (Figure 7.4). On the summit of the alluvial ridge, multiple Hidden Valley points, preforms, end scrapers, and features were piece plotted between 168 cm and 184 cm (Ray and Lopinot 2005c), whereas they occurred at slightly greater depths on the east and west side slopes of the ridge.

Multiple occupations may be represented in the 20-cm-thick deposit that contains the Hidden Valley component. At least three and possibly four activity areas are associated with Hidden Valley. The alluvial ridge summit appears to have been the primary area of occupation (Figure 7.13). Several activities are indicated. Multiple projectile points and end scrapers indicate activities associated with hunting and butchering and hide preparation. Formalized (or specially designed) end scrapers apparently were not produced by Hidden Valley knappers at Big Eddy. Recovered unifacial end scrapers were expedient tools, that is, large, amorphous flakes with minimal retouch on the recurved distal end, whereas bifacial end scrapers were recycled from broken projectile

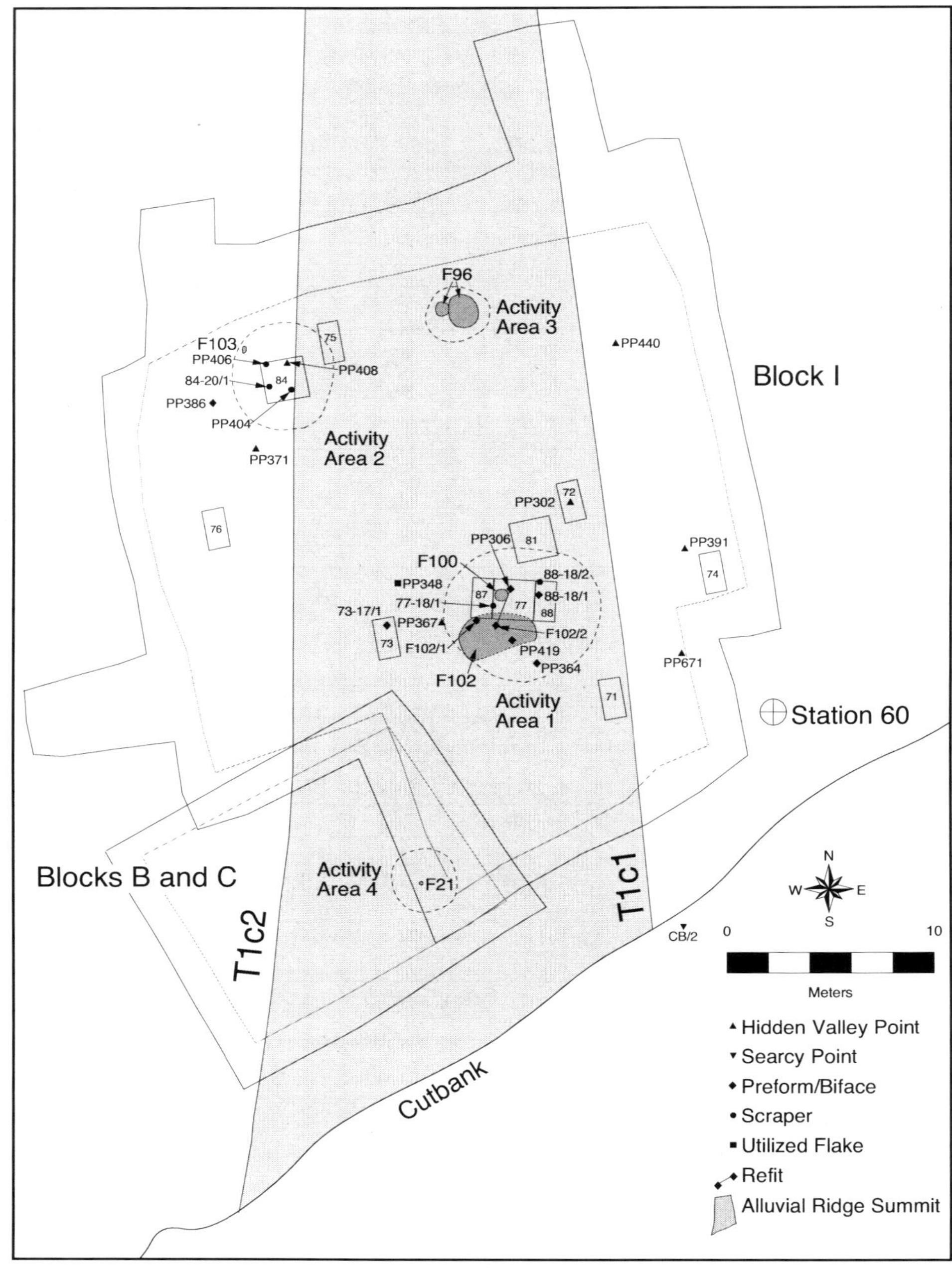

Figure 7.13. Hidden Valley component piece plots, features, and activity areas in relation to excavation units and the alluvial ridge summit.

points. The presence of at least one and possibly two hearths indicates cooking and food preparation.

A major activity conducted at the site was hematite processing. A few pieces of raw hematite were collected from Feature 102, and all of the associated angular sandstone and siltstone fragments were coated with red ocher. Feature 21, located approximately 10–13 m to the southwest of Feature 102 also was associated with the production of hematite powder. It consisted of a concentrated circular deposit of processed (powdered) hematite, possibly cached in a woven bag or a small pit (Ray 1998a:140). Three hematite-stained abraders were recovered from the general vicinity of this feature. Hematite processing appears to have been a very important activity in southwest Missouri during late Early Archaic and early Middle Archaic times (Kay 1982c:570–571; McMillan 1976:225).

The manufacture of chipped-stone tools is indicated by discrete knapping piles, debitage concentrations, and several failed middle- to late-stage preforms. Burlington chert appears to have been the favored local chert resource, although

Chouteau and Jefferson City cherts also were used. Substantial use of heat treatment as a technological aid for improving the working quality of inferior cherts appeared for the first time in the latter part of the Early Archaic period in the Sac River valley (Ray 1998b:257). It was clearly an integral part of the manufacture of Hidden Valley points at Big Eddy. However, heat was applied only to relatively thin, middle- to late-stage, oval-shaped preforms.

Few reliable radiocarbon ages have been associated with Hidden Valley points in the southwestern Ozarks. All previous associated radiocarbon ages have come from caves and rockshelters, which usually produce unreliable dates associated with multiple Early Archaic point types. Examples include Hidden Valley Shelter (Adams 1941, 1949), Miller Cave (Markman 1993), Modoc Rock Shelter (Ahler 1993), Graham Cave (Klippel 1971), Albertson Shelter (Dickson 1991, 2002), and Rodgers Shelter (also see C. Chapman 1975:130–157; O'Brien and Wood 1998:129). Several of these sheltered sites produced Hidden Valley (or Rice Contracting Stemmed) points and Rice Lobed points from the same stratum, suggesting contemporaneity or a single cultural complex. At Albertson Shelter, a large, contracting-stemmed point identified as Hidden Valley was associated with a radiocarbon age of 8200 ± 100 RCYBP (cal 9135 B.P.; Beta-127985) (Dickson 1991: Figure 19d, 2002:86). However, this radiocarbon age as well as three others (Dickson 2003:Table 1) could just as easily date a more intensive Rice Lobed occupation. Several Rice Lobed points were found below, at the same level as, and above the single Hidden Valley point and a Kirk Stemmed–like (Rice Contracting Stemmed) point.

If cultural deposits in sheltered sites are considered good indicators of point type contemporaneity, then deeply stratified alluvial sites in the Sac River valley and elsewhere also should contain both contracting-stemmed points and Rice Lobed points. The Montgomery site produced several Rice Lobed points and other early Early Archaic points, such as Scottsbluff, Hardin, Cache River, and Graham Cave but not one Hidden Valley point. The High Early site (23CE490) also produced several Rice Lobed points and a few Searcy points but no Hidden Valley points. At the Gnat Alley Woods site on the Current River in southeast Missouri, Hidden Valley, Rice Lanceolate (Searcy), and square- and contracting-stemmed (Rice Contracting Stemmed) points were found together stratigraphically above Rice Lobed points (Price et al. 2003:68–69). No reliable radiocarbon ages were obtained for the Gnat Alley Woods site.

Few charcoal fragments were recovered from sediments containing the Hidden Valley component at Big Eddy. Nonetheless, two radiocarbon assays bracket this component. An AMS radiocarbon age of 8190 ± 60 RCYBP (cal 9115 B.P.; AA-29019) was obtained on a wood-charcoal fragment from 190–192 cm, which is slightly lower than the approximate base of the Hidden Valley component. An AMS radiocarbon age of 7300 ± 50 RCYBP (cal 8070 B.P.; AA-56604) was obtained on a piece of wood charcoal found at 160–170 cm bd, at the top of the Hidden Valley component. Thus, a suggested range for the Hidden Valley component at Big Eddy is approximately 7900–7200 RCYBP. The terminal age for Hidden Valley at Big Eddy is compatible with a radiocarbon age of 7090 ± 90 RCYBP (cal 7935 B.P.; Beta-70365) associated with a human burial and a stemmed point (Rice Contracting Stemmed or Hidden Valley) from Great Spirit Rockshelter (Ray 1994b:37).

Searcy

The diagnostic point type of this component was originally called "Rice Lanceolate" (C. Chapman 1975:253; Marshall 1958:103. An alternative name, Searcy, was proposed later by Dickson (1968:5–7) for the same point type in northern Arkansas. The Searcy name is preferred here to reduce potential confusion when dealing with multiple Archaic point types in southwest Missouri that bear the Rice name (C. Chapman 1975; Marshall 1958). Kay (1982b:489–494, Figure 11.31) introduced the name "Rodgers" for a similar, but unserrated lanceolate point at Rodgers Shelter. We agree with O'Brien and Wood (1998:120) that there is little difference between Kay's "Rodgers" type and Rice Lanceolate (or Searcy), except that the "Rodgers" specimens are unresharpened.

Searcy points are lanceolate in form with a contracting stem (Figure 7.14). The base is usually concave, but it may be straight. The stem and basal edges are usually ground. Unresharpened specimens may exhibit slight shoulders above the haft, but the shoulders often are absent as a result of repeated resharpening (Sandstrom and Ray 2004:45). Those with slight shoulders often exhibit a stemmed appearance (C. Chapman 1975:253). Although not always present, moderate to steep bevels (usually on the left side) and serrations often occur on resharpened specimens. Serrations on the blades of Searcy points are more prominent and the spacing between serrations is much wider compared with the fine serrations usually found on the blades of Hidden Valley points.

Figure 7.14. Searcy points: a, 23GR17; b, 23WB382; c–e, 23CN758.

Very little of a Searcy component is extant at Big Eddy. All Searcy points were recovered along the active cutbank south of the excavated area, mostly out of context. However, one in situ Searcy point was found in the cutbank at a depth of approximately 180 cm, which is equivalent to the upper part of the Hidden Valley component. Thus, the Searcy component appears to be contemporaneous with, but spatially separate from, the Hidden Valley component.

Contemporaneity of Searcy and Hidden Valley points also was indicated at the Gnat Alley Woods site (Price et al. 2003:68–69). A comparable incidence of heat treatment of chert tools also is supportive evidence that Searcy and Hidden Valley points are roughly contemporaneous (Ray and Lopinot 2005c). For example, 14 (70 percent) of 20 Searcy points and 11 (73 percent) of 15 Hidden Valley points from the lower Sac River valley were heat treated. This incidence of heat treatment contrasts with projectile points/knives found at lower stratigraphic levels at Big Eddy, such as Rice Lobed, Graham Cave, Cache River, Scottsbluff, and Breckenridge (Ray 2005b).

Radiocarbon ages roughly contemporaneous with Hidden Valley have been obtained from two sheltered sites with stratified Early and Middle Archaic deposits in the southwestern Ozarks. At Albertson Shelter, four Searcy points and an atlatl hook were found in one 3-inch (7.6-cm) level (16A) that yielded a radiocarbon age of 7800 ± 80 RCYBP (cal 8580 B.P.; Beta-127986) (Dickson 1991:59–61, 2003:Table 1). The Searcy points were noted to occur approximately 18–30 cm above levels containing Hidden Valley and Rice Contracting Stemmed points (Dickson 1991:60, 2002:94). Five Searcy points also were recovered from limited test excavations at John Paul Cave (23CN758) in Christian County, Missouri. Three were found between 153 cm and 162 cm bd in Stratum VII (Ray 1995:35), and two were found in younger and apparently displaced contexts (Ray 1997:Table 6). One Graham Cave point also was found in Stratum VII at a depth of 163 cm bd. Two radiocarbon ages were obtained from Stratum VII. One sample from a depth of 155–165 cm bd yielded a radiocarbon age of 7160 ± 180 RCYBP (cal 7960 B.P.; Beta-102272), and the other sample, from a depth of 170–180 cm bd, yielded an age of 7540 ± 90 RCYBP (cal 8365 B.P.; Beta-82220). These ages are too young for Graham Cave and appear to date the Searcy points. If the radiocarbon ages from Albertson Shelter and John Paul Cave are accurate reflections of the age of Searcy points, an approximate age range of 7800–7100 RCYBP may be applicable to Searcy occupations at Big Eddy. This temporal span is essentially contemporaneous with Hidden Valley.

Jakie

Jakie is a common but poorly documented point type in the western Ozarks (Figure 7.15). In general, it is a medium to large expanding-stemmed point with a concave base. The stem and basal areas, however, may vary significantly from deeply concave to slightly concave (Ray 1994a:17–21; Sandstrom and Ray 2004:52). Deeply concave specimens have a swallowtail-like appearance. Stem and basal areas are usually ground. Shoulders are prominent but unbarbed. Blade edges may be serrated or slightly beveled or both, but the beveling is generally much less pronounced than that exhibited by Graham Cave, Rice Lobed, and Searcy points. Although not common, some points exhibit burinated blades (Ray 1994a:23–25). Jakie may be a regional correlate of bifurcate-stemmed points in the East.

Figure 7.15. Jakie points: a, 23MD142; b, 23GR25; c–e, 23NE198.

Very few Jakie points were recovered from the Big Eddy site, and none were found in context. They are commonly found in mixed deposits of caves and rockshelters in the southwestern Ozarks. An undisturbed Early Archaic component at the open-air Casa Blanca site (23NE198) contained primarily Jakie points (Figure 7.15c–e). This site, located on a broad interfluve summit, appears to have served as a seasonal base camp for the extraction of upland resources. Artifact types indicate a diverse and sophisticated economy. Among other hunting-gathering and processing equipment, a large fire-cracked sandstone feature indicated a cooking or roasting facility, and unique ground-stone artifacts with circular holes measuring 4 cm in diameter (one a perforated metate) suggested specialized tools for dehulling walnuts (Ray 1994a:10–16).

Jakie points are generally considered to be Middle Archaic in age (C. Chapman 1975:251; O'Brien and Wood 1998:132), although an age of 8140 ± 150 RCYBP (cal 9040 B.P.; Beta-54304) from the Casa Blanca site (Ray 1994a:13) suggests they may have first appeared during late Early Archaic times. This age, however, may be related to the more limited, earlier Rice Lobed component at that site. Jakie points were found just above Rice Lanceolate (Searcy) and Hidden Valley points at the Gnat Alley Woods site (Price et al. 2003:69–71) and above Rice Lanceolate (Searcy) at John Paul Cave (Ray 1997). At John Paul Cave, charred nutshell from Stratum VI, which contained a Jakie point and a side-notched White River point, yielded radiocarbon ages of 6000 ± 120 RCYBP (cal 6795 B.P.; Beta-82219) and 6300 ± 180 RCYBP (cal 7245 B. P.; Beta-102271) (Ray 1997:34). The incidence of heat treatment of Jakie points and chipped-stone assemblages from southwest Missouri (Ray 1994a:36, 1997:Table 8; Ray and Lopinot 2005c) support a terminal Early Archaic and/or early Middle Archaic affiliation.

Middle Archaic

The Middle Archaic period in the Midwest has traditionally been viewed as an approximately 2,000-year span. In Missouri and other adjoining states west of the Mississippi River, the Middle Archaic is typically dated to 7000–5000 RCYBP (Alex 2000:67; C. Chapman 1975:30; O'Brien and Wood 1995:52, 1998:147) or even 6000–4000 RCYBP (Wyckoff 1984:135). However, some investigators have used the onset of markedly warmer and dryer climatic conditions at ca. 8500–8300 RCYBP as the beginning of the Middle Archaic period and the return to more mesic conditions at ca. 5000–4500 RCYBP as the end of the period (Anderson 1996:157; Kay 1982b:547; McMillan 1976:224–225). In this scheme, the Middle Archaic period is sometimes subdivided into subperiods: Middle Archaic I and Middle Archaic II (McMillan 1976:224–225). We prefer a 2,500-year span of ca. 7000–4500 RCYBP for the Middle Archaic period in the western Ozarks.

The Middle Archaic period in the Midwest is generally related in one manner or another to the Hypsithermal (or Altithermal) Interval (ca. 8300–5000 RCYBP), a mid-Holocene climatic episode marked by warmer and drier conditions. Such climatic changes affected the composition and distribution of plant and animal communities, which, in turn, necessitated new adaptive strategies.

In the upland portions of the western Ozarks, prairie grasslands largely replaced oak-hickory forests and were accompanied by a proliferation of prairie fauna, including bison, pronghorn antelope, jack rabbit, badger, and prairie chicken (McMillan 1976; McMillan and Klippel 1981; Parmalee et al. 1976). The decrease in precipitation may have caused a reduction in springwater discharge in upland areas, which, in turn, probably necessitated an increased focus on major riverine and lacustrine localities. Dramatic effects of Hypsithermal conditions on environmental and cultural patterns were documented by palynological and sedimentological studies at Rodgers Shelter and the lower Pomme de Terre River valley (Kay 1982d; King and Lindsay 1976; McMillan and Klippel 1981; Wood and McMillan 1976).

Although pollen is not well preserved in the acidic soils at Big Eddy, stable carbon isotope data provide compelling evidence for the middle Holocene Hypsithermal episode (Hajic et al. 1998:Figure 7.13). The beginning of this episode is marked by a dramatic shift in the ratio of C_3 (cool temperate forest) to C_4 (warm semiarid grassland) plant communities. Prairie expansion appears to have been underway by about 8200 RCYBP, but it did not peak in the lower Sac River valley until approximately 6500–4500 RCYBP. This is somewhat later than the period of ca. 7000–6000 RCYBP often assigned to the Hypsithermal maximum and peak expansion of the Prairie Peninsula (McMillan and Klippel 1981; Purdue and Styles 1987:146; Webb and Bryson 1972; Wood and O'Brien 1995:44; Wright 1971, 1976), but the Big Eddy isotope record is consistent with findings in the southern High Plains (Hajic et al. 1998:105).

The time span of 7000–4500 RCYBP for the Middle Archaic is characterized in the archaeological record by notable shifts in chipped-stone technology, the proliferation of ground-stone technology, and changes in subsistence and settlement. One shift in chipped-stone technology is illustrated in the blades of Early Archaic and Middle Archaic hafted bifaces. Most large Early Archaic projectile points/knives (e.g., Graham Cave, Rice Lobed, Searcy, Hardin, and Hidden Valley) exhibit beveled and/or serrated edges after resharpening. In contrast, Middle Archaic projectile points/knives (e.g., White River and Calf Creek) were resharpened bifacially and do not exhibit beveled blades.

Another technological shift involved widespread heat treatment of chert to enhance knappability. Although intentional heat treatment of chert in the western Ozarks began during late Early Archaic times, as defined here, the technique was perfected and became commonplace during the Middle Archaic period. Exceptionally high incidences of heat treatment have been noted for Calf Creek points from southwest Missouri and eastern Oklahoma (Neal 1994:245; Neal et al. 1994:303; Ray and Lopinot 2003:15) and for White River points from southwest Missouri (Ray and Lopinot 2003:15).

Although ground-stone technology first appeared during the latter part of the Early Archaic period (Alex 2000:66; C. Chapman 1975:152), it became fully developed in Middle Archaic times. A new type of tool, the full-grooved ax, appeared for the first time during the Middle Archaic (C. Chapman 1975:158). In southwest Missouri, full-grooved axes are generally made of locally available soft, brittle, silty dolostone from the Jefferson City-Cotter Formation, locally called "cottonrock" (Lopinot and Ray 1996), but some were fashioned from igneous rocks obtained either from the St. Francois Mountains area or from the till plains north of the southern limit of glaciation (generally north of the Missouri River). Other ground-stone artifacts typically associated with the Middle Archaic include ungrooved celts, atlatl weights, beads, pitted stones, fishing net weights, and manos (C. Chapman 1975).

Changes in subsistence and settlement patterns also have been documented. Evidence indicates that Middle Archaic occupants of Rodgers Shelter focused more on the procurement of smaller mammals such as rabbits and squirrels than on larger mammals such as deer (McMillan 1976:225). The recovery of several large, notched, flat, cobble net weights from the Hogan Creek site (Lopinot and Ray 1996) suggests that fishing (particularly seining) may have been important. Some archaeologists believe that multiseasonal base camps, permanent habitations, and specialized plant use began during the Middle Archaic as populations became concentrated in major river valleys (Brown and Vierra 1983:167; O'Brien and Wood 1998:52).

Relatively little human activity appears to have taken place at the Big Eddy site during the Middle Archaic period (Ray 1998a:140, 2005a). Middle Archaic artifacts are relatively sparse and pale in comparison to the numbers and varieties of artifacts recovered from Early Archaic and Late Archaic contexts. The relative abandonment of Big Eddy may reflect broader changes in settlement patterns throughout the lower Sac River valley and the western Ozarks, in general. The paucity of Middle Archaic projectile points in private artifact collections indicates that the changes in settlement were valleywide, perhaps involving partial abandonment of the area or even a substantial population decline.

Evidence also indicates that sheltered sites (rockshelters and caves) were inhabited much less frequently, if not abandoned, during certain portions (especially the latter portion) of the Middle Archaic period. For example, Rodgers Shelter was used as a base camp for more than 2,000 years (ca. 8600–6300 RCYBP), from late Early Archaic to early Middle Archaic times (McMillan and Klippel 1981:227–230). Between approximately 6300 and 3000 RCYBP, however, a hiatus in cultural activity occurred at Rodgers Shelter (Kay 1982d; McMillan 1976:225; McMillan and Klippel 1981:230).

John Paul Cave, located at the head of a tributary of the Finley River in northern Christian County, also experienced abandonment, although slightly later and for a shorter period than at Rodgers Shelter (Ray 1995, 1997). Radiocarbon-dated midden deposits in Strata VI and VII indicate that John Paul Cave was utilized intensively from approximately 7550 RCYBP to 6000 RCYBP. Nonmidden Stratum V, which generally exhibited a lighter color and contained fewer artifacts and nutshell fragments than Strata VI and VII, was dated to ca. 5790 ± 130 RCYBP (cal 6620 B.P.; Beta-102270). Midden deposits dating to around 5600 RCYBP occur once again in Stratum IVb. The Middle Archaic deposits (ca. 7500–5000 RCYBP) at Albertson Shelter in Benton County, northwest Arkansas, also contained relatively few artifacts compared with underlying and overlying deposits (Dickson 2002:101).

At least two point types are firmly associated with the Middle Archaic period in the western Ozarks. A side-notched White River type appears to be associated primarily with the early part of the Middle Archaic period, whereas a basal-notched Calf Creek type is associated with the latter part of the Middle Archaic period.

White River

Different names have been applied to unbeveled and often heat-treated Middle Archaic side-notched points in Missouri, including White River (Marshall 1958:114–115), Big Sandy (C. Chapman 1975:242), and Raddatz (O'Brien and Wood 1998:143). The Big Sandy designation, in particular, has been misused. The name Big Sandy should be used sparingly or not at all in Missouri or in areas west of the Mississippi River. The Raddatz type name is used primarily in areas to the east and north of the Ozarks. In southwest Missouri and northwest Arkansas, the White River type name (adapted from Marshall's White River Archaic) is generally applied to the Middle Archaic side-notched type (Dickson 2002:104; Ray and Lopinot 2003:9–12; Sandstrom and Ray 2004:34).

This point type exhibits a wide range of variability with respect to size, stem morphology, and blade treatment. Some White River points can be easily confused with unbeveled Graham Cave points (Ray and Lopinot 2003:11–12). However, White River points generally have a shorter, wider, and thinner blade that was resharpened bifacially. Additionally, most White River points made from Burlington or similar light-colored cherts in the western Ozarks were heat treated (Sandstrom and Ray 2004:34). The base of White River points may be straight (Figure 7.16a–d) or concave (Figure 7.16e–n), and it is often ground. Relative to Cache River points, the notches on White River points are wide, U-shaped, and well defined. Alternate beveling of basal ears, presumably to facilitate haft binding, is a common attribute of White River points at the Bass site (Lopinot and Ray 1995). It also occurs on White River points from the Hogan Creek site but to a lesser extent. Serrations may occur on the blade (Figure 7.16i–k), but they are not common. Unlike Graham Cave points, the blades of White River points were resharpened bifacially, sometimes repeatedly to an exhausted stage (Figure 7.16m, n).

One intensively occupied open-air site in southwest Missouri has yielded a multitude of White River points to the near exclusion of other point types. The Hogan Creek site (23TA601) is located on a high Pleistocene terrace overlooking the confluence of Hogan Creek and the White River (Lopinot and Ray 1996). The site has been severely deflated by shoreline erosion from Bull Shoals Lake since 1951. Many side-notched projectile points/knives have been recovered from this site by private collectors. One collector alone has recovered between 500 and 1,000 White River points. The site was briefly tested in 1996 to evaluate the integrity of remaining deposits, salvage any eroding features, and locate in situ diagnostic artifacts and associated charcoal for radiocarbon dating (Lopinot and Ray 1996). Each of the objectives was realized. The testing demonstrated the presence of intact cultural deposits, including a rock feature of uncertain function and a nearby in situ side-notched point. Five samples of plant material from various contexts below the disturbed surface layer were submitted for AMS dating. Two wood charcoal samples yielded young ages, but three samples of hickory nutshell yielded radiocarbon ages of 6190 ± 50 RCYBP (cal 7120 B.P.; AA-29228), 6180 ± 55 RCYBP (cal 7130 B.P.; AA-29230), and 6100 ± 50 RCYBP (cal 6960 B.P.; AA-29231) (Lopinot and Ray 1996).

Diagnostic artifacts from Hogan Creek represent a remarkably homogeneous assemblage for a surface collection

Figure 7.16. White River points, 23TA601.

from an open-air site. Of 350 diagnostic specimens that have been studied, 315, or 90 percent, are unbeveled White River points. The overwhelming dominance of side-notched points indicates that the Hogan Creek site served repeatedly as a base camp or was intensively occupied by a related group of hunter-gatherers, with only transient use by earlier and later groups. As a result, it is a near-single-component Middle Archaic site in which otherwise nondiagnostic artifacts can be associated with a particular point type, and thus, prehistoric group, with a high degree of confidence (a rare case, indeed, for surface-collected terrace sites in the Ozarks).

Other chipped-stone artifacts in the Hogan Creek assemblage include drills, scrapers, and preforms. Most of the drills were T-shaped, but some with relict side notches represent reworked exhausted projectile points (Figure 7.17a–e). Scrapers were uncommon and apparently served as expedient tools. Two thick (13.5–18.5 mm) unifacial end scrapers were made from minimally retouched, large decortication flakes (Figure 7.17f, g). In comparison with Middle Archaic assemblages found east of the Mississippi River (e.g., assemblages associated with Godar and Matanzas points), broken points reworked into hafted end scrapers are notably absent in the Hogan Creek assemblage. Middle- to late-stage White River preforms exhibit convex sides and straight to slightly concave bases (Figure 7.17h–l).

Several ground, pecked, and otherwise modified artifacts were recovered from the Hogan Creek site. Multiple full-grooved axes (Figure 7.18d, e) were made from cottonrock. These soft axes presumably were used for light-duty chopping. Nevertheless, many cottonrock axes from southwest Missouri exhibit broken and battered bits, and the blades of some axes are entirely exhausted to the full-grooved haft. Other artifacts fashioned from cottonrock were biconically drilled pendant fragments (Figure 7.18b, c), and etched tablets. One tablet measuring approximately 72–75 mm wide and 22 mm thick has crisscross designs on each face. One face has a squared or checked design, whereas the other face is etched diagonally (Figure 7.18a). Several large chunks of hematite exhibit faceted surfaces that formed as the iron ore was ground and processed into red ocher (Figure 7.19c, d). Reddish discolored areas on the grooved tablet might indicate that the tablet was used as a stamp for applying red ocher to hides or other items.

Other lithic tools from Hogan Creek were used in food procurement and processing. Several flat, oblong sandstone and siltstone cobbles apparently were used as fishing net weights (Figure 7.19a, b). These flat river cobbles have a maximum length range of approximately 78–108 mm, a thickness range of approximately 19–37 mm, and weigh between 95 g and 308 g. The only modified areas are pecked semicircular notches approximately 11–15 mm wide and 3–6 mm deep at both ends of the oblong cobbles. The cobbles represent rare extant examples of fishing or seining equipment in the Ozarks. Nut and seed processing equipment included pitted stones (Figure 7.19e) and manos. Several chert hammerstones were found at the site. These are egg-sized, exhausted flaked cores that were recycled as hard hammers and used extensively for percussion knapping (Figure 7.19f).

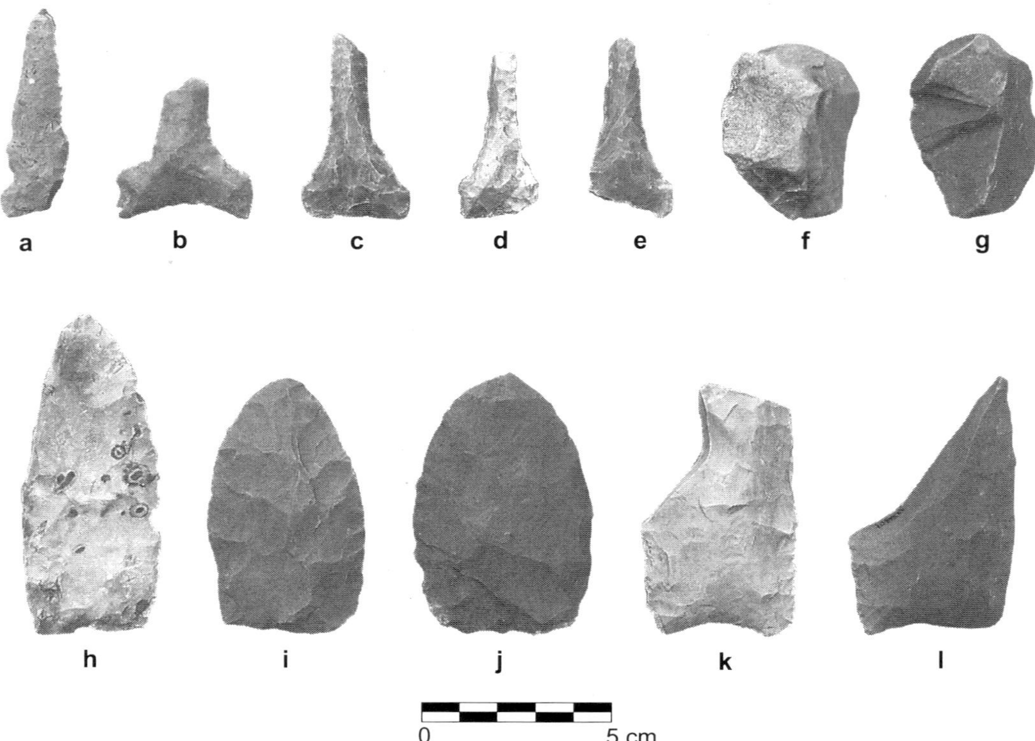

Figure 7.17. Hogan Creek site artifacts: a–e, drills; f, g, scrapers; h–l, preforms.

Figure 7.18. Cottonrock artifacts from the Hogan Creek site: a, etched tablet; b, c, biconically drilled pendant fragments; d, e, full-grooved axes.

Figure 7.19. Ground-stone artifacts from the Hogan Creek site: a, b, net weights; c, d, faceted hematite; e, pitted stone; f, core hammerstone.

Another base camp in southwest Missouri that was used by makers of White River points is the Bass site (23GR41B). The Bass site occupies a Pleistocene terrace in the upper Pomme de Terre River valley. It is situated just east of the Eureka Springs Escarpment. Although multicomponent, the most intensive occupations at this site occurred during Middle Archaic times (Lopinot and Ray 1995; Ray and Lopinot 2003). The Bass site contained numerous diagnostic White River points, but other artifacts such as flake scrapers, core hammerstones, faceted hematite, pitted stones, manos, abraders, metates, and anvilstones could not be reliably associated with a White River occupation.

Calf Creek

Calf Creek points are distributed throughout the southern Plains, but occur primarily in western and central Oklahoma, eastern Texas, and southern Kansas. Although not common, they also occur in the western Ozarks, especially northeast Oklahoma, northwest Arkansas, and southwest Missouri. Adams (1958) was perhaps the first to recognize the distinctive basal-notched type that was later classified as Calf Creek (Dickson 1968, 1970). He reported that these rare basal-notched points are found only occasionally in southwest Missouri with "not more than four pieces of these points ... [from] any one site" (Adams 1958:62).

Calf Creek points (Figure 7.20) exhibit narrow, deep basal notches, a flat, tabular cross section, and systematic fine secondary and tertiary flaking. The stems usually are long and straight, and the edges are sometimes steeply flaked bifacially (Ray and Lopinot 2003:6–7). These attributes distinguish Calf Creek from Late Archaic basal-notched Smith points. The blades of pristine (unresharpened) Calf Creek points, which are rare, are large and convex with long, wide barbs (Figure 7.20a, b). Beveling is absent and serrations are rare, occurring primarily on pristine specimens. Through use and repeated episodes of resharpening, the blade edges become straight, the blade length diminishes substantially, and the barbs become narrower or are broken or lost completely (Figure 7.20c–i).

Figure 7.20. Calf Creek points: a, 23CN864; b, 23CE516; c, 23DG180; d, h, i, 23GR41-E; e, 23GR220; f, 23WB370; g, 23WB163.

The vast majority of Calf Creek points found in southwest Missouri are extensively resharpened, battered, and/or fractured. They often are found as stem fragments with or without blade or barb segments. Extensively reworked Calf Creek points have been noted at sites in Oklahoma (Duncan and Wyckoff 1994; Thurmond and Wyckoff 1999:231; Wyckoff, Neal, and Duncan 1994) and Texas (Ricklis and Collins 1993:5–29). The points appear to have been multipurpose tools. The recent discovery of a Calf Creek point embedded in a bison skull in Oklahoma (Bement et al. 2004) demonstrates that these large, wide-bladed hafted bifaces were being used as projectiles as well as knives. Over much of their range, Calf Creek knappers preferred to use light-colored cherts that were highly amenable to heat treatment (Lopinot and Ray 1995:125–126). In southwest Missouri, they selected for Burlington and Undifferentiated Osagean cherts. Points made from these cherts were almost always heat treated.

Calf Creek points have been firmly associated with the latter part of the Middle Archaic period by multiple radiocarbon ages ranging from 5400 RCYBP to 4600 RCYBP at the Kubik site (Neal 1998, 2001, 2002) and other sites in Oklahoma and Texas (Duncan and Wyckoff 1994:266; Girard and Carr 1994; Ray and Lopinot 2003:Table 3; Wyckoff, Morgan, and Woodard 1994). Bison were part of the economy of Calf Creek hunters on the Plains, but hunters probably focused on more forest and forest-edge species, particularly white-tailed deer, in the western Ozarks.

The Bass site in northeastern Greene County contained the highest concentration of Calf Creek points (n = 53) of any known site in the Ozarks (Ray and Lopinot 2003:15). It apparently represents a rare example of a Calf Creek base settlement in the western Ozarks. Because of the shallow nature of the deposits at this multicomponent site, few other recovered artifacts could be associated with the Calf Creek component. Two exceptions are thin, heat-treated, failed preforms with wide, squared bases and a few notched flakes and bifaces (Ray and Lopinot 2003:Figure 4). The latter artifacts may represent "practice pieces" of young apprentice Calf Creek knappers, "demonstration pieces" of experienced knappers, or pieces used to test a new or rejuvenated notching tool. Similar notched pieces have been reported from sites with Calf Creek components in Missouri (Adams 1958:48, 60), Oklahoma (Duncan 1994:102; Thurmond and Wyckoff 1999:231), and Texas (Ricklis and Collins 1993:5–29).

Late Archaic

The Late Archaic period (ca. 4500–2500 RCYBP) is associated with the end of the Hypsithermal and a return to more mesic climatic conditions similar to those of today. These conditions permitted the reexpansion of forests and resettlement of upland areas. Apparent increases in the number of sites indicate that the western Ozarks were probably more populous than during earlier Archaic periods. The proliferation of Late Archaic point types may reflect a combination of the increasing localization of regional cultural identities and a heightened pace of cultural change (Lopinot 1998:42). A hunting and gathering subsistence strategy based on an even more diverse array of resources than that of Middle Archaic times may have been adopted (Ford 1974).

Nut resources such as hickory, pecan, walnut, and acorn were extensively exploited, along with at least the fruits of persimmon and wild grapes. Additionally, some plants were cultivated during Late Archaic times. These included squash and bottle gourd, both of which were represented in Late Archaic contexts at Phillips Spring in the Pomme de Terre River valley (Chomko and Crawford 1978; Kay et al. 1980). More recently, squash also has been found in Late Archaic contexts at Big Eddy in the Sac River valley (Powell and Lopinot 2005). Other plants that were cultivated in the Ozarks (Fritz 1986, 1997) included sunflower, marsh elder, chenopod, and, possibly, ragweed.

Although early fiber-tempered pottery may have been produced in the Kansas City area (Reid 1983, 1984), there is no evidence of pottery production in the Ozarks during Late Archaic times. Community ceremonial facilities, however, appeared for the first time in the Ozarks. A few rock and earthen burial mounds in the Pomme de Terre River basin have terminal Late Archaic components (Wood 1961:88–89, 102).

The following discussion of Late Archaic in the western Ozarks focuses on recent discoveries in deep, stratified late Holocene alluvial deposits at the Big Eddy site. Excavations in these deposits allowed the delineation of at least four Late Archaic components (Ray and Lopinot 2005b). Each component is represented by a stratigraphically distinct cultural deposit within the thick late submember (Figure 7.21).

Smith-Etley

Extensive excavations in the thick deposits of the late Rodgers Shelter submember at Big Eddy contributed substantial data related to a component containing two large, thick point types: Smith and Etley. The line drawn between these two point types is often a fine one, especially in the western Ozarks, where Etley points often exhibit long barbs that strongly resemble those on Smith points. The direct association of Smith and Etley points may indicate that they are part of a tool kit of a single cultural group. The Smith and Etley categories also may be artificial analytical constructs that do not allow for considerable variability within a single artifact type. Alternatively, Smith and Etley types may have been made by distinct but related contemporaneous Late Archaic groups. The latter explanation of the coexistence of Smith and Etley points implies contemporaneous occupations at Big Eddy by separate but perhaps related groups with overlapping territories and similar settlement and subsistence activities or occasional simultaneous occupations during aggregation events such as fall hunts or trade rendezvous.

Although the single-culture explanation cannot be ruled out, we believe the separate-culture explanation to have some merit given regional distribution and technofunctional differences. First, the ranges of Smith and Etley points differ somewhat. Smith points (Figure 7.22) are most common in the southwestern Ozarks (i.e., northeast Oklahoma, northwest Arkansas, and southwest Missouri). They also can be found in other parts of the Ozarks, including the central and northeastern portions, but they are much less common in those areas where Etley points prevail. Etley points (Figure 7.23) are most common in the greater St. Louis area and the northeastern Ozarks. They are found in portions of the southern Ozarks, but they occur in far fewer numbers than Smith points.

The technology associated with the production of Smith points and that associated with Etley points are similar in several respects. For example, both types exhibit biconvex cross sections, a relative lack of heat treatment, and the same technique of blade thinning. Blade thinning was accomplished by initial random, broad percussion flaking followed by

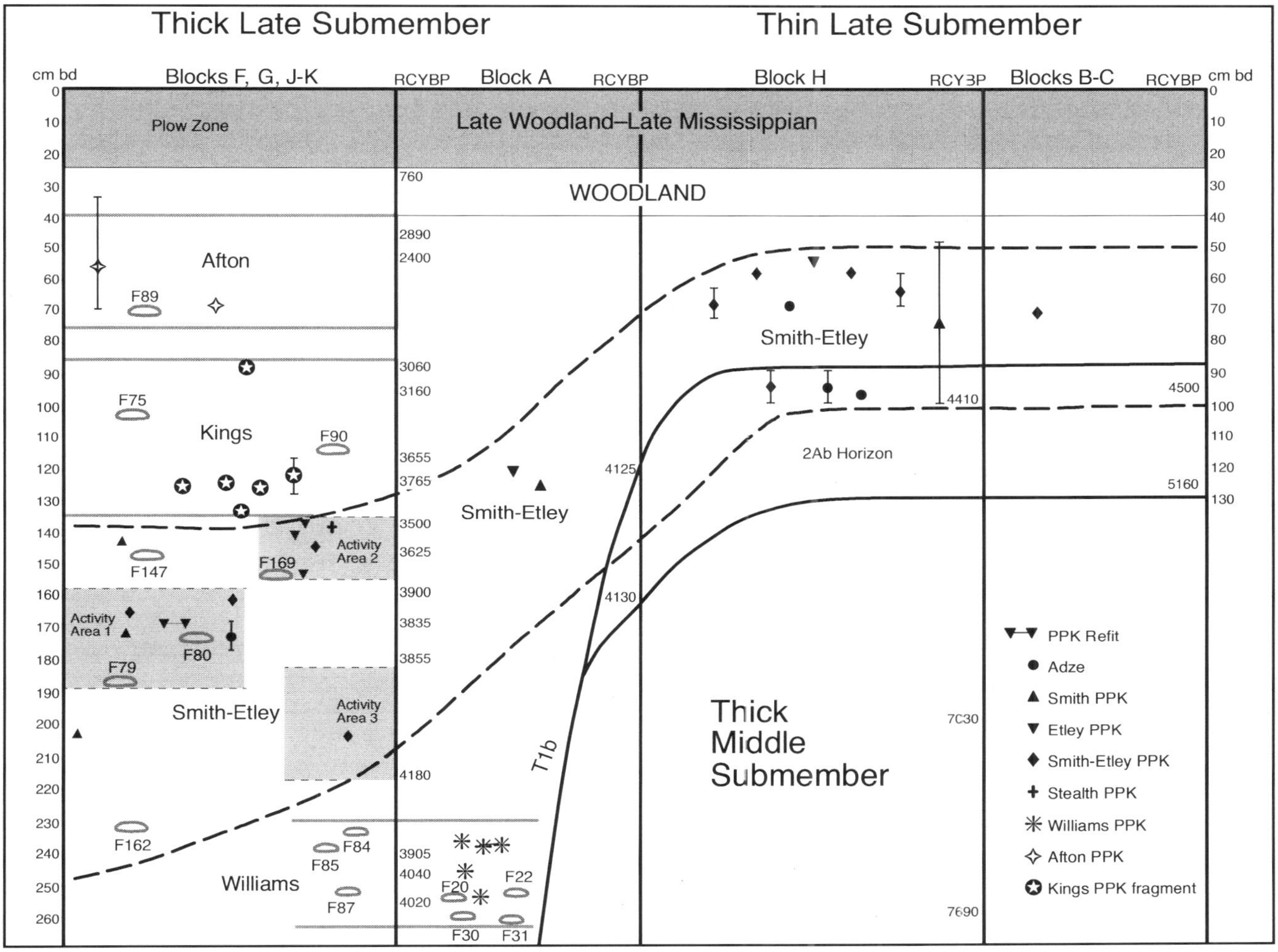

Figure 7.21. Generalized cultural stratigraphic model for the Late Archaic at the Big Eddy site.

Figure 7.22. Smith points: a, 23GR220; b–e, 23CE426.

Figure 7.23. Etley points: a, 23GR705; b–e, 23CE426.

relatively minimal and inconsistent pressure flaking along the margins of the blade (C. Chapman 1975:246; Klippel 1969:7). Etley and Smith points also overlap in maximum thickness, basal width, notch width, and stem and basal morphology (Ray and Lopinot 2005b:Table 9.6). The metric attributes of Big Eddy Etley points compare favorably with those of Etley points from Titterington-phase sites (Cook 1976:137; Fortier 1984:Table 23; Klippel 1969).

Smith and Etley points differ in at least three attributes. All three attributes, presumably functionally related, are associated with the blade. The blade of a typical Etley point (1) is usually longer and more narrow than the blade on a Smith point; (2) is usually recurved rather than excurvate or straight; and (3) often (but not always) exhibits a special-function needlelike tip not typically found on Smith points. Etley specimens with pointed needlelike tips have been found at Big Eddy, Rodgers Shelter, and Phillips Spring in southwest Missouri (Kay 1982b:472; Robinson and Kay 1982:660–661; Ray and Lopinot 2005a), at the Booth site in northeast Missouri (Klippel 1969:Figures 2i, j and 4b, c), and at the Go-Kart North site in western Illinois (Fortier 1984:Plate 7a, m, n). General differences are also evident in the stems of Etley (corner-notched and expanding) and Smith (basal-notched and straight) points, but enough overlap occurs that stem morphology alone is not diagnostic.

As a result of typological problems and subtle gradations from one attribute to another, the hafted bifaces from the Smith-Etley component were classified into four categories. These are Smith, Etley, Smith-Etley, and indeterminate Smith-Etley. The Smith and Etley categories contain specimens most typical of each point type, as generally defined. The Smith-Etley category contains specimens that exhibit stem and/or blade attributes of both types (Figure 7.24). The indeterminate Smith-Etley category contains fragmentary specimens or extensively resharpened specimens of either the Smith or Etley type.

After repeated or extensive resharpening, the length of barbs on Smith points is reduced significantly, and often one or both of the barbs may be missing entirely (Ray 1998a:129–130; Sandstrom and Ray 2004:16). When both barbs are missing, the barbless, square-stemmed form has often been classified as Stone Square Stemmed (C. Chapman 1975:257; O'Brien and Wood 1998:130–131), even though the flaking technology, thickness, and base, stem, and blade attributes are identical to those of Smith points and Etley points. Because of these superficial changes in blade morphology caused by repeated resharpening, "Stone Square Stemmed" recently has been dropped as a formal point type in southwest Missouri (Ray and Lopinot 2005b:176–179; Sandstrom and Ray 2004:11, 16). For the above reasons, large, thick, square-stemmed Late Archaic forms are classified in this discussion as either resharpened Smith or Etley points, depending on the blade shape.

Most archaeologists have assumed that these large hafted tools with wide and relatively thick blades were generally used as knives for cutting, slicing, and butchering. This may be true of many Smith and Etley points, but some also were used as projectile points. For example, at least five of the large hafted bifaces from the Smith-Etley component at Big Eddy exhibit impact fractures, and several more exhibit diagonal and transverse snap fractures across the blade and at the distal end that also could be the result of impact failure.

The reduction technology associated with the production of Smith and Etley points is radically different from that of at least two other Late Archaic point types at Big Eddy (i.e., Williams and Afton). Smith and Etley preforms were produced predominantly by random secondary percussion with a soft billet. This percussion resulted in the removal of large, broad, and often irregular thinning flakes that typically expanded one half the distance across the blade. The preforms were finished by limited pressure flaking along the blade edges and the removal of large notch flakes from the base or corners. Finishing (pressure) flake scars rarely extend more than 15–20 mm from the blade edges, leaving most of the broad secondary flake scars on both faces of the blade.

Another potentially diagnostic artifact associated with Smith and Etley points is the thick, rectanguloid, bifacially flaked chipped-stone adze (Figure 7.25). The bit is beveled.

Figure 7.24. Smith-Etley points, 23CE426.

Figure 7.25. Chipped-stone adzes from the Smith-Etley component at Big Eddy.

Unresharpened specimens often exhibit polished surfaces, presumably as a result of repeated contact with wood. These bifacial chipped-stone adzes are common at Big Eddy and on Sedalia-phase sites, but they occur much less frequently at Titterington-phase sites (Fortier 1984:111, 190). This discrepancy suggests that woodworking activities were undertaken on a more intensive basis in the western Ozarks.

Flake debitage recovered from Smith-Etley contexts reveals a predominant use of Burlington chert and a supplemental role for Jefferson City chert. The data do not reflect intensive selection for Burlington as is the case for a contemporaneous Williams component. The recovery of Smith points made from exotic Reeds Spring chert at Big Eddy and other sites in the Sac River valley (Klinger et al. 1993:Table 96; Ray 1998b:246) indicates at least some contact (trade or seasonal movement) occurred with groups in the lower James and/or upper White River valleys to the south.

Heat treatment was not an integral part of the manufacturing technology used to produce Smith and Etley points (Ray 2005b:310). Less than 10 percent of Burlington chert debitage from Big Eddy was heat modified, which may indicate unintentional thermal alteration. The production of large, thick hafted bifaces from unheated chert is similar to that found in assemblages of the Titterington phase (Cook 1976:66; Fortier 1984:78; Klippel 1971) and the Sedalia phase (Ray 2005b). The same is true for Smith and Etley points from the Truman Reservoir area (Roper 1993a:662). The incidence of heat treatment was reported to be slightly higher at the Hayden site, although Harl (1995:52) noted that some of the heat-altered specimens may have been unintentionally burned. Secondary burning, for instance, through discard into or near hearths or pit fires, was noted at the Go-Kart North site (Fortier 1984:78).

Hematite, as a source of pigment (red ocher), appears to have been extensively processed. At Big Eddy, at least two features of processed hematite and faceted pieces of hematite were directly associated with multiple Smith-Etley occupations. Plant remains indicate that a variety of nuts and other plant foods were being harvested and consumed at the site. Squash and, possibly, chenopod were also being cultivated (Powell and Lopinot 2005).

At Big Eddy, at least three discrete Smith-Etley subcomponents (Activity Areas 1–3) were stratified at depths between approximately 138 cm and 225 cm bd in the rapidly accreted floodplain deposits of the thick late submember (Figures 7.21 and 7.26). Activity Area 1 consisted of a moderate concentration of flake debitage, multiple Smith and Etley points, and a chipped-stone adze between 165 cm bd and 185 cm bd in Block F. The discovery of two refit fragments of a broken Etley point at the same depth (168 cm) and 85 cm apart attests to the integrity of the deposits that compose this Smith-Etley subcomponent. Radiocarbon ages indicate that the discrete concentration of associated tools and debitage in Activity Area 1 was deposited during a relatively short period of time ca. 3900–3800 RCYBP.

Activity Areas 2 and 3 were discovered approximately 30 m north-northeast of Activity Area 1 in Block K. Activity Area 2 was evident between 138 cm and 155 cm bd. It also consisted of a concentration of lithic artifacts. One feature contained fragments of charred squash rind and a large quantity of charred nutshell and wood charcoal. A radiocarbon age from this feature indicated that it was deposited ca. 3620 RCYBP. It represents the youngest habitation level of the Smith-Etley component at Big Eddy.

At the other end of the Smith-Etley temporal continuum was Activity Area 3. It occurred between about 180 cm and 225 cm bd. It was represented by a dense midden deposit of charred plant remains and chipped-stone and ground-stone artifacts. The artifacts suggestive of Smith-Etley origin are one Smith-Etley point and bifacial preforms made from unheated Burlington and other cherts. A radiocarbon age of 4180 ± 40 RCYBP (cal 4740 B.P.; AA-59422) obtained at a depth of 216 cm bd in Block F may date this early Smith-Etley occupation.

Another habitation area was located on higher ground on an adjacent terrace buried by and within terrace-veneer deposits. It contained an assemblage of Smith and Etley points and chipped-stone adzes identical to that found in Block F. The Smith-Etley activity locus in Block H is about 1 m higher than the locus in Block F. This indicates that Smith-Etley activity loci occurred at different elevations on adjacent landforms. Although perhaps a couple of hundred years too early, an AMS radiocarbon age of 4410 ± 40 RCYBP (cal 4970 B.P.; AA-56590) was obtained on a wood charcoal fragment from a depth of 100 cm bd in association with the Smith-Etley occupation in Block H.

Smith-Etley artifacts also occur on a former stream bank or sloping scarp between the floodplain (thick late submember) and the adjacent terrace (thin late submember). They include one Smith point and one refitted Etley point from 120–125 cm bd in Block A. An AMS radiocarbon age of 4125 ± 45 RCYBP (cal 4605 B.P.; AA-29018) is associated with the refitted Etley point (Ray 1998a:130). The location of Smith-Etley artifacts on the terrace, scarp, and floodplain are presented in profile in Figure 7.21.

The intensity of the Smith-Etley occupations was variable through time. Special-use activity areas or nonintensive occupations are represented by Activity Areas 1 and 2, whereas a more intensive occupation is indicated by the development of a 30-cm-thick midden deposit in Activity Area 3. The rapidly aggrading deposits of the thick late submember, however, reduced the likelihood that features would overlap or intrude into one another as a result of intensive and perhaps successive occupations.

Smetley Phase

Initial work in 1997 revealed that the previously defined James River complex (C. Chapman 1975:186) was not applicable to a Late Archaic assemblage from Big Eddy (Ray 1998a:128–131). The poorly defined and overly inclusive

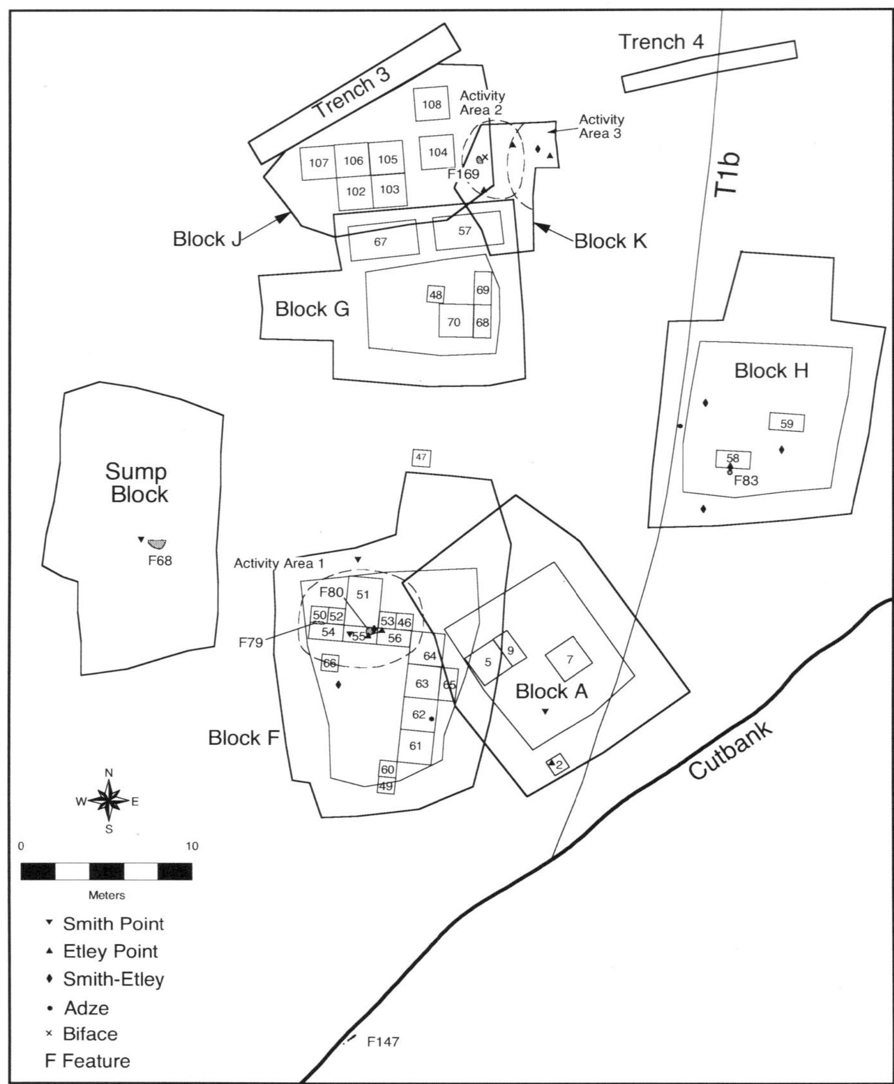

Figure 7.26. Smith-Etley component piece plots, features, and activity areas in relation to excavation units and the T1b stream bank.

James River complex contains diagnostic artifacts such as Smith, Stone (resharpened Smith or Etley), Table Rock Stemmed, and Afton points, whereas the restricted assemblage from deep, stratified deposits at Big Eddy contains only Smith and Etley points. C. Chapman (1975:200–203) also proposed a Sedalia complex that included Sedalia, Smith, and "Stone" points, Clear Fork gouges, and Sedalia diggers for an area surrounding Pettis County in west-central Missouri. C. Chapman (1975:224) redefined the Sedalia complex as a phase when he incorporated similar sites and their assemblages from northeast Missouri (e.g., the Booth site).

Another phase in western Illinois and adjacent parts of eastern Missouri with similar assemblages and temporal range is Titterington (Cook 1976). We believe the local Late Archaic expression in northeast Missouri is best viewed as an extension of the Titterington phase across the Mississippi River and that the Sedalia phase is best expressed in a smaller geographic area centered on Pettis and surrounding counties on the northwest flank of the Ozarks. Certain artifacts that are common to the Sedalia phase are rare to nonexistent in the Titterington phase. For example, one distinctive artifact commonly found on sites of the Sedalia phase that does not occur on sites of the Titterington phase is a specialized, unifacial plano-convex tool known as the Clear Fork gouge (C. Chapman 1975:184).

Although similar in some respects, the Smith-Etley component at Big Eddy does not fit the pattern of Sedalia-phase sites in Pettis and surrounding counties. It differs from the Sedalia phase in at least three respects. First, the Big Eddy site is located in a broad valley setting. Sedalia-phase base camps almost always occur along the shoulders and at the ends of ridge summits and have "greasy black" midden stains arranged in linear fashion (C. Chapman 1975:185, 200; Turner 1965:1).

Second, Sedalia points are much more common on sites in the Sedalia area, where they typically make up 65–70 percent of the projectile points/knives (C. Chapman 1975:200–203; Turner 1965:2–6). Percentages of Sedalia points compared with those of Etley and Smith points are reversed in areas to the east and south of Pettis and Cooper counties. Etley and Etley-like points outnumbered Sedalia points by more than three to one at the Geiger site (23MU91) in Moniteau County (C. Chapman 1975:203) and the Booth site in Monroe County (Klippel 1969). The ratio (10:1) was even higher at Rodgers Shelter in Hickory County (Kay 1982b). Lanceolate Sedalia points are completely absent at Big Eddy. Although a few Sedalia points were recovered from the Phillips Spring site in the Pomme de Terre River valley (Kay 1982a, 1983) and a small number have been recovered from the Sac River valley (see Ray and Lopinot 2005a, 2005b), they are rare in comparison with Smith and Etley points.

Third, Clear Fork gouges do not occur at Big Eddy. These gouges also appear to be absent in assemblages from Rodgers Shelter and Phillips Spring (Kay 1983; Ray and Lopinot 2005b). Additionally, none were noted in extensive private collections from sites in the lower Sac River valley (Ray and Lopinot 2005b).

Kay (1983) extended the range of the Sedalia phase into the Pomme de Terre River valley in southwest-central Missouri primarily on the basis of work at Phillips Spring. While many of the artifacts and features in the Phillips Spring deposits may represent Late Archaic occupations related to the Sedalia phase, a few of the small Woodland-like expanding-stemmed points (Kay 1983: Figures 4.2m–p and 4.3g–i,p) may be intrusive into the former Sedalia-phase habitation horizon via bioturbation, or else they may have been deposited at separate times on a surface that was relatively stable. Certainly, the potential for contamination and intermingling of artifacts from sequential occupations would be relatively high at a base camp located next to a large spring.

The majority of the assemblage from Phillips Spring appears to conform more closely with that found at Big Eddy than with Sedalia-phase assemblages. For example, Smith (including Stone) and Etley points greatly outnumber Sedalia points at Rodgers Shelter (Kay 1982b:454–486); chipped-stone adzes are present and Clear Fork gouges are absent; and some Etley points at Rodgers Shelter and Phillips Spring exhibit needle-sharp tips (Kay 1982b:472; Robinson and Kay 1982:660–661), like those at Big Eddy. We argue here that the Phillips Spring and Big Eddy assemblages are distinct in content from assemblages used to define the Sedalia phase of west-central Missouri.

Accordingly, the Smith-Etley component at Big Eddy appears to be part of a larger cultural entity referred to here as the "Smetley" phase. The Smetley phase is minimally defined for the Sac and Pomme de Terre river valleys in southwest Missouri. Sites containing Smith-Etley components occur primarily along the Springfield Plateau and its eastern and western borders between the Osage River on the north and the Ozarks Divide on the south. A survey of private collections from cutbank locations along the lower Sac River valley (Ray and Lopinot 2005a, 2005b) reveals that Smith-Etley is one of the most common components in the area.

In addition to Rodgers Shelter and Phillips Spring in the Pomme de Terre River valley (Ahler and McMillan 1976; Kay 1983; Robinson and Kay 1982), Smith and Etley points were found at many sites in the Truman Reservoir (Roper 1977, 1993a). A Smith-Etley component also was present at the Little Green Heron site (23GR535) located near the headwaters of the Little Sac River in northern Greene County (Parisi 1985; Ray and Benn 1983).

Components similar to Smith-Etley extend along the Springfield Plateau south of the Ozarks Divide throughout the James River valley and upper White River valley in southwest Missouri (C. Chapman 1975; Chapman and Bray 1960:289–291; Henning 1960:795–813; Ray 1995:39–40, 1997:34; Ray and Benn 1992) and northwest Arkansas (Dickson 2002:109). Etley points and points with attributes of both Smith and Etley, however, become scarce south of the Ozarks Divide (Ray and Lopinot 2005b).

The temporal position of the various Late Archaic phases in Missouri and Illinois that contain Etley points has been well established at ca. 4000 ± 200 RCYBP. For example, the Titterington phase has been firmly dated between 4150 and 3900 RCYBP at the Koster site (Cook 1976:65) and the Go-Kart North site (Fortier 1984: Table 44) in western Illinois, and at the Hayden site (23SL36) in St. Louis County, Missouri (Harl 1995:46). Similarly, a radiocarbon age for the Sedalia-phase Bohon (23CP243) site in Cooper County, Missouri was 3970 ± 60 RCYBP (Eschbacher 1996:8).

Kay (1983:49, Table 4.1) estimated an extended temporal range of approximately 4250–2600 RCYBP for the Pomme de Terre River valley and adjacent areas on the basis of a suite of 30 radiocarbon ages. We consider a span of over 1,600 years to be too long for this phase and suspect that Kay's range probably includes younger terminal Late Archaic components such as Afton and Kings. Our radiocarbon ages from multiple occupations at Big Eddy extend from ca. 4400 to 3600 RCYBP, with six of eight radiocarbon ages ranging between 4180 ± 40 RCYBP (cal 4740 B.P.; AA-59422) and 3765 ± 40 RCYBP (cal 4140 B.P.; AA-60624).

The settlement and subsistence patterns of the Smetley phase are not well documented at this time. Data are available on bottomland sites and plant use in the Sac and Pomme de Terre river valleys, but few comprehensive surveys have been made in upland areas and few Smetley-phase sites with good bone preservation have been excavated. Unlike ridgetop base camps associated with the Sedalia phase, sites containing Smith-Etley components are commonly found on former floodplains and terraces throughout the Sac River and Pomme de Terre river valleys as well as along the Osage River, its tributaries, and adjacent areas in the Truman Reservoir area (Kay 1982b,

1983; Ray and Lopinot 2005a; Roper 1993a). Most of the archaeological investigations have focused on bottomland settings in these areas because of impending impoundments or site erosion. However, a stratified random sample survey of 10 percent of U.S. Army Corps of Engineers fee lands around Truman Reservoir included upland terrain. The results of that survey indicated that (1) Late Archaic sites are well represented throughout the reservoir area, (2) Smith and Etley points are the most common Late Archaic point types, and (3) about 20 percent of the Late Archaic sites are located on upland landforms (Roper 1977:172–176, 1993b:183–199).

More intensive survey of upland areas adjacent to these river valleys might reveal additional temporary or seasonal-use open-air and sheltered field camps for the exploitation of upland resources, but large multiseasonal ridgetop base camps that contain extensive "greasy" midden deposits so characteristic of Sedalia-phase sites (C. Chapman 1975:200–203) have not been reported by professional or avocational archaeologists anywhere in southwest Missouri. One upland site (23SN562) with a substantial number of Smith points was excavated near the confluence of the James and White rivers in southern Stone County, but it contained no features or dark midden deposits (Henning 1960:796).

Base camps of the Smetley phase appear to be located near stream confluences and springs. Examples in the Sac River valley include the Big Eddy site (Activity Area 3), the Bear-Sac site (23CE412), the Obsidian Obsession site (23CE238), and the Old Bear Mouth site (23CE239). Phillips Spring appears to be an example in the Pomme de Terre River valley of a base camp next to a perennial spring (Kay 1983; Robinson and Kay 1982). Extended occupation of the Phillips Spring site is suggested by evidence for plant husbandry (Chomko and Crawford 1978; Kay 1982d). Spring through fall and possible winter occupations were proffered by Kay (1983:61).

Smaller field camps abound in the Pomme de Terre and Sac river valleys. Two good examples are Rodgers Shelter (Kay 1983:57) and the Big Eddy site (Activity Areas 1 and 2). The lack of overlapping or superpositioned storage pit features, midden deposits, and structural remains argues for relatively short-term habitation by a limited number of individuals (e.g., hunting parties or small groups).

Reconstruction of the subsistence system at Big Eddy has been hampered by the poor preservation of faunal remains. Faunal remains from Late Archaic deposits at Rodgers Shelter indicate predominant reliance on white-tailed deer with lesser dependence on other terrestrial mammals, birds (turkey), and fish (Kay 1983:62; Parmalee et al. 1976:Table 9.3).

Archaeobotanical remains from Smetley-phase contexts at Big Eddy are dominated by nutshell fragments, especially from walnuts and thick hickory nuts. The presence of squash rind fragments and the common occurrence of chenopod seeds at Big Eddy (Powell and Lopinot 2005) almost certainly reflect early plant husbandry like that represented at Phillips Spring. Evidence for intensive harvest from wild stands or low-level production of chenopod also has been obtained from coeval sites in western Illinois and eastern Missouri. For example, more than 60 percent of the identifiable seeds from the Titterington-phase component of the Napoleon Hollow site were chenopod, and such seeds were also noted as being common in Titterington-phase assemblages from the Lagoon and Koster sites (Asch and Asch 1985:172). Similarly, 60 percent ($n = 418$) of the total number of identified seeds ($n = 699$) from the Titterington-phase component of the Hayden site also were identified as chenopod (Wright 1995). The chenopod seeds from these sites are biconvex in cross section and have thick testae (Asch and Asch 1985:177; Wright 1995:98), but this does not rule out the possibility of incipient small-scale crop cultivation. On the basis of the relative abundance of chenopod seeds and their testa thicknesses in the Big Eddy assemblage, Powell and Lopinot (2005:336–337) have suggested that chenopod was being harvested from cultivated plots, although the seeds did not yet exhibit clear signs of domestication.

Mortuary sites containing human burials covered with limestone slabs and earthen fill are associated with the Titterington phase in western Illinois (Cook 1976:51–54) but are unknown on the west flank of the Ozarks (i.e., Sedalia- and Smetley-phase areas). Kay (1983:52) mentions a mortuary area at Rodgers Shelter that was associated with a Late Archaic horizon. No direct evidence, however, appears to allow the flexed burials to be assigned to the Smetley phase.

In sum, investigations at many midwestern Late Archaic sites in Missouri and Illinois have delineated three similar and essentially contemporaneous regional phases dating to the interval of ca. 4400–3600 RCYBP, but particularly ca. 4200–3800 RCYBP. All three are located on the flank of the Ozarks. The Titterington phase (located on the eastern border of the Ozarks) and the Sedalia phase (located on the northwest border of the Ozarks) occur along the southern margin of the Prairie Peninsula and may represent adaptations primarily to prairie environments. The Smetley phase occurs in the prairie-forest transition area between the western Ozarks and the eastern edge of the Plains. Adaptations to these border environments resulted in similar but distinct lifeways and tool assemblages that represent variations on a pan-regional theme. Although not conclusive, the oldest dates from Big Eddy and Phillips Spring might indicate that this pan-regional theme originated on the western border of the Ozarks and this cultural adaptation spread eastward with the migration of groups to northeast Missouri and western Illinois (C. Chapman 1975:184; Fortier 1984:186).

Williams

The Williams component differs from all other Late Archaic components at Big Eddy. The distinctions are primarily evident in site use and the technology associated with the production of lithic assemblages. Although at least partially contemporaneous with them, the Williams component differs markedly from at least two of the three Smith-Etley components (Activity Areas 1 and 2). The Williams component appears to represent more intensive site use as a base camp, but over a shorter span of time. The spatial distribution of the occupations also is different from the Smith-Etley occupations. Concentrations of Smith-Etley artifacts occurred on a former terrace surface and an adjacent lower floodplain surface. The Williams midden and associated artifacts were concentrated on the lower floodplain surface, which is more susceptible to flooding. This could be interpreted as differential dry-season use of a lower floodplain during the Williams occupation. However, the Williams archaeobotanical assemblages are quite comparable to the Smith-Etley and include evidence for possible chenopod cultivation as well as intensive nut harvesting.

The Williams component is represented by well-defined midden deposits with abundant wood charcoal, charred nutshell, burned dirt, lithic debris, ocher stains, and occasional calcined bone fragments. The midden deposits vary in density and thickness. Two areas, approximately 20 m apart, contain dense midden deposits that apparently delineate core areas of activity (Figure 7.27). The dense midden deposits (north and south middens) are approximately 30 cm thick. Diffuse midden deposits approximately 15–20 cm thick appear to delineate the midden peripheries separating the dense (or main) midden deposits from nonmidden areas. Several small localized areas within the dense midden were recorded as features and interpreted as concentrated pockets of refuse or possible redeposited fill from hearths (Ray 1998a:136–137).

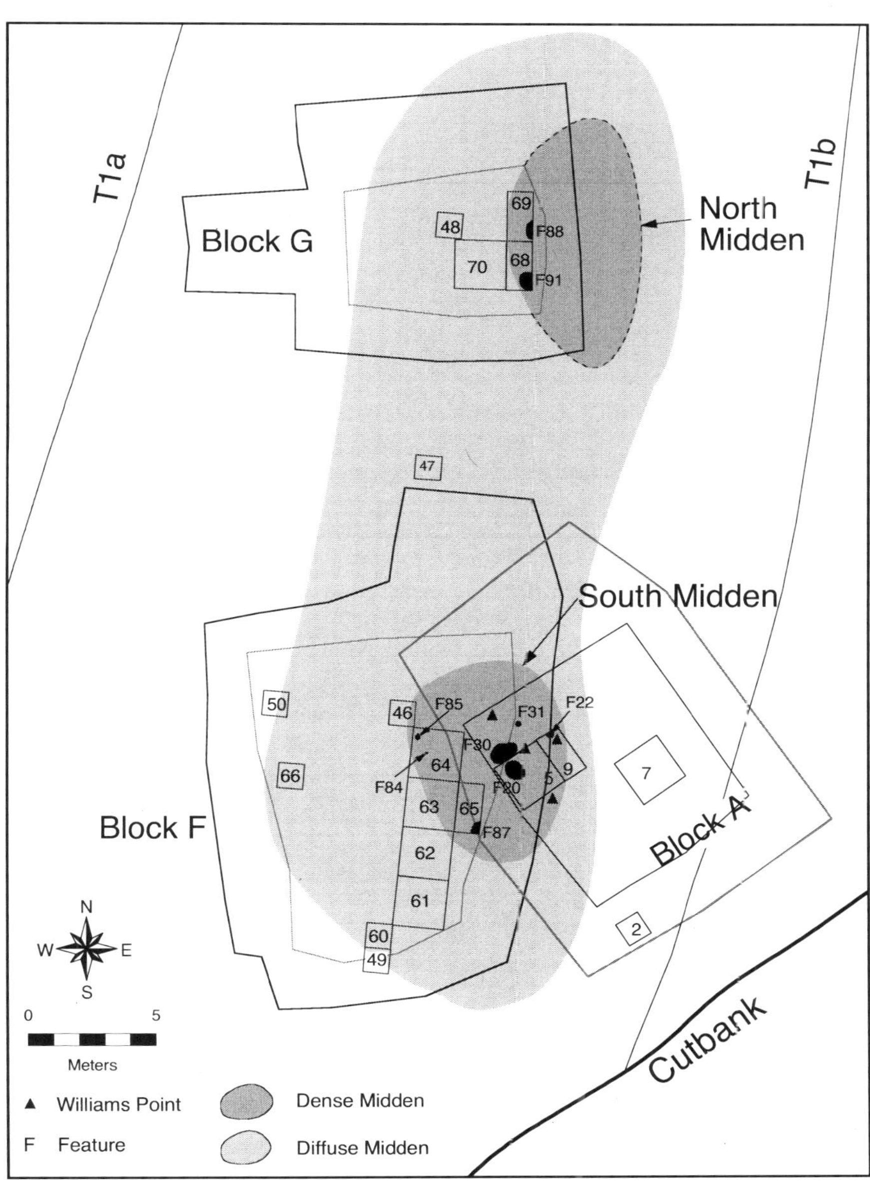

Figure 7.27. Williams-component piece plots, features, and midden deposits in relation to excavation units and the T1a and T1b stream banks.

The roughly circular, dense midden deposits may represent discard of refuse into two primary dump areas located on the floodplain at the base of a terrace scarp, which implies that occupational areas were located elsewhere at the site. The development of thick midden deposits indicates extended habitation and, by implication, the likelihood that domestic structures were present. No structures were evident in sampled deposits of the thin late submember, but it is possible that habitation areas were located outside our areas of excavation.

Two radiocarbon ages of 4020 ± 80 RCYBP (cal 4475 B.P.; Beta-109009) and 4040 ± 100 RCYBP (cal 4520 B.P.; Beta-112984) from the lower and middle portions of the south midden may indicate an occupation of relatively short duration, perhaps a few decades, a little more than 4,000 years ago (Ray 1998a:139). One radiocarbon age from the north midden, however, yielded a slightly younger age of 3905 ± 40 RCYBP (cal 4390 B.P.; AA-56591). This may indicate intermittent or successive occupations during about a century of prehistory. Nevertheless, these radiocarbon ages may represent simultaneous occupations since all three ages overlap one another at one standard deviation.

Several types of lithic artifacts were recovered from the midden deposits. Diagnostics include four Williams projectile points/knives, all of which were recovered from the south midden (Figure 7.28a–d). Williams points are corner notched with an expanding stem and convex to straight base. The corner notches are moderately deep and are usually U-shaped. Unresharpened Williams points exhibit prominent barbs and wide blades with excurvate edges. Repeated resharpenings narrow the blade, and the blade edges become straight to recurved. The recurved distal ends of some points exhibit needlelike tips (Bell 1960:96; Dickson 2002:114; Ray 1998a:134), presumably for use as piercing or etching tools (Ray 1998a:134).

The chipped-stone artifacts from the Williams component differ technologically from those of other Late Archaic components at Big Eddy. These differences reside primarily in specific biface reduction techniques and in the selection and treatment of chert resources. The blades of Williams points were finished by fine, controlled pressure flaking that obliterated most early-stage percussion scars. Flake scars generally terminate at the midline, producing a typical biconvex cross section (Ray 1998a:134). Maximum thickness along the midline is 8.7–9.4 mm (Ray and Lopinot 2005b:204).

Figure 7.28. Williams points, 23CE426.

Williams knappers used Burlington chert to the near exclusion of other local resources. Burlington chert is highly amenable to heat treatment, which was an integral aspect of the manufacture of Williams bifaces. All of the Williams points, most of the middle- to late-stage failed preforms, and approximately 40 percent of the flake debitage exhibit evidence of heat treatment (Ray 2005b:310).

Non-chipped-stone artifacts from the Williams component included fire-cracked rock (presumably used in cooking foodstuffs), one multipurpose mano-nutting stone-hammerstone, and several pieces of hematite and limonite. Most of the iron ore found in the midden deposits is unmodified, but a few pieces exhibit lightly faceted areas that indicate the production of pigment (red ocher). A few pieces appear to have been scratched or etched with a sharp tool. One unusual piece of hematite exhibits a fluted surface 1.24 cm wide and may have been used to coat cylindrical objects of small diameter, such as dart or spear shafts (Ray 1998a:136).

Sac Phase

A distinct cultural unit termed the "Sac" phase has been defined primarily on the basis of the Williams component at Big Eddy (Ray and Lopinot 2005b:208–212). The Sac phase overlaps the Smetley phase spatially and temporally, but, as outlined previously, the Sac phase is technologically distinct from Smetley and other regional Late Archaic phases (and components). At the present time, the Sac phase is based on single-component deposits in a discrete stratigraphic unit at the Big Eddy site. The Big Eddy site appears to be the first location at which a Williams component has been found in direct association with dense midden deposits. Artifacts from the Williams component at Big Eddy also are unmixed with older, contemporaneous, and younger artifacts.

The diagnostic artifact of the Williams component is the Williams point. Williams points occur in southwest Missouri (Ray 1998a:134–135; Sandstrom and Ray 2004:27), northwest Arkansas (Dickson 2002:114), and northeast Oklahoma (Wyckoff 1984:147). They also apparently are found as far west as central Texas and as far east as the Mississippi River valley (Bell 1960:96; Suhm et al. 1954; Turner and Hester 1993:194–195).

The geographic range of the Sac phase is only provisionally defined at this time. At a minimum, it encompasses the Sac River valley and adjacent areas in southwest Missouri. Williams points also have been found in areas to the east and south of the Sac River valley. An unusually large number of points (n = 42) identified as Williams points were recovered from Rodgers Shelter (Kay 1982b:462-464). Although knapped primarily from Jefferson City chert, many had been heat treated. Small numbers of Williams points also have been recovered from sites in Webster, Christian, and Barry counties in southwest Missouri (Ray and Lopinot 2005b:210).

The only regional Late Archaic manifestation that appears to be comparable to the Sac phase is the Lawrence phase in northeast Oklahoma (Wyckoff 1984:146–150). Definition of this phase was based on open-air and sheltered sites centered along the Verdigris and Neosho (or Grand) rivers. The Lawrence phase, which spans approximately 800 years, apparently has early and late components and has been defined as being characterized by multiple large and small point types (including the Williams type). The Lawrence phase, however, does not appear to be a regional correlate of the Sac phase. The Sac phase was defined on the basis of a tight assemblage from a sealed component that contains only one diagnostic projectile point/knife type—Williams. The inclusion of multiple stemmed and corner-notched points indicates that the Lawrence phase probably does not reflect a discrete cultural entity in time and space. The temporal range of the Lawrence phase also is many hundreds of years younger than the Williams component at Big Eddy.

The Williams component at Big Eddy represents a relatively short period of time. The earliest occupations occurred around 4040–4020 RCYBP or slightly earlier. The latest occupations may have occurred about one hundred years later, or around 3900 RCYBP. Few other radiocarbon ages are associated with Williams points. One radiocarbon age from Sugarcamp Rockshelter (23BY629) in Barry County, however, suggests that Williams points may date as late as 3600 RCYBP. At that rockshelter, one Williams point was found directly above a charcoal-rich level that yielded an age of 3620 ± 70 RCYBP (cal 3910 B.P.; Beta-55826) (Ray and Benn 1992:41–45). The Sac phase in southwest Missouri, therefore, may range from approximately 4100 to 3600 RCYBP. The Sac phase is at least partially contemporaneous with the Smetley phase. Significantly, however, no evidence suggests spatial and temporal overlap between the Williams component and the Smith-Etley component at Big Eddy.

Settlement patterns of the Sac phase are poorly understood. Sites that were used as base camps and field camps are common in river valleys in southwest Missouri, but data on the use of upland areas are lacking. The accumulation of dense midden deposits up to 30 cm thick at Big Eddy are indicative of a base camp that experienced intensive or long-term occupations. Given the development of a thick midden and the presence of possible cultigens (e.g., chenopod), the Williams component may represent multiseasonal if not year-round occupation, probably on more than one occasion. Although structural features are lacking, the distribution of dense midden deposits may indicate the existence of unexcavated residential areas. If open-air sites located near the headwaters of Finley Creek and the James River in Webster County and sheltered sites in Christian and Barry counties also are affiliated with the Sac phase, then field camps also were located in open-air and sheltered site settings in smaller tributary valleys.

Flotation-recovered archaeobotanical remains from Big Eddy indicate that, in general, nut resources such as hickory, pecan, and acorn were intensively exploited. Fleshy fruits such as grape, persimmon, and sumac and starchy seeds such as chenopod, panic grass, and purslane also accounted for part of the diet. Some evidence indicates that at least chenopod also was cultivated by the Sac-phase occupants of Big Eddy (Lopinot 1998; Powell and Lopinot 2005). Plant remains from Williams and Smith-Etley contexts are quite similar in content, except for the absence of squash in the former.

Information on the procurement of faunal resources is extremely limited. Several small bone fragments were recovered from midden deposits excavated in 1997 and 2001. The bone, however, was calcined and poorly preserved. The only tentative classifications that could be made were indeterminate medium- to large-size mammal (Ray 1998a:137; Ray and Lopinot 2005b:206). As at other Late Archaic sites in the Ozarks, Big Eddy's Sac-phase occupants probably relied heavily on deer, turkey, and other forest-edge species as well as riparian and aquatic resources such as fish and turtles.

Kings

The Kings point type is poorly defined and often is a classificatory dumping ground for medium-sized dart points with deep corner notches and straight to slightly concave bases (Ray 1998a:126). This has led to its confusion with other corner-notched points, even on a pan-regional scale. For example, O'Brien and Wood (1998:233–234) suggested that numerous corner-notched examples from Missouri fit the criteria of Jack's Reef Corner Notched. Jack's Reef points, however, are only found east of the Mississippi River, and they differ technologically from Kings points. Unlike Kings points, Jack's Reef points are exceedingly thin and flat in cross section and often exhibit a pentagonal outline (Justice 1987:217–219). They date to the late Middle Woodland and Late Woodland periods (Justice 1987:217).

Kings points exhibit corner notches, an expanding stem, and a straight to slightly concave base (Figure 7.29). Prominent small to medium-sized barbs are present on unresharpened specimens, but they are absent on extensively resharpened ones. Some specimens may exhibit fine serrations along the blade edges. Although workmanship varies, final tertiary (pressure) flaking across the blade is generally controlled and perpendicular or diagonal to the long axis of the blade. Flake

Figure 7 29. Kings points: a–d, 23CE426; e, 23WB295.

scars generally terminate at or near the midline, which creates a biconvex cross section. Nearly 70 percent of the Kings points from Big Eddy were manufactured from Burlington chert. Most Kings points are heat treated regardless of chert type. For example, all but one of the Kings points (n = 30) from Big Eddy (Ray and Lopinot 2005b:165) and 95 percent of the Kings points (n = 131) from the Patterson Spring site (Turner and Benn 1986) had been heat treated.

Excavations in the thick late submember at Big Eddy delineated a Kings component between approximately 85 cm and 135 cm bd. It overlies the terminal Smith-Etley component and underlies an Afton component. A low density of debitage compared with that in other Late Archaic components suggests that the primary activities conducted during the Kings occupations were associated with food procurement (i.e., hunting, butchering, and nut collecting), not the procurement of chert and the manufacture of chipped-stone tools. The Big Eddy site may have been used intermittently as a temporary or seasonal field camp during the Kings occupations.

Although numerous Kings points have been recovered from Big Eddy, only a handful were found in context. These include five medial and distal fragments and one unbroken point (Ray and Lopinot 2005b:167–170). All were found between 88 cm and 133 cm bd in the thick late submember. Several features were excavated from the same deposits, but only three were unequivocally cultural in origin.

A definitive age range for the Kings point type has been elusive. Chapman (1980:309) believed it may have first appeared during Archaic times and continued into the Woodland period, whereas others believe it is Middle to Late Woodland in age (O'Brien and Wood 1998:234). If it dates to both terminal Late Archaic and Woodland times, then it either existed as a specific type for a very long time (at least 1,700 years) or two or more, as yet undifferentiated, types are conflated within a generalized Kings corner-notched type.

Several sites in southwest Missouri have yielded predominantly Kings points (Anglen and Angelbeck 1998; Parisi 1985; Turner and Benn 1986; Webb 1995), yet none have produced radiocarbon ages firmly associated only with this corner-notched point type. Two pit features at the Erwin site (23NE212) that yielded radiocarbon ages of 3230 ± 60 RCYBP (cal 3455 B.P.; Beta-69972) and 3120 ± 60 RCYBP (cal 3355 B.P.; Beta-69970) contained several Kings points but also other points interpreted as Late Archaic and Late Woodland or Mississippian (Webb 1995). Radiocarbon ages of 2960 ± 60 RCYBP (cal 3105 B.P.; Beta-11999), 2940 ± 60 RCYBP (cal 3080 B.P.; Beta-12658), and 2350 ± 60 RCYBP (cal 2350 B.P.; Beta-11998) from mixed Late Archaic deposits at the Little Green Heron site (23GR535) were associated with Kings, Little Sac, Smith, and Etley points (Parisi 1985).

Five radiocarbon ages from Big Eddy appear to bracket multiple Kings occupations between approximately 3800 and 3000 RCYBP. One piece of wood charcoal collected near the unbroken Kings point and near the base of the Kings component at 127 cm bd yielded an AMS radiocarbon age of 3765 ± 40 RCYBP (cal 4140 B.P.; AA-60624). Another sample from Feature 90 (115–119 cm bd) yielded a radiocarbon age of 3655 ± 35 B.P. (cal 3970 B.P.; AA-59426). One piece of charred nutshell from Feature 68 yielded an age of 3335 ± 40 B.P. (cal 3570 B.P.; AA-59425). Two samples of wood charcoal collected near the top of the Kings component (96 cm and 89 cm) yielded ages of 3160 ± 40 B.P. (cal 3370 B.P.; AA-59420) and 3060 ± 40 B.P. (cal 3260 B.P.; AA-56587), respectively. Radiocarbon ages from the Erwin and Little Green Heron sites are at the young end of the Kings ages from Big Eddy.

Small- to medium-sized corner-notched points very similar to the Kings type were found at the Labras Lake site in the American Bottom (McElrath et al. 1984:Plate 9). Multiple Late Archaic occupations were identified at this site, and two age ranges of ca. 3900–3400 and 3300–3100 RCYBP were established for a Labras Lake phase (McElrath et al. 1984:46). The Labras Lake phase follows the Titterington phase in the American Bottom. Similarly, the Kings component overlies the youngest component of the Smetley phase at Big Eddy.

Afton

Wood (1961:88–89) defined an Afton complex on the basis of unusually thin and well-crafted points and other artifacts recovered from a limited number of preceramic sites located primarily in the Ozarks and surrounding areas in southwest Missouri and northeast Oklahoma. The distribution was later expanded to include northwest Arkansas (O'Brien and Wood 1998:162).

The most recognizable and, therefore, diagnostic part of the complex is the distinctive Afton point type (Figure 7.30). Afton points have been recovered from a variety of contexts. Many have been found at special-function (ritual or mortuary) sites such as the cache from Afton Springs (Holmes 1903) and burial sites such as Holbert Bridge (Wood 1961) and Coline (Wood 1985:18–20). Many of the Afton points from these ritual or mortuary types of sites are whole or exhibit only minor fractures, which has led some archaeologists to suggest that the function of the points was nonutilitarian (Biddle 1998). However, many Afton points from sheltered and open-air sites in southwest Missouri exhibit fractures, repeated resharpenings, and modifications indicative of everyday use as projectile points/knives as well as for other functions. Some of these sites are Blackwell Cave (Wood 1961), Rodgers Shelter (Robinson and Kay 1982), John Paul Cave (Ray 1995:40), several sites in the Truman Reservoir area (Goldberg and Roper 1993a:60), Big Eddy, and at least six other open-air sites in the lower Sac River valley (Ray and Lopinot 2005a).

The Afton component at Big Eddy occurs stratigraphically above a Kings component and just below a palimpsest

Figure 7.30. Afton points: a, 23CE426; b, c, 23CE418; d, e, 23CE235; f, 23CN758; g, 23WB393.

of younger Woodland and Mississippian deposits. The Afton assemblage consists of a light scatter of lithic debitage and seven diagnostic projectile points/knives. Two Afton points were recovered between depths of 35 cm and 75 cm bd in the thick late submember (Ray and Lopinot 2005b:161). Two more Afton points were recovered from the thin late submember, and the other three points came from disturbed deposits.

Afton points exhibit several distinct attributes. They are thin, flat in cross section, and exhibit controlled secondary and tertiary flaking in parallel and random patterns across the blade. Unresharpened specimens are also usually medium to large in size and exhibit deep, narrow corner notches, prominent barbs, an expanding stem, and a straight to convex base (Sandstrom and Ray 2004:19). Although corner notches are most common, some of the largest and widest Afton points exhibit basal notches. The controlled percussion and pressure flaking across the blade, the thin, flat cross section, the deep, narrow corner notches, and overall size differentiate Afton points from other Late Archaic points such as Kings, Williams, and Etley. Afton points often exhibit a radical shift in the angle of the blade edges. Specifically, the blade is incurvate to straight from the barb to the midpoint, then straight to incurvate from the midpoint to the tip (Figure 7.30b–d, f, g). Although common, the radical shift in blade angle is not always present. For example, 60 percent of the Afton points from the Holbert Bridge Mound (23HI135) exhibited re-angled blade edges (Wood 1961:50).

Until recently, the age of Afton points and the Afton complex was uncertain. Most area researchers presumed a preceramic Late Archaic age (C. Chapman 1975; Kay 1982b:462, 547; O'Brien and Wood 1998:147; Wood 1961:89), but affiliation with the early, middle, or late subperiods was unknown. Afton points were found above a component containing Smith, Etley, Table Rock Stemmed, and Sedalia points at the Cross Timbers site (23HI297) in the Pomme de Terre River valley, but no radiocarbon assays were associated with the component (Goldberg and Oman 1993:611; Goldberg and Roper 1993a:60).

Two radiocarbon samples on unburned bone from a bundle burial at Holbert Bridge Mound yielded ages of 520 ± 135 RCYBP (cal 530 B.P.; GXO-558) and 385 ± 105 RCYBP (cal 475 B.P.; GXO-569), but these young dates were rejected as being impossibly late (Wood 1985:20), perhaps because the bundle burial was intrusive. Although generally considered less reliable than radiocarbon ages, two thermoluminescence (TL) ages from Holbert Bridge Mound reported by Goldberg and Roper (1993b:728) yielded terminal Late Archaic ages. One TL age of 2850 ± 425 B.P. was obtained from a heat-treated Afton point. The second TL age of 2995 ± 200 B.P. was obtained from the dentin of an adult tooth.

A recently obtained AMS age from a small fragment of antler from one of the flintknapping implements found with the large cache of Afton points at Afton Springs (Holmes 1903:247, Plates 24 and 25) appears to corroborate the TL ages from Holbert Bridge Mound. The antler sample yielded a radiocarbon age of 2830 ± 45 RCYBP (cal 2935 B.P.; AA-55199), revealing that Afton points in the Afton Springs cache also date to terminal Late Archaic times (Ray and Lopinot 2005b:164). Two radiocarbon ages from the Afton component at Big Eddy also associate Afton points with terminal Late Archaic times. One AMS sample from 40–50 cm bd yielded an age of 2890 ± 40 RCYBP (cal 2990 B.P.; AA-59419). Another AMS sample from a depth of 89 cm, slightly below the Afton component, yielded an age of 3060 ± 40 RCYBP (cal 3260 B.P.; AA-56587). We conclude, therefore, that the Afton component at Big Eddy dates to terminal Late Archaic times, or ca. 3000–2750 B.P.

Summary

This chapter has focused to a great extent on projectile points and chronology, with little discussion of the people who lived at Big Eddy and manufactured and used various tools. We would like to say more about the changing lifeways of those people, but we know relatively little to nothing about what they ate, how long they stayed and during what season(s), whether they resided in temporary or relatively permanent dwellings, and so on. Despite these limitations, the points and chronology are precisely what make the Big Eddy site such a rare and critical resource. Its relatively clean stratigraphic record provides the data needed to substantially fine-tune the regional chronology, which, in turn, provides a better basis for interpreting survey and excavation findings.

Prehistorians everywhere desire to measure and interpret human adaptations and change, but archaeologists in southwest Missouri have heretofore not been able to establish a good working cultural chronology for this portion of the Midcontinent. Such a chronology is a basic prerequisite for interpreting prehistoric cultural dynamics. Because of the absence of such chronology, it has often been necessary to extrapolate from other regions, some relatively far afield. Rodgers Shelter and other sites in the nearby Pomme de Terre River valley (particularly Phillips Spring) certainly have provided some useful information about regional chronology, past environmental conditions, and settlement-subsistence activities. However, these sites are not without their contextual problems, and the overall clarity of the Archaic sequence is inadequate for establishing a sound and particularized chronological sequence.

The Big Eddy site has provided a substantial number of radiocarbon ages. The ages have been obtained for a variety of purposes, often in some combination—to pin down the ages of projectile points, midden deposits or components, particular landscape configurations, significant geomorphological events, or spikes in carbon isotope curves. The complexities of landform variability within the site and the correlation of various deposits at different elevations within two or all three submembers have necessitated suites of AMS dates. In some cases, the radiocarbon ages have helped greatly in defining the vertical distribution of particular components on a highly variable sequence of landscapes. The distributions of particular diagnostic projectile points in multiple submembers, in turn, have led to a better understanding of sedimentation rates and variability in the development of the geomorphic surfaces and landform geometry through time.

The establishment of a sound chronological record has been easiest for the thick late submember, wherein Late Archaic horizons exhibit the greatest vertical separation and multiple components are marked by midden deposits. The sequence of Early Archaic components has been more difficult to establish, partly because the sampled portion of the site was not intensively used, except when Hidden Valley and Graham Cave points were being produced. The entire Early Archaic sequence is represented in about 1.1 m of sediments within the thin middle submember.

We do not propose a strict one point–one culture scheme, but the record at Big Eddy does dispel the notion of cultural complexes (or aggregates) represented by multiple point styles characterized by different hafting technologies (e.g., an Early Archaic complex that includes side-notched Graham Cave, expanding-stemmed Rice Lobed, and contracting-stemmed Hidden Valley points). We do not, however, rule out the possibility that two point types (as defined by archaeologists) of similar design and haft treatment could be related, contemporaneous, or even part of the same tool kit. Two examples from Big Eddy are the thick-bladed and square-stemmed Etley and Smith points and the contracting-stemmed Hidden Valley and Searcy points. Another example is provided by the side-notched or slightly diagonal-notched Thebes and St. Charles points (Morrow 1996).

We would also like to emphasize here that we do not subscribe to the "have a component, got a phase" approach. The establishment of phases does not preclude considerable refinement, and even "a thin level in a site reflecting no more than a brief encampment" could be defined as a phase (Willey and Phillips 1958:22). However, we are apprehensive about defining phases, even provisional ones, principally on the basis of projectile point styles, a few other tools, small handfuls of debitage, and a radiocarbon age or two, with little or no other information pertaining to settlement and subsistence. We have designated two Late Archaic phases, the Smetley and Sac phases, but we have not defined phases for the Early Archaic as a result of our Big Eddy findings. We suspect, however, that multiple Early Archaic phases could be formulated quite convincingly given additional research at other deep, stratified sites in the lower Sac River valley.

The Big Eddy site appears to have been used intermittently and briefly throughout most of prehistory. Faunal preservation is poor, and little can be inferred with respect to human-plant relations for any but Late Archaic times. Nevertheless, indirect evidence derived from lithic tools indicates that the primary activities throughout most of prehistory at Big Eddy centered on hunting, butchering, and foraging as well as the manufacture and rejuvenation of chipped-stone tools or tool kits. Except during the time span of the Late Paleoindian Dalton-San Patrice component and the series of Late Archaic Smith-Etley and Williams components, the evidence indicates Big Eddy was mostly used as a short-term camp or bivouac. During the Early Archaic period, the site also may have been used on occasion for extended periods of time and, if not frequently and repeatedly on a short-term basis, perhaps even multiseasonally. This can be conjectured for the Graham Cave and Hidden Valley components. The main occupation area for much of Paleoindian and Early Archaic times was perhaps at the southern end of the site, where erosion had taken its toll before the onset of mitigation activities in 1997.

Hickory nuts, walnuts, and perhaps acorns appear to have been important plant food resources throughout Archaic times. Fleshy fruits such as grape and persimmon also were exploited at various times. The archaeobotanical record at Big Eddy points to an emphasis on chenopod harvesting beginning around 4500–4200 RCYBP or shortly thereafter. This is clearly manifested from about 4200–3600 RCYBP during the Smetley and Sac phases. The evidence is suggestive of the cultivation of this starchy seed, or at least the manipulation of the habitats favoring chenopod. Given the presence of squash and gourd at or prior to this interval at Phillips Spring and the presence of squash at Big Eddy during at least the latter part of the Smetley phase, some form of cultivation of chenopod is likely. Pericarp thicknesses lend support to this contention and suggest that chenopod was in the process of becoming domesticated at that time. Thus, in addition to broad-spectrum hunting and gathering, the early Late Archaic occupants at Big Eddy were apparently engaged in low-level food production.

Acknowledgments

Work at the Big Eddy site has been funded by multiple sources. The bulk of funding has been provided by the Kansas City District of the U.S. Army Corps of Engineers. We thank Bob Ziegler and Timothy Meade, past and present archaeologists with the Kansas City District, for overall coordination and assistance with the project. Other funding for the Big Eddy project has been provided by the Historic Preservation Office of the Missouri Department of Natural Resources, the National Geographic Society, the Odyssey Fund, the Green Foundation, and the Tom and Shirley Townsend family. Roy D. Blunt (U.S. House of Representatives) and his assistants Steve McIntosh and Dan Waddlington helped procure additional monies for continued research at Big Eddy. We are deeply indebted to landowner Nina Rosier Brown Howard, who graciously granted access to her property. We also would like to thank the following individuals who allowed us to study and photograph selected specimens in their private collections from southwest Missouri: Terry McCurdy, Dan Long, Charles Collins, Carl Sandstrom, Larry Brown, Marty Horn, Shirley Carpenter, Jack Nunn, and Bob Stringham. Finally, we wish to thank Dustin Thomson, Mike Conner, and Gina Powell for their assistance in producing figures for this chapter.

References Cited

Adams, Lee M.
1958 Archaeological Investigations of Southwestern Missouri. *The Missouri Archaeologist* 20.

Adams, Robert M.
1941 Archaeological Investigations in Jefferson County, Missouri. *Memoir* 1:1–63. Missouri Archaeological Society, Columbia.
1949 Archaeological Investigations in Jefferson County, Missouri. *The Missouri Archaeologist* 11(3–4):1–72.

Ahler, Stanley A.
1970 *Projectile Point Form and Function at Rodgers Shelter, Missouri.* Research Series 8. Missouri Archaeological Society, Columbia.

Ahler, Stanley A., and R. Bruce McMillan
1976 Material Culture at Rodgers Shelter: A Reflection of Past Human Activities. In *Prehistoric Man and His Environments: A Case Study in the Ozark Highland*, edited by W. Raymond Wood and R. Bruce McMillan, pp. 163–199. Academic Press, New York.

Ahler, Steven R.
1993 Stratigraphy and Radiocarbon Chronology of Modoc Rock Shelter, Illinois. *American Antiquity* 58:462–489.

Alex, Lynn M.
2000 *Iowa's Archaeological Past.* University of Iowa Press, Iowa City.

Anderson, David G.
1996 Approaches to Modeling Regional Settlement in the Archaic Period Southeast. In *Archaeology of the Mid-Holocene Southeast*, edited by Kenneth E. Sassaman and David G. Anderson, pp. 157–176. University Press of Florida, Gainesville.

Anglen, Aaron A., and William C. Angelbeck
1998 *Phase I Cultural Resources Survey of Route 160, Greene County and Phase II Testing of Archaeological Sites 23GR838 and 23GR840 (Billings Site).* Cultural Resources Section, Missouri Department of Transportation, Jefferson City.

Asch, David L., and Nancy B. Asch
1985 Prehistoric Plant Cultivation in West-Central Illinois. In *Prehistoric Food Production in North America*, edited by Richard I. Ford, pp. 149–203. Anthropological Papers 75. Museum of Anthropology, University of Michigan, Ann Arbor.

Bell, Robert E.
1960 *Guide to the Identification of Certain American Indian Projectile Points.* Special Bulletin 2. Oklahoma Anthropological Society, Norman.

Bement, Leland, Ernie Lundelius Jr., and Richard Ketchum
2004 Get the Point? Point of No Return, Driving Home a Point. A Date Package from the Arkansas River. Pointing Out the Obvious. A Pointed Comment. Point Taken. *Oklahoma Archeological Society Newsletter* 23(4):1–3.

Biddle, Gregory K.
1998 Some Afton Points from Southwest Missouri: A Holistic Investigation. *Missouri Archaeological Society Quarterly* 15(3):10–14.

Brakenridge, G. Robert
1981 Late Quaternary Floodplain Sedimentation along the Pomme de Terre River, Southern Missouri. *Quaternary Research* 15:62–76.
1984 Alluvial Stratigraphy and Radiocarbon Dating along the Duck River, Tennessee: Implications Regarding Floodplain Origin. *Geological Society of America Bulletin* 95:9–25.
1988 River Flood Regime and Floodplain Stratigraphy. In *Flood Geomorphology*, edited by Victor R. Baker, R. Craig Kochel, and Peter C. Patton, pp. 139–156. Wiley, New York.

Bradley, Bruce A., and George C. Frison
1987 Projectile Points and Specialized Bifaces from the Horner Site. In *The Horner Site: The Type Site of the Cody Cultural Complex*, edited by George C. Frison and Lawrence C. Todd, pp. 199–231. Academic Press, Orlando, Florida.

Bray, Robert T.
1956 Culture-Complexes and Sequence at the Rice Site (23SN200), Stone County, Missouri. *The Missouri Archaeologist* 18(1–2) 47–134.

1960 Standlee Shelter I, 23BY386. In *Archaeological Investigations in Table Rock Reservoir, Part III*, by Carl H. Chapman, Robert T. Bray, and Charles M. Keller, pp. 435–532. University of Missouri, Columbia.

Bretz, J. Harlan
1965 *Geomorphic History of the Ozarks in Missouri*, vol. 41, 2nd series. Geological Survey and Water Resources, State of Missouri, Rolla.

Brown, James A., and Robert K. Vierra
1983 What Happened in the Middle Archaic? Introduction to an Ecological Approach to Koster Site Archaeology. In *Archaic Hunters and Gatherers in the American Midwest*, edited by James L. Phillips and James A. Brown, pp.165–195. Academic Press, New York.

Broyles, Bettye J.
1971 *Second Preliminary Report: The St. Albans Site, Kanawha County, West Virginia*. Report of Archeological Investigations 3. West Virginia Geological and Economic Survey, Morgantown.

Cambron, James W., and David C. Hulse
1975 *Handbook of Alabama Archaeology. Part I, Point Types*. Archaeological Research Association of Alabama, Moundville.

Chapman, Carl H.
1975 *The Archaeology of Missouri, I*. University of Missouri Press, Columbia.
1980 *The Archaeology of Missouri, II*. University of Missouri Press, Columbia.

Chapman, Carl H., and Robert T. Bray
1960 Vaughn I, 23SN203. In *Archaeological Investigations in Table Rock Reservoir, Part II*, by Carl H. Chapman, Richard A. Marshall, Robert T. Bray, W. Raymond Wood, Dale R. Henning, and Bonnie B. Keller, pp. 268–300. University of Missouri, Columbia.

Chapman, Jefferson
1973 *The Icehouse Bottom Site, 40MR23*. Report of Investigations 13. Department of Anthropology, University of Tennessee, Knoxville.
1975 *The Rose Island Site and the Bifurcate Point Tradition*. Report of Investigations 14. Department of Anthropology, University of Tennessee, Knoxville.
1977 *Archaic Period Research in the Lower Little Tennessee River Valley—1975: Icehouse Bottom, Harrison Branch, Thirty Acre Island, Calloway Island*. Report of Investigations 18. Department of Anthropology, University of Tennessee, Knoxville.

Chomko, Stephen A., and Gary W. Crawford
1978 Plant Husbandry in Prehistoric North America: New Evidence for Its Development. *American Antiquity* 43:405–408.

Coe, Joffre L.
1964 *The Formative Cultures of the Carolina Piedmont*. Transactions of the American Philosophical Society 54(5). Philadelphia.

Cook, Thomas G.
1976 *Koster: An Artifact Analysis of Two Archaic Phases in West-central Illinois*. Prehistoric Records 1. Northwestern University Archeological Program, Evanston, Illinois.

Dickson, Don R.
1968 Two Provisional Projectile Point Types. *The Arkansas Amateur* 7(6):5–7.
1970 Excavations at Calf Creek Cave. *The Arkansas Archeologist* 11(3–4):50–82.
1991 *The Albertson Site: A Deeply and Clearly Stratified Ozark Bluff Shelter*. Research Series 41. Arkansas Archeological Survey, Fayetteville.
2002 *Prehistoric Native Americans in the Ozarks*. Special Publication 1. Ozark Resources and Historical Publications, Fayetteville, Arkansas.
2003 Albertson Shelter (3BE174) Radiocarbon Dates. *Missouri Archaeological Society Quarterly* 20(1):12–13.

Duncan, Marjorie
1994 The Williams' Orchard Site: An Analysis of Lithic Procurement. *Bulletin of the Oklahoma Anthropological Society* 40:91–105.

Duncan, Marjorie, and Don G. Wyckoff
1994 The McKellips Site: An Analysis of the Calf Creek Component. *Bulletin of the Oklahoma Anthropological Society* 40:257–275.

Eschbacher, Bill
1996 23PE243, the Bohon Site: An Amateur's Limited Survey/Sample of a Lamine River Late Archaic Sedalia Complex Site in Cooper County. *Missouri Archaeological Society Quarterly* 13(4):4–9.

Fenneman, Nevin M.
1938 *Physiography of the Eastern United States*. McGraw-Hill, New York.

Ford, Richard I.
1974 Northeastern Archaeology: Past and Future Directions. *Annual Review of Anthropology* 3:385–413.

Fortier, Andrew C.
1984 The Go-Kart North Site. In *The Go-Kart North Site and the Dyroff and Levin Sites*, by Andrew C. Fortier and Thomas E, Emerson, pp. 3–197. American Bottom Archaeology FAI-270 Site Reports 9. University of Illinois Press, Urbana.

Fowler, Melvin L.
1959 *Summary Report of Modoc Rock Shelter: 1952, 1953, 1955, 1956*. Report of Investigations 8. Illinois State Museum, Springfield.

Frison, George C.
1978 *Prehistoric Hunters of the High Plains*. Academic Press, New York.
1987 The University of Wyoming Investigations at the Horner Site. In *The Horner Site: The Type Site for the Cody Cultural Complex*, edited by George C. Frison and Lawrence C. Todd, pp. 63–78. Academic Press, New York.

Fritz, Gayle J.
1986 Prehistoric Ozark Agriculture: The University of Arkansas Rockshelter Collections. Ph.D. dissertation, Department of Anthropology, University of North Carolina, Chapel Hill.
1997 A Three-Thousand-Year-Old Cache of Crop Seeds from Marble Bluff, Arkansas. In *People, Plants, and Landscapes: Studies in Paleoethnobotany*, edited by Kristen J. Gremillion, pp. 42–62. University of Alabama Press, Tuscaloosa.

Girard, Jeff, and Helen S. Carr
1994 Calf Creek Bifaces and Middle Archaic Period Occupations in the Bellcow Creek Drainage, Central

Oklahoma. *Bulletin of the Oklahoma Anthropological Society* 40:195–207.

Goldberg, Susan K., and Patricia A. Oman

1993 The Cross Timbers Site—23HI297. In *Prehistoric Cultural Continuity in the Missouri Ozarks: The Truman Reservoir Mitigation Project, 1: Project Background and Field Investigations*, by Donna C. Roper, pp. 569–612. American Archaeology Division, Department of Anthropology, University of Missouri, Columbia.

Goldberg, Susan K., and Donna C. Roper

1993a Projectile Points. In *Prehistoric Cultural Continuity in the Missouri Ozarks: The Truman Reservoir Mitigation Project, 2: Artifact Descriptions and Analyses,* by Donna C. Roper, pp. 1–97. American Archaeology Division, Department of Anthropology, University of Missouri, Columbia.

1993b Results of Radiometric Dating Determinations from Sites in the Harry S. Truman Reservoir. In *Prehistoric Cultural Continuity in the Missouri Ozarks: The Truman Reservoir Mitigation Project, 1: Project Background and Field Investigations*, by Donna C. Roper, pp. 712–736. American Archaeology Division, Department of Anthropology, University of Missouri, Columbia.

Goodyear, Albert C., III

1982 The Chronological Position of the Dalton Horizon in the Southeastern United States. *American Antiquity* 47:382–395.

Hajic, Edwin R.

1990 *Koster Site Archeology I: Stratigraphy and Landscape Evolution*. Research Series 8. Center for American Archeology, Kampsville, Illinois.

2005 Holocene Stratigraphy and Geochronology at Big Eddy. In *Regional Research and the Archaic Record at the Big Eddy Site (23CE426), Southwest Missouri*, edited by Neal H. Lopinot, Jack H. Ray, and Michael D. Conner, pp. 124–132. Special Publication 4. Center for Archaeological Research, Southwest Missouri State University, Springfield.

Hajic, Edwin R., Rolfe D. Mandel, and E. Arthur Bettis III

2000 Stratigraphic and Paleoenvironmental Investigations. In *The 1999 Excavations at the Big Eddy Site (23CE426) in Southwest Missouri*, edited by Neal H. Lopinot, Jack H. Ray, and Michael D. Conner, pp. 26–35. Special Publication 3. Center for Archaeological Research, Southwest Missouri State University, Springfield.

Hajic, Edwin R., Rolfe D. Mandel, Jack H. Ray, and Neal H. Lopinot

1998 Geomorphology and Geoarchaeology. In *The 1997 Excavations at the Big Eddy Site (23CE426) in Southwest Missouri*, edited by Neal H. Lopinot, Jack H. Ray, and Michael D. Conner, pp. 26–35, 74–109. Special Publication 2. Center for Archaeological Research, Southwest Missouri State University, Springfield.

Harl, Joseph L.

1995 *Data Recovery Investigations at the Hayden Site (23SL36) and the Rabanus Site (23SL859), Chesterfield, St. Louis County, Missouri: New Insights into the Titterington/Sedalia Phase in East-Central Missouri*. Research Report 182. Archaeological Services, Department of Anthropology, University of Missouri, St. Louis.

Haynes, C. Vance

1976 Late Quaternary Geology of the Lower Pomme de Terre Valley. In *Prehistoric Man and His Environments: A Case Study in the Ozark Highland*, edited by W. Raymond Wood and R. Bruce McMillan, pp. 47–61. Academic Press, New York.

1985 *Mastodon-Bearing Springs and Late Quaternary Geochronology of the Lower Pomme de Terre Valley, Missouri*. Special Paper 204. Geological Society of America, Boulder, Colorado.

Henning, Dale R.

1960 An Archaic Hill-Top Site, 23SN562. In *Archaeological Investigations in the Table Rock Reservoir Area, Missouri, Part IV*, by Carl H. Chapman, Amy E. Harvey, Dale R. Henning, Richard A. Marshall, Rolland E. Pangborn, and John E. Vincent, pp. 795–813. University of Missouri, Columbia.

Holmes, William H.

1903 *Flint Implements and Fossil Remains from a Sulphur Spring at Afton, Indian Territory*. Report of the U.S. National Museum for 1901, pp. 233–252. Washington, D.C.

Johnson, Donald L., Donna Watson-Stegner, and Patricia R. Wilcock

1993 Aspects of the Soil Geomorphology of the Lower Pomme de Terre River Valley, Missouri, and Surrounding Region. In *Prehistoric Cultural Continuity in the Missouri Ozarks: The Truman Reservoir Mitigation Project, 3: Specialized Studies,* edited by Donna C. Roper, pp. 591–660. American Archaeology Division, Department of Anthropology, University of Missouri, Columbia.

Justice, Noel D.

1987 *Stone Age Spear and Arrow Points of the Midcontinental and Eastern United States*. Indiana University Press, Bloomington.

Kay, Marvin

1982a Overview of the Mitigation Program. In *Holocene Adaptations within the Lower Pomme de Terre River Valley, Missouri*, vol. 1, edited by Marvin Kay, pp. 1–8. Illinois State Museum Society, Springfield.

1982b Stylistic Study of Chipped Stone Points. In *Holocene Adaptations within the Lower Pomme de Terre River Valley, Missouri*, vol. 3, edited by Marvin Kay, pp. 379–559. Illinois State Museum Society, Springfield.

1982c Features and Factors: Activity Area Definition at Rodgers Shelter. In *Holocene Adaptations within the Lower Pomme de Terre River Valley, Missouri*, vol. 3, edited by Marvin Kay, pp. 561–621. Illinois State Museum Society, Springfield.

1982d Project Evaluation and Summary. In *Holocene Adaptations within the Lower Pomme de Terre River Valley, Missouri*, vol. 3, edited by Marvin Kay, pp. 729–742. Illinois State Museum Society, Springfield.

1983 Archaic Period Research in the Western Ozark Highland, Missouri. In *Archaic Hunters and Gatherers in the American Midwest*, edited by James L. Phillips and James A. Brown, pp. 41–70. Academic Press, New York.

Kay, Marvin, Francis [*sic*] B. King, and Christina K. Robinson

1980 Cucurbits from Phillips Spring: New Evidence and Interpretations. *American Antiquity* 45:806–822.

King, James E., and Everett H. Lindsay
1976 Late Quaternary Biotic Records from Spring Deposits in Western Missouri. In *Prehistoric Man and His Environments: A Case Study from the Ozark Highland*, edited by W. Raymond Wood and R. Bruce McMillan, pp. 63–78. Academic Press, New York.

Kinsey, W. Fred
1971 The Middle Atlantic Culture Province: A Point of View. *Pennsylvania Archaeologist* 41:1–8.

Klinger, Timothy C., Steven M. Imhoff, Don R. Dickson, and James E. Price
1993 *Stockton Lake Survey and Assessment*. Report 93–12. Historic Preservation Associates, Fayetteville, Arkansas.

Klippel, Walter E.
1969 *The Booth Site: A Late Archaic Campsite*. Research Series 6. Missouri Archaeological Society, Columbia.
1971 *Graham Cave Revisited, a Reevaluation of Its Cultural Position during the Archaic Period*. Memoir 9. Missouri Archaeological Society, Columbia.

Logan, Wilfred D.
1952 *Graham Cave, an Archaic Site in Montgomery County, Missouri*. Memoir 2. Missouri Archaeological Society, Columbia.

Lopinot, Neal H.
1998 Regional Cultural History. In *The 1997 Excavations at the Big Eddy Site (23CE426) in Southwest Missouri*, edited by Neal H. Lopinot, Jack H. Ray, and Michael D. Conner, pp. 35–47. Special Publication 2. Center for Archaeological Research, Southwest Missouri State University, Springfield.

Lopinot, Neal H., and Jack H. Ray
1995 *Archaeological Excavations at the Bass Site (23GR41B), Northeastern Greene County, Missouri*. Research Report 952. Center for Archaeological Research, Southwest Missouri State University, Springfield.
1996 The Hogan Creek Site and the Problem of Side-Notched Chronology in Southwest Missouri. Poster paper presented at the Southeastern Archaeological Conference, Birmingham, Alabama.

Lopinot, Neal H., Jack H. Ray, and Michael D. Conner (editors)
1998 *The 1997 Excavations at the Big Eddy Site (23CE426) in Southwest Missouri*. Special Publication 2. Center for Archaeological Research, Southwest Missouri State University, Springfield.

Markman, Charles W.
1993 *Miller Cave (23PU2), Fort Leonard Wood, Pulaski County, Missouri: Report of Archaeological Testing and Assessment of Damage*. Research Report 9. Markman and Associates, St. Louis, Missouri.

Marshall, Richard A.
1958 The Use of Table Rock Reservoir Projectile Points in the Delineation of Cultural Complexes and Their Distribution. Master's thesis, Department of Anthropology, University of Missouri, Columbia.

Marshall, Richard A., and Carl H. Chapman
1960 Cultural Materials from Jakie Shelter, 23BY388. In *Archaeological Investigations in the Table Rock Reservoir Area, Missouri, Part V*, by Robert T. Bray, Carl H. Chapman, Richard A. Marshall, and Wayne O. Wallace Jr., pp. 1131–1149. University of Missouri, Columbia.

McElrath, Dale L., Thomas E. Emerson, Andrew C. Fortier, and James L. Phillips
1984 Late Archaic Period. In *American Bottom Archaeology: A Summary of the FAI-270 Project Contribution to the Culture History of the Mississippi River Valley*, edited by Charles J. Bareis and James W. Porter, pp. 34–58. University of Illinois Press, Urbana.

McMillan, R. Bruce
1965 Gasconade Prehistory. *The Missouri Archaeologist* 27(3–4):1–114.
1971 Biophysical Change and Cultural Adaptation at Rodgers Shelter, Missouri. Ph.D. dissertation, Department of Anthropology, University of Colorado, Boulder.
1976 The Dynamics of Cultural and Environmental Change at Rodgers Shelter, Missouri. In *Prehistoric Man and His Environments: A Case Study in the Ozark Highland*, edited by W. Raymond Wood and R. Bruce McMillan, pp. 211–232. Academic Press, New York.

McMillan, R. Bruce, and Walter E. Klippel
1981 Post-Glacial Environmental Change and Hunting-Gathering Societies of the Southern Prairie Peninsula. *Journal of Archaeological Science* 8:215–245.

Morrow, Toby A.
1996 Lithic Refitting and Archaeological Site Formation Processes: A Case Study from the Lower Illinois River Valley. In *Stone Tools: Theoretical Insights into Human Prehistory*, edited by George H. Odell, pp. 345–373. Plenum Press, New York.

Neal, Larry
1994 The Brandon Site, 34TU82, Tulsa County, Oklahoma. *Bulletin of the Oklahoma Anthropological Society* 40:209–247.
1998 Radiocarbon Date from a Large Hearth at the Kubik Site. *Oklahoma Archeological Survey Newsletter* 18(2):3.
2001 Spring 2000 Investigations at the Kubik Site, 34KA354. *Oklahoma Archeological Survey Newsletter* 20(3):3–4.
2002 Activities at the Kubik Site, 2002. *Journal of the Oklahoma Anthropological Society* 50(3):5–7.

Neal, Larry, David Morgan, B. Ross, and Don G. Wyckoff
1994 The Red Clay and Island Locations in Haskell County: Eastern Oklahoma Manifestations of the Calf Creek Horizon. *Bulletin of the Oklahoma Anthropological Society* 40:277–304.

O'Brien, Michael J.
1985 Archaeology of the Central Salt River Valley: An Overview of the Prehistoric Occupation. *The Missouri Archaeologist* 46.

O'Brien, Michael J., and Robert E. Warren
1985 Stratigraphy and Chronology at Pigeon Roost Creek. In *Archaeology of the Central Salt River Valley: An Overview of the Prehistoric Occupation*, by Michael J. O'Brien. *The Missouri Archaeologist* 46:203–225.

O'Brien, Michael J., and W. Raymond Wood
1995 The Prehistoric Archaeological Record. In *Holocene Human Adaptations in the Missouri Prairie-Timberlands*, by W. Raymond Wood, Michael J. O'Brien, Katherine A. Murray, and Jerome C. Rose, pp. 47–77. Research Series 45. Arkansas Archeological Survey, Fayetteville.
1998 *The Prehistory of Missouri*. University of Missouri Press, Columbia.

Parisi, John M.
1985 *The Little Green Heron Site (23GR535): A Late Archaic and Terminal Late Archaic Occupation in Southwest Missouri.* Cultural Resources Management Report 31. Environmental Systems Analysis, Shawnee Mission, Kansas.

Parmalee, Paul W., R. Bruce McMillan, and Frances B. King
1976 Changing Subsistence Patterns at Rodgers Shelter. In *Prehistoric Man and His Environments: A Case Study from the Ozark Highland*, edited by W. Raymond Wood and R. Bruce McMillan, pp. 141–161. Academic Press, New York.

Perino, Gregory
1971 *Guide to the Identification of Certain American Indian Projectile Points.* Special Bulletin 4. Oklahoma Anthropological Society, Oklahoma City.

Powell, Gina S., and Neal H. Lopinot
2005 Archaeobotany. In *Regional Research and the Archaic Record at the Big Eddy Site (23CE426), Southwest Missouri*, edited by Neal H. Lopinot, Jack H. Ray, and Michael D. Conner, pp. 324–351. Special Publication 4. Center for Archaeological Research, Southwest Missouri State University, Springfield.

Price, James E., Mary J. Hastings, and Roger Saucier
2003 Prehistory of the Gnat Alley Woods Site, Ozarks National Scenic Riverways, Missouri. *The Missouri Archaeologist* 64:1–94.

Purdue, James R., and Bonnie W. Styles
1987 Changes in the Mammalian Fauna of Illinois and Missouri during the Late Pleistocene and Holocene. In *Late Quaternary Mammalian Biogeography and Environments of the Great Plains and Prairie*, edited by Russell W. Graham, Holmes A. Semken Jr., and Mary A. Graham, pp. 144–155. Scientific Papers 22. Illinois State Museum, Springfield.

Ray, Jack H.
1994a Casa Blanca: An Early Archaic Upland Base Camp in Southwest Missouri. *The Missouri Archaeologist* 55:2–46.
1994b *Archaeological Investigations at Great Spirit Rockshelter (23SN866) in Dogwood Canyon, Southern Stone County, Missouri.* Research Report 923. Center for Archaeological Research, Southwest Missouri State University, Springfield.
1995 *An Archaeological Investigation at John Paul Cave (23CN758) in Northern Christian County, Missouri.* Research Report 977. Center for Archaeological Research, Southwest Missouri State University, Springfield.
1997 *Additional Excavations at John Paul Cave (23CN758), Christian County, Missouri.* Research Report 1022. Center for Archaeological Research, Southwest Missouri State University, Springfield.
1998a Cultural Components. In *The 1997 Excavations at the Big Eddy Site (23CE426) in Southwest Missouri*, edited by Neal H. Lopinot, Jack H. Ray, and Michael D. Conner, pp. 111–219. Special Publication 2. Center for Archaeological Research, Southwest Missouri State University, Springfield.
1998b Chert Resource Availability and Utilization. In *The 1997 Excavations at the Big Eddy Site (23CE426) in Southwest Missouri*, edited by Neal H. Lopinot, Jack H. Ray, and Michael D. Conner, pp. 221–265. Special Publication 2. Center for Archaeological Research, Southwest Missouri State University, Springfield.
2005a Middle Archaic. In *Regional Research and the Archaic Record at the Big Eddy Site (23CE426), Southwest Missouri*, edited by Neal H. Lopinot, Jack H. Ray, and Michael D. Conner, pp. 214–222. Special Publication 4. Center for Archaeological Research, Southwest Missouri State University, Springfield.
2005b Chert Availability and Use. In *Regional Research and the Archaic Record at the Big Eddy Site (23CE426), Southwest Missouri*, edited by Neal H. Lopinot, Jack H. Ray, and Michael D. Conner, pp. 284–323. Special Publication 4. Center for Archaeological Research, Southwest Missouri State University, Springfield.
2007 *Ozarks Chipped-Stone Resources: A Guide to the Identification, Distribution, and Prehistoric Use of Cherts and Other Siliceous Raw Materials.* Special Publication 8. Missouri Archaeological Society, Springfield.

Ray, Jack H., and David W. Benn
1983 *Phase II Testing of Sites 23GR533, 23GR535, and 23GR537, within the Northwest Interceptor and Treatment Plant Construction Areas, City of Springfield, Greene County, Missouri.* Research Report 600. Center for Archaeological Research, Southwest Missouri State University, Springfield.
1992 *Test Excavations at Selected Sheltered Sites in Flat, Bull, and Swan Creek Drainage Basins in Southwest Missouri.* Research Report 805. Center for Archaeological Research, Southwest Missouri State University, Springfield.

Ray, Jack H., and Neal H. Lopinot
2003 Middle Archaic Components and Chert Use at the Bass Site. *Missouri Archaeological Society Quarterly* 20(2):4–16.
2005a Cutbank Survey. In *Regional Research and the Archaic Record at the Big Eddy Site (23CE426), Southwest Missouri*, edited by Neal H. Lopinot, Jack H. Ray, and Michael D. Conner, pp. 38–102. Special Publication 4. Center for Archaeological Research, Southwest Missouri State University, Springfield.
2005b Late Archaic. In *Regional Research and the Archaic Record at the Big Eddy Site (23CE426), Southwest Missouri*, edited by Neal H. Lopinot, Jack H. Ray, and Michael D. Conner, pp. 156–213. Special Publication 4. Center for Archaeological Research, Southwest Missouri State University, Springfield.
2005c Early Archaic. In *Regional Research and the Archaic Record at the Big Eddy Site (23CE426), Southwest Missouri*, edited by Neal H. Lopinot, Jack H. Ray, and Michael D. Conner, pp. 223–283. Special Publication 4. Center for Archaeological Research, Southwest Missouri State University, Springfield.

Reid, Kenneth C.
1983 The Nebo Hill Phase: Late Archaic Prehistory in the Lower Missouri Valley. In *Archaic Hunters and Gatherers in the American Midwest*, edited by James L. Phillips and James A. Brown, pp. 11–40. Academic Press, New York.

1984 *Nebo Hill and Late Archaic Prehistory on the Southern Prairie Peninsula*. Publications in Anthropology 15. University of Kansas, Lawrence.

Ricklis, Robert A., and Michael B. Collins
1993 *Archaic and Late Prehistoric Human Ecology in the Middle Onion Creek Valley, Hays County, Texas*. Texas Archeological Research Laboratory, University of Texas, Austin.

Robinson, Christine K., and Marvin Kay
1982 Phillips Spring Excavation and Archaeology. In *Holocene Adaptations within the Lower Pomme de Terre River Valley, Missouri*, vol. 3, edited by Marvin Kay, pp. 623–699. Illinois State Museum Society, Springfield.

Roper, Donna C.
1977 *Cultural Resources Survey Harry S. Truman Dam and Reservoir Project, 4: The Archaeological Survey*. American Archaeology Division, Department of Anthropology, University of Missouri, Columbia.
1993a The Prehistory of the Ozark Prairie Border: A Synthesis, 1983. In *Prehistoric Cultural Continuity in the Missouri Ozarks: The Truman Reservoir Mitigation Project, 1: Project Background and Field Investigations*, edited by Donna C. Roper, pp. 647–700. American Archaeology Division, Department of Anthropology, University of Missouri, Columbia.
1993b Field Surveys, 1978–1979. In *Prehistoric Cultural Continuity in the Missouri Ozarks: The Truman Reservoir Mitigation Project, 1: Project Background and Field Investigations*, edited by Donna C. Roper, pp. 163–310. American Archaeology Division, Department of Anthropology, University of Missouri, Columbia.

Sandstrom, Carl B., and Jack H. Ray
2004 *A Point Identification Guide for Southwest Missouri*. Ozarks Chapter, Missouri Archaeological Society, Springfield.

Sherwood, Sarah C., Boyce N. Driskell, Asa R. Randall, and Scott C. Meeks
2004 Chronology and Stratigraphy at Dust Cave, Alabama. *American Antiquity* 69:533–554.

Smith, Lawson M.
1983 Geomorphic Development of Alluvial Fans in the Yazoo Basin, Northwestern Mississippi. Ph.D. dissertation, Department of Geography, University of Illinois, Urbana-Champaign.

Suhm, Dee Ann, Alex D. Krieger, and Edward B. Jelks
1954 *An Introductory Handbook of Texas Archeology*. Bulletin of the Texas Archeological Society 25.

Thurmond, J. Peter, and Don G. Wyckoff
1999 The Calf Creek Horizon in Northwestern Oklahoma. *Plains Anthropologist* 44:231–250.

Turner, Betty Jane, and David W. Benn
1986 Analysis of Chipped Stone Artifacts from the Patterson Spring Site (23CN64), Christian County, Missouri. Unpublished manuscript on file, Center for Archaeological Research, Southwest Missouri State University, Springfield.

Turner, Ellen S., and Thomas R. Hester
1993 *A Field Guide to Stone Artifacts of Texas Indians*. Gulf Publishing, Houston, Texas.

Turner, Richard
1965 *Green Ridge: A Late Archaic Site of the Sedalia Complex in West-Central Missouri*. Research Series 3. Missouri Archaeological Society, Columbia.

Webb, Paul
1995 *Phase III Recovery Excavations at the Erwin Site (23NE212), Newton County, Missouri*. Garrow and Associates, Memphis, Tennessee.

Webb, Thompson, III, and and Reid A. Bryson
1972 Late- and Postglacial Climatic Change in the Northern Midwest, USA: Quantitative Estimates Dervied from Fossil Pollen Spectra by Multivariate Statistical Analysis. *Quaternary Research* 2:70–115.

Willey, Gordon R., and Philip Phillips
1958 *Method and Theory in American Archaeology*. University of Chicago Press, Chicago.

Winters, Howard W.
1967 *An Archeological Survey of the Wabash Valley in Illinois*. Reports of Investigations 10. Illinois State Museum, Springfield.
1969 *The Riverton Culture: A Second Millennium Occupation in the Central Wabash Valley*. Reports of Investigations 13. Illinois State Museum, Springfield.

Wood, W. Raymond
1961 The Pomme de Terre Reservoir in Western Missouri Prehistory. *The Missouri Archaeologist* 23:1–132.
1963 Breckenridge Shelter—3CR2—An Archaeological Chronicle in the Beaver Reservoir Area. In *Arkansas Archeology 1962*, edited by Charles McGimsey III, pp. 67–96. Arkansas Archeological Society, Fayetteville.
1985 The Coline Burial 23PO305. *Missouri Archaeological Society Quarterly* 2(4):18–20.

Wood, W. Raymond, and R. Bruce McMillan (editors)
1976 *Prehistoric Man and His Environments: A Case Study from the Ozark Highland*. Academic Press, New York.

Wood, W. Raymond, and Michael J. O'Brien
1995 Environmental Setting. In *Holocene Human Adaptations in the Missouri Prairie-Timberlands*, edited by W. Raymond Wood, Michael J. O'Brien, Katherine A. Murray, and Jerome C. Rose, pp. 25–46. Research Series 45. Arkansas Archeological Survey, Fayetteville.

Wormington, H. Marie
1957 *Ancient Man in North America*. Popular Series 4. Denver Museum of Natural History, Denver, Colorado.

Wright, Herbert E., Jr.
1971 Late Quaternary Vegetational History of North America. In *The Late Cenozoic Age*, edited by Karl K. Turekian, pp. 425–474. Yale Univesity Press, New Haven, Connecticut.
1976 Pleistocene Ecology—Some Current Problems. In *Ecology of the Pleistocene*, edited by Robert C. West and William G. Haag, pp. 1–12. Geoscience and Man 13. Louisiana State University, Baton Rouge.

Wright, Patti J.
1995 Paleoethnobotanical Analysis. In *Data Recovery Investigations at the Hayden Site (23SL36) and the Rabanus Site (23SL859), Chesterfield, St. Louis County, Missouri: New Insights into the Titterington/Sedalia Phase in East-Central Missouri,* by Joseph L. Harl, pp. 93–104. Research Report 182. Archaeological Services, Department of Anthropology, University of Missouri, St. Louis.

Wyckoff, Don G.
1984 The Foragers: Eastern Oklahoma. In *Prehistory of Oklahoma*, edited by Robert E. Bell, pp. 119–160. Academic Press, Orlando, Florida.
1985 The Packard Complex: Early Archaic, Pre-Dalton Occupations on the Prairie-Woodlands Border. *Southeastern Archaeology* 4:1–26.
1989 Accelerator Dates and Chronology at the Packard Site, Oklahoma. *Current Research in the Pleistocene* 6:24–26.
Wyckoff, Don G., David Morgan, and Lee Woodard
1994 Calf Creek on the Cherokee Prairie, Part I: The Arrowhead Ditch Site (34MS174). *Bulletin of the Oklahoma Anthropological Society* 40:307–327.
Wyckoff, Don G., W. Larry Neal, and Marjorie Duncan
1994 The Primrose Site, 34MR65, Murray County, Oklahoma. *Bulletin of the Oklahoma Anthropological Society* 40:11–65.

8

Dated Projectile Point Sequences from Modoc Rock Shelter and Applications of Assemblage-Based Analysis

Steven R. Ahler and Brad Koldehoff

Modoc Rock Shelter (site 11R5, referred to here as "Modoc") is a National Historic Landmark located at the base of the eastern bluffs of the Mississippi River valley in Randolph County, Illinois (Figure 8.1). Modoc is situated immediately southeast of the emergence of Barbeau Creek onto the Mississippi River floodplain. Sediment eroded from the Barbeau Creek drainage basin forms an alluvial fan at the eastern valley margin, and the lateral edges of this fan have partially contributed to filling of the rockshelter. A more consistent source for sediment is colluvium, which has washed from the steep bluff above the shelter and formed a sloped wedge at the bluff base. The colluvial and alluvial fan sediments constitute the majority of the shelter fill, with aeolian processes contributing minor amounts of sediment. Finally, some sediment containing a wide variety of artifacts is derived from activities conducted by the prehistoric inhabitants of the site, which was occupied between about 9,000 and 3,000 years B.P.

This combination of colluvial, alluvial, aeolian, and anthropogenic processes deposited about 9.3 m of sediment in the rockshelter. Excavations conducted at the site in the 1950s and 1980s recovered thousands of artifacts—including more than 600 projectile points and fragments—and subsistence remains from unmixed, stratified deposits. This chapter presents data on the projectile point assemblages recovered from securely dated stratigraphic contexts and provides a well-dated projectile point sequence for the southern Midwest that can be used for comparison with undated or less well-dated assemblages, including those derived from surface contexts.

Figure 8.1. Location of Modoc Rock Shelter and the Modoc Village site (11R266).

A Brief History of Investigations

The deeply stratified deposits at Modoc were discovered almost by accident when the county highway along the bluff base was improved in the late 1940s and roadbed fill was borrowed from the rockshelter deposits. This exposed artifacts and ash lenses in profile at the edges of the borrow area. In 1952, these features came to the attention of Melvin L. Fowler, then assistant curator of anthropology at the Illinois State Museum, and Irvin Peithman, an amateur archaeologist from Chester, Illinois. Between 1952 and 1956, the Illinois State Museum and the University of Chicago conducted four excavation seasons at Modoc. The report on this early series of excavations (Fowler 1959) demonstrated the antiquity of the Archaic period in the eastern United States (see also Matson 1955) and provided evidence for a sequence of changing artifact styles and adaptive strategies spanning more than 6,000 years.

However, the results were also controversial. Some archaeologists expressed considerable doubt about the age of the deposits and the accuracy of the radiocarbon assays, though these doubts were resolved when other sites in the Midwest and Southeast produced similar age ranges for Archaic materials. Other researchers noted that lanceolate and side-notched points had been found in the same levels at the site (Griffin 1957), which led some to conclude that the deposits were mixed. Methodological questions were also raised regarding the use of arbitrary 1-ft excavation levels as analytical units across the entire site, including in two noncontiguous excavation blocks (Bryan 1965; Griffin 1968). Collectively, these questions created doubts about the stratigraphic integrity of the deposits, and later researchers often excluded large portions of the collection from analyses (e.g., Cook 1976) or minimized the site's importance.

The conditions under which the 1950s excavations were conducted contributed substantively to the later interpretive and analytical controversies. The general site plan (Figure 8.2) shows two separate excavation blocks. The 1952, 1953, and 1955 excavations were conducted in the part of the site now designated the "Main Shelter." Work during the 1952 season was largely sporadic and expedient. The initial assumption was that the majority of the deposits had been removed by the borrow activities, and work was conducted at Modoc only when weather conditions prohibited work at a nearby open-air site. When the base of deposits was not reached in 1952 in the deepest units (extending about 7 ft below the surface of the borrowed area), more intensive work was conducted in 1953 to obtain a sample of the entire vertical range of deposits. A block of units at the west edge of the Main Shelter area provided a sample of the upper deposits (most of which had been removed in the borrow activities), while a smaller group of contiguous units in the center of the Main Shelter (the Central Pit area) was excavated from the surface of the borrow area to bedrock. Collectively, these excavations documented stratified deposits up to 9.3 m in depth. Artifacts assigned to Early Archaic (10,000–8000 B.P.), Middle Archaic (8000–5000 B.P.), and Late Archaic (5000–3000 B.P.) periods were represented in relative stratigraphic position, and the Middle Archaic levels produced the most abundant remains (Fowler et al. 1956).

When radiocarbon assays on charcoal taken from Central Pit units (Libby 1954; Matson 1955) indicated that the deposits were as much as 10,000 years old, two additional excavation seasons were planned. In 1955, from .9 to 1.5 m of the dense Middle Archaic midden were excavated from

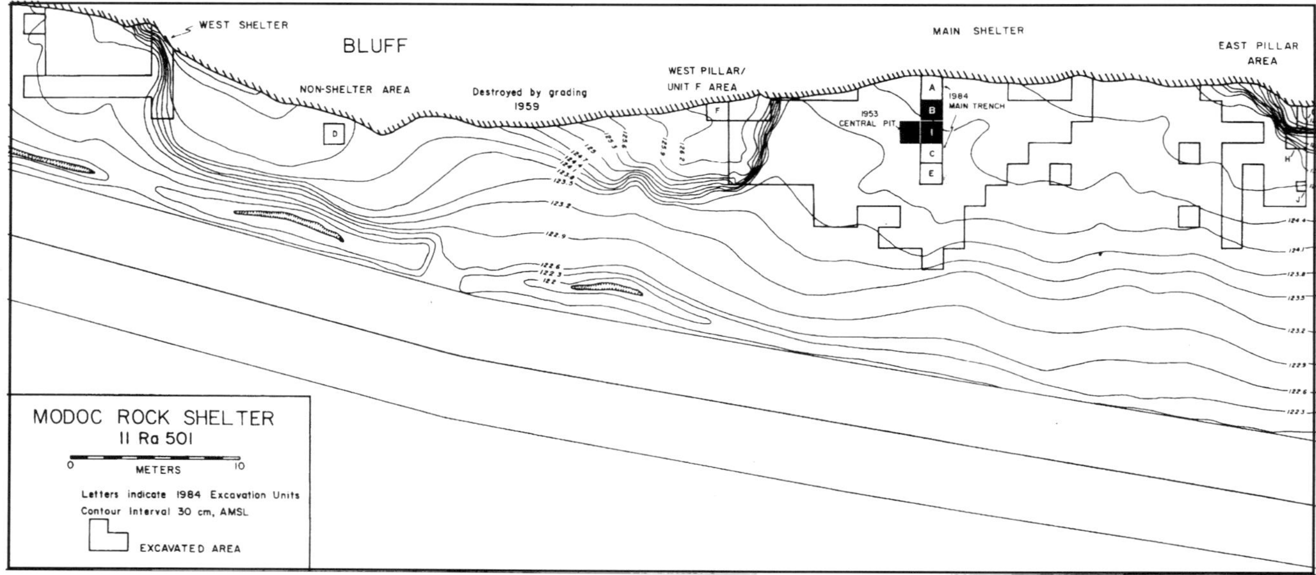

Figure 8.2. Site plan of Modoc Rock Shelter showing excavation areas.

the Main Shelter, providing a large sample of the most artifact-rich deposits in the site. The excavation plan called for the 1956 work to be conducted in the Main Shelter, as well, where a smaller block of units would be excavated down to bedrock, providing a larger sample of the earlier deposits. A misunderstanding with the landowner forced the 1956 excavations to be carried out in a different part of the site, now designated the "West Shelter" and located about 50 m west of the previous excavations. The West Shelter sediments were broadly similar to the strata documented in the Main Shelter, and the highest artifact densities were again associated with Middle Archaic levels. Moreover, a single radiocarbon assay from the West Shelter corresponded closely to dates obtained from the Main Shelter at a similar elevation. On the basis of the overall similarity of the stratigraphy in the two areas and the excellent correlation of the West Shelter radiocarbon assay with those from the Main Shelter at similar depths, the decision was made to combine materials from all excavation seasons into a single sample, which was separated into analytical units based on arbitrary 1-ft excavation levels.

Fowler's (1959) major interpretive and analytical conclusions were not seriously challenged. His 1959 report combined artifact, faunal, and environmental analyses in an interdisciplinary interpretation of changing Archaic-period adaptations, and his conclusions furnished a substantive example of Caldwell's (1958) model of Eastern Woodlands adaptive trends. The shifts documented at Modoc—from generalized to locally intensive to specialized adaptation—were seen as exemplifying long-term trends in Archaic-period culture in the eastern United States (Fowler 1959:56–58).

However, questions were raised about specific aspects of the data and analytical methods. The most serious criticism involved the use of sitewide arbitrary levels as analytical units. With sediment profiles and artifact sequences similar in both the Main and West shelters and the ages of the radiocarbon samples appearing to form a single consistent series of dates when scaled by elevation, combining artifacts into analytical assemblages on the basis of elevation was reasonable. All assays, therefore, were combined in a single sequence, with elevation serving to link the excavation areas. However, as Bryan (1965) points out, combining excavation units from both areas of the site assumed uniform depositional rates in all areas of the site and contemporaneous sediment deposition in both shelters. If these assumptions were not correct, the arbitrary analytical units would appear to contain temporally or stylistically mixed artifact assemblages. This appearance of mixing—created by combining two separate excavation areas for analytical purposes—contributed greatly to the persistent idea that the cultural strata were, in fact, mixed or inverted. This, in turn, led to questions about the integrity of deposits and the accuracy of the radiocarbon assays.

To address some of these persistent questions, another series of excavations was conducted at Modoc in the 1980s. Funded by the Illinois Department of Conservation and the U.S. Department of Interior Heritage Conservation and Recreation Service, the Illinois State Museum and the University of Wisconsin–Milwaukee conducted work in 1980 to provide additional documentation of site stratigraphy, collect samples for radiocarbon assay, recover a stratigraphically controlled excavation sample using water-screening and flotation recovery methods, and conduct interdisciplinary analyses of recovered materials to assess the research potential of the site.

Most work in 1980 was conducted in the West Shelter, though the deep Central Pit excavation area in the Main Shelter was also relocated and documented. Perhaps the most significant results of this work were the detailed documentation of more than 40 linear meters of profiles and 20 natural and cultural strata in the West Shelter (Figure 8.3) and the assay of 10 additional radiocarbon samples from West Shelter contexts. Detailed stratigraphic and chronological data are presented in Ahler (1993), and these results form the basis for the present stratigraphic analyses of projectile points from West Shelter contexts. Expanded discussion and detailed analyses of the 1980 excavations are presented in Styles et al. (1981) and Styles et al. (1983), which also document the potential of the site for continued research.

On the basis of this research potential, the National Science Foundation funded additional excavations in 1984, which focused on obtaining a larger excavation sample from the Middle Archaic occupations documented in the Main Shelter (Styles et al. 1986). Work was conducted in four excavation areas, providing a sample of materials from virtually all stratigraphic contexts documented in the Main Shelter. The principal areas of work were in the Main Trench, where a series of contiguous units provided a sample of materials from Middle and Early Archaic contexts, and in the East Pillar area, where excavations sampled primarily Late Archaic strata (Figure 8.2). The excavations and subsequent analyses documented more than 50 natural and cultural strata that could be correlated among the various Main Shelter excavation areas (Figures 8.4 and 8.5) and added 24 new radiocarbon assays, ranging in age from about 8530 to 4000 B.P. Most major strata are likely continuous across the Main Shelter excavation units, and the overall integrity of these deposits is very good.

One of the most significant findings came from the excavation of a test unit placed in a nonsheltered area between the Main and West shelters (Unit D on Figure 8.2). The strata in Unit D could not be correlated with strata in either shelter. The absence of correlative strata linking the West and Main shelters and the dissimilarity in the radiocarbon sequences indicate that the stratigraphic sequences in each shelter are separate and independent series. Correlation of strata between shelters can be made only through comparison of radiocarbon assays from individual strata. This finding limits the point assemblages that can be analyzed to those from contexts that have been directly dated and those from contexts that are bracketed with acceptable dates.

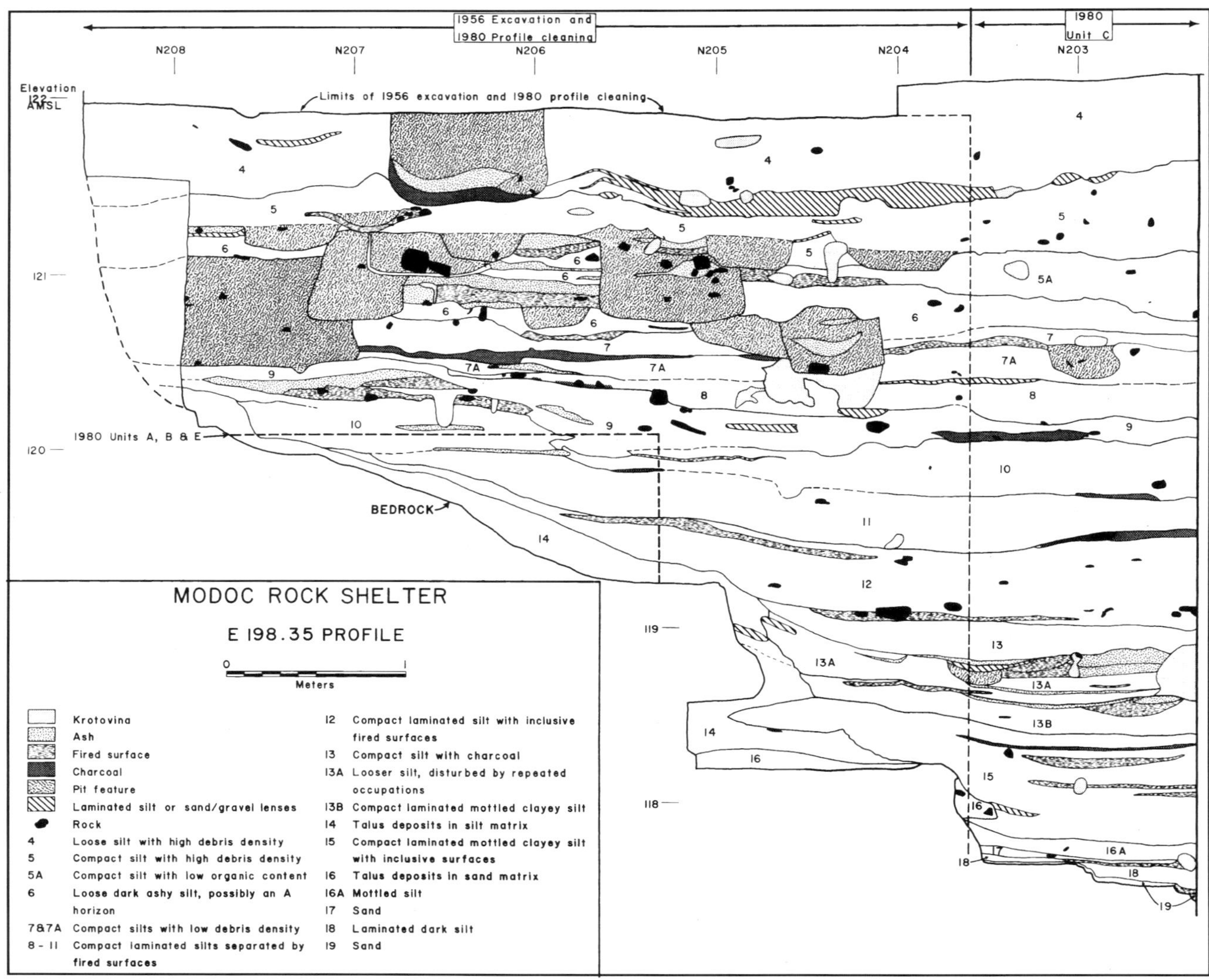

Figure 8.3. West Shelter stratigraphy. Upper portion of stratigraphic sequence showing Strata 1–4 is not shown because these strata are not directly dated.

In 1987, the National Geographic Society funded excavations that obtained a larger sample of Late Archaic material from the East Pillar portion of the Main Shelter (Ahler et al. 1992). Four additional radiocarbon assays were obtained, refining the chronological sequence of this part of the site. Also in 1987, the Illinois State Museum received a grant from the National Endowment for the Humanities (NEH) to reanalyze a portion of the 1950s artifacts. This project also resulted in correlation of all 1950s unit and level data with appropriate 1980s strata, reconstruction of strata on the basis of profile documentation from the 1950s seasons, and reassessment of all radiocarbon assays. The radiocarbon chronology and stratigraphy of the site were summarized and evaluated in Ahler (1993), and the following analyses of projectile point assemblages are based on these published radiocarbon and stratigraphic data, augmented by reconstruction of strata from profiles documented in the 1950s.

Site Stratigraphy and Chronology

The present analyses use the radiocarbon chronology presented in Ahler (1993). The strata descriptions and sequences presented in Ahler (1993) are also used, but additional reconstructed strata are included in the analyses (discussed below). The strata are discussed in detail in the 1993 article, and their attributes are not repeated here. Definitions of all except the reconstructed strata are based on field descriptions compiled by Ahler in the 1980 and 1984 seasons. Major strata were delineated on the basis of differences in texture, structure, and color of sediments and the relative amount and types of associated cultural material. Strata are numbered from top to bottom within each excavation area, with major substrata given letter suffixes. Minor, usually discontinuous substrata are given subscripts. Number designations for strata in the West

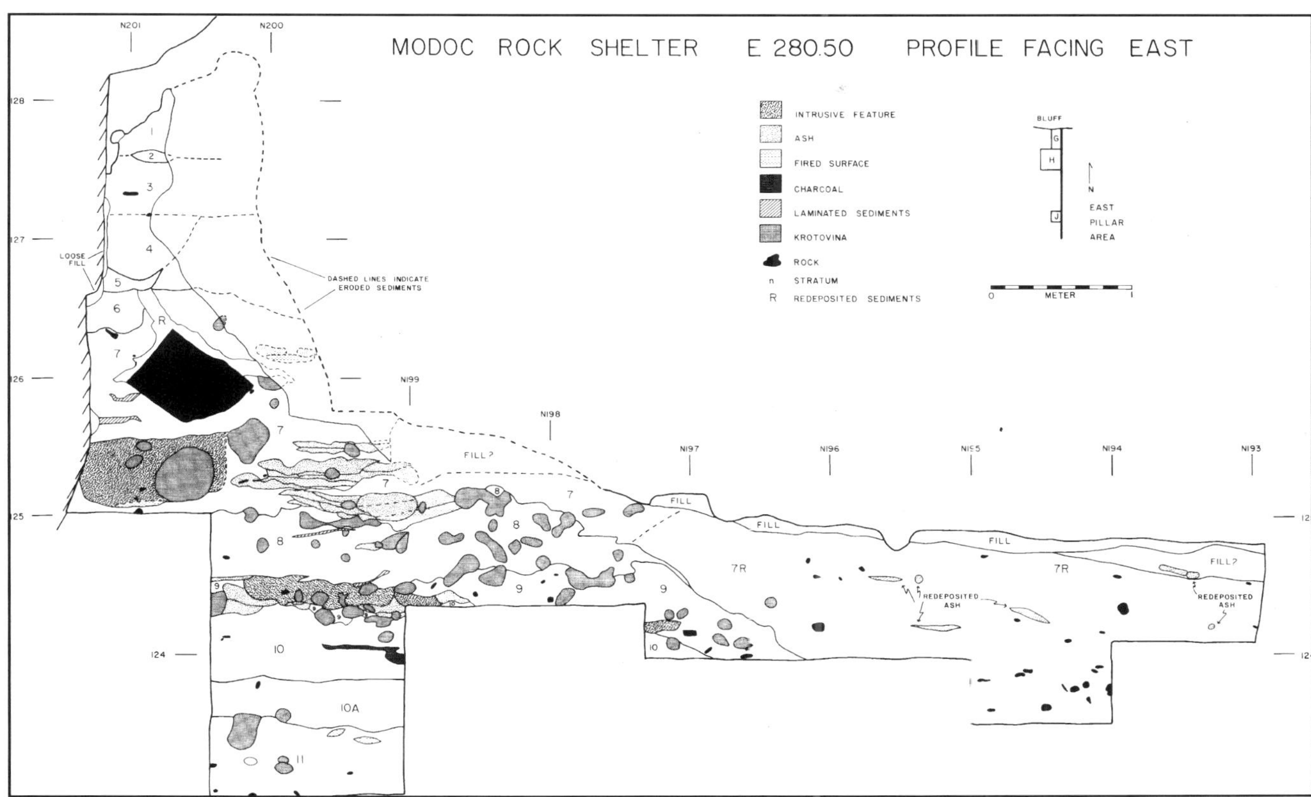

Figure 8.4. Upper portion of Main Shelter stratigraphy showing stratigraphic sequence in the East Pillar area.

Shelter stratigraphic sequence (see Table 8.1) are preceded by a "WS" prefix. The Main Shelter sequence (Table 8.2) is derived from a composite of strata documented in the Main Trench (identified by an "MT" suffix in Table 8.2), East Pillar ("E" suffix), and West Pillar ("F" suffix) portions of the site. For purposes of this chapter, proveniences in the West Pillar-1984 Unit F excavation area within the Main Shelter were combined with correlated strata in the Main Trench.

Level-Stratum Correlations and Reconstructed Strata

Among the major accomplishments of the work conducted under the 1987 NEH grant were reassessment of the 1950s stratigraphy and correlation of 1950s excavation unit and level proveniences with strata described in the 1980 and 1984 seasons. The more recent strata descriptions were much more detailed than those used in the 1950s analyses, and each stratum was a much finer physical subdivision than the four broad stratigraphic zones used in the 1950s interpretations. However, detailed field drawings archived in the 1950s site documentation served as a starting point for correlating the arbitrary excavation levels of the 1950s with 1980s strata. Once some initial correlations were established, by comparing drawings made in the 1950s with the same profiles independently documented in the 1980s seasons, strata could be interpolated between documented profiles or extrapolated with some degree of confidence across the Main Shelter or West Shelter. Detailed profile drawings from the 1950s work had never been published. These profiles and the known correspondences derived from identical profiles documented in the 1950s and 1980s allowed each unit and arbitrary level excavated in the 1950s to be correlated to one or more of the natural or cultural strata documented in the 1980s. Because of sloping strata and arbitrary levels that crosscut natural boundaries, more than one stratum might be represented in a given arbitrary level, especially those from the 1955 and 1956 seasons, when excavations were conducted in 1-ft levels. In these cases, the arbitrary level was correlated with a primary stratum, which contained the majority of the sediment volume, and secondary strata, which contained minor amounts of sediment volume. These level-to-stratum correlations were crucial for the present study, for they enabled most of the projectile points recovered from the 1950s excavations to be assigned to 1980s strata that either had been dated directly or were bracketed by dated strata.

Not all of the strata documented in the 1950s excavations were documented in the 1980s profiles. The 1955 excavations had removed 3 to 5 ft of sediment from most of the Main Shelter, and the 1984 excavations in the Main Trench could not document these excised levels and strata.

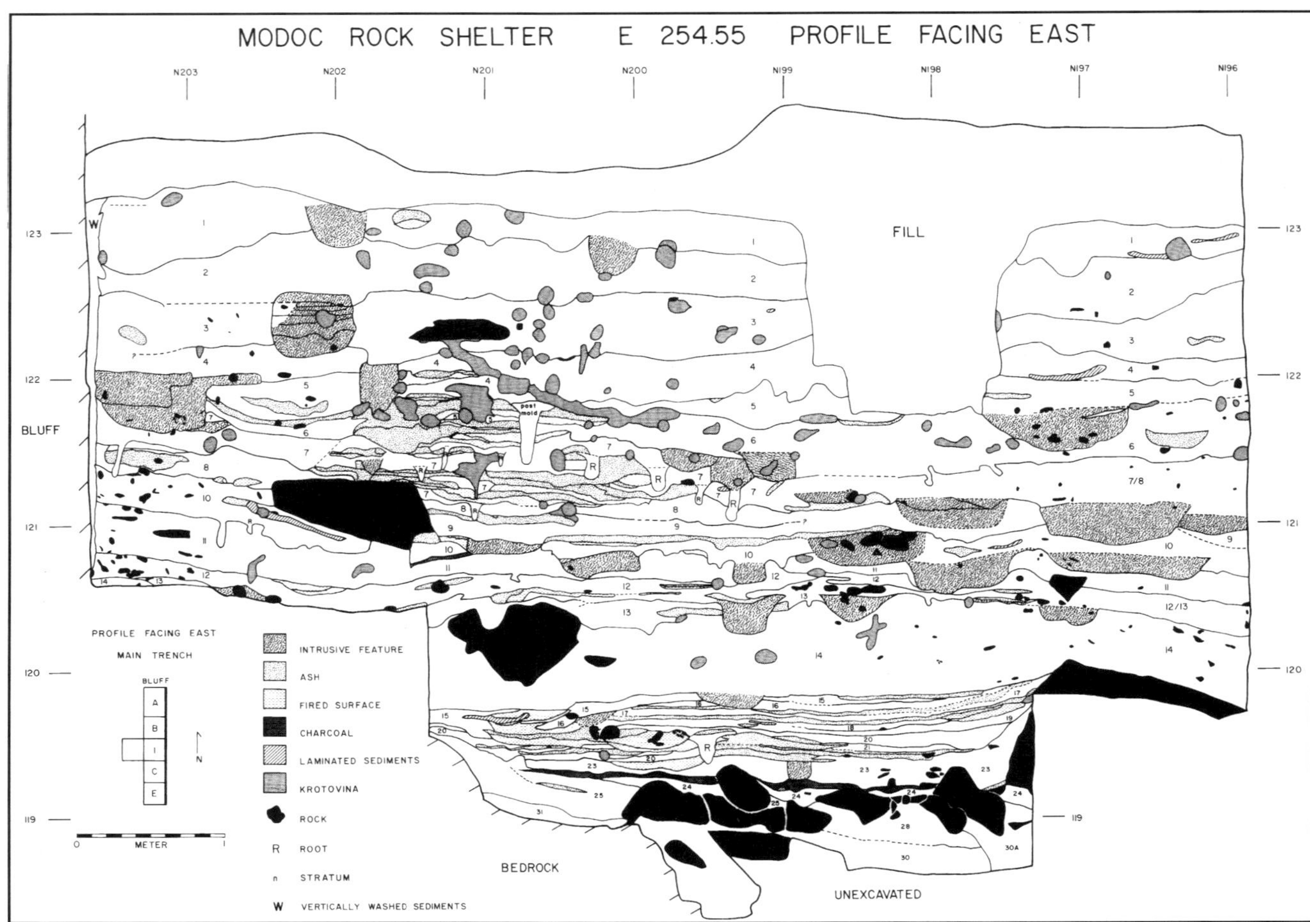

Figure 8.5. Lower portion of Main Shelter stratigraphy showing stratigraphic sequence of the Main Trench.

The 1950s profiles were relied on to reconstruct the upper stratigraphy of the central portion of the Main Shelter, where excavations had removed all evidence of the strata. Detailed descriptions comparable to the 1980s profiles were not available, but, in many instances, the 1950s profiles included brief notes on sediment color and texture. These notes and drawings, along with more detailed descriptions of profiles derived from the field director's notes, were used to define reconstructed strata for the upper part of the Main Shelter sequence. Reconstructed strata were given sequential letter designations, beginning with the lowest reconstructed stratum and proceeding upward in the composite profile. Relevant for this study are reconstructed Strata A, A2, B, C, D, and H. Strata E and F are Terminal Archaic to Woodland in age, while Stratum G likely is an apron of redeposited sediment along the south edge of the Main Shelter excavation area.

Establishing reconstructed strata was crucial to completing the level-stratum correlations since the strata that had been almost entirely removed in the 1955 excavation included material from the late Middle Archaic and early Late Archaic periods, during which the site was occupied most intensively. These strata also had no associated radiocarbon dates but could be bracketed above and below by dated strata. Figures 8.6 through 8.8 show reconstructed strata based on composites of 1950s profiles along selected grid lines. The reconstructed strata were particularly useful for the West Pillar-Unit F portion of the Main Shelter (Figure 8), where grading and backfilling of the site had removed almost all physical evidence of the stratigraphy.

Radiocarbon Sequences

The age ranges for the strata used in this chapter are based on the acceptable radiocarbon assays reported in Ahler (1993). These assays (Tables 8.1 and 8.2) provide accepted dates for the West and Main shelters, respectively. Acceptable dates include those that were not rejected in Ahler (1993) on the basis of possible contamination, use of unsuitable material for assay, radical disagreement with assays from adjacent strata or stratigraphic positions, effects of sample collection or processing techniques, errors in provenience, or outdated laboratory assay

Table 8.1. Strata and Acceptable Radiocarbon Assays from West Shelter Contexts.

Stratum	Provenience	Sample Number[a]	Date (RCYBP)	Calibrated Age B.C. +1σ (centroid[s]) −1σ[b]	Strata Group[c]
WS-1	no dates	—	—	—	not included
WS-2	no dates	—	—	—	not included
WS-3	no dates	—	—	—	not included
WS-3A	no dates	—	—	—	not included
WS-4	no dates	—	—	—	not included
WS-5	1956 Unit 50L190	L-381C	7000 ± 170	6019 (5871, 5858, 5843) 5749	MAR2
WS-5A	1980 Unit C; F507	ISGS-831	7130 ± 180	6205 (5993) 5806	MAR2
	1980 Unit C; F503	ISGS-840	7230 ± 140	6226 (6068, 6035) 5926	MAR2
WS-5A,6,7	1956 mixed units	L-406A	7200 ± 200	6223 (6056, 6042, 6028) 5842	MAR2
WS-6	1980 Unit C; F505	ISGS-813	7580 ± 190	6635 (6437) 6230	MAR1
WS-7A/8	1980 Unit D; F516	ISGS-830	8010 ± 140	7135 (7044) 6662	EAR2
WS-9/10	1984 profile; F20/F22	ISGS-1299	8030 ± 220	7315 (7051) 6642	EAR2
WS-10_1	1980 Unit C	ISGS-808	8270 ± 80	7475 (7445, 7324, 7214) 7142	EAR2
WS-13A	1980 Unit C	ISGS-797	8680 ± 150	7961 (7675, 7651, 7613) 7580	EAR1
WS-13_2	1980 Unit C; F59	ISGS-780	8710 ± 140	8157 (7733, 7691, 7683) 7586	EAR1
WS-15_1	1980 Unit C; F87	ISGS-747	8890 ± 140	8262 (8197, 8119, 8081, 7972) 7754	EAR1
WS-16_1	1980 Units C/G/I; F85	ISGS-740	8920 ± 220	8291 (8202, 8037, 8028) 7655	EAR1

[a]Laboratories: L = Columbia University Lamont Geological Observatory Laboratory; ISGS = Illinois State Geological Survey, Analytical Chemistry Section.
[b]Calibrations are derived from the CALIB revision 4.3 program (Stuiver and Reimer 1993).
[c]EAR = Early Archaic; MAR = Middle Archaic.

procedures. Each of the assays has been discussed in detail in Ahler (1993), and that discussion is not replicated here.

All radiocarbon dates and all age ranges discussed here are based on uncorrected, uncalibrated assays, but calibrated dates are also listed in Tables 8.1 and 8.2. The vast majority of the assays were obtained over a series of years from the Illinois State Geological Survey Isotopic Chemistry Laboratory; this laboratory is considered to be one of the most accurate, consistent, and reliable in the country. All of the radiocarbon assays were obtained using conventional methods rather than the AMS method.

Strata Groups

The total age range for the dated strata in both the Main and West shelters is about 8900 to 4000 B.P., determined on the basis of assay centroids, but the data in Tables 8.1 and 8.2 clearly indicate that occupation was not uniform or consistent for this 5,000-year time span. Some strata are well dated, while others have not been dated, either because no samples were available (e.g., in the case of reconstructed strata) or—more often—only a limited number of samples could be assayed, leaving many undated samples in the curated collections. Assessment of the acceptable dates assigned to various contexts allowed strata defined in different excavation areas within the Main Shelter to be correlated on the basis of age. These correlations were verified when possible by comparing the detailed strata descriptions from the 1980 and 1984 excavation seasons to determine if the overall character of the major strata remained consistent across excavation areas. Minor differences in recorded elevation of these major strata were not considered problematic. All of the strata defined at Modoc have some degree of slope, usually slanting down away from the bluff face, as would be expected for colluvial deposits.

When the reconstructed strata are included in their proper positions relative to strata documented in the 1980 and 1984 seasons, a single master stratigraphic sequence is derived for all of the Main Shelter deposits. This master sequence is reflected in the order in which dates and strata are listed in Table 8.2. Some specific strata correlations warrant discussion. On the basis of strata elevations alone, the lowest stratum in the East Pillar sequence (11E) should correlate with the uppermost stratum in the Main Trench sequence (1MT). However, the attributes of these two strata are not particularly similar, with 11E exhibiting much lower densities of ash, charcoal, and

Table 8.2. Strata and Acceptable Radiocarbon Assays from Main Shelter Contexts.

Stratum[a]	Provenience	Sample Number[b]	Date (RCYBP)	Calibrated Age B.C. +1σ (centroid[s]) −1σ[c]	Strata Group[d]
1E	no dates	—	—	—	not included
2E	no dates	—	—	—	not included
3E	no dates	—	—	—	not included
4E	no dates	—	—	—	not included
7E	1984 Unit H, F1013	ISGS-1298	4100 ± 80	2866 (2856, 2822, 2802) 2497	LAR2
D	no dates	—	—	—	LAR2
C	no dates	—	—	—	LAR2
8E	1987 Unit L/M	ISGS-1982	4330 ± 90	3081 (2916) 2881	LAR2
H	no dates	—	—	—	LAR1
9E	1955 Unit 35R0	M-483	4720 ± 300	3650 (3519) 3355	LAR1
	1987 Unit M; F1131	ISGS-1986	4730 ± 70	3637 (3618, 3608, 3521) 3376	LAR1
	1984 Unit H; F1029	ISGS-1340	4820 ± 130	3708 (3640) 3381	LAR1
	1987 Unit H	ISGS-1983	4850 ± 70	3698 (3644) 3539	LAR1
	1987 Units L, M	ISGS-1987	4890 ± 200	3942 (3657) 3381	LAR1
B	no dates	—	—	—	LAR1
10E	no dates	—	—	—	MAR6
10AE	no dates	—	—	—	MAR6
11E	1955 Unit 35R5	M-484	5280 ± 300	4326 (4216, 4136, 4045) 3960	MAR5[e]
A2	no dates	—	—	—	MAR6
A	1984 Unit 35R5	ISGS-1360	5600 ± 80	4499 (4452, 4417, 4404) 4349	MAR5
A	1984 Unit H	ISGS-1342	5930 ± 70	4902 (4796) 4718	MAR5
1MT	no dates	—	—	—	MAR5
2MT	1984 Unit E; F528	ISGS-1336	6190 ± 150	5316 (5207, 5141, 5080) 4859	MAR4
3MT	1984 Unit A; F526	ISGS-1345	6230 ± 130	5320 (5230, 5211, 5151) 4998	MAR4
	1989 profile	ISGS-1990	6140 ± 70	5227 (5055) 4948	MAR4
4MT	1984 Unit E; F538	ISGS-1389	6510 ± 80	5526 (5477) 5375	MAR3
5MT	1984 Unit E; F540	ISGS-1388	6790 ± 70	5729 (5707, 5685, 5667) 5630	MAR3
6MT	1984 Unit E; F454	ISGS-1485	7200 ± 160	6224 (6056, 6042, 6028) 5907	MAR2
8MT	1984 Unit C; F275	ISGS-1386	7210 ± 70	6196 (6059, 6040, 6030) 5995	MAR2
7/8MT	1989 profile	ISGS-1991	7260 ± 90	6222 (6158, 6143, 6082) 6017	MAR2
9/10MT	1980 profile, F276	ISGS-815	7830 ± 230	7058 (6647) 6441	MAR1
	1984 Unit C; F276	ISGS-1383	7760 ± 70	6647 (6591, 6576, 6574) 6476	MAR1
6F	1984 Unit F; F530	ISGS-1344	7750 ± 130	6688 (6589, 6571, 6533) 6456	MAR1
11MT	no dates	—	—	—	
12MT	1984 Unit C; F244/245	ISGS-1382	8000 ± 80	7062 (7037, 6925, 6870) 6706	EAR2
13MT	1989 profile	ISGS-1994	8240 ± 80	7451 (7309, 7220, 7190) 7082	EAR2
	1984 Unit B; F534	ISGS-1381	8100 ± 130	7306 (7065) 6832	EAR2
7F/8F	1984 Unit F (log)	ISGS-1352	8150 ± 90	7312 (7135, 7113, 7081) 7058	EAR2
15MT	1984 Unit B	ISGS-1376	8190 ± 110	7449 (7284, 7235, 7180, 7142) 7061	EAR2
20MT	1984 Unit B; F261/388	ISGS-1333	8350 ± 100	7538 (7475, 7453, 7380) 7201	EAR2
	1984 Unit C	ISGS-1375	8430 ± 70	7576 (7523) 7381	EAR2
23/24MT	1984 Units B, C; F259	ISGS-1374	8530 ± 120	7604 (7580) 7486	EAR2

[a]A slash (/) in a stratum designation indicates a context at the boundary of the two designated strata.
[b]Laboratories: M = University of Michigan—Phoenix Memorial Project Radiocarbon Laboratory; ISGS = Illinois State Geological Survey, Analytical Chemistry Section.
[c]Calibrations are derived from the CALIB revision 4.3 program (Stuiver and Reimer 1993).
[d]EAR = Early Archaic; MAR = Middle Archaic; LAR = Late Archaic.
[e]Stratum 11E is included in the MAR5 strata group for this analysis because the large standard deviation overlaps both the MAR5 and MAR6 age ranges.

artifacts than are evident in the limited exposure of Stratum 1MT. The eastern edge of the Main Shelter may not have been used as intensively or frequently as the central portion (Main Trench), resulting in a change in stratigraphic attributes over the 25 m that separate these excavation areas. This interpretation is supported by the strata documented in a profile segment running perpendicular to and east of the Main Trench (Figure 8.7). This profile shows the boundary between reconstructed Strata A and A2 becoming variable and less distinct toward the east. On the basis of a combination of elevation data, a limited number of radiocarbon assays, and trends observed in the major strata, Ahler has correlated Stratum 1MT with reconstructed Stratum A. Reconstructed Stratum A2 has no correlate in the 1984 profile of the Main Trench, but it is clearly distinguished from reconstructed Stratum A in most of the 1950s profile drawings. On the basis of elevation,

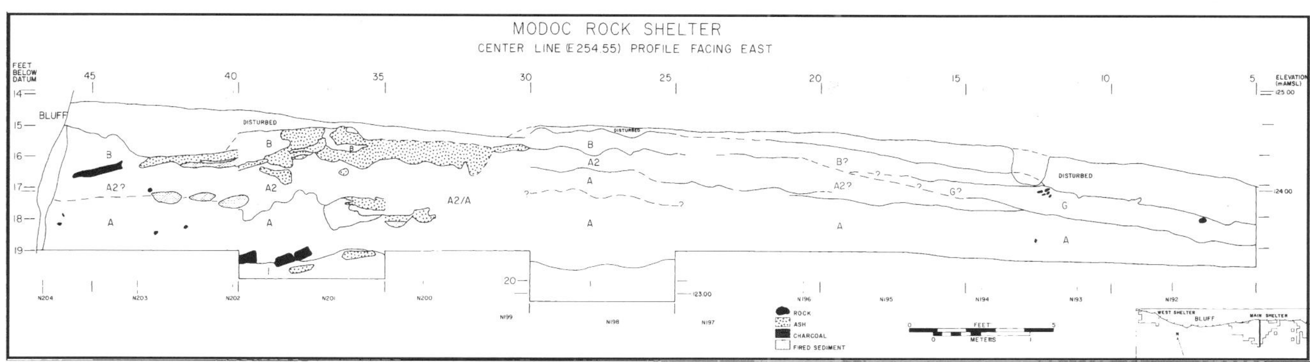

Figure 8.6. Reconstructed strata in the Main Shelter. Data are compiled from individual 1955 profile drawings of units excavated along the primary site center line, which corresponds to the 1984 Main Trench profile.

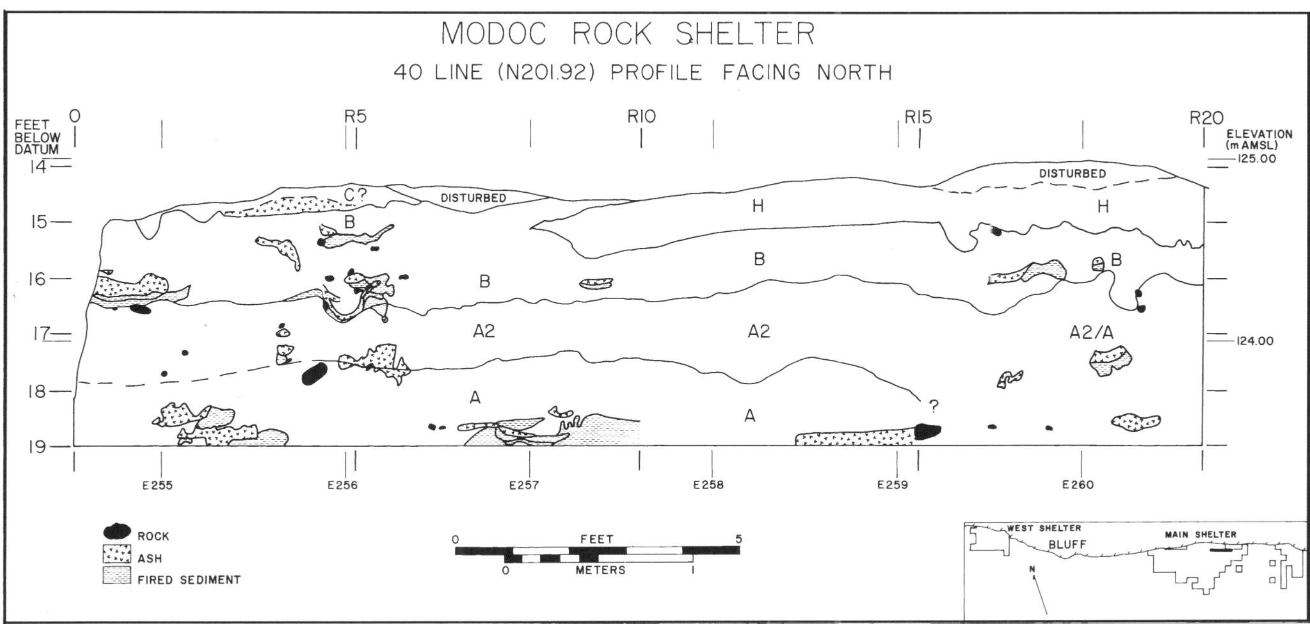

Figure 8.7. Reconstructed strata in the Main Shelter. Illustrated is a series of units forming a composite profile running east, perpendicular to the center line profile shown in Figure 8.6 and parallel to the bluff face.

reconstructed Stratum A2 would correspond to Stratum 10E or 10AE, but, again, artifact densities appear to be much lower in the eastern part of the Main Shelter. Still, these are the most logical correlations, and they are at least partially supported by the radiocarbon dates and projectile points recovered from the lower strata in the East Pillar sequence.

Other correlations can be drawn between reconstructed strata and documented strata. Stratum 9E is strongly correlated with reconstructed Stratum B on the basis of elevation, strata attributes, and projectile point assemblages. Stratum 8CE, which immediately overlies Stratum 9E, is likewise correlated with Stratum H, which is discontinuous across the site. On the basis of the analyses of the East Pillar materials recovered in 1987 (Ahler et al. 1992), Strata 8EC, 9E, B, and H are combined in this analysis as a single strata group. Stratum 7E is a thick stratum that contains Late Archaic materials and corresponds in elevation, characteristics, and associated artifacts to reconstructed Strata C and D. The reconstructed strata are listed in Table 8.2 in their proper position relative to other strata in the master Main Shelter sequence, with reconstructed strata placed just below the documented strata with which they correlate.

Using the array of acceptable radiocarbon assays presented in Tables 8.1 and 8.2, we combined the documented and reconstructed strata in both the West and Main shelters at Modoc into strata groups for the projectile point analyses. Each strata group includes one or more strata and represents a temporal span of about 500 years. Because radiocarbon age is

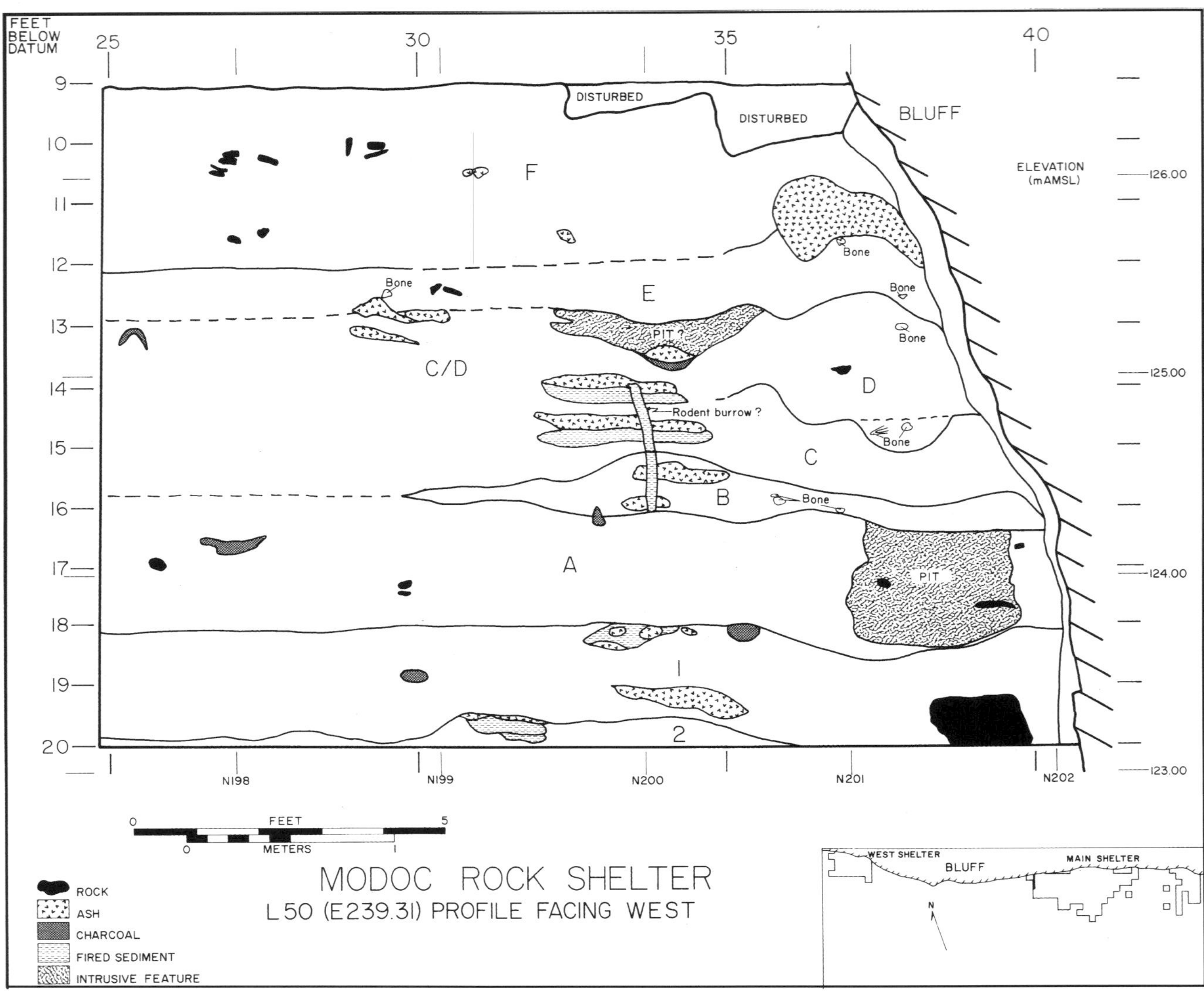

Figure 8.8. Reconstructed strata in the West Pillar portion of the Main Shelter.

the principal criterion for assigning strata to groups, strata from both the West and Main shelters can legitimately be combined. Strata that have no associated radiocarbon assays and that cannot be assigned to an estimated age range (on the basis of radiocarbon dates from adjacent strata) could not be assigned to a temporally based strata group. Limiting the projectile point analyses to directly dated strata and their correlates (or date-bracketed strata and correlates) reduced the assemblage available for analysis, especially from the West Shelter. Strata WS-1 through WS-4 have no associated radiocarbon dates. Yet what is lost by reducing sample size is regained in increased reliability of the strata and age assignments.

The strata groups are listed in Tables 8.1 and 8.2. Strata dated to the Early Archaic period are combined into two strata groups (EAR1 and EAR2, older and younger, respectively). Strata group EAR1 is represented only in the West Shelter, while strata assigned to EAR2 are present in both the West and Main shelters. The Middle Archaic period deposits are divided into six strata groups (MAR1 through MAR6). MAR1 and MAR2 are represented in both the West and Main shelters, while MAR 3 through MAR6 are represented by dated strata found only in the Main Shelter. Given the point types recovered, the likelihood is high that the undated strata WS-3, WS-3A, and WS-4 in the West Shelter correspond to MAR3 through MAR6, but without direct radiocarbon dating of these strata, their assignment to strata groups could not be made with confidence. Late Archaic strata groups LAR1 and LAR2 also include only dated strata from the Main Shelter and their associated reconstructed strata. LAR 1 corresponds to the early Late Archaic period Falling Springs phase (see Ahler et al. 1992; McElrath 1986), while LAR2 is associated with the Late Archaic Titterington phase. Later Late and Terminal Archaic occupations are documented at Modoc, but these strata (1E through 4E and their corresponding reconstructed Strata E and F) have not been directly dated. The most recent radiocarbon date from Modoc is a 4000 B.P. assay

(Titterington phase) from the base of Stratum 7E. The thick Stratum 7E and the correlated reconstructed Strata C and D make up the final strata group used in these analyses.

Projectile Point Assemblages by Strata Group

The projectile points recovered from each of the strata groups are discussed in detail in the following sections. Assemblages are highly variable in size, ranging from two identifiable points to over 100. In each strata group, we focus on identifiable points that can be associated with established point types (see, e.g., Justice 1987; Perino 1985). In several cases, we grouped individual point types into a single cluster of morphologically similar types. For example, the named types Osceola, modal Matanzas, Godar, and Raddatz all have been grouped into a single cluster referred to as the "large side-notched" cluster. This practice has served two purposes. First, it has increased the assemblage size by allowing some fragmentary items to be included in the analyses that might have been eliminated from consideration if they could not be assigned to a specific type. Second, it avoids the pitfall of typological hairsplitting by focusing on the commonalities shared by named types, regardless of whether all analysts would agree on a specific type name for a given specimen.

We accorded special attention to raw material identification and how raw material characteristics were modified by thermal alteration (heat treatment and burning) and patination (weathering). While evidence of intentional heat treatment provides insights into certain aspects of point production, obvious reworking of burned and weathered surfaces provides evidence of earlier points that were found and reused (recycled) by later inhabitants. Such information was used to help verify that earlier points had, in fact, been recycled and redeposited at the shelter by later inhabitants. Similarly, close attention was focused on resharpening strategies. For example, points from a particular strata group that did not conform to resharpening practices that appeared standard for points in that strata group were suspected of having been scavenged for reuse. Finally, the collections included distal and proximal point fragments that had been reworked in an expedient manner to temporarily extend their use life. Specimens that had been expediently "retipped" or "rebased" often confounded typological efforts and were usually considered untyped or unidentifiable.

EAR1 Strata Group (ca. 9000–8500 B.P.)

This strata group includes strata WS-13 through WS-16 (the lowest dated stratum in the West Shelter). Only five points were recovered from this strata group, and of these only three are identifiable. Two of the points are classified as Graham Cave Side Notched (Figure 8.9a, b), while the other identifiable point is a Dalton. The two unidentifiable points are fragments, one of a side-notched point and one whose general hafting mode (side-notched, corner-notched, stemmed, etc.) could not be determined with certainty.

Figure 8.9. Projectile points from EAR1 (a, b) and EAR2 (c–j) contexts: a, Graham Cave, Stratum WS-14; b, Graham Cave, Stratum WS-13A; c, small bifurcate base, Stratum 16MT; d, possible Big Sandy side-notched, Stratum 16MT; e, Rice Lobed (Kirk cluster), Stratum WS-10; f, Rice Lanceolate, Stratum WS-10; g, Stanly, Stratum 19MT; h, small bifurcate base, Stratum WS-8; i, Kirk cluster, Stratum WS-8; j, Hidden Valley, Stratum 14MT.

At this juncture, it is appropriate to discuss the Dalton points recovered from Modoc. One of the most persistent perceptions about the site, that the stratigraphy is mixed or inverted, is largely due to recovery of classic Dalton points from the same levels that produced points known to date much later in time. The issue is discussed in more detail in Ahler (1993), but a summary discussion bears repeating here because of the persistence of this perception. Six Dalton points were recovered from the site, all from West Shelter contexts ranging from strata WS-4 to WS-14. No other Dalton artifacts (e.g., unifacial trapezoidal end scrapers, chipped-stone adzes, or reworked drills) were recovered. Of the points, two show clear signs of patina that has been partially removed by resharpening, and three others have breaks likely incurred during reworking. The probability is high that all of the Dalton points recovered from Modoc were removed from nearby sites and incorporated into the Modoc sediments at a date much later than their original manufacture. These are recycled points that can be excluded from the analyses, as they were not found in their original context of use and discard and make no substantive contribution to the research topic at hand. Dalton points will not be discussed again in connection with later strata groups, but they are included in the summary tables. A few other early point types, besides Dalton points, were apparently recycled from other older contexts; they are mentioned when appropriate in following sections. Dalton points are particularly common surface finds along the Mississippi River bluffs (see Koldehoff 2006) so it should be no surprise that later Early Archaic and Middle Archaic groups found and reused them.

After eliminating the Dalton point from consideration in the EAR1 assemblage, all of the identifiable points are assigned to the Graham Cave Side Notched type. The age of this strata group (8500–9000 B.P.) is generally consistent with the reported date range for this point type (see Justice 1987; Lopinot et al. 1998, 2000; O'Brien and Wood 1998), though it is on the later end of the range.

EAR2 Strata Group (8500–8000 B.P.)

This strata group includes strata from both the West Shelter (WS-7 through WS-12) and Main Shelter (12MT through 28MT). There is apparently a high degree of variability in point types and clusters in this strata group, and the sample size is much larger than that from the EAR1 strata group. Fourteen identifiable points constitute the EAR2 assemblage (Figure 9c–j), representing a wide array of hafting modes; five unidentifiable fragments were found. One unidentified fragment has a burinated basal margin, an attribute commonly found on Decatur points (see Justice 1987). However, the item is too fragmentary for a positive identification. Two recycled points were found—a Dalton and a Hardin Barbed; these are not included in the assemblage totals. The most commonly represented type or cluster from this strata group, with five examples, is the Kirk Corner Notched cluster. This cluster subsumes a variety of corner-notched point types, some of which have a distinct left-hand alternate bevel, including a large point made from nonlocal rhyolite (Figure 8.9e), assigned to the Rice Lobed type, and a smaller example (Figure 8.9i) made from Burlington chert. Included in this assemblage is the only example of a Kirk Stemmed point (not illustrated here) recovered from Modoc. The next most common cluster is the small bifurcate-base cluster, with three specimens (Figure 8.9c, h). Two examples of points assigned to the Rice Lanceolate or Searcy type (Figure 8.9f) were recovered, as were two examples of the broad-bladed, contracting-stem Hidden Valley type (Figure 8.9j). A single example of a small but deeply side-notched specimen (Figure 8.9d) may represent a Big Sandy point, but this item has been heavily reworked, resulting in possible alteration of the haft element. A single thin point with a small square stem is assigned to the Stanly type (Figure 8.9g). Recovery of the small bifurcate-base, Stanly, and possible Big Sandy points suggests that inhabitants of the site during the EAR2 time span may have had connections to the south, as these point types are more commonly found in Tennessee and Kentucky. However, association with more westerly groups is suggested by the Rice Lobed and Rice Lanceolate types, which are more common in Missouri than in areas farther east.

MAR1 Strata Group (8000–7500 B.P.)

This strata group contains strata from both the West Shelter (WS-6) and Main Shelter (9MT to 11MT and 6F to 7F). The variability in point types and clusters that was prevalent in the Early Archaic strata groups is somewhat reduced here, though the sample size is similar to that of the EAR2 assemblage. This assemblage comprises 16 specimens, 11 of which are identifiable to type or cluster (Figure 8.10). Of the unidentifiable fragments, one is likely corner notched, two are possible side-notched fragments, and two could not be assigned even to a gross hafting mode because of their small size. One of the corner-notched fragments may be a portion of a Jakie Stemmed point, but this assignment is extremely uncertain. A recycled Dalton point also was recovered from this strata group.

Of the identifiable points, the most common type, with four specimens, is a large, thick corner-notched point, usually with rounded basal ears (Figure 8.10a). This point is grossly similar to the Cypress Creek I point described by Lewis and Lewis (1961) for the Eva site in western Tennessee. The specimens from Modoc appear to be slightly less well made, and the corner notching is not as pronounced as in the illustrated specimens from Eva (Lewis and Lewis 1961:Plate 9a–f). Still, the points are similar enough to compare favorably with the Cypress Creek I point type. Also in this assemblage are three specimens assigned to the general Kirk Corner Notched cluster (Figure 8.10b, c) and a single example of a small, relatively thick, triangular point with straight base and deep corner notches that form prominent shoulder barbs and basal ears (Figure 8.10d). This point is grossly similar to Merom/Trimble dart points commonly found in late Late Archaic Riverton- or Labras Lake–phase (Yerkes 1987) contexts, and it was initially thought to represent an intrusive item or a point with mislabeled provenience data. However, several examples of similar small points have been recovered from intact stratigraphic contexts dated to the early Middle Archaic period at the Knob Creek site, within the Caesars

Figure 8.10. Projectile points from MAR1 contexts: a, Cypress Creek I, Stratum 9MT; b, Rice Lobed (Kirk cluster), Stratum WS-7; c, Possible Kirk cluster or Cypress Creek, Stratum WS-6; d, small corner-notched dart point, Stratum 9-10MT; e, possible Jakie Stemmed, Stratum WS-6; f, Bass knife, Stratum 10MT.

Palace project area in southern Indiana (see Stafford and Cantin, this volume). The single specimen from Modoc is now viewed as a legitimate part of the MAR1 assemblage and not an intrusive specimen. Other points in the MAR1 assemblage include a probable Jakie Stemmed point (Figure 8.10e) and an elongated specimen with beveled blade and rounded base (Figure 8.10f). This item is similar to beveled bifaces from the Bass site in Grant County, Wisconsin, which were found in close association with Early Archaic Hardin Barbed points (Behm 1985). It is also similar to beveled bifaces from Kirk contexts at the St. Albans site in West Virginia (Broyles 1971) and the James Farnsley site in southern Indiana (Stafford and Cantin, this volume). This single beveled biface from Modoc may represent a recycled Early Archaic point type, but it exhibits no evidence of removal of patina or other direct indications of scavenging and recycling. One unidentified point with an elongated stem may be similar to Campbell Hollow points (Stafford 1985), but the Modoc specimen is too damaged to positively assign to this type. Finally, a Hidden Valley point with partial removal of patina was recovered; this specimen is considered to be recycled from an older context.

The typological and morphological diversity expressed in the MAR1 assemblage is lower than in the preceding EAR2 assemblage. Though fewer categories are represented and the thick Cypress Creek–like point represents the modal type of the identifiable specimens, a wide array of hafting modes and morphological types is present. Recovery of thick Cypress Creek I points in association with the small corner-notched Knob Creek points, along with Kirk and lanceolate, beveled knife forms (if the latter are not recycled) suggests that the points in this strata group are functionally complementary and may be part of a functionally diverse tool kit.

MAR2 Strata Group (7500–7000 B.P.)

This strata group contains strata from both the West Shelter (WS-5 and WS-5A) and Main Shelter (6MT to 8MT). Again, a wide variety of point types and clusters is represented in this assemblage (Figure 8.11), but the sample of identifiable points is larger (n = 26) than those from older strata groups. An additional 16 unidentifiable points were found, including small fragments of side-notched, corner-notched, and stemmed specimens as well as fragments not assignable to any hafting mode. Moreover, three Dalton points excluded from the assemblage totals were recovered from this strata group.

Of the 26 identifiable points, 23 are distributed almost equally among four types or clusters. The Cypress Creek I type (Figure 8.11a) is again well represented, with six specimens. Another six points are assigned to another corner-notched type that is slightly thinner and more carefully flaked than the Cypress Creek I type and that has strongly angled instead of rounded basal corners. This group (Figure 8.11b) is most similar to Cypress Creek II points described by Lewis and Lewis (1961:Plate 9g–l). The relative stratigraphic position of these two types at Modoc is similar to their contexts in the stratified Eva site, where the Cypress Creek II point was slightly later in time. Their ages are also grossly similar at both sites. At Eva, Cypress Creek I points were most common in the Eva component, radiocarbon dated to earlier than about 7200 B.P. Nance (1986) has recovered Cypress Creek I points from contexts dated between about 7100 and 7800 B.P. at the Morrisroe site in western Kentucky. At Modoc this type is most common in the MAR2 strata group, with an age range of 7500 to 7000 B.P. Also well represented in this assemblage are small, deeply side-notched (Figure 8.11c) and larger, deeply side-notched points (Figure 8.11d). The former correspond to the Raddatz or Brannon type, while the latter correspond to the Godar or modal Matanzas type. Other points in this assemblage (not illustrated here) include

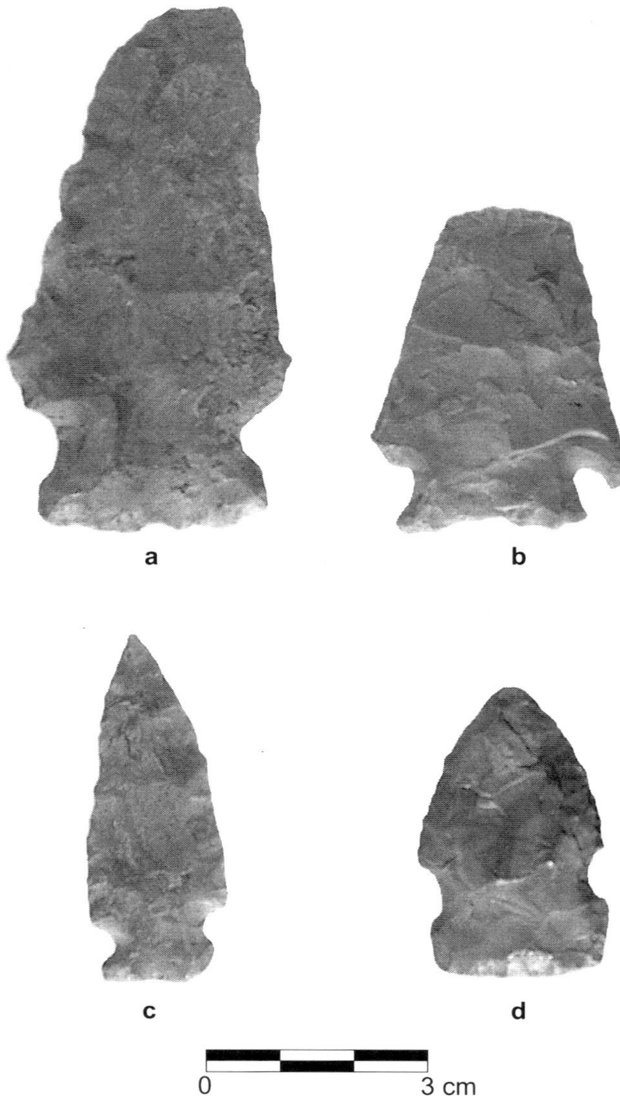

Figure 8.11. Projectile points from MAR2 contexts: a, Cypress Creek I, Stratum 8MT; b, Cypress Creek II, Stratum WS-5; c, small side-notched cluster, Stratum WS-5; d, large side-notched cluster, Stratum WS-5.

single specimens of a possible Jakie Stemmed point, an untyped side-notched to expanding-stem point, and a Hidden Valley point. The latter is likely a recycled item found outside of its original stratigraphic and temporal context.

If all the larger side-notched varieties are grouped together, and if the Hidden Valley point is eliminated as a recycled item, the typological and morphological variation expressed in the MAR2 assemblage is reduced relative to the EAR2 and MAR1 assemblages. Of the 25 remaining specimens, 23 can be placed into four clusters (Cypress Creek I, Cypress Creek II, large side-notched, and small side-notched). Recovery of the corner-notched Cypress Creek points in conjunction with both small and large side-notched points suggests functional complementarity.

MAR3 Strata Group (7000–6500 B.P.)

This strata group (and all subsequent groups) is made up of strata from only the Main Shelter, in this instance Strata 4MT and 5MT. Possibly because of the smaller sample size (total of only 25), a lower variety of point types and clusters is represented in the assemblage from this group. Twelve of the points are unidentifiable and include small fragments of side-notched and corner-notched specimens as well as fragments too small to be assigned to a specific hafting mode.

Of the 13 identifiable points (Figure 8.12), four specimens are placed in the large, deeply side-notched cluster (Figure 8.12a). All of these specimens have concave bases. Another four specimens are classified as small side-notched points (Figure 8.12b). The thinner Cypress Creek II corner-notched type is represented by three specimens (Figure 8.12c). Types represented by single examples include the thicker Cypress Creek I and an expanding-stem to side-notched point (Figure 8.12d) not assignable to a specific named type but still morphologically distinct from other points in the assemblage.

This strata group is clearly dominated by side-notched points. If all specimens identifiable to gross hafting mode are considered, side-notched specimens (regardless of size or detail of haft morphology) constitute 68.4 percent of the assemblage (13 of 19 points). This indicates an overall decrease in the morphological-typological variation in the assemblage relative to preceding strata groups. Corner-notched specimens are still well represented, which supports the interpretation that the side-notched and corner-notched modes may be functionally complementary aspects of the tool kit. The absence of straight- or contracting-stemmed specimens is not surprising, given the smaller sample size and the lower overall representation of these hafting modes. Most of the assemblage diversity in this strata group derives from variations on the general side-notched theme, with a few broad corner-notched items included.

MAR4 Strata Group (6500–6000 B.P.)

This strata group is composed of Strata 2MT and 3MT and correlated strata in other parts of the Main Shelter. The sample size here is larger than from older strata groups (total of 46), but the diversity of point types and clusters represented in this assemblage is lower. Of the total, 13 of the points were unidentifiable, including four small fragments of side-notched specimens as well as specimens too fragmentary to be assigned to a specific hafting mode.

Of the identifiable points (Figure 8.13), the most common ($n = 16$) are those belonging to the large, deeply side-notched cluster, represented by specimens with both straight to convex bases (Figure 8.13a) and concave bases (Figure 8.13b). The second largest group, with 12 specimens, is the cluster of small side-notched points (Figure 8.13c, d). Single specimens of Hidden Valley and Kirk Corner Notched–cluster points were

Figure 8.12. Projectile points from MAR3 contexts: a, large side-notched cluster, Stratum 4MT; b, small side-notched cluster, Stratum 4MT; c, Cypress Creek II, Stratum 5MT; d, untyped expanding-stem/side-notched point, Stratum 4MT.

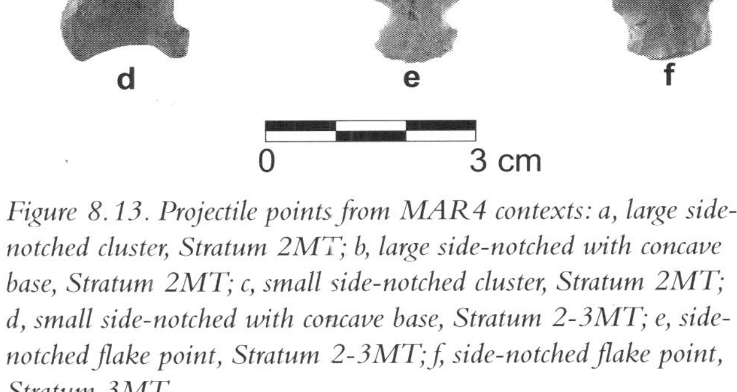

Figure 8.13. Projectile points from MAR4 contexts: a, large side-notched cluster, Stratum 2MT; b, large side-notched with concave base, Stratum 2MT; c, small side-notched cluster, Stratum 2MT; d, small side-notched with concave base, Stratum 2-3MT; e, side-notched flake point, Stratum 2-3MT; f, side-notched flake point, Stratum 3MT.

recovered, but these are likely recycled and out of their proper stratigraphic-temporal contexts. Perhaps the most interesting points in this assemblage are a series of small side-notched points made on marginally modified flakes (Figure 8.13e, f). The three specimens recovered were likely expediently made projectile points, and they conform to the dominant pattern for hafted bifaces recovered from this strata group in that they are clearly and intentionally side notched. If found in a surface context, they would likely be considered Late Woodland flake points. These simple flake points maybe have been nonfunctional ritual or educational items. Miniature points have been recovered from earlier contexts in the Great Lakes region and have been interpreted as ritual items (Ellis 1994). These items may also represent expedient but fully functional projectile points.

Of all the assemblages in this analysis, that from the MAR4 strata group is the most uniform in hafting mode, with side-notched points (regardless of size or basal shape) accounting for 35 of 40 points identifiable to hafting mode, or 87.5 percent of the assemblage. This indicates an overall decrease in the morphological or typological variation in the assemblage relative to preceding strata groups. Only five possibly stemmed fragments provide variability in hafting mode. The material from this strata group, more than any other at Modoc, appears to support the common conception that side-notched points are hallmarks of the Middle Archaic period.

MAR5 Strata Group (6000–5500 B.P.)

This strata group is composed of Strata 1MT, 11E, and reconstructed Stratum A. Though the single radiocarbon date from this strata group falls into the date range of the MAR6 group, the standard deviation for the date is large, overlapping the date ranges for both the MAR5 and MAR6 strata groups. Considering other factors, such as elevation and stratigraphic continuity, Stratum 11E is included in the MAR5 strata group for this analysis. The sample size here is much larger than those from older strata groups (total of 125) because of the extensive volume of Stratum A excavated in the 1955 season. As would be expected, the diversity of point types and clusters represented in this large assemblage is also greater than in those from preceding strata groups. Of the total, 22 points are unidentifiable, including seven small fragments of side-notched points, two small fragments of corner-notched specimens, and seven specimens too fragmentary to be assigned to a specific hafting mode. A single Rice Lanceolate/Searcy point was recovered and is considered to be recycled and out of stratigraphic position.

Of the identifiable points (Figure 8.14), most (41 examples) belong to the large, deeply side-notched cluster, which again includes specimens with both straight to convex bases (Figure 8.14a) and concave bases (Figure 8.14b). The second most common point type, with 31 specimens, is the faintly side-notched Matanzas type, with shallow side notches placed low on the lateral edges (Figure 8.14c). Next most common are points that have straight stems and weak to strong shoulders (Figure 8.14d), depending on the degree of resharpening of the specimens. Though several type names (e.g., Saratoga Stemmed, Saratoga Broad Bladed, and straight-stemmed Matanzas) have been used in reference to this general morphological type, we refer to this as the "Saratoga" cluster (with a tip of the hat to Howard Winters). The straight-stemmed, weak-shouldered Karnak point, with its characteristic double-beveled resharpening pattern, is poorly represented, with only two specimens identified (not illustrated here). Making an initial appearance in this strata group are specimens ($n = 8$) assigned to the Helton cluster (Figure 8.14e, f). Many type names have been coined for the broad array of minor morphological variations that are exhibited within this cluster (e.g., Big Creek, Williams, Helton, Saratoga Expanding Stemmed, and Elko), but here we focus on the common attributes (broad blade, convex base, absence of grinding, and expanding-stem to corner-notched haft shape) that distinguish this cluster from other types and clusters in the Modoc assemblages, and we apply the name used by Cook (1976) for points from the Koster site. Small side-notched points with distinct notches (Figure 8.14g) are not as common as in earlier assemblages ($n = 5$), but they still account for more than a trace of this large assemblage. A single side-notched flake point (not illustrated, but see Figure 8.13f, g) attests to the continued expedient manufacture of side-notched points. Also present in small proportions are two untyped medium-sized points with large and deep corner notches (Figure 8.14h), a single small corner-notched point (Figure 8.14i) with diminutive but pronounced notches, and a single Table Rock point (Figure 8.14j) with characteristic grinding on the expanding-stem margins.

Material from this strata group shows a major increase in hafting variation compared with that from the MAR4 strata group, though some of this diversity derives only from variations on the general side-notched theme. In the MAR5 group, side-notched points (including all types and clusters) still number 77 of 103 points identifiable to hafting mode, or 76 percent of the assemblage. Points with corner-notched to expanding-stemmed hafts are next most common, and straight-stemmed points are also well represented compared with other strata-group assemblages.

MAR6 Strata Group (Helton Phase, 5500–5000 B.P.)

This strata group is composed of reconstructed Stratum A2 and its correlates (10E and 10AE) in the East Pillar area.

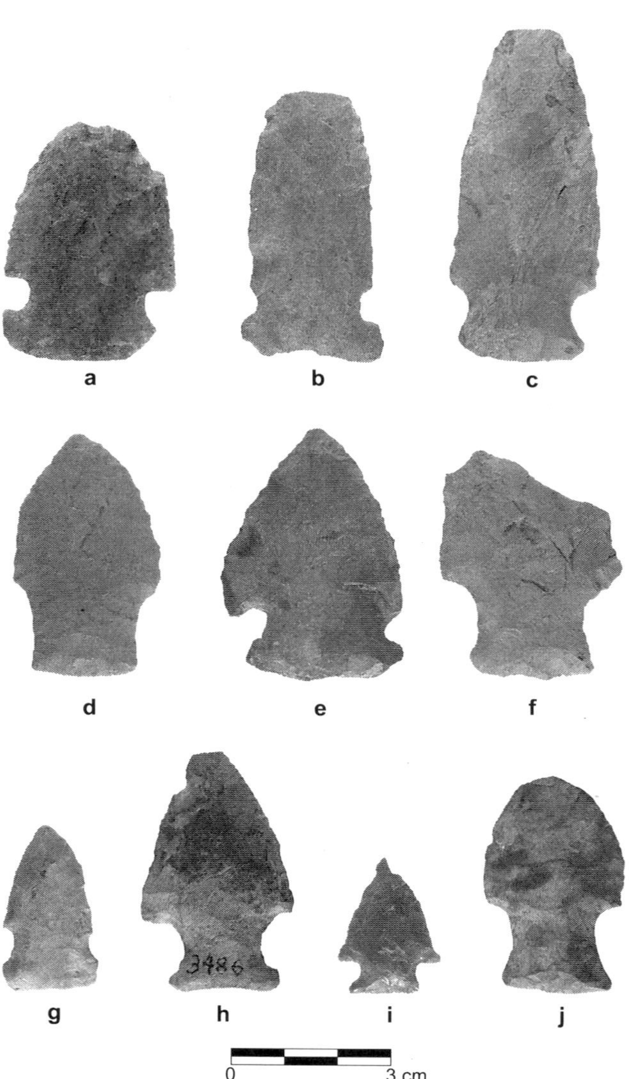

Figure 8.14. Projectile points from MAR5 contexts: a, large side-notched, Stratum 1MT; b, large side-notched with concave base, Stratum A; c, Matanzas, Stratum A; d, Saratoga, Stratum A; e, f, Helton, Stratum A; g, small side-notched, Stratum A; h, medium-sized, deep corner-notched, Stratum A; i, small corner-notched, Stratum A; j, Table Rock, Stratum A.

The sample size from these strata is large ($n = 92$), resulting from the extensive excavations of the 1955 season. The diversity of point types and clusters in this assemblage is also high, but the proportions of specific types and clusters are radically different from those associated with the preceding MAR5 strata group. Of the total, 20 points are unidentifiable, including four fragments of possible contracting-stemmed points, one fragment of a side-notched point, and 13 specimens too fragmentary to be assigned to a specific hafting mode. Single examples of an Etley point and a possible Mule Road point were recovered, but these point types were manufactured much later than the time span represented by this stratigraphic setting. The Mule Road point may be a broken and subsequently rehafted specimen, and the reworking might have considerably altered the original haft morphology.

Of the identifiable points (Figure 8.15), the most common, with 24 examples, belong to the corner-notched to expanding-stemmed Helton cluster (Figure 8.15a). The second most common point type, with 13 specimens, is the faintly side-notched Matanzas type (Figure 8.15b), while the third most common points ($n = 11$) belong to the large, deeply side-notched cluster (Figure 8.15d). Saratoga-cluster (Figure 8.15c) points are fewer in number than in the preceding strata group, but they constitute a slightly higher proportion of the total assemblage. The remaining point types and clusters in this assemblage are represented by three or fewer specimens per type. Small, deeply side-notched points (Figure 8.15f) continue to decrease in representation from earlier contexts, with only three specimens recovered. The straight- to slightly contracting-stem Karnak point (Figure 8.15e) is represented again by only two specimens. Single examples of a medium-sized, deeply corner-notched point (Figure 8.15g), a possible Smith or Eva basally notched point (Figure 8.15h), a side-notched flake point, a possible Apple Blossom Stemmed (Cook 1976), and a Table Rock point make up the remainder of this diverse assemblage.

Like that from MAR5, this strata-group assemblage shows high variability in point morphology compared with earlier MAR2–MAR4 strata-group assemblages. In addition, the proportion of points assignable to the general side-notched hafting mode is markedly lower. This group makes up 28 of 72 points identifiable to hafting mode, or 38.9 percent of the assemblage. Points with corner-notched to expanding-stemmed hafts are almost as common, with 27 examples (37.5 percent). Also well represented are straight-stemmed and contracting-stemmed points, which makes this strata group more diverse than the preceding assemblages.

Figure 8.15. Projectile points from MAR6 contexts; all are from Stratum A2: a, Helton; b, Matanzas; c, Saratoga; d, large side-notched; e, possible Karnak; f, small side-notched; g, medium with deep corner notches; h, possible Smith basal-notched.

LAR1 Strata Group (Falling Springs Phase, 5000–4400 B.P.)

This strata group is composed of Stratum 9E in the East Pillar area (see Ahler et al. 1992) and the correlated reconstructed Strata B and H in the remainder of the Main Shelter. The sample size from these strata is large (total of 95), resulting from the extensive 1955 excavations. The diversity of point types and clusters in this assemblage is relatively high, but the proportions are different relative to the MAR6 strata-group assemblage. Of the total, 29 points are considered unidentifiable. Not included in the point total is a single example of an Early Archaic Hardin Barbed point that is likely recycled from a nearby site.

Of the 66 identifiable points (Figure 8.16), by far the most common cluster represented, with 52 examples, is the corner-notched to expanding-stemmed Helton cluster (Figure 18.16a–d), which exhibits a rather wide variety of hafting widths and basal shapes. Many of these points compare favorably to Falling Springs points, first named by McElrath

Figure 8.16. Projectile points from LAR1 contexts: a, Helton, Stratum B; b, Helton, Stratum B; c, Helton, Stratum B; d, Helton with deep notches and undamaged barbs, Stratum 8E; e, Etley, Stratum B; f, Matanzas, Stratum B.

(1986), but they also are within the general parameters of the Helton cluster as used here. Four points are assigned to the large, generally expanding-stemmed Etley type (Figure 8.16e). Etley points exhibit considerable variation in hafting morphology, but they can be distinguished from other point types of similar age by their greater length and thickness and their flaking patterns. They also exhibit a general lack of heat treatment compared with the routinely heat-treated Helton points. All of the Modoc Etley points are at least 9.8 mm thick. Another four points are included in the Matanzas faintly side-notched type (Figure 8.16f). Though still present, deeply side-notched points account for a much smaller proportion of the assemblage. Only a single point is assigned to the small side-notched cluster, another is assigned to the large side-notched cluster, and a single side-notched flake point was recovered (none are illustrated here, but see Figures 8.14 and 8.15 for examples). Also present are single examples of the basally notched Smith or Eva type, the Saratoga Straight Stemmed type, and the unnamed type with small but pronounced corner notches (none are shown here).

The assemblage from this strata group shows overall high variability in gross point morphology, but it is clearly dominated by points assigned to the Helton cluster. This cluster makes up 78.8 percent of the identifiable assemblage (52 of 66 points). Etley and Matanzas points each constitute 6.1 percent of the assemblage, with four examples. The remaining 9 percent of the assemblage is represented by single examples of six separate types and clusters. Only three side-notched points are present, accounting for 4.5 percent of points identifiable to general hafting mode, and these specimens may have been incorporated into these strata by prehistoric pit excavation or reuse of serviceable points. The data from Modoc strongly indicate that, with few exceptions, side-notched points were, indeed, confined to the Middle Archaic period.

LAR2 Strata Group (Titterington Phase, 4400–3800 B.P.)

This strata group is composed of Stratum 7E (see Ahler et al. 1992) in the East Pillar area and the correlated reconstructed Strata C and D in the West Pillar-Unit F portion of the Main Shelter. The sample size from this group is smaller than for other strata groups (total of 41) because these strata were removed by heavy machinery from the central part of the Main Shelter before professional excavations began. Of the total, nine points are unidentifiable, all of which are specimens too fragmentary to be assigned to a specific hafting mode.

Of the 32 identifiable points (Figure 8.17), the most common type represented, with 17 specimens, is the large, thick, coarsely flaked, expanding-stemmed Etley type (Figure 8.17a–c), which shows considerable variation in haft morphology. The second most common points (nine specimens) belong to the shorter, thinner, expanding-stemmed to corner-notched Helton cluster (Figure 8.17d; note that, because of considerable narrowing of the resharpened blade, this specimen arguably could be placed in the Matanzas category, which illustrates the difficulties of relying on single specimens for temporal or typological assessments). A few examples of broad-bladed, straight-stemmed points could be classified either as Saratoga or as Etley points (Figure 8.17e); they are thinner than the usual Etley points and have narrower stems, and stem bases are often truncated or unworked. The assemblage is completed by single examples of a lanceolate Late Archaic Sedalia point (not illustrated), a broad-bladed point with a diminutive contracting stem (Figure 8.17f) similar to Mule Road points defined by McElrath (1993), a possible late Late Archaic Prairie Lake or Springly point with characteristic expanding stem and lateral asymmetry (not shown), and a Table Rock point. The latter is likely recycled and out of its original stratigraphic context.

The assemblage from this strata group shows overall high variability in point morphology, but it is clearly dominated by Etley points. This type makes up 17 of 32 (53.1 percent) of the identifiable assemblage. Helton points constitute another 28.1 percent of the assemblage. The remaining 19 percent of the assemblage is represented by one or two examples of

Figure 8.17. Projectile points from LAR2 contexts: a–c, Etley, Stratum C; d, Helton, Stratum 7E; e, Etley/Saratoga, Stratum D; f, Mule Road, Stratum 7E.

points assigned to five separate types and clusters. Side-notched points are absent from the assemblage.

Correlations and Trends

The assemblages discussed above are highly variable, which may be a direct function of the sample sizes from the various strata groups. To test for correlation between sample size and diversity, a Simpson diversity-index (D_s [Brower and Zar 1977]) value was calculated for each of the strata-group assemblages. Unidentifiable points and items considered to be out of place stratigraphically were excluded from these calculations. As indicated in the lower two lines in Table 8.3, there is no apparent correlation between assemblage diversity and sample size. The two highest diversity values are associated with relatively low sample sizes, while most of the assemblages have moderately high diversity values (.7 to .8), regardless of sample size.

If assemblage diversity is not a direct function of sample size, there still may be relationships between assemblage diversity and the function of the site in a local settlement system. These relationships are complex and not readily amenable to statistical analyses, but they should be explored. Fowler and Ahler (1991), as well as Ahler and Styles (1998), have presented summary interpretations of changes in the function of Modoc in its local settlement system based on analyses of lithic and faunal assemblage diversity, artifact density, feature types, stratigraphic attributes, and sedimentation rates. These analyses indicate that the EAR1 and EAR2 strata groups are mainly characterized by a series of superimposed short-term use episodes and that, during the time span represented, the site likely served primarily as a residential camp in the local settlement system. EAR1 has the lowest diversity values, while EAR2 has the highest. However, with a sample size of only two for the EAR1 assemblage, the possible diversity values are limited to either 0 (no diversity), if both points belong to the same type or cluster, or 1 (maximum diversity) if the points are different. Combining the EAR1 and EAR2 assemblages gives a composite diversity value of .886. The high diversity in these early assemblages may be related to the variable, short-term use of the site. These occupations generally lack thick midden deposits and exhibit low density and diversity of both lithic and faunal assemblages (see Ahler and Styles 1998; Fowler and Ahler 1991). However, the uppermost stratum in the Main Shelter EAR2 sequence is a thick layer with high lithic and faunal densities and diversities, a variety of surface and pit features, and the earliest burials from the site (Anderson 1991). Collectively, these data indicate a shift in the later part of the EAR2 time span from short-term episodic site use to longer-term use. However, the high diversity value for this strata group suggests continued manufacture of points with a wide range of hafting styles.

The MAR1, MAR2, and MAR3 assemblages derive from strata with attributes that indicate site use alternating between periods of intense or long-term use and episodic or short-term occupation. Yet most of the points in these groups are derived from strata interpreted as representing periods of longer-term site use, likely as a seasonal or multiseasonal base camp. All assemblages are still moderately high in diversity, with values generally steady between .80 and .82, regardless of sample size or a trend toward more intensive use of the site through this time span (8000 to 6500 B.P.). The effects of a strong focus on side-notched hafting are seen in the drop in diversity values for the MAR4 strata-group assemblage. However, the strata in this group have attributes indicative of nearly continuous long-term occupation, so there appears to be no strong correlation between intensity of site use and diversity of point assemblages in the first half of the Middle Archaic period.

The stratigraphy and artifact density data indicate that MAR5, MAR6, and LAR1 strata groups all represent long-term, probably continuous, occupation of the site. Though the diversity indexes for the MAR5 and MAR6 groups are moderately high (.7 to .8), with values consistent with other strata sets indicative of long-term occupations, the LAR1 group has the lowest diversity (.376) of any strata group except for EAR1. This drop in diversity values is not related to assemblage size, and it is also apparently not related to changes in site use. The detailed analyses of the early Late Archaic Falling Springs component (LAR1) conducted by Ahler et al. (1992) present multiple lines of evidence indicating that the site functioned as a long-term base camp during this time span. The point assemblage is clearly dominated by the Helton cluster (Table 8.3), which accounts for the low diversity index. Grouping all the broad corner-notched to expanding-stem points in the LAR1 strata group into the Helton cluster has certainly masked some morphological variation. Detailed analysis of the assemblage shows numerous morphological categories definable by minor variations on the general Helton-cluster theme (see Figure 8.16a–d), but these minor variants have been lumped together in other strata groups (MAR5 and MAR6) without a noticeable decline in the diversity-index values. Early Late Archaic assemblages probably are truly dominated by these broad corner-notched points, similar to the dominance of the deeply side-notched

Table 8.3. Projectile Point Types and Clusters Represented in Each Strata Group.

	Strata Group										
Type or Cluster	EAR1	EAR2	MAR1	MAR2	MAR3	MAR4	MAR5	MAR6	LAR1	LAR2	Total
Mule Road	—	—	—	—	—	—	—	1★	—	1	2
Sedalia	—	—	—	—	—	—	—	—	—	1	1
Prairie Lake/Springly?	—	—	—	—	—	—	—	—	—	1	1
Eva/Smith	—	—	—	—	—	—	—	1	1	—	2
Etley	—	—	—	—	—	—	—	1★	**4**	**17**	22
Apple Blossom Stem	—	—	—	—	—	—	1	1	—	—	2
Karnak Stemmed	—	—	—	—	—	—	2	2	—	—	4
Thin, deep corner notched	—	—	—	—	—	—	2	1	1	—	4
Table Rock	—	—	—	—	—	—	1	1	—	1★	3
Helton	—	—	—	—	—	—	**8**	**24**	**52**	**9**	93
Saratoga	—	—	—	—	—	—	**11**	**10**	1	2	24
Matanzas	—	—	—	—	—	—	**31**	**13**	4	—	48
Side-notched flake point	—	—	—	—	—	3	—	1	1	—	5
Large side-notched	—	—	—	**6**	**4**	**16**	**41**	**11**	1	—	79
Small side-notched	—	—	—	**5**	**4**	**12**	**5**	3	1	—	30
Cypress Creek II (thin)	—	—	—	**6**	**3**	—	—	—	—	—	9
Cypress Creek I (thick)	—	—	**4**	**6**	1	—	—	—	—	—	11
Untyped corner-notched	—	—	—	1	1	—	—	—	—	—	2
Bass Knife	—	—	1	—	—	—	—	—	—	—	1
Jakie Stemmed?	—	—	1	1	—	—	—	—	—	—	2
Small corner-notched dart	—	—	1		—	—	—	—	—	—	1
Hidden Valley	—	**2**	1★	1★	—	1★	—	—	—	—	5
Stanly	—	1	—	—	—	—	—	—	—	—	1
Rice Lanceolate	—	**2**	—	—	—	—	1★	—	—	—	3
Kirk Corner Notched/ Stemmed	—	**5**	**3**	—	—	1★	—	—	—	—	9
Small bifurcate base	—	**3**	—	—	—	—	—	—	—	—	3
Big Sandy?	—	1	—	—	—	—	—	—	—	—	1
Graham Cave	**2**	—	—	—	—	—	—	—	—	—	2
Unidentifiable	2	5	5	16	12	13	22	20	29	9	133
Total	4	19	16	42	25	46	125	90	95	41	503
Not included in assemblage totals[a]											
Hardin Barbed	—	1	—	—	—	—	—	—	1	—	2
Dalton	1	1	1	3	—	—	—	—	—	—	6
N per assemblage	2	14	10	25	13	31	102	68	66	31	
D_s Index value	0	.835	.800	.817	.808	.594	.732	.799	.376	.628	

Note. Items marked with an asterisk (★) denote points that are outside of their expected context and likely have been recycled and redeposited from other contexts. They are excluded from illustrations and assemblage analyses.

[a]These items are definitely recycled and redeposited outside of their original context of manufacture, use, and discard.

clusters shown in the MAR4 assemblage. Finally, the LAR2 strata group represents a shift in site use toward more seasonal or specialized activities, though the site apparently was used intensively throughout the Titterington phase (Ahler et al. 1992; Ahler and Styles 1998). The higher diversity value for this assemblage is comparable to those for the MAR5 and MAR6 assemblages.

These data collectively suggest that assemblage diversity is relatively independent of both gross site function and the intensity or duration of site use. If this is the case, and if diversity is also independent of sample sizes (except for extremely small samples with $n < 4$), then the data presented in Table 8.3 most likely reflect the patterned behavior of cultural practices and choices. This interpretation is supported by the strata-group assemblages that show clear domination by one or two types or clusters and by the often-documented rise and subsequent decline in the proportion of individual types or clusters through time. However, the data also clearly show that (with the exception of the minimal sample from EAR1 contexts) no single point type or cluster is either confined to a single strata group or is the only point type in any given strata group. This finding, relating to a well-dated, stratigraphically refined series of assemblages, strongly indicates the need for assemblage-based analyses that do not rely on a single point type to characterize a given time period. These data also show that the assemblages represented in the Modoc strata groups likely reflect cultural behavior rather than the effects of sample size or site function on assemblage composition. This makes the assemblage more robust when used for comparative purposes and for age estimation of undated assemblages.

The most common points and clusters in each of the strata groups have been designated in bold in Table 8.3. This information is useful for identifying trends through time and also for making comparisons of undated assemblages to the dated assemblages from Modoc (see below). For now, some observations can be made regarding the dated range of some of the more easily identified (and least ambiguous) point types. Graham Cave points are limited to the EAR1 assemblage, which at Modoc dates between about 9,000 and 8,500 years ago. They may also date as early as about 9500 B.P., but contexts dating to this age are not preserved in the excavated sample from Modoc. Stanly, Rice Lanceolate, and small bifurcate-base points are confined to EAR2 contexts (8500 to 8000 B.P.); Hidden Valley points are also probably most strongly related to this time span, though likely recycled Hidden Valley points were recovered from later assemblages. Points assigned to the Kirk Corner Notched cluster are confined to the EAR2 and MAR1 strata groups, giving them a general time range of 8500 to 7500 B.P.

The thicker Cypress Creek I points are most common in MAR1 and MAR2 contexts (8000 to 7000 B.P.), while the thinner and smaller Cypress Creek II are confined to MAR2 and MAR3 strata (7500 to 6500 B.P.). Points in both the large and small side-notched clusters have long histories of manufacture, ranging in age from about 7500 to 5000 B.P. (MAR2 through MAR6). These point clusters, however, comprise the majority of points in both the MAR3 and MAR4 assemblages (7000 to 6000 B.P.), and few other point types or clusters are represented. Saratoga and Matanzas points are most commonly found in MAR5 and MAR6 contexts (6000 to 5000 B.P.), though they may have continued to be made into the LAR1 period. Table Rock and Karnak points, though rare in the Modoc assemblages, are also apparently confined to the MAR5 and MAR6 groups. Points assigned to the Helton cluster began to be made in the MAR5 period, increased in the MAR6 period, and strongly dominate the assemblage from the LAR1 period (5000 to 4400 B.P.). Specimens assigned to this cluster may also be found in LAR2 contexts, but they constitute a much lower proportion of the assemblage. Etley points are present in the LAR1 assemblage but are the most numerous point type in the LAR2 group. Other point types found only in LAR2 contexts at Modoc are Sedalia and possible Mule Road points.

Several trends in raw material procurement and thermal alteration are evident. On the basis of macroscopic characteristics (color, texture, cortex, and inclusions), we sorted 484 points into 17 established raw material types (Tables 8.4 and 8.5). Nineteen points from the total sample were excluded primarily because they were early points recovered from later strata (i.e., recycled or redeposited). Points with ambiguous raw material characteristics were placed into an indeterminate category as were points that were too fragmentary or too severely burned to be identified with confidence. Descriptions of raw material types and their source areas are not presented here but can be found in several other reports (Koldehoff 1985, 2002a, 2002b; Ray 1984, 1998).

The identified raw materials fall into four groups on the basis of source location. The first group includes four chert types with exposures in and along the Mississippi River bluffs in Illinois within 25 km of Modoc Rock Shelter. These are Ste. Genevieve, St. Louis, Salem, and Kinkaid. Combined, these types account for 11.2 percent of the point assemblage. Ste. Genevieve chert is noteworthy because it is exposed within the limestone bedrock that forms the lower part of the shelter and is also common in bluff exposures on the Missouri side of the Mississippi River. However, as noted by Fowler (1959:24) and Ahler et al. (1992:96), the deposit at Modoc itself is narrow and internally fractured, as are nearby exposures. While Ste. Genevieve chert is immediately available, it is of limited utility, especially in terms of biface production (see Table 8.4). However, Ste. Genevieve chert was routinely used for simple flake tools. Archaic inhabitants of the shelter typically maximized the utility of the points and bifaces they brought to the site and relied on Ste. Genevieve chert for expedient tools.

A second group of lithic resources includes Burlington chert, Fern Glen chert, Jefferson City chert, Roubidoux orthoquartzite, and St. Francois rhyolite, all of which occur in Missouri within 45 km of Modoc. In total, these materials represent 62.1 percent of the points in our sample, but

Table 8.4. Summary of Raw Material Types Represented in Strata Groups.

Raw Material	Parent Formation	Geologic System	Distance (km)[a]	N[b]	Percent
Ste. Genevieve chert	Ste. Genevieve	Mississippian	0	23	4.8
St. Louis chert	St. Louis	Mississippian	2	2	.4
Salem chert	Salem	Mississippian	10	18	3.7
Burlington chert	Burlington	Mississippian	10	278	57.6
Fern Glen chert	Fern Glen	Mississippian	10	10	2.1
Jefferson City chert	Jefferson City	Ordovician	20	4	.8
Roubidoux quartzite	Roubidoux	Ordovician	20	2	.4
Blair/St. David chert	Carbondale	Pennsylvanian	25	3	.6
Kinkaid Fossiliferous chert	Kinkaid	Mississippian	25	11	2.3
St. Francois rhyolite	?	Precambrian	45	6	1.2
Bailey chert	Bailey	Devonian	75	20	4.1
Cobden/Dongola chert	St. Louis	Mississippian	90	16	3.3
Kaolin chert	?	Mississippian	90	2	.4
Mill Creek chert	Salem/Ullin	Mississippian	110	1	.2
Elco/Dover chert	Ft. Payne	Mississippian	115	1	.2
Kornthal chert	McNairy	Cretaceous	115	2	.4
Mounds chert	Mounds	Pliocene	120	3	.6
Indeterminate	?	?	?	82	17.0
Total				484	99.9

[a]Approximate straight-line distance to closest or most likely source.
[b]Nineteen points were excluded from raw material analysis.

Burlington by itself makes up 57.6 percent of the total. Burlington chert was clearly the preferred raw material, but it is unlikely that all of the Burlington-chert points in our sample were manufactured from chert gathered from this section of Missouri. Rather, Burlington chert was also probably procured from source areas at Valmeyer in Illinois (36 km northwest of Modoc) and from the Crescent quarries in Missouri (60 km northwest of Modoc). Blair/St. David chert, with scattered exposures 25 km east of Modoc in the interior uplands of Randolph County, represents a third resource, albeit one that was little used. It is represented by only three points (.6 percent of the sample). The fourth group of lithic resources encompasses a series of cherts derived primarily from sources in extreme southern Illinois—Bailey, Cobden/Dongola, Kaolin, Mill Creek, Elco/Dover, Kornthal, and Mounds gravel. Combined, these cherts account for 9 percent of the total sample, indicating that they were never a major resource. Yet their presence indicates persistent long-distance relationships between Modoc and chert resource areas located 75 to 120 km to the southeast.

Overall, the Archaic inhabitants of Modoc Rock Shelter primarily focused on Burlington chert for point production, and this production did not typically occur on-site. Burlington-chert points were manufactured elsewhere and were used, maintained, recycled, and discarded on-site, indicating that Modoc was not routinely visited for its lithic resources. Instead, groups inhabiting the shelter were likely engaging in subsistence activities, using curated lithic tools manufactured at other locations. Less than 10 percent of the points are made from immediately available Ste. Genevieve (n = 23) and St. Louis (n = 2) cherts; most points are made from raw materials with source areas at least 10 km distant from Modoc. However, only 9 percent of the points are made from raw materials with source areas greater than 50 km distant (i.e., the southern Illinois cherts). Thus, raw material procurement for point production largely focused on regionally available resources (what Ahler [1984, 1998] referred to as "semi-local" materials), with Burlington chert being the preferred or central resource. The preeminence of Burlington chert at Modoc—and at most sites in the region—likely stems from a combination of its availability, abundance, and high quality. At most sources, especially at the Crescent quarries, large blocks and nodules of moderate- to high-quality chert are numerous. The array of lesser-used chert types in the sample provides clues to the direction and distance that groups may have moved prior to residing at Modoc or to the locations with which Modoc inhabitants had regular and frequent interactions. Only Bailey (3.9 percent) and Cobden/Dongola (3.3 percent) cherts are present in qualities sufficient to indicate limited but persistent utilization of these resources or limited but persistent interaction with groups that had regular access to these resources.

These patterns are evident at Modoc throughout the time span of its occupation. For example, across all strata groups, Burlington chert is the dominant raw material. However, its popularity increases slightly from the Early Archaic into the Middle Archaic strata, and remains high through the Late Archaic strata (Table 8.5). Likewise, an array of minor chert types is represented in each strata group, but southern Illinois cherts decrease slightly in popularity from the Early Archaic into the Late Archaic levels. Finally, intentional thermal alteration for technological or aesthetic purposes (i.e., heat

Table 8.5. Raw Material Types and Thermal Alteration Condition by Strata Group.

Raw Material	EAR1/ EAR2 n	%	MAR1 n	%	MAR2 n	%	MAR3 n	%	MAR4 n	%	MAR5 n	%	MAR6 n	%	LAR1 n	%	LAR2 n	%	Total
Burlington	10	43.5	8	53.3	22	53.7	14	58.3	26	60.5	72	59.5	51	60.0	55	59.8	20	50.0	278
Fern Glen	1	4.3	—	—	—	—	—	—	—	—	2	1.4	2	2.3	4	4.3	1	2.5	10
Salem	1	4.3	—	—	2	4.9	—	—	5	11.6	7	5.8	—	—	2	2.2	1	2.5	18
St. Louis	—	—	—	—	—	—	—	—	—	—	—	—	—	—	2	2.2	—	—	2
Ste. Genevieve	1	4.3	2	13.3	1	2.4	1	4.2	—	—	8	6.6	5	5.9	3	3.3	2	5.0	23
Kinkaid	—	—	—	—	1	2.4	1	4.2	3	7.0	3	2.5	1	1.2	1	1.1	1	2.5	11
Blair/St. David	—	—	—	—	—	—	—	—	—	—	1	.8	1	1.2	—	—	1	2.5	3
Jefferson City	—	—	—	—	1	2.4	—	—	—	—	1	.8	—	—	1	1.1	1	2.5	4
Roubidoux	—	—	—	—	—	—	—	—	—	—	1	.8	—	—	—	—	1	2.5	2
Rhyolite	1	4.3	—	—	—	—	—	—	—	—	2	1.7	—	—	1	1.1	2	5.0	6
Bailey	3	13.0	1	6.7	2	4.9	—	—	1	2.3	1	.8	4	4.7	5	5.4	3	7.5	20
Cobden/Dongola	1	4.3	—	—	2	4.9	2	8.3	3	7.0	4	3.3	3	3.5	1	1.1	—	—	16
Kaolin	1	4.3	—	—	—	—	—	—	—	—	1	.8	—	—	—	—	—	—	2
Mill Creek	—	—	—	—	—	—	—	—	—	—	—	—	—	—	1	1.1	—	—	1
Elco/Dover	—	—	—	—	—	—	—	—	—	—	—	—	—	—	—	—	1	2.5	1
Kornthal	—	—	—	—	—	—	—	—	—	—	—	—	1	1.2	1	1.1	—	—	2
Mounds	—	—	1	6.7	—	—	—	—	1	2.3	—	—	1	1.2	—	—	—	—	3
Indeterminate	4	17.4	3	20.0	10	24.4	6	25.0	4	9.3	18	14.9	16	18.8	15	16.3	6	15.0	82
Total	23		15		41		24		43		121		85		92		40		484
Thermal Alteration																			
Unaltered	11	47.8	5	33.3	10	24.4	5	20.8	9	20.9	28	23.1	18	21.2	17	18.5	20	50.0	123
Heat treated	1	4.3	5	33.3	10	24.4	5	20.8	12	27.9	40	33.1	30	35.3	37	40.2	9	22.5	149
Burned/charred	11	47.8	5	33.3	21	51.2	14	58.3	22	51.2	51	42.1	34	40.0	36	39.1	10	25.0	204
Indeterminate	—	—	—	—	—	—	—	—	—	—	2	1.7	3	3.5	2	2.2	1	2.5	8
Total	23		15		41		24		43		121		85		92		40		484

treatment) increased markedly through time. It is poorly represented in the Early Archaic strata (4.3 percent), sharply increases in the Middle Archaic strata (33.3 percent), peaks in the LAR1 Falling Springs–phase strata group (40.2 percent), and decreases in the LAR2, or Titterington-phase, strata group (22.5 percent). This trend in thermal alternation is typical of Archaic point assemblages across the region, as is the overall predominance of Burlington chert.

Applying the Modoc Assemblage Data

The well-dated assemblages described for Modoc can be used to provide age estimates for surface collections or other undated assemblages. The assemblages described here, separated into roughly 500-year temporal spans, can provide better age estimates for undated materials than were previously available. We stress that the most useful and accurate way to use the data presented here is to compare assemblages with relatively robust sample sizes, rather than to focus on small assemblages that may be biased by collection strategies, surface visibility, or other factors. To illustrate the utility of the Modoc assemblages, we employ them in this section to obtain an age estimate on a sample of materials obtained from surface collection at the Modoc Village site (11R266), which covers several hectares of bluff crest about 3 km southeast from Modoc Rock Shelter (Figure 8.1). This assemblage is particularly appropriate as a test because of its geographic proximity to Modoc Rock Shelter. In addition, limited excavations at the site documented features that were later radiocarbon dated, providing an independent means of verifying the age estimates based on assemblage comparisons.

The Modoc Village Site

Discovered as a result of the Historic Sites Surveys conducted in 1973 by University of Illinois archaeologists (Porter and Linder 1974), the Modoc Village site is an extensive multi-component habitation area. In 1995 James Marlen, a member of the Cahokia Archaeological Society (CAS), took over ownership and stewardship of the site. Efforts to widen the narrow, entrenched field road that roughly divides the site in half led to a salvage archaeological project. Because Mr. Marlen was sensitive to the research potential of the site, he contacted Koldehoff, who visited the site and made arrangements to conduct volunteer excavations of features that would likely be exposed when the plow zone was stripped from the new field road area. The frequencies of diagnostic artifacts visible in these initial visits led Koldehoff to expect the primary occupations in the vicinity of the field road to be Middle Archaic and Late Woodland.

The new field road area was stripped of plow zone in 1995 and 1996, exposing a total of 66 prehistoric pits in a stripped area of about 750 m^2 (Ahler and Koldehoff 2002). These were excavated by CAS volunteers and by students in Timothy Pauketat's 1996 State University of New York at Buffalo field school. Subsequently, all artifacts and float samples were processed and analyzed. As suggested by the surface collections from this part of the site, most of the pit features were apparently Archaic in age. They contained only lithic artifacts, carbonized nutshells, and a few small calcined bone fragments. Features that produced large ceramic sherds were assigned to the Late Woodland period and are not further considered in this chapter. Three of the features also produced diagnostic Archaic projectile points, discussed below.

Modoc Village Assemblage

Mr. Marlen has made surface collections of the site for several years. These surface materials were made available to Koldehoff for analysis, and they provide an undated point sample to compare to the strata-group assemblages from Modoc Rock Shelter. Table 8.6 shows the Archaic- and Paleoindian-period point types and clusters represented in the surface collections from Modoc Village, sorted by raw material type. The ranges and proportions of raw materials are highly similar in the Modoc Rock Shelter and Modoc Village samples. For instance, Burlington chert is the predominant raw material across all point types and clusters; only modest numbers of points are made from local cherts (Ste. Genevieve, Salem, and St. Louis); and southern Illinois cherts, particularly Bailey and Cobden/Dongola, are represented in low but persistent numbers. The points in this sample suggest that nonlocal materials are more common among earlier point types. Burlington is the most common raw material type, regardless of time period. This is not surprising given the generally high quality of Burlington material and its local availability. Etley, Helton, and large side-notched points are also made on a very wide range of raw materials, which suggests extensive exchange and interregional contact during times when these points were made. We note that very few straight-stemmed Karnak points were identified in the Modoc Rock Shelter assemblage, while the straight-stemmed Saratoga point cluster was not identified in Koldehoff's typological assessment of the Modoc Village assemblage. Most of the straight-stemmed Saratoga points were subsumed into the Etley cluster in Koldehoff's analysis of the Modoc Village materials, and Karnak points were much more frequent in that assemblage than at Modoc Rock Shelter. These differences may partially reflect analysts' preferences for placement of points into various clusters. Regardless, both Saratoga and Karnak points are commonly found in late Middle Archaic contexts and are associated with the MAR5 and MAR6 strata groups (5000 to 6000 B.P.) at Modoc Rock Shelter.

Table 8.6. Surface-Collected Projectile Points from the Modoc Village Site by Type or Cluster and Raw Material.

	Raw Material Type										
Type or Cluster	Burlington	Fern Glen	Salem	St. Louis	Ste. Genevieve	Bailey	Cobden	Jefferson City	Rhyolite	Indeterminate	Total
Clovis	2	—	—	—	—	—	—	—	—	—	2
Dalton	3	1	—	—	—	—	—	—	1	—	5
St. Charles	—	—	—	—	—	—	1	—	—	—	1
Graham Cave	—	1	—	—	—	—	—	—	—	—	1
Kirk Corner-Notch	2	—	—	—	—	1	—	—	—	—	3
Small bifurcate	—	—	1	—	—	—	—	—	—	—	1
Bass Knife	1	—	—	—	—	—	—	—	—	—	1
Large side-notched	57	5	—	—	1	—	—	—	—	3	66
Small side-notched	5	—	—	—	—	—	—	—	—	—	5
Helton	28	6	—	—	—	2	—	1	1	1	39
Matanzas	13	1	—	—	—	—	—	—	—	—	14
Karnak	6	1	1	—	—	3	—	—	—	1	12
Table Rock	1	—	—	—	—	—	—	—	—	—	1
Etley	18	3	—	—	—	3	1	—	—	1	26
Wadlow/Sedalia	1	—	—	—	—	—	—	—	—	—	1
Riverton	6	—	—	—	—	—	—	—	—	2	8
Prairie Lake	4	2	—	1	1	3	—	—	—	1	12
Total	147	20	2	1	2	12	2	1	2	9	198

Note: Points are arranged in rough chronological order.

The Modoc Village assemblage clearly is multicomponent, with the entire range of Archaic subperiods represented. This makes statistical comparison with the Modoc dated assemblages extremely difficult, as there is no way to separate the components in the surface assemblage. Even so, several important observations can be made regarding the overall similarity of the proportions of types and clusters to those in the strata-group assemblages, with the goal of assessing the relative intensity of site use during particular time periods. There is weak but consistent representation of Paleoindian and early Early Archaic points, all of which (Clovis, Dalton, and St. Charles) predate any of the dated assemblages from Modoc Rock Shelter. Dalton points are most common in this temporal span, though they still account for only a small fraction of the total assemblage. The Terminal Archaic Riverton and Prairie Lake periods are better represented in the surface collection, with about 10 percent of the assemblage assigned to these clusters. While a few of these points were recovered from Modoc Rock Shelter, they are from undated strata that overlie the most recent of the dated strata groups.

Points found in the EAR1, EAR2, and MAR1 assemblages at Modoc are also present in the Modoc Village surface collection, but they are represented in relatively low numbers, which indicates low intensity of site use during this temporal span (9000 to 7500 B.P.). Notably absent are Cypress Creek I and II points, which are almost exclusively found in MAR2 and MAR3 strata groups at Modoc Rock Shelter. However, a few examples of these two point types may have been lumped into either the Helton or Kirk Corner Notched clusters. Of most interest is the high proportion of large side-notched points in the surface collection. While high numbers of large side-notched points are characteristic of MAR3 through MAR6 assemblages, their presence at Modoc Village in combination with low proportions of small side-notched points, the absence of the Cypress Creek points, moderate proportions of both Karnak and Matanzas points, and moderately high proportions of Helton points indicate that the site was used most intensively during the MAR5 and MAR6 time ranges (5000 to 6000 B.P.). Recovery of a single Table Rock point, a type found only in the MAR5 and MAR6 strata groups, supports this interpretation. That Helton points are much less common than the large side-notched points suggests that Modoc Village was not used intensively during the LAR1 (Falling Springs phase) time span. Etley-cluster points, by contrast, are well-represented in the surface collections, which indicates reoccupation or increased intensity of site use during the LAR2 (Titterington phase) period. Given these comparisons, the most intensive use of the Modoc Village area probably took place during the late Middle Archaic period, corresponding to the MAR5 to MAR6 strata groups and a time span of 5000 to 6000 B.P.

Verification

If the above interpretations based solely on assemblage attributes are correct, we would expect the features excavated at the Modoc Village site to produce artifacts consistent with the assemblages recovered from the MAR5 and MAR6 strata groups and radiocarbon dates between 5000 and 6000 B.P. Three of the 66 features excavated at the site in 1995–1996 contained temporally diagnostic projectile points. Feature 46 was a deep basin-shaped pit that produced two fragmentary hafted bifaces—a large, deeply side-notched Godar-like point and a point base with broad, shallow notching that might fall into either the Matanzas or Karnak cluster. Feature 65 was a large, shallow basin that produced three hafted bifaces—an intact point with a straight to slightly expanding stem and large barbs, which might be placed in the Helton cluster, an untyped expanding-stem point base, and a drill with an expanding stem that might have been made by reworking a Helton point. Feature 31 was a shallow basin with scattered charcoal; the fill included a basal fragment of a large, deeply side-notched point similar to Godar points. Collectively, this small assemblage of six points is consistent with assemblages recovered from either MAR5 or MAR6 contexts at Modoc Rock Shelter, but the higher numbers of expanding-stem (Helton?) points suggest a closer affinity to the MAR6 assemblage. These data support the inference from the surface collection data that the site was intensively used during the MAR5–MAR6 time span.

The radiocarbon assays obtained from charcoal recovered from these same features provides a more robust verification of the interpretations (see Ahler and Koldehoff 2002). The sample from Feature 46 produced an uncalibrated assay dating to 5430 ± 80 RCYBP (ISGS-4914). A large charcoal sample (17.06 g) from Feature 65 produced an uncalibrated date of 5180 ± 70 RCYBP (ISGS-4915), and a smaller sample of 3.4 g of carbonized nutshell from Feature 31 produced an uncalibrated assay of 5330 ± 70 RCYBP (ISGS-4921). All of these assays fall into the Helton phase, or the time range for the MAR6 strata group at Modoc Rock Shelter, which is consistent with the observations made on the surface-collected materials. The confirmation of the age of this substantial occupation (possibly a base camp) supports previous interpretations of the Middle Archaic record as a period of settlement relocation focused on utilization of major floodplain and valley-margin resources (Ahler 1998; Ahler and Styles 1998).

Conclusions

The projectile point sequence and associated deposits at Modoc Rock Shelter stand as one of the premier records of Archaic chronology, technology, and subsistence in the Midwest and Midsouth. In this chapter, we have taken advantage of this excellent dated stratigraphic sequence to present a synopsis of the points and to highlight their potential for delineating Archaic components in samples from undated contexts. This discussion would not have been possible without the stratigraphic context and radiocarbon sequences (see Ahler 1993) documented through a series of intensive excavations conducted in both the 1950s and the 1980s. Likewise, the interpretations offered here are enhanced by the analyses conducted on the other (perhaps less spectacular but equally important) material classes that are part of the Modoc collections. We hope that we have illustrated the benefits of conducting these kinds of long-term, interdisciplinary investigations, even though the contributions are often many years in the making. Furthermore, we have provided additional regional context for the Modoc sequence by identifying specific chipped-stone raw material types with known source areas and by providing preliminary information about the substantial Archaic occupation at the nearby bluff-top Modoc Village site.

While we hope that this chapter will be useful to other researchers, our efforts here are far from exhaustive. For instance, several critical aspects of the assemblage have been mentioned only in passing if at all, such as metric attributes, detailed comparisons to established types, and technological attributes. These topics require much more space than is available here and are fodder for future articles.

The aspects of the assemblage that we have emphasized, and some of our assumptions, warrant discussion in these concluding remarks, if only as cautionary notes. First, regardless of the quality of the contexts and the number of points in the assemblage, Modoc Rock Shelter is only one site. The collections from this site are but a small sample of the array of projectile points made throughout the time span considered here. Because it is only a sample, it does not contain the entire range of variation of point types documented for the Midwest or Midsouth. For example, the expanding-stemmed Valmeyer points documented from dated Middle Archaic feature contexts at the Strong site (Adams et al. 1997) are apparently not present at Modoc, though these sites are less than 40 km from each other and the raw material sourcing strongly indicates that Modoc inhabitants also visited the Valmeyer locality. Absence of this point type from Modoc does not invalidate either assemblage; it should remind researchers that even the best-dated assemblages are incomplete.

Another important aspect of our interpretations has been the emphasis on assemblages rather than individual point types. This emphasis has taken two forms. First, we have illustrated and discussed all of the identifiable point types (though we have not illustrated each identifiable specimen) in each stratigraphic-chronological unit, and, second, we have relied heavily on the concept of point "clusters" to recognize that many named types are minor variants on a central morphological or typological theme.

This emphasis on the assemblage rather than specific point types that might be considered modal or "typical" of a particular time range is an attempt to acknowledge and account for the morphological variability that is evident in all of the temporal assemblages described here. By acknowledging this variability we make the claim that this variation is a product of the groups that inhabited the site and not an artificial by-product of our analyses, stratigraphic groupings, or the effects of postdepositional translocation of artifacts. In the above discussion, we have inferred that the variation represented in the strata-group assemblages is largely a result of functional complementarity of the hafting styles. However, the variability may be accounted for through a variety of other mechanisms or processes. Some analysts attribute variation in artifact morphology or style to expression of group or ethnic identity. Though we recognize the tendency toward high mobility and large territories for residential groups and the emergence of strong regional typological traditions during the Archaic period, we do not fully subscribe to the notion that a single point type can be equated with a single ethnic or cultural group. Many other factors affect morphological variability in artifact styles, including systematic use of tools for age- or gender-related activities (see, e.g., Benn and Thompson, this volume); use of tools for specific types of kinetic motions or functions (scraping, cutting, drilling, etc.); technological or physical characteristics of the tool; resharpening, recycling, and rehafting during the use life of individual items; and idiosyncratic stylistic expression of individual toolmakers.

Ahler is of the opinion that much of the morphological variability expressed in the Modoc strata-group assemblages is a direct result of technological and functional variation and should not be attributed principally to group identity. However, other well-dated artifact assemblages express low morphological variability (see, e.g., Stafford and Cantin, this volume), and any high degree of artifact similarity in an assemblage needs to be explained, as does the high variability shown in the Modoc assemblages. Technological studies that track tool use life, resharpening, rehafting, and recycling and functional-kinetic studies of hafted bifaces could contribute greatly to this topic by controlling for some of the factors and creating data sets that can correlate morphology with various technological and functional attributes. The Modoc collections could contribute to these types of studies and help assess the meanings of morphological variability. We stress plural *meanings* because all the factors just enumerated can contribute to systematic variability in artifact styles, and none of them are mutually exclusive. However, before group identity or cultural allegiance is ascribed to stylistic differences in hafted bifaces, some of the more concrete and controllable factors (function, technology, and use life) should be accounted for.

We have not contributed new point type names to the glut of nomenclature that is already available. Neither can new date ranges or true refinements in the chronology of existing types be inferred from this analysis and presentation of the Modoc assemblages. However, with the generally large samples available from dated stratigraphic contexts at Modoc, we have been able to shift the focus toward comparison of assemblages, rather than individual specimens or single point types. The Modoc Village data were presented in part to show how an assemblage-based comparison can be made to the dated Modoc assemblages, even using collections from an obviously multicomponent site. However, the Modoc Village site is in close geographic proximity to Modoc Rock Shelter, and we expected the assemblages to be directly comparable. We caution researchers who might use the Modoc Rock Shelter data to derive date ranges for undated assemblages that more severe geographic limits may apply to assemblage-based comparisons than to comparisons based on individual point types. Again, the presence or absence of Valmeyer points in assemblages from sites in relatively close geographic proximity serves to illustrate this cautionary note. Another aspect of the assemblage-based approach is that the researcher necessarily uses multiple lines of evidence. While one point type may be missing, others may be present that will provide needed evidence. The discussions of raw material types provide another means of comparing assemblages as well as indicating additional chronological trends that cross assemblage boundaries.

In the end, after all of these cautions, we are left with the certain knowledge that researchers should use their best judgment when comparing any of the Modoc assemblages discussed here to other assemblages, dated or undated. We hope and trust that the information presented here will help to refine the interpretative frame of that long-ago era we have come to know as the Archaic, an era for which Modoc Rock Shelter has supplied and will continue to supply important insights.

Acknowledgments

The authors would like to thank the Illinois State Museum for providing access to the Modoc collections. We also thank Bonnie Styles and Bruce McMillan (Illinois State Museum) for their support and guidance over the last 20 years of wrestling with the Modoc collections. The granting agencies that have contributed to these analyses include the National Science Foundation, National Endowment for the Humanities, and National Geographic Society; we acknowledge our debt to them. Finally, we recognize the contributions of Melvin Fowler, who was involved in Modoc from the start and who continues to be an inspiration, and we recognize the contributions of the late Howard Winters, who was also there at the start and who was one of the first researchers to develop the notion of point type clusters.

References Cited

Adams, Brian, Gregory R. Walz, Paul P. Kreisa, Kevin P. McGowan, Jacqueline M. McDowell, and Cynthia L. Balek
1997 *Archaeological Investigations for the Relocation of Valmeyer, Monroe County, Illinois: 2. The Strong Site*. Research Report 28. Public Service Archaeology Program, University of Illinois, Urbana.

Ahler, Steven R.
1984 Archaic Settlement Strategies in the Modoc Locality, Southwest Illinois. Ph.D. dissertation, Department of Anthropology, University of Wisconsin, Milwaukee.
1993 Stratigraphy and Radiocarbon Chronology of Modoc Rock Shelter, Illinois. *American Antiquity* 58:462–488.
1998 Early and Middle Archaic Settlement Systems in the Modoc Locality, Southwest Illinois. *Illinois Archaeology* 10:1–109.

Ahler, Steven R., Mary J. Bade, Frances B. King, Bonnie W. Styles, and Paula Thorson
1992 *Late Archaic Excavations at Modoc Rock Shelter, Randolph County, Illinois*. Report of Investigations 48. Illinois State Museum, Springfield.

Ahler, Steven R., and Brad Koldehoff
2002 Archaic Period Radiocarbon Assays from the Modoc Village Site (11R266): 2001 IAAA Field School Grant Results. *Illinois Antiquity* 37:6–7.

Ahler, Steven R., and Bonnie W. Styles
1998 Changes in Archaic Period Subsistence and Site Function at Modoc Rock Shelter, Randolph County, Illinois. *Illinois Archaeology* 10:110–154.

Anderson, Eve
1991 Re-Analysis of Human Skeletal Remains from Modoc Rock Shelter. Paper presented at the 54th Annual Meeting of the Society for American Archaeology, New Orleans, Louisiana.

Behm, Jeffery A.
1985 Identification and Analysis of Stylistic Variation in Hardin Barbed Points. Ph.D. dissertation, Department of Anthropology, University of Wisconsin, Madison.

Brower, James E., and Jerrold H. Zar
1977 *Field and Laboratory Methods for General Ecology*. William C. Brown, Dubuque, Iowa.

Broyles, Bettye J.
1971 *Second Preliminary Report: The St. Albans Site, Kanawha County, West Virginia 1964–1968*. Report of Archaeological Investigations 3. West Virginia Geological and Economic Survey, Morgantown.

Bryan, Alan L.
1965 Paleo-American Prehistory. *Occasional Papers* 16:125–129. Idaho State University Museum, Pocatello.

Caldwell, Joseph R.
1958 *Trend and Tradition in the Prehistory of the Eastern United States*. Memoir 88. American Anthropological Association, Washington, D.C.

Cook, Thomas G.
1976 *Koster: An Artifact Analysis of Two Archaic Phases in Westcentral Illinois*. Prehistoric Records 1. Northwestern University Archaeological Program, Evanston, Illinois.

Ellis, Christopher J.
1994 Miniature Early Paleo-Indian Stone Artifacts from the Parkhill, Ontario, Site. *North American Archaeologist* 15:253–267.

Fowler, Melvin L.
1959 *Summary Report of the Modoc Rock Shelter: 1952, 1953, 1955, 1956*. Reports of Investigations 8. Illinois State Museum, Springfield.

Fowler, Melvin L., and Steven R. Ahler
1991 Modoc Rock Shelter, Randolph County, Illinois: Perspectives on Research Questions, Stratigraphy and Chronology. Paper presented at the 54th Annual Meeting of the Society for American Archaeology, New Orleans, Louisiana.

Fowler, Melvin L., Howard D. Winters, and Paul W. Parmalee
1956 *The Modoc Rock Shelter Preliminary Report*. Reports of Investigations 4. Illinois State Museum, Springfield.

Griffin, James B.
1957 Review of Modoc Rock Shelter: Preliminary Report, by M. L. Fowler and H. Winters. Faunal Analysis by Paul W. Parmalee, Illinois State Museum Report of Investigations, No. 4. *American Antiquity* 23:197.
1968 Observations on Illinois Prehistory in Late Pleistocene and Early Recent Times. In *The Quaternary of Illinois: A Symposium in Observance of the Centennial of the University of Illinois*, edited by Robert E. Bergstrom, pp. 123–137. Special Publication 14. University of Illinois College of Agriculture, Urbana.

Justice, Noel D.
1987 *Stone Age Spear and Arrow Points of the Midcontinental and Eastern United States: A Modern Survey and Reference*. Indiana University Press, Bloomington.

Koldehoff, Brad
1985 Southern Illinois Cherts: A Guide to Siliceous Materials Exploited by Prehistoric Populations in Southern Illinois. Manuscript (1985-6) on file, Center for Archaeological Investigations, Southern Illinois University, Carbondale.
2002a Appendix B: Chipped-Stone Resources of Alexander and Union Counties. In *The Archaeology and History of Horseshoe Lake, Alexander County, Illinois*, by Brad Koldehoff and Mark J. Wagner, pp. 135–139. Research Paper 60. Center for Archaeological Investigations, Southern Illinois University, Carbondale.
2002b Appendix A: Lithic Resources of Salt Lick Point. In *The Woodland Ridge Site and Late Woodland Land Use in the Southern American Bottom*, by Brad Koldehoff, Kathryn E. Parker, Gregory D. Wilson, and John T. Penman, pp. 169–177. Transportation Archaeological Research Report 15. Illinois Transportation Archaeological Research Program, University of Illinois at Urbana–Champaign.
2006 *Paleoindian and Archaic Settlement and Lithic Procurement in the Illinois Uplands*. Research Report 108. Illinois Transportation Archaeological Research Program, University of Illinois, Urbana–Champaign.

Lewis, Thomas M. N., and Madeline K. Lewis
1961 *Eva: An Archaic Site*. University of Tennessee Press, Knoxville.

Libby, W. F.
1954 Chicago Radiocarbon Dates V. *Science* 120:733–741.

Lopinot, Neal H., Jack H. Ray, and Michael D. Connor (editors)
1998 *The 1997 Excavations at the Big Eddy Site (23CE426) in Southwest Missouri*. Special Publication 2. Center for Archaeological Research, Southwest Missouri State University, Springfield.
2000 *The 1999 Excavations at the Big Eddy Site (23CE426)*. Special Publication 3. Center for Archaeological Research, Southwest Missouri State University, Springfield.

Matson, Frederick R.
1955 Charcoal Concentration from Early Sites for Radiocarbon Dating. *American Antiquity* 21:162–169.

McElrath, Dale L.
1986 *The McLean Site*. American Bottom Archaeology FAI-270 Site Reports 14. University of Illinois Press, Urbana.
1993 Mule Road: A Newly Defined Late Archaic Phase in the American Bottom. In *Highways to the Past: Essays on Illinois Archaeology in Honor of Charles J. Bareis*, edited

by Thomas E. Emerson, Andrew C. Fortier, and Dale L. McElrath, pp. 148–157. *Illinois Archaeology* 5.

Nance, Jack D.
1986 The Morrisroe Site: Projectile Point Types and Radiocarbon Dates from the Lower Tennessee River Valley. *Midcontinental Journal of Archaeology* 11:11–50.

O'Brien, Michael J., and W. Raymond Wood
1998 *The Prehistory of Missouri*. University of Missouri Press, Columbia.

Perino, Gregory H.
1985 *Selected Preforms, Points, and Knives of the North American Indians*, vol. 1. Points and Barbs Press, Idabel, Oklahoma.

Porter, James W., and Jean R. Linder
1974 An Archaeological Survey of the Mississippi Valley in St. Clair, Monroe, and Randolph Counties. *Preliminary Report of 1973 Historic Sites Survey*, Part 1, Summary, Section A, pp. 28–34. Illinois Department of Conservation, Springfield.

Ray, Jack H.
1984 An Overview of Chipped Stone Resources in Southern Missouri. In *Lithic Resource Procurement: Proceedings from the Second Conference on Prehistoric Chert Exploitation*, edited by Susan C. Vehik, pp. 225–250. Occasional Papers 4. Center for Archaeological Investigations, Southern Illinois University, Carbondale.
1998 Chipped Stone Resource Availability and Utilization. In *Prehistoric and Historic Properties on Mitigation Lands, Horseshoe Lake Peninsula, Madison County, Illinois*, by Neal H. Lopinot, Michael D. Connor, Jack H. Ray, and Jeffrey K. Yelton, pp. 146–199. St. Louis District (U.S. Army Corps of Engineers) Historic Properties Management Report 56. Center for Archaeological Research, Southwest Missouri State University, Springfield.

Stafford, C. Russell
1985 *The Campbell Hollow Archaic Occupations: A Study of Intrasite Spatial Structure in the Lower Illinois Valley*. Research Series 4. Center for American Archeology, Kampsville, Illinois.

Stuiver, Minze, and Paula J. Reimer
1993 Extended ^{14}C Data Base and Revised CALIB 3.0 ^{14}C Age Calibration Program. *Radiocarbon* 35:215–230.

Styles, Bonnie W., Steven R. Ahler, and Melvin L. Fowler
1983 Modoc Rock Shelter Revisited. In *Archaic Hunters and Gatherers of the American Midwest*, edited by James L. Phillips and James A. Brown, pp. 261–297. Academic Press, New York.

Styles, Bonnie W., Steven R. Ahler, Melvin L. Fowler, Frances B. King, Edwin R. Hajic, Mona L. Colburn, James L. Theler, and David A. Baerreis
1986 Excavations at Modoc Rock Shelter, 1984. Final report to the National Science Foundation. Manuscript on file, Illinois State Museum, Springfield.

Styles, Bonnie W., Melvin L. Fowler, Steven R. Ahler, Frances B. King, and Thomas R. Styles
1981 *Modoc Rock Shelter Archaeological Project, Randolph County, Illinois 1980–1981*. Completion report to the Department of Interior, Heritage Conservation and Recreation Service and the Illinois Department of Conservation. Illinois State Museum, Springfield.

Yerkes, Richard A.
1987 *Prehistoric Life on the Mississippi Floodplain: Stone Tool Use, Settlement Organization, and Subsistence Practices at the Labras Lake Site, Illinois*. University of Chicago Press, Chicago.

9

The Archaic Period in the Lower Illinois River Basin

Michael D. Wiant, Kenneth B. Farnsworth, and Edwin R. Hajic

Introduction

During the 7,500-year-long Archaic period (ca. 10,000 B.P.–2500 B.P. in uncalibrated radiocarbon years), Native American culture changed substantially in the lower Illinois River basin of west-central Illinois and elsewhere in the Eastern Woodlands (e.g., Phillips and Brown 1983). The causes and meaning of these changes have increasingly become the subject of archaeological research. Recent research has clarified archaeologists understanding of cultural developments during the period and has generated a variety of new questions. Continued research promises to shed light on Archaic culture, including aspects that were once thought to be hallmarks of the Woodland period (Winters 1985). In this chapter, we draw on five decades of research to build an overview of our current understanding of Native American culture during the Archaic period in the lower Illinois River basin. Our data are drawn from a roughly 7,100-km^2 area (2,800 mi^2) encompassing the lower 112-km (70-mi) reach of the Illinois River and its drainage.

Since 1959, this area has been the focus of sustained research, first, by the Illinois Valley Archaeological Program and, subsequently, by the Center for American Archeology (CAA, previously known as the Foundation for Illinois Archeology) (Struever 1968, 1969). The discovery in 1969 of a stratified, multicomponent deposit at the Koster site (11GE4; Figure 9.1) focused considerable attention on the Archaic period (Houart 1971; Struever and Holton 1979). A decade-long excavation at Koster unearthed the remains of a suite of Early, Middle, and Late Archaic occupations that established a benchmark sequence of Archaic-period cultural development in the region (Brown and Vierra 1983). Subsequent large-scale excavations at the Campbell Hollow site (11ST144; Stafford 1985; Figure 9.1) and Napoleon Hollow site (11PK500; Wiant et al. 1983; Figure 9.1) and numerous other smaller-scale excavations and site reconnaissance projects have provided additional information with which to evaluate the model of Archaic-period developments offered by Brown and Vierra (1983). Of the more than 2,526 pre-Columbian Native American sites documented in this area, 311 are attributed to the Archaic period. Of these, 26 sites with one or more Archaic-period cultural components have been excavated (Figure 9.1). In many instances, archaeologists have unearthed stratified, well-preserved, multicomponent deposits that provide evidence of environment, technology, subsistence, settlement, the disposition of human remains, and the timing and scope of cultural developments during the Archaic period. Our current understanding of Archaic-period cultural chronology in the region is summarized in Table 9.1; the radiocarbon age determinations discussed throughout the text are presented in uncalibrated radiocarbon years B.P.

Lower Illinois River Basin

The Illinois River rises at the confluence of the Kankakee and Des Plaines rivers in northeastern Illinois and flows 437 km (273 mi) in a westerly and southerly direction, emptying into the Mississippi River at Grafton, Illinois. The lower reach of the river begins near Meredosia, 112 km (70 mi) above the

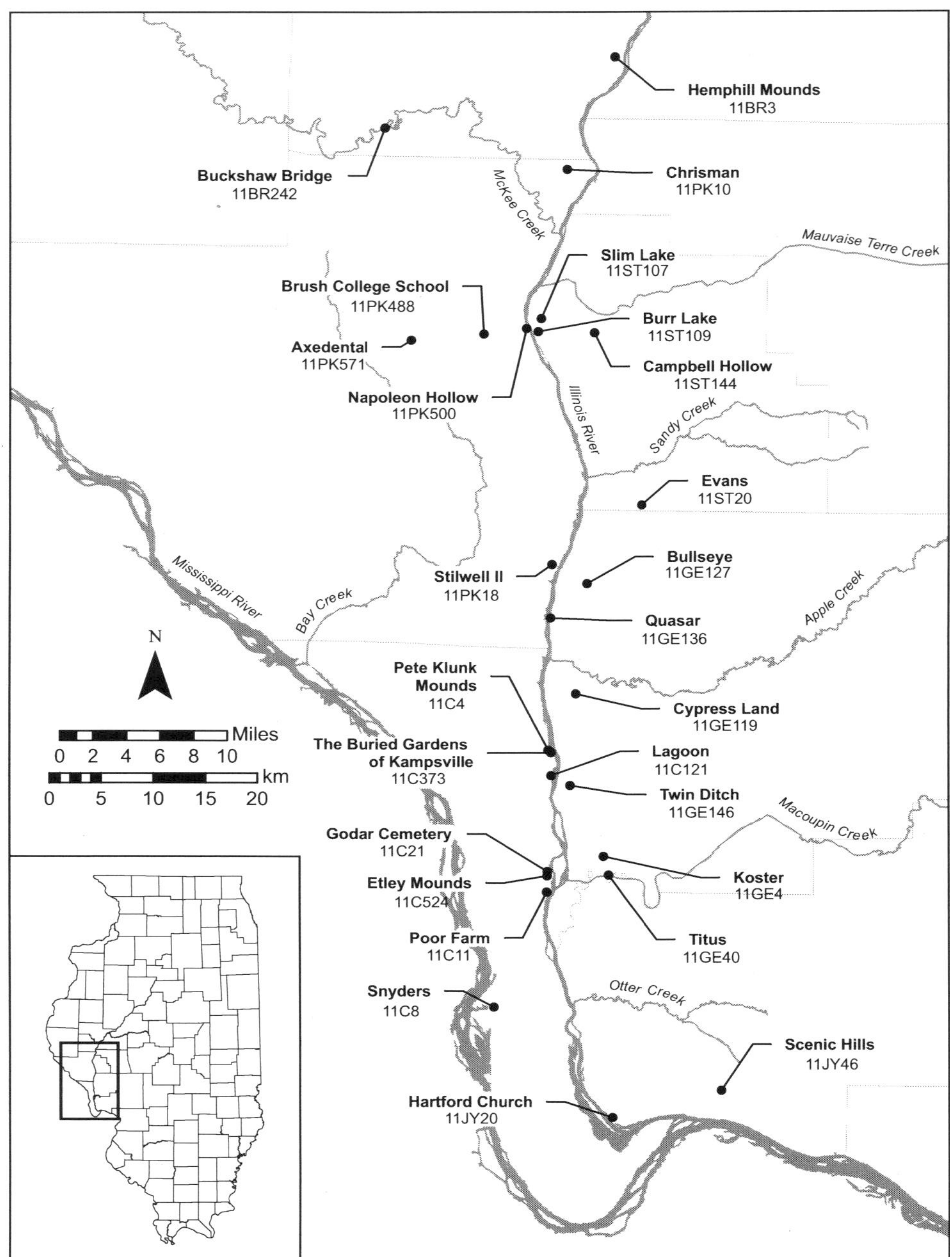

Figure 9.1. Excavated Archaic-period sites in the lower Illinois Valley region.

Mississippi River confluence (Smith 1987). Below Meredosia the river turns due south, and its valley narrows to an average width of 5.6 km (3.5 mi), which it generally maintains to its confluence with the Mississippi River.

In its lower reach, the Illinois River is generally deeply entrenched into Paleozoic limestone bedrock. Precipitous cliffs demarcate the edges of the valley, some rising more than 61 m (200 ft) above the valley floor. Loess, wind-blown silt deposited near the end of the Pleistocene epoch, mantles the bedrock and forms the substrate of the upland surface (Rubey 1952).

The walls of limestone are broken only where tributary streams enter the Illinois River valley and by steep ravines that channel precipitation runoff from small drainage networks reaching onto the upland surface. In many places, particularly where tributaries and small, intermittent streams enter the river valley, sediment eroded from the upland surface has accumulated, creating fans, some of which have lengthy, well-preserved depositional histories. A belt of deeply dissected upland runs parallel to the river's course on each side. To the west, the upland rises until it reaches the drainage divide between the Illinois and Mississippi rivers. To the east, the

Table 9.1. Proposed Archaic Cultural Chronology for the Lower Illinois Valley Region.

Period	Phase	Years B.P. (uncal)	Years B.C. (uncal)	Cal Years B.C.[a]
Paleoindian–Early Archaic Transition	—	ca. 10,000	ca. 8050	ca. 9200
Early Archaic 1	Twin Ditch	9600–8800	7650–6850	8600–8000
Early Archaic 2	Koster	8800–8200	6850–6250	7800–7400
Middle Archaic 1	Campbell Hollow	8200–7600	6250–5650	7200–6400
Middle Archaic 2	Napoleon	7300–6350	5350–4400	6100–5500
Middle Archaic 3	Helton	6350–4400	4400–2450	5500–3800
Late Archaic	Titterington	4200–3800	2250–1850	2800–2400
Terminal Archaic	Kampsville	3250–2550	1300–600	1500–800
Archaic–Early Woodland Transition	—	ca. 2550	ca. 600	ca. 800

[a]All calibrated dates in this chapter use Stuiver and Reimer 1993 (3.03c CALIB Program, University of Washington).

heavily dissected land eventually gives way to rolling then relatively level topography that characterizes the Springfield Plain (Leighton et al. 1948).

The topography of the valley floor is subtle and has relatively little relief, but it belies a depositional history that includes periods of substantially more hydraulic energy than manifest by the present river. Today the Illinois River is an underfit stream with little gradient attempting to transport an overabundance of sediment. As we discuss below, accumulated sediment obscures much of the former topographic relief of the valley floor, and in doing so it has buried a substantial proportion of the Archaic-period landscape.

Paleoenvironmental Research

During the Archaic period, changes in climate had a profound effect on vegetation and landscape evolution in the Midwest (Webb and Bryson 1972). The Prairie Peninsula formed during the Hypsithermal Interval, when warm and dry conditions fostered the expansion of prairie at the expense of forest (Deevey and Flint 1957; Geis and Boggess 1968; Transeau 1935). Archaeologists have long sought to determine how climate change may have figured into cultural development during the Archaic period (e.g., Caldwell 1958; Wood and McMillan 1976). A growing body of paleoenvironmental data from the lower Illinois River valley and elsewhere in the Midwest, especially information on landscape evolution, provides an increasingly detailed context to evaluate the interplay between environmental change and culture.

Archaic Climate Dynamics

According to H. Wright (1968:84), the Hypsithermal was initially conceived of as a period of steady change toward a time of maximum warmth and dryness about 8000 B.P., followed by a reversal that was very slow until about 4500 B.P. and then somewhat faster. Now it appears that there were, in fact, two intervals of warm, dry climate during the Holocene in the Midwest (Grimm and Jacobson 2004; Nelson et al. 2006; Webb et al. 1983). Recent palynological research at Nelson Lake in Kane County (Eric C. Grimm, pers. comm. 2004) and at Chatsworth Bog in Livingston County (Nelson et al. 2006) provides a refined history of Holocene vegetation change in north-central Illinois. Between 10,000 and 8900 B.P., moist conditions advanced the growth of a dense elm forest that dominated the landscape. Relatively arid conditions gradually developed between 8900 and 7600 B.P., fostering the growth of prairie. But increased precipitation ca. 7600 B.P. rejuvenated elm forests at the expense of prairie. Approximately 5,400 years ago, a stronger interval of aridity developed, encouraging an unprecedented expansion of prairie. These conditions persisted until 3200 B.P., when climate became more humid across the entire Prairie Peninsula (Eric C. Grimm, pers. comm. 2004).

Archaic Landscape Systematics

Remains of the Archaic period in the lower Illinois River basin are primarily found in buried contexts as a result of regional landscape evolution during the early to late

Holocene. Many factors, conditions, and events influenced the trajectory of geomorphic evolution of the lower Illinois River, its tributaries, valley-margin slopes, and adjacent upland slopes. A rich history of archaeological, geoarchaeological, geomorphic, and geologic investigations (Butzer 1977, 1978; Hajic 1981a, 1981b, 1983, 1985a, 1985b, 1987, 1990a, 1990b; Hajic and Styles 1982; Styles 1985) has led to the development of Holocene geologic histories of the different depositional subsystems in the lower Illinois River basin (Hajic 1990a). Developmental linkages between these depositional subsystems not only explain why cultural deposits of the Archaic period are mostly buried but also provide information on depositional environments of the Archaic period and where to search for additional intact Archaic deposits.

Valley-margin colluvial hillslopes are preserved in the form of wedge-shaped prisms along the foot of valley walls, small colluvial fans beyond the mouths of hillside swales, and hillside swale fills. The Late Wisconsin Peoria Silt that dominates the colluvial subsystem was redeposited from upland landscape positions largely by sheetflood and creep processes. Investigations of the colluvial subsystem at the Koster (Hajic 1990b), Napoleon Hollow (Styles 1984, 1985), and Campbell Hollow (Hajic 1985a) sites (Figure 9.1) demonstrated that the bulk of colluvial deposits accumulated between about 8450 and 4500 B.P., although sediment accumulated at lower rates before and at progressively lower rates after this interval. Colluvial deposits in these locations contain the remains of multiple buried Archaic (and younger) components that are largely intact; one or more incipient buried soils, with varying degrees of anthropogenic influence, that appear to have developed synchronously throughout the region; and, at the first two locations, evidence of soil erosion (sheetflood and rill and gully erosion) on the surfaces of the youngest middle to late Holocene buried soils. Whereas the overall tempo of deposition of colluvium was in response to a landscape adjusting to postglacial conditions, the timing of regional sediment-soil cycles appears to have been strongly influenced by climate, and the erosion of younger buried soil surfaces was an intrinsic response to the eclipse of a threshold colluvial slope angle (Hajic 1990b), perhaps facilitated by an increased magnitude or frequency of storm runoff or both.

The net result is that largely intact prehistoric cultural deposits, often stratigraphically distinct, are preserved within the colluvial subsystem. The age of the earliest possible cultural deposit is dependent on the paleogeomorphic surface on which a given colluvial deposit rests. Where deposited on terraces no younger than the very early Holocene, Archaic deposits range from deeply buried Early Archaic to shallowly buried Late Archaic.

Colluvial slopes are the first effective storage facility of sediment eroded from upland hillslopes and, to a degree, reflect the net effect of geomorphic processes removing material from those slopes. Away from the Illinois Valley, uplands are flat to gently rolling. Adjacent to the Illinois Valley, the bluff line is dissected by a series of low-order streams, with entrenched higher-order streams occurring periodically. Headwaters of the dendritic network of low-order streams are influenced by disintegrated late Wisconsin ice-wedge polygons (Hajic 1990a). Between low-order drainages along major valley margins, upland spurs descend toward the Illinois and tributary valleys, sometimes in a stepped fashion.

Archaeologists now know that Archaic cultural deposits occur in both surface and shallowly buried upland contexts, depending to a large degree on their hillslope position. However, the frequency, distribution, and age of buried upland Archaic deposits are virtually unknown. Early upland surface surveys recognized a narrow belt of cultural debris extending away from the Illinois and other major tributary-valley bluff lines. The material is largely aceramic, and Early Archaic forms dominate diagnostic artifacts (Luchterhand 1970). Upland surveys at greater distances from the Illinois Valley yielded fewer "sites" (i.e., Asch and Asch 1978). Behavioral explanations were posited for these and similar observed distributions, such as availability and abundance of resources and significance of valley viewsheds (Asch and Asch 1978; Conrad 1981; Esarey 1987; Odell 1984). However, diligent shovel testing during later surveys of loess-mantled upland areas in western Illinois demonstrated that prehistoric cultural deposits were more common than originally believed and perhaps occur in some abundance, buried shallowly beneath the base of plow zones in late Wisconsin loess (Abbott and Tiffany 1986; see also Artz 1993; Nolan and Hickson 1993). Spatial variation of surface versus buried cultural deposits in the uplands was linked to landscape position and hillslope components, with Archaic deposits tending to be surface manifestations on spurs, shoulder slopes, and back slopes where soil downwasting processes have dominated and shallowly buried manifestations where upland summits broaden and are less dissected (Bettis and Hajic 1995; Hajic 1992).

Few data have been generated to specifically address the processes leading to, and the timing of, shallow burial of some upland sites and the nonburial, exposure, or exhumation of others. Hajic (1992) has suggested that the descending spurs, particularly the narrower ones, were dominated by net sediment loss and soil downwasting, effectively resulting in development of a middle Holocene erosion surface bordering the Illinois and major tributary valleys during the Hypsithermal. Eroded loess served as the source for much of the sediment that accumulated downslope on aggrading and prograding colluvial foot and toe slopes. If erosion surfaces did develop, then it is possible, and even likely, that many Archaic deposits on descending spurs are no longer intact. Furthermore, the eroding spurs also may have served as a local source of eolian reentrainment of the loess, depositing it downwind and contributing to burial of Archaic deposits on broader summit areas. Van Nest (2002) hypothesizes that the shallowly buried cultural deposits of broader upland summits resulted from downward movement of artifacts during biomantle formation (Johnson 1990) in the prairie soils with thick organic-rich A horizons that were dominant on the uplands. Soil erosion would have outpaced the rate of biomantle formation in thinner A horizons of forest soils developed on steeper hillslope components.

Sediment production from upland slopes had an impact on the tributary-network depositional subsystems similar to its effect on the colluvial subsystem. The early and middle Holocene record in tributary valleys is dominated by vertical aggradation of silt-dominated sediment derived from loess (Hajic 1985a, 1985b, 1990a). Initially, during the earliest Holocene, valley environments generally were poorly drained, and perhaps stream gradients were altered by beaver dams and ponds. As upland erosion progressed, particularly after the climate shifted to more xeric conditions after about 8500 B.P., aggradation continued at a relatively rapid pace, in places interfingering with colluvial slope deposition. Tributary floodplains became better drained, attracting Archaic peoples. Aggradation of tributary floodplains continued into the late Holocene but at a slower rate, burying nearly all Archaic cultural deposits not located on late Wisconsin or older terrace remnants in tributary valleys. As climatic conditions ameliorated, tributary streams rapidly incised their floodplains between about 2500 and 3000 B.P., effectively rendering them low terraces. As the tributaries created new floodplains at lower levels, their meandering voided through erosion areas of older floodplain sediment assemblages, along with any Archaic cultural deposits that might have been present. Fortunately, postincision lateral movements by most tributaries of the lower Illinois River were limited. Postincision fluvial activity inset below the former floodplain level was dominated by multiple episodes of backfilling and reincision in response to the earlier rapid downcutting of the channel.

The principal tributary floodplain sediment assemblage grades to alluvial fans deposited in the Illinois Valley immediately beyond tributary-valley mouths. The aggradational record of the alluvial fan subsystem beyond the mouths of tributary valleys is similar to that of the tributary valleys and colluvial slopes (Hajic 1990a, 1990b; Wiant et al. 1983). Some of the vast amount of sediment mobilized from upland slopes, beginning in earnest about 8500 B.P., eventually was deposited in the alluvial fans. Archaic cultural deposits are buried, Early Archaic more deeply, Late Archaic more shallowly, within alluvial fans, landforms that would have provided Archaic peoples with well-drained environments intermediate between valley and upland resources. Surface sites on alluvial fans are, with few exceptions, no older than Early Woodland (Asch et al. 1981). As with tributary-valley floodplains, alluvial fans were similarly incised by the tributary creeks during a brief interval of the late Holocene. As a result, perennial tributaries extended their channels beyond the existing fan lobes. In some cases, new fan lobes were deposited, farther removed from the valley walls. More often, tributaries, confined by natural levees newly formed by material eroded during incision, flowed into and through Illinois Valley flood basins occupied by shallow backwater lakes.

As colluvial slope, tributary floodplain, and alluvial fan subsystems were aggrading throughout the Archaic period with sediment eroded from upland slopes, aggradation was also occurring in the lower Illinois River valley but under very different environmental conditions. During the very early Holocene, about 9850 B.P., the Illinois River incised its valley as a result of late deglacial discharge from the Lake Michigan basin through the Chicago Outlet as well as in response to similar downcutting in the Mississippi River valley. After that time, the history of the lower Illinois Valley during the Archaic period effectively was that of a lake slowly infilling with sediment (Hajic 1990a).

Today, the lower Illinois River has one of the lowest gradients of major world rivers, descending less than one inch per mile (Horton 1914). Prior to being confined by artificial levees, the lower Illinois River, bound by natural levees, replenished shallow, intermittent backwater lakes by seasonal flooding. The expansive backwater lakes dominated the valley landscape not occupied by alluvial fans or the river and natural levees. However, the backwater lakes and much of the natural levee system were late Holocene features that simply resulted from the latest phase of valley infilling over the millennia of the early and middle Holocene.

Throughout the early Holocene, and much of the middle Holocene, the lower Illinois Valley was occupied by a lake that extended from valley wall to valley wall, excluding a few terrace remnants and incipient tributary alluvial fans or fan deltas. Terrace remnants, including a now-buried paleogeomorphic surface, increased in percentage of valley area in the upper part of the lower valley. Water was impounded in the low-gradient lower Illinois Valley largely as a result of more rapid aggradation of the Mississippi River valley following deglacial events during the earliest Holocene (Hajic 1990a). The Illinois River initially entered this valley lake upstream of the lower valley. As sediment yield of tributaries increased, the Illinois River extended down-valley into this lake, bounded by initially subaqueous, and eventually, by about 6000 B.P., subaerial natural levees. As the river prograded into the valley lake, deep lateral lakes developed between natural levees and aggrading alluvial fans and fan deltas. Lateral lakes shallowed through this time period with sediment contributions from both the main and tributary rivers. Eventually, lateral lakes filled to the point at which they evolved into shallow, and ultimately intermittent, backwater lakes. This environmental mosaic developed in a down-valley vector in a time-transgressive manner throughout the middle Holocene as the Illinois River extended into the lake.

Early and middle Holocene valley environments thus provided limited options for Archaic habitation sites but an abundant and reliable resource base. The importance of the reliability of this resource base would have been enhanced during the drier climatic intervals of the middle Holocene.

Initially, low terrace remnants and alluvial fans were the loci of Archaic valley occupations. As subaerial natural levees became available during the Middle Archaic, they were also occupied in the upper part of the lower valley (i.e., Goatley 1998). As tributary systems extended beyond their fans into backwater lakes and developed natural levees between about 3000 and 2500 B.P., a second set of Illinois River natural levees also formed (Hajic 1990a). These natural levees were favored locations for Late Archaic and Early Woodland activities.

Climate Change and Illinois River-Basin Biota

Our observations on mid-Holocene climate change and biota are restricted to the Illinois River valley, where archaeological excavations have provided most of the available paleoenvironmental data. Currently, we have insufficient data from the rest of the basin, particularly the uplands, to draw any conclusions concerning climate. With respect to the valley, no differences in the representation of plant and animal species in the Archaic record can at present be definitively attributed to climate change. Drawing on their research into carbonized plant remains from the Koster site, Asch et al. conclude that "climatic regimes . . . did not lead to the replacement of trees that are characteristic of the present-day talus slope" (1972:24). They suggest the topography of the Illinois River valley buffered the effects of climate on local vegetation.

Although no qualitative changes may have occurred in species representation, some evidence, particularly in the geologic record, suggests spatial and quantitative variations in vegetation. Citing an increase in the rate of colluviation at the Koster site ca. 8300 B.P., Butzer (1977, 1978) suggests more open forest and parkland existed on hill slopes. Hajic (1981a; Hajic and Styles 1982) counters that the establishment of prairie grasses on bluff crests could account for the same depositional regime, but both he and Butzer cite changes in local vegetation regimes that promoted sediment mobility.

Variations in snail species from the stratified record at the Koster site also suggest fluctuations in vegetation that correspond with climate dynamics (Jaehnig 1976). On the basis of a comparison of the composition of snail assemblages from contemporary local environments and prehistoric samples, Jaehnig (ca. 1975) proposes a sequence of shifts in moisture and vegetation. At 8500 B.P., the Koster fan was mostly covered by an open, grassy habitat, but evidence of mesic forest occurs in some of the sampling units. Between 7600 and 7000 B.P., evidence indicates forest, perhaps open savanna grassland, was more extensive. The timing of this change corresponds to evidence in the pollen record from northern Illinois of an expansion of elm forest that is attributed to increased precipitation (Eric C. Grimm, pers. comm. 2004; Nelson et al. 2006). After 7000 B.P., open grassland was reestablished as conditions became drier. By 5000 B.P., there was some variation in moisture levels across the site, but species indicative of a xeric talus-slope forest are most common among the snails. After 5000 B.P., most of the site was dry and open, though evidence of moister conditions associated with the presence of trees comes from one portion of the site.

More broadly speaking, correspondence in the geologic and occupational histories of the Koster and Napoleon Hollow sites led Hajic (1981a, 1990b) and Styles (1985; see also Wiant et al. 1983) to link the timing of colluvial fan deposition to climatic changes and biogeomorphic responses.

Floodplain vegetation history is also problematic, but considerable evidence is available relating to the hydrologic evolution of the Illinois River (Hajic 1981a, 1981b, 1983; Hajic and Styles 1982; Styles 1984, 1985). A sequence of fluvial episodes of aggradation and entrenchment controlled by Lake Michigan outlets and the Mississippi River and of terrestrial erosion and deposition controlled by climate transformed the landscape of the Illinois River basin. A consequence of these developments was the enhancement of aquatic resources such as fish and mussels, which became increasingly important components of subsistence during the Archaic period (Styles 1986).

Hill (1975) offers data that suggest changes in river water volume during the mid-Holocene. He identified changes in the ratios of strontium to calcium in the mussel species *Amblema plicata* when he compared modern specimens with those from Koster site Horizons 8, 6, and 4. Hill drew on research that suggested variations in strontium in the shells of freshwater mussels correspond to the element's concentration in their habitat, which, in turn, is directly related to water level. Higher strontium levels in Horizon 8 (ca. 7600–7000 B.P.) specimens indicate low water levels, a correlation that appears to be at odds with the pollen data. The volume of water increased slightly during Horizon 6 (ca. 6000–5000 B.P.) and then substantially by 4000 B.P. (Hill 1975), which corresponds with geological evidence (Hajic 1990a).

Terrestrial resource availability may also have been enhanced during the Hypsithermal. Paleoenvironmental researchers have suggested that dry conditions expanded the prairie-forest ecotone, encouraging population growth in species such as white-tailed deer, which increased in economic importance during the Archaic period in the lower Illinois River basin (Cook 1986; Neusius 1986; Purdue 1986). Mid-Holocene aridity may also have had an adverse effect on deer body size. Purdue (1989) links deer body-size reduction to higher mid-Holocene summer insolation, which shortens the period of availability of high-quality forage.

In sum, current evidence from the lower Illinois River basin suggests a link between climate change, vegetation, and landscape evolution during the Archaic period, but the particulars of this association remain elusive and require more investigation.

Archaeological Research

Scope

As is the case elsewhere in eastern North America, the discovery of grave goods in the Illinois River valley attracted and sustained the attention of those interested in aboriginal history (see Farnsworth 2004). For the most part, early reports chronicle serendipitous discoveries made by those working the land and by avocational archaeologists. Excavations at the Hartford Church/Marquette site (11JY20; Figure 9.1) in Jersey County in 1932 and at the Godar site (11C21; Figure 9.1) and nearby Etley mound group (11C524; Figure 9.1) in the 1940s resulted in the discovery of extraordinary caches of artifacts commingled with human remains stained with red ocher (Farnsworth 1993; Titterington 1950). Eventually, some of these discoveries were described as occurring in nonpottery sites (Titterington 1950), but they would not be attributed to the Archaic period until later. By the mid-twentieth century, little was known about the Archaic period in the lower Illinois River Valley other than what had been gleaned from burials (Wray 1952).

Fieldwork conducted by the University of Illinois at the Chrisman site (11Pk10; Figure 9.1) in Pike County provided some of the first information on an Archaic-period habitation site (McGregor 1954). In the absence of pottery and the presence of grooved axes, distinctive leaf-shaped bifaces, and other artifacts, the assemblage was comparable with one discovered far upstream at Starved Rock and attributed to the Archaic period (Mayer-Oakes 1951).

Gregory Perino did much to advance initial understanding of the Archaic period in the lower Illinois River basin. In two published papers, Perino (1954, 1961) expanded on the information originally documented by Titterington (1950). In 1960, he excavated the Pete Klunk mound group (11C4; Figure 9.1) with the purpose of acquiring evidence of Hopewell and Late Woodland–culture mortuary practices. Beneath Mound 7, he discovered Late Archaic–period interments unlike those reported earlier by Titterington (1950). Later, in an article on the prehistory of Calhoun County, Perino attributed particular point types to Archaic-period horizons, summarized current information on burial components, and reported the unearthing of an Archaic-period village discovered during construction of Hardin High School (Poor Farm site, 11C11; Figure 9.1) (Perino 1961). Then, in 1961, while working at the Koster mound group (11GE546, 11GE547, 11GE548), Perino (1973) excavated a single test pit in a cornfield on the Koster farm. He discovered Late Woodland, Early Woodland, and Late Archaic artifacts and concluded that the remains of one or more major Archaic-period occupations might be present (Struever 1971).

At about the same time, Stuart Struever embarked on what would become an extraordinary program of archaeological research. In 1959, he organized the Illinois Valley Archaeological Program, an enterprise dedicated to intensive, long-term archaeological research in the lower Illinois River valley (Levine 1970; Meyers 1970; Parmalee et al. 1972; Rick 1978; Struever 1968, 1969; Zawacki and Hausfater 1969). The "research universe" of the Illinois Valley Program included the lower 112 km (70 mi) of the Illinois River and approximately 32 km (20 mi) on either side of the river, essentially the Illinois River basin in Calhoun, Greene, Jersey, Pike, and Scott counties. As part of his dissertation research, Struever initiated an archaeological reconnaissance program to identify and document sites in the region. In particular, he drew on the knowledge of artifact collectors, many of whom had amassed substantial collections through surface reconnaissance and, sometimes, excavation. Initially, Struever focused the program on Woodland-period site inventory and excavation, but at the same time he encouraged Kubet Luchterhand to explore the distribution of Early Archaic projectile points, exclusively on the basis of specimens from collectors (Luchterhand 1970). In 1969, Struever turned his attention to the Koster site (11GE4; Figure 9.1). The discovery there of buried, stratified Archaic-period deposits launched a decade-long excavation (Brown and Struever 1973; Houart 1971). Material from Koster has been the subject of a variety of specialized studies, including archaeobotany (Asch et al. 1972), geology (Butzer 1977, 1978; Hajic 1990a), and archaeozoology (Hill 1975; Neusius 1986; Styles 1986), and doctoral dissertations have explored material culture (Carlson 1979; Cook 1976; Doershuk 1989; Lurie 1982; Wolynec 1977), human ecology (Hewitt 1983), and other topics (Brown and Vierra 1983; Wiant et al. 1983). In 1973, while the Koster excavations proceeded, a field-school crew dug several test pits at the Titus site (11GE40), exposing another deeply stratified record of Archaic-period habitation in colluvium (Druhot 1983).

The site reconnaissance program also continued (e.g., Farnsworth 1973, 1976). Beginning in the early 1970s, the Illinois Department of Conservation funded the Historic Sites Survey, a statewide initiative to locate potentially significant sites. Several large-scale surveys throughout the region, all largely dependent on the assistance of artifact collectors and targeted at finding Woodland-period sites, contributed information on hundreds of site locations, many of which had Archaic-period components. Though many sites were discovered and others were revisited, no systematic sampling strategy was implemented. Thus, the inventory of sites constitutes a grab sample of artifact-bearing locations in the lower Illinois River basin (Asch et al. 1981).

Asch et al. (1981) summarized site reconnaissance data as part of an initiative to develop predictive models of site location (Table 9.2). Their tabulation revealed substantial differences in the landscape position (i.e., floodplain, terrace, bluff base, bluff crest, and upland) of sites organized by cultural periods (i.e., Early Archaic, Middle Archaic, Helton phase, Late Archaic, and Terminal Archaic). Scrutiny of the relative proportions of upland sites is illustrative. Whereas 75 percent of the documented Early Archaic sites are located

Table 9.2. Archaic-Period Landscape Position, Lower Illinois River Valley Research Universe (after Asch et al. 1981).

	Archaic Subdivision					
Landscape Position	Early Ct. Col./Row Pct.	Middle Ct. Col./Row Pct	Helton Ct. Col./Row Pct	Late Ct. Col./Row Pct	Terminal Ct. Col./Row Pct	Total Ct. Col./Row Pct
Floodplain	3 6.1/18.8	0 0/0	6 5.4/37.5	1 1.4/6.3	6 16.2/37.5	16 5.9/100
Terrace	2 4.1/3.6	1 16.7/1.8	29 26.1/52.7	12 17.4/21.8	11 29.7/20.0	55 20.2/100
Bluff base	4 8.2/7.8	1 16.7/2.0	23 20.7/45.1	14 20.3/27.5	9 24.3/17.6	51 18.8/100
Bluff crest	3 6.1/27.3	0 0/0	6 5.4/54.5	2 2.9/18.1	0 0/0	11 4.0/100
Upland	37 75.5/26.6	4 66.7/2.9	47 42.3/33.8	40 58.0/28.7	11 29.8/7.9	139 51.1/100
Total	49 100/18.0	6 100/2.2	111 100/40.8	69 100/25.4	37 100/13.6	272 100/100

in the uplands, less than 30 percent of Terminal Archaic sites are found there. Asch et al. acknowledged data limitations, especially concerns with depositional history, that biased their results. Nevertheless, the summary suggests differences in landscape use.

Beginning in the mid-1970s, the development of the CAA cultural resource management program provided new archaeological research opportunities. Work conducted for the Illinois Department of Transportation and the U.S. Army Corps of Engineers, St. Louis District, in particular, catapulted forward understanding of the Archaic period. The path of the Central Illinois Expressway (FAP 408) crosses the Illinois River approximately 45 km (28 mi) north of the Koster site. Eventually, CAA archaeologists had the opportunity to explore several sites with Archaic-period components, including Burr Lake (11ST109; Stafford 1989; Figure 9.1), Campbell Hollow (Stafford 1985), Napoleon Hollow (Wiant et al. 1983; Wiant and McGimsey 1986), and Slim Lake (11ST107; Stafford 1989; Figure 9.1). At the same time, the St. Louis District Corps of Engineers funded geological and archaeological studies of drainage and levee districts along the lower reach of the Illinois River with the purpose of assessing their archaeological site potential. In addition to increasing understanding of the depositional history of the Illinois River and the archaeological potential of various valley landforms (Hajic 1981a, 1981b, 1981c, 1983, 1987; Hajic and Hassen 1980; Hajic and Leigh 1985), the discovery and excavation of several Archaic-period sites such as Bullseye (11GE127; Hassen 1985; Hassen and Farnsworth 1987; Figure 9.1), Quasar (11GE136; Goatley 1998; Hassen 1985; Figure 9.1), and Twin Ditch (11GE146; Hassen and Hajic 1984; T. Morrow 1996; Figure 9.1) contributed important new information on Archaic-period occupations.

The research outlined above has provided a substantial amount of information on the Archaic period in the lower Illinois River basin, but before reviewing that information we must take stock of at least some of the limitations of the data.

Limitations

Information about the Archaic period in the 7,100-km² (2,800-mi²) research universe represents a grab sample, and it must be considered in that light. Though site reconnaissance has been systematic in particular areas, those areas do not constitute a representative sample of the research universe (Asch et al. 1981).

Drawing on contemporary data, 219 sites in the study area have been attributed to the Archaic-period largely on the basis of projectile point types. Of these, 102 have Early Archaic components, 36 have Middle Archaic components, and 81 have Late Archaic components (Table 9.3). Standardized information on each of these sites is recorded in the Illinois Inventory of Archaeological Sites, a Geographic Information System–based tool that we have used to generate information on lower Illinois Valley Archaic-period sites for this chapter. This file has several noteworthy limitations. First, data recorded on paper site forms often do not include information on diagnostic artifacts. Cultural affiliation is noted, but the evidence used to decide affiliation is sometimes not recorded. Thus, one is left to take the cultural-affiliation information at face value or to examine artifacts from each site under consideration. For this discussion, we rely on recorded information for cultural affiliation. Second, new data from revisited sites are not systematically recorded. Thus, the discovery of

Table 9.3. Archaic-Period Landscape Position, Lower Illinois River Valley Research Universe Based on Current Site File Records.

	Archaic Subdivision			
	Early Ct. Col./Row Pct.	Middle Ct. Col./Row Pct.	Late Ct. Col./Row Pct.	Total Ct. Col./Row Pct.
Floodplain	20 17.5/37.7	15 41.7/28.3	18 22.2/34.0	53 22.9/100
Terrace	5 4.4/38.5	2 5.6/15.4	6 7.4/46.2	13 5.6/100
Bluff base	11 9.6/37.9	3 8.3/10.3	15 18.5/51.7	29 12.6/100
Bluff slope	6 5.3/54.5	1 2.8/9.1	4 4.9/36.4	11 4.8/100
Bluff crest	12 10.5/44.4	2 5.6/7.4	13 16.0/48.1	27 11.7/100
Upland	60 61.2/61.2	13 36.1/13.3	25 30.9/25.5	98 42.4/100
Total	114 100/46.6	36 100/15.6	81 100/35.1	231 100/100

an additional cultural component or the reassignment of a particular component may not be reflected by the site record. In the end, we have drawn on the best available data to frame arguments and draw conclusions, but, clearly, more work is required to improve information quality.

We must also consider briefly the Archaic-period chronology used throughout this chapter. Archaeologists studying the Archaic period in the lower Illinois River basin initially subscribed to the chronology established by Griffin (1967): Early Archaic (10,000–8000 B.P.), Middle Archaic (8000–6000 B.P.), and Late Archaic (6000–4000 B.P.). In keeping with this chronology, Cook (1976), drawing on discoveries at the Koster site, identified the Helton phase (6000–5000 B.P.) as Late Archaic. Much of the subsequent research has followed Stoltman's (1973) lead and extended the Middle Archaic period to 5000 B.P. (Brown and Vierra 1983). Thus, the Helton phase is now attributed to the Middle Archaic, a practice that we follow here. But research undertaken for this chapter underscores the need to reconsider the cultural chronology of the Archaic period in this region. The presence of small, side-notched projectiles such as Matanzas and Godar in 4,400-year-old deposits suggests the persistence of what researchers have heretofore considered Middle Archaic culture. Moreover, the inconsistent application of the concepts of Middle and Late Archaic regionally complicate comparison, so we have chosen to organize the presentation of information from excavated sites in temporal terms in lieu of a cultural chronology (Tables 9.4–9.6). However, with respect to settlement distribution drawn from survey data, we are limited to the use of cultural chronology. We regret the potential for confusion, but it simply underscores the state of information.

Much of the excavated data from the lower Illinois River valley comes from sites with buried components, some of which are deeply buried. Under the circumstances, systematic sampling is complicated. The challenge is compounded by commonplace limitations such as funding and project duration, but deep sites pose other problems. In particular, once a commitment is made to expose a deeply buried deposit in one location, expanding the limits of excavation is difficult. In general, excavation methods have evolved considerably since the first 6-ft-x-6-ft squares were excavated to depths exceeding 25 ft at the Koster site. At Campbell Hollow and Napoleon Hollow, we initiated work with geological assessments using tools such as a Giddings soil probe and wheel-mounted backhoes, followed by targeted hand-excavation of pits, to refine our understanding of artifact-bearing deposits. Drawing on these data, we opened modest block excavations to expose broader surfaces in hopes of revealing patterns in midden and the distribution of features. As a result, we have a better qualitative understanding of the context of the excavated portions of these sites, but more robust quantitative measures have not been achieved. This shortcoming is especially troublesome because it limits the

Table 9.4. Early Archaic Radiocarbon Dates from the Lower Illinois River Valley.

Lab No.	Site	Unit/Horizon	Component	Age (B.P.)	S.D.	Uncorrected B.C. Dates	Calibrated[a] B.C. Dates (1 sigma)
Beta-38000	Twin Ditch	22/10	E. Archaic 1	9510	100	7560	8934 (8821, 8820, 8591, 8554, 8537) 8424
Beta-38001	Twin Ditch	25/11	E. Archaic 1	9390	100	7440	8588 (8418) 8269
Beta-37999	Twin Ditch	PM 1	E. Archaic 1	9310	100	7360	8431 (8348, 8284, 8278) 8189
Beta-47002	Twin Ditch	Sq64/lv 08-NE	E. Archaic 1	9200	70	7250	8339 (8322, 8318, 8188) 8088
ISGS-317	Titus	below Horizon 3	E. Archaic 1	9170	110	7220	8341 (8123, 8116, 8096) 8055
Beta-47005	Twin Ditch	Sq67/lv 07-SW	E. Archaic 1	9130	70	7180	8325 (8089) 8054
Beta-47003	Twin Ditch	Sq66/lv 07NW	E. Archaic 1	9120	70	7170	8323 (8088) 8043
Beta-38002	Twin Ditch	30/09	E. Archaic 1	8900	100	6950	8013 (7963) 7747
Beta-47004	Twin Ditch	Sq67/lv 07-SE	E. Archaic 2	8740	70	6790	7917 (7870, 7816, 7707) 7590
ISGS-328	Koster	12	E. Archaic 2	8730	90	6780	7922 (7857, 7820, 7705) 7581
ISGS-236	Koster	11	E. Archaic 2	8480	110	6530	7570 (7501) 7431
ISGS-1762	Koster	11	E. Archaic 2	8470	110	6520	7549 (7499) 7428
ISGS-292	Koster	11	E. Archaic 2	8445	75	6525	7536 (7491) 7430
ISGS-231	Koster	11	E. Archaic 2	8430	100	6480	7538 (7487) 7328
ISGS-230	Koster	11	E. Archaic 2	8430	90	6480	7536 (7487) 7422
ISGS-891	Campbell Hollow	lower occupation	E. Archaic 2	8350	100	6400	7494 (7426) 7268
ISGS-1065	Koster	11	E. Archaic 2	8130	90	6180	7259 (7044) 7007

[a]Dates calibrated using the CALIB 3.03c program (Stuiver and Reimer 1993).

Table 9.5. Middle Archaic Radiocarbon Dates from the Lower Illinois River Valley.

Lab No.	Site	Unit/ Horizon	Component	Age (B.P.)	S.D.	Uncorrected B.C. Dates	Calibrated[a] B.C. Dates (1 sigma)
ISGS-783	Koster	10A	Middle Archaic 1	8230	120	6280	7427 (7261) 7040
ISGS-336	Koster	9D	Middle Archaic 1	8220	75	6270	7413 (7257, 7171, 7149, 7112, 7107) 7045
ISGD-337	Koster	10B	Middle Archiac 1	8130	75	6180	7253 (7044) 7010
ISGS-300	Titus	Horizon 3	Middle Archaic 1	8070	95	6120	7195 (7034) 6777
ISGS-290	Titus	Horizon 3	Middle Archaic 1	7990	75	6040	7034 (6999, 6915, 6903, 6838, 6812, 6790) 6700
ISGS-923	Koster	9B	Middle Archaic 1	7920	150	5970	7034 (6751, 6749, 6706) 6547
ISGS-229	Koster	9A, 9B	Middle Archaic 1	7910	100	5960	7004 (6700) 6596
ISGS-316	Koster	9A	Middle Archaic 1	7800	160	5850	6993 (6595, 6573, 6569) 6453
ISGS-936	Campbell Hollow	n/a	Middle Archaic 1	7670	90	5720	6545 (6460)6412
ISGS-303	Koster	8F	Middle Archaic 1	7670	110	5720	6557 (6460) 6388
ISGS-210	Koster	8E	Middle Archaic 1	7630	210	5680	6608 (6451, 6442, 6428) 6213
ISGS-753	Campbell Hollow	n/a	Middle Archaic	7600	110	5650	6470 (6419) 6260
ISGS-940	Campbell Hollow	n/a	Middle Archaic	7560	80	5610	6454 (6388) 6252
ISGS-859	Koster	8D	Middle Archaic 2	7320	70	5370	6185 (6162, 6136, 6128, 6082, 6076) 6043
ISGS-814	Napoleon Hollow	n/a	Middle Archaic	7050	140	5100	5996 (5940, 5911, 5880) 5724
ISGS-338	Koster	8C	Middle Archaic 2	7020	120	5070	5972 (5923, 5919, 5855) 5716
NRSL-299	Napoleon Hollow	n/a	Napoleon	7000	250	5050	6102 (5838) 5598
ISGS-809	Koster	8B	Middle Archaic 2	7000	80	5050	5950 (5838) 5732
ISGS-800	Koster	8C	Middle Archaic 2	6970	150	5020	5963 (5780) 5667
ISGS-848	Koster	8B	Middle Archaic 2	6960	80	5010	5963 (5772) 5703
ISGS-835	Koster	8A	Middle Archaic 2	6860	80	4910	5755 (5692) 5620
ISGS-817	Napoleon Hollow	n/a	Napoleon	6800	80	4850	5704 (5633) 5590
ISGS-937	Napoleon Hollow	n/a	Napoleon	6730	70	4780	5634 (5593) 5527
ISGS-786	Napoleon Hollow	n/a	Napoleon	6630	100	4680	5593 (5566, 5549, 5524) 5440
ISGS-1000	Koster	8B	Middle Archaic 2	6510	310	4560	5667 (5437) 5086
ISGS-2486	Quasar	4	Middle Archaic 2	6500	100	4550	5520 (5435) 5319
ISGS-1535	Elizabeth Mound 1	n/a	Helton (?)	6340	90	4390	5411 (5270) 5222
ISGS-1278	Quasar	4	Middle Archaic	6320	90	4370	5327 (5263) 5146
ISGS-972	Napoleon Hollow	n/a	Helton	6080	90	4130	5193 (4950) 4853
ISGS-414	Koster	7A	Middle Archaic 3	5825	80	3875	4786 (4714) 4573
ISGS-209	Koster	6B	Middle Archaic 3	5720	75	3770	4684 (4540) 4465
ISGS-806	Napoleon Hollow	n/a	Helton	5670	90	3720	4596 (4496) 4369
ISGS-1325	Elizabeth Mound 6	submound	Helton?	5470	70	3520	4358 (4337) 4248
ISGS-233	Koster	6B	Middle Archaic 3	5440	100	3490	4358 (4327, 4275, 4267) 4159
ISGS-861	Elizabeth Mound 6	submound	Helton?	5420	70	3470	4343 (4319, 4288, 4258) 4164
ISGS-1718	Slim Lake	n/a	Middle Archaic	5380	70	3430	4331 (4237) 4090
ISGS-2978	Quasar	2	Middle Archaic	5360	100	3410	4334 (4228) 4040
ISGS-1719	Slim Lake	n/a	Middle Archaic	5350	70	3400	4319 (4226, 4178, 4166) 4045
ISGS-938	Napoleon Hollow	n/a	Helton	5350	70	3400	4319 (4226, 4178, 4166) 4045
ISGS-2331	Napoleon Hollow	n/a	Helton	5320	70	3370	4244 (4220, 4195, 4151, 4111, 4107) 4006
ISGS-1671	Slim Lake	n/a	Middle Archaic	5310	70	3360	4238 (4218, 4198, 4146, 4116, 4092) 4002
ISGS-237	Koster	6B	Middle Archaic 3	5305	75	3355	4238 (4217, 4200, 4143, 4118, 4088) 3997
ISGS-1038	Napoleon Hollow	n/a	Helton	5280	70	3330	4226 (4212, 4208, 4131, 4130, 4078, 4059, 4046) 3989
ISGS-198	Koster	6A2	Middle Archaic 3	5250	250	3300	4220 (4038, 4015, 4006) 3977
ISGS-3317	Quasar	2	Middle Archaic	5220	80	3270	4216 (4030, 3994) 3961
ISGS-2328	Napoleon Hollow	n/a	Helton	5180	70	3230	4038 (3977) 3950
ISGS-197	Koster	6A2	Middle Archaic 3	5175	85	3225	4070 (3975) 3823
ISGS-1672	Slim Lake	n/a	Middle Archaic	5140	70	3190	3990 (3962) 3812
ISGS-1036	Napoleon Hollow	n/a	Helton	5140	70	3190	3990 (3962) 3812
ISGS-235	Koster	6A2	Middle Archaic 3	5140	75	3190	3992 (3962) 3810
ISGS-199	Koster	6A2	Middle Archaic 3	5070	90	3120	3969 (3934, 3870, 3813) 3772
ISGS-202	Koster	6A1	Middle Archaic 3	4880	250	2930	3958 (3656) 3367
ISGS-1411	Buckshaw Bridge	n/a	Helton	4600	80	2650	3499 (3357) 3124
ISGS-1545	Buckshaw Bridge	n/a	Helton	4510	70	2560	3350 (3303, 3233, 3179, 3163, 3111) 3043

[a]Dates calibrated using the CALIB 3.03c program (Stuiver and Reimer 1993).

Table 9.6. Late Archaic and Terminal Late Archaic Radiocarbon Dates from the Lower Illinois River Valley.

Lab No.	Site	Unit/Horizon	Component	Age (B.P.)	S.D.	Uncorrected B.C. Dates	Calibrated[a] B.C. Dates (1 sigma)
NRSL-303	Lagoon	Titterington	Late Archaic	4300	600	2350	3692 (2906) 2041
ISGS-3839	Quasar	1	Late Archaic	4200	45	2250	2883 (2873, 2798, 2780, 2711, 2709) 2695
ISGS-823	Napoleon Hollow	Tittterington	Late Archaic	4060	75	2110	2855 (2577) 2469
ISGS-804	Lagoon	Titterington	Late Archaic	4030	75	2080	2617 (2563, 2524, 2500) 2462
ISGS-3315	Quasar	1	Late Archaic	4010	70	2060	2587 (2553, 2543, 2493) 2459
ISGS-798	Lagoon	Titterington	Late Archaic	4010	150	2060	2862 (2553, 2543, 2493) 2314
ISGS-1766	Brush College School	Titterington	Late Archaic	4010	70	2060	2587 (2553, 2543, 2493) 2459
ISGS-329	Koster	4B	Late Archaic	3950	75	2000	2561 (2461) 2332
ISGS-933	Napoleon Hollow	Titterington	Late Archaic	3920	90	1970	2553 (2455, 2412, 2409) 2280
ISGS- 1695	Brush College School	n/a	Late Archaic	3680	70	1730	2140 (2035) 1943
ISGS-826	Titus	Horizon 2	Late Archaic	3240	75	1290	1602 (1513) 1421
ISGS-956	Koster	4A	Late Archaic	2980	70	1030	1307 (1251, 1248, 1205) 1062
ISGS-990	Titus	Horizon 2	Late Archaic	2870	80	920	1153 (1009) 916
ISGS-826	Titus	Horizon 2	Terminal Late Archaic	3240	75	1290	1602 (1513) 1421
M-1100	Klunk Mound 7	n/a	Terminal Late Archaic	2870	75	920	1128 (1009) 918
ISGS-990	Titus	Horizon 2	Terminal Late Archaic	2860	80	910	1125 (1004) 910
ISGS-1153	Buried Gardens of Kampsville	n/a	Terminal Late Archaic	2770	70	820	994 (906) 826
ISGS-1758	Axedental	n/a	Terminal Late Archaic	2600	70	650	814 (797) 768
ISGS-1154	Buried Gardens of Kampsville	n/a	Terminal Late Archaic	2550	70	600	801 (778) 539

[a]Dates calibrated using the CALIB 3.03c program (Stuiver and Reimer 1993).

use of standardized measures of artifact density as a basis for interassemblage comparison. Excavated sediment volume is not readily available in many instances, let alone estimates of deposit volume. Some of this information can be generated from existing data, but not all of it.

Finally, we must draw attention to the inconsistency in artifact nomenclature over time, which has hampered clear-cut comparison. We have endeavored to reclassify categories to promote intersite comparison, but a thorough study will require reexamination of specimens and systematic tabulation. Nevertheless, we believe the comparisons offered below are informative.

Archaic-Period Culture History

This overview of the Archaic period in the lower Illinois River basin is divided into five subsections—Paleoindian to Archaic-Period Transition, Early Archaic (9600–8200 B.P.), Middle Archaic (8200–4400 B.P.), Late Archaic (4200–2500 B.P.), and Late Archaic to Early Woodland Transition. The Early, Middle, and Late Archaic subsections are further divided into subperiods or phases where appropriate (Table 9.1). For example, the Early Archaic period is divided into Early Archaic 1 and Early Archaic 2 (Twin Ditch phase and Koster phase) to distinguish apparent differences in the archaeological record. In contrast, following the lead of previous research, the Late Archaic period is subdivided into the Titterington phase (Cook 1976) and Kampsville phase (Farnsworth and Asch 1986), the definitions of which are based on both habitation and mortuary site data.

Paleoindian to Archaic-Period Transition

The beginning of the Archaic period is generally described as a gradual development of Native American culture brought about by the onset of the Holocene and concomitant changes in biota ca. 10,000 B.P. In the Midwest, the transition from the Paleoindian period to the Archaic period is indicated by a succession of hafted-biface designs beginning with fluted lanceolate forms (e.g., Clovis and Folsom) that gave way to unfluted lanceolate forms (e.g., Agate Basin and Dalton) and, finally, to several notched varieties (e.g., Hardin Barbed, St. Charles, and Thebes) (Alex 2000; Birmingham et al. 1997; Griffin 1967; Halsey 1999; Justice 1987; Theler and Boszhart 2003).

Only 18 of the 2,526 sites recorded thus far in the lower Illinois River basin have Paleoindian components, all of which have been identified by the presence of one or more Clovis points. Only two of these sites, Evans (11ST20; Figure 9.1) and Scenic Hills (11JY46; Figure 9.1), also known as Lincoln Hills or Ready (Koldehoff 1983; J. Morrow 1996; Wiant and Winters 1991), appear to be single-component sites; the rest have one or more Archaic-period components. None have been excavated. All but two have been found either on bluff crests or on upland landforms; the others are located on Illinois River valley terraces.

Component Identification

As is the case elsewhere in the Midwest and in other parts of North America, the appearance of lanceolate bifaces such as Dalton (Chapman 1948) and Agate Basin (Wormington 1957) mark the transition from the Paleoindian to the Archaic period in the lower Illinois River basin. Dalton points have been found throughout the region in cultivated fields, but they are not common. In a survey of private collections, Luchterhand (1970) documented only 38 specimens. They also have been found during excavations at Twin Ditch (T. Morrow 1996) and Napoleon Hollow (Wiant et al. 1983). At Twin Ditch, Dalton points were unearthed in Horizon 2. Eight radiometric assays from this context range in age from 9510 ± 100 B.P. (uncalibrated) to 8740 ± 70 B.P. (uncalibrated) (Table 9.4). At Napoleon Hollow, a heavily reworked Dalton was found at a depth of 50 cm in an incipient soil mantling late-glacial Henry Formation gravel. The absence of charcoal in this context precludes an age assessment.

Agate Basin points have also been found in the region. Luchterhand (1970) documented 23 specimens from surface collections, but only two have been found during excavation. At the Titus site (11GE40; Figure 9.1), excavators found the base of an Agate Basin point in Horizon 3, more than 3.9 m below the present-day ground surface (Druhot 1983). Radiometric assays of wood charcoal from Horizon 3 provided an age range estimate of 7990 ± 75 B.P. (uncalibrated) (ISGS-290) to 8070 ± 95 B.P. (uncalibrated) (ISGS-300). This estimate is generally younger than other assessments of the age of Agate Basin (Druhot 1983). Assay of a sample of dispersed wood charcoal below Horizon 3 produced an age of 9170 ± 110 B.P. (uncalibrated) (ISGS-317). An Agate Basin point was also found at Napoleon Hollow in the same stratigraphic context as the Dalton point described above (Wiant et al. 1983).

Early Archaic (9600–8200 B.P.)

We divide the Early Archaic period in the lower Illinois River basin into two subperiods: Early Archaic 1 (9600–8800 B.P.) and Early Archaic 2 (8800–8200 B.P.), following Brown and Vierra (1983) (Table 9.4). Regional survey data (Luchterhand 1970) and excavations at Koster (Brown and Vierra 1983), Napoleon Hollow (Wiant et al. 1983), Titus (Druhot 1983), and Twin Ditch (T. Morrow 1996) provide information about Early Archaic 1. The discovery of Early Archaic 1 components buried in Illinois Valley–margin and tributary-valley-margin colluvium and fans—Koster and Napoleon Hollow in the former landscape position, Titus in the latter—and in Illinois River floodplain settings—Napoleon

Hollow and Twin Ditch—challenges previous conclusions about settlement distribution (cf. Luchterhand 1970). Early Archaic 2 components have been excavated at Campbell Hollow (Stafford 1985), Koster (Brown and Vierra 1983; Houart 1971), Napoleon Hollow (Wiant et al. 1983), and Stilwell II (11PK18; Figure 9.1) (Perino 1970). These sites provide evidence for repeatedly occupied seasonal camps, changes in the organization of lithic technology, use of the atlatl, development of a diverse assemblage of ground-stone tools, and dog domestication. Nine graves containing human remains in Koster site Horizon 11 constitute one of the oldest cemeteries in North America.

Early Archaic 1 (9600–8800 B.P.): Twin Ditch Phase

Twin Ditch–Phase Component Identification. Hardin Barbed (Scully 1951), St. Charles (Scully 1951), and Thebes (Winters 1967) points are generally recognized as the oldest notched biface forms in the region (Luchterhand 1970; Perino 1961). They are relatively common in private collections; Luchterhand (1970), for example, documents 228 of them. Age estimates for the St. Charles and Thebes specimens in Horizon 2 at the Twin Ditch site suggest the transition to notched forms was underway by at least 8700 B.P. (uncalibrated) and as early as 9500 B.P.

At Napoleon Hollow, Hardin Barbed and St. Charles points were found on an extensive paleosurface, buried in some places by 1.8 m of very young alluvium and older sediment probably related to the prograding tip of a colluvial fan (Figure 9.2). Two radiocarbon assays of dispersed wood charcoal from the base of this unit provided age estimates consistent with Middle Archaic artifacts also found in this context (Wiant et al. 1983).

Twin Ditch–Phase Habitation Components. The Twin Ditch site, located in the Illinois River floodplain near the river's east bank, has two stratified, shallowly buried Archaic occupation components. The deepest artifact-bearing component (Horizon 2) has produced the oldest substantial evidence of Early Archaic occupation in the region. In 1980, archaeologists discovered Early Archaic artifacts—Agate Basin, Hardin Barbed, and LeCroy points (Kneberg 1956)—and Middle Archaic artifacts—Matanzas (Munson and Harn 1966) and other side-notched points—in sediment dredged from two drainage ditches in the Illinois River floodplain (Hassen and Hajic 1984). Subsequent excavations here between 1987 and 1990 by a CAA field-school program under the direction of Toby Morrow revealed two artifact-bearing strata on a shallowly buried paleogeomorphic surface called the Columbiana surface (Hassen and Hajic 1984; T. Morrow 1996). Horizon 2 artifacts include Dalton, Holland (Perino 1971), St. Charles, and Thebes points. Radiocarbon assays of Horizon 2 charcoal samples range in age from 9510 B.P. to 8740 B.P. (T. Morrow 1996:347). Only a preliminary analysis of the artifact assemblage and plant and animal remains is available. In addition to the hafted bifaces, the Twin Ditch lithic artifact assemblage includes chipped-stone adzes, end scrapers, side scrapers, gravers, retouched and utilized flakes, bifacial blanks, and debitage. A quantitative breakdown is not presently available. Wood charcoal is common, but few other plant remains have been reported. White-tailed deer and fish dominate the faunal assemblage. Bird bone is common, and some small-mammal elements are also present (T. Morrow 1996). Systematic refitting of lithic debitage and analysis of retouched specimens suggest a series of short-term occupations centered on hearths, each perhaps representing a seasonally reoccupied base camp (T. Morrow 1996).

Figure 9.2. Early Archaic points from Napoleon Hollow site (ca. 9500 B.P.): a, Dalton 33-06-2; b, Hardin Barbed 47-07-1; c, St. Charles 1007-20b-1; d, Agate Basin 1010-ext 1-06-1.

The Napoleon Hollow site is an extensive, multicomponent deposit located at the mouth of Napoleon Hollow, a minor tributary of the Illinois River (Figure 9.3). Here three geomorphic systems—the Illinois River floodplain, the Napoleon Hollow Creek floodplain, and the steep slopes of the river and creek valleys—interface and contribute sediments that coalesce and interfinger to create a series of aggrading landscapes. CAA excavators working on the FAP 408 project unearthed Agate Basin, Dalton, Hardin Barbed, and St. Charles points, all indicative of an Early Archaic 1 component. The points were found in a buried incipient paleosol demarcating an extensive paleosurface mantling a shallowly buried Pleistocene terrace in the Illinois River floodplain (Styles 1985). A piece of uncarbonized white oak from the vicinity of Hardin Barbed and St. Charles points yielded an age of 7050 ± B.P. Evidently, this former surface was available for occupation for at least 2,000 years before being buried by the prograding end of the Russell fan and overbank sedimentation from Illinois River floods.

The Stilwell II site is located on the west side of the Illinois River valley at the base of the bluff north of Pearl in Pike County. It was discovered when a road cut through a colluvial fan was refaced, exposing an artifact-bearing stratum at a depth of 3.8 m. Perino (1970) observed two house floors, one of which included human remains and a dog burial. He returned to the site and excavated a test pit, discovering Early Archaic

Figure 9.3. Three stratified, artifact-bearing paleosols–middens are evident in the west wall of the Napoleon Hollow site excavation unit shown above. From bottom to top, they are the Napoleon component (ca. 6800–6600 B.P.), the Helton component (ca. 6000–5100 B.P.), and the Titterington component (ca. 4000 B.P.).

Agate Basin and LeCroy points and a new corner-notched point form that he designated "Stilwell" (see also Perino 1985:365). There has been no further fieldwork at Stilwell II. The Agate Basin point is indicative of an Early Archaic 1 component, but as we note below, LeCroy and Stilwell points have been found in Early Archaic 2 components.

The Titus site consists of three artifact-bearing strata in the body of a 7.5-m-thick colluvial fan located on the north side of the Macoupin Creek valley, 3.2 km (2 mi) above its opening into the Illinois River valley. A Northwestern University field-school crew excavated here in 1973 (Druhot 1983). The evidence for an Early Archaic 1 component at the Titus site is equivocal and is derived from Horizon 3. Four, or perhaps five, of the excavation units encountered Horizon 3 at depths between 3.93 m and 4.64 m below ground surface. In addition to the Agate Basin point base, an oval bifacial scraper, the base of a biface, and a broken drill bit are the only retouched chipped-stone artifacts from Horizon 3. Animal bones and charcoal were recovered from this horizon, but they have yet to be identified and analyzed. Radiometric assays of dispersed charcoal provided age estimates for Horizon 3 of 7990 ± 75 B.P. (ISGS 290) and 8070 ± 95 B.P. (ISGS 300). The age estimate of a sample of wood charcoal from "immediately below Horizon 3" is 9170 ± 110 B.P. (ISGS 317). It appears that Horizon 3 may contain both Early and Middle Archaic components.

The Koster site is located on the east side of the Illinois River valley in a small, abandoned secondary valley in Greene County. Here 13 distinct cultural horizons were documented in a wedge- or fan-shaped deposit, the deepest of which is 8.6 m below the present-day ground surface (Figure 9.4). Archaic-period components range in age from 8730 ± 90 B.P. to 2980 ± 70 B.P. and represent short- and long-term Early, Middle, and Late Archaic settlements. Well-preserved artifact-bearing deposits provide a substantial amount of information on environment, human ecology, and cultural development. Northwestern University field-school staff and students excavated the Koster site between 1969 and 1978 (Brown and Vierra 1983; Cook 1976; Hajic 1990b; Houart 1971). Horizon 13 is the oldest Archaic-period occupation of the site and the only Early Archaic 1 component. A relative age of ca. 9000 B.P. is estimated from the rate of deposition and the presence of a single Kirk point. A few chert flakes and a block of chert were the only other artifacts discovered in this deposit, suggesting a small encampment (Brown and Vierra 1983).

Twin Ditch–Phase Settlement. An analysis of Early Archaic settlement in the region is limited by several factors: (1) many of the sites Luchterhand used in his 1970 landmark study have not been recorded in the Illinois Inventory of Archaeological Sites and, thus, are not available for analysis; (2) information on the hafted bifaces found at the 102 single-component Early Archaic sites currently listed in the site file is inconsistent, and it is not yet possible to discern any trends in settlement location during the period; and (3) studies of regional geology and geomorphology indicate that a substantial proportion of the Archaic-period landscape in floodplain and valley-margin settings in both Illinois River and tributary valleys is buried (Hajic 1990a; see also *Archaic Landscape Systematics* discussion above). With these caveats in mind, we relate the current state of our understanding.

Luchterhand (1970) considered the regional distribution of Early Archaic types such as Agate Basin, Dalton, Hardin Barbed, St. Charles, and Thebes in the lower Illinois River basin study area, drawing on privately owned artifact collections of specimens found on the ground surface. Roughly four out of every five specimens of all these types were found on the upland landscape, but no significant difference is apparent in the distribution of older forms (Agate Basin and Dalton) when compared with the younger forms (Hardin Barbed, St. Charles, and Thebes). Evidently, the change in biface design (lanceolate vs. notched) does not reflect change in landscape use, though a substantial increase in the number of younger specimens (183 Hardin Barbed, St. Charles, and Thebes vs. 49 Agate Basin and Dalton) may simply reflect a difference in

Figure 9.4. Three stratified, artifact-bearing paleosols–middens are evident in the north wall of the Koster site excavation shown above. From bottom to top, they are Horizon 8 (ca. 7600–6800 B.P.), Horizon 6 (ca. 5700–4800 B.P.), and Horizon 4 (ca. 4000 B.P.).

use of these points, or it may indicate an increase in regional population.

After considering the paucity of points in the Illinois River floodplain and in secondary valleys and concluding that their absence could not be accounted for by alluviation, Luchterhand advanced the hypothesis that the distribution of points reflected hunting practices—specifically the pursuit of white-tailed deer in tributary valleys from base camps on the adjacent upland landscape.

Current data are consistent with Luchterhand's analysis. The landscape position of 71 percent of single-component Early Archaic sites (72 of 102) in the region is listed in the site files as bluff crest or upland, whereas only 13 percent (25 of 102) are listed as occurring on the floodplain or terrace. Asch et al. (1981) also considered the distribution of Early Archaic sites in the lower Illinois River basin, on the Illinois side of the Mississippi River valley between Quincy and the Illinois River confluence, and in the dissected uplands between the Illinois and Mississippi valleys and to the east of the Illinois River valley, although they did not distinguish between points typical of Early Archaic 1 and Early Archaic 2 components. Their findings are consistent with those reported by Luchterhand (1970)—they classified the landscape position of 81 percent of the Early Archaic sites as bluff crest or dissected upland and the rest as Illinois River valley. Asch et al. were aware of the discoveries of buried Early Archaic components in the Illinois River floodplain (Twin Ditch and Napoleon Hollow), in valley-margin colluvial fans (Koster and Napoleon Hollow), and in a colluvial fan along the lower reach of Macoupin Creek, a tributary valley (Titus), and appreciated the probability that a significant proportion of the Early Archaic landscape in both the Illinois Valley and tributary valleys was buried by alluvium or colluvium or both. In the end, the presence of buried Early Archaic sites in the river valley calls into question, but does not necessarily refute, Luchterhand's argument about landscape use. Obviously, more fieldwork is necessary to evaluate the extent of valley-margin and floodplain settlement during the Early Archaic period.

Twin Ditch–Phase Mortuary Component. The presence of a few Early Archaic projectile points among poorly preserved human remains at the Bullseye site (Hassen and Farnsworth 1987; Seddon 1992) has fostered speculation about the possibility of early Holocene graves at the site (Walthall 1999:11).

Early Archaic 2 (8800–8200 B.P.): Koster Phase

Koster-Phase Component Identification. Graham Cave (Logan 1952), Kirk (Coe 1964), LeCroy (Kneberg 1956), and Stilwell (Perino 1970) points are diagnostic of Early Archaic 2 components in the region. A Kirk point (360-068) was found in Koster Horizon 11 (Figure 9.5). The Koster Horizon 11 lithic assemblage also includes three Stilwell points, one of which is made out of Cobden/Dongola chert, which outcrops in southern Illinois (Figure 9.3). The other specimens are made out of local Burlington chert. The Horizon 11 assemblage also includes four Graham Cave points (Figure 9.6), all made out of local Burlington chert, and six bifurcate-base LeCroy points (Figure 9.7). One specimen is made out of a nonlocal dark-black, vitreous chert; the others are local Burlington chert. Four samples of dispersed wood charcoal from Horizon 11 have an average age of 8446 B.P. and are nearly identical when standard errors are considered.

Figure 9.5. Early Archaic Kirk points (a, c–d) and Stilwell point (b) from Koster Horizon 11 (ca. 8500 B.P.): a, 165-065-4; b, 241-062; c, 358-058-1; d, 360-068-2.

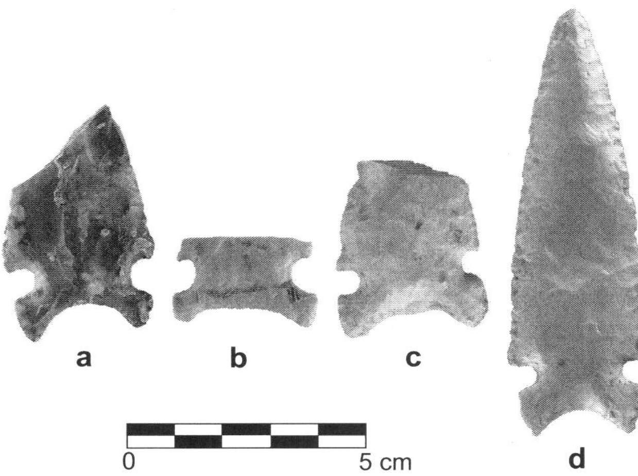

Figure 9.6. Early Archaic Graham Cave points from Koster Horizon 11 (ca. 8500 B.P.): a, 165-066-1; b, 176-078-1; c, 208-071-1; d, 239-056-1.

The Horizon 11 projectile point assemblage is problematic: why is there so much variety in a midden that appears to have accumulated over perhaps only three centuries? There is no evidence of a sequence in point form. A LeCroy point, arguably the youngest in this sequence on the basis of evidence from sites elsewhere (Broyles 1971), was found near the base of the Horizon 11 midden, while specimens thought to be older were found near the top of the midden. Perhaps their distribution is not surprising when one considers the dynamic of midden development through occupation and reoccupation of the site. For those who equate point style with a particular culture or society, the Horizon 11 assemblage has at least three components: Kirk/Stilwell, Graham Cave, and LeCroy. If true, it suggests relatively rapid development of cultural diversity or substantial mobility or influence

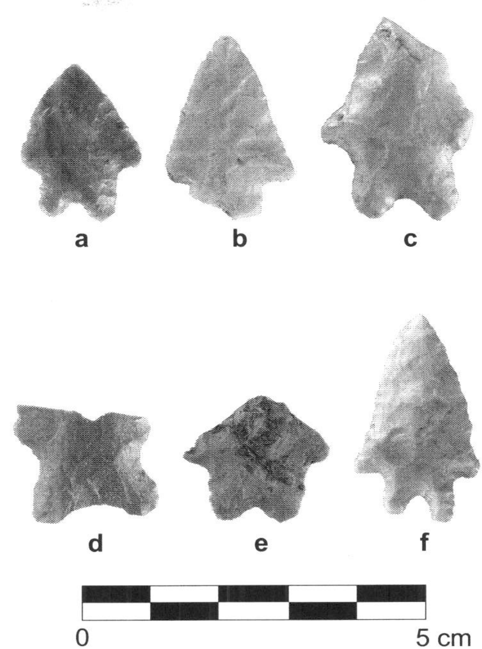

Figure 9.7. Early Archaic LeCroy points from Koster Horizon 11 (ca. 8500 B.P.): a, 161-070-1; b, 192-065-1; c, 267-38-1; d, 237-074-1; e, 211-062; f, F2084b-1.

from traditions to the east (Kirk, Stilwell, LeCroy) and west (Graham Cave) or perhaps a combination of these factors. The assemblage also consists of a variety of reworked hafted bifaces, the forms of which do not correspond to any of the aforementioned types. There are lanceolate, contracting-stem, and side-notched specimens in the assemblage. Such extensive reworking suggests movement in areas where suitable stone resources may not have been readily available (Wiant and Hassen 1984). We are not yet able to reconcile the obvious variety of hafted bifaces with the relatively short duration of Horizon 11 occupation.

Koster-Phase Habitation Components. Koster site Horizon 11 is the most substantial Early Archaic 2 component unearthed to date in the region. Excavated largely by trowel, a 218-m^2 exposure revealed an incipient soil and midden in the floodplain of Koster Creek. A high density of wood charcoal, the preservation of which suggests relatively rapid burial, characterizes the midden, which appears stratified in some locations. Radiometric assays of four charcoal samples average 8446 B.P. (uncalibrated) in age. The principal features are hearths, each of which is marked by concentrations of ash and wood charcoal overlying a patch of highly oxidized loess, suggesting intense fire. Relatively dense scatters of artifacts including chipped-stone debitage, unretouched and retouched tools, and ground-stone implements surround hearths.

From tabulations of the tools now underway, the Koster Horizon 11 chipped-stone tool assemblage is large and diverse. The assemblage sample tabulated thus far consists of adzes, bifaces, cores, drills, gouges, gravers, hammers, projectile points, and scrapers (Table 9.7) (Brown and Vierra 1983). This suggests a variety of activities consistent with longer-term settlements, and it is comparable in diversity to assemblages from Koster Horizon 8C and 6, both Middle Archaic base settlements.

The ground-stone assemblage from Horizon 11 is particularly noteworthy (Table 9.8). In the assemblage sample tabulated so far, there are 70 ground-stone tools, including an adze, hammers, manos, pitted stones, metates, pestles, and what may be an ax or adze preform (Brown and Vierra 1983; Goland ca. 1980). All except the pestles are modified igneous rock; the cylindrical pestles are made from limestone. One of the metates is of the channel-basin style (Cook 1976:193). It has a deep channel or groove, roughly V-shaped in cross section, on obverse and reverse sides, and both surfaces are hematite stained. Two of the pestles have tapered ends that fit into the metate channel, and they too are hematite stained (Figure 9.8). The quantity and variety of implements, especially those that represent a substantial investment in design and production, such as the adze and metates, suggest a mature ground-stone industry. Ground-stone tools such as cylindrical pestles and "mealing" stones have been found in Dalton components in Missouri (e.g., Logan 1952) and in Early Archaic–period sites in Tennessee (Chapman 1973), but the course of the development of ground-stone tool production is not well known. Larger items, such as metates, that are difficult to transport may be what Binford (1978:339) has described as "site-specific 'hardware' " or "furnishings," and they appear to indicate an investment in a particular location periodically revisited over time.

Figure 9.8. A large channel-basin metate found in Horizon 11 at the Koster site. The channeled grooves in both flat sides are roughly V shaped and hematite stained, matching the shape and staining of the distal ends of two unassociated Horizon 11 limestone pestles.

Analysis of plant remains from Horizon 11 is limited to those from a single unit (Asch et al. 1972). Oak (*Quercus* sp.) dominates the wood-charcoal assemblage. Hickory (*Carya* sp.) accounts for 95.7 percent of the nutshell charcoal. Seeds were found in such low density as to indicate that they were not collected for food. Further analysis of Koster Horizon 11 plant remains has been reported (Asch and Asch 1979), but a species breakdown was not included in the report. A larger sample of animal remains from Horizon 11 has been studied (Neusius 1982). The assemblage consists of terrestrial species, especially forest mammals such as deer, squirrel, raccoon, woodchuck, and opossum, and aquatic species such as mussels, fish, semiaquatic turtles, and waterfowl. A broad-spectrum subsistence strategy is indicated, one not concentrated on a particular habitat or species (Neusius 1982).

The Campbell Hollow site is located on the north side of Campbell Hollow in a hillside swale near the embouchure of a small tributary of the Illinois River (Stafford 1985). Here CAA archaeologists working on the FAP 408 project discovered a 4.6-m-thick stratified, two-component deposit in colluvial swale fill and a colluvial fan. The deepest artifact-bearing deposit is a small Early Archaic 2 component covering 100 m^2 at most. A single pit feature was found but no hearths. Chipped-stone implements from the component include a biface, an object similar to a Dalton adze, a blade, a burin, a scraper, and a retouched flake; no hafted bifaces were found. Subsistence remains consist of wood charcoal (elm and oak) and hickory nutshell but no seeds. Animal bone was poorly preserved and fragmented. Small to medium mammals dominate the assemblage. Only two specimens could be attributed to white-tailed deer, and there is some evidence for use of fish (Colburn 1985). C. R. Stafford (1985:250) describes the settlement as a short-term residential camp.

Koster-Phase Settlement. The distribution of Early Archaic 2 settlements has not been studied. Site inventory data often do not identify projectile point type, so research will require firsthand inspection of site assemblages.

Koster-Phase Mortuary Component. Koster Horizon 11 excavators discovered the skeletal remains of nine humans, four infants and five adults (Wright 1987). Most of the graves were found outside a "living" area in which several hearths were located. But two graves within the "living" area suggest repeated occupation. Infants were placed in shallow graves, perhaps on their left side. The remains were then covered with midden. No artifacts appear to have been placed in their graves. The flexed remains of each adult (two females, a male, a probable male, and an individual whose sex could not be ascertained) were placed individually into relatively deep, straight-walled, circular to oval pits (Wright 1987). An artifact was placed with only one individual, the probable male. The object is a cylinder of white-tailed-deer antler, each end of which is cut transversely across the width of the beam. The specimen has also been drilled transversely across the width of the antler. A deer antler tine, the base of which has been drilled to create a socket was pounded into one

Table 9.7. Chipped-Stone Tool Assemblages from Selected Archaic-Period Components in the Lower Illinois River Basin.

Site	Adze	Ax	Biface	Blade	Burin	Chopper	Core	Drill	Gouge	Graver	Hammer	Piece Esquillee	Point	Retouched Flake	Scraper	Uniface	Unknown	Wedge	Total	Source
Koster 11	10	-	76	-	-	-	57	5	2	26	9	-	17	-	125	-	-	-	327	Goland ca. 1980
Campbell EA	1	-	22	2	5	-	-	-	-	-	-	-	-	27	4	-	-	1	62	Stafford 1985:39
Koster 10B	-	-	7	-	-	-	1	-	-	-	1	-	1	4	6	-	-	-	20	Lurie 1982:127–133
Koster 10A	-	-	14	-	-	-	1	-	-	-	-	-	2	9	9	-	-	-	35	Lurie 1982:127–133
Koster 9D	-	-	6	-	-	-	1	-	-	-	-	-	-	6	17	-	-	-	30	Lurie 1982:127–133
Koster 9C	-	-	5	-	-	-	4	-	-	-	-	-	1	5	4	-	2	-	21	Lurie 1982:127–133
Koster 9AB	-	-	18	-	-	-	30	-	-	-	2	-	9	63	97	-	23	-	242	Lurie 1982:127–133
Campbell MA	1	-	196	3	11	2	2	7	-	1	-	2	26	75	38	7	-	10	381	Stafford 1985:39
Koster 8D	-	-	59	-	-	-	3	-	-	-	2	-	4	23	109	-	10	-	210	Lurie 1982:127–133
Koster 8C	-	-	144	-	-	-	91	-	-	-	29	-	57	208	192	-	147	-	868	Lurie 1982:127–133
Koster 8B	-	-	117	-	-	-	85	-	-	-	9	-	53	312	177	-	153	-	906	Lurie 1982:127–133
Napoleon N	-	-	48	2	4	-	17	3	-	1	11	-	8	23	21	1	-	1	140	Odell 1996:247
Napoleon H	-	-	116	8	17	-	46	11	-	8	61	-	43	62	43	7	-	1	423	Odell 1996:247
Koster 6 Lower	-	-	64	-	-	-	103	5	-	-	14	-	24	-	40	-	-	-	250	Cook 1976:76–77
Slim Lake	2	1	449	3	6	-	205	12	1	8	-	-	82	297	37	37	-	2	1142	Stafford 1989:45
Koster 6 Middle	-	-	728	-	-	-		69	-	-	100	-	308	-	851	-	-	-	3,576	Cook 1976:79–81
Elizabeth Submound 6	-	-	71	13	22	1	-	3	-	3	-	-	17	61	28	6	1	-	226	Odell 1988:157
Napoleon T	1	1	93	12	29	-	29	27	-	25	-	-	21	82	48	3	-	7	378	Odell 1996:247
Koster 4	-	-	42	-	-	3	60	6	-	2	6	-	42	-	3	36	-	-	200	Cook 1976:44
Titus	-	-	66	-	-	-	55	13	-	-	13	-	21	-	12	-	-	-	180	Druhot 1983

Note: EA = Early Archaic, MA = Middle Archaic, N = Napoleon phase, H = Helton phase, T = Titterington phase.

Table 9.8. Ground-Stone Tool Assemblages from Selected Archaic-Period Components in the Lower Illinois River Basin.

Site	Abrader	Adze	Ax	Celt	Hammer	Mano	Metate	Pestle	Pitted	Plummet	Worked	Shaped Total	Total	Reference
Koster 11	3	3	1	-	38	8	4	4	12	-	-	73	73	Goland ca. 1980
Campbell EA	-	-	-	-	1	-	-	-	-	-	14	1	15	Stafford 1985:39
Koster 10B	-	-	-	-	1	1	-	1	1	-	-	4	4	Cook 1983
Koster 10A	-	-	-	-	1	2	-	-	-	-	-	3	3	Cook 1983
Koster 9D	-	-	-	-	2	-	-	-	-	-	-	2	2	Cook 1983
Koster 9C	-	-	-	-	-	1	-	2	-	-	-	3	3	Cook 1983
Koster 9AB	-	-	-	-		-	1	2	-	-	83	3	86	Lurie 1982:146–147
Campbell MA	9	-	-	-	10	26	2	-	-	-	31	47	78	Stafford 1985:39
Koster 8D	-	-	-	-	-	-	-	-	-	-	45	0	45	Lurie 1982:146–147
Koster 8C	-	-	1	-	-	-	1	6	-	-	301	8	309	Lurie 1982:146–147
Koster 8B	-	-	3	-	-	1	-	1	-	-	194	5	199	Lurie 1982:146–147
Napoleon N	-	-	-	-	22	18	1	1	-	-	9	42	51	Odell 1996:247
Napoleon H	3	-	11	-	105	68	3	4	1	-	26	221	221	Odell 1996:247
Koster 6 Lower	1	-	3	-	17	7	2	-	19	1	-	49	49	Cook 1976:76–77
Slim Lake	2	-	3	3	80	33	2	-	9	1	26	159	159	Stafford 1989:45
Koster 6 Middle	35	-	40	-	75	152	70	-	88	3	140	460	600	Cook 1976:79–81
Elizabeth	7	1	2	-	17	29	1	-	1	-	21	58	79	Odell 1988:157
Submound 6	-	-	-	-	-	-	-	-	-	-	-	-	-	-
Napoleon T	6	-	5	1	112	24	-	-	-	-	45	148	193	Odell 1996:247
Koster 4	7	-	1	-	6	8	-	-	5	-	-	27	27	Cook 1976:44
Titus	-	-	-	-	3	34	-	-	-	-	-	37	37	Druhot 1983

Note: EA = Early Archaic, MA = Middle Archaic, N = Napoleon phase, H = Helton phase, T = Titterington phase.

end of the antler cylinder, and a piece of antler whittled to a point with a polished proximal end was pounded into the other end. This unusual item was found on the chest of the deceased (Figure 9.9). All of the adult graves were filled with midden, and in a few instances, limestone slabs were placed over the graves.

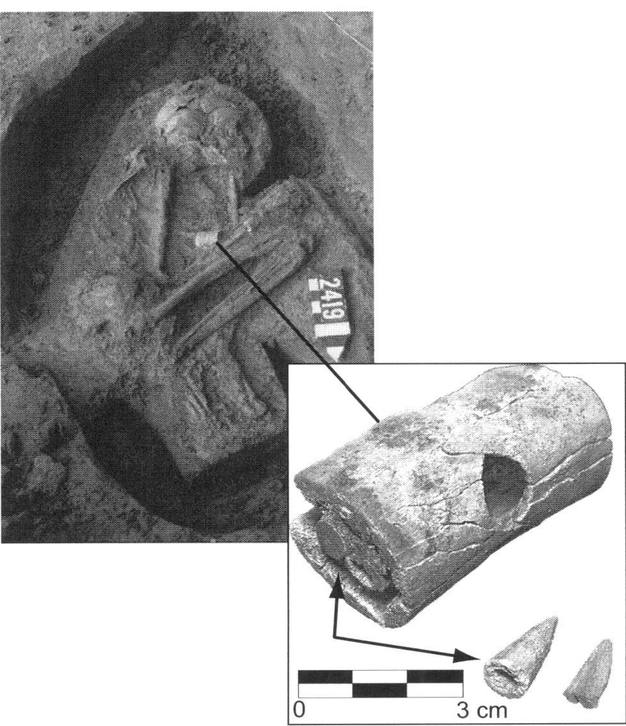

Figure 9.9. The flexed remains of a 35- to 60-year-old male (Burial 80) buried in the Koster Horizon 11 midden. The object lying on the individual's chest (see inset photo) is a cylinder cut from white-tailed-deer antler (Odocoileus virginianus). *A large hole has been drilled transversely across its width and two whittled and polished deer-antler tines have been pounded into each end. In each case, one of the exposed tine ends has been has been smoothed and the other drilled. The object may have been an atlatl totem.*

Early Archaic graves also may have been present at the Bullseye site. Excavators discovered a variety of hafted bifaces, such as Hardin Barbed, St. Charles, Stilwell, and Thebes, but they could not be associated with a particular skeleton because of poor bone preservation and the difficulties of tracing the outline of graves in sandy sediment (Hassen and Farnsworth 1987).

Graves containing the remains of dogs were also found in the Horizon 11 settlement (Morey and Wiant 1993). The evidence of their treatment alone—buried in prepared graves, articulated and nearly complete, no indication of butchering—suggests that they were members of the community (Figure 9.10). Further analysis of their skeletons documented morphological characteristics consistent with domestication (Morey and Wiant 1993).

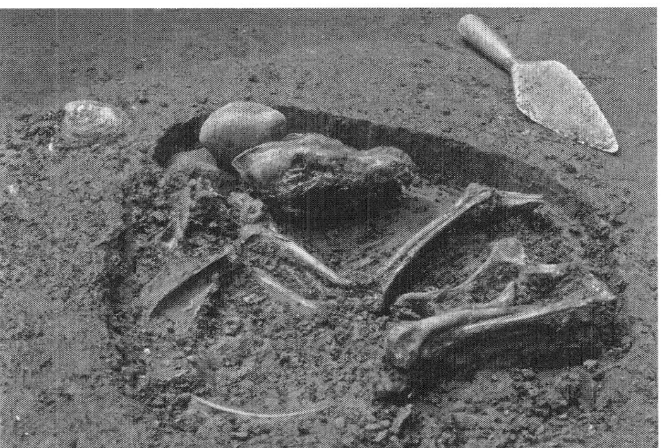

Figure 9.10. The articulated remains of a dog (Canis familiaris) *found in a shallow grave (F2256) in Koster Horizon 11. The dog's head is resting against a mano and metate. Dispersed charcoal from the grave has been radiocarbon dated at 8470 ± 110 B. P. (ISGS-1762).*

Middle Archaic (8200–4400 B.P.)

Brown and Vierra (1983) divided the Middle Archaic period in the lower Illinois River basin into three subperiods: Middle Archaic 1 (8200–7600 B.P.), Middle Archaic 2 (7300–6850 B.P.), and Middle Archaic 3 (5800–4900 B.P.). On the basis of artifacts and radiocarbon assays from Buckshaw Bridge (11BR242; Stafford 1991; Figure 9.1) and Napoleon Hollow, we now believe that the Middle Archaic 3 subperiod should range in age from 6350 to 4400 B.P. These sites provide evidence of the development of large, perhaps multiseason base settlements (Brown 1985; Brown and Vierra 1983; Carlson 1979) and specialized encampments strategically situated to exploit a particular suite of resources (Stafford 1991). They also provide evidence of considerably greater reliance on white-tailed deer (Neusius 1982), aquatic resources (Styles 1986), and hickory nuts (Asch et al. 1972) as well as evidence of cultivated squash (Conard et al. 1983). More elaborate mortuary practices evolved during Middle Archaic 3 times, including the development of the first bluff-crest cemeteries (Charles and Buikstra 1983).

Middle Archaic 1 (8200–7600 B.P.): Campbell Hollow Phase

Information on Middle Archaic 1 is derived from the Campbell Hollow Middle Archaic component (Stafford 1985), Koster Horizons 10B through 8E (Asch and Asch 1978; Brown and Vierra 1983; Carlson 1979; Cook 1983; Lurie 1982; Neusius 1982), and Titus Horizon 3 (Druhot 1983).

Campbell Hollow–Phase Component Identification. A heretofore-unnamed corner-notched to expanding-stem point is the only artifact typical of the Middle Archaic 1 sites excavated in the lower Illinois Valley. We propose the name *Campbell Hollow* for these points, which have been found in the remains of a short-lived settlement at the Campbell Hollow site (Stafford 1985; Figures 9.1 and 9.11). Three charcoal samples from this deposit range in age from 7560 ± 80 B.P. (ISGS-940) to 7670 ± 90 B.P. (ISGS-936). Campbell Hollow points are not the only type of point found in the Middle Archaic component at the Campbell Hollow site. The point assemblage also includes an Early Archaic Neuberger point (Conrad 1981) (Figure 6:9-08-1) and several other unidentified points, many of which have been repaired or reworked. Campbell Hollow points have also been found at Koster in Horizons 10A, 9A/9B, and 9B (Figure 9.12), where they occur with other point types.

Figure 9.11. Middle Archaic Campbell Hollow points from the Campbell Hollow site (ca. 7600 B.P.): a, 62-04a-1; b, 40-02a NE-1; c, 50-04a-2; d, 9-08-1.

Figure 9.12. Middle Archaic points from Koster Horizons 9 and 10 (ca. 7800–8200 B.P.): a, Hz 9B 178-056a Art#3; b, 194-050b-2; c, 262-029-1; d, Hz 10 241-049a-Art#1; e, Hz 9A/B 164-047-Art#1; f, 166-030-11.

At the Koster site, Brown and Vierra (1983) attribute eight components to Middle Archaic 1 (Table 9.5). They range in age from 8230 ± 120 B.P. (ISGS-783) (Horizon 10A—the 10A/10B dates are out of sequence) to 7630 ± 210 B.P. (ISGS-210) (Horizon 8E). The average number of stone tools recovered from Koster Horizons 10B through 9C is only 18 chipped-stone and two ground-stone specimens per horizon. In contrast, there are 199 chipped-stone and 60 ground-stone tools from Horizons 9A and 9B. Unifacially retouched tools—scrapers (*n* = 97) and retouched flakes (*n* = 63)—dominate the chipped-stone tool assemblage (Table 9.7) (Cook 1983; Lurie 1982). Ground-stone tools include hammers, manos, and pestles (Table 9.8) (Carlson 1979; Cook 1983; Lurie 1982). Hearths appear to have been the center of activities and are the only type of feature present. Hickory accounts for 70 percent of the nutshell, except in Horizon 9, where pecan is most abundant. The nutshell-to-wood ratio steadily increases through subsequent Middle Archaic 1 deposits, and evidence indicates major reliance on nuts was established by 7500–7000 B.P., during the Middle Archaic 2 period. Seeds are not common in Middle Archaic 1 charcoal assemblages (Asch and Asch 1978). Residents of the Middle Archaic 1 settlements relied mostly on mammals and mussels and, to a lesser extent, fish. Procurement was opportunistic, focused on forests, and somewhat less on aquatic habitats (Neusius 1982:180–185). On the basis of spatial analysis, Carlson (1979) concludes that these components represent short-term occupations by small bands, though Horizons 9A and 9B, which are characterized by small generalized activity areas surrounded by scattered animal bone and manufacturing debris, may reflect occupation for longer periods of time.

The Campbell Hollow Middle Archaic component compares favorably with the Koster Middle Archaic 1 horizons, especially Horizons 9A and 9B, though there are noteworthy differences. As is the case at Koster, hearths appear to have been the center of activity at Campbell Hollow, but there are also a few shallow basin-shaped pits, which may have been hearth related (Stafford 1985:37). The chipped-stone assemblage is large (*n* = 381) and diverse but dominated by bifaces (*n* = 222), 26 of which are points (Table 9.7). Retouched flakes (*n* = 75) and scrapers (*n* = 38) are numerous but less common (Odell 1996; Stafford 1985). The shaped ground-stone assemblage (*n* = 47) consists of manos (*n* = 26), hammers (*n* = 10), abraders (*n* = 9), and metates (*n* = 2), all grinding and manufacturing tools (Table 9.8) (Odell 1996; Stafford 1985). Black walnut accounts for 69 percent of nutshell in this component, followed by hickory, the dominant nutshell type in the Koster Middle Archaic 1 components, with 20 percent of the total (Asch and Asch 1985:90). Seeds are infrequent (*n* = 11). Animal bone is poorly preserved, but there is a wide range of terrestrial and aquatic mammals, fish, waterfowl, and turtles. Exploitation of white-tailed deer, in particular, is consistent with a trend of increased use of larger-bodied mammals (Colburn 1985:120). C. R. Stafford (1985:254) concludes that this component represents a short-term residential camp, whereas Odell (1996:68) posits a longer-term occupation on the basis of intensive use of debris, though this economizing strategy may reflect local scarcity of lithic resources.

At Titus, four (perhaps five) excavation units encountered Horizon 3 between depths of 3.93 m and 4.64 m below the ground surface. Radiometric assays of charcoal from this stratum indicate occupation during Middle Archaic 1 (Table 9.5), but the only culturally diagnostic artifact is the base of an Agate Basin point. An oval bifacial scraper, the base of an unidentified biface, and a broken drill are the only other chipped-stone artifacts from Horizon 3. Animal bone and charcoal are present in this horizon, but the samples collected have yet to be identified and analyzed.

Campbell Hollow–Phase Settlement. Asch et al. (1981) tabulated the distribution of pre-Helton sites in the region. They did not report what they considered diagnostic artifacts, but at the time of their work, Cook's (1976) Koster-site Helton-phase study had established the prevailing projectile point typology for the region. They identified only six sites with pre-Helton components. Of these, they classified the landscape position of four as dissected uplands and two as valley landforms. The difficulty of identifying distinctive diagnostic artifacts hampers the study of Middle Archaic settlement distribution and whether climate change influenced landscape use.

Campbell Hollow–Phase Mortuary Components. Solitary human graves were discovered in Horizons 10A, 9A, and 8F at the Koster site. Evidently, when a member of the community died, his or her remains were expediently interred.

Middle Archaic 2 (7300–6340 B.P.): Napoleon Phase

Information on Middle Archaic 2 settlements is from Koster site Horizons 8A, 8B, 8C, and 8D (Asch and Asch 1978; Asch et al. 1972; Brown and Vierra 1983; Carlson 1979; Hill 1975; Lurie 1982; Neusius 1982); the Napoleon component at the Napoleon Hollow site (Asch and Asch 1980; Conard et al. 1983; Odell 1996; Wiant 1980); and Quasar (Goatley 1998).

Napoleon Phase–Component Identification. Middle Archaic 2 projectile point assemblages are varied. Although side-notched forms are most common, no particular type stands out as diagnostic of this period. In fact, some types such as Godar (Perino 1963:95) and Matanzas (Munson and Harn 1966:153) appeared during this period for the first time and persisted until at least 4400 B.P. In addition to side-notched points, stemmed forms, including expanding-stem varieties such as Table Rock Stemmed (Bray 1956), are also present in appreciable numbers. There are eight points from Koster Horizon 8D, four of which are side-notched Godar points (Figure 9.13). The rest are type-indeterminate corner-notched points (*n* = 3) and a stemmed variety (*n* = 1). Side-notched varieties such as Godar (*n* = 3) and an Osceola-like form (*n* = 1) also dominate the Koster Horizon 8C assemblage (62 percent, *n* = 10), but two expanding-stem points and three other stemmed points are also present. A fourth stemmed form is a hafted end scraper (Figures 9.14 and 9.15). There are 25 points from Koster Horizon 8B. Side-notched forms, including Godar (*n* = 3) and Matanzas (*n* = 2), account for 32 percent of the points, but expanding-stem (*n* = 8, 32 percent) and other stemmed (*n* = 7, 28 percent) types are also present (Figure 9.16). The same is true for the Napoleon component: half the points are side-notched (*n* = 6), followed in order of frequency by expanding-stem and type-indeterminate points (Figure 9.17). It is noteworthy, however, that hafted end scrapers in the Napoleon-component assemblage are generally stemmed—the same is true for the other Middle Archaic 2 assemblages—and there are three examples of edge-retouched flakes that appear to be expediently produced points. Perhaps haft design was determined by implement function: points are side-notched; end scrapers are stemmed. Many of the specimens are damaged or show evidence of repair. For example, 11 of the 12 specimens in the Napoleon-component assemblage are incomplete, suggesting that they were discarded here, perhaps during the process of retooling. In one instance (specimen NPH35-045), a blade fragment was reworked into a side-notched form.

Figure 9.13. Godar points from Koster Horizon 8D (ca. 7300 B.P.): a, 150-19-Art#1; b, 212-37a-7; c, 254-19-2.

What accounts for the variety in Middle Archaic 2 points? Many of these specimens appear to be small dart points, suggesting increasing use of the atlatl. Is it possible that development of a new form of armament resulted in a greater variety of projectiles? Is the variety attributable to differences in tool function (e.g., spear points, dart points, knives, and end

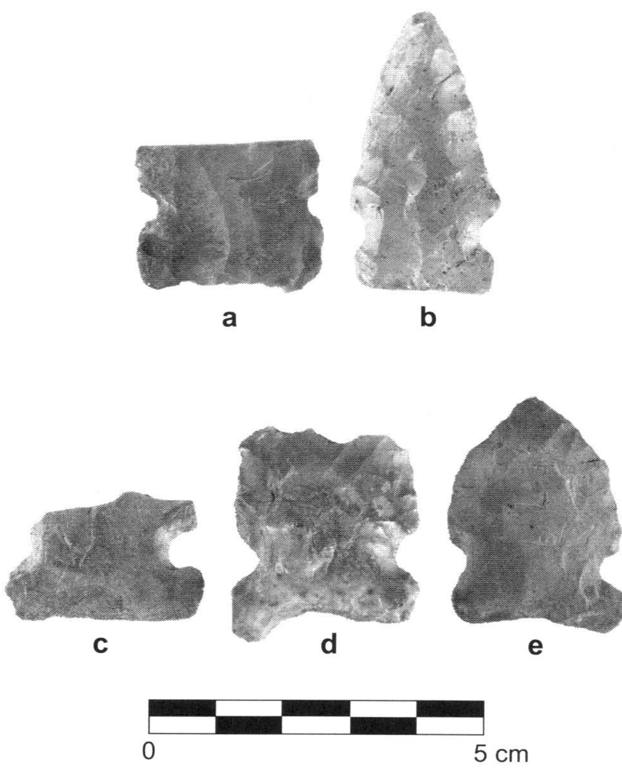

Figure 9.14. Godar/Osceola-like points from Koster Horizon 8C (ca. 7000 B.P.): a, 149-19-2064; b, 249-22-1; c, 250-11-5; d, 251-20-2; e, F1656a-1.

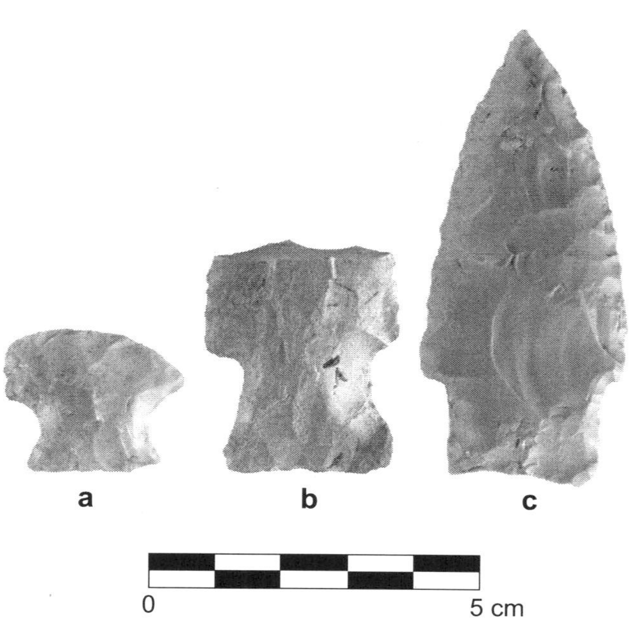

Figure 9.15. Stemmed and expanding-stemmed points from Koster Horizon 8C (ca. 7000 B.P.): a, 206-14-1; b, 221-22-Art#1; c, 221-25-1.

Figure 9.16. Point types from Koster Horizon 8B (ca. 6975 B.P.): a, 6425-Art#1; b, 190-019-1; c, 248-09-1; d, 252-17-1; e, 30-37-Art#1; f, 40-28-Art#2; g, 143-29-2; h, 154-07-1; i, 165-009-Art#1.

Figure 9.17. Napoleon-phase Middle Archaic side-notched and expanding-stemmed points from the Napoleon Hollow site (ca. 6600–6800 B.P.): a, 78-42b-1 (hafted scraper); b, 84-45-1 (hafted scraper); c, 84-48-1; d, 37-59-1; e, 43-39-1; f, 76-42a-1; g, 77-39b-1.

scrapers)? Did some of these varieties persist because they were technically superior to others? More research is necessary to address these questions.

Napoleon-Phase Habitation Components. Koster Middle Archaic 2 components—Horizons 8D, 8C, and 8B—signal a development in settlement strategy: substantial evidence for increasing sedentism (Brown 1985; Brown and Vierra 1983; Carlson 1979; Doershuk 1989; Hewitt 1983) is reflected by the organization of activities (Carlson 1979; Doershuk 1989; Wolynec 1977), intensification of resource use (Asch et al. 1972; Asch and Asch 1978; Hewitt 1983; Neusius 1982; Styles 1986), and technological developments (Lurie 1982).

The organization of the Koster Horizon 8D occupation (7320 ± 70 B.P. [ISGS-817]) is comparable to Middle Archaic 1 settlements: hearths were the focus of a variety of activities, and there is only a single storage pit (Doershuk 1989:182). Edge-retouched chert tools account for 60 percent of the assemblage, twice the proportion of bifacial tools (Table 9.7) (Lurie 1982:127). There are no identifiable ground-stone tools, but 45 pieces of igneous and metamorphic rock are modified (Table 9.8) (Lurie 1982:146). In comparison with the Middle Archaic 1 settlements, evidence indicates a substantial increase in the use of aquatic resources, especially those from rivers and streams rather than backwater lakes, while white-tailed deer dominate the mammalian skeletal remains (Neusius 1982:188, 265), suggesting a more focused hunting-gathering strategy than indicated by the Middle Archaic 1 faunal assemblages (Neusius 1982:252). Hickory accounts for nearly 90 percent of the nutshell, followed in abundance by black walnut and then pecan (Asch and Asch 1979:Figure 3), and seeds are not common, a consistent pattern in Middle Archaic 2 settlements. Horizon 8D represents a series of residential camps (Carlson 1979:350; Doershuk 1989:195).

The sheer number of artifacts and features in Horizon 8C (7020 ± 120 B.P. [ISGS-338], 6970 ± 150 B.P. [ISGS-800]) indicates a more complicated settlement, which is confirmed by analysis of its organization (Carlson 1979; Doershuk 1989). The discovery of eight terraces on the colluvial slope and several post molds is evidence for a fundamental change in settlement, although there is some debate about the interpretation of these features. Carlson (1979:352) finds the number of post molds insufficient to support an argument for the presence of a structure, but Brown and Vierra (1983:184) conclude that the deep post pits represent heavy wall supports for a substantial structure. Interior hearths and a substantial accumulation of debris lend some weight to their argument (see also Doershuk 1989:203).

There are 135 additional features, including 28 hearths, although there is substantial intrasite variability in their distribution and feature patterning does not suggest a particular internal site structure (Doershuk 1989). In comparison with Horizon 8D, the variety of tool forms is more evenly proportioned—biface (23 percent), uniface (18 percent), edge-retouched flake (31 percent) (Table 9.7) (Lurie 1982:127)—and formal rather than expedient tools dominate the assemblage (Lurie 1982). Subsistence procurement concentrated on fewer environmental niches, as indicated by the frequency of mussels, fish, and white-tailed deer (Neusius 1982, 1986; Styles 1986). Hickory nuts account for 92 percent of the carbonized nutshell. There is a greater variety in seeds when compared with Middle Archaic 1 components, but most are fruit seeds, not staples. *Iva* seeds are present, but their size is consistent with natural stands. Goosefoot and maygrass seeds are also present (Asch and Asch 1979). All told, Horizon C represents the remains of a substantial base settlement (Carlson 1979:362).

In Horizon 8B (7000 ± 80 B.P. [ISGS-809], 6960 ± 80 B.P. [ISGS-848]), the debris density is comparable to that of 8C, as is the number of artifacts, but there are fewer features, only three of which show evidence of burning (Carlson 1979:367). Horizon 8B represents another substantial settlement, but parts of the deposit appear to commingle with 8C, thereby obscuring organization of the 8B settlement (Carlson 1979:372). Likewise, a portion of Horizon 8A (6860 ± 80 B.P. [ISGS-835]) is disturbed and ephemeral. The variety of tools suggests more activity than expected for a specialized hunting camp, but the occupation's purpose is not yet understood (Carlson 1979:378).

At Napoleon Hollow, the Napoleon component represents a Middle Archaic 2 occupation that can be compared with the Koster sequence. The Napoleon component was found in a paleosol (Gs-c [Styles 1985]) approximately 2 m below the present-day ground surface. Excavators exposed only 56 m^2 of the deposit. Three radiometric assays of charcoal from this deposit range in age from 7000 ± 250 B.P. (NSRL-299) to 6630 ± 100 B.P. (ISGS-786) (Table 9.5). The chipped-stone tool assemblage is mostly bifacial (Table 9.7; see also Odell 1996:247). On the basis of its variety and an assessment of use wear, Odell (1996) found evidence of butchering and hide scraping, food and animal-hide preparation, woodworking, tool manufacturing, and tool maintenance. Two features, both hearths, appear to have been the focus of activity. Elm accounts for 66 percent of the wood charcoal, whereas oak (44 percent) and ash (23 percent) are most common in Koster Horizon 8 (Asch and Asch 1979; Asch et al. 1972). The proportion and variety of nutshell charcoal from Napoleon Hollow are strikingly different when compared with nutshell from Middle Archaic 2 components at Koster. Thick-shelled hickory (44 percent) is most common, followed by pecan (23 percent) and walnut (27 percent). In contrast, nearly 92 percent of the nutshell from Middle Archaic 2 components at Koster is hickory (Asch et al. 1972). Only 41 seeds have been identified. Wild bean is the most common, followed by giant ragweed. Fragments of cucurbit rind appear to be *C. pepo*. Radiometric assay of a specimen resulted in the age estimate of 7000 ± 250 (NSRL-299) noted above (Conard et al. 1983). Deer account for 78 percent of the number of identified faunal specimens, while fish is a distant second at 8.1 percent. The proportions of fish and medium-sized mammals are comparable to those in the Middle Archaic 2 components at Koster, but a higher proportion of terrestrial turtles is present at Koster and a smaller proportion of deer when compared with the Napoleon-component assemblage (Styles and McMillan Figure 3.10, this volume). Taken together, the evidence from the Napoleon components suggests a settlement more like Koster Horizon 8D than 8C, perhaps a seasonal residential base settlement.

Quasar is the location of a stratified multicomponent deposit exposed at the present-day surface and incorporated in the body of a relict natural levee near the bank of the Illinois River (Goatley 1998). No diagnostic artifacts were found in Stratum 4, but a radiocarbon date of 6320 ± 90 (ISGS-1278) falls within the Middle Archaic 3 interval and a date of 6500 ± 100 (ISGS-2486) falls within the Middle Archaic 2 interval. Analysis is not complete, but some details are available. The lithic-tool assemblage is small (n = 46). The ratio of chipped-stone to ground-stone tools is 14.3 to 1, suggesting an occupation of somewhat limited activity compared with Middle Archaic 2 components at Koster and Napoleon Hollow. Goatley (1998:272) describes each of the six features found at Quasar as a processing pit. Freshwater mussel shell is common, but the remains of white-tailed deer, turtle, and fish—catfish, sucker, bullhead, bowfin, and gar—are reported (Lopinto 1995). Thick-shelled hickory accounts for 94 percent of the nutshell charcoal, a proportion consistent with other Middle Archaic 2 settlements.

Napoleon-Phase Settlement. The study of Middle Archaic 2 settlement patterns falls prey to the same limitations described above for Middle Archaic 1 sites.

Napoleon-Phase Mortuary Components. In Koster Horizon 8D, investigators encountered a solitary human burial among a series of hearths. A grave at Quasar contained the remains of a single flexed individual with a chert core placed on the cranium (Goatley 1998:272).

Middle Archaic 3 (6350–4400 B.P.): Helton Phase

Helton-Phase Component Identification. Cook (1976) defined the Helton phase on the basis of evidence from Koster Horizon 6, a meter-thick, black, multicomponent midden incorporated in a buried paleosol (Butzer 1977, 1978; Hajic 1981a, 1990b). He identified four specific types of projectile points (see below), incised bone pins, and a distinctive channel-basin metate as typical of Helton-phase components (Cook 1976:69, 73–74). Matanzas points, particularly those that Cook (1976:140) identified as "modal" Matanzas (Figure 9.18) and "flared stem" Matanzas (Figure 9.19), along with Godar (Figure 9.20) and Karnak Stemmed points (Winters 1969:25) (Figure 9.21), dominate the Horizon 6 assemblages. Other forms, such as "Helton points" (the name originally used for Matanzas varieties by Houart [1971:36] and later used by Cook [1976:147] in reference to an expanding-stem point), unidentified side- and corner-notched points, and stemmed points, were also found in Horizon 6 (Figure 9.22). Apple Blossom points (Cook 1976:147), some of which were found in the Koster Horizon 6 assemblage, are more common in the older Horizon 8 assemblages. As noted above, Matanzas and Godar points are found in Middle Archaic 2 components (7300–6320 B.P.), but they clearly persisted until at least 4400 B.P. at the Buckshaw Bridge site (Stafford 1991). Karnak Stemmed points appear for the first time in Horizon 6 contexts. This same suite of points—Matanzas, Godar, and Karnak—is found at Napoleon Hollow in Helton-phase components (6100–5000 B.P.) (Figures 9.23–9.26) and at the Quasar site (5300–5200 B.P.).

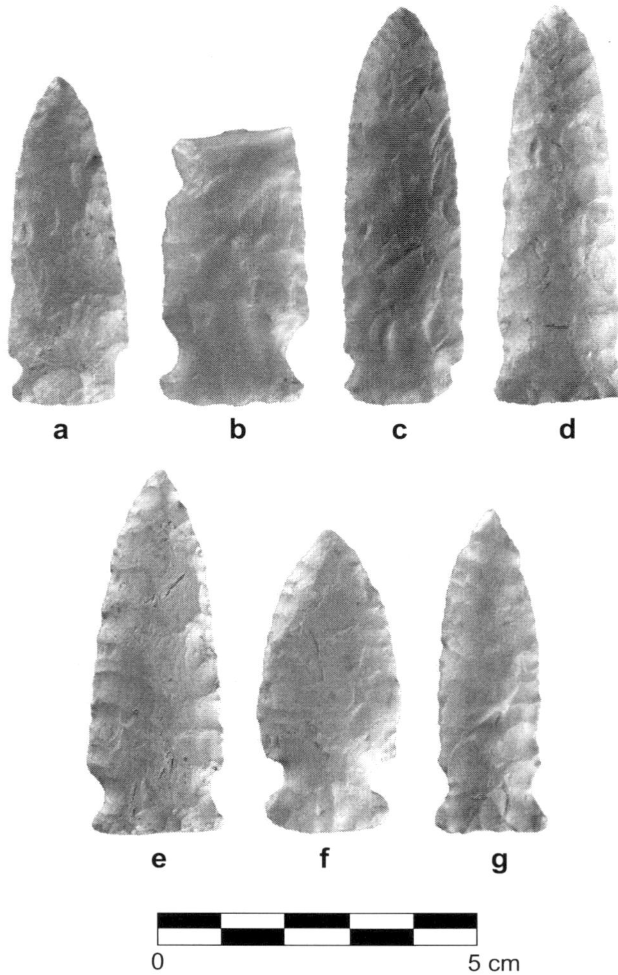

Figure 9.18. Helton-phase Middle Archaic "modal" Matanzas points from Koster Horizon 6 (ca. 5700–4800 B.P.): a, 5-14-3; b, 21-35-1; c, 23-19-3; d, 36-16-195; e, 45-07-2; f, 47-22-3; g, 55-26-3.

Cook (1976:74) also identified bone pins decorated with incised lines applied in several geometric patterns as typical of the Helton phase (Figure 9.27). Koster Horizon 6 artisans made these distinctive decorated pins by splitting, grinding, polishing, and engraving white-tailed-deer bone. No similar engraved bone pins have been found at the Napoleon Hollow or Quasar sites. The third artifact identified by Cook (1976:73)

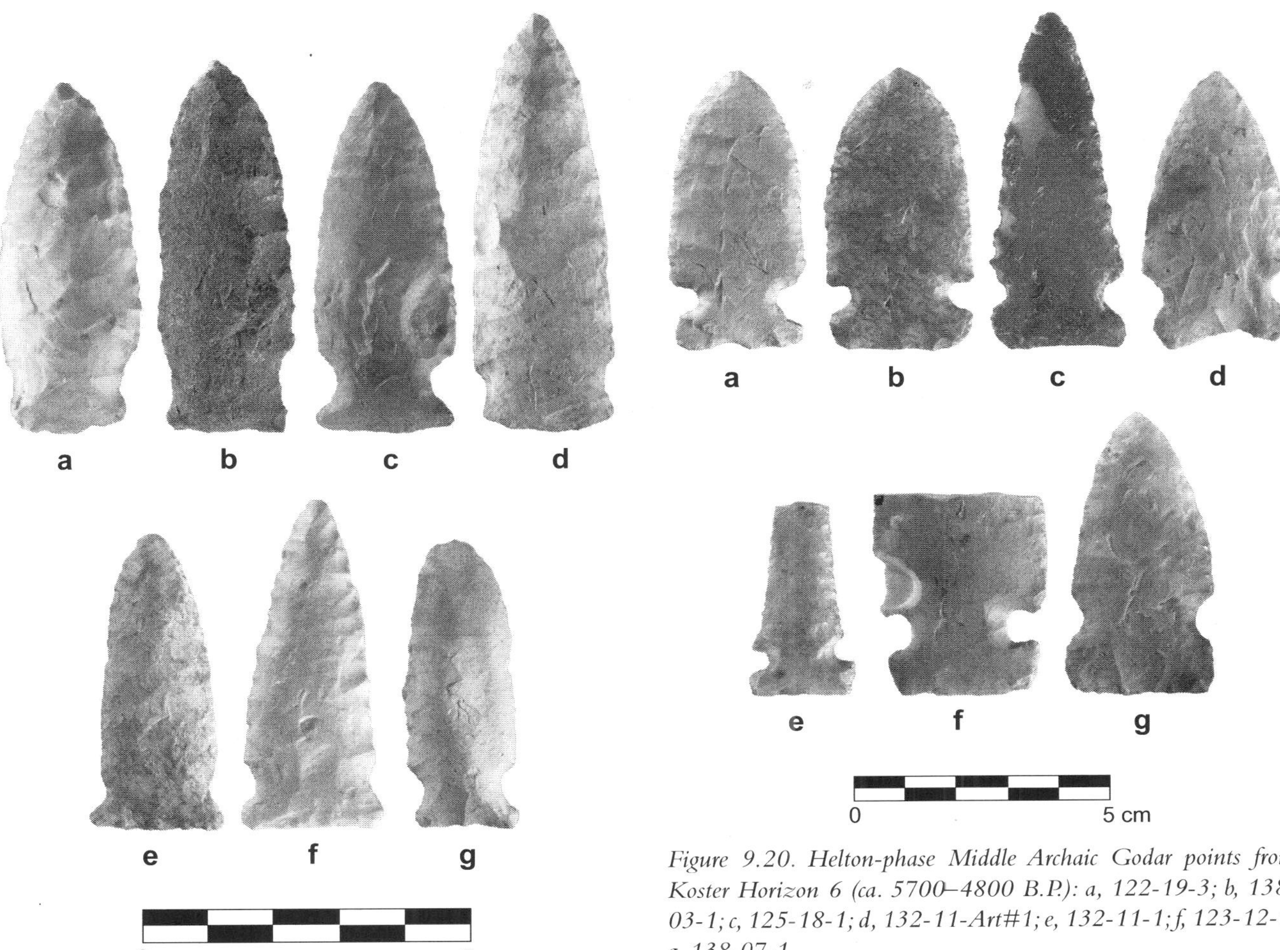

Figure 9.19. Helton-phase Middle Archaic "flared stem" Matanzas points from Koster Horizon 6 (ca. 5700–4800 B.P.): a, 8-35-1; b, 15-25-Art#2; c, 24-26-1; d, 47-20-Art#1; e, 47-23-1; f, 52-15-Art#2; g, 52-24-Art#3.

Figure 9.20. Helton-phase Middle Archaic Godar points from Koster Horizon 6 (ca. 5700–4800 B.P.): a, 122-19-3; b, 138-03-1; c, 125-18-1; d, 132-11-Art#1; e, 132-11-1; f, 123-12-1; g, 138-07-1.

as typical of the Helton phase is the channel-basin metate. This is a very large igneous cobble that has a flat, semipolished grinding surface around an oblong depression. The discovery of a channel-basin metate in the Koster Horizon 11 midden (ca. 8500 B.P.) calls into question the identification of this artifact type as diagnostic of the Helton phase.

Helton-Phase Habitation Components. Although difficult to discern because of the color, density, and thickness of the midden, hundreds of features—hearths, basins, pits, and perhaps house floors—were found throughout Horizon 6 at the Koster site (Wolynec 1977). Comparing the distribution of features in Horizons 8C, 6B, and 6A, Wolynec (1977) concludes that a positive correlation can be drawn between the organization of space and the duration of occupation, a conclusion reached by Carlson (1979) and Doershuk (1989), as well, in their analysis of earlier occupations at Koster.

The Horizon 6 lithic tool assemblage is impressive in sheer size (n = 3,826) and variety (Table 9.7), and it provides a clear measure of the intensity of occupation. The assemblage also includes a variety of bone tools such as antler flakers and bone awls but no evidence of handles or atlatl hooks and only one bone fishhook, artifacts typical of contemporary sites elsewhere (see Jefferies, this volume). The combination of chipped-stone, ground-stone, and bone tools represents a wide range of activities, from resource procurement to tool replacement (Tables 9.7 and 9.8). More than 95 percent of nutshell charcoal is thick-shelled hickory. After analyzing wood charcoal, Asch and Asch (1979:11) observe with interest that hickory is poorly represented in assemblages from earlier settlements occupied during the Hypsithermal Interval. Elm, walnut, and oak are more abundant. Marsh elder accounts for more than 40 percent of the seed assemblage, and goosefoot, knotweed, and maygrass together total less than 15 percent. Marsh elder achene size is consistent with wild stands. The plant may have been cultivated but not yet domesticated (Asch and Asch 1978). The well-preserved animal-bone assemblage indicates a broad-based strategy that included hunting, fowling, fishing, and mussel collecting, with

Figure 9.21. Helton-phase Middle Archaic Karnak points from Koster Horizon 6 (ca. 5700–4800 B.P.): a, 8-34-Sp#1; b, 37-25-4; c, 50-25-Art#2; d, 64-01-4; e, 111-20-Art#1; f, 125-25-Art#1.

Figure 9.22. Helton-phase Middle Archaic shouldered, stemmed points from Koster Horizon 6 (ca. 5700–4800 B.P.): a, 14-35-Art#1; b, 42-21-Art#1; c, 47-16-1; d, 54-25-Art#1; e, 56-18-Art#1; f, 57-17-4; g, 9-12-Art#1; h, 111-21-Art#2.

particular emphasis on aquatic resources (Brown and Vierra 1983:188–189; Hill 1975; Styles 1986). The principal resources from terrestrial habitats included white-tailed deer, raccoon, and turkey, while the pattern of stream and riverine resource use established during Middle Archaic 2 times continued to intensify. But it is evidence of the exploitation of backwater lakes, in particular, that signals a shift in subsistence strategy from earlier times. Hill (1975) documented a substantial increase in backwater fish and mussel species and in migratory waterfowl. Later, Styles (1986), drawing on new Illinois River hydrology evidence (Hajic 1983; Styles 1984, 1985), specifically identified the formation of extensive backwater lakes in Middle Archaic 3 times, and detailed concomitant changes in aquatic-resource exploitation, particularly increases in the use of fish and mussels.

The Helton-phase component at Napoleon Hollow is a thick midden incorporated in a buried paleosol, a situation comparable to that at the Koster site (Wiant et al. 1983). Excavators found evidence of three surfaces within the midden but could not trace them throughout the 56-m^2 exposure. Charcoal from a hearth on the earliest surface yielded an age of 6080 ± 80 B.P. (ISGS-972). The age of a hearth discovered at a higher elevation is 5670 ± 70 B.P. (ISGS-806). Charcoal from a pit descending from the top of the midden-paleosol is dated to 5350 ± 70 B.P. (ISGS-938). Another sample from a nearby pit was assayed at 5140 ± 70 B.P. (ISGS-1036). The lithic tool assemblage consists of 423 chipped-stone and 221 shaped ground tools, a ratio of 1.9 to 1 (Tables 9.7 and 9.8) (Odell 1996:247). There are no bone tools, but their absence appears to be a matter of preservation. On the basis of use-wear analysis, Odell (1996:97–98) identified evidence

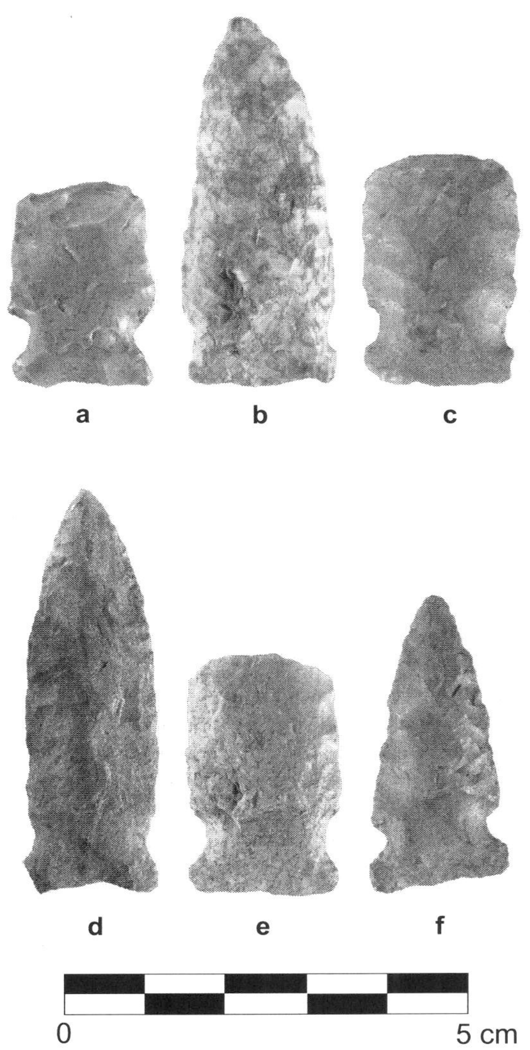

Figure 9.23. Helton-phase Middle Archaic Matanzas points from the Napoleon Hollow site (ca. 5600–4500 B.P.): a, 36-28-5; b, 37-40-1; c, 36b-25-1; d, 77-23-1; e, 84-26-1; f, F31-05c-1.

Figure 9.24. Helton-phase Middle Archaic Karnak points from the Napoleon Hollow site (ca. 5600–4500 B.P.): a, 36-25b-2; b, 75-16-1; c, 75-23b-1.

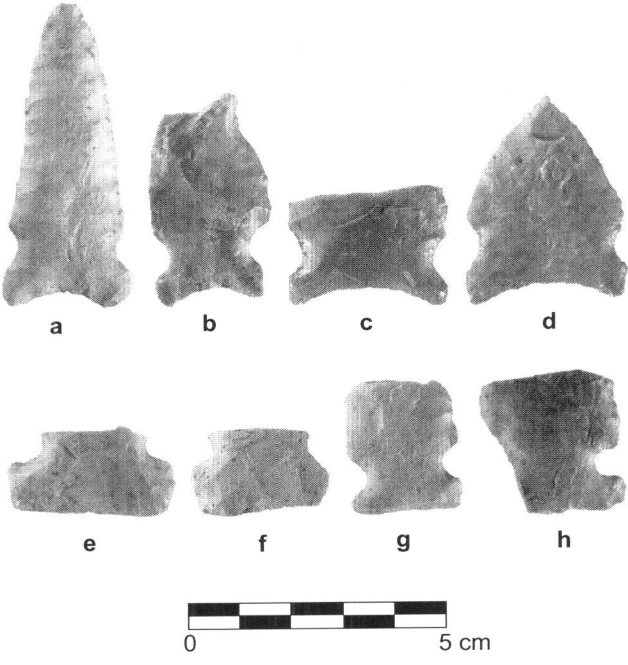

Figure 9.25. Helton-phase Middle Archaic Osceola points (a–d) and Godar points (e–h) from the Napoleon Hollow site (ca. 5600–4500 B.P.): a, 3-22-5; b, 36-28-4; c, 81-30-1; d, 83-31b-1; e, 36-35-1; f, 79-31b-1; g, 80-24-1; h, 84-29-1.

of woodworking, tool maintenance, and butchering, activities that he attributes to a more permanent settlement than indicated by the earlier Napoleon component at the site. Of the 13 features documented, seven are hearths or hearth related and three are pit features—including F-31, a deep, cylindrical pit with a fire-hardened bottom, which was filled with burned limestone. The pit orifice was also surrounded by burned limestone, suggesting stone boiling, perhaps associated with nut processing. Most of the charcoal from the Helton-phase component is nutshell. Thick-shelled hickory accounts for 93 percent of the nutshell charcoal. Seeds are not numerous. Giant ragweed is most common, followed by wild bean (Asch and Asch 1980). A preliminary analysis of faunal remains indicates that fish account for 42 percent of the number of identified specimens, followed by white-tailed deer (29 percent) and medium-sized mammal (15 percent),

Figure 9.26. Helton-phase Middle Archaic Matanzas points (a–c) and Karnak points (d–g) from the Napoleon Hollow site (ca. 5600–4500 B.P.): a, 36-17-1; b, 75-15b-1; c, 81-20-1; d, 75-13-1; e, 76-14-1; f, 77-12-1; g, 77-18-1.

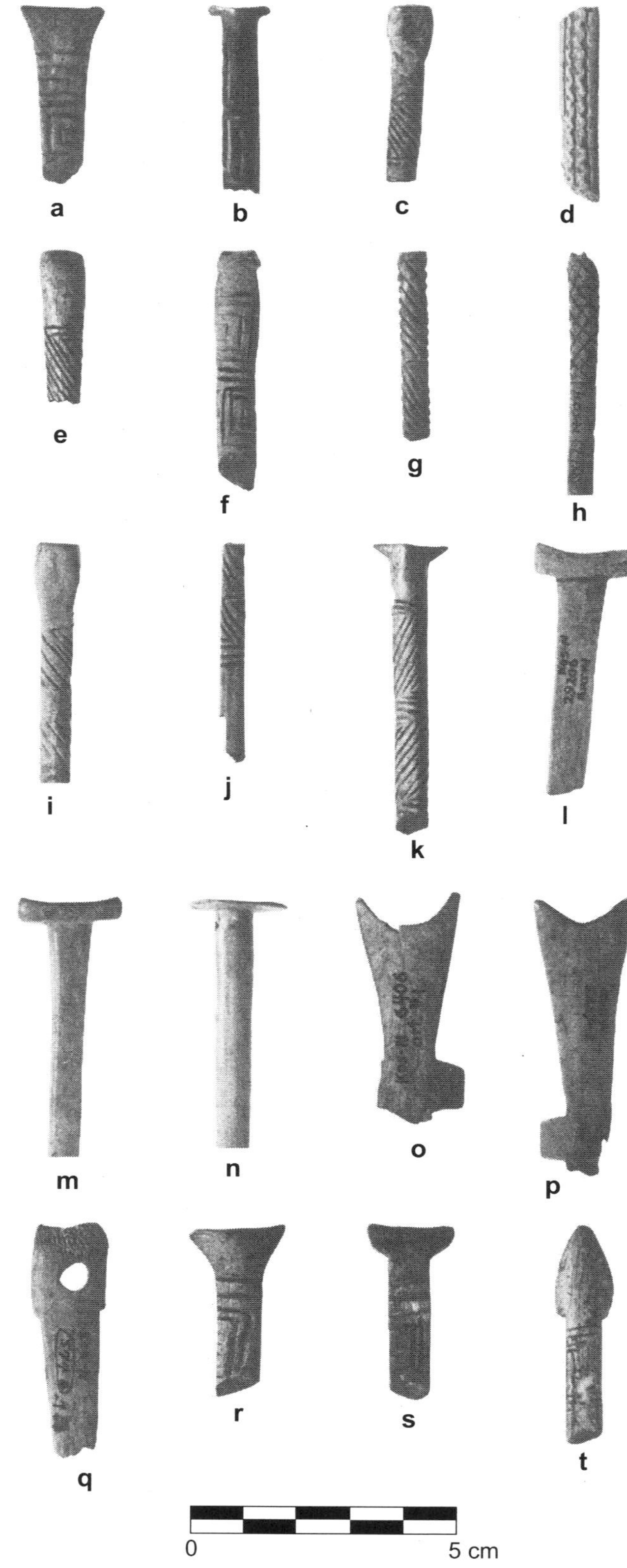

Figure 9.27. The distal ends of a selection of 20 carved bone pins and fragments from Koster site Horizon 6. Flared, concave-flared, crutch-shaped, rectangular, and spatulate carved distal ends are shown.

while the remains of turtles, birds, and small mammals such as squirrels and rabbits are considerably less abundant (Styles and McMillan, this volume). The proportion of fish is comparable to that in Horizon 6, but small mammals are more common in the Napoleon Hollow asemblage and deer are less so (Styles and McMillan Figure 3.11, this volume).

The Elizabeth mound group (11PK512) is perched on the crest of the bluff overlooking Napoleon Hollow. Here a series of 14 Middle Woodland mounds dominated the landscape prior to the construction of Interstate 72 (Charles et al. 1988). There are two Helton-phase components at the site. Excavators discovered evidence of a habitation site beneath Mound 6, and in Mound 1 they found the remains of at least 68 individuals, all attributed to the Helton phase. Isolated bones from mound fill represent 30 to 40 individuals (Charles et al. 1988:29). The lithic tool assemblage from the habitation component consists of 239 specimens, including unretouched blades (Odell 1996:282). Matanzas, Helton, indeterminate stemmed, and side-notched points indicate a Helton-phase affiliation. Bifaces and retouched pieces each constitute approximately 20 percent of the chipped-stone assemblage, but many other forms, such as burins, cores, drills, gravers, and scrapers, are present. In addition, there are 58 shaped ground-stone tools and 21 worked metamorphic or igneous cobbles. Among the shaped tools are abraders, an adze, grooved axes, hammers, and manos (Odell 1988:157, 1996:282). Nutshell makes up 91 percent of the charcoal, with black walnut accounting for 80 percent of the nutshell, in stark contrast to most other Middle Archaic assemblages of plant remains, in which thick-shelled hickory dominates (the exception is the Middle Archaic component at Campbell Hollow, where 69 percent of the nutshell charcoal is black walnut). What accounts for the high proportion of black walnut? After considering natural availability—thick-shelled hickory dominates Helton-component plant remains at the bluff-base Napoleon Hollow site, Asch and Asch (1988:301) attribute the difference to undetermined cultural factors. Similar factors may also be in play at Campbell Hollow. Wood charcoal is ubiquitous, but low in frequency, and only two seeds, both grape, were recovered. No faunal remains are reported for this deposit. On the basis of a preliminary analysis of the stone tool assemblage—a use-wear study was not conducted—Odell (1988, 1996) suggests the Helton-phase component beneath the Elizabeth mounds was a multifunctional base camp.

Two Helton-phase components appear to be present at the Quasar site (Goatley 1998), which is located on a relict natural levee near the bank of the Illinois River. Quasar Stratum 3 was encountered at a depth of approximately 75 cm below the ground surface and is between 55 and 80 cm thick. Isolated scatters of artifacts suggest a series of short-term occupations. Four small side-notched points and one Godar suggest a Helton-phase occupation, but there are no radiocarbon ages for this component. Thick-shelled hickory accounts for 97 percent of the charred nutshell assemblage, while wood charcoal consists of red and white oak and slippery elm (Jennifer Eberlien, pers. comm. 1998). A piece of squash rind and goosefoot seeds also have been identified, but the status of faunal remains has not been reported.

Quasar Stratum 2 (5220 ± 80 B.P. [ISGS-3317], 5360 ± 100 B.P. [ISGS-2978]) was truncated by the plow zone, but what remains is buried as a distinct stratigraphic unit. The projectile point assemblage includes equal numbers of Matanzas ($n = 5$) and Godar points, a large side-notched form, and two Helton points. Two Etley points suggest admixture from a younger cultural horizon (Goatley 1998:Figures 6–10). Excavators recovered a large assemblage of lithic tools ($n = 433$), with a chipped-stone-to-ground-stone ratio of 2.8 to 1, suggesting a variety of activities at the site, including plant-food processing. Features described as food-processing pits dominate the assemblage (24 of 30); none are described as storage pits (Goatley 1998:275). Analysis of subsistence remains is incomplete, but some information is available. Concentrations of mussel shell were found in midden and feature fill. In addition, the remains of fish, turtle, birds, white-tailed deer, and squirrel are present (Lopinto 1995). Thick-shelled hickory nutshell accounts for 97 percent of the nut charcoal. Goosefoot seeds are also reported. All told, Goatley (1998:278) considers the Helton-phase settlement at Quasar to have been a seasonal or multiseasonal residential base camp.

The terminal date of the Helton phase at Koster is 4880 ± 250 B.P. (ISGS-202), but at Napoleon Hollow and Buckshaw Bridge the phase persisted until at least 4400 B.P. The bulk of the Helton-phase component at Napoleon Hollow is associated with an organic buried A horizon. The top of this unit is severely eroded, the paleosol is truncated, and erosional gullies crosscut parts of the upper surface (Styles 1984; Wiant et al. 1983). A posterosion artifact-bearing deposit is identified as the Russell component. At first, researchers were concerned that the Russell component might consist of redeposited Helton-phase material (Asch and Asch 1980), but the discovery of two in situ hearths indicates a subsequent occupation. Karnak Stemmed, Matanzas, and Godar/Osceola points account for 57 percent of the projectile point assemblage in this unit; the remaining points are indeterminate expanding-stem, other stemmed, and side-notched forms. Analysis of charcoal from the Russell component indicates that it is comparable to the Helton-phase assemblage and contrasts with the Titterington-phase assemblage at the site (Asch and Asch 1980).

Located 14 km (8.7 mi) west of the Illinois River valley, the Buckshaw Bridge site sits on a low terrace of a tributary of McKee Creek (Stafford 1991). Excavation revealed 49 pit features, many with evidence of in situ burning and masses of carbonized nutshell. Matanzas and Godar points indicate a Helton-phase occupation. Two radiometric assays—4600 ± 80 B.P. (ISGS-1411) and 4510 ± 70 B.P. (ISGS-1545)—indicate that the Helton phase persisted until perhaps 4400 B.P. The lithic tool assemblage ($n = 555$) is distinctive; ground-stone tools account for 81 percent of the assemblage and include grooved axes ($n = 9$) and metates ($n = 7$) (Stafford 1991). No faunal remains are reported, but a rich charcoal assemblage is consistent with other Helton-phase sites. Oak and hickory make up the sample of wood charcoal; hickory accounts for 95 percent of the nutshell charcoal, and giant ragweed ($n = 42$) is the dominant seed type (Asch and Asch 1987). The high proportion of ground-stone tools, large-volume pits, and high concentrations of hickory nutshell, some of which appears to have been used as fuel, lead C. R. Stafford (1991:218) to conclude that Buckshaw Bridge was a temporary field camp for bulk processing of hickory nuts.

Helton-Phase Settlement. Drawing on surface survey data, Cook (1976) analyzed the distribution of Karnak Stemmed points, Matanzas points, and a class of points including Godar, Raddatz (Wittry 1959), and Faulkner (Winters 1967). At the time, all of these point types appeared to be indicative of the Helton phase, but present evidence suggests that they are also found in Middle Archaic 2 components. For what it is worth, Cook's analysis showed that 71 percent of these projectile point types were found in the Illinois River valley, while the rest came from tributary valleys. Asch et al. (1981) also considered the distribution of Helton-phase sites. They did not report what they considered diagnostic artifacts, but at the time of their work, Cook's (1976) Koster Helton-phase study was the prevailing projectile point typology for the region. Nevertheless, of 334 sites recorded for the Illinois River valley, only two (.006 percent) are attributed to the Helton phase, and of the 671 sites in dissected uplands, 53 (8 percent) are classified as Helton phase. In Asch et al.'s analysis,

Helton-phase sites are nearly evenly distributed between the Illinois River valley and dissected uplands, a finding that sharply contrasts with Cook's (1976). In the end, both studies are limited by the problem of distinguishing Middle Archaic settlements.

Helton-Phase Mortuary Components. Excavated Helton-phase components also provide insight into developments in the ritual treatment and disposition of the dead. Prior to ca. 6000 B.P., human remains were interred in habitation sites, generally in shallow graves excavated into settlement midden, and most often with few, if any, associated artifacts. This practice continued during the Helton phase, but another program evolved, leading to the creation of cemeteries in floodplain and bluff-crest settings.

The Godar site is located on a low terrace at the mouth of a small Illinois River tributary on the west side of the Illinois Valley in Calhoun County. In 1940 and 1941 the landowner, Al Godar, excavated an area about 18 m in diameter to a depth of about 1.2 m. He found a variety of Archaic-period artifacts, including about 400 projectile points—among them many that Perino (1963:95) termed "Godar" points (Figure 9.28; see also Titterington 1950:21, Type 5)—40 T-shaped drills, 25 grooved axes, 24 bannerstones, six plummets, and three stone beads (Figures 9.29, 9.30, and 9.31) commingled in pit fill with poorly preserved human skeletal remains lying on a clay floor and covered with red ocher and limestone (Titterington 1950). The Godar-site artifact assemblage has not been systematically studied to determine its age or cultural affiliation.

Twenty individuals were buried in the Helton-phase midden at Koster (Buikstra 1981). Typically, they were lying on their backs with legs flexed, a position also observed in Koster Horizon 11, although some of the bodies were also buried on their sides in flexed positions. Red ocher was present on the bones in each instance, and some individuals were buried with objects—such as grinding stones, bone awls, stone drills, projectile points, and antler items. Prior to the Helton phase, few objects had been placed in graves. The age distribution of the individuals is strongly bimodal: nearly 50 percent were 10–20 years old and about 30 percent were 50+ years old. Analysis indicates that half of these individuals had serious pathologies that would have limited their normal round of activity (Buikstra 1981:126).

Helton-phase burials were also found beneath the Gibson mounds (Buikstra 1972, 1981; Perino 2006). The Gibson mound group is located on the crest of the Illinois River bluff overlooking Kampsville, Illinois, in Calhoun County. Excavators discovered an Archaic cemetery beneath Mound 1. Godar and Osceola/Hemphill points commingled with the remains indicate a Helton-phase component (Perino 2006). In contrast to the remains found at Koster, the individuals at Gibson were mostly between 20 and 40 years old and do not show signs of severe pathology (Buikstra 1981:129). Buikstra (1981:131) concluded that the individuals buried at Koster had been incapable of performing routine activities during

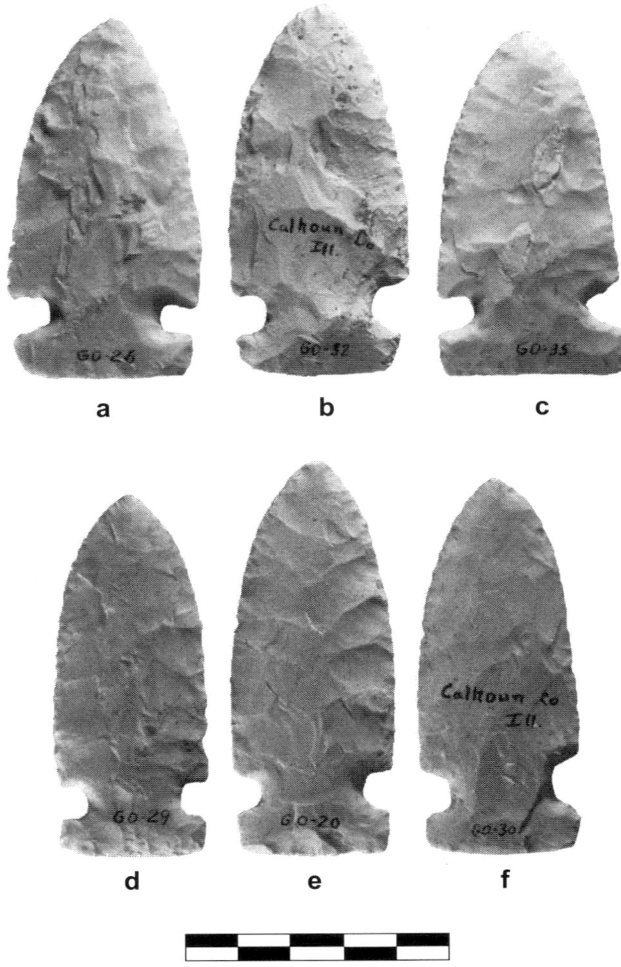

Figure 9.28. A selection of six Godar points from Al Godar's 1941 excavation of the bluff-base Helton-phase Godar cemetery in Calhoun County, Illinois. KBF photos used courtesy of the Gilcrease Museum, Tulsa, OK.

life, while "normal," capable adults were buried in bluff-crest cemeteries.

Beneath Mound 14 at the Pete Klunk mound group, Perino (1968:117–118) discovered a charnel pit with the disarticulated bones of three adults and two Godar points.

At Napoleon Hollow, excavators discovered a disarticulated bundle of human bone in the midden among habitation features. The cranium was missing, but the mandible and 13 teeth were present (Cobb 2005). Postcranial remains consisted of the left scapula, right innominate, sacrum, three thoracic and five lumbar vertebrae, left and right humeri, right radius and ulna, left and right femora, right tibia, right talus, and right navicular (Cobb 2005). Skeletal pathology was minimal. Elsewhere two individual graves contained tightly flexed remains. One individual, Burial 2, showed signs of several pathologies, but none were apparent in the remains of Burial 1 (Cobb 2005). No artifacts were found in the graves or with the bundle burial (Cobb 2005).

Figure 9.29. Titterington-collection bannerstones excavated by Al Godar at the Godar site in 1940–41. KBF photos used courtesy of the Gilcrease Museum, Tulsa, OK.

Figure 9.30. Titterington-collection axes, pebble pendant, and plummet excavated by Al Godar at the Godar site in 1940–41. The "Godar Drilled" plummet in the photo is the only one of six found at the site acquired by PFT. Titterington notebook photo used courtesy of the University of Michigan Museum of Anthropology, Ann Arbor.

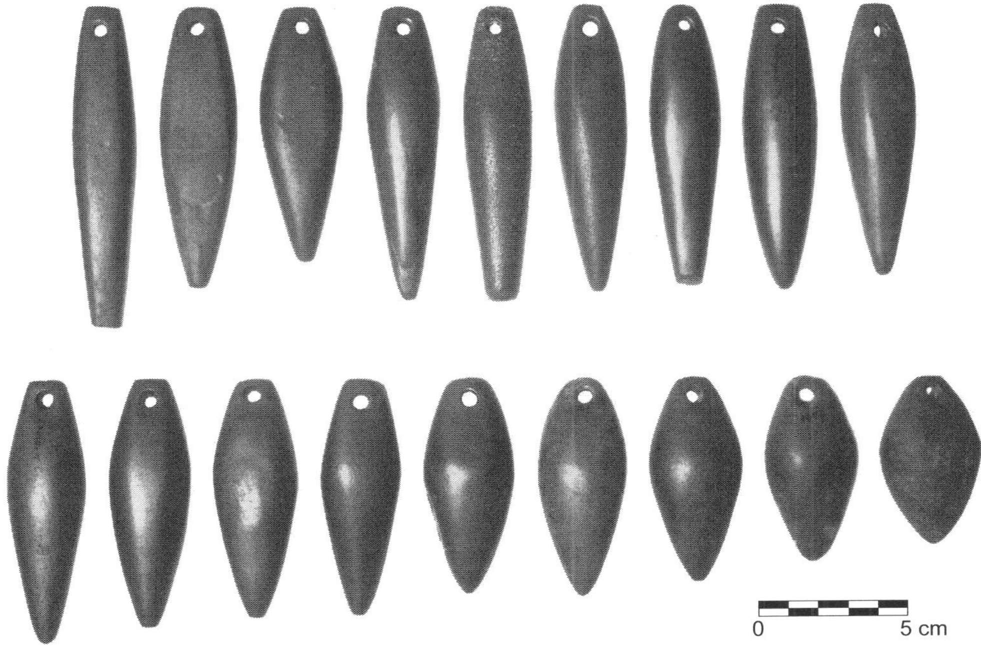

Figure 9.31. Eighteen of 28 Haug-cache Godar Drilled plummets found six miles north of Brussels, southern Calhoun County, in the 1890s (see Goldstein 2004:87–89). Titterington notebook photo used courtesy of the University of Michigan Museum of Anthropology, Ann Arbor.

Excavators also discovered two graves containing human remains at Quasar. In both instances, the bodies were flexed and placed in shallow basins. A deer mandible, a crude chert core, and an unmodified chert flake were placed in the grave of one individual. This is an odd assortment of objects, unlike those reported for other contemporary cemeteries (see Hassen and Farnsworth 1987).

A Helton-phase mortuary component is also present at the Elizabeth mounds (Charles et al. 1988). Burial features included simple graves as well as a large, shallow basin containing the remains of five individuals. All told, the remains of 68 individuals were observed in graves, and another 30–40 individuals are represented by isolated bones found in mound fill (Charles et al. 1988:29). Artifacts placed in graves include Helton, Kirk, and Osceola/Hemphill points, drills, a three-quarter-grooved ax, a bannerstone, a hematite plummet (Godar style), a limestone plummet (Godar style), freshwater-mussel-shell pendants, a marine-shell pendant, antler sockets, and a copper awl (Odell 1988:164). The burial area may have been covered over with a layer of earth, but the evidence is equivocal. A radiometric assay of 6340 ± 90 B.P. (ISGS-1535) for one of the graves suggests that elaborate mortuary practices appeared at the beginning of the Helton phase. The sudden appearance of elaborate mortuary ritual at this early date is surprising and puzzling, especially in light of the evidence for what appears to have been a separate burial program at habitation sites, where few mortuary artifacts accompany burials (Buikstra 1981).

The Bullseye site is located on the eastern margin of the sandy Keach School Terrace in the Illinois River floodplain. The site was known for several years before deep cultivation exposed an extraordinary artifact-bearing deposit (Figure 9.32), prompting a small-scale excavation by the landowner (Hassen and Farnsworth 1987). In 1984 CAA archaeologists working under the auspice of the U.S. Army Corps of Engineers, St. Louis District, hand excavated several 2-x-2-m units. Later, a University of Chicago field-school crew also worked at the site (Seddon 1992). In the end, excavators unearthed poorly preserved human bone and more than 419 Early Archaic, Middle Archaic (Helton phase), and perhaps Late Archaic (Kampsville phase) artifacts including bannerstones, drills, grooved axes, and projectile points, many of which appear to have come from graves, although delineation of these features was complicated in the sandy sediment. There are no radiocarbon ages for the site. The projectile point assemblage is diverse and includes Early and Middle Archaic types, but side-notched forms—Godar, Matanzas, and Osceola/Hemphill—dominate the collection (Hassen and Farnsworth 1987). A Godar plummet also suggests a Helton-phase component. However, a distinctive tubular pipe may be indicative of a Late Archaic Kampsville-phase component. Although it complicates interpretation, the considerable time depth of the site is striking. Bullseye is especially noteworthy because it is a particularly early example of a distinct mortuary area (Buikstra and Charles 1999; Charles 1995; Hassen and Farnsworth1987; see also Milner et al., this volume).

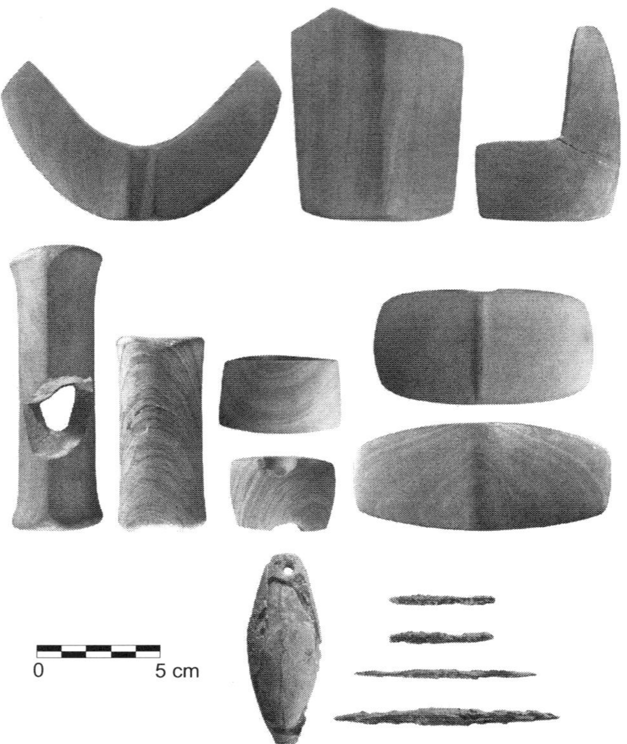

Figure 9.32. Bannerstone styles, square-cross-section copper awls, and Godar Drilled plummet recovered from the Bullseye site (see Hassen and Farnsworth 1987). KBF photos of Wear family collection.

Late Archaic (4200–2600 B.P.)

The Late Archaic period in the lower Illinois River basin is currently divided into two phases: Titterington (Cook 1976) and Kampsville (Farnsworth and Asch 1986). Habitation sites—Koster (Brown and Vierra 1983; Cook 1976), Lagoon (11C121; Cook 1986; Figure 9.1), Napoleon Hollow (Wiant et al. 1983), and Quasar (Goatley 1998); mortuary sites—Etley (Titterington 1950), Hartford Church (11JY20; Farnsworth 1993; Titterington 1950; Figure 9.1), Kampsville (Titterington 1950), and Marquette (Titterington 1950); and surface reconnaissance data (Bartram 1983; Cook 1976) provide information about the Titterington phase.

Farnsworth and Asch (1986:339) define the Kampsville phase on the basis of information from both habitation sites—Buried Gardens of Kampsville (11C373; Kraus 1982; Figure 9.1), Snyders (11C8; Perino 1957; Figure 9.1), and Titus (Druhot 1983)—and mortuary sites—Bell Farm mound (Perino 1968; Poore 1963), Hagen mound (Braun et al. 1982:35–36, 58–59, 154–156; Perino 1961:53; Titterington 1947), Indian Creek Cemetery mound (Fecht 1985), and Pete Klunk mound (11C4; Perino 1968; Figure 9.1).

On the basis of information from Missouri and Illinois, Cook (1976, 1986) describes Titterington-phase settlement as seasonally mobile with nucleated base camps in river and stream valleys and on the upland landscape and smaller, short-term settlements in desired-resource locations. In the lower Illinois River basin, evidence from Koster Horizon 4, Lagoon, and Quasar is consistent with repeated, short-term settlements established for a narrow range of activities, while the Titterington component at Napoleon Hollow represents a season-specific base camp in the Illinois River floodplain (Odell 1996; Wiant et al. 1983). The remains of permanent villages with dwellings have not been found. It is also noteworthy that other than Etley and Wadlow points and grooved axes, artifacts in Titterington-phase burials (e.g., bannerstones, copper implements, and plummets) have not been found in habitation sites.

Although assembled two decades ago, available data on the Kampsville phase remains current (Farnsworth and Asch 1986). At present, few data allow detailed comparison of the Titterington and Kampsville phases, but a stark contrast is apparent in the distribution of settlements (Asch et al. 1981). Compared with Titterington-phase sites, a substantially greater proportion of Kampsville-phase sites are located in the Illinois River valley. With respect to mortuary practices, cremation appears to have been a more common practice during the Kampsville phase (Perino 1968).

Titterington Phase (4200–3800 B.P.)

Titterington-Phase Component Identification. The term *Titterington phase* applies to a particular Native American culture in the central Mississippi River valley and its tributaries ca. 4000 B.P. (Cook 1976; see also Griffin 1952). It is named for pioneer archaeological researcher Dr. Paul Titterington. In a seminal article, Titterington (1950) described "non-pottery" burial sites in the St. Louis region discovered in the 1930s and 1940s. Soon thereafter, Scully (1951) described the Etley point, a large, strongly barbed, stemmed biface, as typical of these sites. Titterington (1950) and, later, Perino (1954, 1961) illustrated large unnotched blades commonly found with Etley points, which Perino (1968) subsequently identified as Wadlow points. In the initial Koster site excavation report, Houart (1971) identified Wadlow points in the Horizon 4 lithic artifact assemblage. After further excavation at the site, Cook (1976) recognized Etley and Sedalia (Seelen 1961) points in the Horizon 4 assemblage as well and asserted that they are typical of Titterington-phase components in the lower Illinois River basin (Figure 9.33). Nebo Hill points (Shippee 1948) were added to the suite of diagnostic artifacts when specimens were found in a 4,000-year-old midden at Napoleon Hollow (Odell 1996) (Figure 9.34). One or more of these point types are found at Titterington-phase habitation sites; Etley and Wadlow have also been found in appreciable numbers at mortuary sites (Perino 1962; Titterington 1950).

Figure 9.33. Titterington-phase Late Archaic points from Koster Horizon 4 (ca. 5600–4500 B.P.): a, Etley F5309b-Art#2; b, Etley 5008-Art#1; c, Sedalia 16-12-2; d, Wadlow 7-15-1.

Figure 9.34. Titterington-phase Late Archaic Etley points (a, b), Sedalia points (c–e), and Nebo Hill point (f) from the Napoleon Hollow site: a, 43-07-1; b, 84-07-5; c, 43-10-1; d, 74-00-1; e, F23-01-1; f, 83-08-1.

Titterington-Phase Habitation Components. Evidence from Koster site Horizon 4B provided the first substantial evidence of a Titterington-phase habitation site in the region. Wadlow points suggested the attribution (Houart 1971), and a subsequent radiometric assay of 3950 ± 75 (ISGS-329) confirmed it (Table 9.6) (Brown and Vierra 1983). Hafted and unhafted bifaces and cores dominate the chipped-stone tool assemblage, which consists of only 200 specimens (Table 9.7) (Cook 1976). Manos, hammers, and abraders constitute the majority of the small (*n* = 27) ground-stone tool assemblage (Table 9.8) (Cook 1976); the paucity of grinding stones is noteworthy. The six Horizon 4 features are hearths or limestone-rich roasting pits (Brown and Vierra 1983; Cook 1976). The density of charcoal is light. Hickory is the most abundant nutshell (90 percent), seeds are rare, and oak and walnut or butternut are the most common types of wood charcoal (Asch et al. 1972). Faunal remains are poorly preserved. Mammal bones account for 88 percent of the remains; white-tailed deer dominate the assemblage. Fourteen species of mussels suggest warm-season collecting (Hill 1975). Poor preservation and small sample size hamper an evaluation of the use of fish (Styles 1986). All considered, the paucity of artifacts, features, and food remains suggests that Horizon 4B was a small-scale, short-term, warm-weather residential camp (Brown and Vierra 1983; Cook 1976).

Excavation of the Lagoon site, located on a small floodplain rise at the embouchure of Crawford Creek, an Illinois River tributary, provided additional data on Titterington-phase habitation (Cook 1983, 1986), but the analysis is not complete. The hafted-biface assemblage—Etley, Sedalia, and Wadlow—and three radiometric assays—4300 ± 600 (NSRL-303), 4010 ± 150 (ISGS-798), and 4030 ± 75 (ISGS-804)—confirm a Titterington-phase occupation. An array of several basin-shaped features occurred over an area of .5 ha, but little more can be said about the function of the site because data on the stone tool assemblage are not available. Analysis of animal bone is hampered by poor preservation, but the remains of white-tailed deer are evident. In contrast, the assemblage of plant remains is substantial. Hickory accounts for 75 percent of the nutshell; 73 percent of the seeds are lamb's-quarters; specimens of squash and marsh elder are probably domesticated varieties (Asch and Asch 1983; Conard et al. 1983). Cook (1986:181) asserts that Lagoon was a "single-group" settlement; the assemblage of plant remains alone suggests a more intensive occupation than at Koster.

The Titterington-phase settlement at Napoleon Hollow provides evidence of a more substantial settlement (Odell 1996; Wiant et al. 1983). Etley, Sedalia, and Nebo Hill points characterize the hafted-biface assemblage (Figure 9.34) (Odell 1996), and two radiocarbon assays, 4060 ± 75 (ISGS-823) and 3920 ± 90 (ISGS-933), confirm the age of the deposit. The chipped-stone tool assemblage is large (*n* = 378), diverse, and indicative of a variety of activities at the site (Table 9.7) (Odell 1996). Igneous hammerstones make up most (76 percent) of the ground-stone tool assemblage (*n* = 148), but grinding tools such as metates and manos are relatively rare, indicative perhaps of a seasonal rather than year-round occupation (Table 9.8). Features are also not common; of the features present, most are shallow basins with evidence of burning (Wiant 1980). There is no evidence for constructed shelters.

Thick-shelled hickory accounts for 89 percent of nutshell, followed in order of frequency by black walnut, pecan, and hazelnut. Feature fill contains more wood charcoal and six times the number of seeds when compared with midden samples. The size of sunflower and lamb's-quarters seeds is consistent with wild forms. Squash rind is present, but the specimens are too small to permit evaluation of the effects of selection under cultivation. But the size of *Iva* achenes is comparable to domesticated specimens from Salts Cave in Kentucky (Asch and Asch 1979; Conard et al. 1983). Faunal remains are poorly preserved. The amount of debitage, number and variety of stone tools, and evidence for cultivation are in stark contrast to Koster Horizon 4, suggesting a more permanent settlement at Napoleon Hollow.

At Quasar, Etley and Sedalia points were found in Stratum 1 or in the plow zone, which truncates Stratum 1 (Goatley 1998). Radiometric assays of charcoal from Stratum 1—4010 ± 70 B.P. (ISGS-3315) and 4200 ± 45 B.P. (ISGS-3839)—are consistent with other Titterington-phase sites, but the presence of Godar, Matanzas, and Osceola points indicates a multicomponent deposit. Analysis of animal and plant remains from the site has not been completed. Goatley (1998:278) speculates that Stratum 1 was the site of a short-term settlement, probably focused on procurement of a single resource. Evidently, the location attracted both Middle Archaic and Late Archaic groups, and the Titterington-phase component, in particular, contributes to understanding of landscape use.

The Brush College School site (11PK488; Figure 9.1) is situated in the dissected uplands between the Illinois River and Blue Creek (Stafford 1994). Of the bifaces that could be classified, half are Sedalia points; the rest are either Early (*n* = 6) or Middle Archaic–period (*n* = 2) types. Radiometric assay of dispersed wood charcoal from two features resulted in estimated ages of 3680 ± 70 B.P. (ISGS-1695) and 4010 ± 70 B.P. (ISGS-1766). Only three features were observed at Brush College School. Charcoal from feature fill consists mostly of wood (81 percent), nutshell accounts for less than 4 percent, and seeds are rare (*n* = 5). No animal bone is reported from the site, perhaps because of a lack of preservation. The paucity of material is consistent with short-term settlement, perhaps to secure a particular resource (Stafford 1994).

Koster Horizon 4B, Lagoon, and Napoleon Hollow appear to represent different types of settlement, but none appear to be multifamily sites (Cook 1986) such as Go-Kart North (11MO552N) in the American Bottom (Fortier 1984).

Titterington-Phase Settlement. Titterington-phase habitation sites are found in the Illinois River and tributary stream valleys and on upland landscapes (Asch et al. 1981; Bartram 1983; Cook 1976). Cook (1976:117–199) compares the geographic distribution of Titterington-phase and preceding Helton-phase sites. Noting that Titterington-phase sites are more evenly distributed in the region and that a greater proportion are found in and around tributary valleys, Cook (1976:119) offers the hypothesis that post-Hypsithermal climate amelioration enriched tributary stream habitats, which in turn encouraged more settlement. This hypothesis has yet to be evaluated.

Asch et al. (1981) classify the landscape position of 39 percent (27 of 69) of Late Archaic Titterington-phase sites as Illinois River valley and 58 percent (40 of 69) as tributary valley. The greater proportion of tributary settlements is consistent with the pattern reported by Cook (1976), but the significance of this finding with respect to Middle Archaic settlement remains problematic.

Titterington-Phase Mortuary Components. One human burial was found at the north end of the Koster Horizon 4 occupation (Brown and Vierra 1983), and, as we describe below, it is not typical of those reported by Titterington (1950).

Given the presence of Etley points, four of the sites reported by Titterington (1950)—Etley, Hartford Church, Kampsville, and Marquette—appear to be Titterington-phase mortuary components (Cook 1976; Montet-White 1968). To the best of our knowledge, no Titterington-phase mortuary site has been reported in the past 50 years.

The Hartford Church site is located on an Illinois River terrace, approximately 6 km (3.7 mi) above the confluence of the Mississippi and Illinois rivers. In 1932, a farmer exposed a limestone-slab-covered pit containing human remains and a variety of artifacts, including grooved axes, bone awls, antler tips, and chipped-stone drills, knives, scrapers, and projectile points (Farnsworth 1993; Titterington 1950). The human remains were covered with red ocher.

While setting up a camp near Kampsville in 1937, fishermen discovered another limestone-covered grave on a terrace at the base of the bluff. Beneath the slab they found two bannerstones, three flint spears—two Wadlow points and an Etley point—and a copper awl (Titterington 1950).

In 1939, Walter Wadlow, a prominent artifact collector in the region, excavated a limestone-slab-covered grave with the remains of two individuals—neither with evidence of red ocher—at the Marquette site. Placed with the remains were two flint knives—a Wadlow and an Etley—two shell ornaments, two grooved axes, and a diorite ball (Titterington 1950).

The Etley site consisted of eight or nine mounds located on the bluff crest overlooking the Illinois River valley. In 1942, Wadlow discovered human remains stained with red ocher in pits marked by limestone slabs (Figure 9.35). Associated artifacts included grooved axes, bannerstones, plummets, copper implements, a tubular pipe, a calcite bead, a perforated stone pendant, a feldspar tablet, and numerous Etley, Wadlow, and Sedalia points (Figures 9.36, 9.37, and 9.38; see Titterington 1950).

Figure 9.35. Limestone-slab-covered burials under excavation at the Etley site bluff-top Archaic cemetery in 1942 (photo misidentified as the floodplain Hartford Church site, Jersey County, in Montet-White 1968:98). University of Michigan Museum of Anthropology photo, used courtesy of UMMA, Ann Arbor.

Kampsville Phase (3250–2550 B.P.)

Perino (1968) used the term *Kampsville focus* to distinguish the characteristics of the Klunk Mound 7 Archaic cemetery. Later, Farnsworth and Asch (1986:339) adopted the term *Kampsville phase* to apply more broadly to Native American culture in the lower Illinois River valley during the final centuries of the Archaic period. It applies to a complex of habitation sites—Cypress Land (11GE119; Figure 9.1), Buried Gardens of Kampsville, Snyders, and Titus—and mortuary sites—Bell Farm mound, Hagen mound, Indian Creek Cemetery mounds, and Klunk mound. Five radiometric assays of charcoal from Kampsville-phase sites range in age from ca. 3250 B.P. to 2550 B.P. Data on the Kampsville phase is generally equivocal; all of the habitation sites are multicomponent, and none but Cypress Land has been systematically analyzed and reported.

Kampsville-Phase Component Identification. Kampsville Barbed projectile points and grooved, teardrop-shaped plummets are indicative of Kampsville-phase components (Farnsworth and Asch 1986; Perino 1968:80, 1985:196). Perino (1968) defined Kampsville Barbed points on the basis of specimens found in 2,800-year-old deposits (2870 ± 75 B.P. [M-1100]) at Klunk Mound 7. Similar specimens were found at the Snyders site (Perino 1962:46) and at the Titus site (Figure 9.32) (Druhot 1983). Grooved, teardrop-shaped plummets, known as Gilcrease Grooved, were also found at Klunk Mound 7 (Perino 1968) and are present in many surface collections in the region (Asch et al. 1981; Goldstein 1971, 2004; Perino 1962).

Kampsville-Phase Habitation Components. Asch et al. (1981) report that 70 percent of Kampsville-phase settlements occur in the Illinois River valley. This concentration is in striking contrast to the Titterington-phase sites, 63 percent of which are located on bluffs overlooking tributary valleys or on the upland landscape (Asch et al.

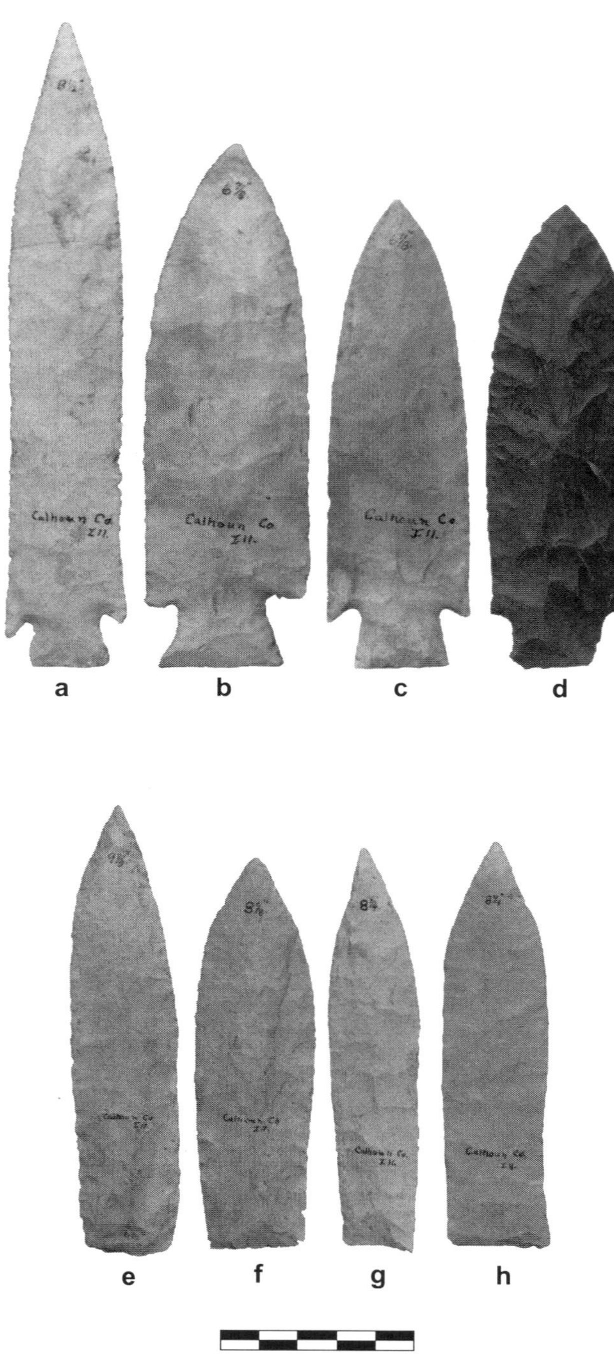

Figure 9.36. Etley points (a–d), Wadlow knives (e, f, h), and a Sedalia point (g) from Walter Wadlow's 1942 excavation of the bluff-top Titterington-phase Etley cemetery in Calhoun County, Illinois. P. F. Titterington photos on file at the University of Michigan Museum of Anthropology, Ann Arbor.

1981). What accounts for this apparent shift in settlement location between the Titterington and Kampsville phases is not yet clear.

Figure 9.37. Square-cross-section copper awl, two of three bannerstones, and three small copper axes recovered during Walter Wadlow's 1942 excavations at the bluff-top Etley cemetery. Bannerstone photos by KBF used courtesy of the Gilcrease Museum, Tulsa, OK. Copper artifacts from Titterington notebook photo used courtesy of the University of Michigan Museum of Anthropology, Ann Arbor.

Information on Kampsville-phase habitation sites comes from the following sites: Axedental (11PK571; Stafford 1994; Figure 9.1), Buried Gardens of Kampsville (Farnsworth and Asch 1986; Kraus 1980, 1982), and Titus (Druhot 1983; Farnsworth and Asch 1986). Understanding of Kampsville-phase habitation sites remains sketchy. Horizon 2 at the Titus site is multicomponent but has a strong Kampsville-phase signature (Figure 9.39). Excavators encountered Horizon 2 in at least seven of 10 units at depths ranging from .6 m below surface to 2.0 m below surface, associated with a paleosol (Druhot 1983; Farnsworth and Asch 1986). Radiocarbon assay of dispersed charcoal—primarily nutshell—from near the top of Horizon 2 resulted in an age estimate of 2860 ± 80 B.P. (ISGS-990). The estimated age of a sample from a depth of 1.4 m below ground surface is 3240 ± 75 B.P. (ISGS-826). A preliminary tabulation of stone tools indicates a chipped-stone assemblage dominated by bifacial tools (e.g., bifaces, drills, and projectile points) (Druhot 1983). The ground-stone assemblage consists of only manos (92 percent) and hammerstones (8 percent). On the whole, the stone tool assemblage is comparable to

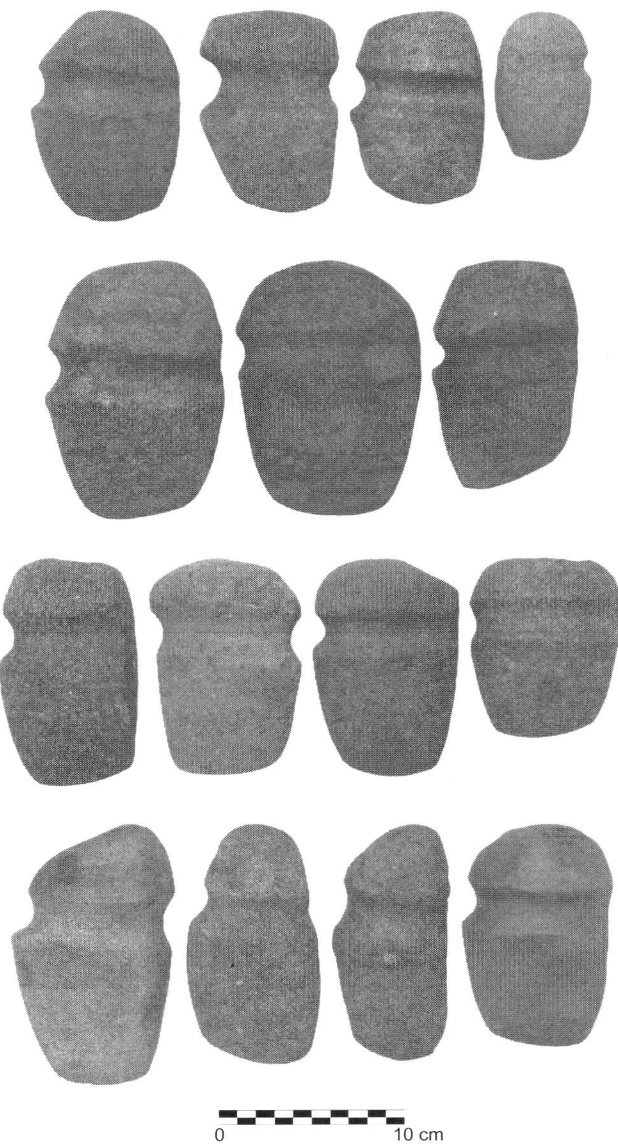

Figure 9.38. Fifteen of 25 grooved axes recovered during Walter Wadlow's 1942 excavations at the bluff-top Etley cemetery. Two are full grooved (both illustrated) and all of the others are three-quarter grooved. Titterington notebook photo used courtesy of the University of Michigan Museum of Anthropology, Ann Arbor.

that from Koster Horizon 4 in size and variety. Nutshell, most of which is thick-shelled hickory, accounts for more than three-quarters of the charcoal by weight recovered by flotation from Titus site Horizon 2. Native seeds are uncommon, and none appear to be from cultivated species (Asch and Asch 1976:21–23, 1978:332–333), an interesting contrast to the evidence for domesticated seeds at the Titterington-phase settlements of Lagoon and Napoleon Hollow. Bone and shell are well preserved and fish bone is abundant in flotation samples, but faunal remains have not been analyzed. A preliminary assessment of data from Titus Horizon 2 suggests a base settlement occupied over a span of several centuries (Farnsworth and Asch 1986:345).

The Buried Gardens of Kampsville site is located on an Illinois River terrace at the base of the valley-margin bluff. It is an extensive, stratified, multicomponent midden, which appears to include a Kampsville-phase component (Farnsworth and Asch 1986; Kraus 1980, 1982). Two radiocarbon assays—2550 ± 70 B.P. (ISGS-1154) and 2770 ± 70 B.P. (ISGS-1153)—date the terminal centuries of the Kampsville phase and the Archaic period. Other than reference to a single Kampsville Barbed point, no information is available on the stone tool assemblage. Nutshell, especially hickory, comprises most of the charcoal from a buried aceramic unit at the site that is recognized as a Kampsville-phase component (Farnsworth and Asch 1986:345). Several carbonized grains of little barley (*Hordeum pusillum*) exhibit characteristics possibly indicating

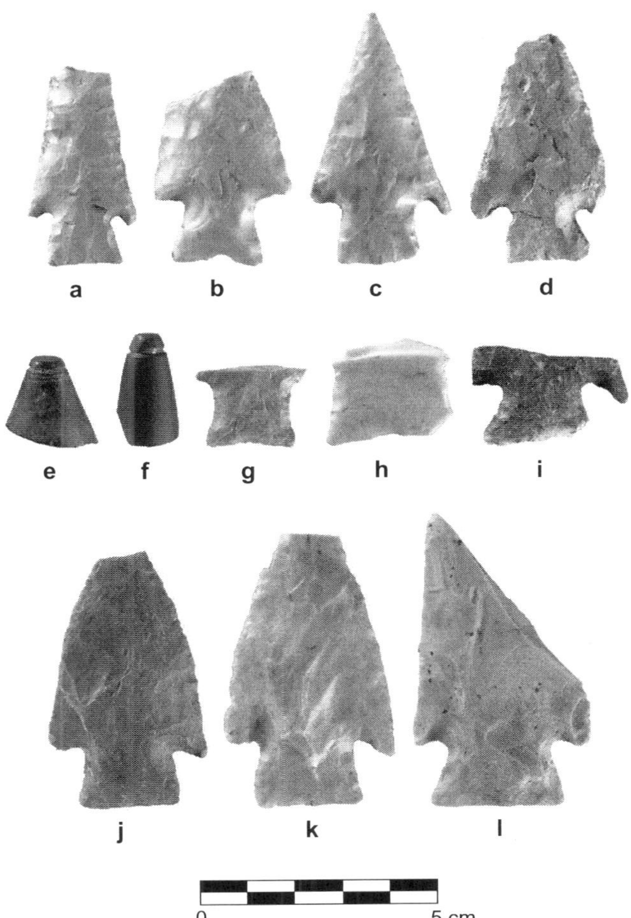

Figure 9.39. Kampsville-phase Terminal Archaic Kampsville Barbed points (a–d, g–l) and hematite plummet fragments (e, f) from the adjacent Titus (a–c, e–l) and Upper Macoupin sites (d): a, TS110-Art#1; b, TS108-Art#1; c, TS109-Art#3; d, TS101-1; e, TS105-4; f, TS108-5; g, TS503-4; h, TS714-1; i, TS716-1; j, TS402-1; k, TS 108-Art#2; l, TS717-Art#4.

cultivation (Asch and Asch 1985:192). Faunal remains from this component have not been analyzed.

The Axedental site is located on an upland knoll overlooking the Blue Creek valley, a tributary of the lower reach of the Illinois River. Artifacts were also found at the base of the knoll in the creek floodplain (Stafford 1994). Five features came to light in the floodplain, and another was found after removing the plow zone of the upland knoll. The deposit is multicomponent—Late Woodland and Archaic—but hickory nutshell from a feature is 2600 ± 70 years old (ISGS-1758) (Stafford 1994:70), and 85 percent of the points from the site are Kampsville Barbed (Stafford 1994:66). Curated tools—bifaces, adzes, axes, choppers, projectile points, and bifacial scrapers—account for 80 percent of the chipped-stone tool assemblage. In addition, the assemblage includes 18 ground-stone tools—hammerstones, manos, and pitted stones (Stafford 1994:40). Thick-shelled hickory nutshell dominates (98 percent) the charcoal found in pit features. Seeds are not abundant, but giant ragweed, marsh elder, sunflower, and knotweed are present (Schroeder 1994:111). No faunal remains are reported. The Axedental site artifact assemblage and subsistence remains are consistent with expectations for a short-term, upland extractive camp (Stafford 1994:149).

Kampsville-Phase Settlement. Asch et al. (1981) consider the landscape positions of Terminal Archaic sites and find that, in comparison with the Titterington phase, a greater proportion of Terminal Archaic sites (70 percent, 26 of 37) are found in the Illinois River valley. The meaning of this apparent shift is not understood.

Kampsville-Phase Mortuary Components. Information about Kampsville-phase mortuary practices comes from Pete Klunk Mound 7 and the Hagen mound. Perino (1968) excavated 14 mounds in the Pete Klunk mound group. Below Mound 7 he found seven Late Archaic crematories covered with limestone slabs and 63 flexed or bundled individuals in graves, some of which were also covered with limestone slabs. Periodically, mortuary activity included blanketing the area with a layer of sediment before proceeding with the addition of more graves, eventually resulting in an accretional mound 1.06 m tall and 9.1 m in diameter. A radiocarbon assay of charcoal from Crematory A resulted in a date of 2870 ± 75 B.P. (M-1160) (Crane and Griffin 1963:232). The artifact assemblage included beads (pearl, marine shell, rolled copper, pipestone, and calcite), plummets (hematite, diorite, limestone, and redstone), stemmed and barbed projectile points (Kampsville Barbed), and a variety of bone tools (Figure 9.40).

Another Kampsville-phase component was documented at the Hagen mound group. In addition to limestone and hematite plummets, excavators unearthed a chisel-shaped slate object similar to a boatstone, a slate gorget fragment, a tubular pipe, galena, a drilled pebble pendant, and copper beads. They also found ocher-covered human skeletal remains, some flexed and others bundled (Braun et al. 1982:35–36, 58–59, 154–156; Farnsworth and Asch 1986:349; Perino 1961:53; Titterington 1947). As is the case with other Kampsville-phase mortuary sites, the Hagen mound group also has Late Archaic and late Middle Woodland components (Farnsworth and Asch 1986:349).

Figure 9.40. Kampsville Barbed projectile points, fragmentary copper-jacketed wooden wand or rattle (with shattered ball-tipped head and a smaller bulbous protrusion at the neck), and 14 Gilcrease Grooved plummets found in Terminal Archaic mortuary context beneath Klunk Mound 7 (see Perino 1968:68–84). KBF photos used courtesy of the Gilcrease Museum, Tulsa, OK.

Terminal Archaic to Woodland-Period Transition

The nature of the transition between Terminal Archaic and Early Woodland culture is not clear. Farnsworth and Asch (1986:352, 439–440) have examined this subject in detail, and their research remains the most comprehensive assessment. Charles et al. (1986) have considered Terminal Archaic–Early Woodland patterns of mortuary activity. Documented Terminal Archaic habitation sites are multicomponent deposits, and all of them—Cypress Land, Buried Gardens of Kampsville, and Titus—appear to be long-term base camps (Conner 1986; Farnsworth and Asch 1986). The Cypress Land site is located on the riverward face of the Keach School Terrace in the Illinois River valley in Greene County (Conner 1986). Excavators recovered well-preserved plant remains and animal bone and a large and diverse artifact assemblage, including specimens diagnostic of Middle Archaic (Helton), Late Archaic (Kampsville), and Early Woodland (Black Sand) components. But they found no evidence of stratification and could only segregate diagnostic artifacts from the deposit (Conner 1986:52). Some stratification is evident at Buried Gardens of Kampsville. Charcoal from an aceramic context associated with Kramer points (Munson and Harn 1966) on a low terrace is ca. 2,600 years old, encouraging speculation that another, as yet undefined phase in the Archaic–Woodland transition may be present (Farnsworth and Asch 1986:440). However, given the current state of the evidence, the circumstances under which ceramic technology was added to the cultural repertoire of the ca. 2600 B.P. inhabitants of the lower Illinois River basin remain obscure.

Archaic-Period Cultural Development

The substantial body of information from Archaic-period sites in the lower Illinois River basin, summarized above, provides us with an opportunity to consider regional developments of Native American culture during the 7,500-year period of Archaic occupation in the area. We begin by addressing radiocarbon chronology and then consider technology, subsistence (see also Styles and McMillan and Simon, this volume), settlement, and mortuary practice (see also Milner et al., this volume). The section concludes with a consideration of Archaic cultural development and climate change.

Archaic Cultural Chronology

With the aid of 85 radiocarbon dates from 14 excavated Archaic sites in the lower Illinois Valley region (see Tables 9.4–9.6), we have substantially revised the Archaic-period cultural chronology proposed over 20 years ago by Brown and Vierra (1983). Obviously, the identification of particular cultural phases remains tentative—we are still only beginning to understand the nature and timing of cultural transitions, and there are substantial gaps in Archaic cultural chronology in the lower Illinois River basin. This is especially apparent when current radiocarbon assays are calibrated (see Table 9.1). For instance, the gap in our lower Illinois Valley radiocarbon chronology between Middle Archaic 3 and Late Archaic times (cal ca. 3800–2800 B.C.) seems to fall in the era of the Hemphill complex proposed by Conrad for the central Illinois Valley area to the north (see Conrad 1981; Farnsworth 1993), and the gap between our Late Archaic and Terminal Archaic Titterington and Kampsville phases (cal 2400–1500 B.C.) seems to be the era of the Falling Springs phase identified for the American Bottom to the south (see McElrath et al., this volume). Nevertheless, it is clearly time to move beyond Koster-site-based subdivisions of the Archaic period in the lower Illinois Valley and begin to build a regional Archaic chronology designed to more widely document episodes of change in cultures and artifact styles and, thus, provide a more meaningful chronological and cultural-phase framework for future regional research.

Technology

In the lower Illinois River basin, the record of Archaic-period technology consists mostly of chipped- and ground-stone artifacts and, where preservation allows, items made from bone and shell. Other material such as wood and fiber must have been used extensively, but there are no examples from this region to date. Arguably, the complete repertoire of stone-tool production and repair was in place during the Early Archaic 2 time span (8800–8200 B.P.), except perhaps the means to drill stone, which seems to have appeared somewhat later (as indicated, e.g., by plummets, bannerstones, pendants, and beads). Evidence for the construction of buildings is equivocal; structures may have been present during Middle Archaic 2 (7300–6320 B.P.) but more certainly by Middle Archaic 3 times (6320–4400 B.P.) (Brown and Vierra 1983). Storage technology is evident in Koster Horizon 8C (Carlson 1979; Wolynec 1977).

Chipped-Stone Technology

Chipped-stone tools dominate Archaic-period artifact assemblages in the region. An assessment of chipped-stone tools from nine components ranging in age from Early Archaic through Late Archaic indicates that raw material was obtained locally. The proportion of Burlington chert ranges from 94 percent of the Koster Horizon 11 and Campbell Hollow Early Archaic 2 assemblages to 98 percent of the Late Archaic Koster Horizon 4 and Napoleon Hollow Titterington components. The proportion of Burlington-chert tools in Middle Archaic assemblages is 97–98 percent (Cook 1976; Odell 1996; Stafford 1989; Stafford 1985). The rare examples of nonlocal chert are generally projectile points, especially those in the Koster Horizon 11 assemblage, which appear to be made from chert found in southern Illinois, Indiana, or Kentucky (Table 9.9).

Taken together, 17 tool types have been identified during the analysis of Archaic-period chipped-stone tool assemblages in the region (Cook 1976; Lurie 1982; Odell 1988, 1996; Stafford 1989; Stafford 1985). Allowing for differences in identification of a particular type, it appears that examples of each type were present since the Early Archaic 2 subperiod (Table 9.7). The exceptions may be the chipped-stone adze, which is present but rare in later assemblages, and the hafted

Table 9.9. Tabulation of Raw Material Type for Selected Early, Middle, and Late Archaic–Period Chipped-Stone Assemblages.

Site	Cultural Phase	Burlington	Other Chert	Total
Koster 11	Early Archaic 2	357	24	381
Campbell Hollow	Early Archaic 2	60	1	61
Campbell Hollow	Middle Archaic 1	362	25	387
Napoleon Hollow	Middle Archaic 3	142	0	142
Napoleon Hollow	Middle Archaic 4	231	6	237
Slim Lake	Middle Archaic 4	1,135	7	1,142
Koster 6	Middle Archaic 4	454	7	461
Napoleon Hollow	Late Archaic	268	5	273
Koster 4	Late Archaic	57	1	58
Total		3,066	76	3,142

scraper, which appears in considerable numbers in Middle Archaic assemblages. Chipped-stone adzes sometimes are considered diagnostic of Early Archaic assemblages. They are also present, if rare, in later assemblages.

A comparison of the relative proportion of bifacial versus unifacial tools for the component assemblages is complicated by a variety of factors including sampling and duration of occupation, but the results are interesting (Table 9.7). Generally speaking, unifacial tools are more common in most of the components dating through the Middle Archaic 2 subperiod, the only exceptions being the Middle Archaic component at Campbell Hollow and the Napoleon component at Napoleon Hollow. Bifacial tools are more common in all of the Middle Archaic 3 components except the assemblage found below Elizabeth Mound 6. Unifacial tools are more common in the Titterington component at Napoleon Hollow, but the reverse is true for Koster Horizon 4. Clearly, more work is needed, but the greater proportion of unifacial, often expedient, tools versus bifacial, often curated, tools in what appear to be shorter-term occupations is consistent with theory based on studies of the organization of lithic technology (Binford 1979).

Although specific point designs correspond to particular periods, they persisted for varying lengths of time and co-occurred with other forms. In some cases, co-occurrence may be attributed to the duration or repetition of occupation, but in other cases, a variety of points appear to have been in use at the same time, reflecting, perhaps, functional differences or circumstances that promoted tool repair over replacement. The variety of points in Middle Archaic assemblages is especially vexing and requires further attention, but the persistence of a variety of co-occurring forms appears to signal the influence of factors not in play during the Early Archaic period.

As is the case elsewhere, projectile point/knife repair and rejuvenation (e.g., blade beveling) varied through time. It is much more common in Early Archaic assemblages than in later ones. The shift in strategy may reflect changes in mobility or the development of the spear-thrower or both. Less recognized are techniques employed to repair broken bifaces. As noted above, in addition to specific diagnostic point specimens in the Koster Horizon 11 assemblage, several specimens are clearly reworked. What is remarkable about this group of points is the variety of haft shapes, including side-notched, corner-notched, and contracting-stem examples. Evidently, Early Archaic flint knappers were aware of different haft designs, and they appear to have employed specific designs when particular situations arose, for example, for hafting distal point fragments. It may be that different factors were in play when a point was manufactured as opposed to when a broken point was repaired.

The diminutive LeCroy points in the Koster Horizon 11 assemblage suggest the use of atlatl darts by at least 8500 B.P. The stem width of these specimens indicates that they were hafted to small-diameter shafts, substantially smaller that those indicated by other hafted-biface forms in the assemblage. A general trend is evident toward smaller point forms through the Middle Archaic, suggesting growing use of the spear-thrower. The abrupt increase in Titterington-phase point size suggests a return to more robust missiles, too heavy to be effectively propelled by an atlatl. The substantial increase in point size was short-lived, perhaps a century or two, after which smaller, lighter forms such as the Kampsville Barbed became typical of Terminal Archaic settlements.

Ground-Stone Technology

Ground-stone implements such as grooved axes, adzes, and grinding stones were made from different varieties of granite found locally in glacial till and redeposited in some tributary valleys. The source(s) of hematite used to produce plummets is not known, but this mineral is found in local till and bedrock outcrops. Objects generally made from nonlocal materials include bannerstones (Hassen and Farnsworth 1987).

Eleven types of ground-stone tools have been identified in tabulated lower Illinois River basin Archaic components (Table 9.8). Among the more formal types, all but celts and plummets have been found in the Early Archaic 2 Koster Horizon 11 component. Ground-stone tools have long been known to be part of the Early Archaic lithic tool assemblage (Griffin 1967), but the diversity of the Koster Horizon 11 assemblage is noteworthy. Variety and the presence of specialized tool forms such as adzes and channel-basin metates suggest a mature ground-stone technology, but the origin of this technology remains obscure.

Plummets appeared after 6300 B.P. and are found in Helton-phase and Kampsville-phase habitation and mortuary sites (Cook 1976; Farnsworth and Asch 1986; Goldstein 1971, 2004). Their apparent absence in Titterington-phase components is noteworthy, but the significance of the observation is not clear.

Bannerstones have been found in Helton- and Titterington-phase mortuary sites (Charles et al. 1988; Hassen and Farnsworth 1987; Titterington 1950). They may represent the first class of artifacts imported in finished form (Farnsworth 1987). Most of those found at Bullseye are described as upper Great Lakes banded slate, although others were made from similarly colored local fine-grained sedimentary rock (Farnsworth 1987:17).

Analysis of the ground-stone assemblages is subject to several limitations, including those related to sampling and tool classification, but comparison of the components is instructive. As is the case with chipped-stone tools, the Horizon 11 ground-stone assemblage contrasts with those from other early components, in particular, most of the Middle Archaic 1 settlements except for Campbell Hollow (Table 9.8). The number and variety of ground tools increased during Middle Archaic 2 and more so during Middle Archaic 3 times, in the large settlements occupied during the Helton phase. The Napoleon Hollow Titterington-component assemblage is comparable in terms of variety and perhaps density, suggesting it, too, represents a longer-term settlement. The Napoleon Hollow block excavation was considerable smaller than that undertaken at Koster.

The ground-stone assemblage includes woodworking, manufacturing, and food-processing tools. Woodworking tools are present in the Horizon 11 assemblage, but not in any of the Middle Archaic 1 or 2 assemblages except for that from Koster Horizon 8B, in which three axes were found. The absence of woodworking tools in Horizon 8C is especially noteworthy given other evidence that it was a long-term settlement. The proportion of woodworking tools is relatively steady for all of the Middle Archaic 3, Helton-phase settlements, but it does not exceed 7 percent. Manufacturing tools (e.g., hammerstones) dominate nearly all of the assemblages, while the proportion of food-processing tools (e.g., manos, metates, pestles, and pitted stones) is highly variable except in Middle Archaic 3 settlements, in which the proportion of manufacturing tools and food-processing tools varies between 40 and 60 percent.

Bone and Mussel-Shell Technology

A variety of bone tools, such as needles, awls, and socketed antler projectile points, occur in the Early Archaic 2 Koster Horizon 11 assemblage, indicating that bone technology was well developed by 8500 B.P. Bone tools are also found in Middle and Late Archaic artifact assemblages. Without further study, especially taking into account preservation bias, the significance of their frequency and variety remains problematic. Incised bone pins appear to be restricted to Helton-phase components.

Subsistence

Although some key components such as Twin Ditch have yet to be systematically analyzed, an extraordinary record is available of plant and animal use during the Archaic period in the lower Illinois River basin (see also Simon, this volume; Styles and McMillan, this volume). Nuts contributed significantly to subsistence throughout the period, with major reliance established ca. 7,500–7,000 years ago. Seeds are rare in assemblages predating 6000 B.P., are not common and are indicative of wild stands in those dating between 6000 B.P. and 4000 B.P., and are more common in those postdating 4000 B.P., when some species, such as *Iva annua*, appear to have been domesticated. Rind fragments of *C. pepo* have been found in two 7,000-year-old components. Exploitation of animal foods from a cross section of valley and upland habitats evidently occurred during the Early Archaic, but hunting, fishing, and collection became more selective and intensive through time as scheduled logistic strategies were implemented.

Plant Remains

From the outset of the Archaic period, hickory nuts were a subsistence staple. Hickory dominates nutshell charcoal in all but three components, Koster Horizon 9 (Middle Archaic 1), in which pecan is more abundant, and Campbell Hollow (Middle Archaic 1) and the Middle Archaic 3 Helton-phase component beneath Elizabeth Mound 6, in which black walnut accounts for 69 and 80 percent, respectively. In every other component, regardless of age, thick-shelled hickory accounts for more than 44 percent of the nutshell, and it often exceeds 90 percent. Nutshell-to-wood ratios indicate that major reliance on nuts was established between 7500 and 7000 B.P. (Asch et al. 1972; Asch and Asch 1976, 1978, 1985, 1987; Asch and Asch 1979, 1980, 1983; Asch et al. 1972; Asch and Sidell 1988; Lopinto 1995; Schroeder 1994).

Seeds were found in such low density in Koster Horizon 11 that they may not represent food (Asch et al. 1972), nor are they common in Middle Archaic 1 or Middle Archaic 2 assemblages (Asch and Asch 1978). Middle Archaic 2 components have a greater variety of seeds, but most are fruit seeds. They also include seeds from native stands of marsh elder (*I. annua*) and a few examples of goosefoot and maygrass seeds. Wild bean and giant ragweed seeds are most common in the Middle Archaic 2 Napoleon component.

Carbonized squash (*Cucurbita* sp.) rind has been found at Koster (Middle Archaic 2, Horizon 8B), Napoleon Hollow (Middle Archaic 2, Napoleon component), and Lagoon. The specimens from Koster and Napoleon Hollow are 7,000 years old, while the piece from Lagoon is 4,300 years old (Conard et al. 1983).

Marsh elder from native though possibly cultivated stands accounts for 40 percent of the seeds from Middle Archaic Helton-phase components at Koster. Goosefoot, knotweed, and maygrass total less than 15 percent (Asch and Asch 1978). Seeds are not numerous in the Helton-phase component at Napoleon Hollow. Giant ragweed and wild bean are most common (Asch and Asch 1980). Only two seeds, both grape, were found in samples from beneath Elizabeth Mound 6.

Seeds from the Titterington-phase component at Napoleon Hollow represent native stands of sunflower and lamb's-quarters, but the size of *Iva* achenes is comparable to domesticated specimens from Salts Cave, Kentucky (Asch and Asch 1980; Conard et al. 1983). Lamb's-quarters accounts for 73 percent of the seeds from Lagoon, and specimens of squash and marsh elder from the site are probably domesticated (Asch and Asch 1983; Conard et al. 1983).

In contrast, native seeds are uncommon in the Kampsville-phase component at Titus, and none appear to be from cultivated species (Asch and Asch 1978), which is surprising given a trend in the evidence of cultivated seeds observed for Late Archaic Titterington-phase components.

Animal Remains

Animal remains from Twin Ditch and Koster Horizon 11 indicate that a variety of aquatic and terrestrial habitats were exploited by 8500 B.P. At Twin Ditch there is evidence of fish, bird, small and large mammals, and the assemblage of faunal remains at Koster consists of fish, mussels, turtles, birds, and forest mammals (T. Morrow 1996; Neusius 1982, 1986). A broad-spectrum strategy of exploitation is indicated (Neusius 1982; Styles and McMillan, this volume).

Faunal remains from Middle Archaic 1 (8200–7600 B.P.) settlements, all of which appear to have been short-term occupations, appear to represent opportunistic procurement (Neusius 1982). Forest species and, to a lesser extent, those from aquatic habitats characterized the Koster Middle Archaic 1 assemblages. Although preservation is a concern, the Campbell Hollow assemblage is consistent with a broad-spectrum strategy: it exhibits substantial variety in terrestrial and aquatic mammals, fish, waterfowl, and turtles (Colburn 1985).

A significant increase in the exploitation of aquatic resources, especially those from rivers and streams, is evident in Middle Archaic 2 (7300–6320 B.P.) components, which suggests more a focused subsistence strategy (Neusius 1982). Fewer environmental niches appear to have been the targets of resource procurement, as indicated by the increase in mussels, fish, and white-tailed deer (Neusius 1982, 1986; Styles 1986). For example, faunal remains from Koster Horizon 8C (ca. 6900 B.P.) indicate the first substantial reliance on backwater-lake resources, which were renewed annually and had a particularly high food density (Hewitt 1983; Hill 1975; Neusius 1982, 1986; Styles 1986). Deer account for 78 percent of the number of identified specimens in the Napoleon-component assemblage, slightly more than for Koster Middle Archaic 2 components, whereas fish total only 8.1 percent of the Napoleon sample (Styles and McMillan Figure 3.10, this volume). Qualitatively speaking, faunal remains from Quasar Horizon 4 are comparable to those reported at Koster and Napoleon Hollow (Lopinto 1995). Variation in the relative proportions of species may be attributable to differences in the location or purpose of a settlement or both. For example, the Napoleon component is within 200 m of the Illinois River bank, while Koster Middle Archaic 2 settlements were within 1.6 km (1 mi) of a backwater lake, 3.5 km (2.2 mi) from the river.

Although the variety of fauna from the Koster Horizon 6 Helton-phase component indicates a broad-based strategy that included hunting, fowling, fishing, and mussel collecting, it also points to increasing reliance on aquatic resources, especially fish and mussels, particularly those found in backwater lakes, such as bullheads and stout floaters (Brown and Vierra 1983; Hill 1975; Styles 1986; Styles and McMillan, this volume). An increase is also evident in the proportion of migratory waterfowl; duck makes up 64 percent of the bird bone (Hill 1975). Styles (1986) attributes these changes to the evolution of increasingly productive backwater lakes. Brown and Vierra (1983:189) emphasize the accessibility of different environmental zones from the Horizon 6 settlement, as indicated by the variety of fauna, and they underscore the combination of differences in environment—the evolution of backwater productivity—and procurement strategy—logistical mobility—in distinguishing the Helton-phase lifestyle from that of the preceding Middle Archaic 2 components.

A similar trend is evident in the data from Napoleon Hollow, in which fish account for 42 percent of the number of identified species in the Helton-phase faunal assemblage, up from 8.1 percent of the Middle Archaic 2 Napoleon component. Mammals remain important, with white-tailed deer representing nearly a third of the number of identified specimens (Styles and McMillan, this volume).

Poor preservation limits analysis of faunal remains from Titterington-phase components at Koster, Napoleon Hollow, and Lagoon (Cook 1983; Hill 1975; Styles 1986). White-tailed deer dominates the Koster Horizon 4 assemblage, accounting for 88 percent of the bones. Mussels are also present (Hill

1975), but the extent to which fish were exploited is not clear (Styles 1986). Neither Napoleon Hollow nor Lagoon contributes any detail to this analysis. Bone and shell are well preserved and fish bone is abundant in the Titus site Kampsville-phase component, but they have yet to be analyzed. Under the circumstances, it is currently not possible to evaluate whether the trend in aquatic resource intensification persisted beyond 5000 B.P.

Settlement

The subject of sedentism has been central to the study of the Archaic period in the lower Illinois River basin. Analysis of the spatial organization of Middle Archaic–period settlements at Koster reveals a trend of increasing complexity consistent with longer-term occupation by more residents (Brown 1985; Brown and Vierra 1983; Carlson 1979; Doershuk 1989; Wolynec 1977). Drawing on the full complement of excavated Archaic-period sites in the region and on evidence for the establishment of base settlements supported by logistical foraging, the argument that sedentism increased in Middle Archaic times is strengthened (Stafford 1991).

Prior to ca. 7000 B.P., settlements in the region appear to have been short-term residential encampments occupied to exploit a generalized suite of resources depending on site location and season of occupation (Brown 1985; Brown and Vierra 1983; Carlson 1979; Doershuk 1989; Hewitt 1983; Neusius 1986). Fire appears to have been the center of domestic activity; discarded tools, debris from tool production and repair, and food remains are concentrated around hearths. Other facilities are rare; shallow basins were used to dispose of hearth contents (Doershuk 1989), and graves contain the remains of humans or dogs. Settlement complexity appears attributable to repeated occupation, not to the duration of occupation. For instance, a series of superimposed surface hearths in Koster Horizon 11 illustrates repeated reoccupation of the same location as the surface of the Koster Creek floodplain aggraded. Evidently, inhabitants of the region found the spring-fed Koster Creek valley attractive over a period of time. Additional evidence of repeated occupation is provided by the complement of heavy grinding tools, which presumably were left at this location as site furniture (Binford 1979) to be used during subsequent visits.

Early Archaic 1 settlements are found throughout the Illinois River basin, although they are underrepresented in floodplains. The discovery of buried components at Napoleon Hollow, Titus, and Twin Ditch suggests that geomorphic factors account for the low visibility of Early Archaic sites in aggrading environments. The distribution of Early Archaic 2 settlements has not been researched but is likely to be strongly correlated with the distribution of buried valley paleogeomorphic surfaces.

A shift in settlement organization occurred ca. 7000 B.P. Though hearths remained fundamental organizational features, the number of pit features and the sheer quantity of artifacts indicate that the Koster Horizon 8C component was a substantial base settlement. In this instance, settlement complexity appears to be attributable to the duration of occupation, the concomitant variety of activity, and, to a lesser extent, the repetition of occupation, and it marks an important threshold in the development of sedentism (Carlson 1979; Doershuk 1989). Key to understanding this transition is the function of the pit features in Horizon 8C. Some appear to be food-processing pits (i.e., pit ovens) (Carlson 1979; Wolynec 1977). But others appear to be food-storage pits, given their volumes (Carlson 1979:360; Doershuk 1989:203). If so, they signal the development of an important means of managing surplus to offset seasonal variations in food availability. Further analysis of the pit features in Koster Horizon 8C will shed light on this important matter.

Subsequent settlements at Napoleon Hollow and Quasar appear less complex in terms of the type and variety of implements, debris, and facilities. For example, there is no evidence of storage pits, but the area of excavation at both settlements is limited. How these components fit into a particular settlement pattern is unclear. Are they the remains of seasonal residential camps or evidence of logistic foraging? At any rate, they suggest that the development of sedentary communities was gradual, perhaps influenced at first by seasonal variations in resource availability.

The distribution of Middle Archaic 1 and Middle Archaic 2 settlements is not known, again in part because of landscape evolution and the burial of most paleolandscape positions of Middle Archaic age. The identification of diagnostic artifacts of Middle Archaic 2 deposits remains problematic, and survey collections have not been reviewed to identify recognized components such as those indicated by the Middle Archaic 1 occupations at Campbell Hollow and Koster Horizons 9 and 10.

The Koster and Napoleon Hollow Helton-phase components also appear to be base settlements. They represent intense occupations, but midden accumulation at Napoleon Hollow with distinct superimposed surfaces marked by features indicates repeated occupation over a period of several hundred years. The number and variety of implements and the amount of debris (e.g., debitage and limestone) in Helton-phase components at Koster and Napoleon Hollow is unprecedented when compared with previous settlements. Clearly, a variety of activities were undertaken at the two sites (Cook 1976; Odell 1996). There is also considerable variety in facilities, which range in shape, size, and function (Brown and Vierra 1983:185; Wolynec 1977). Hearths continued to be at the center of daily life; they are surrounded by a variety of implements and debris. Nearby, one often finds pits for roasting food and processing hickory nuts. Building platforms are evident in Horizon 6 (Brown and Vierra 1983); none are observed elsewhere, but the extent of excavation is considerably smaller than undertaken at Koster. Discrete human burial plots in Horizon 6, in which the remains of 25 individuals were interred, are also consistent with long-term occupations. Though the number of individuals is considerable lower at Napoleon Hollow, the density of graves, three within a 56-m^2 exposure, suggests more burials may be present in this component. Whether these settlements were occupied year-round is not yet clear, but the Helton-phase settlement pattern appears to have included temporary camps to exploit particular resources. According to Stafford (1991:218), Buckshaw Bridge is a short-term Helton-phase camp where residents processed hickory nuts. He offers a compelling argument that this site is consistent with logistical foraging strategies, in which some residents of base settlements set up satellite work camps.

Helton-phase sites are most numerous in Illinois River valley-margin settings (41 percent), with equal numbers in Illinois Valley and secondary-valley settings (29 percent) (Cook 1976:118). As is the case with earlier settlements, geomorphic factors probably influence the visibility of sites.

Late Archaic Titterington-phase settlements in the region are varied in size, function, and duration of occupation. Koster Horizon 4 contrasts sharply with Horizon 6 and appears to have been a short-term logistical camp established for the procurement of white-tailed deer (Cook 1976). Lagoon is described as a "single-group" settlement. The absence of storage pits is noteworthy, especially in light of the evidence for domesticated squash and marsh elder (Asch and Asch 1980; Conard et al. 1983; Cook 1976). The Titterington component at Napoleon Hollow may have been a base settlement, judging from the amount of debris, the number and variety of stone tools, and the evidence for cultivation of marsh elder (Asch and Asch 1980; Odell 1996). The distribution of Titterington-phase sites contrasts with that of Helton-phase sites. Of 72 documented Titterington-phase sites, nearly half (49 percent) are located in secondary valleys, whereas only 29 percent of Helton sites are found in the same settings. Cook (1976:119) advances the hypothesis that climate amelioration renewed the productivity of food resources in secondary valleys and promoted more intensive settlement. This hypothesis remains to be evaluated.

At present, all known Kampsville-phase habitation components are part of mixed, multicomponent deposits. Little is currently known about settlement organization, assemblages of implements, or facilities.

Mortuary Practice

In the lower Illinois River basin, human remains have been discovered in Archaic-period components that range in age from 8500 B.P. to ca. 2800 B.P. There was little difference in the treatment and disposition of the dead between 8500 B.P. and ca. 6300 B.P., when an abrupt change ushered in considerable variation in mortuary ritual during the remainder of the period. Prior to 6700 B.P., burial appears to have been expeditious, leaving behind little material evidence of ritual. An adult corpse, regardless of age or sex, was generally buried in a flexed position in a shallow grave excavated into midden. In a few instances, everyday tools such as projectile points, antler batons, and grooved axes were placed with the remains. The antler object in Koster Horizon 11 Feature 2419 perhaps is a nonutilitarian exception (Figure 9.9). Infants were also placed in shallow graves, but they were not flexed and no artifacts were placed with them. Single graves in subsequent, short-term pre-6300 B.P. Koster settlements are consistent with similar expeditious treatment of remains.

Feature 4 in Elizabeth Mound 1 is a dramatic departure from long-standing expeditious treatment of the deceased. The extended remains of five individuals were placed side by side in a single bluff-crest grave and were accompanied by a variety of objects, including marine shell. At face value, by 6300 B.P., substantial changes appear to have taken place in treatment and disposition of the dead and the ritual that accompanied the process. This early appearance of more-elaborate mortuary ritual is surprising because it predates by at least 200 years the substantial, long-term, Helton-phase settlements at Koster and Napoleon Hollow—whose settled lifestyle likely fostered a more complex society (Charles and Buikstra 1983).

The elaborate treatment accorded the Middle Archaic burials at the bluff-top Elizabeth mounds was part of an increasingly varied mortuary program. Between ca. 6000 B.P. and 5000 B.P., expeditious burial continued on the edge of the Koster Horizon 6 settlement, but individual graves dating to approximately the same time have been found beneath the bluff-crest Gibson mounds and in a long-term cemetery at the Bullseye site, and multiple remains have been found commingled in a single pit at Godar. Red ocher was applied to the remains in many instances, and an assortment of objects was often placed in the graves. Most of the objects—bone tools, grooved axes, grinding stones, drills, projectile points, and plummets—appear to have been everyday tools made out of locally available materials, but some—bannerstones and copper axes and awls—were probably made from nonlocal material, and others—marine-shell pendants—are certainly made from material imported from a long distance. The appearance of more-elaborate and varied mortuary practices corresponds to the development of increasingly sedentary communities, which very early on were engaged in the acquisition of distant resources and perhaps finished objects made elsewhere.

A bundle burial discovered in the Helton component (ca. 5500 B.P.) at the Napoleon Hollow site is the oldest evidence in the lower Illinois Valley of postmortem processing: cut marks are evident on some of the bones. Perhaps disarticulation was necessary to facilitate transport of the body to the settlement. At any rate, such processing represents a new variation in the treatment of the dead. The mortuary record at the Bullseye site is complicated. Graves are difficult to delineate, and bone is poorly preserved at the site. The presence of a few Early Archaic projectile points among the remains has fostered speculation about the possibility that early Holocene graves may be present at the site (Walthall 1999:11). By ca. 5000 B.P., a dense cluster of graves was present at Bullseye, and the site appears to represent a formally designated burial area in the Illinois River floodplain (Buikstra and Charles 1999; Charles and Buikstra 1983; see also Milner et al., this volume). In addition to everyday objects made from local materials, a variety of bannerstones at Bullseye appear to have been made elsewhere.

Variation in mortuary practices is observed in many dimensions. In some instances, a person's physical capability in life influenced where the individual was buried (Buikstra 1981). The treatment of individuals buried at mortuary sites was diverse. Some were interred in a flexed position, and others were buried extended on their backs; the number and types of objects placed with the remains apparently underscored individuals' status. In addition to everyday tools such as projectile points and grooved axes, what may have been ritual or status regalia made from nonlocal or relatively rare materials increased in frequency through the Archaic. For example, occasional copper artifacts appeared for the first time in Titterington-phase mortuary contexts (e.g., Titterington 1950). In some cases, red ocher was applied to the remains. But bluff-crest mortuary sites are multicomponent, and the lack of radiocarbon dates makes it difficult to discern the early chronology of particular cultural practices.

Evidence for Archaic-period mound building at Elizabeth is equivocal, but some evidence suggests that by 4000 B.P. at least some Titterington-phase cemeteries may have been marked by small earthworks. At Etley, for example, a series of bluff-crest mounds cover Archaic graves marked by limestone slabs (Figure 9.35) that entombed red-ocher-stained remains of individuals buried with a variety of artifacts. Given the uncontrolled nature of the early excavations at the site, archaeologists are uncertain whether the mounds are Archaic or later Woodland-period constructions. In general, the Etley artifact assemblage includes the same suite of tools and adornment seen in earlier Helton-phase cemeteries. In some instances, objects such as projectile points and bannerstones were placed with Helton-phase and Titterington-phase burials.

Some aspects of Kampsville-phase mortuary practices are consistent with a long-established trend of bluff-crest cemeteries in which red-ocher-covered human remains were placed in graves in flexed positions. Bundle burials also occur in Kampsville-phase cemeteries. However, there are significant differences in mortuary-artifact associations compared to earlier Archaic contexts. Several regional Red Ocher mortuary contexts (e.g., Elm Point, Collinsville, Rock Creek, and Bunker Hill) include "conspicuous-consumption" deposits of up to 200 or more leaf-shaped blades of various styles—Turkey-tail points and Black Creek knives (see Perino 1985:37, 141), usually well-made from distinctive, glossy, dark gray "hornstones" originating in southern Illinois (Cobden/Dongola chert) and south-central Indiana (Wyandotte chert). Similar deposits of flat-based "Red Ocher" leaf-shaped blades (see Perino 1985:318) are made of local white Burlington cherts (e.g., Farnsworth 2006:50–51; Titterington 1950). A wide range of exotic artifacts made from other nonlocal raw materials (copper, marine shell, and pipestone) frequently accompany Terminal Archaic burials as well. The Riverside Cemetery site near the Wisconsin-Michigan border yielded a block of obsidian wrapped in a strand of copper beads in Red Ocher mortuary context (Pleger 1998:227). Farnsworth's salvage excavations at the Bunker Hill site in Macoupin County produced a calcite-crystal-surfaced grinding stone encrusted with red ocher.

Most Red Ocher artifacts were made and imported specifically to be placed with burials. Because there is almost no overlap between the artifact styles and exotic raw materials found at Terminal Archaic habitation and mortuary sites (except Klunk Mound 7, where a few fire-shattered Kampsville Barbed points were found with the burials; Perino 1968:68–84), precise temporal limits and cultural associations of Red Ocher mortuary ceremonialism are uncertain. There are obvious 1200–900 B.C. Prairie Lake–culture associations (Farnsworth and Asch 1986:339–352), but Red Ocher mortuary activity may have extended into Early Woodland times as well (ca. 800–600 B.C.), at least in some areas (Esarey 1986; Farnsworth and Asch 1986:351; Seeman 1975).

Regional Red Ocher mortuary sites also occur in a variety of settings (Farnsworth 2004:7; Farnsworth and Asch 1986): bluff-top cemeteries are known at the margins of the lower Illinois Valley (Hagen, Klunk, and Hemphill), the adjacent Mississippi Valley (Bell Farm and Indian Creek), and the northern American Bottom (Elm Point and Collinsville), and at least one was mounded (Klunk Mound 7). A Terminal Archaic cemetery is also associated with a bluff-base habitation area (Snyders site) in the Mississippi Valley; the Bunker Hill mortuary site is located some 50 km (31 mi) east of the Illinois Valley (ca. 25 km [15.5 mi] northeast of Alton, Illinois) atop an imposing morainal knob in an interior upland area separating the Piasa and Cahokia Creek drainages.

Red Ocher cemetery structures and burial treatments were more elaborate than those of earlier Archaic times. In addition to the mound-capped Terminal Archaic mortuary at Klunk, some Red Ocher tombs are deeply excavated cylindrical structures that can be over a meter in diameter and over 2 m deep (Bunker Hill and Hemphill). The Bunker Hill tomb also included a simple spiral "stairway" cut into its walls to allow easy access to the deep, cylindrical tomb while it was in use. In addition to bundle burials, a major new element of cremation was included in Red Ocher mortuary activity (e.g., Bunker Hill and Klunk Mound 7). In the case of Bunker Hill, the Black Creek blade cache was arrayed over a pile of cremation ashes brought into the tomb from elsewhere (there was no evidence of in situ burning, but small bits of burned soil and cremated bone were scattered throughout the lower tomb fill). A second group of blades was then placed on top of the scattered cremation fill in a starburst arrangement before the pit was finally capped to ground level (Figure 9.41).

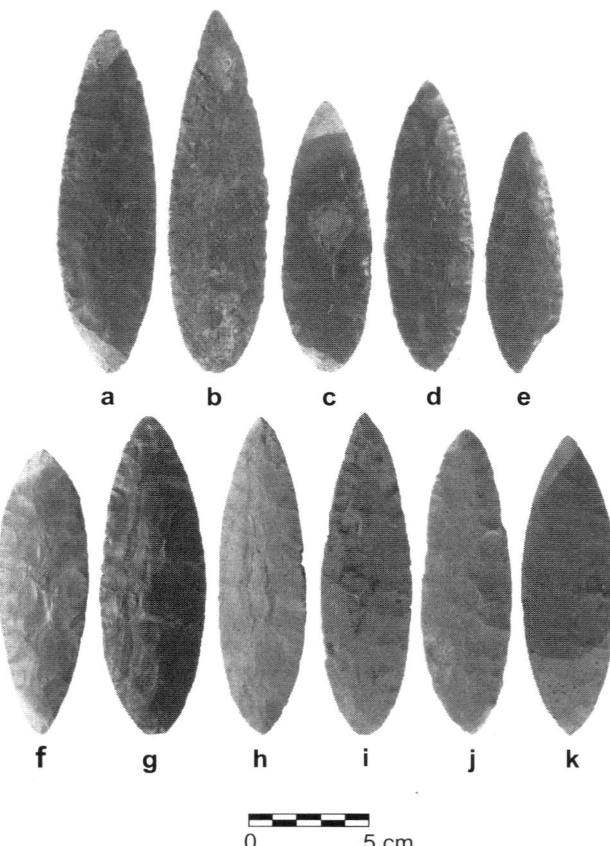

Figure 9.41. Terminal Archaic Black Creek knives from the Bunker Hill cemetery in the interior uplands of Macoupin County. Glossy, gray-chert blades a–e are from the artifact array that capped the primary grave fill. Blades f–k, from the construction-disturbed primary cremation cache on the floor of the pit, illustrate the range of variation in blade shape, cortex use, and raw-material color in the cache. a–e, Center for American Archeology, Kampsville; f–k, private collection.

Some of the artifact types found in Helton-, Titterington-, and Kampsville-phase mortuary contexts have not been found in habitation sites. "Domestic" artifacts (e.g., axes, drills, plummets, and points) are found in habitation sites; other artifacts (e.g., large, lanceolate, hafted bifaces and leaf-shaped blades made of distinctive cherts, bannerstones, calcite beads, copper implements, feldspar tablets, and freshwater shell beads) appear to be largely restricted to mortuary components.

Archaic Cultural Development and Climate Change

The effect of climate change on the development of Archaic culture has long been the subject of archaeological research in the Midwest (Alex 2000; Birmingham et al. 1997; Brown and Vierra 1983; Halsey 1999; Theler and Boszhardt 2003). Other than Luchterhand's (1970) data on Early Archaic sites, there is little information about Archaic settlement distribution from excavated sites in the uplands of the Illinois River basin to compare with regional studies (e.g., Lewis 1983) or draw conclusions about the local effects of climate on culture change. Nevertheless, in our view, some noteworthy correspondence can be traced between the timing of climate events and cultural developments in the Illinois River valley.

From the sparse upland settlement data we have at our disposal (Luchterhand 1970), Early Archaic 1 sites appear to be widely distributed across the landscape, but a shift in mobility strategies seems to have occurred ca. 9000 B.P. Distinctive characteristics of Early Archaic 1 bifaces (e.g., beveling and stem grinding) suggest a society moving across a landscape where lithic resources were irregularly distributed (Goodyear 1979; Wiant and Hassen 1984). At face value, Early Archaic 1 groups appear to have adapted to an elm forest (Eric C. Grimm, pers. comm. 2006; Nelson et al. 2006) in which desirable resources such as white-tailed deer may not have been as densely concentrated as in other contexts and small mammals such as squirrels may have been more available (see Styles and McMillan, this volume). The Early Archaic 1 means of biface rejuvenation, and perhaps the associated way of life, appears to have come to an end at ca. 9000 B.P., at approximately the same time relatively arid conditions began to develop in the Midwest (Eric C. Grimm, pers. comm. 1996; Nelson et al. 2006).

The ca. 8500 B.P. Koster Horizon 11 occupation may represent an adjustment to changing environmental conditions. When compared with the Early Archaic 1 component at Twin Ditch and other Early Archaic 2 sites, qualitative and quantitative differences in Horizon 11 chipped- and ground-stone tool assemblages and evidence for repeated occupation of the Koster Creek valley indicate a substantial reduction in mobility for at least a portion of the annual round. Furthermore, evidence for generalized subsistence (Neusius 1982) may indicate the establishment of a base camp strategically located among a variety of environmental zones, in particular, aquatic habitats. The Horizon 11 occupation may be an example of a first step in the development of an increasingly sedentary way of life. This development was coeval with the first of two intervals of increasing aridity.

All of the excavated Middle Archaic 1 settlements in the Illinois Valley—occupied during the first interval of aridity, ca. 8900 B.P.–7600 B.P.—appear to have been short-duration residential occupations. Quite possibly archaeologists simply have yet to find a Middle Archaic 1 base camp. The number and, perhaps, density of white-tailed deer may have increased during this interval as the forest-prairie ecotone expanded (Hewitt 1983; Neusius 1982). The decrease in projectile point size during the period is generally attributed to the development of atlatl-propelled darts. The development of this technology may be attributable to increased availability of deer.

The Middle Archaic 2 era (7300 B.P.–6850 B.P.) appears to have been a threshold in the development of sedentary life in the lower Illinois valley, and it corresponded to a period of increased precipitation and the expansion of forest (Eric C. Grimm, pers. comm. 2006; Nelson et al. 2006). In terms of subsistence, evidence indicates a more focused hunting-gathering strategy (Neusius 1982; Styles 1986); a significant increase in the use of aquatic resources, especially fish (Styles 1986); and major reliance on nuts, especially hickory (Asch and Asch 1978). In terms of technology, the use of the atlatl improved hunting efficiency, while the development of in-ground storage capacity and the construction of residential shelters indicate increased investment in particular locations.

The period of the most severe mid-Holocene aridity began ca. 5400 B.P. and ameliorated by 3200 B.P. (Eric C. Grimm, pers. comm. 2006; Nelson et al. 2006). The arid conditions affected the landscape of the Illinois Valley, as indicated by the geological record, but the details of their effect on biota remain a matter of research and discussion. The significance of aquatic habitats to the area's human occupants is not in doubt (Brown and Vierra 1983; Hill 1975; Styles 1986), but Hajic (see *Archaic Landscape Systematics*, above), drawing on continuing research, indicates that throughout the early Holocene and much of the mid-Holocene, much of the lower Illinois River valley was occupied by a lake that extended from valley wall to valley wall, inundating everything except for a few elevated landforms such as fans. Deep lateral lakes persisted through the mid-Holocene but eventually succumbed to accumulation of sediment contributed by both the Illinois River and tributary streams. The volume of water in these lakes may have buffered the effects of mid-Holocene climate on aquatic resources, and, possibly, the productivity of the shallow-water lake margins was enhanced. As noted above, the Koster Helton-phase component appears to have been a long-term settlement in which a variety of intense daily activities were undertaken, and, clearly, aquatic resources, the productivity of which was influenced by the evolution of the floodplain and perhaps climate change, were integral to this development.

The Titterington-phase marked an abrupt shift in Archaic culture that did not correspond to any particular shift in mid-Holocene climate but occurred near the end of the long interval of prairie expansion. Cook (1976) noted similarities between Titterington-phase sites in the lower Illinois Valley and Late Archaic sites in Missouri. We wonder if prolonged drought encouraged the expansion of Late Archaic culture from the interior of Missouri into the Mississippi and Illinois River valleys. At present, however, we know of no environmental data to support this idea.

Cook (1976) observed that the proportion of Titterington-phase settlements in tributary valleys was considerably greater than Helton-phase settlements. To account for this difference, he suggested that the amelioration of mid-Holocene climate increased the productivity of tributary valleys and attracted settlement there. At present, environmental data do not support this interpretation.

Geomorphic evidence suggests a significant increase in precipitation ca. 3500–3000 B.P. that resulted in the redeposition of sediment and the formation of natural levees along tributaries and the Illinois River. Although Early Woodland sites are common on these levees (Farnsworth and Asch 1986), the effect of increased precipitation on human settlement during the Terminal Archaic period is not known.

Conclusion

The foregoing overview summarizes our present understanding of the Archaic period in the lower Illinois River basin and the history of Archaic site excavations in the region during the past 50 years. The Archaic era encompassed a long period of dramatic environmental and cultural changes in west-central Illinois. The circumstances and consequences of these changes are becoming increasingly clear, but they also require substantial further archaeological research. If nothing else, we hope this chapter draws attention to important gaps in current understanding and promotes a renewed effort to dig deeper into the data at hand and into the extraordinary archaeological record that is still preserved in the ground in the lower Illinois Valley region.

Much remains to be done if archaeologists are to understand the relationships, if any, between changes in climate and changes in Archaic culture; the culture history of changing Archaic subsistence strategies (such as increased aquatic-resource exploitation) and hunting technologies (such as the use of the spear-thrower); changing Archaic strategies for bulk food storage and for constructing food-storage facilities; through-time changes in Archaic residential mobility, increasing sedentism, and associated developments in residential shelter construction; the factors leading to the Archaic domestication of a variety of native plants and at least one native animal (canines); and the timing, nature, and significance of the elaboration of mortuary practices and structures during Middle and Late Archaic times.

Acknowledgments

This overview is a digest of the considerable labors of many researchers who have explored the Archaic period in the lower Illinois River basin. The regional fieldwork program that produced most of the Archaic data summarized above was an outgrowth of the vision and tireless determination of Stuart Struever. Stuart created a unique place for and approach to archaeological research and persuaded Northwestern University colleagues James A. Brown, Jane E. Buikstra, and Robert K. Vierra to dedicate their considerable talents to the enterprise. They, in turn, encouraged other colleagues and a cadre of graduate and undergraduate students to join them in their search for the past in Stuart's "Kingdom of Lowillva." Many of these students have since contributed to our understanding of the Archaic period, and the references we cite below are acknowledgment of the many important contributions of our Kampsville colleagues to the development of a regional Archaic culture history. We salute them all.

We also acknowledge R. Bruce McMillan, director emeritus of the Illinois State Museum. Bruce created an interdisciplinary research center that has evolved into the museum's Landscape History Program. All of us have been the beneficiaries of the opportunities afforded by the staff and facilities of this program.

Illinois Transportation Archaeological Research Program (ITARP) Director Thomas Emerson served as both editorial hammer and anvil in urging us on to complete this chapter but was also incredibly patient when we stumbled over unforeseen problems in assembling and evaluating the mass of undigested Archaic data from our Illinois Valley study area. Andrew Fortier went far beyond the call of duty in calibrating our assembled radiocarbon dates for us and also offered valuable comments on interregional chronology concerns while we were constructing Table 9.1. Together with editor Dale McElrath, Tom and Andy also helped steer and focus our efforts by offering valuable comments and questions on text, table, and figure drafts along the way.

In addition, ITARP's able production-office staff prepared our chapter illustrations. Linda Alexander took the fine photographs of the projectile points from Koster, Napoleon Hollow, Campbell Hollow, Titus, and Upper Macoupin sites used in this chapter, and Mike Lewis assembled them into finished figures. Mike Farkas designed and produced the regional base map (Figure 9.1). Linda Forman prepared a skilled and detailed technical edit of the final manuscript. Our chapter is greatly enhanced by their efforts.

In the end, we alone are responsible for any errors or omissions in this chapter.

References Cited

Abbott, Larry R., and Joseph A. Tiffany
1986 Archaeological Context and Upland Soil Development: The Midwest, U.S.A. Example. Paper presented at the 24th Midwest Archaeological Conference, Cleveland, Ohio.

Alex, Lynn M.
2000 *Iowa's Archaeological Past*. University of Iowa Press, Iowa City.

Artz, Joe Alan
1993 The Preservation of Cultural Stratigraphy in Loess-Mantled Terrains of Iowa. *Journal of the Iowa Archeological Society* 40:50–62.

Asch, David L.
1978 Predictive Modeling of Archaeological Site Location in the Illinois Upland Prairie Region: A Systematic Survey of the Montgomery County Panhandle. Unpublished manuscript, submitted to the Illinois Department of Conservation, Springfield. Northwestern University Archeological Program, Kampsville, Illinois.

Asch, David L., and Nancy B. Asch
1976 Paleoethnobotany of the Koster Site: An Interim Report. Manuscript on file, Kampsville Archeological Center, Kampsville, Illinois.
1978 The Economic Potential of *Iva annua* and Its Prehistoric Importance in the Lower Illinois Valley. In *The Nature and Status of Ethnobotany*, edited by Richard I. Ford, pp. 301–341. Anthropological Papers 67. Museum of Anthropology, University of Michigan, Ann Arbor.
1985 Archeobotany. In *The Campbell Hollow Archaic Occupations: A Study of Intrasite Spatial Structure in the Lower Illinois Valley*, edited by C. Russell Stafford, pp. 82–107. Research Series 4. Center for American Archeology, Kampsville, Illinois.
1987 *Archeobotany of Buckshaw Bridge, an Archaic Site in Brown County, Illinois*. Archeobotanical Laboratory Report 77. Center for American Archeology, Kampsville, Illinois.
1988 Archeobotany of the Sub-Mound 6 Middle Archaic Occupation. In *The Archaic and Woodland Cemeteries at the Elizabeth Site in the Lower Illinois Valley*, edited by Douglas K. Charles, Steven R. Leigh, and Jane E. Buikstra, pp. 296–302. Research Series 7. Center for American Archeology, Kampsville, Illinois.

Asch, David L., Kenneth B. Farnsworth, H. Carl Udesen, and Ann L. Koski
1981 Upper Mississippi River and Lower Illinois River Units (III-South and VI). In *Predictive Models in Illinois Archaeology: Report Summaries*, edited by Margaret K. Brown, pp. 55–72. Illinois Department of Conservation, Springfield.

Asch, David L., and Nancy Asch Sidell
1988 Archeological Plant Remains: Applications to Stratigraphic Analysis. In *Current Paleoethnobotany: Analytical Methods and Cultural Interpretations of Archaeological Plant Remains*, edited by Christine A. Hastorf and Virginia S. Popper, pp. 86–96. University of Chicago Press, Chicago.

Asch, Nancy B., and David L. Asch
1979 Archeobotany of the Koster Site: The Early and Middle Archaic Occupations. Paper presented at the 44th Annual Meeting of the Society for American Archaeology, Vancouver, B.C. (Archeobotanical Laboratory Report 28. Northwestern University Archeological Program, Kampsville, Illinois.)
1980 *Archeobotany of Napoleon Hollow, a Multicomponent Site in Pike County, Illinois: Initial Report*, edited by Michael D. Wiant, pp. 136–165. Reports of Investigations 76. Submitted to the Illinois Department of Transportation. Contract Archeology Program, Center for American Archeology, Kampsville, Illinois,
1983 The Paleoethnobotany of the Lagoon Site. In The Lagoon Site: The Titterington Component, edited by Thomas G. Cook. Manuscript on file, Kampsville Archeological Center, Kampsville, Illinois.

Asch, Nancy B., Richard I. Ford, and David L. Asch
1972 *Paleoenthnobotany of the Koster Site: The Archaic Horizons.* Reports of Investigations 24. Illinois State Museum, Springfield.

Bartram, Lawrence
1983 The Geomorphology of the Lagoon Site. In The Lagoon Site: The Titterington Component, edited by Thomas G. Cook. Manuscript on file, Kampsville Archeological Center, Kampsville, Illinois.

Bettis, E. Arthur, III, and Edwin R. Hajic
1995 Landscape Development and the Location of Evidence of Archaic Cultures in the Upper Midwest. In *Archaeological Geology of the Archaic Period in North America*, edited by E. Arthur Bettis III, pp. 87–113. Special Paper 297. Geological Society of America, Boulder, Colorado.

Binford, Lewis R.
1978 Dimensional Analysis of Behavior and Site Structure: Learning from an Eskimo Hunting Stand. *American Antiquity* 43:330–361.
1979 Organization and Formation Processes: Looking at Curated Technologies. *Journal of Anthropological Research* 35:255–273.

Birmingham, Robert A., Carol I. Mason, and James B. Stoltman (editors)
1997 Wisconsin Archeology. *The Wisconsin Archeologist* 78.

Braun, David P., James B. Griffin, and Paul F. Titterington
1982 *The Snyders Mounds and Five Other Mound Groups in Calhoun County, Illinois.* Technical Report 19. Museum of Anthropology, University of Michigan, Ann Arbor.

Bray, Robert T.
1956 The Culture-Complexes and Sequence at the Rice Site (235N200) Stone County, Missouri. *Missouri Archeologist* 18(1–2):47–134.

Brown, James A.
1985 Long-Term Trends to Sedentism and the Emergence of Complexity in the American Midwest. In *Prehistoric Hunter-Gatherers*, edited by T. Douglas Price and James A. Brown, pp. 201–231. Academic Press, New York.

Brown, James A., and Stuart Struever
1973 The Organization of Archaeological Research: An Illinois Example. In *Research and Theory in Current Archaeology*, edited by Charles L. Redman, pp. 261–280. John Wiley, New York.

Brown, James A., and Robert K. Vierra
1983 What Happened in the Middle Archaic? In *Archaic Hunters and Gatherers in the American Midwest*, edited by James L. Phillips and James A. Brown, pp. 165–195. Academic Press, New York.

Broyles, Bettye J.
1971 *The St. Albans Site, Kanawha County, West Virginia.* Report of Archaeological Investigations 3. West Virginia Geological and Economic Survey, Morgantown.

Buikstra, Jane E.
1972 *Hopewell in the Lower Illinois Valley: A Regional Approach to the Study of Human Biological Variability and Prehistoric Behavior.* Scientific Papers 2. Northwestern University Archeological Program, Evanston, Illinois.
1981 Mortality Practices, Paleodemography, and Paleopathology: A Case Study from the Koster Site (Illinois). In *The Archaeology of Death*, edited by Robert Chapman, Ian Kinnes, and Klavs Randsborg, pp. 123–132. Cambridge University Press, Cambridge, England.

Buikstra, Jane E., and Douglas Charles
1999 Centering the Ancestors: Cemeteries, Mounds, and Sacred Landscapes of the Ancient North American Midcontinent. In *Archaeologies of Landscape: Contemporary Perspectives*, edited by Wendy Ashmore and A. Bernard Knapp, pp. 201–228. Blackwell, Malden, Massachusetts.

Butzer, Karl W.
1977 *Geomorphology of the Lower Illinois Valley as a Spatial-Temporal Context for the Koster Archaic Site.* Reports of Investigations 34. Illinois State Museum, Springfield.
1978 Changing Holocene Environments at the Koster Site: A Geo-Archaeological Perspective. *American Antiquity* 43:408–413.

Caldwell, Joseph R.
1958 *Trend and Tradition in the Prehistory of the Eastern United States.* Memoir 88. American Anthropological Association, Menasha, Wisconsin.

Carlson, David L.
1979 Hunter-Gatherer Mobility Strategies: An Example from the Koster Site in the Lower Illinois Valley. Ph.D. dissertation, Department of Anthropology, Northwestern University, Evanston, Illinois.

Chapman, Carl
1948 A Preliminary Survey of Missouri Archaeology, Part IV. *Missouri Archaeologist* 10(4):135–164.

Chapman, Jefferson
1973 *The Icehouse Bottom Site 40 MR 23.* Report of Investigations 13. Department of Anthropology, University of Tennessee, Knoxville.

Charles, Douglas K.
1995 Diachronic Regional Social Dynamics: Mortuary Sites in the Illinois Valley/American Bottom Region. In *Regional Approaches to Mortuary Analysis*, edited by Lane A. Beck, pp. 77–99. Plenum Press, New York.

Charles, Douglas K., and Jane E. Buikstra
1983 Archaic Mortuary Sites in the Central Mississippi Drainage: Distribution, Structure, and Behavioral Implications. In *Archaic Hunters and Gatherers in the American Midwest*, edited by James L. Phillips and James A. Brown, pp. 117–145. Academic Press, New York.

Charles, Douglas K., Jane E. Buikstra, and Lyle W. Konigsberg
1986 Behavioral Implications of Terminal Archaic and Early Woodland Mortuary Practices in the Lower Illinois Valley. In *Early Woodland Archeology*, edited by Kenneth B. Farnsworth and Thomas E. Emerson, pp. 458–474. Kampsville Seminars in Archeology 2. Kampsville Archeological Center, Center for American Archeology, Kampsville, Illinois.

Charles, Douglas K., Steven R. Leigh, and Jane E. Buikstra
1988 *The Archaic and Woodland Cemeteries at the Elizabeth Site in the Lower Illinois Valley.* Research Series 7. Kampsville Archeological Center, Center for American Archeology, Kampsville, Illinois.

Cobb, Dawn
2005 A Preliminary Analysis of Human Skeletal Material from the Napoleon Hollow Archaic Components. Manuscript on file, Illinois State Museum, Springfield.

Coe, Joffre
1964 *The Formative Cultures of the Carolina Piedmont.* Transactions of the American Philosophical Society 54(Pt. 5). Philadelphia.

Colburn, Mona L.
1985 Faunal Remains from the Campbell Hollow Archaic Occupations. In *The Campbell Hollow Archaic Occupations: A Study of Intrasite Spatial Structure in the Lower Illinois Valley*, edited by C. Russell Stafford, pp. 108–120. Research Series 4. Kampsville Archeological Center, Center for American Archeology, Kampsville, Illinois.

Conard, Nicholas, David L. Asch, Nancy B. Asch, David Elmore, Harry Gove, Meyer Rubin, James A. Brown, Michael D. Wiant, Kenneth B. Farnsworth, and Thomas G. Cook
1983 Accelerator Radiocarbon Dating of Evidence for Prehistoric Horticulture in Illinois. *Nature* 308:443–446.

Conner, Michael D.
1986 *Cypress Land: A Late Archaic/Early Woodland Site in the Lower Illinois River Floodplain.* Technical Report 2. Kampsville Archeological Center, Center for American Archeology, Kampsville, Illinois.

Conrad, Lawrence A.
1981 *An Introduction to the Archaeology of Upland West Central Illinois: A Preliminary Archaeological Survey of the Canton to Quincy Corridor for the Proposed FAP 407 Highway Project.* Reports of Investigations 2. Archaeological Research Laboratory, Western Illinois University, Macomb.

Cook, Thomas Genn
1976 *Koster: An Artifact Analysis of Two Archaic Phases in Westcentral Illinois.* Prehistoric Record 1. Northwestern University Archaeological Program, Evanston, Illinois.
1983 The Lagoon Site: A Titterington Occupation in the Lower Illinois Valley. Manuscript on file, Center for American Archeology, Kampsville, Illinois.
1986 A Dispersed Harvesting Economy: The Titterington Phase. In *Foraging, Collection, and Harvesting: Archaic Period Subsistence and Settlement in the Eastern Woodlands*, edited by Sarah W. Neusius, pp. 175–200. Occasional Papers 6. Center for Archaeological Investigations, Southern Illinois University, Carbondale.

Crane, H. R., and James B. Griffin
1963 University of Michigan Radiocarbon Dates VIII. *Radiocarbon* 5:228–253.

Deevey, Edward S., Jr., and Richard F. Flint
1957 Postglacial Hypsithermal Interval. *Science* 125:182–184.

Doershuk, John Frederick
1989 Hunter-Gatherer Site Structure and Sedentism: The Koster Site Middle Archaic. Ph.D. dissertation, Department of Anthropology, Northwestern University, Evanston, Illinois.

Druhot, Ray E.
1983 Report of Archaeological Investigations at the Titus and Upper Macoupin Sites in the Lower Illinois Valley. Manuscript on file, Center for American Archeology, Kampsville Archeological Center, Kampsville, Illinois.

Esarey, Duane
1986 Red Ochre Mound Building and Marion Phase Associations: A Fulton County, Illinois Perspective. In *Early Woodland Archeology*, edited by Kenneth B. Farnsworth and Thomas E. Emerson, pp. 231–243. Center for American Archeology Press, Kampsville, Illinois.
1987 The Town Branch Sites: Archaic Encampments on the Bushnell Prairie of West Central Illinois. *The Wisconsin Archeologist* 68:95–124.

Farnsworth, Kenneth B.
1973 *An Archaeological Survey of the Macoupin Valley.* Reports of Investigations 26. Illinois State Museum, Springfield.
1976 *An Archeological Survey of the Lower Illinois River Shoreline.* Reports of Investigations 25. Submitted to the U.S. Army Corps of Engineers, St. Louis District. Contract Archeology Program, Center for American Archeology, Kampsville, Illinois.
1987 Part Two: Preliminary Evaluation of Bannerstones and Other Ground-Stone Artifacts from the Bullseye Site, 11-Ge-127. In *The Bullseye Site: A Floodplain Archaic Mortuary Site in the Lower Illinois Valley*, by Harold Hassen and Kenneth B. Farnsworth, pp. 13–19. Reports of Investigations 42. Illinois State Museum, Springfield.
1993 New Information on 1932 Titterington Salvage Excavations at the Hartford Church Archaic Cemetery. *Illinois Archaeology* 5:141–147.
2004 *Early Hopewell Mound Explorations: The First Fifty Years in the Illinois River Valley.* Studies in Archaeology 3. Illinois Transportation Archaeological Research Program, University of Illinois, Urbana.
2006 Introduction. Gregory Perino's Archaeological Career and Illinois Site Excavations. In *Illinois Hopewell and Late Woodland Mounds: The Excavations of Gregory Perino 1940–1975*, edited by Kenneth B. Farnsworth and Michael D. Wiant, pp. 1–128. Studies in Archaeology 4. Illinois Transportation Archaeological Research Program, University of Illinois, Urbana.

Farnsworth, Kenneth B., and David L. Asch
1986 Early Woodland Chronology, Artifact Styles, and Settlement Distribution in the Lower Illinois Valley Region. In *Early Woodland Archeology*, edited by Kenneth B. Farnsworth and Thomas E. Emerson, pp. 326–457. Center for American Archeology Press, Kampsville, Illinois.

Fecht, William G.
1985 Morse Knives from the Snyders Site, Calhoun County, Illinois. *Central States Archaeological Journal* 16:62–77.

Fortier, Andrew C.
1984 The Go-Kart North Site. In *The Go-Kart North Site and the Dyroff and Levin Sites*, by Andrew C. Fortier and Thomas E. Emerson, pp. 1–197. American Bottom Archaeology FAI-270 Site Reports 9. University of Illinois Press, Urbana.

Geis, James W., and W. R. Boggess
1968 The Prairie Peninsula: Its Origin and Significance in the Vegetational History of Central Illinois. In *The Quaternary of Illinois*, edited by Robert Bergstrom, pp. 89–95. Special Report 14. University of Illinois College of Agriculture, Urbana.

Goatley, Daniel B.
1998 Quasar: A Stratified Archaic Site in the Floodplain of the Lower Illinois River Valley. *Illinois Archaeology* 10:267–293.

Goland, Carol A.
ca. 1980 Tabulation of Koster Horizon 11 Type Collection. Manuscript on file, Illinois State Museum, Springfield.

Goldstein, Lynne
1971 An Analysis of Plummets in the Lower Illinois River Valley. *Illinois Association for the Advancement of Archaeology Quarterly Newsletter* 3:30.

2004 An Analysis of Plummets in the Lower Illinois River Valley. In *Aboriginal Ritual and Economy in the Eastern Woodlands: Essays in Memory of Howard Dalton Winters*, edited by Anne-Marie Cantwell, Lawrence A. Conrad, and Jonathan R. Reyman, pp. 73–112. Scientific Papers 30. Illinois State Museum, Springfield.

Goodyear, Albert
1979 *A Hypothesis for the Use of Cryptocrystalline Raw Materials among Paleo-Indian Groups of North America.* Research Manuscript Series 156. Institute of Archaeology and Anthropology, University of South Carolina, Columbia.

Griffin, James B.
1952 (editor) *Archeology of Eastern United States.* University of Chicago Press, Chicago.

1967 Eastern North American Archaeology: A Summary. *Science* 156:175–191.

Grimm, Eric, and George Jacobson Jr.
2004 Late Quaternary Vegetation History of the Eastern United States. In *The Quaternary Period in the United States*, edited by Alan R. Gillespie, Stephen C. Porter, and Brian F. Atwater, pp. 381–402. Elsevier, Amsterdam.

Hajic, Edwin R.
1981a Geology and Paleopedology of the Koster Archaeological Site, Greene County, Illinois. Master's thesis, Department of Geology, University of Iowa, Iowa City.

1981b *Shallow Subsurface Geology, Geomorphology and Limited Cultural Resource Investigations of the Nutwood Levee and Drainage District, Jersey and Greene Counties, Illinois.* Report of Investigation 108. Submitted to the U.S. Army Corps of Engineers, St. Louis District. Contract Archeology Program, Center for American Archeology, Kampsville, Illinois.

1981c *Shallow Subsurface Geology, Geomorphology and Limited Cultural Resource Investigations of the Hartwell Levee and Drainage District, Greene Counties, Illinois.* Report of Investigation 109. Submitted to the U.S. Army Corps of Engineers, St. Louis District. Contract Archeology Program, Center for American Archeology, Kampsville, Illinois.

1983 *Shallow Subsurface Geology, Geomorphology and Limited Cultural Resource Investigations of the Hillview Levee and Drainage District, Scott and Greene Counties, Illinois.* Cultural Resource Management Report 5. U.S. Army Corps of Engineers, St. Louis District, St. Louis, Missouri.

1985a Geomorphic and Stratigraphic Investigations at Campbell Hollow. In *The Campbell Hollow Archaic Occupations: A Study of Intrasite Spatial Structure in the Lower Illinois Valley*, edited by C. Russell Stafford, pp. 53–81. Research Series 4. Kampsville Archeological Center, Center for American Archeology, Kampsville, Illinois.

1985b Geomorphic and Stratigraphic Investigations. In *Smiling Dan: Structure and Function at a Middle Woodland Settlement in the Lower Illinois Valley*, edited by Barbara D. Stafford and Mark B. Sant, pp. 41–82. Research Series 2. Kampsville Archeological Center, Center for American Archeology, Kampsville, Illinois.

1987 *Environmental Context for Archaeological Sites in the Lower Illinois River Valley.* Historic Properties Management Report 34. U.S. Army Corps of Engineers, St. Louis District, St. Louis, Missouri.

1990a Late Pleistocene and Holocene Landscape Evolution, Depositional Subsystems, and Stratigraphy in the Lower Illinois River Valley and Adjacent Central Mississippi River Valley. Ph.D. dissertation, Department of Geology, University of Illinois, Urbana.

1990b *Koster Site Archeology I: Stratigraphy and Landscape Evolution.* Research Series 8. Center for American Archeology, Kampsville Archeological Center, Kampsville, Illinois.

1992 Model of Holocene Landscape Evolution for Midwestern Dissected Uplands and the Upland Archaeological Record. *Geological Society of America, North-Central Section, Abstracts with Programs* 24(4):18.

Hajic, Edwin R., and Harold Hassen
1980 *Geomorphological, Subsurface, and Limited Cultural Resource Investigations of the Eldred and Spanky Levee and Drainage Districts, Greene County, Illinois.* Reports of Investigations 90. Submitted to the U.S. Army Corps of Engineers, St. Louis District. Contract Archeology Program, Center for American Archeology, Kampsville, Illinois.

Hajic, Edwin R., and David Leigh
1985 *Shallow Subsurface Geology, Geomorphology, and Limited Cultural Resource Investigations of the Meredosia Village and Meredosia Lake Levee and Drainage Districts, Scott, Morgan, and Cass County, Illinois.* Reports of Investigations 158. Submitted to the U.S. Army Corps of Engineers, St. Louis District. Contract Archeology Program, Center for American Archeology, Kampsville, Illinois.

Hajic, Edwin R., and Thomas R. Styles
1982 Dynamic Surficial Geology of the Lower Illinois Valley Region and the Impact on the Archaeological Record. Paper presented at the 47th Annual Meeting of the Society for American Archaeology, Minneapolis, Minnesota.

Halsey, John R. (editor)
1999 *Retrieving Michigan's Buried Past: The Archaeology of the Great Lakes State.* Bulletin 64. Cranbrook Institute of Science, Bloomfield Hills, Michigan.

Hassen, Harold (editor)
1985 *Middle Archaic Investigations along the Illinois River Floodplain: Archaeological Site Evaluations at the Quasar Site (11-Ge-136) and Bullseye (11-Ge127) Site Greene County, Illinois.* Cultural Resource Management Report 18. U.S. Army Corps of Engineers, St. Louis District, St. Louis, Missouri.

Hassen, Harold, and Kenneth B. Farnsworth
1987 *The Bullseye Site: A Floodplain Archaic Mortuary Site in the Lower Illinois River Valley*. Reports of Investigations 42. Illinois State Museum, Springfield.

Hassen, Harold, and Edwin R. Hajic
1984 *Shallowly Buried Archaeological Deposits and Geologic Context: Archaeological Survey in the Eldred and Spanky Drainage and Levee District, Greene County, Illinois*. Cultural Resources Management Report 8. U.S. Army Corps of Engineers, St. Louis District, St. Louis, Missouri.

Hewitt, John
1983 Optimal Foraging Models of the Lower Illinois Valley. Ph.D. dissertation, Department of Anthropology, Northwestern University, Evanston, Illinois.

Hill, Frederick C.
1975 Effects of the Environment on Animal Exploitation by Archaic Inhabitants of the Koster Site, Illinois. Ph.D. dissertation, Department of Zoology, University of Louisville, Louisville, Kentucky.

Horton, A. H.
1914 *Water Resources of Illinois*, pp. 318–319. State of Illinois Rivers and Lakes Commission, Springfield.

Houart, Gail L.
1971 *Koster: A Stratified Archaic Site in the Illinois Valley*. Reports of Investigations 22. Illinois State Museum, Springfield.

Jaehnig, Manfred
1976 Archeo-Malacology in the Lower Illinois Valley: Snails at Koster. Manuscript on file, Center for American Archeology, Kampsville, Illinois.

Johnson, Donald L.
1990 Biomantle Evolution and the Redistribution of Earth Materials and Artifacts. *Soil Science* 149:84–102.

Justice, Noel D.
1987 *Stone Age Spear and Arrow Points of the Midcontinental and Eastern United States*. Indiana University Press, Bloomington.

Kneberg, Madeline
1956 Some Important Projectile Point Types Found in the Tennessee Area. *Tennessee Archaeologist* 12:17–28.

Koldehoff, Brad
1983 Paleo-Indian Chert Utilization and Site Distribution in Southwestern Illinois. *The Wisconsin Archeologist* 64:201–238.

Kraus, Lyn M.
1980 *Archeological Evaluation of the "Buried Gardens of Kampsville."* Report of Investigations 87. Contract Archeology Program, Kampsville Archeological Center, Center for American Archeology, Kampsville, Illinois.
1982 The Buried Gardens of Kampsville Site. Paper presented at the 54th Annual Midwest Archaeological Conference, Cleveland, Ohio.

Leighton, Morris M., George E. Ekblaw, and Leland Horberg
1948 Physiographic Divisions of Illinois. *Geology* 56:16–33.

Levine, Harold
1970 Pre-Modern Vertebrate Fauna of the Lower Illinois River Valley. Unpublished manuscript in possession of the chapter authors.

Lewis, R. Barry
1983 Archaic Adaptations to the Illinois Prairie: The Salt Creek Region. In *Archaic Hunters and Gatherers in the American Midwest*, edited by James L. Phillips and James A. Brown, pp. 99–116. Academic Press, New York.

Logan, Wilfred D.
1952 *Graham Cave: An Archaic Site in Montgomery County, Missouri*. Memoir 2. Missouri Archaeological Society, Columbia.

Lopinto, J.
1995 Middle Archaic Subsistence: A Comparison of Faunal Remains from Quasar, Koster, and Pabst. Center for American Archeology, Education Program, National Science Foundation Young Scholars Program. Center for American Archeology, Kampsville, Illinois.

Luchterhand, Kubet
1970 *Early Archaic Projectile Points and Hunting Patterns in the Lower Illinois Valley*. Reports of Investigations 19. Illinois State Museum, Springfield.

Lurie, Rochelle
1982 Economic Models of Stone Tool Manufacture and Use: The Koster Site Middle Archaic. Ph.D. dissertation, Department of Anthropology, Northwestern University, Evanston, Illinois.

Mayer-Oakes, William J.
1951 Starved Rock Archaic, a Prepottery Horizon from Northern Illinois. *American Antiquity* 16:313–324.

McGregor, John C.
1954 Chrisman Site, Illinois River Valley Archaic Culture. *Illinois State Archaeological Society Journal* 4:12–21.

Meyers, J. Thomas
1970 *Chert Resources of the Lower Illinois Valley*. Reports of Investigations 18. Illinois State Museum, Springfield.

Montet-White, Anta M.
1968 *The Lithic Industries of the Illinois Valley in the Early and Middle Woodland Period*. Anthropological Papers 35. Museum of Anthropology, University of Michigan, Ann Arbor.

Morey, Darcy, and Michael D. Wiant
1993 Early Holocene Domestic Dog Burials from the North American Midwest. *Current Anthropology* 33:224–229.

Morrow, Juliet E.
1996 The Organization of Early Paleoindian Lithic Technology in the Confluence Region of the Mississippi, Illinois, and Missouri Rivers. Ph.D. dissertation, Department of Anthropology, Washington University, St. Louis, Missouri.

Morrow, Toby A.
1996 Lithic Refitting and Archaeological Site Formation: A Case Study from the Twin Ditch Site, Greene County, Illinois. In *Stone Tools: Theoretical Insights into Human Prehistory*, edited by George H. Odell, pp. 345–373. Plenum Press, New York.

Munson, Patrick J., and Alan D. Harn
1966 Surface Collections from Three Sites in the Central Illinois River Valley. *The Wisconsin Archeologist* 47:150–168.

Nelson, David M., Feng Sheng Hu, Eric C. Grimm, Brandon B. Curry, and Jennifer E. Slate

2006 The Influence of Aridity and Fire on Holocene Prairie Communities in the Eastern Prairie Peninsula. *Ecology*, in press.

Neusius, Sarah Ward

1982 Early-Middle Archaic Subsistence Strategies: Changes in Faunal Exploitation at the Koster Site. Ph.D. dissertation, Department of Anthropology, Northwestern University, Evanston, Illinois.

1986 Generalized and Specialized Resource Utilization during the Archaic Period: Implications of the Koster Site Faunal Record. In *Foraging, Collecting, and Harvesting: Archaic Period Subsistence and Settlement in the Eastern Woodlands*, edited by Sarah W. Neusius, pp. 117–144. Occasional Papers 6. Center for Archaeological Investigations, Southern Illinois University, Carbondale.

Nolan, David J., and Robert N. Hickson

1993 Buried Upland Sites: Some Practical Considerations for Archeologists and Cultural Resource Managers. *Illinois Antiquity* 28:4–11.

Odell, George H.

1984 Chert Resource Availability in the Lower Illinois Valley: A Transect Sample. *In Prehistoric Chert Exploitation: Studies from the Midcontinent*, edited by Brian M. Butler and Ernest E. May, pp. 45–67. Occasional Papers 2. Center for Archaeological Investigations, Southern Illinois University, Carbondale.

1988 Preliminary Analysis of Lithic and Other Nonceramic Assemblages. *In The Archaic and Woodland Cemeteries at the Elizabeth Site in the Lower Illinois Valley*, edited by Douglas K. Charles, Steven R. Leigh, and Jane E. Buikstra, pp. 155–190. Research Series 7. Center for American Archeology, Kampsville Archeological Center, Kampsville, Illinois.

1996 *Stone Tools and Mobility in the Illinois Valley: From Hunter-Gatherer Camps to Agricultural Villages*. Archaeological Series 10. International Monographs in Prehistory, Ann Arbor, Michigan.

Parmalee, Paul W., Andreas A. Paloumpis, and Nancy Wilson

1972 *Animals Utilized by Woodland Peoples Occupying the Apple Creek Site, Illinois*. Reports of Investigations 23. Illinois State Museum, Springfield.

Perino, Gregory

1954 Titterington Focus-Red Ochre. *Central States Archaeological Journal* 1:15–18.

1957 The Snyders Village Site. In Illinois Hopewell, by Gregory Perino, 16 pp. Chapter in unpublished manuscript on file, Center for American Archeology, Kampsville Archeological Center, Kampsville, Illinois.

1961 Tentative Classification of Plummets in the Lower Illinois River Valley. *Central States Archaeological Journal* 8:43–56.

1962 Review of Calhoun County, Illinois Prehistory. *Central States Archaeological Journal* 1:15–18.

1963 Tentative Classification of Two Projectile Points and One Knife from West-Central Illinois. *Central States Archaeological Journal* 10:95–100.

1968 The Pete Klunk Mound Group, Calhoun County, Illinois: The Archaic and Hopewell Occupations. In *Hopewell and Woodland Site Archaeology in Illinois*, pp. 9–128. Bulletin 6. Illinois Archaeological Survey, Urbana.

1970 The Stilwell II Site, Pike County, Illinois. *Central States Archaeological Journal* 17:118–121.

1971 *Guide to the Identification of Certain American Indian Projectile Points*. Special Bulletin 4. Oklahoma Anthropological Society, Oklahoma City.

1973 The Koster Mounds, Greene County, Illinois. In *Late Woodland Site Archaeology in Illinois I: Investigations in South-Central Illinois*, edited by James A. Brown. Bulletin 9:141–206. Illinois Archaeological Survey, Urbana.

1985 *Selected Preforms, Points, and Knives of the North American Indians*, vol. 1. Points and Barbs Press, Idabel, Oklahoma.

2006 The 1969 Gibson Mounds Excavations. In *Illinois Hopewell and Late Woodland Mounds: The Excavations of Gregory Perino 1940–1975,* edited by Kenneth B. Farnsworth and Michael D. Wiant, pp. 401–457. Studies in Archaeology 4. Illinois TransportationArchaeological Research Program, University of Illinois, Urbana.

Phillips, James L., and James A. Brown (editors)

1983 *Archaic Hunters and Gatherers in the American Midwest.* Academic Press, New York.

Pleger, Thomas C.

1998 Social Complexity, Trade, and Subsistence during the Archaic/Woodland Transition in the Western Great Lakes (4000–400 B.C.): A Diachronic Study of Copper Using Cultures at the Oconto and Riverside Cemeteries. Ph.D. dissertation, Department of Anthropology, University of Wisconsin, Madison.

Poore, John R. W.

1963 Objects from a Mound Burial, Calhoun County, Illinois. *Central States Archaeological Journal* 10:134.

Purdue, James R.

1986 The Size of White-Tailed Deer (*Odocoileus virginianus*) during the Archaic Period in Central Illinois. In *Foraging, Collection and Harvesting: Archaic Period Subsistence and Settlement in the Eastern Woodlands*, edited by Sarah W. Neusius, pp. 65–96. Occasional Papers 6. Center for Archaeological Investigations, Southern Illinois University, Carbondale.

1989 Changes during the Holocene in the Size of White-Tailed Deer (*Odocoileus virginianus*) from Central Illinois. *Quaternary Research* 32:307–316.

Rick, John Winfield

1978 *Heat-Altered Cherts of the Lower Illinois Valley: An Experimental Study in Prehistoric Technology*. Prehistoric Records 2. Northwestern University Archeological Program, Evanston, Illinois.

Rubey, William W.

1952 *Geology and Mineral Resources of the Hardin and Brussels Quadrangles (in Illinois)*. Professional Paper 218. U.S. Geological Survey, Washington, D.C.

Schroeder, Marjorie B.

1994 Archeobotany. In *Central Illinois Expressway Archeology: Upland Occupations of the Illinois Valley Crossing*, edited by Barbara D. Stafford, pp. 105–120. Technical

Report 5. Kampsville Archeological Center, Center for American Archeology, Kampsville, Illinois.

Scully, Edward G.
1951 Some Central Mississippi Valley Projectile Point Types. Unpublished manuscript, Museum of Anthropology, University of Michigan, Ann Arbor.

Seddon, Matthew T.
1992 Sedentism, Lithic Technology, and Debitage: An Intersite Debitage Analysis. *Midcontinental Journal of Archaeology* 17:198–226.

Seelen, Robert M.
1961 A Preliminary Report of the Sedalia Complex. *Newsletter of the Missouri Archaeological Society* 153.

Seeman, Mark F.
1975 The Prehistoric Chert Quarries and Workshops of Harrison County, Indiana. *Indiana Archaeological Bulletin* 1:47–61.

Shippee, J. Mett
1948 Nebo Hill: A Lithic Complex in Western Missouri. *American Antiquity* 14:29–32.

Smith, Lawson M.
1987 River Basin Evolution and Stream Dynamics. In *Proceedings of Management of the Illinois River System: The 1990s and Beyond*, pp. 134–145. Special Report 16. Water Resources Center, University of Illinois, Urbana.

Stafford, Barbara D.
1989 *Central Illinois Expressway Archeology: Floodplain Occupations of the Illinois Valley Crossing.* Technical Report 4. Center for American Archeology, Kampsville Archeology Center, Kampsville, Illinois.
1994 (editor) *Central Illinois Expressway Archeology: Upland Occupations of the Illinois Valley Crossing.* Technical Report 5. Center for American Archeology, Kampsville Archeology Center, Kampsville, Illinois.

Stafford, C. Russell
1985 (editor) *The Campbell Hollow Archaic Occupations: A Study of Intrasite Spatial Structure in the Lower Illinois Valley*. Research Series 4. Center for American Archeology, Kampsville Archeological Center, Kampsville, Illinois.
1991 Archaic Period Logistical Foraging Strategies in West-Central Illinois. *Midcontinental Journal of Archaeology* 16:212–246.

Stoltman, James
1973 Temporal Models in Prehistory: An Example from Eastern North America. *Current Anthropology* 19:703–746.

Struever, Stuart
1968 Problems, Methods, and Organization: A Disparity in the Growth of Archaeology. In *Anthropological Archeology in the Americas*. Betty J. Meggers, ed., pp. 131–151. Anthropological Society of Washington, Washington, D.C.
1969 Introduction. In *Early Vegetation of the Lower Illinois Valley*, by April Allison Zawacki and Glenn Hausfater, pp. 1–2. Reports of Investigation 17. Illinois State Museum, Springfield.
1971 Foreword. In *Koster: A Stratified Archaic Site in the Illinois Valley*, by Gail L. Houart, pp. ix–x. Reports of Investigations 22. Illinois State Museum, Springfield.

Struever, Stuart, and Felicia Antonelli Holton
1979 *Koster: Americans in Search of Their Prehistoric Past.* Anchor Press/Doubleday, Garden City, New York.

Stuiver, Minze, and Paula J. Reimer
1993 Extended ^{14}C Database and Revised CALIB Radiocarbon Calibration Program. *Radiocarbon* 35:215–230.

Styles, Bonnie W.
1986 Aquatic Exploitation in the Lower Illinois River Valley: The Role of Paleoecological Change. In *Foraging, Collecting, and Harvesting: Archaic Period Subsistence and Settlement in the Eastern Woodlands*, edited by Sarah W. Neusius, pp. 145–174. Occasional Papers 6. Center for Archaeological Investigations, Southern Illinois University, Carbondale.

Styles, Thomas R.
1984 Holocene and Late Pleistocene Geology of the Napoleon Hollow Archaeological Site in Lower Illinois River Valley. Master's thesis, Department of Geology, University of Illinois, Urbana.
1985 *Holocene and Late Pleistocene Geology of the Napoleon Hollow Site in the Lower Illinois Valley*. Research Series 5. Kampsville Archeological Center, Center for American Archeoogy, Kampsville, Illinois.

Theler, James L., and Robert F. Boszhardt
2003 *Twelve Millennia: Archaeology of the Upper Mississippi River Valley*. University of Iowa Press, Iowa City.

Titterington, Paul F.
1947 Caches of Plumbbobs. *Bulletin* 3:18–20. Amateur Archaeologist Club of St. Louis, St. Louis, Missouri.
1950 Some Non-Pottery Sites in the St. Louis Area. *Journal of the Illinois State Archaeological Society* 1:18–31.

Transeau, Edgar N.
1935 The Prairie Peninsula. *Ecology* 16:423–437.

Van Nest, Julieann
2002 The Good Earthworm: How Natural Processes Preserve Upland Archaic Archaeological Sites of Western Illinois, U.S.A. *Geoarchaeology: An International Journal* 17:53–90.

Walthall, John A.
1999 Mortuary Behavior and Early Holocene Land Use in the North American Midcontinent. *North American Archaeologist* 20:1–30.

Webb, Thompson, III, and Reid A. Bryson
1972 Late- and Postglacial Climatic Change in the Northern Midwest, USA: Quantitative Estimates Derived from Fossil Pollen Spectra by Multivariate Statistical Analysis. *Quaternary Research* 2:70–115.

Webb, T., III, E. J. Cushing, and H. E. Wright Jr.
1983 Holocene Changes in the Vegetation of the Midwest. In *Late-Quaternary Environments of the United States: 2. The Holocene,* edited by Herbert E. Wright Jr., pp. 142–165. University of Minnesota Press, Minneapolis.

Wiant, Michael D. (editor)
1980 Napoleon Hollow Interim Report. Manuscript on file, Illinois State Museum, Springfield.

Wiant, Michael D., and Harold Hassen
1984 The Role of Lithic Resource Availability and Accessibility in the Organization of Lithic Technology. In *Lithic Resource Procurement: Proceedings from the Second Conference on Prehistoric Chert Exploitation*, edited by Susan C. Vehik, pp. 101–114. Occasional Papers 4.

Center for Archaeological Investigations, Southern Illinois University, Carbondale.

Wiant, Michael D., Edwin R. Hajic, and Thomas R. Styles
1983 Napoleon Hollow and Koster Site Stratigraphy. In *Archaic Hunters and Gatherers in the American Midwest,* edited by James L. Phillips and James A. Brown, pp. 147–164. Academic Press. New York.

Wiant, Michael D., and Charles R. McGimsey (editors)
1986 *Woodland Period Occupations of the Napoleon Hollow Site in the Lower Illinois River Valley*. Research Series 6. Kampsville Archeological Center, Center for American Archeology, Kampsville, Illinois.

Wiant, Michael D., and Howard D. Winters
1991 The Lincoln Hills Site: A Paleo-Indian Workshop in the Central Mississippi River Valley. Paper presented at the 56th Annual Meeting of the Society for American Archaeology, New Orleans, Louisiana.

Winters, Howard D.
1967 *An Archaeological Survey of the Wabash Valley in Illinois*. Rev. ed. Reports of Investigations 10. Illinois State Museum, Springfield.
1969 *The Riverton Culture*. Reports of Investigation 13. Illinois State Museum, Springfield.
1985 Archaic Hunters and Gatherers. In *Illinois Archaeology*, edited by James Porter, pp. 41–49. Rev. ed. Bulletin 1. Illinois Archaeological Survey, Urbana.

Wittry, Warren L.
1959 The Raddatz Rock Shelter, Sk 5, Wisconsin. *The Wisconsin Archeologist* 40:33–69.

Wolynec, Renata
1977 The Systematic Analysis of Features from the Koster Site, a Stratified Archaic Site. Ph.D. dissertation, Department of Anthropology, Northwestern University, Evanston, Illinois.

Wood, W. Raymond, and R. Bruce McMillan
1976 *Prehistoric Man and His Environments: A Case Study in the Ozark Highlands*. Academic Press, New York.

Wormington, H. Marie
1957 *Ancient Man in North America*. Popular Series 4. Denver Museum of Natural History, Denver, Colorado.

Wray, Donald E.
1952 Archeology of the Illinois Valley: 1950. In *Archeology of Eastern United States*, edited by James B. Griffin, pp. 152–164. University of Chicago Press, Chicago.

Wright, Herbert E., Jr.
1968 History of the Prairie Peninsula. In *The Quaternary of Illinois: A Symposium in Observance of the Centennial of the University of Illinois*, edited by Robert E. Bergstrom, pp. 78–88. Special Publication 14. University of Illinois College of Agriculture, Urbana.

Wright, Lori E.
1987 An Analysis of Early Archaic Skeletal Remains from Horizon 11 at the Koster Site, Illinois. Manuscript on file, Illinois State Museum, Springfield.

Zawacki, April Allison, and Glenn Hausfater
1969 *Early Vegetation of the Lower Illinois Valley*. Reports of Investigations 17. Illinois State Museum, Springfield.

10

Archaic Period Chronology in the Hill Country of Southern Indiana

C. Russell Stafford and Mark Cantin

Introduction

In this chapter, we examine Archaic-period chronological issues in the Southern Hills and Lowlands Region of Indiana (Gray 2000). This region is defined on the north by the maximum extent of the Wisconsin glaciation and is bounded by the Ohio River on the south and the Wabash River on the west. The White River, its east fork, and the Patoka River are the primary drainages within the study area (Figure 10.1), which covers an area of over 35,000 km^2 (Gray 2000:15). The landscape varies from the low, rolling hills of the Wabash Lowland in the west to the heavily dissected and rough terrain of the physiographic regions to the east. As in southern Illinois, extensive Pleistocene lakebeds supporting wetland habitats are found across much of southern Indiana (Gray 1971).

Prior to 1970, Archaic investigations in Indiana were limited to excavation of a few Late Archaic shell-midden sites in southwestern Indiana, including Miller's (1941) work at the McCain site in Dubois County and Winters's (1969) seminal studies at three Riverton shell-midden sites in the lower Wabash River valley. Most archaeological efforts concentrated on later and more visible Woodland- and Mississippian-period sites (see Kellar 1983). Not until the advent of cultural resource management (CRM) archaeology in the 1970s and 1980s was further progress made on Archaic-period chronology and settlement and subsistence strategies. Munson and Cook (Munson 1980b) conducted investigations associated with reservoir construction on the upper Patoka that resulted in the excavation of four Late Archaic sites. On the basis of these studies, they defined the French Lick phase (Munson and Cook 1980b) and proposed a settlement model for the period (Munson 1980b). In the middle 1970s, Higginbotham (1983), as part of his dissertation research, undertook a reconnaissance in the lower Wabash River valley (Gibson and Posey counties) and tested several sites with Archaic components, including the Berry and Moore Bluff Top sites. Indiana University also tested the Ft. Ancient deposits at the Leonard Haag site (12D19) along the Great Miami River and discovered Early Archaic remains underlying the surface midden (Tomak et al. 1980).

Major excavations also took place in Switzerland County in association with construction of the Patriot Generating Station and focused on buried and stratified Archaic components on the Ohio River (McHugh and Michael 1984). Janzen (1977) conducted limited testing on a series of six Late Archaic shell-midden sites in the Falls of the Ohio region during the 1970s, as well. Bellis (1982) tested another shell-midden site, Breeden, in Harrison County, on the Ohio River.

Large-scale systematic site surveys associated with surface coal mining in southwestern Indiana, conducted by R. Pace at Indiana State University (Stafford et al. 1988), resulted in the recording of a large number of Archaic sites (Stafford 1994). At the same time, salvage excavations associated with strip-mining operations were also carried out at the Bluegrass site (Anslinger 1988) in Warrick County and the nearby Millersburg site (Levy n.d.). Several other Early and Late Archaic components were tested on a limited basis during the 1980s (see Kendrick and Pace 1985; Tomak 1979, 1982), including Kirk occupations at the Swan's Landing site on the Ohio River in Harrison County (Mocas and Smith 1995;

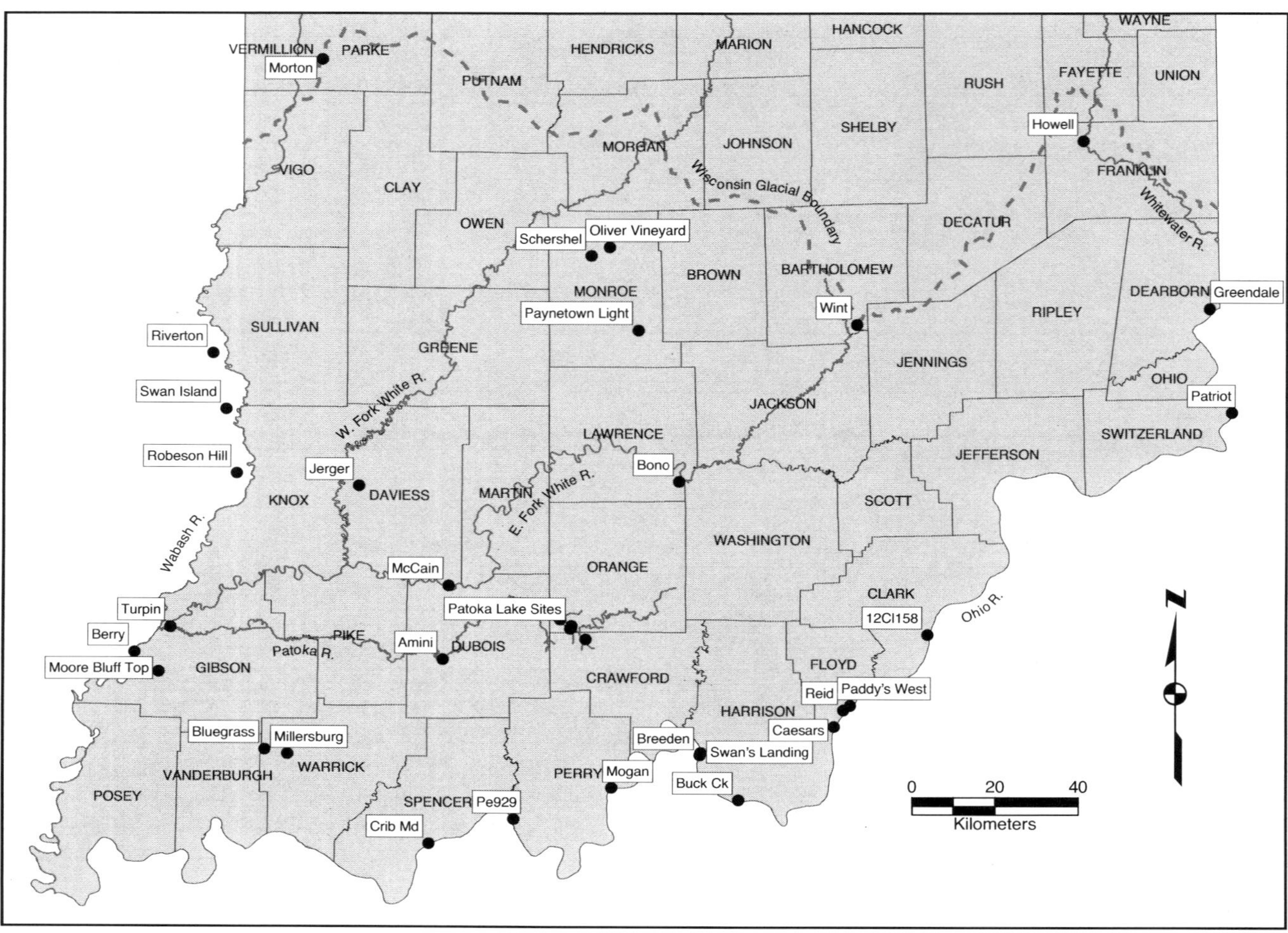

Figure 10.1. Archaic site locations in southern Indiana.

Smith 1986). The results of much of the work from this period are reported in the gray literature or are not otherwise readily available.

In the late 1990s, major excavations at a series of four sites with extensive buried Archaic occupations were conducted for more than 39 months at the Caesars Archaeological Project (CAP), located below the Falls of the Ohio (Stafford 2004). Initial results are reported in this chapter, although analysis of these data is still ongoing.

Despite a substantial quantity of fieldwork on Archaic sites in southern Indiana since 1970, the work of Winters (1969) on Riverton and of Munson and Cook (1980b) on the French Lick phase more than 20 years ago still provides the only formalized chronological framework for the Archaic period. If further advances are to take place in subsistence and settlement (Munson 1980b; Stafford 1994; Stafford et al. 2000) and chert use (Cantin 2000; Munson and Munson 1984) modeling in this region, a more comprehensive Archaic chronology needs to be in place. On the basis of recent investigations conducted as part of the CAP and other CRM-based studies, we attempt in this chapter to provide an updated chronological assessment for the southern part of the state. Our focus is *exclusively* on radiocarbon-dated components and associated diagnostic point forms. When possible, we also examine stratigraphic sequences at buried sites. Moreover, we focus on changing frequencies of point styles in time and space since, from our experience, few examples can be found of single types defining phases.

The CAP is located in Knob Creek bottom 10 km downriver from the Falls of the Ohio in Harrison County, Indiana (Figure 10.1). Extensive excavations of stratified components, along with more than 70 radiocarbon dates spanning most of the Holocene, has resulted in a baseline Archaic record for the lower Ohio River valley region (see Stafford 2004). The project also encompasses two poorly understood Archaic periods in the early (9000–10,000 RCYBP) and middle (6000–7500 RCYBP) Holocene. The CAP has yielded, in most cases, large samples of diagnostic artifacts in association with multiple radiocarbon determinations (Table 10.1). Excavation data from other sites in the lower Ohio Valley provide supplemental support or fill gaps in the CAP stratigraphic record.

Table 10.1. Caesars Archaeological Project Archaic Radiocarbon Ages.

Lab No.	Site	Phase	RCYBP	S.D.	Cal BC 1 Sigma
Beta-152942	12Hr520	Early Side Notched	10,370	190	10,880–9880
ISGS-4898	12Hr520	Early Side Notched	10,100	100	9997–9390
ISGS-4835	12Hr520	Early Side Notched	10,090	120	9966–9311
ISGS-4797	12Hr520	Early Side Notched	10,050	100	9966–9311
Beta-13574	12Hr520	Early Side Notched	10,020	100	9600–9260
ISGS-4897	12Hr520	Early Side Notched	9700	100	9249–8863
Beta-152586	12Hr520	Early Side Notched	9680	170	9270–8780
Beta-153512	12Hr520	Thebes cluster	9490	60	9140–8620
ISGS-4837	12Hr520	Kirk Corner Notched cluster	9420	100	9088–8555
ISGS-4834	12Hr520	Kirk Corner Notched cluster	9350	80	8736–8478
ISGS-5046	12Hr520	Kirk Corner Notched cluster	8900	120	8260–7827
ISGS-5040	12Hr520	Kirk Corner Notched cluster	8810	120	8203–7652
ISGS-5035	12Hr520	Kirk Corner Notched cluster	8780	80	8159–7655
ISGS-4838	12Hr520	Kirk Corner Notched cluster	8740	100	8156–7602
ISGS-5032	12Hr520	Upper Kirk zone	8320	80	7520–7196
ISGS-4955	12Hr484	Knob Ck complex	7220	70	6199–6009
ISGS-4954	12Hr484	Knob Ck complex	7220	70	6199–6009
ISGS-4953	12Hr484	Knob Ck complex	7110	80	6052–5891
ISGS-4980	12Hr484	Knob Ck complex	7170	70	6156–5928
Oxford A-0265	12Hr484	Knob Ck complex	6942	60	5873–5730
Oxford A-0264	12Hr484	Knob Ck complex	6872	56	5798–5714
ISGS-4981	12Hr484	Knob Ck complex	6840	70	5773–5643
ISGS-4996	12Hr484	Knob Ck complex	6780	80	5729–5623
ISGS-4994	12Hr484	Knob Ck complex	6740	90	5722–5561
ISGS-4960	12Hr484	Knob Ck complex	6730	80	5712–5562
Beta-115654	12Hr484	Knob Ck complex	6700	70	5610–5520
ISGS-4973	12Hr484	Knob Ck complex	6670	70	5657–5529
ISGS-4995	12Hr484	Knob Ck complex	6270	70	5316–5082
Beta-113983	12Hr484	late Middle Archaic	5830	90	4800–4565
ISGS-4956	12Hr484	Riverton	3580	70	2027–1781
ISGS-4957	12Hr484	Riverton	3570	70	2021–1777
Beta-192410	12Hr484	Riverton	3550	40	1943–1778
ISGS-4961	12Hr484	Riverton	3430	70	1876–1638
ISGS-4985	12Hr484	Riverton	3400	70	1767–1618
Beta-115655	12Hr484	Riverton	3140	70	1450–1315
ISGS-4983	12Hr484	Buck Creek Barb	2980	70	1369–1053
ISGS-5025	12Hr481	Stilwell Corner Notched	8360	80	7536–7326
ISGS-5024	12Hr481	early French Lick	5360	70	4326–4046
ISGS-5017	12Hr481	early French Lick	5100	70	3974–3796
ISGS-5020	12Hr481	early French Lick	5020	70	3942–3708
ISGS-5018	12Hr481	early French Lick	4990	70	3935–3672
Beta-106189	12Hr481	late French Lick?	4200	50	2885–2680

In addition to work in the Ohio Valley, we review extensive excavations at the Bluegrass site as well as more limited testing at other Archaic sites over the past 20 years in the interior hill country of southern Indiana to the north. We discuss 82 radiocarbon dates reported in CRM or other studies from some 30 Archaic sites in southern Indiana (Table 10.2).

We also draw on an extensive 9,011-ha systematic surface survey of 21 localities (Data Centers) distributed primarily across the Wabash Lowlands in southwestern Indiana. More

Table 10.2. Archaic Radiocarbon Ages from Southern Indiana.

Lab No.	Site	Phase	RCYBP	S.D.	Cal BC 1 Sigma	Reference
Beta-9458	Bluegrass (12W162)	early French Lick	6260	120	5360–5050	this volume
Beta-9459	Bluegrass (12W162)	early French Lick	5130	80	4040–3800	this volume
Beta-33963	Bluegrass (12W162)	early French Lick	5030	110	3940–3710	this volume
Beta-33964	Bluegrass (12W162)	early French Lick	5260	90	4220–3980	this volume
Beta-34580	Bluegrass (12W162)	early French Lick	5220	90	4220–3960	this volume
Beta-34581	Bluegrass (12W162)	early French Lick	5290	70	4220–4000	this volume
UGa-4708	Bluegrass (12W162)	early French Lick	5035	70	3940–3710	this volume
Beta-13129	Amini (12Du323)	early French Lick	5000	90	3940–3700	Kendrick and Pace 1985
UGa-205	Miler A (12Or12)	early French Lick	4700	80	3630–3370	Munson 1980a
UGa-2058	Miler A (12Or12)	early French Lick	4750	85	3640–3380	Munson 1980a
UGa-2062	Miler A (12Or12)	early French Lick	4485	70	3340–3050	Munson 1980a
UGa-2063	Omer Lane (12Or273)	late French Lick?	3410	175	1940–1520	Munson 1980a
UGa-2055	K Branch (12Cr27)	late French Lick?	3615	65	2120–1830	Munson 1980a
UGa-2056	Morganrath (12Or92)	early French Lick	4725	250	3760–3100	Munson 1980a
UGa-2059	Morganrath (12Or92)	late French Lick	4390	85	3310–2900	Munson 1980a
Beta-49082	Mogan (12Pe839)	late French Lick	3920	80	2560–2290	Bader 1994
Beta-49083	Mogan (12Pe839)	?	3530	90	2010–1740	Bader 1994
Beta-6926	Bono (12Lr194)	early French Lick	4920	70	3770–3650	Tomak 1982
Beta-7026	Bono (12Lr194)	early French Lick	4730	70	3630–3380	Tomak 1982
UGa-4549	Schershel (12Mo152)	late French Lick	4595	90	3520–3100	Tomak 1980
Beta-6347	12Sw89	early Middle Archaic	6630	100	5630–5480	McHugh and Michael 1984
Beta-6351	12Sw89	early French Lick	4950	60	3780–3660	McHugh and Michael 1984
Beta-6352	12Sw89	early Middle Archaic	6940	180	5990–5660	McHugh and Michael 1984
Beta-6353	12Sw89	early Middle Archaic	6560	130	5620–5380	McHugh and Michael 1984
Beta-6579	12Sw99	late French Lick	3610	90	2130–1780	McHugh and Michael 1984
Beta-6580	12Sw99	late French Lick	3860	60	2460–2210	McHugh and Michael 1984
Beta-6581	12Sw99	late French Lick	4040	60	2830–2470	McHugh and Michael 1984
Beta-6582	12Sw99	late French Lick	4090	60	2860–2500	McHugh and Michael 1984
Beta-6583	12Sw99	late French Lick	4220	90	2910–2640	McHugh and Michael 1984
Beta-6584	12Sw99	late French Lick	3690	90	2200–1950	McHugh and Michael 1984
Beta-6585	12Sw99	early French Lick	4760	80	3640–3380	McHugh and Michael 1984
Beta-6586	12Sw99	early French Lick	4740	60	3630–3380	McHugh and Michael 1984
Beta-3496	12Sw99	late French Lick	3260	70	1620–1450	McHugh and Michael 1984
Beta-102165	12Pe929	late French Lick	3760	50	2280–2040	Hawkins and Walley 2000
ISGS-3547	12Pe929	late French Lick	3870	70	2460–2210	Hawkins and Walley 2000
ISGS-3495	12Pe929	late French Lick	4000	70	2660–2350	Hawkins and Walley 2000
ISGS-3501	12Pe929	late French Lick	4030	70	2840–2460	Hawkins and Walley 2000
Beta-102167	12Pe929	late French Lick	4050	70	2840–2470	Hawkins and Walley 2000
ISGS-3545	12Pe929	late French Lick	4170	70	2880–2640	Hawkins and Walley 2000
ISGS-3505	12Pe929	late French Lick	4590	130	3520–3100	Hawkins and Walley 2000
Beta-102166	12Pe929	late Middle Archaic	5860	100	4840–4555	Hawkins and Walley 2000
ISGS-3552	12Pe929	late Middle Archaic	5510	120	4490–4170	Hawkins and Walley 2000
ISGS-3500	12Pe929	late Middle Archaic	5670	100	4670–4360	Hawkins and Walley 2000
ISGS-3494	12Pe929	late Middle Archaic	5860	90	4830–4600	Hawkins and Walley 2000
ISGS-2481	Paddy's West (12Fl46)	early Middle Archaic	6620	120	5660–5470	Smith and Mocas 1994
ISGS-2483	Paddy's West (12Fl46)	early Middle Archaic	6530	70	5610–5390	Smith and Mocas 1994
ISGS-2481	Paddy's West (12Fl48)	?	3510	120	2010–1690	Smith and Mocas 1994
Beta-83547	Swan's Landing (12Hr304)	Kirk Corner Notched	9060	70	8410–8200	Mocas and Smith 1995
Beta-83548	Swan's Landing (12Hr304)	Kirk Corner Notched	9090	60	8410–8240	Mocas and Smith 1995
UGa-267	Reid (12Fl1)	early French Lick	4555	70	3480–3100	Janzen 1977
UGa-309	Reid (12Fl1)	early French Lick	5480	90	4450–4230	Janzen 1977
Beta-126551	Greendale (12D511)	early French Lick	5100	60	3960–3800	J. Kerr, pers. comm. 2002
Beta-126522	Greendale (12D511)	early French Lick	5140	60	4040–3800	J. Kerr, pers. comm. 2002
Beta-126553	Greendale (12D511)	early French Lick	5100	60	3960–3800	J. Kerr, pers. comm. 2002
Beta-91281	Greendale (12D511)	early French Lick	4650	80	3620–3350	J. Kerr, pers. comm. 2002
Beta?	Paynetown Light (12Mo193)	late French Lick	3950	100	2620–2290	P. Munson, pers. comm. 2004
UGa-1129	Berry (12Gi11)	early French Lick	5585	105	4540–4340	Higginbotham 1983
UGa-1130	Berry (12Gi11)	early French Lick	5200	95	4220–3820	Higginbotham 1983

Table 10.2. Archaic Radiocarbon Ages from Southern Indiana, continued.

Lab No.	Site	Phase	RCYBP	S.D.	Cal BC 1 Sigma	Reference
RL-514	Berry (12Gi11)	early French Lick	5150	140	4220–3770	Higginbotham 1983
UGa-1131	Berry (12Gi11)	early French Lick	5370	160	4340–4000	Higginbotham 1983
DIC-2367	Breeden (12Hr11)	French Lick?	4200	200	3080–2470	Bellis 1982
Beta-195820	Millersburg (12W81)	early French Lick	5290	50	4220–4000	this volume
Beta-195978	Millersburg (12W81)	late French Lick	4120	80	2860–2580	this volume
UGa-4327	Howell (12Fr157)	late French Lick	4425	120	3330–2920	this volume
Beta-164348	12Cl158	late French Lick	4150	40	2860–2630	White 2002
Beta-164351	12Cl158	late French Lick	4140	40	2860–2620	White 2002
DIC-1018	Oliver Vineyard (12Mo141)	late French Lick	3910	60	2470–2310	Munson 1980a
DIC-1019	Oliver Vineyard (12Mo141)	late French Lick	3960	50	2570–2350	Munson 1980a
I-1463	Riverton (11Cw170)	Riverton	3320	140	1770–1430	Winters 1969
M-1284	Riverton (11Cw170)	Riverton	3110	200	1600–1050	Winters 1969
M-1285	Riverton (11Cw170)	Riverton	3460	250	2140–1460	Winters 1969
M-1286	Riverton (11Cw170)	Riverton	3200	200	1740–1130	Winters 1969
M-1287	Riverton (11Cw170)	Riverton	3270	250	1880–1220	Winters 1969
M-1289	Robeson Hill (11Lw1)	Riverton	3440	200	2030–1520	Winters 1969
M-1288	Robeson Hill (11Lw1)	Riverton	3490	200	2110–1530	Winters 1969
I-1462	Swan Island (11Cw319)	Riverton	3450	120	1920–1620	Winters 1969
I-1461	Swan Island (11Cw319	Riverton	3450	120	1920–1620	Winters 1969
UGa-2070	Wint (12B95)	Riverton	2865	215	1370–830	Anslinger 1986
UGa-2530	Wint (12B95)	Riverton	3405	160	1910–1520	Anslinger 1986
UGa-3146	Wint (12B95)	Riverton	2730	105	1001–800	Anslinger 1986
UGa-1902	Morton (12P80)	Riverton	2760	95	1000–814	Anslinger 1986
UGa-3145	Moore Bluff Top (12Gi7)	Riverton	3045	70	1410–1130	Higginbotham 1983

than 2,100 sites were reported and 922 Archaic points were recovered in these localities under controlled survey conditions (see Stafford 1994).

Radiocarbon ages reported in the text are uncalibrated, although tables show calibrated dates using CALIB version 4.4 (Stuiver and Reimer 1993). Ward and Wilson's (1978) Case II T' statistic was used to test the statistical coherence of clusters of dates and to establish which samples should be used to form pooled means. Calibration results and pooled means are rounded to the nearest 10 years.

In the remainder of the chapter, we discuss the chronology of each Archaic period (Early Archaic, Middle Archaic, Late Archaic, and terminal Late Archaic), evaluating existing phases and tentatively proposing new phases or complexes on the basis of the association of radiocarbon ages with diagnostic tool assemblages (see Figure 10.2). Although chronology is the principal focus of this discussion, we also briefly summarize previously proposed settlement-subsistence strategies and trends in chert utilization and mortuary practices during the Archaic period.

Early Archaic (8000–10,000 RCYBP)

Large-scale excavations at the James Farnsley (12Hr520) site, within the CAP area, revealed a comprehensive stratigraphic record of Early Archaic components, including rarely encountered deposits spanning the period of 9500–10,000+ RCYBP. Occupations are contained within fine-grained alluvium underlying a low early Holocene terrace located along the valley margin (see Stafford 2004). Archaeological deposits were discovered to a depth of more than 5 m below surface (bs).

The basal point bar and overlying overbank units contain large hearths and light scatters of debris associated with an Early Side Notched component. Radiocarbon ages range from 10,100 ± 190 to 9680 ± 170, with one outlier at 10,370 ± 190. Four samples form a statistical cluster with a pooled mean of 10,060 ± 50 RCYBP ($T' = .29, \chi^2_{.05} = 7.81$). Very few diagnostics were recovered from this zone, but a good deal of variation exists in the points collected. Radiocarbon-dated Feature 313, a large surface hearth, produced two points (Figure 10.3a, b) that fall within the enigmatic Early Side Notched class. They have deep diagonal notches, squared ears, and a concave base. One of these hafted bifaces has been shaped into a drill, and the blade of the other, although triangular in shape, has been reworked, as evidenced by several large percussion scars. Two radiocarbon determinations were made on a split sample from the feature and have a pooled mean of 9954 ± 86 RCYBP ($T' = 3.52, \chi^2_{.05} = 3.84$). Although similar in age, the points from this feature are unlike Big Sandy I Side Notched from early southeastern contexts like Dust Cave (Driskell 1996; Sherwood et al. 2004) or Stanfield-Worley Bluff Shelter (DeJarnette et al. 1962) and are more consistent with Thebes-cluster technology and form.

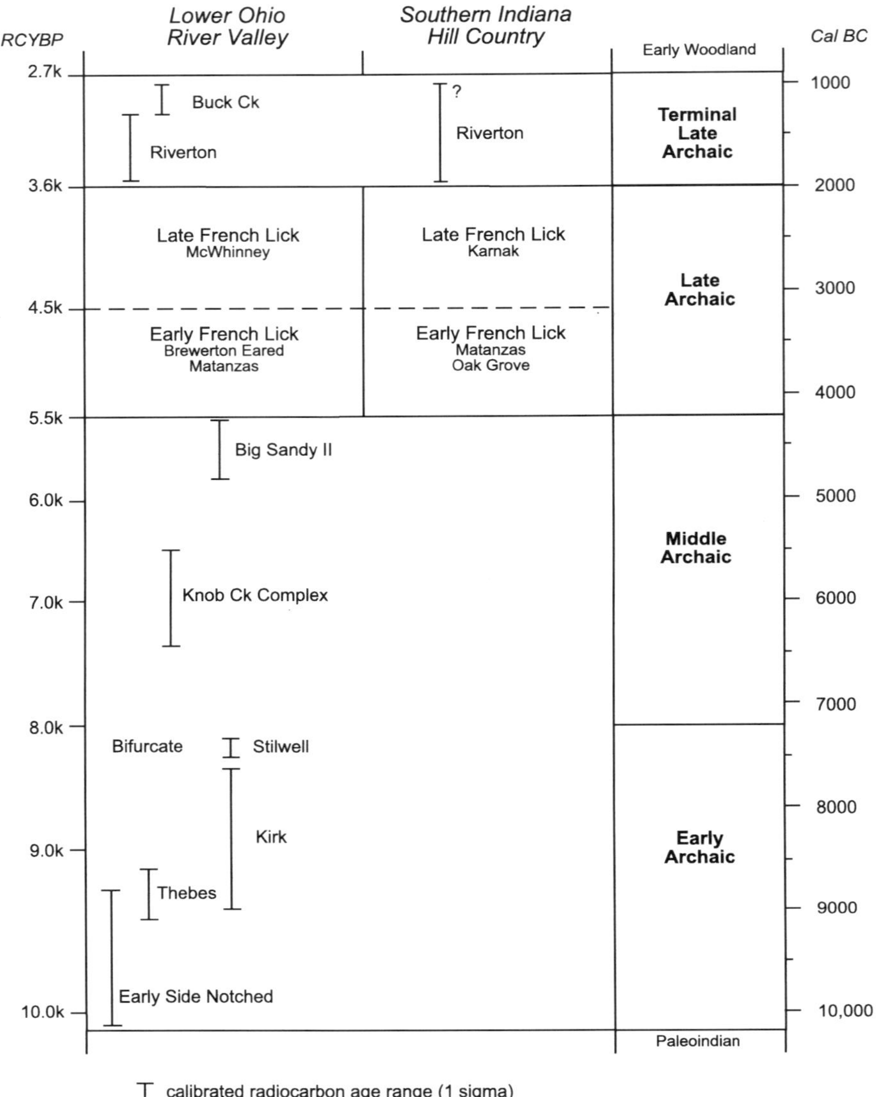

Figure 10.2. Archaic phases and calibrated radiocarbon age ranges for southern Indiana.

Two other largely complete points were recovered from this zone (Figure 10.3c, d). The stem of one has been broken and reworked (Figure 10.3c). The original haft form appears to have been side-notched, and during reworking the base of the stem was beveled. On the second point, the notching is asymmetrical (Figure 10.3d), with side notching on one side and corner notching on the other. The small size and overall blade shape are similar to the Kirk Corner Notched Small variety, but such points in the Kirk zone at the top of the deposit exhibit a more invasive pressure flaking on the blade compared with the percussion flaking on this early point. The period between 9500 and 10,000 RCYBP remains difficult to define stylistically in the Midwest and Midsouth because of the paucity of sites with deposits from this time frame and the lack of standardized point morphologies.

Overlying the Early Side Notched zone is a Thebes/St. Charles component. At the terrace escarpment, St. Charles points (Figure 10.4) were recovered from small clusters of knapping debris. Only one radiocarbon date was obtained from this zone, as little charcoal was available for recovery. An AMS age of 9490 ± 60 RCYBP (Beta 153512) was obtained from refuse scattered in point-bar deposits. The bar deposits slope up to the west, where a Thebes lithic workshop is shallowly buried (.5 m bs). Only Thebes points and drills were recovered from this location (Figure 10.5). No charcoal was present in the highly weathered soil in this zone.

In the upper portion of the overbank deposits are three Kirk Corner Notched occupations. Twenty-two hundred points were recovered along with some 10,000 lithic tools and very high densities of lithic debitage. Other tools recovered

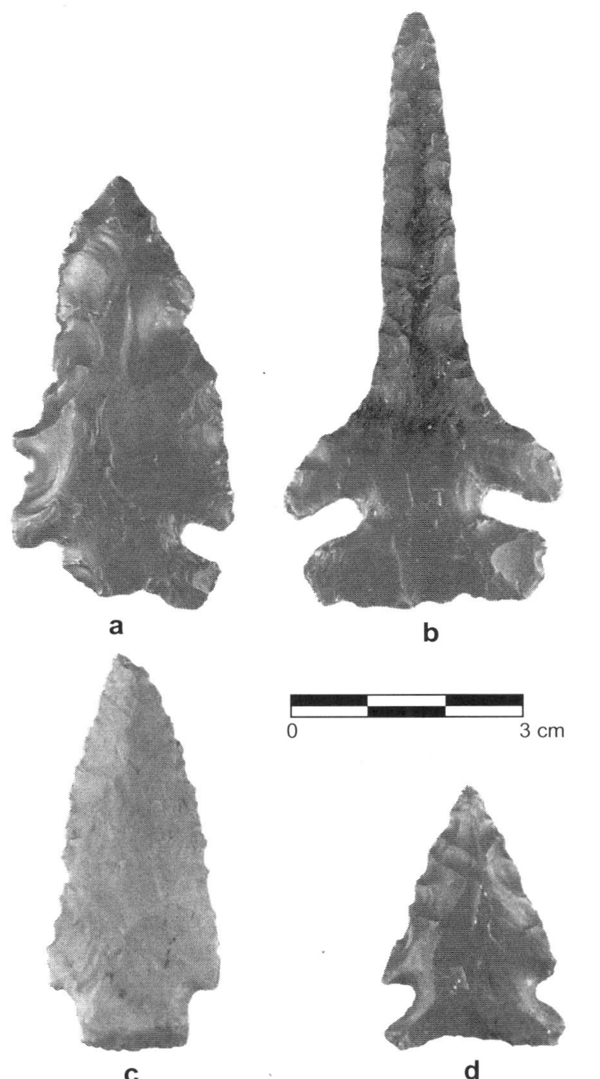

Figure 10.3. Early Side Notched points from the James Farnsley site.

Figure 10.4. St. Charles points from the James Farnsley site.

in association with Kirk Corner Notched points are chipped adzes and celts, unifacial end scrapers, and distinctive long-shanked, bulbous-based drills. Buried on the terrace escarpment is a 30-m-long secondary refuse deposit containing high densities of debitage, tools, and charcoal. Radiocarbon ages obtained (n = 5) from the lower Kirk zone range from 9420 ± 100 to 8780 ± 80 RCYBP. Three of the younger dates cluster at 8815 ± 58 RCYBP (T' = 0.52, $\chi^2_{.05}$ = 5.99). Single ages of 8740 ± 100 RCYBP (ISGS 4838) and 8320 ± 80 RCYBP (ISGS 5032) were obtained from the middle and upper occupation zones, respectively.

The very large sample of Kirk Corner Notched points recovered provides the opportunity to examine stylistic variation within this cluster. We have identified four varieties (Cantin and Stafford 2003): Pine Tree Corner Notched, Kirk Corner Notched Large, Kirk Corner Notched Small, and Stilwell Corner Notched. Pine Tree Corner Notched makes up the vast majority (74 percent) of the collection, followed in frequency by Kirk Large (14 percent), Kirk Small (10 percent), and Stilwell (2 percent). Pine Tree, with its incurvate-recurvate and serrated blade has typically been viewed as a resharpened Kirk Corner Notched Large (Justice 1987; Smith 1986). At Kirk sites in the Southeast, Pine Trees typically make up a small percentage of point assemblages. Although resharpening is a factor in the morphology of Kirk-cluster points from the James Farnsley site, we argue that the Pine Tree form in this region of the lower Ohio River valley represents a stylistically distinctive type because of its technology, especially relative to Kirk Large.

Kirk Point Technology and Stylistic Variability

Cantin and Stafford (2003) have recently examined the relationship between resharpening sequences and technomorphological variability in the Kirk-cluster assemblage from the site. As noted, the Pine Tree form dominates the assemblage from the Kirk zone (Figure 10.6). While resharpened blades occur whose morphology is consistent with the Pine Tree Corner Notched type as defined elsewhere, there is also a Pine Tree style that does not represent a reworked point but, rather, is a pristine form. Pine Tree point blades are relatively long and narrow and usually very well made. Of the complete blades (n = 1,158), the typical shape in pristine forms is recurvate

Figure 10.5. Thebes points from the James Farnsley site.

(65 percent), often with a long medial section that is parallel bladed. A prominent feature is the outswept, flaring barbs, which are isolated from the blade in pristine forms and are even more accentuated through blade maintenance in reworked forms and can lead to a strongly incurvate blade. Of those with measurable notches, almost all (92 percent) have parallel, narrow, deep notches. They are almost always basally ground (87 percent), with grinding extending to the tips of the barbs and within the notches. Another distinctive stylistic feature of the Pine Tree is the exaggerated blade tip.

Perhaps the most striking attribute of Pine Tree points is the use of pressure flaking on the blade, which results in a parallel to chevron flaking pattern (Crabtree 1972). This is related to the production of a serrated blade in which the blade margin is carefully prepared to set up a platform for what Bruce Bradley refers to as "serial pressure flaking" (1997:54) or "serial serration" (pers. comm. 2003) in Dalton points. These serration flakes, regimented in their spacing, carry across the face of the blade and often terminally intersect to form a medial ridge. Serration is installed along the entire blade to the end of the barb. Blade serration is present in 81 percent of all Pine Trees. Of this total, serial serration is recorded for 87 percent.

Serial serration is *not* a resharpening mechanism applied to Kirk Corner Notched Large forms. Although a subset of Kirk Large have a similar outline to Pine Tree, they lack the serial serration. Shape, then, cannot be solely used to differentiate Pine Tree from Kirk Large.

Kirk Corner Notched Large points (Figure 10.7) are usually broad points, typically with excurvate blades. Flaking can be minimally bifacial, at times approaching unifacial. Broad, random percussion flakes dominate the face, which lacks a medial ridge. "Parallel-over-random" flaking—that is, parallel pressure flaking of the margins over a randomly percussion-flaked face—is most common, seen on 71 percent of points, and absolute random flaking is present on 24 percent. Pressure flaking is minimal and noninvasive on the face and is done only to shape the blade margins, not to thin the face. True Pine Tree–like parallel flaking is only observed in 3 percent of Kirk Large. Nearly half of all Kirk Large points are not serrated (48 percent), in stark contrast to Pine Trees. However, 35 percent are serrated, though the procedure used differs somewhat from that applied to Pine Tree. In Kirk Large technology, serration is accomplished by flaking only the blade margin rather than the entire blade face.

While Kirk Corner Notched Small points (Figure 10.8) appear to be diminutive analogs of the Large form, in some technological aspects they are more similar to Pine Tree. The blades are most often excurvate to triangular, with stubby down-swept barbs. Over half (55 percent) have parallel, narrow, deep notches, but 25 percent have broad, open, shallow notches. They are routinely serrated (64 percent) and basally ground (81percent), both attributes occurring in greater frequency than in Kirk Large but in lesser frequency than in Pine Tree. They are often serially serrated (53 percent) with a parallel flaking pattern (68 percent), and parallel-over-random flaking is not unusual (26 percent).

The Stilwell variety (Figure 10.9) is a large, heavy point. It is usually straight or recurvate bladed with an incurvate base, which is often ground (69 percent), and the blade is virtually always serrated (94 percent). Flaking is most typically parallel-over-random (94 percent), reflecting serial serration confined to the margin.

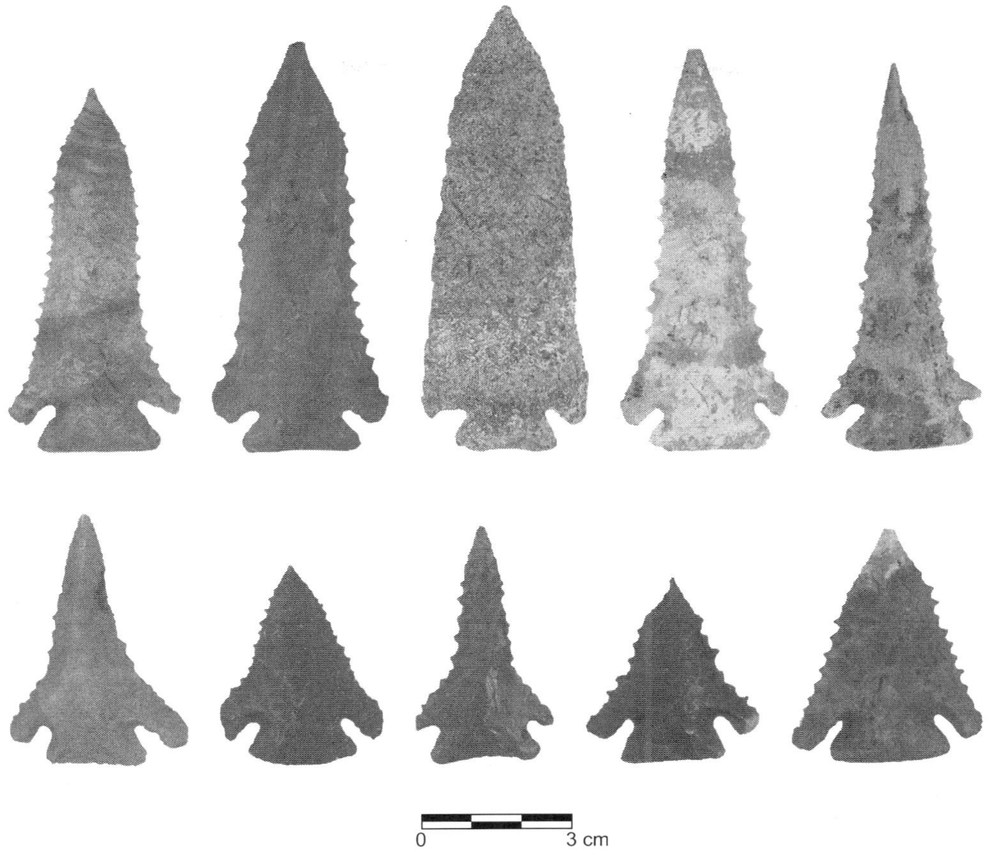

Figure 10.6. Pine Tree Corner Notched points from the James Farnsley site.

Kirk Chronology

Unlike Kirk-cluster stratigraphic sequences elsewhere, no strong shifts in Kirk varieties (i.e., change from Kirk Small to Kirk Large) are stratigraphically detectable through the more than meter-thick deposit at James Farnsley. Stilwell Corner Notched points are associated predominantly with the upper occupation at the site, although Kirk Large and Small co-occur in this zone, as well. At the adjacent Townsend site (12Hr481), a Kirk-cluster occupation underlies a thick Late Archaic rock-filled midden at the terrace surface. Stilwell variety points are by far the most common Kirk form (49 percent), and a radiocarbon age of 8360 ± 80 RCYBP (ISGS 5025) was obtained from a pit feature. This age is consistent with that derived from the upper Kirk zone at James Farnsley. These dates are generally outside the range of Kirk-cluster occupations in the Southeast by 700 years, so it appears likely that this stylistic form of Kirk persisted later in the lower Ohio River valley.

Limited excavations (Mocas and Smith 1995; Smith 1986, 1995) of buried deposits at Swan's Landing (12Hr304) on the west side of Harrison County (Figure 10.1) near the confluence of the Ohio River and Indian Creek have documented early Kirk Corner Notched occupations. Although the sample of points is small ($n = 31$), Pine Tree forms are common (61 percent). Thousands more Pine Tree Corner Notched points reportedly have been recovered by collectors from the eroding bank of the site (Smith 1986, 1995). Pine Tree points dominate the Kirk-cluster points illustrated by Tomak (1994) from one of these collections. Radiocarbon samples from the initial excavations at Swan's Landing were much too young or too old by several millennia (see Smith 1986; Tankersley and Munson 1992), but later excavation (Mocas and Smith 1995) obtained AMS radiocarbon ages of 9060 ± 70 RCYBP (Beta 83547) and 9090 ± 60 RCYBP (Beta 83548), which are well within the range of Kirk ages elsewhere.

Early Archaic Summary

The paucity of data associated with the late Wisconsin–early Holocene transition in the Midwest or Midsouth makes generalization difficult. The Early Side Notched zone at the James Farnsley site hints that lower Ohio River valley point forms are stylistically different from the Big Sandy I type in the Southeast and may be precursors to the Thebes tradition of the Midwest.

Figure 10.7. Kirk Corner Notched Large points from the James Farnsley site.

Figure 10.8. Kirk Corner Notched Small points from the James Farnsley site.

Figure 10.9. Stilwell Corner Notched points from the Townsend site.

At the James Farnsley site, the Thebes-cluster zone is stratigraphically overlain by a series of Kirk-cluster occupations. This is a stratigraphic sequence that has not been documented elsewhere in the Midwest. The earliest Kirk-cluster age at the site is not substantially later than the single Thebes-cluster date, and we, therefore, expect that Thebes and Kirk at least partially overlapped in time. This overlap is also indicated by the Thebes-cluster dates from the Twin Ditch site in the lower Illinois River valley, which range between 9500 ± 100 and 8740 ± 70 (Morrow 1996:347).

The prevalence of a technologically distinctive Pine Tree Corner Notched type at the Farnsley and Swan's Landing sites and its relative rarity elsewhere in the Southeast suggests that a style zone may exist in this part of the lower Ohio River valley.

On a narrower regional scale, Early Archaic points were the second most common Archaic diagnostic artifacts recovered (33.9 percent) in the Data Center Survey in southwestern Indiana. Kirk Corner Notched (20.6 percent) were second only to Matanzas points, while Thebes-cluster points (i.e., Thebes, St. Charles, and Lost Lake) made up 9.1 percent (ranked fourth) of the Archaic points recovered. Bifurcate types ranked seventh (4.2 percent). Excavated Bifurcate sites are rare in southern Indiana but include three mortuary sites: Jerger (Tomak 1979, 1983:70) and Steele (Curtis H. Tomak, pers. comm. 2004), both in Daviess County, and McCullough's Run in Bartholomew County (Cochran et al. n.d).[1] The common occurrence of Early Archaic points, especially Kirk, relative to points of later periods suggests that Archaic populations in southwestern Indiana were prevalent during early Holocene times.

Middle Archaic (5500–8000 RCYBP)

The Middle Archaic has remained a poorly documented period across most of the Midwest and Midsouth, and the lower Ohio River valley is no exception. This is due to a combination of factors, including (1) poorly understood point forms assignable to this period, (2) the low archaeological visibility of the highly mobile hunter-gatherers of the period, and (3) burial of Middle Archaic occupations in alluvial or colluvial contexts. Very few radiocarbon dates span this period in the lower Ohio River valley (see Maslowski et al. 1995).

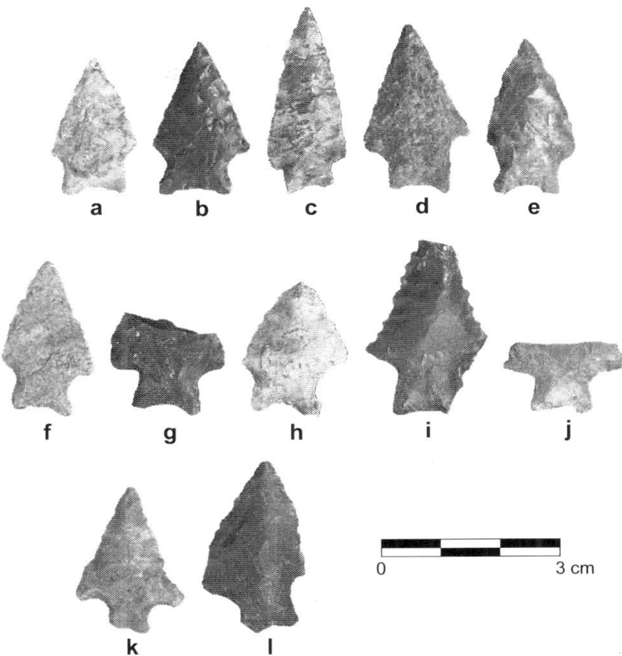

Figure 10.10. Knob Creek Stemmed concave-base variety and bifurcate points from the Knob Creek site.

Middle Archaic Knob Creek Complex

The CAP extensively investigated buried deposits that date to the Middle Archaic at the Knob Creek site (12Hr484). This site is contained within alluvial deposits associated with a late Holocene Ohio River levee, and excavations were conducted along a .5-km segment of the landform. Bar deposits began aggrading as early as 7500 RCYBP, with the levee becoming stable by 2500 RCYBP (Stafford 2004). A Middle Archaic zone exposed between 2.0 and 3.5 m bs was characterized by surface hearths and light-density, circumscribed scatters of lithic debris and tools. Three separate stratified Middle Archaic occupation zones were identified, two of which are associated with the Knob Creek complex.

A relatively large collection of points was recovered from this zone (n = 66), most of which do not fall within currently defined point clusters. Although considerable morphological variety characterizes this sample, the predominant form is a small, short-stemmed point with either a straight or shallow concave base (Figures 10.10 and 10.11), which we term "Knob Creek Stemmed." The concave-base variant is similar to Stanly Stemmed (Coe 1964; Justice 1987) but smaller in size (and seemingly younger in age by 600 years or more; Chapman 1976). The size of Knob Creek Stemmed (mean length = 32.7 mm; n = 22) is more in the range of bifurcate points like Kanawha, St. Albans, or Lake Erie (Justice 1987:246). Knob Creek Stemmed are also roughly similar in morphology and age to Neville points (considered to be a Stanly variant) from the Northeast, but Neville points are larger (Dincauze 1976). Although most Knob Creek Stemmed specimens have a wide stem relative to the blade shoulder, a few have narrow stems and are more spikelike. The shoulder shape varies from weak to barbed.

Figure 10.11. Knob Creek Stemmed straight-base variety from the Knob Creek site.

Limited numbers of several other point types occur in the Middle Archaic zone, including a Lake Erie Bifurcate (Figure 10.10j), Kanawha Stemmed (Figure 10.10k), Kirk Stemmed (Figure 10.10i), and a corner-notched form (Figure 10.11).

Thirteen radiocarbon dates are available for the Middle Archaic zone. They range in age from 7220 ± 70 to 6670 ± 70 RCYBP. Two statistical clusters of dates with pooled means of 7180 ± 20 ($T' = .97, \chi^2_{.05} = 9.49$) and 6770 ± 30 ($T' = 4.11, \chi^2_{.05} = 12.60$) RCYBP are associated with Knob Creek Stemmed points.

Some evidence suggests a temporal shift from the concave-base to straight-base variety of Knob Creek Stemmed. In some portions of the site, there are two Knob Creek occupation zones. The concave variety tends to occur in the lower occupation, which also produced the two Bifurcate points (Figure 10.10), and is associated, with the exception of one date, with the older cluster of radiocarbon ages. Conversely, the straight-base form tends to be higher in the deposit and associated with the younger dates.

Two corner-notched points that were recovered from a feature well within the Middle Archaic zone at first appear out of place, as they could easily be classified as Kirk Corner Notched Small. Both points have triangular, slightly serrated blades (Figure 10.12). An AMS radiocarbon age of 6942 ± 60 RCYBP (Oxford A-0264) was obtained from a wood sample derived from the pit feature containing these points. This age is consistent with the other dates obtained from the Middle Archaic zone and is not stratigraphically lower than Knob Creek Stemmed–associated features or radiocarbon ages.

Figure 10.12. Middle Archaic corner-notched points from the Knob Creek site.

Similar corner-notched forms (Kirk look-alikes) appear to occur in other Middle Archaic contexts in the Ohio River valley. Amos Corner Notched points from the Kanawha River, West Virginia, were originally thought to be apart of the Kirk Corner Notched cluster (Broyles 1971) but have been more recently viewed as a Middle Archaic point type, with ages in the range of 7770 ± 450 to 6315 ± 160 RCYBP from the Amos Power Plant and Charleston Town Center sites (Youse 1983, 1985). At the Hansford site (Wilkins 1985), Amos-like points were recovered in a zone between a stratigraphically higher layer of side-notched points dated at 5680 ± 75 and 5550 ± 80 RCYBP and a lower zone containing Stanly Stemmed (7695 ± 155 RCYBP).

Early Archaic style points have also been recovered from the Paddy's West (north end of Knob Creek bottom) and Patriot Generating Station (Switzerland County) projects in what otherwise appear to be later contexts than expected. At site 12Fl46 in the Paddy's West project (Figure 10.1), Kirk Corner Notched Small points ($n = 8$) were recovered from a buried (ca. 3.5 m bs) overbank context (Smith and Mocas 1995:339). A buried Late Archaic shell midden is stratigraphically above this zone. Two radiocarbon ages were derived primarily from nutshell recovered from two separate well-defined pits (6620 ± 120 [Beta 2481] and 6530 ± 70 [Beta 2483]) (Smith and Mocas 1995:339). The samples are statistically the same ($T' = .31, \chi^2_{.05} = 2.84$). The radiocarbon ages, however, were considered by Smith and Mocas (1995:339) to be several millennia too young, given the presence of Kirk Corner Notched points.

The points recovered from 12Fl46 are similar in morphology to those from the Knob Creek site, with triangular, slightly serrated blades, although they are somewhat larger in size (mean length = 51.8 mm vs. 44.0 mm for Knob Creek). The stratigraphic sequence at 12Fl46 and the radiocarbon ages are consistent with those at the Knob Creek site, and both sites occur in similar late Holocene levees (see Stafford 2004). Site 12Fl46 may represent a Middle Archaic occupation in which a corner-notched point style is present and may be a temporal analog to Amos components in the upper Ohio River valley.

A parallel pattern is present at the Patriot Generating Station project in Mexico Bottom (Figure 10.1). Two late Holocene alluvial ridges adjacent to the modern Ohio River channel contain stratified Archaic occupations (12Sw89 and 12Sw99) (McHugh and Michael 1984). In the interior ridge (12Sw89), a shallowly buried zone containing largely side-notched forms (Matanzas and Brewerton Eared) and some Late Archaic stemmed points overlies a more deeply buried zone containing largely ($n = 11$) bifurcate points (LeCroy and MacCorkle) but also a Kirk Stemmed and corner-notched forms. Three radiocarbon dates were reported from this zone: 6630 ± 100 (Beta 6347), 6560 ± 130 (Beta 6353), and 6940 ± 180 (Beta 6352). These ages form a statistically coherent group ($T' = 2.73, \chi^2_{.05} = 5.99$). Again, the radiocarbon ages and stratigraphic sequence are consistent with a Middle Archaic context.

In sum, the early portion of the Middle Archaic in the southern hills and Ohio River region appears to be characterized by a mix of point styles, including a previously unrecognized type, Knob Creek Stemmed, as well as bifurcate and corner-notched point styles.

A Pre-French Lick Middle Archaic Phase

The earliest French Lick–phase (Munson and Cook 1980b) dates available from Bluegrass and other sites are no older than 5300 RCYBP. Deeply side-notched point forms with squared ears like Big Sandy II or Godar/Raddatz are generally thought to appear earlier than the shallow-side-notched types like Matanzas,[2] but very few dates have been reported for the period 5300 to 6000 RCYBP or earlier. Big Sandy–like points typically make up a small percentage of the point types in French Lick–phase components (< 15 percent) (see below). In the Data Center Survey across southwestern Indiana, Big Sandy II were a minor fraction of the points recovered (4.8 percent).[3]

In the lower Ohio River valley, several sites have buried occupations that may represent a pre-French Lick phase, in which deeply side-notched point forms are the predominant style. At the Knob Creek site, a hint of such a component appeared in the northernmost excavation block. Overlying the Knob Creek component is an ephemeral occupation in which a deeply side-notched Big Sandy II–like point was recovered. In the same unit, a single radiocarbon date of 5830 ± 90 (Beta 113983) was obtained from a hearth.

More substantial buried occupations are represented in Perry County. At site 12Pe929 on the Ohio River floodplain near Tell City (Figure 10.1), test excavations revealed buried and stratified Archaic occupations (Hawkins and Walley 2000). The deepest cultural zone (.8–1.0 m bs) contains deeply side-notched forms (i.e., Big Sandy II; $n = 6$) but also includes Matanzas ($n = 2$) and Brewerton Corner Notched ($n = 2$) (Figure 10.13). Four radiocarbon dates from what was termed "Stratum 4," which contained these points, have an average of 5749 ± 50 RCYBP ($T' = 6.04$, $\chi^2_{.05} = 7.81$). Feature 22, a shallow pit containing two Big Sandy II points, was dated at 5670 ± 100 RCYBP (ISGS 3500). A 20- to 40-cm-thick zone with few artifacts overlies the side-notched stratum, which, in turn, is overlain by a Late Archaic midden (see below).

At the Mogan site (12Pe839) on the eastern side of Perry County (Figure 10.1), a similar buried stratigraphic sequence is present (Bader 1994). The deepest cultural zone (Zone 2), buried between 1.8 and 2.8 m below surface in alluvial ridges of the Ohio River floodplain, contained only Big Sandy II–style points ($n = 12$) (excavators use the term *Faulkner*). No radiocarbon dates are available from this occupation.

As at 12Pe926, a Late Archaic occupation (Zone 3) overlies the deeply side-notched zone and contains a mixed assemblage of Late Archaic forms that include Brewerton Side Notched, Merom, and Table Rock points (see below).

Apparently good stratigraphic evidence at two sites and a clustering of radiocarbon ages from one site (12Pe926) in the lower Ohio River valley indicate that deeply side-notched forms like Big Sandy II can be used to define a pre-French Lick phase (earlier than 5500 RCYBP). What is defined as early Middle Archaic in this study (Knob Creek complex, as recognized at CAP) suggests that the beginning of this phase may have been no earlier than 6300 RCYBP. Given the more recent dating of the French Lick phase from Bluegrass and other sites, this phase should have ended by 5500 RCYBP. Clearly, more data are required to verify this point association, although sites in which deeply side-notched styles predominate appear to be rare in the portion of the lower Ohio River valley considered here and in southern Indiana.

Figure 10.13. Side-notched and expanding-stemmed points from 12Pe929.

Middle Archaic Summary

Few sites from this period have been excavated. One of the factors that makes regional identification of the Middle Archaic difficult is the wide variety of associated point forms. From the Knob Creek site, the best-documented and dated of the sites discussed, the small, stemmed points recovered would most likely be subsumed under types associated with other time periods if found in a surface context or in a mixed assemblage. Bifurcates and corner-notched points similar to Amos (Kirk look-alikes) also apparently occur in Middle Archaic contexts in the lower Ohio River valley.

Although more evidence is needed, more deeply side-notched point forms like Big Sandy II define the latter part of the Middle Archaic but are also associated with the later French Lick phase in small numbers along with Matanzas points.

Late Archaic Period (5500–3600 RCYBP)

Munson and Cook (1980b) proposed the French Lick phase on the basis of excavations at four sites in the Patoka Lake project (Figure 10.1) but also drew on more limited investigations at a series of other southern Indiana sites.[4] Stylistically, the French Lick phase was primarily defined by the presence of Matanzas, Big Sandy II, Karnak, and straight- to expanding-stem point forms (or so-called M-B-K-S points) recovered from the Miler A (12Or12) midden and three other Patoka Lake sites: Morganroth (12Or92), K Branch (12Cr27), and Omer Lane (12Or273). No precise type names were assigned to the miscellaneous straight- and expanding-stem points. Similar styles were recognized at sites like the McCain site (Miller 1941) on the East Fork of the White River and the Turpin site (Morrison 1975) at the mouth of the Patoka River (Figure 10.1). Sites along the Ohio River (Crib Mound, Breeden, and at the Falls of the Ohio) were also included in this phase. Although not recovered from Patoka Lake because of poor bone preservation, engraved bone pins were also viewed as a defining trait of the French Lick phase.

Radiocarbon dates available from Patoka Lake indicate a phase duration from roughly 4800 to 3400 RCYBP (Munson and Cook 1980a:469). Two radiocarbon ages from the K Branch and Omer Lane sites are substantially earlier than the cluster of five dates from the Miler A and Morganroth sites. The later five dates span the period 4800 to 4300 RCYBP. The two oldest samples from Miler A form a statistical cluster with a pooled mean of 4720 ± 60 RCYBP ($T' = .12, \chi^2_{.05} = 3.84$).

Munson and Cook (1980b:736) also noted the similarities in point styles between and the presence of incised bone pins in the French Lick phase and the Illinois Helton phase. Helton-phase dates from Koster (Cook 1976) are, however, substantially earlier (5800–4800 RCYBP) than those available to Munson and Cook in 1980 for the French Lick phase from Patoka Lake (4800–3400 RCYBP).

In the M-B-K-S point group, Matanzas Side Notched forms are by far most common, while other types are relatively rare. Cook's (1980) Matanzas cluster is highly inclusive, however, and incorporates stemmed forms that would now be placed in various Late Archaic straight-stemmed type categories. Point photographs (Cook 1980:410–412) indicate that his Matanzas Straight Stem and Deep Side Notched are more appropriately classified as McWhinney, Saratoga, or Karnak Stemmed (see Justice 1987). We use Munson and Harn's (1966) original definition of Matanzas in this chapter.

Of the 206 points of a faint-side-notched or stemmed variety collected from all Patoka Lake sites, 70 percent are in the reclassified Matanzas cluster and 30 percent are in the Late Archaic stemmed cluster. From the Miler A midden excavations, Matanzas make up 69.4 percent of the 144 M-B-K-S points recovered, while stemmed forms, including Karnak, account for only 12.5 percent and deeply side-notched points (Big Sandy II) make up 7.6 percent.

More recent French Lick–phase site excavations extend the beginning of the phase to about 5300 RCYBP. Extensive investigations at the Bluegrass site in the Pigeon Creek basin and the Townsend site in the Falls of the Ohio region have yielded large point samples that are consistent with the M-B-K-S group observed at Patoka Lake. Testing at the Amini site on the Patoka River and salvage excavations at the Millersburg site in the Pigeon Creek basin near Bluegrass provide additional data on the French Lick phase.

Bluegrass (12W162) is a base camp and cemetery located near Bluegrass Creek (Figure 10.1), a tributary of Pigeon Creek in southwestern Indiana (Stafford et al. 2000). The site consists of a dense rock-filled midden, 132 pits, a minimum of 80 human burials, and 11 dog burials. Engraved bone pins (see Jefferies 1997), atlatl parts, a turtle-shell rattle, a wide array of other bone and antler tools, and hafted end scrapers are also present. A sample of 434 Middle and Late Archaic points was recovered from the site, and seven radiocarbon dates were obtained from the midden and pit features. Six radiocarbon ages fall in the range of 5030 ± 80 to 5290 ±70 RCYBP, with one outlier age of 6260 ± 120 from midden context. The six younger dates form a statistical group with an average of 5170 ± 30 RCYBP ($T' = 6.14, \chi^2_{.05} = 11.1$).

Matanzas-cluster points (Figure 10.14) make up the majority of the point sample (57.4 percent), but Late Archaic stemmed forms contribute a substantially larger percentage (35.9 percent) than at the Miler A site. The Big Sandy II percentage (6.2 percent) is very similar to that at Miler A.

Figure 10.14. Matanzas points from the Bluegrass site.

The Late Archaic stemmed cluster is composed of Karnak Stemmed, Saratoga Broad Stemmed, and McWhinney Heavy Stemmed (Figure 10.15). A fourth stemmed form termed "Oak Grove Stemmed" is also present (Figure 10.16). Schock et al. (1975) first recognized this latter type in Christian County, Kentucky. It is distinct from the other three Late Archaic types in having a slightly expanding and relatively narrow stem (Cantin and Anslinger 1987). Fine pressure flaking is common on the blade edge, and the base is typically bi-beveled with a high incidence of cortex. High-quality cherts like Wyandotte or St. Louis were commonly used. Justice (1987:154) subsumes the Oak Grove from Kentucky under the Saratoga Broad Bladed type, but the examples from Bluegrass are more consistent morphologically and technologically with the Benton cluster. Probable examples of Oak Grove are illustrated in collections from Patoka Lake (Cook 1980:413), McCain (Miller 1941), and Turpin (Morrison 1975).

Cantin and Anslinger (1987) proposed that because of distinct chert utilization patterns and technology, Late Archaic stemmed points like Oak Grove may date later than Matanzas, representing a younger, separate Archaic phase. Radiocarbon dating of features on sites where both side-notched and straight-stemmed types like McWhinney, Karnak, and Oak Grove were recovered suggests that these forms were contemporaneous but that the stemmed forms persisted later in time. At Bluegrass, four pit features were dated that contained exclusively Matanzas, Karnak, or Oak Grove points. The samples were found to be statistically the same at the .05 significance level ($T' = 3.01, \chi^2_{.05} = 7.81$). The Karnak dated feature is younger by 200 years but overlaps the other three ages at two standard deviations. As indicated, all five dates can be considered a single statistical cluster.

The Millersburg site (12W81) is located along Pigeon Creek near Bluegrass (Figure 10.1). Salvage excavations in the late 1980s documented a substantial Late Archaic midden containing large pits and human burials, even though as much as 90 percent of the site had been destroyed by borrowing for a levee and by looting (Levy n.d.). Investigations exposed 345 features in the surviving portions of the site. Twenty-eight graves containing 36 individuals were also encountered.

A small sample of M-B-K-S points was recovered from Millersburg (n = 43) (Figure 10.17). Of these points, 66.6 percent are a part of the Matanzas cluster (including one Brewerton Eared), and 33.3 percent are in the Late Archaic stemmed group that includes Karnak, McWhinney, Oak Grove, and Benton. No Big Sandy II points were found.

Two samples from features were recently submitted for radiocarbon dating. The first is from a burial pit (F141) containing six individuals (an adult male, two adult females, and three subadults). The sample consisted of nutshell from from several hand-picked samples recovered from the burial pit fill. A Matanzas point was found in the scapula of the adult male, and another was recovered from the feature fill. A radiocarbon date of 5290 ± 50 RCYBP (Beta 195820) was obtained.

A second nutshell sample was submitted from a pit (F54) containing fragments of a Karnak point and a McWhinney point and yielded a date of 4120 ± 80 RCYBP (Beta 195978). This date is more than a millennium younger than the Matanzas-associated burial pit ($T' = 85.20, \chi^2_{.05} = 3.84$) and suggests, unlike the case at Bluegrass, that a later phase may be present at the site.

Figure 10.15. Late Archaic stemmed points from the Bluegrass site.

Figure 10.16. Oak Grove Stemmed points from the Bluegrass site.

Figure 10.17. Late Archaic stemmed points from the Millersburg site.

Figure 10.18. Benton-like point from the Millersburg site.

A large Benton-like point (Figure 10.18) was recovered from an extended adult inhumation. It was positioned on the left side of the cranium in association with a partial ring of copper salts. Red ocher was found underneath the skull and elsewhere in the base of the burial pit. This was one of two burials that contained grave goods. The point is similar to Benton points recovered from the Eva site in burial contexts (Lewis and Lewis 1961:36).[5] The stem of the Millersburg point is beveled along the edge, which is a trait consistent with the Eva-site Benton forms (Lewis and Lewis 1961:34).

Small-scale test excavations were conducted in the mid-1980s (Kendrick and Pace 1985) at the Amini site (12Du323) located in Dubois County on the Patoka River (Figure 10.1). A small sample of M-B-K-S points (n = 11), bone pin fragments, and three burials were recovered from a rock-filled midden deposit. At least 17 other burials were reportedly exposed at the site, along with bannerstones (Kendrick and Pace 1985). A radiocarbon date of 5000 ± 90 (Beta 13129) was obtained from charcoal recovered from sub-plow-zone midden deposits. Although the point sample is small, the percentages are consistent with those obtained from Patoka Lake and Bluegrass for this time period. Matanzas-cluster points are in the majority (54 percent), and one Karnak, two straight-stemmed, and two Big Sandy II points were reported.

In the early 1980s, Tomak (1982) tested the Bono site (12Lr194), a shell midden in Lawrence County on the East Fork of the White River (Figure 10.1). M-B-K-S points are illustrated in the report, and two dates were obtained from the midden (4920 ± 70 RCYBP, 4730 ± 70 RCYBP; $T' = 2.12$, $\chi^2_{.05} = 3.84$).

Higginbotham (1983) tested the Berry site (Mussel Knoll; 12Gi11) a Late Archaic shell midden in the Wabash River valley below the Patoka River confluence and reports four radiocarbon dates from the midden, ranging from 5585 ± 105 to 5150 ± 140 RCYBP. Side-notched points (Faulkner) and incised bone pins are reported to have been recovered (Higginbotham 1983:309). No illustrations of the points are provided so how these side-notched forms would be classified under the current system is unclear. The presence of incised bone pins suggests a French Lick–phase site.

The Townsend (12Hr481) site is another Late Archaic rock-filled midden that was excavated as a part of the CAP in the lower Ohio River valley in Harrison County (Figure 10.1). This small (1,000 m^2) but intensively occupied base camp yielded a very large sample ($n = 793$) of M-B-K-S–cluster points. Shallow side-notched (Matanzas and Brewerton Eared) (Figures 10.19 and 10.20) forms dominate the assemblage (> 80 percent). Five radiocarbon dates range from 5360 ± 70 to 4200 ± 50 RCYBP. Three of the ages from pits, however, have a pooled mean of 5036 ± 40 RCYBP ($T' = .76$, $\chi^2_{.05} = 5.99$) and likely provide an age range of 4900–5100 RCYBP for the bulk of the site's occupation. The youngest and oldest ages suggest that, as at the Millersburg site, these rock-filled middens can reflect long occupation histories during the Late Archaic.

Figure 10.20. Brewerton Eared points from the Townsend site.

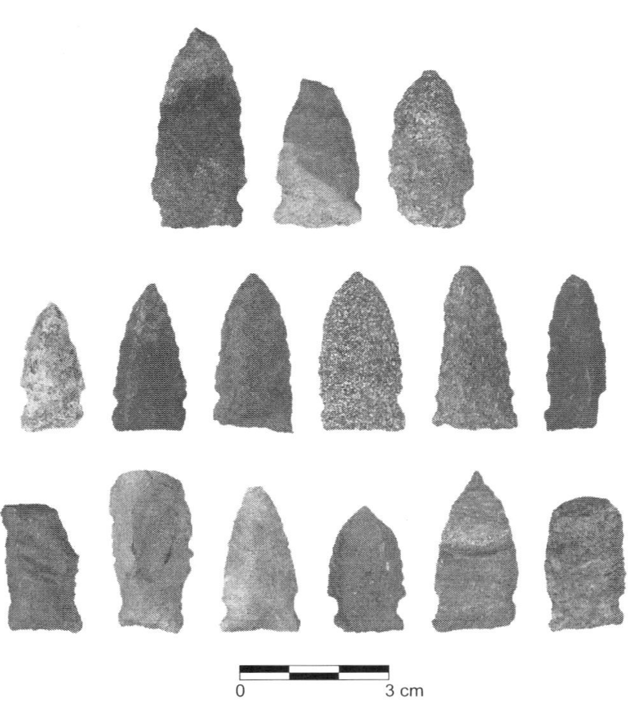

Figure 10.19. Matanzas points from the Townsend site.

In contrast to Bluegrass, Brewerton Eared, a distinctive concave-base and eared variant of the faint-side-notched cluster was the most common point style at the Townsend site, making up 47.7 percent of the Late Archaic points. Matanzas constituted 33.5 percent of the collection recovered. Late Archaic stemmed types like Karnak, McWhinney, and Saratoga were found in much smaller numbers (10.5 percent). Deeply side-notched types (Godar/Raddatz/Big Sandy II) make up less than 2 percent of the sample. The radiocarbon ages suggest an occupation contemporaneous with that at Bluegrass despite the marked differences in point styles and type frequencies.

The radiocarbon ages reported above are from four pits containing Matanzas points, or Brewerton Eared, or both, along with a pit from which a stemmed point (Brewerton Corner Notched) was recovered. As indicated above, they form one statistically coherent group of ages. This result again supports M-B-K-S as a group of associated points defining the French Lick phase.

Munson and Cook (1980b:723), in their review of sites in the lower Ohio River valley, noted the presence of a concave-base type at the Crib Mound and Breeden sites that was not recovered at Patoka Lake. This concave-base style appears to be the form we have identified as Brewerton Eared at the Townsend site. Points similar to Brewerton Eared are rare in the Bluegrass collection, and those that are present were subsumed under the Matanzas cluster in the original classification of the collection. So a clear style zone, as suggested by Munson and Cook, appears to differentiate shallow-side-notched forms in the lower Ohio River valley from those to the north in the hill country of southern Indiana.

Late Middle Archaic remains have been recovered from two other sites (Reid and Paddy's West project) in the Knob Creek bottom. The Reid site (12Fl1), located at the north end of Knob Creek bottom, yielded dates of 4555 ± 70 RCYBP (UGa 267) and 5480 ± 90 RCYBP from Janzen's (1977:133) testing of the 1.8-m-thick stratified shell midden in the 1970s. Little was reported about diagnostic point forms, however. More recent salvage excavations by researchers from Ball State University (Angst 1998) on the northern edge of the site in a dense rock-filled midden recovered points of the M-B-K-S group. Late Archaic stemmed forms make up 61.7 percent of the assemblage (n = 47) and include Karnak/McWhinney, Benton/Elk River, Brewerton Side Notched, and generic Late Archaic stemmed points. Matanzas points are the most common side-notched form. Although not typed as such, a few Brewerton Eared points similar in form to those at the Townsend site are illustrated in the excavation report. No radiocarbon dates are available from the recent investigations.

Janzen (1977) also reports radiocarbon ages from several other sites in the Falls of the Ohio region, including Old Clarkesville (12Cl1), Hoke (12Hr103), Ferry Landing (12Hr3), and Miller (12Hr5), but provides no information on point styles. Ages range from 5480 ± 90 to 4180 ± 180 (Janzen 1977:131).[6] Most of these sites represent shell-, rock-, or shell-and-rock-filled middens.

Salvage excavations at the nearby Paddy's West project encountered a buried Late Archaic shell midden (12Fl46) (Smith and Mocas 1995). A small sample of M-B-K-S points (n = 20) was recovered, and the majority of points are either Matanzas or Brewerton Eared (Smith and Mocas 1995:245–258). No radiocarbon dates were obtained from the shell midden. Nearby, a zone of pit features unrelated to the shell midden produced a date of 3510 ± 120 RCYBP (Beta 2481), but no diagnostic artifacts were recovered.

The Breeden site (12Hr11), located on the western side of Harrison County (Figure 10.1) near the confluence of Indian Creek, is a buried shell midden exposed in the bank of the Ohio River channel (Bellis 1982). Testing of the site revealed a deposit containing M-B-K-S points (n = 48), although the points were typed according to Cook's inclusive Matanzas-cluster scheme. On the basis of an examination of illustrations provided by Bellis (1982:83–85), side-notched points (Matanzas, Big Sandy II, and Brewerton Eared) appear to be more common lower in the deposit and Late Archaic stemmed varieties more prevalent at the top of the cultural unit. A single radiocarbon age of 4200 ± 200 (DIC 2377) was obtained from the lowest of the excavated levels of the site midden. Although this date appears unusually young for the point-type frequencies recovered compared with other sites in the region, the sigma value is substantial. Even so, the sequence suggests a shift from side-notched to stemmed forms through time.

Excavations associated with the Argosy Casino Project (Creasman 1996) investigated the Greendale (12D511) site located in a late Holocene meander belt of the Great Miami River in Dearborn County (Figure 10.1). Light-density occupations originally buried about 2.4 m bs yielded only two diagnostic artifacts—a Matanzas and a Brewerton Side Notched point. Three radiocarbon samples, obtained during Phase III excavations in the middle occupation at the site (J. P. Kerr, pers. comm. 2002), form a statistical group with a pooled average of 5110 ± 30 RCYBP (T' = 2.23, $\chi^2_{.05}$ = 5.99). A fourth sample from a Phase II test trench is younger by 500 years (4650 ± 80 RCYBP, Beta 91281).

In the hill country, 10 radiocarbon ages from three sites have been obtained since the Patoka Lake project; these consistently place the early part of French Lick phase in the 5000 to 5300 RCYPB range. The Bono site dates span the gap between the earliest French Lick ages from Miler A at Patoka Lake. The Patoka Lake ages from the Morganroth site are consistent with the Miler A dates, but those from K-Branch and Omer Lane appear to be beyond the early range of the other dates obtained from French Lick–phase sites. These latter occupations may actually fall within a late French Lick phase, for which the majority of points are of the stemmed variety rather than side notched (see below). Sites in the Ohio River Valley with M-B-K-S points, like Townsend and Reid, also fall within the same age interval.

Early and Late French Lick Phases

At the time Munson and Cook (1980b) formulated the French Lick phase, the only other defined phase in southern Indiana was Winters's Riverton phase (or culture). The younger radiocarbon ages obtained from Patoka Lake did not overlap with known Riverton dates, so the French Lick phase was considered to have persisted later than 4000 RCYBP. More recent excavations and a few radiocarbon ages suggest that the French Lick phase can be subdivided into an early and a late interval on the basis of the increase in the prevalence of Late Archaic stemmed points and the decline of faint-side-notched styles. Whereas Matanzas or similar faint-side-notched styles make up the majority of points in early French Lick assemblages, after 4500 RCYBP, stemmed forms like McWhinney, Saratoga, and Karnak became more common.

The best example of this later manifestation is at the Patriot Generating Station project (McHugh and Michael 1984) in Switzerland County on the Ohio River (see Figure 10.1). Site 12Sw99, a midden deposit almost 2 m below surface in an alluvial ridge, produced largely McWhinney points (n = 130). A suite of seven radiocarbon ages provides a range of 4220 ± 90 to 3610 ± 90 RCYBP. Three of the dates form a statistical cluster with a pooled mean of 4090 ± 40 RCYBP ($T' = 1.74$, $\chi^2_{.05} = 5.99$). This component is underlain (at 2.40+ m bs) by a French Lick–age zone with two radiocarbon ages averaging 4750 ± 50 RCYBP ($T' = .02$, $\chi^2_{.05} = 3.84$). A single side-notched (Big Sandy II) point is apparently associated with this deeper stratum.

As indicated above, site Pe929 contained a zone of Late Archaic stemmed- or corner-notched styles that overlay a deep side-notched component (Hawkins and Walley 2000). Late Archaic Saratoga, Karnak, McWhinney, Brewerton Corner Notched, Table Rock/Bottleneck, and Ledbetter points (n = 16) were recovered from a rock-filled midden buried .3–.4 m bs. No side-notched forms were found in this zone. Eight radiocarbon samples from this component were submitted for dating (Hawkins and Walley 2000:66) and yielded ages ranging from 3260 ± 70 to 4590 ± 130 RCYBP. Four of the dates (excluding the two youngest and two oldest samples) form a statistical cluster with a pooled average of 4060 ± 30 RCYBP ($T' = 3.40$, $X^2_{.05} = 7.81$).

At the Mogan site (12Pe839) in Perry County (Bader 1994), a buried Late Archaic–age occupation zone produced a small, mixed assemblage including Brewerton Side Notched (an expanding-stemmed form; n = 2), Table Rock (n = 3; the report illustration suggests one may be a McWhinney), a Matanzas, a Merom, an unidentifiable corner-notched, and a straight-stemmed point. Two radiocarbon dates, 3920 ± 80 (Beta 49082) and 3530 ± 90 (Beta 49083), which are statistically different ($T' = 7.01$, $\chi^2_{.05} = 3.84$), were obtained from this component. As indicated above, this occupation overlies an undated deeply side-notched component.

Recent excavations at site 12Cl158 (Figure 10.1) in Bethlehem Bottom (Clark County) yielded two AMS dates of 4150 ± 40 (Beta 164348) and 4140 ± 40 (Beta 164351) (White 2002:223). Radiocarbon samples were recovered from pit features containing McWhinney points. Overall, 55 McWhinney points were recovered from the site, 11 of which were from feature contexts, while only one Matanzas was found (White 2002).

In the southern Indiana hill country, a similar temporal trend toward stemmed points appears to be represented. At the Monroe Reservoir on Salt Creek, a tributary of the East Fork of the White River, testing of a rock-filled midden at the Paynetown Light site (12Mo193) (Myers and Munson 1987) produced a point assemblage (n = 29) that is composed predominantly of Late Archaic stemmed forms (n = 23; 79 percent). Karnak stemmed and unstemmed, Saratoga, and generic Late Archaic expanding-stemmed points were identified, along with Matanzas (n = 3) and two other, unidentified, side-notched points. A radiocarbon date of 3950 ± 100 RCYBP (Patrick J. Munson, pers. comm. 2004) was obtained from a pit containing two unstemmed Karnaks (Myers and Munson 1987:20).

The Oliver Vineyard site (12Mo141) has produced two later dates (mean = 3940 ± 40 RCYBP) (Munson and Cook 1980a:475) from pits. No tabulations of the assemblage have been completed, but Late Archaic stemmed points appear to be in the majority, and modal Matanzas points are also common (Patrick J. Munson, pers. comm. 2005).

Testing of the Schershel site (12Mo152), also in northern Monroe County (Tomak 1983), yielded an assemblage that (on the basis of the point forms illustrated) is dominated by Karnak unstemmed and stemmed types (some of the latter might be classified as McWhinney—Tomak [1983:72] refers to the assemblage as containing Schershel and Modesto points). A radiocarbon sample on nutshell from a feature resulted in a date of 4595 ± 90 (UGa 4549) (Tomak 1983:72). Survey and collector interviews in Lawrence County have located sites with undated components in which Karnaks or other Late Archaic stemmed types make up the vast majority of the point assemblages (Meadows and Bair 2000:68–75).

Further east in Franklin County, avocational excavations overseen by Robert E. Pace in the early 1980s at the Howell site (12Fr157) yielded a radiocarbon age of 4425 ± 120 RCYBP from a pit feature (Indiana State University Anthropology Laboratory records). A large surface collection from the site is dominated by Late Archaic stemmed points, including Karnak and McWhinney.

Since Late Archaic stemmed points are associated with both the early and late French Lick phases, discriminating between the two in the Data Center survey results is not possible. Late Archaic stemmed points are common, making up 19 percent of the Archaic points (the third most frequent form) recovered in the Data Center Survey.

Late Archaic Summary

Matanzas points make up the majority of points in early French Lick assemblages, with stemmed points of various types second in frequency, followed by a small percentage of deeply side-notched point forms like Big Sandy II. This assemblage composition dates as early as 5300 RCYBP and appears to have persisted to about 4500 RCYBP. It is coincident with the appearance of rock-filled and shell middens in southern Indiana. Late Archaic stemmed types increased in frequency after about 4500 RCYBP. Along the Ohio River, McWhinney points were common during this later period, along with Saratoga points. By 4000 RCYBP, Late Archaic stemmed points may have been exclusively represented in the Ohio River valley. In the hill country to the north, Karnak (stemmed and unstemmed varieties) appear to dominate some assemblages postdating 4500 RCYBP, indicating a late French Lick phase–age range of 4500 RCYBP to 3600

RCYBP. This geographic division between McWhinney in the Ohio River valley and Karnak in the hill country may represent two separate style zones (or perhaps separate phases). Riverton points define the beginning of the terminal Late Archaic period, dated to post-3600 RCYBP.

Terminal Late Archaic (3600–2700 RCYBP)

Howard Winters's (1963, 1969) seminal study of Riverton culture in the lower Wabash River valley remains the most in-depth treatment of this period. Small expanding-stem (Merom), side-notched (Trimble), and constricted-stem (Robeson) points were recovered from three shell-midden sites (Riverton, Swan Island, and Robeson Hills) in Illinois counties along the Wabash River valley (Figure 10.1). Nine radiocarbon dates obtained from the three sites span the period 3110 ± 120 to 3490 ± 200 (Winters 1969:105). Six samples analyzed by the University of Michigan have large sigmas (200–250 years) compared with those characteristic of today's high-precision radiocarbon dating. Four ages from the Riverton site are from a stratified sequence in the shell midden, and three of the four are the youngest ages from the three sites. One date from Swan Island is from a midden sample, and the remaining four dates are from pits, all of them falling after 3320 RCYBP. The five Riverton site ages have a pooled mean of 3270 ± 90 RCYBP ($T' = 1.35, \chi^2_{.05} = 9.49$), while Robeson Hills (mean = 3470 ± 140 RCYBP; $T' = .03, \chi^2_{.05} = 3.84$) and Swan Island (mean = 3460 ± 90 RCYBP; $T' = .00, \chi^2_{.05} = 3.84$) yielded somewhat older pooled means.

Anslinger (1986) analyzed a substantial Riverton assemblage recovered from the Wint (12B95) site in Bartholomew County, Indiana, on the upper East Fork of the White River (Figure 10.1). In this collection, he observed considerable overlap in morphological attributes of the small points, and, consequently, he simply lumped them into a Riverton cluster rather than attempting to distinguish the individual types identified by Winters. He reported three radiocarbon ages from the site, two of which have a pooled average of 2760 ± 90 RCYBP ($T' = .28, \chi^2_{.05} = 3.84$). The third age is 3405 ± 160 RCYBP.

Anslinger (1986) also reported single ages for samples submitted by Indiana State University from two other Riverton sites in the Wabash River valley. A pit at the Morton site (12P80), a proposed nut processing camp in Parke County (Figure 10.1), yielded an age of 2760 ± 95 (UGa 1902). The Moore Bluff Top site (12Gi17) in Gibson County (Figure 10.1) yielded a date of 3045 ± 70 (UGa 3145).

Two of the ages from the Wint site and the single age from the Morton site are substantially later than the range of Winters's dates (even with the latter's large sigmas). Sample UGa 2530 is from unstratified midden at the Wint site, but UGa 3146 is from a refuse pit within a house post-mold pattern. No significant later components were evident at the Wint site that might have led to mixing of deposits (Anslinger 1986, pers. comm. 2004). The dated pit at Morton contained a Riverton point and an ax (records on file, Indiana State University Anthropology Laboratory). Four Riverton points and an Adena point were recovered from a pit at the Moore Bluff Top site (Higgenbotham 1983:210).

A substantial Riverton occupation was encountered at the Knob Creek (12Hr484) site in the lower Ohio River valley. The Riverton occupation is immediately below an Early and Middle Woodland zone. Seventy-nine features and 325 Riverton points (like Anslinger, we lump them into a single point cluster) were recovered along a .5-km-long levee segment of the Ohio River. Six radiocarbon ages were obtained from pits in this component. Five of the ages statistically cluster, with a pooled mean of 3520 ± 30 RCYBP ($T' = 3.38, \chi^2_{.05} = 9.49$). The youngest age that is not apart of the cluster is 3140 ± 70 RCYBP (Beta 115655). The bulk of the Riverton dates from this site are at the older end of the range of Riverton ages, coinciding well with the dates Winters obtained from Robeson Hills and Swan Island.

Compared with that of Riverton points, the age of Buck Creek Barbed points is poorly understood. Morphologically, Buck Creek Barbed is similar to other terminal Late Archaic barbed points found elsewhere in the Midwest (e.g., Kampsville Barbed, Dyroff, and Springly). This point style was first identified at the Buck Creek site, a large habitation and workshop in Harrison County (Seeman 1975).

At the Knob Creek site, the Buck Creek Barbed occupation is a light-density occupation largely commingled with the Riverton assemblage. No stratigraphic separation is apparent near the top of the levee deposits. Eighty-two Buck Creek Barbed points were recovered from the site, including seven from feature contexts. A single radiocarbon date of 2980 ± 70 RCYBP (ISGS4983) was obtained from a pit feature containing the stem of a probable Buck Creek Barbed point. This age is statistically different from all but the youngest of the Riverton ages at the Knob Creek site. If the Riverton ages from Wint and Morton are accepted, then there may be some overlap in the occurrence of Riverton and Buck Creek points. Additional Buck Creek ages are required to resolve this issue.

In southwestern Indiana, Riverton points outnumber Buck Creek Barbed points in the Data Center Survey. Riverton points rank fifth in abundance (8.9 percent) and Buck Creek eighth (3.35 percent).

The ending of the terminal Late Archaic is indicated by the oldest ages available from Early Woodland occupations. The earliest southern Indiana Marion age is from the Whisman site (Da869) on the West Fork of the White River. A date of 2570 ± 60 was obtained from a Marion pit feature (Munson and Munson 2004:138). At CAP, the Early Woodland component may date to as early as 2780 ± 70 and includes Turkey-tail and Adena points (Mocas n.d.).

Settlement, Subsistence, and Mortuary Trends

In this section, we review general trends in settlement and subsistence systems, chert use, and mortuary practices during the Archaic in southern Indiana.

Settlement and Subsistence

Binford's (1980) forager-collector model has provided the framework for most of the recent settlement and subsistence studies of the Archaic. Though it may be convenient to model foragers and collectors as a dichotomy, Archaic hunter-gatherers clearly fall somewhere along a continuum between the two (Stafford 1994:223). The recent work at CAP suggests that Early Archaic settlement and subsistence, in particular, may have been more complex than the original modeling suggested.

Settlement strategies were identified in the Wabash Lowland of southwestern Indiana by examining the distribution of Archaic points across the landscape (Stafford 1994). Points collected in the Data Center Survey were correlated with stream order, which was used as a proxy for environmental diversity. Results indicated a shift from use of entire drainage basins, including the upper drainage divides, during the Early Archaic to greater concentration on the lower portion of basins near higher-order streams, including large rivers, during the Late Archaic (or late Middle Archaic and Late Archaic, as defined in Stafford 1994). This shift coincided with the appearance of multiseason base camps and a more collector-oriented foraging strategy after 5500 RCYBP (Stafford 1994).

The Bluegrass site is a rock-filled midden and mortuary site that represents one of these multiseason base camps. It is, however, situated in an interior upland location rather than in a large river valley. Although potential wetlands may have existed in poorly drained Pleistocene lakebeds nearby, aquatic resources do not appear to have been abundantly available (or were not emphasized). Analysis of well-preserved faunal remains from Bluegrass indicates a focus on white-tailed deer supplemented by small-bodied animals like squirrel, box turtle, and snake (Stafford et al. 2000). Aquatic taxa including mussel, fish, and duck were of secondary importance. The Bluegrass site is virtually identical to other multiseason base camps located near large rivers or extensive wetlands (e.g., Koster and Black Earth) in the southern Midwest. The faunal composition suggests that the collector strategy associated with these base camps could be implemented in environments where terrestrial animals predominated. Moreover, it implies that aquatic resources were not essential and that small-bodied terrestrial animals could be used as a substitute.

This is not to say that aquatic resources were not important when available. Munson (1980b) discusses the seasonal movement of bands and the use of locations along major rivers like the White and Patoka for shellfish collecting, possibly in the summer.

As in other regions of the Midwest, hickory nuts were used extensively and at least partially account for the development of rock-filled middens after 5500 RCYBP in southern Indiana. At Miler A in the Patoka Lake project, hickory nuts were, by far, the most abundant of the taxa recovered from flotation (Freudenrich 1980). Ninety-two percent of the nutshell recovered from features at Miler A was *Carya* sp. (Freudenrich 1980:539). The remaining nutshell was black walnut (*Juglans nigra*). No formal archaeobotanical analysis has been conducted of the Bluegrass flotation material, but nutshell far outnumbers wood charcoal, and cursory inspection indicates that hickory nutshell is ubiquitous in samples. At the Townsend site in Harrison County, thick-shelled hickory is ubiquitous, making up four-fifths of the nutshell recovered, followed by black walnut (Schroeder 2004).

Stafford et al. (2000) have argued that changes in the density of terrestrial resources by the middle Holocene rather than increases in aquatic resource abundance across the southern Midwest may have triggered the shift to a collector strategy. Given their habitat preferences, the prevalence of gray squirrels in the faunal assemblages from Koster, Modoc, and other sites suggests to Styles (Styles and Klippel 1996; Styles and McMillan, this volume) that a closed-canopy, mixed deciduous forest existed in the early Holocene. By the middle Holocene, a more open oak-hickory forest predominated that was more favorable to nut mast production and denser deer populations. A logistical strategy became more efficient as these terrestrial resources became more abundant. Aquatic resources were added to the diet as lower-ranking foods in large river valleys, just as small-bodied mammals and reptiles were exploited at Bluegrass, in an upland setting (Stafford et al. 2000).

Mortuary Practices

Archaic mortuary data for southern Indiana are limited. Three late Early Archaic mortuary sites are known, but only the Jerger site (Tomak 1979, 1983:70) in Daviess County has been reported in any detail (Figure 10.1). Three features were excavated that contained cremated human remains, pieces of red ocher, bifurcate points (including MacCorkle and St. Albans), broken bifaces, perforated animal teeth, and marine shell. Cremations and bifurcate points are also reported at the Steele site (Curtis H. Tomak, pers. comm. 2004), also in Daviess County, and at McCullough's Run in Bartholomew County (Cochran et al. n.d).

Mayes (1997) conducted bioarchaeological analysis of the Bluegrass human remains. Results indicate a pattern typical of Late Archaic midden cemeteries elsewhere in the Midwest. Excavation of the entire site exposed 80 burials, although an unknown number of graves had been vandalized. A typical age and sex distribution is represented at the site, with infants well represented (13.4 percent). Male mortality peaked in the 40- to 49-year age group and female between 20 and 29 years of age (Mayes 1997:54). Low rates of dental carries and abscesses were observed, and lower than expected rates of arthritis and infectious lesions were found (Mayes 1997:63–72).

Extended, loosely flexed, and tightly flexed burial positions were all represented at the site. There was no association between burial position and age or sex (Mayes 1997:77). Grave goods were found with 34 percent of the burials. Mayes (1997:77) found a statistically significant correlation between burial goods and sex and age. Adult males were more often associated with grave goods and had greater than expected numbers of artifacts. No artifacts were found with infant burials. Males were more often associated with utilitarian items (points, awls, and atlatl parts), while ornaments (shell and bone beads, bone pins, and drilled canines) and red ocher were most often found with females. Of the points recovered from burials, stemmed forms were in the majority (65 percent), and Wyandotte was the favored raw material (65 percent).

The cemetery and habitation area spatially coincide (Figure 10.21). The majority of burials are located on the crest of the ridge, where the highest densities of pit features are also located. A few graves are widely scattered on the southeast flank of the ridge. Dog burials, however, with one exception, are located on the lower part of the slope, away from the main habitation area. One dog was buried with an adult in the central part of the site.

Chert Use

Through the Archaic period, distinct patterns of chert selection and utilization emerged that largely reflect the shift from a residentially mobile forager economy to a more sedentary, logistically organized collector system. This discussion focuses on cherts utilized in projectile point production, using information primarily derived from the Data Center Survey.

Chert is generally abundant in southern Indiana (Cantin 2005; Tankersley 1989; Tomak 1970) though not ubiquitous or uniformly distributed. Thick Mississippian carbonate sequences of the Blue River (Bassett and Powell 1984) and Borden groups incorporate numerous chert types that outcrop in a belt throughout much of the central uplands. The well-known Wyandotte type as well as moderate- to high-quality Allens Creek, Attica, Indian Creek, and Muldraugh types are found in these lithologies. Silurian and Devonian units in the southeast (Laurel and Jeffersonville, respectively) are chert rich, as well. Numerous types outcrop in the Pennsylvanian lowlands of southwest Indiana, though these tend to be circumscribed and of lesser quality, save for the cryptocrystalline Holland type.

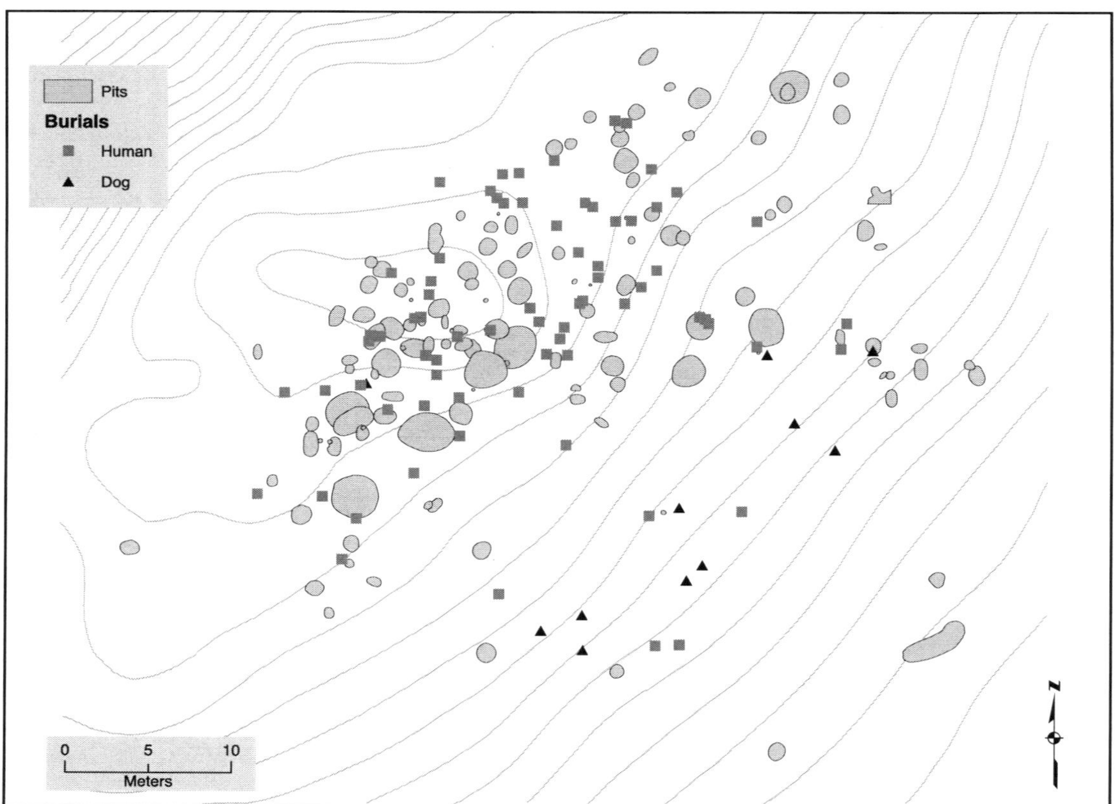

Figure 10.21. Bluegrass site map of pits and human and dog burials (contour interval 30 cm).

Early Archaic groups specifically procured cryptocrystalline materials, notably Holland and Wyandotte cherts, which account for nearly 70 percent of all cherts utilized, according to the Data Center Survey (Cantin 1989, 2000). While Early Archaic groups were relatively mobile, a reduction in mobility is documented from the preceding Paleoindian period (Cantin 1989, 2000). In western Illinois, Paleoindian groups were moving cherts over 300 km from sources in Indiana (Koldehoff and Walthall 2004, this volume). Tankersley (1989) records similar findings in Indiana. However, in southern Indiana, Early Archaic groups seldom transported cherts more than 100 km from sources (but very often beyond 50 km), though Wyandotte was moved as much as 150 km (Cantin 2000; see also Cook 1980; Munson and Munson 1984; Tomak 1981).

At the James Farnsley site (12Hr520), a large, intensive, Kirk-culture residential site and workshop, extensive use was made of the local mid-quality Muldraugh chert. At Swan's Landing, where lithic reduction was also significant, the locally available Wyandotte chert was extensively used in the Kirk occupations (Smith 1995).

Little is known of chert use during the Middle Archaic, as defined here. At the Knob Creek site, Knob Creek Stemmed points are most often manufactured from locally available Muldraugh chert (47 percent), but Wyandotte also makes up a substantial percentage (38 percent) of the assemblage.

During the Late Archaic French Lick phase, there was a greater emphasis on local cherts, regardless of quality (Cantin 1989; Cantin and Anslinger 1987; Cook 1980; Munson and Munson 1984; Tomak 1981), and a greater diversity of chert types was used compared with that seen in the Early Archaic. The Data Center Survey revealed that Wyandotte use dropped significantly (20 percent) and that gravel chert (20 percent) was used with equal frequency during this period (as represented by Matanzas points). Late Archaic stemmed forms like Oak Grove, however, are more likely to be made of Wyandotte (46 percent), as indicated by the Data Center Survey. This trend of increasing use of Wyandotte for some point types (Turkey-tail and Buck Creek Barbed) to the virtual exclusion of other cherts continued into the terminal Late Archaic (Cantin 1989; Tomak 1981). Utilitarian forms are routinely found at distances of over 150 km from Wyandotte sources. Chert consumption patterns in the Riverton culture, however, are very similar to those for French Lick–phase Matanzas points (Anslinger 1986; Tomak 1981). Often, chert pebbles found in alluvium and till were exploited (31 percent gravel chert).

Conclusions

The long stratigraphic record at the CAP and the large number of radiocarbon ages available from other sites in southern Indiana have enabled the construction of a comprehensive chronological sequence for the Archaic.

The Archaic record at the CAP encompasses most of the Holocene and includes two critical and poorly understood periods during the late Wisconsin–early Holocene transition and middle Holocene. Excavations of deeply buried cultural deposits at the James Farnsley site show a unique sequence of Early Side Notched, Thebes cluster, and Kirk Corner Notched components spanning the period 10,000–8000 RCYBP.

Middle Archaic deposits from the Knob Creek site establish a new point type (Knob Creek Stemmed) that might now be recognized in mixed surface assemblages and, thus, provide a greater understanding of the regional distribution of this complex. Clearly, a wide variety of point styles may be encountered in Middle Archaic sites in the lower Ohio River valley, some of which traditionally have been assigned to the Early Archaic period in other regions (e.g., bifurcate points).

Although Munson and Cook's (1980b) characterization of the French Lick phase has not changed significantly, recent radiocarbon ages suggest that the phase can be extended back to as early as 5300 RCYBP. Late and early French Lick phases are proposed on the basis of the change in frequency of faint-side-notched Matanzas to Late Archaic stemmed points after 4500 RCYBP. Big Sandy II side-notched points make up a small percentage of the M-B-K-S group but may be more closely associated with a yet-undefined pre-French Lick Middle Archaic phase (> 5300 RCYBP). Clearly, the French Lick phase represents, with the sudden appearance of rock-filled and shell middens, a significant shift in settlement and subsistence strategies compared with those of the highly mobile populations of the Middle Archaic in southern Indiana (e.g., Stafford et al. 2000).

New ages associated with Riverton sites suggest that this phase may have persisted as late as 2700 RCYBP and may have overlapped in time with the marginally dated Buck Creek Barbed component at the Knob Creek site in the Ohio River valley. However, the bulk of the Riverton ages from CAP coincide with the orginal time frame seen at Winters's (1969) sites in the lower Wabash Valley.

Although substantial progress has been made in fleshing out the chronological sequence in southern Indiana, further work is required on sites dating to the late Wisconsin–early Holocene and the middle Holocene to provide a definitive framework for the Archaic period and to further define stylistic differences between the southern Indiana hill country and the Ohio River valley.

Acknowledgments

We would like to thank Pat Munson, Cheryl Munson, Steve Mocas, Mike Anslinger, and Curt Tomak for freely providing unpublished information and reports on Archaic sites in southern Indiana. We have also benefited from discussions with Steve Mocas on point types as the three of us put together the classification system to be used on the Caesars Archaeological Project. We would also like to thank Cheryl and Pat Munson for extensive comments on an earlier version of this chapter and, particularly, for their suggestions related to the Late Archaic French Lick phase. Thanks to John Schwegman for the artifact photos.

Endnotes

1. In the Indiana-Kentucky border area of the Ohio River, an Early Archaic Bifurcate occupation at the Longworth-Gick site, in Jefferson County, Kentucky, dates to 8420 ± 110 (Collins 1979:579; see Jefferies, this volume).
2. We use the type name *Big Sandy II* to designate these deeply side-notched forms, rather than *Godar* or *Raddatz*, designations for types that appear to date later (i.e., postdate Matanzas) in northern Illinois and Wisconsin (see Nolan and Fishel this volume; Pleger and Stoltman, this volume; and Wiant, this volume).
3. Higginbotham (1983) reports a large number of Faulkner points recovered from survey and excavation in Gibson and Posey counties near the White River-Wabash River confluence. Faulkner points are usually considered to be equivalent to Godar/Raddatz. No point illustrations are included in Higginbotham's study, however, and a Data Center Survey in this area indicates that the points he describes are more likely Matanzas points, by far the most common side-notched form recovered from the nearby Mt. Carmel Data Center or from any other Data Center in our systematic survey.
4. We have previously used the term *late Middle Archaic* as applied in Illinois (Stafford 1994; Stafford et al. 2000) for the early part of this period (i.e., French Lick phase) in southern Indiana. With a better-defined middle Holocene sequence that shows that rock-filled and shell middens appeared after 5500 B.P., in contrast to the ephemeral occupations prior to 5500 B.P., it now seems reasonable to assign these latter components to the Middle Archaic and the former ones to the Late Archaic, as originally specified by Munson and Cook (1980a).
5. Justice (1987:111) states that Benton Stemmed exhibits oblique parallel flaking on the blade; such flaking is absent on this specimen.
6. Two of the younger radiocarbon ages were obtained on bone (4400 ± 185 [UGa 823] and 4365 ± 120 [UGa 843]).

References Cited

Angst, Michael G.
1998 *Archaeological Salvage Excavation at the Reid Site (12-Fl-1), Floyd County, Indiana.* Reports of Investigation 50. Archaeological Resources Management Service, Ball State University, Muncie, Indiana.

Anslinger, C. Michael
1986 The Riverton Culture: Lithic Systems and Parameters. Master's thesis, Department of Anthropology, Washington State University, Pullman.
1988 Bluegrass: A Middle-Late Archaic Site in Southwestern Indiana. Paper presented at the 33d Annual Midwest Archaeological Conference, Urbana, Illinois.

Bader, Ann T.
1994 *A Phase III Archaeological Data Recovery at the Mogan Site, 12Pe839, Perry County, Indiana.* MAAR Associates, Newark, Delaware.

Bassett, John L., and Richard L. Powell
1984 Stratigraphic Distribution of Cherts in Limestones of the Blue River Group in Southern Indiana. In *Prehistoric Chert Exploitation: Studies from the Midcontinent*, edited by Brian M. Butler and Ernest E. May, pp. 239–252. Occasional Papers 2. Center for Archaeological Investigations, Southern Illinois University, Carbondale.

Bellis, James
1982 Test Excavations Conducted at the Breeden Site, 12Hr11, in Harrison County. *Proceedings of the Indiana Academy of Science* 91:78–92. Indianapolis.

Binford, Lewis R.
1980 Willow Smoke and Dogs' Tails: Hunter Gatherer Settlement Systems and Archaeological Site Formation. *American Antiquity* 45:4–20.

Bradley, Bruce A.
1997 Sloan Site Biface and Projectile Point Technology. In *Sloan: A Paleoindian Dalton Cemetery in Arkansas*, edited by Dan F. Morse, pp. 53–57. Smithsonian Institution Press, Washington, D.C.

Broyles, Bettye J.
1971 *Second Preliminary Report: The St. Albans Site, Kanawha County, West Virginia, 1964–1968.* Report of Archaeological Investigations 3. West Virginia Geological and Economic Survey, Morgantown.

Cantin, Mark
1989 Diachronic Model of Hafted Biface Chert Usage in Southwestern Indiana. *Journal of the Steward Anthropological Society* 18:37–71.
2000 Comparative Analysis of Thebes and Kirk Lithic Technology and Home Range Implications in Southwestern Indiana. Master's thesis, Department of Geography, Geology, and Anthropology, Indiana State University, Terre Haute.
2005 *Provenience, Description, and Archaeological Use of Selected Chert Types of Indiana.* Technical Report 05-01. Anthropology Laboratory, Indiana State University, Terre Haute.

Cantin, Mark, and C. Michael Anslinger
1987 Variability within Middle-Late Archaic Projectile Point Morphology and Technology: Implications for the Cultural Chronology of Southwest Indiana. Paper presented at the Annual Meeting of the Indiana Academy of Science, Terre Haute.

Cantin, Mark, and C. Russell Stafford
2003 The Effect of Blade Resharpening on Stylistic Variation in Kirk Cluster Points from the James Farnsley Site. Poster presented at the 68th Annual Meeting of the Society for American Archaeology, Milwaukee, Wisconsin.

Chapman, Jefferson C.
1976 *The Icehouse Bottom Site (40MR23).* Reports of Investigations 13. Department of Anthropology, University of Tennessee, Knoxville.

Cochran, Donald R., Paige Waldron, Ron Richards, Beth McCord, and Debbie Rotman

n.d. *McCulloughs Run: A Bifurcate Tradition Cemetery in Central Indiana.* Report of Investigations 44. Archaeological Resources Management Service, Ball State University, Muncie, Indiana.

Coe, Joffre L.

1964 *Formative Cultures of the Carolina Piedmont.* Transactions of the American Philosophical Society 54. Philadelphia.

Collins, Michael B. (editor)

1979 *Excavations at Four Archaic Sites in the Lower Ohio Valley, Jefferson County, Kentucky.* Occasional Paper in Anthropology 1. Department of Anthropology, University of Kentucky, Lexington.

Cook, Thomas G.

1976 *Koster: An Artifactual Analysis of Two Archaic Phases in Westcentral Illinois.* Prehistoric Records 1. Northwestern University Archaeological Program, Evanston, Illinois.

1980 Typology and Description of Hafted Stone Tools. In *Archaeological Salvage Excavations at Patoka Lake, Indiana: Prehistoric Occupations of the Upper Patoka River Valley,* edited by Cheryl A. Munson, pp. 349–454. Research Reports 6. Glenn Black Laboratory of Archaeology, Indiana University, Bloomington.

Crabtree, Don E.

1972 *An Introduction to Flintworking.* Occasional Papers 28. Idaho Museum of Natural History, Pocatello.

Creasman, Steven D.

1996 *Final Report on the Archaeological Subsurface Reconnaissance of the Indiana Gaming Company, LP and Ameristar Casino Development Area Outside the Lawrenceburg Protective Levee.* Contract Publication Series 96-10. Cultural Resource Analysts, Lexington, Kentucky.

DeJarnette, David L., Edward B. Kurjack, and James W. Cambron

1962 Stanfield-Worley Bluff Shelter Excavations. *Journal of Alabama Archaeology* 8(1–2):1–124.

Dincauze, Dena F.

1976 *The Neville Site: 8,000 Years at Amoskeag, Manchester, New Hampshire.* Peabody Museum of Archaeology and Ethnology, Harvard University, Cambridge, Massachusetts.

Driskell, Boyce N.

1996 Stratified Late Pleistocene and Early Holocene Deposits at Dust Cave, Northwestern Alabama. In *The Paleoindian and Early Archaic Southeast,* edited by David G. Anderson and Kenneth E. Sassaman, pp. 315–330. University of Alabama Press, Tuscaloosa.

Freudenrich, Kathleen L.

1980 Archaeobotanical Remains from Patoka Lake: A Quantitative Analysis. In *Archaeological Salvage Excavations at Patoka Lake, Indiana: Prehistoric Occupations of the Upper Patoka River Valley,* edited by Cheryl A. Munson, pp. 534–554. Research Reports 6. Glenn A. Black Laboratory of Archaeology, Indiana University, Bloomington.

Gray, Henry H.

1971 *Glacial Lake Deposits in Southern Indiana: Engineering Problems and Land Use.* Report of Progress 30. Indiana Geological Survey, Indiana University, Bloomington.

2000 *Physiographic Divisions of Indiana.* Special Report 61. Indiana Geological Survey, Indiana University, Bloomington.

Hawkins, Rebecca A., and Scott A. Walley

2000 *Phase II Investigations at 12PE929, Perry County, Indiana.* Algonquin Archaeological Consultants, Cincinnati, Ohio.

Higginbotham, C. Dean

1983 An Archaeological Survey of the Lower Wabash Valley in Gibson and Posey Counties in Indiana. Ph.D. dissertation, Department of Sociology and Anthropology, Purdue University, West Lafayette, Indiana.

Janzen, Donald E.

1977 An Examination of Late Archaic Development in the Falls of the Ohio River Area. In *For the Director: Research Essays in Honor of James B. Griffin,* edited by Charles E. Cleland, pp. 123–143. Anthropological Papers 61. Museum of Anthropology, University of Michigan, Ann Arbor.

Jefferies, Richard W.

1997 Middle Archaic Bone Pins: Evidence of Mid-Holocene Regional-Scale Social Groups in the Southern Midwest. *American Antiquity* 62:464–487.

Justice, Noel

1987 *Stone Age Spear and Arrow Points of the Midcontinental and Eastern United States.* Indiana University Press, Bloomington.

Kellar, James H.

1983 *An Introduction to the Prehistory of Indiana.* Indiana Historical Society, Indianapolis.

Kendrick, James, and Robert E. Pace

1985 Test Excavations at the Amini Site: A Late Archaic Settlement in Dubois County, Indiana. Paper presented at the Annual Meeting of the Indiana Academy of Science, Bloomington.

Koldehoff, Brad, and John A. Walthall

2004 Settling In: Hunter-Gatherer Mobility during the Pleistocene-Holocene Transition in the Central Mississippi Valley. In *Aboriginal Ritual and Economy in the Eastern Woodlands: Essays in Memory of Howard Dalton Winters,* edited by Ann Marie Cantwell, Lawrence A. Conrad, and Jonathan E. Reyman, pp. 49–72. Scientific Papers 30. Illinois State Museum, Springfield.

Levy, Richard

n.d. Untitled Report on Millersburg site, Warrick County, Indiana. Manuscript on file, Anthropology Laboratory, Indiana State University, Terre Haute.

Lewis, Thomas M. N., and Madeline Kneberg Lewis

1961 *Eva: An Archaic Site.* University of Tennessee Press, Knoxville.

Maslowski, Robert F., Charles M. Niquette, and Derek M. Wingfield

1995 The Kentucky, Ohio, and West Virginia Radiocarbon Database. *West Virginia Archaeologist* 47(1–2):1–71.

Mayes, Leigh Ann

1997 The Bluegrass Site (12W162): Bioarchaeological Analysis of a Middle-Late Archaic Mortuary Site in Southwestern Indiana. Master's thesis, Department of Anthropology, University of Southern Mississippi, Hattiesburg.

McHugh, William P., and Ronald L. Michael
1984 *Archaeological Investigations at Sites 12Sw89 and 12Sw99, IPL Patriot Site, Switzerland County, Indiana*, vols. 1 and 2. GAI Consultants, Pittsburgh, Pennsylvania.

Meadows, William C., and Charles E. Bair
2000 *An Archaeological Survey of High Probability Water Course Development Areas in the East Fork White River Watershed in South Central Indiana*. Reports of Investigations 00-07. Glenn A. Black Laboratory of Archaeology, Indiana University, Bloomington.

Miller, Rex K.
1941 *McCain Site, Dubois County, Indiana*. Prehistory Research Series 2(1). Indiana Historical Society, Indianapolis.

Mocas, Stephen T.
n.d. Early Woodland and Middle Woodland Occupations at the Knob Creek Site (12Hr484). Manuscript on file, Anthropology Laboratory, Indiana State University, Terre Haute.

Mocas, Stephen T., and Edward E. Smith
1995 *Archaeological Subsurface Investigations at the Swan's Landing Site (12Hr304), Harrison County, Indiana*. Reports of Investigations 95-34. Glenn A. Black Laboratory of Archaeology, Indiana University, Bloomington.

Morrison, Gary H.
1975 Archaeological Salvage, Turpin Site: Gibson County, Indiana. Manuscript on file, Anthropology Laboratory, Indiana State University, Terre Haute.

Morrow, Toby A.
1996 Lithic Refitting and Archaeological Site Formation Processes: A Case Study from the Twin Ditch Site, Greene County, Illinois. In *Stone Tools: Theoretical Insights into Human Prehistory*, edited by George H. Odell, pp. 345–373. Plenum Press, New York.

Munson, Cheryl A.
1980a (editor) *Archaeological Salvage Excavations at Patoka Lake, Indiana: Prehistoric Occupations of the Upper Patoka River Valley*. Research Reports 6. Glenn A. Black Laboratory of Archaeology, Indiana University, Bloomongton.
1980b Comments on Subsistence and Settlement in the Upper Patoka Lake Valley. In *Archaeological Salvage Excavations at Patoka Lake, Indiana: Prehistoric Occupations of the Upper Patoka River Valley*, edited by Cheryl A. Munson, pp. 645–683. Research Reports 6. Glenn A. Black Laboratory of Archaeology, Indiana University, Bloomington.

Munson, Cheryl A., and Thomas G. Cook
1980a Chronology of the Excavated Sites: Radiocarbon Dates, Cultural Components, and Stratigraphy. In *Archaeological Salvage Excavations at Patoka Lake, Indiana: Prehistoric Occupations of the Upper Patoka River Valley*, edited by Cheryl A. Munson, pp. 468–503. Research Reports 6. Glenn A. Black Laboratory of Archaeology, Indiana University, Bloomington.
1980b The Late Archaic French Lick Phase: A Dimensional Description. In *Archaeological Salvage Excavations at Patoka Lake, Indiana: Prehistoric Occupations of the Upper Patoka River Valley*, edited by Cheryl A. Munson, pp. 721–740. Research Reports 6. Glenn A. Black Laboratory of Archaeology, Indiana University, Bloomington.

Munson, Patrick J., and Alan D. Harn
1966 Surface Collections from Three Sites in the Central Illinois River Valley. *The Wisconsin Archeologist* 47:150–168.

Munson, Patrick J., and Cheryl A. Munson
1984 Cherts and Archaic Utilization in South-Central Indiana. In *Prehistoric Chert Exploitation: Studies from the Midcontinent*, edited by Brian M. Butler and Ernest E. May, pp. 149–166. Occasional Papers 2. Center for Archaeological Investigations, Southern Illinois University, Carbondale.
2004 Marion Culture (Early Woodland) Occupations in the Wabash and White River Valleys Indiana and East-Central Illinois. In *Aboriginal Ritual and Economy in the Eastern Woodlands: Essays in Memory of Howard Dalton Winters*, edited by Ann Marie Cantwell, Lawrence A. Conrad, and Jonathan E. Reyman, pp. 133–146. Scientific Papers 30. Illinois State Museum, Springfield.

Myers, Jeffery A., and Patrick Munson
1987 *Archaeological Test Excavations at the Paynetown Light Site (12Mo193), Monroe Reservoir, Monroe County, Indiana*. Reports of Investigations 87-56. Glenn A. Black Laboratory of Archaeology, Indiana University, Bloomington.

Schock, James M., William Howell, Mary L. Bowman, Richard Alvey, Dana Beasley, and Joel Stoner
1975 *A Report on the Excavations of Two Archaic Sites (CH302 and CH307) in Christian County, Kentucky*. Bulletin 6–7. Kentucky Archaeological Association, Scottsville.

Schroeder, Marjorie B.
2004 *Carbonized Plant Remains from the Caesars Archaeological Project, Harrison County, Indiana*. Technical Report 2003-1392-11. Landscape History Program, Illinois State Museum, Springfield.

Seeman, Mark F.
1975 Buck Creek Barbed Projectile Points. *Central States Archaeological Journal* 23(3):106–109.

Sherwood, Sarah C., Boyce N. Driskell, Asa R. Randall, and Scott C. Meeks
2004 Chronology and Stratigraphy of Dust Cave, Alabama. *American Antiquity* 69:533–554.

Smith, Edward E.
1986 *An Archaeological Assessment of the Swans Landing Site (12Hr403), Harrison County, Indiana*. Reports of Investigations 86-85F20. Glenn A. Black Laboratory of Archaeology, Indiana University, Bloomington.
1995 The Swan's Landing Site (12Hr304): An Early Archaic (Kirk Horizon) Site in Harrison County, South-Central Indiana. *Midcontinental Journal of Archaeology* 20:192–238.

Smith, Edward E., and Stephen T. Mocas
1995 *Archaeological Investigations at the Paddy's West Substation near New Albany, Floyd County, Indiana*. Reports of Investigations 95-4. Glenn A. Black Laboratory of Archaeology, Indiana University, Blomington.

Stafford, C. Russell
1994 Structural Changes in Archaic Landscape Use in the Dissected Uplands of Southwestern Indiana. *American Antiquity* 59:219–237.
2004 Modeling Soil-Geomorphic Associations and Archaic Stratigraphic Sequences in the Lower Ohio River Valley. *Journal of Archaeological Science* 31:1053–1067.

Stafford, C. Russell, C. Michael Anslinger, Mark E. Cantin, and Robert E. Pace
1988 *An Analysis of Data Center Site Surveys in Southwestern Indiana.* Technical Report 3. Anthropology Laboratory, Indiana State University, Terre Haute.

Stafford, C. Russell, Ronald L. Richards, and C. Michael Anslinger
2000 The Bluegrass Fauna and Middle Archaic Foraging Diversity in the Southern Midwest. *American Antiquity* 65:317–336.

Stuiver, Minze, and Paula J. Reimer
1993 Extended ^{14}C Data Base and Revised CALIB 3.0 ^{14}C Age Calibration Program. *Radiocarbon* 35:215–230.

Styles, Bonnie W., and Walter E. Klippel
1996 Mid-Holocene Faunal Exploitation in the Southeastern United States. In *Archaeology of the Mid-Holocene Southeast*, edited by Kenneth E. Sassaman and David G. Anderson, pp. 115–133. University Press of Florida, Gainesville.

Tankersley, Kenneth B.
1989 A Close Look at the Big Picture: Early Paleoindian Lithic Resource Procurement in the Midwestern United States. In *Eastern Paleoindian Lithic Resource Use*, edited by Christopher J. Ellis and Jonathan C. Lothrop, pp. 259–292. Westview Press, Boulder, Colorado.

Tankersley, Kenneth B., and Cheryl A. Munson
1992 Comments on the Meadowcroft Rockshelter Radiocarbon Chronology and the Recognition of Coal Contamination. *American Antiquity* 57:321–326.

Tomak, Curtis H.
1970 Aboriginal Occupations in the Vicinity of Greene County, Indiana. Master's thesis, Department of Anthropology, Indiana University, Bloomington.
1979 Jerger: An Early Archaic Mortuary Site in Southwestern Indiana. *Proceedings of the Indiana Academy of Science* 88:63–69. Indianapolis.
1980 Scherschel: A Late Archaic Occupation in Southern Indiana with Appended Chert Descriptions. *Central States Archaeological Journal* 27(3):104–111.
1981 Cherts and Their Utilization in an Area of Southwestern Indiana. Paper presented at the Annual Meeting of the Indiana Historical Society, Indianapolis.
1982 *Bono: A Late Archaic Shell Midden in Lawrence County, Indiana.* Proceedings of the Indiana Academy of Science 91. Indianapolis.
1983 A Proposed Prehistoric Cultural Sequence for a Section of the Valley of the West Fork of the White River in Southwestern Indiana. *Tennessee Anthropologist* 8:67–94.
1994 Archaeological Research Project at Swan's Landing, a Buried Early Archaic Site in Harrison County, Indiana. *Tennessee Anthropologist* 19:180–191.

Tomak, Curtis H., Norma J. Tomak, and Van A. Reidhead
1980 The Early Archaic Components at the Leonard Haag Site, Dearborn County, Indiana. *Journal of Alabama Archaeology* 26(1):28–60.

Ward, G. K., and S. R. Wilson
1978 Procedures for Comparing and Combining Radiocarbon Age Determinations: A Critique. *Archaeometry* 20:19–31.

White, Andrew A.
2002 *Survey and Excavations in the Nugent East Area, Clark County, Indiana, 1998–1999.* Reports of Investigations 206. IPFW Archaeological Survey, Indiana University Purdue University, Ft. Wayne.

Wilkins, Gary R.
1985 The Hansford Site: An Archaic Site in Kanawha County, West Virginia. *West Virginia Archaeologist* 37(1):21–26.

Winters, Howard D.
1963 *An Archaeological Survey of the Wabash Valley in Illinois.* Reports of Investigations 10. Illinois State Museum, Springfield.
1969 *The Riverton Culture.* Monograph 1. Illinois Archaeological Survey, Urbana. Reports of Investigations 13. Illinois State Museum, Springfield.

Youse, Hillis J.
1983 Charleston Town Center (46KA165). *West Virginia Archaeologist* 35(1):54–56.
1985 Comments and Corrections Concerning Amos Points. *West Virginia Archaeologist* 37(2):46.

Part 3

The Mississippi River Region

11

The American Bottom: An Archaic Cultural Crossroads

Dale L. McElrath, Andrew C. Fortier, Brad Koldehoff, and Thomas E. Emerson

Introduction

The American Bottom is more famous for its late-period archaeological sites, preeminent among them the World Heritage site of Cahokia, than for its Archaic-period sites. Nevertheless, the region's preceramic period has been a major focus of research from its earliest recognition. The mid-twentieth-century pioneering excavations at the Modoc Rock Shelter (Fowler 1959a, 1959b; Fowler and Winters 1956), in the southern part of the region, served to highlight the great antiquity of cultures in the Eastern Woodlands, and although at times American Bottom Archaic research has been overshadowed by later-period research, the fascination that anthropologists have shown for hunting and gathering societies has served to continually return attention to this epoch of North American history.

The initiation of cultural resource management (CRM) research in the late 1970s led to the involvement of the authors with Archaic research in the American Bottom and laid the groundwork for this chapter. During nearly three decades of excavations and research in the area, our academically formed notions of the nature of the archaeological record have been continually challenged by the sites we have encountered and the materials we have recovered. We are convinced, now more than ever, that a robust chronology and large-scale, ongoing excavations are essential to any understanding of the past and that, even in our region, this process is still in its infancy. With this caveat, we hasten to note that the American Bottom has produced the most detailed regional chronology and one of the largest material assemblages available for the Eastern Woodlands.

History of Research

Recognizing the Archaic

The history of Archaic research in southwestern Illinois is surprisingly recent given the early antiquarian interest in this region of the Midwest; this is attributable to the attention that was initially focused on the impressive and highly visible mounds and villages that dotted the bluffline and floodplains of both the Mississippi and Illinois River valleys. Although Archaic stone points dominate the artifacts in most private and institutional collections, for many years the multicomponent nature of most surface collections and the lack of a chronology supported by excavations precluded a clear delineation of the lengthy Archaic record of habitation in this area. Two institutions, the University of Chicago (UC) and the Illinois State Museum (ISM), often in cooperation, spearheaded much of the early work on Archaic-"pattern" materials in Illinois. MacNeish's (1948; UC) work at the Faulkner site on the Ohio River and Mayer-Oakes's (1951; ISM) work at Starved Rock on the upper Illinois River were important 1940s-era excavations that generated information on the Archaic tradition and also served as the training ground for many of the archaeologists that later rose to prominence in Illinois and midwestern archaeology.

Unable to assess the antiquity of archaeological remains other than in a relative sense, these early researchers nevertheless recognized the existence of preceramic Illinois cultures by comparison with material excavated in caves and stratified open-air sites in the Southeast. Mayer-Oakes (1951) cited the Gypsum Cave excavations, and MacNeish (1948) the work at Stallings Island to infer that prepottery horizons could be pan-regional in the Eastern Woodlands. They both recognized that aceramic sites were potentially "prepottery" in origin. It was an avocational archaeologist from St. Louis, however, who first recognized and published a study of one of these Archaic cultures in southwestern Illinois. We mark the formal beginning of Archaic research in the American Bottom region with the publication of Titterington's (1950) "Some Non-Pottery Sites in the St. Louis Area." His recognition of a large-blade burial complex at several sites in Missouri and Illinois constituted the first formally defined Archaic "focus" or complex of associated tool types for the region.

The 1950s were a pivotal time for Archaic research in the Eastern Woodlands, in general, and for the American Bottom, in particular. The post–World War II period of research witnessed a concerted effort to develop relative cultural sequences from stratified cave and rockshelter sites not only to establish regional chronologies but also to identify cultural relationships between regions. Although efforts were focused both on caves and shelters and on deeply stratified floodplain sites, it was mainly the cave and rockshelter sites that yielded lengthy Archaic sequences. This eventually resulted in the recognition of projectile point types that had regional expressions and that, when recovered from surface sites, could be dated relative to other point types. Indeed, the chronological associations of most Archaic projectile point types are still based on the age ranges from these midcentury cave and shelter excavations (e.g., Stanfield-Worley, Graham, Rodgers, Russell, Modoc, etc.). However, because of their large size and often less specialized material inventories, the deeply stratified open-air floodplain sites that were the focus of much research in the later twentieth century are beginning to offer more refined contextual and chronological information (e.g., Koster, Big Eddy, James Farnsley, Nochta, etc.).

In the mid-1950s, Melvin Fowler began work at the Modoc Rock Shelter. Fortuitously, radiocarbon dating had just become available (Libby 1952). The deep rockshelter sequence revealed by Fowler's Modoc excavations was one of the first to be subjected to systematic radiocarbon dating, yielding the earliest date at the time on archaeological material from the Eastern Woodlands (Fowler 1959a, 1959b). Although this date has since been discounted (Ahler 1993, 1998; Ahler and Koldehoff, this volume), Fowler's Modoc excavations, along with more recent ones at the site (Ahler 1993; Ahler and Styles 1998; Styles et al. 1983), continue to be important for establishing regional chronologies for many of the Early Archaic horizons.

After his early and auspicious efforts at Modoc and minor excavations at the Ferry site (Fowler 1957) and at several other Archaic sites (yet unpublished), Fowler shifted his focus to the region's mound centers. At the same time, interest was growing in the definition of settlement patterns and systems and in cultural ecology. Addressing these issues required systematic and large-scale surveys to acquire the necessary data. During the two decades following the excavations at Modoc, the only significant Archaic research in the region involved documenting and classifying materials recovered from such survey projects. The efforts of Patrick Munson (1971) and Alan Harn (1971) are among the better reported of these projects, but the Historic Sites Surveys that were undertaken in the major river valleys throughout Illinois also added to the database for the American Bottom (Porter 1971, 1972; Porter and Linder 1974). Many Illinois point types were originally recognized by Howard Winters from two important surveys conducted in southern Illinois, the Cache River survey, which remains unpublished to date, and a survey of the Illinois side of the Wabash River (Winters 1967). Shortly after these surveys, Winters (1969) published his instantly famous study of the Riverton culture, a report based on test excavations at three Late Archaic sites on the Wabash River in southeastern Illinois that set the benchmark for Archaic reports in the Midwest. It served as one of the few examples worthy of emulation by later students of the Archaic time period.

The fledgling Archaic studies in the American Bottom during this period were concurrent with work in the lower Illinois Valley by Stuart Struever and his colleagues at the Koster site (Houart 1971). Indeed, because of Struever's ability to nationally promote and attract funding for the work being undertaken in the Kampsville area (Struever and Holton 1979), research there overshadowed much of the archaeology being conducted elsewhere in Illinois and the Midwest. The preliminary results of work at Koster and related Archaic studies (Cook 1976; Houart 1971; Luchterhand 1970; Struever 1973) were only beginning to impact Illinois archaeology when a far stronger force for the investigation of archaeological resources entered the scene in the form of emerging CRM programs. The development of these programs ensured the availability of funds as well as the randomness of the archaeological sites investigated. CRM research also ensures a steady supply of materials from all time periods and continually refreshes archaeologists' approaches to, and understanding and reconstructions of, the past. Although many state and federal agencies are involved in CRM research, in Illinois it is the Department of Transportation (IDOT) that has sponsored the majority of this work, since this agency routinely alters the landscape as part of its mission to provide a reliable and comprehensive transportation network for a mobile public (Emerson and Walthall 2006). It was this force for data acquisition that opened the most recent chapter on Archaic research in southwestern Illinois (McElrath et al. 1984).

Dividing the Archaic

The history and rationale behind the division of the Archaic into three subperiods—Early, Middle, and Late—are obscure, but the subperiods have become enshrined in the lexicon and researchers have imputed meaning to these arbitrary chronological divisions. The differing schools of thought on the timing and intrinsic characteristics of these subdivisions have not only shaped debate on the Archaic but in some cases have also led to unnecessary confusion and hampered communication. Therefore, a brief overview of the scheme's ramifications for the American Bottom sequence is in order.

Prior to the development of radiocarbon dating, temporal assignment of assemblages depended on the recognition of diagnostic projectile points that could be shown to be similar to points recovered from relatively dated assemblages from caves, rockshelters, or stratified floodplain sites. Scully (1951) first attempted to systematically define metric and nonmetric attributes, ages, known variants, and distribution variables for projectile point types from the central Mississippi Valley. He worked with collections acquired during Griffin and Spaulding's (1951) central Mississippi Valley survey project but also relied heavily on contemporaneous literature (primarily Chapman 1948a, 1948b; Titterington 1950). His preradiocarbon sequence reflected the "short-chronology" view then inherent in Eastern Woodlands research. For example, Scully assigned what are now considered Early Archaic points—Hardin, St. Charles, Hidden Valley, and Graham Cave—to the Late Archaic and Dalton points to the generic Archaic period.

During the 1950s, radiocarbon dating quickly expanded the time depth of the Archaic. Excavated materials from stratified deposits at Graham Cave (Logan 1952) and Modoc Rock Shelter (Fowler 1959b; Fowler and Winters 1956) were eventually dated, demonstrating the early placement of many point types (Luchterhand 1970). Luchterhand, in his study of Early Archaic point types in the lower Illinois Valley, added Thebes, Agate Basin, and Dalton to the list of early points. Since Luchterhand's time, Dalton has had an equivocal assignment, either to a transitional Paleoindian time span (largely on the basis of stylistic and production attributes of the points themselves) or to a separate horizon (Smith 1986). In the central Mississippi Valley, it seems best to view Dalton as representing the first Early Archaic horizon (see Koldehoff and Walthall, this volume). The Agate Basin point is more equivocal, and the majority of such points identified in southwestern Illinois may actually fall into the Searcy point type (Ray et al., this volume), which dates to the end portion of the Early Archaic.

The recognition of what constitutes Early Archaic has changed considerably since Ritchie (1951:132) first used a tripartite Archaic division and dated the beginning of his Archaic I period at about 3433 B.C. (uncalibrated). Fowler's subsequent early dates from Modoc Rock Shelter forced a significant reevaluation of Eastern Woodland materials previously thought to be only a few thousand years in age. Fowler (1959a, 1959b) was the first to use a tripartite division of the Archaic in southern Illinois, dividing his (uncalibrated) radiocarbon-dated sequence (8000–2000 B.C.) at Modoc Rock Shelter into three arbitrary 2,000-year periods that, he believed, reflected trends in adaptation to the immediate area. These subdivisions were the "Initial" period (8000–6000 B.C.), a second period (6000–4000 B.C) of "Local Adaptation," and a final period (4000–2000 B.C.) of "Specialized Adaptation." Although he did not refer to these as Early, Middle, and Late Archaic periods, these appellations quickly followed in the literature.

Fowler observed that side-notched points were replaced by expanding-stemmed, corner-notched, and straight-stemmed points in the later levels at Modoc (Fowler 1959a, 1959b; Fowler and Winters 1956), a fact that he used to suggest an uncalibrated date of 2500 B.C. for the Ferry site in southern Illinois (Fowler 1957). This stylistic sequence was later widely adopted to distinguish Middle from Late Archaic projectile points in other contexts, such as surface finds (Ahler 1984, 1998; Ferguson 1997; O'Brien and Warren 1983; Stafford 1985; Warren 1997). Houart (1971), reporting on test excavations at Koster, noted the strong occurrence of side-notched points in Horizon 6. Without benefit of radiocarbon dates, and on the basis of similarities with Lamoka-focus material in New York, she suggested that the horizon dated to 2500–3500 B.C. (uncalibrated) (Houart 1971:49). She referred to the "peculiar" side-notched points as "Helton," a designation that was changed to "Matanzas" (Cook 1976) in view of the points' similarity to a type defined earlier in the central Illinois Valley (Munson and Harn 1966). More extensive excavations at Koster allowed Cook (1976:91) to argue, similarly, that "Matanzas" points at that site were replaced by straight-stemmed points. Similar results were noted at other major sites such as Pigeon Roost (O'Brien and Warren 1983) and Carrier Mills (Jefferies and Lynch 1983).

At some point, which is not clear in the literature, the presumption that side-notched points were earlier than expanding-stemmed and straight-stemmed points became the basis for defining the Middle to Late Archaic shift. This seems to have occurred even though at Koster Cook treated both the side-notched (Helton phase) and later Archaic material (Titterington phase) as Late Archaic and even though the shift in point styles occurred in the middle of the third period (Specialized Adaptation) of Fowler's developmental sequence at Modoc Rock Shelter. One reason side-notched and stemmed hafted bifaces came to denote sequential Archaic subperiods may have been that these artifact categories could be easily recognized in surface collections. Indeed, most archaeologists used basal treatment of hafted bifaces as the basic criterion to assign period affiliation and, thus, study regional settlement patterns (Ahler 1998; Stafford 1985; Warren 1997).

A series of dates from several sites now indicates beyond any doubt that side-notched points were used throughout the Archaic. For example, Graham Cave Side Notched points are Early Archaic (as are Kessell Side Notched, some side-notched Kirks, and certain Thebes variants), other side-notched points (Matanzas, Raddatz, Brannon, and some Karnak varieties) are Middle Archaic, and some (Osceola and Hemphill) are Late Archaic; still others seem to fall in both Middle and Late Archaic periods (e.g., Godar). In fact, the basic descriptive categories employed (e.g., straight, contracting, and expanding stemmed and side and corner notched) in an effort to avoid theoretical concerns with the definition of "types" have not been useful for assigning age since these morphological categories are represented in all periods after fluted points declined and prior to the adoption of the bow and arrow. As a result, in the American Bottom, most researchers have reverted to projectile point type identification, a method that, despite the nihilistic views of some (e.g., Lyman et al. 1997), has a demonstrated utility.

The difficulty of identifying a Middle Archaic subdivision was exacerbated by the theoretical shifts of the early 1970s that were associated with Lewis Binford's New Archaeology. These shifts directly impacted southwestern Illinois Archaic research since two of Binford's UC students, Stuart Struever and James Brown, were instrumental in shaping the Center for American Archeology's (CAA) Koster site research. The CAA became the training ground in the Midwest for the New Archaeology approach. One of the goals of this approach was modeling the relationships between hunter-gatherers and their environments (e.g., Carlson 1979). Archaic-period societies became the focus of much research, as they were viewed as the archaeological correlates of historic and modern hunter-gatherers. This focus dovetailed quite well with and fostered advances in several ancillary sciences, including faunal analysis, botanical analysis, and efforts at environmental reconstruction based on pollen cores and geomorphology. These specialized studies had received a shot in the arm from Struever's (1968) practical new flotation method of retrieving faunal and floral remains from archaeological deposits.

The New Archaeology was decidedly ecological and rejected all earlier, less theoretically informed efforts as of little value; the dominant mantra became adaptation, largely ignoring Fowler's (1959b) earlier use of both ecological and adaptational concepts to describe the archaeological record at Modoc Rock Shelter. Out of a new wave of environmental studies emerged the recognition of the Hypsithermal. Dating to 8500–5100 B.P. (uncalibrated) (Wendland and Bryson 1974), this mid-Holocene drying, warming period fit quite comfortably into the middle of the Archaic sequence. This new climatic model was seen as correlated with, and causally linked to, material shifts in the Archaic sequence. By 1983, Brown and Vierra were able to declare an end to the mystery surrounding the Middle Archaic and suggested that it had "lost some of its vagueness as a long, indefinite transition between the more clearly conceived Early and Late Archaic periods" (1983:165).

Their oft-cited article "What Happened in the Middle Archaic?" was the first widely circulated publication to suggest a relationship between the Hypsithermal and a Middle Archaic abandonment of the Illinois uplands, an idea that Brown and Vierra (1983:167) mistakenly credit to Carmichael (1977). While Carmichael had conducted several surveys in the uplands of Illinois and was concerned with the location of water resources (specifically, glacial kettles) and their impact on human occupation, he never mentioned the Hypsithermal or suggested abandonment during the Middle Archaic period. It was Walter Klippel (Klippel and Maddox 1977) who noted a strong relationship between the time-transgressive nature of changing vegetative patterns and site locations in central Illinois and Lawrence Conrad (1981) who suggested upland abandonment during Middle Archaic times as a direct result of environmental deterioration associated with the Hypsithermal.

The general endorsement of this hypothesis had a solidifying effect on the chronological boundaries used for the Middle Archaic, especially for the interface between the Middle and Late Archaic. The transition prior to 6000 B.C. (uncalibrated) from the securely dated artifact sequences in the Southeast (Broyles 1971; Coe 1964) that terminated with several varieties of Kirk to an enigmatic but remarkably consistent and widespread bifurcate horizon was largely accepted by Midwest archaeologists as representing the Early–Middle Archaic boundary. This dating not only conformed roughly to the original period divisions suggested by Fowler (1959b) for his Initial Archaic period but it also was essentially replicated at the Koster site (Brown and Vierra 1983).

The termination date of the Middle Archaic was extended to about 3000 B.C. to avoid having the Helton phase straddle the Middle and Late Archaic boundary and because of strong differences between Helton-phase and subsequent Titterington-phase materials. The beginning and ending dates have been modified somewhat with ^{14}C calibration, but the assignment of the Helton phase to the Middle Archaic has been standard since Brown and Vierra (1983). The timing, dating, and consequences of the Hypsithermal (Styles and McMillan, this volume; Van Nest 1997) have proven much more difficult to model than expected, and it is unlikely that researchers will be able to continue to view this climatic watershed as the triggering mechanism to explain cultural change during the Archaic. The rationale for the subdivisions of the Archaic in southwestern Illinois remains arbitrary, and attempts to reify these subdivisions as logical evolutionary steps have been futile.

American Bottom Region Physiography

The American Bottom (Figure 11.1) is defined physiographically as the broad expanse of floodplain that extends from below the confluence of the Illinois, Missouri, and Mississippi rivers south to the confluence of the Kaskaskia and Mississippi rivers. As a cultural region, the boundaries are more vague. In the 1970s, researchers began to refer to the bluff line and adjacent uplands that form the valley margin as part of the American Bottom "region," and for the late prehistoric periods, the Silver Creek drainage on the east and the two short forks of the Wood River to the north seem to have formed obvious

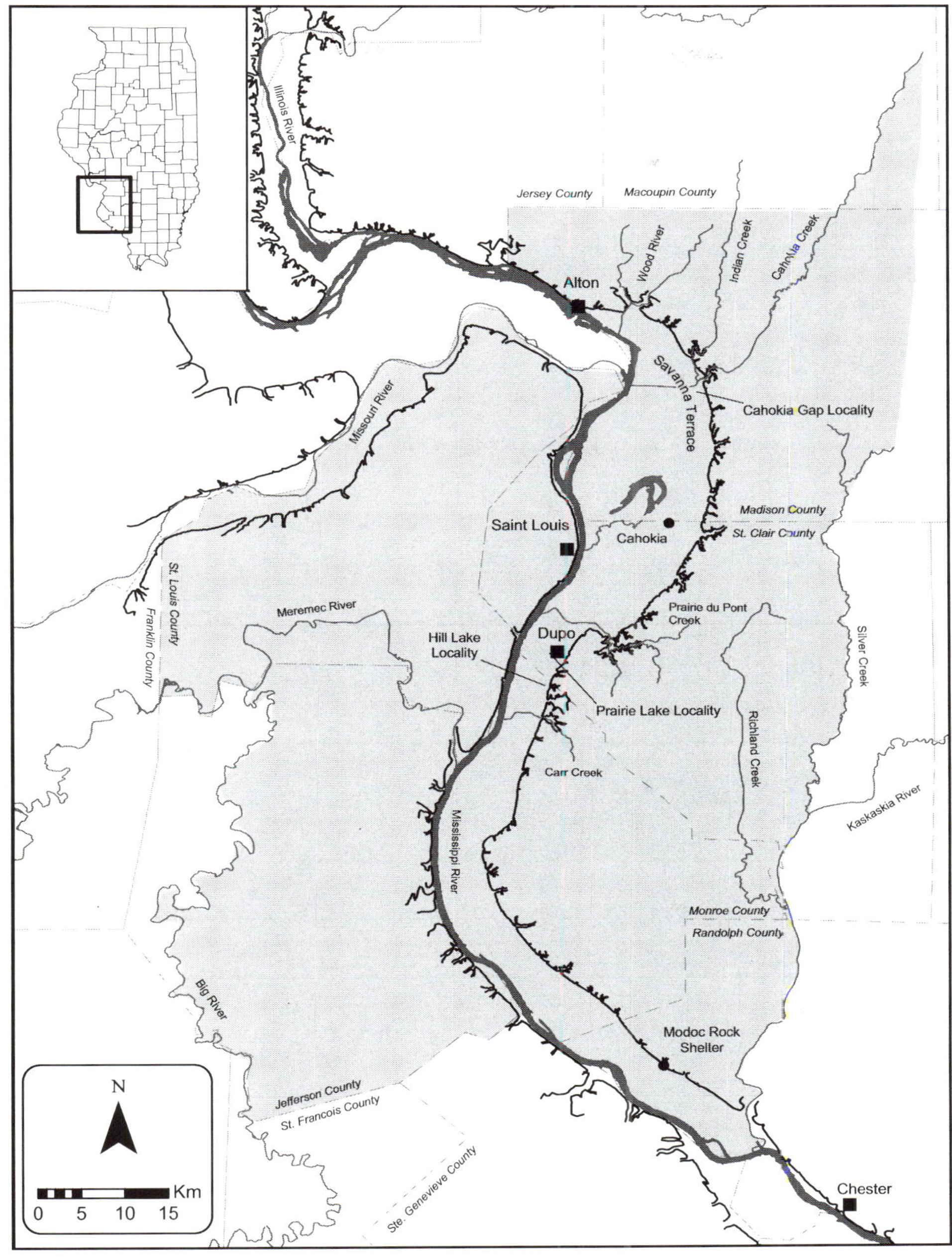

Figure 11.1. American Bottom region.

cultural boundaries. The western boundary is more nebulous, even for later periods, but the St. Louis and Jefferson counties area of northeastern Missouri, extending as far south as the Meramec River, was usually within the area of influence of whatever social milieu characterized the Illinois side of the Mississippi River at any particular point in time. For the Archaic period, these subjective boundaries have considerable fluidity. As we demonstrate below, in prehistoric times this major river confluence area was a crossroads for influences emanating from several areas (e.g., the Plains, Midwest, Midsouth, and Ozark areas), and it fell under the sway of one or the other of these areas throughout the Archaic period. In fact, we argue that the American Bottom was often underpopulated and only at the periphery of cultural developments that unfolded elsewhere; it was only in the later prehistoric period that this region came to dominate, for a short time, the central Mississippi Valley (Emerson 2002; Fortier and McElrath 2002; McElrath et al. 2000; Milner 1998; Pauketat 2004).

The American Bottom comprises diverse physiographic and biotic zones, most of which were utilized by Archaic populations at one time or another (Figure 11.2). Traditionally, the American Bottom has been dichotomized into the flood-

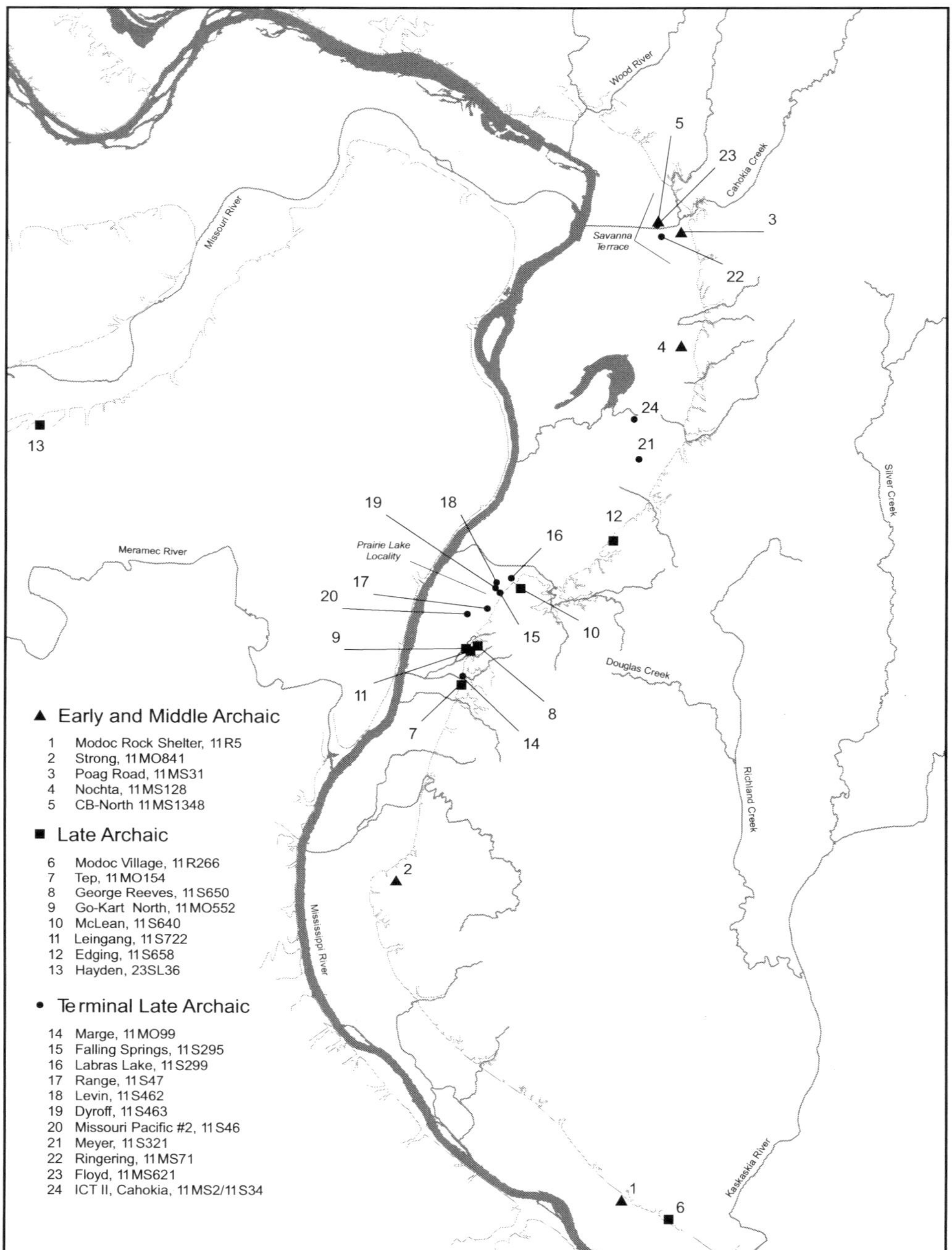

Figure 11.2. American Bottom Archaic sites and major landscape features.

plain regime of the Mississippi River trench and the adjacent uplands. However, these two general units are much more complex and more similar to one another than this division would imply. Many of the significant landscape features of the American Bottom have been detailed elsewhere (Hajic 1993; Hajic et al. 2000; Higgins 1990; Munson 1974; Watters et al. 2001; White et al. 1984; Yerkes 1987), but specific aspects of the geomorphological history are particularly relevant to Archaic research.

The Mississippi River Floodplain

Most of the detailed information regarding the Mississippi River floodplain has been generated by geomorphologists working in tandem with CRM archaeologists on IDOT highway projects (Hajic 1993; Rissing 1991; White et al. 1984). For example, the FAI-270 and FAP-310 projects alone have traversed a nearly 96-km north–south path through the heart of the floodplain and into the adjoining uplands. Thousands of soil cores and many dozens of geomorphological trenches have been placed along these corridors to establish the landscape histories of individual site localities and landscape feature development as well as the historical effect of the Mississippi River on the formation of major landforms. Many of the landforms or soil horizons have been dated, enabling reconstructions of the general histories of many floodplain features. In essence, there are two major landscapes, one centered on the Savanna Terrace in the northern American Bottom and another comprising a vast meander belt south of this terrace formation. Both have complex histories that we can only summarize here.

The most prominent floodplain landscape feature in the northern American Bottom is a massive sand terrace, known as the Savanna Terrace belt (earlier referred to as the Festus or Wood River Terrace). This terrace, a late glacial (late Wisconsinan) remnant, runs from the mouth of Wood River to approximately the midpoint of the McDonough Lake meander scar, 18 km to the south (Flock 1983; Hajic 1993; Hajic et al. 2000). It varies in width but is as much as several kilometers wide in places and rises in elevation 5–6 m above the modern floodplain (Figure 11.3). It was formed around 12,200 B.P. (uncalibrated) and developed over older Henry Formation sands (Hajic 1993:58). The western edge of the terrace is mostly mantled with sand dunes. Most archaeological resources, especially occupations dating to the Archaic, have been buried by duning or eolian processes. A prime example is the Ringering site, a multicomponent Archaic and Early Woodland site situated on the apex of the Savanna Terrace (Evans and Evans 2000), just south of where Cahokia Creek cuts through the terrace; numerous stratified archaeological occupations are buried by dunes above the main terrace. Just 1 km to the north is the terminal Late Archaic Floyd site, a large occupation situated on the outer bank of a Cahokia Creek paleochannel meander (Evans 2001). This site is not buried since it lies within the old Cahokia Creek meander that scoured away the earlier Savanna Terrace sands. Several hundred meters to the north is the Compensatory Basin site, a Paleoindian and Early Archaic site, situated on Savanna Terrace deposits and buried by eolian sand deposits (Evans et al. 1997). These site examples evidence the kind of geomorphological complexity that characterizes the Savanna Terrace remnant.

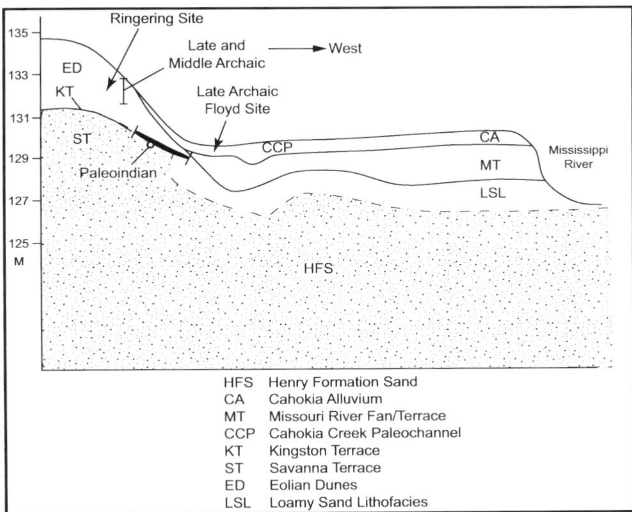

Figure 11.3. Transect of Savanna Terrace (adapted from Hajic et al. 2000:84).

The area to the east, between the Savanna Terrace and the bluff escarpment, is characterized by braided and scoured surfaces resulting from older (late Pleistocene) Mississippi River and subsequent creek meanders of upland origin. Much of the archaeology in this zone has been obliterated, but some buried horizons exist that have been mantled by eroding bluff colluvium, and older surfaces are not visible. It is a complex landscape in its own right and, to date, has been poorly investigated by archaeologists.

Adjacent to the Savanna Terrace to the west, and at a lower elevation, are deposits of the Kingston Terrace, a river-cut terrace formed sometime between 12,300 and 10,400 B.P. (uncalibrated), which has also been mostly buried by eolian dunes. It lies approximately 3–4 m above the modern floodplain. Farther to the west is evidence of a vast fan formed by the Missouri River. It extends from the mouth of Wood River to the McDonough and Edelhardt lakes meander belt complex and slopes downward ca 1.5 m, paralleling the Savanna Terrace; it is truncated by numerous meander scars. Between the Savanna and Kingston terraces and the modern Mississippi River trench is a vast flat feature referred to as the Mississippi River Meander Belt. It was formed by accreted clays and silts from the Mississippi River and is situated 3–3.7 m above the modern floodplain. The accreted clays have effectively buried earlier meander banks, in places up to 3 m. The potential for earlier Archaic or even Paleoindian materials to occur beneath the accreted zone is great but extremely challenging to evaluate archaeologically. Virtually all surficial traces of older meander banks or inner-channel islands, prime locations for Archaic populations in other areas of the American Bottom, are buried. These aspects of landscape formation are in stark contrast to the processes characterizing the central and southern American Bottom floodplain.

The area south of the Edelhardt Lake and Horseshoe Lake meander belt is a sequence of overlapping Mississippi River meander scars. Unlike the case in the northern portion of the American Bottom, individual meander features (e.g., point bars, outer banks, splay ridges, and inner-channel bars) are prominently visible on the modern surface. Some features, including meander channels, are buried beneath river alluvium or, in the case of bluff-base features, under loessal colluvium or creek alluvium. The cut-off dates for many of the meanders have been established, so a partial historical sequence of major channel abandonments can be delineated. Some older features, not related to channel formation, still remain in this area, such as the East St. Louis Rise, a high, unaltered area rimming the northern end of the Prairie Lake locality, and Miles Prairie, an old glacial sand remnant located near Fountain Creek. All of these zones, including the exposed meander banks, offered ideal settlement localities for Archaic populations. In addition, unlike the northern area, the southern and central American Bottom floodplain is skirted by abrupt limestone exposures that offered inhabitants access to chert sources and other rocks as well as places for temporary shelter, for example, Modoc Rock Shelter (Ahler et al. 1992). To date, researchers have identified nearly 70 distinguishable chert types outcropping along the bluff line or exposed in creeks emptying into the Mississippi River floodplain (Koldehoff 2002; McElrath and Emerson 2000).

In addition to the effect of meander scouring, which has resulted in the obliteration of older surfaces in the central meander belt (Munson 1974), many localities have been buried by associated riverine sediments. For example, excavations at the ICT II Cahokia locality revealed a good example of a buried sandy point-bar surface that was subsequently covered by backwater clays deposited by the Spring Lake meander (Nassaney et al. 1983). The Spring Lake meander point-bar surface had been the location of a significant Late Archaic Prairie Lake–phase occupation. There are, no doubt, many similar situations in the central meander belt of the American Bottom.

An important locus of Archaic occupation was associated with the Waterloo-Dupo Anticline. This bedrock uplift and associated dip in topography, occurring just south of the city of Dupo, creates a notable break in the limestone escarpment. The bluffline in this location is low-lying, allowing easy access between the floodplain and adjacent uplands. The Go-Kart North site, a large Titterington-phase occupation, sits at the base of this topographic low on the outer bank of the Hill Lake meander, which represented an active Mississippi River meander at the time of occupation. In addition, just above Go-Kart North along the rim of the bluff line are several Archaic occupations (the George Reeves, Leingang, and Mund House sites), clearly situated here to take advantage of the easy transit between major environmental regimes (McElrath et al. 1984).

Another important locus of Late Archaic occupation in the central portion of the floodplain is found in the Prairie Lake and adjacent Labras Lake localities (McElrath et al. 1984; Yerkes 1987). These localities sustained a relatively large terminal Late Archaic population, as evidenced at the Missouri Pacific #2, Range, Dyroff, Levin, and Labras Lake sites, where excavations by the FAI-270 project in the late 1970s in relatively small areas revealed over 1,200 pit features. So dense are the cumulative occupations that this locality has been referred to in the literature as a terminal Late Archaic base locale (Emerson 1984; Emerson and McElrath 1983). We would add that the setting of the Floyd and Ringering sites near the Savanna Terrace at the far north end of the Bottom has also been characterized as a terminal Late Archaic base locale (see discussion of the Prairie Lake phase below).

The Prairie Lake channel was cut off ca. cal 4300 B.C. (White et al. 1984), but the area was not settled until ca. cal 1400 B.C. during terminal Late Archaic times. At the time of Archaic settlement, the Prairie Lake locality would have essentially been a large paludal oxbow lake and marsh environment and, as such, an ideal source of abundant aquatic resources. As one of the older meander channels in the central floodplain, it was cut off by the Goose Lake Meander to the north and the Hill Lake Meander to the south. For much of the Archaic period, therefore, it would have been a raised island within a vast surrounding marsh. Occupations at the Range site alone extended from about cal 1400 B.C. to A.D. 1300, demonstrating that this was one of the most stable land surfaces in the American Bottom.

Forested Uplands

Equally complex in terms of physiographic and biotic zones are the uplands that bracket the Mississippi River trench and floodplain. We differentiate here between the uplands on the Illinois side of the river and those west of the river in Missouri. Because few modern highway transects have crossed through the uplands, less geomorphic work has been conducted and fewer archaeological sites have been excavated there. Nevertheless, numerous surveys and collector interviews have revealed a multitude of Archaic sites and materials in these environs (Koldehoff 2006).

A major distinction can be made within the Illinois uplands between drainage regimes emptying into the Mississippi floodplain and those draining into the Kaskaskia River to the east. The creek valleys that course through the eastern American Bottom uplands drain into the Kaskaskia and are generally of low relief. From west to east, the most prominent of these creeks are Richland and Silver. Silver Creek has seen a considerable amount of archaeological activity, especially because of the IDOT-sponsored Scott Air Force Base Archaeological Mitigation Project, and, as a result, the Silver Creek environment has been extensively described, with early historic records and soils information used to reconstruct vegetation zones (Watters 2001). This creek extends in a north–south direction for 97 km before it empties into the Kaskaskia River and is the most extensive drainage in the adjacent American Bottom uplands.

Six distinct environmental zones can be defined within the Silver Creek drainage, including slope-edge forest, bottomland forest and marshlands, savanna, flatwoods, prairie, and the Shiloh Uplands (Figure 11.4). The bottomland-marshland zone was the floodplain regime of Silver Creek itself. The greatest plant diversity in the uplands was found here, including sources of nuts and timber for shelter, woodcrafts, and fuel. Fauna were also abundant. Between the floodplain and the highest topography, the Shiloh Uplands, was the slope-edge forest. Relief is sloping, wood and wildlife resources were historically abundant, and the area is better drained than the

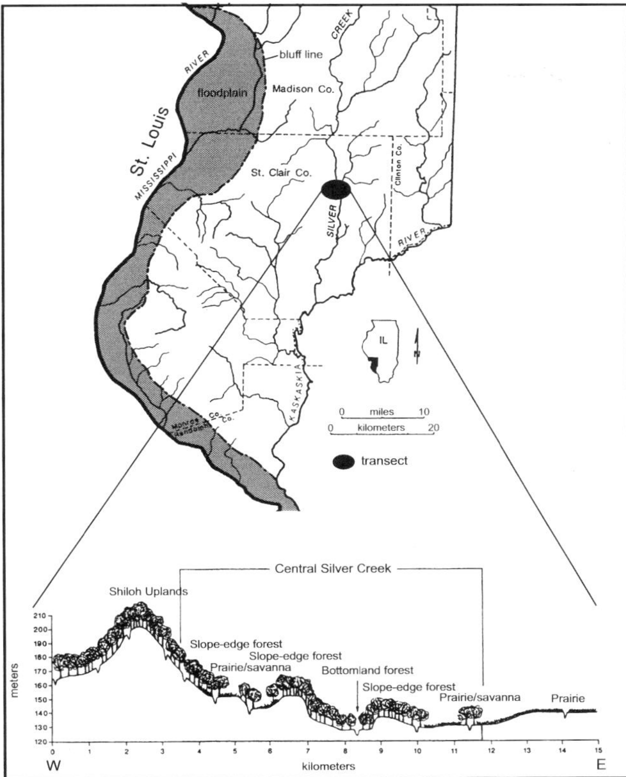

Figure 11.4. Biotic transect of Silver Creek (adapted from Waters 2001).

bottomlands. Most of the archaeological sites found in the Silver Creek drainage are located in this regime. The Shiloh Uplands area, located north and west of Silver Creek, is a landscape of high, well-drained, rolling relief that was once heavily forested. It separates the Silver Creek drainage from the adjacent Richland Creek drainage area. Prairie occurred in various areas but was most extensive east of Silver Creek. It had little timber, and included both poorly drained (wet prairie) and well-drained (dry prairie) areas. The prairie had few resources, and its archaeological signature is low. Between the prairie and bottomlands was the savanna. Viewed as a tension zone between the floodplain and prairie, it was poorly timbered, consisting of small groves and grasslands. Fewer resources occurred than in the bottomlands or slope-edge forest zones, but some faunal resources, such as deer, would have been available here. The flatwoods was a discontinuous zone of small, poorly drained areas typically within savanna. Resources were poor in these environments, and sites are few. The Richland Creek drainage resembled that of Silver Creek but had fewer areas of prairie.

The second upland area on the Illinois side consists of dissected bluff line and interior tributary drainages of the Mississippi River. In the north, these drainages are Piasa, Wood River, Indian, and Cahokia creeks. These drainages have carved out broad floodplains. Many of these creeks carry vast loads of loess that have buried localities within their valleys and formed large alluvial fans extending out into the Mississippi River floodplain. The central American Bottom creeks, including Judy's Branch, Burdick, Canteen, Schoolhouse, and Schoenberger, are similar to those of the north, although their ravines tend to be deep with narrow valleys and associated floodplains, allowing less space for habitation. Finally, the southern drainages include Prairie du Pont, Carr, Hill Lake, Hill Creek, Palmer, Long Slash, Fountain, Fults, and Maeystown creeks, which provide easy access to bluff and upland chert and till resources. These creeks have created alluvial fans in the main valley that may contain deeply buried archaeological resources. These fans and associated valley openings were heavily timbered, as were the bluffs, except for scattered hill prairies and cedar glades.

Another feature of the Illinois uplands is karst, or sinkhole, topography, which is especially prominent along the bluff crests running in a band from Dupo on the north to the mouth of the Kaskaskia River on the south, some 48 km. Karst topography also appears on the Missouri side of the river and extends 65–80 km south of where the Meramec River empties into the Mississippi. Sinkhole ponds provide small patches of aquatic resources and were clearly utilized by prehistoric populations in the area, although little is known about their specific use during the Archaic period.

We include in the American Bottom locality an upland band paralleling the Mississippi River valley in St. Louis and Jefferson counties, Missouri. This zone represents the northeast part of the Ozark Plateau. It is unglaciated and lacks extensive loess deposits. Residual and mostly unweathered chert deposits are common. While spatially restricted, chert from this area was utilized extensively by pre-Columbian people in the Mississippi floodplain. This area of Missouri uplands is particularly rich in the high-quality Burlington chert (Crescent Hills, or Crescent-quarry, chert) that dominates many local Archaic assemblages. In the headwater reaches of the Meramec River, hard hematite, which was used for the manufacture of plummets and pigments, was also easily procured.

Lithic Resources

The floodplain of the Mississippi River, while rich in biotic resources, is a lithic-poor landscape: it is devoid of rock, except in scattered gravel lenses along sand bars and at occasional bedrock exposures along the active channel. In contrast, the adjacent bluff faces and uplands tend to be rich in lithic resources, containing not only various sedimentary rock formations and chert deposits but also concentrations of minerals. The Missouri Ozarks are especially mineral rich. The types of regionally available lithic resources found on archaeological sites as well as extraregional materials (e.g., Cobden chert from southern Illinois) furnish solid clues to the direction, distance, and intensity of prehistoric lithic procurement, which, in turn, furnish insights into settlement mobility and social networks.

On the basis of bedrock geology, the bluffs and adjoining uplands can be divided into three resource zones: the Pennsylvanian uplands, a chert-poor landscape underlain by Pennsylvanian System bedrock; the Mississippian uplands, a chert-rich landscape underlain by Mississippian System bedrock; and the Missouri Ozarks, a chert-rich and mineral-rich landscape underlain primarily by Ordovician and Cambrian System bedrock (Figure 11.5). Across the Missouri Ozarks, chert and quartzite from a series of Ordovician formations are widely available and were routinely used by Archaic groups, especially chert from the Jefferson City Formation (Ray 1985). The bulk of the mineral resources in the Missouri Ozarks fall along the southwest margin of the American Bottom region, and many of these resources are known to have been extensively used by Archaic groups. For instance, galena and hematite were extracted from source areas in Franklin, Washington, and St. Francois counties in addition to adjacent sections of Jefferson and Ste. Genevieve counties (Emerson and Hughes 2000; Holmes 1919; Walthall 1981). Precambrian igneous intrusions in St. Francois County and outliers in Ste. Genevieve County provided hard-rock resources (e.g., basalt, granite, and rhyolite) that were used for both chipped-stone and ground-stone tools (Ray 1985).

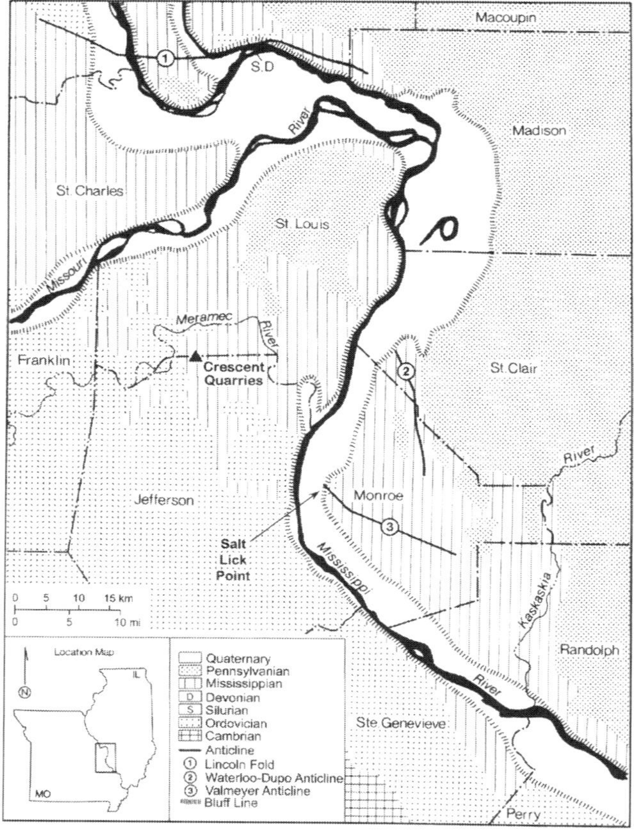

Figure 11.5. Bedrock geology of the American Bottom region (adapted from Koldehoff 1987).

The Mississippian uplands contain numerous exposures of several chert-rich formations: Fern Glen, Burlington, Salem, St. Louis, and Ste. Genevieve. The Burlington Formation is particularly noteworthy because it is endowed with massive layers of chert. In some locations, the Burlington Limestone long ago weathered away, leaving dense, residual layers of moderate- to high-quality chert. Nowhere are these residual deposits richer than in the Crescent Hills area of southern St. Louis and northern Jefferson counties, Missouri (Figure 11.5). Here quarry pits and workshops dot the landscape, and the earliest are undoubtedly Archaic (Fowke 1928; Ives 1975; Titterington 1937). The Crescent quarries, as Fowke noted, represent a chert source of regional importance: "Nearly all of the chipped implements found within 50 miles of St. Louis in any direction are made from this deposit" (1928:532). In Illinois, Burlington-chert exposures are common in the Mississippi River bluffs near Alton and Valmeyer. The bluffs at Valmeyer jut out into the valley, forming a prominent landmark known as Salt Lick Point (Figure 11.5). Here several chert types, in addition to Burlington, are available and were regularly used by Archaic groups (Koldehoff 2002). Salt Lick Point is the southernmost source area for Burlington chert in Illinois. In interior Monroe County, especially around Waterloo (along the Waterloo-Dupo Anticline), chert resources are common, and many were used by Dalton and other Early Archaic groups (Koldehoff 1985, 2002; Walthall and Koldehoff 1999; Woods and Mitchell 1978). Several chert types (Salem, St. Louis, and Ste. Genevieve), in addition to minor deposits of hematite, are available in the uplands of southwest St. Clair County (Booth and Koldehoff 1999:9). These resources are not plentiful or of outstanding quality but are important because they were readily accessible to the sizable Late Archaic populations that inhabited the nearby bottomlands (Emerson and McElrath 1983; Fortier 1983; Yerkes 1987). Finally, at the southern margin of the American Bottom region, the chert-rich Kinkaid Formation is exposed in the Mississippi River bluff in Randolph County, south of the Kaskaskia River.

The Pennsylvanian uplands, compared with the Ozarks and the Mississippian uplands, are less rich. For example, bedrock exposures are uncommon and largely composed of alternating layers of thinly bedded and weakly cemented sandstone, siltstone, limestone, shale, and coal. Chert is uncommon or absent in all of these units. The erodibility of these units accounts for the low elevation of the bluffs and the great breadth of the Mississippi floodplain in Madison and St. Clair counties. Two members of the Carbondale Formation, the St. David Limestone and the Excello Shale, are known to be chert bearing, but chert deposits within these units are undocumented for much of the region. An exception is Blair chert, which is associated with the St. David Limestone in interior Randolph County (Koldehoff 1985).

The uplands in Illinois, unlike those in Missouri (south of the Missouri River), are blanketed by varying amounts of glacial till. In addition to chert cobbles, till deposits hold cobbles of various igneous and metamorphic rock types. These hard-rock cobbles were used for hammerstones and plant-processing tools and were shaped into formal tools and ornaments (e.g., axes, bannerstones, and gorgets). Till deposits on occasion have produced rare and unusual raw materials, like nuggets of native copper (see Goodman 1984). Banded slate, a raw material commonly used in bannerstone production, has been collected from local till exposures (by Koldehoff) as well as from till exposures in the Wabash Valley (Winters 1967:20). Thus, tools and ornaments fashioned from such seemingly exotic raw materials as copper and banded slate may, in fact, be made from locally collected cobbles. Likewise, chipped-stone raw materials from northern Illinois and Wisconsin are potentially available in local till deposits. However, till cherts are of limited utility because of their small cobble size and weathered condition; accordingly, they were little used in the American Bottom region. This latter point is understandable given the number of primary chert sources available in the region.

Archaic Database

In this chapter we reexamine both the excavated Archaic sites in the American Bottom and several large regional surface collections recovered by professional and avocational archaeologists. This redresses one of the limitations of the published American Bottom Archaic record (e.g., McElrath et al. 1984): although it includes an impressive number of systematically excavated, analyzed, and well-dated Archaic sites, it is primarily representative of a small segment of the northwestern margin of the region (the mid-Holocene floodplain meander belt and immediately adjacent bluff line). In the past, we have not had comparably analyzed surface materials that have allowed us to address issues of relative diachronic landscape use (i.e., settlement systems) and overall distribution of Archaic materials at the regional level (i.e., settlement patterns). This database continues to grow with newly excavated materials becoming available on almost an annual basis: the majority of the larger surface surveys, however, took place decades ago and collections have been unanalyzed or underreported. Although large survey projects were undertaken during the 1970s (Ahler 1984; Harn 1971; Kelly et al. 1979; Jackson 1979; Linder et al. 1978; Munson 1971; Porter 1971, 1972; Porter and Linder 1974; Woods and Mitchell 1978), it was not until the 1980s that most of the Archaic chronology was constructed (McElrath et al. 1984). The most recent attempts to examine Archaic settlement patterns took place about two decades ago (Ahler 1984; see also Ahler 1998; Emerson et al. 1986). We have been fortunate for this study to be able to reference several large collections that have recently been made available. The insights gained by comparing the excavated and surface-collected materials have enabled new perspectives on the Archaic occupation and use of American Bottom landscapes.

Excavated Sites

The number of excavated Archaic sites in the American Bottom region continues to grow, but the source of most of the area database remains those sites excavated as part of the FAI-270 highway corridor project and its various extensions. It is perhaps an indication of the state of knowledge prior to that project that almost every site that yielded significant Archaic materials served to define a new phase; this was true of Dyroff-Levin (Prairie Lake phase; Emerson 1980), Go-Kart North (Titterington phase; Fortier 1984), George Reeves (Mule Road phase; McElrath 1993), and Labras Lake (Labras Lake phase; Phillips and Hall 1981). This pattern continued with the Nochta site (Nochta phase; Higgins 1990) and with the Strong site, the first non-highway excavated site to provide information sufficient to name an Archaic phase (Dennis Hollow phase; Walz et al. 1998) in the American Bottom region. In addition to these cornerstones of Archaic research, several excavations have solidified and expanded understanding of the various Archaic phases: Missouri Pacific #2 (McElrath and Fortier 1983), Ringering (Evans and Evans 2000), and Floyd (Evans 2001). The excavation of several small sites—Marge (Fortier 1996), Meyer (Fortier et al. 1998), and Wooded (Abbott 1989)—has improved understanding of the settlement system during specific subperiods. Finally, archaeologists continue to revisit earlier excavations to reassess the significance of material from multicomponent sites such as Range (Fortier 1987), Tep (Moffat 1980), and Leingang (Bentz 1988). Continuing analyses of the materials from the pivotal Modoc Rock Shelter (Ahler 1993, 1998; Ahler et al. 1992; Ahler and Koldehoff, this volume) have expanded understanding of the Archaic sequence, especially in terms of subsistence data.

Because not all sites subject to disturbance are threatened by projects that involve funded investigations, salvage archaeology is alive and well, as illustrated by the excavation of several dozen Archaic-age features from the bluff-top Modoc Village site (Ahler and Koldehoff 2002). We should also point out that our colleagues across the Mississippi River have actively added to the Archaic database for the American Bottom (Harl, this volume); and, finally, we should add that new data continue to be added through excavation, as is true, for example, at the recently excavated Edging site, which contains a significant Falling Springs component (21 McLean points, primarily of heat-treated Burlington chert, were recovered from feature context). Our experience suggests the importance of reexamining previously collected material in light of more recent developments. The insights that can be gained underscore the importance of well-curated assemblages and fully documented site reports with accurate drawings or photographs to identify appropriate diagnostics that can be accessed by future researchers.

Radiocarbon Dates

When the summary *American Bottom Archaeology* volume was published in 1984, 28 uncalibrated Archaic radiocarbon dates from only seven sites were available to researchers (excluding dates from Modoc Rock Shelter), and all were associated with the Late Archaic period (Bareis and Porter 1984:Appendix B). Today there are 69 dates from 19 sites, including 12 dates from Middle and Early Archaic context. Table 11.1 presents all known Archaic dates from the American Bottom region, except for those from the Modoc Rock Shelter (see Ahler and Koldehoff, this volume). These dates have been calibrated using the CALIB 3.03c program, developed at the University of Washington (Stuiver and Reimer 1993:215–230).

All of the cultural dates were run from feature-context material, rather than stratigraphic levels or geomorphic context. When possible, pits with diagnostic material were selected for dating. However, it is extremely rare at most sites to find diagnostic artifacts in Archaic pits. The typical pattern is for artifacts to be distributed about pits, but pits themselves seldom yield diagnostics. So, many of our Archaic dates are derived by association. Materials from pits were deemed suitable for dating when associated with a single cluster of point types representative of a specific phase. For example, at the Go-Kart North site, virtually all

Table 11.1. Calibrated Archaic Dates from the American Bottom.

Lab No.	Site	Phase	B.P.	S.D.	Uncorrected B.C. Dates	Calibrated B.C. Dates (1 sigma)	Reference
ISGS-599	Mo-Pac #2, S46	Prairie Lake	2540	75	590	800 (771) 529	McElrath and Fortier 1983
RL-1287	Labras Lake, S299	Prairie Lake	2670	130	920	922 (814) 771	Yerkes 1987
ISGS-605	Mo-Pac #2, S46	Prairie Lake	2755	75	805	988 (900) 818	McElrath and Fortier 1983
ISGS-3690	Floyd, MS621	Prairie Lake	2790	90	840	1023 (916) 827	Evans 2001
ISGS-588	Mo-Pac #2, S46	Prairie Lake	2800	75	850	1016 (922) 839	McElrath and Fortier 1983
ISGS-3686	Floyd, MS621	Prairie Lake	2810	80	860	1035 (927) 842	Evans 2001
ISGS-3682	Floyd, MS621	Prairie Lake	2820	70	870	1035 (976, 965, 935) 867	Evans 2001
ISGS-3687	Floyd, MS621	Prairie Lake	2830	80	880	1112 (987, 956, 944) 867	Evans 2001
ISGS-3683	Floyd, MS621	Prairie Lake	2850	70	900	1117 (999) 910	Evans 2001
ISGS-3685	Floyd, MS621	Prairie Lake	2850	70	900	1117 (999) 910	Evans 2001
ISGS-601	Mo-Pac #2, S46	Prairie Lake	2860	75	910	1123 (1004) 913	McElrath and Fortier 1983
RL-1291	Labras Lake, S299	Prairie Lake	2880	140	930	1262 (1022) 848	Yerkes 1987
ISGS-3684	Floyd, MS621	Prairie Lake	2890	80	940	1197 (1034) 927	Evans 2001
RL-1292	Labras Lake, S299	Prairie Lake	2900	160	950	1313 (1045) 848	Yerkes 1987
RL-1357	Labras Lake, S299	Prairie Lake	2910	140	960	1306 (1112, 1101, 1064) 905	Yerkes 1987
ISGS-3691	Floyd, MS621	Prairie Lake	2990	80	1040	1376 (1254, 1243, 1213) 1062	Evans 2001
RL-1285	Labras Lake, S299	Prairie Lake	3020	130	1070	1415 (1262) 1034	Yerkes 1987
Beta 5310	Cahokia ICT	Prairie Lake	3110	80	1160	1436 (1396) 1264	Nassaney et al. 1983
RL-1283	Labras Lake, S299	Labras Lake	3120	140	1170	1518 (1401) 1204	Yerkes 1987
Beta 5307	Cahokia ICT	Prairie Lake	3140	100	1190	1513 (1410) 1267	Nassaney et al. 1983
RL-1061	Labras Lake, S299	Labras Lake	3180	140	1230	1606 (1429) 1267	Yerkes 1987
RL-1294	Labras Lake, S299	Labras Lake	3220	130	1270	1626 (1504, 1477, 1462) 1324	Yerkes 1987
RL-1231	Labras Lake, S299	Labras Lake	3220	130	1270	1626 (1504, 1477, 1462) 1324	Yerkes 1987
ISGS-2197	Marge, MO99	Labras Lake	3210	70	1260	1523 (1494, 1486, 1450) 1409	Fortier 1996
Beta 5309	Cahokia ICT	Prairie Lake	3210	60	1260	1520 (1494, 1486, 1450) 1414	Nassaney et al. 1983
ISGS-2196	Marge, MO99	Labras Lake	3300	80	1350	1677 (1527) 1461	Fortier 1996
ISGS-2195	Marge, MO99	Labras Lake	3330	80	1380	1731 (1613) 1515	Fortier 1996
ISGS-2198	Marge, MO99	Labras Lake	3360	70	1410	1737 (1671, 1664, 1636) 1524	Fortier 1996
ISGS-2194	Marge, MO99	Labras Lake	3380	70	1430	1743 (1677) 1529	Fortier 1996
RL-1233	Labras Lake, S299	Labras Lake	3460	140	1510	1936 (1745) 1540	Yerkes 1987

Table 11.1. Calibrated Archaic Dates from the American Bottom, continued.

Lab No.	Site	Phase	B.P.	S.D.	Uncorrected B.C. Dates	Calibrated B.C. Dates (1 sigma)	Reference
ISGS-687	George Reeves, S650	Mule Road	3710	120	1760	1925 (2128, 2080, 2045) 2281	McElrath and Finney 1987
?	Hayden, 23SL36[a]	Titterington	3930	60	1980	2326 (2457) 2475	Harl 1995
?	Hayden, 23SL36[a]	Titterington	3950	70	2000	2337 (2461) 2558	Harl 1995
ISGS-628	Go-Kart North, MO552	Titterington	4020	100	2070	2409 (2558, 2530, 2497) 2850	Fortier 1984
?	Hayden, 23SL36[a]	Titterington	4010	60	2060	2461 (2553, 2534, 2493) 2582	Harl 1995
ISGS-629	Go-Kart North, MO552	Titterington	4060	100	2110	2464 (2577) 2863	Fortier 1984
ISGS-695	Go-Kart North, MO552	Titterington	4060	80	2110	2468 (2577) 2856	Fortier 1984
?	Hayden, 23SL36[a]	Titterington	4080	70	2130	2493 (2586) 2860	Harl 1995
ISGS-698	Go-Kart North, MO552	Titterington	4100	75	2150	2466 (2615) 2867	Fortier 1984
ISGS-693	Go-Kart North, MO552	Titterington	4100	130	2150	2466 (2615) 2879	Fortier 1984
ISGS-697	Go-Kart North, MO552	Titterington	4130	75	2180	2509 (2853, 2822, 2660, 2660, 2625) 2874	Fortier 1984
ISGS-630	Go-Kart North, MO552	Tiitterington	4110	100	2160	2493 (2836, 2829, 2618) 2875	Fortier 1984
ISGS-5751	Edging, S658	unknown	4260	70	2310	2706 (2886) 2915	reported here
ISGS-5814	McLean, S640	Falling Springs	4280	70	2330	2784 (2890) 2920	reported here
ISGS-5811	McLean, S640	Falling Springs	4320	70	2370	2883 (2913) 3022	reported here
ISGS-5813	McLean, S640	Falling Springs	4340	70	2390	2887 (2917) 3033	reported here
ISGS-730	McLean, S640	Falling Springs	4360	120	2410	2881 (2921) 3260	McElrath 1986
ISGS-5749	Edging, S658	unknown	4580	70	2630	3110 (3350) 3491	reported here
ISGS-736	McLean, S640	Falling Springs	4600	75	2650	3131 (3357) 3497	McElrath 1986
Beta 14094	Lone Wolf, 23SL467[a]	Falling Springs	4860	80	2910	3539 (3647) 3706	Hamilton et al. 1986
ISGS-5750	Edging, S658	unknown	4870	70	2920	3547 (3649) 3706	reported here
ISGS-983	Tep, MO154	Tep complex	5150	100	3200	3804 (3965) 4038	Moffat 1980
ISGS-4915	Modoc Village, R266	Falling Springs	5180	70	3230	3950 (3977) 4038	Ahler and Koldehoff 2002
ISGS-769	Leingang, MO722	Tep complex	5290	90	3340	3982 (4217, 4202, 4156, 4154, 4138, 4130, 4047) 4246	Bentz 1988
ISGS-4921	Modoc Village, R266	Tep complex	5330	70	3380	4010 (4222, 4192, 4156) 4311	Ahler and Koldehoff 2002
ISGS-926	Mund House, S695	Tep complex	5360	100	3410	4040 (4228) 4334	reported here
ISGS-4914	Modoc Village, R266	Tep complex	5430	80	3480	4164 (4349, 4323, 4281, 4262) 4349	Ahler and Koldehoff 2002
ISGS-1490	Nochta, MS128	Nochta	6180	120	4230	4942 (5197, 5181, 5133, 5124, 5077) 5256	Higgins 1990
ISGS-1494	Nochta, MS128	Nochta	6450	120	4500	5266 (5420, 5402, 5379, 5356, 5345) 5447	Higgins 1990
ISGS-1573	Nochta, MS128	Nochta	6490	90	4540	5319 (5433) 5448	Higgins 1990
B-74743	Strong, MO841	Dennis Hollow	6560	90	4610	5386 (5445) 5571	Adams et al. 1997
B-84740	Strong, MO841	Dennis Hollow	6630	80	4680	5443 (5566, 5549, 5524) 5588	Adams et al. 1997
B-84742	Strong, MO841	Dennis Hollow	6680	80	4730	5482 (5577, 5541, 5530) 5601	Adams et al. 1997
B-74745	Strong, MO841	Dennis Hollow	6760	70	4810	5579 (5600) 5674	Adams et al. 1997
ISGS-2910	Ringering, MS71	Middle Archaic	6770	140	4820	5524 (5611) 5725	Evans and Evans 2000
B-74744	Strong, MO841	Dennis Hollow	6780	70	4830	5587 (5621) 5686	Adams et al. 1997
B-84741	Strong, MO841	Dennis Hollow	6870	80	4920	5626 (5698) 5765	Adams et al. 1997
ISGS-1492	Nochta, MS128	Nochta	6890	170	4940	5591 (5710) 5944	Higgins 1990
ISGS-A-0597	Kaskaskia Mine, R687	Early Archaic	8050	35	6100	6820 (7030) 6820	reported here

[a]Missouri.

of the point types recovered, such as Etley and Wadlow, are hallmarks of the Titterington phase in the Midwest. A tight cluster of seven dates from pits (lacking Titterington points in their fill) supported a single-component Titterington occupation. In multicomponent situations, the general rule has been not to run radiocarbon dates. An exception to this sampling procedure was made at the Edging site, where two dates were run on suspected Archaic proveniences. Table 1 indicates that these dates fall somewhere in the Archaic sequence, but the chronological placement matches none of the dated Archaic point types recovered from the site. Overall, the 69 radiocarbon dates from the American Bottom have consistently supported the general cultural sequence based on projectile point seriation.

Mortuary Data

Archaic burials are known from only a few sites in the American Bottom, with the best sample obtained from the various Modoc excavations (Anderson 1991; Neumann 1967). A small number of burials date to Early Archaic times. Most have not been reported fully, but Neumann (1967) examined the human remains from the original Modoc Rock Shelter excavations (Fowler 1959b), and Anderson (1991) reexamined the Modoc Rock Shelter specimens subsequent to the 1980s excavations, identifying four individuals (three adults and one infant) from "late Early Archaic" levels. More recently, a burial was removed from the bluff face in Randolph County, where it had been exposed by mining operations. The remains were those of an adolescent (12–15 years of age) of undetermined sex, who had been buried in a flexed position in a pit excavated into the living surface of a rockshelter or cave (Hargrave et al. 2006). Collagen from bone yielded an AMS date of 8050 ± 35 RCYBP (cal 7030 B.C.).

The sample for the Middle Archaic is somewhat larger and includes recognizable burials from open-site context at Nochta (Higgins 1990). Three individuals are represented by interments in domestic pit features; they are poorly preserved, providing little information concerning age, sex, or health status prior to death. Twenty-nine burials are associated with Middle Archaic levels at Modoc, including individuals from all age categories (i.e., infants, children, adolescents, and young and old adults); 13 of these burials were associated with "Helton phase" levels at the rockshelter. Nine individuals were recovered from Late Archaic contexts (Anderson 1991). Full description, dating, and stable carbon and nitrogen analysis of the Archaic individuals from Modoc would considerably enhance, perhaps even revolutionize, understanding of diet during the Archaic period in the American Bottom region.

Survey Data

The information from upland settings that is essential to place excavated sites in and along the Mississippi floodplain within a regional context has been lacking in American Bottom Archaic studies. While numerous large-scale surveys have covered portions of the Mississippi floodplain and Illinois uplands (e.g., Denny 1976; Gums and Kelly 1989; Harn 1971; Holley et al. 2001; Jackson 1980; Kelly et al. 1979; Linder et al. 1978; Munson 1971; Porter 1971, 1972; Porter and Linder 1974), the information presented in the survey reports is variable and was largely recorded prior to the delineation and refinement of the Archaic phases discussed in this chapter. Therefore, to generate information about patterns of settlement and lithic procurement and to create a database in which entries were consistently recorded, Koldehoff (2006) recently examined 2,620 points surface collected from seven upland study areas (Figure 11.6). Because materials from earlier surveys have not been systematically examined in light of currently recognized type diagnostics by phase, we base our discussion of relative occurrence of Archaic points by phase primarily on Koldehoff's survey data.

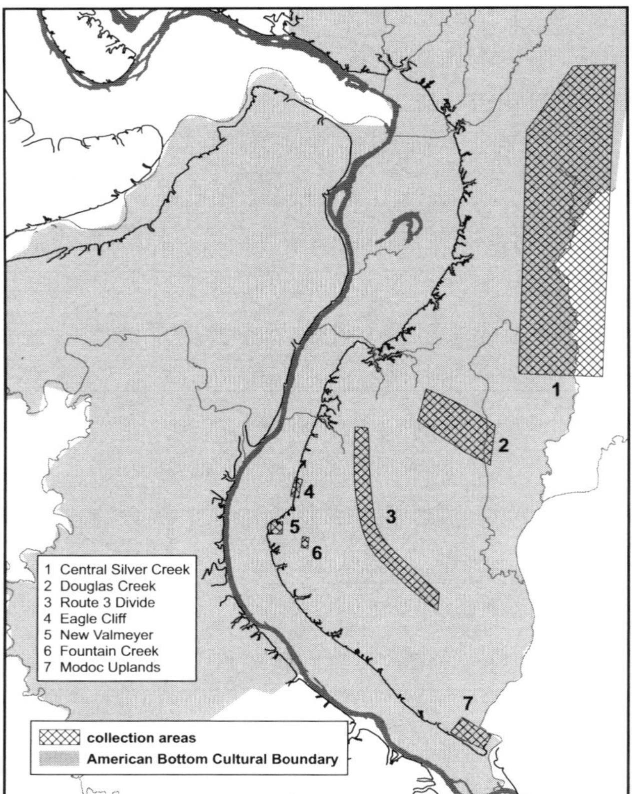

Figure 11.6. American Bottom region upland survey areas.

The Archaic Sequence

Division of the Archaic into archaeological phases has followed its earlier division into three subperiods. Prior to the 1970s, the American Bottom possessed a single defined Archaic phase (i.e., Titterington). The number increased to four during the FAI-270 project (McElrath et al. 1984) then to seven in more recent times (Fortier et al. 2006), and in this chapter we propose one new archaeological complex (Figure 11.7). We also recognize several new point types affiliated with specific phases, and we have established that several point types were previously systematically misidentified, resulting in erroneously constructed chronological and distributional patterns. Three such misidentifications pertain to the present discussion:

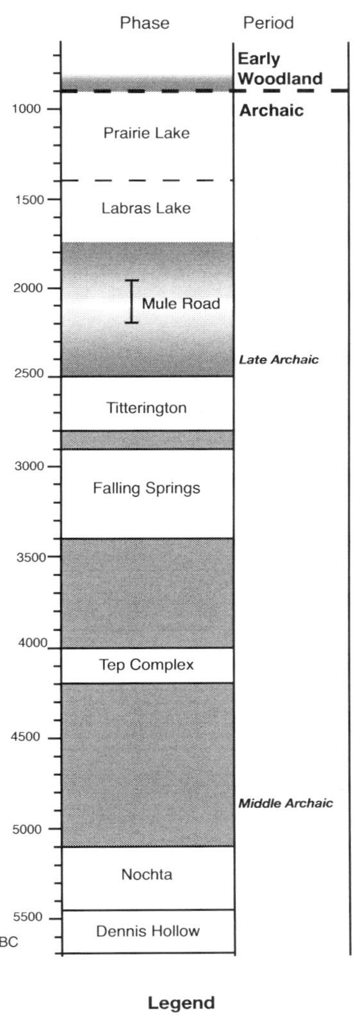

Figure 11.7. American Bottom Archaic chronology chart.

(1) Mund Late Woodland dart points (Fortier et al. 1983) were consistently identified as "Matanzas" points during earlier surveys (Kelly et al. 1979) and we suspect are occasionally so identified even today; (2) the expanding-stemmed Ferry types (see Fowler 1957, 1959b) are demonstrably associated with the Late Archaic Falling Springs phase but were sometimes misidentified as Late Woodland Lowe/Steuben expanding-stemmed types or Middle Woodland Manker and Snyders types; and (3) the straight-stemmed Middle Archaic Karnak points, such as those recovered from the Tep site, were originally thought to be Early Woodland Kramer points (Moffat 1980). Given this level of confusion, one can understand how earlier surveys resulted in ambiguous or even erroneous settlement-pattern reconstruction. We acknowledge that confusion may still surround some less well-dated point types, particularly Early Archaic types for which we lack radiocarbon determinations.

We also acknowledge the importance that point (hafted biface) types play in our understanding of the Archaic record. The existence of point "types" was hotly disputed in recent decades as the type concept became caught up in the "normative" debates of the mid- to late twentieth century (Lyman and O'Brien 2004). After years of struggling with this conundrum, we have chosen to employ point types while at the same time acknowledging the theoretical risk of such an approach. We believe that the recognition of spatially and temporally sensitive attributes allows certain chipped-stone artifacts to be grouped within clusters of affiliated types for the purpose of recognizing de facto population distributions and social group interaction during preceramic times. We think that this approach is suitable for answering some of the questions that arise out of the historical approach that we favor in archaeology (Emerson and McElrath 2001; Fortier and McElrath 2002; McElrath et al. 2000; Pauketat 2001a, 2001b). We believe that the information and insight into the archaeological record generated by this approach will be superior to results obtained through alternative approaches that have been offered.

We do not operate under the assumption that a one-to-one correlation exists between points and people, but we assume that projectile point manufacture was a technique passed down from tutor to student and that lithic technicians tended to conform to recognizable "communities of practice" or ethnic cores (i.e., Emerson and McElrath 2001) that, over time, formed traditions (Pauketat 2001b). We maintain, therefore, as others do in this volume, that point types are sensitive group identity markers and, therefore, should reflect spatial and temporal boundaries conforming to the movement and period of occupation of specific ethnic groups (McElrath et al. ch. 1, this volume). As Emerson and McElrath have put it,

> It seems possible to recognize ethnic groups in the archaeological record, perhaps not as tightly circumscribed, impenetrable material clusters, but as ethnic cores (cf. Van den Berghe 1981) with permeable bounds and as communities of practice that have a material dimension (cf. Lightfoot

> and Martinez 1995:481–482). . . . Whether one frames this research in terms of communities of practice, ethnic cores, boundaries or other models of group interaction, to identify them we must look across broad social and spatial regimes within well-defined chronological and spatial parameters. This requires that archaeologists build strong historical sequences in those areas in which we seek to understand the developments, interactions, and transformations of historical and cultural traditions. [2001:201–202]

As to the problem of "essentialism," which purportedly hampers the point-type classification method, we note that all categories are arbitrary and, as such, do not exist other than as humanly created heuristic devices; therefore, essentialism is "essential" to all organizational schema, whether emic or etic. The advantage that we see in classifying hafted bifaces by type is that the artifacts span the entire Archaic period and provide a common denominator for interregional and chronological comparisons.

Early Archaic

The mid-to-late Holocene age of most of the physiographic features in the American Bottom floodplain generally precludes the surface recovery of Early Archaic materials. Indeed, the surveys by Harn (1971), Munson (1971), and Kelly (Kelly et al. 1979) produced very few Early Archaic diagnostics from floodplain contexts. Earlier surfaces are exposed on the relict Savanna Terrace as well as the adjacent bluffs and uplands. However, in the case of the Savanna Terrace, much duning and reworking has obscured any Early Archaic materials. Along the bluffs and in the uplands, decades of plowing and erosion have turned up many early points and tools, but this process has reduced the likelihood of finding intact features and living surfaces. Although Munson (1971) reports the presence of a Dalton point in one of the private collections that he documented, the vast majority of the sites he referred to as Archaic are, in hindsight, Middle to Late Archaic in age. More recent work has yielded a few fluted points and several Early Archaic points from the Savanna Terrace (e.g., Booth and Dasovich 2006; Evans et al. 1997), but the majority of work along this landform has yielded more recent Archaic materials (Evans 2001; Evans and Evans 2000).

An exception to this generalization is the excavation of early deposits at the deeply buried Nochta site, located at the southern end of the Savanna Terrace. Early and Middle Archaic components were located on a linear sand ridge that was eventually buried by Mississippi River backwater clays from overbank-deposited silt (Figure 11.8). For the most part, Early Archaic features appear to be dug into, or located on, the sand surface of the ridge, while Middle Archaic occupations are in clay deposits downslope from the apex of the ridge. Only a preliminary analysis of this important site has been presented thus far (Higgins 1990). Hundreds of tools and diagnostics from the upper ridge area exhibit some mixing on the buried living surface. This site yielded Dalton, Hardin Barbed, Kirk Corner Notched, and bifurcated points (Figures 11.9 and 11.10) from an areally expansive living surface with associated features (Higgins 1990). Among the best-represented points were several examples that were originally classified as Agate Basin points (Figure 11.10) but were subsequently reclassified as Searcy (or Rice Lanceolate or Titus); Jack Ray verified this reclassification at the 2004 Urbana Archaic Conference. Searcy points are typically made from heat-treated cherts and, with repeated blade resharpening, develop a rather marked left-hand bevel. Additionally, blade edges are often serrated. These points have been stratigraphically dated at Big Eddy and other sites in the Missouri Ozarks to the more recent end of the Early Archaic sequence (cal 6575–5950 B.C.) and may be closely related temporally or culturally to Hidden Valley Stemmed points (Ray et al., this volume).

The temporal relationship between the several Early Archaic occupations at Nochta remains speculative, but the distribution of piece-plotted diagnostics suggests separate but overlapping occupations centering on subtly differing aspects of the site locale. On the basis of geomorphic setting and diagnostic artifact distribution, site excavators estimate that at least 156 features (including hearths, pits, and rock concentrations) located along the upper portion of the sand ridge represent Early Archaic occupations (Figure 11.11). Three Dalton point fragments were recovered from two pit features and a hearth, none of which contained datable charcoal. While none of the numerous diagnostics were recovered from feature context (precluding the association of features with specific point styles; Higgins 1990:74), all can be comfortably assigned to the Early Archaic time period. A large number of ground-stone implements, including grooved axes (Figure 11.12), manos, metates, and pitted cobbles were recovered from the Early Archaic living surface, suggesting the site served as a base camp for at least some part of the Early Archaic period. Tool-grade cobbles were cached at the site, either in anticipation of occupants' return or because such items are rare in the immediate site vicinity. The axes within the Early Archaic area (minimally, eight piece-plotted specimens) are all fully grooved. The association of fully grooved axes with the Early Archaic occupation is supported by their co-occurrence with Early Archaic diagnostic points on the same buried living surface. The chert tool assemblage is impressive, with bifacial preforms, drills, adzes, bifaces, wedges, and dozens of cores having been recovered from the Early Archaic surface, indicating chipped-stone tool production, maintenance, and recycling. A 25-percent sample of the Early Archaic features examined for botanical remains (Parker 1990) indicated use of thick-shelled nuts (hickory, walnut, or both) and some seed plants and consumption of fleshy fruits such as grape, sumac, and black haw (see Simon, this volume). This site has produced the most significant Early Archaic-period materials excavated to date from an open-air context in the American Bottom.

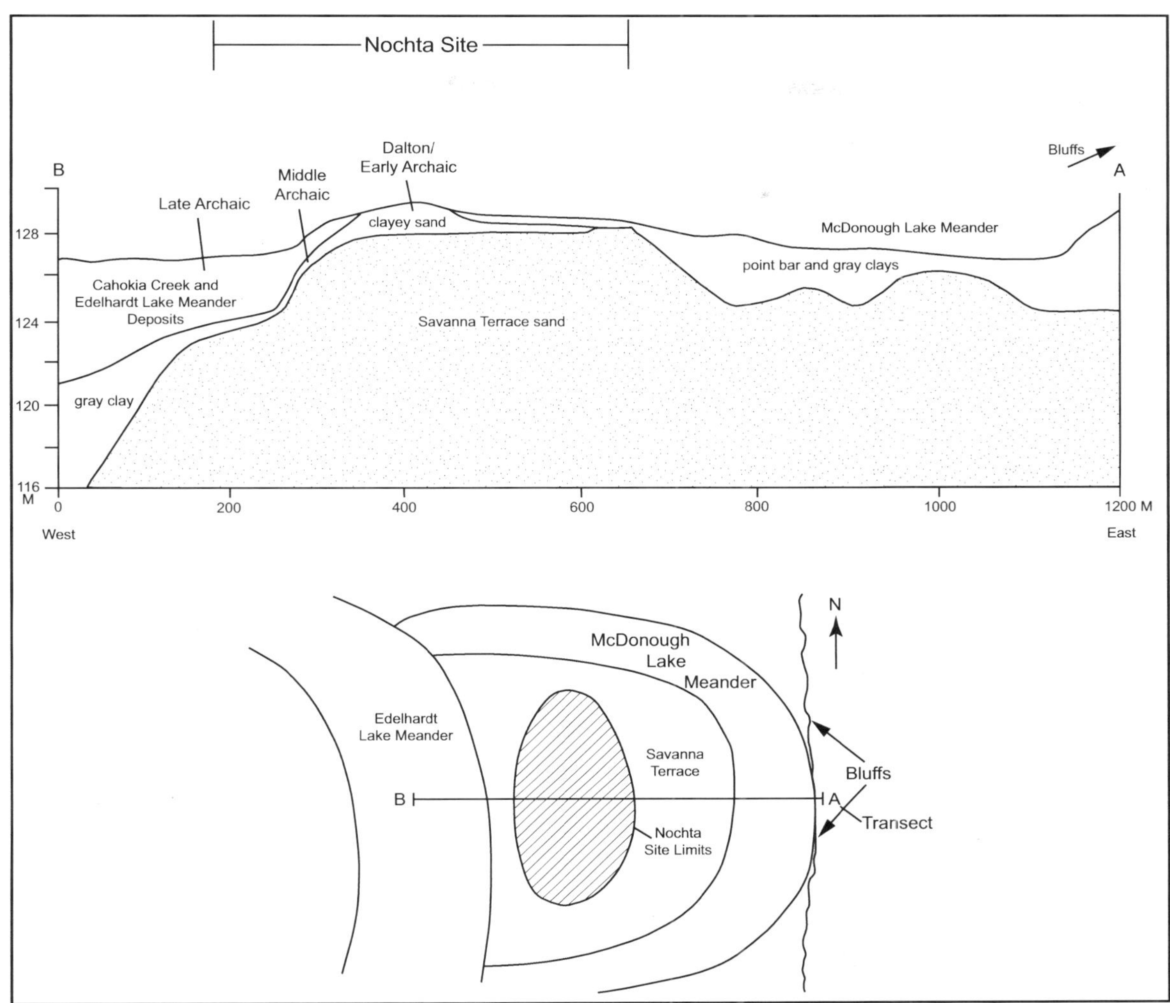

Figure 11.8. Transect of the Nochta site locality (adapted from Higgins 1990).

Early Archaic materials are also represented in the southern American Bottom at the Modoc Rock Shelter (Ahler 1993; Ahler et al. 1992; Ahler and Koldehoff, this volume; Ahler and Styles 1998; Fowler 1959a, 1959b; Fowler and Winters 1956). This site is particularly valuable for the environmental and subsistence data it provides for the American Bottom Early and Middle Archaic periods (Styles and McMillan, this volume). Additionally, many diagnostic Early Archaic point types are datable at the Modoc Rock Shelter. Many of the individual living surfaces sampled at the shelter failed to yield diagnostic points, but by correlating the assemblages from several related strata among the various excavation units, Ahler and Koldehoff (this volume) were able to bracket chronological periods for several of the Early Archaic point types recognized in the American Bottom.

This new analysis demonstrated (Ahler 1993; Ahler and Koldehoff, this volume) that no Dalton occupations occurred at Modoc. Although Dalton points have been recovered from the shelter, they appear to be "found" points that were recycled. Dalton as well as many other Early Archaic points were regularly found and recycled, especially during Middle Archaic times, a situation that attests to the level of cultural (e.g., burning, pit excavation) or natural (e.g., erosion) land disturbance during mid-Holocene times.

Information from Modoc (Ahler and Koldehoff, this volume) indicates that Graham Cave Side Notched points date between 9000 and 8500 B.P. (cal 8100–7600 B.C.), and several point types date between 8500 and 8000 B.P. (cal 7600–7100 B.C.): Kirk Corner Notched cluster, Searcy, Hidden Valley Stemmed, Bifurcate cluster, and a possible Big Sandy side notched. These point types cannot be placed in a sequence, raising the issue of use of single versus multiple point types by a single cultural unit or during a single occupational episode. The excellent separation of cultural horizons at the Big Eddy site supports the single or dual point-type perspective (Ray et al., this volume). Therefore, it is likely that the diversity of early point types at Modoc dated to 8500–8000 B.P. (cal 7600–7100 B.C.) represents

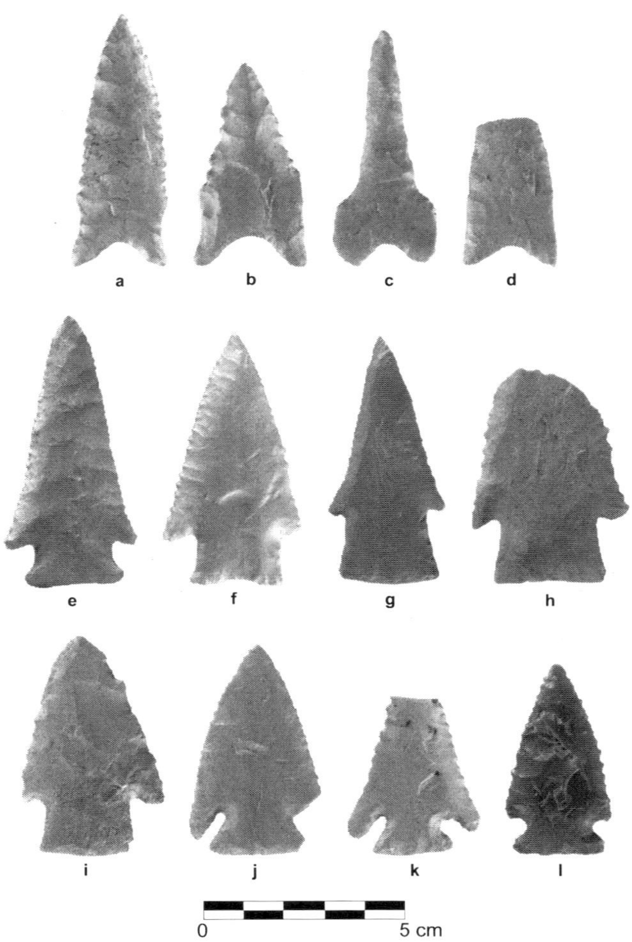

Figure 11.9. Early Archaic points from the Nochta site: a–d, Dalton; e–i, Hardin; j–l, Kirk.

multiple separate but overlapping or mixed occupations. Using the Big Eddy sequence as a template, one can argue that the points in the Kirk Corner Notched cluster, especially those that resemble Rice Lobed points, are remnants of an occupation that postdates Graham Cave and predates Hidden Valley and Searcy. The Rice Lobed horizon at Big Eddy has a date range of 8200–8000 RCYBP, or cal 7185–7035 B.C. (Ray et al., this volume).

Thus, the following sequence for the latter part of the Early Archaic at Modoc and, by extension, the American Bottom, is suggested: Graham Cave Side Notched, Rice Lobed, Hidden Valley Stemmed, and Searcy. Two important questions cannot be easily addressed: (1) where do the Bifurcate-cluster points (and the single Kirk Stemmed point) at Modoc fit into this sequence, and (2) do Rice Lobed points really belong to the Kirk Corner Notched cluster? If the Rice Lobed points are an Ozark expression of the Bifurcate cluster or Kirk Stemmed cluster, then the Rice Lobed and Bifurcate-cluster points at Modoc could be part of the same occupation or series of occupations. Despite these and other uncertainties, we hypothesize (but do not assume) that the points and deposits at Modoc essentially duplicate the later Early Archaic sequence in the Missouri Ozarks; this, of course, must be verified stratigraphically and with radiocarbon dating. Links to the Ozarks are evinced not only by similar point types but also by points fashioned from Ozark raw materials, such as St. Francois rhyolite and Jefferson City chert.

Several well-known very Early Archaic point types are represented in Koldehoff's (2006) survey sample, but few dates from site excavations in the American Bottom region help place them within a sequence. As argued by Koldehoff and Walthall (2004, this volume; also McElrath et al. ch. 1, this volume), we do not see Dalton points and tool kits, and the people who made them, as representing the final florescence of a hunting-foraging tradition derived directly from Clovis. Rather, Dalton groups are best viewed as founders of a newly emerging, more sedentary lifestyle focused on the abundant, seasonally available resources of the early Holocene forests and waterways of the Midcontinent. For example, the development of a robust woodworking tradition, represented by chipped-stone adzes, clearly separates Dalton from Clovis and links it to the rest of the Archaic. As noted previously by Koldehoff and Walthall,

Figure 11.10. Early Archaic points from the Nochta site: top row, Searcy; bottom row, Bifurcates.

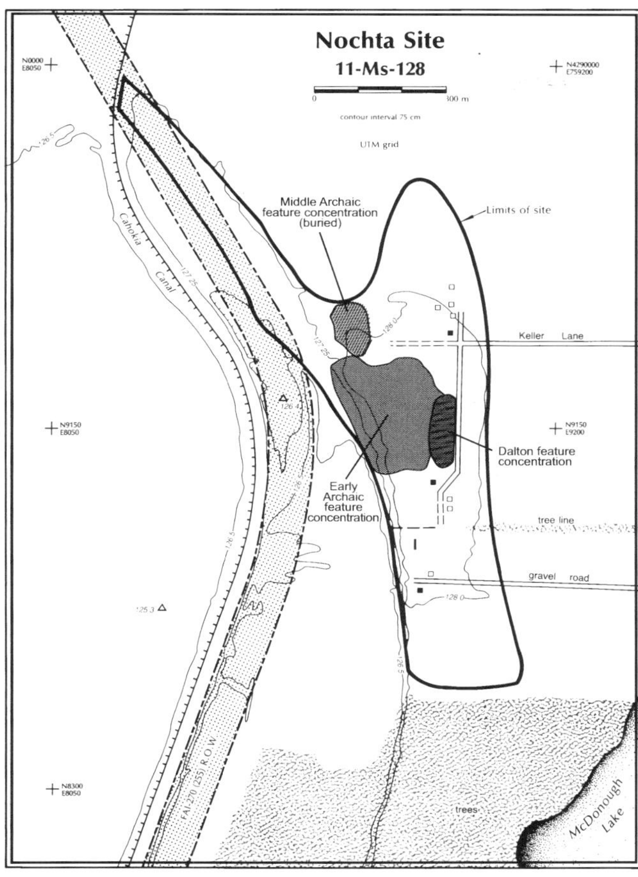

Figure 11.11. Plan map of Early and Middle Archaic feature concentrations at the Nochta site (adapted from Higgins 1990).

Figure 11.12. Early Archaic full-grooved axes from the Nochta site.

> Multiple lines of evidence indicate that Dalton groups represent the population that initially settled into the central Mississippi Valley. With this conclusion, we are not necessarily rejecting the notions of settling in forwarded by Caldwell (1958) for the Late Archaic or by Brose (1979) for the Middle Archaic. We are, however, calling attention to the fact that, as more is learned about early Holocene populations, we can extend further back in time significant technological and social developments previously attributed by researchers to more recent cultural periods. Many of the subsistence strategies, lithic resources, and rockshelters first utilized by Dalton populations remained in use into historic times. Subsequent developments during the Archaic period are, in large part, built on the foraging lifestyle Dalton populations first carved out of the newly emerging and expanding deciduous woodlands. [2004:64]

Ritualized exchange of exceptionally large and finely crafted Sloan-type Dalton points, often found in caches and possible burials, is another important aspect of Dalton culture in the central Mississippi Valley that ties Dalton groups to the rest of the Archaic and illustrates how Dalton groups initiated traditions and practices previously attributed by researchers to Middle or Late Archaic peoples (Walthall and Koldehoff 1998). Byers (2004:160–167; also see Emerson and McElrath, this volume) highlights this issue by pointing out that the Dalton ritual network evidenced by Sloan points shatters prior characterization of the Early Archaic and pushes back notions of ritualized exchange and alliance formation from the Middle Archaic, as argued by Brown (1985), to the Early Archaic. Anderson (2002) and Sassaman (2005), likewise, view the Dalton evidence as possible support for the early emergence of tribal formations and assertions of group or individual identity, while Brookes (2004:107–109) suggests that the oversized Sloan Dalton may have been manufactured by specialists.

However, without the careful excavation and analysis of the Sloan site (Morse 1997), a Dalton cemetery in northeast Arkansas, these inferences and arguments would be difficult to support. This point brings us back to the dearth of well-dated, sealed, and stratified Early Archaic deposits in the American Bottom region. The Big Eddy site in neighboring Missouri once again provides a template for arranging point types (Ray et al., this volume; see also Lopinot et al. 1998, 2000). The Dalton (and San Patrice) dates from Big Eddy generally duplicate those from the terrace deposits at Rodgers Shelter (Kay 1982; Wood and McMillan 1976). Therefore, the Big Eddy dates of ca. 10,500–9800 RCYBP (Ray et al., this volume; see also Lopinot et al. 1998) support the generally accepted time frame for the Dalton horizon (Goodyear 1982). Although the Big Eddy researchers (Ray et al., this volume; see also Lopinot et al. 1998, 2000), along with Morse (1997), Goodyear (1982, 1999), and others, consider Dalton to be Late Paleoindian, this time frame places the Dalton horizon in the Holocene, and available Dalton faunal assemblages reflect the exploitation of only modern species, such as white-tailed deer, wild turkey, squirrel, and certain aquatic resources (see Goodyear 1982, 1999). While technological aspects of Dalton points and tool kits show some similarity to those of Clovis points and tool kits (see Goodyear 1974; Morse 1997), there are important differences: first, Clovis and other fluted-point types were not routinely beveled and serrated or recycled into scrapers, drills, and burins; second, Clovis tool kits do not contain formal woodworking tools, like the Dalton adze (Goodyear 1982, 1999). Therefore, we concur with Goodyear's statement that "Dalton can be considered the beginning of the early Archaic period in the Southeast" (1999:441). The addition of the adze represents a new technology and a key component in a new heavy-duty woodworking industry. Adzes, along with fire, were the tools needed for the manufacture of dugout canoes, a key, we think, to understanding Dalton lifeways (Gaertner 1994; Walthall and Koldehoff 1998; Yerkes and Gaertner 1997).

Ray and his colleagues (this volume) suggest that the Packard point, a variant of Agate Basin, follows Dalton in the Ozark sequence and that it marks the beginning of the Early Archaic in Missouri. On the basis of dates from the Plains (Frison 1991; Holliday 2000; Wyckoff 1985), we would place Packard/Agate Basin points earlier than Dalton, or possibly as Plains contemporaries, but these slender points are technologically and morphologically very different from Dalton points. The Breckenridge Dalton variant follows Packard in the Big Eddy sequence, but few comparable points have been identified in the American Bottom region. Next in the sequence are Scottsbluff points, followed by Cache River side-notched points. Scottsbluff points are extremely rare, if not completely absent, from the American Bottom region, but Hardin Barbed points are common and may be their Eastern Woodlands counterparts (Behm 1985; Justice 1987). Points comparable to the Cache River side-notched type are thinly distributed across the region (Koldehoff 2006). These differences in concentrations of point styles across the landscape may reflect increasing regionalization, population increases, and decreasing population mobility or interaction, perhaps reflecting the enriched environments that were created with Holocene climate maturation and changes associated with early Prairie Peninsula expansion (Styles and McMillan, this volume). While present at the Modoc Rock Shelter site, Graham Cave, Hidden Valley, and Searcy types are minimally represented in the American Bottom region, with the Nochta site having a notable assemblage of 11 Searcy points. The absence or near absence of Thebes, St. Charles, and Kirk Corner Notched–cluster points at Big Eddy and other Ozark and Plains-border sites may also be a reflection of the regionalization process (Justice 1987; Sandstrom and Ray 2004).

So, where do these early corner-notched types fit? At the Kimmswick site, south of St. Louis, a St. Charles point was found in the early Holocene colluvium that caps the Pleistocene terrace and Clovis-mastodon deposits (Graham et al. 1981; Koldehoff and Walthall 2004). At the Little Muddy Rock Shelter in southern Illinois, a Thebes point was found in the basal unit above a Dalton point (Koldehoff 1992). And, at the Twin Ditch site in the lower Illinois Valley, Thebes and St. Charles points were sealed below a bifurcate-point horizon (Morrow 1996). Two Dalton points were discovered with the Thebes and St. Charles points; they may indicate an earlier occupation is present, or they may be "found" points. Five dates from Twin Ditch place the Thebes-St. Charles component at 9400–9100 B.P. (cal 8500–8100 B.C.). These dates generally correspond to those for the Thebes-St. Charles component at the James Farnsley site in southern Indiana, which overlies an early side-notched-point component and, in turn, is overlain by a series of Kirk Corner Notched occupations (Stafford and Cantin, this volume). The early side-notched points are not comparable to Big Sandy points, but they resemble the side-notched points from the American Bottom region that we have classified as Cache River. However, this early side-notched component predates the Cache River component at Big Eddy by a thousand years.

Although these early side-notched points present an interesting chronological problem, the above observations support the placement of Thebes and St. Charles points after Dalton and before Kirk. But where do Hardin points fit into the sequence? This question cannot be easily answered. Important technological similarities exist between Hardin, St. Charles, and Thebes points; for example, their blades are resharpened in the same manner, which creates a strong left-hand bevel, and points are often reworked into scrapers and, occasionally, drills. If Hardin points were contemporary with Scottsbluff points, then the Scottsbluff date at Big Eddy (9525 RCYBP; cal 8785 B.C.) supports the general placement of Hardin points with Thebes and St. Charles. But we are not arguing that Hardin, Thebes, and St. Charles points represent the same people or that they were fully contemporaneous. Later Kirk Corner Notched points characteristically lack the strong beveling seen in Thebes, St. Charles, and Hardin points, but some points we have lumped into the Kirk Corner Notched cluster, like Rice Lobed, do typically have a strong left-hand bevel. More research is needed to better understand the temporal and technological relationships between these corner-notched point types.

We propose the following Early Archaic point-type sequence for the American Bottom region: Dalton, Thebes–St. Charles–Hardin, Kirk Corner Notched cluster, Cache River Side Notched, Graham Cave Side Notched, Bifurcate cluster, Kirk Stemmed cluster, Hidden Valley Stemmed, and Searcy. We exclude Packard/Agate Basin points because they are uncommon in the American Bottom region and because they likely represent a pre-Dalton, Late Paleoindian Plains intrusion. If some side-notched points from the American Bottom region are true examples of the kind of early side-notched points found at the James Farnsley site in southern Indiana, then a post-Dalton, pre-Thebes, side-notched-point horizon may exist. What complicates matters is that Dalton points are uncommon to nonexistent in southern Indiana and eastern Illinois (Koldehoff and Walthall, this volume; Winters 1967).

More early sites need to be located and excavated in the American Bottom, and with luck, they will hold sealed, stratified deposits with ample diagnostic points and charcoal. Clearly, the American Bottom region at this early time was a dynamic cultural landscape, with groups and influences filtering into the region from several directions. This situation is not unexpected and was repeated over the centuries, in large part because the region was a nexus for major overland and riverine transportation routes and lay at the juncture of major biotic and physiographic provinces. Because the fluid nature of groups at this time may have resulted in complex occupation sequences, we have refrained from assigning specific time frames to early point types in our chronology, and we view our attempt at "triangulating" point types on the basis of neighboring regions as having produced a tentative sequence that needs to be verified for our study area through excavation and radiometric determination.

Those point types "indigenous" to the American Bottom region should be the most frequently occurring examples (Koldehoff 2006); of the 813 Early Archaic hafted bifaces (excluding Bass knives) recorded in Koldehoff's (2006) survey areas, the most common are Dalton, Hardin, Kirk Corner Notched cluster, St. Charles, and Thebes (Figures 11.9 and 11.13). Notably, Dalton points ($n = 304$) are two to three times more common than other major Early Archaic point types, like Hardin (n = 173) and St. Charles (n = 85). Bass knives were identified at the Bass site in Grant County, Wisconsin, where they were found in association with Hardin points and early (Dalton-type) adzes (Behm 1985). Conrad (1981) considers similar left-hand-beveled knives to be part of the Thebes cluster (see also Nolan and Fishel, this volume). Early adzes are part of the Thebes-St. Charles component at Twin Ditch, but Bass knives are not reported (Morrow 1996). That Thebes, St. Charles, and Hardin points follow Dalton points chronologically and that they are associated with similar adzes indicates some level of technological continuity as does the edge-maintenance strategy of blade beveling (albeit, the later points exhibit a left-hand rather than right-hand bevel, for whatever reason) and the strategy of converting points into scrapers and other tools. An important change in woodworking technology across the Eastern Woodlands occurred near the close of the Early Archaic: chipped-stone adzes were replaced by ground-stone adzes, celts, and grooved axes. In particular, grooved axes became the dominant Middle Archaic woodworking tool (see discussion of Middle Archaic phases below). Hayden (1989) links this change to economic intensification and reductions in settlement mobility. Sassaman (1996, 2005) argues that the shift was more than technological in that it likely involved aspects of social interaction, such as exchange and displays of group or individual identity. Such interaction may be suggested by bannerstones, which appeared in the Middle Archaic along with other ground-stone tools and ornaments (Brookes 2004).

Figure 11.13. Early Archaic points: a–c, Thebes; d–f, St. Charles; g–i, Bass knives.

Middle Archaic

When the American Bottom summary volume (Bareis and Porter 1984) was published, Middle Archaic dates were only available from four sites: Modoc Rock Shelter, Leingang, Tep, and Mund House. With the extension of the FAI-270 alignment to the north, the Nochta site excavations yielded critical information (Higgins 1990) as did the excavations at the Strong site in advance of the relocation of the town of Valmeyer (Walz et al. 1998). We now have credible evidence for the delineation of two Middle Archaic phases, the Nochta and Dennis Hollow phases. Newly presented information from Modoc Rock Shelter (Ahler and Koldehoff, this volume) adds considerably to the data set for this part of the Archaic sequence. Likewise, with the reanalysis of the Tep (Moffat 1980), Leingang (Bentz 1988), and Modoc Village sites (Ahler and Koldehoff, this volume), we are able to propose the Tep complex.

Middle Archaic deposits were also encountered at the Ringering site (Evans and Evans 2000). This site, located on the Savanna Terrace north of the Nochta site, yielded substantial Archaic and Early Woodland features and materials. The presence of dozens of Early and Middle Archaic diagnostics in lag deposits, which also contained pit features, rock clusters, and hearths, indicates substantial occupations. One point fragment, a possible Searcy or Rice Lanceolate, was recovered from Early Archaic feature context (Evans and Evans 2000:128). We have refrained from demarcating a specific boundary for the Early–Middle Archaic interface until such time that we can associate dated assemblages of appropriate antiquity. The best information thus far is from Modoc (Ahler and Koldehoff, this volume), where dates of around cal 7000 B.C. (youngest at 6925 B.C.) have been obtained from levels containing Kirk Corner Notched and Searcy points.

The earliest reported Middle Archaic date (cal 6947 B.C.) is from levels at Modoc yielding points that are comparable to the Cypress Creek I type from the Midsouth (Ahler and Koldehoff, this volume). Similar but distinct points, with expanding stems rather than corner notches (called "Valmeyer" points), were recovered from dated pit features at the Strong site and are diagnostic of the Dennis Hollow phase (Walz et al. 1998), which postdates the Cypress Creek I horizon at Modoc but chronologically overlaps the Cypress Creek II horizon. Valmeyer points are absent at Modoc. All three point types are represented by only a handful of examples from dated contexts in the American Bottom region; therefore, identification of these types in surface collections has been problematic. For example, points that probably belong to these types have either gone unrecognized or have been misidentified as other better-known point types (e.g., Kirk Corner Notched). Koldehoff identified Valmeyer points in the surface collections he analyzed for this study but not Cypress Creek I and II points because these were not recognized when the analysis was begun. Thus, it is likely that some of the corner-notched points placed in the Kirk Corner Notched cluster and in the McLean type (or Helton type; see discussion of Falling Springs phase below), could be Cypress Creek I and II points. Jakie Stemmed points also likely predate Valmeyer points and the Dennis Hollow phase. Two possible Jakie points were recovered from the Cypress Creek I and II horizons at Modoc, and four possible Jakie points were recorded in surface collections. A few other examples have been identified, including one from the Mund House site (Dale McElrath, pers. comm. 2006), and one from the Ringering site (Evans and Evans 2000:135).

The Helton phase, which has been identified in the lower Illinois Valley (Brown and Vierra 1983; Cook 1976; Wiant et al., this volume) has also been identified at Modoc (Ahler and Koldehoff, this volume) on the basis of the strong presence of Matanzas and Godar points in levels that are grouped as Middle Archaic Stratum 6. We have avoided using the Helton phase designation for the American Bottom chronology until the phase can be distinguished at other excavated sites; we note the strong presence of the Helton (or McLean) point type at Modoc in the same levels as Matanzas and Godar, which we believe date to later times (see discussion of Falling Springs phase below).

Dennis Hollow Phase (cal 5700–5450 B.C.)

The earliest recognized Middle Archaic phase in the American Bottom sequence is the Dennis Hollow phase (Adams et al. 1997; Walz et al. 1998), identified at the Strong site; it has a series of six tightly clustered radiocarbon dates ranging from cal 5698 to 5445 B.C. (similar to the dates obtained for Middle Archaic Stratum 3 at Modoc). The site, located atop Salt Lick Point at the Mississippi Valley margin, contained pit features and a large material assemblage representing chipped-stone and ground-stone tool production as well as maintenance and recycling. The 66 shallow basin-shaped pits were arranged in several clusters and typically contained lithic debris, limestone, and charred nutshell. As is usual for the time period, the botanical remains are dominated by hickory shell but also include black walnut and a few acorn shells. American lotus, rush, grape, and goosefoot seeds were recovered in small numbers. The importance and role of these plants in everyday subsistence is uncertain (Walz et al. 1998:165–167). Faunal evidence from the site is generally lacking.

The occupants of the Strong site had ready access to chert resources, and the majority of the chipped-stone tools are made from local Salem and Burlington cherts. The resulting lithic assemblage contained many examples of expedient tools and unfinished and finished bifaces as well as perforators, scrapers, and wedges. Cobble tools, likely used for plant-food processing, were recovered from feature context, along with sandstone abraders and two axes. The axes, a full-grooved specimen from Feature 16 and a preform from Feature 74, are some of the earliest Middle Archaic ground-stone axes from the region. Numerous finished and unfinished axes were surface collected from the general area around the Strong site as were several crescent-shaped bannerstones and many chipped-stone points and tools (Koldehoff 2002, 2006). The expanding-stemmed Valmeyer points typical of the Dennis Hollow phase (Figure 11.14) are possibly ancestral to the expanding-stemmed and corner-notched point styles that were common throughout much of the Late Archaic, especially McLean (or Helton) points. They are similar to the later points in basic morphology and in that they are commonly made from heat-treated cherts; they are larger, however, and tend to be heavily ground at the base and along the sides of the stem, unlike, for example, McLean points, which lack grinding. Similar points of comparable

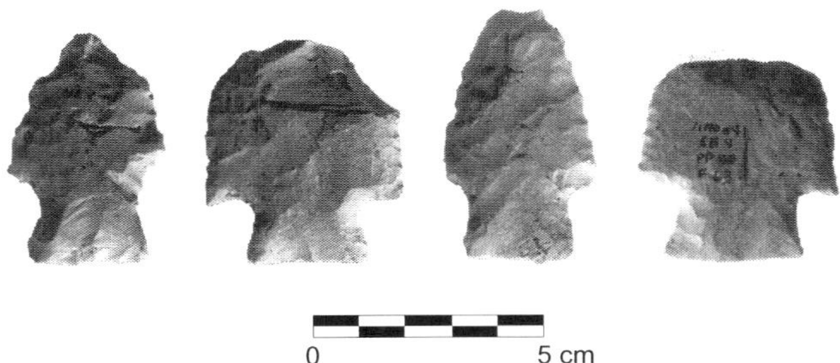

Figure 11.14. Dennis Hollow phase: Valmeyer Corner Notched points.

age have been recognized in the lower Illinois River valley at Campbell Hollow (Stafford 1985) and Napoleon Hollow (Wiant et al., this volume) and are occasionally recognized in surface collections in west-central Illinois between the Mississippi and central Illinois River drainages (Nolan 2004; Nolan and Fishel, this volume).

In his upland survey sample, Koldehoff (2006) identified Valmeyer points in four of the seven study areas, and the majority of the points are from the three bluff-top study areas, including New Valmeyer, where the Strong site was excavated. The Eagle Cliff study area, just north of New Valmeyer is noteworthy because its assemblage of surface artifacts duplicates the surface assemblage from New Valmeyer. For example, nearly identical numbers of Valmeyer points made from the same basic chert types, in particular, heat-treated Burlington, were recovered from both locales. Moreover, numerous finished and unfinished axes were collected as were several finished and unfinished crescent-shaped bannerstones, which may or may not be associated with the Dennis Hollow phase (Koldehoff 2006). Bannerstones of this general configuration are typically found in Middle Archaic deposits (Hassen and Farnsworth 1987; Kwas 1981). At Grassy Lake, on the Wood River Terrace not far from the Nochta and Ringering sites, Titterington documented (in Knoblock 1939:34) the discovery by Standard Oil Company workers of human burials accompanied by 12 broken, or "ceremonially killed" crescent-shaped bannerstones (in Knoblock's typology, knobbed lunate) and eight copper axes (see also Kelly 2000). This discovery affords a glimpse into the social and ritual complexity of the Middle Archaic period, especially as compared with the impoverished Middle Archaic burials discovered at the Noctha site (see below).

Nochta Phase (cal 5450–5100 B.C.)

The Nochta phase (Higgins 1990) is defined on the basis of materials recovered from a sealed living surface and associated pit features and rock clusters at the Nochta site. Early Archaic materials at the site were located along a linear sand ridge, whereas the Middle Archaic materials were primarily confined to lower elevations, buried by over a meter of accretional clay layers that drape the sand ridge; these clay layers are the result of overbank deposits from Mississippi River flood events. The location of the Middle Archaic habitations at lower elevations and their confinement largely to the clay soils may reflect the backwater resource focus and economic orientation of the site's occupants at the time. The site was eventually covered by the Mississippi River (Edelhardt Meander) sometime between cal 3500 and 2500 B.C., which essentially sealed the living surfaces. Over 200 features were identified in a relatively small area (4,000 m^2), and although some, presumably recycled, Dalton diagnostics were recovered from this area, the numerous Middle Archaic diagnostics and the several radiocarbon dates obtained supported the chronological association of this portion of the Nochta site (Higgins 1990). Three of the four radiocarbon dates from feature context bracket a narrow period (cal 5433–5133 B.C.) following closely on the heels of the Dennis Hollow phase. There is a single "outlying" Nochta date of cal 5710 B.C.

Features in the Middle Archaic occupation area of the Nochta site consisted almost exclusively of pits (ca. 220 and one possible structure), in contrast to the Early Archaic sector, which contained pits, rock hearths, and rock concentrations. The Middle Archaic area also contained what are the earliest recognized open-air burials in the American Bottom in the form of three poorly preserved individuals in pits indistinguishable from domestic pits. We also note the existence of a shallow basin that may represent a structure; if so, it is the earliest structure in the American Bottom. Four clusters or contiguous groupings of cobbles (3–12 cobbles per cluster) included recognizable tools used in plant-food processing (pitted stones, manos, or metates). Higgins (1990:100) suggests that the groupings represented caches of tools or tool-quality raw materials. Given the relative scarcity of cobbles and other lithic raw materials in the American Bottom floodplain, one would expect people to have transported such resources to their floodplain base camps. Because of the spatial and stratigraphic separation of the Early and Middle Archaic components, there is little doubt about the Middle Archaic association of the cobble tools and other ground-stone artifacts, several of which were recovered from feature context.

Tools at the Nochta site were dominated by chipped stone, and Higgins (1990:81) notes a reliance on bipolar chipping and the generally small size of the flake tools that characterize the Middle Archaic occupation, especially by comparison with the larger flake tools and more numerous bifacial tools that characterize the Early Archaic occupation. This reliance on small, bipolar-produced tools is understandable not only in the context of sparse lithic resources but also in the context of low settlement mobility. As discussed earlier, Hayden (1989) argues that reductions in mobility made ground-stone woodworking tools, such as grooved axes, useful because they could be easily and repeatedly resharpened by honing the bit with a piece of sandstone, whereas chipped-stone adzes had to be rechipped, shortening their use life. Although only two axes were recovered from Middle Archaic features, a full-grooved specimen from

Feature 308 and a fragment from Feature 259, several other axes were recovered that likely relate to the Middle Archaic occupation. The projectile point assemblage is dominated by side-notched points that were often reworked into scrapers. Higgins (1990) identifies a relatively small side-notched point as belonging to the Robinson type and a slightly larger version as belonging to the Brannon type. He also observes that the smaller version may simply represent reworking of the larger type, as they differ only slightly, mainly in terms of the depth of the side notching; we concur and have used the more traditional Brannon point-type (Figure 11.15) designation for our discussion of surface assemblages representing this phase. Perhaps the most significant observation concerning point types is that none of the larger expanding-stemmed points associated with the Dennis Hollow phase occur at the Nochta site, and it is clear that Dennis Hollow is not directly ancestral to the Nochta phase. This is another example of sequential phases (with solid radiocarbon dating) displaying a remarkable degree of differentiation of point types, possibly indicative of different ethnic-group affiliations. Matanzas points were also minimally represented at the Nochta site as were larger side-notched Godar points. This may indicate some interaction with pre-Helton phase, Matanzas-bearing groups in the lower Illinois Valley or a later Helton-phase occupation. Several of the smaller examples of Brannon points show the very thick basal element and distinctive longitudinal cross section that typify Matanzas points, suggesting that they may represent local precursors of this later type.

Figure 11.15. Nochta phase: Brannon Side Notched points.

Points similar to the Nochta-phase points are present at Modoc Rock Shelter, and Ahler and Koldehoff (this volume) placed them in the small side-notched cluster. These small points are most common in the Middle Archaic 4 Strata Group, which dates to about the same time frame as the Nochta phase (cal 5500–5000 B.C.), but in this strata group, the small side-notched points (n =12) are outnumbered by larger side-notched Godar-like points (n =16). The Nochta phase is represented in Koldehoff's (2006) upland survey sample by small side-notched points that generally correspond to the Brannon type defined by Cook (1976). Brannon points were recorded in six of the seven upland study areas, and they were most common in the Modoc Uplands, where other Middle Archaic side-notched points are well represented. Burlington chert was the preferred raw material at the Nochta site and also at presumably coeval sites in the upland study areas, and heat treatment was common. Middle Archaic points in the uplands, like those at Nochta, were frequently converted into scrapers.

Tep Complex (cal 4200–4000 B.C.)

A gap of almost a millennium occurs in the American Bottom archaeological sequence after the Nochta phase. However, four sites, all situated along the bluff tops, have provided radiocarbon dates that fall within a narrowly defined 200-year period: the Tep (Moffat 1980), Leingang (Bentz 1987), Mund House, and Modoc Village (Ahler and Koldehoff 2002) sites. A fifth, unanalyzed, site, Edging (Galloy 2001), has yielded relevant point types and radiocarbon determinations. We have recognized a suite of presumably associated materials from these sites that we have tentatively designated the "Tep complex."

The Tep site, which lends its name to the complex, was identified in the 1970s and, at the time, generated a great deal of interest as well as confusion. It was the opinion of most American Bottom researchers that the square-stemmed hafted bifaces recovered both from the surface and from excavated pit features were Early Woodland Kramer points, despite the lack of associated pottery (Moffat 1980). Was Tep, as Moffat (1980) surmised, an example of an "aceramic" Early Woodland site with an erroneously early radiocarbon date of cal 3965 B.C., or was there a simpler explanation? In subsequent years, several Marion-phase Early Woodland sites were excavated (Emerson and Fortier 1986; Evans and Evans 2000; Fortier 1985; Stafford 1992; Stafford 1997), and we now have a good sample of contextually secure Kramer points for comparison. On the basis of our reexamination of the Tep site points, we have concluded that they are Karnak points of the stemmed or shouldered variant (Figure 11.16), originally defined by Howard Winters in southern Illinois (see Koldehoff 1992). A weak-shouldered variety is common at Middle Archaic sites in the lower Illinois Valley (Brown and Vierra 1983; Cook 1976; Nolan and Fishel, this volume). Shouldered Karnaks are now recognized from the Leingang site (Bentz 1988), which is best known for its Late Woodland

Figure 11.16. Tep complex: Karnak Straight Stemmed points.

(Rosewood phase) occupation, but over 80 percent of the 57 features excavated at the site yielded no ceramics; given our perspective on the number of aceramic features expected at Woodland occupations in this region, we now believe that the majority of the aceramic features date to Archaic times. The number of straight-stemmed points recovered from the surface, combined with a date (cal 4154 B.C.) similar to the one from the Tep site, argues for Leingang's inclusion in this complex. Consequently, we use the Leingang date as the second bracketing date for this complex.

Because Karnaks are sometimes found on the same sites with Godar-type side-notched points, some possibility exists that these two point types were contemporaneous; indeed, salvage excavations at the Modoc Village site by Ahler and Koldehoff (2002) yielded examples of both from feature contexts with dates that overlap and are slightly earlier (with multiple intercepts falling between cal 4300 and 4000 B.C.) than the Tep and Leingang dates. These dates would only push the dating of the Tep complex back another 100 years, but we remain optimistic that the side-notched points will prove to represent a distinct phase of the Middle Archaic in this region. Similarly, more than 100 Archaic pit features were excavated at the Edging site (Galloy 2001), and features with radiocarbon dates falling within the Late Archaic have yielded points from several recognized phases, including the Tep complex. Features we expected to date to Tep-complex times, however, have yielded younger dates.

This highlights one of the problems of interpreting bluff-top site locations, which were favored throughout prehistory and are usually multicomponent: mixing is a constant concern. For example, mixing probably occurred at the Mund House site, which yielded a date of cal 4228 B.C., indicating a Tep-complex occupation but producing only one Jakie Stemmed point. The Modoc Village and Mund House dates mentioned above would marginally reduce the recognized hiatus after the Nochta phase, but a considerable gap would still separate it from the Tep complex. Strata at Modoc generally contain deeply side-notched (Godar) points along with Matanzas, small side-notched (Brannon), and Cypress Creek types, with no clear separation among them seen at this time. Karnak points are poorly represented at the Modoc Rock Shelter, which further complicates the issue (Ahler and Koldehoff, this volume). Karnak points were recorded in all seven of Koldehoff's upland study areas, but only in modest numbers, except in the Douglas Creek and Modoc Uplands study areas. The Karnak points are typically heat treated and made from Burlington chert and, to a lesser extent, Salem chert. With two exceptions, no more than three Karnak points have been recovered from any particular site; one site in the Douglas Creek study area yielded eight points, and the Modoc Village site, in the Modoc Uplands study area, yielded 12 points. Both of these sites appear to be substantial Middle and Late Archaic base camps. Recent investigations at the bluff-edge Edging site have produced 21 Karnak points. On the basis of the information from these sites, we have tentatively assigned the Karnak shouldered point type to the Tep complex and suggest that the side-notched Godar type may be slightly earlier. Even if the Tep complex remains valid, a hiatus of almost a millennium separates it from the preceding Nochta phase, although some data from Modoc may reflect this period.

Although examples of Matanzas points are occasionally recovered from sites in the American Bottom region, there are no known large Helton-phase habitation sites (or large concentrations of Matanzas points). Four sites in the Douglas Creek study area produced between eight and 13 points, while 14 points were collected from the bluff-edge Modoc Village site. Because of the apparent abundance of Matanzas-style points at sites in the lower Illinois River valley (Cook 1976; Odell 1996), archaeologists had assumed that such components, as yet undiscovered, existed in the American Bottom region (McElrath et al. 1984). That now seems unlikely, given the failure of the upland survey areas (Koldehoff 2006) and recent excavations at the Edging and Modoc Village sites to yield significant Helton-phase habitation areas (unless Godar points date to Helton-phase times?).

At the above-mentioned bluff-top sites and in the uplands study areas, at least twice as many Godar points occur as Matanzas points. Godar points are particularly common in the Modoc Uplands (n =149), with many of the points coming from the Modoc Village site (n = 66). Five sites in the Douglas Creek study area produced eight to 11 points each and, thus, likely represent more than ephemeral campsites. Both Godar and Matanzas points are predominantly made from Burlington chert, are frequently heat treated, and are often converted into scrapers, probably used to work hide (Jefferies 1990). An array of lesser-used regional and extra-regional chert types is represented, and local glacial chert cobbles were used more than in preceding phases (Koldehoff 2006). This pattern likely reflects a localized pattern of lithic procurement consistent with low settlement mobility. Given the presence of Matanzas points at the Nochta site and their presence in pre-Helton levels at Koster (Brown and Vierra 1983), and given the dominance of Godar points in Stratum M5 at Modoc and their occurrence on later Tep-complex sites, we would suggest that the Godar point type reached ascendancy after the Matanzas point type, at least in the American Bottom region. The reverse appears to be true for the lower Illinois Valley (Wiant et al., this volume); it remains to be determined whether this divergence reflects demography or critical issues of taxonomy, context, sample size, or too few relevant radiocarbon determinations.

Late Archaic

The Late Archaic period has been divided into five phases, four of which were defined in the FAI-270 summary volume (McElrath et al. 1984). Except for Table Rock (or Bottleneck) points, which number 44 in all, the Late Archaic point types identified in Koldehoff's upland study areas fit into these five phases. In the absence of contextual information in the American Bottom, we see the smallish, well-made, narrow-stemmed Table Rocks points as Late Archaic rather than Middle Archaic, with possible connections between these points and other small-point traditions (Durst and Riverton). The few Table Rock points recovered from floodplain sites that have been investigated occur in Late Archaic contexts.

Falling Springs Phase (cal 3400–2900 B.C.)

The Falling Springs phase is the earliest designated Late Archaic manifestation in the American Bottom region. Confusion surrounding the derivation of the phase name is worth dispelling. The type site for the Falling Springs complex, defined from surface collections (Kelly et al. 1979:20), was the Falling Springs site, located on a high colluvial terrace and dissected bluff-base ridge adjacent to a prolific spring that emanates from the bluff. Located at the northern end of the Prairie Lake locality, with its numerous Late Archaic sites and components, the Falling Springs site contains materials from several Archaic and Woodland components. Kelly noted the strong presence of side-notched points at this site, and he compared them to Helton-phase Matanzas points from the lower Illinois River valley and to similar points from Modoc Rock Shelter (Fowler 1959b). The stratigraphy at Modoc, as known at that time (Fowler 1959b), suggested these side-notched points were of comparable age to those at the Koster site but could extend back as far as 5000 B.C. (uncalibrated). Kelly also noted the occurrence of several distinctive corner-notched points (Kelly et al. 1979:19) that he likened to ones from a feature at the central Wisconsin Raddatz Rock Shelter site (Wittry 1959) that had been radiocarbon dated to about 3300 B.C. (uncalibrated). Lacking any dated or stratigraphic materials for the Falling Springs complex, he reserved judgment on whether the corner-notched form was part of this complex (Kelly et al. 1979:20). A recent reexamination of the original material by the authors and a previous reassessment by Ahler (1993) confirm the heavy mixing of Archaic materials at the resource-rich, bluff-base Falling Springs site. In retrospect, it is likely that the majority of the Archaic material from the site dates to the Labras Lake phase, the points being similar to the Floyd point type as described by Evans (2001). Ironically, it is unlikely that a significant Falling Springs component exists at the Falling Springs site.

Materials dating to the time period that had been provisionally assigned to the Falling Springs "complex" (Kelly et al. 1979) became available when the McLean site on the bluffs above the Falling Springs and Labras Lake sites was investigated during the FAI-270 project. The primary component at the site consists of 164 pit features with a remarkably uniform material assemblage (McElrath 1986) and can reasonably be considered as truly representing the "type site" for the Falling Springs phase. Five radiocarbon dates (cal 2913, 2917, 2921, 3350, and 3357 B.C.) from features with associated diagnostics are consistent with a Falling Springs–phase age. Falling Springs–age materials have also been recognized from the Modoc Rock Shelter (Ahler et al. 1992; Ahler and Koldehoff, this volume); five dates were obtained from the strata producing these materials (ranging from cal 3519 B.C. to cal 3657 B.C.). These dates indicate a slightly earlier range than those from the McLean site do; we have retained the slightly later dating for this phase, however, because the Modoc Rock Shelter levels yielded point types that were not present in the McLean assemblage (e.g., Matanzas and Saratoga cluster). The Falling Springs phase has not been recognized in the lower Illinois River valley, although similar point styles have been identified at Quasar (Goatley 1998), with a date of cal 2780 B.C., and at Cyprus Land, with dates of cal 3499, 3639, and 3660 B.C. (Conner 1986). Similar materials have also been identified in Missouri at the Lone Wolf site, with a date of cal 3647 B.C. (Hamilton et al. 1986; see also Harl, this volume).

In retrospect, the expanding-stemmed points and scrapers that dominate the McLean assemblage (Figure 11.17) are probably the same type as those recovered by Fowler at both the Ferry site (Fowler 1957) and Modoc Rock Shelter (Fowler 1959a, 1959b; Fowler and Winters 1956), and they are almost certainly the same as the point type originally designated Helton in the lower Illinois River valley (Cook 1976). The Ferry site, however, is clearly multicomponent, and in the lower Illinois Valley, the Helton name was originally used to describe the side-notched point type (Houart 1971) that was eventually redesignated Matanzas; to make matters worse, the term *Helton* was appropriated as the phase designation for the levels in which Matanzas points dominate. Thus, to avoid a situation in which a point type bears the same name as a phase with which it is not associated, we prefer the designation McLean (Evans and Evans 2000; Fortier 1996) for this hafted biface. Not only are the context and dating of the type secure at McLean but the site also has yielded material related to its production trajectory

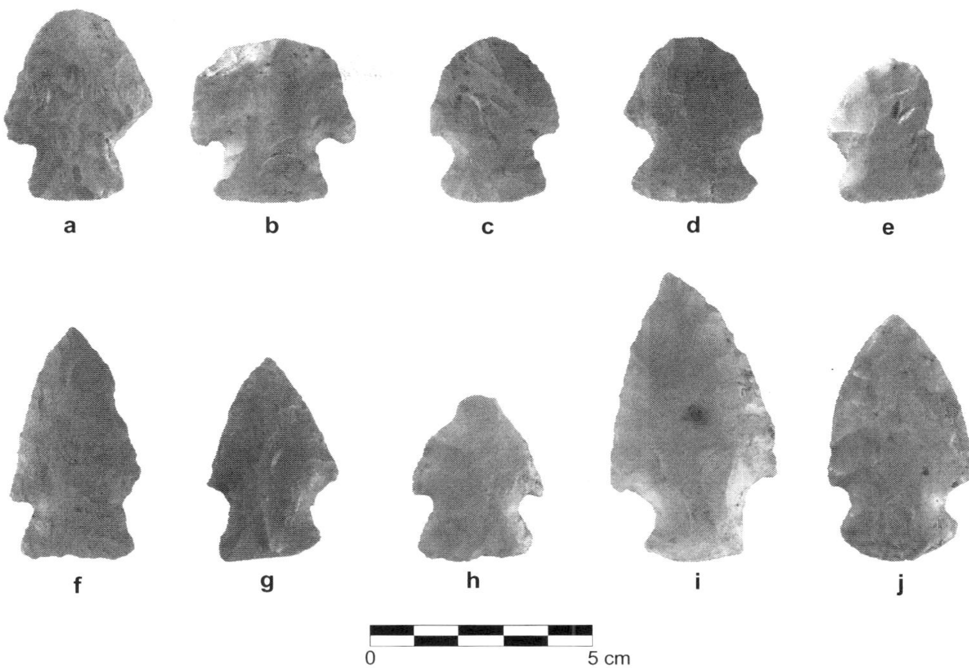

Figure 11.17. Falling Springs phase: a–e, McLean scrapers; f–j, McLean points.

and its metric and nonmetric attributes are well illustrated in the assemblage (McElrath 1986). Another point type that is possibly related to the McLean point is Saratoga Expanding Stemmed, originally defined by Winters as part of the Saratoga cluster along with Saratoga Broad Bladed and Saratoga Parallel Stemmed, although his typology was never fully published (see Justice 1987; Koldehoff 1992; Winters 1967). While the expanding-stem variety is considered a Late Archaic type, it is poorly dated, and Justice (1987, citing the original Modoc data) thought it dated after 2000 B.C. (uncalibrated) and persisted into Early Woodland (i.e., Crab Orchard culture) times. Ahler (1993; Ahler et al. 1992) originally applied the Saratoga Expanding Stemmed type, as well as other Winters types (e.g., Tamms and Elko) to the points that originate from Falling Springs levels of Modoc. Ahler and Koldehoff (this volume) have recently grouped these points into the Helton corner-notched cluster. The only points from Modoc that retain the Saratoga designation have straight stems and are comparable to Cook's (1976) straight-stemmed Matanzas (Ahler and Koldehoff, this volume). At the Little Muddy Rock Shelter, Koldehoff (1992) identified straight- to expanding-stem Saratoga points that date to the Titterington phase and later (2020–1720 B.C., uncorrected). Similar points, often made from southern Illinois chert (Cobden and Bailey) and often exhibiting unworked or truncated bases, are routinely recovered from Titterington-phase sites in the American Bottom region (see discussion of Titterington phase below). Points similar to the McLean type are frequently recovered from southern Illinois sites, but they have not been consistently placed into a single point type or cluster.

We believe that in surface collections from the southern half of Illinois the expanding-stemmed McLean points have been mistaken for Middle–Late Woodland Steuben points and the McLean scrapers for reworked Snyders points. This appears to be the case for several scrapers recovered from the Poag Road and Indian Creek sites (Munson 1971:85, specimens k, n, and o). Indeed, given the presence of these points and the large ovate, corner-notched points (Figure 11.17f, g) that might easily be confused with Affinis Snyders points, we originally thought the McLean site might represent an aceramic Middle Woodland site. This notion was quickly dispelled by the radiocarbon dates and a thorough study of the ethnobotanical remains (Johannessen 1986). McLean points may also be confused with Kirk points, as we believe they were by Odell (1986:165) in reviewing burial associations at the Elizabeth Mound site in the lower Illinois River valley. In this regard, we would point out that Kirk points are rarely heat treated, whereas McLean points are typically heat treated and are usually thicker than Kirk points.

In addition to the McLean points, we also note the strong presence in the Falling Spring–phase assemblage from the McLean site of hafted scrapers (Figure 11.17a–e). These scrapers are made along the same line as the points, and many are clearly retooled points, while in other instances they seem to have been initially manufactured as scrapers. The examples from the McLean site show heavy use and many have been rehafted several times, resulting in a diminutive square-haft element; this heavy use, combined with the fact that virtually every point from the assemblage broken at the midsection showed evidence of use wear along the transverse fracture, suggests that (hide?) scraping was an important activity at the McLean site. We use the term *McLean scraper* to refer to these hafted tools.

Other formal tool types at the McLean site included large unhafted bifaces (some of which may represent production failures and rejects). Drills were also recovered, but they were not as numerous as at sites of other Archaic periods. One artifact type that was not fully appreciated at the time of analysis was the burin. McElrath noted a large number of burination blows on reduction flakes in the debitage from this assemblage, but because he did not know how often these might have occurred accidentally, he did not tabulate them. Given that these tools are rare or nonexistent in other American Bottom lithic assemblages, it is possible that burins are a diagnostic tool type of the Falling Springs phase. Ground-stone implements included two fully grooved axes, numerous cobble tools, and a multiple-pitted sandstone slab. A similar slab was noted at the Ferry site (Fowler 1957:14). This slab would have served well for mass processing of nuts, the remains of which are well represented at the site.

The precise method and sequence of the production of the McLean hafted bifaces have not been explored in detail, but there is no doubt that these points are made on flake blanks. In fact, the assemblage of both formal and informal tools is primarily produced on reduction flakes. The cores indicate a preference for creating platforms that resulted in the detachment of sizable flake blanks. In addition to the multidirectional cores that typify most Archaic-period lithic assemblages, recognizable plano-convex and double-ended cores are present. The better examples of the plano-convex cores approach Middle Woodland polyhedral cores in their symmetry and sophistication. Because cores were so often completely exhausted through reduction and often recycled as scrapers, it is likely that the reduction method was far more systematic than is evidenced by the remnant core fragments. Ahler's (Ahler et al. 1992) study of the patterns of use wear on tools from the Falling Springs horizons at Modoc Rock Shelter suggested that this assemblage (especially the material from Stratum 9E) was used for the most diverse set of tasks and activities of all the Late Archaic components examined.

The botanical remains recovered from Falling Springs–phase sites, as expected, indicate heavy use of nut resources (emphasizing hickory) and lesser quantities of seedy plant remains. Domesticated squash remains were identified at Modoc Rock Shelter but not at McLean. Faunal remains were absent from the McLean site but are well represented at Modoc Rock Shelter. Thorson and Styles (1992) note that a wide spectrum of animals was eaten, including a large number of fish as well as deer and waterfowl, and they view this diversity as the continuation of the pattern established during Middle Archaic times. In this respect, they disagree with Fowler's (1959b) original conclusion that the Late Archaic period represented a more specialized adaptation focusing on deer and waterfowl.

In the American Bottom, this phase is restricted to the valley margin and interior uplands. No significant Falling Spring assemblages have been recovered from the floodplain proper, although there appear to be some on the Savanna Terrace (Evans and Evans 2000:178) and on a recently identified high terrace remnant at the mouth of Prairie du Pont Creek (Booth and Koldehoff 1999). In addition, Fortier (1996:66–69) identified seven McLean points at the Marge site, located at the base of the bluffs near Palmer Creek. None occurred in feature contexts. Fortier (1987:77) also identified several McLean points from the Range site, but the majority of these appear to belong instead to the Floyd type that has since been defined at the Floyd site (see Evans 2001:71) and is associated with the Labras Lake phase (see discussion of Labras Lake phase below). Given the absence of Falling Springs components on the floodplain (except on the fan deposits at Modoc), even though earlier Middle Archaic (Nochta phase) and later Late Archaic materials (Labras Lake and Prairie Lake phases) are well represented, it is possible that the floodplain was too unstable for primary settlements during this period, as is speculated for early Late Woodland times (McElrath and Fortier 2000). It is also possible that yet undiscovered Falling Springs deposits are buried in floodplain contexts.

McLean points are present in all of the upland study areas but generally in small numbers (Koldehoff 2006). However, a notable concentration of 122 points is recorded in the Douglas Creek study area, with more than half of the points ($n = 67$) coming from one large site that probably represents a Falling Springs–phase base settlement that was repeatedly reoccupied. It covers several low, adjacent ridges that extend into the floodplain of Douglas Creek. Cobble tools and chert cores (mainly Burlington and Salem) are common, and several axes have been recovered along with drills and McLean scrapers. This site also contains evidence of two other sizable but considerably smaller Archaic components, represented by 10 Matanzas points and 23 Prairie Lake–phase points. At the McLean site, at the Modoc Rock Shelter, and across the upland study areas, McLean (or Helton) points are consistently made from heat-treated Burlington chert, with small numbers of points manufactured from other regional cherts (e.g., Fern Glen and Salem) as well as extraregional cherts (e.g., Bailey, Cobden, Blair, and Jefferson City).

The McLean point is well represented in the lower Illinois River valley (Conner 1986; Goatley 1998) but is much more rare as one travels north (Conrad 1981; Nolan 2004; Nolan and Fishel, this volume). The contemporaneous Godar occupation at the Tree Row site in the central Illinois River valley (Madeleine Evans, pers. comm. 2004) suggests that a McLean-Godar (i.e., Hemphill horizon-Falling Springs phase) boundary exists somewhere between the central and lower Illinois valleys. McLean points occur in minor numbers at the Tree Row site, and a small number of side-notched points occur at McLean. These collateral point types possibly indicate social interaction or boundary fluidity during this period. In the past, such occurrences have been depicted as indicating the battleship-curve phenomenon of popularity through time rather than drop-off at the margins of spatially defined territories. Similar points are well represented with appropriate dates at the Diana site (Lopinot 1991) at the southern periphery of the American Bottom and, of course, in southern Illinois at the Ferry site (Fowler 1957). In fact, the Falling Springs phase seems to have its strongest affinity with the Midsouth.

Above, we rejected the type Saratoga Expanding Stemmed as a recognizable cognate for the McLean variety for reasons of poor dating and questionable associations. The strong presence of the Saratoga point type in the Midsouth, however, makes it a logical candidate on which to base definition of a type cluster or as either the antecedent or descendant form for the McLean point type. It is usually identified as a Late Archaic point type, and its association with later age contexts may be fortuitous. It is also possible that the Saratoga point was a Midsouth contemporary of the McLean point and lasted somewhat longer, in which case its occurrence in southwestern Illinois may signal an expansion and subsequent contraction of influence from a Midsouth-oriented population into this crossroads area of the Midwest. The distribution of this Late Archaic point type, as provided by Justice (1987:158), may constitute a rough approximation of the true heartland and possible place of origin. We would expand the distribution, however, to include the lower Illinois Valley as far north as Meredosia, beyond which the point declines in occurrence (Nolan and Fishel, this volume).

Titterington Phase (cal 2800–2500 B.C.)

The Titterington phase was the only Archaic phase recognized in southwestern Illinois prior to the inception of the FAI-270 investigations (McElrath et al. 1984). Titterington had defined a burial complex that included several large blade types on the basis of materials from seven sites in adjacent counties in Missouri and Illinois in the St. Louis vicinity, which he concluded "may represent one focus of a large widespread group" (1950:12). He compared and contrasted traits from these sites with those from the Hemphill site in the lower Illinois Valley and the Osceola site in Wisconsin, noting that, while they all shared some elements in common, the latter sites probably represented a separate focus. Although Titterington never named the St. Louis–area focus, it was quickly dubbed the "Titterington focus" by others (Perino 1954; Wray 1952) and retained this status in the American Bottom until investigations undertaken at the Go-Kart North site (Fortier 1983, 1984) yielded extensive information and allowed a phase designation to be applied.

Like many archaeological manifestations, the concept of a Titterington focus expanded beyond its original intent. Titterington originally recognized four (primarily behavioral) traits: the absence of pottery, compound burials, "certain" forms of knives or projectile points, and limestone slabs on top of burials. As an aside, he pointed out that six of the seven St. Louis–area sites showed evidence of red ocher covering the burials, a trait that was not, however, used to define the focus. Wray (1952) chose to draw attention to similarities between these sites and several Early Woodland–period (Roskamp focus) characteristics, noting the use of red ocher and the presence of such other shared characteristics as "the 'turkey-tail' point, laurel leaf blades, copper and hematite plummets, shell spoons, shell gorgets, galena, and stone tubes or pipes" (Wray 1952:158). Montet-White (1969:99–103) inadvertently added to the confusion by citing affiliations with the "Old Copper Culture" but also provided some much needed clarification by recognizing that some of the seven so-called Titterington sites were Late Archaic, while others were more likely Early Woodland.

Misconceptions still persist concerning this highly visible archaeological manifestation. Many of the traits and tool types assigned to this phase may be fortuitous inclusions as a result of the multicomponent nature of some "type" sites. Most of the sites mentioned by Titterington in his original report are bluff-top burial sites. These locations have been the focus of activity throughout the prehistory of this region; bluff tops were especially preferred as burial locations, and sites in these locales are notorious for yielding mixed assemblages. The materials from village sites potentially provide less mixed groups of associated diagnostics, although burial furniture may be largely absent from these locations. We are convinced, however, that some of the traits often associated with this phase are unrelated. For example, a strong case can be made that the production and use of hematite plummets was limited to the terminal Late Archaic Prairie Lake phase rather than associated with the earlier Titterington phase. In the American Bottom, we have recovered dozens of examples of grooved plummets along with production debris from Prairie Lake–phase sites (Emerson and Fortier 1986; McElrath and Fortier 1983; Yerkes 1986). Farnsworth and Asch (1986) have reached this same conclusion for the lower Illinois Valley. The presence of other "exotic" items is less clear; although the Go-Kart North site, a large single-component Titterington occupation, failed to yield bannerstones, copper artifacts, or drilled stone ornaments (Fortier 1984), excavations at the Hayden site in Missouri did recover such items (Harl 1998, this volume; Harl and Wright 1995).

Most researchers today recognize a strong cultural affinity among three related archaeological entities—Titterington, Sedalia, and Nebo Hill (often referred to as "TSN culture"). These archaeological manifestations, which occupy the southern Prairie Peninsula areas of Kansas, Missouri, Iowa, and Illinois, form a recognizable "horizon" and share a focus on the production of large, coarsely flaked, hafted bifaces and blades. Diagnostic hafted bifaces that occur in differing proportions at sites of this age include Etley, Sedalia, and Wadlow blades. We agree with Ray et al. (this volume) that the Stone Square Stemmed designation has lost its utility and should be avoided. The Turkey-tail point that was originally thought to pertain to this phase has also been dropped as a phase marker and tentatively assigned to the Early Woodland period. Red Ocher blades, which are sometimes ascribed to this cultural matrix, have since been found contextually in Early Woodland Marion-phase context (Stafford 1992), which provisionally rules them out as belonging to this decidedly Late Archaic cultural expression. Tool types that are strongly associated, however, with TSN culture include three-quarter-grooved axes (often oversized), small or miniature square celts (Figure 11.18) sometimes manufactured from hematite, massive mortar stones, and chert hammerstones. Other diagnostics that are sometimes associated are the "Clear Fork gouge" and the "Sedalia digger," with the latter more often associated with the Sedalia phase.

Figure 11.18. Titterington-phase diagnostics: a, b, small celts; c, Clear Fork gouge.

Two major sites dating to this period in the American Bottom region have been excavated: the Go-Kart North site (Monroe County, Illinois) and the Hayden site (St. Louis County, Missouri). At the Go-Kart North site, Titterington-age materials dominated the surface collection, and the landowner had amassed a significant collection. Several collectors from the area had also developed large personal collections from the site (Neal Lopinot, pers. comm. 1979). Given the large number of points recovered during excavation and the number of points in the hands of collectors, we can state with certainty that hundreds of large blade points originated from this site. A third site, the Poag Road site (originally reported by Munson 1971), has recently been extensively tested (Booth and Dasovich 2006); the portion of the site examined contained over 1,400 subsurface features dating to Early, Middle, and Late Archaic times. The large number of Titterington-phase artifacts recovered from the surface and plow zone during stripping and from the few excavated pits indicate that many of the features date to the Titterington phase (Don Booth, pers. comm. 2006). Clearly, a Titterington-age base camp or base locale is present at this site.

Although the Go-Kart North site is technically located on the floodplain, it is actually strategically positioned at the base of the Dupo Anticline on the outer bank of a relict channel of the Mississippi River, a convenient access point for exploiting both upland and bottomland resources. Aside from the dozens of projectile points recovered from the plow zone during heavy equipment stripping, 209 pit features were identified and excavated (Fortier 1983, 1984). The radiocarbon dates and associated materials indicate that these features date to the Titterington phase. Eight radiocarbon determinations were run and provide a remarkably tight cluster of seven dates ranging from cal 2829 B.C. to 2530 B.C. (Table 11.1). The features formed identifiable clusters that Fortier (1983, 1984) has suggested represent corporate groups arranged around central focal points (Figure 11.19). A large nonportable grinding mortar (27 kg) was recovered from one of these central points. Given the large number of artifacts recovered, the presence of nonportable site furniture, the formal nature of the site layout, and the failure to identify any comparable Titterington-age floodplain sites in any of our surveys, we believe that Go-Kart North likely represents a large permanent base camp or village.

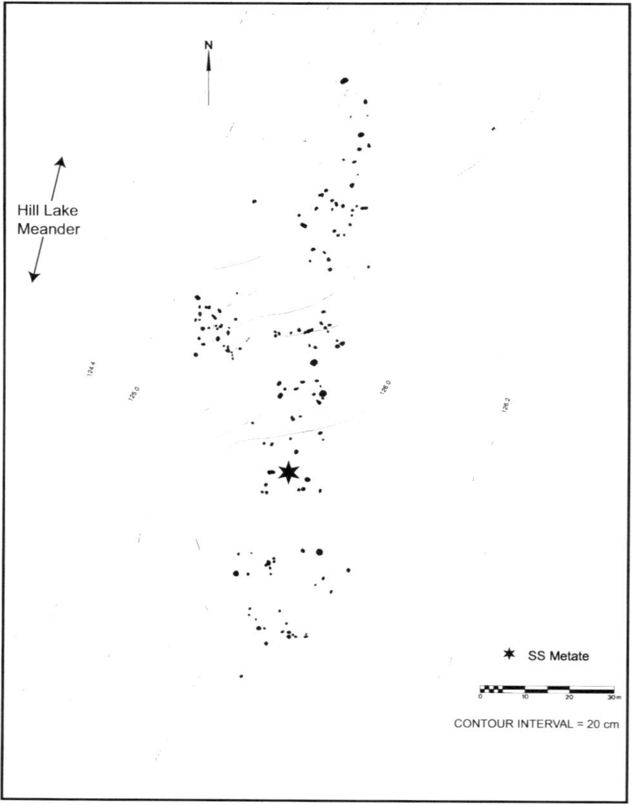

Figure 11.19. Go-Kart North Titterington-phase feature distribution.

The Hayden site is located on the bluff overlooking the Missouri River (Harl 1995, 1998, this volume). The site is multicomponent, yielding a predominance of Titterington-age materials, including 109 features. Four radiocarbon determinations (ranging from cal 2586 to 2457 B.C.) for the Titterington component parallel those from the Go-Kart North site. The points recovered from this site are identical to those from Go-Kart North. Numerous additional Titterington-age sites have been identified on the Missouri side of the American Bottom. Harl (1998, this volume) cites recent surveys documenting 10 Titterington-age sites in St. Charles County and an additional 29 in St. Louis County. He also summarizes excavations at two of the smaller investigated Titterington-phase sites in Missouri, Rabanus and 23SL329. Investigations resulted in the excavation of five features at Rabanus and six features at 23SL329. Although the sites were small, they yielded a significant quantity of lithic tools and debris, suggesting that tool production was important at both locations.

The Titterington people placed a strong emphasis on the production of oversized hafted bifaces, manufacturing some of the largest blades recorded for the Archaic period. It is difficult to believe that they required such hypertrophic specimens to engage in subsistence tasks. The large blades at the Go-Kart North site are consistently made on long flakes that often impart a distinctive "twist" to the blade. Despite the impressive size, the workmanship is often casual, with large, expanding secondary flakes removed to thin the blade; parallel flaking is almost nonexistent. Clearly, the production of these tools was an important ideational element of Titterington society. The production and caching of oversized blades occurred from the earliest times in North American prehistory (Brookes 1999; Gramly 1993; Walthall and Koldehoff 1998), but the intent of such practices is not well understood and may have varied considerably by period and culture. The placement of such implements among burial furnishings has obvious connotations, and we certainly have evidence that this practice occurred during Titterington times (see below), but the majority of the large-blade caches recovered in recent times are from nonburial contexts. It is possible that the blade and tool caches at Go-Kart North and Hayden were associated with burials that had long since deteriorated, but the absence of stone slabs of the type that Titterington noted and the lack of red ocher, copper, stone beads, and other exotics near these caches suggest otherwise.

The likelihood that at least some of the hypertrophic blades served mortuary functions is supported by three early discoveries in the region. One discovery, reported by Blake and Houser (1978), was of 10 Burlington-chert Wadlow blades measuring 20 to 27 cm in length. The blades were found at Jefferson Barracks in south St. Louis County, Missouri, and were subsequently acquired by Henry Whelpley. Little is known about the circumstances surrounding their discovery, but some of the blades bear the notation "grave" on them. The find was made atop a high bluff that overlooks the Mississippi River, which is consistent with known settings for Titterington-phase burial sites, and it is noteworthy that the Go-Kart North site is located just 5 km away. The second discovery, of a single Wadlow blade (24 cm long) of Burlington chert, was made by a farmer who reportedly plowed it out of a low mound near Lebanon, St. Clair County, Illinois, around 1935. The blade was acquired by a local collector and reported by Koldehoff (1980). Even less is known about the third discovery, of a Burlington-chert Wadlow blade (26 cm long) bearing the notation "St. Louis Co., Mo." The artifact was in the Franke Collection (Grimm 1953:41). On average, these blades are longer than most of the Wadlow and Etley (Figure 11.20) points or knives found at the Go-Kart North and Hayden sites and on most other habitation sites in the region, and they are, therefore, possible candidates for mortuary offerings.

The hafted bifaces of this period, however, are not all large; indeed, the majority of the assemblages are made up of morphologically more functional points of the smaller Etley (née Stone Square Stemmed) varieties (Figure 11.21). Several researchers have pointed out that large quantities of production debris typify Titterington-phase sites (Fortier 1984; Harl 1998; Reid 1984). This has led Reid (1984) and Harl (1998) to suggest that groups were "mapping" onto major chert outcrop locations along the Keokuk-Burlington bedrock formation to have convenient access to the raw material necessary to produce the socially valued hypertrophic blades. We agree and note that, while Go-Kart North is not immediately adjacent to a source of tabular chert suitable for large blade production, it was within easy reach (by canoe and land) of the Crescent quarries in Missouri, where both Fern Glen and Burlington cherts are available in large quantities. Aside from these two raw materials, Bailey and Cobden cherts from southern Illinois and rhyolite from the St. Francois Mountains of Missouri often occur in assemblages (see below), suggesting at least minimal interaction or travel between the American Bottom and southern Illinois and southwest Missouri.

The interaction of Titterington-phase groups with contemporaneous populations to the west has been the topic of some discussion for the past three decades. Titterington's original observations focused on the northern American Bottom and the lower Illinois River valley. Klippel (1969) noted the similarity between Titterington material in these areas and Sedalia-complex (Seelen 1961) artifacts from central and northern Missouri. Additional comparisons have been drawn to the earlier-defined Nebo Hill complex (Shippee 1948), especially by Reid (1984), who views the TSN cultural continuum as representing three historically related and interacting groups that shared a "polythetic set" of diagnostic points that they used in differing relative proportions. Harl (1998), in contrast, sees the Titterington and Sedalia phases as representing a single group arbitrarily given different designations as a result of regionally focused archaeological scholarship.

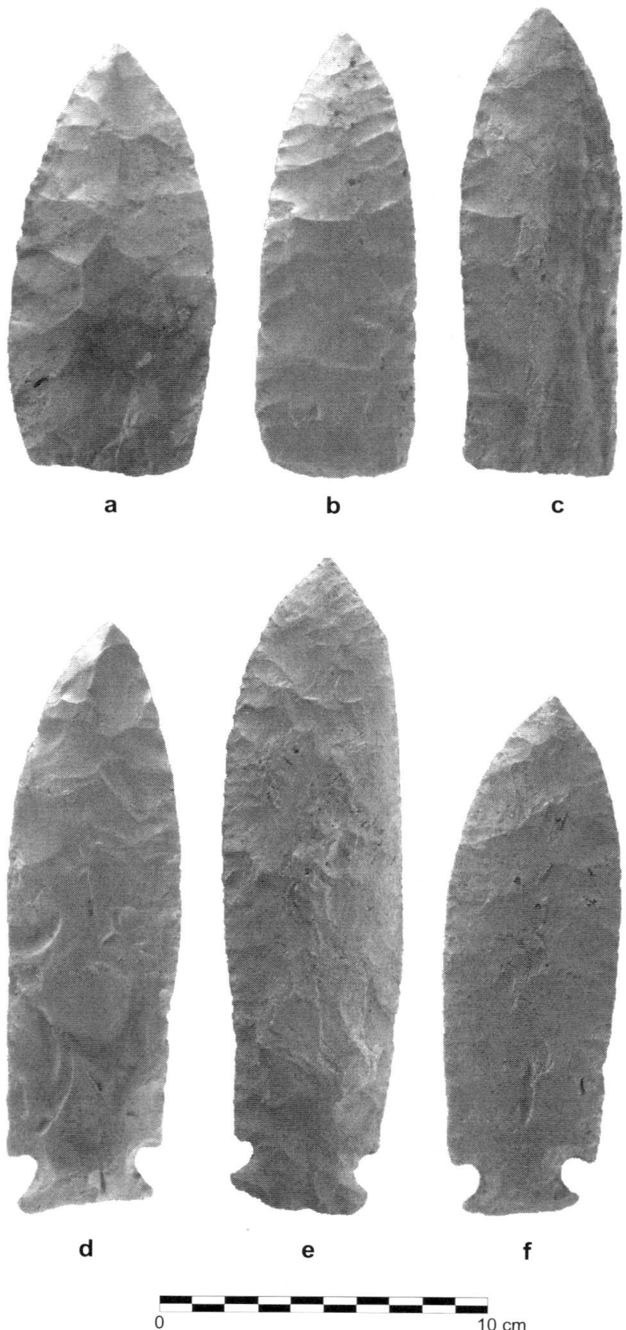

Figure 11.20. Titterington-phase diagnostics: a–c, Wadlow blades; d–f, Etley blades.

At one time, Nebo Hill was thought to predate Sedalia and Titterington (Reid 1984), which would imply a west-to-east spread of the TSN manifestation (Klippel 1969; McElrath 1993), but given the limited number of radiocarbon dates and the often poor context of materials, it is best to withhold judgment on this issue until more data are available (also see Nolan 2004; Nolan and Fishel, this volume). It seems certain, however, on the basis of available dates, that the Sedalia-phase occupation of Missouri continued well after the Titterington occupation in Illinois ceased. This is consistent with a model that proposes a Titterington-phase intrusion into the confluence region of Illinois for a short period, followed by a westward retreat. The dates in Illinois are remarkably consistent, and the area occupied is fairly small; the enigmatic Airport site in Sangamon County (Roper 1978) represents the extreme northeastern extent of this manifestation. This perspective on the age of the Titterington phase differs markedly with the position of most lower Illinois River valley researchers, who postulate a local Titterington-phase emergence from the Helton phase (Brown and Vierra 1983; Cook 1976; Odell 1996; Wiant et al. 1983).

Several researchers have explored the relationship between the TSN culture and the expansion of the Prairie Peninsula during the Hypsithermal (Harl 1998, this volume; Klippel 1969; McMillan 1971; Reid 1984), but the timing and impact of this midcontinental climatic phenomenon (Van Nest 1997) casts doubt on any correlation. The Titterington eastward expansion actually dates to a period long after the termination of the Hypsithermal. Environmental explanations, in general, have come under criticism recently, and generally we concur that environmental shifts, because of their gradual, time-transgressive nature, make poor candidates for triggering mechanisms for cultural change. However, we are not opposed to the concept of a preferential mode of subsistence, or, perhaps more accurately, a well-established and successful economy, flourishing in the context of an expanding favorable environmental setting. We would point out that Reid's suggestion of a population mapping onto outcrops of chert suitable for the production of the socially necessary supersized blades is not dependent on environmental change but on the physical location of suitable chert sources.

Plant-use evidence at the Go-Kart North site (Johannessen 1984) is consistent with that noted for other Late Archaic phases and indicates heavy reliance on nuts. An interesting difference, however, is evident in animal species exploited at this time. In the previous Falling Springs phase, fish, deer, and waterfowl were emphasized (Thorson and Styles 1992), suggesting continuity with earlier periods, and, while fish are represented at both Go-Kart North (Fortier 1984) and in the Titterington-age deposits at Modoc Rock Shelter (Thorson and Styles 1992), an emphasis on deer appears to have been paramount. Also, while birds are present, waterfowl are underrepresented and the birds hunted are indicative of an upland orientation (e.g., turkey). This pattern of upland economic orientation is consistent with the observed rarity of Titterington-age sites and diagnostics on the floodplain. Although actual site distribution mimics that of the preceding Falling Springs phase, a floodplain focus is evident in the floral and faunal remains for the earlier period. Wiant et al. (this volume) identify a similar pattern for the Titterington occupation in the lower Illinois Valley region. This pattern possibly reflects unstable floodplain conditions; more likely, it reflects an economic interest historically developed on the part of TSN-culture groups. In this regard, we have noted

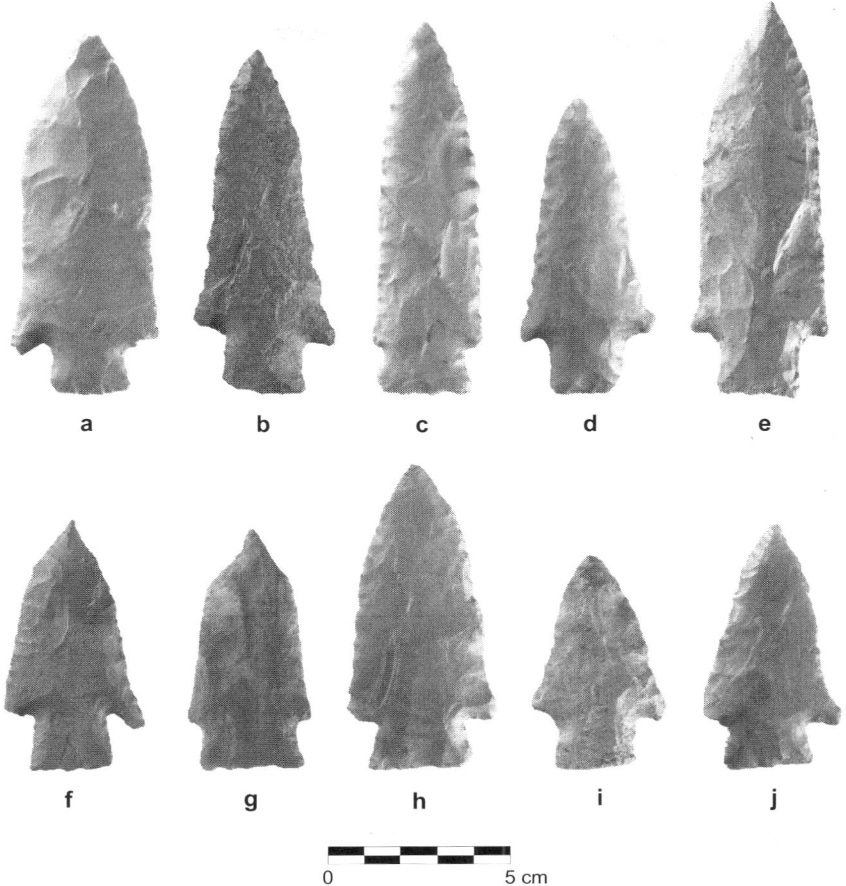

Figure 11.21. Titterington-phase diagnostics: a–e, narrow-bladed Etleys; f–j, broad-bladed Etleys.

that the Go-Kart North site is unique in this locale. It is the only known significant Titterington-phase occupation in the central American Bottom. Its location on the bank of the Mississippi River at a strategic point that allows easy access to the adjacent upland areas may indicate that it was the southeastern outpost of a group centered in northeastern Missouri (around the confluence of the Mississippi, Missouri, and Illinois rivers). The Go-Kart North site may have been a base settlement from which the rich forested upland resources between the American Bottom basin and the Kaskaskia River were exploited.

In Koldehoff's (2006) upland study areas, Titterington-phase bifaces, especially Etley points, are generally well represented. They are uncommon at one of the three bluff-top areas, Eagle Cliff, although they are well represented at both New Valmeyer and the Modoc Uplands. This lends support to the interpretation that the bulk of the ax and bannerstone production at New Valmeyer and Eagle Cliff belongs to the Middle Archaic occupations (see discussion of Dennis Hollow phase above). Away from the bluffs, most Titterington-phase sites are represented by a few diagnostic points, but in the Douglas Creek study area, four sites have produced more than eight diagnostic points each. Two of the sites may represent base camps: one has produced 16 points in addition to a small rectangular ground-stone (basalt) celt and a rectangular Burlington-chert chipped celt or gouge; the other has produced 24 points and several axes. Both sites also have ample amounts of debitage and numerous cobble tools that may be associated with the Titterington components.

As with all of the previous Archaic phases, Burlington chert (especially from the Crescent Hills quarries) is the preferred raw material, but it is seldom heat treated. An assortment of regional and extraregional types is also represented. Three raw materials deserve mention. Points made of Bailey and Cobden cherts from southern Illinois are routinely present in site assemblages, albeit in small numbers (Koldehoff 2006); however, these points are significant because they denote regular interaction with southern groups. These points appear to have been made by southern knappers because they only approximate Etley points; they are typically narrower than "classic" Etleys, usually lack barbs, and often have unworked or truncated bases. In most cases, these points closely match what Koldehoff (1992) identified as Saratoga Stemmed points in the Titterington-age deposits at the Little Muddy Rock Shelter. In those deposits, most points are made from Bailey and Cobden cherts, but a single point made from Crescent Hills Burlington was recovered. The third raw material of interest is St. Francois rhyolite, which has source areas in the Ozarks along the southwestern periphery of the American Bottom region. At the Hayden site in St. Louis County, Missouri, Harl (1995:57) reports, several points are made from these same raw materials. And he also recognizes that the points made from Bailey and Cobden cherts are similar but not identical to Etley points and chooses to call them Stone Square Stemmed. We would argue these latter points should be called Saratoga Stemmed. These patterns of raw material use clearly indicate some type of exchange network involving Titterington groups in the American Bottom region and groups to the south.

Mule Road Phase (cal 2100 B.C.?)

The surmised ca. 300-year Titterington-phase occupation of a small portion of southwestern Illinois was apparently followed by the intrusion of a group from the south that was also seemingly fixated on tabular, unheated cherts for the production of large blades. The Mule Road phase chronologically succeeds the Titterington phase and is best known from the multicomponent George Reeves site (McElrath 1993; McElrath and Finney 1987). Originally, the Mule Road materials were thought to represent a localized variant of the Titterington phase, although a stylistic connection with the Southeast was recognized (McElrath and Finney 1987:10). Although a significant Mule Road–phase occupation occurs at George Reeves, only a single radiocarbon determination has been run on available material, yielding a date with multiple intercepts (cal 2128, 2080, and 2045 B.C.). Mule Road–phase points (Figure 11.22) appear to be cognates of points in the Ledbetter cluster in the South (McElrath 1993). Whether the square-stemmed specimens recovered from George Reeves represent the final versions in a progression from more contracting-stemmed examples is unknown; several points from the site, however, have stems that appear intermediate between the two forms (cf. McElrath and Finney 1987). Dozens of blanks, manufacturing failures, and completed Ledbetter-style points, made primarily from Crescent Hills Burlington chert, were recovered at the George Reeves site, which seems to have served as a lithic workshop area as well as a habitation location (not unlike the Go-Kart North site). The hafted bifaces from this assemblage are somewhat smaller than those from the Go-Kart North site and are made from cores of tabular chert. Also, unlike the Go-Kart North site, the entire production sequence is evident in the production failures recovered from the site (Figure 11.22a–e) The Mule Road lithic tool assemblage, in addition to distinctive hafted bifaces, includes distinctive large, rectanguloid bifaces that have been identified as gouges or adzes (Figure 11.23b), several "bifacially chipped chert hammerstones" (Figure 11.23c), and a single example of an even more distinctive bell-shaped grinding stone or pestle (Figure 11.23a). This type of grinding stone occurs very commonly in the Southeast in Middle and Late Archaic contexts but is rare in the Midwest.

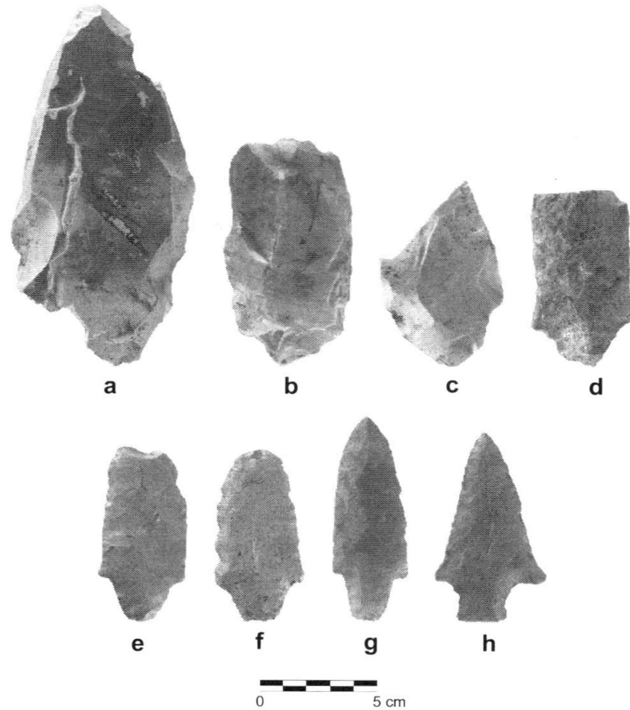

Figure 11.22. Mule Road phase: a–d, Mule Road (Ledbetter) production sequence; e–g, Mule Road points; h, Pickwick point.

Figure 11.23. Mule Road phase: a, bell-shaped pestle; b, rectanguloid adze; c, "bifacial chert hammerstone."

Whereas the immediately preceding Titterington phase appears to represent an intrusion of people from the west (albeit in some contact with southern Illinois groups or with a predilection for the use of southern Illinois cherts), all of the cultural antecedents of the Mule Road phase are clearly to the south (McElrath 1993:154–155). We view this shift not merely as reflecting a shifting sphere of influence but as involving actual population migration. Whether the Ledbetter groups were taking advantage of a region vacated by the Titterington culture or whether they partially coexisted with or actively pushed out the former occupants is not known. In any event, the occupation of the American Bottom region by populations from the south seems to have been rather short-lived. Mule Road–phase sites are the least common Late Archaic–phase sites in the region. Sporadic surface materials have been recovered from floodplain and upland sites in the region, for example, at the Nochta site (Fortier 1990), and at least one sizable site assemblage comes from the Douglas Creek study area (see below). Otherwise, there is no evidence for a major occupation in the American Bottom. Mule Road–phase material has been identified north of the American Bottom in the Mississippi River floodplain (McElrath 1993), but points show up only occasionally in surface collections (Nolan and Fishel, this volume). Winters identified similar points in the Cache River valley of southern Illinois, which he typed as Wetaug points. The scant representation of such points farther north in Illinois may indicate short-lived occupation by a group whose heartland lay considerably farther to the south. Also, the little information available to the north suggests that the equivalent cultural groups show up before the Sedalia-phase groups in the area; since Sedalia is thought to be a variant of the Titterington phase in the American Bottom, this would imply an inverted sequence to the north. Clearly, additional information needs to be developed to address this seemingly paradoxical situation.

Koldehoff (2006) identified small numbers of Mule Road points in six of his seven upland study areas, with the Douglas Creek study area yielding a high of 18 points. Six of these points are from one site that also produced a bell-shaped pestle. This site is the only example of a possible Mule Road base camp or favored hunting camp. As with the Titterington phase, unheated Burlington chert from the Crescent Hills quarries was the preferred raw material for chipped-stone points and tools. Use of extraregional and other regional raw materials is indicated by a small number of points.

Labras Lake Phase (cal 1750–1400 B.C.)

After the apparently brief foray into southwestern Illinois by southern groups represented by the Mule Road phase, the American Bottom region was (re)inhabited by groups that had decidedly more local midwestern and midsouthern ties; in particular, a relationship with the Ohio and Wabash River regions of southeastern Illinois is suggested. This is underscored by the presence in the region of the diminutive points of the Riverton type cluster (Merom, Trimble, and Robeson; Winters 1969) (Figure 11.24a–e). Such points are found sporadically throughout all of Illinois but never seem to predominate except in the Wabash and Ohio River regions of the state. In the American Bottom, Merom points co-occur as a consistent minority with an expanding-stem point type recently termed "Whale-tail" (Figure 11.24). They are well represented at both the Labras Lake (Phillips and Hall 1981; Yerkes 1987) and Floyd (Evans 2001) sites and, although they have not been contextually dated, their occurrence at these two sites and not at Missouri Pacific #2 or Dyroff-Levin suggests that they date to the Labras Lake phase. A third point type, a medium-sized, expanding-stemmed biface that Evans (2001) has designated the Floyd point type (Figure 11.24), shows affinities with the Mo-Pac point type but is apparently associated with the Labras Lake phase, possibly continuing into the succeeding Prairie Lake phase. Floyd points may be a regional cognate of Winters's Robeson point type.

The Labras Lake site, which lends its name to the phase, was the first major open-air Late Archaic site in the American Bottom to be analyzed (Phillips et al. 1980). Over 200 features from several large habitation areas yielding diagnostic Late Archaic materials were excavated. The presence of two distinct components at the site, however, was not appreciated by the initial analysts. The subsequent analysis of assemblages from the neighboring Dyroff-Levin (Emerson 1980) and Missouri Pacific #2 (McElrath and Fortier 1983) sites convinced FAI-270 researchers that the Labras Lake site represented occupations by both Labras Lake and Prairie Lake–phase peoples. Indeed, radiocarbon dates eventually demonstrated the presence of two temporally and spatially discrete occupations dating to late Late Archaic times (Hall 1981:413). Although Phillips

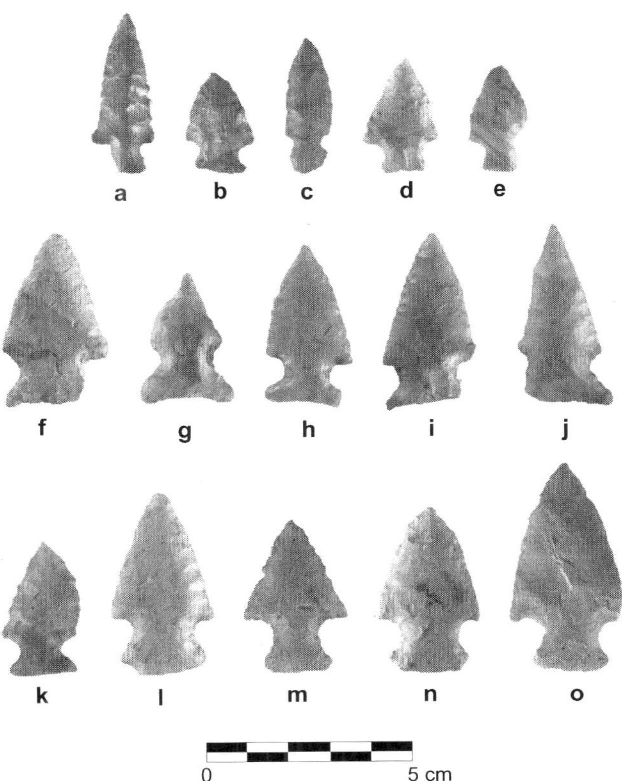

Figure 11.24. Labras Lake phase: a–e, Riverton points; f–k, Whale-tail points; l–o, Floyd points

and Gladfelter (1983) did not distinguish different phases in their discussion of the Labras Lake materials in the influential Phillips and Brown volume (1983), a subsequent reanalysis by Yerkes (1987) recognized and incorporated a division. Yerkes, however, focused on edge-wear analysis of debitage and did not illustrate or describe diagnostic tools in detail or discuss them contextually. The Labras Lake site is the only site that has yielded a substantially large occupation dating to this period for which the individual features can be separated; its reexamination would, therefore, shed considerable light on this period. More recently, the Marge site (Fortier 1996) has yielded features as well as surface diagnostics and five radiocarbon dates for this little-understood archaeological phase. The Marge site occupation includes 33 features: 30 pits, a house structure, and two hearths. The house was an irregular-shaped basin post structure with six interior pits and a prepared-floor hearth. It contained 11 tools, including a "Karnak"-like point, chert scrapers, worked hematite, and several sandstone metates (Fortier 1996:39–44). The house measured roughly 4.8 m x 4.0 m and its basin was 25–30 cm in depth. A date of cal 1554 B.C. was obtained on the house, making it the earliest directly dated structure in the American Bottom.

With its 195 features, the Floyd site, in the Savanna Terrace locality, represents a sizable terminal Late Archaic occupation. Both Labras Lake and Prairie Lake components are present (Evans 2001). The occurrence of 10 Whale-tail and 16 Floyd points, types associated exclusively with the Labras Lake phase, indicates that the Labras Lake component at the site is significant. Ten Labras Lake–phase dates, five each from the Marge and Labras Lake sites, have yielded central intercepts ranging from cal 1745 to 1401 B.C., a date range consistent with Riverton-age materials from the southeastern side of the state (Winters 1969). Because Riverton points are a minority in the suite of points recovered from Labras Lake–phase contexts, the implication is that, unlike the two previous American Bottom phases, which appear to represent cultural transplants from distant places, the Labras Lake phase was a more local development that involved some level of interaction with nearby regions occupied by Riverton-culture groups. Reid (1984) has identified Riverton points on TSN-culture sites west of the Mississippi, suggesting a shared frontier. It is indeed ironic that the TSN culture, with its penchant for oversize points (the largest produced during the Archaic), shared a boundary with the Riverton culture, which produced the smallest known Archaic points. This contemporaneity of hypertrophic and diminutive point types confounds any attempt to place projectile points by size into an evolutionary size-gradient trend (contra Shott 1996). Because the cultural manifestations predating Labras Lake in the American Bottom were territorially limited to the western (Titterington) and southwestern (Mule Road) portions of Illinois, we assume that they were unrelated to coeval social entities in central Illinois and Indiana. The Labras Lake manifestation may represent an expansion into the American Bottom area by or renewed contacts with nearby eastern (i.e., Wabash Valley) groups filling the void left by the retreating Ledbetter (i.e., Mule Road phase) groups.

Little subsistence information has been generated for the Labras Lake phase because of the mixing at most sites and because features were not separated for analysis at the type site. Some insights, however, have been gained from the analysis of plant remains from the Marge site. These remains include nut, wood, and seeds, with nutshell dominant (Simon 1996:79–94). The site's bluff-base locale offered equal access to upland and bottomland wood sources. The seeds, all from nondomesticated plants, include examples of chenopodium, erect knotweed, maygrass, and little barley. A single wild bean was also recovered. No faunal remains were preserved at the site. It is likely that Labras Lake–phase groups followed standard Late Archaic subsistence strategies, with a primary focus on floodplain (wetland) resources; in the case of Marge, nearby upland resources were also targeted. This interpretation is supported by the location of major Late Archaic habitations immediately adjacent to floodplain resources and by the low numbers of Labras Lake–phase points in upland settings (Koldehoff 2006). Most points from Labra Lake contexts are heat treated and manufactured from Burlington chert, but several points manufactured from glacial chert cobbles have been found.

Prairie Lake Phase (cal 1400–900 B.C.)

The terminal Late Archaic Prairie Lake phase is the best-represented Archaic phase in the region. Significant components are described from the Missouri Pacific #2 site (McElrath and Fortier 1983), Dyroff-Levin (Emerson 1984), Floyd (Evans 2001), Labras Lake (Phillips and Hall 1981; Yerkes 1987), Cahokia ICT-II (Nassaney et al. 1983), Range (Fortier 1987), and the smaller Meyer (Fortier et al. 1998) and Wooded sites (Abbott 1989). The phase appears to be indistinguishable from the Kampsville phase in the lower Illinois Valley and the McCraney Creek phase in the Mississippi River valley north of the American Bottom (Farnsworth and Asch 1986), and it is similar to the Logan phase in the LaMoine River valley (Conrad 1986). We have long noted the close morphological similarities between the diagnostic projectile points of the Prairie Lake peoples and points manufactured by inhabitants of the Midsouth (e.g., Emerson and McElrath 1983:227). The resemblance is especially close between American Bottom points and the Buck Creek Barbed point style (Seeman 1975) from southern Indiana and the adjacent Ohio River valley in Ohio and Kentucky. This suggests the contacts established during the Labras Lake phase between the Wabash drainage, the Midsouth, the central Mississippi River valley, and the American Bottom continued and, in fact, expanded during the terminal Late Archaic.

The Prairie Lake phase represents the final Archaic occupation of the American Bottom. Temporal placement is based on 20 radiocarbon determinations from several major sites. The radiocarbon determinations securely date this phase to cal 1400–900 B.C. (Table 11.1). Prior to use of the calibration sequence for establishing temporal parameters, a younger termination date was suggested (Emerson et al. 1986; Emerson and McElrath 1983; McElrath et al. 1984) on the basis of a late date at the Missouri Pacific #2 site. This date, which has a calibrated central intercept of 771 B.C., was obtained from a feature that also yielded the oldest date at the site (central intercept of cal 1004 B.C.). Given the large suite of dates now available, we would question this more recent outlying date, as we would the late fifteenth-century B.C. date from the ICT-II Tract site (Nassaney and Lopinot 1986).

Terminal Prairie Lake–phase hafted-biface diagnostics include the triangular, square-stemmed Dyroff point (Figure 11.25a–e), the somewhat larger, triangular-bladed, square- to expanding-stemmed Springly point (Figure 11.25f–j), and the short, expanding-stemmed Mo-Pac point (Figure 11.25k–o) (Emerson 1980, 1984; Emerson and McElrath 1983; McElrath and Fortier 1983).

Infrequently occurring but diagnostic artifacts are grooved (as opposed to drilled) hematite plummets of the Snyders and Gilcrease varieties (Farnsworth and Asch 1986:342; Goldstein 2004). Plummet manufacturing debris is present in the Prairie Lake–phase components at Labras Lake (Yerkes 1986) and Missouri Pacific #2 (Figure 11.26a–e). Such plummets were originally thought to date to the Titterington phase (Titterington 1950) or even to Middle and Late Woodland times (Perino 1961:55–56), but we agree with Farnsworth and Asch (1986:340) that when found in secure contexts they occur exclusively on Prairie Lake–culture sites (often as burial goods). They occur at Titterington-age sites only where Prairie Lake–phase occupations are also present. Other artifacts associated with the phase include grinding and nutting stones, celts, multiple types of general-utility chert tools, and less usual items such as cloud-blower pipes (or shaman sucking tubes), gorgets, stone beads, and hematite pestles (Figure 11.26).

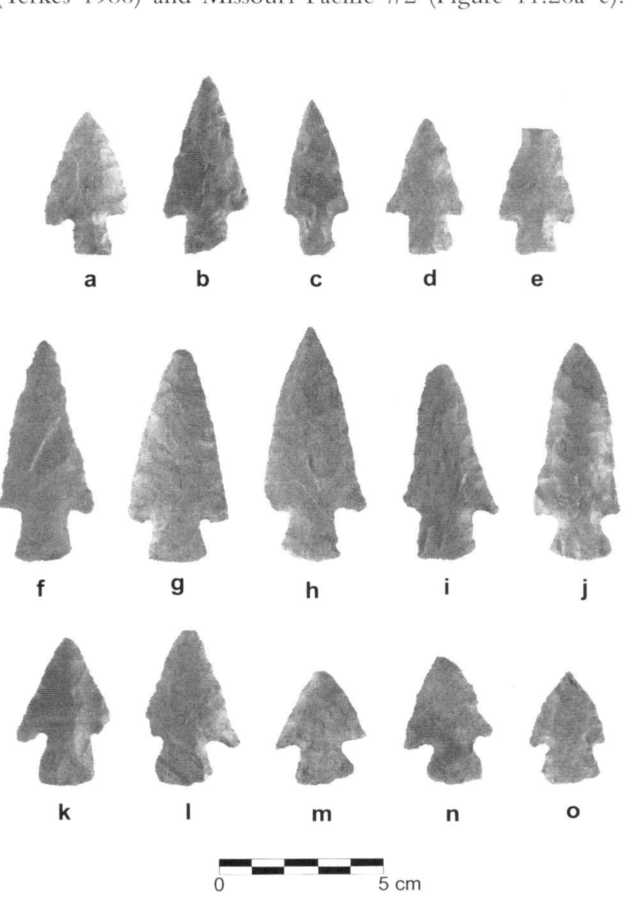

Figure 11.25. Prairie Lake phase: a–e, Dyroff points; f–j, Springly points; k–o, Mo-Pac points.

Figure 11.26. Prairie Lake–phase diagnostics: a–e, plummet production sequence; f, cloud blower pipe; g, gorget.

Terminal Late Archaic sites are rich in many types of features, and just over 2,000 examples have been excavated, primarily from five major Prairie Lake–phase sites. These features are most commonly shallow basins with little evidence of use as fire pits and were presumably used for food processing; a few show evidence of in situ burning, suggesting roasting or cooking. Evans (2001:57–61) reviewed pit features from eight Prairie Lake habitation areas and found they had a mean maximum depth of only 23 cm and lengths ranging from 59 to 76 cm. These shallow depressions typically contain fill similar to that of the extensive sheet middens of fragmentary calcined bone, charred wood and nut fragments, and burned clay that blanket sites of this period. The pits must have been repeatedly cleaned out and reused. The sheet middens suggest that surface hearths were commonly employed for heating and cooking. At the floodplain occupations, the pits are excavated into clay, even when sandy soils occur nearby. This has led some to speculate that these pits served to hold water (perhaps having been lined with dried animal skins). This interpretation is compatible with a method of cooking by heating rocks in a surface fire and transferring them to a water-filled hide, basket, or clay-lined shallow basin. Some researchers have suggested that the innovation of pottery was simply the logical extension of using a clay-lined pit to hold water (Sassaman 1993). We note that when pottery made its appearance in the American Bottom during Early Woodland times, it often appeared in the sandier or siltier habitation locales. The introduction of pottery may have enabled rock boiling nearer to where food resources actually occurred, away from the gumbo clay soil localities that were the focus of Terminal Archaic habitations.

Prairie Lake–phase pits are usually found in spatially discrete clusters that might represent the activity areas of nuclear or extended families (Figure 11.27). Possible domestic structures have been identified at Missouri Pacific #2 (McElrath and Fortier 1983) and Labras Lake (Yerkes 1987). Such facilities are usually recognized as circumscribed activity areas ranging in size from 3 to 16 m^2, sometimes with scattered support posts, and marked by shallow fill zones that include domestic debris, pits, and hearths (e.g., Fortier 1993:260–263). One structure at the Missouri Pacific #2 site is represented by a circular, ca. 10-m-diameter post arbor that circumscribes a cluster of 21 cooking pits (McElrath and Fortier 1983:60). The earliest reported Archaic-age domestic structure is from Middle Archaic times (Higgins 1990); the only other identifiable open-air Archaic structures recognized thus far occur in terminal Late Archaic contexts.

Poor preservation at Terminal Archaic sites has hampered proper understanding of subsistence, but rare insight on plant use is derived from a buried horizon at the ICT Tract at the Cahokia site (Nassaney and Lopinot 1986) that yielded seeds of some 30 plant taxa (including marsh elder, giant ragweed, and chenopod). This pattern is also reflected in the preserved floral remains from the large Prairie Lake–phase occupation at the Floyd site (Parker 2001). As one might expect, nuts were common, especially hickory, walnut, and some acorn. Analysis of the Floyd seed assemblage provided important information on early horticultural practices, including the purposeful harvesting of barnyard grass, chenopod, and little barley. Legumes, fruits, and such aquatic plants as lotus and cattails were also used. Parker (2001) concluded from her analysis that occupants of the Floyd site, and likely those at similar Prairie Lake–phase sites, were practicing incipient gardening and were involved in plant exploitation activities that would have supported multiseasonal use of the occupation area.

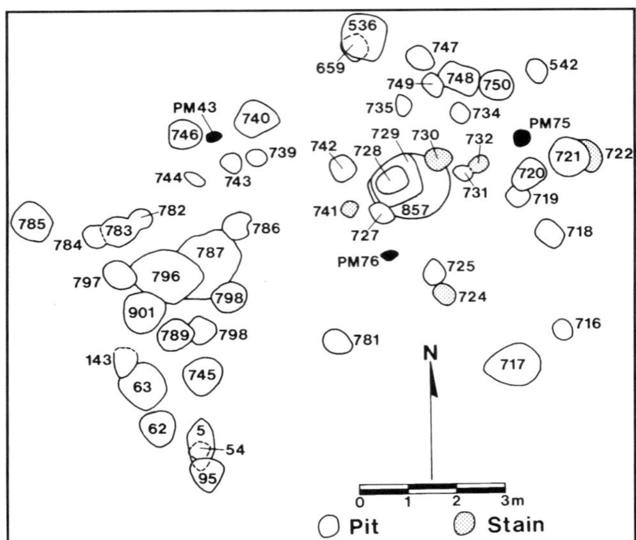

Figure 11.27. Prairie Lake–phase Pit Cluster V at Missouri Pacific #2.

Prairie Lake–phase points were recorded in all of Koldehoff's (2006) upland study areas, with notable concentrations in the interior stream valleys, Silver and Douglas creeks. Fewer points were recorded along the bluff tops and especially along the drainage divides (Route 3 divide and Fountain Creek headwaters). This pattern undoubtedly reflects the riverine and wetland focus of Prairie Lake–phase populations. Most upland sites are represented by only a few points, but several sites along Silver and Douglas creeks have produced more. Most of these sites likely represent brief seasonal encampments, probably associated with deer hunting. However, six sites along Douglas Creek have produced eight or more points each and may represent more substantial or repeated encampments. One site, in particular, may represent a base camp, since 23 points have been recovered along with a hematite Gilcrease Grooved plummet. This site is littered with cobbles, cores, and debitage, but much of the occupation refuse likely belongs to the site's earlier and much larger Falling Springs–phase occupation.

In the uplands as well as at the excavated floodplain sites, Burlington chert, often heat treated, was the preferred raw material for points (Koldehoff 2006). Minor but consistent numbers of points are made from regional (e.g., Salem, Fern Glen, and Ste. Genevieve) and extraregional (Bailey and Cobden) cherts. These extraregional cherts are primarily from southern Illinois, and points made from them often more closely resemble Cypress-cluster points than they do Dyroff or Mo-Pac points. Cypress-cluster points are diagnostic of the Terminal Archaic Au Vase phase defined by Koldehoff (1992) from investigations at the Little Muddy Rock Shelter. This phase is largely coeval with the Prairie Lake phase, and the regular occurrence of points made from southern cherts in American Bottom assemblages indicates routine interaction.

Substantial Prairie Lake–phase sites are rare in the uplands (Emerson et al. 1986; Fortier et al. 1998), suggesting a settlement system of multiseasonal floodplain base camps, likely occupied for most of the year; these occupations are so extensive, often extending for several kilometers along the backwater sloughs of the American Bottom, that they have been referred to as "base locales" (Emerson 1980; Emerson and McElrath 1983; Emerson et al. 1986). These base locales have been characterized as covering many hectares, containing a high density and diversity of artifactual remains (including status and ceremonial items), subsistence evidence of multiseasonal occupations (perhaps year-round), and various structural remains, including pits, houses, and, sometimes, burials. "One of the important features that distinguishes a base locale from a base camp ... is the high probability of having specialized activity zones (which may be used on a seasonal basis) within a base locale. ... In anthropological terms, we would see the base locale as arguing for macroband population (aggregations), as strongly suggestive of territorialism and possibly even of tribalism" (Emerson et al. 1986:251).

Perhaps the most completely investigated example of a base locale is the Prairie Lake locality near Dupo (Emerson et al. 1986:253–256). Here, at the base of the steep limestone bluffs, surveyors have identified over 186 ha of Late Archaic occupational debris distributed along the ridges, swales, banks, and levees associated with Prairie Lake. This Late Archaic habitation zone is interrupted only where the modern development of Dupo or intense later prehistoric occupations have eliminated it (Figure 11.28). During terminal Late Archaic times, Prairie Lake would have been a backwater lake and the course of the Mississippi River would have been immediately adjacent, flowing through the channels of the Goose Lake and Hill Lake paleomeanders (White et al. 1984; Yerkes 1987). The Prairie Lake locality also had two active springs, and several spring-fed streams flowed into it. The uplands were easily accessible via the stream valleys that cut the limestone bluffs.

The FAI-270 corridor ran through the western edge of the 5-km-long, 1-km-wide Prairie Lake locality, providing a unique opportunity for archaeologists to sample this intensely occupied zone. Each of the sampled areas was given a separate site name and number, thus creating the misconception that they were separate entities, rather than segments of a continuous occupation. From south to north, these six sampled areas are referred to as Missouri Pacific #2, Range, Falling Springs, Dyroff, Levin, and Labras Lake. Ultimately, excavations exposed an area of 76,068 m^2, only .04 percent of the likely Late Archaic occupation zone. These excavations have provided some interesting perspectives on the density of the terminal Late Archaic occupation and utilization of this locality. The number of pits per 100 m^2 within the 7.6 ha excavated by FAI-270 crews ranged from 1.8 to 10.8, giving an average of about four pits. A simple calculation suggests that between 33,550 and 200,800 pit features (or a mean of about 74,200 pits) might be present in the undeveloped areas of the Prairie Lake locality, depending on the variable densities and actual habitable area available in terminal Late Archaic times. Despite their limited nature, excavations determined that terminal Late Archaic occupants built structures, dug thousands of processing pits, and produced and used a wide range of both domestic and ritual artifacts in this circumscribed locality.

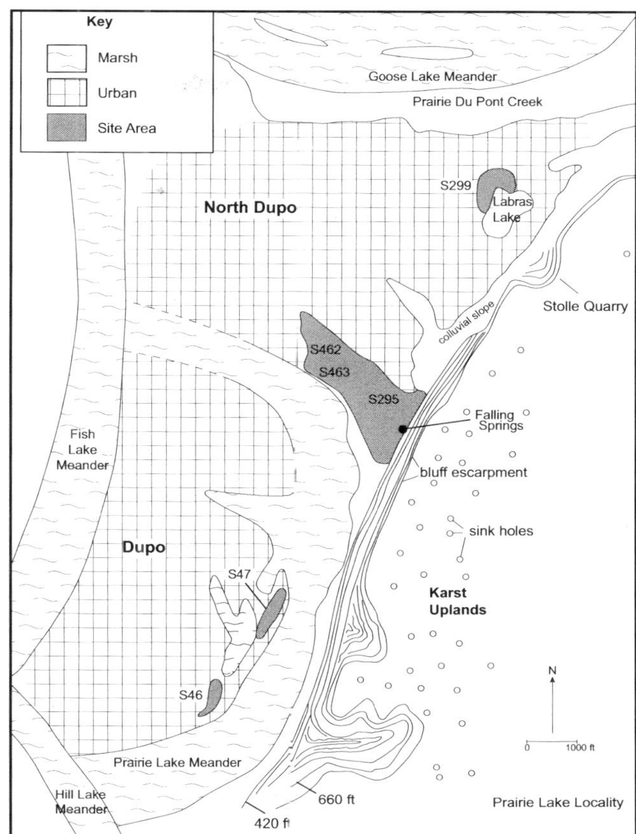

Figure 11.28. Prairie Lake base locale.

A second Prairie Lake base locale has been identified on the Savanna Terrace in the northern American Bottom floodplain, near the confluence of Cahokia and Indian creeks and within the Cahokia Creek Gap (Figure 11.29) locality. Sometime after the formation of the Savanna Terrace or perhaps during its formation, Cahokia Creek incised itself through the Savanna Terrace, creating a broad floodplain loessal mantle that

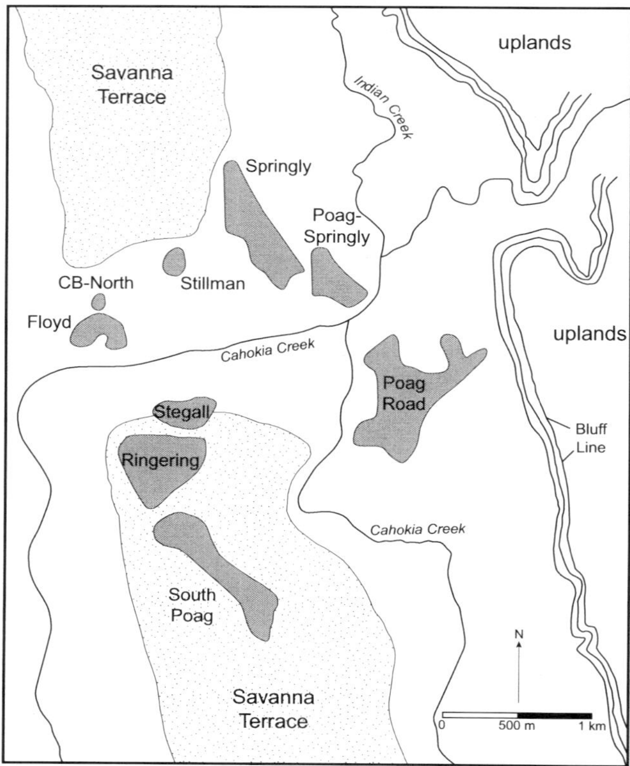

Figure 11.29. Cahokia Creek Gap base locale with known Archaic site locations.

overlies remnants of the older sand terrace. The Ringering (Evans and Evans 2000), Floyd (Evans 2001), and CB-North (Evans et al. 1997) sites, all of which have been excavated, are located in this area, and five other Archaic surface sites are known. The locale covers a several-kilometer-long and wide area with multiple landscapes.

The Poag Road site, situated at the confluence of Indian and Cahokia creeks, has produced a significant scatter of multicomponent Archaic materials. Extensive stripping has revealed over 1,400 features with Early, Middle, and Late Archaic materials (Booth and Dasovich 2006), including Prairie Lake–age materials. Excavations at the Stegall site, although producing no features, yielded evidence of an Early Archaic occupation. Other unexcavated site areas in this locale have produced similar distributions of Archaic artifacts. The Cahokia Creek Gap base locale, therefore, represents long-term, repeated use during the Archaic. The gap's proximity to the floodplain, the higher Savanna Terrace sand ridge, two prominent creeks, and the nearby uplands would have generally allowed access to multiple floodplain and upland resources.

Some researchers (Yerkes 1986) believe that terminal Late Archaic occupants of the American Bottom followed the type of seasonal round that has traditionally characterized highly mobile historic and modern hunter-gather groups. Others (Nassaney and Lopinot 1986) envision Late Archaic subsistence and settlement practices from the perspective of a reduced-mobility model that encompasses a residential-logistical continuum. Terminology aside, Nassaney and Lopinot's concepts of a relatively flexible and fluid pattern of occupation and use of American Bottom landscapes and resources during the Prairie Lake phase do not differ significantly from our past and current interpretations of this period (Emerson et al. 1986; Emerson and McElrath 2001). We have continually stressed the spatial circumscription, the high debris and feature densities, the availability of clustered and rich natural resources, and the evidence of multiseasonal occupation that typify Prairie Lake base locales, and the sparse evidence for occupations outside of these areas. We have interpreted this evidence to suggest that the occupants of such base locales had developed patterns of resource exploitation that allowed a considerable degree of residential stability and social and political mechanisms that allowed macroband aggregations to cohabit areas on a more or less continuous basis. This suggests to us that multiband collectivities (sensu tribes) were present, and the observed floodplain spatial circumscription may imply the existence of bounded territories.

The people of the terminal Late Archaic Prairie Lake phase clearly stand out from earlier Archaic groups in the American Bottom in terms of their subsistence practices, which included incipient cultivation of both Mesoamerican cultigens and native seed plants; their long-term occupation of especially resource-rich localities; their increasing production, acquisition, and use of ceremonial and ritual items; and their markedly greater overall population size and larger population aggregations. Their lifeway is even more distinctive because of its sudden collapse and eventual replacement by transitory Early Woodland groups in the mid-first millennium B.C.

The end of the large Terminal Archaic settlements along the length of the American Bottom floodplain appears, from the archaeological evidence, to have been fairly rapid and decisive. Most regional researchers have noted the strong correlation of Terminal Archaic site locations with the large active or recently abandoned channels that formed the backwater lakes along the bluff base, which still put them within easy reach of the Mississippi River channel (Emerson and Fortier 1986; Evans 2001; Evans and Evans 2000:385–388). Emerson and Fortier (1986:517) have suggested that changing hydrological conditions related to regional falling water levels in the first half of the first millennium B.C. may have negatively impacted these rich backwater-lake microenvironments. Additional research by Hajic (1990) has indicated that this period was marked by increased rainfall and flooding. These events caused the cutoff of meanders of the Mississippi River and its numerous secondary streams, thus, affecting floodplain resource distribution and density. As Evans and Evans (2000:386–387) detail, such hydrological changes would have affected the American Bottom Prairie Lake–phase occupations differentially, for example, flooding the Cahokia ICT area, cutting the Prairie Lake–locality lakes off from frequent replenishment, and shifting the course of the Mississippi far to the west. The

Ringering site area would have been relatively unaffected because of its high elevation, while nearby low-lying Smith Lake, adjacent to the Floyd site, would have been cut off, decreasing its overall biotic richness. The Terminal Archaic lifestyle, as we have discussed, was apparently dependent on the presence of the rich and plentiful resources of the large, seasonally renewed floodplain lakes. Any factors that affected that economic base placed the pattern of multiseasonal occupations by large groups of people in jeopardy. Such forces seem to have been active in the area between about cal 1000 and cal 500 B.C.

The evidence of the American Bottom Terminal Archaic to Early Woodland transition (if such an abrupt shift can be thought of as transitional) cannot be accommodated in a model that perceives Early Woodland cultures as simply Archaic lifestyles plus pottery (Emerson and Fortier 1986; Emerson and McElrath 2001; Fortier 2001). We have suggested that the appearance of Early Woodland groups took the form of a series of intermittent intrusions into the American Bottom by groups both from the north and the south. We only briefly discuss these groups here to suggest the flavor of the significant Archaic–Woodland shift in the region. Small Carr Creek–phase (Emerson and Fortier 1986) sites date to about cal 800 B.C. and represent the local variant of the broadly northern Marion culture. These family-sized sites contain Kramer points, evidence of limited ceramic manufacturing, rare cucurbit remains, and single structures and are found across all physiographic zones. The sites appear to represent residential camps of families who foraged widely across the landscape. Peripheral evidence of intrusive, likely southern-derived Ringering-phase, Black Sand–related families has been identified at a few locations in the floodplain and dates to about cal 750 to 800 B.C. (Evans and Evans 2000). These ephemeral camps are distinct from the Marion-culture sites, usually yielding a few fragments of diagnostic incised-over-cordmarked pottery and contracting-stem points.

Later in the Early Woodland period, more southern groups moved into the American Bottom, practicing a distinctive riverine-oriented lifestyle and bearing grog-tempered conoidal and subconoidal vessels decorated with fingernail or stab-and-drag designs. Their lithic tool kit includes contracting-stem points, Goose Lake knives, humpbacked scrapers, and many other scraping, drilling, and cutting tools. The one large Florence-phase (Emerson et al. 1983; Emerson and Fortier 1986) site excavated on the bank of the then active Mississippi River included a large wigwam-type structure and massive stone hearths covering up to 16 m^2. Related groups have been found up the Illinois River (Farnsworth and Asch 1986) and the Missouri River (Fishel 2005). In the American Bottom, they were apparently succeeded by the poorly understood Columbia-phase groups (ca. cal 200 to 150 B.C.), who appear to have possessed a diminished material inventory, perhaps derived from the earlier Florence phase (Evans and Evans 2000; Fortier 2001).

Discussion

Research into the Archaic occupation of the American Bottom has begun to provide insights into many of the issues that surround this little-understood portion of the archaeological record. In this section, we compare what we know of the various Archaic subperiods against the dominant paradigms used to explain the histories of the people who occupied the Midcontinent for nearly three-quarters of prehistory. Evidence generated by American Bottom researchers bears on several commonly discussed themes relevant to settlement and technological practices. In particular, we focus on ethnic identities, occupational histories, population movements, domestic activities, stone tool use and distribution, and economic practices in the context of patterns of land use and social interaction.

We suggested in this chapter that projectile point styles were likely tied to ethnic cores or communities of practice. The accurate recognition of the artifacts produced by any given practicing community of lithic knappers, then, can serve to define the areal extent of that community through time. Given this context, the comparative representations of point types at the regional level should serve as a (very) approximate marker of the relative intensity of occupation and interaction by groups for any given study area. A host of issues surrounds this bold assertion; aside from the obvious difficulties associated with point-type identification and the problem of achieving comparable survey coverage for landscape surfaces of varying age, the issue of how much time is represented in a given region by a specific point type remains unresolved. For example, numerical dominance of particular types is potentially a reflection of both population size (and density) and length of occupation. This begs the question, of course, of whether points were equivalent in purpose and use life. Clearly, the use of projectiles varied with hunting technique, game targeted, and weaponry employed (lances, darts, or even bows and arrows). Despite this variability, we can proportionally measure relative occupation "intensity" on the basis of point type and time to explore historical patterning of group interaction and establish a baseline of Archaic regional settlement history for the American Bottom.

For this purpose, we used only the surface survey data Koldehoff collected from the seven sampled upland areas (Figure 11.6). Although this data set does not incorporate the floodplain, it should be temporally representative because it is derived from landscape surfaces that were available for occupation or use during all of the periods to be compared. We chose to use only hafted bifaces in our calculations (so, e.g., we excluded Bass knives). We calculated point types as percentages of total points for each of the three arbitrary periods, Early, Middle, and Late Archaic. We also determined the number of points in the sample deposited per annum for each point type or defined phase as well as the mean for each period (Figure 11.30).

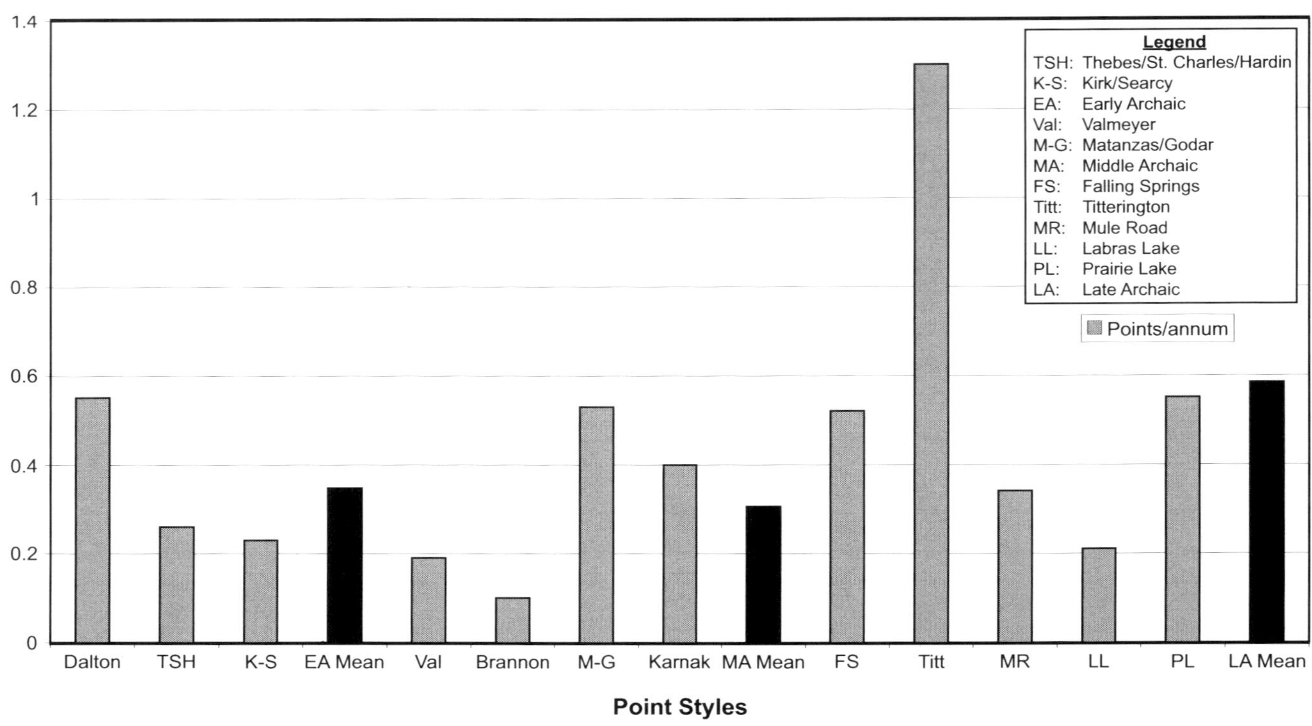

Figure 11.30. Relative per annum distribution of American Bottom Archaic projectile points.

Our tentative reconstruction of the Early Archaic sequence as reflected by point types (n = 813 artifacts) is as follows: Dalton, Thebes–St. Charles–Hardin, Kirk Corner Notched cluster, Cache River Side Notched, Graham Cave Side Notched, Bifurcate cluster, Kirk Stemmed cluster, Hidden Valley Stemmed, and Searcy. Because we lack directly dated examples of most of these point types in the American Bottom, and to avoid the issue of contemporaneity of point types, we grouped suites of points into generally accepted time brackets to reveal evidence of use through time. Dalton is the least well-dated horizon in the Midwest, but most researchers assign it a time frame of about 500 years. The Theban–St. Charles–Hardin (TSH) suite has slightly more reliable dates, and if we use the time frame supplied by Nolan and Fishel (this volume), we assume a 1,200-year duration. We have more locally applicable information for the Kirk Corner Notched through Searcy (K–S) points at Modoc (Strata EA 1 and EA 2), giving us a time frame of a millennium for this suite of point types (Ahler and Koldehoff, this volume). Daltons account for about 34 percent (n = 273) of all Early Archaic points recovered from the sampled survey areas. The THS suite has a similar level of representation (n = 306; ca. 38 percent). The remaining Early Archaic point types appear in decreasing numbers and, combined, represent less than 30 percent (n = 234) of the survey sample. The numbers of points deposited per annum is as follows: Dalton, .55; TSH, .26; and K–S, .23.

Our reconstructed Middle Archaic sequence of points is Valmeyer, Brannon, Matanzas, Godar, and Karnak. This sequence has a greater degree of reliability than the Early Archaic sequence because it is regionally anchored at either end, with the first two point types associated with dated archaeological phases (Dennis Hollow and Nochta phases) and the last assigned to a dated complex (Tep complex). The temporal relationship between the Matanzas and Godar types is more speculative, and their occurrence at Modoc and at Koster may or may not imply contemporaneity; given the occurrence of Godar points at open-air sites that date to slightly later Middle Archaic times (e.g., Tep complex) in the American Bottom, we prefer a Matanzas–Godar ordering but are open to alternative scenarios. The percentage occurrence of Middle Archaic–period point types (n = 642 artifacts) in the survey sample is as follows: Dennis Hollow phase, Valmeyer points, n = 52, 8 percent; Nochta phase, Brannon points, n = 35, 5 percent; Matanzas points, n = 164, 26 percent; Godar points, n = 311, 48 percent; and Karnak points, n = 80, 12 percent.

Basing the deposition rates for individual point types on the available date ranges for the respective phases, and by arbitrarily dividing the 900-year hiatus between the Nochta phase and the Tep complex evenly between Matanzas and Godar types, we derive the following deposition rates: Valmeyer points, .19 per annum; Brannon points, .10 per annum; Matanzas points, .36 per annum; Godar points, .69 per annum; Karnak points, .40 per annum. If the Godar and Matanzas points were, indeed, contemporaneous, they would account for a combined per annum deposition rate of .53.

Again, for the Late Archaic, we have more assurance that our sequence is correct, with all point types identified falling provisionally into defined and dated phases. The points (n = 1,059), grouped by phase, show the following levels of occurrence: Falling Springs, n = 262, 25 percent; Titterington, n = 400, 38 percent; Mule Road, n = 34, 3 percent; Labras Lake, n = 84, 8 percent; and Prairie Lake, n = 273, 26 percent. By assigning an arbitrary span of 100 years to the Mule Road phase, which is represented by only a single radiocarbon date, the following deposition rates are evident: Falling Springs, .52 per annum; Titterington, 1.30 per annum; Mule Road, .34 per annum; Labras Lake, .34 per annum; and Prairie Lake, .55 per annum.

Despite all of the perceived analytical limitations of the hafted-biface data sets, several aspects of the sample command our attention. For example, the Dalton occupation that presumably represents the founding Archaic population in the American Bottom region demonstrates the highest rate of deposition for the Early Archaic period and one of the higher rates for the entire sequence. It matches the rate of deposition noted for the Terminal Archaic Prairie Lake phase, which is thought to represent a very intense occupation, perhaps involving socially complex groups (cf. Emerson and McElrath 2001). Other comparable or higher peaks occur for Middle Archaic (Matanzas and Godar) times and again for Late Archaic (Titterington phase) times. The Titterington-phase peak is surprising because, to date, the Go-Kart North site is the only known Titterington base camp in the central American Bottom region on the east side of the Mississippi River and one of only two known within the American Bottom floodplain (the other is the Poag Road site). Titterington use of the forested uplands was intense, almost double that of other peak uses. On the basis of survey-transect evidence, then, we see comparable levels of settlement or use of upland landscapes at Dalton, Matanzas-Godar, Fallings Springs, Titterington (large increase), and Prairie Lake times. As we noted, Dalton use is comparable to terminal Late Archaic use. It is difficult to reconcile this landscape history either with Brown and Vierra's (1983) reconstruction of landscape usage in the Lower Illinois valley or, in fact, with any identifiable trend of consistent or steady population growth or use. It should be noted that our examination of valley-margin upland sites does not provide a fully adequate test of the model proposed by Brown and Vierra (1983) concerning the abandonment of the prairie uplands in favor of the floodplain during Middle Archaic times, but information generated at the greater pan-regional scale does not seem to support their model (see McElrath and Emerson, this volume).

A pattern previously identified earlier for the Late Archaic period (Emerson and McElrath 2001; Emerson et al. 1986; Fortier 1983; McElrath 1993) that can now be documented for the Early and Middle Archaic periods, as well, is major shifts in the historical connections of the resident populations in the American Bottom. At times during the Early Archaic, the American Bottom was occupied by groups maintaining strong ties to the west of the Mississippi River, while at other times the ties were decidedly more eastern (Figure 11.31). During Middle Archaic times, there was a strong shift to more midwestern connections (Figure 11.32a) followed by a Midsouth orientation for the Falling Springs phase (Figure 11.32b) and what has been well documented now as an intrusion from the west with the Titterington phase (Figure 11.32c). This was followed by a southern intrusion (Figure 11.32c) of the Ledbetter culture (Mule Road phase) and eventually a return to more parochial ties to a southern and eastern Illinois, Riverton-related culture during Labras Lake times (Figure 11.32d). The terminal Late Archaic phase shows much affinity with the Midsouth, with the square-stemmed barbed point type cluster evident in the Prairie Lake phase (Figure 11.32d).

It is also possible to identify trends in patterns of chert acquisition and stone tool production in the region and to observe how these compare with patterns elsewhere in eastern North America. In fact, one of the hallmarks of the Archaic period is the emergence of a robust woodworking industry. Significant shifts in woodworking technology are evident in the Archaic record of the American Bottom region as they are across the Eastern Woodlands (Boydston 1989; Hayden 1989; Sassaman 1996). Heavy-duty woodworking tools appeared for the first time as part of the Dalton tool kit. These heavy-duty tools are chipped-stone adze blades fashioned from chert and hafted onto wooden handles (Gaertner 1994; Morse and Goodyear 1973; Yerkes and Gaertner 1997). These adze blades required chipping to resharpen the bits, and, when exhausted or snapped, they were often recycled into other tools (Goodyear 1974). Similar chert adzes were employed by subsequent groups until late in the Early Archaic period, when hard-rock (e.g., basalt and diorite) ground-stone adzes and grooved axes and, possibly, celts (ungrooved axes) appeared for the first time.

In the American Bottom region, the earliest ground-stone woodworking tools are the full-grooved axes found at the Nochta site. Although the context is clearly Early Archaic, the multicomponent nature of the site does not allow a more precise temporal assignment. Grooved axes of various sizes are common surface finds on large Middle and Late Archaic sites in the region, and they have been recovered from feature context at both the Strong site (Dennis Hollow phase) and at Nochta (Nochta phase) as well as from Middle and Late Archaic strata at Modoc and Koster (Brown and Vierra 1983; Cook 1976; Fowler 1959a, 1959b). Numerous grooved axes as well as the remnants of their production (unfinished axes, chert hammers, and sandstone hones) have been surface collected from the bluff-top study areas: Modoc Uplands, New Valmeyer, and Eagle Cliff. In the Modoc Uplands, these materials are most common at the Modoc Village site (where hematite plummet production was also undertaken). Several sites within the New Valmeyer and Eagle Cliff study areas have produced axes and related manufacturing rejects and by-products (in addition to unfinished bannerstones).

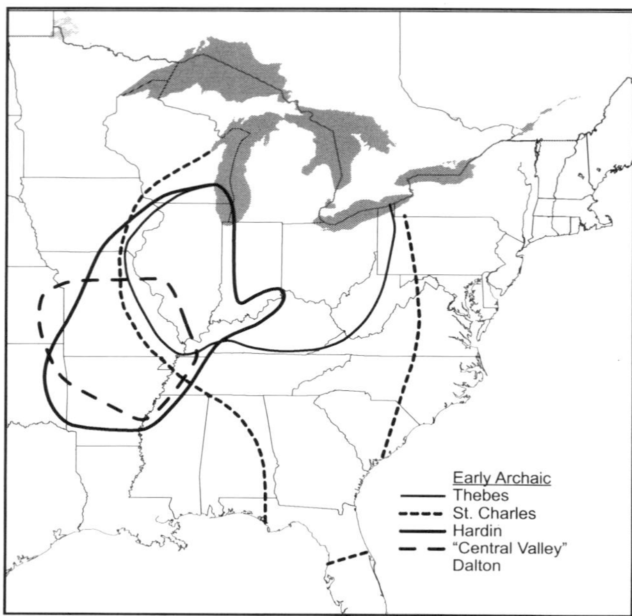

Figure 11.31a. Early Archaic point type distribution; early Early Archaic American Bottom cultural affiliation.

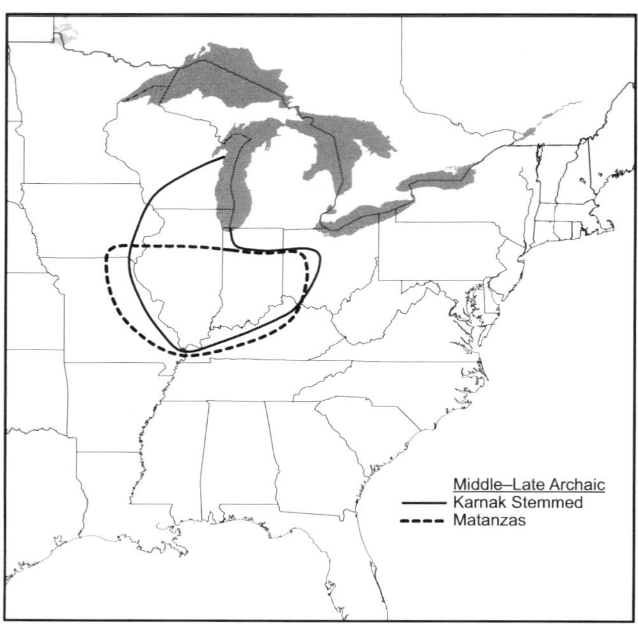

Figure 11.32a. Middle and Late Archaic cultural affiliation and distribution ca. 5th–6th millennium B.C.

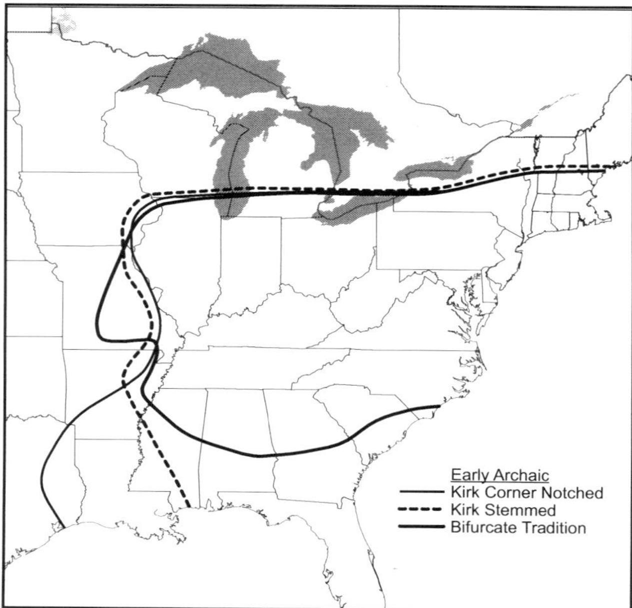

Figure 11.31b. Early Archaic point type distribution; late Early Archaic American Bottom cultural affiliation.

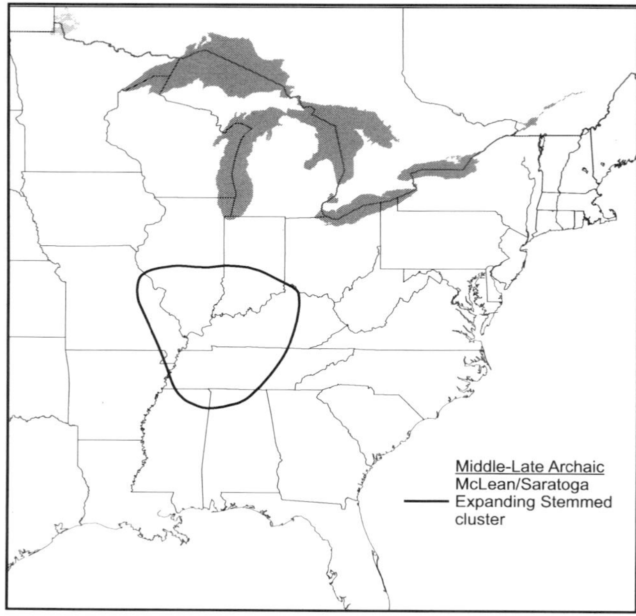

Figure 11.32b. Middle and Late Archaic cultural affiliation and distribution ca. 4th millennium B.C.

It appears glacial cobbles, rather than igneous bedrock from the St. Francois Mountains, were selected for ax production. This observation is supported by the variety of different igneous and metamorphic rock types used in production and by the patches of cobble cortex preserved on both finished and unfinished axes.

The use and manufacture of these heavy-duty groundstone woodworking tools was preceded in both study areas by substantial evidence of Dalton chipped-stone adze production and use (Koldehoff and Walthall 2004:56–57). In fact, Walthall and Koldehoff (1999) note that valley-margin chert sources, like those at Valmeyer, were ideally situated

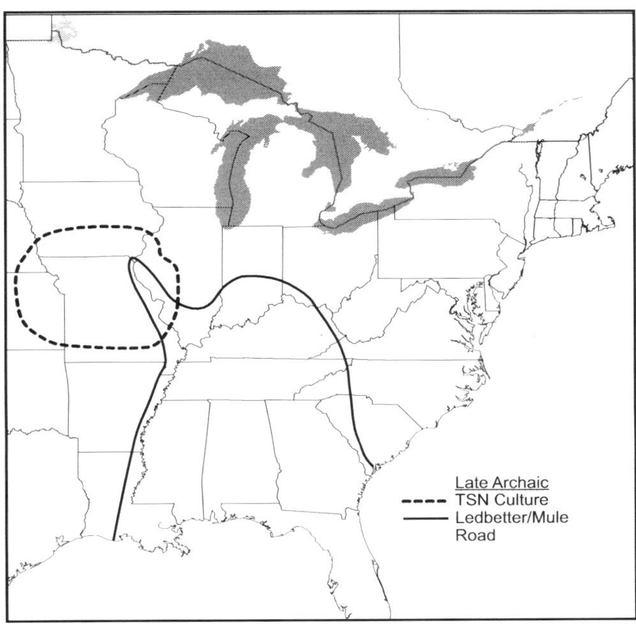

Figure 11.32c. Late Archaic cultural affiliation and distribution ca. 3rd millennium B.C.

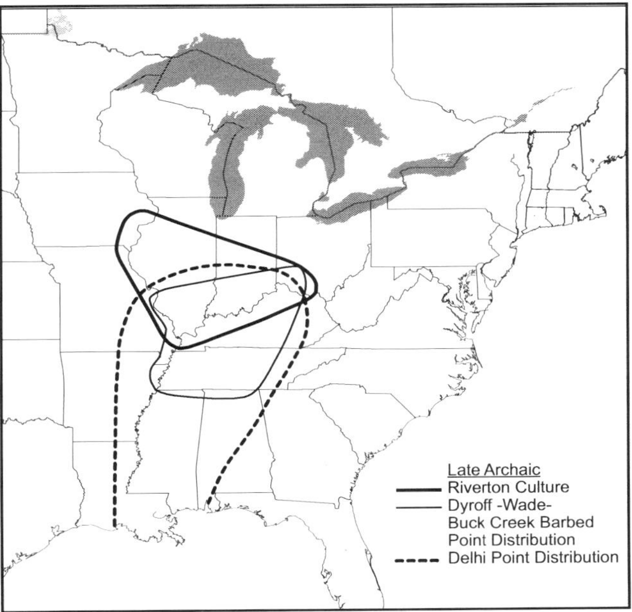

Figure 11.32d. Late Archaic cultural affiliation and distribution ca. 2nd millennium B.C.

from the perspective of Dalton groups to use for retooling whenever they moved back and forth from the bottomlands to the interior uplands. Moreover, such locations are likely spots for dugout-canoe production, given the juxtaposition of chert sources, suitable timber (especially white oak), and bottomland streams and lakes. The shift from chert adzes to primarily ground-stone axes, as previously discussed, increased tool use-life, a significant advantage for groups who had limited access to high-quality chert (Hayden 1989). With a little time, a hammerstone or two, and some sandstone, ground-stone axes could be fashioned from the glacial cobbles available in most upland streams. The widespread availability of glacial cobbles meant that Middle and Late Archaic groups had more latitude in conducting major woodworking projects even though they may have lacked primary access to major chert sources. At the Modoc Village site, where nearby chert resources are limited but glacial cobbles and sandstone are not, there is little evidence of Early Archaic adze production and use, but there is ample evidence of Middle and Late Archaic ground-stone ax production and use.

Valley-margin locations, with their easy access to both upland and bottomland biotic resources, are well recognized as ideal settings for base settlements as well as workshop activities. The local availability of chert and other lithic resources only added to the attractiveness of these locations. Besides sites in the bluff-top study areas, extensive bluff-base habitation areas with evidence of workshop activities occur in the Prairie Lake and Labras Lake locales. These locales are examples of resource-rich floodplain settings, with chert (Salem, St. Louis, and Ste. Genevieve), sandstone, glacial cobbles, and hematite available in the adjacent uplands.

Two Late Archaic valley-margin sites situated just south of these locales, Go-Kart North (Titterington phase) and George Reeves (Mule Road phase), are noteworthy because they have produced ample evidence of chipped-stone tool production, but the predominant chert type used in this production is nonlocal—it is Burlington chert from the Crescent quarries. While Burlington chert was the preferred raw material of all Archaic groups (Koldehoff 2006), it is clear that numerous block cores and early-stage bifaces were transported, probably by canoe, to these two sites for further reduction. As we have noted in this chapter, Titterington and Mule Road populations were especially focused on Burlington chert from the Crescent quarries (25 km west). And while there is abundant evidence of the regular and often intensive utilization of Burlington chert from the Crescent quarries by other Archaic groups, the bulk transport of Crescent Burlington by foot and dugout canoe by Go-Kart and George Reeves site residents appears unequaled elsewhere in the Archaic record.

Lack of heat treatment also distinguishes the lithic assemblages of these two Late Archaic phases from those of the rest of the Late Archaic and from all Middle Archaic phases. In the American Bottom region, heat treatment of points became routine late in the Early Archaic, and this practice continued into the Woodland period. But unlike other Archaic knappers, Titterington and Mule Road–phase knappers did not routinely employ heat treatment. The large size of most Titterington and Mule Road–phase points is another factor that separates these two phases from the rest of the Late Archaic. A major distinction between the two, however, involves the method of production; whereas the Titterington flintknappers used flakes to produce large blades, Mule Road stoneworkers preferred a core production technique. While these distinctive technological and lithic-procurement practices may have involved subtle adaptive properties that we cannot readily determine, these practices probably were influenced more by cultural traditions or sociological factors than by functional considerations. This disjuncture with earlier and later Archaic populations is inconsistent with the notion of a smooth, unbroken, in-place evolution of local populations and technological systems.

During the Titterington phase, ground-stone celts appeared, apparently for the first time as a regular component of tool kits. These small, rectangular tools have chipped-stone counterparts, and both types were probably hafted (in socketed handles) and used for woodworking and, possibly, for other tasks. What necessitated the addition of these small (ungrooved) woodworking tools is unclear because grooved axes (primarily three-quarter grooved) of various sizes were still in use. Grooved axes continued to be used until the Terminal Archaic Prairie Lake phase, when celts were the only ground-stone woodworking tools. This shift from grooved axes to celts is noteworthy because from this point forward—throughout the subsequent Woodland and Mississippian periods—only ground-stone celts were used (in addition to some chert adzes). Celts, with their socketed handles, were perhaps better designed for the tasks associated with the expanding role of horticulture (Simon, this volume). For instance, it is possible that celts, when dulled or broken, were more easily removed from handles and replaced than grooved axes, which were probably lashed to their handles. This ease of replacement may have taken on added importance once ringing trees and cutting brush to clear garden plots in the forest became more frequent and extensive. These "hatchet"-like celts may also have functioned more as tools for breaking up fallen limbs and branches for firewood than for the heavy lumbering activities implied by the larger grooved axes. By contrast, the larger celts that are recovered from later prehistoric (especially Mississippian) times were certainly designed to fell trees.

Although there is much we still do not fully understand about American Bottom Archaic-period technology, we have highlighted two important shifts in heavy-duty woodworking: the change from chipped-stone adzes to ground-stone grooved axes and then to ground-stone celts. At the most general level, these changes likely reflect changes in settlement mobility and increasing reliance on cultigens. We have also highlighted the pivotal role valley-margin locales played throughout the Archaic period in terms of settlement systems, resource procurement, and tool production. It is likely that the interior uplands were used by groups that had base settlements positioned, at times, in this zone. Data from Koldehoff's upland study areas indicate that the uplands were accessed, to some extent, throughout the Archaic period, probably most often for hunting. But during certain times, the uplands appear to have been more fully exploited, most notably during the initial part of the Early Archaic, particularly by Dalton populations, then during the Middle Archaic by groups that used side-notched points (especially Godar), and finally during the Late Archaic by Falling Springs, Titterington, and Prairie Lake–phase groups. There does not seem to be a consistent trend of either increasing or decreasing use of the upland valley-margin locales; rather, the pattern seems to have been a cyclical one, the determinants for which are not readily apparent.

The raw materials used in point manufacture are fairly consistent across time periods and study areas: Archaic knappers preferred Burlington chert, which ranges in frequency from just over 50 percent of the Prairie Lake–phase sample to 80 percent of the Nochta-phase sample (Koldehoff 2006). The majority of this chert probably came from the Crescent quarries, but groups in the northern American Bottom likely procured Burlington chert from deposits in the Alton area; likewise, groups in the southern American Bottom likely procured Burlington chert from deposits at Salt Lick Point. Cherts from southern Illinois, like Cobden and Bailey, are represented in most phases in minor amounts. These cherts represent 8.8 percent of the Early Archaic sample, 16.8 percent of the Tep-complex sample, 17.1 percent of the Titterington-phase sample, and 20.0 percent of the Prairie Lake–phase sample. These percentages indicate a substantial connection with southern Illinois, which increased through time. It is surprising that these connections were strongest in the Late Archaic, not the Early Archaic, when populations have been portrayed as more mobile and having larger seasonal ranges. However, the southern cherts primarily occur as finished points, and as we have noted, these points stand out stylistically, which indicates that they were probably made by southern Illinois knappers and were items of exchange or that they were distributed through some other mechanism of interaction. Chipped-stone resources from the Missouri Ozarks are poorly represented and primarily occur in Early Archaic and again in Late Archaic Falling Springs and Titterington samples. These materials, especially St. Francois rhyolite, are most common in Titterington-phase contexts, and likely represent trade items.

Some details of the American Bottom lithic data seem relevant to the shift from dry, open-hearth roasting to moist cooking that has been proposed for Middle Archaic times (Brown 1989; Brown and Vierra 1983; Sassaman 1993). Although the American Bottom offered Archaic groups several advantages, including strategic location at the confluence of three major rivers—Missouri, Mississippi, and Illinois—that served as conduits to the Plains, upper Midwest, and Great Lakes, respectively, and access to major, high-quality chert resources on both sides of the Mississippi, it generally lacks good-quality igneous and metamorphic rock in the form of glacial cobbles that would have been suitable for use as hearth stones. Although this lack was not disabling, because both sandstone and limestone are abundant and could have been used for hearth rock material, it would have been a major disadvantage for groups who practiced stone boiling (Wisseman 2005). This may have been one of the aspects of the local environment that made the American Bottom less attractive than the lower and central Illinois Valley during Middle Archaic (i.e., Helton phase) times. A second limiting factor may have been the sparse mussel resources (Bartsch 1916) that seemed to be a focus of exploitation during Middle Archaic times in the Midwest and Midsouth. In any event, the eventual development during Late Woodland times of ceramic vessels that could be directly heated put the American Bottom back on the map during later prehistoric periods (McElrath and Fortier 2000).

In addition to the changing external affiliations or points of origin of the various Archaic cultures that inhabited the American Bottom region, and the shifting patterns of movement through time, our surveys and excavations indicate that the use of the region was often spatially differentiated and that specific peoples focused on specific locales to the exclusion of many other apparently suitable habitats. For example, the Matanzas occupation was contained within the southern American Bottom. The Titterington occupation seems to have focused on two floodplain sites (Go-Kart North and Poag Road) that together may have controlled access within their specific locales to the uplands. In the uplands, small Titterington sites are common, but few obvious base camps are represented. Two Mule Road–phase base camps, one at the margin of the valley and the other in the interior, have been identified, indicating how rare such sites are, by comparison, for example, with Prairie Lake–phase base locales and associated camps. Yet even for Prairie Lake times, we are only aware of two locales with evidence of intense settlement. This suggests that, even in the best of times, American Bottom Archaic populations were small in terms of overall numbers, even if they might have achieved moderately high densities in localized instances, such as in the Prairie Lake base locale. Thus, we conclude that, during Archaic times, while much or perhaps most of the floodplain and adjacent upland forests were used, they were only sparsely occupied.

We have interpreted the stylistic relationships and local settlement and landscape use to reflect human population and social dynamics that varied across space and time. Dalton occupation of the American Bottom, for example, represents a clearly intrusive, founding population in the area. We suggest that other intrusions are marked by the appearance of Titterington and Mule Road peoples. At times, the American Bottom was occupied by people who participated in a larger stylistic network and may have represented longer-term residence, for example, during Graham Cave Side Notched, Hidden Valley, and Searcy times, when the area was tied to the Ozarks. We see little evidence in other periods for any resident populations, and unlike other archaeologists who equate such lack of information with data gaps, we suggest that the valley during these periods was sparsely used or empty. Unlike many of our colleagues, we are reluctant to extrapolate a complete evolutionary prehistoric sequence where the evidence is absent. This means we see a dynamic human-landscape relationship through time, a landscape variously filled with people, abandoned, lightly utilized, traversed but not settled, and so forth. The scenario that demonstrably is not supported by the archaeological evidence is one postulating thousands of years of in situ human adaptation to changing environmental settings, accompanied by steadily increasing population density and steadily diminishing group mobility.

In addition to the evidence for cultural or ethnic group affiliation, population movements, and shifting influences, we have amassed considerable evidence relating to the arrangement of domestic and social activities during the various Archaic periods. In a very few cases, the evidence consists of actual house construction; more often, it involves site patterning that suggests forms of community organization. We have identified no formal domestic structures thus far that date to the Early Archaic period. Socially defined spaces are suggested archaeologically by the arrangement of features and by perceived spatial divisions at specific site locations. In the American Bottom, the earliest such examples are at Nochta, which contains evidence of several Early Archaic occupations, consisting of about 160 features, including about 90 pits and over 70 rock-cluster caches. Early Archaic point and artifact types are distributed over the entire occupation area and overlap to such an extent that assigning component affiliations to the various feature clusters is not possible. There does appear, however, to be a small cluster of pits relating to a Dalton occupation. This cluster contains two large hearths that appear, on the basis of size, to have functioned as communal cooking facilities (Figure 11.33). The Early Archaic component at the site includes a large number of cached grinding stones and small metates as well as fully grooved axes, suggesting either permanent or periodic occupation at various times during the Early Archaic.

Single sites representative of the Middle Archaic Dennis Hollow (Strong site; Walz et al. 1998) and Nochta phases (Nochta site; Higgins 1990) yielded combinations of features that reflect some level of social grouping or activity areas or both. At the Nochta site, a single large basin near the midpoint in the Middle Archaic occupation area (Figure 11.34; Ms-128) was interpreted as a structure; it is the earliest structure identified thus far in the American Bottom region. At the Modoc Rock Shelter, Ahler (2000) has identified several postmold patterns in Middle Archaic levels, arranged in lines or arcs that suggest the construction of windbreaks, screens, or domestic structures.

We have considerably more evidence for site patterning during Late Archaic times. We identified two major Late Archaic base locales, one in the Prairie Lake locality, the other in the Cahokia Creek Gap locality. The Prairie Lake locality and sites around it have been more thoroughly investigated and have yielded important information on terminal Late Archaic community organization and order. Evidence that domestic structures were present in this locality date to the Labras Lake phase. The Marge site (Fortier 1996) yielded a basin structure with several associated post molds (Figure 11.34; Mo-99). Several "domestic areas" and a few houses

Figure 11.33. Dalton hearths at the Nochta site.

have been identified at the Labras Lake site; the houses all appear to date to Prairie Lake–phase times. At least one large nonbasin post structure and one small shallow-basin structure have been identified at the Missouri Pacific #2 site (McElrath and Fortier 1983).

However, clusters of pits dominate the large terminal Late Archaic communities in base locales. Although domestic structures occur at the Range, Missouri Pacific #2, Labras Lake, and Marge sites, they represent minor components of the community layout. The more typical site layouts consist of variously sized pit clusters that include open hearths and cooking pits. These clusters may represent functional work groups or social groupings. Sometimes, such as at the Go-Kart North site (Titterington phase), the clusters are clearly demarcated by open areas, suggesting intentional spacing between work or socially defined areas. These open areas typically contain major concentrations of artifacts; in one case, a large metate marked an open area. The McLean site had a pit layout that suggested a four-part division of the occupation area (McElrath 1986). Do these open areas represent activities generated by aggregate community groups or overflow from more localized activities within the pit clusters or both? Does the overall spatial patterning of pit clusters reflect a larger social pattern? The evidence is ambiguous at best.

Various kinds of houses or living areas are associated with terminal Late Archaic occupations. At the Labras Lake site, small irregular basin structures occur alongside so-called domestic areas that, while not structural units per se, were discrete activity foci. At Marge, a single basin structure located some distance away from three pit clusters yielded evidence of activity (pits, hearths, tools) that differed from that represented by the pit clusters. Was the house the focus of the community, or were the pit clusters products of more aggregate social activity? Other house types, such as the ones identified at Range and Missouri Pacific #2, are clearly isolates. These structures typically have no associated artifacts or interior features and may not represent domestic units at all. They are similar to the Middle Archaic structure identified at Nochta. They may represent temporary storage facilities for subsistence items, such as nut masts, hides, dried meats, and so forth, but as living or sleeping facilities they could have accommodated only a half-dozen or so individuals. We presume that multiple families produced the extensive habitation debris and pit remains we have observed at open-air Archaic sites in the region; consequently, the sites should have yielded numerous domestic structures. It is possible that shelters consisted of temporary windbreaks, tents, or lightly built wigwams that have not been preserved. But at the Nochta Middle Archaic occupation, which was sealed from the plow by nearly a meter of clay, it is not clear why more structures were not identified. Perhaps Archaic-period community organization was not structure based. We might add that this pattern holds true for most Early Woodland occupations in the American Bottom. Where structures dating to that time period have been found (e.g., the Florence Street site), only single examples occur. Not until the Hopewell period did houses define community configurations (e.g., the Holding site; Fortier et al. 1989).

We have yet to determine if feature patterns identified at Archaic sites reflect socially significant divisions or if they are the result of fortuitous grouping relating to multiple site occupations. At least in some cases, there is good reason to suspect that spatially discrete feature clusters represent the remains of recognizable social or work groups. The problem is establishing a chronological or functional link between such clusters. To date, the subsistence information retrieved from these sites indicates summer through fall occupations, but this must be weighed against the fact that there are no reliable winter indicators. It seems just as reasonable to suggest that the sites were occupied on a long-term, multiseasonal basis as that they represent cyclical abandonment on a seasonal basis. We believe models that posit "traditional" seasonal rounds are based more on discredited models of hunter-gather settlement than on the available archaeological evidence. Aside from short-term visits to the upland areas of the valley margin, or perhaps movement to more protected secondary valley locations during the winter, we can think of no reason or evidence to suggest that there was a gradual trend to either decreasing or increasing periods of site habitation.

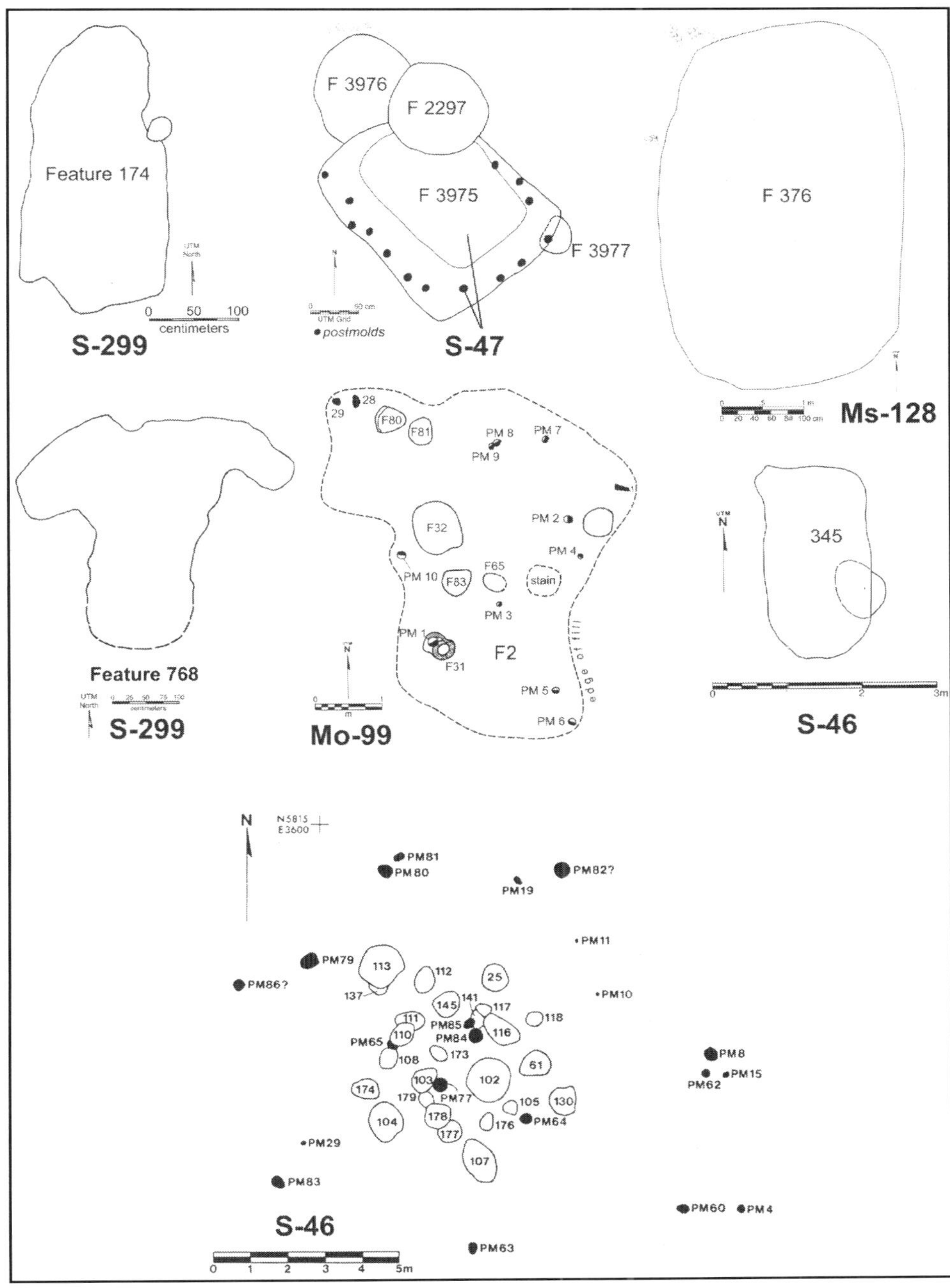

Figure 11.34. Selected American Bottom Archaic structures.

Ideas about plant and animal resource utilization during Archaic times have been generated by a model of highly mobile hunter-gatherers who were attracted to increasingly productive floodplain resources in areas where they eventually became more sedentary and developed cultivated plant resources. The scant data developed here offer little support for this scenario (see also Simon, this volume; Styles and McMillan, this volume). The earliest levels at Modoc revealed use of fish, squirrel, and deer. We have already questioned the upland-abandonment model proposed by Brown and Vierra (1983) and suggest that a focus on the major river valleys is evident from the earliest Archaic (i.e., Dalton) times onward, given the location of base camps and site distribution.

In sum, in the American Bottom region, threads of continuity run through the entire Archaic period: basic technologies and land-use strategies, developed by founding Dalton populations, persisted for millennia. The same chert sources, landform settings, and biotic resources were utilized, often in the same fashion. However, this continuity was punctuated by periodic changes in technology and material culture, which, at one level, appear to have been linked to new or shifting patterns of land use, for example, related to the expanding role of plant cultivation, but, at another level, appear to have been more socially driven. For example, changes in heavy-duty woodworking tools appear to be tied to clearing garden plots and reflect major shifts in human-land interactions, whereas changes in points—in haft elements or heat treatment—may have been driven by varying expressions of group identity or learned traditions. It is difficult to identify and evaluate the causes of change, but we can document that such changes occurred in human practices, technology, and material culture. And unlike our predecessors, we believe more was involved in such changing human practices than adaptational improvements or increasing technological efficiency. Rather, we see a long history of shifting relationships between Archaic peoples and their social and physical landscape, driven at least partially by dynamic population movements and changing intra- and interregional contacts and interactions, a situation that made the American Bottom region a cultural crossroads that was continually traversed during the entire Archaic period.

Acknowledgments

The authors wish to gratefully acknowledge the many people, both professional and avocational colleagues, who provided the necessary assistance, information, and expertise over the years that made the creation of this chapter possible. As always, we have benefited from our many discussions with colleagues who share a passion for the Archaic period, including, John Walthall, Dave Nolan, Madeleine Evans, Bryant Evans, Mary Simon, Larry Conrad, Steve Ahler, Jack Ray, Neal Lopinot, Ken Farnsworth, and the many participants in the 2004 Urbana Archaic conference. In addition, Larry Conrad (WIU) made available the material from the Tep site for presentation, and Paul Kreisa (PSAP) provided the images of the Dennis Hollow artifacts. A special thanks is extended to John Walthall (IDOT Chief Archaeologist) for his encouragement and support during the preparation and production of this chapter and the volume in which it is presented. Linda Alexander photographed most of the artifacts, while Mera Hertel photographed several of the Early Archaic points; Mike Farkas and Mera Hertel constructed the many site location and regional maps, and Mike Lewis developed the figure layouts and the chronological chart. Linda Forman, as always, added coherence to our text. The vast majority of this research was conducted and funded under the auspices of the Illinois Department of Transportation's cultural resources program.

References Cited

Abbott, Larry R.
1989 *Archaeological Investigations at the Wooded Site (11-MS-587), Madison County Illinois.* Research Report 35. Resource Investigation Program, Department of Anthropology, University of Illinois, Urbana.

Adams, Brian, Gregory R. Walz, Paul P. Kreisa, Kevin P. McGowan, Jacqueline M. McDowell, and Cynthia L. Balek
1997 *Archaeological Investigations for the Relocation of Valmeyer, Monroe County, Illinois.* Research Report 28. Public Service Archaeology Program, Department of Anthropology, University of Illinois, Urbana.

Ahler, Steven R.
1984 Archaic Settlement Strategies in the Modoc Locality, Southwest Illinois. Ph.D. dissertation, Department of Anthropology, University of Wisconsin–Milwaukee.
1993 Stratigraphy and Radiocarbon Chronology of Modoc Rock Shelter, Illinois. *American Antiquity* 58:462–488.
1998 Early and Middle Archaic Settlement Systems in the Modoc Locality, Southwest Illinois. *Illinois Archaeology* 10:1–109.
2000 Postmolds and Possible Domestic Structures at Modoc Rock Shelter, Illinois. In *Mounds, Modoc, and Mesoamerica: Papers in Honor of Melvin L. Fowler*, edited by Steven R. Ahler, pp. 57–74. Scientific Papers 28. Illinois State Museum, Springfield.

Ahler, Steven R., Mary J. Bade, Frances B. King, Bonnie W. Styles, and Paula J. Thorson
1992 *Late Archaic Components at Modoc Rock Shelter, Randolph County, Illinois.* Reports of Investigations 48. Illinois State Museum, Springfield.

Ahler, Steven R., and Brad Koldehoff
2002 Archaic Period Radiocarbon Assays from the Modoc Village Site (11R266) 2001 IAAA Field School Grant Results. *Illinois Antiquity* 37(2):6–7.

Ahler, Steven R. and Bonnie W. Styles
1998 A Summary of Changes in Archaic Period Subsistence and Site Formation at Modoc Rock Shelter. *Illinois Archaeology* 10:110–154.

Anderson, David G.
2002 The Evolution of Tribal Social Organization in the Southeast. In *The Archaeology of Tribal Societies*, edited by William A. Parkinson, pp. 246–277. Archaeological Series 15. International Monographs in Prehistory, Ann Arbor, Michigan.

Anderson, Eve
1991 New Perspectives on Archaic Mortuary Behavior at Modoc Rockshelter. Paper presented at the 56th Annual Meeting of the Society for American Archaeology, New Orleans, Louisiana.

Bareis, Charles J., and James W. Porter (editors)
1984 *American Bottom Archaeology: A Summary of the FAI-270 Project Contribution to the Culture History of the Mississippi River Valley.* University of Illinois Press, Urbana.

Bartsch, Paul
1916 The Missouri River as a Faunal Barrier. *The Nautilus* 30:92.

Behm, Jeffery A.
1985 Identification and Analysis of Stylistic Variation in Hardin Barbed Points. Ph.D. dissertation, Department of Anthropology, University of Wisconsin, Madison.

Bentz, Charles
1988 The Rosewood Phase Occupation at the Leingang Site. In *Late Woodland Sites in the American Bottom Uplands*, edited by Charles Bentz, Dale L. McElrath, Fred A. Finney, and Richard B. Lacampagne, pp. 17–73. American Bottom Archaeology FAI-270 Site Reports 18. University of Illinois Press, Urbana.

Blake, Leonard W., and James G. Houser
1978 *The Whelpley Collection of Indian Artifacts*. Transactions of the Academy of Sciences of St. Louis 12(1). St. Louis, Missouri.

Booth, Don, and Steve Dasovich
2006 The Poag Road Site (11MS31): Recent Investigations. Poster presented at the Midwest Archaeological Conference, Urbana, Illinois.

Booth, Donald L., and Brad Koldehoff
1999 *The EWP Project: Archaeological Investigations for the 1998 Metro East Ditch Cleanout Project in Madison and St. Clair Counties, Illinois*. Research Reports 62. Illinois Transportation Archaeological Research Program, University of Illinois, Urbana.

Boydston, Roger A.
1989 A Cost Benefit Study of Functionally Similar Stone Tools. In *Time, Energy, and Stone Tools*, edited by Robin Torrence, pp. 66–77. Cambridge University Press, Cambridge, England.

Brookes, Samuel O.
1999 Prehistoric Exchange in Mississippi, 10,000 B.C.–A.D. 1600. In *Raw Materials and Exchange in the Mid-South: Proceedings of the 16th Annual Mid-South Archaeological Conference, Jackson, Mississippi, June 3–4, 1995*, edited by Evan Peacock and Samuel O. Brookes, pp. 27–43. Mississippi Department of Archives and History, Jackson.
2004 Cultural Complexity in the Middle Archaic of Mississippi. In *Signs of Power: The Rise of Cultural Complexity in the Southeast*, edited by Jon L. Gibson and Philip J. Carr, pp. 97–113. University of Alabama Press, Tuscaloosa.

Brose, David S.
1979 A Speculative Model for the Role of Exchange in the Prehistory of the Eastern Woodlands. In *Hopewell Archaeology: The Chillicothe Conference*, edited by David S. Brose and N'omi Greber, pp. 3–8. Kent State University Press, Kent, Ohio.

Brown, James A.
1985 Long-Term Trends to Sedentism and the Emergence of Complexity in the American Midwest. In *Prehistoric Hunter-Gatherers: The Emergence of Cultural Complexity*, edited by T. Douglas Price and James A. Brown, pp. 201–231. Academic Press, New York.
1989 The Beginnings of Pottery as an Economic Process. In *What's New? A Closer Look at the Process of Innovation*, edited by Sander E. van der Leeuw and Robin Torrence, pp. 203–224. Unwin Hyman, London.

Brown, James A., and Robert K. Vierra
1983 What Happened in the Middle Archaic? Introduction to an Ecological Approach to Koster Site Archaeology. In *Archaic Hunters and Gatherers in the American Midwest*, edited by James L. Phillips and James A. Brown, pp. 165–196. Academic Press, New York.

Broyles, Bettye J. (editor)
1971 *Second Preliminary Report: The St. Albans Site, Kanawha County, West Virginia*. West Virginia Geological and Economic Survey, Morgantown.

Byers, A. Martin
2004 *The Ohio Hopewell Episode: Paradigm Lost and Paradigm Gained*. University of Akron Press, Akron, Ohio.

Caldwell, Joseph
1958 *Trend and Tradition in the Prehistory of the Eastern United States*. Memoir 88. American Anthropological Association, Menasha, Wisconsin.

Carlson, David Lee
1979 Hunter-Gatherer Mobility Strategies: An Example from the Koster Site in the Lower Illinois Valley. Ph.D. dissertation, Department of Anthropology, Northwestern University, Evanston, Illinois.

Carmichael, David L.
1977 Preliminary Archeological Survey of Illinois Uplands and Some Behavioral Implications. *Midcontinental Journal of Archaeology* 1:219–251.

Chapman, Carl H.
1948a A Preliminary Survey of Missouri Archaeology Part III: Woodland Cultures and the Ozark Bluff Dwellers. *The Missouri Archaeologist* 10:95–132.
1948b A Preliminary Survey of Missouri Archaeology Part IV: Ancient Cultures and Sequence. *The Missouri Archaeologist* 10:133–164.

Coe, Joffre Lanning
1964 *The Formative Cultures of the Carolina Piedmont*. Transactions of the American Philosophical Society (New Series) 54, pt. 5. Philadelphia.

Conner, Michael D.
1986 *Cypress Land: A Late Archaic/Early Woodland Site in the Lower Illinois River Valley Floodplain*. Technical Report 2. Center for American Archeology, Kampsville Archeological Center, Kampsville, Illinois.

Conrad, Lawrence A.
1981 *An Introduction to the Archaeology of West Central Illinois: A Preliminary Archaeological Survey of the Canton to Quincy Corridor for the Proposed FAP 407 Highway Project*. Reports of Investigations 2. Archaeological Research Laboratory, Western Illinois University, Macomb.
1986 The Late Archaic/Early Woodland Transition in the Interior of West-Central Illinois. In *Early Woodland Archeology*, edited by Kenneth B. Farnsworth and Thomas E. Emerson, pp. 301–325. Kampsville Seminars in Archeology 2. Center for American Archeology, Kampsville, Illinois.

Cook, Thomas Genn
1976 *Koster: An Artifact Analysis of Two Archaic Phases in West-central Illinois*. Prehistoric Records 1, Koster Research Reports 3. Northwestern Archaeological Project, Evanston, Illinois.

Denny, Sidney G.
1976 A Report of Archaeological Inventory Reconnaissance for the Proposed Richland Creek Flood Abatement Project in the Vicinity of Belleville, Illinois. Submitted to the Illinois Department of Transportation, Springfield. Department of Anthropology, Southern Illinois University, Edwardsville.

Emerson, Thomas E.
1980 *The Dyroff and Levin Sites: A Late Archaic Occupation in the American Bottom*. FAI-270 Archaeological Mitigation Report 24. Department of Anthropology, University of Illinois, Urbana–Champaign.
1984 The Dyroff and Levin Sites. In *The Go-Kart North Site and the Dyroff and Levin Sites*, by Andrew C. Fortier and Thomas E. Emerson, pp. 199–362. American Bottom Archaeology FAI-270 Site Reports 9. University of Illinois Press, Urbana.
2002 An Introduction to Cahokia 2002: Diversity, Complexity, and History. In *Cahokia 2002: Diversity, Complexity, and History*, edited by Thomas E. Emerson and Timothy R. Pauketat, pp. 127–148. *Midcontinental Journal of Archaeology* 27.

Emerson, Thomas E., and Andrew C. Fortier
1986 Early Woodland Cultural Variation, Subsistence, and Settlement in the American Bottom. In *Early Woodland Archeology*, edited by Kenneth B. Farnsworth and Thomas E. Emerson, pp. 475–522. Kampsville Seminars in Archeology 2. Center for American Archeology, Kampsville, Illinois.

Emerson, Thomas E., and Randall E. Hughes
2000 Figurines, Flint Clay Sourcing, the Ozark Highlands, and Cahokian Acquisition. *American Antiquity* 65:79–101.

Emerson, Thomas E., and Dale L. McElrath
1983 A Settlement-Subsistence Model of the Terminal Late Archaic Adaptation in the American Bottom, Illinois. In *Archaic Hunters and Gatherers in the American Midwest*, edited by James L. Phillips and James A. Brown, pp. 219–242. Academic Press, New York.
2001 Interpreting Discontinuity and Historical Process in Midcontinental Late Archaic and Early Woodland Societies. In *The Archaeology of Tradition: Agency and History Before and After Columbus*, edited by Timothy R. Pauketat, pp. 195–217. University Press of Florida, Gainesville.

Emerson, Thomas E., Dale L. McElrath, and Joyce A. Williams
1986 Patterns of Hunter-Gatherer Mobility and Sedentism during the Archaic Period of the American Bottom. In *Foraging, Collecting, and Harvesting: Archaic Period Subsistence and Settlement in the Eastern Woodlands*, edited by Sarah W. Neusius, pp. 247–273. Occasional Papers 6. Center for Archaeological Investigations, Southern Illinois University, Carbondale.

Emerson, Thomas E., George R. Milner, and Douglas K. Jackson
1983 *The Florence Street Site*. American Bottom Archaeology FAI-270 Site Reports 2. University of Illinois Press, Urbana.

Emerson, Thomas E., and John A. Walthall
2006 Building on the Past: The Archaeology of Large-Scale Transportation-Related Corridors. In *Landscapes under Pressure: Theory and Practice of Cultural Heritage Research and Preservation*, edited by Ludomir R. Lozny, pp. 163–182. Springer Press, New York.

Evans, J. Bryant
2001 *The Floyd Site: A Terminal Archaic Habitation in the Northern American Bottom*. Transportation Archaeological Research Reports 11. Illinois Transportation Archaeological Research Program, Department of Anthropology, University of Illinois, Urbana–Champaign.

Evans, J. Bryant, and Madeleine G. Evans
2000 *The Ringering Site and the Archaic-Woodland Transition in the American Bottom*. Transportation Archaeological Research Reports 8. Illinois Transportation Archaeological Research Program, Department of Anthropology, University of Illinois, Urbana–Champaign.

Evans, J. Bryant, Madeleine G. Evans, and Edwin R. Hajic
1997 Paleoindian and Early Archaic Occupations at the CB North Site, Madison County, Illinois. *Midcontinental Journal of Archaeology* 22:159–196.

Farnsworth, Kenneth B., and David L. Asch
1986 Early Woodland Chronology, Artifact Styles, and Settlement Distribution in the Lower Illinois Valley Region. In *Early Woodland Archeology*, edited by Kenneth B. Farnsworth and Thomas E. Emerson, pp. 326–457. Kampsville Seminars in Archeology 2. Center for American Archeology, Kampsville, Illinois.

Ferguson, Jacqueline A.
1997 Native American Settlement and Chert Use in Starved Rock State Park. *Illinois Archaeology* 9:220–256.

Fishel, Richard L.
2005 The Gill Site (23RY102): An Early Woodland Encampment in Northwest Missouri. *Journal of the Iowa Archeological Society* 52:1–19.

Flock, Mark A.
1983 The Late Wisconsinan Savanna Terrace in Tributaries to the Upper Mississippi River. *Quaternary Research* 20:165–176.

Fortier, Andrew C.
1983 Settlement and Subsistence at the Go-Kart North Site: A Late Archaic Titterington Occupation in the American Bottom. In *Archaic Hunters and Gatherers in the American Midwest*, edited by James L. Phillips and James A. Brown, pp. 243–260. Academic Press, New York.
1984 The Go-Kart North Site. In *The Go-Kart North Site and the Dyroff and Levin Sites*, by Andrew C. Fortier and Thomas E. Emerson, pp. 1–197. American Bottom Archaeology FAI-270 Site Reports 9. University of Illinois Press, Urbana.
1985 *Selected Sites in the Hill Lake Locality*. American Bottom Archaeology FAI-270 Site Reports 13. University of Illinois Press, Urbana.
1987 The Archaic Occupation. In *The Range Site: Archaic through Late Woodland Occupations*, edited by John E. Kelly, Andrew C. Fortier, Steven J. Ozuk, and Joyce A. Williams, pp. 34–113. American Bottom Archaeology FAI-270 Site Reports 16. University of Illinois Press, Urbana.
1990 Investigations in the Mainline Portion of the Nochta Site. In *The Nochta Site: The Early, Middle, and Late*

Archaic Occupations, edited by Michael J. Higgins, pp. 163–230. American Bottom Archaeology FAI-270 Site Reports 21. University of Illinois Press, Urbana.

1993 American Bottom House Types of the Archaic and Woodland Periods: An Overview. In *Highways to the Past: Essays on Illinois Archaeology in Honor of Charles J. Bareis*, edited by Thomas E. Emerson, Andrew C. Fortier, and Dale L. McElrath, pp. 260–275. *Illinois Archaeology* 5.

1996 *The Marge Site: Late Archaic and Emergent Mississippian Occupations in the Palmer Creek Locality*. American Bottom Archaeology FAI-270 Site Reports 27. University of Illinois Press, Urbana.

2001 A Tradition of Discontinuity: American Bottom Early and Middle Woodland Culture History Reexamined. In *The Archaeology of Traditions: Agency and History Before and After Columbus*, edited by Timothy R. Pauketat, pp. 174–194. University Press of Florida, Gainesville.

Fortier, Andrew C., Thomas E. Emerson, and Kathryn E. Parker

1998 The Meyer Site: A Terminal Late Archaic Residential Camp in the American Bottom. *Illinois Archaeology* 10:195–228.

Fortier, Andrew C., Fred A. Finney, and Richard B. Lacampagne

1983 *The Mund Site*. American Bottom Archaeology FAI-270 Site Reports 5. University of Illinois Press, Urbana.

Fortier, Andrew C., Thomas O. Maher, Joyce A. Williams, Michael C. Meinkoth, Kathryn E. Parker, and Lucretia S. Kelly

1989 *The Holding Site: A Hopewell Community in the American Bottom*. American Bottom Archaeology FAI-270 Site Reports 19. University of Illinois, Urbana.

Fortier, Andrew C., and Dale L. McElrath

2002 Deconstructing the Emergent Mississippian Concept: The Case for the Terminal Late Woodland in the American Bottom. *Midcontinental Journal of Archaeology* 27:172–215.

Fowke, Gerard

1928 Archaeological Investigations, Part II. *Annual Report for 1926–1927*, pp. 299–540. Bureau of American Ethnology, Smithsonian Institution, Washington, D.C.

Fowler, Melvin L.

1957 *Ferry Site, Hardin County, Illinois*. Scientific Papers 8(1). Illinois State Museum, Springfield.

1959a Modoc Rock Shelter: An Early Archaic Site in Southern Illinois. *American Antiquity* 24:257–270.

1959b *Summary Report of Modoc Rock Shelter 1952, 1953, 1955, 1956*. Report of Investigations 8. Illinois State Museum, Springfield.

1973 The Cahokia Site. In *Explorations into Cahokia Archaeology*, pp. 1–30. Bulletin 7. Illinois Archaeological Survey, Urbana.

Fowler, Melvin L., and Howard D. Winters

1956 *Modoc Rock Shelter Preliminary Report*. Reports of Investigations 4. Illinois State Museum, Springfield.

Frison, George C.

1991 *Prehistoric Hunters of the High Plains*. Academic Press, New York.

Gaertner, Linda M.

1994 Determining the Function of Dalton Adzes from Northeast Arkansas. *Lithic Technology* 19:97–109.

Galloy, Joseph M.

2001 *Archaeological Investigations at 11S658 (Edging Site) for the Visitors Center, Our Lady of the Snows Shrine Project*. Archaeological Testing Short Report 63. Illinois Transportation Archaeological Research Program, University of Illinois, Urbana–Champaign.

Goatley, David B.

1998 Quasar: A Stratified Archaic Site in the Floodplain of the Lower Illinois River Valley. *Illinois Archaeology* 10:267–293.

Goldstein, Lynne

2004 An Analysis of Plummets in the Lower Illinois River Valley. In *Aboriginal Ritual and Economy in the Eastern Woodlands: Essays in Memory of Howard Dalton Winters*, edited by Anne-Marie Cantwell, Lawrence A. Conrad, and Jonathan E. Reyman, pp. 73–112. Scientific Papers 30. Illinois State Museum, Springfield.

Goodman, Claire Garber

1984 *Copper Artifacts in Late Eastern Woodlands Prehistory*. Center for American Archeology, Northwestern University, Evanston, Illinois.

Goodyear, Albert C.

1974 *The Brand Site: A Techno-Functional Study of a Dalton Site in Northeast Arkansas*. Research Series 7. Arkansas Archeological Survey, Fayetteville.

1982 The Chronological Position of the Dalton Horizon in the Southeastern United States. *American Antiquity* 47:382–395.

1999 The Early Holocene Occupation of the Southeastern United States: A Geoarchaeological Summary. In *Ice Age People of North America: Environments, Origins, and Adaptations*, edited by Robson Bonnischen and Karen L. Turnmire, pp. 432–481. Oregon State University Press, Corvallis.

Graham, Russell W., C. Vance Haynes, Donald L. Johnson, and Marvin Kay

1981 Kimmswick: A Clovis Mastodon Association in Eastern Missouri. *Science* 213:1115–1117.

Gramly, Richard Michael

1993 *The Richey Clovis Cache: Earliest Americans on the Columbia River*. Persimmon Press, Buffalo, New York.

Griffin, James B., and Albert C. Spaulding

1951 The Central Mississippi Valley Archaeological Survey, Season 1950—A Preliminary Report. *Journal of the Illinois State Archaeological Society* 1:75–80.

Grimm, Robert C.

1953 *Prehistoric Art: A Picture Study of Ancient America thru Tools and Artifacts*. Greater St. Louis Archaeological Society, St. Louis, Missouri.

Gums, Bonnie L., and John E. Kelly

1989 Preliminary Report of Phase I Reconnaissance Survey for FAP-14 or Illinois Route 3 from Columbia to Waterloo in Monroe County, Illinois. Submitted to the Illinois Department of Transportation, Springfield. Contract Archaeology Program, Southern Illinois University, Edwardsville.

Hajic, Edwin

1990 *Koster Site Archeology I: Stratigraphy and Landscape Evolution*. Research Series 8. Center for American Archeology, Kampsville, Illinois.

1993 Geomorphology of the Northern American Bottom as Context for Archaeology. In *Highways to the Past: Essays on Illinois Archaeology in Honor of Charles J. Bareis*, edited by Thomas E. Emerson, Andrew C. Fortier, and Dale L. McElrath, pp. 54–64. *Illinois Archaeology* 5.

Hajic, Edwin R., Sheena K. Beaverson, and Andrew K. Freeman
2000 Archaeological Geology of the Ringering Site and Vicinity. In *The Ringering Site and the Archaic-Woodland Transition in the American Bottom*, pp. 65–117. Transportation Archaeological Research Reports 8. Illinois Transportation Archaeological Research Program, Department of Anthropology, University of Illinois, Urbana–Champaign.

Hall, Robert L.
1981 Radiocarbon Chronology for the Labras Lake Site. In *Labras Lake: Investigations into the Prehistoric Occupations of a Mississippi Floodplain Locality in St. Clair County, Illinois*, edited by James L. Phillips and Robert L. Hall, pp. 383–414. Department of Anthropology, University of Illinois at Chicago Circle.

Hamilton, M. Colleen, Patti J. Wright, Hanna Stazewska-Kruel, Joseph M. Nixon, and Neal H. Lopinot
1986 *Extensive Archaeological Testing at the Lone Wolf Site, 23SL467, South St. Louis County, Missouri*. Archaeological Survey Research Report 41. University of Missouri–St. Louis.

Hargrave, Eve, Kristin Hedman, and Rebecca Wolf
2006 *Isolated Human Burial at the Kaskaskia Mine Site (11R487), Randolph County, Illinois*. Research Reports 104. Illinois Transportation Archaeological Research Program, University of Illinois, Urbana–Champaign.

Harl, Joseph L.
1998 The Titterington Phase in East-Central Missouri and Archaeology of the Hayden Site: Evidence of Long-Term Occupation in the Late Archaic. *Illinois Archaeology* 10:229–266.

Harl, Joseph L., and Patti J. Wright
1995 *Data Recovery Investigations at the Hayden Site (23SL36) and the Rabanus Site (23SL859), Chesterfield, St. Louis County, Missouri: New Insights into the Titterington/Sedalia Phase in East Central Missouri*. Archaeological Services Research Report 182. University of Missouri–St. Louis.

Harn, Alan D.
1971 An Archaeological Survey of the American Bottoms in Madison and St. Clair Counties. In *An Archaeological Survey of the American Bottom and Wood River Terrace*, edited by Patrick J. Munson and Alan D. Harn, pp. 21–42. Reports of Investigations 21. Illinois State Museum, Springfield.

Hassen, Harold, and Kenneth B. Farnsworth
1987 *The Bullseye Site: A Floodplain Archaic Mortuary Site in the Lower Illinois River Valley*. Reports of Investigations 42. Illinois State Museum, Springfield.

Hayden, Brian
1989 From Chopper to Celt: The Evolution of Resharpening Techniques. In *Time, Energy, and Stone Tools*, edited by Robin Torrence, pp. 7–16. Cambridge University Press, Cambridge, England.

Higgins, Michael J.
1990 *The Nochta Site: The Early, Middle, and Late Archaic Occupations*. American Bottom Archaeology FAI-270 Site Reports 21. University of Illinois Press, Urbana.

Holley, George R., Mikels Skele, Harold W. Watters, Kathryn E. Parker, Elizabeth M. Scott, Joyce A. Williams, Donald L. Booth, Julie N. Harper, Alan J. Brown, Christina L. Fulton, and Laura L. Harmon
2001 *Introduction to the Prehistoric Archaeology of the Scott Joint-Use Archaeological Project*. Office of Contract Archaeology, Southern Illinois University, Edwardsville.

Holliday, Vance T.
2000 The Evolution of Paleoindian Geochronology and Typology on the Great Plains. *Geoarchaeology: An International Journal* 15:227–290.

Holmes, W. H.
1919 *Handbook of Aboriginal American Antiquities: Part I, Introductory, the Lithic Industries*. Bulletin 60. Bureau of American Ethnology, Smithsonian Institution, Washington, D.C.

Houart, Gail L.
1971 *Koster: A Stratified Archaic Site in the Illinois Valley*. Reports of Investigations 22. Illinois State Museum, Springfield.

Ives, David J.
1975 *The Crescent Hills Prehistoric Quarrying Area*. Museum Brief 22. Museum of Anthropology, University of Missouri, Columbia.

Jackson, Douglas K.
1979 An Archaeological Survey of the Wood River Basin, Madison County, Illinois. Submitted to the State of Illinois Department of Transportation. Department of Anthropology, University of Illinois, Urbana.

Jefferies, Richard W.
1990 A Technological and Functional Analysis of Middle Archaic Hafted Endscrapers from the Black Earth Site, Saline County, Illinois. *Midcontinental Journal of Archaeology* 15:3–36.

Jefferies, Richard W., and B. Mark Lynch
1983 Dimensions of Middle Archaic Cultural Adaptations at the Black Earth Site, Saline County, Illinois. In *Archaic Hunters and Gatherers in the American Midwest*, edited by James L. Phillips and James A. Brown, pp. 299–322. Academic Press, New York.

Johannessen, Sissel
1984 Plant Remains. In *The Go-Kart North Site*, by Andrew C. Fortier, pp. 166–178. American Bottom Archaeology FAI-270 Site Reports 9. University of Illinois Press, Urbana.
1986 Plant Remains. In *The McLean Site*, by Dale L. McElrath, pp. 85–100. American Bottom Archaeology FAI-270 Site Reports 14. University of Illinois Press, Urbana.

Justice, Noel D.
1987 *Stone Age Spear and Arrow Points of the Midcontinental and Eastern United States*. Indiana University Press, Bloomington.

Kay, Marvin (editor)
1982 *Holocene Adaptations within the Lower Pomme de Terre River Valley, Missouri*, vol. 3. Illinois State Museum Society, Springfield.

Kelly, John E.
2000 The Grassy Lake Site: An Historical and Archaeological Overview. In *Mounds, Modoc, and Mesoamerica: Papers in Honor of Melvin L. Fowler*, edited by Steven R. Ahler, pp. 141–178. Scientific Papers 38. Illinois State Museum, Springfield.

Kelly, John E., Jean R. Linder, and Theresa J. Cartmell
1979 *An Archaeological Intensive Survey of the FAI-270 Alignment in the American Bottom Region of Southern Illinois.* Illinois Transportation Archaeology Scientific Reports 1. Illinois Department of Transportation, Springfield.

Klippel, Walter E.
1969 *The Booth Site: An Archaic Campsite.* Research Series 6. Missouri Archaeological Society, Columbia.

Klippel, Walter E., and James Maddox
1977 The Early Archaic at Willow Branch. *Midcontinental Journal of Archaeology* 2:99–130.

Knoblock, Byron W.
1939 *Bannerstones of the North American Indians.* Privately published, LaGrange, Illinois.

Koldehoff, Brad
1980 An Inventory of Prehistory in Southwestern Illinois: The Russell Fischer Collection. *Rediscovery* 1:1–9.
1985 Southern Illinois Cherts: A Guide to Silicious Materials Exploited by Prehistoric Populations in Southern Illinois. Manuscript on file, Center for Archaeological Investigations, Southern Illinois University, Carbondale.
1987 The Cahokia Flake Tool Industry: Socioeconomic Implications for Late Prehistory in the Central Mississippi Valley. In *The Organization of Core Technology,* edited by Jay K. Johnson and Carol A. Morrow, pp. 151–185. Westview Press, Boulder, Colorado.
1992 Lithic Analysis. In *The Little Muddy Rock Shelter: A Deeply Stratified Prehistoric Site in the Southern Till Plains of Illinois*, edited by Charles E. Moffat, Brad Koldehoff, Mary Carol Masulis, and Mary R. McCorvie, pp. 279–374. Cultural Resources Management Report 186. American Resources Group, Carbondale, Illinois.
2002 *The Woodland Ridge Site and Late Woodland Land Use in the Southern American Bottom.* Transportation Archaeological Research Reports 15. Illinois Transportation Archaeological Research Program, University of Illinois, Urbana.
2006 *Paleoindian and Archaic Settlement and Lithic Procurement in the Illinois Uplands.* Research Reports 108. Illinois Transportation Archaeological Research Program, University of Illinois, Urbana–Champaign.

Koldehoff, Brad, and John A. Walthall
2004 Settling In: Hunter-Gatherer Mobility during the Pleistocene-Holocene Transition in the Central Mississippi Valley. In *Aboriginal Ritual and Economy in the Eastern Woodlands: Essays in Memory of Howard Dalton Winters*, edited by Anne-Marie Cantwell, Lawrence A. Conrad, and Jonathan E. Reyman, pp. 49–72. Scientific Papers 30. Illinois State Museum, Springfield.

Kwas, Mary
1981 Bannerstones as Chronological Markers in the Southeastern United States. *Tennessee Anthropologist* 6:144–171.

Libby, W. F.
1952 *Radiocarbon Dating.* University of Chicago Press, Chicago.

Lightfoot, Kent G., and Antoinette Martinez
1995 Frontiers and Boundaries in Archaeological Perspective. *Annual Review of Anthropology* 24:471–492.

Linder, Jean R., Theresa J. Cartmell, and John E. Kelly
1978 *Preliminary Archaeological Reconnaissance of the Segments under Study for FAP-413 in Madison County, Illinois.* Illinois Department of Transportation, Fairview Heights, Illinois.

Logan, Wilfred D.
1952 *Graham Cave, an Archaic Site in Montgomery County, Missouri.* Memoir 2. Missouri Archaeological Society, Columbia.

Lopinot, Neal H.
1991 The Diana Site (11-R-331), an Archaic and Woodland Settlement in Southwestern Illinois. *Illinois Archaeology* 3:113–202.

Lopinot, Neal H., Jack Ray, and Michael D. Conner (editors)
1998 *The 1997 Excavations at the Big Eddy Site (23CE426) in Southwest Missouri.* Center for Archaeological Research, Southwest Missouri State University, Springfield.
2000 *The 1999 Excavations at the Big Eddy Site (23CE426).* Center for Archaeological Research, Southwest Missouri State University, Springfield.

Luchterhand, Kubet
1970 *Early Archaic Projectile Points and Hunting Patterns in the Lower Illinois Valley.* Reports of Investigations 19. Illinois State Museum, Springfield.

Lyman, R. Lee, and Michael J. O'Brien
2004 A History of Normative Theory in Americanist Archaeology. *Journal of Archaeological Method and Theory* 11:369–396.

Lyman, R. Lee, Michael J. O'Brien, and Robert Dunnell
1997 *The Rise and Fall of Culture History.* Plenum Press, New York.

MacNeish, Richard S.
1948 The Pre-Pottery Faulkner Site of Southern Illinois. *American Antiquity* 13:323–324.

Mayer-Oakes, William J.
1951 Starved Rock Archaic, a Prepottery Horizon from Northern Illinois *American Antiquity* 17:313–324.

McElrath, Dale L.
1986 *The McLean Site (11-S-640).* American Bottom Archaeology FAI-270 Site Reports 14. University of Illinois Press, Urbana.
1993 Mule Road: A Newly Defined Late Archaic Phase in the American Bottom. In *Highways to the Past: Essays on Illinois Archaeology in Honor of Charles J. Bareis*, edited by Thomas E. Emerson, Andrew C. Fortier, and Dale L. McElrath, pp. 148–157. *Illinois Archaeology* 5.

McElrath, Dale L., and Thomas E. Emerson
2000 Toward an "Intrinsic Characteristics" Approach to Chert Raw Material Classification: An American Bottom Example. *Midcontinental Journal of Archaeology* 25:215–244.

McElrath, Dale L., Thomas E. Emerson, and Andrew C. Fortier
2000 Social Evolution or Social Response? A Fresh Look at the "Good Grey Cultures" after Four Decades of

Research in the Midwest. In *Late Woodland Societies: Tradition and Transformation across the Midcontinent*, edited by Thomas E. Emerson, Dale L. McElrath, and Andrew C. Fortier, pp. 3–36. University of Nebraska Press, Lincoln.

McElrath, Dale L., Thomas E. Emerson, Andrew C. Fortier, and James L. Phillips
1984 Late Archaic Period. In *American Bottom Archaeology: A Summary of the FAI-270 Project Contributions to the Culture History of the Mississippi River Valley*, edited by Charles J. Bareis and James W. Porter, pp. 34–58. University of Illinois Press, Urbana.

McElrath, Dale L. and Fred A. Finney
1987 *The George Reeves Site (11-S-650).* American Bottom Archaeology FAI-270 Site Reports 15. University of Illinois Press, Urbana.

McElrath, Dale L., and Andrew C. Fortier
1983 *The Missouri Pacific Site #2: A Late Archaic Occupation in the American Bottom.* FAI-270 Archaeological Mitigation Project Report 34. Department of Anthropology, University of Illinois, Urbana.
2000 The Early Late Woodland Occupation of the American Bottom. In *Late Woodland Societies: Tradition and Transformation across the Midcontinent*, edited by Thomas E. Emerson, Dale L. McElrath, and Andrew C. Fortier, pp. 97–121. University of Nebraska Press, Lincoln.

McMillan, R. Bruce
1971 Biophysical Changes and Cultural Adaptation at Rodgers Shelter, Missouri. Ph.D. dissertation, Department of Anthropology, University of Colorado, Boulder.

Milner, George R.
1998 *The Cahokia Chiefdom: The Archaeology of a Mississippian Society.* Smithsonian Institution Press, Washington, D.C.

Moffat, Charles E.
1980 The Tep Site (11-Mo-154). In *Final Report of the Investigations of Three Archaeological Sites in Luhr Brother's Borrow Pit #4, Monroe County, Illinois*, edited by Duane Esarey and Charles E. Moffat, pp. 12–40. FAI-270 Archaeological Mitigation Project Report 35. Department of Anthropology, Western Illinois University, Macomb.

Montet-White, Anta
1968 *The Lithic Industries of the Illinois Valley in the Early and Middle Woodland Period.* Anthropological Papers 35. Museum of Anthropology, University of Michigan, Ann Arbor.

Morrow, Toby A.
1996 Lithic Refitting and Archaeological Site Formation Processes: A Case Study from the Twin Ditch Site, Greene County, Illinois. In *Stone Tools: Theoretical Insights into Human Prehistory*, edited by George H. Odell, pp. 345–373. Plenum Press, New York.

Morse, Dan F. (editor)
1997 *Sloan: A Paleoindian Dalton Cemetery in Arkansas.* Smithsonian Institution Press, Washington, D.C.

Morse, Dan F., and Albert C. Goodyear
1973 The Significance of the Dalton Adze in Northeast Arkansas. *Plains Anthropologist* 18:316–322.

Munson, Patrick J.
1971 An Archaeological Survey of the Wood River Terrace and Adjacent Bottoms and Bluffs in Madison County Illinois. In *An Archaeological Survey of the American Bottoms and Wood River Terrace*, edited by Patrick J. Munson and Alan D. Harn, pp. 1–18. Reports of Investigations 21. Illinois State Museum, Springfield.
1974 Terraces, Meander Loops, and Archaeology in the American Bottoms, Illinois. *Transactions of the Illinois State Academy of Science* 67:384–392. Springfield.

Munson, Patrick J., and Alan D. Harn
1966 Surface Collections from Three Sites in the Central Illinois River Valley. *The Wisconsin Archeologist* 47:150–169.

Nassaney, Michael S., and Neal H. Lopinot
1986 The Significance of a Short-Term Late Archaic Occupation in the American Bottom. In *Foraging, Collecting, and Harvesting: Archaic Period Subsistence and Settlement in the Eastern Woodlands*, edited by Sarah W. Neusius, pp. 201–224. Occasional Papers 6. Center for Archaeological Investigations, Southern Illinois University, Carbondale.

Nassaney, Michael S., Neal H. Lopinot, Brian M. Butler, and Richard W. Jefferies
1983 *The 1982 Excavations at the Cahokia Interpretive Center Tract, St. Clair County, Illinois.* Research Paper 37. Center for Archaeological Investigations, Southern Illinois University, Carbondale.

Neumann, Holm Wolfram
1967 *The Paleopathology of the Archaic Modoc Rock Shelter Inhabitants.* Reports of Investigations 11. Illinois State Museum, Springfield.

Nolan, David J. (editor)
2004 *Archaeological Investigations in the Mississippi Valley Uplands of West Central Illinois: Final Report of the FAP 407 and FAP 506 Projects in Adams and Hancock Counties.* Illinois Transportation Archaeological Research Program, University of Illinois, Urbana.

O'Brien, Michael J., and Robert E. Warren
1983 An Archaic Projectile Point Sequence from the Southern Prairie Peninsula: The Pigeon Roost Site. In *Archaic Hunters and Gatherers in the American Midwest*, edited by James L. Phillips and James A. Brown, pp. 71–98. Academic Press, New York.

Odell, George H.
1986 Preliminary Analysis of Lithic and Other Nonceramic Assemblages. In *The Archaic and Woodland Cemeteries at the Elizabeth Site in the Lower Illinois Valley*, edited by Douglas K. Charles, Steven R. Leigh, and Jane E. Buikstra, pp. 155–190. Research Series 7. Center for American Archeology, Kampsville, Illinois.
1996 *Stone Tools and Mobility in the Illinois Valley: From Hunter-Gatherer Camps to Agricultural Villages.* Archaeological Series 10. International Monographs in Prehistory, Ann Arbor, Michigan.

Parker, Kathryn E.
1990 Early Archaic Archaeobotany. In *The Nochta Site: The Early, Middle, and Late Archaic Occupations*, edited by Michael J. Higgins, pp. 231–236. American Bottom Archaeology FAI-270 Site Reports 21. University of Illinois Press, Urbana.

2001 Botanical Remains Recovered from Flotation at the Floyd Site. In *The Floyd Site: A Terminal Archaic Habitation in the Northern American Bottom*, edited by J. Bryant Evans, pp. 151–202. Transportation Archaeological Research Reports 11. Illinois Transportation Archaeological Research Program, Department of Anthropology, University of Illinois, Urbana.

Pauketat, Timothy R.
2001a Practice and History in Archaeology: An Emerging Paradigm. *Anthropological Theory* 1:73–98.
2001b A New Tradition in Archaeology. In *The Archaeology of Traditions: Agency and History Before and After Columbus*, edited by Timothy R. Pauketat, pp. 1–16. University Press of Florida, Gainesville.
2004 *Ancient Cahokia and the Mississippians*. Cambridge University Press, Cambridge, England.

Perino, Gregory
1954 The Titterington Focus-Red Ochre. *Central States Archaeological Journal* 1:15–17.
1961 Tentative Classification of Plummets in the Lower Illinois River Valley. *Central States Archaeological Journal* 8:43–56.

Phillips, James L., and Bruce G. Gladfelter
1983 The Labras Lake Site and the Paleogeographic Setting of the Late Archaic in the American Bottom. In *Archaic Hunters and Gatherers in the American Midwest*, edited by James L. Phillips and James A. Brown, pp. 197–218. Academic Press, New York.

Phillips, James L., and Robert L. Hall (editors)
1981 *Labras Lake: Investigations into the Prehistoric Occupations of a Mississippi Floodplain Locality in St. Clair County, Illinois*. Department of Anthropology, University of Illinois at Chicago Circle.

Phillips, James L., Robert L. Hall, and Richard W. Yerkes (editors)
1980 *Investigations at the Labras Lake Site*. Department of Anthropology, University of Illinois at Chicago Circle.

Porter, James W.
1971 An Archaeological Survey of the Mississippi Valley in St. Clair, Monroe, and Randolph Counties. In *Preliminary Report of 1971 Historic Sites Survey Archaeological Reconnaissance of Selected Areas in the State of Illinois*, Part 1, Summary, Section 4, pp. 28–34. Illinois Archaeological Survey, Department of Anthropology, University of Illinois, Urbana.
1972 An Archaeological Survey of the Mississippi Valley in St. Clair, Monroe, and Randolph Counties. In *Preliminary Report of 1972 Historic Sites Survey Archaeological Reconnaissance of Selected Areas in the State of Illinois*, Part 1, Summary, Section A, pp. 25–33. Illinois Archaeological Survey, Department of Anthropology, University of Illinois, Urbana.

Porter, James W., and Jean Linder
1974 An Archaeological Survey of the Mississippi Valley in St. Clair, Monroe, and Randolph Counties. In *Preliminary Report of 1973 Historic Sites Survey Archaeological Reconnaissance of Selected Areas in the State of Illinois*, Part 1, Summary, Section A, pp. 28–34. Illinois Archaeological Survey, Department of Anthropology, University of Illinois, Urbana.

Ray, Jack
1985 An Overview of Chipped Stone Resources in Southern Missouri. In *Lithic Resource Procurement: Proceedings from the Second Conference on Prehistoric Chert Exploitation*, edited by Susan C. Vehik, pp. 225–250. Occasional Papers 4. Center for Archaeological Investigations, Southern Illinois University, Carbondale.

Reid, Kenneth C.
1984 *Nebo Hill and the Late Archaic Prehistory of the Southern Prairie Peninsula*. Publications in Anthropology 15. University of Kansas, Lawrence.

Rissing, Joseph
1991 *Report on the Geomorphology along the 5.8 Mile Extension of FAI 270(255)*. FAI-270 Archaeological Mitigation Report, Geomorphological Report 1. Department of Anthropology, University of Illinois, Urbana.

Ritchie, William A.
1951 A Current Synthesis of New York Prehistory. *American Antiquity* 17:130–136.

Roper, Donna C.
1978 *The Airport Site: A Multi-Component Site in the Sangamon River Drainage*. Papers in Anthropology 4. Illinois State Museum, Springfield.

Sandstrom, Carl B., and Jack H. Ray
2004 *A Point Identification Guide for Southwest Missouri*. Ozarks Chapter, Missouri Archaeological Society, Springfield.

Sassaman, Kenneth E.
1993 *Early Pottery in the Southeast: Tradition and Innovation in Cooking Technology*. University of Alabama Press, Tuscaloosa.
1996 Technological Innovation in Economic and Social Contexts. In *Archaeology of the Mid-Holocene Southeast*, edited by Kenneth E. Sassaman and David G. Anderson, pp. 57–74. University Press of Florida, Gainesville.
2005 Structure and Practice in the Archaic Southeast. In *North American Archaeology*, edited by Timothy R. Pauketat and Diana DiPaolo Loren, pp. 79–107. Blackwell, Malden, Massachusetts.

Scully, Edward G.
1951 Some Central Mississippi Valley Projectile Point Types. Unpublished manuscript, Museum of Anthropology, University of Michigan, Ann Arbor.

Seelen, Robert M.
1961 *A Preliminary Report of the Sedalia Complex*. Missouri Archaeological Society Newsletter 153.

Seeman, Mark F.
1975 Buck Creek Barbed Projectile Points. *Central States Archaeological Journal* 22:106–108.

Shippee, J. M.
1948 Nebo Hill, a Lithic Complex in Western Missouri. *American Antiquity* 14:29–32.

Shott, Michael J.
1996 Innovation in Prehistory: A Case Study from the American Bottom. In *Stone Tools: Theoretical Insights into Human Prehistory*, edited by George H. Odell, pp. 279–309. Plenum Press, New York.

Simon, Mary
1996 Late Archaic Plant Remains. In *The Marge Site: Late Archaic and Emergent Mississippian Occupations in the Palmer Creek Locality (11-Mo-99)*, by Andrew C. Fortier, pp. 79–94. American Bottom Archaeology FAI-270 Site Reports 27. University of Illinois Press, Urbana.

Smith, Bruce D.
1986 The Archaeology of the Southeastern United States: From Dalton to de Soto, 10,500–500 B.P. In *Advances in World Archaeology*, vol. 5, edited by Fred Wendorf and Angela E. Close, pp. 1–92. Academic Press, New York.

Stafford, Barbara D.
1997 *Early Woodland Occupations at the Bushmeyer and Nearby Sites in the Sny Bottom of West-Central Illinois*. Research Series 11. Kampsville Archeological Center, Center for American Archeology, Kampsville, Illinois.

Stafford, C. Russell (editor)
1985 *The Campbell Hollow Archaic Occupations: A Study of Intrasite Spatial Structure in the Lower Illinois Valley*. Research Series 4. Kampsville Archeological Center, Center for American Archeology, Kampsville, Illinois.
1992 *Early Woodland Occupations at the Ambrose Flick Site in the Sny Bottom of West-Central Illinois*. Research Series 10. Kampsville Archeological Center, Center for American Archeology, Kampsville, Illinois.

Struever, Stuart
1968 Flotation Techniques for the Recovery of Small-Scale Archaeological Remains. *American Antiquity* 33:353–362.
1973 Chert Utilization in Lower Illinois Valley Prehistory. In *Variation in Anthropology: Essays in Honor of John C. McGregor*, edited by Donald W. Lathrap and Jody Douglas, pp. 61–73. Illinois Archaeological Survey, Urbana.

Struever, Stuart, and Felicia A. Holton
1979 *Koster: Americans in Search of Their Prehistoric Past*. Doubleday, New York.

Stuiver, Minze, and Paula J. Reimer
1993 Extended ^{14}C Database and Revised CALIB Radiocarbon Calibration Program. *Radiocarbon* 35:215–230.

Styles, Bonnie W., Steven R. Ahler, and Melvin L. Fowler
1983 Modoc Rock Shelter Revisited. In *Archaic Hunters and Gatherers in the American Midwest*, edited by James L. Phillips and James A. Brown, pp. 261–297. Academic Press, New York.

Thorson, Paula J., and Bonnie W. Styles
1992 Analysis of the Plant Remains. In *Late Archaic Components at Modoc Rock Shelter, Randolph County, Illinois*, edited by Steven R. Ahler, pp. 52–80. Reports of Investigations 48. Illinois State Museum, Springfield.

Titterington, Paul F.
1937 Flint Quarries. *The Missouri Archaeologist* 3:3–6.
1950 Some Non-Pottery Sites in the St. Louis Area. *Journal of the Illinois State Archaeological Society* 1:18–31.

Van den Berghe, Pierre L.
1981 *The Ethnic Phenomenon*. Elsevier, New York.

Van Nest, Julienne
1997 Late Quaternary Geology, Archeology and Vegetation in West-Central Illinois: A Study of Geoarcheology. Ph.D. dissertation, Department of Geology, University of Iowa, Iowa City.

Walthall, John A.
1981 *Galena and Aboriginal Trade in Eastern North America*. Special Paper 17. Illinois State Museum, Springfield.

Walthall, John A., and Brad Koldehoff
1998 Hunter-Gatherer Interaction and Alliance Formation: Dalton and the Cult of the Long Blade. *Plains Anthropologist* 43:257–273.
1999 Across the Divide: Dalton Land Use in the Southern Till Plains. *Illinois Archaeology* 11:27–49.

Walz, Gregory R., Brian Adams, Paul P. Kreisa, Kevin P. McGowan, and Jacqueline M. McDowell
1998 The Strong Site and the Dennis Hollow Phase: A New Perspective on Middle Archaic Chronology, Technology and Subsistence. *Illinois Archaeology* 10:155–194.

Warren, Robert F. (editor)
1997 *Environment and Human Settlement along Interstate 39 in North Central Illinois*. Quaternary Studies Program, Illinois State Museum, Springfield.

Watters, Harold W., Jr., George R. Holley, and Donald L. Booth
2001 Physical and Cultural Setting of the Project. In *Introduction to the Prehistoric Archaeology of the Scott Joint-Use Archaeological Project*, by George R. Holley, Mikels Skele, Harold W. Watters, Kathryn E. Parker, Elizabeth M. Scott, Joyce A. Williams, Donald L. Booth, Julie N. Harper, Alan J. Brown, Christine L. Fulton, and Laura L. Harmon, pp. 7–39. Office of Contract Archaeology, Southern Illinois University, Edwardsville.

Wendland, Wayne M., and Reid A. Bryson
1974 Dating Climatic Episodes of the Holocene. *Quaternary Research* 4:2–24.

White, William P., Sissel Johannessen, Paula G. Cross, and Lucretia S. Kelly
1984 Environmental Setting. In *American Bottom Archaeology: A Summary of the FAI-270 Project Contribution to the Culture History of the Mississippi River Valley*, edited by Charles J. Bareis and James W. Porter, pp. 15–33. University of Illinois Press, Urbana.

Wiant, Michael D., Edwin R. Hajic, and Thomas R. Styles
1983 Napoleon Hollow and Koster Site Stratigraphy: Implications for Holocene Landscape Evolution and Studies of Archaic Period Settlement Patterns in the Lower Illinois River Valley. In *Archaic Hunters and Gatherers in the American Midwest*, edited by James L. Phillips and James A. Brown, pp. 147–164. Academic Press, New York.

Winters, Howard D.
1967 *An Archaeological Survey of the Wabash Valley in Illinois*. Reports of Investigations 10. Illinois State Museum, Springfield.
1969 *The Riverton Culture*. Reports of Investigations 13. Illinois State Museum, Springfield.

Wisseman, Sarah
2005 True Grit: Middle Woodland Cooking and Pot Production. *Illinois Archaeology* 17:189–200.

Wittry, Warren L.
1959 The Raddatz Rockshelter, Sk5, Wisconsin. *The Wisconsin Archeologist* 40:33–69.

Wood, W. Raymond, and R. Bruce McMillan (editors)
1976 *Prehistoric Man and His Environments: A Case Study from the Ozark Highland*. Academic Press, New York.

Woods, William I., and Robert D. Mitchell
1978 A Survey of Aboriginal Chert Sources in the Waterloo, Illinois Area. Submitted to the Illinois Department of Transportation. Southern Illinois University, Edwardsville.

Wray, Donald E.
1952 Archeology of the Illinois Valley: 1950. In *Archeology of Eastern United States*, edited by James B. Griffin, pp. 152–164. University of Chicago Press, Chicago.

Wyckoff, Don G.
1985 The Packard Complex: Early Archaic, Pre-Dalton Occupations on the Prairie-Woodlands Border. *Southeastern Archaeology* 4:1–26.

Yerkes, Richard W.
1987 Late Archaic Settlement and Subsistence on the American Bottom. In *Foraging, Collecting, and Harvesting: Archaic Period Subsistence and Settlement in the Eastern Woodlands*, edited by Sarah W. Neusius, pp. 225–245. Occasional Papers 6. Center for Archaeological Investigations, Southern Illinois University, Carbondale.

Yerkes, Richard W., and Linda M. Gaertner
1997 Microwear Analysis of Dalton Artifacts. In *Sloan: A Paleoindian Dalton Cemetery in Arkansas*, edited by Dan F. Morse, pp. 58–71. Smithsonian Institution Press, Washington, D.C.

12

Archaic Period of East-Central Missouri

Joseph L. Harl

Numerous Archaic sites have been identified in Missouri, but the majority have been described only on the basis of displaced surface evidence. With archaeological investigations generally driven by cultural resource management studies, in which pleasing the client often is paramount, many of these sites are routinely dismissed as "not significant," regardless of their age or potential for subsurface remains. Consequently, despite over 25 years of relatively intensive professional investigations, little information exists from intact subsurface remains at Archaic sites. The limited excavations that have been performed, however, are beginning to provide interesting insights into this remarkable time in prehistory.

This chapter deals with Archaic sites in east-central Missouri, near the confluence of the Missouri River with the Mississippi River (Figure 12.1; see Ray et al., this volume, for a description of Archaic sites in the Missouri Ozarks). Located near the center of the United States, this region is at the margin of four major physiographic provinces: the woodlands to the east, the prairies to the west, the ancient Ozark highlands to the south, and the glaciated till plains to the north. As a result, a diversity of resources was easily accessible to the Archaic inhabitants. Galena and hematite were available along the upper ends of the Meramec River and along the fringes of the Ozark highlands. Granite, gabbro, and basalt, which could have been used for ground-stone tools, were also available in that region. Saline springs were present at a diversity of locations, providing salt and attracting wildlife. Most of the region is underlain by Mississippian and Pennsylvanian geologic formations providing limestone, sandstone, shale, and chert for different uses. Formations of high-quality Burlington cherts, which could be easily worked into a wide variety tools, were present near the surface across a large portion of the area. This chert was used by Archaic groups for their own tool production as well as traded to other regions. In addition to mineral resources, prairie, forest, and riverine faunal and floral resources were within easy access of most Archaic communities. The availability of these resources changed over the years because of fluctuations in the climate and technological developments. As the confluences of several major rivers (Missouri, Mississippi, and Illinois) are located in east-central Missouri, resources and ideas from across a large portion of the country eventually came to this area, influencing the Archaic groups here and their cultures.

The Archaic period covers a large portion of prehistory, and most sites were repeatedly occupied, so surface information can convey a misleading picture of Archaic lifeways at any one time. Generally, only sites producing intact features are discussed below, as they provide more definitive data on Archaic activities. Some portions of the Archaic period have been further divided into regional and temporal phases. However, much work still needs to be performed to better define the subtle changes underlying these divisions. Thus, the phases used are only tentative until more information is available from a greater number of excavated sites.

Early Archaic Period (7900–6000 B.C.)

The first attempt to describe the Early Archaic period in Missouri was that of Carl Chapman (1975; Chapman and

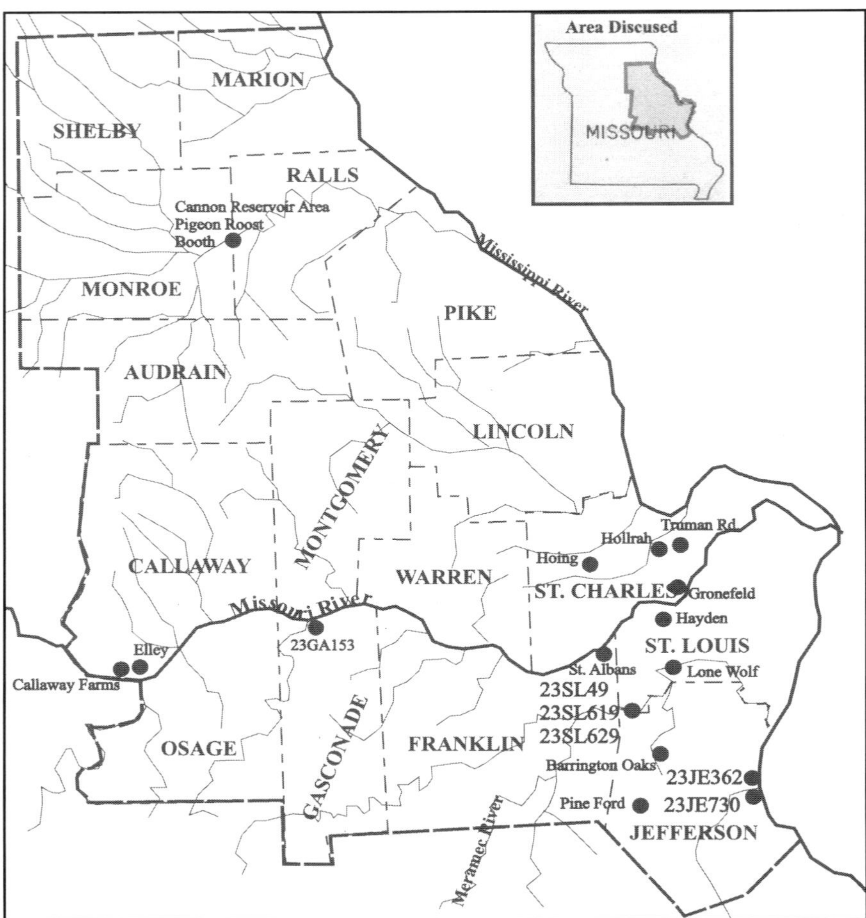

Figure 12.1. Locations of east-central Missouri sites discussed in text.

Chapman 1972), who reviewed the archaeological data available to him from surface finds and excavations. He believed that the Early Archaic period represented a transitional time from a "hunting-forager" to a "forager" tradition. Chapman suggests that

> early in the Archaic Period numbers of people living and working together were small like those in the Paleo-Indian and Dalton periods, perhaps fewer than 100 in a group, and during much of the year may have been divided into extended families made up of 10–25 members. An extended family or two (10–50 people) might hunt or collect together utilizing the same camping place as a base of operation for their particular activities. ... Foragers using the camps were still placing a great deal of emphasis upon hunting as one of the means of gaining their livelihood. [1975:125–126]

The best Early Archaic materials available to Chapman were from excavations at caves and rockshelters, in particular, Graham Cave in Montgomery County, Arnold Rock Shelter in Callaway County, and Hidden Valley Shelter in Jefferson County. These locations appear to have been used sporadically by hunting parties who left behind fire hearths and a scatter of lithic tools such as choppers, scrapers, knives, and spear points. Chapman (1975:136, 145) suggested that plano-convex scrapers became less common than during the earlier Dalton period because of a "change in emphasis from hunting deer to more diversified hunting and trapping of small game animals" (1975:145). He also noted variability in the types of projectile points used in this region, with Graham Cave Notched projectile points (named for the type site, Graham Cave) common at sites along the Missouri River near central Missouri. Other projectile points used in this area included various lanceolate, small Rice Lobed, St. Charles Notched, and Thebes points. Hidden Valley and Hardin Barbed points tended to be more common along the Mississippi River valley.

O'Brien and Wood criticized Chapman's conclusions, noting that the materials within Graham Cave and Arnold Rock Shelter were mixed because of the "friable nature of the deposits ... and [that] the incredible amount of mixing ... was evident during excavation" (1998:109–110).

Their reanalysis of the Early Archaic, however, did not substantially change the conclusions reached by Chapman, although it more clearly indicated when certain styles of projectile points were favored. Further, they suggested that during the Early Archaic period, a "revolution" occurred in projectile point design, with the lanceolate-style tools produced during the Paleoindian period giving way to a wide range of hafting styles, including contracting stemmed (e.g., Hidden Valley and Rice Lanceolate), straight stemmed (e.g., Scottsbluff and Alberta), expanding stemmed (e.g., Hardin Barbed), basal notched (e.g., Calf Creek), corner notched on small- to large-bladed points (e.g., Lost Lake and St. Charles), and side notched on small to large blades (e.g., Cache River, Graham Cave, and Thebes) (O'Brien and Warren 1983; O'Brien and Wood 1998:147–149).

In recent years, extensive surface surveys have brought further insights into the Early Archaic settlement pattern. A systematic survey was performed for the proposed Cannon Reservoir project along the Salt River in northeastern Missouri in Ralls and Monroe counties (Morrow et al. 1995; O'Brien and Wood 1998:152–160; Warren 1982). The research revealed that, at the start of the Early Archaic, the prairie grasslands were first invading the interior upland portions of the Salt River drainage basin. The grasslands, however, were not extensive, as forests covered most of the area. Early Archaic sites were found to be small and scattered across the landscape, situated on stream terraces, at the margins of ridgetops, along interior portions of smaller streams, and within the interior uplands. These sites indicated that Early Archaic people resided in small groups, as first suggested by Chapman, utilizing a mobile foraging economic strategy. Only one of these sites, the Pigeon Roost Creek site, was excavated. The lower levels of this stratified site contained a Dalton–Early Archaic horizon dated at cal 7500 B.C. (Table 12.1), which produced large quantities of hickory (*Carya*) nuts, followed by black walnut (*Juglans nigra*), hazelnut (*Corylus americana*), one giant ragweed seed (*Ambrosia trifida*), and a portion of a groundnut tuber (*Apios americana*). Warren (1982:365) proposed that the Early Archaic groups in this region used a three-part seasonal round incorporating summer bottomland encampments, fall upland encampments coordinated with the collection of nuts, and winter upland encampments principally coordinated with the massing of deer and other large vertebrates.

An archival review of Early Archaic sites reported on either side of the confluence of the Missouri River within St. Louis and St. Charles counties produced similar results (Harl 1995; Harl et al. 1997). Like those of the previous Dalton period, however, the majority of Early Archaic sites were clustered in areas where the better-quality Burlington chert was readily available at the surface.

In more recent years, only one site that may date to the Early Archaic period has been excavated in east-central Missouri (Sturdevant 1997). The Barrington Oaks site (23JE600A), near the center of Jefferson County, is situated on a ridge crest overlooking Big River to the west. Limited shovel tests suggested that two locations at this site (Areas A and B) could have subsurface features. Only the southern area (A) was to be impacted by a proposed housing development and was investigated. Test units and mechanical stripping exposed four features. Feature 1 was a shallow, oval-shaped basin measuring 20 x 59 cm and approximately 10 cm deep. Its fill contained flaking debris, fire-cracked rock, a piece of galena, and fragments of "catlinite pipe." Just outside the feature were two portions of a broken side-notched point identified by Sturdevant (1997:31) as a "Graham Cave" point.

Feature 2, found immediately to the southwest, was also a basin-shaped pit measuring 12 x 36 cm and 10 cm deep. This shallow feature contained "a cache of Early Archaic points with unusual rock forms lying at each end of the cache, an undefined soft rock with a 'fish' shape at the bottom of the stack of points, a 6 ounce piece of melted lead next to the point cache, a geode, and an hourglass shaped natural piece of fine-grained dolomite" (Sturdevant 1997:26). The stack contained five projectile points lying atop each other with the blades facing in the same direction, toward the southeast. The stack included two Hardin Barbed points, one Rice Lanceolate variant, one St. Charles Notched point, and one side-notched lanceolate. The fishlike object found under the cache measured 13.0 x 5.7 x 1.8 cm. It was produced from a soft stone that "has a mica-like consistency" (Sturtevant 1997:26). Two grooves were placed on the sides of the stone and the ends had also been smoothed. A waterworn cobble of local Jefferson City chert with a roughly hourglass shape was found near the proximal end of the point cache.

The other two features contained only a small number of artifacts, consisting primarily of chert flakes. Feature 3 was defined as a "post mold." This conical-shaped pit had a circular opening about 20 cm in diameter and was about 40–50 cm deep. It was filled with charcoal. Similar conical pits have been found at various prehistoric sites within the Meramec River drainage basin (including Big River); however, these have been identified as roasting pits because their fills contained charcoal and burned clay and the walls showed evidence of having been scorched by fire (Harl and Nixon 1992). Feature 4 was another shallow basin that also contained fire-cracked rock. Despite the unusual contents of Feature 2 and the possible early age of the site, more extensive archaeological investigations were not deemed necessary and the Area A portion of the site has been destroyed by development.

Fortunately, the artifacts recovered from this site were reanalyzed by Terrell Martin (2001), providing new insights (Figure 12.2). He found that the seven broken "catlinite pipe" fragments in Feature 1 were made from rhyolitic welded tuff from the St. Francois Mountains about 55 km to the south. Further, the fragments were not from a pipe stem but from a "saddle shaped tube" bannerstone. The broken side-notched point next to Feature 1 was reidentified as a Godar point, indicative of the Middle Archaic period. Two other side-notched Middle Archaic points were found in the

Table 12.1. Radiocarbon Dates from Archaic Sites in East-Central Missouri.

Lab No.	Site	Phase	B.P.	S.D.	Uncorrected B.C. Dates	Calibrated[a] B.C. Dates (1 sigma)	Reference
ISGS-4543	Callaway Farms 23CY227	Prairie Lake?	2570	70	620	816 (790) 544	Harl et al. 2001
ISGS-4544	Callaway Farms 23CY227	Prairie Lake?	2620	70	670	895 (800) 595	Harl et al. 2001
ISGS-4546	Callaway Farms 23CY227	Prairie Lake?	2640	70	690	897 (805) 773	Harl et al. 2001
ISGS-4547	Callaway Farms 23CY227	Prairie Lake?	2550	70	600	803 (785) 541	Harl et al. 2001
ISGS-4548	Callaway Farms 23CY227	Prairie Lake?	2540	70	590	800 (780) 537	Harl et al. 2001
ISGS-4549	Callaway Farms 23CY227	Prairie Lake?	2650	80	700	921 (805) 763	Harl et al. 2001
ISGS-4550	Callaway Farms 23CY227	Prairie Lake?	2550	70	600	803 (785) 541	Harl et al. 2001
ISGS-4557	Callaway Farms 23CY227	Prairie Lake?	2650	80	700	921 (805) 763	Harl et al. 2001
ISGS-4558	Callaway Farms 23CY227	Prairie Lake?	2550	80	600	805 (785) 538	Harl et al. 2001
ISGS-4559	Callaway Farms 23CY227	Prairie Lake?	2560	70	610	807 (790) 543	Harl et al. 2001
ISGS-4560	Callaway Farms 23CY227	Prairie Lake?	2680	80	730	917 (825) 793	Harl et al. 2001
ISGS-4561	Callaway Farms 23CY227	Prairie Lake?	2630	70	680	898 (805) 672	Harl et al. 2001
ISGS-4562	Callaway Farms 23CY227	Prairie Lake?	2760	70	810	996 (887) 829	Harl et al. 2001
B-111170	Callaway Farms 23CY227	Prairie Lake?	2530	70	580	795 (775) 525	Harl et al. 2001
ISGS-4545	Pine Ford 23JE764	Labras Lake	2790	100	840	1035 (916) 822	Meinkoth in press
ISGS-4533	Pine Ford 23JE764	Labras Lake	2910	70	960	1251 (1101) 993	Meinkoth in press
ISGS-4545	Pine Ford 23JE764	Labras Lake	3050	80	1100	1406 (1306) 1139	Meinkoth in press
ISGS-4523	Elley 23CY562	Labras Lake	3370	70	1420	1740 (1674) 1527	Meinkoth in press
ISGS-4525	Elley 23CY562	Labras Lake	3450	70	1500	1876 (1742) 1677	Meinkoth in press
N.A.	Hayden 23SL36	Titterington	4080	70	2130	2857 (2628) 2496	Harl and Wright 1995
N.A.	Hayden 23SL36	Titterington	4010	60	2060	2620 (2530) 2462	Harl and Wright 1995
N.A.	Hayden 23SL36	Titterington	3950	70	2000	2568 (2448) 2314	Harl and Wright 1995
N.A.	Hayden 23SL36	Titterington	3930	60	1980	2548 (2403) 2309	Harl and Wright 1995

[a]Calibrated using CALIB 4.4 (Stuiver et al. 2004).

Table 12.1. Radiocarbon Dates from Archaic Sites in East-Central Missouri, continued.

Lab No.	Site	Phase	B.P.	S.D.	Uncorrected B.C. Dates	Calibrated[a] B.C. Dates (1 sigma)	Reference
B-86679	Truman Road 23SC924	Falling Springs	4490	50	2540	3335 (3273) 3098	Harl 1999b
B-89879	Truman Road 23SC924	Falling Springs	4000	70	2050	2656 (2529) 2354	Harl 1999b
B-90315	Truman Road 23SC924	Falling Springs	4230	70	2280	2911 (2755) 2681	Harl 1999b
B-90314	Truman Road 23SC924	Falling Springs	4300	70	2350	3078 (2949) 2785	Harl 1999b
B-89878	Truman Road 23SC924	Falling Springs	4600	80	2650	3516 (3462) 3104	Harl 1999b
B-90313	Truman Road 23SC924	Falling Springs	4610	80	2660	3518 (3424) 3121	Harl 1999b
B-90312	Truman Road 23SC924	Falling Springs	4890	70	2940	3764 (3675) 3543	Harl 1999b
N.A.	St. Albans 23FR334B	Helton	5470	100	3520	4450 (4313) 4167	Harl and Wright 1992
B-14094	Lone Wolf 23SL467	Helton	4860	80	2910	3757 (3641) 3525	Hamilton et al. 1986
B-14095	Lone Wolf 23SL467	Helton	5640	80	3690	4543 (4489) 4363	Hamilton et al. 1986
N.A.	Pigeon Roost Creek	unknown Middle Archaic phase	4840	440	2890	4217 (3578) 2939	O'Brien and Warren 1985
N.A.	Pigeon Roost Creek	unknownMiddle Archaic phase	5370	350	3420	4550 (4166) 3781	O'Brien and Warren 1985
N.A.	Pigeon Roost Creek	unknownMiddle Archaic phase	5850	210	3890	4945 (4702) 4458	O'Brien and Warren 1985
N.A.	Pigeon Roost Creek	unknown Middle Archaic phase	6050	190	4100	5228 (4976) 4724	O'Brien and Warren 1985
N.A.	Pigeon Roost Creek	unknownMiddle Archaic phase	6130	170	4180	5279 (5047) 4814	O'Brien and Warren 1985
N.A.	Pigeon Roost Creek	unknownMiddle Archaic Phase	6190	320	4240	5469 (5126) 4782	O'Brien and Warren 1985
N.A.	Pigeon Roost Creek	unknownMiddle Archaic phase	6370	100	4420	5472 (5367) 5262	O'Brien and Warren 1985
B-69187	23GA153	unknown early Middle Archaic Phase	6780	90	4830	5700 (5620) 5580	Anglen 1994
B-69188	23GA153	unknown early Middle Archaic phase	6730	110	4780	5680 (5600) 5510	Anglen 1994
N.A.	Pigeon Roost Creek	unknown Early Archaic phase	8500	220	6550	7937 (7561) 7185	O'Brien and Warren 1985

[a]Calibrated using CALIB 4.4 (Stuiver et al. 2004).

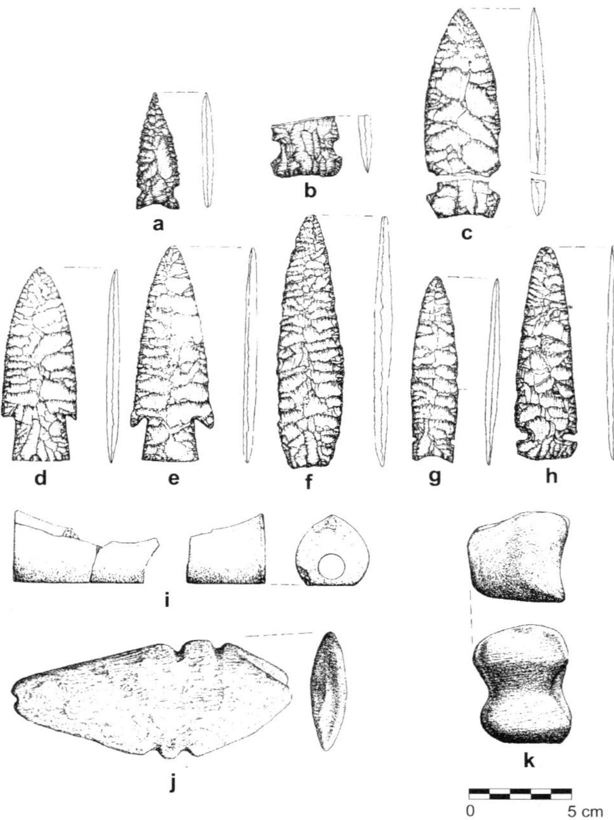

Figure 12.2. Selected artifacts recovered from the Barrington Oaks site: a, side-notched point, outside features; b, Godar, outside features; c, Godar, near Feature 1; d, e, Hardin Barbed, Feature 2; f, Rice Lanceolate, Feature 2 cache; g, side-notched lanceolate, Feature 2 cache; h, Graham Cave Notched, Feature 2 cache; i, bannerstone; j, ground stone; k, unmodified Jefferson City chert (provided by Terrell Martin).

surrounding soils near the features. The presence of Middle Archaic projectile points led Martin (2001) to suggest that the site may have been occupied during that time, with the cache of Early Archaic points and other special objects in Feature 2 possibly representing a Middle Archaic shaman's kit. Martin also reported that Sturdevant had found two clusters (5–10 cm wide) of witchhazel (*Hamamelis vernalis*) seeds, one placed adjacent to Feature 1 and one inside Feature 2, suggesting that both features were used at the same time. The seeds were subsequently lost, and no radiocarbon date was ever run on the other carbonized material from this unique site. Thus, it is still unclear whether this site had multiple occupations, one during the Early Archaic period and one during the Middle Archaic, or just a single Middle Archaic use. Caches, such as the ones found at the Barrington Oak site, typically are placed near burials (Martin 2001:104–106).

Middle Archaic Period (6000–3500 B.C.)

During the Middle Archaic period, people were adapting to a changing climate. This period coincided with the Hypsithermal climatic episode, when temperatures were slightly warmer than today. Chapman suggests that:

> sites of Foragers continued to be small during the Middle Archaic period, and though there were changes in the tool kits, indicating a greater diversity of activities, specialization, or exceptional emphasis on any one exploitive subsistence activity, was not evident. Hunting and associated activities continued to be very important. No one location, in relation to the topography, was indicative of the settlement pattern, which was not significantly different from that in the Early Archaic Period. [1975:158]

He proposes that, for portions of Missouri, especially within the Ozark highlands and the northern prairies, the "population density must have been thin and their existence precarious" (Chapman 1975:172).

O'Brien and Wood (1998) reevaluated this period in Missouri on the basis of more recent data. They also suggested that Middle Archaic groups altered their settlement and economic strategy in response to the Hypsithermal climatic episode but that the effects of this drier climate were not as drastic as suggested by Chapman. It did not trigger a movement of populations out of regions of Missouri; instead, people modified their settlement strategy, clustering within or near the forested bottomlands. As O'Brien and Wood write,

> Middle Archaic settlement-subsistence systems . . . are difficult to interpret with available data, though the small size of the sites and redundancy in functional classes of the stone tools suggest that groups moved from place to place to occupy temporary camps in localities with nondepleted resources rather than establishing more permanent settlements out of which smaller groups traveled to perform specific tasks. Thus, Middle Archaic groups appear to have been foragers, though site contexts were different from those of the Early Archaic period, and specific exploitation patterns probably changed. [1998:158]

The prairies expanded during this time, covering large portions of the uplands and broader portions of the bottoms near the rivers. Although prairies are not devoid of floral or faunal resources, a greater abundance was present within the forests or along the increasing margins between these two zones. Marginal species, such as deer, probably increased in numbers or were more accessible during this time. The dropping water table also made more terraces available for habitation without threat of occasional inundation. Certain riverine species, for example, mollusks, also increased in quantity.

Warren (1982), analyzing sites identified during the Cannon Reservoir survey in northeastern Missouri, suggested that Middle Archaic groups continued to utilize a mobile foraging strategy but established most of their seasonal camps within the forested bottoms near waterways or at the marginal zones between the forests and prairies where the greatest quantity of resources was available. Although the greater number of sites indicates a slight population increase over Early Archaic times, the majority of the sites continued to be small, occupied by only small groups of people (probably fewer than 50 individuals). Information is slight, but these groups seem to have keyed on certain resources. For example, analysis of the floral remains from the Middle Archaic horizon at the Pigeon Roost Creek site, dated between cal 5300 and 4500 B.C., revealed 90 percent hickory nutshells, 4–6 percent black walnut, and 4 percent hazelnut, suggesting Middle Archaic groups' preference for hickory nuts. A greater diversity of ground-stone tools was also present, including various manos, metates, mauls, and full-grooved axes, and, by the end of the Middle Archaic, three-quarter-grooved axes and hematite plummets. Projectile points did not represent the wide diversity of styles popular during the Early Archaic but consisted primarily of side-notched forms. A reanalysis of the projectile points recovered during the Cannon Reservoir project suggested that the point styles utilized may have varied slightly through the Middle Archaic period. Side-notched Raddatz and Robinson and corner-notched Jakie Stemmed styles were popular during the first part of the Middle Archaic (6000–4500 B.C.), with side-notched Godar (Big Sandy), Matanzas, Osceola, Hemphill, expanding-stemmed Table Rock (Apple Blossom), and corner-notched Helton common during the later portion of the Middle Archaic identified as the Helton phase (Morrow et al. 1995:623).

A site tested in Gasconade County seems to have been used during the early portion of the Middle Archaic. Site 23GA153 was identified at the base of the bluffs near the confluence of the Gasconade River with the Missouri River (Anglen 1994; Anglen et al. 1993). Portions of three fire hearths were found approximately 90–100 cm below the surface. One of the hearths was completely lined with large sandstone slabs, the largest measuring 15 x 20 x 5 cm. Two radiocarbon samples taken from the hearth indicated that it was used around cal 5600 B.C. Associated with the hearths were various flakes, cores, and bifaces as well as three metates and one mano. One of the metates had a red stain from grinding hematite; five pieces of ground hematite were found in the general area. Three large bifaces were also recovered, all exhibiting edge wear suggesting they were used as woodworking implements. Portions of seven projectile points were also found, but only three of these were large enough to be identified. These include a deeply side-notched Godar point, a Faint Side Notched Matanzas or Robinson-like point, and a slightly contracting-stemmed point with a short blade (Figure 12.3).

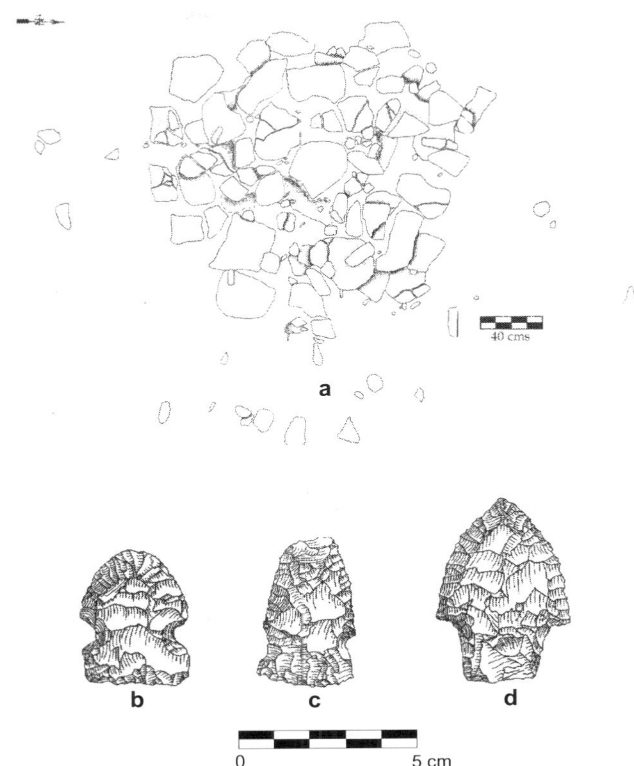

Figure 12.3. Selected remains from site 23GA153: a, Feature 1, rock-lined fire hearth; b, Godar point; c, Matanzas or Robinson-like point; d, Rice Contracting Stemmed point (Anglen 1994).

Most of the other Middle Archaic sites excavated in east-central Missouri were associated with the Helton phase. At these sites, Helton points were the preferred style (Figure 12.4). The Lone Wolf site (23SL467), near the confluence of Keifer Creek with the Meramec River in western St. Louis County (Hamilton et al. 1989; Hamilton et al. 1986), produced a buried Helton-phase horizon (40–100 cm below the surface) containing two medium-deep (approximately 45- and 55-cm-deep), straight-walled pit features. Tools recovered included six Helton projectile points, eight bifacial knives, seven denticulates (likely hide-scraping tools), a nutting stone, a mano, a hammerstone, and 25 utilized flakes of various kinds. Flotation samples recovered from the features produced only a small number of unidentifiable animal bones but had a greater quantity of carbonized plant remains. The plant remains consisted of 1,673 nutshell fragments, dominated by thick-shelled hickory (*Carya*). Thin-shelled pecan or bitternut varieties were also common. Other nutshells recovered included 17 acorn (*Quercus* spp.) pieces, four black walnut (*Juglans nigra*), and 14 hazelnut (*Corylus americana*). In addition to nuts, four groundnut (*Apios americana*) tubers were recovered. These were cut longitudinally, suggesting that the tubers were prepared by slicing. Two radiocarbon dates, cal 4500 and 3600 B.C., were obtained from the carbonized plant remains from the features. Typical of most Helton-phase sites found in east-central Missouri, the Lone Wolf site was small,

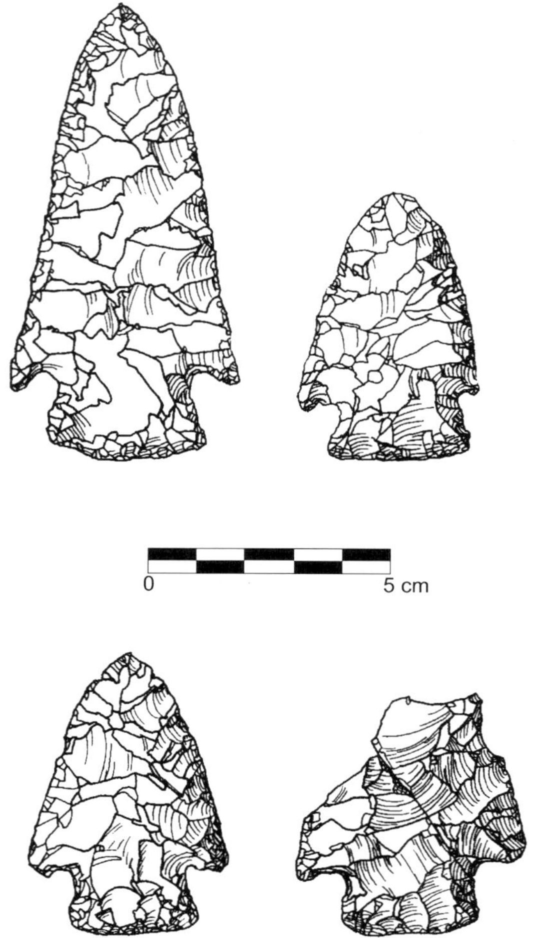

Figure 12.4. Helton projectile points from the Lone Wolf site (Hamilton et al. 1986:114, Figure 14).

representing a short-term habitation, probably used during a part of a seasonal round.

Two additional Middle Archaic sites (23JE362 and 23JE730) were investigated in conjunction with proposed improvements to Interstate 55 in Jefferson County, Missouri, for the Missouri Department of Transportation (MoDOT) and Federal Highways Administration (FHWA). Site 23JE362 was identified on a ridgetop overlooking a major tributary of Joachim Creek and on the back portion of the Mississippi River bluffs. This site was first recorded by Father Benedict Ellis from the nearby St. Pius X Monastery, who found, "relatively high concentration of cultural materials" including tools used for cutting, digging, and scraping as well as projectile points (Ellis 1965). The majority of the 30 projectile points illustrated on the site form filed by Father Ellis had broad blades with straight to excurvate edges, distinctively barbed shoulders, and corner-notched stems with convex bases similar to Helton forms. One of Father Ellis's points was a small corner-notched Late Woodland arrow point, suggesting a second occupation. Only the western edge of this site was to be impacted by the proposed interstate improvements and was tested (Harl 1999a). Two shallow (10-cm-deep) basin features were uncovered about 24 cm below the surface. The top of Feature 1 contained a limestone cobble (8 cm long), and two larger cobbles (18 cm long) were found about 28 cm to the north. This pit contained only four flakes and charcoal flecks. Feature 2, immediately to the west, produced only three flakes and charcoal flecks. Four tools were found at the same level as the features and included a broken biface, which was reworked into an adze, and three projectile points. One point is similar to a Koster or Scallorn form, typical of the Late Woodland period, one is a small, expanding-stem point similar to a Table Rock, and one is a small, straight-stemmed point similar to a Matanzas variety or a small Stone Square Stemmed point.

Below the features, approximately 44 cm beneath the surface, a lithic pile was uncovered measuring about 10 cm in diameter and 7 cm high. The pile contained 15 flakes, one core fragment, three biface fragments (at various stages of working), and two limestone fragments. Two early-stage bifaces (one complete) were found just outside the lithic pile, possibly suggesting that it was left by a knapper. The depth of this lithic pile suggested that it was older than the features. Whether the overlying features were related to the Helton-phase Middle Archaic component or to a Late Woodland component, however, was unclear. The lack of pottery could support the former. If so, the lithic pile must date to an even earlier occupation. Flotation samples were taken but were not analyzed. No samples were submitted for radiocarbon dating because it was anticipated that the data-recovery investigations would soon be performed. However, the proposed interstate improvements and, thus, additional data recovery, were put on hold.

Testing operations were also performed at site 23JE730, situated on a high ridgetop immediately south of Joachim Creek (Harl 1999a). Systematic shovel testing produced numerous flakes, a biface, a core, a piece of hematite, and burned limestone and clay, the latter materials indicative of the presence of earth ovens or fire hearths. Test units uncovered portions of three basin-shaped features, two of them over 2 m long. The pits contained only small numbers of flakes and biface fragments (from five to 33), but only a portion of each was excavated. Two side-notched projectile points found just outside the features are similar to Godar or Big Sandy forms, supporting a Middle Archaic use possibly prior to the Helton phase. Data recovery investigations of this site have been put on hold.

A more substantial Helton-phase occupation was found at the St. Albans site, 23FR334. This site is situated on a high secondary terrace, near the outfall of Tavern Creek onto the Missouri River bottoms, within northeastern Franklin County. The land developer had hoped to turn this location into a borrow pit and a lake. Test units and six mechanically excavated trenches exposed two clusters of Helton-phase features, one (Area A) containing two features and the other

(Area B) containing 10 features (Harl and Wright 1992). The majority of the features ($n = 7$) were shallow, basin-shaped pits, probably used for storage, but the quantity of nutshells in some of these pits could indicate that they were used in nut processing. As suggested by McElrath,

> Most techniques of processing larger quantities of nuts involve parching and/or boiling. These methods are not necessary for processing walnuts or hickory nuts since they can be eaten raw simply by cracking the nuts open and picking out the meat. As several researchers have pointed out, however, this is not an economical way of capturing energy because of the length of time necessary to process a relatively small amount of nuts. It is much more efficient to boil the already cracked nuts, which will serve to separate the nut oil which can be skimmed off the surface, and which will cause the nut meat to float in suspension for easy straining. [1986:83–84]

Shallow basin pits work best for this processing. These could have been lined with hides and then filled with water, but given the clayey nature of the soils at site 23FR334, unlined pits could have held the water.

The larger cluster within Area B also included five medium-deep (22–66 cm) features with inslanting walls. The ratio of nutshell to wood was nearly equal in these pits (unlike the basins, which contained predominantly nutshell), and they contained relatively high quantities of lithic debris. These pits could have been used for storage and later served as places to discard trash. Two of the pits, however, also contained large quantities of burned limestone cobbles, burned clay, and charred faunal remains, suggesting they served as earth ovens.

Various activities were performed at this location, including hunting, as indicated by projectile points. Among the points were 10 corner-notched forms with broad blades and distinctive shoulders similar to Helton points, three Stone Square Stemmed forms, six side-notched Godar or Big Sandy forms, and one with a bifurcated, distinctively lobed base similar to a Jakie Stemmed point. A local collector recovered the middle portion of a bannerstone made from a nonlocal banded slate from near the road within Area A (Figure 12.5). The outer edges of this stone were notched, giving them a denticulate appearance. Other activities carried out at the site included hide working (scrapers), wood- or bone working (bone scrapers, spokeshaves, adzes, and a wedge), food processing (cutting tools, nut-processing features, and earth ovens), and tool manufacturing and maintenance. Examination of flotation samples revealed that nutshells constituted the majority (91 percent) of the floral remains recovered. Hickories dominated, and a small quantity (.8 percent) of black walnut shells was present. Only four seeds were recovered: one grape pip and three persimmon seeds.

Late Archaic Period (3500–600 B.C.)

The most common artifacts reported by collectors and professional archaeologists in Missouri are associated with the Late Archaic period, yet a great deal is not known about this time. Within the past 10 years, however, an increasing number of sites have been tested, and a few have even had more complete data-recovery investigations. These investigations are providing some of the first information on the Late Archaic lifestyle within east-central Missouri.

With the improving environmental situation at the start of the Late Archaic period, Chapman suggests, people made many changes in their societies:

> The greatest change occurred in the Late Archaic period in the prairie regions as demonstrated by the larger size of base camps, the great amount of stone that had been brought to them, and the specialized tools that were manufactured. The prairie Foragers consistently settled on ridges or hilltops. There was limited use of dart points, indicating that little

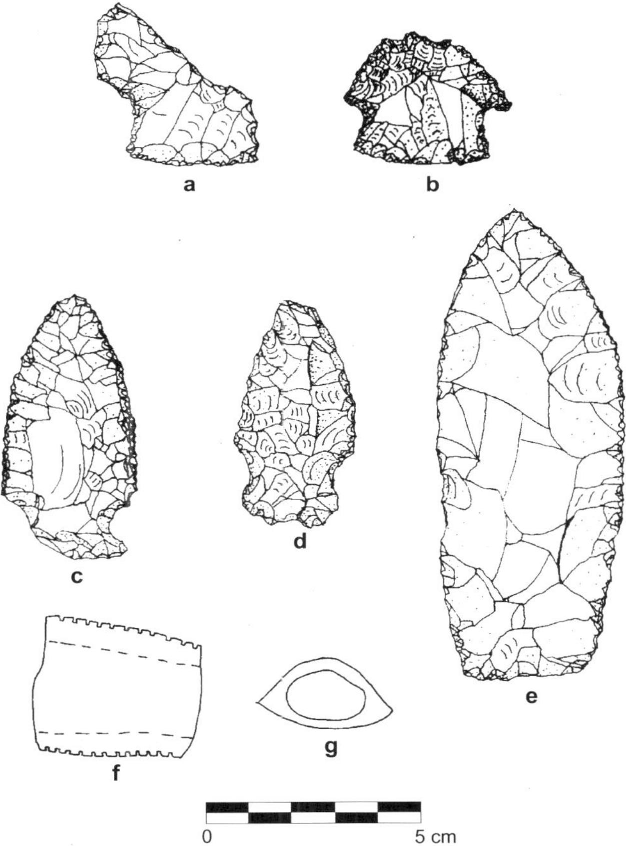

Figure 12.5. Selected artifacts from the St. Alban site: a, b, Helton points; c, d, Godar or Big Sandy points; e, Wadlow bifacial blank; f, g, bannerstone, dorsal view and cross section (Harl and Wright 1992).

> time was devoted to hunting. For the most part except in special hunting camps such as caves, there is little evidence of animal bones. Probably as a result of the deemphasis on hunting, there was little or no bone-working industry. Much stress was placed on ceremony in connection with the burial of the dead as evidenced by specially constructed cemeteries, use of red ochre to cover the bones, and the inclusion in the graves of tools and ornaments made of exotic materials such as copper. According to Winters (1968) extensive trade networks may have developed during this period to replenish supplies of exotic materials. [1975:227–228]

O'Brien and Wood also suggest that the settlement strategy changed during the Late Archaic, as

> site contexts continued to diversify in settings, despite a decline in proportion of upland sites. Also some Late Archaic sites apparently functioned as (a) residential sites, defined as locations with high artifact densities indicative of intensive and/or recurrent occupation and artifact assemblages that represent light domestic activity, and (b) specialized nonresidential procurement-processing locations, defined as sites with low artifact densities and assemblages that represent resource extraction and/or heavy processing activities. These latter sites represent the first *domesticated* appearance of the kind of site in the regional archaeological record. They occur in uplands and in two different bottomland contexts ... and are consistent with the interpretation derived from faunal ... remains, that a semisedentary settlement system had been adopted in which small task groups were more likely to conduct extractive tasks away from residential camps or villages. [1998:159]

O'Brien and Wood further suggest that, during the Late Archaic, plants became a more important part of people's diet. Some became incidental domesticates as humans protected dispersed native species, promoting their concentration around habitation sites and favoring certain morphological attributes, for example, thinner seed coats and larger seeds. But, O'Brien and Wood believe, only after the Early Woodland period did groups begin to depend on domesticated plants. After that time, humans and plants became mutually dependent, with plants grown far beyond their natural ranges and requiring more active care (e.g., weeding, storing, and watering). The intensification of resources afforded through cultivation allowed groups to occupy settlements for longer periods of time and increase their population levels (O'Brien and Wood 1998:215).

The growing amount of data being collected has allowed for the Late Archaic period in east-central Missouri to be divided into various phases. Tentative phase names similar to those originally proposed from the greater number of excavated sites within the American Bottom of western Illinois have been used. Clear differences exist between some aspects of the sites in Missouri and those of similar phases in Illinois, but further work is needed before these local differences can be more clearly defined and possible new phase names proposed.

Falling Springs Phase (3500–2700 B.C.)

The first phase of the Late Archaic period has been identified as Falling Springs (McElrath et al. 1984:36–40). Expanding stemmed points similar to Heltons and side-notched forms such as Godar and Big Sandy continued to be used, but in east-central Missouri Etley and Stone Square Stemmed varieties became popular.

Sites dating to the Falling Springs phase generally tend to be small, probably occupied by fewer than 50 people. These places were occupied for short durations as part of a seasonal round. An archaeological field school in 1979 and 1980 conducted by the University of Missouri-St. Louis investigated one of these seasonal camps, the Hollrah site (23SC424). Test units at the site, which is situated on the Mississippi River bluff top in St. Charles County, exposed four fire hearths, four (20- to 30-cm-deep) basins, one deep (ca. 96-cm-deep) pit possibly used as an earth oven, and a conical pit filled with nearly 2,000 snail shells. The snail shells were large, nearly 2 cm in diameter, suggesting that they had been purposely selected, and they had a slightly red color, indicating that they had been roasted within the shell, probably in the conical pit.

Another Falling Springs site, the Hoing site (23SC834), was unusual, as it was located within the prairie uplands near a plugged sinkhole (Martin 2005). Late Archaic groups seem to have been particularly drawn to sinkholes in St. Louis and St. Charles counties, but Hoing is the only one of these sites to have been further investigated. Data-recovery investigations performed at the Hoing site uncovered 21 pit features, clustered near the southwestern edge of the ponded sinkhole. The majority of these features consisted of large (1- to 3-m-long) basin-shaped pits 30–50 cm deep. Ed Hajic, who performed the geomorphological investigations, suggested that the depressions could represent buffalo wallows (Martin 2005:Appendix C). On the whole, a sparse scatter of lithic debris was recovered from the site, but the materials suggested that various activities were performed here, including hunting (projectile points), hide working (scrapers), woodworking (drills), food processing (manos and metates, nutting stones, and fire-cracked rock), and tool maintenance and production. Five pieces of hematite were recovered, which could have been used to produce a red pigment for decoration or ceremonial activities. The projectile points consisted of a variety of styles (Figure 12.6), including 12 long-bladed Etley or Stone Square Stemmed forms, 10 side-notched forms similar to Raddatz, eight corner-notched forms with short blades—some possibly reworked Etley points—and an unusual point with a narrow stem (Figure 12.6f). In addition, six Wadlow bifaces were recovered that may represent blanks for Etley points, but one was interpreted as a possible

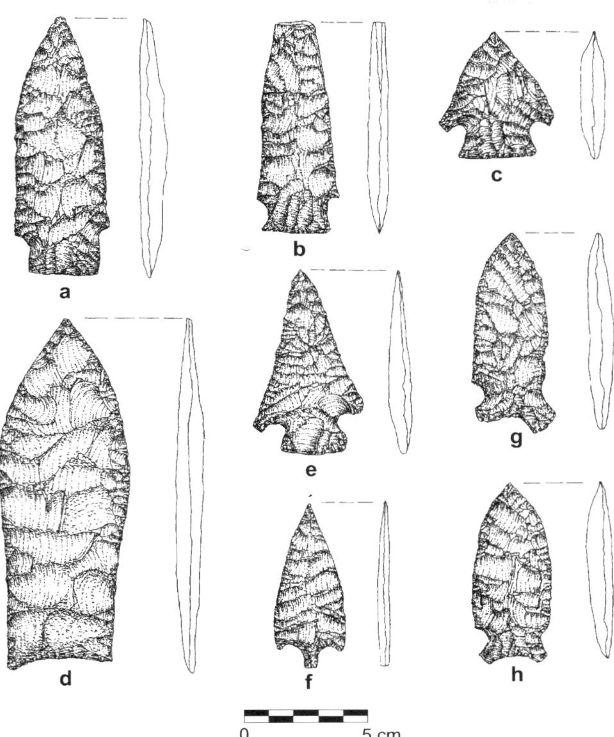

Figure 12.6. Selected projectile points from the Hoing site: a, b, Etley or Stone Square Stemmed; c, e, corner-notched forms; d, Wadlow; f, unknown narrow-stemmed form; g, h, Godar or Big Sandy (Martin 2005).

Sedalia Lanceolate. Radiocarbon samples were taken that will more clearly indicate when this site was occupied, but they have not been processed at this time. The small number of features uncovered, their close position to each other, and the mixture of projectile point styles recovered from the pits suggest that this was a single occupation and not a multicomponent site. A cursory examination of the faunal and floral remains did not support the use of this site to hunt buffalo, but it may have been used for short durations to process resources available from the ponded sinkhole and the surrounding area.

Larger sites occupied by a greater number of people also existed during the Falling Springs phase. Data-recovery investigations were performed at one of these sites (23SL49) situated atop a "Lost Hill" formation within the Meramec River valley of western St. Louis County (Harl and Nixon 1992). Just under a third of the site was excavated, uncovering 39 features. These pits included shallow basin features ($n = 6$) that were used for storage. Feature 9, for example, contained items that could have been used in tool production, such as cores, large flakes, a complete biface, sandstone that could have been used as an abrader, a hammerstone, and a quartzite cobble that could also have been used as a hammerstone (Figure 12.7). Other basins were used for processing nuts. One of these, Feature 4, contained numerous pieces of nutshell and a heated limestone cobble, suggesting that heated stones may have been used to make the water boil, aiding in separating the nutmeat and oils from the shells. This feature also contained a spadelike limestone object that had been flaked (Figure 12.7). It may have been used as a digging implement, but more likely the stone was hafted and used to stir the water-nut solution, aiding in the separation process.

Site 23SL49 also had features that were used as fire hearths ($n = 4$). The majority of the features ($n = 21$) were conical pits resembling large, deep post molds, but they were widely dispersed across the site and were not aligned as to suggest buildings. The fill of these pits contained a mixture of burned soil and carbonized materials—wood and nutshells. The outer edges were scorched by fire, indicating that these narrow pits served as roasting pits (Figure 12.7). The narrowness of the features would not have allowed for much oxygen, but the confined walls would have radiated heat for long periods. Groundnut tubers were found, suggesting that these items may have been roasted in these features. Conical roasting pits seem to have been popular with groups along the Meramec River valley from the Archaic into Mississippian times.

Site 23SL49 may have been occupied during the late summer to fall, as suggested by the presence of nut-processing pits, although wood was found in greater quantity than nuts, indicating that the site may have been abandoned before the peak of the nut harvest. Charred seeds of sumac, blackberry or black raspberry, grape, knotweed, and grass also reflect an occupation during the summer to fall. The large size of the site, numerous features, and pits containing stored items suggest that several families used this location as part of a seasonal round and stored items here to be used the following year.

Other Falling Springs–phase sites may have served as base camps where several families gathered to spend the fall and winter together. One of these base camps was identified at the Truman Road site (23SC924), situated within a construction right-of-way on the lower portion of a bluff slope at the outfall of Sandfort Creek onto the Mississippi River bottom in St. Charles County (Harl 1999b). This site, radiocarbon dated to cal 3500–3000 B.C., was covered by a deep midden and contained at least 178 features. Additional features likely existed to the north and south, beyond the construction limits. Many of the pits were superimposed, suggesting a repeated use of this site. The features consisted of fire hearths, shallow-basin storage pits, basin-shaped nut-processing pits, medium-deep (30–50 cm) storage pits, and deep (75–100 cm) earth ovens containing burned limestone cobbles and food remains.

Flora was dominated by hickory nuts, with lesser quantities of acorns, walnuts, black walnuts, and hazelnuts (in order of occurrence). A small quantity of other plants ($n = 19$) was recovered; this material included nearly equal numbers of chenopodium seeds, persimmon seeds, and groundnut tuber fragments. One grape pip and one grass (Poaceae) seed were also found. All of these appear to have been from nondomesticated species. Unlike most Archaic sites, the Truman

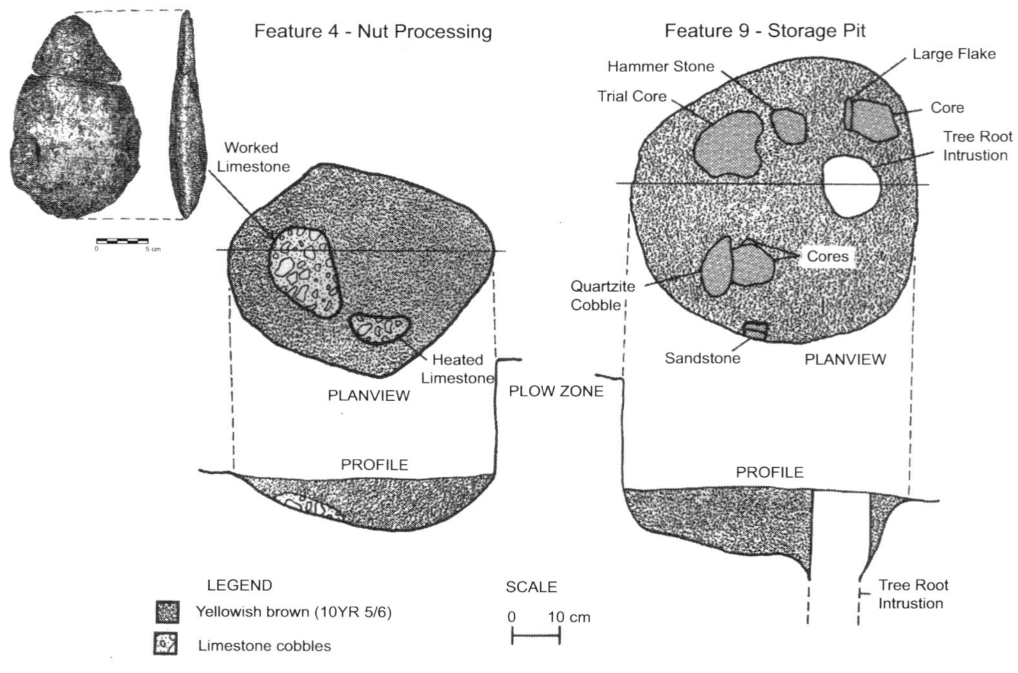

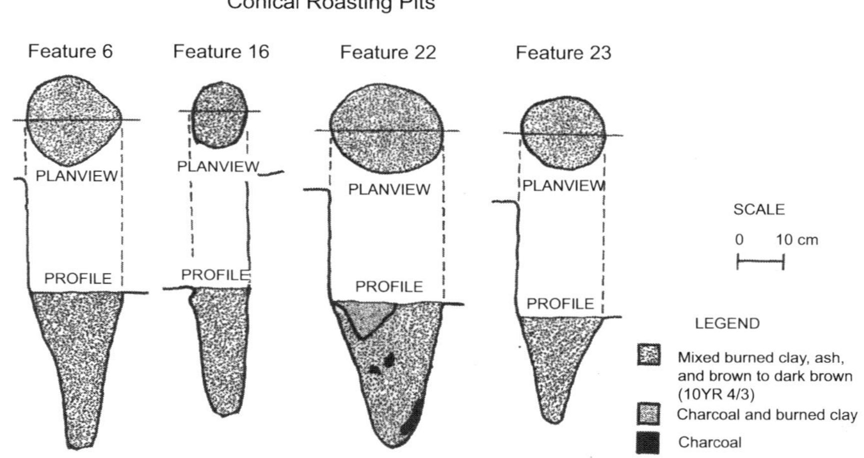

Figure 12.7. Details of selected features, site 23SL49 (Harl and Nixon 1992:68, Figure 18).

Road site had excellent bone preservation, and numerous samples were collected. These indicated that the occupants of this site tended to key on riverine species, including fish (smallmouth or black buffalo, bigmouth or buffalo, bullhead, white bass, and gar), freshwater mussels, birds (various ducks, Canada goose, American coot, and rail), muskrat, and various aquatic frogs and turtles. The fish varied in size, suggesting they were caught using nets. Terrestrial taxa included prairie species, such as greater prairie chicken, and forest or forest-edge species, especially white-tailed deer, but also turkey and various other smaller birds, striped skunk, squirrel, raccoon, and various terrestrial reptiles, especially box turtles.

Artifacts further suggested that a variety of activities were performed or initiated at the Truman Road site. The projectile points reflected hunting, and various styles were used by the site's inhabitants. The majority of the points (n = 90) were long-bladed Stone Square Stemmed or Etley forms. Older varieties of side-notched projectile points (n = 26) continued to be used as did a small number (n = 7) of expanding-stemmed Helton forms. A bannerstone produced from an igneous stone was recovered from the midden. Unfinished hematite plummets and a rounded dolomite cobble with a groove around it could have been used as net weights for fishing. Other activities performed at this site included hide processing (scrapers and bone awls), wood- and bone working (drills, gravers, adzes, and three-quarter- and full-grooved axes), food processing (manos, metates, pestles, mauls, and pitted [nutting] stones), and tool manufacturing and maintenance. In addition to objects suggesting these activities, a stone pendant made from river gravel with a hole drilled through it was probably used for personal adornment or as a charm.

Human remains were found buried within the cluster of cooking and storage pits. No grave goods were left with these burials. Some of the remains were inadvertently cut into when the site's later inhabitants were digging storage or cooking pits. Apparently, no attempt was made to replace or protect the human bones encountered in the features, and the displaced bones were discarded into a nearby pit along with rubbish. This may reflect attitudes about death for this particular group such that after burial there was no longer a perceived need to protect the body. Some of the graves suggest that intergroup relationships were not always congenial. Feature 182 contained the remains of four individuals, three adults and a four- to five-year-old child, that were missing their heads and arms as well as most of their legs. During excavations, the tip of a projectile point was found within the cervical column of the child. According to the forensic analysis performed by George Milner, after being imbedded in the spine, the spear was apparently twisted, breaking the point, clear evidence that the child was not killed as the result of an accident but was purposely murdered. Although the other three individuals did not show similar signs of traumatic death, their placement in this feature and the missing body parts suggest that they all died in a similar fashion.

Also found at this site were five large slabs of limestone. The largest, discovered at the base of the midden, measured 190 cm in diameter and 50 cm thick. The large stones may have been carried to this site either from Sandfort Creek about 80 m to the east or from the exposed bedrock on the steep bluff slope about 200 m to the west. Moving the stones would have been a difficult but certainly not an impossible task, requiring cooperative effort. How the stones were used is unclear, but the larger stone appears to have been placed upright, possibly marking some celestial event.

Evidence at the Truman Road site suggests that scattered groups may have come together during the late summer or fall and used this site throughout the winter. Winter gatherings may have had social importance, serving to bind together scattered groups. Objects and information may have been exchanged, which could account for the presence of distantly procured goods such as Cobden and Bailey cherts from southern Illinois, and hematite, galena, and rhyolite from the Missouri Ozarks. These distant goods were probably obtained by local groups through down-the-line exchanges between neighbors. Ceremonial activities and cooperative efforts (such as the movement of the large limestone slabs) would have promoted group harmony and unity.

Sedalia or Titterington Phase (2700–1900 B.C.)

The next phase of the Late Archaic period is known as Sedalia in Missouri (Chapman 1975:200) or Titterington in Illinois (McElrath et al. 1984:40–46). Projectile points popular during this phase continued to be the long-bladed, stemmed varieties such as Etley and Stone Square forms. These long-bladed points varied in length from 7 to 14 cm, but smaller versions—probably heavily resharpened points—have been recovered. Lanceolates—for example, Sedalia—were also common at these sites as well as large bifacial blanks and preforms such as Wadlow and Red Ocher. These artifacts are often found in caches of two or more. Kay (1983:44) suggests that the *Sedalia* phase label be used to refer to sites within the Prairie Peninsula area of western Missouri and *Titterington* for sites along the Mississippi River. He argues that the difference between these two is in the percentage of lanceolate versus long-bladed stemmed forms, with lances more common to the Prairie Peninsula and stemmed forms more common along the Mississippi River. Information from east-central Missouri seems to support this conclusion (Harl 1995; Harl and Wright 1995).

The long-bladed projectile point styles and lanceolates resembled similar points used on spears by Plains tribes, leading some to suggest an eastward movement of people from the Plains into Missouri. Chapman (1975:184) speculated that the Sedalia-Titterington phase developed from the Nebo Hill complex near the Kansas City area, with groups spreading to the north and east. McMillan (1971:187) and Chapman indicate that the cause of this migration was

> the warmer period, called xerothermic by paleoclimatologists, began perhaps as early as 7000 B.C. and reached its maximum shortly before 2000 B.C. Prairies had shifted to the east, and the forest with its food supply of plants and animals had been diminished. The western part of Missouri and the related prairies may have been abandoned as a place of permanent abode during the preceding period. ... The climatic changes that had taken place may have brought about transfer of cultural phases from the western regions to those further east. The tool kits of the Sedalia complex, assuming that they derived from the Nebo Hill aggregate, are evidence that Foragers as far east as the Northeast Prairie Region had adapted to a prairie-forest- edge environment. [1975:184]

Present archaeological information, however, suggests that the effects of this drier climatic episode climaxed around 5000 B.C. and had subsided by 3500 B.C. Archaeological investigations within the Plains further indicate that, although some local changes in the settlement system occurred, no mass movement of groups out of that region took place during the Hypsithermal climatic episode (Fagan 1991:121–122).

Cook (1976) indicates that, during the Sedalia-Titterington phase, people used a "dispersed harvesting economy," living in small, widely scattered groups, utilizing a variety of upland and bottomland resources. He further suggests that deer hunting was particularly important. On the basis of these traits, Emerson et al. (1991) argued that Sedalia-Titterington groups may not have been indigenous, recalling earlier suggestions of the movement of people from the Plains into this region.

Short-term, special-function camps were prevalent during this time. For example, site 23SL329, situated just southwest of Falling Springs site 23SL49 on the same Lost Hill formation, represented a short-term camp (Harl and Nixon 1992:136–153). Less than half of the site was scraped, exposing six pit features: two shallow-basin storage pits, two conical roasting pits, and two medium-deep earth ovens. In addition, a pile of lithic debris was found just north of the features. The lithic pile contained flakes, a core, an ovoid-shaped biface, two broken digging tools, and a partial Stone Square Stemmed or Etley point. All of this material is of Burlington chert, which was being quarried from the ridge just to the east.

Klippel (1969) excavated the Booth site, located on a ridgetop along the South Fork of the Salt River in Monroe County, Missouri. This site produced numerous artifacts typical of the Sedalia-Titterington phase, with the majority of the materials (28 percent) consisting of Etley points. Other artifacts recovered included Stone Square Stemmed varieties, Sedalia Lanceolates, long bifacial blades, rectangular preforms, three-quarter-grooved axes, Sedalia diggers, Clear Fork gouges, and rubbed hematite. The presence of several pitted stones, manos, and metates led Klippel (1969:52) to suggest that the Booth site was used for short periods of time to process plants gathered from the surrounding region.

Although most of the sites that have been excavated are small, special-function camps, they suggest that, other than adopting lanceolates, Sedalia-Titterington groups did not have lifestyles radically different from those of previous groups in this region. For example, at site 23SL629, conical roasting pits were identified, similar to those used by the Falling Springs inhabitants at nearby site 23SL49 (Harl and Nixon 1992). Overall, nuts (predominantly hickory) continued to be the dietary staple at all of these sites. If groups had moved to this region from the Plains or other regions, their lifestyles and tools should reflect cultural practices developed in those regions. Larger settlements were utilized during the Sedalia-Titterington phase, which appear to have been occupied on a semipermanent if not a permanent basis.

Data-recovery investigations were performed at a possible long-term habitation at the Hayden site (23SL36). The Hayden site was situated on a bluff top along Bonhomme Creek in western St. Louis County (Harl and Wright 1995). It contained a diversity of features and artifacts reflecting the various activities that were performed or initiated there. Artifacts were indicative of hunting (projectile points and a bannerstone), hide working (scrapers and perforators), butchering and food processing (knives, nutting stones, manos, and metates), wood- and bone working (spokeshaves, gouges, drills, sandstone abraders, adzes, and a three-quarter-grooved ax), plant gathering and feature construction (digging tools), personal adornment and ceremonial activity (ground hematite, galena, stone pendants, and gorgets), and tool manufacturing and maintenance. Features included shallow-basin storage and nut-processing pits and medium-deep storage pits. Some of the features were large (over 1-m-deep) earth ovens or storage facilities. The earth ovens showed evidence of repeated utilization and often occurred in pairs, with the second oven replacing the first when it was no longer usable. These dual pits could indicate that the Hayden site was occupied for multiple seasons, perhaps year-round.

Flotation samples revealed that, as at most Archaic sites, bone preservation was poor, and only a few molars from deer and deer long bones were present. Floral remains included wood from a wide variety of trees that would have been available on the surrounding bluff top or in the bottomlands. Nuts were the predominant plant food, with hickory most prevalent, followed by walnut, acorns, black walnut, and hazelnut. A variety of other plant remains were recovered from the float samples, including chenopodium and knotweed seeds. The diameters and testae thicknesses of these starchy seeds suggest that they were from wild, not domesticated, species. Also recovered were oily seeds from marsh elder and giant ragweed, also gathered from wild species. Fleshy fruits included pawpaw, persimmon, grape, and sumac. Legumes were represented by fragments from hog peanut, but only one groundnut tuber was found in Feature 11. Floral remains were used to obtain four radiocarbon dates, which indicated use of the Hayden site between cal 2600 and 2400 B.C.

A noteworthy aspect of the Hayden site is that Burlington chert, obtained from a bed exposed at the base of the bluffs by Bonhomme Creek, was preliminarily worked next to the creek and then the stones were brought to the Hayden site to be finished into tools. The remains of at least 14 lithic work stations were still intact beneath the plow zone away from the features to the south. Two caches of blanks were also identified, one containing seven bifaces and the other 14 bifaces. In all, 555 bifaces, in various stages of production, were recovered from the lithic clusters and features, and additional bifaces were piece plotted between these locations. The same distribution characterized projectile points: 282 were recovered from the features and lithic scatters, and nearly as many were piece plotted outside those areas. Many more projectile points and bifaces were noted in the disturbed plow zone, but these were not collected unless they differed from those found in undisturbed contexts.

The points consisted mostly of long-bladed Etley (n = 172) and Stone Square Stemmed (n = 75) forms (Figure 12.8). Projectile points with convex bases similar to Burkett (n = 9) forms were also found. These three styles have similar attributes, suggesting that the expanding-stemmed Etley form may have been the archetypal point being produced but because of flaws in the chert or mistakes in knapping, a straight-stemmed (Stone Square Stemmed) or convex-based (Burkett) point was sometimes produced. Other points had

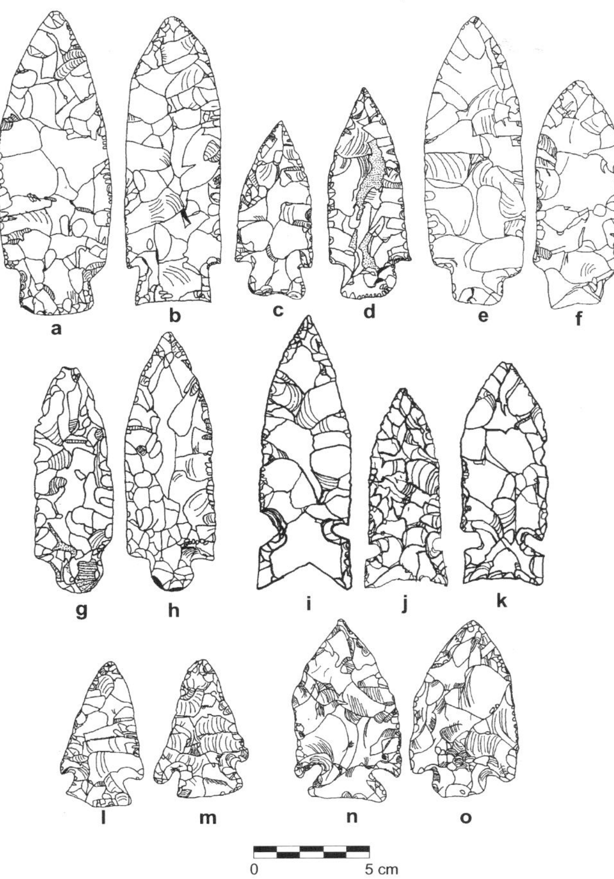

Figure 12.8. Selected projectile points from the Hayden site: a–d, Etley; e, f, Stone Square Stemmed; g, h, Burkett; i–j, Osceola; l, m, corner-notched forms; n, o, Afton (Harl and Wright 1995).

smaller blades and resembled forms typically identified as Afton corner notched (*n* = 5) or other expanding-stemmed (*n* = 14) styles, but these may, in fact, be repeatedly resharpened Etley forms. Also recovered were side-notched points similar to Osceola and Godar (*n* = 7). Within one small pit, an Etley point was found lying directly on top of an Osceola point. The flaking and size of the blades of both points were nearly identical. The only difference between the two was their hafting elements. Both points likely were made by the same knapper.

The quantity of projectile points and bifacial blanks recovered from below the plow zone suggests that they were produced not just for the site inhabtants' own use but for exchange with other regions. In return, the residents received points made from southern Illinois cherts (i.e., Cobden and Bailey) or rhyolite from the Ozarks. Clearly, projectile points made from other stones were not needed by the inhabitants of the Hayden site. These points, with their different colors, would have been conspicuous compared with the lighter-colored Burlington cherts, bringing their owner increased social esteem. Other exotic goods acquired by the inhabitants of the Hayden site included hematite, galena, granite, and steatite. The presence of bannerstones and gorgets suggested not only the spread of goods but ideas, as well.

Also associated with the Titterington-phase occupation at the Hayden site was a mound placed on Bonhomme Creek's floodplain, near the exposed chert bed. To one passing through the narrow gap in the Missouri River bluffs, the mound would have been immediately visible within the Bonhomme Creek valley. The earthwork may have reflected not only the growing influence of the community's leaders but also changing attitudes about land use. It may have represented a territorial marker signifying the Hayden site inhabitants' control of surrounding resources, especially the Burlington chert bed.

A similar permanent community was destroyed during the construction of a housing subdivision on the Missouri River bluffs, just downstream from the Hayden site. Local collectors recovered numerous bifaces in various stages of production, long-bladed projectile points, and other tools as the Gronefeld site (23SC51) was scraped. They also observed many features representing the habitation area on the bluff top. Just to the northeast of the features, burials were identified as early as the 1940s. These graves were reported to have "badly disintegrated burials covered with red ocher and limestone slabs" (Titterington 1950:26). Associated with the graves were "49 flints, 3 grooved axes, a small squared flair bitted celt or spud-like object and a bow-tie bannerstone of granite" (Titterington 1950:26), reflecting the growing influence of the community elite. The housing development has likely destroyed other graves at this site.

Another marked burial ground was identified in Lincoln County at site 23LN11 (Bacon and Miller 1957). The burials appeared to have been placed randomly across the bluff crest, although at some locations two or three interments were placed on top of each other, separated by burned limestone slabs. The slabs, however, appeared to have been heated at a different location, for there was no evidence of in situ burning. The bones were poorly preserved but seemed to represent bundle burials of at least 40 individuals, with the long bones either placed alongside each other or stacked. Each burial was associated with grave goods placed in a cache near the bones or just under them. The burial offerings included three-quarter-grooved and full-grooved axes, bifacial blanks, Etley and Stone Square Stemmed projectile points, and smaller blade varieties similar to Heltons and other expanding-stemmed forms. In addition, hematite, hammerstones, and flakes were also found, but whether these were grave goods or items unintentionally brought in with the fill was unclear.

At the confluence of the Missouri River with the Mississippi in St. Louis and St. Charles counties, a greater number of Sedalia-Titterington-phase sites (*n* = 39) have been identified than Falling Springs (*n* = 14). This could suggest a population increase during Titterington-Sedalia times, although the longer blade forms such as Etley and Stone Square Stemmed are easier to find and more likely to be reported. Sedalia-Titterington-phase sites identified in this region tend to be clustered where Burlington chert is exposed at the surface and are often located near chert quarries, further suggesting that these groups were taking advantage of the exchange potential of this highly desired resource (Harl 1995; Harl et al. 1997).

Labras Lake Phase (1900–900 B.C.)

During the following Labras Lake phase, the preferred projectile point style changed, and smaller corner-notched or expanding-stemmed forms were favored over long-bladed ones. Testing operations performed at the Pine Ford site (23JE764) in Jefferson County exposed a buried Labras Lake component but did not uncover any features (Meinkoth in press). This component, which produced small corner-notched forms similar to Mo-Pac points, was radiocarbon dated to approximately cal 1300–900 B.C.

Another Labras Lake phase site was investigated in Callaway County. The Elley site (23CY562) was situated on a terrace at the base of the bluffs near the confluence of the Middle River with the Missouri River. A midden approximately 10–20 cm thick and approximately 40 pit features were uncovered about 100 cm below the surface. The pits had been excavated into dense gray clay and included 17 small, shallow basins, seven large, shallow basins, six post molds, and two hearths; one flake concentration was also defined. The analysis of this site is still ongoing, but artifacts include flakes, cores, bifaces, hammerstones, nutting stones, metates, fire-cracked rock (both limestone and sandstone), hematite, and projectile points. One Etley point was recovered, but the other points ($n = 6$) consisted of small, corner-notched forms (three with concave bases). Two radiocarbon dates indicated that this site was utilized around cal 1700 B.C. (Aaron Anglen and Michael Meinkoth, pers. comm. 2005).

Another Labras Lake–phase site investigated in western St. Louis County is site 23SL619, situated just northeast of site 23SL629 and east of site 23SL49 on the Lost Hill formation along the Meramec River (Harl and Nixon 1992:112–135). The inhabitants used various small dart points such as Mo-Pac and Merom (Figure 12.9). People also constructed various pit features like those used during the earlier two phases, including shallow-basin storage or nut-processing pits, medium-deep storage pits and earth ovens, hearths, and conical roasting pits.

The remains of buildings were also identified. Although houses were certainly constructed prior to the Labras Lake phase, they are rarely identified because they were only meant to be temporary structures used during the seasonal round. By the Labras Lake phase, sites were used for longer durations and houses were of more substantial construction so were more likely to leave behind archaeological evidence. Two large, circular (ca. 5- to 6-m-diameter) buildings defined by a single row of post molds were found just east of the pits. The buildings lacked any evidence of interior features, but a basin-shaped pit was found just outside of one of the buildings. A smaller structure (ca. 2 m in diameter), identified just to the east, had been separated from the other buildings by a row of posts, possibly suggesting that this smaller structure was purposely screened off from the larger ones. This structure had a conical pit near its center, which contained various lenses of burned soil and charcoal. Ash was scattered around the top of this pit, suggesting that it had been repeatedly cleaned out. Ethnographic studies of historic hunting-and-gathering societies have reported similar buildings, the larger ones representing residences and the smaller ones used as sweat lodges, menstrual huts, birthing huts, places for children to play, storage facilities, or for other special purposes.

Prairie Lake Phase (900–600 B.C.)

The trend toward permanent and larger communities continued into the Prairie Lake phase. Projectile points typically

Figure 12.9. Small dart-form projectile points (Mo-Pac and Merom) recovered from site 23SL619 (Harl and Nixon 1992:130, Figure 41).

associated with Prairie Lake sites included small, slightly expanding-stemmed varieties such as Dyroff, Springly, and Mo-Pac. Only one site dating to the terminal Late Archaic period has been extensively investigated in east-central Missouri (Harl et al. 2001). MoDOT and FHWA sponsored data-recovery investigations at the Callaway Farms site (23CY227) in advance of highway construction. This buried site (approximately 40–50 cm below the surface) was situated on a sandy natural levee near an abandoned channel of the Missouri River at the base the bluffs in Callaway County.

The Callaway Farms site is unique in that it not only produced the remains of houses but also represented an early permanent, organized community (Figure 12.10). A long-term occupation is indicated by the amount of effort that went into the residential construction. The buildings averaged around 6 m in diameter and were placed into basins excavated 25 to 50 cm below the surface. The houses contained numerous storage pits around their inside edges, many of them superimposed, supporting long-term use of these buildings (Figure 12.11). Only a few storage pits were probably open at any one time, with older pits being filled in with trash and sediments and new storage pits constructed nearby. Later pits were eventually dug into older ones. The doorways faced south, as suggested by the sloping sides, approximately 1 m wide, on the southern sides of the house basins and fewer pit features in those areas. The center of each building contained one to four shallow basins, some with burned limestone cobbles, possibly used to heat the buildings or to process nuts or other foods. Four post molds near the center of the floor marked supports for the roof. No evidence of post molds for the walls was found around the edges of the basins. Posts could have been placed into the fill removed from the basins and the sediments then washed away by floodwaters after the houses were abandoned, destroying evidence of the post molds. The basin fill may also have been used to slope the earth around the homes, preventing rainwater from flowing into these partially subterranean buildings. Given the sediments around the homes, there would have been very little space between each building.

Only the northern end of the community was within the MoDOT right-of-way and could be investigated. The five buildings uncovered may have been placed in either a zig-zag, circular, or semicircular pattern (Figure 12.10). Immediately to the east was a larger building with a more rectangular shape that was set into a deeper basin (ca. 75 cm deep). A bench appears to have been placed along the northern wall of this building, with storage pits placed beneath the bench. This building had a keyhole-style entrance facing west toward the residences. Post molds just outside the northern portion of this building may have marked locations of supports used to extend the roof, producing a covered veranda, or the locations of decorated poles around the building. Decorated posts, depicting ancestors or spirits, were used by eastern tribes, as reported by the early British and French settlers.

Artifacts suggest that a wide range of activities were conducted or initiated at this site, including hunting (projectile points), hide working (scrapers and perforators), wood- and bone working (adzes, axes, gouges, gravers, and drills), food processing (cutting tools, mauls, manos, and metates), and tool manufacturing and repair. Most activities were performed inside the buildings or immediately outside them. Every residence was associated with an earth oven. One building (Structure 3) differed from the others in that it had three large earth ovens placed near the center of its floor, a large storage pit attached to its side, and six nut-processing pits in two rows of three just to the east. This structure also contained the greatest number of manos and metates (n = 18) found at the site, possibly suggesting that it was not a residence but a

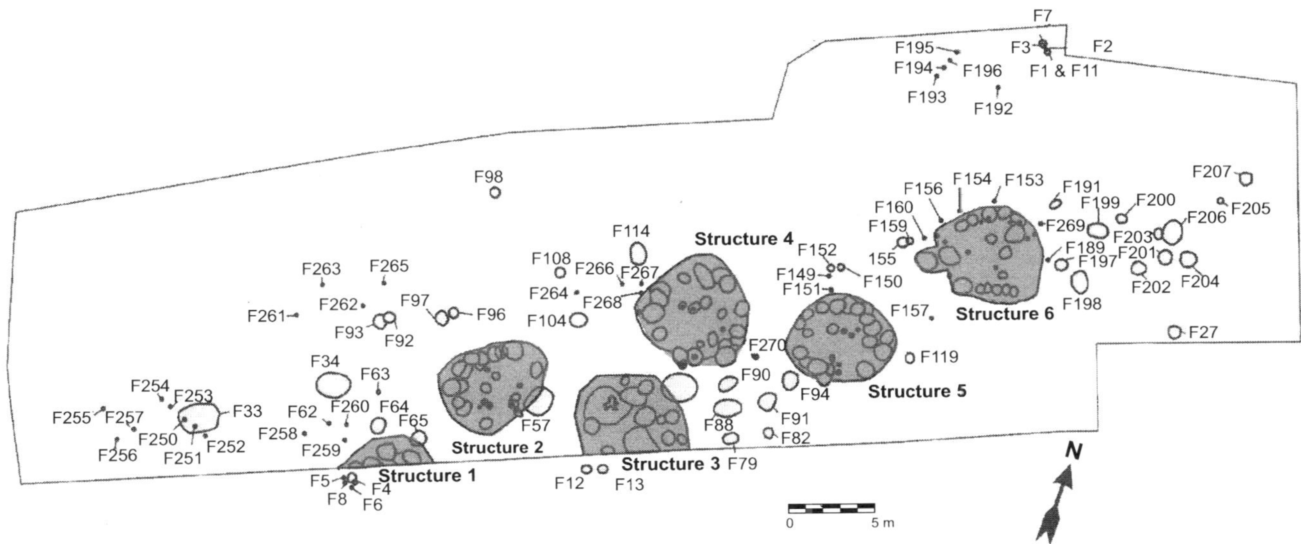

Figure 12.10. Northwest quarter of the Callaway Farms site showing structures and pit features (Harl et al. 2001:45, Figure 11).

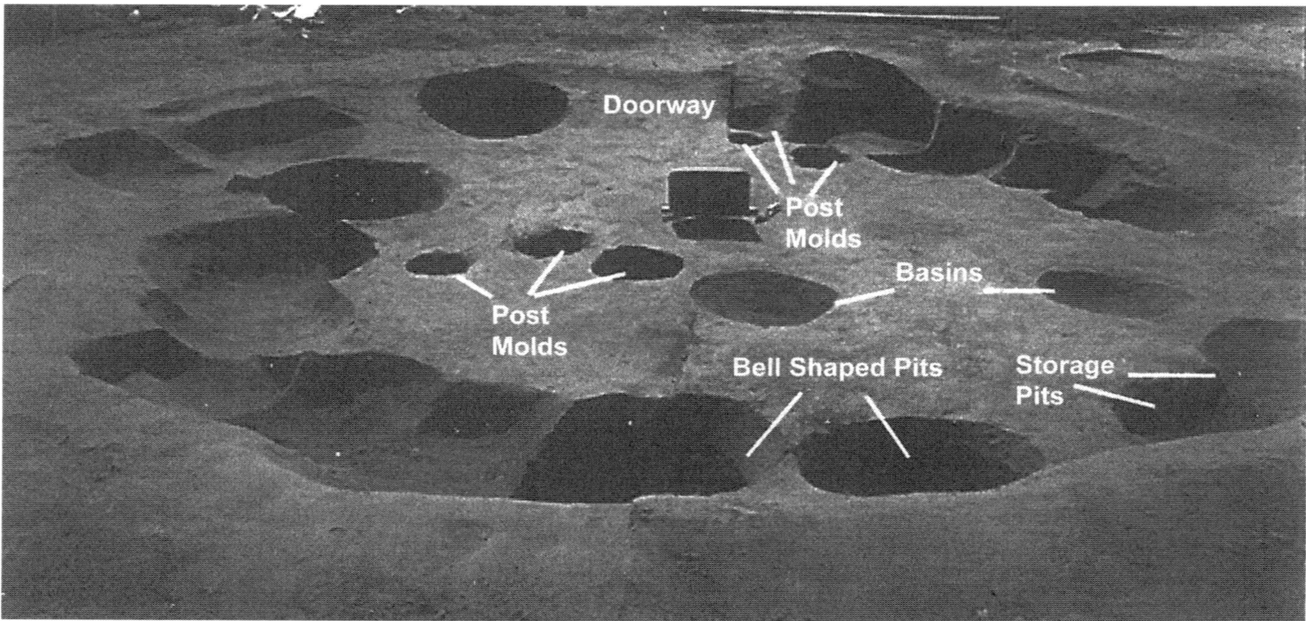

Figure 12.11. Detail of Structure 5, Callaway Farms site (Harl et al. 2001:69, Photo 29).

place where communal cooking was sometimes performed. A small number of earth ovens, storage pits, and processing pits were found to the north of the buildings.

Another cluster of features was found to the east, and a natural depression used to discard rubbish separated that area from the residential one. Similar artifacts and radiocarbon dates suggest that this eastern area was utilized by the inhabitants living in the homes to the west. The eastern feature cluster contained earth ovens, storage pits, nut-processing pits, fire hearths, and a pile of lithic debris from tool manufacturing. A structure 2 m in diameter was found in this area. This building contained only a shallow basin (less than 10 cm deep), probably formed from use. The floor of this building was also criss-crossed by numerous rodent burrows, not very different than what is typically found beneath historic granaries. The burrows could indicate that the structure was used for food storage.

Flotation samples indicated that the occupants of this settlement obtained most of their foods from the Missouri River bottoms or the adjacent bluff tops. Nuts were important foods, especially hickory and black walnut. The distribution of these two nuts varied across the western portion of the site, with hickory nuts more common within the buildings and walnuts outside them. Marjorie Schroeder (Harl et al. 2001:135), who conducted the paleoethnobotanical analysis, speculated that this distribution may indicate that the walnuts were given as a treat to children (as suggested by ethnographic record) or possibly to persons gathered socially outside of houses. Other nuts used at the site in smaller quantities included thin-shelled butternut hickories or pecans, hazelnuts, and acorns. The Callaway Farms site clearly showed that, by the terminal Late Archaic period, several starchy- and oily-seed plants were used. Some of these plants, such as maygrass and marsh elder, were domesticated, the maygrass far beyond its natural range. Chenopodium, amaranth, panic grass, and Poaceae were also common. These did not appear to have been domesticated; the grasses could have been used for food, in house construction, or to line storage pits. Oily seeds (not domesticated) were represented by sunflowers and giant ragweed. Faunal remains were poorly preserved, consisting mostly of long bones and teeth from white-tailed deer. Other animal elements that were found included various bird remains, including turkey, turtle (both pond and box), cottontail rabbit, and a worn fox molar.

These people hunted with various styles of projectile points. The preferred point seems to have been a broad-bladed form, with distinctly barbed shoulders, an expanding stem, and a convex base ($n = 51$). This point was similar to Helton (or Williams) forms, generally common at the end of the Middle Archaic period (Figure 12.12). Recently, similar points (Floyd hafted) were reported in small numbers at the Floyd site within the northern American Bottom of Illinois (Evans 2001:70–74). The Floyd points, however, are generally smaller than those found at the Callaway Farms site. Smaller-bladed forms typical of the terminal Late Archaic period (such as Mo-Pac, Dyroff, and Springly), recovered from the surface of other sites in east-central Missouri, were missing from the Callaway Farms site. Other projectile point styles that were used at this site consisted of long-bladed Etley and Stone Square Stemmed forms ($n = 17$), Smith Basal Notched ($n = 2$) forms, and side-notched forms ($n = 7$). More surprising was the presence of ovate points similar to Manker Stemmed ($n = 11$), popular during the Middle Woodland period (Figure 12.12).

Figure 12.12. Selected projectile points from the Callaway Farms site (Harl et al. 2001).

The artifacts could indicate at least two or possibly three occupations at the Callaway Farms site. A series of 13 radiocarbon dates was processed from features containing projectile points of various styles and from different locations across the site. The samples all came back with nearly identical dates of ca. cal 800 B.C., suggesting that this was a single occupation. Thus, caution should be taken when relying on projectile point styles alone for dating sites. The Callaway Farms site further reflects how poor archaeologists' understanding still is of projectile point typologies that have been developed over 75 years in this portion of Missouri.

Few exotic trade goods were identified at the Callaway Farms site. Burlington chert, the stone preferred for tool production, while not present in the immediate vicinity, was available less than 16 km away and could be collected by work parties. People used various cherts for different purposes at this site, with the local Jefferson City accounting for most of the cores, suggesting this stone was used to produce expedient tools, while Burlington chert was typically used in the production of formal tools. Hematite was probably obtained southeast of the Missouri River and east of the Osage River by work parties or through exchanges with nearby groups. The most distant resources, Kaolin and Kincaid chert from Illinois, were represented by only a few flakes probably removed from formal tools. Exotic objects could represent down-the-line exchanges, with the tools having passed from one group to the next. They could also represent heirloom items left over when more extensive trading was taking place during the Titterington phase. As do other terminal Late Archaic sites, Callaway Farms suggests a hiatus in the long-distance exchange of exotic goods that was so prominent during the middle portion of the Late Archaic period (Sedalia-Titterington phase). This would suggest that long-distance trade was not necessary for permanent settlements to exist.

The lack of trade in exotic goods could indicate that this society was basically egalitarian, with symbols of power or wealth being unimportant. This is not to suggest that community leaders did not exist; certainly an unfinished gorget found in the communal Structure 6 would suggest such a status, but this position was probably achieved by a person, not inherited. The residences at this site were of similar construction, reflecting the equal status of families. Evidence suggests that each family was responsible for cooking its own food and for other work-related activities, although communal cooking (as suggested by Structure 3) and other activities likely took place, binding this group into a whole.

Summary

The data obtained from sites in east-central Missouri allow for some generalizations to be made concerning the Archaic period. As first suggested by Chapman, Early Archaic groups in Missouri seem to have established set territories and utilized a seasonal round, moving to where resources were best at different times of the year. As indicated by extensive surface surveys conducted as part of the Cannon Reservoir project in Ralls and Monroe counties and near the Missouri-Mississippi confluence within St. Louis and St. Charles counties, some Early Archaic sites are present far into the interior uplands, which would have been forested at the time. People typically lived in small groups, as suggested by the small size of the identified sites. Since these places were occupied for only short durations, few remains were typically left behind.

By the Middle Archaic period, the effects of the Hypsithermal climatic episode resulted in the expansion of the prairies across large portions of the uplands and broader river valleys. Although the prairies were certainly not devoid of resources, the forests offered a greater range of resources as well as wood needed for fuel and construction. Most sites were placed within the bottoms of large waterways, on the ridgetops immediately overlooking these areas, or on the forest-prairie boundary. The sites identified within east-central Missouri are small, containing few remains, suggesting that people resided within small groups consisting of only a few families and continued to use a seasonal round, occupying sites for only short durations. These groups, however, seemed to have keyed on certain resources, such as hickory nuts. Use of riverine resources, in general, appears to have increased during the Middle Archaic.

At the start of the Late Archaic period, people were still following a seasonal round and living in small groups. The environmental situation had improved by the beginning of this period, and people should have returned to a lifestyle similar to that used during the Early Archaic period, establishing a residential mobility settlement scheme to exploit newly available resource areas, especially within the uplands. Instead, as shown by the intensive archaeological investigations that were performed along the Salt River in northeastern Missouri as part of the Cannon Reservoir project (O'Brien et al. 1982), Late Archaic groups continued to cluster within the river valleys. Concerning these sites, Warren writes,

> Given these environmental changes, the relative decrease in numbers of upland sites during the Late Archaic-Early Woodland period is anomalous from the perspective of changing resource distribution. If the Middle Archaic settlement-subsistence pattern had persisted, there should have been a proportional increase in upland sites, rather than a decline. Thus, observed trends indicate that there was a significant change after the Middle Archaic, either in the kinds of resources exploited or in the settlement strategy used to house and sustain communities. Moreover, contrasts between site contexts of the Early Archaic and Late Archaic-Early Woodland periods suggest that selection for settlement-subsistence pattern change after the Hypsithermal involved *cultural factors* rather than environmental ones. [1982:351–352, emphasis added]

Changes made in subsistence technologies during the Middle Archaic and early Late Archaic periods allowed people to gather larger quantities of foods from a predictable source within a more confined area and to more efficiently process these resources. By the start of the Late Archaic period, sites such as Truman Road indicate that some scattered groups began to coalesce during the late summer or fall at locations where they spent the winter together. From these base camps, work groups were sent out to hunt and gather plant resources, but probably more important were the social activities that these gatherings afforded. The scattered groups could exchange information about the availability of resources or new ideas (e.g., attempts at plant domestication). These gatherings also allowed people to establish social ties by exchanging exotic items or marrying their children to members of other groups. These marriages alleviated the harmful effects of inbreeding, but, more importantly, the affinal ties established mechanisms for intergroup cooperation.

The greatest challenge for hunting and gathering societies was maintaining information on resource availability. If resources became scarce, it was important for people to have backup alternatives within their territory or the surrounding regions. Groups could gather information by monitoring their environment or exploring new areas. One of the benefits of hunting was not only catching prey but also—because of the mobility involved—identifying new food or raw material sources and monitoring known resources. Another option for survival was networking with others. Winter base camps afforded the opportunity to establish social ties and learn of new ideas or innovations. Establishing friendship and affinal ties with other groups allowed people to move without encountering conflict if resources became scarce in a certain area or if social unrest developed between group members.

By the second half of the Late Archaic period, some base camps were occupied on a permanent basis, especially sites near stable and highly desired resources. These long-term communities were marked by the presence of larger, more permanent dwellings and larger storage facilities. These communities were also more organized, with trash discarded away from high-use areas. Even the dead were moved further away from the living into separate, marked, burial areas.

During the first part of the Late Archaic, the Truman Road site suggests that protecting graves was not an important consideration, perhaps reflecting attitudes about death held by the site's early Late Archaic occupants. They excavated storage and processing pits into preexisting graves at the site, but instead of replacing the displaced bones, they simply discarded them into a nearby pit. By the start of the Sedalia-Titterington phase (ca. 2700 B.C.), treatment of the dead changed, as their graves were separated from living and work areas and often covered with limestone slabs, further protecting them. Sedalia-Titterington-phase burials also contain grave goods, reflecting a different attitude about death.

Another change during the Sedalia-Titterington phase of the Late Archaic period was an increased exchange of goods over long distances. Burlington chert became more common at sites in the central Ozarks of Missouri and western Illinois during this time, often present in caches as cores or long-bladed preforms. Longer-bladed projectile points, such as Etley and Stone Square Stemmed became more popular, their larger size making the points more conspicuous and giving the user increased esteem. Although chert and other useful items were traded, most goods exchanged appear to have been important because of the increased prestige that they brought the users. Walthall (1981) found that galena from the upper Meramec River valley in Missouri was present at sites as far away as the mouth of the Mississippi River. Burials with exotic goods suggest that some individuals may have had more access to trade goods than others, indicating the beginnings of social differentiation. Mounds were occasionally constructed, possibly reflecting the growing influence of certain community leaders as well as changing attitudes about the land, with the earthworks serving as territorial markers. The trade in exotic goods seems to have waned by the end of the Titterington phase (ca. 1900 B.C.), although highly desired resources, such as Burlington chert and hematite, likely were exchanged on a local basis.

The reasons people shifted from a semimobile seasonal round to permanent settlements have long been debated. Traditionally, archaeologists assumed that hunters and gatherers only changed their behavior when a declining environment or overpopulation forced them to rely on a decreasing territory or resource base. It was suggested that, to improve their economy, these groups purposely modified certain plant and animal species, increasing their productivity beyond what the natural environment could normally support. The development of horticulture, making available more food within a smaller space, caused people to establish permanent communities to care for and protect these resources. With declining mobility, trade became necessary to obtain minerals and foods that could no longer be directly acquired. As groups established a more sedentary lifestyle, pottery vessels were favored over grass baskets.

> These assumptions, however, are questioned because agriculture is no longer necessary for the development of cultural complexity. ... Sedentary modes of life were once thought to be naturally beneficial. When the necessary conditions were present, sedentism was adopted out of preference. But investigations since the 1960s have reduced the viability of this idea. Sedentism is presently regarded as making a fundamental break with the long-established residential mobility of the past. ... Because a highly mobile strategy is now regarded as adaptive in its own right, much more is required of explanations of sedentism than establishing its logical preconditions. As a consequence, all theorizing now takes into account the advantages of residential stability. [Brown 1985:201–202]

Population- and food-pressure models have produced a biased view of past human behavior, depicting prehistoric people as passively reacting to changes in their environment as would any plant or animal species. Past humans appear "as predictable automata, driven by covering laws ... controlled by ritual according to universal expectations; there is no sense in which they actively manipulate and negotiate ideologies" (Hodder 1986:25). Past models also fail to account for the opportunity costs—the initial start-up costs—incurred when adopting a new strategy. These costs can be material as well as social and psychological (Limp 1977; Schneider 1974). A group in a declining economy, such as predicted by the population- and food-pressure models, would find it difficult to take on these added costs. People more often make changes to take advantage of new economic opportunities. These do not have to be directly related to survival but can represent improvements in social or perceived spiritual standing. The economy of the Late Archaic period may not have been declining but actually expanding through improved food technologies—for example, utilizing pits to more effectively process nuts (McElrath 1986:83–84; Stafford 1991), increasing reliance on riverine resources, and experimenting with growing plants. These innovations were not rapidly adopted but were experimented with and gradually added to the existing subsistence system over several hundred years. This is certainly not the situation suggested by the population-pressure or environmental-decline models. The change toward a sedentary settlement pattern was not prompted by the environment but was a conscious decision by humans on the basis of social and economic factors.

The exchange of goods during the Late Archaic period is still poorly understood; however, it does not appear to have been necessary for the survival of permanent settlements. After the Titterington phase, these exchanges were drastically reduced or ceased altogether. Yet settlements continued to be permanently occupied and, as suggested by the Callaway Farms site, became larger and more organized.

Archaeological investigations at Archaic sites in east-central Missouri further indicate how little researchers still know about these people and the artifacts they used. Even objects as well studied as projectile points are still not clearly understood chronologically or functionally. Caution should be taken when using a single projectile point to date sites, as a wide variety of styles were utilized during the Early Archaic period and again during the Late Archaic period. For example, artifacts at the Late Archaic Hayden site suggested that older styles (side-notched points resembling Middle

Archaic forms) continued to be produced by the people living there, with one individual likely making a side-notched form at about the same time as a more typical Late Archaic Etley form. The inhabitants of the Callaway Farms site also seem to have preferred styles resembling older broad-bladed, expanding-stemmed Helton forms over the smaller dart forms popular at many other terminal Late Archaic sites. Some of the points they produced even resemble ovate Manker or Snyders forms, popular during the Middle Woodland period. The presence of these ovate points alongside more typical Archaic styles and similar radiocarbon dates show that these various styles were produced by the terminal Late Archaic inhabitants of Callaway Farms. Much work is still needed to understand why people produced different forms of Archaic points and how they used them.

Prehistoric groups are often depicted as unable to control their destinies, maintaining the status quo and changing only to avoid starvation, every day being a struggle to survive. Yet anthropological studies of hunters and gatherers have shown that they can easily survive even within the most restrictive environments. Information from Archaic sites in east-central Missouri suggests that obtaining food and other items needed for survival was not a problem; in fact, by the Middle Archaic period, people were even selective about which resources they used from the rich array available to them in this part of Missouri. Determining the impetus for change and understanding why change occurred during the Archaic period allows for better understanding of human behavior, both in the past and at the present, which is the ultimate goal of archaeology. Further extensive archaeological excavations are needed at Archaic sites—both large and small—to better understand the people of that time and their societies, before the sites they occupied are lost forever.

Acknowledgments

I would like thank members of the Cultural Resources Section of the Missouri Department of Transportation, directed by Robert Reeder, for their continued support of archaeological investigations across the state and for readily agreeing to share their information. In particular, I would like to express my gratitude to Michael Meinkoth and Aaron Anglen, who provided information on the Pine Ford and Elley sites prior to the completion of the formal site reports. I would also like to express my thanks to Terry Martin, who provided a preliminary draft of the Hoing site report so that information on this important site could be included in this summary. He also shared information on his reanalysis of the unique Barrington Oaks site. Further, I would like to thank Valerie Altizer, Janet Kneller, and Meredith McLaughlin of the Archaeological Research Center of St. Louis for taking time out of their busy schedules to edit early versions of this summary and for providing valuable insights.

References Cited

Anglen, Aaron A.
1994 *Extended Phase II Archaeological Testing of Site 23GA153, Missouri Route 100, Gasconade River Replace Bridge K-974, Gasconade County.* Job No. J6S0691. Cultural Resources Section, Missouri Department of Transportation, Jefferson City.

Anglen, Aaron A., David C. Austin, and William W. Martin
1993 *Phase I Cultural Resources Survey of the Gasconade River Bridge Project Corridor, MHTD Job No. J650691, Route 100, Gasconade County, Missouri, and Phase II Archaeological Testing and Evaluation of Site 23GA153.* Cultural Resources Section, Missouri Department of Transportation, Jefferson City.

Bacon, Willard S., and William J. Miller
1957 Notes on the Excavation of a Burial Area in Northeastern Missouri. *The Missouri Archaeologist* 19(3):19–33.

Brown, James A.
1985 Long Term Trends to Sedentism and the Emergence of Complexity in the American Midwest. In *Prehistoric Hunter-Gatherers: The Emergence of Cultural Complexity*, edited by T. Douglas Price and James A. Brown, pp. 201–234. Academic Press, Orlando, Florida.

Chapman, Carl H.
1975 *Archaeology of Missouri, I.* University of Missouri Press, Columbia.

Chapman, Carl H., and Eleanor F. Chapman
1972 *Indians and Archaeology of Missouri.* University of Missouri Press, Columbia.

Cook, Thomas G.
1976 *Koster: An Artifact Analysis of Two Archaic Phases in West-central Illinois.* Prehistoric Records 1, Koster Research Report 3. Northwestern University Archaeological Program, Evanston, Illinois.

Ellis, Father Benedict
1965 Site 23JE362 form. On file, State Historic Preservation Office, Jefferson City, and Archaeological Survey of Missouri, Columbia.

Emerson, Thomas, Joyce Williams, and Paula Cross
1991 Late Archaic Cultures of Northern Periphery of the Mid-South. In *The Archaic Period in the Mid-South*, edited by Charles McNutt, pp. 15–22. Archaeological Report 24. Mississippi Department of Archives and History, Jackson.

Evans, J. Bryant
2001 *The Floyd Site: A Terminal Archaic Habitation in the Northern American Bottom.* Research Report 11. Illinois Transportation Archaeological Research Progam, Department of Anthropology, University of Illinois, Urbana–Champaign.

Fagan, Brian M.
1991 *Ancient North America: The Archaeology of a Continent.* Thames and Hudson, London.

Hamilton, M. Colleen, Joseph L. Harl, and Joseph M. Nixon
1989 *Report of Phase II Level Testing at Sites 23SL226 and 23SL466, and Phase III Level Mitigation of the Lone*

Wolf Site, 23SL467, South St. Louis County, Missouri. Archaeological Survey Research Report 88. University of Missouri–St. Louis.

Hamilton, M. Colleen, Patti J. Wright, Hanna Stazewska-Kruel, Joseph M. Nixon, and Neal H. Lopinot

1986 *Extensive Archaeological Testing at the Lone Wolf Site, 23SL467, South St. Louis County, Missouri.* Archaeological Survey Research Report 41. University of Missouri–St. Louis.

Harl, Joseph L.

1995 *Master Plan for the Management of Archaeological Cultural Resources within St. Louis City and County, Missouri.* Archaeological Services Research Report 203. University of Missouri–St. Louis.

1999a *Phase II Testing of Sites 23JE362 and 23JE730 for the Proposed Improvements to Interstate 55, Jefferson County, Missouri.* Research Report 68. Archaeological Research Center of St. Louis, St. Louis, Missouri.

1999b *Data Recovery Investigations at the Truman Road Site (23SC924) within St. Charles County, Missouri.* Research Report 7. Archaeological Research Center of St. Louis, St. Louis, Missouri.

Harl, Joseph L., Mary Jo Cramer, Cynthia L. Balek, Marjorie B. Schroeder, and Elizabeth M. Scott

2001 *Data Recovery Investigations at the Callaway Farms Site (23CY227): A Terminal Late Archaic Village within Callaway County, Missouri.* Research Report 96. Archaeological Research Center of St. Louis, St. Louis, Missouri.

Harl, Joseph L., Dennis Naglich, and John Fulmer

1997 *Master Plan for the Management of Archaeological Resources within St. Charles County, Missouri.* Research Report 51. Archaeological Research Center of St. Louis, St. Louis, Missouri.

Harl, Joseph L., and Joseph M. Nixon

1992 *Phase III Mitigation of Sites 23SL49, SL619, and SL629, Lost Hill Airport Site, St. Louis County, Missouri.* Archaeological Survey Research Report 119. University of Missouri–St. Louis.

Harl, Joseph L., and Patti J. Wright

1992 *Report of Phase II Testing of Site 23FR334, Franklin County, Missouri.* Archaeological Survey Research Report 148. University of Missouri–St. Louis.

1995 *Data Recovery Investigations at the Hayden Site (23SL36) and the Rabanus Site (23SL859), Chesterfield, St. Louis County, Missouri: New Insights into the Titterington/Sedalia Phase in East Central Missouri.* Archaeological Services Research Report 182. University of Missouri–St. Louis.

Hodder, Ian

1986 *Reading the Past: Current Approaches to Interpretation in Archaeology.* Cambridge University Press, Cambridge, England.

Kay, Marvin

1983 Archaic Period Research in Western Ozark Highlands, Missouri. In *Archaic Hunters and Gatherers in the American Midwest*, edited by James L. Phillips and James H. Brown, pp. 41–70. Academic Press, New York.

Klippel, Walter E.

1969 *The Booth Site: A Late Archaic Campsite.* Research Series 6. Missouri Archaeological Society, Columbia.

Limp, W. Fredrick

1977 The Economics of Agricultural Dispersal. Paper presented at the 42nd Annual Meeting of the Society for American Archaeology, New Orleans, Louisiana.

Martin, Terrell L.

2001 The Barrington Site: A Middle Archaic Cache from the St. Louis Area. *Plains Anthropologist* 46:96–108.

2005 *Phase III Data Recovery at the Hoing Archaeological Site (23SC834), Route 40, St. Charles County, Missouri.* Job No. J6P0672D, Cultural Resources Section, Missouri Department of Transportation, Jefferson City.

McElrath, Dale L.

1986 *The McLean Site.* American Bottom Archaeology FAI-270 Site Reports 14. University of Illinois Press, Urbana.

McElrath, Dale L., Thomas E. Emerson, Andrew C. Fortier, and James L. Phillips

1984 Late Archaic Period. In *American Bottom Archaeology: A Summary of the FAI-270 Project Contributions to the Culture History of the Mississippi River Valley*, edited by Charles J. Bareis and James W. Porter, pp. 34–58. University of Illinois Press, Urbana.

McMillan, R. Bruce

1971 Biophysical Change and Cultural Adaptation at Rogers Shelter. Ph.D. dissertation, Department of Anthropology, University of Colorado, Boulder.

Meinkoth, Michael

In press *The Pine Ford Site (23JE764): Cultural Resources Investigations at the Big River Bridge Replacement, Route Y, Jefferson County, Missouri.* Cultural Resources Section, Missouri Department of Transportation, Jefferson City.

Morrow, Julie, Daniel S. Glover, George P. Kincaid III, Eugene A. Marino, and Michael J. O'Brien

1995 *Historic Properties Data Synthesis Mark Twain Lake, Missouri*, vol. 1. Management Report 47. U.S. Army Corps of Engineers, St. Louis District, St. Louis, Missouri.

O'Brien, Michael J., and Robert E. Warren

1983 An Archaic Projectile Point Sequence from the Southern Prairie Peninsula: The Pigeon Roost Creek Site. In *Archaic Hunters and Gatherers in the American Midwest*, edited by James L. Phillips and James A. Brown, pp. 165–196. Academic Press, New York.

1985 Stratigraphy and Chronology of Pigeon Roost Creek. In *Archaeology of the Central Salt River Valley: An Overview of the Prehistoric Occupation*, by Michael J. O'Brien. *The Missouri Archaeologist* 46:203–225.

O'Brien, Michael J., Robert E. Warren, and Dennis E. Lewarch, editors

1982 *The Cannon Reservoir Human Ecology Project: An Archaeological Study of Cultural Adaptation in the Southern Prairie Peninsula.* Academic Press, New York.

O'Brien, Michael J., and W. Raymond Wood

1998 *The Prehistory of Missouri.* University of Missouri Press, Columbia.

Schneider, Harold

1974 *Economic Man.* Free Press, New York.

Stafford, C. Russell

1991 Archaic Period Logistical Foraging Strategies in West-Central Illinois. *Midcontinental Journal of Archaeology* 16:212–246.

Sturdevant, Craig
1997 *Cultural Resource Investigations Phase II Testing—23JE600-A, Barrington Oaks, Jefferson County, Missouri.* Environmental Research Center of Missouri, Jefferson City.

Stuiver, M., P. J. Reimer, and R. Reimer
2004 CALIB Radiocarbon Calibration, Version 4.4, September 27, 2004. Quaternary Isotope Laboratory, University of Washington, Seattle.

Titterington, Paul F.
1950 Some Non-Pottery Sites in the St. Louis Area. *Journal of the Illinois State Archaeological Society* 1:18–31.

Walthall, John A.
1981 *Galena and Aboriginal Trade in Eastern North America.* Scientific Papers 17. Illinois State Museum, Springfield.

Warren, Robert E.
1982 Prehistoric Settlement Patterns. In *The Cannon Reservoir Human Ecology Project: An Archaeological Study of Cultural Adaptation in the Southern Prairie Peninsula,* edited by Michael J. O'Brien and Robert E. Warren, pp. 337–368, Academic Press, New York.

13

Archaic Cultural Variation and Lifeways in West-Central Illinois

David J. Nolan and Richard L. Fishel

The view that there is a continent-wide Archaic stage leads only to the collecting of type fossils and contributes little to the understanding of the types of variation among these hunting-and-gathering societies and the reasons for the variations.

—Howard Winters

The old adage "variety is the spice of life" is applicable to the study of preceramic cultural adaptations in west-central Illinois. While many early considerations of the Archaic period or stage in the Midwest painted a picture of a rather static way of life that progressed, almost imperceptibly, in a unilinear fashion toward increasingly more sophisticated and sedentary existences, we share the view of Winters (1974:xxiv) and find significance in the inter- and intraperiod variation that is evident across the region. Not only is this variety the "spice" but it is also a key ingredient for providing a more accurate reconstruction of the lifeways and history of Archaic peoples, which were much more complex than accounted for by earlier models.

The term *Archaic* was first used in the United States by Ritchie (1932), who applied it to the aceramic Lamoka complex of New York. He later lumped all nonceramic and nonhorticultural cultures in that area under the Archaic umbrella (Ritchie 1944). Griffin (1952) went on to define the Archaic as a stage for all of the eastern United States, breaking it down into Early and Late periods, and, in the mid- to late 1950s, Willey and Phillips (1955, 1958) refined the term, giving it its present definition.

As currently defined, the Archaic period subsumes two-thirds of the ca. 13,000 years of documented human prehistory in west-central Illinois. Preceded by a much less intensive, ca. 1,300-year span of Late Glacial (Paleoindian) utilization, the 8,800-year-long Archaic period was followed by a 2,750-year span that is broken minimally into Woodland, Mississippian, Protohistoric, and Historic periods. The Archaic period is normally divided into often vaguely defined Early, Middle, and Late segments, each of which encompasses 2,000–3,000 years. The beginning and ending dates for each Archaic segment are often debated, and the division to which certain cultures are relegated can be confusing, especially when one is dealing with the Middle Archaic.

Because of this ambiguity, we propose that the Archaic period no longer be discussed in Early, Middle, and Late terms but, instead, be viewed against the backdrop of climatic change (cf. Conrad 1987). Bryson et al. have proposed a series of worldwide "quasi-stable climatic episodes separated by rather rapid transitions" (1970:72) on the basis of radiocarbon data "indicating discontinuities" in "recurrence surfaces, stratigraphic breaks, sea level maxima and minima, and taxon or species maxima" (1970:54). On the basis of more than 600 radiocarbon dates, they postulate six key dates when "quasi-stable" postglacial climate patterns changed: 10,500, 9650, 8450, 4680, 2890, and 1690 B.P. (Bryson et al. 1970:Table 2). They termed these quasi-stable episodes the Pre-Boreal (10,500–9650 B.P.), Boreal (9650–8450 B.P.), Atlantic (8450–4680 B.P.), Sub-Boreal (4680–2890 B.P.), and Sub-Atlantic (2890–1690 B.P.) (Bryson et al. 1970:Table 2). A summary of the climatic conditions that prevailed during these episodes, and an earlier model of the chronological framework we employ here, can be found in Conrad (1987), while midwestern pollen summaries that form the basis of most climatic models can be found in, for example, Brush (1967), Durkee (1971), Gruger (1972), Webb and Bryson (1972), King and Allen (1977), King (1986), and Royall et al. (1991).

Bryson et al. recognize "major difficulties in the application of the[ir] concept on a more sophisticated level" and that the "march of the seasons in Arizona is not like that in New Mexico, and certainly not like that in Nebraska" (1970:55).

We are, likewise, aware that macroclimatic changes cannot always be applied on a microlevel, that is, that not all areas undergo change at the same time or to the same extent. However, because we view climate as a backdrop for, and not a determining factor of, culture change, we see the human response or nonresponse to microclimatic change that may occur in isolated areas as a moot point. For example, a dramatic increase in herb and grass pollen and a decrease in deciduous tree pollen can be dated to 8300 B.P. at Chatsworth Bog in northeastern Illinois (King 1986). These changes are interpreted as marking the point when prairie vegetation was established across Illinois, suggesting that climatic conditions had become drier by 8300 B.P. Thus, that date likely marks the approximate beginning of the Atlantic episode in Illinois. This dry period reached its maximum expression around 7000 B.P. (Webb and Bryson 1972), and the archaeological record of western Illinois from that approximate time until the Helton horizon ca. 1,000 years later contains few firmly dated projectile point styles.

Our goals in this chapter are straightforward: (1) to present an updated regional Archaic cultural chronology that is based on the recovered artifact assemblages and associated radiocarbon determinations or relative dates and (2) to summarize the available information, much of which exists within the "gray" literature of contract reports and paper presentations at professional meetings. To accomplish these goals, we build and expand on the foundations provided by Conrad (1981, 1987) and others working in the adjacent portions of the lower Illinois Valley (e.g., Brown and Vierra 1983). We begin by defining and briefly describing the study region, the history of archaeological research undertaken there, and the data sets that provide the information used to construct this summary.

Study Region

For our purposes, west-central Illinois includes portions or all of 18 counties (Figure 13.1) in the Mississippi and Illinois river valleys and the intervening and adjacent uplands and tributary valleys from the Green River drainage near the Quad Cities on the north to an arbitrarily chosen line between Jacksonville, Illinois, and Hannibal, Missouri, on the south (cf. the Interstate 72 corridor). The upland portion of the area coincides primarily with a physiographic region known as the Galesburg Plain (Leighton et al. 1948). The Galesburg Plain, which correlates well with Schwegman's (1973) Galesburg

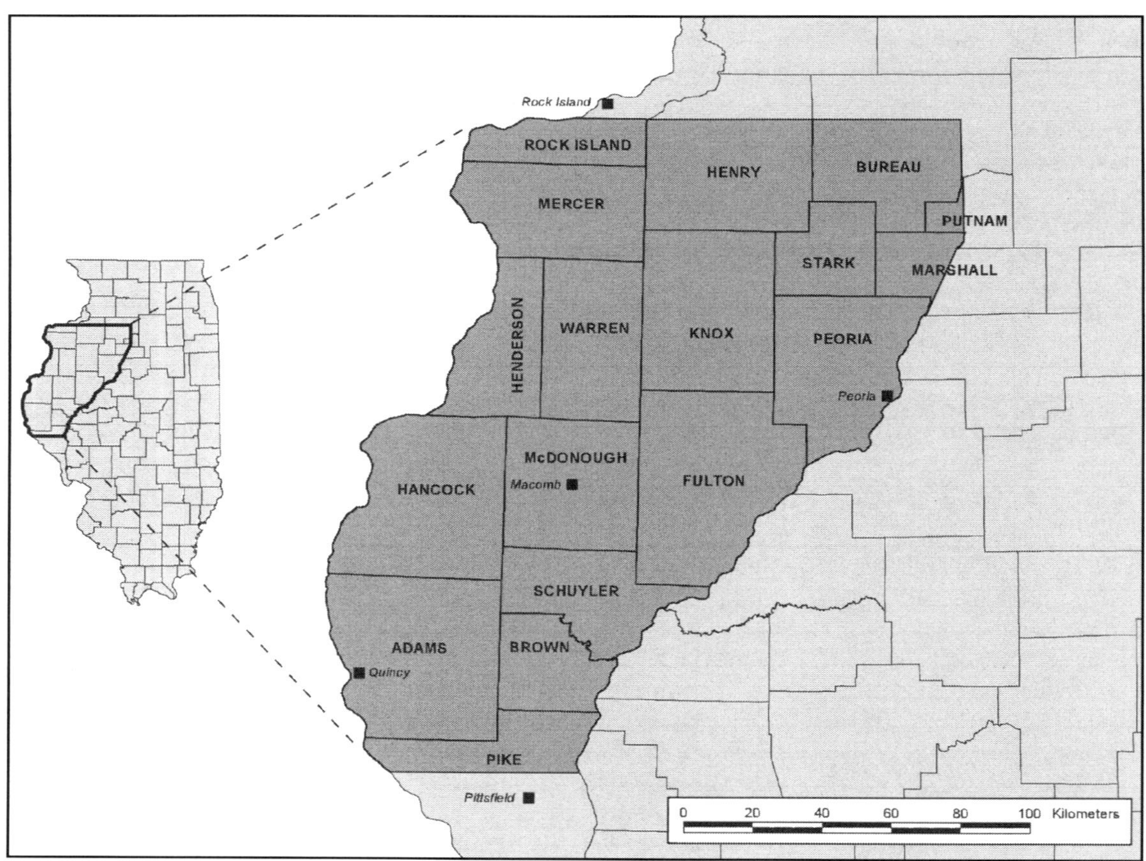

Figure 13.1. Location of west-central Illinois study area.

Section of the Western Forest-Prairie Division of Illinois, covers an area of approximately 20,700 km^2; its maximum dimensions are 240 km north–south and 160 km east–west (Caspall 1965; Leighton et al. 1948). The Galesburg Plain was formed by the deposition of at least two thick loess mantles that altered the pre-Wisconsinan topography. Because the area was not glaciated during Wisconsinan times (aside from the extreme northeastern margin), it generally does not exhibit any relatively modern glacial deposits other than stream-terrace deposits and eolian loess. Two major Illinoian terminal moraines cross the Galesburg Plain within the study area: the Table Grove and Mendon moraines. While a few landforms are higher, relief on the uplands is normally less than 15 m (Conrad 1987). More detailed overviews of the Galesburg Plain, including discussions of the geology, physiography, hydrology, flora, and fauna, can be found in Green and Nolan (2000:346–347) and Conrad (1987).

As will be seen in the following pages, west-central Illinois appears to be divisible into three broadly conceived cultural subregions, the boundaries of which were fluid throughout prehistory. The northernmost encompasses the area between the Quad Cities and Galesburg, the southern subregion consists approximately of the area between Jacksonville to just north of Quincy, and the central area is situated between the other two. As would be expected, the northern subregion contains cultural complexes similar to those found in northern Illinois and Iowa, while those in the southern subregion show strong affinities to the lower Illinois Valley and American Bottom.

Lithic Landscape

Western Illinois has varied floral and faunal assemblages, discussed in Green and Nolan (2000) and Conrad (1987), and the lithic landscape is remarkably rich and relatively diverse. The availability of chipped-stone raw material was vital to the economy of Archaic peoples, who largely relied on hunting to provide their principal sources of dietary protein. In contrast to the deer and other game that supplied these dietary resources, lithic sources are fixed on the landscape and exerted strong but diachronically variable influence on the settlement and mobility of regional aboriginal groups. Thus, understanding the distribution of lithic resources (Figure 13.2) is fundamental to the study and reconstruction of Archaic lifeways and settlement patterns.

Several important studies of regional chert availability have been undertaken in western Illinois and areas immediately beyond its limits. Noteworthy in this regard is the work of

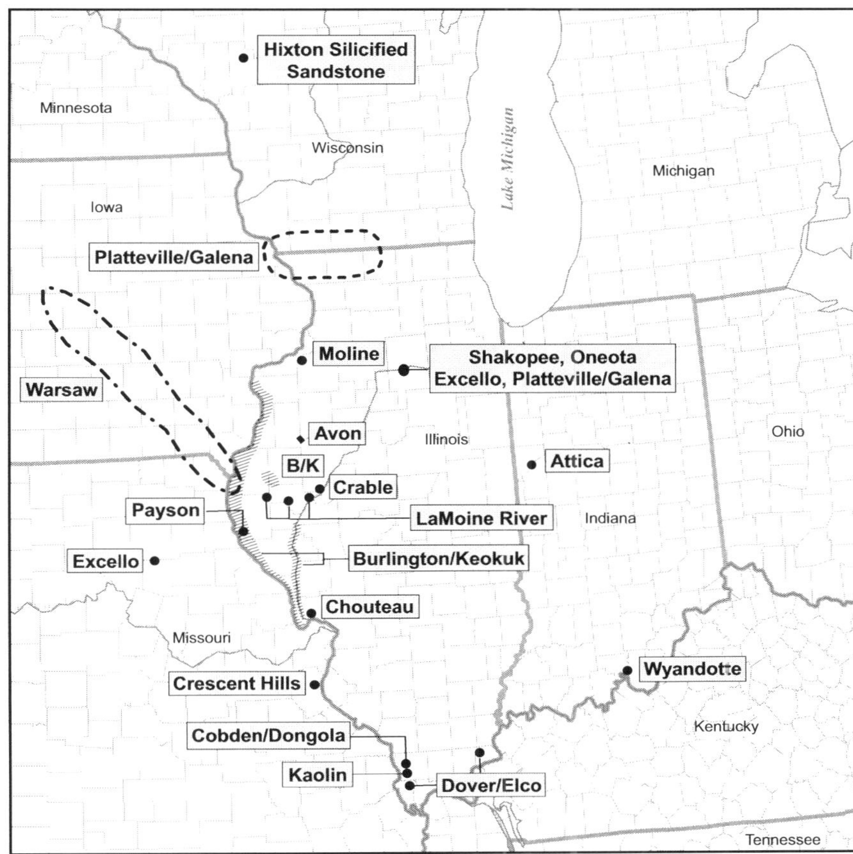

Figure 13.2. Locations of west-central Illinois raw-material outcrop areas.

Esarey (1983) in western Illinois, Odell (1984) in Pike and Adams counties, Myers (1970) and Rick (1978) in the lower Illinois Valley, Ferguson and Warren (1992) near the Big Bend in the central Illinois Valley, Birmingham and Van Dyke (1981) in the lower Rock River, and Morrow (1994) in eastern Iowa. Relevant single-source studies from western Illinois include those describing Payson (Fishel 1992), Moline (Birmingham and Van Dyke 1981), and LaMoine River (Cross 1998; Green 1977a) cherts, and relevant source studies and chert descriptions from outside the study area focus on Hixton silicified sandstone from southwest Wisconsin (Porter 1961), Knife River flint from western North Dakota (Clayton et al. 1970), Attica and Wyandotte cherts from Indiana (Bassett and Powell 1984; Munson and Munson 1984; Winters 1969), Chouteau chert from near the mouth of the Illinois River (Willman et al. 1975:131), Excello chert from northeast Missouri (Ray 1983), and Crescent Hills chert from southwest of St. Louis (Ives 1984). Willman et al. (1975) provide descriptions of the bedrock stratigraphy, including the chert-bearing units, for all of Illinois.

In this study, raw material types are grouped into the following three categories on the basis of their probable point of origin in relation to sites within west-central Illinois: local, regional, and exotic. Local raw materials are those that could be collected within a day's round-trip from a specific site area, that is, those within a 15-km radius, while regional raw materials are those whose collection likely involved one overnight stay, that is, all materials that fall within a 15- to 30-km radius. Exotic materials are those that were obtained beyond this 30-km radius.

Burlington/Keokuk chert (see Morrow 1994:123–124 and Willman et al. 1975:137–138 for descriptions), the most common and abundant chipped-stone raw material in our study area, must therefore be considered a local or regional resource across most of west-central Illinois. Only in the northern portion of our project area, specifically in all or most of Peoria, Stark, Marshall, Putnam, Bureau, and Henry counties as well as smaller segments of Fulton, Knox, and Rock Island counties, is Burlington/Keokuk considered an exotic material (Burlington/Keokuk outcrops across such a wide area, however, that chert from the northern outcrop areas technically would be considered "exotic" in the southern outcrop region and vice versa, but without trace-element analysis, the precise area of origin cannot be distinguished). Often cited as a source for a specific variety of Burlington/Keokuk chert commonly exhibiting grayish blue streaking and mottling are the so-called Avon quarries located along Cedar Creek in the upper Spoon River drainage (Esarey 1983). Chert raw materials are also exposed in many stream cuts in areas where Burlington/Keokuk does not outcrop, and Conrad (1986a) suggests that the prehistoric inhabitants were "quarrying" the till exposed in these stream cuts. While *quarrying* may be too extreme a term in most cases, area inhabitants were nonetheless collecting and exploiting the exposed glacial material from these streambeds.

Two of the raw material types that are found in the region but that are considered exotic across most of the study area are Payson (Fishel 1992; Nolan and Hansen 1995) and Moline (Birmingham 1985; Birmingham and Van Dyke 1981) chert, both of which were commonly utilized by the Archaic peoples of west-central Illinois. Payson chert was recognized as early as the 1960s, when local collectors and rockhounds referred to it as "Adams County flint" (Fishel 1992:74), but it was not formally defined until the early 1990s (Fishel 1992). The only documented source area of Payson is in southeastern Adams County, Illinois, where it occurs as a residual deposit.

With a few exceptions, Payson chert was almost exclusively utilized by Late Glacial and early Holocene hunters. In fact, the chert is so closely associated with Hardin Barbed points that collectors sometimes refer to it as "Hardin" chert (Lawrence Conrad, pers. comm. to Fishel 1991). For example, in Nolan and Hansen's study of 119 projectile points manufactured from Payson chert, 68 percent are Hardin Barbed points, followed by Neuberger points at 8 percent (Nolan and Hansen 1995:Table 4.2). More than 95 percent of Nolan and Hansen's (1995) Payson projectile points are either Late Glacial or Pre-Boreal in age.

Moline chert is a Pennsylvanian-age material that primarily outcrops in the dissected upland area southwest of the Rock River-Green River confluence, east of Moline, Illinois (Birmingham 1985; Birmingham and Van Dyke 1981), and is also found as residual deposits within streambeds of that area. Archaeologists first recognized the source of Moline chert in the mid-1970s (Fowler and Birmingham 1975). While Moline chert was utilized throughout prehistory in the Quad Cities area (Birmingham and Van Dyke 1981:353), it is more commonly associated with Pre-Boreal and Boreal peoples across the remainder of the study region. It occurs infrequently, if at all, in contexts dating to the rest of the Archaic period.

Research History

West-central Illinois was one of the most intensively utilized regions in the Midwest throughout prehistory. As of December 2004, more than 12,000 sites had been documented in this part of Illinois, representing almost 25 percent of the total recorded in the state. The central Illinois Valley was especially densely populated during the Middle Woodland and Mississippian time periods. The large number of extensive Middle Woodland and Mississippian mounds within and adjacent to the central Illinois Valley drew people from abroad during the late 1800s to excavate and collect artifacts (see, e.g., Adams 1883; Chapman 1879; McClelland 1883; Morse 1963: Appendixes F–H; Shallenberger 1883; Walton 1962), and in the early 1900s the lure of these mounds and associated villages brought archaeologists there in an attempt to "make the past live again" (Cole and Deuel 1937:1; see also Deuel 1933; Schoenbeck 1948; Simpson 1934, 1936; Snyder 1908). Don F. Dickson's excavations in the late 1920s at what would become known as Dickson Mounds drew additional attention to the area, "stimulating further research in the immediate vicinity" (Harn 1980:1) of this mound group. The University of Chicago's excavations in Fulton County during the early 1930s (Cole and Deuel 1937) resulted in the "delineation of the basic Midwestern cultural sequence" (Jennings 1974:365), and Illinois Valley town and landowner names were soon applied to numerous pottery types and point styles (e.g., Havana, Morton, Liverpool, Canton, Maples Mills, Dickson, and Matanzas). In the early 1950s, the University of Illinois continued the tradition of Illinois Valley surveys, identifying more than 300 sites (McGregor 1957).

While the Illinois Valley has received a large amount of archaeological attention since the early 1900s, professional archaeological investigations occurred sparingly and sporadically within the interior uplands and adjacent Mississippi Valley (see, e.g., Griffin 1933, 1991; Neumann 1991; Thomas 1894:117–121; Thurber 1935; Ullman 1991; Wedel 1943) until the advent of cultural resource management (CRM) driven investigations in the 1970s (Figure 13.3). One of the first major surveys within this region was conducted by Western Illinois University (WIU) in the late 1970s in conjunction with the proposed FAP 407 highway project between Quincy and Canton (Conrad 1981). This survey covered 20,250 ha and recorded 3,600 archaeological sites; it also provided the first comprehensive statement about the age and distribution of Archaic sites in the region. Other extensive surveys completed around this time include two of areas totaling 3,380 ha by the Upper Mississippi Valley Archaeological Research Foundation in Schuyler and Fulton counties in 1975 and 1976 in conjunction with proposed coal mines (Littleton and Ipava fields) (Green 1977a, 1977b); a survey of 850 upland hectares by WIU in McDonough and Schuyler counties in connection with proposed strip mines (Industry Field) (Conrad 1978); a Historic Sites Survey (HSS) in the LaMoine basin (Holstein et al. 1975), a survey along U.S. 34 (FAP 404) between Galesburg and Monmouth (Dwyer and Burge 1978), and a highway survey (FAP 405) between Mossville and Peoria (Dwyer and Harn 1978), all conducted by Dickson Mounds Museum; and an 860-ha survey in the Sugar Creek drainage of Schuyler and Fulton counties conducted by Holstein (1978) as part of his dissertation research. The mid- to late 1970s also saw the initiation of the FAP 408 (aka Central Illinois Expressway, now Interstate 72) Phase I survey, the final results of which have never been published.

The last two decades of the twentieth century brought an increase in road construction and improvements in west-central Illinois and, as a result, an increase in the number of archaeological surveys associated with these projects. Some of the more extensive surveys (Figure 13.3) conducted at the time include those completed in conjunction with FAP 407-Route 336 (Hansen 1995, 1996; Hansen and Hickson 1993; Hickson 1990, 1991; Hickson and Katz 1992; Nolan 2004; Nolan and Hansen 1994), FAP 506-Route 96 (Nolan 1990, 1991a, 1993, 2004), FAP 408-Route 36 (Conner 1984; Stafford 1994, 1997), FAP 310-Route 67 (Cross 1998), FAP 10-Route 67 (Conrad 1986a; Fishel 1993a), and the FAP 315-Macomb Bypass (Nolan et al. 1997) as well as work

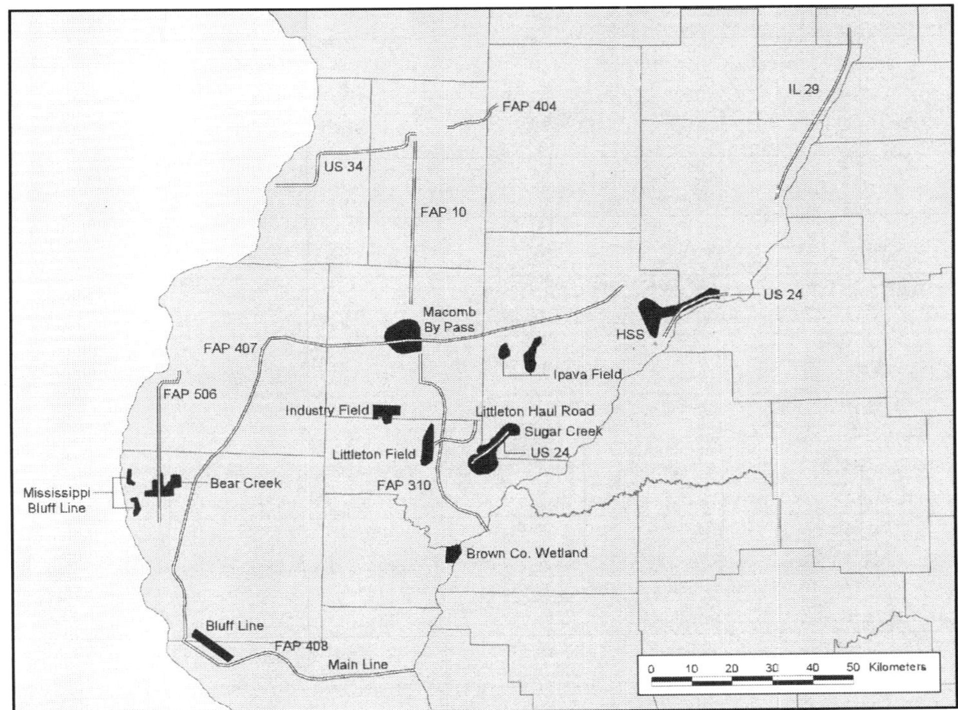

Figure 13.3. Locations of selected west-central Illinois survey areas mentioned in text.

along large segments of Illinois 29 (Fishel et al. 2004), U.S. 34 (Goatley 1998b; Nolan et al. 2003), and U.S. 24 (O'Gorman 1999; Studenmund 1995).

While many of the above-mentioned surveys recovered abundant Archaic-age projectiles and knives, prior to the late 1980s the majority of archaeological excavations in west-central Illinois were directed at ceramic-producing sites. This was in part due to research designs geared toward examining the wealth of artifacts and information found in many Woodland and Mississippian mounds and villages but also to the commonly held assumption that the upland landscape, where the majority of Archaic diagnostics were found, consisted of erosional features with little to no potential to contain in situ deposits. Upland Archaic sites were assumed by many archaeologists and some bureaucrats to be solely surface remnants possessing little to no significance.

The view that the uplands were solely erosional has always been closely tied to the concept of the Archaic period and its associated remains. Wray (1952) was among the first to use the term *Archaic* to describe pre-Woodland-period artifacts in western Illinois, and his description of Archaic sites implied relatively low research potential: "At least one presumed pre-pottery cultural tradition appears in a series of campsites which are typically located in the small tributary valleys. *These sites are limited in area and shallow*, suggesting brief occupation or a mode of living which did not leave quantities of refuse. *This complex is known only through surface collecting*" (Wray 1952:152, emphasis added).

Despite the lack of excavation, researchers assumed and accepted that the dominant process operating on this ancient landscape was, and had always been, erosional. Additionally, they rightly believed that this process had been greatly accelerated in modern times by agricultural practices. In this scenario, intact sub-plow-zone remains could only be expected to occur in pit features that intruded further into the subsoil than materials deposited on a stable living surface, assumed to be located at or near the modern surface. This traditional viewpoint of an erosional upland landscape became part of the collective archaeological subconscious, and it guided study in these areas for most of the three decades that followed Wray's statement. Stafford and Hajic perhaps summed up this viewpoint best:

> In the uplands themselves, it is apparent that a degrading surface is present which has been available for occupation since the Pleistocene. As has been demonstrated by previous surveys, cultural material from Paleo-Indian times onward can be expected. Agricultural practices have had a dramatic impact in terms of soil erosion on upland surfaces and, concomitantly, on cultural resources. *Only in an exceptional case (within the rim of a sink hole) would buried deposits be expected.* [1983:18, emphasis added]

With this type of ruling theory in place, archaeologists believed that repeated surface collecting was the best way to extract information from upland Archaic sites (e.g., Conrad 1981:21, 1982:53–54; Esarey 1987:99–101). Most of the small number of upland Archaic sites that were "tested" during the 1970s and early 1980s were investigated using randomly or statistically placed test units that were generally terminated at the plow zone-subsoil contact, unless some type of obvious subsurface feature stain was observable. If scattered artifacts were found below the plow zone outside of noticeable feature limits, they were typically discounted as a by-product of trampling or some other form of bioturbation. Test-unit excavations generally were not followed by wholesale topsoil removal or machine scraping unless pit features were found during hand excavations. In short, the inherited wisdom concerning the surficial nature of upland Archaic sites was never questioned, and no attempts were made to understand site-formation processes or to test the stable-eroding landscape hypothesis.

The earliest reference to buried or intact upland Archaic deposits in western Illinois appears to be in a 1978 draft CRM report detailing the WIU excavations at 11WA23 for the Illinois Department of Transportation (IDOT) FAP 404-U.S. 34 Monmouth to Galesburg highway project (Conrad and Jones 1978). The results of this study indicated that Archaic-period projectile points and lithic debris were

> naturally buried in an apparently undisturbed loess deposit. As the site was located on the highest point in the vicinity there was no opportunity for alluvial deposition. Since it is assumed loess deposition would probably not have compensated for erosion on the knoll during the period when the artifacts were deposited, we must assume the artifacts in some way moved downward relative to the surface of the loess. [Conrad and Jones 1978:26]

Although the report does not provide detailed excavation results or stratigraphic information, it offers provisional insights into site-formation processes that are surprisingly consistent with the most up-to-date explanatory devices used to account for buried upland sites (see Van Nest 1997). Conrad (1986b:69–70) was one of the first to point out that the recurrent recovery of large, pristine Archaic projectile points from the plowed surface of upland fields in western Illinois indicated that these artifacts had only recently been brought up from some type of previously undisturbed subsurface context.

Among the seminal works relating to the potential for, and discovery of, buried upland sites in the Midwest are a 1978 article on Shriver, a buried upland fluted-point site in northwest Missouri (Reagan et al. 1978) and papers presented by Abbott (1980) at the Iowa Academy of Science and Abbott and Tiffany (1986) at the Midwest Archaeological Conference. The last line of Abbott's Iowa Academy presentation included the subtle warning that "the once dubbed 'sterile subsoil,' or the B and C-horizons, may warrant closer attention by archaeologists" (1980:11). This work did little to change the prevailing archaeological viewpoint in Illinois, although Abbott and his associates at the University of Illinois Resource Investigation Program (RIP) continued to amass limited evidence for the widespread occurrence of buried upland sites during the late 1980s and early 1990s in conjunction with their ongoing, IDOT-sponsored statewide testing program (Abbott 1987, 1989; Alvey 1991, 1993; Jackson 1993). Concurrent with the Illinois work, and also partially spurred by Abbott's research, archaeologists with the Iowa Office of the State Archaeologist began looking for, and finding, buried upland sites throughout that state (e.g., Artz 1992, 1993a, 1993b; Collins 1990; Perry 1983, 1986).

Although the traditional viewpoint of the archaeological potential of upland Archaic sites proved difficult to dismiss, changes in compliance were instituted by the Illinois State Historic Preservation Officer during the mid-1980s (Thomas Emerson, pers. comm. 2005) that complemented the work of Abbott and his colleagues, and word soon filtered down through several other regional Illinois CRM programs. Buried upland sites subsequently began to be documented on an ad hoc basis as a result of ongoing IDOT-sponsored highway projects and some small-scale contract work undertaken for local municipalities. Several buried Archaic lithic scatters were encountered by the Center for American Archeology (CAA) in 1986 at the Brush College School (11PK488) and Elledge (11PK477) sites during the FAP 408 project, but their contribution to buried upland archaeology was not "officially" recognized until much later (Stafford 1994; Van Nest 1993). In 1988, WIU undertook block excavation at the Cadwell #3 site (11HA679) and found evidence for shallowly buried, and perhaps weakly stratified, Archaic deposits (Nolan 1991b). The following year, the CAA excavated the Penstone site (11PK727), an upland Sedalia flintknapping locus buried in a small ravine on the side of a principal divide (Studenmund and Graham 1999; Van Nest 1993).

The recurrent recovery of sub-plow-zone artifacts with preserved spatial patterning challenged the long-held upland paradigm and began to change the way Archaic-period sites were investigated in western Illinois. This soon led to the discovery of additional buried upland sites in Pike County (Fishel 1993b; Goatley and Atwell 1993; Van Nest 1993), Warren County (Conrad 1990; Fishel 1993a; Hansen and Nolan 1998), and elsewhere as well as to the formulation of the FAP 407-Route 336 and the FAP 506-Route 96 research designs of the early 1990s (Nolan 2004), which resulted in the discovery and excavation of numerous buried Archaic upland sites, some of which are discussed in this chapter. These excavations demonstrated that if intact soil horizons exist between the Bt horizon and the plow zone, then the potential also exists for intact sub-plow-zone archaeological materials to be present. As will be seen, many of these components exhibited no surface expression and would have been overlooked using traditional pedestrian survey techniques. As of December 2004, 37 buried upland Archaic sites had been documented in west-central Illinois (Table 13.1).

Data Sets

As of the beginning of 2005, investigations in west-central Illinois had resulted in the acquisition of 62 Archaic-age radiocarbon dates from 29 sites (Figure 13.4 and Table 13.2). The dates range from 8490 ± 100 RCYBP (cal 7570, 7560, 7540 B.C.) at the Dittmer site (11A1252) to 2600 ± 70 RCYBP (cal 800 B.C.) at the Axedental site (11PK751). We present these dates in the standard form of radiocarbon years before present (RCYBP) and in calendrical years B.C., using the Stuiver and Reimer (1993) calibration program, version 4.3. As suggested by Stuiver and Riemer, all calibrated dates are rounded to the nearest 10 years.

Reports on most of the professional survey projects and excavated sites that provide much of the data discussed in this chapter are readily available and are not reviewed here; numerous collector and avocational surveys over the years have also produced a wealth of data regarding the spatial patterning of specific point styles. The strength of our database certainly lies in the distributional realm, but we also have substantive excavated data from more than 50 sites that evidence a wide range of components and feature types. These data sets comprise thousands of projectile points, knives, and other tools (see Appendixes 13.A and 13.B for selected point attributes), many of which have been personally examined by at least one of the chapter authors. Many of the excavated sites referred to in the text are currently being analyzed and reported, so we present more base-line information in the data summary sections than may be typical of other chapters in this volume. However, two of the more complex, multicomponent sites excavated in the 1980s, Eagle Slough and Tree Row, have not been formally reported to date and are briefly summarized below to avoid repetition in the data summaries.

Eagle Slough

The Eagle Slough site (11PK787) lies along the northeastern bank of Eagle Slough, an anabranch of the Snycartee River, within the Mississippi floodplain in western Pike County. Multiple Woodland and Archaic components exist at the site within approximately 1.5 m of cumulic midden deposits. Limited excavations conducted at the site by the CAA in 1987 and 1988 in advance of the FAP 408-Route 36 highway construction primarily focused on the near-surface Woodland components. Several test units and backhoe trenches, however, were excavated through the dense Archaic deposits. Seventy-one Late Woodland features, three Early Woodland features, and six Archaic features were excavated at Eagle Slough; two human burials could not be assigned a cultural affiliation but are likely attributable to middle Holocene Archaic activity, given their stratigraphic placement.

The Archaic occupations at the site predate the formation of the Eagle Slough, which occurred sometime around

Table 13.1. Buried Upland Archaic Sites in West-Central Illinois.

Site Name	IAS No.	Diagnostics	RCYBP	Reference
Early Holocene				
Dittmer	11A1252	Payson chert	8490 ± 100	Nolan 1994, 2003
Cochran 10	11WA140	Theban-cluster points	-	Fishel 1993a; Hansen and Nolan 1998
Alta Guthrie	11A1260	EH scraper	-	Nolan 1995
Ruth Andrew	11A1051	EH scrapers	-	Nolan 1993, 2003
Wesley Dedert	11A332	adze, EH scrapers, Theban knife	8140 ± 70	Nolan 1992, 2003
West Fair	11A1241	Dalton, EH end scraper	-	Nolan 1992, 2003
Wittler's Twister	11A1334	EH scraper	-	Nolan 2003
Schuerman	11A1057	Payson chert	-	Nolan 1993, 2003
Whitefield	11A1054	Payson chert	-	Nolan 1993, 2003
Boyd	11PK951	Theban preform/knife	-	Goatley and Atwell 1993
Pittsfield Prison	11PK993	bifaces, EH scrapers	-	Studenmund and Schroeder 1997
Mohr	11RI562	Thebes point	-	Jones 1994
Kewanee	11HY126	St. Charles point	-	Abbott 1987
Segregation	11PK458	EH preforms	-	Nolan, pers. obs.
Cadwell #3	11HA679	Kirk	-	Nolan 1991b
Stoney Point	11PK736	Payson biface	-	Fishel 1993b
Roberts	11A1029	Kirk	-	Kruger 1988
Elledge	11PK477	LeCroy point, serrated blade	-	Stafford 1994
Middle Holocene				
Wittler's Twister	11A1334	side-notched points	-	Nolan 2003
Quiche	11A1268	side-/corner-notched point, full-grooved ax	-	Nolan 2003
Lecroitip	11A1146	Matanzas points	-	Nolan 1995, 2003
Cadwell #3	11HA679	Matanzas points	-	Nolan 1991b
Elledge	11PK477	side-notched points	5890 ± 70, 5440 ± 90	Stafford 1994
Chenoweth	11MD771	bifaces	-	Nolan and Felix 2004
Read's Point	11PK724	Osceola-like points	-	Studenmund et al. 1998
Titterington Horizon				
Ruth Andrew	11A1051	Sedalia points	4170 ± 120	Nolan 1993, 2003
Brush College School	11PK488	Sedalia points	4010 ± 70, 3680 ± 70	Stafford 1994
Shoemaker	11A1142	Sedalia points	3770 ± 70, 3760 ± 70, 3740 ± 70	Nolan 1995, 2004
Penstone	11PK727	Sedalia points	3700 ± 90	Studenmund and Graham 1999
Lecroitip	11A1146	Sedalia points	-	Nolan 1995, 2003
Tent Town	11HA771	Sedalia points	-	Nolan 1993, 2003
Terminal Archaic				
Seiwell	11P344	barbed point	2940 ± 70	Alvey 1993
Cornjulio	11A1332	barbed point	-	Nolan 2003
Type Indeterminate Archaic				
Hunter's View	11A1144	midsection	-	Nolan 1995
Monmouth Industrial Park	11WA110	debitage	-	Conrad 1990
Awesome	11PK746	debitage	-	Katz et al. 1992
Pottstown	11P531	debitage	-	Atwell and Goatley 1993
Teddy	11A1052	debitage	-	Nolan 1993, 2003
—	11WA22	variety of Archaic points	-	Conrad and Jones 1978
—	11WA23	variety of Archaic points	-	Conrad and Jones 1978
Macomb Industrial Park Tower	—	debitage	-	Conrad, pers. comm. 1993
East Rock	11A1183	biface	-	Nolan 1994

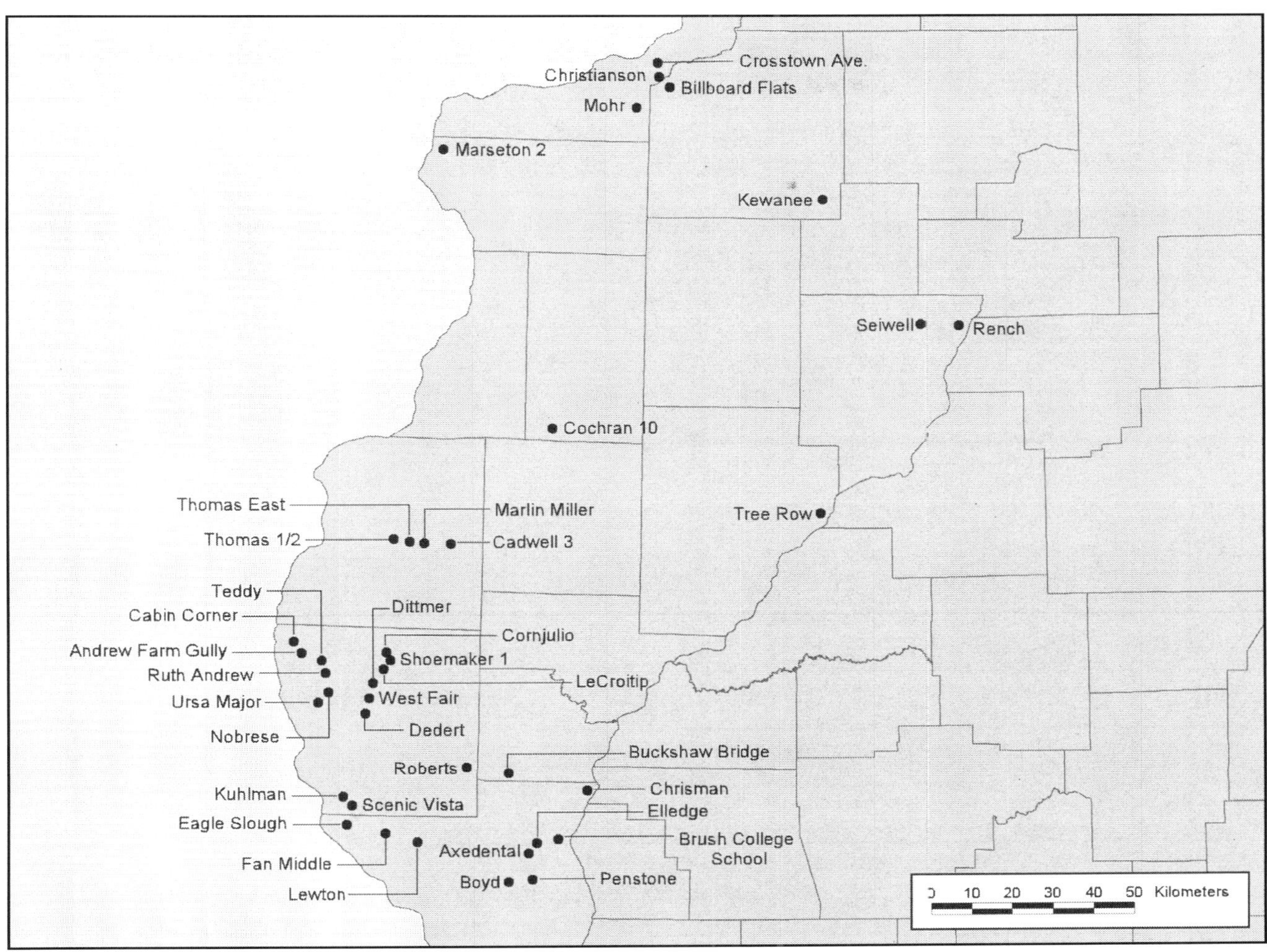

Figure 13.4. Locations of selected west-central Illinois Archaic sites mentioned in text.

3080 ± 180 RCYBP (cal 1380, 1330, 1320 B.C.) (ISGS-1893) (Van Nest 1997:61). Two buried soils are present, both of which are capped by a ca. 40-cm-thick "modern" surface soil (designated Soil 1 in Van Nest 1997) that contains predominantly stratified Woodland deposits. The uppermost buried soil, designated Soil 2, is ca. 30 cm thick and contains stratified Sub-Boreal (Late Archaic) through Early Woodland materials, while the lowermost buried soil, designated Soil 3, is approximately 75 cm thick and contains stratified Atlantic (Middle Archaic) through Sub-Boreal materials. Soil 3 apparently began to form by at least 5810 ± 90 RCYBP (cal 4690 B.C.) (ISGS-1985; the date is from a feature intruded into the subsoil), and, the point styles found in the two buried soils suggest that Soil 2 started forming around 2000 B.C. A date of 5240 ± 90 RCYBP (cal 4020 B.C.) (ISGS-2381) was obtained from midden charcoal found midway through Soil 3, and a date of 4720 ± 70 RCYBP (cal 3520 B.C.) (ISGS-2382) was obtained from a feature apparently originating within Soil 3. Dates of 1330 ± 70 (cal A.D. 670) (ISGS-1997) and 1340 ± 70 (cal A.D. 670) (ISGS-1998) have been obtained from two Eagle Slough Late Woodland features (Van Nest 1997:Table 7).

None of the Eagle Slough artifact assemblage has previously been analyzed and reported. However, we examined the formal chipped-stone tools from the site to better understand the cultural stratigraphy and chronological placement of the Eagle Slough Archaic components. Several identifiable Archaic point types are present at Eagle Slough as well as a few unidentifiable specimens. From earliest to youngest, the identifiable types (Figure 13.5) include Karnak Stemmed, Matanzas, Falling Springs/McLean, Osceola, Etley, Riverton, Kampsville Barbed, and Mo-Pac. The most common of these are Osceola ($n = 8$), Matanzas ($n = 6$), and McLean ($n = 4$) points. In addition to these hafted bifaces, an undrilled Wisconsin winged bowtie bannerstone or gorget was found in the same arbitrary level as a Riverton point, and a pebble pendant was recovered from the same level that produced the Osceola points.

The earliest identifiable points found in context at Eagle Slough are Karnak Stemmed (Figure 13.5o), which occurred

Table 13.2. Archaic Radiocarbon Dates from West-Central Illinois Sites.

Site Name	IAS Site Number	Cultural Association	Sample (ISGS #)	RCYBP	STD (±)	Calibrated B.C.[a]	1 Sigma Range B.C.[a]	Reference
West Central Illinois Dates								
Dittmer	11A1252	Hardin horizon?	A0004	8490	100	7570, 7560, 7540	7600–7480	Nolan 1994, 2004
Wesley Dedert	11A332	unassigned	2997	8140	70	7110, 7080	7300–7060	Nolan 1993, 2004
Andrew Farm Gully	11A1578	unassigned	5700	7720	140	6530, 6500	6680–6440	Nolan 2004
Andrew Farm Gully	11A1578	unassigned	A0577	7360	35	6220	6230–6110	Nolan 2004
Chrisman	11PK10	Helton horizon	M-76[b]	6490	150	5480	5610–5320	McGregor 1954
Tree Row	11F53	unassigned	2091	6340	170	5320	5480–5150	Evans 2001
Elledge	11PK477	unassigned	1754	5890	70	4770, 4750, 4730	4840–4690	Stafford 1994
Eagle Slough	11PK787	unassigned	1985	5810	90	4690	4780–4550	Van Nest 1997
Tree Row	11F53	unassigned	2342	5530	240	4350	4670–4050	Evans 2001
Rench	11P4	unassigned	857	5500	130	4340	4460–4180	McConaughy 1993
Elledge	11PK477	Helton	1755	5440	90	4330, 4270, 4260	4360–4170	Stafford 1994
Tree Row	11F53	unassigned	2343	5410	380	4320, 4290, 4250	4710–3790	Evans 2001
Eagle Slough	11PK787	Helton?	2381	5240	90	4040, 4020, 4000	4220–3960	Van Nest 1997
Tree Row	11F53	unassigned	2240	4820	150	3640	3780–3380	Evans 2001
Eagle Slough	11PK787	Falling Springs/Hemphill	2382	4720	70	3520	3640–3370	Van Nest 1997
Buckshaw Bridge	11BR116	Falling Springs/Hemphill	1411	4600	80	3360	3500–3140	Stafford 1991
Tree Row	11F53	Hemphill	2105	4580	70	3360	3490–3140	Evans 2001
Tree Row	11F53	Hemphill	2106	4580	130	3360	3510–3050	Evans 2001
Tree Row	11F53	Hemphill	2120	4570	150	3360	3510–3040	Evans 2001
Tree Row	11F53	Hemphill	2122	4520	130	3340, 3210, 3190, 3150, 3140	3380–2940	Evans 2001
Buckshaw Bridge	11BR116	Falling Springs/Hemphill	1545	4510	70	3330, 3210, 3190, 3160, 3120	3360–3040	Stafford 1991
Cabin Corner	11A1392	Hemphill horizon	5240	4500	70	3330, 3220, 3170, 3160, 3120, 3110	3360–3030	Nolan and Graham 2004
Tree Row	11F53	Hemphill	2121	4500	160	3330, 3220, 3170, 3160, 3120, 3110	3490–2920	Evans 2001
Rench	11P4	unassigned	1230	4470	70	3260, 3240, 3100	3350–3020	McConaughy 1993
Tree Row	11F53	Hemphill	2088	4390	80	3020, 2980, 2970, 2950, 2940	3290–2920	Evans 2001
Tree Row	11F53	Hemphill	2239	4390	100	3020, 2980, 2970, 2950, 2940	3300–2910	Evans 2001
Tree Row	11F53	Hemphill	2107	4380	170	3010, 2980, 2960, 2950, 2930	3340–2780	Evans 2001
Tree Row	11F53	Hemphill	2209	4360	90	2920	3100–2900	Evans 2001
Tree Row	11F53	Hemphill	2118	4250	100	2880	3010–2700	Evans 2001
Tree Row	11F53	Hemphill	2086	4210	160	2880	3020–2580	Evans 2001
Ruth Andrew	11A1051	Titterington horizon	3850	4170	120	2860, 2810, 2780, 2770, 2760, 2720, 2710	2900–2500	Nolan 1993, 2004
Rench	11P4	Hemphill horizon	981	4160	100	2860, 2810, 2760, 2720, 2700	2890–2580	McConaughy 1993
Rench	11P4	Hemphill horizon	974	4120	100	2830, 2820, 2660, 2650, 2630	2880–2500	McConaughy 1993
Lewton	11PK445	Titterington horizon	1833	4060	70	2620, 2580	2840–2470	notes on file, CAA
Brush College School	11PK488	Titterington horizon	1766	4010	70	2560, 2540, 2500	2620–2460	Stafford 1994
Crosstown Ave.	11RI693	Titterington horizon	5173	4010	70	2560, 2540, 2500	2620–2460	Vanderford 2005

[a]Calibration from Stuiver and Reimer 1993, Version 4.3, rounded to the nearest 10 years.
[b]Suspect date.

Table 13.2. Archaic Radiocarbon Dates from West-Central Illinois Sites, continued.

Site Name	IAS Site Number	Cultural Association	Sample (ISGS #)	RCYBP	STD (±)	Calibrated B.C.[a]	1 Sigma Range B.C.[a]	Reference
Kuhlman	11A162	Titterington horizon	982	4010	130	2560, 2540, 2500	2890–2350	Hassen 1991
Cabin Corner	11A1392	Titterington horizon	5247	3980	70	2480	2580–2410	Nolan and Graham 2004
Crosstown Ave.	11RI693	Titterington horizon	5172	3970	70	2470	2570–2350	Vanderford 2005
Crosstown Ave.	11RI693	Titterington horizon	5175	3970	70	2470	2570–2350	Vanderford 2005
Marseton #2	11MC71	unassigned	5642	3950	70	2470	2560–2350	Fishel 2003
Fan Middle	11PK1562	Titterington horizon	1835	3930	70	2460	2550–2300	Studenmund and Graham 1999
Fan Middle	11PK1562	Titterington horizon	1836	3900	70	2460, 2450, 2430, 2420, 2400, 2360, 2350	2470–2240	Studenmund and Graham 1999
Ursa Major	11A1006	Titterington horizon	1114	3900	70	2460, 2450, 2430, 2420, 2400, 2360, 2350	2470–2240	Esarey 1982
Scenic Vista	11A51	Titterington horizon	1422	3880	70	2400, 2380, 2350	2470–2200	Hassen 1991
Rench	11P4	unassigned	796	3800	80	2270, 2260, 2230, 2200	2400–2070	McConaughy 1993
Fan Middle	11PK1562	Titterington horizon	1715	3780	70	2200	2300–2050	Studenmund and Graham 1999
Shoemaker #1	11A1142	Titterington horizon	3846	3770	70	2200, 2160, 2150	2300–2040	Nolan 1995, 2004
Shoemaker #1	11A1142	Titterington horizon	3841	3760	70	2200, 2170, 2140	2290–2040	Nolan 1995, 2004
Teddy	11A1052	Titterington horizon	3173	3760	70	2200, 2170, 2140	2290–2040	Nolan 1993, 2004
Shoemaker #1	11A1142	Titterington horizon	3837	3740	70	2140	2280–2030	Nolan 1995, 2004
Billboard Flats	11HY289	Titterington horizon	A0544	3730	35	2140	2200–2040	Fishel 2004
Penstone	11PK727	Titterington horizon	2399	3700	90	2130, 2080, 2040	2200–1950	Studenmund and Graham 1999
Brush College School	11PK488	Titterington horizon	1695	3680	70	2110, 2100, 2040	2190–1950	Stafford 1994
Ursa Major	11A1006	Titterington horizon	1111[b]	3450	180	1740	2010–1520	Esarey 1982
Cochran 10	11WA140	Riverton horizon	3155	3280	70	1520	1680–1460	Hansen and Nolan 1998
Christianson	11RI42	unassigned	3770	3040	70	1370, 1360, 1310	1400–1130	Evans and Womac 1997
Seiwell	11P344	Prairie Lake horizon	1699	2940	70	1210, 1190, 1180, 1150, 1140, 1130	1290–1010	Alvey 1993
Christianson	11RI42	unassigned	3769	2910	80	1110, 1100, 1090, 1060, 1050	1260–980	Evans and Womac 1997
Thomas 1/2	11HA326	Logan phase	5691	2890	70	1050	1210–940	Fishel and Nolan 2004
Nobrese	11A1113	unassigned	3154	2620	70	800	830–790	Nolan 1993, 2004
Axedental	11PK751	Kampsville phase	1758	2600	70	800	820–760	Stafford 1994
Other Illinois Dates								
Campbell Hollow	11ST144	Early Archaic	891	8350	100	7480, 7460, 7450, 7390, 7380	7540–7200	Stafford 1985
Campbell Hollow	11ST144	early Middle Archaic	936	7670	90	6470	6590–6440	Stafford 1985
Campbell Hollow	11ST144	early Middle Archaic	753	7600	110	6440	6500–6390	Stafford 1985
Campbell Hollow	11ST144	early Middle Archaic	936	7560	80	6430	6460–6270	Stafford 1985
Napoleon Hollow	11PK500	unassigned	814	7050	140	5980, 5950, 5920	6050–5750	Wiant et al. 1983
Napoleon Hollow	11PK500	lower Middle Archaic	817	6800	80	5710, 5680, 5670	5730–5630	Wiant et al. 1983
Napoleon Hollow	11PK500	lower Middle Archaic	937	6730	70	5640	5710–5560	Wiant et al. 1983
Napoleon Hollow	11PK500	unassigned	949	6710	170	5630	5730–5480	Wiant et al. 1983
Napoleon Hollow	11PK500	lower Middle Archaic	786	6630	100	5610, 5590, 5560	5660–5480	Wiant et al. 1983
Elizabeth	11PK512	Helton/Falling Springs	1535[b]	6340	90	5320	5460–5210	Charles et al. 1988

[a]Calibration from Stuiver and Reimer 1993, Version 4.3, rounded to the nearest 10 years.

[b]Suspect date.

Table 13.2. Archaic Radiocarbon Dates from West-Central Illinois Sites, continued.

Site Name	IAS Site Number	Cultural Association	Sample (ISGS #)	RCYBP	STD (±)	Calibrated B.C.[a]	1 Sigma Range B.C.[a]	Reference
Napoleon Hollow	11PK500	upper Middle Archaic	972	6080	90	4960	5210–4810	Wiant et al. 1983
Barton-Milner	11LS863	unassigned	Beta-29920	5920	75	4780	4900–4700	Ferguson and Warren 1993
Napoleon Hollow	11PK500	Helton	938	5670	90	4500, 4470, 4460	4600–4370	Wiant et al. 1983
Elizabeth	11PK512	Helton	1325	5470	70	4340	4360–4250	Charles et al. 1988
Elizabeth	11PK512	Helton	861	5420	70	4320, 4290, 4250	4340–4170	Charles et al. 1988
Slim Lake	11ST107	Helton	1718	5380	70	4250	4330–4050	Stafford 1989
Napoleon Hollow	11PK500	Helton	938	5350	70	4220, 4180, 4170	4320–4050	Wiant et al. 1983
Slim Lake	11ST107	Helton	1719	5350	70	4220, 4180, 4170	4320–4050	Stafford 1989
Slim Lake	11ST107	Helton	1671	5310	70	4220, 4200, 4160, 4150, 4140, 4120, 4110, 4100, 4070, 4060, 4050	4250–4040	Stafford 1989
Napoleon Hollow	11PK500	Helton	1038	5280	70	4220, 4200, 4140, 4130, 4050	4220–3980	Wiant et al. 1983
Slim Lake	11ST107	Helton	1672	5140	70	3960	3990–3810	Stafford 1989
Napoleon Hollow	11PK500	Helton	1036	5140	70	3960	3990–3810	Wiant et al. 1983
Napoleon Hollow	11PK500	Titterington phase	823	4060	75	2620, 2580	2840–2470	Wiant et al. 1983
Napoleon Hollow	11PK500	Titterington phase	933	3920	90	2460	2560–2240	Wiant et al. 1983

[a]Calibration from Stuiver and Reimer 1993,Version 4.3, rounded to the nearest 10 years.
[b]Suspect date.

Figure 13.5. Selected points from the Eagle Slough site: a, Mo-Pac; b, Kampsville Barbed; c, Riverton; d, Titterington-horizon stemmed cognate; e, Etley; f–i, Osceola; j, k, Falling Springs/McLean; l–n, Matanzas; o, Karnak Stemmed; p, unidentified: q, possible Campbell Hollow cognate.

35 cm above the base of the cumulic midden. A radiocarbon date of ca. cal 4020 B.C. was obtained from midden charcoal within this horizon. A yet-unnamed corner-notched point style (Campbell Hollow cognate?) (Figure 13.5q) occurred below the Karnak Stemmed points, and the blade of an unidentified point was recovered from the feature producing the cal 4690 B.C. date, which originated below the Karnak Stemmed levels. This pit was the lowermost feature encountered at Eagle Slough, and the associated radiocarbon date is assumed, for the time being, to date the initial stages of midden formation. Matanzas points (Figure 13.5l–n) occurred 45 cm above the base of the middle Holocene midden and consistently above the levels producing the Karnak Stemmed points and the radiocarbon date of ca. cal 4020 B.C. Several unidentified side-notched points were associated with the Matanzas points.

Titterington diagnostics occurred within the same arbitrary excavation levels as both the Osceola/McLean and the Kampsville Barbed points, while both Late Archaic stemmed and unidentified side-notched forms occurred within the

Riverton-point-producing levels. Other Archaic point types found during backhoe trenching or in an otherwise disturbed context that could not be assigned a specific provenience include two possible Campbell Hollow cognates, a Sedalia, and a Table Rock. Point types found outside their "normal" stratigraphic placement include a Hardin Barbed recovered from the middle Holocene midden, a Dalton point from near the site's surface, and a Kirk point from a Late Woodland feature. Sedalia, Matanzas, and Osceola points were among the materials recovered from six Woodland features (one Early Woodland and five Late Woodland).

Tree Row

The Tree Row site (11F53) is a 15-acre habitation and burial area located on and within the alluvial fan of an unnamed creek along the western edge of the Illinois Valley in Fulton County. Excavations at the site in 1989 by RIP in advance of and during borrow operations for U.S. 24 improvements uncovered more than 420 features, 99 human burials, and three dog burials and revealed three primary components: Sub-Boreal-Late Archaic (Hemphill horizon), Early Woodland (Black Sand/Morton), and Mississippian (Orendorf phase). Artifacts attributed to more ephemeral components (Late Glacial-Paleoindian, Boreal-Early Archaic, Atlantic-Middle Archaic, and Late Woodland) were also found at the site. The majority of the features, including the human burials, are affiliated with the Hemphill occupation. Mainly on the basis of this large number of burials and a low density of chert tool-manufacturing debris, Evans (2001) suggests that Tree Row functioned not only as a Sub-Boreal-Late Archaic cemetery but also as a "ceremonial site for the local population."

Twelve of the 15 Archaic dates from the site (Table 13.2) fall between cal 2880 and 3640 B.C., suggesting that the primary occupation occurred during the Hemphill horizon. Two of the remaining assays are more consistent with Helton-horizon dates but may simply reflect statistical error, while the third denotes a poorly understood early Holocene component that was discovered beneath the borrow pit limits. The majority of the points associated with the Hemphill component are identified as Godar variants ($n = 140$); five other points are identified as McLean/Falling Springs and two as Osceola (Figure 13.6). Twenty three-quarter-grooved axes and one full-grooved ax, all attributed to the Hemphill component, were also recovered during the 1989 excavations (Evans 2001); numerous grooved axes had been found at the site prior to the 1989 excavations. A copper fishhook and a copper awl found during the RIP investigations are also attributed to the Hemphill occupation(s).

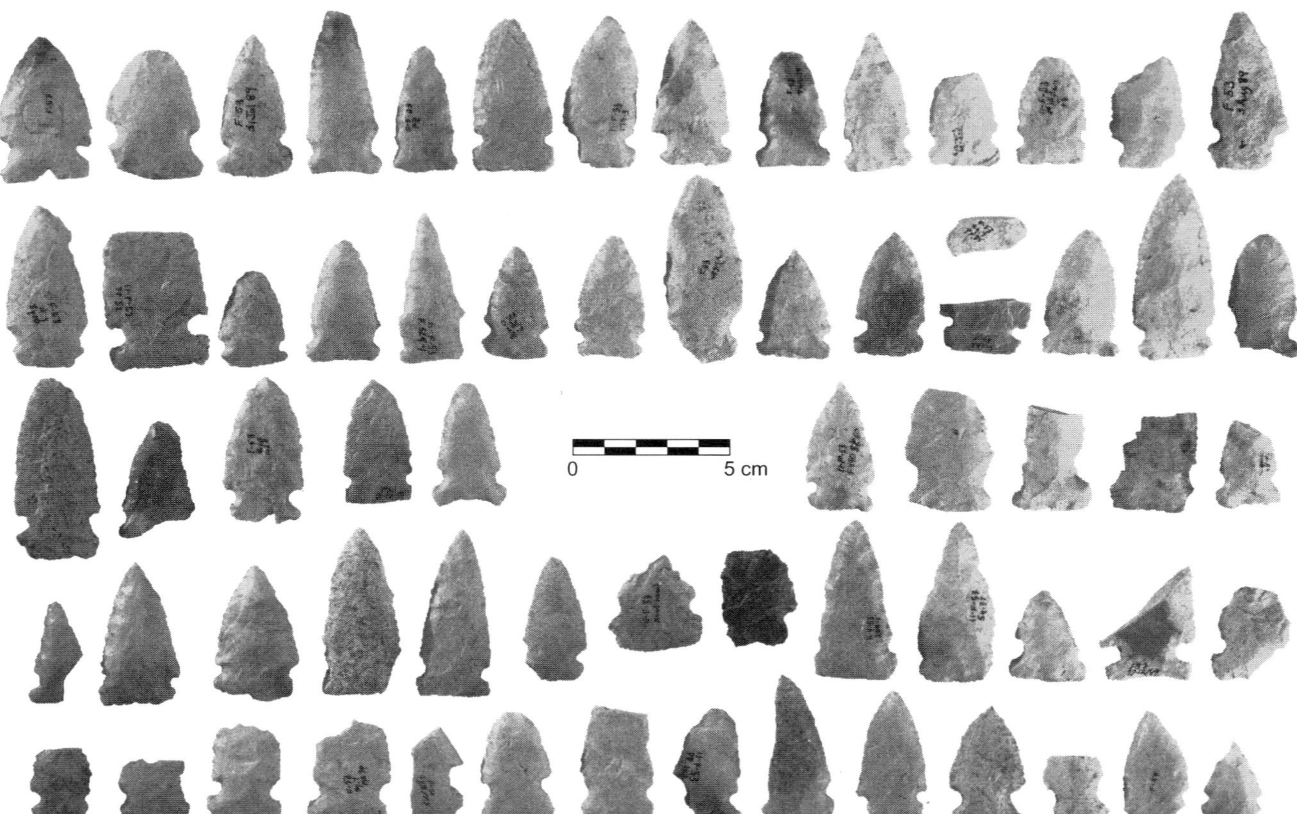

Figure 13.6. Selected points from the Hemphill-horizon component at the Tree Row site.

Archaic History of West-Central Illinois

In this section, we present an overview of the Archaic history of west-central Illinois (Figure 13.7) in the context of climatic change (cf. Conrad 1987). We subscribe to the viewpoint that distinctive projectile point/knife type clusters are horizon markers that denote the presence of specific cultural referents. While a few archaeological phases have been defined, given the state of our data, we feel it is most prudent at this time to discuss Archaic cultural complexes as horizons (sensu Willey and Phillips 1958), pending further refinement.

The temporal parameters we posit for these cultural horizons should, of course, be treated as estimates and will certainly be revised in the future, as more information becomes available. Both local ^{14}C dates and relative chronology were employed to affix these parameters (see Figure 13.7). The dates for the climatic periods are taken from Bryson et al. (1970) (their dates also should be treated as estimates or, in their words, as "tentative" [see Bryson et al. 1970:Table 3], given the large standard deviations) and have been calibrated using CALIB 4.3 (Stuiver and Reimer 1993). We present dates in uncorrected radiocarbon years before present (B.P.) to provide some sense of correspondence with earlier considerations of these data.

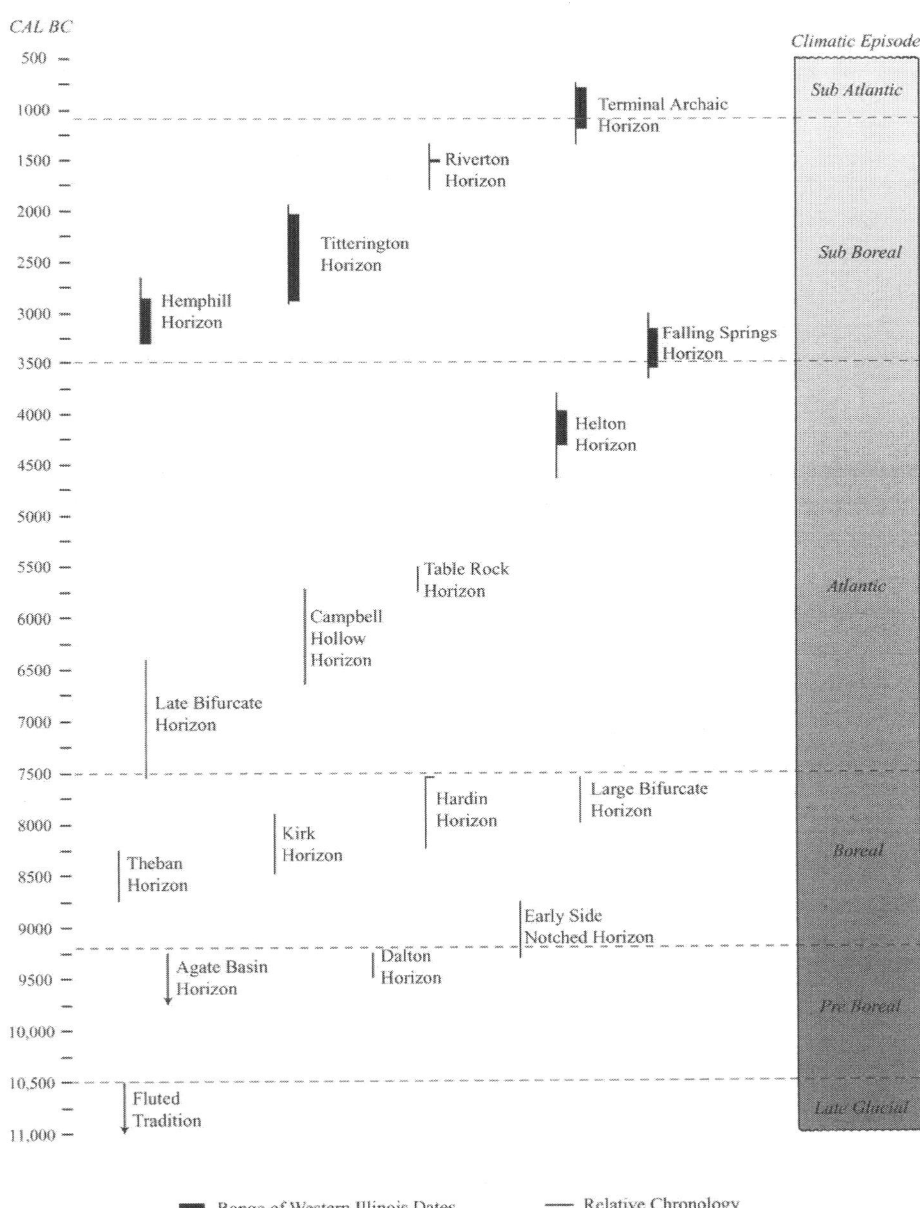

Figure 13.7. West-central Illinois Archaic chronology.

Because this volume focuses on the Archaic, we only briefly mention those western Illinois materials that are indicative of an earlier Paleoindian lifestyle (Clovis, Folsom, and Agate Basin) to set the stage for our discussion of subsequent Holocene adaptations. Fluted points are the earliest recognized cultural diagnostics from the study region and are attributable to the waning centuries of the last glacial episode. Clovis points and other named variants, such as Gainey, appeared in eastern North America around 13,000 years B.P., and a variety of fluted-point types (e.g., Lincoln Hills, Folsom, Cumberland, and Hi-Lo) were produced for approximately the next millennium (see Anderson et al. 1996; Deller and Ellis 1988; Ellis and Lothrop 1989; Haynes 1987; Tankersley and Isaac 1990). The limited evidence available from eastern North America suggests that caribou or mastodons or both were hunted by these groups (Funk et al. 1970; Graham et al. 1981; MacDonald 1968; Martin 1958; Palmer and Stoltman 1976; Wittry 1965), although economies were likely broad based. Diagnostics attributable to the Fluted tradition are infrequently encountered in the study area and are generally quite rare across most of western Illinois (see Conrad 1981, 1987; Munson 1990; Nolan 2003, 2004; Wiant 1993). They appear to be the products of transient peoples who used the area in a fleeting (nonresidential) fashion.

Pre-Boreal Episode (10,500–9650 B.P., cal 10,500–9200 B.C.)

Agate Basin Horizon (10,500–9800 B.P., cal ?–9250 B.C.)

Agate Basin–cluster lanceolate points are part of the Plano tradition (Frison and Stanford 1982; Irwin 1971). While commonly found on the Plains at bison kill and butchering sites, Agate Basin points occur east at least as far as the Illinois River in Illinois and the Lake Michigan shoreline in Wisconsin (Fishel 1988), a distribution that likely represents free-ranging populations extending their transient Plains Paleoindian lifestyle east of the Mississippi. There are no regional dates for the Plano tradition, so the beginning and ending dates for Agate Basin in western Illinois rely on radiocarbon assays from the High Plains (Frison 1978; Irwin 1971:47). Few Agate Basins have been found during professional surveys in west-central Illinois, but they are common in some local collections (Conrad 1987; Fishel 1988; Nolan 2004). Some western Illinois Agate Basin points are manufactured from raw materials from distant sources, including Hixton silicified sandstone, Knife River flint, and Moline chert (Fishel 1988), suggesting high levels of group mobility.

Dalton Horizon (10,300–9800 B.P., cal 9500–9250 B.C.)

This cultural complex witnessed the shift from Late Glacial lifeways to those traditionally regarded as Archaic and has been viewed as either Late Paleoindian or Early Archaic, depending on the criteria employed. The migratory life of the initial midwestern Late Glacial populations began to give way to a more regionally settled, yet still highly mobile type of existence during Dalton times. This long-term process of settling in to specific parts of the landscape is attested to by the dramatic rise in the number of Dalton sites compared with Paleoindian sites (see Conrad 1987), the presence of regionally distinctive point styles, and less frequent use of exotic chert types, which can be interpreted as reflecting smaller, more fixed home ranges (e.g., Nolan 2004). The fluted and unfluted lanceolate points of the preceding Paleoindian period were replaced by more shouldered or waisted lanceolate forms, which constitute the Dalton type cluster (see Justice 1987 for a review). The curated bifacial and flake tool assemblages of Paleoindian peoples also persisted into the Pre-Boreal and Boreal periods, with significant technological additions (see below).

The temporal parameters for the Dalton horizon rely on radiocarbon assays and stratigraphic information that are available from extraregional archaeological sites (e.g., Coe 1964; Driskell 1996; Goodyear 1982; Gramly and Funk 1991; Lopinot et al. 1998) since regionally excavated contexts have not yet produced corroborative dates. Therefore, no way currently exists for determining whether the three distinctive Dalton-cluster point styles recognized in western Illinois and discussed in the following section are generally contemporaneous or are the products of some type of developmental sequence.

The Pike County/Beaver Lake Dalton variant is typically considered to be Late Paleoindian and, technologically, appears intermediate in morphology between earlier fluted points, like Folsom, which are found in the study region (Munson 1990; Nolan 2003; Perino 1985), and classic Mississippi Valley Daltons. In the Midsouth, broadly similar point types have been recovered from the same strata as or underlying Central Mississippi Valley (CMV) Daltons and are presumed to have an ancestral relationship to the more prototypical Dalton-style points (Driskell 1996). In contrast, the morphology of the Northern Mississippi Valley (NMV) variant (Nolan 2004) appears to be intermediate between CMV Daltons (see below) and Neuberger points (Conrad 1981), the latter constituting a regionally distinctive variant of the Boreal-period Kirk Corner Notched–cluster point, which has a similarly limited geographic distribution in western Illinois.

Tools and Other Artifacts. Certainly the most archaeologically distinctive Dalton tools are projectile points/knives (hereafter simply referred to as "points"), which comprise several eared lanceolate forms that typically exhibit pronounced shoulders or an otherwise well-demarcated, incurving haft area. In western Illinois, several named variants are included in our Dalton type cluster: Pike County/Beaver Lake (Perino 1985) (Figure 13.8a–e), the CMV variety (cf. Walthall and Koldehoff 1999) (Figure 13.8f–k), and the NMV variety (Anderson 1989; Evans and Womac 1998; Nolan 2004) (Figure 13.8p–v).

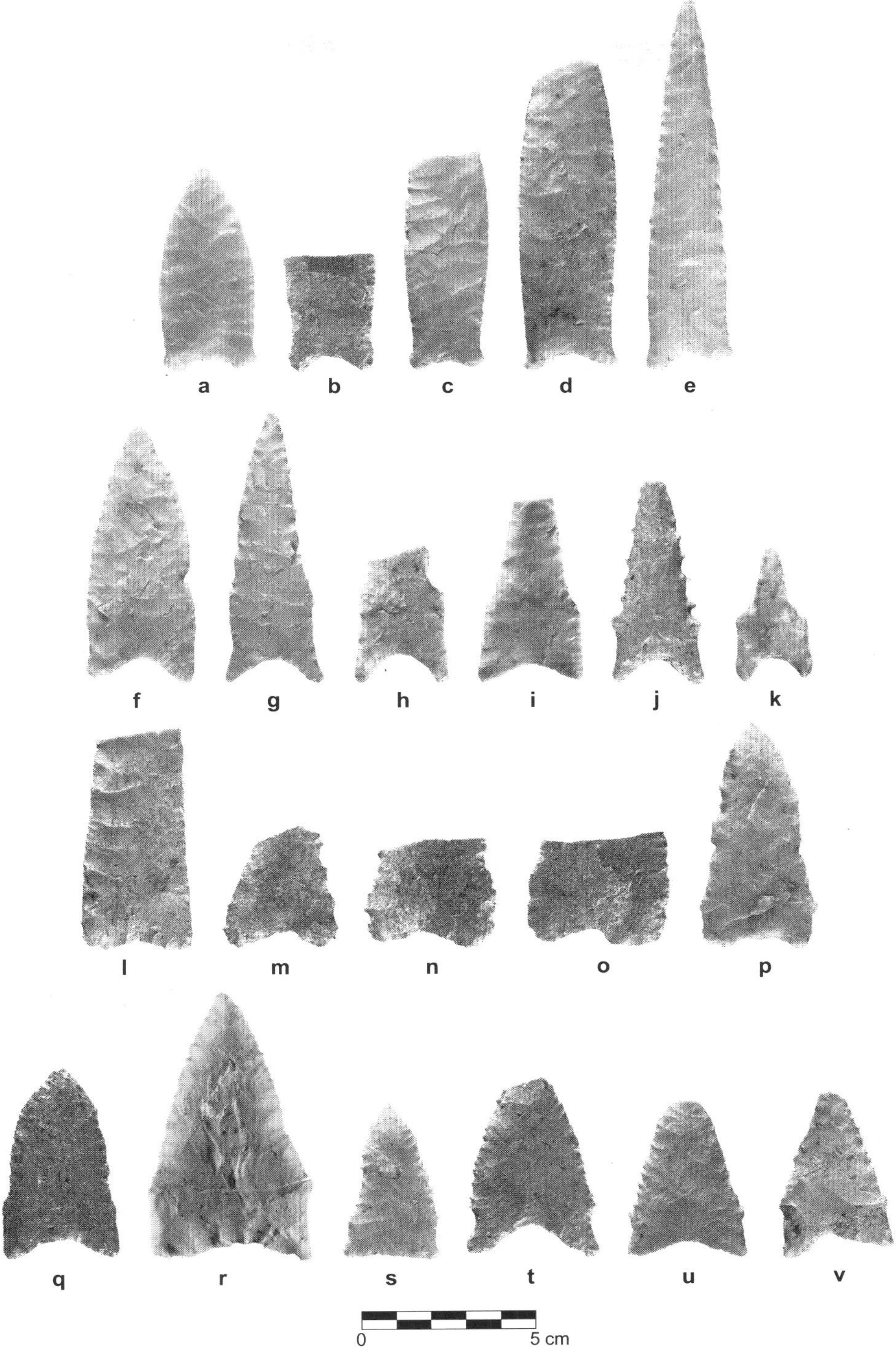

Figure 13.8. Dalton-horizon points: a–e, Pike County/Beaver Lake; f–k, Central Mississippi Valley variant; l–o, Mendon knives (initial-stage Northern Mississippi Valley variant); p–v, Northern Mississippi Valley variant.

We also view Conrad's (1981:321–323) Mendon knife (Figure 13.8l–o), which is similar to Coe's (1964) Hardaway blade, as a completed, unresharpened preform or initial-stage variant of the NMV Dalton variety (sensu Goodyear 1974:24–26). The NMV variant can generally be distinguished from the classic CMV Dalton by its wider haft area (see Appendix 13.A), less elongated and gracile overall appearance, thinner cross section, and rather distinctive resharpening pattern, which typically does not result in alternately beveled blade edges, markedly serrated margins, or awl-like exhausted forms (in this respect, the NMV Daltons exhibit types of rejuvenation similar to the more lanceolate-shaped, and perhaps earlier, Pike County variant). The use of alternate blade beveling, which is believed to be a tool-conservation method (Christenson 1977; Solberger 1971; Wiant and Hassen 1985), and blade serration, indicative of specialized butchering techniques (Michie 1973), are two of the technological innovations that serve to distinguish CMV Dalton implements from earlier Late Glacial-Paleoindian tool kits (see Appendix 13.B).

In addition, a distinctive bifacial chipped-stone adze or gouge added to the tool kit during Dalton times exhibits a plano-convex cross section, facial polish, and heavy lateral grinding indicative of hafting modification. These tools are frequently referred to in the literature as "Dalton" adzes (Morse and Goodyear 1973), although their manufacture and use clearly continued throughout the Boreal episode, or Early Archaic period (Behm 1985; Brooke 1979; Broyles 1966; Morrow 1989; Nolan 1994a:63, 65). Examination of the deeply stratified records of the Midcontinent suggests that this particular adze type abruptly disappeared from aboriginal tool kits sometime prior to 7500 B.P., during the Atlantic climatic episode. Use-wear analysis indicates that these early Holocene (EH) adzes were employed as heavy-duty woodworking tools, most likely used to fell burned trees and hollow out charred logs, perhaps as part of the manufacture of dugout canoes, wooden containers, or shelters (Yerkes and Gaertner 1997:59–66).

The Dalton tool kit also is characterized by formal flake tools, including end scrapers, side scrapers, and flake knives that are difficult to distinguish from those found in earlier Late Glacial, or Paleoindian, and subsequent Boreal, or Early Archaic, contexts (cf. Goodyear 1974). The various chipped-stone tools that make up the Dalton tool kit are typically manufactured from regionally available cherts of quite variable quality. Extraregional or exotic chert types appear to have been infrequently used in western Illinois during Dalton times, although the examples that have been identified (i.e., Moline chert, Hixton silicified sediment or orthoquartzite, and Warsaw Banded and other possible Iowa cherts) suggest northern or northwestern contact or influences (Conrad 1981, 1987; Fishel et al. 2004; Nolan 1994a, 2004).

Settlement and Subsistence Data. As mentioned above, few Dalton-age components have been tested or excavated in western Illinois, so the bulk of these data come from inferences drawn from abundant surface collections. However, two regional sites have produced subsurface Dalton remains, and both appear to be affiliated with the NMV variant. The West Fair site (11A1241) is located 10 km east of the Mississippi Valley on a high Illinoian end moraine situated in lightly dissected uplands, and the Christianson site (11RI42) is found approximately 20 km upstream of the Rock and Mississippi river confluence on a series of stepped terraces associated with the Rock (Evans and Womac 1997, 1998; Nolan 1994a).

West Fair is a single-component, buried upland site that produced the remains of a small, temporary encampment minimally comprising three dense, closely spaced, semicircular flintknapping features (each ca. 5 cm thick and covering < 5 m^2). These features primarily yielded late-stage flaking debris indicative of tool finishing, maintenance, and replacement (Hansen 1994:119–151; Nolan 1994a:15–36). An NMV Dalton point base was recovered from the plow zone immediately above the northernmost flintknapping concentration, and a formal flake end scraper, manufactured from a bladelike flake struck from a prepared core, was directly associated with the subsurface expression of this same deposit. The majority of the artifacts and debitage from the West Fair site are manufactured from regionally available Burlington/Keokuk chert (> 95 percent), although Moline-chert flakes and a side scraper were recovered from two of the subsurface features and the site surface, respectively. The site has been interpreted as a temporary bivouac or camp, perhaps a hunting stand (sensu Binford 1978), used by a small number of individuals who undertook tool repair, maintenance, and replenishment in addition to a few other activities, perhaps involving hide scraping and cutting (Nolan 1994a).

In contrast, the multicomponent Christianson site appears to be the location of a much more durable Dalton habitation-aggregation site, given its riverine setting, much larger size (6.75 ha), and greater variety and density of tool forms. Numerous avocational surface collections and some small-scale hand- and machine-excavated tests (that together examined a 500-m^2 subsurface area) document nearly 50 NMV Dalton-cluster points (termed "Chesrow-like" by Evans and Womac 1998 [see their Figures 4 and 5]), five more deeply concave-based points that seem to have greater affinities with CMV Daltons, and several EH adzes, preforms/bifaces, and formal flake tools from the site area. One of the smaller, but more deeply concave CMV-like Dalton point fragments was found in a pit feature discovered in a buried Bt soil horizon; a complete NMV Dalton was plotted in this same horizon near the feature (Evans and Womac 1998:338–342). These buried Pre-Boreal, early Holocene deposits also produced Moline- and Burlington-chert debitage (81 percent and 17 percent, respectively), two cores (both Moline), a formal flake end scraper, and several informal cobble tools.

Several other substantive Dalton sites as well as numerous small camps and hunting-loss locations have been reported in western Illinois as a result of both professional and avocational surveys. Nolan (2004) identifies several possible residential sites in the uplands bordering the Mississippi Valley. The two densest examples (11A1082 and 11HA789) were found on west-facing slope segments of upland ridges located adjacent to small, possibly spring-fed, tributary streams. Multiple walkovers of the E. E. Andrew '40' SE site (11A1082) produced eight fragmentary CMV Dalton points (Figure 13.8h, k) in different stages of use or manufacture (cf. Goodyear 1974:24–26), numerous EH adze fragments (some reused as cores and scrapers) and preforms, a variety of formal unifacial flake end scrapers (one possibly of extralocal Warsaw chert), a possible blade core and several bladelike flakes, and bifaces, cores, and debitage manufactured from local cherts. The total size of the Dalton habitation area is unknown but probably covers no more than 3,200 m^2 (Nolan 2004), suggesting it is unlikely to be the product of repeated use. At least five sites within a 1-km radius of 11A1082 have produced similar CMV Dalton diagnostics (Figure 13.8g) but nowhere near the density or variety of associated tools and other remains, suggesting the site may have functioned as a residentially oriented operational base for activities conducted in this part of the Bear Creek drainage. During a much larger, regionwide study, Conrad (1987:134) noted the tendency for Dalton components to cluster.

Site 11HA789 is located southeast of Carthage, in a rolling upland area historically dominated by prairie-grass vegetation, near the confluence of an intermittent stream with Slater Creek. Two walkovers of this site produced fragments of two Pike County/Beaver Lake–variant points, at least eight EH adze fragments (including two manufactured from a "cottonrock"-like material probably derived from a Mississippi Valley Warsaw–dolomitic or Salem-chert source, and another broken Burlington specimen that was refurbished into a use-polished end scraper), several formalized discoid and teardrop-shaped end scrapers (one unidentified possible exotic chert example), a backed unifacial blade, a subpyramidal core, and numerous bifacial blanks and tools (Nolan 2004). Unlike the 11A1082 locality, no other Dalton remains have been found in the area, although survey coverage and intensity have admittedly been much less comprehensive. Considered on its face, the Slater Creek site appears to have been a focal point for local Pre-Boreal settlement.

Several other dense upland Dalton sites have been brought to researchers' attention by local avocational archaeologists and collectors. Conrad (1986d) notes a site in the McKee Creek basin that reportedly produced 63 unspecified types of Dalton points for several collectors in a single season! This site is located in southeastern Adams County on a north-facing bluff that overlooks the sinuous, bedrock-lined course of McKee Creek, near the confluence of several large tributaries that drain to the south and west. Little else is known about this important site. The Kathay site (11MD1261) is located south of Colmar on a north-facing bluff spur that overlooks bedrock deposits of medium-grade Burlington/Keokuk chert that are exposed in the south bank of the LaMoine River. Although multiple prehistoric components are represented, one of the more substantial uses of the locality related to NMV Dalton activity. Repeated collection of the site has produced fragments of six initial-stage Dalton point bases (or Mendon knives, one of LaMoine River chert); one complete, exhausted NMV variant with vestigial serration; three reworked, broken point bases; three Dalton medial fragments; one relatively narrow and lanceolate-shaped initial-stage Dalton proximal-medial fragment; an alternately right-beveled, terminal-stage Dalton distal fragment; at least eight Dalton preform fragments (six proximal and two distal); and numerous other indeterminate bifaces that could conceivably relate to Dalton manufacture. In addition, the collection contains nine EH adzes manufactured from cobble cherts (six essentially complete, two fragmentary, and one recycled specimen), approximately two dozen distinctive flake end scrapers (many exhibiting cobble cortex on their dorsal surface or platform or both), and one exotic Moline-chert flake.

One of the focal points for the Dalton occupation of the Kathay site involved chert procurement and retooling, although the recovered assemblage also indicates that generalized habitation activities probably were undertaken. No adze preforms are apparent in the collection, perhaps suggesting that cobble cherts were preferred over local tabular resources for the manufacture of these tools. Evidence for EH adze manufacture has been found at the aforementioned E. E. Andrew '40' SE site and at 11A1009, located on a south-facing high terrace remnant in the Burton Creek valley southeast of Quincy. Abundant chert cobbles have been observed in the streams adjacent to both locations, which may have influenced site location.

Pre-Boreal use of the sandy late Pleistocene terrace remnants found in the major river valleys also appears to have been relatively intensive, and some of these sites likely represent durable residential occupations, if not actual base camps. The East Island site (11A1582) has produced five fragmentary Pike County/Beaver Lake points (Figure 13.8b), at least one EH adze, and distinctive end scrapers. Thale Island (11A42) has produced a similar assemblage associated with the NMV Dalton variant. Both of these sites are located along east-facing, former backwater lake shorelines in the Lima Lake locality of the Mississippi Valley (Nolan 2004). The School 48 site complex, located on the Keach School Terrace in the Illinois River valley in Scott County, appears to be a broadly similar type of Pike County/Beaver Lake site, although heavy multicomponency certainly hinders artifact association (Stafford 1989). Perhaps the densest lowland Dalton habitation we are aware of in the study area (aside from Christianson) is the Wilcox/Fieldhouse site complex (11A1562), which occupies a bluff-base location on a sinuous Savanna Terrace remnant situated near Bear Creek's entrance into the Mississippi Valley. Evidence for intermittent CMV Dalton activity is found along the entire length of the exposed terrace and includes multiple EH adzes and classic Dalton points (Figure 13.8i) recovered from several spatially discrete surficial concentrations of material. At least a dozen CMV Dalton points were found on the site by a local collector (Nolan 2004), but they are no longer available for inspection.

In short, the densest Dalton sites in the study area generally seem to occur low on the landscape relative to the principal divides and moraines but clearly are not limited to the principal river valleys. Yet the elevated, stream-lined terrace remnants in the major river valleys appear to be the best candidates for Dalton base locales (sensu Emerson 1984) since evidence for intermittent and often relatively intense Dalton activity is sometimes strung out along the entire length of some of these landforms (e.g., Christianson, Wilcox). Nevertheless, much smaller and perhaps even denser Dalton sites have also been documented in the uplands (e.g., E. E. Andrew '40' SE, 11A1082, Slater Creek, Kathay, and McKee Creek), generally in protected settings near good supplies of water and lithic resources. These sites also appear to be residentially oriented locations that may have functioned as either base or field camps, perhaps on a seasonal basis.

However, many upland scatters appear to simply be the remains of low-intensity hunting camps, similar to that encountered at the West Fair site. Sites that have produced the CMV variant are generally located on forest soils not far from large, perennial stream courses. Classic Dalton points are rarely found in the study area on level to gently rolling upland areas that were historically dominated by prairie-grass vegetation, although Pike County points and NMV Daltons are occasionally encountered in these settings (Conrad 1981; Nolan 2004; Nolan and Graham 2003). This distribution may suggest that CMV Dalton hunting territories were smaller and more focused than those of groups using the Pike County and NMV variants, perhaps more closely tethered to the larger stream valleys.

In addition to hunting-loss locations and ephemeral habitation scatters, the bluff tops of some of the larger tributary streams that traverse the upland interior also have produced multiple Dalton points as well as a low number of presumably related EH adzes and scrapers (e.g., 11MD1260), although the associated scatters are generally not as well defined or exceptionally concentrated as the examples mentioned earlier. Most of these sites appear to denote some type of less intensive use of favored landforms than more obvious base or field camps like the Kathay site, mentioned above. Walthall and Koldehoff (1999:45) interpret similarly diffuse Dalton site configurations from the southern Illinois interior as the remains of temporary residential locations that were serially used during periodic upland hunting forays staged from base camps located closer to the larger stream and river valleys.

While this interpretation seems plausible and is perhaps applicable to some of the broadly similar study-area sites, we would be surprised if most of the latter are the remains of winter hunting camps, as suggested by Walthall and Koldehoff. We believe it improbable that a locally based population familiar with western Illinois would have chosen such exposed locations for cold-weather occupation, given the harsh winter winds and temperatures. Sites like E. E. Andrew '40' SE would appear to be better candidates for interpretation as seasonal residential bases or field camps, given their dense surface remains (including numerous adzes that may have been used in the production of shelters) and relatively low, protected settings.

Geographic Distribution. The various Dalton-cluster points have overlapping distributions in the central portion of the study area, and in at least one instance possible examples of all three types were found in close surficial association in the Mississippi Valley uplands (11A332 [Nolan 2004]), suggesting possible contemporaneity. Additionally, Conrad (1986d) reports the surficial co-occurrence of unspecified Dalton and Pike County points on three sites in the McKee Creek basin that were repeatedly visited by a local collector. However, the aforementioned examples appear to be exceptional cases; the majority of the sites in the study area are dominated by a single Dalton variety, so the relationship between the different "types" is far from clear.

Examination of the available survey data indicates that the distribution of CMV Dalton sites abruptly attenuates along the Mississippi within the Lima Lake locality (Nolan 2004), where considerable overlap occurs in the distribution of all three Dalton varieties. CMV Daltons are not commonly found anywhere in the Illinois Valley above Pike County, although apparently isolated site-unit intrusions (e.g., Dolltone [11MD1260]) are present in the upland interior south of Macomb and elsewhere. Pike County/Beaver Lake points predominate in the northern portion of the lower Illinois Valley but appear to become increasingly uncommon to the north above the Spoon River confluence. However, they occur at least as far north as southern Hancock County along the Mississippi drainage (Conrad 1981; Nolan 2004). Dalton components, including some with points that fit within the range of the CMV variant, are commonly found in the Spoon River basin, where, Conrad (1987:130) notes, they are oriented toward the river, generally occurring at lower elevations relative to the divides and other upland topographic highs.

Sites found in the more northerly reaches of the study area clearly appear to be dominated by the NMV Dalton variant, although occasional cognates of the other two variants are sometimes found as collateral point types on some of the largest sites (e.g., Evans and Womac 1998:Figure 6). NMV Daltons have been reported in Rock Island (Anderson 1989; Evans and Womac 1998), Henry (Anderson 1989; Shepard 1993), Marshall (Fishel et al. 2004), Warren (Conrad and Jones 1978:Plate 5c; Dwyer and Burge 1978:Figures 24b, 28a), Adams (Nolan 2004:Figure 3.5f, h), Hancock (Conrad 1987:132; Hansen 1996:Figure 5.1d; Nolan 2004:Figure 3.5g), McDonough (Conrad 1978:Plate 7L; Nolan and Graham 2003; this chapter), Fulton (Conrad 1981:Plate 4; Green 1977a:Plate 1a), Schuyler (Cross 1998:Figure 29a; Esarey 1982:Appendix B, Figure 1a), and northern Pike counties (Nolan, pers. obs. 1999; Studenmund et al. 1998:Figure 5). The latter examples come from an area dominated by the Pike County variant, whose distribution extends southward along the Illinois drainage to at least Grafton or the general Illinois-Mississippi-Missouri confluence area, where CMV Daltons are also quite common (Robert Monroe, pers. comm. to Nolan 2004).

Given the changing composition of the Pre-Boreal forests, perhaps a time-transgressive movement of Dalton people is reflected in the north–south differences in the distribution of some or all of the various point types making up the cluster.

Conrad (1981:33, 1987) suggests that Pre-Boreal and Boreal people followed the movement of the oak-hickory forest northward and that this accounts for the limited expression of Dalton-horizon artifacts near the northern margins of the study area and beyond. If correct, this might hint that some of the NMV Daltons, which are the sole evidence for Dalton culture in the northern parts of the study area, may be slightly younger than the period of the CMV Dalton florescence. This hypothesis is congruent with the morphology of NMV Daltons, which, as noted above, appears to be intermediate between CMV Daltons and Boreal-period Neuberger points. If a transition from CMV to NMV Dalton forms occurred, one would expect to find the best evidence for this near the Lima Lake locality, where the distributional and morphological overlap appears to be the greatest. However, if the various Dalton point varieties were largely contemporary, as possibly indicated by the surface remains from 11A332, then the data are suggestive of overlapping territories, fluctuating social boundaries, instances of band-level interaction or aggregation, or some combination thereof.

Figure 13.9. Early Holocene side-notched points: a–f, Big Sandy/Cache River; g, Graham Cave; h, i, Kessell cognate.

Early Side-Notched Point Horizon (9900–9500 B.P., cal 9300–8750 B.C.)

Stratified sites excavated south of the study area document that, while the basic hunting and gathering economy of later Pre-Boreal peoples changed little from that of their predecessors, the lanceolate-shaped Dalton projectile point form was initially replaced by several named varieties of broadly similar concave-based, side-notched points (Broyles 1966; DeJarnette et al. 1962; Driskell 1996; Fowler 1959; Lopinot et al. 1998). The curated bifacial and flake tool technology of the Dalton horizon continued to be employed during the Boreal episode, with few appreciable additions or notable changes. Our dating for this cultural complex relies on stratigraphic information and radiocarbon assays amassed some distance from the study area. Regional dates are available from the largely unreported Koster Horizon 11 (Brown and Vierra 1983:181–183; Wiant et al., this volume) but do not seem to correspond to those associated with the earliest expression of the type cluster in the Southeast. Thus, the temporal parameters we employ here are largely based on data from Big Eddy, Dust Cave, and other early side-notch components. We also note that the dating of these forms overlaps the initial centuries provided for the Boreal episode (Bryson et al. 1970), indicating that they were produced at a time when the climate and forests of the area possibly were undergoing change.

Tools and Other Artifacts. The only distinctive tools that can be definitely attributed to this cultural complex are the points themselves, although they sometimes have proven difficult to distinguish from broadly similar side-notched forms that were commonly used several millennia later in the same area (see Conrad 1987 for a review of this problem). Pre-Boreal-episode side-notched point types (Figure 13.9) include cognates of the Graham Cave (C. Chapman 1975; Scully 1951), Kessell (Broyles 1966), and Big Sandy/Cache River (Cambron and Hulse 1975:14–15; Kneberg 1956:25; Perino 1985:58) types, which appear to be transitional between the earlier shouldered lanceolate forms of the Pre-Boreal and subsequent notched and stemmed points of the Theban and Kirk traditions. However, data from Koster and other sites suggest that some Graham Cave points may actually have been coeval with or postdated some Theban and Kirk forms, indicating this type may be a less than reliable diagnostic indicator. Thus, Graham Cave points may prove to be datable only to the Pre-Boreal or Boreal episode (early Holocene), in general.

Graham Cave (Figure 13.9g) is a medium- to large-bladed, side-notched type that typically displays a deeply concave haft area that extends all the way across the basal margin to the interior edges of delicate, downward-projecting ears. The blades of well-used Graham Cave points frequently exhibit fine serration and alternate beveling, similar to characteristics found on earlier CMV Dalton forms. Local Kessell point cognates (Figure 13.9h–i) are generally thinner than and quite distinctive from Graham Cave points, having an ovate triangular blade and low, angled notches that frequently narrow toward the center of the biface. These points are typically widest near the shoulder and have lateral basal margins that constrict or converge toward a more modestly concave base than that found on Graham Cave points. In contrast, Big Sandy/Cache River points (Figure 13.9a–f) appear to be smaller and narrower than either Graham Cave or the Kessell-like points and generally have narrow triangular blades and notches set closer to the base, which varies from nearly straight to markedly concave. These points also sometimes exhibit alternate blade beveling (Cambron and Hulse 1975).

Western Illinois Pre-Boreal–Boreal side-notched points typically are manufactured from locally or regionally available cherts, although Conrad (1986d) reports that a possible Graham Cave point manufactured from Hixton silicified sediment was found by a local collector on the bluff of McKee Creek. While this specimen was not available for our examination, Conrad (1987) has demonstrated that regional use of the exotic Hixton material ended during the middle of the Boreal episode, since no examples of Hardins, bifurcates, or later Archaic point types have been identified as manufactured from it. In addition to the points themselves, we expect that other typical Pre-Boreal implements, such as adzes and formal flake scrapers, formed part of the tool kit of the time, but direct associations are currently lacking.

Settlement and Subsistence Data. No Pre-Boreal-period side-notched point sites have yet been excavated in western Illinois, nor are we aware of any sizable surface assemblages suggestive of anything more than transient use of the area for hunting. We can only speculate on the reason for the relative rarity of side-notched points, since no regional data (i.e., stratified sites) corroborate the Dalton to notched-point transition documented in the Southeast. Certainly we expect that a generally similar type of transition in point morphology or style occurred in this part of the Midwest. However, the possibility remains that much of western Illinois was largely peripheral to these developments, or perhaps the densest sites are deeply buried by colluvial or alluvial deposits in the principal valleys. Without additional data, we cannot currently say whether the dearth of Pre-Boreal side-notched sites is the result of regional abandonment, a substantive change in the settlement pattern, survey bias (many of the sites dating to this time period could be buried), archaeologists' inability to consistently identify specimens that date to this interval, or a combination of these factors.

Another possible factor that could be negatively shaping the data is that the points that typify this part of the Pre-Boreal were used for a shorter period relative to the types that apparently bracket this span. Recent dating of the Bolen Beveled point type, a southeastern Theban cognate, at 9730 ± 120 RCYBP (Dunbar et al. 1989) could suggest that some Theban-cluster points were used earlier in western Illinois than is indicated by the weighted average of the Twin Ditch dates from the Lower Illinois valley (see below). Additionally, the possibility exists that the NMV Dalton variant dates more recently than the CMV Daltons (see above), which would certainly fill in some, or all, of the apparent chronological gap. Clearly, more information is needed about this transitional period. At present we can only say that side-notched point forms similar to those documented from Pre-Boreal contexts elsewhere in the Midwest are present in the study region.

Geographic Distribution. Although all Pre-Boreal side-notched points occur in low numbers in western Illinois, some are reported more frequently than others. Graham Cave points appear to be more common in the western portion of the study area, reflecting their predominance in Missouri and along the Mississippi southward to the St. Louis area. Nolan et al. (1997:Figure 30f) illustrate a classic example of the type from central McDonough County, and Nolan (2004) reports other serrated Big Sandy and Graham Cave points or cognate forms from private collections amassed from both upland and lowland contexts in the Mississippi drainage in Adams and Hancock counties. Conrad (1981) identified 14 Big Sandy points from 12 different upland sites in the Spoon and LaMoine river drainages during the FAP 407 survey but later backed away from this identification (Conrad 1987). Another possible Big Sandy point from a site in Warren County is illustrated in Dwyer and Burge (1978: Figure 10b). Several other early side-notched points from eastern Schuyler County are illustrated in Esarey (1982:Appendix B, Figure 7c, f). As can be seen from this partial listing, Big Sandy–like points have a relatively wide but apparently unfocused distribution in western Illinois. Examples of local Kessell point cognates, which are the rarest of the three varieties under consideration, have been found in the uplands immediately west of the Illinois Valley in Pike, Brown, and Schuyler counties (e.g., Stafford and Nolan 1990:Table 3.3) but also are present along the Mississippi River (Nolan 2004). Thus, the various Pre-Boreal side-notched "types" appear to have overlapping distributions in western Illinois.[1]

Boreal Episode (9650–8450 B.P., cal 9200–7500 B.C.)

Theban Horizon (9500–9000 B.P., cal 8750–8250 B.C.)

This Boreal cultural tradition is typified by a group of generally large, hafted projectile points and knives that characteristically exhibit alternately left-beveled blades (often serrated), narrow but deep diagonal corner to side notches, and heavy haft grinding (Figure 13.10). In western Illinois, the Theban type cluster (Conrad 1981) includes several named varieties, such as the Thebes knife or Cache Diagonal Notched (Perino 1971;

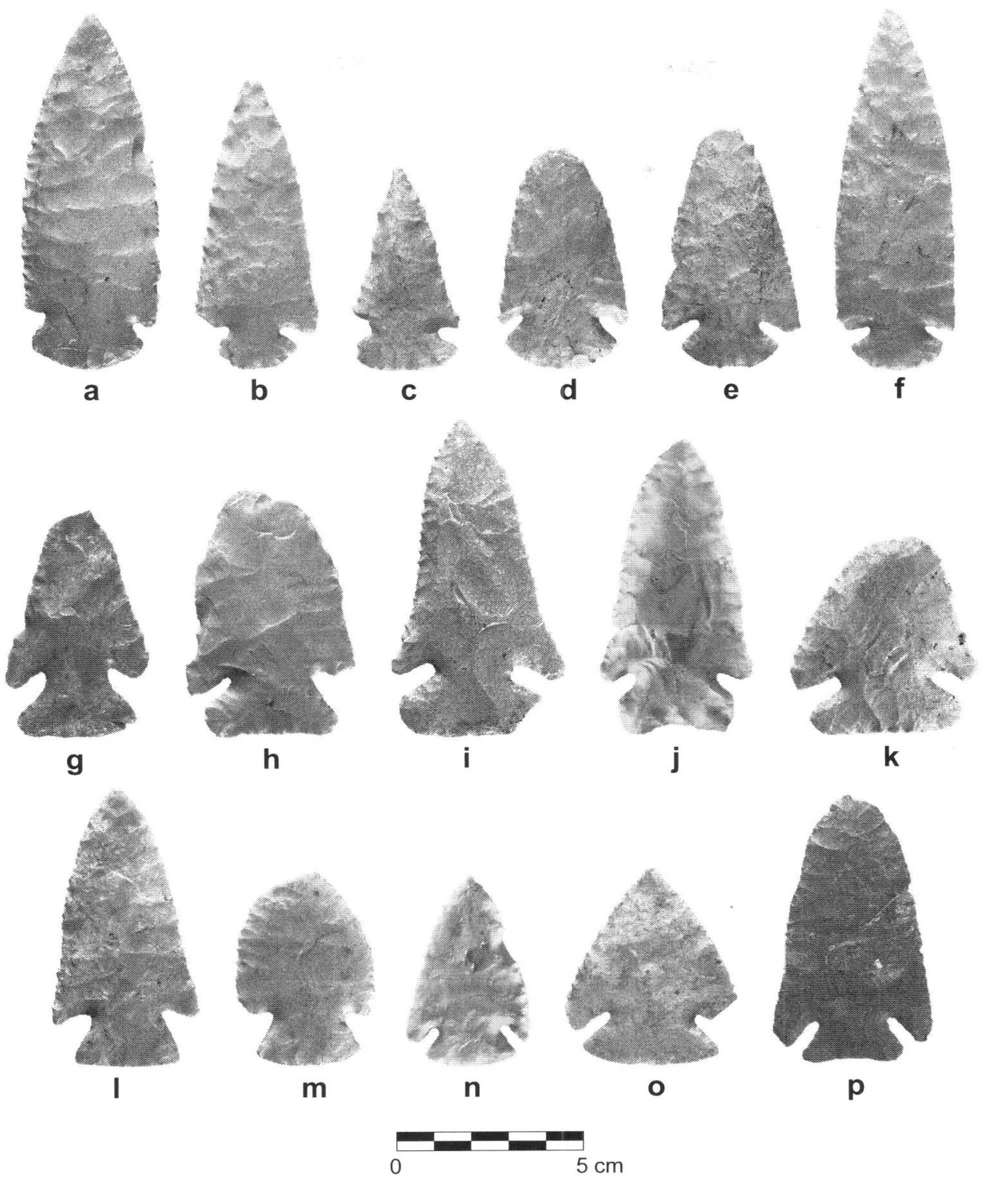

Figure 13.10. Theban-horizon points: a–f, St. Charles/Dovetail; g–k, Thebes knife; l, m, "Hardoves"; n–p, Pulaski.

Winters 1963) (Figure 13.10g–k), St. Charles (aka Dovetail [Luchterhand 1970; Scully 1951]) (Figure 13.10a–f), Pulaski (Winters 1963) (Figure 13.10n–p), and Sampson (Conrad 1987). Our temporal parameters for the Theban horizon are based on a suite of dates ranging from 9500 to 9000 RCYBP returned from stratified buried floodplain contexts at the Twin Ditch site in the lower Illinois Valley (Morrow 1989, 1996). These dates support and clarify earlier assays of 9290 ± 300 RCYBP (cal 8550, 8490, 8480 B.C.) and 9470 ± 400 RCYBP (cal 8740 B.C.) returned from a cultural zone at the Graham Cave site in east-central Missouri that also produced Thebes and St. Charles points (Klippel 1971:22, 27–28).

Tools and Other Artifacts. The most distinctive Theban tools are projectile points and knives, which, in an unexhausted state, typically display large blades, pronounced rounded shoulders, and distinctive haft areas exhibiting fine marginal pressure flaking and visible edge dulling (Figure 13.10). On the basis of the incidence of impact fractures and additional macroscopic edge-wear observations, Morrow (1988, 1989, 1996) and others suggest that classic Thebes generally were used as multifunctional hafted knives, whereas the more elongated and gracile St. Charles were used as both projectiles and multipurpose cutting tools. The other point varieties appear to have functioned similarly but have not been subjected to as much scrutiny because they occur less commonly than Thebes knives and St. Charles. Theban-cluster points were sometimes reworked into hafted scrapers after breakage or were serially resharpened until an awl- or drill-like terminal form was produced. Conrad (1981:81) also notes that a surprising number of St. Charles points are "backed," presumably enabling their use for controlled cutting or engraving.

The Theban tool kit appears to be strongly oriented toward a bifacial technology. Point or knife preforms are rather distinctive, generally thick and subtriangular in outline shape. Distinctive, elongated rectangular knives or preforms also have been reported from several single-component Theban sites located on the Bushnell Prairie (Esarey 1987:Figures 7a, 9c; Hansen and Nolan 1998:Figure 4a, b, and d), and several of these artifacts exhibit incipient beveling. On the basis of his study of the Bass knife, which is a broadly similar but slightly later unnotched knife form, Behm (1985) suggests these tools were handheld rather than hafted.

Bifacial chipped-stone adzes are also commonly associated with some Theban components (Morrow 1996). Their presence appears to denote woodworking tasks that are unlikely to have been undertaken at most temporary upland hunting camps but that are expected to have occurred with increasing regularity at durable residential loci or base camps. This supposition is based on the fact that adzes were the most common formal artifact type (n = 40) recovered from the Theban deposits in Horizon 2 at Twin Ditch (Morrow 1996). Specific morphological or metric attributes that can be used to distinguish Theban adzes from other EH varieties have not yet been identified or disseminated.

Not only did bifaces function as preforms for adzes and points/knives but they also frequently served as the cores or parent pieces for many of the flake tools employed at Twin Ditch (Morrow 1996:349) and other sites. However, Hansen and Nolan (1998:307) report flake tools derived from simple core reduction at Cochran 10, indicating some technological variability. Theban end scrapers form a significant part of the tool kit and are typically manufactured from thick, triangular flake blanks. Simple gravers have also been reported from Twin Ditch and Cochran 10, along with invasively retouched, formal flake side scrapers. Twin Ditch has produced the only bone tools currently associated with Theban technology, and these fragmentary examples appear to represent either awls or pins (Morrow 1989). The ground-stone industry of Theban peoples appears underdeveloped compared with that of later Archaic peoples, consisting of cobbles that were selected from nearby till or stream exposures for use as hammerstones, anvils, and pitted stones.

This apparently casual cobble procurement strategy contrasts markedly with the evidence for relatively intensive exploitation of regional and more distant chert sources. Compared with earlier Dalton peoples, Theban groups used much more exotic chert, although the recovered specimens made of nonlocal materials still constitute only a small percentage of the total number of points found in the study area. While northern raw materials (Moline, Prairie du Chien, and Hixton) continued to be used by Theban peoples, high-quality southern sources (Cobden/Dongola and Crescent) were exploited nearly equally for the first time since early in the Late Glacial, or Paleoindian, period (Nolan 2004). We suspect that some of the generalized Burlington-chert Theban points also were manufactured great distances from their ultimate discard or loss locations, but accurately sourcing these specimens is nearly impossible using only macroscopic observation.

In addition to these well-documented raw-material types, we are aware of study-area Thebes and St. Charles points manufactured from Attica/Indiana Green and Dover/Elco chert, respectively. A distinctive Attica-chert specimen (Figure 13.10g) was found adjacent to a glacial kettle south of Macomb and appears to be an exhausted "Ohio Variety" of Thebes (sensu Perino 1985:378), suggesting it was not made by regionally based populations. Rare examples of Attica-chert Theban points are found east of the Illinois River valley in central Illinois (Brad Koldehoff, pers. comm. to Nolan 2004); and the Macomb-area point is the westernmost example yet reported. The Dover/Elco specimens were found in the Spoon River drainage in Knox County and on the Mississippi bluffs in Adams County (Kelvin Sampson, pers. comm. to Nolan 2004; Steve Tieken, pers. comm. to Nolan 2004), but their morphology does not clearly diverge from that of other regional St. Charles points. This chert type is not represented in any other Archaic context in western Illinois to our knowledge but has been reported in association with late-prehistoric Oneota surface remains in the Lima Lake locality (Nolan and Conrad 1998).

Settlement and Subsistence Data. The Theban horizon is currently the earliest cultural manifestation to have produced substantive excavated data from western Illinois, although the associated remains are still meager compared with those from most later Archaic- and Woodland-period occupations. Five regional sites have produced intact Theban deposits to date: Twin Ditch (11GE146), Cochran 10 (11WA140), Kewanee (11HY126), Wesley Dedert (11A332 [Block 200 area]), and Boyd (11PK951). Additional probable subsurface Theban deposits have been reported at Mohr (11RI562), an extensive multicomponent Moline-chert workshop located near Coal Valley in the Quad Cities (Jones 1994). Twin Ditch is buried under Holocene alluvium in the lower Illinois River valley, whereas the remaining sites were shallowly buried in a variety of upland settings as a result of biomantle formation processes (Abbott 1987; Fishel 1993a; Goatley et al. 1996; Hansen and Nolan 1998; Jones 1994; Morrow 1989; Nolan 1995:4–7).

Twin Ditch, which is located immediately southeast of the study area (Morrow 1988, 1989, 1996; also see Wiant et al., this volume), is the most thoroughly reported and dated Theban site in the Midwest. The buried remains from Horizon 2 have been interpreted as a seasonal base camp that was used for a relatively short duration on more than one occasion. Activities appear to have been hearth focused and included tool production, use, and maintenance as well as basic subsistence-oriented pursuits. White-tailed-deer and fish remains dominate the recovered faunal assemblage, although birds and small mammals are also represented (Morrow 1996:349). The ecofacts have not been fully analyzed or reported to date.

The feature assemblage at Twin Ditch includes simple, unprepared hearths, artifact or tool caches, a possible structure, an ocher concentration, a possible smudge pit or shallow basin, and artifact accumulations of varying size, depth, and composition. Shallow hearths ranging from .5 to 1.5 m in diameter and from 3 to 5 cm thick, accompanied by adjacent clean-out areas composed of charcoal and ash, were distributed in a linear fashion along the low crest of the early Holocene paleosol surface. "These hearth areas were routinely circled by moderate-to-dense concentrations of stone tools and tool fragments, chipped stone manufacturing debris, and faunal remains" (Morrow 1996:347–348). Immediately west of these features, a possible house floor, measuring approximately 2.0–2.5 m in diameter, was indicated by an oval-shaped arc of post molds. Task-specific activity areas are suggested by the distribution of artifacts and specialized features, such as the red-ocher stain, which may denote hide working.

The upland-oriented Theban components at Kewanee, Wesley Dedert, and Boyd exhibit a much simpler site structure compared with Twin Ditch, generally composed of only one or a few closely spaced concentrations of flintknapping debris and associated tools and artifacts. These sites typically produce few formal tools, no animal bone, and little charcoal and have failed to provide evidence for purposefully constructed facilities. However, various forms of open-air degradation may mitigate against the preservation or identification of shallow surface hearths in upland settings. The former locations of hearths can sometimes be deduced by the distribution of burned debitage and tools (e.g., Hansen 1994; Nolan 1994a), but this type of analysis has not been undertaken on these particular site components.

Although generally similar in its overall character and content, the Cochran 10 Boreal component diverges somewhat from the pattern identified at the other upland components, which may simply be a function of the larger area that was excavated (> 1,000 m^2). The Theban component(s) at Cochran 10 is composed of at least three separate buried activity areas, each comprising several closely spaced concentrations of flaking debris of varying size and density. These arcing or semicircular concentrations of chert are primary refuse deposits that appear to denote the locations of individual flintknappers, who apparently worked in close proximity to one another. Each activity area produced Theban diagnostics and was separated from adjacent loci by 15–20 m of relatively open and artifact-free space (Hansen and Nolan 1998:Figure 10). Given the wide spacing between the various occupation or activity loci, Hansen and Nolan suggest the site was serially used on at least three different occasions during the period when St. Charles and Thebes points/knives were made. No purposefully constructed facilities were identified, suggesting the site was task specific and used for relatively brief periods of time in each instance.

Small concentrations of tools or artifacts have been reported from both Twin Ditch and Cochran 10. The former site produced three later-stage bifaces and another cluster consisting of two complete Thebes knives, an intact adze, and a hammerstone (Morrow 1989:11). Cochran 10 yielded several concentrations of apparently unused or lightly used cobbles and minimally flaked chert (Hansen and Nolan 1998:307), suggestive of intentional caching of tool-fabrication materials. In each instance, these materials appear to have been stored in anticipation of future site revisits and use, suggesting both Cochran 10 and Twin Ditch were "persistent places" (sensu Schlanger 1992:92) in regional Theban settlement systems. However, the sites clearly represent markedly different occupation types, Twin Ditch a seasonal floodplain base camp and Cochran 10 a temporary upland encampment focused on tool refurbishment and maintenance.

While an exceptionally large database exists for examining the spatial distribution of Theban diagnostics in western Illinois (e.g., Conrad 1981, 1986d, 1987; Fishel et al. 2004; Nolan 2004; Nolan and Graham 2003), little appreciable information is available about the various site types that make up the settlement pattern. Generally, only a small number of artifacts can be confidently associated with the recovered Theban points because relatively few unmixed or substantive surface collections are available; multicomponency is a serious limitation. Few sites in the region have produced multiple Theban points and other types of associated tools suggestive of residentially oriented use, although Twin Ditch is an example of this type of site. Thus, little information exists about what types of sites are represented, in a functional sense, and how they articulate with others in the region. The relative homogeneity of site types implied by survey data certainly masks significant functional and chronological variability that is critical to the assessment of the Theban settlement pattern. However, several salient observations can be offered on the basis of these data sets.

First, the number of Theban sites is markedly higher than the numbers of earlier Dalton and Boreal side-notched components. Conrad (1987:196, 283) calculates a seventeenfold increase in the number of points and a thirteenfold increase in the number of sites in the upland portion of the study area during the Boreal period. Nolan (2004), using a more culturally and geographically restricted sample, notes the number of Theban components is more than double the number of recorded Dalton components in the Mississippi Valley uplands of Adams and Hancock counties. Conrad (1981:33, 1987:196–197) interprets this as evidence for a dramatic rise in population made possible by the changing composition of the region's deciduous forests and a concomitant rise in nut mast. The pronounced spike in Boreal-period component frequency may or may not reflect population growth, but it almost certainly is a by-product of intensive reuse of persistent places (sensu Hansen and Nolan 1998) within a geographically bounded home range. Thus, the larger number of Theban components (and Kirk; see below) relative to the bracketing temporal spans may be more indicative of differing settlement patterns than increasing or fluctuating population, although it could easily be a function of both.

Second, several lines of evidence indicate that Theban peoples used the regional landscape in a manner that was qualitatively different from earlier Dalton peoples. While Dalton sites of various types are typically found in close proximity to the larger stream courses that traverse the study area, Theban components are less frequently found in these areas but, instead, are commonly recorded some distance from permanent water sources, on principal divides and relatively level upland expanses that were historically covered by prairie (Nolan 2004). These locations appear to have generally been avoided by Dalton and later Archaic peoples, suggesting Theban peoples had larger and less bounded home ranges than their predecessors or successors. Additional evidence for greater Theban mobility, and perhaps home-range size, can be found in the use of exotic cherts, noted above. The sources of these materials suggest that regional populations had some type of regular, albeit perhaps infrequent, contact with areas located 150–350 km to the north and south, whereas Dalton chert use appears to have been much more regionally focused, with a more northerly orientation.

The recovery near Macomb (see above) of an eastern Theban point variant manufactured from an Indiana chert type may indicate that limited forays were undertaken in the study region by different social groups based east of the Illinois Valley, once again suggesting that rather expansive territories were exploited by Boreal peoples as part of their seasonal round. Given this, we wonder whether some or all of the points of southern Illinois chert (Cobden/Dongola, Crescent, and Dover/Elco) also could relate to hunting losses or tool discard by nonlocal Theban social groups based outside of the study region. Most of these examples are St. Charles points rather than Thebes knives, which may reinforce the view that the former were used principally as projectiles and were therefore subject to more frequent loss. Theban-cluster points manufactured from northern cherts, especially Moline, are found as far south as the northern bluff line of the Sny Bottom in the Mississippi Valley but occur most frequently in the central and northern portions of the study area (e.g., Conrad 1987; Nolan 2004). These distributional data suggest that northern chert sources may have been more regularly exploited by a regionally based population with a home range that extended for 150–250 km, which seems to be more in line with that postulated for other contemporary midwestern groups (Cantin 1994). If this is accurate, then we expect that the eastern and southern fringes of the study area may be located at or near the interface of other Boreal-period band territories.

Geographic Distribution. Theban sites have a wide geographic distribution in western Illinois, and Theban bifaces are frequently the most commonly recovered diagnostics encountered in upland surveys (Conrad 1981; Fishel et al. 2004; Nolan 2004). These components have a much more restricted distribution in the major river valleys, which no doubt reflects floodplain aggradation and site burial. However, Theban components are not well represented on the sandy late Pleistocene terraces of the Lima Lake locality (Nolan 2004), despite heavy use of these high, stable landforms during much of the Archaic period. The majority of the Thebes points found in this area have been dredged out of what are today low-lying floodplain deposits, perhaps signaling the presence of buried site locations similar to Twin Ditch. In contrast, Theban components appear to be more common on the surface of ancient floodplain features in the Illinois Valley (Fishel et al. 2004; Moffat et al. 2001:Table 4; Munson and Harn 1966:Figure 3a, b; Nolan et al. 1992:7–14; Stafford 1989:Table 3.19), although this observation should be regarded as impressionistic because fewer relevant collections from the Illinois Valley have been systematically examined.

Kirk Horizon

(9300–8800 B.P., cal 8500–7900 B.C.)

This Boreal cultural tradition may have been partially contemporaneous with, but also clearly postdated, portions of the Theban horizon, raising the possibility that different social or ethnic groups occupied western Illinois at roughly the same time. However, the lack of regional Kirk dates is problematic; our dating of this cultural complex relies on stratigraphic information and radiocarbon assays derived from areas located south and east of the study area (Broyles 1971; J. Chapman 1975, 1977, 1985; Coe 1964; Collins 1979). Evidence from these stratified sites suggests the earliest Kirk forms (e.g., Charleston, Plevna, Lost Lake, etc.) are the most Theban-like, exhibiting alternate blade beveling and heavily ground bases (Kimball 1996:157–159). Kimball (1996:157–159) and others have identified a tentative chronological, and perhaps developmental, sequence for the southeastern Kirk tradition by cross-referencing trends that are evident in the region's stratified sites. This sequence is, from earliest to latest, Lower Kirk (Theban variants), Kirk Corner Notched Small Variety (Palmer/Neuberger), Kirk Corner Notched Large Variety (Stilwell) (Figure 13.11), and various bifurcated-base points, which generally diminished in size through time (St. Albans/MacCorkle to LeCroy to Kanawha). The bifurcated-base points supplanted Kirk as the dominant hafted-biface forms sometime around 8800 B.P. (Chapman 1985).

Early Kirk variants, such as Charleston, have not been reported from western Illinois but apparently occur in the American Bottom (Higgins 1990:Plate 14). Slightly later Kirk Corner Notched forms are found in abundance in the study region and appear to be very similar to those recovered from southern and eastern sites. Thus, the western Illinois Kirk sequence may be foreshortened compared with that of the southeastern Kirk heartland, perhaps indicating actual minimal temporal overlap with regional Theban populations,

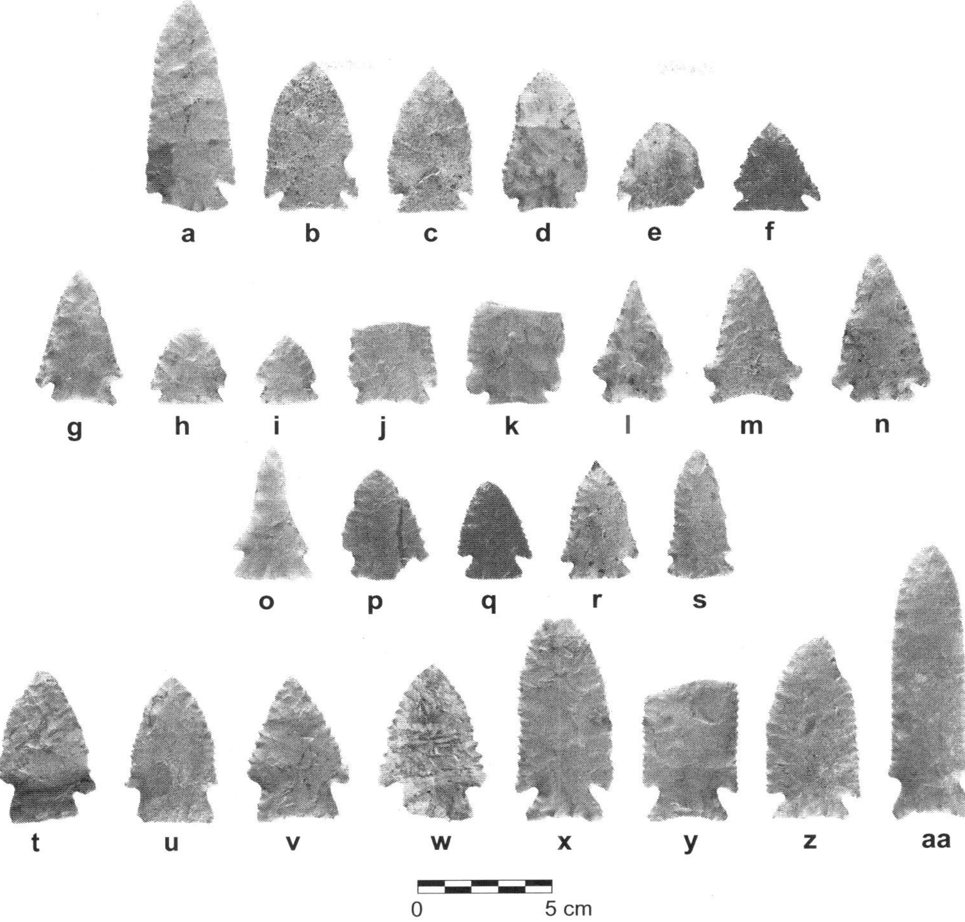

Figure 13.11. Kirk-horizon points: a–j, Neuberger; k–n, Decatur; o–s, Kirk Corner Notched Small Variety; t–w, Kirk Corner Notched Large Variety; x–aa, Stilwell.

who probably were present in the region prior to the influx of Kirk peoples, technology, or ideas.

Some stratigraphic evidence for the temporal priority of Theban-cluster points was found at the Twin Ditch site. Horizon 1, which is separated from the underlying Theban deposits (Horizon 2) by a .3- to .5-m-thick layer of sterile alluvial sand, is perched on a deflated, buried early Holocene terrace that produced a wide range of Boreal- and Atlantic-period points, including nine Kirks, during limited test excavations (Morrow 1989:3). Associated radiocarbon dates are lacking from Horizon 1, however. These data minimally suggest that at least some of the Kirk-cluster points were produced later than Theban forms; this interpretation is strengthened by the recovery of Kirk points in ca. 9000 B.P. contexts at the nearby Koster site (Brown and Vierra 1983:181–182). Given these data, we tentatively date the regional Kirk horizon between 9300 and 8800 B.P., pending the availability of local radiocarbon dates from unmixed contexts. Although the possibility remains that the various Kirk subtypes were used for relatively restricted periods of time relative to the type cluster's overall duration of use in the Boreal period, they generally are considered together in the following discussions for the sake of brevity.

Tools and Other Artifacts. As is the case with most Archaic-period cultural complexes, projectile points and knives are the most distinctive Kirk artifacts (Figure 13.11). A variety of named subtypes are included in our Kirk cluster, including both small and large varieties of Kirk Corner Notched (Coe 1964:69–70) (Figure 13.11o–w), Neuberger (Conrad 1981) (Figure 13.11a–j), Decatur (Cambron 1957:17) (Figure 13.11k–n), and Stilwell (Justice 1987:72–77; Perino 1970:119–121) (Figure 13.11x–aa). Western Illinois Kirk points can be distinguished from Theban-cluster variants by their distinctive form, thinner cross sections, more broadly or openly corner-notched haft elements, less heavily ground bases, and more markedly serrated blades, which were typically resharpened using patterned bifacial retouch rather than alternate beveling.

Decatur points, however, which are perhaps the least common Kirk variant in the study area (see below), were resharpened in a more Theban-like fashion that resulted in alternately beveled blade edges. These points also exhibit distinctively truncated or burinated barbs and bases that are not characteristic of other midwestern Kirk forms but that are similar to attributes observed on some St. Charles points from Kentucky (Perino 1985:101). In addition, Decatur and St. Charles are the two types of points found in the study area that are most frequently manufactured from Hixton silicified sandstone, the most distant tool stone represented in regional Boreal-period collections. These data could suggest that Decatur points were contemporary with or descendant from St. Charles. Evidence from the deeply stratified sites in the Southeast is inconclusive in this regard because relatively few Decatur points have been recovered and they occur in a wide variety of strata and contexts (J. Chapman 1975, 1977).

In addition to projectile points, the Kirk tool kit is composed of typical Boreal-period chipped-stone implements, including bifaces, preforms, adzes, end scrapers, and other flake tools. Few of these tools have been found in direct association with Kirk points in the study region, so few specific details about the technology can be forwarded at this time. Both bifaces and expedient cores appear to have been used to produce the flake blanks that were ultimately used to manufacture formal tools (cf. Nolan 1993, 2004), however. End scrapers tend to be teardrop shaped to nearly rectangular but vary considerably in size and outline form, depending on the degree of use and resharpening. In general, Kirk preforms appear to be more rectangular shaped and thinner than Theban point blanks, although smaller, more oval-shaped, refined bifaces of unknown function have also been recovered with Kirk points (Nolan 1995:Figure 3.24g, i, and m). Nolan (1995:242) depicts a complete EH adze recovered in close association with Kirk artifacts and describes the butt of another fragmentary example from the same deposit, but these artifacts are not sufficiently distinctive to differentiate them from others made during the Boreal and Pre-Boreal periods.

The chipped-stone tools used by Kirk people generally were manufactured from medium- to higher-grade examples of regionally available chert types, although points made from both northern and southern exotic sources have been found in low numbers throughout western Illinois. As mentioned previously, Decatur points, which are the rarest of the regional Kirk variants, are the only examples manufactured from Hixton silicified sandstone, the most distant source represented in the Boreal sample. Of the fewer than a dozen Kirk Corner Notched points manufactured from southern Illinois Cobden/Dongola chert, one was recovered from intact subsoil contexts at the Serpentine Ridge site (11A1165 [Nolan 2004]) in the Bear Creek drainage (see below). Moline chert was frequently used in the northern half of the study area, including at sites located 100 km beyond where it typically outcrops. Similar patterns of use are evident for Payson and LaMoine River cherts (Conrad 1987; Nolan 2004; Nolan and Hansen 1995) as well as some distinctive varieties of Burlington/Keokuk chert, such as the purple-blue mottled material from sources near St. Augustine in Knox County and Stronghurst in Henderson County.

Settlement and Subsistence Data. As alluded to above, no substantive excavated Kirk assemblages have been reported from the region. Nonetheless, important information has been recovered as a result of several small-scale test excavation projects and the extensive survey and collector interview work that has been undertaken in the area. The only subsurface features that can arguably be demonstrated to relate to Kirk occupation were found at the Roberts site (11A1029), which is located in southeastern Adams County (Kruger 1988), and Cadwell #3 (11HA679), located in the LaMoine basin west of Macomb (Nolan 1991b). However, in each case the associations are not particularly strong, since multiple EH point types were found in the subsurface deposits at Cadwell and none were directly associated with the sub-plow-zone remains at Roberts.

Two subsurface lithic concentrations were encountered at the Roberts site: Feature 1 was dominated by fire-cracked rock (FCR) and interpreted as the remains of a rock hearth (< 1 m^2); Feature 2 was similar in size but was poorly defined and produced apparently unburned rough rock and chert (Kruger 1988:9–10). A possible Kirk point found in the backdirt was the only diagnostic recovered from the site, but its association with Features 1 and 2 cannot be empirically demonstrated. Cadwell #3 is a multicomponent, buried upland site that exhibits some weak evidence that cultural stratigraphy may be preserved (Nolan 1991b). The lowermost Archaic-period remains were discovered in the EB soil horizon and consisted of scattered flaking debris and two lithic concentrations: a tight cluster of FCR (< .5 m^2) interpreted as a hearth and a possible cobble-tool cache comprising a pitted anvil, a hammerstone, and a coarse-grained igneous stone found piled together. These same deposits produced the blade of a sizable, heavily serrated large Kirk variant, the medial portion of another untyped, notched, early point, and the concave, eared base of a well-made lanceolate (Titus/Angostura cognate), although none of these points were found in relatively close proximity to the two lithic features (Nolan 1991b:92). Clearly, neither site provides much tangible information about the nature of regional Kirk occupations.

However, two multicomponent sites recorded in the Bear Creek drainage basin as part of the Illinois Route 336/96 project in Adams County, Serpentine Ridge (11A1165) and Tuttle (11A1059), have produced spatially discrete Kirk assemblages. A relatively tight concentration of Kirk artifacts was discovered on the shoulder of a narrow, high terrace remnant or bluff spur at Serpentine Ridge during Phase II testing (Nolan 1995:225–244). Although most of these remains were plow disturbed, a Cobden/Dongola-chert Kirk Corner Notched point, a distolaterally retouched Burlington-chert end scraper, and small amounts of debitage manufactured from similar types of high-quality regional cherts were recovered from subsurface contexts in the EB–BE soil horizon. The other materials were confined to a 112-m^2 area surrounding the intact remains, suggesting these artifacts were plowed directly out of this same deposit. The plow-disturbed remains include a pitted granitic anvil or mano, three medium-sized subrectangular to subovoid-shaped bifaces or preforms, a complete EH chert adze, the butt portion of another similar adze, a small projectile point tang fragment, several invasively retouched flakes, and low amounts of debitage, all manufactured from relatively fine-grained varieties of Burlington/Keokuk chert except the adze butt, which is an unidentified brown, lower-grade chert (Salem?). The relative abundance and diversity of recovered tool types at Serpentine Ridge is rather remarkable considering the small area involved and its low overall material density.

In contrast, the Tuttle site, which is located on a prominent upland divide far from permanent water sources, produced a sharply bounded heavy-density scatter of lithic debris and tools. This linearly oriented surface scatter (240-m^2 area) was subjected to a nonsystematic collection followed by a comprehensive point-provenienced pick-up the following year. These collections produced two similar Kirk Corner Notched points, two preforms, several biface fragments in various stages of manufacture, a possible adze preform, five flake end scrapers, a crude side scraper, other informal or expedient flake tools, and an abundance of manufacturing waste (cores, debitage, and an igneous hammerstone) attributable to locally available chert sources (Nolan 1993:99).

Although the Tuttle assemblage is rather diverse, formal tools are infrequent relative to number of pieces of debitage (1:85 formal-tool-to-debitage ratio; 1:40 overall tool-to-debitage ratio), which contrasts with the pattern observed at Serpentine Ridge (1:7 formal-tool-to-debitage ratio; 1:5 overall tool-to-debitage ratio). However, both curated and expedient tool technologies are in evidence at each site. The curated tools are consistently made from higher grades of Burlington/Keokuk chert or exotic materials, suggesting they were produced elsewhere and were discarded on-site only after they were exhausted or broken. Conversely, the early-stage bifaces, cores, and most of the debitage from Tuttle probably were produced on-site since these artifacts are primarily made from the same lower- to medium-grade, local variety of chert (Nolan 2004). The small size of the Tuttle Kirk component and signature of the recovered remains suggest the site is more likely the product of some types of intensive, short-term logistical activities (e.g., retooling) than of habitation per se. The lower tool-to-debitage ratio in evidence at Serpentine Ridge indicates it may be an altogether different type of site, perhaps representing a more residentially oriented individual household or camp.

Although possible residentially oriented Kirk sites have generally proven difficult to identify during regional survey, they apparently are not restricted to the larger stream or river valleys. Site 11MD1001 was discovered on a flattened upland expanse north of Macomb, near the headwater reaches of a small, dry stream course that formerly traversed a low, relatively sheltered setting between several prominent glacial-drift ridges (Nolan et al. 1997:40, 42–43). The site has been surface collected on two different occasions, each time under excellent conditions, as part of separate investigations for the IDOT-sponsored Macomb Bypass project (Nolan and Graham 2003; Nolan et al. 1997). As a result, nearly 800 artifacts have been recovered from the site's surface, including three Kirk Corner Notched points, several other untyped EH point fragments, nearly 20 fragmentary and whole bifaces in various stages of manufacture (including one LaMoine River–chert preform and another indeterminate exotic specimen), a wide variety of flake tools, including multiple examples of end scrapers, side scrapers, burins, gravers, and spokeshaves; at least 20 cores; abundant debitage; six cobble fabricating tools; two ocher fragments; and a few pieces of FCR.

The scatter density, size (> 11,000 m^2), and overall tool diversity of 11MD1001 contrast markedly with other sites found in the surrounding area, which generally can be characterized as small, ephemeral early Holocene lithic scatters or special-purpose sites, such as hunting, hide-processing, and butchering loci (Nolan and Graham 2003). Relative to most of these locations, 11MD1001 is positioned lower on the rolling till-plain landscape, in a relatively sheltered setting blocked from the prevailing winds by ridged drift that rises 10 or more meters above the site elevation in each direction. Considered together, these data suggest the site may have been a durable residential site of some type, perhaps a seasonal field or base camp (sensu Binford 1980). If so, some of the outlying special-purpose sites, several of which produced Kirk points, may represent activities that were undertaken or provisioned from 11MD1001 or another nearby habitation.

Most of the other Kirk components that have been recorded in western Illinois either have not produced comparable assemblages or are hopelessly mixed as a result of multicomponent aboriginal use. Thus, the available survey data are best suited for simple distribution studies. We briefly summarize and expand on several salient observations made by Conrad (1981, 1987) and Nolan (2004) on the basis of the distribution of Kirk components in western Illinois. First, Kirk points are as common as those of the Theban cluster in western Illinois, which may denote a spike in, or maintenance of, Boreal-period population levels relative to those of the Pre-Boreal Dalton and Early Side-Notched horizons. However, Nolan (2004) found fewer Kirk points than Theban-cluster diagnostics in areas historically dominated by prairie on the Mississippi slope; in his sample, Kirk points generally appear to be more common in formerly forested upland locales located closer to tributary streams or on terraces and other elevated features in the major stream and river valleys, much like earlier Dalton components. However, Conrad's (1987) regionwide data suggest this distribution is either a localized phenomenon or reflects sampling error because Kirks are commonly found on the prairies to the east of the Mississippi slope. Neuberger appears to be the Kirk variant that is found most frequently in remote upland settings, perhaps signifying that diachronic differences in landscape use or natural vegetation or both occurred during the period when Kirk points were made.

Second, subtle differences in the use of exotic cherts by Kirk and Theban populations may provide information about possible variation in landscape use and home-range size or territoriality (Nolan 2004), although the samples are admittedly small. In general, Kirk points made from exotic or extralocal chert appear to be less common, emanate from fewer identifiable sources, and do not seem to have been discarded or lost as far from procurement locations as Theban points. This could relate to technology as much as settlement pattern or home-range size, although the two probably were inextricably related. While points of both type clusters represent heavily curated tools (sensu Binford 1979), Kirks generally are thinner on average than their Theban counterparts and were serially resharpened in a manner that typically resulted in more rapid blade-width reduction than produced by the alternate-beveling technique (e.g., Christenson 1977; Sollberger 1971). Given this, Kirk points may have been exhausted more rapidly and could, therefore, be expected to have entered the archaeological record much closer to source areas than Theban-cluster points made from the same materials; such eventualities probably were accounted for in local settlement systems.

The distribution scenario just sketched for exotic Kirk-cluster points may also hold for Stilwell and Neuberger points, all of which have so far been identified as manufactured from cherts that outcrop in the study region (no obvious extraregional southern or northern exotic sources are represented). All of the Payson-chert Stilwell points that we are aware of have been recovered within 50 km of the known Adams County source (cf. Nolan and Hansen 1995). They are even closer to a putative but yet-unsubstantiated Brown County source of this material. The Payson-chert Neuberger points from the Mississippi Valley were found similar distances (< 60 km) from the known source; some examples, however, occur in the Illinois drainage, much further afield (140–150 km). Few Theban-cluster points were manufactured from this material, although the examples that are known seem to have been discarded at similar, relatively short, distances from the primary source.

In contrast, regional Theban-cluster points manufactured from Dover/Elco, Moline, and Prairie du Chien cherts have been recovered 200–250 km from the known source areas; the few examples of Kirk points made from Moline have been found approximately 100–125 km from the source area. These data suggest that some regional Kirk populations were exploiting smaller, yet geographically overlapping, areas compared with those of Theban people, who may have had more extensive and differently oriented home ranges or settlement areas. This suggestion may be supported by apparent evidence for greater use of southern exotic cherts, like Cobden/Dongola, by regional Kirk populations than by Theban groups, although both samples are admittedly quite small. Whatever their meaning, the differences noted between the Kirk and Theban traditions may extend beyond mere technology and settlement systems, perhaps indicating significant social distinctions, as well.

Geographic Distribution. Kirk points are exceptionally common and occur throughout western Illinois, much like their Theban counterparts. However, some of the distinctive subtypes appear to have more restricted geographic distributions. For example, the classic Stilwell point, the largest and perhaps most recent Kirk variant, appears to be most common along the Illinois drainage in the southeastern part of the study area. Examples manufactured from Payson chert have been reported in Schuyler and Brown counties (Nolan and Hansen 1995:312–313, Table 4.4), whereas numerous Burlington/Keokuk-chert specimens have been observed in these same areas as well as in the eastern half of Pike County (e.g., Stafford and Nolan 1990). Stilwell points occur rarely along the Mississippi drainage north of Quincy (see Nolan 2004) and have not been identified in the HSS collections at WIU or collections from the Illinois 29 surveys in the northern part of the central Illinois Valley (Fishel et al. 2004). Additionally, Nolan does not recall observing them in any of the private collections he examined from Macomb northward.

As mentioned above, Decatur points are quite rare in all parts of western Illinois but have a distribution that appears to be heavily skewed toward the east-southeastern part of the study area. The majority of these are made from Burlington/Keokuk cherts, although at least five Hixton-silicified-sandstone Decatur points have been documented from the area. Three Hixton Decatur points were observed in three separate private collections amassed from upland portions of the LaMoine drainage in northern Schuyler and southern McDonough counties (Nolan, pers. obs. 1995). Two other examples have been reported, a black specimen from the Copperas Creek drainage and another classic example from the Spoon River drainage (Conrad 1987:156–157). Conrad (1982:28, Appendix B, Figure 2f, 1987:156–157) reports 26 Decatur points manufactured from regional cherts have been found along the West Branch of Duck Creek (n = 1), the central Spoon River drainage (n = 21, including multiple examples from several sites), the upper portion of the Sugar Creek drainage (n = 2), and the central LaMoine basin (n = 2), although only a few of these exhibit burinated margins. Two classic Decatur points (Figure 13.11k, l) have been found by an avocational archaeologist at the Kathay site on the LaMoine River bluff in southwestern McDonough County, and two others have been reported from eastern Pike County, one from the bluff top of McKee Creek (Stafford and Nolan 1990:Table 3.3). A less confidently typed specimen with a distinctive alternate right-hand bevel was noted in a private collection amassed from the Rock Creek drainage in Adams County; this is the only possible example of the type documented west of the LaMoine basin in the study area.

In contrast, Neuberger points, which Conrad (1981) views as a regional Decatur variant, appear to be widely distributed throughout the study area, much like the more generalized small and large varieties of Kirk Corner Notched. Neuberger points are commonly found in the Mississippi drainage (Conrad 1987; Nolan 2004), unlike Decatur points, which appear to be either completely absent or poorly represented at best. Although they appear to be more geographically widespread, Neuberger points have a distribution similar to that of the NMV Dalton variant, as previously noted.

Hardin Horizon
(9000–8500 B.P., cal 8250–7550 B.C.)

This cultural tradition is typified by well-made stemmed bifaces (Figure 13.12) that appear to be eastern, or Prairie Peninsula, correlates of Scottsbluff points, which form part of the Cody complex on the Great Plains and in the western

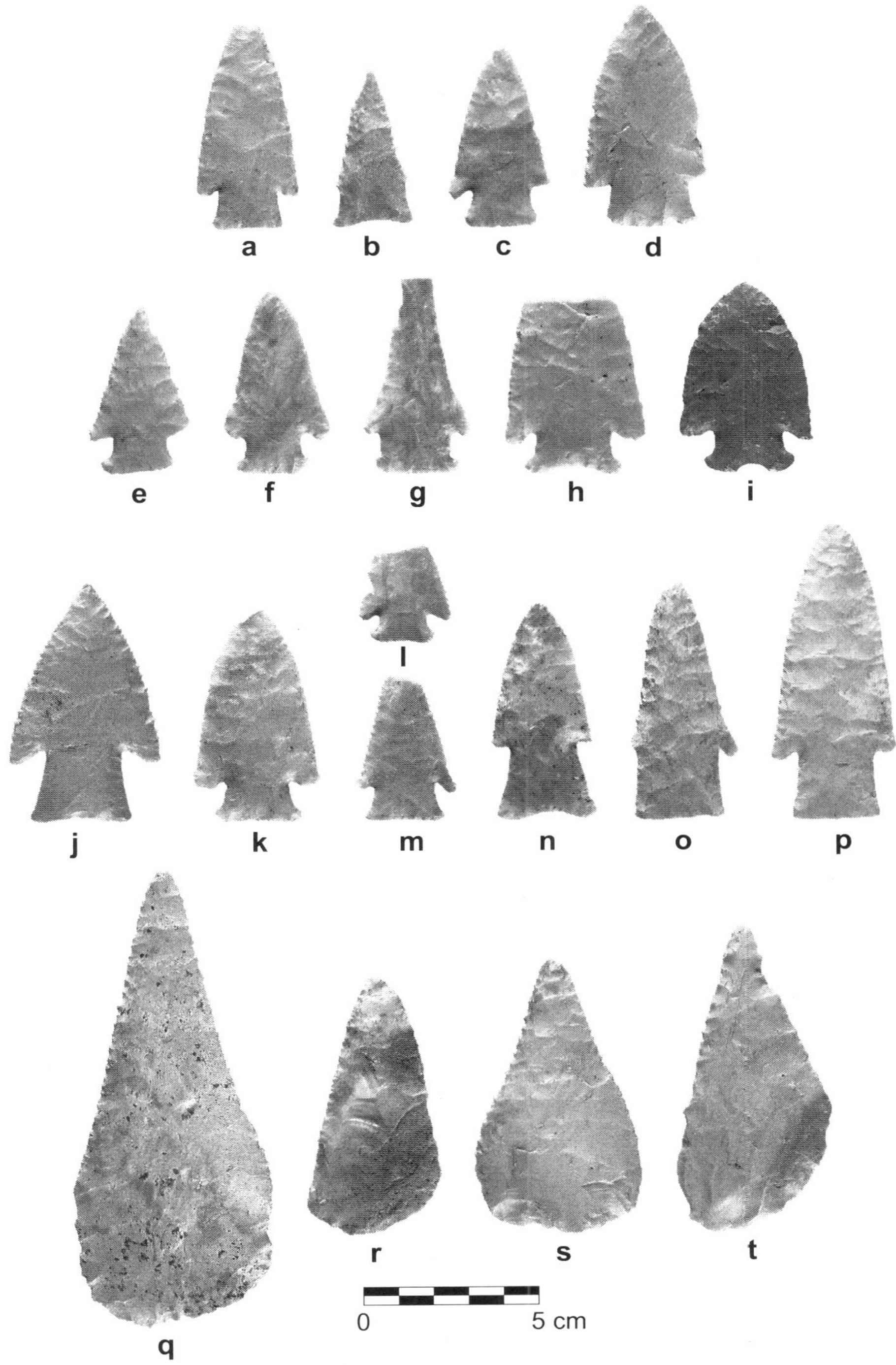

Figure 13.12. Hardin-horizon artifacts: a–d, short-stemmed variety; e–i, eared-base variety; j–n, expanded-notched variety; o, p, long-stemmed variety; q–t, Bass knives.

Great Lakes area (Irwin 1971; Luchterhand 1970; Munson 1967). Although the chronological position of Hardin Barbed points has not been directly established by radiocarbon dates, those that are available for Scottsbluff, ca. 9000–8500 RCYBP (Frison 1978:23, 33–34; Irwin 1971; Irwin-Williams et al. 1973), appear to be reasonable age estimates. The general contemporaneity of the two point types has been established at the Bass site in southwestern Wisconsin, an extensive single-component Galena-chert quarry and workshop site, where examples of both Hardin Barbed and Scottsbluff were found in the same stratigraphically "sealed" upland context (Behm 1985:47–48).

Hardin Barbed points exhibit a variety of stemmed basal configurations, although their morphology, flaking, heavy haft grinding, and use of alternate blade beveling suggest they are technologically "Theban." The close morphological relationship between some St. Charles and Hardin points has long been noted by Perino (1985:170, 277) and other professional and avocational archaeologists, and "hybrid" forms (e.g., "Hardoves") (Figure 13.10l, m) that appear to be intermediate in overall form between the two types have been repeatedly observed in collections from western Illinois. These data suggest that Hardin Barbed points may derive from an ancestral Theban form. As previously mentioned, the Twin Ditch site in the lower Illinois Valley provides stratigraphic evidence for the primacy of Thebes knives and St. Charles points relative to Hardin and Kirk forms (Morrow 1989:3).

Tools and Other Artifacts. Hardin Barbed points (Perino 1985:170–171; Scully 1951) are the most diagnostic artifacts attributable to this Boreal-period tradition. However, evidence from the Bass site suggests that a distinctive unnotched knife form (Figure 13.12q–t), named after this site, can also be attributed to this cultural complex with confidence (Behm 1985:61–65). As mentioned above, a variety of basal configurations are evident within the Hardin Barbed point type. Behm (1985:39–42, 144–147), expanding on the work of Perino, Luchterhand (1970:27), and Conrad (1981:95–96, 102–105), identifies four Hardin varieties defined by distinctive haft configurations: Short Stemmed (Figure 13.12a–d), Long Stemmed (Figure 13.12o, p), Expanded Notched (Figure 13.12j–n), and Eared Base (Figure 13.12e–i). The first two varieties are distinguished entirely on the basis of haft length, with 15 mm the maximum length of the Short Stemmed specimens. Expanded Notched Hardins are identified by the presence of concave-sided, slightly flaring hafts, whereas Eared Base Hardins have small, distinct projections, or "feet," on both lateral margins at the base of the point (Behm 1985:144–147). All four varieties are present in western Illinois (see Conrad 1981:Plates 19, 20; Nolan and Hansen 1995:Figure 4.3, Table 4.4).

Although Hardin Barbed points were typically manufactured from Burlington/Keokuk cherts, regional exotic cherts were frequently used, most commonly Payson and Moline. Nolan and Hansen's (1995) study demonstrates that nearly 70 percent of the points manufactured from Payson chert can be classified as Hardin Barbed, and another 7 percent are related Bass knives. Fewer than 6 percent of all the Hardin Barbed points that Nolan and Hansen examined from western Illinois were made of Payson chert, suggesting it was a rather minor lithic source compared with the much more ubiquitous Burlington/Keokuk cherts. However, since over 95 percent of the points manufactured from Payson chert are attributable to various Early Archaic types, use of this raw material outside the source area is viewed as diagnostic of the Boreal period, in general, and Hardin occupations, in particular (Nolan and Hansen 1995).

As mentioned, Bass knives are distinctively large, oval to triangular-shaped implements that form a significant part of the Hardin tool kit (although they are perhaps not exclusive to that tool kit). These artifacts exhibit no evidence for hafting (i.e., edge grinding) but frequently display heavy alternate (left) blade beveling, suggesting they may have been handheld cutting tools. Although Bass knives generally were bifacially made, largely unifacial examples are also known (Behm 1985), including specimens manufactured from Payson chert (Fishel 1992; Nolan and Hansen 1995:Figure 4.4f). Since Hardin Barbed points probably functioned as both hafted projectiles and knives, Behm (1985:64–65) speculates that Bass knives were multipurpose sawing, cutting, and scraping tools.

Unifacial flake scrapers also form part of the Hardin tool kit but have generally proven difficult to consistently distinguish from other late Pleistocene and Boreal types. On the basis of the Bass site data, Behm (1985:65–67) notes that some exhibit bifacial flaking similar to that observed on earlier Paleoindian end scrapers; such flaking typically was undertaken to thin the bulb area to facilitate hafting but sometimes also covers the entire ventral surface. A variety of Payson-chert scrapers have been found in western Illinois, including double-bitted and distolateral end scrapers, teardrop-shaped unifacial end scrapers, side scrapers, and a broken EH adze recycled into a hafted end scraper (Nolan and Hansen 1995). Several other adzes have been found in association with Hardin materials (e.g., Behm 1985) but were apparently infrequently made of Payson chert, since only four examples are known, including two from a workshop adjacent to the source (Nolan and Hansen 1995:Tables 4.4, 4.5). Of the aggregate Payson chert recovered from nonsource areas, more than half of the formal tools are projectile points, whereas generalized bifaces or preforms and various flake tools make up between a quarter and a third of the total each. By extension, these data suggest that Hardin tool kits were strongly oriented toward a bifacial technology, much like potentially ancestral Theban technologies.

Settlement and Subsistence Data. No incontrovertible Hardin sites have been excavated in the study area, although several buried upland scatters that produced Payson chert or other distinctive artifacts appear relevant to discussions of settlement and subsistence. Chief among these is the Dittmer site (11A1252), which was located on a narrow ridge spur associated with the Mendon Moraine, a high interior landform historically covered by tallgrass prairie that was used almost exclusively during the early Holocene period (Nolan 2004; Nolan and Hickson 1992). Hardin Barbed points and Bass knives as well as Payson- and Moline-chert artifacts have been recovered from sites found atop this moraine, which extends from the Mississippi rapids near Keokuk into southeastern Adams County close to the Payson source area, suggesting it may have been used as a favored route for inland travel (Nolan 2004).

The Dittmer site was excavated as part of the Route 336 project and produced the remains of three contiguous but spatially separate subsurface lithic concentrations (Nolan 1994a, 2003). Given the distance between adjacent clusters (ca. 20 m), it is unlikely that these activity areas relate to a single occupational event. Rather, they appear to be products of similar short-term, serial uses of this landform. However, some shared assemblage characteristics suggest these features are the products of technologically, and perhaps culturally or temporally, related occupations. Each cluster produced evidence for the production or use of expedient tools from locally available chert cobbles as well as high-quality, late-stage chert detritus probably derived from sharpening curated tools (Hansen 1994). Payson chert made up 25 percent of the site's surface assemblage and was recovered from both the northern and western lithic concentrations. Burlington and Moline cherts were also recovered from subsurface and plow-zone contexts near these two scatters. The southernmost scatter produced an expedient cobble-chert end scraper, Burlington-chert sharpening flakes, and carbonized nutshell. A black-walnut fragment from the southern artifact concentration was submitted for AMS dating and returned a calibrated intercept of 7500 B.C. (ISGS-A0004).

This date corroborates the suspected Boreal-period age of the remains and is attributable to a temporal span when, comparative data suggest, Hardin Barbed and large bifurcate points or knives were in vogue. Given the presence of Payson and Moline cherts on-site, the potential Hardin Barbed association at Dittmer is particularly compelling. Nolan (2004) documents that Hardin Barbed points are by far the most frequent points manufactured from Payson (11 of 14 instances) and Moline (8 of 11 instances) cherts in the uplands surrounding the site; no exotic-chert bifurcated-base points were recorded during the Route 336 project, and they occur in extremely low numbers across all of western Illinois (see below). While a direct association is obviously lacking, the cal 7500 B.C. date from Dittmer is the closest to an actual Hardin date currently available from the Midwest.

Several other sites discovered as part of this same project provide additional information about possible Hardin site types and landscape use. The Curtis Asher site (11HA748), located at the margin of the Mendon Moraine near Warsaw, produced a tightly concentrated (1,000 m^2), apparently single-component scatter. Two walkovers of the site resulted in the recovery of a functionally diverse assemblage, including a terminally resharpened (awl-like) Short Stemmed Hardin manufactured from Moline chert, a fragmentary Bass knife, two side scrapers, an end scraper, several subrectangular preform fragments, and a unidirectional core, all of Burlington chert, as well as a small amount of high-quality chert debitage, including several examples of Payson chert and an unidentified dark gray-blue fossiliferous (Pennsylvanian?) material (Nolan 1991a:17–26). The relatively high tool-to-debitage ratio (1:6), small site size, and diversity of discarded implements suggest the Curtis Asher site represents the remains of some type of residential site. This site appears to have been used in a markedly different fashion than Dittmer, despite both sites' remote landform settings and the presence of the same general suite of exotic materials.

The multicomponent Voss #3 site (11A1244), located several kilometers southeast of Dittmer on the same high moraine crest, may represent an altogether different type of landform use, having produced four Hardin Barbed points (three largely complete examples, including one of Moline) during a single walkover and a Bass knife on a subsequent site visit. Several Kirk-cluster points and exotic varieties of chert debitage (Payson, Moline, LaMoine, and Cobden/Dongola) were also recovered during these walkovers, but few EH end scrapers or other bifaces or tools aside from knives or projectiles (one biface fragment of possible Crescent chert was recovered). A similar site occupies a high drift ridge located south of Macomb in the Willow Creek drainage. Multiple walkovers of that site under excellent survey conditions have resulted in the recovery of a dozen largely complete Hardin Barbed points, but little debitage and relatively few other tools have been observed or collected. Several additional productive Hardin sites have been identified elsewhere on the apex of this same landform and on ridge spurs located along its margins.

The Willow Creek and Voss #3 sites are both situated on some of the highest topography found in their respective areas, on long, linear landforms adjacent to chert sources that were frequently used by Hardin people (Mendon Moraine: Payson; Willow Creek: Burlington/Keokuk). These data suggest to us that Hardin (and other EH) people serially revisited such locations while traveling through the upland interior along the principal divides. However, little basic habitation debris occurs on these sites; projectile points, some of which appear to be in usable condition, are the predominant artifact type recovered from these locations (perhaps cached in these settings in anticipation of future use?). Given the prominence of points, the sites do not appear to be strictly residential in nature; they may represent temporary rendezvous areas where disparate groups of hunters met to coordinate activities.

Spent or broken projectile points are also frequently recovered from various quarry and workshop sites distributed across the study area and are often manufactured from materials different from those actually procured at these locations. While this pattern occurs at sites dating throughout the Boreal period, Hardin points occur in unusually large numbers at some of these locations. For example, at least 32

Hardin Barbed points have been found at one of the Payson workshops (Nolan and Hansen 1995), and several sites located at or near the "Avon quarries" have produced from 11 to 22 specimens apiece (Conrad 1987:182–183). A similar pattern of occurrence was observed at the Bass site in southwestern Wisconsin, where at least 37 Hardin Barbed points are reported (Stoltman et al. 1984:202; also see Behm 1985:47). These data suggest that Hardin people either used some chert sources more frequently or more intensively than other EH peoples or that they employed widely different patterns of tool discard and replacement in the course of their seasonal round.

Although use of unspecified Burlington/Keokuk sources once again predominated, use of exotic cherts appears to have been more prevalent in the study area during the Hardin period than during the bracketing temporal spans. As a group, Hardin Barbed points display an unusually diverse array of colors, reflective of the exploitation of different regional and exotic chert sources. Hardin people may have been selecting cherts in part on the basis of their distinctive colors, although the represented source locations indicate these people had a bounded home range that did not regularly bring them into contact with some of the other colorful cherts that were exploited during earlier portions of the Boreal period. For example, we have not seen a single Hardin point of Hixton silicified sandstone or Cobden/Dongola chert from the study region,[2] although a possibly related Boreal (Bass) knife, identified by Toby Morrow as manufactured from southern Illinois Kaolin chert, was found on the surface of the Penstone (11PK727) site in Pike County (Sarah Studenmund, pers. comm. to Nolan 1998), near the southern extreme of our study area.

The most thoroughly documented use of a particular chert source area is of Payson, which is located southeast of Quincy in the upper reaches of several short-order tributaries to the Mississippi (Fishel 1992; Nolan and Hansen 1995). Payson-chert Hardin points or related Bass knives have been recorded from every county located on the Galesburg Plain west of the Illinois River except for those situated near the northern extreme (Rock Island, Henry, and Bureau) of the study area, where survey or collector information is most limited. The greatest numbers of Payson-chert Hardin points have been found within an approximately 125-km area located to the north and east of the known source, which is generally coincident with the northernmost sources of high-quality Burlington chert. This may suggest that an embedded form of chert procurement (sensu Binford 1979) played a significant role in shaping regional Hardin settlement.

Moline-chert Hardins are frequently found in the northern part of the study area as well as in the general vicinity of the Payson source area in Adams and Hancock counties (Nolan 2004). Curiously, none have been identified at any of the Payson workshop locations adjacent to the actual source (cf. Fishel 1992; Nolan and Hansen 1995). However, several exotic, Galena-chert specimens have been recovered from one of these workshop areas and a Payson-chert Hardin was found among Galena-chert workshop debris at the Bass site in southwestern Wisconsin (Toby Morrow, pers. comm. to Nolan 1991). We expect that Payson Hardins ultimately will be found or recognized near sources of Moline chert, but few firm data are available from this area at present (cf. Jones 1994). Nevertheless, several Payson-chert artifacts, including Hardin points, have been noted in both private and professional collections from Mercer, Rock Island, and Whiteside counties (Nolan, pers. obs. 2004), the area surrounding the Moline sources.

These exotic-chert data suggest possible reciprocal movement of Hardin people between northwestern Illinois and the southwestern portion of the study area. The apparent complementary distribution of Hardin points manufactured from Payson, Moline, and Galena cherts may denote the approximate northern boundaries of a distinctive regional-band or ethnic-group territory. Given the locations of these chert sources, this hypothesized territory could extend for approximately 250–300 km paralleling the Mississippi Valley and an unknown distance into the western Illinois interior, perhaps as far as the Illinois Valley itself, where Payson Hardins are also relatively common (see Nolan and Hansen 1995). The apparent absence of southern Illinois cherts from our Hardin sample appears significant in this respect and contrasts with the Theban and Kirk exotic-chert distributional data. This may suggest that regional Hardin populations had limited contact with areas located south of the study area or that they had settlement ranges with a more northerly focus than earlier Boreal populations.

However, we currently do not know how to interpret individual Payson-chert Hardin points found well beyond this core distribution area, such as the aforementioned example from the Bass site in Wisconsin, one from an upland site near Danville (Calentine et al. 2004), and another from Grafton (Robert Monroe, pers. comm. to Nolan 2000), near the confluence of the Illinois and Mississippi rivers. In the absence of other data tying these distant locations to the study area, we suspect that these points denote less regular contact with the Payson source, whether directly or indirectly, by contemporary Hardin groups based outside the region.

Some support for this interpretation is provided by Behm's (1985:321–323) analysis of stylistic variation in midwestern Hardin Barbed points. The results of this study suggest that the geographic distance separating various Hardin populations was the primary factor that shaped interaction intensity. Simply put, Hardin people who lived closer to one another were more likely than more distant groups to have produced points with a similar morphology and "look." Clearly, more attention needs to be paid to the distribution of the various Hardin subvarieties, especially in light of the compelling exotic-chert data summarized above. The distribution of these varieties could help identify distinctive Hardin social territories, for which Behm (1985:321–323) found no real evidence (aside from a possible fluid ethnic boundary with northern Cody-complex peoples and a potentially related northerly skew to the distribution of the Eared Base variety).

However, one factor that Behm may not have considered is that specific basal configurations or "types" may have been in vogue at *different* times over the approximate 500-year span when Hardin Barbed points were made. Thus, time-transgressive movement rather than contemporary interaction could also explain some of the simple clinal distributional relationships among the various subtypes observed by Behm.

Geographic Distribution. Hardin Barbed points and Bass knives are found across most of the study area uplands but apparently occur relatively infrequently on landforms of suitable age in the major river valleys (cf. Luchterhand 1970 for lower Illinois Valley examples). Stafford (1989:Table 3.19) reports three Hardins from as many sites located in the Illinois Valley–crossing portion of the FAP 407 project. Nolan (2004) notes a similarly low number of Hardin points from high-terrace remnants in the Lima Lake locality. Others are certainly present, but we are unaware of any dense Hardin surface sites from the larger valleys. However, several examples of the type have been excavated from buried floodplain contexts in the region (e.g., Eagle Slough, Napoleon Hollow, and Twin Ditch Horizon 1), albeit from mixed or uncertain contexts in each case, suggesting many sites of this period, perhaps the largest ones in the settlement system, are surficially undetectable because they are covered by relatively thick mantles of alluvial or colluvial deposits.

As mentioned, Hardin diagnostics have been found in nearly every county in the study area in what currently can only be described as a random pattern. However, Nolan and Hansen (1995:306, 311) observed that Short Stemmed Hardins were more frequently manufactured from Payson chert than the Long Stemmed variant, especially among examples recovered from the Mississippi drainage. Data such as these indicate that more attention needs to be paid to the distribution of the various Hardin subtypes since it could denote the movement of distinct social groups or chert technicians. Most archaeologists working in Illinois and adjacent states (ourselves included) frequently lump Hardin Barbed points together for reporting purposes and often do not illustrate the recovered examples, perhaps masking significant information that may prove critical to future studies concerned with unlocking possible ethnic boundaries or settlement territories associated with Hardin-producing Boreal peoples.

Large Bifurcate Horizon (8900–8500 B.P., cal 8000–7550 B.C.)

Deeply stratified sites in the southeastern United States document that large bifurcated-base point forms "evolved" from the latest Kirk Corner Notched forms (large variety) as a result of simple stylistic change or technological innovation (Broyles 1971; J. Chapman 1975, 1977, 1985; Kimball 1996), the latter perhaps linked in some way to developments relating to the atlatl. Although Large Bifurcates have not been directly dated in western Illinois, we confidently place them within the 8900–8500 B.P. period on the basis of stratigraphic and radiometric evidence available from southeastern sites. Our Large Bifurcate–point cluster includes several named variants, including St. Albans Side Notched/MacCorkle Stemmed (Broyles 1966, 1971; Chapman 1985:148), Jerger (Tomak 1979), and Keithley (Conrad 1987:192–194) (Figure 13.13).

Figure 13.13. Large Bifurcates.

Large Bifurcate points generally share such attributes as notched basal margins and lobed ears, although some also exhibit distinctive features suggesting that separate types actually may be represented in the study region. The primary difference observed among most of these variants can be attributed to resharpening and other forms of attrition, which result in widely different blade shapes. This has led Chapman (1985:148) and others (e.g., Kimball 1996:159) to consider the MacCorkle Stemmed type a large variant of the St. Albans Side Notched type. Jerger points appear to represent a cognate form, and Justice (1987:90) subsumes them under the MacCorkle type. This leaves Conrad's (1987:192–193) Keithley point as perhaps the most distinctive regional subtype found in western Illinois.[3] Keithley points typically have more elongated, lanceolate blades than St. Albans/MacCorkle/Jerger as well as longer, narrower, and less markedly bifurcated bases. In some respects, these points resemble Coe's (1964) Kirk Stemmed type, although they never appear to be as deeply serrated. While Keithley points have not been directly dated, Conrad (1987:193) notes they are more like other Large Bifurcates and Kirks than like LeCroys or subsequent forms, suggesting relative contemporaneity with the St. Albans/MacCorkle variants.

Tools and Other Artifacts. The only distinctive artifacts that can definitely be associated with the Large Bifurcate horizon are the projectile points themselves. However, Jefferson Chapman (1985:148) notes that, while southeastern bifurcate lithic assemblages share much in common with earlier Kirk assemblages, they appear to be characterized by less formalized end scrapers, increased numbers of bipolar tools, and an apparent reduction in the raw number of unifacial tools. Data gathered from the projectile points recovered from western Illinois suggest that Large Bifurcate peoples typically relied on regionally available Burlington/Keokuk cherts and apparently used exotic chert much less frequently than contemporary Hardin groups did. Only one exotic-chert Keithley point is currently known (a Moline-chert example from 11HY180), and we are aware of one unidentified but likely exotic, black-chert specimen (Excello?), a Cobden/Dongola-chert specimen (Figure 13.13d), and three Payson-chert examples of St. Albans/MacCorkle points from the central portion of the study region (Nolan and Hansen 1995).

Settlement and Subsistence Data. Currently no Large Bifurcate components have been excavated in the region, and substantive surface assemblages are also lacking. Therefore, most of what is known about this cultural complex derives from patterns gleaned from abundant survey and collector interview data. Although they occur relatively infrequently overall, Large Bifurcates have been found on a variety of landform and soil types throughout the study area, much like other Boreal-period points. Nolan (2004) notes that his small sample of Large Bifurcates emanates from landforms located in relatively close proximity to perennial upland stream valleys, generally within 15 km of the Mississippi trench. However, Conrad's (1987:189–195) regionwide sample has produced evidence for more remote upland utilization as well as the only sites where more than one example of specific Large Bifurcate types have been recovered. Two Jerger and four Keithley points have been recovered from one of the major Avon workshop areas (11KX158), whereas two other sites in the same part of the Spoon River drainage produced three of the former (from an upland lobe) and four of the latter (Little Coal Creek bluff), respectively. All of the Large Bifurcates in Conrad's sample are manufactured from Burlington/Keokuk cherts. The apparent underrepresentation of exotic-chert use by the people making Large Bifurcate points may imply a reduction in home-range size relative to that of Hardin and earlier Theban/Kirk groups, although sampling error may also be involved.

One of the most striking aspects of the Large Bifurcate data is the precipitous drop in the raw numbers of points and sites in upland contexts relative to earlier Kirk and roughly contemporary Hardin components. For example, on the basis of an extremely large database amassed from the central portion of the study area, Conrad (1987) reports 55 Large Bifurcate points from 44 sites, 315 Large Kirk points (representing what appears to be the most recent variant) from 185 sites, and 379 Hardin Barbed points from 197 sites. Nolan (2004) documents a similar trend in a smaller yet still sizable data set from the Mississippi Valley uplands, which overlaps with and includes some of the data from the western end of Conrad's study area. Our review of other survey collections and reports suggests this is a regionwide phenomenon. This decline in numbers may partly reflect manufacture of Large Bifurcates for a shorter period of time relative to Kirk and Hardin, but the results are striking nonetheless. Little information about the corresponding Large Bifurcate distribution is available in the major valleys that could shed light on what minimally appears to have been a changing settlement pattern. Available information does not appear to indicate a rise in the number of Large Bifurcates found on ancient landforms in the Mississippi or Illinois Valley, although the potential for substantial buried sites in both areas is great.

Considered together, the lower overall number of components and apparent reduction in exotic- chert exploitation suggest that Kirk-derived Large Bifurcate populations were using the uplands in a different way than either their predecessors or contemporaries. Some of this could be tied to technological change (more prevalent bone tool industry or earlier atlatl developments?), smaller populations, or less extensive home ranges; few obvious differences appear in overall site location or landscape use. Deteriorating climatic conditions or changing upland vegetation and resources could also be related causal factors, but if so, they do not seem to have had a similar effect on Hardin peoples. Whatever the explanation, the precipitous drop in the raw number of Large Bifurcate components is an important phenomenon that is worthy of further study because it presaged continuing reduction of upland habitation and use that ultimately reached its nadir during the subsequent Atlantic climatic episode.

Geographic Distribution. Large Bifurcate components are widely distributed across the study area, much like other Boreal occupations. However, Keithley points primarily have been found in the Spoon River basin, leading Conrad (1987:192–194) to speculate that the distribution possibly defines an ethnic boundary between their makers and the people who manufactured St. Albans points, limited to the LaMoine basin in Conrad's sample. However, since Conrad defined the type, additional Keithley points have come to light in the Mud Creek drainage in Henry County (Shepard 1993) and in the Mississippi Valley uplands in Adams County (Nolan 2004). Additionally, the distinctions between St. Albans and MacCorkle/Jerger points have since been largely rejected or minimized (cf. Chapman 1985; Justice 1987). Thus, the overall distributions of Keithley and St. Albans/MacCorkle/Jerger now appear to overlap considerably, although the clustering of the former in the Spoon drainage (30 of 33 known specimens) still may prove significant.

The other Large Bifurcate cognates, such as St. Albans, MacCorkle, and Jerger, have been reported or observed in nearly every county in the central portion of the study-area uplands and beyond (e.g., Conrad 1978:Plates 6a, 7x, 1981: Plate 21, 1987; Cross 1998:Figure 29d; Esarey 1982:Appendix B, Figure 1b, 1987:Figure 10g; Nolan 1991b:Figure 5.1e, 2004: Figure 3.19a, b; Stafford and Nolan 1990:Table 3.3) but seem to occur sparingly on the ancient landforms found in the major river valleys. For example, Nolan (2004) reports only a few MacCorkle cognates from late Pleistocene Kingston Terrace remnants in the Lima Lake locality, and Studenmund (1992:64–66) documents a single reworked example from a sandy floodplain feature at the HomerVance site near Meredosia. None were identified during large-scale surveys undertaken along the northern part of the central Illinois Valley (Fishel et al. 2004), in a 600-ha bottomland tract located near the mouth of the LaMoine (Moffat et al. 2001), along the Mississippi Valley margin in the northern Sny Bottom (Conner 1984), or during a corridor study running through the Mississippi Valley near Burlington (Goatley 1998b; Nolan et al. 2003), although examples have been found in the uplands adjacent to these localities. These data suggest that the major sites dating to this period may be buried in valley fills. Conversely, the reduced number of Large Bifurcate sites may simply reflect a lower regional population density, perhaps influenced in some way by the appreciable numbers of apparently contemporary Hardin people that occupied the area.

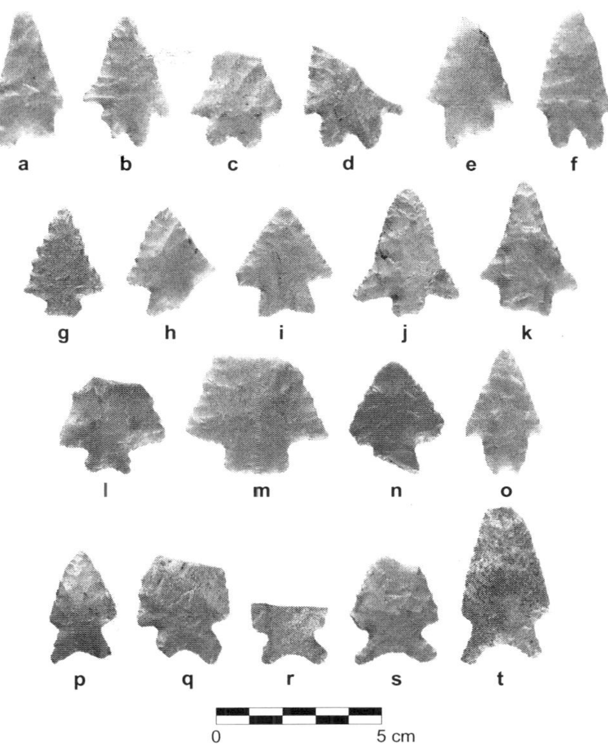

Figure 13.14. Late Bifurcate point types: a–f, LeCroy; g–k, Kanawha; l–n, Stanly Stemmed; o, type indeterminate; p–t, Jakie Stemmed.

Atlantic Episode (8450–4700 B.P., cal 7500–3500 B.C.)

Late Bifurcate Horizon (8450–7500 B.P., cal 7550–6400 B.C.)

The initial portion of the Atlantic climatic period generally witnessed a continuation of the technological and stylistic traditions of the preceding Boreal (Early Archaic) period, although a marked reduction in the overall size of the diagnostic projectile points occurred. The period is characterized by small, bifurcated-base point types like LeCroy, Kanawha, and Stanly Stemmed (Broyles 1966, 1971; Coe 1964; Kneberg 1956) (Figure 13.14), which are the last observable manifestations of the southeastern Kirk/Bifurcate developmental sequence in the study area. The deeply stratified sites where these points have been recovered indicate LeCroy points were the earliest of these forms (ca. 8450 B.P.), followed by Kanawha at ca. 8150 B.P. and then by Stanly Stemmed at 7750 B.P. (Chapman 1985: Table 7-1), although components containing these forms exhibit considerable overlap in dates and assemblages. While many consider Stanly Stemmed points to be Middle Archaic because their associated radiocarbon assays cross the arbitrary line or set of temporal parameters that were affixed for this span, we discuss them with the Late Bifurcates because they appear to be technologically, and perhaps culturally, related; in fact, determining whether broken blade fragments found during survey are Kanawha or Stanly points is very difficult. Significantly, these points appear to mark the end of the southeastern influence that was prevalent in the region from the Pre-Boreal period on (Conrad 1987).

Jakie Stemmed (Marshall 1958) is another bifurcated-base-type point that appears relevant to discussions about this temporal span. Ray (1994:13) reports a radiocarbon date of 8140 ± 150 RCYBP from a hearth unearthed on a buried upland site in southwestern Missouri that produced a large number of Jakie Stemmed points along with other related late Boreal- to early Atlantic-period points (e.g., Rice Lobed and Rice Contracting Stemmed). Jakie Stemmed points are medium-sized Ozark or Missouri bifurcates attributable to a different developmental sequence than the Kirk-derived forms mentioned above. Unlike those types, Jakie Stemmed points occasionally exhibit alternate blade beveling (Ray 1994), which is much more characteristic of midwestern Theban/Hardin variants.

Tools and Other Artifacts. The bifurcated-base points themselves are the most diagnostic objects that can be attributed to this span.[4] Most of the Kirk-derived bifurcates appear to be manufactured on flake blanks derived from regionally available cherts of varying quality. LeCroy points (Figure 13.14a–f) are transitional in size and form between earlier St. Albans/MacCorkle and later Kanawha types. They typically exhibit pointed rather than rounded basal ears, have barbed or rather obtuse shoulders, and are much more deeply bifurcated than either Kanawha or Stanly points. Kanawha Stemmed points (Figure 13.14g–k) have shorter and more rounded, but less markedly bifurcated, stems than LeCroys. However, their most distinctive feature is their prominent shoulders, which tend to have a flared appearance as a result of invasive, patterned bifacial resharpening. Incurving blade margins and lateral serration are two attributes common to both Kirk-cluster and small-bifurcate points. Burlington/Keokuk chert was primarily used in the manufacture of small bifurcates in the study area, although several LeCroy points made of LaMoine River chert have been identified (e.g., McNerney et al. 1991:Figure 8d); no examples of extraregional exotic chert have been observed to date.

In contrast to the smaller Kirk-derived bifurcates, Jakie Stemmed points (Figure 13.14p–t) were produced on moderate-sized bifacial blanks, as were the St. Albans/Keithley variants. They typically have pronounced, unbarbed shoulders and lightly ground (and sometimes beveled), stemmed basal configurations that range from moderately concave to markedly bifurcated, occasionally giving the haft area a "swallowtail-like appearance" (Ray 1994:17). The basal ears vary from rather pointed to moderately well rounded to indistinct. Jakie point blades are infrequently serrated or beveled, the latter apparently as the result of a more ad hoc or desultory technique than the distinctive alternate beveling technique that is a hallmark of Theban-cluster points (cf. Ray 1994:21). All of the Jakie Stemmed points identified to date are manufactured from Burlington/Keokuk chert, and several appear to be intentionally heat treated.

Few other formal artifacts can be attributed with confidence to Late Bifurcate assemblages, although we expect that the tool kit was more similar to that of the Boreal period than not. As mentioned above, Jefferson Chapman (1985:148) indicates that southeastern bifurcate lithic assemblages appear to be characterized by less formalized end scrapers, an increase in bipolar tools, and an apparent reduction in the raw number of unifacial tools compared with Kirk components. Some regional evidence for the first of these propositions was found at the Wesley Dedert site (11A332), which is the only excavated component dating to this period in western Illinois (Nolan 1994a:57–79). Seven scrapers were recovered, and all are characterized by less invasive, regular, or well-controlled retouch than that noted on definite Boreal-period scrapers; several specimens are retouched on the ventral rather than the dorsal surface, which is completely anomalous in this regard compared with Boreal-period scrapers. This buried upland assemblage also produced a fragmentary EH adze, suggesting that this tool form may have continued to be manufactured into the early Atlantic period (cf. Stafford 1985:25). Despite rather radical changes in the size of the weaponry, early Atlantic bifurcate technology appears to be Early Archaic in nearly all respects.

Settlement and Subsistence Data. As noted, the only regionally excavated early Atlantic-period site is Wesley Dedert,[5] whose Block 100 area yielded the remains of a short-term, buried upland occupation that produced an associated calendrical date of cal 7045 B.C. (ISGS-2997) (Hansen 1994; Nolan 1994a:57–79, 2003:31). This ephemeral encampment was discovered in the AB–BA soil horizon of a prominent, prairie-covered drainage divide during test excavations for the Route 336 project. While this part of the site had almost no surficial expression, a Jakie-like point (see Nolan 1992: Figure V-29e), the only diagnostic recovered from the site surface that plausibly dates within the age range of the Block 100 remains, was found on the eroding slope of the landform immediately north of the buried deposits.

Subsequent hand excavation of a 112-m^2 area revealed that the Block 100 occupation area contained two bounded, closely spaced material concentrations that had scattered artifacts located between and surrounding them (Nolan 1994a:57–79). The smaller and more ephemeral western activity area produced only debitage, although an EH adze-bit fragment was recovered nearby. The eastern activity area produced seven EH scraper fragments (both end and side), a small but diversified tool assemblage that included an igneous cobble hammerstone or mano, two bifaces, a point edge fragment, and several expediently produced retouched flake tools as well as abundant chert debitage and a dispersed concentration of carbonized black-walnut shells (used for ^{14}C dating). Considering that burned debitage was confined to the excavated units that surrounded this charcoal concentration, the nutshell probably was used as fuel and likely marked the location of a poorly preserved hearth. All of the tools found in the buried deposits, except the adze, were recovered from this area, suggesting the hearth location was the focal point for this relatively brief occupation. Analysis of the recovered debitage indicates that both expedient tool manufacture and the maintenance of curated tools were undertaken in each activity area (Hansen 1994:134–142). This, along with the character of the recovered tools, suggests the site was used as some type of short-term camp where generalized cutting and scraping activities were undertaken along with some limited tool refurbishment and basic subsistence pursuits. The presence of two closely spaced activity areas, including one that was clearly hearth focused, and the discard of a moderate number of implements (1:33 tool-to-debitage ratio) reflecting various functions, including an adze suggestive of woodworking activities, may indicate the site was more residentially oriented.

Aside from this site, the remaining information about this period is derived from observations of the points themselves and their distribution. The dearth of Payson and other exotic-chert small bifurcates suggests that regional later bifurcate people had a home-range size that was much smaller than that evident during most of the previous Boreal period. Perhaps the most striking thing about this span is the relatively low number of later bifurcate types found in the uplands compared with Hardin points (Conrad 1981, 1987; Nolan 2004), which have no obvious regional antecedent or related forms. However, in contrast to the Hardin and Large Bifurcate distributions, the Kirk-derived small bifurcates appear in greater numbers in or near the major valleys, suggesting a shift in settlement preference. Nolan (2004) notes that Kanawha and Stanly points are regularly found on the sandy late Pleistocene terrace remnants in the Lima Lake locality of the Mississippi; several sites have produced relatively large numbers of them for local collectors. All of Conrad's (1987) Stanly points were found within or immediately adjacent to the central Illinois Valley, as well. We also note that some of the densest later bifurcate sites currently known in Illinois are found near Wisconsinan glacial kettles and other types of upland impoundments located to the east and southeast of the study region (Robert Monroe, pers. comm. to Nolan 1997; Winters 1982).

The general reduction in upland-oriented components may indicate that early Atlantic populations had become more focused on valley-oriented or riverine-lacustrine resources than their Boreal predecessors apparently were, although base camps of both groups likely were located in close proximity to the same productive lowland resource niches. We note that this apparent reduction in upland use is coincident with the traditionally held dates for the onset of the Hypsithermal (Wright 1968), but we will leave discussions of the causal factors to the paleoclimatologists, geomorphologists, and palynologists, since the timing and effects of the Hypsithermal have been called into question (e.g., Van Nest 1997).

Geographic Distribution. As mentioned, the Kirk-derived Late Bifurcates are found in small numbers throughout the study area (Conrad 1978, 1981, 1982, 1986a, 1986d, 1987; Fishel et al. 2004; Green 1977a, 1977b; McNerney et al. 1991; Munson and Harn 1966:Figure 3e; Neal and McNerney 1994; Nolan 2004; Nolan et al. 1992; Nolan and Graham 2003; Nolan et al. 1997; Nolan et al. 2003; Stafford 1989, 1994). LeCroy and Kanawha points occur in both upland and lowland settings, but Stanly Stemmed cognates (Figure 13.14l–n) have only been reported to date from the southern half of the study area in contexts closely associated with the major valleys (e.g. Conrad 1987; Nolan 2004). Classic Jakie Stemmed points are similarly rare but appear to be most common along the Mississippi slope, particularly in the Lima Lake locality, where Nolan has documented at least one moderately productive floodplain site and several others that have produced individual specimens. The presence of Jakie Stemmed points suggests that some Ozark-derived peoples migrated into the study region at this time, perhaps pushed into the area by the deteriorating climatic conditions that prevailed in their homeland to the south and west. Also noteworthy is that Fox Valley points (Justice 1987:96–97; Perino 1985:136; Ritzenthaler 1961), a Late Bifurcate style commonly found to the north and east of the study area and believed to be generally contemporary with Kanawha points, are rarely if ever found in western Illinois. This suggests a social or ethnic boundary may be definable; clearly, more information is needed about the type composition and distribution of Late Bifurcate points in the northern portion of the study area.

Campbell Hollow Horizon

(7800–6800 B.P., cal 6650–5700 B.C.)

A suite of expanding-stemmed to corner-notched points found at the Campbell Hollow and Koster sites in the lower Illinois River valley appear to denote the presence of a poorly defined, yet regionally distinctive, early Atlantic-period cultural complex. The relevant assemblages from these sites are dominated by medium-size, expanding-stemmed points with open corner notching of the haft area. However, we view several of the more heterogeneous forms in the Campbell Hollow assemblage as earlier point types (Stafford 1985:Figure 1.10c, e, Figure 1.11a) that probably were deposited in the associated strata as a result of the mixing effects of fan formation processes or scavenging by the chert-poor site occupants. Evidence for such scavenging behavior seems implicit in the high degree of tool recycling and the raw-material conservatism documented at the site (see Odell 1985; Stafford 1985). Given this evidence, only the expanding-stemmed varieties from the site are viewed as diagnostic of the Campbell Hollow horizon, although the presence of other corner- to side-notched points at the type site indicates potential for recognizing other collateral point types in the future.

Certainly Campbell Hollow–like points can only be *demonstrated* to be typical of the 7800–7500 B.P. period, on the basis of the associated radiocarbon dates from Koster and Campbell Hollow, and apparently were supplanted by other unnamed expanding-stemmed and side-notched varieties sometime shortly thereafter at the former site (cf. Brown and Vierra 1983). However, recent excavations at the multicomponent Strong site (11MO841) in the American Bottom yielded broadly similar, expanding-stemmed to corner-notched hafted bifaces termed "Valmeyer Corner Notched," whose associations with dated pit features suggest they were made as recently as 6780 ± 70 B.P. (Walz et al. 1998:177–181). Walz et al. (1998:183–184) provisionally set the age range for the corresponding Dennis Hollow phase between 6900 and 6500 B.P. on the basis of other radiometrically dated features at the site, despite the lack of associated diagnostic materials. Given the lower Illinois Valley sequence and Walz et al.'s reference to similar points found in the Modoc Middle Archaic strata dating between 7800 and 6800 B.P., we suspect that the Strong site dates are most representative of the waning centuries of the span when Campbell Hollow–like points or antecedent forms were commonly made and used in western Illinois.

Tools and Other Artifacts. The only diagnostics that can be attributed with some confidence to this cultural complex are expanding-stemmed to corner-notched points similar to those found at Campbell Hollow, Koster, and Strong (Figure 13.15). This type cluster appears to be broadly analogous to Cypress Creek I points from the Wabash-Ohio river confluence area, which generally date between 7800 and 7500 B.P. (Lewis and Lewis 1961; Nance 1986). Campbell Hollow and Valmeyer Corner Notched points typically exhibit broad, biconvex blades and relatively short, expanding stems that have slightly convex to straight basal margins. One of the more distinguishing features of the Campbell Hollow type sample is the heavy haft grinding, which extends relatively unbroken from the basal margin to under the lower shoulder (cf. Stafford 1985; Walz et al. 1998). Similarly extensive haft

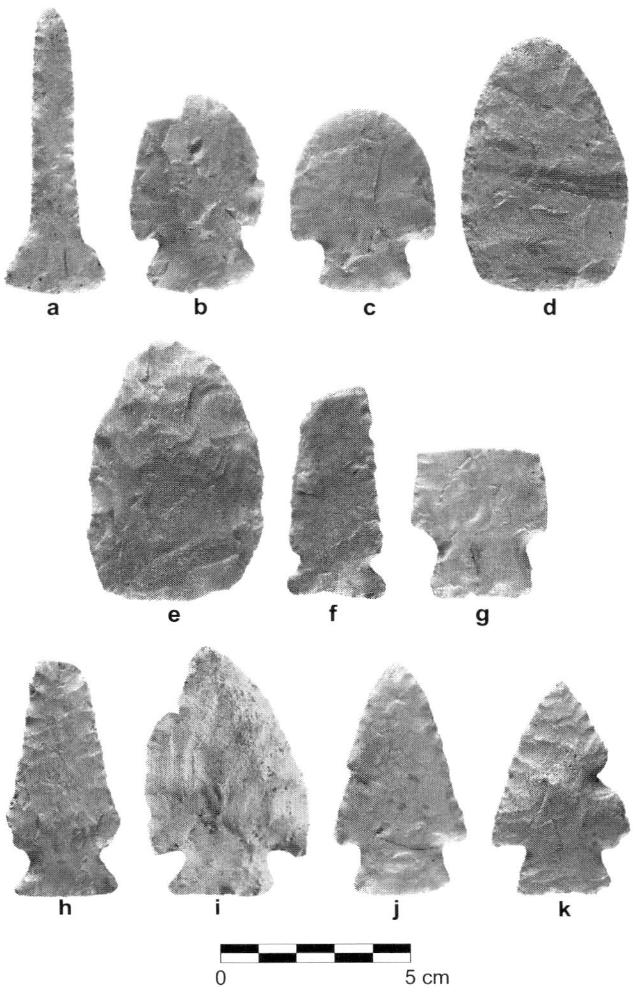

Figure 13.15. Campbell Hollow–horizon artifacts.

grinding is also manifest on earlier regional Theban-cluster points and subsequent Atlantic-period Table Rock points but is not characteristic of later side-notched types like Matanzas or Osceola. Evidence for heat treatment routinely occurs in the Campbell Hollow assemblage (Stafford 1985:Tables 1.10, 1.12), marking a significant departure from most earlier regional Boreal-period chipped-stone technologies, which generally did not produce much evidence for intentional heat alteration of formal tools.

Settlement and Subsistence Data. No excavated sites aside from Campbell Hollow (see Stafford 1985 and Wiant et al., this volume) are currently attributable to this cultural complex in western Illinois, and relatively few points have been identified as belonging to the type cluster during regional surveys. However, a few possible Campbell Hollow cognates were found in disturbed contexts at the Eagle Slough site (see discussion under *Data Sets* above), and an apparently isolated tool cache that may also relate to this cultural complex was recently found in subsoil contexts at the Marlin Miller site (11HA318) (Figure 13.15a–d). In addition, a human burial salvaged from an eroding midden at the stratified Andrew Farm Gully site (11A1578) in northwestern Adams County may also prove relatable because recent ^{14}C dating places it within the inclusive temporal span.

The Marlin Miller feature (Feature 44) was discovered on the western lip of a high terrace that overlooks the West Fork of the LaMoine River during a mitigation project undertaken by Illinois Transportation Archaeological Research Program (ITARP) personnel for the Route 336 project. The principal subsurface component relates to a sizable early Late Woodland Weaver occupation (Nolan 1991b), although a few scattered Archaic artifacts have been recovered from subsurface and disturbed contexts, including an EH chipped-stone adze, a rare example of a ground-stone granitic adze, and a probable EH scraper. The subsurface tool kit consists of a thin, subovate preform, two expanding-stemmed hafted scrapers (one heat treated), and another expanding-stemmed point reworked to an awl or drill-like form, all manufactured from similar pieces of a local Burlington/Keokuk chert (Figure 13.15a–d). Although Feature 44 cannot be absolutely dated, the basal configurations of the three hafted artifacts are internally consistent and are quite similar to Campbell Hollow forms, although they are not as heavily ground as examples from the type site. These expanding-stemmed bifaces do not comfortably fit into any other preexisting later Archaic point types, and their flaking characteristics are reminiscent of earlier Boreal-period forms.

The authors salvaged the Andrew Farm Gully burial in 1985 after postcranial skeletal remains were found exposed in an erosional cutbank located in a small side valley situated at the base of the Mississippi bluffs north of Quincy (Nolan 2004 and notes and collections on file at the WIU Archaeological Research Laboratory). Burial 1 consisted of a tightly flexed adult male that was interred at the base of a ca. .25-m-thick organic midden; pit outlines could not be discerned, and no definitive grave goods were interred with this individual. However, an untyped expanding-stemmed point with some broad similarities to specimens recovered from Campbell Hollow (e.g., Stafford 1985:Figure 1.10d) (Figure 13.15f) was found approximately 8 cm above the right leg during excavation; a full-grooved granitic ax and a distinctive preform (Figure 13.15e) were recovered from nearby midden contexts. No other information about the cultural affiliation of the midden or burial was obtained prior to the return of radiocarbon dates of 7720 ± 140 RCYBP (cal 6530, 6500 B.C. [ISGS-5700]) and 7360 ± 35 RCYBP (cal 6220 B.C. [ISGS-A0577]). While these are surprisingly early dates, we believe the association with the Campbell Hollow horizon must be considered provisional pending additional information about this particular site component.

Nolan (2004) reports three or four Burlington/Keokuk-chert Campbell Hollow cognates from the surfaces of three sites located on high terraces in the Bear Creek valley: 11A1073, 11A1076, and 11A1164. Each of these sites is located in close proximity to outcrops and residual deposits of medium-grade Burlington/Keokuk chert. In fact, two of the Campbell Hollow cognates were recovered from 11A1076, a substantial chert workshop. One example is a medium-sized, expanding-stemmed point that exhibits a heavily ground haft area and intentional heat treatment (Figure 13.15g). The other specimen is a heavily ground, stemmed point that was reworked into an extensively use-polished hafted "blunt" or scraper; it is similar to an unreworked example pictured by Stafford (1985:Figure 1.10h). Fishel et al. (2004) report a possible heat-treated example of the type from 11MA176, located on a floodplain landform in the central Illinois Valley. Nolan also observed a few possible examples from private collections in the LaMoine River drainage south and west of Macomb (Figure 13.15h).

The only pattern that emerges from these data is that Campbell Hollow and other early Atlantic-period points are greatly underrepresented in institutional and private collections from strict upland contexts in western Illinois. This dearth cannot simply be explained by a lack of named types, as Stafford (1985:31) and others have suggested, although recognition and accurate identification remain problematic. However, we have been looking for Campbell Hollow points in collections for several years now, and the total number of actual or possible specimens is not appreciably greater than it was when Stafford first offered these remarks. In our opinion, the underrepresentation of points dating to this span probably *does* reflect the diminishing role of upland utilization in a settlement system that had seemingly become more focused on lowland locations and resources. This supposition is underscored by the recovery of most of the identified points from the larger stream valleys in the region. The meager number of upland Campbell Hollow–horizon components must also be viewed in the context of a preexisting trend of decreasing component frequency observed for the late Boreal to early Atlantic bifurcate tradition. To what extent these changes in upland utilization and settlement were determined by deteriorating climatic conditions or the "pull" of more productive floodplain aquatic habitats can not be assessed with the data at hand, although these remain some of the most widely cited causal factors (e.g., Brown and Vierra 1983; Conrad 1981).

Table Rock Complex (6900–6500? B.P., cal 5750–5500 B.C.)

The dating of Table Rock, or Bottleneck Stemmed, points (Bray 1956; Converse 1973) is much debated, even between the authors of this chapter, although Nolan feels that some must have been produced by at least 6860 ± 80 B.P., given their presence in Koster Horizon 8. The Koster examples were subsumed by Cook (1976:147–148) under the heterogeneous Apple Blossom Stemmed type (which should be dropped as a type name). This chronological position is also consistent with the similarities noted between Campbell Hollow and Table Rock points (stemmed basal configuration, marked to obtuse shoulders, heavy haft grinding, and consistent heat treatment), suggesting the former could be an ancestral form.

No firm terminal dates are currently available for Table Rock points, since examples have been found in Koster Horizon 6 and elsewhere (see, e.g., Fishel 2000; Lensink 1986) in apparent Late Archaic (Sub-Boreal) contexts (Justice [1987:124] estimates they range from ca. 5000 to 3000 B.P., which is more in line with the view of Fishel). While tradition lag is a possible explanation for the late occurrences, Nolan views the recovery of these points in post-6000 B.P. contexts as likely reflecting aboriginal scavenging or the presence of mixed deposits associated with repeatedly used locations. This view is based on the Table Rock points having rarely if ever been recovered in association with Matanzas points, except in Koster Horizon 6, where the latter are the dominant form (Cook 1976). Additionally, if the recently dated Nochta site remains from the American Bottom are representative of what was happening at the same time in western Illinois, then small side-notched forms like Robinson and Brannon would appear to have been dominant between 6500 and 6100 B.P. (Higgins 1990). However, no regional data allow us to summarize what cultural complexes, if any, were present in the area between ca. 6500 and 5800 B.P., although side-notched points similar to Robinson and Brannon have been found.

Tools and Other Artifacts. The Table Rock Stemmed (née Bottleneck) point (Figure 13.16) is the sole diagnostic that can currently be associated with this cultural complex. We should note, however, that the type, as used today, bears little resemblance to the original examples described and illustrated from the Table Rock Reservoir in Missouri (Bray 1956:127–128, Figure 23, Row 3). Table Rocks are commonly believed to be a product of Sub-Boreal–Sub-Atlantic small-point traditions like the Riverton, Durst, and Lamoka complexes (e.g., see Justice 1987:124), but western Illinois examples are typically manufactured from bifacial preforms rather than flake blanks and can be 7.5 to 10+ cm long in a pristine state; they only take on a diminutive appearance as a result of various forms of attrition, damage, and rejuvenation. Table Rock points are well made, medium to small-sized projectiles that exhibit a moderately broad, shouldered, symmetrical blade and a distinctive, heavily ground "bottleneck-shaped" haft area (Justice 1987:124). Technologically speaking, these points appear to be most similar to Campbell Hollow variants, given their their heavy haft grinding, expanding-stemmed basal configuration, consistent heat treatment, and moderate overall size.

Table Rock points are typically manufactured from heat-altered Burlington/Keokuk chert, although examples of colorful, unidentified and presumably exotic sources and poorer-quality LaMoine River chert are known. Additionally, a quartz specimen was observed in a collection amassed from the Henderson Creek drainage near Gladstone. Perino (1985:371) notes that some Table Rock points from unspecified Illinois locations were made of Knife River flint from the Dakotas. We have observed several other regional examples made from local cherts that have been facially worn or polished to such a degree that the flake scars are nearly or wholly

Figure 13.16. Table Rock–horizon points.

obliterated. While these data suggest that Table Rock points probably were heavily curated tools, relatively few appear to have been refurbished as hafted end scrapers after they were broken, a common feature of later Atlantic-period Matanzas and Karnak points. However, several Table Rock points found in western Illinois exhibit impact fractures, which are perhaps more indicative of use as projectiles.

Settlement and Subsistence Data. Although Table Rock points are commonly found in western Illinois, no definitive regional Table Rock component has been identified as a result of excavation, to our knowledge; as noted above, Koster has produced the only specimens from buried contexts. Thus, most of what is known about this cultural complex derives from site distribution data. Like many earlier Pre-Boreal and Boreal types, Table Rock points are frequently recovered as isolated finds, suggesting loss or discard during hunting or other types of transient activities. For example, at least 60 percent of the Route 336/96 Table Rock components were either true find spots or single specimens located at the fringes of potentially unrelated, multicomponent scatters. One of the points from the latter category at 11A284 was extensively damaged by an impact fracture, and several others exhibit damage consistent with hunting loss (Nolan 2004).

In the Mississippi trench area adjacent to the Route 336/96 corridor, Table Rock points are regularly found (e.g., Conrad et al. 1986; Cripe 1988; Nolan 1987; Nolan and Scott 1996), although their distribution appears to be heavily skewed toward the late Pleistocene terrace remnants, alluvial fans, and bluff crests located at the eastern margin of the valley. However, a few scattered Table Rock components have also been identified on sandy terrace remnants located near the western margin of the floodplain. Overall, this distribution is similar to that of subsequent Helton-horizon components but is quite dissimilar to that of other later point forms, like Falling Springs and Godar/Osceola, which are found in greater frequency within and immediately surrounding Lima Lake, near the center of the floodplain (Nolan 2004). These principal-valley Table Rock components have not produced projectile point assemblages that are quantitatively different from their upland counterparts, which is another striking contrast between these components and later Atlantic and Sub-Boreal occupations.

Data from other regional surveys and collector interviews corroborate the observation that Table Rock components are geographically diverse and quite widespread. Table Rocks are typically among the most common post-Boreal Archaic point types observed in local private collections amassed from upland contexts in the study area. Conrad (1981:131–133, 1987:211–217) suggests that these points are more commonly found in the eastern portion of the study area, as he recognized only three Table Rock components from the Mississippi slope portion of the original FAP 407 survey: two from the Rock Creek bluffline (11A676 and 11A202) and another from a prairie-dominated upland divide located between that stream and Ursa Creek (11A809). However, Nolan's reexamination of the FAP 407 type-collection materials suggests potentially a half dozen more components are represented by points that were originally attributed to Durst or Riverton types. The majority of these points were recovered from upland divides or interfluves that have modern soils suggestive of various types of native vegetation: hardwood forest, savannah, and prairie; one point was found on a formerly forested low terrace immediately adjacent to Rock Creek (Nolan 2004).

Recent investigations at a multicomponent upland site in Henderson County (11HE382) produced six Table Rock points (Nolan and Graham 1999:Figure 1), marking it as one of the most productive middle Atlantic-period properties identified to date. This site was discovered after unauthorized brush clearing for a proposed county road had compromised or destroyed portions of the artifact scatter. Although some subsurface projectile points and lithic concentrations were discovered and removed from the EB–BE soil horizon in less disturbed parts of the site, none could be empirically demonstrated to relate to the Table Rock component (Nolan and Graham 1999). Conrad (1987:213–214) reports three other sites from the Spoon River drainage where repeated surface collection has resulted in the recovery of three, four, and seven Table Rock points, respectively. The site yielding seven points is an extensive, multicomponent chert workshop associated with the "Avon" chert source. Site 11HE382 is also located in an area characterized by relatively abundant outcrops of high-quality Burlington/Keokuk chert (the Ellison-Honey Creek source area; see Esarey 1983), although it clearly was not a point of procurement or extensive workshop per se.

A general lack of identified Table Rock assemblages or specific site types prohibits settlement reconstruction. Certainly, archaeologists' inability to isolate the side-notched point varieties that might have coexisted or predominated during this poorly defined interval limits understanding of this and other Atlantic-period cultural complexes. However, this situation is not so problematic in the Mississippi Valley uplands because few side-notched points of any type have been recovered there, and Table Rock components do not appear to be strongly associated with any other obvious point types (Nolan 2004). This contrasts with the situation observed in the lower Illinois Valley, where a proliferation of side- and corner-notched styles apparently co-occur in the same contexts (e.g., Goatley 1998a).

Conspicuously dense, artifact-rich Table Rock sites, like those observed on the major stream bluff tops and other landforms during the subsequent Helton horizon (see below), have not been documented in the study region. These data suggest that the primary residences of Table Rock peoples must have been situated low on the landscape and are now subsumed by alluvial or colluvial deposits that effectively mask their locations. The sites that have been recorded to date probably are the remains of extractive camps, hunting loci, or other short-term activity areas associated with more intensively occupied but yet-undocumented residential locations.

Geographic Distribution. Table Rock components exhibit a rather remarkable locational diversity in view of the limited distributional information that is available for the Atlantic-period cultural complexes that apparently bracket this span. Table Rock components have been found on forest, prairie, and transitional or savannah types of soils throughout the uplands and principal valleys of the study area (Conrad 1981, 1982, 1986d, 1987; Evans and Womac 1997; Green 1977a, 1977b; Munson and Harn 1966; Nolan 2004; Nolan et al. 1992; Stafford 1989, 1997; Stafford et al. 1983; Stafford and Nolan 1990). Nonetheless, use of relatively unbroken upland prairie areas appears to have been limited at best. If Table Rock points are correctly dated, the survey data indicate that mid-Atlantic-period upland utilization probably resurged to levels approaching those documented for the latter part of the Boreal (Conrad 1981, 1987; Nolan 2004). However, we disagree with Conrad's (1981:132, 1987) assertion that the distribution of Table Rock points is markedly skewed toward the eastern portion of the study area. Recent data collection indicates that these points are quite common in the western part of the study area (Nolan 2004; Nolan and Graham 2003; Nolan et al. 2003), and they are common in eastern Iowa, as well (Morrow 1984:45), suggesting that their distribution cannot be used to track the east to west amelioration of climatic conditions associated with the retreat of the dry Pacific Air Mass, as Conrad (1981:132, 1987) previously suggested.

Helton Horizon (5800–5000 B.P., cal 4650–3800 B.C.)

This cultural complex is typified by Matanzas and Karnak points (Figure 13.17), which are the principal nonperishable diagnostics of the Helton phase in the lower Illinois Valley (Brown and Vierra 1983; Cook 1976; Munson and Harn 1966). We refer to this temporal span as the "Helton horizon" because potentially significant variation (actually, much less variation) is evident in the point assemblages found across much of the study area compared with those from the lower Illinois Valley. Such variation may signify that multiple phases or distinctive cultural complexes are represented in the large geographic expanse under consideration here. In addition, few radiocarbon dates or sizable excavated assemblages are available from areas located north of the Helton-phase heartland in the lower Illinois River valley. While these more northerly cultural complexes may not be completely defined or synchronous, we expect them to be generally contemporary with lower Illinois Valley Helton on the basis of relative dating.

Although the lower Illinois Valley Helton phase, or "late Middle Archaic," is relatively well known and much discussed (e.g., Brown and Vierra 1983; Cook 1976; Stafford 1991), it has become a taxonomic black hole of sorts, with some researchers pulling in or including a variety of assemblages dating within half a millennium of it (Conner 1986:24; Stafford 1991), including points found in entirely different localities or regions. We take a much more parsimonious view of the data and consider sites like Buckshaw Bridge and Cypress Land, which have fairly distinctive projectile point assemblages and carbon dates that clearly postdate Helton, as representative of Atlantic–Sub-Boreal cultural complexes similar to the Falling Springs complex defined in the American Bottom (McElrath 1986).

Our dating of the Helton horizon is largely based on radiocarbon assays derived from obvious single-component sites in the adjacent lower Illinois Valley, like Slim Lake (Stafford 1989), and the dense organic middens present in Koster Horizon 6 Middle and the uppermost surfaces of the

Figure 13.17. Helton-horizon points: a–f, Matanzas hafted scrapers; g–m, Matanzas; n–q, Karnak hafted scrapers; r–x, Karnak.

Napoleon Hollow "Upper Middle Archaic" strata (Cook 1976; Wiant et al. 1983; also see Wiant et al., this volume). Dates from these particular contexts range from ca. 5500 to 5000 B.P., which probably denotes the "core" of the Helton phase. However, we remain skeptical of deposits used to denote either end of the total span originally attributed to Helton because the associations appear to be spurious, or at the very least, poorly reported.

For example, a date of 5890 ± 70 RCYBP (cal 4770, 4750, 4730 B.C.) was returned from a subsurface nutshell concentration at the Elledge site (11PK477) (Stafford 1994) and was attributed to the Helton phase despite the lack of directly associated diagnostics and the presence of other untyped (perhaps earlier?) side-notched Archaic points at the site (Stafford 1994:Table 3.12). However, another nearby nutshell concentration produced a "typical" Helton date of 5440 ± 90 RCYBP (cal 4330, 4270, 4260 B.C.), although our review of the site collections failed to identify any classic Matanzas points (contra Stafford). Given this ambiguity, we feel no firm basis currently exists for assigning the older of the two Elledge dates to Helton, or for calling any other pre-5800 B.P. date Helton, for that matter, since Cook (1976:Tables 16, 17) reports no examples of Matanzas or Karnak points from Koster Horizon 6 Lower/Horizon 7, which has been dated to 5720 ± 75 B.P. (Brown and Vierra 1983). While we believe that the Helton horizon was probably restricted for the most part to the 5500 to 5000 B.P. period, we view the 5800 B.P. date used by Brown and Vierra from Koster for its inception with some reservation. The terminal date of 5000 B.P. we offer for Helton is based on the aforementioned Koster and Napoleon Hollow dates considered in light of the earliest Falling Springs radiocarbon assays from sites in the lower Illinois Valley and American Bottom.

Tools and Other Artifacts. As mentioned, the most diagnostic Helton-horizon chipped-stone tools are Matanzas (Figure 13.17g–m) and Karnak cluster (Figure 13.14r–x) points. Our use of the former type follows Munson and Harn's (1966) original definition, which was based on a sample of points derived from the central Illinois River valley. Cook (1976) defined several subtypes within the Matanzas cluster, using samples derived from multiple living surfaces at Koster, and in doing so, in our opinion, he considerably watered down the original definition. Cook's Modal and Faint Side-Notched Matanzas appear to be most compatible with Munson and Harn's original definition of the type and are the most recognizable and dominant forms in the study area. These Matanzas points typically exhibit narrow, moderately thick, bullet-shaped blades and shallow to almost imperceptible side notches set low on the preform. Both Matanzas and Karnak points were frequently reworked into hafted end scrapers (Figure 13.17a–f, n–q, respectively) and other tool forms, such as awls, drills, and bi-bitted "scrapers," after they were broken.

Cook (1976, 1980) defined two varieties of Karnak points on the basis of the presence or absence of a well-defined shoulder and stem. Most of the Karnak points found in western Illinois are narrow, unstemmed lanceolate forms that are often difficult to distinguish from Matanzas when the haft element is missing; unbroken examples typically exhibit a squared to slightly eared trapezoidal base. These points/knives are sometimes erroneously typed as Nebo Hill points in western Illinois (e.g., McConaughy 1993:Figure 4.9h; Neal and McNerney 1994:43–44, 62–63) but clearly are attributable to the Helton horizon on the basis of flaking characteristics, heat treatment, and their consistent association with Matanzas. We simply refer to this probable knife form as a Karnak "point" since local examples appear to have attributes diagnostic of both varieties defined by Cook. However, distinctive stemmed variants that differ from the more typical lanceolate form are occasionally found on some of the larger sites and are referred to as "Karnak Stemmed." Some of these stemmed forms may actually derive from reworking or rehafting more typical Karnak points.

Contra Cook (1976) and following Conrad (1981, 1987), we do not view Godar points as particularly representative of regional Helton artifact assemblages, although clearly some generic, broadly side-notched forms were manufactured at this same time, especially south of the study area (e.g., Koster, Black Earth, etc.). Conrad (1981) has demonstrated that Matanzas and Godar points have markedly different surface distributions in western Illinois, and recent dating of single-component sites dominated by Godar/Osceola points demonstrates that they clearly postdate the Helton florescence by more than a half a millennium (see Hemphill-horizon summary below). We also do not view Helton points (Cook 1976:147) as particularly representative of the cultural complex they are named for, since they constitute less than 2 percent of the points found in Koster Horizon 6 and appear to be absent from single-component sites like Slim Lake (Stafford 1989:Table 3.19). Similar forms found in western Illinois are considered to be McLean cognates (see McElrath et al., this volume) and are believed to be representative of a subsequent cultural complex (see below). The more-lanceolate-bladed Helton points found in Koster Horizon 6 may, in fact, exemplify a transitional form relative to Matanzas and subsequent McLean points.

Matanzas and Karnak points are both frequently made from heat-treated regional cherts such as Burlington/Keokuk and Illinois Agate. However, LaMoine River chert, which is relatively coarse grained, appears to have been preferred for the manufacture of Karnak points, perhaps because they were used as knives and needed to be durable. Conrad (1982b:77) reports that 64 percent of the Karnak points from the Littleton Field survey were manufactured from LaMoine River chert as opposed to only 7 percent of Matanzas points, despite equal numbers of both types (n = 14). LaMoine River–chert Karnak points are also found some distance from the known source area, suggesting they may have been traded between local groups. Evidence for more extensive extraregional interaction is also present in a few collections. A Cobden/Dongola Karnak point is reported from Pike County (Stafford and Nolan 1990:Table 3.3), and another less confidently typed (Matanzas?) hafted scraper of similar but patinated raw material was observed in the Chrisman (111PK10) site collections by the authors, along with two lower Illinois Valley Chouteau-chert Karnak Stemmed variants (one refurbished as a double-bitted scraper). In addition, a large, unusual Benton-like stemmed point manufactured from southern Illinois Kaolin chert may be relatable because it was recovered from the surface of a relatively dense upland Karnak site located south of Macomb in the Grindstone Creek drainage. These are the only examples of exotic materials currently identified from study-area Helton sites, although Cook (1976:Table 21) and Brown and Vierra (1983:185) report copper and galena objects from Koster.

Aside from hafted bifaces, few other nonperishable artifact forms can definitely be associated with regional Helton technology. McGregor (1954:16–17) describes three-quarter-grooved axes that were found in surficial relationship with Helton materials at Chrisman as short in relation to their width and as having rather convex sides. This form appears to be distinctive from Titterington-horizon axes (see below) but has uncertain diagnostic potential vis-à-vis other Atlantic-period cultural complexes. Other nondiagnostic tools that are frequently found on Helton-horizon sites include chert hammers, pitted manos, and metates or grinding mortars. Conrad (1986d:28) relates a collector report of a fine engraved bone pin found at Chrisman, which, if confirmed, is one of the northernmost examples now known (cf. White 2003). A wide array of bone ornaments and tools were recovered from Helton-phase deposits at Koster (Brown and Vierra 1983; Cook 1976) but typically are underrepresented in surface collections and on ephemeral upland habitation sites from the study area, where preservation is generally poor.

Settlement and Subsistence Data. Although Helton-horizon sites are fairly numerous in the region, astonishingly few have been tested or excavated outside the lower Illinois Valley. Subsurface remains have been encountered at five sites located north and west of Napoleon Hollow, Elizabeth, and Slim Lake, which are located within the southeastern edge of the study area (see Wiant et al., this volume). The five are the Chrisman (11PK10), Cadwell #3 (11HA679), Eagle Slough (11PK787), Elledge (11PK477), and Lecroitip (11A1146) sites (McGregor 1954:12–21; Nolan 1991b:73–99, 1995:92–125, 2003:22–26; Stafford 1994). Cadwell #3, Elledge, and Lecroitip are multicomponent buried upland scatters, whereas Eagle Slough and Chrisman are located in the Mississippi and Illinois valleys, respectively.

Chrisman was the first Archaic-period habitation site to be tested and radiometrically dated in the study region. It is located near several backwater lakes on a relict channel of McKee Creek that traverses the western side of the Illinois River floodplain. The site produced Karnak and a few Matanzas-cluster points from surface and subsurface contexts as well as the remains of an extensive sub-plow-zone shell heap or midden (McGregor 1954:13–14). Some of the shell from this deposit was used to obtain a radiocarbon assay, although the date of cal 5480 B.C. appears unreliable today in light of the temporal parameters that have more recently been established for Helton in the lower Illinois Valley. The Eagle Slough site is located along an anabranch of the Sny within the Mississippi River floodplain in the northwestern corner of Pike County (Van Nest 1997). Limited testing by the CAA revealed 1.5-m-thick, stratified Woodland- and Archaic-period midden deposits with associated features (see discussion of Eagle Slough in *Data Sets* above). Karnak Stemmed and Matanzas points were recovered from the lowermost midden deposit (Soil 3), which produced a dispersed charcoal date of 5240 ± 90 RCYBP (cal 4040, 4020, 4000 B.C.). Since Eagle Slough has never been formally studied or reported, pit and artifact associations have not yet been worked out to any degree, so we can only note that Helton artifacts occur in what appears to be their correct stratigraphic placement relative to Falling Springs and Hemphill diagnostics.

The upland scatters were each found on bluff tops or other formerly forested landforms located in close proximity to the valley margin of perennial streams, such as the LaMoine River, Bear Creek, and Blue Creek. Cadwell #3 produced the remains of three apparently hearth-focused activity areas (ranging from 4 m^2 to ca. 24 m^2) arranged in a linear, east–west trending distribution through the center of the excavated portion of the site. These hearth areas were defined in the E soil horizon by concentrations of FCR and burned debitage but did not contain any associated charcoal or oxidized soil. Matanzas and Karnak points were found around the periphery of each rock concentration, generally within a 1-m radius (Nolan 1991b:95–96), but few other tools aside from biface fragments were recovered, suggesting that hunting and generalized cutting and piercing activities were integral to site function. The relevant subsurface features at Lecroitip consist of several concentrations of colorfully heat-treated, late-stage chert debitage and associated Matanzas points found in the lower E and upper EB soil horizons (Nolan 2003:22–26). The only features that can arguably be attributed to Helton activity at the Elledge site are the two dated nutshell concentrations (ranging from .32 to .45 m^2 in diameter and from .13 to .23 m deep) mentioned above, which were located approximately 8–10 m apart in the EB–BE soil horizon. Feature 14 was dominated by thick-shelled hickory nut, and Feature 21 produced primarily black walnut (Stafford 1994:70–76). Given their overall depth and profile shapes, both features appear to be the remains of poorly preserved Archaic pits.

These upland sites produced evidence for what appear to have been short-term Helton occupations; Cadwell #3 and Lecroitip appear focused on general hunting-related activities, such as tool maintenance and replacement, whereas Elledge has produced evidence for some low-intensity nut processing but cannot be characterized further. The low overall density of associated artifacts and features does not suggest that these are the remains of residential sites per se; rather, they appear to relate to general foraging activities undertaken by small groups of people (e.g., Stafford 1991). While survey data suggest such small-sized Helton occupations are common in some upland settings (e.g., Conrad 1981, 1982, 1987), such occupations may have been tethered to larger and more optimally located habitation sites. Most upland sites appear to be associated with formerly forested areas; little or no evidence suggests intensive use of level, former prairie areas.

On the basis of surface data derived from both the principal valley and the adjacent uplands, Nolan (2004) suggests that the Helton settlement pattern in the Lima Lake locality was centered on large residential sites located along the bluff and valley margins of the Mississippi and its major tributaries, like Bear Creek. A key variable in primary residential site location appears to have been access to productive floodplain environments. These principal settlements appear to have been provisioned by smaller, extractive types of sites located within a several-kilometer radius. Similarly large and dense Helton sites have been documented along the bluffs of the central LaMoine River valley (Nolan 1991b; Nolan and Graham 2003; Nolan et al. 1997) and on a variety of landforms located near the western valley margin of the central Illinois River (Lawrence A. Conrad, pers. comm. to Nolan 2004), suggesting this pattern may have been quite widespread.

One of the more unusual LaMoine River Helton components is the Kathay site, where a local avocational archaeologist reports finding several dark, plowed-out, house-sized stains that produced Karnak points and three-quarter-grooved axes. In all, the site has yielded nearly two dozen finished or spent Karnak points and a full range of production failures relating to this type. The Kathay site Helton occupants clearly were exploiting the abundant Burlington/Keokuk resources that were available within several kilometers, and the site likely represents a residential camp where Karnak points were produced. The Nelson site (11HA934) is another sizable bluff-top habitation located in the LaMoine drainage; at least 50 Matanzas and Karnak points were observed in a collection amassed from this property (Nolan 1991b:97). Other dense, but less conspicuous Helton sites have also been documented on the LaMoine bluffs near Macomb (Nolan and Graham 2003), suggesting the preference for high, stable landforms may have been quite widespread in the drainage. Currently, little surficial evidence indicates use of the high terraces or flood-basin deposits in the central LaMoine drainage.

Large Helton-horizon sites, however, apparently are not limited to areas located within or immediately adjacent to the larger tributary valleys. We are aware of several sizable Karnak sites from upland contexts south of Macomb. The densest (11MD36) is located on the summit of a principal divide that overlooks an expanse of bottomland associated with the sinuous course of Grindstone Creek, a tributary of the LaMoine. Multiple walkovers of this extensive multicomponent site by the same avocational archaeologist have resulted in the recovery of nearly three dozen Karnak points (some of which are the largest examples we have seen), several Matanzas points, and five three-quarter-grooved axes. Several smaller yet remarkably productive sites have also been recorded nearby on the apexes of high, linearly oriented glacial-drift ridges that are not situated in close proximity to any obvious permanent water sources (some obviously infilled glacial kettles are present elsewhere, though, in the vicinity). These sites have produced abundant FCR and from four to a dozen Karnak points apiece during multiple revisit surveys made by the same individual. While we currently do not know what types of occupations these latter sites signify, they raise an interesting question. What significance should be given to the predominance at some study-area Helton sites of only one of the two associated hafted-biface types?

While Matanzas points are found in at least low numbers on most Helton sites in western Illinois, the more lanceolate-shaped Karnak forms typically outnumber them on some of the largest sites found in the central part of the study area (e.g., Duke, Chrisman, and Kathay), whether they are located in the Mississippi, LaMoine, or Illinois drainage. We are aware of few sites that are dominated by Matanzas points or that have produced large numbers of both types, although the former may be the common pattern in the lower Illinois Valley, if Koster, Slim Lake, Quasar, and other sites are typical (Cook 1976:Table 17, Figure 18; Goatley 1998a:Table 3; Stafford 1989:Table 3.19). Could these disparities simply be a product of differing site functions, or is some type of spatial-temporal variation also evident? What patterns, if any, are present in the northern part of the study area? We currently cannot address these questions but think they are worthy of further investigation.

Geographic Distribution. While Helton-horizon diagnostics are broadly distributed throughout western Illinois, assessing their overall distribution on the basis of contract reports, site forms, or other types of secondhand information is becoming increasingly difficult because many researchers misapply the type name *Matanzas*. This is especially critical in the northern part of the study region (and beyond) because the distributional limits for a distinctive western Illinois cultural complex or phase(s) probably occur in this area. For example, we are unaware of any Karnak points found north of the Rench site in the central Illinois drainage (e.g., Fishel et al. 2004), although Matanzas-cluster points reportedly are found as far north as the Quad Cities along the Mississippi and into the interior (Ferrel Anderson, pers. comm. to Nolan 2004; Nolan et al. 2003; Shepard 1993:Figure 13e). If Helton correlates exist in the northern part of the study area, we expect that they denote a different cultural complex than that evidenced in the central portion (summarized above), because Karnak points do not seem to form a dominant or consistent part of the tool kit. At least some of the northern side-notched forms resemble Brewerton-cluster points (Justice 1987:115–124) as much as Matanzas, again suggesting distinctive populations may be represented by these archaeological remains.

Determining the spatial or geographic limits of the various Helton-age phases represented in western Illinois is a considerable undertaking and beyond the scope of this review. However, we suspect that the Helton phase has its northern limits in or near Pike County and is principally centered on areas located to the south and east in the lower Illinois Valley. One or more distinctive phases may be represented in the central portion of the western Illinois study area, and other contemporary cultural complexes may be definable to the north, in Rock Island, Henry, and Mercer counties.

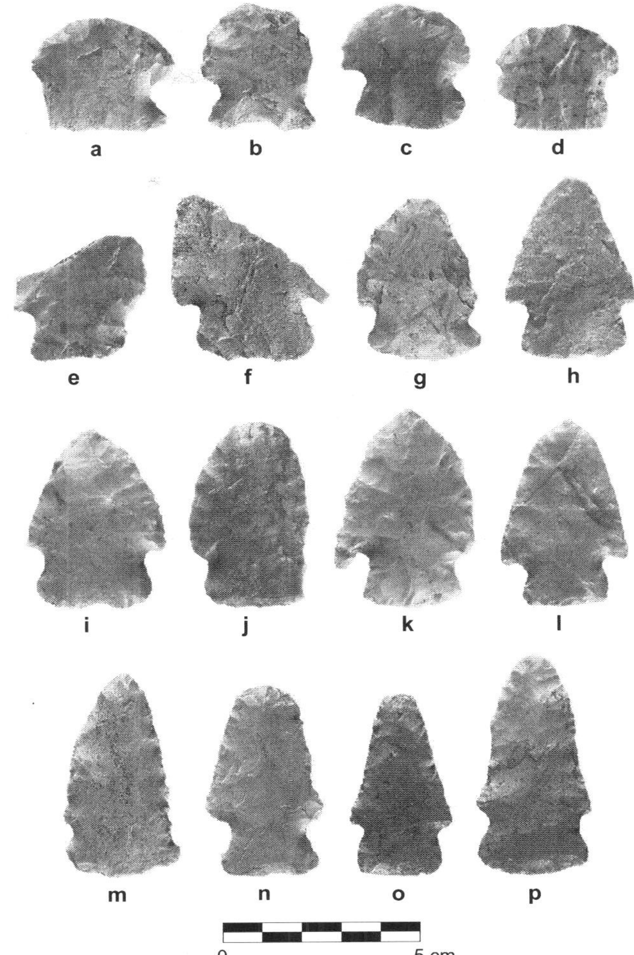

Figure 13.18. Falling Springs–horizon points.

Falling Springs Horizon (4900–4400 B.P., cal 3650–3000 B.C.)

The beginning of the post-Helton period in parts of western Illinois is typified by expanding-stemmed to open corner-notched point forms (Figure 13.18) that appear to be local correlates of those found in Falling Springs–phase contexts in the American Bottom (McElrath 1986). McElrath et al. (this volume) refer to them as McLean points, although this type cluster certainly includes what were formerly called "Helton" points at Koster (Cook 1976) as well as Ferry, Barbeau Stemmed, Saratoga Expanding Stemmed, and Williams points (Brown and Vierra 1983; Fowler 1957, 1959; Winters 1963). Radiocarbon dates associated with the Falling Springs phase primarily cluster between approximately 4900 and 4500 B.P. (Ahler et al. 1992; McElrath 1986). The weighted average of Falling Springs–phase dates from Strata 9E and 8EC at the Modoc Rock Shelter is ca. 4800 B.P., although a single assay from a stratigraphically separate later component of this phase is 4330 ± 90 RCYBP (Ahler et al. 1992:33–34). The assays from the McLean site fall within the Modoc range of dates (McElrath 1986:106) as do those from the Cypress Land site in the lower Illinois Valley, despite the latter contexts having been originally erroneously attributed to the Helton phase (Conner 1986:22–25). Thus, the majority of the radiocarbon assays from the expanding-stemmed components from Illinois do not appear to overlap with those available for the Hemphill complex (Conrad 1981; see below), although the number of sites involved is admittedly small.

However, a recent AMS date returned from an expanding-stemmed-point horizon wedged in between Helton- and Titterington-phase components at the stratified Quasar site in the lower Illinois Valley has produced a ca. 4200 B.P. age (Goatley 1998a). We are unsure what significance should be applied to this assay since it derives from "midden" charcoal found on a "living surface" that also produced Hemphill-complex and Titterington-phase points (Goatley 1998a:277). This assay, along with the one from the upper Falling Springs component at Modoc, overlaps the dates for the Hemphill horizon and could be interpreted as representative of the terminal portions of the Falling Springs phase, but the data are currently too equivocal to assess whether expanding-stemmed forms were partly coeval with the boldly side-notched points or not (also see below).

More excavated data are needed to resolve questions about the possible associations between the two study-area point traditions that typify the millennia marking the Atlantic–Sub-Boreal transition. However, a few boldly side-notched points were found as a collateral type at McLean, and a few expanding-stemmed points occurred at the Hemphill-complex Tree Row site in the central Illinois River valley (see below). In addition, both styles have been recovered from the same approximate depths in the cumulic midden deposits at Eagle Slough (see *Data Sets* section above) and from eroding midden contexts at the Andrew Farm Gully (11A1578) site, located in the Lima Lake locality north of Quincy. Thus, if there was temporal overlap between the Falling Springs and Hemphill cultural complexes, we expect it to have occurred around the time when these sites were occupied, ca. 4500 B.P.

Tools and Other Artifacts. The only distinctive artifacts that can currently be associated with Falling Springs–horizon occupations are expanding-stemmed points, which are often easily confused with some corner-notched to stemmed Middle Woodland and early Late Woodland types, such as Manker and Steuben (e.g., Conner 1986). Given their morphology and flaking characteristics, McLean points (see McElrath et al., this volume) appear to derive from an ancestral side-notched form, perhaps Matanzas, which exhibits a similarly flaring haft area. In a pristine state, McLean-cluster points appear to be moderately thick and have relatively wide, somewhat parallel-sided shoulders that taper toward a narrow tip. With repeated sharpening, the modest barbs found at the shoulders are removed and the blade becomes more rounded and triangular, giving these points an excurvate overall appearance (McElrath 1986:21–30). Many of these points ultimately were refurbished as hafted end scrapers. These expanding-stemmed points are typically made from regionally available cherts, principally those from the Burlington/Keokuk formation, and are frequently heat treated.

Settlement and Subsistence Data. Few excavated contexts in western Illinois can be attributed to the Falling Springs horizon with confidence, although three sites are relevant to this discussion. The Eagle Slough site produced several classic McLean points (Figure 13.5j–k) from a portion of a cumulic floodplain midden that also yielded more boldly side-notched Hemphill-complex forms. A pit feature that originated in the levels producing these points returned a radiocarbon date of 4720 ± 70 RCYBP (cal 3520 B.C.), which is consistent with those available for the Falling Springs phase in the American Bottom (see McElrath et al., this volume). However, no additional information about this component or feature is available since the site has never been formally analyzed or reported.

Another occupation that may be relevant is Buckshaw Bridge (11BR116), which was excavated by the CAA as part of a small salvage project in the McKee Creek drainage in southwestern Brown County. Machine stripping exposed 49 Archaic-period features oriented in a series of linear clusters perpendicular to the edge of the low terrace on which they were located; areas of sheet midden were also encountered along the terrace margin (Stafford 1991:215–218). Nearly two-thirds of the features were steep-sided pits that had an average volume of 150 liters; they generally exhibited greasy middenlike fills but had quite variable depths (< .45 m). Given the features' high concentration of nutshell (74 g/10 liters), low frequency of wood charcoal (nutshell-to-wood ratio of 101:1), and predominance of ground-stone tools, for example, three-quarter-grooved axes, manos, metates, and pitted anvils, the site has been interpreted as a temporary field camp that was repeatedly used for the bulk processing of hickory nuts to extract nutmeat and oils for transport back to a base camp (Stafford 1991:215–218).

While Buckshaw Bridge has been attributed to late Middle Archaic (Atlantic) occupation by Stafford, our review of the recovered artifacts and dates indicates the site has a substantial post-Helton, Falling Springs–age component. The projectile point assemblage is relatively heterogeneous compared with that from the American Bottom type site and includes specimens that appear to be intermediate between expanding-stemmed and broadly side-notched forms, like Godar (Figure 13.19). While many of these appear relatable to the McLean type cluster, narrow-bladed specimens found in Features 5 and 15 ($n = 2$) seem to be examples, or derivatives, of Matanzas and Karnak points (Figure 13.19n–q). The lack of Falling Springs diagnostics in these same pits raises the possibility that the feature assemblage is attributable to multicomponent Atlantic-period site use.

However, the two dated features (Features 3 and 33) produced assays of 4600 ± 80 RCYBP (cal 3360, 3330, 3210, 3190, 3160 B.C.) and 4510 ± 70 RCYBP (cal 3120 B.C.), which are completely congruent with other Falling Springs assays from Illinois. Expanding-stemmed hafted bifaces, including one of the aforementioned intermediate McLean/Godar forms, were the only types recovered from these two features; they also occurred in other pit and near-surface contexts. These data suggest to us that Buckshaw Bridge primarily dates to the Falling Springs horizon, rather than the "late Middle Archaic" Helton phase, much like the Cypress Land site in

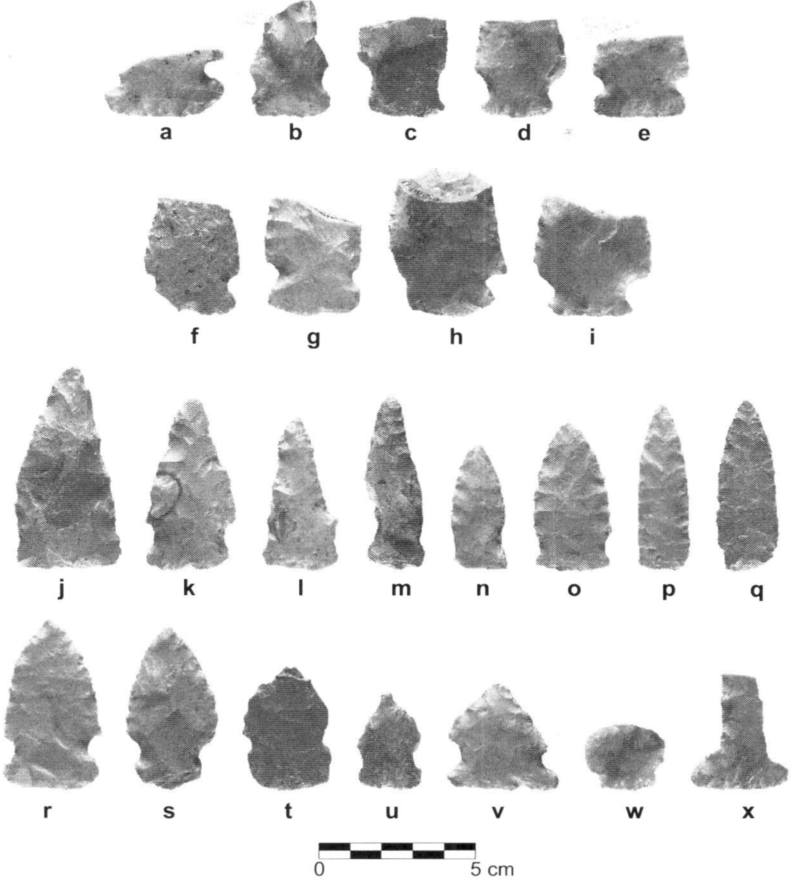

Figure 13.19. Selected artifacts from the Buckshaw Bridge site.

the lower Illinois Valley. However, the variability in these two sites' projectile point assemblages may be sufficient to warrant consideration of distinctive regional phases, with Cypress Land displaying closer affinities to, and perhaps denoting a northward extension of, the American Bottom Falling Springs phase. The diverse projectile point assemblage from Buckshaw Bridge could be interpreted as reflecting interaction with Hemphill-horizon peoples or could be seen as transitional between these two cultural complexes.

Another site located on the Illinois bluffs near the southeastern margin of the study area, Elizabeth (11PK512), has produced what appear to be Falling Springs horizon ("Helton") points in direct association with Archaic-period burials. The remains of five articulated individuals (Burial 32) were discovered on a buried B horizon, beneath a Middle Woodland mound that was constructed on the side of a knoll or ridge overlooking Napoleon Hollow (Albertson and Charles 1988:33–38). Four of the skeletons had beaded *Anculosa* shell "belts" encircling their waists and expanding-stemmed points within their chest cavities; each of the five individuals also had *Anculosa* bead "bracelets" on at least one wrist. All of the illustrated points, except one (Odell 1988: Figure 9.4i) recovered from the individuals in Burial 32, appear to be rather pristine, local McLean cognates (contra Odell 1988:162–166), although the cal 5320 B.C. bone date derived from this feature appears to be nearly two millennia too early for this typological context. Stratigraphically above or possibly intruding on Burial 32 was a mass of disarticulated human bone (Burial 24) representing five individuals (Albertson and Charles 1988:36). Several Hemphill-complex artifacts, including an Osceola point, two drilled (Godar-variety) plummets, a three-quarter-grooved ax, and an antler handle, were found interspersed among the bones associated with Burial 24, providing at least one instance in which stratigraphy suggests Falling Springs–horizon remains are older than Hemphill, although that is far from clear.

Aside from the few excavated contexts summarized above, the Falling Springs cultural complex is primarily known from survey, although this data set is similarly meager. Some of this apparent paucity can be blamed on misidentification of points; McLean points typically have been attributed to either Helton assemblages or Middle Woodland–Early Late Woodland components (e.g., Conner 1986:Figure 15f–l; Hassen and Batura 1983) or languish as type-indeterminate examples (Stafford et al. 1983:Figure 11). However, they have been identified more frequently in several recent survey reports, and we have observed other specimens in older, well-illustrated contract reports. Nolan (2004) reports several McLean occupations in the Lima Lake locality, including what appear to be extensive components on the western shoreline of the former lake and on a narrow, sandy terrace remnant located along the banks of an interior slough course, near the western edge of the floodplain. Smaller numbers of McLean points have also been identified on Kingston Terrace remnants situated in the middle of what was formerly Lima Lake. Studenmund (1992: Figure 4.8d) illustrates an example from a sandy floodplain feature at the Homer Vance site in the Illinois Valley near Meredosia. These sites all are located in close proximity to what would have been productive lowland habitats, such as backwater lakes and sloughs. Similar settings were occupied in the lower Illinois Valley during the preceding Helton phase (e.g., Stafford 1989; Stafford 1991:218–219).

Examination of regional survey and collector data suggests that Falling Springs components occur relatively rarely in upland contexts. For example, Conrad (1981:131, Plate 25b) reports only a single example of a "Helton" point in a sample derived from over 5,000 sites; this specimen was found in the LaMoine River drainage. Stafford and Nolan (1990:Table 3.3) recorded an example in a private collection amassed from an upland area located immediately adjacent to the Illinois Valley in Pike County. Nolan (2004) identified only one possible component east of the Mississippi bluff, located in an unusually culturally diverse upland area surrounding several prominent natural springs and glacial kettles. However, he also observed a few expanding-stemmed points in private collections amassed from small streambeds and cutbanks located throughout the tributary valleys that traverse portions of the upland interior adjacent to the Mississippi trench. These data suggest that much of the upland archaeological record associated with the Falling Springs complex may prove to be surficially undetectable because the components are buried within tributary stream alluvium or colluvial drape. Similarly masked occupations are likely represented in the floodplains of the larger valleys, too, as indicated by sites like Eagle Slough.

Geographic Distribution. The distribution of Falling Springs–horizon sites appears to be heavily skewed toward the southern half of the study area, which may suggest close connections with contemporary lower Illinois Valley and American Bottom populations. In the Mississippi Valley, the number of sizable Falling Springs sites appears to drop off dramatically north of Lima Lake (Nolan 2004), although scattered expanding-stemmed points have been identified as far north as Warsaw. Much less is known about the distribution of sites in the Illinois Valley. An avocational archaeologist has brought several examples to our attention from floodplain landforms in Schuyler and southern Fulton counties, but these specimens do not appear to denote the presence of dense habitation sites. Falling Springs habitation sites seem to occur more regularly along the backwater lakes of the lower Illinois Valley, perhaps as far north as Meredosia (Conner 1986; Hassen and Batura 1983; Stafford et al. 1983; Studenmund 1992).

Nonetheless, apparently isolated McLean-cluster points are found beyond the areas where large habitation sites have heretofore been documented, in association with boldly side-notched points. For instance, Benn (1987:Figure 4.10g) reports a single example from an excavated Hemphill component at the Sand Run West site (13LA38) in southeast Iowa. As previously mentioned, a similar situation is evident at the Tree Row site (11F53), where five expanding-stemmed points were found among the 142 boldly side-notched forms associated with the Hemphill component (Evans 2001). On the basis of a corresponding situation in the American Bottom involving a small number of Hemphill-complex points found on the Falling Springs–phase type site (McElrath 1986:30–31), McElrath (pers. comm. to Nolan 2004) suggests these "collateral" forms may be evidence for contact or interaction among contemporary groups. The overlap in radiocarbon assays associated with the Falling Springs and Hemphill horizons (see below) certainly indicates that this is possible. However, more work clearly needs to be done before archaeologists can address the geographic limits of the Falling Springs horizon and the nature of the social landscape during the millennia marking the Atlantic–Sub-Boreal transition.

Sub-Boreal Episode (4700–2900 B.P., cal 3500–1100 B.C.)

Hemphill Horizon (4600–4100 B.P., cal 3350–2650 B.C.)

Hemphill is the earliest cultural complex in the study area to have sizable excavated collections that are securely dated by multiple radiocarbon assays. Conrad (1981:125–130, 143–144) defined the Hemphill complex prior to most excavation of Hemphill components. He observed that Godar/Raddatz and Osceola points, which Cook (1976) subsumed under the Helton phase, formed less than 9 percent of the assemblage from Koster Horizon 6 (no Osceola points were identified), yet they were the only side-notched point types found in association with Archaic cemeteries considered by Cook and others (e.g., Charles and Buikstra 1983) to be representative of that phase (e.g., Klunk submound 14, Gibson submound 1, Hemphill, and Godar). Given this pattern of occurrence and the fact that the FAP 407 survey data showed that Godar/Raddatz and Osceola points have the same distribution—quite different from that of Helton diagnostics—Conrad (1981:143–144) postulated that a cultural complex typified by boldly side-notched forms was temporally intermediate between Helton and Titterington. This hypothesis was confirmed by excavations at Sand Run West (13LA38) in Iowa and at the Elizabeth Mounds (11PK512) and Tree Row (11F53) sites in the Illinois Valley. We therefore consider boldly side-notched forms, such as Godar/Raddatz and Osceola points, to denote the Hemphill horizon.[6] We simply refer to these points and related materials as "horizon markers" because we suspect that multiple phases could be represented across the broad geographic expanse under consideration here.

The Hemphill cultural complex is relatively well dated in this part of the upper Mississippi basin, with assays available from at least four sites, Tree Row, Sand Run West, Cabin Corner (11A1392), and Rench (11P4), located within or immediately adjacent to the study area. Tree Row is exceptionally well dated; 11 of the 14 dates from suspected Hemphill contexts cluster between 4580 and 4210 B.P., with a weighted average of 4438.7 ± 33.2 B.P. (Evans 2001; also see Table 13.2). The Cabin Corner Hemphill date falls within this span, although the Sand Run West and Rench dates are slightly younger (Table 13.2) and appear to overlap the early end of the Titterington phase of the Illinois-Mississippi-Missouri river confluence area (e.g., Fortier 1984). This dating is essentially congruent with our expectations since some of the larger Osceola points we have examined exhibit similar types of blade flaking and overall morphology as Titterington diagnostics. Additionally, such oversized forms have been found in association with mortuary caches consisting of Etley, Wadlow, and Sedalia/Nebo Hill points (Reid 1983; Roper 1978; Titterington 1950), suggesting at least some measure of contemporaneity and culture contact (cf. Conrad 1987).

Tools and Other Artifacts. Projectile points are the most diagnostic artifacts associated with this cultural complex. However, Conrad (1981:143) notes that Wisconsin winged and triangular-shaped bannerstones and copper spearheads also can be confidently attributed to the Hemphill complex on the basis of their co-occurrence at the Hemphill Mound Group in Brown County and at the Osceola site in Grant County, Wisconsin (e.g., Knoblock 1939:201–210; Ritzenthaler 1946, 1957; Titterington 1950:26–31; Wittry and Ritzenthaler 1957). To this list, we would add drilled Godar-variety plummets (Perino 1961), which were found with an Osceola burial at Elizabeth Mounds (Albertson and Charles 1988) and are associated with Godar points at the type site in the lower Illinois Valley (Titterington 1950:22).

Hemphill-horizon projectile points consist of boldly side-notched forms, such as Godar/Raddatz (Cook 1976:145–146; Perino 1963:95; Wittry 1959:44–46) and Osceola (Ritzenthaler 1946:63) (Figures 13.6 and 13.20), which characteristically have deep, squared to U-shaped notches that were removed perpendicular or at a slight angle to the long axis of the blade. Points of the former type cluster also typically display squared haft areas, biconvex cross sections, and parallel to convergent-sided blades that were shaped by a combination of percussion and pressure flaking. While Osceola points generally display similar manufacturing attributes, they usually are much larger, or at least more robust, than Godar/Raddatz types and have basal margins that vary from straight to markedly concave, with some lateral "earing" evident. Heat treatment, haft grinding, and weakly developed blade serration are attributes that sometimes are associated with all Hemphill-complex points, even though the frequency of these traits varies considerably from sample to sample. Most of the points are manufactured from regionally available cherts, especially varieties of Burlington/Keokuk, although a possibly related Excello-chert specimen was recovered from the Grace site (11PK490) in Pike County during the FAP 408 survey (Stafford and Nolan 1990:7, Table 2.51) and a Cobden/Dongola side-notched(?) form was noted in a private collection amassed from Tree Row.

Aside from the points and aforementioned burial objects, few other tool or artifact forms can be confidently associated with the Hemphill complex. A variety of hafted bifacial drill or awl types, including so-called T-drills, which may represent terminally resharpened side-notched points, have been recovered from Sand Run West and Cabin Corner. Three-quarter-grooved axes appear to have been the predominant form; 20 were found at Tree Row (Evans 2001), two at Cabin Corner, and one apiece from Osceola burials excavated at the Elizabeth (Odell 1988:Figure 9.6d) and Hemphill (Titterington 1950: Figure 5 no. 3) sites. Our impression is that these ax forms exhibit tapering bits and asymmetrically rounded poll areas that vary in overall shape. However, we think consistently distinguishing these axes from other Atlantic and early Sub-Boreal specimens, such as those found in Helton and Falling Springs contexts, would be difficult.

Settlement and Subsistence Data. Fewer than a dozen sites in western Illinois have produced evidence for subsurface habitation remains, in one case with associated mortuary features, that appear relatable to this cultural complex. In addition, two other excavated sites have yielded what apparently are isolated Hemphill-complex cemeteries. Only a few of these sites have been adequately reported to date (Albertson and Charles 1988:29–40; Knoblock 1939:201–210; McConaughy 1993:57–60; Titterington 1950:26–30); the others are in the process of being analyzed and written up, so we can only broadly characterize the remains at this time.

The multicomponent Tree Row site (11F53) yielded the remains of the largest Hemphill habitation and associated cemetery yet encountered. This component produced hundreds of features and over 90 human burials; several dog burials may also be related. Nearly 150 boldly side-notched points (Figure 13.6) were recovered during the RIP excavations, the overwhelming majority of which were identified as belonging to the Godar/Raddatz type cluster. On the basis of the large number of burials and relatively low density of chert tool-manufacturing debris, Evans (2001) tentatively proposes that the site functioned not only as a Late Archaic–Sub-Boreal cemetery but also as a "ceremonial site for the local population."

Some Hemphill cemeteries were also located away from obvious habitation areas on the bluff tops of the major valleys. A variety of interments with associated Osceola points were found beneath Middle Woodland Mound 1 at the Elizabeth site in eastern Pike County, including a possible bundle burial

(Burial 24) comprising five individuals; individuals placed primarily on their backs in shallow pits ("Flat Cemetery") excavated into the subsoil of the natural ridge (e.g., Burial 19); and flexed (e.g., Burial 7), extended, and disarticulated burials placed on a prepared floor or intruded below the base of a large basin feature (Feature 7) (Albertson and Charles 1988:36–38; Charles et al. 1988:248–253; Odell 1988: Figures 9.5, 9.6).

Aside from their having produced spectacular artifacts (see Knoblock 1939 and Titterington 1950 for details), little is known about the Hemphill Mound burials located on the Illinois River bluffs in Brown County because they were not systematically excavated or reported. The landowners of the site "ransacked" two plowed-down mounds of uncertain construction or age during the 1930s. Each mound produced two primary burials, which had been placed on subsoil and covered with red ocher; these burials were subsequently capped with earth and limestone slabs, but their relationship to the mounded fill is uncertain (Charles and Buikstra 1983: Table 7.1; Knoblock 1939:201–210). Although only one of the mounds produced an Osceola point, several others share artifact types, such as large calcite beads and quartz or calcite gorgets, which suggests the burials are attributable to a single cultural complex.

Elizabeth and Hemphill contain some of the earliest bluff-top cemeteries documented in the region. Their locations may denote increasing population and levels of social interaction or competition among late Atlantic and Sub-Boreal native peoples living in the major valleys. The placement of the dead in knolls or mounds occupying highly visible landforms like bluff tops is believed to reflect the marking of group territory or hereditary rights (sensu Charles and Buikstra 1983). Clearly, given the large number of burials found at the bluff-base Tree Row site as well as other possiblly contemporary floodplain cemeteries in the lower Illinois Valley (e.g., Hassen and Farnsworth 1987; Titterington 1950:22), not all individuals or groups were accorded burial in prominent bluff-top cemeteries, nor were they always accompanied by abundant cached grave offerings, irrespective of their location. We are not in a position to address the possible meaning of these differences and refer the reader to Charles and Buikstra (1983) for more detailed insights into regional Archaic-period mortuary patterns and behavior (also see Milner et al., this volume).[7]

Clearly, not all Hemphill sites that have been investigated have produced evidence for associated mortuary activity. However, most investigations have examined much less area than at Tree Row, so what is present in the parts of the sites that have not been professionally excavated is not known. A Hemphill site that has not produced evidence of mortuary activity is the stratified Cabin Corner site (11A1392), located on the Buel Branch alluvial fan in the Lima Lake locality of the Mississippi Valley (Nolan and Farkas 1998; Nolan and Graham 2005). This site's buried Hemphill-horizon component only came to archaeologists' attention after unauthorized borrow removal associated with road construction had destroyed most of the overlying fan stratigraphy, exposing a dense habitation deposit on the floor of the borrow pit. IDOT halted work at the site, and ITARP personnel conducted small-scale identification and stabilization so that what remained could be preserved in place. These investigations sampled a nutshell-rich midden area, which provided a date of 4500 ± 70 RCYBP (cal 3330, 3220, 3170, 3160, 3120, 3110, 3110 B.C.), and removed several Hemphill features. A large number of cobble tools, including axes, manos, metates, and two larger grinding mortars, were piece plotted on the exposed paleosol surface along with Godar/Raddatz and Osceola points, some of which were refurbished as awls or drills (Figure 13.20) (Nolan and Graham 2005). The Cabin Corner Hemphill component appears to be the remains of a durable bluff-base habitation where a variety of tasks were undertaken, although processing hickory nuts was clearly a central activity in the investigated site area.

Figure 13.20. Selected Hemphill-horizon artifacts from the Cabin Corner site.

Two other Hemphill components have been identified as result of small-scale hand-excavated tests (< 50-m^2-area examined) at the Eagle Slough and Rench sites in the Sny Bottom and central Illinois Valley, respectively. The former site produced eight Osceola points (Figure 13.5f–i), most of which are from the same general midden levels as Falling Springs–age McLean points; they were the most common diagnostics recovered from the Archaic-period strata. Little more can currently be offered about this component since Eagle Slough has not been formally analyzed or reported.

The Rench site is located north of Peoria at the foot of the Illinois bluffs on the Dickison Run alluvial fan. A buried Archaic-period component was located approximately .75 m below the modern fan surface along a former distributary channel of Dickison Run. This occupation, termed "Late Archaic Occupation #1" by McConaughy (1993:57–60), appears attributable to Hemphill-horizon activity, as an Osceola point base was recovered from an area surrounding, and at the same depth as, a large (> 100 liters), rock-filled, basin-shaped pit that produced radiocarbon dates of 4160 ± 100 RCYBP (cal 2700 B.C.) and 4120 ± 100 RCYBP (cal 2830, 2820, 2660, 2650, 2630 B.C.). This component also yielded a small, reworked lanceolate point or knife (termed "Nebo Hill" in the original report), the distal end of some type of excurvate, broad-bladed point, another small pit feature (< 32 liters), and several post molds. The majority of the ecofacts came from nonfeature contexts in Paleosol A, and the overall diversity of remains suggests that an array of habitats and a broad spectrum of plant and animal species were exploited (McConaughy 1993:60). This limited sample has a relatively high wood-to-nutshell ratio.

Two additional, apparently small-sized, buried upland sites may also be attributable to this cultural complex: Read's Point (11PK724) and Pottstown (11P531) (Atwell and Goatley 1993; Studenmund et al. 1998). However, the affiliation of each of these buried components cannot be demonstrated since the relationship between the recovered boldly side-notched Osceola-like points and intact features (rock-lined hearths in each case) is unclear. The former site is located in the McGee Creek drainage in northern Pike County, while the latter was found on the Kickapoo Creek bluff in Peoria County after it had been disturbed by heavy machinery.

Aside from these excavated remains, the primary source of information about this cultural complex stems from professional survey and collector interview. During the FAP 407 survey (Conrad 1981:145–147), Godar/Raddatz and Osceola points were primarily found on forest soils in dissected upland contexts; while none were found on large former prairie expanses, 8 percent of the components were situated on dark Alfisols near lighter-colored timber soils. Conrad noted that both point types tend to cluster together near the larger upland stream drainages, such as Rock and Bear creeks near the Mississippi, the West Fork of the LaMoine near the center of the survey transect, and the Spoon River and Big Creek at the eastern end. However, no Hemphill-horizon points were found along the East Fork of the LaMoine during the FAP 407 survey, although a few examples have since been reported from this part of the drainage in the Macomb area (Nolan and Graham 2003; Porubcan and Lurie 2000). In addition, a sizable habitation (11MD989) covered with FCR has been documented southwest of Macomb on the Killjordan Creek bluff (Nolan et al. 1997:39–41, Figure 20c–f), which drains to the West Fork. Ephemeral, apparently hunting-related sites have also been documented to the south in the uplands between Willow and Grindstone creeks (e.g., Conrad 1978: Plate 7I–K; McNerney et al. 1991:Figure 11B), which are tributaries of the former stream, and to the north and east along streams that drain to the Spoon and the Illinois (Esarey 1982:Appendix B, Figure 7e, g; Green 1977a:Plate 7e–h, 1977b:Plate 2i–n).

Nolan (2004) notes that most of the Hemphill sites encountered in the Mississippi Valley uplands between Quincy and Keokuk occur on the terraces and bluff tops of the larger streams. However, a few components were also documented several kilometers east of the Mississippi trench near a lightly dissected but hydrologically unique area marked by the presence of several productive natural springs and glacial kettles. A local collector reported another site from this particular area that purportedly produced dozens of boldly side-notched points and several grooved axes, although its existence has never been verified by professional survey. Several other amateurs and collectors working in the uplands of Adams and Hancock counties have reported finding Godar/Raddatz and Osceola points in stream gravel bars, suggesting sites dating to this span are eroding from buried floodplain contexts. While ephemeral hunting-related sites are common, these data attest that the more substantial upland Hemphill components tend to be located in close proximity to productive aquatic resource niches.

Given this distribution, the presence of sizable Hemphill sites in the major valleys is not surprising, although many, like Cabin Corner and Eagle Slough, are buried under late Holocene alluvium. However, Nolan (2004) reports that several dense sites occupy sandy Kingston Terrace remnants in the Lima Lake locality; dozens of boldly side-notched points have been recovered from at least three sites, one of which purportedly produced nearly 50 grooved axes after it was first cleared and farmed in the 1930s (Sterling Snowden, pers. comm. to Nolan 1998). Much less is known about the distribution of Hemphill-horizon components in the Illinois trench since Godar points have historically been considered part of the Helton phase or were subsumed under the broadly eclectic Middle Archaic Side Notched "type" by most lower Illinois Valley researchers (e.g., Hassen and Batura 1983; Stafford 1989; Stafford et al. 1983). However, examples are clearly present on or buried within floodplain features of sufficient age (see Goatley 1998a; Stafford 1989:Table 3.19).

Geographic Distribution. As can be seen from the previous discussion, Hemphill components are found throughout western Illinois and have a near-continuous distribution that extends up to and beyond the Quad Cities into the Tri-State portions of the upper Mississippi River valley (Benn et al. 1994:66; also see Benn and Thompson, this volume). Both excavated and surface sites are known from the Sny and Lima Lake localities (e.g., Morgan and Stafford 1986:Figure 4.1e, f; Nolan 2004; Nolan and Graham 2005), and others have been identified during survey and collector interview undertaken in the Henderson County portion of the valley to the north (Goatley 1998b; Nolan et al. 2003). Collections housed at ITARP suggest that a sizable Hemphill component is present in the lower Rock River drainage at the Crawford Farm site (11RI81) (Shane Vanderford, pers. comm. to Nolan 2004). To date, the largest excavated component is located in the central Illinois Valley (Tree Row), where other buried (Rench) and surface sites have been identified (Fishel et al. 2004). Boldly side-notched points appear to have an unbroken distribution from this point southward into at least the northern part of the lower Illinois Valley (Stafford 1989; Stafford and Nolan 1990; Stafford et al. 1983) but appear to be generally atypical of post-5000 RCYBP contexts in the American Bottom region (see McElrath et al., this volume). However, published reports (e.g., Hassen and Batura 1983; Hassen and Farnsworth 1987) suggest that Osceola points are much less common than Godar south of the study area in the lower Illinois Valley, a phenomenon that warrants further research because it could denote the presence of distinctive phases whose limits may prove useful in the reconstruction of social or ethnic boundaries.

Titterington Horizon (4200–3600 B.P., cal 2650–2050 B.C.)

The Titterington horizon equates to a temporal span occupied by several related Illinois and Missouri phases, including Titterington, Sedalia, and Nebo Hill as well as the recently named Mule Road phase of the American Bottom region (C. Chapman 1975; Conrad 1981; Cook 1976, 1986; Fortier 1984; McElrath 1993; Reid 1983, 1984; Titterington 1950). These phases are characterized by a polythetic group of large hafted bifaces that seems to vary in composition from locality to locality. The principal diagnostics of these phases are Etley, Wadlow, Sedalia, Nebo Hill, Stone Square Stemmed, and Mule Road/Ledbetter-cluster points as well as other distinctive tools such as the Clear Fork gouge and Sedalia digger (Figure 13.21). McElrath (1993:150) suggests this sharing of diagnostic forms is the result of interaction between contemporary but regionally distinctive peoples. He believes these disparate but similar remains denote a definable "culture" (termed the "Titterington-Sedalia-Nebo Hill," or "TSN" culture), using the term similarly to the way other archaeologists speak of a "Havana" Middle Woodland culture. TSN within-culture interaction probably had its most overt expression in the movement of large distinctive bifaces, often in caches, through trade into areas where these types generally do not make up significant parts of the local assemblages (cf. Reid 1983:20–21; Roper 1978). Such trade or interaction likely solidified intergroup relationships, although its archaeological effect is to blur the boundaries of what may be regionally distinctive cultural complexes.

This is especially true of the Titterington "phase," which exerted a magnetlike pull on TSN assemblages from various parts of western Illinois. This phase has traditionally been attributed to the 4200 to 3850 RCYBP time span on the basis of available radiocarbon assays (see Cook 1986:189–190 and McElrath et al., this volume, for a review of the formative dates). However, recent work in the study region indicates variability in the dates and assemblages that are routinely, and often unhesitatingly, assigned to this "phase." It seems clear today that the once-monolithic Titterington phase of western Illinois comprises multiple phases or complexes, which remain rather poorly defined, despite the availability of relatively large assemblages and associated radiocarbon dates. Much of this ambiguity relates to the startling diversity in the composition of the projectile point assemblages, even within relatively small geographic areas, which has constrained attempts to taxonomically rein them in. This diversity is especially characteristic of the study area; we make no attempt to define Titterington-horizon phases because much of the analysis and reporting that will be required to support their definition is currently underway.

If the Titterington "phase" is to be retained as a local taxon, it should be applied to archaeological assemblages dominated by Etley points and Wadlow knives, which are found near the Illinois-Missouri-Mississippi river confluence area in the Lincoln Hills section of the lower Illinois Valley and American Bottom regions (Cook 1976, 1986; Fortier 1984) but occur rarely in the rest of western Illinois (cf. Conrad 1981:148; Nolan 2004).[8] Given this distribution, this phase is probably only represented in the southernmost part of our study area (i.e., Pike County). However, very little is known about the artifact composition of most of the Titterington-phase sites in Illinois south of the study area, aside from Go-Kart North and Koster, because relatively little attention appears to have been given to any assemblage variation that was evident. For example, Sedalia points are casually regarded as typical of the phase but are absent from or form only a small part of some site assemblages (e.g., Cook 1976, 1986; Fortier 1984; also see McElrath et al., this volume).

Across much of western Illinois, these lanceolate forms constitute the dominant point style and represent the common denominator among most local TSN assemblages. Noting this, Conrad (1987) defined two sequential cultural complexes, which he termed "Macomb" and "Bear Creek," on the basis of the assumption that Nebo Hill points or cognate forms date more recently than Sedalia; nonetheless, he noted that both types were sometimes found on the same site and that they had considerable distributional overlap (Conrad 1981:162–167). Nolan (2004), armed with hindsight gained from nearly two decades of additional survey, regional excavations, and new ^{14}C dates, collapsed these two provisional cultural complexes into a single, more broadly conceived, yet-unnamed taxonomic unit. This cultural complex was defined on the basis of data from the Lima Lake locality of the Mississippi Valley, which indicated that both lanceolate types form parts of local assemblages (Figure 13.22); their distinctive but covarying morphology is believed to be attributable to differing tool functions, resharpening patterns, or perhaps extraregional interaction, rather than a strict temporal or cultural dichotomy.

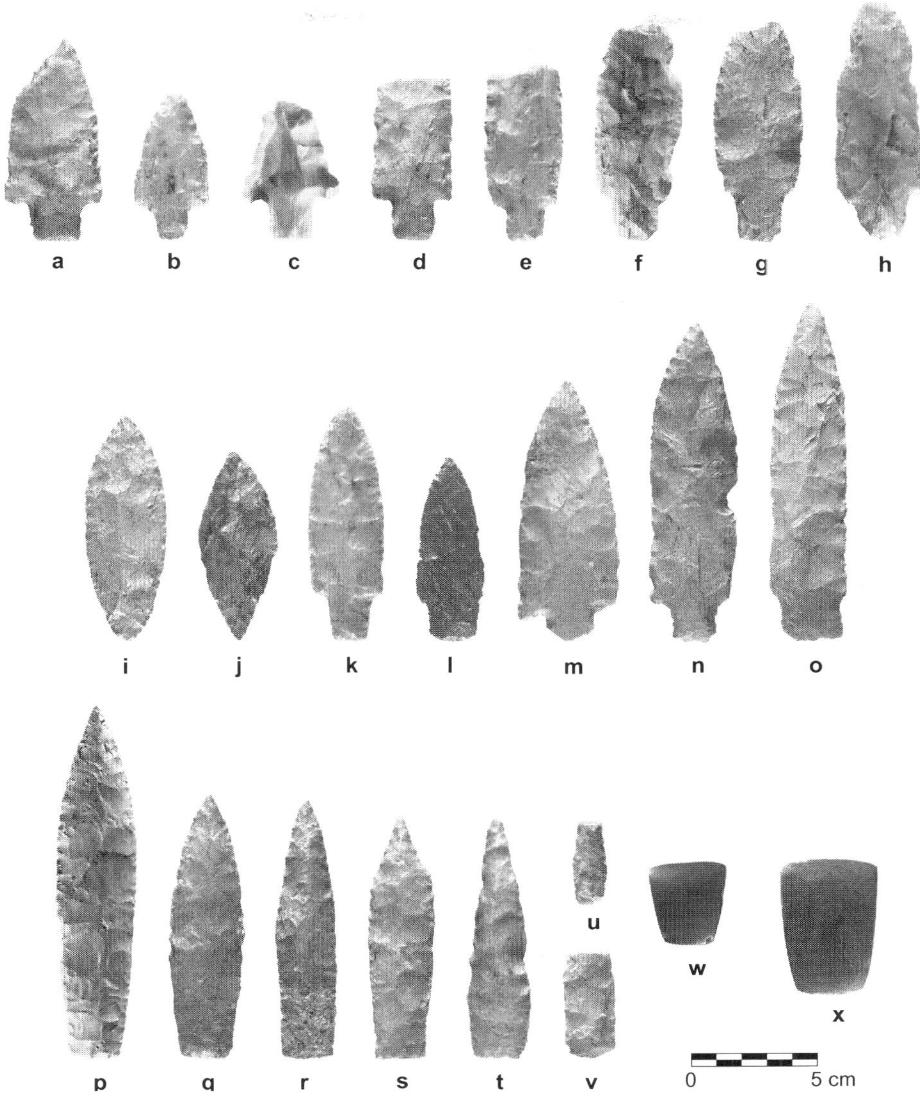

Figure 13.21. Titterington-horizon diagnostics from western Illinois: a–h, k–o, stemmed variants; i, j, leaf-shaped bifaces; p–s, Sedalia/Nebo Hill; t–v, bifacial awls or drills; w–x, hematite celts or adzes.

In addition to these lanceolate forms, Nolan (2004) noted that some TSN sites in the Lima Lake locality produced stemmed points similar to those ascribed to the Mule Road phase in the American Bottom and the Sedalia phase in Missouri (C. Chapman 1975:200–219, 224; McElrath 1993). We have observed similar stemmed point types in other TSN assemblages from the Sny Bottom, the lower and central Illinois Valley, the Spoon, and the lower Rock River drainage of western Illinois (Conrad 1987; Fishel 2004; Studenmund et al. 1998), indicating that similar or related cultural complexes may be present across much of the study area. However, these stemmed forms are not found on all sites that produce Sedalia/Nebo Hill lanceolates, and they are the predominant point types in relatively few components.

One site where stemmed points predominate is the Ursa Major site (11A1006), located north of Quincy on a low floodplain terrace in the Ursa Creek drainage (Esarey 1982). Stemmed Mule Road–like points vastly outnumber the lanceolate forms at this site, although examples of both types were recovered from the same stratigraphic context during test excavations. Two radiocarbon assays are available from adjacent pit features with a shared projectile point refit, the more reliable of which appears to be 3900 ± 70 RCYBP (cal 2460, 2450, 2430, 2420, 2400, 2360, 2350 B.C.). Other sites and assays summarized below indicate that most of these stemmed points are not appreciably younger than the Titterington *phase*, although a recently excavated stemmed-point-producing site from the Quad Cities area (Billboard

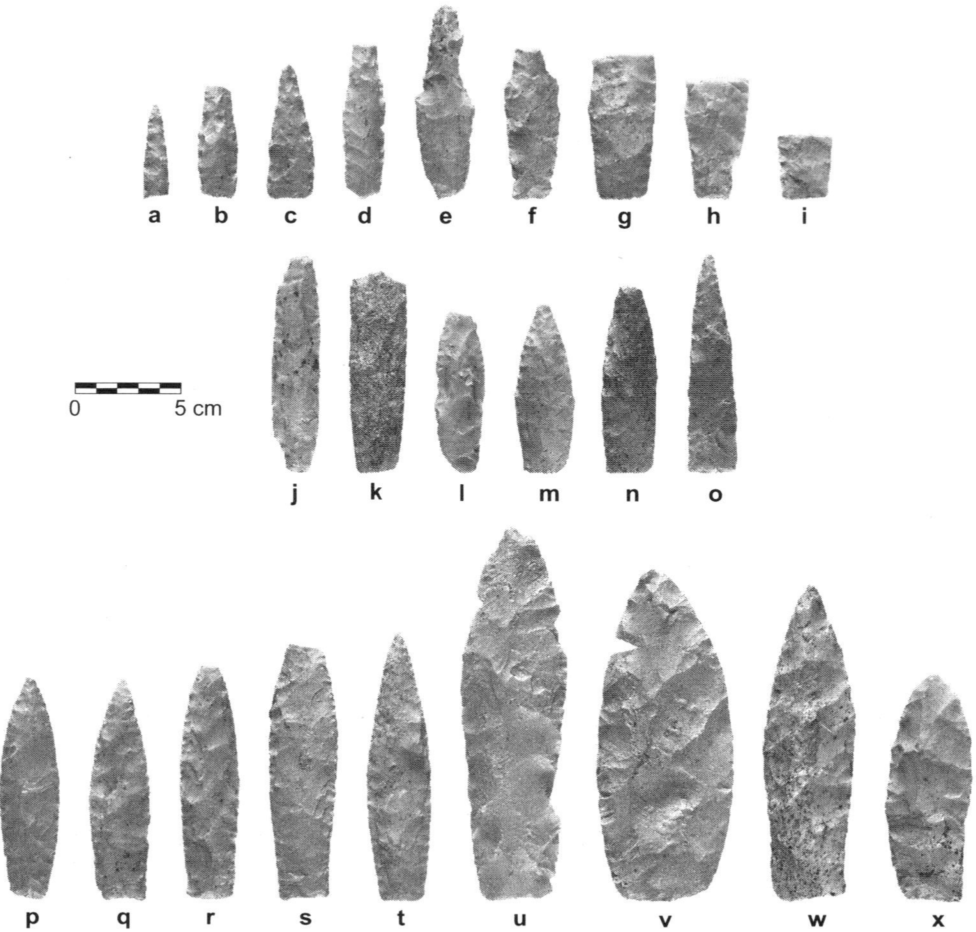

Figure 13.22. Selected Titterington-horizon artifacts from the Shoemaker site.

Flats, 11HY289) and some single-component sites yielding only Sedalia/Nebo Hill–cluster points date as recently as 3700 RCYBP (Fishel 2004; Nolan 2003).

Currently, 23 radiocarbon dates are either directly associated with, or fall within the temporal span attributed to, the Western Illinois Titterington horizon (excluding those from Napoleon Hollow, which are summarized by Wiant et al., this volume). These dates range from 4170 ± 120 RCYBP at the Ruth Andrew site (11A1051) to 3450 ± 180 RCYBP at Ursa Major. However, these two particular dates are outliers and may not be completely reliable, given their high standard deviations. This is almost certainly true of the Ursa Major assay, which is much too young and directly tied to an acceptable date, mentioned above. The remaining assays cluster between 4060 ± 70 (cal 2620, 2580 B.C.) and 3680 ± 70 RCYBP (cal 2110, 2100, 2040 B.C.), which equates to a roughly 600-year period using calendar ages (Table 13.2). Many of these assays actually postdate the Titterington *phase*, as expressed in the American Bottom and lower Illinois Valley (see McElrath et al., this volume), which may be related to the absence of assemblages dominated by Etley points from areas located north of the Sny Bottom in the Mississippi and of McKee Creek in the Illinois drainage.

Tools and Other Artifacts. While the predominant tool types associated with western Illinois Titterington-horizon assemblages are the projectile points or knives, these are the first assemblages postdating the late Boreal–early Atlantic in which appreciable numbers of other associated implements and distinctive patterns of raw material or artifact use can be recognized. Sedalia/Nebo Hill–cluster points/knives are the most recognizable artifacts associated with western Illinois TSN sites. These large lanceolate forms are shaped by the removal of broad percussion flakes and typically exhibit little marginal retouch, although individual specimens show considerable variation and some well-made examples are known. The basal margins are frequently straight, but convex and concave examples also occur, the latter perhaps resulting from reworking the haft area after damage. Nebo Hill–like forms are typically narrower and have a more diamond-shaped cross section than Sedalia points, which are more lenticular in cross section, with the widest part of the biface generally toward the distal third. On larger sites, both "types" are represented and the full range of variation is often evident (Figure 13.22).

In addition to these lanceolate forms, some sites also produce stemmed variants that generally exhibit broad blades with obtuse to barbed shoulders (e.g., Esarey 1982:Figures 10–14) (Figure 13.21); narrower examples are also known that appear to be Sedalia points on which stems were fashioned in an ad hoc manner. The stems of these points are generally short relative to overall blade length and width and have a squared to somewhat rounded or contracting appearance. In contrast to most Sedalia/Nebo Hill points, some of the stemmed variants exhibit light marginal haft grinding. Some of these points are similar to Mule Road variants found in the American Bottom area (McElrath 1993; McElrath et al., this volume), while others have been shoehorned into the broadly conceived Stone Square Stemmed or Smith Basal Notched types (C. Chapman 1975:245–257). Given their stemmed configuration, smaller examples are also sometimes confused with Early Woodland Kramer points.

However, recent dating of a feature from the Billboard Flats site, which produced a small unbarbed, Moline-chert stemmed point (Figure 13.21l), to cal 2140 B.C. (Fishel 2004) casts doubt on the Early Woodland association that is frequently attributed to smaller stemmed types in the Quad Cities area (e.g., Markman and Kriesa 1986; Neller 1998: Figures 5a, 6a), even in the absence of associated Marion ceramics. The Quad Cities examples generally are thicker and less regularized than classic Kramer points. Additionally, the stems are shorter and lack the alternate beveling and pronounced grinding that is frequently associated with the haft elements of Kramer points (Munson 1966:111; Perino 1985:212; also see Stafford and Stafford 1992 for variation in these attributes). These forms are similar to the other Titterington-horizon stemmed points described above, although they typically do not appear as robust in overall blade length, width, and thickness. This stemmed variant may represent a distinctive Titterington-horizon point type found in the lower Rock River drainage. Assemblages comprising lanceolate points or knives have also been found in this area (Ferrel Anderson and Shane Vanderford, pers. comms. to Nolan 2004). These lanceolates appear similar to but are slightly more diminutive than, the Sedalia/Nebo Hill–cluster bifaces that are characteristically found in the central and southern parts of the study area.

In addition to the projectile points or knife forms, other implements can be attributed with confidence to western Illinois Titterington-horizon tool kits. Chief among these are narrow, pointed bifacial objects commonly referred to as "drills" (Esarey 1982:Figure 19; Studenmund et al. 1998: Figure 29) (Figure 13.21t–v), which may have actually functioned as knives or as awls or punches. While Sedalia/Nebo Hill and stemmed projectile points were sometimes reworked to produce drill-like forms (Figure 13.21t), most examples are smaller than the points (Figure 13.22a–d) and appear to have been fashioned for specific purposes. These narrow bifacial tools are common on some Titterington-horizon sites, especially those producing stemmed points; the most distinctive examples have parallel sides with squared to rounded basal configurations. Three separate examples of the type were recovered from Feature 1 at the Cabin Corner site (11A1392) in association with a crude contracting-stemmed point and a radiocarbon assay of 3980 ± 70 RCYBP (cal 2480 B.C.). Others have been recovered from Fan Middle, Billboard Flats, Crosstown Avenue, Shoemaker #1, Ursa Major, and Frazier I (Esarey 1982; Fishel 2004; Nolan 2004; Studenmund et al. 1998).

Additional distinctive chipped-stone objects include Sedalia diggers and Clear Fork gouges described by Carl Chapman (1975), and relatively thin, bipointed, leaf-shaped blades or knives (Figure 13.21i, j). The former occur sporadically in western Illinois (Esarey 1982:Figure 25b; Nolan 2004; Stafford and Nolan 1990:86) but have been reported from some larger sites, suggesting their use may have been primarily tied to durable habitations. While also quite rare, the bipointed bifaces have a similarly wide and diffuse distribution that extends from the Quincy area to the Quad Cities (Fishel 2004; Neller 1998:Figure 5c; Nolan 2004). Chert hammerstones fashioned from cores are also commonly found on Titterington-horizon sites although they are not expressly diagnostic.

Most of the Titterington-horizon chipped-stone artifacts are manufactured from medium to higher grades of regionally available Burlington/Keokuk chert, although variety is sometimes evident. Some of the material attributed to these sources may actually derive from Salem limestone bedrock sources (Brad Koldehoff, pers. comm. to Nolan 2004), suggesting either the presence of undocumented local exposures or extraregional contacts. The only definite exotic-chert Titterington point we are aware of from the study area is the blade of an Etley point from the Choda site (11PK844) in Pike County that Toby Morrow identified as manufactured from Wyandotte chert. Several flakes of a similar exotic gray "hornstone" material were identified from a dated Titterington-horizon pit (F2) excavated at the adjacent Brush College School site (Stafford 1994:43).

Use of other regionally available chert types is also evident. A few LaMoine River–chert artifacts have been found in the Bear Creek drainage in Adams County, and debitage from another dark, untyped fossiliferous Pennsylvanian chert, perhaps emanating from the Ursa Major site area (Esarey 1983), has been recovered from other Adams County sites (e.g., Cabin Corner Feature 1 [Nolan and Graham 2005]). Moline chert was used in the lower Rock River area, albeit in smaller amounts than one would anticipate, given its wide availability (e.g., Fishel 2004). It has not been found in Titterington contexts outside the general Quad Cities area, however. In the Lima Lake locality, Warsaw chalcedonic chert, which naturally occurs in ball-shaped, geodelike form, was used for expedient flake tool and some projectile point manufacture. Localized Warsaw bedrock sources also produce quartz-filled geodes that were apparently exploited to extract their crystals (see below) (Nolan 2003). Others (Cook 1976; Fortier 1984) have viewed the lack of intentional heat treatment of chert as characteristic of Titterington lithic technology, and the western Illinois data strongly support this, although angular, thermally shattered chert fragments are exceedingly common in some assemblages (e.g., Nolan and Graham 2005; Stafford 1994).

In addition to chipped stone, Titterington contexts feature distinctive ground-stone tools, including axes and celts as well as shaped grinding mortars and pestles. The predominant, or at least most recognizable, ax form appears to be an elongated, parallel-sided, three-quarter-grooved form often referred to as the "western rectangular axe" (C. Chapman 1975). Small, rectangular-shaped hematite celts or adzes (Figure 13.21w, x) are also associated with Sedalia/Mule Road forms in the Lima Lake locality and perhaps as far north as the general Quad Cities area, where several examples have been found in surficial association with lanceolate points (Ferrel Anderson, pers. comm. to Nolan 2004). At least five fragmentary hematite celts or adzes have been recovered from Frazier I (11A1085), and flakes removed from the bit of an adze were found in Feature 1 at the Cabin Corner site (Nolan and Graham 2005). Hematite (and limonite [see Fishel 2004]) use, in general, appears to have been common, but the source of this material is unknown. While some of it may denote extraregional exchange or procurement, local amateurs suggest outcrops are present near Camden in tributaries of the LaMoine (Glen Hanning, pers. comm. to Nolan 2001); Fishel has also collected palm-sized tabular pieces of hematite southwest of Rushville from the bed load of a tributary of Town Branch, which drains to the LaMoine.

Extremely large, cupped grinding mortars, smaller pecked and shaped sandstone metates, and bell-shaped pestles are also believed to be associated with Titterington-horizon peoples, given their surficial co-occurrence with Sedalia/Mule Road points. McElrath (1993:153) identifies the latter as particularly diagnostic of Mule Road occupations. At least five examples of bell-shaped grinding stones have been documented in private and institutional collections amassed between Quincy and Keokuk in the Mississippi drainage (Nolan 2004; Steven Tieken, pers. comm. to Nolan 2003); they are all but unknown from other parts of the study area.

Settlement and Subsistence Data. Currently, 18 sites in western Illinois have produced subsurface remains that are relatable to the Titterington horizon; 14 of these have associated radiocarbon assays (Table 13.2). This total excludes Napoleon Hollow, which relates to the lower Illinois Valley Titterington phase and is ably summarized by Wiant et al. (this volume). Another site that is excluded is Marseton #2 (11MC71), which produced a large, rock-filled basin that was radiometrically dated to this span but lacked associated diagnostics (Fishel 2003); this component is not discussed further, although ongoing analyses may ultimately prove it to be directly relatable since stemmed points have been recovered from the site.

A variety of occupation types appear to be represented by the remains encountered at these 18 sites, ranging from short-term encampments to slightly larger and perhaps seasonal residences to what appear to be large, heterogeneous base-camp settlements. The sites occupy a range of different landform types, including upland interfluves and the bluff tops and terraces of tributary streams that traverse the interior as well as the bluffs, fans, and floodplains of the major river valleys. Since these sites were not totally excavated, we cannot be sure that sampled areas accurately portray the overall diversity of remains or site function, although we feel the data are broadly representative. These excavated data are supplemented by an abundance of survey information from the region (e.g., Conrad 1981, 1987; Nolan 2004), which provides additional insights into settlement location and overall landscape use or preference.

Three shallowly buried sites have been tested or excavated in the upland interior away from the immediate environs of perennial water sources: Penstone (11PK727), Tent Town (11HA771), and Lecroitip (11A1142) (Nolan 1993, 1995, 2003; Studenmund and Graham 1999; Van Nest 1993). These components are characterized by a simple site structure comprising primary refuse accumulations resulting from short-term occupation. No intentionally constructed facilities are evident, although concentrations of burned rock or scattered carbonized materials may denote the locations or presence of poorly preserved, low-intensity hearths. Projectile points or knives are the predominant tools found at each of these sites, and the assemblages generally are characterized by a low number and limited diversity of formal tool types. Botanical remains are similarly meager and primarily reflect the use of locally available wood and nutshell resources, including hazelnut, which is indicative of the exploitation of savanna or prairie-forest ecotones (Schroeder 1998:14).

While these may be the remains of hunting camps, tool manufacture and maintenance or repair appear to have been important activities that were undertaken at each site, as indicated by the presence of multiple concentrations of flaking debris. The best example of this is the Penstone site, where dense piles of subsurface chipping debris and production failures relating to the manufacture of Sedalia points were found (Studenmund and Graham 1999). Brush College School (11PK488), located several kilometers to the northeast of Penstone on a bluff top overlooking the same stream course, produced similarly large and dense scatters of subsurface flaking debris and bifaces relating to the production of Sedalia points (Stafford 1994). However, several pit features and a wider variety of tool types were found at this site, perhaps indicating it was a more residentially oriented, or seasonally reoccupied, habitation than the others, albeit still short-term.

Examples of denser habitation sites that have produced pit features and sheet-midden deposits have been documented on the bluff tops of the larger tributary streams and principal valleys: Kuhlman Village (11A162) and Scenic Vista (11A51) overlook the Sny Bottom, Crosstown Avenue (11RI693) occupies a prominent location above the confluence of the Rock and Green rivers, and Shoemaker #1 (11A1142), Ruth Andrew (11A1051), and Teddy (11A1052) are situated on or near the upland margin above Bear Creek (Hassen 1991; Nolan 1993, 2003; Vanderford 2005). These sites have produced variable remains but generally have low numbers of pit features (up to two dozen), including large rock-filled basins (Shoemaker, Teddy, Crosstown Avenue, Scenic Vista) that apparently functioned as roasting pits and smaller, simple basin-shaped pits, probably used to process basic subsistence resources.

In addition, shallowly buried sheet-midden deposits were associated with the Ruth Andrew and Shoemaker sites. The former was characterized by overlapping concentrations of FCR, chert reduction debris, and tool discards; some of these concentrations appear to represent the remains of aboriginally scattered hearths, whereas others may be secondary refuse accumulations (Nolan 2003). The sheet-midden deposits at Shoemaker principally comprised manufacturing debris and tool discards but also included burned rock. They occurred in opposing parts of the site adjacent to or surrounding two loose concentrations of pit features. Two relatively unique living-surface features were also associated: a small thin, oval (.04-m^2) smear of heavily reduced red ocher and a concentration of thermally shattered geodes that appear to have been intentionally heated and split, perhaps to extract the quartz crystals contained within them (Nolan 2003). Small amounts of quartz and geode detritus have been recovered from several Titterington-horizon sites in the area, including Ruth Andrew, Teddy, Tent Town, and Cabin Corner, suggesting the exploitation of this raw material was patterned.

The artifact and ecofact assemblages recovered from these bluff-top sites vary considerably (Hassen 1991; Nolan 1993, 2003; Vanderford 2005). The sites from Adams and Pike counties are dominated by Burlington/Keokuk chert, while Crosstown Avenue principally yielded Moline and other related local cherts. Lanceolate Sedalia-cluster points are the predominant diagnostic forms, although a few Wadlow-like knives were also found at Kuhlman, Scenic Vista, and Shoemaker. The Teddy site produced the only obvious stemmed point fragment, which appears to be a somewhat atypical form and is the sole chipped-stone Titterington-horizon diagnostic found there. Bifacial drills or punches and ax fragments have been found at all of these sites but in relatively low numbers; Scenic Vista may have considerably more but they have not been formally reported (cf. Hassen 1991). Large grinding mortars or metates suggestive of intensive plant-food processing were recovered at Shoemaker and Scenic Vista.

However, the botanical assemblages from these bluff-top sites are not appreciably more dense or varied than those from the apparent short-term occupations mentioned above and can be described as having moderately low overall charcoal concentrations (Schroeder 1998:10–14). Wood charcoal predominates at all sites, although a variety of nutshell and a few bramble or weedy seeds are typically represented. Crosstown Avenue is notable for producing only a single nut variety: hazelnut (Shane Vanderford and Leighann Calentine, pers. comms. to Nolan 2004). Additionally, two large features at Scenic Vista that yielded Sedalia point fragments and another sizable facility from which only nondiagnositc lithics were recovered produced the remains of unidentified, carbonized tubers (Hassen 1991).

Small-scale tests have been conducted at Titterington-horizon sites located within the major river and tributary stream valleys, including Cabin Corner (11A1392), Fan Middle (11PK1562), Rench (11P4), Eagle Slough (11PK787), Hot Bend (11A1158), Lewton (11PK445), Ursa Major (11A1006), and Billboard Flats (11HY289). The initial three listed are located on alluvial fans in the Mississippi and Illinois valleys, Eagle Slough is buried in the Mississippi floodplain, and the remainder were found on terrace remnants situated in a variety of secondary drainages (Esarey 1982; Fishel 2004; McConaughy 1993; Nolan 1995; Nolan and Graham 2005; Studenmund and Graham 1999; Studenmund et al. 1998; notes and data on file at the CAA). All of these sites have yielded stemmed-point variants, although Rench, Cabin Corner, and Billboard Flats failed to produce any associated lanceolate forms, which may be attributable to small sample size in the first two cases. In addition, Eagle Slough produced one of the only definite Etley points (Figure 13.5e) recovered from excavated context in the study area.[9]

These data indicate that most of the lowland sites have more heterogeneous projectile point assemblages than occupations located in the uplands. Aside from this, relatively little is known about any given site because such small areas were investigated. The sites located on alluvial fans and in flood-basin deposits are buried at depths greatly exceeding the modern plow zone; as such, they have little or no surface expression, so the size and intensity of occupation is difficult to discern. All that can be said at this time regarding the Titterington component at Eagle Slough is that points have generally been found in their correct stratigraphic positions relative to other Archaic-period diagnostics recovered from this cumulic midden deposit. Cabin Corner produced a single rich feature (an earth oven?) and sparse living-surface debris (Nolan and Graham 2005). The Rench Late Archaic Occupation #2 produced more than a dozen overlapping, unprepared hearths, and several rock, artifact, and charcoal concentrations (including two piles of charred logs).[10] A similarly sized area at Fan Middle comprised a tight arc of pit features (including possible earth ovens yielding carbonized tubers, chenopod seeds, and a variety of nutshell) and hearths located upslope of a dense midden deposit yielding abundant FCR, burned sedimentary stone, charcoal, and lenses of flaking debris (Studenmund and Graham 1999:7–8).

Unlike the fan and flood-basin sites, all of the sites tested to date on stream terraces had some type of surface expression, consisting of light to heavy-density lithic scatters. The excavated areas at two of these terrace sites, Lewton and Hot Bend, appear to be peripheral to the densest parts of each site, and therefore the remains encountered are probably not representative. The former contained two apparently isolated pits (notes and data on file at the CAA), and the latter produced several subsurface concentrations of burned rock and postdepositionally disturbed sheet-midden deposits (Nolan 1995:126–162, 2003:26–29). At the Billboard Flats site, 10 closely spaced processing and storage features were found within a 304-m^2 portion of a late Pleistocene-age landform that bordered a former marsh located in the Green River lowlands (Fishel 2004). Fishel believes these features were used by a small group of people to process nuts and tubers during a short-term occupation that probably occurred in the late summer or early fall.

In contrast, Ursa Major appears to represent a large, dense base locale (sensu Emerson 1984). The site is situated on a south-facing floodplain terrace in the Ursa Creek drainage, in close proximity to dense bedrock exposures and bed-load deposits of Burlington/Keokuk chert. Through repeated surface collection and small-scale subsurface testing of the site, using both hand- and machine-excavated units, 36 stemmed and lanceolate Titterington-horizon points were recovered from intact and plow-disturbed contexts along with 54 untyped point fragments, at least 30 bifaces or blanks, 37 drills, nearly 70 thin bifaces or knives, three leaf-shaped blades, five rectangular gouges, a small number of flake tools, and a large amount of chert waste (Figure 13.23) (Esarey 1982:23). In addition, ground-stone tools were common and consisted of numerous manos and pitted cobbles, some ground or faceted hematite, sandstone abraders (both grooved and planar), a large sandstone metate, and an exceptionally large granitic grinding mortar weighing 55 kg. Esarey (1982:24–25, Figures 26, 27) reports seven pit features that appear to be associated with the Titterington-horizon component, including two large rock-filled basins similar to those found in blufftop contexts elsewhere, a regionally unique, .75-m-deep, multizoned bell-shaped pit (Feature 13.6), and several simple basin-shaped pits. An incompletely exposed arc of post molds, possibly representing a structure (Esarey 1982:Figure 27), was encountered at one end of a hand-excavated test unit. Sub-plow-zone sheet midden or living-surface debris was also common throughout Stratigraphic Component C, the Titterington-horizon occupational zone.

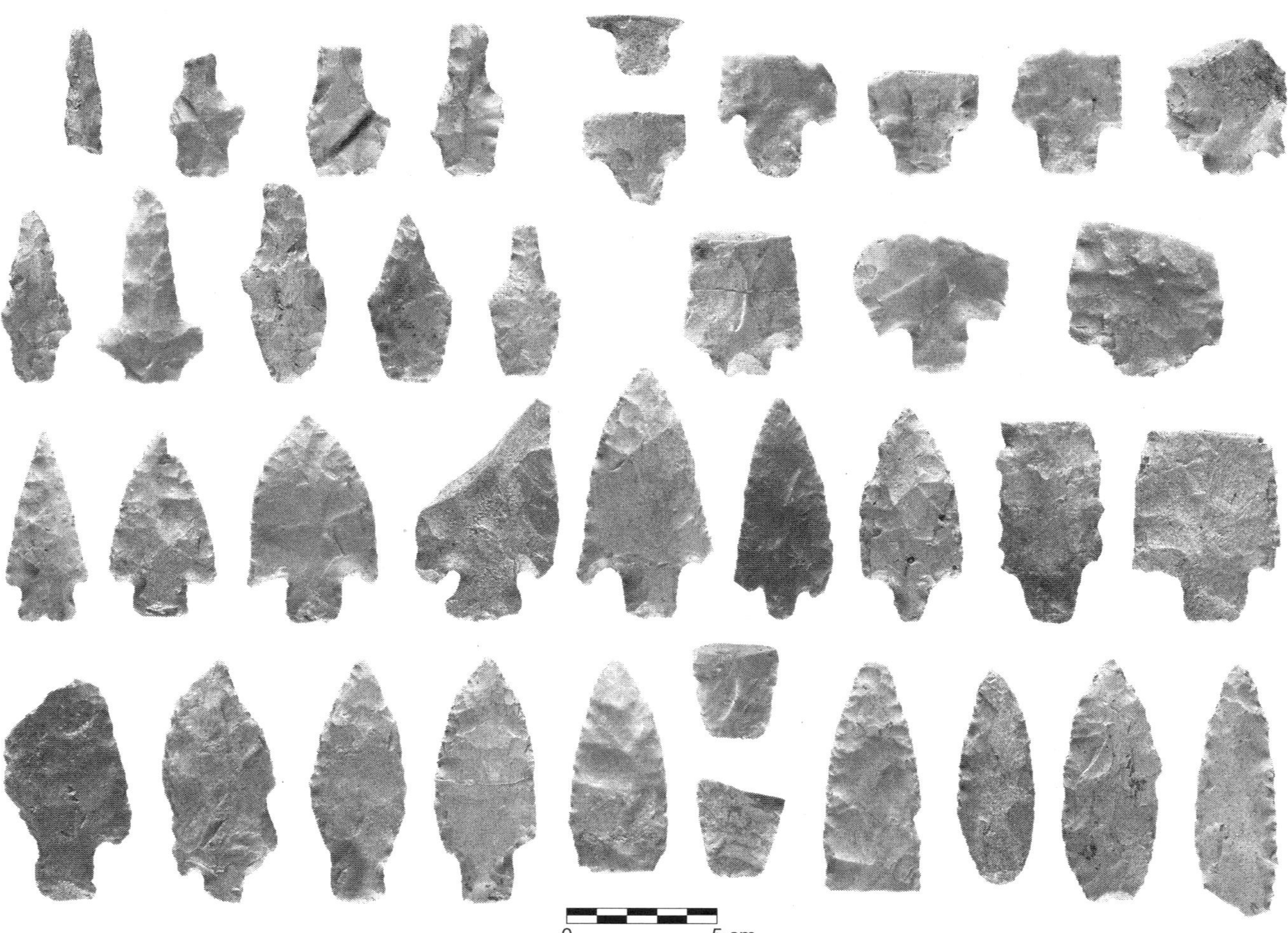

Figure 13.23. Selected Titterington-horizon artifacts from the Ursa Major site.

As mentioned, Ursa Major is the most durable Titterington-horizon residential settlement for which we have evidence. We note its overall size, protected setting, density of remains, relative feature diversity, heterogeneous point/knife assemblage, and evidence of varied site activities: hunting (points/knives), butchering or cutting (knives and flake tools), quarry and workshop-related tasks (hammerstones, bifaces or blanks, cores and debitage, and adjacent raw-material source), woodworking (gouges), plant-food processing (manos, large grinding mortar and metate, and basin pits), leather or hide work (numerous drills or perforators), possible storage of perishable resources (deep bell-shaped pit), large-scale (communal?) cooking or roasting (large rock-filled basins), and shelter construction (arc of post molds). Similarly dense and diverse surface sites have also been identified during regional survey, although they appear to be the exception rather than the rule.

The densest sites known from the upland area adjacent to Ursa Major are Frazier I (11A1085) and Eleanor Hilgenbrink #3 (11A1583) (Nolan 2004). The former site occupies a high, narrow terrace remnant in the Bear Creek valley and has produced large numbers of both Sedalia and stemmed Mule Road variants in surficial association with leaf-shaped blades, drills or perforators, grooved axes, hematite celts, an exceptionally large mortar, other shaped metates, numerous cores (including discoid-shaped examples used as hammers), rubbed and faceted hematite, and an array of tool and debitage types. The relative abundance of hematite artifacts and presence of LaMoine River–chert bifaces may be indicative of extralocal contacts, perhaps with the LaMoine River drainage area in Schuyler County, where Titterington-horizon components are common and local informants suggest these raw materials naturally occur (Glen Hanning, pers. comm. to Nolan 1990).

Eleanor Hilgenbrink #3 is situated on a high terrace or bluff top overlooking Bear Creek's entrance into the Mississippi Valley. Systematic professional survey has recovered a modest assemblage of Sedalia points and functionally specific ground- and chipped-stone tool types, but no obvious stemmed points have been found at the site, to our knowledge. However, this site has been heavily combed over as a result of decades of local collecting activity, so the samples derived from systematic surveys may not be completely representative. Local individuals report that it has been especially productive of lanceolate ("spike") points, grooved axes, and bannerstones (Ed Wilcox, pers. comm. to Nolan 1995). The prominent and strategic site location and unusual artifact composition suggest a significant mortuary component may be associated, although this remains purely speculative.

Ursa Major, Frazier I, Eleanor Hilgenbrink #3, and other sites mentioned above form part of a database from the upland portion of the Lima Lake locality that consists of at least 91 professionally recorded Titterington-horizon components and numerous others known only from collector interview (Nolan 2004). The distributional data clearly reveal that the focal points for the regional TSN settlement were the secondary stream valleys that traverse this area. Nearly two-thirds of the components are located on or within the walls of these valleys, and many others were documented on divides situated immediately beyond their margins. The densest sites in this sample are found on the bluff tops and terraces of these streams, including closely spaced, linearly oriented habitation scatters that parallel the banks of the South Fork of Bear Creek (e.g., 11A1156, 1157, and 1158). However, sites that produced stemmed Mule Road–like points appear to be more heavily nucleated west of the Mendon Moraine in the lower reaches of streams located closer to the Mississippi Valley (Nolan 2004:Figure 3.30), perhaps indicating they have a more limited interior distribution than those yielding primarily Sedalia/Nebo Hill points. The lack of identifiable components from the till-plain expanses located in the northern third of the Route 336/96 study area and their association with formerly forested locales or edge-opening areas indicate that local Titterington peoples generally avoided extensive prairie expanses, which is congruent with previous considerations of TSN settlement patterns (Cook 1986).

The most startling aspect of the site distribution pattern in the adjacent portion of the Mississippi Valley is the virtual absence of conspicuous residential sites, despite rather broad survey coverage (see Conner 1984; Conrad et al. 1986; Cripe 1988; Nolan 1987, 1994; Nolan and Scott 1996). While site burial is a limiting factor (e.g., Eagle Slough), Titterington-horizon diagnostics are also largely absent from stable Kingston and Savannah Terrace remnants and other ancient floodplain landforms that were heavily utilized throughout most of prehistory. These data suggest that sandy terraces were largely avoided for intensive occupation by Titterington peoples, perhaps because they were covered by prairie grasses or their coarse substrates may have proven unsuitable for the excavation of subterranean storage and processing pits (Dale McElrath, pers. comm. to Nolan 2003). The recovery of occasional diagnostic points from the surface of alluvial and colluvial fans or from ditches cutting through them (e.g., Joe Bartholomew, pers. comm. to Nolan 1993; Conner 1984; Nolan 1987; Nolan and Scott 1996; Steve Tieken, pers. comm. to Nolan 2003) probably indicates that substantial buried components, like the one hinted at by the remains encountered at Cabin Corner, are common along the valley margin.

The only sizable, principal-valley floodplain occupation we are aware of in the Mississippi Valley was documented southwest of Quincy during a waterline survey undertaken by WIU. This multicomponent site (W. Dobbs, 11A53) occupies a clayey terrace remnant, located not far from the bluff base adjacent to a former backwater lake, a setting quite analogous to Go-Kart North in the American Bottom (see Fortier 1984; McElrath et al., this volume). Site 11A53 is the largest and densest TSN *floodplain* site yet recorded in the study area. Two walkovers of the site produced multiple Sedalia points, some stemmed variants, several three-quarter-grooved ax fragments, an exceptionally large cupped grinding mortar, a grooved maul, and an abundance of FCR and chert debitage. Examination of the relevant survey reports indicates that near-surface Titterington-horizon sites appear to be rare in the central Illinois Valley, as well (Conrad 1981; Fishel et al. 2004; Moffat et al. 2001), although Studenmund (1992:64–68) identifies two Etley points and a related gouge or digger from a private collection reportedly amassed from the Homer Vance site, situated adjacent to Meredosia Lake. Stafford (1989:Table 3.19) likewise reports no Sedalia/Nebo Hill points from the FAP 408 floodplain crossing. In addition, we are aware of at least one apparently sizable, or at least dense, bluff-base site near the LaMoine River confluence in Schuyler County (Lucille Ray, 11SC65), where an avocational archaeologist has recovered a suite of stemmed and lanceolate Titterington-horizon point bases similar to those observed at Frazier I in the Lima Lake locality.

In summary, the most conspicuous sites in the local TSN settlement system demonstrate that neither base locales nor smaller residences are closely associated with a single landform type or setting, as Cook (1986) previously suggested, although sites tend to be located near permanent water sources. Cook postulated that such locational variability might suggest that Titterington-horizon peoples in western Illinois employed a more residentially mobile pattern of seasonal aggregation and dispersal (which he termed a "dispersed harvesting economy"). Given the overlap in their dating and distribution, one could argue, distinctive, heterogeneous assemblages comprising both stemmed and lanceolate points from large, protected possible base locales like Ursa Major (11A1006), Frazier I (11A1085), W. Dobbs (11A53), and Lucille Ray (11SC65) are evidence for population aggregation. Correspondingly, the predominance of only one point type or unequally weighted mixtures of both Sedalia/Nebo Hill and Mule Road–like points from smaller upland sites might arguably relate to seasonal dispersal, perhaps by distinctive social groups.

However, these data might also be reasonably used to make a case for sequential phases having similar or coincident settlement patterns (with lanceolate forms predominating later), like that postulated for the American Bottom Titterington and Mule Road remains, or even a functional dichotomy between the two hafted-biface types. Until a larger body of regionally excavated data sets and formal analyses becomes available, the relationship between the lanceolate and stemmed points that currently typify the western Illinois Titterington horizon, as well as the constituent site types in the settlement pattern, will continue to be speculatively discussed. Nevertheless, we feel the recognition and identification of such variability represents an important leap forward in the study of Titterington peoples and lifeways.

Geographic Distribution. Titterington-horizon sites in western Illinois tend to be heavily nucleated in areas where abundant chert resources are available, as Conrad (1987:247) previously noted, but they appear to be poorly represented or absent altogether from intervening areas, especially those locales dominated by prairie-grass vegetation. Some of these intervening areas appear to have been used in a peripheral manner for hunting and other transient activities but currently provide little evidence for substantive habitation. For example, Titterington-horizon sites are virtually absent from the East Fork of the LaMoine near Macomb and from upland areas located to the north in McDonough and Warren counties (Conrad 1981, 1986a, 1987; Dwyer and Burge 1978; Nolan and Graham 2003; Nolan et al. 2003; Nolan et al. 1997; Porubcan and Lurie 2000). South of Macomb, no more than a dozen Sedalia/Nebo Hill–cluster point fragments have been identified in an avocational survey collection amassed from more than 350 sites in the upper reaches of the Willow and Grindstone creek drainages. Conrad (1987) notes that Titterington-horizon remains are similarly rare to the east in the Sugar Creek drainage, and we are unaware of any sizable collections of Sedalia/Nebo Hill points from the Fulton County portion of the Illinois trench, which is chert poor (however, see Montet-White 1968:Figure 46a, b for possibly related stemmed forms from Liverpool). Surveys conducted to the north of this area in the Illinois Valley and adjacent uplands (Conrad 1987; Fishel et al. 2004; Green 1975; O'Gorman 1999) have not identified any substantive near-surface Titterington components, although an unknown number of associated sites could be buried in the bottoms, as the remains from Rench indicate.

Titterington components have a largely unbroken distribution in the southern portion of the study area across much of Adams, Pike, Brown, and Schuyler counties (Conrad 1986d; Cross 1998; Stafford 1994; Stafford et al. 1983; Stafford and Nolan 1990). The sites are generally found in formerly forested upland locations in close proximity to Burlington/Keokuk-chert exposures. In addition to Sedalia/Nebo Hill–cluster points, which predominate, some of these sites also produce Etley points. However, only a single classic Etley has been observed north of Quincy along the Mississippi (Nolan 2004), and the type's distribution appears to drop off considerably north of Pike County along the Illinois, although apparently isolated specimens or cognate forms have been reported as far north in the interior uplands as the central McKee Creek drainage (Conrad 1986d:31). These data suggest that the southern part of the study area is located at or near the interface between Titterington *phase* peoples of the Lincoln Hills plateau region and peoples of one or more unnamed local phases characterized by the predominance of Sedalia/Nebo Hill points, variable representation of stemmed forms, and a dearth of classic Etley points.

Sites characterized by Sedalia/Nebo Hill–cluster and potentially related stemmed points are found along the Mississippi Valley from the Sny Bottom as far north as the general Quad Cities area (Nolan 2004; Nolan et al. 2003; Ferrel Anderson and Shane Vanderford, pers. comms. to Nolan 2004) but seem to become much rarer in the interior farther to the north. The Quad Cities Titterington-horizon peoples made both lanceolate and stemmed points out of Burlington and Moline cherts, the latter of which outcrops in the area, although diagnostic points manufactured from the Moline have never been found south of Henderson Creek, to our knowledge. The data suggest these people may have had little, if any, contact with the central or southern parts of the study area and likely denote the presence of one or more distinctive Titterington-horizon complexes in the general Quad Cities locality.

Several other seemingly isolated areas of nucleated Titterington-horizon settlement are suggested by Conrad's (1987) extensive survey database. A small number of productive bluff-top sites that have apparently yielded only Sedalia/Nebo Hill lanceolates were recorded in a private collection amassed from the area surrounding the relatively chert-rich confluence of the East and West forks of the LaMoine River. These sites produced nearly all the specimens in Conrad's sample; only two possible Sedalia points were recovered during the original FAP 407 survey of this area (Conrad 1981). An even denser area of Titterington-horizon settlement and activity has been documented in the Spoon River drainage (Conrad 1981, 1987), from the general "Avon" (Burlington) chert source locality in the central portion at least as far downriver as Duncan Mills, where Nolan has noted typical lanceolate and stemmed point variants in a private collection. This area is notable for producing both lanceolate and stemmed point variants, including examples of what Conrad (1987) believes are Smith points, but no classic Etley points. If this pattern is valid, it would be further evidence that these isolated areas of nucleated Titterington-horizon settlement warrant consideration as the remains of distinctive archaeological phases. However, the overall geographic limits of both the LaMoine and Spoon River site concentrations are currently poorly understood; excavated remains and detailed assemblage information are completely lacking from these areas.

Riverton Horizon (3500–3100 B.P., cal 1800–1350 B.C.)

This cultural complex is denoted by the presence of projectile points fitting the descriptions of those found in excavated Riverton- and Labras Lake–phase contexts south of the study area, in the Wabash Valley and the American Bottom, respectively (McElrath et al. 1984; Phillips et al. 1980; Winters 1969; also see McElrath et al., this volume). However, given the great distance from these areas, the Riverton-like materials in west-central Illinois seem to represent poorly defined regional populations rather than geographic extensions of the more southerly phases. We follow Conrad (1981:174, 1987:253) and consider these artifacts to be horizon markers for an undefined cultural entity, pending the recovery of regionally dated assemblages that clarify their relationship to the aforementioned cultural complexes. The presence of these diagnostics suggests that contact, influence, or perhaps an actual population influx from the Midsouth came either directly or indirectly into the region via sources located to the south or east, perhaps the American Bottom itself. Midsouth contacts appear to have been in place in the study area prior to this, since the local Falling Springs and Titterington-horizon Mule Road point cognates suggest strong ties to these areas during the Sub-Boreal period.

The principal diagnostics of the Riverton horizon are several small-sized point types, such as Merom Expanding Stem and Trimble Side Notched (Winters 1969) (Figure 13.24), which have been collectively referred to as "Riverton" or "Merom-cluster" points (Conrad 1987; Justice 1987). These and other cognate forms have been radiometrically dated between 3110 ± 200 and 3490 ± 200 RCYBP at the type sites for which the Riverton and Labras Lake phases were named (Phillips et al. 1980; Winters 1969; Yerkes 1987). In addition, Evans (2001:66–70) suggests a newly identified hafted-biface type, referred to as "Whale-tail" by virtue of its

Figure 13.24. Riverton-horizon points.

distinctively flaring-eared basal configuration, is also associated with Labras Lake–phase tool kits. However, Whale-tail points have only been recovered from nonfeature contexts on sites with both Labras Lake- and subsequent Prairie Lake–phase components, so their temporal association is far from clear. We too suspect that these points are attributable to later Archaic-period occupation and note that cognate forms are present in the study area, specifically in collections amassed from the Lima Lake locality of the Mississippi Valley.

Tools and Other Artifacts. As mentioned, the only artifacts that can be confidently associated with this cultural complex are the projectile points themselves, although fragmentary examples are often difficult to distinguish from larger Late Woodland arrowheads. The Merom type is a small, triangular-bladed point that exhibits a side-notched to expanding-stemmed basal configuration that ranges from slightly to markedly flaring (Winters 1969:151). Points of this type are further characterized by triangular cross sections that probably reflect the shape of the original flake blank, which was modified by only minimal secondary flaking, sometimes resulting in serrated-looking or irregular blade margins. Trimble Side Notched points are somewhat better made than Merom, frequently exhibiting a more lenticular cross section and regular margins. Although they are also small, they are characterized by longer, narrower blades than Merom and have side notches placed low on the biface perpendicular to its long axis (Winters 1969:152–153).

Some of the points attributed to this complex in the study area do not conform to the classic Riverton template described by Winters (1969) because they appear to be somewhat better made, often on bifacial preforms, and frequently exhibit more pronounced (light) haft grinding than the type sample. However, these attributes may simply reflect the ready availability of tool-grade chert in our area and, thus, no need for a micropoint and tool technology exactly like that employed in the Wabash Valley. Western Illinois Merom and Trimble points are typically manufactured from regionally available cherts, such as Burlington/Keokuk, LaMoine River, and Illinois Agate, but we are unaware of any obvious exotic-chert specimens from the region.

Settlement and Subsistence Data. Although Riverton points occur in a variety of physiographic settings and are geographically widespread, very little evidence exists for actual Riverton-horizon occupation within the study area. The only excavated remains come from the Eagle Slough site and Cochran 10, the latter of which is located in the uplands north of Macomb. All that can be currently said about the former site is that Riverton points were found in buried Soil 2, stratigraphically above earlier Atlantic and Sub-Boreal types like Falling Springs and Osceola and below Woodland remains emanating from Soil 1 (cf. Van Nest 1997). At Cochran 10, several small-sized dart points were recovered from the same plow-disturbed contexts in which four basin-shaped Archaic pit features originated. One of these, a burned rock-lined basin (Feature 1), produced a radiocarbon assay of 3280 ± 70 RCYBP (cal 1520 B.C.) (Hansen and Nolan 1998:300) that is consistent with the dating of the Riverton and Labras Lake phases south of the study area. This near-surface component also yielded an abundance of cobble tools and FCR (some in distinct sub-plow-zone concentrations that may represent material cleaned out of nearby pits), suggesting heat-aided bulk processing, presumably of plant or nut resources, was a primary site activity. The Riverton-horizon occupation of Cochran 10 appears to have been brief and quite focused, given its restricted areal size, low overall artifact density, and limited tool diversity.

The remainder of what is known about this cultural complex is derived from site distribution data. Examination of regional survey and collector-interview information confirms that Riverton points are widely distributed in western Illinois, but they are underrepresented compared with those of the preceding Titterington horizon. Nolan (2004:Table 3.20) documented only 11 components from the Mississippi uplands (compared with 91 Titterington horizon), although these sites and find spots were distributed across a variety of formerly wooded landform types and settings. He also noted that specimens are found on the Savannah and Kingston Terrace remnants located in the Lima Lake bottoms (e.g., Nolan 1994b:Figure 6b, e), although prolific Riverton sites have yet to be identified in the Mississippi Valley. Their apparent absence is somewhat surprising since the majority of the known Labras Lake settlements in the American Bottom are located in the Mississippi trench (Emerson et al. 1986:262, Table 10-1; Evans 2001) and there are strong similarities between the cultural developments in both the Lima Lake and American Bottom localities during much of the Atlantic and Sub-Boreal periods.

Conrad's (1987:253–258) larger regionwide sample produced slightly more than 100 examples from approximately 90 sites (compared with more than 300 Titterington-horizon points). However, the largest number recovered from any one location was five from 11KX158, the extensively collected chert workshop located in the "Avon quarry" district. Moreover, better than half of this sample emanates from the Hook-Sampson-Keithley collections, amassed from repeatedly visited locations within an approximately 30-km^2 area centered on the middle Spoon River valley and adjacent uplands. Clearly, the elevated sample size reflects the intensity of collection as much as anything. Conrad (1987:258) found that the distribution of Riverton points was largely similar to that noted for points of the preceding Titterington horizon, except along relatively minor streams in the Lower Spoon River and Sugar Creek basins, where the latter points were more common, and in the LaMoine basin, where small dart points were rare.

So few data are available concerning local Riverton-horizon settlement that patterns have not yet emerged. All of the known components contain only one or a few points that cannot be confidently associated with any other diagnostic artifacts. Thus, no sizable assemblages or habitation sites are known, although the remains from Cochran 10 suggest it is an extractive site tied to some type of nearby residence. Perhaps these presumed residences are strongly nucleated in settings that are often masked by soil aggradation, such as the tributary stream and river valleys. Heavily nucleated settlement appears to have been characteristic of some local Sub-Boreal and Sub-Atlantic populations (see Conrad 1986c, 1987; Conrad et al. 1986) and remains a distinct possibility in this case. Another limiting factor could be a failure on archaeologists' part to consistently recognize Riverton diagnostics, which can be easily confused with both earlier and later point types.

One of the more vexing facets of Riverton-horizon subsistence relates to the unique chipped-stone tools. Riverton points represent a striking technological and stylistic departure from the oversized lanceolate and broad-bladed stemmed tools of the preceding TSN culture and the barbed and stemmed points used by subsequent Terminal Archaic peoples. This technology has no clear cultural antecedents or descendants, suggesting its intrusion into the area, whether through the diffusion of traits or an actual influx of foreign peoples. This raises a number of questions, such as what happened to local Titterington peoples, who also appear to have migrated into the area from a southern or western source. Did these people retreat to a homeland area and, if so, why? While we cannot currently answer the questions we raise, we note that the Sub-Boreal period appears to be marked by little if any group continuity, suggesting large-scale regional migration and abandonment may have played a key role in aboriginal settlement at this time.

Geographic Distribution. Riverton points are widespread in the study region, although little is known about their presence or absence from the northern subarea. They have been recorded from the Sny Bottom at Eagle Slough and along the valley margin (Conner 1984:Table 13). They are present in appreciable numbers in some Pike County collections (cf. Stafford and Nolan 1990:86, Table 3.3) but generally appear to be poorly represented or inconsistently identified in other surveys reported from the southern part of the study area (e.g., Stafford 1989, 1994; Stafford et al. 1983). Scattered examples have been identified at least as far north in the central Illinois Valley as Chillicothe (Fishel et al. 2004; McConaughy 1993:Figure 4.9g) and appear to have an unbroken distribution southward into Fulton County (Behm and Green 1982; Conrad 1981; Munson and Harn 1966:Figure 3; Nolan et al. 1992:12). The central part of the study area below Conrad's (1981) FAP 407 corridor has also produced low but consistent numbers of Riverton points (Conrad 1978:Plate 7a–f, 1986d; Esarey 1982:Appendix B, Figure 12; Green 1977a; Studenmund 1995). As mentioned, the distribution continues into the Mississippi Valley (Nolan 2004) at least as far north as Burlington (Nolan et al. 2003). However, the data from the Christianson site (Evans and Womac 1997) suggests cognate forms extend up to the general Quad Cities area. Nevertheless, sites like Cochran 10 and several others located not far north of the site in the Town Branch drainage (Esarey 1987:Figure 10b, c) have yielded some of the northernmost Riverton points identified to date in the interior uplands, along with those previously mentioned by Conrad (1987) from Knox County.

Sub-Boreal Episode (4700–2900 B.P., cal 3500–1100 B.C.)–Sub-Atlantic Episode (2900–1700 B.P., cal 1100 B.C.–A.D. 350)

Terminal Archaic Horizon (3100–2600 B.P., cal 1350–800 B.C.)

The Sub-Boreal to Sub-Atlantic transition is marked by the appearance of a complex of thin, distinctively barbed projectile points that are attributable to the Prairie Lake culture of the central Mississippi drainage. Subsumed under this rubric are several previously named phases, including the Prairie Lake phase of the American Bottom, the Kampsville phase of the lower Illinois Valley, and the Logan phase of west-central Illinois (Conrad 1986c; Emerson 1984; Emerson and Fortier 1986; Farnsworth and Asch 1986; also see McElrath et al., this volume; Wiant et al., this volume). A fourth taxon, termed the "McCraney Creek phase" by Farnsworth and Asch (1986:340), was tentatively proposed on the basis of a single small assemblage found in surficial contexts along a tributary of the Sny but has not been fleshed out to date. We feel it most parsimonious at this time to refer to McCraney Creek as an archaeological complex rather than a phase, because its spatial, temporal, and physical dimensions have not been sufficiently defined.

The chronological placement of the Prairie Lake culture has already been established through relative dating and radiocarbon assays that are available from the adjacent lower Illinois Valley and American Bottom localities (Emerson 1984; Emerson and Fortier 1986; Emerson and McElrath 2001; Farnsworth and Asch 1986). However, six dates have recently been obtained from sites excavated in western Illinois that provide a local basis for the calendar ages provided above in the subheading for this section (Table 13.2). Only the assays from Axedental and Seiwell are directly associated with obviously related diagnostic points and assemblages; the other four are attributable to occupations producing more meager or ambiguous subsurface remains.

While we are confident that the assemblages discussed here date within the inclusive temporal span, different suites of diagnostics may characterize assemblages recovered from some of the more poorly known localities or subregions, such as the lower Rock River. These cultural complexes are referred to as "Terminal" Archaic because they appear to represent the last identifiable assemblages known from western Illinois prior to the introduction of pottery, which is traditionally viewed as one of the hallmarks of the Woodland period in our study area. Few substantive data have been collected from the study area since the publication of *Early Woodland Archeology* (Farnsworth and Emerson 1986) that would allow for expansion on, or additions to, existing models of the Archaic to Woodland transition as well as the possible relationship of Red Ocher and Glacial Kame materials to Terminal Archaic cultures in west-central Illinois. We therefore refer the reader to the articles contained in that volume (e.g., Esarey 1986) for information about this subject (also see Conrad 1987).

Tools and Other Artifacts. Barbed, triangular-bladed, straight- to expanding-stemmed projectile points (Figure 13.25), grouped under the Springly type cluster, are the most diagnostic artifacts of the Prairie Lake culture, along with grooved plummets and tubular pipes, which occur much more rarely.

Figure 13.25. Terminal Archaic points.

At least three varieties compose this Terminal Archaic point cluster: Springly (Munson and Harn 1971:24), Dyroff (Emerson 1984:262–266), and Mo-Pac (McElrath and Fortier 1983:119–120), although the recently named Floyd point (Evans 2001:70–74) may also be attributable to this cultural complex, or possibly the preceding Labras Lake phase, in the American Bottom. Another distinctive form, Kampsville Barbed (cf. Farnsworth and Asch 1986), has been named on the basis of examples recovered from the lower Illinois Valley area and is also clearly associated. Since these types are ably described elsewhere, we refer the reader to the works cited above for more detailed information (also see McElrath et al., this volume). We follow Conrad (1986c:303) and refer to these points collectively as belonging to the Springly type cluster, pending more detailed analysis and description of *local* assemblages. However, we must note that much of the same variability identified for these particular point types is represented in the study area, along with some additional variation that could denote regionally distinctive expressions. For example, some classic barbed specimens found in the Lima Lake locality and elsewhere occasionally exhibit distinctively concave, stemmed bases; some local collectors refer to these points as "swallowtails" (Figure 13.25n).

While narrow stemmed (Dyroff) and expanding stemmed (Mo-Pac) point forms occur in the area, it is our impression that most specimens could be accommodated in the Springly or Kampsville Barbed types. These points are sometimes erroneously typed as Hardin Barbed, which is broadly similar in outline form only, and are also difficult to sort from some early Late Woodland stemmed forms (Steuben/Mund), especially when specimens have been heavily reworked. Examples of the Floyd type may be present in the Lima Lake locality, but we are not familiar enough with them to make an empirical assessment. However, we think consistently distinguishing them from earlier McLean-cluster points would be difficult. An expanding-stemmed point recovered from a pit cluster at the Christianson site (see Evans and Womac 1997:Figure 4.4a) is a case in point; the dating of this feature cluster suggests the point could be relatable to the Floyd type, although the illustration in the report suggests it is much more robust and rounded, like earlier McLean-cluster points.

Springly-cluster points are typically manufactured from regionally available chert types, primarily Burlington/Keokuk, although examples made from LaMoine River and Moline are found near the sources of these raw materials. No definite exotic-chert Springly-cluster points have been identified in the study area. Evidence exists for the heat treatment of some Burlington/Keokuk specimens, but its frequency has not been formally assessed. Some light haft grinding has also been noted, but analysts have also not consistently recorded this attribute, perhaps because of the subjectivity involved in its recognition.

As mentioned above, grooved plummets and tubular pipes also appear to be diagnostic of this cultural complex, although we are aware of only a few examples of the latter from unprovenienced private collections. The plummets typically are teardrop shaped, although more elongate and bulbous-ended examples are known. They generally conform to the Gilcrease Grooved type (Perino 1961), although examples of Perino's Snyders Grooved type are now also believed to be associated with the Terminal Archaic (see Farnsworth and Asch 1986). These plummets are characteristically manufactured from hematite or limonite, although examples made from granitic stone (Nolan 2004; Stafford 1989:Figure 3.6c), limestone, and Sterling, or Rock River, pipestone (Farnsworth et al. 2004) also are known (see, e.g., the Christianson site [Evans and Womac 1997]). These artifacts are commonly assumed to be net weights used for fowling or fishing, but no data speak to their function other than their distribution, which, aside from their inclusion in burials (e.g., Farnsworth and Asch 1986; Perino 1961), seems to primarily be confined to lowland contexts and, so, is congruent with this interpretation (Goldstein 2004:101–104).

Settlement and Subsistence Data. While an abundance of survey data relates to the Terminal Archaic, only eight sites produced some type of subsurface remains that can be attributed to this cultural complex with varying degrees of certainty. Four of these components (Axedental [11PK751], Eagle Slough [11PK787], Heineken [11PM20], and Nobrese [11A1113]) had no surface expression because they were buried under younger alluvial or colluvial deposits. While three of the remaining sites had vestiges that could be detected during standard pedestrian survey, each one (Christianson [11R142], Cornjulio [11A1332], and Seiwell [11P344]) was masked to some degree by aeolian or biomantle deposits (Alvey 1991, 1993; Evans and Womac 1997; Farnsworth 2003; Nolan 1993, 2003; Stafford 1994). The final site, Thomas 1/2 (11HA326), is located on an eroding loess-mantled terrace but failed to produce evidence for Terminal Archaic occupation prior to excavation.

Another tested site that could prove relevant to discussions of Terminal Archaic settlement and subsistence is Sale Barn Road (11HY125), located in the uplands near Kewanee, which produced a Gilcrease Grooved hematite plummet from the surface and five subsurface features (Barr 1986). However, an Archaic side-notched point was also found on the surface, and the subsurface facilities failed to produce diagnostics. The subsurface facilities included two small rock-filled basins and three concentrations of FCR, possibly representing surface hearths (Barr 1986). Two widely separated features apparently produced unmodified hematite. The botanical assemblage was dominated by wood charcoal, but walnut and hazelnut shell was also recovered.

The eight confidently assigned excavated components have produced widely disparate remains, ranging from projectile points or plummet caches found in what appears to be correct stratigraphic placement in poorly sampled cumulic midden deposits (Eagle Slough and Heineken) to relatively ephemeral upland and lowland camps (Cornjulio, Seiwell, and Thomas 1/2) to buried floodplain habitations with preserved features or midden or both (Axedental, Christianson, and Nobrese). At Eagle Slough and Heineken, only a few limited tests were excavated into or through what appear to be quite substantial stratified Woodland- and Archaic-period deposits. Eagle Slough produced several examples of Springly and Mo-Pac points from Soil 2, but little other information is currently available. Farnsworth's (2003) analysis of the notes and collections stemming from Struever's 1958–1959 test excavations at the bluff-base Heineken site (11PM20), located in the central Illinois River valley near Putnam, documents the recovery of a cache of four Gilcrease Grooved plummets. These objects were found together approximately 75–105 cm below the modern ground surface. While the lithic artifacts from these excavations are no longer in the CAA collections, photographs and descriptions of the plummets suggest one is hematite and the other three are either limonite or limestone (Farnsworth 2003:8, Figure 7). Little else is currently known about this potentially important Terminal Archaic component.

The two upland components produced shallowly buried deposits from prominent, formerly forested divides or bluff tops located in close proximity to sizable tributary stream valleys with well-developed floodplains. While both of these components are rather ephemeral, they appear to represent functionally divergent occupation types. The Cornjulio site, located immediately south of Loraine, produced the remains of three closely spaced, but spatially separate (5–10 m apart), bounded lithic concentrations primarily comprising late-stage flaking debris indicative of tool maintenance (Nolan 2003). The northernmost scatter produced a fragmentary Springly-cluster point and was associated with a small discolored subsoil anomaly that may have been the remains of a poorly preserved pit hearth; botanical analysis revealed this feature was entirely composed of carbonized wood and bark (Schroeder 1998:15–17). A possibly related, broken subtriangular preform or knife manufactured from a distinctive yet unidentified chert was found in the southern concentration, and a large, retouched flake of LaMoine River chert, a raw material exotic to the area, was associated with the central activity area. Flakes removed from the distinctive knife or preform were recovered from both southern and central lithic concentrations, indicating they probably accumulated at the same time (Nolan 2003). The data suggest that this formerly forested divide was used by Terminal Archaic people on one or more occasions as a temporary encampment probably associated with hunting-related activities.

The Seiwell site is located south of Dunlap, on a bluff top overlooking Kickapoo Creek. The excavated portion of the site produced three large multizoned, rock-filled roasting pits, which were somewhat evenly spaced across the site, two smaller and more widely scattered, shallow, basin-shaped pits, and four centrally located sheet hearths dominated by FCR exhibiting fractures produced by slow, dry heating (Alvey 1991, 1993). Only the larger roasting pit features produced carbonized botanical remains, which were dominated by oak wood charcoal; a few pieces of nutshell attributable to the walnut family were also found in two of the pits (Alvey 1991:27, 32). Grinding stones were recovered from both pit and subsoil contexts; relatively few chipped-stone tools are represented, and the debitage is suggestive of tool maintenance rather than production (Alvey 1993:164–165). A radiocarbon date of 2940 ± 70 RCYBP (cal 1210, 1190, 1180, 1150, 1140, 1130 B.C. [see Table 13.2]) was returned from one of the pits and, along with the recovery of a Mo-Pac-like point and two other expanding-base hafted-biface fragments from the E soil horizon during machine stripping (Alvey 1991:25–26), is indicative of a Terminal Archaic affiliation. On the basis of the prevalence of baking, roasting, or parching features and cobble grinding tools, Alvey (1993:164) suggests the site functioned as an extractive camp that was focused on plant-processing activities.

The excavated remains encountered in lowland contexts at the Thomas 1/2, Nobrese, Axedental, and Christianson sites also vary considerably as do their landform settings. Thomas 1/2 (11HA326) is a multicomponent site located east of Carthage on a narrow, heavily eroded, loess-mantled terrace remnant situated adjacent to the West Fork of the LaMoine River and a floodplain oxbow lake. Recent hand excavations and extensive machine stripping (1,550 m^2) produced the remains of 12 subsurface features that were dispersed down the spine of the terrace. These features included shallow pits (average volume of 13 dm^3), deeper, steep-walled basins (average volume of 104 dm^3), a dense subsurface lithic concentration, and two possible cobble-tool caches (Fishel and Nolan 2004). A wide range of Archaic point styles was recovered from the site, but none were found in secure pit feature context. However, a large Springly-cluster point was recovered from the subsurface lithic concentration, another was found in plow-disturbed contexts, and one of the steep-walled pit features (Feature 10) returned a radiocarbon assay of 2890 ± 70 RCYBP (cal 1050 B.C.). This feature and an identical nearby pit are confidently associated with the Terminal Archaic occupation and produced relatively abundant hickory nutshell charcoal and several grinding or pounding tools indicative of plant processing (Fishel and Nolan 2004).

The Nobrese site was discovered north of Ursa during geoarchaeological backhoe trenching undertaken in the Jenkins Creek floodplain as part of a < 5-m-wide highway-widening project. Stratified Late Woodland- and Archaic-period deposits were discovered beneath a mantle of historic alluvium, the latter contained within a 2Bw horizon ca. .75 m below the modern surface (Nolan 1993:8–32). Sparse buried living-surface debris and the remains of two closely spaced features were associated with this component, which appears to represent an occupation of an inner-channel bar deposit. One of the features (Feature 6) was a small (.13-m^2) basin-shaped pit, and the other (Feature 5) was a large (1.5 m north–south x .8+ m east–west), .2-m-deep, flat-bottomed basin that was truncated along one end by the existing road ditch. A small (.13-m^2), circular intramural concentration of fibrous, carbonized charcoal was discovered inside the southwestern wall of this feature during excavation and produced a radiocarbon date of 2620 ± 70 RCYBP (cal 800 B.C.) (Nolan 1993:31–32, 2003:2–3). Botanical analysis indicates nutshell exceeds wood in both features and comprises 35 percent of the tabulated charcoal from the sampled living surface and midden deposits. The feature samples are dominated by hazelnut, with hickory and black walnut occurring in diminishing frequency. In contrast, hickory nut predominates in the midden samples, with black walnut and hazelnut occurring in nearly equal frequency, followed by trace amounts of butternut (Schroeder 1998:15–17).

Given the small area excavated (< 30 m^2), the meager amount of associated lithic remains, and the complete absence of formally shaped tools, interpreting or characterizing the Nobrese Terminal Archaic component is difficult. However, the feature density is relatively high as are the charcoal concentrations encountered in the pits and living surface. The larger truncated feature (Feature 5) described above is similar to a sizable, rectanguloid facility excavated at the Axedental site (Feature 22, see below) that produced a nearly identical radiocarbon date (Stafford 1994:66–71). The size and morphology of these features correspond well to other Terminal Archaic facilities found in the American Bottom that have been interpreted as pit houses or temporary shelters (Fortier 1993:260–261). If Feature 5 at Nobrese represents a domestic structure, which is arguable, the site may prove attributable to some type of residentially oriented floodplain settlement.

Although the excavated sample produced much denser buried remains than Nobrese, the areal limits of the Axedental site, located southwest of Griggsville, have, likewise, never been firmly established.[11] The buried Kampsville-phase Terminal Archaic component was discovered approximately .85 m below the modern surface in a 2Bw horizon during geoarchaeological trenching undertaken in the Blue Creek floodplain, near the valley wall (Stafford 1994:205–206). A block area < 50 m^2, composed of nine hand-dug test units, was opened off the trench walls and produced the remains of three modest-sized pit features (volumes ranging from 23 to 53 liters) and the large rectangular, possible domestic facility mentioned above. These features were embedded within a relatively dense, unplowed living surface or midden. One hundred two chipped- and ground-stone tools were recovered from the excavated buried component, including parts of 24 projectile points (Figure 13.26), 37 unspecified bifaces or fragments thereof, two drills, three chipped-stone woodworking tools (referred to as "adzes" and "axes") (Figure 13.26q, s), a chopper, 17 generalized flake tools, 10 manos, six hammerstones, and two pitted stones (Stafford 1994:Table 3.5). While Kampsville Barbed points dominate the projectile assemblage (Stafford 1994: Figure 3.1f–i, k) (Figure 13.26a–n), a heat-altered lanceolate knife (dagger?) similar to one found at Dyroff-Levin in the American Bottom (Emerson 1984:Figure 20e), a broadly

Figure 13.26. Selected Kampsville-phase artifacts from the Axedental site: a–n, Kampsville Barbed; o, pick(?); p, lanceolate point/biface fragment; q, s, chipped-stone adzes or axes; r, preform fragment.

notched Riverton-like point (Stafford 1994:Figure 3.1e), and a robust Archaic side-notched point (Stafford 1994: Figure 3.1d) were also recovered.[12]

Hickory nutshell dominates the botanical assemblage from the Kampsville-phase component at Axedental and is ubiquitous, with nutshell frequencies similar in both feature and midden contexts. Seeds are common, as well, especially in the midden deposits, and include an array of plant types, although the concentration is low relative to the overall amount of charcoal recovered (Schroeder 1994:110–113). Several of these plants appear to have been important to the inhabitants, including domesticated sunflower, marsh elder, American lotus, and giant ragweed, which, along with tubers and native fruits, supplemented other dietary sources (there was no bone preservation). Overall, the site exhibits high concentrations of charcoal (features = 111.5 g/liter, midden = 12.9 g/liter [seed counts of 2.63 and 2.49 g/liter, respectively]) with nutshell-to-wood ratios of better than 40:1 for both feature and midden contexts (Schroeder 1994:Table 8.1). Primarily on the basis of the tremendous amount of nutshell, but also its "small" size, Stafford (1994:149) interprets the site as a short-term upland extractive camp. However, we must note that the limits of the site were never established by either excavation or survey and that interpretations are based on information from the small block arbitrarily superimposed over a portion of the occupation area. While we, too, believe that nut processing was an important site activity (with the shell commonly used as a fuel source), we find it difficult to view the incredibly large and diverse chipped- and ground-stone tool assemblage, given the potential range of tasks represented, as reflecting something less than a durable residential site, if not an actual base locale (sensu Emerson 1984). This interpretation seems all the more reasonable in light of the spartan assemblages recovered from Seiwell and Cornjulio, which appear to be representative of short-term, upland-oriented Terminal Archaic extractive sites.

The Christianson site Terminal Archaic component is also difficult to interpret since only a small portion of what is clearly a much larger site was subjected to test excavations. This component, which occupies the margin of a high sandy slackwater terrace in the Rock River valley, comprises two nearby but noncontiguous feature clusters, one consisting of 18 and the other of six basin-shaped pits (Evans and Womac 1997:4–7), the largest number from any Terminal Archaic site in our sample. The larger cluster (Feature Cluster I) provided two ^{14}C dates (Table 13.2) and a variety of hearth, earth oven, and processing facilities but few formal tools of any type; FCR dominates the recovered remains. Feature Cluster II produced primarily processing pits, although a hearth and an earth oven or hearth were also identified. Artifact density was much lower in the Cluster II pits, with FCR much less common than in Cluster I, but the number of tools was similarly low (Evans and Womac 1997:30–39). Possibly associated tools that have been recovered from the site surface by local avocational archaeologists and collectors include two plummets (one mentioned above) and a small number of projectile points.

Botanical analysis of the floral remains indicates that both pit clusters have low concentrations of charcoal (.09 g/liter), with the quantity of nutshell nearly doubling that of wood (1.9:1 ratio). While hazelnut dominates the nutshell assemblage, every mast-producing species that would have been available in the general site area is represented (Parker 1998:6). Few seeds or other plant remains were found, although the identifiable specimens include possible domesticated sunflower and marsh elder along with a cucurbit rind fragment. While the two feature clusters have nearly identical charcoal densities and reflect the same general economy, the recovered remains suggest that a greater range of subsistence-related activities occurred in the vicinity of Cluster I, where all the hazelnut charcoal was found and a greater diversity of wood species was noted (Parker 1998:13).

Overall, the site activities that were undertaken during the Terminal Archaic occupation of Christianson include the procurement of Moline chert and the initial stages of reduction, tool maintenance (tertiary flakes), substantial harvesting and processing of the locally available hazelnut mast, small-scale gardening (oily domesticates and cucurbit), limited faunal exploitation (fowling or fishing, suggested by plummets, and hunting, by points), and wide-ranging fuelwood collection (Evans and Womac 1997:37–39; Parker 1998:8–13).

Considered together, the excavated sample of Terminal Archaic sites suggests that residential sites are located in both the larger river (Christianson) and smaller tributary stream (Axedental and Nobrese) valleys but appear to be quite variable in content and configuration, although the data are strongly conditioned by the small-sized areas investigated in every case. However, durable residential sites have not been identified on upland ridges, where simple extractive sites (Cornjulio and Seiwell) have been encountered. These sites are located not far from the valleys themselves, generally immediately above or adjacent to sizable floodplain expanses, suggesting they may have provisioned or were otherwise tethered to nearby residential bases located in the bottoms. This hypothesis will prove hard to test since the work undertaken to date has shown that the largest sites in the settlement system are frequently buried under Holocene alluvium or colluvium.

Nonetheless, regional survey data strongly support the idea that Terminal Archaic settlement tended to be heavily nucleated near productive streams (cf. Conrad 1986c), although the distributional pattern seems more widespread and includes much smaller interior drainages than originally thought. Since Conrad has already outlined the LaMoine and Haw Creek (Spoon River) settlement concentrations in some detail, we briefly focus our attention on data that have come to light since his original summary statement.

As expected (e.g., Conrad et al. 1986), evidence for Terminal Archaic occupation in the Mississippi trench is abundant. Nolan (2004) reports that sites are nucleated along the western shoreline of Lima Lake as well as an interior slough belt located to the northwest, although components are also found on other nearby landforms, including the adjacent bluff top. Hematite plummets have been recovered from some of these sites, mainly those clustered along the former lake shoreline and located off the edges of terrace remnants that once formed islands within the lake (Ed Wilcox, pers. comm. to Nolan 2000). On the bluff top adjacent to Lima Lake, collectors reportedly recovered four hematite plummets associated with an adult male burial (Stephens 1951:18–19), which is the only possible Terminal Archaic mortuary feature reported from the study area. Additional site concentrations were noted by Nolan (2004) in the northern part of the Lima Lake bottoms near Warsaw and elsewhere; they also appear to be present in the Sny, as indicated by the recovery of diagnostic points at Jug Run, McCraney Creek, Bushmeyer, Eagle Slough, and possibly Fan Middle (cf. Conner 1984; Farnsworth and Asch 1986; Morgan et al. 1984; Stafford 1997; Stafford 1992:295; Studenmund et al. 1998). Another area of nucleated settlement may exist in the floodplain opposite Burlington, Iowa, where professional survey and collector interview have identified Springly-cluster points (Goatley 1998b:Figure 3.20d; Nolan et al. 2003).

Terminal Archaic diagnostics appear to occur sparingly in the uplands adjacent to these localities, however. Nolan

(2004) recorded only 10 examples from the Mississippi slope near the Lima Lake locality; half of these were located on terraces or floodplains within the tributary valleys, and four others were found on perennial stream bluffs overlooking these same bottomland expanses. No obvious Springly-cluster points were found in the uplands adjacent to the Burlington bottoms (Goatley 1998b; Nolan et al. 2003); they are similarly absent from the bluff top and immediate environs of the eastern margin of the Sny valley (Conner 1984). These data again suggest a tendency toward nucleation, with outlying sites perhaps representing extractive activities (i.e., hunting) relating to the larger valley residences.

One of the more intriguing patterns that has emerged is use of smaller-sized valleys located in the upland interior, perhaps best expressed by the Axedental site, which is located in a narrow portion of the Blue Creek drainage. Given the distance from the principal river valleys (12 km in the Axedental case), these upland sites seem unlikely to have provisioned occupations located in the main trenches, although they arguably could represent dispersed groups from the same populations. Perhaps the most extreme examples of this pattern come from an avocational survey collection amassed from a series of upland locations south-southwest of Macomb. Compared with materials from other upland surveys, these collections contain unusually large (yet still modest) numbers of Springly-cluster points. Two concentrated areas of settlement appear to be indicated in the data.

The first of these is located in the Troublesome Creek drainage, where three adjacent bluff-slope sites have each produced one or more examples of Springly-cluster points. This part of the drainage is marked by a broad floodplain that contains several oxbows, which appear to have been attractive to Terminal Archaic settlement. Survey in other portions of this drainage as part of the FAP 407 and Route 336 Carthage to Macomb projects failed to locate a single Terminal Archaic specimen (Conrad 1981; Hansen 1996); the surveyed areas typically did not exhibit strong floodplain development, however. Conrad (1986c) reports only one Springly-cluster point from the entire Macomb area, although several more are now known from the East Fork of the LaMoine (Nolan and Graham 2003; Simon 1985:Figure 5), which is located well north of the Troublesome Creek concentration. The second possible site concentration is located in the uplands between the Willow and Grindstone creek drainages, both of which are tributaries of the LaMoine. The avocational collection from this area includes nearly a dozen examples from the bluff tops and divides overlooking each valley. These data suggest to us that these sites represent the remains of temporary extractive activities, likely hunting related, undertaken in areas adjacent to more concentrated stream-valley settlements that have eluded discovery perhaps because they are buried by Holocene alluvium.

Geographic Distribution. Terminal Archaic diagnostics are found across the study area, albeit in physiographically restricted areas. The following discussion focuses on the Illinois basin since the data have not already been presented above. Stafford et al. (1983:A-9, Figure 8) identify two Kampsville Barbed points from an inner channel bar in the floodplain and another isolated specimen from an unidentified floodplain location near the northern end of the lower Illinois Valley. Additional occupations are indicated by the recovery of a Kampsville Barbed point and two plummets (one hematite and one granitic) from the Burr Lake site and an additional hematite plummet from the Slim Lake site (Stafford 1989:64–65, Table 3.19), both located along the shorelines of former backwater lakes. In the adjacent uplands, a Kampsville Barbed point was recovered from the Dead Chevy site (11PK750), which is located on the bluff top immediately east of Axedental, and 11 other examples were identified in a private collection amassed from an upland area located to the east, within 5 km of the Illinois trench (Stafford and Nolan 1990:Tables 2.51, 3.3).

In the central Illinois Valley, Terminal Archaic diagnostics are frequently found on the natural levee of the river (Esarey 1990; Nolan et al. 1992), but their frequency elsewhere has not been formally assessed. However, a possible Springly-cluster point base has been identified from an alluvial fan site (11BR428) located near the LaMoine-Illinois river confluence (Moffat et al. 2001), and two others (including a classic Mo-Pac) were found by an avocational archaeologist in a similar setting not far to the north at the Lucille Ray site (11SC65). Fishel et al. (2004) report finding four Springly-cluster points from as many sites during the Illinois 29 survey north of Peoria, and McConaughy (1993:Figure 4.9i) and Farnsworth (2003) identify Terminal Archaic diagnostics from bluff-base settings at Rench (Springly-cluster point) and Heineken (plummet cache).

Concluding Remarks

Western Illinois was used throughout the Archaic period by both resident and migrant populations of hunter-gatherers. The cultural chronology that we have developed is based on observations of local assemblages and should not be interpreted as reflecting unilinear development. The archaeological record of the region clearly can be viewed in historical terms, with a variety of peoples or groups coming and going throughout the long interval under consideration. While significant periods of cultural continuity are evident (i.e., during the second half of the Atlantic episode into the Sub-Boreal), some cultural complexes appeared and disappeared from the area without evidence for any obvious antecedents or descendants. At times portions of the study area may have been largely abandoned or perhaps were peripheral to cultural developments occurring in other parts of this or adjacent regions.

This sizable and physiographically diverse study region could realistically be broken into perhaps three or more culturally distinctive subregions, each with quite variable archaeological data sets. However, most of the area is covered by the Galesburg Plain and is either bordered or drained by the Mississippi and Illinois basins. These river valleys, with their abundant natural resources, appear to have served as the economic base for the entire region, and they also provided natural routes for the movement of peoples, ideas, and resources. Some cultural complexes that are evident in or immediately adjacent to these valleys appear to have few to no parallels in the upland interior, suggesting settlement and interaction was at times strongly river oriented; this appears especially true of the Mississippi Valley. As mentioned, both subtle and overt diachronic differences are also sometimes apparent from north to south in the study area. We believe that recognition of this variation is important to the reconstruction of Archaic-period lifeways because it may denote the presence of distinctive populations or social groups (i.e., archaeological phases).

Our understanding of the northernmost subregion, generally located between Galesburg and the Quad Cities, is the poorest overall. This largely results from the lack of long-term institutional study as well as biases derived from the authors' work history and research interests. The southernmost portion of the study region corresponds to the northern limits of the rugged Lincoln Hills section, or the driftless area (Schwegman 1973) traditionally referred to as the lower Illinois Valley region. This area has been subjected to relatively intensive archaeological study, although the preexisting culture history and chronology were somewhat underdeveloped or compressed compared with other nearby regions (i.e., the American Bottom). The bulk of the information used in this study comes from the central subregion (those portions of the Galesburg Plain and adjacent river valleys located between Mt. Sterling and Galesburg), which has exceptional site distribution data supplemented by a modest but growing number of excavated contexts and ^{14}C dates.

As might be expected, the northern subregion appears to have had close affinities with northern Illinois and the adjacent portion of Iowa, whereas the cultural developments in the southern subregion closely paralleled those in the lower Illinois Valley and the American Bottom. The central subregion evidences contact or influence from each of the aforementioned areas at various times but also was the scene of regionally distinctive cultural developments. In fact, broad diachronic trends are evident in the data and are briefly summarized below.

The Pre-Boreal climatic episode witnessed the shift from Late Glacial, or Paleoindian, lifeways to those traditionally regarded as Early Archaic. These cultural adaptations coincided with documented changes in the climate and biota of the region (e.g., Anderson et al. 1996; Bryson et al. 1970; Conrad 1981, 1987). At the time, the migratory way of life of the "initial" colonizing populations of the Midwest began to give way to a more regionally settled, yet still highly mobile, type of existence. This long-term process of settling in to specific portions of the landscape is manifested by the identification of regionally distinctive point styles or variants (within the broader pan-southeastern U.S. point traditions) and a dramatic rise in the number of local archaeological sites, the latter also perhaps signaling rising population levels. The earlier fluted and unfluted lanceolate points of the Late Glacial were initially replaced by more "shouldered" lanceolates (Dalton cluster), which subsequently gave way to notched and stemmed varieties during the Pre-Boreal and Boreal episodes (Early Side-Notched, Theban, Kirk, Hardin, and Large Bifurcate clusters). The highly curated chipped-stone tool kits of these early Holocene peoples were quite similar to those of Late Glacial groups, but exhibited significant technological innovations, including recognizable woodworking (adze) and butchering components.

The regular use of exotic raw materials by Boreal peoples is viewed as evidence for group mobility (rather than exchange) since these materials were employed for utilitarian items that were discarded in mundane contexts after clearly being used and broken or exhausted (cf. Binford 1979; Meltzer 1989). The data encoded in their heavily curated tools suggest that these people had rather extensive home ranges that allowed for fairly regular contact with areas located 100–200 km away and less frequent but observable connections (whether direct or indirect) beyond these limits. We must note, however, that few identifiable differences are discernible in the archaeological remains associated with particular Boreal point clusters across most of the study region, indicating that, if cultural phases were to be defined, their spatial limits would be much more extensive than those of Atlantic-period and later Archaic complexes. A strong possibility also exists that distinctive groups of people coexisted in western Illinois for some or all of the Boreal climatic episode (i.e., Theban and Kirk cultural complexes or traditions).

During the early Holocene, aboriginal settlement appears to have consisted of a complex interplay of both logistical and residential patterns of movement. Upland areas were used extensively for hunting and related activities that ultimately may have been tied to more durable residences located in the larger tributary stream and river valleys. Buried sites like Twin Ditch and Koster Horizon 11 are currently the only excavated examples of durable residences known from the region, although this rarity may simply relate to the undetectability of primary habitation locales as a result of more recent sediment accumulation. In contrast to the view of many, the artifact signatures of most early Holocene upland scatters imply to us that they are not the remains of entire family or social groups (as predicted by high residential mobility). Rather, they appear to reflect a low number of specific activities (hide scraping, tool sharpening and maintenance, and butchering) that could have been undertaken by a few individuals over a relatively short period, generally a single day or less.

The onset of the Atlantic climatic period coincided with dramatic changes that are evident in the settlement patterns and technology of western Illinois Archaic peoples. At the beginning of this warm, dry interval, the site distributional data seem to indicate, the dissected uplands were largely being abandoned, with an apparent corresponding rise in the number and density of Late Bifurcate sites in the adjacent valleys as well as in the wet, rolling till-plain areas located to the north and east of the study region (cf. Winters 1982). Much smaller bifurcated-base forms, such as LeCroy, Kanawha, and Stanly, which represent a distinctive technological departure, initially replaced the larger projectile points and knives of the Boreal; these points also mark the severance of observable influence from the southeastern United States (subsequent southeastern forms like Eva and Morrow Mountain are absent from the region).[13] Exotic-chert use, the EH adze form, the alternate-blade-beveling technique, and the formalized flake tool industry characteristic of Boreal-episode technologies also disappeared sometime during the initial half-millennium of the Atlantic episode; ground-stone tool forms and technologies appeared to expand, however. These changes seem to clearly indicate that a major cultural disruption took place at this time, with migration or perhaps group consolidation occurring in some areas at the expense of others, possibly in part as a response to changing climatic conditions and vegetation.

Innovations in food processing also occurred in the Midwest at approximately this same time, with the introduction of stone boiling evidenced archaeologically by large quantities of FCR (cf. Fishel 2000; Fishel et al. 2003). The initial part of the Atlantic climatic episode has historically been viewed as a time of dietary unpredictability brought about by prolonged drier conditions that undoubtedly had a detrimental effect on the oak-hickory forest and upland fauna in many areas. As a response to this, the exploitation of hickory nuts may have intensified to take full advantage of dwindling resources. Stone boiling was a highly effective and efficient bulk-processing technique that yielded higher quantities of nutmeat (and oil) than were previously achieved by hand separating the nutmeat from the shell (Talalay et al. 1984:355). Besides the processing of nuts, stone boiling was also used in the manufacture of bone grease (see Vehik 1977). The fat content of bone is generally higher in autumn and early winter (Vehik 1977), or at approximately the same time that nuts become available, suggesting that stone boiling may have been primarily a fall activity.

While hickory and other nuts had been a minor constituent of the diet prior to the beginning of the Atlantic episode, it is in Campbell Hollow–horizon contexts that nutshell charcoal becomes abundant. For example, at Koster, nutshell represents 2 percent of the charcoal assemblage in Horizon 11 (ca. 8500 B.P.) but increases to 68 percent by Horizon 8A (ca. 6900 B.P.) (Asch and Asch 1985). After 7500 B.P., "specialized nut harvesting" also began in the Koster area (Brown and Vierra 1983:188). Likewise, at the Campbell Hollow site, hickory nutshell comprises 90 percent or more of the nutshell charcoal during the Atlantic-episode (MA1) occupation (Asch and Asch 1985). Sites dating to this period are quite rare in western Illinois, and for the most part are limited to the larger tributary and principal river valleys. These data indicate that people retreated to the lowlands,[14] perhaps because these areas were buffered from the negative effects of the warm, dry conditions of the Hypsithermal or otherwise were so productive that they had a magnetlike pull on settlement and subsistence systems.

For the period from ca. 7000 to 5800 RCYBP, little appreciable information is available about regional site locations or settlement types because of the lack of clearly recognizable horizon markers or excavated site remains. The assemblages from adjacent regions are characterized by a variety of side-notched points (see McElrath et al., this volume; Wiant et al., this volume), which are not exceptionally common in the central part of the study region but do occur. Nolan believes Table Rock points may also date to part of this span, but the data are far from clear. If this hypothesis proves correct, then the projectile point distributions suggest a greatly renewed interest in upland utilization, perhaps reflecting amelioration in the warm and dry climatic conditions traditionally associated with the Hypsithermal (cf. Conrad 1981:132) or at least changing adaptive responses.

The forested portions of the uplands were clearly reoccupied during the subsequent Helton horizon, although the character of the constituent sites appears to have changed considerably from that evidenced by earlier Archaic utilization. Large, dense habitation sites were for the first time located in the interior, typically along the bluff tops of tributary streams near productive floodplain environments or other aquatic resource niches. Similarly dense habitation sites or base camps were also situated along the margins of the principal valleys, as they apparently had been for more than a millennium in the lower Illinois Valley (Brown and Vierra 1983; also see Wiant et al., this volume). In fact, the Helton-horizon settlement system appears to represent the culmination of long-term trends during the Atlantic episode involving diminishing overall group mobility, fewer and more fixed site locations, and more logistically oriented resource procurement. This profile also certainly appears to characterize the ensuing Falling Springs horizon. Sites associated with this cultural complex are almost exclusively found in the major river valleys in the south-central and southern parts of the study area and are closely associated with backwater lakes and other productive floodplain features.

The presence of large, stable populations in the major valleys at the end of the Atlantic appears to have coincided with the use of prominent bluff-top locations for burying the dead. This has been interpreted as reflecting a greater awareness of territoriality, and perhaps rising social complexity, that may have stemmed from an increased competition for resources caused by population packing (cf. Charles and Buikstra 1983). Although Hemphill-horizon diagnostics have been identified from the uplands and are geographically widespread, all of the major sites that are known, including prominent cemeteries, are located in the principal valleys, like the partially contemporary Falling Springs–horizon sites. Distinctive phases and perhaps related social boundaries may ultimately prove definable for this period in western Illinois. For example, both Falling Springs– and Hemphill-horizon sites are found in the Lima Lake locality of the Mississippi Valley, but only the latter seem to occur both north and south of this area. A similar pattern seems to prevail in the northern part of the lower Illinois Valley, perhaps suggesting that the central part of the study area was a tension zone between two distinctive, temporally overlapping cultural traditions or social groups. Conversely, these data could also be interpreted as reflecting time-transgressive behavior, marking the northern limits of late Atlantic-episode, Falling Springs–horizon cultural complexes.

The cultural continuity that appears to have been in place in the region during the latter portion of the Atlantic period seems to have given way to a pattern of more punctuated use and abandonment of portions of the study area starting in the Sub-Boreal. The Titterington horizon clearly seems to represent the remains of an influx of nonlocal peoples or ideas, most likely from the lower Illinois Valley-American Bottom region or eastern Missouri or both. These people possessed a chipped-stone technology that required large pieces of chert and deemphasized intentional heat treatment, which represents a significant departure from the technology associated with the regional side-notched to expanding-stemmed point traditions in place for the preceding two millennia. Taken on their face, the oversized points and knives that typify Titterington-horizon tool kits are suggestive of substantive changes in either hunting or butchering techniques and perhaps in the prey being sought, although the dearth of tool edge-wear studies and general lack of preserved faunal remains preclude definitive assessment. The corresponding settlement pattern also appears quite different, with a much greater emphasis on the chert-rich tributary stream valleys of the interior and apparently more limited use of the major valleys and intervening chert-poor upland areas. Seasonal dispersal and aggregation also may have played a more significant role in regional settlement systems than was the case earlier (cf. Cook 1986).

Subsequent Riverton-horizon assemblages share little in common with those of the preceding Titterington horizon, especially in terms of their primary weaponry, which are often described as darts or micropoints. Additionally, no current evidence suggests substantive Riverton habitation sites occur in the region, leaving open the possibility that some or all of the scattered remains relate to more transient use of the study area by nonresident groups. In contrast, Terminal Archaic Prairie Lake–culture sites are heavily nucleated in productive floodplain environments in western Illinois. Relatively dense habitation sites, some with well-developed middens, have been identified from both surficial and buried contexts in stream valleys of differing sizes, ranging from the principal valleys to relatively minor upland streams. Nutshell is exceedingly common at these sites, which have also produced evidence for gardening, if not actual horticulture. The dissected uplands appear to have been used sparingly, seemingly to extract resources needed to provision nearby lowland base locales.

The appearance of pottery in the region was "sudden," and the associated chipped-stone tools do not closely resemble those of local Terminal Archaic groups, although landscape use continued to be focused on productive floodplain environments or lowland areas. However, Early Woodland Marion settlement was not strongly nucleated in most of western Illinois; the sites are generally small and widely scattered across the landscape (Conrad 1981, 1986c; Harn 1986; Nolan 2004), suggesting relatively high group mobility. Given this dispersed pattern, we suspect that pottery-making technology (i.e., Marion culture) was brought into the area as part of an influx or migration of new ideas, if not people. This hypothesis will require additional testing but is generally consistent with how the region had been used for much of the preceding two millennia: as a "revolving" door by apparently unrelated cultural groups who occupied the area (and possibly co-occupied it, in some instances) and then disappeared from the local archaeological record without obvious descendants. The appearance of pottery marks the end of this pattern, however, and the beginning of an episode of apparent widespread regional group continuity during the Early and Middle Woodland periods.

Acknowledgments

The authors wish to thank the following individuals, who contributed to the success of this undertaking. Foremost among these is Lawrence A. Conrad, who graciously shared unpublished data, ideas, and collections amassed from four decades of work in western Illinois; Larry also provided numerous comments that improved earlier drafts of this chapter. We also gratefully acknowledge the support and encouragement of the IDOT and ITARP, especially John A. Walthall, Thomas E. Emerson, and Dale L. McElrath. Several institutions provided access to collections and records used in this study, including the CAA, the Dickson Mounds Museum, ITARP, and the WIU Archaeological Research Laboratory. Our research in these facilities was greatly aided by Linda Alexander, Larry Conrad, Stephanie Daniels, Duane Esarey, Wendy Smith French, Amy Graham, Laura Kozuch, Kelvin Sampson, and Jason Titcomb. We have also benefited from the help of numerous individuals who freely provided information, advice, and access to collections used in this study. They include Ferrel Anderson, Tom Bainter, Joe Bartholomew, Larry Conrad, Madeline Evans, Ken Farnsworth, Andrew Fortier, Glen Hanning, Robert Hickson, Brad Koldehoff, Ike Billingsly, June Galbraith, Gerald James, Dick Lambeth, Patsy Lantz, Tom Moore, Tom Loebel, Don Logan, Dale McElrath, Robert Monroe, Rodney Richardson, Kelvin Sampson, Sterling Snowden, Joe Stambaugh, Terry Stumpf, Steve Tieken, Shane Vanderford, and Ed Wilcox.

Marcia Martinho created all the maps and illustrations accompanying this report, with the exception of Figures 13.6 and 13.7, which were ably produced by Linda Alexander and Amy Graham, respectively. Susan Nolan helped record point metrics and assisted in the accompanying data entry. Last but certainly not least, Dave would like to thank Sue and his children, who gave up the numerous weekends and evenings that were needed to complete this chapter.

Endnotes

1. An apparently localized expression of the Packard complex (9900–9400 B.P., cal 9300–8700 B.C.) was present in the northwestern part of the study region at approximately the same time as the Early Side-Notched horizon (see Ray et al., this volume).
2. Conrad (pers. comm. 2004) reports that a Hixton silicified sandstone Scottsbluff or Hardin variant was recovered by a local collector immediately north of the Quad Cities (and of our study-area limits), near Hampton, Illinois.
3. A few contemporary Rice Lobed (Marshall 1958) specimens, uniquely beveled, Ozark-area large bifurcates, have been observed in collections amassed near the Mississippi trench in the western part of the region. However, they occur so infrequently that we suspect they are the result of either trade or periodic forays into the region by nonlocal groups based in Missouri.
4. Several other point types generally dating to this temporal span are occasionally found in the region, including Hidden Valley Stemmed, Titus/Angostura lanceolates, and others, but they either occur, or are reported, so infrequently that we can do little aside from note their presence at this time.
5. A LeCroy point was recovered from a subsurface lithic concentration at the Elledge site (11PK477) during excavations conducted by the CAA for the FAP 408 project (Stafford 1994), but its relationship to the buried remains is ambiguous at best.
6. Although we do not include Godar points in our Helton artifact complex, we recognize, as Conrad did, that some broadly side-notched forms were manufactured in Helton times, especially at sites like Black Earth (Jefferies and Lynch 1983), and others may have continued to be manufactured into early Titterington times. However, data from a variety of excavated contexts within or immediately adjacent to the study area, such as Tree Row, Sand Run West, and Cabin Corner, indicate that boldly side-notched points like Godar and Osceola are primarily found in contexts that clearly postdate the Helton florescence. The question is, should generalized side-notched points found in Helton or pre-Helton contexts be called "Godar" points, or should they be given different type names? Clearly more attention needs to be paid to any variation that may be evident among the Archaic side-notched point forms found in the Midwest.
7. We should note, however, that we disagree with Charles and Buikstra's (1983) assignment of a Helton affiliation for the pre-Titterington components.
8. The senior author's reexamination of the original FAP 407 Adams and Hancock County Wadlow specimens (Conrad 1981:148, 155–161) suggests that none are obviously attributable to this type. Most of these artifacts appear to represent earlier Archaic-period preforms, although the example from 11A933 may be a Sedalia preform or related knife form. Some wider, recurved Wadlow-like knife forms are found at some study-area sites, such as Shoemaker #1, but they appear to represent a minority type, at best.
9. McConaughy (1993:Figure 4.6a) typed a crude, broad-bladed, contracting-stemmed point found in the Late Archaic Occupation #2 at Rench as an Etley point, but we feel this specimen has greater affinities with roughly contemporary Mule Road variants. Additionally, a small, squared biface fragment recovered from this horizon (Figure 4.6c) is possibly the base of a Sedalia-cluster or related point.
10. These logs were used to produce a radiocarbon date of 4470 ± 70 RCYBP (ISGS-1230), which McConaughy and we believe is too early to be used to affix the age of the occupation; McConaughy speculates that these logs reflect "contamination with older organic materials" (1993:62).
11. Since the site has no surface expression, assessing its overall limits is difficult. We suspect it could be extensive, especially along its north–south axis, as a Kampsville Barbed point was found embedded in a stream cutbank located less than 150 m to the north of the Axedental excavation block.
12. We should note that Stafford (1994:Figure 3.1, Table 3.12) provides different type assignments for some of these points; those listed in this chapter reflect our interpretation, not hers. Additionally, Stafford recognized that the specimen in her Figure 3.1j is a Hardin Barbed point, which was found on the bluff-top part of the site and not the buried component, but the figure caption contains a typographical error indicating it is a Kampsville Barbed point
13. Nolan is aware of a single possible Morrow Mountain or Eva cognate found on the Illinois River bluffs near Browning in Schuyler County. This short, squat, contracting-stemmed point is manufactured from an unidentified, very dark gray to black variety of chert.
14. *Retreat* may be a misleading term since it is our view that the largest sites in most Archaic settlement systems were probably always located in or near the larger valleys, as posited by the editors of this volume. Taken on their face, the western Illinois data are suggestive of an extensive reduction in the settlement and use of strict upland areas at this time, however.

References Cited

Abbott, Larry R.
1980 Upland Soil Development in Iowa. Paper presented at the 92nd Annual Meeting of the Iowa Academy of Science, Indianola.
1987 *Archaeological Investigations at the Kewanee Site (11-HY-126), Henry County, Illinois.* Research Reports 27. Resource Investigation Program, University of Illinois, Urbana.
1989 *Archaeological Investigations at the Wooded Site (11-MS-587), Madison County, Illinois.* Research Reports 35. Resource Investigation Program, University of Illinois, Urbana.

Abbott, Larry R., and Joseph A. Tiffany
1986 Archaeological Context and Upland Soil Development: The Midwest U.S.A. Example. Paper presented

at the 24th Annual Midwest Archaeological Conference, Cleveland, Ohio.

Adams, W. H.
1883 Mounds in the Spoon River Valley. *Annual Report of the Board of Regnts of the Smithsonian Institution for 1881*, pp. 558–563. Government Printing Office, Washington, D.C.

Ahler, Steven R., Mary J. Bade, Frances B. King, Bonnie W. Styles, and Paula J. Thorson
1992 *Late Archaic Components at Modoc Rock Shelter, Randolph County, Illinois*. Reports of Investigations 48. Illinois State Museum, Springfield.

Albertson, Donald G., and Douglas K. Charles
1988 Archaic Mortuary Component. In *The Archaic and Woodland Cemeteries at the Elizabeth Site in the Lower Illinois Valley*, edited by Douglas K. Charles, Steven R. Leigh, and Jane E. Buikstra, pp. 29–40. Research Series 7. Center for American Archeology, Kampsville, Illinois.

Alvey, Richard L.
1991 *Archaeological Investigations at the Seiwell Site (11-P-344), Peoria County, Illinois*. Research Reports 36. Resource Investigation Program, University of Illinois, Urbana.
1993 The Seiwell Site: A Terminal Archaic Site in the Illinois Uplands. *Illinois Archaeology* 5:158–166.

Anderson, David G., Lisa D. O'Steen, and Kenneth E. Sassaman
1996 Environmental and Chronological Considerations. In *The Paleoindian and Early Archaic Southeast*, edited by David G. Anderson and Kenneth E. Sassaman, pp. 3–15. University of Alabama Press, Tuscaloosa.

Anderson, Ferrel
1989 Dalton Points from Rock Island and Henry County, Illinois. *Illinois Antiquity* 22:3–6.

Artz, Joe Alan
1992 *Archaeology and Geomorphology of a Portion of Muscatine Island and Adjacent Uplands: A Phase I Archaeological Survey of Primary Roads Project F-61-4(55)--20-70, a.k.a. PIN 92-700040-1, Muscatine County, Iowa*. Project Completion Report 15(63). Office of the State Archaeologist, University of Iowa, Iowa City.
1993a The Preservation of Cultural Stratigraphy in Loess-Mantled Terrains of Iowa. *Journal of the Iowa Archeological Society* 40:50–62.
1993b *Phase II Archaeological Investigations at 13RN59: A Late Archaic Campsite in Ringgold County, Iowa*. Project Completion Report 16(53). Office of the State Archaeologist, University of Iowa, Iowa City.

Asch, David L., and Nancy B. Asch
1985 Archeobotany of the Campbell Hollow Archaic Occupations. In *The Campbell Hollow Archaic Occupations: A Study of Intrasite Spatial Structure in the Lower Illinois Valley*, edited by C. Russell Stafford, pp. 82–107. Research Series 4. Center for American Archeology, Kampsville, Illinois.

Atwell, Karen A., and Daniel B. Goatley
1993 *Archaeological Testing Short Report for the Pottstown Site, Peoria County, Illinois*. Report prepared for the Illinois Department of Transportation. Center for American Archeology, Kampsville, Illinois.

Barr, Kenneth A.
1986 *Archaeological Investigations at the Sale Barn Road Site (11HY125), Henry County, Illinois*. Research Reports 24. Resource Investigation Program, University of Illinois, Urbana.

Bassett, John, and Richard L. Powell
1984 Stratigraphic Distribution of Cherts in Limestones of the Blue River Group in Southern Indiana. In *Prehistoric Chert Exploitation: Studies from the Midcontinent*, edited by Brian M. Butler and Ernest E. May, pp. 239–251. Occasional Papers 2. Center for Archaeological Investigations, Southern Illinois University, Carbondale.

Behm, Jeffery A.
1985 Identification and Analysis of Stylistic Variation in Hardin Barbed Points. Ph.D. dissertation, Department of Anthropology, University of Wisconsin, Madison.

Behm, Jeffery A., and William Green
1982 Collections from the Copperas Creek Site (11-F-100), a Multicomponent Site in the Central Illinois Valley. *Rediscovery* 2:31–66.

Benn, David W.
1987 *Archaeology in the Mississippi River Floodplain at Sand Run Slough, Iowa*. CAR 690. Center for Archaeological Research, Southwest Missouri State University, Springfield.

Benn, David W., Jeffrey D. Anderson, and E. Arthur Bettis III
1994 *Archaeological and Geomorphological Surveys in Pools 21-22, Upper Mississippi River*. Submitted to the U.S. Army Corps of Engineers, Rock Island. Bear Creek Archaeology, Cresco, Iowa.

Binford, Lewis R.
1978 Dimensional Analysis of Behavior and Site Structure: Learning from an Eskimo Hunting Stand. *American Antiquity* 43:330–361.
1979 Organization and Formation Processes: Looking at Curated Technologies. *Journal of Anthropological Research* 35:255–273.
1980 Willow Smoke and Dogs' Tails: Hunter-Gatherer Settlement Systems and Archaeological Site Formation. *American Antiquity* 45:4–20.

Birmingham, Nancy Ryden
1985 Lithic Assemblages of the Moline Chert Source Area, Rock Island and Henry Counties, Illinois. In *Lithic Resource Procurement: Proceedings from the Second Conference on Prehistoric Chert Exploitation*, edited by Susan C. Vehik, pp. 133–152. Occasional Papers 4. Center for Archaeological Investigations, Southern Illinois University, Carbondale.

Birmingham, Robert A., and Allen P. Van Dyke
1981 Chert and Chert Resources in the Lower Rock River Valley-Illinois. *The Wisconsin Archeologist* 62:347–360.

Bray, Robert T.
1956 The Culture-Complexes and Sequence at the Rice Site (23SN200), Stone County, Missouri. *The Missouri Archaeologist* 18:45–134.

Brooke, Samuel O.
1979 *The Hester Site, an Early Archaic Site in Monroe County, Mississippi: A Preliminary Report*. Mississippi Department of Archives and History, Jackson.

Brown, James A., and Robert K. Vierra
1983 What Happened in the Middle Archaic? Introduction to an Ecological Approach to Koster Site Archaeology. In *Archaic Hunters and Gatherers in the American Midwest*, edited by James L. Phillips and James A. Brown, pp. 165–195. Academic Press, New York.

Broyles, Bettye J.
1966 Preliminary Report: The St. Albans Site (46KA27), Kanawha County, West Virginia. *West Virginia Archaeologist* 19:1–43.
1971 *Second Preliminary Report: The St. Albans Site, Kanawha Valley, West Virginia*. Report of Archaeological Investigations 3. West Virginia Geological and Economic Survey, Charleston.

Brush, G. S.
1967 Pollen Analysis of Late-Glacial and Postglacial Sediments in Iowa. In *Quaternary Paleoecology*, edited by E. J. Cushing and H. E. Wright Jr., pp. 99–115. Yale University Press, New Haven, Connecticut.

Bryson, Reid A., David A. Baerreis, and Wayne M. Wendland
1970 The Character of Late-Glacial and Post-Glacial Climatic Changes. In *Pleistocene and Recent Environments of the Central Great Plains*, edited by Wakefield Dort Jr., and J. Knox Jones Jr., pp. 53–74. University Press of Kansas, Lawrence.

Calentine, Leighann, Dale L. McElrath, and Jamey Zehr
2004 *Phase I Archaeological Survey of the Proposed Danville Beltline*. Research Report 101. Illinois Transportation Archeological Research Program, University of Illinois, Urbana.

Cambron, James W.
1957 Some Early Projectile Point Types from the Tennessee Valley. *Journal of Alabama Archaeology* 3(2):17–19.

Cambron, James W., and David C. Hulse
1975 *Handbook of Alabama Archaeology: Part I, Point Types*. Archaeological Research Association of Alabama, Huntsville.

Cantin, Mark
1994 Comparative Analysis of Thebes and Kirk Lithic Traditions and Implications of Home Ranges. Paper presented at the Joint Meeting of the 51st Southeastern Archaeological Conference and the 39th Midwest Archaeological Conference, Lexington, Kentucky.

Caspall, Fred C.
1965 Parallel Drainage in West-Central Illinois. Master's thesis, Department of Geography, Western Illinois University, Macomb.

Chapman, Charles C.
1879 *History of Fulton County, Illinois*. Charles C. Chapman, Peoria, Illinois.

Chapman, Carl H.
1975 *The Archaeology of Missouri, I*. University of Missouri Press, Columbia.

Chapman, Jefferson
1975 *The Rose Island Site and the Bifurcate Point Tradition*. Report of Investigations 14. Department of Anthropology, University of Tennessee, Knoxville.
1977 *Archaic Period Research in the Lower Little Tennessee River Valley, 1975: Icehouse Bottom, Harrison Branch, Thirty Acre Island, Calloway Island*. Report of Investigations 18. Department of Anthropology, University of Tennessee, Knoxville.
1979 *Archaeological Investigations at the Howard (40MR66) and Calloway Island (40MR41) Sites*. Report of Investigations 27. Department of Anthropology, University of Tennessee, Knoxville.
1985 Archaeology and the Archaic Period in the Southern Ridge-and-Valley Province. In *Structure and Process in Southeastern Archaeology*, edited by Roy S. Dickens and H. Trawick Ward, pp. 137–153. University of Alabama Press, Tuscaloosa.

Charles, Douglas K., and Jane E. Buikstra
1983 Archaic Mortuary Sites in the Central Mississippi Drainage: Distribution, Structure, and Behavioral Implications. In *Archaic Hunters and Gatherers in the American Midwest*, edited by James L. Phillips and James A. Brown, pp. 117–145. Academic Press, New York.

Charles, Douglas K., Steven R. Leigh, and Jane E. Buikstra
1988 *The Archaic and Woodland Cemeteries at the Elizabeth Site in the Lower Illinois Valley*. Research Series 7. Center for American Archeology, Kampsville, Illinois.

Christenson, Andrew L.
1977 Some Trends in Biface Technology in Central Illinois. *Plains Anthropologist* 22:283–290.

Clayton, L., W. B. Bickley Jr., and W. J. Stone
1970 Knife River Flint. *Plains Anthropologist* 15:282–290.

Coe, Joffre L.
1964 *The Formative Cultures of the Carolina Piedmont*. Transactions of the American Philosophical Society 54, Part 5. Philadelphia.

Cole, Fay-Cooper, and Thorne Deuel
1937 *Rediscovering Illinois: Archaeological Explorations in and around Fulton County*. University of Chicago Press, Chicago.

Collins, James M.
1990 *Human Adaptations to Holocene Landscapes in the Iowa River Greenbelt: A Phase I Archaeological Survey of Primary Roads Project F-20-5(53)--20-42, Relocated U.S. 20, Hardin and Grundy Counties, Iowa*. Contract Completion Report 290. Office of the State Archaeologist, University of Iowa, Iowa City.

Collins, Michael B.
1979 *Excavations at Four Archaic Sites in the Lower Ohio Valley, Jefferson County, Kentucky*. Occasional Papers in Anthropology 1. Department of Anthropology, University of Kentucky, Lexington.

Conner, Michael D.
1984 *An Archaeological and Geomorphological Assessment of the FAP 408 Illinois Bluffline Borrow Area*. Report of Investigations 152. Center for American Archeology, Kampsville, Illinois.
1986 *Cypress Land: A Late Archaic/Early Woodland Site in the Lower Illinois River Floodplain*. Technical Report 2. Center for American Archeology, Kampsville, Illinois.

Conrad, Lawrence A.
1978 *Final Report of an Archaeological Survey of the Freeman United Coal Mining Companies' Properties in McDonough and Schuyler Counties, near Industry, Illinois*. Archaeological Research Laboratory, Western Illinois University, Macomb.
1981 *An Introduction to the Archaeology of Upland West Central Illinois: A Preliminary Archaeological Survey of the Canton to Quincy Corridor for the Proposed FAP 407 Highway*

Project. Reports of Investigations 2. Archaeological Research Laboratory, Western Illinois University, Macomb.

1982 Update on the Archaic Period in the Littleton Project Area. In *Final Report on Phase II Archaeological Investigations on Portions of Amax's Proposed Littleton Mine Field and Littleton Haul Road, Schuyler, McDonough, and Fulton Counties, Illinois*, by Duane Esarey, pp. 16–62. Reports of Investigations 4. Archaeological Research Laboratory, Western Illinois University, Macomb.

1986a *A Survey of Prehistoric Archaeology of a 1000-Foot-Wide Transect Between Good Hope and Monmouth Illinois*. Reports of Investigations 9. Archaeological Research Laboratory, Western Illinois University, Macomb.

1986b (editor) *A Cultural Resources Overview and Reconnaissance Survey of Two Dry Reservoirs, Tazewell County, Illinois*. Reports of Investigations 8. Archaeological Research Laboratory, Western Illinois University, Macomb.

1986c The Late Archaic/Early Woodland Transition in the Interior of West-Central Illinois. In *Early Woodland Archeology*, edited by Kenneth B. Farnsworth and Thomas E. Emerson, pp. 301–325. Seminars in Archeology 2. Center for American Archeology, Kampsville, Illinois.

1986d *An Archaeological Survey of Siloam Springs State Park and of Portions of the Lower and Middle McKee Creek Basin in Adams, Brown, and Pike Counties, Illinois*. Archaeological Research Laboratory, Western Illinois University, Macomb.

1987 Man, Land, and Climate in Upland West Central Illinois, 11,500–3000 BP. Draft manuscript on file, Archaeological Research Laboratory, Western Illinois University, Macomb.

1990 *Archaeological Survey Short Report on the Monmouth Industrial Park Investigations*. Submitted to the Illinois Department of Transportation. Archaeological Research Laboratory, Western Illinois University, Macomb.

Conrad, Lawrence A., Susan L. Gardner, and J. Joe Alford

1986 A Note on the Late Archaic, Early Woodland, and Early Middle Woodland Occupations of the Lima Lake Locality, Adams and Hancock Counties, Illinois. In *Early Woodland Archeology*, edited by Kenneth B. Farnsworth and Thomas E. Emerson, pp. 191–206. Seminars in Archeology 2. Center for American Archeology, Kampsville, Illinois.

Conrad, Lawrence A., and Debi Jones

1978 *A Preliminary Report on Sub-Surface Testing of Four, and Mitigation of Two Archaeological Sites Affected by IDOT District 4 Project EBRF-404-1 in Sections 94-16A and 94-16B (HB), in Warren County, Illinois*. Submitted to the Illinois Department of Transportation. Archaeological Research Laboratory, Western Illinois University, Macomb.

Converse, Robert N.

1973 *Ohio Flint Types*. 6th ed. Archaeological Society of Ohio, Columbus.

Cook, Thomas Genn

1976 *Koster: An Artifact Analysis of Two Archaic Phases in Westcentral Illinois*. Prehistoric Record 1. Northwestern University Archaeological Program, Evanston, Illinois.

1980 Typology and Description of Hafted Stone Tools. In *Archaeological Salvage Excavations at Patoka Lake, Indiana: Prehistoric Occupations of the Upper Patoka River Valley*, edited by Cheryl A. Munson, pp. 349–454. Research Reports 6. Glenn A. Black Laboratory of Archaeological Research, Indiana University, Bloomington.

1986 A Dispersed Harvesting Economy: The Titterington Phase. In *Foraging, Collecting, and Harvesting: Archaic Period Subsistence and Settlement in the Eastern Woodlands*, edited by Sarah W. Neusius, pp. 175–200. Occasional Papers 6. Center for Archaeological Investigations, Southern Illinois University, Carbondale.

Cripe, Donald B.

1988 Comparison of Holocene Climatic Periods and Archaeological Materials: A Study in Lima Lake Geoarchaeology. Master's thesis, Department of Geography, Western Illinois University, Macomb.

Cross, Paula

1998 *Phase I Archaeological Survey for the FAP 310 North Project*. 2 vols. Report of Investigations 225. Center for American Archeology, Kampsville, Illinois.

DeJarnette, David L., Edward B. Kurjack, and James W. Cambron

1962 Excavations at the Stanfield-Worley Bluff Shelter. *Journal of Alabama Archaeology* 8:1–124.

Deller, D. Brian, and Christopher J. Ellis

1988 Early Paleo Indian Complexes in Southwestern Ontario. In *Late Pleistocene and Early Holocene Paleoecology and Archaeology of the Eastern Great Lakes Region*, edited by Richard S. Laub, Norton G. Miller, and David W. Steadman, pp. 251–263. Bulletin 33. Buffalo Society of Natural Sciences, Buffalo, New York.

Deuel, Thorne

1933 Cultural Sequence in Fulton County. *Transactions of the Illinois State Academy of Science* 25:96–97. Springfield.

Driskell, Boyce N.

1996 Stratified Late Pleistocene and Early Holocene Deposits at Dust Cave, Northwestern Alabama. In *The Paleoindian and Early Archaic Southeast*, edited by David G. Anderson and Kenneth E. Sassaman, pp. 315–330. University of Alabama Press, Tuscaloosa.

Dunbar, James S., S. David Webb, and Dan Cring

1989 Culturally and Naturally Modified Bones from a Paleoindian Site in the Aucilla River, North Florida. In *Bone Modification*, edited by Robson Bonnichsen and Marcella H. Sorg, pp. 473–497. Center for the Study of the First Americans, Oroño, Maine.

Durkee, L. H.

1971 A Pollen Profile from Woden Bog in Northcentral Iowa. *Ecology* 52:837–844.

Dwyer, James P., and Thomas L. Burge

1978 *Archaeological Investigations in the Cedar Creek Drainage, West Central Illinois*. Illinois State Museum, Springfield.

Dwyer, James P., and Alan D. Harn

1978 *An Archaeological Reconnaissance of the Proposed FAP-405 Corridor Between Mossville and Peoria, Illinois*. Illinois State Museum, Springfield.

Ellis, Christopher J., and Jonathan C. Lothrop (editors)
1989 *Eastern Paleoindian Lithic Resource Use.* Westview Press, Boulder, Colorado.

Emerson, Thomas E.
1984 The Dyroff and Levin Sites: A Late Archaic Occupation in the American Bottom. In *The Go-Kart North Site and the Dyroff and Levin Sites*, by Andrew C. Fortier and Thomas E. Emerson, pp. 199–362. American Bottom Archaeology FAI-270 Site Reports 9. University of Illinois Press, Urbana.

Emerson, Thomas E., and Andrew C. Fortier
1986 Early Woodland Cultural Variation, Subsistence, and Settlement in the American Bottom. In *Early Woodland Archeology*, edited by Kenneth B. Farnsworth and Thomas E. Emerson, pp. 475–522. Seminars in Archeology 2. Center for American Archeology, Kampsville, Illinois.

Emerson, Thomas E., and Dale L. McElrath
2001 Interpreting Discontinuity and Historical Process in Midcontinental Late Archaic and Early Woodland Societies. In *The Archaeology of Traditions: Agency and History Before and After Columbus*, edited by Timothy R. Pauketat, pp. 195–217. University Press of Florida, Gainesville.

Emerson, Thomas E., Dale L. McElrath, and Joyce Williams
1986 Patterns of Hunter-Gatherer Mobility and Sedentism during the Archaic Period in the American Bottom. In *Foraging, Collecting, and Harvesting: Archaic Period Subsistence and Settlement in the Eastern Woodlands*, edited by Sarah W. Neusius, pp. 240–266. Occasional Papers 6. Center for Archaeological Investigation, Southern Illinois University, Carbondale.

Esarey, Duane
1982 *Summary of Phase II Investigations at the Ursa Major Site (11-A-1006), Ursa, Illinois.* Archaeological Research Laboratory, Western Illinois University, Macomb.
1983 *Chert Availability and Aboriginal Utilization in West Central Illinois: A Geographic Overview.* Archaeological Research Laboratory, Western Illinois University, Macomb.
1986 Red Ocher Mound Building and Marion Phase Associations: A Fulton County, Illinois Perspective. In *Early Woodland Archeology*, edited by Kenneth B. Farnsworth and Thomas E. Emerson, pp. 231–243. Seminars in Archeology 2. Center for American Archeology, Kampsville, Illinois.
1987 The Town Branch Sites: Archaic Encampments on the Bushnell Prairie of West Central Illinois. *The Wisconsin Archeologist* 68:95–124.
1990 *An Archaeological Survey of the Banks of the Illinois River from Naples to Starved Rock Lock and Dam.* Technical Report 90-557-7. Quaternary Studies Center, Illinois State Museum, Springfield.

Evans, J. Bryant, and Kevin T. Womac
1997 *The Christianson Site (11RI42): Paleoindian through Late Archaic Occupations of the Lower Rock River, Rock Island County, Illinois.* Research Reports 56. Illinois Transportation Archaeological Research Program, University of Illinois, Urbana.
1998 The Christianson Site (11RI42): A Paleoindian Occupation in the Lower Rock River Valley, Illinois. *Illinois Archaeology* 10:331–355.

Evans, Madeleine G.
2001 Implications of the Archaic Lithic Assemblage at the Tree Row Site in Fulton County, Illinois. Paper presented at the 47th Annual Midwest Archaeological Conference, LaCrosse, Wisconsin.

Farnsworth, Kenneth B.
2003 Stuart Struever's 1958–59 Excavations at the Heineken Site, Putnam County, Illinois. Manuscript on file, Illinois Transportation Archaeological Research Program, Macomb.

Farnsworth, Kenneth B., and David L. Asch
1986 Early Woodland Chronology, Artifact Styles, and Settlement Distribution in the Lower Illinois Valley Region. In *Early Woodland Archeology*, edited by Kenneth B. Farnsworth and Thomas E. Emerson, pp. 326–457. Seminars in Archeology 2. Center for American Archeology, Kampsville, Illinois.

Farnsworth, Kenneth B., Thomas E. Berres, Randall E. Hughes, and Duane M. Moore
2004 Illinois Platform Pipes and Hopewellian Exchange: A Mineralogical Study of Archaeological Remains. In *Aboriginal Ritual and Economy in the Eastern Woodlands: Essays in Memory of Howard Dalton Winters*, edited by Anne-Marie Cantwell, Lawrence A. Conrad, and Jonathan E. Reyman, pp. 182–213. Scientific Papers 30. Illinois State Museum, Springfield.

Farnsworth, Kenneth B., and Thomas E. Emerson (editors)
1986 *Early Woodland Archeology.* Seminars in Archeology 2. Center for American Archeology, Kampsville, Illinois.

Ferguson, Jacqueline A., and Robert E. Warren
1992 Chert Resources of Northern Illinois: Discriminant Analysis and an Identification Key. *Illinois Archaeology* 4:1–37.
1993 Artifact Distribution and Chert Use at the Barton-Milner Site: A Middle Archaic Occupation in North-Central Illinois. *Illinois Archaeology* 5:130–140.

Fishel, Richard L.
1988 Preliminary Observations on the Distribution of the Agate Basin Projectile Point East of the Mississippi River. *The Wisconsin Archeologist* 69:125–138.
1992 Payson Chert: A Distinct Lithic Raw Material from Adams County, Illinois. *Illinois Archaeology* 4:74–84.
1993a *Phase II Archaeological Survey and Limited Subsurface Testing of Prehistoric Cultural Resources of the FAP 10 RT 67 Project Area in McDonough and Warren Counties, Illinois.* Report of Investigations 200. Center for American Archeology, Kampsville, Illinois.
1993b *The Pike County Highway 1 Project: Late Woodland and Mississippian in Far West-Central Illinois.* Report of Investigations 201. Center for American Archeology, Kampsville, Illinois.
2000 *Phase III Archaeological Data Recovery at the Smith Bottom Site (13HA181) and the Allen Fan Site (13HA385): The Middle and Late Archaic of Hardin County, Iowa, NHS-520-5(53)--19-42, a.k.a. PIN 94-42060-2.* Contract Completion Report 692. Office of the State Archaeologist, University of Iowa, Iowa City.

2003 *Archaeological Investigations at Site 11MC71 (Marseton Site II) for the CH14/New Boston Road Project.* Archaeological Testing Short Report 112. Illinois Transportation Archaeological Research Program, University of Illinois at Urbana–Champaign.

2004 *Archaeological Investigations at Site 11HY289 (Billboard Flats Site) for the FAU 5822/Milan Beltway Extension-West River Crossing, Green River Wetland Mitigation Site Project.* Archaeological Testing Short Report 160. Illinois Transportation Archaeological Research Program, University of Illinois at Urbana–Champaign.

Fishel, Richard L., Rhett B. Felix, and James M. Pisell

2004 *Executive Summary for IL Route 29 and IL Route 29 Addendum Phase I Archaeological Surveys in Peoria, Marshall, Putnam, and Bureau Counties, Illinois.* Research Reports 90. Illinois Transportation Archaeological Research Program, University of Illinois, Urbana.

Fishel, Richard L., Rolfe D. Mandel, James M. Collins, and Michael T. Dunne

2003 *The Archaic Occupations of the Allen Fan Site (13HA385) in the Iowa Valley of Central Iowa.* Memoir 34. Plains Anthropological Society, Lincoln, Nebrsksa.

Fishel, Richard L., and David J. Nolan

2004 *Archaeological Investigations at Site 11HA326 (Thomas 1/2 Site) for the FAP 315/IL 336 Wetland Project.* Archaeological Testing Short Report 196. Illinois Transportation Archaeological Research Program, University of Illinois, Urbana.

Fortier, Andrew C.

1984 The Go-Kart North Site. In *The Go-Kart North Site and the Dyroff and Levin Sites*, by Andrew C. Fortier and Thomas E. Emerson, pp. 1–197. American Bottom Archaeology FAI-270 Site Reports 9. University of Illinois Press, Urbana.

1993 American Bottom House Types of the Archaic and Woodland Periods: An Overview. *Illinois Archaeology* 5:260–275.

Fowler, Melvin L.

1957 *Ferry Site, Hardin County, Illinois.* Scientific Papers (8)1. Illinois State Museum, Springfield.

1959 *Summary Report of Modoc Rock Shelter: 1952, 1953, 1955, 1956.* Reports of Investigations 8. Illinois State Museum, Springfield.

Fowler, Melvin L., and Robert A. Birmingham

1975 An Archaeological Survey of the Rock River in Illinois. In *Preliminary Report of 1974 Historic Site Survey Archaeological Reconnaissance of Selected Areas in the State of Illinois*, pp. 72–78. Illinois Archaeological Survey, Urbana.

Frison, George C.

1978 *Prehistoric Hunters of the High Plains.* 2nd ed. Academic Press, New York.

Frison, George C., and Dennis J. Stanford

1982 *The Agate Basin Site: A Record of the Paleoindian Occupation of the Northwestern High Plains.* Academic Press, New York.

Funk, R. E., D. W. Fisher, and E. M. Reilly Jr.

1970 Caribou and Paleo-Indian in New York State: A Presumed Association. *American Journal of Science* 268:181–186.

Goatley, Daniel B.

1998a Quasar: A Stratified Archaic Site in the Floodplain of the Lower Illinois River Valley. *Illinois Archaeology* 10:267–293.

1998b *Preliminary Phase I Archaeological Survey of the Proposed US 34 Expansion between Monmouth and Gulfport, in Henderson and Warren Counties, Illinois.* Report of Investigations 253. Center for American Archeology, Kampsville, Illinois.

Goatley, Daniel B., and Karen A. Atwell

1993 *Archaeological Testing Short Report on the Boyd Site, Pike County, Illinois.* Submitted to the Illinois Department of Transportation. Center for American Archeology, Kampsville, Illinois.

Goatley, Daniel B., Karen A. Atwell, and Shannon Chappell

1996 *The Boyd Site: A Debitage Analysis from a Buried Upland Site in Pike County, Illinois.* Report of Investigations 232. Center for American Archeology, Kampsville, Illinois.

Goldstein, Lynne

2004 An Analysis of Plummets in the Lower Illinois River Valley. In *Aboriginal Ritual and Economy in the Eastern Woodlands: Essays in Memory of Howard Dalton Winters*, edited by Anne-Marie Cantwell, Lawrence A. Conrad, and Jonathan E. Reyman, pp. 73–112. Scientific Papers 30. Illinois State Museum, Springfield.

Goodyear, Albert C.

1974 *The Brand Site: A Techno-Functional Study of a Dalton Site in Northeast Arkansas.* Research Series 7. Arkansas Archeological Survey, Fayetteville.

1982 The Chronological Position of the Dalton Horizon in the Southeastern United States. *American Antiquity* 47:382–395.

Graham, R. W., C. V. Haynes, D. L. Johnson, and M. Kay

1981 Kimmswick: A Clovis-Mastodon Association in Eastern Missouri. *Science* 213:1115–1117.

Gramly, Richard Michael, and Robert E. Funk

1991 Olive Branch: A Large Dalton and Pre-Dalton Encampment at Thebes Gap, Alexander County, Illinois. In *The Archaic Period in the Mid-South: Proceedings of the 1989 Mid-South Archaeological Conference*, edited by Charles H. McNutt, pp. 23–33. Archaeological Report 24. Mississippi Department of Archives and History, Jackson. Occasional Paper 16. Anthropological Research Center, Memphis State University, Memphis, Tennessee.

Green, William

1975 An Archaeological Survey of Strip Mine Lands and Adjacent Areas in West Central Illinois. In *Preliminary Report of 1974 Historic Sites Survey, Archaeological Reconnaissance of Selected Areas in the State of Illinois*, Part I, Summary, Section B, pp. 151–158. Illinois Archaeological Survey, Urbana.

1977a *Final Report of Littleton Field Archaeological Survey, Schuyler County, Illinois.* Reports on Archaeology 1. Upper Mississippi Valley Archaeological Research Foundation, Macomb, Illinois.

1977b *Final Report of Ipava Field Archaeological Survey, Fulton County, Illinois.* Reports on Archaeology 2. Upper Mississippi Valley Archaeological Research Foundation, Macomb, Illinois.

Green, William, and David J. Nolan
2000 Late Woodland Peoples in West-Central Illinois. In *Late Woodland Societies: Tradition and Transformation across the Midcontinent*, edited by Thomas E. Emerson, Dale L. McElrath, and Andrew C. Fortier, pp. 345–386. University of Nebraska Press, Lincoln.

Griffin, James B.
1933 Archaeological Remains in Adams County, Illinois. *Transactions of the Illinois State Academy of Science* 25:97–98. Springfield.
1952 Culture Periods in Eastern United States Archeology. In *Archeology of Eastern United States*, edited by James B. Griffin, pp. 352–364. University of Chicago Press, Chicago.
1991 The Parker Heights Mound at Quincy, Illinois. In *The Kuhlman Mound Group and Late Woodland Mortuary Behavior in the Mississippi River Valley of West-Central Illinois*, edited by Karen A. Atwell and Michael D. Conner, pp. 276–291. Research Series 9. Center for American Archeology, Kampsville, Illinois.

Gruger, E.
1972 Late Quaternary Vegetation Development in South-Central Illinois. *Quaternary Research* 2:217–231.

Hansen, Eric G.
1994 Lithic Analysis of Three Buried Sites. In *1993–1994 Excavations on the FAP 407-Route 336 Quincy to Mendon Priority Segment,* edited by David J. Nolan and Eric G. Hansen, pp. 119–151. Report of Investigations 197E. Center for American Archeology, Kampsville, Illinois.
1995 (editor) *1994–1995 Interim Report of the FAP 407-Route 336 Project: Tested Sites in the Bear Creek Segment; Geological Overview; and a Study of Payson Chert.* Report of Investigations 197F. Center for American Archeology, Kampsville, Illinois.
1996 (editor) *Cultural Resources Overview and Limited Phase I Archaeological Survey for the Route 336 Carthage to Macomb Right-of-Way.* Report of Investigations 227. Center for American Archeology, Kampsville, Illinois.

Hansen, Eric G., and Robert N. Hickson (editors)
1993 *Progress Report on the FAP 407-Route 336 Project: Archaeological Survey Completion and Site Testing.* Report of Investigations 197D. Center for American Archeology, Kampsville, Illinois.

Hansen, Eric G., and David J. Nolan
1998 Was the Cochran 10 Site (11-Wa-140) a Theban Persistent Place? Assemblage Structure and Settlement Patterns in the Early Archaic of West Central Illinois. *Illinois Archaeology* 10:294–330.

Harn, Alan D.
1980 *The Prehistory of Dickson Mounds: The Dickson Excavation.* Reports of Investigations 35. Illinois State Museum, Springfield.
1986 The Marion Phase Occupation of the Larson Site in the Central Illinois River Valley. In *Early Woodland Archeology*, edited by Kenneth B. Farnsworth and Thomas E. Emerson, pp. 244–279. Center for American Archeology, Kampsville, Illinois.

Hassen, Harold (editor)
1991 *Late Archaic and Late Woodland Archeology in the Sny Bottom Region of the Mississippi River Valley: Archeological Investigations at the Kuhlman Habitation and Scenic Vista Sites.* Center for American Archeology, Kampsville, Illinois.

Hassen, Harold, and James M. Batura
1983 *Archaeological Investigations along the Lower Illinois River Floodplain: Cultural Resource Surveys of the Hartwell and Nutwood Levee and Drainage Districts, Jersey and Greene Counties, Illinois.* Cultural Resource Management Report 4. U.S. Army Corps of Engineers, St. Louis District, St. Louis, Missouri.

Hassen, Harold, and Kenneth B. Farnsworth
1987 *The Bullseye Site: A Floodplain Archaic Mortuary Site in the Lower Illinois River Valley.* Reports of Investigations 42. Illinois State Museum, Springfield.

Haynes, C. Vance, Jr.
1987 Clovis Origin Update. *Kiva* 52:83–93.

Hickson, Robert N.
1990 *Progress Report on FAP 407 Archaeological Surveys Route 336 Quincy to Carthage Segment, Hancock and Adams Counties.* Report of Investigations 197A. Center for American Archeology, Kampsville, Illinois.
1991 *Progress Report on the FAP 407 Archaeological Survey of the Priority Alternate Segment Combination E-1 Route 336 Quincy to Carthage Segment, Adams and Hancock Counties.* Report of Investigations 197B. Center for American Archeology, Kampsville, Illinois.

Hickson, Robert N., and Susana R. Katz (editors)
1992 *Progress Report on the FAP 407 Route 336 Archeological Survey and Prehistoric Site Testing along the Priority Quincy to Mendon Alternate Segment in Adams County, Illinois.* Report of Investigations 197C. Center for American Archeology, Kampsville, Illinois.

Higgins, Michael J.
1990 *The Nochta Site: The Early, Middle, and Late Archaic Occupations (11-Ms-128).* American Bottom Archaeology FAI-270 Site Reports 21. University of Illinois Press, Urbana.

Holstein, Harry O.
1978 Sugar Creek: An Archaeological Investigation and Survey of a Minor Secondary Tributary in Central Illinois. Ph.D. dissertation, Department of Anthropology, University of Pittsburgh, Pittsburgh, Pennsylvania.

Holstein, Harry, Jerry Fairchild, and Wayne Shields
1975 An Archaeological Survey of the Lower Central Illinois and LaMoine River Drainages. In *Preliminary Report of 1974 Historic Sites Survey Archaeological Reconnaissance of Selected Areas in the State of Illinois*, Part I, Summary, Section A. Pp. 56–64. Illinois Archaeological Survey, Urbana.

Irwin, Henry T.
1971 Developments in Early Man Studies in Western North America, 1960–1970. *Arctic Anthropology* 8:42–67.

Irwin-Williams, Cynthia, Henry Irwin, George Agogino, and C. Vance Haynes Jr.
1973 Hell Gap: Paleo-Indian Occupation on the High Plains. *Plains Anthropologist* 18:40–53.

Ives, David J.
1984 The Crescent Hills Prehistoric Quarrying Area: More than Just Rocks. In *Prehistoric Chert Exploitation:*

Studies from the Midcontinent, edited by Brian M. Butler and Ernest E. May, pp. 187–195. Occasional Papers 2. Center for Archaeological Investigations, Southern Illinois University, Carbondale.

Jackson, Douglas K.
1993 The Determann Borrow Site: A Mississippian Occupation on the Silver Creek Drainage. *Illinois Archaeology* 5:355–364.

Jefferies, Richard W., and B. Mark Lynch
1983 Dimensions of Middle Archaic Cultural Adaptation at the Black Earth Site, Saline County, Illinois. In *Archaic Hunters and Gatherers in the American Midwest*, edited by James L. Phillips and James A. Brown, pp. 299–322. Academic Press, New York.

Jennings, Jesse D.
1974 *Prehistory of North America*. 2nd ed. McGraw-Hill, New York.

Jones, Douglas W.
1994 Preliminary Results from Test Excavations at 11-Ri-562, a Multicomponent Site near Coal Valley, Illinois. Paper presented at the 106th Annual Meeting of the Iowa Academy of Science, Davenport.

Justice, Noel D.
1987 *Stone Age Spear and Arrow Points of the Midcontinental and Eastern United States*. Indiana University Press, Bloomington.

Kimball, Larry R.
1996 Early Archaic Settlement and Technology: Lessons from Tellico. In *The Paleoindian and Early Archaic Southeast*, edited by David G. Anderson and Kenneth E. Sassaman, pp. 149–186. University of Alabama Press, Tuscaloosa.

King, James E.
1986 Chatsworth Bog: A Woodfordian Kettle. In *Quaternary Records of Northeastern Illinois and Northwestern Indiana*, edited by Ardith K. Hansel and W. Hilton Johnson, pp. 17–21. Guidebook 22. Illinois State Geological Survey, Urbana.

King, James E., and William H. Allen Jr.
1977 A Holocene Vegetation Record from the Mississippi River Valley, Southeastern Missouri. *Quaternary Research* 8:307–323.

Klippel, Walter E.
1971 *Graham Cave Revisited: A Reevaluation of Its Cultural Position during the Archaic Period*. Memoir 9. Missouri Archaeological Society, Columbia.

Kneberg, Madeline
1956 Some Important Projectile Point Types Found in the Tennessee Area. *Tennessee Archaeologist* 12:17–28.

Knoblock, Byron W.
1939 *Bannerstones of the North American Indian*. Published by the author, LaGrange, Illinois.

Kruger, Robert P.
1988 *Archaeological Investigations at the Roberts Site (11-A-1029), Adams County, Illinois*. Research Report 29. Resource Investigation Program, University of Illinois, Urbana.

Leighton, M. M., G. E. Ekbaw, and C. L. Horberg
1948 Physiographic Divisions of Illinois. *Journal of Geology* 56:16–33.

Lensink, Stephen C. (editor)
1986 *Archaeological Investigations along the F-518 Corridor*. Iowa Quaternary Studies Contribution 9. University of Iowa, Iowa City.

Lewis, Thomas M. N., and Madeline Kneberg Lewis
1961 *Eva: An Archaic Site*. University of Tennessee Press, Knoxville.

Lopinot, Neal H., Jack H. Ray, and Michael D. Conner (editors)
1998 *The 1997 Excavations at the Big Eddy Site (23CE426) in Southwest Missouri*. Special Publication 2. Center for Archaeological Research, Southwest Missouri State University, Springfield.

Luchterhand, Kubet
1970 *Early Archaic Projectile Points and Hunting Patterns in the Lower Illinois River Valley*. Reports of Investigations 19. Illinois State Museum, Springfield.

MacDonald, George F.
1968 *A Paleo-Indian Site in Central Nova Scotia*. Anthropological Papers 16. National Museum of Canada, Ottawa.

Markman, Charles W., and Paul P. Kreisa
1986 Early Woodland Adaptation along the Lower Rock River, Illinois. In *Early Woodland Archeology*, edited by Kenneth B. Farnsworth and Thomas E. Emerson, pp. 179–190. Seminars in Archeology 2. Center for American Archeology, Kampsville, Illinois.

Marshall, Richard A.
1958 The Use of Table Rock Reservoir Projectile Points in the Delineation of Cultural Complexes and Their Distribution. Master's thesis, Department of Anthropology, University of Missouri, Columbia.

Martin, Paul S.
1958 Pleistocene Ecology and Biogeography of North America. In *Zoogeography*, edited by C. L. Hubbs, pp. 375–420. Memoir 51. American Association for the Advancement of Science, Washington, D.C.

McClelland, M. A.
1883 Antiquities of Knox County, Illinois. *Annual Report of the Board of Regents of the Smithsonian Institution for 1881*, pp. 554–556. Government Printing Office, Washington, D.C.

McConaughy, Mark A. (editor)
1993 *Rench: A Stratified Site in the Central Illinois River Valley*. Reports of Investigations 49. Illinois State Museum, Springfield.

McElrath, Dale L.
1986 *The McLean Site*. American Bottom Archaeology FAI-270 Site Reports 14. University of Illinois Press, Urbana.
1993 Mule Road: A Newly Defined Late Archaic Phase in the American Bottom. *Illinois Archaeology* 5:148–157.

McElrath, Dale L., Thomas E. Emerson, Andrew C. Fortier, and James L. Phillips
1984 Late Archaic Period. In *American Bottom Archaeology: A Summary of the FAI-270 Project Contribution to the Culture History of the Mississippi River Valley*, edited by Charles J. Bareis and James W. Porter, pp. 34–58. University of Illinois Press, Urbana.

McElrath, Dale L., and Andrew C. Fortier
1983 *The Missouri Pacific #2 Site*. American Bottom Archaeology FAI-270 Site Reports 3. University of Illinois Press, Urbana.

McGregor, John C.
1954 The Chrisman Site: Illinois River Valley Archaic Culture. *Journal of the Illinois State Archaeological Society* 4:12–21.
1957 Prehistoric Village Distribution in the Illinois River Valley. *American Antiquity* 22:272–279.

McNerney, Michael J., James Ross, Wesley Neal, and Jane K. Johnston
1991 *A Phase I Cultural Resource Survey of Freeman-United Coal Mining Company's Industry Mine, McDonough County, Illinois*. Cultural Resources Management Report 148. American Resources Group, Carbondale, Illinois.

Meltzer, David J.
1989 Was Stone Exchanged among Eastern North American Paleoindians? In *Eastern Paleoindian Lithic Resource Use*, edited by Christopher J. Ellis and Jonathan C. Lothrop, pp. 11–39. Westview Press, Boulder, Colorado.

Michie, James
1973 A Functional Interpretation of the Dalton Projectile Point in South Carolina. *South Carolina Antiquities* 5(2):26–36.

Moffat, Charles, David J. Nolan, Ryan Gifford, Amy K. Graham, and Jennifer Logan
2001 Archaeological Survey Short Report of the Brown County Wetland Mitigation Bank, Wessel Property. Submitted to the Illinois Department of Transportation. Illinois Transportation Archaeological Research Program, University of Illinois, Urbana.

Montet-White, Anta
1968 *The Lithic Industries of the Illinois Valley in the Early and Middle Woodland Period*. Anthropological Papers 35. Museum of Anthropology, University of Michigan, Ann Arbor.

Morgan, David T., Christine E. Grebey, and Raymond M. Perkins
1984 *Archaeological Test Excavations at the McCraney Creek Site (PK-321), Pike County, Illinois*. Report of Investigations 67. Center for American Archeology, Kampsville, Illinois.

Morgan, David T., and C. Russell Stafford (editors)
1986 *Early Late Woodland Occupations in the Fall Creek Locality of the Mississippi Valley*. Technical Report 3. Center for American Archeology, Kampsville, Illinois.

Morrow, Toby A.
1984 *Iowa Projectile Points*. Special Publication. Office of the State Archaeologist, University of Iowa, Iowa City.
1988 Thebes Knives: Experimental Applications to Archaeological Data. Manuscript on file, Center for American Archeology, Kampsville, Illinois.
1989 Twin Ditch: Early Archaic Settlement and Technology in the Lower Illinois Valley. Manuscript on file, Center for American Archeology, Kampsville, Illinois.
1994 A Key to the Identification of Chipped-Stone Raw Materials Found on Archaeological Sites in Iowa. *Journal of the Iowa Archeological Society* 41:108–129.
1996 Lithic Refitting and Archaeological Site Formation Processes: A Case Study from the Twin Ditch Site, Greene County, Illinois. In *Stone Tools: Theoretical Insights into Human Prehistory*, edited by George H. Odell, pp. 345–373. Plenum Press, New York.

Morse, Dan F.
1963 *The Steuben Village and Mounds: A Multicomponent Late Hopewell Site in Illinois*. Anthropological Papers 21. Museum of Anthropology, University of Michigan, Ann Arbor.

Morse, Dan F., and Albert C. Goodyear
1973 The Significance of the Dalton Adz in Northeast Arkansas. *Plains Anthropologist* 18:316–321.

Munson, Patrick J.
1966 The Sheets Site: A Late Archaic-Early Woodland Occupation in West-Central Illinois. *Michigan Archaeologist* 12:111–120.
1967 Hardin Barbed Projectile Points: Analysis of a Central Illinois Sample. *Central States Archaeological Journal* 14(1):16–19.
1990 Folsom Fluted Projectile Points East of the Great Plains and Their Biogeographical Correlates. *North American Archaeologist* 11:255–272.

Munson, Patrick J., and Alan D. Harn
1966 Surface Collections from Three Sites in the Central Illinois River Valley. *The Wisconsin Archeologist* 47:150–168.
1971 *An Archaeological Survey of the American Bottoms and Wood River Terrace*. Reports of Investigations 21. Illinois State Museum, Springfield.

Munson, Patrick J., and Cheryl Ann Munson
1984 Cherts and Archaic Chert Utilization in South-Central Indiana. In *Prehistoric Chert Exploitation: Studies from the Midcontinent*, edited by Brian M. Butler and Ernest E. May, pp. 149–166. Occasional Papers 2. Center for Archaeological Investigations, Southern Illinois University, Carbondale.

Myers, J. Thomas
1970 *Chert Resources of the Lower Illinois Valley*. Reports of Investigations 18. Illinois State Museum, Springfield.

Nance, Jack D.
1986 The Morrisroe Site: Projectile Point Types and Radiocarbon Dates from the Lower Tennessee Valley. *Midcontinental Journal of Archaeology* 11:11–50.

Neal, Wes, and Michael J. McNerney
1994 *Phase II Archaeological Testing and Assessment at Sites 11-Md-44, 11-Md-45, 11-Md-46, 11-Md-53, 11-Md-56, 11-Md-58, 11-Md-62, 11-Md-64, 11-Md-65, 11-Md-66, 11-Md-69, and 11-Md-73, at Freeman United Coal Mining Company's Industry Mine, McDonough County, Illinois*. Cultural Resources Management Report 246. American Resources Group, Carbondale, Illinois.

Neller, Earl
1998 *Archaeological Investigations at Site 11R1541 for the FAP 595/Borrow 2/3 (Teske Borrow Pit) Project*. Archaeological Testing Short Report 35. Illinois Transportation Archaeological Research Program, University of Illinois, Urbana-Champaign.

Neumann, Georg
1991 Report on an Archaeological Survey of Illinois, 1929. In *The Kuhlman Mound Group and Late Woodland*

Mortuary Behavior in the Mississippi River Valley of West-Central Illinois, edited by Karen A. Atwell and Michael D. Conner, pp. 292–309. Research Series 9. Center for American Archeology, Kampsville, Illinois.

Nolan, David J.

1987 The Ioway in Illinois? An Historic Archaeological Approach. Master's thesis, Department of History, Western Illinois University, Macomb.

1990 *A Progress Report on the FAP 506 Archaeological Survey: Rt 96 Ursa to Hamilton Segment, Adams and Hancock Counties, Illinois*. Reports of Investigations 17. Archaeological Research Laboratory, Western Illinois University, Macomb.

1991a *Supplemental Conclusions to the Progress Report on the FAP 506-Rt 96 Archaeological Survey in Adams and Hancock Counties, Illinois*. Report of Investigations 196C. Center for American Archeology, Kampsville, Illinois.

1991b *Final Report of Phase II Testing on the FAP 53 (U.S. Route 136) Project: Archaic and Weaver Occupations in the Confluence Area of the LaMoine River*. Report of Investigations 24. Archaeological Research Laboratory, Western Illinois University, Macomb.

1992 Summary of Phase II Testing of Prehistoric Sites in the Quincy to Mendon Priority Segment of the FAP 407-Rt 336 Right-of-Way. In *Progress Report on the FAP 407 Route 336 Archaeological Survey and Prehistoric Site Testing along the Priority Quincy to Mendon Alternate Segment in Adams County, Illinois*, edited by Robert N. Hickson and Susanna R. Katz, pp. 75–179. Report of Investigations 197C. Center for American Archeology, Kampsville, Illinois.

1993 *Archaeological Investigations along the FAP 506-Rt 96 Right-of-Way: A Report of Progress for the 1992–1993 Field Season*. Report of Investigations 196D. Center for American Archeology, Kampsville, Illinois.

1994a Description of Excavated and Tested Sites. In *1993–1994 Excavations on the FAP 407-Route 336 Quincy to Mendon Priority Segment*, edited by David J. Nolan and Eric G. Hansen, pp. 8–118. Report of Investigations 197E. Center for American Archeology, Kampsville, Illinois.

1994b *A Summary of Known Archaeological Resources along the Meyer Road, in Adams County, Illinois*. Reports of Investigations 27. Archaeological Research Laboratory, Western Illinois University, Macomb.

1995 Description of Tested Sites in the Bear Creek Section. In *1994–1995 Interim Report of the FAP 407-Route 336 Project: Tested Sites in the Bear Creek Segment; Geological Overview; and a Study of Payson Chert*, edited by Eric G. Hansen, pp. 68–287. Report of Investigations 197F. Center for American Archeology, Kampsville, Illinois.

2003 A Summary of Excavated Site Contexts from the Route 336 and 96 Projects. Manuscript on file, Illinois Transportation Archaeological Research Program, Macomb.

2004 (editor) *Archaeological Investigations in the Mississippi Valley Uplands of West Central Illinois: Final Report of the FAP 407 and FAP 506 Projects in Adams and Hancock Counties*. Research Reports 98. Illinois Transportation Archaeological Research Program, University of Illinois, Urbana.

Nolan, David J., and Lawrence A. Conrad

1998 Characterizing Lima Lake Oneota. *The Wisconsin Archeologist* 79(2):116–145.

Nolan, David J., Lawrence A. Conrad, and Sarah J. Studenmund

1992 *Preliminary Cultural Resource Identification and Predictive Modeling for the Chautauqua, Cameron, and Meredosia National Wildlife Refuges, Mason, Marshall, Morgan, and Cass Counties, Illinois*. Reports of Investigations 22. Archaeological Research Laboratory, Western Illinois University, Macomb.

Nolan, David J., and Michael G. Farkas

1998 The Archaeology of Lima Lake Alluvial Fans: Initial Observations. Paper presented at the Annual Meeting of the Illinois Archaeological Survey, Springfield.

Nolan, David J., and Rhett B. Felix

2004 *Archaeological Investigations at Site 11MD771 (Chenoweth Site) for the IL 336/US 136 Frontage Road Project*. Archaeological Testing Short Report 197. Illinois Transportation Archaeological Research Program, University of Illinois, Urbana.

Nolan, David J., and Amy K. Graham

1999 Archaeological Survey Short Report for TR 197 Borrow 1/1, Henderson County. Submitted to the Illinois Department of Transportation. Illinois Transportation Archaeological Research Program, University of Illinois, Urbana.

2003 Archaeological Survey Short Report for the FAP 315/IL 336 Macomb Bypass Project, McDonough County. Submitted to the Illinois Department of Transportation. Illinois Transportation Archaeological Research Program, University of Illinois, Urbana.

2005 *Archaeological Investigations at Site 11A1392 (Cabin Corner Site) for the FAS 1600/North Bottom Road Project*. Archaeological Testing Short Report 207. Illinois Transportation Archaeological Research Program, University of Illinois, Urbana.

Nolan, David J., Amy K. Graham, and Bruno A. Calgaro

2003 *U.S. 34 Phase I Archaeological Survey, Henderson and Warren Counties, Illinois*. Research Reports 87. Illinois Transportation Archaeological Research Program, University of Illinois, Urbana.

Nolan, David J., and Eric G. Hansen

1994 (editors) *1993–1994 Excavations on the FAP 407-Route 336 Quincy to Mendon Priority Segment*. Report of Investigations 197E. Center for American Archeology, Kampsville, Illinois.

1995 The Payson Chert Toolkit: Scale of Mobility and Technological Organization in the Early Archaic of West Central Illinois. In *1994–1995 Interim Report of the FAP 407-Route 336 Project: Tested Sites in the Bear Creek Segment; Geological Overview; and a Study of Payson Chert*, edited by Eric G. Hansen, pp. 288–360. Report of Investigations 197F. Center for American Archeology, Kampsville, Illinois.

Nolan, David J., and Robert N. Hickson

1992 Phase I Results. In *Progress Report on the FAP 407-Route 336 Archaeological Survey and Prehistoric Site Testing along the Priority Quincy to Mendon Alternate Segment in Adams County, Illinois*, edited by Robert N.

Hickson and Susanna R. Katz, pp. 40–68. Report of Investigations 197C. Center for American Archeology, Kampsville, Illinois.

Nolan, David J., and Michael J. Scott
1996 *Phase I Survey of the North Bottom Road (FAS 1600) in Adams and Hancock Counties, Illinois.* Center for American Archeology, Kampsville, Illinois.

Nolan, David J., Kyle Ullman, and Julieann Van Nest
1997 *Preliminary Archaeological Overview Study of the Macomb Bypass Alternates in McDonough County, Illinois.* Report of Investigations 241. Center for American Archeology, Kampsville, Illinois.

Odell, George H.
1984 Chert Resource Availability in the Lower Illinois Valley: A Transect Sample. In *Prehistoric Chert Exploitation: Studies from the Mid-Continent*, edited by Brian M. Butler and Ernest E. May, pp. 45–67. Occasional Papers 2. Center for Archaeological Investigations, Southern Illinois University, Carbondale.
1985 Lithic Use-Wear Analysis of the Archaic Occupations. In *The Campbell Hollow Archaic Occupations: A Study of Intrasite Spatial Structure in the Lower Illinois Valley*, edited by C. Russell Stafford, pp. 121–157. Research Series 4. Center for American Archeology, Kampsville, Illinois.
1988 Preliminary Analysis of Lithic and Other Nonceramic Assemblages. In *The Archaic and Woodland Cemeteries at the Elizabeth Site in the Lower Illinois Valley*, edited by Douglas K. Charles, Steven R. Leigh, and Jane E. Buikstra, pp. 155–190. Research Series 7. Center for American Archeology, Kampsville, Illinois.

O'Gorman, Jodie (editor)
1999 *Banner to Kingston Mines: Phase I Archeological Survey along U.S. 24 in Fulton and Peoria Counties, Illinois.* Report of Investigations 255. Center for American Archeology, Kampsville, Illinois.

Palmer, Harris A., and James B. Stoltman
1976 The Boaz Mastodon: A Possible Association of Man and Mastodon in Wisconsin. *Midcontinental Journal of Archaeology* 1:163–178.

Parker, Kathryn E.
1998 *Macrobotanical Remains from Archaeological Excavations at the Christianson Site (11-RI-42).* Great Lakes Ecosystems, Indian River, Michigan.

Perino, Gregory
1961 Tentative Classification of Plummets in the Lower Illinois River Valley. *Central States Archaeological Journal* 8:43–56.
1963 Tentative Classification of Two Projectile Points and One Knife from West Central Illinois. *Central States Archaeological Journal* 10(3):95–100.
1970 The Stilwell II Site, Pike County, Illinois. *Central States Archaeological Journal* 17(3):118–121.
1971 The Mississippian Component at the Schild Site (No. 4), Greene County, Illinois. In *Mississippian Site Archaeology in Illinois I: Site Reports from the St. Louis and Chicago Areas*, edited by James A. Brown, pp. 1–148. Bulletin 8. Illinois Archaeological Survey, Urbana.
1985 *Selected Preforms, Points, and Knives of the North American Indians*, vol. 1. Points and Barbs Press, Idabel, Oklahoma.

Perry, Michael J.
1983 *Phase II Investigations at 13HN48, BROS-9044(2), Henry County Local Roads.* Project Completion Report 7(193). Office of the State Archaeologist, University of Iowa, Iowa City.
1986 *Phase II Test Investigations at 13LC17, Primary Roads Project BRF-65-2(3), Lucas County, Iowa.* Project Completion Report 9(182). Office of the State Archaeologist, University of Iowa, Iowa City.

Phillips, James L., Robert L. Hall, and Richard W. Yerkes
1980 *Investigations at the Labras Lake Site, 1: Archaeology.* Department of Anthropology, University of Illinois at Chicago Circle.

Porter, James
1961 Hixton Silicified Sandstone: A Unique Lithic Material Used by Prehistoric Cultures. *The Wisconsin Archeologist* 42:78–85.

Porubcan, Paula J., and Rochelle Lurie
2000 *Results of a Phase I Archaeological Reconnaissance Survey of the 340 Acre Envirofil of Illinois, Inc. Disposal Facility in Macomb Township, McDonough County, Illinois.* Cultural Resource Management Report 888b. Midwest Archaeological Research Services, Harvard, Illinois.

Ray, Jack H.
1983 Excello Chert: An Undescribed Chert Resource in North Central Missouri. *Missouri Archaeological Society Newsletter* 375–376:9–14.
1994 Casa Blanca: An Early Archaic Upland Base Camp in Southwest Missouri. *The Missouri Archaeologist* 55:1–46.

Reagan, Michael J., Ralph M. Rowlett, Ervan G. Garrison, Wakefield Dort Jr., Vaughan M. Bryant Jr., and Chris J. Johannsen
1978 Flake Tools Stratified below Paleo-Indian Artifacts. *Science* 200:1272–1275.

Reid, Kenneth C.
1983 The Nebo Hill Phase: Late Archaic Prehistory in the Lower Missouri Valley. In *Archaic Hunters and Gatherers in the American Midwest*, edited by James L. Phillips and James A. Brown, pp. 11–39. Academic Press, New York.
1984 *Nebo Hill and Late Archaic Prehistory on the Southern Prairie Peninsula.* Publications in Anthropology 15. University of Kansas, Lawrence.

Rick, J. W.
1978 *Heat-Altered Cherts of the Lower Illinois Valley, an Experimental Study in Prehistoric Technology.* Prehistoric Records 2. Northwestern University Archaeological Program, Evanston, Illinois.

Ritchie, William A.
1932 The Lamoka Lake Site: The Type Station of the Archaic Algonkin Period in New York. *Researches and Transactions of the New York State Archaeological Association* 7(4):79–134. Rochester.
1944 *The Pre-Iroquoian Occupations of New York State.* Memoir 1. Rochester Museum of Arts and Sciences, Rochester, New York.

Ritzenthaler, Robert
1946 The Osceola Site: An "Old Copper" Site near Potosi, Wisconsin. *The Wisconsin Archeologist* 27:53–70.
1957 The Osceola Site: An "Old Copper" Site near Potosi, Wisconsin. *The Wisconsin Archeologist* 38:186–203.
1961 Truncated Barb Points from Dodge County. *The Wisconsin Archeologist* 42:90–91.

Roper, Donna C.
1978 *The Airport Site: A Multicomponent Site in the Sangamon River Drainage*. Papers in Anthropology 4. Illinois State Museum, Springfield.

Royall, P. Daniel, Paul A. Delcourt, and Hazel R. Delcourt
1991 Late Quaternary Paleoecology and Paleoenvironments of the Central Mississippi Alluvial Valley. *Bulletin* 103:157–170. Geological Society of America, Denver, Colorado.

Schlanger, S. H.
1992 Recognizing Persistent Places in Anasazi Settlement Systems. In *Space, Time, and Archaeological Landscapes*, edited by Jacqueline Rossignol and LuAnn Wandsnider, pp. 91–112. Plenum Press, New York.

Schoenbeck, E.
1948 Steuben Village Site, a Hopewellian Village of Central Illinois. *Transactions of the Illinois Academy of Science* 41:19–21. Springfield.

Schroeder, Marjorie B.
1994 Archaeobotany. In *Central Illinois Expressway Archeology: Upland Occupations of the Illinois Valley Crossing*, edited by Barbara D. Stafford, pp. 105–120. Technical Report 5. Center for American Archeology, Kampsville, Illinois.
1998 *Upland Site Archeobotany, Adams and Hancock Counties, Illinois*. Technical Report 98-1044-6. Quaternary Studies Program, Illinois State Museum, Springfield.

Schwegman, John E.
1973 *Comprehensive Plan for the Illinois Nature Preserves System, Part 2: The Natural Divisions of Illinois*. Illinois Nature Preserves Commission, Rockford.

Scully, Edward G.
1951 Some Central Mississippi Valley Projectile Point Types. Unpublished manuscript, Museum of Anthropology, University of Michigan, Ann Arbor.

Shallenberger, T. M.
1883 Mounds in Henry and Stark Counties, Illinois. *Annual Report of the Board of Regents of the Smithsonian Institution for 1881*, pp. 522–525. Government Printing Office, Washington, D.C.

Shepard, Kristopher S.
1993 *An Archaeological Survey of Mud Creek and Its Tributaries, Henry County, Illinois*. Archaeological Research Laboratory, Western Illinois University, Macomb.

Simon, Mary L.
1985 *Archaeological Investigations at the East Fork Site (11-MD-829), McDonough County, Illinois*. Research Reports 22. Resource Investigation Program, University of Illinois, Urbana.

Simpson, Anson M.
1934 Kingston (Illinois) Focus of the Mississippi Culture. *Transactions of the Illinois State Academy of Science* 27(2):55. Springfield.
1936 Archaeological Survey of Peoria County. *Transactions of the Illinois State Academy of Science* 29(2):50–51. Springfield.

Snyder, John Francis
1908 Prehistoric Illinois: The Brown County Ossuary. *Journal of the Illinois State Historical Society* 1(2–3):33–43.

Sollberger, J. B.
1971 A Technological Study of Beveled Knives. *Plains Anthropologist* 16:209–218.

Stafford, Barbara D.
1989 *Central Illinois Expressway Archeology: Floodplain Archaic Occupations of the Illinois Valley Crossing*. Technical Report 4. Center for American Archeology, Kampsville, Illinois.
1994 (editor) *Central Illinois Expressway Archeology: Upland Occupations of the Illinois Valley Crossing*. Technical Report 5. Center for American Archeology, Kampsville, Illinois.
1997 *Early Woodland Occupations at the Bushmeyer and Nearby Sites in the Sny Bottom of West-Central Illinois*. Research Series 11. Center for American Archeology, Kampsville, Illinois.

Stafford, Barbara D., and David J. Nolan
1990 *Archaeological Survey and Testing of Small Upland Sites from the Illinois River to Highway 107, FAP-408 Project*. Report of Investigations 191. Center for American Archeology, Kampsville, Illinois.

Stafford, Barbara D., and C. Russell Stafford
1992 Lithic Assemblage. In *Early Woodland Occupations at the Ambrose Flick Site in the Sny Bottom of West-Central Illinois*, edited by C. Russell Stafford, pp. 150–176. Research Series 11. Center for American Archeology, Kampsville, Illinois.

Stafford, C. Russell
1991 Archaic Period Logistical Foraging Strategies in West-Central Illinois. *Midcontinental Journal of Archaeology* 16:212–246.
1985 (editor) *The Campbell Hollow Archaic Occupations: A Study of Intrasite Spatial Structure in the Lower Illinois Valley*. Research Series 4. Center for American Archeology, Kampsville, Illinois.
1992 (editor) *Early Woodland Occupations at the Ambrose Flick Site in the Sny Bottom of West-Central Illinois*. Research Series 10. Center for American Archeology, Kampsville, Illinois.

Stafford, C. Russell, Ronald W. Deiss, Edwin R. Hajic, and David S. Leigh
1983 *Archeological Survey and Limited Soil Coring and Test Excavations of Cultural Resources in the FAP 408 Flint and Blue Creek Alternates of the Illinois Crossing, Pike and Scott Counties, Illinois*. Report of Investigations 140. Center for American Archeology, Kampsville, Illinois.

Stafford, C. Russell, and Edwin R. Hajic
1983 An Overview of Geomorphic Variation in the Project Area. In *Archeological Survey and Limited Soil Coring and Test Excavations of Cultural Resources in the FAP 408 Flint and Blue Creek Alternates of the Illinois Crossing, Pike and Scott Counties, Illinois*, by C. Russell Stafford, Ronald W. Deiss, Edwin R. Hajic, and David

S. Leigh, pp. 15–20. Report of Investigations 140. Center for American Archeology, Kampsville, Illinois.

Stephens, B. W.
1951 Middle Mississippi Valley Plummets. *Journal of the Illinois State Archaeological Society* 2:17–22.

Stoltman, James B., Jeffery A. Behm, and Harris A. Palmer
1984 The Bass Site: A Hardin Quarry/Workshop in Southwestern Wisconsin. In *Prehistoric Chert Exploitation: Studies from the Midcontinent*, edited by Brian M. Butler and Ernest E. May, pp. 197–224. Occasional Papers 2. Southern Illinois University, Carbondale.

Studenmund, Sarah J.
1992 Meredosia Unit. In *Preliminary Cultural Resource Identification and Predictive Modeling for the Chautauqua, Cameron, and Meredosia National Wildlife Refuges, Mason, Marshall, Morgan, and Cass Counties, Illinois*, by David J. Nolan, Lawrence A. Conrad, and Sarah J. Studenmund, pp. 42–74. Reports of Investigations 22. Archaeological Research Laboratory, Western Illinois University, Macomb.
1995 *US 24, Fulton and Schuyler Counties: Phase I Cultural Resource Investigations.* Report of Investigations 215. Center for American Archeology, Kampsville, Illinois.

Studenmund, Sarah J., and Amy K. Graham
1999 Penstone: Site Function at a Titterington Phase Occupation in West-Central Illinois. Paper presented at the 45th Annual Midwest Archaeological Conference, East Lansing, Michigan.

Studenmund, Sarah J., Amy K. Graham, and Wesley James
1998 New Perspectives on Archaic Period Upland Occupations in West-Central Illinois. Paper presented at the 44th Annual Midwest Archaeological Conference, Muncie, Indiana.

Studenmund, Sarah J., and Marjorie B. Schroeder
1997 *Phase III Archaeological Investigations at 11-PK-993, Pike County, Illinois.* Report of Investigations 237. Center for American Archeology, Kampsville, Illinois.

Stuiver, Minze, and Paula J. Reimer
1993 Extended ^{14}C Database and Revised CALIB Radiocarbon Calibration Program. *Radiocarbon* 35:215–230.

Talalay, Laurie, Donald R. Keller, and Patrick J. Munson
1984 Hickory Nuts, Walnuts, Butternuts, and Hazelnuts: Observations and Experiments Relevant to Their Aboriginal Exploitation in Eastern North America. In *Experiments and Observations on Aboriginal Wild Plant Food Utilization in Eastern North America*, edited by Patrick J. Munson, pp. 338–359. Preliminary Research Series 6(2). Indiana Historical Society, Indianapolis.

Tankersley, Kenneth B., and Barry L. Isaac
1990 *Early Paleoindian Economies of Eastern North America.* Research in Economic Anthropology, Supplement 5. JAI Press, Greenwich, Connecticut.

Thomas, Cyrus
1894 *Report on the Mound Explorations of the Bureau of Ethnology.* Twelfth Annual Report of the Bureau of Ethnology, 1890–1891. Smithsonian Institution, Washington, D.C.

Thurber, O. D.
1935 A New Type of Burial Mound near Quincy, Illinois. *Transactions of the Illinois State Academy of Science* 28:67–68. Springfield.

Titterington, Paul F.
1950 Some Non Pottery Sites in the St. Louis Area. *Journal of the Illinois State Archaeological Society* 1(1):18–31.

Tomak, Curtis H.
1979 Jerger: An Early Archaic Mortuary Site in Southwestern Indiana. *Proceedings of the Indiana Academy of Science* 88:63–69. Indianapolis.

Ullman, Kyle
1991 Spencer Mound Group. In *The Kuhlman Mound Group and Late Woodland Mortuary Behavior in the Mississippi River Valley of West-Central Illinois*, edited by Karen A. Atwell and Michael D. Conner, pp. 310–318. Research Series 9. Center for American Archeology, Kampsville, Illinois.

Vanderford, K. Shane
2005 *Archaeological Investigations at Site 11RI693 (Crosstown Avenue Site) for the FAP 595/IL 5, Crosstown Road Extension and Frontage Road RS at the IL 5 and Crosstown Avenue Intersection Project.* Archaeological Testing Short Report 18C. Illinois Transportation Archaeological Research Program, University of Illinois at Urbana-Champaign.

Van Nest, Julieann
1993 Geoarchaeology of Dissected Loess Uplands in Western Illinois. *Geoarchaeology* 8:281–311.
1997 Late Quaternary Geology, Archeology and Vegetation in West-Central Illinois: A Study in Geoarcheology. Ph.D. dissertation, Department of Geology, University of Iowa, Iowa City.

Vehik, Susan C.
1977 Bone Fragments and Bone Grease Manufacturing: A Review of Their Archaeological Use and Potential. *Plains Anthropologist* 22:169–182.

Walthall, John A., and Brad Koldehoff
1999 Across the Divide: Dalton Land Use in the Southern Till Plains. *Illinois Archaeology* 11:27–49.

Walton, Clyde C. (editor)
1962 *John Francis Snyder: Selected Writings.* Illinois State Historical Society, Springfield.

Walz, Gregory R., Brian Adams, Paul P. Kreisa, Kevin P. McGowan, and Jacqueline M. McDowell
1998 The Strong Site and the Dennis Hollow Phase: A New Perspective on Middle Archaic Chronology, Technology, and Subsistence. *Illinois Archaeology* 10:155–194.

Webb, Thompson, III, and Reid A. Bryson
1972 Late- and Postglacial Climatic Change in the Northern Midwest, USA: Quantitative Estimates Derived from Fossil Pollen Spectra by Multivariate Statistical Analysis. *Quaternary Research* 2:70–115.

Wedel, Waldo R.
1943 *Archaeological Investigations in Platte and Clay Counties, Missouri.* Bulletin 183. Smithsonian Institution, Washington, D.C.

White, Andrew A.
2003 Temporal Variation in Late Middle Archaic Bone Pins. *Midcontinental Journal of Archaeology* 28:49–72.

Wiant, Michael D.
1993 Exploring Paleoindian Site Distribution in Illinois. *Illinois Archaeology* 5:108–118.

Wiant, Michael D., Edwin R. Hajic, and Thomas R. Styles
1983 Napoleon Hollow and Koster Site Stratigraphy: Implications for Holocene Landscape Evolution and Studies of Archaic Period Settlement Patterns in the Lower Illinois River Valley. In *Archaic Hunters and Gatherers in the American Midwest*, edited by James L. Phillips and James A. Brown, pp. 147–164. Academic Press, New York.

Wiant, Michael D., and Harold Hassen
1985 The Role of Lithic Availability and Accessibility in the Organization of Lithic Technology. In *Lithic Resource Procurement: Proceedings from the Second Conference on Prehistoric Chert Exploitation*, edited by Susan C. Vehik, pp. 101–114. Occasional Papers 4. Center for Archaeological Investigations, Southern Illinois University, Carbondale.

Willey, Gordon R., and Philip Phillips
1955 Method and Theory in American Archeology II: Historical-Developmental Interpretation. *American Anthropologist* 57:723–819.
1958 *Method and Theory in American Archaeology*. University of Chicago Press, Chicago.

Willman, H. B., Elwood Atherton, T. C. Buschbach, Charles Collinson, John C. Frye, M. E. Hopkins, Jerry A. Lineback, and Jack A. Simon
1975 *Handbook of Illinois Stratigraphy*. Bulletin 95. Illinois State Geological Survey, Urbana.

Winters, Howard D.
1963 *An Archaeological Survey of the Wabash Valley in Illinois*. Reports of Investigations 10. Illinois State Museum, Springfield.
1969 *The Riverton Culture: A Second Millennium Occupation in the Central Wabash Valley*. Reports of Investigations 13. Illinois State Museum, Springfield.
1974 Introduction to the New Edition. In *Indian Knoll*, by William S. Webb, pp. v–xxvii. University of Tennessee Press, Knoxville.
1982 Laws Farm Site. Manuscript on file, Illinois Transportation Archaeological Research Program, Macomb.

Wittry, Warren L.
1959 The Raddatz Rockshelter SK5, Wisconsin. *The Wisconsin Archeologist* 40:33–69.
1965 The Institute Digs a Mastodon. *Cranbrook Institute of Science Newsletter* 35(2):14.

Wittry, Warren L., and Robert Ritzenthaler
1957 The Old Copper Complex: An Archaic Manifestation in Wisconsin. *The Wisconsin Archeologist* 38:311–329.

Wray, Donald E.
1952 Archaeology of the Illinois Valley: 1950. In *Archeology of Eastern United States*, edited by James B. Griffin, pp. 152–164. University of Chicago Press, Chicago.

Wright, H. E., Jr.
1968 History of the Prairie Peninsula. In *The Quaternary of Illinois*, edited by Robert E. Bergstrom, pp. 78–88. Special Report 14. University of Illinois College of Agriculture, Urbana.

Yerkes, Richard W.
1987 *Prehistoric Life on the Mississippi Floodplain: Stone Tool Use, Settlement Organization, and Subsistence Practices at the Labras Lake Site, Illinois*. University of Chicago Press, Chicago.

Yerkes, Richard, and Linda M. Gaertner
1997 Microwear Analysis of Dalton Artifacts. In *Sloan: A Paleoindian Dalton Cemetery in Arkansas*, edited by Dan F. Morse, pp. 58–71. Smithsonian Institution Press, Washington, D.C.

Appendix 13.A. Selected Point Metrics.

	Axial Length (mm)	Blade Length (mm)	Maximum Thickness (mm)	Shoulder Width (mm)	Stem Length (mm)	Stem Width (mm)	Basal Width (mm)	Concavity Depth (mm)	Weight (g)
NMV Dalton									
Number	35	35	49	44	47	44	44	15	44
Range	43.80–83.52	23.40–64.54	5.35–9.14	21.5–46.0	9.40–24.17	20.3–43.95	23.10–44.96	1.31–8.87	1.7–23.0
Average	57.78	41.40	6.69	29.74	17.03	28.52	29.27	4.70	10.45
Std Dev	10.49	10.52	1.11	6.40	5.34	5.48	5.21	2.14	5.38
Mendon knives									
Number	—	—	6	5	5	5	6	5	5
Range	—	—	8.21–10.15	31.79–42.11	20.59–28.91	37.23–39.49	33.92–44.77	1.08–6.00	10.9–25.0
Average	—	—	9.12	37.53	25.17	38.61	37.20	2.78	15.16
Std Dev	—	—	1.45	10.29	5.09	8.35	7.01	2.18	7.98

	Axial Length (mm)	Blade Length (mm)	Stem Length (mm)	Maximum Thickness (mm)	Shoulder Width (mm)	Basal Width (mm)	Weight (g)
Neuberger[a]							
Number	12	16	17	34	12	9	10
Range	36–79	27–73	5–10	4–9	27–43	18–31	7–21
Average	63.67	55.25	7.18	6.44	34.08	23.22	14.4
Std Dev	12.49	13.40	1.33	1.05	4.40	3.80	4.67

	Axial Length (mm)	Maximum Width (mm)	Maximum Thickness (mm)	Bit Thickness[b] (mm)	Shoulder Width (mm)	Neck Width (mm)	Basal Width (mm)	Bit Width (mm)	Weight (g)
Matanzas									
Number	23	30	30	9	15	28	26	23	30
Range	29.93–75.17	16.49–25.50	7.42–11.22	5.22–7.85	6.77–25.23	14.27–22.45	14.19–23.83	11.11–23.69	4.4–18.1
Average	46.67	20.64	8.92	6.90	18.70	18.96	17.73	18.73	8.91
Std Dev	11.18	2.28	.87	.92	5.06	2.22	2.51	2.50	2.84
Karnak									
Number	48	74	76	19	63	1	33	52	80
Range	24.19–101.65	9.17–29.40	7.25–25.83	6.49–11.38	6.49–26.46	—	14.57–24.53	9.46–26.10	3.6–34.1
Average	56.81	22.08	10.61	8.33	22.27	14.28	17.67	17.51	12.87
Std Dev	17.92	3.82	2.43	1.49	2.33	—	2.31	2.86	6.89

[a]From Conrad 1981:Table 3.
[b]Hafted scraper variety.

Appendix 13.B. Selected Point Attributes.

Point Type/Cluster	North Subregion	Central Subregion	South Subregion	Heat Treatment	Serration	Alternate Beveling	Haft Grinding
Pike County	x	+	+	u	u	u	t
NMV Dalton	x	+	x	u	⋆	⋆	t
CMV Dalton	x	x	+	u	t	t	t
Early Holocene Side-Notch	x	x	x	u	t	⋆	t
Theban	+	+	+	u	t	t	t
Kirk Corner Notch	+	+	+	u	t	u	t
Neuberger	+	+	+	u	t	u	t
Decatur	a	x	x	u	t	t	t
Stilwell	a	x	+	u	t	u	t
Hardin	+	+	+	u	t	t	t
St. Albans/MacCorkle	a	+	+	u	t	u	t
Keithley	x	+	a	u	t	u	t
LeCroy	a	+	+	u	t	u	t
Kanawha	a	+	+	u	t	u	u
Stanly Stemmed	a	x	x	⋆	t	u	u
Campbell Hollow	a	x	x	t	⋆	u	t
Table Rock	+	+	+	t	u	u	t
Matanzas	x	+	+	t	u	u	t
Karnak	a	+	+	t	⋆	u	t
McLean	a	x	+	t	u	u	u
Osceola	+	+	+	u	⋆	u	t
Godar/Raddatz	+	+	+	t	⋆	u	t
Sedalia/Nebo Hill	+	+	+	u	u	u	u
Etley	a	x	+	u	u	u	u
Titterington Stemmed	+	+	+	u	u	u	t
Riverton	+	+	+	t	u	u	t
Springly	+	+	x	t	u	u	u
Dyroff	a	x	x	t	u	u	u
Mo-Pac	a	x	x	t	u	u	u
Kampsville Barbed	a	x	+	t	u	u	u

Note. + = common; x = rare; a = absent or unreported; t = typical; u = uncharacteristic; ⋆ = infrequent.

14

Archaic Periods in Eastern Iowa

David W. Benn and Joe B. Thompson

Introduction

The initial, intensive effort to analyze the cultural processes of the Middle Archaic period in the Midwest was instigated when Brown and Vierra (1983:165) asked, "What happened in the Middle Archaic [period]?" Theirs was an ecological perspective drawn from James Brown's (1965) career association with environmental studies and the excellent state of preservation of floral and faunal remains in the colluvial sediments at the Koster site. Iowa archaeologists have not been lucky enough to chance upon a "Koster" site that could yield such a long Archaic sequence,[1] and understanding of this lengthy and important era has languished accordingly. Yet Iowa is an excellent place to examine relationships between environment and culture change during the Holocene era since it was at the forefront of the Prairie Peninsula's eastward expansion. Meanwhile, contract, or cultural resource management (CRM), archaeology has been plodding inexorably across Iowa for three decades, and enough data have accumulated to take a stab at "what happened" during the Archaic periods in eastern Iowa.

When evaluating Archaic site records, it is prudent to keep two geologically induced biases in mind: deep site burial and site destruction by stream erosion. Modern models of Archaic settlement patterns (e.g., Ahler 1998; Emerson and McElrath 1983; Luchterhand 1970; Nassaney and Lopinot 1986) exhibit ambivalence concerning the problem of deeply buried sites. Either this issue, and geomorphic contexts, in general, are ignored or the ramifications of sampling biases associated with deep site burial are discussed and then settlement models are constructed that ignore data from buried sites. Ahler's (1998:37) sampling survey of the Modoc locality is an example of the latter approach, despite his explicit discussion of this bias in the floodplain tracts of that locality.[2] Of course, deeply buried Archaic sites are known in Illinois and appreciated for their stratigraphic integrity, with the Koster (Brown and Vierra 1983), Napoleon Hollow (Odell 1996), and Quasar sites (Goatley 1998) being a few of the examples with useful sequences. Such sites are cited as representative examples of part of the Archaic settlement model in Illinois (e.g., base camps in Horizon 6 at Koster), and we are not arguing that existing settlement models are necessarily incorrect because buried site data were not considered in their formulations. Where the models fall short is in attempting to develop relative *frequencies* of the various site types and settlement patterns within natural habitats without accounting for landform changes and differential site preservation.

The largest body of data about the Archaic periods in Iowa has emerged from buried contexts both in alluvial settings and in loess-covered uplands (Bettis and Hajic 1995). Our initial impression is that buried sites exhibit similarities to the surface-site settlement types—seasonal base camps, procurement sites, and so on—analyzed in the Illinois Archaic models. Yet site burial preserves the cultural record on its original land surface without interference from plows and usually with less mixing from other cultural components, thus, providing a clearer picture of the habitation "surface." Many recent excavation reports describe piece plotting all artifacts, defining shelter locations, and analyzing household activity areas within buried sites. What emerges from these kinds of data are understandings about the size and composition of resident bands in addition to seasonality and length of stay for bivouacs, seasonal base camps, and villages. Many of these discoveries have been "reburied" in the unpublished "gray" CRM literature. We make such data available in Appendix 14.C, which summarizes the following buried or unplowed sites: Allen Fan (13HA385), Bash (13MR228), Lost Creek High Terrace (13MK357), Fett (13LE597), Garden (13DB493), McNeal Fan (13MC15d), Riley (13HN373), Edgewater Park (13JH1132), and Sand Run West (13LA38). Reasonably intact terrace and upland sites summarized in Appendix 14.C include Davis Creek (13WS122), Ed's Meadow (13DM712), Overberg (13HN318), Prymek (13WS65), and Jasper County site 13JP87. From the few excavations of buried sites, we realize that older components—that is, Paleoindian through Early Archaic—lie beneath the mitigation zone in some excavation blocks. This is true at McNeal Fan and the Garden site and probably at the Bash, Riley, and Sand Run West sites. Systematic surveys employing bucket-auger tests in the upper Mississippi Valley and along highway corridors within Iowa's tributary valleys demonstrate that buried Archaic sites are common in early and mid-Holocene sediments; thus, the existing sample of excavated components is extremely small and problematically representative. Efforts in this chapter to model Archaic cultural patterns and to explain cultural processes should be viewed as heuristic proposals.

Our analysis of Archaic culture change builds on theories that focus on the shift in the mobility strategies of hunters and gatherers. The basic notion espoused by Binford (1980) is that the evolution from mobile hunting and gathering to sedentary horticultural life entailed fundamental changes in strategies of residential mobility. In Illinois this happened gradually during the Archaic periods (Brown and Vierra 1983). Between the stage of "residential mobility" (cf. Binford 1980), in which hunters and gatherers moved their places of residence from one resource patch to another, and the stage of full sedentism during the Woodland periods, there must have been a stage of "logistic mobility" (cf. Binford 1980) or a "collector" stage (Odell 1996:9), when hunters and gatherers established base-camp residences and conducted collecting forays to resource patches within corporate territories. In Iowa, environmental context is central to understanding how and when this change in residential strategy occurred. The next section of this chapter presents evidence that hardwood forest replaced the periglacial conifer forest by ca. 9000 B.P. in eastern Iowa and that the boundary of the Prairie Peninsula crossed east of the Mississippi River by ca. 6000 B.P. (Bettis et al. 1992). Spreading prairies increased plant and animal diversity for human hunters and gatherers because forest edges proliferated (the "edge effect"; see Odum 1971). Stream channels stabilized as prairies were advancing, and the subsequent aggradation of river floodplains resulted in formation of backwater lakes teeming with aquatic resources. We present evidence that, by 4000 B.C.,[3] Middle Archaic folks had either borrowed or developed the technology necessary to take full advantage of an increasingly diverse environment. Family bands began to aggregate in seasonal base camps after 3000 B.C., that is, during the "logistical mobility" stage, and large residential base camps appeared in the larger river valleys where vast forest and riparian resources were available. Those aggregate bands established "corporate" territories (see Charles and Buikstra 1983) around permanent base camps. During the Late Archaic period, the trend toward aggregation was undone as aggregate bands fragmented to pursue forest-edge habitat into medium- and small-sized tributary valleys, which had the effect of dispersing corporate territories throughout the drainage network. Regionalization seems to have evolved from Late Archaic settlement patterns. This constitutes our heuristic model of cultural change.

Natural and Cultural Contexts

Archaeologists cannot afford to view landforms and the natural environment as static backdrops for cultural modeling. Landscapes, vegetation communities, and climatic conditions have changed dramatically during the last ca. 10,000 years and form a baseline on which models of Archaic cultures must be constructed. Foremost among these changes has been development of the Prairie Peninsula (Transeau 1935) across the Midcontinent, centering on Iowa (Figure 14.1).

Physiography and Geology

Eastern Iowa spans four geological regions (Prior 1991), whose ages of formation range from a youthful ca. 14,000 years to more than a million years (Figure 14.1).[4] The Paleozoic Plateau region, the oldest landscape in Iowa, is marked by deeply dissected stream valleys, sinuous uplands, and extensive exposures of limestone and sandstone bedrock but very little glacial till (Hallberg et al. 1984). The Southern Iowa Drift Plain in the southern half of the state is hundreds of thousands of years old and is marked by broad, rolling upland plains and a mature drainage network that exposes Illinoian and pre-Illinoian glacial tills as well as chert-bearing sedimentary bedrock. Between these two regions in east-central Iowa is the Iowan Surface, a youthful region of level uplands, stepped interfluves, and shallow valleys formed in loess, pre-Illinoian till, or eolian sand. The Mississippi Alluvial Plain on the eastern side of Iowa is a glacial outwash valley filled with sediments from episodes of alluviation during the late Wisconsinan and Holocene eras. This great valley is a patchwork floodplain of backwater lakes and marshes, seasonally wet terraces, yazoo streams, and sandy ridges flanked by high terraces and alluvial fans (Bettis et al. 1996). The fourth region is the Des Moines Lobe in north-central Iowa, which was created during the last ca. 14,000 years. This geologically immature landscape of moraine ridges, closed depressions, marshes and lakes, and

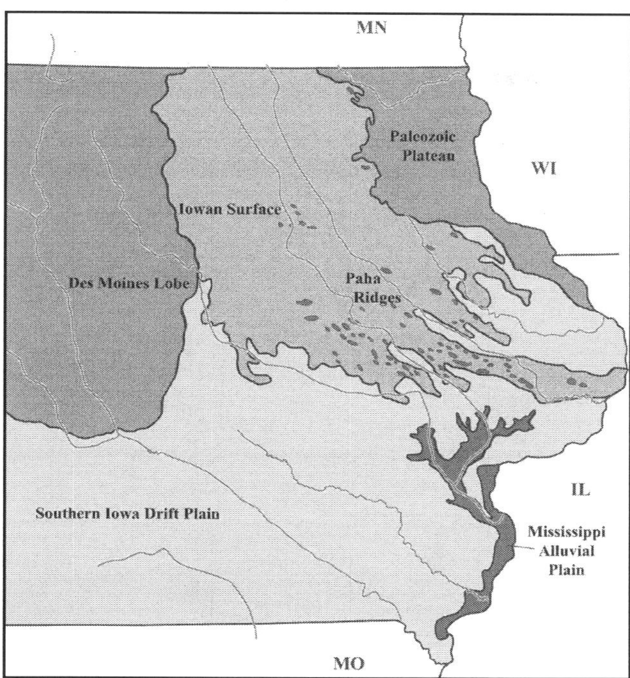

Figure 14.1. Regional landforms of Iowa (after Prior 1991).

shallow stream valleys is dissected by a single major valley containing the Des Moines River.

One reason the age and geographic character of Iowa's landform regions are significant for prehistoric cultures is that chert outcrops occur in greatest abundance along incised stream valleys, where bedrock is not obscured by unconsolidated sediments. Some subregions lack sources of good-quality chert, and the best cherts—for example, Burlington—come from specific areas favored by prehistoric people of every culture period. Morrow's (1994) overview of chert resources revealed that Pennsylvanian strata exposed in the Southern Iowa Drift Plain contain poor-quality chert and that the glacial till yields only small pieces of workable chert. Roper (1984), among others, suggested that the relative paucity of local chert caused prehistoric people in chert-poor areas to establish long-distance trade relationships to obtain quality material. The Iowan Surface of east-central Iowa yields low- to medium-quality cherts (e.g., Blanding, Hopkinton, Wapsipinicon, Grand Meadow, and Rapid) from Silurian- and Devonian-age strata, which are largely buried by till and loess. By contrast, the massively exposed Ordovician limestones of the Paleozoic Plateau region contain large amounts of cherts like Prairie du Chien and Galena/Platteville. These low- to medium-quality cherts were heavily exploited locally but do not seem to have been widely traded (Morrow 1994:108). It is the Mississippian bedrock of central and southeastern Iowa that yields abundant assortments of high-quality cherts (e.g., Maynes Creek, Wassonville, Burlington, Croton/Warsaw, and Verdi/Salem) that were widely traded.

Glacial till that covers so many chert sources was itself the source of igneous rock for making cobble and ground-stone tools. The oldest Quaternary glacial deposit across southern Iowa is pre-Illinoian glacial till, while the latest glacial advance from the Lake Michigan basin occurred during the early portion of the Illinois glacial advance (Hallberg 1980a, 1980b; Willman and Frye 1970). Our field experience shows that Illinoian tills contain few cherts and little hematite useful for human exploitation. The older pre-Illinoian till contains substantial amounts of high-quality metallic hematite but little chert. More quality hematite is available from the Pennsylvanian bedrock in the same region (Thompson 1999). The Laurentide ice sheet that covered north-central Iowa deposited a thick layer of till that contains large amounts of good-quality chert and small pieces of hematite. Glacial cobbles occur in small amounts but are rare enough in the streambeds of the Paleozoic Plateau region of northeastern Iowa to have been considered a valued resource by Archaic people. Lacking igneous rock, the people of northeastern Iowa substituted limestone (see Benn 2007). Access to glacial till sources is limited in the uplands of every region except the Des Moines Lobe by a surface layer of wind-blown deposits of fine sediments, including silts and sands, that blanketed eastern Iowa during two episodes of the Wisconsinan era before 12,500 B.P. (Bettis 1987; Bettis and Kemmis 1992; Hallberg et al. 1978; Leigh and Knox 1993; Ruhe 1969). Archaic sites always occur on top of the principal loess layer. Dunes along the upper Mississippi Valley and the Iowa and Cedar river valleys also date to the midperiod of Peoria Loess deposition (Bettis and Autin 1997), but dune sand moves and may bury Archaic components in local areas.

Late Wisconsinan and Holocene alluvial and colluvial deposits in Iowa are classified and mapped as Landform Sediment Assemblages (LSA) in the upper Mississippi Valley (Bettis et al. 1996) and as members of the DeForest Formation (Bettis and Littke 1987) in all other valleys. As glacial ice waned during the latter half the Woodfordian era, outwash sediments accumulated in the major river valleys of eastern Iowa that originated in the Des Moines ice lobe and, in the case of the Mississippi Valley, in the Lake Superior region (Figure 14.1). The thickest (5–8 m) of these sand and gravel deposits (capped by loess) was deposited ca. 22,000–18,000 B.P. in the Mississippi Valley and lower tributaries and is the Savanna Terrace. A younger, thinner sandy outwash that covers the floors in large river valleys is called the "Kingston" LSA in the Mississippi Valley (Bettis et al. 1996) and is known by other names in smaller valleys (i.e., Low Terrace in the Iowa Valley [Esling 1984] and Beaver Creek II Terrace in the central Des Moines Valley [Bettis and Benn 1984]). Both the Savanna and Kingston terraces lack caps of Holocene alluvium, except for alluvial-fan materials; therefore, Archaic sites usually occur on their surfaces. After ca. 10,000 B.P., episodic cycles of aggradation and erosion in tributary valleys either buried or eroded Archaic-age deposits (Bettis and Hajic 1995). These alluvial and colluvial sediments belong to the DeForest Formation

(Bettis and Littke 1987). Cyclical aggradation in alluvial fans (Corrington Member) and the floodplain (Gunder Member) began ca. 8500 B.P. and ceased by ca. 3000–2000 B.P., when streams entrenched (Bettis et al. 1992). The Corrington and Gunder members are contexts in which Archaic sites tend to be buried the deepest, 2–3 m deep in the Gunder Member and as much as 6 m deep in fans along the Mississippi River trench. Aggradation filled stream meander belts during the last ca. 3,000 years, forming the Roberts Creek Member (Bettis and Hallberg 1985). Only the youngest Archaic materials occur at the bottom of Roberts Creek deposits, and this alluvium also can bury the Gunder Member.

Climate Change and Environment

For a few decades during the mid-twentieth century, environmental factors and climate change (Bryson et al. 1968–69) were viewed by many archaeologists as significant if not determinant influences on prehistoric economies and on the process of cultural change (e.g., Griffin 1960). Most of this environmental determinism has been ameliorated, except among some of the evolutionary theorists (e.g., O'Brien and Holland 1992), by a renewed focus on historical process (Pauketat 2001:74), although the impacts habitat changes had on the archaeological record have continued to be the subjects of much analysis and debate, with no clear consensus emerging. Researchers concede, for instance, that the disappearance of most Pleistocene megafauna, many types of which were hunted by humans (e.g., Anderson and Semken 1980; Graham 1980), and the desiccating effects of the Altithermal, which changed vegetation patterns and the geomorphic responses of fluvial systems (e.g., McMillan and Klippel 1981), influenced Archaic cultures (Wolverton 2005). But environments change over long periods of time—longer than human memory—and people make their own history. Direct causation between environment and culture change cannot be assumed; instead, this relationship must be investigated at local and regional scales (instead of a continental scale) to make sense of the feedback cycle between the two systems.

The late Quaternary climatic record for the North American Midcontinent is securely framed by proxy data from pollen records (Delcourt and Delcourt 1981; Webb and Bryson 1972; Wendland 1978). The Webb and Bryson (1972) climatic sequence showed that glacial conditions of colder, moister, and cloudier weather dominated the northern Midwest until ca. 11,300 B.P. The shift to a postglacial pattern (warmer, longer growing season and increased moisture stress in July) was rapid and widespread in regions south of Minnesota, and by ca. 9500 B.P., drier, warmer Pacific airflow was well established across Iowa. Pacific air continued to dominate over moister Gulf air and the colder, drier Arctic air mass throughout a period of maximum effect until ca. 6200 B.P. (Altithermal). For example, pollen data from the upper Midwest indicated that precipitation decreased by 10–25 percent, and the mean July temperature rose by .5–2.0° C between ca. 9000 and 7000 B.P. (Bartlein et al. 1984). After ca. 6200 B.P., conditions ameliorated with the influx of moister Gulf air. Significant decreases in the Pacific airflow and increases in Arctic and Gulf air masses were recorded by the Kirchner Marsh pollen diagram at ca. 5500 and 4700 B.P. As the average annual temperature and moisture patterns trended toward the modern regime, climatic oscillations occurred at a lower amplitude than during the Altithermal maximum.

Familiar effects of climatic change on vegetation patterns in the upper Midwest included the northward retreat of periglacial habitats at the beginning of the Holocene era and eastward movement of the Prairie Peninsula during the Altithermal maximum (Borchert 1950; Bryson and Wendland 1967; Transeau 1935; Wendland 1978). The shift from periglacial to temperate climatic conditions is recorded by pollen and macrofossil records from eastern Iowa. In the Iowa River valley at Iowa City, the general picture of the local forest at ca. 10,000 B.P. is of mixed stands of temperate species like *Carya* (hickories), *Ostrya-Carpinus* (ironwood-blue beech), *Quercus* (oaks), *Ulmus* (elm), and *Fraxinus* (ash) along with conifer-hardwood (boreal) species like *Picea* (spruce), *Larix* (larch), *Betula* (birch), and *Abies* (fir) (Baker et al. 1993:211). Baker and colleagues contend that boreal species were relics of the departed ice age and remained for a while in the protected environs of large river valleys, which acted as conduits for the northward migration of temperate species after ca. 12,000 B.P. Farther east in the Mississippi River valley, spruce, larch, and fir pollen held on in the record of ca. 11,000–10,000 B.P. (on the east-facing valley wall) and then gave way to oak and elm pollen during the ca. 10,000–7500 B.P. time frame (Bettis et al. 1992:53). Temperate forests spread from the south (King 1981; McMillan and Klippel 1981), but tracing a time line for the spread of this forest "front" northward across eastern Iowa is problematic. Studies from northeastern Iowa (Baker et al. 2001) and southeastern Minnesota (Baker et al. 2002:119) place the time of forest transition shortly before ca. 10,000 B.P. Specifically, cold-boreal environmental conditions are indicated at 11,450 B.P. by predominantly spruce-larch forest, but shortly before ca. 10,000 B.P., temperate forest species like the oaks, elm, ironwood, maples (*Acer*), and basswood (*Tilia*) moved in (Baker et al. 2001:288). Although some boreal species hung on for millennia as relics in cool, protected microhabitats, especially in northeastern Iowa, mesic deciduous forest covered almost all of eastern Iowa by ca. 10,000 B.P. (Bettis et al. 1992:53). Butternut (*Juglans cinerea*) and possibly black walnut (*Juglans nigra*) seem to have preceded the appearance of the hickories by at least a thousand years (i.e., Early Archaic period) in the upper Mississippi River basin (Bettis et al. 1992:53), and pecans were present by the eighth millennium near Muscatine, Iowa (Bettis et al. 1990). Human collectors may have had something to do with the spread of pecans.

The Prairie Peninsula crossed the western boundary of Missouri and advanced across the northern portion of the state shortly after ca. 9000 B.P. (McMillan and Klippel 1981:239). In eastern Iowa the advent of prairie pollen is documented slightly later at several locations, with a time line indicating that prairie vegetation moved in an east-northeasterly direction (Wendland 1980). A pollen profile from the Cedar Rapids locality indicated prairie with few trees was present by ca. 6000 B.P. (Baker et al. 1990). Farther east at Gast Spring Fan and Klum Lake in the Mississippi Valley, tree pollen decreased shortly after ca. 7600–7300 B.P., although a hiatus in the middle Holocene record at these sites prevents precise dating of this shift (Bettis et al. 1992:53; Nations and Baker 1991). Baker (Bettis et al. 1992:57) suggested that prairie may have invaded broad terraces and fans in the Mississippi Valley, although they were drought-resistant habitats with a high water table. Perhaps researchers should be looking for evidence of natural and human-induced fire as one of the agents causing forest to be replaced by prairie-edge habitats. A few tens of miles north and east of Cedar Rapids, the Two Bridges locality in the Mud Creek basin yielded pollen and macrofossil data showing a habitat dominated by mesic forest (i.e., hickory, basswood, black walnut, butternut, elm, and ironwood-blue beech) at ca. 6100 B.P. (Bettis et al. 1992:16). This portion of the Mud Creek basin is a fairly dissected landscape where prairie would have been allocated to upland ridges. Still farther northeast in Iowa, at Roberts Creek, and in southeastern Minnesota, the pollen and macrofossil assemblages illustrate a dramatic shift from deciduous forest to prairie species beginning ca. 6100 B.P. (Baker et al. 2001:288, 2002:119). *Quercus macrocarpa* (burr oak) pollen increased at this juncture, indicating this drought-tolerant oak spread as a component of oak openings in the upland prairie. After ca. 3500 B.P., prairie habitat decreased somewhat from its maximum as the oak-hickory forest moved from valley sanctuaries upstream and uphill throughout first-order tributaries, although fire played an important role in maintaining prairies on the uplands (Baker et al. 2002:120). This patchwork vegetation pattern engendered prodigious amounts of edge habitat, where deer, turkeys, rabbits, edible birds, fruits, and nuts would have been common. Rivers, small streams, and backwater wetland habitats provided other sources of diverse sustenance for prehistoric hunters and gatherers. Aside from fish, turtles, waterfowl, and aquatic mammals, wetlands contained tubers (e.g., arrowhead root), cattail, and even wild rice, dating in the Mississippi Valley as early as ca. 7300 B.P. (Nations and Baker 1991).

Archaeological Potential in Eastern Iowa Landforms

Preservation of the archaeological record is a dependent variable in geomorphic processes and soil formation (Bettis and Benn 1984; Thompson and Bettis 1982). It took most of the twentieth century for researchers to fully appreciate and to apply this principle to discovery and evaluation of the archaeological record (e.g., Abbott and Bettis 1975; Brakenridge 1981; Hajic 1982; Hoyer 1980; Knox et al. 1981; Schmits 1978; Stafford 1981; Sterns 1915; Wood and McMillan 1976). Ancient cultural records cannot be preserved if their original landscape setting has been eroded by deflation of the ground surface or by lateral movement by a stream. By starting with the complex responses of geologic systems (Schumm 1976), investigators can develop principles for determining the preservation potential of archaeological landscapes. In a seminal article, Bettis and Hajic (1995) called on almost 20 years of experience with archaeological site preservation to conjure a location model for Archaic site preservation within medium-scale landscapes in the upper Midwest. They looked at uplands and hillslopes, colluvial slopes and alluvial fans, and small and large valley floodplains.

In upland-hillslope contexts (see Ruhe and Walker 1968), the Illinois data compiled by Bettis and Hajic (1995:91) revealed that Early and Middle Archaic–period sites are more numerous on back slopes, shoulders, and upland spur summits than is statistically expected, while the same kinds of sites occur less frequently on major upland summits. While these authors grant that cultural preference might have played some part in this distribution pattern, they argue that extensive erosion of hillslopes during the early middle Holocene era (the Altithermal) exposed Paleoindian and Early Archaic sites and may have displaced materials downslope. At the same time, Archaic and Paleoindian materials are less common than later sites on upland summits, a relationship they explain by reasoning that older sites are more likely to be intact because of burial by eolian sediment (e.g., loess and dust fall; Artz 1991) and biotic upbuilding (Johnson 1990; Van Nest 1993). The same argument—deep site burial—also explains very low numbers of sites on foot slopes and toe slopes in their survey data.

Data from eastern Iowa can be used to test part of the Bettis-Hajic hypothesis. Data from eight highway projects in the uplands (Stanley 1994:220–221, Table D8) produced a combined site-density figure of one site per 46 surveyed acres (18.5 surveyed hectares). The comparable figure for all landforms on 6,000+ ac (2,425 ha) in the Odessa bottomland of the upper Mississippi Valley in Louisa County is one site per 104 ac (43 ha) (Benn and Bettis 1999). Finding that prehistoric sites are more than twice as common in the uplands as in a "prime" zone of backwater lakes in the Mississippi Valley is an outcome that, at first, seems surprising, but this finding matches the Illinois site data (Bettis and Hajic 1995:91). Many floodplain sites are buried too deeply to be exposed on the surface, while upland sites are easily found under optimal survey conditions on weathered, plowed surfaces with high visibility. The chances of finding small ("flake") sites are much better in the uplands than in the forested floodplains of river valleys, where almost everything must be found with a shovel or by bankline survey. We anticipate that current calculations of site densities in river valleys are too low by a factor of two to four.

What about the representation of upland sites by site type and culture period? Our breakdown of 284 highway survey sites by functional type (see *Settlement Modeling* below) is 65 percent resource-procurement stations, 32 percent bivouacs, and 2 percent seasonal base camps (Stanley 1994:220, Table D8). The data seem to show that prehistoric people went to the uplands most of the time for short-term visits. The same site sample breaks down by culture period in this way: Paleoindian and Dalton 6 percent, Early Archaic 19 percent, Middle Archaic 8 percent, Late Archaic 33 percent, Early Woodland 9 percent, Middle Woodland 6 percent, and Late Woodland and Mississippian 19 percent (Stanley 1994:221, Table D8). These figures are significant if one assumes that prehistoric populations generally increased throughout the Holocene era and that hillslope erosion during the Holocene era has influenced site visibility (cf. Bettis and Hajic 1995). For example, the proportions of Early Archaic and Late Woodland and Mississippian sites are the same, yet far fewer people lived in the area during the Early Archaic period. Upland geomorphic factors cannot be controlling this relationship since Early Archaic components are generally less than 20–30 cm beneath Woodland artifacts in upland soils. Thus, relatively few Early Archaic folks must have visited the uplands much more often than more numerous Late Woodland or Mississippian people. The Middle Archaic representation, at 8 percent of the sites, seems "low," considering this period spanned almost 30 percent of prehistory. Both upland site burial and a preference for valley settlement must be weighed as possible explanations for this low number. A different set of variables seems to be working to produce the 33 percent of Late Archaic sites since this period spanned only 14 percent of prehistoric time. Late Archaic sites are near enough to the surface to be plowed to the surface, so there must be a *lot* of these sites.

The colluvial slopes and alluvial-fan contexts evaluated by Bettis and Hajic (1995:92) are depositional environments in which sedimentation rates have been roughly synchronous with those across the Midwest. The sedimentation rate decreased gradually as the climatic regime changed from a dryer, warmer middle Holocene to a moister late Holocene era. According to coincident radiocarbon dates, cycles of sedimentation-soil formation commenced in these landforms ca. 10,000, 8500, 6500, 4100, and 2500 B.P. (e.g., Bettis et al. 1992; Bettis and Hajic 1995:Figure 3; Bettis et al. 1996; Hoyer 1980). An important condition of archaeological context in these depositional landforms is that "the density of archaeological materials is likely to be greater in the upper, pedogenically altered deposits of each sediment-soil cycle because the sedimentation rate is slowest there" (Bettis and Hajic 1995:93). This tells archaeologists to look carefully at Archaic middens in the upper soil profile, for they may represent reoccupations of a location rather than a single long-term base camp. The culturally significant aspect of Corrington Member fans is that they provided well-drained occupation surfaces that lay *above* expected flood levels. In the Lake Odessa survey area (Benn and Bettis 1999) on the Mississippi River, the alluvial-fan landform (FANCO LSA; Bettis et al. 1996) yielded the highest site density (6.4 percent of all acreage) of any landform, although, spatially, fans make up the smallest zone (4.0 percent of the bottomland). Even this density figure underestimates site coverage because many recorded sites are merely "find spots" that add little to the total site area but represent larger, deeply buried habitation sites. So far, no one knows how many Early Archaic components rest on the bottom of fans because survey techniques rarely extend to 4- to 6-m depths.

The archaeological record in small valleys (fourth order or smaller) where the loess layer is thin or absent has been affected by episodes of downcutting and deposition of terrace fills (Bettis and Hajic 1995:94; Bettis and Littke 1987). A period of stream entrenchment and increased lateral channel migration occurred between ca. 4000 and 2500 B.P. Resultant erosion of the early to middle Holocene sediment package (Gunder Member) depended on the degree of lateral stream meandering within a given segment of a valley; that is, Gunder deposits tended to be voided from narrow valleys, while the lower reaches of larger valleys retained unpaired Gunder terrace remnants (e.g., Bettis and Hallberg 1985). An example of voiding of early Gunder sediment can be found in the Fett site, where the Graham Cave component occurred on a deflated till surface (see Appendix 14.C). Inset below the Gunder and covering much of the modern floodplain of small valleys are late-Holocene-age terraces of the Roberts Creek Member (Hudak 1987). Because the Roberts Creek deposits are so extensive, Late Archaic remains are likely better preserved than Early and Middle Archaic sites in small valleys.

Large valleys (i.e., larger than fourth order) were all directly or indirectly affected by late Wisconsinan glaciation, which shaped valley contours and laid coarse-grained sediments on valley floors (Bettis and Hajic 1995:94–95). The period between ca. 10,500 and 3000 B.P. witnessed an episode of net storage of sediment in large river valleys, with alluvial fans prograding at tributary mouths and a thick, fine-grained terrace forming atop the proglacial sediments on the valley floor (Bettis et al. 1984; Hoyer 1980; Knox et al. 1981; Wiant et al. 1983). The Mississippi River north of Hannibal shifted from a braided to an island-braided pattern (Bettis 1988:72–73), while its larger tributaries assumed a meandering pattern after ca. 10,000 B.P. This change in flow patterns created abandoned channels, and the resultant patchwork of oxbow lakes and wetlands became depositional basins for sediment (Bettis and Hajic 1995:96). Deep (3+ m), fine-grained deposits of mid-Holocene age formed on the valley floors, for example, EMHOL2 LSA in the upper Mississippi Valley (Bettis et al. 1996) and the High Terrace (TH) in the Des Moines Valley (Bettis and Benn 1984). Intervals of surface stabilization and soil development cycled through this aggradation episode, creating one or more buried soil horizons in river terraces and alluvial fans. The Odessa Soil Sequence, a stack of two or more buried soils in the EMHOL2 in the upper Mississippi Valley (Benn et al. 1988), is an example of this process creating stratigraphic contexts for Archaic cultural deposits. Lateral meandering of the master stream, often at confluences with larger tributaries, caused many early to middle Holocene sediment packages to be eroded during the last ca. 4,000 years (Benn et al. 1988).

We can calculate the fraction of the early to middle Holocene landforms preserved today with data from archaeological investigations in the U.S. Army Corps of Engineers Rock Island District (i.e., Hannibal, Missouri, to Guttenburg, Iowa) of the upper Mississippi Valley. For the entire district, 35 percent of the original late Pleistocene and early Holocene landforms (i.e., Savanna Terrace, Kingston Terrace, and early to middle Holocene sediments) are preserved on the valley floor. The other 65 percent of those landforms have been voided by lateral movements of the Mississippi channel during the middle to late Holocene. However, this does not mean that 65 percent of the Paleoindian and Early Archaic sites on those landform units were destroyed by natural processes because habitation sites tended to cluster around rich aquatic habitats relatively close to the bluffline (Benn et al. 1988). Data from the Lake Odessa bottomland (Benn 1998; Benn and Bettis 1999) suggest that somewhat less than 50 percent of those desirable habitats and associated sites have been voided by river meandering. Backwater-lake contexts are most likely to have younger sediments overlapping the early Holocene landscapes; thus, the potential for Early Archaic materials to be deeply buried within lacustrine environments is "high." About 55 percent of the original mid-Holocene alluvium is preserved on the valley floor within the Rock Island District. Following the reasoning for wetland habitats, we estimate that somewhat less than 30 percent of Middle Archaic sites have been destroyed by river erosion. Site-destruction proportions for interior river valleys may be comparable, depending on the stability of the meander belt. Today, most riverbanks in the upper Mississippi Valley are eroding at an ever-increasing rate (Benn 1998), and so the rate of site destruction is accelerating.

Settlement Modeling

Interpretation of the Archaic lifeway is founded on the assumption that the economy was based on a hunting and gathering mode of production. The precise composition of this mode of production in Iowa varied according to the kinds of prey animals that were available during various climatic episodes, the incipient practice of horticulture, and the political context of everyday social life (see Alex 2000). Given the variety of habitats and change of seasons, mobile hunters and gatherers should have created different kinds of habitation and mortuary site types with characteristic archaeological signatures. The site types vary in their geographic distributions because they were created by different labor processes and lengths of occupation. Site types are distinguished archaeologically by functional (use-wear) artifact types and distribution of recovered cultural materials. Less reliable are relative artifact densities since they can be affected by sample size. Others (e.g., Morrow and Artz 1997:251) have criticized the use of site-type models that are based on Phase I survey data, principally because multicomponent sites cannot be classified reliably. This is a cogent argument that we respect by classifying only sites with excavation data. Models of hypothetical site function are useful for organizing and interpreting assemblages of sites within a region; they are not considered to be actual reconstructions of cultural patterns. When "enough" sites have been recorded to establish a picture of regional assemblages, comparing assemblages of site types by cultural period should be possible. The site typology described here has been adapted from historical models proposed by Keyes (1927, 1951) and Wedel (1961), from behavioral models proposed by Binford (1983), and from archaeological survey data recorded by Benn (Benn 1987; Benn and Bettis 1979) and Collins (1990:19). Here we describe six site types we have employed during two decades of CRM work.

Resource-procurement stations produce very limited varieties of artifact types, usually in low numbers, at places where specific resources were likely to have been collected for transport elsewhere. These sites produce artifacts consisting of a few flakes and expedient tools (e.g., flake tools, bifaces, cobble tools, choppers, or hammerstones) from which a single task or related tasks can be inferred. Quarries belong to this category and may yield more artifacts than other procurement sites. Fire-cracked rock (FCR) and hearth evidence are absent, indicating people did not camp very long at these locations. Some stations were revisited, and artifacts multiplied but did not diversify. Collins (1990:19) calls this site type a "limited activity site."

Bivouacs have thin surface hearths or lightly fired FCR, suggesting brief heating activities occurred. Tools and flaking debris not exceeding three or four types can be present and reflect a narrow range of use-wear types. Structural and storage features are absent. Bivouacs apparently were associated with resource-procurement activities and may have been visited by the entire domestic unit. Bivouac sites with a large quantity of FCR or multiples of a few types of artifacts scattered over a large area are indicative of multiple bivouac episodes, but spatial organization is lacking in larger sites. Collins (1990:19) defines the type "specialized activity site," which is similar to the bivouac.

Temporary base camps were occupied for a longer duration than bivouacs, and structures must have been present to shelter the domestic unit. These occupations typically represent residence for one principal reason, such as procurement of a prolific resource or ceremonial activity. Evidence for domestic processing and consumption, manufacture and maintenance of equipment (weapons and clothing), leisure activities, and the affirmation of social relationships also occurs. Artifact types include heavily used FCR, flaking debris, multiple broken tools, animal and plant remains reflecting particular seasons, and specialized tool kits consisting of hide scrapers, flake tools and cores, gravers, spokeshaves, or ground-stone tools. Evidence of processing pits exists, but storage features are not common. Collins (1990:20) calls this site type a "short-term occupation site."

Seasonal base camps contain a full range of tool types, debris, and multiples of different types of expended tools. The occupation zone contains multiple houses and evidences episodes of *reoccupation*. Depending on the degree of preservation, cache pits, structural features, middens, heavily used FCR, a diverse array of tool types, the entire lithic-reduction sequence, and ceremonial equipment should be present. Camp location, coupled with floral and faunal remains, reflects seasonal preferences, usually dichotomized in terms of "warm" or "cold" seasons of occupation. These sites are similar to temporary base camps in content but are distinguished by large amounts of tool manufacturing debris as well as expended tools, reuse of activity areas, and reoccupation of substantial structures. Collins (1990:20) uses the terms *extended residence* and *extensive habitation site*, depending on the amounts of material, for this kind of archaeological deposit.

Villages are long-term habitations representing one or more human generations living at the same place. People may have traveled to other site types but returned to villages during an annual economic cycle. One would expect to find debris middens, evidence of permanent structures and special-use structures, storage pits, heavily used FCR, and a complete range of tools as well as pipes and other ceremonial equipment. Burials are anticipated in or near villages. Villages exhibit planning in their layouts. Collins (1990:20) also applies the term *village* to the site type just described.

Burial sites contain human remains in formal deposits or other indications of mortuary activities, such as caches of specialized artifacts, or both.

Iowa Archaic Database

Appendix 14.A is the result of an initial attempt to formulate a comprehensive database from records of Archaic sites in eastern Iowa. Data collecting in this instance followed a different path to the cultural overview than an approach based on records of a few familiar excavated sites (e.g., Alex 2000) because the search gathered hundreds of isolated bits of information scattered among existing site forms and curated collections. Here is what we have learned from one gleaning of the site records.

Hafted Biface Styles, Distributions, and Lithic–Reduction Trajectories

Examination of information at the Iowa Office of the State Archaeologist (OSA) commenced with a search of all records attributed to "Archaic" periods. This search produced a listing of about 740 site records within the eastern Iowa study area. Many site forms lack the cultural identification line (only "prehistoric" period is checked). Therefore, we also reviewed reports of large-scale CRM projects (Phases I–III) referred to as "gray literature." Then, the senior author examined all hafted bifaces cited in the records, either by handling the curated artifacts or by viewing photographs and drawings in reports, to confirm that biface styles were identified consistently. Sites lacking diagnostic artifacts and those with incorrect artifact identifications were deleted from the database.[5] An estimated 80 percent or more of the archaeological citations and site forms contain what we perceive to be correct (or nearly correct) biface type identifications. Problematic identifications usually involved base fragments and small side-notched (Late Woodland) and corner-notched (barbed) styles that were often attributed incorrectly to the Archaic time span. In general, we only tabulated bifaces with complete haft elements and at least part of the blade. The final database (Appendix 14.A) contains 147 Early Archaic, 258 Middle Archaic, and 203 Late Archaic–period site records (Figure 14.2). Radiocarbon and thermoluminescence (TL) dates from Archaic contexts are presented in Appendix 14.B.

When radiocarbon dating has not been done and no datable geomorphic context exists, archaeologists rely exclusively on hafted-biface typologies to identify Archaic-period sites. The typology of diagnostic hafted bifaces is shared by the authors of this volume and has been published in familiar formats inside and outside Iowa (e.g., Morrow 1984b; Justice 1987; Sandstrom and Ray 2004). Do other tool types (e.g., adzes, grooved axes, winged drills, distinctive end scrapers, core types, and flaking debris with certain characteristics) have diagnostic value? Can archaeologists relatively date sites lacking hafted bifaces by associating other characteristics of the chipped- and ground-stone tool assemblages with specific Archaic periods? Does recognition of a characteristic bifacial reduction sequence assist in identifying particular Archaic-period assemblages?

Early Archaic Period

This period is poorly known (Alex 2000:61), so the 147 entries in the database constitute a greater number than we expected prior to commencing this research. Dalton, the earliest style straddling the Paleoindian transition, occurs along the Mississippi River valley, especially in the southeastern corner of the state, and at a small cluster of locations at the southern terminus of the Des Moines Lobe in central Iowa (Figure 14.3). Hardin Barbed sites are similarly distributed along the Mississippi Valley and also occur along major interior rivers (e.g., Flanders 1977)—Upper Iowa, Cedar, Skunk, and Des Moines rivers. The thin-bladed, notched styles like Kirk, Cache River, Palmer, and Decatur/Neuberger are distributed along the big rivers in the manner of the Hardin style but cluster in central and southern Iowa and close to the Mississippi Valley in northeastern Iowa (Figure 14.4). The St. Charles style clusters in northeastern and southeastern Iowa, again, close to the Mississippi Valley (Figure 14.5). Heavier Thebes points and associated Grundy

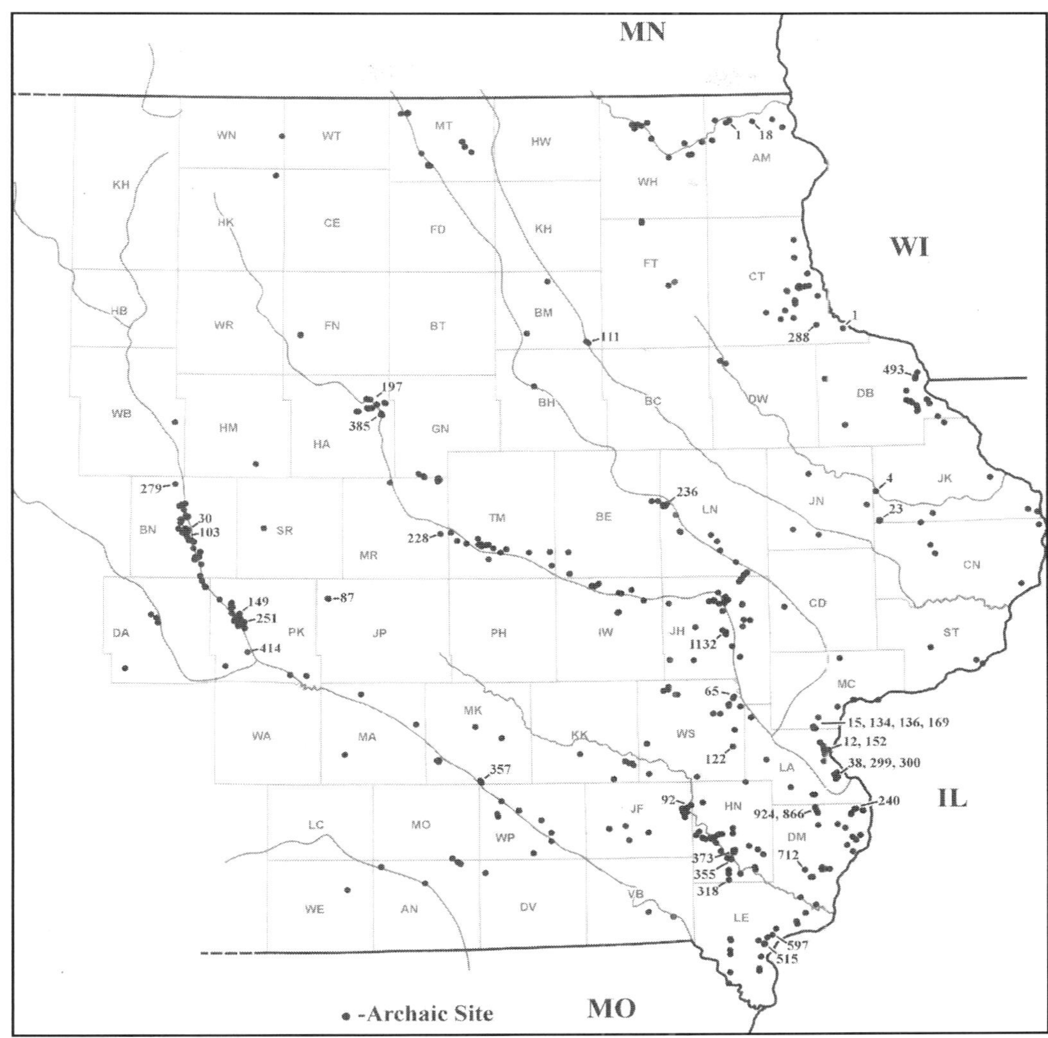

Figure 14.2. Locations of all Archaic sites included in the database compiled for this chapter.

preforms (Morrow 1984b:88) are widely distributed along the Des Moines and Iowa-Cedar river valleys, especially in east-central Iowa. Distinctive large bifacial adzes made on flake blanks (Figure 14.6) and associated with Paleoindian, Dalton, and St. Charles points occur at a cluster of locations in the uplands near the confluence of the Mississippi Valley and the lower Skunk River basin (Figure 14.5). In sum, all of the stemmed and corner-notched styles that were the products of sophisticated bifacial reduction (see below) and that date to the early half of the Early Archaic period appear to have been introduced into the state in the upstream direction via the Mississippi Valley corridor. Morrow (1981b:29) noticed that a small number of the St. Charles points he studied were manufactured from exotic cherts from southern sources. Distribution of heavier, side-notched styles, like Stilwell, Graham Cave, MacCorkle, and Greenbrier, which date to the latter half of this period, is more widespread, as if these styles had been incorporated by resident populations (Figure 14.7). A small side-notched style, Wolf Creek, is distributed in east-central Iowa, indicating it was an indigenous variant of the larger types.

Less is known about nondiagnostic lithic artifacts in the Early Archaic assemblage because so few sites have been excavated, for a poor artifact return. The small assemblage from the Graham Cave component at the Fett site (13LE597; Appendix 14.C) contained early-stage bifaces, cores, and very few bifacial thinning flakes. A small lithic assemblage recovered immediately beneath that component yielded lamellar flakes, small unfinished bifaces, and polymorphic cores probably dating to the Late Paleoindian period (authors' report pending). Other intriguing assemblages came from upland sites in Des Moines and Henry counties in southeastern Iowa. This region contains bedrock outcrops of high-quality Burlington and Verdi/Salem cherts. Surface scatters at Dalton site 13DM924, lanceolate-point site 13DM866, and St. Charles site 13HN355 yielded examples

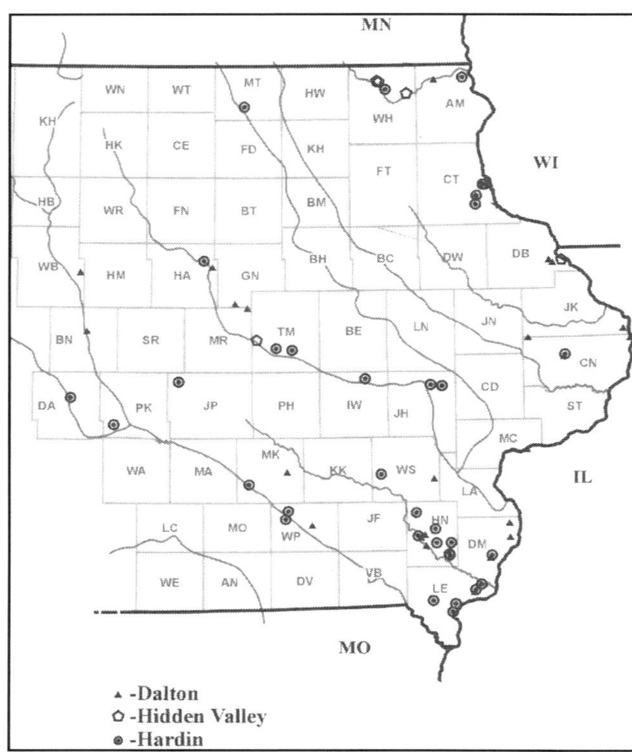

Figure 14.3. Early Archaic–period sites with Dalton, Hidden Valley, and Hardin bifaces.

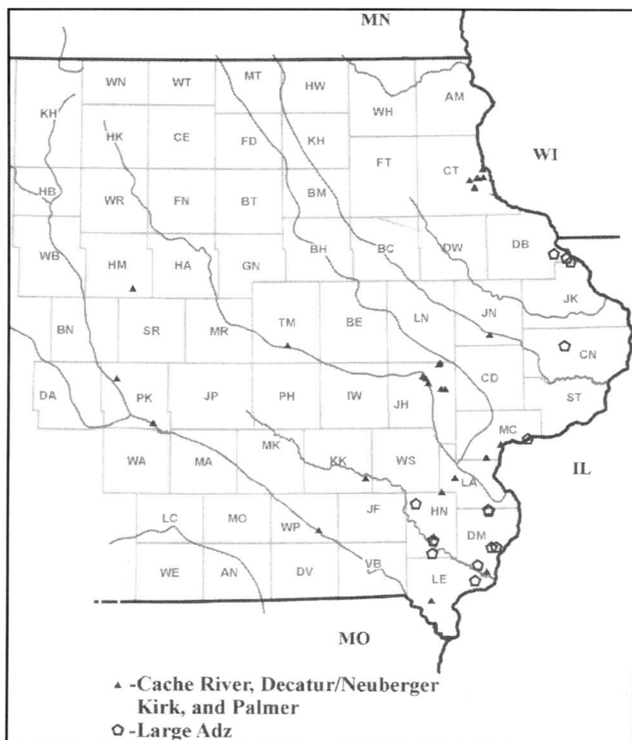

Figure 14.4. Early Archaic–period sites with Cache River, Decatur/Neuberger, Kirk, Palmer, and adze bifaces.

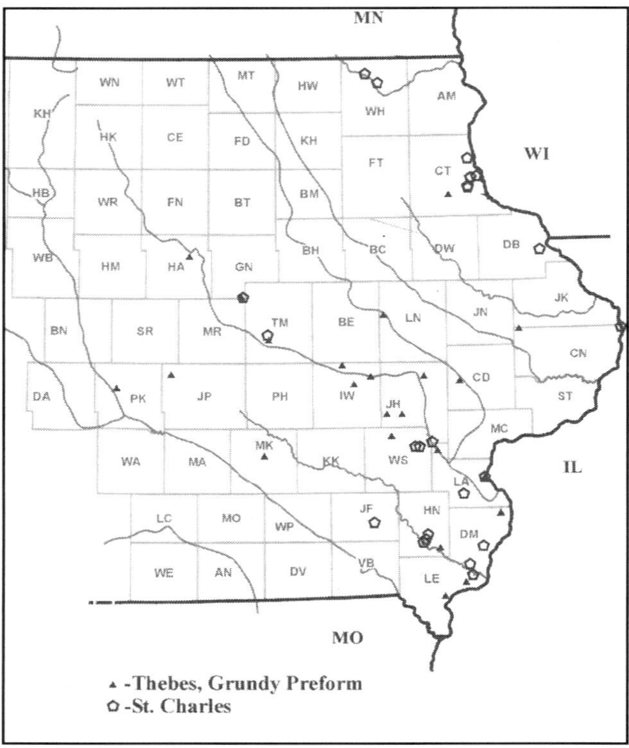

Figure 14.5. Early Archaic–period sites with Thebes, Grundy preform, and St. Charles bifaces.

Figure 14.6. Early Archaic adzes: right, finished; left, preforms.

of large Burlington primary flakes, large bifaces, heavy scrapers, and adzes (Figure 14.8; Morrow et al. 1995; Morrow and Artz 1997). The adzes (Figure 14.6), bifacial scrapers, and projectiles were formed from large, thin bifaces or primary (some of them decortication) flakes subsequently shaped by antler-billet percussion. Morrow and Artz (1997) considered this a Paleoindian lithic reduction technology recognizable at other sites in the locality, even when hafted bifaces were absent from surface collections. Another effort to distinguish Early Archaic technology was pursued at the

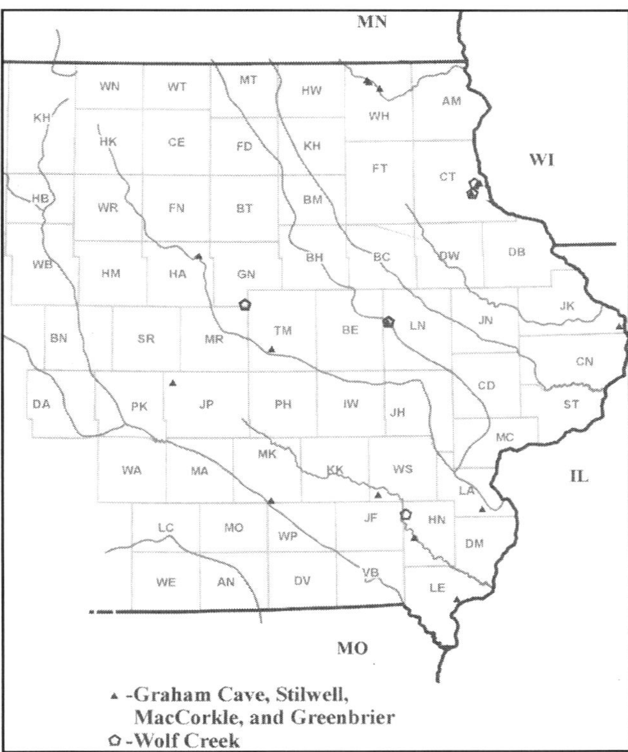

Figure 14.7. Early Archaic–period sites with Graham Cave, Stilwell, MacCorkle, Greenbrier, and Wolf Creek bifaces.

Overberg site (13HN318: Appendix 14.C), a resource-procurement or bivouac camp located in the same region. A large adze made from Keokuk chert was recovered from this upland site during a Phase I survey (Morrow et al. 1995), and, subsequently, a crew from the Louis Berger Group undertook excavation of the site (Fiedel et al. 2004). A TL date of 6096 B.C. and a radiocarbon date of 6690 B.C. place this occupation at the end of the Early Archaic period. The Berger Group recovered a large late-stage biface similar to the Grundy style, which Morrow (1984b:88) associated with the Thebes bifacial-reduction strategy, and seven bladelike (lamellar) flakes. The rest of the 3,300+ pieces of debitage, almost all of which were of local cherts and 18 percent of which were heat treated, were not distinguishable as relating to a Paleoindian technology.

The key aspects of Paleoindian technology—that is, large, thin bifacial cores as blanks for making adzes and projectiles, production of large, thin bifacial thinning flakes exhibiting use wear, and a low incidence of polymorphic cores (Boldurian 1991:291; Muniz 2004:270–271), are observed in the Early Archaic site collections. Morrow (1984a:100–103) observed from his study of Wolf Creek (Grundy County) sites that the largest flake tools and hafted bifaces tended to occur in Paleoindian and Early Archaic assemblages, which also revealed a consistent selection of higher-quality cherts not requiring heat treatment. The larger hafted bifaces like Hardin, St. Charles, and Thebes were made from good-quality local cherts, such as Burlington and Maynes Creek, and were infrequently heat treated. Morrow reasoned that because heat treatment increases

Figure 14.8. Nondiagnostic Early Archaic surface material, all from 13DM50: a–d, hard-hammer flakes of Burlington chert and basalt; e, Kirk-like biface blade of Moline chert; f, lanceolate base; g, oval biface; h, end scraper; i, bifacially retouched flake.

the brittleness of chert, high-quality cherts not requiring heat treatment were preferred for making large bifaces to lower the failure rate in production. But, this reasoning is not consistently borne out in Early Archaic technologies. Dalton points were made from a wide variety of cherts, often heat treated, and exhibited less refined workmanship than other early biface forms (Morrow 1981b:28–30). This may have something to do with function, as Dalton bifaces were multipurpose tools like the later side-notched bifaces.

Middle Archaic Period

There is no way to draw absolute distinctions among the traits of heavy-bodied, side-notched bifaces that go by the names Godar, Big Sandy, Raddatz, and Osceola (Figure 14.9). Justice (1987:60) placed all within the Large Side Notched cluster. Although Osceola specimens from the Mississippi Valley are notably larger and more deeply concave across the base than Raddatz, these types exhibit a continuum of attributes that mirrors gradations between the Godar and Raddatz styles. Big Sandy (Chapman 1975:272) is a southern-region name for the large side-notched style that resembles Turin (Morrow 1984b:62) in Iowa. Godar and the corner-notched Helton type have not been identified as often in Iowa as elsewhere and neither has the small side-notched Brannon type. The Matanzas type, with its distinctive narrow blade and shallow side notches, is recognized all over the state. Our impression is that all eight of the relatively large side-notched points mentioned above are widely distributed in eastern Iowa and into Wisconsin (Stoltman 1986:221), Missouri (Chapman 1975), and the lower Illinois River valley (Conrad 1981; Cook 1976).

Distributions of side-notched bifaces exhibit some possible temporal and regional patterns. Turin and Brewerton styles with distinctive basal ears are concentrated in east-central Iowa, while Jakie occurs only in southern Iowa (Figure 14.10). Turin and Brewerton bear a strong resemblance to two styles from Missouri, (respectively) Jakie Stemmed and Big Sandy notched (Chapman 1975:242, 250; Marshall 1958: Figure 20). Brewerton occurred with Matanzas points at the Garden site (13DB493), so it may date later than Turin. Jakie has been placed at the end of the Early Archaic period as vaguely related to Dalton (Ray 1994; Sandstrom and Ray 2004), while Big Sandy is part of the broad Middle Archaic horizon in Missouri. A Turin point was found in Horizon I (5300 B.C.) at the Cherokee site (Anderson and Semken 1980:Figure 9.3c), and a side-notched point with flaring ears occurred with human remains and is associated with a 5070 B.C. date at 14DO417 in Kansas (Hoard et al. 2004:722, 726).

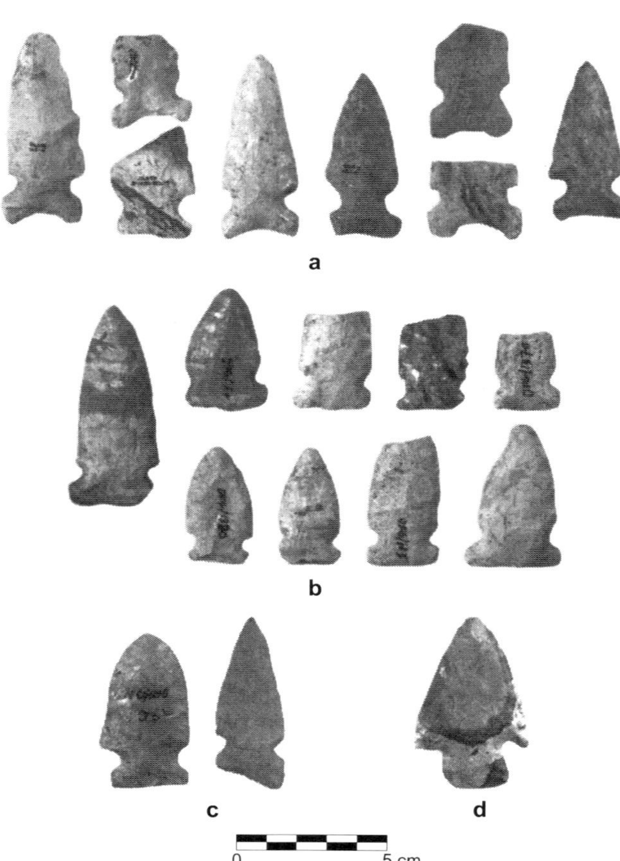

Figure 14.9. Large Middle Archaic hafted bifaces: top row, a, Osceola, 13LA38; b, Raddatz, 13LA12; c, Godar, 13LA12, 13IW94; d, Helton, 13LA38.

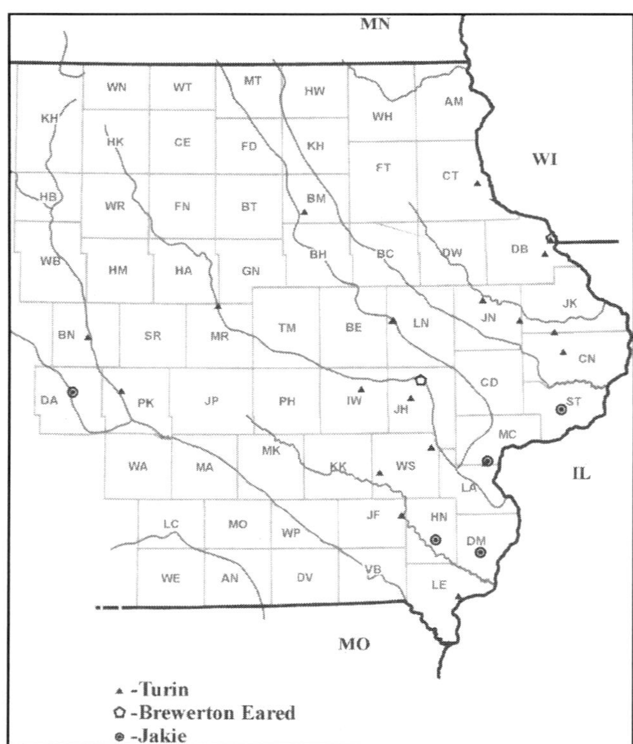

Figure 14.10. Middle Archaic–period sites with Turin, Brewerton Eared, and Jakie bifaces.

Thus, the Turin style probably was produced early in the Middle Archaic period, generally predating the horizon of the Large Side Notched cluster. Tama and Little Sioux/Simonsen styles are small to medium-size points (Morrow 1984b), with the narrow-bladed Tama style the eastern Iowa version and the wider-bladed Little Sioux/Simonsen type the western Iowa version (Figure 14.11). Both types tend to be smaller than those grouped in the Large Side Notched cluster,[6] and, more significantly, their haft elements are thinner and narrower than the shoulders and their bases are always concave. Little Sioux points were recovered from Early Archaic Horizon II (6225 B.C.) at the Cherokee bison-kill site in northwestern Iowa (Anderson and Semken 1980:Figure 9.4a–e), Tama points were dated to 5825 B.C. at Allen Fan (13HA385; Collins and Mandel 1999), and a Tama point was recovered beneath the Matanzas component at the Fett site (13LE597), indicating they belong to the earlier half of the Middle Archaic period. The Raddatz and Matanzas types, along with scattered instances of Brannon and Big Sandy points, are the dominant styles throughout eastern Iowa (Figure 14.12) and represent the basic design of Middle Archaic weapon tips. Wide, boldly notched points like Godar and Helton are Illinois types, and recorded examples occur along the Des Moines and Iowa-Cedar river valleys proximate to Illinois (Figure 14.13). The coeval Osceola style is also concentrated on the eastern side of Iowa, especially along the Iowa-Cedar and Upper Iowa

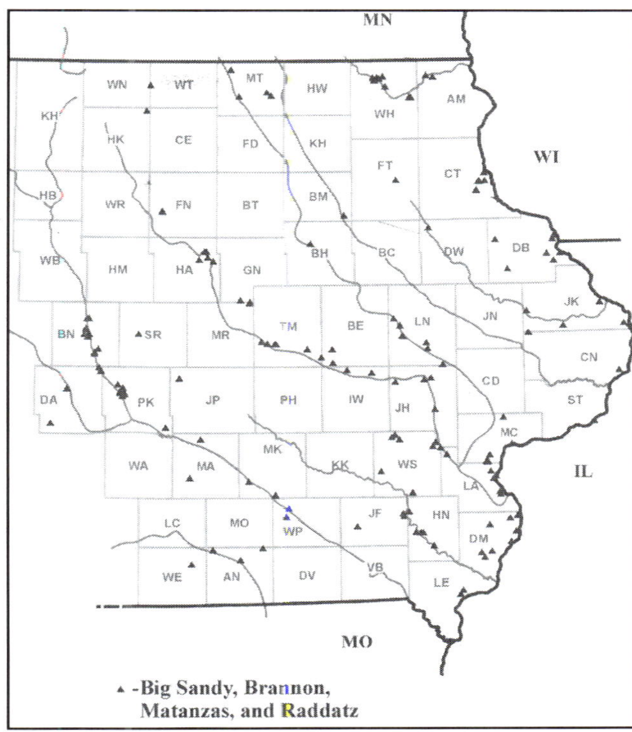

Figure 14.12. Middle Archaic–period sites with Big Sandy, Brannon, Matanzas, and Raddatz bifaces.

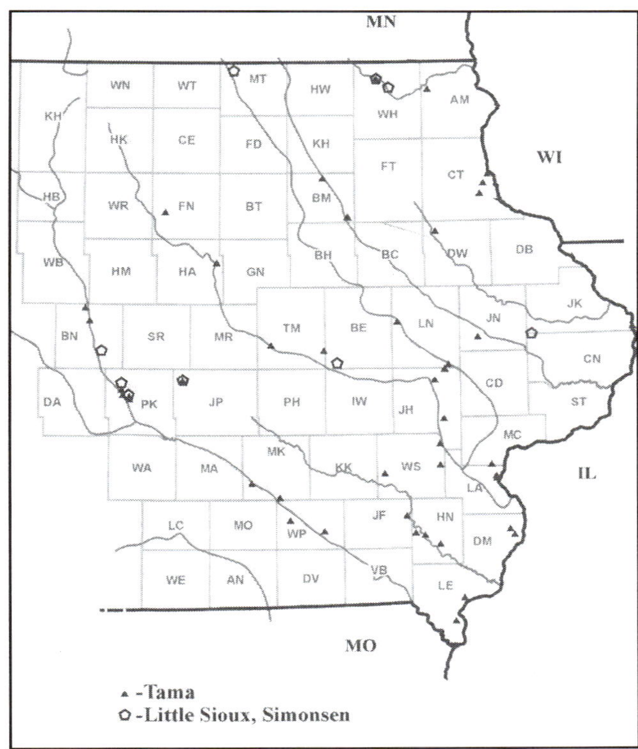

Figure 14.11. Middle Archaic–period sites with Tama, Little Sioux, and Simonsen bifaces.

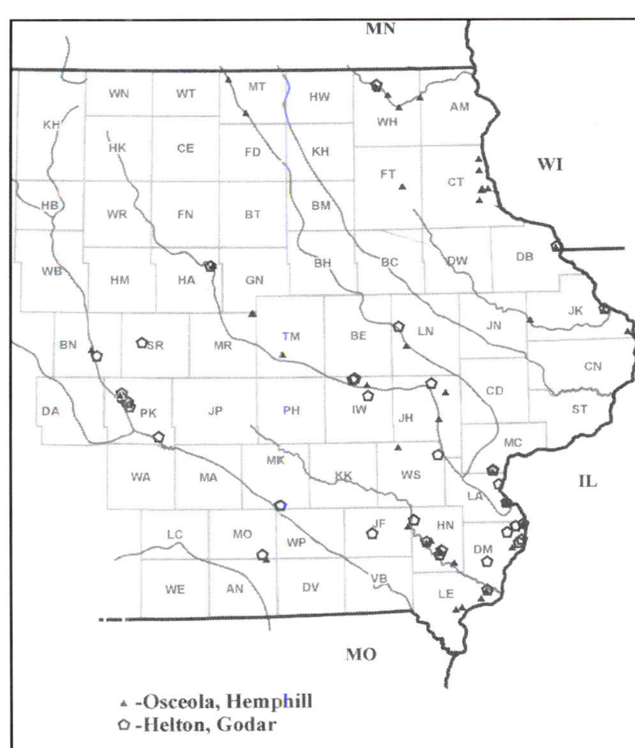

Figure 14.13. Middle Archaic–period sites with Osceola, Hemphill, Helton, and Godar bifaces.

valleys (Figure 14.13). Prolific numbers of Osceola bifaces occur on many sites within the Mississippi Valley (Overstreet 1988), particularly where there is a broad floodplain with extensive backwaters. The Osceola style is firmly dated at the end of the Middle Archaic period, to around 2700 ± 200 B.C. (Benn et al. 1987; Thompson 2006; see Appendix 14.B).

The information tabulated in Table 14.1 compares a series of Archaic assemblages and two typical Late Woodland flake-tool assemblages. Looking at the chipped-stone tool numbers, Archaic assemblages tend to have proportionally fewer unifacial and flake tools than Woodland assemblages. For example, the averages for the Archaic chipped-stone tools (n = 1,716) are 44 percent unifaces and flake tools, 32 percent bifaces, and 24 percent cores, and for Late Woodland chipped-stone tools (n = 896) the averages are 69 percent unifaces and flake tools, 19 percent bifaces, and 12 percent cores. Archaic assemblages exhibit higher proportions of bifaces and cores, with many of the late-stage bifaces having been developed from reduced cores. This is a bifacial reduction strategy used by Archaic knappers. Heat treatment apparently was applied at various stages of bifacial reduction; for instance, at the Garden site 10–15 percent of cores versus 58

Table 14.1. Comparisons of Archaic- and Late Woodland–Period Tool Inventories.

Period, Site, Area Excavated		Cores	Bifaces	Unifaces and Flake Tools	Cobble Tools
Middle Archaic period					
Garden site (13DB493)[a]	n =	53 (36%)	64 (43%)	31 (21%)	7
468 m²	density	.11	.14	.07	.01
Allen Fan (13HA385)[b]	n =	16 (9%)	30 (16%)	137 (73%)	51+
145 m²	density[c]	.11	.21	.94	.35
Sand Run West (13LA38)[d]	n =	48 (17%)	82 (30%)	147 (52%)	65
28 m²	density[c]	1.7	2.9	5.2	2.3
McNeal Fan (13MC150)[e] Stratum IId	n =	96 (32%)	105 (35%)	100 (33%)	309
650 m²	density	.15	.16	.15	.48
Ed's Meadow (13DM712)[f]	n =	0 (0%)	4 (40%)	6 (60%)	3
20 m²	density[c]	0	.2	.3	.15
Mixed Archaic periods					
Fett (13LE597) levels 18–30[g]	n =	85 (44%)	47(24%)	61(32%)	80
360 m²	density[c]	.23	.13	.17	.22
13MC134, levels 5–6[h]	n =	7 (8%)	16 (18%)	65 (74%)	15
300 m²	density	.02	.05	.22	.05
13MC136, levels 5–6[i]	n =	33 (18%)	66 (37%)	80 (45%)	81
310 m²	density	.11	.21	.26	.26
Merrimac Mills (13JF92) sub-Ap[j]	n =	32 (36%)	18 (20%)	39 (44%)	40
140 m²	density	.22	.13	.29	.29
Late Archaic period					
13MK357 U.Terr.[k]	n =	22 (22%)	35 (35%)	44 (44%)	220
ca. 600 m²	density	.04	.06	.07	.37
Davis Creek (13WS122)[l]	n =	22 (15%)	79 (54%)	46 (31%)	5
507 m²	density	.04	.16	.09	.01
Late Woodland period					
Horseshoe (13LA27)[m]	n =	61 (14%)	83 (19%)	299 (67%)	31
100 m²	density[c]	.61	.83	2.99	.31
Cross (13LA309)[n]	n =	46 (10%)	89 (20%)	318 (70%)	35
200 m²	density	.23	.45	1.89	.18

[a]Benn 2007; [b]Fishel et al. 2000; [c]backdirt screened; [d]Benn et al. 1987; [e]Thompson 2006; [f]Morrow 1998; [g]unpublished data on file, Bear Creek Archeology, Inc.; [h]Benn 2002a; [i]Benn 2002b; [j]Finn 1981, 1982; [k]Thompson 1999; [l]Lensink 1986; [m]Benn et al. 1999; [n]Benn et al. 2001.

percent of the bifaces had been heat treated. At Allen Fan, all nine projectile points and 60 percent of the other bifaces had been heat treated, while at Sand Run West, only 8 percent of the debitage had been heated. The heat-treatment figures for the reduction sequence at McNeal Fan were 22 percent of cores, 25 percent of debitage, 46 percent of tools, and 56 percent of bifaces.

The five discrete Middle Archaic components (i.e., Garden, Allen Fan, Sand Run West, McNeal, and Ed's Meadow) exhibit considerable variability in lithic-tool densities compared with the relatively uniform tool densities from the four mixed Archaic assemblages (i.e., 13MC134, 13MC136, Merrimac Mills, and Fett). The bivouac occupations at Ed's Meadow have very low tool densities, while the base camp or village at the Sand Run West site produced very high densities in all four tool categories. The McNeal village and Allen Fan base camp yielded relatively high densities of some tool categories (i.e., cobble tools and unifaces and flake tools, respectively), perhaps reflecting a degree of activity specialization during the occupations. By contrast, the Garden base camp has uniformly low tool densities, which may be a reflection of its single componency. Thus, while one can try to derive a conceptually "typical" Middle Archaic lithic assemblage of chipped- and cobble and ground-stone tools and by-products, the existence of seasonally specialized sites complicates the attempt because only part of the whole cultural complex is present at these sites or the sites have multiple components.

What all of the Middle Archaic sites have in common is a diverse tool inventory, with base camps producing multiple examples of a wide variety of tools types like side and end scrapers, meat knives, spokeshaves, shredders, drills, gravers, burins, choppers, hammerstones and pounders, grinding slabs, manos, and axes. McNeal Fan and Sand Run West villages are prime examples of this diversity. In general, Middle Archaic assemblages have smaller flake inventories and higher frequencies of heat-treated bifaces than Early Archaic assemblages (Morrow 1984a:100–103).

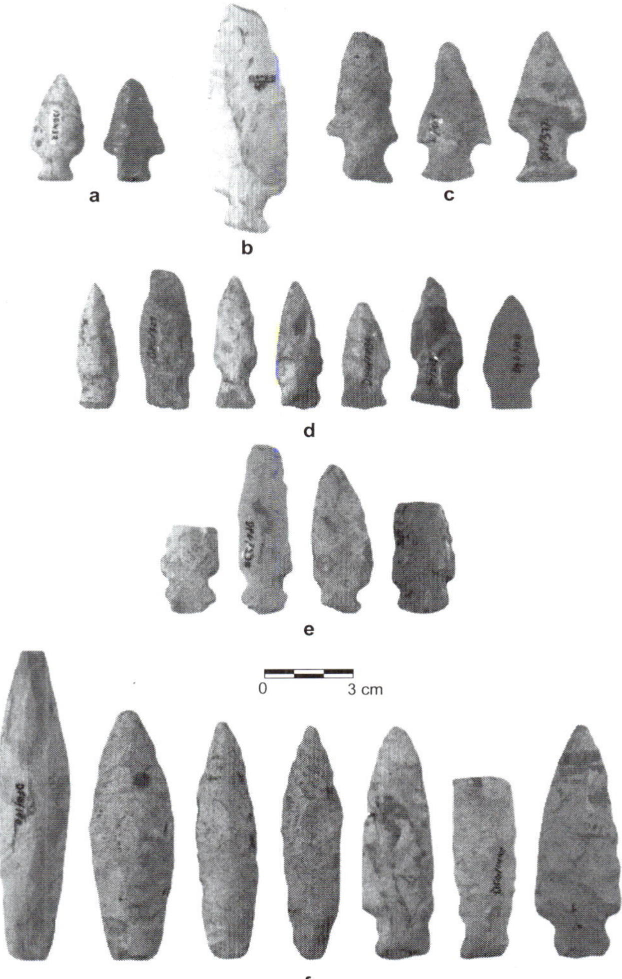

Figure 14.14. Late Archaic–period stemmed bifaces: a, b, Table Rock; c, Tipton; d, Durst; e, Atalissa; f, Sedalia and Karnak/Etley.

Late Archaic Period

Diversification was a general trend of hafted-biface manufacture during the Late Archaic period, and the array of styles cannot be "pigeonholed" comfortably into types. Very different Atalissa and Tipton styles (Figure 14.14) may have been contemporaries early in the period, but the sample of these types is too small to know if they are only distributed across the center of the state (Figure 14.15). Apple Blossom Stemmed shows no consistent distribution pattern (Figure 14.16), perhaps because this type is shaped like and confused with the Woodland-period Pelican Lake type. The larger stemmed and barbed style called "Etley" or "Ledbetter" is consistently found in southeastern Iowa, especially along the Des Moines and Skunk rivers, where the Titterington-Sedalia-Nebo Hill (TSN) complex lanceolate types—Karnak, Nebo Hill, Sedalia, and Wadlow—are concentrated (Figure 14.17). Etley/Ledbetter as well as Smith Basal Notched and Stone Square Stemmed probably are related to an unnamed TSN manifestation in Iowa. The small to medium-size expanding-stem points so characteristic of the Late Archaic period are widely distributed, with the larger styles (Epps, Fort Dodge, Table Rock, and Poag) tending to occur in the southern half and the smaller styles (Durst and Merom/Trimble) in the northeastern quadrant (Figures 14.15, 14.18). There is a continuum of sizes and haft shapes among these stemmed points, and size rather than shape may be the temporal indicator (i.e., small = later). The youngest cluster of Late Archaic bifaces includes small to medium-size barbed styles: Vosburg, Mule Road, Springly, Wade, and unnamed barbed, corner-notched types (Figure 14.19). Barbed points cluster in extreme southeastern Iowa and in central Iowa but are nearly absent from northeastern Iowa, where Durst is common (Figure 14.16). Given that barbed points often lost their barbs through breakage and resharpening, the Durst category possibly is a catch-all for other styles with broken and reworked hafts.

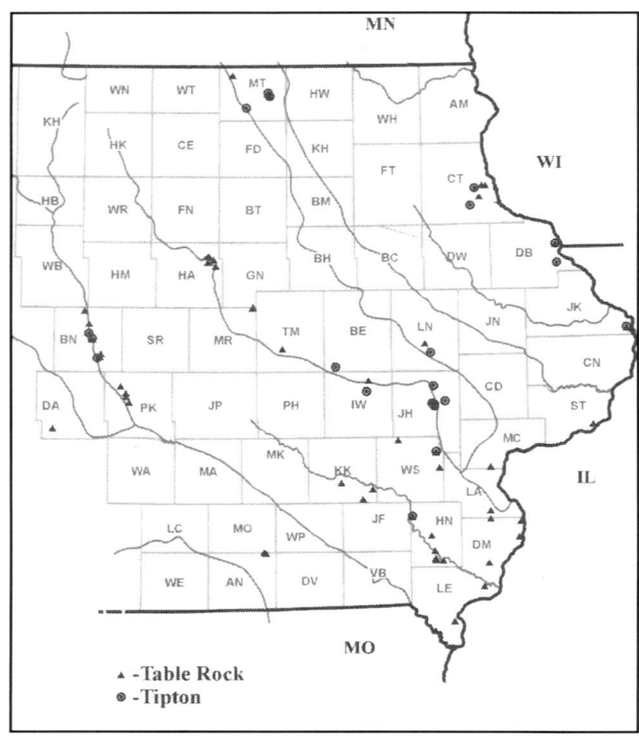

Figure 14.15. Late Archaic–period sites with Table Rock and Tipton bifaces.

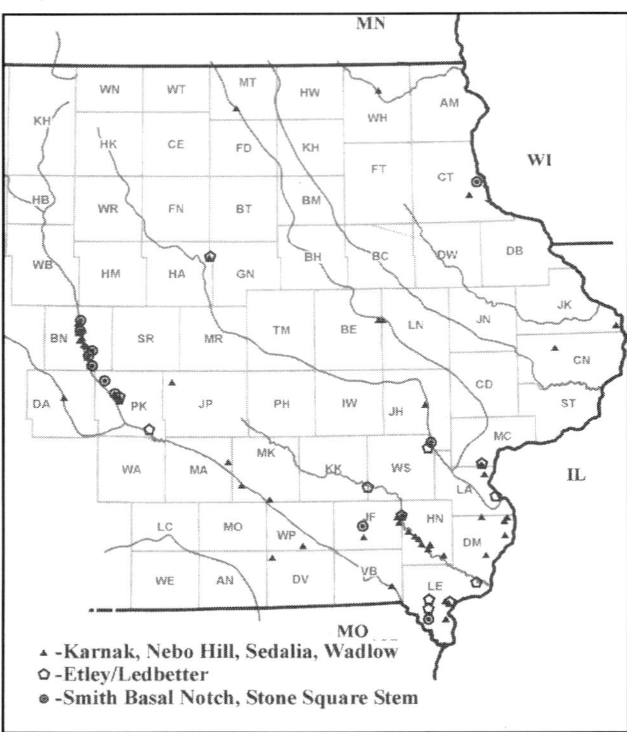

Figure 14.17. Late Archaic–period sites with Karnak, Nebo Hill, Sedalia, Wadlow, Etley/Ledbetter, Smith Basal Notched, and Stone Square Stemmed bifaces.

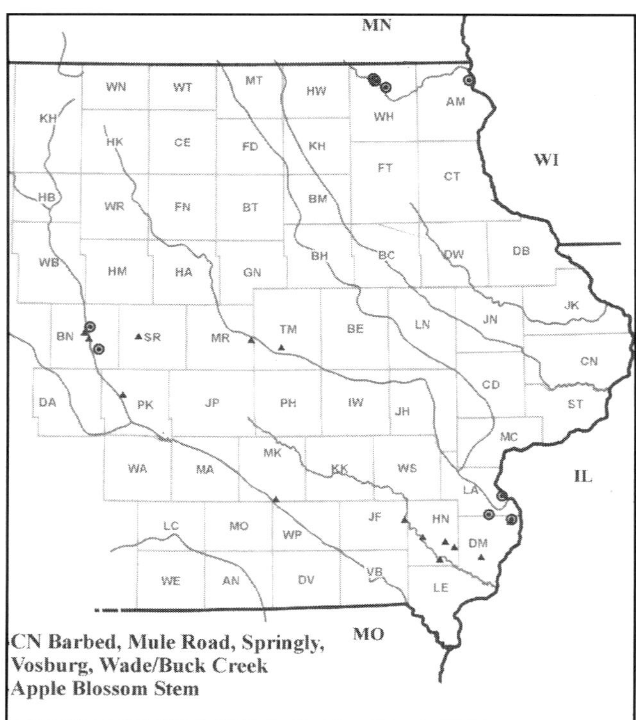

Figure 14.16. Late Archaic–period sites with corner-notched barbed, Mule Road, Springly, Vosburg, Wade, and Apple Blossom Stemmed bifaces.

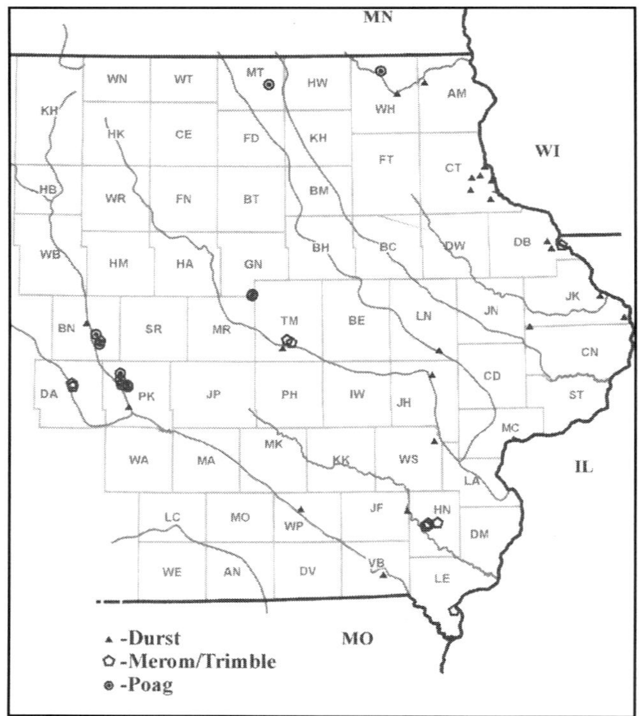

Figure 14.18. Late Archaic–period sites with Poag, Merom/Trimble, and Durst bifaces.

Figure 14.19. Late Archaic bifaces: a, b, Apple Blossom Stemmed, 13LA38; c–e, corner-notched barbed, 13LA12, 13LA38.

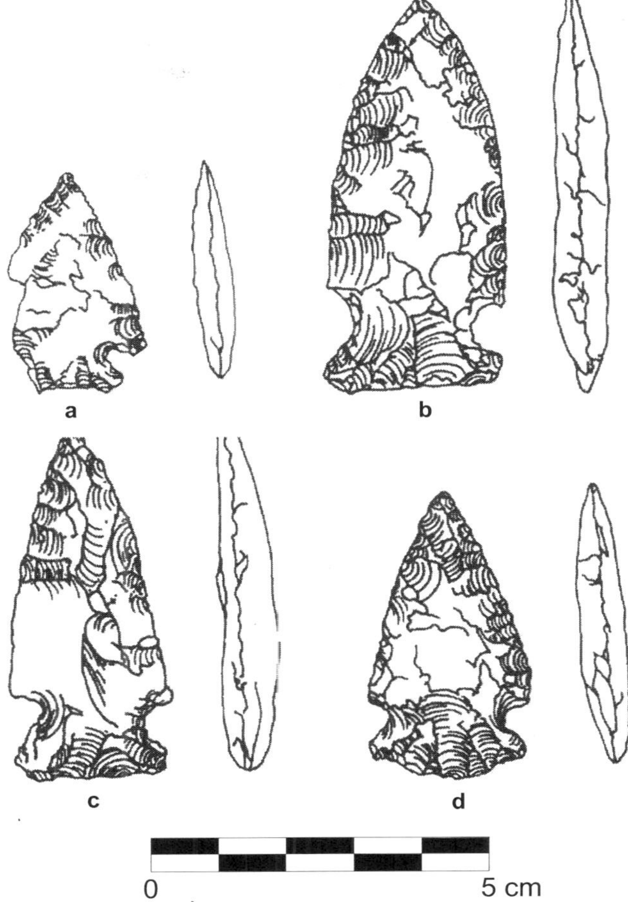

Figure 14.20. Hafted bifaces from Lost Creek Upper Terrace Component II: a, Vosburg; b, Godar; c, d, Raddatz-like (after Thompson 1999:Figure 14 22).

It follows that Durst and barbed styles may be less mutually exclusive than their distributions indicate.

This diversity of Late Archaic hafted-biface styles likely results from chronological variation and regionalization, although this hypothesis cannot be examined in detail because of an inadequate sample of excavated stratified contexts. The two excavated Late Archaic sites available for comparison are Lost Creek Upper Terrace (13MK357; Thompson 1999) and Davis Creek (13WS122; Lensink 1986). Hafted bifaces from both sites fall into a narrow range of forms developed from a single style theme. The four small to medium-sized specimens from 13MK357 are designed around a thin-based, corner-notched format (Figure 14.20), although three type names—*Vosburg*, *Raddatz*, and *Godar*—have been given to these points. All 23 hafted bifaces from Davis Creek were placed in the expanding-stem Table Rock type (Lensink 1986:178), although one resembles the Tipton type, with barbs and a relatively long stem, and two others have short, contracting stems (Figure 14.21). The bifaces in each of these assemblages could have been hafted by a single method (see *Weaponry, Hafted Biface Styles, and Gender*, below). Both sites yielded relatively low tool densities in most categories (Table 14.1), the lowest densities of any of the base camps and lower than even most of the bivouacs. Are low tool densities an indication of temporary-base-camp occupations? Perhaps, but with such a limited sample of sites, there is no way to quantify the effect of size and volume of excavation blocks. Despite its "low" density, site 13MK357 yielded a wide variety of lithic tool types, including large numbers of cores, unfinished bifaces, flake knives, flake scrapers, cobble abraders, manos, cobble pounders and hammerstones, and cobble scrapers and spokeshaves as well as fewer chipped-stone drills, choppers, spokeshaves, shredders, and a digger (Appendix 14.C). The assemblage from Davis Creek, while not subjected to use-wear analysis, appeared to be less varied. Although it contained very large numbers of finished and unfinished bifaces (many produced elsewhere), Davis Creek yielded only three end scrapers, 43 flake tools, 14 hammerstones, and five other cobble tools (Appendix 14.C).

Weaponry, Hafted Biface Styles, and Gender

Hafted bifaces were mounted on thrusting spears or javelins, dart foreshafts, or handles for use as weapons or handheld processing tools. Judging by the diversity of haft shapes, total lengths, weights, and blade widths, stone tips were engineered for specific functions. Researchers have expended considerable effort, ranging from detailed metric analysis and study of archaeological specimens to field tests with measuring devices and real animals, to reconstruct aboriginal weaponry

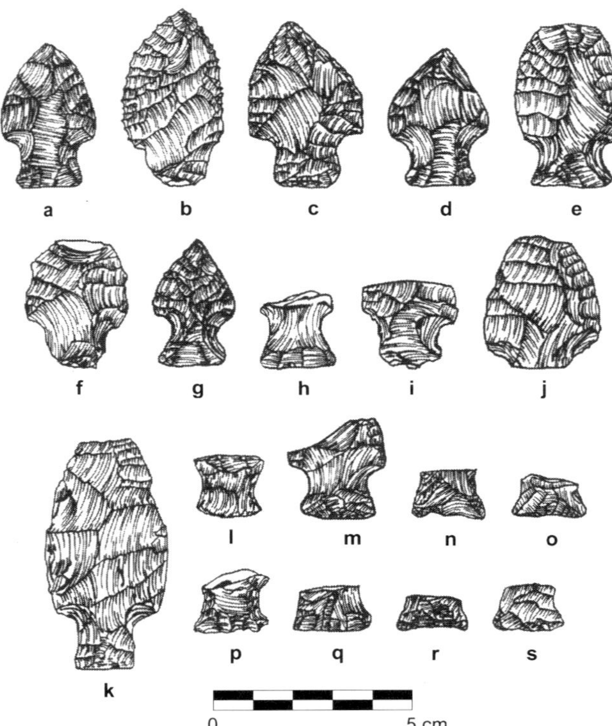

Figure 14.21. Table Rock bifaces from 13WS122 (after Lensink 1986:Figure 9-11).

and understand performance characteristics (e.g., Frison 1989; Hutchings 1997; Knecht 1997; Shott 1997). Most of these analyses have focused on differentiating the technologies of the dart or javelin versus the bow and arrow (e.g., Blitz 1988; Hitchcock and Bleed 1997; Shott 1993; Thomas 1978) because of the social and economic implications this change had for prehistoric societies (see Hall 1980). There should have been equally significant social and economic relationships tied to use of javelins and darts during the Archaic periods. Consider the relative efficiency of weapons used by historically recorded hunting groups. Ethnographic data provided by Shott (1993:436–437) and Ellis (1997:63) suggested that spears were employed more often to kill large-bodied animals taken relatively infrequently. By contrast, bows and arrows were used to kill a wide variety of species, generally smaller animals taken in large numbers. Thus, while the bow and arrow is an accurate weapon with a high ratio of successful kills, the spear also is an effective weapon for bringing down large animals because of its weight (Hitchcock and Bleed 1997:355). Habitat context, that is, grassland versus forest, was not taken into account by Shott (1993) but was by Ellis (1997:64), who was informed by San hunters that light spears with foreshafts and replaceable tips were effective at long distances in open areas. By analogy, because it is a heavy high-velocity projectile (Hutchings 1997), the dart is a more efficient weapon than the javelin or thrusting spear for a variety of prey sizes. Shott's (1993:438) perspective, derived from his analysis, is that various hunting techniques had complementary functions and that the "efficiency" of various weapons was conceptually related to the types of animals being hunted. Nelson (1997:374–375) categorized "flexible" projectile designs as ones that could undergo modification (e.g., resharpening) and still be effective, while "versatile" projectile designs had more specific functions related to specific attributes.

Although hard data on performance characteristics of weapons are meager, ethnographic descriptions of weapon attributes have been reviewed by various authors in Knecht (1997). Hutchings (1997) presented useful data from archaeological, ethnographic, and modern weaponry based, among other measurements, on the "lithic fracture velocity" of stone projectiles. He concluded that the spear-thrower (atlatl) was used in North America during the Paleoindian (Clovis) period. His analysis showed that darts can be delivered with 185 percent of javelin velocity and, therefore, can strike more distant targets, and, because they can be made much heavier than arrows, darts delivered at a velocity of 50–60 m per second can strike a target with up to four times the kinetic energy of an arrow traveling at greater velocity (Hutchings 1997:136–137). This makes the spear-thrower–dart combination an effective weapon, albeit one that is dependent on the skill and stealth of the hunter, because high kinetic energy increases the shock effect (lethality) to the prey. Among the San of Africa, javelins and thrusting spears were preferred for dispatching large, solitary game animals (Ellis 1997:64; Hitchcock and Bleed 1997:349). A hand-thrown javelin with a long shaft should be an effective weapon in a tundra setting, while high-velocity darts with lighter shafts should work well in the forest. Hutchings's (1997:73, 78) experienced informant, who hunted wild boars with darts in Georgia, accumulated a 47 percent rate for "hits" in wooded and open terrain, with successful (disabling or fatal) throws averaging 15 m (s = 8.5 m) and misses averaging 24 m (s = 14.3 m). This informant used a dart 221 cm long, weighing 240 g, and tipped with a Clovis-style point weighing 20–30 g. Kalahari hunters on foot (often using dogs) achieved a 67 percent success (kill) rate with spears (Hitchcock and Bleed 1997:359). George Frison's (1989) African elephant experiment showed the best penetration came from a dart with a 44.7-g Clovis-style point fitted on a foreshaft. The entire weapon with shaft weighed 475 g.

The efficiency of darts and javelins can be varied by modifying shaft length, weight, and thickness, adding a foreshaft of various materials and weight, sizing the stone tip, designing the haft structure, and employing fletching (Nelson 1997:377)—all characteristics that are related in some way to the form and weight of hafted bifaces. Since almost all of the organic components of weapons have long since vanished from the Paleoindian and Archaic archaeological records in the Midwest, we turn to Christenson (1986) for technological interpretations of projectile sizes derived from the metric attributes of the hafted bifaces and modern experiments in aerodynamics. Christenson's (1986:116–119) conclusions are fivefold:

1. The flight stability of a dart depends on keeping the "center of pressure" behind the center of mass on a weapon shaft, so the weight of the stone tip will covary with the use of fletching: For example, lighter-weight stone tips can be coupled with heavier (bone) foreshafts, heavier stone tips are needed on plain wooden shafts and fletching reduces the need for weight at the stone tip.
2. Narrow stone tips will penetrate deeper than wider barbed points, which make a larger wound.
3. Unfletched darts create less drag and fly farther, while fletched darts are more accurate. "Hunting techniques that could consistently place the hunter within a few meters of the target would substantially reduce the need for careful design of the projectile for extended, accurate flight" (Thomas Kehoe, cited in Christenson 1986:118).
4. Projectile biface durability was a secondary consideration to accuracy, killing power, and range of weaponry.
5. Projectile neck width correlates with shaft or foreshaft diameter, with smaller diameters indicating the absence of a foreshaft. Use of a foreshaft allows for use of lighter-weight stone tips (see 1 above).

Christenson (1986:120–121) employed these principles to analyze the prehistoric projectile point sequence in the Sangamon Valley of Illinois, and below we apply his conclusions to the data from eastern Iowa to look for trends in weaponry.

When viewing the cultural sequence, consider that there are two basic methods of hafting stone tips. Side- or corner-notched bifaces can be *permanently* fastened to a split shaft by securing with pitch or blood glue and binding with crossover wrapping (Figure 14.22). Fixed to a foreshaft in this manner, the biface can be used and resharpened as a knife, scraper, or drill. The second method involves inserting a biface stem into a hollow shaft then wrapping the insertion zone to tighten the haft (Figure 14.22). This method permits rapid removal of the biface from its foreshaft (Boszhardt 2002), either to refurbish the weapon with a new tip or to allow for the tip to separate from the shaft inside the prey.

Figure 14.22. Haft reconstructions: left, side-notched hafting; right, stemmed hafting.

The wide size variation of Early Archaic projectiles in Illinois (Christenson 1986) also characterizes Iowa bifaces. Dalton is a medium-size biface with a relatively wide neck that likely was mounted by a tight binding on a dart foreshaft in the manner of other Late Paleoindian point types. Dalton points usually exhibit extensive attrition because of impact or snap fractures and resharpening (Morrow 1981b:33). Beveling and use wear are indicative of a variety of cutting, sawing, and drilling functions (Goodyear 1974); thus, Dalton points were truly all-purpose weapons and fabricating tools. Hardin and Thebes types are relatively large, heavy (20–40 g) bifaces with wide necks, indicating they were mounted on thick javelin shafts or detachable foreshafts. At this juncture, we depart somewhat from Christenson's conclusions and differentiate the functional interpretations of Thebes and Hardin types. Thebes points in Illinois and Iowa (Morrow 1981b:33) show extensive attrition on the blade although the heavy barbs often remain intact (Figure 14.23), indicating intensive use as handheld tools and less use as projectiles, when barbs would have been broken. Thebes points would have had to be tightly bound to heavy foreshafts, and we agree with Christenson (1986:120) that the heavy weight and broad blade of Thebes projectiles means they would have been effective weapons only if thrown at high velocity across a relatively short range in the early Holocene forests. In general, Thebes points likely were multipurpose handheld tools and were generalized hunting weapons only until attrition reduced them below the weight of effective projectiles. Some Iowa Hardin points also display blade resharpening, but many are missing tips, probably the result of impact fractures (Figure 14.24). The flaring shape of Hardin stems (and perhaps other infrequent types like Rice Lobed,

Figure 14.23. Early Archaic Grundy preform (left), 13LA12, and Thebes bifaces, from left to right, 13JH1003, 13IW97, 13IW199.

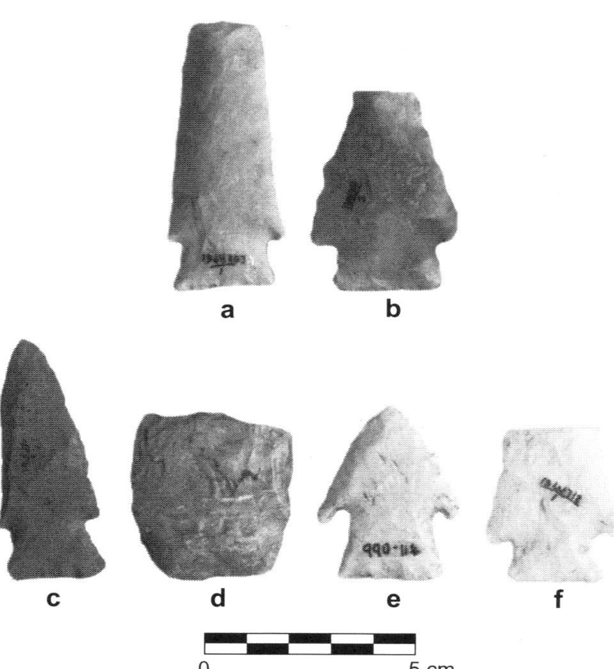

Figure 14.24. Early Archaic Hardin bifaces and one adze, 13JH1107.

Figure 14.25. Early Archaic thin corner-notched bifaces: left, St. Charles, 13DM555; above right, Kirk, 13JH622, 13HN355; below right, Cache River and Hardaway, 13LA12.

MacCorkle, and Hidden Valley) suggests hafting by insertion in a split shaft held by a temporary binding, allowing either for quick replacement of the weapon tip or for the point to detach from its shaft inside the game animal (Boszhardt 2002:58). The Hardin style seems to represent a refined version of the dart projectile design whose foremost use was as a weapon. Many sites in Iowa yielded large numbers of mostly unscathed Hardin points, perhaps because these weapons were produced in bundles for communal hunting. Other biface styles like St. Charles, Kirk, Cache River, Decatur, and so on, are much thinner (and lighter: 10–20 g) projectiles, according to Christenson, but have wide necks (Figure 14.25). They appear to have been securely hafted through corner notches, and because of their lighter weight, may have been attached to fletched dart shafts. Since fletching stabilizes flight and increases accuracy, these thin bifaces would have represented refinements of projectile design. Their thinness precludes extensive use as handheld tools that needed resharpening (Morrow 1981b:33). The evolution of Early Archaic hafted bifaces is characterized by increasingly formalized knapping sequences, careful crafting of the blade proportions and haft elements, specialized hafting adaptations, and routine attrition sequences—all indicators of specialized knapping and hunting techniques. If men exclusively were doing the hunting for large game, then obtaining quality chert and manufacturing sophisticated tools were men's tasks. This speculation leaves us wondering if women used tools like Thebes knives, if women made and used expedient flake tools, or if a gendered division of labor characterized chipped-stone production (see Nelson 1997).

By the end of the Early Archaic period, new forms of side-notched, eared bifaces came into use. Types like Graham Cave, Greenbrier, Stilwell, and Wolf Creek are relatively thick-bodied (15–40 g) styles with side-notched hafts designed to be firmly lashed to a moderately thick foreshaft or javelin (Figure 14.26). This technological format proliferated during the Middle Archaic period in types like Raddatz, Helton, Tama, Matanzas, Brannon, Osceola, Conrad, and so on. Christenson (1986:120–121) observed that many of these types have long enough blades and are thick enough to be resharpened many times, even when broken at midblade. Weight reduction through resharpening would have changed the center of mass and, therefore, the flight characteristics of the projectile. Thus, judging by the high frequency of reshaping on many of the large Middle Archaic types, the specifications for projectiles must have been at least equally balanced with the requirements for the handheld functions (i.e., more flexible design; Nelson 1997:374). As noted above, resharpening projectiles *in the haft* changes their flight characteristics; therefore, accuracy probably was not a critical aspect of these weapons. Group hunting (drives) and use of dogs are ways of compensating for reduced accuracy of darts.

Subtle differences in size (weight), blade shape, and resharpening evidence indicate that side-notched bifaces of different styles may have been designed for different functions. For instance, shorter, narrower points like Matanzas, Little

Figure 14.26. Early Archaic side-notched bifaces: left three, Wolf Creek, 13GN32, 13GN354; center two, Graham Cave, 13LE597, 13LA12; right two, Stilwell/Greenbrier, 13IW97, 13LA12.

Sioux, and Tama are relatively thick but exhibit low frequencies of resharpening (Figure 14.27). Their lighter weights derive from narrow blades and small bases, suggesting they were designed to be securely hafted to foreshafts and used primarily as projectiles, perhaps on fletched darts (Christenson 1986:116). Again, if one identifies men with hunting, then these projectiles were primarily men's tools. Jakie retained the straight-stem design of some Early Archaic types and seems to be the single example of a point that was inserted in the dart shaft and intended for dislodging inside the prey. The rest of the side-notched assemblage—Graham Cave, Greenbrier, Stilwell, and Wolf Creek from the late Early Archaic period and Raddatz, Big Sandy, Helton, Godar, Conrad, Turin, Osceola, and Brannon—are medium- to large-sized hafted bifaces with blades that are long and thick enough to absorb minor breakage and resharpening and remain functional. In Iowa, the Raddatz, Conrad, Turin, Osceola, and, probably, Wolf Creek types represent the best examples of this design, for unblemished specimens are rarely recovered. Wolf Creek bifaces always have been shortened by blade beveling (Figure 14.26), Raddatz blades are typically asymmetrical because of resharpening, and Osceola bifaces often are foreshortened by

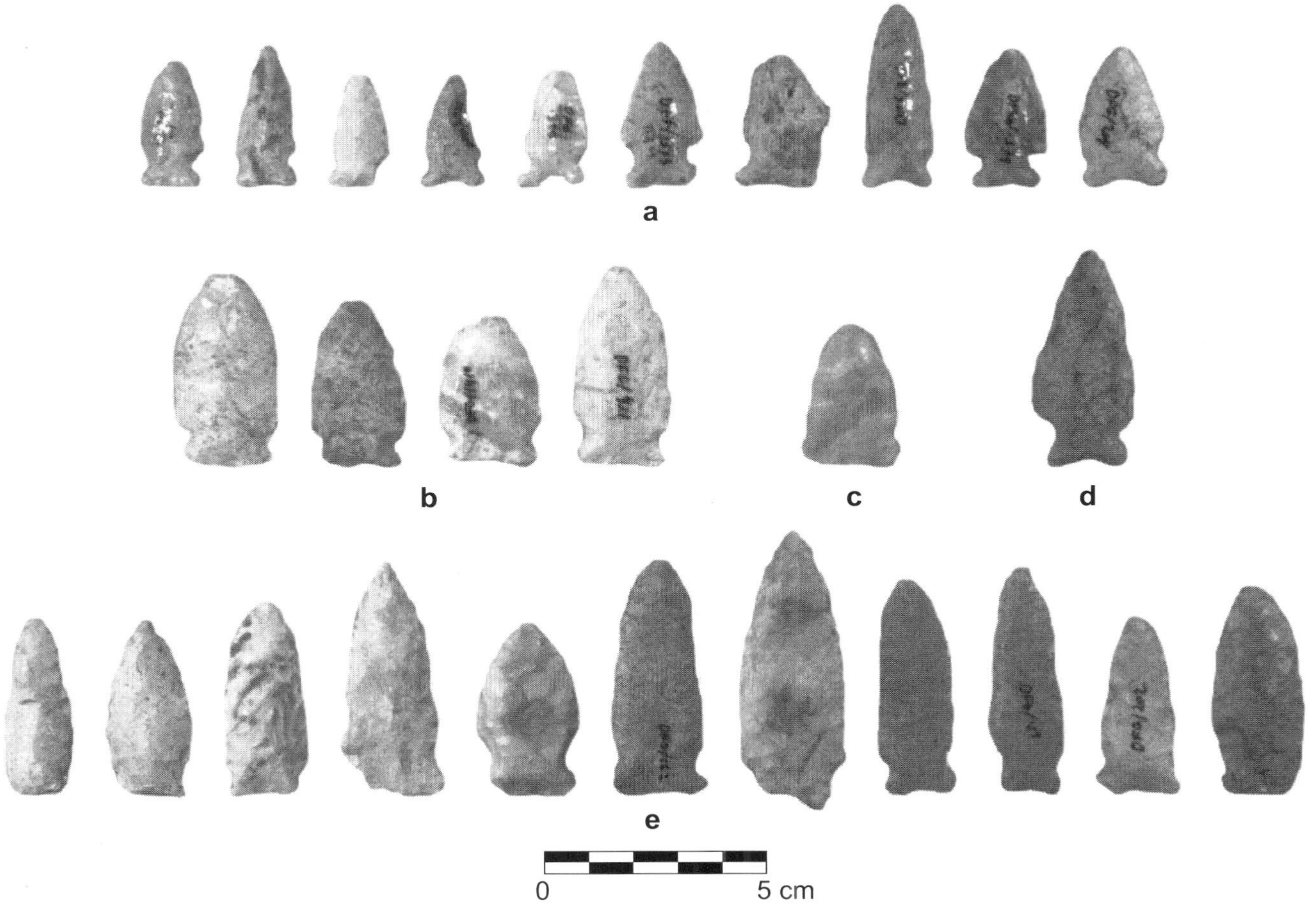

Figure 14.27. Middle Archaic bifaces: top row, Tama, 13BN512, 13LA12; middle row, left four, Brannon, 13LA12; middle row, right two, Little Sioux and Turin, 13LA12; bottom row, Matanzas, 13LA12.

resharpening if the blade is not already snapped above the haft element. These larger side-notched points were securely lashed to a foreshaft and either mounted on darts as weapons or used as handheld, multipurpose domestic tools (see Ellis 1997:53). Large side-notched bifaces also were shaped into drills and end scrapers (i.e., Logan Creek scraper, Appendix 14.A) and mounted on handles or foreshafts (Odell 1996:90, 195). End scrapers are supposed to have been women's tools; thus, it seems likely that women and men used the same kinds of large hafted bifaces. In sum, we postulate that development of a variety of transgender chipped-stone tools characterized the Middle Archaic period. The predominance of unspecialized (polymorphic) cores, probably made by men and women, is congruent with this view.

According to Christenson (1986:121), Late Archaic points in the Sangamon Valley are 30 percent smaller than points in his Middle Archaic sample. This generalization is not applicable to at least half of the Late Archaic hafted bifaces in Iowa. Stone, Ledbetter, Etley, Table Rock, Tipton, and Atalissa—all straight- or expanding-stem styles—are the same size as half or more of the Middle Archaic types, and TSN lanceolates like Karnak, Nebo Hill, Sedalia, and Wadlow are even larger (Figure 14.14). All these large bifaces date to the early half of the Late Archaic period. Other styles like Epps, Durst, Merom, Vosburg, Afton, Delhi, Springly, Mule Road, and corner-notched barbed, which fall within the latter half of this period, *are* smaller by degrees. The entire array of Late Archaic hafted bifaces is evidence for more diversity in weaponry hafting strategies than we reconstructed for the Middle Archaic period or than Christenson (1986) and Boszhardt (2002) postulated. Basically, these authors focused on size changes and concluded that diminished biface sizes indicate that small stone tips were mounted on wooden foreshafts (Boszhardt 2002:58) and may have been combined with fletched darts (Christenson 1986:121). Christenson called these fletched darts "light, fast projectiles" (1986:121), leading us to speculate that these weapons were designed for accuracy and use by lone hunters. Heavier bifaces with expanding stems used during the early Late Archaic period probably were securely mounted on foreshafts, like Middle Archaic side-notched types, for use as both projectiles and handheld tools. Very large TSN bifaces appear to have been designed for variable functions, and all four types must have been mounted on large-diameter shafts with extensive bindings. Nebo Hill bifaces are narrow and thick, making them poorly designed for cutting functions but perhaps a good design for drilling; this style may have been used predominantly as a projectile mounted directly on the dart shaft in group-hunting situations. Karnak, Sedalia, and Wadlow bifaces are wider, heavier, and exhibit more damage from use wear and resharpening than Nebo Hill. These likely were mounted on foreshafts or handles and used principally as handheld tools. Smaller Late Archaic types, especially Durst, Merom/Trimble, and Poag, exhibit little use wear and may have functioned strictly as projectiles (Boszhardt 2002). Lacking barbs, they likely were slotted in fletched dart shafts. The late-period barbed types do not evidence much resharpening but often have broken barbs, indicating they functioned as projectiles most of their use lives. Barbed styles are wide and tend to be stemmed; thus, they may have been mounted loosely in the dart shaft to facilitate detachment inside the prey animal. Following prey mortally wounded by a barbed projectile is a technique used by single or small groups of hunters (e.g., the San of Africa; Hitchcock and Bleed 1997).

The diversity of Late Archaic biface hafting and functional categories leads us to postulate that bifaces were designed for relatively (but not exclusively) specialized uses associated with the division of labor (by gender). Large and small hafted bifaces lacking much resharpening were projectiles used by men, while other large and small bifaces with resharpening were hafted in foreshafts or handles and used men and women. Women probably manufactured some of their own bifaces (they certainly must have resharpened their own tools) and (re)mounted them in handles fashioned by men. In this system, both men and women worked chipped stone in parallel patterns but for divergent functions.

Archaic Patterns in Eastern Iowa

The Archaic tradition has not been chronologically subdivided in Iowa beyond the traditional tripartite scheme of early, middle, and late periods applied in other parts of the Midwest. Current concepts of culture change are built around this borrowed chronology (Alex 2000), which is only tenuously supported by data sets and has no basis in reconstruction of culture change. Borrowed taxonomy consisting of the Middle Archaic Helton and Late Archaic Titterington phases (Brown and Vierra 1983) found application to societies in southeastern Iowa two decades ago (see Benn et al. 1987), but this taxonomy is incomplete without consideration of cultural boundaries in the rest of the state. We offer some remedies for this situation by building a cultural framework around the chronology and by developing notions of cultural processes from evidence of changes in settlement patterns and tool assemblages.

Early Archaic Period (ca. 10,000–8500 B.P.)

The current assemblage of Iowa Early Archaic sites presents a "low" archaeological profile, for more than one reason. Upland sites appear more common than we think they should be (see *Archaeological Potential in Eastern Iowa Landforms*) given the sparse population they represent (Figure 14.28), but CRM archaeologists have hesitated to commit excavation dollars to the uplands when site preservation below the plow zone is uncertain (e.g., Morrow and Artz 1997). Only one deeply buried component in alluvium has

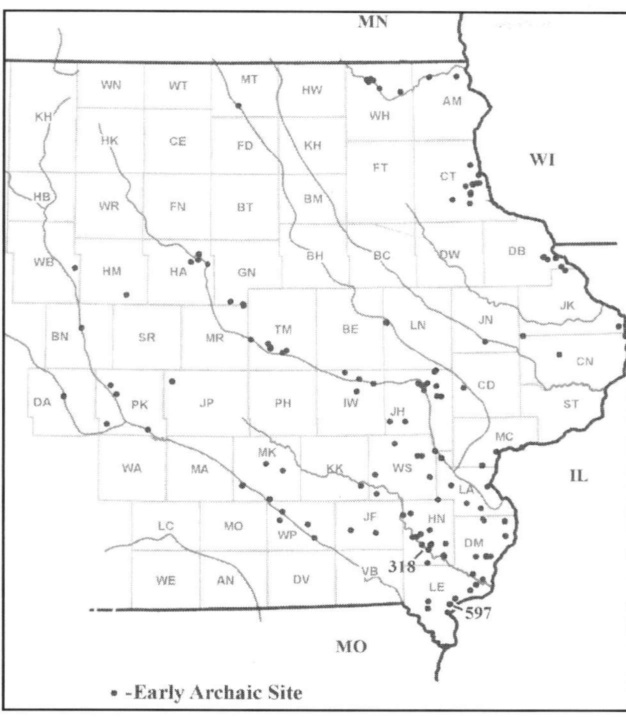

Figure 14.28. All Early Archaic–period database sites.

been excavated (Fett site; Appendix 14.C); other sites not already destroyed by stream erosion are yet to be discovered below the water table.

Dating the Dalton horizon between ca. 10,500 and 9900 B.P. (Goodyear 1982) positions it during the era of major floral changes in the upper Midwest. In eastern Iowa, spruce, larch, and fir pollen maintain a presence in coring records dating to ca. 10,000 B.P. (see *Climate Change and Environment*), then pollen of hardwood-forest species (elm, maple, basswood, ironwood, and oak) fills the record. Butternut probably preceded the hickories by about 1,000 years in the hardwood forest. No hard evidence from excavated sites in the forms of tool use wear or carbonized nutshell demonstrates a direct correlation between the appearance of the Dalton or other Archaic modes of production and the northward movement of hardwood forest in Iowa.[7] However, adequate artifact evidence demonstrates that sweeping technological changes appeared by ca. 10,000 B.P., and some of this evidence relates to exploitation of hardwood forests. Hardwood forests and their edge environments are, after all, more productive for foraging humans than boreal forests are (Odum 1971). The heavy adzes associated with early Early Archaic (and possibly Late Paleoindian) assemblages (see *Hafted Biface Styles, Distributions, and Lithic-Reduction Trajectories*) distributed along the Mississippi River trench are woodworking tools (with bit polish). Large adzes do not occur in later Archaic contexts. Eventually, use-wear analysis should show that other large flakes and bifacial tools in the Early Archaic assemblages functioned as fabricating tools for making handles, darts, and other wooden implements. Dalton, Hardin, and St. Charles sites occur along the Mississippi trench and some of its larger tributaries in central and southeastern Iowa, which we take to be indications of the northward diffusion of this technology through the state as the hardwood forest became established. Paleoindians had been present in Iowa (Anderson and Tiffany 1972), but early Early Archaic sites far outnumber Paleoindian sites, such that some northward population movement is inferred. A Dalton point made from Crowley's Ridge chert (from northeastern Arkansas), found by a private collector in the Mississippi Valley below Muscatine, reveals this movement (Bettis et al. 1990).

One issue we do not resolve in this chapter is whether lanceolate hafted-biface styles persisted during the Early Archaic period. Alex (2000:58) depicted broad-bladed bifaces like Browns Valley and Angostura as part of the assemblage postdating St. Charles and Thebes, and Morrow (1984b:28) placed the Meserve type in the Early Archaic period. The senior author has observed stubby Burroughs-type (Morrow 1984b:21) bifaces in collections of mixed Archaic forms from Saylorville Lake in central Iowa (Benn and Rogers 1985:Figure A2). None of these lanceolate styles have been recovered from stratigraphic or dated contexts in a demonstrable association with the Early Archaic period, nor do any use-wear studies demonstrate lanceolate bifaces from Early Archaic sites were utilized as projectiles instead of merely being Stage 3–4 preforms. Observe, for instance, the range of lanceolate, stemmed, and faint-side-notched forms from the Matanzas component at the Fett site (Figure 14.29). The dating of these forms is an important issue, because lanceolate bifaces require different hafting methods (implying different functions) than side- or corner-notched bifaces.

Figure 14.29. Varieties of Matanzas bifaces, 13LE597.

By the time large side-notched styles (Graham Cave, MacCorkle, and Wolf Creek) appeared after ca. 8800 B.P., hunting territories in Iowa were "filling," judging by the dispersal of sites throughout the interior valleys of eastern Iowa. We postulate that an indigenous population adopted new projectile/knife forms by borrowing technical ideas from outside the state and applying those notions to local raw materials (chert). The question arises, why change hafting styles? An answer might lie in the turn toward a broad-spectrum subsistence base that hunters and gatherers were making by the end of the Early Archaic period (Brown and Vierra 1983; Odell 1996:9–11). Odell reasoned that the lithic-tool assemblage was diversified as people settled for longer intervals in temporary base camps (see Shott 1986:29). The rigid hafting of large, thick, side-notched bifaces made these tools useful for an array of functions as knives, scrapers, drills, and so on, that could be resharpened *in the haft* (Odell 1994) in addition to performing a generalized projectile function.

Middle Archaic Period (ca. 8500–4500 B.P.)

A continuum of projectile point forms distinguishes the heart of the Middle Archaic period in eastern Iowa, including Big Sandy, Matanzas, Godar, Osceola/Hemphill, Raddatz, Turin, Conrad, Brewerton, Brannon, Tama, Helton, and Little Sioux (see Appendix 14.A). Ed's Meadow (13DM712) in Des Moines County (Figure 14.30) is the only excavated site to yield a Jakie Stemmed point from a Middle Archaic context

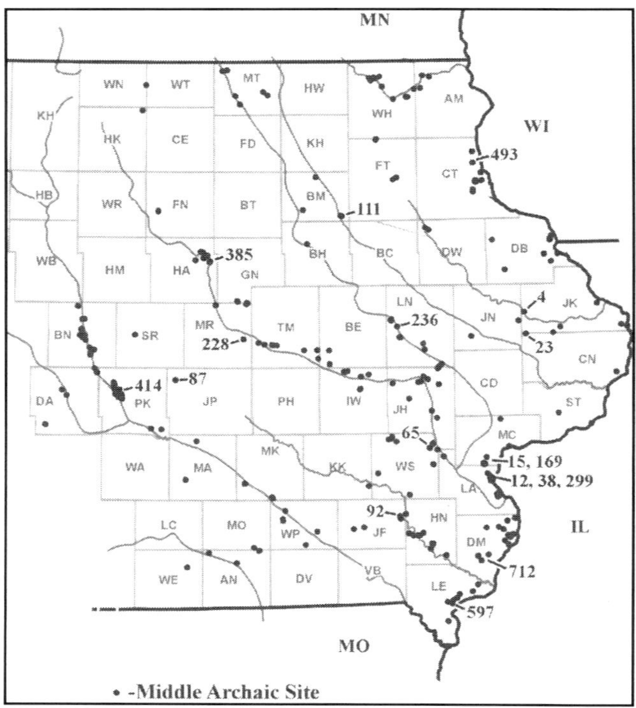

Figure 14.30. All Middle Archaic–period database sites.

(Morrow 1998). Jakies are otherwise very rare in Iowa as are large stemmed (e.g., Hidden Valley) and small bifurcate-stemmed (e.g., LeCroy) points. Broad corner-notched bifaces like MacCorkle, along with Jakie and LeCroy, might be indicators of a very early Middle Archaic horizon, but no excavated material confirms this in Iowa. Instead, small and medium-size side-notched types like Tama, Raddatz, and Little Sioux are widespread (Figures 14.11, 14.12) and appear to represent the initial dominance of the side-notched technology tradition. Examples of these types in context are a Raddatz point recovered beneath the Matanzas component at the Garden site (13DB493) that predates ca. 4300 B.C. (Benn 2007); a Tama basal fragment from beneath the Matanzas component at the Fett site (13LE597); a Raddatz basal fragment at Ed's Meadow (13DM712) associated with FCR on which Morrow (1998:30) obtained a TL date of 5316 B.C.; and a broken, small side-notched point (Little Sioux?) from a deeply buried bivouac habitation at Sweet Jane Fan (13BN279) associated with a date of 5115 B.C. (Benn 1986:42). Tama and Raddatz styles were made throughout the middle of the Middle Archaic period, when a full range of styles like Matanzas, Big Sandy, Brewerton, Brannon, and Turin appeared in a horizon coeval with the Helton phase (Cook 1976) in Illinois. We are wary, however, of naming a cultural phase for Iowa without geographic site coverage.

Geologic contexts are crucial with regard to dating the Early–Middle Archaic transition (Bettis and Hajic 1995). At the Fett site (13LE597), the authors excavated through a 3-m-thick Gunder Member terrace, a sediment package assumed to span the Holocene era, ca. 9000–2000 B.P. (Bettis and Hallberg 1985). The Matanzas component proved to be the most intensive Archaic occupation in this stratified site, while earlier Tama and Graham Cave components had lighter artifact scatters. Traceable in the Fett sequence, and complicating interpretation of the cultural record, is the DeForest Gap (Bettis and Autin 1997; Thompson and Bettis 1982), an early phase of the Gunder record that involved voiding or deflation of the sedimentary record in certain reaches of small valleys. The Early–Middle Archaic boundary spanned that gap in eastern Iowa; thus, a datable sedimentary record is unavailable in many terraces for calculating the relative density of artifacts in Early Archaic components. By contrast, the Middle Archaic period was a time of heavy sedimentation in Midwest valleys (Bettis and Hajic 1995; Bettis et al. 1996), so remains of this period are well preserved at Fett, McNeal Fan (13MC15), Sand Run West (13LA38), Garden (13DB493), Allen Fan (13HA385; Appendix 14.C), and numerous other sites. At McNeal Fan, the late Middle Archaic component was 2 m below surface and the ca. 6000 B.P. component was 6 m below surface (Artz 1995:40). The deeper component probably is well preserved but is too deeply buried to reach during a CRM project with finite funding!

Because of geologic contextual problems, we maintain skepticism about the perceived correlation between the proliferation of Middle Archaic habitation sites in large river valleys and the eastward advance of the Prairie Peninsula (Odell 1996:10). In her review of Iowa prehistory, Alex (2000:68) does not promote this correlation, citing the bison-hunting campsites around glacial lakes (see Lensink 1984) as an adaptation to the prairie in north-central Iowa. Nevertheless, the upland highway-survey data cited above (*Archaeological Potential in Eastern Iowa Landforms*) gave the Early Archaic period a higher proportion (19 percent) of sites than the Middle Archaic period (8 percent), which was twice as long. This is a proxy indicator that Middle Archaic settlement gravitated toward river valleys, and certainly the big Middle Archaic sites are situated within large river valleys. The critical time span is ca. 7600–6000 B.P., when, pollen cores show, prairie species and burr oak trees increased dramatically in eastern Iowa (see *Climate Change and Environment*). Side-notched hafting of bifaces appears to have become the dominant technology at this time, but only one excavated base camp with side-notched bifaces supports this proposition. This is the Garden site (13DB493), a warm-season base camp that yielded a slim assemblage (because of preservation problems) of forest and riparian resources (Benn 2007).

Mid–Middle Archaic habitation sites are distinctive because they contain large numbers and varieties of lithic tools (see *Hafted Biface Styles, Distributions, and Lithic-Reduction Trajectories*). Private collectors know this by the great numbers of side-notched points, grooved axes, and other commercially valued relics gleaned from plowed sites. Archaeologists have reacted to this high visibility by recording more Middle Archaic components (n = 262, Appendix 14.A; Figure 14.30) than components of other periods in Iowa. Most of the sites are multicomponent, and either too little digging has been done or the sites are too mixed to be certain about the habits of the inhabitants. Middle Archaic points noted in CRM site records include the Little Sioux point from Keystone Rock Shelter (13JK23; Anderson 1987); Raddatz and Osceola points from the Levsen Rock Shelter (13JK4; Marcucci et al. 1993); Raddatz-style bifaces from open site 13BH30 (Billeck 1987); Raddatz, Tama, and Matanzas points from 13BM111 (Thompson 1996); a Big Sandy point from 13AM1 (Stanley 1993); Helton and Turin points from 13LN236 (Perry 1985, 1991); Raddatz and Osceola points from Merrimac Mills (13JF92; Finn 1981, 1982); and Matanzas, Turin, and Brannon types from 13MC169 (Blikre 2003:23–24). Archaeologists have not yet figured out how to mine these kinds of site records for insightful cultural reconstructions.

The mixed-context issue is particularly problematic with regard to grooved axes and other elaborate ground-stone objects. "Thousands" of grooved axes have been found on the surface of Iowa (Filbrandt 1997; Keyes 1931), but a very small number have been excavated by professionals and most come from mixed contexts (e.g., Blikre 2003:38, 44). Only the half-grooved Keokuk type and three-quarter-grooved axes from the McNeal Fan Osceola component (Figure 14.31) have been securely dated, to ca. 2850 ± 100 B.C. (Thompson 2006:131). A well-made three-quarter-grooved ax from 1.6 m below surface in the Des Moines River cutbank at 13PK414 was associated with a carbon date of 4005 B.C. (Benn 1983; Benn and Harris 1983:20, 84). Morrow (1998:12–13) suggested that the full-grooved form constituted the initial ax design (during the Early or early Middle Archaic period?) followed by the round-polled, three-quarter-grooved and, then, the flat-polled, three-quarter and half-grooved styles—all distributed mainly in southeastern Iowa. As for northeastern and central Iowa, the senior author combed the Keyes

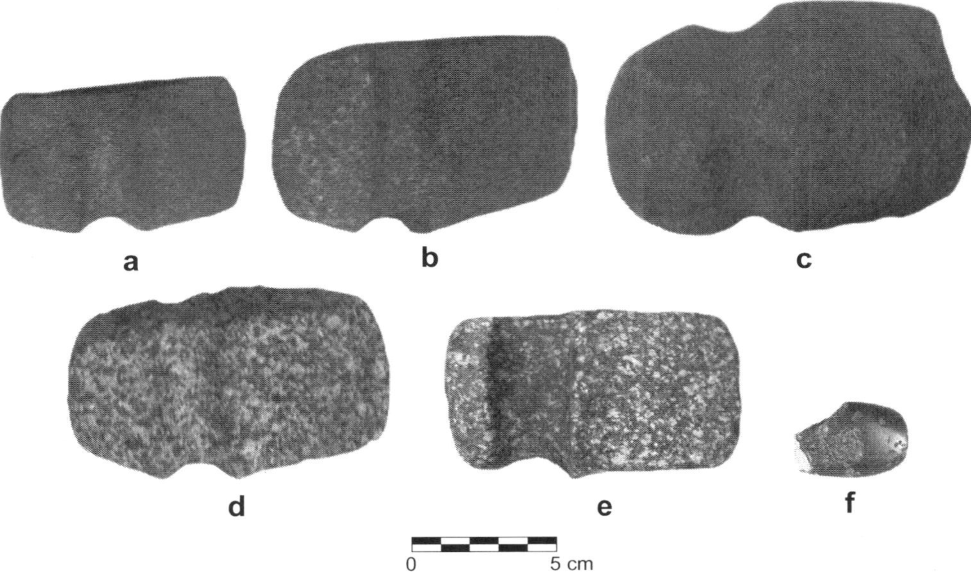

Figure 14.31. Ax styles: a,b,d, three-quarter grooved; c, full-grooved (Tama Co., Keyes Collection); e, half-grooved Keokuk, 13MC15; f, hematite ax, 13JP87.

Collection at the OSA for a sample of axes and located a total of 51 examples from six counties (Figure 14.31). Nine of these (18 percent) were full grooved (all but one had round polls), 40 (78 percent) were three quarter grooved, of which more than twice as many had flat as opposed to fluted edges, and only two (4 percent) were vaguely half grooved. The three-quarter-grooved category contained a high proportion of well-made or polished axes with flat or fluted edges. Did changes in shape and finish constitute refinements in ax design to increase functional effectiveness, or were finely crafted axes a form of surplus production?

Does the term *surplus* also apply to bannerstones, plummets, hematite objects, and galena crystals? Galena is not common in Archaic contexts, and a piece from the Sand Run West site is the only excavated crystal known to occur outside the source region around Dubuque. Only one bannerstone fragment has been professionally excavated. It is also from Sand Run West, from the Middle Archaic Stratum III (Benn et al. 1987). Private collectors find "bowtie" bannerstones in southeastern Iowa, such as the examples from Monroe (Spears 1979:2) and Johnson (Anonymous 1977:10) counties. The authors' search of the Keyes Collection at the OSA turned up five "bowtie" bannerstones (Figure 14.32), four from Tama County and one from Benton County (associated with a Thebes point?)—all within the Iowa River valley. A possible "tube" bannerstone (Anonymous 1977:10) also came from Tama County. Elaborate ground-stone objects, notably Keokuk and other polished axes as well as bannerstones, represent a significant labor investment, perhaps the most substantial for all late Middle Archaic tool types. Morrow (1981) produced axes experimentally, making a rounded full-grooved ax in 2.5 hours and a small, more refined three-quarter-grooved ax in six hours. Larger axes and more polishing would require 10–15 hours. Social "value" (i.e., power, influence, obligation, etc.) is embedded in this kind of "surplus" labor. The Keokuk ax and "bowtie" bannerstone distribution covers the southeastern quadrant of Iowa, while adjacent portions of west-central Illinois and northeastern Missouri also have Keokuk axes (Filbrandt 1997). This distribution pattern nearly matches that of the Helton biface style (Figure 14.13). Was this region a zone of cultural interaction involving the exchange of specific styles of surplus objects?

The rest of the cobble assemblage from mid–Middle Archaic sites consists of minimally shaped and expedient tools like hammerstones, manos, grinders, pounders, anvils, and so on, and large amounts of FCR. While quantification of these tools for comparison with sites of other culture periods is problematic given the small excavated sample, in general terms, a huge increase is observable in the numbers of cobble tools and the weights of FCR in Middle Archaic sites. Early Archaic surface scatters encountered during highway surveys have produced barely noticeable amounts of FCR (Benn and Bowers 1994; Morrow and Artz 1997). Excavation at the Overberg site yielded only 16 pieces of FCR (Fiedel et al. 2004), and the Fett site (13LE597) produced handfuls of small pieces of FCR. Except for hammerstones and an occasional mano, cobble tools seem to be few in number and type on Early Archaic sites. The tabulations of all lithic tool categories in Table 14.1 reveal that cobble tools occur in densities approaching or higher than cores or bifaces in all of the Middle Archaic sites except Garden (13DB493). But, the Garden site is situated in the Paleozoic Plateau region,

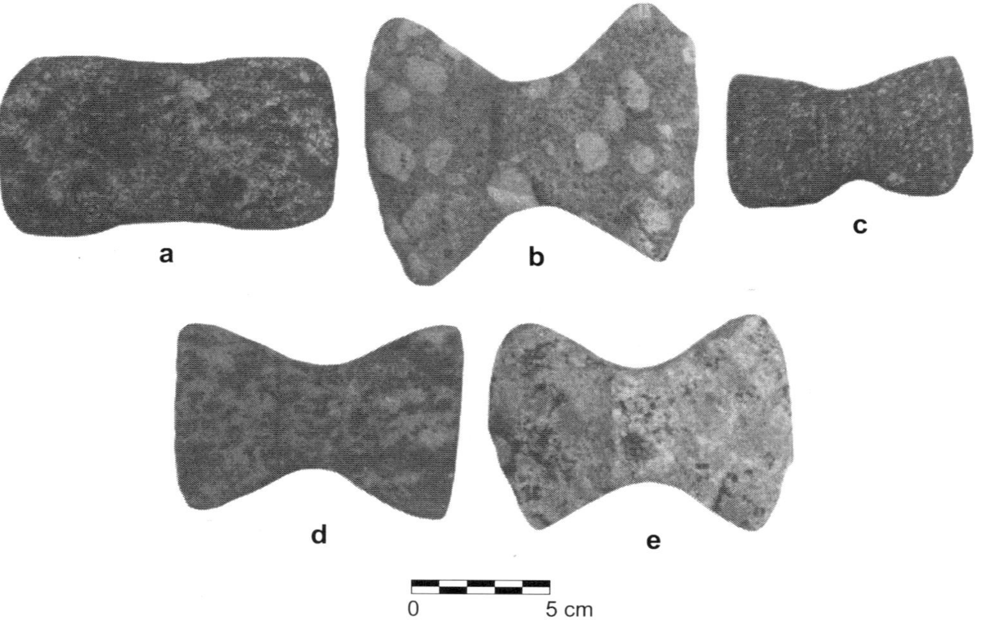

Figure 14.32. Bannerstones (Keyes Collection): a, TA67k; b, TA49k; c, TM107; d, TM260; e, BE248; BE248 and TM107 not drilled; TM107 also double-bitted (ax?); other three partially drilled.

where glacial rocks, the usual raw material for cobble tools and FCR, are not available in significant amounts. Add elaborate ground-stone tools to the Middle Archaic cobble assemblage, and it is clear that a great deal of labor was expended in the procurement, shaping, and use of glacial cobbles to process foods and fabricate other kinds materials like bone, wood, hematite, and fiber. We view proliferation of a cobble-tool industry as a labor strategy for expanding the range of exploitable resources (i.e., diversification) as well as increasing the efficiency (i.e., specialization) of processing natural and cultivated resources.

Other indications exist of site specialization in the Middle Archaic period. Collins (1995; Collins et al. 1991) examined a large assemblage of freehand cores, bipolar cores, decortication and primary flakes, hammerstones, anvils, and early-stage bifaces at the Bash site (13MR228), a multicomponent Maynes Creek quarry in Marshall County (Figure 14.2). Significant quarries must also be present within the Burlington-chert region of southeastern Iowa (see Collins and Zalucha 1997), but quarry sites have not been systematically investigated in Iowa. Fishel (Fishel et al. 2000; Fishel et al. 2003) reported on a bone-grease manufacturing station apparently associated with a base camp at the Allen Fan (13HA385) in Hardin County. This station produced large numbers of bifaces, few cores and projectile points, and considerable numbers of hammerstones, metates, and FCR. If bison and elk were common ungulates of the mid-Holocene prairies in east-central Iowa, then kill sites and meat- and grease-processing camps exist and await excavation.

Enough information has accumulated to identify a late Middle Archaic phase for southeastern Iowa. The *Van Buren phase* is named for the county on the Des Moines River where the largest number of recorded Keokuk axes has been found (Filbrandt 1997:xii). The Keokuk ax itself is not the basis for the definition of this phase; rather, Van Buren County is near the center of the distributions of several distinctive artifacts. Component IId at McNeal Fan (13MC15; Thompson 2006) and Stratum III at Sand Run West (13LA38; Benn et al. 1987) are typical Van Buren–phase base camps with dense artifact middens, large roasting pits, and large, oval house patterns (at McNeal Fan; Appendix 14.C). Both sites are positioned near backwaters and may have been occupied year-round. Aside from deer, raccoons, and nuts, the diet of the sites' occupants probably included significant amounts of aquatic foods (fish, turtles, muskrat, beaver, wild rice, and mussels[?]), birds (turkey and aquatic species), and mostly wild versions of starchy and oily seeds. Other large sites (e.g., 13LA12 and 13LA299) have been recorded as surface scatters on fans and in the floodplain of the Mississippi Valley between Muscatine and Burlington. Van Buren sites likely occur as much as 100 miles up major tributaries like the Des Moines, Skunk, and Iowa-Cedar rivers, and judging by the distribution of Keokuk axes, sites of this phase will be identified in western Illinois (Hemphill?) and northeastern Missouri. Characteristic Van Buren artifacts include large, side-notched hafted bifaces (Godar, Helton, and Osceola types), winged drills, hafted end scrapers, well-made three-quarter-grooved and Keokuk axes, hematite items, bannerstones, and probably other specialized ground-stone tools like pestles. The proportions of other biface types in this assemblage, like Raddatz, Matanzas, Brannon, and, possibly, Wadlow stemmed, are uncertain. The cluster of 11 flexed burials, including subadults and both genders, within the Sand Run West habitation (Benn et al. 1992) is the only known cemetery, although bluff-top cemeteries are suspected on the basis of artifact finds by private collectors around the mouth of the Iowa River (see Benn et al. 1988). Most of the calibrated radiocarbon dates from McNeal Fan and Sand Run West fall between 2920 and 2685 B.C., so it seems reasonable to bracket the Van Buren phase between 3000 and 2500 B.C. The Van Buren phase postdated the Helton phase as it is known in the southern Illinois River valley (Cook 1976:69) and probably is manifested in some form in eastern Iowa (e.g., Garden site). Van Buren was contemporary with the Hemphill phase of west-central Illinois (Benchley et al. 1997:74; Conrad 1981). Perhaps a variant (Green 1996) should be named to encompass the Van Buren and Hemphill phases. The variant taxon also could be applied to the Helton and Titterington manifestations in the Midwest.

Late Archaic Period (ca. 4500–2500 B.P.)

Two hundred sixty-two Middle Archaic sites are listed in Appendix 14.A but only 206 Late Archaic sites (Figure 14.33).

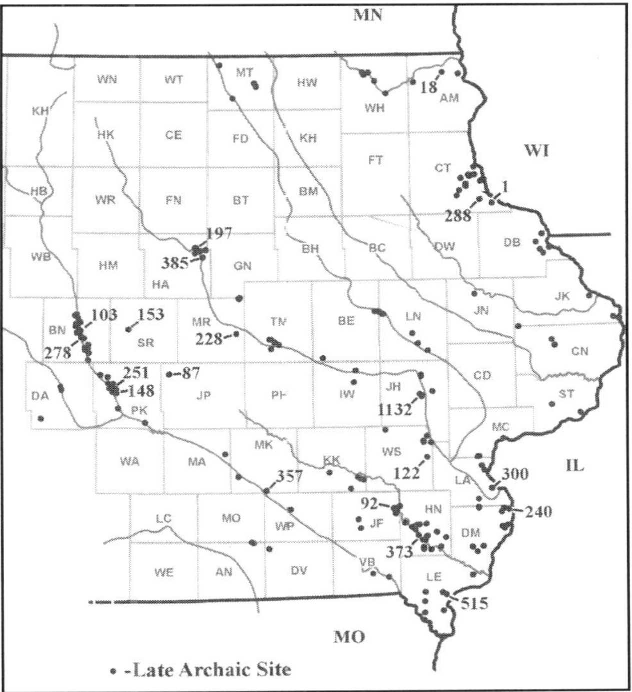

Figure 14.33. All Late Archaic–period database sites.

Although the Middle Archaic period was twice as long as the Late Archaic, if the Late Archaic population was increasing, then these numbers should be more equal. The independent variable impeding efforts to identify a reliable sample of Late Archaic sites is, again, their geomorphic context within the voluminous mid- to late Holocene sediment package (Bettis and Hajic 1995:Table 2). The same sedimentation episode buried Middle Archaic sites. It follows that buried Middle and Late Archaic sites should be archaeologically visible in roughly the same proportions, but not *if Late Archaic components were smaller and more dispersed* on low terraces in large valleys (Benn et al. 1989), in smaller tributary valleys (Bettis and Hajic 1995: Table 1), and throughout the uplands (see *Archaeological Potential in Eastern Iowa Landforms*). One example of the influence of geomorphic processes has been documented by large-scale surveys on the floor of the upper Mississippi Valley of Iowa and Illinois (Benn et al. 1989:174; Benn et al. 1988:143). During the fieldwork, dozens of Middle and Late Archaic projectile points were viewed in private collections obtained from the surfaces of high (old) terraces, fans, and the uplands, and it was not difficult to locate some of those Middle Archaic habitations on fans and the floodplain. Almost 20 years later, archaeologists are still looking for equally conspicuous Late Archaic habitation sites. It was outcrops of Archaic materials in cutbanks—a piece of FCR here, a biface or grooved ax there—and occasional radiocarbon dates (e.g., 13CT228 [Green 1988a, 1988b, 1990]; 13LA300 [Benn 1998]) that told a story of small, deeply buried Late Archaic components in the floodplain. Alluvial burial also is a common occurrence in smaller valleys of northeastern Iowa (Bettis and Hallberg 1985) and southern Iowa (Ray and Benn 1988). Many Late Archaic components rest below the water table for most of the year (e.g., 13JH1132; Appendix 14.C). In terms of CRM investigations, water-table components tend to be "out of sight, out of planning" (Thompson and Bettis 1982).

The variety of hafted-biface styles from surface collections and sites tested or excavated in the last 20 years (e.g., Anderson 1987; Benn 2005; Blikre 2003; Finn 1981; Green 1988b; Lensink 1986; Thompson 1999) has provided barely enough information to subdivide the Late Archaic period stylistically into four horizons (technological complexes) with vague chronological and regional parameters (Benn et al. 1987). Alex (2000:73–74) summarized the four complexes with respect to their artifact inventories and settlement characteristics. We take this opportunity to critique and revise this cultural sequence, first by moving what now is called the "Van Buren phase" (above) from the Late Archaic period, where it has languished uncomfortably, to the late Middle Archaic period.

The Late Archaic artifact inventory dating to the time span of ca. 4500–3800 B.P. does not constitute a distinctive technical complex because it includes little excavated material from unmixed contexts. Hafted-biface types likely consisted of modified side-notched forms developed from Middle Archaic technology, of which the stemmed forms are the most difficult to pin down chronologically. For instance, Morrow (1984b:46) placed the stemmed, notched Atalissa style at the end of the Late Archaic period and in the Early Woodland period, but we suspect some form of Atalissa dates earlier, along with other types like Tipton stemmed, Fort Dodge side notched, and Conrad side notched. These four types have similar distributions (Figure 14.34) across a large area of east-central Iowa, and Atalissa points often co-occur with other Archaic styles (see Appendix 14.A). An assemblage of Fort Dodge, Motley, and Conrad types was recovered from mixed contexts at Brassica Bench (13PK251 and 13PK251W), where the earliest TL and radiocarbon dates were (respectively) 1290 B.C. and 2670 B.C. (Benn 1986; Osborn and Gradwohl 1981). The Fort Dodge biface from the Buchanan site (13SR153) was found in the stratum bracketed by dates ranging from 3400 to 3200 B.P. (Alex 2000:74), and three Conrad points came from Level 6 at 13PK149, which produced a radiocarbon date of 975 B.C. (Osborn and Gradwohl 1981:131). Thus, available dates for these notched and stemmed styles span most of the period. Other artifact types have equally problematic time horizons. For instance, Morrow (1998:12–13) proposed that flat- or trough-bottomed ("fluted") three-quarter-grooved axes were being made at this time.

A mid–Late Archaic technical complex for which there is some contextual information is distinguished by the Wadlow, Karnak, Sedalia, Etley/Ledbetter, and Nebo Hill biface styles. Archaeological records have been muddied by instances of

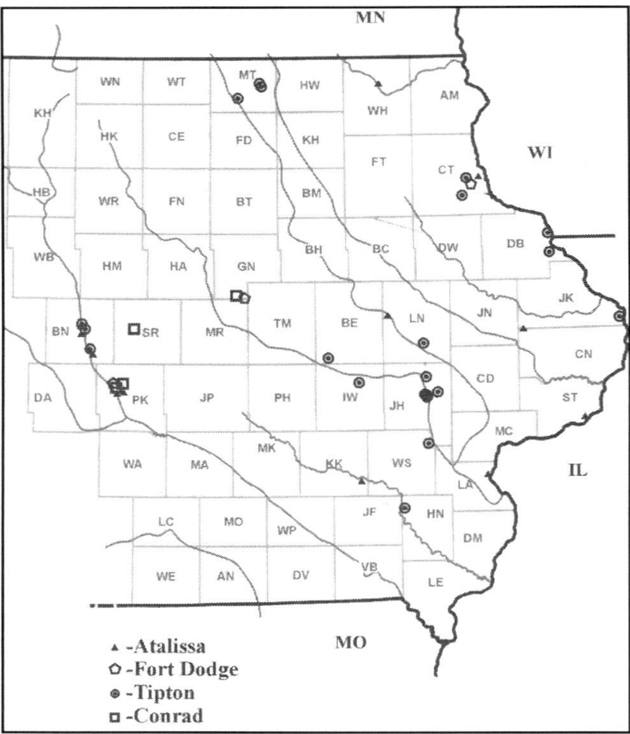

Figure 14.34. Distributions of problematic Middle–Late Archaic bifaces: Atalissa, Fort Dodge, Tipton, and Conrad.

classificatory confusion among the late Paleoindian lanceolate points and preforms and the Wadlow and Sedalia styles. Additionally, the Wadlow type, which also may have been a preform for the Etley type (Banks 2002), apparently developed during the late Middle Archaic period, for it shows up in the Helton phase in Illinois (Cook 1976), and one Wadlow biface was recovered from the Osceola component at McNeal Fan (13MC15; Thompson 2006). The Late Archaic lanceolate-biface complex was coeval with the Sedalia phase (Chapman 1975; Harl 1998; Seelen 2002) and Nebo Hill phase (O'Brien and Wood 1998:122) in Missouri and the Titterington phase in Illinois (Benchley et al. 1997:74; Cook 1976) and has been designated the Titterington-Sedalia-Nebo Hill (TSN) culture in the American Bottom (McElrath et al. 1993:150). The problem with naming an indigenous phase for the TSN complex in Iowa is that no site with an array of the diagnostic tools has been recorded or excavated. Diagnostic artifacts often occur one per site. A date of 1135 B.C. came from a knapper's activity area with Sedalia/Wadlow bifaces at the Riley site (13HN373; Foradas 2004), a Sedalia point from the west lobe of the Allen Fan was associated with a date of 3440 B.C. (Collins 1990), and a Sedalia point occurred within the stratum bracketed at 3000–3500 B.P. at the Buchanan site (13SR153; Alex 2000:74; Hainlin 1992). Recently, the authors obtained a date of 2290 B.C. from a Sedalia house site at 13LE628. Some candidate sites have been recorded that could fill the TSN bill: For example, site 13HA197 has produced a Clear Fork gouge and Sedalia "digger" (Collins 1990), site 13DM240 has yielded an array of bifaces and other tools (Benn et al. 1988), and Sedalia and Nebo Hill points have been recovered from site 13LE515 (Morrow and Artz 1997). All three sites are situated on benches or terraces within large river valleys. A look at the biface distribution map (Figure 14.17) suggests the TSN complex, including the Stone Square Stemmed type, is spread across southeastern Iowa, especially along the Des Moines, Skunk, Mississippi, and Iowa-Cedar valleys as far upstream as Hardin County (Collins 1990). This distribution includes the region of Burlington and Keokuk chert outcrops—favored materials for diagnostic tools of the TSN complex. Artifact types believed to be part of this complex include bifacial drills, Sedalia "diggers," gouges, heavy end scrapers, three-quarter-grooved axes, abraded hematite, grinding equipment, a wide array of cobble tools, bannerstones, probably plummets, and occasional Stone Square Stemmed and Smith Basal Notched bifaces (Alex 2000:73; Benn et al. 1988). How many of the Late Archaic lanceolate bifaces actually were hafted is an open question. Broad-bladed forms like Wadlow and Sedalia are large enough to have been handheld or hafted for use as knives that could be resharpened. By the same reasoning, Nebo Hill appears to have been designed as a projectile tip, being too narrow to allow for much resharpening. Late Archaic lanceolates constitute an assemblage of multiple-use tools appropriate for the activities of both genders. Specialized dart tips may not have been commonly used.

A second stylistic horizon dating within the latter half of the Late Archaic period is represented by a range of stemmed biface styles, including Table Rock, Tipton, Poag, Durst, and Merom/Trimble (Benn et al. 1988). This complex, at least the Durst assemblage, conforms stylistically and chronologically to the Durst phase in Wisconsin (Stoltman 1986). In northeastern Iowa, testing at 13CT228, a multicomponent site buried in the Turkey River floodplain, produced a Durst Stemmed point associated with a date of 785 B.C. (Green 1988b:254, 1990). At 13BN103 in the central Des Moines River valley, a soil buried approximately 1.5 m below surface yielded two Durst points and a radiocarbon date of 2465 B.C. (Osborn and Gradwohl 1981:599), although this site also produced lanceolate points of the Karnak style along with other Archaic types. Twenty-one Table Rocks and one Tipton point were recovered from the Davis Creek site (13WS122; Lensink 1986:178), and the TL date of 1650 B.C. from a roasting feature was judged to be more reliable (for technical reasons) than a younger radiocarbon date (Lensink 1986:198–199). Most of the 21 Table Rock bifaces brought to this seasonal base camp were used as projectiles, yet the collection also included 57 unfinished bifaces—most made on-site—three end scrapers, and 43 flake tools. Three smaller versions of the Table Rock style were associated with a date of 680 B.C. from the Late Archaic component at the Allen Fan (13HA385) in the central Iowa River valley (Fishel et al. 2003). The last available date, of 1815 B.C. (Beta-179291, unpublished), was derived recently from the Edgewater Park site (13JH1132) in the Iowa River floodplain, where Table Rock points, a Tipton point, and stemmed styles resembling the Genesee/Saratoga style were recovered (Johnson, 2003:5).

A third stylistic horizon is recognized by small to medium-size stemmed bifaces with conspicuous barbs, like Vosburg, Delhi, Springly, Mule Road, possibly Afton, Apple Blossom Stemmed, and an unnamed stubby, corner-notched style with flaring barbs (Figure 14.19). Several examples of barbed points, grouped under the Pelican Lake type by the analyst (Hainlin 1992:54) but conforming to Late Archaic styles, were recovered from a stratum dating to 500 B.C. at the Buchanan site (13SR153). A barb from an unknown corner-notched version was dated at 2675 B.C. in a sealed bivouac habitation at 13BN278 (Benn 1986:119). In the American Bottom, a comparable manifestation, the Prairie Lake phase (ca. 1100–700 B.C.; McElrath et al. 1984:49–58; Fortier et al. 1998:210), is distinguished by Dyroff, Springly, Mo-Pac, and Apple Blossom points with stems and barbed shoulders, along with celts, grinding stones, plummets, galena, and worked hematite. No Iowa sites have been excavated with similar assemblages, and plummets are extremely rare in the state.

The western Great Lakes manifestation known as the Old Copper complex is identified by heavy, socketed tools (adzes and projectiles), awls, fishhooks, spatulas, crescent knives, and bracelets made of native copper from northern Michigan (Pleger 2000). Most of this material belongs to the

Late Archaic period, although ages from the copper region are being pushed into the Middle Archaic period (see Pleger and Stoltman, this volume). Scattered Old Copper artifacts have been found mostly in northeastern Iowa (Alex 2000:75); unrelated copper awls and adzes have turned up in Woodland mounds and Oneota burials (Logan 1976). While a few copper objects probably were traded into Archaic societies in eastern Iowa, the numbers are not sufficient and the proveniences are too unclear to justify extending the Old Copper–culture taxon to Iowa. Eventually, researchers may learn about the social context of these trade items.

Look back now at the Late Archaic period discussion and consider the distribution patterns of all hafted-biface styles to evaluate the integrity of each horizon style. The TSN complex dating to the early half of this period is distributed along the Mississippi River and up the large river valleys in southeastern Iowa, concentrated around the Burlington-chert outcrops in Jefferson, Henry, and Des Moines counties (Figure 14.17). This pattern looks like it represents an interacting population (e.g., ethnic group, tribe, or part of a confederacy), but no one has yet excavated a complete assemblage that would justify a new phase name for Iowa. Another distinct pattern shows up in the distribution of the terminal Late Archaic barbed styles, which occur in extreme southeastern Iowa (Figure 14.16) and probably extend into Illinois and Missouri. Barbed styles occur in the American Bottom (McElrath et al. 1984), suggesting the technology producing these points was part of an interaction sphere. The distributions of various stemmed-biface styles dating to the latter half of the Late Archaic period coalesce in a broad pattern across all of eastern Iowa (Figures 14.15, 14.18). The Table Rock style tends to be distributed across the southwestern half of this area, while the Durst style clusters toward the northeast. The Tipton style is scattered between Table Rock and Durst distributions, while Poag and Merom/Trimble cover central Iowa. All of these patterns correlate roughly with the landform regions of Iowa, raising the possibility that each industrial complex represented specific adaptations to regional resources. The dichotomy between Durst and Table Rock types amounts to *size*, and Tipton points are merely variants of these two styles. Poag and Merom/Trimble probably were mounted on hollow shafts, a slightly different hafting technology than used for Durst and Table Rock.

The cultural manifestation filling the transition from the Archaic to the Early Woodland period is the Red Ocher complex. In northeastern Iowa, Red Ocher mound burial merges into the Ryan phase (Logan 1976), whose associated habitation sites have produced Marion Thick pottery (Benn and Stadler 2004). More examples of Red Ocher sites have been found in southern Wisconsin (see Boszhardt et al. 1986; Stoltman 1986), where typical traits include communal burials; instances of mound building; and offerings of exotic materials like heavy copper beads and celts, stone gorgets, galena, marine shell beads, and layers of red ferric pigment (ocher). These traits were seen at three of the Turkey River mounds (13CT1) in Clayton County, where diagnostic artifacts included a ground-stone bar amulet, a copper "dagger" (see also the copper "bar" from Ryan Mound 4 [Orr 1936:103]), and marine-shell beads (Green and Schermer 1988). The headless central burial (No. 4) in Turkey River Mound 37 was associated with charcoal that assayed to 2550 ± 60 B.P. (WIS-2049; William Green, pers. comm. 1989). This date is very close to the "suspect" solid carbon result of 2500 ± 250 B.P. (M-308) from Mound 43 at Sny Magill (13AM18; Beaubien 1953b), dating the boundary of the Late Archaic–Early Woodland periods. At conical Mound 43, Beaubien (1953b:57–60) found two prepared surfaces with red-ocher layers centered in the mound, one at the premound surface where the topsoil had been cut away and another in the lower third of the mound fill. Red-stained bifaces, thick copper beads, and bundled burials were associated with the upper layer. The two largest bifaces, with long unnotched stems (Beaubien 1953a:Figure 21d, e), are the Red Ocher style (see Stoltman 1986:Figure 4-11), not the Turkey-tail style. Three smaller stemmed points (Beaubien 1953a:Figure 21b, f), one of which appears to be Hixton silicified sediment from the Wisconsin source, resemble Late Archaic Table Rock and Durst styles and the Early Woodland Kramer style (Beaubien 1953a:Figure 21c).

Ryan-phase artifacts are in every way comparable in terms of style and exotic materials to artifacts from Red Ocher mounds in the central Illinois River valley (Esarey 1986). Green and Schermer (1988:158–159) used the westernmost distribution of Turkey-tail bifaces in the Turkey River mounds to argue for the existence of a pan-midwestern sphere of Red Ocher ceremonialism. We conclude that Red Ocher ritual in northeastern Iowa retained ancestral ties with Late Archaic technology but was the initial horizon of the Woodland mound-burial tradition. A Late Archaic precursor to Red Ocher in the form of blufftop cemeteries, possibly involving mound building, will probably be identified in the upper Mississippi Valley in Iowa.

Community and Settlement Patterns

We now turn attention to mapping settlement patterns and to reconstructing *communities*, which we define as a congregation of two or more contemporary habitation units at a single locale. Data from the Middle Archaic period are more abundant than for the Early and Late Archaic periods, thanks to recent CRM projects.

The highway survey data from upland contexts (see *Archaeological Potential in Eastern Iowa Landforms*) recorded 19 percent of the sites as Early Archaic, the second highest percentage after Late Archaic sites. About 67 percent of the Early Archaic sites listed in the Appendix 14.A database are in the uplands—almost 50 percent more than the proportions of Middle or Late Archaic upland sites. Although geologic processes have buried many Archaic sites of all three periods in valley settings, we hypothesize these data accurately reflect an Early Archaic settlement pattern that saw habitation and procurement sites relatively evenly distributed across forested upland and valley-floor settings. Most recorded sites consist of a few bifaces, discarded or cached at various stages of reduction, associated with a couple of other tools (e.g., scrapers, knives, or hammerstones) and relatively light scatters of debitage. The rest of the recorded sites are represented by single diagnostic bifaces from multicomponent artifact scatters. No Early Archaic houses have been found; features at two sites (Fett and Overberg; Appendix 14.C) consist of hearths and knapping concentrations, not pits. These settlement and site patterns were created by small, mobile groups (families) changing campsites frequently to follow seasonal resources and move into unexploited territories. Very few sites have yielded more than one or two diagnostic points, and two or more points from a single site usually belong to the same technical style. Men hunting alone probably were responsible for this evidence (see *Weaponry, Hafted Biface Styles, and Gender*). Early Archaic sites with several finished bifaces, especially expended weapons, are rare, indicating that campsites tended not to be periodically revisited. This means that band territories were not "fixed" in the landscape. By contrast, localities prolific with chert, like the Burlington quarries in southeastern Iowa, attracted bands throughout the Early Archaic period even as campsites were moved often (Morrow and Artz 1997). Perhaps small kin groups congregated briefly for social interacting and to conduct communal hunts. Judging by the regionally distinct distribution patterns of many of the biface types (see *Hafted Biface Styles, Distributions, and Lithic-Reduction Trajectories*), we postulate that people arranged themselves in band-based territories as the period progressed, gradually filling the richest upland and valley habitats by 6500 B.C.

Forty-eight percent of the Middle Archaic sites listed in Appendix 14.A are located in upland and 50 percent in valley settings (terraces, fans, and benches). The shift toward valley settings during the Middle Archaic entailed the creation of larger communities that left denser debris scatters (indicating longer stays) with a higher "visibility" to archaeological survey methods. We believe the settlement shift began during the seventh millennium B.C. and may have been encouraged by the expansion of prairie across the uplands (Wolverton 2005), while the development of extended seasonal occupations and coalescence of large communities took longer.

The Garden site (13DB493; Appendix 14.C) was a fourth-millennium B.C. occupation with Matanzas, Brewerton, and Brannon biface styles on a side valley of the upper Mississippi River in the Paleozoic Plateau region (Figure 14.2). Three complete households were excavated at the site, each consisting of a round structure (bark- or skin-covered) surrounded by a dense artifact scatter and pits, hearths, and artifact dumps (Figure 14.35). The size of the three houses fits within the range of Middle and Late Archaic structures adequate for a "nuclear family," as determined by Sassaman and Ledbetter (1993) from a review of eastern U.S. data. We prefer the term *family band* to describe the inhabitants of each of the Garden houses, as each nuclear family likely included other dependents, such as unmarried uncles or aunts, widowed parents, or orphaned children. Reconstruction of intrasite spacing indicated Households 1 and 3 were contemporary, and Household 6 was a separate occupation but close in time to the other two. The Garden "community" consisted of two households arranged so that they overlapped the feature cluster and their house entryways faced one another. Concurrent occupations by brothers, sisters, or father and son and their respective family members are possible scenarios. This community was small enough to have been supported by one or two large-game hunters, as implied by the Matanzas projectile technology (see *Weaponry, Hafted Biface Styles, and Gender*). Household 6 was occupied for the same economic purposes but did not appear to have shared space with another household.

The mid–Middle Archaic Garden community of two family bands occupied a well-drained alluvial fan within the floodplain forest and adjacent to a wetland. The families dwelled here for several months, at least long enough to collect local chert and to manufacture considerable numbers of cores and bifaces, often heat treating these objects at various stages of the reduction sequence. The residents apparently arrived with ready-made hafted bifaces made from nonlocal cherts because flaking debris from these cherts was rare at the site, and they carried away bifacial tools made on-site out of local material. The mesic forest resources recovered from the site point to a warm-season (late summer–fall) but not year-round occupation. There is evidence in the three households for at least four storage pits, that is, pits with large volumes and restricted orifices. In a provocative article on subterranean storage, sedentism, and surplus, DeBoer argues that, "rather than a marker of full sedentism, subterranean storage is more likely to indicate seasonal settlement abandonment" (1988:14).[8] This reasoning fits nicely with the seasonal bone, nutshell, and seed evidence from Garden, where storage pits could have been packed with a winter supply of nuts, dried flesh, and vegetable products, ready-to-finish bifaces, and nonportable tools for later retrieval.

Similar habitation evidence was exposed on the Gast Spring fan site (13LA152) located along the Mississippi River valley wall a few miles south of Muscatine (Figure 14.2). Here, a house basin identified in a backhoe trench yielded dates of 4535 B.C. and 4590 B.C. (Bettis et al. 1992:39). In the context of the residential models proposed by Illinois researchers, the Garden site and other base camps best fit with the "seasonal base camp" type (Evans et al. 2001:128), which is also called a "residential camp" by Brown and Vierra (1983:188) and by Ahler (1998:27) and "residential extractive camp" by Emerson et al. (1986:257). The concept embedded in all three terms is that family bands maintained temporary and seasonal residential sites for the extraction and processing of a variety of resources and that one of these base camps functioned as the territorial focus of the seasonal round. This model, emphasizing *permanency* of one of the base camps, has been criticized by Yerkes (1987:233) for failing to demonstrate that habitation

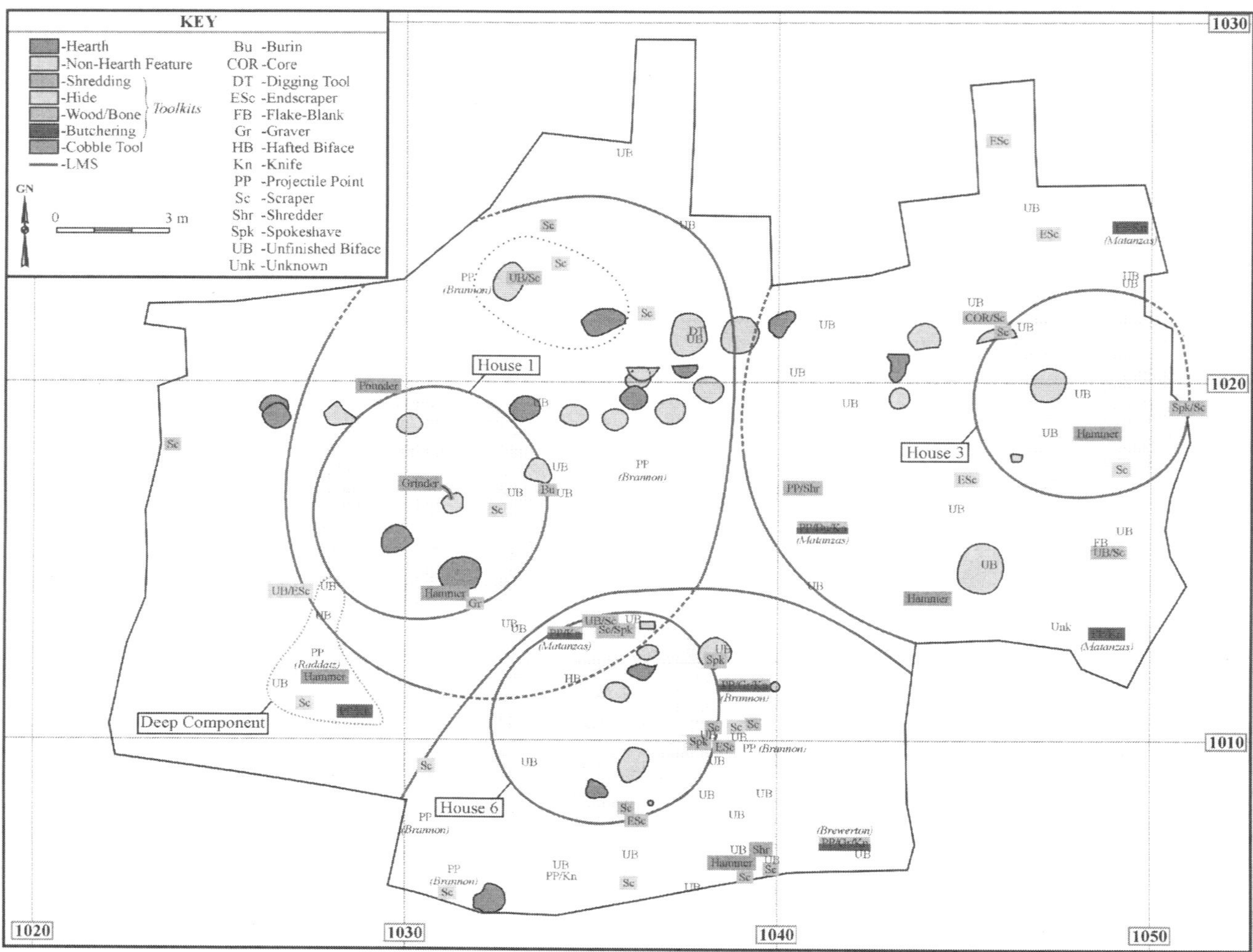

Figure 14.35. Garden site (13DB493) household plans.

sites with dense artifact scatters, called "base camps," did *not* result from repeated reoccupation of the same locus, leading to a build-up of tool types. One way to answer Yerkes's critique is to piece plot *all* habitation materials, so that households like the ones at the Garden site can be separated and the nature of the community defined. Other supporting evidence would come from locating a "residential extractive camp," also called a "temporary base camp," in Iowa (Benn 1987).

The Fett site (13LE597) Matanzas component looked like a temporary base camp. This component contained a 3-m-diameter "house" basin surrounded by a moderately dense lithic scatter and associated with surface hearths *but no big pits*. The tool inventory consisted of five complete Matanzas points (not manufactured on-site), a few hammerstones, cobble abraders, pounders, and flake tools with use wear indicative of (in descending order) working soft wood or bone, hard wood or bone, hair, meat, plant materials, and hides. Small amounts of nutshell were recovered by flotation. Although the site lacks faunal evidence, the tool types and site location point to use of this component as a wintering camp by both men and women but not long enough for debris to accumulate, features to be superimposed, or storage pits to be dug. The Matanzas technology suggests a lone hunter supported this camp (see *Weaponry, Hafted Biface Styles, and Gender*). Similar assemblages of artifacts probably were present (but were largely unexcavated) in Middle Archaic components at Merrimac Mills (13JF92), a possible temporary base camp. Middle Archaic components at Fett, Prymek (13WS65), and Ed's Meadow (13DM712) contained too few artifact types to have been base camps and qualify as short-term occupations, that is, bivouacs.

Near the end of the Middle Archaic period (ca. 3000–2500 B.C.), a considerable proportion of the Iowa population had committed itself to long-term habitations in big river valleys. McNeal Fan (13MC15) Component IId was one of these residential base camps (villages) consisting of at least seven large, oval houses oriented around a "commons" area (Figure 14.36; see Appendix 14.C). The charcoal-enriched sheet midden containing hundreds of features, some superimposed on houses, attests to the permanence of this occupation. Sand Run

Figure 14.36. McNeal Fan (13MC15) village plan.

West (13LA38), located a few miles south, and 13MC15 are situated on alluvial fans along the valley wall and adjacent to wetlands. Floral and faunal remains from Sand Run revealed a year-around occupation for maximizing exploitation of forest and aquatic habitats on the valley floor and adjoining upland oak forest-prairie edges. One significant feature type at McNeal Fan and Sand Run West was big (.7- to 2-m-diameter) roasting pits. McNeal Fan contained 56 of these pits within 1,200 m^2 of excavation block. While specific evidence is missing for what was processed in the McNeal features, they represent a substantial labor investment in collecting large volumes of resources, digging large holes, and redistributing the heated products to large groups. No other Early or Late Archaic–period community effort reflects this degree of labor commitment. Other indicators of settled (village) life are the communal burial ground and the dog interments at 13LA38. Such practices attest to territorial permanence promulgated by rituals like feasting and communal mortuary activity.

Our site sample for the Late Archaic period (Appendix 14.A) records a slightly larger proportion of sites with valley settings (57 percent) than it does for the preceding period. This difference is not analytically significant, although Late Archaic people may have positioned more seasonal base camps in small valleys and upland settings than Middle Archaic folks chose to do. The only two excavated seasonal base camps are Davis Creek (13WS122; Appendix 14.C), a Table Rock component whose pit and hearth features spread over a bench slope gave an impression of multiple households, and Lost Creek Upper Terrace (13MK357; Appendix 14.C). Two Lost Creek house patterns, at 46 m^2 each (Figure 14.37), were twice the size of the Garden site houses. Sassaman and Ledbetter (1993:94) suggested that such large spaces (e.g., 40–100 m^2) may not have been completely enclosed but had roofed shelters at opposite ends. The Lost Creek households were large enough to support multiple families, which we would interpret as extended family units including the spouses, children, and a

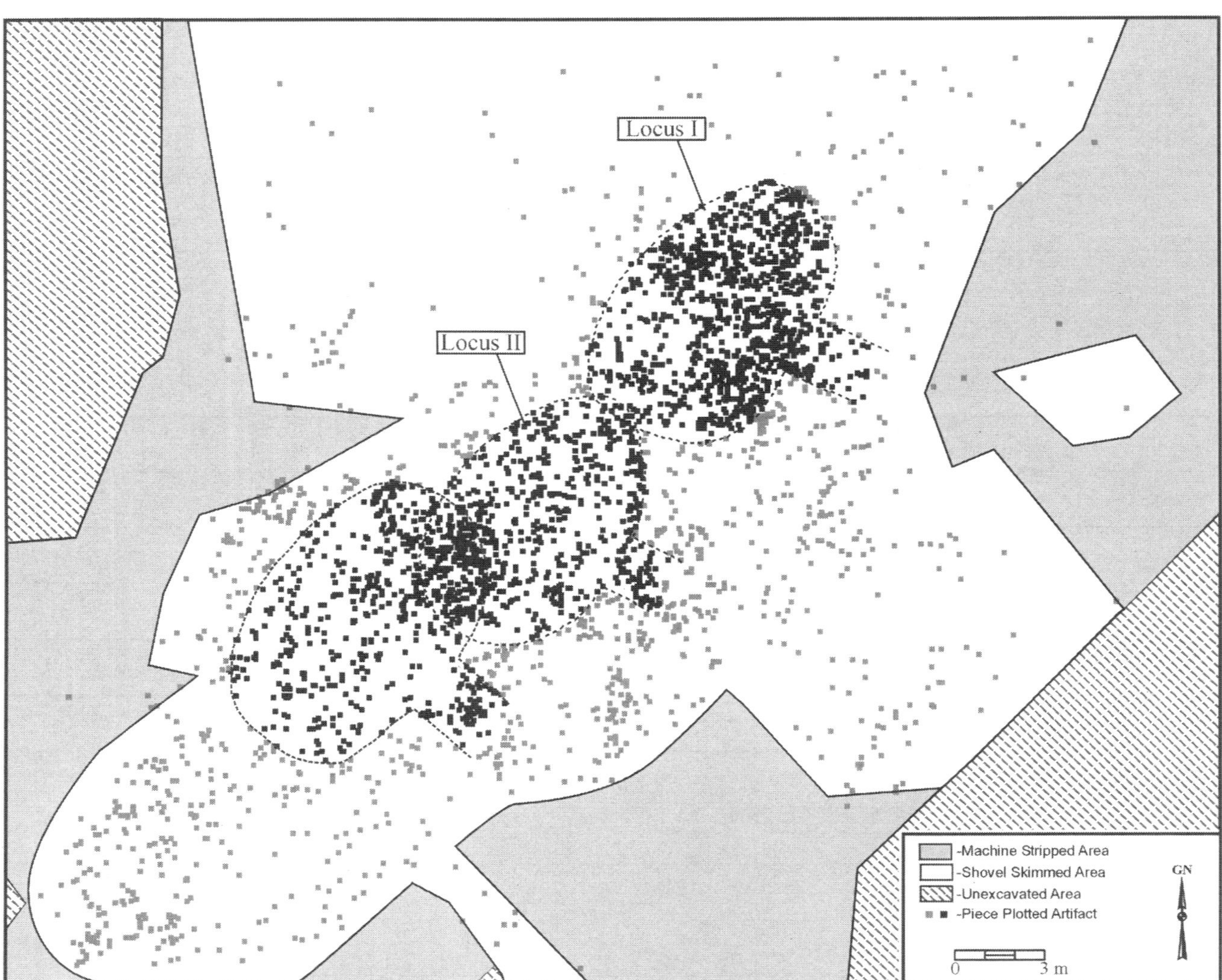

Figure 14.37. Lost Creek Upper Terrace (13MK357) house plans.

widowed parent of two brothers or sisters. Only one roasting pit and several lithic reduction concentrations were found at Davis Creek, and Lost Creek had surface hearths and small pits. While two or more extended family bands inhabited each of these base camps, there were no indications of an extended stay (i.e., more than one season). The terminal Late Archaic component at 13PK149 (D.U.III), situated in the floodplain in the central Des Moines Valley, contained one or, possibly, two round to oblong "house" features about 45 m apart (Osborn and Gradwohl 1981:127–129). Pits and a heavily burned hearth associated with the round house stain, in addition to projectiles, 21 end scrapers, and a variety of bifaces and flake tools, indicate this base camp was seasonally occupied for purposes of hunting, hide working, and collecting plant and animal resources from the floodplain forest. Other Late Archaic bivouacs at Prymek (13WS65), Merrimac Mills (13JF92), and Fett (13LE597; Appendix 14.C), where very small (2-m) house basins occurred on the side slope of a small valley, did not yield enough information for reconstruction of community patterns.

Late Archaic habitation sites are recorded (but have not been studied) throughout the gently rolling prairies and gallery forests of interior Iowa and the prairie lakes region of the Des Moines Lobe (Alex 2000:78). Mallam (Mallam and Bettis 1980) and Lensink (1984) postulated that societies in the prairie-lakes region did not change their dispersed settlement patterns or technologies to any great degree during the Archaic millennia, perhaps because the harsh winters exercised a leveling effect on population aggregation. At 13JP87 (Appendix 14.C) in the Skunk River basin on the edge of the Des Moines Lobe, the Middle Archaic habitations (Figure 14.38) included household patterns with heavy organic accumulation, roasting and basin-hearth features, huge amounts of FCR, and large numbers of projectile bifaces, end scrapers, flake tools, and cobble tools (Benn 2005). These were seasonal but not year-round base camps. By contrast, the Late Archaic TSN component at 13JP87 was a much less intensive occupation and probably constituted a bivouac.

Culture Change

What is striking about finding Early Archaic bifaces, such as Dalton, Kirk, St. Charles, Hardin, Hardaway, Thebes, Cache River, and so on, in Iowa is that these types occur in the same sophisticated technical format throughout the eastern and southern United States. Such pan-continental styles must have been introduced to the upper Midwest. The stylistic distribution patterns illustrated for eastern Iowa suggest many of these biface types entered the state from the south-southeastern direction, that is, the Mississippi River valley. These weapon tips were carried by bands of hunters and gatherers moving northward apparently with the advancing hardwood forest. The indigenous Paleoindian population either moved northward with the retreating boreal forest or blended with the new residents and took up the technology of notched projectiles. Whether used as weaponry (darts) or hafted on foreshafts for use as knives, corner-notched bifaces were manufactured by sophisticated knapping techniques that also produced heavy tools (scrapers, knives, gravers, and adzes) made from prepared cores of selected, high-quality local cherts. We believe men were largely responsible for this specialized technology, which was a holdover from the Paleoindian tradition. The corner-notched projectiles are thin, wide, and mostly barbed, a design that causes traumatic wounds in large prey animals and works well for men who hunt alone or in pairs and track mortally wounded animals. Women seem to have utilized other types of tools fashioned by male knappers, for example, end scrapers, hafted bifaces (Dalton and Thebes), perforators, and flake tools. while exclusively women's tools (e.g., FCR and grinders) are not conspicuous elements in the early archaeological record. Early Archaic sites were relatively small, short-term (bivouac) habitations that left behind few bifaces; we believe these sites were occupied by family bands who aggregated periodically with other bands in upland and valley settings for communal hunts or to quarry and exchange fine cherts. This is a residential-mobility settlement pattern (Binford 1980).

As the Early Archaic period waned, tool types proliferated (cf. Brown and Vierra 1983:181; Esarey 1986; Klippel and Maddox 1977) to include more kinds of bifacial knives, end and side scrapers, drills, choppers, multiple kinds of flake tools, and varied grinding and pounding equipment. The side-notched bifaces that came into use—for example, Graham Cave, Stilwell, MacCorkle, and Wolf Creek—were manufactured by less formalized core-reduction techniques than characterized previous Paleoindian technology and were designed for multiple resharpening in their hafts. An expansion in the range of uses for hafted bifaces suggests women wielded the same tools in the sphere of domestic production that men employed as projectile tips. Obviously, women also resharpened these tools. The proliferation of tool types leads us to infer that women's roles diversified in the food production system. Other authors have related diversification of the tool inventory to subsistence patterns shifting toward exploitation of a wider range of the plants and animals in the expanding, upland oak-hickory forest and in the maple forest and riparian biomes of the valley floor (Alex 2000:56; Klippel and Maddox 1977; Luchterhand 1970; Odell 1996:220; Stoltman 1986). The logical postulate of these economic processes is that family bands gradually settled into stable territories, where a broad spectrum of plants and animals could be exploited more effectively by women gatherers with diversified tools and by groups of men taking single large animals (deer) with relatively unspecialized (i.e., variable-size) dart tips.

Now we return to the question, what happened during the Middle Archaic period in Iowa? Price and Brown (1985:8) proposed three conditions that fostered the development of complexity during the Middle Archaic period in Illinois: (1) A condition of social circumscription developed as producer

Figure 14.38. Site 13JP87 "house" and feature distributions.

groups (bands) packed into established territories and opportunities for emigration closed; (2) resource abundance in larger valleys allowed for the creation of social surpluses; and (3) increasing population placed stress on subsistence strategies (collecting) based on wild resources. The general response to perceived subsistence stress was to focus on a narrow range of resources, that is, the most productive "patches," by occupying residential sites for longer periods and by developing more intensive food production systems through logistical organization of work groups (Brown and Vierra 1983:168–169; Cohen 1985:102; Warren and O'Brien 1982:94). By the late Middle Archaic period, these patterns are displayed in Iowa by production of starchy and oily native seeds at Sand Run West and by proliferating storage and large roasting pits at the McNeal village, Sand Run West, and site 13JP87. The production of elaborate artifacts also can be a response to socioeconomic stress (Suttles 1960). In Iowa, indelible lithic items that display "elaboration" beyond use-value include polished grooved axes, hematite items, and bannerstones; bone pins, shell, and fabrics probably would be present if preservation were better. In prestate societies, "surplus" objects are produced to fulfill social obligations ("debts"; see Bender 1985), and exchange of such objects yields a guarantee of reciprocal assistance during times of stress. The term *surplus* is used here to designate *labor-value* (cf. Marx 1906:588–589) expended for social purposes other than the simple use-value (consumption) of objects and materials.

The aspect of social organization in which changes in the Middle Archaic mode of production should have been the starkest, although it remains archaeologically almost invisible, is gender-based activities. After all, the locus of *intensive exploitation of a narrower range of resource patches* was in the realm of traditional women's work in Indian societies: for example, seed and nut collecting, gathering aquatic creatures, and processing various meat and plant foods. Likewise, the manufacture and trading of exotic commodities like ground-stone axes and bannerstones, copper, crafted bone and shell, hematite objects, and red ocher were traditional male activities. Yet another range of activities like netting fish, snaring small to medium-size animals and birds, and participating in communal game drives likely was shared by men and women. We see the broadening of the range of male and female activities evident not only in the proliferation of tool types but also in the generalization of lithic knapping patterns and in the design of side-notched bifaces. Women probably made some of their own flake tools and resharpened their own bifacial tools, so the combination of men and women knappers led core and bifacial reduction technologies to became "generalized." Hafted bifaces probably still made by full-time knappers (men) were designed for a variety of functions; large bifaces were securely hafted on foreshafts for use on unfletched darts by men or as handheld knives and scrapers by men and women, while smaller projectiles were fitted to fletched darts. We suspect that big-game hunting often was a communal activity, for example, a deer drive, because the big projectiles were relatively unspecialized in form, were not detachable, and lacked barbs (see *Weaponry, Hafted Biface Styles, and Gender*). Projectiles with fletching are designed for accuracy in tight (forested) places but are less likely to remain inside the wounded prey—an effective communal hunting technique when large numbers of accurate shots are launched.

Now for some thoughts about storage. At 13JP87, 35 deep basins and pits average 92 cm in diameter and a bulky .16 m^3 in volume. Some of these were heating pits in which burn evidence has disappeared, but others probably functioned as storage pits, as indicated by their straight sides and relatively large volumes. The Garden and Sand Run West sites contained similar large pits, and the McNeal Fan village had dozens of large pits. Since cultigens were developed only by the end of the Archaic period (Asch and Green 1992; Dunne and Green 1998), why would bands of Middle Archaic hunters and collectors need storage pits? DeBoer (1988) plumbed ethnographic and archaeological literature and disclosed that people do not need pit storage unless they seasonally abandon the production site and, therefore, need to conceal dried foodstuffs until they return and retrieve cached supplies during seasons of shortage (i.e., winter–early spring in the Midwest). Holman and Krist (2001), citing historical sources, refer to hunters and gatherers in Michigan who stated there was no need to conceal supplies from other bands (i.e., other people did not steal from caches); instead, protecting cached supplies from predators like wolves (and coyotes in Iowa) was more important. This debate over the motivations for concealing cached supplies is tangential to the fact that quantities of food (and tools) seem to have been processed and stored at seasonal base camps, not just in permanent habitations. Geographic analysis by Holman and Krist (2001:15–18) concluded that preserved foods and other supplies were cached at locations of production situated along familiar trails, where bands expected to retrace their paths during subsequent seasons. Caches, then, are part of a logistically organized settlement pattern.

What foods were stored in cache pits and processed in large roasting pits? Actual evidence for foodstuffs in the form of floral and faunal remains is absent from most Iowa sites, although incipient cultigens were recovered from Sand Run West. Asch and Green (1992) showed that the native seed complex appeared during the Late Archaic period throughout eastern Iowa (see Dunne and Green 1998). Indirect evidence for food processing exists in the large numbers of hammer and anvil implements for breaking hard objects and the huge amounts of FCR in the primary (roasting pits) and secondary (midden) contexts. We assume part of the hammering equipment was used to process nuts and to smash bones for grease. Wandsnider's (1997:28) analysis of pit-hearth (roasting-pit) cooking methods sheds more light on the food question by concluding that (1) pit-hearth cooking was used to process foods for long periods of time at high heat; (2) foods were cooked in large quantities; and (3) this method tended not to be used on lean meats and starchy plant foods. The third criterion applied in cases in which large amounts of seasonally fat meats (e.g., beaver, bear, muskrat, and goose) were processed to supply large groups of people. Using Wandsnider's analysis, we argue that deep roasting pits in late Middle Archaic sites were used to stone boil fatty meats, cook large amounts of leaner meats (e.g., deer and elk), and roast tubers like Jerusalem artichoke (*Helianthus tuberosus*) and arrowhead root (*Alisma* sp.). The other obvious uses for pit hearths were slow drying or smoking meat and parching seeds. Bone-grease manufacture should leave behind evidence in the form of pounding and anvil stones (Fishel et al. 2003:65). Supplies of dried meat and fruits, bone grease, nuts, and tubers would have been cached in pits similar in size to the roasting pits.

Another characteristic of the late Middle Archaic settlement pattern in Iowa is a diversity of site types. The combination of villages, temporary and seasonal base camps, short-term bivouacs (or residential extractive camps), and resource-extraction locations (e.g., quarries and kill sites) constitutes an outline of a logistical settlement strategy (Binford 1980) for the Middle Archaic mode of production. So far, this is only a postulated model of the settlement system because very few of the example sites in the Iowa database are situated in the same county and, so, cannot be territorially associated with one another. Archaeologists do not know how far up the major river systems large seasonal base camps (villages) are distributed beyond the Mississippi Valley. Furthermore, we know nothing about the settlement system of the bison hunters who apparently inhabited the Des Moines Lobe region of north-central Iowa. Because bison are migratory creatures, bison hunting requires a different kind of settlement pattern than the one described here. The other site type absent from our modeling is the cemetery. Communal burial grounds are a critical aspect of community life and a place for depositing surplus accumulation for territorially based aggregate bands (Charles and Buikstra 1983). "Village" life probably does not exist without maintaining appropriate sacred space for a society's dead.

How people communicated beyond their communities about territorial, economic, and social aspects of life is an interesting question. Direct long-distance communication or down-the-line trading by Middle Archaic peoples undoubtedly happened, with the current evidence in Iowa consisting of a handful of chert types from sources more than 100 miles distant, one or two pieces of galena, the sharing of hafted-biface styles, and the distribution of refined artifacts like polished axes, bannerstones, and hematite objects. The frequency of exotic material and the consistent appearance of specific kinds of commodities are *much* higher in Early and Middle Woodland–period sites than in Middle Archaic–period sites. Thus, the interaction between folks in the upper Mississippi basin appears to have been less formalized and frequent during the Middle Archaic period than 2,000 years hence. This has implications for localized surplus production; after all, elaborate ground-stone axes and bannerstones that exhibit far more labor-value than functional value occur in the Van Buren phase. Producing surplus from local materials rather than trading regionally for exotic commodities indicates that the political organization of Middle Archaic cultures was not developed at the level of pan-regional complexity, in contrast to the cult-centered trading organizations of the Middle Woodland period or the tribal or stratified societies of the Mississippian period.

The number of Late Archaic sites recorded in four Mississippi River pool surveys (Benn et al. 1988, 1989) was slightly larger than the number of Middle Archaic sites, and the Late Archaic sites were more widely distributed on all landforms. Likewise, our sample of sites listed in Appendix 14.A indicates widespread distribution of Late Archaic sites throughout interior Iowa, including small valleys. This proliferation of Late Archaic components has been noticed by many researchers working in the Mississippi River valley (Asch et al. 1981:62; Billeck and Benchley 1982:7; Dudzik 1974:16; McElrath et al. 1984:58; Odell 1996:221) and along the Iowa River valley (Collins 1990). We believe most of these sites are relatively small and have light artifact scatters, suggesting that Late Archaic people either congregated in smaller numbers or resided for shorter periods of time at base camps than their Middle Archaic predecessors did. The house patterns at Lost Creek (13MK357; Appendix 14.C) may be typical of what was happening; that is, large houses for extended-family bands were occupied for no more than a single season. The proliferation of Late Archaic components suggests bands were filling the available space in valleys as well as establishing new upland niches as oak forests advanced into the prairies. Brown and Vierra (1983) and others (e.g., Price and Brown 1985) have made this point in recent years, and Bender (1985) used this kind of evidence to imply that a condition of "social closure" had developed in Late Archaic societies. By "social closure," she meant that corporate groups were becoming socially packed and circumscribed so that male hunters and women collectors had fewer choices about moving or changing allegiance. "Allegiance" is something that may be reflected in the record of regional biface styles. Men probably developed specialized hafting styles (i.e., insertion, split-shaft hafting, and fletching) for projectile tips and a variety of foreshafts and handles, while women focused their energies on the proliferation of native seed horticulture. Archaeologists should be looking for evidence of band allegiance and territoriality in bluff-top cemeteries, which have not been recognized in eastern Iowa yet because of the cessation of excavations in mound groups in Iowa.[9] Bluff-top cemeteries dating to the Late Archaic period occur in western Iowa (Anderson et al. 1978; see 13MN2 and 13PW5 in Appendix 14.B) and have been found beneath Woodland mounds in the central and lower Illinois Valley (Charles et al. 1988). Many unexcavated mounds occur on bluff tops along Iowa's Mississippi Valley.

Conclusions

This overview of eastern Iowa Archaic periods is a first attempt at gleaning the archaeological records. More unanalyzed data are buried in obscure contract reports, generalized records of "prehistoric" sites, and private collections all over the state. Construction of geographic information system databases for site records, surveys, and collections that specify artifact types is a first step to making this information accessible for manipulation and interpretation. Rapid expansion of information technologies makes this feasible, when it would have been far more difficult to do 20 years ago, and continued expansion of the database will happen with participation by the entire community of archaeologists, paraprofessionals, and collectors. One of the ironies of the information age is that huge quantities of data are being generated by CRM work, but little interpretation is coming out in reports. Another limitation is that many sites are still being excavated with traditional methodologies (i.e., square holes) that do not allow archaeologists to address questions about community patterns, including what type of habitation is evidenced. Not being able to identify habitation types and community patterns is a barrier to anthropological interpretation (viz. Gibbon 1984:140). Archaeologists need to reconsider why we are excavating sites: to address questions about prehistoric community life, to salvage doomed cultural deposits and place the material in repositories, or to maintain our own job security.

In this chapter, we designated the first named phase for the Archaic era in eastern Iowa: the late Middle Archaic Van Buren phase. Other information hints at the existence of other phases for the mid–Middle Archaic period (coeval with the Helton phase) and for the Late Archaic period (coeval with the Titterington and Durst phases), but too little is known about the related tool complexes and their geographic distribution patterns to designate names unique to Iowa. Concrete geophysical boundaries (e.g., river basins and landform regions) need to be traced across all of Iowa to create these taxons. Are the phases from western Illinois, northern Missouri, and southwestern Wisconsin applicable to eastern Iowa? Do familiar manifestations, like Old Copper, not occur in eastern Iowa?

Intensive site excavations are vital sources of information about Archaic subsistence, albeit sites from this era typically have poor paleobotanical and faunal records. To glean more information from scant records, researchers need to move from mere sampling of Archaic features to subjecting all feature matrix to flotation. We also have to increase systematic sampling in middens to obtain more environmental data. One benefit of increased sampling for fine screening would be to multiply the amount of carbonized material available for radiocarbon dating. Producing larger samples of biological remains means more money would be spent on botanical and faunal analysis, and always-finite CRM funds could be shifted away from stone analysis, especially of redundant flaking debris. When more sampling does not produce additional faunal remains, sophisticated analyses (e.g., blood residue, amino acid, DNA, etc.) need to be instituted to determine the uses of stone tools. Traditional use-wear analysis of lithic tools needs to be applied to all excavation projects. We would like to see more frequent TL dating of FCR and burned chipped-stone debitage, which is ubiquitous on Archaic sites. To examine community patterns, archaeologists must excavate large enough portions of habitation sites to visualize what is going on. Short of inventing remote sensing machines that can consistently and accurately identify house loci across an array of soil conditions, researchers have to explore habitation sites for complete household patterns, extramural activity areas, and community boundaries by piece plotting all artifacts.

Archaeologists know virtually nothing about the religion, ideology, and cosmology of Archaic cultures in Iowa beyond a single glimpse into the Red Ocher complex afforded by the Turkey River mounds. The Middle Archaic cemetery at Sand Run West is the only other excavated site with human remains in eastern Iowa, but bone preservation was poor and no grave inclusions were found at this site. Few mortuary sites are likely to be exhumed under the current burial law regime, so the rituals of peoples predating the Woodland-era mound builders are not likely to be known in Iowa as they are becoming known elsewhere, as least in the foreseeable future. We believe that formal cemeteries associated with earthworks were created by Iowa Archaic people. Learning about the material life—technologies and community patterns—of Archaic people but not about their ideology is unacceptable.

Acknowledgments

John Cordell and Colleen Eck (OSA) provided invaluable assistance for the senior author's search of site records and curated collections. Mark Anderson (OSA) prepared the hafted-biface reconstruction and offered suggestions about the functionality of darts. Site data from the central Des Moines and Mississippi river valleys was produced from surveys and excavations contracted by the Rock Island District, U.S. Army Corps of Engineers. Most of the Archaic site excavations summarized here were projects funded by the Iowa Department of Transportation, for which much of the credit goes to Randy Faber. Randy Withrow (Louis Berger and Associates) offered site reports for review. Derek Lee (Bear Creek Archeology [BCA]) prepared excellent digital versions of the figures. James M. Collins (OSA) and Lowell Blikre (BCA) reviewed the manuscript and generously provided comments. The chapter's second author contributed most of the excavation data, while the senior author is principally responsible for the content and cultural interpretations.

Endnotes

1. Although the Cherokee Sewer site (Anderson and Semken 1980) had very good faunal and floral preservation in fan sediments.
2. In fairness to the research team at Kampsville, the Modoc survey was conducted prior to the period of rising concern for deeply buried sites. The team did utilize bucket augering to survey heavily vegetated areas.
3. Throughout this text, B.P. dates are uncalibrated. B.C. dates have been calibrated using the CALIB5 program. Calibrated ranges for each date are provided in Appendix 14.B, while a median date for each assay range is used in this text.
4. Much of the contextual information in this geological overview has been adapted from Art Bettis's contribution in Thompson (2001:10–12).
5. Sites and components dated only by radiocarbon assays or relatively dated by geological context but lacking bifaces are excluded from the database.

6. Some Tamas are arrowpoint size, although Tama is included in the Large Side Notched cluster by Justice (1987:69).
7. On the other side of this "coin," no clear correlation can be drawn between types of Paleoindian artifacts and boreal or hardwood forest; both types of forests covered portions of North America prior to ca. 11,000 B.P.
8. DeBoer also noted that storage pits can be viewed as "a powerful signal of resistance to a new social order" and that they "indicate the precariousness of all external relationships" (1988:14). These comments take us too far out on the limb of sociopolitical analysis given what we actually know about Middle Archaic culture.
9. State law prohibits excavation of aboriginal mounds and human remains except in cases of emergency.

References Cited

Abbott, Larry R., and E. Arthur Bettis III
1975 Erickson Creek Drainage: A Preliminary Report of Geological, Pedological, and Archaeological Potential of the Area. Manuscript on file, Iowa State University Archaeological Laboratory, Ames.

Ahler, Steven R.
1998 Early and Middle Archaic Settlement Systems in the Modoc Locality, Southwestern Illinois. *Illinois Archaeology* 10:1–109.

Alex, Lynn M.
2000 *Iowa's Archaeological Past*. University of Iowa Press, Iowa City.

Anderson, Adrian, and Joseph A. Tiffany
1972 Rummells-Maske: A Clovis Find-Spot in Iowa. *Plains Anthropologist* 17:55–59.

Anderson, Duane C.
1987 The Keystone Site (13JK23): A Multicomponent Rockshelter in Jackson County, Iowa. *Journal of the Iowa Archeological Society* 34:1–6.

Anderson, Duane C., Michael Finnegan, John Hotopp, and Alton K. Fisher
1978 The Lewis Central School Site (13PW5): A Resolution of Ideological Conflicts at an Archaic Ossuary in Western Iowa. *Plains Anthropologist* 23:183–219.

Anderson, Duane C., and Holmes A. Semken (editors)
1980 *The Cherokee Excavations: Holocene Ecology and Human Adaptations in Northwestern Iowa*. Academic Press, New York.

Anderson, Mark L.
1996 *A Phase I Archaeological Survey of Primary Roads Project NHS-63-1(39)--19-26 a.k.a. PIN91-26030-1 Davis and Wapello Counties, Iowa*. Project Completion Report 19(12). Office of the State Archaeologist, University of Iowa, Iowa City.

Anonymous
1977 Bannerstones. *Newsletter of the Iowa Archeological Society* 85:10.

Artz, Joe Alan
1991 Site Formation Processes and Soil Evolution: A Case Study from Southeastern Iowa. Paper presented at the 49th Plains Anthropological Conference, Lawrence, Kansas.

1994 *Archaeology in the Montrose Bottom: A Supplemental Phase I Archaeological Survey of Primary Roads Project F-61-1(55)--20-56 a.k.a. PIN 79-56046-1, Lee County, Iowa*. Project Completion Report 17(20). Office of the State Archaeologist, University of Iowa, Iowa City.

1995 *Archaeology of the Eisele's Hill Locality: Phase II Test Excavations at Six Sites in Muscatine County, Iowa, Primary Roads Project NHS-61-4(55)--20-70, a.k.a. PIN 92-70040-1*. Project Completion Report 18(30). Office of the State Archaeologist, University of Iowa, Iowa City.

Artz, Joe Alan, Cherie E. Haury, Michelle Berg Vogel, and Gregory Vogel
1995 *Phase II Archaeological Test Excavations at 11 Archaeological Sites in the Montrose Bottom, Primary Roads Project F-61-1(55)--20-56 a.k.a. PIN 79-56040-1, Lee County, Iowa*. Project Completion Report 18(23). Office of the State Archaeologist, University of Iowa, Iowa City.

Asch, David L., Kenneth B. Farnsworth, H. Carl Udesen, and Ann L. Koski
1981 Upper Mississippi River and Lower Illinois River Units (III-South and VI). In *Predictive Models in Illinois Archaeology Report Summaries*, edited by Margaret K. Brown, pp. 55–72. Illinois Department of Conservation, Division of Historic Sites, Urbana.

Asch, David, and William Green
1992 *Crops of Ancient Iowa: Native Plant Use and Farming Systems*. Report prepared for the Leopold Center for Sustainable Agriculture. Office of the State Archaeologist, University of Iowa, Iowa City.

Baker, Richard G., E. A. Bettis III, R. F. Denniston, and L. A. Gonzalez
2001 Plant Remains, Alluvial Chronology, and Cave Speleothem Isotopes Indicate Abrupt Holocene Climatic Change at 6 ka in Midwestern USA. *Global and Planetary Change* 28:285–291.

Baker, R. G., E. A. Bettis III, R. F. Denniston, L. A. Gonzalez, L. E. Strickland, and J. R. Krieg
2002 Holocene Paleoenvironments in Southeastern Minnesota—Chasing the Prairie-Forest Ecotone. *Palaeogeography, Palaeoclimatology, Palaeoecology* 177:103–122.

Baker, R. G., E. A. Bettis III, and D. G. Horton
1993 Late Wisconsinan-Early Holocene Riparian Paleoenvironment in Southeastern Iowa. *Geological Society of America Bulletin* 105:206–212.

Baker, R. G., C. A. Chumbley, P. M. Witinok, and H. K. Kim
1990 Holocene Vegetational Changes in Eastern Iowa. *Journal of the Iowa Academy of Science* 97(4):167–177.

Banks, Alan
2002 Some Information on the Etley Point. *Missouri Archaeological Society Quarterly* 19(1):12–18.

Bartlein, P. J., T. Webb III, and E. Fleri
1984 Holocene Climatic Change in the Northern Midwest: Pollen-Derived Estimates. *Quaternary Research* 22:361–374.

Beaubien, Paul L.
1953a Some Hopewellian Mounds at the Effigy Mounds National Monument, Iowa. Manuscript on file, National Park Service, Midwest Archeological Center, Lincoln, Nebraska.

1953b Cultural Variation within Two Woodland Mound Groups of Northeastern Iowa. *American Antiquity* 19:56–66.

Benchley, Elizabeth D., Blane Nansel, Clark A. Dobbs, Susan M. Thurston Myster, and Barbara H. O'Connell

1997 *Archeology and Bioarcheology of the Northern Woodlands.* Research Series 52. Arkansas Archeological Survey, Fayetteville.

Bender, Barbara

1985 Emergent Tribal Formations in the American Midcontinent. *American Antiquity* 50:52–56.

Benn, David W.

1979 *A Sampling Survey of Prehistoric Cultural Resources in Mitchell County, Iowa.* Luther College Archaeological Research Center, Decorah, Iowa.

1983 Another Three-Quarter Grooved Ax from Polk County. *Iowa Archeological Society Newsletter* 33(106):3.

1986 *Site Testing for the Interpretive Cultural Overview, Saylorville Lake, Iowa*, vol 3. CAR-627. Center for Archaeological Research, Southwest Missouri State University, Springfield.

1987 (editor) *Big Sioux River Archaeological and Historical Resources Survey, Lyon County, Iowa.* CAR-705. Center for Archaeological Research, Southwest Missouri State University, Springfield.

1998 *Phase II Archeological Testing of 14 Sites, Lake Odessa Habitat Rehabilitation and Enhancement Project, Upper Mississippi River System, Pools 17 and 18, Iowa.* BCA 466. Report submitted to the Rock Island District Corps of Engineers. Bear Creek Archeology, Cresco, Iowa.

2002a (editor) *Phase III Data Recovery Excavations at 13MC134, U.S. Highway 61, Muscatine County, Iowa,* vol. 2. BCA 628/629. Report submitted to the Iowa Department of Transportation. Bear Creek Archeology, Cresco, Iowa.

2002b (editor) *Phase III Data Recovery Excavations at 13MC136, U.S. Highway 61, Muscatine County, Iowa,* vol. 3. BCA 628/629. Report submitted to the Iowa Department of Transportation. Bear Creek Archeology, Cresco, Iowa.

2005 (editor) *Data Recovery Excavations at Multi-Component Historic and Prehistoric Sites 13JP86 and 13JP87, Jasper County, Iowa.* BCA 867. Bear Creek Archeology, Cresco, Iowa.

2007 (editor) *Data Recovery Excavations at Middle Archaic Site 13DB493, Dubuque Township, Dubuque County, Iowa.* 2 vols. BCA 847. Bear Creek Archeology, Cresco, Iowa.

Benn, David W., Jeffrey D. Anderson, Robert C. Vogel, and Lawrence Conrad

1989 *Archaeology, Geomorphology and Historic Surveys in Pools 13-14, Upper Mississippi River.* CAR-752. Center for Archaeological Research, Southwest Missouri State University, Springfield.

Benn, David W., and E. Arthur Bettis III

1979 Archeological Investigations and Cultural-Historical Interpretations in the Volga Lake Project, Fayette County, Iowa. Prepared for the Iowa Conservation Commission and the Division of Historic Preservation. Report on file, Luther College Archaeological Research Center, Decorah, Iowa.

1999 Holocene Landscapes & Prehistoric Settlement Patterns: Upper Mississippi River Valley. Paper presented at the 64th Annual Meeting of the Society for American Archaeology, Chicago.

Benn, David W., E. Arthur Bettis III, Arthur Hoppin, Lucretia S. Kelly, Neal H. Lopinot, and David G. Stanley

1987 *Archaeology in the Mississippi River Floodplain at Sand Run Slough, Iowa.* CAR-690. Center for Archaeological Research, Southwest Missouri State University, Springfield.

Benn, David W., E. Arthur Bettis III, and Robert C. Vogel

1988 *Archaeology and Geomorphology in Pools 17-18, Upper Mississippi River.* CAR-714. Report submitted to the Rock Island District, U.S. Army Corps of Engineers. Center for Archaeological Research, Southwest Missouri State University, Springfield.

Benn, David W., Lowell R. Blikre, Arne J. Hengesteg, Derek V. Lee, Jeffrey R. Straka, E. Arthur Bettis III, Neal Lopinot, and Gina Powell

2001 *Data Recovery Excavations at the Late Woodland Cross Site (13LA309), Louisa County, Iowa.* BCA 746. Report submitted to the Rock Island District, U.S. Army Corps of Engineers. Bear Creek Archeology, Cresco, Iowa.

Benn, David W., Lowell R. Blikre, Arne J. Hengesteg, Jeffrey R. Straka, and Patti Wright

1999 *Data Recovery Excavations at the Late Woodland Horseshoe Site (13LA27), Louisa County, Iowa.* BCA 646. Report submitted to the Rock Island District, U.S. Army Corps of Engineers. Bear Creek Archeology, Cresco, Iowa.

Benn, David W., and Martha Bowers

1994 *Survey Report of Highway 34, Mt. Pleasant to Fairfield.* Louis Berger and Associates, East Orange, New Jersey.

Benn, David W., and Suzanne Harris

1983 *Testing Nine Archaeological Sites in the Downstream Corridor, Saylorville Lake, Iowa: 1982.* Center for Archaeological Research, Southwest Missouri State University, Springfield.

Benn, David W., and David M. Hovde

1976 *Archaeological Remains in the Pleasant Creek Reservoir, Iowa.* Luther College Archaeological Research Laboratory, Decorah, Iowa.

1981 *Intensive Survey of Archaeological Site 13AN52, Rathbun Lake, Iowa.* U.S. Army Corps of Engineers, Kansas City District, Purchase Order DACW41-77-M-1672. Luther College Archaeological Research Center, Decorah, Iowa.

Benn, David W., Gina Powell, E. Arthur Bettis III, William Isenberger, and Derek Lee

2007 *Data Recovery Excavations at the Terminal Late Woodland Period Union Bench Site (13DB497), Dubuque County, Iowa.* BCA 847. Bear Creek Archeology, Cresco, Iowa.

Benn, David W., and Leah D. Rogers

1985 *Interpretive Overview of Cultural Resources in Saylorville Lake, Iowa*, vol. 2. CAR-627. Center for Archaeological Research, Southwest Missouri State University, Springfield.

Benn, David W., Shirley Schermer, and Jonathan Sellars

1992 *Excavations of Human Remains from the Sand Run West Site (13LA38), Louisa County, Iowa.* BCA 150. Report submitted to the Rock Island District, U.S. Army

Corps of Engineers. Bear Creek Archeology, Cresco, Iowa.

Benn, David W., and Scott Stadler
2004 *Effigy Mounds National Monument Archeological Overview and Assessment.* BCA 1087. Bear Creek Archeology, Cresco, Iowa.

Benn, David W., Joe B. Thompson, and Derek V. Lee
1999 Prehistoric Households in Iowa. *The Wisconsin Archeologist* 80:161–210.

Benn, David W., and Robert C. Vogel
1996 *Phase I Cultural Resources Investigation of the Proposed Water Supply and Treatment Facilities, City of Iowa City, Johnson County, Iowa.* BCA 435. Bear Creek Archeology, Cresco, Iowa.

Bettis, E. Arthur, III
1987 History of the Upper Mississippi Valley. *Iowa Geology* 12:12–15.
1988 Quaternary History, Stratigraphy, Geomorphology, and Pedology. In *Archaeology and Geomorphology in Pools 17-18 Upper Mississippi River*, by David W. Benn, E. Arthur Bettis III, and Robert C. Vogel, pp. 18–91. CAR-714. Center for Archaeological Research, Southwest Missouri State University, Springfield.

Bettis, E. Arthur, III, Jeffrey D. Anderson, James S. Oliver, David W. Benn, and Michael D. Wiant
1996 *Landform Sediment Assemblage (LSA) Units in the Upper Mississippi River Valley, United States Army Corps of Engineers, Rock Island District.* 2 vols. Technical Report 95-1004-11b. Quaternary Studies Program, Illinois State Museum Research and Collections Center, Springfield.

Bettis, E. A., III, and W. J. Autin
1997 Complex Response of a Midwestern, USA Drainage System to Late Wisconsinan Sedimentation. *Journal of Sedimentary Research* 67:740–748.

Bettis, E. Arthur, III, Richard G. Baker, William Green, Mary K. Whelan, and David W. Benn
1992 *Late Wisconsinan and Holocene Alluvial Stratigraphy, Paleoecology, and Archaeological Geology of East-Central Iowa.* Guidebook Series 12, Iowa Quaternary Studies Group Contribution 51. Iowa Geological Survey Bureau, Iowa City.

Bettis, E. Arthur, III, Richard G. Baker, Brenda K. Nations, and David W. Benn
1990 Early Holocene Pecan, *Carya illinoensis*, in the Mississippi River Valley near Muscatine, Iowa. *Quaternary Research* 33:103–107.

Bettis, E. Arthur, III, and David W. Benn
1984 An Archaeological and Geomorphological Survey in the Central Des Moines River Valley, Iowa. *Plains Anthropologist* 29:211–227.

Bettis, E. Arthur, III, and Edwin R. Hajic
1995 Landscape Development and the Location of Evidence of Archaic Cultures in the Upper Midwest. In *Archaeologial Geology of the Archaic Period in North America*, edited by E. Arthur Bettis III, pp. 87–113. Special Paper 297. Geological Society of America, Boulder, Colorado.

Bettis, E. Arthur, III, and George R. Hallberg
1985 Quaternary Alluvial Stratigraphy and Chronology of Roberts Creek Basin, Northeastern Iowa. In *Pleistocene Geology and Evolution of the Upper Mississippi Valley*, coordinated by R. S. Lively, pp. 44–45. Minnesota Geological Survey and University of Minnesota, Minneapolis.

Bettis, E. Arthur, III, Bernard E. Hoyer, and Edwin R. Hajic
1984 Alluvial/Colluvial Fan Development in the American Midwest. *Program and Abstracts*, p. 13. American Quaternary Association Eighth Biennial Meeting, University of Colorado, Boulder.

Bettis, E. Arthur, III, and Timothy J. Kemmis
1992 Effects of the Last Glacial Maximum (21,000–16,500 B.P.) on Iowa's Landscapes. *Abstracts with Programs* 24:5. North-Central Section of the Geological Society of America 26th Annual Meeting, Boulder, Colorado.

Bettis, E. Arthur, III, and John P. Littke
1987 *Holocene Alluvial Stratigraphy and Landscape Development in Soap Creek Watershed, Appanoose, Davis, Monroe, and Wapello Counties, Iowa.* Open File Report 87-2. Geological Survey Bureau, Iowa Department of Natural Resources, Iowa City.

Billeck, William T.
1987 Functional Variation at Two Short-Term Multi-Component Sites in Black Hawk County. *Journal of the Iowa Archeological Society* 34:7–21.

Billeck, William T., and Elizabeth D. Benchley
1982 *Regional Summary Northern Illinois.* Archaeological Research Laboratory, University of Wisconsin–Milwaukee.

Binford, Lewis R.
1980 Willow Smoke and Dogs' Tails: Hunter-Gatherer Settlement Systems and Archaeological Site Formation. *American Antiquity* 45:4–28.
1983 *In Pursuit of the Past.* Thames and Hudson, New York.

Blikre, Lowell
1997 *An Extended Cultural Resource Survey of 13MK392 along Proposed IA 137 Corridor, Harrison Township, Mahaska County, Iowa.* BCA 508. Bear Creek Archeology, Cresco, Iowa.
2003 (editor) (draft) *Archeology in the Eisele's Hill Locality: Phase II Data Recovery Excavations at 13MC169, U.S. Highway 61, Muscatine County, Iowa.* BCA 628/629. Report prepared for the Iowa Department of Transportation. Bear Creek Archeology, Cresco, Iowa.

Blitz, John H.
1988 Adoption of the Bow in Prehistoric North America. *North American Archaeologist* 9:123–145.

Boldurian, Anthony T.
1991 Folsom Mobility and Organization of Lithic Technology: A View from Blackwater Draw, New Mexico. *Plains Anthropologist* 36:281–295.

Bond, Eyan, and David G. Stanley
2002 *Phase I Cultural Resource Survey for a Proposed Bridge Replacement, Clear Creek Township, Johnson County, Iowa.* BCA 1040. Bear Creek Archeology, Cresco, Iowa.

Borchert, J. R.
1950 The Climate of the Central North American Grassland. *Annals of the Association of American Geographers* 40:1–39.

Boszhardt, Robert F.
2002 Contracting Stemmed: What's the Point? *Midcontinental Journal of Archaeology* 27:35–67.

Boszhardt, Robert F., James L. Theler, and Thomas F. Kehoe
1986 The Early Woodland Stage. In *Introduction to Wisconsin Archeology*, edited by William Green, James B. Stoltman, and Alice B. Kehoe, pp. 243–262. *The Wisconsin Archeologist* 67.

Brakenridge, G. Robert
1981 Late Quaternary Floodplain Sedimentation along the Pomme de Terre River, Southern Missouri. *Quaternary Research* 15:62–76.

Brown, James A.
1965 The Prairie Peninsula: An Interaction Area of the Eastern United States. Ph.D. dissertation, Department of Anthropology, University of Chicago.

Brown, James A., and Robert K. Vierra
1983 What Happened in the Middle Archaic? Introduction to an Ecological Approach to Koster Site Archaeology. In *Archaic Hunters and Gatherers in the American Midwest*, edited by James L. Phillips and James A. Brown, pp. 165–195. Academic Press, New York.

Bryson, Reid A., David A. Baerreis, W. D. Frankforter, Amy E. Henning, Dale R. Henning, William R. James, Gerhard B. Lee, Harvey Nichols, and Martin Q. Peterson
1968–69 Climatic Change and the Mill Creek Culture, Parts I and II. *Journal of the Iowa Archeological Society* 15.

Bryson, Reid A., and Wayne M. Wendland
1967 Tentative Climatic Patterns for Some Late Glacial and Post-Glacial Episodes in Central North America. In *Life, Land and Water*, edited by William J. Mayer-Oakes, pp. 271–298. University of Manitoba Press, Winnipeg.

Chapman, Carl H.
1975 *The Archaeology of Missouri, I.* University of Missouri Press, Columbia.

Charles, Douglas K., and Jane E. Buikstra
1983 Archaic Mortuary Sites in the Central Mississippi Drainage: Distribution, Structure, and Behavioral Implications. In *Archaic Hunters and Gatherers in the American Midwest*, edited by James L. Phillips and James A. Brown, pp. 117–145. Academic Press, New York.

Charles, Douglas K., Steven R. Leigh, and Jane E. Buikstra (editors)
1988 *The Archaic and Woodland Cemeteries at the Elizabeth Site in the Lower Illinois Valley*. Research Series 7. Kampsville Archeological Center, Center for American Archeology, Kampsville, Illinois.

Christenson, Andrew L.
1986 Projectile Point Size and Projectile Aerodynamics: An Exploratory Study. *Plains Anthropologist* 31:109–128.

Cohen, Mark Nathan
1985 Prehistoric Hunter-Gatherers: The Meaning of Social Complexity. In *Prehistoric Hunter-Gatherers: The Emergence of Cultural Complexity*, edited by T. Douglas Price and James A. Brown, pp. 99–119. Academic Press, New York.

Collins, James M.
1990 *Human Adaptations to Holocene Landscapes in the Iowa River Greenbelt*. Contract Completion Report 290. Office of the State Archaeologist, University of Iowa, Iowa City.
1995 Lithic Technology and Temporal Variation at a Chert Workshop in Central Iowa. *Journal of the Iowa Archeological Society* 42:8–20.

Collins, James M., E. Arthur Bettis III, and Timothy J. Kemmis
1991 *Archaeological and Geomorphological Investigations at the Bash Site*. Project Completion Report 14(85). Office of the State Archaeologist, University of Iowa, Iowa City.
1994 Archaeological Geology at the Bash Site. *Illinois Archaeology* 6:98–149.

Collins, James M., and Rolfe Mandel
1999 *Phase II Archaeological Testing at Three Sites in the Iowa River Greenbelt: Primary Roads Project NHS-520-5(57)--19-42 a.k.a. PIN 94-42060-4, Hardin County, Iowa.* Project Completion Report 22(2). Office of the State Archaeologist, University of Iowa, Iowa City.

Collins, James M., and Anthony Zalucha
1997 *Prehistoric Archaeology of the Marriott Site: Archaeological Data Recovery at 13VB455, Van Buren County, Iowa.* Research Papers 22(2). Office of the State Archaeologist, University of Iowa, Iowa City.

Conrad, Lawrence A.
1981 *An Introduction to the Archaeology of Upland West Central Illinois: A Preliminary Archaeological Survey of the Canton to Quincy Corridor for the Proposed FAP-407 Highway Project.* Reports of Investigations 2. Archaeological Research Laboratory, Western Illinois University, Macomb.

Cook, Thomas G.
1976 *Koster: An Artifact Analysis of Two Archaic Phases in Westcentral Illinois.* Prehistoric Records 1 and Koster Research Reports 3. Northwestern University Archaeological Program, Evanston, Illinois.

DeBoer, Warren R.
1988 Subterranean Storage and the Organization of Surplus: The View from Eastern North America. *Southeastern Archaeology* 7:1–20.

Delcourt, Paul A., and Hazel R. Delcourt
1981 Vegetation Maps for Eastern North America: 40,000 Yr BP to the Present. In *Geobotany II*, edited by Robert C. Romans, pp. 123–166. Plenum Publishing, New York.

Dudzik, Mark J.
1974 Aboriginal Subsistence-Settlement Systems in the Upper Mississippi River Valley. Master's thesis, Department of Anthropology, University of Wisconsin–Milwaukee.

Dunne, Michael T., and William Green
1998 Terminal Archaic and Early Woodland Plant Use at the Gast Spring Site (13LA152), Southeast Iowa. *Midcontinental Journal of Archaeology* 23:45–88.

Eddins, John, K. Kris Hirst, Todd L. Butler, James G. Foradas, Randall Withrow, and Todd Hejlik
2004 (draft) *Archaeological Investigations at the Jennings Bottom Site (13HN177), Henry County, Iowa.* Report prepared for the Iowa Department of Transportation. Louis Berger Group, Marion, Iowa.

Ellis, Christopher J.
1997 Factors Influencing the Use of Stone Projectile Tips: An Ethnographic Perspective. In *Projectile Technology*, edited by Heidi Knecht, pp. 37–78. Plenum Press, New York.

Emerson, Thomas E., and Dale L. McElrath
1983 A Terminal Late Archaic Settlement-Subsistence Model. In *Archaic Hunters and Gatherers in the American Midwest*, edited by James L. Phillips and James A. Brown, pp. 219–242. Academic Press, New York.

Emerson, Thomas E., Dale L. McElrath, and Joyce A. Williams
1986 Patterns of Hunter-Gatherer Mobility and Sedentism during the Archaic Period in the American Bottom. In *Foraging, Collecting, and Harvesting: Archaic Period Subsistence and Settlement in the Eastern Woodlands*, edited by Sarah W. Neusius, pp. 247–273. Occasional Papers 6. Center for Archaeological Investigations, Southern Illinois University, Carbondale.

Esarey, Duane
1986 Red Ochre Mound Building and Marion Phase Associations: A Fulton County, Illinois Perspective. In *Early Woodland Archeology*, edited by Kenneth B. Farnsworth and Thomas E. Emerson, pp. 231–243. Kampsville Seminars in Archeology 2. Center for American Archeology, Kampsville, Illinois.

Esling, Steven Paul
1984 Quaternary Stratigraphy of the Lower Iowa and Cedar River Valleys, Southeast Iowa. Ph.D. dissertation, Department of Geology, University of Iowa, Iowa City.

Evans, J. Bryant, Madeleine G. Evans, and Kathryn E. Parker
2001 *The Floyd Site: A Terminal Archaic Habitation in the Northern American Bottom*. Transportation Archaeological Research Reports 11. Illinois Department of Transportation Research Program, University of Illinois, Champaign–Urbana.

Fiedel, Stuart J., K. Kris Hirst, and Laura J. Elsinger
2004 *Phase III Data Recovery Investigations at the Overberg Site (13HN318), Henry County, Iowa.* Report prepared for the Iowa Department of Transportation. Louis Berger Group, Marion, Iowa.

Filbrandt, Bruce
1997 *Keokuk Axes.* Hynek Printing, Richland Center, Wisconsin.

Finn, Michael R.
1981 *13JF92: An Archaic Site in Southeast Iowa, RS-7721, COE: NCROD-S-070-0X6-1-07107, Jefferson County Secondary Roads.* Project Completion Report 4(79). Office of the State Archaeologist, University of Iowa, Iowa City.
1982 The Merrimac Mills Site (13JF92): A Study of Site Positioning and Mobile Strategy of an Upland Archaic Site in Southeast Iowa. Master's thesis, Department of Anthropology, University of Iowa, Iowa City.

Fishel, Richard, James M. Collins, Michael T. Dunne, Rolfe Mandel, David Stephenson, Richard W. Slaughter, J. Wendt, and Brian J. Witzke
2000 *Phase III Archaeological Data Recovery at the Smith Bottom Site (13HA181) and the Allen Fan Site (13HA385): The Middle and Late Archaic of Hardin County, Iowa.* Contract Completion Report 692. Office of the State Archaeologist, University of Iowa, Iowa City.

Fishel, Richard L., Rolfe D. Mandel, James M. Collins, and Michael T. Dunne
2003 *The Archaic Occupations of the Allen Fan Site (13HA385) in the Iowa Valley of Central Iowa.* Memoir 34. Plains Anthropological Society, Lincoln, Nebraska.

Flanders, Richard E.
1977 The Soldow Site, 13BH1: An Archaic Component from North Central Iowa. *Journal of the Iowa Archeological Society* 24:125–147.

Foradas, James G.
2004 (draft) *Phase III Archaeological Data Recovery at the Riley Site (13HN373).* Report prepared for the Iowa Department of Transportation. Louis Berger Group, Marion, Iowa.

Fortier, Andrew C., Thomas E. Emerson, and Kathryn E. Parker
1998 The Meyer Site: A Terminal Late Archaic Residential Camp in the American Bottom. *Illinois Archaeology* 10:195–228.

Frison, George C.
1989 Experimental Use of Clovis Weaponry and Tools on African Elephants. *American Antiquity* 54:766–784.

Gibbon, Guy
1984 *Anthropological Archaeology.* Columbia University Press, New York.

Goatley, Daniel B.
1998 Quasar: A Stratified Archaic Site in the Floodplain of the Lower Illinois River Valley. *Illinois Archaeology* 10:267–293.

Goodyear, Albert C.
1974 *The Brand Site: A Techno-Functional Study of a Dalton Site in Northeast Arkansas.* Research Series 7. Arkansas Archeological Survey, Fayetteville.
1982 The Chronological Position of the Dalton Horizon in the Southeastern United States. *American Antiquity* 47:382–395.

Graham, Russell W.
1980 *Final Report on Paleontological and Archaeological Excavations and Surface Surveys at Mastodon State Park.* Illinois State Museum, Springfield.

Green, William
1988a (editor) *Archaeological and Paleoenvironmental Studies in the Turkey River Valley, Northeastern Iowa.* Research Papers 13(1). Office of the State Archaeologist, University of Iowa, Iowa City.
1988b Investigations at 13CT228: A Buried Prehistoric Site on the Lower Turkey River. In *Archaeological and Paleoenvironmental Studies in the Turkey River Valley, Northeastern Iowa*, edited by William Green, pp. 249–268. Research Papers 13(1). Office of the State Archaeologist, University of Iowa, Iowa City.
1990 Durst Style Artifacts Dated to about 600–800 B.C. *Newsletter of the Iowa Archeological Society* 40(4):4.
1996 Employing the "Variant" Taxon to Refine Effigy Mound Systematics. Paper presented at the Effigy Mounds Workshop, Beloit, Wisconsin.

Green, William, and Shirley Schermer
1988 The Turkey River Mound Group (13CT1). In *Archaeological and Paleoenvironmental Studies in the Turkey River Valley, Northeastern Iowa*, edited by William Green, pp. 131–198. Research Papers 13(1). Office of the State Archaeologist, University of Iowa, Iowa City.

Griffin, James B.
1960 A Hypothesis for the Prehistory of the Winnebago. In *Culture in History: Essays in Honor of Paul Radin*, edited by Stanley Diamond, pp. 809–865. Columbia University Press, New York.

Hainlin, Sheila Willoughbe

1992 Analysis of the Archaic Lithic Artifacts from the Buchanan Site (13SR153), Ames, Iowa. Master's thesis, Department of Anthropology, Iowa State University, Ames.

Hajic, Edwin R.

1982 Holocene Landscape Evolution and Archaeological Site Location in the Lower Illinois Valley Region, USA. *Abstracts*, p. 142. Eleventh International Congress of Sedimentology, McMaster University, Hamilton, Ontario.

Hall, Robert L.

1980 An Interpretation of the Two-Climax Model of Illinois Prehistory. In *Early Native Americans: Prehistoric Demography, Economy, and Technology*, edited by David L. Browman, pp. 401–462. Mouton, The Hague.

Hallberg, George R.

1980a (editor) *Illinoian and Pre-Illinoian Stratigraphy of Southeast Iowa and Adjacent Illinois.* Technical Information Series 11. Iowa Geological Survey, Iowa City.

1980b *Pleistocene Stratigraphy in East-Central Iowa.* Technical Information Series 10. Iowa Geological Survey, Iowa City.

Hallberg, George R., E. Arthur Bettis III, and Jean C. Prior

1984 Geologic Overview of the Paleozoic Plateau Region of Northeastern Iowa. *Proceedings of the Iowa Academy of Science* 91(1):5–11.

Hallberg, George R., Thomas E. Fenton, G. A. Miller, and A. J. Lutenegger

1978 The Iowan Erosion Surface: An Old Story, an Important Lesson, and Some New Wrinkles. In *42nd Annual Tri-State Geological Conference Guidebook*, edited by R. Anderson, pp. 2-1–2-94. Iowa Geological Survey, Iowa City.

Harl, Joe

1998 The Titterington Phase of East-Central Missouri and Archaeology of the Hayden Site: Evidence of Long-Term Occupation in the Late Archaic. *Illinois Archaeology* 10:229–266.

Hedden, John G., Michael J. Perry, Mark L. Anderson, David A. May, and Todd N. Threet

2000 *Phase I Archaeological Survey of the Old Military Trail, Johnson and Linn Counties, Iowa, Primary Roads Project STP-1-5(64)--2C-52, a.k.a. PIN94-52012-1.* Project Completion Report 23(2). Office of the State Archaeologist, University of Iowa, Iowa City.

Hitchcock, Robert, and Peter Bleed

1997 Each According to Need and Fashion: Spear and Arrow Use among San Hunters of the Kalahari. In *Projectile Technology*, edited by Heidi Knecht, pp. 345–370. Plenum Press, New York.

Hoard, Robert J., William E. Banks, Rolfe D. Mandel, Michael Finnegan, and Jennifer E. Epperson

2004 A Middle Archaic Burial from East Central Kansas. *American Antiquity* 69:717–739.

Hollinger, R. Eric

2001 Lithic Artifact Analysis. In *Paleoindian, Archaic, and Woodland Period Occupations on the Wever Terrace*, pp. 44–66. Archaeological Data Recovery for the U.S. 61 Wever Bypass, Lee County, Iowa. Iowa Department of Transportation No. DE-61-1(24)--2A-56. Louis Berger Group, Marion, Iowa.

Holman, Margaret B., and Frank J. Krist Jr.

2001 Late Woodland Storage and Mobility in Western Lower Michigan. *The Wisconsin Archeologist* 82:7–32.

Hoppin, Art, and David G. Stanley

2000 *Phase I Cultural Resource Survey for a Proposed Road Improvement and Bridge Replacement Project on County Road H-16 in Morning Sun Township, Louisa County, Iowa.* BCA 802. Bear Creek Archeology, Cresco, Iowa.

Hoyer, Bernard E.

1980 The Geology of the Cherokee Sewer Site. In *The Cherokee Excavations: Holocene Ecology and Human Adaptations in Northwestern Iowa,* edited by Duane C. Anderson and Holmes A. Semken Jr., pp. 21–66. Academic Press, New York.

Hudak, Curtis M.

1987 Quaternary Landscape Evolution of the Turkey River Valley, Northeastern Iowa. Ph.D. dissertation, Department of Geology, University of Iowa, Iowa City.

1990 (editor) *Phase I Cultural Resources Investigation of the Des Moines to Burlington Highway Corridor: Section II, Iowa Counties Mahaska, Wapello, Monroe and Jefferson, DE-163-2(11)--24-62.* Report submitted to the Iowa Department of Transportation. BRW, Minneapolis, Minnesota.

Hummell, Glenn R.

1982 The Keokuk Axe. *Iowa Archeological Society Newsletter* 101:3–10.

Hutchings, Wallace Karl

1997 The Paleoindian Fluted Point: Dart or Spear Armature? The Identification of Paleoindian Delivery Technology through the Analysis of Lithic Fracture Velocity. Master's thesis, Department of Archaeology, University of Toronto, Toronto, Ontario.

Johnson, Donald L.

1990 Biomantle Evolution and the Redistribution of Earth Materials and Artifacts. *Soil Science* 149:84–102.

Johnson, Rebecca Lynn

2003 *Phase II Archaeological Evaluation of 13JH1132 (a.k.a. the Edgewater Park Site), Section 4, T79N, R6W, City of Coralville, Johnson County, Iowa.* Contract Completion Report 1103. Office of the State Archaeologist, University of Iowa, Iowa City.

Justice, Noel D.

1987 *Stone Age Spear and Arrow Points of the Midcontinental and Eastern United States.* Indiana University Press, Bloomington.

Keyes, Charles R.

1927 Prehistoric Man in Iowa. *The Palimpsest* 8:185–229.

1931 Grooved Axes of the Keokuk Type. *The Wisconsin Archeologist* 10:128–131.

1951 Prehistoric Indians of Iowa. *The Palimpsest* 32:281–344.

King, J. E.

1981 Late Quaternary Vegetational History of Illinois. *Ecological Monographs* 51:43–62.

Klippel, Walter E., and James Maddox

1977 The Early Archaic of Willow Branch. *Midcontinental Journal of Archaeology* 2:99–130.

Knecht, Heidi (editor)
1997 *Projectile Technology.* Plenum Press, New York.

Knox, J. C., P. F. McDowell, and W. C. Johnson
1981 Holocene Fluvial Stratigraphy and Climatic Change in the Driftless Area, Wisconsin. In *Quaternary Climatic Change,* edited by W. C. Mahaney, pp. 107–127. Geo Abstracts, Norwich, England.

Leigh, D. S., and J. C. Knox
1993 AMS Radiocarbon Age of the Upper Mississippi Valley Roxana Silt. *Quaternary Research* 39:282–289.

Lensink, Stephen C.
1984 A Quantitative Model of Central-Place Foraging among Prehistoric Hunter-Gatherers. Ph.D. dissertation, Department of Anthropology, University of Iowa, Iowa City.
1986 *Archaeological Investigations along the F-518 Corridor: Phase III Mitigation of 13WS61, 13WS65, 13WS122, 13WS126.* Iowa Quaternary Studies Contribution 9. University of Iowa, Iowa City.

Logan, Wilfred D.
1976 *Woodland Complexes in Northeastern Iowa.* Publications in Archaeology 15. National Park Service, Washington, D.C.

Lopinot, Neal H.
1987 Archaeobotany. In *Archaeology in the Mississippi River Floodplain at Sand Run Slough, Iowa,* by David W. Benn, E. Arthur Bettis III, Arthur Hoppin, Lucretia S. Kelly, Neal H. Lopinot, and David G. Stanley, pp. 203–225. CAR-690. Center for Archaeological Research, Southwest Missouri State University, Springfield.

Luchterhand, Kubet
1970 *Early Archaic Projectile Points and Hunting Patterns in the Lower Illinois Valley.* Reports of Investigation 19 and Illinois Valley Archaeological Program Research Papers 5. Illinois State Museum, Springfield.

Mallam, R. Clark, and E. Arthur Bettis III
1980 *The Iowa Northern Tier Archaeological Project.* Luther College Archaeological Research Center, Decorah, Iowa.

Mallam, R. Clark, and Mary Housker
1976 *A Cultural Resource Survey of the Volga Lake and Recreation Area, Fayette County, Iowa.* Luther College Archaeological Research Center, Decorah, Iowa.

Marcucci, Derrick J., Susan L. Gade, Julie Morrow, and Toby Morrow
1993 An Introduction to the Prehistory and History of Maquoketa, Jackson County, Iowa. Association of Iowa Archaeologists 1993 Field Trip Guide, June 4–5, 1993. On file, Office of the State Archaeologist, University of Iowa, Iowa City.

Marshall, Richard A.
1958 The Use of Table Rock Projectile Points in the Delineation of Cultural Complexes and Their Distribution. Master's thesis, Department of Sociology and Anthropology, University of Missouri, Columbia.

Marx, Karl
1906 *Capital: A Critique of Political Economy.* Modern Library, New York.

McElrath, Dale L.
1993 Mule Road: A Newly Defined Late Archaic Phase in the American Bottom. In *Highways to the Past: Essays on Illinois Archaeology in Honor of Charles J. Bareis,* edited by Thomas E. Emerson, Andrew C. Fortier, and Dale L. McElrath, pp. 148–157. *Illinois Archaeology* 5.

McElrath, Dale L., Thomas E. Emerson, Andrew C. Fortier, and James L. Phillips
1984 Late Archaic Period. In *American Bottom Archaeology: A Summary of the FAI-270 Project Contribution to the Culture History of the Mississippi River Valley,* edited by Charles J. Bareis and James W. Porter, pp. 34–58. University of Illinois Press, Urbana.

McElrath, Dale L., and Andrew C. Fortier
1983 *The Missouri Pacific #2 Site (11-S-46).* American Bottom Archaeology FAI-270 Site Reports 3. University of Illinois Press, Urbana.

McMillan, R. Bruce, and Walter E. Klippel
1981 Post-Glacial Environmental Change and Hunting-Gathering Societies of the Southern Prairie Peninsula. *Journal of Archaeological Science* 8:215–245.

Morrow, Julie, and Joe Alan Artz
1997 *In Small Sites Forgotten: A Phase I Archaeological Survey for Primary Roads Project NHS-61-2(50)--19-29 Des Moines County, Iowa.* Project Completion Report 20(2). Office of the State Archaeologist, University of Iowa, Iowa City.

Morrow, Toby A.
1981a An Analysis of the Conrad Archaic Site (13GN21). Manuscript on file, Office of the State Archaeologist, University of Iowa, Iowa City.
1981b Late Paleo-Indian and Early Archaic Projectile Points: A Perspective from the Keyes Collection. Manuscript on file, Office of the State Archaeologist, University of Iowa, Iowa City.
1984a Cultural Change and Continuity in Eastern Iowa Prehistory: A Perspective from the Wolf Creek Valley. Master's thesis, Department of Anthropology, University of Iowa, Iowa City.
1984b *Iowa Projectile Points.* Special Publication. Office of the State Archaeologist, University of Iowa, Iowa City.
1994 A Key to the Identification of Chipped-Stone Raw Materials Found on Archaeological Sites in Iowa. *Journal of the Iowa Archeological Society* 41:108–129.
1998 *Phase III Excavations at the Ed's Meadow Site (13DM712), Local Systems Project P-64, a.k.a. FHWA 143160, Des Moines County, Iowa.* Contract Completion Report 480. Office of the State Archaeologist, University of Iowa, Iowa City.

Morrow, Toby A., Rolfe D. Mandel, and Ronald W. Mayer
1995 *Phase I Archaeological Survey of Avenue of the Saints between Mount Pleasant and the Missouri Line, Linn and Henry Counties, Iowa.* Contract Completion Report 430. Office of the State Archaeologist, University of Iowa, Iowa City.

Muniz, Mark P.
2004 Exploring Technological Organization and Burial Practices at the Paleoindian Corgon Creek Site (5LR99), Colorado. *Plains Anthropologist* 49:253–279.

Nassaney, Michael S., and Neal H. Lopinot
1986 The Significance of a Short-Term Late Archaic Occupation in the American Bottom. In *Foraging, Collecting, and Harvesting: Archaic Period Subsistence and Settlement in the Eastern Woodlands,* edited by Sarah W. Neusius, pp. 201–224. Occasional Papers 6. Center for Archaeological Investigations, Southern Illinois University, Carbondale.

Nations, Brenda K., and Richard G. Baker
1991 Klum Lake Pollen Cores. In *Paleoenvironments and Archaeology of the Mississippi Valley in Southeastern Iowa,* Appendix F. Association of Iowa Archaeologists 1991 Field Trip Guide. On file, Office of the State Archaeologist, University of Iowa, Iowa City.

Nelson, Margaret C.
1997 Projectile Points: Form, Function, and Design. In *Projectile Technology*, edited by Heidi Knecht, pp. 371–384. Plenum Press, New York.

O'Brien, Michael J., and Thomas D. Holland
1992 The Role of Adaptation in Archaeological Explanation. *American Antiquity* 57:3–59.

O'Brien, Michael J., and W. Raymond Wood
1998 *The Prehistory of Missouri.* University of Missouri Press, Columbia.

Odell, George H.
1994 Prehistoric Hafting and Mobility in the North American Midcontinent: Examples from Illinois. *Journal of Anthropological Archaeology* 13:51–73.
1996 *Stone Tools and Mobility in the Illinois Valley.* Archaeological Series 10. International Monographs in Prehistory, Ann Arbor, Michigan.

Odum, Eugene
1971 *Fundamentals of Ecology.* W. B. Saunders, Philadelphia.

Orr, Ellison
1936 Sundry Archaeological Papers and Memoranda, 1936. Vol. V. Iowa Archaeological Reports 1934 to 1939. Evaluation and Index by Marshall McKusick. In Archives of Archaeology. Society for American Archaeology, Microcard Series 20 (1963), edited by David Baerreis. University of Wisconsin Press, Madison. Original documents on file, National Park Service, Effigy Mounds National Monument, Harpers Ferry, Iowa.

Osborn, Nancy M., and David M. Gradwohl
1981 *Saylorville Stage 2 Contract Completion Report: Archaeological Investigations in the Saylorville Lake Project, Iowa.* Archaeological Laboratory, Iowa State University, Ames.

Overstreet, David F.
1988 Osceola Revisited: Archaeological Investigations on the Potosi Terrace, Grant County, Wisconsin. *The Wisconsin Archeologist* 69:1–61.

Pauketat, Timothy R.
2001 Practice and History in Archaeology. *Anthropological Theory* 1:73–98.

Perry, Michael J.
1982 *Phase II Investigation GRS-8028(2) Louisa County Roads.* Project Completion Report 5(41). Office of the State Archaeologist, University of Iowa, Iowa City.
1985 *Phase II Excavations at Sites 13LN226 and 13LN236, RS-4834(5), Linn County, Local Roads.* Project Completion Report 8(228). Office of the State Archaeologist, University of Iowa, Iowa City.
1991 Middle Woodland Field Camps in the Cedar Valley. *Journal of the Iowa Academy of Science* 98:109–117.

Pleger, Thomas C.
2000 Old Copper and Red Ochre Social Complexity. *Midcontinental Journal of Archaeology* 25:169–190.

Price, T. Douglas, and James A. Brown
1985 Aspects of Hunter-Gatherer Complexity. In *Prehistoric Hunter-Gatherers: The Emergence of Cultural Complexity*, edited by T. Douglas Price and James A. Brown, pp. 5–20. Academic Press, New York.

Prior, Jean C.
1991 *Landforms of Iowa.* University of Iowa Press, Iowa City.

Ray, Jack H.
1994 Casa Blanca: An Early Archaic Upland Base Camp in Southwest Missouri. *The Missouri Archaeologist* 55:1–46.

Ray, Jack H., and David W. Benn
1988 *Historic Properties Survey in the Soap Creek Watershed, South-Central Iowa* CAR-723. Center for Archaeological Research, Southwest Missouri State University, Springfield.

Roggman, Arnold D.
1990 Durst Points Found in Northeast Iowa Site Explored by IAS Member. *Iowa Archeological Society Newsletter* 49(4):1–3.

Roper, Donna C.
1984 *Cultural Resources Reconnaissance at Lake Red Rock, Iowa.* Report R-2596. Commonwealth Associates, Jackson, Michigan.

Ruhe, Robert V.
1969 *Quaternary Landscapes of Iowa.* Iowa State University Press, Ames.

Ruhe, R. V., and P. H. Walker
1968 Hillslope Models and Soil Formation: I. Open Systems. *Transactions of the 9th Congress of Soil Scientists* 4:551–560. Adelaide, Australia.

Ruppé, Reynold J.
1954 An Archaic Site in Olin, Iowa. *Journal of the Iowa Archeological Society* 3(4):12–15.

Sandstrom, Carl B., and Jack H. Ray
2004 *A Point Identification Guide for Southwest Missouri.* Ozarks Chapter, Missouri Archaeological Society, Springfield.

Sassaman, Kenneth E., and R. Jerald Ledbetter
1993 Middle and Late Archaic Architecture. In *Archaeology of the Mid-Holocene Southeast*, edited by Kenneth E. Sassaman and David G. Anderson, pp. 75–95. University Press of Florida, Gainesville.

Schmits, Larry J.
1978 The Coffey Site: Environmental and Cultural Adaptation at a Prairie Plains Archaic Site. *Midcontinental Journal of Archaeology* 3:69–185.

Schumm, S. A.
1976 Episodic Erosion: A Modification of the Geomorphic Cycle. In *Theories of Landform Development*, edited by W. N. Melhorn and R. C. Flemal, pp. 69–85. George Allen and Unwin, London.

Seelen, Robert M.
2002 A Preliminary Report of the Sedalia Complex. *Missouri Archaeological Society Quarterly* 19(2):14–16. Expanded version of original published 1961, Missouri Archaeological Society, Columbia.

Sellars, Jonathan R., and Leslie A. Ambrosino
2000 *Archaeological Investigations for the Proposed Lake MacBride Restoration, Johnson County, Iowa.* Consulting Archaeological Services, Creston, Iowa.

Shott, Michael J.
1986 Technological Organization and Settlement Mobility: An Ethnographic Examination. *Journal of Anthropological Research* 42:15–51.
1993 Spears, Darts, and Arrows: Late Woodland Hunting Techniques in the Upper Ohio Valley. *American Antiquity* 58:425–443.
1997 Stones and Shafts Redux: The Metric Discrimination of Chipped-Stone Dart and Arrow Points. *American Antiquity* 62:86–101.

Spears, D. G.
1979 Plano—Archaic Tradition in Southeast Iowa. *Newsletter of the Iowa Archeological Society* 92:2–5.

Stafford, Thomas, Jr.
1981 Alluvial Geology and Archaeological Potential of Texas Southern High Plains. *American Antiquity* 46:548–565.

Stanley, David G. (editor)
1993 *Archeological Investigations of the Bear Creek Locality, Allamakee County, Iowa.* 3 vols. HCRC 155. Highland Cultural Research Center, Highlandville, Iowa.
1994 *Phase I and Extended Phase I Cultural Resources Investigation of the Des Moines to Burlington Corridor, Section III, Henry and Des Moines Counties, Iowa.* BCA 209. Report submitted to the Iowa Department of Transportation. Bear Creek Archeology, Cresco, Iowa.

Stanley, David G., and Arthur Hoppin
1987 Lithic Analysis. In *Archaeology in the Mississippi River Floodplain at Sand Run Slough, Iowa*, edited by David W. Benn, pp. 101–187. CAR-690. Center for Archaeological Research, Southwest Missouri State University, Springfield.

Sterns, F. H.
1915 Stratification of Cultures in Eastern Nebraska. *American Anthropologist* 17:121–127.

Stevens, J. Sanderson, and Blane Nansel
1976 *Intensive Archaeological Investigations at the Cedar Rapids Water Pollution Control Facilities.* Contract Completion Report 42. Office of the State Archaeologist, University of Iowa, Iowa City.

Stevens, J. Sanderson, and Joseph A. Tiffany
1977 *The Williams Site (13HN10): A Multicomponent Village in Southeast Iowa.* Research Papers 2(7). Office of the State Archaeologist, University of Iowa, Iowa City.

Stoltman, James B.
1986 The Archaic Tradition. *The Wisconsin Archeologist* 67:207–238.

Straka, Jeff, and David W. Benn
2001 *Phase I Cultural Resource Survey of the Proposed Mad Creek Borrow and the Hershey Borrow for the Mad Creek Section 205 Project, Muscatine County, Iowa.* BCA 902. Bear Creek Archeology, Cresco, Iowa.

Stuiver, Minze, and Paula J. Reimer
1993 Extended ^{14}C Database and CALIB Radiocarbon Calibration Program. *Radiocarbon* 35:215–230.

Suttles, Wayne Prescott
1960 Affinal Ties, Subsistence, and Prestige among Coast Salish. *American Anthropologist* 62:296–305.

Thomas, David Hurst
1978 Arrowheads and Atlatl Darts: How the Stones Got the Shaft. *American Antiquity* 43:461–472.

Thompson, Dean M., and E. Arthur Bettis III
1982 Out of Site Out of Planning: Assessing and Protecting Cultural Resources in Evolving Landscapes. *Contract Abstracts and CRM Archeology* 2(3):16–22.

Thompson, Joe B.
1996 *A Phase I Cultural Resource Survey of Aldo Leopold Wetland Complex, Franklin Township, Bremer County, Iowa.* BCA 438. Bear Creek Archeology, Cresco, Iowa.
1999 (editor) *Phase III Data Recovery at the Eddyville Locality: Lost Creek Sites 13MK355, 13MK357, 13MK403, Mahaska County, Iowa.* BCA 492. Report submitted to the Iowa Department of Transportation, Project NHS-137-3(5)--19-62. Bear Creek Archeology, Cresco, Iowa.
2001 *Phase II Archeological Testing of Seven Prehistoric Sites along County Road H16, Morning Sun Township, Louisa County, Iowa.* BCA 829. Report prepared for the Office of the Louisa County Engineer. Bear Creek Archeology, Cresco, Iowa.
2006 *Phase III Archeological Data Recovery from the McNeal Fan (13MC15), Eisele's Hill Locality, Muscatine County, Iowa.* BCA 629. Report prepared for the Iowa Department of Transportation. Bear Creek Archeology, Cresco, Iowa.

Thompson, Joe B., and David W. Benn (editors)
2007 (draft) *Data Recovery Excavations at the Fett Site (13LD597), Lee County, Iowa.* BCA-1130. Bear Creek Archeology, Cresco, Iowa.

Till, Anton
1984 Area XV Cultural Resource Surveys: Wapello County Archaeology. Manuscript on file, Office of Historic Preservation, Des Moines, Iowa.

Till, Anton, and Blaine Nansel
1981 Area XV Cultural Resource Surveys: Jefferson County Archaeology. Manuscript on file, Office of Historic Preservation, Des Moines, Iowa.
1983a Area XV Cultural Resource Surveys: Mahaska County Archaeology. Manuscript on file, Office of Historic Preservation, Des Moines, Iowa.
1983b Area XV Cultural Resource Surveys: Keokuk County Archaeology. Manuscript on file, Office of Historic Preservation, Des Moines, Iowa.

Titus, Steve, Jane K. Johnston, Charles R. McGimsey, and Jeffrey D. Anderson
1991 (draft) *Phase II Archaeological Investigations within the Northern Border Pipeline Expansion/Extension Project Corridor: Harper, Iowa, to the Mississippi River.* Cultural Resources Management Report 168. American Resources Group, Carbondale, Illinois.

Titus, Steve, Jane K. Johnston, James S. Ross, Michael J. McNerney, and Todd A. Ogier
1990 (draft) *Phase I Archaeological Survey and Assessment of the Northern Border Pipeline, Ventura to Kingston, Iowa.* Cultural Resources Management Report 147. American Resources Group, Carbondale, Illinois.

Transeau, E. N.
1935 The Prairie Peninsula. *Ecology* 16:423–437.

Van Nest, Julianne
1993 Geoarchaeology of Dissected Loess Uplands in Western Illinois. *Geoarchaeology* 8:281–311.

Wandsnider, LuAnn
1997 The Roasted and the Boiled: Food Composition and Heat Treatment with Special Emphasis on Pit-Hearth Cooking. *Journal of Anthropological Archaeology* 16:1–48.

Warren, Robert E., and Michael J. O'Brien
1982 Models of Adaptation and Change. In *The Cannon Reservoir Human Ecology Project*, edited by Michael J. O'Brien, Robert E. Warren, and Dennis E. Lewarch, pp. 85–100. Academic Press, New York.

Webb, Thompson, III, and Reid A. Bryson
1972 Late- and Postglacial Climatic Change in the Northern Midwest, USA: Quantitative Estimates Derived from Fossil Pollen Spectra by Multivariate Statistical Analysis. *Quaternary Research* 2:70–115.

Wedel, Mildred M.
1961 Indian Villages on the Upper Iowa. *The Palimpsest* 62:561–592.

Wendland, Wayne M.
1978 Holocene Man in North America: The Ecological Setting and Climatic Background. *Plains Anthropologist* 23:273–287.
1980 Holocene Climatic Reconstructions on the Prairie Peninsula. In *The Cherokee Excavations, Holocene Ecology and Human Adaptations in Northwestern Iowa,* edited by Duane C. Anderson and Holmes A. Semken Jr., pp. 139–148. Academic Press, New York

Wiant, Michael D., Edwin R. Hajic, and Thomas R. Styles
1983 Napoleon Hollow and Koster Site Stratigraphy: Implications for Holocene Landscape Evolution and Studies of Archaic Period Settlement Patterns in the Lower Illinois Valley. In *Archaic Hunters and Gatherers in the American Midwest*, edited by James L. Phillips and James A. Brown, pp. 147–164. Academic Press, New York.

Willman, H. B., and J. C. Frye
1970 *Pleistocene Stratigraphy of Illinois.* Bulletin 94. Illinois State Geological Survey, Urbana.

Withrow, Randall M., Jeffrey Anderson, Henry Holt, Marie-Lorraine Pipes, and Seppo Valppu
1998 *Archaeological Investigations at Napoleon Park and the South River Corridor, Iowa City, Iowa.* Report prepared for the City of Iowa City. Cultural Resource Group, Louis Berger and Associates, Marion, Iowa.

Wolverton, Steve
2005 The Effects of the Hypsithermal on Prehistoric Foraging Efficiency in Missouri. *American Antiquity* 70:91–106.

Wood, W. Raymond, and R. Bruce McMillan
1976 *Prehistoric Man and His Environment: A Case Study in the Western Ozark Highland.* Academic Press, New York.

Yerkes, Richard W.
1987 *Prehistoric Life on the Mississippi Floodplain: Stone Tool Use, Settlement Organization, and Subsistence Practices at the Labras Lake Site, Illinois.* University of Chicago Press, Chicago.

Appendix 14.A. Eastern Iowa Archaic Sites.

Site Number	Early Archaic	Middle Archaic	Late Archaic	Landform	Hafted Biface Types	OSA Catalog Number	Reference
13AM1		X		terrace	Big Sandy		Stanley 1993
13AM24	X			terrace	sub-Hardin	31	Sampson coll.
13AM319		X		terrace	Raddatz		Stanley 1993
13AM344			X	terrace	Apple Blossom Stemmed?	4062	
13AM35		X	X	terrace	Tama, Durst		Sampson coll.
13AM415	X			upland	Dalton		
13AN52		X		terrace	Raddatz, Brannon	370-52, 6044	Benn and Hovde 1981
13AN69		X		upland	2 Big Sandy	6048	
13AN94		X	X	terrace	Raddatz, Osceola, Table Rock	6769	Ray and Benn 1988
13BE109			X	upland	Sedalia		
13BE115			X	terrace	Sedalia-Nebo Hill-Wadlow		
13BE130		X		upland	Raddatz	9914	
13BE99		X	X	upland	Simonsen-like, Big Sandy/Godar, Tipton		
13BH30		X		terrace	Raddatz/Robinson		Billeck 1987
13BM104		X		bench	Tama	6517	
13BM111		X		terrace-dune	Raddatz, Tama, Matanzas?		
13BM114		X		terrace	Tama		
13BM54		X		upland	Turin small	3611	
13BN103		X	X	terrace	Matanzas, Karnak, Tipton, Atalissa		Benn and Rogers 1985
13BN103					Stone Square Stemmed, Durst		
13BN110		X	X	terrace	Karnak, Atalissa		Benn and Rogers 1985
13BN114		X		terrace	Matanzas		Benn and Rogers 1985
13BN121		X		terrace	Matanzas		Benn and Rogers 1985
13BN125			X	fan	corner-notched barbed		Benn and Rogers 1985
13BN127			X	terrace	Turin		Benn and Rogers 1985
13BN129			X	terrace	Sedalia/Nebo Hill		Benn and Rogers 1985
13BN132		X		bench	Osceola		Benn and Rogers 1985
13BN133			X	terrace	Atalissa		Benn and Rogers 1985
13BN14			X	terrace	Karnak, Poag		Benn and Rogers 1985
13BN140		X	X	upland	Little Sioux, Matanzas, Apple Blossom Stemmed		Benn and Rogers 1985
13BN140					Table Rock, Poag, Stone Square Stemmed		
13BN146			X	terrace	Karnak		Benn and Rogers 1985
13BN148		X		terrace	Raddatz		Benn and Rogers 1985
13BN162			X	terrace	Sedalia/Nebo Hill		Benn and Rogers 1985
13BN172		X		upland	Brannon/Matanzas		Benn and Rogers 1985
13BN187		X	X	bench	Matanzas, Karnak		Benn and Rogers 1985
13BN203		X	X	fan	Matanzas, Atalissa		Benn and Rogers 1985
13BN206			X	fan	Apple Blossom Stemmed		Benn and Rogers 1985
13BN210			X	terrace	Sedalia		Benn and Rogers 1985
13BN216		X		fan	Matanzas		Benn and Rogers 1985
13BN233			X	upland	Afton		Benn and Rogers 1985
13BN244	X			bench	Dalton		Benn and Rogers 1985
13BN259			X	terrace	Smith Basal Notched		Benn and Rogers 1985
13BN260		X		terrace	Godar		Benn and Rogers 1985
13BN27		X	X	fan-bench	Matanzas, Karnak, Table Rock, Tipton	146, 5426	Benn and Rogers 1985
13BN278			X	terrace	corner-notched barbed		Benn 1986
13BN279		X		fan	small side-notched, sub-Table Rock	5437	Benn 1986
13BN302			X	upland	Karnak		Benn and Rogers 1985
13BN32		X	X	upland	Matanzas, Tama, Sedalia/Nebo Hill, Table Rock		Benn and Rogers 1985
13BN32					Smith Basal Notched		
13BN37			X	upland	Rice Corner Notched, Table Rock, Poag		Benn and Rogers 1985
13BN38		X	X	terrace	Matanzas, Karnak, Tipton, Stone Square Stemmed	5427	Benn and Rogers 1985
13BN40			X	terrace	Table Rock	3236	Benn and Rogers 1985
13BN43			X	terrace	Karnak		Benn and Rogers 1985

Appendix 14.A. Eastern Iowa Archaic Sites, continued.

Site Number	Early Archaic	Middle Archaic	Late Archaic	Landform	Hafted Biface Types	OSA Catalog Number	Reference
13CD99	X			upland	Thebes		
13CN49	X		X	upland	3 Hardin, adzes, Dalton, Turin		Hudak 1990
13CN51			X	upland	Sedalia/Red Ocher		Hudak 1990
13CN8	X			upland	Dalton, St. Charles		Benn et al. 1989
13CN95		X		terrace	Raddatz?		
13CT112	X	X		upland	Dalton, Raddatz		Roggman coll.
13CT113	X	X		upland	St. Charles, Cache River, MacCorkle, Raddatz, Matanzas		Roggman coll.
13CT114	X	X		upland	St. Charles, Osceola		Roggman coll.
13CT116	X	X		upland	Cache River, Matanzas, Osceola		Roggman coll.
13CT117		X	X	upland	Raddatz, Durst		Roggman coll.
13CT119	X	X		upland	St. Charles, Cache River, Osceola		Roggman coll.
13CT120	X	X		upland	Hardaway, Wolf Creek, Osceola		Roggman coll.
13CT121		X		upland	Raddatz		Roggman coll.
13CT121		X	X	upland	Osceola, Table Rock		Roggman coll.
13CT123	X	X	X	upland	Cache River, St. Charles, Hardin, Hardaway, Wolf Creek		Roggman coll.
13CT123					Tama, Osceola, Table Rock, Sedalia		
13CT124			X	upland	Tipton		Roggman coll.
13CT125	X		X	upland	Cache River, Durst		Roggman coll.
13CT129	X	X	X	upland	Decatur, Raddatz, Matanzas, Tama, Durst		Roggman coll.
13CT130		X	X	upland	Raddatz, Fort Dodge		Roggman coll.
13CT131	X		X	upland	MacCorkle, Hardin, Table Rock, Smith Basal Notched		Roggman coll.
13CT132	X		X	upland	St. Charles, Hardin, Atalissa		Roggman coll.
13CT132	X	X		upland	MacCorkle, Kirk/MacCorkle, Hardin, Raddatz, Osceola		Roggman coll.
13CT137	X	X	X	upland	Cache River, Turin, Osceola, Tama, Durst		Roggman coll.
13CT144	X			upland	Cache River		Roggman coll.
13CT145		X		upland	Osceola	398	
13CT228			X	fan	Durst	228, 1626	Green 1988b, 1990
13CT281			X	upland	Durst	3865	
13CT311	X			upland	Thebes		collector
13CT312			X	upland	Tipton		collector
13CT47			X	terrace	Durst	7603	Roggman 1990
13CT98	X			upland	Hardin		Roggman coll.
13DA288		X	X	upland	Raddatz, Table Rock	4958	
13DA311	X	X	X	terrace	Hardin, Jakie, Nebo Hill, Merom	6821	
13DA324		X		upland	Raddatz	6829	collector
13DA451			X	fan	Merom		collector
13DA5		X		terrace	Matanzas		Benn and Rogers 1985
13DA6		X		terrace	Brannon/Matanzas, Raddatz		Benn and Rogers 1985
13DB20		X		terrace	Raddatz		
13DB346		X		cave	Raddatz		
13DB365		X		upland	Raddatz		
13DB367	X			upland	barbed-stem (Hidden Valley?)		
13DB44			X	upland	Merom?	931-44	
13DB457			X	upland	Durst	4426	
13DB493		X		fan	Raddatz, Brannon, Brewerton Eared, Matanzas		Benn 2007
13DB497		X	X	bench	Godar, Osceola, Turin, Table Rock, Tipton		Benn et al. 2007
13DB511	X			upland	adze-Dalton like	6644	
13DB512	X			upland	adze with Gainey point	6645	
13DB593	X			upland	Dalton	7438	
13DB627				terrace	Paleoindian, adze	9493	
13DB694		X		upland	Raddatz, Turin	9106	
13DB697	X			upland	St. Charles		

Appendix 14.A. Eastern Iowa Archaic Sites, continued.

Site Number	Early Archaic	Middle Archaic	Late Archaic	Landform	Hafted Biface Types	OSA Catalog Number	Reference
13DB704	X			upland	Dalton-like		
13DB706			X	upland	Durst?		
13DB722			X	upland	Tipton		
13DB739		X		upland	Raddatz?		
13DB80		X		terrace	Raddatz/Osceola	931-80, 1811	
13DM117		X		terrace	Raddatz	929-117	
13DM129		X		upland	Osceola	929-159	
13DM230			X	terrace	Rice Corner Notched		Benn et al. 1988
13DM234			X	terrace	Nebo Hill		Benn et al. 1988
13DM240	X	X	X	fan	Dalton, Grundy, Godar, Matanzas, Apple Blossom Stemmed		Benn et al. 1988
13DM240					Nebo Hill, Sedalia, Springly		
13DM241	X			terrace	Grundy		Benn et al. 1988
13DM291	X	X	X	fan	Dalton, Tama, Nebo Hill		Benn et al. 1988
13DM292		X	X	terrace	Helton, Rice Corner Notched		Benn et al. 1988
13DM333		X		upland	Godar		Titus et al. 1990
13DM35		X	X	terrace	Matanzas, Godar, Osceola, Table Rock		Benn et al. 1988
13DM353		X		upland	Tama		Titus et al. 1990
13DM50	X			upland	lanceolate base, Kirk fragment?, large flakes	929-50 pics	
13DM555	X			upland	St. Charles, adze	4298	
13DM648		X	X	terrace	Matanzas, Godar, Table Rock	6754 pic	Titus et al. 1991
13DM692		X		upland	Big Sandy	5225	Stanley 1994
13DM696			X	upland	Table Rock	5229 pic	Stanley 1994
13DM712	X	X		upland	Jakie, Helton, Raddatz		Morrow et al. 1995
13DM719	X			upland	serrated biface	5784	
13DM728	X			upland	adze preform	6919, 8930	
13DM729	X			upland	Dalton early	6920	
13DM734		X		upland	Matanzas	6925	
13DM799		X		upland	Matanzas	6990, 8912	
13DM866	X			upland	adzes, preforms, large flakes	7057	
13DM871			X	upland	Sedalia	7062	
13DM888			X	upland	Sedalia	7122	
13DM889	X			upland	Dalton, Stanfield/St. Charles, Hardin	7123	
13DM90	X			upland	adze		
13DM924	X			upland	adze	7158	
13DV45			X	terrace	Nebo Hill		
13DW50		X		terrace	Tama	7187-88	
13DW51		X		upland	Matanzas	5335	
13FN75		X		upland	Raddatz, Tama (small)	8849	
13FN77		X		upland	Matanzas	8851	
13FT22		X		upland	Raddatz		Mallam and Housker 1976
13FT30		X		bench	Osceola		Mallam and Housker 1976
13GN2	X			upland	Grundy, Wolf Creek		Morrow 1984b
13GN21		X		terrace	Raddatz, Matanzas		Morrow 1984b
13GN32	X	X	X	terrace	Wolf Creek, Raddatz, Table Rock, Poag	1057 pic	Morrow 1981a
13GN354		X		terrace	Conrad	733 pic (serrated)	
13GN37	X			terrace	St. Charles		Morrow 1984b
13GN5		X	X	upland	Dalton,Raddatz, Osceola, Brannon, Table Rock, Poag	478	
13GN59	X			terrace	Dalton		Morrow 1984b
13GN6			X	bench	Fort Dodge		Morrow 1984b
13GN92		X		terrace	Osceola		Morrow 1984b
13HA185	X			lake terrace	Thebes	2247	Collins 1990

Appendix 14.A. Eastern Iowa Archaic Sites, continued.

Site Number	Early Archaic	Middle Archaic	Late Archaic	Landform	Hafted Biface Types	OSA Catalog Number	Reference
13HA193		X		upland	Matanzas	2255	Collins 1990
13HA194		X	X	bench?	Matanzas, Table Rock		
13HA197			X	bench	Sedalia digger, Clear Fork gouge		Collins 1990
13HA198			X	upland	Etley?		Collins 1990
13HA21		X		upland	Matanzas	2226, 399-21	Collins 1990
13HA212		X		upland	Tama?	399-212, 2263, 7621	Collins and Mandel 1999
13HA25		X		terrace	Godar		Collins 1990
13HA322	X			upland	Hardin	2273	Collins 1990
13HA323			X	upland	Table Rock	2274	Collins 1990
13HA38	X		X	upland	MacCorkle, Delhi/Stone Square Stemmed, Vosburg	399-38, 2233	Collins 1990
13HA38					Table Rock		
13HA385		X	X	fan	Tama, Raddatz, Logan Creek scraper, Table Rock	7414	Fishel et al. 2003
13HA50		X	X	upland	Osceola, Table Rock, Delhi		Collins 1990
13HA65	X			upland	Dalton	2234	Collins 1990
13HA84		X		upland	Matanzas	2240	Collins 1990
13HK96		X		upland	Matanzas	4783	
13HM27	X			upland	Decatur	7866	
13HN10			X	terrace	Table Rock, Wade/Buck Creek Barbed, corner-notched barbed		Stevens and Tiffany 1977
13HN101			X	upland	Springly		Benn and Bowers 1994
13HN104	X			terrace	Hardin, Stilwell		Till and Nansel 1981
13HN108		X		terrace	Logan Creek scraper		Benn and Bowers 1994
13HN113			X	terrace	Sedalia	413	
13HN135	X			terrace	Hardin		
13HN177		X		terrace	Godar, Tama, Raddatz		Eddins et al. 2004
13HN185			X	upland	Merom/Trimble	8440	Benn and Bowers 1994
13HN187			X	upland	Table Rock		Benn and Bowers 1994
13HN201			X	upland	Merom/Trimble	8456	Benn and Bowers 1994
13HN204		X		upland	Osceola		Benn and Bowers 1994
13HN205	X			upland	Dalton	8460	Benn and Bowers 1994
13HN214			X	upland	Merom/Trimble	8469	Benn and Bowers 1994
13HN216		X		terrace	Raddatz	8470, 10024	Benn and Bowers 1994
13HN224			X	terrace	Sedalia		Benn and Bowers 1994
13HN228			X	upland	Merom/Trimble	8479	Benn and Bowers 1994
13HN229	X	X		upland	Dalton, Osceola	8480	Benn and Bowers 1994
13HN230		X		upland	Raddatz	8481	Benn and Bowers 1994
13HN232		X		upland	Matanzas	8483	Benn and Bowers 1994
13HN24	X			upland	Hardin, adzes		
13HN251			X	upland	Mule Road class II	5152	Stanley 1994
13HN261	X			upland	Hardin	5162 pic	Stanley 1994
13HN281			X	upland	Mule Road class I	5182	Stanley 1994
13HN318	X			upland	adze	9540	
13HN335			X	upland	Table Rock	5005	Morrow et al. 1995
13HN341			X	terrace	Table Rock		Morrow et al. 1995
13HN342			X	upland	Vosburg	5012	Morrow et al. 1995
13HN354	X	X	X	terrace	St. Charles, adze, Godar, Sedalia	5023	Fiedel et al. 2004
13HN355	X	X		terrace?	St. Charles/Neuberger, adze, Godar, Matanzas, Raddatz	5024	Morrow et al. 1995
13HN37		X	X	upland	Godar, Tama, Nebo Hill	5050, 944-37	Morrow et al. 1995
13HN373			X	terrace	Sedalia/Wadlow		Foradas 2004
13HN379	X			upland	Kirk	5047	Morrow et al. 1995
13HN380		X		upland	Osceola	5048	Morrow et al. 1995
13HN383	X			upland	St. Charles?	5388	

Appendix 14.A. Eastern Iowa Archaic Sites, continued.

Site Number	Early Archaic	Middle Archaic	Late Archaic	Landform	Hafted Biface Types	OSA Catalog Number	Reference
13HN384		X		upland	Jakie	5389	
13HN385	X			upland	Hardin	5390 (patinated)	
13HN426			X	terrace	Table Rock		
13HN433			X	upland	Nebo Hill		
13HN512		X		upland	Tama	8910	
13HN535	X		X	bench	Dalton, Sedalia		collector
13HN551	X	X	X	upland	Hardin, Thebes, Osceola, Karnak		
13HN552	X			upland	Hardin		
13HN96			X	terrace	copper point/knife		file correspondence, 20.8 cm
13IW199	X			fan	Thebes	1807 pic	
13IW204	X		X	upland	Hardin, Table Rock		Titus et al. 1990
13IW289		X		upland	Raddatz		
13IW53		X		upland	Osceola	600-53	
13IW67		X		upland	Matanzas	600-67	
13IW68		X		upland	Helton	600-68	
13IW83	X	X		terrace	Grundy?, Turin	600-83	
13IW87		X	X	upland	Helton, Tipton	600-87	
13IW94		X		upland	Godar	600-94 pic	
13IW97	X			upland	Thebes	600-97 pic	
13JF10		X	X	terrace-fan	Helton, Stone Square Stemmed	8485	Benn and Bowers 1994
13JF123			X	upland	Nebo Hill, Sedalia		Till and Nansel 1981
13JF21			X	terrace	Durst		Till and Nansel 1981
13JF3		X	X	terrace	4 Big Sandy, Tama, Matanzas, Turin, Nebo Hill	436-3	Till and Nansel 1981
13JF33			X	bench	Motley-Springly		Till and Nansel 1981
13JF36		X		bench	Raddatz, Osceola		Till and Nansel 1981
13JF370	X			upland	St. Charles	8497	Benn and Bowers 1994
13JF387	X	X		upland	Pulaski, Matanzas	8514	Benn and Bowers 1994
13JF43			X	terrace	Etley	436-43	
13JF92	X	X	X	upland	Wolf Creek, Godar, Raddatz, Table Rock, Tipton		Finn 1981
13JF92					Nebo Hill, Sedalia		
13JF98			X	terrace	Sedalia	436-98 pic	
13JH1003	X			upland	Thebes	8588	
13JH1066	X			upland	Thebes	9046	
13JH1078		X		upland	Tama, Raddatz	9067	Sellars and Ambrosino 2000
13JH1107	X			upland	Hardin	9615	
13JH1114		X		terrace	Turin		Bond and Stanley 2002
13JH1132			X	terrace	Tipton	9601	
13JH1132			X	terrace	Tipton		
13JH1140	X			upland	Thebes		
13JH122		X		terrace	Brewerton	952-122	
13JH250		X		terrace	Raddatz, Osceola		Withrow et al. 1998
13JH286			X	upland	Sedalia	232, 8967	Benn and Vogel 1996
13JH362	X			terrace	Kirk	952-362	
13JH406			X	upland	Tipton		
13JH457		X		terrace	Matanzas	1884	
13JH496		X		upland	Godar (crude)	5526	
13JH502		X		upland	Tama	1272, 3486 pic	
13JH622	X	X		upland	Kirk-Decatur, Matanzas	4581 pic	
13JH626	X			upland	Kirk-like	4585	
13JH644	X			terrace	Kirk	4563	
13JH650	X			upland	Kirk	4608	
13JH660			X	terrace	Tipton	4902	

Appendix 14.A. Eastern Iowa Archaic Sites, continued.

Site Number	Early Archaic	Middle Archaic	Late Archaic	Landform	Hafted Biface Types	OSA Catalog Number	Reference
13JH663			X	upland	Durst		Sellars and Ambrosino 2000
13JH715			X	upland	Tipton		Benn and Vogel 1996
13JH813			X	terrace	Tipton	7710	Hedden et al. 2000
13JH824	X			upland	Kirk		Hedden et al. 2000
13JH864		X		upland	Osceola	7760	
13JH866	X			upland	Hardin?	7762	Hedden et al. 2000
13JH876	X			upland	Kirk	7782	Hedden et al. 2000
13JK111		X		terrace	Turin		
13JK146		X	X	terrace	Raddatz, Tama, Osceola, Table Rock		Benn et al. 1989
13JK147	X	X	X	terrace	Dalton, Graham Cave, Raddatz, Osceola, Table Rock		Benn et al. 1989
13JK147					Sedalia, Tipton, Durst		
13JK220		X		upland	Raddatz-like, Matanzas		
13JK23	X	X	X	shelter	Dalton, Thebes, Little Sioux, Raddatz, Atalissa		Anderson 1987
13JK23				shelter	Durst		
13JK4		X		shelter	Raddatz, Osceola		Marcucci et al. 1993
13JK91		X	X	terrace	Raddatz, Osceola, Godar, Durst		Benn et al. 1989
13JN1	X			terrace	Kirk, copper pin		Ruppe 1954
13JN232		X		upland	Tama	8374	
13JN323			X	terrace	Turin	8231	
13JN81		X		upland	Turin	1495	
13JP86	X			terrace	Thebes		Benn 2005
13JP87	X	X	X	terrace	Hardin, Stilwell, Little Sioux, Raddatz, Tama		Benn 2005
13JP87					Matanzas, Karnak, Nebo Hill, Eva II		
13KK114			X	upland	Table Rock		Till and Nansel 1983b
13KK31			X	upland?	Table Rock		Till and Nansel 1983b
13KK359	X		X	upland	Decatur, Atalissa	2805	
13KK404			X	upland	Table Rock	3665, 4892, 4532 pic	
13KK66			X	terrace	Etley		Till and Nansel 1983b
13KK80		X		bench?	Godar scraper		Till and Nansel 1983b
13LA12	X	X	X	fan			collector
13LA246	X	X		upland	sub-Thebes, Matanzas		
13LA249	X			upland	Thebes, St. Charles	958-249, 616	Perry 1982
13LA273	X			upland	Kirk		Titus et al. 1990
13LA275		X		terrace	Raddatz	3516	Benn et al. 1988
13LA281		X		terrace	Matanzas	3521	Benn et al. 1988
13LA282		X		terrace	Matanzas		Benn et al. 1988
13LA284		X	X	terrace	Helton, Tama, Atalissa		Benn et al. 1988
13LA285		X		terrace	Tama		Benn et al. 1988
13LA293		X		terrace	Matanzas	3523, 5271, 6404, 7497	Benn et al. 1988
13LA299		X		terrace	Osceola		Benn et al. 1988
13LA300		X		terrace	Osceola drill	7499	Benn et al. 1988
13LA340	X			upland	St. Charles?		Titus et al. 1990
13LA364	X			upland	Kirk		Titus et al. 1991
13LA373			X	upland	Table Rock, Apple Blossom Stemmed	3958, 7161	
13LA38		X	X	fan	Matanzas, Helton, Raddatz/Godar, Osceola, Etley		Benn et al. 1987, 1988
13LA38				terrace	Apple Blossom Stemmed		Benn et al. 1987, 1988
13LA437		X		terrace	Osceola	6416	
13LA462		X	X	upland	Raddatz, Wadlow/Sedalia	7105, 7237	
13LA488			X	upland	Table Rock		Hoppin and Stanley 2000
13LA495	X			upland	Graham Cave?		

Appendix 14.A. Eastern Iowa Archaic Sites, continued.

Site Number	Early Archaic	Middle Archaic	Late Archaic	Landform	Hafted Biface Types	OSA Catalog Number	Reference
13LE110	X	X	X	terrace	Hardin, St. Charles, Helton, Osceola, Table Rock		Hollinger 2001
13LE110					Etley		
13LE137	X			terrace	Dalton, Hardin, Thebes, adzes, Keokuk ax		collector (proven?)
13LE326			X	terrace	Nebo Hill, Merom/Trimble, Table Rock		Artz et al. 1995
13LE340		X		upland	Tama	4130	Artz 1994
13LE351	X			terrace-dune	Hardin	4352 pic	Artz 1994
13LE368			X	terrace	Table Rock		Morrow et al. 1995
13LE382			X	upland	Stone Square Stemmed	4623	Morrow et al. 1995
13LE407			X	terrace	Etley		Morrow et al. 1995
13LE416	X			upland?	White Springs (sub-Kirk)	4657	Morrow et al. 1995
13LE478			X	upland	Etley		Morrow et al. 1995
13LE480	X			upland	Hardin		Morrow et al. 1995
13LE513			X	terrace	Wadlow	6858	Morrow and Artz 1997
13LE515	X		X	terrace	Thebes, Sedalia, Sedalia digger, Etley	6860	Morrow and Artz 1997
13LE520	X			terrace	Hardin	6865	Morrow and artz 1997
13LE550		X		upland	Raddatz		collector
13LE586		X		fan	Osceola	9790, 9847	
13LE597	X	X		terrace	Graham Cave, Tama, Matanzas, Turin		
13LE612		X	X	terrace	Osceola, Nebo Hill, Sedalia		
13LE628		X		upland	Osceola?	9744, 9765	
13LN132		X		upland	Turin		Benn and Hovde 1976
13LN133		X	X	terrace	Logan Creek scraper, Atalissa		Benn and Hovde 1976
13LN136		X		terrace	Tama?		Benn and Hovde 1976
13LN141		X	X	terrace	Raddatz-Godar, Tipton	957-141	Stevens and Nansel 1976
13LN236		X		terrace	Helton, Turin		Perry 1985
13LN255			X	terrace	Durst	1742	
13LN29	X			terrace	Thebes, MacCorkle		Benn and Hovde 1976
13LN36	X			terrace	Wolf Creek		Benn and Hovde 1976
13LN37			X	upland	Atalissa		Benn and Hovde 1976
13LN41	X			upland	MacCorkle		Benn and Hovde 1976
13LN44		X		terrace	Matanzas		Benn and Hovde 1976
13LN51	X			terrace	Wolf Creek/Tama, MacCorkle		Benn and Hovde 1976
13LN657			X	terrace	Table Rock		
13LN713		X		upland	Tama	7785	Hedden et al. 2000
13LN715		X		upland	Tama	7787	Hedden et al. 2000
13LN717		X		upland	Tama scraper		Hedden et al. 2000
13LN718	X			upland	Kirk/Hardin	7790	Hedden et al. 2000
13LN723		X		terrace	Raddatz	7795	
13LN750		X		terrace	Tama	8011, 8532	
13LN824		X		terrace	Matanzas?		
13LN826		X		terrace?	Raddatz, Osceola?		
13LN85		X		terrace	Matanzas	5438	
13LN862		X		upland	Matanzas?		
13MA542		X		upland	Raddatz-Matanzas?		
13MA552		X		fan	Big Sandy/Conrad?	8046	
13MA566			X	terrace	Sedalia	8200	
13MC10		X		upland	Raddatz	609	
13MC134		X	X	upland	Matanzas, Table Rock		Benn 2002a
13MC136	X	X	X	upland	Palmer, Kirk/Graham Cave, Raddatz, Brannon		Benn 2002b
13MC136					Matanzas, Table Rock		
13MC15	X	X	X	fan	Kirk, Jakie, Godar, Raddatz, Brannon, Matanzas		Thompson 2006
13MC15					Tama, Osceola, Wadlow, Table Rock		
13MC158			X	fan	Durst	3822	
13MC160		X		fan	Matanzas	3824	

Appendix 14.A. Eastern Iowa Archaic Sites, continued.

Site Number	Early Archaic	Middle Archaic	Late Archaic	Landform	Hafted Biface Types	OSA Catalog Number	Reference
13MC169		X	X	upland	Godar, Brannon, Matanzas, Turin, Nebo Hill, Karnak		Blikre 2003
13MC169					Etley/Helton		
13MC222	X			upland	Kirk	8875	Straka and Benn 2001
13MC46	X			upland	Dalton, small thin adze	120-46	
13MC54		X		upland	Raddatz		
13MC61		X		upland	Raddatz/Osceola	970-61	
13MK145	X			bench?	Meserve/Dalton		Till and Nansel 1983a
13MK355	X	X		terrace	MacCorkle/St. Charles, Tama, Godar/Helton	5243	Thompson 1999
13MK357		X	X	terrace	Raddatz, Godar, Vosburg, Nebo Hill		Thompson 1999
13MK385	X			upland	Thebes	5310	
13MK392		X		terrace	Raddatz?	8926	Blikre 1997
13MK396		X	X	upland	Tama, Sedalia	7690	
13MK422	X			upland	Rice Lobed/MacCorkle	7684	
13MK426		X		upland	Raddatz	7688	
13MK427	X			upland	Hardin	7689	
13MO61			X	terrace	Table Rock	6777	Ray and Benn 1988
13MO64		X		terrace	Godar	6780	Ray and Benn 1988
13MR123			X	upland	barbed point?		
13MR95		X		terrace	Turin	964-95	
13MT105			X	terrace	Tipton, Nebo Hill?		Benn 1979
13MT107		X		upland	Osceola		Benn 1979
13MT117		X		bench	Little Sioux, Matanzas		Benn 1979
13MT123			X	bench	Table Rock		Benn 1979
13MT127		X	X	bench	Matanzas, Poag		Benn 1979
13MT128			X	bench	Tipton, Table Rock?		Benn 1979
13MT132		X		upland	Raddatz		Benn 1979
13MT136			X	upland	Table Rock? Tipton		Benn 1979
13MT137			X	upland	Table Rock		Benn 1979
13MT141	X			upland	sub-Hardin		Benn 1979
13MT145		X		bench	Osceola?		Benn 1979
13MT27		X		upland	Raddatz/Matanzas		Benn 1979
13MT49		X		terrace	Matanzas	8118	Benn 1979
13PK103	X	X	X	upland	Kirk, Godar, Ledbetter		Benn and Rogers 1985
13PK107		X		bench	Helton/Godar, Brannon, Raddatz		Benn and Rogers 1985
13PK109		X	X	bench	Turin, Sedalia/Nebo Hill		Benn and Rogers 1985
13PK111		X	X	bench	Brannon/Matanzas, Table Rock, Atalissa		Benn and Rogers 1985
13PK112		X	X	terrace	Helton, corner-notched barbed		Benn 1986
13PK113	X			bench	Thebes		Benn and Rogers 1985
13PK114		X	X	fan	Matanzas, Ledbetter		Benn and Rogers 1985
13PK122		X	X	terrace	Little Sioux, Table Rock, Poag		Benn and Rogers 1985
13PK146			X	upland	Sedalia/Nebo Hill		Benn and Rogers 1985
13PK149		X		terrace	Matanzas, Conrad		Benn and Rogers 1985
13PK150		X	X	bench	Tama, Poag		Benn and Rogers 1985
13PK153		X		terrace	Raddatz		Benn and Rogers 1985
13PK154		X	X	bench	Raddatz, Brannon, Table Rock		Benn and Rogers 1985
13PK155			X	terrace?	corner-notched barbed		Benn and Rogers 1985
13PK158		X	X	upland	Tama, Poag		Benn and Rogers 1985
13PK163			X	terrace	Sedalia/Nebo Hill		Benn and Rogers 1985
13PK165		X	X	terrace	Helton/Godar, Tama, Sedalia/Nebo Hill, Table Rock		Benn and Rogers 1985
13PK175		X	X	terrace	Helton/Godar, Logan Creek scraper, Tama, Poag		Benn and Rogers 1985
13PK186			X	bench	Smith Basal Notched		Benn and Rogers 1985
13PK197		X	X	upland	Little Sioux, Poag		Benn and Rogers 1985
13PK221		X		upland	Helton/Godar		Benn and Rogers 1985

Appendix 14.A. Eastern Iowa Archaic Sites, continued.

Site Number	Early Archaic	Middle Archaic	Late Archaic	Landform	Hafted Biface Types	OSA Catalog Number	Reference
13PK225	X			upland	Kirk		Benn and Rogers 1985
13PK235		X		upland	Matanzas		Benn and Rogers 1985
13PK251		X	X	bench	Brannon, Conrad, Stone Square Stemmed, Fort Dodge, Motley		Benn 1986
13PK265		X		upland	Brannon/Matanzas	5452	Benn and Rogers 1985
13PK265		X		upland	Matanzas		Benn and Rogers 1985
13PK273		X	X	fan	Matanzas, sub-Atalissa	5457	
13PK29		X		upland	Brannon/Matanzas, Osceola		Benn and Rogers 1985
13PK480			X	terrace	Durst-like		
13PK525	X			upland	Hardin		
13PK742		X		upland	Raddatz		
13SR153		X	X	terrace	Tama, Raddatz, Godar, Conrad/Raddatz, corner-notched barbed		Hainlin 1992
13ST129		X		terrace	Raddatz		
13ST140		X	X	upland	Jakie, Rice Corner Notched		
13ST42			X	upland	Atalissa, Table Rock		
13TM102		X		upland	Raddatz	986-102	
13TM16		X		upland	Tama	603-16, 9928	
13TM191		X	X	upland	Osceola, Table Rock		
13TM196			X	upland	Merom/Trimble	8390	
13TM200	X		X	upland	Kirk, Merom/Trimble		
13TM213			X	terrace	Springly	8398	
13TM26		X		upland	Matanzas	603-26	
13TM280		X		upland	Raddatz, Tama		
13TM302			X	terrace	Durst		
13TM337		X		upland	Raddatz		
13TM339		X		upland	Matanzas		
13TM345	X			upland	St. Charles		
13TM370	X			upland	Hardin		
13TM375	X			upland	Thebes	8415	
13TM419		X		upland	Raddatz		
13TM528	X			upland	Stilwell?		
13TM530	X			upland	Hardin?		
13TM58	X			terrace	Hidden Valley?	603-58	
13VB401			X	terrace	Sedalia	1437	
13VB580			X	upland	Durst		
13WB248	X			terrace	Dalton/Meserve	994-248	
13WE152		X		fan	Matanzas		
13WH1		X	X	terrace	Osceola, Durst		Sampson coll.
13WH10	X	X	X	terrace	Graham Cave? Simonsen, St. Charles, Helton, Raddatz		Sampson coll.
13WH10					Matanzas, Tama, Osceola, Little Sioux, Apple Blossom Stemmed		
13WH11	X			terrace	large stemmed (Hidden Valley)		Sampson coll.
13WH13		X		terrace?	Raddatz		Sampson coll.
13WH132		X		fan	Logan Creek scraper		
13WH134		X		terrace	Logan Creek scraper		
13WH14		X		terrace	Raddatz		Sampson coll.
13WH18		X		upland	Osceola		Sampsoncoll.
13WH33	X	X	X	upland	large stemmed (Hidden Valley), Big Sandy, Poag-like		Sampson coll.
13WH37	X	X		rockshelter	large stemmed (Hidden Valley), fishtail, Raddatz		Sampson coll.
13WH38	X	X	X	terrace	Hardin, Graham Cave, Simonsen, St. Charles, Osceola		Sampson coll.
13WH38					Karnak, Atalissa		

Appendix 14.A. Eastern Iowa Archaic Sites, continued.

Site Number	Early Archaic	Middle Archaic	Late Archaic	Landform	Hafted Biface Types	OSA Catalog Number	Reference
13WH38					Matanzas, Raddatz/Godar, Brannon, Apple Blossom Stemmed		
13WH41	X	X	X	terrace	Graham Cave, Brannon, Osceola, Apple Blossom Stemmed		Sampson coll.
13WH8		X		upland	Raddatz		Sampson coll.
13WH9		X	X	terrace	Raddatz, Matanzas, Osceola, Apple Blossom Stemmed		Sampson coll.
13WN13		X		lake terrace	Matanzas	6839 pic	
13WP114	X	X		terrace	Hardin, Raddatz/Big Sandy	990-114 pic	
13WP288	X			upland	Kirk		
13WP3	X			terrace	Dalton		
13WP330		X		terrace	Nebo Hill	6024	Anderson 1996
13WP363			X	upland	Durst		
13WP413		X		upland	Tama	9913	
13WP67	X	X		upland	Hardin, Big Sandy	439-67	Till 1984
13WP82		X		terrace	Tama	439-82	
13WS122			X	bench	Table Rock, Tipton		Lensink 1986
13WS132		X		upland	Raddatz		
13WS148		X	X	fan	Tama, Smith Basal Notched		site form
13WS154		X		upland	Matanzas		collector
13WS155	X			upland	Thebes		collector
13WS165		X		upland	Hemphill		collector
13WS168		X	X	terrace	Raddatz/Godar, Table Rock		collector
13WS169		X		upland	Raddatz		collector
13WS177	X			upland	St. Charles		collector
13WS184	X	X	X	fan	St. Charles, Raddatz, Epps		collector
13WS187	X			upland	St. Charles		collector
13WS262		X	X	upland	Tama, Table Rock		Titus et al. 1990
13WS276	X	X		terrace	Hardin, Tama, Matanzas, Turin		Titus et al. 1991
13WS28	X			upland	Dalton		
13WS291	X			fan	Greenbrier	3240	
13WS384		X		upland	Matanzas		
13WS65		X	X	upland	Matanzas/Brannon, Godar, Turin, sub-Etley, Durst		Lensink 1986
13WS712		X	X	upland	Jakie, Raddatz, corner-notched		Morrow 1998

Appendix 14.B. Iowa Archaic-Era Archaeological and Geological Radiocarbon and Thermoluminescence Dates.

Context	County	Site Name	Site Number	RC/TLYBP[a]	Date B.C. (calibrated)	Lab Sample No.
Archaeological						
C14	Boone		13BN27	3920 ± 80	2490–2290	Beta-12911
TL	Boone		13BN27	3410 ± 440	1460	Alpha-2071
C14	Boone		13BN103	3975 ± 80	2580–2345	Wis-1220
TL	Boone		13BN277	4200 ± 1300	2250	Alpha-2072
C14	Boone		13BN278	4190 ± 100	2820–2530	Beta-11115
C14	Boone	Sweet Jane Fan	13BN279	3190 ± 190	1690–1250	Beta-11116
C14	Boone	Sweet Jane Fan	13BN279	3900 ± 70	2475–2285	Beta-11117
C14	Boone	Sweet Jane Fan	13BN279	4610 ± 80	3520–3330	Beta-11118
C14	Boone	Sweet Jane Fan	13BN279	5490 ± 80	4400–4310	ISGS-1359
C14	Boone	Sweet Jane Fan	13BN279	6200 ± 260	5380–4845	Beta-11119
C14	Cedar	Rock Run	13CD10	3660 ± 60	2060–1955	WIS-384
C14	Cedar	Rock Run	13CD10	4180 ± 70	2815–2670	WIS-317
C14	Cedar	Rock Run	13CD10	4300 ± 65	3020–2880	WIS-383
C14	Cedar	Rock Run	13CD10	4730 ± 50	3630–3575	WIS-392
C14	Cherokee	Cherokee Sewer	13CK405	6300 ± 90	5375–5205	UCLA-1877B
C14	Cherokee	Cherokee Sewer	13CK405	6500 ± 200	5635–5295	UCR-492
C14	Cherokee	Cherokee Sewer	13CK405	6800 ± 190	5885–5550	UCR-491
C14	Cherokee	Cherokee Sewer	13CK405	7145 ± 75	6080–5975	WIS-891
C14	Cherokee	Cherokee Sewer	13CK405	7370 ± 100	6370–6205	UCLA-1877C
C14	Cherokee	Simonsen	13CK61	8430 ± 520	8010–6905	I(UW)-79
C14	Clayton		13CT228	2580 ± 60	815–750	Wis-2051
C14	Dallas	Foxtail	13DA180	2930 ± 70	1166	ISGS-5880
TL	Des Moines	Ed's Meadow	13DM712	3035 ± 243	1313	U. of Mis-
TL	Des Moines	Ed's Meadow	13DM712	6341 ± 373	5316	U. of Mis-
TL	Des Moines	Ed's Meadow	13DM712	9320 ± 601	9550	U. of Mis-
C14	Dubuque	Garden	13DB493	4000 ± 40	2570–2515	Beta-152119
C14	Dubuque	Garden	13DB493	4430 ± 70	3115–3005	Beta-147212
C14	Dubuque	Garden	13DB493	5250 ± 400	4520–3635	Beta-147213
C14	Dubuque	Garden	13DB493	5400 ± 600	4945–3630	Beta-146199
C14	Dubuque	Union Bench	13DB497	4000 ± 40	2570–2515	Beta-152119
C14	Hardin	Allen Fan	13HA385	2570 ± 70	810–550	ISGS-4487
C14	Hardin	Allen Fan	13HA385	4650 ± 70	3520–3360	ISGS-4169
C14	Hardin	Allen Fan	13HA385	6960 ± 70	5900–5750	ISGS-A-0028
C14	Henry	Riley	13HN373	2830 ± 40	1035	Beta-172982
C14	Henry	Riley	13HN373	2920 ± 40	1135–1050	Beta-172981
C14	Henry	Overberg	13HN318	7890 ± 40	6780–6655	Beta-183870
TL	Henry	Overberg	13HN318	8100 ± 640	6095	Quat. TL Serv.
C14	Jackson	Robert Battey	13JK21	7240 ± 80	6210–6045	WIS-938
C14	Jasper		13JP87	3720 ± 70	2205–2025	ISGS-4864
C14	Jasper		13JP87	3880 ± 100	2475–2205	ISGS-4866
C14	Jasper		13JP87	4185 ± 62	2815–2680	A-0014
TL	Jasper		13JP86	6295 ± 629	4345	UW-681
C14	Johnson	Edgewater Park	13JH1132	3510 ± 40	1855–1770	Beta-179291
C14	Lee	(2Ab)	13LE186	3650 ± 160	2210–1870	Beta-15074

Appendix 14.B. Iowa Archaic-Era Archaeological and Geological Radiocarbon and Thermoluminescence Dates, continued.

Context	County	Site Name	Site Number	RC/TLYBP[a]	Date B.C. (calibrated)	Lab Sample No.
C14	Lee	Fett	13LE597	2500 ± 120	790–510	ISGS-5471
C14	Lee	Fett	13LE597	2670 ± 70	900–795	ISGS-5484
C14	Lee	Fett	13LE597	3710 ± 70	2200–2020	ISGS-5529
C14	Lee	Fett	13LE597	7605 ± 35	6470–6435	ISGS-A0482
C14	Lee		13LE628	3820±40	2290	Beta-216664
C14	Louisa	Sand Run West	13LA38	4140 ± 110	2875–2620	Beta-18293
C14	Louisa	Sand Run West	13LA38	4270 ± 90	3020–2850	Beta-17937
C14	Louisa	Gast Spring	13LA152	2800 ± 45	1010–900	AA-24943
C14	Louisa	Gast Spring	13LA152	3060 ± 70	1415–1260	Beta-103260
C14	Louisa	Gast Spring (structure)	13LA152	5680 ± 90	4620–4445	Beta-51682
C14	Louisa	Gast Spring (structure)	13LA152	5730 ± 90	4690–4490	Beta-51468
C14	Louisa	Heidelbaugh	13LA300	3900 ± 80	2480–2280	Beta-108161
C14	Louisa		13LA499	3090 ± 50	1420–1310	Beta-145805
C14	Mahaska	Component II upper terrace	13MK357	2210 ± 50	360–270	Beta-106531
C14	Mahaska	Component II upper terrace	13MK357	2930 ± 50	1215–1050	Beta-110836
C14	Mahaska	Component III upper terrace	13MK357	3610 ± 60	2035–1890	Beta-106530
C14	Mahaska	Component IV level 9	13MK355	5650 ± 50	4545–4445	Beta-106527
C14	Monona	Turin	13MN2	4720 ± 250	3715–3260	M-932
C14	Muscatine	McNeal Fan	13MC15	4050 ± 120	2710–2465	ISGS-2439
C14	Muscatine	McNeal Fan	13MC15	4110 ± 70	2705–2575	ISGS-3201
C14	Muscatine	McNeal Fan	13MC15	4100 ± 110	2775–2570	ISGS-2440
C14	Muscatine	McNeal Fan	13MC15	4160 ± 70	2815–2665	Beta-127683
C14	Muscatine	McNeal Fan	13MC15	4170 ± 70	2815–2665	ISGS-3202
C14	Muscatine	McNeal Fan	13MC15	4160 ± 80	2820–2660	Beta-127680
C14	Muscatine	McNeal Fan	13MC15	4220 ± 70	2905–2740	Beta-127686
C14	Muscatine	McNeal Fan	13MC15	4330 ± 70	3025–2890	Beta-127681
C14	Muscatine	McNeal Fan	13MC15	4350 ± 80	3025–2890	Beta-127685
C14	Muscatine	McNeal Fan	13MC15	4450 ± 80	3335–3015	Beta-127684
C14	Muscatine	McNeal Fan	13MC15	4880 ± 100	3790–3625	Beta-127682
C14	Muscatine	McNeal Fan	13MC15	6400 ± 120	5480–5290	ISGS-3020
C14	Muscatine	McNeal Fan	13MC120	3590 ± 80	2040–1875	ISGS-3204
C14	Muscatine		13MC136	2780 ± 90	1025–825	Beta-127577
C14	Muscatine		13MC169	3880 ± 50	2460–2330	Beta-127582
TL	Polk	Klein (FCR feature)	13PK112	4130 ± 430	2180	Alpha-1281
C14	Polk	Darr-es-Shalom III	13PK149	2820 ± 65	1055–890	WIS-905
C14	Polk	Darr-es-Shalom IV	13PK149	3045 ± 65	1405–1255	WIS-880
C14	Polk	Darr-es-Shalom IV	13PK149	3095 ± 65	1435–1290	WIS-901
C14	Polk	Brassica Bench	13PK251	4100 ± 70	2705–2570	WIS-1083
TL	Polk	Brassica Bench west	13PK251W	3240 ± 400	1290	Alpha-1517
C14	Polk		13PK414	5190 ± 100	4075–3935	Beta-2634
TL	Pottawattamie	Lewis Central School	13PW5	2815 ± 60	955	UCLA-2105
C14	Story	Buchanan (C 130–140cm)	13SR153	2450 ± 100	595–410	Beta-30338
C14	Story	Buchanan (B 60–70 cm)	13SR153	3000 ± 140	1405–1055	Beta-44529
C14	Story	Buchanan (C 170–185 cm)	13SR153	4230 ± 160	3025–2575	Beta-30337
C14	Story	Buchanan (B 170–190 cm)	13SR153	5220 ± 70	4975–3960	Beta-39670

Appendix 14.B. Iowa Archaic-Era Archaeological and Geological Radiocarbon and Thermoluminescence Dates, continued.

Context	County	Site Name	Site Number	RC/TLYBP[a]	Date B.C. (calibrated)	Lab Sample No.
C14	Story	Buchanan (B 220–230 cm)	13SR153	5480 ± 170	4375–4045	Beta-39899
C14	Story	Buchanan (B 200–210 cm)	13SR153	5560 ± 110	4060–3785	Beta-39672
C14	Story	Buchanan (B 120–140 cm)	13SR153	5600 ± 140	4610–4325	Beta-44068
C14	Story	Buchanan (C 200–206 cm)	13SR153	5570 ± 60	4455–4355	Beta-51683
C14	Story	Buchanan (B 250–260 cm)	13SR153	5820 ± 190	4855–4460	Beta-44069
C14	Story	Buchanan (A 210 cm)	13SR153	6000 ± 120	5040–4765	Beta-18028
C14	Story	Buchanan (B 225–240 cm)	13SR153	6120 ± 240	5320–4780	Beta-25037
TL	Washington	Davis Creek	13WS122	2995 ± 330	1010	U. of Missouri
TL	Washington	Davis Creek	13WS122	3633 ± 360	1650	U. of Missouri
C14	Washington	Goose Creek	13WS126	2520 ± 70	695–540	Beta-12686
Geological						
C14	Boone	Sweet Jane Fan VII	13BN279	5430 ± 100	4365–4225	Beta-11120
C14	Boone	Sweet Jane Fan VII	13BN279	5680 ± 90	4620–4445	Beta-10884
C14	Boone	Sweet Jane Fan VII	13BN279	6200 ± 100	5235–5040	ISGA-1357
C14	Boone	soil 5Ab	13BN27	6170 ± 170	5310–4930	Beta-12912
C14	Des Moines	EMHOL1	13DM648	6210 ± 150	5315–4930	Beta-21876
C14	Dubuque	Garden (fan base)	13DB493	10,380 ± 60	10,430–10,175	Beta-150345
C14	Dubuque	Garden (fan base)	13DB493	10,750 ± 80	10,900–10,785	Beta-150344
C14	Hardin	Allen Fan	13HA385	4215 ± 40	2805–2755	ISGS-A-0136
C14	Henry	Riley	13HN373	5380 ± 60	4330–4225	Beta-172986
C14	Henry	Riley	13HN373	5590 ± 50	4455–4365	Beta-172987
C14	Jackson	Henry Schnoor Rock Shelter	13JK20	3680 ± 70	2140–1960	WIS-407
C14	Lee	Hoenig Alluvial Fan (5Ab)	13LE42	10,530 ± 70	10,725–10,445	ISGS-5539
C14	Lee	Hoenig Alluvial Fan (4Ab)	13LE42	10,210 ± 70	10,105–9857	ISGS-5545
C14	Louisa	Gast Spring (3ABb)	13LA152	3770 ± 110	2345–2030	Beta-41518
C14	Louisa	Gast Spring (4Ab)	13LA152	3830 ± 110	2460–2190	Beta-41517
C14	Louisa	Gast Spring (3Ab)	13LA152	4840 ± 50	3665–3535	Beta-44380
C14	Louisa	Gast Spring (4.7 m)	13LA152	5680 ± 90	4620–4445	Beta-51682
C14	Louisa	Gast Spring (Fea. G)	13LA152	5730 ± 90	4690–4490	Beta-51468
C14	Louisa	Gast Spring (5ABb)	13LA152	6215 ± 70	5180–5065	Beta-41210
C14	Louisa	Gast Farm Fan	13LA12	4730 ± 50	3630–3380	Beta-77382
C14	Louisa	Gast Farm Fan	13LA12	5400 ± 70	4340–4230	Beta-77383
C14	Louisa	Klum Lake	paleochannel	7290 ± 90	6235–6060	Beta-23635
C14	Louisa	Klum Lake	paleochannel	7330 ± 100	6260–6070	Beta-22804
C14	Louisa	Klum Lake	lake sediment	10,410 ± 80	10,450–10,175	Beta-22806
C14	Louisa	Klum Lake	lake sediment	12,210 ± 510	13,015–11,690	Beta-22805
C14	Muscatine	McNeal Fan	IIf soil	6400 ± 120	5480–5295	ISGS-3020
C14	Story	Buchanan	13SR153 bank	3095 ± 55	1430–1305	Beta-44070

[a]One-sigma ranges calibrated using CALIB5 program (Stuiver and Reimer 1993).

Appendix 14.C. Iowa Site Data

Many Archaic sites have been excavated in Iowa during the past two decades as a result of CRM projects. Analytical reports for most of these sites reside in the "gray literature," and few site summaries have reached publication. We offer annotated site summaries of these data along with modest interpretations of the projectile point and settlement types to support analyses in our chapter.

McNeal Fan. The largest excavation of Archaic deposits to date in eastern Iowa has taken place at McNeal Fan (13MC15) in the Mississippi Valley in Muscatine County (Figure 14.2). The late Middle Archaic component in Stratum IId was buried over 1.5 m deep within this large alluvial fan at the base of the west valley wall (Thompson 2006). The cultural zone was marked by an organic- and charcoal-enriched midden approximately 30–40 cm thick, covering more than 1,300 m^2, and encompassing no fewer than seven house loci, more than 130 features, and thousands of artifacts. About three-quarters of the village was excavated. Most notable among the features were 55 large (1- to 2.5-m-diameter) roasting pits filled with burned soil and charcoal layers. The orientation of the house loci around a heavily trampled "commons area" suggests household contemporaneity in this village (Figure 14.36). Eleven radiocarbon dates from this late Middle Archaic component ranged from cal 2530 to 3655 B.C. (Appendix 14.B). The oldest date is an anomaly, over 400 years earlier than the next earliest. Dropping this date produces an age range of 2585–3175 B.C., and a cluster of six dates between 2740 and 2960 B.C. best documents the interval of village occupation(s).

Within an interval of 200 years at the beginning of the third millennium B.C., the McNeal Fan was the locus of intensive habitations, where hundreds of cultural features were dug for stone boiling, roasting and cooking, refuse deposition, chert heat treating, and other activities. Widespread pit excavation, coupled with intensive reuse of cooking facilities, resulted in a completely homogenized midden draped over the fan apex. The "house" features consisted of shallow, irregular oval-shaped basins extending from the bottom of the midden (Figure 14.36), but too few post molds were found to provide a basis for interpreting the actual building plan and orientation of these houses.

Incorporated into this midden and the features were several thousand artifacts, about two-thirds of which were pieces of heavily reduced FCR. The remainder were chipped-stone flaking debris, cores, and tools; unmodified stones; and over 250 cobble and ground-stone tools. Not surprisingly, flaking debris (70.1 percent) dominated the chipped-stone inventory, which was predominantly local materials like Burlington chert and other cherts available in local streams as residual cobbles from the Illinoian glacial till. The presence of nonlocal cherts from northeastern Iowa and southeastern Minnesota (Blanding, Galena, Shapokee, and Grand Meadow), central Iowa (Maynes Creek), east-central Iowa (Scotch Grove, Wapsipinicon, and Rapid), and across the Mississippi River in Illinois (Moline and Cobden; see Morrow 1984b, 1994) indicates resident interaction on a regional scale. Among the chipped stone are a few hundred flake tools, unifaces, and bifaces. Twenty-five bifaces conform to types identified in the regional literature (e.g., Justice 1987; Morrow 1984b). The majority are Osceola-style points, which were used for a variety of activities, as projectiles and for drilling and cutting (Table 14.C1; Figure 14.9). Except for a Wadlow blade, the other diagnostic points—Raddatz, Godar, Brannon, Jakie, and Matanzas—appear to have been used as projectiles. One Kirk Corner Notched, a type commonly attributed to the Early Archaic period, probably was recycled by the villagers, while the Table Rock point seems to have intruded from another habitation stratigraphically higher in the fan profile (a second Table Rock point was found in the overlying Early Woodland Marion component).

Table 14.C1. Diagnostic Bifaces from the McNeal Fan Archaic Component.

Biface Style	Count	Use Activities
Osceola	13	projectiles, drills, knives
Raddatz Side Notched	2	projectile, unfinished
Godar	2	projectiles
Brannon Side Notched	2	projectiles
Jakie Stemmed	1	projectile?
Karnak Stemmed	1	projectile
Wadlow	1	knife
Table Rock Stemmed	1	projectile
Matanzas	1	projectile
Kirk Corner Notched[a]	1	projectile

[a]Curated Early Archaic type?

Macroscopic use-wear patterns indicate chipped-stone tools were used on a range of materials, notably wood, followed by bone, meat, fiber, and hide (Table 14.C2). These chipped-stone tools probably were not used in isolation but in tandem with other implements made from wood, bone, and shell, but preservation conditions precluded the recovery of organic implements as well as faunal remains. The excavation did produce an assemblage of roughly 250 cobble tools, as noted above, and several ground-stone axes. The cobble tools, most no more than rounded igneous stones unmodified before use, served as hammers, pounders, grinders or manos, grinding slabs, bipolar hammers, and anvils. Some exhibiting minimal knapping or representing angular fragments are coarse, heavy-duty choppers, scrapers, and spokeshaves likely used for woodworking and similar heavy fabricating activities. The ground-stone axes are well-made full- and three-quarter-grooved styles fashioned from igneous stones (Figure 14.31).

Of special note are two axes classified as "Keokuk," a type with a limited geographic range centered in extreme southeastern Iowa, northeastern Missouri, and adjacent areas of western Illinois (Filbrandt 1997; Hummell 1982).

Table 14.C2. McNeal Fan Archaic Village Chipped-Stone Tool Activities.

	Material Worked				
Activity[a]	Wood	Hide	Bone	Fiber	Meat
Shredding	–	–	–	3	–
Splitting	5	–	–	–	–
Cutting	2	–	–	9	19
Sawing	2	–	–	–	–
Stripping	6	–	5	–	–
Scraping	25	10	10	2	–
Splitting	–	–	5	–	–
Drilling	4	1	–	–	–
Chopping	1	–	1	–	–
Engraving/etching	8	–	4	–	–
Total	53	11	25	14	19

[a]Some tools were used for multiple activities and on multiple materials.

Other artifacts providing evidence of on-site activities at the McNeal village include numerous center-pitted hammers and anvils suggestive of processing hard-shell nuts, such as thick-shelled hickory and black walnut, recovered in roughly equal amounts from flotation samples. Seed processing was indicated by several sets of grinding equipment, although paltry numbers of seed remains were recovered from the flotation samples. Among the potential taxa being processed with these tools were giant ragweed (*Ambrosia trifida*) and undomesticated chenopod. The numerous, giant roasting pits indicate communal cooking was taking place, probably during multiple seasons. A rind fragment identified as probable squash (*Cucurbita* sp.) could be one of many foodstuffs processed in these features, and some large-volume foodstuff was probably systematically processed. Possible uses of these pits include steaming mussels or fish, boiling nuts for oil, cooking meat from communal deer hunts, baking tubers, and preparing combinations of these resources in layers.

The location of this residential base camp (village) at the base of the Mississippi Valley wall meant that resources in the nearby upland prairies and oak openings and on the adjoining valley floor were readily available within an hour's walk. Analysis of the carbonized remains confirms that McNeal Fan residents exploited both zones for fuel and food resources. Positioning of larger Middle Archaic habitation sites at valley margins within easy reach of multiple biomes may be patterned, as other examples of base-camp habitations are reported at the Sand Run West (Benn 1987) and Gast Spring sites (Bettis et al. 1992).

A series of 1980s excavation projects by the OSA on four multicomponent sites along the modern route of U.S. 218 in Washington County, southeastern Iowa (Figure 14.2), produced extensive but uneven evidence for Archaic habitations (Lensink 1986). The Davis Creek site contained the most intensive and best-documented habitations, while the Prymek and Goose Creek site components were more ephemeral. Both Davis and Goose creeks are tributaries of the Iowa River.

Davis Creek Site. This multicomponent site (13WS122) situated on a loess-mantled bench overlooking Davis Creek (Figure 14.2) contained Late and Middle Woodland and Late Archaic components scattered from the plowed surface to a depth of about 36 cm within an Alfisol (Lensink 1986:158–159). The Late Archaic component in the E2 horizon about 20–36 cm below surface produced 22 Table Rock Stemmed points (Figure 14.21) and several early-stage bifaces along with a suite of flaking debris, FCR, and cobble tools (Lensink 1986:177–193). Forty-four cultural features, mostly lithic concentrations and at least one hearth or roasting pit, were assigned to the Archaic component (Lensink 1986:160–166). FCR from the cooking feature produced a TL date of 1650 B.C. A second TL date of 1010 B.C. came from a piece of heat-treated flaking debris, but because no background radiation soil sample was taken from the vicinity of the flake, the site investigator concluded that a third date of 1236 B.C. date may not accurately place the Table Rock component (Lensink 1986:198–199). The sparse amounts of carbonized remains from the features included hickory (*Carya*) hull fragments and a few pieces of hawthorn (*Crataegus*) fruit (Lensink 1986:202–203).

Billeck (Lensink 1986:178) reported that 16 of the 22 Table Rock points were made of nonlocal Maynes Creek cherts, a material from east-central Iowa perhaps 50 miles distant, with the remainder of locally available Wassonville and unidentified gray or black cherts. The fragmentary nature of the points, along with evidence for impact fractures, indicates that most of these Table Rock points were used as projectiles. However, a few specimens with noticeably asymmetrical (resharpened) blades appear to have been used additionally as knives (Lensink 1986:Figure 9-11). Wassonville chert dominates the assemblage of flaking debris, nondiagnostic flake tools, and early-stage bifaces (Lensink1986:Table 9-22, Appendix E-17), accounting for 98.9 percent of the chipped stone by weight (Lensink 1986:204). Thus, the sparseness of Maynes Creek flaking debris suggests that production of most of the Table Rock points took place elsewhere. The Davis Creek Table Rock points follow the general trends noted by Morrow (1984b:45) for such points in Iowa; that is, they display a high frequency of heat treatment and production from Maynes Creek or Burlington chert. Both chert types predominate in the Iowa, Skunk, and Des Moines river valleys in the southeastern quadrant of the state.

Use-wear analysis of the other Davis Creek site tools, including three end scrapers, 57 bifaces (Stages 2–4), and 43 flake tools, was not comprehensive. For example, the three end scrapers had evidence of use on hides, while only eight of the 43 flake tools were so identified (six soft-material knives, one spokeshave, and one soft-material scraper). Unused Stage 2 specimens account for over two-thirds of the nondiagnostic bifaces (Lensink 1986:Table 9-20). Billeck reported the Stage 4 bifaces often exhibited use wear but suggested no specific activities (e.g., cutting, chopping, etc.) or use with hard or soft materials (Lensink 1986:182). We wonder if most of the Stage 2–4 bifaces were utilized as processing or fabricating tools, since they were not being fashioned into Table Rock projectiles.

The distribution of the Table Rock–component features around an oval-shaped open area in the southern part of the excavation block suggested to Lensink (1986:204) that an activity area possibly including a structure might have been present. At the Late Archaic component on the Missouri Pacific #2 site in the American Bottom, features were similarly clustered around circular open areas no more than 10 m in diameter. At least one of these circular clusters was encompassed by a similarly shaped structure defined by a scatter of post molds (McElrath and Fortier 1983). On the Davis Creek site, however, no structural evidence in the form of post molds was identified. The large-scale community pattern at the Davis Creek site may have consisted of features scattered in a broad arc beginning at the aforementioned oval-shaped cluster and extending some 30–40 m to the northwest (Lensink 1984: Figure 9-10). Virtually all of these features were concentrations of lithic debris, primarily from the processing of locally obtained Wassonville chert. The artifact assemblages indicate various domestic and tool-production tasks took place on-site, although knapping workshops are the most prevalent activity areas. The large quantity of Wassonville chert, coupled with the large number of early-stage bifaces, suggested to Lensink (1986:204) that the material was quarried locally and returned to the site for reduction. Perhaps this was the principal reason for occupying this location, although the range of tool types and potential domestic activities indicates Davis Creek was a seasonal base camp.

Prymek Site. The second U.S. 218 site, Prymek (13WS65), was a multicomponent property located on a loess-mantled interfluve about .5 km north of Davis Creek (Figure 14.2). The site contained a Middle–Late Archaic component from 30 to 50 cm below surface in the Bw1, Bt2, and upper Bt3 horizons (Lensink 1986:123, Table 8-3). Among the diagnostic artifacts from this component are a large, corner-notched, flat-based (nonground) specimen resembling the Etley style of the Late Archaic Sedalia phase in Missouri, a Durst point, and several points assigned to the Middle Archaic period. Among the Middle Archaic styles are a shallow-side-notched point with a heavily ground, flat base (Matanzas/Brannon), a Turin point, and at least one Godar point. Little information is presented in the report on use wear on these tools (many are fragments, some of which were produced during manufacture), although the sporadic appearance of impact fractures indicates their primary use as projectiles. Another reworked projectile point was tentatively identified as Calf Creek, usually assigned to the early half of the Middle Archaic period (Lensink 1986:127–131). Use wear on this tool suggested it was used as a cutting implement (Lensink 1986:127–131). Additional bifaces and flake tools used as knives and scrapers may be associated with the Archaic components but were not differentiated from the Woodland component (Lensink 1986:131–135). Overall, the Archaic components did not produce significant information on community patterns because of the absence of cultural features. The excavators interpret the Prymek site as the location of repeated visits over several thousand years, with chipped-stone-tool production and a limited range of domestic activities associated with short-term habitations commonplace (Lensink 1986:141–142). In contrast to the nearby Davis Creek site, a property situated closer to the stream channel where lithic workshops predominated, the Prymek site encompassed less active knapping areas associated with briefer habitations, that is, bivouacs.

Goose Creek Site. The Goose Creek site (13WS126) is located several kilometers south of the other Davis Creek properties (Figure 14.2). Positioned on a stream terrace south of the channel, multiple Woodland components and a possible Late Archaic–Early Woodland component were identified (Lensink 1986). The Late Archaic–Early Woodland component, located about 50 cm below surface, produced no diagnostic artifacts or flaking debris but apparently did contain an FCR-filled feature probably used as a roasting pit (Lensink 1986:216–218). Carbonized elm wood (*Ulmus americana*) from this feature produced a radiocarbon age of cal 695–540 B.C. (Lensink 1986:224). Little can be concluded about the nature of the Late Archaic–Early Woodland habitation on the Goose Creek site other than it apparently was ephemeral and of short duration.

Ed's Meadow Site. The loess-mantled uplands south of Flint Creek in Des Moines County provided the setting for the Ed's Meadow site (13DM712; Figure 14.2), a multicomponent property containing Middle Archaic to Late Woodland components between the surface and a maximum depth of 50 cm. The main concentration of artifacts was within the E horizon of an Alfisol (Morrow 1998:27). The excavation consisted of two blocks, labeled "A" and "B." The most informative, Block A, contained what the excavator termed a "Jakie" point, which resembles the Turin style in Iowa, and an untyped (Helton-like) corner-notched point, along with a few early-stage bifaces and several flake tools. Use-wear analysis indicated that the two Stage 2 bifaces were unfinished and the Jakie-style biface was a projectile. Four flake tools were single-purpose specimens: two knives used on soft materials (e.g., meat, hides, or vegetal matter), one used as a spokeshave (hard material?), and one wedge presumably used on hard material such as bone or wood. The other flake tools were multipurpose: one knife-scraper (soft material-hard material) combination and one knife-wedge (soft material-hard material?) combination. Also present were small collections of chipped-stone tools, flaking debris, FCR, cobble tools, and hematite materials. One cobble tool was used as an abrader and one as a hammer or mano. Three ground hematite pieces indicate the processing of this material for pigment or perhaps as a desiccating agent for hides. Block A also contained Feature 1, a small circular concentration of flaking debris (Morrow 1998:28). Morrow (1998:37) concluded that Block A exposed a single component dating to the early Middle Archaic period, although TL dates on rocks from Feature 1 assayed at 1313 B.C. and 9550 B.C. (Morrow 1998:28–30). Much of the cultural material is flaking debris in proximity to Feature 1. Morrow (1998:47) interpreted this feature to have been a knapping locus where three or four bifaces were initially prepared. Found within a meter radius of this feature were the stone hammer and two bifaces, while five projectile points (Jakie/Turin, Helton-like, and point fragments) and a few flake tools were found within a few meters (Morrow 1998:Figure 18). Another, less dense, concentration of cultural material was located about 3 m to the south-southwest, and Morrow (1998:47) suggested this area was either within or immediately adjacent to the primary habitation area, most of which remained unexcavated outside Block A. Block B yielded a Raddatz point base and FCR that gave a TL date of cal 5316 B.C. Our impression of data from Ed's Meadow is that they indicate short-term habitations by very small groups of people, which we would term "bivouacs."

Merrimac Mills Site. The Merrimac Mills site (13JF92) is positioned on an upland interfluve above the Skunk River valley in Jefferson County (Figure 14.2). Surface collecting and excavation produced 18 projectile points (Finn 1981, 1982) dating from the Late Paleoindian through Woodland periods. Four projectiles are lanceolate-shaped specimens resembling Scottsbluff, Agate Basin, and Eden styles dating to the Late Paleoindian period. Archaic projectiles reidentified by the senior author include the Early Archaic–period Wolf Creek style, Middle Archaic–period Godar and Raddatz types, which the site investigator attributed to Osceola (Finn 1981:27–28, 1982:47–49), and Late Archaic Table Rock, Tipton, Sedalia, and Nebo Hill styles.

Only three features were found in the 140 m^2 excavated at the Merrimac Mills site, indicating either a relatively low-intensity occupation or poor preservation. Two are hearths, one (Feature 4) producing a dense scatter of 260 pieces of FCR across a 1.8-x-1-m area in two visible concentrations (Finn 1981:Figure 6). Another hearth encompassed a smaller but tightly packed cluster of FCR measuring 40 x 70 cm (Finn 1981:Figure 12). Along with the FCR, a moderately large collection of flaking debris, cores, flake tools, bifacial tools, cobble tools, and ground hematite was recovered (Finn 1982:Table 9). Significantly, 77 cores and tested cobbles were found in the sub–plow zone (and presumably Archaic levels) of the excavation block, with the majority representing either fragments or exhausted specimens (Finn 1982:54–55). Tool classification for this site collection was based on morphology (e.g., projectiles, bifacial knives, scrapers, choppers, etc.), not use-wear analysis, and "utilized/retouched flakes" were identified by the presence of macroscopic edge wear or resharpening. Thirty of these tools were found in the vicinity of the Feature 4 hearth and 19 within the Feature 5 area (Finn 1981:24). Modeling the distribution of these items, especially the tools, around the hearths revealed these areas to have been the loci of food-preparation and tool-processing activities, including cooking, heat treating cores, grinding or pounding, and possibly butchering. Initial and final stages of lithic reduction for chipped-stone-tool production were indicted by the flaking debris. Finn (1982:81) suggested that the Merrimac Mills site, having no evidence of a large midden, extensive storage facilities, or other indicators of long-term habitations, was created by a series of seasonal occupations of relatively short duration by small groups. These encampments were hypothesized to have been seasonal base camps from which residents went on foraging tours and hunting forays, most likely in the fall of the year, when upland resources would have been optimal (Finn 1982:86–87). But, because it lacks storage facilities or processing pits, we find it difficult to conceive of the Merrimac Mills site functioning as a base camp for any length of time. Additionally, the site is multicomponent with evidence of numerous episodes of occupation during all of the Archaic periods. Although it may have been a base camp, this site just as likely represents numerous bivouac occupations for differing purposes during the Paleoindian and Archaic periods.

Fett Site. The setting for the Fett site (13LE597) in Lee County (Figure 14.2) is the colluvial foot slope of a small side valley behind the Mississippi Valley bluff line. Colluvium (Flack Member, DeForest Formation) prograded with Gunder Member alluvium at this location, forming stratified sediments interdigitated with stream channels that spanned the early–middle Holocene era. Recent archaeological data recovery directed by the authors produced evidence for multiple prehistoric occupations dating from the Late Paleoindian through Late Woodland periods in this sequestered location (Thompson and Benn 2007). During the Early–Middle Archaic occupations, a series of small (2-x-4-m), roughly oval to circular basins were dug into the gentle foot slope, although too few post molds were located to demonstrate that anything other than wickiup structures were placed over the basins. Associated with these shelters were one or two small hearths or pits located on the downslope side of each of the basins in extramural activity areas. Additionally, a deeper, 3-m-diameter "house" basin contained several Middle Archaic Matanzas points. Small to moderately sized inventories of flaking debris (mostly locally obtained Burlington chert), cobble tools (hammers, abraders, pounders, and one three-quarter-grooved ax), flake tools used as scrapers, knives, and gravers for hide, wood, or bone working and butchering, and projectile points were found (Tables 14.C3, 14.C4). The projectile points, mostly made from Burlington chert, include Graham Cave, a diminutive Tama, three varieties of Matanzas, Turin, and Nebo Hill (Figure 14.29) and occurred in stratigraphic sequence. Four radiocarbon dates from the same stratigraphic sequence range from 635 to 6440 B.C.; these enigmatic assays appear to be 2–3,000 years too young

Table 14.C3. Use-Wear Analysis Counts on Fett Site Bifaces.

	Soft Wood/ Bone	Hide	Dry Hide	Hard Bone/ Wood	Meat	Multiple Materials	Unknown/ None
Adze	1	–	–	–	–	–	–
Awl	–	1	–	–	–	–	–
Drill	1	–	1	–	–	–	–
Graver	1	–	–	–	–	–	–
Knife	–	–	–	–	1	5	1
Scraper	–	–	–	1	–	–	–
Unfinished	–	–	–	–	–	–	25
Projectile	–	–	–	–	–	–	12
Totals[a]	3	1	1	1	1	5	38

[a]Some tools were used on multiple materials.

Table 14.C4. Use-Wear Analysis Counts on Fett Site Flake Tools and Unifaces.

	Soft Wood/ Bone	Hide	Dry Hide	Hard Bone/ Wood	Meat	Multiple Materials	Plant Materials	Hair	Unknown
Awl	–	1	–	–	–	–	–	–	–
Drill	–	–	–	–	–	–	–	–	–
Graver	4	–	–	2	–	–	–	–	–
Knife	–	–	–	–	8	1	5	–	–
Scraper	11	4	3	8	–	–	–	14	1
Denticulate	–	–	–	–	–	–	3	–	–
Burin	1	–	–	–	–	–	–	–	–
Chopper	–	–	–	1	–	–	–	–	–
Spokeshave	1	–	–	3	–	–	–	–	–
Totals[a]	17	5	3	14	8	1	8	14	1

[a]Some tools were used on multiple materials.

for the associated points. In the basal gravels covering the eroded glacial till surface at the bottom of the Gunder sediments (3-m depth) we recovered some relatively large, heavily patinated lamellar and other primary flakes and nondiagnostic biface fragments along with FCR. In one area, large glacial cobbles formed a 3-m-diameter ring around a hearth and debitage, and we hypothesize that a temporary skin structure (with the cobbles acting as weights for the skin) was erected at this location. Because this habitation is located *beneath* the Gunder Member, which began accumulating during the early Holocene (Bettis and Littke 1987), and because of the patination on the flake tools, this component undoubtedly dates to the Late Paleoindian period, making it one of the earliest habitations excavated in Iowa.

The Fett Archaic artifact assemblages indicate a relatively narrow range of domestic and tool-production tasks was taking place during each of the several habitations on the site, including hide, bone, and woodworking, early-stage biface production, and expedient flake-tool production. The Matanzas occupation contained at least six refurbished projectile points, several bifaces and cores, and flake tools with most of the use-wear categories listed in Tables 14.C3 and 14.C4. The time-transgressive nature of these occupations, coupled with the presence of family-size (or smaller?) house loci, suggests that the type of occupation was fairly constant throughout the Early–Late Archaic periods: that is, hunting parties or single families occupying one or two houses at a given time. We think most of these habitations were bivouacs, although the Matanzas component might be considered a temporary base camp. The site was sheltered from the elements in its deep valley, prompting speculation that these were wintertime occupations. The Mississippi Valley was readily accessible for garnering a variety of resources. White-tailed deer were available around the site, while workable chert cobbles and potable water were readily available in the stream outside the entryways of the houses. The Fett site must have been a logistically well-situated and comfortable place for small groups to camp during the cold months of the year.

Sand Run West. The Sand Run West site (13LA38) was tucked against the Mississippi Valley wall on a small alluvial fan in the Lake Odessa bottoms of Louisa County in southeastern Iowa (Figure 14.2). This multicomponent property was initially excavated by the senior author with Southwest Missouri State University (SMSU) in 1986 (Benn 1987). Small block excavations exposed components dating from the Late Woodland to the late Middle Archaic periods. Multiple Archaic occupations separated by fan sediments (Stratum III) contained an assortment of artifacts, including large quantities of FCR, flaking debris, and expedient and formal chipped-stone tools as well as large (1-m-diameter), deep storage and roasting pits. Among the projectile points from the Middle Archaic component were Godar/Raddatz Side-Notched, Helton, Matanzas, and Osceola, with the latter predominating (Stanley and Hoppin 1987). The two radiocarbon dates—2685 B.C. and 2890 B.C.—(Benn 1987:20–21) fix the period of the Osceola style and are coeval with the suite of dates from the residential base camp on the McNeal Fan. A lesser Late Archaic component represented by Etley and Apple Blossom Stemmed styles was mixed with materials of other ages.

Early-stage bifacial tools in the Middle Archaic component were used predominantly for heavy-duty cutting and scraping activities on multiple kinds of usually hard materials. Several digging tools were among the early-stage bifaces (Stanley and Hoppin 1987:133–138). These items could have been used for digging pit features and extracting tubers and other subterranean foodstuffs. The later-stage bifaces were dominated by drills (n = 16), used on hard materials such as bone, wood, and antler, and projectiles, many of which were used as knives (n = 47) and were heavily resharpened (see Table 14.C5). The flake-tools and unifaces in Stratum III (n = 189) were primarily used for cutting (n = 103), scraping (n = 67), and engraving (n = 48), with minor instances of stripping (n = 3) and perforating (n = 6) (Benn 1987:Table 4.14; some tools listed in the table were used for multiple activities).

Sand Run West was the first Archaic site in Iowa to be systematically fine screened for biological remains. Faunal remains were poorly preserved, although the deeper Stratum III contained enough organic midden material, especially within pit features, to neutralize the acidic soil and preserve a range of heavy-walled as well as fine bones (Benn 1987:226). The conspicuously low number of deer elements in the collection (Table 14.C6) suggests differential preservation was at work, perhaps due to aboriginal processing techniques and disposal in pits or the midden. The species list for the late Middle Archaic component is heavily weighted in favor of floodplain-forest creatures like squirrels, raccoon, and turkey, although deer predominate, as they always do in prehistoric sites in eastern Iowa. There were two dog burials. Muskrat, beaver, and duck bones reflect the nearness of the slough to the site, and the assemblage includes large numbers of turtles, notably the aquatic softshell, and fish. Mussel shell was not preserved. A study of 200 fish vertebrae growth rings found that roughly one-third of individuals died during each of three divisions of the year—March–June, July–October, and November–February—indicating year-round occupation of the site. In the large assemblage of floral remains (Lopinot 1987), nutshell predominated over wood charcoal. Charcoal must have come from wood growing around the site, including oak, hickory, ash, hackberry or elm, and cottonwood or willow. Lopinot (1987:208) converted nutshell remains to nutmeat equivalents, giving these ratios for the late Middle Archaic component: hickory (*Carya* spp.) 65.3 percent, walnut (*Juglans* spp.) 14.8 percent, acorns (*Quercus* spp.) 17.6 percent, and hazelnut (*Corylus americana*) 2.3 percent. The seed-to-nut ratio for 11 features from this Archaic component was lower than the one for the Middle Woodland component at this site. Nevertheless, noteworthy ubiquity indexes indicate exploitation of the following seed species during the Middle Archaic period: *Chenopodium* spp. (primarily *berlandieri*) 72.7 percent, wild rice (*Zizania aquatica*) 45.4 percent, ragweed (*Ambrosia* spp.) 27.3 percent, *Amaranthus* spp. 18.2 percent,

Table 14.C5. Late-Stage Bifaces from Stratum III, Sand Run West Site.

Biface Style	Count	Use-Activities
Apple Blossom Stemmed	1	unknown
Godar/Raddatz Side Notched	7	projectiles(?), knives
Helton	1	knife
Matanzas, deep side notched	4	knife, unknown (knives?)
Matanzas, faint side notched	2	knives
Matanzas, flared stem	2	unknown (knives?)
Osceola	9	projectiles, knives
Koster[a]	2	knives
Steuben[a]	1	drill, scraper, knife
Nondiagnostic fragments	18	unknown
Total	47	

[a]Intrusive Woodland type.

Table 14.C6. Faunal Elements from Sand Run West, Stratum III.

Species	General Excavation	Flotation
Indeterminate small rodents	–	8
Squirrels (*Sciurus* spp.)	3	–
Muskrat (*Ondatra zibethicus*)	–	2
Raccoon (*Procyon lotor*)	5	–
Beaver (*Castor canadensis*)	5	–
Dogs (*Canis* spp.)	1 (+2 dog skeletons)	7
Deer (*Odocoileus virginianus*)	50	6
Elk (*Cervus canadensis*)	–	–
Indeterminate mammal	–	66
Duck (*Anas* spp.)	3	1
Turkey (*Meleagris gallopavo*)	1	16
Indeterminate bird	1	–
Softshell turtle (*Trionyx* sp.)	6	–
Indeterminate turtle	10	24
Indeterminate snake	2	20
Gar (*Lepisosteus* sp.)	–	3
Bowfin (*Amia calva*)	–	16
Ictaluridae	5	61
Bullhead (*Ictalurus* sp.)	–	27
Minnows (Cyprinidae)	–	1
Catostomidae	–	7
Buffalo sucker (*Ictiobus* sp.)	–	2
Centrarchidae	–	7
Sunfish (*Lepomis* sp.)	–	2
Bass (*Micropterus* sp.)	–	1
Drum (*Aplodinotus grunniens*)	2	6
Indeterminate fish	44	1,063

and knotweed (*Polygonum* sp., not *erectum*) 18.2 percent. One feature that produced many chenopod seeds also yielded four wild sumpweed seeds (*Iva* sp.) and seven sunflower achenes (*Helianthus* sp.), including one fragment that appears to have been large enough to have been a domesticate.

The SMSU excavation crew returned to Sand Run West in 1991 after human remains were reported by a local resident to be eroding from the bank of the slough. The remains of 10–11 flexed and bundle burials were exhumed from the Osceola component (Benn et al. 1992:1–4). An isolated skull had been recovered during the previous excavation of the habitation midden and proved to be part of this cemetery; thus, the two radiocarbon dates from that project date the entire cemetery. These Archaic burials, among the oldest recorded in eastern Iowa, included adult and subadult individuals in bundles and an ossuary pit containing the jumbled remains of at least five persons. Most of these poorly preserved burials were of indeterminate sex, but male and females were tentatively identified. Collectively, these burials presumably formed a large part of a corporate cemetery, as suggested by spacing and limited superposition of the remains. The cemetery may have been active for a few years either during the Middle Archaic habitation or immediately after it ended (Benn et al. 1992:5–16). The excavated part of the Sand Run West cemetery did not contain grave goods, in contrast to similarly aged interments elsewhere in the Midwest. Perhaps the portion of the cemetery destroyed along the Lake Odessa shoreline once contained utilitarian grave goods, because a great number of whole Osceola points had been found by private collectors over the years prior to the excavation (Benn et al. 1992:24).

As much as 75 percent of the Sand Run West habitation had been destroyed by bank erosion prior to the excavations. The terrace portion of this larger site contained a 20- to 40-cm-thick Middle Archaic midden, while the fan sediments preserved stratified remains of domestic activity areas (households) composed of large roasting pits, FCR scatters, and lithic fabricating tools in addition to the cemetery. Viewed as a whole, this habitation had all of the earmarks of a seasonal base camp, and if its houses were occupied year-round, as the fish vertebrae indicate, the term *village* may also apply.

Bash Site. Bash (13MR228) is a chert-procurement, lithic-reduction station and campsite of unknown duration on a tributary of the Iowa River in central Iowa (Figure 14.2). Lithic-activity areas on outwash and Holocene terraces (DeForest Formation) represent numerous visits during the Early–Middle Archaic through Late Woodland periods (Collins 1995; Collins et al. 1991, 1994). Although no radiocarbon dates fix the time of any of the occupations, the value of the site-testing (Phase II) investigation lies in Collins's careful analysis of lithic-reduction sequences represented by more than 58,500 artifacts. During the middle of the Archaic period, nodules tended to be stripped of cortex first and then heat treated as cores, while at the end of the Archaic and throughout the Woodland periods, raw nodules tended to be heat treated prior to being worked into cores (Collins et al. 1991:81). Also, the overall frequency of heat treatment was lower during the middle of the Archaic period than at its end (Collins 1991:84). Bash Test Unit 1 yielded a higher proportion of freehand cores from the earlier Archaic component(s) than the later Archaic–Woodland components, where bipolar cores increased dramatically (Collins et al. 1991:87). One of the explanations for this shift toward bipolar technology late in the Archaic period is that some of the previously quarried and discarded chert chunks were being recycled with the more efficient bipolar technique.

Edgewater Park Site. Site 13JH1132 was excavated during the late fall of 2004, and the analytical report is in production. The testing report (Johnson 2003) and information provided by John Doershuk of the OSA (pers. comm., December 2004) demonstrate this site to be buried at least a meter within a middle–late Holocene alluvial terrace near the bank on the Iowa River (Figure 14.2). Excavation uncovered FCR and debitage features from within the seasonal water table. From this apparent single-component habitation, the excavators recovered several Table Rock points, a Tipton-like point, and two straight-stemmed points that resemble the Genesee/Saratoga styles (see Justice 1987:154, 159). An AMS date of cal 1770–1855 B.C. (Beta-179291) on carbon from the cultural zone helps to fix the age of the stemmed-point styles in Iowa.

Lost Creek Upper Terrace. Component III at this unplowed site (13MK357) on a Wisconsinan outwash terrace in south-central Iowa (Figure 14.2) was uncovered by machine stripping the sod and shovel skimming the AE soil horizon, which exposed three Late Archaic household patterns (Figure 14.37). No structural evidence or dark-stained basin fill was evident to assist with house definitions, which was accomplished by tracing the "crisp borders" in the scatters of almost 4,000 piece-plotted artifacts along with 10 hearths, small pits, and rock concentrations (Benn et al. 1999:168; Thompson 1999). The most discrete household loci, I and II, had dimensions of roughly 9 x 6 m (60–70 m^2) with east-facing entryways and two hearths in the same half of each "house" (Figure 14.37). AMS radiocarbon dates of 2210 ± 50 and 2930 ± 50 B.P. were obtained from bits of charcoal recovered from two of the households, and the older one, calibrated at 1080 B.C., seems the likely age for this component (a Late Woodland component is present and may be mixed). This date correlates with the two Vosburg projectiles found in the household scatters, but this component also yielded a Raddatz-like and larger Godar point (Figure 14.20). The wide array of tool types from the entire Late Archaic assemblage (600 m^2) included 22 cores (19 unpatterned), a high frequency (n = 21) of unfinished bifaces, 11 Stage 5 (hafted) bifaces, three heavy choppers for hard material, four flake drills for hard material, one digger (hoe), two spokeshaves, three flake shredders for plant materials, nine flake knives for soft material (meat or skins), 14 flake scrapers for soft material, two end scrapers for hide working, 15 flake scrapers for hard material, and one graver (multiple-use tools are counted multiple times). The chipped-stone assemblage was composed principally of local cherts, about 45 percent of which had been heat treated. Among the large assemblage of informal cobble tools were (by use wear) 30 abraders, 51 grinders (manos), 89 heavy pounders, 27 hammerstones, 41 scrapers, 31 spokeshaves, and four or fewer anvils, choppers, and cutting tools. Metallic hematite also was worked extensively at the site. The households are interpreted to have functioned as sequentially occupied seasonal base camps for multiple families or a large extended-family-sized group, who passed the (winter) season conducting all manner of domestic tasks and fabricating clothing and tools of wood and bone.

Garden Site. A small alluvial fan in an abandoned outwash valley of the Mississippi River at Dubuque was the location for Middle Archaic habitations (Figure 14.2). The Garden site (13DB493) consisted of a discrete midden with little contamination from other culture periods in a buried soil about 1.2 m below surface (Benn 2007). Four radiocarbon dates ranged from 2530 to 4290 B.C., with the principal occupation occurring during the fourth millennium. Three circular houses with internal areas of 18.1 m^2 (House 3), 26.2 m^2 (House 1), and 31.2 m^2 (House 6) were defined by organic stains and piece-plotted artifact scatters. Houses 1 and 3 had entryways facing one another and appeared to have shared extramural activity areas (households) consisting of hearths, small processing pits, and a few larger "storage" pits (Figure 14.34). Projectile point types from this occupation consisted of four Matanzas in three varieties along with six Brannon Side Notched and two Brewerton Eared, almost all of which had been utilized as knives, gravers, burins, and, likely, other tools besides spear tips. Two Paleoindian points represented recycled artifacts. A large Raddatz point was recovered from the component beneath this habitation. The chipped-stone assemblage was composed overwhelmingly (98 percent) of local Galena and Blanding cherts, yet at least 10 percent of the formal chipped-stone tools were made from imported cherts. About 10–15 percent of all cores and debitage had been heat treated, while 58 percent of all bifaces had received such treatment. Almost all of the 52 cores were unpatterned. Bifaces tended to have been made by reducing tabular chert cores, not flake blanks. The 24 flake tools were used as gravers, burins, spokeshaves, plant shredders, side and end scrapers, and knives. The cobble-tool assemblage was small and consisted of one grinder, five expedient hammerstones, one heavy pounder, and a scanty collection of FCR pieces. Igneous (glacial outwash) rocks are not common in the Paleozoic Plateau region of northeastern Iowa. The archaeobotanical analysis identified wood from floodplain species like elm, walnut, and willow. The residents frequently exploited walnuts and hickory nuts and also gathered some acorns and a few hazelnuts. They also gathered the fruits of plums or black cherries and grapes. One of their campfires carbonized a violet seed, which, along with the nuts and fruits, indicates late summer through early fall seasons of occupation. The relative absence of FCR may mean that there was no need for heat retention (i.e., for roasting foods and warming people), which bolsters the argument that this was a warm-season occupation. The very sparse remains of animals (only calcined bone) indicate the Garden residents hunted mammals, fished, and gathered turtles. According to the use wear on their lithic tool kits, the residents spent their hours in residence fabricating tools of wood and bone, processing hides for shelter or clothing, and butchering animals for consumption and dry storage. Considerable time was spent processing hematite powder. The Garden site was interpreted to have been a seasonal base camp occupied during the late summer and fall.

Allen Fan. This alluvial fan site (13HA385) in the Iowa River valley in Hardin County, central Iowa, was excavated by the OSA (Collins and Mandel 1999; Fishel et al. 2000, 2003). The east and west lobes of the site contained three Archaic components buried in the topsoil (Figure 14.2). Testing on the east lobe (Collins and Mandel 1999) produced a Sedalia point associated with a pit dated to 3440 B.C. On the west lobe, Component VI was a partially uncovered Late Archaic campsite of unknown duration dated to 790 B.C. The three "small" versions of Table Rock points recovered from this component apparently correlate with this relatively late dating result. The points were found with extensive FCR features apparently used to process hazelnuts, which were recovered from flotation samples. Fifty-two percent of the lithic assemblage of 415 pieces was local chert (Maynes Creek), 5 percent was cherts from southeastern Minnesota, 5 percent was cherts from southeastern Iowa, and the heat-treatment rate was 48 percent. The FCR assemblage included 20 cobble tools: four hammerstones and the rest unidentified tool fragments. Middle Archaic Component VII was uncovered more extensively at 70 cm below surface and dated to cal 5010 B.C. This component yielded five Tama and four Raddatz points along with a large debitage assemblage made up of 65 percent local chert (Maynes Creek), 13 percent southeastern Minnesota cherts, and 7 percent southeastern Iowa cherts; the heat-treatment rate was 61 percent. Other tools in the lithic assemblage include 30 bifaces (mostly fragments), 18 scrapers (mostly end scrapers, three of them hafted), 119 utilized flakes, 16 unpatterned cores (most of them nuclei), 42 cobble hammerstones, 10 anvil stones, and 10 unidentified cobble-tool fragments. Flotation produced a small amount of walnut shell (*Juglans* sp.), one little barley seed (*Hordeum pusillum*), one knotweed achene (*Polygonum* sp.), panic grass seeds (*Panicum* sp.), and single fruits of *Rubus* sp., feverwort (*Triosteum* cf. *perfoliatum*), grape (*Vitis* sp.), and Rosaceae. The site investigators (Fishel et al. 2003:63) interpreted the Middle Archaic component to have been the remains of a bone-grease-processing and stone-boiling station associated with an adjacent seasonal base camp.

Jasper County 13JP87. This multicomponent midden (Paleoindian–Late Woodland) was situated on a sand dune on a tributary of the Skunk River in central Iowa (Figure 14.2). Although materials of every cultural period were thoroughly mixed and cannot be segregated into discrete assemblages, the large excavation block (1,100 m^2) exposed almost 300 features and 20 house or household loci (Figure 14.38; Benn 2005). It is the clusters of features within households and the associations of projectiles and absolute dates that provide significant information. A dozen large FCR-filled roasting pits were present, and three of these yielded radiocarbon dates with calibrated ranges of 2205–2025 B.C. (Fea. 81), 2475–2205 B.C. (Fea. 179), and 2815–2580 B.C. (Fea. 157) (nearby site 13JP86 yielded a TL date of 4345 B.C. on another deep, FCR-filled pit). Locus 5, a 5-x-8-m oval, basin-shaped stain with a central hearth, produced two of these Late Archaic dates (Fea. 157 and 179), and 5-m-diameter Locus 11 yielded the third Late Archaic date (Fea. 81). Scattered around the site but not directly associated with these loci were Matanzas, Karnak, Nebo Hill, and Eva II–type points along with a full-grooved ax, a wide range of cobble tools (e.g., hammerstones, grinders, grinding slabs, abraders, choppers, and pounders), drills, scrapers of all types, gravers, burins, knives, and so on. Locus 3, while not directly dated, produced the clearest evidence for a Middle Archaic household. This 6-x-10-m stain contained large roasting pits, hearths, and basin pits and a high proportion of Tongue River silica (source areas northwest of the site) associated with Raddatz, Matanzas, and Tama points and beveled and serrated broken bifaces. While rock-filled roasting pits were associated with the Middle–Late Archaic habitations, most of the deeper storage pits probably belonged to the Early–Late Woodland components. While site 13JP87 was visited numerous times by Archaic and other people, the conspicuous Archaic habitations were associated with the mapped households, which constituted seasonal base camps probably used by extended-family-sized groups.

Overberg Site. This site (13HN318) in Henry County (Figure 14.2) yielded a chipped-stone adze from a lithic-reduction station uncovered during the testing investigation (Morrow and Artz 1997). Subsequently, a Phase III excavation uncovered three more lithic stations from a single layer in the EB and Bt horizons on an upland ridge slope (Fiedel et al. 2004). The assemblage, which did not include any projectile points, consisted of a late-stage biface that resembled an Early Archaic Grundy point (Morrow 1984a:88), more than 3,300 pieces of debitage (90 percent local chert), only three or four cores, seven bladelike (lamellar) flakes, a metate or anvil stone, a multipurpose abrader-mano-hammerstone, and only 16 pieces of FCR. The heat-treatment rate for the debitage was about 18 percent. A TL date of 6095 B.C. on FCR was close to the radiocarbon date of 6690 B.C., and the error of ± 640 years on the TL date would place it within one sigma of the end date for the Early Archaic period. Fiedel et al. (2004) termed this site a single-component extractive camp, that is, resource-procurement stations within a bivouac habitation, in our terminology.

Riley Site. This multicomponent habitation (13HN373) on a natural levee of Big Creek in Henry County (Figure 14.2) contained an intact Late Archaic component below Woodland components (Foradas 2004). A Tipton point was taken from this site, and Sedalia/Wadlow bifaces were associated with a knapper's activity area where bifaces were manufactured in the vicinity of hearth Feature 48. A radiocarbon date from this activity area assayed at 1090 B.C., and a second date from aceramic Feature 42 came in at 1035 B.C. About 77 percent of the debitage from this component was locally derived Keokuk chert.

Part 4

The Ohio River Region and Southeast

15

The Ohio Archaic: A Review

Matthew P. Purtill

Although research within Ohio has played a prominent role in the historical development of New World archaeological thought (Trigger 1989), Archaic studies within the state have been sparse and largely reactive to developments occurring elsewhere. Significantly, while William Webb and William Ritchie formalized the eastern Archaic concept during the first half of the twentieth century (e.g., Ritchie 1932; Webb 1946), Ohio scholars retained an almost myopic focus on Adena, Hopewell, and Fort Ancient–related issues. Aside from the brief mention of state materials in several pan-regional syntheses (e.g., Cunningham 1948; Didier 1967; Mayer-Oakes 1955), Ross Moffett's 1949 report on the Raisch-Smith site in Preble County represented the only major discussion of the Ohio Archaic until the mid- to late 1960s. This disinterest profoundly affected the direction of Archaic studies for years to come. Instead of developing state-specific cultural models, archaeologists commonly ascribed Ohio sites to either Webb's Indian Knoll culture or Ritchie's Laurentian tradition (e.g., Britt 1967; Geistweit 1970; McKenzie 1967; Moffett 1949; Morgan 1952; Prufer and Sofsky 1965). This "simplistic either-or proposition," as James Murphy (1975:80) has termed it, resulted in an approach laden with unwarranted cultural implications such as perceived ethnic affiliation and population movements. Although more recent fieldwork has made advances in combating the "either-or" mentality, archaeologists still struggle with the temptation of applying neighboring state models to regional data (e.g., Prufer and Long 1986; Purtill 2001).

Since the late 1960s, archaeologists have made advances in understanding the Archaic concept in Ohio. In 1970, two statewide syntheses of Archaic-period data were completed (Blank 1970; Geistweit 1970). Each study was successful at providing some structure to the record, but both were poorly circulated and marred by the limited number of sites excavated with good temporal control. Regional surveys—first by academic institutions and more recently through federally mandated studies (cultural resources management, or CRM)—have documented the widespread abundance of Archaic materials across the state. Over the past 20 years, CRM projects undeniably have provided the primary source of new raw data regarding Archaic chronology, settlement, subsistence, technology, and demography. As William Gardner has observed, CRM studies have forced archaeologists "into habitats and areas which most archaeologists ignored in the past" (1978:5), resulting in a clearer, more representative, picture of occupations statewide. As of June 2004, over 7,000 Archaic components, representing all 88 Ohio counties, had been recorded on Ohio Archaeological Inventory (OAI) forms filed at the Ohio Historic Preservation Office (OHPO) in Columbus. No attempts at synthesizing these data from a statewide perspective have been attempted since 1970.

The start of the twenty-first century continues to see Ohio Archaic research as poorly focused and mired in normative thought. Archaic societies often are described within a simple evolutionary framework. The initial stages of the Archaic are said to have featured low populations and high mobility. As time progressed, populations increased, mobility decreased, and the technology and subsistence base expanded. To date, few archaeologists have attempted to test the validity of such assertions or to see if they are represented equally across the state.

This chapter provides an updated review of Archaic manifestations within the state on the basis of current data. It is the first statewide synthesis of the Archaic period since Blank's and Geistweit's efforts of 1970. To provide a data-rich synthesis, a theoretical approach that is largely culture-historical in design and descriptive in content is employed. This study draws on previous efforts described in published, unpublished, and limited-circulation CRM sources. In addition, the results of new research undertaken by the chapter author specifically for this review are presented. This review is intended to provide a foundation on which to base future research. As will be demonstrated, Ohio's Archaic record holds substantial promise for addressing broader anthropological themes, especially ones that relate to hunter-gatherer studies.

Time and Cultural Taxonomy

The Archaic in Ohio has been described both as a stage (e.g., Blank 1970) and a temporal unit (e.g., Geistweit 1970). For this review, the Archaic will be presented as a temporal unit dated between cal 10,950 and 2650 B.P. with three subdivisions: Early (cal 10,950–8450 B.P.), Middle (cal 8450–5950 B.P.), and Late (cal 5950–2650 B.P.).[1] This framework breaks with more traditional views that posit a cal 9950–2950 B.P. time frame for midwestern Archaic societies (e.g., Griffin 1967). As will be demonstrated, the proposed temporal revisions outlined above better account for current information regarding diachronic shifts in hafted-biface styles, demographic levels, climate, and settlement and subsistence patterns. This chapter considers the full-scale adoption of side- and corner-notched hafted bifaces as marking the start of the Archaic period in Ohio. Recent recalibration of radiocarbon assays associated with the earliest hafted bifaces indicates that many types commonly associated with "Archaic" societies, such as Thebes or Kirk Corner Notched (e.g., Justice 1987), date significantly earlier than cal 9950 B.P. (see also Sherwood et al. 2004; Stafford 2004). Accordingly, if more traditional temporal frameworks were followed here, then many of the assemblages long thought to represent Early Archaic societies would need to be reclassified as Paleoindian. Such an approach would hamper comparisons between past research programs and, overall, would confuse the matter. Instead, the Early and Middle Archaic subperiods were redefined to account for the current temporal data. Dalton hafted bifaces, which clearly are a transitional type and are rare in the state, are assigned to the preceding Paleoindian period and will not be discussed.

The terminus of the Archaic period also has been revised in this review, placing it at cal 2650 B.P., or approximately 300–800 years younger than in most traditional schemes. As has long been recognized, many of the traits originally used to differentiate between Archaic and Woodland "stages," such as the introduction of fired-clay ceramics and domesticated plants, are now known to have had their origins in the Middle and Late Archaic periods across much of the Midcontinent (e.g., Stoltman 1978). In Ohio, several archaeologists have noted that, although traditional Woodland traits are found in contexts dating prior to cal 2950 B.P., their full-scale adoption did not occur until sometime after cal 2650 B.P. (e.g., Prufer and Sofsky 1965; Purtill 2004a; Stothers and Abel 1993). Importantly, the introduction of such traits into native societies does not appear to have significantly altered the generalized Archaic lifeway to any measurable degree. Only those changes in material culture, subsistence and settlement regimes, and (to a lesser degree) ceremonial practices that postdate cal 2650 B.P. appear significant enough to be characterized as Woodland. Similar arguments have been advanced elsewhere in the Midwest (e.g., Brown 1986; Emerson and Fortier 1986; Stoltman 1978).

Beginning in the mid-1960s, Ohio archaeologists espoused a series of phases, traditions, horizons, and complexes to describe Archaic assemblages (Abel et al. 2001; Blank 1970; Bowen 1991; Geistweit 1970; Litfin 1993; McKenzie 1967; Prufer and Sofsky 1965; Stothers and Abel 1993; Stothers, Abel, and Schneider 2001; Vickery 1976, 1980) (Figure 15.1). Many of these taxonomies are replete with problems related to the inadequate and sometimes inappropriate manner by which cultural units have been defined and applied. Little agreement exists among Ohio archaeologists regarding the appropriate application of such categories. The use of the "phase-tradition" concept has been especially troublesome in Ohio studies, with some archaeologists defining phases on the basis of diachronic changes in material culture (e.g., Vickery 1976), while others utilized strict temporal and spatial boundaries to define taxa (Bowen 1991; Stothers and Abel 1993). Moreover, many constructs have been based on limited data from multicomponent sites with poor temporal control. To avoid some of these classification pitfalls, and to maximize interregional comparability, this discussion emphasizes spatial variation within the Early, Middle, and Late temporal subdivisions discussed above. Physiographic regions (discussed below) present an effective means of partitioning space for this area.

Natural Setting and Paleoenvironment

Ohio is characterized by five major physiographic regions: Till Plains, Lake Plains, Unglaciated Plateau, Glaciated Plateau, and Lexington Plain (Fenneman 1938) (Figure 15.2). Each region is distinctive in geologic history, relief, drainage systems, climatic patterns, and biotic communities. Presumably, this interregional variation presented varying challenges to early Ohioans. For this study, the Lexington Plain region, which is spatially restricted to Adams and southeastern Brown counties, has been subsumed into the Till Plains region.

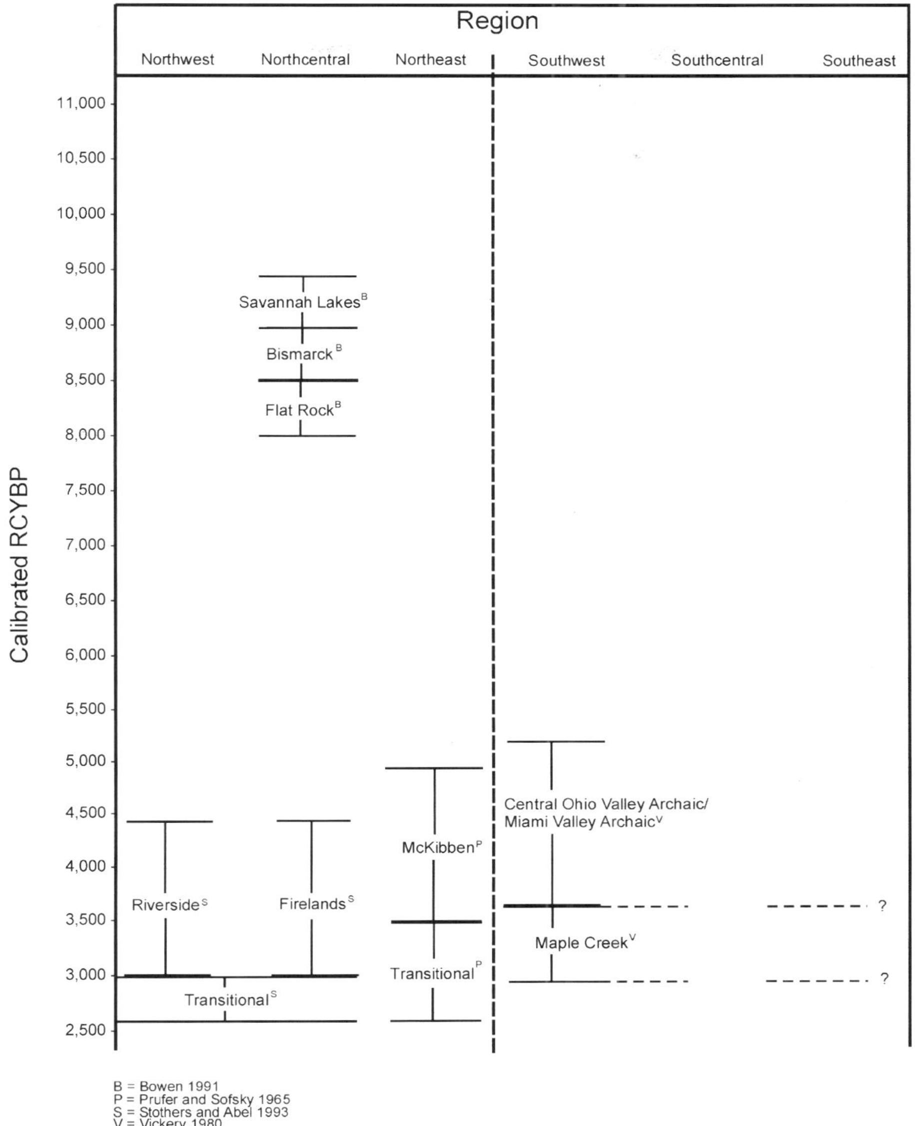

Figure 15.1. Previously proposed cultural-temporal units for the Archaic period in Ohio.

The Lake and Till plains are part of the Central Lowlands Province that extends westward into Indiana. The Lake Plains include level areas of low relief that surround modern-day Lake Erie. This region includes relict lake beds and beach ridges associated with Glacial Lake Maumee. During the Archaic period, the interaction between climate and tectonic factors resulted in highly variable water levels in postglacial Lake Erie (Coakley 1999; Forsyth 1973). Much of the Lake Plains region was a vast elm-ash wetland swamp historically referred to as the "Black Swamp" (Gordon 1969). The Till Plains region, which includes most of west-central and southwestern Ohio, formed as a result of Wisconsin-age glacial advances and retreats. This region is relatively flat, having been scoured by advancing glaciers, with low areas infilled by outwash and drift. Numerous glacial features dot the region.

Eastern Ohio is part of the Appalachian Plateau or Highland Province and consists of two main physiographic regions: Glaciated and Unglaciated plateaus. Elevations, on average, are about 100 m higher in the Appalachian Plateau region than in the Lake and Till plains. The Glaciated Plateau is situated in northeastern Ohio and is an area of gently rolling upland hills. Glacially derived kettle lakes and bogs and fens are abundant. The Unglaciated Plateau is located in the southeastern portion of the state and typically features narrow, deeply dissected river valleys.

Over the past 40 years, several regional and site-specific paleoenvironmental reconstruction studies within the state have been published (e.g., Ogden 1966; Shane 1987, 1994; Shane et al. 2001). These studies revealed that the Archaic period was characterized by variable climate regimes,

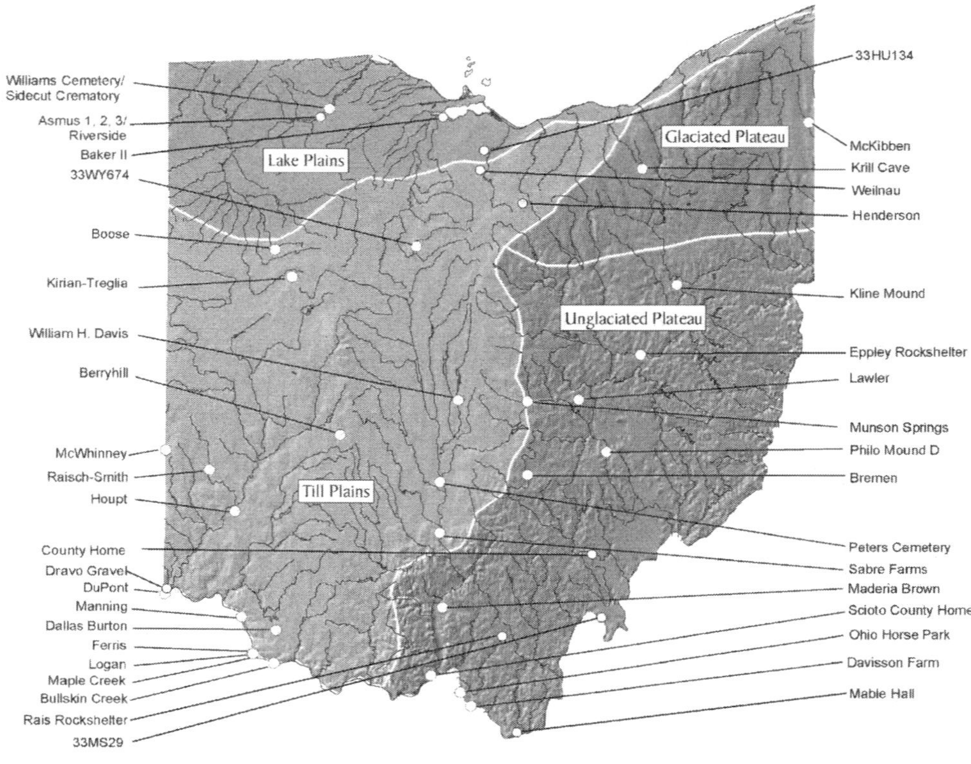

Figure 15.2. Physiographic regions map of Ohio and important Archaic sites.

precipitation levels, and vegetation communities. At the start of the Early Archaic period—ca. cal 11,000–10,000 years B.P.—forests across the state had just undergone a south-to-north transition from a conifer forest to a mixed deciduous woodland dominated by oak and hickory trees (Shane 1987, 1994; Shane et al. 2001). Between cal 11,500 and 7750 B.P., evidence indicates, conditions were warmer and dryer across most of the state (Shane et al. 2001:29). The Lake and Till plains regions consisted of relatively open forests, whereas the Appalachian Plateau region continued to be densely wooded (Shane 1987; Shane et al. 2001).

For the interval cal 7750–4500 B.P., pollen profiles are variable and contradictory. Shane et al. characterize this period as one of "extensive vegetation change across the region, with much local variability in evidence" (2001:30). The oak-dominated forests declined as species variability increased, including an increase in nonarboreal plants. Although complex and not completely understood, current evidence suggests that between cal 7750 and 6000 B.P. moisture levels likely were slightly higher than today. Between cal 6000 and 4500 B.P., however, a dramatic reduction in beech pollen occurred, which, coupled with an increase in nonarboreal pollen, suggests a general warming and drying episode that likely was associated with the pan-regional Hypsithermal, or Xerothermic, Interval (Ogden 1966; Shane et al. 2001).

Between cal 4500 and 2650 B.P., vegetation and climatic patterns roughly assumed modern conditions statewide (Shane et al. 2001). Oak and hickory forests again dominated, although the western Till and Lake plains continued to be more open and may have housed true prairies, especially in south-central Ohio. Assuming that forest composition during this time was similar to that encountered by European settlers in the 1700s, a great deal of interregional variability in tree species was present across the state during the Late Archaic period (Gordon 1969).

Chronology and Material Culture

An accurate picture of Archaic chronology and material culture is slowly emerging in Ohio. Although early studies intimated the complete abandonment of Ohio during significant portions of the Early and Middle Archaic periods (e.g., Morgan 1952; Prufer and Sofsky 1965), Archaic components are now recognized as abundant and distributed statewide. As of December 2004, 204 absolute dates (radiocarbon [^{14}C], oxidizable carbon ratio [OCR], and thermoluminescence [TL]) from 100 sites have been reported for Ohio (Appendix 15.A).

They include five Early Archaic, five Middle Archaic, and 194 Late Archaic dates.

The Early Archaic period (cal 10,950–8450 B.P.) is marked by the full-scale adoption of side- and corner-notched hafted bifaces into native tool kits. Over 20 defined hafted-biface types have been categorized into seven "horizons" for this discussion (Figure 15.3). Similar to Justice's (1987:6–9) use of the term *cluster, horizon* denotes morphologically similar biface styles that were contemporary in use. In rough chronological order, Early Archaic hafted-biface horizons include Early Side Notched, Charleston, Thebes, Kirk/Palmer, Kirk Stemmed, Large Bifurcate, and Small Bifurcate. Only a few of these types have been directly dated in Ohio (Table 15.1). Collectively, these horizons represent artifacts manufactured until ca. cal 8000 B.P., perhaps even as late as cal 7600 B.P. if late dates for St. Albans Side Notched forms from Pennsylvania are accepted (Cowin 1991).

There are two lines of thought regarding the cultural significance of the various Early Archaic hafted-biface types, especially ones with similar temporal spans. Some researchers, especially Vickery (1980) and Litfin (1993), view distinct types as representing separate ethnic groups, each group manufacturing a single type. The second approach assumes that groups used multiple types for different functions. Large bifaces such as Thebes and MacCorkle, for example, supposedly were used as knives, while smaller types such as Palmer Corner Notched

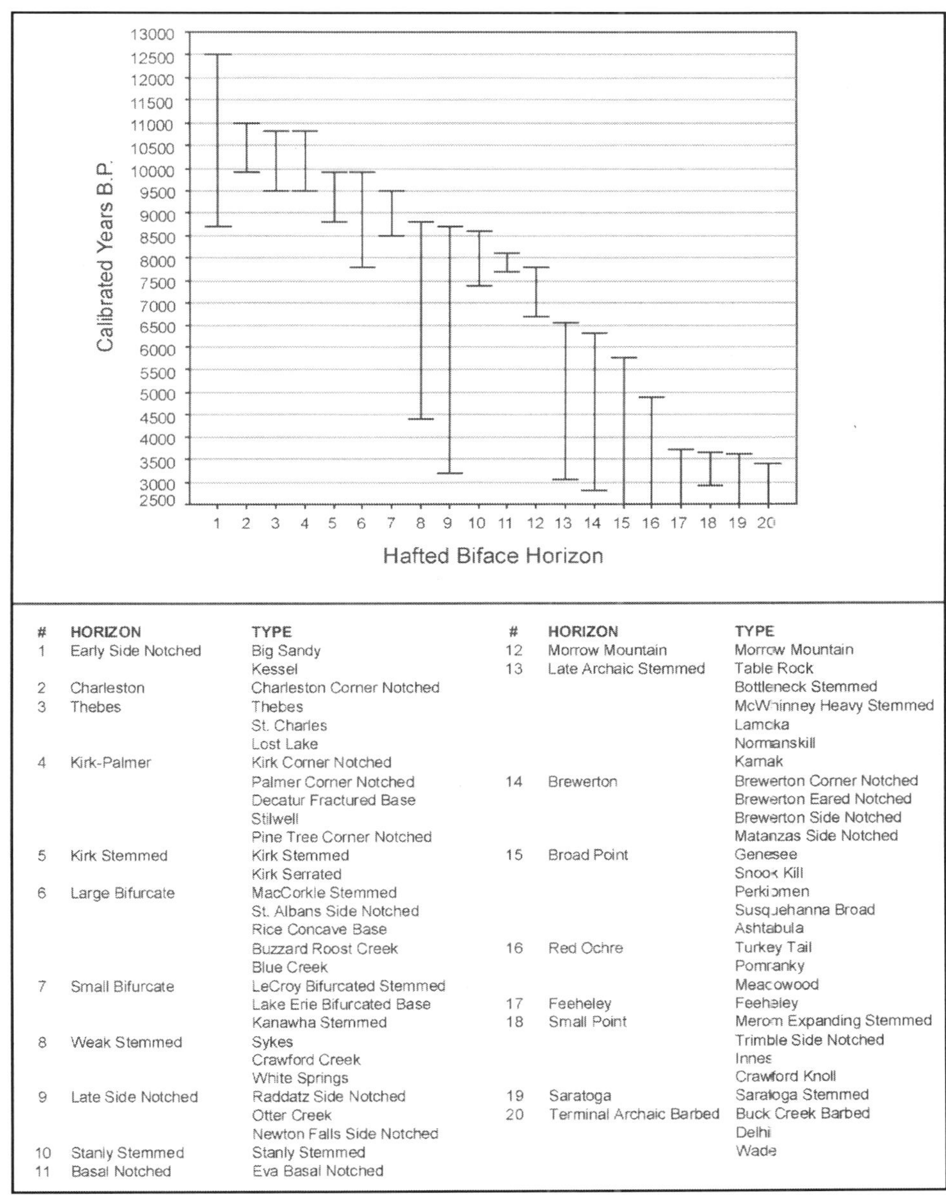

Figure 15.3. Hypothesized date ranges of hafted-biface horizons for the Ohio area.

Table 15.1. Inventory of All Directly Dated Archaic Hafted-Biface Artifacts from Ohio.

Horizon	Type	RCYBP (1 Sigma)	Site	Context	Reference
Kirk/Palmer	Kirk Corner Notched	10,100[a]	Manning (33CT476)	Occupation 3	Lepper 1994
—	Hardin Barbed	8106–7790	Burrill Farm (33LN15)	pit feature (?)	Brose 1978
Stanly	Stanly Stemmed	8106–7790	Burrill Farm (33LN15)	pit feature (?)	Brose 1978
Late Side Notched	Raddatz Side Notched–like	3635–3476	Krill Cave	Feature 5	Prufer et al. 1989
Brewerton	Brewerton Corner Notched	5452–4849	Hendricks Cave	hearth	Pedde and Prufer 2001
Brewerton	Brewerton Corner Notched	3205–2473	Eppley Rockshelter (33CS442)	Unit F-5, Level 7	Brush 1990
Brewerton	Brewerton Eared Notched	5929–5749	Davisson Farm (33LE619)	Feature 45	Purtill 2001
Brewerton	Brewerton Side Notched	2994–2792	Davisson Farm (33LE619)	Feature 111	Purtill 2001
Late Archaic Stemmed	Lamoka	3549–3378	Maderia Brown (33PK153)	Feature 45	Church 1995
Late Archaic Stemmed	Lamoka	3680–3476	Maderia Brown (33PK153)	Feature 45	Church 1995
Late Archaic Stemmed	Lamoka Cluster	3828–3588	Maderia Brown (33PK153)	Feature 14	Church 1995
Late Archaic Stemmed	Lamoka	3888–3636	Maderia Brown (33PK153)	Feature 43	Church 1995
Late Archaic Stemmed	Karnak	4524–4423	Ohio Horse Park (33SC421)	Feature 44a	Purtill, site notes
Broad Point	Ashtabula	3350–3079	Johnson Site II (33TU57)	Feature 1	Brown 1996
Broad Point	Ashtabula	3159–2873	Johnson Site II (33TU57)	Feature 1	Brown 1996
Small Point	Merom Cluster	3549–3378	Maderia Brown (33PK153)	Feature 45	Church 1995
Small Point	Merom Cluster	3680–3476	Maderia Brown (33PK153)	Feature 45	Church 1995
Small Point	Merom Expanding Stemmed	3632–3468	Houpt (33BU477)	Feature 12	Duerksen and Doershuk 1998
Small Point	Merom-like	3468–3271	33MS29	Feature 16	Keener and Pecora 2003
Small Point	Merom-like	3553–3388	33MS29	Feature 18	Keener and Pecora 2003
Small Point	Trimble Side Notched	3826–3553	33CT525	Feature 15	Jackson et al. 1990
Small Point	Trimble Side Notched	3209–3003	County Home (33AT40)	Feature 9	Heyman et al. 2005
Red Ocher	Turkey-tail	5026–4654	Grandstaff and Davis Cache	pit feature	Grandstaff and Davis 1985
Saratoga	Saratoga Stemmed	3549–3378	Maderia Brown (33PK153)	Feature 45	Church 1995
Saratoga	Saratoga Stemmed	3680–3476	Maderia Brown (33PK153)	Feature 45	Church 1995

[a]This date represents an estimate derived from calculating the sediment accumulation rate from other dated soil horizons presented in Lepper 1994.

bifaces represent dart or spear points (Bowen 1994; DeRegnaucourt 1992; Stothers 1996). Recent use-wear analysis of the MacCorkle type in northern Ohio indicates that these bifaces functioned as both knives and projectiles during their use lives (Miller 2002). Miller concluded that MacCorkles longer than 5 cm in axial length tended to be used for general cutting tasks. In contrast, smaller and heavily resharpened forms exhibit wear consistent with use as projectiles.

Early Archaic chipped-stone assemblages also contained a variety of both unifacial and bifacial tool types. The abundance of steep-edged end scrapers, often with gravers or spurs, suggest continuity with earlier Paleoindian times (Figure 15.4f, g). At the Ferris site, for example, Theler and Dalbey (1974) recovered over 80 of these artifacts, approximately half with at least one graver or spur. Several other chipped-stone tool types are known from Early Archaic assemblages, including large blades and blade cores, drills, burins, bifacially chipped adzelike tools, and unifacially beveled and crescent-shaped bifaces (Kozarek et al. 1994; Lepper 1994; Theler and Dalbey 1974) (Figure 15.4).

During the initial stages of the Early Archaic (cal 10,950–9500 B.P.), raw material use was dominated by a few, widely distributed, high-quality bedrock chert sources. Ohio's Upper Mercer and Ohio Flint Ridge cherts, Indiana's Harrison County (Wyandot) chert, and Kentucky's Paoli chert were most intensively utilized in Ohio. Other chert sources commonly reported for Ohio sites include Onondaga (Michigan, Ontario), Pipe Creek (Ohio), Ten Mile Creek (Ohio), Bayport (Michigan), Kettle Point (Ontario), Burlington (Illinois), Crescent (Missouri), and Knox (Tennessee).

In the Lake Plains, central to northern Till Plains, and Glaciated Plateau regions, Upper Mercer chert was the most heavily utilized material during both Paleoindian and Early Archaic times (e.g., Bowen 1994; Kingsley 1988; Prufer and Baby 1963; Stothers 1996; Stothers, Abel, and Schneider 2001). Bowen (1994) reports that over 90 percent of Large Bifurcate–horizon bifaces from these areas were manufactured from Upper Mercer chert. Other hafted-biface types also were manufactured from Upper Mercer but in lower proportions (Stothers 1996:199–200). Notably, northern

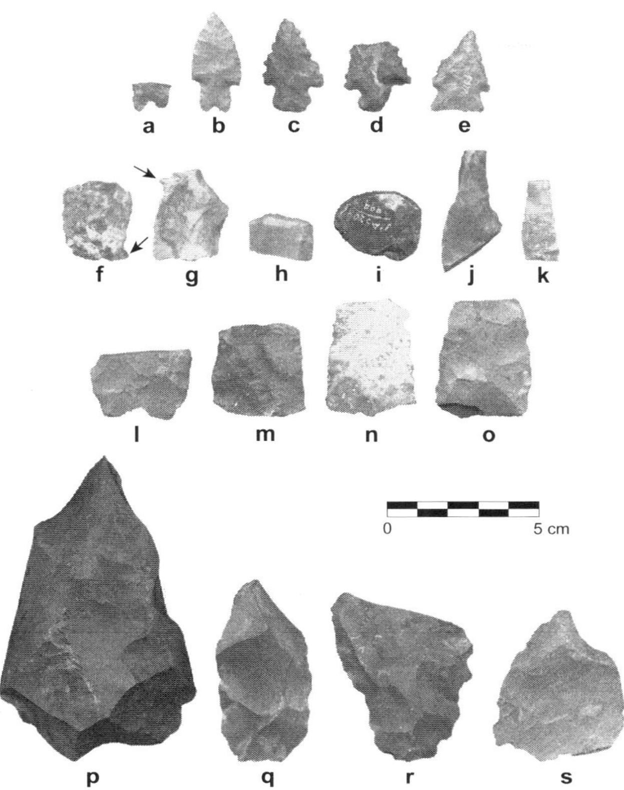

Figure 15.4. Early Archaic artifacts from the Henderson site (33AS206): a, b, Small Bifurcate–horizon hafted bifaces; c–e, Palmer Corner Notched hafted bifaces; f, steep-edged end scraper; g–i, end scrapers; j, k, bifacial drills; l–o, late-stage bifaces; p, q, cores; r, s, early-stage bifaces. Arrows denote locations of spurs.

Ohio Thebes bifaces tend *not* to be manufactured from Upper Mercer chert. Instead, northern Bayport and Kettle Point cherts were used extensively (e.g., Davis 2000; Stothers 1996). Stothers also documents that two "local" northern Ohio chert types, Pipe Creek and Ten Mile Creek, were heavily utilized.

The extensive use of Upper Mercer chert led Bowen to postulate an Upper Mercer "lithic supply zone" for northern Ohio and beyond. Borrowing the concept from Seeman (1994), Bowen documented the distribution of Upper Mercer Early Archaic bifaces over 250,000 km^2 of land in Ohio, western Pennsylvannia, southern Michigan, southern Ontario, and eastern Indiana. Intensive use of this material was restricted to an 80,000 km^2 area in north-central Ohio; Upper Mercer outcrops are located in the extreme southeastern sector of this zone. Some archaeologists view these distributions as reflecting territorial boundaries used by bands during annual, seasonal rounds (Bowen 1994; Stothers 1996:199). Others interpret the sudden appearance of previously undocumented chert types (e.g., Kanawha Black [West Virginia]) as a sign of new populations migrating into the region from the south (e.g., Stothers, Abel, and Schneider 2001).

Bowen (1994) interprets the lack of Upper Mercer manufacturing debris at northern sites as evidence that frequent retooling trips back to Upper Mercer outcrops were needed. He postulates that most tools were manufactured near quarry sites prior to being transported elsewhere. Not all Early Archaic sites show this pattern, however. The Early Archaic Henderson site in Ashland County was characterized by extensive use of Upper Mercer chert to manufacture several tool types, including Palmer Corner Notched bifaces (Kozarek et al. 1994) (Figure 15.4). Although the nearest outcrop is located nearly 100 km to the south, excavations yielded cores, early- to late-stage bifaces, and abundant debitage, all of Upper Mercer chert (Figure 15.4). Long-distance transportation of minimally modified raw material is indicated. This assemblage, plus several Upper Mercer biface cache sites recently reported for Ohio (e.g., DeRegnaucourt 2002:24), suggests that groups did not anticipate returning to quarry sites on a regular basis and transported ample raw material for later use.

Stothers (1996), Bowen (1991), and Ellis et al. (1991) documented a second, smaller, lithic supply zone tethered to northern Ohio's Pipe Creek outcrops. This material was used extensively for the manufacture of Kirk/Palmer–horizon bifaces at several north-central Ohio sites (e.g., 33HU134) and southern Ontario sites (e.g., Nettling) within an area stretching nearly 200 linear kilometers. Transportation routes likely included areas that were dry lake plains during the Early Archaic period but are now inundated by Lake Erie (Forsyth 1973).

The high frequency of cal pre-9500 B.P. Harrison County chert bifaces in southwestern Ohio led Bowen (1994) to postulate a third lithic supply zone that extended into Ohio's southern Till Plains from the southwest. This zone encompassed close to 100,000 km^2 of land and partially overlapped with the Upper Mercer supply zone in the upper Miami River area. Litfin (1993) and DeRegnaucourt (1992, 2002) also have documented extensive regional use of Harrison County chert in this area, although not to the exclusion of other varieties.

Without formally defining it, I would suggest that a fourth lithic supply zone can be recognized for south-central to southeastern Ohio, especially along the Ohio River corridor. Here, Early Archaic assemblages are dominated by Paoli chert (e.g., Purtill 2004b; Theler and Dalbey 1974), which outcrops in nearby Carter County, Kentucky. Artifacts in these assemblages often are extensively resharpened (Figure 15.5). Modest amounts of Harrison County chert also occur in this area, likely representing westward transport up the Ohio River. The presence of both Paoli and Brush Creek cherts in southwestern Ohio indicates downriver transport, as well (Picklesimer 1999; Theler and Dalbey 1974). Significantly, the southern Unglaciated Plateau region along the Ohio River is characterized by an almost total absence of Upper Mercer and Ohio Flint Ridge material—this despite ample evidence of both materials in the lower reaches of several local drainages (e.g., the Hocking River valley; see Abrams and Freter 2005).

Figure 15.5. Palmer Corner Notched hafted bifaces from the Ferris site (33CT31), all made from Paoli chert. Note heavy blade resharpening on three specimens to the right. Artifacts made available for documentation by the University of Cincinnati, Department of Anthropology.

The presence of the rugged Unglaciated Plateau region appears to have served as a buffer to the southern transport of this material despite the presence of several southward-draining rivers (e.g., the Hocking and Muskingum).

By cal 9500–9000 B.P., increased use of local cherts at the expense of nonlocal, high-grade material apparently occurred statewide (Litfin 1993; Stothers 1996; Stothers, Abel, and Schneider 2001). This shift corresponds with the adoption of Small Bifurcate–horizon hafted bifaces. Most researchers speculate that reduced mobility accounted for this change, although small artifact size may have eliminated the need for large bedrock outcrops (Bowen 1994).

Although long thought to represent a Middle to Late Archaic innovation, ground- and pecked-stone technology has been documented at several Ohio Early Archaic sites. Manos (several with pitted surfaces), pitted stones, and other miscellaneous ground-stone "abrading" tools have been recovered at Manning (Lepper 1994), Ferris (Theler and Dalbey 1974), and Cooper Hollow (Brose 1975). At Manning, ground-stone tools, including manos and pitted stones, were recovered from three deeply buried strata (Occupations 1–3). Occupation 3, which was characterized by Kirk/Palmer–horizon bifaces and was thought to date to ca. cal 9900 B.P., contained the majority of these implements. The underlying Occupation 2, which was radiocarbon dated to cal 11,120 B.P., contained a single large sandstone mortar with a pitted surface.

Large Middle Archaic assemblages are unknown for Ohio, as only a few sites have been securely dated to this period (Appendix 15.A). Middle Archaic tool kits primarily are characterized by two hafted-biface types: medium to large side-notched forms, variously identified as either Raddatz, Otter Creek, Big Sandy, or Newtown Falls Side Notched, and the medium-sized, triangular-bladed Stanly Stemmed. Other forms recovered in lesser frequency include Sykes, Crawford Creek, White Springs, Eva Basal Notched, and Morrow Mountain. Although side-notched forms generally are assigned to the Raddatz, Otter Creek, or Big Sandy types, a great deal of confusion exists over the correct classification and temporal placement of such artifacts (Morton and Carskadden 1975; Purtill 2004b; Stothers, Abel, and Schneider 2001). Southwestern Ohio assemblages, for example, are replete with thick, shallow-notched, hafted bifaces with square stems and straight bases. DeRegnaucourt (1992) has argued that these side-notched hafted bifaces—which he terms "Big Sandy"—can be distinguished from earlier "true" Big Sandy types by the lack of quality workmanship, beveling, and concave bases. DeRegnaucourt posits a Middle Archaic date for these artifacts, although the repeated co-association of side-notched forms with McWhinney Heavy Stemmed bifaces in southwestern Ohio (e.g., Converse 2004) suggests continued manufacture into Late Archaic times, as well. A Late Archaic placement of these bifaces also has been suggested for sites in the Muskingum River valley, where small side-notched bifaces have been indirectly associated with radiocarbon dates of cal 4650 and 3430 B.P. at the Lawler site (Morton and Carskadden 1975).

Late Archaic artifact assemblages show significant regional differences that likely reflect increased sedentism and parochialism. Statewide, chipped-stone tool assemblages include drills, minimally retouched flakes and scrapers, cores, and bifacial "knives," blanks, and preforms. Hafted-biface scrapers, which appear to be recycled artifacts, are very common and are often recovered by the hundreds at certain sites (e.g., Converse 2004) (Figure 15.6). In southwestern Ohio, Vickery (1976, 1980) also documented a well-developed, microtool industry including gravers, perforators, and drills on flakes and the presence of "Maple Creek knives," defined as bifaces with one straight and one excurvate edge (Vickery 1980:35).

For the cal 5200–2650 B.P. time span in southwestern Ohio, high frequencies of McWhinney Heavy Stemmed (Figure 15.6), untyped side-notched, and Merom/Trimble hafted-biface styles are reported. Other types include the Brewerton series, Vosburg, Motley, Robeson Constricting Stem, Lamoka, Normanskill, Snook Kill, and Ashtabula (Vickery 1980). At Maple Creek, Vickery (1976, 1980) documented the co-occurrence of McWhinney Heavy Stemmed and Merom/Trimble forms from sub-plow-zone contexts dated to ca. cal 3500 B.P. He suggested that McWhinney Heavy Stemmed forms were manufactured over a broad span of time in southwestern Ohio and that they represented the principal hafted-biface type in both his Central Ohio Valley Archaic (cal 5200–3700 B.P.) and Maple Creek (cal 3700–2950 B.P.) phases. Whether McWhinney Heavy Stemmed and Merom/Trimble forms were contemporary in the mid-Ohio Valley is still open to debate, however. Several researchers argue that McWhinney Heavy Stemmed bifaces significantly predated Merom/Trimble forms at most sites (e.g., Boisvert 1986; Duerksen and Doershuk 1998; Ledbetter and O'Steen 1991). In contrast, CRM investigations at the Driving Range site in Hamilton County recovered both a McWhinney Heavy Stemmed and a Merom/Trimble from

Figure 15.6. Chipped-stone hafted bifaces and hafted scrapers from the McWhinney site (33PR9): rows 1 and 2, McWhinney Heavy Stemmed hafted bifaces; rows 3 and 4, hafted-biface scrapers (all McWhinney Heavy Stemmed type). Artifacts made available for documentation by the Dayton Society of Natural History, Anthropology Department.

an undated burial (Kreinbrink et al. 1992), suggesting at least some temporal overlap between the two types.

The temporal placement of Merom/Trimble forms is more established in southern Ohio. Merom/Trimble bifaces have been recovered from seven directly dated contexts (Table 15.1). These dates tightly cluster between cal 3800 and 3000 B.P., suggesting an approximate 800-year manufacturing range of the type by southern Ohio groups.

In the southeastern Unglaciated Plateau region, tool assemblages, especially hafted-biface forms, seem to reflect multidirectional cultural relationships (e.g., Geistweit 1970; Purtill 2004a). This is true along the Ohio River, where groups would have had easy access to multiple regions and, so, chances for interaction. So-called Laurentian Archaic hafted-biface types, perhaps reflecting northeastern influence, are most common and include the full Brewerton series as well as Lamoka, Genesee, and Vosburg forms. Minor numbers of Merom/Trimble, McWhinney Heavy Stemmed, Matanzas Side Notched, Karnak Stemmed, Ledbetter Stemmed, Snook Kill, Robbins, and Saratoga Broad Blade also have been identified (DaRe 2002; Purtill 2004b). Perhaps significantly, Purtill (2001, 2003a, 2003b, 2004a, 2004b) has demonstrated that a great deal of interassemblage variability existed among hafted-biface types at contemporary sites in this region. Sites such as Davisson Farm in Lawrence County were dominated by Brewerton Eared Notched forms, whereas other similarly dated area sites, including Grayson in northeastern Kentucky and site 33MS29 in Meigs County, were dominated by Merom/Trimble forms (Keener and Pecora 2003; Ledbetter and O'Steen 1991). Such disparate assemblages led Purtill (2004a) to speculate that distinct ethnic groups may have been operating in this segment of the Ohio Valley during portions of the Late Archaic period.

In the Glaciated Plateau region, Prufer and Long (1986) and Prufer (2001) report hafted-biface assemblages dominated by the full range of Brewerton series types. Lamoka, Vosburg, Genesee, Steubenville Stemmed, Susquehanna Broad, Perkiomen, Orient Fishtail, and Ashtabula also are found in lesser frequencies. Similar tool assemblages are documented in the central to northern Till Plains and Lake Plains regions (Stothers and Abel 1993; Stothers, Abel, and Schneider 2001). Within Ohio, corner-notched Feeheley bifaces occur primarily in the Lake Plains region, although Purtill (2004a) reports one at Davisson Farm along the Ohio River. Innes and Crawford Knoll hafted bifaces, which appear to be technologically equivalent to Merom/Trimble types, also are abundant in later Late Archaic assemblages in the northwestern part of the state.

Stothers and Abel (1993) also have documented a chipped-stone argillite industry in northwestern Ohio. Argillite was used to manufacture a variety of Broad Point–horizon forms, especially ones best ascribed to the Genesee type. Commonly identified as belonging to the Satchell complex, these bifaces are proposed to have been part of a specialized tool kit for processing large game, principally white-tailed deer (Stothers and Abel 1993).

Throughout Ohio, Late Archaic assemblages reflect the increased use of locally available cherts. Evidence indicates that procurement strategies were not uniform at all sites, however. In southwestern Ohio, for example, Hill-Ariens (2003) documented distinct utilization patterns between the more western Dupont Village and Dravo Gravel sites (Hamilton County) and contemporary eastern neighbors in Clermont

County (Bullskin and Maple Creek). Although heavy reliance on local cherts is evident at all sites, Clermont County locales contained an unexpectedly high percentage of Kentucky cherts, including Boyle, Kentucky Flint Ridge (i.e., Breathitt), and Paoli (Hill-Ariens 2003). The use of Kentucky cherts by some Late Archaic groups in southwestern Ohio may reflect a continuation of earlier procurement strategies, albeit to a lesser degree. Continued cultural ties with southern groups also are indicated. In contrast to the Clermont County sites, DuPont Village was characterized by a focal procurement plan based almost entirely on Laurel chert, which outcrops nearby in southeastern Indiana and was available locally in stream-pebble form.

Where preservation is good, Late Archaic components yield extensive bone and shell tool inventories. Vickery (1980) lists a range of polished, perforated, and ground or pecked bone tools, including awls, fishhooks, shuttles, flakers and punches, perforated animal and human teeth (necklaces or pendants?), bone and shell beads, pins, beamers, needles, antler atlatl hooks, bird-bone flutes, and turtle-carpace containers (Figure 15.7). Rich bone-tool industries also were noted at the Scioto County Homes site along the lower Scioto River (Bowen 1987) and at the upland Krill Cave site in Summit County (Prufer et al. 1989).

A well-developed ground- and pecked-stone tool industry was in use by cal 5950 B.P. Hard-stone material types, including granite, quartzite, tillite, slate, hematite, siltstone, sandstone, and limestone, were utilized. Most materials are available statewide, except in the Unglaciated Plateau region, where hard stone is rare. Common tool types include sandstone tubular pipes (cloud-blower type), celts and adzes, pitted stones, notched-pebble net sinkers, roller- and bell-shaped pestles, and three-quarter- to full-grooved axes (Murphy 1975; Prufer 2001; Purtill 2004a; Stothers, Abel, and Schneider 2001; Vickery 1980) (Figure 15.8). Grinding stones, abraders, mortars, and manos are infrequently recovered.

Several other Late Archaic ground- or pecked-stone tool types and material sources were used only in portions of the state. Hematite, which outcrops in southeastern Ohio, is common in the Unglaciated Plateau region but rarely found elsewhere. This material was used to manufacture a range of artifacts, including plummets, miniature celts, and hemispheres, all of which continued to be made well into Woodland times. Although rarely dated in Ohio, a hematite hemisphere from a sub-plow-zone context was recovered adjacent to a Late Archaic pit feature at the Ohio Horse Park site in southern Scioto County that yielded a cal 3277 B.P. age (Purtill 2003c; see Appendix 15.A).

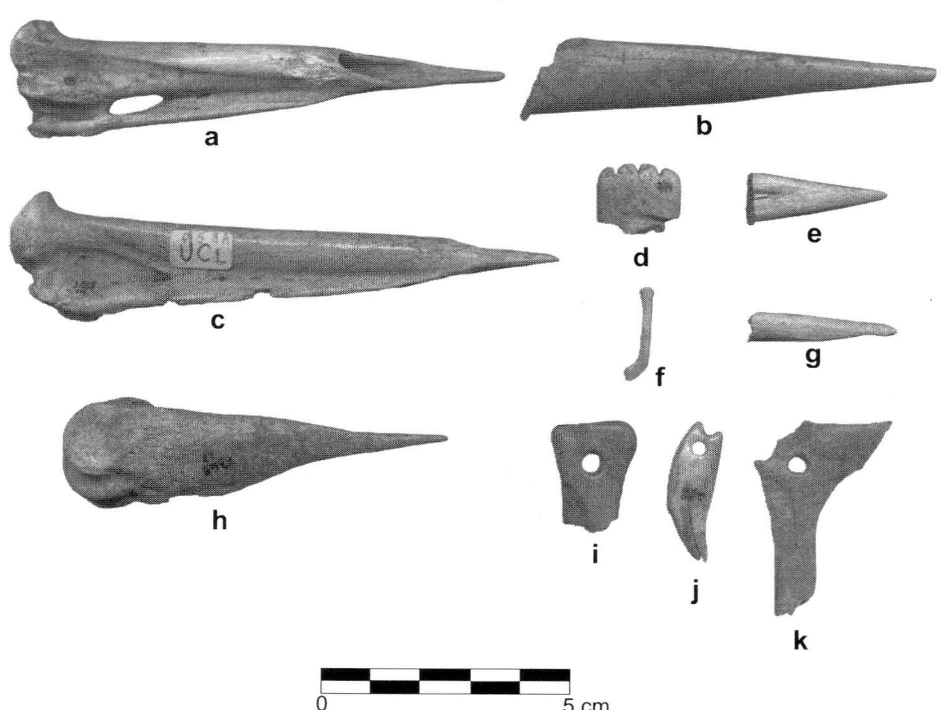

Figure 15.7. Late Archaic bone tools from the DuPont Village site (33HA11): a–c, h, bone awls; d, polished and notched hairpin head; e, g, bone awl or pin tip; f, bone fishhook; i, perforated pin or shuttle head; j, polished perforated and notched animal canine; k, polished and perforated turtle bone. Artifacts made available for documentation by the University of Cincinnati, Department of Anthropology.

Figure 15.8. Ground-stone tools from the McWhinney site (33PR9): left, bell-shaped pestle; middle and right, three-quarter-grooved axes. Artifacts made available for documentation by the Dayton Society of Natural History, Anthropology Department.

Figure 15.9. Chipped-slate bars and pendant from the McWhinney site (33PR9). Artifacts made available for documentation by the Dayton Society of Natural History, Anthropology Department.

Along the lower Scioto River valley, "ironstone," which is a local siltstone material cemented with hematite and goethite, was used to manufacture chipped-stone hoes employed in generalized digging tasks (Lindner 1982). Primarily used during the Late Archaic period, these "ironstone hoes," as they are called, appear to have been used without hafting in most cases. Spatially, they are restricted to the lower Scioto River valley and surrounding counties along the Ohio River. In southwestern Ohio, Vickery (1976, 1980) has documented a local tillite industry primarily for manufacturing steep-edged "scraper planes," presumably for use in woodworking tasks. Vickery has assigned these tools to his Central Ohio Valley Archaic phase (cal 5200–3700 B.P.), and they are abundant only in the Little and Great Miami river valleys.

Slate artifacts include bannerstones, birdstones, pendants and gorgets, disk "knives," rectangular and subrectangular bars, and various other miscellaneous items (Figure 15.9). The widespread distribution of crude, unfinished slate bannerstone and birdstone specimens on Ohio sites indicates that these enigmatic artifacts were manufactured locally and do not represent long-distance trade items. Bannerstones are common statewide except in the southeastern and central regions (Whaley 1992). Over 90 percent of Ohio specimens were manufactured from locally available green-banded slate. Whaley (1992) found that various forms (e.g., notched ovates and geniculates) were patterned in their regional distributions, suggesting that they may have been emblematic of distinct bands or tribes. The only well-dated bannerstone artifact in Ohio, a fragment, derives from DuPont Village in Hamilton County and was associated with a burial dating between cal 5130 and 4650 B.P. (Vickery 1980).

Slate bar-style, bust-style, and pop-eyed-style birdstones are recovered in abundance from the central to northern Till Plains and Lake Plains regions (Figure 15.10). These artifacts undoubtedly had ceremonial significance and occasionally have been reported with red ocher staining (Townsend 2003:190–192). Recovery of two bar-style birdstones from the head region of an isolated adult Late Archaic burial at the Baker II site in Sandusky County indicates that such artifacts were included, at least in one instance, as grave offerings (Stothers and Abel 1993). The Baker II burial yielded a date of cal 2820 B.P., placing it in the terminal Late Archaic period. As seen at the well-dated Williams Cemetery site in Wood County (Abel et al. 2001), birdstone artifacts continued to be manufactured well into the Early Woodland period.

An additional slate artifact type is a rectangular or subrectangular bar (Figure 15.9) and was recovered en masse from Late Archaic sites in the upper reaches of the Great and Little Miami rivers in southwestern Ohio (Converse 2004). These artifacts, typically associated with so-called Miami Valley Archaic–complex sites (Converse 2004), may represent preforms for pendants or gorgets. Sometimes they are referred to as slate "knives" or "axes," but rarely are they notched. They tend to be associated with McWhinney Heavy Stemmed and untyped side-notched hafted-biface forms in Ohio.

Durable-container technology, both in the form of carved-stone bowls and fired-clay pottery, was introduced into Ohio by around cal 4500 B.P. Carved-stone containers are primarily steatite bowls and appear to represent items traded in from the Middle Atlantic area. Although not directly dated in Ohio, steatite vessels typically date between cal 4500 and 3500 B.P. in the Southeast, Northeast, and along the eastern coast (e.g., Sassaman 1993). Gartley (1976) reports steatite sherds in at least three undated conical mounds thought to represent Adena-period edifices. This association may indicate that steatite technology continued to be used in Ohio well into the Woodland period. The overall infrequent recovery of steatite sherds from Ohio sites, however, suggests that such vessels were not a principal component of Late Archaic assemblages. Although steatite sherds have been reported for

Figure 15.10. Distribution of birdstone artifacts across Ohio. Data based on a sample of 483 specimens compiled from review of Ohio Archaeologist *1969–72, 1975–98, 1999 (Issue 1), 2000, and Townsend's* Birdstones of North America *(1959).*

all areas of Ohio, Gartley (1976) has shown that they tend to be largely restricted to the southeast and northeast segments of the state.

Although not well studied, steatite vessel shape consistently is described as round- to flat-bottomed, oblong-shaped bowls with semicircular lug handles located a few centimeters below the lip. Gartley (1976) reports a thickness of between 8 and 9 mm. Decorations are rare and restricted to vertical, parallel, incised lines or notches. Kreinbrink et al. (1992) report vertical incising on the lug itself in Hamilton County, whereas notched, vertical lines on the lip section have been reported in Muskingum County (Gartley 1976). The presence of repair holes suggests curation or recycling of damaged vessels.

Fired-clay pottery, long believed to mark the beginning of the Woodland period or stage (e.g., Griffin 1967), is now commonly reported in assemblages dating between cal 4500 and 2650 B.P. in Ohio (Table 15.2). Although early pottery is noted in assemblages from all four physiographic regions, most finds have been reported from sites located in the Unglaciated Plateau. This distribution might indicate the direction from which pottery technology initially entered Ohio (i.e., from the southeast). Early pottery typically is recovered in low frequency, suggesting that it was not a major component of native technologies until sometime after cal 2650 B.P., when its use expanded noticeably (Stothers and Abel 1993).

Table 15.2. Reported Occurrences of Cal Pre-2650 B.P. Ceramics from Directly Dated Deposits.

Site	County	Physiographic Region	Context	Published Description	Cal B.P. Date (1 Sigma)	Reference
Bremen (33FA1460)	Fairfield	Unglaciated Plateau	Feature 2	grit-tempered, highly eroded sherdlets (n = 2)	4527–4302	Pecora and Burks 2005
Hoffaker (33TR58)	Trumbull	Glaciated Plateau	Feature 14	thick, interior/exterior cordmarking (n = 92)	4508–3997	Seeman 1986
Rais Rockshelter (33JA159)	Jackson	Unglaciated Plateau	strata—38 inches	thick, grit-tempered, plain-surface ceramics, 8–11 mm in thickness; comparable to Dominion Thick pottery type	3962–3574	Seeman 1986; Shane 1971
Rais Rockshelter (33JA159)	Jackson	Unglaciated Plateau	strata—31 inches	thick, grit-tempered, plain-surface ceramics, 8–11 mm in thickness; comparable to Dominion Thick type	3975–3593	Seeman 1986; Shane 1971
Kendera (33ER3)	Erie	Lake Plains	Feature ?	thick, interior/exterior cordmarking; classified as Leimbach Thick pottery type	3678–3396	Stothers and Abel 1993
Bremen (33FA1460)	Fairfield	Unglaciated Plateau	Feature 3	grit-tempered, highly eroded sherdlets (n = 17)	3679–3382	Pecora and Burks 2005
Maple Creek (33CT52)	Clermont	Till Plains	strata ?	thick, grit tempered, plain surface	4406–2749	Vickery 1976, 1980
Maderia Brown (33PK153)	Pike	Unglaciated Plateau	Feature 39	not described, suggested that it could be intrusive	3564–3384	Church 1995
33MS29	Meigs	Unglaciated Plateau	Feature 18	plain-bodied, grit/grog-tempered pottery (n = 1)	3553–3388	Keener and Pecora 2003
Possum Hollow (33CT645)	Clermont	Till Plains	Feature 44	pottery "crumbs" directly dated; additional pottery recovered from features thought to be contemporary	3360–3473[a]	Anne Lee, pers. comm. 2004
33MS29	Meigs	Unglaciated Plateau	Feature 16	eroded, grit-tempered pottery (n = 1)	3468–3271	Keener and Pecora 2003
Continental Construction (33RO348)	Ross	Till Plains	Feature ?	classified as Dominion Thick pottery type	3447–3085	Carr 1988; Pacheco 1987, 1991
Ohio Horse Park (33SC421)	Scioto	Unglaciated Plateau	Feature 2	split sherdlet, grit tempered (n = 1)	3339–3212	Purtill 2003c
Philo Group: Mound D (33MU77)	Muskingum	Unglaciated Plateau	Feature 1	thick, grit tempered, plain surface; lug handles	3322–3003	Morton and Carskadden 1987
Rais Rockshelter (33JA159)	Jackson	Unglaciated Plateau	strata—27–28 inches	comparable to Dominion Thick pottery type	3376–2869	Seeman 1986; Shane 1971
Seaman's Fort (33ER85)	Erie	Lake Plains	Feature ?	Leimbach series pottery type	3448–2777	Stothers and Abel 1993
Stanford Knoll (33LA2)	Lake	Lake Plains	?	thick-walled pottery	2850 ± 300[b]	Lee 1986
Possum Hollow (33CT645)	Clermont	Till Plains	Feature 4 (Trench 1)	pottery "crumbs" directly dated; additional pottery recovered from features thought to be contemporary	2985–2846	Anne Lee, pers. comm. 2004
Rais Rockshelter (33JA159)	Jackson	Unglaciated Plateau	strata—27–28 inches	comparable to Dominion Thick pottery type	3058–2780	Seeman 1986; Shane 1971
Danbury (33OT16)	Ottawa	Lake Plains	Feature 04-13	37 grit-tempered sherds (min. of 5 vessels); exterior and interior cordmarking, flat bases; wall thickness range of 8.4–20.4 mm, average 13.2 mm; comparable to Dominion Thick type	2990–2890[a]	Redmond 2005
Weilnau (33ER409)	Erie	Lake Plains	Feature ?	Leimbach series pottery type	2946–2788	Stothers and Abel 1993
Gregory's Field-Fort Ancient (33WA2)	Warren	Till Plains	Feature 274; Lot 17	thick-walled ceramics	2856–2751[a]	Cowan et al. 2004
Mabel Hall (33LE97)	Lawrence	Unglaciated Plateau	strata ?	thick, grit tempered, plain surface	2775–3115	Seeman 1986
Meek I (33CS93)	Coshocton	Unglaciated Plateau	Feature 1	quartz-, shist-, and mica-tempered ceramics (n = 19), thickness between 8.1 and 9.6 mm.	2920–2740	Bush et al. 1987
Munson Springs (33LI251)	Licking	Glaciated Plateau	Feature 116	thick, grit-tempered (primarily crushed granite), plain surfaced, thickness averaging 11.03 mm (n = 103); rims have a flattened lip and slight outward flaring and average 8.6 mm in thickness; lug handles are present; comparable to Dominion Thick type	3057–2779 (estimate)	Pacheco and Burks 2002

[a] This date represents a late addition to this analysis; it is not listed in Appendix 15.A.
[b] This assay represents a TL date and was not subject to calibration.

Early pottery assemblages are small in number, often highly eroded, and poorly described. Temper includes large pieces of undifferentiated grit, although quartz, shist, and mica also have been reported at the Meek I site in Coshocton County (Bush et al. 1987). Average sherd thickness ranges between 8 and 13 mm. At the Hoffaker and Kendera sites in northern Ohio, interior and exterior cordmarking was observed, although most sherds are undecorated or exhibited exterior cordmarking only. Rims are flattened and necks show a straight to slightly outward-flaring profile. Thickness of rim-neck sections is noticeably thinner than the body of the vessel. Lug handles are common.

Most analysts indicate that cal pre-2650 B.P. pottery assemblages compare favorably to one of two previously defined ceramic types: Dominion Thick (Cramer 1989) and Leimbach Thick (Shane 1967) (see Table 15.2). Both of these types were proposed to represent Early Woodland pottery and initially were not thought to date prior to cal 2650 B.P. in Ohio. The Dominion Thick type, which appears to represent a variant of the Fayette Thick type (Griffin 1943), is most often cited when describing assemblages deriving from central to southern Ohio. This type is defined as thick, plain surfaced, and barrel shaped, with little neck curvature. Lug handles are common, and at least one example of a riveted lug is known. Rims are flattened to slightly beveled. Leimbach Thick was defined in north-central to northeastern Ohio by Shane (1967) and appears stylistically similar to the above-described Dominion Thick type. Leimbach Thick wares are grit tempered with cordmarked exteriors. Vessel shape ranges from semiconoidal (globular) to canted, with rounded to flat bases. Cordmarking is seen on lip sections, and thickness ranges from 8 to 22 mm. "Door knob" lug handles also are reported (Shane 1967:108).

Settlement Patterns, Distribution, and Demography

The Data

Few studies of statewide settlement patterns, site distribution, and demographic levels for the Ohio Archaic have been conducted. To reveal diachronic trends for this overview, a review of the published literature was supplemented by an examination of three distinct data sets. First, an inventory of all known absolute dates between cal 10,950 and 2650 B.P. was compiled (Appendix 15.A). Second, a database of over 2,400 Early–Middle Archaic hafted bifaces from all four physiographic regions was assembled. Finally, information on over 7,000 Archaic-period components as reported on OAI site inventory forms was considered.

Each data set presents information at different levels of detail. Absolute dates, for example, can be considered "fine-grained" data, as they represent precise temporal indicators. Yet absolute dates in isolation provide little cultural information. Diagnostic hafted bifaces provide good temporal and cultural data but often are difficult to interpret (e.g., do variable hafted-biface styles represent ethnic or functional differences?). The OAI database is unique in its size, list of variables, and broad statewide representation. These data are limited, however, when one searches for trends *within* temporal periods (e.g., Early Archaic), as short-duration cultural shifts may be obscured. Although each data set presents information at various scales of detail, consideration of all three data sets in concert helps to strengthen arguments put forth regarding settlement dynamics.

The remainder of this section discusses the significant trends revealed through examination of these three data sets. For continuity's sake, observed trends are considered separately below, and a more thorough discussion with reference to published literature follows. Ohio boasts a robust absolute date inventory, as 204 assays dating to the Archaic period have been reported (Appendix 15.A). Figure 15.11 presents a high-low graphic illustrating the calibrated age ranges (at one sigma) of all reported dates. For comparative purposes, all reported Ohio Paleoindian dates also were included in this graphic. Significant variation in the distribution and density of reported dates is evident. Both the Early and Middle Archaic periods are represented by five dates each, or .2 assays per 100 years. The Late Archaic period is represented by a dramatic increase both in the total number of dates (n = 194) and number of dates per 100-year subperiod (5.9 assays). Overall, the most unanticipated trend seen in Figure 15.11 is the significant reduction in the number of dates representing the period between cal 10,500 and 6300 B.P.

When cal post-6300 B.P. date ranges are considered by physiographic region (Figure 15.12), three additional trends are evident. First, southern provinces are characterized by significantly higher numbers of absolute dates than contemporary sites in the north (157 vs. 40). Second, the majority of assays dating between cal 6300 and 5000 B.P. derive from southern sites, especially in the Unglaciated Plateau region, where a continuous span of dates is shown between cal 6300 and 2650 B.P. Finally, the composition of *what* is being dated differs between northern and southern sites. Whereas pit features and hearths account for 66 percent of all assays in the Till Plains and Unglaciated Plateau regions, such features only account for 28 percent of all dates on northern sites. Although this distribution may reflect sampling bias, cultural factors arguably account for this variance.

The hafted-biface database assembled for this chapter included over 2,400 artifacts derived from several sources (Blank 1970; Boedy 1980; Bowen 1990, 1992; Brush 1990; Carskadden et al. 2004; Carskadden, Felumlee, and Morton 2003; Carskadden et al. 2004a, 2004b, 2004c; Carskadden and Morton 2004; Carskadden, Morton, and Gartley 2003;

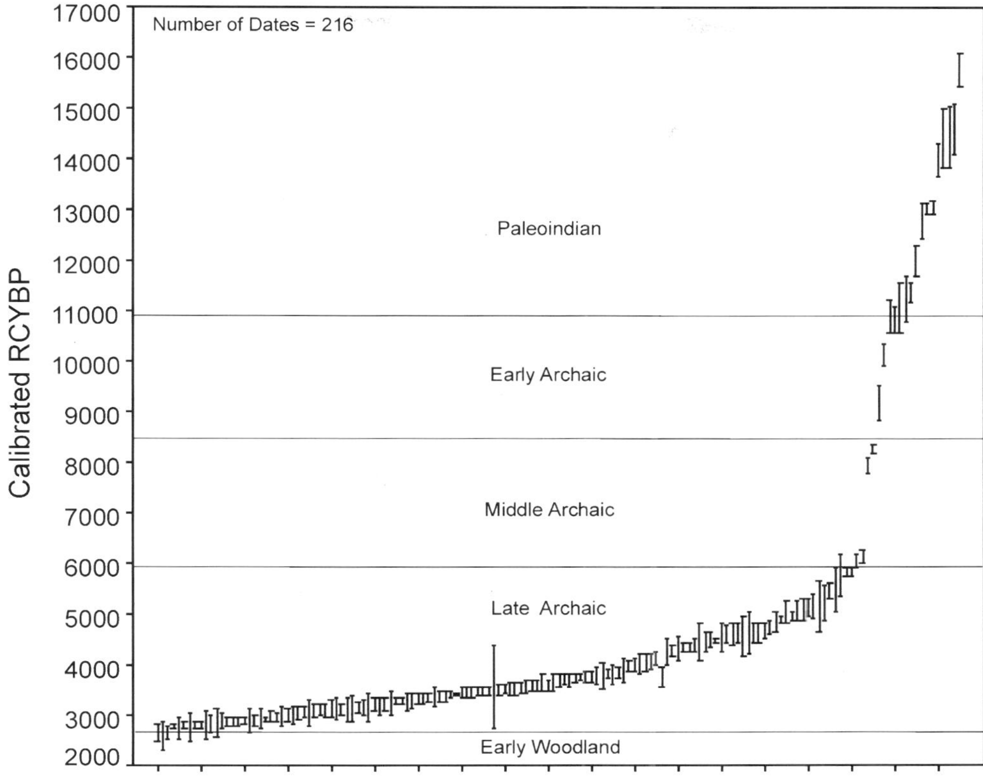

Figure 15.11. Paleoindian and Archaic calibrated absolute date ranges for Ohio sites.

Coughlin 1991; DeRegnaucourt 1992; Litfin 1993; Morton and Carskadden 2004a, 2004b, 2004c; Morton et al. 2004; Purtill 2003a, 2003b; Stothers 1996; as well as information contained in select OAI forms and at the Cincinnati Museum Center). The database included artifacts from all four physiographic provinces. As seen in Table 15.3, the earliest Early Archaic styles (Early Side Notched, Charleston, and Thebes horizons) were not distributed evenly across the state. Early Side Notched–horizon bifaces, for example, are present almost exclusively in the Unglaciated Plateau region of Ohio, although Stothers, Schneider, and Pape (2001) recently have documented small numbers of these artifacts in several collections in the Glaciated Plateau area, as well. Thebes-horizon bifaces also show uneven statewide distribution, being heavily represented in the western Till and Lake plains regions and less so in the more mountainous plateau areas. Table 15.3 illustrates that Kirk/Palmer–horizon bifaces are recovered in great frequency across all portions of the state. These artifacts represent the first biface horizon to be distributed in near-equal proportions across all four physiographic regions, a trend that is seen in subsequent Early–Middle Archaic biface horizons.

When compared, Early–Middle Archaic hafted-biface frequencies exhibit significant variation. Figure 15.13 demonstrates substantial reduction in hafted-biface frequency through time in all regions. The Lake and Till plains, especially, show dramatic reduction in biface frequency, whereas the plateau province, principally the Glaciated Plateau region, saw only modest decline.

Because several hafted-biface types significantly overlap in time, possibly overinflating frequency data, a subsample of selected biface types thought to represent a contiguous span of time was inspected to see if additional trends could be detected (Figure 15.14). This subsample included Kessell (cal 12,200–10,500 B.P.), Kirk/Palmer (cal 10,800–9500 B.P.), MacCorkle (cal 9800–9700 B.P.), LeCroy (cal 9500–8500 B.P.), and Stanly Stemmed (cal 8700–7300 B.P.) types. As seen in Figure 15.14, a continued reduction in hafted-biface counts is evident in all four regions, although at different scales. Some caution is needed when analyzing this plot, given the variable lengths of currently accepted manufacturing ranges for each type. If total biface counts are standardized by discard rates per 100 years, this dramatically increases the relative number of MacCorkles, which are reported to have had an extremely short life span (100 years). Given the paucity of dated MacCorkle samples in the mid-Ohio Valley (see Justice 1987), such an approach should be viewed with caution, however.

The OAI site inventory is the most extensive of the three databases examined. Traditionally, OAI data quality has been questioned, but recent recoding efforts by the OHPO staff have increased its reliability. The data set's chief limitation with regard to this discussion is the lack of strict temporal guidelines by which sites are assigned Early, Middle, or Late Archaic

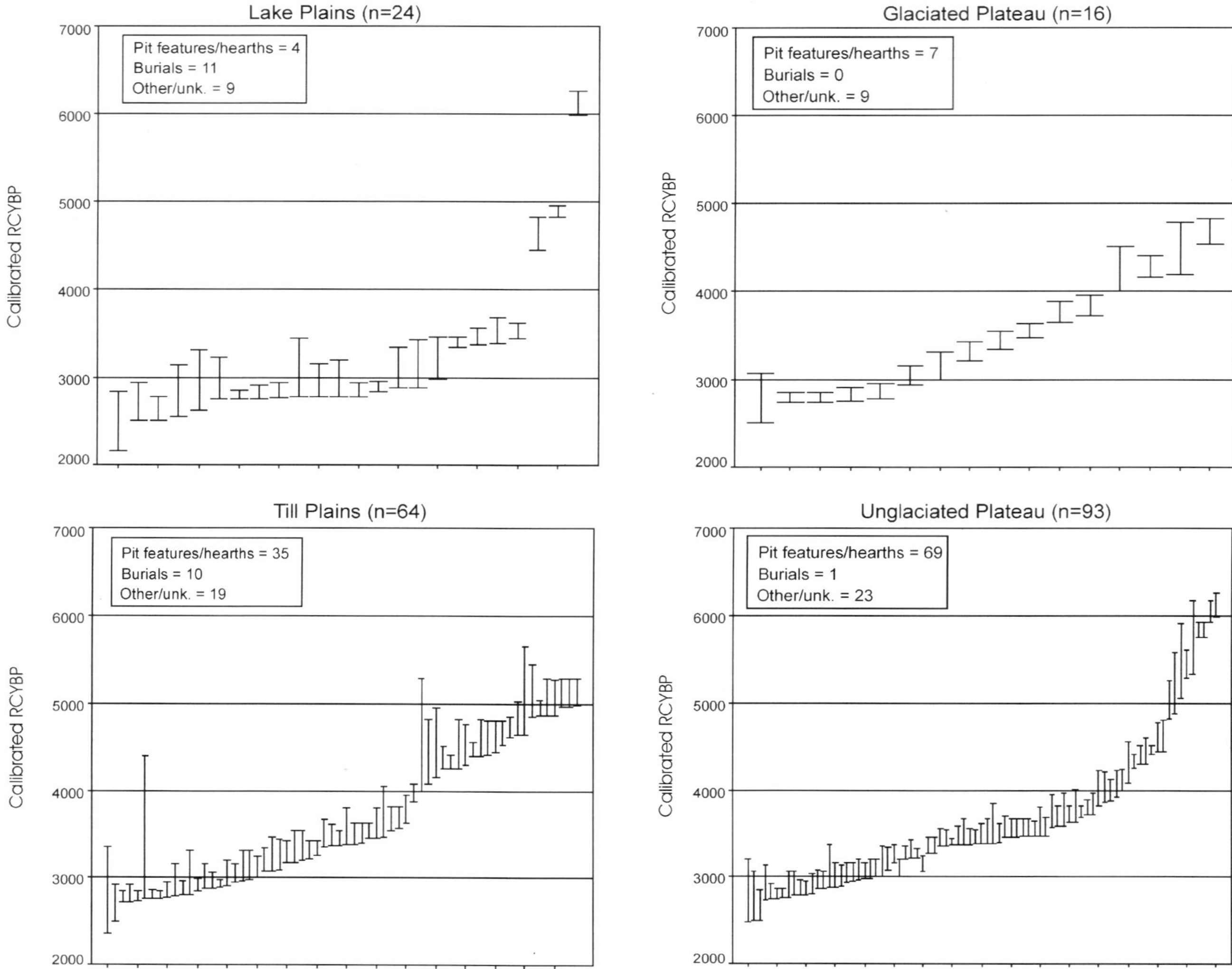

Figure 15.12. Cal post-6300 B.P. absolute date ranges for Ohio sites by physiographic region.

status. Regardless, the OAI database provides a view of broad, statewide patterns that cannot be achieved through inspection of the hafted-biface or absolute-date inventories.

Figure 15.15 illustrates relative percentages of OAI-derived Early, Middle, and Late Archaic components per county. Data were standardized to control for uneven survey coverage between counties by dividing the number of sites for each Archaic subperiod (Early, Middle, and Late) by the total number of prehistoric sites reported for each county (minus "unassigned prehistoric"). A relative percentage for each county was generated and plotted on Figure 15.15. When all three Archaic subperiods are considered, a dramatic decrease in components assigned to the Middle Archaic period is seen. This decrease is evident not only in counties where significant alluviation might mask Archaic components (e.g., along the Ohio River) but also in counties characterized by extensive tracts of primarily stable, nonaccreting landforms (e.g., uplands). Of Ohio's 88 counties, only one (Lake County) contained proportionately more Middle Archaic (13 percent) than Early Archaic (4 percent) components (an extremely small county sample size [n = 4] might account for this anomaly). Early Archaic sites are heavily distributed along the edge of Lake Erie, whereas Late Archaic populations were dispersed more equitably throughout the state.

A Pearson's chi-square test (SPSS Base 8.0) calculated between subperiod (Early, Middle, and Late Archaic) and physiographic region disclosed significant variation for statewide site distributions ($\chi 2 = 49.123$, $df = 6$, $p < .001$) (Table 15.4). Inspection of cross-tabulated adjusted residual scores helped reveal the nature of this variation.[2] Low residual scores for Early Archaic components in the Unglaciated (−3.7) and Glaciated (−3.0) Plateau regions indicate low density, whereas the score for the Till Plains (+5.4) indicates higher than expected frequencies. Middle Archaic sites are slightly overrepresented (+2.2) in the Unglaciated Plateau. Finally, Late Archaic sites are slightly overrepresented in the

Table 15.3. Early–Middle Archaic Hafted-Biface Horizon Distribution by Physiographic Setting.

Hafted-Biface Horizon	Proposed Time Range (RCYBP)	Unglaciated Plateau	Glaciated Plateau	Lake Plain	Till Plain	Total
Early Side Notched	12,500–8700	110 (12)	—	4 (3)	17 (2)	131
Charleston	11,000–9900	29 (3)	—	1 (< 1)	26 (3)	56
Thebes	10,800–9500	98 (10)	30 (8)	42 (30)	208 (21)	378
Kirk/Palmer	10,800–9500	200 (21)	75 (20)	34 (24)	246 (25)	555
Kirk Stemmed	9900–8800	102 (11)	30 (8)	6 (4)	60 (6)	198
Large Bifurcate	9900–7800	97 (10)	15 (4)	25 (18)	99 (10)	236
Small Bifurcate	9500–8500	131 (14)	67 (18)	20 (14)	174 (18)	392
Weak Stemmed	8800–4400	4 (< 1)	9 (2)	—	7 (< 1)	20
Late Side Notched	8700–3100	103 (11)	134 (36)	3 (2)	81 (8)	321
Stanly Stemmed	8600–7400	77 (8)	3 (< 1)	5 (4)	38 (4)	123
Basal Notched	8100–7700	2 (< 1)	9 (2)	1 (< 1)	19 (2)	31
Morrow Mountain	7800–6700	—	—	—	11 (1)	11
Total		953	372	141	986	2,452

Note: Count followed by percentage in parentheses. Percentage represents proportion of total bifaces within each physiographic region.

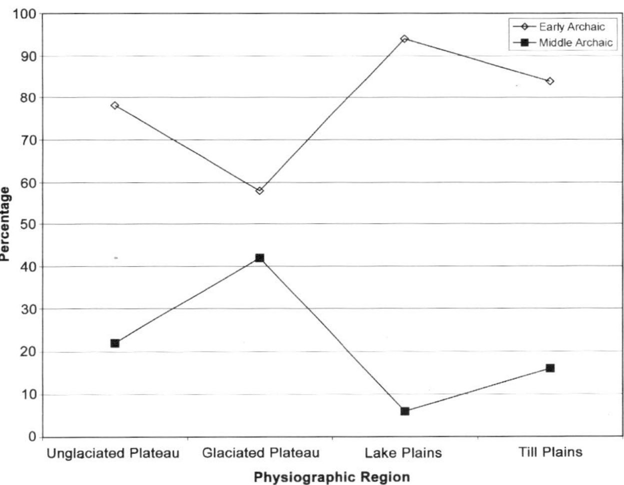

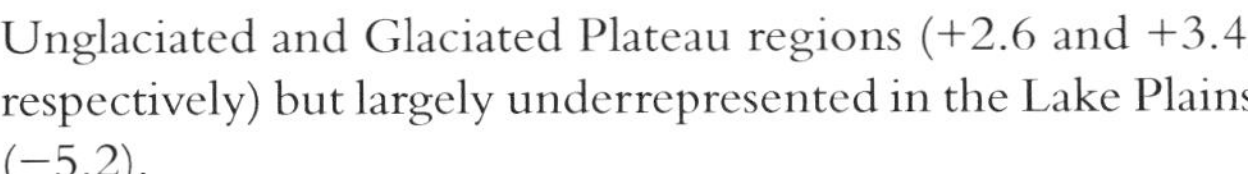

Figure 15.13. Plot of Early and Middle Archaic hafted-biface percentages by physiographic region.

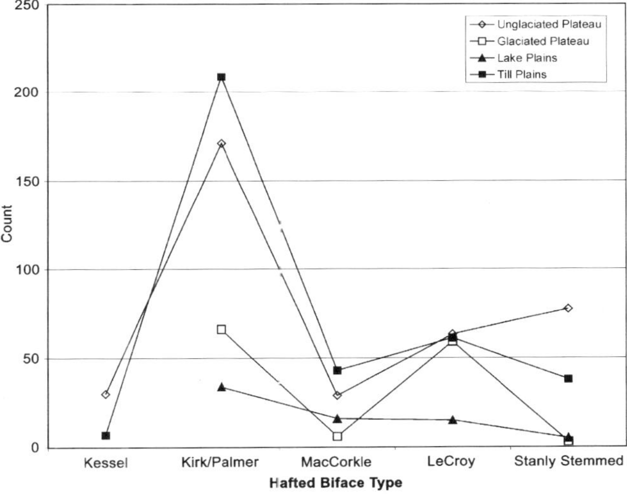

Figure 15.14. Plot of selected hafted-biface frequencies representing Early through Middle Archaic times by physiographic region.

Unglaciated and Glaciated Plateau regions (+2.6 and +3.4, respectively) but largely underrepresented in the Lake Plains (−5.2).

Table 15.5 presents OAI data regarding the distribution of sites by subperiod and landform type. Somewhat surprisingly, no significant variation between subperiod and landform type was noted ($\chi 2 = 4.414$, $df = 4$, $p < .353$). This may indicate that landform utilization patterns remained fairly constant through time. Finally, the OAI data revealed only slight variation in the average distance to water by subperiod. Early Archaic components were located an average of 246.98 m from a permanent water source, whereas Middle Archaic (244.83 m) and Late Archaic (240.01 m) sites were situated only slightly closer.

Discussion

Current information suggests that Early Archaic groups intensively occupied the generally level Till and Lake Plain regions of Ohio. Limited use of the rolling Glaciated Plateau region is seen, as well. The rugged Unglaciated Plateau area, however, was largely avoided by early groups until ca. cal 10,500 B.P., as evidenced by significant numbers of Kirk/Palmer–horizon

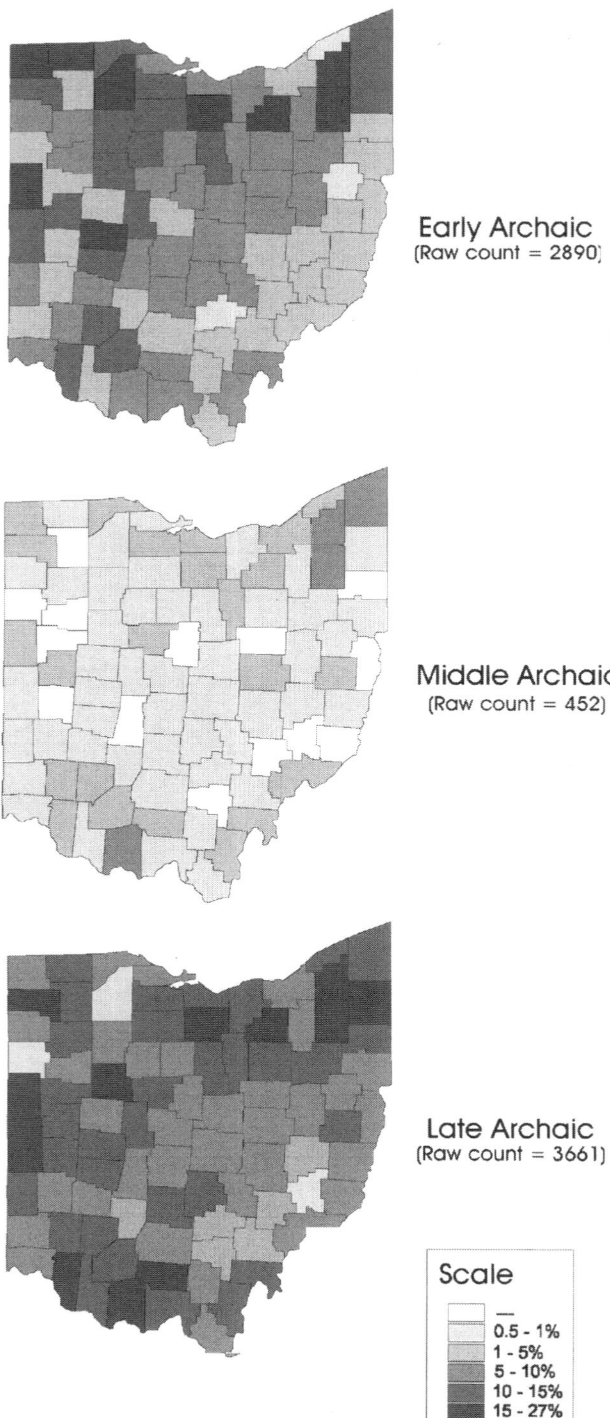

Figure 15.15. Distribution map of Early, Middle, and Late Archaic sites based on OAI site inventory form data.

bifaces in local assemblages dating to that time. Similar distributions are reported for Ohio Paleoindian groups (Prufer and Baby 1963; Seeman and Prufer 1982), suggesting some continuity in settlement patterns through time.

On the basis of the wide distribution of a few preferred chert sources, most authors view Early Archaic groups as highly mobile but tethered to a select number of outcrops. High-quality bedrock chert sources, such as Upper Mercer, were used to manufacture tools that had a wide distribution across the Midwest. Whether the use of nonlocal chert reflects population migration or the use of expansive band territories is still poorly understood.

As early as cal 10,800 B.P., evidence suggests, local populations were beginning to settle into areas all across the state and population expansion was underway. These trends are most evident in the sudden increase in the number of Kirk/Palmer–horizon bifaces and their widespread distribution across all four physiographic regions. Individual sites commonly contain unusually high numbers of Kirk/Palmer bifaces, especially when compared with biface totals of other types. For example, Bowen (1991) reports over 200 Kirk/Palmer bifaces (Nettling variety) from site 33HU134 in north-central Ohio. Fifty-seven bifaces, primarily Palmer Corner Notched types, were recovered from the Ferris site in southwestern Ohio (Theler and Dalbey 1974).

In addition to greater frequencies of hafted bifaces, several sites dated to this period also show evidence of longer-term use and tool-kit diversity. At the Manning site in Clermont County, for example, a 10- to 12-cm-thick midden deposit containing Kirk Corner Notched bifaces was documented (Lepper 1994). This site also contained a variety of tool types, including ground-stone implements, and nutshell. Lepper concluded that the site was occupied for substantial periods of time and may have represented a seasonal base camp. Significantly, earlier occupations at Manning failed to disclose intensive utilization, and they were interpreted as short term and likely task specific. Although the possible use of seasonal base camps such as Manning may indicate involvement in a "collecting" settlement strategy (after Binford 1980), the true nature of Early Archaic settlement patterns remains difficult to assess.

In contrast to the argument that significant population expansion and settlement occurred across the state between cal 10,800 and 9500 B.P., the period between cal 9500 and 6300 B.P. appears to have witnessed substantial population reduction and relocation. Evidence for population loss derives from the drastic decline in the frequency of hafted bifaces, absolute dates, and archaeological components dating to this temporal period. This trend is most obvious in the Lake Plains region where both OAI and hafted-biface data sets illustrate steep declines in components and bifaces over preceding Early Archaic times. Although population decrease is postulated throughout Ohio, the decline in the Plateau region, particularly the Unglaciated section, appears comparatively moderate. As reflected in OAI data, the Unglaciated Plateau region actually contained proportionately higher population densities during the Middle Archaic when compared with other regions (see Table 15.4). This suggests either (1) that population shifts from the Till and Lake plains to the

Table 15.4. Percentage of Archaic Sites within Physiographic Regions.

	Unglaciated Plateau	Glaciated Plateau	Lake Plain	Till Plain
Early Archaic	5.44	7.90	11.80	10.16
Middle Archaic	1.56	1.24	1.42	1.26
Late Archaic	9.56	11.38	11.12	11.58

Source: Based on OAI Site Inventory Data; n = 7,003.
Note: $\chi^2 = 49.123$, $df = 6$, $p < .001$ (based on raw count data).

Table 15.5. Archaic-Period Sites by Landform Type.

	Floodplain	Terrace	General Upland
Early Archaic	221 (17)	678 (54)	365 (29)
Middle Archaic	41 (18)	132 (58)	54 (24)
Late Archaic	332 (18)	967 (53)	533 (29)

Source: Based on OAI Site Inventory Data; n = 3,323.
Note: Count followed by percentage in parentheses. Percentage represents proportion of sites within time period. $\chi^2 = 4.414$, $df = 4$, $p = .353$.

Plateau region occurred during the Middle Archaic or (2) that population loss through low birth rates was moderated in the Plateau region.

Several additional lines of evidence can be cited that support the idea of decreased populations during this time. First, evidence derived from rockshelters where long occupation spans have been documented indicates limited habitation during most of the terminal Early and Middle Archaic periods. With the exception of the controversial Squaw Rockshelter (Brose 1989; see Prufer 2001), little to no evidence of Middle Archaic occupation of Ohio rockshelters is available despite ample evidence of Early and Late Archaic materials at such sites (e.g., Brush 1990; Prufer et al. 1989). In the well-dated Eppley Rockshelter in Coshocton County, for example, radiocarbon dates suggest continuous occupation between cal 14,000 and 11,300 B.P. and again between cal 5000 and 1300 B.P. (Brush 1990). No evidence of occupation between cal 11,300 and 5000 B.P. was found. Moreover, in his examination of 25 rockshelters in the Killbuck Creek drainage area, Brush (1990:280) reported recovering 21 Early Archaic and 34 Late Archaic bifaces but no Middle Archaic types.

Survey data along the Ohio River terrace system further support the idea of reduced population densities during the Middle Archaic period. Recent survey of several Pleistocene-age terraces associated with the Ohio River in Lawrence and Scioto counties failed to identify large numbers of Middle Archaic biface forms despite comparatively high frequencies of both Early and Late Archaic types (Purtill 2003a, 2003b, 2004b). Purtill reports the recovery of 10 Early Archaic, five Middle Archaic, and 60 Late Archaic bifaces from these terraces. Since these terraces were not inundated on a regular basis during the Holocene period, Middle Archaic sites, if present, should not be deeply buried or have been destroyed by high-velocity flood events. Instead, proportions of Middle Archaic artifacts in surface deposits along these terraces should accurately reflect their densities prehistorically.

In contrast to the Middle Archaic, abundant Late Archaic data are available for settlement patterning and site organization. By cal 6300 B.P., both OAI and absolute date information suggest, populations began to rebound and expand substantially. The number of absolute dates per 100 years rises from .2 for the Middle Archaic to 5.9 for the Late Archaic. If one considers absolute date ranges, the Unglaciated Plateau region appears to have experienced the earliest population increase, at ca. cal 6000 B.P. Subsequent population increases occurred in the southern Till Plains about 500 years later. Population growth in northern Ohio appears to have occurred significantly later, sometime around cal 4800 B.P. in the Glaciated Plateau and then around cal 3700 B.P. in the Lake Plains region. By cal 3700 B.P., Late Archaic groups were utilizing all physiographic regions on a near-equal basis (see Table 15.4), and they began to develop regionally specific settlement and subsistence strategies.

As reflected by the number of absolute dates, site density was at its peak in southern Ohio between cal 4500 and 2650 B.P. Currently, it is possible to recognize two primary site types along the Ohio River: (1) semiannual to year-round occupations with midden development, feature clusters, house structures, and burials placed within domestic zones; and (2) seasonal, late summer–early winter, domestic base camps from which bulk-food processing was undertaken. Additional specialized site types such as lithic extraction locales and ephemeral hunting, collecting, and processing camps also are known (e.g., Abrams and DeAloia 2005; Pecora and Burks 2005) but are poorly reported.

Only a few major settlements thought to represent semiannual to year-round occupation are known. These sites are located along major river corridors (e.g., the Ohio River), especially on elevated terraces and near confluences with secondary creeks or streams. Vickery (1980) has documented several in southwestern Ohio, including Maple Creek, Dravo Gravel, Bullskin Creek, and DuPont Village. Of these, the DuPont Village site appears the most extensively occupied and has the best evidence for year-round settlement. In south-central Ohio along the lower Scioto River, Bowen (1987) documented the Scioto County Homes site, a year-round base camp with shell-midden development. Radiocarbon dates indicate that the site was occupied between cal 5750 and 3500 B.P.

The second site type includes seasonally occupied bulk-food processing centers, principally used to parch, roast, or otherwise process nut resources for consumption during cold months. Evidence for bulk meat processing at such sites is rare but not unknown (e.g., County Home site [Heyman et al. 2005]). Seasonal indicators at such sites suggest occupation during the late summer through late fall, although several researchers have postulated spring occupation, as well (e.g., Abrams and Freter 2005). Researchers speculate that these sites were occupied by one to three family units for several weeks to possibly as long as a few months. In the Hocking River valley, Heyman et al. (2005) have argued that the County Home site was regionally unique and represented a macroband aggregation event for communal processing, feasting, and exchange of ideas, materials, and mates. Midden development is rare at the majority of these sites, and no burials have been reported.

Current evidence suggests that Late Archaic sites in northern Ohio are much smaller than their southern counterparts (on average), generally lacking extensive midden development or dense feature clusters (Prufer 2001; Prufer and Long 1986; Stothers and Abel 1993; Stothers, Abel, and Schneider 2001). Nut processing, although present, does not appear to have been overly intensive, especially in the northwestern section of the state where mast-producing trees were not abundant (Gordon 1969).

Starting around cal 3800 B.P., population densities began to rise in the northern Till Plains and Lake Plains regions. Stothers, Abel, and Schneider (2001) and Stothers and Abel (1993) have proposed a seasonal settlement system for this area based on spring to summer coalescence around riverine settings and fall through winter dispersal into uplands for nut collecting and deer harvesting. They recognize three site types: interaction centers, base camps, and extractive camps. Interaction centers included sites thought to represent special-purpose population aggregation events, perhaps on a seasonal basis and as part of an annual settlement cycle. These were primarily easily accessible cemetery sites, often located at the intersection of major drainages and close to abundant seasonal food sources (e.g., fish runs).

Base camps were seasonal coalescence settlements occupied during the spring and summer months and are thought to have included several nuclear or extended families. Base camps were located in site clusters often in close proximity to an interaction center. Individual clusters are dispersed, and parent populations exploited nonoverlapping catchment zones approximately 10–15 km in diameter. Extractive camps, including hunting and collecting camps, quarries, fishing stations, and animal processing sites, are postulated to have existed (Stothers, Abel, and Schneider 2001).

Site Organization

Few studies of site organization have been conducted on Early–Middle Archaic sites in Ohio, primarily because of the lack of known single-component locales. A basin-shaped feature identified as a late fall to winter Early–Middle Archaic domestic structure was identified at the Weilnau site in north-central Ohio (Abel 1994). Excavations revealed a 2.6-x-2.2-m semisubterranean basin that contained a rock-lined hearth and 25 post molds oriented in a roughly circular pattern. One Stanly Stemmed-like and four Lake Erie Bifurcate bifaces were recovered, suggesting a cal 8650–8450 B.P. occupation date.

Considerable north–south variation is observable in the size and density of nonmortuary sites in Ohio that postdate 6000 B.P. Late Archaic sites situated in the northern Till Plains, Lake Plains, and the Glaciated Plateau regions are spatially restricted, lack midden, and yield few features. In Wyandot County, for example, mechanical stripping of about 24 percent of the site area (2,033 m^2) at 33WY674 revealed only six prehistoric pit features, one post mold, and no evidence of midden (Rutter et al. 2000). Although Prufer (2001) has attributed the dearth of features in northeastern Ohio to the results of historic-period deep plowing, functional differences may better account for the lack of features on northern sites.

In contrast to northern sites, southern Late Archaic occupations, especially those along the Ohio River, tend to be significantly larger, with increased artifact counts and feature densities (Figure 15.16). Seasonally occupied sites often are extensive, their size resulting from multiple occupations over extended periods of time. Sites such as Davisson Farm in Lawrence County and 33MS29 in Meigs County are mantled with hundreds of pit features (Keener and Pecora 2003; Purtill 2004a). These sites often occupy prominent landforms, such as terrace edges or natural levees, and repeated occupation resulted in linear site development through time.

No evidence of spatial segregation of function-specific activity loci (e.g., tool production, butchering or hide working, etc.) has been discovered at such sites (e.g., Purtill 2004a). At Davisson Farm, Purtill compared debitage subassemblages from various portions of the site and found no statistically significant differences. Purtill (2004a) interpreted the site as representing a series of discrete, slightly overlapping, reoccupations that were functionally similar.

A range of domestic features, including basin-shaped pits, stone-lined hearths, surface hearths or burned areas, post molds, fire-cracked-rock (FCR) clusters, and thermally unaltered rock piles, has been reported for Late Archaic sites statewide. In many cases, compound pit features (e.g., basin-shaped pits with internal hearths or posts) have been noted (Purtill 2001, 2004a). Nonstructural posts directly associated with pit features—interpreted as spits, windbreaks, and drying racks—also have been found at southern Late Archaic sites (e.g., Crowell et al. 2005:90; Purtill 2001, 2004a; Vickery 1978) (see Figure 15.16).

On Late Archaic sites, oval to round, basin-shaped pit features, usually with gently sloping to flattened bases and variable densities of FCR (but little else), are abundant. Although often referred to as "trash" or "storage" pits, they

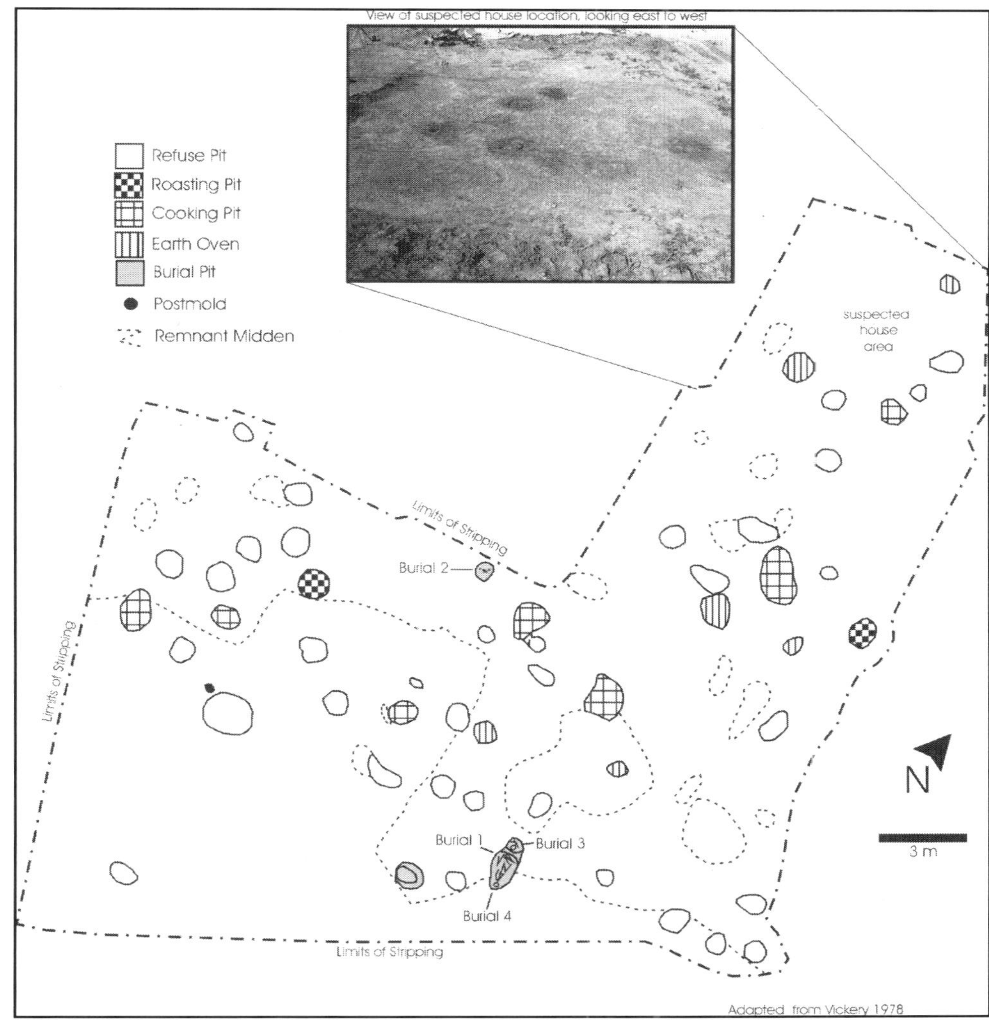

Figure 15.16. Plan view of salvage excavations at the Dravo Gravel site in Hamilton County, Ohio.

almost undoubtedly served as cooking and roasting facilities initially and only secondarily as trash pits. CRM investigations in southern Ohio have provided an opportunity to analyze these features (Purtill 2001, 2002a, 2003c, 2004a). Purtill recognizes two basic classes of pit features: small basin-shaped pits, defined as circular to oval in plan and having a maximum axial length of less than 1 m, and large basin-shaped pits, typically oval in plan and having an axial length of 1 m or greater. This basic "small" versus "large" pit dichotomy also has been recognized by other Ohio Valley archaeologists (e.g., Baker 1979; Ledbetter and O'Steen 1991). Analysis of feature dimensions, depths, and volumes indicates highly standardized design for small basin-shaped pits, especially regarding diameter and volume specifications. In contrast, large basin-shaped pits were more variable in size and less structured in shape (Purtill 2004a).

Attempts at ascertaining pit function and use history also were made. Initially, it was believed that standardized measures of feature content could reliably predict feature function. High instances of FCR, so it was argued, should represent either intact or heavily utilized cooking facilities with relatively high food yields (in this case, nuts). A nonparametric correlation test (Kendall's Tau-*b*) was calculated for paired variables, including FCR versus nutshell weights ($\tau_b = .199; p = .138$) and FCR weight versus seed count densities ($\tau_b = .136; p = .352$) (Purtill 2004a). No correlation was found between FCR weight and food-item density, which led Purtill to postulate that feature fill principally represented redeposited contents. Further, although in situ burned earth was rare, water flotation analysis of feature soils commonly revealed small "bits" of burned earth, which Purtill suggested was evidence of wall scraping and feature reuse. Alternatively, Heyman et al. (2005) have interpreted the presence of burned clay "pellets" from features as possible evidence that small game or shelled animals were prepared for cooking by coating them with a clay slurry to help limit moisture and nutrient loss. What appears obvious is that such features rarely are intact and that they represent heavily reused facilities.

Both circular–oval and C-shaped (i.e., open on one side) post patterns, interpreted as house locations, have been noted at several sites, including 33MS29 (Keener and Pecora 2003), Lawler (Morton and Carskadden 1975), 33LE680 (Purtill 2002b), Davisson Farm (Purtill 2004a), Stubbs (Cowan and Sunderhaus 2002), Mabel Hall (Baker 1979), Raisch-Smith (Geistweit 1970), Riverside, Asmus 2, and Asmus 3 (Stothers and Abel 1993), and Maple Creek (Vickery 1980). At Dravo Gravel in southwestern Ohio, Vickery (1978, 1980) has argued, a C-shaped ring of processing pit features surrounding an empty area likely represents the location where a house structure existed, although no post molds were located (see Figure 15.16). Several potential house patterns also were identified at the County Home site in Athens County, although complete house patterns were not preserved, making exact shape and dimensions difficult to ascertain (Crowell et al. 2005). Some structures have evidence of rebuilding or erection of secondary support posts (see Stothers and Abel 1993:54). At some sites, both circular and C-shaped patterns have been documented. Recent magnetometry survey at site 33MS29, for example, has revealed several clustered post mold–like features representing up to four possible structures (Keener and Pecora 2003). Although only limited testing was conducted, several suspected post mold locations were confirmed through excavation. One structure is circular in plan, and the remaining three appear C shaped. Vickery (1980) suggests that C-shaped structures may reflect temporary lean-to shelters. Interior floor space of reported structures ranges between 3 and 12 m in diameter, but averages between 4 and 8 m.

Subsistence and Health

Early–Middle Archaic subsistence evidence is especially sparse in the state and must be inferred indirectly through tool assemblages and site locations. The persistence of many tool forms from earlier Paleoindian times, especially steep-edged spurred end scrapers, in addition to the maintenance of large band territories (discussed above), may indicate continuation of caribou hunting, at least during the initial stages of the Archaic (Stothers 1996; see also Picklesimer 1999:47). In the northwestern Lake Plains region, cal 8800 B.P. is postulated as the time at which local populations shifted focus to white-tailed deer, elk, and perhaps moose (Blank 1970:343; Stothers 1996). Stothers sees the increased use of local chert types as evidence of reduced mobility, which would have eliminated the ability to hunt northward-migrating caribou populations.

In the hilly Glaciated and Unglaciated Plateau regions of Ohio, Early–Middle Archaic subsistence likely focused on white-tailed deer and perhaps elk and moose (Blank 1970:342). Utilization of aquatic resources during this time is undetermined, although it may be the case that high river-flow velocities and lowered lake levels negatively impacted aquatic habitat productivity, as suggested for other areas of the Midwest (e.g., Brown and Vierra 1983).

Most scholars have postulated that plant foods represented only a minor part of the subsistence diet for Early Archaic populations (e.g., Griffin 1967). This idea is based on the perceived absence of ground-stone technology. Evidence of plant use, however, has been observed at some early sites, including Manning, where black walnut and hickory nutshell was associated with ground-stone tools from deposits dated to between cal 12,000 and 10,100 B.P. (Lepper 1994). Assuming that nutshell remains represent food and not fuel, this evidence indicates at least some early exploitation of seasonally available nut resources.

After cal 5950 B.P., Late Archaic subsistence strategies were focally based on intensive exploitation of seasonally available food resources, including nuts, fish, and shellfish, as well as the continuation of generalized hunting practices (Bowen 1987; Purtill 2004a; Stothers, Abel, and Schneider 2001; Vickery 1980). Seasonal exploitation of nut resources (primarily hickory, black walnut, hazelnut, and acorn) was widespread, particularly between cal 3550 and 2650 B.P. along the Ohio River corridor (e.g., Church 1995; Purtill 2004a). Seasonal reoccupation of favorable locales over extended periods of time (upward of 2,000 years) is indicated (e.g., Purtill 2003c, 2004a) and may reflect ecologically rich biomes such as high-yield, mast-producing tree stands. Purtill (2004a) feels that such sites were used to generate food surpluses in anticipation of lean winter months.

A range of wild plant remains has been reported from southern Ohio sites. The quantity of wild plant remains, however, is generally low at individual sites. The list of wild plant remains includes bean (Fabaceae), bedstraw (*Galium* spp.), chenopodium (*Chenopodium* spp.), pigweed (*Amaranthus* spp.), grape (Vitaceae), grass (Poaceae), knotweed (*Polygonum* spp.), mustard (*Brassica* spp.), pokeweed (*Phytolacca americana*), purslane (*Portulaca* spp.), sunflower (*Helianthus annuus*), and sida (*Sida spinosa*) (e.g., Church 1995; Purtill 2004a). How many of these plants represent food items is unclear at this time. Significantly, none of these plants show evidence of domestication during the Archaic period in Ohio.

Squash (*Cucurbita* cf. *pepo*) remains the only known domesticated plant used during the Archaic period in Ohio. Only the rind section of the plant has been documented in Ohio contexts. Squash rind is assumed to represent the remains of food and not portions of containers or rattles. Late Archaic squash only has been documented in southern Ohio along the Scioto and Ohio rivers, although a possible occurrence of early squash from the Leimbach site in north-central Ohio has been reported (Struever and Vickery 1973:1201). Three sites have yielded evidence of domesticated squash from well-dated contexts: Maderia Brown in Pike County (Church 1995), Davisson Farm in Lawrence County (Purtill 2004a), and Ohio Horse Park in Scioto County (Purtill 2003c). The

Maderia Brown site yielded squash rind from several features radiocarbon dated to between cal 3700 and 3510 B.P. (Church 1995). At Davisson Farm, seven pieces of squash rind were recovered from several pit features, one of which (Feature 26) was directly dated to cal 3540 B.P. At the Ohio Horse Park site, a single piece of squash rind was recovered from Feature 2, which yielded a date of cal 3277 B.P. Collectively, early evidence of domesticated squash in Ohio closely coincides with age ranges reported from eastern Kentucky, where squash has been dated to between cal 4300 and 3510 B.C. at several rockshelter sites (Cowan 1997).

A wide range of vertebrate and invertebrate animal remains has been identified at Late Archaic sites. Table 15.6 presents the vertebrate faunal assemblage from three environmentally distinct locales, including Bullskin Creek, which is located on a high terrace overlooking an Ohio River tributary in the southern Till Plains region (Slawson 1977; Vickery 1980); Krill Cave, which is an upland rockshelter in the Glaciated Plateau province of northeastern Ohio (Prufer et al. 1989); and Scioto County Homes, which is a shell midden site located on the upper floodplain of the Scioto River in the Unglaciated Plateau region of southern Ohio (Bowen 1987). At all three sites, white-tailed deer remains dominate the vertebrate assemblages, indicating its dietary importance. Aquatic vertebrate resources—such as fish, reptiles, amphibians, and waterfowl—are only minimally represented at Bullskin Creek and Krill Cave but are present in modest frequencies at Scioto County Homes, where they account for over 20 percent of the entire assemblage. The Scioto County Homes site also was uniquely characterized by a large number of freshwater mussel shells (over 8,000) derived from a thick shell midden (Feature 9). Shell midden accumulation is rare in Ohio and only has been documented at Scioto County Homes and perhaps Sloane (Littlecott and Fair 1969). A heavy reliance on aquatic resources also is suggested by the documentation of elevated strontium levels in human bone from the northwestern Ohio Williams Cemetery site (Price 1985; Stothers, Abel, and Schneider 2001). These levels suggest a strong reliance on fish in addition to terrestrial animals by northwestern populations.

Over the past 25 years, Paul Sciulli of The Ohio State University and his colleagues have conducted numerous studies involving Late Archaic skeletal populations from Ohio (e.g., Sciulli and Aument 1987; Sciulli et al. 1982; Sciulli and Heilman n.d.; Sciulli et al. 1991; Sciulli and Schuck 2001; Tatarek and Sciulli 2000; among others). These studies have demonstrated that Late Archaic populations in west-central and northwestern Ohio were likely part of a single, large regional population base. Overall health was good, with few cases of infectious disease, dietary deficiency, or disease stress, although high occurrences of degenerative joint disease likely reflecting a "strenuous and mobile life-style of hunter-gatherers" (Sciulli and Schuck 2001:36) was observed. Stature estimates indicate that members of Ohio Late Archaic populations were robust and, on average, taller than their contemporaries in surrounding regions (Sciulli et al. 1991). Finally, the documentation of blunt and piercing trauma on human bones from several sites suggests that violent conflict was not unknown among Late Archaic groups (Sciulli and Schuck 2001).

Ceremonial and Mortuary Systems

Ceremonial and mortuary practices for Early–Middle Archaic groups are largely undocumented for Ohio. A possible late Early Archaic cremation burial was reported in northern Tuscarawas County near the town of Bolivar by Nigel Brush (as cited in Stothers, Abel, and Schneider 2001). The site consisted of three dark features, one of which contained cremated human remains and four broken St. Albans hafted bifaces, indicating a date between cal 9900 and 7800 B.P. Little additional information is available on this site. In 1989, David Brose reported an Early Archaic burial from the Squaw Rockshelter in Cuyahoga County. Although Brose suggested that these remains were associated with a cal 10,780 B.P. date, recent reanalysis returned two bone-derived AMS dates indicating a post–2400 RCYBP age for the interment (Prufer 2001:186).

Beginning around cal 5700 B.P., mortuary ceremonialism increased in complexity and regionalization. Two primary trends are witnessed in Late Archaic mortuary systems: (1) interment within habitation zones and (2) the use of mortuary processing and burial areas separate from domestic areas. Current evidence suggests that burial within habitation areas was restricted to southern Ohio, primarily along the Ohio River and associated drainages (e.g., Scioto River). At least 10 such sites dated between cal 5700 and 3500 B.P. have yielded modest numbers (< 35; mean = 10 per site) of burials indiscriminately located among midden and other nonmortuary features (Bowen 1987; Dancey 1995; Kreinbrink et al. 1992; Nass et al. 1990; Vickery 1980) (see Figure 15.16). In some cases, burial features were disturbed by later pit construction, suggesting a lack of site planning or cognitive "mapping" of burial vaults through time (see Vickery 1980). Significantly, no evidence of burial within habitation areas postdates cal 3500 B.P. in Ohio.

Burial practices at these sites were not overly complex, nor are interments replete with exotic grave furniture. Most individuals were buried on one side or the other in the flexed position. Both the Dravo Gravel (Burial 3; see Figure 15.16) and DuPont Village sites in southwestern Ohio contained burials recovered in upright, sitting positions (Vickery 1978, 1980). At the Overly Tract site (33RO110) in Ross County, a single male in his midthirties was hastily buried face down with his legs bent backward to accommodate the confines of a small burial pit feature (Dancey 1995). Grave offerings are modest and utilitarian in design. Reported items include bone fishhooks, bone pins, bird-bone flutes, bone beads, perforated-bone shuttles, tillite scraper planes, roller pestles, pitted

Table 15.6. Faunal Assemblage Composition from Selected Late Archaic Sites.

Group Name	Common Name	Scientific Name	Bullskin Creek (33CT29)	Krill Cave (33SU18)	Scioto County Homes (33SC17)
Fish	freshwater drumfish	*Aplodinotus grunniens*	.31	.1	12.68[a]
Fish	freshwater catfish	*Ictalurus* sp.	.00	.00	12.68[a]
Fish	redhorse	*Moxostoma* sp.	.00	.00	12.68[a]
Fish	gar	*Lepisosteus* sp.	.00	.00	12.68[a]
Fish	pike	*Esox* sp.	.00	.00	12.68[a]
Fish	largemouth bass	*Micropterus* sp.	.00	.00	12.68[a]
Reptile	cottonmouth snake	*Agkistrodon* sp. (cf.)	.04	.00	.00
Reptile	timber rattlesnake	*Crotalus horridus* (cf.)	.04	.00	.00
Reptile	unidentified snake	—	.16	< .01	.00
Reptile	soft-shell turtle	*Trionyx* sp.	.31	.0	.00
Reptile	box turtle	*Terrapene carolina*	.05	.16	9.03[a]
Reptile	painted turtle	*Chrysemis picta*	.00	.10	9.03[a]
Reptile	turtle	*Chelydra* sp.	.00	.00	9.03[a]
Reptile	unidentified turtle	—	.25	.00	.00
Amphibian	toad	*Bufo* sp.	.00	<.01	.00
Amphibian	frog	*Rana* sp.	.00	<.01	.00
Bird	turkey	*Meleagris gallopavo*	.00	.9	3.05
Bird	mallard	*Anas platyrhynchos*	.00	.21	.00
Bird	duck	*Anas* sp.	.00	.16	<.01
Bird	blue-winged teal	*Anas discors*	.00	.16	.00
Bird	passenger pigeon	*Ectopistes migratorius*	.00	.42	.00
Bird	red-tailed hawk	*Buteo jamaicensis*	.00	.21	.00
Bird	eagle	*Haliaeetus leucocephalus*	.00	.00	< .01
Bird	unidentified bird	—	.48	< .01	2.78
Mammal	white-tailed deer	*Odocoileus virginianus*	92.51	63.98	43.75[b]
Mammal	gray squirrel	*Sciurus carolinensis*	.31	.85	.00
Mammal	eastern chipmunk	*Tamias striatus*	.08	< .01	.00
Mammal	eastern cottontail	*Sylvilagus floridanus*	.18	1.12	.00
Mammal	gray fox	*Urocyon cinereoargenteus*	.45	1.06	.00
Mammal	opossum	*Didelphis marsupialis*	.87	.00	<.01
Mammal	raccoon	*Procyon lotor*	.93	11.19	3.25
Mammal	beaver	*Castor canadensis*	3.03	6.72	< .01
Mammal	bobcat	*Lynx rufus*	.00	3.2	.00
Mammal	dog	*Canis familiaris*	.00	1.6	.00
Mammal	unidentified canid	*Canis* sp.	.00	1.6	<.01
Mammal	mink	*Mustela vison*	.00	.00	<.01
Mammal	otter	*Lutra canadensis*	.00	.00	<.01
Mammal	skunk	*Mephitis mephitis*	.00	.53	.00
Mammal	muskrat	*Ondatra zibethica*	.00	.45	.00
Mammal	woodchuck	*Marmota monax*	.00	4.8	1.32
Mammal	flying squirrel	*Glaucomys volans*	.00	< .01	.00
Mammal	squirrel	*Sciurus* spp.	.00	.42	2.32
Mammal	meadow vole	*Microtus pennsylvanicus*	.00	< .01	.0-
Mammal	vole	*Microtus* sp.	.00	< .01	.00
Mammal	deer mouse	*Peromyscus maniculatis*	.00	< .01	.00
Mammal	shrew	*Blarina brevicauda*	.00	< .01	.00
Mammal	unidentified small rodent	—	.00	< .01	< .01
Mammal	bat	*Myotis* sp.	.00	< .01	.00
Mammal	unidentified rabbit	*Sylvilagus* sp.	.00	.00	< .01

Note: Percentage of total elements based on raw counts.

[a]Actual percentage for some groups was not available since Bowen (1987) combined counts for a number of species.

[b]This percentage undoubtedly is underrepresented because of the high number of "unidentified mammal" bones reported (Bowen 1987).

stones, drilled animal and human bone, and small numbers of hafted bifaces, among other items (Vickery 1980). Red and yellow ocher sprinkled over burials and grave goods is documented but rare.

Burial away from habitation zones is manifested in three ways in Ohio. First, formal cemeteries were established on, or in, prominent landforms (e.g., elevated glacial features, as at the Duff site [Sciulli and Aument 1987]). Second, open sites typified by burial pit features, "empty" pit features of unknown function, prepared hearths, and post molds are found (e.g., William H. Davis Mound site [Baby and Mays 1959]). In some cases, later Woodland populations erected earthen burial mounds overtop existing Late Archaic components (e.g., Philo Mound D [Carskadden 1989]). Finally, the erection of low mounds atop burial pits by Late Archaic groups is infrequent but not unknown within the state (e.g., Kline Mound [Richards and Shane 1974]).

Formal cemetery areas, principally in west-central and northwestern Ohio, usually are ascribed to the Glacial Kame "culture" or "complex" (e.g., Converse 1982; Moorehead 1909). These cemeteries were established as early as cal 5120 B.P., as in the case of Peters Cemetery in Pike County, but were not widespread until sometime after cal 3300 B.P. (see Appendix 15.A). Cemetery areas are found disassociated from habitation sites, although few surveys in areas immediately surrounding known cemeteries have been conducted. Absolute dates from several larger sites (e.g., Williams Cemetery; Abel at el. 2001) indicate that cemeteries were in use, at least on a sporadic basis, for extended periods of time bridging the Late Archaic and Early Woodland periods. The florescence of cemetery use in west-central and northwestern Ohio appears to have coincided with the decline in the southern Ohio practice of interment within habitation zones, which, as noted, did not occur after cal 3500 B.P. Although some researchers suggest that elaborate mortuary ceremonialism seen in formal cemetery construction and maintenance indicates the nascent development of complex, perhaps even ranked, societies (e.g., Stothers, Abel, and Schneider 2001), others suggest a continuation of an egalitarian social system on the basis of nonstatus burial practices (Sciulli and Schuck 2001:40).

Formal cemeteries contain evidence of complex ceremonialism, such as exotic, long-distance trade items included as grave offerings. Typical grave offerings include artifacts manufactured from marine shell, such as sandal-sole gorgets, circular disks, and bar gorgets; discoidal-, tubular-, and barrel-shaped conch shell beads; copper beads; cannel coal beads; slate birdstones; sandal-sole, coffin-shaped, and humpback-shaped slate gorgets; tubular pipes; constricted-center gorgets; copper awls and celts; modified animal cranium masks (bear and wolf); incised antler and bone artifacts (Figure 15.17); preform cache bifaces; and various bifaces, including Feeheley, Crawford Knoll, Merom/Trimble, and Innes types (Abel et al. 2001; Converse 1982, 2004; Sciulli and Aument 1987). Many of the marine-shell gorgets may have been worn as hair barrettes

Figure 15.17. Incised antler handle and bone inset from the Late Archaic Berryhill Cemetery site (33CL17). Photograph courtesy of Dayton Society of Natural History, Anthropology Department.

(Sciulli and Schuck 2001). Quite often these assemblages were sprinkled with powdered red and yellow ocher.

Factors determining the nature or process of the distribution of grave offerings are poorly understood. Grave goods do not appear to be positively correlated with any sex or age group, although subadult burials contain slightly "richer" assemblages in many cases (e.g., Sciulli and Schuck 2001). Moreover, a statistically significant association was found at Kirian-Treglia between the use of red ocher and the presence of subadult burials (Sciulli et al. 1993). Importantly, the presence of exotica in subadult burials suggests that the quality and quantity of grave offerings was not directly tied to status level, as is the case in "big man" societies.

Principles guiding cemetery placement across the landscape are poorly known. Preference for prominent landforms such as glacial kames and eskers, however, is obvious. Such locations may have provided high visibility for some distance along the generally flat Till and Lake plains regions. Burial population size for each cemetery is variable, ranging from fewer than 30 interments (e.g., Berryhill [Sciulli and Heilman n.d.]; McKee [Sowder 1972]) to well over 600 (e.g., Williams Cemetery [Sciulli et al. 1982]; Richardson-Ridgeway [Converse 2004]). Burials tend to be situated within round to oval pits excavated deep into glacial gravels (e.g., 6.7 m at the Zimmerman site [Converse 1982]). At the Kirian-Treglia cemetery, burial depth was positively correlated with individuals' ages (i.e., children tended to be buried at shallower depths than adults) (Sciulli et al. 1993). Burial pits commonly overlapped one another, suggesting periodic reuse of such locales.

Typical cemetery burials were in the flexed to semiflexed position (Converse 1982). Hand placement tended to be on, or near, the face region (Sciulli and Schuck 2001), and the head was oriented to all cardinal directions with the possible exception of east. At Berryhill, cranial deformation, a trait witnessed later in the Early Woodland period (Webb and Snow 1945), was documented for several individuals (Sciulli and Heilman n.d.).

Perhaps the most unusual of the Late Archaic cemetery sites is the Williams Cemetery and nearby Sidecut Crematory located on the banks of the Maumee River in Wood County (Abel et al. 2001; Stothers and Abel 1993). To date, 20 burial features that contained between 600 and 1,000 interments (Sciulli et al. 1982) have been excavated from an estimated 25 percent of the site. Most burial pits were stratified, showing layers of human bone and ash interrupted by sterile sand banding. More than 90 percent of the recovered human remains at the site were cremated.

The Sidecut Crematory site, which is located on the opposite bank of the Maumee (and slightly upstream) from the Williams site, is argued to represent a contemporary locale at which human remains to be buried at Williams Cemetery were first cremated and otherwise prepared (Abel et al. 2001). Burned limestone slabs associated with calcined human bone and several artifact caches, including 18 bipointed knives or performs and three Turkey-tail bifaces, were documented at Sidecut Crematory.

Twenty-one radiocarbon assays have been processed from the Williams Cemetery site. These dates demonstrate continuous, or near-continuous, use of the cemetery for over 1,000 years between cal 3250 and 1928 B.P. Importantly, this date range indicates some cultural continuity in northwestern Ohio between Late Archaic and Early Woodland populations.

Williams Cemetery site burials contained an abundance of grave offerings, indicating to Stothers, Abel, and colleagues that the site operated as an interregional trade fair (Abel et al. 2001; Stothers, Abel, and Schneider 2001). Borrowing the concept from Jackson (1991:266), they view the "trade fair" as representing a periodic gathering of distinct cultural or ethnic groups to exchange items, mates, and ideas and bury deceased members of each band or tribe. Support for the interregional scope of the site may be found in a recent biological population study by Tatarek and Sciulli (2000) that demonstrated a high degree of osteological (i.e., biological) variation for the Williams Cemetery burial population when compared with surrounding cemeteries. This variation supports the idea of interregional visitation of the site by groups from across portions of the Midwest, perhaps at predetermined times, as envisioned in the trade-fair scenario.

Another distinctive aspect of burial practice in central and northern Ohio was the use of mortuary processing sites. These sites usually contain several burial pits in association with "domestic"-looking features of unknown function. Such sites are seen in both open and rockshelter locations. At Krill Cave in Summit County, for example, excavations by Olaf Prufer identified human remains associated with radiocarbon dates of cal 4400 and 3570 B.P. (Prufer et al. 1989). Several partially intact burials were recovered, and numerous stray human bones were located throughout the Archaic levels of the site. Analysis revealed that the partial remains of at least 15 individuals had been disposed of in the rockshelter. Robert Mensforth, who conducted the osteological analysis, concluded that "it remains a possibility that the cave may have intermittently served as a funeral house or preparation area for human remains which were destined to be interred elsewhere as secondary burials" (Prufer et al. 1989:51). Similar situations have been documented for other rockshelter and sinkhole sites across Ohio (e.g., Pedde and Prufer 2001).

In many cases, Late Archaic mortuary areas were selected by later Woodland-period groups as locations to construct earthen burial mounds. Mound placement directly over Late Archaic mortuary pits and domestic-looking features suggests knowledge of earlier components and the deliberate association of Woodland-period burials with earlier "ancestor" groups. At the William H. Davis Mound site in Franklin County, for example, salvage excavations of a 5.4-m-tall Adena mound by Raymond Baby revealed 27 interments dating to the Early Woodland. Directly beneath the mound, however, were nine Late Archaic domestic-like processing features and burial pits dated to cal 3350 B.P. (Baby and Mays 1959; Geistweit 1970; Seeman 1986). The Late Archaic component included 25 individuals within four circular pits. Both flexed and bundle burial methods were used. A wealth of grave offerings, both utilitarian and exotic, were documented in the Late Archaic component of the site, including mussel-shell pendants; shell, copper, and bone beads, drilled and worked animal bone; bone awls; tubular pipes; hematite plummets; a slate gorget; hammerstones; bell pestles; disk-shaped bifaces; and several broad-bladed, stemmed, hafted bifaces. A similar circumstance was noted at Mound D of the Philo Mound Complex in Coshocton County (Carskadden 1989; Morton and Carskadden 1987), where several Late Archaic domestic features were located below the Woodland-period Mound D.

The final Late Archaic burial practice included construction of low earthen mounds on top of domestic features or burial pits. Although evidence of cal pre-2650 B.P. mound construction is known for areas outside of Ohio (e.g., Russo 1996), its commencement within the state has been poorly studied. Radiocarbon evidence suggests that mound construction, at least in a nascent form, may date to as early as cal 4500 B.P. in the state. To date, six mound sites have produced cal pre-2650 B.P. assays, including Phillips Mound I (cal 4590 B.P.), Byler (cal 3320 B.P.), Toepfner (cal 2910 B.P.), Munson Springs (cal 2890–2790 B.P. [Pacheco and Burks 2002]), Kline (cal 2800 B.P. [Richards and Shane 1974]), and McCoy (cal 2760 B.P.). Of these, two sites—Kline and Munson Springs—represent particularly strong cases for cal pre-2650 B.P. mound construction.

The Kline Mound in Tuscarawas County was a low mound measuring 15 m in diameter by 1 m in height (Richards and Shane 1974). Below the mound, nine Late Archaic features were located. They included a hearth, three pit features of unknown function, and five burial pits containing the partial remains of eight individuals. The Kline Mound also was characterized by an extensive array of grave offerings, including bone and copper beads, a conch-shell pendant, both unfinished and finished plummets (many of which were manufactured from unusual materials such as slate, granite, and petrified wood), limestone tubular pipes, a grooved sandstone "plug," a copper awl, hematite bars, and triangular bifaces. Burials 4 and 8, both subadults, contained especially rich assemblages. Burial 8 contained a copper bead necklace and bracelet. Burial 4 was directly dated to cal 2800 B.P.

At Kline, the overlying mound fill was nearly devoid of artifacts and contained no burials of later periods. This suggests that the mound construction was not a post-Archaic event at this site but, instead, that the limited mound capping of mortuary processing pits took place in Archaic times. The overall low height of the mound (1 m) suggests that substantial mound mantling, as seen later in time, was not undertaken by site builders.

Similar to the Kline Mound, Munson Springs, located in Licking County, was a low mound measuring approximately 14 m in diameter by 1 m in height (Pacheco and Burks 2002). Excavation revealed six distinct strata, including a submound floor. Two separate radiocarbon assays of cal 2890 and 2990 B.P. are thought to date the primary mound-building episodes. The overlying Stratum V at Munson Springs yielded dates of cal 2267 B.P. (Beta-35275), and Stratum VI contained diagnostic Hopewell artifacts, collectively indicating periodic earth mantling of the mound well into the Middle Woodland period (Pacheco and Burks 2002).

Ceremonial artifact caching also appears widespread in Ohio after cal 4900 B.P. Primarily restricted to the western half of the state, caches of exotic materials and artifact types have commonly been ascribed to the Red Ocher "culture" or "complex" (e.g., Converse 2004; Ritzenthaler and Quimby 1962). At least 13 cache sites have been reported in Ohio (Converse 2004; Grandstaff and Davis 1985; Holzapfel 1993). Typical artifact caches include Turkey-tail hafted bifaces manufactured exclusively from Harrison County chert (Justice 1987). Most caches were deposited away from domestic or other mortuary settings, although association with human burials is known (Seeman 1986:570). Such caches are thought to date to between cal 3800 and 3400 B.P. The Grandstaff and Davis Cache, discussed in more detail below, is the only dated cache in Ohio and returned a somewhat surprisingly early date of cal 4860 B.P.

Artifact cache size varies considerably from small caches containing fewer than a dozen artifacts to large assemblages containing over 300, as in the case of the Patrick Cache in Brown County (Murphy and Morton 1978). Most typically, Turkey-tail bifaces were intentionally "killed," that is, fractured or fire damaged. The recovery of only partial sections of Turkey-tail bifaces in many caches suggests that artifacts may have been broken elsewhere and then transported. Additional artifact classes include gneiss bar amulets, rectangular slate gorgets, hematite celts and hemispheres, slate pendants, and gneiss rectangular tablets (Converse 2004). The use of powdered red ocher to cover artifacts was common.

The Grandstaff and Davis Cache site, located in Ross County, was excavated by two avocational archaeologists (Grandstaff and Davis 1985). A single circular pit measuring approximately 2 m in diameter and 30 cm in depth was exposed in an agricultural field along Paint Creek. The pit's periphery was lined with sandstone cobbles. The cache within the pit consisted of three gneiss tablets, approximately 10 Turkey-tail bifaces, a slate gorget, and a gneiss bar amulet. Seven complete Turkey-tail bifaces, all oriented north to south, were situated on top of one of the gneiss tablets in the approximate center of the feature. Abutting this tablet was a gneiss bar amulet that was heavily burned and fragmented. A second gneiss tablet was found to the north of the first tablet and was characterized by intense burning to one face. This second tablet was situated on its side, perpendicular to the first tablet. Fragmented pieces of a third gneiss tablet, along with several pieces of charcoal and bone, were found to the south of the first tablet. Pieces of two to four additional Turkey-tail bifaces also were recovered between the first and second tablets. Red ocher was sprinkled over many of these pieces.

Discussion

By the start of the Holocene, Early Archaic groups were beginning to adapt to an environment transitioning from a conifer forest to mixed oak-hickory communities with dense forest cover in the east and more open spaces in the west. Forest transition occurred rapidly, spreading from south to north. OAI and hafted-biface data show that native groups primarily occupied the Till Plains, Lake Plains, and Glaciated Plateau regions of the state; however, hafted-biface data suggest that sometime after cal 10,500 B.P., populations began to exploit the Unglaciated Plateau area, as well. Similarities in site distribution, settlement patterns, tool-kit design, and chert procurement strategies point to a great deal of continuity between Paleoindian and Early Archaic systems. Although several authors have suggested that these two groups represented distinct populations that arrived in Ohio during multiple migrations (e.g., Blank 1970; Litfin 1993; Stothers, Abel, and Schneider 2001), settlement, subsistence, and technological similarities appear to indicate cultural continuity (Brose 1975; Kozarek et al. 1994).

Although little direct evidence of subsistence patterns for the Early Archaic is available, similarities with Paleoindian systems may indicate a continued reliance by Archaic groups on large herding game, principally caribou, which may have roamed in the relatively open forests of western Ohio. A shift in focus to deer, elk, moose, and various smaller game populations occurred by cal 9500–9000 B.P. (Blank 1970; Stothers, Abel, and Schneider 2001). Southern Ohio Early Archaic groups, however, may have relied more heavily on plant foods, as evidenced by ground-stone and nutshell remains from some early sites (e.g., Manning [Lepper 1994]).

Current evidence, primarily low frequencies of Early Side Notched and Charleston-horizon bifaces, suggests low population densities at the start of the Early Archaic. In fact, the first few hundred years of the Archaic likely witnessed no substantial population increase over preceding Paleoindian times. In local assemblages dating to 10,500 to 9500 B.P., however, hafted-biface frequencies (primarily Thebes and Kirk/Palmer) increase by 79 percent, suggesting that population had begun to expand. The presence of substantial numbers of Kirk/Palmer–horizon bifaces in the Unglaciated Plateau indicates the earliest sustained exploitation of this region. Collectively, these trends are viewed as representing a "settling-in" period in which early groups successfully adapted to the newly established environment and vegetation communities.

Between cal 10,500 and 9500 B.P., evidence suggests, more intensive occupation occurred at some sites, as witnessed by higher artifact densities, midden development, and tool-kit diversity. Lepper (1994) has suggested that Occupation 3 at the Manning site represented an intensively utilized base camp during this period. Parenthetically, I would add that Manning is not an isolated occurrence in the mid-Ohio Valley, as several other contemporary sites, such as St. Albans in West Virginia (Broyles 1971) and Longworth-Gick in Kentucky (Collins 1979), also contain evidence of substantial occupation in association with Kirk/Palmer–horizon bifaces. Whether these intensively used sites were true base camps in the sense of Binford's (1980) collector system remains debatable. It seems likely, however, that groups operating in the mid-Ohio Valley during this time were involved in some form of logistically organized settlement system. A similar argument has been made by Stafford (1994) for southwestern Indiana, although he posits the shift from foraging to collecting somewhat later, at 7000 RCYBP (uncalibrated).

Major settlement and technological changes occurred throughout Ohio by as early as cal 9500 B.P. Procurement of chert from long-distance sources greatly diminished, a trend that is seen equally statewide. Instead, more local cherts were used to manufacture slightly smaller hafted-biface forms, including Small Bifurcate–horizon types. Several authors have suggested that the increased use of local cherts reflects reduced band territories and increased sedentism (e.g., Stothers, Abel, and Schneider 2001). Although terminal Early Archaic groups may have been operating within smaller territories, little evidence exists to suggest that individual sites were being occupied for longer periods of time. Early Archaic sites characterized by hafted bifaces manufactured after cal 9500 B.P. typically are not represented by large numbers of artifacts, diverse tool-kits, or midden development, as was the case in earlier times. These trends suggest that although exploitative territories were reduced in size, mobility within these territories actually may have increased when compared with that of earlier Thebes and Kirk/Palmer–horizon populations.

Many have suggested that Middle Archaic sites are rare within the state as a result of sampling bias or archaeologists' inability to completely distinguish Middle Archaic biface forms. Research presented in this chapter suggests that the paucity of sites is real and a result of substantial settlement and subsistence disruption and population reduction or relocation. This assertion is strengthened by converging lines of evidence from all three assembled data sets (absolute dates, hafted-biface frequencies, and site frequencies). These data suggest that population reduction first occurred during the terminal Early Archaic period ca. cal 9500 B.P. Assuming that OAI, absolute-date, and hafted-biface frequencies provide an accurate picture of demographic trends, Middle Archaic populations may have been reduced in size by upward of 80 percent versus earlier times.

To understand significant trends in Ohio population densities during the Middle Archaic period, recognizing environmental trends in the region is imperative. Although Hypsithermal-like warming and drying episodes are documented for the Middle Archaic in more western states (e.g., Missouri), Ohio actually witnessed precipitation *increases* across most regions between cal 7750 and 6000 B.P. (Shane et al. 2001). General warming and drying trends did not occur in Ohio until sometime after 6000 B.P. This led Vickery astutely to recognize that "perhaps most pertinent to an understanding of later Middle and Late Archaic lifeways is the west to east transgression of the Hypsithermal/Xerothermic Interval, the effects of which are manifested in different areas at different times" (1999:8). Because this climatic change moved slowly up the Ohio Valley and did not uniformly affect all regions at the same time, it might be best to consider the cultural and environmental factors that led to the rise of the "Middle Archaic" in places such as Illinois as more comparable to factors that precipitated the "Late Archaic" in Ohio. Indeed, substantial western Middle Archaic sites such as Black Earth (Jefferies and Lynch 1983) and Koster Horizon 6A/6B (Brown and Vierra 1983) in Illinois have no contemporary parallels in Ohio and appear most similar to Late Archaic sites, including DuPont Village and Maple Creek (Vickery 1980), despite the latter being occupied between 500 and 1,500 years later.

Although the Hypsithermal does not appear to have been responsible for the perceived population reduction during this time, variable climatic patterns and changing vegetation communities likely generated stress on local settlement and subsistence systems that relied on predictable food sources. Assuming that change was not gradual, such factors would have resulted in an uncertain food base because of unpredictable year-to-year fluctuations. To combat this, local populations would have been forced to either (1) alter existing settlement and subsistence strategies or (2) migrate to more stable areas. Current evidence supports the latter alternative, as groups appear to have largely left Ohio for areas yet unspecified. Remaining groups may have found refuge in the Plateau region, especially the Unglaciated Plateau, which appears to have been somewhat buffered from environmental fluctuations because of its higher elevation and eastern-leading lake effect (Shane et al. 2001:25–26; see also Fredlund 1989:23 for a discussion of a similar buffering effect in West Virginia associated with the Ohio River). Hafted-biface data support the notion that depopulation was less severe in this area, whereas OAI data suggest that the Middle Archaic occupation of the Unglaciated Plateau region was disproportionately higher compared with other areas across the state.

By the beginning of the Late Archaic (cal 5950 B.P.), warming and drying trends were occurring across most parts of the state. This resulted in the reduction of beech trees statewide and an expansion in oak-hickory forests in the Plateau region, especially along bottomland areas associated with the Little Miami, Great Miami, Scioto, and Ohio rivers. Repopulation of the state occurred from south to north in accordance with the sudden expansion of mast-producing trees and a stabilizing environment that assumed modern conditions by cal 4500 B.P. According to absolute date information, the southeastern Unglaciated Plateau region witnessed the first substantial population increase ca. cal 6000 B.P., as local groups began exploiting increased volumes of seasonally available nut resources along the major river valleys. Population increase in the north was slower and occurred about 1–2,000 years later. Importantly, the Late Archaic period is characterized by increased parochialism of cultures, as populations expanded and began to adapt to local environments. Such regional differentiation is seen both in domestic-related tool assemblages (hafted-biface types) and ceremonial artifact styles (e.g., bannerstones [Whaley 1992]). Increased sedentism is evident, and groups throughout the state appear to have been operating within a collector-based system (after Binford 1980), utilizing both semiannual to year-round settlements and seasonal sites to exploit bulk food resources. In the south, collection of wild plants (mostly nut sources), hunting, and some fishing and incipient horticulture appear to have been practiced. Similar strategies were employed to the north, except nut processing was less intensive and aquatic resources appear more important, at least in the northwestern section of the state. Squash appears to have been the only plant domesticated during the Archaic period in Ohio. Domesticated squash dating to as early as cal 3700 B.P. has been identified at several southern Ohio sites.

Between cal 5200 and 3500 B.P., groups living along the Ohio River were establishing large base camps characterized by midden development and human interment within habitation zones. These trends largely predate the widespread use of distinct cemetery areas seen in western Ohio between cal 3300 and 2650+ B.P. The development and continued use of cemeteries suggests the growth of corporate identity and land ownership among western Ohio populations during this time (Charles and Buikstra 1983; Saxe 1970). In extreme southern Ohio, the lack of known Late Archaic burials at sites dating later than cal 3500 B.P. is difficult to interpret. Potentially, southern groups also were participating in ceremonial practices seen to the north and west and made frequent trips to regional cemeteries to bury their dead and perhaps interact with northern neighbors. Osteological evidence from these cemeteries suggests that the individuals buried there shared close biological relationships and were part of a larger population base with frequent interaction (e.g., Sciulli and Aument 1987). Whether extreme southern Ohio groups were part of this larger population base is uncertain at this time.

A second interpretation of the lack of Late Archaic burials in southern Ohio is that significant portions of the region were utilized only on a seasonal basis between cal 3500 and 2650 B.P. Absolute dates obtained from seasonal bulk-food processing centers indicate that such sites were intensively used during this period, which is significantly later than the time of the last known permanent settlement. Whether more permanent settlements were relocated elsewhere is unclear. It may be the case that settlement systems again changed, perhaps in response to rising population pressures, and that mobility increased during these terminal times. Again, these issues await further study.

Many of the traits and trends initiated during the later part of the Archaic period flourished into the Woodland cultural pattern. Chief among these were the initiation of distinct burial areas and incipient mound construction, establishment of widespread trade networks, domestication of plant species, and the adoption of fired-clay technology. In some parts of Ohio, such as the northwest, direct cultural continuity between Archaic and Woodland groups is seen in the uninterrupted suite of radiocarbon dates that span both periods at major sites (e.g., Williams Cemetery). The penchant for Early Woodland groups to erect earthen mounds atop Late Archaic burial areas in central to northeastern Ohio also may suggest cultural continuity. In other parts of the state, such as the southeast, continuity is less evident. Purtill (2003a, 2003b) documented that, although the period between cal 3700 and 2650 B.P. was characterized by a continuous series of absolute date ranges in Lawrence and Scioto counties, post–cal 2650 B.P. dates are more sporadic and show considerable time gaps. Additional research is needed to better document this important transition within the state.

Concluding Remarks

In his 2001 review of the Archaic of northeastern Ohio, Olaf Prufer grimly concluded that the Archaic represented "a rather monotonous cultural pattern through time ... what we are left with is an essentially boring situation in which, as far as I can tell, only those devoted to the investigation of minutiae could be interested" (2001:195). The results of the current review have demonstrated, I hope, that the Archaic temporal period was not a "monotonous cultural pattern" locked into a gradual evolutionary path across the state—let alone the Midcontinent—in equal proportions. Instead, the Archaic period clearly was a culturally dynamic time of demographic fluctuation, intrastate population movement and growth, and shifts in settlement and subsistence strategies. These shifts all occurred within transitional climatic patterns that may have precipitated cultural change. Going forward, Ohio archaeologists should not blindly accept normative views of Archaic life, especially ones based on data derived from other regions. Instead, we should read the archaeological record for what it contains and what it lacks, and accept that significant spatial and temporal variation was a reality for prehistoric native life.

Endnotes

1. All dates are reported as calibrated radiocarbon years B.P., unless otherwise indicated. Calibrations are based on Stuiver et al. 1998 (IntCal98.c14; Version 4.4html). To conserve space, standard deviations and lab numbers of absolute dates are not reported in the text; instead, this information is available in Appendix 15.A.
2. Residual scores, or adjusted residuals, represent the difference between observed and expected counts in cross-tabulation cells after being standardized to have a variance of 1. Residual scores below −2 or above +2 identify cells that depart markedly from the model of independence (SPSS 1998:71).

Acknowledgments

The author wishes to thank the many individuals, both professional and avocational, that contributed information and ideas to this project. The Ohio Historic Preservation Office, notably Brent Eberhard and David Snyder, was instrumental in providing access to CRM report files and the electronic OAI database. I also wish to thank Elliot Abrams, Jarrod Burks, Jeff Carskadden, Brian DaRe, Ruth Myers, Robert Genheimer, Carly Meyer, Casey Fagin, Craig Keener, William Kennedy, Anne Lee, the Ohio Department of Transportation, Albert Pecora, Tommy Martin, the University of Cincinnati, Mark Seeman, Jeremy Norr, Andrew Sewell, Lynn Simonelli, and Alan Sullivan, for various contributions. Gray & Pape, Inc., also supported this endeavor by providing me with logistic and graphic support. Dr. Jennifer Reiter-Purtill and Dr. Jarrod Burks graciously edited early drafts of this article. Finally, thanks to the volume editors for inviting me to participate in the worthwhile conference that inspired this overview.

References Cited

Abel, Timothy J.
1994 An Early Archaic Habitation Structure at the Weilnau Site, North-Central Ohio. In *The First Discovery of America: Archaeological Evidence of the Early Inhabitants of the Ohio Area*, edited by William S. Dancey, pp. 61–76. Ohio Archaeological Council, Columbus.

Abel, Timothy J., David M. Stothers, and Jason M. Koralewski
2001 The Williams Mortuary Complex: A Transitional Archaic Regional Interaction Center in Northwestern Ohio. In *Archaic Transitions in Ohio and Kentucky Prehistory*, edited by Olaf H. Prufer, Sara E. Pedde, and Richard S. Meindl, pp. 290–327. Kent State University Press, Kent, Ohio.

Abrams, Elliot M., and Sara DeAloia
2005 The Walker Site: An Archaic/Woodland Hunting-Collecting Site in the Hocking Valley. In *The Emergence of the Moundbuilders: The Archaeology of Tribal Societies in Southeastern Ohio*, edited by Elliot M. Abrams and AnnCorinne Freter, pp. 59–66, Ohio University Press, Athens.

Abrams, Elliot M., and AnnCorinne Freter (editors)
2005 *The Emergence of the Moundbuilders: The Archaeology of Tribal Societies in Southeastern Ohio*. Ohio University Press, Athens.

Baby, Raymond S., and Asa Mays Jr.
1959 Exploration of the William H. Davis Mound. *Museum Echoes* 32:95–96.

Baker, Stanley W.
1979 Fieldnotes on the Mabel Hall site excavation. Notes on file, Department of Archaeology, Ohio Historical Society, Columbus.

Binford, Lewis R.
1980 Willow Smoke and Dogs' Tails: Hunter-Gatherer Settlement Systems and Archaeological Site Formation. *American Antiquity* 45:4–20.

Blank John E.
1970 The Ohio Archaic: A Study in Culture History. Ph.D. dissertation, Department of Anthropology, University of Massachusetts, Amherst.

Boedy, Randall D.
1980 A Preliminary Archaeological Survey of a Late Pleistocene Lake in Medina County, Ohio. Master's thesis, Department of Anthropology, Kent State University, Kent, Ohio.

Boisvert, Richard A.
1986 Late Archaic Settlement Models in the Middle Ohio Valley: A Perspective from Big Bone Lick, Kentucky. Ph.D. dissertation, Department of Anthropology, University of Kentucky, Lexington.

Bowen, Jonathan E.
1987 Late Archaic Occupations at the Scioto County Homes Site (33SC17). *Ohio Archaeologist* 37(1):15–17.
1990 Early Archaic of the Lower Sandusky River Drainage. *Ohio Archaeologist* 40(3):32–36.
1991 The Early Archaic Savannah Lakes Phase of North-Central Ohio. *Ohio Archaeologist* 41(1):24–29.
1992 Early/Middle Archaic Occupations of the Sandusky River, Green Creek, and North Ridge Survey Tracts in Sandusky County, Ohio. *Ohio Archaeologist* 42(3):20–25.
1994 *Upper Mercer Flint Large Bifurcates of the Ohio Region*. Sandusky Valley Chapter, Archaeological Society of Ohio, Upper Sandusky.

Britt, Claude J.
1967 Archaic Occupation of West-Central Ohio. Master's thesis, Department of Geology, Bowling Green State University, Bowling Green, Ohio.

Brose, David S.
1975 Botanical Archaeology at the Norman P Site in Ohio: A Method for the Identification of Recently Disturbed Stratigraphy at an Early Alluvial Floodplain Occupation. *Journal of Field Archaeology* 2:293–305.

1978 Archaeological Investigations at the Burrill Farm Site, Lorain County, Ohio: Prehistoric and Historic Evidence. Report on file, Lorain County Metropolitan Park District, LaGrange, Ohio.

1989 The Squaw Rockshelter (33CU34): A Stratified Archaic Deposit in Cuyahoga County. *Kirtlandia* 44:17–53.

Brown, James A.

1986 Early Ceramics and Culture: A Review of Interpretations. In *Early Woodland Archeology*, edited by Kenneth B. Farnsworth and Thomas E. Emerson, pp. 598–608. Kampsville Seminars in Archeology 2. Center for American Archeology Press, Kampsville, Illinois.

Brown, James A., and Robert K. Vierra

1983 What Happened in the Middle Archaic? Introduction to an Ecological Approach to Koster Site Archaeology. In *Archaic Hunters and Gatherers in the American Midwest*, edited by James L. Phillips and James A. Brown, pp. 165–191. Academic Press, New York.

Brown, Jeffrey D.

1996 The Johnson Site II: Terminal Archaic Points and Pottery. *Ohio Archaeologist* 46(2):4–7.

Broyles, Bettye J.

1971 *Second Preliminary Report: The St. Albans Site, Kanawha County, West Virginia, 1964–1968*. Report of Archaeological Investigations 3. West Virginia Geological and Economic Survey, Morgantown.

Brush, Nigel R.

1990 Developing an "Archaeology of Place": A Debitage Analysis of Rockshelter Utilization in the Lower Killbuck Valley of Holmes and Coshocton Counties, Ohio. Ph.D. dissertation. Department of Anthropology, University of California at Lost Angeles.

Bush, David R., M. A. Kollecker, and J. E. Thomas

1987 Phase III Assessment Testing of Three Prehistoric Sites in Coshocton County, Ohio. Report prepared by David R. Bush, Inc., on file, Ohio Historic Preservation Office, Columbus.

Carr, Christopher

1988 Correspondence with Brad Baker, Collections Manager, on file, Ohio Historical Society, Columbus.

Carskadden, Jeff

1989 Excavation of Mound D at the Philo Mound Group, Muskingum County, Ohio. *Ohio Archaeologist* 39:4–8.

Carskadden, Jeff, Jeff Brown, Gary Felumlee, and James Morton

2004 *A Survey of Prehistoric Archaeological Sites in Rich Hill Township, Muskingum County, Ohio*. Occasional Papers in Muskingum Valley Archaeology 30. Muskingum Valley Archaeological Survey, Zanesville, Ohio.

Carskadden, Jeff, Gary Felumlee, and James Morton

2003 *A Survey of Prehistoric Archaeological Sites in Newton Township, Muskingum County, Ohio*. Occasional Papers in Muskingum Valley Archaeology 21. Muskingum Valley Archaeological Survey, Zanesville, Ohio.

Carskadden, Jeff, Steve House, and James Morton

2004a *A Survey of Prehistoric Archaeological Sites in Perry Township, Muskingum County, Ohio*. Occasional Papers in Muskingum Valley Archaeology 23. Muskingum Valley Archaeological Survey, Zanesville, Ohio.

2004b *A Survey of Prehistoric Archaeological Sites in Blue Rock Township, Muskingum County, Ohio*. Occasional Papers in Muskingum Valley Archaeology 24. Muskingum Valley Archaeological Survey, Zanesville, Ohio.

2004c *A Survey of Prehistoric Archaeological Sites in Salt Creek Township, Muskingum County, Ohio*. Occasional Papers in Muskingum Valley Archaeology 29. Muskingum Valley Archaeological Survey, Zanesville, Ohio.

Carskadden, Jeff, and James Morton

2004 *A Survey of Prehistoric Archaeological Sites in Wayne Township, Muskingum County, Ohio*. Occasional Papers in Muskingum Valley Archaeology 27. Muskingum Valley Archaeological Survey, Zanesville, Ohio.

Carskadden, Jeff, James Morton, and Richard Gartley

2003 *A Survey of Prehistoric Archaeological Sites in Brush Creek Township, Muskingum County, Ohio*. Occasional Papers in Muskingum Valley Archaeology 22. Muskingum Valley Archaeological Survey, Zanesville, Ohio.

Charles, Douglas K., and Jane E. Buikstra

1983 Archaic Mortuary Sites in the Central Mississippi Drainage: Distribution, Structure, and Behavioral Implications. In *Archaic Hunters and Gatherers in the American Midwest*, edited by James L. Phillips and James A. Brown, pp. 117–141. Academic Press, New York.

Church, Flora

1995 The Results of Data Recovery at Site 33 Pk 153 for the PIK-SR.32-13.55 Project in Pike County, Ohio. Report prepared by ASC Group, Inc., on file, Ohio Historic Preservation Office, Columbus.

Coakley, John P.

1999 Lake Levels in the Erie Basin: Driving Factors and Recent Trends. In *Proceedings of the Great Lakes Paleo-Levels Workshop: The Last 4000 Years*, edited by Cynthia E. Sellinger and Frank H. Quinn, pp. 24–29. NOAA Technical Memorandum ERL GLERL-113. Great Lakes Environmental Research Laboratory, Ann Arbor, Michigan.

Collins, Michael B. (editor)

1979 *Excavations at Four Archaic Sites in the Lower Ohio Valley, Jefferson County, Kentucky. 2 vols.* Occasional Papers in Anthropology 1. Department of Anthropology, University of Kentucky, Lexington.

Converse, Robert N.

1982 *The Glacial Kame Indians*. Archaeological Society of Ohio, Plain City.

2004 *The Archaeology of Ohio*. Archaeological Society of Ohio, Plain City.

Coughlin, Sean P.

1991 Prehistoric Population and Land Utilization in the Central Scioto River Valley: An Analysis of the Robert L. Harness, Jr. Collection. Honors thesis, Department of Anthropology, Kent State University, Kent, Ohio.

Cowan, C. Wesley

1997 Evolutionary Changes Associated with the Domestication of *Cucurbita pepo*: Evidence from Eastern Kentucky. In *People, Plants, and Landscapes: Studies in Paleoethnobotany*, edited by Kristen J. Gremillion, pp. 63–85. University of Alabama Press, Tuscaloosa.

Cowan, Frank L., and Ted S. Sunderhaus

2002 Dating the Stubbs "Woodworks." *Ohio Archaeological Council Newsletter* 14(1):11–16.

Cowan, Frank, L., Ted S. Sunderhaus, and Robert A. Genheimer
2004 Earthwork Peripheries: Probing the Margins of the Fort Ancient Site. In *The Fort Ancient Earthworks: Prehistoric Lifeways of the Hopewell Culture in Southwestern Ohio*, edited by Robert P. Connolly and Bradley T. Lepper, pp. 107–124. Ohio Historical Society, Columbus.

Cowin, Verna L.
1991 The Middle Archaic in the Upper Ohio Valley. *Journal of Middle Atlantic Archaeology* 7:43–52.

Cramer, Ann C.
1989 The Dominion Land Company Site: An Early Adena Mortuary Manifestation in Franklin County, Ohio. Master's thesis, Department of Anthropology, Kent State University, Kent, Ohio.

Crowell, David, Elliot M. Abrams, AnnCorinne Freter, and James Lein
2005 Woodland Communities in the Hocking Valley. In *The Emergence of the Moundbuilders: The Archaeology of Tribal Societies in Southeastern Ohio*, edited by Elliot M. Abrams and AnnCorinne Freter, pp. 82–97, Ohio University Press, Athens.

Cunningham, Wilbur M.
1948 *A Study of the Glacial Kame Culture in Michigan, Ohio, and Indiana*. Occasional Contributions 12. Museum of Anthropology, University of Michigan, Ann Arbor.

Dancey, William S.
1995 Original unpublished field and laboratory notes from the Overly Tract site (33RO110), Ross County, Ohio. Notes on file, Department of Anthropology, the Ohio State University, Columbus.

DaRe, Brian
2002 Towards a More Comprehensive Understanding of Archaic Settlement Patterns for Eastern Ohio. *Ohio Archaeological Council Newsletter* 14(1):4–7.

Davis, Jeremy Todd
2000 Early Archaic Land Use Patterns at Nobles Pond: Evaluating the Fit of Two Settlement Models. Master's thesis, Department of Anthropology, Kent State University, Kent, Ohio.

DeRegnaucourt, Tony
1992 *A Field Guide to the Prehistoric Point Types of Indiana and Ohio*. Occasional Monographs 1. Upper Miami Valley Archaeological Research Museum, Ansonia, Ohio.
2002 The Early Archaic of the Upper Miami River Valley and Environs in Western Ohio. *Ohio Archaeologist* 52(4):22–27.

Didier, Mary Ellen
1967 A Distributional Study of the Turkey-Tail Point. *The Wisconsin Archeologist* 48:3–73.

Duerksen, Ken, and John F. Doershuk
1998 The Houpt Site and the Late Archaic of Southwestern Ohio. *Midcontinental Journal of Archaeology* 23:101–112.

Ellis, Chris J., Stanley Wortner, and William A. Fox
1991 Nettling: An Overview of an Early Archaic "Kirk Corner-Notched" Cluster Site in Southwestern Ontario. *Canadian Journal of Archaeology* 15:1–34.

Emerson, Thomas E., and Andrew C. Fortier
1986 Early Woodland Cultural Variation, Subsistence, and Settlement in the American Bottom. In *Early Woodland Archeology*, edited by Kenneth B. Farnsworth and Thomas E. Emerson, pp. 475–519. Kampsville Seminars in Archeology 2. Center for American Archeology, Kampsville, Illinois.

Fenneman, Nevin M.
1938 *Physiography of Eastern United States*. McGraw-Hill, New York.

Forsyth, Jane L.
1973 Late Glacial and Postglacial History of Western Lake Erie. *The Compass of Sigma Gamma Epsilon* 51(1):16–26.

Fredlund, Glen G.
1989 *Holocene Vegetational History of the Gallipolis Locks and Dam Project Area, Mason County, West Virginia*. Contract Publication Series 89-01. Cultural Resource Analysts, Lexington, Kentucky.

Gardner, William M.
1978 Comparison of Ridge and Valley, Blue Ridge, Piedmont, and Coastal Plain Archaic Period Site Distributions: An Idealized Transect. Paper presented at the 77th Annual Meeting of the American Anthropological Association, Washington, D.C.

Gartley, Richard
1976 Distribution of Steatite Vessels in Ohio. *Ohio Archaeologist* 26(2):28–29.

Geistweit, Barbara Ann
1970 Archaic Manifestations in Ohio and the Ohio Valley. Master's thesis, Department of Anthropology, the Ohio State University, Columbus.

Gordon, Robert B.
1969 *The Natural Vegetation of Ohio in Pioneer Days*. Bulletin of the Ohio Biological Survey 3(2). The Ohio State University, Columbus.

Grandstaff, Barry, and Gary Davis
1985 Another Red Ocher Discovery in Ross County. *Ohio Archaeologist* 35(3):26–27.

Griffin, James B.
1943 Adena Village Site Pottery from Fayette County, Kentucky. In *The Riley Mound, Site Be15 and the Landing Mound, Site Be17, Boone County, Kentucky with Additional Notes on the Mt. Horeb Site, Fa1 and Sites Fa14 and Fa15, Fayette County, Kentucky*, edited by William S. Webb, pp. 666–670. Reports in Anthropology and Archaeology 5(7). University of Kentucky, Lexington.
1967 Eastern North American Archaeology: A Summary. Prehistoric Cultures Changed from Small Hunting Bands to Well-Organized Towns and Tribes. *Science* 156:175–191.

Heyman, Marjorie, Elliot M. Abrams, and AnnCorinne Freter
2005 Late Archaic Community Aggregation and Feasting in the Hocking Valley. In *The Emergence of the Moundbuilders: The Archaeology of Tribal Societies in Southeastern Ohio*, edited by Elliot M. Abrams and AnnCorinne Freter, pp. 67–81. Ohio University Press, Athens.

Hill-Ariens, Alicia Jean
2003 Chert Availability and Exploitation at Three Late Archaic Sites in Southwestern Ohio. Master's thesis, Department of Anthropology, University of Cincinnati, Cincinnati, Ohio.

Holzapfel, Elaine
1993 A Study of Prehistoric Flint Caches in the Ohio Area. *Ohio Archaeologist* 43(3):30–37.

Jackson, H. Edwin
1991 The Trade Fair in Hunter-Gatherer Interaction: The Role of Intersocietal Trade in the Evolution of Poverty Point Culture. In *Between Bands and States*, edited by Susan A. Gregg, pp. 265–286. Occasional Papers 9. Center for Archaeological Investigations, Southern Illinois University, Carbondale.

Jackson, Kenneth E., Ruth G. Meyers, and Matthew J. Steinkamp
1990 Phase IV Archaeological Data Recovery at Site 33CT525, Clermont County, Ohio. Report prepared by Gray & Pape, Inc., on file, Ohio Historic Preservation Office, Columbus.

Jefferies, Richard W., and B. Mark Lynch
1983 Dimensions of Middle Archaic Cultural Adaptation at the Black Earth Site, Saline County, Illinois. In *Archaic Hunters and Gatherers in the American Midwest*, edited by James L. Phillips and James A. Brown, pp. 299–321. Academic Press, New York.

Justice, Noel D.
1987 *Stone Age Spear and Arrow Points of the Midcontinental and Eastern United States*. Indiana University Press, Bloomington.

Keener, Craig S., and Albert Pecora
2003 Phase II Archaeological Assessment of Site 33Ms29 Located at the Proposed Ohio River Boat Access in Racine, Sutton Township, Meigs County, Ohio. Report prepared by Professional Archaeological Services Team, on file, Ohio Historic Preservation Office, Columbus.

Kingsley, Ronald F.
1988 A Regional Study of Six Archaic Sites in the Mahoning Valley of Northeastern Ohio. *North American Archaeologist* 9:285–298.

Kozarek, Sue Ellen, William S. Dancey, Thomas J. Minichillo, and W. Kevin Pape
1994 Phase IV Data Recovery of an Early Holocene Lithic Cluster in North Central Ohio. In *The First Discovery of America: Archaeological Evidence of the Early Inhabitants of the Ohio Area*, edited by William S. Dancey, pp. 157–166. Ohio Archaeological Council, Columbus.

Kreinbrink, Jeannine, Timothy King, Karl Huebchen, Patricia Hartman, Steve Roberts, and Laura Clifford
1992 Prehistoric Discoveries at the Driving Range Site 33Ha586, Newtown, Ohio. Report prepared by KEMRON Environmental Services, on file, Ohio Historic Preservation Office, Columbus.

Ledbetter, Jerald R. and Lisa D. O'Steen
1991 The Grayson Site: Phase III Investigations of 15CR73, Carter County, Kentucky. Report prepared by Southeastern Archaeological Services, Inc., on file, Office of State Archaeology, Lexington, Kentucky.

Lee, Alfred M.
1986 Archaeological Recovery of Early, Middle and Early Late Woodland Remains from the Excavation of the Stanford Knoll Site in the Cuyahoga Valley National Recreation Area. Report prepared by the Cleveland Museum of Natural History, on file, Midwestern Archaeological Center, National Park Service. Lincoln, Nebraska.

Lepper, Bradley T.
1994 Locating Early Sites in the Middle Ohio Valley: Lessons from the Manning Site (33CT476). In *The First Discovery of America: Archaeological Evidence of the Early Inhabitants of the Ohio Area*, edited by William S. Dancey, pp. 145–156. Ohio Archaeological Council, Columbus.

Lindner, Christopher R.
1982 Ironstone Hoes of South-Central Ohio: Their Technology, Utilization, Distribution, and Cultural Affiliation. Master's thesis, Department of Anthropology, University of Cincinnati, Cincinnati, Ohio.

Litfin, James C.
1993 Early Archaic Band Territoriality: A Projectile Point and Chert Raw Material Perspective. Master's thesis, Department of Anthropology, University of Cincinnati, Cincinnati, Ohio.

Littlecott, Harry A., and Martin L. Fair
1969 The Sloane Site, Toronto, Ohio. *Ohio Archaeologist* 19(1):20–26.

Mayer-Oakes, William J.
1955 *Prehistory of the Upper Ohio Valley: An Introductory Archaeological Study*. Annals, Anthropological Series 2. Carnegie Museum, Pittsburgh, Pennsylvania.

McKenzie, Douglas H.
1967 The Archaic of the Lower Scioto Valley, Ohio. *Pennsylvania Archaeologist* 37(1–2):33–51.

Miller, Michael J.
2002 A Lithic Reduction Strategy of the Archaic: Manufacturing and Use Traces in the MacCorkle Bifurcate Tradition of Ohio. Paper presented at the 2002 Midwest Archaeological Conference, Columbus, Ohio.

Moffett, Ross
1949 The Raisch-Smith Site, an Early Indian Occupation in Preble County, Ohio. *Ohio Archaeological and Historical Quarterly* 58:428–441.

Moorehead, Warren K.
1909 A Study of Primitive Culture in Ohio. In *Putnam Anniversary Volume. Anthropological Essays Presented to Frederic Ward Putnam in Honor of His Seventieth Birthday, April 16, 1909*, edited by Franz Boas, pp. 137–150. G. E. Stechert, New York.

Morgan, Richard G.
1952 Outline of Cultures in the Ohio Region. In *Archeology of Eastern United States*, edited by James B. Griffin, pp. 83–98. University of Chicago Press, Chicago.

Morton, James, and Jeff Carskadden
1975 Excavation of an Archaic Open Site. *Ohio Archaeologist* 25(2):16–19.
1987 Test Excavations at an Early Hopewellian Site near Dresden, Ohio. *Ohio Archaeologist* 37(1):8–12.
2004a *A Survey of Prehistoric Archaeological Sites in Jackson Township, Muskingum County, Ohio*. Occasional Papers in Muskingum Valley Archaeology 25. Muskingum Valley Archaeological Survey, Zanesville, Ohio.
2004b *A Survey of Prehistoric Archaeological Sites in Meigs Township, Muskingum County, Ohio*. Occasional Papers in Muskingum Valley Archaeology 26. Muskingum Valley Archaeological Survey, Zanesville, Ohio.
2004c *A Survey of Prehistoric Archaeological Sites in Hopewell Township, Muskingum County, Ohio*. Occasional Papers

in Muskingum Valley Archaeology 26(a). Muskingum Valley Archaeological Survey, Zanesville, Ohio.

Morton, James, Jeff Carskadden, and Steve House
2004 *A Survey of Prehistoric Archaeological Sites in Washington Township, Muskingum County, Ohio*. Occasional Papers in Muskingum Valley Archaeology 33. Muskingum Valley Archaeological Survey, Zanesville, Ohio.

Murphy, James L.
1975 *An Archeological History of the Hocking Valley*. Ohio University Press, Athens.

Murphy, James L., and James Morton
1978 A Brown County Turkey-Tail Cache. *Ohio Archaeologist* 28(3):24.

Nass, John P., Jr., Flora Church, Annette Erickson-Latimer, and Myra Giesen
1990 Phase IV Data Recovery at the Sabre Farms (33RO385), a Multicomponent Prehistoric Site in Ross County, Ohio. Report prepared by ASC Group, Inc., on file, Ohio Historic Preservation Office, Columbus.

Ogden, J. G.
1966 Forest History of Ohio: Radiocarbon Dates and Pollen Stratigraphy of Silver Lake, Logan County, Ohio. *Ohio Journal of Science* 66:287–400.

Pacheco, Paul J.
1987 Salvage Excavations at the Continental Construction Site (33Ro348), Chillicothe, Ohio. Paper presented at the Midwestern Archaeological Conference, Milwaukee, Wisconsin.
1991 Woodland Period Archaeology in Central Ohio. *Ohio Archaeological Council Newsletter* 3(2):4–9.

Pacheco, Paul J., and Jarrod Burks
2002 Early Woodland Ceremonialism in Context: Results of LCALS' Research at the Munson Springs Site (33Li251). In Transitions: Archaic and Early Woodland Research in the Ohio Country, edited by Martha Otto. Unpublished manuscript, Ohio Archaeological Council, Columbus.

Pecora, Albert M., and Jarrod Burks
2005 The Bremen Site: A Terminal Late Archaic Period Upland Occupation in Fairfield County, Ohio. In *The Emergence of the Moundbuilders: The Archaeology of Tribal Societies in Southeastern Ohio*, edited by Elliot M. Abrams and AnnCorinne Freter, pp. 39–58. Ohio University Press, Athens.

Pedde, Sara E., and Olaf H. Prufer
2001 Hendricks Cave, Rockshelters, and Late Archaic Mortuary Practices in Ohio. In *Archaic Transitions in Ohio and Kentucky Prehistory*, edited by Olaf H. Prufer, Sara E. Pedde, and Richard S. Meindl, pp. 328–354, Kent State University Press, Kent, Ohio.

Picklesimer John W.
1999 Early Archaic of Southern Ohio: A Comparative Analysis of Early Holocene Subsistence and Settlement in the Little Miami Drainage System of Southwestern Ohio and the Hocking River Drainage System of Southeastern Ohio. Master's thesis, Department of Anthropology, Kent State University, Kent, Ohio.

Price, Thomas D.
1985 Late Archaic Subsistence in the Midwestern United States. *Journal of Human Evolution* 14:449–459.

Prufer, Olaf H.
2001 The Archaic of Northeastern Ohio. In *Archaic Transitions in Ohio and Kentucky Prehistory*, edited by Olaf H. Prufer, Sara E. Pedde, and Richard S. Meindl, pp. 183–209. Kent State University Press, Kent, Ohio.

Prufer, Olaf H., and Raymond S. Baby
1963 *Paleo-Indians of Ohio*. Ohio Historical Society, Columbus.

Prufer, Olaf H., and Dana A. Long
1986 *The Archaic of Northeastern Ohio*. Kent State Research Papers in Archaeology 6. Kent State University Press, Kent, Ohio.

Prufer, Olaf H., Dana A. Long, and Donald J. Metzger
1989 *Krill Cave: A Stratified Rockshelter in Summit County, Ohio*. Kent State Research Papers in Archaeology 8. Kent State University Press, Kent, Ohio.

Prufer, Olaf H., and Charles Sofsky
1965 The McKibben Site (33TR-57), Trumbull County, Ohio: A Contribution to the Late Paleo-Indian and Archaic Phases of Ohio. *Michigan Archaeologist* 11:9–40.

Purtill, Matthew P.
2001 Eastern Maple Creek, Laurentian Archaic, or What? Preliminary Results of Investigations at a Late Archaic Occupation along the Ohio River Valley in Lawrence County, Ohio. Paper presented at the Ohio Archaeological Council Fall Membership Meeting and Symposium "Current Research in Ohio Archaeology 2001," Highbanks Park, Columbus, Ohio.
2002a Phase III Archaeological Investigations of the Davisson Farm Site (33Le619) in Support of the Proposed Hanging Rock Energy Facility, Hamilton Township, Lawrence County, Ohio. 2 vols. Report prepared by Gray & Pape, Inc., on file, Ohio Historic Preservation Office, Columbus.
2002b Phase II Archaeological Investigations at Sites 33Le680, 33Le683, 33Le684, and 33Le685 within the Proposed South Point Industrial Park, Lawrence County, Ohio. Report prepared by Gray & Pape, Inc., on file, Ohio Historic Preservation Office, Columbus.
2003a Notes and Observations on Several Large-Scale CRM Projects in South-Central Ohio. Paper presented at the Ohio Archaeological Council Fall Membership Meeting and Symposium "Current Research in Ohio Archaeology 2003," Highbanks Metro Park, Columbus, Ohio.
2003b From Beginning to End: Key Findings from Recent CRM Excavations along the Ohio River in Lawrence and Scioto Counties, Ohio. Paper presented at the 48th Midwest Archaeological Conference, Milwaukee, Wisconsin.
2003c Phase III Archaeological Investigations of the Ohio Horse Park Site (33Sc421) in Support of the Proposed Texas Eastern Hanging Rock Lateral Pipeline Project, Lawrence and Scioto Counties, Ohio. Report prepared by Gray & Pape, Inc., on file, Ohio Historic Preservation Office, Columbus.
2004a Down on the River: Late Archaic through Terminal Archaic Dynamics at the Davisson Farm Site (33Le619), Lawrence County, Ohio. In Transitions: Archaic and Early Woodland Research in the Ohio

Country, edited by Martha Otto. Unpublished manuscript, Ohio Archaeological Council, Columbus, Ohio.

2004b The Documentation of the Robert Davisson Sr. Prehistoric Artifact Collection, Hanging Rock, Lawrence County, Ohio. Unpublished report on file, Ohio Historic Preservation Office, Columbus.

Redmond, Brian G.

2005 *A Report of Archaeological Investigations at the Danbury Site (33OT16): 2004 Season.* Archaeological Research Reports 146. Cleveland Museum of Natural History, Cleveland, Ohio.

Richards, E., and O. C. Shane III

1974 Tuscarawas County's Kline Mound. *Ohio Archaeologist* 24(3):4–8.

Ritchie, William A.

1932 *The Lamoka Lake Site: The Type Station of the Archaic Algonkian Period in New York.* Researches and Transactions 7(4). New York Archeological Association, Albany.

Ritzenthaler, Robert E., and George I. Quimby

1962 The Red Ochre Culture of the Upper Great Lakes and Adjacent Areas. *Fieldiana, Anthropology* 36:243–275.

Russo, Michael

1996 Southeastern Archaic Mounds. In *Archaeology of the Mid-Holocene Southeast*, edited by Kenneth E. Sassaman and David G. Anderson, pp. 259–287. University Press of Florida, Gainesville.

Rutter, William E., Andrew M. Schneider, and Jason M. Koralewski

2000 Site 33Wy674: A Preliminary View of a Multicomponent, Transitional Late Archaic/Woodland Extractive Site in Wyandot County, Ohio. *Ohio Archaeological Council Newsletter* 12(1):10–14.

Sassaman, Kenneth E.

1993 *Early Pottery in the Southeast: Tradition and Innovation in Cooking Technology.* Tuscaloosa: University of Alabama Press.

Saxe, Arthur A.

1970 Social Dimensions of Mortuary Practices. Ph.D. dissertation, Department of Anthropology, University of Chicago, Chicago.

Sciulli, Paul W., and Bruce W. Aument

1987 Paleodemography of the Duff Site (33LO111), Logan County, Ohio. *Midcontinental Journal of Archaeology* 12:117–144.

Sciulli, Paul W., Bruce Aument, and Lenny Piotrowski

1982 The Williams (33WO7A) Red Ochre Cemetery: Preliminary Description and Comparative Analysis of Acquired Dental Pathology. *Pennsylvania Archaeologist* 52(3–4):17–24.

Sciulli, Paul W., and James M. Heilman

n.d. Terminal Late Archaic Mortuary Practices: Berryhill (33Cl17). Manuscript on file, Boonshoft Museum of Discovery, Dayton, Ohio.

Sciulli, Paul W., Paul J. Pacheco, and Charles A. Sanini

1991 Variation in Limb Bones of Terminal Late Archaic Populations in Ohio. *Midcontinental Journal of Archaeology* 16:247–271.

Sciulli, Paul W., and Ray Schuck

2001 Terminal Late Archaic Mortuary Practices II. The Boose Cemetery. *Pennsylvania Archaeologist* 71(1):29–42.

Sciulli, Paul W., Ray Schuck, and Myra J. Geisen

1993 Terminal Late Archaic Mortuary Practices at Kirian-Treglia (33AL39). *Pennsylvania Archaeologist* 63(2):53–63.

Seeman, Mark F.

1986 Adena "Houses" and Their Implications for Early Woodland Settlement Models in the Ohio Valley. In *Early Woodland Archeology*, edited by Kenneth Farnsworth and Thomas E. Emerson, pp. 564–595. Kampsville Seminars in Archeology 2. Center for American Archeology Press, Kampsville, Illinois.

1994 Inter-Cluster Patterning at Nobles Pond: A Case for "Disembedded" Procurement among Early Paleoindian Societies. *American Antiquity* 59:273–287.

Seeman, Mark F., and Olaf H. Prufer

1982 An Updated Distribution of Ohio Fluted Points. *Midcontinental Journal of Archaeology* 17:155–169.

Shane, Linda C. K.

1987 Late-Glacial Vegetational and Climatic History of the Allegheny Plateau and the Till Plains of Ohio and Indiana, U.S.A. *Boreas* 16:1–20.

1994 Intensity and Rate of Vegetation and Climatic Change in the Ohio Region between 14,000 and 9,000 14C YBP. In *The First Discovery of America: Archaeological Evidence of the Early Inhabitants of the Ohio Area*, edited by William S. Dancey, pp. 7–22. Ohio Archaeological Council, Columbus.

Shane, Linda C. K., Gordon G. Snyder, and Katherine H. Anderson

2001 Holocene Vegetation and Climate Changes in the Ohio Region. In *Archaic Transitions in Ohio and Kentucky Prehistory*, edited by Olaf H. Prufer, Sara E. Pedde, and Richard S. Meindl, pp. 11–58. Kent State University Press, Kent, Ohio.

Shane, Orrin C., III

1967 The Leimbach Site: An Early Woodland Village in Lorain County, Ohio. In *Studies in Ohio Archaeology*, edited by Olaf H. Prufer and Douglas H. McKenzie, pp. 64–98. Kent State University Press, Kent, Ohio.

1971 Comments. In *Adena: The Seeking of an Identity*, edited by B. K. Swartz, pp. 27, 60–162. Ball State University, Muncie, Indiana.

Sherwood, Sarah C., Boyce N. Driskell, Asa R. Randall, and Scott C. Meeks

2004 Chronology and Stratigraphy at Dust Cave, Alabama. *American Antiquity* 69:533–554.

Slawson, Laurie V.

1977 Faunal Analysis: A Study of the Methods and Their Application to the Late Archaic Bullskin Creek Site, 33Ct29, Clermont County, Ohio. Master's thesis, Department of Anthropology, University of Cincinnati, Cincinnati, Ohio.

Sowder, Richard

1972 McKee Site: Report on Human Skeletal Material—Determination of Individuals Represented. Manuscript on file, Boonshoft Museum of Discovery, Dayton, Ohio.

SPSS

1998 *SPSS Base 8.0 Applications Guide.* SPSS, Chicago.

Stafford, C. Russell
1994 Structural Changes in Archaic Landscape Use in the Dissected Uplands of Southwestern Indiana. *American Antiquity* 59:219–237.
2004 Modeling Soil-Geomorphic Associations and Archaic Stratigraphic Sequences in the Lower Ohio River Valley. *Journal of Archaeological Science* 31:1053–1067.

Stoltman, James B.
1978 Temporal Models in Prehistory: An Example from Eastern North America. *Current Anthropology* 19:703–746.

Stothers, David M.
1996 Resource Procurement and Band Territories: A Model for Lower Great Lakes Paleoindian and Early Archaic Settlement Systems. *Archaeology of Eastern North America* 24:173–216.

Stothers, David M., and Timothy J. Abel
1993 Archaeological Reflections of the Late Archaic and Early Woodland Time Periods in the Western Lake Erie Region. *Archaeology of Eastern North America* 21:25–109.

Stothers, David M., Timothy J. Abel, and Andrew M. Schneider
2001 Archaic Perspectives in the Western Lake Erie Basin. In *Archaic Transitions in Ohio and Kentucky Prehistory*, edited by Olaf H. Prufer, Sara E. Pedde, and Richard S. Meindl, pp. 233–289. Kent State University Press, Kent, Ohio.

Stothers, David M., Andrew M. Schneider, and Mark Pape
2001 Early Archaic Side-Notched Points from East-Central Ohio. In *Archaic Transitions in Ohio and Kentucky Prehistory*, edited by Olaf H. Prufer, Sara E. Pedde, and Richard S. Meindl, pp. 184–210. Kent State University Press, Kent, Ohio.

Struever, Stuart, and Kent D. Vickery
1973 The Beginnings of Cultivation in the Midwest-Riverine Area of the United States. *American Anthropologist* 75:1197–1220.

Stuiver, Minze, Paula J. Reimer, Edouard Bard, J. Warren Beck, G. S. Burr, Konrad A. Hughen, Bernd Kromer, Gerry McCormac, Johannes van der Plicht, and Marco Spurk
1998 INTCAL98 Radiocarbon Age Calibration 24,000–0 cal BP. *Radiocarbon* 40:1041–1083.

Tatarek, Nancy E., and Paul W. Sciulli
2000 Comparison of Population Structure in Ohio's Late Archaic and Late Prehistoric Periods. *American Journal of Physical Anthropology* 112:363–376.

Theler, James L., and Timothy S. Dalbey
1974 Chert Utilization at the Ferris Site, 33Ct31, an Early Archaic Camp in Southwestern Ohio. Paper presented at the Ohio Valley Archaeological Conference, Normandy Reservoir, Tennessee.

Townsend, Earl C., Jr.
2003 *Birdstones of the North American Indians*. Reprinted, Hart Publishers, Huntington, Indiana. Originally published 1959 by Earl C. Townsend Jr., Indianapolis, Indiana.

Trigger, Bruce G.
1989 *A History of Archaeological Thought*. Cambridge University Press, Cambridge.

Vickery, Kent D.
1976 An Approach to Inferring Archaeological Variability. Ph.D. dissertation, Department of Anthropology, Indiana University, Bloomington.
1978 A Preliminary Report on the Dravo Gravel Site Excavations, 1977 Field Season. Manuscript in possession of chapter author.
1980 Preliminary Definition of Archaic "Study Units" in Southwestern Ohio. Prepared for the State Archaeological Preservation Plan Meeting, Columbus, Ohio.
1999 The Ohio Archaic: Problems and Prospects. Paper presented at the Eastern States Archaeological Federation/Ohio Archaeological Council Conference, Kings Island.

Webb, William S.
1946 *Indian Knoll, Site Oh 2, Ohio County, Kentucky*. Reports in Anthropology and Archaeology 4(3). University of Kentucky, Lexington.

Webb, William S., and Charles E. Snow
1945 *The Adena People*. Reports in Anthropology and Archaeology 6. University of Kentucky, Lexington.

Whaley, Marie Annala
1992 The Regional Distribution of Bannerstones in Ohio: A Statewide Survey. Master's thesis, Department of Anthropology, Kent State University, Kent, Ohio.

Appendix 15.A. Inventory of Absolute Dates from the Archaic Period in Ohio.

Site No.[a]	Site Name	Site Type[b]	Physio. Region	Lab No.[c]	RCYBP	Calibrated B.P. Date (Median)[d]	Calibrated B.C. Date Range (1 Sigma)[d]	Calibrated B.P. Date Range (1 Sigma)[d]
AT521	Boudinot 4	O	Unglaciated Plateau	Beta-26743	2610 ± 80	2710	896–554	2845–2493
LN7	Leimbach	O	Lake Plains	OWU250	2460 ± 260	2720	892–204	2841–2153
DL14	Arthur James Mound	M	Till Plains	OWU331	2630 ± 115	2720	966–541	2915–2490
WO7	Williams Cemetery	CE	Lake Plains	DIC-948	2600 ± 55	2730	831–563	2780–2512
PI28	McCoy Mound	M	Till Plains	PITT0110	2630 ± 55	2760	891–764	2840–2713
BU477	Houpt	O	Till Plains	Beta-71185	2640 ± 60	2760	896–780	2845–2729
WO7	Williams Cemetery	CE	Lake Plains	DIC-949	2660 ± 110	2770	1000–560	2945–2508
LI251	Munson Springs	M	Glaciated Plateau	Beta-36276	2670 ± 75	2790	910–790	2857–2740
LI252	LIC79.1/Hale House	O	Glaciated Plateau	Beta-27446	2670 ± 70	2790	900–800	2848–2745
CL17	Berry Hill	CE	Till Plains	I17707	2670 ± 90	2790	970–770	2919–2714
LE619	Davisson Farm	O	Unglaciated Plateau	Beta-161296	2670 ± 70	2790	900–800	2848–2745
TU40	Kline Mound	M	Unglaciated Plateau	GX-2842	2690 ± 180	2800	1110–540	3062–2490
WY1	Thomas Reber Kame	CE	Till Plains	DIC-3070	2700 ± 55	2810	900–810	2846–2760
CS93	Meek I	O	Unglaciated Plateau	Beta-17264	2690 ± 90	2810	970–790	2920–2740
MU685	—	O	Unglaciated Plateau	Beta-133129	2690 ± 70	2810	900–800	2852–2749
SA (?)	Baker II	IB	Lake Plains	Beta-46639	2710 ± 60	2820	900–810	2852–2758
RO616	—	O	Till Plains	not reported	2700 ± 70	2820	910–800	2856–2751
TR58	Hoffaker	O	Glaciated Plateau	not reported	2710 ± 150	2830	1130–560	3075–2513
TR58	Hoffaker	O	Glaciated Plateau	not reported	2730 ± 75	2840	970–810	2918–2758
WO17c	Asmus 3	O	Lake Plains	DIC-229	2730 ± 75	2840	970–810	2918–2758
CS442	Eppley Rockshelter	RS/C	Unglaciated Plateau	UCLA-2589B	2720 ± 235	2840	1260–520	3205–2473
LA (?)	Stanford Knoll	O	Lake Plains	A2622 (TL)	2850 ± 300			
WO7	Williams Cemetery	CE	Lake Plains	DIC-420	2750 ± 75	2860	1000–830	2945–2774
HO65	Park	O	Unglaciated Plateau	DIC-1749	2730 ± 145	2860	1190–780	3134–2724
AL39	Kirian-Treglia	CE	Till Plains	I11681	2755 ± 85	2870	1000–830	2946–2775
ER409	Weilnau	O	Lake Plains	Beta-45513	2780 ± 60	2880	1000–840	2946–2788
SC421	Ohio Horse Park	O	Unglaciated Plateau	Beta-174756	2780 ± 60	2880	1000–840	2946–2788
LI251	Munson Springs	M	Glaciated Plateau	Beta-36273	2785 ± 70	2890	1000–840	2950–2785
WY674	—	O	Till Plains	GX-26430	2790 ± 60	2890	1000–840	2950–2791
LE619	Davisson Farm	O	Unglaciated Plateau	Beta-161297	2790 ± 70	2890	1000–840	2953–2784
WO7	Williams Cemetery	CE	Lake Plains	DIC-950	2800 ± 45	2896	1004–897	2953–2846
FR43	Toepfner Mound	M	Till Plains	C-492	2780 ± 410	2910	1410–410	3361–2360
CT645	Possum Hollow	O	Till Plains	Beta-192490	2810 ± 50	2910	1036–897	2985–2846
LE97	Mabel Hall	O	Unglaciated Plateau	UGA-3047	2775 ± 115	2910	1110–810	3056–2754
LE619	Davisson Farm	O	Unglaciated Plateau	Beta-161299	2810 ± 70	2920	1050–840	2994–2792

Appendix 15.A. Inventory of Absolute Dates from the Archaic Period in Ohio, continued.

Site No.[a]	Site Name	Site Type[b]	Physio. Region	Lab No.[c]	RCYBP	Calibrated B.P. Date (Median)[d]	Calibrated B.C. Date Range (1 Sigma)[d]	Calibrated B.P. Date Range (1 Sigma)[d]
WO7	Williams Cemetery	CE	Lake Plains	GX-10261	2785 ± 230	2930	1370–670	3319–2622
JA159	Rais Rockshelter	RS/C	Unglaciated Plateau	GX-1454	2805 ± 100	2930	1110–830	3058–2780
AT40	County Home	O	Unglaciated Plateau	Beta-139636	2820 ± 70	2930	1108–843	3057–2792
WY783	—	O	Till Plains	Beta-??	2840 ± 25	2935	1016–933	2965–2882
LE97	Mabel Hall	O	Unglaciated Plateau	not reported	2835 ± 75	2950	1130–900	3074–2850
CS282	—	O	Unglaciated Plateau	Beta-65614	2840 ± 60	2950	1110–910	3060–2860
CT525	—	O	Till Plains	Beta-38538	2850 ± 60	2970	1210–1000	3062–2870
WO7	Williams Cemetery	CE	Lake Plains	GX-10259	2825 ± 200	2980	1290–800	3238–2751
WO7	Williams Cemetery	CE	Lake Plains	GX-10262	2830 ± 150	2980	1210–830	3159–2779
RO616	—	O	Till Plains	not reported	2830 ± 130	2980	1210–830	3155–2783
DL1080	—	O	Till Plains	not reported	2870 ± ? (100)	3010	1210–916	3159–2865
LE680	—	O	Unglaciated Plateau	Beta-169121	2880 ± 60	3010	1190–940	3137–2890
WO7	Williams Cemetery	CE	Lake Plains	GX-10260	2860 ± 180	3020	1260–830	3209–2782
TU57	Johnson Site II	O	Unglaciated Plateau	I-14219	2880 ± 90	3020	1210–920	3159–2873
CU402	Plateau Picnic	O	Glaciated Plateau	Beta-109156	2900 ± 60	3040	1210–1000	3159–2948
AL39	Kirian-Treglia	CE	Till Plains	I11680	2900 ± 80	3040	1260–950	3204–2894
CT525	—	O	Till Plains	Beta-38540	2900 ± 60	3040	1110–920	3159–2948
AT521	Boudinot 4	O	Unglaciated Plateau	Beta-27478	2900 ± 60	3040	1210–1000	3159–2948
CS282	—	O	Unglaciated Plateau	Beta-65619	2900 ± 70	3040	1210–980	3160–2925
LE618	—	O	Unglaciated Plateau	Beta-155080	2910 ± 40	3047	1207–1017	3156–2966
CT525	—	O	Till Plains	Beta-38535	2890 ± 190	3050	1600–1430	3316–2792
SC421	Ohio Horse Park	O	Unglaciated Plateau	Beta-174757	2920 ± 60	3070	1250–1010	3197–2961
LE403	—	O	Unglaciated Plateau	Beta-175880	2940 ± 40	3097	1256–1052	3205–3001
LE683	—	O	Unglaciated Plateau	Beta-169123	2940 ± 70	3100	1260–1020	3208–2972
LO111	Duff	CE	Till Plains	DIC-3177	2950 ± 115	3110	1370–1000	3316–2953
ER85	Seaman's Fort	O	Lake Plains	OWU-265	2955 ± 290	3120	1500–830	3448–2777
AL1	Boose	CE	Till Plains	GX25552	2960 ± 80	3120	1295–1045	3244–2994
HI203	—	O	Till Plains	not reported	2960 ± 100	3120	1370–1020	3315–2971
AT40	County Home	O	Unglaciated Plateau	Beta-143697	2960 ± 40	3126	1260–1054	3003–3209
WO7	Williams Cemetery	CE	Lake Plains	GX-10257-G	2965 ± 195	3130	1410–940	3355–2887
JA159	Rais Rockshelter	RS/C	Unglaciated Plateau	GX-1247	2970 ± 220	3140	1430–920	3376–2869
SC421	Ohio Horse Park	O	Unglaciated Plateau	ACT 6365 (OCR)	3157 ± 94			
MU77	Philo Group:Area D	O	Glaciated Plateau	TX2347	2990 ± 80	3160	1370–1050	3322–3003
WO7	Williams Cemetery	CE	Lake Plains	GX-10258	3005 ± 210	3170	1490–940	3436–2889

Appendix 15.A. Inventory of Absolute Dates from the Archaic Period in Ohio, continued.

Site No.[a]	Site Name	Site Type[b]	Physio. Region	Lab No. [c]	RCYBP	Calibrated B.P. Date (Median)[d]	Calibrated B.C. Date Range (1 Sigma)[d]	Calibrated B.P. Date Range (1 Sigma)[d]
BU477	Houpt	O	Till Plains	Beta-71184	3010 ± 100	3180	1400–1130	3345–3074
PK153	Maderia Brown	O	Unglaciated Plateau	Beta-75497	3020 ± 110	3190	1410–1060	3357–3004
TU57	Johnson Site II	O	Unglaciated Plateau	I-14218	3030 ± 90	3210	1400–1130	3350–3079
WO7	Williams Cemetery	CE	Lake Plains	GX-10257A	3075 ± 195	3250	1520–1040	3471–2992
SC421	Ohio Horse Park	O	Unglaciated Plateau	Beta-167103	3060 ± 40	3277	1390–1263	3339–3212
LE619	Davisson Farm	O	Unglaciated Plateau	Beta-161298	3070 ± 60	3280	1410–1260	3358–3210
SC421	Ohio Horse Park	O	Unglaciated Plateau	Beta-174761	3070 ± 60	3280	1410–1260	3358–3210
AT40	County Home	O	Unglaciated Plateau	Beta-141234	3080 ± 80	3280	1432–1215	3381–3164
AT40	County Home	O	Unglaciated Plateau	Beta-136254	3070 ± 60	3280	1409–1269	3358–3210
RO348	Continental Construction	O	Till Plains	ETH3312	3100 ± 105	3290	1500–1130	3447–3083
CL17	Berry Hill	CE	Till Plains	I17706	3100 ± 90	3300	1490–1220	3440–3167
WY674	—	O	Till Plains	not reported	3110 ± 150	3300	1520–1190	3472–3078
AL1	Boose	CE	Till Plains	BX25553	3105 ± 75	3310	1490–1260	3436–3211
TR1	Byler/Buyler Mound	M	Glaciated Plateau	SI-1150	3115 ± 80	3320	1490–1260	3441–3212
LE97	Mabel Hall	O	Unglaciated Plateau	UGA-3048	3115 ± 85	3320	1490–1260	3442–3211
FR38	William H. Davis Mound	M	Till Plains	DIC-2838	3130 ± 60	3350	1490–1320	3442–3265
FR38	William H. Davis Mound	M	Till Plains	unknown	3150 ± 120	3360	1600–1220	3548–3170
HU (?)	Bores	IB	Till Plains	Beta-5906	3150 ± 110	3360	1600–1260	3545–3210
SC434	—	O	Unglaciated Plateau	Beta-167101	3160 ± 70	3380	1520–1320	3466–3270
MS29	—	O	Unglaciated Plateau	Beta-179832	3170 ± 70	3390	1520–1320	3468–3271
WO86	Freeworth	O	Lake Plains	DIC-2589	3190 ± 65	3410	1520–1400	3471–3349
LE619	Davisson Farm	O	Unglaciated Plateau	Beta-155079	3190 ± 40	3413	1500–1430	3452–3377
LE619	Davisson Farm	O	Unglaciated Plateau	Beta-155077	3190 ± 40	3413	1500–1430	3452–3377
MU29	Lawler	O	Glaciated Plateau	not reported	3210 ± 80	3430	1600–1400	3551–3351
AT40	County Home	O	Unglaciated Plateau	Beta-141235	3220 ± 70	3440	1600–1411	3549–3360
SC148	Teneco Site #2	O	Unglaciated Plateau	Beta-174752	3220 ± 90	3450	1620–1410	3564–3356
PK153	Maderia Brown	O	Unglaciated Plateau	Beta-75488	3230 ± 60	3450	1600–1430	3549–3378
CT525	—	O	Till Plains	Beta-38543	3240 ± 60	3460	1880–1600	3550–3382
LE680	—	O	Unglaciated Plateau	Beta-169120	3250 ± 40	3466	1600–1449	3549–3398
WO16	Riverside	O	Lake Plains	DIC-2595	3250 ± 80	3480	1620–1440	3564–3384
BU477	Houpt	O	Till Plains	Beta-71183	3250 ± 90	3480	1670–1430	3626–3378
LE619	Davisson Farm	O	Unglaciated Plateau	Beta-155078	3250 ± 90	3480	1680–1430	3626–3378
MS29	—	O	Unglaciated Plateau	Beta-179833	3250 ± 70	3480	1600–1440	3553–3388
PK153	Maderia Brown	O	Unglaciated Plateau	Beta-75484	3250 ± 80	3480	1620–1440	3564–3384

Appendix 15.A. Inventory of Absolute Dates from the Archaic Period in Ohio, continued.

Site No.[a]	Site Name	Site Type[b]	Physio. Region	Lab No.[c]	RCYBP	Calibrated B.P. Date (Median)[d]	Calibrated B.C. Date Range (1 Sigma)[d]	Calibrated B.P. Date Range (1 Sigma)[d]
CT52	Maple Creek	O	Till Plains	UGA-327	3260 ± 330	3500	1950–1050	4406–2749
PK153	Maderia Brown	O	Unglaciated Plateau	Beta-76007	3270 ± 90	3510	1680–1440	3628–3392
PK153	Maderia Brown	O	Unglaciated Plateau	Beta-76013	3280 ± 70	3510	1680–1460	3628–3408
LU10	Gladieux	O	Lake Plains	DIC-796	3290 ± 70	3520	1680–1500	3630–3449
FR895	Marsh Run	O	Till Plains	Beta-48079	3290 ± 80	3530	1680–1460	3631–3411
RO385	Sabre Farms	O	Till Plains	Beta-28771	3290 ± 140	3530	1740–1410	3688–3363
WA78	Pipeline	O	Till Plains	DIC-1035	3290 ± 110	3530	1690–1440	3636–3391
FA1460	Bremen	O	Unglaciated Plateau	Beta 146167	3290 ± 120	3530	1730–1430	3679–3382
ER (3?)	Kendera	O	Lake Plains	Beta-45510	3300 ± 110	3540	1730–1450	3678–3396
BU477	Houpt	O	Till Plains	Beta-71186	3310 ± 70	3540	1680–1520	3632–3468
LE619	Davisson Farm	O	Unglaciated Plateau	Beta-155076	3300 ± 130	3540	1740–1430	3687–3382
SC17	Scioto County Homes	SM	Unglaciated Plateau	Beta-18093	3300 ± 110	3540	1730–1450	3678–3396
SU18	Krill Cave	RS/C	Glaciated Plateau	DIC-317	3340 ± 65	3570	1690–1530	3635–3476
SC421	Ohio Horse Park	O	Unglaciated Plateau	Beta-174754	3330 ± 130	3570	1770–1450	3687–3382
MU1228	Conn	O	Unglaciated Plateau	Beta-171964	3340 ± 60	3570	1690–1530	3635–3477
WA4	Anderson Village	O	Till Plains	DIC-777	3330 ± 145	3580	1860–1440	3805–3387
PK153	Maderia Brown	O	Unglaciated Plateau	Beta-75489	3340 ± 90	3580	1740–1520	3687–3469
PK153	Maderia Brown	O	Unglaciated Plateau	Beta-75487	3350 ± 70	3580	1730–1530	3680–3476
PK153	Maderia Brown	O	Unglaciated Plateau	Beta-75474	3350 ± 60	3580	1730–1530	3677–3477
PK153	Maderia Brown	O	Unglaciated Plateau	Beta-76016	3350 ± 90	3590	1740–1520	3688–3471
PK153	Maderia Brown	O	Unglaciated Plateau	Beta-76008	3350 ± 80	3590	1740–1530	3684–3474
PK153	Maderia Brown	O	Unglaciated Plateau	Beta-75494	3360 ± 100	3600	1770–1520	3715–3468
PK153	Maderia Brown	O	Unglaciated Plateau	Beta-76012	3360 ± 90	3600	1740–1530	3688–3474
HA17	Sand Ridge	O	Till Plains	UGA-1334	3370 ± 110	3610	1860–1520	3807–3470
PK153	Maderia Brown	O	Unglaciated Plateau	Beta-76011	3380 ± 70	3620	1740–1530	3693–3480
PK153	Maderia Brown	O	Unglaciated Plateau	Beta-75472	3390 ± 90	3640	1860–1530	3808–3478
CT525	—	O	Till Plains	Beta-38536	3410 ± 90	3660	1370–840	3826–3553
PK153	Maderia Brown	O	Unglaciated Plateau	Beta-75478	3440 ± 80	3700	1880–1640	3828–3588
WA92	Wood-73	O	Till Plains	DIC-1038	3450 ± 90	3710	1880–1640	3832–3586
SC282	Ira Bays	RS/C	Unglaciated Plateau	Beta-19812	3460 ± 80	3730	1880–1680	3831–3633
WN412	—	O	Unglaciated Plateau	not reported	3490 ± 40	3758	1878–1748	3827–3697
PK153	Maderia Brown	O	Unglaciated Plateau	Beta-75486	3490 ± 100	3760	1940–1690	3888–3636
MU304	Hunter I	O	Glaciated Plateau	Beta-37361	3510 ± 80	3780	1940–1700	3887–3648
JA159	Rais Rockshelter	RS/C	Unglaciated Plateau	GX-1248	3510 ± 130	3790	2030–1640	3975–3593

Appendix 15.A. Inventory of Absolute Dates from the Archaic Period in Ohio, continued.

Site No.[a]	Site Name	Site Type[b]	Physio. Region	Lab No. [c]	RCYBP	Calibrated B.P. Date (Median)[d]	Calibrated B.C. Date Range (1 Sigma)[d]	Calibrated B.P. Date Range (1 Sigma)[d]
RO186	Harness 28	O	Till Plains	ETH-3069	3525 ± 95	3800	2010–1700	3957–3644
CS442	Eppley Rockshelter	RS/C	Unglaciated Plateau	UCLA-2589D	3495 ± 290	3800	2200–1450	4151–3398
PK153	Maderia Brown	O	Unglaciated Plateau	Beta-76010	3540 ± 60	3820	1940–1770	3893–3718
AS (?)	Ringler (dugout canoe)	O	Glaciated Plateau	DIC-612	3550 ± 70	3830	2010–1770	3957–3719
RO385	Sabre Farms	O	Till Plains	Beta-29168	3540 ± 130	3830	2110–1700	4057–3473
CS442	Eppley Rockshelter	RS/C	Unglaciated Plateau	UCLA-2589A	3580 ± 65	3880	2030–1780	3978–3729
PK153	Maderia Brown	O	Unglaciated Plateau	Beta-75985	3580 ± 190	3900	2200–1690	4147–3636
CT525	—	O	Till Plains	Beta-38542	3660 ± 70	3980	2140–1940	4086–3891
LE683	—	O	Unglaciated Plateau	ACT 6781 (OCR)	4004 ± 120			
LE165	Brady Run Rockshelter 3	RS/C	Unglaciated Plateau	Beta-35340	3680 ± 130	4020	2280–1880	4228–3832
PK153	Maderia Brown	O	Unglaciated Plateau	Beta-76015	3690 ± 100	4030	2270–1920	4216–3871
PK153	Maderia Brown	O	Unglaciated Plateau	Beta-76009	3730 ± 90	4080	2280–1980	4233–3928
SC282	Ira Bays Rockshelter	RS/C	Unglaciated Plateau	Beta-19813	3730 ± 90	4080	2280–1980	4233–3928
SC421	Ohio Horse Park	O	Unglaciated Plateau	ACT 6366 (OCR)	4127 ± 123			
JA159	Rais Rockshelter	RS/C	Unglaciated Plateau	GX-1249	3790 ± 140	4170	2460–2040	3962–3574
TR58	Hoffaker	O	Glaciated Plateau	not reported	3860 ± 150	4270	2560–2050	4508–3997
MU304	Hunter I	O	Glaciated Plateau	Beta-37355	3870 ± 70	4290	2460–2210	4409–4160
TU02	Riker	O	Unglaciated Plateau	GX-1741	3905 ± 160	4330	2620–2140	4568–4087
LE396	—	O	Unglaciated Plateau	Beta-121122	3910 ± 40	4342	2466–2314	4415–4263
CT648	—	O	Till Plains	Beta-191925	3920 ± 50	4350	2470–2312	4419–4261
CT525	—	O	Till Plains	Beta-38534	3960 ± 90	4410	2580–2310	4526–4257
FR810	—	O	Till Plains	Beta-67413	3970 ± 270	4420	2880–2140	4824–4090
SU18	Krill Cave	RS/C	Glaciated Plateau	DIC-317	3980 ± 130	4440	2840–2240	4788–4192
FA1460	Bremen	O	Unglaciated Plateau	Beta 146168	3980 ± 60	4440	2580–2350	4527–4302
FR1521	—	O	Till Plains	Beta-129508	4000 ± 60	4470	2620–2460	4569–4407
PI467	Peters Cemetery	CE	Till Plains	Beta-36271	4000 ± 75	4470	2830–2350	4775–4302
AT521	Boudinot 4	O	Unglaciated Plateau	Beta-26472	4000 ± 70	4470	2660–2350	4605–4303
SC421	Ohio Horse Park	O	Unglaciated Plateau	Beta-182663	4020 ± 40	4484	2575–2474	4524–4423
HI182	—	O	Till Plains	not reported	4030 ± 180	4510	2870–2310	4820–4263
LE623	—	O	Unglaciated Plateau	Beta-155082	4060 ± 40	4538	2830–2494	4779–4443
CT52	Maple Creek	O	Till Plains	UGA-306	4065 ± 150	4560	2880–2460	4824–4413
CT525	—	O	Till Plains	Beta-38537	4070 ± 100	4580	2860–2470	4807–4422
FR63	Phillips Mound I	M	Till Plains	OWU-147	4095 ± 255	4590	3010–2210	4959–4156
LN07	Leimbach	O	Lake Plains	GX-1250	4105 ± 140	4610	2880–2500	4825–4444

Appendix 15.A. Inventory of Absolute Dates from the Archaic Period in Ohio, continued.

Site No.[a]	Site Name	Site Type[b]	Physio. Region	Lab No.[c]	RCYBP	Calibrated B.P. Date (Median)[d]	Calibrated B.C. Date Range (1 Sigma)[d]	Calibrated B.P. Date Range (1 Sigma)[d]
CT30	Logan	O	Till Plains	UGA-579	4115 ± 455	4610	3340–2050	5286–3995
HA45	DuPont	O	Till Plains	UGA-1343	4100 ± 65	4620	2860–2500	4809–4451
SC17	Scioto County Homes	SM	Unglaciated Plateau	Beta-18091	4110 ± 70	4640	2860–2500	4811–4453
MU29	Lawler	O	Glaciated Plateau	I-7604	4130 ± 100	4650	2870–2580	4819–4530
HA45	DuPont	O	Till Plains	UGa-1342	4125 ± 65	4650	2860–2580	4812–4531
CT525	—	O	Till Plains	Beta-38541	4220 ± 70	4730	2900–2680	4851–4627
—	Grandstaff and Davis	CS	Till Plains	not reported	4290 ± 80	4860	3080–2710	5026–4654
HY97	—	O	Lake Plains	Beta-10023(?)	4320 ± 40	4880	3013–2884	4962–4833
CS442	Eppley Rockshelter	RS/C	Unglaciated Plateau	UCLA-2589F	4355 ± 95	4960	3310–2880	5255–4829
WA83	Oglesby-Harris	O	Till Plains	DIC-1037	4400 ± 50	4980	3090–2921	5039–4870
HA45	DuPont	O	Till Plains	Uga-1344	4435 ± 70	5050	3330–2920	5275–4873
WA83	Oglesby-Harris	O	Till Plains	DIC-1037	4450 ± 150	5090	3340–2920	5289–4872
CT29	Bullskin Creek	O	Till Plains	UGA-931	4470 ± 75	5120	3340–3030	5285–4977
PI467	Peters Cemetery	CE	Till Plains	Beta-36270	4470 ± 75	5120	3340–3030	5285–4977
HA45	DuPont	O	Till Plains	UGA-928	4485 ± 75	5130	3340–3040	5290–4992
—	Hendricks Cave	RS/C	Till Plains	BGS-1922	4493 ± 220	5130	3500–2900	5452–4849
CT29	Bullskin Creek	O	Till Plains	UGA-930	4550 ± 355	5170	3700–2710	5648–4658
VI (?)	Wheelabout Rockshelter	RS/C	Unglaciated Plateau	OWU-258	4570 ± 240	5210	3630–2930	5576–4879
SC421	Ohio Horse Park	O	Unglaciated Plateau	ACT 6367 (OCR)	5452 ± 163	N/A	N/A	N/A
GA16	Bob Evans Rockshelter	RS/C	Unglaciated Plateau	CWRU-109	4810 ± 300	5500	3960–3100	5908–5053
SC17	Scioto County Homes	SM	Unglaciated Plateau	Beta-17170	5010 ± 270	5750	4220–3380	6168–5333
LE619	Davisson Farm	O	Unglaciated Plateau	Beta-161294	5120 ± 70	5850	3980–3800	5929–5749
MS8	John Cleek	O	Unglaciated Plateau	Beta-189000	5130 ± 50	5860	3980–3805	5929–5754
SC421	Ohio Horse Park	O	Unglaciated Plateau	Beta-174759	5240 ± 50	6000	4218–3976	6167–5925
HY97	—	O	Lake Plains	Beta-10001(?)	5330 ± ? (100)	6100	4317–4042	6266–5991
AT653	Allen	O	Unglaciated Plateau	Beta-66178	5330 ± 80	6100	4311–4043	6260–5992
LN15	Burrell Orchard	O	Lake Plains	DIC-734	7120 ± 125	7930	6160–5840	8106–7790
CU34	Squaw Rockshelter	RS/C	Glaciated Plateau	DIC-321B	7450 ± 85	8260	6400–6230	8344–8181
HU10	Willard Mastodon	O	Till Plains	not reported	8260 ± 230	9200	7580–6870	9527–8822

Note: This inventory represents the raw count of absolute dates reported for Ohio as of December 2004. To conserve space, reference citations and contextual information are not included but are available on request.

[a]All site numbers have the prefix 33 (Ohio).

[b]O = open; CE = cemetery; M = mound; RS/C = rockshelter/cave; IB = isolated burial; SM = shell midden; CS = cache site.

[c]All dates represent radiocarbon assays except where otherwise noted (OCR = oxidizable ratio carbon; TL = thermoluminescence).

[d]Calibration based on IntCal98.c14 (Stuiver et al. 1998).

16

Land between the Rivers: The Archaic Period of Southernmost Illinois

Brian M. Butler

Introduction

What is today southern Illinois offered a rich and varied landscape to the Native American hunter-gatherers who occupied it for nine millennia. Modern political boundaries have little relevance to the remote past, but southernmost Illinois, framed in large part by the convergence and confluence of two major rivers, does have a certain geographic coherence as a research area. The physiographic variation is impressive, including segments of three major river valleys and the confluences of five major rivers, large tracts of swampy lowlands, rugged bedrock uplands, and glaciated terrain with little available rock. The region also straddles a border zone of sorts between the Midsouth and southern Midwest, a distinction that began to have some significance in the latter part of the Archaic period as cultures became more regionalized. The primary focus of this chapter is the ca. 8,600-year period from the end of Dalton culture to the arrival of pottery in the region—9200 to 600 cal B.C. Although I will make a few comments on the immediately preceding Dalton culture, that culture is not a major topic of discussion here.

This chapter begins with a description of the region in environmental terms followed by a brief discussion of the research history. Next, the data sources and the current state of knowledge are characterized. Following that is a lengthy presentation on the chronology and systematics, and finally, a discussion of long-term trends in settlement, demography, and subsistence adaptation. Unless otherwise indicated, chronology is discussed in terms of calendar years based on tree-ring-calibrated radiocarbon dates. To simplify the discussion, single values are generally used for radiocarbon dates rather than one- or two-sigma ranges. When individual dates are given, they represent the calibrated intercept rounded to the nearest 100 years. In the case of multiple intercepts, the intercept most central to the two-sigma range is used (see below). References to the chronological sequence of the American Bottom Archaic use the dates provided in this volume (chapter 11).

The Land

The term *southern Illinois* is sufficiently vague and inclusive that some clarification is required here. As a physiographic unit, the southern Illinois study area is framed by the convergence of major rivers—the Mississippi on the west and the lower Wabash and Ohio rivers to the east and south (Figure 16.1). The northern limit of "southernmost Illinois" is open to various interpretations, but since the northern margins of this area currently provide little information on the Archaic period other than surface survey data, a precise boundary is not an issue. The northern part of the study area as defined here consists of the Saline, Big Muddy, and Mary's River drainages as well as the lands south and east of the lower Kaskaskia River in Washington, St. Clair, and Randolph counties. This "northwest frontier" at the Kaskaskia River is quite arbitrary, but it has the advantage of preserving the American Bottom to the north as a single study unit for the purposes of this volume. To the east, the lower portions of the Little Wabash

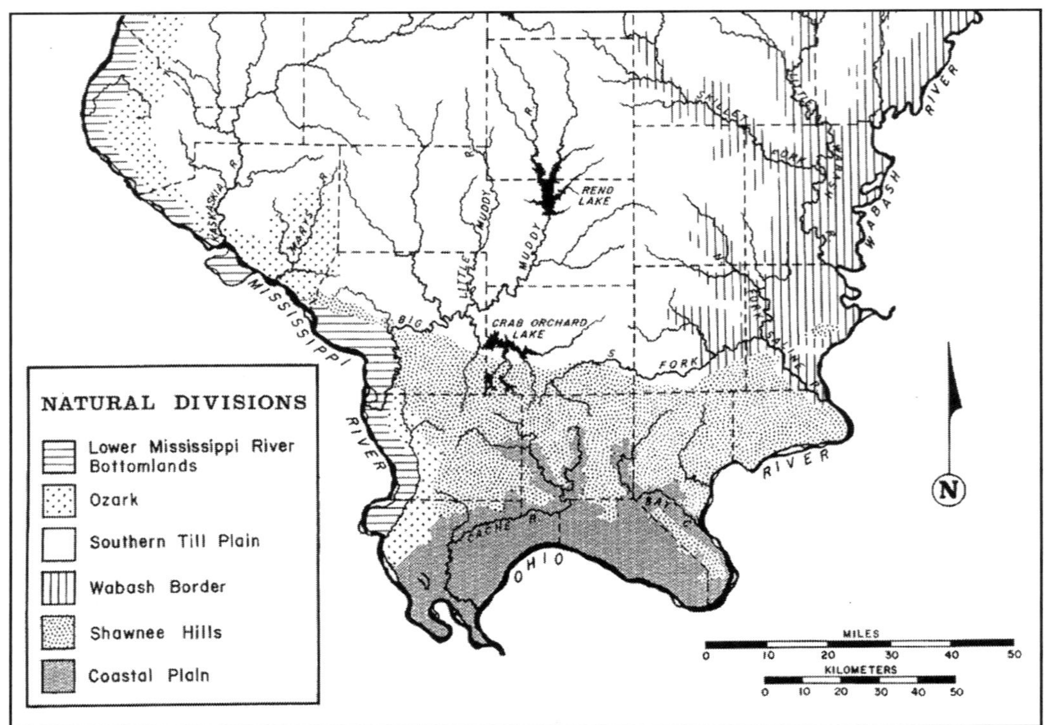

Figure 16.1. Map of southern Illinois showing physiographic divisions, county boundaries, and major drainages.

drainage and its Skillet Fork, about which little is known archaeologically, are excluded. In the rest of this chapter the term *southern Illinois* is used with this more restricted meaning. Given that other contributions to this volume deal with adjacent areas, my discussion will stray only occasionally outside the limits of southernmost Illinois. The lower Wabash Valley, which is better known archaeologically on its Indiana side, is discussed by Russell Stafford and Mark Cantin, although I include some discussion of the Riverton materials here. Western Kentucky, except for the immediate Ohio River corridor, is left to Richard Jefferies's presentation.

As defined here, the region encompasses portions of 19 counties and approximately 17,000 km^2. Within these boundaries the area can be described as consisting of a series of east–west physiographic zones bordered to the east, west, and south by major river valleys (see Harris et al. 1977). In the north it consists of the level to rolling, glaciated terrain of the Southern Till Plains drained by the Kaskaskia, Mary's, Big Muddy, and Saline rivers. Immediately south is a broad east–west band of highly dissected hill country consisting of the Shawnee Hills and the easternmost extension of the Ozark uplift. This area has extensive bedrock exposures, and rockshelters are plentiful in many localities. The bedrock exposures in many parts of the hill country abound in usable cherts.

South of the hill country is a feature of particular importance to hunter-gatherers—the Cache River-Bay Creek drainage, a former paleochannel of the Ohio River. It forms a broad alluvial corridor that extends all the way across southern Illinois, connecting the Ohio and Mississippi drainages (Figure 16.2). Until modern clearing and drainage efforts, it was an expanse of swampy timbered lowlands that contained shallow lakes and ponds. Separating the Cache River-Bay Creek drainage and the Ohio River to the south is a band of low, rolling uplands capped by unconsolidated deposits of Pliocene age bordered on the south by a series of Pleistocene terraces along the Ohio River.

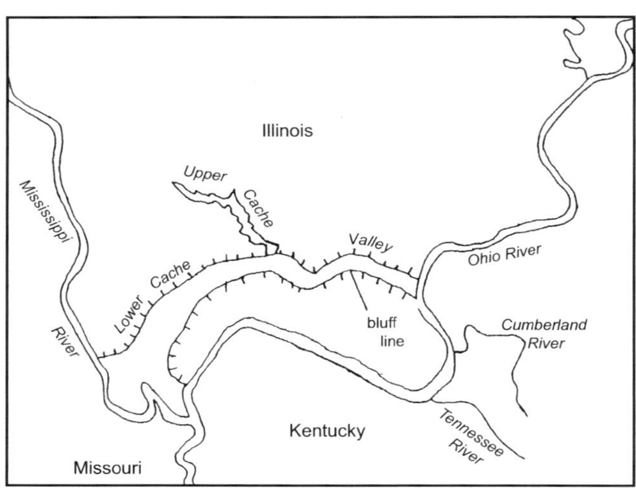

Figure 16.2. Schematic map of the Cache River valley (adapted from Graham 1985).

The lower Ohio River has been a relatively stable river system during the Holocene, with the active channel often abutted directly by uplands or high terraces, especially on the Illinois side. Until reaching the Thebes Gap, the Mississippi meanders (or meandered) within a broad but deeply entrenched valley flanked by markedly higher uplands. South of the gap, the uplands recede, and one is in the northernmost extremity of the Lower Mississippi Alluvial Valley. The Ohio-Mississippi River confluence area south of the Thebes Gap is a complex alluvial terrain additionally complicated by the western end of the Cache River valley.

The environmental conditions at the beginning of the Archaic period have not been documented in any detail in the region, but large-scale studies of pollen cores suggest that the region was generally covered by a mixed hardwood forest (Delcourt and Delcourt 1981, 1983). This inference is supported by small samples of botanical remains from Dalton and Early Archaic levels in local rockshelters (Cremin 1992; Parker 2000). The progressive expansion of grasslands in the early and middle Holocene, the formation of the Prairie Peninsula (Transeau 1935; Wright 1968), transformed the northern part of the study area into a mosaic of prairie and forest, with prairie becoming more expansive toward the north. Elsewhere, the region was always forested, even if the species composition varied somewhat from what exists today. Essentially modern environmental conditions and faunal distributions were reached at the beginning of the Late Archaic period around 3500 cal B.C.

Research History

The study area abounds in late prehistoric earthen mounds, which were usually the focus of early archaeological efforts (Thomas 1894), but it lacks the Archaic shell middens that so fascinated early excavators in the Green River valley of western Kentucky (Moore 1916). Thus, Archaic sites in the region were not investigated during the early period of mound exploration. The first systematic investigation of an Archaic site in the region was a part of the University of Chicago field program that operated in and around the Black Bottom of the Ohio River between 1934 and 1944 (Cole et al. 1951). Although primarily known for its investigation of the Kincaid site, the Chicago program actually sought to develop a complete cultural sequence in the locality. To that end, R. S. MacNeish excavated the prepottery Faulkner site, Mx^{v}-34 (Figure 16.3, No. 6). The site was located on the southern edge of the Pleistocene-age Brownfield Terrace, overlooking the interior of the Black Bottom. MacNeish (1948) defined a prepottery Faulkner focus from that work, a term that appears in the early literature of the midwestern Archaic (see also Cole et al. 1951:211–225). Today, archaeologists recognize that the site was a poor choice for defining a cultural

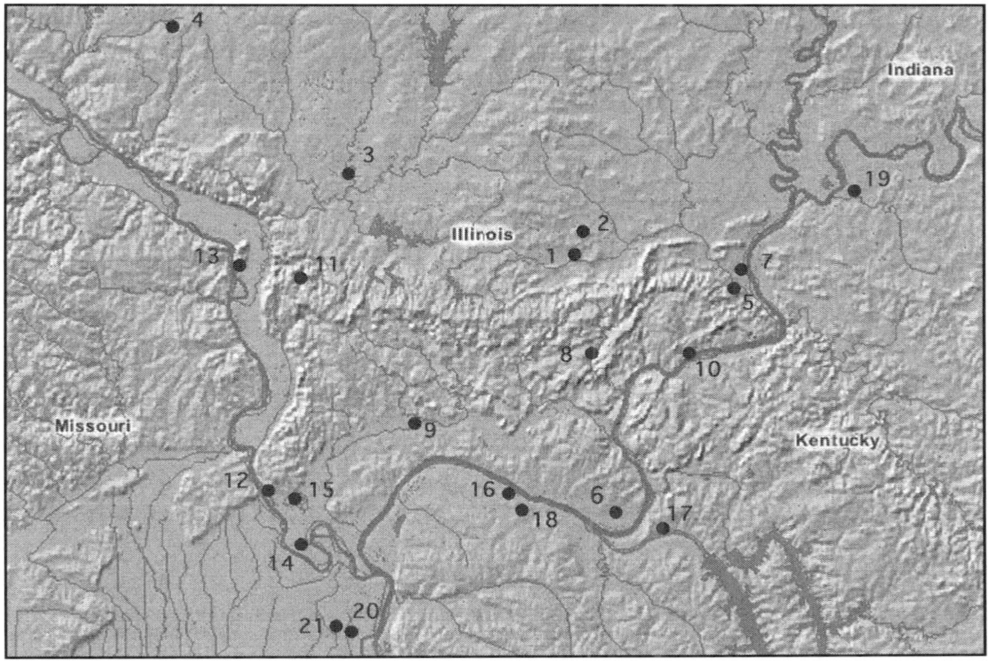

Figure 16.3. Locations of sites, localities, and projects discussed in the text: 1, Carrier Mills Project; 2, West Harrisburg Project; 3, Little Muddy Rock Shelter; 4, Diana; 5, Ferry; 6, Faulkner; 7, Fitzgibbons; 8, Hills Branch Rock Shelter; 9, 11JS321; 10, Rose Hotel; 11, Cave Creek Rockshelter; 12, Olive Branch; 13, Grand Tower Power Plant Project; 14, Dogtooth Bend; 15, Horseshoe Lake; 16, 15MCN20; 17, Morrisroe; 18, Hedden; 19, Highland Creek; 20, Burkett; 21, Weems.

or temporal unit, being poorly stratified and containing a mix of Archaic occupations as well as some younger components. But it was a start.

In the early 1950s professional attention on the Archaic was focused on the Mississippi Valley, where Melvin Fowler's Modoc Rock Shelter excavations were taking place in the southern American Bottom (Fowler 1959). In 1954, Fowler took a break from the Modoc excavations to excavate an unusual Ohio River site. The Ferry site (Fowler 1957; Muller 1986:68–70) was an eroded lithic scatter on a hilltop overlooking the Saline River just above its confluence with the Ohio (Figure 16.3, No. 5). The site was of interest because of the large number of atlatl weights that collectors had obtained from there, many of them elaborate forms. Excavation recovered a temporally mixed array of Archaic projectile points and chert tools, numerous grinding tools, and 22 atlatl-weight fragments. The high frequency still stands out as quite unusual, even 60 years later.

Howard Winters was an influential figure in Archaic-period research, and, although his formal publications were few, he left a major imprint on archaeology in Illinois (see Cantwell et al. 2004). During his tenure at the Southern Illinois University (SIUC) Museum from 1955 to 1960, Winters was strongly focused on the Archaic and directed a great deal of survey in the Cache River valley. Winters credited the Cache River Survey Project to his boss, J. Charles Kelley, a specialist in northern Mexico (Winters 1959:2), but there is little doubt that it was really Howard's project to execute. That survey recorded large numbers of sites in the Cache Valley and recovered large collections of hafted bifaces, which were studied to establish a typology. Winters also directed the 1958–59 Duran Rock Shelter (11U146) excavations in Union County (an early highway project) in the hope that the site would provide a stratified cultural sequence like Modoc. The site had some stratification but did not fulfill the expectation of a deep or cleanly stratified sequence. Winters left SIUC shortly thereafter, and only a brief description of the Duran excavations was prepared (Winters 1959). Winters never published the Cache survey work, although he refers to some of its results in his Wabash Valley study (Winters 1967). The importance of the southern Illinois survey in his experience is, however, reflected in the numerous projectile point types he defined with southern Illinois place names: Thebes, Belknap, Cache, Saratoga, Karnak, Tamms, and Cypress (Winters 1967). Although he collected a large body of descriptive and metric data on these types, Winters never published detailed descriptions of them, a situation that, through the years, has resulted in a great deal of latitude in their definition.

In 1960, Winters was hired by the Illinois State Museum to direct survey work in the Wabash Valley, a project that eventually resulted in a published monograph (Winters 1967). An outgrowth of the survey project was his excavation of three Late Archaic middens in the central Wabash Valley, from which he defined the Riverton culture (Winters 1969). His comprehensive monograph based on this work was very influential in North American archaeology and is still considered by many to be one of the best site reports ever done.

Since the onset of cultural resource management (CRM) based research in the 1970s, four projects in the region stand out for their contribution to Archaic-period research. The first is the Carrier Mills Project in the late 1970s (Jefferies and Butler 1982; Jefferies and Lynch 1983). The focus was a cluster of three intensively occupied sites situated on ridges around the edge of a relict lake system on the South Fork of the Saline River (Figure 16.3, No. 1). The Black Earth site (11SA87), especially Area A, with its rich, deep midden, numerous burials, and excellent bone preservation, was the centerpiece, but the adjacent 11SA88, also contributed importantly. The project provided a wealth of new data and a new understanding of the late Middle Archaic occupations of the region.

Less well known is the more recent West Harrisburg Project (Hargrave and Butler 1994a), which dealt with three sites on the Bankston Fork of the Saline River only 9 km northeast of the Carrier Mills Project (Figure 16.3, No. 2). These sites were generally comparable to site 11SA88 in the Carrier Mills District, with shallow midden accumulations and many intrusive Woodland pits. While lacking the depth and preservation of the Black Earth site, these three sites—Wasson No. 1 (11SA50), Funkhouser (11SA217), and Kottmeyer (11SA234)—represented the same occupation sequence as the Carrier Mills sites and provided both amplification of and contrasts with the Carrier Mills data.

The Diana site (11R331) is situated on the small interior drainage of Plum Creek, a southern tributary of the lower Kaskaskia River (Figure 16.3, No. 4). It is located near the northern boundary of this study unit and is presently the only major source of information on Archaic occupations from that area. The site consists of a series of shallow, plow-disturbed midden deposits along the margins of high ground overlooking the creek valley (Lopinot 1991a, 1991b). Radiocarbon dates and diagnostic artifacts document Middle and Late Archaic occupations ranging from around 4200 to 900 cal B.C.

Archaeological work in the region has involved the excavation of an appreciable number of rockshelters, but the one that stands out for its informational contribution is the Little Muddy Rock Shelter, (11J814; Moffat et al. 1992). This is a rare example of a rockshelter site in the till plains region. Located just north of Carbondale (Figure 16.3, No. 3), this site yielded a deep, stratified sequence extending back to Dalton times, but it is especially important for yielding a stratified series of Middle and Late Archaic deposits.

Landforms and the Archaeological Record

The Archaic period is abundantly represented in the region. Throughout the region Archaic sites occur predominantly as surface scatters on upland landforms, and midden accumulations are rare. Site file data from the 19 counties contained wholly or partially within the study area list 1,707 Archaic components, of which 1,095 (64 percent) are identified simply as "Archaic" (data from the Illinois site files, Illinois State Museum). The remaining 612 components are characterized as either Early, Middle, or Late Archaic. This high incidence of generic identification reflects, in part, the abundance of short-term occupations that left few diagnostic pieces and, in part, the recording of many sites during a time when little attention was paid in survey work to separating the Middle and Late Archaic subperiods.

Understanding the geological character of the archaeological record is especially important for the Archaic period. In particular, this involves a consideration of landform and evolving landscapes. The evolution of landscapes during the Holocene had profound implications for Archaic groups as it does today for the archaeologists who study them. In some cases, valley settings, in particular, geomorphological processes have substantially restricted the consultable site record. In the Till Plains, the major streams developed in what were formerly glacial lake basins. These streams typically have low-gradient, sinuous courses that meander through poorly drained valleys. Because of the poor drainage and frequent inundation, the valley bottoms and low terraces rarely yield prehistoric archaeological remains. Bedrock exposures are rare, except in the Mary's River drainage, and rockshelters are largely unknown, the previously mentioned Little Muddy Rock Shelter being a notable exception.

The hill country abounds in Archaic sites on upland ridges and slopes, and occupied rockshelters are common in many areas. In the valley bottoms and major floodplains, the Archaic-period record is more problematic. Upland valleys in southern Illinois, particularly in unglaciated areas, have filled dramatically during the Holocene. Coring studies in the upper Cache Valley have documented early Holocene surfaces in the 8,000-RCYBP range that are from 5.5 to over 8 m below the present surface (Graham 1985). The valley fill in smaller drainages is not so dramatic but is still sufficient to put many Archaic sites that existed in upland valley-floor settings beyond easy archaeological discovery.

The Cache River lowlands are an important feature of the study area. The Ohio River's capture of the lower Tennessee and Cumberland rivers and its abandonment of the Cache Valley is not well dated; it is generally thought to have been about the time of the Maumee Flood about 14,000 years ago (Esling et al. 1995), although some place the event somewhat later (Hughes 1987). Once the Ohio ceased to flow through the Cache corridor, the valley began to fill rapidly with sediment from local tributaries, creating a generally level surface on which the modern underfit drainages of the Cache River and Bay Creek developed. These small sinuous streams flow in opposite directions—the Cache River to the west, entering the Ohio (originally) just east of Horseshoe Lake, and Bay Creek to the east, joining the Ohio at Bay City. The higher ridges and sediment dams of the former Ohio River regime (essentially, the Henry Formation) remained above the fill, however. Thus, the ridges in the Cache lowlands have an extensive and abundant record of Paleoindian- and Archaic-period settlement, but those sites generally lack stratification.

As one would expect, Archaic-period sites are rarely found at or near the surface in the Mississippi floodplain. Channel meanders have doubtless erased a considerable portion of the record, but remnants of older Holocene depositional units survive within the floodplain, albeit with deeply buried surfaces. This segment of the valley has not received much geomorphological study, although recent work has occurred in the Jackson County bottoms (McDonald 1995; Snyder et al. 2002; Straffin and McGimsey 1995). Snyder et al. (2002:65–73) describe geomorphological transects in a remnant early- to mid-Holocene depositional unit just south of Fountain Bluff, excavated as part of archaeological work for the Grand Tower Power Plant (Figure 16.3, No. 13). Here, stable surfaces dating from 7800 to 5900 cal B.C. were found at depths of around 2.5 m. Although some indications of human settlement were found, none of these surfaces had a well-defined archaeological component. Some mid-Holocene occupation was documented higher in these deposits in a well-developed paleosol that extended upward to about 1.4 m below the present surface. Organic sediment dates on this paleosol range from 5300 to 4400 cal B.C. In the overlying alluvium, Late Archaic and Woodland cultural features were identified in near-surface contexts, apparently originating from the same general surface. One of these pit features, containing a Late Archaic Etley point, yielded a date of 2500 cal B.C. (Snyder et al. 2002:390–391).

The prevailing lack of Archaic sites on the surface of the Mississippi floodplain does not hold true in the Ohio-Mississippi River confluence area, where the evolution of floodplain features has been affected by the convergence of the Ohio River channel and the proximity of the mouth of the Cache Valley. In the older, north end of the Dogtooth Bend meander locality (Figure 16.3, No. 14), Middle Archaic sites have been found on the highest terrace remnant, and Late Archaic sites exist on the surface of several ridges to the south (Stephens 1995). To the east, adjacent to the late Holocene Cache River channel, is a relict meander scar of the Mississippi—Horseshoe Lake (Figure 16.3, No. 15)—where late Middle and Late Archaic sites exist on the surface around its margins and on the island in the middle of the lake (Cobb and Jefferies 1983; Koldehoff and Wagner 2002).

During the Holocene, the lower Ohio River has exhibited much greater channel stability than the Mississippi (Alexander 1974; Alexander and Prior 1968, 1971; see also Leach and Jackson 1987), although it, too, has migrated to one side or the other of its valley. To date, no deeply stratified sites have been identified along this portion of the Ohio River, although they must exist, and they obviously exist on the Tennessee River near its Ohio confluence (Nance 1986, 1987a). Within the study area, most of the alluvial floodplain is along the Kentucky side of the river, and the Illinois side is flanked largely by either bedrock uplands or remnant Pleistocene terraces. Only two large expanses of alluvial floodplain occur along the Illinois side of the river: the area between the mouths of the Wabash and Saline rivers (ca. 19 river miles) and the Black Bottom opposite Paducah, Kentucky (ca. 15 river miles).

Late Archaic sites are found on or near the surface of the Ohio River floodplain, but they are not common. Site 15MCN20 and the Highland Creek site (15UN127) are examples. Site 15MCN20 (Butler et al. 1981) is situated in sandy alluvial deposits one ridge inside the active bank (Figure 16.3, No. 16), whereas Highland Creek is located on an interior drainage within the floodplain but distant from the active channel (Figure 16.3, No. 19) (Maggard and Pollack 2000). The above examples are on the Kentucky side of the river, where alluvial surfaces are more plentiful. In the older interior portion of the Black Bottom, scattered Late Archaic materials have been found on the present surface, but no Archaic sites have been found in the outer band of the bottom, where only Late Woodland and Mississippian occupations are found at the surface. At the Kincaid mound center on Avery Lake, the earliest occupations on the underlying landforms are Early and Middle Woodland (Baumer), and these are overlain by alluvium and thick Mississippian deposits (Cole et al. 1951:184).

Upstream from the Black Bottom, survey and testing work on the Illinois side of the Smithland Pool identified Late Archaic components in relatively deep alluvial deposits adjacent to the current bank line (Ahler et al. 1980; Butler et al. 1979). Generally, these appear to be the downslope margins of habitation areas located further inland at lesser depths. Away from the riverbank, stratified Middle and Late Archaic deposits have been found at depths of between 50 cm and 1 m. Here the Fitzgibbons site (11G12) is worth noting (Figure 16.3, No. 7). Located on a prominent alluvial ridge of the Ohio River south of Shawneetown, the site was briefly investigated to repair damage caused by looting (Robison 1986). A rich late Middle Archaic midden with burials, dated to 4000 cal B.C., was found at the base of the site, buried under a meter of more recent alluvial and cultural deposits.

To summarize, the Archaic-period record in southern Illinois, and certainly its most informative excavated sites, derives primarily from upland and interior drainage contexts, which include numerous rockshelters. The southern part of the Saline River drainage has yielded some of the best information to date. The Mississippi and Ohio alluvial valleys are seriously underrepresented in the research and doubtless have great untapped research potential, but most of the sites there are buried and are not easily found or excavated.

Chronology and Systematics

The chronology and cultural systematics of the study area are not well developed, largely because of the scarcity of well-stratified or, at least, dated single-component contexts. A large portion of the most useful data derives from a small number of localities and projects. Thus, a set of defined phase units that apply to the region cannot be offered. Because of that, this discussion necessarily deals more with the specifics of individual dated sites and site groups. The framework presented is crude but consistent with the available data, although it may not agree in detail with chronological sequences developed in adjoining areas.

As a part of this review, an effort was made to compile all of the Archaic-period radiocarbon dates obtained from the study area since around 1980. Dates from geomorphology studies were not included. The undertaking produced a list of 76 radiocarbon dates from archaeological contexts, and these are listed in Table 16.1. Because of the difficulty of locating all of the relevant gray literature, the listing is not complete, but it includes the vast majority of available dates from the region. Dates were included regardless of whether they were thought by individual investigators to accurately date the specific contexts from which they were derived. The dates are grouped by subperiod but are otherwise grouped by site and, thus, are not listed in chronological order. All dates in Table 16.1 were either produced or recalibrated by Beta Analytic, Inc. Recalibration was required in the case of dates for which isotopic correction was not done or for which that information was not given in published sources. Beta Analytic, Inc., recalibrated those dates using the INTCAL98 calibration and an estimated value for the stable isotopes ratio (Stuiver et al. 1998; Talma and Vogel 1993). If calibration produced more than one date range, the one-sigma ranges given in the table represent the total spread all the ranges.

The calibrated intercepts of these dates are displayed graphically in Figure 16.4. The primary value of the figure is to show the temporal distribution of dated contexts for the Archaic period. The figure indicates continuous occupation of the region throughout the Archaic period. As expected, dates on the Early Archaic and early Middle Archaic are scarce, with only a trickle falling between 9000 and 5000 cal B.C. and only two in the 9000 to 7000 cal B.C. span. Dates become more numerous for the period beginning around 4500 cal B.C., the onset of the late Middle Archaic, a time marked by a major change in the character and visibility of settlements and by a corresponding increase in archaeological attention over earlier time spans. Generally speaking there is a solid distribution of dates between 4500 cal B.C. and about 2000 cal B.C. The last segment of the period, 1000 to 600 cal B.C., is also well represented by dates. The number of dates in the Late Archaic implies a better command of the cultural chronology than is really the case, as a significant number of those dates are not associated with a specific cultural component or with cultural diagnostics. Curiously, the 2000 to 1000 cal B.C. interval is poorly represented. This could reflect sampling error, but I suspect it has something to do with the archaeological visibility of occupations dating to that time. This result may reflect a reduced regional population or changes in settlement pattern or artifact styles such that components are less frequently identified and dated by archaeologists.

Table 16.1. Calibrated Radiocarbon Dates from Archaic Sites in Southernmost Illinois and Western Kentucky.

Lab No.	Site	Temporal Unit	B.P.	S.D.	Calibrated B.C. Range (1 sigma)	Reference
Beta 141573	Hills Branch,[a] PP508	E. Archaic	9130	200	8595 (8290) 8205	Wagner and Butler 2000
SFU 271	Morrisroe, 15LV156	E. Achaic Strat 4	8220[b]	100	7450 (7280,7230,7190) 7080	Nance 1987b
Beta 10477	Morrisroe, 15LV156	E. Archaic Strat 3 lw	7840[b]	100	6810 (6660) 6560	Nance 1986, 1987b
SFU 130	Morrisroe, 15LV156	E. Archaic Strat 3 lw	7530[b]	130	6480 (6410) 6230	Nance 1986, 1987b
SFU 29	Morrisroe, 15LV156	M. Archaic Strat 3	7450[b]	150	6440 (6360,6310,6260) 6180	Nance 1986, 1987b
Beta 10476	Morrisroe, 15LV156	M. Archaic Strat mid	6630[b]	110	5640 (5550) 5480	Nance 1986, 1987b
SFU 121	Morrisroe, 15LV156	M. Archaic Strat 3 up	7110[b]	250	6220 (5990) 5730	Nance 1986, 1987b
SFU 270	Morrisroe, 15LV156	M. Archaic Strat 3 up	7180[b]	130	6200 (6020) 5910	Nance 1986, 1987b
Beta 10474	Morrisroe, 15LV156	M. Archaic Strat 2	5580[b]	100	4500 (4380) 4340	Nance 1987b
Beta 10475	Morrisroe, 15LV156	M. Archaic Strat 2	6440	110	5490 (5450,5410,5390) 5310	Nance 1987b
Beta 20098	Little Muddy,[a] 11J814	E. or M. Archaic	7260	210	6380 (6080) 5910	Moffat 1992
Beta 20100	Little Muddy,[a] 11J814	M. Archaic	5480	60	4360 (4340) 4260	Moffat 1992
UGa 2703	Black Earth Area A, SA87	Middle Archaic	4860[b]	80	3700 (3650) 3540	Jefferies 1982
UGa 2710	Black Earth Area A, SA87	Middle Archaic	5060[b]	80	3960 (3920,3870,3810) 3760	Jefferies 1982
UGa 2704	Black Earth Area A, SA87	Middle Archaic	5680[b]	70	4580 (4500) 4450	Jefferies 1982
UGa 2705	Black Earth Area A, SA87	Middle Archaic	5640[b]	70	4530 (4460) 4370	Jefferies 1982
UGa 2706	Black Earth Area A, SA87	Middle Archaic	5900[b]	80	4830 (4760) 4700	Jefferies 1982
UGa 2707	Black Earth Area A, SA87	Middle Archaic	5540[b]	120	4480 (4360) 4260	Jefferies 1982
UGa 2708	Black Earth Area A, SA87	Middle Archaic	5560[b]	80	4460 (4360) 4340	Jefferies 1982
UGa 2709	Black Earth Area A, SA87	Middle Archaic	5280[b]	140	4320 (4050) 3960	Jefferies 1982
Beta 39621	Diana, 11R331	Middle Archaic	4870[b]	110	3760 (3650) 3530	Lopinot 1991a, 1991b
Beta 39622	Diana, 11R331	Middle Archaic	5110[b]	110	3990 (3950) 3780	Lopinot 1991a, 1991b
Beta 39623	Diana, 11R331	Middle Archaic	5060[b]	100	3970 (3920,3870,3810) 3710	Lopinot 1991a, 1991b
Beta 39624	Diana, 11R331	Middle Archaic	5350[b]	80	4320 (4230) 4050	Lopinot 1991a, 1991b
Beta 39626	Diana, 11R331	Middle Archaic	5150[b]	90	4040 (3960) 3810	Lopinot 1991a, 1991b
Beta 14783	Fitzgibbons, 11G12	Middle Archaic	5160	90	4040 (3970) 3810	Robison 1986

[a]Rockshelter.
[b]C13/C12 value estimated.
[c]Aux Vase phase.

Table 16.1. Calibrated Radiocarbon Dates from Archaic Sites in Southernmost Illinois and Western Kentucky, continued.

Lab No.	Site	Temporal Unit	B.P.	S.D.	Calibrated B.C. Range (1 sigma)	Reference
Beta 73400	Funkhouser, 11SA217	Middle Archaic	5440	70	4350 (4330) 4240	Stephens 1994
Beta 73401	Funkhouser, 11SA217	Middle Archaic	5170	70	4020 (3970) 3950	Stephens 1994
Beta 73405	Funkhouser, 11SA217	Middle Archaic	4910	80	3780 (3690) 3640	Stephens 1994
Beta 73406	Funkhouser, 11SA217	Middle Archaic	5090	130	4000 (3840,3850,3830) 3730	Stephens 1994
Beta 116925	Cave Creek,[a] 11J822	Middle Archaic	4990	80	3930 (3775) 2925	Butler and DelCastello 2000
Beta 22418	Little Muddy,[a] 11J814	Late Archaic I	4540[b]	150	3510 (3340) 3010	Moffat 1992
Beta 20099	Little Muddy,[a] 11J814	Late Archaic I	4440[b]	150	3360 (3090) 2900	Moffat 1992
Beta 22417	Little Muddy,[a] 11J814	Late Archaic II	3970[b]	90	2580 (2470) 2340	Moffat 1992
Beta 20097	Little Muddy,[a] 11J814	Late Archaic II	6410[b]	120	5480 (5370) 5290	Moffat 1992
Beta 20096	Little Muddy,[a] 11J814	Late Archaic II	6160[b]	200	5320 (5060) 4810	Moffat 1992
Beta 20095	Little Muddy,[a] 11J814	Late Archaic III	3670[b]	70	2140 (2030) 1940	Moffat 1992
Beta 20092	Little Muddy,[a] 11J814	Late Archaic[c]	3360[b]	80	1740 (1650) 1530	Moffat 1992
Beta 20094	Little Muddy,[a] 11J814	Late Archaic[c]	2990[b]	80	1380 (1250) 1100	Moffat 1992
UGa 2984	11SA86	Late Archaic	3790[b]	200	2480 (2210) 1940	Lynch and Jefferies 1982
Beta 39628	Diana, 11R331	Late Archaic	2750[b]	50	930 (900) 830	Lopinot 1991a, 1991b
Beta 39627	Diana, 11R331	Late Archaic	4700[b]	60	3620 (3510,3420,3390) 3370	Lopinot 1991a, 1991b
Beta 15271	Fitzgibbons, 11G12	Late Archaic	4160	90	2890 (2860,2810,2750,2720,2700) 2580	Robison 1986
Beta 73397	Wasson No. 1, 11SA50	Late Archaic	2690	140	980 (820) 780	Hargrave and Butler 1994
Beta 73398	Wasson No. 1, 11SA50	Late Archaic	3840	120	2470 (2290) 2130	Hargrave and Butler 1994
Beta 73399	Funkhouser, 11SA217	Late Archaic	4290	90	2930 (2900) 2780	Hargrave and Butler 1994
Beta 73408	Kottmeyer, 11SA234	Late Archaic	4020	80	2600 (2550,2540,2490) 2460	Hargrave and Butler 1994
Beta 73410	Kottmeyer, 11SA234	Late Archaic	4630	80	3510 (3360) 3340	Hargrave and Butler 1994
Beta 73411	Kottmeyer, 11SA234	Late Archaic	3690	90	2190 (2040) 1930	Hargrave and Butler 1994
Beta 116924	Cave Creek,[a] 11J822	Late Archaic	4440	70	3310 (3070) 2925	DelCastello and Butler 1998
Beta 177170	Kerr C'yon # 10,[a] 11U128	Late Archaic	4500	40	3340 (3320,3220,3120) 3100	Koldehoff et al. 2003
Beta 134856	11JS321	Late Archaic	2710	60	910 (835) 810	DelCastello and Butler 2000

[a]Rockshelter.
[b]C13/C12 value estimated.
[c]Aux Vase phase.

Table 16.1. Calibrated Radiocarbon Dates from Archaic Sites in Southernmost Illinois and Western Kentucky, continued.

Lab No.	Site	Temporal Unit	B.P.	S.D.	Calibrated B.C. Range (1 sigma)	Reference
Beta 134229	Highland Creek, 15UN127	Late Archaic	4580[b]	80	3500 (3360) 3120	Maggard and Pollack 2000
Beta 134230	Highland Creek, 15UN127	Late Archaic	4380[b]	70	3090 (3000,2980,2940) 2900	Maggard and Pollack 2000
Beta 134231	Highland Creek, 15UN127	Late Archaic	4470[b]	80	3350 (3100) 3010	Maggard and Pollack 2000
Beta 134232	Highland Creek, 15UN127	Late Archaic	4440[b]	70	3330 (3090) 2930	Maggard and Pollack 2000
Beta 134233	Highland Creek, 15UN127	Late Archaic	4130[b]	70	2870 (2850,2820,2670) 2580	Maggard and Pollack 2000
Beta 134234	Highland Creek, 15UN127	Late Archaic	4310[b]	70	3000 (2900) 2880	Maggard and Pollack 2000
Beta 141782	Case, 11G190	Late Archaic	3820	60	2340 (2280) 2150	Titus et al. 2001
Beta 152611	Case, 11G190	Late Archaic	3900[b]	70	2470 (2430) 2290	Titus et al. 2001
Beta 93733	Hedden, 15MCN81	Late Archaic	4420[b]	60	3270 (3030) 2920	Rossen 2000
Beta 93734	Hedden, 15MCN81	Late Archaic	4520[b]	50	3350 (3340,3200) 3100	Rossen 2000
Beta 93738	Hedden, 15MCN81	Late Archaic	4030[b]	50	2590 (2570,2520,2500) 2480	Rossen 2000
Beta 93735	Hedden, 15MCN81	Late Archaic	4300[b]	60	2920 (2900) 2880	Rossen 2000
Beta 93737	Hedden, 15MCN81	Late Archaic	5130[b]	50	3980 (3960) 3820	Rossen 2000
Beta 93736	Hedden, 15MCN81	Late Archaic	3850[b]	50	2130 (2300) 2210	Rossen 2000
Beta154027	Ameren 1, 11J1148	Late Archaic	2810	60	1020 (940) 900	Snyder et al. 2002
Beta154028	Ameren 1, 11J1148	Late Archaic	2720	40	900 (840) 820	Snyder et al. 2002
Beta154029	Ameren 1, 11J1148	Late Archaic	2870	130	1410 (1020) 800	Snyder et al. 2002
Beta154030	Ameren 1, 11J1148	Late Archaic	3190	60	1520 (1440) 1410	Snyder et al. 2002
Beta154031	Ameren 1, 11J1148	Late Archaic	2480	70	780 (760,680,550) 400	Snyder et al. 2002
Beta154032	Ameren 1, 11J1148	Late Archaic	2710	120	990 (830) 790	Snyder et al. 2002
Beta154033	Ameren 1, 11J1148	Late Archaic	2570	60	800 (830) 770	Snyder et al. 2002
Beta154034	Ameren 1, 11J1148	Late Archaic	2490	60	780 (760,640,560) 430	Snyder et al. 2002
Beta154037	Ameren 2, 11J1149	Late Archaic	2910	40	1140 (1100) 1020	Snyder et al. 2002
Beta154465	Hileman, 11J1150	Late Archaic	3980	70	2580 (2480) 2450	Snyder et al. 2002

[a]Rockshelter.
[b]C13/C12 value estimated.
[c]Aux Vase phase.

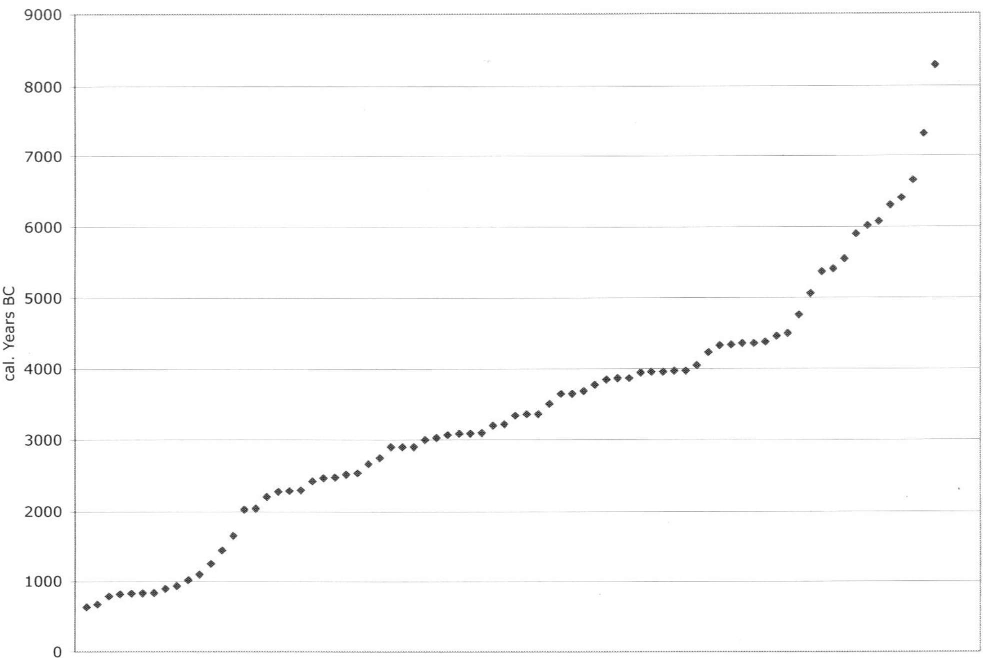

Figure 16.4. Intercepts (cal years B.C.) for 76 Archaic radiocarbon dates from southern Illinois and western Kentucky.

Dalton (ca. 10,000 to 9200 cal B.C.)

Many researchers feel that Dalton should be considered the beginning expression of the Archaic period even though its principal diagnostic tools show a clear legacy from older Paleoindian forms. The Dalton culture is discussed in greater detail in this volume by Koldehoff and Walthall (see also Koldehoff and Walthall 2004), and I make only a few comments here. Dalton occupations are well represented in the study area, both in surface finds and from the basal levels of rockshelters. To date, the rockshelter occurrences are Dalton tools either found in mixed stratigraphic contexts or from deep levels where excavation yielded only minimal remains. Hills Branch Rock Shelter (11PP508) in the eastern Shawnee Hills (Wagner and Butler 2000) and the Little Muddy Rock Shelter (11J814) in the Till Plains north of Carbondale (Koldehoff 1992:319–320) are two examples, but there are others. A genuine concentration of Dalton settlement appears to have occurred in the uplands immediately adjacent to the Mississippi River around the Thebes Gap in Alexander and Union counties (Webb et al. 1989:138–142), and this appears to be one aspect of a regionwide tethering of Dalton occupations to the Mississippi River in the central Mississippi Valley corridor (Koldehoff and Walthall 2004:60–65).

The Thebes Gap is also the location of the spectacular but poorly understood Olive Branch site, 11AX267 (Gramly 2002), an intensively occupied settlement on a small bedrock spur at the base of a bluff just a short distance from the bank of the Mississippi River (Figure 16.3, No. 12). This is also the only carbon-dated Dalton occupation in the study area. Of the site's seven dates, three fall within the Late Archaic or Early Woodland periods, and three others fall between 8000 to 8500 cal B.C. and, thus, are too recent for the Dalton occupation. Only one sample, taken from near the base of the deposit, yielded an appropriate age: 9975 ± 125 RCYBP (AA 4805) (Gramly 2002:72). A calibrated date is not given in the site report, but the application of CALIB 4.3 suggests that the intercepts should fall between 9300 and 9400 cal B.C.

Early Archaic (ca. 9200 to 6500 cal B.C.)

The Early Archaic is defined here as beginning with the post-Dalton era. In the study area, there are few well-dated contexts for the Early Archaic period, but given the representation of point styles locally, I rely heavily on the chronological framework developed in the Ohio River valley and Midsouth (Anderson et al. 1996; Broyles 1971; Chapman 1977, 1985; Driskell 1994; Nance 1978b), especially as recently summarized by Sherwood et al. (2004:542–550) for Dust Cave in northwest Alabama. The temporal boundary between the Early and Middle Archaic periods is, to my mind, not well fixed. The threshold used here (6500 cal B.C.) largely reflects the systematics of the Middle Archaic in the Midsouth; it is not based on any firm chronostratigraphic data from southern Illinois.

The Early Archaic in the study area is well documented only in survey data. The settlement record is one of numerous but scanty components generally yielding only a few diagnostics and little associated debris, most often comingled with later artifacts. Chert assemblages are characterized by a high diversity of raw materials and a high frequency of items made from cherts not available in the immediate vicinity (Butler 1983). The pattern is one of classic foraging (see Brown and Vierra 1983; Stafford 1994). Rockshelter occupations are common, but to date, the materials have most often been found in mixed contexts rather than cleanly stratified deposits. The region currently lacks the rich body of stratified data on the Early Archaic that has been developed elsewhere in the Ohio River valley (see Stafford and Cantin as well as Jefferies, this volume).

For those who want to see the Early Archaic period resolved into discrete temporal units characterized primarily by single projectile point styles, this discussion will provide little satisfaction. A basic projectile point sequence can be stipulated, but with the current data, judging the extent of overlap in certain point styles is difficult, and differences may also exist between the Ohio River drainage and areas to the north. The sequence of major Early Archaic point types and type clusters recognized in the area is as follows: Early Side Notched, Thebes/St. Charles, Kirk Corner Notched, bifurcate points (chiefly LeCroy), and, finally, Kirk Stemmed and large side-notched forms (Graham Cave). Additional types, such as the Hardin Barbed and Agate Basin, occur in smaller numbers.

As other authors in this volume demonstrate, side-notched points are the real bane of an orderly projectile-point-based chronology for the Archaic. The chronology of such points has long been confusing because of their great longevity and their apparent disappearance and reappearance at various points in time in the Early and Middle Archaic. The Early Side Notched cluster—part of Justice's (1987) Large Side Notched cluster—is represented in the area, especially along the Ohio River, where specimens are generally typed as Big Sandy (DelCastello and Butler 1999:190). In the Tennessee Valley the Big Sandy type was originally defined as a Middle Archaic point style, but later work at Stanfield-Worley (DeJarnette et al. 1962) showed that a basally ground side-notched point form was nearly contemporaneous with Daltons. The problem was resolved by splitting the Big Sandy type into two forms—an Early Archaic Big Sandy I and a Middle Archaic Big Sandy II (Cambron and Hulse 1964:A-10, A-11). O'Brien and Wood (1998:139–143) have described the confused chronology of side-notched forms in Missouri, where the small Cache River points (an Arkansas type name not used in Illinois) were contemporaneous with the early Big Sandy, with the Graham Cave point, which does occur in southern Illinois, falling later in the period. Radiocarbon dates from Dust Cave suggest that the Early Side Notched points immediately postdate the Dalton/Quad/Beaver Lake component at around 9300 cal B.C. (Sherwood et al. 2004:546–547).

Comparable early forms are present in southern Illinois, but they are underrecognized in the study area because of confusion with the later side-notched forms. The Graham Cave form is not directly dated in the study area, but if it follows the Missouri pattern, it comes later in the Early Archaic and extends into the early Middle Archaic. The Thebes/St. Charles point cluster is common in southern Illinois but currently undated. It should co-occur to some extent with both the Early Side Notched and the later Kirk Corner Notched clusters.

One component of the Kirk Corner Notched horizon (8500–7800 cal B.C.) was excavated in a tiny rockshelter in the upper Bay Creek drainage in the eastern Shawnee Hills, the Hills Branch Rock Shelter (11PP508; Wagner and Butler 2000) (Figure 16.3, No. 8). Here the basal cultural deposit was a deflated layer that yielded a Dalton point and Dalton blades, a Beaver Lake point, and a Greenbrier point (Figure 16.5a–d), but it was dominated by a Kirk Corner Notched component (Figure 16.6). Wood charcoal from the layer yielded a very acceptable date of 9130 ± 200 B.P. or ca. 8300 cal B.C. (Beta 141573). The assemblage also included one example of a "large Kirk Variant" (Figure 16.5e), a type that is considered to be a younger form, closer in age to the Kirk Stemmed (DelCastello 2000:88, 92; French 1998). Other early diagnostics found at this site, but not in appropriate contexts, included Hardin Barbed (Figure 16.5f), LeCroy (Figure 16.7a), St. Charles, and Kirk Stemmed (Figure 16.8e) points. Howard

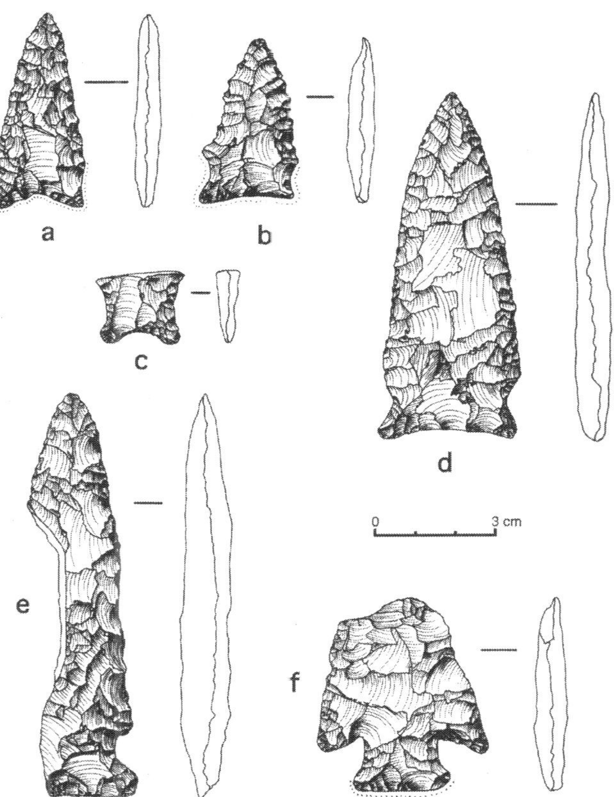

Figure 16.5. Dalton cluster and Early Archaic points from the Hills Branch Rock Shelter: a, b, Dalton; c, Beaver Lake; d, Greenbrier; e, Kirk Corner Notched, large variety; f, Hardin Barbed (adapted from DelCastello 2000).

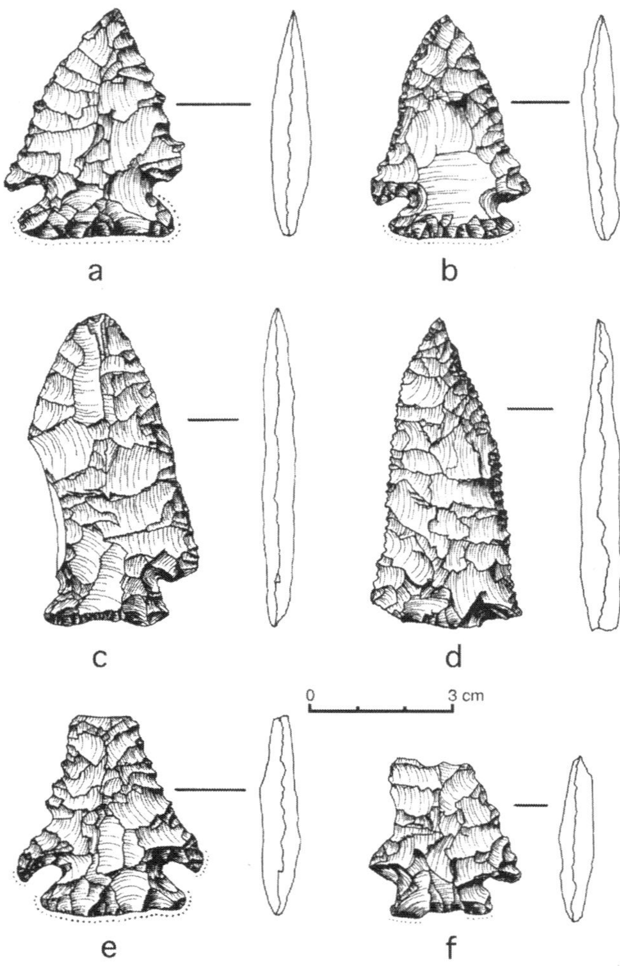

Figure 16.6. Kirk Corner Notched points from the Hills Branch Rock Shelter (adapted from DelCastello 2000).

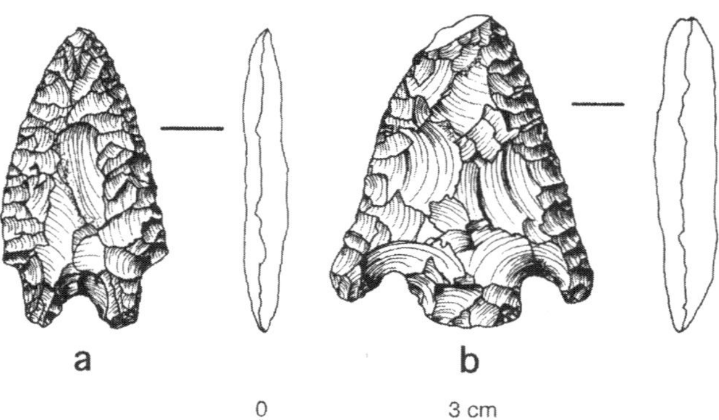

Figure 16.7. LeCroy and Eva/Morrow Mountain points from the Hills Branch Rock Shelter (adapted from DelCastello 2000).

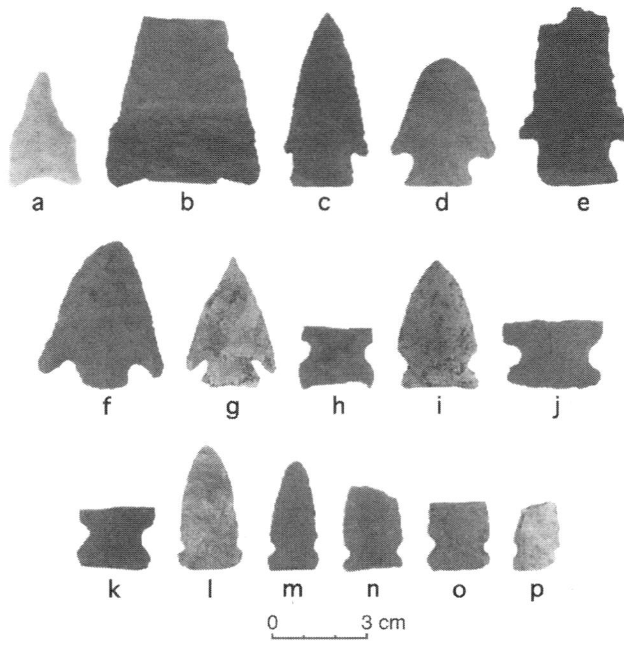

Figure 16.8. Early and Middle Archaic points from the Kottmeyer site: a, Dalton; b, Thebes Corner Notched; c, d, Hardin Barbed; e, Kirk Stemmed; f, Eva/Morrow Mountain; g, Barbee Corner Notched; h–k, Godar; l–p, Matanzas (adapted from Stephens 1994).

Winters (1967:19) defined the Barbee Corner Notched, a seldom-used type that appears to be a Kirk variant (Figure 16.8g). The Decatur point, a technologically distinctive Kirk variant with a burinated base (Cambron and Hulse 1964:A-31; Justice 1987:81–82) has a rare but persistent occurrence in the area. This point has been securely dated largely in the Little Tennessee Valley (Chapman 1977:48–49, 1985) in contexts that would place it locally with the more abundant Kirk Corner Notched materials.

Bifurcated points are relatively rare but occur widely, and they are most often typed as LeCroy (DelCastello and Butler 2000:93–94). At Dust Cave the LeCroy and Kanawha forms date from 7800 to 6600 cal B.C. (Sherwood et al. 2004:546). Whether the same sequence of bifurcated forms that is documented elsewhere (Broyles 1971; Chapman 1977) occurs locally is not clear, but without stratified and dated contexts, there is no incentive to subdivide these forms. Typologically, local points (Figure 16.7a) generally seem to fit the LeCroy definition, but they often lack serrations, a relatively common feature of Midsouth specimens. Occasional examples of the later Kanawha (Broyles 1971) and Stanly points (Coe 1964) are found (Nance 1986; Pulcher 1977:164–165), but they have rarely been identified as such. In the Midsouth, the youngest bifurcate form (Stanly) is usually considered early Middle Archaic.

The only excavated example of a buried Early Archaic component in a large floodplain setting is the Morrisroe site (15LV156; Figure 16.3, No. 17) at the edge of the study area. The site (also discussed by Jefferies, this volume) is located on the lower Tennessee River near its confluence with the Ohio (Nance 1986, 1987a, 1987b). Here, a cutbank exposure revealed a series of buried Archaic strata. The Early Archaic stratum (Morrisroe 4) represents considerable time depth, yielding both Kirk Corner Notched and Kirk Stemmed/Serrated forms as well as a lone Stanly, but the Kirk Stemmed forms were predominant. The investigator concluded that the layer primarily represented the end of the Early Archaic period. The 7300 cal B.C. date from the layer (Nance 1986:42) is early for the Kirk Stemmed, according to Midsouth chronology (ca. 6900–6300 cal B.C.) but may be acceptable, as the chronological relationship between the later bifurcate forms and Kirk Stemmed/Serrated forms is not established locally.

Large side-notched points (Graham Cave or an equivalent) are not directly dated in southern Illinois, but they seem to have appeared toward the end of the Early Archaic and may co-occur with the Kirk Stemmed points in contexts dating to the end of the Early Archaic sequence. As noted earlier, the temporal boundary between Early and Middle Archaic is not clearly fixed in this region. Indeed, in the Midsouth, the Kirk Stemmed/Serrated forms are considered by some to be Middle Archaic (Sherwood et al. 2004:548). A later threshold for Middle Archaic (6500 cal B.C.) is used here, but the distinction is not one of consequence.

The "intrusive" western and northern styles of the Early Archaic include the Agate Basin (or a younger look-alike) and the Hardin Barbed, both of which are associated elsewhere with groups inhabiting areas dominated by grasslands (O'Brien and Wood 1998:86–89, 125–128). O'Brien and Wood (1998:117–120) assert that most of the Agate Basin points reported east of the Plains are actually younger forms, but researchers disagree as to the proper chronology of these forms in Missouri (see Ray et al., this volume). The Agate Basin (or younger look-alike) specimens are extremely rare in this region, and none have been found in dated contexts. Over the years, I have seen a few in private collections, mostly from the western half of the area and made from exotic cherts. A broken specimen was recovered from the Dalton deposits at the Olive Branch site (Gramly 2002:208–209). Given that these points are so rare and almost always made of cherts from distant sources, it seems reasonable to conclude that these are trade pieces.

Hardin Barbed points (Figures 16.5f and 16.8c, d) (Luchterhand 1970) are much more common in the region and occur throughout the entire study area, although never in large numbers and none, so far, in dated contexts. These are frequently made of nonlocal cherts but not invariably so. Projected dates for the Hardin vary widely (see Justice 1987). O'Brien and Wood (1998:128) date these to the time span immediately following the Dalton horizon; if that is correct, the points would have been contemporaneous with Early Side Notched points and probably St. Charles/Thebes-cluster points. At least two examples were recovered from the Dalton deposits at Olive Branch, where they appeared to be intrusive (Gramly 2002:180–181).

Middle Archaic (ca. 6500 to 3000 cal B.C.)

Early Middle Archaic (6500 to 4500 cal B.C.)

The early Middle Archaic in the area is as murky and ill defined as much of the Early Archaic, lacking, for the most part, stratified and dated contexts. The Early Archaic stratum at the Little Muddy Rock Shelter yielded a Dalton and a Thebes point, but the radiocarbon date obtained from the upper part of the layer is early Middle Archaic (6100 cal B.C.) (Moffat 1992:100, 102, 108), and, indeed, the investigators regarded the date as marking the end of the Early Archaic occupation. Brown and Vierra (1983) suggest that the shift to more logistically based settlement patterns began in the Illinois Valley somewhat before 6000 cal B.C.; increased emphasis on nut harvesting also began at about the same time. Sometime in this interval, new ground-stone tool forms also appeared—grooved axes and atlatl weights. To date, however, major sites comparable to the early Middle Archaic Horizon 8 sequence at Koster (ca. 5700–5800 cal B.C.) (Wiant et al. 1983) have not been identified in this region.

Typologically, the early Middle Archaic is marked by a variety of side-notched and undefined expanding-stemmed forms that have yet to be adequately dated. Side-notched points appear to have been present for much of the Middle Archaic, with the larger forms, such as Graham Cave, present at the beginning but evolving into the Godar and Matanzas forms that dominated the late Middle Archaic.

In the Ohio River drainage, Eva/Morrow Mountain (Figures 16.7b and 16.8f) and Cypress Creek points occur, types more at home in the lower Tennessee Valley. At Morrisroe, the early Middle Archaic stratum (Morrisroe 3 upper and lower) yielded primarily Eva II and Cypress Creek I points, here referring to the lower Tennessee Valley typology (Lewis and Kneberg 1959; Lewis and Lewis 1961). The Cypress Creek points decreased in frequency from lower to upper levels, whereas the Eva/Morrow Mountain points increased. Also present in these strata were some less distinctive "stemmed-barbed points" (Nance 1986). The Morrisroe 3 carbon dates accord reasonably well with the 6300 to 5400 cal B.C. range for the Eva/Morrow Mountain component at Dust Cave (Sherwood et al. 2004).

Some medium- to large-sized straight- and expanding-stem points also seem to belong in this interval, although there are no broadly recognized type names for these forms. These stemmed points are better known in areas adjacent to southern Illinois. As noted above, the Morrisroe 3 stratum yielded stemmed points in association with Eva and Cypress Creek points (Nance 1986). The previously noted Ferry site (Hardin County) predominantly yielded medium-sized expanding-stem points (Fowler 1957:10–13). These are undated, but the character of the other artifacts recovered from the site suggests that they are probably early Middle Archaic. In the southern American Bottom (Monroe County), Walz et al. (1998) proposed the Dennis Hollow phase (5700 to 5500 cal B.C.), an early Middle Archaic unit that is characterized by large, strongly shouldered expanding-stemmed points called "Valmeyer Corner Notched." The Rose Hotel site on the Ohio yielded two similar points from Middle Archaic contexts (DelCastello and Butler 1999:192), although these artifacts are also not directly dated.

Although later side-notched forms are common in the lower Tennessee Valley (Lewis and Kneberg's [1959] Big Sandy phase), the Sykes/White and Benton point clusters that so dominate the middle and lower Tennessee Valley and adjacent areas of the Southeast (see Meeks 2000), are extremely rare along the lower Ohio River. Over the years, I have noted only a handful of surface-collected examples that could possibly be placed in these types.

Late Middle Archaic (ca. 4500 to 3500 cal B.C.)

This period witnessed a striking expansion in settlement aggregation and settlement intensity, with the first appearance of large, intensively occupied, long-term base camps that began to resemble, at least for some intervals, sedentary settlements. These sites provide the earliest contexts with good preservation, abundant floral and faunal materials, and numerous burials. The chert utilization reflects an increasing familiarity with the available resources and a marked localization in the use of raw materials, which resulted in decreased diversity of the cherts used for tools (Butler 1983).

Present understanding of the period comes largely from the Carrier Mills sites in the Saline River valley. The Black Earth site (11SA87), especially Area A, where a meter of cultural deposits accumulated on a ridgetop in about a millennium, is especially impressive (Jefferies and Butler 1982; Jefferies and Lynch 1983). This period is also well represented in rockshelters, which also seem to have experienced an upsurge in the intensity of use.

Good suites of radiocarbon dates are available from the Carrier Mills sites, the West Harrisburg Project (Hargrave and Butler 1994a), and the Diana site (11R331) at the northern edge of the study area (Lopinot 1991a, 1991b) as are useful individual dates from several rockshelters. The 11SA87 Area A chronology is the primary basis for defining the temporal limits of the late Middle Archaic period in the study area. Midden accumulation began there around 4500 cal B.C. and ended sometime after 3700 cal B.C. (Jefferies 1982a:102, dates recalibrated). The suite includes an earlier date of 4800 cal B.C., but it is stratigraphically out of sequence and not considered reliable. Dates from the West Harrisburg Project and other sites (see Hargrave and Butler 1994b:195–203) suggest that the terminal date for this unit should be set at around 3500 cal B.C.

Stylistically, the southern Illinois sites, as well as others like the Bluegrass site in southwest Indiana (Stafford et al. 2000), strongly resemble the Horizon 6 occupations at the Koster site, which Cook (1976) described as the Helton phase. All of these sites represent a well-defined regional cultural tradition present in the lower Ohio Valley and southern Illinois as well as the lower Illinois Valley and eastern margins of Missouri. This regional culture is also defined by the presence of a variety of elaborately engraved bone pins, whose similarities suggest an active exchange network and a considerable degree of social connectedness over a large area (Jefferies 1995, 1996, 1997; White 2003). The similarities among these various assemblages are undeniable, but whether the sites in deep southern Illinois belong in the same phase construct as Illinois Valley sites is less clear.

Typologically, the late Middle Archaic is dominated by side-notched forms of the Godar (Figure 16.8h–k) and Matanzas (Figure 16.8l–p) types, with Godar having earlier origins (Cook 1976; also Justice 1987). These points were frequently reworked into hafted end scrapers, which often dominate tool assemblages (Jefferies 1990). Although these side-notched points are predominant, small numbers of other forms are present, at least in materials from the later part of the interval.

The chief minority point type is the Karnak (Cook 1976; May 1982; Winters 1967:25), a thick, narrow-stemmed point with steep retouch and weakly defined shoulders (Figures 16.9 d–f and 16.10c, the latter a classic specimen). In southern Illinois the Karnak exhibits slight shoulders and a straight stem, but Cook applied the type to a virtually stemless point found in Illinois Valley sites. In southern Illinois the Karnak persisted into the early part of the Late Archaic (Koldehoff 1992:324–325). At Area A of the Black Earth site, so-called early Karnaks comprised only 1.4 percent of the Middle Archaic hafted bifaces (Jefferies 1982a:211), although the typological basis for the separation from "Late Archaic" specimens is questionable. Given the stratigraphic distribution of Karnaks, their true frequency in late Middle Archaic deposits is more likely around 3 percent. The production and discard circumstances at this long-term base camp probably resulted in the Karnak's understated importance in the tool inventory.

At Koster, Cook (1976) described three other stemmed and notched points as minority members of the Helton complement: Helton, Apple Blossom Stemmed, and Brannon Side Notched. Although comparable points have not been documented in unambiguous late Middle Archaic contexts in southern Illinois, they may well exist as minority forms.

Late Archaic (ca. 3500 to 600 cal B.C.)

The beginning of the Late Archaic is defined by the end of the intensively occupied Late Middle Archaic settlements (middens) in the Saline Valley. That date is an approximation and may need to be revised as more detailed information is obtained. Given the present state of knowledge, the Late Archaic of southern Illinois could be appropriately described as the "good gray culture." Although the Late Archaic is often the most frequently represented time period in terms of identified components in large survey compilations, the period has not

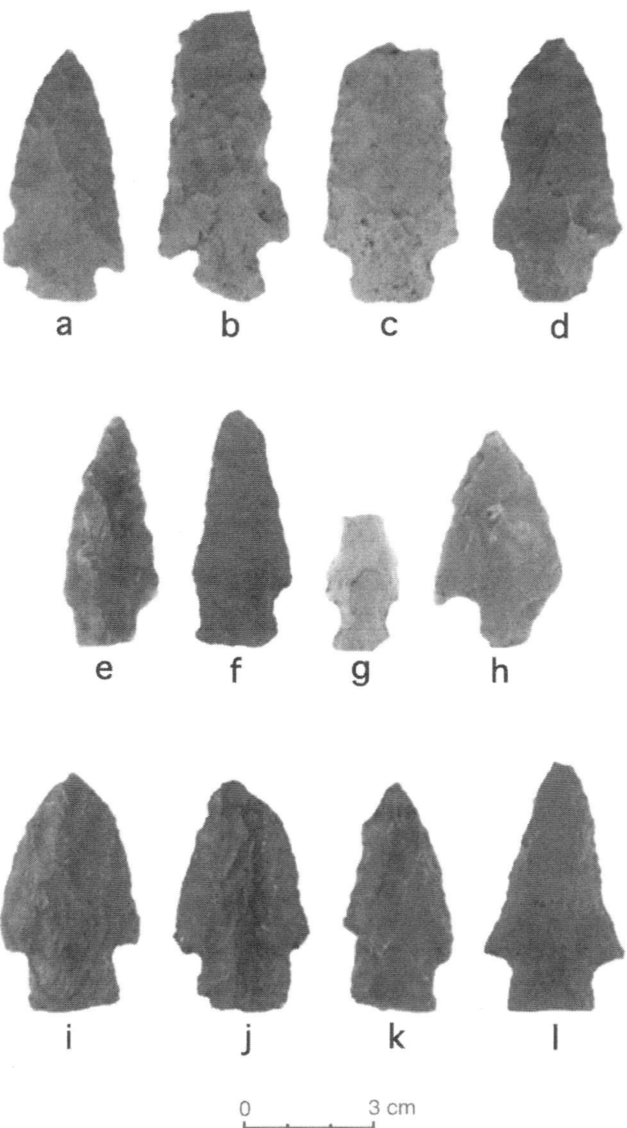

Figure 16.9. Late Archaic points from the Kottmeyer site: a–c, Etley and Etley-like; d–f, Karnak Stemmed; g, h, untyped points; i–l, Saratoga (adapted from Stephens 1994).

received intensive study. The Late Archaic period witnessed a return to a more even distribution of settlement over the landscape and fewer intensively occupied sites. Chert source exploitation was localized but not as strongly as in the late Middle Archaic, and a high diversity of resources with minor and often poor raw materials was used. Some of the increased diversity in raw material use may be a result of increased local exchange (Butler 1983).

Late Archaic occupation is abundantly represented at both Carrier Mills and the West Harrisburg sites, but the deposits show little stratification and are heavily mixed with both older and younger materials. A similar situation prevails at the Rose Hotel site (11HN116), perched on a bedrock lobe at the edge of the Ohio River (Wagner and Butler 1999) (Figure 16.3, No. 10). Here, a thin Middle and Late Archaic midden lies below an intensive Middle Woodland occupation. Recent work across the river in Kentucky has provided data from two largely single-component Late Archaic sites, Highland Creek in the Ohio floodplain near the Wabash confluence (15UN127; Maggard and Pollack 2000) and Hedden (15MCN81) (Figure 16.3, No. 18) in the Ohio floodplain west of Paducah, although in the latter case only the botanical and radiocarbon data have been reported (Rossen 2000).

Recent research in and around the American Bottom has provided a detailed Late Archaic phase sequence (McElrath et al. 1984; see McElrath et al., this volume). That sequence cannot yet be matched in southern Illinois, although the available data suggest substantial parallels.

Typologically, the local Late Archaic sequence is characterized primarily by stemmed rather than notched projectile points. The straight-stemmed Saratoga points dominate the early and middle sequence, and the Karnak is a minority form. There is also apparently some carryover of the side-notched Matanzas point. The large but less common Etley, Ledbetter, and Pickwick forms appear midsequence, perhaps as early as 3000 cal B.C. along the Ohio River, but these forms seem to be later in the northern part of the region. The latter two types reflect a broad horizon style more at home in the Midsouth. Sometime after 2000 cal B.C., a Riverton-like suite of small stemmed and notched forms appeared in the area as part of a broad horizon style in the southern Midwest. Whether they

Figure 16.10. Late Archaic points from the Hills Branch Rock Shelter: a, b, Saratoga; c, Karnak Stemmed; d, e, Cypress Straight Stemmed; f, Motley; g, Wade/Buck Creek Barbed (adapted from DelCastello 2000).

displaced other point styles as a unit or were merely added to the local complement is not clear. In the latter half of the period, Saratoga points "morphed" into slightly smaller stemmed forms with strongly developed shoulders and barbs (Justice's [1987] Terminal Archaic Barbed cluster). Contracting-stemmed (Cypress) and barbed points (Wade, Buck Creek Barbed, and Motley) came to dominate and persisted into the local Woodland sequence. No major shift in point styles is associated with the Late Archaic to Early Woodland transition, although some temporally useful form distinctions may be exhibited by the contracting-stemmed points.

The only useful stratigraphic sequence from the region is from the Little Muddy Rock Shelter (Moffat et al. 1992), and that sequence is used here as a basis for discussion. Work at Little Muddy identified five Late Archaic components (Koldehoff 1992; Moffatt 1992), but the number of diagnostics from any one component is small and the radiocarbon dates do not always cleanly separate the components. The earliest (Late Archaic I), with radiocarbon dates of 3300 and 3100 cal B.C., yielded no diagnostic points, but some point fragments exhibited flaking typical of Karnaks and some Matanzas points. Typologically, one could argue that the Late Archaic I component could just as easily be classified as terminal Middle Archaic. Comparable radiocarbon dates were obtained on deposits from the end of late Middle Archaic and the early Late Archaic from another rockshelter (the Cave Creek Rockshelter [Butler and DelCastello 2000]) but were not associated with diagnostic points.

The Black Earth site exhibited some horizontal stratification in that the heaviest Late Archaic usage shifted eastward from Area A to Area B of the site, where a Late Archaic occupation zone could be roughly isolated in two excavation levels (2 and 3). This occupation was defined typologically by a predominance of broad, straight-stemmed Saratoga points in addition to small numbers of Cypress and Karnak points (Jefferies 1982a:341–349). Saratoga points from the West Harrisburg project (Figure 16.9i–l) and the Hills Branch shelter (Figure 16.9a, b) are illustrated here.

The Highland Creek site (15UN127) near the Ohio River, yielded six carbon dates ranging between 3400 and 2700 cal B.C., although three of the six group tightly between 2900 and 3100 cal B.C. The small number of associated diagnostics included Etley and Pickwick points as well as one Saratoga specimen (Maggard and Pollack 2000).

At Little Muddy, the Late Archaic II component evidenced some mixture with older materials (and two older dates) but yielded one acceptable date of 2500 cal B.C. Diagnostics included straight-stemmed Saratoga points and one Karnak. This component is thought to be coeval with the Titterington phase of the lower Illinois Valley and American Bottom (Cook 1976), which does not exist in the study area. Koldehoff (1992:327) has suggested that the "classic" Etley points found in southern Illinois, which are often made of Burlington chert, are probably trade pieces from the north. Etley and Etley-like points are illustrated in Figure 16.9a–c.

Late Archaic III yielded Saratoga points similar to those found in Late Archaic II as well as one Etley point and a carbon date of 2000 cal B.C. The date of 2500 cal B.C. on an Etley point from a buried context near Fountain Bluff has previously been noted (Snyder et al. 2002:390–391). Titus et al. (2001:138) report a date of 2400 cal B.C. from the Case site in Gallatin County (11G190), with a Saratoga point in direct association.

At some point, contracting-stemmed points become important in southern Illinois, although the exact chronology is not yet known. In the American Bottom, Cypress and Ledbetter-like contracting-stemmed forms, as well as Pickwick-like points, are present in the post-Titterington Mule Road phase (2500 to 1750 cal B.C.), which McElrath (1993) links to the Ledbetter phase of the Midsouth (Lewis and Kneberg 1959). Nance (1987b:139) dates the Ledbetter and Pickwick types in the lower Tennessee Valley to between 2200 and 1800 cal B.C., which is comparable to the Mule Road phase. Presently, no comparable phase unit in southern Illinois bridges the intervening area. Ledbetter and Pickwick-like points have yet to be found in any coherent dated context in southern Illinois.

The Late Archaic IV component at Little Muddy is dated to 1700 cal B.C., only slightly younger than Late Archaic III, but it yielded a very different array of projectile points: small stemmed and notched points of the Merom, Trimble, and Riverton types. These points are characteristic of the Riverton culture (phase) that Winters (1969) defined in the central Wabash River valley. Typologically, the Late Archaic IV component has been equated with the Labras Lake phase in the American Bottom (McElrath et al. 1984), where Riverton-like points occur but do not dominate assemblages. The Little Muddy date of 1700 cal B.C. falls right at the start of the Labras Lake phase (1750 to 1400 cal B.C.). Merom/Trimble and Riverton points were not abundant at the Carrier Mills sites, but they were at 11SA217 and 11SA234 in the West Harrisburg Project, where they represented one of the more intensive occupational episodes, as indicated by biface deposition rates (Hargrave and Butler 1994c; Stephens 1994) (Figures 16.11a–l and 16.12a–d).

Although technically outside of the area discussed in this chapter, Winters's (1969) original Riverton construct deserves some comment here. The unit was defined from work at three major sites in the central Wabash Valley: Robeson Hills, Swan Island, and Riverton. The middens at these sites have the depth and character of those at the older Middle Archaic sites but are Late Archaic (ca. 2000 to 1500 cal B.C.) and, thus, seem to defy the Late Archaic settlement trends noted in central and southern Illinois. These sites are also unusual (for Illinois) in containing appreciable amounts of shellfish remains. Although Winters described them as shell middens, they do not exhibit the massive concentrations of shell that characterize the well-known Archaic sites on the Green and Tennessee rivers.

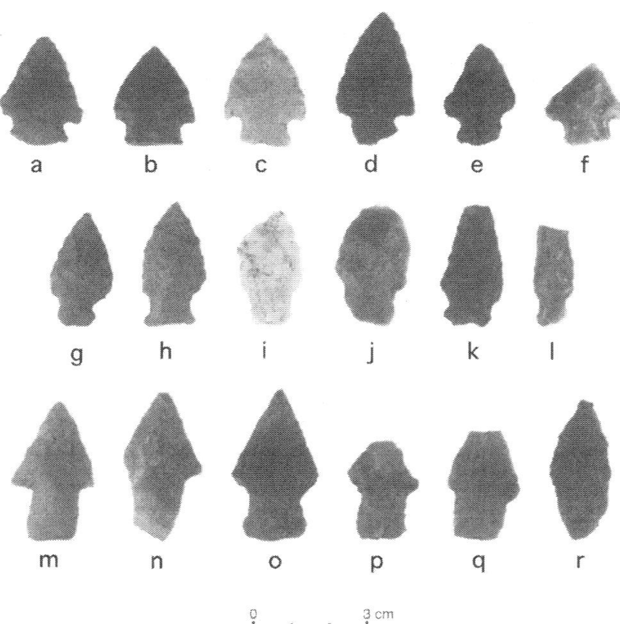

Figure 16.11. Late Archaic points from the Funkhouser site: a–f, Merom; g–j Riverton; k, l, Trimble; m–r, Cypress Straight Stemmed (adapted from Stephens 1994).

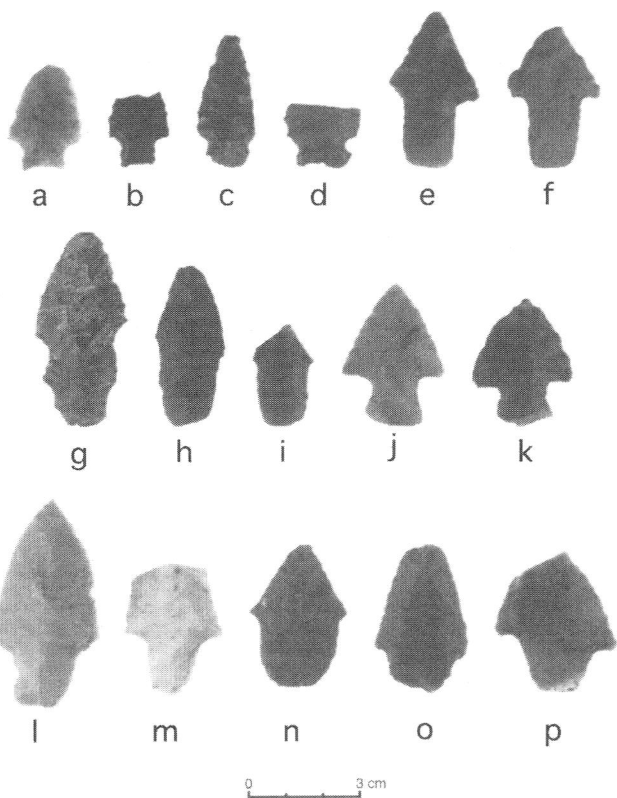

Figure 16.12. Late Archaic points from the Kottmeyer site: a, b, Riverton; c, d, Trimble; e–i, Cypress Straight Stemmed; j, k, Motley; l, m, Cypress Contracting Stemmed; n–p, Adena/Dickson (adapted from Stephens 1994).

Although originally defined in the central Wabash, the Riverton phase has been used for similar manifestations with Riverton, Merom, and Trimble points in southern Indiana and around the Falls of the Ohio. In these areas more recent work has suggested a longer persistence of these point types, to around 1200 cal B.C. (see Jefferies and Stafford and Cantin, this volume). It is now clear that a Riverton-like point complex occurs throughout a large area of the southern Midwest, including large portions of the Ohio Valley and all of southern Illinois. This complex is, in effect, a horizon style. Bradbury (1997) has suggested that these points are really arrow tips and that this group of small stemmed and notched points (as well as some small Matanzas points) represents an early appearance of bow-and-arrow technology. This view is still not widely accepted, but the rapid spread of these distinctive points in the Late Archaic suggests that they may be linked to some kind of technological or behavioral innovation. Outside of the Wabash Valley, the approximate time interval of the Riverton lithic complex is poorly documented in southern Illinois. One wonders if demographic shifts or perhaps some modification in settlement patterns tend to obscure these occupations.

At the Little Muddy shelter, a Terminal Archaic component was defined with an associated date of 1300 cal B.C. The occupation is marked primarily by straight- and contracting-stemmed Cypress points. The Cypress type is essentially its own type cluster, encompassing a wide range of variation in points with contracting (Figure 16.12l, m) or elongated, straight-stemmed hafting elements (Figures 16.10d, e, 16.11m–r, and 16.12e–i). Winters's (1967) vague type definition has led to multiple attempts at defining variants, which usually distinguish simple contracting-stemmed forms from those with long, straight stems, or distinct shoulder barbs, or both (Denny 1972; Trotter and McNerney 1984). Locally, these points are often grouped with Adena-like forms (Figure 16.12n–p) into an Adena/Cypress cluster or as part of Justice's even larger Dickson cluster (1987:189–198).

The final members of the area's Late Archaic projectile point suite are small- to medium-sized points with prominent barbed shoulders and straight or expanding stems. These are variously called "Wade" or "Buck Creek Barbed" (Figure 16.10g) (DelCastello 2000:95–98), types that constitute a large part of Justice's (1987:187–194) Terminal Archaic Barbed cluster. These points are not well dated locally but, at a minimum, seem to co-occur and overlap with Cypress points. Indeed, many of the Cypress Straight Stemmed points with shorter stems can just as readily be typed as Buck Creek Barbed or Wade. Similar strong-shouldered and barbed points figure importantly in the Labras Lake and Prairie Lake phases in the American Bottom (McElrath et al. 1984). Points with wide notches and sharply expanding stems are often typed as Motley (Figures 16.10f, 16.12j, k). Although not included in the Barbed cluster, the Motley point (Justice 1987:198–201) is clearly a related form.

Koldehoff (1992:332–333) uses the Terminal Archaic occupation at Little Muddy to define an Au Vase phase for the Big Muddy basin, which is a rough equivalent to the Prairie Lake phase in the American Bottom sequence (1400 to 900 cal B.C.). In the Grand Tower Power Plant project, the Ameren No. 1 site (11J1148) yielded a nice suite of radiocarbon dates, ranging from ca. 1400 to 600 cal B.C., but only a few diagnostic artifacts, primarily Cypress and Saratoga points (Snyder et al. 2002). In the Cache Valley a good Terminal Archaic date of 800 cal B.C. was obtained from a pit at site 11JS321 (Figure 16.3, No. 9) (DelCastello and Butler 2000). Terminal Archaic points (Cypress Stemmed and a Wade) were the most common forms found at this site, although no diagnostics occurred in the dated feature.

The end of the local Late Archaic is defined by the arrival of the first pottery in the region. The latter event is not well dated, but it appears to have been around 600 cal B.C. (Butler and Jefferies 1986). The date is tenuous because ceramics were initially rare in the region and do not commonly occur on many sites predating 300 cal B.C., at which point they are clearly identifiable as Crab Orchard. Currently, few dated sites fall at or near the Late Archaic–Early Woodland boundary.

Although both the contracting-stemmed and barbed points characterize the last part of the Archaic sequence, they are not very reliable markers outside of sealed or dated contexts. These points and their typological kin also dominate the Crab Orchard (Early and Middle Woodland) sequence until around cal A.D. 1 (Butler and Jefferies 1986; Maxwell 1951:129–132). The Motley type belongs with these other late forms, as it, too, shows up in early Crab Orchard contexts. The persistence of these types is responsible for so many sites in the region being identified in survey records as Late Archaic–Early Woodland. Cypress-like contracting-stemmed points even persisted in diminutive form into the latter portion of the Late Woodland sequence (DelCastello and Butler 2002:129; Koldehoff 1992:332).

The Late Archaic South of the Mississippi-Ohio Confluence Region

The alluvial valley adjacent to and immediately south of the Ohio-Mississippi River confluence at Cairo deserves some comment. This area was part of an important geographic nexus for communication and trade between the deep South and the Midwest. The influence of Poverty Point culture is archaeologically traceable here, and temporal units and point types derived from the lower Mississippi Valley abruptly confront those from the Midwest and Midsouth, usually with rather jarring results for the analyst. In the Cairo Lowlands and adjacent alluvial areas, the Late and Terminal Archaic are currently encapsulated in the O'Bryan Ridge phase, a local unit assigned to the lower Mississippi Valley's Poverty Point period because of the presence of distinctive baked-clay objects and lapidary items (Lafferty and Price 1996:3, 19–26). Here, archaeological efforts have focused on a small number of major sites on remnants of older, higher alluvial ridges. Recent investigations of three major sites, Burkett (11MI20) and its neighbor Weems (23MI25) on O'Bryan Ridge (Figure 16.3, Nos. 20 and 21) (Thomas et al. 2004) and the Clifford LaPlant site (23NM561) on Barnes Ridge (just off the lower edge of Figure 16.3) (Buchner et al. 2003), have documented intensive Late Archaic occupations that date from ca. 2000 to 1000 cal B.C., with some later occupation to around 500 cal B.C. This work reaffirmed the expected ties with the Poverty Point culture. Burkett also had the basal remnants of a badly damaged earthen mound, whose original construction phase *may* have started in the Late Archaic. The mound's interpretation, however, is clouded by multiple earthquake liquefaction events reflected in the stratigraphy and by derivation of the mound chronology from oxidizable carbon ratio (OCR) dates (Thomas et al. 2004:120–125).

Given the date range, these occupations are fittingly characterized by a diverse array of stemmed and notched point types. The sites are not well stratified, however. The same basic suite of Late Archaic point styles that occurs in southern Illinois appears to be present, although different type names are used. Some southern Illinois cherts are present, indicating exchange with groups to the north. Likewise, a few Poverty Point objects have been reported on the Mississippi River in extreme southern Illinois at the Olive Branch site (Gramly 2002:216), although their context and exact age (Late Archaic or Early Woodland) are uncertain.

Patterns and Trends

Overview

Numerous researchers have addressed middle Holocene changes in subsistence and settlement patterns and residential mobility. Early Archaic and early Middle Archaic groups are characterized as having had high residential mobility, small group size, and strongly curated technology. In the middle Holocene, and roughly in concert with the later portion of the so-called Hypsithermal climatic interval, a general shift occurred toward logistically organized settlement systems with greater residential stability. In some localities at this time large, intensively occupied, long-term base camps appeared. These seem to have been occupied year-round or nearly so, at least by parts of the population and during some periods of time. In the southern Midwest, this horizon is defined as the late Middle Archaic, which, in this study area, began about 4500 cal B.C. and lasted for about a millennium.

The intensity of use at the Carrier Mills sites decreased markedly around 3500 cal B.C., and this signaled the beginning of the Late Archaic in the local scheme. This threshold also seems to have coincided roughly with the arrival of modern climatic and biotic patterns (Ahler and Styles 1998; Lopinot 1982a). Greater dispersal of settlement is apparent archaeologically, with habitation more evenly distributed over the landscape. These changes in Late Archaic settlement patterns have also been seen as reflecting, in part, an increased regional population, which restricted band territories and required a more even distribution of population over the landscape (Ford 1974). Under such circumstances, one would expect to see some increase in diet breadth as restrictions in range would have demanded a more comprehensive exploitation of available food resources.

Two large-scale, multistate studies using site file records in the Southeast and Midwest have looked at the issue of population growth during the Archaic period (Anderson 1996; Milner 2004:28–29). These studies support the idea of a general trend of increasing population during the Archaic period, with an obvious increase in the Late Archaic period. The data suggest episodic variation in population size at different times and places. As the studies' authors admit, site file data are an extremely crude measure that also embody variation resulting from changing residential patterns, changing environmental circumstances, and differing quantities and refinement of the archaeological work.

The survey data from southern Illinois are somewhat contradictory. Site file data from the 19 counties contained wholly or partially within the study area yield a total of 612 components that are qualified as being Early, Middle, or Late Archaic (data from the Illinois site files provided by the Illinois State Museum). Of these 612 Archaic components, 183 (29.9 percent) are Early Archaic, 132 (21.6 percent) are Middle Archaic, and 297 (48.5 percent) are Late Archaic. Adjusted for the number of centuries within each unit, the components-per-century values are 6.8, 4.4, and 10.2, respectively. Taken at face value, these data suggest a possible decrease in Middle Archaic populations in the region, but several other factors are at play. Numbers of components do not always equate directly with population, as periods of settlement aggregation (which the late Middle Archaic period is thought to have been) would yield proportionally fewer sites. Also, there is a recognition issue. Early Archaic diagnostic points come in diverse styles and are readily identified, but side-notched points are generally used as the markers for the Middle Archaic to the exclusion of other forms, and, thus, Middle Archaic components are likely to be underenumerated. There are more helpful data from several large survey projects within the region involving variable landforms or large expanses of stream valley margins. These surveys, which also reflect greater attention to component definition than older work did, typically yield either roughly equal numbers of Early and Middle Archaic components or slightly more Middle Archaic components and notably increased numbers for the Late Archaic (Canouts et al. 1984:23; Neusius and Remley 1988; Stephens 1990). Thus, the combined information supports a long-term trend of population growth through the Archaic—gradual through the Early and Middle Archaic but more pronounced in the Late Archaic.

Subsistence and Settlement Patterns

To date, southern Illinois sites have yielded almost no subsistence data from the Early Archaic and the early Middle Archaic periods. Small, unremarkable samples of botanical data (nuts and wood charcoal) have been reported from Early Archaic deposits in two rockshelters (Cremin 1992; Parker 2000). The oldest detailed records of Archaic subsistence patterns come from the late Middle Archaic components at Carrier Mills, Little Muddy, and West Harrisburg.

Researchers have known for some time that nuts and white-tailed deer were generally the most important dietary components for these late Middle Archaic societies, at least in terms of overall dietary contribution (Stafford et al. 2000; Styles and Klippel 1996). That certainly appears to have been the case at Carrier Mills (Breitburg 1982:932; Lopinot 1982b), although at the Black Earth site riparian and aquatic habitats made an appreciable contribution, between 8 and 10 percent of the estimated meat weight (Breitburg 1982:932). Analysis of microremains from midden column samples further suggests that the contribution of small fish was underestimated by faunal analyses based on standard screened recovery (Oetelaar 1982).

Archaeobotanical analyses have documented the use of various wild plants foods as well as the intensive use of nuts, but they have found little evidence for plant manipulation or cultivation on Archaic sites in the region other than cucurbit rind (*Cucurbita pepo*). Notably, the Little Muddy shelter yielded cucurbit rind in both its Middle and Late Archaic strata, with a notable increase in the Terminal Archaic component (Cremin 1992). By contrast, no cucurbits were recovered from either Middle or Late Archaic contexts at the Carrier Mills sites (Lopinot 1982b) or from Late Archaic components along the Ohio River (Rossen 2000), which probably indicates a preservation bias in open sites.

Available subsistence data do not suggest any major changes in basic subsistence practices until the end of the Late Archaic. Seeds from the starchy- and oily-seeded plants (sunflower, chenopod, marsh elder, maygrass, little barley, and erect knotweed) show up sporadically in Late Archaic contexts in the Ohio drainage, but the evidence generally suggests that these are not cultivated varieties (Rossen 2000).

Residential Mobility, Settlement Aggregation, and the Hypsithermal

In southern Illinois, these circumstances are best illustrated by the impressive Carrier Mills (Jefferies and Butler 1982; Jefferies and Lynch 1983) and West Harrisburg sites (Hargrave and Butler 1994a). These sites are situated in the southern portion of the Saline River drainage near the northern edge of the Shawnee Hills. The Carrier Mills sites are located around the margins of shallow lakes that are relicts of the late Pleistocene Lake Saline (Frye et al. 1972; Heinrich 1982). Area A of the Black Earth site, with its meter of late Middle Archaic deposits, is clearly something special. The other areas of the Black Earth site and site 11SA88, its neighbor on the adjacent ridge (Lynch and Jefferies 1982), would be major Archaic sites in any other locality, but they pale in comparison with Area A of SA87. The Carrier Mills data are available in great detail, and I will not belabor them here, but a few comments from a regional perspective are appropriate.

In terms of settlement patterns, a classic "hub-and-spoke" settlement model is indicated, in which groups were tethered to major settlements near the lakes and wetlands, seasonally dispersing and task groups radiating outward for some distance (Jefferies 1982b). Indeed, chert-procurement studies suggest that Carrier Mills occupants were ranging widely to the south and west into the hill country, including occasional trips to the major chert source localities in the western Shawnee Hills (Union County) between 60 and 70 km away (Morrow and Jefferies 1989). This fact suggests a high degree of contact and interaction among the late Middle Archaic population of the region, an interpretation bolstered by the previously noted shared styles in engraved bone pins. Long-distance exchange involving exotics from distant regions, however, was minimal. Only a few items of copper and marine shell were recovered from the Carrier Mills sites (Jefferies 1982b).

What is interesting from a regional perspective is that the South Fork and Bankston Fork of the Saline River are the only places in the region where such a concentration of Middle Archaic settlement is documented, both in terms of numbers of impressive sites and levels of usage. The concentration of intensive Middle Archaic occupation in the southern Saline River basin is especially impressive when one notes that the Black Earth site was only the last survivor of several comparable sites, lost to early strip mining, that were located around nearby lakes and wetlands. Nothing comparable has been found in the Kaskaskia Valley, the Big Muddy basin, or elsewhere in the southern Till Plains, Shawnee Hills, or even the Cache Valley. There is no lack of Middle Archaic occupation in these areas, but few known sites approach the occupational intensity of even the lesser sites of the Carrier Mills and West Harrisburg groups.

A great deal of discussion has been directed at the reasons for the dramatic change in settlement patterns and the appearance of the large, aggregated settlements in certain locales during the Middle Archaic, and much of that has focused on the effects of the so-called Hypsithermal, the warm, dry interval that is associated with the expansion of the prairies (Wright 1968). The Hypsithermal is now understood to have been a complex, time-transgressive phenomenon whose timing and environmental effects depended on location, especially latitude (Baker et al. 1992). The warm, dry conditions in the southern Midwest were originally thought to have peaked around 6000 cal B.C., but more recent studies emphasizing different climatic indicators suggest a later peak at around 5000 cal B.C. (Webb et al. 1993).

Major human responses to these conditions, however, do not appear to have occurred in this region until perhaps five centuries after the peak conditions. Both "push" and "pull" environmental arguments have been made in explaining the Middle Holocene shift to more logistically organized settlement systems (see Brown 1985; Brown and Vierra 1983). Some rearchers have seen the desiccation of upland areas and resulting reduction of the resources there as "pushing" populations into the well-watered and forested riverine corridors; others have pointed to the evolving hydrological regimes in the major valleys, and the emergence of large backwater lakes and sloughs, as "pulling" groups into these new, high-resource areas. In their article on the lower Illinois River valley, Brown and Vierra (1983) argued persuasively for the environmental "pull" scenario. This article was widely read and very influential, especially among archaeologists who did not work with Archaic culture in the Midwest and who took its interpretation as the last word on the Middle Archaic in that region.

The problem with this scenario is that it may work well for the Illinois River valley, but it does not work well in other localities, where different river and hydrological circumstances existed in the middle Holocene. At Carrier Mills, the sites are located on a series of shallow lakes and wetlands that are remnants of a late Pleistocene lake system. Thus, rich aquatic environments existed there well before the late Middle Archaic. Early Archaic and early Middle Archaic groups would have been aware of the resource potential of the area but did not focus settlement there to any great degree.

More recently, Stafford (1994; Stafford et al. 2000) has framed the discussion of these changes in a more useful way. His review of survey data from the southern Midwest examines the significant shift in settlement patterns taking place in the late Middle Archaic, in which upper drainage and headwater areas were largely abandoned in favor of areas on lower drainages and locales near major stream outlets. The changes in settlement pattern structure and mobility are seen as a general response to the increased heterogeneity (patchiness) of resources in the environment resulting from the climatic changes. Specifically, he suggests that the shifts in settlement strategy were a result of changes in the abundance of terrestrial resources brought about by a shift from a closed mesic forest to a more open, xeric oak-hickory forest (Stafford et al. 2000). More open forest conditions would have increased the deer population (as well as various types of small game that thrive in forest-edge environments) as well as promoted mast production.

The pivotal importance of areas with high aquatic and riparian resource potential lies not in these resources' bulk contribution to diet but in their key addition to the dependability and reliability of the total resource base. The point is that, while not contributing as much to the overall diet, aquatic and riparian resources played a crucial role in providing a dependable dietary increment that helped underwrite long-term economic and residential stability against the vagaries of mast production and hunting success. In upland and small stream-valley settings, small-bodied mammals and reptiles could replace the contribution of aquatic resources, a situation documented in Stafford's Bluegrass site analysis (Stafford et al. 2000).

In southern Illinois one finds Late Archaic sites in virtually all topographic settings as well as a very high level of rockshelter use. Detailed stratigraphic data from Modoc Rock Shelter show that the Late Archaic components there continue to reflect a predominantly logistically organized system, although duration and intensity of use varied considerably (Ahler and Styles 1992, 1998). The Carrier Mills and West Harrisburg sites were still heavily used, but the intensity or frequency of use was less than before, and there is much less midden accumulation. These Late Archaic components are still major sites; they appear unimpressive only in comparison with the Middle Archaic components in the southern Saline River basin.

Mortuary Patterns

No Archaic burial mounds are documented in extreme southern Illinois, unlike other parts of the state. Most of the burials have been recovered from heavily used base-camp settlements, typified by the Carrier Mills and West Harrisburg sites, but some are known from rockshelters. The burials are virtually all primary inhumations. The large late Middle Archaic burial sample from the Black Earth site exhibits considerable variation in body placement, with flexed interments only slightly more prevalent than extended ones (Jefferies and Lynch 1983:318). One unusual mortuary treatment was the use of clay caps to cover interments, eight examples of which were found (Lynch 1982:1133). Grave goods, consisting mostly of utilitarian items, were relatively common, but the mortuary data are consistent with a lack of ascribed statuses (Jefferies and Lynch 1983; Lynch 1982).

The previously noted Ferry site, located on a hilltop near the confluence of the Saline River with the Ohio, was always unusual for the abundance of atlatl weights it yielded, especially in comparison to the modest amounts of occupation debris (Fowler 1957). No direct evidence of burials was found, but the abundance of atlatl weights suggests that burials, or caches, or both may have been present but were obliterated by plowing. In the context of more recent work, the Ferry site is quite similar to the Bullseye site in the lower Illinois Valley, which is an Early and Middle Archaic cemetery situated in the Illinois River floodplain and which also produced many atlatl weights (Hassen and Farnsworth 1987). The Ferry site example suggests that at least some Archaic cemeteries likely are located apart from major habitation sites. The Ferry site and its abundance of atlatl weights, and the scarcity of these artifacts in the Carrier Mills and West Harrisburg sites, implies an aspect of Archaic mortuary behavior in the region that archaeologists do not yet understand.

Social Organization and Complexity

It has long been an article of faith that the Archaic-period peoples of the Midcontinent were egalitarian societies, essentially band level or, at best, low-level tribal entities. In the Eastern United States the Late Archaic Poverty Point culture (Ford and Webb 1956; Gibson 2000) was always seen as the great exception, but the recent discovery of even older mound complexes in the lower Mississippi Valley (Saunders et al. 2005) and elsewhere in the Southeast (Russo 1996) has made it clear that Poverty Point was not a one-time fluke, but the culmination, in some sense, of a long tradition of earthwork construction. Clearly, rather complex social and political formations were achieved by some nonagricultural groups in the Southeast, even if the nature of those formations is not presently clear to archaeologists. In later prehistory, such mound constructions are seen as the hallmark of chiefdoms, but such an interpretation may not be appropriate here, and some see the development of complex forms of community organization and labor mobilization as not driven by the power concerns of aggrandizing chiefs (Gibson 2000; Sassaman and Heckenberger 2004).

In contrast, the archaeological record of the late Middle Archaic in the southern Midwest does not provide any obvious evidence of social hierarchy or larger-scale forms of societal organization and labor mobilization. Earthworks and public architecture are lacking—as far as one can tell—and mortuary patterns offer little evidence of ascribed status.

That said, archaeologists now recognize distinct regional cultures in the Middle Archaic of the southern Midwest and Midsouth that participated in the widespread exchange of visually distinctive and, possibly, symbolically potent artifacts. This recognition has raised the issue of whether these regional cultures embodied some kind of larger-scale social, political, or religious organization (Jefferies 1995, 1996, 1997). The term *complex hunter-gatherers* was in vogue for a time, primarily emphasizing the perspective of horizontal complexity rather than vertical complexity or social stratification (see Price and Brown 1985), and more recently the idea of "transegalitarian" communities has been explored (Hayden 1995). The new Archaic mound revelations have raised the "complexity question" anew (Brookes 2004; Jefferies 2004), although researchers still need to agree on what is meant by *complex* in these societies.

I am not suggesting that Archaic chiefdoms and mound centers have existed unseen in the southern Midwest. My point here is that the archaeological record of the midwestern Archaic may yet hold surprises. It is at least possible that some of these Archaic societies had more complex social, political, or ritual arrangements than once thought. Building earthen constructions had a long tradition in eastern North America, but could there have been monumental and symbolically meaningful constructions that did not use earth or stone? How readily would archaeologists recognize and date large woodhenges or similar constructions built by Archaic peoples? The surviving stone tools and ornaments have always given the Archaic societies a strong utilitarian cast, but could there have been a rich symbolic landscape defined by carved trees, wooden posts, and statues? Archaeologists have marveled at the wooden artifact finds from Key Marco in Florida (Gilliland 1975), but were such representations limited only to the later prehistory of Florida? Perhaps we, as researchers, have had our vision narrowed too greatly by preservation conditions and by a reliance on the archaeological and ethnohistorical record of much later societies.

Summary

In this chapter I have sketched the Archaic period of a region that occupies an important geographic position astride the convergence of the Mississippi, Ohio, Tennessee, and Cumberland rivers and that also lies along the border region between the southern Midwest and the Midsouth. The archaeological record in southernmost Illinois appears to fit the broad regional trends of the adjacent areas, but the local record is not well developed except in a few localities. The best data come from interior drainages and upland areas, especially the Carrier Mills and West Harrisburg areas in the southern Saline River basin, and from a small number of rockshelter excavations. Presently, only minimal information is available concerning Archaic-period utilization of the Mississippi floodplain. The Archaic period has generally not been the object of long-term research in the region, and, indeed, no excavation of a major Archaic site has taken place since about 1990, with the exception of one Dalton site (Gramly 2002). A great deal of additional work will be needed to refine the local chronology and cultural units, but great research potential is there. The Archaic-period sites that lie buried in the floodplains of the Mississippi and Ohio rivers are a largely untapped resource, and these sites have the potential to radically revise understanding of Archaic-period societies in the region.

Acknowledgments

I would like to specifically thank the conference organizers (and volume editors) for their efforts in creating a relaxed, stimulating, and intellectually productive conference. Michael Wiant and Nicholas Klobuchar of the Illinois State Museum provided data on Archaic sites of the study region, assembled from the Illinois archaeological site file administered by their institution. Their assistance is gratefully noted. Mr. Darden Hood of Beta Analytic, Inc., recalibrated many of the radiocarbon dates given in Table 16.1. The projectile point illustrations in Figures 16.5–16.7 were prepared from original drawings by Brian DelCastello. The base map for Figure 16.3 was prepared by Mr. Kevin Davie of Morris Library, SIUC.

References Cited

Ahler, Steven R., Jon Muller, and Joel Rabinowitz
1980 *Archaeological Testing for the Smithland Pool, Illinois.* Research Paper 13. Center for Archaeological Investigations, Southern Illinois University, Carbondale.

Ahler, Steven R., and Bonnie W. Styles
1992 Summary and Integration. In *Late Archaic Components at Modoc Rock Shelter, Randolph County, Illinois*, by Steven R. Ahler, Mary J. Bade, Frances B. King, Bonnie S. Styles, and Paula J. Thorson, pp. 124–129. Reports of Investigations 48. Illinois State Museum, Springfield.
1998 A Summary of Changes in Archaic Period Subsistence and Site Function at Modoc Rock Shelter. *Illinois Archaeology* 10:110–154.

Alexander, Charles S.
1974 *Some Observations on the Late Pleistocene and Holocene History of the Lower Ohio Valley*. Occasional Publications of the Department of Geography 7. Geography Graduate Student Association, University of Illinois, Urbana–Champaign.

Alexander, Charles S., and Jean Cutler Prior
1968 The Origin and Function of the Cache Valley, Southern Illinois. In *The Quaternary of Illinois*, edited by Robert E. Bergstrom, pp. 19–26. Special Publication 14. College of Agriculture, University of Illinois, Urbana–Champaign.
1971 Holocene Sedimentation Rates in Overbank Deposits in the Black Bottom of the Lower Ohio River, Southern Illinois. *American Journal of Science* 270:361–372.

Anderson, David G.
1996 Approaches to Modeling in the Archaic Period Southeast. In *Archaeology of the Mid-Holocene Southeast*, edited by Kenneth E. Sassaman and David G. Anderson, pp. 157–166. University Press of Florida, Gainesville.

Anderson, David G., Lisa D. O'Steen, and Kenneth E. Sassaman
1996 Environmental and Chronological Considerations. In *The Paleoindian and Early Archaic Southeast*, edited by David G. Anderson and Kenneth E. Sassaman, pp. 3–15. University of Alabama Press, Tuscaloosa.

Baker, Richard G., Louis J. Maher, Craig A. Chumbley, and Kent L. Van Zant
1992 Patterns of Holocene Environmental Change in the Midwestern United States. *Quaternary Research* 37:379–389.

Bradbury, Andrew
1997 The Bow and Arrow in the Eastern Woodlands: Evidence for an Archaic Origin. *North American Archaeologist* 18:207–233.

Breitburg, Emanuel

1982 Analysis of Area A Fauna. In *The Carrier Mills Archaeological Project: Human Adaptation in the Saline Valley, Illinois*, vol. 2, edited by Richard W. Jefferies and Brian M. Butler, pp. 861–957. Research Paper 33. Center for Archaeological Investigations, Southern Illinois University, Carbondale.

Brookes, Samuel O.

2004 Cultural Complexity in the Middle Archaic of Mississippi. In *Signs of Power: The Rise of Cultural Complexity in the Southeast*, edited by Jon L. Gibson and Phillip J. Carr, pp. 97–113. University of Alabama Press, Tuscaloosa.

Brown, James A.

1985 Long Term Trends to Sedentism and the Emergence of Complexity in the American Midwest. In *Prehistoric Hunter-Gatherers: The Emergence of Cultural Complexity*, edited by T. Douglas Price and James A. Brown, pp. 201–231. Academic Press, Orlando, Florida.

Brown, James A., and Robert K. Vierra

1983 What Happened in the Middle Archaic? Introduction to an Ecological Approach to Koster Site Archaeology. In *Archaic Hunters and Gatherers in the American Midwest*, edited by James L. Phillips and James A. Brown, pp. 165–198. Academic Press, New York.

Broyles, Bettye J.

1971 *Second Preliminary Report: The St. Albans Site, Kanawha County, West Virginia*. Report of Archaeological Investigations 3. West Virginia Geological and Economic Survey, Morgantown.

Buchner, C. Andrew, Eric S. Albertson, Emanuel Breitburg, Gina S. Powell, and Neal H. Lopinot

2003 *Data Recovery Excavations at the Clifford LaPlant Site (23NM561) on Barnes Ridge, New Madrid County, Missouri*. Panamerican Consultants, Memphis, Tennessee.

Butler, Brian M.

1983 Patterns of Chert Source Utilization in Southern Illinois. Paper presented at the 48th Annual Meeting of the Society for American Archaeology, Pittsburgh, Pennsylvania.

Butler, Brian M., and Brian G. DelCastello

2000 The Cave Creek Rockshelter (11J-822), and Seasonal Settlement in the Western Shawnee Hills. *Illinois Archaeology* 12:277–314.

Butler, Brian M., Glen P. Harrell, and Mary C. Hamilton

1979 *An Archaeological Reconnaissance of the Illinois Portions of the Smithland Pool of the Ohio River*. Research Paper 5. Center for Archaeological Investigations, Southern Illinois University, Carbondale.

Butler, Brian M., and Richard W. Jefferies

1986 Crab Orchard and Early Woodland Cultures in the Middle South. In *Early Woodland Archeology*, edited by Kenneth B. Farnsworth and Thomas E. Emerson, pp. 523–534. Kampsville Seminars in Archaeology 2. Center for American Archeology, Kampsville, Illinois.

Butler, Brian M., JoAnne M. Penny, and Cathy A. Robison

1981 *Archaeological Survey and Evaluation for the Shawnee 200 M.W.A.F.B.C. Plant, McCracken County, Kentucky*. Center for Archaeological Investigations, Southern Illinois University, Carbondale.

Cambron, James W., and David C. Hulse

1964 *Handbook of Alabama Archaeology: Part 1 Point Types*. Edited by David L. DeJarnette. Archaeological Research Association of Alabama, University, Alabama.

Canouts, Valetta, Ernest E. May, Neal H. Lopinot, and Jon D. Muller

1984 *Cultural Frontiers in the Upper Cache Valley, Illinois*. Research Paper 16. Center for Archaeological Investigations, Southern Illinois University, Carbondale.

Cantwell, Anne-Marie, Lawrence A. Conrad, and Jonathan E. Reyman (editors)

2004 *Aboriginal Ritual and Economy in the Eastern Woodlands: Essays in Memory of Howard Dalton Winters*. Scientific Papers 30. Illinois State Museum, Springfield.

Chapman, Jefferson

1977 *Archaic Period Research in the Lower Little Tennessee River Valley*. Reports of Investigations 18. Department of Anthropology, University of Tennessee, Knoxville.

1985 Archaeology and the Archaic Period in the Southern Ridge and Valley Province. In *Structure and Process in Southeastern Archaeology*, edited by Roy S. Dickens Jr. and H. Trawick Ward, pp. 137–153. University of Alabama Press, Tuscaloosa.

Cobb, Charles R., and Richard W. Jefferies

1983 *Archaeological Investigations at the Milar Site, Alexander County, Illinois*. Research Paper 40. Center for Archaeological Investigations, Southern Illinois University, Carbondale.

Coe, Joffre L.

1964 The Formative Cultures of the Carolina Piedmont. *Transactions of the American Philosophical Society* 54(5). Philadelphia.

Cole, Fay-Cooper, Robert Bell, John Bennett, Joseph Caldwell, Norman Emerson, Richard MacNeish, Kenneth Orr, and Roger Willis

1951 *Kincaid, a Prehistoric Illinois Metropolis*. University of Chicago Press, Chicago.

Cook, Thomas G.

1976 *Koster, an Artifact Analysis of Two Archaic Phases in Westcentral Illinois*. Prehistoric Records 1. Northwestern University Archaeological Program, Evanston, Illinois.

Cremin, William M.

1992 Botanical Analysis. In *The Little Muddy Rock Shelter: A Deeply Stratified Prehistoric Site in the Southern Till Plains of Illinois*, by Charles R. Moffat, Brad Koldehoff, William M. Cremin, Terrance J. Martin, Mary Carol Masulis, and Mary R. McCorvie, pp. 375–426. Cultural Resources Management Report 186. American Resources Group, Carbondale, Illinois.

DeJarnette, David L., Edward B. Kurjack, and James W. Cambron

1962 The Stanfield-Worley Bluff Shelter. *Journal of Alabama Archaeology* 8:1–111.

DelCastello, Brian G.

2000 Analysis of Lithic Artifacts. In *Archaeological Investigations at Dixon Springs State Park: The Hills Branch Rock Shelter, Pope County, Illinois*, by Mark J. Wagner and Brian M. Butler, pp. 60–123. Technical Report 00-2. Center for Archaeological Investigations, Southern Illinois University, Carbondale.

DelCastello, Brian G., and Brian M. Butler
1999 Lithic Analysis. In *Archaeological Investigations at the Rose Hotel (11-HN-116), Hardin County, Illinois*, edited by Mark J. Wagner and Brian M. Butler, pp. 125–190. Technical Report 99-3. Center for Archaeological Investigations, Southern Illinois University, Carbondale.
2000 *Archaeological Investigations at 11Js-321, Cache River Scenic Natural Area Visitor Center, Johnson County, Illinois.* Technical Report 00-1. Center for Archaeological Investigations, Southern Illinois University, Carbondale.
2002 Analysis of Lithic Artifacts. In *The Giant City Stone Fort (11J-35), Jackson County, Illinois*, by Brian M. Butler, Mark J. Wagner, Brian G. DelCastello, Richard L. Herndon, and Kathryn E. Parker, pp. 109–170. Technical Report 02-02. Center for Archaeological Investigations, Southern Illinois University, Carbondale.

Delcourt, Paul A., and Hazel R. Delcourt
1981 Vegetation Maps for Eastern North America: 40,000 Years Bp to Present. In *Geobotany II*, edited by Robert C. Romans, pp. 123–165. Plenum Press, New York.
1983 Late Quaternary Vegetational Dynamics and Community Stability Reconsidered. *Quaternary Research* 19:265–271.

Denny, Sidney G.
1972 The Archaeology of the Big Muddy River Basin of Southern Illinois. Ph.D. Dissertation, Department of Anthropology, Southern Illinois University, Carbondale.

Driskell, Boyce N.
1994 Stratigraphy and Chronology at Dust Cave. *Journal of Alabama Archaeology* 40:17–34.

Esling, Steven P., Eric Sloneker, Richard C. Graham, and Leon R. Follmer
1995 The Cache Valley. In *Quaternary Sections in Southern Illinois and Southeast Missouri*, edited by Steven P. Esling and Michael D. Blum, pp. 3.1–3.27. Guidebook for Midwest Friends of the Pleistocene 42nd Annual Meeting. Department of Geology, Southern Illinois University, Carbondale.

Ford, James A., and Clarence H. Webb
1956 *Poverty Point, a Late Archaic Site in Louisiana.* Anthropological Papers 46, pt. 1. American Museum of Natural History, New York.

Ford, Richard I.
1974 Northeastern Archaeology: Past and Future Directions. *Annual Review of Anthropology* 3:385–413.

Fowler, Melvin L.
1957 *Ferry Site, Hardin County, Illinois.* Scientific Papers8(1). Illinois State Museum, Springfield.
1959 *Summary Report of Modoc Rock Shelter, 1952, 1953, 1955, 1956.* Reports of Investigations 8. Illinois State Museum, Springfield.

French, Michael W.
1998 Early Archaic Settlement Mobility, Lithic Resource Use, and Technological Organization in the Lower Ohio River Valley: A Perspective from the Longworth-Gick Site (15JF243). Master's thesis, Department of Anthropology, University of Kentucky, Lexington.

Frye, John C., A. Byron Leonard, H. B. Willman, and H. D. Glass
1972 *Geology and Paleontology of Late Pleistocene Lake Saline, Southeastern Illinois.* Circular 471. Illinois State Geological Survey, Urbana.

Gibson, Jon L.
2000 *The Ancient Mounds of Poverty Point, Place of Rings.* University Press of Florida, Gainesville.

Gilliland, Marion S.
1975 *The Material Culture of Key Marco, Florida.* University Presses of Florida, Gainesville.

Graham, Richard C.
1985 The Quaternary History of the Upper Cache Valley. Master's thesis, Department of Geology, Southern Illinois University, Carbondale.

Gramly, Richard M.
2002 *Olive Branch: A Very Early Archaic Site on the Mississippi River.* Special Publication. American Society for Amateur Archaeology, North Andover, Massachusetts.

Hargrave, Michael L., and Brian M. Butler
1994a (editors) *Archaeological Investigations on the Bankston Fork of the Saline River: The AMAX West Harrisburg Project.* Technical Report 1994-3. Center for Archaeological Investigations, Southern Illinois University, Carbondale.
1994b Stratigraphy, Features, and Radiocarbon Dates. In *Archaeological Investigations on the Bankston Fork of the Saline River: The AMAX West Harrisburg Project*, edited by Michael L. Hargrave and Brian M. Butler, pp. 117–209. Technical Report 1994-3. Center for Archaeological Investigations, Southern Illinois University, Carbondale.
1994c Summary and Conclusions. In *Archaeological Investigations on the Bankston Fork of the Saline River: The AMAX West Harrisburg Project*, edited by Michael L. Hargrave and Brian M. Butler, pp. 511–541. Technical Report 1994-3. Center for Archaeological Investigations, Southern Illinois University, Carbondale.

Harris, Stanley E., C. William Horrell, and Daniel Irwin
1977 *Exploring the Land and Rocks of Southern Illinois.* Southern Illinois University Press, Carbondale.

Hassen, Harold, and Kenneth B. Farnsworth
1987 *The Bullseye Site: A Floodplain Archaic Mortuary Site in the Lower Illinois River Valley.* Reports of Investigations 42. Illinois State Museum, Springfield.

Hayden, Brian
1995 Pathways to Power: Principles for Creating Socioeconomic Inequalities. In *Foundations of Social Inequality*, edited by T. Douglas Price and Gary M. Feinman, pp. 15–86. Plenum Press, New York.

Heinrich, Paul V.
1982 Geomorphology and Sedimentology of Pleistocene Lake Saline, Southern Illinois. Master's thesis, Department of Geology, University of Illinois, Urbana–Champaign.

Hughes, W. B.
1987 The Quaternary History of the Lower Cache Valley, Southern Illinois. Master's thesis. Department of Geology, Southern Illinois University, Carbondale.

Jefferies, Richard W.
1982a The Black Earth Site. In *The Carrier Mills Archaeological Project: Human Adaptation in the Saline Valley, Illinois,* vol. 1, edited by Richard W. Jefferies and Brian M. Butler, pp. 75–452. Research Paper 33. Center for Archaeological Investigations, Southern Illinois University, Carbondale.
1982b Archaeological Overview of the Carrier Mills District. In *The Carrier Mills Archaeological Project: Human Adaptation in the Saline Valley, Illinois*, vol. 2, edited by Richard W. Jefferies and Brian M. Butler, pp. 1459–1509. Research Paper 33. Center for Archaeological Investigations, Southern Illinois University, Carbondale.
1990 A Technological and Functional Analysis of Middle Archaic Hafted Endscrapers from the Black Earth Site, Saline County, Illinois. *Midcontinental Journal of Archaeology* 15:3–36.
1995 Late Middle Archaic Exchange and Interaction in the North American Midcontinent. In *Native American Interactions, Multiscalar Analyses and Interpretations in the Eastern Woodlands*, edited by Michael S. Nassaney and Kenneth E. Sassaman, pp. 73–99. University of Tennessee Press, Knoxville.
1996 The Emergence of Long-Distance Exchange Networks in the Southeastern United States. In *Archaeology of the Mid-Holocene Southeast*, edited by Kenneth E. Sassaman and David G. Anderson, pp. 222–234. University Press of Florida, Gainesville.
1997 Middle Archaic Bone Pins: Evidence of Mid-Holocene Regional Scale Social Groups in the Southern Midwest. *American Antiquity* 62:464–488.
2004 Regional-Scale Interaction Networks and the Emergence of Cultural Complexity along the Northern Margins of the Southeast. In *Signs of Power: The Rise of Cultural Complexity in the Southeast*, edited by Jon L. Gibson and Phillip J. Carr, pp. 71–85. University of Alabama Press, Tuscaloosa.

Jefferies, Richard W., and Brian M. Butler (editors)
1982 *The Carrier Mills Archaeological Project: Human Adaptation in the Saline Valley, Illinois.* 2 vols. Research Paper 33. Center for Archaeological Investigations, Southern Illinois University, Carbondale.

Jefferies, Richard W., and B. Mark Lynch
1983 Dimensions of Middle Archaic Cultural Adaptation at the Black Earth Site, Saline County, Illinois. In *Archaic Hunters and Gatherers in the American Midwest,* edited by James L. Phillips and James A. Brown, pp. 299–322. Academic Press, New York.

Justice, Noel
1987 *Stone Age Spear and Arrow Points of the Midcontinental and Eastern United States.* Indiana University Press, Bloomington.

Koldehoff, Brad
1992 Lithic Analysis. In *The Little Muddy Rock Shelter: A Deeply Stratified Prehistoric Site in the Southern Till Plains of Illinois*, by Charles R. Moffat, Brad Koldehoff, William M. Cremin, Terrance J. Martin, Mary Carol Masulis, and Mary R. McCorvie, pp. 279–374. Cultural Resources Management Report 186. American Resources Group, Carbondale, Illinois.

Koldehoff, Brad, Dawn E. Cobb, and Jack R. Nawrot
2003 The Eastern Woodrat (*Neotoma floridana*) and Its Archaeological Significance: A Southern Illinois Case Study. *Illinois Archaeology*, in press.

Koldehoff, Brad, and Mark J. Wagner
2002 *The Archaeology and History of Horseshoe Lake, Alexander County, Illinois.* Research Paper 60. Center for Archaeological Investigations, Southern Illinois University, Carbondale.

Koldehoff, Brad, and John A. Walthall
2004 Settling In: Hunter-Gatherer Mobility during the Pleistocene-Holocene Transition in the Central Mississippi Valley. In *Aboriginal Ritual and Economy in the Eastern Woodlands: Essays in Memory of Howard Dalton Winters,* edited by Anne-Marie Cantwell, Lawrence A. Conrad, and Jonathan E. Reyman, pp. 49–72. Scientific Papers 30. Illinois State Museum, Springfield.

Lafferty, Robert H., III, and James E. Price
1996 Southeast Missouri. In *Prehistory of the Central Mississippi Valley*, edited by Charles H. McNutt, pp. 1–45. University of Alabama Press, Tuscaloosa.

Leach, Elizabeth K., and Michael J. Jackson
1987 Geomorphic History of the Lower Tennessee and Cumberland Valleys. *Southeastern Archaeology* 6:100–106.

Lewis, Thomas M. N., and Madeline Kneberg
1959 Archaic Culture in the Middle South. *American Antiquity* 25:161–183.

Lewis, Thomas M. N., and Madeline Kneberg Lewis
1961 *Eva, an Archaic Site.* University of Tennessee Press, Knoxville.

Lopinot, Neal H.
1982a A Summary of Late Pleistocene and Holocene Palynology. In *The Carrier Mills Archaeological Project: Human Adaptation in the Saline Valley, Illinois*, vol. 1, edited by Richard W. Jefferies and Brian M. Butler, pp. 72–74. Research Paper 33. Center for Archaeological Investigations, Southern Illinois University, Carbondale.
1982b Plant Macroremains and Paleoethnobotanical Implications. In *The Carrier Mills Archaeological Project: Human Adaptation in the Saline Valley, Illinois*, vol. 2, edited by Richard W. Jefferies and Brian M. Butler, pp. 671–860. Research Paper 33. Center for Archaeological Investigations, Southern Illinois University, Carbondale.
1991a *The Diana Site (11-R-331), Randolph County, Illinois.* Report prepared for Peabody Coal Company. Archaeology Program Research Report 7. Contract Archaeology Program, Southern Illinois University, Edwardsville.
1991b The Diana Site (11-R-331), an Archaic and Woodland Settlement in Southwestern Illinois. *Illinois Archaeology* 3:1–113.

Luchterhand, Kubet
1970 *Early Archaic Projectile Points and Hunting Patterns in the Lower Illinois Valley.* Reports of Investigations 19. Illinois State Museum, Springfield.

Lynch, B. Mark
1982 Mortuary Behavior in the Carrier Mills Archaeological District. In *The Carrier Mills Archaeological Project: Human Adaptation in the Saline Valley, Illinois*, vol. 2, edited by Richard W. Jefferies and Brian M. Butler, pp. 1115–1232. Research Paper 33. Center for Archaeological Investigations, Southern Illinois University, Carbondale.

Lynch, B. Mark, and Richard W. Jefferies
1982 Sa-88 Investigations. In *The Carrier Mills Archaeological Project: Human Adaptation in the Saline Valley, Illinois*, vol. 1, edited by Richard W. Jefferies and Brian M. Butler, pp. 583–670. Research Paper 33. Center for Archaeological Investigations, Southern Illinois University, Carbondale.

MacNeish, Richard S.
1948 The Pre-Pottery Faulkner Site of Southern Illinois. *American Antiquity* 13:232–243.

Maggard, Greg, and David Pollack
2000 *Archaeological Investigation of the Highland Creek Site in Union County, Kentucky*. Research Report 5 (draft). Kentucky Archaeological Survey, Lexington.

Maxwell, Moreau S.
1951 *The Woodland Cultures of Southern Illinois: Archaeological Investigations in the Carbondale Area*. Bulletin 7. Logan Museum Publications in Anthropology. Beloit College, Beloit, Wisconsin.

May, Ernest E.
1982 Analysis of Carrier Mills Projectile Points. In *The Carrier Mills Archaeological Project: Human Adaptation in the Saline Valley, Illinois*, vol. 2, edited by Richard W. Jefferies and Brian M. Butler, pp. 1347–1379. Research Paper 33. Center for Archaeological Investigations, Southern Illinois University, Carbondale.

McDonald, Timothy A.
1995 Quaternary Geology around Fountain Bluff. In *Quaternary Sections in Southern Illinois and Southeast Missouri*, edited by Steven P. Esling and Michael D. Blum, pp. 5.1–5.32. Guidebook for Midwest Friends of the Pleistocene 42nd Annual Meeting. Department of Geology, Southern Illinois University, Carbondale.

McElrath, Dale L.
1993 Mule Road: A Newly Defined Late Archaic Phase in the American Bottom. *Illinois Archaeology* 5:148–157.

McElrath, Dale L., Thomas E. Emerson, Andrew C. Fortier, and James L. Phillips
1984 Late Archaic Period. In *American Bottom Archaeology: A Summary of the FAI-270 Project Contribution to the Culture History of the Mississippi River Valley*, edited by Charles J. Bareis and James W. Porter, pp. 34–58. University of Illinois Press, Urbana.

Meeks, Scott C.
2000 *The Use and Function of Late Middle Archaic Projectile Points in the Midsouth*. Reports of Investigations 77. Office of Archaeological Services, University of Alabama Museums, Moundville.

Milner, George R.
2004 *The Moundbuilders, Ancient Peoples of Eastern North America*. Thames and Hudson, London.

Moffat, Charles R.
1992 Stratigraphy, Cultural Sequence, Features, and Chronology. In *The Little Muddy Rock Shelter: A Deeply Stratified Prehistoric Site in the Southern Till Plains of Illinois*, by Charles R. Moffat, Brad Koldehoff, William M. Cremin, Terrance J. Martin, Mary Carol Masulis, and Mary R. McCorvie, pp. 71–138. Cultural Resources Management Report 186. American Resources Group, Carbondale, Illinois.

Moffat, Charles R., Brad Koldehoff, William M. Cremin, Terrance J. Martin, Mary Carol Masulis, and Mary R. McCorvie
1992 *The Little Muddy Rock Shelter: A Deeply Stratified Prehistoric Site in the Southern Till Plains of Illinois*. Cultural Resources Management Report 186. American Resources Group, Carbondale, Illinois.

Moore, Clarence B.
1916 Some Aboriginal Sites on Green River, Kentucky. Certain Aboriginal Sites on the Lower Ohio River. *Journal of the Academy of Sciences of Philadelphia* (2nd series) 16(3):431–511.

Morrow, Carol A., and Richard W. Jefferies
1989 Trade or Embedded Procurement? A Test Case from Southern Illinois. In *Time, Energy, and Stone Tools*, edited by Robin Torrence, pp. 27–33. Cambridge University Press, Cambridge, England.

Muller, Jon
1986 *Archaeology of the Lower Ohio River Valley*. Academic Press, New York.

Nance, Jack D.
1986 The Morrisroe Site: Projectile Point Types and Radiocarbon Dates from the Lower Tennessee Valley. *Midcontinental Journal of Archaeology* 11:11–50.
1987a Research into the Prehistory of the Lower Tennessee-Cumberland-Ohio Region. *Southeastern Archaeology* 6:93–99.
1987b The Archaic Sequence in the Lower Tennessee-Cumberland Region. *Southeastern Archaeology* 6:129–139.

Neusius, Phillip, and Juliet E. Remley
1988 *Historic Properties Data Synthesis: Compliance Document, Rend Lake, Illinois*. U.S. Army Corps of Engineers, St. Louis District, St. Louis, Missouri.

O'Brien, Michael J., and W. Raymond Wood
1998 *The Prehistory of Missouri*. University of Missouri Press, Columbia.

Oetelaar, Gerald A.
1982 An Analysis of Microremains in an Area A Column Sample. In *The Carrier Mills Archaeological Project: Human Adaptation in the Saline Valley, Illinois*, vol. 2, edited by Richard W. Jefferies and Brian M. Butler, pp. 989–1007. Research Paper 33. Center for Archaeological Investigations, Southern Illinois University, Carbondale.

Parker, Kathryn E.
2000 Plant Remains from the Hills Branch Rock Shelter. In *Archaeological Investigations at Dixon Springs State Park: The Hills Branch Rock Shelter, Pope County, Illinois*, by Mark J. Wagner and Brian M. Butler, pp. 145–154. Technical Report 00-2. Center for Archaeological Investigations, Southern Illinois University, Carbondale.

Price, T. Douglas, and James A. Brown (editors)
1985 *Prehistoric Hunter-Gatherers: The Emergence of Cultural Complexity*. Academic Press, Orlando, Florida.

Pulcher, Ron
1977 *Final Report on the "Delta Mine Expansion" Archaeological Survey, Saline County, Illinois.* Report prepared for AMAX Coal Company. Southern Illinois University Museum, Carbondale.

Robison, Cathy A.
1986 *Archaeological Excavations at the Fitzgibbons Site, Gallatin County, Illinois.* Research Paper 53. Center for Archaeological Investigations, Southern Illinois University, Carbondale.

Rossen, Jack
2000 Archaic Plant Utlilization at the Hedden Site, McCracken County, Kentucky. In *Current Archaeological Research in Kentucky*, vol. 6, edited by David Pollack and Kristen J. Gremillion, pp. 1–24. Kentucky Heritage Council, Frankfort.

Russo, Michael
1996 Southeastern Archaic Mounds. In *Archaeology of the Mid-Holocene Southeast*, edited by Kenneth E. Sassaman and David G. Anderson, pp. 259–287. University Press of Florida, Gainesville.

Sassaman, Kenneth E., and Michael J. Heckenberger
2004 Roots of the Theocratic Formative of the Archaic Southeast. In *Hunters and Gatherers in Theory and Archaeology*, edited by George M. Crothers, pp. 423–444. Occasional Papers 31. Center for Archaeological Investigations, Southern Illinois University, Carbondale.

Saunders, Joe W., Rolfe D. Mandel, C. Garth Sampson, Charles M. Allen, E. Thurman Allen, Daniel A. Bush, James K. Feathers, Kristen J. Gremillion, C. T. Hallmark, H. Edwin Jackson, Jay K. Johnson, Reca Jones, Roger T. Saucier, Gary L. Stringer, and Malcolm F. Vidrine
2005 Watson Brake, a Middle Archaic Mound Complex in Northeast Louisiana. *American Antiquity* 70:631–668.

Sherwood, Sarah C., Boyce N. Driskell, Asa R. Randall, and Scott C. Meeks
2004 Chronology and Stratigraphy at Dust Cave, Alabama. *American Antiquity* 69:533–554.

Snyder, Jim, Steve Titus, Chris Koeppel, Jeff Anderson, Blaine Ensor, Elizabeth Scott, and Kathryn Parker
2002 *Phase II and Phase III Archaeological Investigations at the Ameren 1 (11J1148), Ameren 2 (11J1149), and Hileman (11J1150) Sites, Ameren Grand Tower Power Plant, Jackson County, Illinois.* Cultural Resources Management Report 1046. American Resources Group, Carbondale, Illinois.

Stafford, C. Russell
1994 Structural Changes in Archaic Landscape Use in the Dissected Uplands of Southwestern Indiana. *American Antiquity* 59:219–237.

Stafford, C. Russell, Ronald L. Richards, and C. Michael Anslinger
2000 The Bluegrass Fauna and Changes in Middle Holocene Hunter-Gatherer Foraging in the Southern Midwest. *American Antiquity* 65:317–336.

Stephens, Jeanette E.
1990 Archaeological Surveys of the Crab Orchard Lake Shoreline and Selected Borrow Areas, Crab Orchard National Wildlife Refuge. Report prepared for the U.S. Fish and Wildlife Service. Manuscript 1990-6 on file, Center for Archaeological Investigations, Southern Illinois University, Carbondale.
1994 Lithic Assemblages from the Funkhouser, Kottmeyer, and Wasson No. 1 Sites. In *Archaeological Investigations on the Bankston Fork of the Saline River: The AMAX West Harrisburg Project*, edited by Michael L. Hargrave and Brian M. Butler, pp. 332–447. Technical Report 1994-3. Center for Archaeological Investigations, Southern Illinois University, Carbondale.
1995 *An Archaeological Survey of the Dogtooth Bend of the Mississippi River in Alexander County, Illinois.* Historic Properties Management Report 45. U.S. Army Corps of Engineers, St. Louis District, St. Louis, Missouri.

Straffin, Eric C., and Charles R. McGimsey
1995 Geomorphic Controls on the Mississippi River Landscape near Fountain Bluff. In *Quaternary Sections in Southern Illinois and Southeast Missouri*, edited by Steven P. Esling and Michael D. Blum, pp. 5.33–5.38. Guidebook for Midwest Friends of the Pleistocene 42nd Annual Meeting. Department of Geology, Southern Illinois University, Carbondale.

Stuiver, Minze, Paula J. Reimer, Edouard Bard, J. Warren Beck, G. S. Burr, Konrad A. Hughen, Bernd Kromer, Gerry McCormac, Johannes van der Plicht, and Marco Spurk
1998 INTCAL98 Radiocarbon Age Calibration, 24,000–0 cal BP. *Radiocarbon* 40:1041–1083.

Styles, Bonnie W., and Walter E. Klippel
1996 Mid-Holocene Faunal Exploitation in the Southeastern United States. In *Archaeology of the Mid-Holocene Southeast*, edited by Kenneth E. Sassaman and David G. Anderson, pp. 115–133. University Press of Florida, Gainesville.

Talma, A. S., and J. C. Vogel
1993 A Simplified Approach to Calibrating ^{14}C Dates. *Radiocarbon* 35:317–322.

Thomas, Cyrus
1894 *Report on the Mound Explorations of the Bureau of American Ethnology*. Annual Report 12. American Bureau of Ethnology, Smithsonian Institution, Washington, D.C.

Thomas, Prentice M., Jr., L. Janice Campbell, and James R. Morehead
2004 The Burkett Site (23MI20), Implications for Cultural Complexity and Origins. In *Signs of Power: The Rise of Cultural Complexity in the Southeast*, edited by Jon L. Gibson and Phillip J. Carr, pp. 114–128. University of Alabama Press, Tuscaloosa.

Titus, Steve, Keith Keeney, Kathryn Parker, and Elizabeth Scott
2001 *Phase III Data Recovery at the Case (11G190) and Poole (11G200) Sites within Black Beauty Coal Company's Cottage Grove Mine Permit Area, Gallatin County, Illinois.* Cultural Resources Management Report 944. American Resources Group, Carbondale, Illinois.

Transeau, E. N.
1935 The Prairie Peninsula. *Ecology* 16:423–437.

Trotter, Charles, and Michael J. McNerney
1984 A Reexamination of Cypress Projectile Point/Knives. In *The Archaeology and History of White Walnut Creek*

Perry County, Illinois: Phase I Survey and Phase II Test Excavations at Deep Strip #3, Burning Star Mine #2, Consolidation Coal Company, by Michael J. Higgins, Michael J. McNerney, and K. R. Moore, Appendix C. Preservation Series 1. American Resources Group, Carbondale, Illinois.

Wagner, Mark J., and Brian M. Butler

1999 *Archaeological Investigations at the Rose Hotel (11Hn-116), Hardin County, Illinois.* Technical Report 1999-3. Center for Archaeological Investigations, Southern Illinois University, Carbondale.

2000 *Archaeological Investigations at Dixon Springs State Park: The Hills Branch Rock Shelter, Pope County, Illinois.* Technical Report 00-2. Center for Archaeological Investigations, Southern Illinois University, Carbondale.

Walz, Gregory R., Brian Adams, Paul P. Kreisa, Kevin P. McGowan, and Jacqueline McDowell

1998 The Strong Site and the Dennis Hollow Phase: A New Perspective on Middle Archaic Chronology, Technology, and Subsistence. *Illinois Archaeology* 10:155–194.

Webb, Paul A., Michael L. Hargrave, and Dennis B. Blanton

1989 *Archaeological Investigations in the Thebes Gap Vicinity, Alexander County, Illinois.* Research Paper 55. Center for Archaeological Investigations, Southern Illinois University, Carbondale.

Webb, Thompson, III, Patrick J. Bartlein, Sandy P. Harrison, and Katherine N. Anderson

1993 Vegetation, Lake Levels, and Climate in Eastern North America for the Past 18,000 Years. In *Global Climates since the Last Glacial Maximum*, edited by H. E. Wright Jr., John E. Kutzbach, Thompson Webb III, William F. Ruddiman, F. Alayne Street-Perrott, and Patrick J. Bartlein, pp. 415–467. University of Minnesota Press, Minneapolis.

White, Andrew A.

2003 Temporal Variation in Late Middle Archaic Bone Pins. *Midcontinental Journal of Archaeology* 28:49–72.

Wiant, Michael D., Edwin R. Hajic, and Thomas R. Styles

1983 Napoleon Hollow and Koster Site Stratigraphy: Implications for Holocene Landscape Evolution and Studies of Archaic Period Settlement Patterns in the Lower Illinois River Valley. In *Archaic Hunters and Gatherers in the American Midwest*, edited by James L. Phillips and James A. Brown, pp. 147–164. Academic Press, New York.

Winters, Howard D.

1959 *Archaeological Salvage Report No. 1, District 9, Illinois Division of Highways: The Duran Rock Shelter, 24D2-137.* Southern Illinois University Museum, Carbondale.

1967 [1963] *An Archaeological Survey of the Wabash Valley in Illinois.* Reports of Investigations 10. Illinois State Museum, Springfield.

1969 *The Riverton Culture: A Second Millennium Occupation in the Central Wabash Valley.* Reports of Investigations 13. Illinois State Museum, Springfield.

Wright, H. E., Jr.

1968 History of the Prairie Peninsula. In *The Quaternary of Illinois*, edited by Robert E. Bergstrom, pp. 78–88. Special Publication 14. College of Agriculture, University of Illinois, Urbana–Champaign.

17

Archaic Cultures of Western Kentucky

Richard W. Jefferies

Introduction

The Commonwealth of Kentucky lies along the southern margin of the Midwest, separated from the core area to the north by the Ohio River (Figure 17.1). Because of its location, Kentucky's prehistoric people shared cultural traits with groups that lived north of the Ohio River in the southern Midwest as well as with those who resided further south in the interior Southeast (Nance 1988:147). Clearly, this land now called "Kentucky" has held a border status for far longer than modern historians may realize.

Extending more than 650 km east to west, Kentucky's borders encompass a highly diverse physical and cultural landscape (McFarland 1943). The Cumberland Plateau, with its rugged mountains and steep, narrow valleys, covers much of eastern Kentucky. The rolling Interior Low Plateau, including the Bluegrass, Knobs, Mississippian Plateau, and Western Coalfield regions, comprises much of the central and western Kentucky landscape. Extreme western Kentucky, including the Ohio-Mississippi confluence, lies in the northern part of the low-lying Coastal Plain (Pollack 1990:7). The Tennessee and Cumberland rivers link southern and western Kentucky with the interior Southeast, while the Ohio River and its tributaries connect the southern Midwest and upper Southeast with the Northeast.

As in other parts of the Midwest, highly mobile Paleoindian hunter-gatherers had filtered into Kentucky by the end of the Pleistocene. The widely scattered, stylistically similar fluted projectile points left by these groups suggest that they shared a similar cultural tradition.

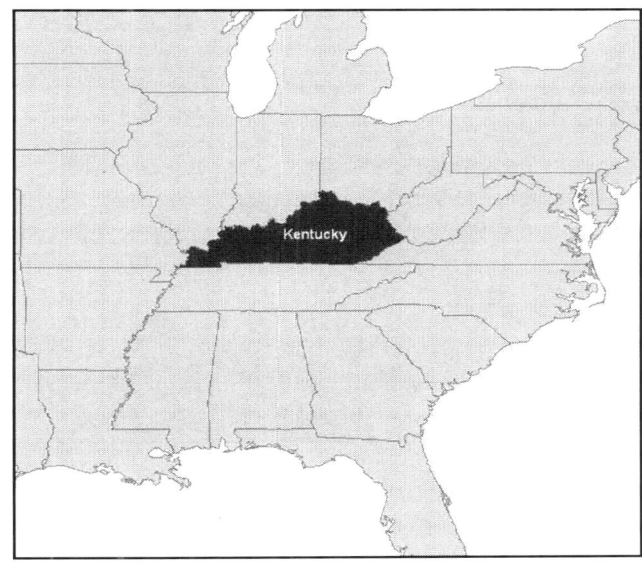

Figure 17.1. Location of Kentucky in the North American Midcontinent.

By the early Holocene, Kentucky experienced a significant population increase, with groups of hunter-gatherers rapidly filling the commonwealth's highly diverse landscape (Milner 2004:28). The appearance of geographically distinctive projectile point styles throughout the Midwest about this time suggests the development of regional cultural traditions.

Throughout the subsequent roughly 8,800 years of prehistory, commonly called the "Archaic" period, Kentucky's hunter-gatherers pursued variable paths of cultural development. By the late Holocene, thousands of years of interaction between these groups and their social and physical surroundings led to the creation of a highly diverse cultural landscape inhabited by hunting and gathering societies of variable size and complexity.

Despite Kentucky's border status, the eastern half of the commonwealth is geographically isolated from most of the Midwest. Cultural relationships among Kentucky's prehistoric residents appear to reflect this isolation, there being little evidence for intensive interaction between eastern Kentucky Archaic groups and those that lived in the Midwest (Jefferies 1997:483). Therefore, this chapter focuses on Archaic societies that inhabited the central and western parts of the state, primarily in the area along and adjacent to the Ohio River from the Falls of the Ohio, near modern-day Louisville, Kentucky, to the Ohio-Mississippi river confluence near Cairo, Illinois (Figure 17.2). This area contains that part of Kentucky lying within roughly 100 km of the Ohio River, including the lower portions of the Salt, Green, Tradewater, Cumberland, and Tennessee rivers. These river systems served as important communication and transportation routes for western Kentucky's hunter-gatherer societies, facilitating the flow of information, goods, and people among the region's dispersed population (Muller 1986:25).

Over the past 100 years, names like Moore, Nelson, Webb, Rolingson, Schwartz, Winters, Marquardt, Watson, Nance, Granger, Collins, and Janzen have become associated with the study of Kentucky's Archaic people. Research done by these and other archaeologists has had a major impact on current understanding of prehistoric North American hunter-gatherers. Initial work helped to define the Archaic concept (Ritchie 1932), while subsequent investigations provided important insights on the emergence of hunter-gatherer cultural complexity (Price and Brown 1985).

Dates used in this chapter were calibrated using the CALIB Rev 4.4.2 radiocarbon calibration program (Stuiver and Reimer 2004). The dates given in the text represent the median probability for the one-sigma range. A comprehensive list of Kentucky lower Ohio Valley Archaic radiocarbon dates is presented in Table 17.1. If calibration provided more than one intercept, the one with the highest probability was included in the table. The date in parentheses is the median probability for all intercepts. Information used to construct Table 17.1 was obtained from original site documentation, supplemented by data from Turnbow (1981) and Maslowski et al. (1995).

Environmental Setting

The Ohio River is one of the longest rivers in North America, stretching nearly 1,600 km from the confluence of the Allegheny and Monongahela rivers in Pennsylvania to the juncture of the Ohio and Mississippi rivers near Cairo, Illinois. The lower Ohio River region comprises the lower one-third (ca. 600 km) of the river valley, extending from the Falls of

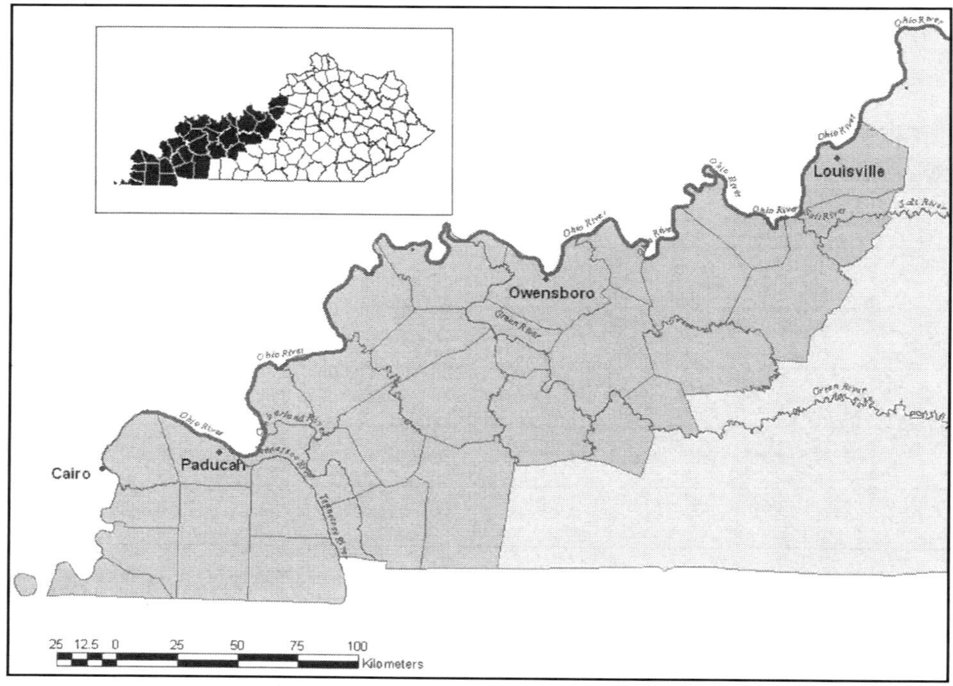

Figure 17.2. The lower Ohio Valley region of western Kentucky.

Table 17.1. Radiocarbon Dates from Western Kentucky Sites.

Site Number	Site Name	Lab Number	C14 age (B.P.)	Sigma	Uncalibrated B.C. Date	Calibrated B.C. Dates	Reference(s)
15JF243	Longworth-Gick	TX-3012	9490	230	7540	9186(8834)8598	Collins et al. 1979:1024; Turnbow 1981
15LY48	Whalen	Beta-15080	9430	100	7480	8813(8736)8551	Nance 1988:132
15LY48	Whalen	SFU-221	8500	460	6550	8226(7562)7055	Nance 1988:132
15JF243	Longworth-Gick	TX-3011	8440	380	6490	7971(7476)7036	Collins et al. 1979:1024; Turnbow 1981
15JF243	Longworth-Gick	UGA-1336	8440	125	6490	7595(7475)7447	Collins et al. 1979:1024; Turnbow 1981
15JF243	Longworth-Gick	TX-2951	8420	110	6470	7582(7459)7448	Collins et al. 1979:1024; Turnbow 1981
15LV156	Morrisroe	SFU-271	8220	100	6270	7334(7253)7110	Nance 1986:42
15LV156	Morrisroe	Beta-10477	7840	100	5890	6825(6718)6587	Nance 1986:42
15MCL11	Ward	Not reported	7750	50	5800	6594(6562)6503	Mensforth 1996
15LY48	Whalen	SFU-249	7670	630	5720	7326(6642)5980	Nance 1988:132
15LV156	Morrisroe	SFU-130	7530	150	5580	6525(6365)6524	Nance 1986:42
15TR33	Lawrence	UGA-286	7470	85	5520	6401(6319)6242	Mocas 1985:84–85
15BT5	Carlston Annis	C-180	7375	500	5425	6770(6294)5718	Arnold and Libby 1951:114; Marquardt and Watson 1974:7
15TR33	Lawrence	UGA-436	7325	125	5375	6260(6181)6055	Mocas 1985:84–85
15McL12	Kirkland	ISGS-2299	7320	80	5370	6235(6170)6070	Haskins 1988
15TR3	Lawrence	UGA-240	7265	305	5315	6417(6136)5841	Mocas 1985:84–85
15LV156	Morrisroe	SFU-270	7180	130	5230	6114(6041)5969	Nance 1986:42
15LV156	Morrisroe	SFU-121	7110	250	5160	6115(5983)5737	Nance 1986:42
15LY48	Whalen	SFU-252	7100	600	5150	6609(6014)5457	Nance 1988:132
15LV156	Morrisroe	Beta-10476	6630	110	4680	5638(5562)5478	Nance 1986:42
15McL12	Kirkland	ISGS-2298	6600	80	4650	5562(5544)5480	Haskins 1988
15LV156	Morrisroe	Beta-10475	6440	110	4490	5483(5401)5302	Nance 1986:42
15WA601	unknown	UGA-1713	6310	105	4360	5374(5268)5208	Brandau 1977
15McN18	Crawford Lake	ISGS-2153	6150	150	4200	5262(5076)4919	Maslowski et al. 1995
15ED175	Lee Cave Interior	UCLA-1729B	6050	60	4100	5001(4940)4899	Watson 1974:215, 236
15BT5	Carlston Annis	UAZ-1	5730	640	3780	5322(4575)3942	Haskins and Herrmann 1989
15BU33	unknown	UGA-806	5690	70	3740	4616(4530)4455	Janzen 1977:131
15MCL12	Kirkland	Beta-82081	5650	80	3730	4616(4521)4449	Claassen 1996
15MCL4	Barrett	Beta-131956	5620	40	3670	4422(4439)4395	Herrmann 2002
15MCL11	Ward	AA-31192	5600	100	3650	4536(4442)4343	Herrmann 2002
15LV156	Morrisroe	Beta-10474	5580	100	3630	4504(4423)4334	Nance 1986:42
15ED371	McCoy Hollow Shelter	Beta-31384	5470	100	3520	4402(4297)4223	Prentice 1990
15WA601	unknown	UGA-1714	5465	75	3515	4363(4296)4224	Schock 1979
15SP8	unknown	UGA-821	5390	220	3440	4404(4208)3977	Janzen 1977:131
15Bt92	York/Render	Beta-47624	5370	100	3420	4127(4186)4049	Crothers 1999

Table 17.1. Radiocarbon Dates from Western Kentucky Sites, continued.

Site Number	Site Name	Lab Number	C14 age (B.P.)	Sigma	Uncalibrated B.C. Date	Calibrated B.C. Dates	Reference(s)
15BT5	Carlston Annis	WIS-1302	5350	80	3400	4130(4170)4047	Marquardt and Watson 1983
15OH2	Indian Knoll	C-254	5302	300	3352	4401(4120)3789	Winters 1974
15JF60	Hornung	M-2461	5220	230	3270	4254(4036)3794	Janzen 1977:131
15ED69	Jagger Ridge Shelter	Beta-31383	5175	70	3225	4045(3980)3937	Prentice 1990
15BT5	Carlston Annis	C-116	5149	300	3199	4255(3955)3651	Winters 1974
15BT92	York/Render	Beta-47623	5140	100	3190	4004(3933)3887	Crothers 1999
15ED371	McCoy Hollow Shelter	Beta-31117	5130	95	3180	3998(3917)3888	Prentice 1990
15MCN81	Hedden	Beta-93737	5130	50	3180	3864(3914)3805	Rossen 2000
15MCL11	Ward	AA-30520	5120	90	3170	3986(3902)3887	Herrmann 2002
15JF60	Hornung	UGA-401	5100	75	3150	3882(3877)3799	Janzen 1977:131
15JF60	Hornung	UGA-390	5085	85	3135	3965(3869)3788	Janzen 1977:131
15BT11	Haynes	Beta-102648	5080	90	3130	3967(3866)3780	Crothers 1999
15BT5	Carlston Annis	UGA-3393	5030	85	3080	3941(3829)3837	Marquardt and Watson 1983
15JF267	KYANG	Beta-29627	5010	90	3060	3818(3807)3706	Bader and Granger 1989
15JF60	Hornung	M-2464	5000	200	3050	3998(3800)3629	Crane and Griffin 1972:162; Janzen 1977:133–134
15BT5	Carlston Annis	C-251	4900	250	2950	3967(3676)3940	Winters 1974
15JF60	Hornung	M-2460	4900	200	2950	3944(3686)3515	Crane and Griffin 1972:162
15BT11	Haynes	Beta-102650	4850	60	2900	3704(3644)3630	Crothers 1999
15BT92	York/Render	Beta-59057	4830	90	2880	3707(3601)3517	Crothers 1999
15MCL11	Ward	AA-30521	4800	65	2850	3652(3571)3520	Herrmann 2002
15JF630	Railway Museum	Beta-70350	4780	80	2830	3647(3556)3511	Anslinger et al. 1994
15BT6	DeWeese	Beta-104498	4760	70	2810	3640(3544)3515	Crothers 1999
15BT5	Carlston Annis	WIS-1301	4760	90	2810	3641(3539)3503	Marquardt and Watson 1983
15JF630	Railway Museum	Beta-70351	4720	70	2770	3435(3508)3378	Anslinger et al. 1994
15BT92	York/Render	Beta-59054	4710	110	2760	3473(3482)3370	Crothers 1999
15BT92	York/Render	Beta-59055	4700	100	2750	3475(3475)3369	Crothers 1999
15BT92	York/Render	Beta-59053	4680	100	2730	3537(3456)3361	Crothers 1999
15BT5	Carlston Annis	UGA-3391	4670	85	2720	3325(3455)3360	Marquardt and Watson 1983
15OH2	Indian Knoll	T0-8791	4670	70	2720	3521(3460)3366	Morey et al. 2002
15BT5	Carlston Annis	UGA-3395	4655	540	2705	3980(3320)2833	Marquardt and Watson 1983
15BT11	Haynes	Beta-102649	4650	60	2700	3517(3450)3398	Crothers 1999
15BT6	DeWeese	Beta-104497	4650	50	2700	3511(3452)3413	Crothers 1999
15UN127	Highland Creek	Beta-134229	4580	80	2630	3379(3298)3307	Maggard and Pollack 2000
15BT6	DeWeese	Beta-104496	4570	80	2620	3375(3273)3306	Crothers 1999

Table 17.1. Radiocarbon Dates from Western Kentucky Sites, continued.

Site Number	Site Name	Lab Number	C14 age (B.P.)	Sigma	Uncalibrated B.C. Date	Calibrated B.C. Dates	Reference(s)
15OH2	Indian Knoll	AA-31194	4570	75	2620	3375(3272)3306	Herrmann 2002
15SP8	unknown	UGA-820	4550	85	2600	3243(3236)3099	Janzen 1977:131
15BT92	York/Render	Beta-59056	4530	100	2580	3368(3219)3088	Crothers 1999
15MCN81	Hedden	Beta-93734	4520	50	2570	3238(3212)3168	Rossen 2000
15MCL4	Barrett	Beta-131957	4520	40	2570	3236(3212)3170	Herrmann 2002
15BT11	Haynes	Beta-106447	4520	60	2570	3238(3211)3168	Crothers 1999
15BT5	Carlston Annis	UCLA-2117I	4500	60	2550	3341(3201)3258	Marquardt and Watson 1983
15JF550	Habich	Beta-50950	4480	80	2530	3340(3175)3206	Granger et al. 1992
15UN127	Highland Creek	Beta-134231	4470	80	2520	3337(3165)3208	Maggard and Pollack 2000
15OH2	Indian Knoll	TO-8792	4460	90	2510	3337(3153)3208	Morey et al. 2002
15UN127	Highland Creek	Beta-134232	4440	70	2490	3104(3115)3013	Maggard and Pollack 2000
15MCN81	Hedden	Beta-93733	4420	60	2470	3102(3072)2921	Rossen 2000
15UN127	Highland Creek	Beta-134230	4380	70	2430	3096(3023)2906	Maggard and Pollack 2000
15JF10	Lone Hill	UGA-841	4365	185	2415	3348(3030)2866	Janzen 1977:131
15BT5	Carlston Annis	UGA-3390	4350	85	2400	3097(3001)2882	Marquardt and Watson 1983
15BT5	Carlston Annis	C-739	4333	450	2383	3536(2942)2456	Winters 1974
15BT6	DeWeese	Beta-104499	4320	50	2370	2932(2947)2884	Crothers 1999
15JF60	Hornung	UGA-262	4315	60	2365	2939(2946)2882	Janzen 1977:131
15UN127	Highland Creek	Beta-134234	4310	70	2360	3026(2942)2877	Maggard and Pollack 2000
15OH2	Indian Knoll	TO-8794	4300	70	2350	3024(2921)2873	Morey et al. 2002
15MCN81	Hedden	Beta-93735	4300	60	2350	2940(2919)2877	Rossen 2000
15BT5	Carlston Annis	C-738	4289	300	2339	3351(2907)2564	Winters 1974
15OH2	Indian Knoll	C-740	4282	250	2332	3124(2903)2576	Winters 1974
15BT5	Carlston Annis	UCLA-1845A	4250	80	2300	2816(2811)2671	Marquardt and Watson 1983
15JF60	Hornung	UGA-261	4240	95	2290	2819(2802)2663	Janzen 1977:131
15MCL12	Kirkland	ISGS-2306	4240	150	2290	3021(2825)2618	Haskins 1988
15OH2	Indian Knoll	TO-8793	4230	80	2280	2815(2788)2674	Morey et al. 2002
15ED175	Lee Cave Interior	UCLA-1729A	4200	65	2250	2815(2765)2675	Watson 1974:215, 236
15MCL11	Ward	not reported	4140	60	2190	2865(2724)2806	Mensforth 1996
15ED1	Mammoth Cave	UCLA-1730A	4120	70	2170	2705(2698)2617	Watson et al. 1974:235-236
15BT5	Carlston Annis	Beta-175338	4080	40	2130	2669(2624)2567	Marquardt and Watson 2005c:Table 6.1
15OH13	Bowles	UAZ-2	4060	220	2110	2887(2595)2296	Haskins and Hermann 1989
15BT5	Carlston Annis	UCLA-1845B	4040	180	2090	2787(2571)2400	Marquardt and Watson 1983

Table 17.1. Radiocarbon Dates from Western Kentucky Sites, continued.

Site Number	Site Name	Lab Number	C14 age (B.P.)	Sigma	Uncalibrated B.C. Date	Calibrated B.C. Dates	Reference(s)
15BT5	Carlston Annis	Beta-175337	4030	40	2080	2579(2542)2488	Marquardt and Watson 2005b:Table 6.1
15MCN81	Hedden	Beta-93738	4030	50	2080	2582(2551)2472	Rossen 2000
15MCL12	Kirkland	ISGS-2304	3990	160	2040	2698(2504)2288	Haskins 1988
15OH2	Indian Knoll	C-741	3963	350	2013	2905(2465)2008	Winters 1974
15JF10	Lone Hill	UGA-842	3935	95	1985	2501(2418)2288	Janzen 1977:131
15MCN81	Hedden	Beta-93736	3850	50	1900	2353(2316)2271	Rossen 2000
15MCL12	Kirkland	ISGS-2297	3830	80	1880	2353(2282)2196	Haskins 1988
15OH2	Indian Knoll	NSEC	3800	80	1930	2349(2240)2135	Herrmann 2002
15AD70	unknown	Beta-16932	3560	110	1610	2033(1904)1743	DiBlasi 1987
15OH2	Indian Knoll	AA-31193	3500	60	1550	1889(1819)1740	Herrmann 2002
15HT4	Salts Cave	GAK-2767	3490	110	1540	1952(1814)1683	Watson 1974:235–236
15JF550	Habich	Beta-42898	3480	100	1530	1923(1802)1683	Granger et al. 1990
15BT10	Read	ISGS-2245	3470	200	1520	1984(1807)1524	Haskins 1988
15OH13	Bowles	UCLA-2117G	3440	80	1490	1829(1750)1681	Marquardt and Watson 1983
15OH94	Peter Cave	UGA-3454	3415	105	1465	1784(1720)1603	Marquardt and Watson 1983
15HT4	Salts Cave	GAK-2766	3410	200	1460	1780(1713)1603	Watson 1974:235–236
15BT10	Read	ISGS-2246	3400	100	1450	1777(1701)1600	Haskins 1988
15HT4	Salts Cave	GAK-2764	3360	220	1410	1946(1669)1405	Watson 1974:235–236
15BT10	Read	ISGS-2249	3350	70	1400	1690(1635)1598	Haskins 1988
15BT5	Carlston Annis	UCLA-2117B	3330	80	1380	1690(1615)1520	Marquardt and Watson 1983
15HT4	Salts Cave	M-1589	3140	150	1190	1536(1390)1211	Crane and Griffin 1968
15JF4	Spadie	TX-3013	3090	150	1140	1518(1324)1188	Boisvert 1979:881; Turnbow 1981
15HD41	Bland Cave	M-561	3030	250	1080	1520(1256)969	Crane and Griffin 1958:1123
15BU___	Riverwood	M-2462	2870	150	920	1220(1077)896	Janzen 1977:131, 136
15WA916	unknown	UGA-1708	2860	270	910	1414(1065)791	Schock 1979
15BT5	Carlston Annis	UCLA-2117D	2515	80	565	724(622)537	Marquardt and Watson 1983
15OH13	Bowles	UCLA-2117F	2420	200	470	799(530)357	Marquardt and Watson 1983

the Ohio near present-day Louisville, Kentucky, to the Ohio-Mississippi river confluence. The Falls of the Ohio was selected as the eastern boundary of the area under consideration here because, prior to modern navigation improvements, it was the only significant natural barrier to river transportation and appears to have coincided with some kind of Archaic-period social boundary (Jefferies 1997, 2004).

The lower Ohio River flows through a constantly changing physical landscape (Figure 17.3). In Kentucky, its eastern portion is bordered by the gently rolling Outer Bluegrass region. This area of low to moderate relief is cut by many steep valleys, resulting in little flat land (McGrain 1983:66). The Salt River drains much of this part of the commonwealth.

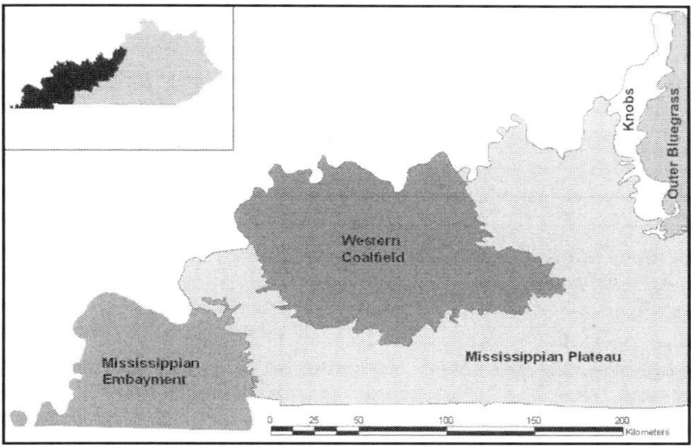

Figure 17.3. Major physiographic regions of western Kentucky.

Downriver, the western edge of the Outer Bluegrass is separated from the Mississippian Plateau by a narrow band of steep conical hills known as the "Knobs" (McDowell 1986:66–67). The plateau's limestone plains are marked by thousands of sinkholes, springs, and caves, creating a karst topography with a poorly developed drainage system (Kentucky Geological Survey 2002). Prior to the introduction of modern agriculture, portions of the Mississippian Plateau were covered by "barrens," a pioneer-era term that referred to grassland prairies (McDowell 1986:67).

Further west, the hilly terrain of the Western Coalfield is dissected by streams flowing though wide, poorly drained, swampy valleys. Extensive beds of Pennsylvanian sandstone, shale, and coal underlie this part of the commonwealth. Rockshelters often form where sandstone strata are exposed to weathering. Much of the Western Coalfield is drained by either the Tradewater or Green River. During the Pleistocene, the lower portion of the Ohio River was choked by glacial outwash, creating extensive, shallow slackwater lakes in the lower Green and Tradewater valleys (Pollack 1990:10).

The Dripping Springs Escarpment, a narrow band of sandstone ridges, separates the Western Coalfield from the western section of the Mississippian Plateau (McDowell 1986:68). The many rockshelters found along the escarpment were available for temporary shelters (Pollack 1990:10). This far-western part of the Mississippian Plateau is drained by tributaries of the lower Tennessee River.

As the Ohio River approaches its juncture with the Mississippi River, it enters the Mississippian Embayment region. The Embayment, a northward extension of the Gulf Coastal Plain, is generally flat and subject to frequent and extensive flooding. Oxbow lakes and meander loops are particularly common in this part of the valley, as are other kinds of wetland habitats (swamps, ponds, and sloughs) (Pollack 1990:9). The Embayment is drained by tributaries of the Tennessee, Ohio, and Mississippi rivers (Kentucky Geological Survey 2002).

The plants and animals that inhabited the prehistoric Kentucky landscape varied according to regional and local environmental conditions. Because of the rapidly changing Holocene environment (Delcourt and Delcourt 1981), direct correlations between physical landscapes inhabited by Archaic hunter-gatherers and those encountered by early Euro-American visitors to the commonwealth are, at best, risky. Nevertheless, early historical accounts can provide a general idea of the diversity of western Kentucky's prehistoric plant and animal communities.

In the eastern part of the study area, including parts of the Outer Bluegrass and Knobs, white and red oak, sugar maple, tuliptree, beech, black walnut, and shagbark hickory dominated the forests. Early travelers also reported lots of cane, rye, and clover, reflecting the presence of open forests and sizable grasslands (Braun 1950:125–131). Oak, oak-hickory, and oak-chestnut communities grew on the drier slopes and uplands of the Knobs. Wetter areas hosted oak-tulip forests, while pines, red cedar, and a variety of prairie vegetation grew in drier areas (Braun 1950:136–151).

The Mississippian Plateau was covered by a mosaic of different plant communities. In the east, forests resembled those that grew in the Knobs and Outer Bluegrass. In the west, oak forest grew on the rolling plateau surface, while the isolated hills were covered by oak-hickory forests. Prairie vegetation was common, drier upland slopes hosted cedar barrens, and swamp forests grew in the wet flatlands (Braun 1950:151–152).

Mississippian Embayment plant communities included many species commonly associated with the Gulf Coastal Plain, including swamp, oak-hickory and mixed mesophytic forests, and prairies. Dense stands of willow, swamp chestnut, pin and water oaks, cottonwood, elm, sycamore, and pecan trees once grew in the wet alluvial valleys. Deeper swamps hosted bald cypress trees (Braun 1950:157–159).

The diverse nature of the lower Ohio Valley landscape meant that Archaic hunter-gatherers had access to wide variety of foods. In addition, they could, hunt, trap, or fish for the many animal species associated with those plant communities.

History of Archaic Period Research

Interest in Kentucky's prehistoric people and their way of life can be traced back nearly 200 years (Lewis 1996; Schwartz 1967). Many early explorers, naturalists, and scientists who came to the commonwealth in the early nineteenth century noted the numerous large and impressive mounds and earthworks that dotted the rolling landscape (Rafinesque 1824, cited in Lewis 1996:7; Squier and Davis 1848). The architecture and contents of these earthen constructions fascinated many people, and their age and origin were the subjects of intense intellectual debates for many years (Silverberg 1968; Thomas 1894).

Archaeological investigations increased in frequency during the late nineteenth century, but most continued to focus on what archaeologists now recognize as the products of Woodland or Late Prehistoric groups (Thomas 1894). Largely because of the absence of monumental architecture, most sites attributable to earlier Archaic-period hunter-gatherers were missed or ignored by these early "archaeological" endeavors.

By the beginning of the twentieth century, a growing cadre of scientists was starting to realize that these "mound-building" societies were not Kentucky's earliest prehistoric inhabitants. In 1916, C. B. Moore, known for his many archaeological forays along the rivers of the Midwest and Southeast, published a report describing his "excavations" at 10 Green River sites in west-central Kentucky. Along with his site descriptions, Moore also published high-quality illustrations, a few in color, showing some of the many artifacts that he unearthed. Moore's photographs and drawings showed that, while the age of the implements, ornaments, and ritual objects was uncertain, their technological complexity and stylistic sophistication indicated that the hunter-gatherers who made them lived a life that was hardly "solitary, poore, nasty, brutish, and short" (Hobbes 1990:89).

Moore (1916) and his energetic crew opened sizable portions of some of the Green River Archaic sites. For example, they removed nearly 300 human burials in 20 days while visiting Indian Knoll (15Oh2) (Funkhouser and Webb 1928:155). In his 1916 report, Moore (1916:432–437) described the artifacts that he found at Indian Knoll as well as incorrectly speculated that the many stone atlatl weights and antler atlatl hooks found there were used to make fish nets. The perceived function of these stone and antler objects would be a topic of discussion for many years to come (Webb 1981).

Nels C. Nelson (1917) visited Mammoth Cave about the same time that Moore was working along the Green River. His investigations at the cave and at other nearby sites clearly demonstrated that Archaic people had once lived in the area (Nelson 1917:Figures 1 and 15). Nelson recognized that these people were more primitive and older than the "Mound Builder" groups. He perceptively suggested that these ancient people subsisted by hunting, collecting, and fishing and that they were the cultural and biological antecedents of the region's later agriculture-based societies (Nelson 1917:68–69).

By the mid-1920s, William S. Webb and William D. Funkhouser, two University of Kentucky professors, started their career-long interest in Kentucky's Archaic cultures. In 1924, the two budding archaeologists traveled to the Green River to visit the Indian Knoll and Chiggerville shell middens, excavating several trenches to collect information about the sites. Like C. B. Moore, they, too, were intrigued by the atlatl hooks and weights that they also interpreted as net-making implements (Webb and Funkhouser 1928). The middens' abundant shell suggested to Funkhouser and Webb (1928:153) that their inhabitants were fishermen and boatmen, so the two referred to them as "River People."

In 1928, Funkhouser and Webb published their views on Kentucky prehistory in *Ancient Life in Kentucky*. They divided the commonwealth's prehistoric archaeological record, then of unknown duration, into six "cultures," which they gave archaeological, tribal, or linguistic names. Although none of the six really corresponded to what researchers now call the "Archaic" tradition, some of the "Algonquin" group's cultural attributes were rather Archaic-like (Schwartz 1967:31–34). Funkhouser and Webb (1928:67) proposed that the many large shell middens along and west of the Green River marked the former presence of these Algonquin groups.

Webb and Funkhouser refined their views on Kentucky's prehistoric culture areas for their 1932 publication, *Archaeological Survey of Kentucky*. They renamed the part of the state where the "River People" once lived the "Shell Mound Area." They proposed that the mounds were among the oldest evidence of mound occupancy in Kentucky and that their inhabitants subsisted entirely on hunting and fishing (Webb and Funkhouser 1932:425). Despite Webb's and Funkhouser's exhaustive shell-mound research, the formal definition of an "Archaic" culture did not take place until Ritchie (1932) published his Lamoka Lake report (Schwartz 1967:80).

During the 1930s and early 1940s, federal legislation designed to help pull the country out of the Great Depression, like the Emergency Relief Act, greatly contributed to the refinement of the Archaic concept. While these measures were not specifically designed to assist archaeologists, the labor-intensive nature of archaeological fieldwork made it a particularly effective way to put unemployed people back on the payroll, particularly in rural areas where other sources of employment were hard to find. The use of large field crews made large-scale excavations possible for the first time, while standardized field and laboratory techniques facilitated consistent data collection and analysis. Given the conditions under which the work was done, the results were of remarkably high quality (Milner and Smith 1986).

From 1937 to 1941, Webb and his associates, using largely Works Progress Administration (WPA) crews, excavated many now-famous Green River middens, including Indian Knoll (Webb 1946), Carlston Annis (Webb 1950a), Ward (Webb and Haag 1940), Kirkland (Webb and Haag 1940), Read (Webb

1950b), Chiggerville (Webb and Haag 1939), Jimtown Hill (Rolingson 1967), and Barrett (Webb and Haag 1947). These endeavors yielded thousands of artifacts, features, and burials attributable to the repeated occupation of these sites by Archaic hunter-gatherers. Webb developed elaborate trait lists with which to investigate the cultural relationships among the Green River Archaic sites as well as between the Green River region and other parts of the Midcontinent (Webb 1946:235–240).

In 1940, Webb and Haag (1940:109) concluded that the Archaic inhabitants of the Read and Kirkland sites, known as the "Cypress Creek villages," were hunter-gatherer-fisher people who built "rude" habitation structures, used the atlatl to hunt animals, did not make pottery vessels, and did not grow gardens. They estimated that the Cypress Creek villages were between 1,000 and 2,000 years old.

The entry of the United States into World War II abruptly ended archaeological research in Kentucky. The 1950s brought with them a return to near-pre-Depression levels of archaeological research. Left in the wake were data from more than a dozen Green River Archaic sites that needed to be analyzed, synthesized, and integrated into a broader regional framework (Fowler 1959; Lewis and Kneberg 1959; Miller 1950). In some cases, reports on these unfinished projects were completed once the country returned to a peacetime footing (Webb 1946, 1950a, 1950b; Webb and Haag 1947).

As a consequence of these developments, along with the advent of radiocarbon dating, information on the Kentucky Archaic sites, primarily those along the Green River, was incorporated as part of several regional syntheses of Archaic research (Fowler 1959; Lewis and Kneberg 1959; Miller 1950). Among these syntheses, Lewis and Kneberg's (1959) analysis of the Midsouth's Archaic cultures, including the Green River Archaic, was particularly relevant for Kentucky researchers. Their analysis of data from Indian Knoll, Carlston Annis, Read, Ward, Chiggerville, and Parrish Village resulted in these sites' assignment to either the Midcontinent or Eastern Archaic tradition.

Fowler's (1959) synthesis of the Modoc Rock Shelter data also drew on information from the Green River shell middens. On the basis of his comparison of Modoc Rock Shelter assemblages with those from Parrish, Read, Carlston Annis, Ward, Butterfield, Kirkland, and Barrett, Fowler (1959:57) concluded that assemblage variability reflected seasonally specific occupations and that the seasonal food procurement cycle was fully developed by ca. 3800 cal B.C.

During the 1960s, western Kentucky Archaic research continued to focus on the analysis or reanalysis of Depression-era excavated sites and artifacts, interspersed with a few new reservoir salvage and dam construction projects (Clay and Schwartz 1963; Coe and Fischer 1959; Duffield 1966; Morse 1962). In 1966, Rolingson and Schwartz published the results of their analysis of Paleoindian and Archaic materials from the Henderson (15Ly27) and Roach (15Tr10) sites in the lower Tennessee-Cumberland Valley and the Morris (15Hk49) and Parrish (15Hk45) sites in the Tradewater watershed (1966:145). On the basis of artifacts from Henderson and the lower levels of Morris and Roach, they defined the hunting-based Henderson phase. They proposed that by ca. 4300 cal B.C., Henderson-phase groups had developed into seasonally specialized hunter-gatherers identified archaeologically as the Late Archaic Green River and Ledbetter phases in Kentucky and Tennessee, respectively (Rolingson and Schwartz 1966:162).

Martha Rolingson's 1967 analysis of the Green River shell-midden data represented the first systematic reexamination of that material in nearly 30 years. On the basis of her projectile point distribution analysis, she concluded that the midden artifacts spanned much of the prehistoric era but that most were more than 4,000 years old. She proposed that the middens gradually formed as a consequence of repeated occupation by hunter-gatherer groups (Rolingson 1967:418–419).

In the late 1960s, Winters extended his study of Archaic settlement patterns and systems (1967, 1969) to the Green River valley (1974). He described the "Indian Knoll Culture" as a harvesting economy and characterized Read, Chiggerville, and Ward as "settlements"; Kirkland, Barrett, and Carlston Annis as "base camps"; Butterfield as a "transient camp"; and Kirkland as a "hunting camp" (1974:xii–xvi). Unfortunately, Winters's analyses were severely impaired by his overemphasis on tool function, which he determined on the basis of tool morphology rather than use-wear analysis.

Winters (1968) also conducted the first systematic analysis of lower Ohio Valley Late Archaic mortuary practices and regional exchange, using data from the Green River middens. He noted that exotic items, primarily marine-shell beads and a few copper objects, occurred with only a few burials, which he interpreted as reflecting the differential distribution of wealth within this hunter-gatherer society (Winters 1968:209).

In 1972, William Marquardt and Patty Jo Watson initiated the Shell Mound Archaeological Project (SMAP) at the Carlston Annis site (15Bt5) in the Green River's Big Bend. The initial purpose of the SMAP was to compare the subsistence strategies of the shell middens' Archaic inhabitants with those of the prehistoric mineral miners of Mammoth (Watson 1974) and Salts (Watson et al. 1969) caves (Marquardt and Watson 1983:323–324).

Over the years, Marquardt and Watson continued to expand the scope of the SMAP. Additional research at Carlston Annis, along with field investigations at the Bowles (15Oh13) site, revealed that the middens were the products of very complex depositional processes. To learn more about how they formed, Marquardt and Watson developed a multifaceted research program that focused on a broad spectrum of issues, including geomorphology (Stein 1980), lithic and faunal remains (Hensley-Martin 1986; White 1990), human skeletal biology (Haskins and Herrmann 1996; Herrmann 2002), and settlement and subsistence (Crothers 1999; Crothers and Bernbeck 2004; Hensley 1994; Wagner 1996) (see Carstens and Watson

1996 for additional details). Publication of the SMAP's final report (Marquardt and Watson 2005a) represents the most comprehensive overview of middle Green River hunter-gatherers yet produced.

The Green River region has not been the only part of western Kentucky to yield important information about Archaic hunter-gatherers. In 1969, Donald E. Janzen (1977) initiated research on Holocene hunter-gatherer adaptation at the Falls of the Ohio. On the basis of excavations at several large Falls-area Archaic middens (Old Clarksville [12Cl1], Reid [12Fl1], Ferry Landing [12Hr3], and Miller [12Hr5] in Indiana and Hornung [15Jf60] and Lone Hill [15Jf10] in Kentucky), he proposed that the region's environmental diversity allowed Late Archaic hunter-gatherers to adopt a mobility strategy resembling a hub-and-spoke or semisedentary-wandering settlement model.

Complementing Janzen's research, Granger's (1988:179) study of Falls-area Archaic hunter-gatherers led to the definition of the late Middle Archaic Old Clarksville (ca. 4820 to 2970 cal B.C.) and the Late Archaic Lone Hill (ca. 2970 to 1422 cal B.C.) phases. Old Clarksville and Lone Hill–phase site distribution data provided a means for investigating diachronic trends in hunter-gatherer settlement and landscape use during the middle to late Holocene (Granger 1988).

In 1978, Jack Nance (1987) initiated the Lower Cumberland Archaeological Project (LCAP) to study the cultural and natural histories of the lower portions of the Cumberland, Tennessee, and Ohio rivers. The LCAP's long-range objectives included developing a detailed regional culture history, with emphasis on the Archaic period, employing areal sampling and informal site survey, excavating selected sites, documenting regional lithic resources, investigating geomorphic and environmental history, and conducting bioarchaeological research (Nance 1987:96).

Much of what was learned about hunter-gatherer activity in the lower Tennessee-Cumberland region came from the excavation of deeply stratified floodplain sites like Morrisroe (15Lv56) and Whalen (15Ly48) (Nance 1986, 1988). Excavation of the thick early Middle Archaic midden zone at Morrisroe yielded artifacts and charcoal for radiocarbon dating that helped clarify this poorly documented part of lower Ohio Valley prehistory (Conaty 1985; Nance 1986:25).

During the past 25 years, much of what archaeologists have learned about the Archaic occupation of Kentucky's lower Ohio Valley has resulted from cultural resource management–related projects spawned by the passage of federal and state environmental legislation. For example, archaeological investigations conducted prior to the construction of the Southwest Jefferson County Flood Protection project (Collins 1979a), just downriver from the Falls of the Ohio, identified four sites (Longworth-Gick [15Jf243], Villier [15Jf110], Rosenberger [15Jf18], and Spadie [15Jf14]) of National Register significance.

One of these sites (Longworth-Gick) contained deeply buried cultural strata representing at least six Early Archaic components (Collins 1979b). The other three sites were not as deeply stratified as Longworth-Gick but still provided abundant data on Early through Late Archaic adaptive strategies (Bovisert 1979; Driskell 1979; Robinson and Smith 1979).

Work done for the Railway Museum project (Anslinger et al. 1994) at the Falls of the Ohio and the Shawnee Power Plant project (Butler et al. 1981) in far western Kentucky also has yielded important data on the Kentucky Late Archaic.

Archaic Hunter–Gatherers of Western Kentucky

For purposes of this chapter, the Archaic "period" in western Kentucky is defined as the approximately 8,800 years extending from ca. 9500 to 650 cal B.C. This period generally coincides with the early through late Holocene in geological terminology. The beginning of the early Holocene (ca. 12,000 to 7000 cal B.C.) coincides with the melting of the Laurentide ice sheet; the start of the middle Holocene (ca. 7000 to 3800 cal B.C.) equates with the beginning of the Hypsithermal Interval; and the late Holocene (ca. 3800 cal B.C. to the present) coincides with the end of the Hypsithermal Interval (Smith 1986:6).

Regional archaeologists traditionally divide the Archaic period into Early, Middle, and Late subperiods on the basis of technological, subsistence, and settlement criteria. Some researchers have defined a "Terminal" Archaic subperiod consisting of the last part of the Late Archaic time span. However, because of local variation in the Midwest's cultural and physical landscape, the exact timing of the events and processes associated with these subperiods, along with the starting and ending dates of the subperiods, vary across the region (Stoltman 1978:708). The following temporal framework is used for this chapter: Early Archaic: ca. 9500 to 7000 cal B.C.; Middle Archaic: ca. 7000 to 3800 cal B.C.; Late Archaic: ca. 3800 to 1200 cal B.C.; Terminal Archaic: ca. 1200 to 650 cal B.C.

Early Archaic (ca. 9500 to 7000 cal B.C.)

The early Holocene brought with it significant changes in regional vegetation, animal populations, and the number and distribution of people over the landscape. Pollen records from Jackson Pond in west-central Kentucky, indicate that about 11,000 cal B.C., the region's spruce and jack-pine forests were gradually replaced by mesic, open-canopy forests dominated by oak, ash, and other deciduous trees (Wilkins et al. 1991:235). The region also experienced a decrease in the diversity of its mammal population, so that by roughly 9500 cal B.C., essentially the same animals lived in western Kentucky that did at the time of European settlement. Short-term environmental fluctuations undoubtedly resulted in diachronic variation in the frequency and distribution of some species (Semken 1983:192).

Technology and Chronology

As in other parts of the Midwest, much of what is known about the western Kentucky Early Archaic is based on the distribution of temporally diagnostic projectile points (Figure 17.4). These bifaces largely consist of a variety of stemmed and corner- and basal-notched types like Hardin Barbed (ca. 9400 to 6300 cal B.C.); Kirk Corner Notched (ca. 8700 to 8100 cal B.C.), Stemmed (ca. 8100 to 6900 cal B.C.), and Serrated (ca. 8100 to 6900 cal B.C.); Thebes Diagonal Notched (ca. 9400 to 6900 cal B.C.); Pine Tree Corner Notched (ca. 8700 to 8100 cal B.C.); MacCorkle Stemmed (ca. 8200 to 7500 cal B.C.); and LeCroy Bifurcated Stem (ca. 7500 to 6600 cal B.C.) (Justice 1987). Most examples come from temporally mixed surface contexts, but in a few cases, deeply stratified floodplain sites and rockshelters have yielded specimens from relatively undisturbed, temporally discrete contexts (Collins 1979a; Nance 1986). The dating of similar biface types from deeply stratified sites in adjacent parts of the Midwest and Southeast has clarified the temporal placement of these widely distributed point types (Brown and Vierra 1983; Broyles 1971; Chapman 1975, 1976; Coe 1964; Styles et al. 1983).

In addition to projectile points, Early Archaic assemblages also included flaked-stone bifaces reflecting different stages of reduction, hafted and unhafted drills and side and end scrapers,

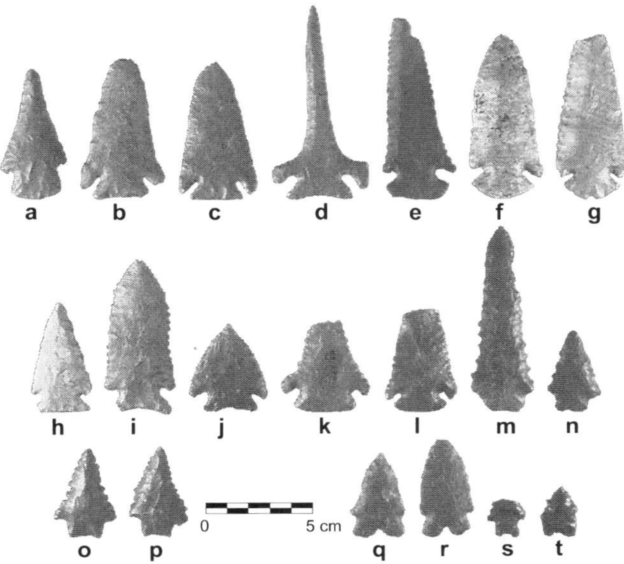

Figure 17.4. Early Archaic hafted bifaces from Kentucky's lower Ohio Valley region: a, Hardin Barbed cluster; b–g, Thebes cluster; h–l, Kirk Corner Notched cluster; m–p, Kirk Stemmed cluster; q, r, MacCorkle Stemmed; s, t, LeCroy cluster (Justice 1987).

knives, gravers, denticulates, perforators, and retouched flakes. A limited variety of ground-stone tools were also manufactured. Early Holocene hunter-gatherers undoubtedly made many tools out of wood, bone, and fiber, but these materials are seldom preserved on Kentucky Early Archaic sites.

Settlement

The Kentucky site file contains information on 342 Early Archaic components (137 components/1,000 years) in the study area (Figure 17.5). This compares with only 38 dating to the Late Paleoindian period (76 components/1,000 years). Although variation in component frequency cannot always be equated with demographic change, the substantial increase in numbers of Early Archaic sites suggests a considerable population increase. Early Archaic hunter-gatherers exploited a wide range of environments but preferred upland habitats (44 percent of sites) (Figure 17.6). Floodplain settings were also important (27 percent of sites), and fewer components were located on terraces (16 percent) and hillsides (12 percent).

Recent archaeological survey along Cypress Creek, a major Green River tributary, has helped to clarify diachronic trends in western Kentucky Archaic settlement (Jefferies et al. 2005). Although the Cypress Creek watershed is not representative of the entire lower Ohio Valley region, it typifies areas located away from the river's main channel.

Drawing on new survey data, museum collections, and site-file data, researchers identified 98 Cypress Creek Archaic components situated in four environmental zones. Early Archaic components accounted for 27 percent of the 98 Cypress Creek Archaic components. Early Archaic components are widely distributed throughout the Cypress Creek region. While Early Archaic activities were extensive, they were not intensive—most components are represented by one or two projectile points and a light debitage scatter.

A general distribution of sites yielding low artifact densities is consistent with what would be expected of hunter-gatherers who inhabited widely scattered sites for short periods of time. Early Archaic hunter-gatherers made greater use of the uplands relative to other environmental settings than did later hunter-gatherers. The few sites having intensive Early Archaic occupations were apparently situated in resource-rich areas that would have supported the periodic aggregation of otherwise scattered, mobile groups.

Archaeological investigations at several deeply stratified western Kentucky sites have helped clarify Early Archaic temporal and cultural parameters. Excavation of the Longworth-Gick site (Figure 17.7, No. 11), situated on a low floodplain ridge just downriver from the Falls of the Ohio (Collins 1979b), revealed eight deeply buried Early Archaic strata. The lower components (Zones XIII–VII) contained small varieties of Kirk points dating from approximately 9230 to 7640 cal B.C. Large-variety Kirks from the overlying zone (Zone V) dated to ca. 7640 cal B.C. The assemblage also contained bifaces in different stages of reduction, drills,

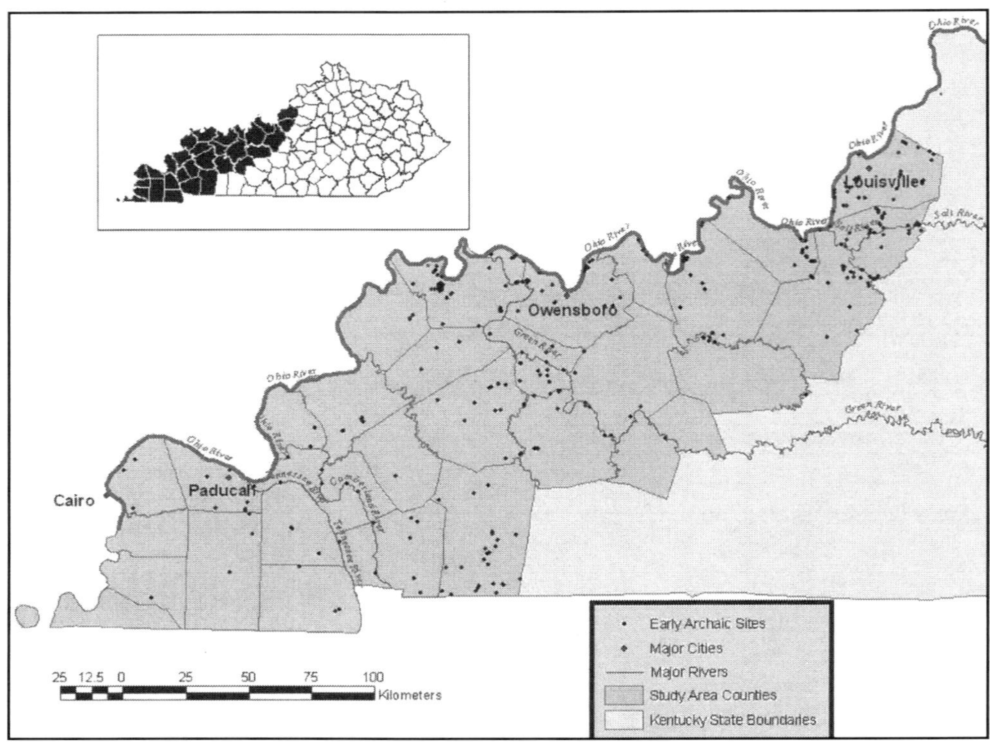

Figure 17.5. Early Archaic site distribution in western Kentucky.

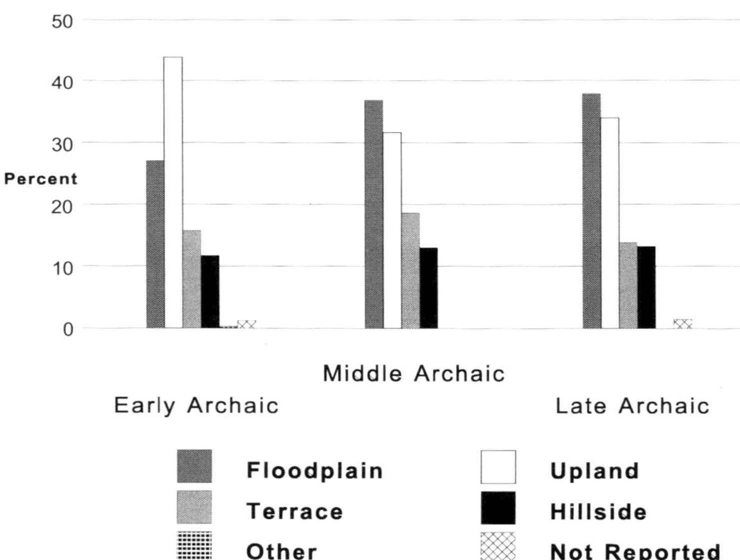

Figure 17.6. Percentage distribution of Kentucky lower Ohio Valley Archaic sites by landform type.

unifacial end scrapers, retouched flakes, and a small amount of ground stone (Collins 1979b:Table 5.17). The uppermost Early Archaic zone (Zone III), also dating to about 7640 cal B.C., yielded very small bifurcate-stemmed LeCroy and Kanawha points, representing a significant stylistic break with the earlier Kirk types. Stylistic changes were attributed by the excavator to changes in biface function (Collins 1979b:581).

Artifact and geomorphological data suggest that Early Archaic use of the Longworth-Gick site was brief but intensive. These occupations, marked by numerous charcoal-filled pits and burned areas, probably took place during the late

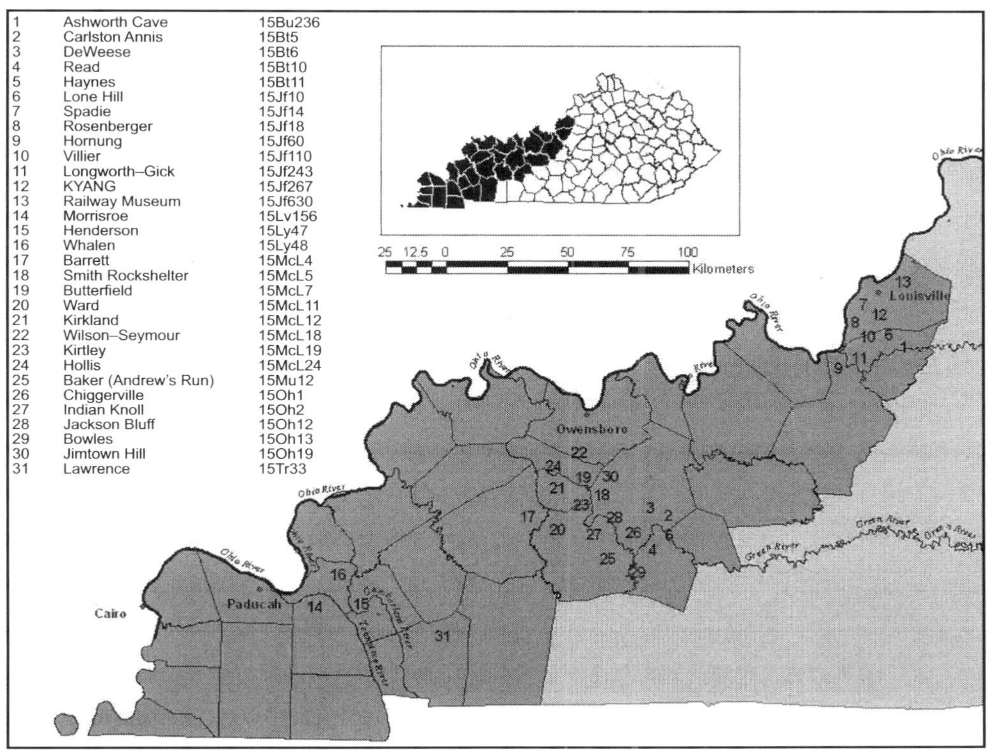

Figure 17.7. Major Kentucky lower Ohio Valley Archaic sites.

summer, fall, and early winter, when flooding was less likely (Collins and Driskell 1979:1024–1026).

The functional and technological attributes of the Longworth-Gick Early Archaic assemblages suggest that flaked-stone tool diversity, along with the tasks for which the tools were used, increased over time. An increase in the number of implements used to process plant foods (pitted stones and digging tools) relative to those associated with hunting suggests the increasing use of plant foods during the Early Archaic occupation (Collins 1979b:582).

Nance's research at the Morrisroe site, done as part of the LCAP, has done much to clarify the Archaic cultural sequence at the Tennessee-Cumberland-Ohio confluence (Conaty 1985; Nance 1986,1987, 1988). Prior to the LCAP, most of what was known about the area's Early Archaic culture was based on Lewis and Kneberg's (1961) work at the Eva site in western Tennessee (Nance 1986:12–13). The LCAP research has shown that, in western Kentucky, most Early Archaic projectile points generally fall into the Kirk Stemmed and Kirk Serrated types. Older types, including Kirk Corner Notched and Bifurcate Stem points, have been documented but do not commonly occur (Nance 1986).

The Morrisroe site (Figure 17.7, No. 14) is located in a high-deposition setting on the north bank of the lower Tennessee River (Nance 1986, 1988). The earliest-known occupation of the site is represented by a Kirk component containing Kirk Stemmed and Kirk Serrated projectile points. Older Kirk Corner Notched and Bifurcate Stem types were rare, leading Nance to conclude that the deeply buried stratum dated to the "tail end" of the Early Archaic. The presence of an early Middle Archaic Stanly point and a radiocarbon date of ca. 7270 cal B.C. support his temporal placement (Nance 1986:22–23).

The LCAP documented additional evidence of Early Archaic hunter-gatherer activity at the nearby Whalen site (Figure 17.7, No. 16), situated on the east bank of the lower Cumberland River (Nance 1988:129–135). Excavation revealed a Kirk component dating to approximately 7560 cal B.C. buried by nearly 3 m of alluvium. Mussel shell impressions associated with this Early Archaic zone represent the only known evidence for mussels on any lower Tennessee-Cumberland Archaic site (Nance 1988:132).

Data from the Morrisroe and Whalen sites suggest that late Early Archaic (post–ca. 7530 cal B.C.) settlement in the Lower Tennessee-Cumberland region consisted of nonintensive, short-term occupations (Nance 1988:129–135). Little data exist for the earlier times, but little difference would be expected.

Subsistence

Western Kentucky Early Archaic sites have yielded little botanical or faunal material with which to refine general regional subsistence models. Early Archaic groups appear to have exploited western Kentucky's early Holocene plant and animal communities using a mobile foraging strategy that incorporated base camps that were strategically located with respect to subsistence resources along with smaller extractive camps situated near seasonally available food sources. They continued to practice a broad-based subsistence strategy similar to that of Late Paleoindian groups, hunting a variety of large and small game and supplementing these resources with an assortment of plant foods. Nuts, particularly hickory and acorn, assumed an increasingly significant role in the Early Archaic diet. Implements associated with plant-food processing (nutting stones, manos, and metates) occur on some Early Archaic sites, supporting the inference of an increased significance of plant foods (Gremillion 2003:31–32; Meltzer and Smith 1986:17–18).

Faunal material from the Early Archaic strata at Ashworth Cave (15Bu236), located in the Knobs region (Figure 17.7, No. 1), suggests that site inhabitants focused their subsistence efforts on aquatic and forest animal communities, hunting deer, squirrel, and raccoon, collecting aquatic and terrestrial turtles, and fishing for drumfish (DiBlasi 1981). These animals provided important dietary protein and fat as well as bone, antler, and hides to manufacture needed implements, clothing, and items of personal adornment.

Social Organization and Mortuary Practices

Early Archaic site attributes, along with the distribution of those sites, indicate that western Kentucky's early Holocene hunter-gatherers were organized into small, highly mobile groups. Little is known about the composition of those groups, but they probably consisted of related kin and their spouses.

Brief glimpses of these societies' social and demographic characteristics come from the very few burials that have been professionally investigated. For example, a young adult female buried face down at the back of Ashworth Cave met her death by means of the large corner-notched projectile point embedded in her third thoracic vertebra. The point entered the woman's body with sufficient force to split the vertebra in half, resulting in excessive blood loss, traumatic shock to the nervous system, and possible paralysis of her respiratory muscles (DiBlasi 1981:74–75). This case illustrates that Early Archaic groups buried their dead in caves that also served as domestic spaces. In addition, the nature of the woman's trauma demonstrates that interpersonal violence was a risk faced by early Holocene hunter-gatherers, regardless of their age or gender.

A second example of Early Archaic mortuary behavior comes from the Lawrence site (15Tr33) located in the uplands east of the Cumberland River (Figure 17.7, No. 31) (Mocas 1977, 1985). Excavation of a pit feature exposed the flexed remains of two adult males between the ages of 22 and 28 years. One individual was accompanied by a heavily resharpened Kirk Serrated projectile point and a tool cache containing Kirk Corner Notched points, spokeshaves, drills, and scrapers. Both men wore necklaces made from beaver incisors and dog canines and were sprinkled with red ocher (Mocas 1985). A radiocarbon date of ca. 6170 cal B.C. places this burial feature slightly later in time than would the accepted dates for Kirk points.

Clearly, these two isolated examples of Early Archaic mortuary behavior have limited value in terms of what they say about early Holocene social organization. However, they underscore the ever-present danger to Early Archaic people from interpersonal conflict as well as providing information about the organization of Early Archaic technology (tool-kit composition) and personal adornment.

Middle Archaic (ca. 7000 to 3800 cal B.C.)

The Middle Archaic was a time of major environmental and culture change throughout much of eastern North America (Sassaman and Anderson 1996). In the Midwest, this segment of prehistory (ca. 7000 to 3800 cal B.C.) coincides with the middle Holocene (Sandweiss et al. 1999), characterized by generally warmer and drier conditions associated with the Hypsithermal Interval, or Climatic Optimum (Deevy and Flint 1957). These regional-scale climatic trends are expressed locally by seasonally fluctuating water levels, warmer water temperatures, and reduced water depth at Jackson Pond in LaRue County. Mesic trees gradually disappeared from the forests that surrounded Jackson Pond during the middle Holocene, replaced by oak-hickory-chestnut forests that thrived in the drier Hypsithermal conditions (Wilkins et al. 1991:236).

The Middle Archaic also was a time of major culture change for hunter-gatherers living in the lower Ohio Valley region. During the first half of the Middle Archaic, small, highly mobile groups of hunter-gatherers continued to inhabit the region. In most respects, their material culture, subsistence strategies, and socioeconomic organization closely resembled that of their Early Archaic predecessors (Jefferies 1996).

In contrast, by about 5400 cal B.C., some western Kentucky hunter-gatherers were experiencing major changes to their way of life that eventually led to decreased group mobility, reorganization of settlement and subsistence strategies, use of formal mortuary areas, elaboration of interregional exchange networks, and increased importance of cultivated plants (Price and Brown 1985). These developments parallel similar changes in adjacent parts of the Midwest about the same time (Brown and Vierra 1983; Jefferies et al. 2005; Stafford 1994).

Technology

Diagnostic early Middle Archaic projectile points include the types Stanly Stemmed (ca. 6900 to 5800 cal B.C.), Cypress Creek I and II (ca. 6600 to 5800 cal B.C.), Eva I and II (ca. 6900 to 2500 cal B.C.), and Morrow Mountain I (ca. 5800 to 5400 cal B.C.) (Figure 17.8). Most of these types were defined on the basis of work done in Tennessee (Lewis and

Lewis 1961) and North Carolina (Coe 1964), so the lower Ohio Valley lies along the western margin of their distribution (Justice 1987:Figures 42–45).

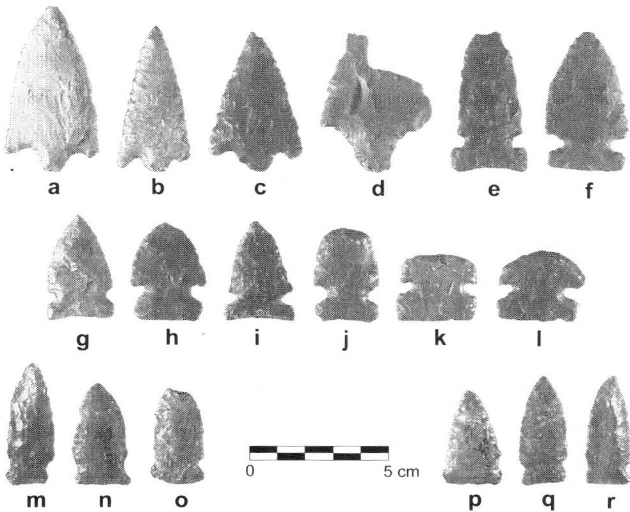

Figure 17.8. Middle Archaic hafted bifaces from Kentucky's lower Ohio Valley region: a–d, Eva cluster; e–l, Godar/Big Sandy II; m–r, Matanzas cluster (Justice 1987).

The Morrisroe site has a substantial early Middle Archaic Cypress Creek-Eva component (Stratum 3) dating from approximately 6560 to 5920 cal B.C. Cypress Creek I points, morphological correlates of Kirk Corner Notched points, appeared to span the temporal gap between Kirk and bifurcate-stem types and the later Eva types (Nance 1986:25–26). Eva II points were manufactured at Morrisroe as early as 6620 cal B.C., pushing back their first appearance in the region by at least several hundred years. At the nearby Lawrence site, the association of Kirk Serrated and Kirk Stemmed points with radiocarbon dates ranging from ca. 6320 to 6140 cal B.C. suggests that these varieties were manufactured well into the Middle Archaic (Mocas 1977:84–85).

Late Middle Archaic projectile points include side-notched types like Big Sandy II, Matanzas, and Salt River along with some Benton, White Springs, and Karnak varieties (Figure 17.8). Radiocarbon dates associated with the side-notched types generally range from 7000 to 3800 B.C., but later dates suggest that they were manufactured until the early Late Archaic (Justice 1987:119–120). Benton and White Springs points also span the Middle–Late Archaic temporal border (Justice 1987:108, 111).

Late Middle Archaic hunter-gatherers made an assortment of ground-stone items (Figure 17.9), such as grooved axes, pitted cobbles (i.e., nutting stones), pestles, grinding stones, abraders, pendants, and beads (Bader and Granger 1989). The appearance of ground-stone atlatl weights (Figure 17.10), often manufactured from nonlocal stone, marked the introduction of the atlatl weapon system that greatly extended a hunter's effective killing range (Burdin 2004). Middle Archaic hunter-gatherers made a diverse inventory of implements from bone (Figure 17.11), antler (Figure 17.12), and shell, but knowledge of their technological significance at most sites is limited because of poor preservation conditions. The late Middle Archaic Old Clarksville assemblage from the KYANG site (Figure 17.7, No. 12) near the Falls of the Ohio contained carved and engraved bone pins, needles, awls, and gouges; antler was used to make projectile points, atlatl hooks, and flakers (Bader and Granger 1989:IV-13, 1992).

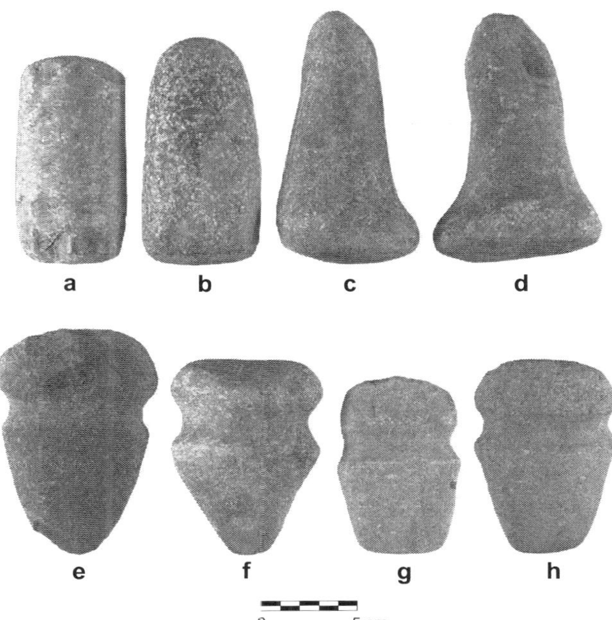

Figure 17.9. Ground stone from the Middle Green River region: a–d, pestles; e–h, grooved axes.

Figure 17.10. Ground-stone atlatl weights, or bannerstones, from the Middle Green River region. The two upper left specimens are unfinished.

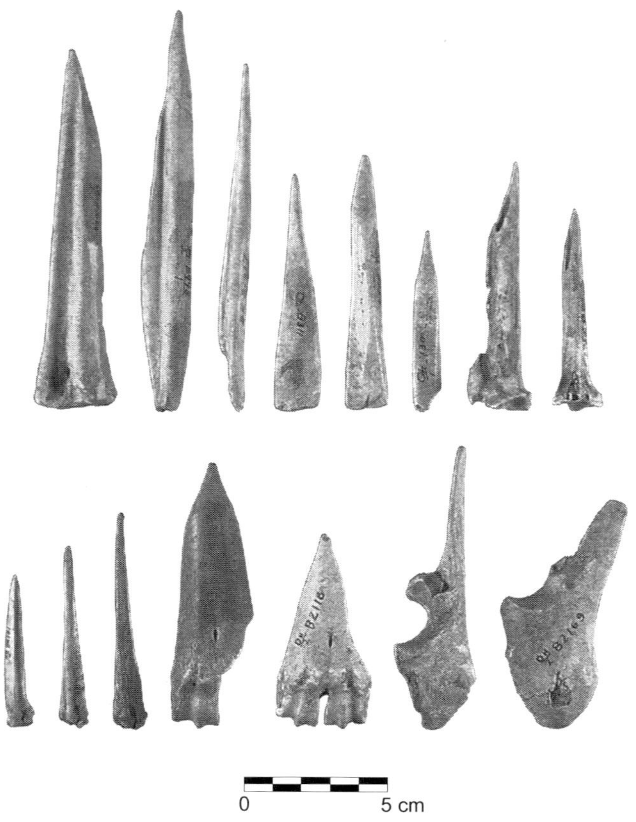

Figure 17.11. Bone awls and perforators from the Middle Green River region.

Settlement

The Kentucky site file reports fewer lower Ohio Valley Middle Archaic sites than Early Archaic ones (341 vs. 251) (Figure 17.13). The decrease in component frequency may be attributable to actual demographic changes, but other factors also may influence site counts.

First, for many years, most Kentucky archaeologists used the date of ca. 4820 cal B.C. to mark the end of the Middle Archaic (Granger 1988:153), conforming to Griffin's (1967) temporal framework for eastern North America. More recently, many researchers have used later dates for the division (ca. 3800 to 3100 cal B.C.) that are based on research in other parts of the Midwest (Brown and Vierra 1983:185; Jefferies and Morrow 1982:19–20; Stafford 1994:227). Consequently, many sites having diagnostic artifacts dating to 4820 to 3730 cal B.C. (many of them late Middle Archaic side-notched points) were classified as Late Archaic instead of late Middle Archaic. This is purely a taxonomic problem, but it affects the number of sites that are classified as Middle Archaic.

Second, identifying diagnostic early Middle Archaic projectile points is problematic. Recent investigation of sealed early Middle Archaic components on the Indiana side of the Ohio River recovered projectile points that would probably be dated earlier or later on the basis of their morphology (Stafford 2004). Failure to recognize these point types in surface collections could significantly contribute to an underenumeration of Middle Archaic components.

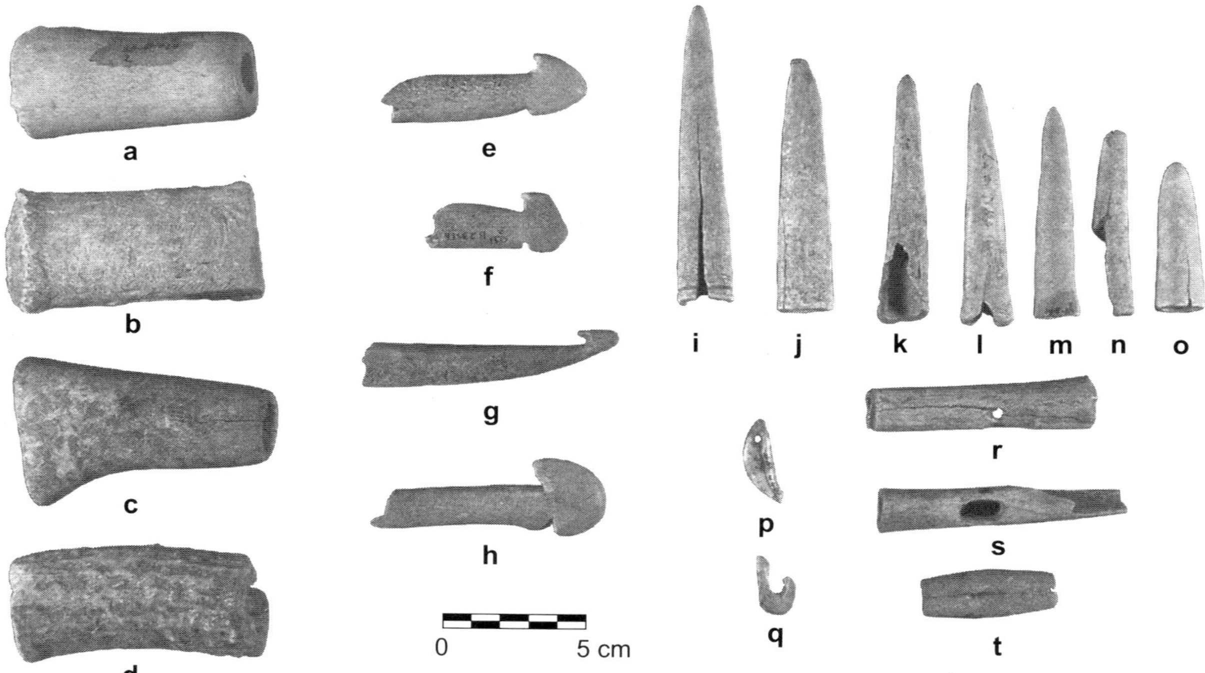

Figure 17.12. Antler and bone artifacts from the Middle Green River region: a–d, antler atlatl handles; e–h, antler atlatl hooks; i–o, antler projectile points; p, drilled canine bead; q, bone fishhook; r, s, drilled bone tubes; t, antler barrel-shaped bead.

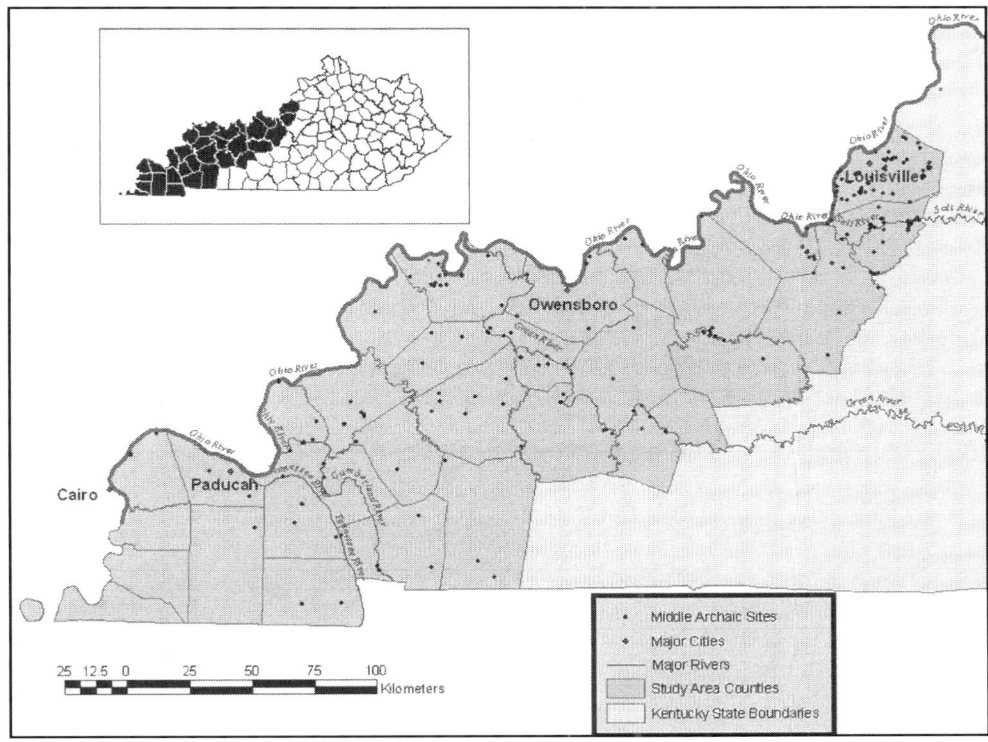

Figure 17.13. Middle Archaic site distribution in western Kentucky.

Comparison of Early and Middle Archaic site locations shows a marked decrease in the percentage of Middle Archaic sites in upland settings and a substantial increase in the percentage of floodplain sites (Figure 17.6). Little change is apparent in the use of other landform types. The increased use of floodplain habitats conforms to a regional trend toward the increased use of wetlands that became more pronounced during the late Middle Archaic (Brown 1985; Jefferies et al. 2005; Stafford 1994).

The Cypress Creek site data reflect this broad regional trend (Jefferies et al. 2005). Here, 68 percent of the Middle Archaic components occurred in wetland areas compared with just 46 percent of Early Archaic sites. Thirty-eight percent of all Middle Archaic sites were located next to the Green River, with many others situated near other kinds of wetland habitats.

The Cypress Creek data also illustrate differences between early Middle and late Middle Archaic settlement strategies. Very few early Middle Archaic components were documented, suggesting continuation of a highly mobile Early Archaic way of life well into the Middle Archaic. Stafford (1994) has documented a similar trend just across the Ohio River in southwestern Indiana.

In contrast, the number of late Middle Archaic components is sharply higher, these components occurring at 51 percent of the sites. Sites were situated in all environmental zones, but many clustered near wetland resources. Late Middle Archaic components at some of the Green River middens (Ward, Butterfield, and Jimtown Hill) reflect the gradual transition to a more sedentary way of life and the favoring of resource-rich locations for base camps. Other sites characterized by low artifact densities reflect shorter, less intensive occupations. Late Middle Archaic people also occasionally used rockshelters (e.g., Smith Rockshelter) (Jefferies et al. 2005).

Aside from site survey data like those used in the Cypress Creek Archaeological Project, most other Middle Archaic settlement data come from the excavation of Middle Archaic middens along the lower Ohio River, its tributaries, and nearby wetlands (Bader and Granger 1989; Granger 1988; Janzen 1977; Nance 1988).

Because of the difficulty in locating intact components, little is known about hunter-gatherers who lived in the lower Ohio Valley during the early part of the Middle Archaic period. Some of the best information comes from the Cypress Creek-Eva component (Stratum 3) at the Morrisroe site, dating from ca. 6620 to 5940 cal B.C. (Nance 1986, 1988). Site investigators used radiocarbon dates and temporally diagnostic artifacts to define three early Middle Archaic artifact assemblages (H, I, and J) (Conaty 1985:Table 33). Using assemblage attributes, Conaty was able to examine the contents of each assemblage and identify patterns of diachronic variability in the kinds of activity conducted by Morrisroe's Archaic inhabitants. Since the Morrisroe excavations consisted of five deep 2-x-2-m units, they provided few insights into intrasite activity patterning.

Morrisroe's early Middle Archaic assemblages contained an abundant and diverse inventory of extractive, processing, manufacturing, and maintenance tools along with their production residues (Conaty 1985:Appendix D). Flaked-stone artifacts included gravers, notches, unhafted and hafted bifaces, drills, steeply retouched flakes, and reworked bifaces. Production residues included cores, angular fragments, cortical and secondary flakes, bifacial thinning flakes, and bipolar by-products. Tool kits also included ground-stone mortars, pestles, and pitted and battered cobbles.

Conaty's analysis of Archaic technological organization suggested that assemblages dating to the earlier part of the Middle Archaic contained abundant debitage representing the entire biface production trajectory. Later Middle Archaic assemblages represented shorter trajectories, suggesting a more restricted range of tool production and maintenance activities. Also, earlier groups apparently used more ground-stone and pecked and battered artifacts than their later counterparts. Overall, early Middle Archaic assemblage attributes suggest that Morrisroe was occupied for relatively long periods and was the locus of a wide range of activities (Conaty 1985:339–340).

More than 50 years of research along the Falls of the Ohio has identified many late Middle Archaic middens that today are classified as Old Clarksville–phase (ca. 4820 to 2970 cal B.C.) base camps (Granger 1988). Situated 10 km south of the Ohio River floodplain, the KYANG site (Figure 17.7, No. 12) represented one of the last relatively well-preserved "inland" Old Clarksville–phase middens (Bader and Granger 1989; Granger 1988:175). Prior to urban development, the marshes and sluggish streams that covered this area made it one of the richest seasonal catchment zones in the vicinity (Granger 1988:173, 179).

The Old Clarksville component, the lower of the site's two Archaic cultural zones, consisted of a thick midden capped by a shell layer. Diagnostic Old Clarksville projectile points included various side-notched specimens classified as Big Sandy, Salt River Side Notched, and Brewerton types (Granger 1988:190). A single radiocarbon date placed the occupation at ca. 3810 cal B.C. (Bader and Granger 1989: Appendix C). Feature types included hearths, stone clusters, earth ovens, and storage pits. Thirty-two Old Clarksville burials, all in flexed positions, were placed in deep, bowl-shaped pits. Many of the graves contained flaked-stone tools; antler atlatl hooks; ground-stone axes, beads, and pendants; carved and engraved bone pins; and deer, bear, and wolf tooth necklaces (Granger 1988:175).

Botanical and faunal remains indicate that KYANG's inhabitants had a marsh-oriented economy. The site was minimally occupied in the late summer and fall while the inhabitants hunted white-tailed deer and small marsh animals, collected freshwater mussels, and fished (Granger 1988:179). Because of the absence of seasonal indicators, Granger (1988:179) proposed that the inhabitants left KYANG for the Outer Bluegrass in the winter.

Recent reanalyses of hafted bifaces from some Green River middens indicate that late Middle Archaic side-notched bifaces are well represented at the Andrews (Baker), Ward, Butterfield, Jimtown Hill, Jackson Bluff, and Barrett sites (Hensley 1994:Table 42; Jefferies et al. 2005:Table 2). The presence of these projectile points indicates that trends toward increased sedentism and the extended occupation of locations in resource-rich areas were also underway in this part of the lower Ohio Valley by the late middle Holocene (Hensley 1994:Figure 43; Jefferies et al. 2005).

Subsistence

Compared with some parts of the Midwest, relatively little is known about the subsistence practices of western Kentucky's Middle Archaic hunter-gatherers. Excavation of Stratum 3 at Morrisroe, much of which dates to the early Middle Archaic, yielded hickory, black walnut, and acorn shell along with grape, hawthorn, honey locust, black cherry, knotweed, and possible sumac seeds (Wymer 1987). Hickory was the predominant nut species (Wymer 1987:Table 2).

A partial analysis of the KYANG faunal material indicated that deer was the primary meat source (Hill n.d., cited in Bader 1992:17). Site inhabitants also collected freshwater mussels, hunted small mammals, and fished for species that lived in shallow, standing water near the site. Charred nut remains were common in the midden soil (Bader 1992:17).

On the basis of these very limited data, it appears, not surprisingly, that the subsistence strategies used by Middle Archaic hunter-gatherers in Kentucky's lower Ohio Valley paralleled those employed by contemporary groups living in southern Illinois (Breitburg 1982; Lopinot 1982) and southern Indiana (Stafford et al. 2000). Of course, the relative importance of specific plant and animal foods would have varied according to a group's locally available resources.

Social Organization and Mortuary Practices

As for Early Archaic hunter-gatherers, there is little information on Middle Archaic social organization or mortuary practices. Few Middle Archaic mortuary areas are known for central or western Kentucky, and those that have been studied have produced small samples from disturbed sites (Bader and Granger 1989).

The 32 Old Clarksville–phase burials from the KYANG site represent the largest and most thoroughly documented Middle Archaic mortuary program in Kentucky's lower Ohio Valley (Bader and Granger 1989). The KYANG burials consisted of either single or double inhumations placed in deep, bowl-shaped pits. Most of the individuals were flexed; however, several bundle burials were present. Grave goods were common and included engraved bone pins; bear, deer, and wolf tooth necklaces; ground-stone pendants and beads; adzes; antler atlatl hooks and flakers; an assortment of flaked-stone implements; and red ocher (Bader and Granger 1989).

Treatment of the deceased at the KYANG site closely paralleled that observed at contemporary sites in other parts of the lower Ohio Valley (Lynch 1982; Mayes 1997). Such treatment has generally been interpreted as representing an egalitarian social organization in which an individual's social position was largely determined by his or her personal accomplishment while living (Lynch 1982; Mayes 1997; Stafford et al. 2000).

Perhaps the most distinctive KYANG burial goods were the carved and engraved bone pins (Bader 1992:Figures 6.16–6.19; Bader and Granger 1989:Figure IV-6). Some of these highly stylized pins are quite similar to specimens found on late Middle Archaic sites in southern Indiana and southern Illinois (Jefferies 1997), suggesting that KYANG inhabitants interacted with distant groups that lived north of the Ohio River.

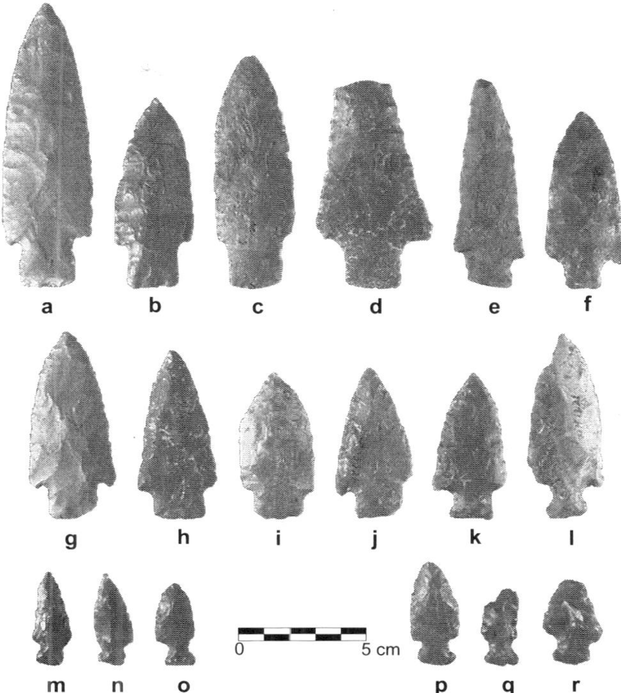

Figure 17.14. Late Archaic hafted bifaces from Kentucky's lower Ohio Valley region: a–k, Late Archaic stemmed; l, Motley cluster; m–r, Merom cluster (Justice 1987).

Late Archaic (ca. 3800 to 1200 cal B.C.)

By the beginning of the Late Archaic, essentially modern environmental conditions and vegetation patterns were established throughout the lower Ohio Valley. As Muller (1986:51) cautions, however, this did not mean that there was no environmental variation, only that the general resources available did not significantly change. An increase in the percentage of grass pollen and the appearance of prairie vegetation at Jackson Pond suggest that the mixed prairie and deciduous forest mosaic encountered by the first Euro-Americans was also established by this time (Wilkins et al. 1991:236).

Technology

Late Archaic tool kits suggest a range of activities similar to that indicated by Middle Archaic tool inventories, but in many cases, formal tools replaced more expediently produced ones. For example, the many conical, bell-shaped, and cylindrical pestles found at Green River middens (Figure 17.9) (Webb 1946:Figure 39B–D) probably were used to do many of the same tasks for which Middle Archaic grinding stones were employed.

Perhaps the most noticeable technological change was the transition from side-notched to stemmed biface-hafting technology (Figure 17.14). So far, the technological significance of this change is unclear, but it may have been associated with the increased use of the atlatl.

Most Late Archaic hafted bifaces are relatively large with straight, contracting, or expanding stems. Justice (1987:133–158) assigns many of these types to the Late Archaic Stemmed cluster, which includes a variety of regionally specific types like Karnak Stemmed (Winters 1967); McWhinney Heavy Stemmed (Vickery 1972); Ledbetter Stemmed (Kneberg 1956); Pickwick (DeJarnette et al. 1962:66); Saratoga Broad Bladed, Parallel Stemmed, and Expanding Stemmed (Winters 1967); and Rowlett (Duffield 1966; Granger 1988:Figure 5). Radiocarbon dates indicate that these types were manufactured from about 4300 to 800 cal B.C. While regionally distinct stylistic differences exist, much of the morphological variation within types is attributable to raw material differences and the extent of resharpening.

Smaller stemmed and notched Merom/Trimble types (Winters 1969), dating to ca. 1900 to 1200 cal B.C. (Justice 1987:130), also occur in the lower Ohio Valley. Terminal Archaic (ca. 1200 to 500 cal B.C.) straight-stemmed, barbed Wade points occur on some lower Tennessee River Late Archaic sites (Cambron and Hulse 1969). Brewerton-like points (Ritchie 1961), commonly associated with central and upper Ohio Valley Late Archaic manifestations, occasionally are found in the Falls area (Collins and Driskell 1979:1026).

Late Archaic flaked-stone tool inventories also included hafted and unhafted drills and end scrapers, side scrapers, gravers, choppers, and reamers (Webb 1946:237). Late Archaic tool makers used ground-stone technology to make stylistically variable atlatl weights, three-quarter- and full-grooved axes, grooved mauls, pestles, hoes, hammerstones, and abraders (Figures 17.9 and 17.10), as well as ornamental items like beads and pendants (Webb 1946:237).

The number and diversity of bone, antler, and shell items found on some Kentucky Late Archaic sites reminds archaeologists of how biased our interpretations are when estimates of site activity diversity are based just on stone tools (Figures 17.11 and 17.12). Some tasks done with bone and antler implements paralleled those for which stone tools were used; many others did not. Mammal, bird, reptile, and fish bone was used to make awls, pins, fishhooks, projectile points, rattles, and flutes. Antler provided raw material to make projectile points, atlatl hooks and handles, flakers, awls, and chisels (Webb 1946:238–239). Many ornamental items (gorgets, pendants, and beads) were made from riverine or marine shell as were atlatl weights and cups (Webb 1946:239–240).

Settlement

Six hundred fifty-one Late Archaic sites have been recorded in Kentucky's lower Ohio Valley (Figure 17.15), more than twice the number known for the Middle Archaic (n = 251). If more sites can be equated with more people, then the increase in regional population parallels trends seen in other parts of eastern North America about this same time (Milner 2004:Figure 13). The distribution of Late Archaic sites by landform is very similar to that of Middle Archaic sites, with 37.8 percent in the floodplains and 33.9 percent in the uplands (Figure 17.6).

Throughout parts of the lower Ohio Valley, settlement strategies initiated in the late Middle Archaic continued well into the Late Archaic (Marquardt and Watson 2005a). In contrast, activities at some intensively occupied Middle Archaic sites, like Morrisroe, became more sporadic during the Late Archaic, suggesting short-term, intermittent site use (Nance 1988). At the same time, lower Tennessee-Cumberland Late Archaic hunter-gatherers appear to have expanded their use of the uplands, where hunting-related activities predominated (Nance 1977:11–13).

In the Cypress Creek area, Late Archaic components occurred at 75 percent (n = 43) of all Archaic sites, representing a significant increase over the Middle Archaic rate. Late Archaic hunter-gatherers intensively occupied several large shell middens near Cypress Creek and the Green River (Butterfield, Hollis, and Wilson-Seymour), representing a continuation of settlement-subsistence practices started by their late Middle Archaic predecessors (Marquardt and Watson 2005a). A broad range of activities is suggested by the number and diversity of artifacts, burials, and features at these sites. Archaic groups presumably stayed for considerable periods of time at midden-bearing sites, from which small task groups made forays to exploit distant, scattered resources (Jefferies et al. 2005).

Large, midden-bearing sites are also found in interior upland settings (Ward and Kirkland). The presence of carbonized goosefoot, marsh elder, and pigweed at some upland sites suggests that these habitats offered plant foods not commonly found closer to the Green River (Bonzani 2002).

Cypress Creek Late Archaic hunter-gatherers occupied many of the same sites that late Middle Archaic groups did, suggesting similar preferences for nearby resources. Other sites were first occupied during the Late Archaic, particularly those situated in the uplands near their interface with

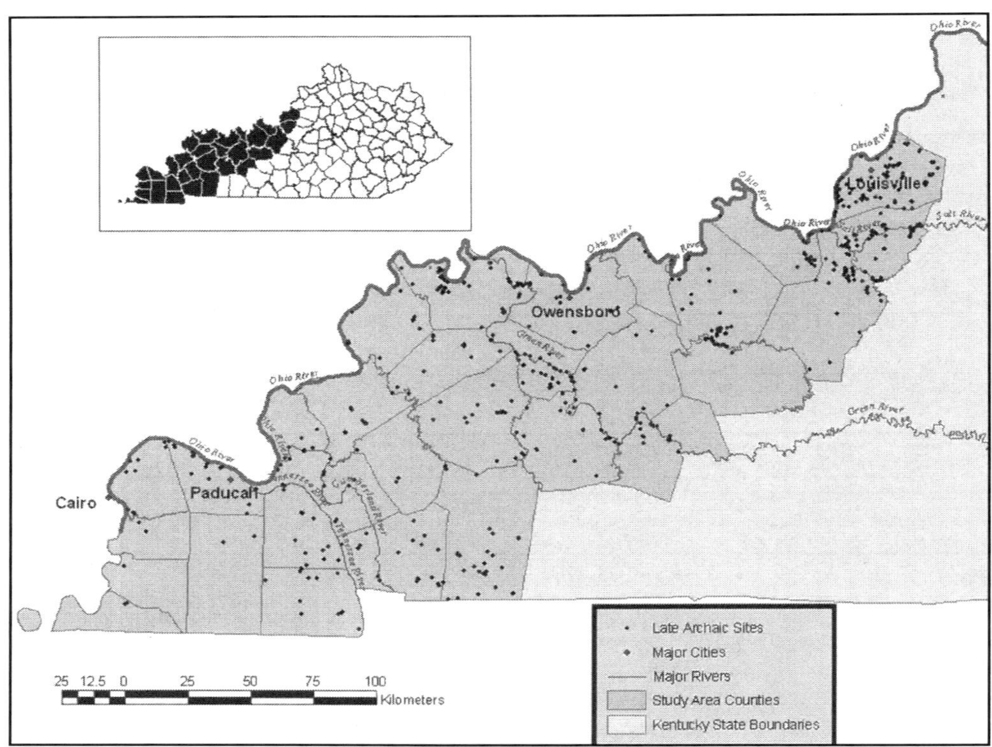

Figure 17.15. Late Archaic site distribution in western Kentucky.

interior wetlands. An increase in the use of the resource-rich interior wetlands is consistent with more people living in the area. Newly occupied sites are characterized by light artifact scatters, suggesting that small groups stayed there for short periods (Jefferies et al. 2005).

The frequency and distribution of Cypress Creek Late Archaic sites are consistent with an increasing population that experienced greater pressure to use all of its environmental resources. No longer were sites distributed uniformly across similar environmental settings. Instead, Late Archaic sites were clustered in riverbank and swamp-edge habitats, underscoring the disproportionate use of these habitats. Over time, some of these sites acquired cultural significance as traditionally favored places for people to congregate and perform important rituals (Jefferies et al. 2005).

Late Archaic Regional Variants

Much more is known about the number and distribution of Late Archaic sites than about those of earlier hunter-gatherers, but most are represented by light lithic scatters disturbed by later prehistoric or historical activities. In contrast, sites situated along some of western Kentucky's rivers, particularly the Green, Ohio, and Tennessee-Cumberland, have yielded abundant data on Late Archaic technology, settlement, subsistence, social organization, and economy. This section draws on that wealth of information to illustrate specific aspects of lower Ohio Valley Late Archaic life.

Green River Region

The archaeological significance of the Green River "shell" middens has been recognized for nearly 100 years (Moore 1916). From 1937 to 1941, William Webb directed excavations at many of these sites, helping to define and understand the nature of Archaic hunting-gathering societies (Figure 17.16). Today, nearly 50 prehistoric shell, earth, and rock middens are known along the Green River (Hockensmith et al. 1985; Pedde and Prufer 2001).

Diagnostic artifacts indicate that some of the Green River middens were initially occupied during the Early or Middle Archaic (Jefferies et al. 2005). However, radiocarbon dates (ca. 4500 to 600 cal B.C.) indicate that much of the midden-producing activity is attributable to Late Archaic hunter-gatherers (Marquardt and Watson 2005b:631).

Starting in the early 1970s, Patty Jo Watson and William H. Marquardt (Marquardt and Watson 2005a) initiated a new phase of shell-mound investigation with the inauguration of the SMAP. Much of this work focused on the famous Carlston Annis midden (Webb 1950b) and nearby sites (Figures 17.7 and 17.17). More than 30 years of research by dozens of SMAP investigators has led to a new understanding of the mid- to late-Holocene "Green River Shell Mound Archaic."

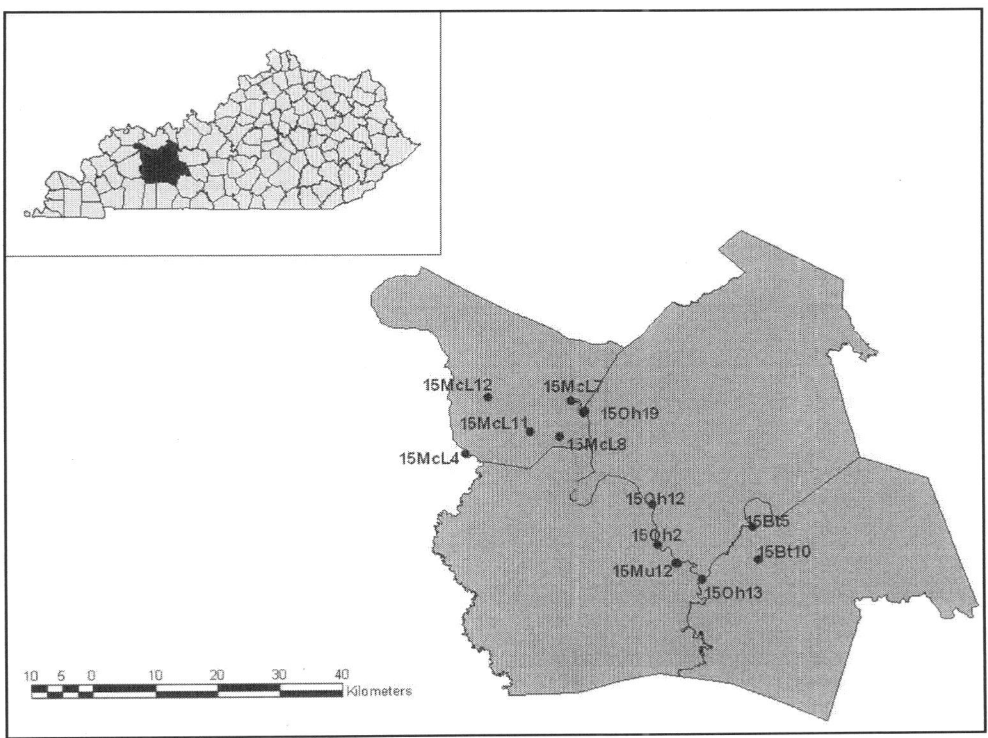

Figure 17.16. Major Middle Green River Archaic sites.

Figure 17.17. Depression-era block excavation at the Carlston Annis site (15Bt5) showing the site's major shell deposits. (Courtesy of the William S. Webb Museum of Anthropology, University of Kentucky.)

The following draws heavily on that research (Marquardt and Watson 2005a).

The Shell Mound Archaic (SMA) cultural landscape consisted of midden mounds containing varying amounts of shell, rockshelters, ephemeral camps, and extraction loci. Midden mounds vary in size, but most range from 50 to 130 m long, 40 to 80 m wide, and .5 to 2.5 m thick. Rockshelters occur in the sandstone bluffs away from the Green River, while camps and extractive loci, ranging from small lithic scatters to extensive but thin sheet middens, existed throughout the region. Although earlier radiocarbon dates exist, most SMA dates range from ca. 4600 to 1800 cal B.C. (Marquardt and Watson 2005b:631).

Marquardt and Watson (2005b:633) suggest that Late Archaic hunter-gatherers aggregated at riverside midden sites, like Carlston Annis, for several months during the summer and fall, possibly every year for many generations. During the winter and spring, they dispersed to rockshelters and ephemeral camps situated in different environmental settings. A similar pattern of seasonal rounds was probably followed by hunter-gatherers that lived at the nearby DeWeese, Haynes, Bowles, Chiggerville, and Indian Knoll sites (Marquardt and Watson 2005b:635).

The Carlston Annis midden consists of shell (17 percent), sandstone (15 percent), inorganic matrix (23 percent), and air in pore spaces (45 percent). Some middens have more shell than the one at Carlston Annis does, but others have almost none. Midden contents include charcoal, ash, cracked rock, mollusk shells, animal bones, human and dog burials, and artifacts made of ground and polished stone, flaked stone, bone, and antler. Shell artifacts (beads, pendants, atlatl weights, and drinking vessels) are usually associated with human burials rather than general midden contexts (Marquardt and Watson 2005b:632).

Despite evidence for their multiseason occupation, shell middens have yielded little evidence for dwelling structures. While occupation surfaces have been identified, post molds are rare as are formal hearths. A variety of heat-related features may represent mussel-steaming or roasting or baking facilities (Marquardt and Watson 2005b:632).

Extensive analyses of Green River shell-midden human remains and mortuary programs have provided important insights into Late Archaic paleodemography, health, social organization, and trade and interaction. The average life expectancy for a newborn SMA person was about 20 years. As expected for hunter-gatherers, infant mortality was quite high, with one in every five children dying within its first year. If a person survived to the age of 15 years, he or she could expect to live about 20 more years (Mensforth 2005).

Typical of many midwestern Archaic populations (Bassett 1982), SMA people experienced heavy dental wear caused by the grit contained in their food. On the positive side, they had few caries compared with groups that had an agriculture-based diet (Powell 1996; Ward 2005:496). Like many people today, many SMA hunter-gatherers had to deal with the pains of osteoarthritis (Marquardt and Watson 2005b:632).

A high percentage of SMA males had external auditory exostoses, suggesting that they spent time in the river with their heads below water, possibly while collecting shellfish. Since these bony growths are caused by immersion in cold water, their prevalence supports occupation of the midden sites during cooler seasons of the year (Herrmann 2002; Mensforth 2005:465–467).

Evidence for interpersonal trauma, consisting of projectile points embedded in bones, scalping-related cut marks, and certain kinds of fractures (Mensforth 2001, 2005:Table 20.13), along with evidence of trophy taking, suggest that SMA people were familiar with the consequences of interpersonal violence. Such trauma may have been associated with decreased group mobility and the need to maintain and defend food procurement territories (Marquardt and Watson 2005b:634–635; Mensforth 2005:472).

Subsistence remains indicate that SMA people were hunters, gatherers, fishers, and gardeners (Marquardt and Watson 2005b:633). Game animals, including deer, raccoon, and turkey, were hunted using the atlatl or spear. SMA people captured large fish, like drum, catfish, and bowfin, using hooks-and-lines or gorges; smaller species were collected using nets. Land and aquatic turtles were also eaten. Of course, mollusks played a major role in the subsistence strategy, and at least 36 species of unionids and five species of aquatic gastropods are represented in the middens.

Acorn and hickory nuts were the most important plant foods, supplemented by seasonally available wild plant foods that included blackberry, grape, strawberry, honey locust, persimmon, knotweed, little barley, foxtail grass, wild rice, and chenopod. SMA people grew squashlike gourds, but some plants grown elsewhere in the Midwest, like sumpweed, apparently were not cultivated in the Green River region (Marquardt and Watson 2005b:633).

The technologies used by SMA people to collect and process resources were probably quite similar to those used by other midwestern Late Archaic hunter-gatherers (see above). SMA people used local cherts (Vienna, St. Louis, and Ste. Genevieve) to make flaked-stone tools (Hensley 1996). Initial reduction took place near the source areas, but later-stage manufacturing activities occurred at the river-edge sites and rockshelters. They used unmodified flakes struck from amorphous cores for cutting and scraping; however, bladelets or bladelike flakes were occasionally produced. The ground-stone tool inventory resembled those documented in other parts of the Midwest. Bone was occasionally used to make flutes, whistles, and other kinds of musical instruments (Marquardt and Watson 2005b:633). Bone and antler implements were used for many of the same tasks as flaked-stone tools.

The small amount of copper, abundant marine shell, and the bones of a few exotic animals (marten and fisher) (Watson 2005:634) are indicative of the SMA people's participation in regional-scale social networks (Goad 1980; Jefferies 1995; Johnson and Brookes 1989). The few pieces of copper (13 items from three WPA-excavated sites) and exotic animal bone could have been brought to the Green River region from the Lake Superior area by one person making one trip. In contrast, the thousands of marine-shell beads, cups, and gorgets suggest sustained interaction with south Atlantic or Gulf Coast groups (Marquardt and Watson 2005b:637). The abundance of marine shell relative to the amount of material originating from north of the Ohio River suggests that SMA social interaction was more intensive with hunter-gatherers who lived to the south.

Comparison of bone hairpin styles from Green River SMA sites with those from sites north of the Ohio River revealed few similarities, supporting the southern orientation of SMA society (Jefferies 2004). Nance (1988:147) also suggests that by the Late Archaic, the Green River area was developing into a "regional sphere of influence" that was most closely affiliated with groups that lived to the south.

Excavation of thousands of SMA burials has provided important insights into the social aspects of these hunting and gathering societies. Most individuals were interred in a flexed or semiflexed position, either in middens or the hardpan underlying middens (Watson 2005:550).

Grave goods are associated with burials at most middle Green River middens. However, the percentage of individuals with associated objects varies considerably, ranging from 6 percent at Kirkland to 55 percent at Carlston Annis (Watson 2005:560). Researchers have examined the distribution of grave goods by age and gender to discern patterns of social variability within the SMA burial populations (Rothschild 1979; Thiel 1979; Winters 1968). Particular emphasis has been placed on the distribution of items made from copper and marine shell.

SMA grave goods include a variety of utilitarian (projectile points, drills, scrapers, awls, pestles, abraders, and atlatl parts), ornamental (shell and stone beads, gorgets, pins, and pendants), and ritual objects (rattles, flutes, and whistles) (Marquardt and Watson 2005b). Clustered artifacts that appear to have been medicine bundles (Webb 1950a:336–434) were found with a few individuals (Marquardt and Watson 2005b:633–635). Grave goods accompanied many of the Carlston Annis burials, ranging from about 35 percent of infants (up to one year) and older adults (over 40 years) to about 60 percent of adolescents (13–17 years) and subadults (18–20 years) (Watson 2005:558–560).

The treatment of the SMA burials is usually interpreted as reflecting an egalitarian society within which few social differences existed. A person's status appears largely to have been based on age, gender, and personal abilities (Rothschild 1979:672). Contemporary hunter-gatherer mortuary programs in nearby parts of the Ohio Valley suggest a similar level of social organization (Cook et al. 1996; Lynch 1982; Mayes 1997).

Falls of the Ohio

Essentially modern environmental conditions had developed in the Falls area by the start of the late Holocene. The Ohio River floodplain was covered by numerous sloughs and lakes, creating habitats for many different kinds of wetland plants and animals. Dense riverine and upland forests covered much of the region. Undoubtedly, these diverse habitats provided an abundant, diverse, and reliable food supply for Late Archaic hunter-gatherers (Collins and Driskell 1979:1036). Janzen (1977) proposed that the Falls of the Ohio region contained at least five environmental zones and that many Late Archaic sites were positioned to take advantage of one or more of those zones.

As in many other parts of Kentucky's lower Ohio Valley, the Falls of the Ohio area experienced a dramatic increase in site density during the Late Archaic (Figure 17.15). Sites are situated along the floodplains, in the uplands, and adjacent to swampy interior lowlands. Large middens, some containing shell, occur along the river floodplains as well as away from the rivers in areas that were once covered by extensive wetlands. Upland site types are generally shallow lithic scatters and rockshelter occupations (Granger et al. 1992:32).

Granger (1988:199–203) identified at least six Archaic site clusters in the Falls area, largely consisting of Late Archaic components. Site clusters are associated with discrete ecological settings, possibly representing different components of Late Archaic settlement systems.

Falls-area Late Archaic components are assigned to either the Lone Hill (ca. 2970 to 1420 cal B.C.) or Riverton (ca. 1900 to 900 cal B.C.) phase, primarily on the basis of changes in projectile point manufacturing technology (Anslinger et al. 1994:25). Lone Hill projectile points include a variety of stemmed types (Granger 1988), while Riverton points consist of smaller notched and stemmed varieties (Winters 1969).

Important Lone Hill–phase components have been investigated at the Spadie, Rosenberger, and Villier sites (Figure 17.7, Nos. 7, 8, and 10), all near the Ohio River just downstream from the Falls (Granger 1988:Figure 16). Late Archaic hunter-gatherers that inhabited these sites appear to have focused their activities on local resources, as indicated by the absence of exotic materials. The hunting, fishing, and collecting of local food resources occupied most of their attention, but they also conducted other tasks of everyday life, like making tools and burying their dead (Collins and Driskell 1979:1026).

Diagnostic Lone Hill artifacts from these Falls-area sites include three-quarter-grooved axes, atlatl weights, and McWhinney, Rowlett, Lamoka-like, and Brewerton projectile points (Collins and Driskell 1979:1026). Numerous burials, some containing grave goods, are reported for some Lone Hill–phase sites (Anslinger et al. 1994:25). Lone Hill burials appear to have been interred in areas of deep midden, coinciding with dense concentrations of other features (Granger et al. 1992:137). This contrasts with the late Middle Archaic Old Clarksville mortuary practice of interring the deceased in deep pits (Anslinger et al. 1994:136; Bader and Granger 1989:VI-8, Figure IV-5).

Large, intensively occupied Riverton sites have not been investigated on the Kentucky side of the Falls (Anslinger et al. 1994:26), but some sites have substantial Riverton components (Robinson and Smith 1979). In contrast, recent research in southern Indiana has documented large Riverton components a short distance down the Ohio River (Stafford and Cantin, this volume).

Riverton lithic technology is based on the expedient acquisition of raw materials and production of flaked-stone implements. These expediently produced tools show little evidence of extensive resharpening or other indications of tool curation (Anslinger et al. 1994:26).

The Rosenberger site (15Jf18), located along a 250 m-section of a high floodplain ridge, was strategically situated so that Late Archaic hunter-gatherers would have easy access to the floodplain's riverine and wetland resources (Figure 17.7, No. 8). High-quality chert sources were close by, as were highly productive stands of nut-producing hickory trees (Driskell 1979:802).

Rosenberger was occupied throughout much of the Late Archaic, as indicated by the presence of McWhinney, Brewerton-like, and Merom/Trimble points (Driskell 1979:800). The predominance of McWhinney points suggests that the most intensive period of activity was during the early Late Archaic. Intensive site use is indicated by the more than 400 features, consisting of large and small circular pits, burned areas, and artifact scatters, along with hundreds of human burials. Subsistence data suggest multiseasonal site use, minimally during the fall (nuts) and spring (fetal deer) (Driskell 1979:801–102).

Slightly more than 50 percent of the analyzed burials contained grave goods, which varied considerably in quantity and type. Nearly all of the mortuary artifacts were "technological" items, consisting of projectile points; drills; cores; hammerstones; stone, bone, and antler atlatl parts; grooved axes; net weights; and bone fishhooks. The few ornamental items included a drilled canine tooth and some worked bone. Most of the grave goods were associated with adults, so the site excavator inferred that status was more commonly achieved than ascribed (Driskell 1979:774).

Late Archaic inhabitants of the nearby Spadie site (15Jf14), located on a low ridge between the Ohio River and a narrow slough, conducted a wide range of hunting, fishing, plant-food processing and flaked-stone tool manufacturing activities (Figure 17.7, No. 7). Activity diversity suggests that Spadie functioned as a base camp. Diagnostic projectile points (Lamoka and Brewerton-like) and radiocarbon dates suggest that the site was occupied from about 2500 to 1200 cal B.C. (Boisvert 1979:880–882).

The Villier site (15Jf110) was located on the first terrace of the Ohio River, immediately adjacent to the riverbank (Figure 17.7, No. 10). Late Archaic cultural deposits cover a roughly 700-x-180-m area (Robinson and Smith 1979:590), suggesting that the site area was repeatedly occupied during the middle to late Holocene. The Villier assemblage includes a high percentage of Merom/Trimble points, indicating relatively heavy site use by Riverton-phase groups during the Terminal Archaic (ca. 1200 to 650 cal B.C.). The site appears to have served as a seasonally or intermittently occupied camp (Robinson and Smith 1979:656).

Recent archaeological investigations at the Railway Museum site (15Jf630) (Anslinger et al. 1994) has helped to refine understanding of Late Archaic hunter-gatherer adaptation (Figure 17.7, No. 13). The site, located just upstream from the Falls of the Ohio, consists of a large midden deposit containing numerous features and human burials. Analyses of hafted bifaces suggest that the site contains three discrete Late Archaic components, each represented by a distinctive projectile point type.

The most intensive occupation is represented by broad-barbed, stemmed points and hafted scrapers. In many ways, the haft elements of these points are reminiscent of those on Titterington-phase bifaces from the central Mississippi Valley (Fortier 1984:81). Similar bifaces are reported from nearby Lone Hill–phase sites (Anslinger et al. 1994:129; Granger 1988:Figure 15).

A few McWhinney projectile points represent a second Late Archaic component. These bifaces are morphologically and technologically distinct from the broad-barbed points, as well as having been made from different cherts. The third component, characterized by Riverton and Lamoka points, dates to the terminal Late Archaic (Anslinger et al. 1994:129).

The number and diversity of Railway Museum artifacts and features, combined with the sizable midden, suggest that a variety of extractive and maintenance tasks were intensively conducted there during much of the Late Archaic. The presence of human burials (n = 17), consisting of people of all ages and both genders, may reflect occupation of the site by family groups. Collectively, these site characteristics conform to what would be expected at a Lone Hill–phase base camp (Anslinger et al. 1994:136).

Excavations at the KYANG site, situated 10 km south of the Ohio River, have provided important information about Lone Hill–phase activities outside of the floodplain (Bader and Granger 1989). The site once sat adjacent to an extensive shallow wetland containing a great abundance of subsistence resources.

The Lone Hill component, restricted to the upper of two cultural strata, was represented by diagnostic Lone Hill–phase projectile points, a few features, and nine burials. The KYANG mortuary program generally conforms to those seen at other Lone Hill sites (Driskell 1979:774), with most individuals placed in the midden (not in pits) near the center of the site (Granger et al. 1992:227). Burials generally lacked elaborate grave goods (Granger 1988:175).

Summary

As in other parts of the Midwest, the more than 8,000 years constituting the Archaic period was a time of considerable change for central and western Kentucky's hunter-gatherer population. Most Early and early Middle Archaic groups appear to have pursued a way of life that was, in many ways, like that of earlier Paleoindian hunter-gatherers. The general absence of intensively occupied sites suggests that these people lived in small, highly mobile groups that did not focus on any one specific set of resources.

In contrast, a variety of archaeological indicators suggests that by the late Middle Archaic, some hunter-gatherer groups were starting to exhibit indications of greater cultural complexity (Marquardt 1985). This trend is reflected by decreased group mobility, the repeated occupation of food-rich locations, the elaboration of regional social networks, a more complex technology, and, in some places, experimentation with plant cultivation. These trends are particularly well expressed by the SMA groups, but similar changes are apparent in the Falls of the Ohio area and elsewhere in the commonwealth.

From a broader perspective, indications of increased hunter-gatherer cultural complexity seen in Kentucky's lower Ohio Valley reflect trends seen throughout the southern Midwest and Southeast. To fully understand the nature of this diachronic culture change, Kentucky data must be placed in a broader regional cultural framework. Clearly, the commonwealth's Archaic hunter-gatherers did not live in isolation from groups that inhabited the surrounding region. As archaeologists, we cannot hope to understand regional histories and processes by looking just at the individual parts of the puzzle. Instead, we need to work at the same regional scale as did the Archaic hunter-gatherers that we are studying. This volume represents a major step in that direction.

Acknowledgments

I would like to acknowledge George Crothers, George Milner, Phil Mink, Chris Moore, David McBride, David Pollack, Paul Ramey, and Victor Thompson for their valuable help in assembling the data and illustrations contained in this chapter. I am indebted to the many archaeologists who have collected the information on which this chapter is based. In particular, I would like to thank Patty Jo Watson and Bill Marquardt for providing a draft of their report on their Middle Green River research. Brian Butler and Rus Stafford provided me with "advance" copies of their chapters on the southern Illinois and southern Indiana Archaic, respectively. Much of the historical background is based on research by Douglas W. Schwartz (1967). Some of the contents of this chapter incorporate and expand on earlier discussions of the Kentucky Archaic published by the Kentucky Heritage Council (Jefferies 1990) and the University Press of Kentucky (Jefferies 1996).

References Cited

Anslinger, Michael, Albert M. Pecora, Charles M. Niquette, and Jonathan P. Kerr
1994 *Salvage Excavations at the Railway Museum Site (15Jf630), Jefferson County, Kentucky.* Contract Publication 94-15. Cultural Resource Analysts, Lexington, Kentucky.

Arnold, J. R., and W. F. Libby
1951 Radiocarbon Dates. *Science* 2927:113–114.

Bader, Anne T.
1992 An Analysis of Bone and Antler Tool Use Patterns from the Kentucky Air National Guard Site. Master's thesis, Department of Anthropology, University of Kentucky, Lexington.

Bader, Anne T., and Joseph E. Granger
1989 *Recent Archaeological Investigations on the Kentucky Air National Guard Site (15Jf267), Jefferson County, Kentucky.* Granger Consultants, Louisville, Kentucky.

Bassett, Everett J.
1982 Osteological Analysis of Carrier Mills Burials. In *The Carrier Mills Archaeological Project: Human Adaptation in the Saline Valley, Illinois*, vol. 2, edited by Richard W. Jefferies and Brian M. Butler, pp. 1029–1114. Research Paper 33. Center for Archaeological Investigations, Southern Illinois University, Carbondale.

Boisvert, Richard A.
1979 Excavations at the Spadie Site (15Jf14). In *Excavations at Four Archaic Sites in the Lower Ohio Valley, Jefferson*

County, Kentucky, vol. 1, edited by Michael B. Collins, pp. 804–882. Occasional Papers in Anthropology 1. Department of Anthropology, University of Kentucky, Lexington.

Bonzani, Renee M.
2002 Plant Remains from Test Excavations at the Ward site. In *Cypress Creek Archaeological Project: Archaic Adaptive Strategies in West Central Kentucky*, by Richard W. Jefferies, Victor D. Thompson, and George R. Milner, pp. 158–174. Department of Anthropology, University of Kentucky, Lexington.

Brandau, Betty Lee
1977 Correspondence from the author. University of Georgia, Athens. In *Cultural Radiocarbon Determinations of Kentucky*, by Christopher A. Turnbow. Occasional Papers in Anthropology 3. Department of Anthropology, University of Kentucky, Lexington.

Braun, Lucy E.
1950 *Deciduous Forests of Eastern North America*. Blakiston, Philadelphia.

Breitburg, Emanuel
1982 Analysis of Area A Fauna. In *The Carrier Mills Archaeological Project: Human Adaptation in the Saline Valley, Illinois*, vol. 2, edited by Richard W. Jefferies and Brian M. Butler, pp. 863–934. Research Paper 33. Center for Archaeological Investigations, Southern Illinois University, Carbondale.

Brown, James A.
1985 Long-Term Trends to Sedentism and the Emergence of Complexity in the American Midwest. In *Prehistoric Hunter-Gatherers: The Emergence of Cultural Complexity*, edited by T. Douglas Price and James A. Brown, pp. 201–231. Academic Press, Orlando, Florida.

Brown James A., and Robert K. Vierra
1983 What Happened in the Middle Archaic? Introduction to an Ecological Approach to Koster Site Archaeology. In *Archaic Hunters and Gatherers in the American Midwest*, edited by James L. Phillips and James A. Brown, pp. 165–195. Academic Press, New York.

Broyles, Bettye J.
1971 *Second Preliminary Report: The St. Albans Site, Kanawha County, West Virginia*. Archaeological Investigation Report 3. West Virginia Geological and Economic Survey, Morgantown.

Burdin, Sheldon R.
2004 Interaction, Exchange, and Social Organization among Hunter-Gatherers in the Midcontinent—Evidence from the Lower Ohio River Valley: Bannerstone Use from 6500 to 3000 B.P. Master's thesis, Department of Anthropology, University of Kentucky, Lexington.

Butler, Brian M., JoAnne M. Penney, and Cathy A. Robison
1981 *Archaeological Survey and Evaluation for the Shawnee 200 MW A.F.B.C. Plant McCracken County, Kentucky*. Research Paper 21. Center for Archaeological Investigations, Southern Illinois University, Carbondale.

Cambron, James W., and David C. Hulse
1969 *Handbook of Alabama Archaeology: Part I Point Types*. Archaeological Research Association of Alabama, Huntsville.

Carstens, Kenneth C., and Parry Jo Watson (editors)
1996 *Of Caves and Shell Mounds*. University of Alabama Press, Tuscaloosa.

Chapman, Jefferson
1975 *The Rose Island Site and the Bifurcate Point Tradition*. Report of Investigations 14. Department of Anthropology, University of Tennessee, Knoxville.
1976 The Archaic Period in the Lower Little Tennessee River Valley: The Radiocarbon Dates. *Tennessee Anthropologist* 1:1–12.

Claassen, Cheryl P.
1996 A Consideration of the Social Organization of the Shell Mound Archaic. In *Archaeology of the Mid-Holocene Southeast*, edited by Kenneth E. Sassaman and David G. Anderson, pp. 235–258. University Press of Florida, Gainesville.

Clay, R. Berle, and Douglas W. Schwartz
1963 The Archaeology of Barkley Basin and Adjacent Regions: A Synthesis. Manuscript on file, W. S. Webb Museum of Anthropology, University of Kentucky, Lexington.

Coe, Joffre L.
1964 *The Formative Cultures of the Carolina Piedmont*. Transactions of the American Philosophical Society 54, pt. 5. Philadelphia.

Coe, Michael D., and F. William Fischer
1959 Barkley Reservoir—Tennessee Portion, Archaeological Excavations 1959. Manuscript on file, National Park Service, Regional Office, Richmond, Virginia.

Collins, Michael B.
1979a (editor) *Excavations at Four Archaic Sites in the Lower Ohio Valley, Jefferson County, Kentucky*. Occasional Papers in Anthropology 1. Department of Anthropology, University of Kentucky, Lexington.
1979b The Longworth-Gick Site (15Jf243). In *Excavations at Four Archaic Sites in the Lower Ohio Valley, Jefferson County, Kentucky,* vol. 1, edited by Michael B. Collins, pp. 471–589. Occasional Papers in Anthropology 1. Department of Anthropology, University of Kentucky, Lexington.

Collins, Michael B., and Boyce N. Driskell
1979 Summary and Conclusions. In *Excavations at Four Archaic Sites in the Lower Ohio Valley, Jefferson County, Kentucky,* vol. 1, edited by Michael B. Collins, pp. 1023–1042. Occasional Papers in Anthropology 1. Department of Anthropology, University of Kentucky, Lexington.

Conaty, Gerald T.
1985 Middle and Late Archaic Mobility Strategies in Western Kentucky. Ph.D. dissertation, Department of Archaeology, Simon Fraser University, Burnaby, British Columbia.

Cook, Della Collins, Sandra K. Parker, Robert G. McCollough, Timi L. Barone, Gregory Cook, Douglas S. Blank, Christine Shaneyfelt, Kristin Hedman, and Christine A. Marvin
1996 Little Pigeon Creek Cemetery (12W340): An Archaic Midden-Mound in Warrick County, Indiana. Electronic document, http://www.gbl.indiana.edu/abstracts/86/cook_et.al_86.html, accessed October 2004.

Crane, H. R., and James B. Griffin
1972 University of Michigan Radiocarbon Dates XIV. *Radiocarbon* 14:155–194.

Crothers, George M.
1999 *Prehistoric Hunters and Gatherers, and the Archaic Period Green River Shell Middens of Western Kentucky*. Ph.D. dissertation, Washington University. University Microfilms International, Ann Arbor, Michigan.

Crothers, George M., and Reinhard Bernbeck
2004 The Foraging Mode of Production: The Case of the Green River Kentucky, Archaic Shell Middens. In *Hunters and Gatherers in Theory and Archaeology*, edited by George M. Crothers, pp. 401–422. Occasional Papers 31. Center for Archaeological Investigations, Southern Illinois University, Carbondale.

Deevy, Edward S., and Richard F. Flint
1957 Postglacial Hypsithermal Interval. *Science* 125:182–184.

DeJarnette, David L., Edward B. Kurjak, and James W. Cambron
1962 Excavations at the Stanfield-Worley Bluff Shelter. *Journal of Alabama Archaeology* 8:1–124.

Delcourt, Paul A., and Hazel R. Delcourt
1981 Vegetation Maps for Eastern North America: 40,000 Years B.P. to the Present. In *Geobotany II*, edited by Robert C. Romans, pp. 123–166. Plenum Press, New York.

DiBlasi, Philip J.
1981 A New Assessment of the Archaeological Significance of the Ashworth Site (15Bu236): A Study in the Dynamics of Archaeological Investigation in Cultural Resource Management. Master's thesis, Interdisciplinary Studies, University of Louisville, Kentucky.
1987 Rogers Cave, Glyph Passage. National Register of Historic Places nomination form, on file, Kentucky Heritage Council, Frankfort.

Driskell, Boyce N.
1979 The Rosenberger Site (15Jf18). In *Excavations at Four Archaic Sites in the Lower Ohio Valley, Jefferson County, Kentucky*, vol. 1, edited by Michael B. Collins, pp. 697–803. Occasional Papers in Anthropology 1. Department of Anthropology, University of Kentucky, Lexington.

Duffield, Lathel F.
1966 The Robert Dudgeon Site: A Stratified Archaic Site in the Green River Reservoir, South Central Kentucky. Manuscript on file, Museum of Anthropology, University of Kentucky, Lexington.

Fortier, Andrew C.
1984 *The Go-Kart North Site*. In *The Go-Kart North Site and the Dyroff and Levin Sites*, by Andrew C. Fortier and Thomas E. Emerson, pp. 1–197. American Bottom Archaeology FAI-270 Site Reports 9. University of Illinois Press, Urbana.

Fowler, Melvin L.
1959 *Summary Report of Modoc Rock Shelter: 1952, 1953, 1955, 1956*. Report of Investigations 8. Illinois State Museum, Springfield.

Funkhouser, William D., and William S. Webb
1928 *Ancient Life in Kentucky*. Geologic Reports Series 6, Volume 34. Kentucky Geological Survey, Lexington.

Goad, Sharon I.
1980 Patterns of Late Archaic Exchange. *Tennessee Anthropologist* 5:1–16.

Granger, Joseph E.
1988 Late/Terminal Archaic Settlement in the Falls of the Ohio River Region of Kentucky: An Examination of Components, Phases, and Clusters. In *Paleoindian and Archaic Research in Kentucky*, edited by Charles Hockensmith, David Pollack, and Thomas Sanders, pp. 153–204. Kentucky Heritage Council, Frankfort.

Granger, Joseph E., Edgar E. Hardesty, and Anne T. Bader
1992 *Phase III Data Recovery: Archaeology at Habich Site (15Jf550) and Associated Manifestations at Gutherie Beach, Jefferson County, Kentucky*. Report of Investigations 90-2. Archaeology Resources Consultant Services, Louisville, Kentucky.

Gremillion, Kristen J.
2003 Eastern Woodlands Overview. In *People and Plants in Ancient Eastern North America*, edited by Paul E. Minnis, pp. 17–49. Smithsonian Books, Washington, D.C.

Griffin, James B.
1967 Eastern North American Archaeology: A Summary. *Science* 156:175–191.

Haskins, Valerie A.
1988 The Prehistory of Prewitts Knob, Kentucky. Master's thesis, Department of Anthropology, Washington University, St. Louis, Missouri.

Haskins, Valerie A., and Nicholas P. Herrmann
1989 Shell Mound Bioarchaeology: An Overview of Past Research from the Green River Region, and Preliminary Observations on New Data from the Read Site, 15BT10. Paper presented at the 46th Annual Meeting of the Southeastern Archaeological Conference, Tampa, Forida.
1996 Shell Mound Bioarchaeology. In *Of Caves and Shell Mounds*, edited by Kenneth C. Carstens and Patty Jo Watson, pp. 107–118. University of Alabama Press, Tuscaloosa.

Hensley, Christine K.
1994 The Archaic Settlement System of the Middle Green River Valley, Kentucky. Ph.D. dissertation, Department of Anthropology, Washington University, St. Louis, Missouri.
1996 Lithic Materials from the Read Shell Mound. In *Of Caves and Shell Mounds*, edited by Kenneth C. Carstens and Patty Jo Watson, pp. 94–106. University of Alabama Press, Tuscaloosa.

Hensley-Martin, Christine K.
1986 A Reanalysis of the Lithic Industry from the Read Site, Butler County, Kentucky. Master's thesis, Department of Anthropology, Washington University, St. Louis, Missouri.

Herrmann, Nicholas P.
2002 Biological Affinities of Archaic Period Skeletal Populations from West-Central Kentucky and Tennessee. Ph.D. dissertation, Department of Anthropology, University of Tennessee, Knoxville.

Hill, Fredrick N.
n.d. Preliminary Faunal Analysis of the KYANG Site (15Jf267). Manuscript on file, Program of Archaeology, University of Louisville, Louisville, Kentucky.

Hobbes, Thomas
1990 [1651] *Leviathan*. Edited by Richard Tuck. Cambridge University Press, Cambridge, England.

Hockensmith, Charles D., Thomas N. Sanders, and David Pollack
1985 The Green River Shell Middens of Kentucky. National Register of Historic Places thematic nomination form, on file, Kentucky Heritage Council, Frankfort.

Janzen, Donald E.
1977 An Examination of Late Archaic Development in the Falls of the Ohio River Area. In *For the Director: Research Essays in Honor of James B. Griffin*, edited by Charles E. Cleland, pp. 123–143. Anthropological Paper 61. Museum of Anthropology, University of Michigan, Ann Arbor.

Jefferies, Richard W.
1990 Archaic Period. In *The Archaeology of Kentucky: Past Accomplishments and Future Directions*, edited by David Pollack, pp. 143–246. Kentucky Heritage Council, Frankfort.
1995 Late Middle Archaic Exchange and Interaction in the North American Midcontinent. In *Native American Interactions: Multiscalar Analyses and Interpretations in the Eastern Woodlands*, edited by Michael S. Nassaney and Kenneth E. Sassaman, pp. 73–99. University of Tennessee Press, Knoxville.
1996 Hunters and Gatherers after the Ice Age. In *Kentucky Archaeology*, edited by R. Barry Lewis, pp. 39–77. University Press of Kentucky, Lexington.
1997 Middle Archaic Bone Pins: Evidence of Mid-Holocene Regional-Scale Social Groups in the Southern Midwest. *American Antiquity* 62:464–487.
2004 Regional Scale Interaction Networks and the Emergence of Cultural Complexity along the Northern Margins of the Southeast. In *Signs of Power: The Rise of Cultural Complexity in the Southeast*, edited by Jon L. Gibson and Philip J. Carr, pp. 71–85. University of Alabama Press, Tuscaloosa.

Jefferies, Richard W., and Carol A. Morrow
1982 The Carrier Mills Archaeological Project: An Introduction. In *The Carrier Mills Archaeological Project: Human Adaptation in the Saline Valley, Illinois*, vol. 2, edited by Richard W. Jefferies and Brian M. Butler, pp. 1–33. Research Paper 33. Center for Archaeological Investigations, Southern Illinois University, Carbondale.

Jefferies, Richard W., Victor D. Thompson, and George R. Milner
2005 Archaic Hunter-Gatherer Landscape Use in West-Central Kentucky. *Journal of Field Archaeology* 30:3–23.

Johnson, Jay K., and Samuel O. Brookes
1989 Benton Points, Turkey Tails, and Cache Blades: Middle Archaic Exchange in the Southeast. *Southeastern Archaeology* 8:134–145.

Justice, Noel D.
1987 *Stone Age Spear and Arrow Points of the Midcontinental and Eastern United States*. Indiana University Press, Bloomington.

Kentucky Geological Survey
2002 Kentucky Geological Survey. Electronic document, http://www.uky.edu/KGS/, accessed October 2004.

Kneberg, Madeline
1956 Some Important Projectile Point Types Found in the Tennessee Area. In *Ten Years of Tennessee Archaeologist Selected Subjects, 2: 1954–1963*, pp. 17–26. Tennessee Archaeological Society, Knoxville.

Lewis, R. Barry
1996 Introduction. In *Kentucky Archaeology*, edited by R. Barry Lewis, pp. 1–20. University of Kentucky Press, Lexington.

Lewis, Thomas M. N., and Madeline K. Kneberg
1959 The Archaic Culture in the Middle South. *American Antiquity* 25:161–183.
1961 *Eva: An Archaic Site*. University of Tennessee Press, Knoxville.

Lopinot, Neal H.
1982 Plant Macroremains and Paleoethnobotanical Implication. In *The Carrier Mills Archaeological Project: Human Adaptation in the Saline Valley, Illinois*, vol. 2, edited by Richard W. Jefferies and Brian M. Butler, pp. 671–860. Research Paper 33. Center for Archaeological Investigations, Southern Illinois University, Carbondale.

Lynch, B. Mark
1982 Mortuary Behavior in the Carrier Mills Archaeological District. In *The Carrier Mills Archaeological Project: Human Adaptation in the Saline Valley, Illinois*, vol. 2, edited by Richard W. Jefferies and Brian M. Butler, pp. 1113–1231. Research Paper 33. Center for Archaeological Investigations, Southern Illinois University, Carbondale.

Maggard, Greg, and David Pollack
2000 *Archaeological Investigation of the Highland Creek Site in Union County, Kentucky*. Research Report 5. Kentucky Archaeological Survey, University of Kentucky, Lexington.

Marquardt, William H.
1985 Complexity and Scale in the Study of Fisher-Gatherer-Hunters: An Example from the Eastern United States. In *Archaic Hunter-Gatherers: The Emergence of Cultural Complexity*, edited by T. Douglas Price and James A. Brown, pp. 59–98. Academic Press, New York.

Marquardt, William H., and Patty Jo Watson
1974 The Green River, Kentucky, Shell Mound Archaeological Project. Paper presented at the 73rd Annual Meeting of the American Anthropological Association, Mexico City.
1983 The Shell Mound Archaic of Western Kentucky. In *Archaic Hunters and Gatherers in the American Midwest*, edited by James L. Phillips and James A. Brown, pp. 323–339. Academic Press, Orlando, Florida.
2005a (editors) *Archaeology of the Middle Green River Region, Kentucky*. Institute of Archaeological and Paleoenvironmental Studies Monograph 5. Florida Museum of Natural History, University of Florida, Gainesville.
2005b The Green River Shell Mound Archaic: Conclusions. In *Archaeology of the Middle Green River Region, Kentucky*, edited by William H. Marquardt and Patty Jo Watson, pp. 629–647. Institute of Archaeological and Paleoenvironmental Studies Monograph 5. Florida Museum of Natural History, University of Florida, Gainesville.
2005c SMAP Investigations at the Carlston Annis Site, 15Bt5. In *Archaeology of the Middle Green River Region, Kentucky*, edited by William H. Marquardt and Patty Jo Watson, pp. 87–120. Institute of Archaeological and

Paleoenvironmental Studies Monograph 5. Florida Museum of Natural History, University of Florida, Gainesville.

Maslowski, Robert F., Charles M. Niquette, and Derek M. Wingfield

1995 The Kentucky, Ohio and West Virginia Radiocarbon Database. *West Virginia Archeologist* 47 and electronic document, http://www.crai-ky.com/education/reports/c14-database.html, accessed October 2004.

Mayes, Leigh Ann

1997 The Bluegrass Site (12W162): Bioarchaeological Analysis of a Middle-Late Archaic Mortuary Site in Southwestern Indiana. Master's thesis, Department of Anthropology and Sociology, University of Southern Mississippi, Hattiesburg.

McDowell, Robert C.

1986 *The Geology of Kentucky: A Text to Accompany the Geologic Map of Kentucky*. U.S. Geological Survey Professional Paper. U.S. Geological Survey, Department of Interior, Washington, D.C.

McFarland, Arthur C.

1943 *Geology of Kentucky*. University of Kentucky, Lexington.

McGrain, Preston

1983 *The Geologic Story of Kentucky*. Special Publication 8, Series XI. Kentucky Geological Survey, Lexington.

Meltzer, David J., and Bruce D. Smith

1986 Paleoindian and Early Archaic Subsistence Strategies in Eastern North America. In *Foraging, Collecting, and Harvesting: Archaic Period Subsistence and Settlement in the Eastern Woodlands*, edited by Sarah W. Neusius, pp. 3–21. Occasional Papers 6. Center for Archaeological Investigations, Southern Illinois University, Carbondale.

Mensforth, Richard P.

1996 Observations on Antiquity, Geographic Distribution, and Theoretical Significance of Violent Injuries, Scalping and other Trophy-Taking Behaviors among Archaic Hunter-Gatherers of the Eastern United States (abstract). *American Journal of Physical Anthropology* 22:166.

2001 Warfare and Trophy Taking in the Archaic Period. In *Archaic Transitions in Ohio & Kentucky Prehistory*, edited by Olaf H. Prufer, Sara E. Pedde, and Richard S. Meindl, pp. 110–138. Kent State University Press, Kent, Ohio.

2005 Paleodemography of the Skeletal Population from the Carlston Annis Site, 15Bt5. In *Archaeology of the Middle Green River Region, Kentucky*, edited by William H. Marquardt and Patty Jo Watson, pp. 453–487. Institute of Archaeological and Paleoenvironmental Studies Monograph 5. Florida Museum of Natural History, University of Florida, Gainesville.

Miller, Carl F.

1950 Early Cultural Horizons in the Southeastern United States. *American Antiquity* 15:273–288.

Milner, George R.

2004 *The Moundbuilders: Ancient People of Eastern North America*. Thames and Hudson, London.

Milner, George R., and Virginia G. Smith

1986 *New Deal Archaeology in Kentucky: Excavations, Collections, and Research*. Occasional Papers in Anthropology 5. Program for Cultural Resource Assessment, University of Kentucky, Lexington.

Mocas, Stephen T.

1977 *Excavations at the Lawrence Site, 15Tr3, Trigg County, Kentucky*. University of Louisville, Louisville, Kentucky.

1985 An Instance of Middle Archaic Mortuary Activity in Western Kentucky. *Tennessee Anthropologist* 10:76–91.

Moore, Clarence B.

1916 Some Aboriginal Sites on Green River, Kentucky. Certain Aboriginal Sites on Lower Ohio River. Additional Investigations on Mississippi River. *Journal of the Academy of Natural Sciences of Philadelphia* 16:431–511.

Morey, Darcy F., George M. Crothers, Julie K. Stein, James P. Fenton, and Nicholas P. Herrmann

2002 The Fluvial and Geomorphic Context of Indian Knoll, an Archaic Shell Midden in West-Central Kentucky. *Geoarchaeology* 17:521–553.

Morse, Dan. F.

1962 Report of 1962 Excavations in the Stewart County, Tennessee Portion of the Lake Barkley Reservior. Manuscript on file, F. H. McClung Museum, University of Tennessee, Knoxville.

Muller, Jon

1986 *Archaeology of the Lower Ohio River Valley*. Academic Press, Orlando, Florida.

Nance, Jack D.

1977 Aspects of Late Archaic Culture in the Lower Tennessee/Cumberland River Valleys. *Tennessee Archaeologist* 33:1–15.

1986 The Morrisroe Site: Projectile Point Types and Radiocarbon Dates from the Lower Tennessee River Valley. *Midcontinental Journal of Archaeology* 11:11–50.

1987 The Archaic Sequence in the Lower Tennessee-Cumberland-Ohio Region. *Southeastern Archaeology* 6:129–140.

1988 The Archaic Period in the Lower Tennessee-Cumberland-Ohio Region. In *Paleoindian and Archaic Research in Kentucky*, edited by Charles D. Hockensmith, David Pollack, and Thomas N. Sanders, pp. 127–152. Kentucky Heritage Council, Frankfort.

Nelson, Nels C.

1917 Contributions to the Archaeology of Mammoth Cave and Vicinity, Kentucky. *Anthropological Papers* 22:1–73. American Museum of Natural History, New York.

Pedde, Sara E., and Olaf H. Prufer

2001 The Kentucky Green River Archaic as Seen from the Ward Site. In *Archaic Transitions in Ohio & Kentucky Prehistory*, edited by Olaf H. Prufer, Sara E. Pedde, and Richard S. Meindl, pp. 59–86. Kent State University Press, Kent, Ohio.

Pollack, David

1990 Introduction. In *The Archaeology of Kentucky: Past Accomplishments and Future Directions*, edited by David Pollack, pp. 1–24. Kentucky Heritage Council, Frankfort.

Powell, Mary L.

1996 Health and Disease in the Green River Archaic. In *Of Caves and Shell Mounds*, edited by Kenneth C. Carstens and Patty Jo Watson, pp. 119–131. University of Alabama Press, Tuscaloosa.

Prentice, Guy

1990 *Mammoth Cave Archeological Inventory Project Interim Report—1989 Investigations*. National Park Service, Southeast Archeological Center, Tallahassee, Florida.

Price, T. Douglas, and James A. Brown

1985 Aspects of Hunter-Gatherer Complexity. In *Prehistoric Hunter-Gatherers: The Emergence of Cultural Complexity*, edited by T. Douglas Price and James A. Brown, pp. 3–20. Academic Press, Orlando, Florida.

Rafinesque, Constantine S.

1824 *Ancient History, or Annals of Kentucky: with a Survey of the Ancient Monuments of North America, and a Tabular View of the Principal Languages and Primitive Nations of the Whole Earth*. Privately printed, Frankfort, Kentucky.

Ritchie, William A.

1932 *The Lamoka Lake Site*. Researches and Transactions 7. New York State Archaeological Association, Rochester.

1961 *A Typology and Nomenclature for New York Projectile Points*. Bulletin 384. New York State Museum and Science Service, Albany.

Robinson, Kenneth W., and Steven D. Smith

1979 The Villier Site (15Jf110 Complex). In *Excavations at Four Archaic Sites in the Lower Ohio Valley, Jefferson County, Kentucky*, vol. 1, edited by Michael B. Collins, pp. 590–696. Occasional Papers in Anthropology 1. Department of Anthropology, University of Kentucky, Lexington.

Rolingson, Martha A.

1967 *Temporal Perspective on the Archaic Cultures of the Middle Green River Region, Kentucky*. Ph.D. dissertation, University of Michigan. University Microfilms, Ann Arbor, Michigan.

Rolingson, Martha A., and Douglas W. Schwartz

1966 *Late Paleo-Indian and Early Archaic Manifestations in Western Kentucky*. Studies in Anthropology 3. University of Kentucky Press, Lexington.

Rossen, Jack

2000 Archaic Plant Utilization at the Hedden Site, McCracken County, Kentucky. In *Current Archaeological Research in Kentucky*, vol. 6, edited by David Pollack and Kristen J. Gremillion, pp. 1–24. Kentucky Heritage Council, Frankfort.

Rothschild, Nan A.

1979 Mortuary Behavior and Social Organization at Indian Knoll and Dickson Mounds. *American Antiquity* 44:658–675.

Sandweiss, Daniel H., Kirk A. Maasch, and David G. Anderson

1999 Climate and Culture: Transitions in the Mid-Holocene. *Science* 283:499–500.

Sassaman, Kenneth E., and David G. Anderson (editors)

1996 *Archaeology of the Mid-Holocene Southeast*. University Press of Florida, Gainesville.

Schock, Jack M.

1979 Ten Carbon-14 Dates from Prehistoric Indian Sites in Southern Kentucky. Manuscript on file, Office of State Archaeology, University of Kentucky, Lexington.

Schwartz, Douglas W.

1967 *Conceptions of Kentucky Prehistory: A Case Study in the History of Archaeology*. Studies in Anthropology 6. University of Kentucky Press, Lexington.

Semken, Holmes A.

1983 Holocene Mammalian Biogeography and Climatic Change in the Eastern and Central United States. In *Late-Quaternary Environments of the United States: 2. The Holocene*, edited by H. E. Wright Jr., pp. 183–207. University of Minnesota Press, Minneapolis.

Silverberg, Robert

1968 *Mound Builders of Ancient America: The Archaeology of a Myth*. New York Graphic Society, Greenwich, Connecticut.

Smith, Bruce D.

1986 The Archaeology of the Southeastern United States: From Dalton to de Soto, 10,500–500 B.P. In *Advances in World Archaeology*, vol. 5, edited by Fred Wendorf and Angela E. Close, pp. 1–92. Academic Press, New York.

Squier, Ephraim G., and Edwin H. Davis

1848 *The Ancient Monuments of the Mississippi Valley*. Contributions to Knowledge 1. Smithsonian Institution, Washington, D.C.

Stafford, C. Russell

1994 Structural Changes in Archaic Landscape Use in the Dissected Uplands of Southwestern Indiana. *American Antiquity* 59:219–237.

2004 Modeling Soil-Geomorphic Associations and Archaic Stratigraphic Sequences in the Lower Ohio Valley. *Journal of Archaeological Science* 31:1053–1067.

Stafford, C. Russell, R. L. Richards, and C. Michael Anslinger

2000 The Bluegrass Fauna and Changes in Middle Holocene Hunter-Gatherer Foraging in the Southern Midwest. *American Antiquity* 65:317–336.

Stein, Julie K.

1980 *Geoarchaeology of the Green River Shell Mounds, Kentucky*. Ph.D. dissertation, University of Minnesota. University Microfilms International, Ann Arbor, Michigan.

Stoltman, James B.

1978 Temporal Models in Prehistory: An Example from Eastern North America. *Current Anthropology* 19:703–746.

Stuiver, Minze, and Paula Reimer

2004 *CALIB REV 4.4.2 Radiocarbon Calibration Program*. Electronic document, http://calib.qub.ac.uk, accessed October 2004.

Styles, Bonnie W., Steven R. Ahler, and Melvin L. Fowler

1983 Modoc Rock Shelter Revisited. In *Archaic Hunters and Gatherers in the American Midwest*, edited by James L. Phillips and James A. Brown, pp. 261–297. Academic Press, Orlando, Florida.

Thiel, Barbara

1979 The Distribution of Grave Goods with Infants and Children at Indian Knoll. Manuscript on file, Office of State Archaeology, Lexington, Kentucky.

Thomas, Cyrus

1894 *Report on Mound Explorations of the Bureau of Ethnology*. Annual Report 12. Bureau of Ethnology, Smithsonian Institution, Washington, D.C.

Turnbow, Christopher (editor)
1981 *Cultural Radiocarbon Determinations of Kentucky*. Occasional Papers in Anthropology 3. Department of Anthropology, University of Kentucky, Lexington.

Vickery, Kent
1972 Projectile Point Type Descriptions: McWhinney Heavy Stemmed. Paper presented at the 29th Southeastern Archaeological Conference, Morgantown, West Virginia.

Wagner, Gail E.
1996 Botanizing along the Green River. In *Of Caves and Shell Mounds*, edited by Kenneth C. Carstens and Patty Jo Watson, pp. 88–93. University of Alabama Press, Tuscaloosa.

Ward, Steven C.
2005 Dental Biology of the Carlston Annis Shell Mound Populations. In *Archaeology of the Middle Green River Region, Kentucky*, edited by William H. Marquardt and Patty Jo Watson, pp. 489–503. Institute of Archaeological and Paleoenvironmental Studies Monograph 5. Florida Museum of Natural History, University of Florida, Gainesville.

Watson, Patty Jo
1974 Prehistoric Horticulturalists. In *Archeology of the Mammoth Cave Area*, edited by Patty Jo Watson, pp. 233–238. Academic Press, New York.
2005 WPA Excavations in the Middle Green River Region: A Comparative Account. In *Archaeology of the Middle Green River Region, Kentucky*, edited by William H. Marquardt and Patty Jo Watson, pp. 515–628. Institute of Archaeological and Paleoenvironmental Studies Monograph 5. Florida Museum of Natural History, University of Florida, Gainesville.

Watson, Patty Jo, Richard A. Yarnell, Harold Meloy, William Benninghoff, Eric Callen, Aidan Cockburn, Hugh Cutler, Paul Parmalee, Lionel Prescott, and William White
1969 *The Prehistory of Salts Cave, Kentucky*. Reports of Investigations 16. Illinois State Museum, Springfield.

Webb, William S.
1946 Indian Knoll, Site Oh2, Ohio County, Kentucky. *Reports in Anthropology and Archaeology* 4(3):115–365. Department of Anthropology and Archaeology, University of Kentucky, Lexington.
1950a The Carlson Annis Mound, Site 5, Butler County, Kentucky. *Reports in Anthropology* 7(4):267–354. Department of Anthropology, University of Kentucky, Lexington.
1950b The Read Shell Midden, Site 10, Butler County, Kentucky. *Reports in Anthropology* 7(5):357–401. Department of Anthropology, University of Kentucky, Lexington.
1981 *The Development of the Spearthrower*. Occasional Papers in Anthropology 2. Department of Anthropology, University of Kentucky, Lexington.

Webb, William S., and William D. Funkhouser
1932 *Archaeological Survey of Kentucky*. Reports in Archaeology and Anthropology 2. University of Kentucky, Lexington.

Webb, William S., and William G. Haag
1939 The Chiggerville Site, Site 1, Ohio County, Kentucky. *Reports in Anthropology and Archaeology* 4(1):1–62. Department of Anthropology and Archaeology, University of Kentucky, Lexington.
1940 Cypress Creek Villages, Sites 11 and 12, McLean County, Kentucky. *Reports in Anthroplogy* 4(2):67–110. Department of Anthropology and Archaeology, University of Kentucky, Lexington.
1947 Archaic Sites in McLean County, Kentucky. *Reports in Anthropology* 7(1):4–46. Department of Anthropology, University of Kentucky, Lexington.

White, Karli E.
1990 An Analysis of Bone Tools from the Carlston Annis Site (15Bt5), Kentucky. Master's thesis, Department of Anthropology, Washington University, St. Louis, Missouri.

Wilkins, Gary R., Paul A. Delcourt, Hazel R. Delcourt, Frederick W. Harrison, and Manson R. Turner
1991 Paleoecology of Central Kentucky since the Last Glacial Maximum. *Quaternary Research* 36:224–239.

Winters, Howard D.
1967 *An Archaeological Survey of the Wabash Valley in Illinois*. Reports of Investigations 10. Illinois State Museum, Springfield.
1968 Value Systems and Trade Cycles of the Late Archaic in the Midwest. In *New Perspectives in Archeology*, edited by Sally R. Binford and Lewis R. Binford, pp. 175–221. Aldine, Chicago.
1969 *The Riverton Culture: A Second Millennium Occupation in the Central Wabash Valley*. Reports of Investigations 13. Illinois State Museum, Springfield.
1974 Introduction to the New Edition. In *Indian Knoll*, by William S. Webb, pp. iii–xxvii. University of Tennessee Press, Knoxville.

Wymer, Dee Ann
1987 The Paleoethnobotanical Record of the Lower Tennessee-Cumberland Region. *Southeastern Archaeology* 6:124–129.

18

The View from the Southeast

Tristram R. Kidder and Kenneth E. Sassaman

All too frequently, the Archaic peoples, who were greatly diversified culturally through space and time, are treated as though they were a homogeneous array of hunters and gatherers, and as though they were idiots savants capable only of changing styles of artifacts, producing an occasional nicely ground piece of stone, continuously foraging for a precarious and uncertain subsistence, and in general doing little beyond surviving as noble and unspoiled primitives.

—Howard Winters, 1968

This is an exciting time to be studying Archaic societies in eastern North America. A wealth of new data provides evidence that the Archaic was a time of unprecedented social, political, economic, and technological variability. New data are proving Winters correct; the Archaic of the Southeast (Figures 18.1 and 18.2) was not the uniform, homogeneous phenomenon it was once seen to be. Archaic people were not all living a Hobbesian existence confined to a short, nasty, and brutish life. Trends evident among Archaic populations, such as increasing sedentism, greater site density, population increase, long-distance trade, social differentiation, and technological innovation, are leading archaeologists to

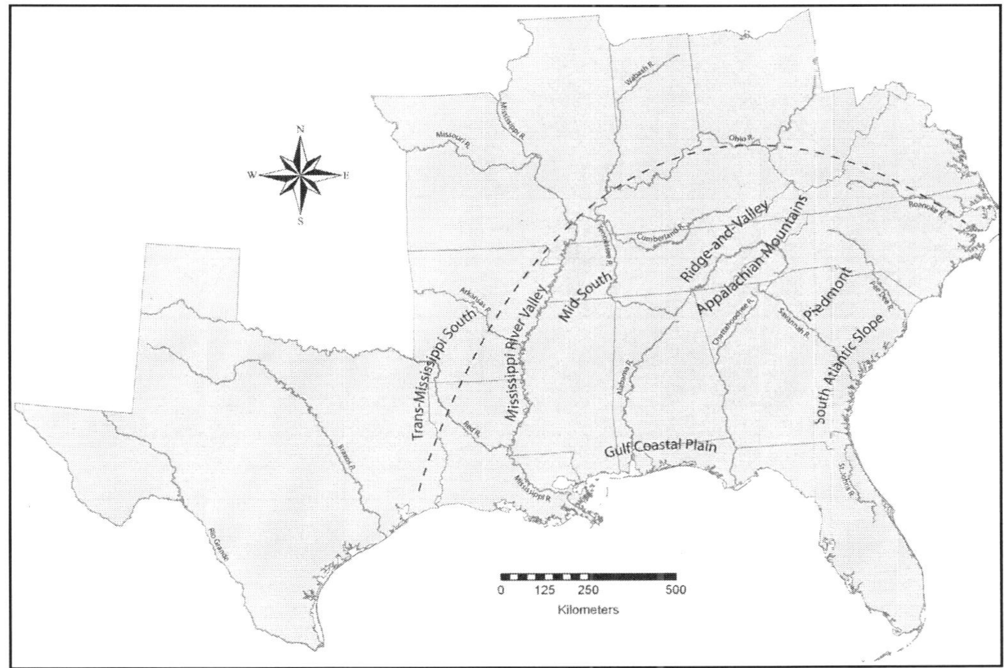

Figure 18.1. The southeastern United States with major geographic and culturally relevent areas indicated. The dashed line indicates the approximate boundary of the archaeologically defined Southeast.

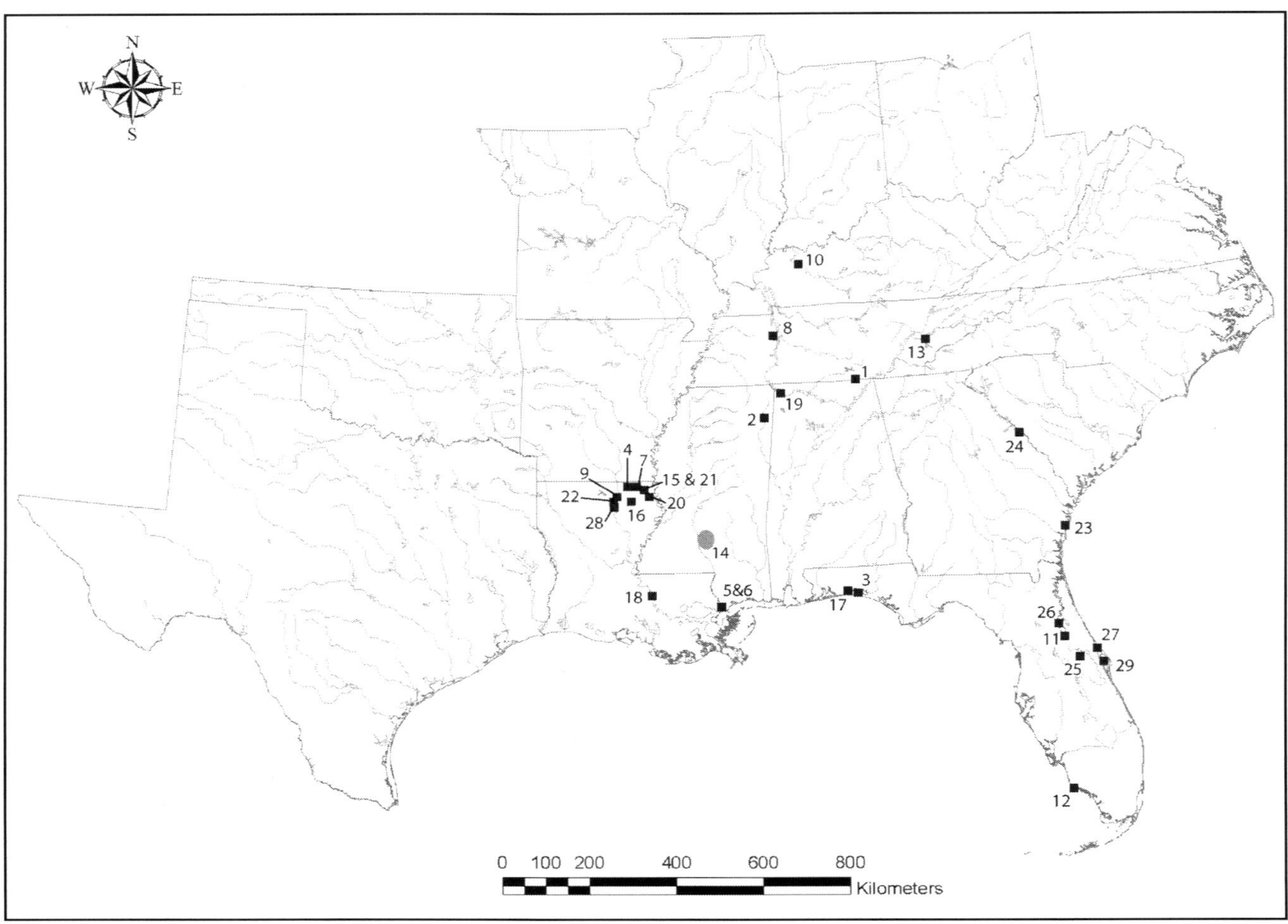

Figure 18.2. The southeastern United States showing the locations of archaeological sites mentioned in the text: 1. Bailey (40GL26); 2. Beech site; 3. Buck Bayou Mound (8WL90); 4. Caney Bayou (16CT5); 5. Cedarland (22HA30); 6. Claiborne (22HA35); 7. Denler (16MO106); 8. Eva (40BN12); 9. Frenchman's Bend (16OU259); 10. Green River sites; 11. Hontoon Island (8VO214); 12. Horr's Island (8CR205–209, 211); 13. Iddins (40LD38); 14. Kennan Bead Cache (approximate location); 15. Lower Jackson (16WC10); 16. Metz Midden (16RI105); 17. Miegs Pasture (8OK102); 18. Monte Sano (16EBR17); 19. Mulberry Creek (1CT27); 20. Nolan (16MA201); 21. Poverty Point (16WC5); 22. Plum Creek Archaic (16OU89); 23. Sapelo Island (9MI23); 24. Stallings Island (9CB1); 25. Thornhill Lake (8VO58); 26. Tick Island (Harris Creek) (8VO24); 27. Tomoka (8VO81); 28. Watson Brake (16OU175); 29. Windover (8BR246).

reassess their views of this period of Native American history. Archaic societies can no longer be assumed a priori to have been somehow less complex than the Woodland tribes and Mississippian chiefdoms that followed. Although most populations across the Southeast started out looking if not behaving the same at the beginning of the Archaic, this relative egalitarianism did not last long. By the Middle Archaic, the construction of planned communities, monumentalization of architecture, modification of the landscape, and embodiment of symbolic meaning in material culture demonstrated Archaic social, political, and ideological complexity. These patterns were elaborated during the Late Archaic, when hunter-forager-fisher groups throughout the Southeast showed trends of increasing social, political, and economic differentiation.

In this chapter we review new or recently reinterpreted data to explore notions of Archaic cultural history and evolution in the Southeast. The chronological and cultural boundaries used here follow Anderson and Sassaman (2004) and Sassaman and Anderson (2004). The Early Archaic is generally synonymous with the early Holocene and is dated ca. 11,450–8900 cal B.P.[1] The Middle Archaic is largely the same as the middle Holocene and is considered here to span the period ca. 8900–5700 cal B.P. The Late Archaic developed during the early part of the late Holocene and dates to ca. 5700–3200 cal B.P. To accommodate the chronology of the Poverty Point culture, we extend our discussion of the Late Archaic to ca. 3000 cal B.P.

Early Archaic (ca. 11,450–8900 cal B.P.)

The Early Archaic was largely coincident with the early Holocene and was a period of remarkable environmental transformation in eastern North America (Anderson 2001; Ellis et al. 2004; Kneller and Peteet 1999; Shuman et al. 2002; Webb et al. 1993; Yu 2000; Yu and Wright 2001). Global temperatures were rising steadily at this time. Plant and animal life like that seen today was established by ca. 11,500 cal B.P., but evidence indicates that seasonal and annual temperature and precipitation varied significantly from today; north-to-south and east-to-west spatial differences in biota also existed that are not present in the modern Southeast. Sea levels were considerably lower than at present, and rivers were undergoing rapid changes as they adjusted to changing base levels. Although the early Holocene is notable mostly for gradual environmental change, the final collapse of the Laurentide ice sheet ca. 8200 cal B.P. (Alley et al. 1997; Barber et al. 1999; Shuman et al. 2002) caused a brief but relatively extreme decline in global temperatures. Because this event was brief, at least in geological terms, its impact on human populations is not obvious, but given the magnitude of climate change during this event, it is hard to imagine that it did not have some effect on the people living in the Southeast.

Throughout the Southeast, initial Early Archaic societies were using tool types derived from those produced during the Paleoindian period. Ground-stone tools appeared for the first time, and notched, stemmed, and notched and stemmed bifaces replaced lanceolate forms after ca. 11,500 cal B.P. Although spatial and temporal variation is evident, biface morphology is generally similar across large parts of the region. An "early Side-Notched horizon" is recognized and comprises types such as Big Sandy, Bolen, Kessell, Taylor, and San Patrice *var. St. Johns* (Anderson and Sassaman 2004). At present archaeologists do not know if these different types represent actual ethnic or cultural differences or if they are simply part of an expected range of morphological or typological variation across space and through time. Wear patterns suggest these tools were used for a variety of activities, including hunting, butchering, skinning game, hide working, and woodworking. Side-notched points were largely replaced by corner-notched forms such as Kirk, Palmer, and Hardin Stemmed by ca. 10,500 cal B.P. These corner-notched forms were, in turn, replaced by bifurcate-stemmed points (e.g., MacCorkle, St. Albans, LeCroy, and Kanawha) after ca. 10,000 cal B.P.

Changes in point morphology reflect other changes in technology and society following the end of the Paleoindian period. Early Archaic archaeological sites are more numerous than Paleoindian, suggesting a substantial population increase. Population distributions, however, were not uniform across space, and evidence indicates that some areas were more heavily populated than others at given times. Population concentrations tended to focus on locations where resources were both abundant and seasonally predictable. The middle Tennessee River valley and the South Atlantic Slope are places where Early Archaic populations were especially concentrated relative to other parts of the Southeast. Clusters of Early Archaic material in the uplands along the Mississippi River and its tributaries indicate this area may have supported a considerable Early Archaic population (Jeter and Williams 1989; Saunders and Allen 1997); much of the data that would allow archaeologists to understand the distribution of sites in the alluvial valley are either deeply buried or have been eroded.

Coupled with greater populations was a long-term trend for resource procurement, most notably, of lithic raw material, to be focused increasingly on locally available resources. A shift in technology also occurred; this transformation was marked by changes in hafting morphology and a decreasing emphasis on formal tools. Early Archaic social, settlement, and subsistence practices were designed to take advantage of the increasingly diverse fauna and flora of the Southeast and to cope with decreased territorial ranges imposed by growing populations. A strong correlation is evident between increasing group size, decreasing territorial range, and changes in climatic conditions in the early Holocene. Anderson (1996b:49–53) argues that in some parts of the Southeast a shift occurred from initial colonizing Paleoindian societies that emphasized logistical mobility strategies and collector-based technologies to Early Archaic societies that emphasized a pattern based on forager adaptations characterized by expedient lithic technologies and significant residential mobility (see also Anderson and Sassaman 2004:88, 90). Available evidence suggests considerable and perhaps overlapping variations in settlement and subsistence strategies during the early Holocene, but long-term economic changes from Paleoindian to Early Archaic emphasize a shift from specialized hunting to increasingly generalized foraging. Despite fluctuations among local and regional settlement and subsistence strategies, increasing populations, changes in climate (and, thus, fauna and flora), and emerging social networks appear to have dictated the gradual entrenchment of logistical mobility strategies over the course of the Early Archaic.

The band-macroband model is most commonly invoked to explain how societies organized themselves in the Early Archaic (Anderson and Hanson 1988; cf. Daniel 1998). This model is most fully developed for the South Atlantic Slope. Populations lived in small bands of roughly 25 to 150 persons for the majority of the annual cycle and are assumed to have exploited most parts of the landscape on a regular basis. These band-level groups probably had annual ranges largely restricted to single river drainages. Periodically, macroband population aggregations of 500–1,500 persons formed for the purpose of practicing rituals or exchanging information, raw materials, and mates. These macrobands were not formally organized and did not have permanent mechanisms for promoting group identity; their existence was temporary and depended on the cooperative behavior of constituent bands.

Macroband aggregation probably took place at or near the Fall Line, productive quarry locations, or at the mouths of rivers along the coast.

Site distributions, raw material acquisition and utilization practices, and site types all indicate that Early Archaic lifeways were based on very fluid social practices and emphasized settlement mobility (whether logistical or residential in nature). Mobility may have been variable over a given annual cycle, with local climatic and environmental conditions influencing specific patterns and timing of movements. Sites are limited in diversity and consist primarily of small, presumably short-term camps and larger, more densely occupied settlements often associated with specific resource concentrations (e.g., shoals and quarries). Settlement variability is minimal across the entire region, and much of what has been detected may be a function of the temporal span(s) of occupation(s) rather than any inherent social distinction within or between communities or groups.

Artifact types within Early Archaic communities emphasized utilitarian needs and were designed for reliability and efficiency. When possible, high-quality raw materials were sought out, and substantial evidence indicates that materials were transported over long distances and across river drainages. These data suggest that group foraging ranges were considerable. Artifacts that might denote social status and differentiation are almost entirely absent from sites of this time period. No indications in artifacts, site features, or settlement patterns suggest institutionalized or permanent social, political, or economic status differences. Ceremonial uses of large and elaborate bifaces, such as those of the Late Paleoindian Dalton horizon (Morse 1997; Walthall and Koldehoff 1998), are rarely duplicated in Early Archaic horizons.

The growing (but still not common) utilization of groundstone tools at this time points to increasing exploitation of plant foods, most likely nuts, grasses, and wild starchy seeds. Bone tools were being used in greater numbers (or they are more often preserved). Hunting of deer and small mammals was evidently the primary source of animal protein; fishing was not a significant activity at this time perhaps because interior rivers were still adjusting to post-Pleistocene sea-level changes; coastal areas that may have been occupied are now drowned (e.g., Faught 2004), and, thus, archaeologists are missing an important source of information on subsistence and settlement.

Middle Archaic (8900–5700 cal B.P.)

Humans living in the Southeast during the middle Holocene are usually thought to have adapted to the climate interval known alternatively as the Hypsithermal or mid-Holocene Climatic Optimum (Deevey and Flint 1957; Ganopolski et al. 1998; O'Brian et al. 1995; Ruddiman and Mix 1993; Steig 1999). This era was once seen as a time of uniformly increased global temperature, but it is now understood as a period of significant climatic variability in eastern North America. Current data suggest that seasonality was more pronounced across the region; summers were, on average, warmer than at present and winters were cooler. Precipitation varied considerably, both seasonally and annually.

Across much of the Midwest and Midsouth, average rainfall appears to have been lower than today. The prairie-forest margin shifted eastward, indicating warmer, dryer conditions (Anderson et al. 1989; Baker et al. 2002; Bradbury and Dean 1993; Bradbury et al. 1993; King 1981; Webb et al. 1993; Whitehead and Sheehan 1985). Reduced vegetation in upland settings led to greater soil erosion and floodplain aggradation (Bettis 2003; Bettis and Hajic 1995; Brown and Vierra 1983; Schuldenrein 1996). Lake levels were generally lower at this time, suggesting that permanent water sources would have been favorable settlement locations. Although average conditions may have been dryer, periods of increased rainfall and flooding in the Midwest and the lower Mississippi Valley indicate greater climatic variability than previously recognized (Brown et al. 1999; Knox 1985, 1987, 1999; Royall et al. 1991). No evidence suggests this was a period of significant overall climatic deterioration or destabilization, although in some instances local environments were greatly affected. In some parts of the Southeast, notably the South Atlantic Slope, climatic conditions were wetter than at present (Goman and Leigh 2004). Here, groundwater recharge exceeded evapotranspiration and lake levels rose; large interior swamps such as the Everglades and Lake Okeefenokee expanded (Watts et al. 1996). Sea levels were fluctuating at this time, but the general trend of rising sea levels persisted (Törnqvist et al. 2004).

Middle Archaic is often diagnosed by the appearance of new artifact forms and technologies. Chipped-stone projectile points and knives are the most useful for delineating Middle Archaic temporal and cultural units. In comparison with Early Archaic, Middle Archaic formal biface technology is more varied and morphological characteristics are more regionally specific and may indicate increasingly circumscribed ethnic and territorial units. Variation is notable between the eastern and western parts of the lower Southeast; west of the Mississippi River, projectile point forms share morphological affinities with those used by populations in Texas and the eastern Plains. In the eastern parts of the region, Early Archaic notched and bifurcate-stem points were replaced by square and contracting-stem forms, such as Kirk Stemmed, Stanly Stemmed, and Morrow Mountain Types I and II. In the Midsouth, these same forms are present along with Crain, Denton, Sykes, and Benton (Brookes 2004; McGahey 2000). In the Mississippi Valley and to the west, the point styles are varied and not as well dated but are thought to include Bulverde, Carrolton, Ensor, Epps, Jones Creek, Kent, Marshall, Wells, Williams, and Yarborough (Jeter and Williams 1989; Schambach 1998; Webb et al. 1963). The Evans point is perhaps the best-dated form in this region and is placed in the period ca. 5700–5000 cal B.P. (Saunders and Allen 1997; Webb 1981).

Chipped-stone tool assemblages at sites west of the Appalachians include diverse formal tools such as adzes, picks, drills, end and side scrapers, and knives. Ground-stone tool use increased greatly at this time. Full- and three-quarter-grooved axes are found in many areas, and large tools such as pestles, mortars, nutting stones, manos and metates, and net sinkers are widely distributed at sites west of the Appalachians. Bone and antler tools were used in large numbers; bone awls, needles, scrapers, fishhooks, and antler woodworking tools have been recovered at sites throughout the region. The functional diversity and morphological variation in these artifact types indicate that Middle Archaic people were intensively exploiting the full range of biota available in the Southeast. Increasing emphasis was being placed on plant and plant-food processing equipment, woodworking and forest clearance was progressively more important, and fishing was evidently a major subsistence pursuit.

In addition, the Middle Archaic is well known for a variety of artifacts and artifact forms associated less directly with subsistence and functional pursuits (Figure 18.3). Famous among these categories are oversize bifaces (Brookes 1997, 2004; Deter-Wolf 2004; Johnson and Brookes 1989; McGahey 2000), bannerstones, beads (Brookes 2004; Connaway 1982; Crawford 2003; Dowd 1989; Gibson 1968; Johnson 2000; Saunders et al. 1997), "cloud-blower" pipes (Dowd 1989; Lewis and Kneberg 1961), bone pins (Jefferies 1997), and pendants. Most often these artifacts are made of stone, but beads of bone, cannel coal, shell, and copper also occur. Zoomorphic effigy beads have a widespread distribution in the Mississippi Valley and the Midsouth and have been infrequently recovered farther east and north (Crawford 2003).

Many of these artifacts, including some in the chipped-stone category, are so finely made or so large as to be lacking utilitarian function. These artifacts are sometimes recovered in isolated caches; for example, the Beech site cache consisted of 11 ceremonially broken bifaces (Brookes 2004), while the Keenan Bead cache included 449 unmodified pebbles, preforms, and bead blanks (including zoomorphic effigy forms) (Connaway 1982). They are also found in burials and have been unearthed in midden contexts (Craig 1958; Deter-Wolf 2004; Dowd 1989; Gibson 1968; Lewis and Kneberg 1961).

Changes in material culture are one reflection of the many social, cultural, technological, and political changes that occurred during the Middle Archaic. Anderson and Sassaman point out that "ceremonial shell and earthen mound construction was initiated in several areas, long-distance exchange networks spanning much of the region appeared ... and there is increased evidence for interpersonal violence or warfare" (2004:95). Considerable evidence of settlement variability exists beyond the use of mounded architecture, and a hallmark of the Middle Archaic in some regions is extensive elaboration in mortuary behavior and grave furnishings. The available evidence indicates the pace of change was increasing rapidly and was especially marked during the later part of the Middle Archaic, or by 6800–5700 cal B.P.

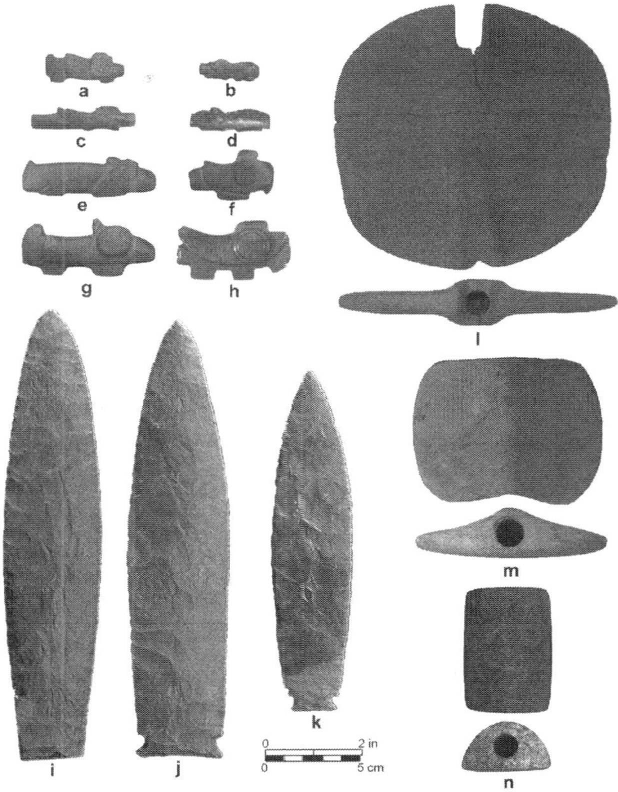

Figure 18.3. Zoomorphic beads, oversized bifaces, and bannerstones of the Archaic-period Southeast. Zoomorphic beads: a, Carpenter Cache, 22GR781, Grenada County, Mississippi; b, Denton 136, 22QU522, Quitman County, Mississippi; c, Moore 3, 1LU11, Lauderdale County, Alabama; d, Denton 62, 22QU522, Quitman County, Mississippi; e, Crisler, 22CB576, Claiborne County, Mississippi; f, Monte Sano, 16EBR17, East Baton Rouge Parish, Louisiana; g, Hoover, 16TA5, Louisiana; h, Lemley, Lafayette County, Arkansas; all photographs courtesy of Jessica F. Crawford (Crawford 2003:146–158). Oversized Benton-era bifaces from Mississippi: i, cache blade; j, oversized Benton; k, double-notched Turkey-tail–like blade; all photographs courtesy of Jay K. Johnson. Bannerstones: l, Notched Southern Ovate preform, Stallings Island, 9CB1, Columbia County, Georgia (note that only one of two notches has been pecked from this preform and the longitudinal hole remains incomplete); m, Hinge-type or Southern Ovate, Edgefield County, South Carolina; n, Southern Humped, Stallings Island, 9CB1, Columbia County, Georgia; all photographs courtesy of Asa Randall and used with permission of the Peabody Museum of Archaeology and Ethnology, Harvard University.

This was not, however, a period of cultural homogeneity, and many of the characteristics inferred to reveal increasing social, economic, or political differentiation are found in different temporal contexts or in different places and often do not co-occur. For example, the people who built the earthen mound sites in the Mississippi Valley were not involved in far-reaching, long-distance exchange systems, as might be anticipated given their extensive investment in monumental architecture. Similarly, elaborate burials that contain large amounts of marine shell in the Tennessee Valley and adjacent areas are not accompanied by any obvious ceremonial or monumental architecture (cf. Claassen 1992, 1996). Furthermore, although this is a time noted for seemingly remarkable and complex behaviors in some areas of the Southeast, many if not most inhabitants of the region were carrying on a lifeway not especially far removed from that of their Early Archaic ancestors.

While perhaps the majority of people were living lives little changed from previous eras, some populations were engaging in very distinctive settlement and social behaviors. This process is most notable in the creation of monumental architecture that has a limited distribution in the Mississippi River valley and in peninsular Florida. In both of these areas, populations engaged in the construction of large earthen or shell mounds and associated architectural features as early as 6000 cal B.P. In some instances, these mound settlements are arranged around a central open space or plaza. These settlements are distinctive because of the use of monumental architecture and because they display clear evidence of planning and labor mobilization. Further, in both regions the erection of these sites was coupled with the emergence of sedentary or nearly sedentary resident populations.

In the Mississippi Valley, more than a half dozen mound sites are securely dated as early as 6000 cal B.P. and as late as 4800 cal B.P. (Anderson 2002; Anderson and Sassaman 2004; Saunders et al. 2005:662–663). These settlements range in size from 11 mounds with a circular embankment over 250 m in diameter at Watson Brake (Figure 18.4) (Saunders et al. 2005) to one mound at Caney Bayou. Mound heights range from 7.5 m (Watson Brake, Nolan) to less than a meter. These mounds apparently were built rapidly and were in use at the same time. Site occupations lasted from as long as 800 years at Watson Brake to as briefly as 400 years at the Nolan site. Sites are found mostly on upland terraces overlooking rivers and floodplains. The Nolan site, a four-mound complex with an apparently linear earthen embankment, is located on a relict channel of the Arkansas River in the modern floodplain of the Mississippi River. The discovery of this site, which is buried by up to 5 m of recent alluvium, indicates

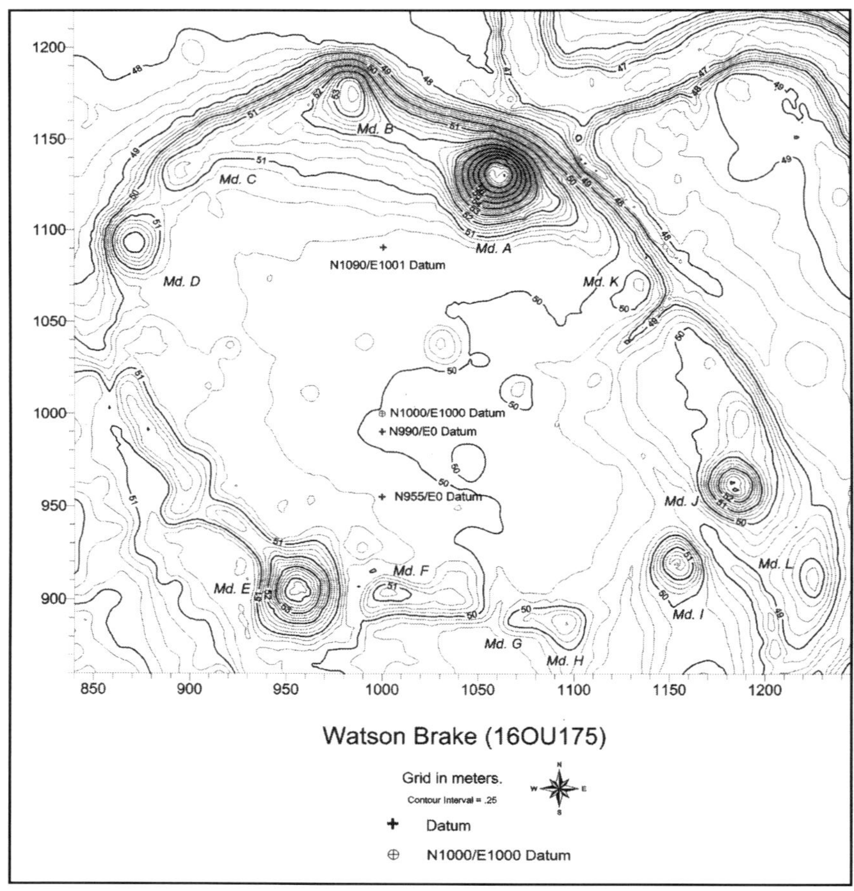

Figure 18.4. Topographic map of the Watson Brake site, Ouachita Parish, Louisiana (courtesy of Dr. Joe Saunders and the Regional Archaeology Program, Department of Geosciences, University of Louisiana-Monroe, and the Louisiana Division of Archaeology).

that large parts of the Middle Archaic landscape in the Mississippi Valley are buried or have been destroyed by erosion (Arco et al. 2006).

The only Middle Archaic site in the lower Mississippi Valley that has yielded evidence for human burials is Monte Sano. A rectangular structure measuring 10 m on a side was built on the ground surface. This building was dismantled, and a low rectangular platform roughly .5 m high was built, covering most of the rectangular structure. The surface of this platform was burned and was overlain by a layer of charcoal and burned bone, "most probably the remains of human cremations" (Kuttruff 1997:5). A small (ca. .4-m-high by 1.5-m-diameter) dome-shaped mound was built on this platform; two layers of charcoal and redeposited cremated human bone were found in this mound. A final mantle covered the primary and secondary platforms. Artifacts included an oversized biface of northern flint, two tubular jasper beads, and a jasper "bird" effigy bead. Radiocarbon dates place Monte Sano squarely in the Middle Archaic (Hays 1995; Kuttruff 1997; Saunders 1994).

Although the Poverty Point site (Figure 18.5) is known because of its Late Archaic occupation, recent work in this area suggests a more substantial Middle Archaic occupation than previously thought. Saunders et al. (2001) demonstrated that the Lower Jackson mound was constructed during the Middle Archaic, and contemporary artifacts have been recovered from the "Mound B field" at the northern and western ends of the site. Four of seven radiocarbon dates from the so-called Deep Six occupation at the edge of Macon Ridge were rejected by Greene (1985, 1989) as too early to be included in the accepted range of Poverty Point dates. Greene argued that the most plausible explanation for these "anomalously" early dates was the presence of lignite or unrecognized rootlet contamination. This conclusion was not based on the actual identification of contaminants but, rather, on the early ages of the dates. However, these four dates fall in the Middle Archaic as now understood at sites throughout northeast Louisiana. When the Deep Six dates are examined by depth, they reveal a pattern suggesting two occupations, one Middle Archaic and one early in the Poverty Point–age occupation (Greene 1985). Given what archaeologists now know about Middle Archaic earth moving, the materials from Deep Six could represent a Middle Archaic occupation or construction event that has only been revealed because it is

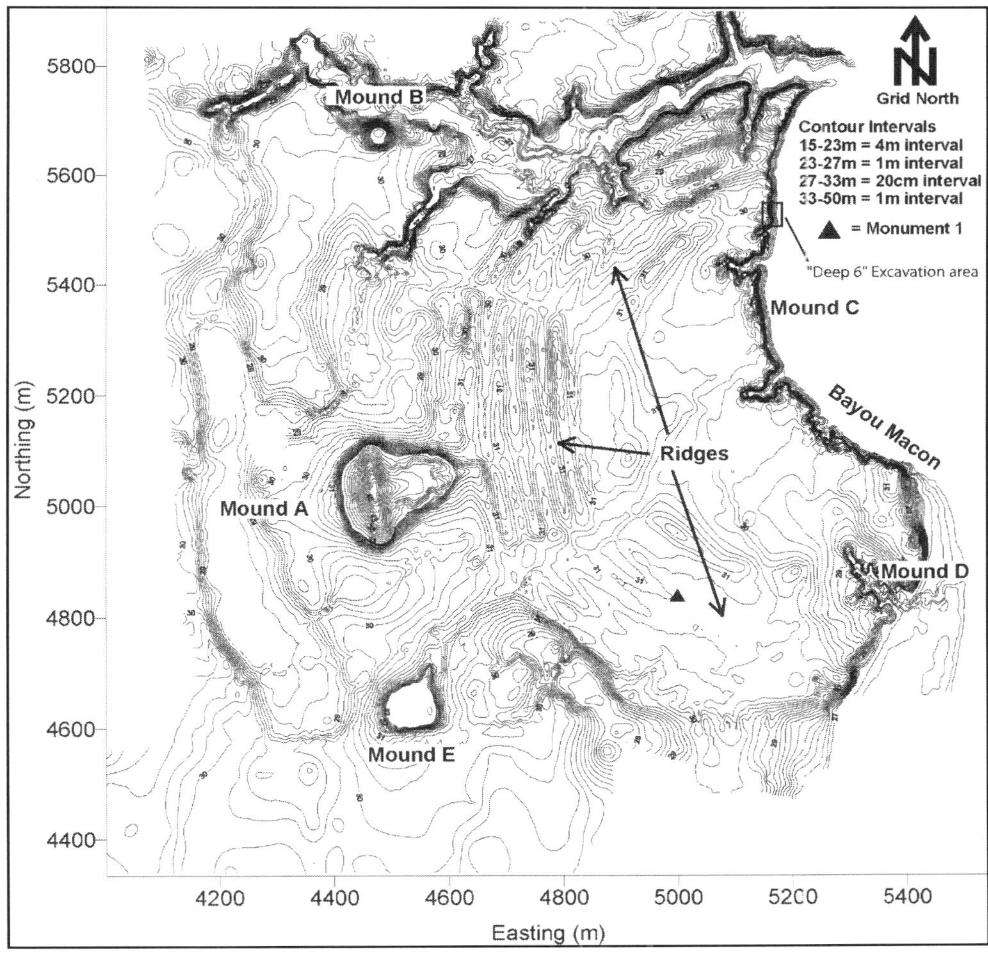

Figure 18.5. Topographic map of Poverty Point site, West Carroll Parish, Louisiana (after Ortmann 2003).

exposed along the bank of Bayou Macon (Connolly 2003a, 2003b:92–95, Figure 20).

Further, recent work by Ortmann and Kidder at Mound A suggests that part of this massive mound may date as early as the Middle Archaic (Ortmann 2003). Coring in the western conical part of the mound revealed that the fill of this part was very different from the fill of the eastern platform. The fill in the cone is highly weathered and shows extensive pedogenesis. In contrast, the platform is composed of unweathered sediments that were rapidly deposited and buried in a series of construction episodes. These sediments are varied in color and texture, unlike the cone, where the sediments are homogenized by pedogenic processes. Furthermore, coring indicates that the platform was constructed after the cone had been formed; sediments from the platform uncomformably lie over those composing the cone. At a minimum, the evidence indicates that the sediments from the cone and platform were derived from different sources or have been emplaced for different amounts of time.

While mounds were clearly important locations on the lower Mississippi Valley landscape, smaller occupations occurred, as well. Excavations at Plum Creek and Metz Midden indicate Middle Archaic habitation sites existed outside of mound sites (J. Saunders 2004). Denler, located on a sandy ridge overlooking the floodplain of the Boeuf River, shows that these small sites were widely distributed across the landscape. The site was badly eroded, and no intact midden deposits were recovered. However, surface collections turned up Middle Archaic projectile points (Evans, Sinner, Big Creek-like, Burkette-like), a triangular atlatl weight made of red jasper (?), three ground-stone celts, several pitted nutting stones, and small amounts of nonlocal lithic debitage, all indicating that the site was more than a short-term hunting camp (Kidder 1986).

Although Middle Archaic mound sites are remarkable for their early monumental architecture, the material culture of the occupants is not as elaborate as the architecture. The majority of material found on these mound sites is replicated at the few nonmound communities identified to date. Moreover, almost no evidence at these sites suggests extensive long-distance trade (Johnson 2000). Denler is unusual in having modest quantities of nonlocal lithic materials. Many ritual or ceremonial artifacts seen elsewhere in the Southeast (e.g., bannerstones, oversize bifaces, marine shell, etc.) are absent or have not been found. Tubular chipped- and ground-stone beads are recovered at some sites, and bead working was evidently practiced at Watson Brake, but these sites cannot be seen as economic centers (J. Saunders 2004). Faunal and floral remains at Watson Brake indicate that the site was occupied over multiple seasons, but whether that site was a fully sedentary occupation is impossible to say (Saunders et al. 2005; Saunders et al. 1997).

In Florida, mound building involved the purposeful accumulation of earth and shell, often associated with human interments. The best example thus far comes from Tick Island on the middle St. Johns River (Aten 1999). Burials salvaged by Bullen from a basal component of a shell-mound complex known as Harris Creek, dating to ca. 6300 cal B.P., were set in a stratum of white sand beneath a shell midden and a second mortuary layer dating to ca. 6000–5750 cal B.P. Successive layers of shell midden, clean shell, and earth spanning subsequent periods capped the remnant of the mound. This same pattern of successive mound episodes interspersed with midden, over a period of at least 4,000 years, was documented recently at several other mounds on and near Hontoon Island, to the south of Tick Island (Randall and Sassaman 2005; Sassaman 2003a) (Figure 18.6).

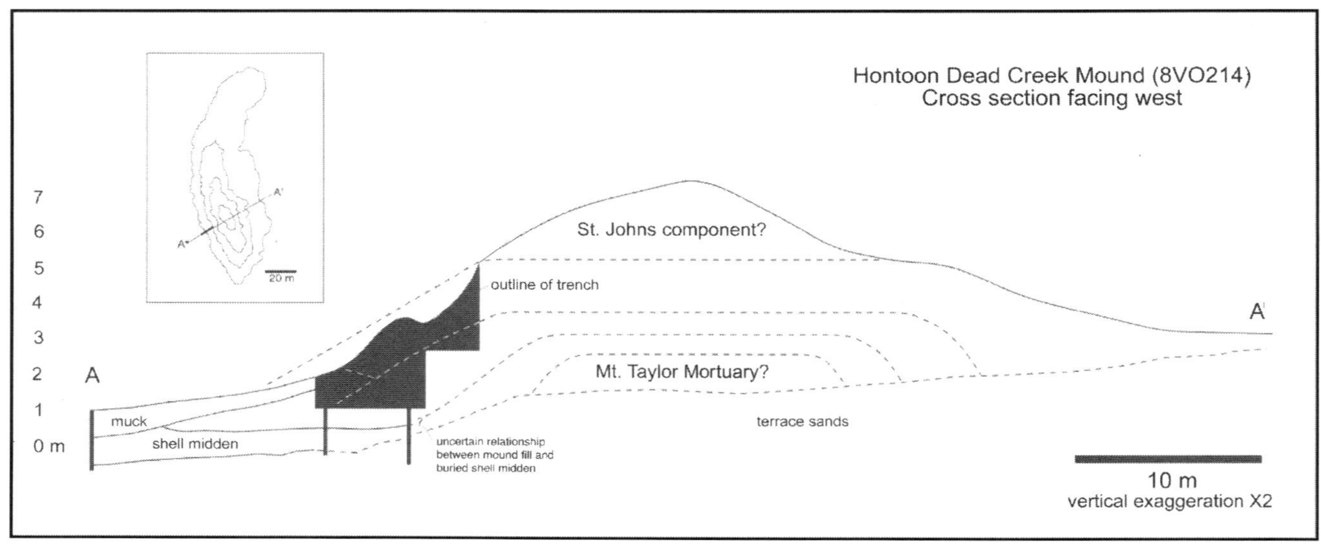

Figure 18.6. Cross section of Hontoon Dead Creek Mound (8VO214) showing relationship between St. Johns component and the hypothesized earlier Mt. Taylor mortuary. Bullen (see Aten 1999) recorded a similar mound construction sequence at Harris Creek (8VO24) on Tick Island.

Other earthen and shell mounds in northeast Florida contained mortuary or cached items with geographical origins to the far north and west. Jasper beads at Thornhill Lake (Goggin 1952; Moore 1999) almost certainly came from producers in Mississippi (Brookes 1999), while bannerstones at this riverine site and at Tomoka Mounds on the coast (Moore 1999; Piatek 1994) likely came from north Georgia or South Carolina (Sassaman 1998). These early patterns of long-distance exchange portended the more intensive interactions of Poverty Point times (see below).

Middle Archaic mound building, although limited spatially, is an indication of the increasing presence of humans as agents of landscape change and modification. This process was possibly inadvertent as people living in increasingly large communities for greater periods of time altered their environment by accumulating refuse and by harvesting plants and animals for food and wood for fuel. In some localities humans affected local environments by altering habitats, changing local topography, or differentially selecting plants and animals (Kidder 1998). The most obvious effects, however, are the result of deliberate practices of landscape manipulation. Mound building as a monumental practice is a substantial change from practices of earlier times. Mounds are not only an indication of the capacity to move dirt or to mobilize labor but they are also a social and conceptual statement by the builders that they are capable of re-creating the landscape to suit their needs and to fulfill their vision of how the physical and symbolic world should be constructed. Earthen ridges connecting mounds, borrow pits, and open plazas are additional elements of built landscapes at some sites.

The specific purposes of this built environment elude archaeologists for the most part. Undoubtedly, some of the reasons for expending energy were strictly functional, such as providing habitation surfaces, elevating residences above wet soils, or providing elevations from which to secure a better vantage. However, these mundane functions are certainly not the only reasons for building mounds and earthworks. One can point to the labor and effort needed to plan and erect these mounds as one example of the departure from strict functionality. Clearly, Middle Archaic people in many other parts of the eastern United States were content to live their lives on the ground and with a minimal investment in labor efforts to modify their environment. Even in the Mississippi Valley, the existence of nonmound habitation sites at this time indicates that the mound sites were conceptually if not economically and socially distinct. But another factor should not be overlooked. While these early mounds were built to provide activity surfaces, these same surfaces were interred after they were used. At Watson Brake, Monte Sano, Frenchman's Bend, and probably Nolan as well as many northeast Florida sites, mound stages were erected over occupation surfaces or, as at Frenchman's Bend and Monte Sano, over buildings. These mound caps were not built as platforms for future constructions but as final events that buried the contents of the mounds. Outside of Florida, only limited evidence so far suggests that these earthen features were regularly used for entombing bodies.

Mound building, as we see it, was apparently the end product of behaviors that were either unique to the time and place or were being enacted and demarcated in a unique fashion relative to the rest of the Southeast. These actions demonstrate the creation and perpetuation of a ritual landscape. The monuments need not be seen as the products of a highly complex or elaborate economic or political hierarchy, however (J. Saunders 2004). They clearly indicate the existence of leadership positions, given the need to plan, mobilize labor for, and execute the construction of these features. The absence of markers of permanent economic inequality or political ranking suggests that these apparently complex behaviors were embedded within cosmological or ideational realms without being manifest in permanent structures of political authority or economic control. Considerable debate revolves around the extent, nature, and configuration of economic, political, and social differentiation manifest in the construction, use, and maintenance of Middle Archaic monumental architecture, and many questions are still unresolved (Gibson and Carr 2004).

Across much of the Southeast, social organization appears for the first time to have been increasing in relative complexity. Although most populations were living in small groups and were probably only differentiated by age, sex, and ability, evidence from burials and in the form of monumental architecture, long-distance exchange, and specific exotic or nonfunctional artifacts suggests that some people or groups had a status that was socially and, possibly, politically distinctive. Some people were being buried with more goods, and their graves or grave furniture was more elaborate than the rest of the population. At present, whether these graves represent specific sex-gender distinctions within the community or mark achieved or ascribed status is unclear. The mobilization of labor for the construction of large earthen or shell mounds and the planning of these communities indicate the presence of leadership roles not seen in the Early Archaic. No evidence, however, indicates these distinctions were institutionalized or perpetuated by a limited subset of the population over appreciable periods of time. The more common use of nonperishable goods exchanged over very long distances suggests intergroup interaction was also changing. Coupled with increased evidence of sedentism, long-distance trade appears to have supplanted group mobility as a mechanism for the movement of ideas and, possibly, as a medium for exchanging mates and cementing alliances.

Trade or exchange was used to create or promote social and ceremonial or ritual identity. Nonutilitarian lithic tools, beads, pendants, and bannerstones were, on occasion, made with raw materials imported over long distances. The rarity of these raw materials and their use in specific forms is inferred to reflect ritual behaviors that spanned large areas and that served to mediate alliance formation and to promote risk-reduction strategies by binding ethnically or territorially diverse populations together by a shared iconography or ritual worldview. The Benton Interaction Sphere (Figure 18.7) is perhaps the best-articulated example of this process (Brookes 1997; Johnson and Brookes 1989; Meeks 1999). Exchange mechanisms were not, however, apparently uniformly successful in buffering intergroup stresses, as it is in Middle Archaic sites that archaeologists see the first evidence of interpersonal violence (Smith 1995, 1996, 1997).

Populations were increasing slowly from earlier times, and most habitation sites were small and probably supported band-sized groups. Larger communities may have served as seasonal aggregation points, but in a few instances people were living in the same community year-round or nearly so. Increasingly through this period, evidence suggests, populations were making more use of aquatic and riverine resources for their subsistence. This pattern reflects the increasing stabilization of floodplains as a consequence of rising sea levels (Smith 1986); the slowing of sea-level rise probably allowed the exploitation of coastal resources as a major part of the diet. Shellfish were especially important for the first time during the Middle Archaic, and large accumulations of shellfish refuse in inland river settings as well as along the south Atlantic coast suggest populations were likely targeting these resources because they were abundant and predictable. Although plant foods constituted a growing part of the diet, at present no secure evidence indicates the domestication of plant species. Nuts were clearly important, and intensive exploitation of wild oily seed plants such as chenopodium and little barley occurred for the first time (Saunders et al. 1997). Wild squashes were being utilized, possibly for their seeds but more likely as containers. The presence of bottle gourd in a burial at the Windover site in eastern Florida is the only example of a possible domesticate at this time (Doran et al. 1990).

Explanations for social change in the Middle Archaic often focus on human response to climatic fluctuations (Anderson 2004; Anderson and Sassaman 2004; Brookes 2004). Climate changes are inferred to have had several effects on the Middle Archaic populations of the Southeast. Middle Holocene climates were certainly dryer than early Holocene. Increased aridity may have forced populations into resource-rich areas such as river valleys and coastal zones,

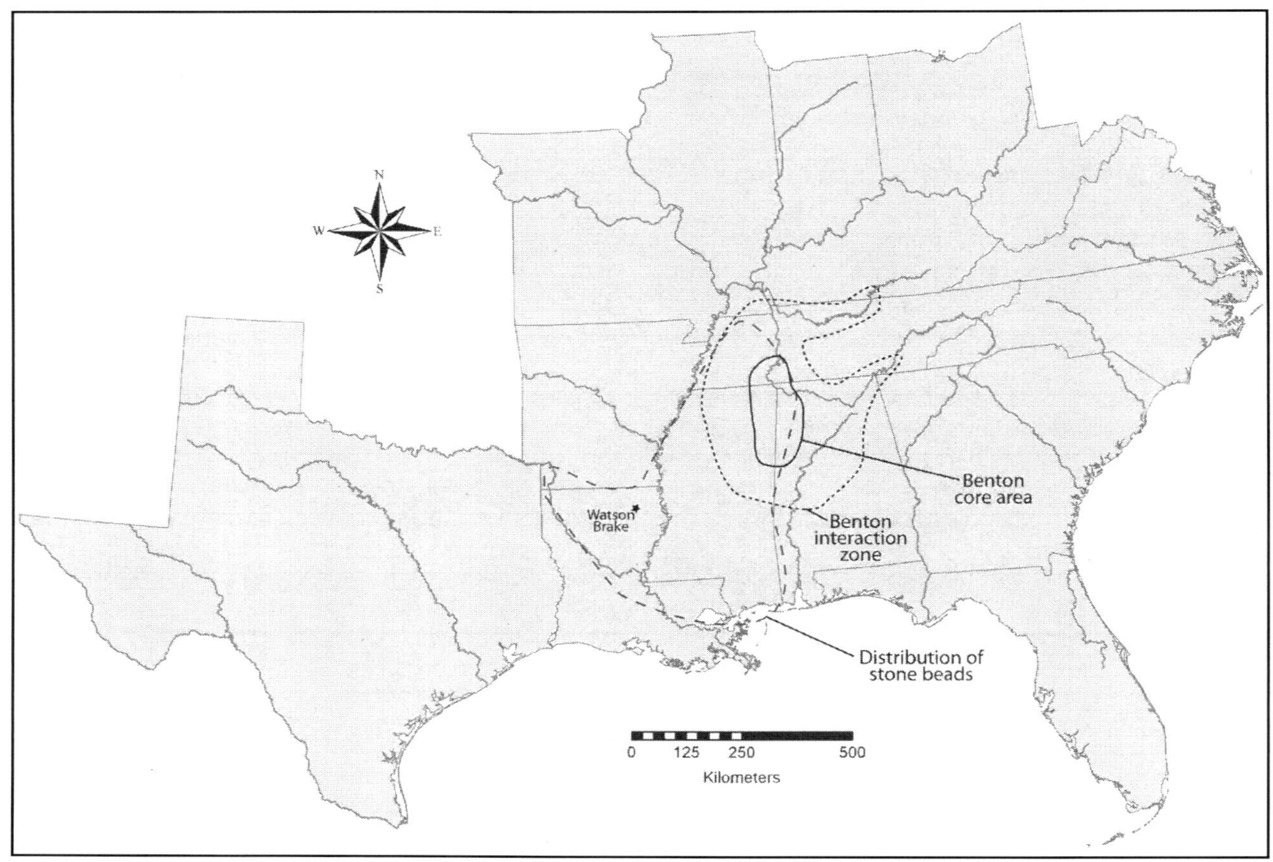

Figure 18.7. Boundaries of the Benton Interaction Sphere and the distribution of stone beads in the Southeast. The Benton core area is defined in accordance with Johnson and Brooks (1989) and is noted for the presence of cached oversize Benton and Turkey-tail points. The broader Benton Interaction Sphere is defined by the use of Benton and similar points in caches and burials (see Deter-Wolf 2004). The distribution of stone beads follows Crawford (2003).

placing increasing pressure on resources in these localities. Human groups, their mobility already restricted by rising population pressure resulting from natural demographic increase, would have encountered greater competition for restricted or scarce resources. Greater population, coupled with restricted resources and limited mobility, may possibly account for the greater evidence of interpersonal violence in comparison with the Early Archaic.

While competition may have increased, it was not always manifest in violent or hostile relationships. Brookes and Johnson (Brookes 2004; Johnson and Brookes 1989) argue the Benton Interaction Sphere and its attendant behaviors represent a means of risk reduction by increasing information flow and integrating diverse populations over long distances. The extensive bead production and exchange practices in the western Southeast may have been part of a similar strategy that encompassed a different territory or population than that included in the Benton Interaction Sphere (see Figure 18.7). Increased hypertrophy of artifact forms may reflect a related strategy using material symbols to mediate and emphasize ritualized cooperative behaviors. Exchange networks reconciled resource stress by moving ritual or ceremonial goods and fostering the flow of information and encouraging cooperation. Exchange products probably were more valued as a medium of communication than for their practical or commodity value. Mound building may have served a similar purpose, either by redirecting (re)productive energy and, thus, alleviating population stresses (Hamilton 1999) or by encouraging cooperative behavior among populations living within a given territory. For some archaeologists, these developments mark the origins of tribal societies in the Southeast (Anderson 2002, 2004). Risk reduction and cooperative behaviors seem to have been favored but not exclusive strategies during the Middle Archaic.

Although many of the seemingly complex behaviors first observed in the Middle Archaic may have served to lessen the effects of environmental fluctuations or to dampen risk, not all developments at this time can be attributed to this function alone. Complex-looking behaviors, such as construction of shell and earth monumental architecture, expansion of exchange networks, and the manufacture, exchange, and use of elaborate and nonutilitarian artifacts, are not uniformly evident across the region. Much of the elaboration of cultural behavior appears to have been in areas where food resources were relatively abundant (e.g., coastal regions and interior river valleys). Historical contingency, including local political developments, demographic patterns, the accumulation of cultural knowledge, ritual innovation, and local environmental history, no doubt played crucial roles in the formation of social groups, their expression(s) of identity, and their success through time. If complexity is defined by an increase in the number of parts and their interaction, then, not surprisingly, the Middle Archaic is more complex looking than the Early Archaic.

Late Archaic (5700–3200 cal B.P.)

Although climate systems were still fluctuating considerably (Little 2003; O'Brian et al. 1995; Wurster and Patterson 2001), largely modern physical environments had been established by the onset of the Late Archaic period, and, thus, sites of the period map onto contemporary zones of inhabitable land and favorable resources. A 40-percent increase in the number of known sites over the Middle Archaic period reflects regionwide population growth (Anderson 1996a; Steponaitis 1986). Locations underpopulated during the Middle Archaic period, notably portions of the Gulf and Atlantic coastal plains, were again intensively occupied, and coastal zones became major centers of settlement.

The continued expansion of wetland habitat that started in the middle Holocene occurred on two major fronts: along rivers of the interior Southeast, as terraces stabilized with lowered channel gradients compared with the middle Holocene (Schuldenrein 1996), and in coastal zones, as the diminishing rate of sea-level rise after 6000 RCYBP enabled the establishment of increasingly stable and productive estuarine habitat. Likewise, groundwater levels rose as near-surface aquifers responded to rising seas, resulting in a mosaic of freshwater wetland habitat in lower coastal plain environs and peninsular Florida.

Developments along interior rivers of the lower Midwest are summarized elsewhere by Jefferies (1995, 1996b, 2004). Rather than duplicate his efforts, we simply point out here some parallel developments along rivers of the Midsouth. As noted earlier, the origins of freshwater shell exploitation and attendant riverine settlement can be traced back some 7,000 years in the Midsouth to a tradition known as the "Shell Mound Archaic" (Marquardt and Watson 1983, 2005). The use of freshwater shellfish intensified during the Late Archaic period, leading to large accumulations of midden deposits at sites along rivers of the Interior Lowlands. Despite enormous accumulations of human refuse, unequivocal evidence for permanent occupation is lacking. Rather, a seasonal settlement round involving cool-season dispersal into interriverine upland zones and warm-season aggregation at locations along major rivers likely characterized the settlement patterns of most Late Archaic groups (Bowen 1977; Dye 1996; Prentice 1994).

Evidence for permanent architecture and community patterning at shell-midden sites is especially sparse (cf. Winters 1969). Nonetheless, the large number of human interments at sites on the Green and middle Tennessee rivers (e.g., Webb 1946, 1950a, 1950b; Webb and DeJarnette 1942; Webb and Haag 1940, 1947) provides evidence for long-term, repeated use of locations for purposes other than food gathering. The prevalence of burials at certain Shell Mound Archaic sites led Claassen (1991a, 1991b) to suggest shell was sometimes deposited for expressly mortuary purposes. Others view burials as incidental to routine habitation (Hensley 1994; Milner and Jefferies 1998).

Some of the best data available on Late Archaic shell middens of the Midsouth come from sites along the Green River of Kentucky (Crothers 1999, 2004; Marquardt and Watson 1983). A second major venue of the Shell Mound Archaic is the middle Tennessee River valley of northern Alabama and Tennessee. Although shellfish collection began as early as 7800 cal B.P. at Eva (Lewis and Kneberg 1961) and Mulberry Creek (Webb and DeJarnette 1942), most shell deposits date to Late Archaic times or later. Despite intensified use of sites for shellfishing, Late Archaic groups of the middle Tennessee, like those of the Green River, apparently abandoned shell-midden sites during the cool seasons, when climate was generally wetter, and relocated to adjacent upland tributaries such as Bear Creek in Alabama (Futato 1983) and Yellow Creek in Mississippi (Johnson 1981).

A noteworthy aspect of the Shell Mound Archaic in the middle Tennessee River valley is the adoption of ceramic vessel technology after 3700 cal B.P. Known as "Wheeler" fiber-tempered pottery (Haag 1939; Sears and Griffin 1950), this early ware is assigned to the Gulf Formational stage (Walthall and Jenkins 1976), which is divided into an early phase, characterized by Wheeler, and a late phase (ca. 2800–2100 cal B.P.), when the sand-tempered Alexander pottery series appeared (Jenkins and Kraus 1986:43). Little is known about the actual uses of this early pottery or its consequences for the subsistence economy. Soapstone and sandstone vessels also occur in middle Tennessee River shell middens and sites in the adjacent uplands, sometimes in burials (e.g., Webb and DeJarnette 1948). Despite the presumed temporal precedence of stone vessels over pottery (e.g., Bense 1994; Caldwell 1958; Smith 1986:30; Steponaitis 1986:373–374; Walthall 1980:70), recent dating of soot from soapstone bowls suggests that most often pottery predated its stone counterparts (Sassaman 1997, 1999, 2006).

Sites located along tributaries of the Tennessee River show that some Late Archaic populations maintained relatively permanent settlement with reliance on aquatic resources other than shellfish. Located on a tributary terrace of the Elk River only 30 km from the Wheeler Dam of the middle Tennessee River, the Bailey site was a locus of seemingly year-round habitation from ca. 5750 to 5100 cal B.P. (Bentz 1988). An assemblage of pit features included large storage features and postholes for five structures. Along with an assemblage of fish bone dominated by suckers, catfish, sunfish, and drum were other aquatic resources, such as turtles and waterfowl, as well as terrestrial game, mostly white-tailed deer and turkey. Hickory and walnut shell dominated the assemblage of plant remains.

The lower Little Tennessee River valley of eastern Tennessee provides additional information on riverine settlement outside the core area of the Shell Mound Archaic. Late Archaic occupation in the area through ca. 3800 cal B.P. was substantial but not especially dense. During the Iddins phase (3800–3150 cal B.P.) the number of sites increased fourfold, with four-fifths of them located in the alluvial valleys of the Little Tennessee and Tellico rivers (Davis 1990:223–225). Located on a terrace at the end of a series of shoals, the namesake Iddins site appears to have been the locus of spring fish harvests from ca. 3800 to 3400 cal B.P. (Chapman 1981). Over 450 notched cobbles similar to those described as net weights among historic Indians were recovered from Iddins. Also found were scores of rock-filled basins, which Chapman (1981) interprets as hearths for smoking fish. The remains of cultivated gourd and squash, wild forms of sunflower and marsh elder, and grape and walnut reflect additional subsistence activities through the summer and early fall. Soapstone bowls were routinely used at the site for direct-heat cooking and represent one of the truly unequivocal occurrences of this technology prior to the local adoption of pottery.

Despite the dominance of shellfishing economies along its coast, the South Atlantic Slope supported comparatively few riverine populations that chose to collect freshwater shellfish. One of the few examples is found in the middle Savannah River valley of Georgia and South Carolina, home to the fourth millennium B.P. Stallings culture. Noteworthy foremost for the innovation of pottery, Stallings-culture populations accumulated the remains of freshwater clam at habitation sites along the lower half of the Savannah River. A parallel development is found in the St. Johns River valley of northeast Florida, home to Late Archaic populations who continued the Middle Archaic tradition of collecting and mounding freshwater snails and bivalves and added the innovation of fiber-tempered pottery. Known locally as "Orange" fiber-tempered pottery (Bullen 1972), this ware appeared at about 4700 cal B.P. and became the chief diagnostic artifact of the ensuing millennium of intensive riverine and coastal settlement. Unlike the middle Savannah sequence, the St. Johns tradition of riverine shellfishing did not terminate in the fourth millennium but, instead, continued well into late prehistoric times.

Both the south Atlantic and Gulf coasts supported large, stationary populations, but until recently, these were believed to date no earlier than ca. 4700 cal B.P., when the rate of sea-level rise slowed sufficiently to promote relatively stable barrier island and estuarine environments (Crusoe and DePratter 1976; DePratter and Howard 1980). New evidence places the onset of intensive coastal occupation as early as 6500 cal B.P. on the south Atlantic coast and perhaps several centuries earlier on the Gulf Coast (Mikell 2001; Russo 1996a; Russo et al. 1993; Saunders and Mikell 2004).

Arcuate or ringlike configurations of shell along the Atlantic and Gulf coasts (Figure 18.8) reflect a long-standing Late Archaic tradition of intensive, possibly specialized, coastal settlement. Referred to widely as "shell rings," such sites along the Atlantic are distributed intermittently from Cape Canaveral, Florida, to just south of the Santee River in South Carolina (Russo and Heide 2001). Debate over the formation and function of shell rings has continued since the 1960s, when Waring and Larson opined that a shell ring on Sapelo Island "very likely represents a ceremonial or social arrangement" (1968:273). They also recognized that the

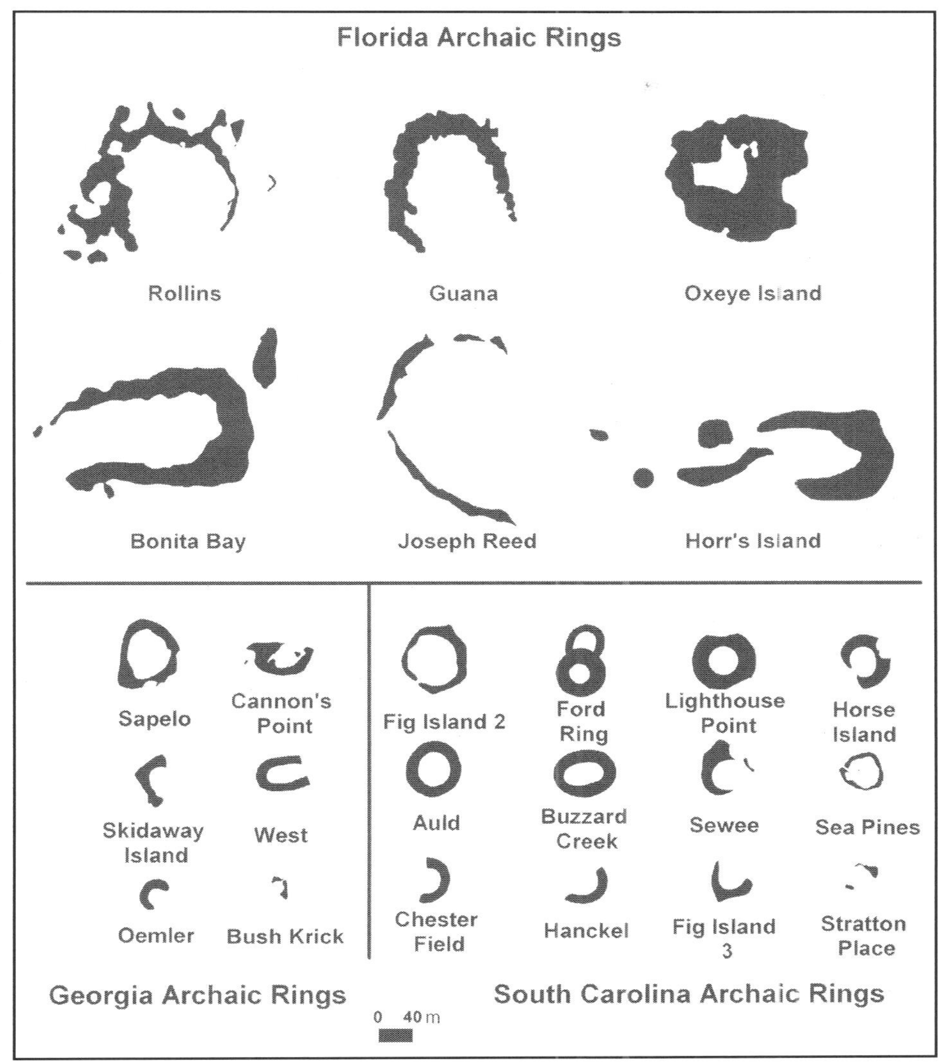

Figure 18.8. Representative plans of coastal shell arcs and rings along the Atlantic and (more rarely) Gulf coasts of the southeastern United States (courtesy of Dr. Michael Russo).

shell deposits accumulated from the everyday refuse of small habitations, a supposition later confirmed by Trinkley (1980, 1985). The most recent work supports the notion that shell rings resulted from ceremonial activities, notably, communal feasts (Russo 2002, 2004; Saunders 2002).

That shell and earthen mounds on the south Atlantic coast were, indeed, deliberate constructions is perhaps best exemplified by the Tomoka Mound complex near Daytona (Piatek 1994; Russo 1996b:274–276). Located on the mainland side of a coastal lagoon, the Tomoka complex includes nine mounds surrounded by a midden consisting chiefly of coquina and oyster. Charcoal from the base of the 3-m-high Mound 6 returned an uncalibrated ^{14}C assay of 4460 ± 70 B.P. (5297–4946 cal B.P.) (Piatek 1994). A coeval preceramic mound and midden complex is located on the Gulf coast of southwestern Florida. Dating from ca. 5500–4450 cal B.P., Horr's Island is an extensive shell-ringed village with at least three ceremonial mounds (Russo 1991). The largest, Mound A, rises more than 12 m above the water level at its base. The associated village midden consists largely of oyster, up to 5 m thick, lying on dune crests and slopes among the mangrove swamps that circumscribe the island. Within the midden, Russo (1991) uncovered successive living floors with hundreds of postholes representing the remains of small structures estimated at 3 m in diameter. Analysis of saltwater shellfish (scallop, clam, and oyster) and estuarine fishes (hardhead catfish, pinfish, and threadfin herring) for seasons of capture led Russo to conclude that Horr's Island was occupied year round.

Other major shell ring or arc sites on the Gulf Coast generally postdate 4450 cal B.P., and several have historical connections to the Poverty Point culture of northeast Louisiana (see below). Two such sites, Cedarland and Claiborne, occupy a bluff overlooking a salt marsh near the mouth of the Pearl River in Mississippi (Bruseth 1991; Gagliano and Webb 1970). The Late Archaic–period Cedarland site is a semicircular oyster midden measuring 165 m in diameter, encompassed by a 3- to 5-m-high earth and shell embankment. A variety of nonlocal raw materials, including Great Lakes copper and Arkansas quartz crystals, attest to extensive trade relations. Claiborne is a semicircular ridge of midden some 250 m in diameter with artifacts of Poverty Point affiliation: gorgets, plummets, celts, Jaketown perforators, soapstone vessels, baked-clay objects, and Motley points.

Four clusters of sites in the Choctawhatchee Bay of northwest Florida are assigned to the Elliott's Point complex, defined by Lazarus (1959) as a local expression of Poverty Point culture (Thomas and Campbell 1991). One of the chief sites, Buck Bayou Mound, is a 2-m-thick semicircular shell deposit over 150 m in diameter. Small shell middens dot the landscape surrounding Buck Bayou Mound, suggesting a possible settlement hierarchy or, alternatively, functional differentiation between habitation and extractive loci. A second cluster of small sites surrounding the horseshoe-shaped Miegs Pasture midden mirrors the Buck Bayou pattern, although at a smaller scale. Radiometric dates for all Elliott's Point sites range from about 4450 to 2650 cal B.P. (Thomas and Campbell 1991).

Late Archaic sites tend to be small and widely scattered in the intervening coastal areas between clusters of shell mounds and rings. For instance, investigations in the Apalachicola-lower Chattahoochee area of northwest Florida have yielded evidence for scores of Late Archaic sites, but mounded shell is limited to low, linear deposits of clam shell (White 2003, 2004). Similar small sites in coastal Alabama occasionally containing plain fiber-tempered pottery are presumed to date ca. 3800–3150 cal B.P. (Saunders and Hays 2004).

Poverty Point

The pinnacle of cultural elaboration for the Archaic period is the Poverty Point culture of northeast Louisiana (Gibson 1996b, 2000; Webb 1982). Emerging after ca. 4000 cal B.P. and developing over several ensuing centuries, the Poverty Point culture involved unprecedented levels of mound construction and interregional exchange centered on the type site, Poverty Point, a 3-km^2 complex of nearly 765,000 m^3 of mounded earth in six nested, elliptical half rings, two massive mounds, and a few smaller conical and flat-topped mounds (Ford and Webb 1956; Gibson 2000; Kidder 2002; Kidder et al. 2004; Ortmann 2003) (see Figure 18.5). Other settlements of Poverty Point affiliation were distributed across a 1,813-km^2 area centered on the type site, with more distant communities (such as Claiborne and Elliott's Point, noted above) participating through exchange with core groups (see Byrd 1991). Although neither long-distance exchange nor mound construction can be considered an innovation of Poverty Point culture, the scale of both activities eclipsed anything that came before.

A 1,000-year hiatus in mound building occurred between ca. 4800 and 3800 cal B.P. In contrast to the Middle Archaic data, which show mounds to have been surprisingly common, Poverty Point mound building is unequivocally documented only at Poverty Point and at Lake Enterprise in southeast Arkansas (Jackson and Jeter 1991, 1994). Many more Poverty Point mound sites probably existed, and further research into this subject is urgently needed. As the details of Poverty Point life continue to accumulate through sustained field research, explanations for its genesis, reproduction, and eventual demise remain elusive. For instance, archaeologists continue to disagree over the level of sociopolitical organization underwriting such massive, coordinated efforts at mound building and exchange.

Perhaps the most debated aspect of the earthworks at Poverty Point is their implications for population size and sociopolitical complexity. Clearly an earth-moving project of this magnitude and sophistication, no matter how protracted over time, required not only a large pool of labor but also formal orchestration. Ford and Webb (1956) asserted that Poverty Point was home to thousands of people, whose houses were distributed along each of the six nested ridges. Evidence for an advanced level of sociopolitical complexity, much less a large resident population, has not been forthcoming. Repeated efforts to locate domestic architectural evidence have failed (Connolly 2002). The subsistence economy centered on the intensive use of aquatic resources, especially fish, while the use of native cultigens was negligible (Fritz and Kidder 1993; Jackson 1986, 1989; Ward 1998). The importation of raw materials from as far away as the Great Lakes and the Appalachians, while impressive in volume and diversity, was often geared toward the production of mundane items: soapstone for cooking vessels; granite, basalt, and greenstone for celts; hematite and magnetite for plummets; and various cherts for projectiles and cutting tools, to name but a few. Coupled with the ubiquitous baked-clay objects, hearths, pits, and midden accumulation, the inventory of material related to subsistence technology clearly shows that Poverty Point was a place of residence (Gibson 2000:157), but the size of the resident population, its level of permanence, and, of course, its sociopolitical make-up remain unknown.

The regional constitution of Poverty Point culture is no less certain. Obviously, members of local populations were well connected to the outside world through trading partnerships stretching hundreds of kilometers in virtually all directions (Gibson 1996a, 2000; Jackson 1982, 1986). However, the organization of such exchange is poorly known. Communities in a 1,813-km^2 area centered on the type site share much of the material inventory that is distinctively Poverty Point, yet the degree of similarity is not simply a function of distance proximity to the core (Gibson and Griffing 1994; Johnson 1991, 1993; Kidder 1991). This suggests to Gibson (2000) that communities were economically and politically autonomous. Temporal variation that is not yet fully understood may also be relevant (Thomas et al. 2004). It follows that Poverty Point was foremost a shared belief system, organized at a corporate level for public works and ritual but underwritten by an ethos of egalitarianism (Gibson 2004). Certainly, the symbolism of the earthworks and associated charms and fetishes point to a complex worldview of supernatural forces and spirits (Gibson 1998, 2000, 2004). Advances in understanding of Poverty Point sociopolitical organization may benefit from deeper consideration of the relationship between cosmology encoded in its mounds and material symbols and the relations among people in ritualized practice (Clark 2004; Sassaman and Heckenberger 2004). Although a host of economic, social, and political factors likely contributed to the demise of Poverty Point, an abrupt shift in the river channels near the main site appears to have precipitated its abandonment (Kidder 2006).

The End of the Archaic?

Poverty Point and its elaborate trade and mound building ceased at about 3100–3000 cal B.P. (Kidder 2006; Saunders and Allen 2003). At roughly the same time, people living on the south Atlantic coast stopped constructing shell rings, and a gap between ca. 3000 and 2500 cal B.P. appears in the archaeological record of many parts of the Midcontinent. A generally unasked but clearly significant question is, what became of the Archaic? The shift from Late Archaic to Early Woodland is one of the most prominent culture-historical transformations recorded in eastern North America (Anderson 2001; Sassaman and Anderson 2004:111–113). The Late Archaic–Early Woodland transition in much of eastern North America is indicated by a sudden disruption in regional, local, and site occupations and notable transformations in settlement, economy, and society. In contrast to the Late Archaic, Early Woodland societies are considered less complex looking and are characterized by apparently lower population densities, more restricted ranges of settlements and settlement types, less long-distance trade, and decreased architectural, burial, and artifact diversity (Bense 1994; Emerson and Fortier 1986; Emerson and McElrath 2001; Farnsworth and Asch 1986; Farnsworth and Emerson 1986; Fiedel 2001; Neuman 1984; O'Brien and Wood 1998).

For many archaeologists, the transition was not a discrete event or events but simply a gradual locally and regionally in situ process of evolutionary change (Garland 1986; Lewis 1986; Tiffany 1986). In this model, Early Woodland populations practiced Late Archaic lifeways with the addition of some key traits, most notably, ceramic vessels (Farnsworth and Emerson 1986; Griffin 1986). Others argue the Late Archaic to Early Woodland transition was accomplished by the physical or biological replacement of earlier Late Archaic populations by immigrants into the region who brought with them emerging ceramic technology and, perhaps, associated subsistence knowledge (Emerson and McElrath 2001). This model explicitly challenges the prevailing notion of cultural continuity and argues that punctuated equilibrium rather than gradualism better describes the process of social change in this part of North America (Emerson and McElrath 2001; Fortier 2001).

Gibson (1974, 1996b, 1999, 2000) argues that Poverty Point was so large, had such complex architecture, economy, and social institutions, and was so regionally interconnected through trade and exchange that an exceptional form of social and political organization was required to develop, organize, and maintain it. The historical inability of Poverty Point leadership to sustain this complexity led to the rapid demise of the site and the transformation of the associated culture into the local Early Woodland Tchula culture. A final model proposed by Fiedel (2001) argues that, for northeastern North America, climate change may have been a causal factor in the shift from Late Archaic to Early Woodland. He argues that the shift from Late Archaic to Early Woodland and the subsequent decline in human populations correlate well with evidence for climate change resulting in a period of cooler temperatures and increased precipitation.

The climate-change model receives support from multiple sources. Examination of an increasingly large body of high-resolution climate data suggests that an episode (or multiple brief episodes) of global climate change involving significant changes in temperature and precipitation occurred during the period ca. 3150–2600 cal B.P. (Baier et al. 2004; Berglund 2003; Bond et al. 1997; Bradley et al. 2003; Calvo et al. 2002; Huntley et al. 2002; Kaplan et al. 2002; Lücke et al. 2003; Marshall et al. 2001; Schulz and Paul 2002; Wefer et al. 2002). The effects of altered climate systems are apparent in data from throughout the northern hemisphere and are also visible in some records from the southern hemisphere (Binford et al. 1997; Moseley 1999; Sandweiss et al. 1999; Van Buren 2001). Evidence for climate change at this time in North America has been found in New Mexico, California, the Midwest, the Great Lakes, the Southeast, the Northeast, and the Mississippi Valley (Armour et al. 2002; Baker et al. 2002; Booth and Jackson 2003; Booth et al. 2002; Kaplan et al. 2002; Kidder 2006; Little 2003; Polyak and Asmerom 2001; Willemse and Törnqvist 1999).

A disjunction or hiatus in archaeologically visible occupations in the alluvial portions of the Mississippi River basin dates to ca. 3150–2600 cal B.P. This dramatic decline in sites (and populations?) correlates with global climate data showing significantly cooler and wetter climates during this same interval. The paleoclimatic evidence indicates that the North American Midcontinent was affected by storm and flood events of increased frequency and amplitude. All, or at least most, of the Mississippi River basin was evidently affected, and parts of the basin experienced floods of historically unprecedented size and duration.

Changes in the course of the Mississippi River and some of its tributaries and in the deposition of thick sediment packages in the areas immediately east of the Poverty Point site coincided with the end of Poverty Point occupation in the Mississippi Valley. Because Poverty Point people were extensively engaged in a complex web of long-distance trade and exchange (Gibson 2000; Webb 1982), massive flooding at the local and regional (and even basinwide) scale probably disrupted the flow of goods to and from Poverty Point sites in the lower Mississippi Valley. If, as is hypothesized, long-distance trade goods provided much of the rationale for the remarkable cultural developments of the Poverty Point culture (Gibson 1996b, 1996c, 1998, 2000; Webb 1982), then a sustained disruption of the trade in goods, information, and associated cultural baggage may have been catastrophic for populations across the Southeast. At least for the lower Mississippi Valley, and perhaps elsewhere in the Southeast, broad-scale restructuring of climate and the hydrologic landscape was likely a chief factor in the transformation of Archaic lifeways, in general.

The Late Archaic–Early Woodland transition in the Southeast was a complex phenomenon with multiple causes and varying outcomes. The spatial breadth and limited temporal duration of this transition shows that large-scale factors affected populations throughout the Mississippi River basin and eastern North America. Global climate changes in the period ca. 3150–2600 cal B.P. greatly increased flood frequencies and magnitudes in the Mississippi River watershed and played an important role in the processes underlying the shift from Late Archaic to Early Woodland in this area. These same climate changes probably played a role in some other parts of the Southeast, notably in the south Atlantic coastal area, where rising sea levels may have forced the abandonment of large shell-ring sites and led to reorganization of settlement and subsistence pursuits.

Conclusions

It is abundantly evident today, as it was to Howard Winters in 1968, that the Archaic was a time of remarkable cultural variability and complexity. Archaeological research in the last 10 years has provided new information on Archaic societies and has provided impetus to reexamine old collections for new ideas. While no short summary can do justice to the rich and varied lifeways of Archaic people in the Southeast, we conclude by emphasizing some of the larger trends that we feel are evident in the archaeological record.

Climate change has always been seen as a powerful force affecting Archaic populations, and this notion persists today. In the past, however, climate changes have been seen as largely homogeneous within subdivisions of the Holocene. Thus, the middle Holocene has been equated with the Hypsithermal and is assumed to have been a time when human populations were adapting to warmer temperatures and reduced surface-water availability. Similarly, the onset of the late Holocene is often considered the time when modern climate conditions emerged. Archaeological consideration of human responses to these uniform and generalized climate models has emphasized equilibrium-seeking processes. Early Archaic people were adapting to immediate postglacial environments, Middle Archaic people to the Hypsithermal, and Late Archaic folks to the modern climate regime.

However, as is now fully evident, climate changes during the entire Holocene have not been uniform; in fact, available evidence suggests that climate changes during the Holocene have never been spatially or temporally coherent. Instead, researchers now recognize a dynamic, mosaic climate pattern in which temperature and precipitation have varied over time and across space. Nowhere is this more evident than in current understanding of the Hypsithermal, in which the paradigm of a uniform warm trend has been replaced by one that recognizes seasonally unpredictable and spatially uneven climate variability within a generalized trend of increased warmth. The implications for the archaeology of the Middle Archaic period are enormous and suggest that, rather than considering human adaptation to be equilibrium focused, archaeologists should consider, instead, that cultural responses were geared to risk reduction in the face of long-term climate unpredictability and uncertainty. Cordell (2000; see also Dean 1996) makes a similar suggestion for the later Holocene Southwest. Similarly, researchers should be wary of the idea that the Late Archaic was a time of so-called modern climate conditions. Late Holocene climates were highly variable, and evidence for periodic climate perturbations is abundant. Large-scale atmospheric reorganization after ca. 3150 cal B.P. demonstrates that modern conditions did not truly emerge during the Late Archaic.

Another common theme expressed in summaries of the Archaic is that of an overall increase in population. Judging from changes in site frequencies or numbers of diagnostic artifacts, this trend seems obvious (Anderson 1996b). However, this observation must be tempered by several caveats. Foremost is biased site discovery resulting from changes in the landscape over the course of the Holocene. We have already mentioned the drastic resculpting of the lower Mississippi Valley and Atlantic coast in the post-Pleistocene era, and we can add to this the aggradation of interior floodplains that deeply buried early Holocene surfaces. Other landforms, such as the interriverine zones of the Georgia-Carolina Piedmont, have been so eroded by Euroamerican agricultural practices that the intensity of upland land use is disproportionately represented in an abundance of surface finds. All such recovery biases require better analytical control.

Even if sample biases were fully controlled, neither sites nor artifacts can be equated directly with personnel if changes in settlement reorganization and technology affected rates of occupational duration and tool replacement. For instance, a relative increase in the forager component of a settlement strategy (sensu Binford 1980) has the potential to increase both the number of sites occupied annually and the rate of tool discard per capita without an increase in population. The mid-Holocene shift from collector to forager settlement in the Georgia-Carolina Piedmont can explain the increase in Middle Archaic sites and artifacts without a net gain in regional population (Sassaman and Anderson 1995).

In related fashion, the settlement permanence of people on the landscape is perhaps more relevant to an understanding of cultural stability and change than are the absolute numbers of people. As Carneiro (1970) theorized long ago, population circumscription, not growth per se, is the key variable in processes of state formation. Tethered to particular features or resources on the landscape, populations incapable of relocating to offset local stresses undergo rapid structural change, notably, the emergence of institutionalized hierarchy. Many circumscriptive circumstances may have affected Archaic populations, including exogenous factors such as limited surface water as well as the unintended consequences of cultural practices like mound construction. That institutions of social inequality and political control never emerged is testimony to the persistence of mobility as a way of life throughout the Archaic. Few Archaic populations in the Southeast outside of certain coastal areas and, possibly, parts of the Mississippi Valley have been demonstrated to be entirely stationary over the year, let alone for decades or generations.

That populations routinely relocated in response to all manner of ecological and social stress is implicit in models of seasonal mobility and environmental change. Much less consideration is given to larger-scale population movements that reconfigured the regional distribution of people with differing histories and cultural experiences. Serious consideration of the sorts of migratory and ethnogenetic "events" that Ritchie (1969) envisioned in his original definition of the "Archaic" became anathema in the neo-evolutionary perspectives of late-twentieth-century Americanist archaeology. This point of view is especially unfortunate given the growing evidence for more than one ancestral population in ancient North America. The sea change in technology and cultural adaptations usually attributed to environmental change in parts of the Southeast (i.e., reduction in formalized unifacial technology, shift from notched to stemmed bifacial forms, increase in polished-stone media, notably bannerstones, and first intensive use of shellfish) may very well signal broad-scale, eastward movement of populations with no direct relation to indigenous Paleoindian and Early Archaic populations. This is a highly controversial supposition, charged with political overtones as regards Native American ancestry and patrimony, but it is, nonetheless, an increasingly important factor to consider in any understanding of the Archaic period. Archaeologists cannot assume that local or even regional historical trajectories were enacted by people with direct cultural lineages tracing back to the Pleistocene; even if these historical trajectories merely reflect reshuffling of regional populations of close biological affinity, the respective histories almost certainly involved deeply entrenched differences in matters as mundane as the edibility of food and the appropriate means of refuse disposal as well as less prosaic concerns such as disposal of the dead and rites of passage into adulthood.

Irrespective of the particular populations involved, one unequivocal trend in Archaic flaked-stone technology is the pattern of decreased style ranges associated with specific morphological forms. Early Archaic biface styles were widespread over large regions and serve as pan-regional horizon markers perhaps associated with group mobility or widely distributed kin networks. As suggested by style markers, the spatial extent of group ranges and the sharing of stylistic and technological characteristics progressively diminished, perhaps as a result of increasing population size and decreased mobility.

Artifact assemblages generally became increasingly elaborate over time. New tool forms and new raw materials, notably, bone and ground stone, were added to technological repertoires. The increasing employment of nonutilitarian artifacts is another example of greater material culture elaboration and diversity. Changes in technology were commonly geographically localized as groups adapted to available raw materials or developed specific tools to satisfy particular needs (e.g., microlithic technology in Middle and Late Archaic contexts in the Mississippi Valley).

Among the more conspicuous changes in technology is the advent of ceramic vessels. Dating from ca. 5100 cal B.P., the Stallings series of the Savannah River valley and coastal Georgia-Carolina remains the oldest in the region, followed closely by the Orange series of Florida and, after ca. 3800 cal B.P., by the Wheeler series of the Midsouth and local wares of the Poverty Point culture area. Hypotheses of South American origins for early pottery in the Southeast (e.g., Ford 1969; cf. Clark and Knoll 2005) have been overshadowed in recent decades by models of indigenous change emphasizing the economic demands of increasingly permanent settlement (e.g., Smith 1986). However, three new findings undermine any simplistic model of local, microeconomic evolution of pottery. First, the heretofore-presumed precursors of pottery, stone vessels, either postdated or accompanied the onset of pottery manufacture across most of the region (Gibson 1996a; Sassaman 1997, 1999, 2006). Second, sequences of presumed change in early pottery, based largely on stratigraphic contexts, have not held up to modern dating. This is most apparent in the Orange series of Florida, in which variations in fiber-tempered wares and certain sponge spiculate wares are now demonstrably synchronic, not evolutionary (Cordell 2004; Sassaman 2003b). Third, a growing body of evidence suggests that the innovation of pottery was a response to growing demands for serving vessels, not cooking vessels (Sassaman 2004; R. Saunders 2004). This new perspective is consonant with emerging data for feasting at shell-bearing sites along the Atlantic coast, the Savannah River, and the St. Johns River (Russo 2002; Sassaman et al. 2006; R. Saunders 2002, 2004). Increased demand for serving vessels does not, however, explain the intensified use of stone vessels at the close of the Late Archaic period. Both sandstone and soapstone vessels are often sooted on exterior surfaces, attesting to their use in direct-heat cooking. Even so, the long-distance exchange and caching of stone vessels at places like Poverty Point and Claiborne, as well as their use in mortuary contexts of Terminal Archaic and Early Woodland age in the Midsouth, serve notice that durable vessel technology of any sort cannot be explained by the local circumstances of domestic economies (Truncer 2004) but, rather, by the interregional alliances and political-economic imperatives that are defining traits of the Archaic Southeast, in general (Sassaman 2006).

Subsistence patterns shifted slowly, and, for all the other changes noted at this time, hunter-fishing-foraging undoubtedly was the only mode of food production in the Southeast. Archaic hunter-gatherers were largely generalists. Through time some populations focused increasing energy on limited numbers of food sources, most often stable, predictable ones such as fish and shellfish. In no instance, however, is there evidence of any populations specializing in a particular mode of subsistence. Seasonal food-procurement specialization may have existed in some areas, but these practices were at best limited in time and space. A notable trend in some areas was year-round site occupation, or at least yearly returns to the same loci, where resource density would support it. The adoption of pottery in the Late Archaic did not coincide with any major changes in daily subsistence. Although some populations undoubtedly were increasingly interfering with plant breeding and were manipulating plant resources to a significant extent, Archaic peoples in the Southeast only occasionally crossed the threshold of plant domestication or even obvious cultivation. The only exception to this statement is the frequent use of squash, but evidence for phylogenetic alteration of cucurbits in Archaic times is not yet documented.

The most novel and exciting finding in Archaic-period archaeology in recent decades is the multifaceted evidence for nascent cultural complexity. The growing record of early mound building in the lower Mississippi Valley and Florida, coupled with increasing recognition for elaborate material culture, long-distance exchanges, and mortuary ceremonialism, is causing regional specialists to discard the shopworn models of cultural evolutionism that privileged food production as a prerequisite for complexity. Nothing in the record of everyday Archaic life points to the existence of institutionalized structures of political or economic authority, and yet conventional models of egalitarian society are inadequate to explain the emergence and reproduction of cultural practices that led to the construction of Watson Brake and the organization of the Benton Interaction Sphere, not to mention Poverty Point. The numerous contradictions between the Archaic archaeological record and extant models point to the fundamental fallacy of the dichotomy between simple and complex societies. The Archaic record, like that of many so-called complex hunter-gatherers, encourages archaeologists to liberate complex sociocultural processes and structures from the material realm of politics and economies and relocate them in the realm of cosmology, ideology, and ritual practice. This is what Ford (1969) was promoting in his model of the Theocratic Formative, and it is inherent in recent anthropological models that demonstrate how nonegalitarian structures are embedded within so-called egalitarian societies (Flanagan 1989; Weissner 2002). In related fashion, the Archaic record of seemingly corporate actions, such as mound building and ritual feasting, must be rethought as translocal processes that integrated and perhaps ranked disparate cultural elements in shared belief systems, as in Pintupi men's cults (Myers 1986), Hopewell religion (Seeman 1995), and even Cahokian mound building (Pauketat and Alt 2003). All such processes have real material consequences in the allocation of labor, regional distribution of people, and direct ceremonial costs, but they can hardly be considered epiphenomenal to economic and political structures, as they are, indeed, the processes that reproduced Archaic societies at large.

The varied and at times remarkable history of Archaic peoples in the Southeast did not develop in a geographic or cultural vacuum. Evidence indicates that from the beginning of the Archaic widespread and extensive trade, exchange, and interaction occurred among people in the Southeast and between groups in this region and populations in the Northeast, Midwest, and eastern Plains. In Dalton times, Burlington and gray midwestern cherts were being transported into Arkansas and beyond; marine shell was being moved northward from 7800 cal B.P. on, while copper was sent southbound as early as 6800 cal B.P. By the Middle Archaic, extensive evidence indicates, exchange systems mediated the movement of goods and presumably intangible ideas and information across the southeastern-midwestern "boundary" (Jefferies 1995, 1996a, 1997, 2004). Similar but less well understood systems may have been operating between the Southeast and the Northeast (Bourque 1995) and along the western boundary between the Southeast and the Plains (Gregory and Curry 1978; Jeter and Williams 1989; Johnson 1989).

The existence of Paleoindian and Early Archaic stylistic horizons spanning the entire Eastern Woodlands is historical testimony to exchange and interaction processes that bridged vast amounts of space (Tuck 1974). These horizons may reflect connections between biologically related peoples or the movement of prized raw materials. By Middle Archaic times, interaction appears to have been a vehicle for information exchange and the movement of socially valued commodities used for developing and maintaining social identity and differentiation. The Benton Interaction Sphere, zoomorphic beads, engraved bone pins, and trade in rare, exotic lithics, copper, and marine shell all reflect processes that linked populations across geographic and environmental boundaries and that served to distinguish groups and individuals in relation to adjacent populations. That this elaboration in long-distance trade and exchange took place at the same time that environments were becoming increasingly unpredictable is no real surprise.

Late Archaic interaction centered on the Poverty Point culture. Poverty Point represents the first time that a single area, indeed, a single site, emerged as the nexus of social, economic (?), and, possibly, political processes in the Southeast. Populations elsewhere in the Southeast and Midwest were involved in this widespread interaction network, to be sure, but little evidence outside of Poverty Point and related sites suggests the accumulation of trade goods as markers of social identity and differentiation. Perhaps the people of Poverty Point took all the diversity that had developed since the time of pan-continental horizons and brought it all back together through shared ritual. The end of the Archaic is in part diagnosed by the collapse of inter- and intraregional trade and exchange. The demise of the Archaic may have been hastened by climate change, but it was effected because, for the first time in over 5,000 years, people throughout eastern North America were no longer interacting with one another in a regular and sustained fashion, at least not over long distances without intervening personnel.

Understanding the Archaic of the Southeast requires recognizing the different threads that were woven together by Native Americans over thousands of years of history. Climate, demographics, subsistence, technology, sociopolitical elaboration, and long-distance interaction were intertwined processes that gave shape to the Archaic of the Southeast. As new data emerge, researchers learn more about the remarkable and varied lives of these people and further recognize that theirs were not "simple" societies.

Endnote

1. For the purposes of standardizing dates in this chapter, we converted any date range or other time referent that was established on the basis of conventional ^{14}C to cal B.P. using median values for two-sigma ranges as provided in the latest CALIB program online (CALIB v. 4.4.2) (Stuiver et al. 1998; Stuiver et al. 2004).

References Cited

Alley, Richard B., Paul A. Mayewski, T. Sowers, Minz Stuiver, K. C. Taylor, and P. U. Clark

1997 Holocene Climatic Instability: A Prominent, Widespread Event 8200 yr Ago. *Geology* 25:483–486.

Anderson, David G.

1996a Approaches to Modeling Regional Settlement in the Archaic Period Southeast. In *Archaeology of the Mid-Holocene Southeast*, edited by Kenneth E. Sassaman and David G. Anderson, pp. 157–176. University Press of Florida, Gainesville.

1996b Models of Paleoindian and Early Archaic Settlement in the Lower Southeast. In *The Paleoindian and Early Archaic Southeast*, edited by David G. Anderson and Kenneth E. Sassaman, pp. 29–57. University of Alabama Press, Tuscaloosa.

2001 Climate and Culture Change in Prehistoric and Early Historic Eastern North America. *Archaeology of Eastern North America* 29:143–186.

2002 The Evolution of Tribal Social Organization in the Southeast. In *The Archaeology of Tribal Societies*, edited by William A. Parkinson, pp. 246–277. Archaeological Series 15. International Monographs in Prehistory, Ann Arbor, Michigan.

2004 Archaic Mounds and the Archaeology of Southeastern Tribal Societies. In *Signs of Power: The Rise of Complexity in the Southeast*, edited by Jon L. Gibson and Philip J. Carr, pp. 270–299. University of Alabama Press, Tuscaloosa.

Anderson, David G., and Glen Hanson

1988 Early Archaic Settlement in the Southeastern United States: A Case Study from the Savannah River Valley. *American Antiquity* 53:262–286.

Anderson, David G., and Kenneth E. Sassaman

2004 Early and Middle Holocene Periods, 9500–3750 B.C. In *Southeast*, edited by Raymond D. Fogelson, pp. 87–100. Handbook of North American Indians, vol. 14, William C. Sturtevant, general editor. Smithsonian Institution, Washington, D.C.

Anderson, T. W., R. W. Mathewes, and C. E. Schweger

1989 Holocene Climatic Trends in Canada with Special Reference to the Hypsithermal Interval. In *Quaternary Geology of Canada and Greenland*, edited by Robert J. Fulton, pp. 520–528. Geology of Canada 1. Geological Survey of Canada, Ottawa.

Arco, Lee J., Katherine A. Adelsberger, Ling-yu Hung, and Tristram R. Kidder

2006 Alluvial Geoarchaeology of a Middle Archaic Mound Complex in the Lower Mississippi Valley, U.S.A. *Geoarchaeology* 21:591–614.

Armour, Jake, Peter J. Fawcett, and John W. Geissman

2002 15 k.y. Paleoclimatic and Glacial Record from Northern New Mexico. *Geology* 30:723–726.

Aten, Lawrence E.

1999 Middle Archaic Ceremonialism at Tick Island, Florida: Ripley P. Bullen's 1961 Excavations at the Harris Creek Site. *The Florida Anthropologist* 52:131–200.

Baier, J., Andreas Lücke, Jörg F. W. Negendank, Gerhard H. Schleser, and Bernd Zolitschka

2004 Diatom and Geochemical Evidence of Mid- to Late Holocene Climatic Changes at Lake Holzmaar, West-Eifel (Germany). *Quaternary International* 113:81–96.

Baker, R. G., E. A. Bettis III, R. F. Denniston, L. A. Gonzalez, L. E. Strickland, and J. R. Krieg

2002 Holocene Paleoenvironments in Southeastern Minnesota—Chasing the Prairie-Forest Ecotone. *Palaeogeography, Palaeoclimatology, Palaeoecology* 177:103–122.

Barber, D. C., A. Dyke, C. Hillaire-Marcel, A. E. Jennings, J. T. Andrews, M. W. Kerwin, G. Bilodeau, R. McNeely, J. Southon, M. D. Morehead, and J-M. Gagnon

1999 Forcing of the Cold Event of 8,200 Years Ago by Catastrophic Drainage of Laurentide Lakes. *Nature* 400:344–348.

Bense, Judith A.

1994 *Archaeology of the Southeastern United States*. Academic Press, San Diego, California.

Bentz, Charles
1988 The Late Archaic Occupation of the Bailey Site (40GL26), Giles County, Tennessee. *Tennessee Anthropological Association Newsletter* 13(5):1–20.

Berglund, Björn E.
2003 Human Impact and Climate Changes—Synchronous Events and Causal Link? *Quaternary International* 105:7–12.

Bettis, E. Arthur, III
2003 Patterns in Holocene Colluvium and Alluvial Fans across the Prairie-Forest Transition in the Midcontinent USA. *Geoarchaeology* 18:779–797.

Bettis, E. Arthur, III and Edwin R. Hajic
1995 Landscape Development and the Location of Evidence of Archaic Cultures in the Upper Midwest. In *Archaeological Geology of the Archaic Period in North America*, edited by E. Arthur Bettis III, pp. 87–113. Special Paper 297. Geological Society of America, Boulder, Colorado.

Binford, Lewis R.
1980 Willow Smoke and Dogs' Tails: Hunter-Gatherer Settlement Systems and Archaeological Site Formation. *American Antiquity* 45:4–20.

Binford, Michael W., Alan L. Kolata, Mark Brenner, John W. Janusek, Matthew T. Seddon, Mark B. Abbott, and Jason H. Curtis
1997 Climate Variation and the Rise and Fall of Andean Civilization. *Quaternary Research* 47:235–248.

Bond, Gerard, William Showers, Maziet Cheseby, Rusty Lotti, Peter Almasi, Peter deMenocal, Paul Priore, Heidi Cullen, Irka Hajdas, and Georges Bonani
1997 A Pervasive Millennial-Scale Cycle in North Atlantic Holocene and Glacial Climates. *Science* 278:1257–1266.

Booth, Robert K., and Stephen T. Jackson
2003 A High-Resolution Record of Late-Holocene Moisture Variability from a Michigan Raised Bog, USA. *The Holocene* 13:863–876.

Booth, Robert K., Stephen T. Jackson, and Todd A. Thompson
2002 Paleoecology of a Northern Michigan Lake and the Relationship among Climate, Vegetation, and Great Lakes Water Levels. *Quaternary Research* 57:120–130.

Bourque, Bruce J.
1995 *Diversity and Complexity in Prehistoric Maritime Societies: A Gulf of Maine Perspective*. Plenum Press, New York.

Bowen, Rowe
1977 A Reevaluation of Late Archaic Subsistence and Settlement Patterns in the Western Tennessee Valley. *Tennessee Anthropologist* 2:100–120.

Bradbury, J. Platt, and Walter E. Dean (editors)
1993 *Elk Lake Minnesota: Evidence for Rapid Climatic Change in the North-Central United States*. Special Paper 276. Geological Society of America, Boulder, Colorado.

Bradbury, J. Platt, Walter E. Dean, and Roger Y. Anderson
1993 Holocene Climatic and Limnologic History of the North-Central United States as Recorded in the Varved Sediments of Elk Lake, Minnesota: A Synthesis. In *Elk Lake, Minnesota: Evidence for Rapid Climatic Change in the North-Central United States*, edited by J. Platt Bradbury and Walter E. Dean, pp. 309–328. Special Paper 276. Geological Society of America, Boulder.

Bradley, R. S., K. R. Briffa, J. Cole, M. K. Hughes, and T. J. Osborn
2003 The Climate of the Last Millennium. In *Paleoclimate, Global Change and the Future*, edited by K. D. Alverson, R. S. Bradley, and T. F. Pederson, pp. 105–141. Springer-Verlag, Berlin.

Brookes, Samuel O.
1997 Aspects of the Middle Archaic: The Atassa. In *Results of Recent Archaeological Investigations in the Greater Mid-South: Proceedings of the 17th Annual Mid-South Archaeological Conference, Memphis, Tennessee, June 29–30, 1996*, edited by Charles H. McNutt. Occasional Paper 18. Anthropological Research Center, University of Memphis, Memphis, Tennessee.
1999 Prehistoric Exchange in Mississippi, 10,000 B.C.–A.D. 1600. In *Raw Materials and Exchange in the Mid-South: Proceedings of the 16th Annual Mid-South Archaeological Conference, Jackson, Mississippi, June 3–4, 1995*, edited by Evan Peacock and Samuel O. Brookes, pp. 29–43. Archaeological Report 29. Mississippi Department of Archives and History, Jackson.
2004 Cultural Complexity in the Middle Archaic of Mississippi. In *Signs of Power: The Rise of Complexity in the Southeast*, edited by Jon L. Gibson and Philip J. Carr, pp. 97–113. University of Alabama Press, Tuscaloosa.

Brown, James A. and Robert K. Vierra
1983 What Happened in the Middle Archaic? Introduction to an Ecological Approach to Koster Site Archaeology. In *Archaic Hunters and Gatherers in the American Midwest*, edited by James L. Phillips and James A. Brown, pp. 165–195. Academic Press, New York.

Brown, Paul, James P. Kennett, and B. Lynn Ingram
1999 Marine Evidence for Episodic Holocene Megafloods in North America and the Northern Gulf of Mexico. *Paleoceanography* 14:498–510.

Bruseth, James E.
1991 Poverty Point Development as Seen at the Cedarland and Claiborne Sites, Southern Mississippi. In *The Poverty Point Culture: Local Manifestations, Subsistence Practices, and Trade Networks*, edited by Kathleen M. Byrd, pp. 7–25. Geoscience and Man 29. Louisiana State University, Baton Rouge.

Bullen, Ripley P.
1972 The Orange Period in Peninsular Florida. *The Florida Anthropologist* 25(2):9–23.

Byrd, Kathleen M. (editor)
1991 *The Poverty Point Culture: Local Manifestations, Subsistence Practices, and Trade Networks*. Geosciences and Man 29. Louisiana State University, Baton Rouge.

Caldwell, Joseph R.
1958 *Trend and Tradition in the Prehistory of the Eastern United States*. Memoir 88. American Anthropological Association, Springfield, Illinois.

Calvo, Eva, Joan Grimalt, and Eystein Jansen
2002 High Resolution U^{k}_{37} Sea Surface Temperature Reconstruction in the Norwegian Sea during the Holocene. *Quaternary Science Reviews* 21:1385–1394.

Carneiro, Robert L.

1970 A Theory of the Origin of the State. *Science* 169:733–738.

Chapman, Jefferson

1981 *The Bacon Bend and Iddens Sites: The Late Archaic Period in the Lower Little Tennessee River Valley*. Report of Investigations 31, Department of Anthropology, University of Tennessee, Knoxville; Publications in Anthropology 25, Tennessee Valley Authority, Knoxville, Tennessee.

Claassen, Cheryl P.

1991a Gender, Shellfishing, and the Shell Mound Archaic. In *Engendering Archaeology: Women and Prehistory*, edited by Joan M. Gero and Margaret W. Conkey, pp. 276–300. Basil Blackwell, Oxford.

1991b New Hypothesis for the Demise of the Shell Mound Archaic. In *The Archaic Period in the Mid-South*, edited by Charles H. McNutt, pp. 66–71. Archaeological Report 24. Mississippi Department of Archives and History, Jackson.

1992 Shell Mounds as Burial Mounds: A Revision of the Shell Mound Archaic. In *Current Archaeological Research in Kentucky*, vol. 2, edited by David Pollack and A. Gwynn Henderson, pp. 1–11. Kentucky Heritage Council, Frankfort.

1996 A Consideration of the Social Organization of the Shell Mound Archaic. In *Archaeology of the Mid-Holocene Southeast*, edited by Kenneth E. Sassaman and David G. Anderson, pp. 235–258. University Press of Florida, Gainesville.

Clark, John E.

2004 Surrounding the Sacred: Geometry and Design of Early Mound Groups as Meaning and Function. In *Signs of Power: The Rise of Complexity in the Southeast*, edited by Jon L. Gibson and Philip J. Carr, pp. 162–213. University of Alabama Press, Tuscaloosa.

Clark, John E., and Michelle Knoll

2005 The American Formative Revisited. In *Gulf Coast Archaeology: The Southeastern United States and Mexico*, edited by Nancy M. White, pp. 281–303. University Press of Florida, Gainesville.

Connaway, John M.

1982 The Keenan Bead Cache, Lawrence County, Mississippi. *Louisiana Archaeology* 8:59–71.

Connolly, Robert P.

2002 The 1980–1982 Excavations on the Northwest Ridge 1 at the Poverty Point Site. *Louisiana Archaeology* 25:1–92.

2003a *2003 Annual Report: Station Archaeology Program at Poverty Point State Historic Site*. Louisiana Division of Archaeology, Baton Rouge.

2003b *2003 Poverty Point Site (16WC5) Research Design*. Louisiana Division of Archaeology, Baton Rouge.

Cordell, Ann S.

2004 Paste Variability and Possible Manufacturing Origins of Late Archaic Fiber-Tempered Pottery from Selected Sites in Peninsular Florida. In *Early Pottery: Technology, Function, Style, and Interaction in the Lower Southeast*, edited by Rebecca Saunders and Christopher T. Hays, pp. 63–104. University of Alabama Press, Tuscaloosa.

Cordell, Linda

2000 Aftermath of Chaos in the Pueblo Southwest. In *Environmental Disaster and the Archaeology of Human Response*, edited by Garth Bawden and Richard M. Reycraft, pp. 179–193. Anthropological Papers 7. Maxwell Museum of Anthropology, Albuquerque, New Mexico.

Craig, A. B.

1958 A Dwarf Burial from Limestone County, Alabama. *Journal of Alabama Archaeology* 4:15–17.

Crawford, Jessica

2005 Archaic Effigy Beads: A New Look at Some Old Beads. Master's thesis, Department of Sociology and Anthropology, University of Mississippi, Oxford.

Crothers, George M.

1999 Prehistoric Hunters and Gatherers, and the Archaic Period Green River Shell Middens of Western Kentucky. Ph.D. dissertation, Department of Anthropology, Washington University in St. Louis, St. Louis, Missouri.

2004 The Green River in Comparison to the Lower Mississippi Valley during the Archaic: To Build Mounds or Not to Build Mounds. In *Signs of Power: The Rise of Complexity in the Southeast*, edited by Jon L. Gibson and Philip J. Carr, pp. 86–96. University of Alabama Press, Tuscaloosa.

Crusoe, Donald L., and Chester B. DePratter

1976 A New Look at the Georgia Coastal Shellmound Archaic. *The Florida Anthropologist* 29(1):1–23.

Daniel, I. Randolph, Jr.

1998 *Hardaway Revisited. Early Archaic Settlement in the Southeast*. University of Alabama Press, Tuscaloosa.

Davis, R. P. Stephen, Jr.

1990 *Aboriginal Settlement Patterns in the Little Tennessee River Valley*. Report of Investigations 50, Department of Anthropology, University of Tennessee, Knoxville; Publications in Anthropology 54, Tennessee Valley Authority, Knoxville, Tennessee.

Dean, Jeffrey S.

1996 Demography, Environment and Subsistence Stress. In *Evolving Complexity and Environmental Risk in the Prehistoric Southwest*, edited by Joseph A. Tainter and Bonnie Bagley Tainter, pp. 25–56. Proceedings 25. Santa Fe Institute Studies in the Sciences of Complexity. Addison-Wesley, Reading, Massachusetts.

Deevey, Edward S., and Richard F. Flint

1957 Postglacial Hypsithermal Interval. *Science* 125:182–184.

DePratter, Chester B., and James D. Howard

1980 Indian Occupation and Geologic History of the Georgia Coast: A 5000 Year Summary. In *Excursions in Southeastern Geology: The Archaeology-Geology of the Georgia Coast*, edited by James D. Howard, Chester B. DePratter, and Robert W. Frey, pp. 1–65. 2 vols. Guidebook 20. Geological Society of America, Boulder, Colorado.

Deter-Wolf, Aaron

2004 The Ensworth School Site (40DV184): A Middle Archaic Benton Occupation along the Harpeth River Drainage in Middle Tennessee. *Tennessee Archaeology* 1(1):18–35. Electronic document, http://histpres.mtsu.edu/tennarch/V1I1Deter.pdf, accessed December 7, 2004.

Doran, Glen H., David N. Dickel, and Lee A. Newsom
1990 A 7,290-Year-Old Bottle Gourd from the Windover Site, Florida. *American Antiquity* 55:354–360.

Dowd, John T.
1989 *The Anderson Site: Middle Archaic Adaptation in Tennessee's Central Basin*. Miscellaneous Papers 13. Tennessee Anthropological Association, Knoxville.

Dye, David H.
1996 Riverine Adaptation in the Midsouth. In *Of Caves and Shell Mounds*, edited by Kenneth C. Carstens and Patty Jo Watson, pp. 140–158. University of Alabama Press, Tuscaloosa.

Ellis, K. G., H. T. Mullins, and W. P. Patterson
2004 Deglacial to Middle Holocene (16,600 to 6000 calendar years BP) Climate Change in the Northeastern United States Inferred from Multi-Proxy Stable Isotope Data, Seneca Lake, New York. *Journal of Paleolimnology* 31:343–361.

Emerson, Thomas E., and Andrew C. Fortier
1986 Early Woodland Cultural Variation, Subsistence, and Settlement in the American Bottom. In *Early Woodland Archeology*, edited by Kenneth B. Farnsworth and Thomas E. Emerson, pp. 475–522. Kampsville Seminars in Archeology 2. Center for American Archeology Press, Kampsville, Illinois.

Emerson, Thomas E., and Dale L. McElrath
2001 Interpreting Discontinuity and Historical Process in Midcontinental Late Archaic and Early Woodland Societies. In *The Archaeology of Traditions: Agency and History Before and After Columbus*, edited by Timothy R. Pauketat, pp. 195–217. University Press of Florida, Gainesville.

Farnsworth, Kenneth B., and David L. Asch
1986 Early Woodland Chronology, Artifact Styles, and Settlement Distribution in the Lower Illinois Valley Region. In *Early Woodland Archeology*, edited by Kenneth B. Farnsworth and Thomas E. Emerson, pp. 326–457. Kampsville Seminars in Archeology 2. Center for American Archeology Press, Kampsville, Illinois.

Farnsworth, Kenneth B., and Thomas E. Emerson (editors)
1986 *Early Woodland Archeology*. Kampsville Seminars in Archeology 2. Center for American Archeology Press, Kampsville, Illinois.

Faught, Michael K.
2004 The Underwater Archaeology of Paleolandscapes, Apalachee Bay, Florida. *American Antiquity* 69:275–289.

Fiedel, Stuart J.
2001 What Happened in the Early Woodland? *Archaeology of Eastern North America* 29:101–142.

Flanagan, James G.
1989 Hierarchy in Simple "Egalitarian" Societies. *Annual Review of Anthropology* 18:245–266.

Ford, James A.
1969 *A Comparison of Formative Cultures in the Americas: Diffusion or the Psychic Unity of Man*. Smithsonian Contributions to Anthropology 11. Smithsonian Institution Press, Washington, D.C.

Ford, James A., and Clarence H. Webb
1956 *Poverty Point, a Late Archaic Site in Louisiana*. Anthropological Papers 46, pt. 1. American Museum of Natural History, New York.

Fortier, Andrew C.
2001 A Tradition of Discontinuity: American Bottom Early and Middle Woodland Culture History Reexamined. In *The Archaeology of Traditions: Agency and History Before and After Columbus*, edited by Timothy R. Pauketat, pp. 174–194. University Press of Florida, Gainesville.

Fritz, Gayle J., and Tristram R. Kidder
1993 Recent Investigations into Prehistoric Agriculture in the Lower Mississippi Valley. *Southeastern Archaeology* 12:1–14.

Futato, Eugene M.
1983 *Archaeological Investigations in the Cedar Creek and Upper Bear Creek Reservoirs*. Report of Investigations 29. Office of Archaeological Research, Tuscaloosa, Alabama.

Gagliano, Sherwood M., and Clarence H. Webb
1970 Archaic-Poverty Point Transition at the Pearl River Mouth. In *The Poverty Point Culture*, edited by Betty J. Broyles and Clarence H. Webb, pp. 47–72. Bulletin 12. Southeastern Archaeological Conference, Morgantown, West Virginia.

Ganopolski, Andrey, Claudia Kubatzki, Martin Claussen, Victor Brovkin, and Vladimir Petoukhov
1998 The Influence of Vegetation-Atmosphere-Ocean Interaction on Climate During the Mid-Holocene. *Science* 280:1916–1919.

Garland, Elizabeth B.
1986 Early Woodland Occupations in Michigan: A Lower St. Joseph Valley Perspective. In *Early Woodland Archeology*, edited by Kenneth B. Farnsworth and Thomas E. Emerson, pp. 47–83. Kampsville Seminars in Archeology 2. Center for American Archeology Press, Kampsville, Illinois.

Gibson, Jon L.
1968 Cad Mound: A Stone Bead Locus in East Central Louisiana. *Bulletin of the Texas Archaeological Society* 38:1–17.
1974 The Rise and Decline of Poverty Point. *Louisiana Archaeology* 1:8–33.
1996a The Orvis Scott Site: A Poverty Point Component on Joes Bayou, East Carroll Parish, Louisiana. *Midcontinental Journal of Archaeology* 21:1–48.
1996b Poverty Point and Greater Southeastern Prehistory: The Culture That Did Not Fit. In *Archaeology of the Mid-Holocene Southeast*, edited by Kenneth E. Sassaman and David G. Anderson, pp. 288–305. University Press of Florida, Gainesville.
1996c Religion of the Rings: Poverty Point Iconology and Ceremonialism. In *Mounds, Embankments, and Ceremonialism in the Midsouth*, edited by Robert C. Mainfort and Richard Walling, pp. 1–6. Research Series 46. Arkansas Archeological Survey, Fayetteville.
1998 Broken Circles, Owl Monsters, and Black Earth Midden: Separating the Sacred and Secular at Poverty Point. In *Ancient Earthen Enclosures of the Eastern Woodlands*, edited by Robert C. Mainfort Jr. and Lynn P. Sullivan, pp. 17–30. University Press of Florida, Gainesville.
1999 *Poverty Point: A Terminal Archaic Culture in the Lower Mississippi Valley*. 2nd ed. Anthropological Study 7. Department of Culture, Recreation and Tourism,

Louisiana Archaeological Survey and Antiquities Commission, Baton Rouge.

2000 *The Ancient Mounds of Poverty Point: Place of Rings.* University Press of Florida, Gainesville.

2004 The Power of Beneficent Obligation in First Mound-Building Societies. In *Signs of Power: The Rise of Complexity in the Southeast*, edited by Jon L. Gibson and Philip J. Carr, pp. 255–269. University of Alabama Press, Tuscaloosa.

Gibson, Jon L., and Philip J. Carr

2004 Big Mounds, Big Rings, Big Power. In *Signs of Power: The Rise of Complexity in the Southeast*, edited by Jon L. Gibson and Philip J. Carr, pp. 1–9. University of Alabama Press, Tuscaloosa.

Gibson, Jon L., and David L. Griffing

1994 Only a Stone's Throw Away: Exchange in the Poverty Point Hinterland. In *Exchange in the Lower Mississippi Valley and Contiguous Areas at 1100 B.C.*, edited by Jon L. Gibson. *Louisiana Archaeology* 17:207–250.

Goggin, John M.

1952 *Space and Time Perspective in Northern St. Johns Archaeology, Florida.* Yale University Publications in Anthropology 42. Yale University Press, New Haven, Connecticut.

Goman, M., and D. S. Leigh

2004 Wet Early to Middle Holocene Conditions on the Upper Coastal Plain of North Carolina, USA. *Quaternary Research* 61:256–264.

Greene, Glen S.

1985 *The Deep Six Paleosol: The Incipient Poverty Point Occupation 1983 Excavations.* Office of the State Archaeologist, Baton Rouge, Louisiana.

1989 *Cultural Stratigraphy and Pedology at Poverty Point: The Emergence of the Incipient Settlement Surface during the Late Archaic-Early Formative Stage.* Stratigraphic Series 2. The Research Institute, College of Pure and Applied Sciences, Northeast Louisiana University, Monroe.

Gregory, Hiram F., Jr. and H. K. Curry

1978 *Natchitoches Parish Cultural and Historical Resources, Prehistory.* Natchitoches Parish Planning Commission, Natchitoches, Louisiana.

Griffin, James B.

1986 Comments on the Kampsville Early Woodland Conference. In *Early Woodland Archeology*, edited by Kenneth B. Farnsworth and Thomas E. Emerson, pp. 609–620. Kampsville Seminars in Archeology 2. Center for American Archeology Press, Kampsville, Illinois.

Haag, William G.

1939 Pottery Type Descriptions. *Newsletter of the Southeastern Archaeological Conference* 1(1).

Hamilton, Fran E.

1999 Southeastern Archaic Mounds: Examples of Elaboration in a Temporally Fluctuating Environment? *Journal of Anthropological Archaeology* 18:344–355.

Hays, Chris

1995 *1995 Annual Report for Management Units IV and V.* Louisiana Division of Archaeology, Baton Rouge.

Hensley, Christine K.

1994 The Archaic Settlement System of the Middle Green River Valley. Ph.D. dissertation, Department of Anthropology, Washington University in St. Louis, St. Louis, Missouri.

Huntley, Brian, Michael G. L. Baillie, Jean M. Grove, Claus U. Hammer, Sandy P. Harrison, Stefanie Jacomet, Eystein Jansen, Wibjön Karlén, Nalân Koç, Jürg Luterbacher, Jörg Negendank, and Jörg Schibler

2002 Holocene Paleoenvironmental Changes in North-West Europe: Climatic Implications and the Human Dimension. In *Climate Development and the History of the North Atlantic Realm*, edited by Gerold Wefer, Wolfgang H. Berger, Karl-Ernst Behre, and Eystein Jansen, pp. 313–326. Springer-Verlag, Berlin.

Jackson, H. Edwin

1982 Recent Research on Poverty Point Subsistence and Settlement Systems: Test Excavations at the J. W. Copes Site in Northeast Louisiana. *Louisiana Archaeology* 8:73–86.

1986 Sedentism and Hunter-Gatherer Adaptations in the Lower Mississippi Valley: Subsistence Strategies during the Poverty Point Period. Ph.D. dissertation, Department of Anthropology, University of Michigan, Ann Arbor.

1989 Poverty Point Adaptive Systems in the Lower Mississippi Valley: Subsistence Remains from the J. W. Copes Site. *North American Archaeologist* 10:173–204.

Jackson, H. Edwin, and Marvin D. Jeter

1991 Late Archaic Settlement and Poverty Point Connections in the Lowlands of Southeast Arkansas: An Initial Assessment. *Mississippi Archaeology* 26:33–55.

1994 Preceramic Earthworks in Arkansas: A Report on the Poverty Point Period Lake Enterprise Mound (3AS379). *Southeastern Archaeology* 13:153–162.

Jefferies, Richard W.

1995 Late Middle Archaic Exchange and Interaction in the North American Midcontinent. In *Native American Interactions: Multiscalar Analysis and Interpretations in the Eastern Woodlands*, edited by Michael S. Nassaney and Kenneth E. Sassaman, pp. 73–99. University of Tennessee Press, Knoxville.

1996a The Emergence of Long-Distance Exchange Networks in the Southeastern United States. In *Archaeology of the Mid-Holocene Southeast*, edited by Kenneth E. Sassaman and David G. Anderson, pp. 222–234. University Press of Florida, Gainesville.

1996b Hunters and Gatherers after the Ice Age. In *Kentucky Archaeology*, edited by R. Barry Lewis, pp. 39–77. University Press of Kentucky, Lexington.

1997 Middle Archaic Bone Pins: Evidence of Mid-Holocene Regional-Scale Social Groups in the Southern Midwest. *American Antiquity* 62:464–487.

2004 Regional-Scale Interaction Networks and the Emergence of Cultural Complexity along the Northern Margins of the Southeast. In *Signs of Power: The Rise of Complexity in the Southeast*, edited by Jon L. Gibson and Philip J. Carr, pp. 71–85. University of Alabama Press, Tuscaloosa.

Jenkins, Ned J., and Richard A. Kraus

1986 *The Tombigbee Watershed in Southeastern Prehistory.* University of Alabama Press, University.

Jeter, Marvin D., and G. Ishmael Williams Jr.
1989 Lithic Horizons and Early Cultures. In *Archeology and Bioarcheology of the Lower Mississippi Valley and Trans-Mississippi South in Arkansas and Louisiana*, edited by Marvin D. Jeter, Jerome C. Rose, G. Ishmael Williams Jr., and Anna M. Harmon, pp. 71–110. Research Series 37. Arkansas Archeological Survey, Fayetteville.

Johnson, Jay K.
1981 *Lithic Procurement and Utilization Trajectories: Analysis*. 2 vols. Archaeological Paper 1. Center for Archaeological Research, University, Mississippi.
1991 Lithic Technology and Cultural Complexity in the Poverty Point Period. In *The Poverty Point Culture: Local Manifestations, Subsistence Practices, and Trade Networks*, edited by Kathleen M. Byrd, pp. 181–186. Geoscience and Man 29. Louisiana State University, Baton Rouge.
1993 Poverty Point Period Quartz Crystal Drill Bits, Microliths, and Social Organization in the Yazoo Basin, Mississippi. *Southeastern Archaeology* 12:59–64.
2000 Beads, Microdrills, Bifaces, and Blades from Watson Brake. *Southeastern Archaeology* 19:95–104.

Johnson, Jay K., and Samuel O. Brookes
1989 Benton Points, Turkey Tails, and Cache Blades: Middle Archaic Exchange in the Midsouth. *Southeastern Archaeology* 8:134–145.

Johnson, LeRoy, Jr.
1989 *Great Plains Interlopers in the Eastern Woodlands during Late Paleo-Indian Times*. Report 36. Office of the State Archaeologist, Texas Historical Commission, Austin.

Kaplan, Michael R., Alexander P. Wolfe, and Gifford H. Miller
2002 Holocene Environmental Variability in Southern Greenland Inferred from Lake Sediments. *Quaternary Research* 58:149–159.

Kidder, Tristram R.
1986 *Final Report on Archaeological Test Excavations in the Central Boeuf Basin, Louisiana, 1985*. Bulletin 10. Lower Mississippi Survey, Peabody Museum of Archaeology and Ethnology, Harvard University, Cambridge, Massachusetts.
1991 New Directions in Poverty Point Settlement Archaeology: An Example from Northeast Louisiana. In *Poverty Point Culture: Its Local Manifestations, Subsistence Practices, and Trade Networks*, edited by Kathleen Byrd, pp. 27–53. Geoscience and Man 29. Louisiana State University, Baton Rouge.
1998 The Rat That Ate Louisiana. In *Advances in Historical Ecology*, edited by William L. Balée, pp. 141–168. Columbia University Press, New York.
2002 Mapping Poverty Point. *American Antiquity* 67:89–101.
2006 Climate Change and the Archaic to Woodland Transition (3000–2500 cal B.P.) in the Mississippi River Basin. *American Antiquity* 71:195–231.

Kidder, Tristram R., Anthony L. Ortmann, and Thurman Allen
2004 Mounds B and E at Poverty Point. *Southeastern Archaeology* 23:98–113.

King, James E.
1981 Late Quaternary Vegetational History of Illinois. *Ecological Monographs* 51:43–62.

Kneller, Margaret, and Dorothy Peteet
1999 Late-Glacial to Early Holocene Climate Changes from a Central Appalachian Pollen and Macrofossil Record. *Quaternary Research* 51:133–147.

Knox, James C.
1985 Responses of Floods to Holocene Climatic Change in the Upper Mississippi Valley. *Quaternary Research* 23:287–300.
1987 Stratigraphic Evidence of Large Floods in the Upper Mississippi Valley. In *Catastrophic Flooding*, edited by Larry Mayer and David Nash, pp. 155–180. Allen and Unwin, Boston.
1999 Long-Term Episodic Changes in Magnitudes and Frequencies of Floods in the Upper Mississippi River Valley. In *Fluvial Processes and Environmental Change*, edited by Anthony G. Brown and Timothy A. Quine, pp. 255–282. John Wiley and Sons, Chichester, England.

Kuttruff, Carl
1997 Louisiana's Lost Heritage: The Monte Sano Mounds. *Louisiana Archaeological Conservancy* 7(2):4–6.

Lazarus, William C.
1959 A Poverty Point Complex in Florida. *The Florida Anthropologist* 2(1):23–32.

Lewis, R. Barry
1986 Early Woodland Adaptations to the Illinois Prairie. In *Early Woodland Archeology*, edited by Kenneth B. Farnsworth and Thomas E. Emerson, pp. 171–178. Kampsville Seminars in Archeology 2. Center for American Archeology Press, Kampsville, Illinois.

Lewis, Thomas M. N., and Madeline Kneberg
1961 *Eva: An Archaic Site*. University of Tennessee Press, Knoxville.

Little, Keith J.
2003 Late Holocene Climatic Fluctuations and Culture Change in Southeastern North America. *Southeastern Archaeology* 22:9–32.

Lücke, Andreas, Gerhard H. Schleser, Bernd Zolitschka, and Jörg F. W. Negendank
2003 A Lateglacial and Holocene Organic Carbon Isotope Record of Lacustrine Paleoproductivity and Climatic Change Derived from Varved Lake Sediments of Lake Holzmaar, Germany. *Quaternary Science Reviews* 22:569–580.

Marquardt, William H., and Patty Jo Watson
1983 The Shell Mound Archaic of Western Kentucky. In *Archaic Hunters and Gatherers in the American Midwest*, edited by James L. Phillips and James A. Brown, pp. 323–339. Academic Press, New York.
2005 (editors) *Archaeology of the Middle Green River Region, Kentucky*. Monograph 5. Institute of Archaeology and Paleoenvironmental Studies, University of Florida, Gainesville.

Marshall, John, Yochann Kushner, David Battisti, Ping Chang, Arnaud Czaja, Robert Dickson, James Hurrell, Michael McCartney, R. Saravanan, and Martin Visbeck
2001 North Atlantic Climate Variability: Phenomena, Impacts and Mechanisms. *International Journal of Climatology* 21:1863–1898.

McGahey, Samuel O.
2000 *Mississippi Projectile Point Guide*. Archaeological Report 31. Mississippi Department of Archives and History, Jackson.

Meeks, Scott C.
1999 The "Function" of Stone Tools in Prehistoric Exchange Systems: A Look at Benton Interaction in

the Mid-South. In *Raw Materials and Exchange in the Mid-South: Proceedings of the 16th Annual Mid-South Archaeological Conference, Jackson, Mississippi, June 3–4, 1995*, edited by Evan Peacock and Samuel O. Brookes, pp. 29–43. Archaeological Report 29. Mississippi Department of Archives and History, Jackson.

Mikell, Gregory A.
2001 Recent Data Concerning Late Archaic Period Estuarine Adaptation on the Northern Gulf Coast of Florida. Paper presented at the 58th Annual Meeting of the Southeastern Archaeological Conference, Chattanooga, Tennessee.

Milner, George R., and Richard W. Jefferies
1998 The Read Archaic Shell Midden in Kentucky. *Southeastern Archaeology* 17:119–132.

Moore, Clarence B.
1999 *The East Florida Expeditions of Clarence Bloomfield Moore (originally 1892–94)*, edited and with an introduction by Jeffrey M. Mitchem. University of Alabama Press, Tuscaloosa.

Morse, Dan F.
1997 *Sloan: A Paleoindian Dalton Cemetery in Arkansas.* Smithsonian Institution Press, Washington, D.C.

Moseley, Michael E.
1999 Convergent Catastrophe: Past Patterns and Future Implications of Collateral Natural Disasters in the Andes. In *The Angry Earth: Disaster in Anthropological Perspective*, edited by Anthony Oliver-Smith and Susanna M. Hoffman, pp. 59–71. Routledge, New York.

Myers, Fred R.
1986 *Pintupi Country, Pintupi Self: Sentiment, Place, and Politics among Western Desert Aborigines.* Smithsonian Institution Press, Washington, D.C.

Neuman, Robert W.
1984 *An Introduction to Louisiana Archaeology.* Louisiana State University Press, Baton Rouge.

O'Brian, S. R., Paul A. Mayewski, L. David Meeker, Debra A. Meese, M. S. Twickler, and S. I. Whitlow
1995 Complexity of Holocene Climate as Constructed from a Greenland Ice Core. *Science* 270:1962–1964.

O'Brien, Michael J., and W. Raymond Wood
1998 *The Prehistory of Missouri.* University of Missouri Press, Columbia.

Ortmann, Anthony L.
2003 Project 2/01: Results of 2001 and 2002 Field Seasons at Poverty Point. Report on file, Louisiana Division of Archaeology, Baton Rouge.

Pauketat, Timothy R., and Susan M. Alt
2003 Mounds, Memory, and Contested Mississippian History. In *Archaeologies of Memory*, edited by Ruth M. Van Dyke and Susan E. Alcock, pp. 151–179. Blackwell, Oxford.

Piatek, Bruce J.
1994 The Tomoka Mound Complex in Northeast Florida. *Southeastern Archaeology* 13:109–118.

Polyak, Victor J., and Yemane Asmerom
2001 Late Holocene Climate and Cultural Changes in the Southwestern United States. *Science* 294:148–151.

Prentice, Guy
1994 A Settlement Pattern Analysis of Prehistoric Sites in Mammoth Cave National Park, Kentucky. Ph.D. dissertation, Department of Anthropology, University of Florida, Gainesville.

Randall, Asa R., and Kenneth E. Sassaman
2005 *St. Johns Archaeological Field School 2003–2004: Hontoon Island State Park.* Technical Report 6. Laboratory of Southeastern Archaeology, Department of Anthropology, University of Florida, Gainesville.

Ritchie, William A.
1969 *The Archaeology of New York State.* Rev. ed. Natural History Press, Garden City, New Jersey.

Royall, P. Daniel, Paul A. Delcourt, and Hazel R. Delcourt
1991 Late Quaternary Paleoecology and Paleoenvironments of the Central Mississippi Alluvial Valley. *Geological Society of America Bulletin* 103:157–170.

Ruddiman, W. F., and A. C. Mix
1993 The North and Equatorial Atlantic at 9000 and 6000 BP. In *Global Climates since the Late Glacial Maximum*, edited by H. E. Wright Jr., John E. Kutzbach, Thompson Webb III, William F. Ruddiman, F. Alayne Street-Perrott, and Patrick J. Bartlein, pp. 94–125. University of Minnesota Press, Minneapolis.

Russo, Michael
1991 Archaic Sedentism on the Florida Coast: A Case Study from Horr's Island. Ph.D. dissertation, Department of Anthropology, University of Florida, Gainesville.
1996a Southeastern Mid-Holocene Coastal Settlements. In *Archaeology of the Mid-Holocene Southeast*, edited by Kenneth E. Sassaman and David G. Anderson, pp. 177–199. University Press of Florida, Gainesville.
1996b Southeastern Preceramic Archaic Ceremonial Mounds. In *Archaeology of the Mid-Holocene Southeast*, edited by Kenneth E. Sassaman and David G. Anderson, pp. 259–287. University Press of Florida, Gainesville.
2002 Architectural Features at Fig Island. In The Fig Island Ring Complex (38CH42): Coastal Adaptation and the Question of Ring Function in the Late Archaic, edited by Rebecca Saunders and Michael Russo, pp. 85–97. Report prepared for the South Carolina Department of Archives and History, Grant #45-01-16441. Louisiana State University Baton Rouge, and National Park Service, Tallahassee, Florida.
2004 Measuring Shell Rings for Social Inequality. In *Signs of Power: The Rise of Complexity in the Southeast*, edited by Jon L. Gibson and Philip J. Carr, pp. 26–70. University of Alabama Press, Tuscaloosa.

Russo, Michael, Ann S. Cordell, and Donna L. Ruhl
1993 The Timucuan Ecological and Historical Preserve, Phase III Final Report. Report submitted to the Southeast Archeological Research Center, Contract CA-5000-9-8001. National Park Service, Tallahassee, Florida.

Russo, Michael, and G. Heide
2001 Shell Rings of the Southeast US. *Antiquity* 75:491–492.

Sandweiss, Daniel H., Kirk A. Maasch, and David G. Anderson
1999 Transitions in the Mid-Holocene. *Science* 283:499–500.

Sassaman, Kenneth E.
1997 Refining Soapstone Vessel Chronology in the Southeast. *Early Georgia* 25(1):1–20.

1998 Crafting Cultural Identity in Hunter-Gatherer Economies. In *Craft and Social Identity*, edited by Cathy Lynne Costin and Rita P. Wright, pp. 93–107. Archeological Papers 8. American Anthropological Association, Washington, D.C.

1999 A Southeastern Perspective on Soapstone Vessel Technology in the Northeast. In *The Archaeological Northeast*, edited by Mary Ann Levine, Kenneth E. Sassaman, and Michael S. Nassaney, pp. 75–95. Bergin and Garvey, Westport, Connecticut.

2003a *St. Johns Archaeological Field School 2000–2001: Blue Spring and Hontoon Island State Parks.* Technical Report 4. Laboratory of Southeastern Archaeology, Department of Anthropology, University of Florida, Gainesville.

2003b New AMS Dates on Orange Fiber-Tempered Pottery from the Middle St. Johns Valley and Their Implications for Culture History in Northeast Florida. *The Florida Anthropologist* 56(1):5–14.

2004 Common Origins and Divergent Histories in the Early Pottery Traditions of the American Southeast. In *Early Pottery: Technology, Function, Style, and Interaction in the Lower Southeast*, edited by Rebecca Saunders and Christopher T. Hays, pp. 23–39. University of Alabama Press, Tuscaloosa.

2006 Dating and Explaining Soapstone Vessels: A Comment on Truncer. *American Antiquity* 71:141–156.

Sassaman, Kenneth E., and David G. Anderson

1995 *Middle and Late Archaic Archaeological Records of South Carolina: A Synthesis for Research and Resource Management.* Savannah River Archaeological Research Papers 6. South Carolina Institute of Archaeology and Anthropology, University of South Carolina, Columbia.

2004 Late Holocene Period, 3750–650 B.C. In *Southeast*, edited by Raymond D. Fogelson, pp. 101–114. Handbook of North American Indians, vol. 14, William C. Sturtevant, general editor, Smithsonian Institution, Washington, D.C.

Sassaman, Kenneth E., Meggan E. Belssing, and Asa R. Randall

2006 Stallings Island Revisited: New Evidence for Occupational History, Community Patterning, and Subsistence Technology. *American Antiquity* 71:539–561.

Sassaman, Kenneth E., and Michael J. Heckenberger

2004 Crossing the Symbolic Rubicon in the Southeast. In *Signs of Power: The Rise of Complexity in the Southeast*, edited by Jon L. Gibson and Philip J. Carr, pp. 214–233. University of Alabama Press, Tuscaloosa.

Saunders, Joe W.

2004 Are We Fixing to Make the Same Mistakes Again? In *Signs of Power: The Rise of Complexity in the Southeast*, edited by Jon L. Gibson and Philip J. Carr, pp. 146–161. University of Alabama Press, Tuscaloosa.

Saunders, Joe, and Thurman Allen

1997 The Archaic Period. *Louisiana Archaeology* 22:1–30.

2003 Jaketown Revisited. *Southeastern Archaeology* 22:155–164.

Saunders, Joe, Thurman Allen, Dennis LaBatt, Reca Jones, and David Griffing

2001 An Assessment of the Antiquity of the Lower Jackson Mound. *Southeastern Archaeology* 20:67–77.

Saunders, Joe W., Rolfe D. Mandel, C. Garth Sampson, Charles M. Allen, E. Thurman Allen, Daniel A. Bush, James K. Feathers, Kristen J. Gremillion, C. T. Hallmark, H. Edwin Jackson, Jay K. Johnson, Reca Jones, Roger T. Saucier, Gary L. Stringer, and Malcolm F. Vidrine

2005 Watson Brake, A Middle Archaic Mound Complex in Northeast Louisiana. *American Antiquity* 70:631–668.

Saunders, Joe W., Rolfe D. Mandel, Roger T. Saucier, E. Thurman Allen, C. T. Hallmark, Jay K. Johnson, Edwin H. Jackson, Charles M. Allen, Gary L. Stringer, Douglas S. Frink, James K. Feathers, Stephen Williams, Kristen J. Gremillion, Malcom F. Vidrine, and Reca B. Jones

1997 A Mound Complex in Louisiana at 5400–5000 Years Before the Present. *Science* 277:1796–1799.

Saunders, Rebecca

1994 The Case for Archaic Period Mounds in Southeastern Louisiana. *Southeastern Archaeology* 13:118–134.

2002 Summary and Conclusions. In The Fig Island Ring Complex (38CH42): Coastal Adaptation and the Question of Ring Function in the Late Archaic, edited by Rebecca Saunders and Michael Russo, pp. 154–159. Report prepared for the South Carolina Department of Archives and History, Grant #45-01-16441. Louisiana State University, Baton Rouge, and National Park Service, Tallahassee, Florida.

2004 Spatial Variation in Orange Culture Pottery: Interaction and Function. In *Early Pottery: Technology, Function, Style, and Interaction in the Lower Southeast*, edited by Rebecca Saunders and Christopher T. Hays, pp. 40–62. University of Alabama Press, Tuscaloosa.

Saunders, Rebecca, and Christopher T. Hays

2004 Introduction: Themes in Early Pottery Research. In *Early Pottery: Technology, Function, Style, and Interaction in the Lower Southeast*, edited by Rebecca Saunders and Christopher T. Hays, pp. 1–22. University of Alabama Press, Tuscaloosa.

Saunders, Rebecca, and Gregory A. Mikell

2004 Coastal Dynamics and Cultural Complexity on Choctawhatchee Bay. Report submitted to National Science Foundation, Award 0003933. Louisiana State University, Baton Rouge, and Panamerican Consultants, Tampa, Florida.

Schambach, Frank F.

1998 *Pre-Caddoan Cultures in the Trans-Mississippi South.* Research Series 53. Arkansas Archeological Survey, Fayetteville.

Schuldenrein, Joseph

1996 Geoarchaeology and Mid-Holocene Landscape History. In *Archaeology of the Mid-Holocene Southeast*, edited by Kenneth E. Sassaman and David G. Anderson, pp. 3–27. University Press of Florida, Gainesville.

Schulz, Michael, and André Paul

2002 Holocene Climatic Variability on Centennial-to-Millennial Time Scales: 1. Climate Records from the North Atlantic Realm. In *Climate Development and History of the North Atlantic Realm*, edited by G. Wefer, W. Berger, K.-E. Behre, and E. Jansen, pp. 41–54. Springer-Verlag, Berlin.

Sears, William H., and James B. Griffin

1950 Type Descriptions: Fiber Tempered Pottery. In *Prehistoric Pottery of the Eastern United States*, edited by

James B. Griffin, pp. 1–12. Museum of Anthropology, University of Michigan, Ann Arbor.

Seeman, Mark F.
1995 When Words Are Not Enough: Hopewell Interregionalism and the Use of Material Symbols at the GE Mound. In *Native American Interactions: Multiscalar Analysis and Interpretations in the Eastern Woodlands*, edited by Michael S. Nassaney and Kenneth E. Sassaman, pp. 122–143. University of Tennessee Press, Knoxville.

Shuman, Bryan, Patrick J. Bartlein, Nathaniel Logar, Paige Newby, and Thompson Webb III
2002 Parallel Climate and Vegetation Responses to Early Holocene Collapse of the Laurentide Ice Sheet. *Quaternary Science Reviews* 21:1793–1805.

Smith, Bruce D.
1986 The Archaeology of the Southeastern United States: From Dalton to De Soto, 10,500 B.P.–500 B.P. In *Advances in World Archaeology,* vol. 5, edited by Fred Wendorf and Angela Close, pp. 1–92. Academic Press, Orlando, Florida.

Smith, M. O.
1995 Scalping in the Archaic Period: Evidence from the Western Tennessee Valley. *Southeastern Archaeology* 14:60–68.
1996 Bioarchaeological Inquiry into Archaic Period Populations of the Southeast: Trauma and Occupational Stress. In *Archaeology of the Mid-Holocene Southeast*, edited by Kenneth E. Sassaman and David G. Anderson, pp. 134–154. University Press of Florida, Gainesville.
1997 Osteological Indications of Warfare in the Archaic Period of Western Tennessee Valley. In *Troubled Times: Violence and Warfare in the Past*, edited by Debra L. Martin and David W. Frayer, pp. 241–265. Gordon and Breach, Amsterdam.

Steig, Eric J.
1999 Mid-Holocene Climate Change. *Science* 286:1485–1487.

Steponaitis, Vincas P.
1986 Prehistoric Archaeology in the Southeastern United States, 1970–1985. *Annual Review of Anthropology* 15:363–404.

Stuiver, Minze, Paula J. Reimer, Edouard Bard, John W. Beck, George S. Burr, Konrad A. Hughen, Bernd Kromer, F. Gerry McCormac, Johannes van der Plicht, and Marco Spurk
1998 INTCAL98 Radiocarbon Age Calibration 24,000-0 cal B.P. *Radiocarbon* 40:1041–1083.

Stuiver, Minze, Paula J. Reimer, and Ron Reimer
2004 CALIB Radiocarbon Calibration (version 4.4.2). Electronic document, http://radiocarbon.pa.qub.ac.uk/calib, accessed December 7, 2004.

Thomas, Prentice M., Jr. and L. Janice Campbell
1991 The Elliot's Point Complex: New Data Regarding the Localized Poverty Point Expression on the Northwest Florida Gulf Coast, 2000 B.C.–500 B.C. In *The Poverty Point Culture: Local Manifestations, Subsistence Practices, and Trade Networks*, edited by Kathleen M. Byrd, pp. 103–119. Geoscience and Man 29. Louisiana State University, Baton Rouge.

Thomas, Prentice M., Jr., L. Janice Campbell, and James R. Morehead
2004 The Burkett Site (23MI20): Implications for Cultural Complexity and Origins. In *Signs of Power: The Rise of Complexity in the Southeast*, edited by Jon L. Gibson and Philip J. Carr, pp. 114–128. University of Alabama Press, Tuscaloosa.

Tiffany, Joseph A.
1986 The Early Woodland Period in Iowa. In *Early Woodland Archeology*, edited by Kenneth B. Farnsworth and Thomas E. Emerson, pp. 159–170. Kampsville Seminars in Archeology 2. Center for American Archeology Press, Kampsville, Illinois.

Törnqvist, Torbjörn E., Arie F. M. de Jong, C. W. Kurnik, Juan L. González, Linda A. Newsom, and Klaas van der Borg
2004 Deciphering Holocene Sea-Level History on the U.S. Gulf Coast: A High-Resolution Record from the Mississippi Delta. *Bulletin of the Geological Society of America* 116:1026–1039.

Trinkley, Michael B.
1980 Investigations of the Woodland Period along the South Carolina Coast. Ph.D. dissertation, Department of Anthropology, University of North Carolina, Chapel Hill.
1985 The Form and Function of South Carolina's Early Woodland Shell Rings. In *Structure and Process in Southeastern Archaeology*, edited by Roy S. Dickens and H. Trawick Ward, pp. 102–118. University of Alabama Press, Tuscaloosa.

Truncer, James
2004 Steatite Vessel Age and Occurrence in Temperate Eastern North America. *American Antiquity* 69:487–513.

Tuck, James A.
1974 Early Archaic Horizons in Eastern North America. *Archaeology of Eastern North America* 2:72–80.

Van Buren, Mary
2001 The Archaeology of El Niño Events and Other "Natural" Disasters. *Journal of Archaeological Method and Theory* 8:129–149

Walthall, John A.
1980 *Prehistoric Indians of the Southeast.* University of Alabama Press, Tuscaloosa.

Walthall, John A., and Ned J. Jenkins
1976 The Gulf Formational Stage in Southeastern Prehistory. *Southeastern Archaeological Conference Bulletin* 19:43–49.

Walthall, John A., and Brad Koldehoff
1998 Hunter-Gatherer Interaction and Alliance Formation: Dalton and the Cult of the Long Blade. *Plains Anthropologist* 43:257–273.

Ward, Heather D.
1998 The Paleoethnobotanical Record of the Poverty Point Culture: Implications of Past and Current Research. *Southeastern Archaeology* 17:166–174.

Waring, Antonio J., Jr., and Lewis H. Larson Jr.
1968 The Shell Ring on Sapelo Island. In *The Waring Papers: The Collected Works of Antonio J. Waring, Jr.*, edited by Stephen Williams, pp. 263–278. Papers of the Peabody Museum of Archaeology and Ethnology 58. Harvard University, Cambridge, Massachusetts.

Watts, William A., Eric C. Grimm, and T. C. Hussey
1996 Mid-Holocene Forest History of Florida and the Coastal Plain of Georgia and South Carolina. In *Archaeology of the Mid-Holocene Southeast*, edited by Kenneth E. Sassaman and David G. Anderson, pp. 28–38. University Press of Florida, Gainesville.

Webb, Clarence H.
1981 *Stone Points and Tools of Northwestern Louisiana*. Special Publication 1. Louisiana Archaeological Society, Baton Rouge.
1982 *The Poverty Point Culture*. 2nd ed., revised. Geoscience and Man 17. Louisiana State University, Baton Rouge.

Webb, Clarence H., James A. Ford, and Sherwood M. Gagliano
1963 Poverty Point and the American Formative. Manuscript on file, Center for Archaeology, Tulane University, New Orleans, Louisiana.

Webb, Thompson, III, Patrick J. Bartlein, Sandy P. Harrison, and Katherine H. Anderson
1993 Vegetation, Lake Levels, and Climate in Eastern North America for the Past 18,000 Years. In *Global Climates since the Late Glacial Maximum*, edited by H. E. Wright Jr., John E. Kutzbach, Thompson Webb III, William F. Ruddiman, F. Alayne Street-Perrott, and Patrick J. Bartlein, pp. 415–467. University of Minnesota Press, Minneapolis.

Webb, William S.
1946 *Indian Knoll, Site Oh 2, Ohio County, Kentucky*. Reports in Anthropology and Archaeology 4(3, pt. 1). University of Kentucky, Lexington.
1950a Carlston Annis Mound, Site 5, Butler County, Kentucky. *Reports in Anthropology and Archaeology* 7(4):267–354. University of Kentucky, Lexington.
1950b *The Read Shell Midden, Site 10, Butler County, Kentucky*. Reports in Anthropology and Archaeology 7(5). University of Kentucky, Lexington.

Webb, William S., and David L. DeJarnette
1942 *An Archeological Survey of the Pickwick Basin in the Adjacent Portions of the States of Alabama, Mississippi and Tennessee*. Bulletin 129. Bureau of American Ethnology, Washington, D.C.
1948 *The Flint River Site, Ma°48*. Museum Paper 23. Alabama Museum of Natural History, University.

Webb, William S., and William G. Haag
1940 Cypress Creek Villages. *Reports in Anthropology and Archaeology* 4(2):67–110. University of Kentucky, Lexington.
1947 Archaic Sites in McLean County, Kentucky. *Reports in Anthropology and Archaeology* 7(1):1–48. University of Kentucky, Lexington.

Wefer, Gerold, Wolfgang H. Berger, Karl-Ernst Behre, and Eystein Jansen (editors)
2002 *Climate Development and the History of the North Atlantic Realm*. Springer-Verlag, Berlin.

Weissner, Polly
2002 The Vines of Complexity: Egalitarian Structures and the Institutionalization of Inequality among the Enga. *Current Anthropology* 43:233–270.

White, Nancy M.
2003 Late Archaic in the Apalachicola/Lower Chattahoochee Valley of Northwest Florida, Southwest Georgia, Southeast Alabama. *The Florida Anthropologist* 56(2):69–90.
2004 Late Archaic Fisher-Foragers in the Apalachicola-Lower Chattahoochee Valley, Northwest Florida-South Georgia/Alabama. In *Signs of Power: The Rise of Complexity in the Southeast*, edited by Jon L. Gibson and Philip J. Carr, pp. 10–25. University of Alabama Press, Tuscaloosa.

Whitehead, Donald R., and Mark C. Sheehan
1985 Holocene Vegetational Changes in the Tombigbee River Valley, Eastern Mississippi. *American Midland Naturalist* 113:122–137.

Willemse, Nico W., and Torbjörn E. Törnqvist
1999 Holocene Century-Scale Temperature Variability from West Greenland Lake Records. *Geology* 27:580–584.

Winters, Howard D.
1968 Value Systems and Late Archaic Trade Cycles. In *New Perspectives in Archeology*, edited by Sally R. Binford and Lewis R. Binford, pp. 175–222. Aldine, Chicago.
1969 *The Riverton Culture: A Second Millennium Occupation in the Central Wabash Valley*. Reports of Investigations 13. Illinois State Museum, Springfield.

Wurster, Christopher M., and William P. Patterson
2001 Late Holocene Climate Change for the Eastern Interior United States: Evidence from High-Resolution $\delta^{18}O$ Values of Sagittal Otoliths. *Palaeogeography, Palaeoclimatology, Palaeoecology* 170:81–100.

Yu, Zicheng
2000 Ecosystem Response to Lateglacial and Early Holocene Climate Oscillations in the Great Lakes Region of North America. *Quaternary Science Reviews* 19:1723–1747.

Yu, Zicheng, and H. E. Wright Jr.
2001 Response of Interior North America to Abrupt Climate Oscillations in the North Atlantic Region during the Last Deglaciation. *Earth Science Reviews* 52:333–369.

Part 5

The Great Lakes

19

The Archaic Tradition in Wisconsin

Thomas C. Pleger and James B. Stoltman

Introduction: Defining the Archaic in Wisconsin

The term *Archaic* has a long history of variable usage in the literature of American archaeology. In eastern North America it first appeared in the 1920s, pertaining to local prehistoric expressions in New York State (see Stoltman 1992), later to be incorporated as a pan-eastern "pattern" into the Midwest Taxonomic System championed by Will C. McKern (1939, 1942). Patterns in the Midwestern Taxonomic System were defined solely on the basis of formal properties (cultural practices) and were independent of time. Archaic, as a pattern, thus, came to apply mainly to cultures in eastern North America lacking pottery and horticulture. In their well-known *Method and Theory in American Archaeology*, Willey and Phillips (1958) adopted this basic formal usage of the Archaic concept but expanded its geographic scope to include the entire New World and redesignated it a "stage."

After initially demurring at the Archaic concept in 1946, James B. Griffin, in his influential 1952 synthesis of eastern U.S. prehistory, redefined it as a "period," that is, a temporal rather than a formal taxon. In contrast to this usage, Gordon Willey, in his monumental 1966 text, synthesized eastern U.S. prehistory in terms of a series of formally defined "traditions," one of which was the Archaic. Thus, since the late 1950s, the "Archaic" taxon has been used variously to apply to a period (Griffin 1952; Phillips and Brown 1983), a stage (Willey 1966), and also a tradition (Stoltman 1986, 1992, 1997) in the eastern United States.

In this chapter, the Archaic is conceptualized as a tradition, an approach that has been used previously in Wisconsin (Stoltman 1986, 1997). As such, it is a formal taxon composed of prehistoric cultures that share several distinctive properties that co-occur as a polythetic set; that is, "no single attribute is both sufficient and necessary to the aggregate membership" (Clarke 1968:42). The main properties of this polythetic set are (1) various stemmed and notched chipped-stone bifaces that tipped knives, spears, or darts (but not arrows), (2) broad-spectrum, hunter-gather subsistence, (3) the appearance of cemeteries and other evidence of increasing sedentism, and (4) an increase in interregional exchange and social complexity when compared with preceding Paleoindian cultures.

The Archaic tradition in Wisconsin has been traditionally subdivided into three stages (Early, Middle, and Late) on the basis of detectable changes in lifestyle represented by the appearance or disappearance of specific types of material culture. These stages were sequential in the order of their appearance but may have overlapped temporally because of the time-transgressive onset of the defining properties (Figure 19.1; Table 19.1). The calendrical ages for each of the stages are provided in this discussion, but as secondary descriptors rather than as defining properties of the stages. They should be understood to be provisional estimates only, subject to revision in light of new archaeological data. The earliest evidence of the Archaic tradition in Wisconsin is denoted by the appearance of bevel-resharpened bifaces that are dated farther to the south to the eighth millennium RCYBC. The terminus of the Archaic in Wisconsin is marked, arbitrarily

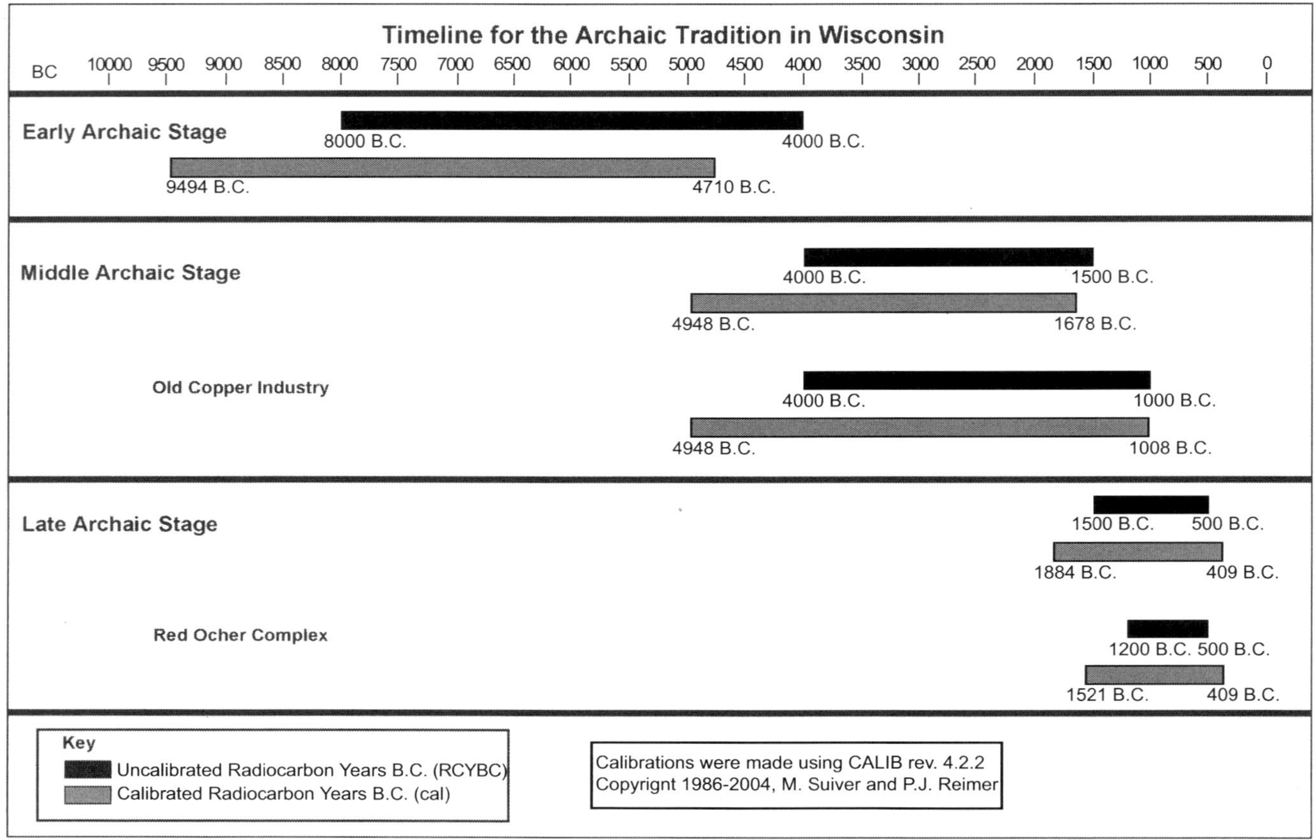

Figure 19.1. Time line for the Archaic tradition in Wisconsin.

to be sure, by the appearance of Early Woodland pottery in the first millennium RCYBC. Both the beginning and end of Archaic lifeways unfolded in time-transgressive fashion across the state, appearing earlier in the south and persisting later in the north (Figure 19.2).

The Early Archaic Stage: 8000–5500 B.C. to 4000 B.C. (RCYBC) (cal ca. 9500 B.C.–5000 B.C.)

Evidence for the earliest Archaic occupation of Wisconsin is extremely sparse. Early Archaic cultural practices also apparently overlapped in time and space with Late Paleoindian Plano lifeways. The main basis for recognizing the Early Archaic stage is through diagnostic stemmed and notched bifaces (Luchterhand 1970) that have turned up widely in surface collections, especially in the southern two-thirds of the state (Behm 1985). Their association with the Early Archaic stage in Wisconsin is based on typological resemblances to bifaces from Illinois and other states to the south, where the early Holocene age of such forms is well established.

Reliable indicators of the Early Archaic stage include the following point types: Thebes Notched and St. Charles Notched ("Dovetails"; see Figure 19.3), Hardin Barbed, and the bifurcate-base family of points (Figure 19.4). Assuming that the radiocarbon ages for these point types at the Twin Ditch site in west-central Illinois pertain to the Wisconsin examples, as well, it can be suggested that the Thebes and St. Charles point types (Thebes cluster) date to a range of 7750–7000 RCYBC (Morrow 1996). The Hardin Barbed type probably dates to the early to middle 6000s RCYBC, and the bifurcates probably date to the late 6000s RCYBC. What projectile point types (and, thus, archaeological cultures) should be assigned to the 6000–4000 RCYBC interval in Wisconsin is a dilemma, for this interval is a virtual void in the state's current archaeological record. The present 4000 B.C. boundary separating the Early and Middle Archaic stages will probably eventually be revised as the archaeology of the mid-Holocene becomes better known. The results of Kuehn's (2002) recent study of Archaic radiocarbon dates from both cultural resource management (CRM) reports and journal articles for southern Wisconsin further support the notion that 4000 RCYBC conforms nicely to the temporal boundary for the appearance of the Middle Archaic stage in the archaeological record.

Table 19.1. Significant Calibrated Archaic Dates from Wisconsin and the Riverside Cemetery, Upper Peninsula of Michigan.

Lab Number	Site Name	Site Number	C^{14} Age Years B.P.[a]	Standard Deviation	Uncalibrated RCYBC Dates B.C.	Calibrated Age Ranges B.C.[b] 68.3% (1 Sigma)[c]	Probability Distribution	Sample References
WIS-720	Dwyer	47JA21	9405	90	7455	8800–8540	.935	Stoltman 1997
C-837 / C-839	Oconto	47OC45	7510	600	5560	7080–5780	1.000	Pleger 2001
Beta-134256	Vilas County	47VI46	7690	40	5740	6510 –6460	.663	Bruhy, pers. comm. 2004
WIS-600	Brogley Rockshelter	47GT156	7460	80	5510	6390–6240	1.000	Kuehn 2002
AA-31977/WG-613	Vilas County	47VI320	7305	60	5355	6220–6160	.534	Bruhy, pers. comm. 2004
C-836	Oconto	47OC45	5600	600	3650	5079–3788	.974	Pleger 2001
AA-19678 / WG-2404	Oconto	47OC45	6020	60	4070	4960–4830	.841	Pleger 2001
M-813	Raddatz Rockshelter	47SK5	5200	400	3250	4460–3630	.957	Kuehn 2002; Stoltman 1997
AA-20281 / WG-2413	Oconto	47OC45	5250	110	3300	4170–3960	.833	Pleger 2001
GAK	Oconto	47OC45	4900	65	2590	3710–3640	.750	Pleger 2001
Beta-80613	Murphy	47DA736	4960	150	3010	3950–3640	1.000	Kuehn 2002; Stoltman 1997
WIS-593	Brogley Rockshelter	47GT156	4785	65	2835	3650–3520	.971	Kuehn 2002; Stoltman 1997
WIS-592	Brogley Rockshelter	47GT156	4780	65	2830	3640–3520	.950	Kuehn 2002; Stoltman 1997
Beta-77821	Murphy	47DA736	4780	60	2830	3640–3520	1.000	Kuehn 2002; Stoltman 1997
WIS-590	Brogley Rockshelter	47GT156	4655	75	2705	3520–3360	.993	Kuehn 2002; Stoltman 1997
Beta-106254	Crow Hollow	47CR598	4330	80	2380	3040–2880	.887	Kuehn 2002
M-1440	Price III	47RI4	4180	150	2230	2920–2560	.951	Kuehn 2002
WIS-368	Governor Dodge Rockshelter	47IA1	4170	65	2220	2820–2670	.792	Kuehn 2002; Stoltman 1997
Beta-180022	Carcajou Point	47JE02	4200	40	2250	2810–2750	.579	Jeske et al. 2002
TO-3983	Chautauqua	47MT71	4210	60	2260	2810–2700	.735	Stoltman 1997
WIS-591	Brogley Rockshelter	47GT156	4145	65	2195	2710–2660	.267	Kuehn 2002; Stoltman 1997
WIS-1706	Osceola	47GT24	4080	70	2130	2700–2560	.623	Kuehn 2002; Stoltman 1997
WIS-367	Governor Dodge Rockshelter	47IA1	3820	65	1870	2350–2220	.790	Kuehn 2002; Stoltman 1997
M-644	Reigh	47WN1	3660	250	1710	2350–1740	.942	Stoltman 1997
Beta-164355	Casey Kawlewski	47PT263	3790	70	1840	2310–2140	.854	Kuehn 2002
M-1444	Price III	47RI4	3710	150	1760	2310–1890	1.000	Kuehn 2002; Stoltman 1997
M-1441	Price III	47RI4	3620	150	1670	2150–1860	.754	Kuehn 2002
WIS-2269	Rainbow Dam	47ON179	3630	60	1680	2040–1910	.812	Moffat and Speth 1999
M-1443	Price III	47RI4	3540	150	1590	2040–1690	.929	Kuehn 2002; Stoltman 1997
M-643	Osceola	47GT24	3450	250	1500	2040–1490	.906	Kuehn 2002; Stoltman 1997
P-2469	Lawrence I Rockshelter	47VE154	3500	70	1550	1890–1740	.923	Kuehn 2002; Stoltman 1997
Beta-180025	Carcajou Point	47JE02	3450	50	1500	1780–1730	.402	Jeske et al. 2002
M-1442	Price III	47RI4	3280	150	1330	1740–1400	1.000	Kuehn 2002
P-2468	Lawrence I Rockshelter	47VE154	3150	260	1200	1690–1050	.993	Kuehn 2002; Stoltman 1997
WIS-2270	Rainbow Dam	47ON180	3270	80	1320	1620–1490	.785	Moffat and Speth 1999
P-2467	Lawrence I Rockshelter	47VE154	3090	260	1140	1620–1000	.994	Kuehn 2002; Stoltman 1997
P-2465	Lawrence I Rockshelter	47VE154	3040	250	1090	1520–970	.953	Kuehn 2002
Beta-180024	Carcajou Point	47JE02	3180	50	1230	1500–1410	1.000	Jeske et al. 2002
Beta-189658	Carcajou Point	47JE02	3090	40	1140	1360–1310	.512	Jeske et al. 2002
WIS-2237	Bobwhite	47RI185	2970	60	1020	1260–1110	.816	Kuehn 2002
M-1445	Price III	47RI4	2920	130	970	1260–970	.897	Kuehn 2002; Stoltman 1997
WIS-941	Preston Rockshelter	47GT157	2780	65	830	1000–890	.729	Kuehn 2002
WIS-946	Preston Rockshelter	47GT157	2710	65	760	910–810	1.000	Kuehn 2002
P-2466	Lawrence I Rockshelter	47VE154	2570	70	620	650–540	.491	Kuehn 2002
Calibrated Archaic Dates from Riverside Cemetery, Menominee, Michigan								
M-658	Riverside	20ME01	3040	150	1090	1430–1110	.898	Pleger 1998, 2000
AA-19679 / WG2405	Riverside	20ME01	2960	50	1010	1260–1110	.896	Pleger 1998, 2000
AA-19685 / WG-2411	Riverside	20ME01	2850	50	900	1050–970	.620	Pleger 1998, 2000
AA-19680 / WG-2406	Riverside	20ME01	2790	50	840	1000–900	.881	Pleger 1998, 2000
AA-19677 / WG-2403	Riverside	20ME01	2780	65	830	1000–890	.729	Pleger 1998, 2000
AA-19684 / WG-2410	Riverside	20ME01	2710	50	760	900–820	1.000	Pleger 1998, 2000
AA-19686 / WG-2412	Riverside	20ME01	2690	60	740	860–800	.699	Pleger 1998, 2000
AA-19682 / WG-2408	Riverside	20ME01	2605	45	655	830–770	1.000	Pleger 1998, 2000
AA-19683 / WG-2409	Riverside	20ME01	2605	50	655	830–760	.925	Pleger 1998, 2000
AA-20282 / WG-2414	Riverside	20ME01	2495	65	545	770–540	.961	Pleger 1998, 2000
M-1719	Riverside	20ME01	2460	140	510	600–410	.561	Pleger 1998, 2000
AA-19681 / WG-2407	Riverside	20ME01	2380	50	430	520–390	.912	Pleger 1998, 2000
M-1717	Riverside	20ME01	2190	140	240	390–90	.945	Pleger 1998, 2000
M-1718	Riverside	20ME01	2080	140	130	210 B.C.–A.D. 60	.833	Pleger 1998, 2000
M-1716	Riverside	20ME01	2050	130	100	200 B.C.–A.D. 80	.931	Pleger 1998, 2000
M-1715	Riverside	20ME01	1949	130	A.D. 1	90 B.C.–A.D. 230	1.000	Pleger 1998, 2000

[a]Years Before Present (A.D. 1950 = 0 B.P.); [b]Dates are rounded to the nearest 10 years; [c]Calibrations were made using CALIB rev. 4.4.2 software (copyright 1986-2004, M. Stuiver and P.J Reimer.); the calibration data set used was intcal98.14C.

Whether the establishment of the Archaic tradition in Wisconsin involved the readaptation of local people to new environmental conditions or the arrival of new peoples from the south is uncertain. Probably both processes were involved.

Early Archaic groups existed during a time of rapid and substantial environmental changes that accompanied the progressive northward retreat of glacial ice sheets into Canada. The most dramatic changes on the Wisconsin landscape during early postglacial times involved a progressive northward expansion of new plant communities into the state as well as substantial fluctuations in lake levels in the Lake Michigan basin. The period from about 8000 RCYBC to 4000 RCYBC was a time of warming (although still cool compared with the present)

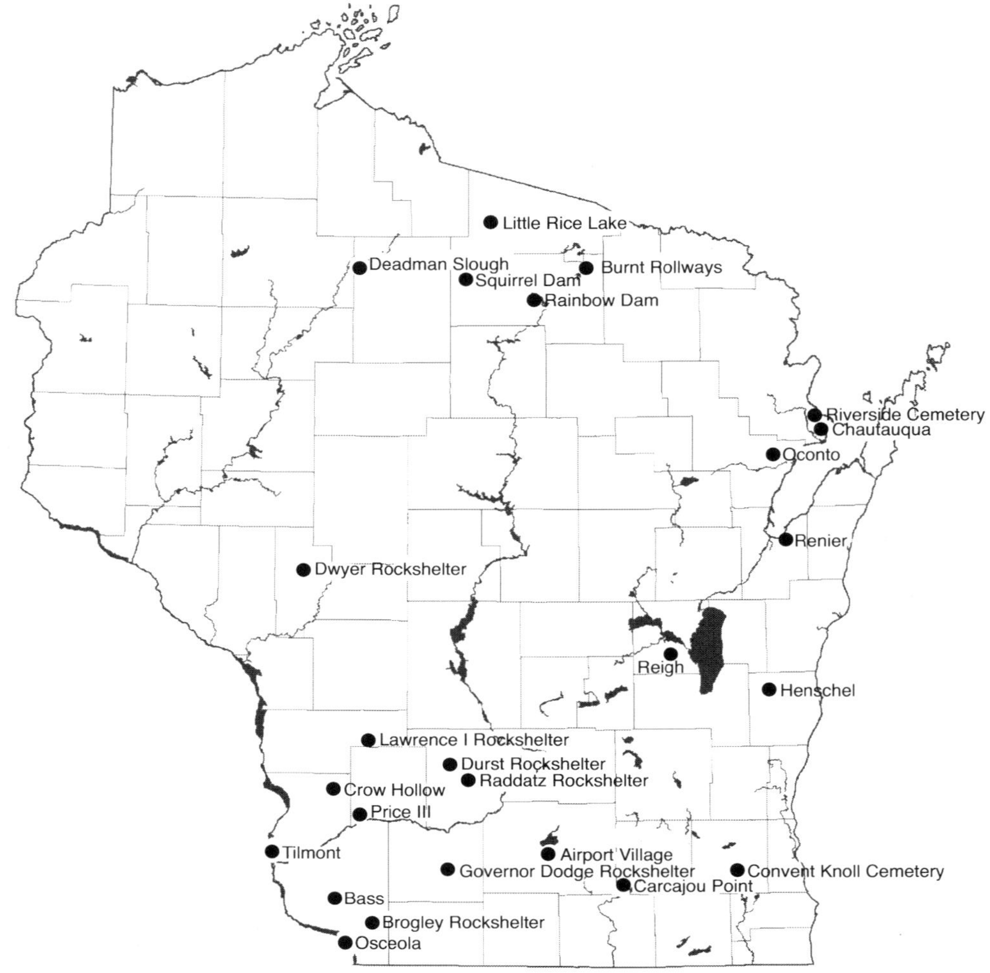

Figure 19.2. Locations of Archaic sites discussed in the text.

Figure 19.3. Thebes (top row) and St. Charles/Dovetail (bottom row) points (surface finds from southern Wisconsin).

and moist climatic conditions. Studies of fossil pollen spectra from northeastern Iowa across southern Wisconsin indicate that this was a time of peak abundance of such deciduous hardwood species as elm, hornbeam, basswood, and sugar maple, along with a rising abundance of oak (Baker et al. 1992; Chumbley et al. 1990; Maher 1982; Winkler et al. 1986). What is especially notable about this early to mid-postglacial "mesic deciduous forest" (Baker et al. 1992) is that it seems to have been associated with moist, rather than warm and dry, climatic conditions and that it was probably not an especially attractive environment for humans. Its thick canopy probably produced so much shade that shrubs and other ground cover on which browsing animals like white-tailed deer and elk depend would have been sparse, and there was little edible nut mast other than acorns, which require special preparation to render them nontoxic for humans.

Figure 19.4. LeCroy Bifurcated Stem projectile points (surface finds from southern Wisconsin).

At the same time, the removal of the enormous "plug" of glacial ice from the north rim of Lake Michigan left the bedrock so deeply depressed that lake waters were able to drain northeastward into Lake Huron rather than southward into the Illinois Valley, as they had formerly done when the glaciers had dammed the northern outlets. As a result of these changes in drainage directions, lake levels in Lake Michigan (which today stand at 177 m [580 ft] above mean sea level [amsl]) dropped drastically from about 184 m (605 ft amsl) around 8000 RCYBC to as low as about 70 m (230 ft amsl) by 7500 RCYBC. From this time—the Chippewa low-water stage—until after 4000 RCYBC, levels in Lake Michigan were significantly lower than the present time. Thus, any Archaic peoples living along the Lake Michigan shorelines between about 7500 RCYBC and 4000 RCYBC would have dwelled in locations that are today completely inundated. These two factors—the reduced capacity of the early to mid-Holocene mesic deciduous forest to sustain large human populations of hunter-gatherers and the drowned shorelines of early to mid-Holocene Lake Michigan—likely have contributed significantly to the reduced visibility of Early Archaic archaeological sites in Wisconsin.

What life was like for the Early Archaic occupants of Wisconsin can only be speculatively inferred since the archaeological record is so meager. No villages or major campsites are known, nor have any pure Early Archaic cemeteries been identified. Radiocarbon dates from two rockshelters—Dwyer in Jackson County (7455 ± 90 RCYBC [WIS-720]) and Brogley in Grant County (5510 ± 80 RCYBC; Figure 19.2 and Table 19.1) document (because of their association with definite stone artifacts) the earliest evidence of rockshelter habitation in the state. No diagnostic artifact types were recovered from these early occupation levels, so the dates cannot be positively associated with any known culture.

However, several sites exhibit a mixing of Late Paleoindian and Early Archaic technologies. The Renier site in Brown County (northeastern Wisconsin; see Figure 19.2) was excavated by Ronald Mason and Carol Irwin Mason in 1959 (Mason and Irwin 1960). This site produced a series of fire-shattered biface and tool fragments with a small amount of cremated human remains. The majority of the bifaces are of the Eden-Scottsbluff or Cody-complex cluster. The lithics had been subjected to intense heat and were likely the grave furniture from a single cremation of one small individual. Almost all of the tools are made of Hixton silicified sandstone, a material from western Wisconsin. The Masons also recovered one fire-fractured, side-notched point made from a dull, black chert (Figure 19.5). They interpreted this point as evidence of culture contact between Plano and Archaic peoples:

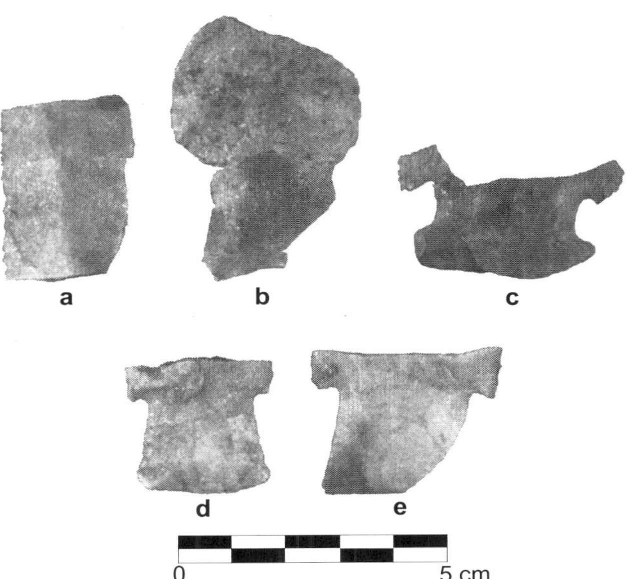

Figure 19.5. Sample of biface fragments from the Renier site: a, b, d, e, Cody point fragments; c, side-notched point base. Courtesy of the Neville Public Museum of Brown County, Green Bay, Wisconsin.

> We believe the evidence is sufficient to warrant considering the side-notched point and the Eden-Scottsbluff quartzite points as contemporaneous and definitely associated with the burial activity at the site. We do not believe, however, that the two projectile point traditions are directly related or that the two radically different kinds of points were made by members of the same group—they are too clearly separated in the contexts of shape and flaking technique. For this reason we believe that some sort of culture-contact, rather than developmental, situation is represented, one between Archaic and paleo-Indian traditions. [Mason and Irwin 1960:47–48]

Renier has not been radiocarbon dated, but accepting the side-notched point as evidence of Early Archaic interaction with Late Paleoindian people, a temporal range of 6500–4000 RCYBC has been postulated for the site (Mason 2002:121). The mixing of both cultural patterns could be viewed as an anomaly if Renier were the only site exhibiting such an assemblage, but it is not. Similar mixing of Archaic and Late Paleoindian projectile point types has been documented at the Gorto site, another possible Late Paleoindian–Early Archaic crematory mortuary site in the Upper Peninsula of Michigan (Buckmaster and Paquette 1988). At Gorto, the assemblage consisted of heat-fractured Cody-like materials along with side-notched, Archaic-looking bifaces.

A similar mixed assemblage was also encountered at the Deadman Slough site in Price County in northern Wisconsin (Meinholz and Kuehn 1996). The Museum Archaeology Program at the State Historical Society of Wisconsin excavated the site (Figure 19.2) as part of a CRM highway project. The site is extremely important given that it produced faunal remains from layers associated with mixed Paleoindian and Early Archaic materials. The mixed assemblage includes diagnostic Plano (Agate Basin) and side- and corner-notched bifaces. The notched points include examples that fall within the range of the Thebes cluster and within general Archaic side-notched varieties. The flaked-stone-tool raw materials are dominated by Hixton silicified sandstone. Quartz, local quartzite, rhyolite, and a variety of cherts are also represented. The excavators report that "ten points were recovered from the Main Ridge. They include a lanceolate point, corner- and side-notched points, stemmed points and a small flake point. With the exception of the flake point and a small stemmed point, the projectile point assemblage from Main Ridge includes a variety of styles commonly identified at Late Paleoindian/Early Archaic sites" (Meinholz and Kuehn 1996:50).

Besides the projectile points, a variety of scrapers, including some with graver spurs, were recovered along with a series of heat-fractured Hixton silicified sandstone biface blanks that have been interpreted by the investigators as representing some type of cremation activity (Meinholz and Kuehn 1996:184). Additional lithic tools associated with the Late Paleoindian–Early Archaic deposits include four complete and four fragments of chipped and ground adzes made from siltstone, basalt, and graywacke.

Deadman Slough also yielded several features associated with the Late Paleoindian–Early Archaic occupation. They consisted of shallow, oval basins, small, shallow stains, and a deep basin. Feature contents included small amounts of charcoal, burned bone, fire-cracked rock, lithic tools and debris, and heat-shattered biface fragments. Faunal remains from this occupation were fragmentary and generally in poor condition. However, large mammals (tentatively identified as white-tailed deer) and small mammals, turtle, and bird were identified (Meinholz and Kuehn 1996:187). This variety is significant in that it suggests a fairly broad-based subsistence strategy that incorporated a diverse set of resources.

Although no radiocarbon dates were run on materials associated with the Late Paleoindian–Early Archaic deposits, Meinholz and Kuehn (1996:188) suggest a temporal range of 6000–4000 RCYBC for this component. To date, Deadman Slough has provided the most comprehensive subsistence data available for sites of this age in Wisconsin; how representative it is of Early Archaic cultures is difficult to know.

Besides Deadman Slough, the only other site within the state of Wisconsin to produce significant evidence about the Early Archaic stage is the Bass site (Figure 19.2), a Galena chert quarry-workshop located in the uplands of Grant County (Stoltman et al. 1984). Field research conducted here by the University of Wisconsin (UW)-Madison during the summer of 1976 defined an area of 43 ha (nearly 100 ac) that was literally paved with debitage associated with the quarrying and initial shaping of countless chert nodules that occur in a residual layer on top of the local dolomitic bedrock and beneath up to 2.4 m (8 ft) of late-glacial, wind-deposited loess that blankets the landscape of the Driftless Area of southwest Wisconsin.

The vast size and richness of the Bass site are formidable obstacles to attempting a comprehensive evaluation of the site. Only one season of fieldwork has been conducted there (in 1976), and the resulting study must be considered preliminary at best. The 1976 fieldwork had two major components: (1) a 100-m by 200-m area (2 ha) near the center of the plowed portion of the site was gridded into 10-m squares and then all objects on the surface were collected from each of the 200 10-m squares in a controlled surface collection, and (2) a total area of 55 m^2 was excavated in an unplowed portion of the site.

Perhaps the most surprising finding of this research is that, despite the seemingly endless supply of chert available at the site, the location seems to have been exploited intensively only during a single cultural episode. Of the 44 identifiable projectile points recovered from the site, 38 are of a single type, Hardin Barbed (Figure 19.6). These data were especially surprising since, at the time of the excavation, Hardin Barbed was hardly known to exist in Wisconsin. The collection of Hardin Barbed points from the Bass site remains the largest sample recovered from a single site anywhere in the Midcontinent.

What accounts for the presence and unusual richness of the Bass site? A speculative interpretation of the site is as follows: For early postglacial time, when climatic conditions were cooler and moister than present, there is solid geological evidence within the Driftless Area of southwestern Wisconsin that lateral and headward erosion by streams was widespread (Knox et al. 1981). From this evidence, it can be surmised that the small stream that bisects the Bass site, like other Driftless Area streams, had eroded headward until it was cutting deeply into the flanks of the main ridge on which the site is situated. There, after cutting through the loess cap, it exposed the chert-rich residuum that lay sandwiched between the loess above and the uneroded bedrock below. Presumably, at

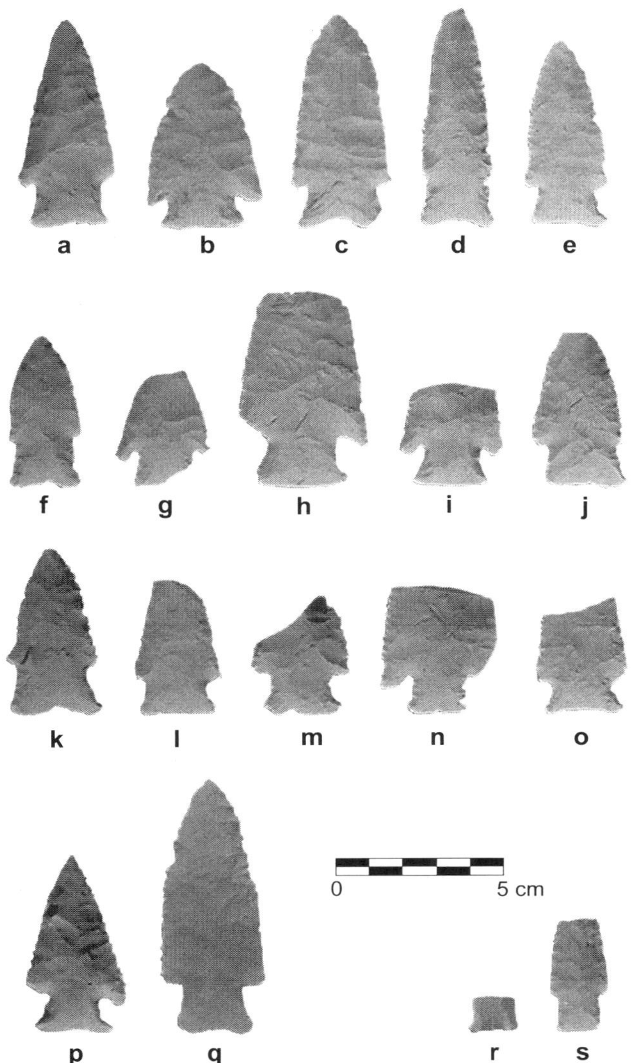

Figure 19.6. Projectile points from the Bass site: a–q, Hardin Barbed; r, s, Scottsbluff.

that time Hardin foragers happened on the recently exposed chert, literally lying on the ridge flanks for the picking. They simply collected the raw chert nodules from the gullies along the ridge flanks, took them to convenient loci nearby (e.g., on top of the ridge), and trimmed them into more portable cores, blanks, and preforms for easy transport during the remainder of their seasonal round of mobile hunting and gathering. In this fashion, their chippage was scattered over the surrounding countryside, far beyond the gullies where the nodules must actually have originated.

As one would surmise from this interpretation, the most abundant items recovered from both the surface collections and the excavations were nodules, cores, preforms, and flakes. Indeed, from the 2-ha area of the controlled surface collection, which constitutes just 5 percent of the site area, over 75,000 such chert artifacts were recovered. Included among the items from both the surface collections and the excavations were igneous-cobble hammerstones that must have been carried to the site by the flintknappers because no igneous rocks occur in the sediments that underlie the uplands of the Driftless Area. Clearly, the Hardin people were well prepared for their visits to the quarry.

The excavations, which were intended to expose undisturbed campsite areas, encountered massive amounts of chipping debris. Considering that the vast majority of activities at the site were related to quarrying and roughly shaping chert nodules, a surprising number of finished artifacts were recovered. Besides the projectile points (and excluding the cores, preforms, and unfinished flakes), thousands of carefully retouched flake tools were recorded, including a substantial number of distinctive bifacially worked end scrapers. Despite the obvious focus of the site occupants on extracting the local chert, such exotic materials as Hixton silicified sandstone from western Wisconsin and Moline chert from the Rock River region of Illinois also have turned up at the site, suggesting widespread seasonal movements as well as peaceful cultural exchange with neighboring peoples. Clearly, the Hardin occupants of the site were doing much more than quarrying and reducing chert nodules, but other aspects of their lives still remain largely unknown.

One final point that must be mentioned in connection with the the Bass site data is that the excavations also yielded one Late Paleoindian Scottsbluff biface. This point is made of the same local chert that was exploited by Hardin Barbed peoples. Its presence at Bass, coupled with the presence of mixed Late Paleoindian assemblages at the sites discussed above, further supports the idea that the Late Paleoindian and Early Archaic lifeways were contemporary in Wisconsin during the period 8000–4000 RCYBC.

Mason (1981:126–127) has concluded that Early Archaic and Late Paleoindian assemblages were partly coeval over much of the Great Lakes region. At the same time, he has also commented about the sparseness of Early Archaic sites: "The rarity of Early Archaic sites in the Great Lakes is something of a puzzle. Even when the Late Paleo-Indian components in the western Great Lakes are added, population levels during the 4500 years of the Interregnum do not seem to have risen much, if at all, above those of the pioneering fluted-point period. South of the lakes the Early Archaic population was far higher. Why the difference?" (Mason 1981:131).

Because of the lack of well-excavated sites, archaeologists still know little about Early Archaic peoples in Wisconsin. On the basis of minimal evidence from the few excavated sites in the region, surface surveys, and negative evidence, and considering the environmental setting, it is reasonable to infer that Early Archaic people lived in small, widely scattered family or extended-family groups that had a highly mobile life based on diversified hunting and gathering. Kuehn (1998) examined faunal remains from the few well-excavated Late Paleoindian and Early Archaic sites in Wisconsin. He concluded that "in the Western Great Lakes, it is probable that lake, river, and wetland habitats were heavily exploited by Late Paleoindian and Early Archaic foragers" (Kuehn 1998:471).

In Wisconsin, the Early Archaic pattern is virtually indistinguishable from Late Paleoindian lifeways except for apparent differences in biface technology (Late Paleoindian: Cody-like biface forms; Early Archaic: bevel-resharpened stemmed and notched biface forms). Data from Renier, Gorto, Deadman Slough, and Bass suggest that these two technologies may have coexisted. We assume that the lithic technologies do, indeed, represent different people. If that assumption is true, we do not know the degree and type of interaction between these two distinctive groups. Further research may demonstrate that both technologies were, in fact, used by people of a single culture who gradually shifted to a more Archaic lifeway.

The Middle Archaic Stage: 4000 B.C.–1500 B.C. (RCYBC) (cal ca. 5000–1700 B.C.)

The appearance of the Middle Archaic stage in Wisconsin is marked by the development of several new technologies that include production of side-notched bifaces and ground-stone grooved axes and copper smithing. In addition to the changes in technology, for the first time in the region large (over 100 individuals) cemeteries appeared, suggesting an increase in population and the development of local group territories. The first substantial evidence of rockshelter occupation in Wisconsin also dates to this time. In terms of sheer numbers of sites and artifacts, the Middle Archaic stage is much more abundantly represented in the archaeological record of Wisconsin than the Paleoindian or Early Archaic stages. Surface collections invariably contain at least some evidence of this stage. Collectively, Middle Archaic data suggest a substantial increase in population.

As mentioned above, important technological innovations first appear in Wisconsin's archaeological record in the context of the Middle Archaic stage. These include polished-stone tools such as grooved axes and bannerstones, specialized fishing gear (e.g., hooks, gorges, and harpoons), copper tool manufacture, and ground-stone plant-processing tools (i.e., milling stones). The first direct evidence of shellfish exploitation (shell middens in the Mississippi Valley), the domesticated dog (at the Reigh site), and long-distance trade of exotic materials like marine shell (at the Oconto and Reigh sites) appears in this context. Since virtually all of these innovations and practices appear even earlier in the archaeological record elsewhere in eastern North America, earlier evidence of them may eventually be found in Wisconsin, as well. Meanwhile, as with everything else in the archaeological record, the dating of these Wisconsin "firsts" is accepted only tentatively, subject always to revision in light of new evidence.

The environmental context of these cultural developments was apparently a climatic episode of maximum warmth and dryness compared with both prior and subsequent periods. Paleobotanical research in northeastern Iowa and southern Wisconsin indicates that shortly after 4000 RCYBC, the main elements of the mesic deciduous forest (like elm, hornbeam, and basswood) were on the decline, while dry-adapted herbaceous plants were on the rise (Baker et al. 1992; Chumbley et al. 1990; Maher 1982; Winkler 1985; Winkler et al. 1986). Drier conditions meant more open woodlands interspersed with prairies, a richer habitat for browsing animals like deer and elk, especially in southern Wisconsin.

Fisheries in the Lake Michigan basin may also have improved at this time (Cleland 1982), for, by 3000 RCYBC, the progressively rising lake levels due to the isostatic rebound of the glacier-depressed bedrock along the north shore had reached, and then surpassed, modern levels. Thus, the third millennium RCYBC saw Lake Michigan standing at an elevation of 184 m (605 ft) amsl, over 6 m (20 ft) higher than its current levels, in what is referred to as the "Lake Nipissing high-water stage" (Anderton 1995; Hansel and Mickelson 1988; Larsen 1985).

Biface morphology is what most archaeologists have focused on to identify the presence of a Middle Archaic component. The side-notched point cluster is most often used as diagnostic. This general point style occurs in a number of named types, for example, Matanzas, Raddatz, Osceola, Oconto, Reigh, Madison, and so on, all of which share the general property of bilateral notches placed near the base and directed more or less at right angles to the long axis of the point (Figures 19.7–19.11). This is the earliest relatively well-dated projectile point style in Wisconsin, and nearly 20 radiocarbon dates place it within the interval between 3000 RCYBC and 1200 RCYBC (see Table 19.1).

Figure 19.7. Matanzas Side Notched projectile points from the Crow Hollow site.

The great morphological diversity observed among side-notched points in Wisconsin is likely a reflection of age or regional cultural differences or both. Thus, by careful attention to certain details (e.g., length vs. breadth, overall blade form, or size and placement of notches), temporal and spatial variants of the general side-notched style can probably be recognized and used to differentiate Middle Archaic cultures. However, two major difficulties beset anyone trying to make sense of the morphological diversity observed among large side-notched points: (1) the ranges of physical variation of the named types commonly overlap, so that individual points may simultaneously conform to the definitions of two or more types; and (2) many of the types were originally defined on the basis of small samples or collections that have no stratigraphic or radiometric evidence to confirm their relative or absolute ages.

This latter problem is particularly well illustrated by the Madison Side Notched type, which was originally defined on the basis of five specimens selected from a plow-disturbed, multicomponent site (Baerreis 1953a:154–155) (Figure 19.8). By giving this particular group of points formal, named, type status, archaeologists presumably are expressing the view that they connote a particular age or cultural affiliation distinct from other named types. Yet, no sound stratigraphic or radiometric evidence places these points in a discrete cultural context, while considerable evidence from larger collections at other sites suggests that these points are nothing more than one end of the range of morphological variation that is encompassed within other named types, especially Raddatz Side Notched and Reigh Side Notched (see Ritzenthaler 1957; Wittry 1959a, 1959b).

Figure 19.8. Type specimens of Madison Side Notched projectile points from the Airport Village site (47DA2).

At the present time, a conservative view would be to recognize only three side-notched projectile point types in Wisconsin: (1) Matanzas, (2) Raddatz (which includes Osceola and some Madison variants, as discussed below), and (3) Reigh (which includes Oconto and some Madison variants, also discussed below). This is not to say that no other side-notched types exist but, rather, that these three are associated with the most reliable contextual evidence (not just pure typology) to facilitate the recognition of temporal and spatial patterning among Middle Archaic cultures within Wisconsin.

The Matanzas Side Notched type is a member of a family or "cluster" of point types that is well-represented in Illinois (Cook 1976) but has rarely been recognized in Wisconsin. It is characterized by small, shallow, side notches placed close to the base of a point form that is of generally equal breadth immediately above and below the notches (Figure 19.7). This type is important because in Illinois it is well dated to the millennium 4000 to 3000 RCYBC (e.g., Brown and Vierra 1983; Cook 1976:70; Harris 2002:11). Recent examination of artifact collections from southwestern Wisconsin housed at the Wisconsin Historical Society, coupled with the recovery of this point type in buried contexts beneath Woodland levels at a stratified site in Prairie du Chien, confirms that this point type does, indeed, occur in southern Wisconsin. Additionally, this point type has been recently recovered from the Crow Hollow site, a single-component Middle Archaic site situated on the Kickapoo River floodplain in southwestern Wisconsin. A single uncalibrated radiocarbon date of 2380 ± 80 RCYBC was obtained from one of the five pit features encountered (Kuehn 1997, 2002). This date is somewhat younger than those reported for Matanzas in Illinois: 4000–3000 RCYBC (Harris 2002).

When it comes to the other two side-notched types, much firmer ground exists, for a substantial body of radiocarbon evidence places them within the 4000–1200 RCYBC interval in Wisconsin. The Raddatz Side Notched type is extremely common across the southern half of the state, especially in the southwest, where it occurs in stratified contexts within rockshelters and river valleys as well as in open-air sites in upland settings. Its hallmarks are broad, deep, side notches placed substantially above the base in such a way that the maximum breadth of each point is roughly equal both below and above the notches, while the haft area (below the notches) stands out as broadly rectangular (Figure 19.9). Morphologically, this type overlaps with other named types, both within Wisconsin (especially Osceola, Madison, and even most varieties of Matanzas) as well as elsewhere in the eastern United States. Raddatz projectile points have also been recovered in association with Old Copper artifacts (Stoltman 1997), and, at the Bobwhite site in Richland County, Raddatz projectiles were recovered within a feature containing a copper bracelet and a bannerstone (Finney et al. 1992).

Efforts to define clearly the morphological differences among Raddatz, Osceola, and Madison side-notched types within Wisconsin have so far met with failure. When the full range of side-notched points recovered from the Osceola type site in Grant County (only seven of the 38 side-notched points from the site have been published [Ritzenthaler 1957:199]) is systematically compared with the side-notched points recovered from the Raddatz Rockshelter (Wittry 1959a), no significant differences between them can be documented except that some of the Osceola points are larger. Since Osceola is a mortuary site and Raddatz is a campsite, the size difference observed in some of the points likely reflects nothing more than the difference between specially prepared grave

Figure 19.9. Raddatz Side Notched projectile points from various sites. Top row, Raddatz Rockshelter; bottom row, left two points, Durst Rockshelter; bottom row, right two points, Price III site.

goods and everyday spear points. If the term *Osceola* is to be used for a type, it should be reserved for large, side-notched mortuary bifaces (Figure 19.10). Similarly, the Madison Side Notched type, while different from Raddatz in having smaller, closer-to-the-base side notches and an overall form that has the greatest breadth at the base (rather than being equally broad both above and below the notches), really overlaps the range of variation present at the Raddatz type site (cf. Figures 19.8, 19.9). Until either stratigraphic or radiometric evidence becomes available to document the common inference that Madison Side Notched points postdate the Raddatz type, we prefer to consider these as variants of a single type whose age, on the basis of current radiocarbon evidence, falls within the interval 4000–1200 RCYBC (Table 19.1).

The Reigh Side Notched point type takes its name from a cemetery in Winnebago County (Figure 19.2). Contextual evidence clearly indicates that many of the larger points of this type were knives, but other smaller ones were presumably projectile points (Ritzenthaler 1957:249) (Figure 19.11). While only a few stone projectile points were recovered at the Oconto cemetery, they are closely similar to the Reigh points (Mason 1981:193; Ritzenthaler 1957:234, 249). What the points from the two sites have in common is a form whose breadth is proportionately greater compared to the length, when contrasted with the Matanzas and Raddatz clusters, and relatively shallow notches placed close to the base. In

Figure 19.10. Osceola Side Notched points from the Osceola site.

Figure 19.11. Reigh Side Notched knives and projectile points from the Reigh site.

this last respect, the smaller Reigh and Oconto points overlap with Madison Side Notched. As a generalization, the large side-notched points of eastern Wisconsin—variously called "Reigh," "Oconto," and "Madison"—differ from those of western Wisconsin, especially Raddatz/Osceola, in being broader (i.e., more "triangular") in proportion to their lengths and in having the notches inserted relatively closer to the base.

The Old Copper Industry: 4000 B.C.–1000 B.C. (RCYBC) (cal ca. 5000–1000 B.C.)

The most famous manifestation of the Middle Archaic stage in Wisconsin is the Old Copper industry (Martin 1999; Martin and Pleger 1999; Pleger 1998, 2000, 2001, 2003; Stoltman 1997). The term *Old Copper industry* was originally employed by McKern in 1942 to refer to the heavy copper-tool technology found in Wisconsin. Because such tools were not associated with mound-building or ceramic-producing cultures, he believed (correctly) that they predated the Woodland tradition, a viewpoint and terminology perpetuated by Quimby (1952) in his synthesis a decade later. Eventually, however, the term *culture* was adopted to link together a series of Old Copper mortuary sites with the thousands of surface-collected copper tools that had been previously known (Ritzenthaler 1957). In 1951, Miles argued that Old Copper artifact types did not represent a single culture and that they likely were products of an industry employed by multiple prehistoric societies. Stoltman, in 1986 and 1997, argued that Old Copper should not be conceptualized as a single cultural entity but viewed as a group of related cultures (referred to as a "complex") that shared a common technology. Martin and Pleger (1999) also used the term *complex* to describe Old Copper but stated that the term *industry* is also applicable.

Current data suggest that the Old Copper complex be viewed as a series of regional Middle and Late Archaic–stage cultures that shared a basic copper fabrication technology. The view of a single culture should be abandoned in favor of recognition that a series of cultures, over a 3,000 year span, existed within a large area that included much of the northern and western Great Lakes. We can justifiably call this manifestation old, and we can certainly call it copper, but we cannot call it a culture. Ironically, McKern's original Old Copper industry taxon makes sense even now, because it can be conceptualized as time transgressive, spanning Middle and Late Archaic times. [Martin and Pleger 1999:70]

Accordingly, in this chapter we return to McKern's original usage. The concept of "industry" is entirely appropriate given that archaeologists now know that Old Copper technology occurred widely in time and space, well beyond the limits of a single archaeological culture.

The Old Copper industry takes its name from the native metal from which a wide range of distinctive tools were fabricated (Figure 19.12). The sources of the copper are well known on the basis of archaeological and geological research in aboriginal mines and metallurgical and trace-element analyses of the copper itself (Griffin 1961; Rapp et al. 1990; West 1929). These studies confirm that the ancient lavas surrounding Lake Superior, especially on the Keweenaw Peninsula and on Isle Royale, where literally thousands of aboriginal open-pit mines occur, were the primary producers of the copper. Aboriginal people freed the copper from its bedrock matrix by lighting fires on top of or adjacent to appropriate rock exposures and then quenching them with cold water, thus, causing the bedrock to spall away. Stone hammers, which occur by the thousands in and around the mines, were then apparently used to finish the process of separating the copper from bedrock. In this manner, veins of copper were followed down from the surface, sometimes to depths of 6 m (20 ft) or more. The copper recovered in this way, referred to as "native" copper, is nearly 100 percent pure copper.

Figure 19.12. Sample of Old Copper tools from western Great Lakes, Menominee County Historical Society, Menominee, Michigan.

The manufacture of artifacts from native copper was done by cold hammering, followed by heating to relieve the accumulated stresses (referred to as "annealing"), then quenching in water, repeating these steps as often as necessary to complete the tool (LaRonge 2001; Vernon 1990). This repetitive process of heating and cooling was the critical discovery in fashioning sharp-edged tools or thin sheets from this material because it prevented the copper from becoming brittle, the normal outcome of prolonged cold hammering alone. One of the ironies of research on the Old Copper industry is that, until recently, virtually no manufacturing sites had been scientifically investigated despite wide recognition as early as 1920 that such sites never occurred at the mines and are best identified not by finished tools but by copper flakes and chips, the main by-products of the manufacturing process (West 1929).

Several possible copper workshop sites have been recently reported in Wisconsin. Moffat and Speth (1999) describe copper-working areas consisting of a series of pit features containing copper scrap and blanks, charcoal, and fire-cracked rock from the Rainbow Dam sites (47ON179 and 180) on the upper Wisconsin River. Although the sites are multicomponent, two radiocarbon dates (1680 ± 60 RCYBC and 1320 ± 80 RCYBC), one from each site, suggest the presence of Archaic occupation (Moffat and Speth 1999:155–156).

The second published report of a copper-working site comes from Little Rice Lake (47VI272) in Vilas County (Hunzicker 2002). The Little Rice Lake site is known from a surface-collected assemblage of finished and unfinished copper tools, two copper pieces in the process of being recycled, and a large quantity of copper scrap. Although no features were observed and no materials have been dated, the copper tools include a classic socketed copper point, suggesting a Middle Archaic affiliation for this assemblage. However, the only diagnostic lithic artifact from the site was an Agate Basin projectile point. Hunzicker postulated that the copper and the Late Paleoindian materials might be associated. Jack Steinbring (1968, 1975) has also proposed a similar association, arguing that some copper projectile points resemble Late Paleoindian Plano forms. However, the acceptability of these associations must still be regarded as problematic.

The copper artifact types considered diagnostic of Old Copper are found primarily in Wisconsin. Pioneer Wisconsin archaeologist George A. West (1929:60) once estimated that at least 20,000 copper artifacts occur in Wisconsin, in contrast to about 1,000 in the Upper Peninsula of Michigan and even fewer in adjacent portions of Minnesota and Ontario. These estimates surely can no longer be taken literally, but they do provide a useful relative scale of regional abundance.

The distribution of Old Copper artifacts within Wisconsin is far from uniform. In a study of some 2,600 selected Old Copper artifacts, Wittry (1957) documented that the vast majority occur in the eastern half of the state. Recently, William Gartner (pers. comm. 2003) has identified a significant number of Old Copper sites in the Stevens Point area, indicating that Wittry's original map does not accurately reflect the distribution of Old Copper materials in north-central Wisconsin. Additionally, as metal-detector availability to the public has increased, thousands of unreported Old Copper artifacts have been recovered by avocational collectors in the western Great Lakes over the last 10 years. Many of these artifacts have been recovered from once-submerged contexts along lake and river shorelines in the northern part of the state.

Old Copper tools are found throughout the entire Great Lakes region, but in the east they are less common than locally made ground-stone counterparts (Mason 2002). Classic Old Copper forms have also been recovered as far away from the Lake Superior basin core area as the eastern Dakotas, northwestern Ontario, Manitoba, and Alberta in the west (Gibbon 1998:45) and Maryland (Curry 2002) and New Jersey (Veit et al. 2004) in the east. Considering the wide dispersal of finished native copper artifacts, sophisticated mechanisms of intersocietal exchange such as formal trade partnerships are surmised to have been in existence by the Middle Archaic stage (Pleger 1998, 2000).

Most Old Copper artifacts appear to be utilitarian forms (i.e., tools and weapons) rather than items of personal adornment or status symbols. Typical artifact types include hunting gear (spear points), fishing gear (hooks, harpoons, and gorges), and woodworking gear (axes, adzes, celts, spuds, chisels, gouges, and wedges) as well as tools for performing such everyday tasks as food preparation or hide working (knives, awls, drills, punches, and spatulas). A wide range of typical Old Copper tools is shown in Figure 19.12. Among the relatively few Old Copper items that served more personal or ornamental purposes are beads, bracelets, rings, clasps (for clothing?), pendants, and, from the Reigh site, a unique headdress composed of a series of sheet-copper replicas of feathers (Ritzenthaler 1957:250–52) (Figure 19.13).

The vast majority of Old Copper artifacts have been recovered as surface finds, so their precise age and cultural context are no longer ascertainable. However, the accelerator mass spectrometry (AMS) technique has opened a new door on the age of the Old Copper industry by allowing dating of small bits of wood or textiles that are often preserved through direct contact with prehistoric copper artifacts. This approach has pushed the use of native copper on the north shore of Lake Superior back nearly to 5000 RCYBC (Beukens et al. 1992) and confirmed that a wooden shaft fragment still adhering to a conical copper point from northeastern Wisconsin dates to at least 2200 RCYBC (Pleger 1992). AMS dating was also used on string and charcoal fragments at Oconto to establish a 4000–3000 RCYBC age for the site (Pleger 1998, 2000, 2001). Recently, William Gartner (pers. comm. 2004) has obtained a series of AMS dates in the 3600s RCYBC on shaft fragments adhering to copper artifacts from north-central Wisconsin. Finally, there are now two yet-unpublished AMS dates from wooden shaft fragments associated with two copper conical points recovered

Figure 19.13. Copper feather-like forms from headdress with Burial 6 at the Reigh site.

as surface finds in Vilas County, Wisconsin (Mark Bruhy, pers. comm. 2004): 7690 ± 40 B.P. (5740 ± 40 RCYBC) from site 47VI46 (Beta 134256 AMS) and 7305 ± 60 B.P. (5355 ± 60 RCYBC) from site 47VI320 (WG613/AA-31977). These dates demonstrate that the beginnings of Old Copper metalsmithing extend back before the fifth millennium RCYBC.

Other than surface finds of diagnostic artifacts, the Old Copper industry is known in Wisconsin primarily from four burial sites. In the 1940s, 1950s, and 1960s, several Old Copper–related cemeteries were professionally excavated in Wisconsin. Three additional Old Copper–related sites were also excavated: one in the Upper Peninsula of Michigan (Riverside—discussed in the Late Archaic section of this chapter) and two on the Ottawa River along the Ontario-Quebec border (Morrison's Island-6 and Allumette Island-1 sites [Kennedy 1966; see Ellis et al., this volume]). Collectively, these sites produced the first undisturbed archaeological evidence about Old Copper mortuary behavior.

The Osceola Site, Grant County, Wisconsin

In 1945, two fishermen discovered artifacts and human remains eroding out of the bank of the Mississippi River near Potosi, Grant County, Wisconsin. Robert Ritzenthaler of the Milwaukee Public Museum subsequently conducted excavations at the site to determine the cultural affiliation of the artifacts (Overstreet 1988; Ritzenthaler 1946, 1957). The excavation revealed a massive burial pit containing human remains; copper tools (particularly awls), projectile points, and some ornamental items; and a series of flaked-stone artifacts. Lithic artifacts included side-notched Osceola points (Figure 19.10), bannerstones, T-shaped drills, and side-notched scrapers. The drills and scrapers appear to be manufactured from reduced Osceola side-notched points. The burial area consisted of a single massive feature filled with black sand. No ceramics were recovered in direct association with the burials, and there was no indication of mound construction. Radiocarbon dates obtained on samples from the burial pit ranged from approximately 2200 to 1250 RCYBC (see Table 19.1).

Human remains (in the form of bundle burials) and grave furniture were dispersed throughout the feature. Although a portion of the site had been destroyed, as many as 500 individuals are estimated to have been buried in this single grave pit. The excavators noted that the grave artifacts appeared to be offerings made to the entire corporate group rather than placed with any particular set of individuals. This pattern could be interpreted as indicative of an egalitarian social system.

The Oconto Site, Oconto County, Wisconsin

In 1952, a 13-year-old boy digging in an abandoned quarry outside of Oconto, Wisconsin, discovered human remains. Two local amateur archaeologists visited the site and recovered a series of copper, bone, stone, and shell artifacts in direct association with human skeletal material. The Milwaukee Public Museum and State Historical Society of Wisconsin were called to the site to excavate the remaining burials (Pleger 1998, 2000, 2001; Ritzenthaler 1957; Ritzenthaler and Wittry 1952; Wittry and Ritzenthaler 1956). Approximately 20 burial features were identified during the professional and amateur excavations. Unlike the Osceola site, here the burials were either single individuals or small groups in isolated graves. Burial modes included primary extended, primary flexed, bundle reburial, and cremation. The remains of approximately 50 individuals were recovered, but the excavators estimate that the cemetery may have contained as many as 200 prior to the quarrying activities. Grave artifacts included flaked, corner-notched projectile points similar to Madison Side Notched, bone and shell artifacts (marine shell and local freshwater shell), and a series of copper artifacts, including knives, awls, a fishhook, projectile points, a spiral, a bracelet, and unformed fragments. Of the bone artifacts, the most notable was a whistle or flute made from the wing bone of a tundra swan (Figure 19.14).

Figure 19.14. Replica of the Oconto flute or whistle from the Oconto Old Copper site.

It was buried with a young child who was accompanied by an adult female.

Pleger's (1998, 2000) analysis of the associated artifacts indicates that they were mostly utilitarian tools and that all but the marine shell could have been obtained locally in the western Great Lakes region. Additionally, the grave artifact distributions showed no dramatic preferential associations by age or sex. On the basis of the relatively uniform distribution and utilitarian nature of the grave artifacts, Pleger (1998, 2000) has suggested that the Oconto society was relatively egalitarian in character. If this community had high-status leaders, one would predict a pattern of dramatic differential treatment of the dead whereby some burials would have significantly more wealth than others. Although the people from Oconto participated in long-distance trade, as evidenced by the presence of marine shell apparently from the Gulf of Mexico, such trade, evidently, was minimal or sporadic.

The original radiocarbon dates (see Table 19.1) from Oconto (one of approximately 5560 RCYBC and a second of 3650 RCYBC) were rejected by some archaeologists, who argued that the site should be younger (see Pleger 2001 for a discussion of the age of the Oconto site). Another date was run in the 1970s on human bone; it indicated an age of approximately 2590 RCYBC. Because of the controversy surrounding the age of the site, Pleger ran two new dates using the more precise AMS radiocarbon technique (Table 19.1). One of these new dates was run on a copper-preserved string fragment. This sample produced a date of 4070 ± 60 RCYBC (AA19678/WG2404). The second date, run on a sample of charcoal, yielded a date of 3300 ± 110 RCYBC (AA20281/WG2413). Pleger (1998, 2000, 2001) argued that the site must date to between 4000 and 3000 RCYBC on the basis of the combined radiocarbon and geological evidence.

The Reigh Site, Winnebago County, Wisconsin

In the mid-1950s, burials were discovered at a quarry in Winnebago County, Wisconsin. Professional excavations were conducted by UW-Madison, and a series of salvage excavations was undertaken by several amateur archaeologists (Baerreis et al. 1954; Ritzenthaler 1957). The UW-Madison excavations revealed 44 individuals. Later salvage work uncovered two additional graves (Ostberg 1956). Burial modes included extended, flexed, bundle, and cremation. Red ocher (ground hematite) was present in some of the burials. Burial pits often contained more than one individual, and one individual was buried with a dog.

Grave artifacts included copper projectile points, awls, beads and necklaces, knives, celts, axes, and a unique headdress. The headdress consisted of a series of hammered copper strips in the shape of feathers (Figure 19.13). They were discovered surrounding the cranium of a male in a manner suggesting that they had originally been attached to a headband. Other grave artifacts included flaked-stone bifaces of the Reigh type (some of the larger ones clearly having served as hand-held knives, other smaller ones presumably projectile points; Figure 19.11), two distinctive elk antler handles (Figure 19.15), antler points and two worked swan humeri (Figure 19.16), three pearl beads, three eagle talons, and at least two marine shell artifacts (Baerreis et al. 1954; Ostberg 1956). One of the shell artifacts, a so-called sandal-sole gorget (Figure 19.16), is a distinctive type associated with burials of the Glacial Kame complex in the Midwest, especially in the contiguous parts of Ohio, Indiana, and Illinois (Cunningham 1948). It was made from marine shell that likely originated either in the Gulf of Mexico or south Atlantic Ocean (Figure 19.16).

Figure 19.15. Elk antler handles from the Reigh site.

The Reigh site has yielded a radiocarbon date of approximately 1700 RCYBC (see Table 19.1). The archaeological evidence at Reigh, unlike at Oconto, Osceola, or Price (see below), suggests that in some Old Copper societies differential statuses existed, presumably a reflection of personal achievements. Whether this evidence of greater intrasocietal differentiation should be viewed as a purely regional practice or the reflection of a temporal trend within later Old Copper societies is presently an open question.

The Price III Site, Richland County, Wisconsin

The Price III site (Figure 19.2) was excavated under the direction of Joan Freeman of the State Historical Society of Wisconsin in 1960 and 1961 as a highway salvage project. The site consisted of 26 features containing 130 individuals

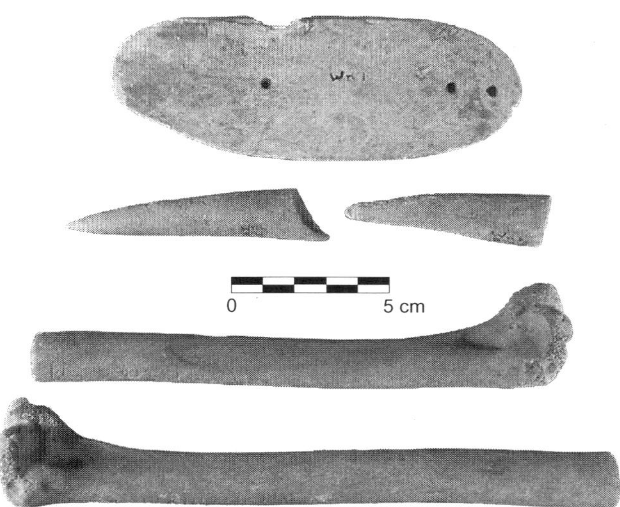

Figure 19.16. Sandal-sole gorget of marine shell (top), conical antler points (middle), and cut and notched swan humeri from the Reigh site.

(Freeman 1966). Burial modes included cremation, flexed primary burials, and bundle reburials. Red-ocher pigment was present with several burials, similar to the case at Reigh, and many burials were covered with a mantle of stone slabs. Feature 25 was the most noteworthy feature at the site. It consisted of a massive multicomponent burial pit containing six levels that three radiocarbon dates indicate represented an interval of time from 1330 ± 150 to 1760 ± 150 RCYBC (Freeman 1966:52–53). This feature contained 88 individuals.

Burial artifacts from Price III were minimal: four chert bifaces and a tip fragment that was embedded in a human vertebra, two conical antler points, a perforated bear canine, two fragments of worked human bone, and a copper fishhook (Freeman 1966:41–45). All of the complete chert bifaces have concave bases. Two are side-notched, one that can be considered to belong to the Osceola type and a smaller one that is a classic Raddatz. Freeman (1966:42–43) refers to a third as "Price Stemmed." Both the Price Stemmed and the fourth point, which has an expanding stem, may be the result of resharpening and may originally have been more similar to the two side-notched bifaces.

Final Observations on Old Copper Populations

Because Old Copper habitation sites are unknown or unrecognized, relatively little information is available about the daily lives of the people. A series of studies and observations made on some of the skeletal remains that were excavated have, however, produced some interesting insights. Susan Pfeiffer's (1977) study of Archaic skeletal biology of the Great Lakes included an examination of several Old Copper sites (Oconto, Osceola, Reigh, Morrison's Island, and Allumette Island) along with other Middle and Late Archaic cemeteries (Hind, Cole, Picton, Frontenac Island, and Riverside) from the Great Lakes. Although her study included both Middle and Late Archaic populations from over a large area, her observations shed light on Middle and Late Archaic lifeways in Wisconsin. She concluded that (with the exception of individuals from Morrison's Island and Allumette Island) adults rarely survived for more than ca. 30 years, and she noted that

> broken bones are common. The effects of disease and nutritional inadequacies are uncommon. The relative frequency of traumatic injury, when combined with the skeletal robusticity commonly noted indicates a very active way of life. Both men and women appear to have led a physically taxing routine. [Pfeiffer 1977:281]

Tre-min Hsu (1970) also observed that relatively few people at the Reigh site (only five of 28) had lived beyond the age of 34. Hsu also observed that teeth showed considerable wear, a condition normally associated with eating lots of gritty plant food. Complementing the latter observation are findings from bone-chemistry analyses of four individuals from Reigh and 53 individuals from Price III suggesting that, while meat was the predominant food eaten, plants could have constituted up to 40 percent of the diet of Old Copper people (Price 1985; Price et al. 1985).

Pleger (1998) analyzed elemental strontium- and barium-to-calcium ratios in human bone samples from Oconto. His results suggest that the Oconto Old Copper diets consisted of a relatively high proportion of animal resources and probably some plants (Pleger 1998:281). One final observation about the skeletal remains recovered from the Old Copper cemeteries pertains to the Price III site, where, as mentioned, a human vertebra was recovered with the tip of a stone projectile point embedded in it (Freeman 1966:43). This is the earliest unequivocal evidence of human assault on other humans in the archaeological record of Wisconsin.

Other than the Old Copper industry, relatively little is known about the Middle Archaic stage in Wisconsin except what can be gleaned from surface collections. The main exception to this generalization occurs in the Driftless Area of southwestern Wisconsin. In this region, rockshelters (Figure 19.2) like Raddatz, Durst, Lawrence I, Brogley, and Governor Dodge (Wittry 1959a, 1959b) have been carefully excavated and have produced excellent Middle Archaic assemblages, many of which have been radiocarbon dated.

The hallmark of these assemblages is the Raddatz Side Notched projectile point, the same type that occurs at both the Osceola and Price III sites. Stratigraphically, the Raddatz levels usually constitute the earliest evidence of intensive human occupation in rockshelters, and they are typically overlain by Late Archaic and Woodland components. Because of dry conditions within the rockshelters, bone preservation is excellent. Human burials are virtually never found there, but, in contrast to the open-air cemeteries, the discarded bones of animals that were butchered and eaten are abundant. These remains are especially informative about diet, and they also can be used to infer the seasons of occupation. Not surprisingly, white-tailed deer is the predominant animal found in these rockshelters, but a wide range of smaller game also occurs (Parmalee 1959). Fish and migratory waterfowl are rare. Deer skulls are typically in the antlerless stage. Male deer shed their antlers in mid-December and remain antlerless until April. The implications of these latter data are that the rockshelters were primarily used as short-term, seasonal encampments, especially in the late fall and winter (Emerson 1979; Parmalee 1959:89). Further support for this view comes from the Brogley Rockshelter in Grant County, where the flotation of soil samples from Middle Archaic levels produced abundant fragments of fall-ripening walnut, hickory, and hazel (Tiffany 1974).

Because copper artifacts are seldom found in the rockshelters—there is but a single reported occurrence of a fragment of an Old Copper spear in one rockshelter (Wittry 1959b:227)—the relationship of the Middle Archaic occupants of the rockshelters to the Old Copper industry has long been regarded as uncertain. Wittry (1959a:65, 1959b:251) took the position that these rockshelter levels were simply seasonal occupation sites of the Old Copper people, who, for whatever reasons, had been careful not to leave any of their precious copper tools behind. This is a reasonable interpretation, particularly when one considers that the same type of stone projectile points turn up in the rockshelters and in the Osceola and Price cemeteries and that the available radiocarbon dates for the Old Copper cemeteries and the "Raddatz" components in the rockshelters fall in the same time interval.

One other possible Middle Archaic–stage occupation site that has been excavated is the Squirrel Dam site, a small, single-component camp in Oneida County (Figure 19.2). The unique assemblage from this site contains at least one side-notched point along with expanding-stemmed points and Old Copper–like tools (Salzer 1974:45–46). Since no radiocarbon dates are available from Squirrel Dam, its age is currently unknown, but on typological grounds, it can reasonably be seen as representing yet another regional variant of the Old Copper industry.

Recent excavations at Carcajou Point in Jefferson County (Figure 19.2) by UW-Milwaukee (Jeske et al. 2002) have led to the first formal recognition of a southeastern Wisconsin variant of the Middle Archaic stage. Termed the "Kelly North phase," it has been identified on the basis of a series of excavated features and stratigraphic layers that have produced assemblages that include Kelly Notched, Matanzas, and Vosburg bifaces, a T-drill, a copper conical point, and a series of awls. Radiocarbon dates from contexts associated with these artifacts suggest a temporal range of 2890–1300 RCYBC (calibrated one-sigma range) (Jeske et al. 2002:26). Lithic materials appear to be primarily of local origin, and the investigators note high levels of heat alteration. The variety of projectile point forms, particularly those not previously recognized in Wisconsin, may represent connections to Illinois. Jeske et al. (2002:26) suggest that, morphologically, the projectile points are similar to Helton-phase materials in Illinois, but they date to the period of the later Titterington phase. Daniel Winkler has recently examined Middle and Late Archaic assemblages from sites in southeast Wisconsin. He has identified sites there and in northeastern Illinois that appear to fit formally and temporally within the proposed Kelly North phase:

> The examination of the sites in southeastern Wisconsin and northeastern Illinois suggests that the transitional Middle to Late Archaic occupations at the Kelly North Tract at Carcajou Point, the Storrs Lake Site, the Garrison Site, and the McGraw Farm Site are all possibly part of the proposed Kelly North Phase. These occupations employed similar lithic procurement strategies, and utilized morphologically similar projectile points. These four sites compose the provisional Kelly North Phase of the Eastern Archaic. . . . The presence of nearby sites with similar lithic economies and projectile points suggests this lithic economy functioned over an area encompassing southeastern Wisconsin and northeastern Illinois between approximately 5000 and 3100 B.P. The transitional Middle to Late Archaic occupations at these sites are provisionally being assigned to the proposed Kelly North Phase of the Archaic, with the Kelly North Tract at Carcajou Point functioning as the type site. [Winkler 2004:283–285]

Further research in southeastern Wisconsin is needed to better understand the relationship of the Kelly North phase to other previously reported Middle and Late Archaic phases in Wisconsin.

The Late Archaic Stage: 1500 B.C.–500 B.C. (RCYBC) (cal ca. 1700 B.C.–400 B.C.)

The Late Archaic stage is marked by the appearance of several new cultural practices. Side-notched biface technology faded from the archaeological record and a variety of new forms emerged, including corner-notched (Preston Notched; Figure 19.17), expanding-stem (Durst Stemmed; Figure 19.18), and straight- and contracting-stemmed varieties (Waubesa Contracting Stem and Kramer Stemmed; Figure 19.19). Terminal Late Archaic peoples produced a variety of ritual biface styles (Turkey-tail and Adena; Figures 19.19–19.21) specifically for mortuary use as grave furniture. These finely crafted knives and projectile points were often made from imported blue-gray (Hornstone varieties) and white (Burlington) cherts. The presence of these exotic materials in Late Archaic graves along with Knife River flint, marine shell, and even obsidian indicates a dramatic increase in trade. Copper continued in use, but there was a shift toward the increased production of personal ornaments rather than tools.

These cultural changes coincided with subtle environmental changes. For example, paleobotanical research in southern Wisconsin documents the replacement of oak savanna by closed

Figure 19.17. Preston Notched/"Monona Stemmed" points from various sites. Top row, Durst Rockshelter; bottom row, left four points, Preston Rockshelter; bottom right, Blackhawk Village type specimen for Monona Stemmed.

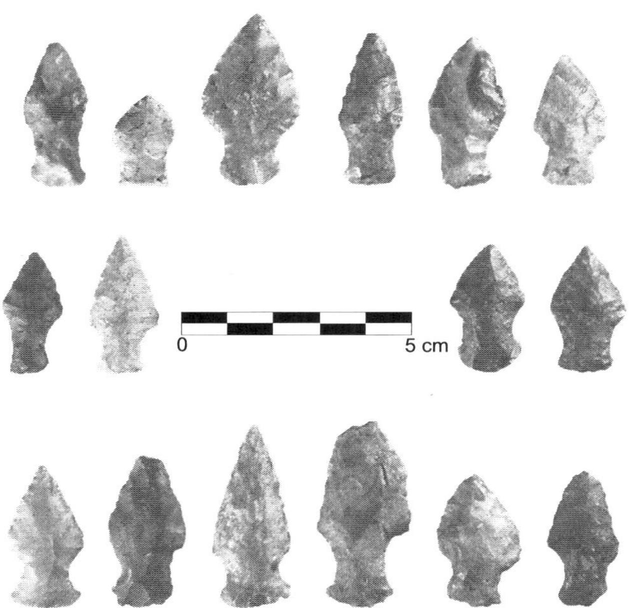

Figure 19.18. Durst Stemmed points from the Durst Rockshelter.

oak forest over much of the area after about 1500 RCYBC, suggesting the establishment of moister, essentially modern, climatic conditions (Baker et al. 1992; Winkler et al. 1986). Similarly, lake levels in the Lake Michigan basin declined from the Nipissing high-water stage after 1500 RCYBC, eventually attaining modern levels shortly before the time of Christ (Larsen 1985). However, these seemingly minor changes in environmental conditions are unlikely to account for the most drastic cultural changes observed at any particular time during the span of the Archaic tradition.

The Late Archaic stage in Wisconsin is known from Red Ocher cemeteries, from rockshelter excavations in the southwestern part of the state, and from what has been gleaned from surface collections and excavations of plow-disturbed sites elsewhere. Two Late Archaic phases can now be recognized, but the contexts on which they are based permit the identification of few differences between them other than projectile point styles.

The earliest-known Late Archaic phase, Preston, is named for a rockshelter in Grant County that was excavated between 1966 and 1969 by Harris Palmer of UW-Platteville. A comprehensive report of these excavations has not been published, but a brief description appears in Stoltman (1997), in which the Preston phase was first proposed.

The excavations, which were halted at a depth of about 3 m (10 ft), apparently well above the base of the archaeological deposits, revealed a deeply stratified site that had been recurrently occupied in prehistory. The uppermost levels contained artifacts from two or three episodes of Woodland occupation, beneath which were two Late Archaic components. Excavations appear to have stopped near the base of the Late Archaic levels. The presence of these two stratigraphically superimposed Late Archaic occupations is unique in Wisconsin and provides the primary basis for distinguishing the Preston from the Durst phase (for a discussion of the latter, see below). On the basis of these data, it can be seen in retrospect that Preston-phase occupations had been encountered previously in other Driftless Area rockshelters but were misidentified as Middle Woodland (see below).

The hallmark of the Preston phase is a small (ca. 4.5 cm [2 inch] long), diagonal- to side-notched projectile point with clear, angular shoulders, here referred to as "Preston Notched" (Figure 19.17). Close analogies for these points occur in the Riverton culture in southern Illinois, where they are variously referred to as Merom Expanding Stem and Trimble Side Notched (Winters 1969). The Riverton culture is well dated by radiocarbon to the interval 1500–1000 RCYBC (Winters 1969:105). The typologically defined Late Archaic Burnt-Rollways phase of northern Wisconsin is also characterized by Preston Notched–like projectile points (Salzer 1974:46–47).

Preston Notched points are abundant at the type site, where their stratigraphic context is consistently below Durst Stemmed points. A charcoal sample from a level that had produced three Preston Notched points along with one Durst Stemmed point yielded a radiocarbon age of 830 ± 65 RCYBC (WIS-941). Given evidence of cultural mixing, this date—the only one currently available that could pertain to the Preston phase—must be regarded with caution. Considering the close cultural affinities to the well-dated Merom Expanding Stem and Trimble Side Notched points of the Riverton culture in Illinois, along with the few available radiocarbon dates for the stratigraphically younger Durst Stemmed type in Wisconsin (see below), an age of 1500 to 1000 RCYBC for the Preston phase seems most appropriate.

Figure 19.19. Additional Red Ocher biface forms. Lawrence University collections.

Figure 19.20. Turkey-tails from Marinette County. Wisconsin Historical Society collections.

The pioneering excavations of Warren Wittry (1959b) at the Knoop and Durst rockshelters in Sauk County apparently encountered evidence of Preston occupations that were mistakenly attributed to Middle Woodland peoples. Wittry erroneously dated the small, notched points that he excavated from these sites, equating them with the poorly known "Monona Stemmed" type. Since the latter was defined on the basis of a single projectile point recovered from a surface context at the multicomponent Blackhawk Village site in Madison (Baerreis 1953b:10), its age was uncertain; moreover, as a single-specimen type, there was really no way to demonstrate objectively how much morphological variability should be included within Monona Stemmed. Systematic comparison of the "Monona Stemmed" points recovered by Wittry from the Knoop and Durst rockshelters with the Preston Notched points from the Preston type site leaves little doubt that they are the same type (see Figure 19.17).

The Late Archaic cultural context for this type is clearly demonstrable at Preston, and the same case can be made for the Durst Rockshelter, as well. The cultural stratigraphy at Knoop and Durst is difficult to interpret because of the sandy soils, which allow easy postdepositional intermixture of artifacts, and because the sites were excavated in arbitrary levels. Only the Durst site had deep enough deposits and yielded large enough artifact samples to allow meaningful inferences to be drawn concerning cultural stratigraphy. If one assumes that the mean depths of artifact types within a site excavated in arbitrary levels offer the most reliable index of relative age, the expected relative depths (thus, ages) of the three main Archaic projectile point types recovered at Durst should be Raddatz Side Notched deepest, Preston Notched ("Monona Stemmed") in the middle, and Durst Stemmed shallowest. As can be seen from the following relative mean depths in inches, this is exactly what occurs: Raddatz, 23.8 inches; Preston, 16.7 inches; Durst, 15.3 inches. Accordingly, it seems reasonable to infer that a Preston component was present at the Durst Rockshelter, just as at the Preston Rockshelter.

Stratigraphically superimposed above the Preston component at the Preston Rockshelter, and presumably also at the Durst Rockshelter, was a second Late Archaic component, one characterized by the distinctive Durst Stemmed projectile point type (Wittry 1959b). Durst Stemmed points are similar in size to Preston Notched but differ in having more rounded, "upturned" shoulders and proportionately narrower basal widths (Figure 19.18). As with Preston Notched, Durst Stemmed has well-known analogies outside of Wisconsin, again raising the possibility of the importance of external influences in the shaping of the Late Archaic stage in the state. Rather than looking to the south, however, it is to the east, in Indiana and Michigan and all the way into New York, that the closest relatives of Durst Stemmed points are to be found, in what is now referred to as the "Lamoka" cluster (Justice 1995:127–130).

Radiocarbon dates from two Driftless Area rockshelters suggest that the Durst phase dates to the interval 1000–500 RCYBC, perhaps lingering on in some places until near the time of Christ. These dates are 110 ± 50 RCYBC (P-2464), 620 ± 70 RCYBC (P-2466), and 620 ± 70 RCYBC (P-2465) for the Lawrence I Rockshelter and 760 ± 65 RCYBC (WIS-946) for the Preston Rockshelter (see Table 19.1 for calibrated dates).

Considering the stylistic dissimilarities between the large, side-notched projectile points that characterize the Middle Archaic stage and the small, notched and stemmed points that are the hallmarks of the Late Archaic stage, it seems reasonable to postulate the appearance of a major technological innovation. Recently, Boszhardt has suggested a likely possibility for what this innovation may have been: "Middle Archaic side-notched tips were fixed directly to main spear shafts, a configuration that gave way in Late Archaic times to compound darts with wood foreshafts armed with 'small' points" (2002:58).

Just as the Archaic tradition began across Wisconsin in a time-transgressive fashion, so, too, it probably ended, earlier in the south, later in the north. The period between

Figure 19.21. Adena and ellipsoidal bifaces from Riverside (20ME01).

500 RCYBC and 100 RCYBC probably saw the replacement of the Archaic tradition by the Woodland tradition across most of Wisconsin. The nature of this cultural transition is poorly understood because of the incompleteness of the archaeological record during this period. The Woodland tradition may have been introduced into parts of southern Wisconsin by an influx of new people or new ideas from the south, but the evidence in this regard is far from conclusive. The vast majority of native Wisconsinites must have continued their basic lifestyles, depending primarily on hunting and gathering, adopting, first, the new technology of pottery manufacture, and only later incorporating the practices of mound burial and plant cultivation into their cultural repertoire.

The Red Ocher Complex—The Transition from Archaic to Woodland: 1200 B.C.–500 B.C. (RCYBC) (cal ca. 1500 B.C.–400 B.C.)

Red Ocher is a term originally applied to hematite-covered burials and associated artifacts recovered from beneath burial mounds in the Illinois River valley, where their Woodland affiliation was postulated (Cole and Deuel 1937:202). The term was subsequently expanded to include mortuary sites extending across the Midwest from southern Ontario and Ohio in the east through the states of Michigan, Indiana, Illinois, and Wisconsin into Iowa and the upper Mississippi River valley in the west (Ritzenthaler and Quimby 1962). Since the preponderance of these latter sites were not associated with either mounds or pottery, a Late Archaic affiliation for at least a portion of the Red Ocher complex was generally accepted (Pleger 1998, 2000, 2003; Ritzenthaler and Quimby 1962:243; Stevenson et al. 1997; Stoltman 1986; Theler and Boszhardt 2003).

Information about Wisconsin's Red Ocher complex is limited almost exclusively to mortuary data. In both Wisconsin and Michigan, Red Ocher sites have been identified primarily by the presence of red ocher powder or a mixture of red ocher and red sand (Mikkola 1970) placed on burials that usually have caches of exotic bifaces, copper beads, and, occasionally, marine-shell beads. Great Lakes cultures earlier than Red Ocher also used red pigment in their burial ceremonies, as seen at Old Copper cemeteries such as Oconto, Reigh, and Morrison's Island.

Many aspects of the Red Ocher mortuary complex are reminiscent of Old Copper. The most common mode of burial is primary interment of the corpse in a flexed position in a pit typically excavated into a natural ridge or knoll. Bundle reburials, multiple burials, and cremations also occur, but unlike Old Copper, primary extended burials are rare or absent. In general, the use of copper for heavy tools decreased during Red Ocher times (Pleger 1998, 2000, 2003). Copper artifacts such as socketed projectile points, woodworking tools, and fishing gear, all common in earlier Old Copper burials, were replaced in Red Ocher cemeteries by copper beads and other ornaments. Copper awls, knives, and celts, however, were still common. Red Ocher burials often contain strands of copper beads made by folding, bending, and hammering strips of copper around cords or dowels. Binford (1962) was the first to suggest that this apparent shift from tools to ornaments reflects an important change in how copper was used, first as a utilitarian raw material and then as an indicator of the higher status of certain individuals. This change suggests growing social complexity and the development of different status levels between individuals and, perhaps, family lineages within Red Ocher communities. Whether Red Ocher cemeteries contain the remains of all members of the society or only those of higher status is not known.

Over 20 probable Red Ocher sites have been reported in Wisconsin and the Upper Peninsula of Michigan (Ritzenthaler and Quimby 1962; Stoltman 1986). Many of them were discovered before the 1940s and were not professionally excavated. Only one site in Wisconsin, Convent Knoll (Figure 19.2) in Waukesha County, has been thoroughly excavated using modern archaeological techniques (Overstreet 1980). Convent Knoll contained four Red Ocher burial features and the remains of eight individuals, several of whom showed evidence of traumatic death, including partial dismemberment. The only other major, professionally excavated Red Ocher site in the region is the Riverside Cemetery located just across the Wisconsin state line in Menominee County, Michigan.

The Riverside Cemetery site is perhaps the most thoroughly studied Red Ocher cemetery site in the Upper Great Lakes (Hruska 1967; Papworth 1967; Pleger 1998, 2000). The Riverside Cemetery represents a Late Archaic society that has elements of both Old Copper and Red Ocher cultural practices (Pleger 1998, 2000). This site lies on a sandy knoll along a bend in the Menominee River near the city of Menominee, Michigan, across the river from Marinette, Wisconsin. The cemetery contained the remains of over 75 individuals and over 80 features. The Riverside and Convent Knoll sites have provided the most comprehensive information to date regarding Red Ocher ceremonialism in Wisconsin and the Upper Peninsula.

As discussed above, Red Ocher burial ceremonialism probably evolved in the region out of Old Copper–related cultures. Supporting evidence comes from burial artifacts found at Riverside, where some burials dating to the first millennium RCYBC contained classic Old Copper–industry artifacts. One burial in particular (Spaulding's Burial No. 6) suggested a transition between Old Copper and Red Ocher. This flexed burial of an adult male was covered with red ocher and contained grave furniture including socketed and tanged copper projectile points, two dog skulls, beaver-tooth tools, hide scrapers, worked animal bones, including a section of caribou antler, a series of scrapers, including two made of Knife River flint, and corner-notched, chipped-stone projectile points (Hruska 1967:149; Pleger 1998:138). Two of the three points resemble Preston Notched, and the third is a deeply corner-notched point (see Figure 19.22). This feature has been radiocarbon dated to 1090 ± 150 RCYBC (M-658) (Pleger 1998:127). A similar deeply corner-notched point was recovered at Convent Knoll (Overstreet 1980:62), and one was found at the McCollum site, an undated Old Copper site on the southeastern shore of Lake Nipigon, Canada (Griffin and Quimby 1961).

Red Ocher ceremonial flaked-stone bifaces range from double-pointed ovals to notched and stemmed varieties such as Turkey-tail and Adena (contracting) stemmed types (Figures 19.19–19.21). In addition to blue-gray hornstone bifaces, Red Ocher sites have yielded elaborately made chipped-stone knives, some over 30 cm (1 ft) long, made of materials that closely resemble Burlington cherts from southeast Iowa or west-central Illinois (Figure 19.22). These artifacts have been found throughout Wisconsin since the late 1800s (see Halsey 1972; Overstreet 1980; Ritzenthaler and Quimby 1962; Stevenson et al. 1997; Stoltman 1986). No debitage of these exotic cherts has been found at Red Ocher sites, suggesting that the artifacts were obtained in finished form by trade. Red Ocher biface caches also probably are representative of an interregional exchange system that focused on the procurment of exotica to reinforce the status of certain individuals and families (Krakker 1997; Pleger 1998, 2000).

Other high-status exotic materials have been reported from Red Ocher–complex mortuary sites. Burials sometimes have contained marine-shell beads and worked shell from the Gulf Coast of Mexico and the southeast Atlantic seacoast. Perhaps the most unusual burial artifact is a 1.46-kg (3.2-lb) block, or core, of obsidian found at the Riverside site (Figure 19.23) that has been identified as deriving from Obsidian Cliff in Yellowstone National Park, Wyoming (Griffin et al. 1969). It was wrapped in bark resting on strands of 102 copper beads covered with red ocher and placed with the cremated remains of a young woman and an infant (Papworth 1967; Pleger 2000). Pleger AMS dated two samples from this feature. One sample consisted of a leather fragment used to string together the copper beads; it produced the following date: 545 ± 65 RCYBC (AA20282/WG2414). The second sample was run on a fragment of the birch bark; it yielded the following date: 830 ± 65 RCYBC (AA19677/WG2403). This is one of the earliest known uses of obsidian in the Great Lakes region outside of the Paleoindian tradition and provides further evidence of a far-reaching trade system during Red Ocher times.

Figure 19.22. Riverside Burial No. 6 Preston-like and corner-notched points, University of Michigan collections.

Besides the use of exotic burial artifacts, additional mortuary patterns indicate that Red Ocher social organization was more complex than that of preceding Old Copper–industry cultures. Riverside's burial population included both adults and juveniles interred with high-status items, and the bulk of the grave goods were buried with young children and adult females (Pleger 2000). At least two child burials contained lavish burial artifacts. One burial of a red-ocher-covered fetus was wrapped in 92 round and tubular copper beads accompanied by a copper celt. Another, in which only the child's teeth survived, contained 110 flaked-stone bifaces

Figure 19.23. Block of obsidian from Riverside (20ME01). University of Michigan collections.

(Hruska 1967; Pleger 1998, 2000). Similar treatment of a juvenile was reported at Convent Knoll, where a child no more than six years old was buried with a 33-cm (13-inch) long ceremonial white chert knife, a corner-notched projectile point, a copper awl, a piece of worked antler, and a strand of shell beads (Overstreet 1980). Interpreting the significance of placing such items with women and children is difficult. Pleger has suggested

> that the Riverside data represent a non-egalitarian society in which there were some high-status males; however, prestige appears to have attached more to young women and children, who were potential mates. This pattern could be interpreted as a reflection of the importance of reproduction and perpetuation of kin-groups. It may also reflect the existence of arranged marriages and the presence of some type of bridewealth system associated with high-status families or lineages. I also suggest that some of the lavish fetus, infant and young child burials at Riverside might reflect a belief in reincarnation. [2000:186]

Several burials at Riverside and Convent Knoll exhibited evidence of violent death, including projectile points embedded in bone. The Convent Knoll burials seem to represent a single episode in which eight people were killed and at least three were partially dismembered (Overstreet 1980). Such evidence of violent death is suggestive of population growth and its resulting stresses as territories were recognized and contested within the region. Late Archaic cultures likely competed for both local and exotic resources.

In Wisconsin, no living sites have been conclusively linked to Red Ocher, and little is known about habitation sites or ways of life during the Archaic-to-Woodland transition. Presumably, subsistence was based on hunting and gathering seasonally available resources such as wild plants, nuts, berries, migrating waterfowl, fish, deer, and other mammals. Fishing gear, in the form of toggle-head harpoons, fixed-barb harpoons, fishhooks, and, possibly, nets, was in use by Red Ocher times (Pleger 1992). These tools provided the means for effectively harvesting a variety of fish, including sturgeon. During the preceding Archaic, Lake Michigan's surface level had fluctuated drastically, by 30 m (100 ft) or more, but by about 500 RCYBC, it had begun to stabilize, perhaps increasing aquatic food resources along lake and river-mouth shorelines. Sturgeon bone was found within grave fills at the Riverside site (Hruska 1967), and a comparison of elemental bone-chemistry signatures between Riverside and Oconto human populations suggests an increase in fish consumption during Late Archaic times (Pleger 1998). A contemporary cremation burial from the Dunn Farm site in Leelanau County, in Lower Michigan, yielded burned grains of wild rice harvested during the late summer (Ford and Brose 1975), the oldest reported account of wild rice in the western Great Lakes. Since the sturgeon and wild rice were from burials, they might have been ceremonial offerings rather than common foods, but they do show that these resources were collected.

As with Old Copper, Red Ocher as a taxon cannot be regarded as an archaeological culture: it is a distinctive set of mortuary practices that recurs cross-culturally through both space and time (Stoltman 1983:220). Its roots may be traced into the Middle Archaic stage (evidence of continuity with Old Copper mortuary practices has already been cited), while its persistence can be documented through the Late Archaic stage (arguably, its primary context within Wisconsin) and, apparently, into the Early Woodland stage.

The association of Red Ocher mortuary ceremonialism with mound construction, a widely accepted hallmark of the Woodland tradition, has been suspected ever since the complex was first recognized (Cole and Deuel 1937). Pottery, that most classic of all Woodland diagnostics, has also been attributed to some Red Ocher sites. Patrick Munson (1966) has long advocated the view that Red Ocher mortuary ceremonialism was associated, in its later stages, with the Early Woodland Marion culture, characterized by its twin hallmarks of Marion Thick pottery and Kramer Stemmed projectile points. In recent years Munson's view has received wide acceptance (e.g., Esarey 1986; Green and Schermer 1988; Stoltman 1983), although not without some dissent (e.g., Ozker 1982).

Further support for the Marion culture-Red Ocher association was uncovered at the Tillmont site near Prairie du Chien in Crawford County, Wisconsin. Here, in a deeply buried paleosol, Marion Thick pottery and Kramer Stemmed projectile points were recovered in association with several red-ocher-stained basins (although with no burials) and seven obsidian flakes (with Obsidian Cliff chemical signatures), all dating to the sixth century RCYBC (Stoltman and Hughes 2004). What is especially important about this assemblage is the association of Obsidian Cliff obsidian in a temporal context virtually identical to that of the only other known occurrence—at the Riverside Cemetery—of obsidian in a pre-Hopewell context in the Eastern Woodlands. At the very least, an interactive relationship must be postulated to have existed between peoples possessing the Red Ocher complex and the Marion culture.

But the relationship between the Red Ocher complex and the Early Woodland stage is even more complicated than the oft-cited Marion-Red Ocher association. Some evidence also suggests that Red Ocher mortuary ceremonialism may have been practiced by peoples who made incised-over-cordmarked pottery. At the Riverside site, such pottery was found within the Red Ocher burial area, although not directly associated with the burials themselves. At the Henschel site in Sheboygan County (Overstreet et al. 1996), a mound with red-ocher-stained human bones also contained incised-over-cordmarked pottery along with contracting-stemmed projectile points, artifact types that characterize the Early Woodland Black Sand culture (e.g., Munson 1982). However, in the absence of direct associations of pottery with Red Ocher burials at Riverside and a total absence of diagnostic Red Ocher artifact types at Henschel (see Ritzenthaler and Quimby 1962), claims of an association of the Red Ocher mortuary complex with any regional variant of Black Sand culture must be viewed with appropriate skepticism.

Discussion and Conclusions

In this chapter, we have discussed the Archaic tradition in Wisconsin as a cultural-historical sequence of a series of related post-Pleistocene cultures that shared, in polythetic fashion, the following cultural practices:

1. Generalized hunting and gathering subsistence strategies
2. Aceramic technology
3. The use of cemeteries for multiple interments without the construction of mounds (burials in natural rises or knolls)
4. The manufacture of chipped-stone bifaces of various diagnostic stemmed and notched types.

While these four diagnostic properties can be inferred to have characterized most cultures dating between 8000 RCYBC and 500 RCYBC in Wisconsin, the archaeological record for this broad interval is so incomplete that the formal assignment of specific sites or cultures to the Archaic tradition has depended heavily on the *presence* of but one of them: diagnostic projectile points. Additionally, the *absence* of pottery and burial mounds has been an important marker, but reliance on such negative evidence is not without its problems. Since the properties used to define the Archaic tradition and to delimit its stages are all cultural in character, their appearance in time and space was variable. Moreover, they did not necessarily appear in any place as a "package," for all had complex, individual histories of their own.

In Wisconsin, the Early Archaic stage is marked by the widespread use of bevel-resharpened biface technology exemplified by the types Hardin Barbed, Thebes, and St. Charles. These projectile points co-occur with Cody-related materials. Archaeologists assume that bevel-resharpened technology represents a different cultural pattern from the Paleoindian pattern, but the presence of these styles together with Late Paleoindian materials is cause to doubt this assumption. A great deal is unknown about the transition from Late Paleoindian to Early Archaic. There are no radiocarbon dates for the Early Archaic in Wisconsin, and no multiple-grave cemeteries have been identified, suggesting that people were still relatively nomadic.

The transition from Middle to Late Archaic can be observed in the archaeological record in the region by the widespread use of side-notched bifaces, the development of the Old Copper industry, and the use of ground-stone tools. These technologies, coupled with the occurrence of multiple-grave cemeteries and the beginnings of long-distance trade, are what we consider formal attributes that demonstrate a change in lifeways during the mid-Holocene. All of these cultural practices were in place by 4000 RCYBC in the region. The projectile point sequence is not completely understood; some recognized types may be regional contemporary variants of larger clusters, while others may represent temporal variation. Rockshelter excavations have identified a consistent temporal sequence of types for southwestern and south-central Wisconsin, but this sequence may not apply to northern and southeastern Wisconsin. The newly identified Kelly North phase is characterized by a Middle to Late Archaic projectile point sequence that is unique to southeast Wisconsin and perhaps northern Illinois.

The best-known and most-studied Middle Archaic manifestation in Wisconsin is the Old Copper industry. Previous investigators have viewed Old Copper as a single culture or as a series of cultures sharing a copper industry. New data suggest that classic Old Copper tools are distributed across wide temporal and spatial boundaries, and the cemetery sites in Wisconsin and adjacent areas indicate that copper technology was shared by many Middle Archaic peoples. Because of these patterns, we argue that Old Copper should be viewed as an industry, much the way McKern (1942) originally conceived the term. Old Copper technology may very well have had its roots in Early Archaic–stage lifeways, but the excavated cemetery sites are clearly linked to Middle and early Late Archaic cultural patterns. A temporal range of 4000–1000 RCYBC is suggested for the widespread use of heavy Old Copper tools, but the use of copper for some tool forms continued into Woodland times and beyond.

Late Archaic–stage lifeways (1500–500 RCYBC) in Wisconsin are observed in the archaeological record by the development of a variety of stemmed and notched projectile point forms. Many of these are smaller in size when compared with their Middle Archaic predecessors. These smaller Late Archaic forms may be indicative of the use of foreshafts (Boszhardt 2002). Late Archaic sites appear to be more numerous and are larger in size than earlier sites. Some evidence indicates that some Late Archaic peoples increased their dependence on fish and other aquatic resources.

The most notable terminal Late Archaic cultural manifestation in the region is the Red Ocher complex. Red Ocher mortuary sites in the region show a dramatic increase in procurement of exotic materials, including marine shell, Knife River flint, blue-gray cherts, and even obsidian. Red Ocher peoples also utilized copper more for ornamentation than for tools. From the perspective of Red Ocher, Late Archaic populations appear to have been more complex in terms of social organization. Red Ocher cultures can be conceptualized as transegalitarian (Hayden 1995) because evidence of personal and corporate status is present at cemeteries. Evidence of violence also occurs, which suggests an increase in competition between groups. Like Old Copper, Red Ocher is known primarily from mortuary data, and no habitation sites have been conclusively linked to the cemeteries.

Widespread mound construction and the use of pottery are still the most useful cultural traits for recognizing the end of Archaic lifeways in Wisconsin, and Red Ocher mortuary practices appear to have included mound building and pottery manufacture at the very end (500 RCYBC). "Although many questions remain about this period of transition, it seems clear that the complex ceremonialism of the Hopewell Interaction Sphere of subsequent Middle Woodland times had its roots in the trade systems and social complexity of the Red Ocher complex" (Stevenson et al. 1997:150).

Acknowledgments

We would like to thank Thomas Emerson and Andrew Fortier for inviting us to participate in this volume. Their editorial comments and suggestions were also greatly appreciated. Richard Baken assisted with the radiocarbon date calibrations and figure and table construction. Janet Speth helped proof various versions of this article.

References Cited

Anderton, John B.
1995 *Paleoshoreline Geoarchaeology in the Northern Great Lakes: An Interdisciplinary Approach to Prehistoric Coastal Settlement.* Ph.D. dissertation, Department of Geography, University of Wisconsin-Madison. University Microfilms, Ann Arbor, Michigan.

Baerreis, David A.
1953a The Airport Village Site, Dane County. *The Wisconsin Archeologist* 34:149–164.
1953b The Blackhawk Village (Da 5), Dane County, Wisconsin. *Journal of the Iowa Archeological Society* 2:5–20.

Baerreis, David A., Hiroshi Daifuku, and James E. Lundsted
1954 The Burial Complex of the Reigh Site, Winnebago County, Wisconsin. *The Wisconsin Archeologist* 35:1–36.

Baker, Richard G., Louis J. Maher, Craig A. Chumbley, and Kent L. Van Zant
1992 Patterns of Holocene Environmental Change in the Midwestern United States. *Quaternary Research* 37:379–389.

Behm, Jeffery A.
1985 *Identification and Analysis of Stylistic Variation in Hardin Barbed Points.* Ph.D. dissertation, Department of Anthropology, University of Wisconsin–Madison, University Microfilms International, Ann Arbor, Michigan.

Beukens, R. P., L. A. Pavlish, R. G.V. Hancock, R. M. Farquhar, G. C. Wilson, P. J. Julig, and W. Ross
1992 Radiocarbon Dating of Copper-Preserved Organics. *Radiocarbon* 34:890–897.

Binford, Lewis R.
1962 Archaeology as Anthropology. *American Antiquity* 28:217–225.

Boszhardt, Robert F.
2002 Contracting Stemmed: What's the Point. *Midcontinental Journal of Archaeology* 27:35–67.

Brown, James A., and Robert K. Vierra
1983 What Happened in the Middle Archaic? In *Archaic Hunters and Gatherers in the American Midwest*, edited by James L. Phillips and James A. Brown, pp. 165–195. Academic Press, New York.

Buckmaster, Marla A., and James Paquette
1988 The Gorto Site: Preliminary Report on a Late Paleo Indian Site in Marquette County, Michigan. *The Wisconsin Archeologist* 69:101–124.

Chumbley, C. A., R. G. Baker, and E. A. Bettis III
1990 Midwestern Holocene Paleoenvironments Revealed by Floodplain Deposits in Northeastern Iowa. *Science* 249:272–274.

Clarke, David L.
1968 *Analytical Archaeology*. Methuen, London.

Cleland, Charles E.
1982 The Inland Shore Fishery of the Northern Great Lakes: Its Development and Importance in Prehistory. *American Antiquity* 47:761–784.

Cole, Fay-Cooper, and Thorne Deuel
1937 *Rediscovering Illinois: Archaeological Explorations in and around Fulton County*. University of Chicago Press, Chicago.

Cook, Thomas Genn
1976 *Koster, an Artifact Analysis of Two Archaic Phases in West-central Illinois.* Prehistoric Records 1. Northwestern University Archaeological Program, Evanston, Illinois.

Cunningham, Wilbur M.
1948 *A Study of Glacial Kame Culture in Michigan, Ohio, and Indiana.* Occasional Contributions 12. Museum of Anthropology, University of Michigan, Ann Arbor.

Curry, Dennis C.
2002 The Old Copper in Maryland? *Maryland Archeology* 38(2):33–34.

Emerson, Thomas E.
1979 Prehistoric Seasonal Exploitation of the White-Tailed Deer in the Driftless Area of Wisconsin: An Example from Brogley Rockshelter (47-GT-156). *The Wisconsin Archeologist* 60:278–292.

Esarey, Duane
1986 Red Ochre Mound Building and Marion Phase Associations: A Fulton County, Illinois Perspective. In *Early Woodland Archeology*, edited by Kenneth B. Farnsworth and Thomas E. Emerson, pp. 231–243. Kampsville Seminars in Archaeology 2. Center for American Archaeology Press, Kampsville, Illinois.

Finney, Fred A., Scott B. Meyer, and Kathryn E. Parker
1992 *Phase III Archaeological Investigation of a Middle Archaic Raddatz Occupation at the Bobwhite Site (47Ri185), Richland County, Wisconsin*. Research Papers 17(2). Office of the State Archaeologist, University of Iowa, Iowa City.

Ford, Richard I., and David S. Brose
1975 Prehistoric Wild Rice from the Dunn Farm Site, Leelanau County, Michigan. *The Wisconsin Archeologist* 56:9–15.

Freeman, Joan E.
1966 Price Site III, RI 4, a Burial Ground in Richland County, Wisconsin. *The Wisconsin Archeologist* 47:33–75.

Gibbon, Guy
1998 The Old Copper in Minnesota: A Review. *Plains Anthropologist* 43:27–50.

Green, William, and Shirley Schermer
1988 The Turkey River Mound Group (13CT1). In *Archaeological and Paleoenvironmental Studies in the Turkey River Valley, Northeastern Iowa*, edited by William Green, pp. 131–198. Research Papers 13(1). Office of the State Archaeologist, University of Iowa, Iowa City.

Griffin, James B.
1946 Cultural Change and Continuity in Eastern United States Archaeology. In *Man in Northeastern North America*, edited by Frederick Johnson, pp. 37–95. Papers of the Robert S. Peabody Foundation for Archaeology 3. Andover, Massachusetts.
1952 Culture Periods in Eastern United States Archaeology. In *Archeology of Eastern United States*, edited by James B. Griffin, pp. 352–364. University of Chicago Press, Chicago.
1961 (editor) *Lake Superior Copper and the Indians: Miscellaneous Studies of Great Lakes Prehistory*. Anthropological Papers 17. Museum of Anthropology, University of Michigan, Ann Arbor.

Griffin, James B., A. A. Gordus, and Gary A. Wright
1969 Identification of Sources of Hopewellian Obsidian in the Middle West. *American Antiquity* 34:1–14.

Griffin, James B., and George I. Quimby
1961 The McCollum Site, Nipigon District, Ontario. In *Lake Superior Copper and the Indians: Miscellaneous Studies of Great Lakes Prehistory*, edited by James B. Griffin, pp. 91–102. Anthropological Papers 17. Museum of Anthropology, University of Michigan, Ann Arbor.

Halsey, John R.
1972 The Molash Creek Red Ocher Burial. *The Wisconsin Archeologist* 53:1–14.

Hansel, Ardith K., and David M. Mickelson
1988 A Reevaluation of the Timing and Causes of High Lake Phases in the Lake Michigan Basin. *Quaternary Research* 29:113–128.

Harris, Wendy G.
2002 Upland Abandonment during the Middle Archaic Period: A View From Northeastern Illinois. *The Wisconsin Archeologist* 83(1):3–18.

Hayden, Brian D.
1995 Pathways to Power: Principles for Creating Socioeconomic Inequalities. In *Foundations of Social Inequality*, edited by T. Douglas Price and Gary M. Feinman, pp. 15–78. Plenum Press, New York.

Hruska, Robert
1967 The Riverside Site: A Late Archaic Manifestation in Michigan. *The Wisconsin Archeologist* 48:145–260.

Hsu, Tse-min
1970 An Analysis of the Reigh Site Old Copper Human Remains. Master's thesis, Department of Anthropology, University of Wisconsin–Madison.

Hunzicker, David A.
2002 Little Rice Lake Site (47VI272): An Old Copper Complex Manufacturing Site in Vilas County, WI. *The Wisconsin Archeologist* 83(1):45–62.

Jeske, Robert J., Daniel M. Winkler, and Chrisie L. Hunter
2002 Paleoindian and Archaic Occupations of the Kelly North Tract at Carcajou Point in Southeast Wisconsin. *The Wisconsin Archeologist* 83(2):5–31.

Justice, Noel D.
1995 *Stone Age Spear and Arrow Points of the Midcontinental and Eastern United States*. Indiana University Press, Bloomington.

Kennedy, Clyde C.
1966 *Preliminary Report on the Morrison's Island-6 Site*. Bulletin 206. National Museum of Canada, Ottawa.

Knox, J. C., P. F. McDowell, and W. C. Johnson
1981 Holocene Fluvial Stratigraphy and Climatic Change in the Driftless Area, Wisconsin. In *Quaternary Paleoclimate*, edited by W. C. Hahaney, pp. 107–127. GeoAbstracts, Norwich, England.

Krakker, James J.
1997 Biface Caches, Exchange, and Regulatory Systems in the Prehistoric Great Lakes Region. *Midcontinental Journal of Archaeology* 22:1–41.

Kuehn, Steven R.
1997 *Archaeological Investigations at the Bell Center Wetland Mitigation Area, Crawford County, Wisconsin*. Research Report in Archaeology 63. Museum Archaeology Program, Wisconsin Historical Society, Madison.
1998 New Evidence for Late Paleoindian-Early Archaic Subsistence Behavior in the Western Great Lakes. *American Antiquity* 63:457–476.
2002 Defining the Temporal Boundaries of the Middle Archaic: Old and New Evidence from Southern Wisconsin. *The Wisconsin Archeologist* 83(1):19–44.

LaRonge, Michael
2001 An Experimental Analysis of Great Lakes Archaic Copper Smithing. *North American Archaeologist* 22:371–385.

Larsen, Curtis E.
1985 Geoarchaeological Interpretation of Great Lakes Coastal Environments. In *Archaeological Sediments in Context*, edited by Julie K. Stein and William R. Farrand, pp. 91–110. Center for the Study of Early Man, Institute for Quaternary Studies, University of Maine, Orono.

Luchterhand, Kubet
1970 *Early Archaic Projectile Points and Hunting Patterns in the Lower Illinois Valley*. Monograph 2. Illinois Archaeological Survey, Springfield.

Maher, Louis J.
1982 The Palynology of Devils Lake, Sauk County, Wisconsin. In *Quaternary History of the Drifless Area*, pp. 119–135. Field Trip Guide Book 5. University of Wisconsin-Extension, Geological and Natural History Survey, Madison.

Martin, Susan R.
1999 *Wonderful Power: The Story of Ancient Copper Working in the Lake Superior Basin*. Wayne State University Press, Detroit, Michigan.

Martin, Susan R., and Thomas C. Pleger
1999 The Complex Formerly Known as a Culture: The Taxonomic Puzzle of "Old Copper." In *Taming the Taxonomy: Toward a New Understanding of Great Lakes Archaeology*, edited by Ronald F. Williamson and Christopher M. Watts, pp. 61–70. Eastend Books and the Ontario Archaeological Society, Toronto.

Mason, Ronald J.
1981 *Great Lakes Archaeology*. Academic Press, New York.
2002 *Great Lakes Archaeology*. 2nd printing. Blackburn Press, Caldwell, New Jersey.

Mason, Ronald J., and Carol Irwin
1960 An Eden-Scottsbluff Burial in Northeastern Wisconsin. *American Antiquity* 26:43–57.

McKern, Will C.
1939 The Midwestern Taxonomic Method as an Aid to Archaeological Culture Study. *American Antiquity* 4:301–313.
1942 The First Settlers of Wisconsin. *Wisconsin Magazine of History* 26:153–169.

Meinholz, Norman M., and Steven R. Kuehn
1996 *The Deadman Slough Site: Late Paleoindian/Early Archaic and Woodland Occupations along the Flambeau River, Price County, Wisconsin*. Archaeology Research Series 4. Museum Archaeology Program, State Historical Society of Wisconsin, Madison.

Mikkola, Paul H.
1970 Physical Properties of Red Ocher. *The Michigan Archaeologist* 16:43–46.

Miles, Suzanne W.
1951 A Revaluation of the Old Copper Industry. *American Antiquity* 16:240–247.

Moffat, Charles R., and Janet M. Speth
1999 Rainbow Dam: Two Stratified Late Archaic and Woodland Habitations in the Wisconsin River Headwaters. *The Wisconsin Archeologist* 80:111–160.

Morrow, Toby A.
1996 Lithic Refitting and Archaeological Site Formation Processes, a Case Study from the Twin Ditch Site, Greene County, Illinois. In *Stone Tools: Theoretical Insights into Human Prehistory*, edited by George H. Odell, pp. 345–373. Plenum Press, New York.

Munson, Partick J.
1966 The Sheets Site: A Late Archaic-Early Woodland Occupation in West Central Illinois. *The Michigan Archaeologist* 12:111–120.
1982 Marion, Black Sand, Morton and Havana Relationships: An Illinois Valley Perspective. *The Wisconsin Archeologist* 63:1–17.

Ostberg, Neil J.
1956 Additional Material from the Reigh Site, Winnebago County. *The Wisconsin Archeologist* 37:28–31.

Overstreet, David F.
1980 The Convent Knoll Site (47Wk327): A Red Ocher Cemetery in Waukesha County, Wisconsin. *The Wisconsin Archeologist* 61:34–90.
1988 Osceola Revisited: Archaeological Investigations on the Potosi Terrace, Grant County, Wisconsin. *The Wisconsin Archeologist* 69:1–61.

Overstreet, David F., Larry Doebert, Gary W. Henschel, Phil Sander, and David Wasion
1996 Two Red Ocher Mortuary Contexts from Southeastern Wisconsin—The Henschel Site (47 SB 29), Sheboygan County and the Barnes Creek Site (47 KN 41), Kenosha County. *The Wisconsin Archeologist* 77(1–2):36–62.

Ozker, Doreen
1982 *An Early Woodland Community at the Schultz Site 20SA2 in the Saginaw Valley and the Nature of the Early Woodland Adaptation in the Great Lakes Region*. Anthropological Papers 70. Museum of Anthropology, University of Michigan, Ann Arbor.

Papworth, Mark L.
1967 *Cultural Traditions in the Lake Forest Region during the Late High-Water Stages of the Post-Glacial Great Lakes*. Ph.D. dissertation, University of Michigan. University Microfilms, Ann Arbor, Michigan.

Parmalee, Paul W.
1959 Animal Remains from the Raddatz Rockshelter, Sk 5, Wisconsin. *The Wisconsin Archeologist* 40:83–90.

Pfeiffer, Susan
1977 *The Skeletal Biology of Archaic Populations of the Great Lakes Region*. Mercury Series Paper 64. Archaeological Survey of Canada, National Museum of Man, Ottawa.

Phillips, James L., and James A. Brown (editors)
1983 *Archaic Hunters and Gatherers in the American Midwest*. Academic Press, New York.

Pleger, Thomas C.
1992 A Functional and Temporal Analysis of Copper Implements from the Chautauqua Grounds Site (47-Mt-71) a Multicomponent Site near the Mouth of the Menominee River. *The Wisconsin Archeologist* 73:160–176.
1998 *Social Complexity, Trade, and Subsistence during the Archaic/Woodland Transition in the Western Great Lakes (4000–400 B.C.): A Diachronic Study of Copper Using Cultures at the Oconto and Riverside Cemeteries*. Ph.D. dissertation, University of Wisconsin–Madison. University Microfilms International, Ann Arbor, Michigan.
2000 Old Copper and Red Ocher Social Complexity. *Midcontinental Journal of Archaeology* 25:169–190.

2001 New Dates for the Oconto Old Copper Culture Cemetery. In *Papers in Honor of Carol I. Mason*, edited by Thomas C. Pleger, Robert A. Birmingham, and Carol I. Mason. *The Wisconsin Archeologist* 82:87–100.

2003 A Brief Introduction to the Old Copper Complex of the Western Great Lakes: 4000–1000 B.C. In *Proceedings of the Twenty-Seventh Annual Meeting of the Forest History Association of Wisconsin*, pp. 10–18. Forest History Association of Wisconsin, Wisconsin Rapids.

Price, T. Douglas

1985 Late Archaic Subsistence in the Midwestern United States. *Journal of Human Evolution* 14:449–459.

Price, T. Douglas, Melissa Connor, and John D. Parsen

1985 Bone Chemistry and the Reconstruction of Diet: Strontium Discrimination in White-Tailed Deer. *Journal of Archaeological Science* 12:419–442.

Quimby, George

1952 The Archaeology of the Upper Great Lakes Area. In *Archeology of Eastern United States*, edited by James B. Griffin, pp. 99–107. University of Chicago Press, Chicago.

Rapp, George, Jr., Eiler Henrickson, and James Albert

1990 Native Copper Sources of Artifact Copper in Pre-Columbian North America. In *Archaeological Geology of North America*, edited by Norman P. Lasca and Jack Donahue, pp. 179–498. Centennial Special Volume 4. Geological Society of America, Boulder, Colorado.

Ritzenthaler, Robert

1946 The Osceola Site: An "Old Copper" Site near Potosi, Wisconsin. *The Wisconsin Archeologist* 27:53–70.

1957 (editor) *The Old Copper Culture.* The Wisconsin Archeologist 38(4).

Ritzenthaler, Robert, and George Quimby

1962 The Red Ocher Culture of the Upper Great Lakes and Adjacent Areas. *Fieldiana Anthropology* 36:243–275.

Ritzenthaler, Robert, and Warren Wittry

1952 The Oconto Site—An Old Copper Manifestation. *The Wisconsin Archeologist* 33:199–223.

Salzer, Robert J.

1974 The Wisconsin North Lakes Project: A Preliminary Report. In *Aspects of Upper Great Lakes Anthropology*, edited by Elden Johnson, pp. 40–54. Minnesota Prehistoric Archaeology Series 11. Minnesota Historical Society, St. Paul.

Steinbring, Jack H.

1968 A Copper Blade of Possible Paleo-Indian Type. *Manitoba Archaeological Newsletter* 5(1–2):3–12.

1975 *Taxonomic and Associational Considerations of Copper Technology during the Archaic Tradition.* Ph.D. dissertation. University of Minnesota. University Microfilms, Ann Arbor, Michigan.

Stevenson, Katherine, Robert F. Boszhardt, Charles R. Moffat, Philip H. Salkin, Thomas C. Pleger, James L. Theler, and Constance Arzigian

1997 The Woodland Tradition. In *Wisconsin Archaeology*, edited by Robert A. Birmingham, Carol I. Mason, and James B. Stoltman. *The Wisconsin Archeologist* 78:140–201.

Stoltman, James B.

1983 Ancient Peoples of the Upper Mississippi River Valley. In *Historic Lifestyles of the Upper Mississippi River Valley*, edited by John Wozniak, pp. 197–255. University Press of America, New York.

1986 The Archaic Tradition. In *Introduction to Wisconsin Archaeology*, edited by William Green, James B. Stoltman, and Alice B. Kehoe. *The Wisconsin Archeologist* 67:207–238.

1992 The Concept of Archaic in Eastern North America Prehistory. *Revista de Arqueología Americana* 5:101–118.

1997 The Archaic Tradition. In *Wisconsin Archaeology*, edited by Robert A. Birmingham, Carol I. Mason, and James B. Stoltman. *The Wisconsin Archeologist* 78:112–139.

Stoltman, James B., Jeffery A. Behm, and Harris A. Palmer

1984 The Bass Site: A Hardin Quarry/Workshop in Southwestern Wisconsin. In *Prehistoric Chert Exploitation: Studies from the Midcontinent*, edited by Brian M. Butler and Ernest E. May, pp. 197–224. Occasional Papers 2. Center for Archaeological Investigations, Southern Illinois University, Carbondale.

Stoltman, James B., and Richard E. Hughes

2004 Obsidian in Early Woodland Contexts in the Upper Mississippi Valley. *American Antiquity* 69:751–759.

Theler, James L. and Robert F. Boszhardt

2003 *Twelve Millennia: Archaeology of the Upper Mississippi River Valley.* University of Iowa Press, Iowa City.

Tiffany, Joseph A.

1974 An Application of Eigenvector Techniques to the Seed Analysis of the Brogley Rockshelter (47-Gt-156). *The Wisconsin Archeologist* 5:2–41.

Veit, Richard, Gregory D. Lattanzi, and Charles A. Bello

2004 More Precious than Gold: A Preliminary Study of the Varieties and Distribution of Pre-Contact Copper Artifacts in New Jersey. *Archaeology of Eastern North America* 32:73–88.

Vernon, William W.

1990 New Archaeometallurgical Perspectives on the Old Copper Industry of North America. In *Archaeological Geology of North America*, edited by Norman P. Lasca and Jack Donahue, pp. 499–512. Centennial Special Volume 4. Geological Society of America, Boulder, Colorado.

West, George A.

1929 Copper: Its Mining and Use by the Aborigines of the Lake Superior Region. *Bulletin of the Public Museum of the City of Milwaukee* 10(1):1–182.

Willey, Gordon R.

1966 *An Introduction to American Archaeology*, vol. 1. Prentice-Hall, Englewood Cliffs, New Jersey.

Willey, Gordon R., and Philip Phillips

1958 *Method and Theory in American Archaeology.* University of Chicago Press, Chicago.

Winkler, Daniel

2004 The Kelly North Phase: Transitional Middle to Late Archaic Lithic Technology at Carcajou Point in Southeastern Wisconsin. Master's thesis, Department of Anthropology, University of Wisconsin–Milwaukee.

Winkler, Marjorie Green

1985 *Late-Glacial and Holocene Environmental History of South-Central Wisconsin: A Study of Upland and Wetland Ecosystems.* Institute for Environmental Studies, University of Wisconsin, Madison.

Winkler, M. G., A. M. Swain, and J. E. Kutzbach
1986 Middle Holocene Dry Period in the Northern Midwestern United States: Lake Levels and Pollen Stratigraphy. *Quaternary Research* 25:235–250.
Winters, Howard D.
1969 *The Riverton Culture*. Reports of Investigations 13. Illinois State Museum, Springfield.
Wittry, Warren L.
1957 A Preliminary Study of the Old Copper Complex. *The Wisconsin Archeologist* 38:204–221.
1959a The Raddatz Rockshelter, Sk 5, Wisconsin. *The Wisconsin Archeologist* 40:33–69.
1959b Archeological Studies of Four Wisconsin Rockshelters. *The Wisconsin Archeologist* 40:137–267.
Wittry, Warren L., and Robert E. Ritzenthaler
1956 The Old Copper Complex: An Archaic Manifestation in Wisconsin. *American Antiquity* 21:244–254.

20

Hunter-Gatherer Adaptations and Alternative Perspectives on the Michigan Archaic: Research Problems in Context

William A. Lovis

In developing this discussion of the Michigan Archaic, I am in the unique and, some would even wager, enviable position of being the only researcher in the state currently undertaking sustained, systematic, and multiyear research into this time period, albeit the majority but not all of my work has been spatially constrained to southern lower Michigan. The cumulative results of this research and that of others have led to several recent syntheses of the Archaic that have provided substantial and detailed information on chronology, subsistence economy, changing technology and assemblage style, mortuary and exchange patterns, and regional settlement systems (Lovis 1999; Lovis 2002a; Robertson et al. 1999; Shott 1999). I therefore take the position that this gives me leave to at least partially depart from this volume's more general themes and cast this discussion in terms of my own perceptions of which Archaic research topics have recently attained importance, why they have achieved this status, and what future directions might be most profitable in pursuing them. In essence, I intend here to provide background information on the environmental context of the Michigan Archaic and a detailed reappraisal of the state's Archaic radiocarbon time scale, after which I address broader themes by providing the theoretical and substantive rationale for specific problem orientations, in effect, proposing what amounts to a multidecade research agenda for the Michigan Archaic. To achieve this end, I introduce each major segment of this chapter with a specific proposition or assertion.

The Environmental Backdrop

Considering the Archaic adaptations that have been documented across Michigan's two peninsulas apart from the macroscale environmental changes taking place between ca. 9000 and 500 cal B.C. is impossible, although assessing the interactive effects of paleoenvironmental changes on the human groups coping with those changes is difficult. While other contributors to this volume take a close look at paleoclimate across the Midcontinent, significant points about the environmental context of the Michigan Archaic nonetheless warrant emphasis here.

First, almost all of the two Michigan peninsulas are surrounded by water (Figure 20.1), specifically Lakes Huron, Michigan, and Superior. The lakes that occupy the Huron and Michigan basins have been joined for much of their evolution since deglaciation and appear subject to similar controlling variables, whereas the lake occupying the Superior basin has often been separated and controlled independently of the other two. Much has been made about the ameliorating effects of these water bodies on adjacent land masses, and such effects have certainly characterized historically documented time. However, it is exceedingly important to recognize that these lakes were not always at their current mean elevations (Figures 20.2 and 20.3); at times they were higher by several meters and at other times substantially lower. Additionally, the

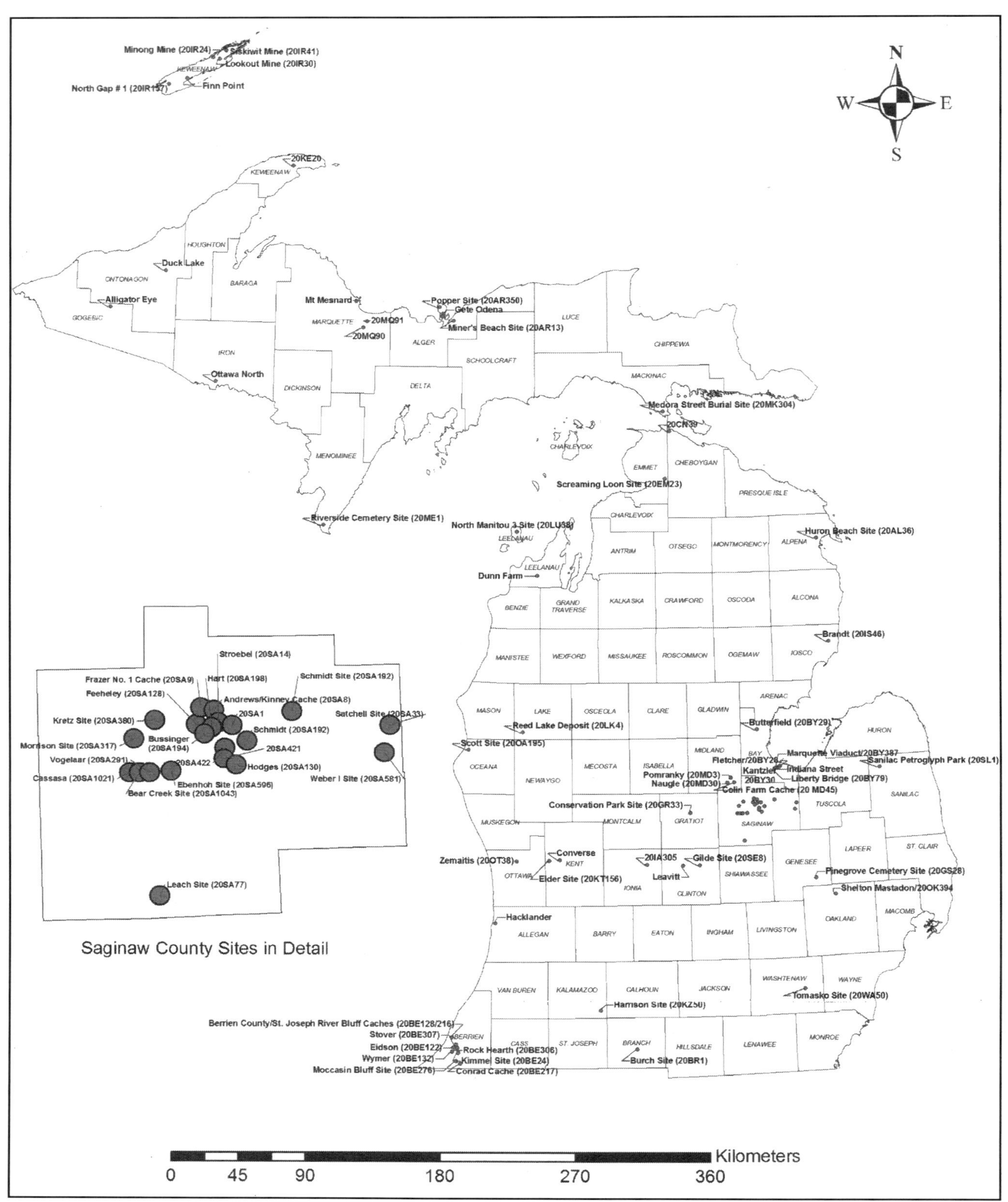

Figure 20.1. Locations of major Archaic-period archaeological sites in Michigan (courtesy Michigan State University).

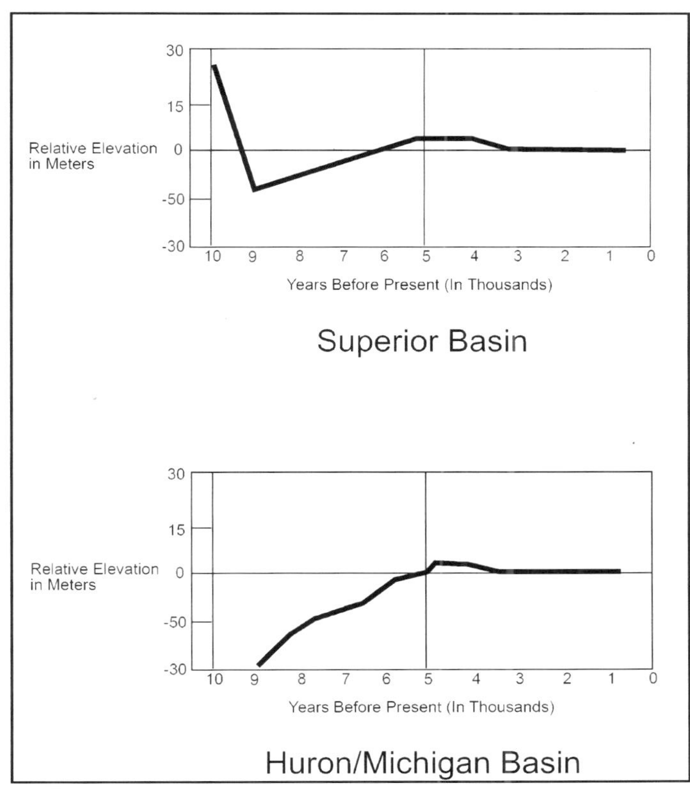

Figure 20.2. Changes in base elevation of the Michigan-Huron and Superior lake basins (after Lovis and MacDonald 1999; courtesy Michigan State University).

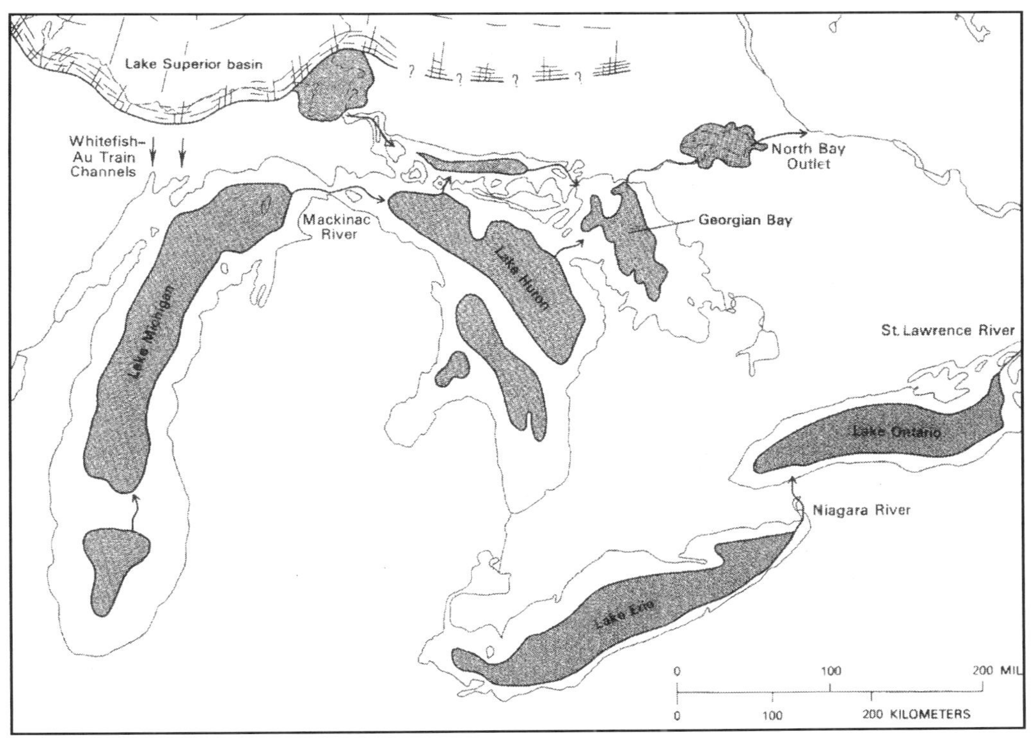

Figure 20.3. Michigan-Huron and Superior lake basins ca. 10,000 B.P. (reproduced from Larsen 1987).

lake occupying the Superior basin was ultimately deglaciated much later than the conjoined Huron-Michigan basins; variations in water elevations between the northern and southern basins were not always synchronous and, at times, were even inverse to one another—one was lower in elevation while the other was higher. Thus, any generalizations about the relative basinwide effects of these water masses on paleoclimate must accommodate their changing surface areas over time. Such correlations have not yet been established, and here it would be foolhardy to do more than speculate that, as these lakes shrank in size, their relative ameliorating effects also diminished and, as they grew larger, their moderating climatic effects increased, as well. The magnitude of such change, however, cannot currently be assessed.

Second, the lowest stage of the Huron and Michigan basins, the Chippewa-Stanley stage, was substantially below modern elevations. This stage occurred ca. 10,000 B.P., at the onset of the Archaic, and resulted in greatly diminished water masses (Figure 20.3). As any long-term student of Great Lakes archaeology will readily know (I hope!), this regression in the lake basins had two key physical consequences. One was an increase in the size of the adjacent and occupiable land masses, especially in Michigan, Wisconsin, and Ontario but also, to a degree, along coastal zones in Illinois, Indiana, and Ohio. The other was that the water barriers present during higher (and modern) lake stages between Wisconsin, Michigan, and Ontario almost literally evaporated, potentially allowing for easier social interactions across a much larger region. As will be evident in succeeding sections of this discussion, these water-level fluctuations have other major implications for both the preservation and the discovery of Archaic site populations as well as for Archaic mobility behavior.

As recent summary statements on the vegetative biogeography of Michigan clearly reveal (Kapp 1999; Lovis and MacDonald 1999), it was with the onset of the Archaic stage that deciduous hardwoods approximated their historical successional states in the Lower Peninsula, whereas this did not occur for at least another millennium in the Upper Peninsula—there was a clear latitudinal lag. The data that underpin these interpretations are drawn from pollen cores available from the currently exposed land masses and may not reflect accurately the plant composition of areas that are currently submerged under the waters of the Michigan-Huron (or Superior) lake basins. Recent data reveal that as late as 6500 B.P. (5500–5300 cal B.C.) mixed conifer-dominated stands were present on what are now the bottomlands of southern Lake Huron, 13 m (40 ft) below modern lake elevations (Hunter 2004), while the effects of Hypsithermal warming appear to have resulted in grassland habitats at higher elevations in the central Lower Peninsula at approximately the same time (Holman 1990). While productive deciduous oak-hickory hardwood forest may well have established itself early in the Archaic, it is increasingly clear that this was a very diverse vegetative environment that warrants more refined consideration if archaeologists are to understand how human populations interacted with it (Lovis 1986).

Calibrating the Michigan Archaic Radiocarbon Chronology

The future of the Michigan Archaic lies in a few good dates.

As a contribution to refining the Archaic-stage chronology in Michigan, I have attempted to compile a comprehensive listing and to calibrate (per CALIB Revision 4.4.2; Stuiver and Reimer 2004) all of the approximately 117 published and unpublished ^{14}C dates for this time period. Earlier attempts to provide such information include the Archaic age dates in Fitting's summary compilation in *The Archaeology of Michigan* (1975); the work by Lovis and Robertson (1989) that dealt primarily with the Archaic of southern Michigan, particularly the Saginaw Valley, and adjacent southern Ontario and Wisconsin; and the ^{14}C citations in chapters by Shott, Lovis, Robertson et al., and Garland and Beld in Halsey's edited volume *Retrieving Michigan's Buried Past* (1999). Additional radiocarbon references may also be found embedded in a recent discussion of site formation and burial processes in southern Michigan by Monaghan and Lovis (2005). As I think will become evident, the spatial clustering of the radiocarbon chronology coupled with problems of poor or nonexistent diagnostic artifact association make some of the results of the current endeavor only partially satisfying. Moreover, many of the available dates recapitulated here derive from the 1950s and 1960s, when the precision of small-sample dating was in its infancy, when extended counts were rare, and when Accelerator Mass Spectrometer (AMS) dating did not exist, which cumulatively resulted in what today are considered unacceptably large sigma values, often in the several-century range.

In tandem with this comprehensive dating effort, I attempted to make consistent the comparative illustrative data for the resultant artifact chronology. To this end, the published images of diagnostic Archaic materials employed here were rescaled for consistent size presentation and were redrawn from the original reports. The redrawn images are presented here in Figures 20.4–20.13 with their original references.

The Upper Peninsula and Isle Royale

Among the more surprising aspects of this undertaking was the relative abundance of absolute dates, both radiocarbon dates and thermoluminescence dates, available for the Upper Peninsula and Isle Royale regions of Michigan (Tables 20.1 and 20.2). A total of 48 absolute dates seemingly provides an abundance of chronological information. Several observations

Table 20.1. Calibrated Archaic Radiocarbon Dates from Isle Royale and the Upper Peninsula of Michigan.

Site Name/ Lab Number	^{14}C Age B.P.	Uncorrected B.C.	Calibrated 1-sigma B.C.	References
20KE20				
Beta-29788	7870 ± 350	5920	7182–6408	Martin 1993, 1999
Beta-29787	3300 ± 60	1350	1637–1518	Martin 1993
Beta-29789	3260 ± 70	1310	1617–1488, 1481–1448	Martin 1993
Popper Site				
Beta-79515	4260 ± 50	2310	2918–2865, 2806–2780	Dunham and Anderton 1999; Dunham and Branstner 1995
Beta-79516	4100 ± 60	2150	2700–2574, 2859–2811, 2749–2723	Dunham and Anderton 1999; Dunham and Branstner 1995
Minong (Isle Royale)				
M-1384	4420 ± 150	2470	3138–2910, 3336–3209	Clark 1995; Crane and Griffin 1965
M-1390	4400 ± 150	2450	3136–2894, 3334–3211	Clark 1995; Crane and Griffin 1965
M-371c	3800 ± 250	1850	2502–1885	Clark 1995; Crane 1956
W-291	3310 ± 200	1360	1831–1390	Clark 1995
M-1388	3460 ± 130	1510	1943–1615	Clark 1995; Crane and Griffin 1965
M-1385	3360 ± 130	1410	1776–1509	Clark 1995; Crane and Griffin 1965
M-1387	3320 ± 130	1370	1742–1486, 1483–1443	Crane and Griffin 1965
M-1389	3310 ± 130	1360	1701–1441	Crane and Griffin 1965
M-320	3000 ± 175	1050	1414–1002	Crane 1956
Lookout Site (Isle Royale)				
M-1275c	2800 ± 120	850	1214–917	Crane and Griffin 1964
M-1275 d,e,f,g	4110 ± 130	2160	2875–2566	Clark 1995; Crane and Griffin 1964
Alligator Eye				
Beta-42441	3640 ± 150	1690	2203–1861	Hill 1994
Beta-42442	3490 ± 110	1540	1952–1683	Hill 1994
Duck Lake				
Beta-099777	3420 ± 50(AMS)	1470	1772–1680	Mark A. Hill, pers. comm. November 15, 2004
Beta-124454	3400 ± 110	1450	1778–1599, 1571–1529, 1876–1841	Mark A. Hill, pers. comm. November 15, 2004
North Gap I/20IR157(Isle Royale)				
Beta-35056	3440 ± 70	1490	1782–1682, 1878–1840, 1827–1794	Clark 1995
Finn Point/20IR5(Isle Royale)				
M-1274	3060 ± 130	1110	1450–1126	Clark 1995
Siskiwit Site (Isle Royale)				
M-386	3370 ± 130	1420	1778–1517	Crane and Griffin 1964
Ottawa North				
Beta-42451	3320 ± 220	1370	1893–1374	Hill 1994
Miner's Beach				
Beta-46964	3150 ± 80	1200	1518–1371, 1342–1317	Clark 1993
Beta-46965	2990 ± 60	1040	1316–1187, 1183–1128	Clark 1993

Table 20.1. Calibrated Archaic Radiocarbon Dates from Isle Royale and the Upper Peninsula of Michigan, continued.

Site Name/ Lab Number	^{14}C Age B.P.	Uncorrected B.C.	Calibrated 1-sigma B.C.	References
Mount Mesnard/20MQ64				
None available	5270	3320		Marla Buckmaster, pers. comm. September 2005
Beta-63729	5280 ± 60	3330	4229–4198, 4172–4088, 4084–4040	Marla Buckmaster, per. comm. September 2005
Silver Lake				
Beta-196214	3150 ± 40	1200	1457–1395, 1492–1478	Marla Buckmaster, pers. comm. September 2005
20MQ90				
Beta-80125	2950 ± 60	1000	1220–1106, 1104–1050, 1259–1230	Robertson et al. 1995
20MQ91				
Beta-79451	3630 ± 90	1680	2068–1883, 2136–2078	Robertson et al. 1995
Gete Odena /20AR348				
Beta-163732	2780 ± 60	830	978–892, 879–839	Skibo et al. 2007
Riverside Site (20ME01)				
M-658	3040 ± 150	1090	1434–1107, 1103–1051	Crane and Griffin 1958
M-1715	1949 ± 130	A.D. 1	92–A.D. 231	Crane and Griffin 1968
M-1716	2050 ± 130	100	204–A.D. 82	Crane and Griffin 1968
M-1717	2190 ± 140	240	391–89	Crane and Griffin 1968
M-1718	2080 ± 140	130	210–A.D. 62, 352–296	Crane and Griffin 1968
M-1719	2460 ± 140	510	597–410, 761–679, 669–609	Crane and Griffin 1968
AA19677/WG2403	2780 ± 65	830	997–892, 879–838	Pleger 2000
AA20282/WG2404	2495 ± 65	545	765–537	Pleger 2000
AA19679/WG2405	2960 ± 50	1010	1261–1111	Pleger 2000
AA19680/WG2406	2790 ± 50	840	1000–896	Pleger 2000
AA19681/WG2407	2380 ± 50	430	521–392	Pleger 2000
AA19682/WG2408	2605 ± 45	655	825–765	Pleger 2000
AA19683/WG2409	2605 ± 50	655	830–761	Pleger 2000
AA19684/WG2410	2710 ± 50	760	899–819	Pleger 2000
AA19685/WG2411	2850 ± 50	900	1052–967, 963–923	Pleger 2000
AA19686/WG2412	2690 ± 60	740	864–804, 896–870	Pleger 2000

Note: Calibrated per Stuiver and Reimer 2004.

Table 20.2. Thermoluminescence Dates from the Trout Point I Site.

Sample Number	Age in Years B.P.	Reference
87-3-UWM-1	2370 ± 215	Benchley et al. 1988
87-3-UWM-2	2300 ± 165	Benchley et al. 1988
87-3-UWM-3	2150 ± 180	Benchley et al. 1988

Note: All samples processed at University of Missouri Thermoluminescence Laboratory.

regarding the dates, however, suggest their judicious use. First, two major series of dates spatially constrain any inferences that might be made. One cluster of dates derives from the Riverside Cemetery site and includes both an early University of Michigan date series as well as more recent AMS assessments by Thomas Pleger. Pleger and James Stoltman (this volume) provide an in-depth evaluation of the Riverside dates in their discussion of the Wisconsin transition from Late Archaic to Early Woodland. The other major date series, derived from multiple sites but focused on the Minong Mine, relates to copper-mining activities on Isle Royale. The value of this date group is in its exposition of the early and continuous nature of copper extraction on Isle Royale (see Clark 1995 for an extended discussion of radiocarbon dates from Isle Royale). This revelation has limited significance in the current context, given Clark's (1995) observation that most of the cultural relationships of Isle Royale were with the northern, Canadian, shore of Lake Superior rather than the Upper Peninsula of Michigan.

The second and far more striking observation about the Upper Peninsula ^{14}C chronology is that few if any diagnostic artifacts are associated with any of the dated sites, let alone with the dated materials (except at the Riverside site). While at least in part this is an issue of taphonomy and preservation, this circumstance makes the chronology itself useful only from the reference or vantage point of understanding relative ages and intensity of occupation across the region—it is almost useless for building a chronology of diagnostic artifact styles. Finally, with respect to such chronology building, while one very early date is available from site 20KE20 on the Keweenaw Peninsula (7182–6408 cal B.C., Beta-29788; Martin 1993), only slightly postdating some of the late Paleoindian Plano materials from the western Upper Peninsula, this date stands in relative isolation. Furthermore, a very large ^{14}C hiatus spans the Early and Middle Archaic periods in the region. Very few ^{14}C assays predate ca. 3300 cal B.C. in the Upper Peninsula, and none are in direct association with diagnostics. On its face, this would suggest that the majority of occupations, or at least the bulk of recorded and investigated sites, date to the Late Archaic. Clearly, understanding the period intervening between the late Paleoindian Plano occupations of the region and the Late Archaic is a major research priority.

The Northern Lower Peninsula

Turning to the northern Lower Peninsula of Michigan, one does not derive much relief from this state of affairs (Table 20.3). The ^{14}C chronology is both limited and spatially dispersed, although in contrast with the Upper Peninsula, diagnostics have been recovered from the few dated sites and can assist in preliminary chronology building. In the northern Lower Peninsula, a feature at the Screaming Loon site, located at post-Nipissing elevations on the Devil's Elbow of the Crooked River, has produced a date of 3360 ± 270 (2031–1371 cal B.C., DIC-650), but the date lacks direct association with diagnostics (Lovis 1990). However, the several projectile points recovered (Figure 20.4) reveal tremendous heterogeneity and clear associations with northeastern Lake

Figure 20.4. Projectile points from the North Manitou #3 and Screaming Loon sites: top row, North Manitou #3 site (illustration by W. Lovis); bottom row, Screaming Loon site (illustration by W. Lovis).

Table 20.3. Calibrated Archaic Radiocarbon Dates from the Lower Peninsula of Michigan.

Site Name/ Lab Number	^{14}C Age B.P.	Uncorrected B.C.	Calibrated 1-sigma B.C.	Reference	Component/Point Type
Andrews					
M-941	5300 ± 150	3350	4254–3976	Crane and Griffin 1960	dates burial
M-659	3170 ± 150	1220	1622–1259	Crane and Griffin 1960	dates Algoma stage
Bear Creek/20SA1043					
Beta-56118/CAMS-3817	2250 ± 50	300	387–351, 299–230	Branstner and Hambacher 1994	elk femur from feature
Beta-56311/CAMS-3835	4250 ± 50	2300	2915–2864, 2807–2778	Branstner and Hambacher 1994	dates large side notched
Beta-56425/CAMS-3836	2510 ± 80	560	724–537	Branstner and Hambacher 1994	charcoal from paleosol
Brandt					
DIC-2501	3090 ± 45	1140	1412–1306	Mead and Kingsley 1985	dates Van Etten points
Conservation Park					
Beta-9644	2560 ± 60	610	804–758, 646–543	Beld and Luke 1985	dates Meadowood
Beta-9645	2400 ± 90	450	759–683, 546–393	Beld and Luke 1985	"
Beta-9646	2530 ± 60	580	796–756, 698–540	Beld and Luke 1985	"
Beta-9648	2760 ± 90	810	1002–824	Beld and Luke 1985	"
Beta-10508	2750 ± 100	800	1002–807	Beld and Luke 1985	"
Beta-10509	2490 ± 100	540	779–517	Beld and Luke 1985	"
GX-5764	2515 ± 145	565	800–503	Beld and Luke 1985	"
Converse/20KT2					
Beta-142610	3060 ± 40	1110	1390–1329, 1323–1291, 1278–1263	Hambacher et al. 2003	Riverton points in close proximity
Dunn Farm/20LU22					
DIC-611A/611Ba	3040 ± 125	1090	1434–1119	Brose and Hambacher 1999	dates cremation pit
Ebenhoff					
Beta-47065	6040 ± 110	4090	5061–4785	Beaverson and Mooers 1993	dates Middle Archaic
Beta-47379	4660 ± 90	2710	3534–3353	Beaverson and Mooers 1993	"
Beta-51001	4720 ± 50	2770	3434–3378, 3629–3580, 3537–3500	Beaverson and Mooers 1993	"
Eidson/20BE122					
Beta-6151	2850 ± 100	900	1130–898	Clark 1990	St. Joseph corner notched
Beta-6152	2940 ± 80	990	1223–1017	Clark 1990	Berrien, Wymer, Sodus
Beta-6462	2960 ± 70	1010	1270–1108, 1104–1056	Clark 1990	dates *Helianthus*
Beta-6463	2730 ± 100	780	980–802	Clark 1990	Eidson side notched
Feeheley					
M-1139	3930 ± 150	1980	2601–2197	Crane and Griffin 1962	dates submidden pit
Fletcher-Marquette Viaduct Locale/ 20BY28					
Beta-154672	3740 ± 50	1790	2202–2116, 2099–2038	Lovis and Phillips 2002	nutshell from feature
Beta-154673	3660 ± 40	1710	2130–2082, 2043–2007, 2003–1960	Lovis and Phillips 2002	dates Satchell point
Beta-154674	3670 ± 70	1720	2139–1947	Lovis and Phillips 2002	dates stratified feature
Beta-154676	3760 ± 60	1810	2234–2126, 2084–2041	Lovis and Phillips 2002	dates pit feature
Beta-154677	2960 ± 60	1010	1262–1109	Lovis and Phillips 2002	dates pit feature

Table 20.3. Calibrated Archaic Radiocarbon Dates from the Lower Peninsula of Michigan, continued.

Site Name/ Lab Number	^{14}C Age B.P.	Uncorrected B.C.	Calibrated 1-sigma B.C.	Reference	Component/Point Type
Green Point/20SA1					
Beta-150203	2820 ± 40	870	1010–912	Monaghan et al. 2006	dates *Cucurbita pepo*
M-1432	2480 ± 120	530	784–515	Wright 1964	dates side notched
Hacklander					
Beta-11988	4770 ± 90	2820	3644–3504, 3427–3381	Bianchi and Heinrich 1992	Brewerton side notched
Kantzler/20BY30					
UGA-3195	4290 ± 75	2340	3022–2865	Larsen and Demeter 1979	reworked Middle Archaic
Leavitt/20CL81					
AA-1223	7886 ± 115	5936	6837–6639, 7031–6962, 6919–6878	Shott 1993	possible bifurcate date
Liberty Bridge/20BY79					
Beta-11130	2880 ± 70	930	1130–971	Monaghan 1993	dates small stemmed
Beta-11131	2770 ± 80	820	997–832	Monaghan 1993	dates small stemmed
Marquette Viaduct/State Street/ 20BY387					
Beta-154678	3980 ± 40	2030	2567–2519, 2499–2462	Lovis and Phillips 2002	narrow expanding stem
Beta-154680	4250 ± 100	2300	2819–2663, 2925–2835	Lovis and Phillips 2002	"
Beta-181524	3840 ± 40	1890	2346–2270, 2258–2204	Monaghan et al. 2006	dates *Cucurbita* rind
Naugle					
CWRU-169	2850 ± 110	900	1131–896	Ozker 1976	dates small stem and Meadowood
North Manitou #3					
M-2402	3030 ± 200	1080	1460–1001	MSU Laboratory Notes	dates stemmed and notched
Pinegrove Cemetery					
N-110	3010 ± 110	1060	1400–1113	Simons 1979	dates Satchell complex
Not reported	3305 ± 135	1355	1739–1434	Simons 1972	dates Satchell complex
Rock Hearth/20BE306					
Beta-6460	2910 ± 60	960	1208–1139, 1135–-1013	Clark 1990	dates smudge pit with fish remains
Beta-5373	3020 ± 140	1070	1419–1110	Clark 1990	Late Woodland ceramics, rejected
Beta-5374	3740 ± 80	1790	2233–2030, 2283–2248	Clark 1990	dates Archaic structure trench (E)
Beta-6461	3750 ± 100	1800	2300–2022	Clark 1990	dates Archaic structure trench (N)
Screaming Loon					
DIC-650	3360 ± 270	1410	2031–1371	Lovis 1990	dates various Late Archaic points
Schmidt					
M-1731	6550 ± 250	4600	5726–5258	Crane and Griffin 1968	rejected
M-1732	6650 ± 250	4700	5791–5356	Crane and Griffin 1968	rejected
M-1733	5400 ± 200	3450	4371–4036	Crane and Griffin 1968	rejected
M-1734	8100 ± 500	6150	7592–6455	Crane and Griffin 1968	rejected
N-1780	2470 ± 370	520	1002–106	Fairchild 1977	rejected
N-1781	4660 ± 740	2710	4250–2459	Fairchild 1977	rejected

Table 20.3. Calibrated Archaic Radiocarbon Dates from the Lower Peninsula of Michigan, continued.

Site Name/ Lab Number	^{14}C Age B.P.	Uncorrected B.C.	Calibrated 1-sigma B.C.	Reference	Component/Point Type
Shelton Mastodon/20OK394					
Beta-10302	9640 ± 120	7690	9012–8810, 9222–9107	Shoshani et al. 1990	LeCroy and Kessell
GX-13682	9490 ± 295	7540	9226–8453	Shoshani et al. 1990	LeCroy and Kessell
Stover/20BE307					
Uga-3552	3410 ± 100	1460	1829–1610, 1878–1839	Clark 1990	dates "firepit"
Vogelaar					
Beta-78825	4780 ± 100	2830	3654–3501, 3432–3379	Branstner and Hambacher eds. 1995	Middle Archaic feature
Weber I/20SA581					
Beta-6804	6230 ± 190	4280	5368–4941	Monaghan et al. 1986	dates large side-notched points
SI-5596	4560 ± 200	2610	3521–3017	Monaghan et al. 1986	"
Beta-5474	2990 ± 60	1040	1316–1187, 1183–1128	Monaghan et al. 1986	dates small notched points
Beta-5473	2990 ± 110	1040	1320–1108	Monaghan et al. 1986	"
Beta-5472	2910 ± 70	960	1133–1001, 1193–1138	Monaghan et al. 1986	"
Wymer					
Beta-3833	2500 ± 70	550	724–537, 785–742	Clark 1990	Oronoko, Sodus, Snyders points
Beta-4205	2280 ± 60	330	296–230, 400–352	Clark 1990	Wymer point
Beta-6464	2920 ± 130	970	1264–970	Clark 1990	Berrien corner-notched point
Zemaitis/20OT68					
Beta-65115	2200 ± 80	250	365–267, 263–174	Brashler and Mead 1996	dates Durst points
20IA305					
Beta-171298	4770 ± 40	2820	3602–3522	Branstner 2004	dates feature
Beta-171299	3560 ± 40	1610	1955–1876, 1841–1826	Branstner 2004	"
Beta-171300	7210 ± 40	5260	6081–6016, 6157–6143	Branstner 2004	"
Beta-171301	4100 ± 40	2150	2683–2577, 2856–2814	Branstner 2004	"

Michigan, eastern Upper Peninsula, and northern Lake Huron styles, thereby suggesting that these areas may have been part of a Straits of Mackinac settlement system. Likewise, the North Manitou #3 site, a multicomponent Woodland and Archaic occupation on North Manitou Island, yielded a ^{14}C date of 3030 ± 200 (1460–1001 cal B.C., M-2402). No diagnostics were directly associated with the sample, although a broad range of Late Archaic notched and stemmed point styles (as well as copper artifacts) were present in the excavations (Figure 20.4). Two tantalizingly early dates from the Dunn Farm site, one on charcoal and one on bone, were reported as an average of 3040 ± 125 (DIC-611A and DIC 611B), 1434–1119 cal B.C., by Brose and Hambacher (1999). Dunn Farm is a multicomponent Late Archaic, Early Woodland, Middle Woodland, and Historic-period site that has yielded a Middle Woodland ^{14}C date on wild rice (*Zizania aquatica*). It is currently difficult to isolate the Archaic component. In general, the late Archaic materials at the site demonstrate a clear focus on the extraction of distinctive primary raw materials from the Pi-wan-go-ning Quarry site at Norwood, Michigan, on the northwest coast of the Lower Peninsula (Cleland 1973; Cleland and Ruggles 1996; Luedtke 1976) as well as use of various cherts extracted from the local glacial till deposits (Lovis 1990).

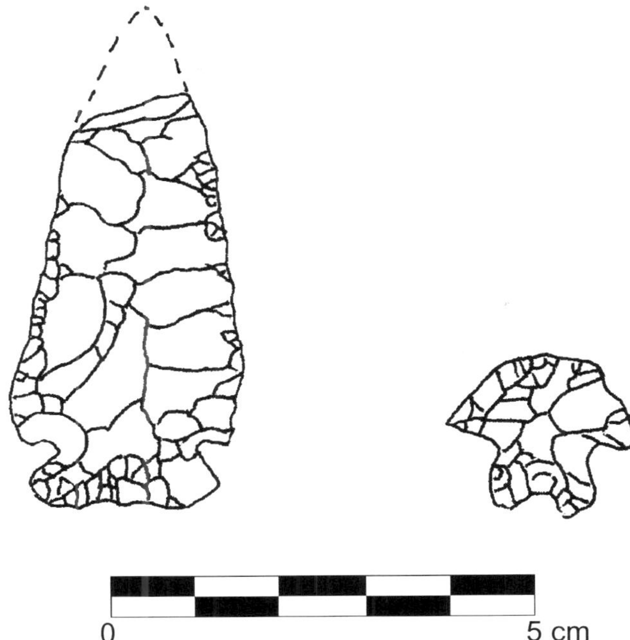

Figure 20.5. Kessell Side Notched and LeCroy bifurcate-base points from site 20OK394 (illustration by W. Lovis, after Shoshani et al. 1990).

Southeastern Lower Peninsula

Without doubt, southeastern lower Michigan is the most depauperate region in terms of usable Archaic-age ^{14}C dates (Table 20.3), although, as will be seen, its minimal record, in fact, provides some of the most significant information on the cultural affinities of the earliest Archaic in southern Michigan. Specifically, the two dates reported from site 20OK394 by Shoshani et al. (1990) are the only absolute dates on diagnostic lithics from Early Archaic context in Michigan (Figure 20.5). Dates of 9640 ± 120 B.P. (9012–9222 cal B.C., Beta-10302) and 9490 ± 295 B.P. (9226–8453 cal B.C., GX-13682) are associated with what have been identified as Kessell Side Notched and LeCroy bifurcate-base points. I agree with the site's investigators on their stylistic attributions as well as the acceptable age of the dates. Moreover, their discussion of Early Archaic LeCroy spatial distributions in southern lower Michigan reveals that components of the Midcontinent Archaic sequence as defined at the St. Albans site are confined largely to the southern third of the lower Michigan peninsula, terminating at a line south of the extent of deciduous hardwood forest (see also Ellis et al., this volume and Shott 1999 for a discussion of Early Archaic in southern Ontario). While not located in southeastern Michigan, the Leavitt site has produced a date of 7886 ± 115 (7031–6639 cal B.C., AA-1223) that, one could argue, potentially dates an Early Archaic component that includes bifurcate-base diagnostics, rather than being an unacceptably late date from the Paleoindian component (Shott 1986, 1993). This proposition needs to be further assessed. The 6157–6016 cal B.C. date (Beta-171300) from site 20IA305 in Ionia County, albeit not in association with diagnostics, also certainly speaks to early activity in central southern Michigan. It is certainly worth considering the information provided by Purtill (this volume) on the Ohio Archaic, particularly northwestern Ohio, in attempting to place the southeastern Michigan Archaic chronology in broader regional perspective.

Saginaw Valley of Southern Lower Michigan

Here, as I have in the past, I isolate the Saginaw Valley Archaic radiocarbon chronology since it, without doubt, represents the most refined view of chronological change in projectile point styles in southern Michigan. Perhaps the most noticeable omission in the record is the complete lack of dated Early Archaic sites in the region.

However, on a relative scale, the Middle Archaic is well represented by dates and assemblages of varying quality from the Weber I, Bear Creek, Ebenhoff, and Leach sites along with various other undated site contexts. These sites have previously been grouped into the Dehmel Road phase (Lovis and Robertson 1989; Robertson et al. 1999). For the current discussion, this phase is bracketed by dates as early as 5368 cal B.C. (Beta-6804) at the Weber I site and as recent as 2778 cal B.C. (Beta-56311) at the Bear Creek site. This range brackets dated contexts lacking diagnostics at the Ebenhoff site. Specific point styles attributed to the Dehmel Road phase (Figure 20.6) include large, square-based points or knives with shallow

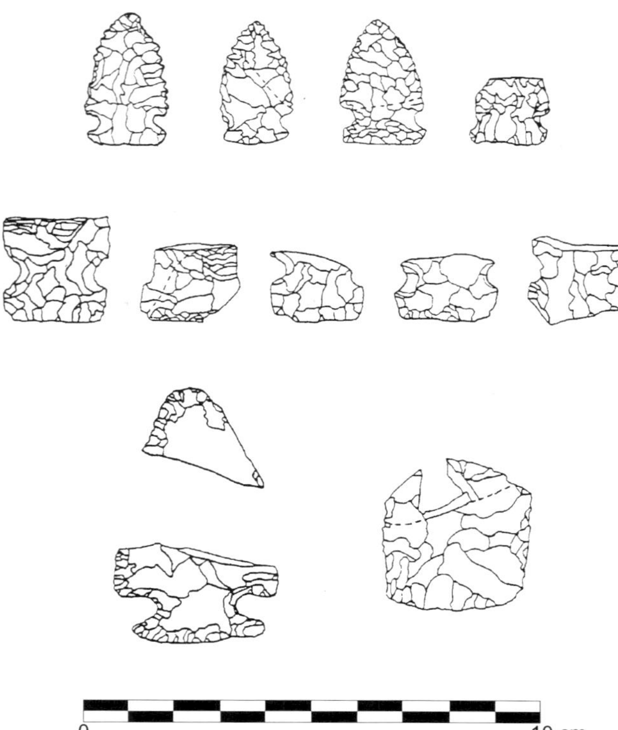

Figure 20.6. Dehmel Road–phase Middle Archaic bifaces from the Weber I site (illustration by W. Lovis, after Robertson 1987).

side notches, similar to Helton, Big Sandy, and Otter Creek. A series of smaller side-notched points with short blades, serrations, and relatively deeper notches occurs in association with the larger series. A single large *affinis* Thebes-cluster point base was also recovered. Occupation Zone II at the Weber I site is bracketed by ^{14}C dates of 5368–4941 cal B.C. (Beta-6804) and 3521–3017 cal B.C. (SI-5596) and should, therefore, date all three point series. A similar large Raddatz Side Notched point recovered from the Bear Creek site caps the upper, or more recent, end of the Dehmel Road–phase continuum, dating between 2915 and 2778 cal B.C. (Beta-56118). At least stylistically, this would signal the end of the Middle Archaic period by ca. 3000 cal B.C. Of note is the dominance of local Bayport chert (Luedtke 1976) in Middle Archaic assemblages, complemented by a variety of quartz, quartzite, and till cherts and only a minor component of exchanged material (see Robertson 1987). While this observation is not terribly surprising given the local distribution of Bayport chert across the Thumb, the mouth of Saginaw Bay, and northwestward into Arenac County, it nonetheless speaks to more restricted exchange relationships during the Middle Archaic than during the ensuing Late Archaic.

Subsequent Late Archaic point styles witness increasing amounts of stylistic diversity and manufacture on a larger array of raw materials, culminating in Early Woodland stemmed varieties such as Adena and Kramer by ca. 600 cal B.C., and are often found in association with thick, coiled ceramics of the Marion and Schultz types. Given substantial recent work since the last major chronological update for the Late Archaic (Robertson et al. 1999), I initiate the larger discussion of this time period with comments on so-called Dustin points. As initially defined, Dustin points were seen as Michigan variants of the Lamoka type from New York State, with narrow, diamond-shaped blades and shallow side to corner notches. It has become clear, however, that Dustin points, as originally defined, actually represent the longer end of a size continuum. The shorter varieties on this continuum often stylistically approach a Crawford Knoll/Innes/Merom-Trimble category (see Kenyon 1989 on the relationships of the Ontario varieties; also Ellis et al., this volume; and see Winters 1969 on Merom and Trimble). Some appear to have been intentionally manufactured as short varieties, and others appear to have been reworked to shorter lengths. Reworking of the blades on the longer varieties often resulted in drills with rather narrow basal haft elements.

The inception of these narrow-bladed styles is best recorded at site 20BY387 in Bay City (Figure 20.7), where an almost homogeneous assemblage has been bracketed by radiocarbon dates of 2925 cal B.C. (Beta-154680) and 2204 cal B.C. (Beta-181524). At the Weber I site, these varieties date as recently as 1001 cal B.C. (Beta-5472). Thus, these expanding-stemmed point styles, whether large or small, enjoyed a period of popularity and use of almost 2,000 years.

However, the narrow-bladed series did not exist in isolation for over two millennia. Feeheley points, with their broad blades and corner notches (Figure 20.8), apparently also made an appearance by ca. 2600–2200 cal B.C. (M-1139).

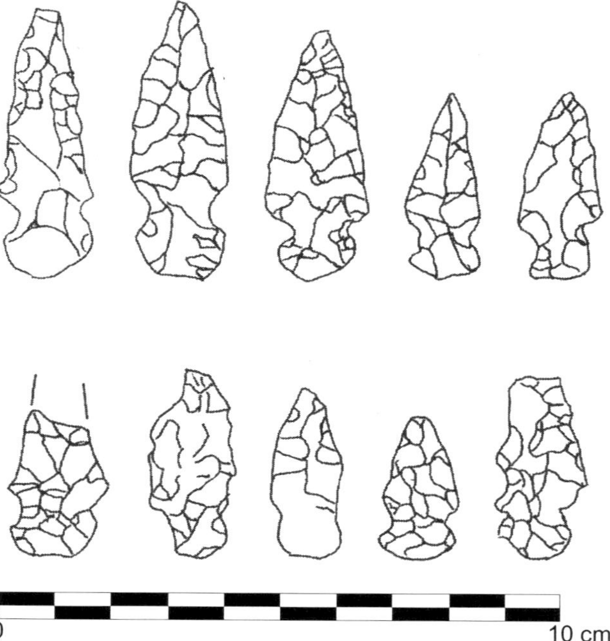

Figure 20.7. Long and short narrow-blade points from Marquette Viaduct site (20BY387) (illustration by W. Lovis, after Cook 2002).

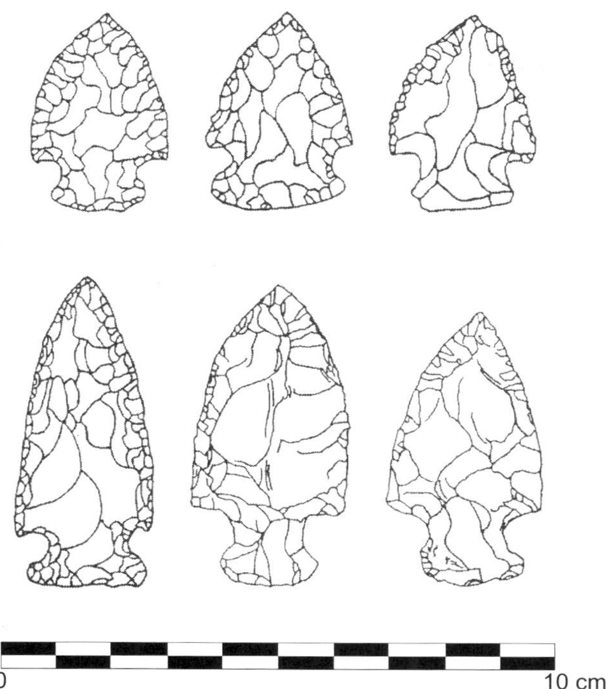

Figure 20.8. Feeheley points from the Feeheley site and Van Etten points from the Brandt site: top row, small Feeheley points (illustration by W. Lovis, after Robertson 1987); bottom row, left, large Feeheley point; center and right, Van Etten points from the Brandt site (illustrations by W. Lovis, after Robertson 1987 and Mead and Kingsley 1985).

Significantly, these, too, express rather substantial size variation and at times almost grade into larger Middle Woodland varieties. They were also periodically reworked into notched, so-called dumbbell, end scrapers (Taggart 1967). Large, expanding-stemmed or corner-removed, broad-blade varieties termed "Van Etten" points (Figure 20.8) appear to date to 1412–1306 cal B.C. (DIC-2501) at the Brandt site, although one must keep in mind the mortuary context of the Brandt site and the possibility that the points are idiosyncratic. In turn, there is temporal overlap of the Brandt-site series with early stemmed varieties attributed to the Satchell complex at the Pinegrove Cemetery site (Figure 20.9), dated to between 1739 and 1113 cal B.C. (N-110, one additional unreported lab number). A stemmed Satchell point on graywacke was also recently recovered from a feature at the Marquette Viaduct locale of the Fletcher site (20BY28) (Figures 20.9 and 20.10) with an age of 2130–1960 cal B.C. This date clearly extends the time range for the Satchell complex back by half a millennium and raises the possibility of this local variant of the Broad Point Archaic having an even earlier date of inception. Satchell-complex stemmed points also have clear similarities with materials from the Adder Orchard and other sites in southern Ontario (see Ellis et al. 1990; Ellis et al., this volume; Kenyon 1983). Thus, one can argue for a rather

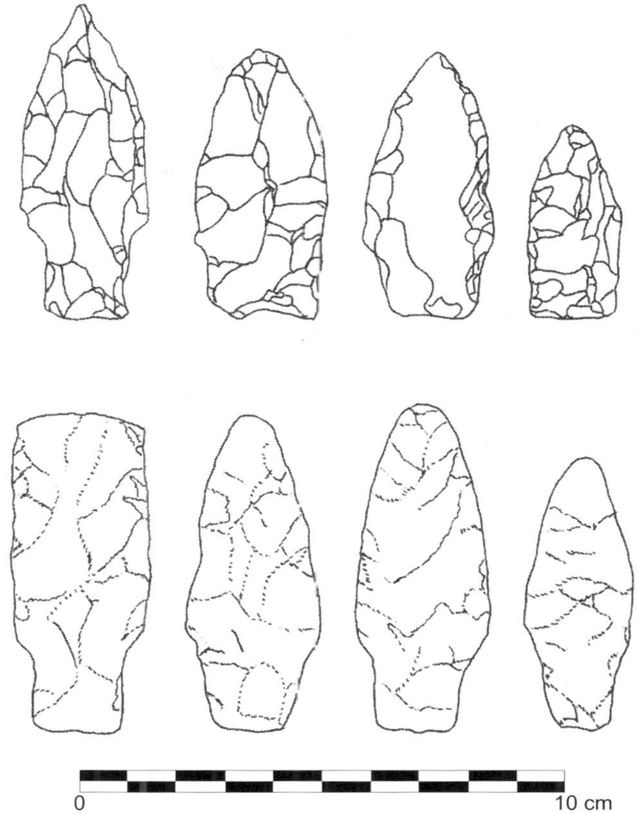

Figure 20.9. Satchell-complex points from Marquette Viaduct locale of Fletcher site (20BY28) and the Pinegrove Cemetery site: top row, Marquette Viaduct locale of Fletcher site (illustration by W. Lovis, after Cook 2002); bottom row, Pinegrove Cemetery (illustration by W. Lovis, after Simons 1972).

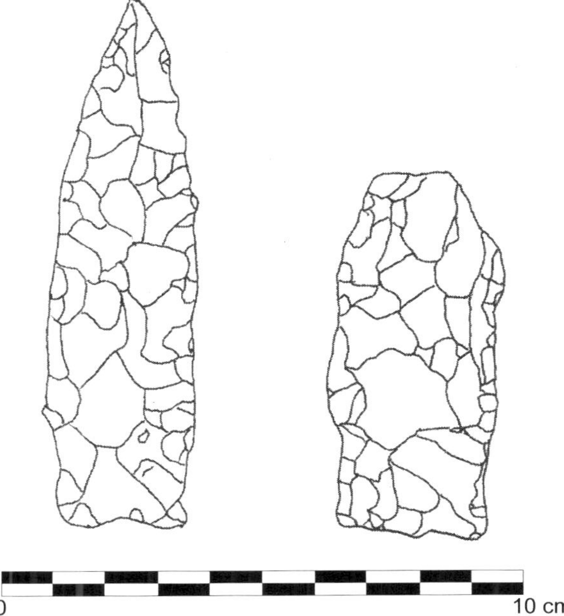

Figure 20.10. Satchell-complex points from Marquette Viaduct locale of Fletcher site (20BY28) (illustration by W. Lovis, after Cook 2002).

heterogeneous grouping of corner-notched, corner-removed, and early stemmed, broad-bladed point types being used in tandem with the narrow-bladed varieties.

A clear stylistic threshold occurred ca. 1200–1000 cal B.C., and a long litany of named point styles had their inception prior to ca. 600–500 cal B.C. and persisted to or past that point into the beginning of the Early Woodland time period. These point types clearly span the transition between the end of Late Archaic lifeways and the onset of ceramic-producing Early Woodland societies in the region and include Meadowood side-notched, Schultz side-notched, Hunt side-notched, Hodges side-notched, Davis side-notched, Hind corner-notched, Durst Stemmed, Pomranky cache blades (actually preforms), and, of course, Turkey-tail "points" or cache blades often manufactured on Wyandotte chert (see Krakker 1997 for discussion of the social implications of such cache materials during the Terminal Archaic). Leaving Durst Stemmed and Turkey-tail cache blades aside for the moment, I explore the relationships between Meadowood, Schultz, Hunt, Hodges, Davis, and Hind further.

To my mind, the highly generalized Pomranky-style cache blade is the initial starting platform for all of the parallel- to ovate-blade, side- and corner-notched varieties present during this waning Late Archaic time period (Figures 20.11 and 20.12; but see Binford 1963a). It is the range of notch variation and blade treatment that has given rise to the different named varieties. Corner notches on a Pomranky-style blade result in Hind or Hind-like points. The combination of side notches of variable width and depth with minor differences in the angle of the blade-base juncture results in the Meadowood/Schultz/Hunt/Hodges/Davis continuum (see Binford 1963b). Serrations on the blades make them Hodges points. At times, the corner-notched Hind and side-notched Meadowood varieties were treated to additional notches above the original series, resulting in specimens with multiple notches (Figure 20.11). Resharpening of blades, probably from their use as knives or cutting implements, resulted in sharply incurvate blades on both side- and corner-notched varieties. Ultimately, some were worked into drills, either T-base forms, on which only the original basal segment remains, or corner- and side-notched drills on which the entire haft segment remains (Figure 20.12).

Some evidence suggests that the corner-notched Hind series, associated with so-called Glacial Kame in Ontario (Spence and Fox 1986), may have had a somewhat earlier inception than the remaining side-notched series. In Michigan the Andrews-site burial assemblages have Hind-like corner-notched varieties with an age of 1622–1259 cal B.C. (M-659). That these continued into later periods is best evidenced by the seven ^{14}C estimates from the Conservation Park site, which have an age range of 1002–503 cal B.C. While Beld (1991) groups a full range of corner-, side-, and multiple-notched variation into a single category that he calls "Meadowood," a broad range of stylistic variation is present in the Conservation Park assemblage. Corroborative ages are available from

Figure 20.11. Hind corner-notched points from the Andrews and Conservation Park sites: top row, Andrews site (illustration by W. Lovis); bottom row, Conservation Park site (illustration by W. Lovis, after Beld 1991).

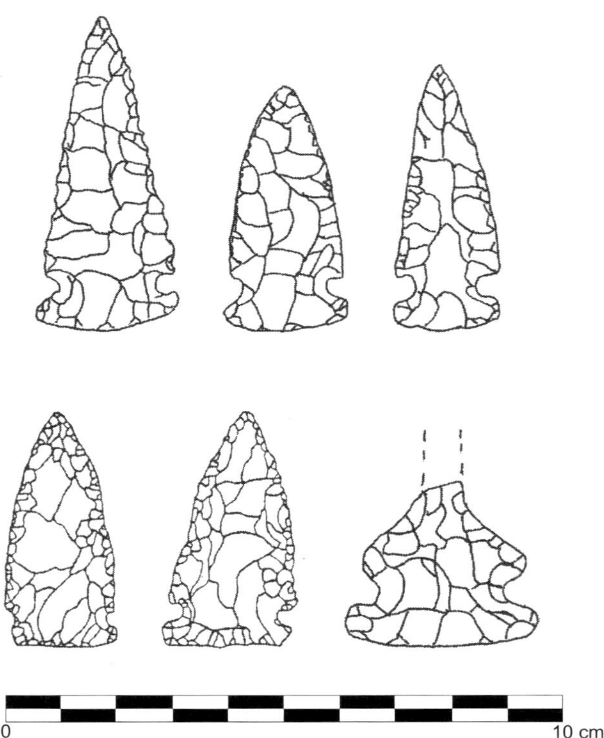

Figure 20.12. Meadowood point variation in the Saginaw Valley (illustration by W. Lovis, after Beld 1991; Binford 1963a, 1963b; Robertson 1997).

the Naugle site, dated to 1131–896 cal B.C. (CWRU-169) and the Green Point (20SA1) site, dated to 1010–515 cal B.C. (Beta-150203, M-1432). While primarily dating small, stemmed points, the two Liberty Bridge (20BY79) age estimates of 1130 and 832 cal B.C. (Beta-11130 and 11131) may also apply to Meadowood and reworked Meadowood side-notched points. Notably, the later end of this age range is consistent with two age estimates from the basal Early Woodland levels at the Schultz site (20SA2), which contained Schultz side-notched points. Clearly, these notched forms persisted into early ceramic-producing periods, at least in the Saginaw Valley, although assemblages during the succeeding Early Woodland came to be dominated by a stemmed-point continuum including Adena, Cresap, and Kramer (Garland and Beld 1999), which is not discussed here.

Expanding-stemmed varieties identified as Durst/Ace of Spades/Innes points (Figure 20.13) also occur during the earlier segment of this continuum (Lovis and Robertson 1989). The dates from the Liberty Bridge (20BY79) and Naugle sites, which provide a range for these varieties of 1140–892 cal B.C., may equally be applied to the earlier end of the Meadowood continuum time span. At a certain level of chronological symmetry it would be parsimonious to have these materials culminate the narrow-bladed point continuum and be supplanted by Hind/Meadowood varieties ca. 1000 cal B.C. At present, however, the Saginaw Valley dates do not allow this, and, in fact, if one turns to the Grand River valley, a date from the Zemaitis site on a buried aceramic stratum with Durst-like stemmed points produced an age of 365–174 cal B.C. (Beta-65115), suggesting that these materials might have continued in use later than initially anticipated.

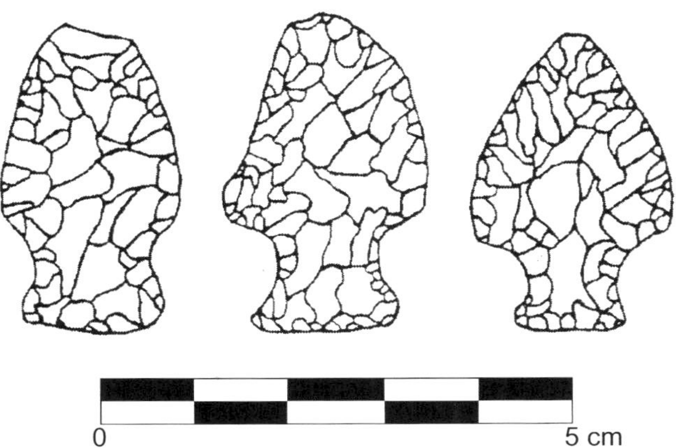

Figure 20.13. Durst/Ace of Spade points from Liberty Bridge site (20BY79) (illustration by W. Lovis, after Robertson 1987).

As mentioned in passing above, Late Archaic groups of the Saginaw Valley incorporated a wide array of raw materials into local-level lithic production, bespeaking greatly expanded social or material exchange relationships compared with earlier groups. This interregional connectivity was broadly based, encompassing an area minimally including southeastern Michigan (Pipe Creek chert), southwestern Ontario (Onondaga and Kettle Point cherts; see Ellis et al., this volume), and northwestern Ohio (Pipe Creek, Ten Mile Creek, Flint Ridge, and Upper Mercer cherts) as well as extending further south to southern Illinois, southern Indiana, and Kentucky (Wyandotte chert, or Indiana hornstone). The latter material occurs almost exclusively as Turkey-tail points (see Krakker 1997; Robertson et al. 1999). Metasediments such as graywacke were employed almost exclusively on Satchell-complex diagnostics. Also of note, low frequencies of Bayport chert as well as finished artifacts are often found in Late Archaic assemblages from both southwestern Ontario and northwestern Ohio. While copper is at times found in Late Archaic burials in the Saginaw Valley region, to my knowledge, lithic materials from western and northern Michigan are so poorly represented that they are essentially invisible, thereby throwing the weight of interregional interaction primarily to the south, potentially vindicating interpretations of certain sites as points of social and ceremonial interaction (Abel et al. 2001).

Southwestern Lower Michigan

Southwestern Michigan has produced multiple Late Archaic ^{14}C dates (Table 20.3), several of which date specific point styles, but these derive almost exclusively from multicomponent sites with subsequent Woodland and Upper Mississippian occupations. Consequently, the radiocarbon dates have, for the most part, been interpreted in terms of pan-regional artifact styles (Clark 1990), although the question has been raised whether it is even possible to apply the nearby Saginaw Valley sequence to southwestern Michigan with any legitimacy (Robertson et al. 1999). That said, Robertson and colleagues make general associations of styles between the two regions; I modify that discussion here with particular attention paid to ^{14}C-dated contexts. Of particular note is the almost exclusive use of local till cherts in the Archaic assemblages from the region, although exceptionally low frequencies of primary-source raw materials from Illinois, Indiana, Ohio, Ontario, and other parts of Michigan can be observed. Lambrix chert, from a series of till deposits in Oceana and Mason counties (Luedtke 1976), and the qualitatively similar Deer Lick Creek chert (see Campbell 1988) likewise did not figure prominently in Archaic raw-material procurement. This suggests that the Archaic inhabitants of southwestern Michigan may have operated in a more insular fashion than their contemporaries in other parts of the state.

Radiocarbon-dated Archaic point types include side-notched (Eidson, Oronoko), corner-notched (Berrien), and expanding-stemmed (Wymer, Sodus) series defined in the St. Joseph River valley sequence (Clark 1990). Of these, the Eidson side-notched series poses the biggest interpretive problem. The series encompasses a broad range of morphological variation that could easily span Middle Archaic through Early

Woodland and even more recent periods if a more refined typology that could discriminate among these periods had been developed. Thus, the single date of 980–802 cal B.C. (Beta-6463) on Eidson side-notched from the Eidson site probably dates the more recent range of variation in this heterogeneous group, making such points earlier than the Meadowood-like Oronoko side-notched points, which are dated to 785–537 cal B.C. at the Wymer site—a range consistent with that of the Meadowood phase in the Saginaw Valley sequence.

Robertson et al. (1999) suggest that the Berrien corner-notched series from southwestern Michigan bears strong metric resemblances to materials discussed above from the Saginaw Valley, including the narrow- and broad-bladed corner-notched series dated to 3000–1000 cal B.C. Berrien points have been dated at the Wymer and Eidson sites to an age range of 1264–970 cal B.C. (Beta-6152 and Beta-6464), consistent with the later end of the corner-notched series in the Saginaw Valley sequence. Moreover, the two defined expanding-stemmed series from southwestern Michigan—Wymer varieties A and B and Sodus (but particularly Wymer)—bear a strong resemblance to Durst expanding-stemmed points. Wymer varieties have been dated at the Wymer and Eidson sites to 400–230 cal B.C. (Beta-4205) and 1223–1017 cal B.C. (Beta-6152), respectively. Sodus expanding-stemmed points have been dated at Wymer to 785–537 cal B.C. (Beta-3833). The age range of the Wymer and Sodus points is closely consistent with the Saginaw Valley and Grand Valley dates on late expanding-stemmed small points.

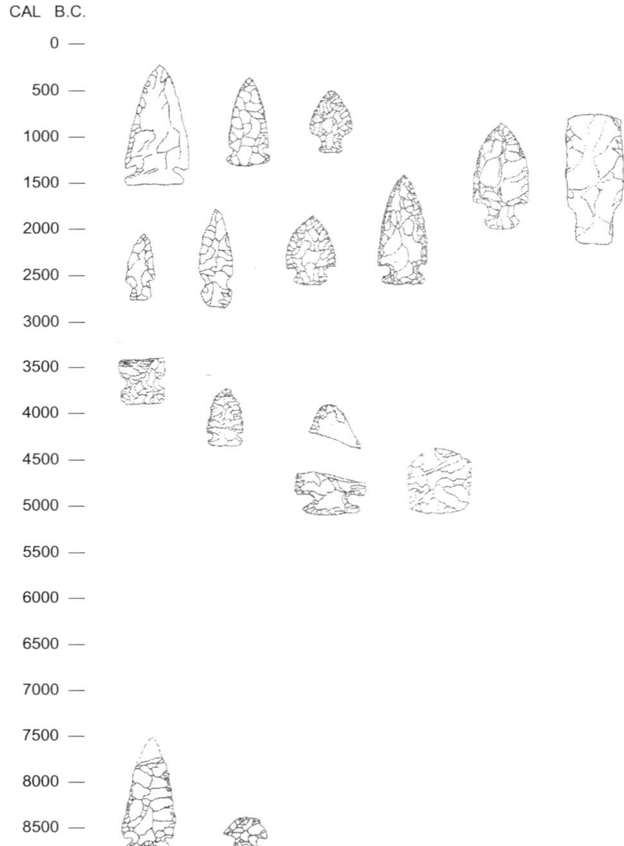

Figure 20.14. Revised Archaic chronology for southern Michigan, 9000 to 500 cal B.C. (illustration by W. Lovis; courtesy Michigan State University).

Calibrated Chronology of the Michigan Archaic

So, what does this intensive calibration and discussion exercise actually reveal about the chronology of the Michigan Archaic?

North of the deciduous hardwood zone in southern lower Michigan almost no dated contexts have directly associated diagnostic points or other objects. The dates from the Riverside Cemetery site in Menominee County aside, the current group of 48 dates reveals only that people began using copper as early as 7182 cal B.C. and that there appears to have been a peak of occupation (at least as reflected in a peak in discovered sites!) between 3000 and 800 cal B.C. It will be almost impossible to either isolate or associate regional cultural traditions on the basis of this type of data. It is abundantly clear that, regardless of the taphonomic processes at work, priority must be placed on establishing direct associations between diagnostics and datable organics or that residues adhering to specific objects should be directly dated, regardless of cost, if this problem is to be solved.

Reappraisal of the 70-date ^{14}C chronology in the deciduous-hardwood-forest zone of southern lower Michigan, nevertheless, has proven highly productive and allows a better-refined chronological sequence of point types (Figure 20.14). Early side-notched and bifurcate-base points clearly date between 9200 and 8400 cal B.C. at the Shelton Mastodon site, and the bifurcate varieties may extend as recently as 7000–6600 cal B.C., if one accepts the previously discarded Leavitt site date. Actually, the Leavitt date is more consistent with the known age ranges for bifurcates in the Midcontinent. A brief hiatus occurs in the radiocarbon chronology between ca. 6600 and 5400 cal B.C.

At least in the Saginaw Valley, the period from ca. 5400 to 3000 cal B.C. (previously defined as the Dehmel Road phase by Lovis and Robertson 1989) is marked by a diagnostic assemblage of large square-based and shallow-side-notched points; smaller side-notched, square-based, serrated varieties; and an *affinis* Thebes-cluster knife base. This pattern is clearly consistent with adjacent traditions across the northeastern United States and Canada. By 3000 cal B.C., several point varieties appear to have developed in tandem, including a continuum of both large and small narrow- and broad-bladed varieties variously categorized as Dustin, Feeheley, Crawford Knoll, Innes, and so on. These persisted to ca. 1000 cal B.C. This cluster was joined by stemmed Satchell varieties (similar to Adder Orchard in Canada) by ca. 2100 cal B.C. at the Fletcher site as well as by larger expanding-stemmed varieties (Van Etten at the Brandt site) by ca. 1400 cal B.C. These latter materials clearly represent a local variant of a Broad Point Archaic horizon.

The transition to the final phases of the Late Archaic began ca. 1600 cal B.C. with parallel-bladed and corner-notched Hind points, as dated at the Andrews site. By ca. 1200 cal B.C., these were joined by side-notched Meadowood and several Meadowood-related varieties that lasted until ca. 500 cal B.C., some undergoing modification in the form of resharpening, multiple notching, and production or recycling into drills. Contemporary with the notched forms were expanding-stemmed varieties best characterized as Durst, appearing ca. 1200 cal B.C. and possibly lasting as late as 200 cal B.C. By 1000 cal B.C., Turkey-tail forms occurred, as well, but rarely in occupation context. By ca. 500 cal B.C., stemmed Early Woodland forms, including Adena, Cresap, and Kramer varieties, dominated southern Michigan assemblages. This closing period of the Michigan Archaic, ca. 1200–500 cal B.C. (or perhaps 1600–500 cal B.C.), has been termed the "Meadowood" phase by multiple authors (Garland and Beld 1999; Lovis and Robertson 1989; Robertson et al. 1999) and was followed by the Early Woodland Schultz phase.

Regional Geoarchaeology and the Nature of Archaic Site Population Preservation

The future of Archaic research in Michigan lies deeply buried on floodplains.

Some time ago, John O'Shea and I collaborated on a discussion of "Major Problem Orientations in Michigan Archaeology" (Lovis and O'Shea 1994). One of the primary themes of that treatise was the nature of the information archaeologists collectively use to understand the past, specifically what we know about the populations of archaeological sites on which we base our interpretations. Are they representative? Under what conditions are they formed and preserved? Do we know where any biases might lie? These taphonomic questions are not easily answered and, in fact, require a detailed understanding of site formation and postdepositional processes to appropriately address. Here, I focus on one aspect of this problem—the formation and burial of Archaic-age sites in alluvial contexts in southern Michigan. While this might not prove particularly insightful to those who work in the well-evolved drainages of the Midwest and Midsouth, it is becoming a more significant focus of research in more northern and younger drainage systems.

Recognition that alluvial contexts preserve deeply buried sites as a consequence of floodplain depositional processes has great time depth across the eastern United States and has led to regional-scale or drainage-system modeling as a predictive device for locating archaeological sites (e.g. Bettis and Hajic 1995). Clearly, ignoring an entire suite of sites (and, consequently, their locations), many of which are not readily visible because of deep burial, skews one's view of overall settlement patterning. Sensitivity to this issue came relatively late in Michigan, largely precipitated by the efforts of Curtis Larsen (1980), Christopher Peebles (1978), and John Halsey in bringing this potential to the attention of the research community.

Catalyzed by this initial work, in the early 1980s, geoarchaeologist G. William "Bill" Monaghan and I set out a field research agenda that we felt would assist in the accumulation of the data necessary to answer questions of floodplain taphonomy and site preservation in southern lower Michigan. This agenda was implemented across all the projects with which we have been associated, both compliance and research based, and ultimately resulted in the accumulation of a large array of comparable data. We recently synthesized this cumulative material into a model of site formation and burial that explains the differential representation of sites of different time periods in the archaeological record of Michigan (Monaghan and Lovis 2006; see also Lovis 2004 for a discussion of urban landscape taphonomy and formation processes).

Of significance to Archaic-period research is that, at least in the Michigan and Huron drainage basins, site burial was an episodic phenomenon, largely keyed to what appear to have been climatically and isostatic rebound-outlet induced fluctuations of lake level. During higher water fluctuations of the lake basins, river drainages graded to a higher elevation, which in turn resulted in the increased deposition of suspended sediments in floodplain contexts. While we can document three such episodes, it is the earliest of these that is of importance here, associated with the Nipissing I and II stages of the postglacial Michigan and Huron lake basins and dated to ca. 4000–3000 RCYBP (ca. 3000–1400 cal B.C.). Multiple buried soil surfaces on several drainage systems in southern lower Michigan have been documented for this time period. Some contain cultural material, and many do not.

To take full advantage of our observations of these phenomena and to better understand the structure of what remains of Archaic site populations, Monaghan and I (2006) have proposed that regular incorporation of an earth-sciences perspective into regional archaeological research be systematically implemented. Only by augmenting observations on the evolution and dynamics of floodplain development across multiple fluvial systems will archaeologists be able to properly assess and refine our knowledge of what time periods, and in what contexts, buried Archaic surfaces are most likely to be preserved. Thus, researchers should have the ability to refine scale, while refining resolution will be contingent on both the methods employed and the intensity of sampling. Monaghan and I view this as a long-term and cumulative research agenda for Michigan archaeology in general, and Archaic-stage research in particular.

Underwater Archaeology and Our Knowledge of the Early and Middle Archaic

The future of Archaic research in Michigan lies underwater.

While I certainly favor various theoretical and problem approaches that diminish the role of environmental or ecological factors in seeking to understand the details of Archaic society (most archaeologists are, of course, anthropologists!), the environmental and landscape evolution of the Great Lakes region ensures that limiting variables will always constrain researchers' ability to apply such approaches. As briefly mentioned above, and as many readers are already aware, the terminal Pleistocene deglaciation of the Great Lakes was a complex process related to the effects of glacial meltwater and its interaction with bedrock and surficial geology, potential drainageways and outlets, and the effects of isostatic readjustment (Larson and Schaetzl 2001; Monaghan and Lovis 2006). Among the most overt outcomes of this interaction, in brief, were marked changes in the base water planes of the major Great Lakes lake basins. These changes resulted at times in water planes many meters above those at present and at times below current planes by as much as 100+ m (330+ ft) (see Figures 20.2 and 20.3). It is largely to these low-water stages, particularly in the Michigan-Huron drainage basin, that much of the ensuing discussion is directed. My approach here is not to provide a detailed evolutionary history of this conjoined basin but, rather, to look at the implications of such low-water stages for interpretation of the Archaic past and to create a polemic for future research. Further, I link this consideration to some of the topical areas discussed below.

In brief, between ca. 11,000 B.P and 6000 B.P., the water planes of the conjoined Michigan-Huron lake basin, while variable, were below the plane of the modern lake (Figures 20.2 and 20.3). In more northern areas, north of a line between Saginaw Bay and Manistee, and subject to isostatic rebound, the shoreline features associated with this period have been raised above the level of the modern lake plane and are available to archaeologists through standard inspection techniques, for example, as is the case with the Samel's Field terminal Paleoindian–Early Archaic occupation (Cleland and Ruggles 1996). To the south of this line, they remain submerged below modern lake levels. Thus, in southern Michigan at least, about 5,000 years of the Early and Middle Archaic record is probably currently submerged under the modern lake. Past analyses of this topic have made a case for both the modeling of submerged shoreline features and better understanding of the attenuated nature of the current terrestrial archaeological record of the Archaic period (Lovis et al. 1995; Lovis et al. 1994; Lovis and MacDonald 1999). Major components of the Early and Middle Archaic record, particularly as it relates to coastal and littoral settlement systems, are currently submerged, whereas what were then "upland" components of the settlement systems are available for inspection and provide the only direct measure of Archaic adaptation. This deficiency needs to be addressed, and the vehicle is underwater archaeology.

My ongoing discussions with Russell Skowronek, Margaret Holman, John O'Shea, and others have led me to the conclusion that regular and systematic professional research effort must be applied to the problem. Recent research in regions with similar underwater potential suggests that, under the proper conditions, submerged Archaic and earlier archaeological sites can be discovered and incorporated into regional analyses of settlement (e.g., Blanton 1996; Faught 2004).

In Michigan and other parts of the upper and lower Great Lakes, researchers have a solid basic knowledge of changing lake elevations during this period (Larsen 1974, 1985, 1987, 1999; Larson and Schaetzl 2001; Monaghan and Lovis 2006). Archaeologists have contributed to this knowledge, and we further know that submerged and intact surfaces can be preserved under the proper conditions (e.g., Hunter 2004). For example, Project Drowned Forest, in southern Lake Huron, has examined one of the more recently discovered of several submerged stands of rooted tree stumps on the bottomlands of the Great Lakes and has produced a suite of radiocarbon dates suggesting that transgressive events between the Stanley low and the Nipissing high lake stages attained elevations of about 165 m (540 ft) amsl (ca. 12 m [40 ft] below modern) by ca. 7000 RCYBP (6000 cal B.C.), during the Middle Archaic (Hunter 2004). To date, archaeologists have not been directly involved with this project. This locale has produced abundant botanical information suggesting that the nature of forests at this time, and at this elevation, was actually quite different than that inferred for the currently exposed uplands on the basis of dated pollen cores. Moreover, the formation processes of this locale are well understood and provide a template for future predictive modeling of preserved surfaces on the bottomlands. Current information points to a linkage between eolian activation, coastal or otherwise, and coastal transgression in relatively protected lee shore locations. These are variables that require substantially more investigation. It is, further, doubtful that this locale is unique and, given the cyclic nature of dune activation (see Loope and Arbogast 2000), that it is only at this elevation and for this time period that such transgressive lakeshore events are preserved on the bottomlands.

The Origins, Dispersal, and Role of Domestic Plants in the Michigan Archaic

Domesticating the Michigan Archaic (?): squash is good.

Researchers debate the timing, impact, and agencies by which domesticates were incorporated into the Archaic economy of the Midwest, particularly different varieties of *Cucurbita pepo*. In more northern latitudes such as those of the Great Lakes region, including Michigan, the evidence for the use of Mesoamerican cultigens has been limited, though not for lack of research effort, including concerted use of fine-scale recovery techniques across a range of sites and projects. Until quite recently, however, the only documented instance of *C. pepo* in the Michigan Archaic record has been a suite of three seeds recovered from adjacent to the Green Point site (20SA1) in the Saginaw drainage more than 40 years ago (Wright 1964). These seeds currently remain undated despite the advent of small-sample AMS techniques. The report on their discovery made an excellent attempt to link these early squash examples with the Terminal Archaic occupation at Green Point, thereby making them the earliest known examples of such cultigens in the state.

Indirect evidence of domestication includes the infamous negative impression of *C. pepo* ssp. *ovifera* in an Early Woodland Schultz Thick pottery coil reported from the Schultz site (20SA2), adjacent to the Green Point site and dated ca. 2500 RCYBP (ca. 780–500 cal B.C.; Ford 1986; Ozker 1982). Thus, the presumed ages of the Green Point and Schultz specimens are close, spanning the Terminal Archaic–Early Woodland transition. More importantly, Ozker (1982:38–42) makes the observation that the *C. pepo* seeds from Green Point are much larger than the Schultz vessel impression, and she goes on to make the case that two varieties of squash were present in the Saginaw Valley during this transitional Archaic–Early Woodland time frame. Presumably, the larger variety from Green Point is *C. pepo* ssp. *pepo*, the Mesoamerican strain. At present, measurements on both the Green Point specimens and the Schultz site impression clearly reveal size differences but are insufficient for making comparison either between sites or with the larger range of *C. pepo* from the Midwest.

Additional data from two other Saginaw basin contexts, and supplementary discussion that bears on the larger argument, have recently been presented by Lovis (2002b), Egan-Bruhy (2002), and Monaghan et al. (2006). Synoptically, we have recovered a squash rind from site 20BY387 in Bay City, Michigan, that may be either wild or domesticated, given its thickness of less than 2 mm. It was recovered from a pit feature containing Late Archaic diagnostics and has been direct AMS dated to 2900 cal B.C. Additionally, a relatively large seed was recovered adjacent to, and in contexts similar to, the reported Green Point specimens. Monaghan, Egan-Bruhy, and I, along with others, concur that this is *C. pepo*. On the basis of seed size and morphology, however, it could be either ssp. *pepo* or ssp. *ovifera*. It has been direct AMS dated to 1000 cal B.C. If ssp. *pepo*, it would be an early occurrence of the Mesoamerican variety This date, further, calls into question the originally inferred age of the other Green Point specimens (they may date differently than the adjacent occupations) as well as the timing of squash introduction in the region. Thus, by at least 2900 cal B.C., Late Archaic populations were using wild or domesticated squash species for food or technological purposes or both. By 1000 cal B.C., a possible Mesoamerican variety was present in sufficient quantity to be recovered on two occasions from contexts adjacent to a Late Archaic occupation. And by 780 cal B.C., eastern varieties were present in sufficient quantities in domestic context to be incorporated into Early Woodland ceramic paste during vessel production (Monaghan et al. 2006).

To date, and despite research on Late Archaic–age sites in southwestern Michigan as well as further north in the Lower Peninsula of Michigan, the only occurrences of Archaic domesticated cucurbits are in the Saginaw Valley, which suggests a rather restricted biogeography and human use. This observation warrants additional and careful scrutiny in future regional work across southern Michigan. Additionally, while recovery frequency suggests low density, repetitive discovery and cultural contexts reveal that cucurbits may have been relatively common around domestic localities, either during technological use, during processing for technological or consumption purposes, or as part of tended garden plots. That said, nothing indicates that domesticated *Cucurbita* had a discernible impact on Late Archaic hunter-gatherer economy, and, in fact, it does not appear to have been a substantial part of the local hunter-gatherer diet until at least the latter part of the Middle Woodland (Monaghan et al. 2006).

This all, of course, begs the question of agency, a salient and long-standing question not only in Michigan but also across the greater Midwest. Context plays an important role in the interpretation presented here (see Monaghan et al. 2006). Given its thickness, the 20BY387 rind fragment is most likely from a wild variety, which would suggest local preadaptation to the use of cucurbits before 4000 B.P. and probably before the introduction of domestic strains. If, however, it is from a domesticated variety, it demonstrates early presence, use, and deposition of the cultigen in habitation debris. All of the large *C. pepo* seeds from the Green Point site come from directly adjacent to the site area but lack association with cultural material and may have been redeposited in floodplain context. In this light, Monaghan, Egan-Bruhy, and I have suggested either (1) that Mesoamerican squash became locally adapted in ruderal stands adjacent to habitation areas, (2) that Late Archaic hunter-gatherers were tending small informal garden plots adjacent to habitation areas on fertile floodplain soils, or (3) that stands of these varieties, either ruderal or tended, were present in sufficient density to result in their downstream dispersal and redeposition at Green Point (see Monaghan et al. 2006). None of these scenarios explains agency of arrival. However, given the absolute lack of archaeological evidence for direct trade with Mexico, we have suggested that down-the-line exchange (Renfrew 1975) was the most likely means of dispersal into the upper Great Lakes.

A parallel line of inquiry involves the incorporation of indigenous cultigens into the Archaic diet. I do not devote much space to that here, however, since the evidence is scant, to say the least. At present, one Archaic site from southwestern Michigan, the Eidson site, has produced evidence for sunflower, *Helianthus annuus* (Garland 1990), dated to 1270–1056 cal B.C. (Clark 1990). At present, no other evidence exists for the incorporation of the standard suite of Eastern Agricultural Complex cultigens into the Michigan Archaic economy or diet (see Egan 1988).

Long-Distance Logistic Mobility and Changing Regional Landscape Use

The future of Archaic research is in supply-train management.

Contrary to the title of this section, I do not intend to engage in semantic argument about whether we are dealing with a collector-forager continuum (Binford 1978, 1980, 1982) or a traveler-processor continuum (Bettinger 1991) or try to characterize the Archaic mobility of Michigan populations as central-based wandering or anything else. Rather, the larger goal here is to frame the discussion relative to the nature and evolution of mobility change over the course of the Archaic, specifically in terms of shorter- or longer-distance movement tied to either activity-specific or multiactivity locations. Further, I attempt to contextualize mobility in relation to changing Great Lakes water planes as well as resource distribution and targeting.

The nature of Archaic mobility cannot be divorced from changing environment in Michigan or other parts of the western Great Lakes. During the Early Archaic and Late Archaic periods, both the size and shape of the Michigan land mass changed markedly as a consequence of fluctuations in the base level of the lake basins. At 10,000 B.P. water planes in the conjoined Michigan-Huron basin were at an all-time low of ca. 42.6 m (139.8 ft), whereas by 4500 B.P. they had risen to 182 m (597 ft), higher than modern levels (Figure 20.2). Basic area estimates reveal that the Lower Peninsula of Michigan was, consequently, almost halved in size between ca. 10,000 B.P. and 4500 B.P., with undoubted impacts on exploitable area and increases in population densities due to packing (Lovis et al. 2005; Lovis and MacDonald 1999). It was also during this period that Michigan felt the effects of Hypsithermal warming in the form of upland desiccation resulting in grassland environments and the support of large herbivores such as elk (e.g., Holman 1990; Holman et al. 1986), while the submerged parts of at least the Huron basin probably supported a mixed conifer forest (Hunter 2004) and, presumably, different animal species. During low-water stages, shoreline environments were at a great distance from interior habitats, whereas by ca. 4500 B.P. (ca. 3200 cal B.C.), they were juxtaposed (Lovis et al. 2005). A better understanding of the interactive coupling of these different variables is essential to clarifying the nature of Archaic mobility in Michigan.

What do archaeologists know about changing mobility in the Michigan Archaic? First, one can argue, we have so few documented Early Archaic sites, and no primary in situ, let alone excavated, Early Archaic sites that we know virtually nothing (Shott 1999). An interesting, but potentially irrelevant, observation, however, is that several reported Paleoindian sites have produced Early Archaic bifurcate-base and notched points in low frequency (Fitting et al. 1966; Shoshani et al. 1990; Shott 1986, 1993). A ^{14}C date of 7886 ± 115 B.P. (7000 cal B.C.; AA-1223; Shott 1986, 1993) at the Leavitt site, which produced excavated bifurcate points and surface materials of a similar age, appears to be a perfectly acceptable Early Archaic date, arguments to the contrary notwithstanding. Does this suggest that components of the preceding Paleoindian settlement and mobility pattern continued into the Early Archaic? Perhaps.

Recent discussion of the Middle Archaic (Lovis 1999; Lovis et al. 2005) presents a more holistic view of mobility during this time period. The record of sites, while not abundant, is better than for earlier periods (see Lovis 1999 for a comprehensive summary), and I also refer the reader to discussion in this chapter related to the modeling of buried alluvial surfaces, which suggests that there is promise in exploring for and finding sites of this age deeply buried in floodplain settings. Additionally, as is true of the Early Archaic, much of the land area available for exploitation currently resides under the waters of Lakes Michigan and Huron. In considering both the Early and Middle Archaic, archaeologists should dispense with current state- and nation-centered political boundaries—there was no significant barrier between Wisconsin and Michigan, or Ontario and Michigan, that would have prohibited settlement systems from extending around and between ponded postglacial Lakes Chippewa and Stanley during the rise to Lake Nipissing levels.

The view that long-distance, task-specific movement of restricted age and gender units during the Middle Archaic might be a valuable heuristic device was borne of multiple considerations. Among these is that Middle Archaic diagnostics are rarely represented in surface collections, particularly from central Michigan. A second, potentially more important consideration is that the ethnographic records of hunter-gatherers in northern boreal forests reveals substantial evidence for regular task-specific movement in the range of about 80 km (50 mi) from a residential location. Low-density task-specific activities would leave a very low-visibility archaeological signature—precisely what one observes in Michigan's central uplands. I have recently collaborated with other researchers to present a hypothesis of long-distance "logistic" mobility (*sensu* Binford, but Bettinger's "travelers" also suffices) for the Saginaw Valley and central uplands of Michigan (Lovis et al. 2005), from which the following discussion is drawn.

In a nutshell, the model we propose for the Middle Archaic argues that, during the period when the lake level in the Michigan-Huron basin was at its lowest, that is, during the Early Archaic, minimal use was made of habitats in what are now the central Michigan uplands (the headwater regions of the Saginaw and Grand River drainage basins). When lake levels rose to elevations about 12 m (40 ft) below modern, ca. 7000 B.P., the central uplands were brought within the range of long-distance, task-specific hunting and collecting activities as ethnographically documented among boreal forest hunters-gatherers. We have evidence for regular use of the lower Saginaw basin at that time primarily during fall. It was also during that time period that, the evidence reveals, increasing, but limited, probably task-specific and low-intensity use of the uplands occurred. We further argue that one segment of the seasonal round was probably on the Huron-Michigan littoral in areas currently submerged in about 12 m (40 ft) of water.

The preceding interpretation divorces interpretation of the exceedingly abundant archaeological record of the succeeding Late Archaic period from the "Garden of Eden" problem (see Fitting 1972; also Keene 1981) as well as the linked population-increase explanation (Cleland 1992) and, in turn, tends to substantiate an approach favoring regular group movement to productive resource patches in the context of more constrained social spaces as population densities increased. One might call this "residential mobility in a foraging context." As I have in past work (Lovis 1999; Lovis et al. 2005; Lovis and O'Shea 1994; Monaghan and Lovis 2006; Robertson et al. 1999), I invoke a multidimensional model developed by Robertson (1987) for the Late Archaic of the Saginaw drainage basin. On the basis of microwear analysis of stone-tool function, reduction strategies, assemblage composition, and site locations, Robertson concludes that mobility within the Saginaw Archaic system was radial along various tributaries of the basin, that sites were fundamentally similar in the range of activities carried out, and that these were clearly multifunctional sites. Moreover, this pattern coincided with water levels higher than present in the Michigan-Huron basin and fits with the observation that Late Archaic diagnostics are well represented in collections from the interior of Michigan and are functionally variable. It stands in contrast to the Early and Middle Archaic pattern and is consistent with increased intensity of use of the reduced lower Michigan land mass by more concentrated populations practicing what Binford would call "residential mobility."

Spatial Organization at the Scale of the Site and Locale

Space, the final frontier in Archaic research in Michigan.

Few have had the temerity to tackle the spatial organization of Archaic sites, and the few case studies that exist are from the Saginaw basin (Egan n.d.; Lovis 1989, 2002a; Robertson 1987). I attribute this situation not to a lack of research interest but, rather, to a lack of large-scale systematic work at the level of the Archaic site and locale. Here, I use the term *locale* to mean a landform or feature that contains either contiguous or separated activity sets; thus, a locale may contain multiple so-called sites in a traditional sense. To a degree, this is distributional archaeology (Ebert 1992), although at a more discrete spatial scale. In most instances large excavated areas are needed to properly understand spatial organization at these scales, and only in limited instances has this level of coverage been achieved in any part of Michigan. To my mind, achieving such coverage and resolution is a clear goal of future Michigan Archaic research. I illustrate this point with a case study (a work still in progress) from a group of Late Archaic sites located in the lower Saginaw Valley in what is now downtown Bay City, Michigan, that have been excavated over a period of 40 years starting in the mid-1960s. The following discussion derives from Lovis et al. (2001) and draws heavily from multiple rounds of fieldwork in the lower Saginaw River area (Lovis 1985; Lovis 1989, 1993, 2002a; Lovis et al. 1996; Robertson 1987).

The Saginaw Valley region has the largest numbers of recorded Archaic sites in Michigan, largely as a consequence of better than a century of concerted avocational and professional involvement (Peebles 1978), and some areas have received substantial attention and have yielded an abundant body of archaeological information. Such is the case with the lower Saginaw River in Bay City (Lovis 2002a, 2004).

For convenience, this discussion of Archaic age sites within the limits of Bay City proceeds from south to north. Importantly, most if not all of the pertinent Archaic components are situated within sites containing multiple occupation episodes. The Archaic occupations range in age from ca. 3000 to 500 cal B.C. Within any given site are occupations of variable intensity, duration, and preservation, and they have data of variable quality associated with them.

The Kantzler site is the southernmost site on the west bank of the Saginaw River. Its surface lies at an elevation of 182 m (597 ft), and the site has about a meter of partially stratified cultural deposits. Archaic-age occupation is limited, as indicated by Crumley's (1973) initial analysis as well as my own. Crumley identified a Perkiomen Broad point from the basal deposits and attributed side-notched Meadowood forms and certain Durst-like materials to subsequent Early and Middle Woodland occupations. I disagree with the latter attributions. As is consistent with other sites in the vicinity, I believe that vertical mixing of components is common, even though some of the gross stratigraphy may be intact. Subsequent work on the site by Commonwealth Associates Inc. produced a ^{14}C date from bedded basal gravels of 4290 ± 90 B.P. (3022–2865 cal B.C.; UGa 3195; Larsen and Demeter 1979). These gravels also contained culturally derived fire-cracked rock, suggesting the presence of pre-Nipissing, Middle Archaic, occupation. Later work by Caminos Associates and Michigan State University recovered side-notched Meadowood projectiles but no ceramics from basal organic horizons. Although I may disagree with Crumley's assignment of the earliest occupations to the Early Woodland, as I believe they are primarily transitional Archaic–Woodland or Late Archaic, I do agree with her interpretation of their seasonality. The Kantzler site is probably a spring–summer fishing camp where final rather than initial artifact processing took place. Significantly, there is clear spatial differentiation of feature activity at the site, with pits and hearths located at lower elevations and the only red-ocher feature at the highest elevation on the terrace.

A spatial hiatus separates the Kantzler and Liberty Bridge sites (20BY79) largely because of impacts from riverfront development. Observations of scattered debitage and point finds in the intervening space, however, reveal that a continuous spatial distribution of cultural materials probably existed between the two. The Liberty Bridge site has been extensively reported by Lovis (1993), Robertson (1987), and others. Primary occupations are associated with both Durst and Meadowood projectile point series at elevations between 181 and 183 m (595 and 600 ft) amsl. Radiocarbon dates of 2880 ± 70 and 2770 ± 80 B.P. uncalibrated (100–800 cal B.C.) reveal that this is the youngest of the Late Archaic occupations and that it is partially contemporaneous with the later occupations at Kantzler. Subsistence remains reveal a late summer to fall occupation. Hearths, smudge pits, caches, and large surface burns characterize the feature assemblage. Robertson (1987) argues for a spatial partitioning of activities at the site. One area, higher on the terrace, appears to be associated with subsistence-related activities, including butchering, cooking, and plant food processing, while another area of the site toward the foot of the terrace was employed for final tool manufacturing or anticipatory retooling. The only material related to ritual activity occurs at the topographically highest, most inland, locations at the site: a cache of Turkey-tail points and a feature containing red-ocher pigment.

The Indiana Street site is poorly and discontinuously preserved. Although at least three institutions have worked at the site, none of this work has produced diagnostic artifacts or ^{14}C dates. Of importance, however, and an observation that I return to shortly, is the presence of large storage pit features along the crest of the 181-m (595-ft) terrace in this location. I believe that this is the southernmost edge of a Late Archaic pit field that dominates Archaic sites further to the north.

The combined Birney Mound/State Street/Marquette Avenue site area is a complex of historically reported and recently excavated locales lying above an elevation of 181 m (595 ft). The State Street site (20BY125) is the southernmost part of the complex and was initially identified by Walter Schmidt, who reported a variety of distinctive Late Archaic artifact forms at the site. These may be largely attributed to burial activities because they include distinctive ground-stone materials such as bannerstones and birdstones that are rarely found in habitation context. The Birney Mound site (20BY63) actually lies within the State Street site. Numerous burials have been reported from the site over time, most recently, Late Archaic Red Ocher burials and traces of red ocher, but Woodland and Historic-period interments are present, as well (State of Michigan Archaeological Site File data). Importantly, recent work did not reveal any occupation debris, hearths, or storage pits, suggesting the site's rather restricted use as a burial locale.

The Marquette Avenue site (20BY387) is the northernmost part of the complex and was the subject of recent mitigation (Lovis 2002a). Among the more significant aspects of 20BY387 are the numerous Late Archaic storage pits, smudge pits, and hearths concentrated along the edge of the 181-m (595-ft) terrace. A suite of radiocarbon dates reveals occupation as early as 4250 B.P. uncalibrated (2900 cal B.C.). This is the oldest dated in situ Archaic occupation. Much like parts of the Liberty Bridge site, the lithic assemblage is dominated by projectile points, some of which reveal armature damage and replacement, as well as by material indicative of initial stages of reduction, that is, decortication and primary flakes (Cook 2002). The pit field does not extend back from the terrace any great distance, and together with the Birney Mound and State Street sites, reveals that the inland part of the terrace was probably reserved primarily for ritual activity involving burials. However, the pit field extends south, along the front of the terrace toward the Indiana Street site.

The northernmost of the Bay City–area remains is the complex consisting of the Marquette Viaduct, Defoe Park, and Fletcher locales of the Fletcher site. This area has undergone multiple episodes of investigation. The site is multicomponent and has ample evidence of Late Archaic occupation in the form of Meadowood, Durst, and so-called Ace of Spades points. The latter are here viewed as a Durst variant (Lovis 1985). Late Archaic occupation appears to have been more intensive at the southern and westernmost edges of the site near Defoe Park. Excavations from 1967 to 1970 failed to provide ^{14}C chronologies or firmly associate features directly with projectiles, but recent work has rectified these deficiencies. A suite of radiocarbon dates, with one exception statistically identical within the two-sigma range (Table 20.3), reveal occupation dating from the period 3760 to 2960 B.P. uncalibrated (2200–1109 cal B.C.), younger than Marquette Avenue and older than Liberty Bridge. The stemmed and side-notched Kramer and Meadowood projectiles from this occupation span are associated with smudge pits, hearths, roasting pit complexes, and storage features. The features occur predominantly at elevations below the Marquette Avenue site (20BY387), apparently on interior parts of the site. Prior work at the Marquette Viaduct locale (Lovis et al. 1996) failed to reveal any intact Archaic occupation closer to the riverbank, although some evidence suggests that earlier occupations may have been eroded out. Thus, the Late Archaic occupation of 20BY28 is spatially restricted. The Marquette Viaduct locale of the site was the locus of later stages of core reduction and tool manufacture, as indicated by the presence of prepared cores and preforms (Cook 2002).

Landscape and Time

The earliest Archaic occupations on the west bank in Bay City are those at the Kantzler (20BY30) and Marquette Viaduct sites (locale 20BY387). Both occur at or above an altitude of 181 m (593 ft) and were initially occupied just after 4500 B.P. (ca. 3200 cal B.C.). Some potentially significant chronological observations are pertinent here. First, the surfaces of both sites lie below that commonly accepted for the Nipissing-stage maximum. This may indicate that Lake Nipissing only briefly stood at its maximum level and then dropped well below the level accepted for the succeeding Algoma stage (G. William Monaghan, pers. comm.).

By ca. 2500 to 3500 B.P., or 700–2000 cal B.C., most of the sites along the west bank of the Saginaw River in Bay City were occupied contemporaneously by groups using Durst, Meadowood, and so-called Dustin/Lamoka/large expanding-stemmed points. These sites occur at elevations between 177 and 183 m (580 and 600 ft) and call into question the age or longevity of the 181-m (593-ft) Algoma stage. Kantzler, Liberty Bridge, and Marquette Avenue (sites 20BY30, 20BY79, and 20BY387) occur above this elevation, but at least one Late Archaic locale of Fletcher (20BY28) occurs below it.

Of potential interest to issues of landscape use over time is the relative chronological position of Late Archaic projectile point styles, a topic previously addressed (Lovis and Robertson 1989; Robertson et al. 1999; see also preceding discussion in this chapter) but that can benefit from the current compendium perspective. The Bay City data reveal a highly consistent association between Meadowood knives and Durst projectiles at Kantzler (20BY30), Liberty Bridge (20BY79), and Marquette Viaduct-Fletcher (20BY28). By contrast, dated Archaic stemmed materials have been recovered from Marquette Viaduct and a Broad-Point-series projectile from Kantzler. Perhaps the single most impressive display of stylistic and spatial partitioning, however, is the large to small expanding-stemmed-point continuum of Marquette Avenue (20BY387). This site also has the earliest ^{14}C dates and the best evidence for early-stage reduction and replacement.

Landscape and Space

The complex of Archaic sites near Bay City was occupied from late spring through fall. Substantial overlap of features further reveals probable short-duration, repetitive reoccupation episodes. Lack of statistical overlap of ^{14}C dates between locales also reveals that different locations were being used at different points in time. Despite this, perceptions of landscape were rather well structured and persisted over time (Figure 20.15 presents a hypothetical reconstruction of such spatial perception). At the Kantzler (20BY30), Liberty Bridge (20BY79), Marquette Avenue (20BY387), Birney (20BY63), and State Street (20BY125) sites, Late Archaic ritual activity took place 20 to 30 m (65 to 100 ft) inland from the terrace edges. Such behavior contrasts with the intensive secular use of terrace edges. Abundant pits, hearths, and occupational debris along the terrace edges, coupled with scant evidence of ritual activity there, reveals a broad binary partitioning of linear spaces into secular and sacred "precincts."

Schematic Representation of Late Archaic Partitioning of Activities and Perceptions of Space

Sacred Precinct
(Burials, Red Ochre Features, Caches)

////////////////////////////// **Note Overlap** //////////////////////////////

Secular Precinct
Residential Space
(Hearths, Storage Pits)

-------------------------- **Terrace Edge** --------------------------

////////////////////////////// **Note Overlap** //////////////////////////////

Secular Precinct
Special Activity Space
(Smudge Pits, Reduction Areas)

-------------------------- **River Edge** --------------------------

Figure 20.15. Hypothesized spatial organization of the secular and sacred spaces from Archaic occupation locales in Bay City, Michigan (courtesy Michigan State University).

Within the secular precincts, and regardless of specific subdivisions of Archaic time, space was further subdivided into areas employed for rehafting and replacement, anticipatory retooling, and subsistence-related tasks such as animal butchering, processing, and preparation. For example, Liberty Bridge (20BY79) and Kantzler (20BY30) were used for anticipatory retooling, while Marquette Avenue (20BY387) and

MarquetteViaduct (20BY28) have evidence of both rehafting and replacement. Marquette Avenue, with its early and distinctive expanding-stemmed point series, was employed for early stages of reduction, whereas the other sites were employed for final, rather than initial, stages of artifact processing. The spatial evidence from Liberty Bridge, furthermore, suggests that manufacturing activities took place lower on the river terrace edge, while subsistence activities took place at topographically higher locations (Robertson 1987).

Finally, just because Archaic sites are situated on river and lake terraces of known geological age does not necessarily mean that the occupations were, in fact, temporally associated with water levels consistent with the establishment of those landforms. If the lower altitudes of the Meadowood/Durst occupation at MarquetteViaduct and Fletcher (20BY28), and the absolute dating of this occupation, can be considered in this context, then the other contemporaneous Meadowood/Durst occupations on landforms at higher and earlier elevations are even further *away* from the riverfront or lakeshore, that is, the occupations are more recent than the landforms (Lovis et al. 2001).

In sum, the model of spatial perception and use presented here has potential to be tested in other locations both within the Saginaw basin and other, adjacent regions, as data quality is augmented and resolution is refined.

Predictive Modeling, Hunter-Gatherers, and the Michigan Archaic

The future of the Michigan Archaic is in the (kilo) calories, my dear; or is it?

Predictive mathematical modeling has not been common in analyses of the Michigan Archaic, or for that matter any time period in Michigan. In fact, I can only point to three such analyses that are directly related to the Archaic period: those of Arnold (1977), Egan (1993), and Keene (1981). Egan's also has Early and Middle Woodland content. Two other works of pertinence to this discussion are related to the Paleoindian period: Krist and Brown (1994) and Krist (2001). Importantly, each of the works cited here has potential application for understanding issues of hunter-gatherer adaptation beyond those related to the Michigan Archaic per se. Here, my intent is to highlight the critical parts of each of these analyses, not to provide detail on the specifics of modeling strategy. Readers are referred to the primary documents for specifics.

The earliest attempt to develop a formal predictive model for any part of the Archaic is found in Jeanne Arnold's senior thesis, published as an appendix to the River Raisin fieldwork conducted in the 1970s by Christopher Peebles, then of the University of Michigan. Arnold employed the then-novel approach developed by Michael Jochim (1976) to model Early Archaic subsistence zones in southeastern Michigan on the basis of the variable monthly distribution and abundance of primary food resources, as inferred from paleovegetation, drainage, and topographic data. Arnold employed the drainage as the extraction area (an approach that she herself questioned) and the entire group as the unit of exploitation, and she expanded on Jochim's approach by concerted incorporation of plant resources. The modeling exercise allowed for the definition of seasonal catchments, estimates of carrying capacity (50–100 Early Archaic individuals), and the development of a seasonal mobility model keyed to resource distribution and abundance. Moreover, her results called into question the proportions of big game, small game and waterfowl, and fish and plants that composed the Early Archaic diet. To date, however, no researcher in Michigan has seen fit to actually try and test any of Arnold's predictions, either in the River Raisin drainage or in other drainages.

Ensuing work by Keene (1981), using the abundant Late Archaic archaeological data from the Saginaw Valley region (a data set that has been remarkably transformed over the past two and one-half decades), was cast in the framework of a linear-programming model employing economic data reconstructed from presettlement forest distributions and fisheries and wildlife data on species richness in given habitats on a monthly or seasonal cycle. Significantly, Keene modeled subsistence choice in a nonmarginal environment on the basis of group-level decisions, and, as is common with such approaches, he considered the input-output ratio of kilocalories and essential nutrients. He also considered raw material requirements (net optimal energy capture). Lowest "cost" choices were rank ordered in terms of preferences, with the result being the low-cost choice for need satisfaction. Keene's work expanded on earlier such approaches in several ways, for example, clearly balancing processing costs in the evaluation of net gain from any particular food, factoring in the costs of storage in terms of nutritional loss from processing decisions, and incorporating nonfood necessities such as hides for clothing.

Keene ultimately derived a monthly suite of primary, secondary, and marginal resources in a model that is constrained by various factors during the winter months. He posited four economic seasons, two narrow spectrum and two broad spectrum, and recognized that plant foods had high value at various points in this cycle (but the absence of nut in the optimal solution, largely as a consequence of processing costs, required a major digression) and that, at times, shellfish were significant resources. Keene then developed models of the archaeological expectations for sites of each season, with important implications for the seasonal representation of Late Archaic site types. Again, however, this heuristic model has only been marginally tested in any systematic fashion with the increased economic data available from the region.

Egan's (1993) is the most recent subsistence and economic modeling exercise directly related to the Michigan Archaic. As one might expect given her paleoethnobotanical bent, her work places important emphases on the role of plant foods in the diet of both Archaic and subsequent Woodland peoples in the Saginaw Valley of Michigan. While Egan is consistent with her predecessors in employing caloric value as the "currency" through which she evaluates the optimality of specific monthly resource choices, she also employs variables such as taste and nutritional needs in her calculations. More importantly, however, and the part of her analysis that I think requires emphasis here, is her departure from the notion of group-level resource choice and extraction to a model that subdivides the larger group into task units of varying age and gender composition. This is accomplished through the concerted use of Great Lakes ethnographic data to reconstruct the social units responsible for seasonal extraction of specific types or sets of resources. The importance of this approach should be self evident—a specific task group, for example, a male hunting group, adult women, older women and children, and so on, will make an independent set of decisions about resource choice that, ultimately, may result in the selection of secondary or even marginal resources as rank ordered in a group's strategy. Not only is this, to my mind, a better reflection of reality than offered by other approaches but it also results in a broader array of optimal resource choices in any given economic month or season. Egan's work deserves to be read more widely and to be systematically assessed against the augmented archaeological and economic record for the Archaic.

I do not intend to belabor Krist's (2001; Krist and Brown 1994) work on Paleoindian adaptations, other than to point out that, at least in Michigan, it has involved some of the more elegant uses of Geographic Information System spatial modeling beyond simple descriptive data displays and associations between site locations and physical environmental features. Krist used paleoenvironmental reconstruction to simulate the spatial distribution of hunter-gatherer activities under three sets of economic conditions: caribou dependent, caribou and mastodon dependent, and general foraging (including exploitation of moose, fish, small and medium mammals, and plants). Rank-order best fits with archaeological distributions revealed that, during the dormant season, general foraging and then caribou dependency explained the observed pattern best, whereas during the growing season, general foraging was the best fit. Moreover, the reconstructed heterogeneous environment and analysis of site locations relative to resource availability suggested to Krist that both residential *and* logistic strategies were probably being employed during different parts of the economic year and in different spatial locations. These collective observations have significant implications for the transition from Paleoindian to Early Archaic since they suggest that broad-spectrum foraging in a highly flexible mobility system was already established by late Paleoindian times (see also Kuehn 1998 on this issue in Wisconsin), thereby placing a rather different perspective on the nature of the economic transition between the two periods. Further, Krist's results suggest that scavenging rather than hunting was the mechanism by which Paleoindian populations engaged with large proboscideans. Collectively, these various modeling approaches have tremendous heuristic value for better understanding the Michigan Archaic.

Topical Foraging and the Future of Archaic Research in Michigan

With one exception, the several assertions I have made to organize my arguments on the Michigan Archaic are largely atemporal in nature; they can just as easily be applied to the Early, Middle, or Late Archaic. Further, while certain of them are specific to particular kinds of environments, for example, bottomlands, floodplains, or areas susceptible to the growth of tropical cultigens, most of these problem directions are interrelated and can be addressed across both the Lower and Upper peninsulas of Michigan, if not more broadly across the upper Great Lakes. In fact, there is tremendous need to generate additional research interest in the Archaic of the upper Great Lakes, in general, and of northern Michigan, in particular.

My primary goal here has been to provide a series of systematic problem orientations through which to contextualize what have been largely idiosyncratic, compliance-initiated, site-level forays into Archaic research. Each of the six areas discussed can easily be viewed as a resource patch for research foraging. They have varying amounts of predictable gain, and, as should be clear, they also have highly differential potential return rates. Some also pose much higher risk of failure than others, and at least one case offers real potential for zero yield. The nature of our collective group composition, however, suggests that this research arena can actually buffer against specific task failures and potentially even allow us to learn from them. Archaic-period research in Michigan will ultimately be stronger as a result.

Acknowledgments

The following individuals assisted tremendously in the compilation of the comprehensive list of Archaic radiocarbon dates presented in Tables 20.1 and 20.3: John Anderton, Mark Branstner, Sean Dunham, John Franzen, Michael Hambacher, Mark Hill, Loreen Lomax, Barbara Mead, and James Skibo. Any contribution this chapter may ultimately make to advancing Archaic research would have been diminished without their considerable help. I also greatly appreciate the invitation by Thomas Emerson, Dale McElrath, and Andrew Fortier to participate in the Urbana Conference on the Archaic Societies of the Midcontinent, which catalyzed my efforts in producing this discussion. Their persistent editorial prodding and advice has enhanced this chapter considerably, and I hope their efforts are evident. Jon Carroll is responsible for creating Figures 20.1 and 20.2 and for digitizing the other illustrations. His assistance in the graphic presentation of the information contained in this chapter is greatly appreciated. Finally, I greatly appreciate the editorial eye of Linda Forman in making my prose clearer and more direct; this chapter has benefited tremendously from her suggestions.

References Cited

Abel, Timothy J., David M. Stothers, and Jason M. Koralweski
2001 The Williams Mortuary Complex: A Transitional Archaic Regional Interaction Center in Northwestern Ohio. In *Archaic Transitions in Ohio and Kentucky Prehistory*, edited by Olaf H. Prufer, Sara E. Pedde, and Richard S. Meindl, pp. 290–327. Kent State University Press, Kent, Ohio.

Arnold, Jeanne E.
1977 Early Archaic Subsistence and Settlement in the River Raisin Watershed, Michigan. In *The River Raisin Archaeological Survey Season 2, 1976: A Preliminary Report*, edited by Christopher S. Peebles and James J. Krakker, pp. 279–376. Museum of Anthropology, University of Michigan, Ann Arbor.

Beaverson, Sheena K., and Howard D. Mooers
1993 *Reconstruction of the Late Glacial and Holocene Paleoenvironmental Setting at 20SA596, Saginaw Valley, Michigan.* Report of Investigations 210. Institute for Minnesota Archaeology, Minneapolis.

Beld, Scott G.
1991 *Two Terminal Archaic/Early Woodland Sites in Central Michigan.* Technical Report 22. Museum of Anthropology, University of Michigan, Ann Arbor.

Beld, Scott G., and J. Tracy Luke
1985 *Radiocarbon Dating in Gratiot County – S84-19: Phase II/Completion.* Report submitted to the Bureau of Michigan History, Michigan Department of State, Lansing. Alma College, Alma, Michigan. On file, Office of the State Archaeologist, Lansing, Michigan.

Benchley, Elizabeth D., Derrick J. Marcucci, Cheong-Yip Yuen, and Kristin L. Griffin
1988 *Final Report of Archaeological Investigations and Data Recovery at the Trout Point I Site, Alger County, Michigan.* Report of Investigations 89. Archaeological Research Laboratory, University of Wisconsin–Milwaukee.

Bettinger, Robert L.
1991 *Hunter-Gatherers: Archaeological and Evolutionary Theory.* Plenum, New York.

Bettis E. Arthur, III, and Edwin R. Hajic
1995 Landscape Development and the Location of Evidence of Archaic Cultures in the Upper Midwest. In *Archaeological Geology of the Archaic Period in North America*, edited by E. Arthur Bettis III, pp. 87–113. Special Paper 297. Geological Society of America, Boulder, Colorado.

Bianchi, Thomas H., and Paul V. Heinrich
1992 Geoarchaeological Evidence of the Lake Nipissing High Lake Phase in the Kalamazoo River Valley of Southwestern Michigan. *The Michigan Archaeologist* 38:189–206.

Binford, Lewis R.
1963a The Pomranky Site: A Late Archaic Burial Station. In *Miscellaneous Studies in Typology and Classification*, by Anta Montet-White, Lewis R. Binford, and Mark L. Papworth, pp. 149–192. Anthropological Papers 19. Museum of Anthropology, University of Michigan, Ann Arbor.
1963b The Hodges Site: A Late Archaic Burial Station. In *Miscellaneous Studies in Typology and Classification*, by Anta Montet-White, Lewis R. Binford, and Mark L. Papworth, pp. 124–148. Anthropological Papers 19. Museum of Anthropology, University of Michigan, Ann Arbor.
1978 *Nunamiut Ethnoarchaeology.* Academic Press, New York.
1980 Willow Smoke and Dogs' Tails: Hunter-Gatherer Settlement Systems and Archaeological Site Formation. *American Antiquity* 45:4–20.
1982 The Archaeology of Place. *Journal of Anthropological Archaeology* 1:5–13.

Blanton, Dennis B.
1996 Accounting for Submerged Mid-Holocene Sites in the Southeast: A Case Study from the Chesapeake Bay Estuary, Virginia. In *Archaeology of the Mid-Holocene Southeast*, edited by Kenneth E. Sassaman and David G. Anderson, pp. 200–218. University Press of Florida, Gainesville.

Branstner, Mark C. (editor)
2004 *Archaeological Data Recovery at 20IA305, Village of Muir, Ionia County, Michigan.* Technical report prepared for the Village of Muir, Michigan, under contract with Gove Associates, Kalamazoo, Michigan. Report 2004-02. Great Lakes Research, Williamston, Michigan.

Branstner, Mark C., and Michael J. Hambacher (editors)
1994 *1991 Great Lakes Gas Transmission Limited Partnership Pipeline Expansion Projects: Phase III Investigations at the Shiawassee River (20SA1033) and Bear Creek Sites (20SA1043), Saginaw County, Michigan.* Report 94-01. Great Lakes Research Associates, Williamston, Michigan.
1995 *1991 Great Lakes Gas Transmission Limited Partnership Pipeline Expansion Projects: Phase III Investigations at the Vogelaar Site (20SA291), Saginaw County, Michigan.* Report 94-02. Great Lakes Research Associates, Williamston, Michigan.

Brashler, Janet G., and Barbara E. Mead
1996 Woodland Settlement in the Grand River Basin. In *Investigating the Archaeological Record of the Great Lakes State: Essays in Honor of Elizabeth Baldwin Garland*, edited by Margaret B. Holman, Janet G. Brashler, and Kathryn C. Parker, pp. 181–249. New Issues Press, Western Michigan University, Kalamazoo.

Brose, David S., and Michael J. Hambacher
1999 The Middle Woodland in Northern Michigan. In *Retrieving Michigan's Buried Past: The Archaeology of the Great Lakes State*, edited by John Halsey, pp. 173–192.

Bulletin 64. Cranbrook Institute of Science, Bloomfield Hills, Michigan.

Campbell, Amy L.
1988 A Comparative Discussion of Lambrix and Deer Lick Creek Cherts. *The Michigan Archaeologist* 34:103–113.

Clark, Caven P.
1990 Typological Assessment of the US-31 Project Projectile Points. In *Late Archaic and Early Woodland Adaptation in the Lower St. Joseph River Valley*, edited by Elizabeth B. Garland, pp. 58–81. Michigan Cultural Resource Investigation Series 2. Michigan Department of State and Michigan Department of Transportation, Lansing.
1993 *Archaeological Survey and Site Testing at Pictured Rocks National Lakeshore, Alger County, Michigan, 1991*. Technical Report 23. Midwest Archaeological Center, National Park Service, Lincoln, Nebraska.
1995 *Archeological Survey and Testing at Isle Royale National Park, 1987–1990 Seasons*. Occasional Studies in Anthropology 32. Midwest Archaeological Center, National Park Service, Lincoln, Nebraska.

Cleland, Charles E.
1973 The Pi-wan-go-ning Prehistoric District at Norwood, Michigan. In *Geology and the Environment: Man, Earth, and Nature in Northwestern Lower Michigan*, edited by W. T. Straw and R. L. Chambers, pp. 85–87. Michigan Basin Geological Society, Ann Arbor.
1992 *Rites of Conquest: The History and Culture of Michigan's Native Americans*. University of Michigan Press, Ann Arbor.

Cleland, Charles E., and David L. Ruggles
1996 Samel's Field Site: An Early Archaic Base Camp in Grand Traverse County, Michigan. In *Investigating the Archaeological Record of the Great Lakes State: Essays in Honor of Elizabeth Baldwin Garland*, edited by Margaret B. Holman, Janet G. Brashler, and Kathryn C. Parker, pp. 55–100. New Issues Press, Western Michigan University, Kalamazoo.

Cook, Robert A.
2002 The Lithic Assemblage from Sites 20BY28 and 20BY387. In *A Bridge to the Past: The Post-Nipissing Archaeology of the Marquette Viaduct Replacement Project Sites 20BY28 and 20BY386*, edited by William Lovis, pp. 3.1–3.111. Michigan State University Museum and Department of Anthropology, Michigan State University, East Lansing.

Crane, H. R.
1956 University of Michigan Radiocarbon Dates I. *Science* 124:664–672.

Crane, H. R., and J. B. Griffin
1958 University of Michigan Radiocarbon Dates III. *Science* 128:1117–1123.
1960 University of Michigan Radiocarbon Dates V. *American Journal of Science, Radiocarbon Supplement* 2:31–48.
1962 University of Michigan Radiocarbon Dates VII. *Radiocarbon* 4:183–203.
1964 University of Michigan Radiocarbon Dates IX. *Radiocarbon* 6:1–24.
1965 University of Michigan Radiocarbon Dates X. *Radiocarbon* 7:123–152.
1968 University of Michigan Radiocarbon Dates XII. *Radiocarbon* 10:61–114.

Crumley, Carole S.
1973 The Kantzler Site (20 BY 30): A Multi-Component Woodland Site in Bay County, Michigan. *The Michigan Archaeologist* 19:183–291.

Dunham, Sean B., and John B. Anderton
1999 Late Archaic Radiocarbon Dates from the Popper Site (FS 09-10-03-825/20AR350): A Multicomponent Site on Grand Island, Michigan. *The Michigan Archaeologist* 45:1–22.

Dunham, Sean B., and Mark C. Branstner
1995 *1994 Phase II Cultural Resurce Evaluations: Hiawatha National Forest*. Report 95-07. Great Lakes Research Associates, Williamston, Michigan.

Ebert, James I.
1992 *Distributional Archaeology*. University of New Mexico Press, Albuquerque.

Egan, Kathryn C.
1988 Middle and Late Archaic Phytogeography and Floral Exploitation in the Upper Great Lakes. *Midcontinental Journal of Archaeology* 13:83–89.
1993 *Hunter-Gatherer Subsistence Adaptation in the Saginaw Valley, Michigan*. Ph.D. dissertation, Michigan State University. University Microfilms International, Ann Arbor, Michigan.
n.d. Spatial Analysis of the Weber I Site Using Dimensional Analysis of Variance. Manuscript on file, Consortium for Archaeological Research, Michigan State University, East Lansing.

Egan-Bruhy, Kathryn C.
2002 Floral Analysis of Sites 20BY28 and 20BY387. In *A Bridge to the Past: The Post-Nipissing Archaeology of the Marquette Viaduct Replacement Sites 20BY28 and 20BY387*, edited by William Lovis, pp. 6.1–6.31. Submitted to City of Bay City and Federal Highway Administration. Michigan State University Museum and Department of Anthropology, Michigan State University, East Lansing.

Ellis, Chris J., Ian Kenyon, and Michael Spence
1990 The Archaic. In *The Archaeology of Southern Ontario to A.D. 1650*, edited by Chris J. Ellis and Neal Ferris, pp. 65–124. Occasional Publication 5. London Chapter, Ontario Archaeological Society.

Fairchild, Jerry D.
1977 The Schmidt Site: A Pre-Nipissing Village in the Saginaw Valley, Michigan. Master's thesis, Department of Anthropology, Western Michigan University, Kalamazoo.

Faught, Michael K.
2004 Underwater Archaeology of Paleolandscapes, Apalachee Bay, Florida. *American Antiquity* 69:275–290.

Fitting, James E.
1972 The Schultz Site in the Saginaw Valley and Beyond. In *The Schultz Site at Green Point: A Stratified Occupation Aea in the Saginaw Valley of Michigan*, edited by James E. Fitting, pp. 267–272. Memoirs 4. Museum of Anthropology, University of Michigan, Ann Arbor.
1975 [1970] *The Archaeology of Michigan*. 2nd ed. Cranbrook Institute of Science, Bloomfield Hills, Michigan.

Fitting, James E., Jerry DeVisscher, and Edward J. Wahla
1966 *The Paleo-Indian Occupation of the Holcombe Beach.* Anthropological Paper 27. Museum of Anthropology, University of Michigan, Ann Arbor.

Ford, Richard I.
1986 Reanalysis of Cucurbits in the Ethnobotanical Laboratory, University of Michigan. In *New World Ethnobotany: Collected Papers in Honor of Leonard W. Blake*, edited by Evan E. Voigt and Deborah M. Pearsall, pp. 13–32. *The Missouri Archaeologist* 47.

Garland, Elizabeth B. (editor)
1990 *Late Archaic and Early Woodland Adaptation in the Lower St. Joseph River Valley.* Michigan Cultural Resource Investigation Series 2. Michigan Department of State and Michigan Department of Transportation, Lansing.

Garland, Elizabeth B., and Scott G. Beld
1999 The Early Woodland: Ceramics, Domesticated Plants, and Burial Mounds Foretell the Shape of the Future. In *Retrieving Michigan's Buried Past: The Archaeology of the Great Lakes State*, edited by John R. Halsey, pp. 125–146. Bulletin 64. Cranbrook Institute of Science, Bloomfield Hills, Michigan.

Halsey, John R. (editor)
1999 *Retrieving Michigan's Buried Past: The Archaeology of the Great Lakes State.* Bulletin 64. Cranbrook Institute of Science, Bloomfield Hills, Michigan.

Hambacher, Michael J., Janet G. Brashler, Kathryn C. Egan-Bruhy, Daniel R. Hayes, B. Hardy, Daniel G. Landis, Terrance E. Martin, G. William Monaghan, Kimmarie Murphy, James A. Robertson, and Diane L. Seltz
2003 *Phase III Archaeological Data Recovery for the U.S. 131 S-Curve Realignment Project, Grand Rapids, Michigan.* Submitted to the Michigan Department of Transportation, Lansing. Report R-0446. Commonwealth Cultural Resources Group, Jackson, Michigan.

Hill, Mark A.
1994 *Ottawa North and Alligator Eye, Two Late Archaic Sites on the Ottawa National Forest.* Cultural Resources Management Series Report 6. United States Department of Agriculture, Forest Service, Ottawa National Forest, Ironwood, Michigan.

Holman, J. Alan
1990 Vertebrates from the Harper Site and Rapid Climatic Warming in Mid-Holocene Michigan. *Michigan Academician* 22:205–218.

Holman, J. Alan, Daniel C. Fisher, and Ronald O. Kapp
1986 Recent Discoveries of Fossil Vertebrates in the Lower Peninsula of Michigan. *Michigan Academician* 18:431–463.

Hunter, R. D.
2004 Project Drowned Forest: A Study of Prehistoric Underwater Forest in Lake Huron, Michigan. Electronic document, http://www2.oakland.edu/biology/files/drownedforest.pdf, accessed February 2, 2006.

Jochim, Michael A.
1976 *Hunter-Gatherer Subsistence and Settlement: A Predictive Model.* Academic Press, New York.

Kapp, Ronald O.
1999 Michigan Late Pleistocene, Holocene, and Presettlement Vegetation and Climate. In *Retrieving Michigan's Buried Past: The Archaeology of the Great Lakes State*, edited by John R. Halsey, pp. 31–58. Bulletin 64. Cranbrook Institute of Science, Bloomfield Hills, Michigan.

Keene, Arthur S.
1981 *Prehistoric Foraging in a Temperate Forest: A Linear Programming Model.* Academic Press, New York.

Kenyon, Ian T.
1983 Late Archaic Stemmed Points from the Adder Orchard Site. *Kewa, Newsletter of the London Chapter, Ontario Archaeological Society* 84(4):2–5.
1989 Terminal Archaic Projectile Points in Southwestern Ontario: An Exploratory Study. *Kewa, Newsletter of the London Chapter, Ontario Archaeological Society* 89(1):2–21.

Krakker, James J.
1997 Biface Caches, Exchange, and Regulatory Systems in the Prehistoric Great Lakes Region. *Midcontinental Journal of Archaeology* 22:1–41.

Krist, Frank J.
2001 *A Predictive Model of Paleo-Indian Subsistence and Settlement.* Ph.D. dissertation, Michigan State University, East Lansing. University Microfilms International, Ann Arbor, Michigan.

Krist, Frank J., and Daniel G. Brown
1994 GIS Modeling of Paleo-Indian Migrations and Viewsheds in Northeastern Lower Michigan. *Photogrammetric Engineering and Remote Sensing* 65:1129–1137.

Kuehn, Steven R.
1998 New Evidence for Late Paleoindian-Early Archaic Subsistence Behavior in the Western Great Lakes. *American Antiquity* 63:457–476.

Larsen, Curtis E.
1974 Late Holocene Lake Levels in Southern Lake Michigan. In *Coastal Geology, Sedimentology, and Management, Chicago and the North Shore*, edited by Charles Collinson, pp. 39–49. Guidebook Series 12. Illinois State Geological Survey, Champaign.
1980 Some Personal Views on Needed Archaeological Research in Michigan Archaeology. In *Major Problem Orientations in Michigan Archaeology: 1980–1984, Phase II Completion Report,* edited by J. Mueller, pp. 1–31. Report R-2134. Commonwealth Associates, Jackson, Michigan.
1985 Lake Level, Uplift and Outlet Incision: The Nipissing and Algoma Great Lakes. In *Quaternary Evolution of the Great Lakes*, edited by P. F. Karrow and P. E. Calkin, pp. 63–77. Special Paper 30. Geological Society of Canada, St. John's, Newfoundland.
1987 *Chronological History of Glacial Lake Algonquin and the Upper Great Lakes.* Bulletin 180. United States Geological Survey, Washington, D.C.
1999 A Century of Great Lakes Levels Research: Finished or Just Beginning? In *Retrieving Michigan's Buried Past: The Archaeology of the Great Lakes State,* edited by John R. Halsey, pp. 1–30. Bulletin 64. Cranbrook Institute of Science, Bloomfield Hills, Michigan.

Larsen, Curtis E., and C. Stephan Demeter
1979 *Archaeological Investigations of the Proposed West River Drive, Bay City.* Report R-2090. Commonwealth Cultural Resources Group, Jackson, Michigan.

Larson, Grahame, and Randall Schaetzl
2001 Origin and Evolution of the Great Lakes. *Journal of Great Lakes Research* 27:518–546.

Loope, Walter L., and Alan F. Arbogast
2000 Dominance of a ~150-Year Cycle of Sand-Supply Change in Late Holocene Dune Building along the Eastern Shore of Lake Michigan. *Quaternary Research* 54:414–422.

Lovis, William A.
1985 The Role of the Fletcher Site and the Lower Basin in the Woodland Adaptations of the Saginaw Valley. *Arctic Anthropology* 22:153–170.
1986 Environmental Periodicity, Buffering, and the Archaic Adaptations of the Saginaw Valley of Michigan. In *Foraging, Collecting, and Harvesting: Archaic Period Subsistence and Settlement in the Eastern Woodlands,* edited by Sarah Neusius, pp. 99–116. Occasional Papers 6. Center for Archaeological Investigations, Southern Illinois University, Carbondale.
1989 (editor) *Archaeological Investigations at the Weber I (20SA581) and Weber II (20SA582) Sites, Frankenmuth Township, Saginaw County, Michigan.* Michigan Cultural Resource Investigation Series 1. Michigan Department of Transportation and Michigan Department of State, Lansing.
1990 Screaming Loon: A Post-Nipissing Site on the Devil's Elbow. *The Michigan Archaeologist* 36:232–252.
1993 (editor) *The Archaic, Woodland and Historic Period Occupations of the Liberty Bridge Locale, Bay City, Michigan.* Michigan Cultural Resource Investigation Series 3. Michigan Department of Transportation and Michigan Department of State, Lansing.
1999 The Middle Archaic: Learning to Live in the Woodlands. In *Retrieving Michigan's Buried Past: The Archaeology of the Great Lakes State,* edited by John R. Halsey, pp. 83–94. Bulletin 64. Cranbrook Institute of Science, Bloomfield Hills, Michigan.
2002a (editor) *A Bridge to the Past: The Post-Nipissing Archaeology of the Marquette Viaduct Replacement Project Sites 20BY28 and 20BY386.* Michigan State University Museum and Department of Anthropology, Michigan State University, East Lansing.
2002b Conclusions. In *A Bridge to the Past: The Post-Nipissing Archaeology of the Marquette Viaduct Replacement Sites 20BY28 and 20BY387*, edited by William A. Lovis, pp. 11.1–11.9. Michigan State University Museum and Department of Anthropology, Michigan State University, East Lansing.
2004 Backyards, Scrap Yards, and the Taphonomy of Riverine Urban Environments: Bay City, Michigan, as a Case Study. In *An Upper Great Lakes Archaeological Odyssey: Essays in Honor of Charles E. Cleland,* edited by William A. Lovis, pp. 127–149. Cranbrook Institute of Science, Bloomfield Hills, Michigan.

Lovis, William A., Randolph E. Donahue, and Margaret B. Holman
2005 Long Distance Logistic Mobility as an Organizing Principle among Northern Hunter-Gatherers: A Great Lakes Middle Holocene Settlement System. *American Antiquity* 70:669–693.

Lovis, William A., Kathryn Egan, G. William Monaghan, Beverley A. Smith, and Earl J. Prahl
1996 Environment and Subsistence at the Marquette Viaduct Local of the Fletcher Site. In *Investigating the Archaeological Record of the Great Lakes State: Essays in Honor of Elizabeth Baldwin Garland,* edited by Margaret Holman, Janet Brashler, and Kathryn E. Parker, pp. 251–306. New Issues Press, Kalamazoo, Michigan.

Lovis, William A., Margaret B. Holman, Mark W. Holley, Kenneth J. Vrana, and Russell K. Skowronek
1995 Saginaw Bay Archaeological Project Pilot Technology Assessment. Submitted to Coastal Zone Management Program, Michigan Department of Environmental Quality (Contract No. 95D-0.07). Michigan State University Museum, East Lansing.

Lovis, William A., Margaret B. Holman, G. William Monaghan, and Russell K. Skowronek
1994 Archaeology, Geology, and Paleoecology: Perspectives on Regional Research Design in the Saginaw Bay Region of Michigan. In *Great Lakes Archaeology and Paleoecology: Exploring Interdisciplinary Initiatives for the Nineties,* edited by Ronald I. MacDonald, pp. 81–94. Quaternary Sciences Institute, University of Waterloo, Waterloo, Ontario.

Lovis, William A., and Ronald I. MacDonald
1999 Archaeological Implications of Great Lakes Paleoecology at the Regional Scale. In *Taming the Taxonomy: Toward a New Understanding of Great Lakes Archaeology*, edited by Ronald F. Williamson and Christopher M. Watts, pp. 125–150. Eastend Books and Ontario Archaeological Society, Toronto.

Lovis, William A., G. William Monaghan, and James A. Robertson
2001 Landscape Change and the Late Archaic Occupation of the Lower Saginaw River in Bay City. Paper presented at the 2001 Midwest Archaeological Conference, Symposium on Archaic Research in the Upper Midwest, LaCrosse, Wisconsin.

Lovis, William A., and John O'Shea
1994 A Reconsideration of Archaeological Research Design in Michigan: 1993. *The Michigan Archaeologist* 39:107–126.

Lovis, William A., and Shaun M. Phillips
2002 Features and Radiocarbon Dates from Sites 20BY387 and 20BY28. In *A Bridge to the Past: The Post-Nipissing Archaeology of the Marquette Viaduct Replacement Project Sites 20BY28 and 20BY386*, edited by William A. Lovis, pp. 10.1–10.24. Michigan State University Museum and Department of Anthropology, Michigan State University, East Lansing.

Lovis, William A., and James A. Robertson
1989 Rethinking the Archaic Chronology of the Saginaw Valley of Michigan. *Midcontinental Journal of Archaeology* 14:226–260.

Luedtke, Barbara E.
1976 *Lithic Material Distributions and Interaction Patterns during the Late Woodland Period in Michigan.* Ph.D. dissertation, University of Michigan. University Microfilms International, Ann Arbor.

Martin, Susan R.
1993 (editor) 20KE20: Excavations at a Prehistoric Copper Workshop. *The Michigan Archaeologist* 39:127–193.

1999 *Wonderful Power: The Story of Ancient Copper Working in the Lake Superior Basin.* Wayne State University Press, Detroit.

Mead, Barbara E., and Robert G. Kingsley
1985 20IS46, a Late Archaic Cemetery in Iosco County, Michigan. *The Michigan Archaeologist* 31:67–81.

Monaghan, G. William
1993 Geology of the Third Street Bridge Right-of-Way, Bay City, Michigan. In *The Archaic, Woodland and Historic Period Occupations of the Liberty Bridge Locale, Bay City, Michigan*, edited by William A. Lovis, pp. 35–40. Michigan Cultural Resource Investigation Series 3. Michigan Department of Transportation and Michigan Department of State, Lansing.

Monaghan, G. William, and William A. Lovis
2006 *Modeling Archaeological Site Burial in Southern Michigan: A Geoarchaeological Synthesis* (with contributions by Michael J. Hambacher). Special Publication 1. Michigan Department of Transportation, Michigan State University Press, East Lansing.

Monaghan, G. William, William A. Lovis, and Kathryn C. Egan-Bruhy
2006 Earliest *Cucurbita* from the Great Lakes, Northern USA. *Quaternary Research* 65:216–222.

Monaghan, G. William, William A. Lovis, and Leslie Fay
1986 The Lake Nipissing Transgression in the Saginaw Bay Region, Michigan. *Canadian Journal of Earth Sciences* 23:1851–1854.

Ozker, Doreen B.
1976 The Naugle Site, 20MD30, Midland County, Michigan. *The Michigan Archaeologist* 22:315–355.
1982 *An Early Woodland Community at the Schultz Site 20SA2 in the Saginaw Valley and the Nature of the Early Woodland Adaptation in the Great Lakes Region.* Anthropological Papers 70. Museum of Anthropology, University of Michigan, Ann Arbor.

Peebles, Christopher S.
1978 Of Archaeology and Archaeologists in Saginaw County, Michigan. *The Michigan Archaeologist* 24:83–129.

Pleger, Thomas
2000 Old Copper and Red Ocher Complexity. *Midcontinental Journal of Archaeology* 25:169–190.

Renfrew, Colin
1975 Trade as Action at a Distance. In *Ancient Civilizations and Trade*, edited by Jeremy Sabloff and C. C. Lamberg-Karlovsky, pp. 1–59. University of New Mexico Press, Albuquerque.

Robertson, James A.
1987 Inter-Assemblage Variability and Hunter-Gatherer Settlement Systems: A Perspective from the Saginaw Valley of Michigan. Ph.D. dissertation, Department of Anthropology, Michigan State University, East Lansing.

Robertson, James A., William A. Lovis, and John R. Halsey
1999 The Late Archaic: Hunters-Gatherers in an Uncertain Environment. In *Retrieving Michigan's Buried Past: The Archaeology of the Great Lakes State,* edited by John R. Halsey, pp. 95–124. Bulletin 64. Cranbrook Institute of Science, Bloomfield Hills, Michigan.

Robertson, James A., G. G. Robinson, K. C. Taylor, and Mary L. Jeakle
1995 *Final Phase II Archaeological Investigation K. I. Sawyer Air Force Base, Marquette County, Michigan.* Commonwealth Cultural Resources Group, Jackson, Michigan, and Earth Tech, Colton, California.

Shoshani, Jeheskel, Henry T. Wright, and Arnold R. Pilling
1990 Ecological Context of Two Early Archaic Projectile Points from Michigan: A LeCroy and a Kessell Point Recovered at 20OK394. *The Michigan Archaeologist* 36:1–20.

Shott, Michael J.
1986 Settlement Mobility and Technological Organization among Great Lakes Paleo-Indian Foragers. Ph.D. dissertation, Department of Anthropology, University of Michigan, Ann Arbor.
1993 *The Leavitt Site: A Parkhill Phase Paleo-Indian Occupation in Central Michigan.* Memoir 25. Museum of Anthropology, University of Michigan, Ann Arbor.
1999 The Early Archaic: Life after the Glaciers. In *Retrieving Michigan's Buried Past: The Archaeology of the Great Lakes State*, edited by John R. Halsey, pp. 71–82. Bulletin 64. Cranbrook Institute of Science, Bloomfield Hills, Michigan.

Simons, Donald B.
1972 Radiocarbon Date from a Michigan Satchell-Type Site. *The Michigan Archaeologist* 18:209–213.
1979 New Data on the Satchell Complex from the Pinegrove Cemetery Site (20-GS-28) in Genesee County, Michigan. Paper presented at the Annual Meeting of the Eastern States Archaeological Federation, Ann Arbor, Michigan.

Skibo, James, M., John G. Franzen, and Eric Drake
2007 Smudge Pits and Hide Smoking Revisited: In *Archaeological Anthropology: Perspectives on Method and Theory*, edited by J. M. Skibo, M. W. Graves, and M. T. Stark, pp. 72–92. University of Arizona Press, Tucson.

Spence, Michael W., and William A. Fox
1986 The Early Woodland Occupations of Southern Ontario. In *Early Woodland Archeology*, edited by Kenneth B. Farnsworth and Thomas E. Emerson, pp. 4–46. Kampsville Seminars in Archeology 2. Center for American Archeology, Kampsville, Illinois.

Stuiver, Minze, and Paula J. Reimer
2004 *CALIB Rev. 4.4.2.* Quaternary Isotope Lab, University of Washington, Seattle.

Taggart, David W.
1967 Seasonal Patterns in Settlement, Subsistence, and Industries in the Saginaw Late Archaic. *The Michigan Archaeologist* 13:153–170.

Winters, Howard D.
1969 *The Riverton Culture, a Second Millenium Occupation in the Central Wabash Valley.* Monograph 1, Illinois Archaeological Survey, Springfield; Reports of Investigations 13, Illinois State Museum, Springfield.

Wright, Henry T.
1964 A Transitional Archaic Campsite at Green Point (20SA1). *The Michigan Archaeologist* 10:17–22.

21

Defining the Archaic in Northern Illinois

Rochelle Lurie, Douglas Kullen, and Scott J. Demel

Introduction

Archaeologists in northern Illinois dream of deeply buried Archaic sites with well-preserved features containing abundant plant and animal remains. The sections of northern Illinois most likely to contain these sought-after deposits, however, have received little archaeological attention. Although Archaic sites have been reported along the major rivers in the Driftless Zone of northwestern Illinois and the Rock River Hill Country of north-central Illinois, none have been extensively excavated. Knowledge of the Archaic, such as it is, derives primarily from survey and testing projects conducted in the last 25 years by cultural resource management (CRM) firms in northeastern Illinois. The rapid pace of development in the counties surrounding Chicago makes northeastern Illinois one of the most intensively surveyed parts of the state. But, given the demands of compliance-driven archaeology, there has been little time or money for developing syntheses of information contained in the gray literature. One of the goals of this chapter is to present as-yet-unpublished information on Archaic sites excavated in recent years.

After a brief consideration of the archaeologically less well-known parts of northern Illinois, this chapter focuses on the northeast part of the state and on recently excavated sites (Figure 21.1). There, Archaic-period manifestations occur across a landscape of youthful river valleys with narrow floodplains, poorly drained morainal uplands with knob-and-kettle terrain, and the Lake Michigan coastal zone of alternating beach ridges, dunes, and lacustrine plains. Prehistorically, the river valleys and the coastal zone contained forest, prairie, and marsh resources used by hunter-gatherers during their seasonal rounds, and the rivers served as important routes for travel and communication. Pollen records available from the many bogs

Figure 21.1. Northeastern Illinois and Archaic-period sites discussed in this chapter.

and basins in this region suggest that the effects of the Hypsithermal were minimal in northeast Illinois. It is our contention that permanent and seasonal wetlands were a major resource draw for Archaic people that induced them to persistently inhabit the area's upland settings throughout the period. A cursory study of 150 tested Archaic sites in northeast Illinois recorded 195 Archaic components. Of these, 77 components (40 percent) were situated on rises adjacent to upland marshes (Lurie 2003a). Twenty of the 77 components were described as Early Archaic, 24 as Middle Archaic, 23 as Late Archaic, and 10 as Late Archaic–Early Woodland.

As of January 1, 2003, more than 5,700 sites of all time periods were listed in the electronic version of the state site files covering northeastern Illinois, and of these, 1,094 were coded as Archaic (Lurie 2003b). These sites include 1,297 Archaic components. Of these, 452 were listed as generalized Archaic, 282 as Early Archaic, 189 as Middle Archaic, and 374 as Late Archaic. Defining Archaic subperiods is problematic because there is little consensus on what projectile point types are characteristic of particular time spans, with the exception of the Early Archaic. This is primarily due to the lack of radiocarbon dates for point types and to researchers' ignorance of variability within point stylistic groupings.

Descriptions of point types and accompanying date ranges are usually based on information from stratified sites to the south or north with suites of radiocarbon dates. But the few reliable Archaic dates available from northern Illinois and southern Wisconsin suggest that the appearance of point styles was time transgressive. Specific point types may have appeared in northern Illinois a thousand years later than in southern Illinois.

Archaic subperiods are very broad heuristic constructs in northeastern Illinois. How one labels sites affects the results of any hypothesis testing about how, when, and if subsistence orientations, settlement patterns, and social organization changed in this area, as they seem to have done elsewhere in the Midwest. If one were going to use the state site files to address cultural stability or change during the Archaic, one would need to make explicit which diagnostic artifacts were used to define Archaic subperiods, to consult the paper files for sites recorded prior to 1993, to reassign components to subperiods on the basis of diagnostic points selected, and to examine survey reports that might contain photographs of artifacts recovered. This is a daunting task, given the number of Archaic sites reported, and is not undertaken here. For now, comparisons with other midwestern regions must be based on the few sites that have been radiocarbon dated and on the more extensively excavated sites that have produced diagnostic Archaic artifacts.

Environmental and Landscape Context

Paleoenvironmental Conditions

The first humans entered northern Illinois following the retreat of the continental ice sheet during the late Pleistocene. By all indications, Paleoindian peoples roamed a dynamically changing landscape for hundreds of years. But by the earliest of Archaic times, woodland had developed across northern Illinois, despite the Valderan ice advance around 10,950 B.P. (Willman 1971:57). A pollen core from Nelson Lake in Kane County documents a closed spruce-larch forest mixed with black ash from around 13,500 to 10,000 B.P., which suggests a climate with cool summers and winters warmer than those characterizing the modern boreal forest (Curry et al. 1999:11). Thus, in Early Archaic times, "the general appearance of the landscape was probably open spruce woodland on the uplands," with denser populations of spruce, fir, and larch around the numerous kettle lakes (King 1981:49). At Volo Bog, in Lake County, spruce woodland began to decline by around 10,900 B.P., to be temporarily replaced by pine, fir, birch, and ash. During this time, elm, oak, walnut, dogwood, and hackberry first appeared. This decline in spruce occurred at Nelson Lake, too, where fir, balsam poplar, black ash, birch, and alder peaked around 10,000–9000 B.P. (Curry et al. 1999:11). The pattern occurs further south, as well, at Chatsworth Bog in Livingston County (King 1981:52).

After 10,300 B.P., pine, fir, birch, and ash declined in turn. Increasingly, the uplands began to support woodlands of oak, hickory, hop hornbeam, walnut, basswood, and silver maple, with some pine. Lowlands and upland bog margins supported small populations of ash, sycamore, beech, and silver maple (King 1981:50). For the next two millennia, cool temperate species like birch, elm, beech, and ash declined as oak grew to dominate the woodlands, both at Volo Bog and at Chatsworth Bog. Grasses increased at this time, too. This transition has been dated to the same time range (ca. 9000–5500 B.P.) at Nelson Lake, where ironwood, elm, oak, hickory, and sugar maple pollen increased along with grass and ragweed pollen (Curry et al. 1999:12; Nelson et al. 2004). These data show that deciduous forest became firmly established during conditions wetter than today's but that some prairie openings were developing at the same time. Although undated, this dramatic shift from mixed coniferous forest to oak woodland has also been documented in pollen cores from Hill's Bog near Huntley on the McHenry-Kane County border (Duerr 1967) and from Lily Lake in central Kane County (Voss 1937). This vegetational change probably corresponds to the withdrawal of the glacial ice front from the Lake Michigan basin and the concurrent draining of the proglacial lakes that occupied the basin.

Dryer climatic conditions of the Hypsithermal Interval are evidenced by changes in the vegetation. Drought-resistant species, such as grasses and weedy plants, began to make up a larger part of the vegetation cover, at the expense of most arboreal and wet-habitat plants. This transition was complete by 8300 B.P. at Chatsworth Bog and by 7900 B.P. at Volo Bog. Recent work with dated pollen cores and ostracod sequences at Nelson Lake and at Crystal Lake, in southeast McHenry County, indicates that the shift to prairie started somewhat earlier in those locations, around 9000 B.P. (Curry et al. 2004). Dry conditions at Nelson Lake peaked after 5500 B.P. (Curry et al. 1999:12; Nelson et al. 2004). From that time onward through the rest of the Archaic period, xeric oak-hickory forest was the dominant type of woodland in northeastern Illinois (King 1981:50).

The period after ca. 5500 B.P. saw the formation of the Prairie Peninsula in Illinois, that great embayment of the western prairie and high plains into the forested woodlands east of the Mississippi. Throughout much of northern Illinois, oak-hickory forest gave way to tallgrass prairie. In northeast Illinois, drought- and fire-resistant oak species survived in the rougher morainal uplands and on the east sides of streams to form savannas of widely spaced trees with a prairie-grass understory (Moran 1980). Elsewhere, lowlands and river valleys retained their forest cover, but since prairie became established in the uplands of central Illinois, it has remained the dominant vegetation cover through the present (King 1981:57). Whereas profound vegetational change characterized more westerly and southerly sections of the Prairie Peninsula, pollen data indicate less dramatic change in the composition of local northeastern Illinois vegetation, such that it may have had a less significant impact on human subsistence.

Physiography

Northern Illinois is physiographically diverse. If we take as our southern boundary a line that roughly follows the Kankakee River valley to the upper Illinois River through the Starved Rock vicinity and then west to the mouth of the Rock River, northern Illinois encompasses four great physiographic divisions. It includes the valleys of four major midwestern rivers, fronts on Lake Michigan, and straddles the subcontinental divide between the Mississippi and Great Lakes watersheds.

Extending southward from Wisconsin, the so-called Driftless Zone covers the extreme northwestern part of northern Illinois. This is a maturely developed land surface of rugged hills, deep interior valleys, and loess-capped bluffs and palisades along the Mississippi River valley (Schwegman 1973:9). Because the area escaped the ravages of the Pleistocene glaciation, ancient landforms are still intact. Deep slope-base colluvium, rockshelters, and even caves are present.

The Rock River Hill Country extends eastward from the Driftless Zone to the line of the Rock River. This section was glaciated, and a relatively thin mantle of glacial drift blankets the rolling hills of the area (Schwegman 1973:10).

Extending southeast from the Rock River Hill Country is a broad expanse of plains known as the Grand Prairie physiographic division of Illinois (Schwegman 1973). Although this area was formerly glaciated, its morainal ridges are relatively low and are separated by wide expanses of fairly level outwash plains and former glacial lake beds. Natural drainage, in general, was very poor in this section. From the Green River lowland in the west, this section extends south beyond the Illinois River valley and eastward to include the Kankakee River valley.

Although relatively flat overall, the Grand Prairie Division contains nearly all of the documented source areas of the several chert types known from northern Illinois. These cherts all occur along river valleys where bedrock outcrops are exposed. Moline chert—a distinctive banded blue-gray to steel-gray material—occurs in ravines exposed in side valleys along the lower Rock River (Birmingham and Van Dyke 1981; Ferguson and Warren 1992). On the lower Vermillion River, Everett chert from the Nachusa Formation and Eagle Point chert from the Dunleith Formation are exposed (Ferguson and Warren 1992:9–10). Not far away, on the upper Illinois River near Starved Rock, Pecatonica, Shakopee, and Oneota cherts all occur (Ferguson and Warren 1992:3–9). At the northeastern margin of the Grand Prairie Division, mottled white and light-gray cherts of the Elwood and Joliet formations occur in the Des Plaines River valley and its tributaries from Joliet upstream to Lemont (Ferguson and Warren 1992:10–11). This chert is variously referred to by archaeologists as "crystal" chert, "sugar" chert, "Harmilda" chert, "Bolingbrook" chert, or, more generically, "Silurian" chert.

Extending eastward in northern Illinois from the Rock River Hill Country and the plains of the Grand Prairie Division are the low, arcuate hills of the Northeastern Morainal Division. This physiographic section contains the most varied terrain in northern Illinois, as the scars of numerous Pleistocene glacial retreats, pauses, and advances mark the landscape. More than a dozen glacial moraines sweep in a great curving arc south from Wisconsin and east into Indiana, roughly paralleling the shoreline of Lake Michigan, from whence the glacial ice advanced during Pleistocene times. The crests of these moraines feature knob-and-kettle terrain, which grows more pronounced toward the north. Trellislike networks of streams flow through the series of north–south valleys that run between the morainal ridges. Along the Des Plaines River and Sag Channel, the valleys have been scoured down to bedrock by torrential glacial floods that drained entire lakes as the Pleistocene ice front shifted. The easternmost and youngest of the moraines are buried in lacustrine sediments deposited on the floor of the Chicago Lake Plain—actually a composite feature that developed beneath a series of shallow proglacial lakes that once existed in the Lake Michigan basin. Ancient beaches, sand bars, spits, and gravel bars stand out on the otherwise flat and marshy lake plain, marking the various former lake levels. In places, current and former lake margins are covered by sand dunes, increasing their prominence above the surrounding plain.

Current understanding of the Late Pleistocene–Early Holocene history of Lake Michigan should be noted here, as much of the lake basin was exposed as dry land during parts of the Archaic period. Glacial Lake Chicago formed in the Lake Michigan basin as the Lake Michigan Lobe of the continental glacier melted and the ice retreated northward during the late Pleistocene. Lake Chicago covered much of what is now dry land on the Chicago Lake Plain, and this proglacial lake drained southward through the Des Plaines River valley. But in time, the glacial margin retreated so far that it opened up a new and lower outlet. The water level in the Lake Michigan basin dropped by approximately 128 m to what is known as the Main Algonquin of Michigan stage (Larsen 1987:24). A swath of dry land, some 40 km wide, was exposed all around the lower end of the lake. This situation lasted for hundreds of years until continued retreat of the glacial margin opened the even lower North Bay outlet. Waters in the Lake Michigan basin drained out until they reached what is termed the "Chippewa" low level at about 55 m amsl. This drained much of the northern end of the Lake Michigan basin but only slightly reduced the size of what had become a separate water body in the southern end of the basin. This situation persisted for centuries until, during the Nipissing I transgression, isostatic rebound lifted the North Bay outlet, and the Lake Michigan basin began refilling (Larsen 1987:24). Eventually, waters in the Lake Michigan and Lake Huron basins rejoined, but the southern end of the Lake Michigan basin was still close to the Chippewa low level. The Nipissing I transgression continued from 4700 B.P. through 4500 B.P. (Fraser et al. 1990; Larsen 1985, 1987), refilling the Lake Michigan basin to a maximum elevation of 183 m amsl and reactivating the Chicago outlet. This latest transgression brought Lake Michigan to 6 m above its modern-day level of 177 m. After a brief drop during the period from 4200 to 4000 B.P., the lake rose again to a maximum of 180.5 m (Larsen 1985:23, 1987:26). This Nipissing II transgression began around 4000 B.P. and lasted until about 3800 B.P. (Larsen 1985), refilling the basin to about 3.5 m above the modern level. Since that time, minor lake-level fluctuations have continued to occur.

Settlement Patterns

Driftless Zone and Rock River Hill Country

As an archaeological subregion of the Midwest, northern Illinois has yielded no comprehensive data for the Archaic period. The Driftless Zone has produced important stratified Archaic deposits across the border in Wisconsin, but the Illinois part of the Driftless Zone has been virtually unexplored. Current understanding of the Archaic in this part of northern Illinois is a complete blank, but the area holds great potential for stratified and well-preserved sites. Archaic sites have been reported in the Rock River Hill Country, but no systematic studies have been undertaken to record and analyze Archaic settlement patterns. Only a few Archaic deposits have been professionally excavated. All of these excavations have been undertaken along the Rock River, on the extreme eastern edge of the Rock River Hill Country. And all of the excavated Archaic deposits were exposed incidentally, during investigations at sites containing more extensive Woodland-period deposits. The interior of the Rock River Hill Country, like Illinois' Driftless Zone, is a virtual unknown as far as the Archaic period is concerned.

Grand Prairie

Many Archaic sites have been reported in the Grand Prairie of northern Illinois, but only a few have been fully investigated. Those that produced Archaic radiocarbon dates or stratified deposits are discussed in the next section. Here we attempt to summarize the more important archaeological surveys that have been undertaken and reported in this physiographic division.

Many systematic surveys have been completed in the Grand Prairie Division, and more are being done every day as urban sprawl pushes outward from the Chicago metropolitan area into the hinterlands of DeKalb, Kane, Kendall, and Will counties. While most of the local compliance surveys cover relatively small areas, results from some of the larger, more extensive surveys can help to shed empirical light on Archaic settlement patterns in the region.

Methodological problems have plagued some large-scale survey efforts in northern Illinois. Despite extensive background research and field efforts, some surveys simply confirmed the rather mundane observation that prehistoric sites tend to cluster near streams and rivers (e.g., Doershuk 1988; Hart and Jeske 1991). Such surveys were unable to distinguish settlement patterning at a resolution that would allow researchers to detect patterns within the subdivisions of the Archaic period or even between general divisions of prehistory as a whole. Such is the case when many sites are found but most lack temporally diagnostic artifacts.

One of the earliest survey efforts in the region was undertaken by professional archaeologists collaborating with amateurs through Northern Illinois University. By repeatedly visiting known sites and systematically surveying to locate new sites, researchers were able to amass temporal data on numerous prehistoric sites along the Kishwaukee River and across the surrounding uplands in DeKalb County, located on the north edge of the Grand Prairie Division. Researchers noted that Early Archaic settlement was "stream oriented," with 65 percent of sites occurring within 800 m of a stream. End moraines were avoided for settlement, except where upland bogs or marshes were present. The general pattern was one of transient hunting camps occupied by hunters who rapidly traversed the area and then returned to sedentary camps located somewhere else, presumably along the Illinois, Rock, or Mississippi rivers (Springer et al. 1978).

Through additional analysis and the acquisition of more survey data, James Springer (1985) later refined and expanded his conclusions regarding prehistoric settlement in the Kishwaukee basin. He concluded that, while the period was poorly known in his study area, very small groups of Early Archaic peoples ranged widely through the area, exploiting a diverse food base and leaving little evidence of a seasonal round of subsistence. Early Archaic sites occur on high elevations, away from major rivers but often near small tributaries or headwater streams (Springer 1985:31). Site patterning did not change much in the Middle and Late Archaic periods. Sites tended to occur on small knolls near large upland bogs or kettle ponds.

A major systematic survey was undertaken by the Illinois State Museum in advance of the construction of Interstate 39, linking Bloomington and LaSalle-Peru. This project provided archaeologists with the opportunity to examine settlement patterns along a broad north–south transect extending across uplands and stream valleys in the Grand Prairie Division (Ferguson et al. 1986). Here again, investigators found that Middle Archaic sites tend to be concentrated near streams and upland kettle ponds. They note that the virtual abandonment of the uplands during the Middle Archaic that has been observed in other parts of the Prairie Peninsula is definitely not seen in north-central Illinois. The reason for this, they suggest, is that the effects of the Hypsithermal may have been milder in central Illinois than in more westerly locations (Ferguson et al. 1986:41–43).

A recent systematic survey of Starved Rock State Park was conducted by the Illinois State Museum along the bluff tops, ravines, and narrow floodplain on the south side of the Illinois River. Investigators managed to document 32 prehistoric sites with temporal diagnostics (Ferguson 1997). Researchers concluded that Early and Middle Archaic sites were relatively sparse compared with those of later periods. Middle Archaic occupations tended to cluster in areas containing soils with moderately slow permeability. This suggested that Middle Archaic groups were exploiting wetland-related resources that had become geographically restricted because of Hypsithermal dry conditions (Ferguson 1997:237–238). Despite this subtle change in settlement patterning, no changes were evident in overall patterns of chert use and lithic technology throughout the entire Holocene. The relatively small numbers of Archaic sites around Starved Rock are attributed either to an actual low population level, the possibility that Archaic sites were scoured away by catastrophic floods, or the possibility that undetected Archaic deposits are deeply buried in the Illinois floodplain or adjacent alluvial fans.

Further east in the Grand Prairie Division, a recent large survey by the University of Illinois was completed for the controversial Peotone Airport project (Harris 1998, 2002). This survey reported some 216 archaeological sites, from which 76 individual prehistoric components could be identified. Nearly half of the Early Archaic components were found within 100 m of water, and all were found within 800 m. Researchers concluded that upland marshes and small streams were extremely important to Early Archaic peoples. Middle Archaic components were few in number and occurred in an unpatterned distribution. Twenty-six Late Archaic components were identified, and their locations mirrored the Early Archaic pattern, with all occurring within 700 m of a marsh or stream. This study was hampered by an "inability to clearly define some Middle Archaic point types" (Harris 2002:11), which casts doubt on all but the most general conclusions regarding diachronic change in settlement patterning.

Northeastern Morainal Division

The Northeastern Morainal Division contains the greater Chicago metropolitan area, which has created an archaeological paradox. Because it is a major center of new infrastructural, commercial, industrial, and residential development, the Chicago area has benefited from much archaeological survey work. This survey work, although extensive, has been performed piecemeal on a project-by-project basis by numerous different investigators and has not been synthesized. Moreover, rigorous compliance standards have only been instituted in the last 25 years, so that much of the area's unique archaeological database has been destroyed without receiving the attention of professional archaeologists. Therefore, while a lot of work has been completed in the Chicago area and a great deal is known, much about local prehistory is still not understood and much will never be known.

The paradoxical nature of archaeological understanding in northeast Illinois is exemplified in Charles Markman's *Chicago before History* (1991), the most recent attempt by an archaeologist to review the entire prehistory of the region. In that summary, the Archaic period is covered in only three pages of text, a quick synopsis of state site file data, and the results of a few surveys providing the bulk of the raw information (Markman 1991:49–59). The potential for buried sites on the Chicago Lake Plain is discussed at some length, but the two sites mentioned as examples received very limited testing and are still unpublished.

Despite these problems, some large-scale and comprehensive surveys have supplemented knowledge of Archaic settlement patterns developed elsewhere in the region. For example, an investigation by the Illinois State Museum for the Superconducting Super Collider project in DuPage and Kane counties gathered data from known sites and from point collections amassed by amateurs (McGimsey et al. 1989). While this approach did not produce statistically viable or systematic survey results, it did confirm an important observation regarding Archaic site locations in northeast Illinois. Archaic sites and isolated finds, in general—and Middle Archaic ones, in particular—occur proportionately more often in upland settings, away from major river valleys, than do later prehistoric sites (McGimsey et al. 1989:108).

David Keene (1989) reported on his 1979 survey in the Cook County preserves (Keene and Karamanski 1980), which covered contrasting landscapes on the Chicago Lake Plain and in the adjacent morainal uplands. Keene's fieldwork was unsystematic, in that he employed "irregular" shovel-testing intervals and ignored areas formerly covered by wet prairie while tracking down previously reported site locations (Keene 1989:141–142), so his results are suspect. Of the 118 prehistoric sites found, 60 percent could not be assigned to even a general time period. Working with the remaining 40 percent, Keene concludes that Woodland and later peoples utilized the lake plain much more intensively than did Archaic peoples, whose sites are underrepresented on beach ridges, perhaps because of deep burial during fluctuations in the level of Lake Michigan (Keene 1989:143–146).

In 1989, Joe Craig examined the distribution of prehistoric sites on the Chicago Lake Plain from a different perspective. He looked at a 241-km^2 section of the lake plain, including the area containing some of the Cook County Forest Preserve sites reported by Keene in 1979. Craig employed multiple regression statistical procedures to isolate key environmental variables, producing results that directly contradict Keene's conclusions. Craig found that on the lake plain, Archaic sites occur most frequently (75 percent) on beach ridges and less frequently (17 percent) in alluvial bottomlands. By contrast, Woodland sites occur throughout the entire range of local topographic settings but are concentrated on both beach ridges and bottomlands, and Mississippian peoples continued the trend toward locating themselves with greater frequency in alluvial bottoms and on the lake bottom itself (Craig 1989:355). Craig proposed an Archaic settlement pattern that maximized access to the extensive wetlands on the lake plain. He suggested that, as Hypsithermal dry conditions took hold, wetlands on the lake plain dried up less than wetlands in the uplands did, and they remained a viable resource throughout the Archaic period (Craig 1989: 359).

Although the character and timing of lake level changes in the Lake Michigan basin is a topic of debate and ongoing research among geologists and climatologists, the issue directly concerns archaeologists, too, since the lifeways of prehistoric peoples in northern Illinois must have been profoundly affected by the changes. Current interpretations suggest that Lake Chicago only began receding around the beginning of the Early Archaic period. Thus, no Paleoindian sites should be expected below the modern lake level. As Lake Chicago receded, associated shoreline sites inhabited by Archaic peoples would have been located progressively downslope into the lake basin. The expectation is that cultural deposits would have been deposited relatively thinly in the wake of the receding coastline, similar to the situation observed on late Pleistocene beaches exposed off the coast of western Canada (Fedje and Christensen 1999:641). The Chippewa low phase, when the lake reached its lowest level, was relatively brief. The basin is thought to have begun refilling during the Early–Middle Archaic transition and continued to do so through the Middle Archaic period. As the lakeshore rose, any Middle Archaic coastal populations would have been pushed back to the west. Any surviving archaeological sites found on the floor of Lake Michigan should date to the Early or Middle Archaic periods. Because the lake restabilized at approximately the modern level during the Middle–Late Archaic transition, no sites younger than this should be inundated.

Fluctuating water levels in the Lake Michigan basin created variable conditions for the formation and preservation of archaeological sites dating to the Archaic period. Erosion of the various shorelines in the basin is a dynamic process that has been underway ever since the continental ice sheet began to melt. Beach erosion has affected each shoreline at every lake-level stage. Because they are the most elevated, the shorelines that formed during the Paleoindian period are relatively intact. An exception occurs in northern Lake County and northward, where older beaches have been erased by erosion. Elsewhere, early sites above 184 m in elevation should be unaffected by lake-level shifts. On some parts of the shoreline below that elevation, as much as three-quarters of a kilometer of land may have eroded away since Late Archaic times (Demel 2000). Along other sections of the lakefront, where sediments accumulated (spits, dunes, and quiet-water estuaries), archaeological deposits may still be preserved.

Within the southern Lake Michigan basin, Early and Middle Archaic shorelines are inundated beneath the lake. These areas must have been seriously affected by beach erosion during refilling of the basin and are either destroyed, buried by near-shore sediments, or submerged. The Barnes Creek locality in Kenosha County, Wisconsin—at an elevation of 183 m—contains a buried forest stratum covered by 3 m of near-shore sediments (Goldstein 1995:109). Twenty-three kilometers out into the lake from Chicago, the submerged Olson-locality forest, however, indicates that remnants of the early and mid-Holocene coast have survived the dynamics of changing lake levels and shoreline displacement events (Chrzastowski et al. 1991). This provides initiative for future underwater research aimed at locating evidence of the Early Archaic and Middle Archaic occupation beneath Lake Michigan.

Shorelines from the time of the Middle–Late Archaic transition are relatively intact above the modern shoreline, but continuous erosion on the west coast of Lake Michigan has no doubt taken its toll. The clustering of Late Archaic sites in the modern coastal zone may be more apparent than real. Because of erosion, most Late Archaic sites now found near the western shore of the lake may represent nonbeach sites—occupations that were originally situated away from the shoreline (Demel 2000). Minor lake-level fluctuations and ongoing coastal erosion since the Late Archaic may have destroyed or reworked deposits from any time period, so the context of any prehistoric cultural materials found in nearshore settings must be examined carefully.

The Illinois site files as well as CRM surveys shed light on the distribution of prehistoric sites in northeast Illinois, even if few Archaic sites can actually be identified. These reports and surveys reinforce our belief that wooded areas, rivers and streams, and upland kettle marshes provided the most attractive resources for prehistoric peoples in all time periods. A few examples are offered here.

The aptly named Moraine Pipeline project resulted in the systematic survey of a 29-km transect extending north–south through the morainal uplands of Lake County to the Wisconsin border (Kullen 1987). The survey encountered four Archaic components, all of which were found in close proximity to upland marshes. The Middle Archaic was well represented by side-notched points. The occurrence of Archaic sites near upland kettle ponds echoes patterns seen elsewhere in northern Illinois.

In 1988, Midwest Archaeological Research Services Inc. (MARS Inc.) surveyed 263 ha of dry land in Lake Villa, Illinois (Lurie and Jeske 1988). The area is typical of the knob-and-kettle topography in Lake County—gently sloping terrain and glacial lakes, kettles, and marshes with poorly defined drainage patterns. General Land Office (GLO) notes described the area as oak forest and savannah interspersed with lakes and marshes. Thirty-five prehistoric sites and 70 isolates were identified. All but three of the sites were on higher ground on the margins of kettles, marshes, or lakes. The other three were situated on intermittent drainages leading into marshes. One Early Archaic, four Middle Archaic, eight Late Archaic–Early Woodland, and five generalized Archaic components were identified, along with six more recent ones. Site density was greater than five sites per 4 ha. Several of these sites in woods or grass are now protected on land owned by the Lake County Forest Preserve District.

In Chain O' Lakes State Park, on the border of Lake and McHenry counties, Northwestern University archaeologists surveyed some 728 ha of dry land, finding eight Early and Late Archaic components but no Middle Archaic ones (Jeske 1988). The absence of a Middle Archaic presence is tentatively attributed to possible fluctuations in local lake levels. Jeske (1988:39–40) argues that these may have been lower during the Middle Archaic, if shifting water levels documented for the Lake Michigan and Lake Huron basins are any proxy for local interior lake levels. Nearly all of the Archaic components at Chain O' Lakes were found on the Fox River or along the shore of Grass Lake, while most of the later prehistoric components are situated on the shores of the much smaller Turner Lake. Jeske (1988:41) points to the need for more archaeological and geomorphological research to understand the reasons for this shift.

At the Fermi National Accelerator Laboratory, in the uplands straddling the watershed between the Fox and DuPage rivers in Kane and DuPage counties, systematic survey of nearly the entire 2,751-ha area began in the 1970s. Jeske (1990) examined the distribution of Archaic and Mississippian components in relation to GLO vegetation data and other topographic variables. His main conclusion was that the Archaic components were distributed relatively evenly across all upland topographic settings, whereas the later components were clustered along the prairie-forest ecotone. This may be explained by noting that the prairie-forest ecotone, as recorded by GLO surveyors ca. A.D. 1840, would not have been a factor relevant to Archaic settlement ca. 7000–3000 B.C. Climatic conditions were changing through the Archaic period and, in response, vegetation patterns were in a state of flux. Solid deciduous forest cover gave way to a patchy mosaic of prairie and oak-hickory woodland as the Prairie Peninsula developed in northeast Illinois. By considering the Archaic period as a single unit, Jeske identified a uniform site distribution across the landscape that probably masks changes in settlement patterns within the Archaic period in response to major mid- to late Holocene vegetational shifts.

As part of his work at the Garrison site, Demel (2000) examined the distribution of Matanzas points in Cook and Lake counties to ascertain evidence of Middle–Late Archaic territoriality. Demel used isolated diagnostic finds in addition to site locations to identify clusters of sites. These site clusters were presumed to indicate territories, each 280 to 311 km^2 in extent. In Lake County, Matanzas sites were preferentially situated within or at the borders of oak savannas. The most common nearby water sources (over 40 percent) were marshes. The most often used location type in the landscape (22 percent of Matanzas sites) was an upland oak savanna knoll next to a marsh. The Matanzas point distribution data suggest seasonal (late summer and fall) use of sites in northeast Illinois as part of a more extensive settlement and subsistence system.

Prairies were undoubtedly traversed by Archaic peoples, and resources within prairies were no doubt exploited as part of prehistoric settlement and subsistence rounds. Yet sites in open prairie settings, away from woods and permanent water sources, are few in number and small in size, suggesting limited use of prairie environments. This seems odd, considering that, if the local paleoenvironmental reconstructions are to be trusted, full prairie conditions did not develop until Middle Archaic times in much of northern Illinois and the effects of the Hypsithermal appear to have been ameliorated in the morainal country of northeast Illinois. One would expect Early Archaic and earlier Middle Archaic occupations to be fairly common across the landscape, regardless of where prairies later developed. Yet this is certainly not the case. Several large surveys illustrate this point.

In Jackson Township, Will County, about 567 ha of former prairie were surveyed (Johnson 2003). The GLO maps show these acres as prairie. Although two permanent streams flow just beyond the north and south edges of the survey area, only intermittent drainages are present within it. Despite excellent ground surface visibility conditions during the survey, only seven isolates and two small prehistoric sites of unknown date (each with fewer than 10 artifacts) were found in the entire area surveyed.

Approximately 716 ha of former wet and dry prairie were surveyed in Sugar Grove Township, Kane County (Higgs and Porubcan 2004a, 2004b, 2004c; Porubcan 2003). Here again, intermittent streams are the main water sources. Only a dozen isolates and five sites—each with 10 or fewer artifacts—were found. Two sites and one isolate date to the Early Archaic. Four sites, including the Early Archaic ones, are situated on a ridge overlooking wetlands.

Another set of surveys in Kane County—these covering 556 ha (Bird 1995; Bird and Kahl 1994; Loebel 1998)—suggests that even the presence of a permanent stream may not have been enough to attract native peoples to some prairie areas. Mill Creek runs through part of this survey area, which is otherwise labeled as prairie on the GLO maps. Nelson Lake lies at the southeast corner of the property. Only nine isolates and one undated prehistoric site (with 11 artifacts) were recorded in the entire area. One of the isolates was an Early Archaic Kirk point. Just beyond that 556-ha survey area, in formerly wooded land adjacent to the eastern shore of Nelson Lake, a separate survey in 1991 (Kullen 1991) documented 14 prehistoric sites (including three Early and three Late Archaic components) on just 35 ha. Many of the sites were large, representing multiple occupations. The site density figure of 1.63 sites per 4 ha is 23 times greater than that of .07 sites per 4 ha for the adjacent larger survey area. The contrast between these surveys demonstrates the attractiveness that both permanent water and wooded terrain held for prehistoric peoples.

Large parts of many townships in Chicago's collar counties have been extensively surveyed, and these surveys, taken in aggregate, provide additional clear contrasts between the drawing power of timbered land versus prairie. For example, substantial development in Grafton Township, McHenry County—especially the sections between Lake-in-the-Hills and Huntley—has resulted in numerous surveys by several private and university-based CRM firms, together covering over 3,076 ha. The GLO map shows that most of this land (64 percent) was prairie. A band of timber covered the northernmost section and part of the southwest corner of the township. Grafton Township contains many intermittent streams, some now channelized, which flow east beyond the township to the Fox River or to the headwaters of the South Branch of the Kishwaukee River in the southwestern corner of the township. Only 14 prehistoric sites or isolates had been reported in Grafton Township as of August 2004. Four of the 14 are located in the timber in the north of the township. Two of these are isolated finds. All but one Woodland-period site are of unknown prehistoric affiliation. Six other prehistoric sites (three of them Archaic) were found in formerly wooded areas in the southwest corner of the township. The remaining four sites were found on knolls overlooking wetlands in the western end of the township (Porubcan 1997). Three of these four were found in forest soils, but no diagnostics were recovered. The fourth site, which produced Middle Archaic diagnostics, was found in prairie soils. It is the only recorded prehistoric site in the township found in prairie soils. Although the GLO map of Grafton Township does not differentiate between dry and wet prairie, examination of soil types from surveys conducted in the middle of the township indicates that much of the area was wet prairie, with few high and dry places for campsites.

Site-by-Site Descriptions

Archaic Burials

Archaic burials are rarely discovered in northeast Illinois, but those that have been found are situated on terraces overlooking major rivers. Most of these sites were found within the Des Plaines River valley and are thought to be affiliated with the Red Ocher Archaic (among them, the Beake, Von Sandy, and Doetsch sites). The Red Ocher Archaic, by most reckonings, is considered transitional Late Archaic–Early Woodland and therefore probably not typical of the bulk of the Archaic cultures that precede it. In any case, none of the Des Plaines Valley red-ocher burials are radiocarbon dated. The only firmly dated Archaic burials are from the McGraw site above the Fox River near Barrington. A brief review of this and the other burial sites follows.

Beake Site (11L3)

Discovered in 1952 during gravel-mining operations in Lake County, the Beake site burials were situated on a high gravel terrace west of the Des Plaines River and north of a small tributary stream (Young et al. 1961). At least 30 cm of topsoil had been removed before gravel mining exposed the burials. At least six burials were found in relatively shallow pits, which extended into the sterile yellow gravel layer below the topsoil (Young et al. 1961:21). While much of the skeletal material was dispersed during mechanical removal of the gravel, one fragmentary skull was still in situ when the find was brought to the attention of professional archaeologists. According to Young et al. (1961:21), all of the burials were flexed and covered in red ocher as were the grave goods.

The grave goods consisted of Turkey-tail projectile points and fragments of a long quartzite blade. This blade was made of a tan- to cream-colored quartzite, perhaps from the Hixton source in northwestern Wisconsin. The Turkey-tails were made of dark blue-gray chert, either from Harrison County, Indiana, or possibly from the Cobden-Dongola quarries in southern Illinois. In 2001, Ms. Pat Otka brought two Turkey-tail points to the Lake County Museum to be identified and subsequently sent Demel photographs of them (Figure 21.2).

As children, she and her brother had lived across the street from the gravel pit, and each took a pair of Turkey-tails from the Beake site. All of the Turkey-tail points reported by Young and colleagues were associated with a single burial, while the quartzite blade was found with another. Presumably, the Otka Turkey-tails came from at least one other burial.

The current location of the skeletal remains and artifacts recovered in 1961 remains a mystery. Searches at the Lake County Museum and inquiries at the Illinois State Museum and at the University of Illinois (Urbana) proved fruitless. The Turkey-tail points and red ocher covering the burials, and the absence of overlying mounds, suggest the burials date to between 1500 and 500 B.C., that is, the Late Archaic.

Figure 21.2. Turkey-tail points from the Beake site.

Von Sande Site (11L1)

In 1955 a crew from the Chicago Natural History Museum, University of Illinois, and University of Chicago tested a known surface site in an agricultural field near the town of Half Day, in Lake County. The Von Sande site was initially discovered and collected by Mr. Erickson, a former antique dealer from Half Day. Over the years, the site yielded several hundred artifacts from a 1.6-ha area. These included 35 side-notched points, 12 stemmed points, one corner-notched point, a full-grooved ax, a celt, a graver, seven ovate blades, two side-notched bunts, and numerous spalls and worked flakes (Young 1961:8). Several of the short, broad, side-notched points were designated Van Sande points, a type name that no longer is used. Test excavations did not reveal any recognizable cultural features or stratigraphic sequence, suggesting that the artifacts were restricted to the plow zone.

The Doetsch brothers bought land on the east side of the Von Sande site. In 1959, burials and a series of post molds were exposed on the Doetsch property when sod was removed prior to gravel mining (Neumann 1961; Young et al. 1961). The burial area is known as the Doetsch site and was at one time assigned its own site number (11L64), but Von Sande and Doetsch are now considered part of the same site—11L1 (Bird and Lurie 1991).

Six burials and one possible structure (represented by post molds) were excavated at the site. The only complete skeleton was that of a 21-year-old female buried in a flexed position in a shallow pit. The bones were covered with red ocher, and two marine-shell gorgets (one in the chest area and one between the legs) were included in the burial pit. The remains of two young children buried in the same pit were accompanied by four rolled, sheet-copper beads. The other burials consisted of fragmentary, unidentifiable remains extensively disturbed by bulldozers. A systematic survey of the western edge of the Von Sande site conducted in 1991 found that a small, unplowed remnant of the habitation portion of the site is preserved (Bird and Lurie 1991). The site area is now owned by the Lake County Forest Preserve District. The materials from the burials are currently stored at the Illinois Transportation Archaeological Research Program facilities on the campus of the University of Illinois in Urbana.

McGraw Farm (11L386)

The McGraw Farm site was found in a plowed field near the crest of a prominent glacial kame overlooking the Fox River. Artifacts recovered from the site surface and from subsurface features and radiocarbon assays indicate the site was occupied from the Late Paleoindian period through the Late Woodland, or possibly Mississippian, period. The site was discovered by MARS Inc. in 1994 (Lurie 1994) and tested and mitigated in 1996 (Porubcan and Lurie 1998). Deep plowing prior to testing had brought human bone to the surface. Mitigation resulted in the identification of 39 subsurface features, including 13 pit basins of indeterminate function, two refuse pits, four possible hearths, one refuse pit or hearth feature, three postholes, one possible smudge pit, seven pit features containing probable cremated human remains, and eight formal mortuary features containing a minimum of 31 individuals (Figure 21.3). Nonburial features contained moderate amounts of lithic debris, tool fragments, pottery, and carbonized plant and animal remains. Charcoal from one of these features, a smudge pit containing a Point Sauble pot, was dated to the Late Woodland period.

Burial features were grouped temporally, spatially, and morphologically into two sets. Archaic burials were concentrated near the ridge crest. Late Woodland burials were spread out along the ridge's upper southern slope. Dr. Anne Grauer of Loyola University supervised the removal of the burials and analyzed the human remains with the help of

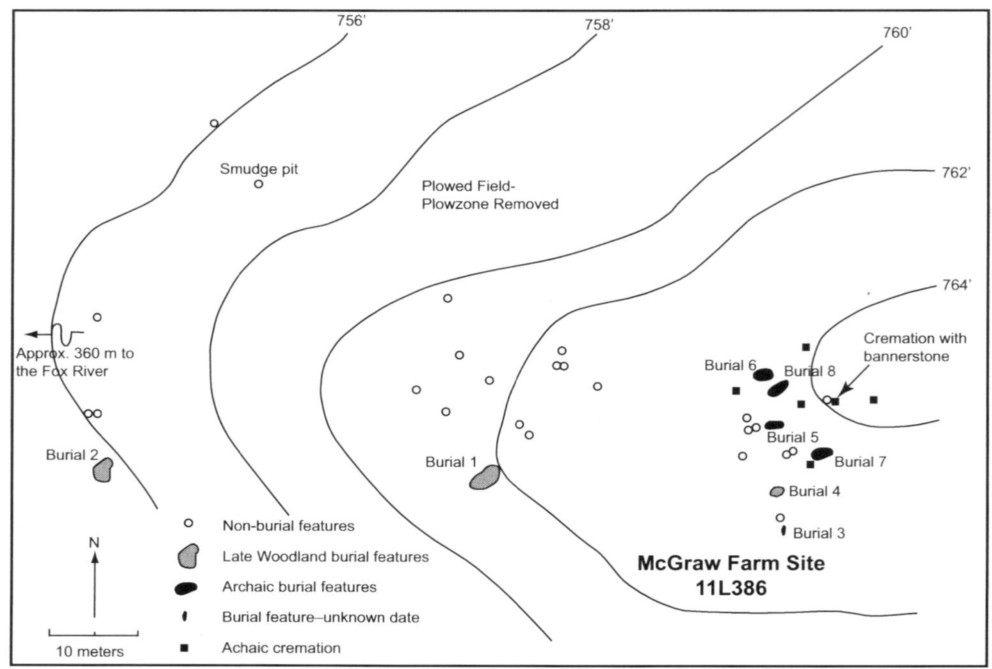

Figure 21.3. McGraw site map showing the concentration of Archaic burial features and cremations.

her laboratory staff and students. Only the Archaic burials are discussed here.

The seven pit features containing probable cremated human remains were clustered near the top of the ridge in the vicinity of four formal Archaic burial facilities. Only a limited number of calcined bones (including cranial and long-bone fragments) in these pits were identifiable as human, but the associated remaining fragments are considered human, as well.

One of these cremation pits contained a Middle Archaic double-edge primary bannerstone (Kwas 1981:147). The bannerstone (Figure 21.4) is made from green pipestone quarried in the vicinity of Sterling, Illinois, approximately 62 km southwest of the McGraw Farm site (Gray 1996). The mineralogical signature of the sample (60 percent berthierine, 7 percent kaolinite, and 33 percent beohmite) is characteristic of the Sterling source (Hughes et al. 1998). The bannerstone is lenticular to diamond shaped in cross section. The shaft diameter is 15 mm at one end and 13.5 mm at the other. The bannerstone is broken in half through the shaft, perhaps intentionally.

Bannerstones are drilled using a hollow reed and sand, producing a cylindrical shaft, or using a stone drill, producing a conical shaft (Webb 1974:68–69). In either case, one might expect to find striations or grooves perpendicular to the shaft, but the McGraw bannerstone has longitudinal striations on the shaft walls. These striations are very fine at the larger end of the shaft and deeper and wider at the smaller end. The deeper gouging may have been an attempt to increase the diameter of the shaft at the narrower end. Similar striations

Figure 21.4. Artifacts from Archaic-period burials: a, McGraw bannerstone found in cremation pit; b, projectile point recovered from Burial 5; c–f, Archaic points and drill found in Burial 7.

were found on a similar bannerstone from the Bobwhite site in Richland County, Wisconsin (Finney and Meyer 1991:43). Fine striations made by some type of abrader can be seen on the ends of the McGraw bannerstone. Small notches are present on the outside edges of one face at both ends. There are seven notches on each side, but more may have been present in the area around the break. The purpose of the notches is unknown.

In a study of bannerstones found in the southeastern United States, Kwas (1981:155) places double-edge bannerstone forms in the early part of the Middle Archaic at around 5800 to 4000 B.C. A possible double-edge bannerstone was found in the Morrow Mountain component (5045 B.C.) at the Ice House Bottom site in Tennessee (Kwas 1981:162). Double-edge bannerstones have been found at the Bullseye site in west-central Illinois (Hassen and Farnsworth 1987: Figures A.22 and A.23). Farnsworth (1987:17) lists bannerstones with double-edge morphology under several reel and shuttle types, which he dates roughly to 5500–4500 B.C. The bannerstone from the Bobwhite site, mentioned above, dates to the Middle Archaic (Finney and Meyer 1991).

Four formal mortuary features (Burials 5 through 8) appear to date to the Middle Archaic. Bone preservation in all of these features was poor (Grauer and Buzon 1998). Burial 5 contained the remains of one tightly flexed adult, the remains of a second adult, and cremated remains. Wood charcoal from this burial produced an AMS date of 4690 ± 50 (Beta-111153; charred material: $\delta^{13}C$ −22.7 ‰) or cal B.C. 3635–3360 (2σ; Stuiver and Reimer 2000) (Table 21.1). The burial feature also contained a Matanzas projectile point (see Figure 21.4).

Burial 7 was the most complicated feature at McGraw Farm. The feature included a bundle burial consisting of the remains of a 45- to 55-year-old (possible) male and fetal or infant bones. The burial feature also contained the commingled remains of at least five individuals (two adults, a juvenile, and two infants) and the blackened and calcined remains of at least one adult and one child. Diagnostic artifacts recovered from Burial 7 include an Early Archaic Kirk-cluster projectile point, a Middle Archaic Raddatz projectile point, a Middle Archaic side-notched point fragment and T-drill, and an Archaic side-notched to expanding-stemmed projectile point (see Figure 4). Animal bone and antler tools, including a polished raccoon baculum, a modified trunk vertebra from an unidentified species of fish, a socketed projectile point fashioned from the tip of a white-tailed-deer antler, an antler awl or pin, a small shaft fragment of worked white-tailed-deer antler (that may have served as a projectile point), and a pressure flaker (or heavy-duty awl or perforating tool) were also found in the feature (Kuehn 1998).

Burial 6 contained the remains of two adults: one tightly flexed and one semiflexed. Burial 8 contained the unburned remains of one juvenile and two adults and a concentration of cremated bone. Neither Burial 6 nor 8 contained diagnostic artifacts, but both were deemed Middle Archaic on the basis of their similarity to Burials 5 and 7 in terms of feature depth, placement of human remains, and type of burial treatment.

According to Grauer and Buzon (1998), the presence of both blackened and calcined bone within a single mortuary facility indicates variations in fire intensity or duration or both. Longitudinal cracking, superficial or curvilinear checking, and marked warping are all present on calcined bone fragments within the same burial feature, indicating that both dry-bone and in-flesh burning occurred. Individuals buried in the Middle to Late Middle Archaic features do not appear to have been accorded differing mortuary treatment on the basis of their ages. The sex of most individuals could not be determined. Skeletal stressors (such as degenerative joint diseases and trauma) and dental diseases (enamel hypoplasia, periodontitis, abscesses, and calculus) were common in the Archaic population at McGraw Farm, but dental caries were absent.

Grauer also noted marked similarities in skeletal stressor frequencies between the Middle Archaic McGraw Farm population and several other known Middle and Late Archaic skeletal populations in Illinois and Wisconsin. All these populations shared similar frequencies of trauma, osteoarthritis, periosteal reaction, and dental diseases. The McGraw Farm

Table 21.1. Calibrated Archaic Dates from Northeastern Illinois.

Lab No.	Site	Associated Diagnostics	Uncorrected B.P. Date	Calibrated Date Range (2 sigma)[a]	Reference
Beta-111153	McGraw	Matanzas	4690 ± 50	3635–3360 B.C.	Porubcan and Lurie 1998
ISGS-4554	Garrison	Matanzas	4620 ± 150	3630–3099 B.C.	Demel 2000
Beta-177045	Gazebo	Godar/Raddatz	5090 ± 50	3980–3770 B.C.	date on file, MARS Inc.
ISGS-3725	11Ck210	none	5120 ± 70	3980–3801 B.C.	date on file, MARS Inc.
Beta-29920	Barton-Milner	Matanzas	5920 ± 75	5045–4665 B.C.[b]	Ferguson and Warren 1993

[a]Dates calibrated using Stuiver and Reimer 2000.
[b]Recalibrated for this chapter.

population fits the pattern described by Pfeiffer (1985) for other Archaic populations in the region, wherein low frequencies of infectious disease and arthritis, together with considerable dental wear but few to no dental caries, suggest a primarily nomadic hunter-gatherer lifestyle.

According to Porubcan and Lurie (1998:203), the Archaic McGraw Farm burials share characteristics with Middle Archaic rather than Late Archaic mortuary facilities in the greater Midwest region. These characteristics include large burial pit facilities containing multiple individuals and the use of multiple mortuary treatments—primary inhumation, bundle reburial, and cremation. There is no evidence for different body treatment based on age or sex, nor is there evidence for internal hierarchy. Grave goods are minimal and usually are utilitarian tools rather than items of personal adornment manufactured from local materials. Grave goods are primarily associated with the grave facility itself rather than with specific individuals. The green pipestone bannerstone suggests the existence of some type of trade network or territory that included part of western Illinois. Lurie suggests here that mortuary treatment of the deceased depended to some degree on the season of death and the distance from the burial site. McGraw Farm would probably have been well marked and could have been accessed either by way of the Fox River or overland. In either case, the site was apparently used repeatedly by Archaic people as a communal burial ground.

Archaic Habitation Sites

Barton-Milner Site (11La863)

The Barton-Milner site was discovered by the Illinois State Museum in 1985 and excavated prior to the construction of Interstate 39 (Ferguson and Warren 1993). This plow-zone site is located on the margins of an upland kettle pond on a ground moraine west of Tonica in LaSalle County. Controlled surface collecting recovered 717 lithic artifacts (flakes, shatter, hammerstones, fire-cracked rock [FCR], and chipped-stone tools). Piece-plot mapping identified nine distinct surface artifact clusters encircling the kettle basin. Surface-collected side-notched Godar and Matanzas points dated some of these clusters to the Middle Archaic period.

Excavations determined that most of the cultural deposits were contained entirely in the plow zone, as is typical of upland sites in northern Illinois. But sub-plow-zone cultural deposits were present in one area, and a complete Matanzas point and carbonized nutshell were found within a ring of 16 post molds that are thought to be the remains of an ovoid structure. AMS dating of the nutshell (Beta-29920; ETH-5036) produced a result of 5920 ± 75 B.P. (5045–4665 B.C. calibrated), which falls solidly within the Middle Archaic (Ferguson and Warren 1993:133).

Photon Site (11Du203)

The Photon site is located on the grounds of Argonne National Laboratory (ANL) in DuPage County, 48 km southwest of Chicago (Elias and Greby 1990; Kullen and Malinowski 1990). The site was discovered in June of 1987 during a Phase I survey by the ANL Cultural Resource Management Group for the Advanced Photon Source (APS) Project. Originally, construction was planned for the site area, but the new facility was redesigned to avoid the site. The site is now surrounded by a chain-link security fence and is undisturbed. The Photon site lies on the Valparaiso Moraine in terrain consisting of low hills and plains interspersed with upland marshes and small kettle lakes. The Des Plaines River valley trench is about one and a half kilometers south of the site.

Shovel test results indicate that the Photon site covers about 140 m^2 and contains a relatively high concentration of artifacts in comparison with the fairly diffuse lithic scatters found at nearby plow-zone sites. Artifact frequencies ranged as high as 76 artifacts per square meter. Artifacts were recovered from an undisturbed 23-cm-thick cultural stratum that was buried up to 7 cm below the ground surface. The high artifact density, the condition of natural soil horizons, and the location of the site in a mature oak-hickory forest suggested that the site had never been plowed. Phase II testing was started in July 1987 and completed in November 1988 (Elias and Greby 1990). In sum, about 53 m^2 (38 percent) of the site was excavated, but no features were encountered (Figure 21.5).

Fieldwork recovered some 1,500 flaked lithics, more than 600 pieces of FCR, and several pecked- or ground-stone artifacts. Many of the FCR fragments from this site are also fragments of ground-stone manos or grinding slabs. The ground-stone tools appear to have been reused as boiling stones or hearth liners. Twenty-one flake and bifacial tools underwent microwear analysis using the methods described by Keeley (1980), but only a few (25 percent) exhibited any wear traces. Two flake tools had been used for light

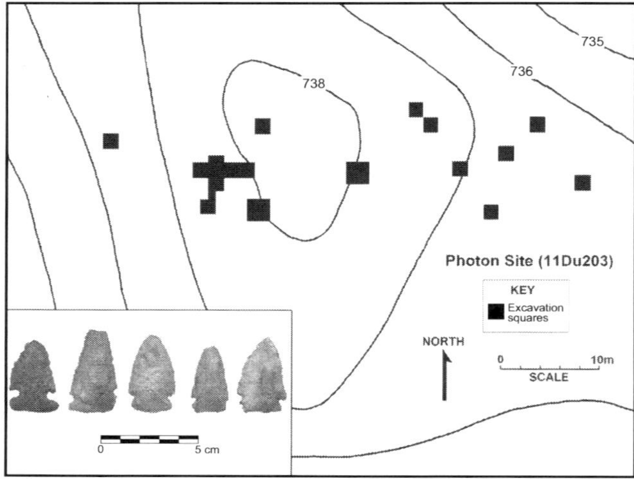

Figure 21.5. Photon site map and artifacts.

butchering, while two bifacial knives had been used for heavier butchering.

Diagnostic artifacts from the Photon site consist of 15 notched points and knives that have narrow to broad triangular blades, half of which have been reworked. One-quarter of the reworked tools are beveled (see Figure 21.5). Blade margins on only two specimens are serrated. About half of these tools have distinct U-shaped or rounded notches set close to the base. These notches are often angled upward and appear as low side notches or corner notches. The rest of these points are irregularly notched, with one notch set close to the base and the other(s) offset, doubled, or absent. Basal margins are irregular, varying from straight to either slightly convex or concave, and basal grinding is generally absent. Three preforms for these tools were found at the site, and they are ovate to subrectangular in outline, with lenticular cross sections. These points were assigned to the Matanzas and Brewerton point styles and are thought to roughly date the Photon site occupation to the Middle–Late Archaic transition around 3000 B.C.

Investigators identified two types of activity areas within the site. Specialized task areas are located on the east edge of the site. One of these covers at least 16 m² and contains a high density of cores, debitage, and dart point fragments. It appears to be a small lithic workshop where new dart points were made from scratch and old hunting tools were refurbished. The other specialized task area covers an area of about 63 m², contains the only intact manos and grinding stones found at the site, and lacks FCR and debitage. It appears to be a nut-grinding workshop area, where the initial processing of nuts took place. A communal task area is located in the center of the site. It covers an area of at least 48 m² and contains high densities of debitage, butchering tools, dart points, hide-processing tools, ground-stone ax fragments, and boiling-stone fragments. The large number of boiling stones indicates that the separation of hickory nutshells from nutmeats probably took place in that area. Meat was butchered there and probably was also smoked or dried. Likewise, hides from butchered animals were tanned in this area. The presence of ax fragments suggests that wood was chopped at this location—perhaps the firewood that all these processing activities would have required. Despite the absence of floral or faunal indicators, the site clearly seems to have been seasonally occupied during the fall.

Gazebo Site (11Du38)

Located in the middle of the Fermi National Accelerator Laboratory property, the Gazebo site was identified by Ann Early in 1970 and tested by her in 1971 (Early 1970, 1971). She recovered cultural material from a plowed field along a gentle slope north of an upland kettle basin and from an adjacent unplowed oak pasture. The pre–Euro-American settlement vegetation of the area was hardwood forest—a remnant of the "Big Woods" that extended through the uplands east of the Fox River. In prehistory, the kettle basin would have been filled with marsh vegetation and standing water, at least seasonally. Early identified a substantial Archaic component along with an ephemeral Upper Mississippian component.

At the time of the 1970 survey, .4 ha of the site was plowed field, and 74 pieces of debitage and 33 stone tools (including 10 projectile points) were recovered. In 1971, four 5-ft² (2.3-m²) test pits were excavated in the oak grove, and one 10-ft² (9.3-m²) test pit was placed in the cultivated field (Figure 21.6). According to Early (1971), 157 pieces of lithic debris and 19 stone tools (including eight projectile points) were recovered. Archaic material was recovered from 1.5 to 1.8 ft (46–55 cm) below the ground surface in the wooded portion of the site. Early commented that this relatively shallow site did not warrant further testing.

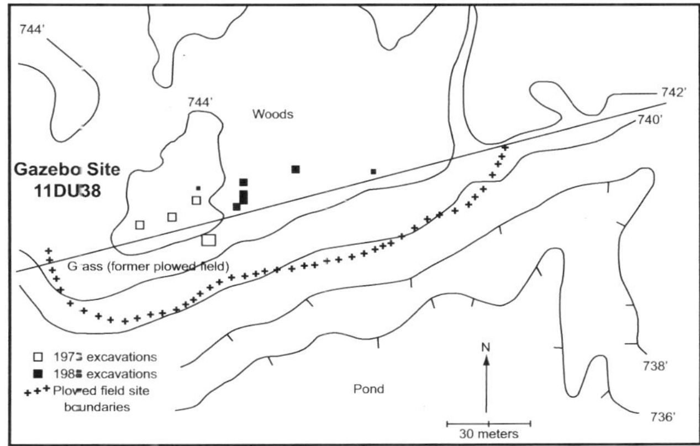

Figure 21.6. Gazebo site map showing the location of 1971 and 1988 excavation units.

But experience has shown that Gazebo is probably as deep a site as is apt to be found in northeastern Illinois. MARS Inc. revisited the site in 1988 and excavated four 2-m² units and one 50-cm² unit within the undisturbed oak grove (Lurie 1990). Although the majority of artifacts were recovered between 20 and 30 cm below the ground surface, some were found up to 40 cm below the surface.

One feature, a concentration of FCR that contained a few charred nutshell fragments, was excavated, as well. A large, reworked side-notched point was found in the same excavation unit as the nutshell. In 2003, .6 g of this nutshell was assayed. This resulted in an AMS date of 5090 B.P. ± 50 (BETA-177045; nutshell; $\delta^{13}C$ −25.8 ‰) or cal 3980 to 3770 B.C. (2σ; Stuiver and Reimer 2000). This sample dates the side-notched point and, by extension, the other shallow- to deep-side-notched Archaic points that make up most of the projectile point assemblage from the site (Figure 21.7).

Altogether, 72 chipped-stone and ground-stone tools and 525 pieces of chipped-stone debris have been recovered during three seasons of work at Gazebo. Tool shapes, edge angles and

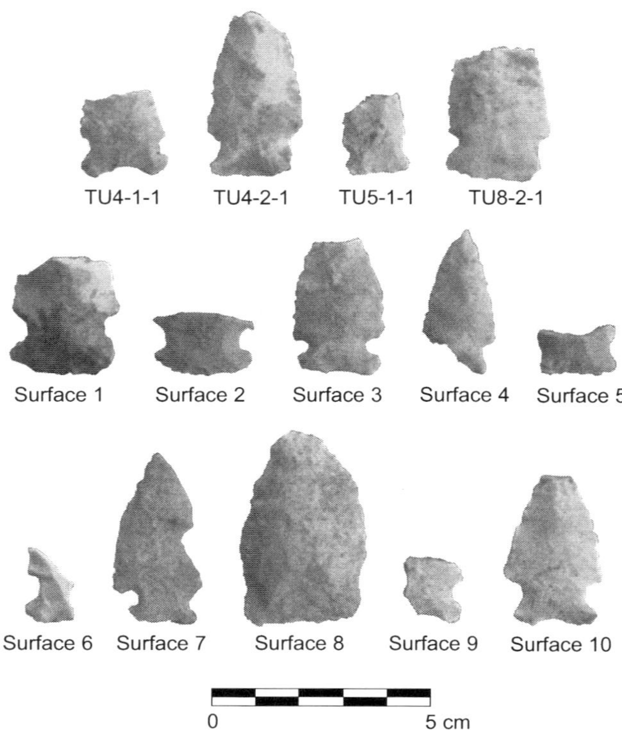

Figure 21.7. Archaic-period artifacts from test units and from the surface of the Gazebo site. Artifact TU8-2-1 was found in the unit yielding the radiocarbon date.

configurations, impact fractures, and small projections indicate that a variety of activities were performed at the site. Tools were used as spears or darts, knives, saws, scrapers, gravers, and wedges (Lurie 1990). The quantity and size range of lithic debris, the virtual lack of cortex on the debitage, and the presence of hammerstones and a possible anvil indicate that tool rejuvenation and all but the initial stages of tool production took place at the site. Six snapped hafting elements and small haft fragments suggest retooling activities.

The presence of cultural material—most of which appears to be Middle Archaic—in undisturbed sediments to a depth of 40 cm and the presence of a feature and of carbonized remains (although limited) mark the Gazebo site as an important Archaic resource. The site is now protected.

Garrison Site (11L337)

The Garrison site was a relatively undisturbed multicomponent site used periodically from the Late Paleoindian–Early Archaic transition through the Late Woodland and Mississippian periods. The site was located east of the North Branch of the Chicago River and just over 3.2 km inland from the modern shoreline of Lake Michigan, in Lake Forest, Lake County. At the time of European settlement the site was covered with oak-hickory forest slightly elevated above the marshes and sloughs on the Chicago River floodplain, a landscape setting that had apparently persisted since as early as 3000 B.C. (Demel 2000).

From 1991 to 1998, the site was tested and mitigated by two CRM firms, by community college field-school students, and by volunteers participating in dissertation research (Adams et al. 1991; Demel 2000; Lurie 1992; Lurie and Demel 1992). While overall site size was 14,110 m², the heart of the site was a 70- by 45-m area (Figure 21.8). The various excavators opened 253.5 m² of the site. More than 425 chipped-stone tools and tool fragments were recovered from the site, along with thousands of pieces of debitage and large quantities of FCR and ground stone.

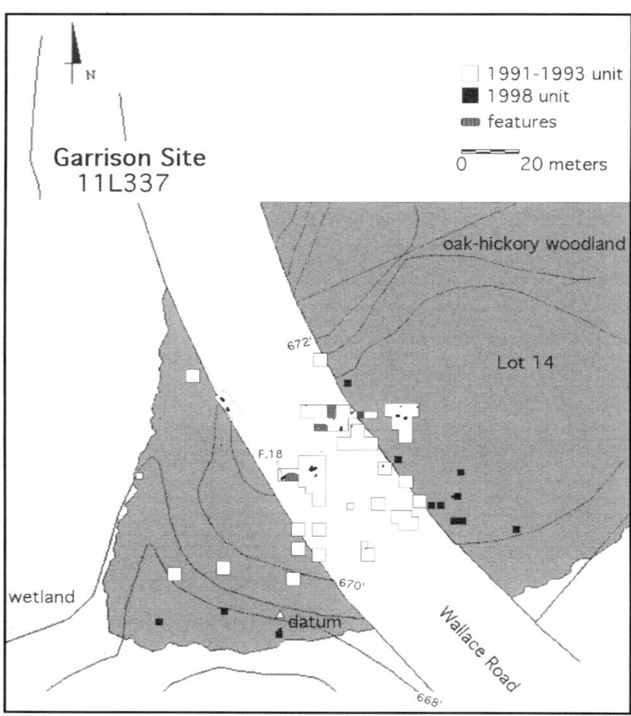

Figure 21.8. Garrison site map showing the location of excavation units and features.

Four Archaic components, defined primarily by diagnostic point types, were identified. The oldest was a substantial Paleoindian–Early Archaic campsite with Plainview/Hi-Lo–like and Big Sandy points (Figure 21.9). A later Early Archaic campsite with Fox Valley, St. Albans, and Kirk Corner Notched points was also defined. A minor Middle Archaic occupation with Godar-like points and a substantial Middle Archaic–Late Archaic residential camp with Matanzas, Madison Side Notched, and Table Rock points were documented. An ephemeral Late Woodland–Mississippian occupation was also present (Demel 2000; Lurie 1992).

Because of the youthful glacial origin of the landscape, the soil profile was relatively shallow. This made it somewhat difficult to make distinctions between cultural horizons. In

Figure 21.9. Garrison site artifacts. Artifact 604-2/611-1 was found in Feature 18 yielding the radiocarbon date.

addition, bioturbation and tree falls affected stratigraphy. There was, however, some horizontal separation among the components, so that activity areas were discernible.

More than 20 features were identified at Garrison. These included post molds and relatively shallow hearths or plant processing pits containing FCR or flanked by FCR clusters (e.g., Feature 18). These were found in both the Late Paleoindian–Early Archaic and Late Archaic–Early Woodland occupations. Floral remains were fairly abundant in features. Carbonized plant remains include American lotus (*Nelumbo lutea*) seed, bulrush seed, rose hips, five kinds of nutshell (acorn, butternut, hazelnut, hickory, and walnut) and unidentified nut fragments and berry pits, and wood charcoal (oak, maple, hickory, hardwood, and resinous wood). Charred materials from a Late Archaic hearth or roasting pit (Feature 10) contained a tuber fragment, two water-lily seeds, and small fragments of charred acorns, hazelnuts, and walnuts. This evidence indicates that the site was periodically used as a base for exploiting local wetland resources and for nut processing—both late summer through fall or early winter activities. Faunal remains were virtually absent because of high soil acidity (Demel 1995).

Microwear analysis indicates that other activities took place at the site, including butchering, meat processing, bone or antler working, woodworking, and, possibly, hide processing. Analysis of tools and chipping debris indicated some spatial partitioning existed within the main part of the site, where areas of primary tool production, tool repair, and tool use were identified (Lurie 1992).

Tool fragments indicate that curation, retooling, and a variety of other activities occurred at the site. Fifty-nine biface haft elements exhibiting impact fractures and haft snaps were found as were many heavily resharpened tools and points broken by overexposure to heat. Other stone artifacts include 20 bipolar cores, gravers, a T-shaped drill, two burins (one with traces of bone polish), several very small flake points, a crude pestle, a hammerstone, and a pecked anvil.

The white, gray, and tan cherts that compose much of the assemblage appear to be local in origin, probably derived from glacial till. Chert nodules from the Lake Michigan beach were apparently collected, and cores of this material were cached at the site. The use of local chert increased during the Middle Archaic and Late Archaic subperiods, perhaps indicating more permanent residence and restricted access to nonlocal chert sources. A pile of 15 unheated cores, some with a smooth caramel-colored cortex, were associated with the Late Paleoindian–Early Archaic concentration, which contained no heat-altered cherts. The use of intentional heat treatment as well as unintentional heat alteration is apparent especially in the Late Archaic materials.

A plethora of FCR was recovered from the Garrison site. The total number approached 4,700 pieces with a total weight of 209.4 kg. The high density of FCR resulted from repeated occupation of the site by small groups and from less frequent occupations by larger groups that used the site as a residential camp. Much of the FCR appears to be associated with the Middle Archaic and Late Archaic occupations. FCR was found scattered throughout most units, occasionally occurring in dense clusters, and was often associated with dark soil stains and pits. The most common features at the site were small piles of FCR associated with relatively shallow pits. The FCR was either contained within the feature stains or the feature stains were flanked by FCR. These features appear to have been either plant or tuber roasting pits (i.e., earth ovens) or boiling-stone heating pits.

Feature 18 is the best example of these shallow pits. The feature was defined as a dark stain in the transition zone between the A and E soil horizons. Numerous large pieces of FCR, debitage, and stone tools were recovered from this level. The feature became larger as it extended deeper into the E soil horizon, and it contained abundant lithic debris and smaller pieces of FCR as well as heat-treated biface fragments that refit into a Matanzas point. Lower down, in the transition zone between the E and B soil horizons, the feature was defined by FCR and a slightly darker stain. FCR and debitage were abundant, and a flotation sample was taken. The feature disappeared at 30 cm below datum. A standard ^{14}C sample of charred nutshell from Feature 18 (Unit 42, Level 5) produced an uncorrected date of 4620 ± 150 (ISGS 4554; $\delta^{13}C$ −26.5) or cal 3630 to 3099 B.C. (2σ; Stuiver and Reimer 2000). The charred plant remains from this feature have been identified as hazelnut, black walnut, butternut, hickory, and walnut shells and a charred herbaceous stem fragment.

During the Late Paleoindian–Early Archaic occupation at the Garrison site, hunters camped briefly. They used stemmed Plainview/Hi-Lo–like points, which were found in association with large, deeply side-notched points. Broken point bases were removed and discarded. Burins were fashioned out of exotic chert and were used to grave bone or antler. Only one small shallow pit feature is possibly associated with the Late Paleoindian–Early Archaic occupation.

A later Early Archaic occupation by people who used bifurcate-base and corner-notched points was more substantial. The number of discarded point bases indicates that hunters returned to this camp, removed broken points from hafts, and retooled. The relatively large numbers of points, the presence of bipolar cores and gravers, evidence for tool resharpening and reuse, and the presence of three shallow pit features that may be associated with this component suggest that this was an Early Archaic residential camp where retooling, bone splitting, and graving took place and semiexotic cherts were used.

The early Middle Archaic occupation at the Garrison site was similar to the late Paleoindian–Early Archaic occupation. Few projectile points were left behind by the Middle Archaic occupants, but one of their side-notched, Godar-like points was resharpened into a hafted scraper, the only scraper recovered at the site. One feature attributed to this component produced three calcined mid- to large-sized mammal vertebra fragments. Hunting-related activities took place, as did hide scraping, at this ephemeral Middle Archaic hunting camp. One other hearth or roasting pit may also be associated with this component.

The transitional Middle–Late Archaic occupation at the site was substantial. A greater diversity of tools was used, and tool curation was more diverse, as well. Cores were cached, and the number of features increased. Tools were manufactured, and the heat treatment of chert was common. Chert was obtained from local and semilocal sources, including pebbles from the glacial till and cobbles from the Lake Michigan shoreline. Nut processing and cooking of semiaquatic plants were part of the Late Archaic subsistence regime. From the terminal Middle Archaic through the Late Archaic, the Garrison site appears to have been a small residential camp within the local settlement system.

Several diagnostic point types represent the Middle–Late Archaic occupation. These include Madison Side Notched and Matanzas varieties. One refitted Matanzas point was associated with the charred nutshell in Feature 18 and, therefore, is datable to 3363 B.C. A single Table Rock Stemmed/Bottleneck Stemmed projectile point was also recovered. This stemmed point appears to represent the terminal Late Archaic at the site.

The Garrison site was a "persistent place," used periodically throughout the Archaic period. According to the most current understanding of Lake Michigan levels, the site could have been a coastal-zone site only during the Late Paleoindian, Late Paleoindian–Early Archaic, and Late Archaic periods, and would have been an upland hunting locale during the Early, Middle, and early Late Archaic periods.

If the Garrison site was a residential camp during the transitional Middle–Late Archaic and Late Archaic, it might indicate a more general settlement shift toward the coastal zone during the Hypsithermal episode, to take advantage of related resources as the Lake Michigan shoreline returned to the general vicinity. The abundance of FCR and related features indicates a reliance on plant processing, which may have been a response to resource stress. Alternatively, the abundance of FCR might suggest that this was a place where plant processing took place for several thousand years. The presence of nuts indicates a fall and possibly winter occupation of the site. The presence of nuts in several features might indicate a prolonged stay at the site and that nut-bearing forests were sought out during periods of resource stress. The coastal zone and forests along the lakeshore and east of the Des Plaines River were likely less influenced than other locales by the climatic changes brought on by the Hypsithermal episode and would have offered greater resources than areas further inland. Even today, microclimates persist along the Lake Michigan shoreline that enable the survival of relict plant communities in a highly mosaic landscape.

95th Street Bridge Site (11Wi897)

The only documented site in northeast Illinois with stratified Early and Middle Archaic components was test excavated by Allied Archeology in 1994 (Kullen 1995). Site 11Wi897—the 95th Street Bridge site—is located in the DuPage River confluence area, in Naperville, northern Will County. The site is located on a low terrace adjacent to the main channel of the DuPage River (Figure 21.10). The setting has received alluvial deposition, which preserved deeply buried Early Archaic deposits intact, despite the adverse effects of cultivation on near-surface sediments.

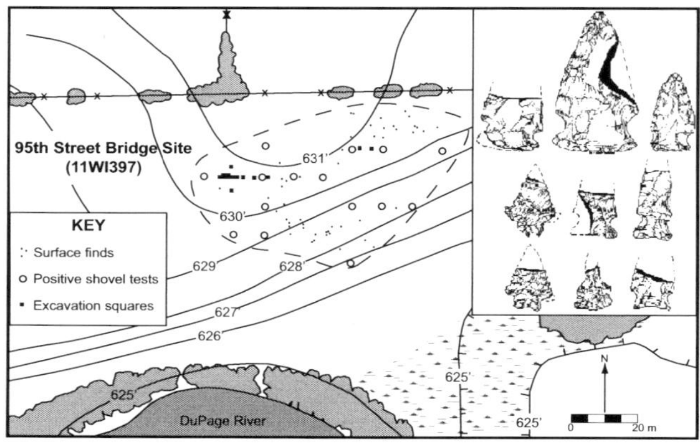

Figure 21.10. 95th Street Bridge site map and artifacts.

The site consists of a series of three Archaic camps. Component 1 produced Brewerton points and seems to date to the Late Archaic. Component 2 produced a Matanzas point, suggesting a Middle–Late Archaic date. These components are spatially separated, but both are contained entirely in the plow zone.

Component 3 has been partially incorporated into the plow zone, but it also contains an intact sub-plow-zone A horizon remnant, which is continuous and varies in thickness from 7 to 18 cm, with an average thickness of about 12 cm. This component produced two distinct Early Archaic projectile point types—the Fox Valley type and a shallow-notched type that bears a superficial resemblance to the Kirk style (see Figure 21.10). These points were found together in situ, demonstrating their contemporaneity.

The number and variety of stone tools (utilized flakes, bifacial knives, scrapers, grinding stone, drill, wedge, etc.) found in each component indicate that domestic tasks, rather than solely the manufacturing of hunting weaponry, were undertaken. This suggests that the prehistoric occupations were of relatively extended duration at what might be termed base camps, rather than hunting camps. Lithic raw materials found in all site components consist mainly of white or mottled light gray and white chert from the Joliet and Elwood formations, which outcrop locally. Site 11Wi897 has been determined eligible for listing on the National Register of Historic Places, but it has not yet been fully excavated.

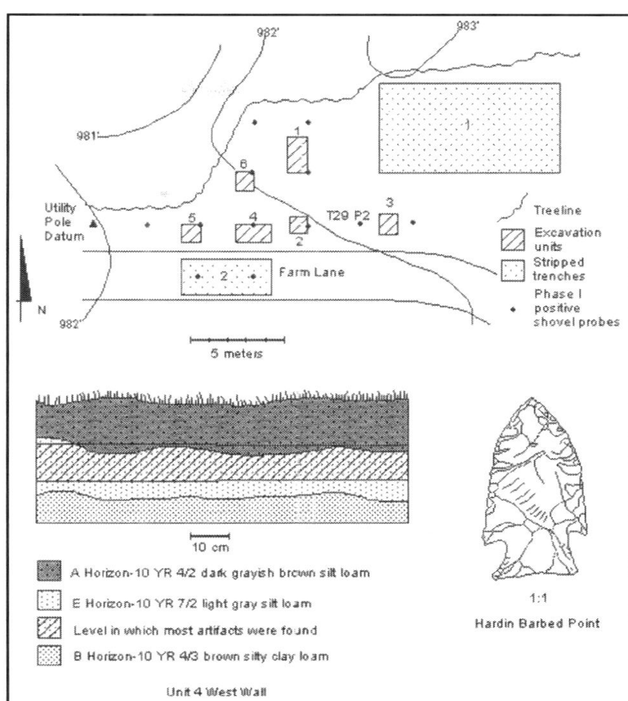

Figure 21.11. 11Mh124 site map, soil profile, and Hardin Barbed point.

Site 11Mh124

Site11Mh124 is a 9-m by 15-m Early Archaic camp found on high ground flanked by a stream and a sedge meadow (Figure 21.11). Soils suggest that the site was once wooded and that the stream was probably bordered by wet forest prehistorically. The site was discovered during a shovel probe survey for a golf course in Alden Township, McHenry County (Lurie et al. 1994) and was subsequently test excavated (Lurie et al. 1996). Shovel probing and 8 m^2 of excavations found seven stone tools and more than 300 pieces of chert debitage in an undisturbed cultural horizon buried 10–20 cm below the ground surface. Despite extensive topsoil stripping, no cultural features were identified. Although the site was deemed ineligible for National Register listing, it has been preserved within the golf course.

One Hardin Barbed projectile point was found, dating the site to the Early Archaic period (Justice 1987:51–53). Three biface fragments (two heat treated), a scraper-graver, a heat-treated scraper, and a unifacial knife were also found. Chert appears to have been collected from local Joliet Formation sources. Debitage analysis concluded that the entire range of lithic reduction took place at the site, from initial knapping of raw cores to production of finished bifaces.

Four large fire-cracked rocks, a burned pebble, and 8 g of charcoal are the only indications of a hearth at the site. This is typical of ancient wooded sites, where the podsolization process has leached out most organic material, dissolving bone and making identification of features difficult. But the absence of features may also be attributed to Early Archaic lifeways, wherein most sites were inhabited briefly and by relatively few individuals. One would not expect storage pits, formal hearths, or permanent types of housing to have been constructed by such transient peoples.

Site11Ck210

In 1983, this multicomponent site in Orland Township was reported to the Illinois Archaeological Survey by Mr. Ed Lace, then a naturalist with the Forest Preserve District of Cook County. Private surface collections from the site include stone points representing Paleoindian through Mississippian time periods (Pfannkuche and Lurie 1996). The site, oriented along the crest of a small hill, overlooks Midlothian Creek, which would have been an extensive swamp in prehistory (Figure 21.12). By the time the site was examined by professional archaeologists, most of it had been destroyed by development (Demel 1997). Only a small portion of the site remained under a large clay stockpile. Three flakes and one biface fragment were noted on the old plow-zone surface following removal of the clay stockpile.

An intact cultural feature was found beneath the plow zone (see Figure 21.12). The feature appeared as a light red

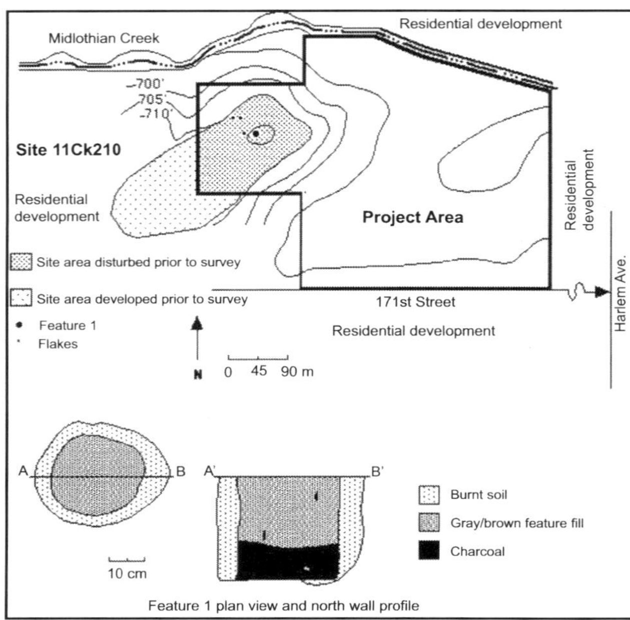

Figure 21.12. 11Ck210 site map and Feature 1 plan view and profile.

circular ring, 38 cm in diameter, with a dark, mottled interior 26 cm in diameter. The exterior ring appeared to be clay matrix that had been exposed to intense heat; the interior dark fill contained charcoal flecks. In profile, the feature was 33 cm deep and had straight sides and a slightly rounded bottom. Burned soil was present at the sides of the feature and under part of the base. A mass of charcoal 10 cm thick was encountered at the bottom of the feature. This was radiocarbon dated to 5120 ± 70 (ISGS-3725; bark and wood charcoal, nutshell; $\delta^{13}C$ −26.4) or cal 3980 to 3801 B.C. (2σ; Stuiver and Reimer 2000).

A flotation sample was collected from the fill. Analysis determined that the sample contained a high density of bark charcoal (2,007 pieces, or 11.86 g/6 liters), a small amount of wood charcoal (three pieces, or .03 g/6 liters), and a moderate density of nutshell, including black walnut (*Juglans nigra*; 17 pieces, or .63 g/6 liters) and walnut family (Juglandaceae; 28 pieces, or .37 g/6 liters). Small fragments of uncarbonized bark were noted in the sample. The bark and wood charcoal were unidentifiable to taxon.

Evidently, black walnut and, perhaps, other kinds of nuts that were readily available in the vicinity of the site were exploited by the site occupants. The density of nuts is comparable to that observed for other Archaic sites in the Upper Great Lakes (e.g., the Weber I site in Michigan, where 18.2 pieces/10 liters were recovered from a Terminal Archaic feature). The high density of bark charcoal strongly suggests that the feature was a smudge pit, a pit used to construct a smoky fire for hide processing. The presence of abundant nutshell probably indicates a fall occupation.

Killdeery I (11Wi2074)

Killdeery I is a 625-m² Early Archaic site located on a low knoll adjacent to wetlands along Lily Cache Creek near Plainfield in Will County. The site was partially tested by MARS Inc. in 2000 (Demel and Lurie 2001). Surface collecting and shovel probing were used to define site limits, and 173 artifacts were recovered in the process. Five blocks and one trench (totaling 197 m², or 31.5 percent of the site area) were stripped of plow zone (Figure 21.13). The 30-m linear trench was excavated across one axis of the site to expose a soil profile extending from the edge of the wetland to the deflated knoll. A very shallow plow zone was revealed at the uphill end of the trench, but a buried plow zone was found downslope, adjacent to the wetland. Block excavations were placed along this trench and in other parts of the site.

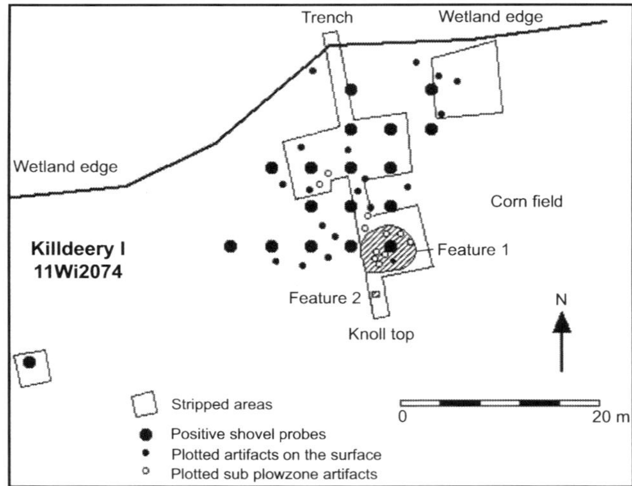

Figure 21.13. Killdeery site map showing stripped areas and sub-plow-zone Feature 1.

Thirty-six artifacts (one projectile point/knife, 24 tertiary flakes, three primary flakes, six blocky chert fragments, and two cores) were recovered from below the plow zone. Although fragmentary, the projectile point belongs to the Kirk Corner Notched cluster, in particular, the Stilwell type (Justice 1987:71–77). The point is made of very distinctive tan-gray "kornthal" chert from Union County, Illinois, some 451 km distant. In contrast, most of the sub-plow-zone debitage is a medium-grained, gray chert with dark gray to dark blue-gray speckles. The source of this chert is unknown, but it most likely outcrops nearby along the Des Plaines River and perhaps some of its tributaries.

A lithic concentration, more than 30 small post molds, and a single larger post mold were noted at the downslope end of the trench. The lithic concentration, found in a 4-m by 5-m area within and below the buried plow zone, primarily contained flakes and biface fragments of the local chert.

Freezing weather and snow prohibited completion of the excavations. The small post molds and all of these artifacts were left in place and covered with plastic and backdirt for future excavation. Testing was scheduled to continue the following spring and site mitigation was anticipated, but changes to federal law governing wetlands brought a halt to the project.

Cement Pond (11Wi2533)

The Cement Pond site was discovered by MARS Inc. during shovel probe survey in the Hillcrest Amusement Park picnic grounds in Romeoville, Will County (Loebel 2001a) (Figure 21.14). The site is on the bluff crest overlooking the Des Plaines River valley trench to the south at the presettlement upland prairie and oak-hickory forest boundary (Tolmie 2003). Testing confirmed that at least part of the site was relatively undisturbed (Loebel and Lurie 2001). Testing and mitigation opened up 48 m² of the 300-m² site area. Thirty-six square meters were excavated within the 50-m² site core (where most of the artifacts were found during testing). Ten square meters of excavations were placed in locations around the periphery. Eighteen chipped-stone tools, including three Middle Archaic projectile point/knife fragments, six cores, and over 7,900 pieces of debitage were recovered. No cultural features were found.

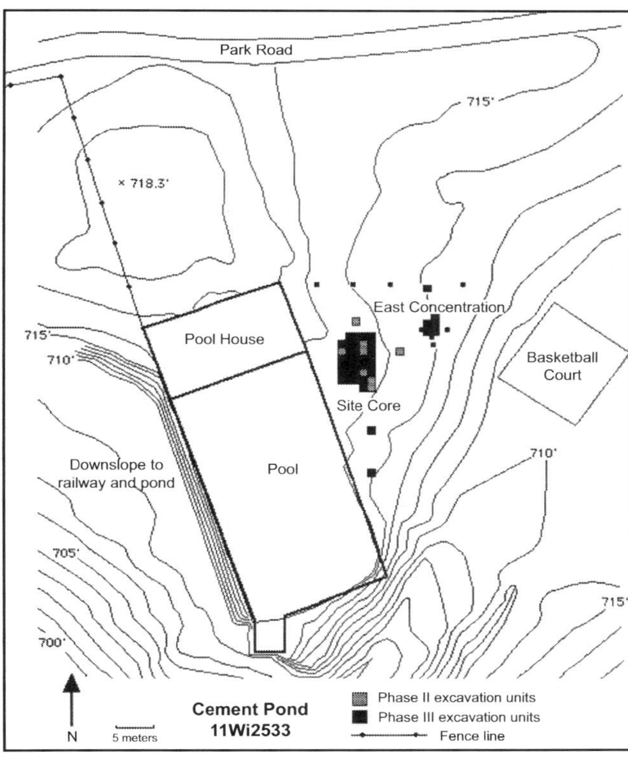

Figure 21.14. Cement Pond site map showing the site core and east concentration of artifacts.

Two concentrations of tool-making debris were defined during mitigation—one in the site core and another approximately 8 m to the east (Johnson and Lurie 2007). In the core area, the low percentage of cortex (especially on large pieces of debris) and the preponderance of small to medium-sized pieces of debris suggested that all but the earliest stages of cobble reduction took place at the site. Evidence for heat treatment was found on only 8.5 percent of the debris. Although several of the larger flakes in the concentration were used as informal tools, formal bifacial tools apparently were made here and then taken from the site. Lithic debris in the outlying concentration was similar in size range and presence of cortex, but fewer blocky fragments were present. A much higher percentage of heat treatment (29.1 percent) was evident, especially among the smaller-sized pieces of debris. The only tools found here were two small biface fragments and a bipolar wedge. No cores were found. Production or repair of heat-treated tools probably took place in this area.

The edges of all formal tools, cores, retouched flakes, and all other flakes over 16 mm in longest dimension were examined for traces of use wear under low-power magnification (10x–30x). At this magnification, eight artifacts appeared to have microflaking wear traces—a Brewerton Notched projectile point (sawing wood) (see Figure 21.15), a biface midsection (scraping soft material), a thumbnail scraper (dry hide scraping), a side scraper (scraping soft material), two utilized flakes (cutting soft materal) and two bipolar wedges (splitting wood or bone). These items were then examined under high power magnification (100x–500x) for traces of polishes and striations (Loebel 2005). At this magnification, wear traces were found on five of the eight tools. No wear was found on the two wedges or on the biface midsection, but wear from cutting and scraping hide and soft tissue was

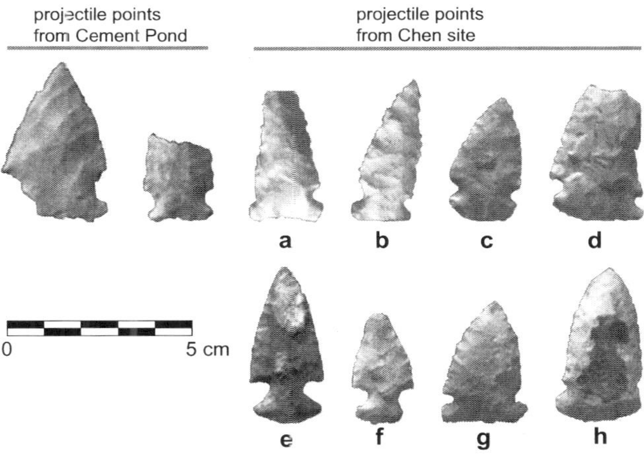

Figure 21.15. Cement Pond and Chen projectile points/knives: a, b, Brewerton Eared Notched; c, d, Matanzas/Brewerton Side Notched points; e, f, Motley points; g, h, Matanzas/Brewerton Side Notched points.

confirmed on the side scraper and utilized flakes; in addition, wood polish was found on the side scraper. Dry hide polish was confirmed on the thumbnail scraper, but soft plant wear and antler haft wear were also noted. The projectile point had polishes suggesting cutting hide and soft tissue and occasional contact with bone, rather than evidence of woodworking.

Cement Pond appears to be a short-term Middle Archaic occupation where retooling using local chert took place. Broken hafted bifaces were discarded, and new ones were manufactured and carried off-site. Some evidence for woodworking suggests that spear shaft manufacture or repair may have occurred, as well. Butchering animals and hide working are represented by wear on several tools. All of these activities would have made use of readily obtainable upland resources.

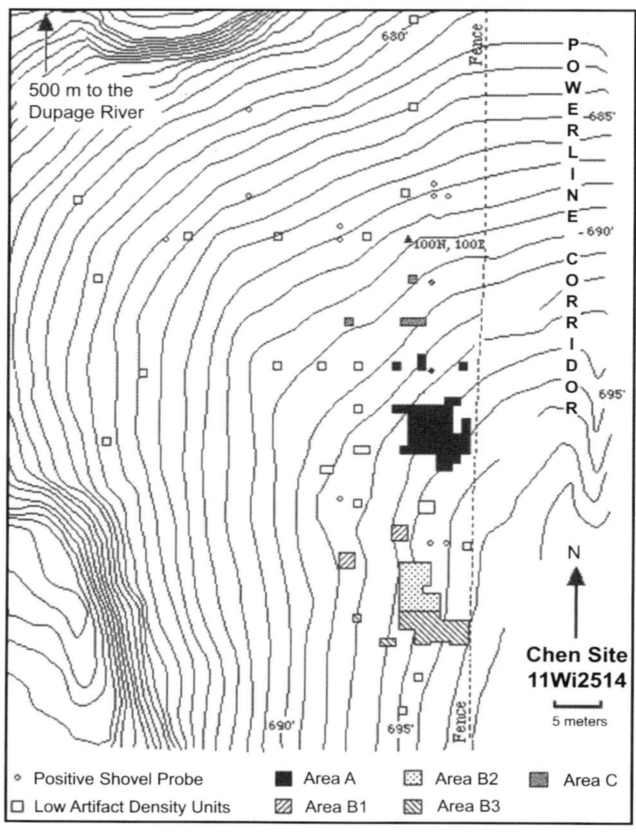

Figure 21.16. Chen site map showing activity areas and low-artifact-density excavation units.

Chen Site (11Wi2514)

The Middle to Late Archaic Chen site was found in a woodlot on a north-facing bluff slope overlooking the floodplain of the East Branch of the DuPage River in Romeoville, Will County. The site was initially recorded by the C.A.V.E. Group in January 2000, but site limits were later defined by MARS Inc. during a Phase I survey conducted in July 2001 (Loebel 2001b). An unknown portion of the site exists to the east of an area scheduled for development. During testing and mitigation, 140 m^2 were excavated (Higgs et al. n.d.). Block excavations were opened in areas of high artifact density to better identify specific activity zones (Figure 21.16). Stratigraphy was consistent across the site, with a silt loam A horizon overlying a silt loam E horizon, in turn, overlying a silty clay loam B horizon. The majority of artifacts were recovered from the E horizon, at around 20 cm below the ground surface, although some were recovered from the A horizon and from well within the B. Root growth, cicada tunneling, and rodent burrowing caused some vertical and horizontal artifact displacement.

More than 17,700 artifacts, including 79 chipped-stone tools, 20 cores, and 17,500 pieces of knapping debris, were recovered. Although the analysis of these artifacts and their distributions is not complete, the site clearly contains three concentrations of artifacts representing five distinct activity zones.

Area A, the densest artifact concentration on the site, yielded more than 6,800 lithics, including 52 stone tools and 12 cores, in 51 m^2 of excavation. One possible pit feature was found, filled with midden from the surrounding area. Biface production was the major activity in this area. Artifacts representing all stages of reduction—edged and thinned bifaces, preforms, and finished bifacial tools—are present. Seven points/knives were recovered, including four Matanzas (or Brewerton Eared Notched) points and three Brewerton Side Notched points (see Figure 21.15). Other tools collected from Area A include a drill tip, a wedge, retouched and used flakes, a hammerstone, and an abrader. Biface-reduction activity was concentrated in the middle of the area, while finished and broken stone tools, block cores, and expedient flake tools were discarded around the periphery. Sixty-five percent of all tools from the site were recovered from Area A. These tools portray a profile typical for a hunter-gather base camp. In terms of microwear, a variety of tool motions and resistance categories have been recorded (Odell 2005:8). These represent an array of domestic and subsistence activities, ranging from construction (digging in the earth; chopping and wedging wood) to tool or facility manufacture (graving, drilling and shaving wood, bone, and antler), butchery (cutting soft animal material and hard substances), food preparation (cutting soft animal and vegetal materials), clothing manufacture (perforating soft animal material), hide processing (soft material scraping), and hunting (projectile use).

More than 3,500 artifacts, including 18 stone tools and tool fragments and six cores, were recovered from the 55 m^2 excavated in Area B. Although most of the artifacts were concentrated in the southern portion of Area B, three separate activity zones (B1, B2, B3) have been defined. A 2-m^2 excavation completed during Phase II testing partially uncovered zone B1, which contained a small knapping concentration and a fragment of a biface used to cut soft vegetable material. B2, a more diffuse scatter of artifacts, produced knapping debris (64 percent of which is heat treated), block cores (none heat treated), and tools (several of them heat treated). Tools include a reworked, heat-treated, side-notched Archaic knife, both halves of another almost-finished, heat-treated, broken biface, and two other heat-treated biface fragments (see Figure 21.15). This activity zone was a workshop for heat-treated biface reduction or heat-treated-tool maintenance or both. In addition, some block cores were used to produce expedient flake tools. Wear traces on tools include those associated with processing soft animal and vegetable materials. B3 yielded knapping debris, a core, and nine stone tools, including two heat-treated Motley points (see Figure 21.15), a heat-treated biface fragment, two abraders, a perforator, two retouched flakes, and a utilized flake. B3 was both a tool production and tool use zone. In addition to processing soft animal and vegetable materials, tools from B3 were used to cut and grave hard organic material such as bone.

Area C was only 5 m² in extent. It produced 182 pieces of debitage and seven stone tools, including a corner-notched biface haft element, a drill, two heat-treated biface fragments, one retouched flake, and two utilized flakes. The tools are made from several different chert cores that are not represented in the debris. Area C appears to be a tool discard area. Wear traces include evidence of graving, cutting, and shaving hard to medium-hard material such as wood, cutting and drilling bone, and cutting soft animal tissue.

The Chen site was ideally situated to take advantage of floodplain, forest, and prairie resources year-round, but its exposure to the prevailing northwest winds makes winter occupation unlikely. Projectile points suggest two occupations—one represented by the Matanzas/Brewerton Eared Notched and Brewerton Side Notched points and another represented by Motley points. However, given the current difficulties in assigning points to specific type categories and the lack of radiocarbon dates for most point types in northern Illinois, the site may represent a single occupation with several distinct activity areas. As with other Archaic-period sites in northern Illinois, the absence of preserved flora and fauna limits interpretations of site function.

Ruby Robin (11Wi2713) and Hunters Home (11Wi398) Sites

These two adjacent sites are located in an unplowed oak savanna remnant on high ground next to the West Branch of the DuPage River in Naperville, northern Will County. In 2002 and 2003, the sites were reported, test excavated, and mitigated by Allied Archeology as part of compliance work for the Washington Woods subdivision (Kullen 2002a, 2002b). The Ruby Robin site covers 800 m², and 432 m² of the site was hand excavated as one contiguous block centered in the areas of highest artifact density, as determined by 2.5-m grid-interval shovel testing (Figure 21.17). Hunters Home is substantially larger, covering 9,300 m² (.9 ha), but most of it extends into adjacent Naperville Park District land, where it is protected. A total of 537 m² within the proposed subdivision

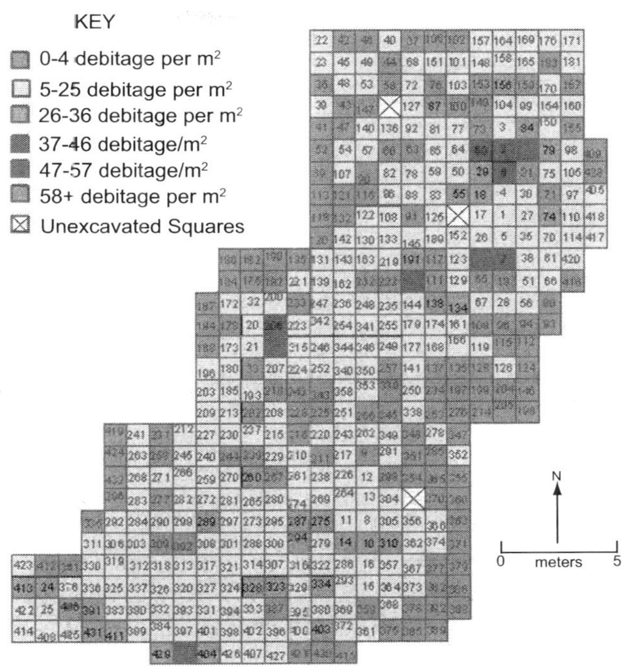

Figure 21.17. Ruby Robin artifact-density map.

was hand excavated in two large blocks. This work represents the most areally extensive hand excavation undertaken to date at any archaeological site in northern Illinois. The intent behind digging in large block-area excavations was to gather detailed data on intrasite activity patterning while maximizing recovery of diagnostic artifacts (Figure 21.18).

As at virtually all undisturbed sites in northern Illinois, all the cultural deposits at both sites were contained in the upper 25 cm of soil, in the topsoil and eluvial horizons. Stratigraphic separation was not evident between components of different age. Neither site is located in a topographic setting in which sediments have accumulated naturally. Soils have experienced no net deposition, and some parts of each site may even have undergone slight sediment loss. Artifactual materials appear to have been worked down into the soil through the gradual processes of bioturbation. Reoccupation of the same general locations over the millennia created a palimpsest of cultural deposits from different prehistoric time periods, the deposits more or less overlapping, but all occurring at the same general depth.

While the cultural deposits were not separated stratigraphically, multiple occupations were indicated by points and pottery ranging from Early Archaic through Late Woodland. No radiocarbon-datable features were encountered, but about 100 notched and stemmed Archaic points were recovered. This sample provides a truly large, well-provenienced collection of hafted bifaces by which a local Archaic stylistic sequence can be ordered (Figure 21.19). This sequence is discussed at length below.

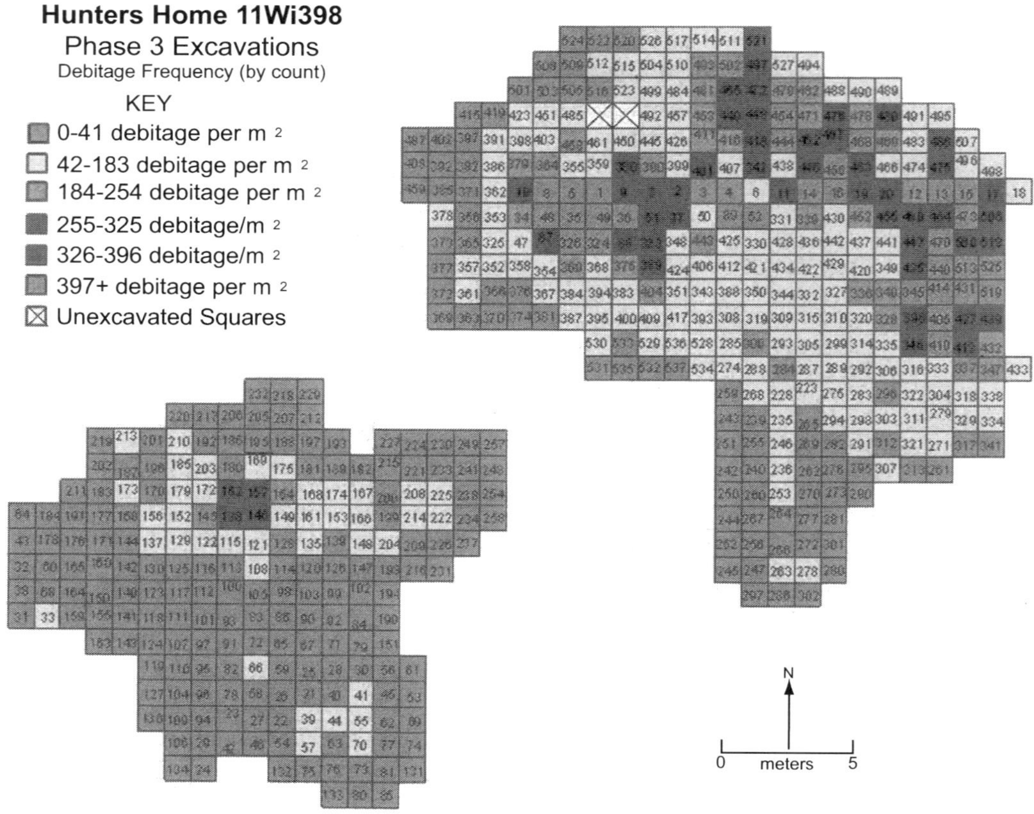

Figure 21.18. Hunters Home artifact-density map.

Point Styles in Northern Illinois

Establishing a basic projectile point chronology for northern Illinois requires assuming that artifact styles change in a certain way over time, that is, that styles are born, grow in popularity for whatever reason (functionality, low production costs, perceptions of beauty, etc.), dwindle in popularity, and then die. This pattern of birth, growth, dwindling, and death can be illustrated via the standard battleship-shaped curves used in seriation studies. The concept does not preclude the simultaneous existence of several different styles at any given moment in time. Some styles, particularly those associated with key technological developments, may grow in popularity very rapidly to replace older, perhaps outmoded, styles. The production of other forms may linger on, for whatever reason (habit, tradition, nostalgia, etc.) long after their heyday has passed.

Our combined experience in dealing with projectile point types in northern Illinois allows us special insight into defining a projectile point chronology for the region. Insight is certainly needed because there are simply not yet enough dated point types, or even documented stratigraphic relationships, from this region to allow researchers to empirically establish a full and complete Archaic point type chronology.

Matanzas Points

A few good dates are available for shallow-side-notched points that are very similar to the Brewerton and Matanzas types. As Brewerton is an eastern style defined for New York State and Matanzas is a style defined around a type collection from central Illinois, we naturally favor the term *Matanzas* for similar points found in northern Illinois.

The Matanzas point style was initially defined by Munson and Harn (1966) in their examination of surface collections from three sites (including the West Matanzas site) located on terraces along the Illinois River in Fulton County, in central Illinois. The type was distinguished from Raddatz points—which also occurred at the same sites—on the basis of their shallow notches set low to the base and a low incidence of basal grinding. From their sample of 27 points, Munson and Harn established ranges and averages for a series of metric attributes. They suggested a Late Archaic affiliation for the style on the basis of its occurrence at the nearby Chrisman site, which had been dated to ca. 3000 B.C. by geological means. They discounted the radiocarbon date of 6490 ± 300 B.P. from Chrisman, which they considered too early (Munson and Harn 1966:153). If this date is calibrated, it produces a two-sigma age range of 5970–4780 B.C.

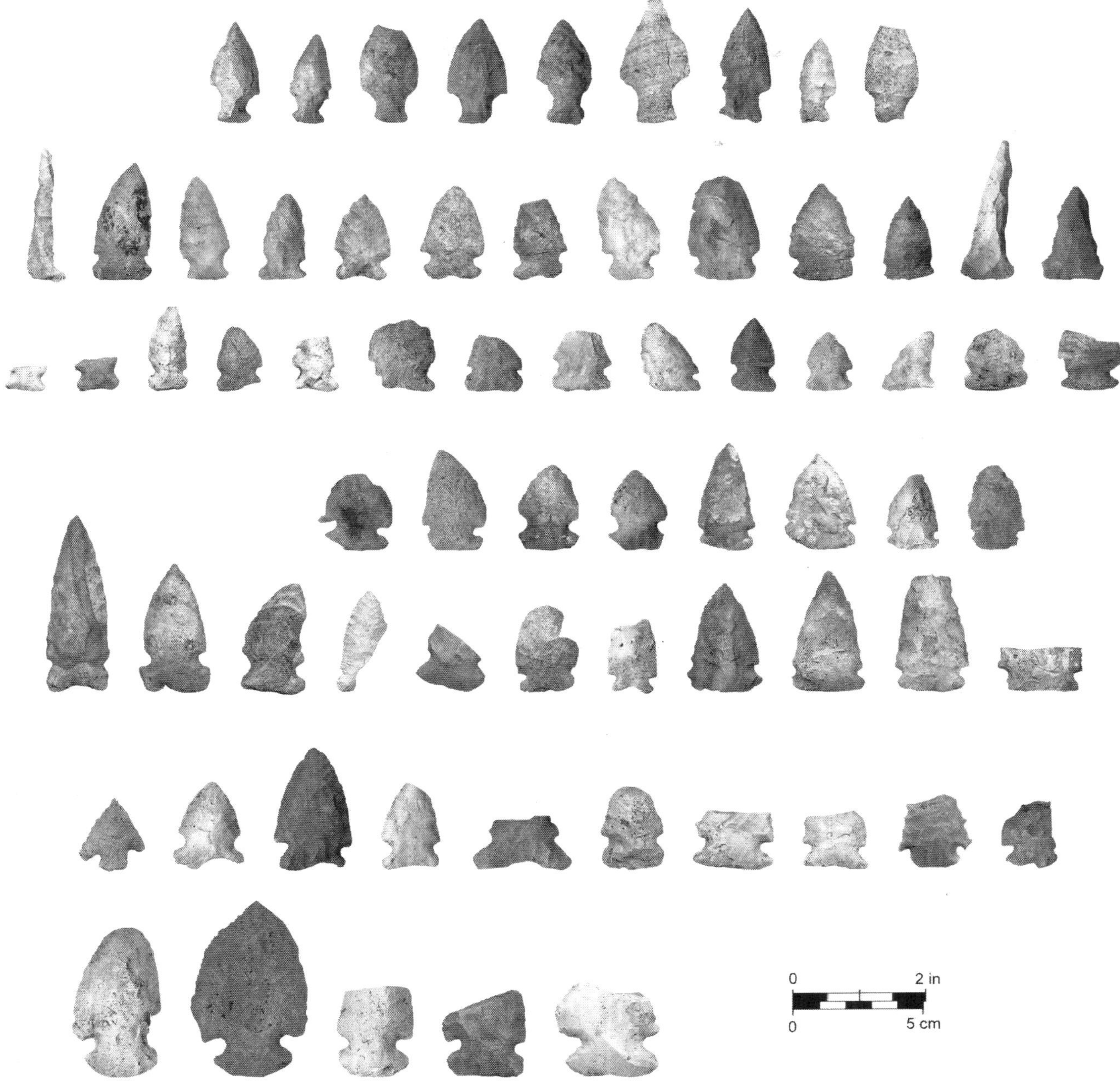

Figure 21.19. Selected points and knives from Ruby Robin and Hunters Home. Large Early Archaic types are at the bottom, Middle Archaic side-notched types are in the middle, and Late Archaic shallow-notched and stemmed types are at the top. Note the transitional forms between these modal types.

Large numbers of Matanzas points were recovered during excavations at the Koster site. Cook (1976) formally analyzed these points as part of an overall stylistic analysis. Aside from the "modal" types, which represent the originally defined form, Cook's analysis included lesser numbers of Matanzas variants. These exhibited a rather wide range of basal morphology beyond the modal form, including deeply notched forms that graded into the Raddatz style, faintly notched forms that appeared almost straight stemmed, straight-stemmed forms with prominent shoulders, and flared-stem forms. These were all assigned to the Helton phase at Koster, which dates from 5233 to 3787 B.C. (calibrated). This age range is based on a series of seven radiocarbon dates obtained from the middle and lower parts of Horizon 6 (Cook 1976:70–71) and five additional Helton-phase dates from other Koster contexts (Wiant et al. 1983:154). These dates place the Matanzas type in the Middle Archaic period.

In northern Illinois, Matanzas-type points from Garrison, McGraw, and Barton-Milner are associated with calibrated date ranges of 3630–3099 B.C., 3635–3360 B.C., and 5045–4665 B.C., respectively, as noted above. The date from Barton-Milner falls solidly within the Helton-phase date range from Koster, but the others are somewhat younger than might be expected, given the Koster dates for the Matanzas style. Probably not coincidentally, Barton-Milner is located some 130 km closer to the central Illinois River valley than the other two sites. The limited evidence suggests that the Matanzas style occurred later in northeast Illinois.

Raddatz Points

Raddatz is the name commonly applied across the Midwest to medium-large bifaces that feature distinct U-shaped side notches, flat bases, and squared basal ears. The name is derived from the Raddatz Rockshelter in Wisconsin, where the type was dated by a combination of radiocarbon and stratigraphic methods (Wittry 1959). After calibration, the Raddatz component from the type site dates from around 4000 to 6000 B.C.

Godar is the central Illinois name for the Raddatz form. In central Illinois, the Godar type has been well dated at the Napoleon Hollow and Koster sites. At both of these sites, the Godar style is considered diagnostic of the Helton phase, and it co-occurs with Matanzas points in the same levels (Wiant et al. 1983:160).

In northern Illinois, one carbon date is available for a Raddatz/Godar point recovered from the Gazebo site. The calibrated date range of 3980–3770 B.C. suggests a slightly older date than the dated Matanzas points, if one ignores the Barton-Milner date. Certainly the date ranges for the Raddatz and Matanzas styles in northern Illinois overlap substantially.

Other Dated Point Types in Northern Illinois

In addition to the four dated points noted above, one instance of stratified Archaic deposits provides evidence relating to projectile point chronology in northern Illinois. At the 95th Street Bridge site, Kirk Corner Notched points were found in direct association in the same undisturbed sub-plow-zone stratigraphic level as a Fox Valley point (Kullen 1995). This association indicates at least a partial temporal overlap between these two point styles. This should not be completely unexpected since both types are thought to date to the Early Archaic. The Kirk style has been dated to around 7500–6900 B.C. (uncalibrated) at sites in North Carolina and West Virginia (Justice 1987:71–77). Fox Valley points are thought to date from the same time range as other small bifurcate-base-tradition points in eastern North America—types such as Kanawha Stemmed, Lake Erie Bifurcated Base, and LeCroy Bifurcated Stem. These all date from around 6500 to 5800 B.C. (uncalibrated) at sites on the Appalachian Plateau in West Virginia, Kentucky, and Tennessee (Justice 1987:91–97).

Northern Illinois Point Styles

An analysis is currently in progress of haft configurations from the large collection of notched and stemmed points recovered at the Ruby Robin and Hunters Home sites (Kullen 2003; Kullen et al. 2007). To facilitate wider comparisons, the database has been supplemented with information from site 11Wi82 and the Chen, 95th Street Bridge, Cement Pond, Photon, Gazebo, and Garrison sites. Cluster analysis of three morphological variables (haft width, stem thickness, and basal convexity) has produced well-defined clusters that parallel known point stylistic groupings. These clusters can be considered to represent the Archaic point types of northeastern Illinois.

On the basis of the few dates and stratigraphic data outlined above, and given known dates from elsewhere in the Midwest, a rough sequence can be arranged. The following stylistic sequence lays out broad, general trends. We fully expect, as more radiocarbon-dated points are obtained from sites in northeast Illinois, that this overview will be corrected and expanded. But for the time being, we must leave it to future researchers, armed with more and better dates, to discover and define the minutiae.

The large and deeply notched St. Charles/Thebes are probably the earliest Early Archaic types, although data on transitional Late Paleoindian forms such as Agate Basin and Plainview are scant. The St. Charles form, with its deep corner notches, grades into the somewhat more recent Kirk Corner Notched form. Fox Valley Truncated Barb points and other serrated, bifurcate-base forms are to some degree contemporaneous with the Kirk type in the Early Archaic, as evidenced by their co-occurrence at the 95th Street Bridge site.

Some Early Archaic stylistic elements continued into the Middle Archaic. The large, corner-notched Kirk style transitioned into the large, side-notched Raddatz style by the Middle Archaic, although these forms continued to overlap stylistically. This overlap is typified by specimens that are both side-notched and corner-notched.

Later in the Middle Archaic, the large corner-notched forms faded away, but the large side-notched forms persisted. Shallow-side-notched Matanzas forms appeared in northern Illinois by 5045–4665 B.C., and these were contemporaneous with the Raddatz style, which persisted until at least 3980–3770 B.C. The Matanzas style in northern Illinois continued through the end of the Middle Archaic, until at least 3630–3099 B.C.

In the Late Archaic, the shallow side-notched form began to transition into stemmed forms. The transition from the Matanzas form to the Durst Stemmed form appears to have been gradual, as evidenced by many subtle gradations from shallow-side-notched to very shallow side-notched to expanding-stemmed forms.

Were some Archaic styles specific to function? Certain Archaic points from northern Illinois exhibit beveled or otherwise reworked blades that indicate they were used as knives or scrapers, rather than projectile points. Many corner-notched Kirk and side-notched Raddatz points are large, with broad, thick stems, while others of the same stylistic types are smaller and thinner but still distinctly corner or side notched. Could the large Kirk types have been used as hafted knives while the contemporaneous Fox Valley points were used as projectile points during the Early Archaic? The same question could be posed for the Middle Archaic types, given that hafted bifaces with broad, thick stems occur alongside smaller, narrowly stemmed bifaces with otherwise identical forms.

Over time, the size of points, in general, tended to decrease. The larger Early Archaic point forms were presumably lashed to the ends of thrusting or throwing spears. The invention of the atlatl by Middle Archaic times increased the range, accuracy, and power of the throwing spear. A premium must have begun to be placed on smaller, lighter points that would not unbalance a throwing spear after the point broke and was resharpened. If so, this might help explain why large side- and corner-notched points were replaced by smaller side- and corner-notched forms, even though both deep- and shallow-side-notched forms were used contemporaneously for a long time through the Middle Archaic period.

During the Late Archaic, point size continued to shrink as shallow-side-notched forms gave way to expanding-stemmed forms. The notably diminutive character of Late Archaic stemmed forms—some of which are nearly as small as early arrow points—can been explained as related to detachable foreshafts used in combination with throwing spears and the atlatl. As Boszhardt explains,

> Alteration of any component requires a compensatory adjustment to others for balance and flight. In the case of darts, it is to be expected that point size would diminish as foreshaft size increased ... reduced point size in the Late Archaic may reflect compensation for the added weight of wooden foreshafts. More specifically, weight adjustments of the dart tip shifted from large (Raddatz) chipped stone points to smaller Preston and Durst tips that were likely mounted in wooden foreshafts. [2002:60]

The Potential for Deeply Buried Sites in Northeast Illinois

Both the Grand Prairie and Northeastern Morainal divisions of northern Illinois were glaciated relatively recently, and they lack the kinds of geomorphological settings in which deeply buried Archaic deposits are found throughout the rest of Illinois. Practically no caves are present because the passage of the continental glacier crushed and scoured out near-surface voids in the bedrock. Rockshelters are absent because bedrock exposures are relatively recent and have had little time to erode into overhangs. Almost all bedrock in these divisions occurs as exposures located immediately adjacent to actively flowing streams, on banks, or in channels. Thus, dependably dry land usually does not occur at the foot of local bedrock exposures, so human habitation sites are not present.

Likewise, river valleys are immature in a geomorphological sense. There are no well-developed levees and slackwater basins. Terraces, where present, are usually remnants of Pleistocene alluviation and are, therefore, positioned well above active floodplains. The Illinois-Des Plaines and Kankakee rivers served as outlets for catastrophic late Pleistocene floods that scoured out the valleys, in some cases all the way down to bedrock. Along sections of these rivers, floodplain sediments consist only of a thin veneer of continuously reworked sands and gravels. Side-stream alluvial fans are present along the margins of some of the river valleys, but they are small and poorly developed. Because upland loess deposition in northeast Illinois was relatively thin, the quantity of silt that accumulated in alluvial fans was substantially less than in other parts of the state.

The glacial landscape does offer possibilities for deeply buried Archaic sites. Of course, in northern Illinois, *deeply buried* is a relative term. In a region where more than 95 percent of the land surface has been cultivated at one time or another, *deeply buried* means sub–plow zone. Three landform types have the potential to contain deeply buried Archaic deposits.

Alluvial fans, often containing mixed colluvium as well, are present along the margins of major rivers. Fans in northern Illinois are typically quite small and may not have presented much of an attraction to prehistoric peoples. No Archaic sites have been excavated in such settings in northern Illinois.

Slope-base settings are more abundant than alluvial fans, and they occur in two different locations. The valley wall or terrace slope–base setting may contain sediments accumulated via slope-wash and colluvial action as well as alluvial deposits from occasional flood events, depending on the position relative to the active floodplain. The Killdeery I and 95th Street Bridge sites are examples of this kind of setting. Archaic materials have recently been reported in colluvial deposits at the Macktown site adjacent to the Rock River in Winnebago County (Amick 2000; Pfannkuche 2005).

The second type of slope-base setting is perhaps the most common topographic setting in which deeply buried Archaic horizons can be expected. This is the upland basin–margin setting. Upland basins, closed depressions, kettle lakes, and prairie potholes—a variety of names denote these glacial features—occur widely in northeast Illinois. In all of them, slopes lead down to a marsh edge from the surrounding higher ground. Typically, this high ground has been cultivated, and sediment from the surrounding farm fields has washed down the slope into the basin. Where the accumulation of such recent sediment was rapid and deep, a protective mantle can cover Archaic cultural deposits, even after the basin has been artificially drained and put to the plow. In settings in which the surrounding slopes are quite steep, sediments may not accumulate at the slope base but may be deposited directly into the basin itself, and thus, the protective mantle does not form. This was found to be the case at the Primavilla site in Lake County, which otherwise contained a Middle Archaic Raddatz component (Kullen 1990). Intact sub-plow-zone Archaic deposits have been found at several sites, including Ls^{v}231 and the Barton-Milner site in LaSalle County (Christenson 1988; Ferguson and Warren 1993) and Killdeery I in Will County (Demel and Lurie 2001).

The third type of geomorphic setting in which intact Archaic deposits might be expected is beneath the surface of Lake Michigan. In the course of some five millennia spanning the Early and Middle Archaic periods, Lake Michigan drained to half its size and refilled again. Presumably, Archaic peoples did not simply stand around the old shoreline and watch this happen. The Chicago and Calumet rivers continued to flow into the basin, and, at the very least, one should expect that Archaic hunters and gatherers would have moved along these streams into the newly drained territory as vegetation became established and was able to support game. The low lake levels persisted for hundreds of years, so one must assume that Archaic people themselves became well established during that time.

The subsequent refilling of the Lake Michigan basin was slow and steady, but any archaeological deposits in the basin left behind by Early and Middle Archaic peoples may no longer be intact. As waters rose, wave action or currents may have eroded them away. Deeply buried Archaic deposits reported from the Torrence Blow Out site (Craig 1988) and the Laughton site (Keene 1987) suggest that some intact, deeply buried Archaic deposits may still survive on subaerial portions of the Chicago Lake Plain. The discovery of in situ tree stumps at the underwater Olson locality and the shoreline Barnes Creek locality offers hope for the survival of cultural deposits in near-shore and underwater settings. Any surviving archaeological deposits beneath Lake Michigan, however, would now be buried to some degree under lacustrine silts and difficult to locate, even though constant saturation and cold temperatures may have allowed for remarkable preservation of wooden and bone artifacts.

Conclusions

At present, none of the universities in northern Illinois has a research-based interest in the Archaic period of the region. Neither does there appear to be any sign on the horizon of an academic research program directed toward locating and testing Archaic sites. This situation has persisted for years and does not appear likely to change. Until the advent of contract archaeology, the Archaic period in northern Illinois was virtually ignored, except when red-ocher burials turned up in gravel pits. Without a commitment to local archaeology by academia, contract archaeology has pushed ahead on its own. CRM has contributed greatly to Archaic studies by dutifully and professionally recording Archaic data as they crop up in archaeological compliance projects. Contract archaeologists with limited funds to develop regional contexts (and without a cadre of graduate students in search of research topics) find in-depth studies of subsistence-settlement patterning and stylistic typology beyond the scope of most contracts but still must find creative ways to synthesize the extensive gray literature.

Much of the current understanding of the Archaic in northern Illinois continues to be drawn substantially from work done in adjacent parts of the Midwest, but some independent perspectives are beginning to develop. Projectile point styles show definite gradations between types, indicating prolonged but uninterrupted stylistic evolution. This, in turn, argues for the presence of highly conservative cultural groups not subject to disruptive intrusions from cultural outsiders. Changes in point types occurred slowly, however, and some documentation supports a time lag in the projectile point stylistic chronology. Archaic hunter-gatherers in northern Illinois had a strong preference for camping near upland marshes and small streams—a preference that equaled, or perhaps exceeded, the attraction of permanent stream valleys. Archaic peoples considered large sections of the landscape unfit for habitation. These areas were flat, wet woods that became wet prairie with the onset of the Hypsithermal. Hunting was always an important part of Archaic subsistence in northern Illinois, but evidence indicates that nut processing occurred during and after the Middle–Late Archaic transition, paralleling developments elsewhere in the Midwest.

Many lessons have been learned regarding methods for excavating Archaic sites in northern Illinois. Sites—even if unplowed—are almost always found in shallow deposits with no vertical stratigraphy. Despite this situation, separate components are commonly offset and can be identified by using careful horizontal controls, such as piece plotting at surface sites and standard hand excavations at buried sites. Mechanical stripping is usually necessary to efficiently locate features, but the technique should be limited to plow-zone sites only and should only be employed after several episodes of plowing (not shallow disking) and surface collecting have adequately sampled the artifact content of the plow zone. Mechanical topsoil stripping at unplowed sites should be avoided at all costs. Even where soils are shallow, cultural deposits in undisturbed topsoil can contain functionally and temporally diagnostic artifacts and evidence for intrasite activity areas.

This essential information may not be contained in features, and Archaic features are rare, in any case. Because Archaic features are few, large portions of Archaic sites need to be excavated. One-percent, 5-percent, or 10-percent samples are not big enough. Fifty, 80, or 100 percent of individual Archaic sites need to be tested or mitigated, if features are to be located. Fortunately, most northern Illinois Archaic sites are not very large, so such sample sizes are not infeasible, especially if the site is in plow-zone context. Hand excavating unplowed sites is expensive and time-consuming, but identifying and evaluating sites early in the planning process will let developers avoid and preserve important sites or give archaeologists sufficient time for careful, but large-scale, excavation when avoidance is not an option.

Even if Archaic features are located, flora and bone are rarely preserved, so indirect techniques must be employed to assess subsistence practices. The most promising of these is high-power lithic microwear analysis, using the techniques outlined by Chicago's own Lawrence Keeley (1980). While a variable percentage of wear traces is typically obscured by patination, as many as 50–80 percent of stone tools still retain some of the minute polishes, striations, and other indications that enable experienced specialists to assign artifacts to highly specific functions, such as dry hide scraping, light butchering, bone and antler graving, and so on. Alternatively, the low-power magnification microwear technique described by Odell (1979), while less specific in identifying the type of material worked, may be suited to the patinated, light-colored chert tools often found on sites in northeastern Illinois.

Given the lack of local academic interest, CRM-based archaeologists must continue to find ways to fill the gaps in archaeologists' knowledge of the Archaic period in northern Illinois. This effort will require greater cooperation among CRM firms and the development of creative ways to conduct research outside the CRM box. Possibilities include working with public land administrators to establish long-term, publicly funded survey and excavation projects, forming partnerships with interested academic archaeologists in adjacent areas to obtain research grants, and encouraging CRM staff members planning on graduate careers to use contract data as thesis or dissertation topics. This chapter is a first step toward synthesizing the data on hand and sharing information on those more extensively investigated sites that have yet to be widely reported.

References Cited

Adams, Keith, Madeleine Garceau, and Douglas Kullen
1991 *Report of Phase I Archeological Survey of the Proposed LeWa Farm Subdivision, Lake Forest, Illinois.* Patrick Engineering, Glen Ellyn, Illinois.

Amick, Daniel S.
2000 *Preliminary Results of the 1999 Field Season at Macktown Shell Midden A (11-WO-256), Macktown Forest Preserve, Winnebago County, Illinois.* Loyola Archaeology Technical Report 2. Department of Sociology and Anthropology, Loyola University of Chicago.

Bird, M. Catherine
1995 *Phase I Archaeological Survey of the Mill Creek Development Wrobel Parcel 83.1 Acres in Blackberry Township, Kane County, Illinois and Phase II Testing of the Baker Cemetery (11-K-321).* Cultural Resource Management Report 457. Midwest Archaeological Research Services, Harvard, Illinois.

Bird, M. Catherine, and Kirsten Kahl
1994 *Archaeological Reconnaissance Survey of the Proposed Mill Creek Development, 1,375 Acres of Land in Central Kane County, Illinois.* Cultural Resource Management Report 336. Midwest Archaeological Research Services, Harvard, Illinois.

Bird, M. Catherine, and Rochelle Lurie
1991 *Muddy Bottoms, Tom-Tom, and Von Sande Site Testing, Des Plaines River Trail, Vernon Township, Lake County, Illinois.* Cultural Resource Management Report 152. Midwest Archaeological Research Services, Harvard, Illinois.

Birmingham, Robert A., and Allen P. Van Dyke
1981 Chert and Chert Resources in the Lower Rock River Valley – Illinois. *The Wisconsin Archeologist* 62:347–360.

Boszhardt, Robert F.
2002 Contracting Stemmed: What's the Point? *Midcontinental Journal of Archaeology* 27:35–67.

Christenson, Andrew L.
1988 Test Excavation at an Upland Prairie Depression, LaSalle County, Illinois. *The Wisconsin Archeologist* 69:334–346.

Chrzastowski, Michael J., Frank A. Pranschke, and Charles W. Shabica
1991 Discovery and Preliminary Investigations of the Remains of an Early Holocene Forest on the Floor of Southern Lake Michigan. *Journal of Great Lakes Research* 17:543–552.

Cook, Thomas G.
1976 *Koster: An Artifact Analysis of Two Archaic Phases in West-central Illinois.* Prehistoric Records 1. Koster Research Reports 3. Northwestern University Archeological Program, Evanston, Illinois.

Craig, Joseph
1988 Prehistoric Occupation of the Chicago Lake Plain: Predictive Modeling of Settlement Location. Master's thesis, Department of Anthropology, Northern Illinois University, DeKalb.
1989 Predictive Modeling of Prehistoric Settlement Patterns in the Chicago Lake Plain. *The Wisconsin Archeologist* 70:347–361.

Curry, B. Brandon, David A. Grimley, and Jay A. Stravers
1999 *Quaternary Geology, Geomorphology and Climatic History of Kane County, Illinois.* Guidebook 28. Illinois State Geological Survey, Champaign.

Curry, B. Brandon, Eric C. Grimm, David M. Nelson, Jennifer Slate, Sallie E. Greenberg, and John W. Scott
2004 Contrasting Hydrological Responses to Holocene Climate at Nelson Lake and Crystal Lake, Northeastern Illinois. Paper presented at the 18th Biennial Meeting of the American Quaternary Association, Lawrence, Kansas.

Demel, Scott J.
1995 Soil pH and the Preservation of Bone. Unpublished manuscript in possession of the author.
1997 *Phase II Archaeological Testing of Site 11-Ck-210, Orland Township, Cook County, Illinois, for Gallagher & Henry Developers.* Cultural Resource Management Report

440b. Midwest Archaeological Research Services, Harvard, Illinois.

2000 Understanding Remnant Archaic Settlement along the Western Coast of Lake Michigan. Ph.D. dissertation, Department of Anthropology, University of Wisconsin–Milwaukee.

Demel, Scott J., and Rochelle Lurie

2001 *Report of Results of Phase II Archaeological Testing of Eight Prehistoric Sites (11-Wi-458, -459, -2062, -2063, -2066, -2067, -2068, and -2074) in DuPage Township, Will County, Illinois*. Cultural Resource Management Report 927b. Midwest Archaeological Research Services, Harvard, Illinois.

Doershuk, John

1988 *Plenemuk Mound and the Archaeology of Will County*. Illinois Cultural Resources Study 3. Illinois Historic Preservation Agency, Springfield.

Duerr, Jon J.

1967 A Study of Succession on an Acid Peat Bog in Kane County, Illinois. Master's thesis, Department of Biological Sciences, Northern Illinois University, DeKalb.

Early, Ann M.

1970 NAL 1970 Archaeological Survey: The Prehistoric Occupations of the National Accelerator Laboratory Site. Manuscript on file, Fermi National Accelerator Laboratory, Batavia, Illinois.

1971 Salvage Excavations National Accelerator Laboratory. Manuscript on file, Fermi National Accelerator Laboratory, Batavia, Illinois.

Elias, J. P., and M. Greby

1990 *Report on the Identification and Evaluation of Site ANL-32 in the Advanced Photon Source Project Area, Argonne National Laboratory*. Environmental Assessment and Information Sciences Division, Argonne National Laboratory, Argonne, Illinois.

Farnsworth, Kenneth B.

1987 Preliminary Evaluation of Bannerstones and Other Ground-Stone Artifacts in the Wear Collection from the Bullseye Site, 11-Ge-127. In *The Bullseye Site 11-Ge-127: A Floodplain Archaic Mortuary Site in the Lower Illinois River Valley*, edited by Harold Hassen and Kenneth B. Farnsworth, pp. 13–19. Reports of Investigations 42. Illinois State Museum, Springfield.

Fedje, Daryl W., and Tina Christensen

1999 Modeling Paleoshorelines and Locating Early Holocene Coastal Sites in Haida Gwaii. *American Antiquity* 64:635–652.

Ferguson, Jacqueline A.

1997 Native American Settlement and Chert Use in Starved Rock State Park. *Illinois Archaeology* 9:220–256.

Ferguson, Jacqueline A., and Robert E. Warren

1992 Chert Resources of Northern Illinois: Discriminant Analysis and Identification Key. *Illinois Archaeology* 4:1–37.

1993 Artifact Distribution and Chert Use at the Barton-Milner Site: A Middle Archaic Occupation in North-Central Illinois. *Illinois Archaeology* 5:130–140.

Ferguson, Jacqueline A., Robert E. Warren, and John A. Walthall

1986 *106-Case Report and Mitigation Plan for the Minonk Prairie Multiple Resource Area FAP-412 Highway Project, North-Central Illinois*. Illinois State Museum, Springfield.

Finney, Fred A., and Scott B. Meyer

1991 *Archaeological Investigations of a Middle Archaic Raddatz Occupation at the Bobwhite Site (47Ri185), Richland County, Wisconsin*. Archaeological Consultants, Middleton, Wisconsin.

Fraser, Gordon S., Curtis E. Larsen, and Norman C. Hester

1990 Climatic Control of Lake Levels in the Lake Michigan and Lake Huron Basins. In *Late Quaternary History of the Lake Michigan Basin*, edited by Allen F. Schneider and Gordon S. Fraser, pp. 75–89. Special Paper 251. Geological Society of America, Boulder, Colorado.

Goldstein, Lynne

1995 Kenosha County: Excavations at the Barnes Creek Site. In *The Southeastern Wisconsin Archaeology Program 1994–1995*, edited by Lynne Goldstein, pp. 64–110. Report of Investigations 125. Archaeological Research Laboratory, University of Wisconsin–Milwaukee.

Grauer, Anne L., and Michele R. Buzon

1998 Skeletal Analysis. In *Results of Phase III Archaeological Mitigation of the McGraw Farm Site (11-L-386), Cuba Township, Lake County, Illinois*, by Paula J. Porubcan and Rochelle Lurie, pp. 102–144. Cultural Resources Management Report 621. Midwest Archaeological Research Services, Harvard, Illinois.

Gray, Jean

1996 The Proof Is in the Pipestone. *Illinois Antiquity* 31:8–10.

Harris, Wendy G.

1998 *The South Suburban Airport: Phase I Archaeological Investigations for the Proposed South Suburban Airport, Will County, Illinois*. Research Reports 45. Illinois Transportation Archaeological Research Program, Department of Anthropology, University of Illinois, Urbana.

2002 Upland Abandonment during the Middle Archaic Period: A View from Northeastern Illinois. *The Wisconsin Archeologist* 83(1):3–18.

Hart, John P., and Robert J. Jeske

1991 Models of Prehistoric Site Location for the Upper Illinois River Valley. *Illinois Archaeology* 3:3–22.

Hassen, Harold, and Kenneth B. Farnsworth (editors)

1987 *The Bullseye Site 11-Ge-127: A Floodplain Archaic Mortuary Site in the Lower Illinois River Valley*. Reports of Investigations 42. Illinois State Museum, Springfield.

Higgs, Andrew S., Rochelle Lurie, and Richard Johnson

n.d. *Phase III Data Recovery of Prehistoric Site11-Wi-2514 on the Kukuen Chen Property (North), DuPage Township, Will County, Illinois*. Cultural Resource Management Report 1140. Midwest Archaeological Research Services, Marengo, Illinois.

Higgs, Andrew, and Paula Porubcan

2004a *A Phase I Archaeological Reconnaissance Survey of 70+ Acres of Land (Parcel A) in Sugar Grove Township, Kane County, Illinois*. Cultural Resource Management Report 1286. Midwest Archaeological Research Services, Marengo, Illinois.

2004b *Phase I Archaeological Reconnaissance Survey of 90+ Acres of Land (Parcel B) in Sugar Grove Township, Kane County, Illinois*. Cultural Resource Management Report 1286.

Midwest Archaeological Research Services, Marengo, Illinois.

2004c *Phase I Archaeological Reconnaissance Survey of 80+ Acres of Land (Parcel C) in Sugar Grove Township, Kane County, Illinois.* Cultural Resource Management Report 1286. Midwest Archaeological Research Services, Marengo, Illinois.

Hughes, R., T. Berres, and D. Moore

1998 Revision of Hopewellian Trading Patterns in Midwestern North America Based on Mineralogical Sourcing. *Geoarchaeology* 13:709–729.

Jeske, Robert J.

1988 *The Archaeology of the Chain O' Lakes Region in Northeastern Illinois.* Illinois Cultural Resources Study 5. Illinois Historic Preservation Agency, Springfield.

1990 Environmental Variation and Site Distribution at the Prairie Peninsula Edge: The View from Fermi National Accelerator Laboratory, Batavia, Illinois. *The Wisconsin Archeologist* 71:137–171.

Johnson, Richard B.

2003 *Results of a Phase I Archaeological Reconnaissance Survey of 1,400± Acres of Land in Jackson Township, Will County, Illinois.* Cultural Resource Management Report 1192. Midwest Archaeological Research Services, Marengo, Illinois.

Johnson, Richard B., and Rochelle Lurie

2007 *Phase III Investigations at the Cement Pond Site (11-Wi-2533) in DuPage Township, Will County, Illinois.* Cultural Resource Management Report 1149. Midwest Archaeological Research Services, Marengo, Illinois.

Justice, Noel D.

1987 *Stone Age Spear and Arrow Points of the Midcontinental and Eastern United States.* Indiana University Press, Bloomington.

Keeley, Lawrence H.

1980 *Experimental Determination of Stone Tool Uses.* University of Chicago Press, Chicago.

Keene, David

1987 Reconstructing Prehistoric Settlement in the Chicago Area. Paper presented at the 86th Annual Meeting of the American Anthropological Association, Chicago.

1989 Reconstructing Prehistoric Settlement Patterns in the Chicago Area. *Illinois Archaeology* 1:137–149.

Keene, David, and Theodore Karamanski

1980 *Cultural Resource Survey of the Cook County Forest Preserve: Palos and Calumet Divisions.* Mid-American Research Center, Loyola University, Chicago.

King, James E.

1981 Late Quaternary Vegetational History of Illinois. *Ecological Monographs* 51:43–62.

Kuehn, Steven R.

1998 Analysis of the Faunal Remains from the McGraw Farm Site (11-L-386), Lake County, Illinois. In *Results of Phase III Archaeological Mitigation of the McGraw Farm Site (11-L-386), Cuba Township, Lake County, Illinois,* by Paula J. Porubcan and Rochelle Lurie, pp. 176–186. Cultural Resource Management Report 621. Midwest Archaeological Research Services, Harvard, Illinois.

Kullen, Douglas

1987 *Final Report of Phase I and Phase II Archeological Investigations along the Proposed Moraine Pipeline Corridor, Lake County, Illinois.* Archeology Division, Patrick Engineering, Glen Ellyn, Illinois.

1990 Excavations at Primavilla, a Paleoindian and Archaic Site in Lake County, Illinois. *The Wisconsin Archeologist* 71:172–191.

1991 *Report of Phase I Archeological Survey on the East Side of Nelson Lake, Kane County, Illinois.* Allied Archeology, Aurora, Illinois.

1995 *Phase II Testing and National Register Evaluation of Site 11Wi897 at the Proposed 95th Street Bridge, Naperville, Will County, Illinois.* Allied Archeology, Aurora, Illinois.

2002a *Phase I Archeological Survey of the Washington Woods Subdivision, Naperville, Will County, Illinois.* Allied Archeology, Aurora, Illinois.

2002b *Phase II Historical Significance Evaluation of Prehistoric Sites 11Wi398 and 11Wi2713, Naperville, Will County, Illinois.* Allied Archeology, Aurora, Illinois.

2003 Observations on Archaic and Woodland Projectile Point Types from the Hunter's Home and Ruby Robin Sites in Naperville, Will County, Illinois. Paper presented at the 49th Annual Midwest Archaeological Conference, Milwaukee, Wisconsin.

Kullen, Douglas, Matt Greby, Melinda Hickman, Rebecca Bria, and Thomas Loebel

2007 *Ruby Robin and Hunters Home: Phase III Data Recovery at Prehistoric Sites 11Wi398 and 11Wi2713 in Naperville, Will County, Illinois.* Allied Archeology, Aurora, Illinois.

Kullen, Douglas, and Lynn Malinowski

1990 The Photon Site: An Archaic Settlement in the Forested Uplands of Northern Illinois. Paper presented at the 35th Annual Midwest Archaeological Conference, Evanston, Illinois.

Kwas, Mary L.

1981 Bannerstones as Chronological Markers in the Southeastern United States. *Tennessee Archaeologist* 6(2):144–171.

Larsen, Curtis E.

1985 *A Stratigraphic Study of Beach Features on the Southeastern Shore of Lake Michigan: New Evidence of Holocene Lake Level Fluctuations.* Environmental Geology Notes 112. Illinois State Geological Survey, Urbana.

1987 *Geological History of Glacial Lake Algonquin and the Upper Great Lakes.* Bulletin 1801. U.S. Geological Survey, Washington, D.C.

Loebel, Thomas J.

1998 *Results of a Phase I Archaeological Reconnaissance Survey of the 320± Acre Nursery Portion of Shodeen's Mill Creek Development, Blackberry and Geneva Townships, Kane County, Illinois.* Cultural Resource Management Report 745. Midwest Archaeological Research Services, Harvard, Illinois.

2001a *Report on a Phase I Archaeological Reconnaissance Survey of the 83 Acre Davey Road Site Development, DuPage Township, Will County, Illinois.* Cultural Resource Management Report 1017. Midwest Archaeological Research Services, Harvard, Illinois.

2001b *A Phase I Archaeological Reconnaissance Survey of Site 11-Wi-2514 in the 2.47 Acre Wood Lot on the Kukuen Chen Property (North) to Amend Previous Investigations, DuPage Township, Will County, Illinois.* Cultural Resource

Management Report 1027. Midwest Archaeological Research Services, Harvard, Illinois.
2005 Microwear Analysis of Select Tools from 11Wi2533 MARS, Inc. Project 1149. Manuscript on file, Midwest Archaeological Research Services,Marengo, Illinois.

Loebel, Thomas J., and Rochelle Lurie
2001 *Phase II Archaeological Testing of Eight Prehistoric Sites Located within DuPage Township, Will County, Illinois*. Cultural Resource Management Report 1025. Midwest Archaeological Research Services, Harvard, Illinois.

Lurie, Rochelle
1990 *Report on the Wooded Areas Survey, Gazebo Site Testing, Collector Interviews, and Review of the Prehistoric Site Status and Location at Fermi National Accelerator Laboratory, Batavia, Illinois*. Cultural Resource Management Report 56. Midwest Archaeological Research Services, Harvard, Illinois.
1992 *Preliminary Report of Phase III Investigations at the Garrison Site 11-L-337 in Lake Forest, Lake County, Illinois*. Cultural Resource Management Report 174. Midwest Archaeological Research Services, Harvard, Illinois.
1994 *An Archaeological Reconnaissance Survey of the McGraw Property—Three Parcels of Land in Cuba Township, Lake County, Illinois*. Cultural Resource Management Report 358. Midwest Archaeological Research Services, Harvard, Illinois.
2003a A Compilation of Phase II and Phase III Reports for Archaic Period Sites in Northeastern Illinois. Paper presented at the 49th Annual Midwest Archaeological Conference, Milwaukee, Wisconsin.
2003b So Many Sites, So Few Insights: The Archaic in Northeastern Illinois. Paper presented at the 68th Annual Meeting of the Society for American Archaeology, Milwaukee, Wisconsin.

Lurie, Rochelle, M. Catherine Bird, and Richard Johnson
1996 *Phase II Archaeological Testing on Five Sites in Alden Township, McHenry County, Illinois*. Cultural Resource Management Report 520. Midwest Archaeological Research Services, Harvard, Illinois.

Lurie, Rochelle, M. Catherine Bird, and Sara L. Pfannkuche
1994 *Results of an Archaeological Reconnaissance Survey of Portions of an Approximately 220 Acre Parcel of Land in Alden Township, McHenry County, Illinois*. Cultural Resource Management Report 407. Midwest Archaeological Research Services, Harvard, Illinois.

Lurie, Rochelle, and Scott J. Demel
1992 *Results of Phase II Testing on Four Prehistoric Sites of the LeWa Farm Subdivision, Lake Forest, Illinois*. Cultural Resource Management Report 174. Midwest Archaeological Research Services, Harvard, Illinois.

Lurie, Rochelle, and Robert J. Jeske
1988 *Results of Phase I Archaeological Investigations of the Cedar Shores Development Property, Lake County, Illinois*. Cultural Resource Management Report 34. Midwest Archaeological Research Services, Evanston, Illinois.

Markman, Charles W.
1991 *Chicago before History: The Prehistoric Archaeology of a Modern Metropolitan Area*. Studies in Illinois Archaeology 7. Illinois Historic Preservation Agency, Springfield.

McGimsey, Charles R., Erich K. Schroeder, Michael D. Wiant, Misty M. Jackson, and Ray Druhot
1989 *An Assessment of Cultural Resources in the Superconducting Super Collider Project Area, DuPage, Kane, Kendall, and Will Counties, Illinois*. Anthropology Section Technical Report 89-276-26. Quaternary Studies Program, Illinois State Museum, Springfield.

Moran, Robbin C.
1980 Presettlement (1830) Vegetation of DeKalb, Kane, and DuPage Counties, Illinois. Master's thesis, Department of Botany, Southern Illinois University, Carbondale.

Munson, Patrick J., and Alan D. Harn
1966 Surface Collections from Three Sites in the Central Illinois River Valley. *The Wisconsin Archeologist* 47:150–168.

Nelson, David, Feng Sheng Hu, and Eric Grimm
2004 Dynamics of Middle-Holocene Climate, Vegetation, and Fire on the Northern Prairie Peninsula. Paper presented at the 2004 American Quaternary Association Meeting, University of Kansas, Lawrence. Abstract published in *American Quaternary Association Program and Abstracts of the 18th Biennial Meeting*, pp. 53–55.

Neumann, Georg K.
1961 The Skeleton from the Doetsch site, Lake County, Illinois. In *Chicago Area Archaeology*, edited by E. A. Bluhm, pp. 29–34. Bulletin 3. Illinois Archaeological Survey, Urbana.

Odell, George H.
1979 New and Improved System of the Retrieval of Functional Information from Microscopic Observations of Chipped Stone Tools. In *Lithic Use-Wear Analysis*, edited by Brian Hayden, pp. 329–344. Academic Press, New York.
2005 Lithic Use-Wear Analysis of a Sample of Tools from the Chen Site, Northern Illinois. Manuscript on file, Midwest Archaeological Research Services, Marengo, Illinois.

Pfannkuche, Sara L.
2005 *Report on the 2003 Field Season at Macktown: A Return to Shell Midden A*. Cultural Resource Management Report 1212. Midwest Archaeological Research Services, Marengo, Illinois.

Pfannkuche, Sara L., and Rochelle Lurie
1996 *Report on an Archaeological Reconnaissance Survey of Fairmont Village Unit 3, Approximately 50 Acres of Land in Orland Township, Cook County, Illinois*. Cultural Resource Management Report 440a. Midwest Archaeological Research Services, Harvard, Illinois.

Pfeiffer, Susan
1985 *The Skeletal Biology of the Archaic Populations of the Great Lakes Region*. Mercury Series Paper 64. Archaeological Survey of Canada, National Museum of Man, Ottawa.

Porubcan, Paula J.
1997 *Results of a Phase I Archaeological Survey of the Proposed Par Development Boulder Ridge Country Club—West Nine Holes in Grafton Township, McHenry Co., Illinois*. Cultural Resource Management Report 649. Midwest Archaeological Research Services, Harvard, Illinois.

2003 *A Phase I Archaeological Reconnaissance Survey of the Proposed 1,535 Acre Settler's Ridge Development in Sugar Grove Township, Kane County, Illinois.* Cultural Resource Management Report 1192. Midwest Archaeological Research Services, Marengo, Illinois.

Porubcan, Paula J., and Rochelle Lurie

1998 *Results of Phase III Archaeological Mitigation of the McGraw Farm Site (11-L-386), Cuba Township, Lake County, Illinois.* Cultural Resource Management Report 621. Midwest Archaeological Research Services, Harvard, Illinois.

Schwegman, John E.

1973 *Comprehensive Plan for the Illinois Nature Preserves System: 2. The Natural Divisions of Illinois.* Illinois Nature Preserves Commission, Rockford.

Springer, James W.

1985 Site Distribution, Environmental Adaptation, and Environmental Change along the Northern Edge of the Prairie Peninsula. *The Wisconsin Archeologist* 66:1–46.

Springer, James W., Claude C. Karch, and William F. Harrison

1978 Early Archaic Hafted Stone Tools from Northern Illinois. *The Wisconsin Archeologist* 59:277–309.

Stuiver, M., and P. J. Reimer

2000 University of Washington Quarternary Isotope Lab Radiocarbon Calibration Program, Version 4.3. Seattle, Washington.

Tolmie, Clare

2003 Catchment Analyses for the Archaic Period Chen and Cement Pond Sites. Paper presented at the 49th Annual Meeting of the Midwest Archaeological Conference, Milwaukee, Wisconsin.

Voss, John

1937 Comparative Study of Bogs on Cary and Tazewell Drift in Illinois. *Ecology* 18:119–135.

Webb, William S.

1974 *Indian Knoll.* University of Tennessee Press, Knoxville.

Wiant, Michael D., Edwin R. Hajic, and Thomas R. Styles

1983 Napoleon Hollow and Koster Site Stratigraphy: Implications for Holocene Landscape Evolution and Studies of Archaic Period Settlement Patterns in the Lower Illinois River Valley. In *Archaic Hunters and Gatherers in the American Midwest*, edited by James L. Phillips and James A. Brown, pp. 147–164. Academic Press, New York.

Willman, H. B.

1971 *Summary of the Geology of the Chicago Region.* Circular 460. Illinois State Geological Survey, Urbana.

Wittry, Warren L.

1959 The Raddatz Rockshelter, Sk5, Wisconsin. *The Wisconsin Archeologist* 40:33–69.

Young, Philip D.

1961 Evidence for an Archaic Tradition in the Chicago Area. In *Chicago Area Archaeology*, edited by Elaine A. Bluhm, pp. 7–12. Bulletin 3. Illinois Archaeological Survey, Urbana.

Young, Philip D., David J. Wenner, and Elaine A. Bluhm

1961 Two Early Burial Sites in Lake County. In *Chicago Area Archaeology*, edited by Elaine A. Bluhm, pp. 21–28. Bulletin 3. Illinois Archaeological Survey, Urbana.

22

At the Crossroads and Periphery: The Archaic Archaeological Record of Southern Ontario

Christopher Ellis, Peter A. Timmins, and Holly Martelle

We provide an overview here of the Archaic occupations of southern Ontario. This area includes that vast region of Ontario south of the Canadian Shield (Figure 22.1), although we have left the boundary somewhat flexible to accommodate developments that do not fit neatly within such an arbitrary geographic subdivision. We focus particularly on research developments since the late 1980s, when the last major Archaic synthesis of the region was written (Ellis, Kenyon, and Spence 1990), and on events that tie the Ontario record into that of surrounding regions. Since New York was one of the first areas to be studied and to provide data on Archaic sites and sequences (e.g., Ritchie 1932b,

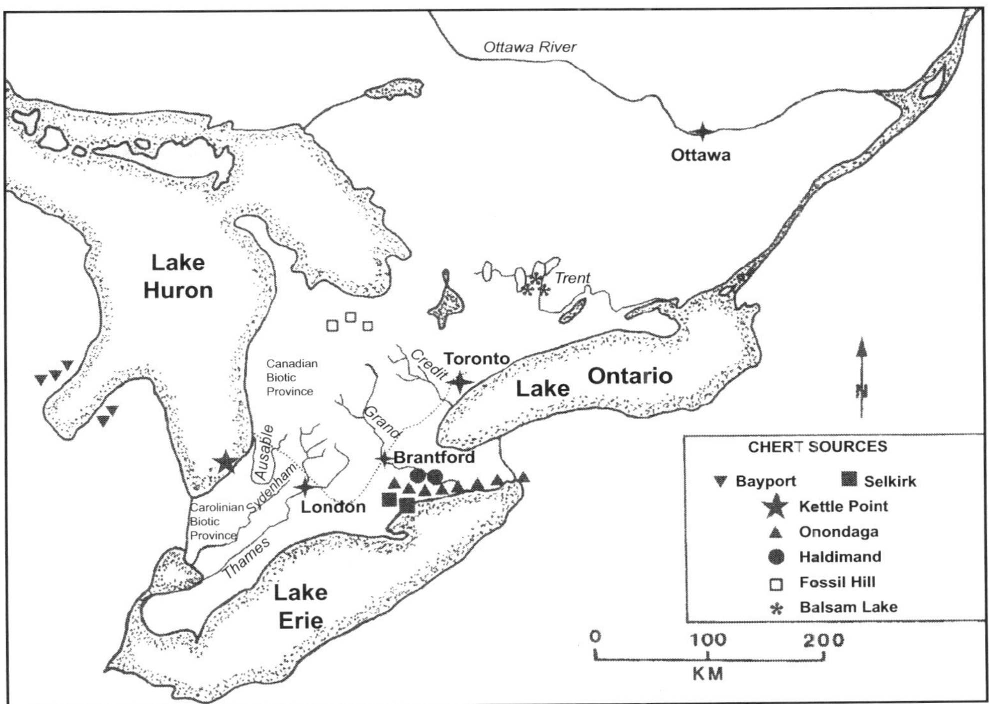

Figure 22.1. Southern Ontario historic landscape features.

1944, 1969, etc.), traditionally, archaeological developments in adjacent southern Ontario had been related to the data from that state. However, as has become increasingly clear, in earlier time periods and, spatially, particularly in southwestern Ontario (e.g., from the Michigan border to the west end of Lake Ontario), developments seem to have been more closely related to events in the Midwest and Southeast.

Archaic Parameters

Age and Subdivisions

For purposes of this discussion, we conceive of the Archaic in terms of basic characteristics of the archaeological record, such as artifact forms and site types, rather than in much-debated inferred sociocultural terms (for explicit statements of this rationale, see Ellis 2004a; Ellis and Deller 2002:138–139; Ellis, Kenyon, and Spence 1990:65–67). In practical terms this conception leads to a somewhat arbitrary definition of the Archaic as that segment of the archaeological record marked on the early end by certain assemblages dominated by notched or markedly stemmed point forms dating to around 10,000 RCYBP and on the late end by the introduction of ceramics around 2800 RCYBP. The Ontario Early Archaic has generally been seen to extend until 8000 RCYBP, which follows the usage of most researchers elsewhere (e.g., Chapman 1975; Fowler 1959; Griffin 1964), but we note that such a division may actually arbitrarily divide up a temporal continuum, at least in terms of point style changes. Somewhat paradoxically, because the end dates for the Middle Archaic used in regions such as New York and Illinois arbitrarily divide up what is a continuous sequence in Ontario, placement of the Ontario Middle–Late Archaic boundary has varied over time and differed from that in use in some nearby areas. The most recent writers, following the practice in adjacent Michigan, have tended to end the Middle Archaic around 4500 RCYBP (Ellis, Kenyon, and Spence 1990:93), a date that corresponds to some major formal shifts in items such as projectile points and also to a major geological event, the beginning of the recession of the high-water levels in the eastern Great Lakes called the "Nipissing phase" (see below).

The Setting

Southern Ontario encompasses an area of some 75,000 km^2 (30,000 mi^2). This area has little in the way of bedrock at the surface and, therefore, little potential for stratified cave deposits. Moreover, the surficial deposits since the last glaciation have tended to be shallow, and over much of the area the land surface at the end of the Pleistocene was the same one seen today. In addition, the area is the most populated, deforested, industrialized, and intensively cultivated part of Canada. The result is that archaeological assemblages in southern Ontario come mainly from shallow, disturbed surface deposits.

One exception is largely littoral areas near the Great Lakes, particularly Lake Huron, where aeolian processes have often resulted in buried, and in some cases stratified, albeit relatively shallow, sites (e.g., Kenyon 1959; Ramsden 1976; Wright 1972b). Other locations that might favor buried and protected sites are not as well studied. Stewart (2002) has noted the potential for preserved sites to be present in Holocene river terraces, and demonstrably preserved middle Holocene soils in some areas such as the Rouge River valley may contain archaeological deposits. In addition, as in the Midwest, the potential exists for deposits to occur at the base of bluffs, covered as a result of colluvial and aeolian processes, but these settings have not been examined in Ontario. Also, buried deposits may exist in areas flooded by high lake levels such as those of the Nipissing phase in the Huron basin (see below).

Major river valleys obviously have the potential to harbor preserved and stratified sites. However, studies of such Ontario locations, particularly as they apply to the preservation and discovery of archaeological sites, are very much in their infancy. The few studies available have not been encouraging with regard to the discovery of deeply buried sites with many stratified occupation layers laid down in relatively rapid succession, thus, affording very fine temporal control, such as are seen to the south and into the Midwest (e.g., Broyles 1971; Chapman 1975). In comparison with those of other areas, many of Ontario's major rivers are smaller in scale and low energy, with little gradient in their lower courses, and their sediment sources are more cohesive silts and clays that limit the supply of sediment available. Hence, although some major rivers such as the Grand River (Figure 22.1) seem to have stable watercourses and floodplains formed largely by vertical accretion of deposits, the thickness of those deposits and their potential to contain deeply buried and highly stratified (e.g., many layers in rapid succession) sites are limited (see Walker et al. 1997). Other river floodplains, such as the Thames (Figure 22.1), at least in the middle to late Holocene, seem to have been formed by different processes such as slow lateral accretion (Stewart and Desloges 2002). This process has resulted in relatively shallow deposits, with most archaeological finds, regardless of whether they are 8,000 or 2,000 years old, occurring at the surface, although given the lateral movement of the riverbank and a tendency for people to camp adjacent to that riverbank, a potential exists for some horizontal separation of components. In all cases, an underlying theme of these studies is that southern Ontario rivers have mixed boundaries of both glacial sediments (e.g., cohesive clay-till beds) and alluvial (more erodible) sediments. Therefore, southern Ontario rivers may behave differently from midwestern rivers, possibly being more stable vertically and laterally, resulting in distinct kinds of deposits.

While such processes may limit the potential for deeply stratified, profusely layered sites, nonetheless, the probability that buried components have escaped modern land use practices is very high, and floodplains represent some of the areas with the best potential to contain such components. We are encouraged by growing evidence that such components exist. As an example, at the Grand Banks site on the lower Grand River, the lower of two paleosols encountered seems to include occupations dating to the Late Archaic, ca. 3000 RCYBP (Crawford et al. 1998). Similarly, at the Johnson Flats site located just upstream from Grand Banks, a buried paleosol that represented the surface prior to European land clearing yielded Late Archaic and Woodland diagnostics, while what may be an underlying paleosol yielded, among other things, Middle Archaic points of various forms (Parker 1995). On the Thames River near Delaware, Ontario, excavation by the late William B. Roosa found a sub-plow-zone paleosol that contained a Late Archaic Broad Point component overlain by a Middle Woodland midden established on the same surface (University of Western Ontario Collections). Finally, at the George Davidson site on the lower Ausable River, Ian Kenyon (1980a) reported a buried paleosol that contained an intact Late Archaic Broad Point component, which was protected by silt deposited in subsequent historic flooding events.

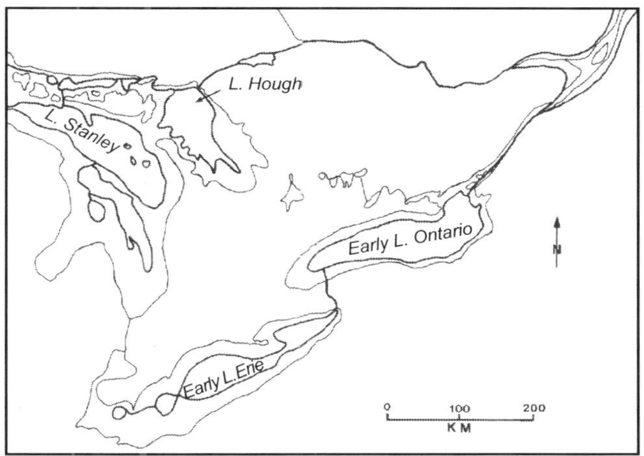

Figure 22.2. Great Lakes levels, ca. 10,000–5500 B.P.

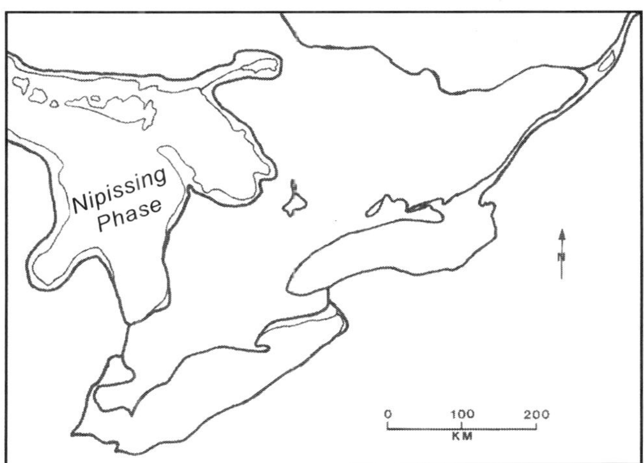

Figure 22.3. Great Lakes levels at the time of the Nipissing phase, ca. 5500–4500 B.P.

Changing Lake Levels

Southern Ontario is bordered on its western and southern margins by Lakes Huron, Erie, and Ontario, whose levels have varied considerably over time (see Jackson et al. 2000; Karrow and Calkin 1985; Karrow and Warner 1990). Thus, understanding the Archaic record of southern Ontario requires a knowledge of those levels. By 10,000 RCYBP in the Lake Huron basin, two interconnected water bodies called "Stanley" and "Hough" drained down the Ottawa River valley on the east (Figure 22.2). Early Lake Erie did not get the outflow from Huron that it does today, but it did follow modern drainage patterns in that it drained into the Ontario basin. Levels in all basins were much below modern, and, conservatively, an additional 30,000 km^2 of land surface was available for occupation. Phrased another way, at the minimum levels, at least 40 percent of the area available for human occupation at that time is now underwater, and, clearly, a substantial part of the earliest Archaic record is not easily examined. Of course, such now-inundated areas included lakeshores that in later times were magnets for occupation, so areas of probably some of the densest occupation are invisible to researchers.

Water levels in the Huron and Erie basins remained below modern levels until about 5000–5500 RCYBP. With isostatic uplift, the outlet to the Ottawa River was closed off and water levels rose until they were above modern levels, forming in the Huron basin what is called the "Nipissing phase" (Karrow 1980; Larsen 1985; see Figure 22.3). Water levels were high enough that the Huron basin could drain south into Lake Erie, as it does today, and corresponding rises above modern levels occurred in the Erie basin. The areas flooded by this event were comparatively small, but some sites were submerged and some altered (e.g., Ellis and Deller 1986). Although no sites sealed and buried by the water-level rise have yet to be reported from Ontario, the documentation of such sites in adjacent Michigan (e.g., Lovis 1989) indicates potential for finding these sites in the future. With erosion downward of the outlet at Port Huron, water levels lowered from the Nipissing-phase maximum beginning around 4500 RCYBP, eventually reaching levels approximating modern ones.

In the Ontario basin, water levels rose relatively continuously over time as the isostatic process lifted the outlets at the eastern end leading into the St. Lawrence River. Because of the differential and distorting effects of the rebounding surface, modern levels were achieved at different times throughout the basin (Anderson and Lewis 1985; Coakley and Karrow 1994). In some areas, such as the north-central shore, the historic level was achieved as early as 6000 RCYBP, whereas in other areas, stable levels approximating the modern were not achieved until 4000 RCYBP or slightly thereafter. The greater outflow from the Erie basin during the Nipissing phase also apparently led to slight rises above modern levels in the western Lake Ontario basin for a brief period prior to 4000 RCYBP.

Vegetation History

Although spruce seems to have persisted as a common species in southeastern Ontario (e.g., the area north of Lake Ontario), by 10,000 RCYBP pine was a major component of the vegetation of the rest of the study area, and it would remain so until the beginning of the Middle Archaic (Karrow and Warner 1990; McAndrews 1981, 1994; Muller 1999: Figures 9–14). Nonetheless, even during the Early Archaic, evidence suggests various deciduous tree species were entering and replacing pine, such that, after peaking around 10,000–9500 RCYBP in southwestern Ontario and 9500–9000 RCYBP in the rest of the area, pine clearly declined. The deciduous species entered the area at different times. Oak and maple were the earliest and may have been present before 10,000 RCYBP. They were followed by elm and ash around 9000 RCYBP and hemlock, beech, hickory, and basswood by 8000 to 7500 RCYBP. Fluctuations in certain species occurred after that date, as evidenced notably by the hemlock decline that occurred around 5000 to 4000 RCYBP and that is often attributed to a disease that struck that species, but an essentially modern vegetation was present by 7500 RCYBP throughout the area.

Deciduous species entered southwestern Ontario first and only later spread northeasterly into other areas, including the area north of Lake Ontario. Moreover, some coniferous species have remained relatively common until the present day, particularly in more northern and easterly areas, because of climatic and soil differences. The combined result of these factors was environmental differences between the southwestern area and southeastern areas throughout the Archaic (see Karrow and Warner 1990). During the Early Archaic, a mixed coniferous-deciduous forest was found in the southwest, whereas to the southeast, the forest was dominated more by conifers. In subsequent times, and extending to the present, the southwestern part, or roughly the area south of a line drawn from the west end of Lake Ontario to the southeastern corner of Lake Huron, was a deciduous forest historically referred to as the "Carolinian Biotic Province" (Dice 1943) (see Figure 22.1) or "Deciduous Forest Zone" (Rowe 1972). The remainder, often referred to as the "southeastern portion," was a mixed coniferous-deciduous (e.g., northern hardwoods such as maple) forest referred to as the "Canadian Biotic Province" (Dice 1943) (see Figure 22.1) or "Great Lakes-St. Lawrence Forest Region" (Rowe 1972). These gross environmental distinctions have been and continue to be used to explain variability in the Archaic archaeological record across the region.

Research

Despite its equation with the bulk of the Ontario archaeological record, the Archaic remains much more poorly known than both the preceding Paleoindian and succeeding Woodland periods. One might attribute this fact to a simple lack of interest, as almost no pure research projects in the last 15 years have been devoted to the study of Archaic materials. The main exceptions are the projects of a few M.A. students (e.g., Fisher 1997; Lackowicz 1996; McMillan 2003; Snarey 2000; Woodley 1990), most of which involved analyses of already-existing collections. Other studies resulting from research-oriented projects have also largely involved publication of data from sites investigated many years before (e.g., Donaldson and Wortner 1995; Ellis et al. 1991) or have reported on Archaic material discovered incidental to research focused on other developments (e.g., Ellis 1998; Ellis and Deller 1991; Ellis et al. 1990).

The bulk of recent Archaic fieldwork and publication has resulted from cultural resource management (CRM) projects, and, to be sure, some important insights have resulted from that work. However, one can complain that, relative to the insights provided into Paleoindian and Woodland developments, comparatively little knowledge has been generated for the Archaic. The smaller size of Archaic sites, their poorer preservation, and their lack of diagnostics such as ceramics easily explain why the Woodland, and particularly the Late Woodland time span, has received the bulk of CRM attention. Yet, these characteristics do not explain why more Paleoindian than Archaic material seems to be found, examined, and reported in CRM research. One reason for this difference may be that Paleoindian sites and finds are seen as rare, whereas Archaic material is seen as common and does not have the exotic cachet of that from the more ancient sites. As a result, many Archaic sites receive cursory treatment in reports or remain hidden, either unpublished or mentioned only in the gray CRM literature. Another important reason for the disparity is that the landscape during Paleoindian times was relatively unstable or changing, whereas in the Archaic it was relatively stable. As a result, Archaic site locations tended to be used for longer periods of time and to be multicomponent. Moreover, as noted above, the bulk of the southern Ontario landscape consists of shallow deposits heavily impacted by modern activities, including agricultural use, so materials representing thousands of years of time can be hopelessly intermingled. To be sure, many Paleoindian sites also have later components, but even in these cases, the earlier materials can be isolated because Paleoindians produced a large number of hafted and heavily resharpened—and, therefore, more formed and easily assignable—tools, often made on very exotic materials. In contrast, Archaic stone artifacts tend to be nondescript, and assemblages are dominated by simple expedient tools and by more site-local raw materials, making recognition and sorting out of finds associated with particular periods of site use difficult. These sorts of problems have led to the suggestion that proportionally real and lasting insights into the Archaic will necessitate both (1) greater attempts by archaeologists to publish the results of CRM site investigations and (2) the development of focused research-based projects that target the specific sites and areas most likely to contain undisturbed deposits (especially the floodplains), rather than relying on the luck of the draw associated with CRM-based research projects (Ellis 2003).

The Early Archaic

Largely on the basis of comparative point typologies, particularly from areas in the Southeast, the Early Archaic is seen to begin at ca. 10,000 RCYBP. As discussed above, the Early Archaic is seen here to begin with the appearance of assemblages in which notched and markedly stemmed point forms predominate as opposed to the more lanceolate, occasionally slightly stemmed items that characterize "Paleoindian" assemblages. In southern Ontario, some of these Paleoindian assemblages include unfluted point forms that, although certainly exhibiting differences, most closely resemble types seen in the West, such as Agate Basin and Hell Gap. We call these unfluted forms "Plano" points here. If comparisons with western types are accurate, then these points actually date to a period ranging from ca. 10,500 to 9500 RCYBP or later. One occasionally finds these point forms in southernmost Ontario, but find spots are common and actual sites known only at the northerly fringes of the area considered here, ranging from the southeastern Huron basin (Deller 1976; Ellis and Deller 1986) east to the area of Lake Simcoe (Dibb 2004; Stewart 1983, 1984).

Early Archaic assemblages are recognized by point forms that closely resemble those from the well-known and well-dated sequences of the southeastern United States derived through the studies of Coe (1964), Broyles (1971), and Chapman (1975, 1976, 1980). These include point forms resembling those that define the four time-sequential "Early Archaic" horizons recognized by Tuck (1974) and Chapman (1975): Dalton, Big Sandy, Kirk, and Bifurcate. In Ontario, although the term *Bifurcate* is retained, the earlier horizons have tended to be called by the more local or neutral terms Hi-Lo, Side-Notched, and Corner-Notched, respectively (e.g., Ellis, Kenyon, and Spence 1990). Only the Bifurcate horizon is directly dated in southern Ontario, but the formal attributes of the earlier points and dates from adjacent areas such as New York State (e.g., Fergusson 1996; Funk and Wellman 1984:84) suggest comparable ages to the southeastern U.S. forms, thus, indicating an overall date range of ca. 10,500 to 8000 RCYBP for all of these assemblages.

The earliest part of this range clearly overlaps that of the Plano assemblages noted earlier, suggesting some degree of contemporaneity. Moreover, although more detailed studies are necessary, the only substantial reported sites with point forms attributed to the earlier Archaic horizons are, in contrast to Plano, found in areas relatively close to Lake Erie, or the more southerly parts of the area considered here. Also, in the few studies in which distributions of isolated points have been examined, forms such as Hi-Lo, Bifurcates, and so on, while not restricted to the south (see, e.g., Stewart 2004a), are clearly more common in those same areas (Wright 1978). In sum, these assemblages seem to be concentrated in different areas than the Plano Paleoindian assemblages noted above, and these distribution differences have been used to suggest they are, in fact, geographically contemporary variants (Ellis, Kenyon, and Spence 1990:68–70). Given the transgressive nature of environments across the area, this would also suggest an association of the more Archaic-looking material with increasing amounts of deciduous vegetation. In fact, across the Northeast and Great Lakes regions, lanceolate point–dominated assemblages seem to persist in areas of more coniferous dominated vegetation (e.g., Sanger et al. 1992:157–159).

Hi-Lo and Side-Notched Horizons

Named after a site in Michigan (Fitting 1963), Hi-Lo seems the best Great Lakes analogue to Dalton (Ellis and Deller 1982) and is probably the earliest of the horizons to be discussed here. Assemblages lumped under this rubric have had a "schizophrenic" history, with some regarding them as Paleoindian (Ellis and Deller 1982; Fitting 1963), others as Early Archaic (Wright 1995:71–73), and some as both (Ellis 2004a; Ellis and Deller 1990:57–58; Ellis, Kenyon, and Spence 1990:71). Part of the problem is that comparisons are often drawn to Dalton, which itself has been variously classified and, in terms of point forms, often broadly defined to include everything from almost fluted to side-notched points. Also, the arguments for Dalton as Early Archaic boil down to the presence of what are often seen as Archaic traits, such as large adzes, cemeteries, and so on (see Walthall and Koldehoff, this volume), which are not associated with Hi-Lo components. Compounding the problem is that the most diagnostic indicator, the Hi-Lo point, like Dalton, also has been a rather broadly and "loosely defined type" (Mason 1981:114).

Hi-Lo points (Figure 22.4) share much in common that serves to distinguish them from all other early point forms in the region. Shared traits, notably, include a thinned, ground, concave base with broad thick ears that have rounded apexes; a thick cross section (6–10 mm); a distinctive pattern of frequent lateral foresection resharpening that results in alternate left bevels; and consistent recycling, not seen in earlier assemblages, into drills, specialized "side scrapers" beveled on only one foresection margin, end scrapers, notches, and gravers (Ellis 2004a). However, despite these commonalities, they differ in basal form in certain ways. Some have generally lanceolate overall forms and lack stems, and, so, most closely resemble apparently earlier Late Paleoindian point forms such as Holcombe (hence, they are increasingly being referred to as "Hi-Ho" points; e.g., Timmermans 1999). Still others, which are the "Classic" forms, clearly have distinct, slight stems, or, phrased another way, their foresections are wider than their haft areas, although often, with lateral resharpening, most of the stem demarcation is removed. The lateral edges of the stem tend to be slightly concave. Finally, clear shallowly side-notched examples are known (Figures 22.4 and 22.5). These variants may actually represent a time series. The implications are (1) that the side-notched forms represent the earliest notched points in the area and, by definition, would be seen as Early Archaic, whereas the other variants would be seen as Late Paleoindian; and (2) that the presumed earlier forms such as the Hi-Ho variant represent stylistic continuity from earlier Holcombe points. However, since few researchers have seen fit to make such distinctions in reporting sites and since the time-series idea is only informed speculation, we treat Hi-Lo as a single entity here.

Figure 22.4. Hi-Lo points, Snow Hill and Double Take sites.

Figure 22.5. Hi-Lo points and fragments, Welke-Tonkonah, Area C. Reproduced courtesy of the London Chapter, Ontario Archaeological Society from Ellis (2004b).

As will become a familiar refrain throughout this chapter, few sites have been excavated. Most Hi-Lo sites are small and multicomponent and lack organic and feature preservation. However, some largely or definitively single-component sites or site areas have either been recently reported or excavated (see Figure 22.6 and Table 22.1); examples are Caradoc (Deller and Ellis 2001; Ellis and Deller 2002), Welke-Tonkonoh Area C (Ellis 2004b), Stelco 1 (Timmins 1995), and Snow Hill and Double Take (Timmins Martelle Heritage Consultants 2004b).

The Caradoc site consists mainly of a deposit of 62 siliceous artifacts, including tools, tool preforms, and flake blanks, almost all of which are on Bayport, Michigan, chert from over 175 km away. Most of the items were purposefully broken, indicating that the site was the location of a sacred, ritual offering. The single point recovered was unbroken but conforms to the Hi-Ho variant and may suggest an early date within the Hi-Lo time span. The recovered artifacts include items such as large biface cores and large side scrapers, confirming the similarities to Paleoindian tool production and tool kits suggested by earlier research (Ellis and Deller 2002).

The Welke-Tonkonoh site is a large Hi-Lo site with at least five or more discrete activity areas distributed over some 20 ha (Ellis and Deller 1982). Area A covers 1,500 m^2 and was apparently repeatedly used, but most of the other areas are half that size or less. All areas are plowed and most are also multicomponent, which makes them difficult to assess, but Area C, covering about 300–400 m^2, seems to represent an almost pure Hi-Lo assemblage (Ellis 2004b). A small 16-m^2 area in the center of the concentration was excavated in 1979. Including the surface collections at that time, a total of 20 tools and preforms was recovered. Subsequent surface collections in the 1980s resulted in the recovery of an additional 12 tools. Almost all the tools and preforms (27 of 32, or 81.3 percent) are on Haldimand chert from bedrock outcrops, the nearest sources of which are 175 km southeast of the site. This is a material that was almost never used by other groups in the site vicinity but was favored by Hi-Lo and subsequent Early Archaic groups in south-central Ontario (see below). Aside from a single microsherd that seems to have originated in a small Late Woodland component to the north, all of the diagnostic items, including five points or fragments and a point recycled into a drill, are side-notched examples (Figure 22.5). Other notable recoveries include six small, oval to trianguloid end scrapers (Figure 22.7), three of which have spurs on lateral margins and one of which may be a result of recycling, two side scrapers, several simple tools such as beaks and gravers, and combination tools incorporating

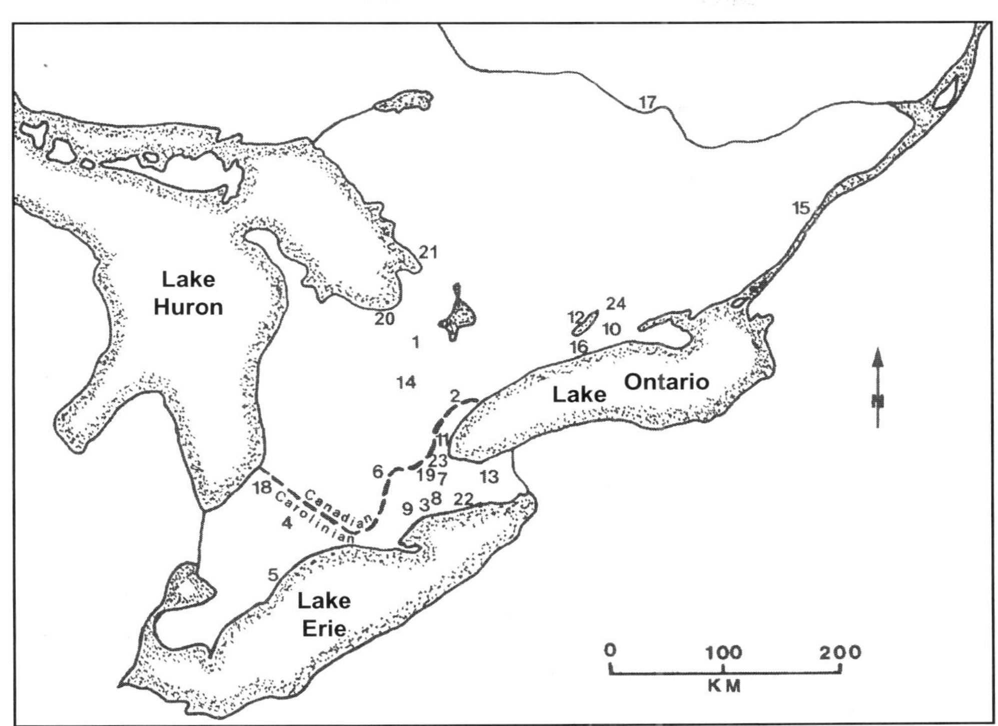

Figure 22.6. Locations of Early and Middle Archaic sites in southern Ontario. For key to site names, see Table 22.1.

Table 22.1. Early and Middle Archaic Sites in Ontario.

Site	Map No.[a]	Designation	References
Stelco 1	3	Hi-Lo (Side-Notched)	Timmins 1995
Stewart	4	Hi-Lo	Ellis and Deller 1982
Stephenson	4	Hi-Lo (Side-Notched)	Ellis and Deller 1982
Welke-Tonkonoh	4	Hi-Lo (Lanceolate and Side-Notched)	Ellis and Deller 1982
Caradoc	4	Hi-Lo (Lanceolate)	Ellis and Deller 1982
ENL-Hi-Lo	16	Hi-Lo	Roberts 1985
Witz Locus C	23	Hi-Lo	Woodley 1997
Snow Hill	19	Hi-Lo (Lanceolate and Side-Notched)	this chapter
Double Take	19	Hi-Lo	this chapter
Allan	8	Hi-Lo (Side-Notched)	Parker 1986a, 1986b
Ageing Maple	2	Hi-Lo (Side-Notched)	Murray 1997
McKean	20	Early Archaic: Side/Corner-Notched horizon?	Lennox 2000
Welke-Tonkonoh	4	Corner-Notched and Bifurcate horizons; Middle Archaic: Stemmed Point horizon	Ellis and Deller 1982; Ellis, Kenyon, and Spence 1990: Figure 4.4e
Coates Creek	1	Early Archaic: Side-Notched horizon	Storck 1978
Nettling	5	Early Archaic: Corner-Notched horizon	Ellis et al. 1991
Culloden Area B	4	Early Archaic: Corner-Notched horizon	Ellis and Deller 1991
Trail	6	Early Archaic: Corner-Notched horizon	Dodd 1997
Cherry Hill	13	Early Archaic: Corner-Notched horizon	Wilson et al. 1997
Huson	13	Early Archaic: Corner-Notched horizon?	Stewart 2004b
Kassel	6	Early Archaic: Bifurcate horizon	Lennox 1993:4–19
Blue Dart	6	Early Archaic: Bifurcate horizon	Lennox 1993:19–24

Table 22.1. Early and Middle Archaic Sites in Ontario, continued.

Site	Map No.[a]	Designation	References
Laphroaig	7	Early Archaic: Bifurcate horizon	Woodley 1996
Slack-Caswell	9	Early Archaic: Bifurcate horizon	William Fox, pers. comm.
Baxter	21	Early Archaic: Bifurcate horizon	Dodd 1996; Lennox 2000
Morrow	10	Early Archaic: Bifurcate horizon; Middle Archaic: Laurentian	Ellis, Foster, and Jesmer 1990:350
Northoway 2	11	Middle Archaic: Stemmed horizon	Fisher et al. 1997
Poison Ivy	12	Middle Archaic: Stemmed horizon and Laurentian	Kenyon 1973; Lawrence Jackson, pers. comm.
Crowfield	4	Middle Archaic: Stemmed horizon	Deller and Ellis 1984
Farrugie	19	Middle Archaic: Stemmed horizon	this chapter
Leschuk-Weisz	19	Middle Archaic: Stemmed horizon	this chapter
Johnson Flats	22	Middle Archaic: Stemmed horizon	Parker 1995
Paget 1, 2, and 3	13	Middle Archaic: Eva-like basally notched points	Ellis 1997
Milton-Thomazi	14	Middle Archaic: unknown affiliation	Katzenberg and Sullivan 1979
East Sugar Island	12	Middle Archaic: Laurentian	Ritchie 1949
Parker	12	Middle Archaic: Laurentian	Leechman and deLaguna 1949; Ritchie 1949
Brockville	15	Middle Archaic: Laurentian	Reynolds 1856
McIntyre	12	Middle Archaic: Laurentian	Johnston 1984
ENL Otter Creek/ Brewerton	16	Middle Archaic: Laurentian	Roberts 1985:212–227
Allumette-1	17	Middle Archaic: Laurentian	Clermont et al. 2003; Kennedy 1966
Morrison's 6	17	Middle Archaic: Laurentian	Clermont and Chapdelaine 1998; Kennedy 1966
Bell	13	Middle Archaic: non-Laurentian	Williamson et al. 1994
Pascoe	18	Middle Archaic: non-Laurentian	Ellis and Deller 1986:48–52
Rentner	20	Middle Archaic: Laurentian?	Lennox 2000
Healy Falls	24	Middle Archaic: Laurentian	Ross et al. 2000
Little Shaver	23	Middle Archaic: Laurentian?	Timmins 1996
South Bend	18	Middle Archaic: non-Laurentian	this chapter

[a]Map no. refers to location on Figure 20.6.

Figure 22.7. Hi-Lo end scrapers, Welke-Tonkonah, Area C. Reproduced courtesy of the London Chapter, Ontario Archaeological Society from Ellis (20004b).

massive borers, notches, and denticulated edges. Several of the unifacial tools are made on large flakes from biface cores as well as smaller biface-thinning flakes, a typical Paleoindian trait. Moreover, some tools are clearly made on small flakes that, by the most stringent morphological definition, are small blades or apparent blade fragments. Such blanks are also reported for other Hi-Lo sites or site areas (Ellis 2004a; Timmermans 1999).

Little or no flaking debris was visible on the surface, probably because, as the excavation sample indicates, almost all of the debris is small thinning, retouch, or resharpening flakes. The excavated flaking debris assemblage included only 17 pieces, among which are two early-stage reduction flakes on Kettle Point chert weighing 2.79 and 3.25 g, which seem to represent rather expedient use of till sources. Yet all other flakes weigh under .68 g and average under .30 g. Moreover, the debris-to-tool ratio in the excavated area was only 1.8:1. The small size of flakes is also a characteristic of earlier Paleoindian sites distant from quarries, and one can argue that this indicates a strategy was followed to minimize wastage of transported raw materials by only transporting highly reduced preforms, tool blanks, and finished tools. Also, the low debris-to-tool ratio is consistent with Paleoindian sites dominated by unifacial tools. Restricting retouch and resharpening to such items would produce only the tiniest flakes, most of which are so small they are difficult to recover in even 1/8-inch (3.2-mm) mesh (for discussion, see Deller and Ellis 1992:87–88; Ellis and Deller 2000:224). However, as we discuss below, other sites suggest that the Hi-Lo staging of core-reduction activities in relation to lithic source locations was more complex and perhaps differed from that suggested for earlier assemblages. In short, some Hi-Lo sites with extensive evidence of core-reduction activities are not located at, or very near, the lithic sources employed.

The Stelco I site is partially in a plowed field near the mouth of the Grand River (Figure 22.6, No. 3) and covers some 600 m^2 (Timmins 1995). In addition to surface collection of the plowed surface, some 18 m^2 of the unplowed west edge of the site, which extended into a highway right-of-way, was excavated. This work resulted in the recovery of a homogeneous assemblage of 242 pieces of flaking debris and some 38 tools, which, with the exception of one waste flake on Onondaga chert, were made on Haldimand chert, the nearest outcrops of which are only some 21 km away. The use of Haldimand is particularly surprising as several outcrops and plentiful secondary deposits of Onondaga chert, the most commonly used material in all of southern Ontario prehistory, occur throughout the area. The nearest outcrops actually occur closer to the site than the Haldimand sources (they lie only 13 km away but in the same direction). Most of the tools are simple expedient forms, but a side-notched Hi-Lo point and tools identical to those at Welke-Tonkonoh Area C were found, the latter including three finely flaked gravers and three small end scrapers, two of which have abrupt corners or spurs at the distal end. Unlike Welke-Tonkonoh, evidence of core reduction, in the form of several larger flakes and a single core, was recovered.

The Snowhill and Double Take sites are just beginning to be analyzed, but some preliminary observations are possible. Unlike the assemblages previously described, the sites bear evidence of extensive primary reduction and have very large assemblages (each yielded over 30,000 artifacts, including flaking debris). Although both sites are multicomponent, a substantial portion of the artifacts can be attributed to the Hi-Lo occupation, and certain site areas have evidence of little occupation other than in Hi-Lo times. These are both plow-disturbed sites situated on raised terraces fronting the Grand River in Brantford, Ontario (Figure 22.6, No. 19). As is typical of many Hi-Lo sites in this region, over 95 percent of the artifacts from each assemblage are manufactured on Haldimand chert from near the mouth of the Grand River 50 km to the south.

Unlike other Hi-Lo assemblages, these collections are dominated by chipping debris (both primary and secondary) and bifaces in various stages of reduction. The presence at Snowhill of numerous cores and exhausted projectile points, many of which are shallowly side notched (Figure 22.4), suggests that early-stage tool and blank production, not just finishing and resharpening, was an important activity at the site. In contrast to the Snowhill site, end scrapers are a predominant tool type at Double Take. These resemble the end scrapers from the Hi-Lo sites described above in that they are relatively small and often made on biface thinning flakes or "blades."

As noted above, Hi-Lo assemblages exhibit considerable variability in point forms and presumably in temporal placement, and we cannot rule out the possibility of significant temporal change within these assemblages. Nonetheless, on the basis of reported assemblages, including those with side-notched points, some generalizations seem possible. What we know about the tool kits suggests similarities to Paleoindian tool kits in terms of artifact forms as well as lithic production methods, including the use of standardized core forms such as the large bifacial forms. The pending analyses of the Snowhill and Double Take debris will clarify this issue. Raw material procurement methods are also reminiscent of Paleoindian, in that one can find assemblages made predominantly on raw materials obtained at distances approaching 200 km away, as at Caradoc, where Bayport was used, or at Welke-Tonkonoh Area C, where Haldimand was the main material used. Parker (1986a, 1986b) carried out excavations at the Allen site, associated with a known Haldimand outcrop, that yielded mainly Early Archaic point forms ranging from Hi-Los to bifurcates. He also examined diagnostic points in local collections. His research indicates Haldimand chert was favored in Late Paleoindian to Early Archaic times in an extensive area of south-central Ontario but was little used before or after except in the immediate source area. The reasons for such preferences can be debated. However, sites such as Stelco I, Snowhill, and Double Take are instructive. Here Hi-Lo peoples used Haldimand to the almost total exclusion of Onondaga. Onondaga is a much more plentiful material that has better flaking qualities, outcrops closer at hand or at about the same distance as Haldimand, and unlike Haldimand was extensively used by earlier fluted point–producing groups. Yet within south-central Ontario, when Onondaga was used, as at Welke-Tonkonoh Area C or at the small Witz Locus C site just west of Lake Ontario (Woodley 1997) (Figure 22.6, No. 19), it usually appears to have been derived from secondary sources and may represent more expedient use, in contrast to the effort involved in procuring Haldimand. The focus on Haldimand seems to support Ellis's (1989) arguments that factors such as simple availability, flaking quality of materials, or lack of knowledge of sources were not the primary reasons governing raw material choice among these early groups. Certain materials seem to have been deliberately selected to the exclusion of others and for reasons that are not self-evident. Like Paleoindian, Hi-Lo sites also can contain some small amounts of even more exotic materials. For example, Bayport chert from Michigan is reported in some small site assemblages around the western end of Lake Ontario, such as Witz and Ageing Maple (see Murray 1997; Woodley 1997) (Figure 22.6, Nos. 19, 23), that are 300+ km from that source. Exotic material is also seen on earlier sites and suggests relatively wide-ranging interaction networks.

While the Hi-Lo assemblages seem to have much in common with Paleoindian, differences exist. A potential small-blade industry or, at the very least, a preference for selecting small, linear flakes for tool use and the consistently small size and oval shape of many end scrapers are not seen in presumably earlier assemblages, particularly on fluted-point sites, or even in possibly contemporary lanceolate-point assemblages concentrated more to the north. Both, however, are characteristic of presumably earlier Holcombe assemblages, including even the use of the small "blades" for the same tool forms, such as concave side scrapers (see Fitting et al. 1966: Figures 8r–w, 9e–i). This evidence, along with the similarities in point forms, reinforces the idea that, somehow, Hi-Lo technology is closely related to and derived from Holcombe assemblages. In short, continuity appears to exist between lanceolate- and notched-point industries in this area. Very little evidence suggests connections between Hi-Lo and normal conceptions of the Archaic. In fact, aside from point notching and foresection edge beveling, only limited characteristics of Hi-Lo assemblages are more Archaic-like. One such characteristic is the frequency of these assemblages. Where more detailed data are available, and taking into account biases in frequency because of extensive excavations at some fluted-point sites, Hi-Lo points are five to six times more common than any earlier or possibly contemporary form (e.g., Deller 1989; Roberts 1985:82–83; Williamson et al. 2002:Table 2). Whether this is due to population increases or simply to a longer period of use and use for more tasks (recall that Hi-Lo points are often laterally beveled and recycled into other uses) cannot be determined. Another difference concerns the suggestions of extensive primary lithic reduction activities some 50 km from the quarries, as evident at the Snowhill and Double Take sites. No earlier Paleoindian sites with such evidence are known beyond about 25 km from the source used (e.g., Storck and von Bitter 1989:176). However, these Hi-Lo sites may be exceptions because of their geographic situation: They are located on a major water route, the aptly named Grand River, that links them directly to the main sources of Haldimand chert to the south. In sum, direct access using watercraft may have obviated the need to highly reduce the chert and transform it into more portable forms prior to transporting it away from source locations.

Aside from the Hi-Lo variants, other probable Early Archaic side-notched forms that may date in the general pre–9000 RCYBP period are not well documented. Large side-notched points have been found that are steeply beveled and sometimes serrated and that correspond to, or closely resemble, midwestern types like Thebes (e.g., Allen and Ellis 2004; Ellis and Deller 1986:Figure 10d) or more southeastern types such as Big Sandy (e.g., Ellis, Kenyon, and Spence 1990:Figure 4.4e, f). The only potential pre-9000 site with such points is McKean (Lennox 2000) located near Georgian Bay on Lake Huron (Figure 22.6, No. 20). The investigator interprets the site as a single component, and one point with a steep bevel and a second foresection with serrated edges seem comfortable as Early Archaic forms. Moreover, several finely made gravers, side scrapers, and end scrapers occur, which would not be inconsistent with such an assignment (Lennox 2000:Figures 20, 21). Nevertheless, some of the other notched-point basal fragments recovered (Lennox 2000:Figure 19e, f), although related by the investigator to midwestern Early Archaic types such as St. Charles points, would not be out of place in later Archaic assemblages. The examples are quite fragmentary and could easily be related to later corner-notched styles such as the ca. 8,000-year-old corner-notched Swanton points of western New England (Thomas 1992:Figure 5) or even to later Middle Archaic Brewerton-style points. The Middle Archaic assignment is also supported by the only date reported from a feature, 4700 ± 170 RCYBP, which is consistent with Brewerton dates elsewhere (see below). The feature lacked diagnostics, although the spatially closest diagnostic was a corner-notched point. Regardless, at present we do not think it easy to consider this a single-component Early Archaic site.

The only other potential early side-notched site is Coates Creek (Storck 1978), located in the same area of Ontario as McKean. The points include not only a single large, side-notched form but also two lanceolate Paleoindian ones as well as some gravers. The point is not particularly diagnostic, so the site may be multicomponent with both a Paleoindian and a later component, or it may be an example, better known from the upper Great Lakes (e.g., Mason and Irwin 1960), of the occasional production of side-notched points by predominantly lanceolate-point users. However, the styles of Paleoindian points found at upper Great Lakes sites seem to much postdate 9000 RCYBP, suggesting they are unrelated to the earliest side-notched points of concern here.

Corner-Notched Horizon

Basic aspects of whole Early Archaic stone tool kits are best known for the Corner-Notched horizon, and this is largely due to work at one site in southwestern Ontario, Nettling (Ellis, Kenyon, and Spence 1990:73–78; Ellis et al. 1991; McMillan 2003). Now just inland from the modern shore of Lake Erie (Figure 22.6, No. 5), at the time of the occupations, given the lowered water levels in that basin, it would have been 25 km or more inland. The site is in a plowed field and, aside from brief test excavations, is known through surface collections, which began in the 1960s. The site collection now includes over 1,675 tools and preforms. Most of the projectile points—over 175 diagnostic corner-notched and serrated points—relate to the Kirk Corner-Notched type cluster (Figure 22.8). Material at the site clusters on two small knolls beside an ephemeral, now-dry, third-order streambed. Called Nettling "North" and "South," these areas are separated from each other by about 10 m and cover 800 m^2 and 600 m^2, respectively. A much smaller cluster of material lies about 15 m to the south and is called the "peripheral" cluster. Traces of Late Woodland site use occur in both the north and south clusters, and a single Hi-Ho point, five bifurcate-based points, and a few Early and Middle Woodland diagnostics have come from Nettling North. No evidence of later occupations has been found in the peripheral cluster.

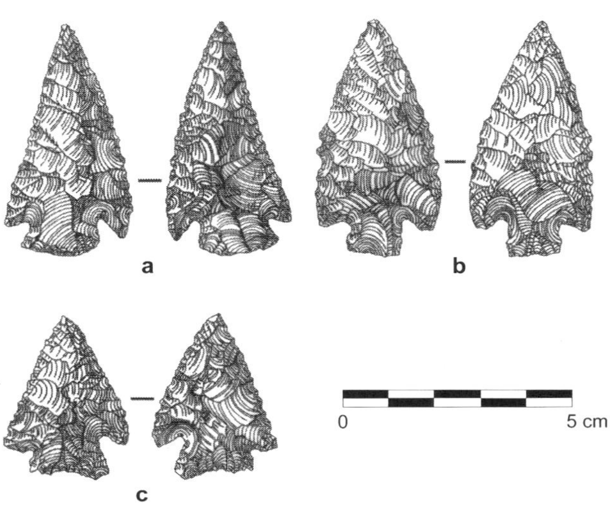

Figure 22.8. Corner-notched serrated points, Nettling site. Drawings by Janie Ravenhurst.

The most characteristic items at the site are identical to those reported from Kirk Corner Notched–cluster sites in the Southeast (compare with Chapman 1975, 1978; Coe 1964; etc.) and include items on both cherts and coarse-grained rocks: large trianguloid bifacial knives (n = 27; Figure 22.9a); expanding-based to notched "drills" (n = 28); small, teardrop-shaped end scrapers (n = 133; Figure 22.9d, e), often with "all-over" dorsal flaking; celts (n = 32) and celt preforms (n = 6) that have been pecked, if on slate, or flaked, if on metasediments, into their basic shape and then had only their bits ground (Figure 22.10a); large ovate chopper-scrapers (n = 2); and a host of other less diagnostic forms such as denticulates and used flakes. These detailed tool-kit similarities to the classic southeastern assemblages leave no doubt about the site's affinities, but two distinctive and relatively common artifact forms from Nettling have not been reported from the Corner-Notched horizon in the Southeast.

One such form (n = 20) is a hafted, concave side scraper (Figure 22.9b, c). These have an extensively flaked stem, in rare cases even bifacially, to aid fitting in a handle. The foresection has an extensively retouched concave margin,

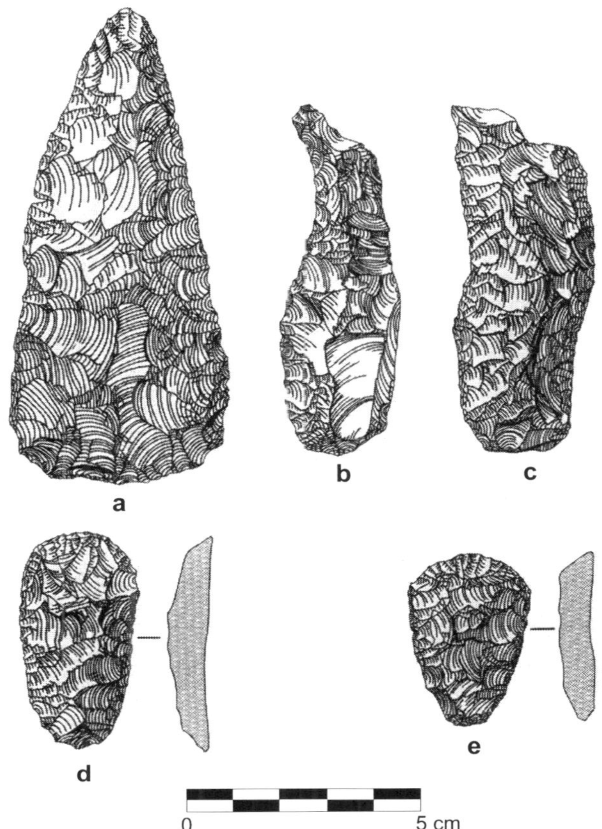

Figure 22.9. Nettling site flaked-stone tools: a, trianguloid biface; b, c, hafted concave side scrapers; d, e, end scrapers with all-over dorsal flaking. Drawings by Janie Ravenhurst.

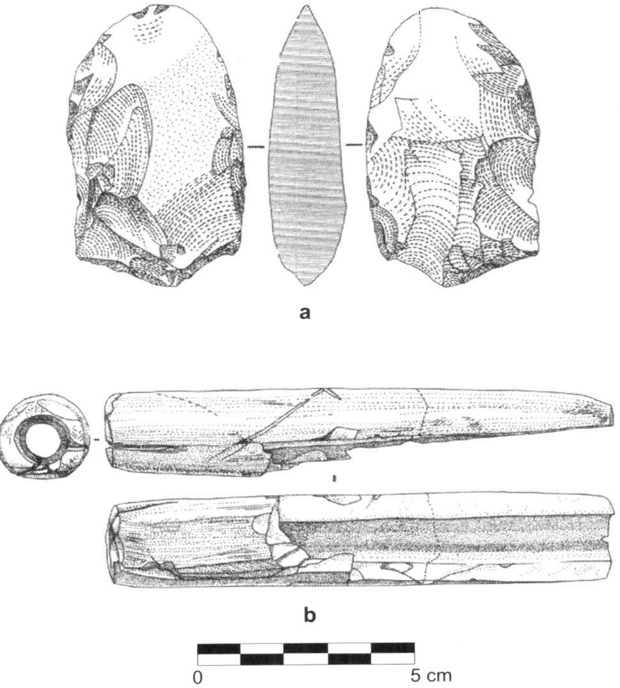

Figure 22.10. Nettling site ground stone; a, chipped celt with ground bit; b, ground-stone tube. Drawings by Janie Ravenhurst.

which almost always is on the left foresection edge when the items are viewed dorsally with the base to the bottom. While exact duplicates may not be reported from Kirk sites, virtually identical items occur in Dalton and other lanceolate point–related assemblages, in which they are variously called "backed" unifaces (Morse 1997:Figure 3.15a; Redfield and Moselage 1970:Figure 6h) or "Hendrix" scrapers-knives (Purdy 1986:18). Also, many Early Archaic sites also yield concave-edge tools with notched, rather than stemmed, bases, such as the Edgefield scraper (Michie 1973). More surprising is a second form found at Nettling: fully ground and polished slate tubes (Figure 22.10b). These are represented by six complete items as well as seven preforms, which range from simple pecked-out, elongated forms to examples broken in drilling. The finished items are not just simple circular tubes in cross section but have been deliberately flattened along one side. The drill holes average 12 mm in diameter. The number of such items and the presence of preforms indicate they are not isolated losses. While they might relate to possible later occupations at the site, the dominance of classic Kirk notched material at Nettling, the recovery of the tubes from all three known concentrations of Kirk material, including the peripheral cluster, the lack of any consistent diagnostics in all three areas other than the Kirk material, and an actual absence of later occupations in one of those areas suggest an Early Archaic association. Also, an absence of reports of anything remotely resembling these tubes in association with the few later diagnostics at the site reinforces, to us, the idea that this is a real association. If so, these would be among the earliest fully ground stone tools in the East.

The Nettling site is also of interest for what it says about lithic source preferences. Excluding unidentified materials, on the basis of the totals as of 1991, 60 percent of the chert tools and preforms and 76 percent of the flaking debris are on Selkirk and Onondaga cherts, which are derived mainly from secondary deposits, presumably near the site. The remaining materials are mainly on exotic Ohio-source materials, predominantly Pipe Creek chert (21 percent tools and preforms, 17 percent debris) from across Lake Erie some 175+ km away, and Upper Mercer chert from south-central Ohio (19 percent tools and preforms, 7 percent debris) over 300 km away. The high percentages of the Ohio cherts suggest, at the very least, extensive interaction networks and may even indicate extensive mobility patterns. In fact, by examining relative frequencies of certain artifact categories, patterns emerge that suggest mobility or range covered is at least partially responsible for the high percentages of Ohio cherts.

For example, if one examines unfinished bifaces or preforms, one finds that 85 percent are on the local Ontario cherts, but only 43 percent of the finished bifaces are of local material. In contrast, the Ohio cherts are represented among only 14 percent of the preforms but 55 percent of the finished bifaces. Comparable patterns are seen among the unifaces, with more formal hafted and, one presumes, curated tools such as end scrapers more often on Ohio cherts (71 percent), whereas simpler, handheld, and more expedient tools such as denticulates are predominantly on local Ontario cherts (61 percent). This pattern is highly suggestive of a cyclical movement between the Ohio and Ontario source areas. At Nettling, as worn-out and more often-curated finished tools on Ohio cherts were discarded, they were being replaced by tools made on-site on local cherts. Such cyclical movement between different source areas seems characteristic of much of the Archaic and, although not necessarily at the huge geographic scale implied here, in terms of simple direct-line distances to sources, might suggest a range mobility much beyond that of groups of all other time periods save the very earliest Paleoindians.

The Nettling site is of interest, as well, for the large amount of material recovered, considering it is represented only by a surface collection. The large number of items from the small area of the site (more than one item per square meter) is much beyond that found at any earlier sites that have been extensively excavated, and this information could be used (and has been, e.g., Ellis et al. 1998:162) to speculate on longer residential stays and, consequently, reduced residential mobility or patterns of movement involving more consistent return to the same site location (e.g., entrenched mobility; Graham and Roberts 1986). However, such inferences should be treated with caution. A large percentage of the recovered items are preforms or probable fragments thereof (50 percent), most of which, as noted above, are on site-local cherts; so the great density of material may be due to the site having served partially as a gearing-up locality where knappers took advantage of local sources to replenish tool kits, discarded lots of rough outs in the process, and may even have cleaned out tool kits of exhausted or nearly exhausted tools. Since many of the bifaces are complete and show no apparent cause for discard, they may also represent caches, hence, inflating artifact totals. Perhaps the large numbers of stone tubes recovered are also from caches, perhaps sacred ones, for example, from burials, but this is absolute speculation.

All other sites that have been reported tend to be small, ephemeral, and mainly, although not exclusively, from plowed fields, and we describe here some typical examples. One small site is Culloden Acres Area B, which was discovered accidentally during examination of a fluted-point component at the same site (Ellis and Deller 1991) (Figure 22.6, No. 4). Excavation of a 14-m^2 area uncovered nine tools and 71 pieces of flaking debris. Included were two points, a preform, a graver, and, of special note since they confirm associations suggested at other sites, a fragment of a hafted concave side scraper and two distinctive, dorsally flaked end scrapers. Almost all of the material (> 90 percent) was on Onondaga chert, apparently derived from secondary deposits, the nearest sources of which seem to occur about 20 km east of the site in the Thames River valley. The remainder, including one of the points, was on Kettle Point chert from 50 km to the northwest. Two concentrations of debris seem to be present, one including the end scrapers and graver and the other the bifaces and concave scraper. The same spatial separation of artifact forms was seen in the earlier Paleoindian component.

Another example is the Trail site (Dodd 1997) on the Grand River (Figure 22.6, No. 6). Excavation of a 40 m^2 area yielded a single point, a biface edge fragment, and six expedient unifaces as well 286 pieces of flaking debris. A point and two unifaces are of Haldimand chert, but all of the rest of the material, including all of the flaking debris, is Onondaga. This is one of the few sites where an attempt has been made to identify whether the Onondaga is from bedrock outcrops or secondary deposits, and the results suggest that both were used but predominantly the bedrock sources. The closest sources of all materials are about 80 km south of this site.

Similar to the Trail site is the Cherry Hill site on the Niagara Peninsula south of Lake Ontario (Wilson et al. 1997). Although traces of Late Archaic Lamoka occupation occurred on the periphery, the main cluster of material appears to be Early Archaic, was concentrated in an area of about 50 m^2, and tended to be below the plow zone, for reasons that are not clear. The depth could simply reflect that the site is of sufficient age for natural processes to have led to some movement of artifacts down into the B soil horizon, as has been suggested at some other sites (e.g., Anderton 1999; Creemens 2003). The artifact assemblage (n = 9) included three corner-notched and serrated points, two biface preforms, an end scraper and a drill similar to those reported from other components, a concave side scraper, and an expedient uniface. One of the points was on Selkirk chert, but all of the other items, plus 661 pieces of flaking debris dominated by late-stage thinning and resharpening flakes, were on Onondaga chert. While primary and secondary sources of Onondaga occur about 25 km south of the site, the nearest Selkirk sources are about 120 km away to the west.

Located near Cherry Hill is the Huson site (Stewart 2004b). Situated in a woodlot, the excavation of 56 m^2 produced 27 formed artifacts and over 9,000 pieces of flaking debris, all of Onondaga chert, the nearest sources of which are about 40 km south of the site. The recovered artifacts included a drill with a squared-off base, four preform fragments, two typical end scrapers, a graver, and several expedient tools and fragments. No points were recovered, but the end scraper and drill forms are very distinctive. Three discrete concentrations were isolated by piece plotting all of the debris in the central site area, which seem to be feature remnants, the best preserved of which included only Zone 2 pollen (e.g., pine-dominated), supporting an early Holocene age for the occupation. As at Culloden B, the unifaces seem to cluster spatially separate from the bifaces at this site.

The above assemblages do not provide much of a basis for generalization, but some comments are in order. Some continuity from earlier assemblages is clearly suggested. The high quality of the workmanship is one example, as is the use of exotic raw materials, at least, at Nettling, which suggests extensive social networks, a high distance mobility, or both. Nonetheless, differences from those earlier assemblages are also clear. The density of material at Nettling might be used to argue for reduced residential mobility or more entrenched patterns of movement. As cautioned above, generalizing from a single site is difficult, and the number of preform rejects made on site-local cherts may inflate assemblage size versus those sites where such an activity was not carried out. Even excluding the preforms, however, the over 800 items from the site are clearly more than from any other early Ontario site of comparable size, and we note that other sites similar to Nettling probably exist. On the basis of the frequency of points in local amateur collections, we know of other very productive sites in southwestern Ontario, along and just inland from the modern north Erie shore, but they have not been examined at the level of detail or attention to maintaining a strict provenience as has Nettling. Moreover, most of those sites seem to have many extensive later components, which make comparable analyses difficult. Also, whereas the emphasis on the exotic cherts at Nettling may be used to argue for high mobility by the users of that site, for every other site, including surface-collected ones, for which we have information, the cherts used are not from such *extreme* distances, and most assemblages are based on relatively local Ontario cherts. The focus on more local cherts is also evident in adjacent New York State to the east (Smith et al. 1998:21). The use of exotics may have been characteristic only of those groups who used southwesternmost Ontario, or Nettling may represent a relatively early Corner-Notched-horizon site, occupied when more extensive range mobility was characteristic. Some Ohio researchers, noting the close resemblances of this material to southeastern assemblages, want to see it as reflecting population intrusions from the south (e.g., Stothers and Abel 1991). While we are not convinced of this, one could argue that a site such as Nettling dates to the earliest period of occupation of groups extending their ranges into Ontario from Ohio, so not just normal settlement mobility was involved.

Regardless, with the exception of Nettling, more local source use appears to have been typical, and this could suggest some changes from earlier times. Even so, some of the Ontario sources, particularly Onondaga, are available over a wide area in both extensive primary and secondary deposits; recall that both seem to have been used at certain sites, such as Trail. This distribution means that Early Archaic assemblages in which such material is common could actually represent groups who moved over fairly extensive areas, at least equivalent to those suggested for occupants of Hi-Lo sites. For example, if a group exploited an area from west of the Grand River east into the Niagara Peninsula or even beyond, into New York State, a linear distance of 200 km+, it could have exploited Onondaga sources throughout that whole range. We also believe that some evidence, to be discussed below, could even suggest Late Archaic groups ranged fairly widely. Note also that earlier groups, including Hi-Lo, seem to have ignored certain available sources, whereas during the later Early Archaic, these preferences declined. Therefore, by limiting source use, the earlier groups were forced to move certain materials over longer distances, whereas the later groups did not. In sum, researchers may be dealing with apparent contrasts here that have nothing to do directly with the mobility of people but, instead, with the mobility of lithics. Nonetheless, whatever one concludes about mobility, the absence of even small amounts of very exotic materials at sites other than Nettling is not suggestive of widespread interaction networks.

While Ellis (1989) may have overstressed the use of primary sources by Paleoindians in the area, they certainly seem to have relied far more on primary sources than Corner-Notched-horizon peoples, and in that horizon one can begin to document a more laissez-faire attitude toward lithic procurement. This is signaled not just by more extensive use of secondary deposits but also by the use of more coarse-grained materials. While it is certainly true that even Paleoindians used coarser-grained materials on occasion for more expedient tools (e.g., Deller and Ellis 1992:87; Woodley 2004), sites such as Nettling evidence much more extensive use of these materials than anything seen on earlier sites and in wider contexts (e.g., for less expedient tools). Finally, the Nettling site, with its mix of local Ontario and exotic Ohio materials, suggests serial visits to, and extensive use of, multiple sources of raw materials, something archaeologists have not yet been able to demonstrate very easily, if at all, on earlier sites, particularly fluted-point ones. Of note, as well, is that at some of the small sites described above, such as Trail, Cherry Hill, and Culloden B, points seem to be made on different materials more often than the rest of the assemblage. Very similar patterns are noted in later Archaic assemblages, and this pattern might also be used to argue for serial source use or, perhaps, as suggested for earlier Paleoindian materials (e.g., Deller 1989), that such items were circulated more often in exchange systems.

Numerous other changes are evident in Early Archaic tool kits compared with those of earlier times. An increasing reliance on more expedient flaked-stone tools is apparent, and items such as side scrapers are generally rare unless they are hafted or concave forms that required more extensive shaping to haft or to produce the desired working edge. The introduction of probable atlatl weights (e.g., the tubes) and larger, formal woodworking tools such as celts are other obvious differences. There are also suggestions of differences in tool production from earlier assemblages. One difference is the use of ground stone, but there are others, as well. The best evidence of changing production techniques comes from the work of McMillan (2003), who carried out detailed comparisons of the large Nettling site end-scraper assemblage with several earlier, largely fluted point–related, assemblages of these tools. These studies suggest that in comparison with at least the very earliest fluted-point assemblages (Clovis-like or Gainey), end scrapers from Nettling had been resharpened less or were less exhausted at discard. Yet, in terms of haft standardization, they exhibit as little variability as the most standardized of Paleoindian industries and are even more standardized compared with some of the later Paleoindian assemblages. They really differ from all the Paleoindian samples in how that standardization was achieved. Most Paleoindian scrapers have little postblank detachment modification and exhibit largely marginal retouch; they were shaped on the core often through standardized core-reduction techniques. In direct contrast, the Nettling scrapers were extensively shaped after blank detachment, and the most obvious examples of this production strategy are those varieties with the extensive all-over dorsal flaking. All of these new technological characteristics are clearly seen as Archaic ones by most investigators, so little basis exists from an artifact perspective for seeing these Ontario assemblages as little different from Paleoindian ones, as some have suggested for other areas (e.g., Gardner 1977). Corner-Notched-horizon assemblages clearly are different in southern Ontario and even seem to differ from Hi-Lo and Side-Notched assemblages, trending in a more Archaic "direction."

Finally, Corner-Notched-horizon materials, in comparison with all earlier assemblages are very common. Whenever point samples are compared, corner-notched and serrated forms are consistently 10–15 times as common as earlier forms such as Hi-Lo and Side-Notched and 100+ times as common as fluted points (Roberts 1985:Table AI-3; Williamson et al. 2002:Table 2; Wright 1978). This increase in number does not seem to be due to a longer period of use. Taking into account late Pleistocene fluctuations in atmospheric carbon, if anything, each of the earlier classes was used for a longer period of time than the corner-notched materials, which, on the basis of southeastern dates, seem to have been used for about 600 radiocarbon years, at most. Neither can the frequency of these items be related to extensive use in different contexts, as very little evidence other than a few drills suggests that the notched points were recycled or used extensively for varied tasks any more than points in earlier Hi-Lo assemblages. In fact, using the Nettling site as a guide, only about 23 percent have (slight) alternate beveling as opposed to the steep lateral beveling seen on many more Hi-Lo points (69 percent at sites such as Welke-Tonkonoh). This evidence suggests, at a minimum, some very different patterns of tool use and discard than those seen among earlier groups or, we think just as likely, population increases. Some have argued that the arrival of the "pine pollen zone," and an inferred sterile pine forest, led to actual population declines in the area from Paleoindian to Early Archaic times (e.g., Fitting 1968; Ritchie 1971a). In agreement with investigators such as Wright (1978:69) and Roberts (1985:250), we think the nature of these environments has been overgeneralized and see little or no evidence for a population decline in southern Ontario, especially considering that a substantial part of the Early Archaic record is probably now under the waters of the eastern Great Lakes.

Bifurcate Horizon

Because of their distinctive basal morphology, bifurcate-based points were the first definitive Early Archaic point forms recognized in Ontario (Noble 1975). Nonetheless, little is yet known about these materials. Compilations of isolated finds in various collections suggest in some cases that they occur with about the same frequency as earlier corner-notched forms (Wright 1978), but in others, as is the case in adjacent areas of Ohio to the south (e.g., Stothers 1996) and New York to the east (Smith et al. 1998:25), they actually appear to be rarer, sometimes less than half as common, as the earlier forms (Roberts 1985:Table AI-3; Williamson et al. 2002: Table 2). If anything, we think bifurcate frequency is overestimated, as the tendency has been to call almost any small, stemmed, concave-based point "bifurcated," and this creates difficulties in distinguishing them from subsequent early Middle Archaic stemmed and concave-based points. Certainly no large sites comparable to Nettling have been reported, nor do we know of any local collections suggesting comparable sites exist. Excavated sites are rare, have largely been reported within the last 10 years, and are uniformly small, resembling most of the small Corner-Notched-horizon components describer earlier.

Two of the sites, Kassel and Blue Dart (Lennox 1993), are located about a kilometer apart and were excavated in advance of highway construction. Both are situated on small, sandy ridges or points of land surrounded by wetlands bordering a tributary of the Grand River (Figure 22.6, No. 6). They were in woodlots at the time of construction, although they may have been plowed shallowly in the past. Kassel covers about 170 m^2, most of which was excavated. The 79 tools and preforms recovered included seven points, 15 preforms or fragments, four stemless, rodlike bifaces, 18 side and end scrapers, and a range of other simpler, expedient tools. The points have relatively short, broad stems that lack lateral grinding; show narrow, pointed corners, rather than more lobate ears; have deeply notched bases formed usually by several small flake removals; and exhibit straight to slightly concave foresections (Figure 22.11a–c). They seem to be good analogs for the LeCroy Bifurcated Stem points of the Southeast, as defined by Broyles (1971:69). Two of the rodlike bifaces have pointed tips and diamond-shaped cross sections and were referred to by the site investigator as "drills," whereas two others, which were made on flakes and were only marginally retouched on the interior face, were relatively short and broad with rounded working ends and a more biconvex cross section and were placed with other items in a "retouched bladelet" category (Lennox 1993:8, 14–15). Neither form is reported from earlier Ontario sites such as Nettling, but the first form noted occurs in apparent Corner-Notched- and Bifurcate-horizon sites in the Southeast (e.g., Chapman 1977:77–78). The end scrapers recovered are all very small (< 26 mm long), relatively oval in shape, and relatively poorly made and do not closely resemble any of the Nettling examples. However, they are very similar to, and at face value would seem to be difficult to distinguish from, later end-scraper forms extending even into the Late Archaic. Excepting five of the scrapers, which are on Kettle Point chert from the northwest (see Figures 22.1 and 22.6), the remaining items (93 percent) are on Onondaga chert, which had to have come from sources at least 80 km to the south. The 1,084 pieces of flaking debris recovered are dominated by later-stage reduction debris (cores are absent) and are also predominantly (96 percent) on Onondaga.

The Blue Dart site covers only 25 m^2 and was completely excavated. Only six tools were recovered, including a point, an obvious trianguloid preform for a similar point, a large biface knife, and three expedient unifaces. The point and preform

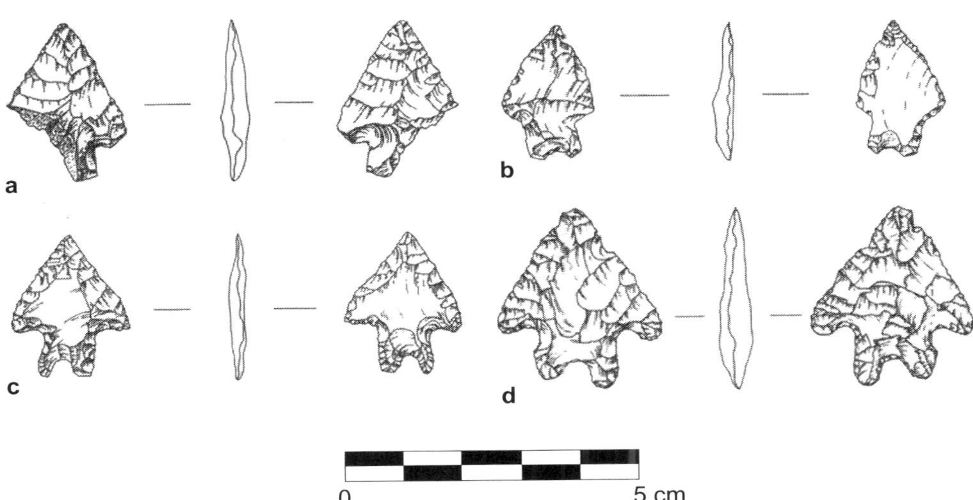

Figure 22.11. Bifurcate-base points, Kassel and Blue Dart sites. Drawings by John MacDonald. Reproduced courtesy of Paul Lennox and with the permission of the Main Body, Ontario Archaeological Society, Inc., Toronto, Ontario, from Lennox (1993).

are of Onondaga chert, the knife of Haldimand, and the three unifaces of Kettle Point. In contrast, 86 percent of the debris, which is dominated by later-stage thinning and retouch flakes, is Onondaga, and only trace amounts of the other materials occur. The point is a stemmed LeCroy-like form identical to those seen at the nearby Blue Dart site (Figure 22.11d). A notable discovery at the site was a single feature containing sugar maple and pine charcoal as well as flaking debris, which corresponded to the most dense topsoil concentration of debris. The pine charcoal yielded an AMS date of 8320 ± 60 RCYBP (see Table 22.2), essentially identical to the dates reported for LeCroy components in the Southeast (e.g., Chapman 1976). Hence, Blue Dart is the earliest directly dated archaeological site in southern Ontario.

Another important component is found at the Baxter site (Dodd 1996; Lennox 2000:57) located near the Severn River near the eastern shore of Georgian Bay (Figure 22.6, No. 21). The site is located in a depression between two surface bedrock exposures and is predominantly a substantial Middle Woodland site. However, in the northern part of the site a scatter of items included a bifurcate-based point; three bifaces, two of which are linear and bipointed; a pointed drill bit; four expedient unifaces; and 44 pieces of debris, including a bipolar core. The point is expanding stemmed with lobed stem corners and a 5-mm-deep basal notch, and has a trianguloid foresection with slightly concave edges. It seems most similar to the Kanawha Stemmed type, the latest-dating bifurcate type in the Southeast (Broyles 1971:59; Chapman 1975). The Baxter site is notable for two reasons. First, all of the artifacts have a brown patina, and some are demonstrably water rolled; it is these characteristics that allow the artifacts to be isolated from the Middle Woodland component. The patina is probably limonite precipitated during submergence in the shallow, oxygen-rich waters of the Nipissing phase, which rose to cover the locality around 5500–5000 RCYBP. This patina is comparable to that seen at a series of sites and finds on and below the maximum Nipissing-phase strand in the southeastern Lake Huron basin area reported earlier by Ellis and Deller (1986). No bifurcates were found in that more southerly area, but earlier Corner-Notched-horizon points

Table 22.2. Radiocarbon Dates for Ontario Early and Middle Archaic Sites.

Site	Point Form	Lab No.	RCYBP	S.D.	Uncalibrated B.C. Dates	Calibrated B.C. Dates[a]	Reference
Blue Dart	Bifurcate, LeCroy	TO-2592	8320	60	6370	7520–7200	Lennox 1993
Milton-Thomazi	Burial; no artifacts	GX-5193G	5910	165	3960	4960–4550	Katzenberg and Sullivan 1979
Allumettes	Otter Creek (Vergennes)	S-509	5240	80	3290	4230–3960	Wright 1972a
Allumettes	Otter Creek (Vergennes)	Beta-141985	5440	40	3490	4340–4245	Clermont and Chapdelaine 1998
Allumettes	Otter Creek (Vergennes)	Beta-141986	5270	40	3320	4220–3990	Clermont and Chapdelaine 1998
Allumettes	Otter Creek/ Brewerton?	Beta-141987	4680	40	2730	3520–3370	Clermont and Chapdelaine 1998
Morrison's Island	Brewerton series	Beta-88725	4620	40	2670	3500–3350	Clermont et al. 2003
Morrison's Island	Brewerton series	Beta-88852	4630	40	2680	3500–3350	Clermont et al. 2003
Morrison's Island	Brewerton series	GSC-162	4700	150	2750	3700–3100	Kennedy 1966
Morrison's Island	Brewerton series	Beta-88851	4860	50	2910	3710–3540	Clermont et al. 2003
McKean	Brewerton series?	TO-6096	4700	170	2750	3700–3100	Lennox 2000
Rentner	Brewerton series?	BGS-1718	5900	90	3950	4910–4540	Lennox 2000

[a]Calibrated dates are one-sigma ranges derived from Oxcal Program v3.9, University of Oxford, Radiocarbon Accelerator Unit (Ramsey 2003).

and a single Thebes-like point as well as subsequent Middle Archaic materials (see below) were found. In short, these sites, including Baxter, provide direct Ontario evidence of a pre-Nipissing age for bifurcate and other points. Baxter is also important because of its location. It is the northernmost bifurcate site ever reported.

To sum up, in contrast to all earlier horizons, no use of very exotic cherts is evident at Bifurcate-horizon sites, and no direct evidence from straight-line distance to source preferences suggests extensive range mobility or interaction networks. Debris samples and detailed technological analyses are limited, but there also seems to be little evidence of standardized core reduction. Unifacial assemblages, including the end-scraper forms produced, are not that distinctive and seem little different than the better-known later Archaic developments. Some evidence from sites such as Baxter suggests that Early Archaic groups of this time were ranging farther north, but at the same time, bifurcate sites and finds seem rarer than those of earlier times. This might be a reflection of changing use contexts or frequencies of use of points rather than a measure of population decline. The apparent decrease may not reflect temporal duration, as these tool forms seem to have been used for almost a thousand radiocarbon years, estimated on the basis of information from elsewhere. Most finds in Ontario are of forms approximating later bifurcate types such as LeCroy or Kanawha Stemmed, so the duration of use may have been truncated. Also, as is becoming clear, bifurcates were not the only points in use at this time in areas just to the east, such as Vermont. For example, at the Well's Bridge site, there are corner-notched points well dated to around 7800–8200 RCYBP (Thomas 1992:191–194) that, we suspect, if found in Ontario would be largely lumped in with later types such as Brewerton. In sum, if types other than bifurcates were in use in some areas such as eastern Ontario, the frequency of the bifurcate points is not a good indicator of population trends.

The Middle Archaic

Middle Archaic prior to 5500 RCYBP

The Middle Archaic is, as noted earlier, defined here as encompassing assemblages dated between ca. 8000 and 4500 RCYBP. The earliest developments, prior to 5500 RCYBP, are very poorly known, such that we consider that period the "black hole" of Ontario archaeology. The main suggestions of occupation are, as in the preceding Bifurcate horizon, the presence in local collections of certain point styles resembling those found elsewhere and the very occasional, small, apparently single-component site. The earliest material probably includes stemmed points related to developments dated elsewhere to ca. 8000 to 7500 RCYBP and assigned to point types such as Kirk Stemmed and Kirk Serrated (Chapman 1980:127; Coe 1964; Sherwood et al. 2004) or the Stanly Stemmed of the Southeast (Coe 1964) and Neville Stemmed (Dincauze 1975) of New England. While the Kirk Stemmed and Serrated variants are extremely rare, the other stemmed point styles actually seem to be relatively common in local collections. Also, multiple excavated examples have been recovered from multicomponent sites across southern Ontario, such as Poison Ivy in southeastern Ontario, where they occurred intermixed with later Laurentian Archaic and Woodland materials (Kenyon 1973 and personal observation), and Crowfield in southwestern Ontario, better known for its Paleoindian as well as Late Woodland components (Deller and Ellis 1984). While we may relate points from these sites to Stanly or Neville forms, the Ontario points are certainly not classic examples of either type, and one can also debate whether they should be classified as bifurcates or as subsequent Middle Archaic stemmed forms. Three sites of note in this regard are Laphroaig (Woodley 1996) and Farrugie and Leschuk-Weisz (Timmins Martelle Heritage Consultants 2003).

Laphroaig is near the Grand River at Brantford, Ontario (Figure 22.6, No. 7) and was found in advance of highway construction. Although located in a formerly plowed area, and although a Middle Woodland point was found on the periphery, most of the site material formed a nice, tight cluster encompassing about 40 m^2, all of which was excavated. Finds included five points or fragments thereof and 32 other artifacts, among which were five preforms, a biface knife, an end scraper, and several expedient unifaces. Most of the tools at the site are actually expedient ones, and the cores recovered include bipolar and random forms suggesting unstructured and relatively informal core-reduction practices. Thirty-eight percent of these artifacts were on Haldimand and 54 percent on Onondaga cherts; the closest sources of both are near the mouth of the Grand River some 50 km to the south. Comparable frequencies of these materials were found among the detritus recovered (39 percent and 46 percent, respectively).

The Laphroaig site points are suggested by the site investigator to most closely resemble Lake Erie Bifurcated–type points and are referred to the Early Archaic (Woodley 1996:50–51). Just what defines a Lake Erie Bifurcate, however, is not clear, as there have been many varying definitions (compare Converse 1973; Justice 1987:92–95; Payne 1982:49; Prufer and Sofsky 1965:31–32), and some consider it a "semi-discredited" type (Smith et al. 1998:29). The points have short, broad, relatively parallel-sided stems. The basal ears are slightly flaring and pointed to somewhat lobate, but still quite narrow in plan. Foresections are small and narrow with triangular outlines, and only one example is serrated. Comparable points have had a somewhat variable classification history. A few investigators, such as Funk and Wellman (1984:Plate 6, 36–39) refer to them as "Kanawha-like," but they deviate from the classic Kanawha forms as defined by Broyles (1971:59) in that they can have parallel-sided stems and lack the broad, lobate ears.

Most investigators actually seem to see closer relationships to types such as Stanly points, usually attributed to the Middle Archaic. For example, Chapman (1977:35, Figures 15g and 16a) illustrates points from the Icehouse Bottom site in Tennessee that are exactly the same size and have exactly the same attributes (short, broad stem; slightly flaring, narrow corners) as the Laphroaig points. He notes that they "share many attributes with the Stanly Stemmed type" (Chapman 1977:35) and that most were actually recovered in the same stratigraphic levels as definitive Stanly materials and above the layers containing the definitive bifurcate types. Moreover, Wright (1978:62–64) discusses identical finds of stemmed points from southern Ontario and Smith et al. (1998) from adjacent western New York, which they also relate to Stanly as well as Neville types. These finds do deviate from classic Stanly and Neville forms in that the stems are parallel rather than contracting, in a tendency toward narrower, smaller blade sections, and in having slightly flared ears. However, for our purposes, and especially since the bases at Laphroaig are not noticeably "bifurcated" (e.g., they do not appear "notched" but are simply broadly and shallowly concave), we follow Wright's (1978) lead and assign sites with these kinds of points to the Middle Archaic, with a date beginning somewhere around 8000 RCYBP.

The Leshcuk-Weisz and Farrugie sites are located on a sandy terrace overlooking the Nith River (Figure 22.6, No. 19). The sites are in plow-disturbed fields and are clustered around two small relict watercourses separated by a distance of approximately 150 m. The Leschuk-Weisz site is a small base camp measuring 132 m^2, while the Farrugie site consists of three considerably smaller loci or activity areas (70 m^2, 22 m^2, and 19 m^2 in size). That all four areas produced early Middle Archaic Stanly-like points suggests that all four occupations were likely contemporary, but the artifact assemblage from the Leschuk-Weisz site is more diverse than that from the other three loci, whether considered individually or together.

As hinted above, the projectile points are also not easy to classify. Morphologically, as do the points from Laphroaig, they appear transitional between late Early Archaic bifurcate types like Kanawha Stemmed (Broyles 1966:27) and early Middle Archaic Stanly and Neville forms (Figure 22.12). Like earlier bifurcates, these tools are small (between 2.5 and 3 cm in length), with thin, triangular blades and somewhat rounded or lobate ears. In fact, they are somewhat more lobate than the Laphroaig examples. Similar to Stanly and Neville points, they have well-defined stems and "Christmas tree-like" blades (Ellis 1987) with straight to slightly excurvate lateral edges. Unlike most classic Neville points, the stems of these specimens are straight rather than tapered and can have slight corner flaring, but, nevertheless, this flaring is minimal in comparison with that seen on classic Kanawha points. The basal concavity is also minimal in comparison with Kanawha specimens and has only what some refer to as "weak" or "shallow" bifurcation (Justice 1987:97; Smith et al. 1998:32). In this case, the concavity is produced through the removal of a series of long thinning flakes, rather than notching per se. In some instances, the basal concavity is pronounced, resulting from extensive basal thinning; in others it is far more subtle, reflecting a comparable degree of variability seen in Neville forms. Several of the points have serrated edges and barbed shoulders from extensive resharpening. Whereas Dincauze (1976) considers edge serration to be a temporal marker of the early Middle Archaic, Cross interprets it as "an individual preference or a way to compensate for a reduction in relative edge thinness during a Stanly/Neville point's use life" (1999:68).

Figure 22.12. Stemmed points from the Leschuk-Weisz and Farrugie sites.

Over 3,000 artifacts were recovered from the Leschuk-Weisz site, representing a diversity of tool forms, including five projectile points and fragments, nine drills and perforators, three spokeshaves, one wedge, 12 scrapers, and 25 bifaces. Many of these were clustered in one central area around an "invisible" feature that, despite no obvious evidence of soil discoloration, produced fragments of calcined bone and a high quantity of artifacts within the subsoil. Only 1,505 artifacts were collected from the three loci of the Farrugie site. Although the majority of these were flakes and expedient flake tools, the assemblage also includes six bifaces, four cores, five end (?) scrapers, and two hammerstones. Four of the scrapers (Figure 22.13) were recovered from a single locus and, like those from the Laphroaig site described above, are small, are roughly made, and appear much less standardized than earlier forms such as those from Corner-Notched-horizon sites. A trend to less standardized scrapers in the Middle Archaic has been posited by other researchers (Chapman 1979:40).

Over 95 percent of the flakes and tools in the two site assemblages show signs of thermal alteration in the form of pop outs, discoloration, surface pitting, and shearing. Although artifacts with various degrees of thermal alteration are commonly found on sites in the Great Lakes region, such intense and widespread burning is rarely if ever documented. Such extensive burning is known for this general time period, although it is generally restricted to mortuary or ceremonial sites. For example, the Early Archaic Jerger site in southwestern Indiana produced an extensive quantity of burned flakes and tools in association with cremated human bone and red ocher (Tomak 1979). At Leschuk-Weisz, however, there are no associated mortuary remains, nor is there other evidence of ritual activity of any kind. Neither is there

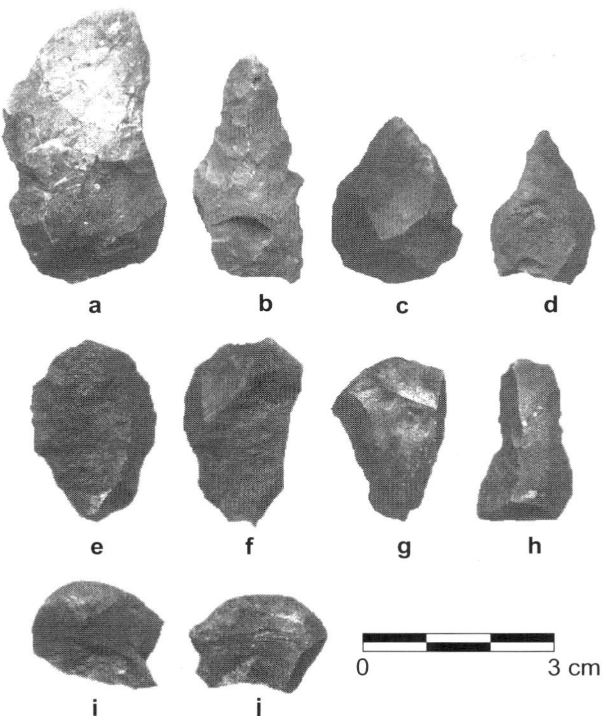

Figure 22.13. Flaked-stone artifacts, Leschuk-Weisz and Farrugie sites: a, biface; b–d, drills and perforators; e–j, end scrapers.

evidence that burning relates to the intentional heating of the chert to improve workability. The unburned specimens are typically made on Onondaga chert, a locally available yet high-quality raw material. Nevertheless, many of the tools have been extensively damaged, and many are missing proximal, distal, or lateral portions that were sheared off at very high temperatures. This is particularly noticeable in the scraper assemblage, as many tools are represented by only a working edge (Figure 22.13), a pattern that also appears at the Jerger site. That many highly exhausted cores have spalls on the flake-scar surfaces suggests the burning was postdiscard. Such widespread postdepositional burning may have been associated with a forest or grass fire.

Another site with a stemmed-point component is Johnson Flats (Parker 1995) on the lower Grand River, briefly mentioned earlier. Excavations of a 46-m^2 area to be impacted by a pipeline uncovered a paleosol capped by about a 50-cm-thick layer of topsoil and silts representing deposition since European land clearing. The old paleosol contained cultural diagnostics representing Late Archaic and Woodland occupations. Beneath this paleosol was a 30- to 50-cm-thick stratum whose source was not clearly determined, according to the preliminary report, but which may be another paleosol remnant. The only diagnostics from that lower level were lithics, and they included only two Middle Archaic points. Besides a classic Brewerton-style corner-notched point reworked into an end scraper, a point with a relatively wide triangular blade and narrow (10 mm), short (5 mm) stem was found. The item has a shallow basal concavity (< 2 mm) and slightly flaring corners and is very reminiscent of the Stanly type cluster, to which it was related by the site investigator. A comparable point was also recovered nearby, albeit in the plow zone. Faunal remains were present in this lower level, including deer and sucker, but given the level's multicomponent and diffuse nature, associations are not clear.

The Northoway 2 site is a stemmed-point component located in a cultivated field near the west end of Lake Ontario (Fisher et al. 1997). Excavation of a 68.5-m^2 area recovered two stemmed points, four fragmentary bifaces, 19 used flakes, and 2,360 pieces of detritus, including 10 random cores. Except for two pieces of flaking debris on the relatively site-local and low-quality Ancaster chert, all of the items were on Onondaga chert, the nearest sources of which are near Lake Erie, 60 km to the south. The points are identical to those at the previously discussed sites and have relatively short and narrow stems with slightly flaring corners and shallow basal concavities. One pit feature, coinciding with a dense concentration of flaking debris, was noted, but no organics were recovered.

The time period from 7500 to 5500 RCYBP remains the poorest known of the Ontario Archaic time span. Some point forms found in surface collections may date to this time. One form includes distinctive basally notched points, most closely resembling those of the Eva types. To the South, these types as a whole seem to date to the ca. 7500–7000 RCYBP time (Lewis and Lewis 1961; Nance 1986). Although the odd example is known from eastern Ontario (e.g., Ross and D'Annibale 2000:160), most of these points are reported in the Niagara Peninsula and adjacent areas just to the west (Borland and Poulton 1997:Figure 7d; Ellis 1997; Wright 1978:67). Yet the points are so rare as to be almost nonexistent. Also, in areas to the east, as in northern New England, it is becoming clear that assemblages can contain ground-stone items such as rods or gouges but often lack stone points altogether (e.g., Sanger 1996). If this is the case in some parts of Ontario where stone rods are also known to occur (e.g., Lackowicz 1996), it would clearly make identification of assemblages of this age difficult in the absence of any good contextual information. Many of the broad-bladed side-notched points reported from Ontario collections (e.g., Roberts 1985) may also date to prior to 5500 RCYBP, especially since they are present in contexts so dated in surrounding areas such as southeast Michigan (Lovis 1989), Illinois (Brown and Vierra 1983), and upper New York State (the "proto-Laurentian"; Funk 1976, 1993:188). However, virtually identical side-notched point forms continued to be used after 5500 RCYBP in these same areas, so these earlier-dating items would be difficult to distinguish in simple surface artifact collections. An isolated, flexed burial of a 50+-year-old male from the Milton-Thomazi site in south-central Ontario is directly dated to 5910 ± 165 RCYBP, but that individual was unaccompanied by any grave goods (Katzenberg and Sullivan 1979).

Middle Archaic after 5500 RCYBP

Better-known assemblages postdate 5500 RCYBP. The earliest of these include broad-bladed, side-notched (5000–5500 B.P.) points usually related to those of the Otter Creek type, and later assemblages include corner- to side-notched (ca. 4500–5000 RCYBP) points assigned to Brewerton types or their variants (see Ritchie 1971b). As discussed by Tuck (1977), some investigators have tended to refer to this development as a whole, and even subsequent post-4500 RCYBP developments, as the "Laurentian Archaic" (Wright 1972a, 1995:217), while others (Ellis, Kenyon, and Spence 1990:85; Funk 1988; Ritchie 1969:79–83) have used the term in a more restricted sense to refer to pre-4500 RCYBP developments found only in eastern Ontario north of Lake Ontario and in adjacent areas of Quebec, New York, and New England. Following Ritchie's (1940:96) original definition, the latter researchers define Laurentian not simply on the basis of point styles but also on the basis of associated tool kits that are said to be distinctive in that they include a wide range of ground-stone artifacts. Such artifacts include points that often have laterally barbed and serrated stems, large knives or spearpoints ("bayonets"), "plumb-bobs," and semilunar knives ("ulus") as well as a wide range of woodworking tools, including gouges, adzes, and chisels, although grooved axes are noticeably absent. In Ontario, sites yielding this range of artifacts *in association* are reported solely in the eastern half of the province. Past distributional studies of individual slate artifact types have tended to show that several of those types are more common in those same eastern areas (Popham and Emerson 1954:13–15; Vastokas 1970:148; Watson 1990; Wintemberg 1931:79–80; Wright 1962). The most recent and comprehensive study is that of Lackowicz (1996). Although it displays some sampling biases, that study confirms that ground-stone forms such as points, bayonets, gouges, plummets, and ulus, while not totally absent from southwestern Ontario, are more common in the eastern areas. In addition, the grooved axe, not traditionally seen as a Laurentian trait, is certainly more common in areas to the west.

The meaning of such distributions is much debated. Some see Laurentian as a cultural-ethnic or even linguistic (e.g., as Iroquoian; Tuck 1977; Wright 1984) construct, whereas others, noting its correlation with mixed conifer-hardwood forests (e.g., the Canadian biotic province more characteristic of eastern Ontario), tend to see the distinctive characteristics as representing, or also reflecting, an adaptation to those kinds of environments (e.g., Funk 1988; Ritchie 1969; but see Ramsden 1997:9 for a dissenting view). Other interpretations are also possible. For example, eastern Ontario and adjacent areas have a paucity of good, flakable, cryptocrystalline sources, so the emphasis on coarser-grained rocks and grinding could be related to raw material availability. This explanation, however, does not help in understanding why items such as ground-stone points were not used much by earlier or subsequent groups in the same area. Notably, individual artifact forms are distributed beyond the Laurentian heartland although often in different frequencies and directions. For instance, plummets tend to be more common to the east of Ontario in developments such as the "Maritime Archaic," while certain forms of gouges, such as fully longitudinally grooved ones, are actually just as common in southwestern Ontario as in the southeastern "Laurentian" heartland. Using these differential distributions and ethnoarchaeological work such as that of Lemonnier (1986) in New Guinea, which shows that the distribution of different technical traits does not necessarily correlate with the distribution of different ethnic groups, Lackowicz (1996:28–46) implies that the apparent distinctiveness of "Laurentian" sites in eastern Ontario may simply reflect their location in an area where the relatively independently determined distributions of diverse slate objects and broad-bladed points overlap.

Whatever one calls these materials or assumes is their significance, clearly, the best-known sites with at least the broad-bladed flaked-stone point forms are in eastern Ontario and immediately adjacent areas and have been traditionally called "Laurentian" (see Ellis, Kenyon, and Spence 1990:85–92). Most of the longer-known "Laurentian" sites, almost all of which appear to be large and associated with major waterways, have proven to be multicomponent, and markedly so, with the Middle materials intermixed with subsequent Late Archaic and Woodland assemblages (e.g., Johnston 1984; Leechman and DeLaguna 1949; Ritchie 1949). Very few other sites have seen work in recent years, and, again, some are markedly multicomponent, which does not facilitate easy interpretation. Nonetheless, some exceptions occur, and certain of the multicomponent sites can provide detailed insights.

One site of note is Rentner, located just inland from the modern Lake Huron shore (Figure 22.6, No. 20) in a plowed field (Lennox 2000:16–40). The site is on a bluff overlooking the abandoned lakebed of the Nipissing phase and was probably contemporary with that high-water level. Over 20 points were recovered, of which five are ground-slate points or fragments thereof and 11 are Brewerton Corner- or Side-Notched forms. Traces of later occupations, from Late Archaic to Late Woodland, are suggested by two point recoveries and small concentrations of ceramics. Most of the Middle Archaic notched points are made on Onondaga chert, and the same material is common in the flaking debris as well as among biface preforms, despite having to be obtained from at least 200 km away. Its common occurrence among the debris might actually suggest a relatively high distance mobility for populations using the site. Since the nearest Onondaga chert sources occur in an area traditionally not seen as Laurentian, if Rentner site occupants traveled to those sources to acquire the material, the Laurentian-non-Laurentian distinction is blurred. Other exotic materials, such as some Michigan cherts, occur at Rentner, albeit in small amounts, and represent the first good evidence for long-distance interaction since the earliest Archaic.

Several subsoil features were found at Rentner, and two, Features 2 and 6, are notable in that they contained Brewerton point forms. Feature 2 also contained a slate point and over 3,000 faunal bones, including 752 fish bones, 529 mammal bones, and six bird bones. Most of the bone was unidentifiable to more specific taxa; a few small mammal species, deer, and whitefish were the only identified species. That fish species tends to be inshore during spawning in the early fall and its presence may indicate site use during that time. Feature 2 returned an AMS date of 5900 ± 90 RCYBP, which seems somewhat early for a Brewerton occupation. Feature 6 was not dated, but it also contained faunal remains (n = 715), including 198 fish bones and 145 mammal bones. Catfish, freshwater drum, and sucker remains were identified as well as a single whitefish bone, and the investigator suggests the remains indicate spring to summer use of the feature.

Another notable site in eastern Ontario is at Healey Falls (Figure 22.6, No. 24) on the Trent River (Ross and D'Annibale 2000:160–162; Ross et al. 1999:156–159, 2000:123–126). This particular site has yielded both Otter Creek and Brewerton points as well as many ground-stone points and woodworking tools. Especially notable is the presence of large amounts of flaking debris from roughing out the ground-stone tools and of many preforms for ground-stone points and celts discarded in manufacture. This evidence suggests the site may have been a major production center for the ground-stone items. Unfortunately, the site is multicomponent and includes evidence of Late Archaic and Woodland occupations as well as traces of even earlier use by Middle Archaic peoples making stemmed and basally notched points.

Among "Laurentian" sites that have been known for some time, those with the least admixture and the best potential for insights are located on islands in the Ottawa River separating Ontario and Quebec, and they actually fall within the latter province: Allumette Island and Morrison's Island (Figure 22.6, No. 17). These sites were investigated some time ago by the late Clyde Kennedy (1966) but have only recently been reported in detail (Clermont and Chapdelaine 1998; Clermont et al. 2003).

Alumettes covers about 1,600 m^2, of which 635 m^2 was excavated. At least 14 burial features were uncovered through the center of the site, where they were widely distributed and occurred in areas with occupation debris; they do not appear to represent cemeteries in the sense of areas put aside solely for the interment of the deceased. Few patterns are evident in the burials, other than they tend to be in flesh and that a broad cross section of the population is represented. There seem to be few or no grave goods, but the burials here are so disturbed by plowing that it is hard to reach firm conclusions. The site has yielded predominantly side-notched points approximating the Otter Creek type (Figure 22.14), several of which are on local cherts and metasediments but many of which are, despite a rarity among the flaking debris, on Onondaga chert (39 percent), traded in as finished forms from southwestern Ontario or New York State 500 km away. Also indicative of long-distance interaction, and an outstanding characteristic of the site, is the presence of a large number of objects made on native copper that analyses confirm are derived from the Lake Superior area over 1,000 km to the west. Over 1,000 such artifacts were recovered, which, except for 12 beads and a single pendant, are utilitarian items, with points, gorges, barbs, awls, fishhooks, and needles being especially common. There are also over 900 pieces of copper scrap, indicating on-site repair and manufacture. Most original pieces of copper were apparently small and suggest importation in an already highly processed form. Production and use of bone tools was also important, and, as is the case with the copper items, excepting a few pendants and beads, most objects are utilitarian, including 184 multibarbed and unilaterally barbed harpoons (Figure 22.15), 204 eyed needles, and other forms. The harpoons, fishhooks, and so on, certainly suggest fishing was important, but a broad range of faunal species, available from April to November, were recovered (Cossette 2003:276–277). Four radiocarbon dates

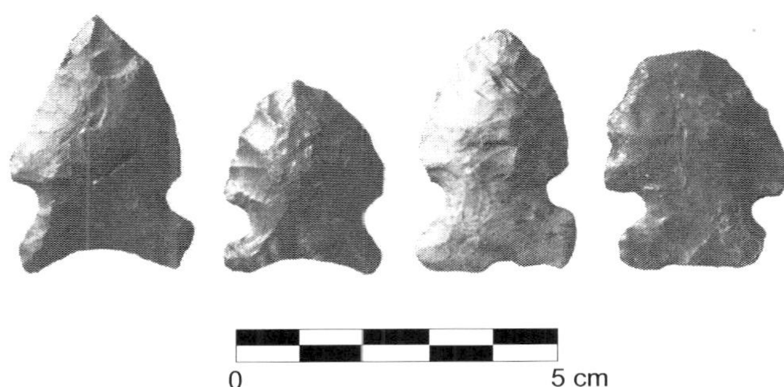

Figure 22.14. Otter Creek–type points, Allumette Island. Courtesy of Claude Chapdelaine.

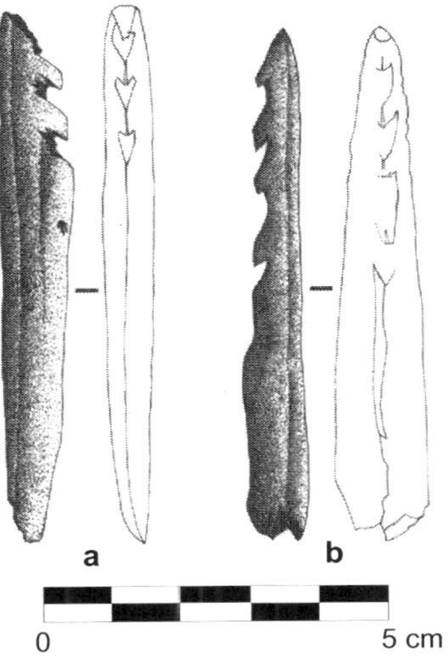

Figure 22.15. Harpoons from Allumette Island. Drawings by Sophie Limoges. Reproduced with permission, courtesy of Claude Chapdelaine from Clermont et al. (2003).

are now available, all from burials. One later date of 4680 ± 40 RCYBP was obtained, but the three others all suggest an age between 5500 and 5000 B.P. (see Table 22.2), in line with date estimates for comparable points (Vergennes phase) from the adjacent United States (see Funk 1988).

The nearby Morrison's Island site has predominantly yielded forms resembling the Brewerton Side- and Corner-Notched types (Ritchie 1971b) (Figure 22.16), although it has also produced smaller, stemmed forms that may postdate the broader, notched types. As at Allumettes, many points are on Onondaga chert (24 percent). The site seems to have covered less than 400 m^2, most of which was excavated (374 m^2). Copper items are rarer than at Allumettes, numbering 284 modified pieces as well as an almost equal number of scrap pieces. Much the same as at Allumettes, items such as barbs, gorges, fishhooks, eyed needles, awls, and points predominate, although the specific forms of objects can vary. For example, conical copper points are very common at Allumettes, whereas they are nonexistent at Morrison's. Morrison's has also yielded a considerable number of bone and antler items, including 86 unilaterally barbed harpoons with and without line holes, 132 eyed needles, and 699 worked beaver incisors. At least 21 burial features occur at Morrison's, but these do not seem to form a separate cemetery, as they are distributed across the site and occur in areas with occupation debris. Moreover, even where there are suggestions of several bodies in close juxtaposition, burials crosscut one another, suggesting the placement is somewhat fortuitous. A broad cross section of the population is represented, with both males and females and young and old reported. Seventeen of the graves contained artifacts; in several cases these include waste flakes, which suggests some objects may have been accidentally included when the individuals were interred in areas with occupation debris. Nonetheless, there are some suggestions of ritual activity or grave goods associated with the burials. For example, red ocher was present in at least nine of the graves. In one case, a very large stone gouge was laid on an individual's chest in a cluster of red ocher flecks, and a turtle-shell rattle was placed on the chest of another individual. Two burials included pairs of copper bracelets. Since only one other bracelet was reported from the site, these are clearly deliberate inclusions. Regardless, if all of the tools and completed items found were deliberate grave inclusions, they are dominated by utilitarian forms, and few grave goods were associated with particular individuals, perhaps seven or eight objects at most. Several of the burials have been directly dated, and the dates all indicate an age consistent with Brewerton sites in New York of ca. 4500 to 5000 RCYBP (Table 22.2).

Figure 22.16. Brewerton Corner Notched points from Morrison's Island. Courtesy of Claude Chapdelaine.

The traditional view of Laurentian subsistence is that groups aggregated at larger encampments along major waterways in the warmer months and then dispersed into more interior areas in the fall to winter (see Ellis, Kenyon, and Spence 1990:91–92; Ritchie and Funk 1973:339–341). However, the faunal material at Morrison's, as well as the site's restricted overall size, does not easily fit that stereotype. The faunal material is dominated by the remains of beaver and, especially, eels. Eels can be intercepted in quantity during their migrations by the site in the early fall. In sum, the evidence suggests the site was used in the late summer to fall by a relatively small number of individuals who focused on taking eels and beaver and preparing and refurbishing hunting equipment, probably as preparation for colder-weather activities.

Turning to southwestern Ontario, points similar to Brewerton and Otter Creek forms certainly occur in that area. As noted above, some use the occurrence of such points to argue for a Laurentian presence in that region. We are not so sure this is an apt characterization not only because of an absence of sites with a variety of ground-stone items but also because comparable side- and corner-notched points dated to the same time also occur to the west, from Illinois to Michigan (e.g., Cook 1976b:Table 16; Jefferies 1987:41; Lovis 1989; McElrath et al. 1984:37–40). There, where good samples are available, they are often associated with very different kinds of objects, such as grooved axes, drilled plummets, and engraved pins, suggesting very different interaction networks, and are found in contexts such as formal cemeteries, suggesting somewhat different lifestyles. Comparable broad-bladed points do occur in southwestern Ontario, and direct evidence indicates that at least the Brewerton-like points date to this era, as they have been recovered in surface collections on the abandoned beach of the highest Nipissing-phase level in the southeastern Lake Huron basin at sites such as Pascoe (Ellis and Deller 1986:48–52) (Figure 22.6, No. 18). These objects are stained and waterworn and, hence, must predate or be contemporary with the lake level at ca. 4500–5000 RCYBP. Few sites have been investigated, and most finds are from multicomponent sites in cultivated fields (e.g., Steiss et al. 1997), but there are some exceptions.

Located in a plowed field in the interior of the Niagara Peninsula (Figure 22.6, No. 13) near the headwaters of a small creek, the Bell site covers under 200 m^2, of which 132 m^2 was excavated (Williamson et al. 1994). All of the points from the site are side-notched to eared forms that, although somewhat at the small end of the range, are assigned to Brewerton types. Two hundred twenty-two formed stone objects were recovered, of which bifaces, presumably largely preforms discarded in manufacture, and simple used or retouched flakes were the dominant forms (33% and 41%, respectively). The most common formal tools (9 %) were 19 small, relatively roughly made end scrapers, and no ground-stone items were found. Four features were located, and, in addition to flaking debris, wood charcoal, and the odd stone tool, they contained charred butternut fragments, charred raspberry seeds, and calcined bone. The bone from the site definitely included white-tailed deer, beaver, otter, wild turkey, and cottontail rabbit. The soils in the immediate site vicinity are sandy loams, which are generally rare throughout the region and are optimal for rich mast-producing forests. Arguing that the site area would have been especially attractive in the fall to animals such as deer and turkey and noting the recovery of the butternut shell, the site investigators suggested a predominantly fall, roughly September to December, occupation. Assuming the end scrapers are hide-working tools, accumulation of foods for the winter and preparation of hides for clothing and shelter are seen as major activities.

The Little Shaver site (Figure 22.6, No. 23) also yielded a small collection of four Brewerton-like points (Timmins 1996). Although this small site is multicomponent, careful spatial analysis using models derived from the ethnoarchaeological work of Binford (1978, 1983) and others strongly suggested a hearth-centered Middle Archaic activity area at the north end. Other tool forms from the north end of the site that are attributed to the Middle Archaic occupation (on the basis of provenience) include a semilunar biface, a wedge, two retouched flakes, one denticulate, and 19 utilized flakes, most made of Onondaga chert (Timmins 1996:58). The lack of formal scrapers and the concurrent high frequency of utilized flakes suggest that expedient tools were being used for scraping and cutting activities. Ground-stone tools are absent, but one chipped-slate celt preform was recovered. The small faunal assemblage comprises mainly the bones of medium to large animals that are not identifiable to species but probably are deer. On the basis of an artifact assemblage dominated by projectile points and associated manufacture and maintenance debris and containing no formal scrapers but several informal tools, the site is interpreted as a logistical hunting and retooling camp occupied by a small task group.

Another site, called South Bend, has been recently investigated through CRM projects, and it has considerable potential to fill in knowledge of this time span. The site is located near the southeastern corner of Lake Huron (Figure 22.6, No. 18) on a low sand ridge that was formed as a baymouth bar across the mouth of the Thedford embayment during the high-water levels of the Nipissing phase (Cooper 1979). Recent excavations have revealed a buried paleosol overlain by sterile sand, which, in turn, was overlain by a plow zone that contained Early Woodland diagnostics. The paleosol yielded a series of side- and corner-notched points that are probably contemporary with the Nipissing phase. The high-water level of the Nipissing phase is marked by beaches at 184 m asl, while the sand ridge on which the site is located lies at 185 m asl. Thus, if the South Bend site was occupied during the Nipissing stage, the area around it would have been inundated and the sand ridge may have been either a low-lying island or a long northeast–southwest peninsula or sand spit. The inundated areas around the site would have formed a shallow lagoonlike body of water, undoubtedly rich in waterfowl and other aquatic resources.

While the analysis of the South Bend data is ongoing, some preliminary results are of interest. The points from the paleosol are very similar to the (Class II) notched points from the nearby and above-mentioned Pascoe site, located along the southern margin of the Nipissing beach embayment just to the south (Ellis and Deller 1986:50, Figure 11). Like the South Bend points, the Pascoe points vary from corner to side notched and include both straight-based and concave-based varieties (Ellis and Deller 1986; Timmins Martelle Heritage Consultants 2004a) (see Figure 22.17). As noted above, the Pascoe artifacts are waterworn and stained by Nipissing I waters and have to be at least contemporary with that lake level. Two of the South Bend points exhibit similar staining or patination, suggesting that they may have been water rolled or deposited in a wet environment (Figure 22.17b, h).

Morphological correlates to the South Bend points can be found throughout the lower Great Lakes region, the Midwest, and beyond. The straight-based points (Figure 22.17d–g) are similar to the small, side-notched points from the lower stratum at the Weber I site, Michigan, which is of pre-Nipissing age, ca. 6240–4560 RCYBP (Lovis and Robertson 1989b:217). These points are also similar to the Matanzas Side Notched type, common in Illinois and Indiana and dated ca. 5700–4000 RCYBP (Justice 1987:119–120). The concave-based forms (Figure 22.17a–c, h) bear striking similarities to the Brewerton Eared-Notched and Brewerton Eared-Triangle points, defined by Ritchie (1971b) and grouped by Justice (1987:122–123) within the Matanzas cluster. However, they are also akin to the White River type found in Missouri and Kansas (Hoard et al. 2004). At the Hogan Creek site, White

Figure 22.17. Brewerton-like points from the South Bend site.

River points have been dated to ca. 6150 RCYBP (Hoard et al. 2004:724). Finally, morphological correlates that parallel the projectile point variation observed in the South Bend collection can be found in the extensive Middle Archaic lithic collections from the Morrison's Island site located on the Ontario-Quebec border and discussed above, and from several Laurentian Archaic collections in New York State (e.g., Ritchie 1940:30, 1969:93).

The South Bend paleosol excavations yielded an assemblage of bifacial and unifacial tools that offer insight into Middle Archaic tool kits in southwestern Ontario. This collection includes large, early-stage, ovate bifaces (Figure 22.18a–d) and smaller, more refined triangular bifaces (Figure 22.18e), some of which are obviously projectile point preforms. All of the 10 scrapers from the paleosol are end scrapers (Figure 22.18j–m), usually made on expanding flakes of Kettle Point chert. The contracting proximal ends of these scrapers suggest that they may have been hafted, but they show no obvious hafting modifications other than limited lateral retouch, usually on only one edge. The only complete drill from the paleosol is a straight-based triangular form with markedly concave lateral edges (Figure 22.18f). The chipped-stone tool kit also includes large and small triangular wedges (Figure 22.18h, i) and informal utilized flakes. A well-preserved faunal sample from South Bend has not yet been analyzed but holds potential to greatly enhance understanding of the subsistence practices of the occupants, while radiocarbon dating of the paleosol will provide an independent line of evidence on the age of the occupation.

Figure 22.18. South Bend stone artifacts: a–e, bifaces; f, g, drills; h, i, wedges; j–m, end scrapers.

As a whole, the record of the late Middle Archaic seems much more substantial than that of earlier times. In areas where there has been detailed documentation, such as in the Trent-Severn waterway of eastern Ontario (Ellis, Foster, and Jesmer 1990), sites dating in the ca. 5500–4500 RCYBP period seem 10 to 15 times more common than earlier Middle Archaic materials, although the use of multiple diagnostics, including not only the flaked-stone points but also ground-stone objects such as points and ulus, results in a clear bias toward reporting these "Laurentian" sites. Nevertheless, where there have been studies of large point collections from various areas, such as the Ruthven collection from the lower Grand River in south-central Ontario (Williamson et al. 2002:Table 2) and the collections examined by Roberts (1985:Table 8) on the north shore of Lake Ontario, the later Middle Archaic point forms are also 10 to 15 times as common than what are apparently combined samples of bifurcate-based and early Middle Archaic stemmed points. If these figures can be taken as proxy measures of population, then some growth seems to have occurred. However, several cautions must accompany such estimates.

Some of the points, especially broad-bladed, side-notched forms, may actually predate 5500 RCYBP. In addition, it is worth noting that the Brewerton point category has often been a grab-bag one used to conveniently hold about any relatively large side- or corner-notched point, such that the numbers of these forms are probably overestimated. The use of individual point totals also may be misleading. For example, although apparently many more later Middle Archaic points (21 percent) occur in the Ruthven sample in comparison with Early Archaic (8 percent), the number of sites represented is the same for both periods (7 percent; Williamson et al. 2002:Table 1). Nonetheless, the larger number of points does suggest more substantial use of individual Middle Archaic sites in that vicinity and the same results have been suggested in other comparative studies (e.g., Stewart 2004a:109). Also, looking at site, rather than point, frequency in Roberts's (1985) sample from eastern Ontario, the later Middle Archaic sites are about six times more common than the earlier sites of concern here. Again, that the frequency of those point forms is much higher than the frequency of the sites themselves suggests that the late Middle Archaic sites are more substantial, on average. Even if one accepts these totals as indicating a more dense population in later times, this need not indicate real population growth but, just as likely, could indicate more population packing. The 5500 to 4500 RCYBP era corresponds to the rise in water levels associated with the Nipissing transgression. This event inundated significant areas, which must have forced populations into smaller land areas (Lovis et al. 2005). Moreover, the prime areas for occupation in earlier times, where one would expect population concentrations, such as littoral zones, are today inundated and inaccessible. Such events also make it difficult to assess the meaning of site and point frequency.

If one ignores the organic components and copper objects found at sites such as Allumettes and Morrison's Island, given the larger number of points per site indicated in data noted above, the stone assemblages alone are still very substantial. These assemblages may indicate reduced settlement mobility (e.g., longer residential stays at some sites), more entrenched mobility (e.g., more constant return year after year to the same site locations), occupation by larger groups, or some combination thereof. The small spatial extent of sites like Morrison's suggests more entrenched mobility, rather than larger population aggregations, may have played at least some role. Also, given the small size of that site and even of Allumettes, the large number of burials is notable. Given annual known death rates among modern hunter-gatherers (see Spence 1986), and inferring, using site size, a relatively small occupying group, the sheer number of burials suggests multiyear use. Entrenched mobility might be expected because of the population packing forced by the Nipissing water-level rise, which, in turn, would have restricted the number of suitable seasonal locations for settlement use.

However, interpretation is not so clear-cut. One could argue that what little evidence exists from sites such as Rentner indicates that Middle Archaic groups in easternmost Ontario may have been moving over large areas (at least 200 km in a straight line to preferred lithic sources), which is not that suggestive of population packing. Also, these large suggested ranges might not have been compatible with entrenched patterns of mobility; that is, people may have been moving over such large areas that they would have gained access to an increased number of productive resource locales. This evidence related to chert procurement, in turn, along with the small spatial extent of sites, might suggest more reduced residential mobility was playing the predominant role. Again however, there are complications with such an interpretation. Aside from very inadequate samples, the emphasis on Onondaga chert might not have been due solely to procurement during large-scale normal settlement moves. The raw materials could have been procured by task groups at some point in the annual round, even when groups were farther south and somewhat closer to the source. If that material was superior enough that it was probably exchanged to sites farther afield, like Allumettes, such procurement ventures on a periodic basis when exploiting areas nearer the source may have been worth the trouble. Also, the evidence for Morrison's suggesting more restricted seasonal use by a small population would tend to favor entrenched mobility as a primary determining factor of site structure, as would the fact that the sites yield more items such as points on average.

Irrespective of settlement mobility, the presence of Onondaga chert and copper at the upper Ottawa River valley sites and of Michigan cherts at Rentner certainly suggests widespread interaction networks, most probably exchange systems, involving the distribution of what largely seem to be materials used in utilitarian manners. This is the best evidence for long-distance interaction since the Early Archaic Corner-

Notched horizon and, of course, even earlier Paleoindian times, when quite exotic cherts made into everyday items were circulating over larger areas. However, the reasons for the Middle Archaic movement, particularly of the cherts, seem to be different than for the earlier movement. The earlier movement of exotic cherts involved small amounts between areas where there are plenty of more-local cherts. If any of that movement reflects exchange, it seems more compatible with gift exchange (Luedtke 1976:66) or simply the hand-to-hand movement of small amounts of materials to maintain social ties. While the presence of some of the exotic cherts in certain Middle Archaic assemblages, such as the Bayport chert at Rentner, could conceivably be attributed to the same process, the relatively larger amounts at sites such as Morrison's Island and Allumette and the lack of good, higher-quality flakable materials in the upper Ottawa Valley make utilitarian exchange (Luedtke 1976:56) a more likely explanation.

The burials with actual grave goods and use of red ocher are also of note. In southern Ontario, except for some *possible* Paleoindian burials that date much earlier (e.g., Deller and Ellis 1984, 2001), no good direct evidence exists for such activity at an earlier time. Indeed, the only known earlier-dating burial had no evidence of ritual associated with the interment (Katzenberg and Sullivan 1979). Hamilton (2004), however, has recently reported several burials with red ocher from sites in northwestern Ontario close to modern Hudson Bay dated by radiocarbon to 6500–7000 RCYBP. Also, at least one burial with grave goods, including several bone objects, a winged bannerstone, and an engraved stone plaque with a facial image, is reported from Quebec just 20 km east of the southeastern Ontario border near the St. Lawrence River (Marois 1987). This burial has a date of 6600 RCYBP and, along with the northwestern Ontario evidence, suggests there may be earlier evidence of burial ritual in southern Ontario that has so far eluded archaeologists.

The Late Archaic

As noted earlier, we use the appellation "Late Archaic" to cover developments dating from ca. 4500 RCYBP until the introduction of ceramics at ca. 2800 RCYBP. In line with earlier syntheses (e.g., Ellis, Kenyon, and Spence 1990; Funk 1983), we divide the Late Archaic into three broad complexes distinguished largely on the basis of point form and call these "Narrow Point," "Broad Point," and "Small Point."

Narrow Point Archaic

This complex is distinguished by the presence of relatively poorly made narrow, thick points with shallow side notches or expanding stems referable to types such as Lamoka and Normanskill (Ritchie 1971b). The archetypal Narrow Point development, and, in fact, the archetypal Archaic development, given that Ritchie (1932a, 1932b) based his concept of the Archaic on it, is Lamoka. In western to central New York, radiocarbon dates suggest these Narrow Point materials date to ca. 3800 to 4500 RCYBP (Hayes and Berg 1969; Ritchie 1969). Despite its seminal role, the Narrow Point Archaic remains poorly understood in Ontario. Narrow points had been reported across southern Ontario and west into adjacent Michigan. In Michigan they were referred to as "Dustin" points and said to be related to Lamoka (e.g., Binford 1963). However, more recent researchers have suggested that points assigned to types such as Lamoka in eastern Ontario and Dustin in Michigan are more similar to Small Point and other post-3500 RCYBP examples (Ellis, Kenyon, and Spence 1990:119–120; Lovis and Robertson 1989a; Robertson et al. 1999:100). Ritchie (1944, 1969) always regarded Lamoka as extending into Ontario, and especially the Niagara Peninsula, where its other inorganic diagnostic, the Lamoka adze with beveled lateral margins, also occurs. However, there was no suggestion it extended throughout all of southern Ontario and, as will be discussed below, throughout some of its time range, apparently contemporary groups in southwestern Ontario were using much different point forms, specifically, those associated with the earliest Broad Point Archaic.

Very few Ontario sites yielding narrow points have been excavated and, again, those that have been investigated tend to be multicomponent and from disturbed, plowed contexts (see Table 22.3). Only two seemingly pure components have been reported in recent years: Canada Century (Lennox 1990) and Winter (Ramsden 1990). Canada Century, on the south bank of the Welland River in the Niagara Peninsula (Figure 22.19, No. 1), consists of a single lithic cluster covering about 200 m^2. Three features were encountered at the cluster peripheries, and one yielded hickory and butternut or walnut shell, but the single date on one of the features (980 ± 70 RCYBP) suggests this particular evidence should be treated with caution. The lithic assemblage is dominated by used flakes, bipolar pieces and wedges, and points and preforms, and all of the last named ($n = 11$) are assignable to the Lamoka type or variants thereof (see Ellis, Kenyon, and Spence 1990:Figure 4.9). It also includes a few drills and a single ground-stone celt. The flaked-stone tools are almost exclusively on Onondaga chert from sources in the southern part of the Niagara Peninsula, about 20 km away on the Lake Erie shore. However, those sources possibly were still under the receding waters of areas initially flooded during Nipissing times, and, in fact, Lennox (1990) presents evidence that secondary pebbles of material from west of the Grand River, at least 40 km away, were being used, rather than the nearby outcrops.

A distributional analysis of the Canada Century debris, specifically, of transects across the main site concentration, suggested a denser central cluster with slight peaks in debris toward the cluster margins. Lennox (1986) had noted the same sorts of patterns at the later Small Point Archaic Innes

Table 22.3. Late Archaic Sites in Southern Ontario.

Site	Map No.[a]	Designation	References
Canada Century	1	Narrow Point	Lennox 1990
Winter	2	Narrow Point	Ramsden 1990
Rideau Lake sites	3	Broad Point	Watson 1981
McIntyre	4	Broad Point and other	Johnston 1984
McFarlane #1	5	Broad Point	Ellis, Foster, and Jesmer 1990:96–121
Parkhill	7	Broad Point	Fisher 1987
Davidson, Sadler, etc.	8	Broad Point	Kenyon 1980a, 1980b
Adder Orchard	9	Broad Point	Fisher 1997
Brodie, etc.	10	Broad Point	Fisher 1987; Kenyon 1980b
Hamilton Golf Club	11	Broad Point	Kenyon 1980b
Britannia Road site	12	Broad Point	Roberts 1985:227
Johnson Flats (upper level)	29	Broad Point	Parker 1995
Surma/Peace Bridge site	6	Narrow, Broad, and Small Point	Emerson and Noble 1966; Kenyon 1981; Robertson et al. 1997
Hillerman	34	Small Point	Fisher 2004
Thistle Hill	11	Small Point	Woodley 1990
Masterson Heights	33	Small Point	Esler 2002
Innes	13	Small Point	Lennox 1986
Inverhuron	14	Small Point	Kenyon 1959
Rocky Ridge	14	Small Point	Ramsden 1976
Knechtel I	15	Small Point	Wright 1972b
Thedford II	8	Small Point	Deller and Ellis 1992:4–5; Ellis et al. 1990; Ellis and Spence 1997
Welke-Tonkonoh	16	Small Point	Muller 1989; Ellis and Spence 1997
Sunnydale	30	Small Point	Martelle 2001
Fregg	31	Small Point	Wilson 2002
Crawford Knoll	17	Small Point	Kenyon and Snarey 2002
AgHc-82	18	Small Point	Park and Karaba 1997
Tegis	32	Small Point (?)	Burgar 1997
Collins Bay	19	Small Point—Glacial Kame	Ritchie 1955
Picton	20	Small Point—Glacial Kame	Donaldson and Wortner 1995:58–66; Ritchie 1949; Wintemberg 1928
Trenton Mountain/Mount Pelion	21	Small Point—Glacial Kame	Donaldson and Wortner 1995:57–58; Wintemberg 1928
Finlan	21	Small Point—Glacial Kame	Donaldson and Wortner 1995:52–57
Port Franks/Pinery Park	22	Small Point—Glacial Kame	Donaldson and Wortner 1995:46–51; Jury 1978
Blackfriar's Bridge	23	Small Point—Glacial Kame	Donaldson and Wortner 1995:51–52; Wintemberg 1928
Zimmer	24	Small Point—Glacial Kame	Donaldson and Wortner 1995:44–46
Hind	25	Small Point—Glacial Kame	Donaldson and Wortner 1995:6–30; Pfeiffer 1977; Varney and Pfeiffer 1995
Meredith-Goodall	24	Small Point—Glacial Kame	Donaldson and Wortner 1995:38–44
Caron 2	26	Small Point—Glacial Kame	Donaldson and Wortner 1995:37–38
Sartori	27	Small Point—Glacial Kame	Donaldson and Wortner 1995:30–37
Rikley	26	Small Point—Glacial Kame (?)	Donaldson and Wortner 1995:37
Schweitzer	18	Small Point—Glacial Kame	Donaldson and Wortner 1995:52
Bruce Boyd	28	Small Point—other burials	Ellis and Spence 1997; Spence and Fox 1986:8–11; Spence et al. 1978

[a]Map no. refers to site locations on Figure 22.19.

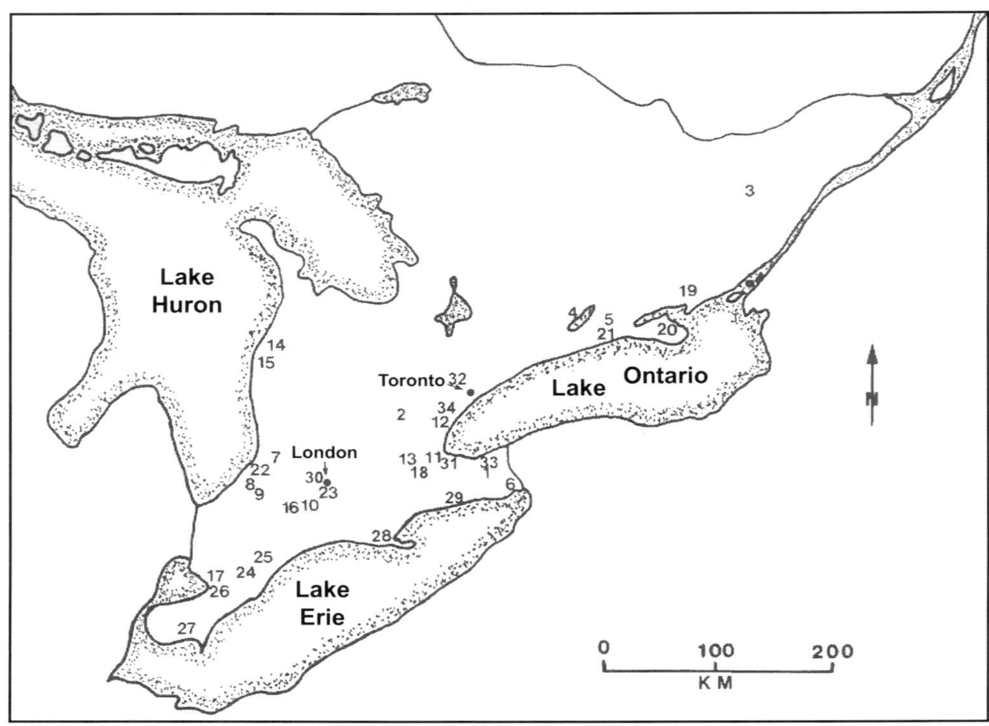

Figure 22.19. Map of Late Archaic site locations in southern Ontario. For key to site names, see Table 22.3.

site (see below) and attributes the pattern at Canada Century to the presence of a large structure, at least 7 by 13 m in size, which had central activity areas and debris accumulating around the periphery against the walls. However, these patterns seem too large to represent house structures and are easily interpreted in other ways. For example, they could indicate that activities were focused in the site center, the peripheral concentrations constituting evidence of sweeping or tossing of debris to the site margins.

Winter is located near Guelph, Ontario, adjacent to and overlooking a broad and swampy tributary creek (Figure 22.19, No. 2). The site covers an estimated 300 m^2, of which only 20 m^2 was excavated, uncovering four pits. The pits were located in two areas, one of which also had some scattered post molds. Both areas were coextensive with concentrations of lithic debris, leading the investigator to suggest the presence of two activity areas or possible structures, each with a radius of about 2 m. The site assemblage seems similar to that at Canada Century, in that it is on Onondaga chert, the tool assemblage is dominated by used flakes, bipolar pieces and wedges, and points and preforms, and a few drills and fragments of ground-stone tools are present. Although one broadly side-notched point was recovered, the other five finished points and point fragments recovered fall within the range of Lamoka points. Floral and faunal remains were absent, but, on the basis of the relatively high frequency of points, the sheltered site locale, and an analysis of the surrounding site catchment, Ramsden (1990:34–36) suggests the site was ideally situated with regard to deer habitat and may represent fall to winter activities.

Broad Point Archaic

Materials assigned to the Broad Point or "broadspear" (e.g., Witthoft 1953) horizon occur throughout southern Ontario (e.g., Ellis, Foster, and Jesmer 1990; Kenyon 1980a; Watson 1981) and clearly tie the Ontario Archaic record to well-known developments farther to the south, such as Stalling's Island (Stoltman 1974). The main distinguishing criterion is the presence of relatively large, stemmed points. Some Ontario forms (see Figure 22.20), such as those assigned to the Genesee type (Ritchie 1971b:24–25), are very broad bladed, as the appellation infers, but in actuality, researchers in Ontario have also applied the term such that it includes some examples with narrow blades, referred to as "Adder Orchard." In fact, some more narrow-bladed, stemmed points that occur in the Midwest, such as Etley points of the Titterington phase, have also been related to the Broad Point complex (Cook 1976a). In view of such connections, a "large stemmed-point horizon" may be a more apt general characterization.

Currently, Genesee or related point forms seem to be the most widespread, while other Broad Point forms seem more spatially restricted. The somewhat different narrower forms, such as Adder Orchard, are relatively common but are concentrated in southwesternmost Ontario and also frequently

Figure 22.20. Examples of different Broad Point types from southern Ontario: a, Adder Orchard; b, Genesee; c, Perkiomen. University of Western Ontario Collections.

occur in adjacent Michigan (see Kenyon 1983; Simons 1972). Forms apparently later in time than Genesee (e.g., after ca. 3400 RCYBP), such as Susquehanna and Perkiomen (Witthoft 1953), do occur in Ontario (e.g., Figure 22.20c), but they are rare and seem to be found largely in areas near the northeastern side of Lake Erie. The only possible Perkiomen site is Chaingate located at the western end of Lake Ontario. Although called a Perkiomen site by its investigator, only two of the points reported seem to marginally fit that taxon (Bursey 1994:Figure 2a, c), and even those examples lack some of the most distinctive features of the type, notably the rounded or upsloping shoulders and lobate stem corners (see Ritchie 1971b:42–43; Witthoft 1953), making their assignment debatable. Also, one point with a contracting stem and concave base seems to be a good example of a Neville or Stanly Stemmed variant (Bursey 1994:Figure 2d), and other notched and stemmed points were recovered that are certainly not Perkiomen forms and suggest the site is multicomponent (Bursey 1994:Figure 2e, f). Therefore, we reserve judgment on the affiliation of that site.

Unlike most earlier Archaic developments, broad points are often made on coarse-grained rocks, including metasediments such as subgraywacke. Large lanceolate points on such materials have in the past been assigned to a putative Paleoindian-age taxon called the "Satchell complex" in southwestern Ontario and adjacent areas (e.g., Cufr 1973; Fitting 1970; Peske 1963). However, in the 1980s, Ian Kenyon (1979, 1980a, 1980b, 1983) demonstrated that the Satchell complex was of Late Archaic age and not Paleoindian and that it was not a distinct "culture." Following the earlier arguments of Witthoft (1953), Ian Kenyon (1980b) argued that the production of these large bifaces required large, flaw-free pieces of material. In areas where fine-grained materials were in short supply, broad-point makers switched to using the flakable but coarser-grained rocks. The current understanding is that Broad Point sites in southern Ontario date from just before 4000 to around 3400 RCYBP or later.

In recent years, two significant Broad Point sites have been examined and reported in some detail. One site is Adder Orchard, just inland from Lake Huron (Figure 22.19, No. 9). Ian Kenyon (1983) briefly test pitted the site, and, subsequently, more extensive excavations, although still limited, were carried out by Fisher (1997). The site covers almost 5,000 m² on an elevated, shallowly plowed peninsula of land that extends out onto the floodplain of the Ausable River. It is actually only one of a whole series of very extensive Broad Point sites in the area, several of which have Genesee as opposed to Adder Orchard components (Kenyon 1980a, 1980b). Excavations were placed in two areas. One area encompassed some of Ian Kenyon's (1983) test units and the area excavated totalled only 105 m². Nonetheless, even within that small area, often-overlapping pits (n = 25) and hearths (n = 2) were found, suggesting intensive and repetitive site use. The only diagnostics excavated in the area included the distinctive Adder Orchard points (n =10; see Figure 22.21). Over 50 large bifaces or fragments, obviously preforms for such points, were also found. Bone was not well preserved, and deer was the only identified animal present. Aside from wood charcoal, nut remains were recovered, and, although few pieces could be identified, butternut, black walnut, and oak nut meat was present. Along with a hawthorn seed, these plants suggest a predominantly fall use. Charred raspberry seeds may indicate either summer use or, perhaps, use of stored berries. In all, four statistically identical radiocarbon dates of around 4000 RCYBP were obtained from features in the excavated area (see Table 22.4).

As noted above, the Adder Orchard points are relatively narrow bladed and also sometimes exhibit small spurs at the basal corners. They closely resemble types reported elsewhere, such as Stringtown and Satchell, which are often seen, erroneously, as Paleoindian (see also Fisher 1997; Kenyon 1983:13). Very comparable Late Archaic points dating to a similar time occur elsewhere, although they are not always related by investigators to the Broad Point phenomenon. They include, notably, the Steubenville Stemmed of the Panhandle Archaic of West Virginia (Mayer-Oakes 1955) and, as previously mentioned, the more narrow-bladed forms of the Titterington phase in Illinois (Cook 1976b). In addition to T-based and oval-stemmed drills, a few scrapers, and simple flake tools, the excavations at Adder Orchard recovered a small circular ground-stone bead, and surface collections yielded a faceted-spine winged bannerstone such as are reported in association with broad points elsewhere (e.g., Claflin 1931:Plate 46; Dincauze 1972). Some of the Adder Orchard points are on subgraywacke, but there is more emphasis on cherts such as Kettle Point from sources just 20 km to the northwest and, assuming secondary source use, Onondaga from sources as near as 65 km to the south. Unlike the larger Genesee-style broad points, the

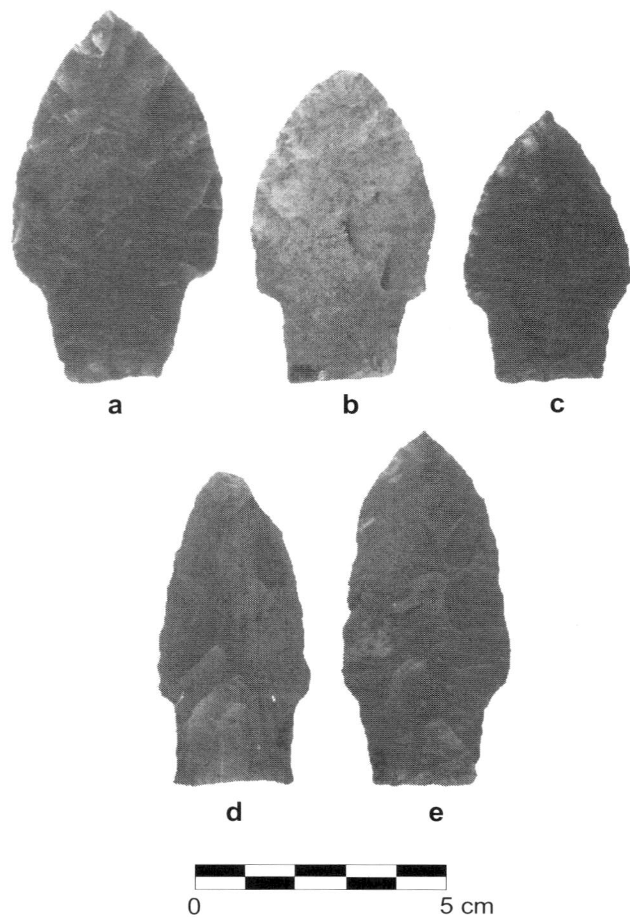

Figure 22.21. Points from the Adder Orchard site. Reproduced courtesy of Jacqueline Fisher and with permission of the London Chapter, Ontario Archaeological Society from Fisher (1997).

smaller Adder Orchard forms could be made more often on cherts such as Kettle Point rather than Onondaga. Kettle Point is more difficult to obtain in sizable, flaw-free pieces (Kenyon 1983). Fisher (1997:Table 3.6) shows that Onondaga commonly appears among finished points (40 percent) as well as later-stage preforms but, among earlier-stage bifaces and other tools such as unifacial ones, the more local Kettle Point is much more common (> 88 percent). Similar variability between points and other artifact classes in raw material usage is seen on subsequent (post-3500 RCYBP) Small Point sites, as well, and we will discuss its potential significance when we consider those sites in a later section.

A second major Broad Point excavation at the Surma, or Peace Bridge, site (Figure 22.19, No. 6) also relates to more extensive excavation at a site briefly investigated earlier. In the 1960s, excavations for a hotel in downtown Fort Erie exposed a series of Late Woodland burials as well as abundant evidence of a Genesee occupation associated with use of abundant local outcrops of Onondaga chert (Emerson and Noble 1966; Kenyon 1981). In the 1990s, additional CRM work was carried out in the same vicinity related to the upgrading of the Peace Bridge linking Fort Erie to nearby Buffalo, New York, and of its associated customs facilities. This work exposed a large area of densely packed precontact features and artifactual material and confirmed the existence of extensive occupation debris covering a total of 24 ha lining the Niagara River (Williamson and MacDonald 1997, 1998). Many components are present, including substantial post-Archaic ones. The area seems to have been inundated by Lake Erie during the Nipissing high-water stage until around 4000–4500 RCYBP, after which it became available for occupation. Therefore, not surprisingly, the earliest evidence for site use consists of Lamoka points, but these are very rare, and the most common Archaic materials relate to a Genesee occupation and include not only the distinctive points but also several stemmed "drills" reworked from points as well as numerous large pentagonal preforms (Williamson and MacDonald 1997) (see Figure 22.22). The intensive use of the area led to many later features intruding on earlier ones and incorporating earlier materials. Nonetheless, several features yielding solely Genesee diagnostics seem to have survived, and in an area adjacent to the bridge itself (Area 4), over 25 Genesee pits and hearths were documented. In some

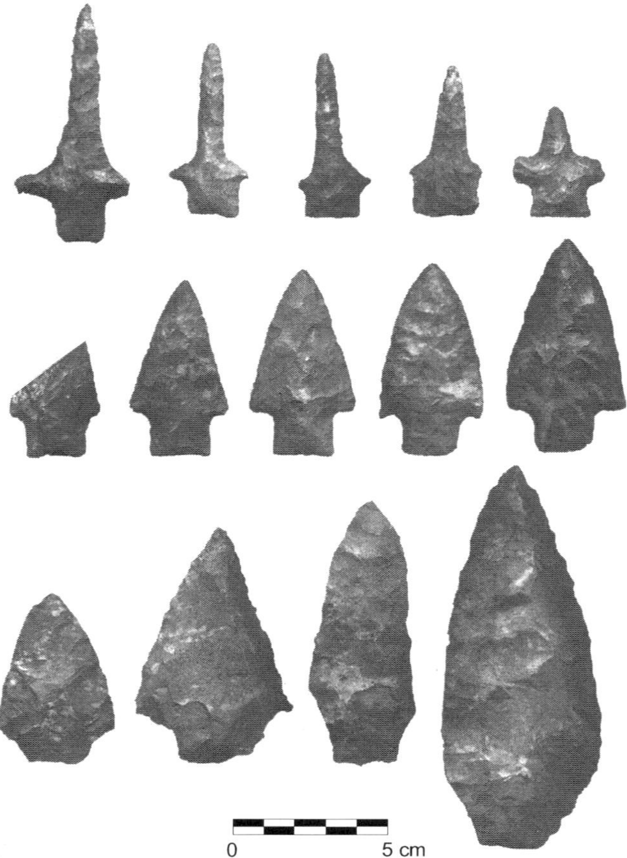

Figure 22.22. Genesee points and drills from the Peace Bridge site. Courtesy of Ronald Williamson.

Table 22.4. Radiocarbon Dates for Ontario Late Archaic Sites.

Site	Point Form	Lab No.	RCYBP	S.D.	Uncalibrated B.C. Dates	Calibrated B.C. Dates	Reference
Adder Orchard	Adder Orchard	WAT-23080	3950	130	2000	2630–2200	Fisher 1997
Adder Orchard	Adder Orchard	WAT-23079	4000	90	2050	2840–2340	Fisher 1997
Adder Orchard	Adder Orchard	WAT-23081	4040	100	2090	2860–2460	Fisher 1997
Adder Orchard	Adder Orchard	I-12480	3850	90	1900	2460–2200	Fisher 1997
George Davidson	Genesee	I-10313	3780	85	1830	2400–2030	Kenyon 1980a
Peace Bridge	Genesee	I-6305	3580	60	1630	2030–1770	Robertson et al. 1997
Peace Bridge	Genesee	I-6307	3470	60	1520	1880–1690	Robertson et al. 1997
Crawford Knoll	Crawford Knoll	TO-920	3480	120	1530	1960–1620	Kenyon and Snarey 2002
Knechtel I	Crawford Knoll	S-504	3250	90	1300	1680–1420	Wright 1972b
Knechtel I	Crawford Knoll	BGS-35	3690	45	1740	2140–1970	Wright 1972b
Knechtel I	Crawford Knoll	BGS-37	3040	40	1090	1380–1210	Wright 1972b
Parkhill, Area D	Crawford Knoll	I-8866	3400	210	1450	2000–1400	Ellis 1998
Parkhill, Area D	Crawford Knoll	I-8867	>2980	105	>1030	>1380–1040	Ellis 1998
Parkhill, Area D	Crawford Knoll	I-8868	>2485	100	>535	>770–410	Ellis 1998
Innes	Innes	I-13062	2620	80	670	900–550	Lennox 1986:265
Innes	Innes	I-13061	3350	195	1400	1890–1410	Lennox 1986:265
Thistle Hill	Innes	not given	3440	75	1490	1880–1630	Woodley 1990
Knechtel I	Hind?	BGS-34	2888	45	938	1190–990	Wright 1972b
Thedford II	Hind	BGS-1427	3020	80	1070	1400–1120	Ellis et al. 1990a
Rocky Ridge	Hind	Gak-2851	<3100	120	<1150	<1520–1130	Ramsden 1976:44
Inverhuron "M"	Hind	S-60	2850	60	900	1130–920	Wilmeth 1978:125
Hind	Hind	Gak-3974b	2920	170	970	1370–920	Donaldson and Wortner 1995
Hind	Hind	S-1061	2875	75	925	1210–920	Donaldson and Wortner 1995

Note: Excludes some dates from Adder Orchard, Rocky Ridge, Knechtel I, Innes, Crawford Knoll, Thistle Hill, and Hind that appear much too early or late. Also excludes dates of Late Archaic age from the McIntyre site in eastern Ontario (Johnston 1984:74) because cultural associations are unknown. Calibrated dates are one-sigma ranges derived from Oxcal Program v3.9, University of Oxford, Radiocarbon Accelerator Unit (Ramsey 2003).

cases they form dense, oval concentrations 2.5 to 5.5 m across, which include the odd post mold and which the investigators suggest are possible house floors.

Those features containing only Genesee diagnostics included artifacts such as net sinkers as well as at least one mortar and pestle. Several features yielded abundant flaking debris as well as core nuclei or preforms, suggesting intensive knapping activities (see also Williamson and MacDonald 1998:108). This activity is not surprising. Thick outcrops of relatively flaw-free Onondaga chert, necessary to make the large Genesee points, occur at the site, and there is even evidence of actual "mining" of such outcrops. Charred nutshell, predominantly walnut but also including hickory, was found in several features (Monckton 1997). Other feature contents include the odd seed, including grape, and calcined mammal bone. Identified species include deer, several small mammals, canid, passenger pigeon, turtle, and sauger or walleye (Thomas 1997). Overall, the faunal and floral remains suggest early spring to fall site use. However, interpretation is complicated by the possibility of the use of stored food products and the possibility of mixing of material from later deposits.

Also encountered at the Peace Bridge site were dog and human interments. However, determining definitively if these are associated with the Genesee component is difficult. The presence of dog burials is not surprising, as they are also reported from another Genesee component at the George Davidson site in Ontario (Kenyon 1980a:19). One cremation, Feature 44, included not only calcined human bone but also burned and unburned animal remains, including deer, felid (probably bobcat), and Canada goose as well as a bone needle, a bone bead, and a modified antler tine. No definitive Genesee diagnostics occurred in that feature, but the investigators draw parallels to well-known cremations from New England Broad Point sites, which sometimes include food offerings (Robertson et al. 1997:499). Another feature, 157a, also yielded a large amount of calcined animal bone, including deer and passenger pigeon, and may represent the same activity as Feature 44. Feature 157a also included a

Genesee point tip. However, the only definitive human remains recovered included a single molar, making identification as a cremation quite tentative.

Two dates, 3580 ± 60 RCYBP and 3470 ± 60 RCYBP (see Table 22.4), are reported from Peace Bridge features, and these are in line with previously reported dates from sites with Genesee or related components, suggesting an age of roughly 3800–3400 RCYBP (e.g., Funk and Rippeteau 1977:21; Kenyon 1980a, 1980b; Ritchie 1969:136; Snow 1975:53). These dates actually overlap somewhat with the earliest assays on Small Point Archaic assemblages, to be described below, and raise the possibility of some contemporaneity. In fact, some researchers have suggested that the large broad points of the Genesee type are specialized tools such as knives or spear tips used by peoples who otherwise were using Small Point and other point forms (e.g., Stothers 1983; Stothers et al. 2001:238). At Peace Bridge, two of the four Lamoka narrow points, the only two complete examples from the site, were recovered in an otherwise Genesee feature, and the investigators suggest that this could indicate some overlap between the very latest Narrow Point and the earliest Genesee point use (MacDonald and Steiss 1997:324). Such overlap is plausible, although the co-occurrence could also indicate multicomponent mixing. We are much less convinced of an association of broad points such as Genesee with small points, believing the small points to date later (see below). Broad points are the sole forms to occur at large sites such as George Davidson and several other sites in Ontario (see Kenyon 1980a) and are found in pure components much beyond Ontario and immediately adjacent areas, as in New England (Dincauze 1972). Moreover, Small Point–related developments also occur as pure components in other areas such as the Midwest (see below and Winters 1969; Wittry 1959). In addition, as discussed by Snarey (2000:27–28), most dates for Small Point components are later than 3400 RCYBP, and no known Small Point sites are dated much in excess of 3500 RCYBP, so the overlap may be merely statistical or minimal, at best. If the burials at the Peace Bridge turn out to be typical of Broad Point, the emphasis on cremations and interment within occupation areas is much different than, as we will detail below, the use of discrete cemeteries and inclusion of unburned grave goods seen in Small Point, suggesting a deep split in sacred belief systems. We believe it plausible that some broad-point forms that are dated later elsewhere, such as Perkiomen and Susquehanna (see Witthoft 1953), date to the same age range as the earliest Ontario small points but, as noted above, forms like Perkiomen and Susquehanna are not significantly represented in Ontario.

Regardless, Ian Kenyon (1983) once suggested that Genesee was the earliest broad-point type in Ontario and was the base from which two regional variants developed: Adder Orchard in southwesternmost Ontario and, to the east, in areas such as the Niagara Peninsula, assemblages with broad points more similar to Genesee, such as Snook Kill. However, the radiocarbon dates from Adder Orchard sites and the similarities of that point form to those seen in developments such as Titterington suggest it predates Genesee in areas where both co-occur, such as southwestern Ontario. Moreover, these Adder Orchard dates are so early (e.g., ca. 4000 RCYBP) as to strongly suggest contemporaneity with the classic narrow point–using cultures of the time, such as Lamoka, in the Niagara Peninsula and adjacent New York State (Fisher 1997:92–93).

Small Point or Terminal Archaic

The term *Small Point* was coined by Spence and Fox (1986) to subsume several Terminal Archaic developments in southwestern Ontario dating to ca. 3500–2800 RCYBP and previously referred to by terms such as the *Inverhuron Archaic* (Kenyon 1959) and the *Haldimand* (Spence and Fox 1986) and *Glacial Kame* (Cunningham 1948) burial complexes. The points related to these developments are relatively small, and this difference is emphasized when they are contrasted with the notably large broad points. However, as noted above with respect to the designation *Broad Point*, the term *Small Point* is a bit of an oxymoron. Just as the former category includes some relatively narrow points, some relatively large point styles are subsumed in the Small Point category. As it currently stands, the Small Point Archaic is known primarily from southwestern Ontario and along the immediate north shore of Lake Ontario west of Toronto, and the exact classification and affiliation of assemblages farther to the east and north is not clear (see, e.g., Ellis, Kenyon, and Spence 1990:119–120). The tendency certainly has been to relate points from eastern Ontario more to the types defined by Ritchie (1971b) for immediately adjacent New York State. Moreover, many of these typological assignments were made prior to the more recent research leading to the recognition and definition of small-point types, work that has been concentrated in southwestern Ontario. The overall result has been a tendency to minimize the potential presence of Small Point–related developments in the eastern area when, in fact, comparable point forms seem to be present. For example, several points from the McIntyre site in eastern Ontario are related by the site investigator to Narrow Point types like Lamoka and Normanskill or are unassigned typologically (Johnston 1984). Yet, they appear to be somewhat wide for narrow points and, in terms of size and outline shape, many actually resemble quite closely small-point types to be described below, such as those in the Innes/Durst cluster (e.g. Johnston 1984:Figures 11d, j, 13i). In addition, mortuary components associated with small-point types occur in eastern Ontario (Ritchie 1949:24–45), and even in bordering areas of New York State (e.g., Feature 4 at the Muskalonge Lake site; Ritchie 1955:Plate 11), also suggesting a Small Point presence in that area.

In contrast to earlier materials, a considerable number of Small Point Archaic sites and assemblages have been reported or more fully described. Hence, discussing each site in detail is not possible. We list many of those sites in Table 22.3 but restrict ourselves here to discussing ideas and interpretations that have appeared in the last 15 years and how certain selected components have added to or changed our viewpoint of this development.

Point Types and Age

Several distinct point types are recognized within the Small Point designation (Ellis, Kenyon, and Spence 1990; Kenyon 1989), the most common being Crawford Knoll, Innes, and Hind. Crawford Knoll, named after a site in southwestern Ontario, includes very small, notched forms, sometimes with edge serrations (Figure 22.23), that closely resemble midwestern types such as Merom Expanding Stemmed and Trimble Side Notched, associated with the Riverton culture (Winters 1969). Innes points, named after a site near Brantford, Ontario (Lennox 1986) (see Figure 22.24), are medium-sized forms with expanding stems and closely resemble Late Archaic types elsewhere, notably the Durst Stemmed of Wisconsin (Wittry 1959:179–180). Co-occurring at the same sites are broader, and usually much rarer, forms referred to as "Ace of Spades" (Lovis and Robertson 1989a:229), which may be a functional variant such as a knife or spear tip. However, at the Innes site itself, the more broad-bladed points were associated with one of two clusters, whereas the narrower, more Durst-like forms were associated with the other cluster. This distribution may suggest that more than a simple functional difference is involved. Hind points (Figure 22.25) resemble those called "Feeheley" in adjacent areas such as Ohio (Stothers and Abel 1993) and are named after finds from the Hind cemetery on the Thames River (Donaldson and Wortner 1995). They are corner notched and tend to be larger on average than the other types. Ian Kenyon (1989) showed that there were two size variants of these points and the larger points seem to have been specially made as grave inclusions.

Ontario archaeologists believe at least some of the variation in these point forms represents change through time within the Small Point Archaic. At least the Ontario dates for Hind-style points suggest they date near the end of Small Point times, or around 2800–3100 RCYBP (Table 22.4). Too, there are clear similarities in artifact forms between sites with Hind points, including Glacial Kame burials, and subsequent Early Woodland developments, notably Meadowood, which also suggests a somewhat later temporal placement (Ellis, Kenyon, and Spence 1990; Ritchie 1969; Spence and Fox 1986). These similarities include continuity in artifact forms such as cache blades, tubular pipes, rectanguloid gorgets, birdstones, and even the points themselves. Hind points are very similar to Meadowood forms, the most notable difference being that they are corner rather than side notched. Moreover, continuity and a closer temporal relationship are also indicated by the consistent presence of burials in close juxtaposition, often in the same cemetery, indicating use both in Hind Late Archaic and Meadowood times (e.g., Abel et al. 2001; Ritchie 1955;

Figure 22.23. Crawford Knoll points from the Bruce Boyd site, Burial Feature No. 9. Courtesy of Michael Spence.

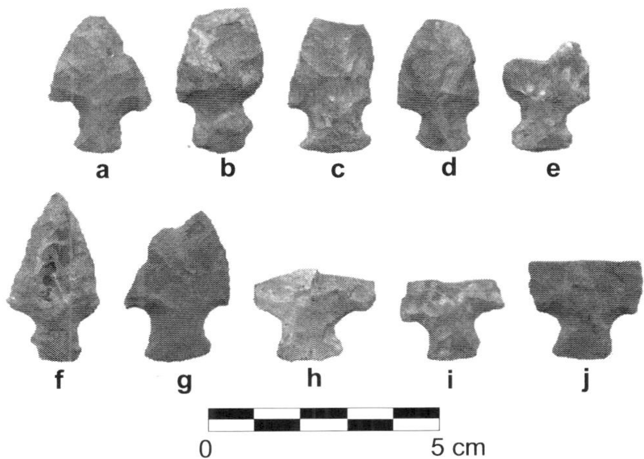

Figure 22.24. Innes points from the Innes site. Ontario Ministry of Culture Collections.

Figure 22.25. Hind points, Welke-Tonkonah site. University of Western Ontario Collections.

Williamson 1978). At the opposite extreme, and although there are some exceptions, Crawford Knoll points are the only ones with any dates in the 3400 to 3500 RCYBP range (Table 22.4). This led Ian Kenyon (1989) to suggest they date earlier. The Innes-point dates are more problematic, as a range of plausible dates is reported, sometimes from the same site, as from Innes itself (Table 22.4).

Darts or Arrows?

As has been suggested to explain the shift to comparable small-point types such as Merom Expanding Stemmed and Trimble Side Notched in the Midwest (Bradbury 1997), the marked reduction in size from the earlier broad points to the much smaller Crawford Knoll–style points might represent a shift from spear-thrower and dart use to the use of the bow and arrow (Ellis, Kenyon, and Spence 1990:106). This shift would also be consistent with the disappearance of bannerstones, which are not reported from the Terminal Archaic sites. To evaluate this idea, Snarey (2000) carried out detailed analyses of points from all of the major Small Point sites in southwestern Ontario as well as of comparative samples from earlier (Broad Point) and subsequent Early Woodland (Meadowood) sites. Several means were used to evaluate this proposition, but discriminant function analyses were emphasized. These functions have been developed by several researchers on the basis of preserved or ethnographic samples of definitive darts and arrows, but since Shott's (1997) results were based on the largest samples, and, hence, we believe are the most accurate, we include only those results here (Table 22.5). Shott (1997) actually developed several functions—what he called "four variable," "three variable," and so on, classification functions. The four-variable function used length, shoulder width, thickness, and neck width; the three-variable eliminated length, as that is often not preserved on archaeological specimens; the two-variable eliminated neck width because it seemed to be synonymous with shoulder width and also could not be recorded on unnotched point varieties; and the one-variable used only shoulder width. Shott (1997) found shoulder width to be the best predictor of actual tool use and noted that, as a rule of thumb, most points over 20 mm wide at the shoulder are darts, whereas most below are arrows.

Table 22.5 presents the results of Snarey's (2000) analyses arranged in roughly chronological order. Depending on the discriminant function used, from 58 to 94 percent of the points dating to the start of the Small Point time span (e.g., Crawford Knoll) are classified as arrows. Only one of the earlier broad points (e.g., Adder Orchard and Genesee) is classified as an arrow, and this is a heavily reworked item. At face value, this suggests that the bow and arrow may have been introduced at the beginning of Small Point times. However, fewer of the other, and probably later-dating, small points, such as Innes and Hind, are classified as arrow tips, nor are many subsequent Meadowood points classed as such—percentages are so low for Meadowood that one could argue for no arrow use at all (Table 22.5). This trend seems contradictory and, indeed, it leads one to question whether even the earlier forms like Crawford Knoll were arrow tips. One possibility for the apparent trend is that the arrow totals may be inflated for Crawford Knoll points. The samples of known origin used to actually derive the discriminant functions may have been biased toward larger, more pristine forms: museum specimens that had never been used and points from caches from archaeological sites such as dry caves. If the archaeological samples used here were more exhausted, one would expect reworking to have reduced size, especially length, and this would have resulted in more items classified as arrows, thus inflating the totals. Since length would be most affected, given the somewhat elongated shape of the points, it is interesting that the only function that includes length, namely Shott's (1997) four-variable, actually assigns more Crawford Knoll

Table 22.5. Classification of Ontario Archaic Points as Arrows.

Function	Adder Orchard	Genesee	Crawford Knoll	Innes	Ace of Spades	Hind	Meadowood
Shott 4v	1/22 (4.5%)	0/9 (.0%)	45/48 (93.8%)	4/7 (57.1%)	0/0 (.0%)	1/5 (20.0%)	7/33 (21.2%)
Shott 3v	0/33 (.0%)	0/15 (.0%)	34/51 (66.7%)	6/17 (35.3%)	0/2 (.0%)	0/7 (.0%)	2/53 (3.8%)
Shott 2v	0/34 (.0%)	0/15 (.0%)	31/52 (59.6%)	5/17 (29.4%)	0/2 (.0%)	0/7 (.0%)	3/56 (5.6%)
Shott 1v	0/35 (.0%)	0/15 (.0%)	32/55 (58.2%)	4/21 (19.1%)	0/4 (.0%)	0/7 (.0%)	3/61 (4.9%)

Source: Snarey 2000.
Note: 4v, 3v, etc. indicate four-value, three-value, etc., discriminant functions.

points to the arrow category (Table 22.5), perhaps indicating that reworking is biasing these totals. Nevertheless, examination of the Crawford Knoll point samples used did not reveal any evidence of extensive reworking. Moreover, the Crawford Knoll point samples include items from grave lots and caches from the Bruce Boyd cemetery, which are probably little affected by resharpening and, perhaps, more comparable to the samples of known weapon systems used to derive the functions. For that site, the overall percentage classified as arrows is comparable to the total sample, ranging from 55 to 92 percent. When length is not used (one- to three-variable functions), lower percentages of items are classified as arrows (55 to 65 percent). When length is included in the Shott four-variable function, 92 percent of the Bruce Boyd points are classified as arrows, which leads us to believe resharpening is not that much of a factor in the functional identification of these points, at least. In fact, some of these Crawford Knoll points are so tiny, many having neck widths under 10 mm, that it is difficult not to believe they tipped arrows. Among reported definitive darts, few are known with such widths under 10 mm.

Snarey (2000) concluded that darts and arrows were both being used from the Small Point period on, and continuing analyses are providing additional evidence that that may have been the case for the Crawford Knoll–type points, at least. For example, the Bruce Boyd grave caches suggest a bimodal distribution of points in terms of the single variable Shott (1997) found to be the best discriminator, namely, width. Moreover, the two modes are on either side of the measure that he found distinguished darts and arrows: 20 mm (Figure 22.26). If one accepts these inferences, the almost total lack of items assigned to the arrow category among certain later Early Woodland Meadowood samples is perplexing. Several explanations are possible. For example, Meadowood points were made on cache blades, which were widely exchanged and, unlike Terminal Archaic points, recycled in high percentages into non-projectile-tip uses as drills, perforators, end scrapers, side scrapers, gravers, knives, and many other imponderables (Ellis and Spence 1997:Table 10). These other uses may have required a slightly more massive biface, especially if hafted. Although Meadowood points served as arrow tips, their use for other purposes could have been much more or equally important. One might be willing to accept a slightly larger and perhaps somewhat inefficient point as an arrow tip if flexibility of use was more important than precision of application.

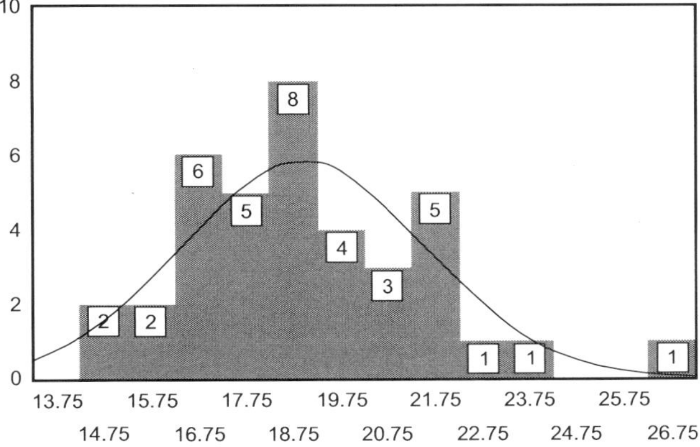

Figure 22.26. Distribution of shoulder width (in mm), Bruce Boyd site Crawford Knoll point caches.

Settlement-Subsistence Systems

Aside from mortuary components, the earliest Small Point domestic sites investigated were located in littoral areas, notably those at Inverhuron (see Kenyon 1959; Ramsden 1976; Wright 1972b) (Figure 22.19, Nos. 14, 15), and were clearly warm-weather occupations. Subsequently, sites were reported in interior areas, with the first detailed study being that by Lennox (1986) at the Innes site near Brantford (Figure 22.19, No. 13). Although no faunal material was preserved at Innes and elderberry, cherry, and raspberry seeds were recovered, the presence of walnut shell suggested fall site use, and the location of the site in an area of both lowland black-ash swamp and a rolling upland, oak-dominated forest led to the suggestion that the site was a cold-weather occupation. The observed dominance of points and end scrapers in the flaked-stone tool kit, the latter presumed to be hide-working tools, was used to reinforce the presumption of an emphasis on hunting and the seasonal inferences. Subsequently, similar locational and artifact evidence was used to argue for cold-weather occupation at other interior sites (e.g., Muller 1989). The result was the development of a model of settlement-subsistence that involved late spring to summer residence in littoral areas and movement into the interior in the fall to winter (Ellis, Kenyon, and Spence 1990). In addition, since both kinds of sites are relatively small and suggest occupation by limited populations, on the assumption that all hunter-gatherers aggregate at some point, Ian Kenyon (in Ellis, Kenyon, and Spence 1990:114–115) drew an analogy with certain later Middle Woodland populations who gathered in early spring at favored fishing locales on major rapids to exploit the runs of sucker and walleye. He suggested that the presence of discrete mortuary sites near these locales, the earliest true cemeteries known in southern Ontario, indicates they were used during, and associated with, such aggregations. This inference still remains totally speculative, as no such aggregation sites have been documented. We note, though, that some of the same sites used to exploit such fishing runs in subsequent Middle Woodland times, such as Brodie on the Thames River, have yielded surface collections including small points and broad points (University of Western Ontario collections), suggesting the early spring aggregration scenario at least may be plausible.

Research since the 1980s has tended to support some aspects of this reconstruction or to question it and suggest, as might be expected, that the situation is somewhat more complex. The only other littoral sites that have been reported are Crawford Knoll (Figure 22.19, No. 17) and Peace Bridge. A small part of the Crawford Knoll site, about 40 m², was excavated by Ian Kenyon in the late 1970s, and more detailed published reports on certain aspects of the site have now appeared (Kenyon and Snarey 2002; Thomas 1988). The site is situated on a small knoll, which, at the time it was occupied, would have been surrounded by marshland. The inhabitants camped on the top of the knoll, where several large, basin-shaped pit features were found. They tossed their refuse down the south side of the knoll into the marsh, where it accumulated to form a midden, the bottom 10 cm of which escaped subsequent plowing. The flaked-stone artifact assemblage from the site is small and includes mainly points and small, trianguloid preforms, with only a few scrapers and other tools. In fact, and as shown in Table 22.6, points and preforms make up a higher percentage of the flaked-stone tool kit than at almost any other site reported. We note that, if not for the good organic preservation, which suggests many activities were carried out at the site, such as fishing and trapping (see below), the stone assemblage alone would suggest a very specialized occupation. Regardless, this flaked-stone artifact evidence by itself seems to contradict the idea of an emphasis on hunting only at interior sites and will receive more discussion below. Other Crawford Knoll stone artifacts include a net sinker and a tubular bead, and several bone and antler artifacts were recovered, including bone gorges, awls, a harpoon barb, and two beads. About 12 m² of the midden was excavated and yielded over 12 kg of faunal remains, the analysis of which suggests occupation from spring to fall. Muskrat are especially common and, on the basis of fusion of epiphyses, Stephen C. Thomas (1988) argued these were taken in the early spring as well as at other times. Fish remains such as those of drum and bowfin as well as the presence of turtle suggest summer occupation, and fall use is indicated by nutshell and a high incidence of antlered deer remains.

In contrast to the Broad Point component, evidence of Small Point use of the Peace Bridge site is relatively ephemeral, and few features were encountered. Nonetheless, Feature 16 in Area 1 at that site, which contained two Crawford Knoll points (MacDonald and Stiess 1997:328), yielded a range of floral and faunal materials. Among the floral remains were walnut and hickory shell as well as acorns, and the seeds recovered included grape and goosefoot (Monckton 1997). The faunal material included deer, bear, elk, chipmunk, and fish species such as walleye or sauger, sucker, and bass (Thomas 1997). Overall, and as at Crawford Knoll, the range of materials suggests broad spring to fall use by, apparently, relatively small groups.

The interior sites, several more of which have now been investigated, are proving even more complex. One site of note is Thistle Hill near Brantford (Woodley 1990) (Figure 22.19, No. 11), which yielded over 400 tools, including several Innes-type points, from an area of 175 m². Woodley (1990:33–38) questioned the cold-weather use of that site, arguing that the site vicinity had a variety of resources that could have supported a small group at any time of the year. However, a notable discovery at the site was two semisubterranean house features, each measuring about 3 by 4 m, which had been truncated by site cultivation (e.g., Figure 22.27). The bottom 28–29 cm of the house depressions were still preserved as were the tips of several surrounding 5- to 10-cm-diameter stains representing locations of poles that supported the superstructure. The houses had interior hearths and a few pits and contained concentrated areas of flaking debris. Ellis and Spence (1997:130) noted the thermal retention properties of semisubterranean features, the interior hearths, and evidence of indoor flintknapping and have argued that this evidence actually suggests cold-weather use. Moreover, a pit just outside the end of one structure is very reminiscent of what appear to be exterior cold-storage pits seen on later precontact winter sites (e.g., Murphy 1991; Murphy and Ferris 1990:252–254).

Table 22.6. Flaked-Stone Tools on Ontario Small Point Sites.

Site	Points/Preforms	End Scrapers	Other	Totals	Ratio Points/ Preforms to Scrapers
Crawford Knoll	25 (86.2%)	3 (10.3%)	1 (3.5%)	29	8.33 to 1
Masterton Heights	29 (11.3%)	8 (3.1%)	220 (85.6%)	257	3.63 to 1
Innes	78 (48.1%)	22 (13.6%)	62 (38.3%)	162	3.55 to 1
Welke-Tonkonoh	13 (39.4%)	7 (21.2%)	13 (39.4%)	33	1.86 to 1
Thedford II	30 (33.0%)	17 (18.7%)	44 (48.4%)	91	1.76 to 1
Tegis	21 (17.2%)	12 (9.8%)	91 (74.6%)	122	1.75 to 1
Thistle Hill	51 (11.9%)	62(?)(14.5%)	316 (73.7%)	429	.82 to 1
Fregg	17 (22.1%)	1 (1.3%)	59 (76.6%)	77	17 to 1
Sunnydale	17 (65.4%)	0	9 (34.6%)	26	N/A
Hillerman	11 (61.1%)	0	7 (38.9%)	18	N/A

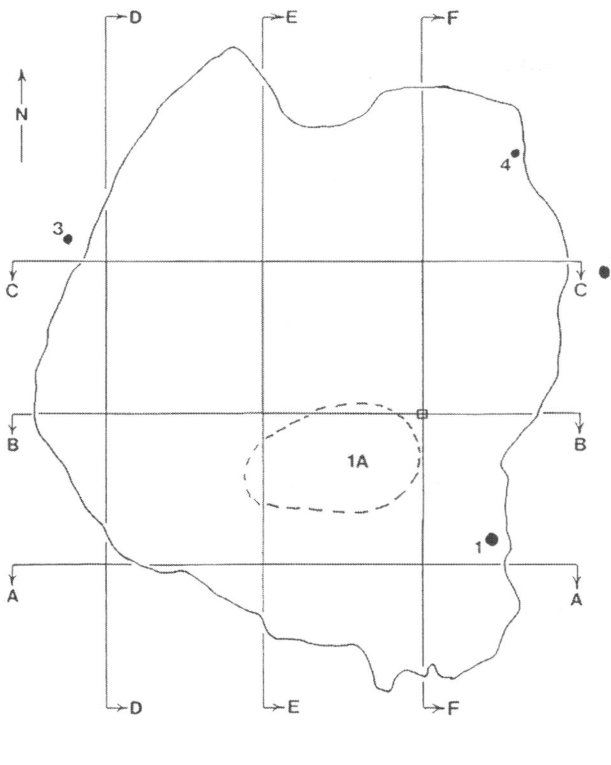

Figure 22. 27. Feature 1 (house structure), Thistle Hill site. Feature 1A is an interior hearth. Each square measures 1 m. Reproduced courtesy of Philip Woodley and with the permission of Peter Ramsden and Copetown Press from Woodley (1990).

As hinted above, while points and preforms are common at interior sites, they are actually present in lower overall frequencies than at definitive warm-weather occupations such as Crawford Knoll. For example, only 11.9 percent of the Thistle Hill flaked-stone tool assemblage consists of points, as opposed to almost 86.9 percent at Crawford Knoll (see Table 22.6), which, at the very least, might suggest hunting was important year round. However, it is difficult to treat these frequencies at face value. Of most importance, the items other than points in these assemblages predominantly include simple "used or retouched flakes," and all archaeologists are aware of the idiosyncratic recognition and reporting of such items. While variation in recognition would also affect the recognition of preforms and end scrapers, one would expect at least more consistency in the sorting of those tool forms. Of note in this regard, what distinguishes many of the interior sites such as Innes and Thistle Hill from the definitive warm-weather occupation at Crawford Knoll is not only a high percentage of stone-tool artifacts other than points and preforms but also an often-higher percentage of end scrapers. The ratio of points to end scrapers is, correspondingly, usually relatively low. If the latter are hide-scraping tools, their relatively high frequency indeed may be evidence of cold-weather use.

At some interior sites however, end scrapers are rare to nonexistent. A good example is the Hillerman site near Mississauga, Ontario (Fisher 2004) (Figure 22.19, No. 34). The site cannot be considered interior in the strictest sense, as it is not far inland from the Lake Ontario shore, being located about 1.5 km up Cooksville Creek. Although a single Early Woodland point was recovered in a peripheral area, the main plowed site area, covering only 60 m^2, yielded the bases of six Innes-style points, several preform fragments, and a few used flakes (Figure 22.28). There were no end scrapers. All of the stone artifacts were concentrated around a hearth feature. Also recovered above and around the feature were 461 pieces of calcined bone, among which were deer and turtle—probably painted turtle. The turtle suggests warm-weather site use. The presence of deer, the small size of the site, and the high percentage of points and preforms, which again exceeds that at presumed cold-weather camps (Table 22.6), have led to the suggestion the site was probably a special-purpose one, occupied by a small warm-season hunting task group that had a residential base elsewhere, one presumes on the nearby Lake Ontario shore.

Two other reported small, interior sites are of note: Sunnydale near London (Martelle 2001) and Fregg near

Figure 22.28. Stone artifacts from the Hillerman site: a–c, j, bifaces and fragments; d, Meadowood point from peripheral site area; e, drill; f–i, l–n, Innes points, bases, and fragments; k, bipolar core or wedge. Reproduced courtesy of Jacqueline Fisher and with permission of the London Chapter, Ontario Archaeological Society from Fisher (2004).

Ancaster (Wilson 2002) (see Figure 22.19, Nos. 30, 31). The single excavated area at Sunnydale covers about 150 m^2 but yielded relatively few flaked-stone tools (Table 22.6). As at the Crawford Knoll site, a single Innes or Ace of Spades point was recovered, but most of the points (n = 3) can be assigned to the Crawford Knoll type. An additional seven point tips and all the preforms recovered (n = 4) also clearly represent, or were intended to be made into, the very small points of the Crawford Knoll type. Fregg consisted of two concentrations. Locus "A" covered 120 m^2 and was somewhat ephemeral, and recovered artifacts included only 12 tools or preforms, among which was a single Innes point. Locus "B" was somewhat larger (400 m^2), but only 65 tools and preforms were recovered. Most artifacts were simple used flakes, but four Innes or Ace of Spades points were recovered as well as at least nine biface preforms or fragments of a size and morphology suggesting they were intended to be made into the same styles of projectile tips.

Neither Sunnydale nor Fregg has any reported floral or faunal remains, so any inferences as to the nature of the site occupations must be made on other bases. The sites are in topographic situations similar to the classic interior encampments, on raised areas overlooking marshy areas in regions of rolling topography. However, the sites' investigators stress that the artifact assemblages differ somewhat from those at sites such as Innes and Welke-Tonkonoh, which have previously been argued to be cold-weather encampments. Notable at both Sunnydale and Fregg is an almost total absence of end scrapers (see Table 22.6). In fact, Sunnydale's flaked-stone artfact inventory includes almost solely points and preforms (Table 22.6), suggesting, if that inventory alone can be trusted (see above comments on Crawford Knoll), a rather specialized occupation. Also, Sunnydale is unique among reported sites in that it has ground-stone woodworking tools and no fewer than six examples of celts and adzes. These artifacts also suggest somewhat specialized activities. No features were reported from either site, and despite their comparable spatial extent, relatively low amounts of material were recovered, in contrast to many other extensively excavated and explored interior sites such as Innes and Thistle Hill (Table 22.6). These attributes do not seem indicative of the long-term seasonal residential use of such locations, for example, during the extensive winter period.

Overall, the previously suggested settlement-subsistence system of warm-weather littoral and cold-weather interior occupation seems to have some merit, as indicated by the Thistle Hill data. However, sites such as those described above suggest that this model is greatly oversimplified and that other kinds of logistical as well as residential camps undoubtedly exist, particularly in interior areas. However, until more of these are investigated, including ones with good floral and faunal preservation, and until use studies are carried out of tools such as end scrapers, adequately evaluating such propositions will be difficult.

Mortuary Sites

The Small Point Archaic represents the earliest documented use of true cemetery burial in southern Ontario (Spence 1986). That is, there is evidence of multiple burials in repeatedly used locations reserved solely for burial and associated ritual activities. In fact, as hinted above, these cemeteries are not immediately adjacent to any extensive occupation areas but occur as separate sites. The apparently earliest burials are those from the Bruce Boyd site on Lake Erie (Spence and Fox 1986; Spence et al. 1978) (Figure 22.19, No. 28). This cemetery was used into later times, notably during the Early Woodland Meadowood phase. The site has not been fully reported, but the definitive Small Point–associated burials include three individuals accompanied by offerings of Crawford Knoll points (Figure 22.23) and preforms and, additionally, in one case, by some rolled copper beads. Aside from these examples, however, no other burials associated with the groups producing that style of point are reported.

More common are apparently slightly later-dating sites that comfortably fit into the taxon often referred to as "Glacial Kame" (Cunningham 1948; see Ellis, Kenyon, and Spence 1990:115–119; Spence and Fox 1986). Artifacts seen as most typical of Glacial Kame *in the region* include corner-notched Hind-style points and associated trianguloid preforms or cache blades, T-based drills, tubular cloud-blower stone pipes, eyeless bar-type birdstones, circular and sandal-sole marine-shell gorgets, bear maxilla masks, paired copper adzes with gougelike bits, and deposits of green clay. Sites contain from single to upward of 20 burial features but nonetheless suggest use by relatively small groups overall (see Spence 1986).

No new reported Glacial Kame burials have been reported in the last ten years. However, a major contribution has been the detailed publication of the report on the Hind cemetery on the Thames River in southwestern Ontario (Figure 22.19, No. 25), the only such cemetery, outside of some burials at the Picton site (Ritchie 1949), investigated using more contemporary methods of excavating and recording data (Donaldson and Wortner 1995). In addition, Varney and Pfeiffer (1995) did an updated and more extensive analysis of the skeletal remains that had been reported on previously by Pfeiffer (1977). Donaldson and Wortner (1995) also did a major service by summarizing data on, and illustrating material from, more than 13 other sites across southern Ontario, some discovered as long ago as 1849. In many cases, such as the Blackfriar's Bridge site in London (Figure 22.19, No. 23), these materials represent sites that had not been previously published in detail elsewhere.

The Hind site excavations exposed 19 Late Archaic burial features containing the remains of 34 individuals, about half of whom were cremated and many of whom were accompanied by red ocher deposits or staining. Most graves contained only one or two individuals, but a single cremation deposit of seven individuals (Burial 7) is reported. Of the 22 individuals whose osteology was studied in detail, 16 were adults and the remainder subadults. Of those adults whose sex could be determined, seven were males and seven were females. Average age at death was 35 years, with only one individual surviving until close to 60 years of age. Osteoarthritis was common as was evidence of poor dental health, such as abscesses. Harris lines, suggesting periods of interruption of growth and, probably, malnutrition, were found among half the adolescents and virtually all of those over one year of age. Among the adults, males had a surfeit of grave goods, especially Burials 15A (two birdstones, a circular marine-shell gorget, a rectanguloid stone gorget, and iron pyrites), and 20 (a point, cache blades, a drill, a black bear mask, 283 shell beads, and numerous animal bones, including deer, martin, raccoon, and even snake). Two other richly accompanied graves were of adolescents of indeterminate sex. Burial 15 goods included 32 items. In addition to a necklace of 108 copper beads that had preserved fabric and fur adhering, the goods included a bear mask, several cut jaws of raccoon, marten, and fisher, a stone pipe, and several flaked-stone tools such as a drill and a point (Figure 22.29). Burial 18A was accompanied by a relatively large number of flaked-stone artifacts, including five drills and five points, a stone gorget, freshwater mollusk valves, and a large number of animal bone and antler objects including a probable conical antler point blank and several awls.

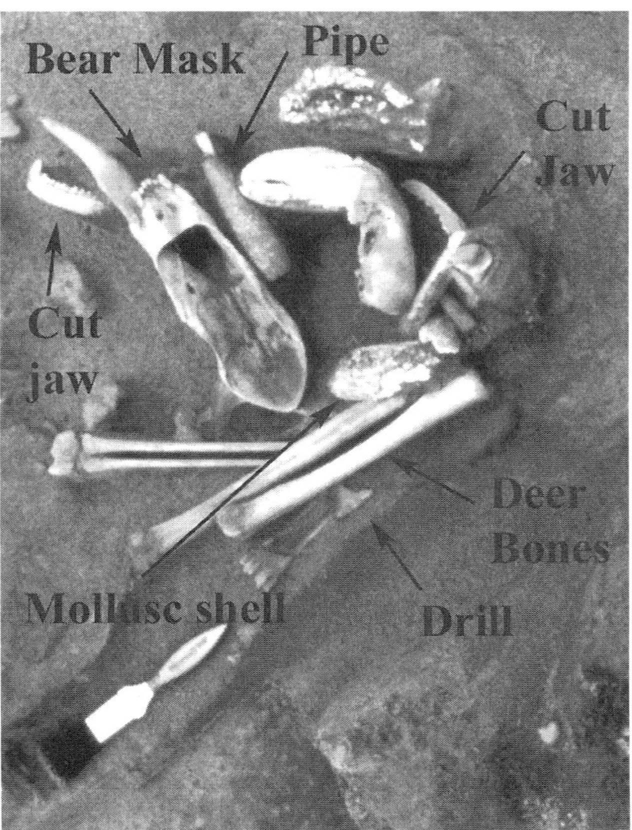

Figure 22.29. Grave goods with Burial 15, Hind site. Only some items pinpointed. Courtesy of Stanley Wortner.

Lithic Raw Material Source Use

Since several Small Point sites are now known and reported, it has been possible to begin examining in more detail how their occupants organized their flaked-stone lithic procurement and transport practices. Ellis and Spence (1997) carried out a detailed comparative study of material from six of the major excavated assemblages. An intriguing pattern that emerged from this study is that a high percentage of the points, and, sometimes, the preforms as well, are often made predominantly on a different chert source(s) than those dominating the rest of the assemblage, including the flaking debris. For example, at the Crawford Knoll site, most of the assemblage, including just about half the points and preforms as well as most of the other tools, were on Kettle Point chert from about 100 km to the northeast, whereas the remaining points and preforms were mainly on Onondaga chert from elsewhere in Ontario. A few points were made of material from more exotic sources in Michigan. The diversity of materials from exotic sources at this littoral site led Ellis and Spence (1997) to suggest that the warm season was the time of movement and interaction, including long-distance travel involving visiting and movement of individuals between widespread social groups.

At other sites however, the points and preforms tended to be almost all on material from a single source, different than that of the rest of the assemblage, a pattern that is more difficult to see as due to interaction alone. For example, almost all of the points and preforms from Welke-Tonkonoh (Muller 1989) are on Onondaga chert, probably from outcrops some 50+ km away to the southeast, whereas the unifaces and debris are almost all on Kettle Point chert from 55 km to the northwest. Yet, at the Thedford II site, while most of the preforms, unifaces, and flaking debris are on Kettle Point chert from only about 20 km away, Onondaga chert from 80+ km to the southeast is common among the points (Ellis and Spence 1997:Table 4). Similar to the case at Thedford II, among the Bruce Boyd grave lots, Haldimand chert from 60 to 70 km away is common as points, but most of the other tools are on Onondaga, which is more local to the site as secondary deposits and closer as outcrop sources (Ellis and Spence 1997:Tables 6–8).

This pattern of difference in raw material frequencies between preforms and points and the rest of the assemblages is one not restricted to these Late Archaic assemblages. As described earlier, similar differences can be seen in earlier Broad Point Archaic ones such as that from Adder Orchard and, in fact, are even seen on Early Archaic sites such as Nettling and Trail. There are two plausible explanations for these patterns. One explanation is that such patterns are a measure of serial procurement, or the visiting of several lithic sources throughout the annual round. Ellis and Spence (1997:121–122) suggest that of all the tool types produced by Small Point Archaic peoples, only points required relatively large, flaw-free blanks. Other tools, which are all quite simple, could be made on almost any blank and on flakable raw materials of any quality. They suggested therefore, that to avoid shortfalls in tool availability, specifically in points, as well as to produce a surplus of bifaces for use in other activities, such as mortuary activities, preforms were overproduced during periodic and episodic visits to lithic procurement locales. As a result, preforms and points on materials so collected remained in an individual's tool kit longer, long after other sources had been visited and were used for the simpler tools and came to dominate flaking debris assemblages. As illustrated schematically in Figure 22.30, after a source was visited, supplies of unifacial tools made on chert from that source would be exhausted first, followed by preforms and, finally, by points. This explanation implies that groups could regularly move long distances (100 to 150+ km) in Ontario during their annual rounds, such that they directly exploited more than one source in different areas or, alternatively, they made trips, albeit perhaps over relatively short distances, from certain points in their annual ranges to obtain lithic materials.

The alternative explanation is that the dominance of one material among the points indicates such items were favored in exchange relationships (see, e.g., Deller 1989). Sites such as Peace Bridge show that, at least in earlier Broad Point times, groups were residing near or at outcrops such as the Onondaga ones and producing apparently prodigious numbers of bifaces, perhaps to exchange to groups in other areas. Moreover, at Middle Archaic sites in the upper Ottawa River valley, such as Allumettes and Morrison's Island, described earlier, a significant number of points occur on Onondaga, which, given the distances involved, seem more than likely to have been obtained by exchange with groups in the source areas of that chert. In southwestern Ontario during Small Point times, however, the distances were not so extreme that normal settlement mobility can be ruled out, and evidence of extensive production of small points on Onondaga at outcrops is lacking, unlike that seen in the Broad Point assemblages. Moreover, in contrast to Broad Point times, when large, flaw-free blanks were required, and in contrast to the eastern Ontario Middle Archaic area, where there are no good sources of flakable stone locally, there was no advantage to exploiting Onondaga over sources such as Kettle Point. We believe it also unlikely that the Late Archaic groups would have relied almost entirely on exchange for points and preforms, as is implied by some Small Point Archaic assemblages such as Welke-Tonkonoh. In addition, the raw material that predominates among points versus the rest of the assemblages shifts from site to site, indicating that groups had to shift from using one material for unifaces to using others for points, material obtained by exchange depending on the group's location. Also, at some sites, notably Thistle Hill (Woodley 1990), the raw material used for points and preforms, Ancaster chert, is actually more local than the material used for the rest of the tool kit (Onondaga). Here, the use of that material for points and preforms does not seem parsimonious with exchange.

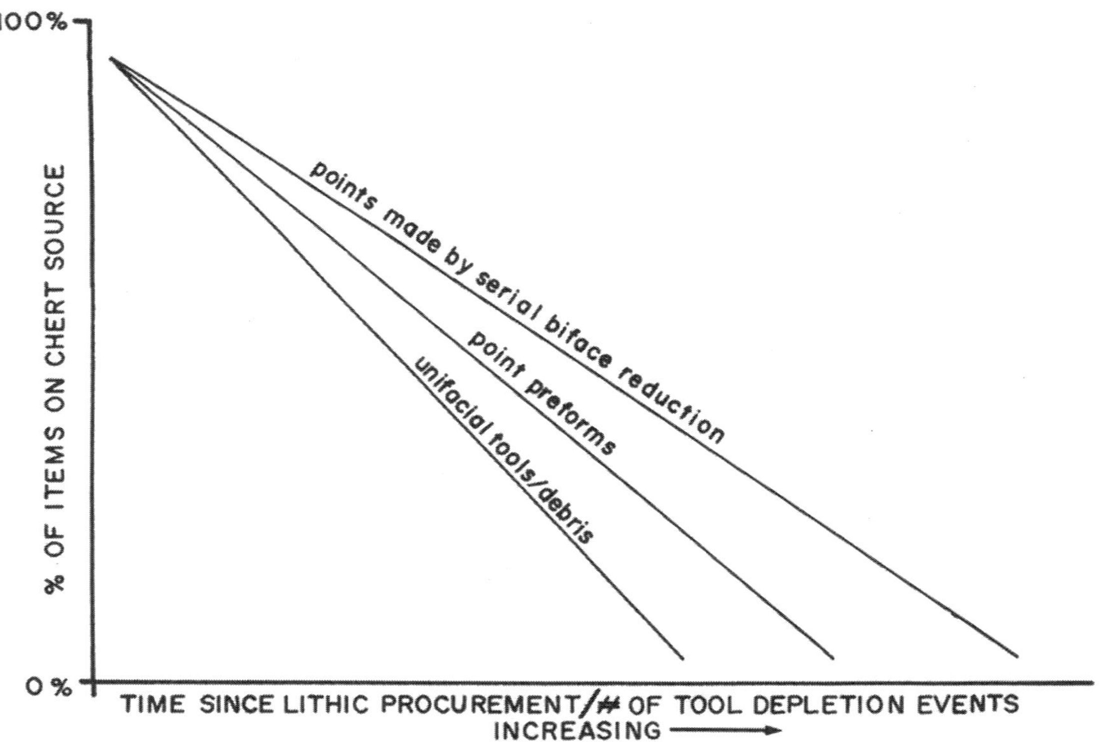

Figure 22.30. Model of varying degrees of tool-kit exhaustion by tool/debris class.

Summary

While researchers could certainly use much more data on Small Point Archaic sites, the number of such sites that are well reported exceeds that for earlier periods, and the implication is that Small Point sites are much more common. However, few detailed comparative studies are available to confirm such an inference. Also, the exact frequencies of items such as points cannot be taken at face value because some earlier types are easier to recognize (e.g., Broad Point types) than others (e.g., Brewerton) and because certain developments, such as Lamoka, are represented only marginally in Ontario. Nonetheless, the few studies available suggest that points from the brief Small Point time period are more common than all earlier point styles excepting perhaps those in the Brewerton Middle Archaic series (Williamson et al. 2002:Table 2).

The number of better-reported sites has allowed some development of subsistence and settlement models as well as ideas about weapon use and lithic procurement strategies, at least within the Small Point heartland of southwestern Ontario. A major change is certainly the presence of specialized mortuary sites, which are unknown for earlier times. Increasing social complexity (e.g., increasing status differentiation) is suggested by the clear association of more grave goods with certain individuals, and the appearance for the first time of exotic goods, such as marine-shell gorgets, green-clay deposits, and ritual or decorative copper objects, which can be seen as evidence of trade in valuables, rather than simply utilitarian exchange. Also, the presence of discrete cemeteries alone suggests probable increases in territoriality (e.g., Charles and Buikstra 1983; Pardoe 1988). It may also indicate increasing sedentism, that is, fewer residential moves. However, since several of the burials are cremations or bundles, the bodies could have been transported from elsewhere. Spence (1986) has suggested that burial features at sites such as Hind represent annual use of these cemeteries, during which all of the deceased from a given year were taken to the mortuary locales. Moreover, if the inferences as to serial use of different lithic sources are reliable, extensive areas were still being exploited; that is, distance mobility, or the distance between successive residential locales, was still relatively high.

Conclusions

We have titled this chapter "At the Crossroads and Periphery." The notion of southern Ontario as a crossroads is meant to convey the idea that the Archaic record indicates changing relationships to various external areas over time. In some time periods, the ties were to the east and the New York-New England record, as during later Broad Point times, whereas in other periods, the ties were to the Midwest, as reflected in the point forms and, to some extent, burial practices, seen in the Small Point Archaic. At still other times, relationships were with areas to the more immediate south, as suggested by the close resemblances in point forms between the earliest (Adder Orchard) broad points and the Panhandle Archaic of West Virginia and the narrower broad points of Illinois, such as Etley. Of course, whole Early Archaic tool kits exhibit similarities to those of the southeastern U.S. record. The record is clearly more complex in terms of possible external relationships than was recognized in the past, when the tendency was, as noted in the introduction, to relate everything to New York State.

In a sense, the Ontario record is also peripheral in that, unlike the emerging record for the Eastern Archaic in other areas, it lacks good archaeological evidence for emerging social and ritual complexity at a very early date, as seen in the building of mounds and other elaborate structures (e.g., Russo 1996). Neither is there direct evidence of discrete cemeteries suggestive of increasing territoriality until the very end of the Late Archaic, in contrast to evidence from other areas dating back to the Middle Archaic and beyond (e.g., Charles and Buikstra 1983). In addition, although long-distance movement of certain raw materials, such as copper, employed for utilitarian or gift-exchange purposes, can be documented in the Ontario Middle Archaic record, no compelling evidence suggests extensive movement of exotic goods in networks of valuables exchange or for mortuary purposes, as seen elsewhere (e.g., Jefferies 1996), until the Terminal Archaic.

On the basis of such evidence, one might be tempted to view the archaeological record of southern Ontario as conforming to a progressivist or unidirectional view of change during Archaic times. In fact, a previous synthesis (Ellis, Kenyon, and Spence 1990) displayed a definite tendency to view the Archaic from such a perspective. Not only was change seen toward increasing social complexity, greater territoriality, and more complex exchange networks but several other unidirectional trends were also inferred, including increasing use of more diverse resources, decreasing distance mobility, more entrenched mobility, increasing sedentism, and, consequently, fewer residential moves, steadily increasing populations, and so on. The idea that this change was unidirectional in the region is, however, questionable and, in fact, may be misleading, as several investigators have argued for hunter-gatherers, in general, or the Archaic in particular (e.g., Brown 1986; Hantman 1990:135; Rowley-Conwy 2001).

For example, on present evidence, although the frequencies should not be taken at face value, residential sites such as the surface-collected Early Archaic Nettling site are larger and have as much or more lithic debris than any excavated Small Point Archaic site reported in southern Ontario. Indeed, even if one excludes the preforms from that site, as they may tend to inflate artifact totals, there are still two to three times more tools at Nettling than at even the largest reported Small Point site. Also, the largest Small Point assemblages are dominated much more by expedient tools than by the highly formalized and, one presumes, more curated tools such as points, scrapers, and celts that predominate at Nettling. This evidence may suggest comparable degrees of residential mobility or entrenched mobility early on, as in the latest times. Also, while lithic preferences at Nettling suggest relatively high range mobility, no comparable evidence has derived from any other Corner-Notched-horizon site in Ontario. In addition, because it is plausible to interpret the lithic preferences seen at the Terminal Archaic sites as due to a persisting high degree of range mobility (Ellis and Spence 1997), one would be hard pressed to conclusively demonstrate a significant difference in the ranges exploited from most earlier sites, some Hi-Lo sites and Nettling excepted. With current evidence, suggestions of the annual movement through very small ranges cannot be seen until the Middle Woodland, for which analyses suggest the annual settlement system of local groups focused on certain river drainages, particularly their lower reaches (e.g., Finlayson 1977).

The idea of steadily increasing populations is also questionable. As noted, some apparent increases may actually have been due to population packing rather than growth, a packing forced by rising water levels, as in the later Middle Archaic. Also, although Early Archaic sites and finds may be fewer than later Middle Archaic sites in some areas, one must remember that the prime occupation areas in littoral regions for all of the earlier periods are now under the Great Lakes. With the paucity of present evidence one could argue that there were fewer people in southern Ontario during the 8000–5500 RCYBP period than in the Early Archaic. Of course, one could argue that archaeologists simply have not yet determined how to recognize the earlier Middle Archaic sites. That may be true, but unless one presupposes a progressivist stance, it is far from demonstrated. The same could be said for the lack of direct evidence of burial ritual in earlier time periods. A view of changes as unidirectional would tend to see the existing evidence that way and is consistent with a more evolutionary viewpoint. Yet, increasing evidence for more complex Early to Middle Archaic burial practices, including use of cemeteries and accompanying ritual, has come from almost all surrounding areas (e.g., Hamilton 2004; Marois 1987; Robinson 1992; Tomak 1979), and the absence of such evidence in southern Ontario may simply reflect investigators not having yet found that evidence.

Whatever the case, southern Ontario archaeologists are far from being in a position to rigorously evaluate such suggestions, whether they ultimately demonstrate more evolutionary or historical processes at play. We are still plagued by problems highlighted over 15 years ago that do not seem to want to go away (Ellis, Kenyon, and Spence 1990:122–124). More attention needs to be focused on investigating, determining the significance of, and reporting Archaic sites, and we still need to work at developing better means of assessing ideas, including more precision in measuring various kinds of settlement mobilities, estimating population densities, and determining site seasonality.

Acknowledgments

This review would not have been possible without the support and aid of several individuals. We especially thank Rick Baskey, Claude Chapdelaine, Brian Deller, Joseph Desloges, Christine Dodd, Darcy Fallon, Neal Ferris, Jacqueline Fisher, Bill Fox, Paul Lennox, Andrew Nelson, Peter Ramsden, Kristy Snarey, Mike Spence, Andrew Stewart, Steve Timmermans, Frank Wight, Ron Williamson, Phil Woodley, and Stan Wortner. Ellis dedicates his contributions to this review to the memory of a good friend, whose enthusiasm for the Archaic knew no bounds: Ian Thomas Kenyon.

References Cited

Abel, Timothy J., David M. Stothers, and Jason M. Koralewski
2001 The Williams Mortuary Complex: A Transitional Archaic Regional Interaction Center in Northwestern Ohio. In *Archaic Transitions in Ohio and Kentucky Prehistory*, edited by Olaf H. Prufer, Sara E. Pedde, and Robert S. Meindl, pp. 290–327. Kent State University Press, Kent, Ohio.

Allen, William A., and Christopher J. Ellis
2004 A Thebes Point from Mersea Township, Essex County. *Kewa* 04(2–3):23–24.

Anderson, Thane W., and C. F. Michael Lewis
1985 Postglacial Water-Level History in the Lake Ontario Basin. In *Quaternary Evolution of the Great Lakes*, edited by Paul F. Karrow and Parker E. Calkin, pp. 231–253. Special Paper 30. Geological Association of Canada, St. John's, Newfoundland.

Anderton, John
1999 The Soil-Artifact Context Model: A Geoarchaeological Approach to Paleoshoreline Site Dating in the Upper Peninsula of Michigan, USA. *Geoarchaeology* 14:265–288.

Binford, Lewis R.
1963 The Pomranky Site: A Late Archaic Burial Station. In *Miscellaneous Studies in Typology and Classification*, by Anta White, Lewis R. Binford, and Mark Papworth, pp. 149–192. Anthropological Papers 19. Museum of Anthropology, University of Michigan, Ann Arbor.
1978 *Nunamuit Ethnoarchaeology*. Academic Press, New York.
1983 *In Pursuit of the Past: Decoding the Archaeological Record*. Thames and Hudson, New York.

Borland, Mark, and Dana R. Poulton
1997 The Cider Site: A Small Point Late Archaic Component in the Town of Ancaster. *Kewa* 97(1):2–24.

Bradbury, Andrew P.
1997 The Bow and Arrow in the Eastern Woodlands: Evidence for an Archaic Origin. *North American Archaeologist* 18:207–233.

Brown, James A.
1986 Food for Thought: Where Has Subsistence Analysis Gotten Us. In *Foraging, Collecting, and Harvesting:*

Archaic Period Subsistence and Settlement in the Eastern Woodlands, edited by Sarah W. Neusius, pp. 315–330. Occasional Papers 6. Center for Archaeological Investigations, Southern Illinois University, Carbondale.

Brown, James A., and Robert Vierra
1983 What Happened in the Middle Archaic? Introduction to an Ecological Approach to Koster Site Archaeology. In *Archaic Hunters and Gatherers in the American Midwest*, edited by James L. Phillips and James A. Brown, pp. 165–195. Academic Press, New York.

Broyles, Bettye J.
1966 Preliminary Report: The St. Albans Site (46Ka 27), Kanawha County, West Virginia. *West Virginia Archaeologist* 19:1–43.
1971 *Second Preliminary Report: The St. Albans Site, Kanawha County, West Virginia, 1964–1968*. Report of Archaeological Investigations 3. West Virginia Geological and Economic Survey, Morgantown.

Burgar, Robert W. C.
1997 Points of View from the Tegis Site (AkGv-118): A Newly Defined Archaic Component in South-Central Ontario. In *Preceramic Southern Ontario*, edited by Phillip Woodley and Peter Ramsden, pp. 3–27. Occasional Publications in Northeastern Archaeology 9. Copetown Press, Hamilton, Ontario.

Bursey, Jeff
1994 Chaingate (AhGw-11): A Late Archaic Site in Burlington, Ontario. *Ontario Archaeology* 57:45–63.

Chapman, Jefferson
1975 *The Rose Island Site and the Cultural and Ecological Position of the Bifurcate Point Tradition in Eastern North America*. Report of Investigations 14. Department of Anthropology, University of Tennessee, Knoxville.
1976 The Archaic Period in the Lower Little Tennessee River Valley: The Radiocarbon Dates. *Tennessee Anthropologist* 1:1–12.
1977 *Archaic Period Research in the Lower Little Tennessee River Valley—1975*. Report of Investigations 18. Department of Anthropology, University of Tennessee, Knoxville.
1978 *The Bacon Farm Site and a Buried Site Reconnaissance*. Report of Investigations 23. Department of Anthropology, University of Tennessee, Knoxville.
1979 *The Howard and Calloway Island Sites*. Report of Investigations 27. Department of Anthropology, University of Tennessee, Knoxville.
1980 The Early and Middle Archaic Periods: A Perspective from Eastern Tennessee. In *Proceedings of the Conference on Northeastern Archaeology*, edited by J. A. Moore, pp. 123–132. Research Report 19. Department of Anthropology, University of Massachusetts, Amherst.

Charles, Douglas K., and Jane E. Buikstra
1983 Archaic Mortuary Sites in the Central Mississippi Drainage: Distribution, Structure and Behavioral Implications. In *Archaic Hunters and Gatherers in the American Midwest*, edited by James L. Phillips and James A. Brown, pp. 117–145. Academic Press, New York.

Claflin, William H.
1931 *The Stallings Island Mound, Columbia County, Georgia*. Papers of the Peabody Museum of American Archaeology and Ethnology 14(1). Harvard University, Cambridge, Massachusetts.

Clermont, Norman, and Claude Chapdelaine
1998 *Île Morrison: Lieu sacré et atelier de l'Archaïque dans l'Outaouais*. Paléo-Québec 28. Musée Canadien des Civilisations et Recherches Amérindiennes au Québec, Montreal.

Clermont, Norman, Claude Chapdelaine, and Jacques Cinq-Mars (editors)
2003 *Île aux Allumettes: l'Archaïque supérieur dans l'Outouais*. Paléo-Québec 30. Musée Canadien des Civilisations et Recherches Amérindiennes au Québec, Montreal.

Coakley, John P., and Paul F. Karrow
1994 Reconstruction of Post-Iroquois Shoreline Evolution in Western Lake Ontario. *Canadian Journal of Earth Sciences* 31:1618–1629.

Coe, Joffre L.
1964 *The Formative Cultures of the Carolina Piedmont*. Transactions of the American Philosophical Society 54(5). Philadelphia.

Converse, Robert N.
1973 *Ohio Flint Types*. Archaeological Society of Ohio, Columbus.

Cook, Thomas G.
1976a Broad Point: Culture, Phase, Horizon, Tradition, or Knife? *Journal of Anthropological Research* 32:337–355.
1976b *Koster: An Artifact Analysis of Two Archaic Phases in Westcentral Illinois*. Prehistoric Records 1. Northwestern University Archaeological Program, Evanston, Illinois.

Cooper, Andrew J.
1979 *Quaternary Geology of the Grand Bend-Parkhill Area, Southern Ontario*. Ontario Geological Survey Report 188. Ontario Ministry of Natural Resources, Toronto.

Cossette, Évelyne
2003 Étude de l'assemblage zooarchéologique du site BkGg-11. In *Île aux Allumettes: l'Archaïque supérieur dans l'Outouais*, edited by Norman Clermont, Claude Chapdelaine, and Jacques Cinq-Mars, pp. 265–286. Paléo-Québec 30. Musée Canadien des Civilisations et Recherches Amérindiennes au Québec, Montreal.

Crawford, Gary W., David G. Smith, John R. Desloges, and A. M. Davis
1998 Floodplains and Agricultural Origins: A Case Study in South-Central Ontario. *Journal of Field Archaeology* 25:123–137.

Creemens, David L.
2003 Geoarchaeology of Soils on Stable Geomorphic Surfaces: Mature Soil Model for the Glaciated Northeast. In *Geoarchaeology of Landscapes in the Glaciated Northeast*, edited by David L. Creemens and John P. Hart, pp. 49–60. Bulletin 497. New York State Museum, Albany.

Cross, John R.
1999 "By Any Other Name …": A Reconsideration of Middle Archaic Lithic Technology and Typology in the Northeast. In *The Archaeological Northeast*, edited by Mary Ann Levine, Kenneth Sassaman, and Mark Nassaney, pp. 57–73. Bergin and Garvey, Westport, Connecticut.

Cufr, Robert J.

1973 Satchell Complex Sites in Northern Ohio and Monroe County, Michigan. *Toledo Area Aboriginal Research Club Bulletin* 2(3):1–25.

Cunningham, Wilbert M.

1948 *A Study of the Glacial Kame Culture in Michigan, Ohio and Indiana*. Occasional Contributions 12. Museum of Anthropology, University of Michigan, Ann Arbor.

Deller, D. Brian

1976 The Heaman Site: A Preliminary Report on a Paleo-Indian Site in Middlesex County, Ontario. *Ontario Archaeology* 27:13–28.

1989 Interpretation of Chert Type Variation in Paleoindian Industries, Southwestern Ontario. In *Eastern Paleoindian Lithic Resource Use*, edited by Christopher Ellis and Jonathan Lothrop, pp. 191–220. Westview Press, Boulder, Colorado.

Deller, D. Brian, and Christopher J. Ellis

1984 Crowfield: A Preliminary Report on a Probable Paleo-Indian Cremation in Southwestern Ontario. *Archaeology of Eastern North America* 12:41–71.

1992 *Thedford II: A Paleo-Indian Site in the Ausable River Watershed of Southwestern Ontario*. Memoirs 24. Museum of Anthropology, University of Michigan, Ann Arbor.

2001 Evidence for Late Paleo-Indian Ritual from the Caradoc Site (AfHj-104), Southwestern Ontario, Canada. *American Antiquity* 66:267–284.

Dibb, Gordon C.

2004 The Madina Phase: Late Pleistocene-Early Holocene Occupation along the Margins of the Simcoe Lowlands in South-Central Ontario. In *The Late Palaeoindian Great Lakes: Geoarchaeological and Archaeological Studies of Late Pleistocene and Early Holocene Environments*, edited by Lawrence J. Jackson and Andrew Hinshelwood, pp. 117–161. Mercury Series Paper 165. Archaeological Survey of Canada, Canadian Museum of Civilization, Gatineau.

Dice, Lee R.

1943 *The Biotic Provinces of North America*. University of Michigan Press, Ann Arbor.

Dincauze, Dena F.

1972 The Atlantic Phase: A Late Archaic Culture in Massachusetts. *Man in the Northeast* 4:40–61.

1975 The Late Archaic Period in Southern New England. *Arctic Anthropology* 12(2):23–34.

1976 *The Neville Site: 8,000 Years at Amoskeag*. Monograph 4. Peabody Museum of Archaeology and Ethnology, Harvard University, Cambridge, Massachusetts.

Dodd, Christine F.

1996 An Archaeological Assessment of Highway 69 and Excavation of the Baxter, Bentley and Bressette Sites in Georgian Bay Township, Ontario. Licence report on file, Ontario Ministry of Culture, Toronto.

1997 The Trail Site: A Nettling Camp on the Grand River. In *Preceramic Southern Ontario*, edited by Phillip Woodley and Peter Ramsden, pp. 65–75. Occasional Publications in Northeastern Archaeology 9. Copetown Press, Hamilton, Ontario.

Donaldson, William, and Stanley Wortner

1995 The Hind Site and the Glacial Kame Burial Complex in Ontario. *Ontario Archaeology* 59:5–95.

Ellis, Christopher J.

1987 Stanly/Neville Points. *Kewa* 87(9):21.

1989 The Explanation of Northeastern Paleoindian Lithic Procurement Patterns. In *Eastern Paleoindian Lithic Resource Use*, edited by Christopher Ellis and Jonathan Lothrop, pp. 139–164. Westview Press, Boulder, Colorado.

1997 Some Sites/Artifacts I Have Known: The Paget Sites. *Kewa* 97(5):8–12.

1998 The Pits (Part III) or Evidence from the Parkhill Site Pertaining to the Age of Late Archaic "Smallpoints." *Kewa* 98(7–8):18–24.

2003 Review of *Great Lakes Archaeology*, by Ronald J. Mason. *Canadian Journal of Archaeology* 27:326–329.

2004a Hi-Lo: An Early Lithic Complex in Southern Ontario. In *The Late Palaeoindian Great Lakes: Geoarchaeological and Archaeological Studies of Late Pleistocene and Early Holocene Environments*, edited by Lawrence J. Jackson and Andrew Hinshelwood, pp. 57–83. Mercury Series Paper 165. Archaeological Survey of Canada, Canadian Museum of Civilization, Gatineau.

2004b The Hi-Lo Component at the Welke-Tonkonoh Site, Area C. *Kewa* 04(5):1–19.

Ellis, Christopher J., and D. Brian Deller

1982 Hi-Lo Materials from Southwestern Ontario. *Ontario Archaeology* 38:3–22.

1986 Post-Glacial Lake Nipissing "Waterworn" Assemblages from the Southeastern Huron Basin Area. *Ontario Archaeology* 45:39–60.

1990 Paleo-Indians. In *The Archaeology of Southern Ontario to A.D. 1650*, edited by Chris J. Ellis and Neal Ferris, pp. 37–63. Occasional Publication 5. London Chapter, Ontario Archaeological Society.

1991 A Small (But Informative) Early Archaic Assemblage from the Culloden Acres Site, Area B. *Kewa* 91(8):2–17.

2000 *An Early Paleo-Indian Site near Parkhill, Ontario*. Mercury Series Paper 159. Archaeological Survey of Canada, Canadian Museum of Civilization, Gatineau.

2002 *Excavations at the Caradoc Site (AfHj-104): A Late Paleoindian Ritual Artifact Deposit*. Occasional Publication 8. London Chapter, Ontario Archaeological Society.

Ellis, Christopher J., D. Brian Deller, Carl Murphy, and Christine Dodd

1990 The Pits Part I: A Radiocarbon-Dated "Small Point" Late Archaic Feature from the Thedford II Site. *Kewa* 90(7):8–12.

Ellis, Christopher J., Gary Foster, and Michael Jesmer

1990 *A Preliminary Evaluation of Native Cultural History of the Trent-Severn Waterway*. Environment Canada, Parks Service, National Historic Parks and Sites Branch Report. Canadian Parks Service, Archaeological Research Branch, Ottawa.

Ellis, Christopher J., Albert C. Goodyear, Dan F. Morse, and Kenneth Tankersley

1998 Archaeology of the Pleistocene-Holocene Transition in Eastern North America. *Quaternary International* 49–50:151–166.

Ellis, Christopher J., Ian T. Kenyon, and Michael W. Spence

1990 The Archaic. In *The Archaeology of Southern Ontario to A.D. 1650*, edited by Chris J. Ellis and Neal Ferris, pp.

65–124. Occasional Publication 5. London Chapter, Ontario Archaeological Society.

Ellis, Christopher J., and Michael W. Spence
1997 Raw Material Variation and the Organization of "Small Point" Archaic Lithic Technologies in Southwestern Ontario. In *Preceramic Southern Ontario*, edited by Phillip Woodley and Peter Ramsden, pp. 119–140. Occasional Publications in Northeastern Archaeology 9. Copetown Press, Hamilton, Ontario.

Ellis, Christopher J., Stanley Wortner, and William Fox
1991 Nettling: An Overview of an Early Archaic "Kirk Corner-Notched Cluster" Site in Southwestern Ontario. *Canadian Journal of Archaeology* 15:1–34.

Emerson, J. Norman, and William C. Noble
1966 The Surma Site, Fort Erie, Ontario. *Ontario Archaeology* 9:68–88.

Esler, James
2002 The Masterson Heights Site (AgGt-105): A Late Archaic Period Site in St. Catherines, Ontario. *Kewa* 02(5–6):1–30.

Fergusson, John P.
1996 The Haviland Site: The Early Archaic in Schoharie County. *Bulletin of the New York State Archaeological Association* 110:1–15.

Finlayson, William D.
1977 *The Saugeen Culture: A Middle Woodland Manifestation in Southwestern Ontario*. Mercury Series Paper 61. Archaeological Survey of Canada, National Museum of Man, Ottawa.

Fisher, Jacqueline A.
1987 Brodie and Parkhill: An Analysis of Two Late Archaic Broadpoint Samples from Southwestern Ontario. *Kewa* 87(8):3–21.
1997 *The Adder Orchard Site (AgHk-16): Lithic Technology and Spatial Organization in the Broad Point Late Archaic*. Occasional Publication 3. London Chapter, Ontario Archaeological Society.
2004 The Hillerman Site (AjGv-51) A Small Point Warm Season Interior Camp, Mississauga, Ontario. *Kewa* 04(2–3):1–22.

Fisher, Jacqueline A., James S. Molnar, and W. Bruce Stewart
1997 Northoway 2: An Early Middle Archaic Stanly/Neville Site, Burlington, Ontario. In *Preceramic Southern Ontario*, edited by Phillip Woodley and Peter Ramsden, pp. 77–87. Occasional Publication in Northeastern Archaeology 9. Copetown Press, Hamilton, Ontario.

Fitting, James E.
1963 The Hi-Lo Site: A Late Paleo-Indian Site in Michigan. *The Wisconsin Archeologist* 44:87–96.
1968 Environmental Potential and Post-Glacial Readaptation in Eastern North America. *American Antiquity* 33:441–445.
1970 *The Archaeology of Michigan*. Natural History Press, New York.

Fitting, James E., Jerry DeVisscher, and Edward Wahla
1966 *The Paleo-Indian Occupation of the Holcombe Beach*. Anthropological Papers 27. Museum of Anthropology, University of Michigan, Ann Arbor.

Fowler, Melvin
1959 *Summary Report of Modoc Rock Shelter: 1952, 1953, 1955, 1956*. Reports of Investigations 8. Illinois State Museum, Springfield.

Funk, Robert E.
1976 *Recent Contributions to Hudson Valley Prehistory*. Memoir 22. New York State Museum, Albany.
1983 The Northeastern United States. In *Ancient North Americans*, edited by Jesse D. Jennings, pp. 303–371. W. H. Freeman, San Francisco.
1988 The Laurentian Concept: A Review. *Archaeology of Eastern North America* 16:1–42.
1993 *Archaeological Investigations in the Upper Susquehanna Valley, New York State*, vol. 1. Persimmon Press, Buffalo, New York.

Funk, Robert E., and Bruce Rippeteau
1977 *Adaptation, Continuity and Change in Upper Susquehanna Prehistory*. Occasional Publications in Northeastern Anthropology 3. George's Mills, New Hampshire, Man in the Northeast.

Funk, Robert E., and Beth Wellman
1984 The Evidence of Early Holocene Occupations in the Upper Susquehanna Valley, New York State. *Archaeology of Eastern North America* 12:81–109.

Gardner, William A.
1977 Flint Run Paleoindian Complex and Its Implications for Eastern North American Prehistory. *Annals of the New York Academy of Sciences* 288:257–263.

Graham, Martha, and A. Roberts
1986 Residentially Constrained Mobility: A Preliminary Investigation of Variability in Settlement Organization. *Haliksa'i: University of New Mexico Contributions to Anthropology* 5:105–116.

Griffin, James B.
1964 The Northeast Woodlands Area. In *Prehistoric Man in the New World*, edited by Jesse D. Jennings and Edward Norbeck, pp. 223–258. University of Chicago Press, Chicago.

Hamilton, Scott
2004 Early Holocene Human Burials at Wapekeka (FlJi-1), Northern Ontario. In *The Late Palaeoindian Great Lakes: Geoarchaeological and Archaeological Studies of Late Pleistocene and Early Holocene Environments*, edited by Lawrence J. Jackson and Andrew Hinshelwood, pp. 337–368. Mercury Series Paper 165. Archaeological Survey of Canada, Canadian Museum of Civilization, Gatineau.

Hantman, Jeffrey L.
1990 The Early and Middle Archaic in Virginia: A North American Perspective. In *Early and Middle Archaic Research in Virginia: A Synthesis*, edited by Theodore R. Reinhart and Mary Ellen N. Hodges, pp. 133–153. Archeological Society of Virginia, Richmond.

Hayes Charles F., and L. Bergs
1969 A Progress Report on an Archaic Site on the Farrell Farm: The Cole Gravel Pit. *Bulletin of the New York State Archaeological Association* 47:1–12.

Hoard, Robert J., William E. Banks, Rolfe D. Mandel, Michael Finnegan, and Jennifer E. Epperson
2004 A Middle Archaic Burial from East Central Kansas. *American Antiquity* 69:717–739.

Jackson, Lawrence J., Christopher J. Ellis, Alan V. Morgan, and John H. McAndrews

2000 Glacial Lake Levels and Eastern Great Lakes Palaeo-Indians. *Geoarchaeology* 15:415–440.

Jefferies, Richard W.

1987 *The Archaeology of Carrier Mills: 10,000 Years in the Saline Valley of Illinois.* Southern Illinois University Press, Edwardsville.

1996 The Emergence of Long-Distance Exchange Networks in the Southeastern United States. In *Archaeology of the Mid-Holocene Southeast*, edited by Kenneth E. Sassaman and David G. Anderson, pp. 222–234. University Presses of Florida, Gainesville.

Johnston, Richard B. (editor)

1984 *The McIntyre Site: Archaeology, Subsistence and Environment.* Mercury Series Paper 126. Archaeological Survey of Canada, National Museum of Man, Ottawa.

Justice, Noel D.

1987 *Stone Age Spear and Arrow Points of the Midcontinental and Eastern United States: A Modern Survey and Reference.* Indiana University Press, Bloomington.

Jury, Wilfred

1978 *A Red Ochre Burial from Port Franks, Ontario.* Museum Notes 1. Museum of Indian Archaeology, London, Ontario

Karrow, Paul F.

1980 The Nipissing Transgression around Southern Lake Huron. *Canadian Journal of Earth Sciences* 17:1271–1274.

Karrow, Paul F., and Parker E. Calkin (editors)

1985 *Quaternary Evolution of the Great Lakes.* Special Paper 30. Geological Association of Canada, St. John's, Newfoundland.

Karrow, Paul F., and Barry Warner

1990 The Geological and Biological Environment for Human Occupation in Southern Ontario. In *The Archaeology of Southern Ontario to A.D. 1650*, edited by Chris Ellis and Neal Ferris, pp. 5–35. Occasional Publications 5. London Chapter, Ontario Archaeological Society.

Katzenberg, M. Anne, and Norman C. Sullivan

1979 A Report on the Human Burial from the Milton-Thomazi Site. *Ontario Archaeology* 32:27–34.

Kennedy, Clyde C.

1966 Preliminary Report on the Morrison's Island-6 Site. *Bulletin* 206:100–125. National Museum of Man, Ottawa, Ontario.

Kenyon, Ian T.

1979 The Sub-Greywacke Lanceolate Biface in the Ausable River Valley. *Kewa* 79(4):2–8.

1980a The George Davidson Site: An Archaic "Broad Point" Component in Southwestern Ontario. *Archaeology of Eastern North America* 8:11–28.

1980b The Satchell Complex in Ontario: A Perspective from the Ausable Valley. *Ontario Archaeology* 34:17–43.

1981 Making Genesee Points by the Niagara River. *Kewa* 81(1):2–5.

1983 Late Archaic Stemmed Points from the Adder Orchard Site. *Kewa* 83(2):7–14.

1989 Terminal Archaic Projectile Points in Southwestern Ontario: An Exploratory Study. *Kewa* 89(1):2–21.

Kenyon, Ian T., and Kristy Snarey

2002 The Crawford Knoll Site. *Kewa* 02(1):1–19.

Kenyon, Walter

1959 *The Inverhuron Site.* Occasional Paper 1. Art and Archaeology Division, Royal Ontario Museum, Toronto.

1973 *Relatives They Did Not Know.* Archaeological Newsletter (n.s.) 94. Royal Ontario Museum, Toronto.

Lackowicz, Robert

1996 *An Attribute and Spatial Analysis of Several Ground Stone Artifact Types from Southern Ontario.* Master's thesis, Trent University, Peterborough, Ontario. University Microfilms, Ann Arbor, Michigan.

Larsen, Curtis E.

1985 Lake Level, Uplift and Outlet Incision, the Nipissing and Algoma Great Lakes. In *Quaternary Evolution of the Great Lakes*, edited by Paul F. Karrow and Parker E. Calkin, pp. 63–77. Special Paper 30. Geological Association of Canada, St. John's, Newfoundland.

Leechman, Douglas, and Frederica DeLaguna

1949 The Parker Site. In *Annual Report of the National Museum for the Fiscal Year 1947–48.* Bulletin 113:29–30. National Museum of Canada, Ottawa.

Lemonnier, Pierre

1986 The Study of Material Culture Today: Toward an Anthropology of Technical Systems. *Journal of Anthropological Archaeology* 5:147–186.

Lennox, Paul A.

1986 The Innes Site: A Plow-Disturbed Archaic Component, Brant County, Ontario. *Midcontinental Journal of Archaeology* 11:221–268.

1990 The Canada Century Site: A Lamoka Component Located on the Niagara Peninsula, Ontario. *Ontario Archaeology* 51:31–52.

1993 The Kassel and Blue Dart Sites: Two Components of the Early Archaic Bifurcate Base Projectile Point Tradition, Waterloo County, Ontario. *Ontario Archaeology* 56:1–31.

2000 The Rentner and McKean Sites: 10,000 Years of Settlement on the Shore of Lake Huron, Simcoe County, Ontario. *Ontario Archaeology* 70:16–65.

Lewis, Thomas M. N., and Madeline K. Lewis

1961 *Eva: An Archaic Site.* University of Tennessee Press, Knoxville.

Lovis, William A. (editor)

1989 *Archaeological Investigations at the Weber I (20SA581) and Weber II (20SA582) Sites, Frankenmuth Township, Saginaw County, Michigan.* Michigan Cultural Resource Investigation Series 1. Michigan Department of State and Michigan Department of Transportation, Lansing.

Lovis, William A., Randolph E. Donahue, and Margaret B. Holman

2005 Long-Distance Logistical Mobility as an Organizing Principle among Northern Hunter-Gatherers: A Great Lakes Middle Holocene Settlement System. *American Antiquity* 70:669–693.

Lovis, William A., and James A. Robertson

1989a Rethinking the Archaic Chronology of the Saginaw Valley, Michigan. *Midcontinental Journal of Archaeology* 14:226–260.

1989b The Archaic of the Saginaw Valley: The View from Weber I. In *Archaeological Investigations at the Weber I (20SA581) and Weber II (20SA582) Sites, Frankenmuth Township, Saginaw County, Michigan*, edited by William A. Lovis, pp. 217–223. Michigan Cultural Resource Investigation Series 1. Michigan Department of State and Michigan Department of Transportation, Lansing.

Luedtke, Barbara E.
1976 *Lithic Material Distribution and Interaction Patterns during the Late Woodland Period in Michigan*. Ph.D. dissertation, University of Michigan. University Microfilms, Ann Arbor, Michigan.

MacDonald, John
1997 The Deercrest Site: A Late Archaic Collingwood Chert Assemblage. In *Preceramic Southern Ontario*, edited by Phillip Woodley and Peter Ramsden, pp. 89–96. Occasional Publications in Northeastern Archaeology 9. Copetown Press, Hamilton, Ontario.

MacDonald, Robert I., and Deborah Steiss
1997 Artifact Analysis. In *In the Shadow of the Bridge: The Archaeology of the Peace Bridge Site (AfGr-9), 1994–1996 Investigations*, edited by Ronald F. Williamson and Robert I. MacDonald, pp. 323–332. Occasional Publications 1. Archaeological Services, Toronto.

Marois, Roger
1987 Souvenirs d'antan: Les sépultres Archaïques de Couteau-du-Lac, Québec. *Recherches Amérindiennes au Québec* 17(1–2):7–31.

Martelle, Holly
2001 The Sunnydale Site: AgHh-53. A Small Point Archaic Camp in North London. *Kewa* 01(5):1–14.

Mason, Ronald J.
1981 *Great Lakes Archaeology*. Academic Press, New York.

Mason, Ronald J., and Carole Irwin
1960 An Eden-Scottsbluff Burial in Northeastern Wisconsin. *American Antiquity* 26:43–57.

Mayer-Oakes, William J.
1955 *The Globe Shell Heap (Site 46Hk34-1) Hancock County, West Va.* Publication 3. West Virginia Archaeological Society, Moundsville.

McAndrews, John H.
1981 Late Quaternary Climate of Southern Ontario: Temperature Trends from the Fossil Pollen Record. In *Quaternary Paleoclimate*, edited by William C. Mahaney, pp. 319–333. Geoabstracts, Norwich, England.
1994 Pollen Diagrams for Southern Ontario Applied to Archaeology. In *Great Lakes Archaeology and Paleoecology: Exploring Interdisciplinary Initiatives for the Nineties*, edited by Robert I. MacDonald, pp. 179–195. Publication 10. Quaternary Sciences Institute, University of Waterloo, Waterloo, Ontario.

McElrath, Dale, Thomas Emerson, Andrew Fortier, and James Phillips
1984 Late Archaic Period. In *American Bottom Archaeology: A Summary of the FAI-270 Contribution to the Culture History of the Mississippi River Valley*, edited by Charles J. Bareis and James W. Porter, pp. 34–58. University of Illinois Press, Urbana.

McMillan, Katherine
2003 Hafted Diagnostic End Scrapers from the Nettling Site: Assessing Technological Change in the Paleoindian-Early Archaic Transition (ca. 9,000 to 10,000 B.P.). Master's thesis, Department of Anthropology, University of Western Ontario, London.

Michie, James L.
1973 The Edgefield Scraper: Its Inferred Antiquity and Use. *The Chesopiean* 11:2–10.

Monckton, Stephen G.
1997 Plant Remains. In *In the Shadow of the Bridge: The Archaeology of the Peace Bridge Site (AfGr-9), 1994–1996 Investigations*, edited by Ronald F. Williamson and Robert I. MacDonald, pp. 427–440. Occasional Publications 1. Archaeological Services, Toronto.

Morse, Dan F.
1997 *Sloan: A Paleoindian Dalton Cemetery in Arkansas*. Smithsonian Institution Press, Washington, D.C.

Muller, Joseph P.
1989 A "Smallpoint" Archaic Component at the Welke-Tonkonoh Site, Ontario. *Kewa* 89(3):3–22.
1999 The McLeod Site: A Small Paleo-Indian Occupation in Southwestern Ontario. Master's thesis, Department of Anthropology, McMaster University, Hamilton, Ontario.

Murphy, Carl R.
1991 A Western Basin Winter Cabin from Kent County, Ontario. *Kewa* 91(1):3–17.

Murphy, Carl R., and Neal Ferris
1990 The Late Woodland Western Basin Tradition of Southern Ontario. In *The Archaeology of Southern Ontario to A.D. 1650*, edited by Chris J. Ellis and Neal Ferris, pp. 189–278. Occasional Publications 5. London Chapter, Ontario Archaeological Society.

Murray, Andrew
1997 The Ageing Maple Site: The Importance of Being Small. In *Preceramic Southern Ontario*, edited by Phillip Woodley and Peter Ramsden, pp. 59–63. Occasional Publications in Northeastern Archaeology 9. Copetown Press, Hamilton, Ontario.

Nance, Jack D.
1986 The Morrisroe Site: Projectile Point Types and Radiocarbon Dates from the Lower Tennessee River Valley. *Midcontinental Journal of Archaeology* 11:11–50.

Noble, William C.
1975 Canadian Prehistory: The Lower Great Lakes-St. Lawrence Region. *Canadian Archaeological Association Bulletin* 7:96–121.

Pardoe, Colin
1988 The Cemetery as Symbol. The Distribution of Prehistoric Aboriginal Burial Grounds in Southeastern Australia. *Archaeology in Oceania* 23:1–16.

Park, Robert W., and Lori A. Karaba
1997 Debitage Analysis and AgHc-82. In *Preceramic Southern Ontario*, edited by Phillip Woodley and Peter Ramsden, pp. 47–57. Occasional Publications in Northeastern Archaeology 9. Copetown Press, Hamilton, Ontario.

Parker, Lawrence R.
1986a Haldimand Chert: A Preferred Raw Material in Southwestern Ontario during the Early Holocene Period. *Kewa* 86(4):4–21.
1986b *Haldimand Chert and Its Utilization during the Early Holocene Period in Southwestern Ontario*. Master's thesis,

Trent University, Peterborough, Ontario. University Microfilms, Ann Arbor, Michigan.
1995 The Johnson Flats Site (AgGx-214): A Stratified Prehistoric Occupation on the Lower Grand River Floodplain. *Kewa* 95(1):2–19.

Payne, James H.
1982 The Western Basin Paleo-Indian and Early Archaic Sequences. Bachelor's thesis, Department of Sociology, Anthropology and Social Work, University of Toledo, Toledo, Ohio.

Peske, Robert G.
1963 Argillite of Michigan: A Preliminary Projectile Point Classification and Temporal Placement Based on Surface Materials. *Papers of the Michigan Academy of Science, Arts, and Letters* 48:557–566.

Pfeiffer, Susan
1977 *The Skeletal Biology of Archaic Populations of the Great Lakes Region*. Mercury Series Paper 64. Archaeological Survey of Canada, National Museum of Man, Ottawa.

Popham, Robert E., and J. Norman Emerson
1954 Manifestations of the Old Copper Industry in Ontario. *The Pennsylvania Archaeologist* 24:3–19.

Prufer, Olaf H., and Charles Sofsky
1965 The McKibben Site (33TR-57), Trumbull County, Ohio: A Contribution to the Late Paleo-Indian and Archaic Phases of Ohio. *The Michigan Archaeologist* 11(1):9–40.

Purdy, Barbara A.
1986 *Florida's Prehistoric Stone Technology*. University Presses of Florida, Gainesville.

Ramsden, Peter G.
1976 *Rocky Ridge: A Stratified Archaic Site Near Inverhuron, Ontario*. Research Report 7. Historical Planning and Research Branch, Ontario Ministry of Culture and Recreation, Toronto.
1990 The Winter Site (AkHb-2): A Late Archaic Campsite near Guelph, Ontario. *Ontario Archaeology* 50:27–38.
1997 Laurentian Archaic in the Kawartha Lakes and Haliburton. In *Preceramic Southern Ontario*, edited by Phillip Woodley and Peter Ramsden, pp. 141–147. Occasional Publications in Northeastern Archaeology 9. Copetown Press, Hamilton, Ontario.

Ramsey, Christopher Bronk
2003 *Oxcal Program v3.9. Radiocarbon Accelerator Unit, University of Oxford*. Electronic document, http://www.rlaha.ox.ac.uk/orau/oxcal.html, accessed January 7, 2005.

Redfield, Andrew, and John Moselage
1970 The Lace Place, a Dalton Project Site in the Western Lowland in Eastern Arkansas. *The Arkansas Archaeologist* 11(2):21–44.

Reynolds, Thomas
1856 Discovery of Copper and Other Early Indian Relics, near Brockville. *The Canadian Journal* (n.s.) 64:265–287.

Ritchie, William A.
1932a The Algonkian Sequence in New York. *American Anthropologist* 43:406–415.
1932b The Lamoka Site: The Type Site of the Archaic Algonkian Period in New York. *New York State Archaeological Association Researches and Transactions* 7(4):79–134. Rochester.
1940 *Two Prehistoric Village Sites at Brewerton, New York*. Research Records 5. Rochester Museum of Arts and Sciences, Rochester, New York.
1944 *The Pre-Iroquoian Occupations of New York State*. Memoir 1. Rochester Museum of Arts and Sciences, Rochester, New York.
1949 *An Archaeological Survey of the Trent Waterway in Ontario Canada*. New York State Archaeological Association Researches and Transactions 12(1). Rochester.
1955 *Recent Discoveries Suggesting an Early Woodland Burial Cult in the Northeast*. Circular 40. New York State Museum and Science Service, Albany.
1969 *The Archaeology of New York State*. Natural History Press, New York.
1971a The Archaic in New York. *Bulletin* 52:2–12. New York State Archaeological Association, Rochester.
1971b *A Typology and Nomenclature for New York Projectile Points*. Bulletin 384. New York State Museum and Science Service, Albany.

Ritchie, William A., and Robert E. Funk
1973 *Aboriginal Settlement Patterns in the Northeast*. Memoir 20. New York State Museum and Science Service, Albany.

Roberts, Arthur B.
1985 *Preceramic Occupations along the North Shore of Lake Ontario*. Mercury Series Paper 132. Archaeological Survey of Canada, National Museum of Man, Ottawa.

Robertson, David A., Ronald F. Williamson, Robert I. MacDonald, Robert H. Pihl, and Martin S. Cooper
1997 Interpretations and Conclusions. In *In the Shadow of the Bridge: The Archaeology of the Peace Bridge Site (AfGr-9), 1994–1996 Investigations*, edited by Ronald F. Williamson and Robert I. MacDonald, pp. 493–510. Occasional Publications 1. Archaeological Services, Toronto.

Robertson, James A., William A. Lovis, and John R. Halsey
1999 The Late Archaic: Hunters and Gatherers in an Uncertain Environment. In *Retrieving Michigan's Buried Past: The Archaeology of the Great Lakes State*, edited by John R. Halsey, pp. 95–124. Cranbrook Institute of Science, Bloomfield Hills, Michigan.

Robinson, Brian S.
1992 Early and Middle Archaic Period Occupation in the Gulf of Maine Region: Mortuary and Technological Patterning. In *Early Holocene Occupation in Northern New England*, edited by Brian S. Robinson, James B. Petersen, and Ann K. Robinson, pp. 63–117. Occasional Publications in Maine Archaeology 9. Maine Historic Preservation Commission, Augusta.

Ross, Brian D., and Cesare D'Annibale
2000 National Parks and Native Sites Archaeology, Parks Canada, Ontario Service Centre: 1999. *Annual Archaeological Report for Ontario* (n.s.) 11:151–169. Ontario Heritage Foundation, Toronto.

Ross, Brian D., Cesare D'Annibale, and Kristen Spence
1999 National Parks and Native Sites Archaeology, Parks Canada, Ontario Service Centre: 1997. *Annual Archaeological Report for Ontario* (n.s) 9:151–169. Ontario Heritage Foundation, Toronto.
2000 National Parks and Native Sites Archaeology, Parks Canada, Ontario Service Centre: 1998. *Annual*

Archaeological Report for Ontario (n.s.) 10:113–130. Ontario Heritage Foundation, Toronto.

Rowe, John S.
1972 *Forest Regions of Canada*. Publication 1300. Canadian Forest Service, Ottawa.

Rowley-Conwy, Peter
2001 Time, Change and the Archaeology of Hunter-Gatherers: How Original is the 'Original Affluent Society'? In *Hunter-Gatherers: An Interdisciplinary Perspective*, edited by Catherine Panter-Brick, Robert H. Layton, and Peter Rowley-Conwy, pp. 39–72. Cambridge University Press, Cambridge, England.

Russo, Michael
1996 Southeastern Archaic Mounds. In *Archaeology of the Mid-Holocene Southeast*, edited by Kenneth E. Sassaman and David G. Anderson, pp. 259–287. University Presses of Florida, Gainesville.

Sanger, David W.
1996 Gilman Falls Site: Implications for the Early and Middle Archaic of the Maritime Peninsula. *Canadian Journal of Archaeology* 20:7–28.

Sanger, David, William R. Belcher, and Douglas C. Kellogg
1992 Early Holocene Occupation at the Blackman Stream Site, Central Maine. In *Early Holocene Occupation in Northern New England*, edited by Brian S. Robinson, James B. Petersen, and Ann K. Robinson, pp. 149–161. Occasional Publications in Maine Archaeology 9. Maine Historic Preservation Commission, Augusta.

Sherwood, Sarah C., Boyce N. Driskell, Asa R. Randall, and Scott C. Meeks
2004 Chronology and Stratigraphy at Dust Cave, Alabama. *American Antiquity* 69:533–554.

Shott, Michael J.
1997 Stones and Shafts Redux: The Metric Discrimination of Chipped Stone Dart and Arrow Points. *American Antiquity* 58:425–443.

Simons, Donald B.
1972 Radiocarbon Date from a Michigan Satchell Site. *The Michigan Archaeologist* 18:209–214.

Smith, Kevin P., N. O'Donnell, and John D. Holland
1998 The Early and Middle Archaic in the Niagara Frontier: Documenting the "Missing Years" in Lower Great Lakes Prehistory. *Bulletin* 36:1–79. Buffalo Society of Natural Sciences, Buffalo, New York.

Snarey, Kristy
2000 The Adoption of the Bow and Arrow in Southwestern Ontario: A View from the Smallpoint Archaic. Master's thesis, Department of Anthropology, University of Western Ontario, London.

Snow, Dean R.
1975 The Passadumkeag Sequence. *Arctic Anthropology* 12(2):46–59.

Spence, Michael W.
1986 Band Structure and Interaction in Early Southern Ontario. *Canadian Journal of Anthropology* 5(2):83–95.

Spence, Michael W., and William A. Fox
1986 The Early Woodland Occupations of Southern Ontario. In *Early Woodland Archeology*, edited by Kenneth B. Farnsworth and Thomas E. Emerson, pp. 4–46. Seminar in Archaeology 2. Center for American Archeology Press, Kampsville, Illinois.

Spence, Michael W., Ronald Williamson, and John Dawkins
1978 The Bruce Boyd Site: An Early Woodland Component in Southwestern Ontario. *Ontario Archaeology* 29:33–46.

Steiss, Deborah A., Ronald F. Williamson, Carole N. Ramsden, and W. Bruce Welsh
1997 Archaic Ancaster: The Archaeology of the Meadowlands. In *Preceramic Southern Ontario*, edited by Phillip Woodley and Peter Ramsden, pp. 97–118. Occasional Publications in Northeastern Archaeology 9. Copetown Press, Hamilton, Ontario.

Stewart, Andrew
1983 Hell Gap: A Possible Occurrence in Southern Ontario. *Canadian Journal of Archaeology* 7:87–92.
1984 The Zander Site: Paleo-Indian Occupation of the Southern Holland Marsh Region of Ontario. *Ontario Archaeology* 42:45–79.
2002 Review of *Geoarchaeology of Landscapes in the Glaciated Northeast*, edited by David L. Creemens and John P. Hart. *Ontario Archaeology* 73:43–47.
2004a Intensity of Land-Use around the Holland Marsh: Assessing Temporal Change from Regional Site Distributions. In *The Late Palaeoindian Great Lakes: Geoarchaeological and Archaeological Studies of Late Pleistocene and Early Holocene Environments*, edited by Lawrence J. Jackson and Andrew Hinshelwood, pp. 85–116. Mercury Series Paper 165. Archaeological Survey of Canada, Canadian Museum of Civilization, Gatineau.
2004b Stage 3 and 4 Archaeological Excavation of the Huson Site (AgGt-111), Mountain Road, City of Thorold, Regional Municipality of Niagara, Ontario. Report on file, Archaeological Services, Toronto.

Stewart, Andrew, and John Desloges
2002 Floodplain Formation in Southern Ontario: Sediments and Archaeology on the Lower Thames River. Paper presented at the annual meeting of the Ontario Division of the Canadian Association of Geographers, University of Western Ontario, London.

Stoltman, James B.
1974 *Groton Plantation: An Archaeological Study of a South Carolina Locality*. Monographs 1. Peabody Museum of Archaeology and Ethnology, Harvard University, Cambridge, Massachusetts.

Storck, Peter L.
1978 The Coates Creek Site: A Possible Late Paleo-Indian–Early Archaic Site in Simcoe County, Ontario. *Ontario Archaeology* 30:25–46.

Storck, Peter L., and Peter von Bitter
1989 The Geological Age and Occurrence of Fossil Hill Formation Chert: Implications for Early Paleo-Indian Settlement Patterns. In *Eastern Paleoindian Lithic Resource Use*, edited by Christopher J. Ellis and Jonathan C. Lothrop, pp. 165–189. Westview Press, Boulder, Colorado.

Stothers, David M.
1983 The Satchell Complex: Tool Kit or Culture? *Arch Notes* 83(3):25–27.
1996 Resource Procurement and Band Territories: A Model for Lower Great Lakes Paleoindian and Early Archaic Settlement Systems. *Archaeology of Eastern North America* 24:173–216.

Stothers, David M., and Timothy J. Abel
1991 Earliest Man in the Western Lake Erie Basin: A 1992 Perspective. *North American Archaeologist* 12:195–242.
1993 The Late Archaic and Early Woodland Culture History of the Western Lake Erie Drainage. *Archaeology of Eastern North America* 21:25–110.

Stothers, David M., Timothy J. Abel, and Andrew M. Schneider
2001 Archaic Perspectives in the Western Lake Erie Basin. In *Archaic Transitions in Ohio and Kentucky Prehistory*, edited by Olaf H. Prufer, Sara E. Pedde, and Richard S. Meindl, pp. 233–289. Kent State University Press, Kent, Ohio.

Thomas, Peter A.
1992 The Early and Middle Archaic Periods as Represented in Eastern Vermont. In *Early Holocene Occupation in Northern New England*, edited by Brian S. Robinson, James B. Petersen and Ann K. Robinson, pp. 187–203. Occasional Publications in Maine Archaeology 9. Maine Historic Preservation Commission, Augusta.

Thomas, Stephen C.
1988 The Muskrat: A Lean-Season Resource in the Late Archaic of Southwestern Ontario. In *Diet and Subsistence: Current Archaeological Perspectives*, edited by Brenda V. Kennedy and Genevieve M. LeMoine, pp. 349–355. Proceedings of the Nineteenth Annual Conference of the Archaeological Association of the University of Calgary, Calgary, Alberta.
1997 Faunal Analysis. In *In the Shadow of the Bridge: The Archaeology of the Peace Bridge Site (AfGr-9), 1994–1996 Investigations*, edited by Ronald F. Williamson and Robert I. MacDonald, pp. 441–492. Occasional Publications 1. Archaeological Services, Toronto.

Timmermans, Steven
1999 The Southwinds Site: A Late Paleo-Indian 'Hi-Ho' Encampment in Middlesex County. *Kewa* 99(8):4–14.

Timmins, Peter A.
1995 Stelco 1: A Late Paleo-Indian Hi-Lo Site in the Region of Haldimand-Norfolk. *Kewa* 95(5):2–22.
1996 The Little Shaver Site: Exploring Site Structure and Excavation Methodology on an Unploughed Site in the Region of Hamilton-Wentworth, Ontario. *Ontario Archaeology* 61:45–81.

Timmins Martelle Heritage Consultants
2003 Stage 4 Archaeological Assessment AhHc-131–The Farrugie Site and AhHc-132–The Leschuk-Weisz Site, Farrugie Subdivision Part of Lot 9, Concession 1, Geographic Township of Brantford, Town of Paris, Brant County, Ontario. Manuscript on file, Department of Anthropology, University of Western Ontario, London.
2004a Stage 4 Archaeological Assessment, Municipality of Lambton Shores New Transmission Watermain: The South Bend Site (AhHk-97) and the Wheat Site (AhHk-98) Lambton County, Ontario. Manuscript on file, Department of Anthropology, University of Western Ontario, London.
2004b Stage 4 Executive Summary AgHb-238: Blue Box Site, AgHb-239: Snowhill Site, AgHb-240: Double Take Site, Hampton Estates Subdivision, Part of Lots 22 & 23, Concession 3, Brantford Township, City of Brantford, Brant County, Ontario. Manuscript on file, Department of Anthropology, University of Western Ontario, London.

Tomak, Curtis
1979 Jerger: An Early Archaic Mortuary Site in Southwestern Indiana. *Proceedings of the Indiana Academy of Science* 88:62–69. Indianapolis.

Tuck, James A.
1974 Early Archaic Horizons in Eastern North America. *Archaeology of Eastern North America* 2:72–80.
1977 A Look at Laurentian. In *Current Perspectives in Northeastern Archaeology, Essays in Honor of William A. Ritchie*, edited by Charles F. Hayes, pp. 33–40. Researches and Transactions of the New York State Archaeological Association 17(1). Rochester.

Varney, Tamara L., and Susan Pfeiffer
1995 The People of the Hind Site. *Ontario Archaeology* 59:96–108.

Vastokas, Romas
1970 *Aboriginal Use of Copper in the Great Lakes Area*. Ph.D. dissertation, Columbia University, New York. University Microfilms, Ann Arbor, Michigan.

Walker, Ian J., John R. Desloges, Gary A. Crawford, and David G. Smith
1997 Floodplain Formation Processes and Archaeological Implications at the Grand Banks Site, Lower Grand River, Southern Ontario. *Geoarchaeology* 12:865–887.

Watson, Gordon D.
1981 A Late Archaic Broad Point Phase in the Rideau Lakes Area of Eastern Ontario. *Arch Notes* 4:7–20.
1990 Palaeo-Indian and Archaic Occupations of the Rideau Lakes. *Ontario Archaeology* 50:5–26.

Williamson, Ronald F.
1978 *Report of Investigations at the Early Woodland Liahn II Site (AcHo-2) and Test Excavations at the Peterkin Site (AcHo-9), Mitchell's Bay, Ontario*. Research Report 8. Museum of Indian Archaeology, London, Ontario.

Williamson, Ronald F., and Robert I. MacDonald
1997 (editors) *In the Shadow of the Bridge: The Archaeology of the Peace Bridge Site (AfGr-9), 1994–1996 Investigations*. Occasional Publications 1. Archaeological Services, Toronto.
1998 *Legacy of Stone: Ancient Life on the Niagara Frontier*. Eastend Books, Toronto.

Williamson, Ronald F., Eva M. MacDonald, Robert H. Pihl, Robert I. MacDonald, Deborah A. Steiss, and David A Robinson
2002 Ruthven and the Collection of Andrew Thompson: A Case Study of a Nineteenth Century Antiquarian. *Arch Notes* (n.s.) 7(2):7–34.

Williamson, Ronald F., Stephen C. Thomas, and Deborah A. Steiss
1994 The Middle Archaic Occupation of the Niagara Peninsula: Evidence from the Bell Site (AgGt-33). *Ontario Archaeology* 57:64–87.

Wilmeth, Roscoe
1978 *Canadian Archaeological Radiocarbon Dates*. Mercury Series Paper 77. Archaeological Survey of Canada, National Museum of Man, Ottawa.

Wilson, James
2002 The Fregg Site (AhGx-390), A Small Point Archaic Occupation in Ancaster, Ontario. *Kewa* 02(8):1–16.

Wilson, James, Brent Wimmer, and Anthony Figura
1997 Cherry Hill: A Kirk Corner-Notched Site at Fonthill, Ontario. *Kewa* 97(7):2–12.

Wintemberg, William J.
1928 Artifacts from Ancient Graves and Monuments in Ontario. *Proceedings and Transactions of the Royal Society of Canada* (Series 3) 22:175–206. Ottawa.
1931 Distinguishing Characteristics of Algonkian and Iroquoian Cultures. In *Annual Report for 1929*, pp. 65–126. Bulletin 67. National Museum of Canada, Ottawa.

Winters, Howard D.
1969 *The Riverton Culture: A Second Millennium Occupation in the Wabash Valley*. Monograph 1. Illinois State Museum, Springfield.

Witthoft, John H.
1953 Broad Spearpoints and the Transitional Period Cultures in Pennsylvania. *The Pennsylvania Archaeologist* 23(1):4–31.

Wittry, Warren L.
1959 Archaeological Studies of Four Wisconsin Rockshelters. *The Wisconsin Archeologist* 40:137–267.

Woodley, Philip J.
1990 *The Thistle Hill Site and Late Archaic Adaptations*. Occasional Papers in Northeastern Archaeology 4. Copetown Press, Dundas, Ontario.
1996 The Early Archaic Occupation of the Laphroaig Site, Brant County, Ontario. *Ontario Archaeology* 62:39–62.
1997 The Witz and Koeppe II Sites, Ancaster, and the Hi-Lo Occupation of Southern Ontario. In *Preceramic Southern Ontario*, edited by Phillip Woodley and Peter Ramsden, pp. 149–171. Occasional Publications in Northeastern Archaeology 9. Copetown Press, Hamilton, Ontario.
2004 The Fowler Site: A Holcombe Camp near Lake Simcoe, Ontario. In *The Late Palaeoindian Great Lakes: Geoarchaeological and Archaeological Studies of Late Pleistocene and Early Holocene Environments*, edited by Lawrence J. Jackson and Andrew Hinshelwood, pp. 163–199. Mercury Series Paper 165. Archaeological Survey of Canada, Canadian Museum of Civilization, Gatineau.

Wright, James V.
1962 A Distributional Study of Some Archaic Traits in Southern Ontario. In *Contributions to Anthropology, 1960, Part I*, pp. 124–142. Bulletin 180. National Museum of Canada, Ottawa.
1972a *The Shield Archaic*. Publication in Archaeology 3. National Museum of Canada, Ottawa.
1972b *The Knechtel I Site, Bruce County, Ontario*. Mercury Series Paper 4. Archaeological Survey of Canada, National Museum of Canada, Ottawa.
1978 The Implications of Probable Early and Middle Archaic Projectile Points from Southern Ontario. *Canadian Journal of Archaeology* 2:59–78.
1984 The Cultural Continuity of Northern Iroquoian Speakers. In *Extending the Rafters: Interdisciplinary Approaches to Iroquois Studies*, edited by Michael K. Foster, Jack Campisi, and Marianne Mithun, pp. 283–299. State University of New York Press, Albany.
1995 *A History of the Native People of Canada, Volume 1: 10,000–1,000 B.C.* Mercury Series Paper 152. Archaeological Survey of Canada, Canadian Museum of Civilization, Gatineau.

Part 6

Concluding Comments

23

Concluding Thoughts on the Archaic Occupation of the Eastern Woodlands

Dale L. McElrath and Thomas E. Emerson

Rather than propose new models or attempt to present a series of general trends typifying the Archaic period, we prefer, in these concluding thoughts, to highlight selected issues that we think deserve further consideration. We believe that the resolution of these issues would make a significant contribution to the emerging historical reconstruction of Archaic social, political, and economic developments in the Eastern Woodlands. We would be the first to admit that this project is daunting, and some would say that the data are insufficient to accomplish the task. Despite the large number of radiocarbon determinations that appear in this volume, the period under consideration is too long, the individual cultures are too poorly defined, and the local and regional chronologies are too sketchy to permit accurate historical reconstruction. Archaeologists are often unable to assess the significance of variability between potentially related assemblages or to resolve whether the various point types in a "cluster" represent historically related contemporaneous groups or indicate a trajectory of population movement across the landscape. Studying the lives of people who lived during the Archaic period is undoubtedly one of the more challenging endeavors in North American archaeology.

Because of the lack of basic information about the cultural context and chronology of most recognized hafted-biface clusters and defined horizons, summarizing the midcontinental Archaic in a conventional manner would force us to resort to the same frustratingly ambiguous neo-evolutionary "trends" critiqued in this volume's introductory chapter. That said, broad patterns can be observed in the archaeological record. For example, for most of the Archaic, researchers recognize a south-to-north progression in point types. In other words, the same point types that appeared either in the Midsouth or the southeastern United States often appeared in the Midwest somewhat later. A similar, east-to-west, pattern is apparent in the Great Lakes region; that is, the same point types date earlier in the New York area than in the western Great Lakes. An east–west axial relationship can also be traced between the upper Midwest and the Plains, but the directional flow of cultural influences is not always clear; in fact, it likely varied by period. While archaeologists can document the spatial and chronological aspects (to some extent) of these shifting, spreading patterns of point-type use, we have not been able to effectively explain them. We have not been able to determine if such patterns result from the adoption of new forms by neighboring groups, the spread of technological innovation, or the movement of people.

Additionally, a combination of natural and cultural factors documented in the various volume chapters has significantly complicated the form of the archaeological evidence for all periods prior to Late Prehistoric times. Natural processes have clearly buried or eroded away Early and Middle Archaic remains in the floodplains and potentially exposed such remains to modern disturbances in upland areas. These processes have skewed the evidence for early human occupation of the Midwest. Moreover, past cultural practices have seemingly exaggerated the densities of later Archaic occupations. We believe that these biases contributed, to some degree, to the initial development of the upland-abandonment model and also encouraged the persistence of a neo-evolutionary perspective positing gradual change among resident populations. In contrast to this perspective, we believe that the Archaic developments in the Midwest are better viewed as the result of a patterned (re)occupation of the interior by colonizing riverine populations with well-developed technologies and social skills. Such a view does not rely on a founding population of big-game hunters who, over a millennium or more, adapted to new Archaic lifestyles and who reinvented the complex material assemblages and practices their ancestors possessed many millennia earlier, before they ever entered the High Plains and became hunters of megafauna. It also does not depend on a generalized concept of evenly distributed populations across multiple regions somehow simultaneously achieving critical threshold levels, triggering predictable reformulations of mechanisms of social interaction and political complexity.

Recognizing the First Boat People

None of the identifiable trends we note, however, shed much light on what appears to have been the foundational episode in Archaic cultural development in the central Mississippi Valley and Midwest—that is, the advent of the Dalton culture and regionally related groups (e.g., Greenbrier, Quad, Beaver Lake, Hardaway, San Patrice, etc.). Recent work (Koldehoff and Walthall 2004, this volume; Walthall 1998; Walthall and Koldehoff 1998) leaves little doubt about the position of this cultural expression within the Archaic culture-historic framework. Considerable questions, however, remain concerning the historical relationship between Dalton and Paleoindian societies, particularly Clovis. Researchers seem largely split on this issue, and given the overall lack of dates for both cultural horizons, virtually any position could be taken or challenged. The argument for a Clovis–Dalton historical connection seems to be largely based on the view that Eastern Woodlands Clovis manifestations represent residual big-game-hunter dead enders who were the victims of downsizing of their prey and eventually were forced to adopt a more locally sustainable lifestyle, resulting in the regionalization of point-type forms recognizable to some as Dalton variants; this position relies heavily on the "transitional" appearance of the Dalton point itself. The problem with this scenario, aside from the grievous lack of radiocarbon dates to support a temporal interface between the two cultures, lies in the drastically different lifestyle and subsistence orientation of Dalton compared with Clovis.

Although there is considerable doubt about the primary focus of Clovis hunting efforts—whether now-extinct megafauna or modern species were pursued—there is little doubt that they were oriented toward land mammals. By contrast, while Dalton hunters may have had a strong interest in deer, evidence of tool design and use-wear analysis of adzes indicate they were also concerned with manufacturing dugout canoes (Morse and Goodyear 1973). Reliably associated faunal remains are nonexistent on Dalton sites in the Midwest, but Dalton is widely thought to represent the earliest occupation of floodplain rockshelters and cave sites (Walthall 1998), and some circumstantial subsistence evidence is available to support this view. Assuming that early levels at cave sites in the Midwest region represent Dalton-era activities, or use by only slightly later groups, we note that early Holocene faunal remains indicate use of both fish and squirrel (Styles and McMillan, this volume); and while we do not know the complete food pyramid consumed by these river-oriented folk, it is unlikely that they went to the effort of building canoes for the purpose of hunting squirrels! Styles and McMillan (this volume) infer from the small size of fish represented in the early cave levels that mass-harvesting techniques (poison, nets, or seines) were deployed sometime in the early Holocene. While little of this subsistence evidence can be directly laid at the doorstep of Dalton peoples, it reasonably points to them as boat people possessing the first riverine-based economies in the Midwest.

Some subsistence models have emphasized the growing importance of nut harvesting for Archaic populations (e.g., contributors in Neusius 1986). While we have never doubted the importance of nuts to past societies, experiments conducted by Limp and Reidhead (1979) clearly show that fish would have been a far more easily harvested and productive food source than nuts would have been. This is not meant to argue that these early groups did not avail themselves of multiple resources but, rather, to suggest that archaeologists should consider the ramifications of a river-oriented settlement system in the interior Midwest by Dalton times, rather than the broad upland-oriented settlement systems that have been posited thus far. We contend that an economic focus on fishing, combined with a well-defined Dalton heartland in the Mississippi River valley (Koldehoff and Walthall, this volume), supports this interpretation. Although fish may have been the mainstay of the Dalton diet, no doubt hunting (presumably of white-tailed deer) was important to these riverine pioneers of the Mississippi.

Other notable Dalton cultural practices included the manufacture of hypertrophic blades, possibly by lithic specialists (Walthall and Koldehoff 1998). Such behavior is not unknown for Paleoindian groups (Gramly 1993), but in the case of Dalton groups, such blades show up in the context of large cemeteries (Morse 1997). Bioarchaeologists (e.g., Charles and Buikstra 1983; Milner et al., this volume) have considered cemeteries to be evidence of defined and defended territories and long-term settlement, but the Dalton-age Sloan cemetery seldom seems to have been so viewed. Perhaps because of its early age, its questionable position vis-à-vis the Paleoindian–Archaic interface, and the scant (but chemically definitive) evidence for human bone (Morse 1997), Dalton-age funerary customs have not received the critical attention necessary to properly evaluate the social implications of such practices. Even so, Dan Morse has concluded that the Dalton settlement system involved habitation of sedentary villages. We are aware that the concept of low-mobility river-dwelling inhabitants in the Midwest at about 10,000 B.C. raises considerable issues for those favoring a Clovis big-game origin for Dalton culture or, for that matter, for interpretations favoring a slow, gradual evolution of settlement systems and adaptive economies; but the circumstantial evidence for the idea is persuasive, if not conclusive.

The overall lack of regionally comprehensive or contextually reliable dates and assemblages has had a crippling effect on attempts to trace the origin, relatedness, and directional spread of Dalton groups. If we are correct about their subsistence focus and village orientation, Dalton groups may have derived historically from societies with a robust fishing economy in the lower Mississippi Valley or possibly a mixed riverine and maritime coastal economy in the Gulf Coastal area. Sites of such age along the coast would now be drowned (Kidder and Sassaman, this volume), placing the assessment of this proposition beyond the reach (hopefully temporarily) of archaeologists. It may be noteworthy that historic Gulf Coastal cultures that embraced maritime fishing economies were more reliant on bone, shell, and wood as raw sources for tools than on lithic materials. Because interior riverine habitats, by contrast, are less prolific in terms of the variety and size of bone and shell available, stone—which is abundantly available there—would have formed a more than adequate substitute for the shell, sharks' teeth, and fish spines used for cutting, slicing, and piercing on the coast.

The idea that dugout canoes date to this early period can only be circumstantially argued, but a large number of canoes were recently unearthed in Florida that date to the early Middle Archaic period. Researchers were surprised to find that these were not primitive precursors of the several known Late Archaic specimens but, rather, very sophisticated and well-designed watercraft not far removed technologically from their much later counterparts (Wheeler et al. 2003). This information points to the antiquity of the watercraft industry and adds credence to already strong circumstantial evidence for dugouts in Dalton times. We argue that the dugout canoe was not only Dalton peoples' preferred means of transportation but that it was also the key to the foundation of the Early Archaic Mississippi River valley economies that subsequently flourished in the Midwest. The tool kits of the subsequent Early Archaic cultures are not well documented at present, but excavations (McElrath et al., this volume; Stafford and Cantin, this volume) provide evidence for the use of stone axes, celts, and adzes, which indicates a continuity in woodworking technology and, presumably, boat-production capability.

If Dalton culture was based on a village-oriented fishing economy originating in coastal regions farther south, then one should not presuppose the level of social complexity to have been that of a band or even macroband of the type invariably posited for post-Paleoindian groups. North American maritime-fishing groups, and other similar groups across the world, were very complex at the time of their contact by Europeans (see, e.g., Beardsley et al. 1956; Binford 1980). Researchers have not traced the cultural development of coastal groups in sufficient detail to determine whether they were organized in complex societies at an early time, although good evidence certainty exists of complex behavior by Middle Archaic groups along the Atlantic coast (Kidder and Sassaman, this volume). If, on the one hand, the Dalton immigrants were descendants of Clovis hunters who reached the coast and adopted a surf-and-sand economic orientation, then Dalton would represent the independent invention of watercraft and coastal-riverine adaptations by specialized big-game hunters several centuries or millennia removed from their roots. If, on the other hand, as some have argued (e.g., Dixon 1999), the coastal adaptation occurred separately and potentially much earlier than the time of the specialized hunters represented by the fluted-point traditions, then the Dalton expansion inland may have been the end result of a long period of earlier and continuous complex social development. In this scenario, early peoples moved down the western coast of North America, crossed the Central American isthmus, and expanded northward along the Gulf Coast and eventually up the Mississippi River valley. Whatever the historical sequence, a flourishing, well-developed sedentary fishing economy would seem to indicate, at the very least, some level of complexity in a group's social and, possibly, political organization.

The use of the canoe, we feel, may also be key to understanding the distribution of subsequent Early Archaic sites in the interior uplands of the Midwest. As Winters (1961) pointed out long ago, large Early Archaic sites in the uplands of Illinois are located adjacent to *navigable* streams. This focus better accounts for the distribution of Early Archaic sites across the landscape than does the notion that they were occupied primarily by upland-oriented hunters and foragers. Thus, while the main river valleys were certainly the central focus of fishing, hunting, and gathering, the larger tributaries may have been as productive in terms of easily collected fish and mollusks and perhaps were even more densely packed with a broader variety of plant and other animal resources. The large number of complete Early Archaic points recovered as isolated finds in the interior of Illinois certainly attests to the importance that hunting forays played during this time. Archaeologists have no idea how the use of terrestrial resources compared to the use of aquatic resources, but hunting may have been geared as much toward the collection of usable animal skins to provide warm clothing for the more northerly winters as it was toward extracting the caloric value of the meat alone.

The main base camps, however, judging by the modest but growing evidence, were oriented toward the main river valleys. Such long-term camps have been identified in the lower Illinois Valley (Wiant et al., this volume), the Mississippi River valley (McElrath et al., this volume), and the Ohio River valley (Stafford and Cantin, this volume). In retrospect, this distribution makes perfect sense, because the main river valleys contained the most attractive features for these early colonizing fisher-hunter-gatherers. The value of Early Archaic–period river valleys in terms of access to wood, multiple plant and animal communities, shelter in winter, and, of course, easily accessible drinking and cooking water should not be underestimated (even if the valleys did become even more productive later in time). The waterways provided quick access to new hunting or fishing territories within a few miles of the base camp when game was depleted close by. The use of a dugout, aside from the obvious advantages for fishing, considerably reduced the "freight" cost of returning meat, even of large game animals, to the base settlement (especially if hunting was conducted upriver). The deeply cut rock escarpments in the valleys were the main source, and indeed in many areas the only source, of abundant high-quality chert for the manufacture of sometimes oversized early Holocene blades. The valleys also provided convenient sheltered bluff faces and rock overhangs for use, with minimal modification, as both windbreaks and fire-heat reflectors (Winters 1961) during long winter nights.

Ironically, the post-Dalton Early Archaic groups may have been less sedentary than their descendants. Humanly induced burning and, eventually, the drying associated with the Hypsithermal appear to have steadily improved hunting opportunities in the uplands, making a significant portion of the Prairie Peninsula even more attractive than it had been for Dalton-era immigrants. A more seasonally regulated use of resources may have been the opportunistic response to improved habitat conditions during subsequent Archaic periods. There are suggestions in the distribution of particular point-type clusters and variants that new territories and social boundaries were emerging along with potentially distinct habitat preferences (e.g., Nolan and Fishel, this volume). The degree to which these can be spatially or temporally defined has yet to be answered. It may well be that a variety of settlement systems were operating in the Midwest contemporaneously. Prime locations near good chert sources and with abundant river and adjacent upland resources would have been highly prized and defended.

Abandoning the Upland–Abandonment Model

What happened during Middle Archaic times that caused, or seems to have caused, a major shift in settlement systems? The original evidence for the timing of the Hypsithermal led, perhaps unavoidably given the cultural-ecological paradigm, to the conclusion that it somehow played a significant role in both the demise of Early Archaic settlement systems and the emergence of a new lifestyle and associated settlement system that better fit the changing plant and animal communities associated with the new climatic regime. One of the most influential adaptational models of midwestern Archaic societies is, in fact, based on this premise. It suggests that small upland-oriented hunter-gatherer groups become attracted to the increasingly productive major river floodplains during mid-Holocene times. Brown and Vierra argue that this process began around 7500 B.P. (uncalibrated), after which,

> occupations begin to lengthen in duration at strategic locations in response to rising availability of prime foods in the floodplain. This began the trend that continued over the succeeding thousands of years towards greater reliance on those foods from this highly productive resource area while becoming increasingly more sedentary. In our view, the key factor in this development was the growth of the food-rich slack-water environment of the valley to the point where the valley pulled hunter gatherer subsistence and settlement strategies predominantly toward this area to the exclusion of alternatives. With increasing floodplain productivity, this zone came to dominate, and with this came sedentism and economic intensification. [1983:190]

This model, with minor variations and significant elaboration of the ramifications and consequences involved (Brown 1985, 1986), remains largely intact today. The Archaic adaptationist model has never been seriously contested in the Midwest, although we have raised several theoretical issues, questioning the grounds on which the model rests (see Emerson and McElrath 2001, this volume; see also Emerson and McElrath, this volume, and McElrath et al. ch. 1, this volume). Many of the criticisms of the conceptual underpinnings of cultural evolution, gradualism, and adaptation are applicable, but few researchers have directed their attention specifically to the components of the lower Illinois Valley environmentally driven model of increasing sedentism in the floodplain. In fact, Archaic and Paleoindian studies have largely been ignored by postprocessualist theoreticians and continue to be the mainstay of cultural evolutionists and adaptationists. The scenario of gradual upland abandonment during Middle Archaic times in favor of expanding slack-water floodplain resources is still the preferred interpretation among midwestern Archaic researchers today (including contributors to this volume, e.g., Ahler and Koldehoff; Benn and Thompson; Nolan and Fishel; Ray et al.; Stafford and Cantin). The conflation of this prehistoric trajectory with the hypothesized switch (Binford 1980) from residential mobility (foraging) to logistical mobility (collecting) formed a powerful and apparently logical argument to "explain," from a cultural-ecological perspective, the foundations of sedentism (Brown 1985, 1986; Brown and Vierra 1983; Carlson 1979) and the rise of complex societies.

We contend that the available evidence is open to alternative explanations and that the model can be challenged on many grounds. For example, Brown and Vierra assert,

> It has been proposed that the strength and duration of the Hypsithermal forced hunter-gatherers out of the uplands and into the major river valleys (Carmichael 1977). Survey data superficially support this conclusion. Several systematic surveys of the prairie uplands show there are fewer Middle Archaic sites than Early Archaic (Carmichael 1977; Conrad 1981; Klippel and Maddox 1977; Lewis 1977). [1983:167]

The model explicitly recognizes two major physiographic habitat zones, the "major river valleys" and the "prairie uplands." The major river valleys would certainly include the Mississippi, Illinois, and possibly the Rock, all of which exhibit floodplains wide enough to have allowed development of slack-water lakes, the growth of which was essential to the model for enhanced aquatic resource habitats during the mid-Holocene. This category, however, would presumably not include many large tributaries, even those that might have contained marshy slough areas, unless they were broad enough to contain large shallow lakes. Brown and Vierra (1983) clearly viewed such tributary streams as falling within the prairie-uplands habitat given that two of the "upland" surveys they refer to involved the Salt Fork (Lewis 1977) and Willow Branch (Klippel and Maddox 1977), both tributaries of the Sangamon River. Floodplain breadth seems to constitute a reasonable criterion for distinction, and we note that the prairie uplands of Illinois are crisscrossed by a series of meandering streams that eventually flow into the larger river trenches. Also, it is important to note that the term *prairie uplands*, as characterized in the model, does not refer to the bluff tops or valley margins adjoining the major floodplains but, rather, to the interior uplands. This is clear from the remaining two sources cited in support of Middle Archaic upland abandonment, which were based on major upland surveys, one in west-central Illinois between the towns of Canton and Quincy involving major expanses of formerly prairie habitat (Conrad 1981) and the other in the ridge drift and morainal areas of south-central Illinois (Carmichael 1976, 1977). There is a distinct inconsistency, however, between the conclusions reached by the individual authors of the surveys cited and Brown and Vierra's portrayal and interpretation of them. For example, Brown and Vierra credit Carmichael with the observation that Hypsithermal drying resulted in abandonment of the upland regions during Middle Archaic times. In fact, Carmichael never mentions the Hypsithermal in the article cited, nor does he identify a Middle Archaic abandonment, arguing instead for a post-Archaic abandonment resulting in a focus on the floodplain by Woodland groups (Carmichael 1977:233).

Likewise, Lewis's survey (1977) of the Salt Fork, cited by Brown and Vierra as confirming Middle Archaic abandonment, concludes just the opposite; in fact, Lewis summarizes the same survey data for an article for the Phillips and Brown *Archaic Hunters and Gatherers in the American Midwest* volume and states that he was unable to separate Middle Archaic materials from Late Archaic materials, concluding, "I do not feel that this difficulty reflects a possible lack of Middle Archaic sites. I prefer the explanation that our current taxonomies handle the Middle Archaic poorly" (1983:105). Ironically, Lewis cites many of the same reports that Brown and Vierra do to demonstrate that, "in the Illinois Prairie itself, most surveys do not support the post-Early Archaic abandonment argument (e.g., Asch et al. 1978; Barth 1982; Carmichael 1977, 1978; Clouse 1975; Lewis 1977)" (1983:105).

In fact, other lower Illinois Valley researchers were contemporaneously coming to the opposite conclusions from Brown and Vierra's. In a predictive-modeling exercise using site survey data from Montgomery County in west-central Illinois, Asch et al. conclude that,

> in contrast to Klippel and Maddox's findings from survey of Willow Creek (Sangamon drainage), the Montgomery County panhandle region shows little change in Archaic occupational intensity until 2,500 B.C.—i.e. there is no apparent decrease of occupation intensity during the Hypsithermal, and if a decline occurs at all, it is subsequent to the time of major prairie expansion. The differences between Willow Branch and the Montgomery panhandle show there is a regional diversity in prehistoric upland prairie utilization. No single region can be assumed representative of the Prairie Peninsula as a whole. [1978:47]

We cite these differing interpretive positions to underscore the continuing difficulty that researchers face in attempting to understand the Early to Middle Archaic transition (or lack thereof). A significant part of the dilemma stems from the ambiguity of the environmental evidence and variations in its interpretation and dating (for a summary, see Styles and McMillan, this volume, as well as various chapters). Another part of the problem is the difficulty in assigning component designations, especially on the basis of post–Early Archaic hafted bifaces from surface collections in Illinois (e.g., Harris 2002). It is clear that each of the studies cited employed differing criteria for component assignment. In fact, we acknowledge that the most comprehensive data accumulated thus far indicate a diminished use of upland areas through time, at least in the upland stretches between the Mississippi and Illinois drainages (cf. Conrad 1981; Nolan and Fishel, this volume); elsewhere in the state, the patterns are less clear (e.g., Butler, this volume; Lurie et al., this volume).

Although we concur that there seems to have been more Early Archaic activity in the uplands of some areas (e.g., west-central Illinois) than in subsequent times, the pattern is not universal and how this variability is to be interpreted is a matter of conjecture. There is a notable lack of obvious Early Archaic base camps in the uplands, and one could reasonably conclude that the upland point finds largely represent hunting camps or isolated point losses; indeed, the large number of complete hafted-biface specimens recovered would support such an interpretation. Moreover, the Early Archaic sites that have the appearance of base settlements occur in the floodplain, not the uplands. We would cite the impressive assemblage from Koster Horizon 11 (Brown and Vierra 1983; Struever and Holton 1979; Wiant et al., this volume) as representing a clear candidate for such a designation. The presence of multiple human and dog burials (Morey and Wiant 1992; Wiant et al., this volume) as well as nonportable furniture and a robust ground-stone industry (Struever and Holton 1979; Wiant et al., this volume) argues strongly in this direction. To this we would add the large Early Archaic assemblages from the deeply buried Nochta site in the American Bottom (Higgins 1990; McElrath et al. ch. 11, this volume), which indicate multiple substantial Early and Middle Archaic occupations with a wide variety of stone tools and features. An even better example of an Early Archaic base camp, in our opinion, is the James Farnsley site in the Ohio River valley (Stafford and Cantin, this volume). The recovery of 2,200 hafted bifaces and 10,000 tools from the excavated area of three Kirk-horizon components leaves little doubt as to the cultural assignment and intensive use of this locality during Early Archaic times. Some of the earlier and much of the newly emerging evidence, then, is compatible with a settlement system involving substantial long-term camps located in the major floodplains combined with specialized, perhaps seasonal use of the scattered resources found in the uplands. It also fundamentally alters how archaeologists view the data currently available and the directions future inquiries should take.

The time-transgressive nature of the Hypsithermal and the complex and variable effects experienced by plant and animal communities across such a broad multistate area make it difficult to identify this climatic event as a triggering mechanism to explain the hypothesized shift toward settlement based on logistical collecting from a pattern of residentially mobile foraging, as suggested by adaptationist models. Yet many archaeologists believe a significant and fundamental change is evident in the archaeological record and that it corresponds generally with this phenomenon. Of course, the approximate chronological correlation of such events says nothing about causal relations, and the evidence to date on the supposed climate-culture shift is circumstantial rather than conclusive. Researchers must recognize that major climatic shifts are necessarily slow processes and, because of their pace, do not act as cultural triggering mechanisms. Human societies succeed or fail, people live and die, in terms of several years, not centuries or millennia. And while ecotonal shifts would have been engendered by climatic shifts and might be reflected by the locations of hunting losses across the landscape (as codified in the archaeological record), these ecotonal shifts would have occurred on a time scale that may never have affected the real-life histories of the people who relied on these imperceptibly migrating locations for seasonal game.

How did the Hypsithermal and the associated expansion of the prairie affect midwestern biotic regimes and interested populations? The emerging picture of the timing, pace, and extent of Prairie Peninsula progression into Iowa, Minnesota, Wisconsin, Illinois, and Indiana becomes progressively more subtle and complex as new data are compiled. Styles and McMillan (this volume) provide a comprehensive, detailed, state-of-the-art summary that underscores the variability evident in local, regional, and macroregional patterns of response that resulted from the ever-changing plant and animal makeup for any given locality. Clearly, one of the more influential factors involved was humanly induced fire, which played a role as early as the onset of the Hypsithermal if not earlier and served to expand and perpetuate prairie conditions in the face of climatic conditions that would have favored arboreal expansion. In general, the expansion of the prairie and the human agency involved in burning improved conditions for the area's native inhabitants by creating and expanding habitat for several species of plants and animals that were exploited by local groups. Nevertheless, expansive stretches of prairie overran some localities, and, while such grasslands are not without prolific wildlife, they would have lacked the variable mosaic of plants and animals that preferred the open meadows and tree groves that were so abundant along the advancing periphery of the prairie wedge. These open grasslands also would have lacked the large exploitable nut masts found in forested areas, not to mention easily obtainable firewood. However, bison may have offset the loss associated with diminishing economic biodiversity. Bison seem to have intermittently inhabited major portions and fringe areas of the Prairie Peninsula, and their presence may be poorly reflected in the archaeological record (McMillan 2006; Styles and McMillan, this volume).

At the same time that the uplands were experiencing positive changes from the standpoint of biodiversity and economic potential, the floodplains were also benefiting. We concur with lower Illinois River valley researchers (Brown and Vierra 1983; Hajic 1990; Styles and McMillan, this volume; Wiant et al., this volume; Wiant et al. 1983) on the many positive effects the Hypsithermal had for major river valleys, including the accumulation of rich alluvium and the development of significant marshy areas and broad, shallow slack-water lakes. The increase of aquatic wildlife would have dramatically expanded the already plentiful strategic floodplain resources available for use. However, archaeologists need to take into account the timing of these changes and that the net effect varied between valleys. For example, Styles and McMillan (this volume) suggest that the Mississippi River valley may have experienced many of these changes earlier than the Illinois River valley. Also, the backwater lakes in at least the American Bottom section of the Mississippi Valley were less suitable for mussel populations, mainly because the sediment discharge from the Missouri River oversilted the water flow, creating less favorable conditions for most mussel species (Bartsch 1916). This may have been one reason why Middle Archaic sites seem to be less well represented in the American Bottom basin (McElrath et al. ch 11, this volume). The other main waterway in this region, the Ohio River valley, had yet a different hydrologic history during this period (e.g., Butler, this volume; Jefferies, this volume, Purtill, this volume; Stafford and Cantin, this volume).

One major outcome of this dry-weather-related phenomenon, from the archaeological standpoint, was the profound impact it had on the visibility of earlier site locations. While channel cutting and tributary-stream erosion may have destroyed many sites (occasionally even during their occupation), it buried others. The depth at which these sites can be sought is just now being appreciated (e.g., Benn and Thompson, this volume; Higgins 1990; Ray et al., this volume; Stafford and Cantin, this volume; Wiant et al., this volume). That researchers have acquired the sample they have thus far is remarkable. It is sobering to consider that the few times archaeologists have made concerted efforts to investigate deeply buried habitations, they have actually encountered them. One method used to characterize relative population densities of different periods is based on the overall number of burials represented (e.g., Milner et al., this volume). If we are correct that the main river valleys were the primary locations of base camps and, therefore, of burials for all three Archaic subperiods, a proportional comparison based on the percentage of area examined archaeologically by reference to landform age in these valleys might indicate amazingly high, even model-defying levels for Early Archaic populations.

Archaeologists have argued for some time that buried land surfaces in the major valleys have had a skewing effect on apparent archaeological site distribution (e.g., Yerkes 1986). The potential for sites to be buried in upland areas has only been recently appreciated (Abbott 1987; Bettis and Hajic 1995; Nolan and Fishel, this volume; Van Nest 1997; Warren 1997). The possibility that Early Archaic sites are buried in upland prairie settings is still a matter of conjecture (Nolan and Fishel, this volume), but a potentially biasing effect may have resulted from stream-valley erosion and infilling there. These phenomena are well understood in Iowa (Benn and Thompson, this volume; Bettis and Hajic 1995) but are less often considered east of the Mississippi. If we are correct about the significance of navigable waterways as the prime focus for Archaic seasonal hunting, the desiccation and erosional infilling of formerly navigable streams may have buried much evidence of early camping and hunting activities. These processes would have had a differential impact on sites by age and location across the landscape.

A twofold effect on the archaeological record is possible under this scenario. Early Archaic hunting losses may seem to be scattered across the prairie, but they actually may have occurred at the edge of former tree groves and at stream valley margins long since defunct. Later sites may have been close to the streams of the larger drainage basins that survived the drying episode (and that are still active today). But as these streams rebounded during subsequent wetter periods, the sites may have been buried or eroded in the rapidly infilling stream drainages. Archaeological surveyors in Illinois and Iowa are painfully aware of the depth of postsettlement alluvium, especially in smaller stream valleys where, often, several meters of historic fill mantle the earlier ground surface. Some support for the scenario just outlined is supplied by avocational archaeologists. Those who search active stream bottoms for artifacts have often acquired collections that seem to be more representative of a variety of time periods than are collections of those who prefer walking freshly plowed fields (Nolan and Fishel, this volume). Some researchers in Illinois (Lurie et al., this volume) have identified related but situationally distinct factors that may also have contributed to burial of Archaic-period sites.

The biases discussed thus far are largely restricted to the interior Midwest. Several contributors to this volume who work in other parts of the Eastern Woodlands have identified even more onerous conditions that bias the archaeological record of earlier time periods (e.g., Ellis et al.; Kidder and Sassaman; Lovis). Many earlier Archaic sites should occur in drowned or waterlogged conditions in coastal areas and along lakeshores, and while their investigation may pose formidable problems (Purdy 1988), the level of preservation expected at such sites may offer abundant opportunities for the recovery of normally perishable remains (Doran et al. 2002; Kay et al. 1980). It may well be that many of the questions posed by researchers concerning the antiquity and choice of weapon systems, as well as a host of technology-related issues, will be resolved to a degree not possible for the later, less well-preserved sub-plow-zone sites that form the current mainstay of research in eastern North America.

Not all of the biases in the archaeological record are the result of natural factors. Sometime during the Middle Archaic there seems to have been a shift in preferred cooking methods. The method of spit- or rack-roasting food over an open fire, which was and still is commonly practiced worldwide, was largely replaced, at least in some areas, by moist cooking techniques. One of these methods ("clambake") involves heating rocks and placing them in a pit basin over which the food is layered and covered with mats, bark, or leaves. The food is steam cooked by pouring water over the covered pit. An alternative method ("rock boiling") involves placing heated rocks in a water-filled basin lined with animal skins. Use of these methods is readily identifiable archaeologically by the jagged appearance of the rock fragments that results when the heated stones are submerged in water. Moist cooking methods quickly contribute to a rapid accumulation of debris, often resulting in deep middens. The rock used quickly degrades and cannot be easily recycled for dry-hearth cooking. Heating the stones on the ground surface near pit basins requires much wood fuel that is soon reduced to ashes. The steaming effect on meat tends to cook the flesh but leave the bone essentially unmodified. The bone and shell quickly accumulate along with the wood ash, all of which creates a superior environment for midden development and enhanced preservation.

The "clambake" method is well suited to aquatic resources, particularly mussels, and no doubt was a reflection of a focus on such food sources; it may have much greater antiquity to the south, especially along the eastern seaboard and Gulf Coast where both salt and freshwater resources were exploited from the earliest times. The stone-boiling method (which may have been more prevalent in later times) may have resulted in experimentation with the use of stews and gruels using both plant and animal products to best advantage. Some have argued that the invention of pottery was conceptually based on the skin-lined pit excavated in a clay matrix (Sassaman

1993). The American Bottom has failed, thus far, to produce evidence of deep Middle Archaic middens. One reason, as noted, appears to be the high silt load carried by the Missouri River, which discharges into the Mississippi River immediately to the north, creating a situation less favorable for many species of mussels (Bartsch 1916), which were favored resources throughout much of the Middle Archaic in the Eastern Woodlands. To judge by the location of major commercial shell-button production in historic times, the most productive locations for mussel shells in the Midwest were the upper Mississippi River around Muscatine, Iowa, and along the central and lower Illinois River (Coker 1919). The American Bottom also lacks good sources of glacial cobbles for "clambake" cooking (McElrath et al. ch. 11, this volume); although sandstone and limestone abound in the region, they are inferior to glacial cobbles for such use because they degrade quickly and impart grit to any liquids that they are used to boil (Wisseman 2005).

This emphasis on cooking-pit construction and associated heavy buildup of midden deposits fostered several conditions that affected the archaeological record and the inferences that are drawn from it. Frequent pit excavation systematically intruded into earlier cultural deposits, churning up unrelated artifacts and debris and contributing to the mixing of diagnostics by level, which in turn would have created an artificially flavored battleship curve of artifact types. This was particularly true in rockshelters and cave sites (Walthall 1998), where activities were focused in confined areas and natural soil buildup was often slow. Researchers who believe in the "points equal people" maxim cite this mixing as a primary reason for the false impression of contemporaneous co-occurring point types (McElrath and Emerson 2000). A second problem associated with the shift in cooking methods concerns the issue of relative intensity of occupation. The unusually fast accumulation of debris associated with moist cooking and the enhanced preservation conditions have the potential of making it appear as if the later occupations were considerably more intense (i.e., more sedentary), which is certainly a possibility but cannot be proven simply on the basis of quantitative comparisons of cooking-material densities.

A Spectacular Decline

The Late Archaic is certainly the best-known and explored period of the Archaic. Because the ground surface that was available to the historic European pioneers was established during the late Holocene, the landscape occupied by Late Archaic populations was essentially the same as that settled and utilized by the colonizing immigrants from the Old World, especially on the major floodplains. More remains from the Late Archaic time period have been recovered than from earlier time periods, with the possible exception of hunting losses dating to the Early Archaic period. Certainly, Archaic habitation sites that have been investigated date primarily to this late portion of the Archaic period. We would argue that the material assemblage changed little from the Middle to the Late Archaic period (unless one accepts the assertion that the bow and arrow was adopted at this time). In particular, the "diagnostic" point types that are present in Late Archaic sites can usually be stylistically traced back to Middle Archaic times, at least on a macroregional level. For example, the Matanzas point, which clearly dates to Middle Archaic times in western Illinois, occurs in Late Archaic sites in southern Indiana (Stafford and Cantin, this volume). The Late Archaic Mule Road point from western Illinois can be traced back to the Middle Archaic Ledbetter tradition of the Southeast (McElrath 1993; Thorne et al. 1981).

Whereas during Early Archaic times there seems to have been considerable interaction, judging by the widespread occurrence of point-type clusters, often displaying an almost pan–Eastern Woodlands distribution (Smith 1986), the Middle and Late Archaic evidence suggests regionalization of point types and presumably the emergence of multiple ethnic cores (e.g., Emerson and McElrath 2001; Sassaman 2005). The Late Archaic to Early Woodland transition does not seem to have involved, as was once thought, simply the addition of pottery to a Late Archaic lifestyle. Major disruptions are documented in settlement systems and lifestyle (Farnsworth and Emerson 1986). The source, timing, and nature of this discontinuity have yet to be explained. Late Archaic groups were focused on floodplain resources, a fact virtually all midwestern archaeologists agree on, and it is possible that major changes in the hydrologic regime of one or more of the major river systems disrupted well-established economies, resulting in a major reorientation of predictable resources and the methods used to take advantage of them (see also Kidder and Sassaman, this volume). Archaeologists working in the American Bottom have argued (McElrath et al., ch. 11, this volume) that there was a hiatus between the terminal Late Archaic (Prairie Lake culture) populations and the eventual reoccupation of the area by Early Woodland groups associated with Marion and Black Sand cultures (Emerson and Fortier 1986; Emerson and McElrath 2001). Early Woodland sites in the confluence area of the Mississippi, Missouri, and Illinois rivers are much smaller and more ephemeral, suggesting lower population levels, altered economies, and less intensive use of the floodplain resources. Neither do Early Woodland populations appear to have merely shifted emphasis toward the uplands, as sites are fairly rare along the bluffs and in the interior drainages. Many Early Woodland sites occupy lower elevations on the floodplain, and many more could be buried or drowned, as is surmised for many of the earlier Archaic-period sites.

Finally, the potential early colonization of the interior Midcontinent by expanding populations from coastal areas of the Southeast is clearly only part of the historical picture. While cultures in the upper Midwest and Great Lakes areas may have been influenced by contact and interaction with more southerly oriented populations (e.g., Lovis, this volume), the overall cultural milieu within which they developed demonstrates largely distinct social relationships from their southern counterparts (e.g., Ellis et al., this volume). Although we are much less familiar with this northern area, we wonder if similar historic factors were not involved there. Researchers have noted the east-to-west flow of projectile point types (Mason 1981), especially during Late Archaic times. Cleland pointed out a strong pattern of seasonal fishing from Late Archaic through historic times in the Great Lakes region: "It is argued that the unique prehistoric fishery, which was extant in this region during European contact and survived through most of the historic era, provides the most important organizing concept for understanding the cultural development of this region" (1982:761). That early sites in this area were drowned raises the possibility that this pattern extended further back into antiquity. This northern Archaic pattern demonstrates, even within the limited region examined in this volume, how strongly populations were affected by *local* physiography and climate and suggests, as we have stressed in our discussion, that historical trajectories of individual Archaic groups and regional sequences are best comprehended in that context, rather than in terms of broad neo-evolutionary models.

Skipping over thousands of years of native history from the inception to the termination of Archaic lifeways, we continue many of the themes raised above—for example, riverine adaptations, large long-term settlements, and social and political complexity. We are especially interested in the termination of the Archaic because it so clearly, from our restricted perspective of the American Bottom, serves as a contradiction to the all-pervasive neo-evolutionary models. In his 1967 Eastern Woodlands summary, Griffin could speak in glowing terms of the Late Archaic cultures with their increasing populations, long-distance interregional exchange, copper working, woodworking tools, stone bowls, and the expansion of many other new technologies. He noted the end of the Archaic and the beginning of the Early Woodland period as marked by the appearance of "ceramics, burial mounds, and agriculture." This transition was marked most dramatically by Adena ceremonialism. For several decades archaeologists have known that this transition was not so abrupt as it is sometimes portrayed. We now know that squash and native plants were regularly cultivated by Late Archaic peoples (Simon, this volume). Ceramic manufacture as well as stone-bowl carving along the Atlantic coast and inland began well before the beginning of the Early Woodland period (Kidder and Sassaman, this volume; Purtill, this volume). Burial ceremonialism, including the sporadic use of burial mounds (Ellis et al., this volume; Esarey 1986; Purtill, this volume), was in place and elaborated by Late Archaic times.

So what did the Early Woodland period contribute to the evolution of social, political, and economic complexity in the Eastern Woodlands? We would have to answer, very little. Examining the Late Archaic–Early Woodland transition in detail was not a task we set for the authors in this volume. The Early Woodland period is thoroughly reviewed in Farnsworth and Emerson (1986). The research presented in that volume and in this one make it apparent that the terminal Late Archaic to Early Woodland shift involved political, economic, and social collapse in many if not most locations (e.g., Ellis et al., this volume; McElrath et al., ch. 11, this volume; Purtill, this volume). If we use the American Bottom as a case example of this shift, the change was fairly dramatic. The terminal Late Archaic period was marked by the clustering of large population aggregates about the rich meander lakes of the floodplain, especially those near the bluff bases (Emerson 1984; Emerson and Fortier 1986; Emerson and McElrath 1983, 2001; Fortier 2001; McElrath and Fortier 1983). These sites include thousands of shallow cooking pits, houses, and a wide array of tools as well as ceremonial objects. We have argued that these "base locales" represent long-term, multiseasonal bluff-base settlements. Despite spatially extensive surveys and excavations, the only terminal Late Archaic sites found outside the base locales are small hunting and gathering camps. Terminal Late Archaic sites just north of the American Bottom also display evidence of mortuary ceremonialism that may have been associated with cemeteries and, perhaps, low mound construction (Farnsworth and Asch 1986). These activities and archaeological remains indicate to us that this period was marked by the presence of territorially restricted groups who may have been organized at a tribal level (Emerson and McElrath 2001). Shortly after the end of the first millennium, all evidence indicates, these large groups disappeared, and we can only assume their social and political and, perhaps, economic lifestyle collapsed. Subsequent Early Woodland utilization and occupation of the area is marked by a thin scattering of small, family-sized campsites. There is no evidence for mortuary ceremonialism, no large population aggregations, no long-term settlements, no exotic items, and none of the other elaborations that mark the terminal Late Archaic societies. Furthermore, we suggest that the Early Woodland groups represent a pattern of discontinuous intrusions into the American Bottom region by outside groups and that they were not "descendants" of the earlier Prairie Lake peoples. We contend that this pattern of social, political, and economic downsizing and population movement was, in fact, typical of much of the terminal Late Archaic to Early Woodland transition in much of the Eastern Woodlands (e.g., Kidder and Sassaman, this volume; Purtill, this volume).

The idea of Early Woodland complexity, in fact, seems to have been based very much on the anticipated importance of attributes that were associated with the period's inception—thought to involve agriculture, burial mounds, and ceramics. Cultural evolutionists saw the importance of these attributes in later periods and assumed they would have had transformational effect when they first appeared (i.e., during Woodland times), but archaeologists now know this was not the case. Data have been slowly accumulating that indicate domestication, ceramic technology, and mortuary ceremonialism predated Early Woodland times. On most fronts, Early Woodland societies are now known to have been less complex economically and socially than their terminal Late Archaic predecessors. The confirmation of declining complexity in Eastern Woodlands societies after the terminal Late Archaic is not new. However, like the discovery of Middle Archaic monumental earthworks, this evolutionary involution seems to have done little to impact the conventional neo-evolutionary paradigm. If there is a single example of the power of a paradigm over contrary evidence, this might be it.

Discussion

The recent study of Archaic-period societies has been characterized by various researchers as "much to do about nothing." The dependence on modern hunter-gather analogies and broad-scale economic and ecological modeling has redirected many researchers from much-needed studies of archaeological material culture, cultural context, and chronological settings. These are the building blocks at the heart of archaeological research, and without them archaeologists are reduced to musings about the past, no matter how sophisticated we contend our models are. Much Archaic-period archaeological discussion resembles the famous apocryphal medieval deliberations on the question "How many teeth does a horse have?"—deliberations that, in the specific exclusion of available data, could continue ad infinitum since they had no reference to reality. Even more than ever, archaeologists need to design and execute field excavations and studies that will address the tremendous data gaps that are what really prevent us from moving beyond mere counting of stone tools and reconstructing of environments to the actual people who give such exercises meaning. The potential of such field studies to illuminate the Archaic past is indicated by several discussions in this volume, for example, the discovery of Atlantic coast and lower Mississippi River valley monumental architecture (Kidder and Sassaman), the presence of large, dense early settlements (e.g., Stafford and Cantin; Wiant et al.), and the excavation of many ceremonial and ritual sites (e.g., Ellis et al.), which force researchers to rethink many of the foundational precepts of Archaic studies.

The foundational concepts of Archaic studies have tended to depict human societies as mere cultural reflections of the environmental constraints of only broadly understood climatic and physiographic patterns. Such ecologically directed approaches obscure social variation and homogenize human actions in favor of a behaviorist approach. If there is one message readers should take away from the chapters included in this volume it is that the Archaic period, from its earliest to its latest manifestations, is characterized by dramatic variation and diversity. It is apparent that ecological parameters allowed for a broad range of human responses and are best characterized as having provided multiple opportunities rather than crippling limits. Where sufficient evidence exists, it is also apparent that, from earliest times, native populations employed a wide array of adaptations, some verging on what neo-evolutionary archaeologists like to think of as only feasible for later "complex" societies, that is, sedentism, ceremonialism, craft specialization, and monumental earthworks. If anything is evident in these many chapters, it is that human history during the nine- to ten-millennia-long Archaic period was more complex and less evolutionary than archaeologists have been led to believe.

We can only conclude that the neo-evolutionary and cultural-ecological paradigms that have been consistently employed to explain developments in the Eastern Woodlands during Archaic times are no longer (and never have been) fully compatible with the evidence at hand. In particular, several aspects of these paradigms have seriously fettered researchers' ability to independently evaluate the data and accurately reconstruct the historical record of Archaic native societies: (1) the inherent assumption that indigenous groups, at the time of European arrival, were at or near their peak in terms of social complexity and that all earlier groups were, by necessity, simpler and less complex (e.g., Muller 1997); (2) acceptance that the social, political, and economic attributes of modern hunter-gatherer groups living in marginal environments are valid analogs for precontact fisher-hunter-gatherer folks living in temperate North America (Brown and Vierra 1983); and (3) the cultural ecologists' view (e.g., Binford 1965) that native populations were inescapably one with their environments and were essentially locked in a permanent stasis from which they only infrequently escaped when forced to make technological innovations in reaction to environmental change.

There is no reason to believe that Archaic populations were not socially, politically, and economically dynamic and variable. The homogenization of such folks into *simple* hunting and gathering societies does them a disservice. While there is little doubt that population sizes were greater at the time of European contact than in Archaic times, it can also be assumed that population levels (and more importantly, densities) at the local, regional, macroregional, and even culture-area levels would have fluctuated because of both natural and cultural factors, such as shifting environmental conditions, catastrophic natural events (in particular, flooding), economic resource shifts, political variation, and warfare or opportunistic predatory expansion. These factors would have resulted not only in regional population expansions and declines but also in both large- and small-scale population movements. We believe such factors are self-evident archaeologically in view of the hydrologic record of the major river basins (Brown et al. 1999; Knox 1985, 1993), the appearance and subsequent disappearance of monumental architecture (Kidder and Sassaman, this volume), the evidence for shifting hunting and fishing patterns (Styles and McMillan, this volume), the incidence of violence recorded on human skeletal remains from the Early Archaic period on (Milner et al., this volume), and perhaps, most obviously, in the examination of the historical diversity and distribution of native language groupings in North America (Mithun 2001).

We think two points are of special importance in reformulating Archaic histories because they represent the negative impact of current dominant theories. These two points revolve about, first, the early colonization of eastern North America and, second, the termination of Archaic lifestyles and their replacement by Woodland groups. We contend that the colonization of the Midwest by Archaic populations began at least in Dalton times (10,000–9000 cal B.C.) and represented an actual population migration or expansion into largely unpopulated areas. We further question the idea that the ancestral populations for these people were the specialized Clovis and Folsom hunters of the High Plains. We see no credible evidence to demonstrate this link. As a footnote to the history of Archaic studies, Fowler (1959) came to the same conclusion, using a different line of reasoning, several decades ago. Dalton groups may have come into sporadic or even regular contact with "Late Paleoindian" groups who relied on a specialized bison-oriented hunting lifestyle in the Plains and eastward into the Prairie Peninsula. The major river trenches were the primary focus of subsequent Early Archaic development stemming from the Dalton cultural matrix and were the avenues by which people expanded into new territories. Subsequent Early Archaic populations may have expanded into the major tributary drainages and even up into smaller, navigable stream valleys to take advantage of the ever-increasing exploitable animal populations. Ironically, the post-Dalton Early Archaic populations may have utilized more seasonally oriented settlement systems than their Dalton-age counterparts. This pattern of a systematic and continual northward push of Archaic groups was the result of population pressure created by expanding groups along the Gulf Coast and in the lower Mississippi Valley. Eventually, groups expanding northward encountered other groups following the margins of the Great Lakes and ultimately originating among peoples with prolific fishing economies developed along the Atlantic seaboard.

This riverine focus of Archaic groups made them susceptible to unexpected changes in hydrological regimes that, at times, forced them out of the floodplains and onto the higher terraces and bluff lines; seasonally or in longer cycles, upland hunting may have been more heavily relied on to provide suitable animal hides for clothing during periods of extremely cold winters or to replace the protein loss resulting from disruption of fish stock during catastrophic flooding. The pattern of upland hunting has been erroneously interpreted as representing the residue of highly mobile hunting-gathering groups that were eventually attracted to the increasingly productive floodplains during mid-Holocene times (Brown 1985; Brown and Vierra 1983; and several authors in this volume). This much-modeled switch appears to us to be unsupported by the evidence in the Midwest. If anything, the reverse appears to be true, in that fishing-based groups may have been attracted to productive forest-edge habitat created by prairie expansion and human burning that opened up the closed-canopy forests during mid-Holocene times.

This view of an early emphasis on floodplain habitats is compatible with a growing body of data on the Archaic period in the Eastern Woodlands and elsewhere, specifically, on early net construction (Chapman and Adovasio 1977; Frison et al. 1986); the early use, spread, and eventual domestication of gourds, which is compatible with their industrial (sensu Moseley 1975) value as net floats (Fritz 1999; Hart et al. 2004); the use of techniques to harvest fish en masse (through nets, seining, or poisoning) during the early Holocene (Styles and McMillan, this volume); and finally, early canoe making, as indicated by the recent recovery of a large number of Middle and Late Archaic canoes in Florida (Wheeler et al. 2003). As an aside, we note that recent discoveries in California (Rick et al. 2001) have resulted in a similar reappraisal of the antiquity and sophistication of fishing techniques on the Pacific Coast, pushing back such techniques as boat and hook-and-line fishing and the ability to exploit a variety of aquatic habitats to cal 9500 B.C., at which time, fishing is estimated to have accounted for over 50 percent of the diet.

Evidence for substantial Early Archaic settlements is strong in the Ohio River valley (Stafford and Cantin, this volume), the Illinois River valley (by Kirk-horizon times [ca. 7000–6000 cal B.C.]; Wiant et al., this volume), and the American Bottom (McElrath et al. ch. 11, this volume); and we think that these "base camps" demonstrate the same level of long-term occupation as their Middle and Late Archaic successors. Additionally, there is compelling evidence that this pattern was already established during Dalton times (10,000–9000 cal B.C.), namely, strong circumstantial evidence for watercraft construction and the creation of bounded cemeteries (Morse 1997), and evidence for sophisticated fish-harvesting techniques dates to slightly later periods (Styles and McMillan, this volume).

Some cultural neo-evolutionists have tended to treat native North American societies as if they were so attuned to their environment that the archaeological record can be largely viewed as if individual populations were creatures of habitat. However romantic this may sound, it is the same expectation that ecologists have of their plant and animal subjects and would seem to imply that native societies were less than human. Conversely, there has been a tendency on the part of some recent theorists to treat the same groups as transcending their environment. Such a view fosters the impression that the inhabitants were incapable of failure, that they eschewed politics and united effortlessly into communalistic groups for the purpose of constructing ritual landscapes. Again, however romantic this may sound, it is the same expectation that hagiographers might have for their subjects and would seem to imply that such societies were more than human. Either perspective results in dehumanized subjects. We prefer to believe that native societies embodied all of the human capacities, emotions, and motives of their equally human

Old World cousins and therefore produced history, enjoying successes and suffering setbacks in ways not predictable from even the most careful consideration of the spatial configuration of economic resources and changing weather patterns. We argue that while all human societies have been subject to the exigencies of habitat and the vicissitudes of climate, when it comes to interpreting the archaeological record, history trumps habitat, tradition trumps technology, and action trumps adaptation.

In answer to the rhetorical question posed by Prufer, and cited in the volume introduction, there now exists compelling evidence that Archaic groups (even the earliest ones) were not the archaeological corollaries of modern hunting and gathering bands; they were, instead, the tribal and possibly chiefdom-level precursors of the highly complex societies noted, for example, in Florida and on the coast of Georgia (Marquardt 1987) in historic times. Rather than view the Eastern Woodlands Archaic as the laboratory for the study of hunting-gathering groups, archaeologists should instead view the Archaic as an ideal laboratory for the study of the development of complex fishing-hunting-gathering societies. We side with Kidder and Sassaman (this volume) in affirming that "a wealth of new data provides evidence that this was a time of unprecedented social, political, economic, and technological variability." The rich temperate and subtropical riverine and coastal habitats offered by much of the Eastern Woodlands provided the stage for the iconoclastic societies that rocked the boats of early social anthropologists as they attempted to categorize cultures, and their ancient predecessors continue to do the same for present-day cultural neo-evolutionists.

References Cited

Abbott, Larry R.

1987 *Archaeological Investigations at the Kewanee Site (11-HY-126), Henry County, Illinois.* Research Reports 27. Resource Investigation Program, Department of Anthropology, University of Illinois, Urbana.

Asch, David L., Kenneth B. Farnsworth, H. Carl Udesen, and Ann L. Koski

1978 *Development of Preliminary Predictive Models of Regional Prehistoric Settlement in the Lower Illinois and Adjacent Mississippi River Drainages (IDOC Regions III & VII).* Submitted to the Illinois Department of Conservation, Springfield. Reports of Investigation 45. Center for American Archeology, Kampsville, Illinois.

Barth, Robert J.

1982 The Allison-Lamotte and Vincennes Cultures: Cultural Evolution in the Wabash Valley. Ph.D. dissertation, Department of Anthropology, University of Illinois, Champaign.

Bartsch, Paul

1916 The Missouri River as a Faunal Barrier. *The Nautilus* 30:92.

Beardsley, R. K., Preston Holder, A. D. Kreiger, B. J. Meggars, and John Rinaldo

1956 *Functional and Evolutionary Implications of Community Patterning.* Memoir 11. Society for American Archaeology, Salt Lake City, Utah.

Bettis, E. Arthur, III, and Edwin Hajic

1995 *Landscape Development and the Location of Evidence of Archaic Cultures in the Upper Midwest.* Special Paper 297. Geological Society of America, Boulder, Colorado.

Binford, Lewis R.

1965 Archaeological Systematics and the Study of Culture Process. *American Antiquity* 31:203–210.

1980 Willow Smoke and Dogs' Tails: Hunter-Gatherer Settlement Systems and Archaeological Site Formation. *American Antiquity* 45:4–20.

Brown, James A.

1985 Long-Term Trends to Sedentism and the Emergence of Complexity in the American Midwest. In *Prehistoric Hunter-Gatherers: The Emergence of Cultural Complexity*, edited by T. Douglas Price and James A. Brown, pp. 201–231. Academic Press, New York.

1986 Food for Thought: Where Has Subsistence Analysis Gotten Us? In *Foraging, Collecting, and Harvesting: Archaic Period Subsistence and Settlement in the Eastern Woodlands*, edited by Sarah W. Neusius, pp. 315–327. Occasional Papers 6. Center for Archaeological Investigations, Southern Illinois University, Carbondale.

Brown, James A., and Robert K. Vierra

1983 What Happened in the Middle Archaic? Introduction to an Ecological Approach to Koster Site Archaeology. In *Archaic Hunters and Gatherers in the American Midwest*, edited by James L. Phillips and James A. Brown, pp. 165–196. Academic Press, New York.

Brown, Paul, James P. Kennett, and B. Lynn Ingram

1999 Marine Evidence for Episodic Holocene Megafloods in North America and the Northern Gulf of Mexico. *Paleoceanography* 14:498–510.

Carlson, David Lee

1979 Hunter-Gatherer Mobility Strategies: An Example from the Koster Site in the Lower Illinois Valley. Ph.D. dissertation, Department of Anthropology, Northwestern University, Evanston, Illinois.

Carmichael, David

1976 *Archaeological Survey of Uplands Adjacent to the Middlefork of the Vermilion River.* Report submitted to the Illinois Department of Conservation, Springfield. Department of Anthropology, University of Illinois, Urbana.

1977 Preliminary Archeological Survey of Illinois Uplands and Some Behavioral Implications. *Midcontinental Journal of Archaeology* 1:219–251.

1978 *Archaeological Survey of the Chicap Pipeline Easement, Central and Northeastern Illinois.* Report submitted to Nalco Environmental Sciences and Union Oil Company, Chicago. Department of Anthropology, University of Illinois, Urbana.

Chapman, B. J., and J. M. Adovasio

1977 Textile and Basketry Impressions from Icehouse Bottom, Tennessee. *American Antiquity* 42:620–625.

Charles, Douglas K., and Jane E. Buikstra
1983 Archaic Mortuary Sites in the Central Mississippi Drainage: Distribution, Structure, and Behavioral Implications. In *Archaic Hunters and Gatherers in the American Midwest*, edited by James L. Phillips and James A. Brown, pp. 117–145. Academic Press, New York.

Cleland, Charles E.
1982 The Inland Shore Fishery of the Northern Great Lakes: Its Development and Importance in Prehistory. *American Antiquity* 47:761–784.

Clouse, Robert A.
1975 An Archaeological Assessment and Impact Statement for the Amax Coal Company "Ayrcat" Coal Strip Mine, Vermilion County, Illinois. Manuscript on file, Department of Anthropology, University of Illinois, Urbana.

Coker, Robert E.
1919 Fresh-Water Mussels and Mussel Industries of the United States. *Bulletin of the Bureau of Fisheries* 36:13–89. Government Printing Office, Washington, D.C.

Conrad, Lawrence A.
1981 *An Introduction to the Archaeology of West Central Illinois: A Preliminary Archaeological Survey of the Canton to Quincy Corridor for the Proposed FAP 407 Highway Project*. Reports of Investigations 2. Archaeological Research Laboratory. Western Illinois University, Macomb.

Dixon, James E.
1999 *Bones, Boats, and Bison: Archeology and the First Colonization of Western North America*. University of New Mexico Press, Albuquerque.

Doran, Glen H. (editor)
2002 *Windover: Multidisciplinary Investigations of an Early Archaic Florida Cemetery*. University Press of Florida, Gainesville.

Emerson, Thomas E.
1984 The Dyroff and Levin Sites. In *The Go-Kart North Site and the Dyroff and Levin Sites*, by Andrew C. Fortier and Thomas E. Emerson, pp. 199–362. American Bottom Archaeology FAI-270 Site Reports 9. University of Illinois Press, Urbana.

Emerson, Thomas E., and Andrew C. Fortier
1986 Early Woodland Cultural Variation, Subsistence, and Settlement in the American Bottom. In *Early Woodland Archeology*, edited by Kenneth B. Farnsworth and Thomas E. Emerson, pp. 475–522. Kampsville Seminars in Archeology 2. Center for American Archeology, Kampsville, Illinois.

Emerson, Thomas E., and Dale L. McElrath
1983 A Settlement-Subsistence Model of the Terminal Late Archaic Adaptation in the American Bottom, Illinois. In *Archaic Hunters and Gatherers in the American Midwest*, edited by James L. Phillips and James A. Brown, pp. 219–242. Academic Press, New York.
2001 Interpreting Discontinuity and Historical Process in Midcontinental Late Archaic and Early Woodland Societies. In *The Archaeology of Tradition: Agency and History Before and After Columbus*, edited by Timothy R. Pauketat, pp. 195–217. University Press of Florida, Gainesville.

Esarey, Duane
1986 Red Ochre Mound Building and Marion Phase Associations: A Fulton County, Illinois Perspective. In *Early Woodland Archeology*, edited by Kenneth B. Farnsworth and Thomas E. Emerson, pp. 231–243. Kampsville Seminars in Archeology 2. Center for American Archeology, Kampsville, Illinois.

Farnsworth, Kenneth B., and David L. Asch
1986 Early Woodland Chronology, Artifact Styles, and Settlement Distribution in the Lower Illinois Valley Region. In *Early Woodland Archeology*, edited by Kenneth B. Farnsworth and Thomas E. Emerson, pp. 326–457. Kampsville Seminars in Archeology 2. Center for American Archeology, Kampsville, Illinois.

Farnsworth, Kenneth B., and Thomas E. Emerson (editors)
1986 *Early Woodland Archeology*. Kampsville Seminars in Archeology 2. Center for American Archeology, Kampsville, Illinois.

Fortier, Andrew C.
2001 A Tradition of Discontinuity: American Bottom Early and Middle Woodland Culture History Reexamined. In *The Archaeology of Traditions: Agency and History Before and After Columbus*, edited by Timothy R. Pauketat, pp. 174–194. University Press of Florida, Gainesville.

Fowler, Melvin L.
1959 Modoc Rock Shelter: An Early Archaic Site in Southern Illinois. *American Antiquity* 24:257–270.

Frison, George C., R. L. Andrews, J. M. Adovasio, R. C. Carlisle, and Robert Edgar
1985 A Late Paleoindian Animal Trapping Net from Northern Wyoming. *American Antiquity* 51:352–361.

Fritz, Gayle J.
1999 Gender and the Early Cultivation of Gourds in Eastern North America. *American Antiquity* 64:417–429.

Gramly, Richard Michael
1993 *The Richey Clovis Cache: Earliest Americans on the Columbia River*. Persimmon Press, Buffalo, New York.

Hajic, Edwin
1990 *Koster Site Archeology I: Stratigraphy and Landscape Evolution*. Research Series 8. Center for American Archeology, Kampsville, Illinois.

Harris, Wendy G.
2002 Upland Abandonment during the Middle Archaic Period: A View from Northeastern Illinois. *The Wisconsin Archeologist* 83(1):3–18.

Hart, John P., Robert A. Daniels, and Charles J. Sheviak
2004 Do *Cucurbita pepo* Gourds Float Fishnets? *American Antiquity* 69:141–148.

Higgins, Michael J.
1990 *The Nochta Site: The Early, Middle, and Late Archaic Occupations*. American Bottom Archaeology FAI-270 Site Reports 21. University of Illinois Press, Urbana.

Kay, Marvin, Frances B. King, and Christine K. Robinson
1980 Cucurbits from Phillips Spring: New Evidence and Interpretation. *American Antiquity* 45:806–822.

Klippel, Walter E., and James Maddox
1977 The Early Archaic of Willow Branch. *Midcontinental Journal of Archaeology* 2:99–130.

Knox, James C.
1985 Responses of Floods to Holocene Climatic Change in the Upper Mississippi Valley. *Quaternary Research* 23:287–300.
1993 Large Increases in Flood Magnitude in Response to Modest Changes in Climate. *Nature* 361:430–432.

Koldehoff, Brad, and John A. Walthall
2004 Settling In: Hunter-Gatherer Mobility during the Pleistocene-Holocene Transition in the Central Mississippi Valley. In *Aboriginal Ritual and Economy in the Eastern Woodlands: Essays in Memory of Howard Dalton Winters*, edited by Anne-Marie Cantwell, Lawrence A. Conrad, and Jonathan E. Reyman, pp. 49–72. Scientific Papers 30. Illinois State Museum, Springfield.

Lewis, R. Barry
1977 *Archaeological Densities and Distributions in East Central Illinois*. Report submitted to the Illinois Department of Conservation, Springfield. Department of Anthropology, University of Illinois, Urbana.
1983 Archaic Adaptations in the Illinois Prairie: The Salt Creek Region. In *Archaic Hunters and Gatherers in the American Midwest*, edited by James L. Phillips and James A. Brown, pp. 99–116. Academic Press, New York.

Limp, W. Frederick, and Van A. Reidhead
1979 An Economic Evaluation of the Potential of Fish Utilization in Riverine Environments. *American Antiquity* 44:70–78.

Marquardt, William H.
1985 Complexity and Scale in the Study of Fisher-Gatherer-Hunters: An Example from the Eastern United States. In *Prehistoric Hunter-Gatherers: The Emergence of Cultural Complexity*, edited by T. Douglas Price and James A. Brown, pp. 59–98. Academic Press, New York.

Mason, Ronald J.
1981 *Great Lakes Archaeology*. Academic Press, New York.

McElrath, Dale L.
1993 Mule Road: A Newly Defined Late Archaic Phase in the American Bottom. In *Highways to the Past: Essays on Illinois Archaeology in Honor of Charles J. Bareis*, edited by Thomas E. Emerson, Andrew C. Fortier, and Dale L. McElrath, pp. 148–157. *Illinois Archaeology* 5(1–2).

McElrath, Dale L., and Thomas E. Emerson
2000 Toward an "Intrinsic Characteristics" Approach to Chert Raw Material Classification: An American Bottom Example. *Midcontinental Journal of Archaeology* 25:215–244.

McElrath, Dale L., and Andrew C. Fortier
1983 *The Missouri Pacific #2 Site*. American Bottom Archaeology FAI-270 Site Reports 3. University of Illinois Press, Urbana.

McMillan, R. Bruce
2006 Perspectives on the Biogeography and Archaeology of Bison in Illinois. In *Records of Early Bison in Illinois*, edited by R. Bruce McMillan, pp. 67–147. Scientific Papers 31. Illinois State Museum, Springfield.

Mithun, Marianne
2001 *Languages of Native North America*. Cambridge University Press, Cambridge, England.

Morey, Darcy F., and Michael D. Wiant
1992 Early Holocene Domestic Dog Burials from the North American Midwest. *Current Anthropology* 33:224–229.

Morse, Dan F.
1997 *Sloan: A Paleoindian Dalton Cemetery in Arkansas*. Smithsonian Institution, Washington, D.C.

Morse, Dan F., and Albert C. Goodyear
1973 The Significance of the Dalton Adze in Northeast Arkansas. *Plains Anthropologist* 18:316–322.

Moseley, Michael
1975 *The Maritime Foundations of Andean Civilization*. Cummings, Menlo Park, California.

Muller, Jon
1997 *Mississippian Political Economy*. Plenum, New York.

Neusius, Sarah W. (editor)
1986 *Foraging, Collecting, and Harvesting: Archaic Period Subsistence and Settlement in the Eastern Woodlands*. Occasional Papers 6. Center for Archaeological Investigations, Southern Illinois University, Carbondale.

Purdy, Barbara A. (editor)
1988 *Wet Site Archaeology*. Telford Press, Caldwell, New Jersey.

Rick, Torben C., Jon M. Erlandson, and Rene L. Vellonoweth
2001 Paleocoastal Marine Fishing on the Pacific Coast of the Americas: Perspectives from Daisy Cave. *American Antiquity* 66:595–614.

Sassaman, Kenneth E.
1993 *Early Pottery in the Southeast: Tradition and Innovation in Cooking Technology*. University of Alabama Press, Tuscaloosa.
2005 Poverty Point as Structure, Event, Process. *Journal of Archaeological Method and Theory* 12:335–364.

Smith, Bruce D.
1986 The Archaeology of the Southeastern United States: From Dalton to de Soto, 10,500–500 B.P. In *Advances in World Archaeology*, vol. 5, edited by Fred Wendorf and Angela E. Close, pp. 1–92. Academic Press, New York.

Struever, Stuart, and Felicia A. Holton
1979 *Koster: Americans in Search of Their Prehistoric Past*. Doubleday, New York.

Thorne, Robert M., Bettye J. Broyles, and Jay K. Johnson
1981 *Yellow Creek Archaeological Project*. Tennessee Valley Authority Publications in Anthropology 1. Center for Archaeological Research, University of Mississippi, University.

Van Nest, Julieann
1997 Late Quaternary Geology, Archeology and Vegetation in West-Central Illinois: A Study of Geoarcheology. Ph.D. dissertation, Department of Geology, University of Iowa.

Walthall, John A.
1998 Rockshelters and Hunter-Gatherer Adaptations to the Pleistocene/Holocene Transition. *American Antiquity* 63:223–238.

Walthall, John A., and Brad Koldehoff
1998 Hunter-Gatherer Interaction and Alliance Formation: Dalton and the Cult of the Long Blade. *Plains Anthropologist* 43:257–273.

Warren, Robert F. (editor)
1997 *Environment and Human Settlement along Interstate 39 in North Central Illinois.* Technical Report 92-396-10. Quaternary Studies Program, Illinois State Museum, Springfield.

Wheeler, Ryan J., James J. Miller, Ray M. McGee, Donna Ruhl, Brenda Swann, and Melissa Memory
2003 Archaic Period Canoes from Newnans Lake, Florida. *American Antiquity* 68:533–552.

Wiant, Michael D., Edwin R. Hajic, and Thomas R. Styles
1983 Napoleon Hollow and Koster Site Stratigraphy: Implications for Holocene Landscape Evolution and Studies of Archaic Period Settlement Patterns in the Lower Illinois River Valley. In *Archaic Hunters and Gatherers in the American Midwest*, edited by James L. Phillips and James A. Brown, pp. 147–164. Academic Press, New York.

Winters, Howard D.
1961 The Archaic Period. In *Illinois Archaeology*, pp. 9–16. Bulletin 1. Illinois Archaeological Survey, Urbana.

Wisseman, Sarah
2005 True Grit: Middle Woodland Cooking and Pot Production. *Illinois Archaeology* 17, in press.

Yerkes, Richard W.
1986 Late Archaic Settlement and Subsistence on the American Bottom. In *Foraging, Collecting, and Harvesting: Archaic Period Subsistence and Settlement in the Eastern Woodlands*, edited by Sarah W. Neusius, pp. 225–245. Occasional Papers 6. Center for Archaeological Investigations, Southern Illinois University, Carbondale.

Index

D

E

F

G

H

I

J

K

L

M

U

V

W